D0384477

CANADIAN EDITION

AUTOMOTIVE TECHNOLOGY

Principles, Diagnosis, and Service

CANADIAN EDITION

AUTOMOTIVE TECHNOLOGY

Principles, Diagnosis, and Service

James D. Halderman
Sinclair Community College

Chase D. Mitchell, Jr.
Utah Valley State College

Jim Marchant
British Columbia Institute of Technology

Roger Davey
Algonquin College

Toronto

Library and Archives Canada Cataloguing in Publication

Automotive technology : principles, diagnosis, and service / James D. Halderman ... [et al.]. — Canadian ed.

Includes index.
ISBN 0-13-124890-1

1. Automobiles—Maintenance and repair—Textbooks.
I. Halderman, James D., 1943–

TL152.A99 2006 629.28'72 C2005-900310-3

0-13-124890-1

Vice President, Editorial Director: Michael J. Young
Executive Editor: Dave Ward
Marketing Manager: Toivo Pajo
Developmental Editor: John Polanszky
Production Editor: Mary Ann McCutcheon
Copy Editor: Jim MacLachlan
Production Manager: Wendy Moran
Manufacturing Coordinator: Susan Johnson
Page Layout: Carlisle Communications, Ltd.
Photo and Permissions Research: Nicola Winstanley
Art Director: Julia Hall
Cover Design: Anthony Leung
Cover Image: The Image Bank/GettyImages

1 2 3 4 5 10 09 08 07 06

Printed and bound in the United States of America.

Portions of materials contained herein have been reprinted with permission of General Motors Corporation, Service and Parts Operations, License Agreement #0410850.

Brief Contents

SECTION I

Introduction 1

SECTION II

Engine Repair 71

SECTION 

Electrical/Electronic Systems 259

SECTION 

Heating and Air Conditioning 498

SECTION 

Engine Performance 542

SECTION 

Brakes 772

SECTION 

Suspension and Steering 925

SECTION 

Manual Drive Trains and Axles 1017

SECTION 

Automatic Transmissions and Transaxles 1171

APPENDIXES
(Sample Red Seal Certification Tests)

Contents

20

Accessory Circuits Operation and Diagnosis 457

21

Audio System Operation and Diagnosis 488

SECTION IV

Heating and Air Conditioning 498

22

Heating, Ventilation, and Air-Conditioning Principles 499

23

Heating and Air-Conditioning Diagnosis and Service 524

SECTION V

Engine Performance 542

24

Ignition System Operation, Diagnosis, and Service 543

34

35

36

37

38

39

SECTION VII

40

50

Tech Tips, Frequently Asked Questions, Diagnostic Stories, High Performance Tips, and Safety Tips

13

Electrical and Electronic Principles and Circuits 260

14

Meters, Scopes, Wiring, and Schematics 294

15

Batteries and Battery Testing 340

16

Cranking System Operation, Diagnosis, and Service 363

17

Charging System Operation, Diagnosis, and Service 388

18

Lighting and Signalling Circuit Operation and Diagnosis 421

19

Dash Instruments Operation and Diagnosis 437

20

Accessory Circuits Operation and Diagnosis 457

21

Audio System Operation and Diagnosis 488

22

Heating, Ventilation, and Air-Conditioning Principles 499

23

Heating and Air-Conditioning Diagnosis and Service 524

24

Ignition System Operation, Diagnosis, and Service 543

31

Engine Performance Diagnosis and Testing 739

32

Brake System Principles and Operation 772

33

Master Cylinders and the Hydraulic System 785

34

Wheel Bearings and Service 817

35

Drum Brake Operation, Diagnosis, and Service 834

36

Disc Brake Operation, Diagnosis, and Service 853

43

Wheel Alignment Principles, Diagnosis, and Service 1013

44

Clutches 1047

45

Manual Transmissions/Transaxles 1065

46

Drive Shafts and CV Joints 1095

47

Differentials 1124

48

Four-Wheel Drive and All-Wheel Drive 1147

49

50

Photo Sequences

Preface

The Canadian edition of *Automotive Technology: Principles, Diagnosis, and Service* is organized around eight test areas and is correlated to the Automotive Service Technician (AST) Task List. Terminology throughout the text reflects the SAE J1930 standard.

Diagnostic Approach

The primary focus of this textbook is to satisfy the need for problem diagnosis. Time and time again, the authors were told that technicians require more training in diagnostic procedures and skill development. To meet this need and to help illustrate how real problems are solved, diagnostic stories are included throughout. Each new topic covers the parts involved plus their purpose, function, and operation, as well as how to test and diagnose each system.

Multimedia System Approach

The multimedia CD-ROM that accompanies and supplements the textbook is informative and also makes learning more fun for the student. The CD includes:

1. Live action videos and animation to help students understand complex systems.
2. A glossary of automotive terms.
3. Sample interprovincial Red Seal test questions with immediate correct answer feedback.
4. Diagnostic aids including a waveform library.

Worktext Approach

A separate worktext accompanies the book. Each worktext page is correlated to the AST Task List. The worksheets included in the worktext help instructors and students apply the material presented to everyday-type activities and typical service and testing procedures. The worksheets show typical results and a listing of what could be defective if the test results are not within the acceptable range. These sheets help build diagnostic and testing skills.

Chapter Components

- Each chapter opens with a list of learning *objectives* including the AST content area covered by the chapter. These objectives identify the topics covered and goals to be achieved in the chapter.
- Most chapters contain *tech tips, diagnostic stories, frequently asked questions, high-performance tips,* and *safety tips.*
- All chapters contain a *summary* at the end that highlights the material covered in the chapter.
- *Review questions* (discussion-type questions) are offered at the end of each chapter.
- Each chapter contains *interprovincial Red Seal certification-type questions.*

Type Styles Used in This Text

Various type styles are used throughout this text to emphasize words, identify important terms, and highlight figure references. *Italic type* is used to emphasize words and terms. For example, the word *not* is often printed in italic type when it is important that an operation be avoided. New terms appear in **bold type** at first usage. These terms are defined when introduced, and most are listed in the glossary at the back of the text.

Troubleshooting Charts

Troubleshooting charts have been added to the end of each service chapter. These charts will help the reader diagnose and repair common problems.

Colour Use

Colour is used extensively throughout this text to enhance understanding and highlight important information. Hundreds of colour photographs help students grasp the subject material.

New Features of the Canadian Edition

1. All eight AST areas are thoroughly covered and correlated.
2. AST objectives are included at the beginning of each chapter.
3. Canadian content including references to WHMIS safety regulations, Red Seal certification, and sample Red Seal-type examination questions.
4. Hundreds of new colour photographs and line drawings help students understand the content material and bring the subject alive.
5. Expanded electrical and electronic content.
6. Expanded coverage of OBD II and I/M 240.
7. Expanded coverage on manual and automatic transmissions.
8. Many new photo sequences help to explain service procedures.
9. New topics covered include improved metric, diesel engines, diesel fuel injection, expanded import information, advanced vehicles, newer fuel injection systems, current manifold designs, improved diagnostics, and current trends.
10. Each technical topic discussed in one place or chapter. Unlike other textbooks, this book is written so that the theory, construction, diagnosis, and service of a particular component or system are presented in one location. There is no need to search through the entire book for other references to the same topic.
11. Improved theory and principles of operation.

Instructor Package

This instructor package includes the following:

- Instructor CD-ROM with suggested student activities, a test bank, photo library with hundreds of digital colour photos, Power Point presentations, answers to all questions in the textbook, as well as many other useful elements for the classroom.

ACKNOWLEDGMENTS

A large number of people and organizations have cooperated in providing the reference material and technical information used in this text. The authors wish to express sincere thanks to the following organizations for their special contributions:

Accu Industries, Inc.
Allied Signal Automotive Aftermarket
Arrow Automotive
ASE
Autolite Spark Plugs
Automotion, Inc.
Automotive Engine Rebuilders Association (AERA)
Automotive Parts Rebuilders Association (APRA)
Automotive Transmission Rebuilders Association (ATRA)
Ballard Power Systems Inc.
Battery Council International (BCI)
Bear Automotive
Bendix
British Columbia Institute of Technology
British Petroleum (BP)
Cadillac Motor Car Division, General Motors Corporation
Camosun College: Victoria, BC
Camwerks Corporation
Castrol Incorporated
Champion Spark Plugs, Cooper Automotive, Cooper Industries
Chevron Canada Ltd.
Classic Engine Supplies Inc.
Clayton Associates
Cooper Automotive Company
DaimlerChrysler Canada Inc.
Dana Corporation, Perfect Circle Products

Defiance Engine Rebuilders, Incorporated
Delphi Chassis, GMC
The Dow Chemical Company
Duralcan USA
EIS Brake Parts
Envirotest Systems Corporation
Fel-Pro Incorporated
Fluke Corporation
FMSI
Ford Motor Co. of Canada Ltd.
General Electric Lighting Division
General Motors of Canada Ltd.
Goodson Auto Machine Shop Tools and Supplies
Greenlee Brothers and Company
Hennessy Industries
Honda Canada Inc.
Hunter Engineering Company
Ignition Manufacturers Institute
Jasper Engines and Transmissions
John Bean Company
McCord Manufacturing Inc.
Mitsubishi Motor Co.
Modine Manufacturing Company
Neway
Northstar Manufacturing Company, Inc.
Oldsmobile Division, GMC
Optima Batteries
OTC Division: SPX Corporation
Pacific Vehicle Testing Technologies: AirCare
Panasonic Energy Co.
Parsons and Meyers Racing Engines
Perfect Hofmann-USA
Raybestos Brake Parts, Inc.
Reynolds and Reynolds Company
Robert Bosch Corporation
Rottler Manufacturing
Shimco International, Inc.
SKF USA, Inc.
Snap-On Tools
Society of Automotive Engineers (SAE)
Speciality Products Company
Sun Electric Corporation: division of Snap-On Tools
Sunnen Products Company
Toyota Motor Corporation
TRW Inc.
Volkswagen Canada Inc.
Wurth USA, Inc.

Technical and Content Reviewers

The following people reviewed the manuscript before production and checked it for technical accuracy and clarity of presentation. Their suggestions and recommendations were included in the final draft of the manuscript. Their input helped make this textbook clear and technically accurate while maintaining the easy-to-read style:

Al Playter, Centennial College
Phil Johnston, Vancouver Community College
Jeremy Anderson, Algonquin College
Cam McRobb, Okanagan University College
Mark Daigle, St. Lawrence College
Steve Best, Centennial College
Dennis Peter, Northern Alberta Institute of Technology
Oldrich Hajzler, Red River College
John Mercer, Loyalist College
Ron Smith, Canadore College
Larry Rhodenizer, Kwantlen University College
Corey Bransfield
Andre Ooievaar, Camosun College
David Yeo, Holland College
Vito Ialungo, BCIT

Features of This Text

To enhance readability and understanding, as well as making study more enjoyable, this text is packed with many special features.

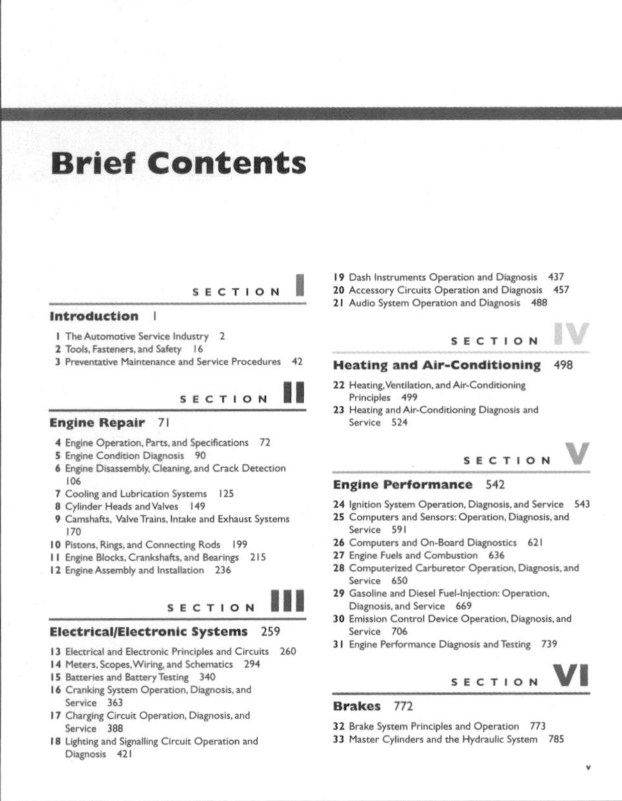

Brief Contents

v

Automotive Technology: Principles, Diagnosis, and Service, Canadian Edition, is arranged into nine major sections. The first is an introductory section. The next eight sections correspond to the eight Automotive Service Technician (AST) categories.

Photo Sequences show in detail the steps involved in performing a test or service procedure. The Photo Sequences reinforce classroom instruction by allowing students to view the important elements in an automotive procedure as they learn about a particular topic.

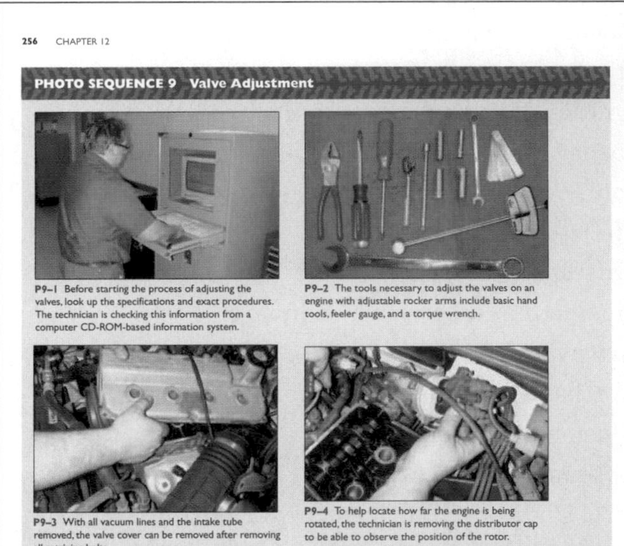

256 CHAPTER 12

PHOTO SEQUENCE 9 Valve Adjustment

P9–1 Before starting the process of adjusting the valves, look up the specifications and exact procedures. The technician is checking this information from a computer CD-ROM-based information system.

P9–2 The tools necessary to adjust the valves on an engine with adjustable rocker arms include basic hand tools, feeler gauge, and a torque wrench.

P9–3 With all vacuum lines and the intake tube removed, the valve cover can be removed after removing all retaining bolts.

P9–4 To help locate how far the engine is being rotated, the technician is removing the distributor cap to be able to observe the position of the rotor.

P9–5 The engine is rotated until the timing marks on the front of the crankshaft line up with zero degrees—top dead centre (TDC)—with both valves closed on #1 cylinder.

P9–6 With the rocker arms contacting the base circle of the cam, insert a feeler gauge of the specified thickness between the camshaft and the rocker arm. There should be a slight drag on the feeler gauge if the clearance is the same as the thickness of the feeler gauge.

More than 2200 **photos** and **illustrations,** most in full colour, graphically depict critical components and procedures much better than just words could explain. In fact, the illustrations could almost stand alone as a teaching tool.

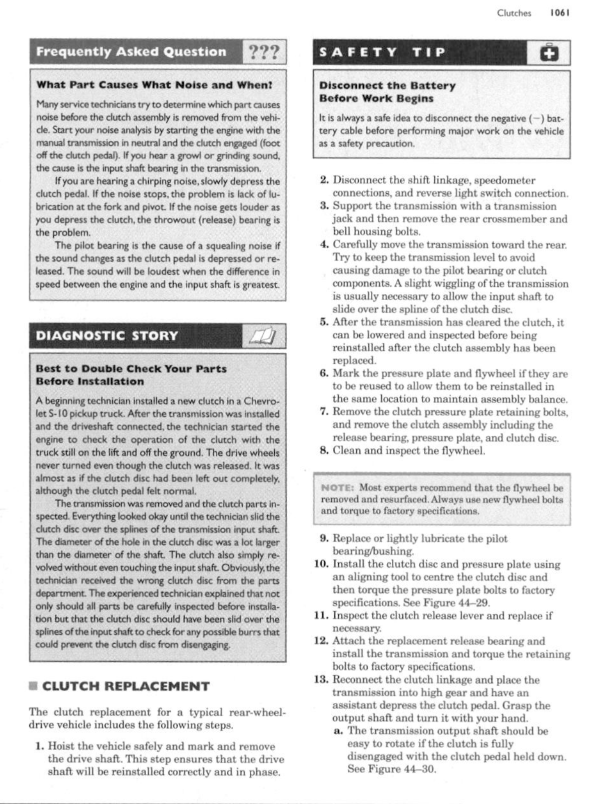

Clutches 1061

Frequently Asked Question ???

What Part Causes What Noise and When?

Many service technicians try to determine which part causes noise before the clutch assembly is removed from the vehicle. Start your noise analysis by starting the engine with the manual transmission in neutral and the clutch engaged (foot off the clutch pedal). If you hear a growl or grinding sound, the cause is the input shaft bearing in the transmission.

If you are hearing a chirping noise, slowly depress the clutch pedal. If the noise stops, the problem is lack of lubrication at the fork and pivot. If the noise gets louder as you depress the clutch, the throwout (release) bearing is the problem.

The pilot bearing is the cause of a squealing noise if the sound changes as the clutch pedal is depressed or released. The sound will be loudest when the difference in speed between the engine and the input shaft is greatest.

DIAGNOSTIC STORY

Best to Double Check Your Parts Before Installation

A beginning technician installed a new clutch in a Chevrolet S-10 pickup truck. After the transmission was installed and the driveshaft connected, the technician started the engine to check the operation of the clutch with the truck still on the lift and off the ground. The drive wheels never turned even though the clutch was released. It was almost as if the clutch disc had been left out completely, although the clutch pedal felt normal.

The transmission was removed and the clutch parts inspected. Everything looked okay until the technician slid the clutch disc over the splines of the transmission input shaft. The diameter of the hole in the clutch disc was a lot larger than the diameter of the shaft. The clutch also simply revolved without even touching the input shaft. Obviously, the technician received the wrong clutch disc from the parts department. The experienced technician explained that not only should all parts be carefully inspected before installation but that the clutch disc should have been slid over the splines of the input shaft to check for any possible burrs that could prevent the clutch disc from disengaging.

CLUTCH REPLACEMENT

The clutch replacement for a typical rear-wheel-drive vehicle includes the following steps.

1. Hoist the vehicle safely and mark and remove the drive shaft. This step ensures that the drive shaft will be reinstalled correctly and in phase.

SAFETY TIP

Disconnect the Battery Before Work Begins

It is always a safe idea to disconnect the negative (−) battery cable before performing major work on the vehicle as a safety precaution.

2. Disconnect the shift linkage, speedometer connections, and reverse light switch connection.
3. Support the transmission with a transmission jack and then remove the rear crossmember and bell housing bolts.
4. Carefully move the transmission toward the rear. Try to keep the transmission level to avoid causing damage to the pilot bearing or clutch components. A slight wiggling of the transmission is usually necessary to allow the input shaft to slide over the spline of the clutch disc.
5. After the transmission has cleared the clutch, it can be lowered and inspected before being reinstalled after the clutch assembly has been replaced.
6. Mark the pressure plate and flywheel if they are to be reused to allow them to be reinstalled in the same location to maintain assembly balance.
7. Remove the clutch pressure plate retaining bolts, and remove the clutch assembly including the release bearing, pressure plate, and clutch disc.
8. Clean and inspect the flywheel.

NOTE: Most experts recommend that the flywheel be removed and resurfaced. Always use new flywheel bolts and torque to factory specifications.

9. Replace or lightly lubricate the pilot bearing/bushing.
10. Install the clutch disc and pressure plate using an aligning tool to centre the clutch disc and then torque the pressure plate bolts to factory specifications. See Figure 44–29.
11. Inspect the clutch release lever and replace if necessary.
12. Attach the replacement release bearing and install the transmission and torque the retaining bolts to factory specifications.
13. Reconnect the clutch linkage and place the transmission into high gear and have an assistant depress the clutch pedal. Grasp the output shaft and turn it with your hand.
    a. The transmission output shaft should be easy to rotate if the clutch is fully disengaged with the clutch pedal held down. See Figure 44–30.

The **Frequently Asked Question** feature was included at the request of students and faculty to provide answers to questions that many students and beginning service technicians have when studying technical automotive topics.

Each **Diagnostic Story** presents a problem or situation that the service technician might face. These stories tell about the steps taken to arrive at a solution to a technical problem.

The **Safety Tip** feature is new to this edition. This feature warns students about possible hazards on the job and how to avoid harm.

Troubleshooting Guides have been added to the end of each service chapter. These guides help students diagnose and repair common problems. In addition, the **Review Questions** and **Red Seal Certification-Type Questions** at the end of each chapter will help students gain confidence in their ability to pass tests and achieve the certification they will need to qualify for automotive technician positions in the automotive service industry.

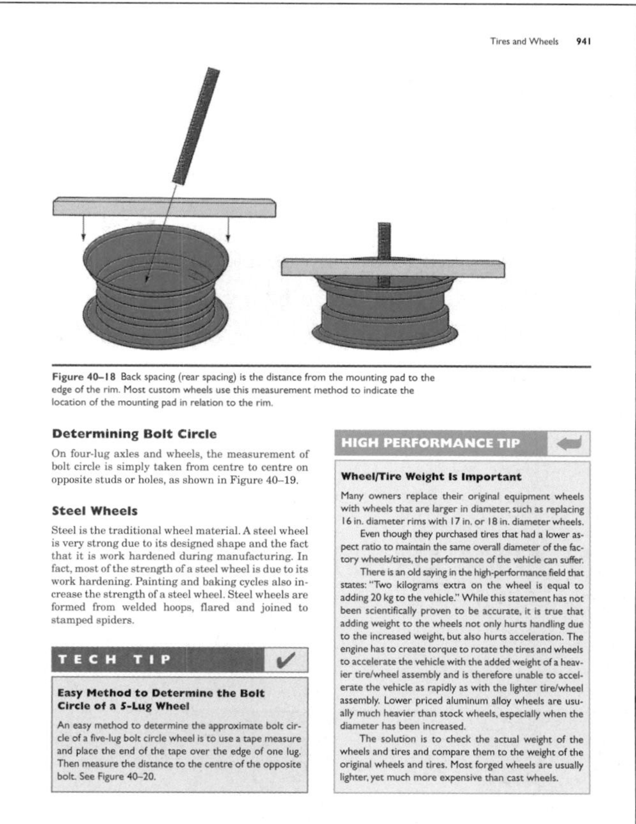

Tires and Wheels 941

Figure 40–18 Back spacing (rear spacing) is the distance from the mounting pad to the edge of the rim. Most custom wheels use this measurement method to indicate the location of the mounting pad in relation to the rim.

Determining Bolt Circle

On four-lug axles and wheels, the measurement of bolt circle is simply taken from centre to centre on opposite studs or holes, as shown in Figure 40–19.

Steel Wheels

Steel is the traditional wheel material. A steel wheel is very strong due to its designed shape and the fact that it is work hardened during manufacturing. In fact, most of the strength of a steel wheel is due to its work hardening. Painting and baking cycles also increase the strength of a steel wheel. Steel wheels are formed from welded hoops, flared and joined to stamped spiders.

TECH TIP

Easy Method to Determine the Bolt Circle of a 5-Lug Wheel

An easy method to determine the approximate bolt circle of a five-lug bolt circle wheel is to use a tape measure and place the end of the tape over the edge of one lug. Then measure the distance to the centre of the opposite bolt. See Figure 40–20.

HIGH PERFORMANCE TIP

Wheel/Tire Weight Is Important

Many owners replace their original equipment wheels with wheels that are larger in diameter, such as replacing 16 in. diameter rims with 17 in. or 18 in. diameter wheels.

Even though they purchased tires that had a lower aspect ratio to maintain the same overall diameter of the factory wheels/tires, the performance of the vehicle can suffer.

There is an old saying in the high-performance field that states: "Two kilograms extra on the wheel is equal to adding 20 kg to the vehicle." While this statement has not been scientifically proven to be accurate, it is true that adding weight to the wheels not only hurts handling due to the increased weight, but also hurts acceleration. The engine has to create torque to rotate the tires and wheels to accelerate the vehicle with the added weight of a heavier tire/wheel assembly and is therefore unable to accelerate the vehicle as rapidly as with the lighter tire/wheel assembly. Lower priced aluminum alloy wheels are usually much heavier than stock wheels, especially when the diameter has been increased.

The solution is to check the actual weight of the wheels and tires and compare them to the weight of the original wheels and tires. Most forged wheels are usually lighter, yet much more expensive than cast wheels.

Tech Tips help readers gain insight into specific situations that they might encounter on the job and are based on real-life experiences.

High Performance Tips focus on techniques often used in motor sport racing to improve vehicle performance.

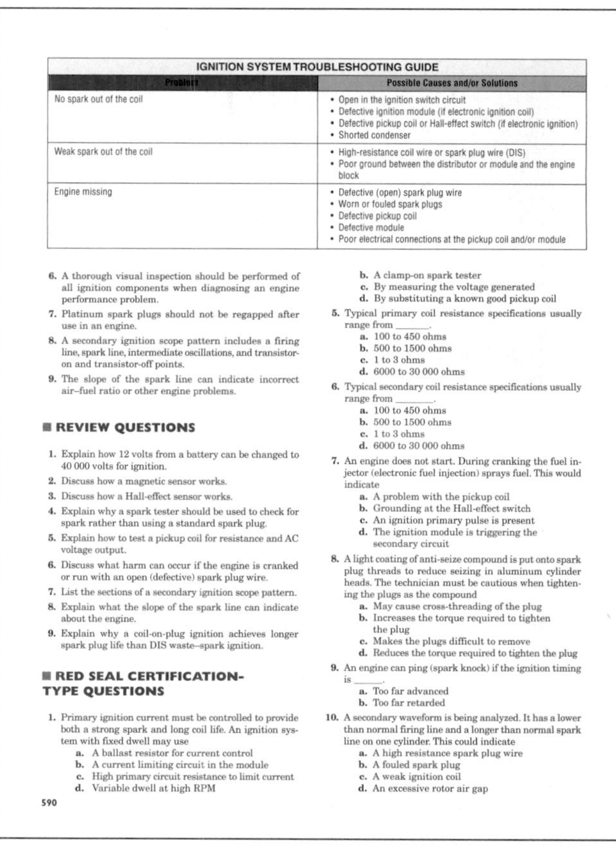

IGNITION SYSTEM TROUBLESHOOTING GUIDE	
Problem	Possible Causes and/or Solutions
No spark out of the coil	• Open in the ignition switch circuit • Defective ignition module (if electronic ignition coil) • Defective pickup coil or Hall-effect switch (if electronic ignition) • Shorted condenser
Weak spark out of the coil	• High-resistance coil wire or spark plug wire (DIS) • Poor ground between the distributor or module and the engine block
Engine missing	• Defective (open) spark plug wire • Worn or fouled spark plugs • Defective pickup coil • Defective module • Poor electrical connections at the pickup coil and/or module

6. A thorough visual inspection should be performed of all ignition components when diagnosing an engine performance problem.
7. Platinum spark plugs should not be regapped after use in an engine.
8. A secondary ignition scope pattern includes a firing line, spark line, intermediate oscillations, and transistor-on and transistor-off points.
9. The slope of the spark line can indicate incorrect air–fuel ratio or other engine problems.

REVIEW QUESTIONS

1. Explain how 12 volts from a battery can be changed to 40 000 volts for ignition.
2. Discuss how a magnetic sensor works.
3. Discuss how a Hall-effect sensor works.
4. Explain why a spark tester should be used to check for spark rather than using a standard spark plug.
5. Explain how to test a pickup coil for resistance and AC voltage output.
6. Discuss what harm can occur if the engine is cranked or run with an open (defective) spark plug wire.
7. List the sections of a secondary ignition scope pattern.
8. Explain what the slope of the spark line can indicate about the engine.
9. Explain why a coil-on-plug ignition achieves longer spark plug life than DIS waste–spark ignition.

RED SEAL CERTIFICATION-TYPE QUESTIONS

1. Primary ignition current must be controlled to provide both a strong spark and long coil life. An ignition system with fixed dwell may use
    a. A ballast resistor for current control
    b. A current limiting circuit in the module
    c. High primary circuit resistance to limit current
    d. Variable dwell at high RPM

590

    b. A clamp-on spark tester
    c. By measuring the voltage generated
    d. By substituting a known good pickup coil
5. Typical primary coil resistance specifications usually range from ______.
    a. 100 to 450 ohms
    b. 500 to 1500 ohms
    c. 1 to 3 ohms
    d. 6000 to 30 000 ohms
6. Typical secondary coil resistance specifications usually range from ______.
    a. 100 to 450 ohms
    b. 500 to 1500 ohms
    c. 1 to 3 ohms
    d. 6000 to 30 000 ohms
7. An engine does not start. During cranking the fuel injector (electronic fuel injection) sprays fuel. This would indicate
    a. A problem with the pickup coil
    b. Grounding at the Hall-effect switch
    c. An ignition primary pulse is present
    d. The ignition module is triggering the secondary circuit
8. A light coating of anti-seize compound is put onto spark plug threads to reduce seizing in aluminum cylinder heads. The technician must be cautious when tightening the plugs as the compound
    a. May cause cross-threading of the plug
    b. Increases the torque required to tighten the plug
    c. Makes the plugs difficult to remove
    d. Reduces the torque required to tighten the plug
9. An engine can ping (spark knock) if the ignition timing is ______.
    a. Too far advanced
    b. Too far retarded
10. A secondary waveform is being analyzed. It has a lower than normal firing line and a longer than normal spark line on one cylinder. This could indicate
    a. A high resistance spark plug wire
    b. A fouled spark plug
    c. A weak ignition coil
    d. An excessive rotor air gap

The Pearson Education Canada **COMPANION WEBSITE**

A Great Way to Learn and Instruct Online

The Pearson Education Canada Companion Website is easy to navigate and is organized to correspond to the chapters in this textbook. Whether you are a student in the classroom or a distance learner you will discover helpful resources for in-depth study and research that empower you in your quest for greater knowledge and maximize your potential for success in the course.

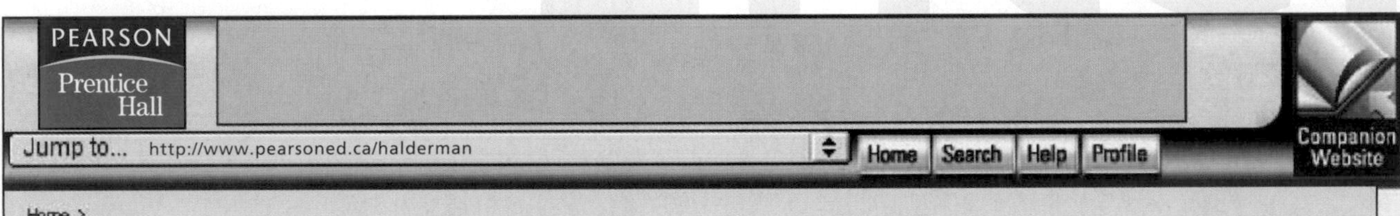

PEARSON Prentice Hall

Jump to... http://www.pearsoned.ca/halderman | Home | Search | Help | Profile

Companion Website

Home >

PH Companion Website

Automotive Technology: Principles, Diagnosis, and Service, Canadian Edition, by Halderman, Mitchell, Marchant, and Davey

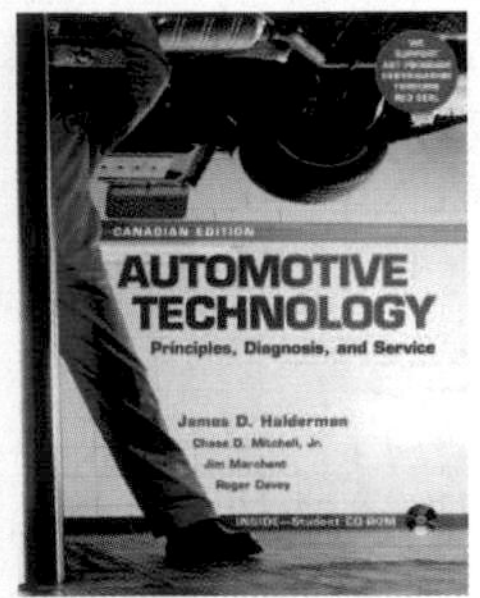

Student Resources

The modules on this section provide learning objectives, practice tests, and web links to help students prepare for the interprovincial Red Seal examination.

Topics covered include

- Engine Repair
- Automatic Transmission/Transaxle
- Manual Drive Trains and Axles
- Suspension and Steering
- Brakes
- Electrical/Electronic Systems
- Heating and Air Conditioning
- Engine Performance

In the practice tests students can send answers to the grader and receive instant feedback on their progress through the Results Reporter.

Instructor Resources

A link to this book on the Pearson Education Canada online catalogue (vig.pearsoned.ca) provides instructors with additional teaching tools. Downloadable PowerPoint Presentations and an Instructor's Manual are just some of the materials that may be available. The catalogue is password protected. To get a password, simply contact your Pearson Education Canada Representative or call Faculty Sales and Services at 1-800-850-5813.

SECTION I

Introduction

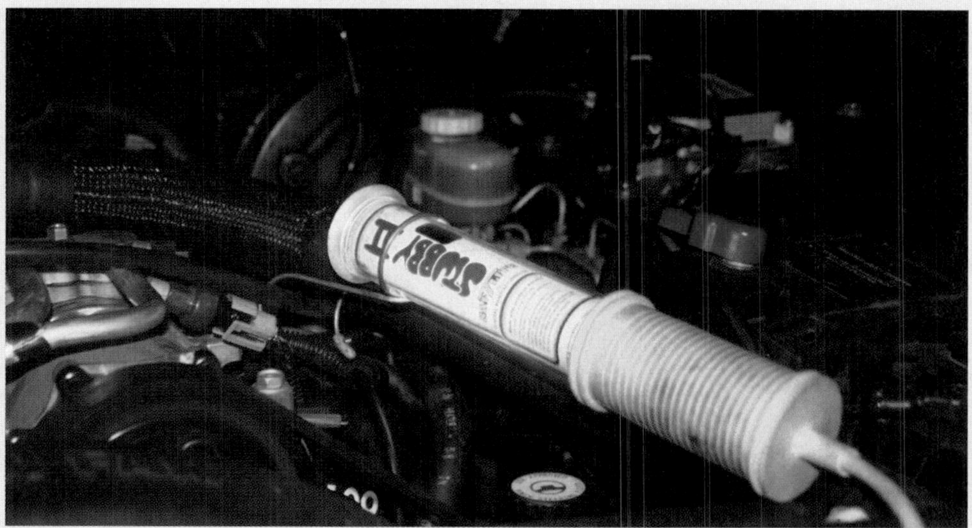

1 The Automotive Service Industry
2 Tools, Fasteners, and Safety
3 Preventative Maintenance and Service Procedures

The introduction to automotive service includes material needed by the beginning service technician that is beyond what is included under the seven areas of the interprovincial (IP) Red Seal certification. Chapter 1 describes the various opportunities within the automotive service industry and introduces terms and procedures used throughout the industry. Chapter 2 includes tools and safety. All basic hand tools are shown as well as information on fasteners and the safe methods of hoisting a vehicle. Chapter 3 describes typical preventative maintenance and service procedures.

1

The Automotive Service Industry

OBJECTIVES: After studying Chapter 1, you should be able to:

1. Prepare for the interprovincial Red Seal certification examination in Appendix I (Engine Repair) on the topics covered in this chapter.
2. Explain the role of the service advisor, shop foreman, and service manager.
3. Describe the role of a service technician.
4. List the various types of automotive service facilities that employ service technicians.
5. Explain how the flat-rate pay plan works.
6. List the flow of parts from the manufacturer to the end customer.

Figure 1–1 Chassis being welded by robotic machinery on an assembly line at Saturn plant. (Courtesy of Saturn Corporation)

The automotive industry is huge. It incorporates new vehicle manufacturing and service as well as maintenance and repair of all of the existing vehicles on the road today.

VEHICLE CONSTRUCTION

Vehicles are assembled in factories (also called *plants*) from parts and components manufactured at other factories. For example, a vehicle may use stamped-steel body panels shipped from a steel-stamping company and then welded into a finished body at the assembly plant. See Figure 1–1.

Assembly plants also have subassembly lines where many smaller components are combined into larger components that are eventually assembled to form the finished vehicle. Examples of a subassembly line include:

- Instrument panel and dash assembly
- Steering column assembly
- Engine and transmission/transaxle assembly

Many component parts of a vehicle are assembled before being installed in a vehicle, which is the reason some parts are difficult to remove after the vehicle has been assembled.

FRAME CONSTRUCTION

Frame construction usually consists of channel- or tube-shaped steel beams welded and/or fastened

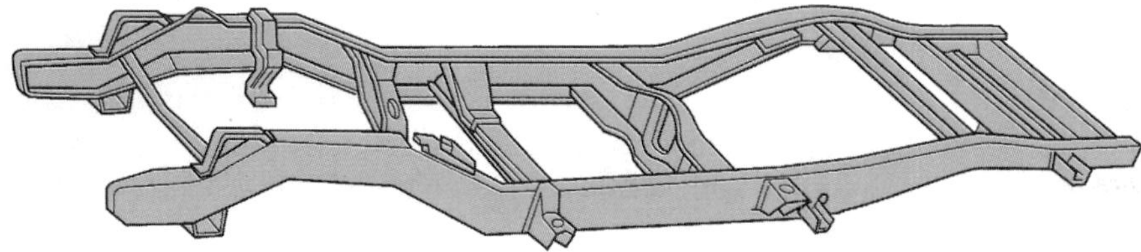

Figure 1–2 Typical frame of a vehicle.

together. Vehicles with a separate frame and body are usually called body-on-frame vehicles (BOF) or full-frame vehicles. Many terms are used to label or describe the frame of a vehicle including:

Ladder Frame

A ladder frame is a common name for a type of perimeter frame where the transverse connecting members are straight across, as in Figure 1–2.

Perimeter Frame

A perimeter frame consists of welded or riveted frame members around the entire perimeter of the body. See Figure 1–3.

Stub-Type Frames

A stub frame is a partial frame often used on unit-body vehicles to support the power train and suspension components. This frame is also called a *cradle* on many front-wheel drive vehicles. See Figure 1–4.

UNIT-BODY CONSTRUCTION

Unit-body construction (sometimes called *unibody*) is a design that combines the body with the structure of the frame. The body is composed of many individual stamped-steel panels welded together. The strength of this type of construction lies in the *shape* of the assembly. The typical vehicle uses 300 separate stamped-steel panels that are spot-welded together to form a vehicle's body. See Figure 1–5.

Figure 1–3 Perimeter frame.

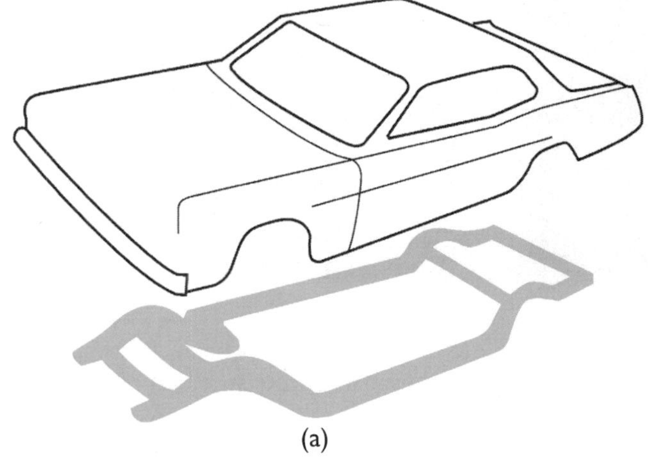

(a)

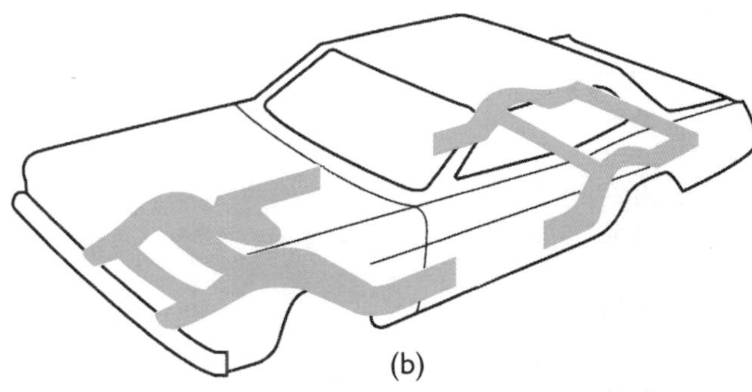

(b)

Figure 1–4 (a) Separate body and frame construction. (b) Unitized construction—the small frame members are for support of the engine and suspension components. Many vehicles attach the suspension components directly to the reinforced sections of the body and do not require the rear frame section.

> **NOTE:** A typical vehicle contains about 10 000 separate individual parts.

SPACE-FRAME CONSTRUCTION

Space-frame construction consists of formed sheet steel used to construct a framework of the entire vehicle. The vehicle is driveable without the body, which uses plastic or steel panels to cover the steel framework. See Figure 1–6.

Figure 1–5 Note the ribbing and the many different pieces of sheet metal used in the construction of this body.

VEHICLE ASSEMBLY

After the body and chassis are constructed, the other vehicle components are assembled to form a completed vehicle. The sequence of assembly usually includes:

1. Attaching the suspension to the frame or subframe
2. Completing the body with the interior, dash, seats, and all wiring
3. Attaching the engine to the frame (if a body-on-frame vehicle) or installing it into the body (if unit-body construction)
4. Attaching all other parts and components such as wheels and tires, front grill, hood, and fenders
5. Starting and driving the completed vehicle off the assembly line into an area where the wheel alignment is checked and adjusted as necessary and then "driving" the vehicle on rollers where it is driven through its normal operating range of gears and speeds while the vehicle computer is checked to be sure everything is okay
6. Loading the vehicles onto rail cars or transport trucks to be delivered to the local new vehicle dealers

Figure 1–6 A Corvette without the body. Notice that the vehicle is complete enough to be driven. This photo was taken at the Corvette Museum in Bowling Green, Kentucky.

VEHICLE DEALER PREPARATION

When a new vehicle arrives at the dealership, it must be cleaned and made ready for sale. See Figure 1–7. This process is usually called *pre-delivery inspection* and involves removing all of the protective plastic and installing the components such as wheel covers, floor mats, etc. that are not installed until the vehicle is ready to sell.

VEHICLE SERVICE JOBS

There are many jobs in the vehicle service industry. In smaller service facilities, the duties of many positions may be combined in one job. A large city dealership may have all of the following vehicle service positions.

Service Advisor

A service advisor, also called a **service writer,** is the person at the dealership or service facility designated to communicate the needs of the customer and accurately complete a **repair order.** A repair order is often referred to as an **R.O.** or a **work order.** See Figure 1–8 for an example of a typical R.O. A typical service advisor is not a service technician but is usually a person who can easily talk with people and accurately write on the R.O. exactly what the customer needs or says about how the vehicle is acting. See Figure 1–9. The service advisor's duties include

1. Recording the vehicle identification number (**VIN**) of the vehicle on the R.O.
2. Recording the make, model, year, and mileage on the R.O.
3. Carefully recording what the customer's complaint (concern) is so that the service technician can verify the complaint and make the proper repair
4. Keeping the customer informed as to the progress of the service work

Service Technician

An R.O. is assigned to a technician who is best qualified to perform the work. The technician gets the keys and drives the vehicle to an assigned **service bay** (also called a **stall**), gets the necessary parts from the parts department, and completes the repair. The vehicle is then driven by the service technician to verify the repair.

Shop Foreman

A shop foreman (usually employed in larger dealerships and vehicle repair facilities) is an experienced service technician who is usually paid a salary (so

Figure 1-7 A typical auto service department. (Courtesy of Roger Davey)

HOME TOWN PONTIAC
100 N. MAIN ST.

8993

COST		QUAN.	PART NUMBER / DESCRIPTION	PRICE	
		1	Battery Interstate 60 Month Battery	74	00
		1	Oil filter	11	25
		1	Air filter	36	59
		1	Seal Ring		25
		1	Ant Mast	67	97
				190	06
			ALL PARTS ARE NEW UNLESS SPECIFIED OTHERWISE		
			SUBLET REPAIRS		
			GALS. GAS @		
			QTS. OIL @		
			LBS. GREASE @		
			TOTAL GAS - OIL - GREASE		

NAME: MR CUSTOMER — DATE RECEIVED: 1/9/97
ADDRESS: 444 W. 3rd St. — COMPLETION DATE
CITY — STATE — ZIP — MILEAGE IN: 52084
VIN: 1G2NW51A6SC201 — ENGINE NO.: 3.1 V-6 — MAKE: PONTIAC — MILEAGE OUT
TYPE OR MODEL: GRAND AM — YEAR: 98 — LICENSE NUMBER: BQU449 — PHONE WHEN READY: YES ☐ NO ☐
TERMS — ORDER ACCEPTED BY — PHONE

	LABOR CHARGE	
LUBRICATE ☐		
CHANGE OIL ☐		
CHANGE OIL FILTER CART. ☐		
CHANGE TRANS. OIL ☐		
CHANGE DIFF. OIL ☐		
PACK FRONT WHEEL BRGS. ☐		
ADJUST BRAKES ☐		
X TIRES ☐		
WASH ☐		
SAFETY INSPECTION ☐		

OPER. NO.	INSTRUCTIONS:		
1.0	45 K Service	450	00
.6	Check Battery Replace	22	50
.5	Ant Mast	22	50
.5	Check left front Headlight	22	50

REPLACED PARTS WILL BE RETURNED FOR YOUR INSPECTION. IF YOU DO NOT WANT THEM, PLEASE CHECK THE BLOCK BELOW.
☐ DISCARD REPLACED PARTS

I hereby authorize the repair work herein set forth to be done by you, together with the furnishing by you of the necessary parts and other material for such repair, and agree: that you are not responsible for any delays caused by unavailability or delayed availability of parts or material for any reason; that you neither assume nor authorize any other person to assume for you any liability in connection with such repair; that you shall not be responsible for loss of or damage to the above vehicle, or articles left therein, in case of fire, theft or other cause beyond your control; that an express mechanic's lien is hereby acknowledged on the above vehicle to secure the amount of repairs thereto; that your employees may operate the above vehicle on streets, highways or elsewhere for the purpose of testing and/or inspecting such vehicle.
I HEREBY ACKNOWLEDGE RECEIPT OF A COPY HEREOF.
X ______

ESTIMATE
(UNDER OHIO LAW) YOU HAVE THE RIGHT TO AN ESTIMATE IF THE EXPECTED COST OF REPAIRS OR SERVICES WILL BE MORE THAN TWENTY-FIVE DOLLARS. INITIAL YOUR CHOICE.
____ WRITTEN ESTIMATE ____ ORAL ESTIMATE
____ I DO NOT REQUEST AN ESTIMATE

DISCLAIMER OF WARRANTIES
THE SELLER, HEREBY EXPRESSLY DISCLAIMS ALL WARRANTIES, EITHER EXPRESSED OR IMPLIED, INCLUDING ANY IMPLIED WARRANTY OF MERCHANTABILITY OR FITNESS FOR A PARTICULAR PURPOSE, AND NEITHER ASSUMES NOR AUTHORIZES ANY OTHER PERSON TO ASSUME FOR IT ANY LIABILITY IN CONNECTION WITH THE SALE OF SAID PRODUCTS.

ORIGINAL ESTIMATE $ ______ — CUSTOMERS ACCEPTANCE ______ INITIAL HERE
AUTHORIZED ADDITIONS $ ______ — DATE ______ TIME ______ BY ______

In the event that you, the customer, authorize commencement but do not authorize completion of a repair or service, a charge will be imposed for disassembly, reassembly or partially completed work. Such charge will be directly related to the actual amount of labor or parts involved in the inspection, repair or service.

		SALE	
TOTAL LABOR		517	50
TOTAL PARTS		190	06
GAS, OIL & GREASE			
SUBLET REPAIRS			
		707	56
TAX	6.5%	45	99
TOTAL		753	55

Figure 1–8 Typical repair order (RO). (Courtesy of The Reynolds and Reynolds Company)

much a week, month, or year). Typical shop foreman duties include:

- Test driving the customer's vehicles to verify the customer complaint
- Assigning work to the service technicians
- Assisting the service technicians
- Assisting the service manager
- Verifying that the repair is completed satisfactorily

Service Manager

The service manager rarely works on a vehicle but instead organizes the service facility and keeps it operating smoothly. The service manager typically handles all of the paper work associated with operating a service department. Typical service manager's duties include:

- Establishing guidelines to determine the technician's efficiency
- Supervising any warranty claims submitted to the vehicle manufacturer
- Evaluating and budgeting for shop tools and equipment
- Establishing service department hours of operation and employee schedules
- Assigning working hours and pay for technicians and others in the service department
- Service department promotions

Parts Manager

The parts manager and other parts personnel such as the parts **counter person** are responsible for getting the correct part for the service technician. The specific duties of a parts manager usually include:

- Ordering parts from the vehicle manufacturers and aftermarket companies
- Organizing the parts department in a clear and orderly fashion

Figure 1–9 A service advisor, also called a service writer or service consultant, is the person that greets the customers and prepares the repair order for the service technician. Note that this service advisor is wearing a cordless telephone and is therefore always in touch regardless of where he is in and around the dealership.

- Developing contacts with parts departments in other local dealerships so that parts that are not in stock can be purchased quickly and at a reasonable cost

TECHNICIAN WORK SITES

Service technician work takes place in a variety of work sites including:

New Vehicle Dealerships

Most dealerships handle one or more brands of vehicle, and the technician employed at dealerships usually has to meet minimum training standards. The training is usually provided at no cost to the technician at regional training centres. The dealer usually pays the service technician for the day(s) spent in training as well as provides or pays for transportation, meals, and lodging. See Figure 1–10.

Figure 1–10 A service technician working on the brakes of a vehicle in a new-vehicle dealership service department. (Courtesy of Ogle-Tucker Buick)

Independent Service Facilities

These small- to medium-size repair facilities usually work on a variety of vehicles. Technicians employed at independent service facilities usually have to depend on aftermarket manufacturers' seminars or the local vocational school or college to keep technically up-to-date. See Figure 1–11.

Figure 1–11 A typical independent service facility. Independent garages often work on a variety of vehicles and perform many different types of vehicle repairs and service. Some independent garages specialize in just one or two areas of service work or in just one or two makes of vehicles.

Mass Merchandiser

Large national chains of vehicle repair facilities are common in most medium- and large-size cities. Some examples of these chains include Canadian Tire, Sears, Goodyear, and Firestone, as shown in Figure 1–12. Technicians employed by these chains usually work on a wide variety of vehicles. Many of the companies have their own local or regional training sites designed to train beginning service

Figure 1-12 An auto parts store may also have a garage for service work. (Courtesy of Roger Davey)

technicians and to provide update training for existing technicians.

Specialty Service Facilities

Specialty service facilities usually limit their service work to selected systems or components of the vehicle and/or to a particular brand of vehicle. Examples of specialty service facilities include Midas, Speedy, and Mister Transmission. Many of the franchised specialty facilities have their own technician training for both beginning and advanced technicians.

Fleet Facilities

Many city, county, and provincial governments have their own vehicle service facilities for the maintenance and repair of their vehicles. Service technicians are usually employees of the city, county, or province and are usually paid by the hour rather than on a commission basis.

TECHNICIAN PAY METHODS

Straight-Time Pay

When the particular service or repair is not covered or mentioned in a flat-rate guide, it is common practice for the technician to **clock-in** and use the actual time spent on the repair as a basis for payment. The technician uses a flat-rate time ticket and a time clock to record the actual time. Being paid for the actual time spent is often called **straight time** or **clock time.** Difficult engine-performance repairs are often calculated using the technician's straight time.

Flat-Rate Pay Methods

Beginning service technicians are usually paid by the hour. The hourly rate can vary greatly depending on the experience of the technician and type of work being performed. Most experienced service technicians are paid by a method called **flat-rate.** The flat-rate method of pay is also called **incentive** or **commission pay.** "Flat-rate" means that the technician is paid a set amount of time (flat-rate) for every service operation. The amount of time allocated is published in a flat-rate manual. For example, if a bumper requires replacement, the flat-rate manual may call for 1.0 hour (time is always expressed in tenths of an hour). The service technician would therefore get paid one hour of pay regardless of how long it actually took to complete the job. Often, the technician can "beat flat-rate" by performing the operation in less time than the published time. It is therefore important that the technician not waste time and work efficiently to get paid the most for a day's work. The technician also has to be careful to perform the service procedure correctly because if the job needs to be done again due to an error, the technician does the repair at no pay. Therefore, the technician needs to be both fast and careful at the same time.

The vehicle manufacturer determines the flat-rate for each labour operation by having a team of technicians perform the operation several times. The average of all of these times is often published as the allocated time. The flat-rate method was originally developed to determine a fair and equitable way to pay dealerships for covered warranty repairs. Because the labour rate differs throughout the country, a fixed dollar amount would not be fair compensation. However, if a time could be established for each operation, then the vehicle manufacturer could reimburse the dealership for the set number of hours multiplied by the labour rate approved for that dealership. For example, if the approved labor rate is \$60.00 per hour and:

Technician A performed
6.2 hours × \$60.00 = \$372.00
Technician B performed
4.8 hours × \$60.00 = \$288.00
The total paid to the dealership
by the manufacturer = \$660.00

Does this mean that the service technician gets paid \$60.00 per hour? Sorry, no! This means that the dealership gets reimbursed for labour at the \$60.00 per hour rate. The service technician usually gets paid a lot less than half of the total labour charge.

Depending on the part of the country and the size of the dealership and community, the technician's flat-rate per hour income can vary from \$10.00 to \$25.00 or more per flat-rate hour. Remember, a high pay rate (\$25 for example) does not necessarily mean that the service technician will be earning \$1000.00 per week (40 hours × \$25.00 per hour = \$1000.00). If the dealership is not busy or it is a slow time of year, maybe the technician will only have the opportunity to "turn" 20 hours per week. So it is not really the pay rate that determines what a technician will earn but rather a combination of all of the following:

- Pay rate
- Number of service repairs performed
- Skill and speed of the service technician
- Type of service work (a routine brake service may be completed faster and more easily than a difficult engine performance problem)

A service technician earns more at a busy dealership with a lower pay rate than at a smaller or less busy dealership with a higher pay rate.

Customer Pay

Customer pay (CP) means that the customer will be paying for the service work at a dealership rather than the warranty. Often the same factory flat-rate number of hours is used to calculate the technician's pay, but CP often pays the service technician at a higher rate. For example, a service technician earning $15.00 per flat-rate hour for warranty work may be paid $18.00 per hour for CP work. Obviously, service technicians prefer to work on vehicles that require CP service work rather than factory-warranty service work.

Nondealership Flat-Rate

Technicians who work for independent service facilities or at other nondealership locations use one or both of the following to set rates of pay:

- *Mitchell Parts and Time Guide*
- *Motors Parts and Time Guide*

Both of these guides contain service operation and flat-rate times. Generally, these are about 20% higher (longer) than those specified by the factory flat rate to compensate for rust or corrosion and other factors of time and mileage that often lengthen the time necessary to complete a repair. Again, the service technician is usually paid a dollar amount per flat-rate hour based on one of these aftermarket flat-rate guides. The guides also provide a list price for the parts for each vehicle. This information allows the service advisor to accurately estimate the total cost of the repair.

Additional Service Technician Benefits

Many larger dealerships and service facilities often offer some or all of the following:

- Paid uniforms/cleaning
- Vacation time
- Update training (especially new vehicle dealerships)
- Some sort of retirement program
- Health and dental insurance (usually not fully paid)
- Discounts on parts and vehicles purchased at the dealership or shop

Not all service facilities offer all of these additional benefits.

Frequently Asked Question ???

What Can a Service Technician Do to Earn More Money?

Because service technicians are paid on a commission basis (flat-rate), the more work that is completed, the more hours the technician can "turn." Therefore, to earn the most money, the service technician could do the following to increase the amount of work performed:

- Keep up-to-date and learn the latest technical information
- Practice good habits that help avoid errors or incomplete repairs
- Learn from experienced and successful fellow technicians and try to approach the repair the same way the successful technician does
- Purchase the proper tools to do the work efficiently

NOTE: This does not mean that every technician needs to purchase all possible tools. Purchase only those tools that you know you will need and use.

FLAGGING AN R.O.

When a service technician completes a service procedure or repair, a sticker is completed indicating the following:

- Technician number (number rather than a name is often used not only to shorten the identification but also to shield the actual identity of the technician from the customer)
- R.O. number
- Amount of time allocated to the repair expressed in hours and tenths of an hour

The application of the service technician's sticker to the back of the R.O. is often called **flagging the R.O.**

NOTE: The actual assignment of the time is often done by another person at the dealership or service facility. This procedure assures that the correct number of hours is posted to the R.O. and to the technician's ticket.

SUBLET REPAIRS

Often a repair (or a part of a repair) is performed by another person or company outside the dealership or service facility. For example, an engine needing repair that also has a defective or leaking radiator would be repaired by the original repair facility, but the radiator might be sent to a specialty radiator repair shop. The radiator repair cost is then entered on the R.O. as a sublet repair.

PARTS REPLACEMENT

Parts replacement is often called **R & R,** meaning **remove and replace.**

NOTE: R & R can also mean **remove and repair,** but this meaning is generally not used as much now as it used to be when components such as starters and air conditioning compressors were repaired rather than replaced as an assembly.

R & I is often used to indicate **remove and inspect** to check a component for damage. The old replaced part is often returned for remanufacturing and is called a **core.** A **core charge** is often charged by parts stores when a new (or remanufactured) part is purchased. This core charge usually represents the value of the old component. Because it is needed by the remanufacturer as a starting point for the remanufacturing process, the core charge is also an incentive to return the old part for credit (or refund) of the core charge.

Original Equipment Parts

Parts at a new vehicle dealership come either directly from the vehicle manufacturer or a regional dealership. If one dealership purchases from another dealership, the cost of the part is higher, but no waiting is required. If a dealership orders a part from the manufacturer directly, the cost is lower, but there is often a seven- to ten-day waiting period. **Original equipment** parts, abbreviated **OE,** are generally of the highest quality because they have to meet performance and durability standards not required of replacement parts manufacturers.

NOTE: Many service technicians will use only OE parts for certain critical systems such as fuel injection and ignition system components because, in their experience, even though the price is often higher, the extra quality seems to be worth the cost not only to the owner of the vehicle but also to the service technician, who does not have to worry about having to replace the same part twice.

Aftermarket Parts

Parts manufactured to be sold for use after the vehicle is made are often referred to as **aftermarket parts** or **renewal parts.** Most aftermarket parts are sold at automotive parts stores or **jobbers.** A jobber or parts retailer usually gets parts from a large regional **warehouse distributor.** The warehouse distributor can either purchase parts directly from the manufacturer or from an even larger central warehouse. Because each business needs to make a profit (typically, 35%), the cost to the end user may not be lower than it is for the same part purchased at a dealership (a two-step process instead of the typical three-step process) even though it costs more to manufacture the original equipment part. To determine what a 35% margin increase is for any product, simply divide the cost by 0.65. To illustrate how this works, look at the chart below and compare the end cost of a part (part A) from a dealership and a parts store.

NOTE: The cost of the part to the customer where service work is performed is increased about 35% over the base cost of the part. For example, a part that cost the repair facility $40.23 will be billed to the customer at about $60.00. The retail service customer at the dealer may pay $59.17 ($38.46 ÷ 0.65 = $59.17).

New Versus Remanufactured Parts

New parts are manufactured from raw materials and have never been used on a vehicle. A remanu-

Retail Parts Store (for Part A)	New Vehicle Dealership (for Part A)
Manufacturer's selling price = $17.00	Manufacturer's selling price = $25.00
Warehouse distributor's selling price = $26.15 ($17.00 ÷ 0.65 = $26.15)	Parts department selling price = $38.46 ($25.00 ÷ 0.65 = $38.46)
Retail store selling price = $40.23 ($26.15 ÷ 0.65 = $40.23)	

factured component (also called **rebuilt**) has been used on a vehicle until the component wore out or failed. A remanufacturer totally disassembles the component, cleans, machines, and performs all the necessary steps to restore the part to a "like new" look and function. If properly remanufactured, the component can be expected to deliver the same length of service as a new component part.

The cost of a remanufactured component is often less than the cost of a new part.

CAUTION: Do not always assume that a remanufactured component is less expensive than a new component. Due to the three-step distribution process, the final cost to the end user (you) may be close to the same!

Used Parts

Used parts offer another alternative to either new or remanufactured parts. The cost of a used component is typically one-half the cost of the component if purchased new. Wrecking and salvage yards use a Hollander manual that lists original equipment part numbers and cost and cross-references them to other parts that are the same.

TECHNICIAN CERTIFICATION IN CANADA

Apprenticeship is one of the oldest ways of combining formal education and practical training. Over the years, it has adopted the term "earn while you learn" because the student moves between the classroom and job-site training throughout the course of the contract. By completing both on-the-job and classroom training, a student in Canada can become a certified journeyperson and receive a Certificate of Qualification.

In Canada, apprenticeship training is the responsibility of individual provinces or territories under the term "designated trades." For this reason, apprenticeship programs will differ slightly from province to province. In some instances, training is completely funded whereas in other provinces, the student and employer each pay a portion. Provincial regulations outline the terms and conditions of the training as well as the various methods of registration, curriculum, certification, and accreditation; they also determine what occupations will be designated for apprenticeship.

About 15% of the overall training is provided in a training institution. The in-school training is offered in various formats. It is possible to attend school for as little as one day per week over the course of a year or as much as every day for a series of weeks. Some provinces offer distance-education delivery through correspondence or on-line learning. The in-school hours vary from 480 to 620 hours, depending on the province or territory. The total length of time a student will be studying/working as an apprentice ranges from 3 to 5 years, depending on the student.

Once the student has achieved the in-school and on-site requirements of the program, the next and final step in most jurisdictions is to apply to write the Interprovincial Standards Examination. If a mark of 70% or more is achieved, the student will receive a Certificate of Qualification bearing the Interprovincial Red Seal. In all provinces and territories except Quebec and Nunavut, the Interprovincial Red Seal Certificate is required.

The Red Seal program was established to give Canadian skilled workers more mobility. The Red Seal allows qualified trades persons to practice their trade in any province or territory in Canada where the trade is designated, without having to write further examinations. Red Seal examinations are administered through the provincial and territorial certificate and apprenticeship offices. For more detailed province-specific information contact your local provincial government website or the federal government site for Red Seal trades at http://www.red-seal.ca.

SAFETY TIP 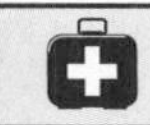

Infection Control Precautions

Working on a vehicle can result in personal injury, including the possibility of being cut or hurt enough to cause bleeding. Some infections such as hepatitis B, HIV (which can cause acquired immunodeficiency syndrome AIDS), hepatitis C virus, and others are transmitted in the blood. These infections are commonly called **bloodborne pathogens.** Report any injury that involves blood to your supervisor and take the necessary precautions to avoid coming in contact with blood from another person.

NOTE: A valid driver's licence is a must for any automotive service technician, as is a high school graduation diploma, or equivalent.

TECH TIP

Work Habit Hints

The following statements reflect the expectations of service managers or shop owners for their technicians:

1. Report to work every day on time. Being several minutes early every day is an easy way to show your service manager and fellow technicians that you are serious about your job and career.
2. If you *must* be late or absent, call your service manager as soon as possible.
3. Keep busy. If not assigned to a specific job, ask what activities the service manager or supervisor wants you to do.
4. Report any mistakes or accidents *immediately* to your supervisor or team leader. *Never* allow a customer to be the first to discover a mistake.
5. Never lie to your employer or to a customer.
6. Always return any borrowed tools as soon as you are done with them and in *clean* condition. *Show* the person you borrowed the tools from that you are returning them to the toolbox or workbench.
7. Keep your work area neat and orderly.
8. Always use fender covers when working under the hood.
9. Double check your work to be sure that everything is correct.
   - **a.** Remember: "If you are forcing something, you are probably doing something wrong."
   - **b.** Ask for help if unclear as to what to do or how to do it.
10. Do not smoke in a customer's vehicle.
11. Avoid profanity.
12. DO NOT TOUCH THE RADIO! If the radio is turned on and prevents you from hearing noises, turn the volume down. Try to return the vehicle to the owner with the radio at the same volume as originally set.

> **NOTE:** Some shops have a policy that requires employees to turn the radio off.

13. Keep yourself neatly groomed including:
    - **a.** Shirt tail tucked into pants
    - **b.** Daily bathing and use of deodorant
    - **c.** Clean hair, regular haircuts, and hair tied back if long
    - **d.** Men: daily shave or keep beard and/or mustache neatly trimmed
    - **e.** Women: make-up and jewellery kept to a minimum

AUTOMOTIVE SERVICE TECHNICIAN 310S

Interprovincial Red Seal Certificate of Qualification Examination

Examination Plan

Summary	
1. Work Practices, Procedures and Safety in the Workplace	7%
2. Internal Combustion Engine	14%
3. Engine Management System	22%
4. Drive Line System	14%
5. Electrical, Electronic and Emission Control Systems	20%
6. Steering, Suspension and Brake Systems	18%
7. Body Hardware Trim and Accessories	5%

The Certification of Qualification examination evaluates ability to perform skills within the trade. As a designated Red Seal trade, the Automotive Service Technician examination is based on the skills as identified and agreed to by all participating provinces and territories.

Both metric and imperial measurements may be used. (You will not be required to convert the measurements from one system to the other.)

> **NOTE:** This document is subject to change. You may wish to contact the local Apprenticeship office to confirm that this exam plan is current. However, you will receive the current exam plan when you schedule to write the exam.

Section	Title	Percentage
1	**Work Practices, Procedures and Safety** • Safe working practices • Preliminary diagnosis • Accesses service manuals • Operates hand, cutting and power tools, and shop equipment • Welds	7%
2	**Internal Combustion Engine** • Inspects/tests/repairs valve train components, cylinder block assemblies and engine cooling systems • Installs engines	14%
3	**Engine Management System** • Inspects/tests/repairs emission control systems, ignition systems, fuel delivery systems, air induction systems and diesel fuel systems.	22%
4	**Drive Line System** • Inspects/tests/repairs automatic transmissions/transaxles, clutches, manual transmission/transaxles, transfer cases, drive lines and differentials.	14%
5	**Electrical, Electronic and Emission Control Systems** • Tests/replaces batteries • Inspects/tests/repairs electrical, electronic and emission control systems	20%
6	**Steering, Suspension and Brake Systems** • Inspects/tests/repairs braking systems; tires, wheels, steering linkages; suspension systems; power steering gears; and steering columns	18%
7	**Body Hardware Trim and Accessories** • Inspects/repairs trim and body hardware • Installs and services accessories	5%

TYPES OF JOBS IN THE AUTOMOTIVE SERVICE INDUSTRY

There is a wide variety of jobs in the automotive service industry depending on the type of service facility.

New Vehicle Dealerships

- New vehicle preparation duties usually include:
  1. Removing plastic protective coverings
  2. Washing the vehicle
  3. Installing roof racks, running boards, or other add-on or dealer-installed options
- Routine service technician duties usually include:
  1. Changing oil and oil filters
  2. Lubricating the chassis
  3. Checking tire pressure
  4. Helping other service technicians
- Used vehicle technician duties usually include:
  1. Repairing all types of faults including interior and mechanical components
  2. Cleaning or detailing the exterior and interior of a vehicle
  3. Performing routine service checks
- Specialist (journey-level) technician (experienced service technician) duties are limited only by the knowledge, skills, and interests of the technician. In larger dealerships, there may be specialists in the following areas:
  1. Engine repair
  2. Automatic transmissions
  3. Steering, suspension, and alignment
  4. Electrical
  5. Engine performance and driveability
  6. Other areas that may be seasonal such as air conditioning

Independent Service Facilities

Because the work at independent service facilities involves many different types of work on a wide variety of vehicles, the beginning technician is usually

TECH TIP 

How to Become an Entrepreneur

An entrepreneur is a person who organizes and manages his or her own business, assuming the risk for the sake of a profit. Many service technicians have the desire to own their own repair facility. The wise business owner (entrepreneur) seeks the advice of the following people when starting and operating a business.

- **Attorney (lawyer)**—This professional will help guide you to make sure that your employees and your customers are protected by community, provincial, and federal regulations.
- **Accountant**—This professional will help you with the journals and records that must be kept by all businesses and help you with elements such as payroll taxes, unemployment taxes, and workmen's compensation that all businesses have to pay.
- **Insurance agent**—This professional will help you select the coverage needed to protect you and your business from major losses.

assigned routine service procedures that can be quickly learned and mastered, such as

- Oil and oil filter changes
- Tire repair, mounting, balancing, and rotation
- Assisting other technicians performing a wide variety of service work

PAYROLL TAXES AND DEDUCTIONS

Gross earnings are the total amount you earned during the pay period. The paycheck you receive will be for an amount called **net** earnings. Taxes and deductions that are taken from your paycheck may include all or most of the following:

- Employment Insurance deductions
- Federal income tax
- Provincial income tax
- Health/dental/eye insurance deductions
- Canada Pension Plan deductions

In addition to the above, uniform costs, savings plan deductions, parts account deductions, as well as weekly payments for tools, may also reduce the amount of your net or "take home" pay.

SUMMARY

1. Vehicle designs include frame, unit-body, and space-frame construction. A full-frame vehicle is often stronger and quieter and permits the towing of heavier loads. Unit-body and space-frame designs are often lighter and more fuel efficient.
2. Vehicle assembly does not necessarily follow the same sequence as would be followed by a service technician while servicing a vehicle. For example, during assembly the engine is usually attached to the chassis before the body is attached. In the field, it is normal for the engine to be removed from a vehicle without having to remove the body.
3. The service advisor writes down what service work the customer says is needed on a repair order, commonly abbreviated R.O.
4. A service technician performs the service work as specified on the repair order.
5. A shop foreman is usually the most highly skilled technician in the shop and is usually assigned to help other technicians and the service manager.
6. A service manager handles all personnel and organizational details of the service facility.
7. Service technicians can work in new vehicle dealerships, independent service facilities, mass merchandisers, specialty service facilities, or fleet facilities.
8. Service technicians are usually paid by the hour (sometimes called *straight time*), on commission, or by the flat-rate method. The flat-rate method pays the service technician a fixed amount for each repair regardless of how long it actually takes to complete.
9. Parts replacement is often called R & R, meaning *remove and replace.*
10. The U.S. National Institute for Automotive Service Excellence, usually abbreviated ASE, sets the internationally known standards for vehicle service technician certification.
11. Service work varies depending on the type of business (dealership, independent garage, etc.) as well as the skill level of the technician.

REVIEW QUESTIONS

1. Describe the type of vehicle construction that would be best to have for towing a large trailer and explain why.
2. List the steps that are followed to assemble a new body-on-frame vehicle.
3. List the duties of the service advisor.
4. Explain the difference in duties between a shop foreman and the service manager.
5. Describe how a service technician gets paid on the flat-rate pay plan.

■ RED SEAL CERTIFICATION-TYPE QUESTIONS

1. What does unit-body construction utilize?
   a. Ladder frame
   b. Stub frame
   c. Body and frame combined
   d. Space frame
2. A customer explains what needs to be serviced to the ___________.
   a. Shop foreman
   b. Service manager
   c. Service advisor
   d. Service technician
3. Which pay method is best suited financially for a technician who can perform repairs effectively and efficiently?
   a. Straight time
   b. Flat rate
   c. Customer pay
   d. Warranty repairs
4. The customer usually only talks to the ___________.
   a. Shop foreman
   b. Service manager
   c. Service advisor
   d. Service technician
5. What type of repair facility would work on all brands and vehicle systems?
   a. Dealerships
   b. Specialty repair shops
   c. Wholesale ports distributors
   d. Independent service facility
6. Midas, Speedy, and Mister Transmission are examples of ___________.
   a. An independent service facility
   b. A mass merchandiser
   c. A specialty service facility
   d. A fleet facility
7. A service technician gets paid 4 hours for repair. The shop rate is $100 per hour; the technician gets paid 30% of the shop rate. How much does the technician get paid?
   a. $100
   b. $90
   c. $140
   d. $120
8. How many skills sections will the technician be tested on when writing the interprovincial Red Seal exam?
   a. 1
   b. 7
   c. 10
   d. 5
9. Customer pay usually pays more to the service technician than does warranty work.
   a. True
   b. False
10. Who should the apprentice approach for technical information?
   a. Shop foreman
   b. Service advisor
   c. Parts manager
   d. Service manager

2

Tools, Fasteners, and Safety

OBJECTIVES: After studying Chapter 2, you should be able to:

1. Prepare for the interprovincial Red Seal certification examination in Appendix I (Engine Repair) on the topics covered in this chapter.
2. Explain the strength ratings of threaded fasteners
3. Identify hazardous materials
4. Describe how to safely hoist a vehicle
5. Discuss how to safely use hand tools

THREADED FASTENERS

Most of the threaded fasteners used on engines are cap screws. They are called **cap screws** when they are threaded into a casting. Automotive service technicians usually refer to these fasteners as **bolts,** regardless of how they are used. In this chapter, they are called bolts. Sometimes, studs are used for threaded fasteners. A **stud** is a short rod with threads on both ends. Often, a stud will have coarse threads on one end and fine threads on the other end. The end of the stud with coarse threads is screwed into the casting. A nut is used on the opposite end to hold the parts together. See Figure 2–1.

The fastener threads *must* match the threads in the casting or nut. The threads may be measured either in millimetres or in fractions of an inch (called fractional). The size is measured across the outside of the threads, called the **crest** of the thread.

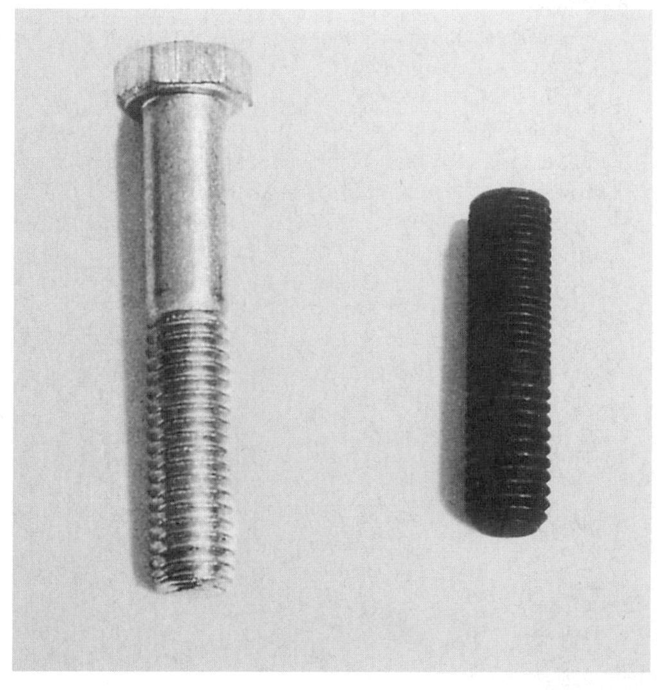

Figure 2–1 Typical bolt on the left and stud on the right. Note the different thread pitch on the top and bottom portions of the stud.

Fractional threads are either coarse or fine. The coarse threads are called Unified National Coarse (UNC), and the fine threads are called Unified National Fine (UNF). Standard combinations of sizes and number of threads per inch (called **pitch**) are used. Pitch can be measured with a thread pitch gauge as shown in Figure 2–2. Bolts are identified by their diameter and length as measured from below the head as shown in Figure 2–3.

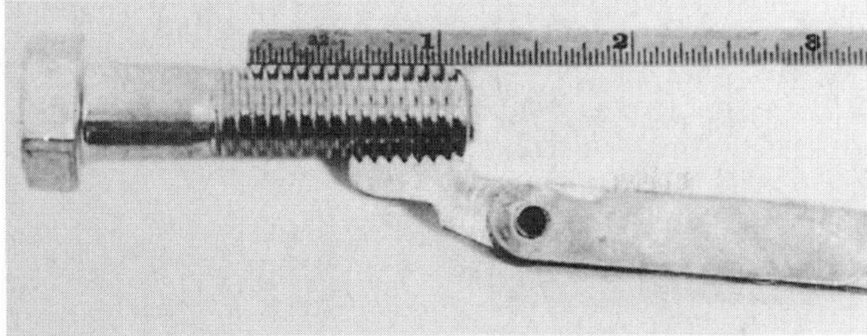

Figure 2–2 Thread pitch gauge used to measure the pitch of the thread. This is a ½-inch-diameter bolt with 13 threads to the inch (½-13).

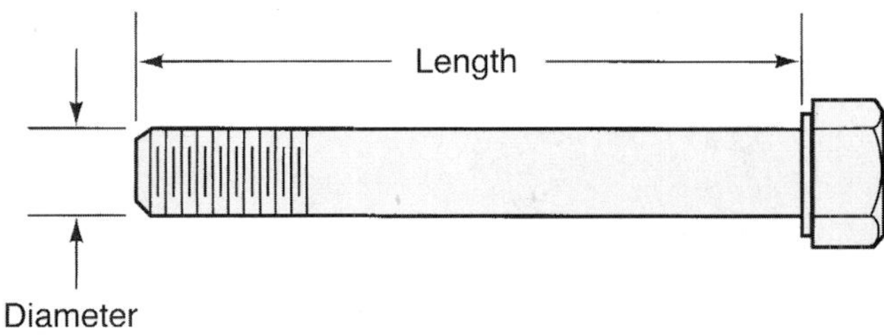

Figure 2–3 Bolt size identification.

Fractional thread sizes are specified by the diameter in fractions of an inch and the number of threads per inch. Typical UNC thread sizes would be 5⁄16-18 and ½-13. Similar UNF thread sizes would be 5⁄16-24 and ½-20.

METRIC BOLTS

The size of a metric bolt is specified by the letter *M* followed by the diameter in millimetres (mm) across the outside (crest) of the threads. Typical metric sizes would be M8 and M12. Fine metric threads are specified by the thread diameter followed by *X* and the distance between the threads measured in millimetres (M8 X 1.5).

GRADES OF BOLTS

Bolts are made from many different types of steel, and for this reason some are stronger than others. The strength or classification of a bolt is called the **grade.** The bolt heads are marked to indicate their grade strength. Fractional bolts have lines on the head to indicate the grade, as shown in Figures 2–5 and 2–6.

The actual grade of bolts is two more than the number of lines on the bolt head. Metric bolts have a decimal number to indicate the grade. More lines or a higher grade number indicate a stronger bolt. In some cases, nuts and machine screws have similar grade markings.

Figure 2–4 Synthetic wintergreen oil can be used as a penetrating oil to loosen rusted bolts or nuts.

TECH TIP

The Wintergreen Oil Trick

Synthetic wintergreen oil, available at drugstores everywhere, makes an excellent penetrating oil. So the next time you can't get that rusted bolt loose, head for the drugstore. See Figure 2–4.

TECH TIP 

A ½-Inch Wrench Does Not Fit a ½-Inch Bolt

A common mistake made by persons new to the automotive field is to think that the size of a bolt or nut is the size of the head. The size of the bolt or nut (outside diameter of the threads) is usually smaller than the size of the wrench or socket that fits the head of the bolt or nut. Examples are given in the following table:

Wrench Size	Thread Size
7⁄16 in.	¼ in.
½ in.	5⁄16 in.
9⁄16 in.	⅜ in.
⅝ in.	7⁄16 in.
¾ in.	½ in.
10 mm	6 mm
12 mm or 13 mm*	8 mm
14 mm or 17 mm*	10 mm

*European (Système International d'Unités-SI) metric.

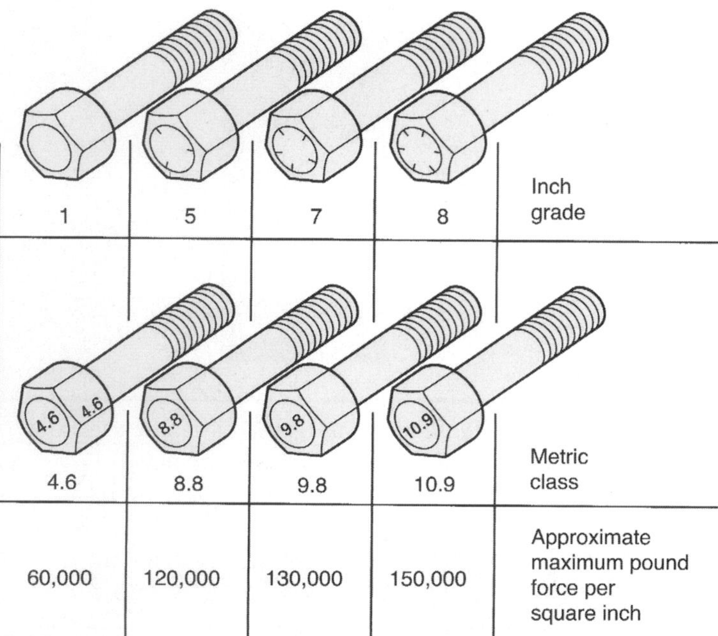

1
5
7
8
Inch grade
4.6
8.8
9.8
10.9
Metric class
60,000
120,000
130,000
150,000
Approximate maximum pound force per square inch

Figure 2–5 Typical bolt (cap screw) grade markings and approximate strength.

Figure 2–6 Every shop should have an assortment of high quality bolts and nuts to replace those damaged during vehicle service procedures.

CAUTION: *Never* use hardware store (nongraded) bolts, studs, or nuts on any vehicle steering, suspension, or brake component. Always use the exact size and grade of hardware that is specified and used by the vehicle manufacturer.

NUTS

Most nuts used on cap screws have the same hex size as the cap screw head. Some inexpensive nuts use a hex size larger than the cap screw head. Metric nuts are often marked with dimples to show their strength. More dimples indicate stronger nuts. Some nuts and cap screws use interference fit threads to keep them from accidentally loosening. This means that the shape of the nut is slightly distorted or that a section of the threads is deformed. Nuts can also be kept from loosening with a nylon washer fastened in the nut or with a nylon patch or strip on the threads. See Figure 2–7.

NOTE: Most of these *locking nuts* are grouped together and are commonly referred to as prevailing torque nuts. This means that the nut will hold its tightness or torque and not loosen with movement or vibration. Most prevailing torque nuts should be replaced whenever removed to ensure that the nut will not loosen during service. Always follow manufacturer's recommendations. Anaerobic sealers, such as Loctite, are used on the threads where the nut or cap screw must be both locked and sealed.

Figure 2–7 Types of lock nuts. On the left, a nylon ring; in the centre, a distorted shape; and on the right, a castle for use with a cotter key.

SAFETY TIP

Personal Safety Equipment

There is no better tool for a service technician than safety glasses. See Figure 2–8. The wise technician should always wear safety glasses and an additional face shield if performing any grinding operations.

Another often overlooked item of safety equipment is a pair of steel-toed shoes. See Figure 2–9. Heavy engine or suspension parts could break toe or other foot bones if not protected.

WASHERS

Washers are often used under cap screw heads and under nuts. Plain flat washers are used to provide an even clamping load around the fastener. Lock washers are added to prevent accidental loosening. In some accessories, the washers are locked onto the nut to provide easy assembly.

BASIC TOOL LIST

Hand tools are used to turn fasteners (bolts, nuts, and screws). The following is a list of hand tools every automotive technician should possess. Specialty tools are not included. See Figures 2–10 through 2–34.

Tool chest
¼-inch drive socket set
¼-inch drive ratchet
¼-inch drive 2-inch extension
¼-inch drive 6-inch extension
¼-inch drive handle
⅜-inch drive socket set
⅜-inch drive Torx set
⅜-inch drive 13/16-inch plug socket
⅜-inch drive ⅝-inch plug socket
⅜-inch drive ratchet
⅜-inch drive 1 ½-inch extension
⅜-inch drive 3-inch extension
⅜-inch drive 6-inch extension
⅜-inch drive 18-inch extension
⅜-inch drive universal
½-inch drive socket set
½-inch drive ratchet
½-inch drive breaker bar
½-inch drive 5-inch extension
½-inch drive 10-inch extension
⅜-inch to ¼-inch adapter
½-inch to ⅜-inch adapter
⅜-inch to ½-inch adapter
⅜-through 1-inch combo wrench set
10 mm through 19 mm combo wrench set
1/16-inch through ¼-inch hex wrench set
2 mm through 12 mm hex wrench set
⅜-inch hex socket
13 mm to 14 mm flare nut wrench
15 mm to 17 mm flare nut wrench
5/16-inch to ⅜-inch flare nut wrench
7/16-inch to ½-inch flare nut wrench
½-inch to 9/16-inch flare nut wrench
Diagonal pliers
Needle pliers
Adjustable-jaw pliers
Locking pliers
Snap-ring pliers
Stripping or crimping pliers
Ball-peen hammer
Rubber hammer
Dead-blow hammer
Five-piece standard screwdriver set
Four-piece Phillips screwdriver set
#15 Torx screwdriver
#20 Torx screwdriver
Crowfoot set (fractional inch)
Crowfoot set (metric)
Awl
Centre punch

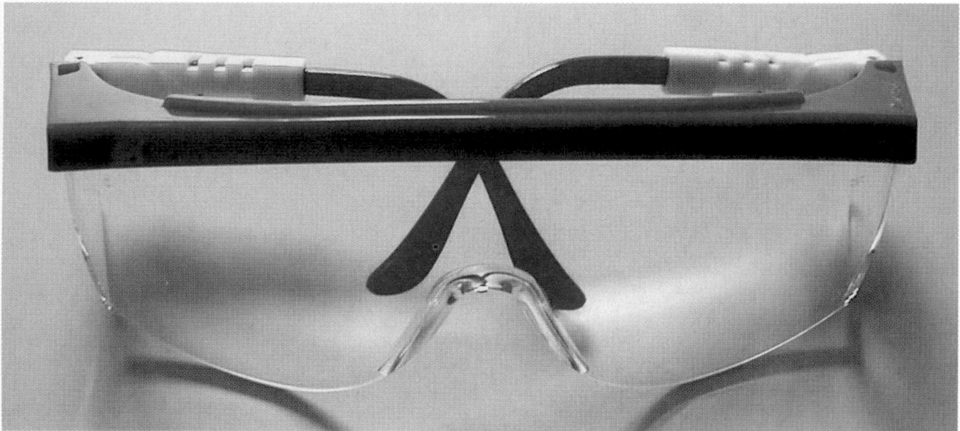

Figure 2–8 Safety glasses should be worn at all times when working on or around any vehicle or servicing any component.

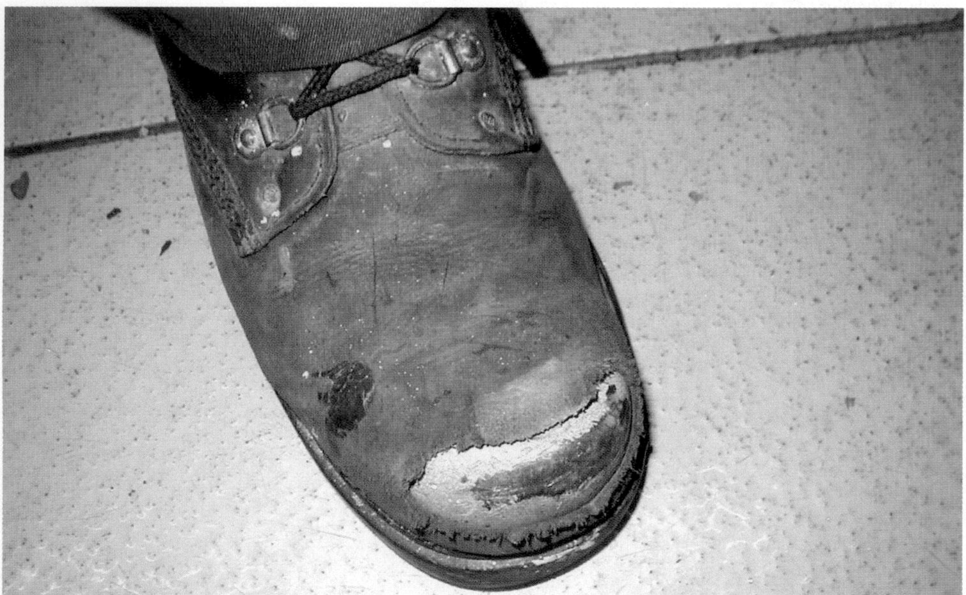

Figure 2–9 Steel-toed shoes are a worthwhile investment to help prevent foot injury due to falling objects. Even these well-worn shoes can protect the feet of this service technician.

Pin punches (assorted sizes)
Chisel
Utility knife
Valve core tool
Coolant tester
Filter wrench (large filters)
Digital volt-ohm meter
Filter wrench (smaller filters)
Safety glasses
Circuit tester
Feeler gauge
Scraper
Pinch bar
Magnet

Figure 2–10 Combination wrench. The openings are the same size at both ends. Notice the angle of the open end to permit use in close spaces.

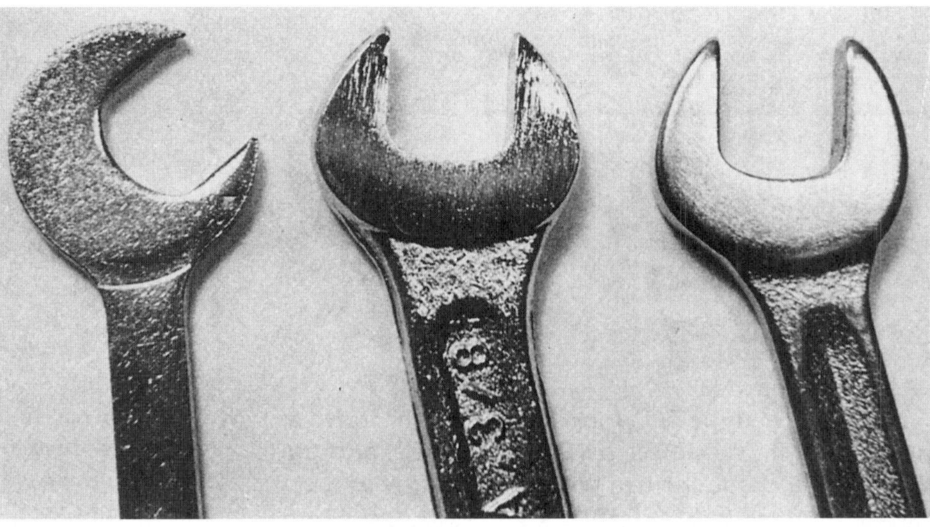

Figure 2–11 Three different qualities of open-end wrenches. The cheap wrench on the left is made from weaker steel and is thicker and less accurately machined than the standard in the centre. The wrench on the right is of professional quality (and price).

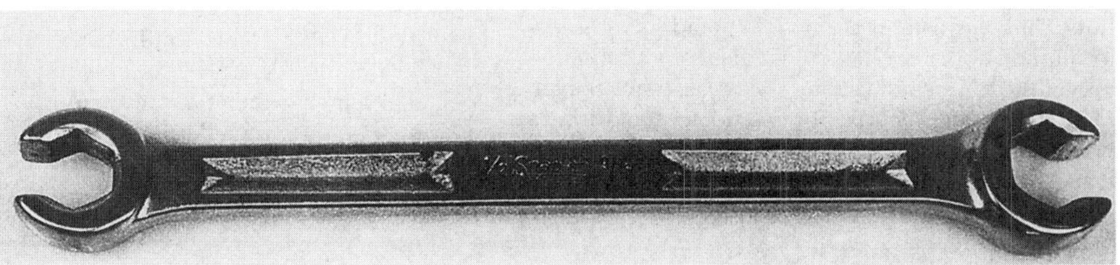

Figure 2–12 Flare-nut wrench. Also known as a *line wrench, fitting wrench,* or *tube-nut wrench.* This style of wrench is designed to grasp most of the flats of a six-sided (hex) tubing fitting to provide the most grip without damage to the fitting.

Figure 2–13 Box-end wrench. Recommended to loosen or tighten a bolt or nut where a socket will not fit. A box-end wrench has a different size at each end and is better to use than an open-end wrench because it touches the bolt or nut around the entire head instead of at just two places.

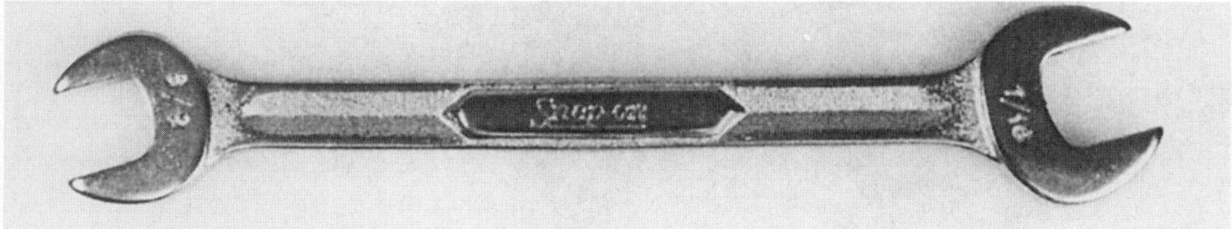

Figure 2–14 Open-end wrench. Each end has a different-sized opening and is recommended for general usage. Do not attempt to loosen or tighten bolts or nuts from or to full torque with an open-end wrench because it could round the flats of the fastener.

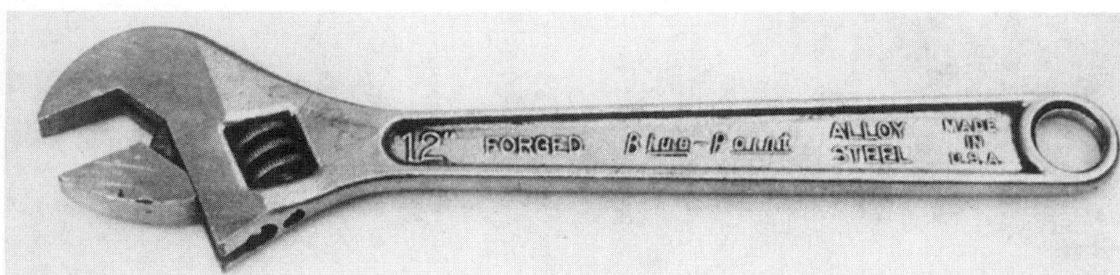

Figure 2–15 Adjustable wrench. The size (12 inches) is the *length* of the wrench, not how far the jaws open!

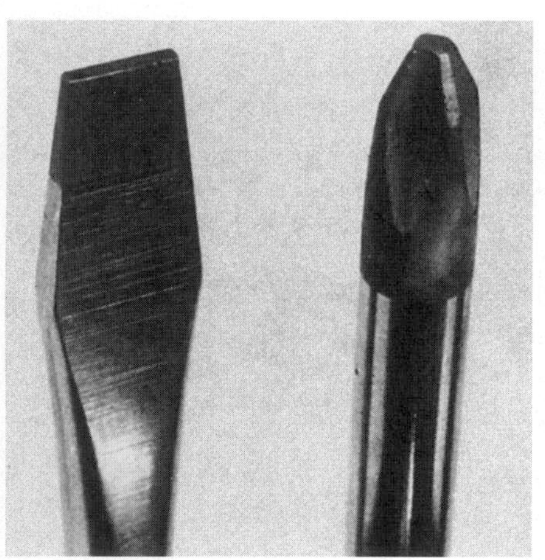

Figure 2–16 A flat-blade (or straight-blade) screwdriver (on the left) is specified by the length of the screwdriver and width of the blade. The width of the blade should match the width of the screw slot of the fastener. A Phillips-head screwdriver (on the right) is specified by the length of the handle and the size of the point at the tip. A #1 is a sharp point, #2 is most common (as shown), and a #3 Phillips is blunt and is only used for larger sizes of Phillips-head fasteners.

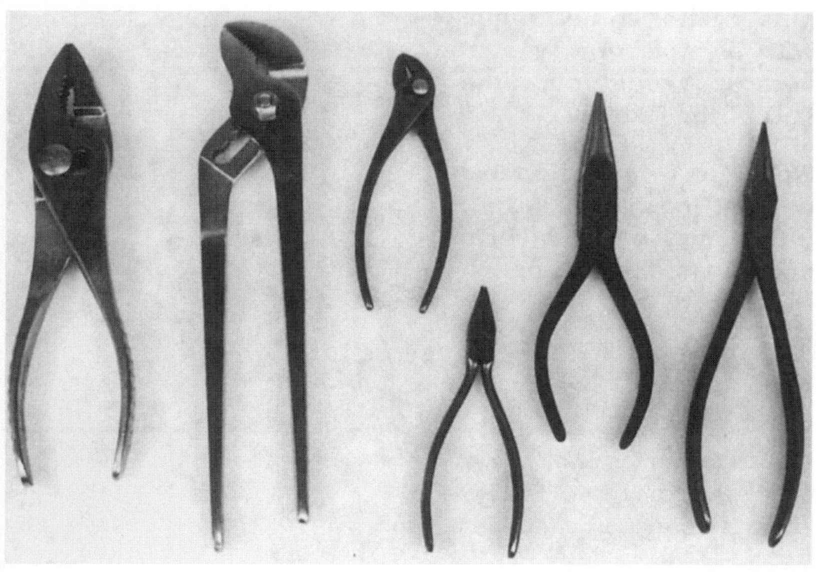

Figure 2–17 Assortment of pliers. Slip-joint pliers (far left) are often confused with water pump pliers (second from left).

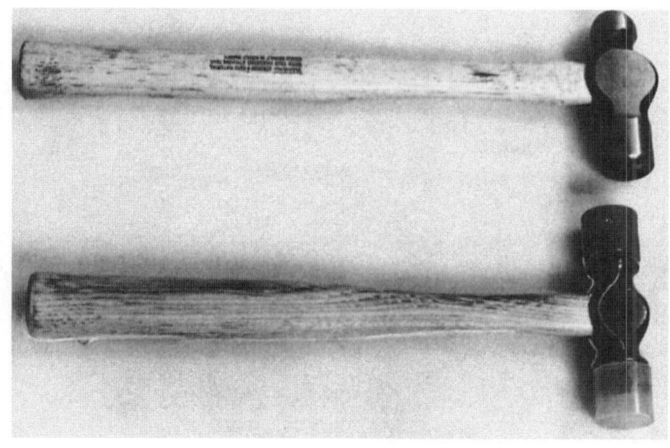

Figure 2–18 A ball-peen hammer (top) is purchased according to weight (usually in ounces) of the head of the hammer. At bottom is a soft-faced (plastic) hammer. Always use a hammer that is softer than the material being driven. Use a block of wood or similar material between a steel hammer and steel or iron engine parts to prevent damage to the engine parts.

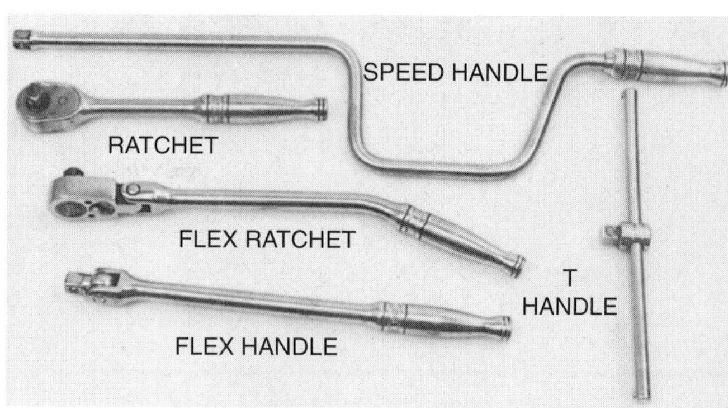

Figure 2–19 Typical drive handles for sockets.

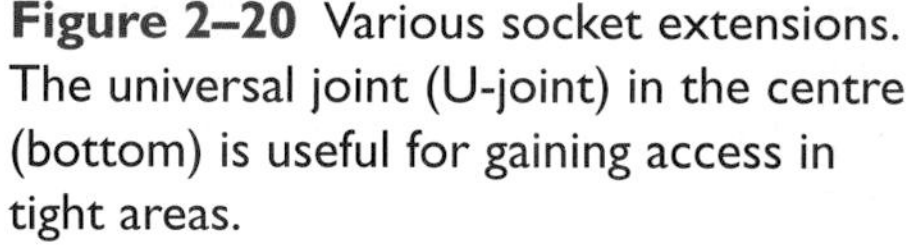

Figure 2–20 Various socket extensions. The universal joint (U-joint) in the centre (bottom) is useful for gaining access in tight areas.

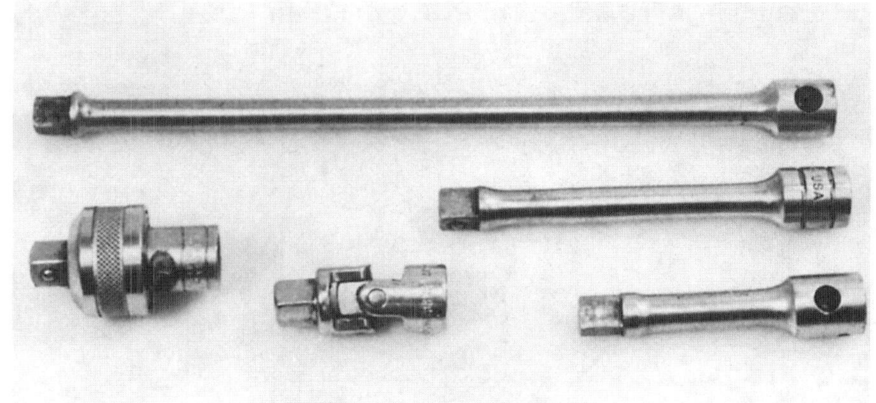

Figure 2–21 Socket drive adapters. These adapters permit the use of a ⅜-inch drive ratchet with ½-inch drive sockets, or other combinations as the various adapters permit. Adapters should *not* be used where a larger tool used with excessive force could break or damage a smaller-sized socket.

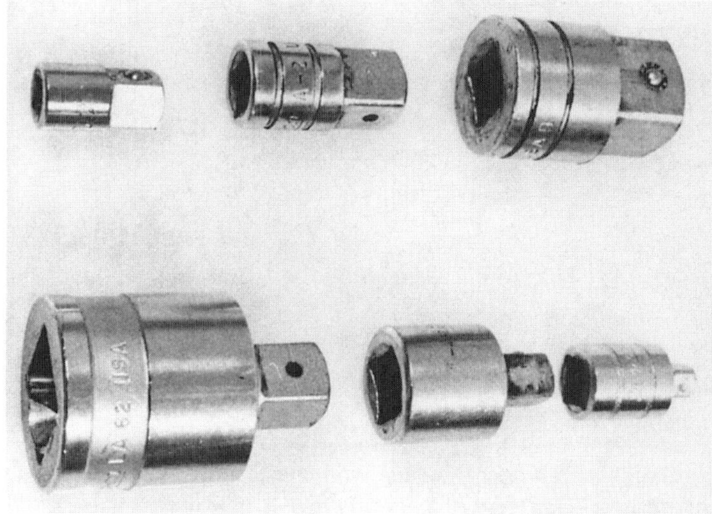

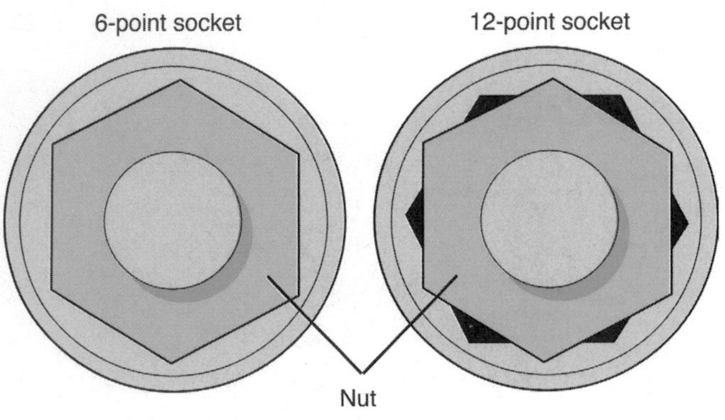

Figure 2–22 A six-point socket fits the head of the bolt or nut on all sides. A twelve-point socket can round off the head of a bolt or nut if a lot of force is applied.

Figure 2–23 Standard twelve-point short socket (left), universal joint socket (centre), and deep-well socket (right). Both the universal and deep well are six-point sockets.

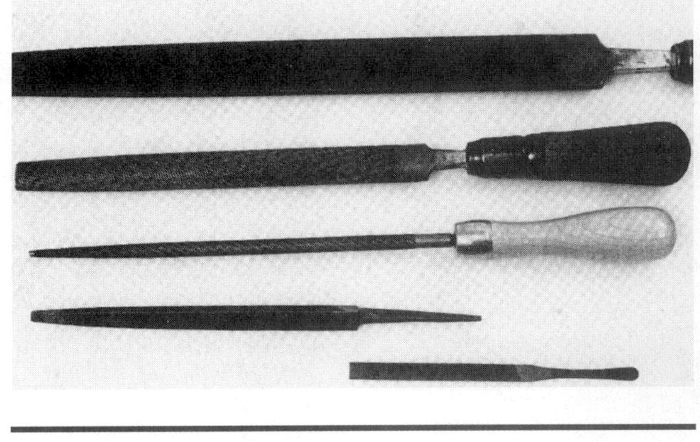

Figure 2–25 Typical files.

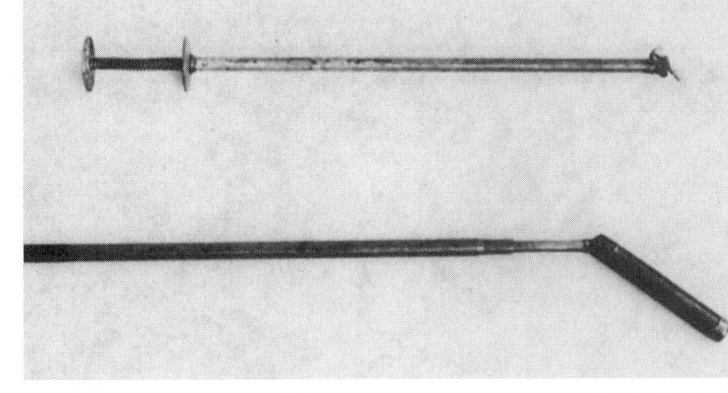

Figure 2–26 Mechanical pickup finger (top) and extendible magnet (bottom) are excellent tools to have when a nut drops down into a small area where fingers can never reach.

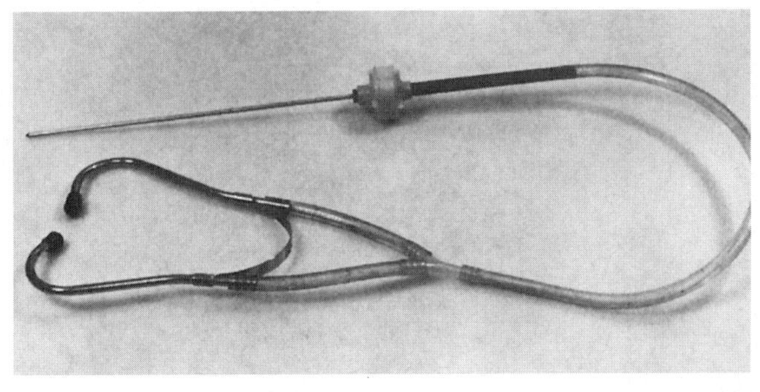

Figure 2–27 Stethoscope used by technicians to listen for the exact location of the problem noise.

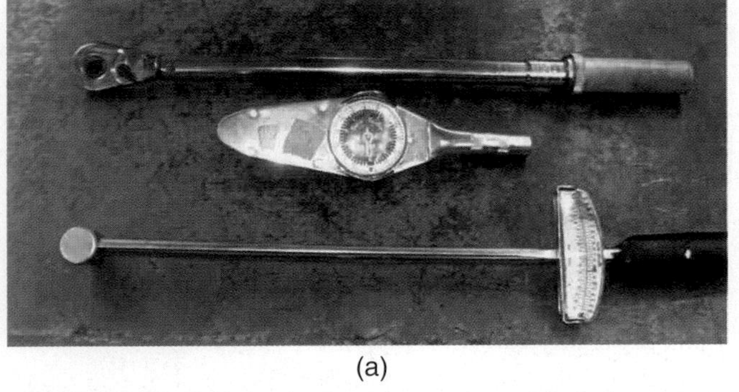

(a)

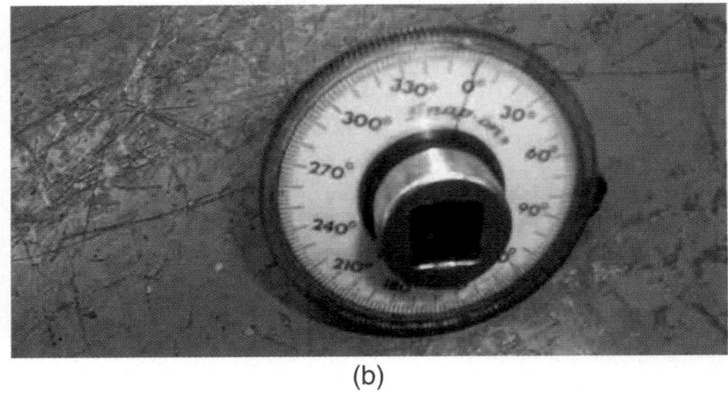

(b)

Figure 2-24 (a) Typical torque wrenches can measure torque in newton-metres, pound-feet, or pound-inches. (b) A torque angle gauge. (Courtesy of Roger Davey)

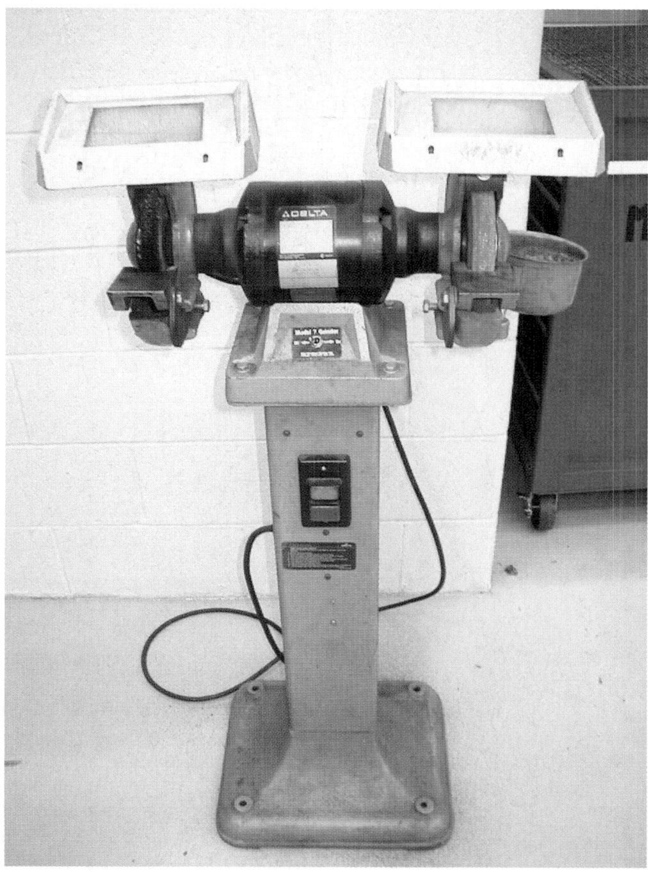

Figure 2–28 Pedestal grinder with shields. This type of grinder should be bolted to the floor. A face shield should also be worn whenever using a grinder or wire wheel.

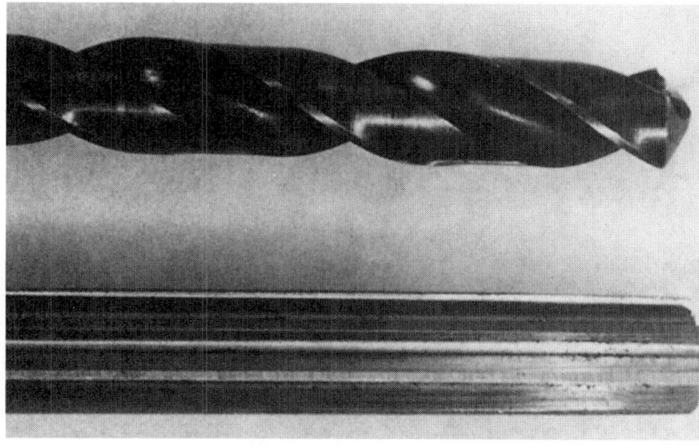

Figure 2–30 Drill bit (top) with twisted flutes (grooves) and a reamer (bottom) with straight flutes.

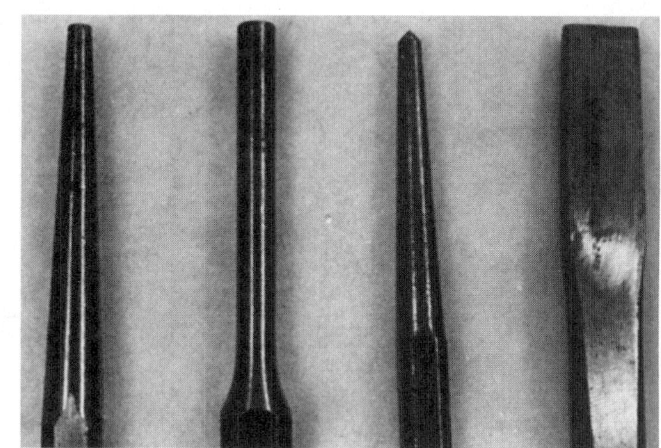

Figure 2–31 Various punches on the left and a chisel on the right.

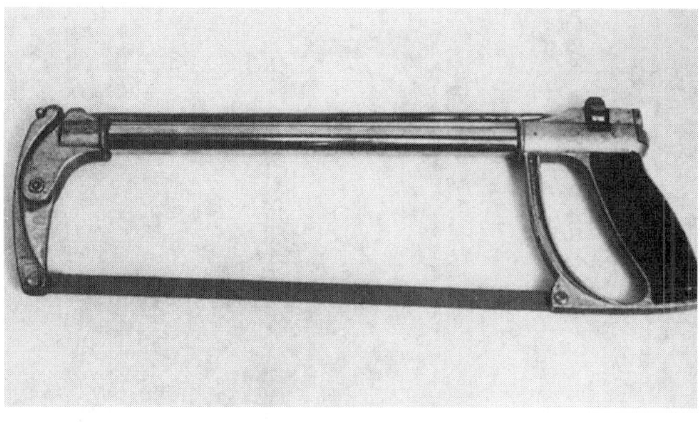

Figure 2–29 Hacksaw. The teeth of the blade should point away from the handle. The thinner the material being cut, the finer should be the blade teeth.

Figure 2–32 Using a die to cut threads on a rod.

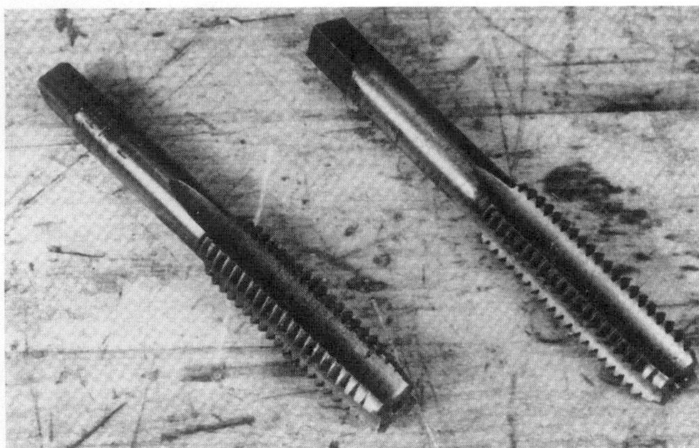

Figure 2–33 A standard and a bottoming tap. These taps are commonly used to *chase* or clean existing threads in blocks.

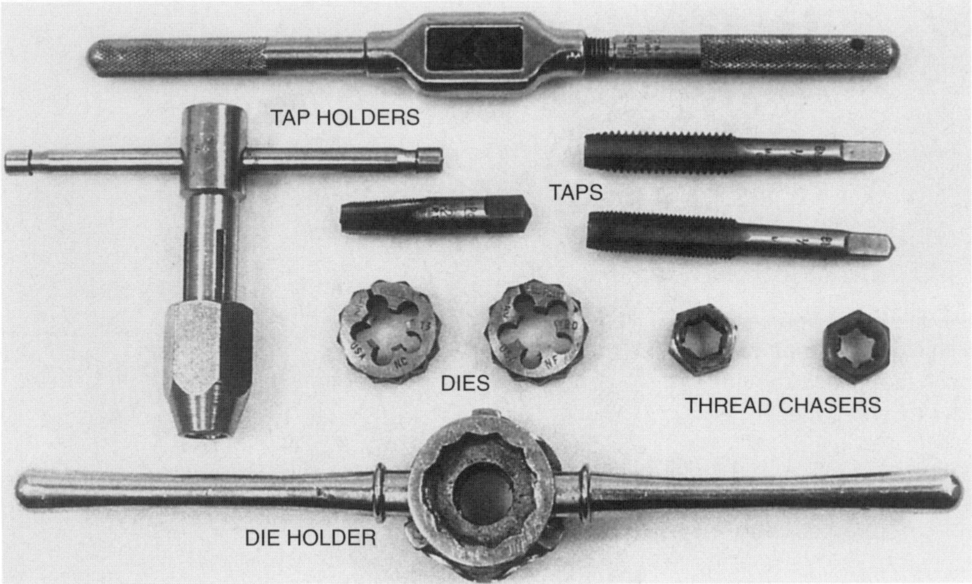

Figure 2–34 Dies are used to make threads on the outside of round stock. Taps are used to make threads inside holes. A thread chaser is used to clean threads without removing metal.

TECH TIP 

Hide Those from the Boss

An apprentice technician started working for a dealership and put his top tool box on a workbench. Another technician observed that along with a complete set of good-quality tools, the box contained several adjustable wrenches. The more experienced technician said, "Hide those from the boss." If any adjustable wrench is used on a bolt or nut, the movable jaw often moves or loosens and starts to round the head of the fastener. If the head of the bolt or nut becomes rounded, it becomes that much more difficult to remove.

TECH TIP 

Need to Borrow a Tool More Than Twice? Buy It!

Most service technicians agree that it is okay for a beginning technician to borrow a tool occasionally. However, if a tool has to be borrowed more than twice, then be sure to purchase it as soon as possible. Also, whenever a tool is borrowed, be sure that you return the tool clean and show the technician you borrowed the tool from that you are returning the tool. These actions will help in any future dealings with other technicians.

TOOL SETS AND ACCESSORIES

A beginning service technician may wish to start with a small set of tools before spending a lot of money on an expensive, extensive tool box. See Figures 2–35 through 2–37.

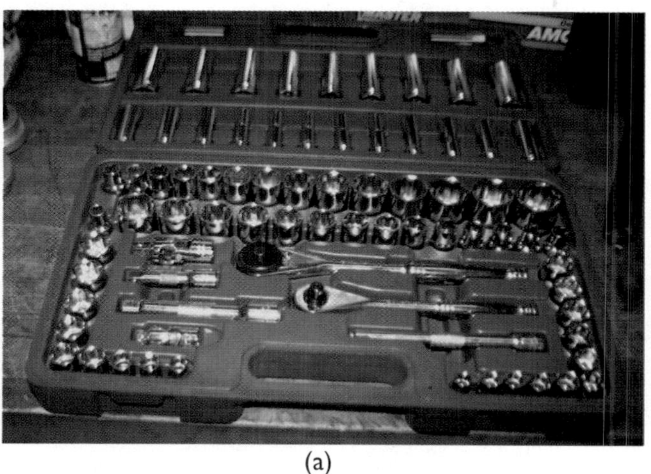

(a)

(b)

Figure 2–35 (a) A beginning technician can start with some simple basic hand tools. (b) An experienced, serious technician often spends several thousand dollars a year for tools such as found in this large (and expensive) tool box.

TECH TIP

The Valve Grinding Compound Trick

Apply a small amount of valve grinding compound to a Phillips or Torx screw or bolt head. The gritty valve grinding compound grips the screwdriver or tool bit and prevents the tool from slipping up and out of the screw head. Valve grinding compound is available in a tube from most automotive parts stores.

Figure 2–36 An inexpensive muffin tin can be used to keep small parts separated.

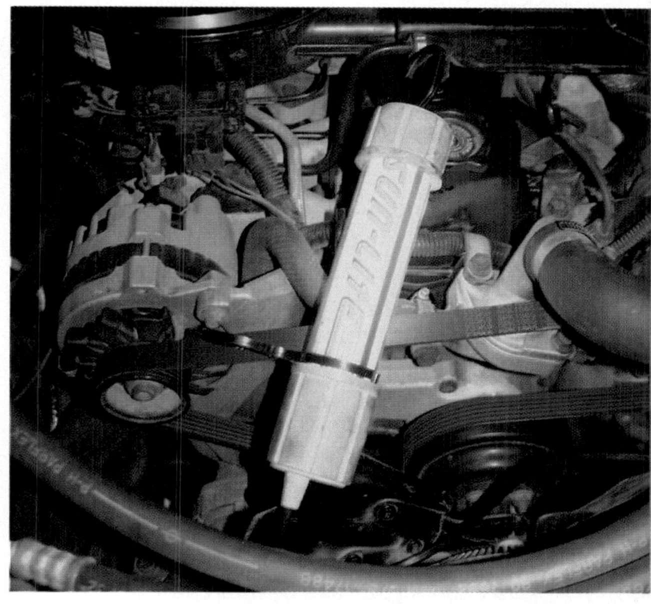

Figure 2–37 A good fluorescent trouble light is essential. An operating fluorescent light is cooler than an incandescent light and does not pose a fire hazard, as when gasoline is accidentally dropped on an unprotected incandescent bulb used in some trouble lights.

BRAND NAME VERSUS PROPER TERM

Technicians often use slang or brand names of tools rather than the proper term. This results in some confusion for new technicians. Some examples are given in the following table.

Brand Name	Proper Term	Slang Name
Crescent wrench	Adjustable wrench	Monkey wrench
Vise Grips	Locking pliers	
Channel Locks	Water pump pliers or multigroove adjustable pliers	Pump pliers
	Diagonal cutting pliers	Dikes or side cuts

TECH TIP 

It Just Takes a Second

Whenever removing any automotive component, it is wise to screw the bolts back into the holes a couple of threads by hand. This ensures that the right bolt will be used in its original location when the component or part is put back on the vehicle. Often, the same diameter of fastener is used on a component, but the length of the bolt may vary. Spending just a couple of seconds to put the bolts and nuts back where they belong when the part is removed can save a lot of time when the part is being reinstalled. Besides making certain that the right fastener is being installed in the right place, this method helps prevent bolts and nuts from getting lost or kicked away. How much time have you wasted looking for that lost bolt or nut?

SAFETY TIPS FOR USING HAND TOOLS

The following safety tips should be kept in mind whenever you are working with hand tools:

- Always *pull* a wrench toward you for best control and safety. Never push a wrench.
- Keep wrenches and all hand tools clean to help prevent rust and for a better, firmer grip.
- Always use a 6-point socket or a box-end wrench to break loose a tight bolt or nut.
- Use a box-end wrench for torque and the open-end wrench for speed.
- Never use a pipe extension or other type of "cheater bar" on a wrench or ratchet handle. If more force is required, use a larger tool or use penetrating oil and/or heat on the frozen fastener. (If heat is used on a bolt or nut to remove it, always replace it with a new part.)
- Always use the proper tool for the job. If a specialized tool is required, use the proper tool and do not try to use another tool improperly.
- Never expose any tool to excessive heat. High temperatures can reduce the strength (draw the temper) of metal tools.
- Never use a hammer on any wrench or socket handle unless you are using a special "staking face" wrench designed to be used with a hammer.
- Replace any tools that are damaged or worn.

MEASURING TOOLS

The purpose of any repair is to restore the engine or vehicle to factory specification tolerance. Every repair procedure involves measuring. The service technician must measure twice:

- The original engine or vehicle components must be measured to see if correction is necessary to restore the component or part to factory specifications.
- The replacement parts and finished machined areas must be measured to ensure proper dimension before the engine or component is assembled or replaced on the vehicle.

Micrometer

A micrometer is the most used measuring instrument in engine service and repair. See Figure 2–38. The **thimble** rotates over the **barrel** on a screw that has 40 threads per inch. Every revolution of the thimble moves the **spindle** 0.025 inch. The thimble is graduated into 25 equally spaced lines; therefore, each space represents 0.001 inch.

Metric Micrometer

The parts of a metric micrometer are the same as those of an inch (imperial) micrometer (Figure 2–38). On a 25 mm micrometer the screw has 50 threads in that length. One revolution of the thimble moves the spindle 0.5 mm. The thimble is graduated by 50 equally spaced lines, making each space represent 0.01 mm.

Every micrometer should be checked for calibration on a regular basis. See Figure 2–39. See Figures 2–40a and 2–40b for examples of imperial and metric micrometer readings.

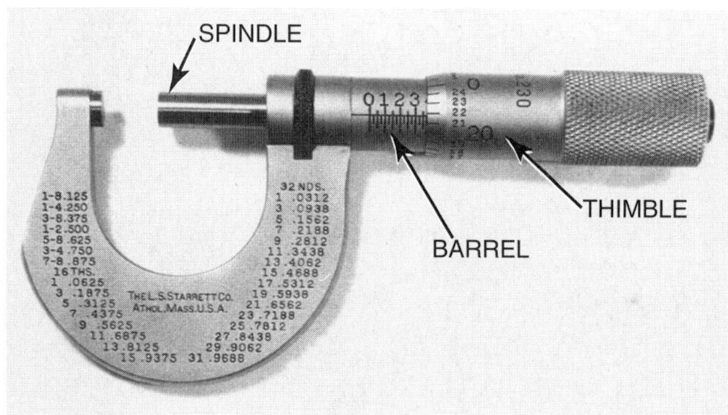

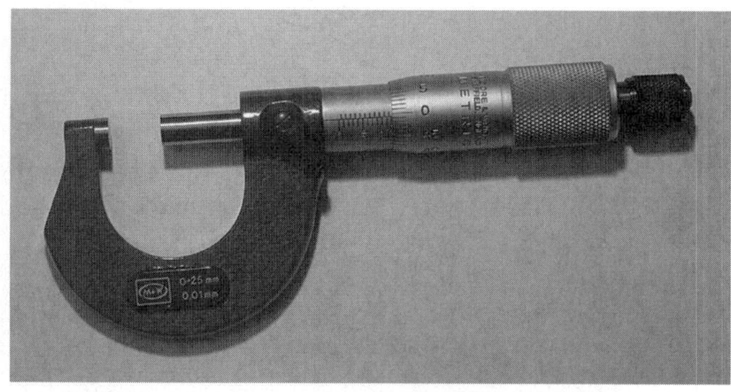

Figure 2–38 Typical micrometers used for dimensional inspection. (Courtesy Roger Davey)

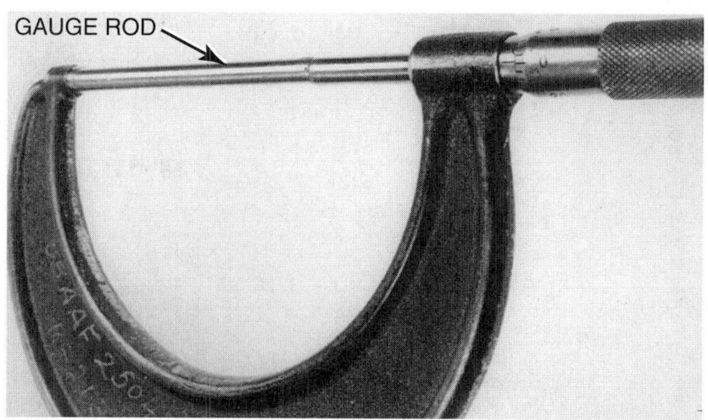

Figure 2–39 All micrometers should be checked and calibrated as needed using a gauge rod.

Telescopic Gauge

A telescopic gauge is used with a micrometer to measure the inside diameter of a hole or bore.

Cylinder Bore

The cylinder bore can be measured by inserting a telescopic gauge into the bore and rotating the handle lock to allow the arms of the gauge to contact the inside bore of the cylinder. Tighten the handle lock and remove the gauge from the cylinder. Use a micrometer to measure the telescopic gauge. See Figure 2–41. A telescopic gauge can also be used to measure the following:

- Camshaft bearing
- Main bearing bore (housing bore) measurement
- Connecting rod bore measurement

Small-Hole Gauge

A small-hole gauge (also called a **split-ball gauge**) is used with a micrometer to measure the inside diameter of small holes such as a valve guide in a cylinder head. See Figures 2–42 and 2–43.

Vernier Dial Caliper

A vernier dial caliper is normally used to measure the outside diameter or length of a component such as a piston diameter or crankshaft and camshaft bearing journal diameter. See Figures 2–44a and 2–44b.

Feeler Gauge

A feeler gauge (also known as a thickness gauge) is an accurately manufactured strip of metal that is used to determine the gap or clearance between two components. See Figure 2–45. A feeler gauge can be used to check the following:

- Piston ring gap—see Figure 2–46
- Piston ring side clearance
- Piston to cylinder wall clearance
- Connecting rod side clearance

Straightedge

A straightedge is a precision ground metal measuring gauge that is used to check the flatness of engine components when used with a feeler gauge. A straightedge is used to check the flatness of the following:

- Cylinder heads—see Figure 2–47
- Cylinder block deck
- Straightness of the main bearing bores (saddles)

Dial Indicator

A dial indicator is a precision measuring instrument used to measure crankshaft end play, crankshaft runout, and valve guide wear. See Figure 2–48.

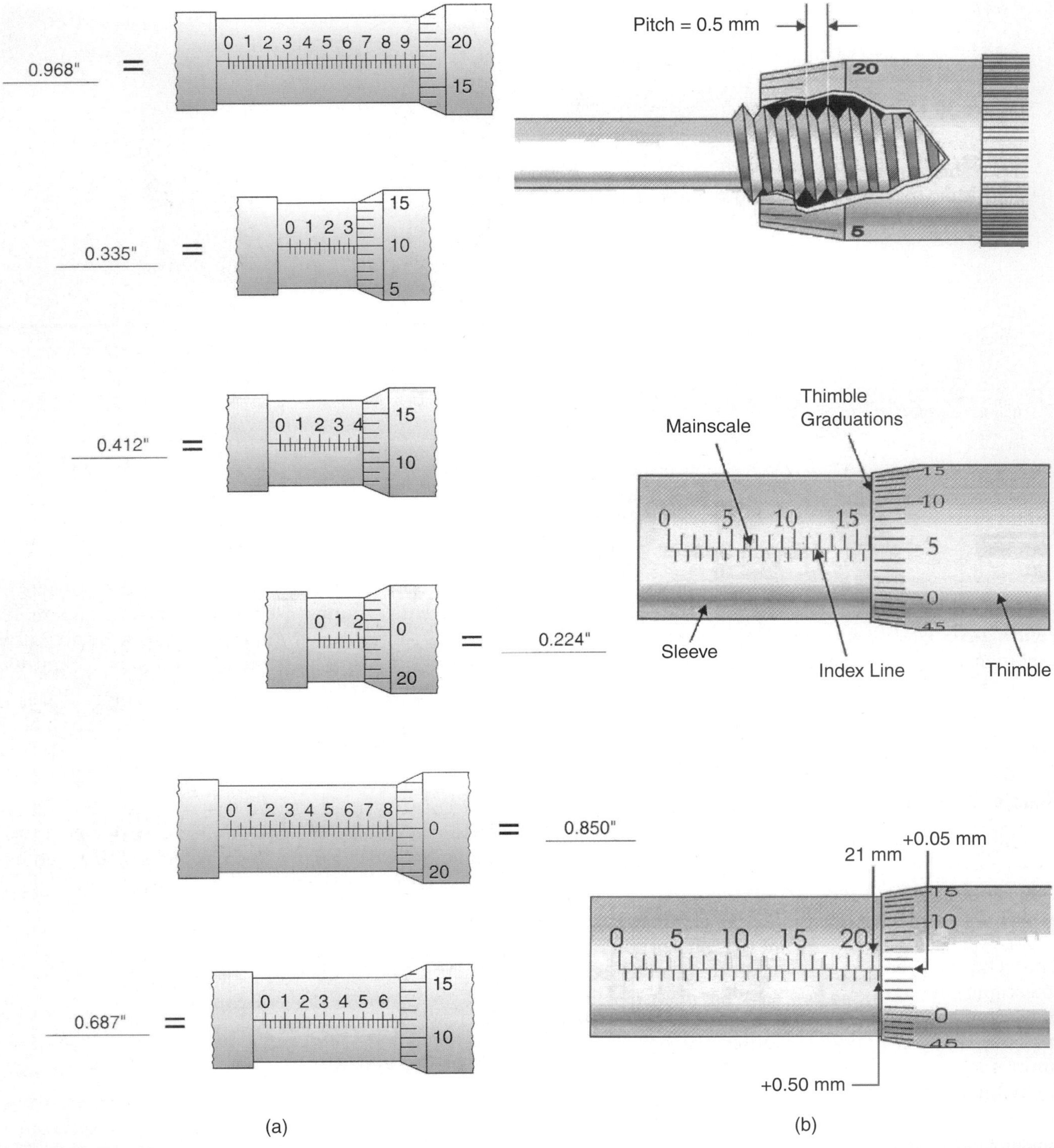

Figure 2-40 (a) Readings on an inch micrometer. The numbers on the barrel represent steps of 0.1 in. Each smaller division is 0.025 in. In the first example, "9" gives 0.9 in. The next two divisions make 0.05 in more. Then the thimble at 18 thousandths gives 0.018 in more, for a total of 0.968 in. Check the other five examples in the same way. (b) A metric micrometer measures to the nearest 0.01 mm. There are 50 turns on the screw over a distance of 25 mm, making the pitch of the screw 0.5 mm. On the sleeve (or barrel) the thimble advances 0.5 mm in one rotation. With 50 marks on the thimble, each space represents 0.01 mm. The middle micrometer shows 16.05 mm, and the bottom one, 21.55 mm. (Figure 2-40b from Northern Alberta Institute of Technology, *Individual Learning Modules for Automotive Technicians*)

(a)

(b)

Figure 2–41 (a) A telescopic gauge being used to measure the inside diameter (ID) of a camshaft bearing. (b) An outside micrometer is used to measure the telescopic gauge.

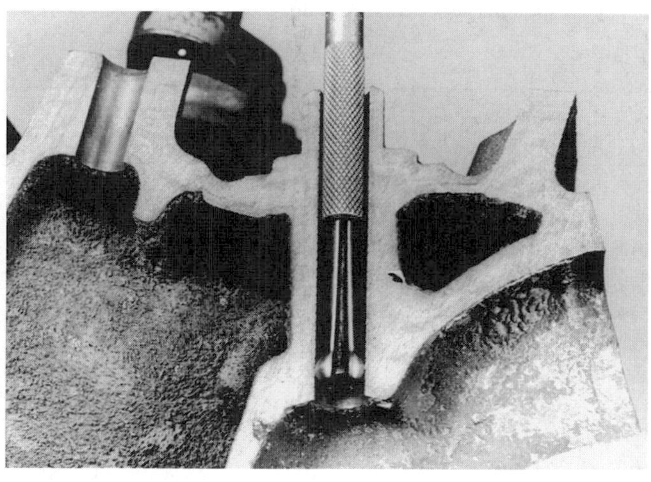

Figure 2–42 Cutaway of a valve guide with a hole gauge adjusted to the hole diameter.

Figure 2–43 The outside of a hole gauge being measured with a micrometer.

Dial Bore Gauge

A dial bore gauge is an expensive, but important, gauge used to measure cylinder taper and out-of-round as well as main bearing (block housing) bore for taper and out-of-round. See Figure 2–49. A dial bore gauge has to be adjusted to a dimension such as the factory specifications; then the reading on the dial bore gauge indicates plus (+) or minus (−) readings from the predetermined dimension. This is why a dial bore is best used to measure taper and out-of-round, because it shows the difference in cylinder or bore rather than an actual measurement.

SAFETY TIPS FOR TECHNICIANS

Safety is not just a buzzword on a poster in the work area. Safe work habits can reduce accidents and injuries, ease the workload, and keep employees pain free. Suggested safety tips include the following:

- *Wear safety glasses at all times while servicing any vehicle.*
- Watch your toes—always keep your toes protected with steel-toed safety shoes. If safety

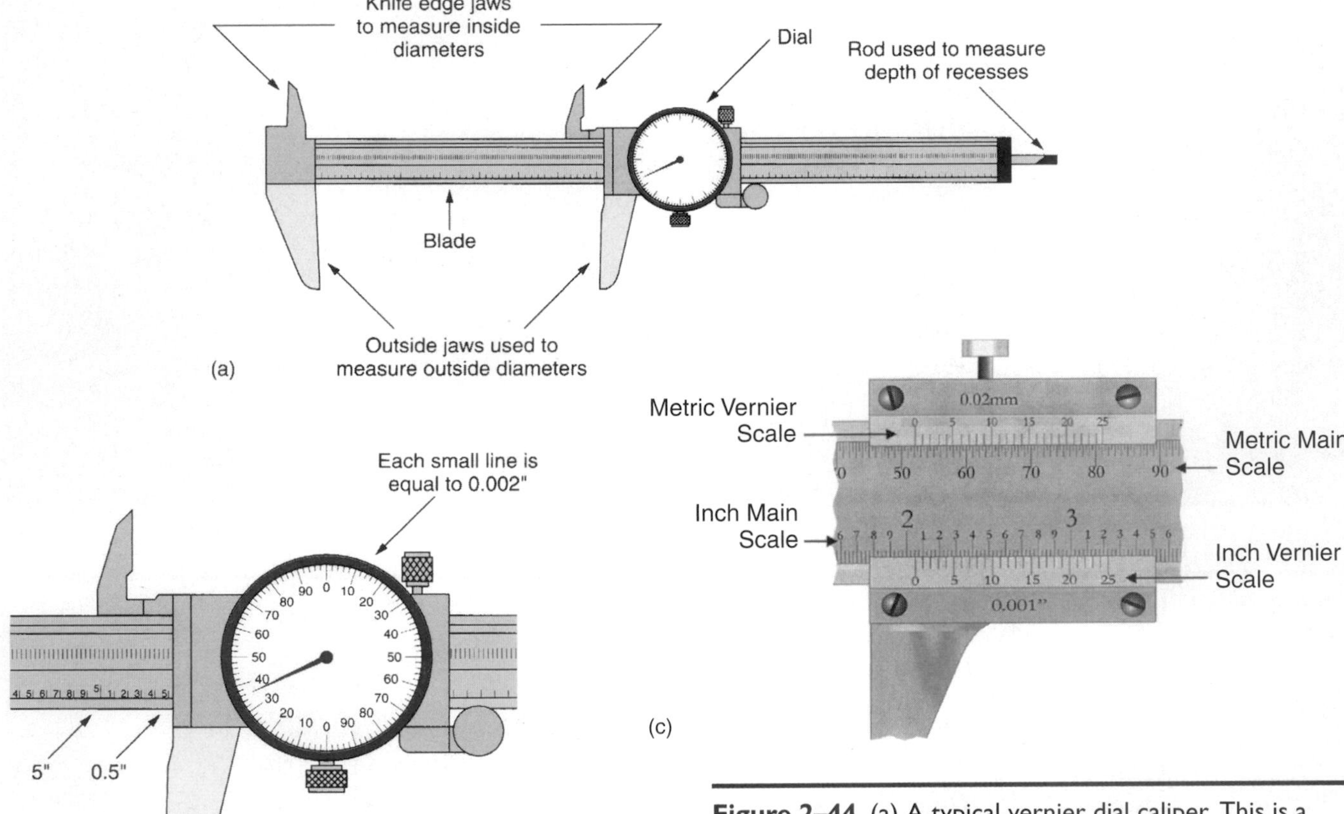

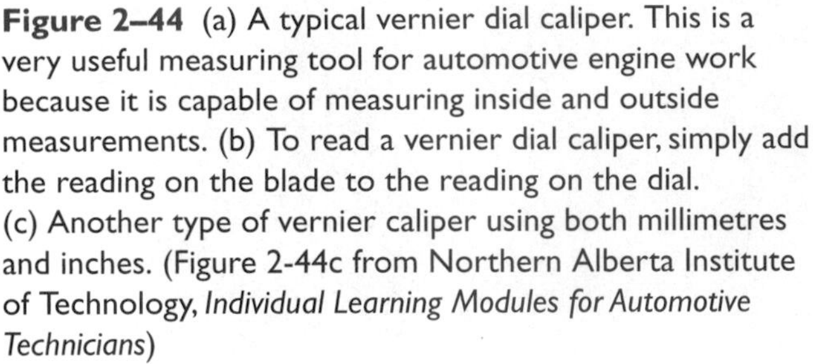

Figure 2–44 (a) A typical vernier dial caliper. This is a very useful measuring tool for automotive engine work because it is capable of measuring inside and outside measurements. (b) To read a vernier dial caliper, simply add the reading on the blade to the reading on the dial.
(c) Another type of vernier caliper using both millimetres and inches. (Figure 2-44c from Northern Alberta Institute of Technology, *Individual Learning Modules for Automotive Technicians*)

shoes are not available, then leather-topped shoes offer more protection than canvas or cloth.

- Wear gloves to protect your hands from rough or sharp surfaces. Thin rubber gloves are recommended when working around automotive liquids such as engine oil, antifreeze, transmission fluid, or any other liquids that may be hazardous.
- Service technicians working under a vehicle should wear a **bump cap** to protect the head against under-vehicle objects and the pads of the lift.
- Remove jewellery that may get caught on something or act as a conductor to an exposed electrical circuit.
- Avoid loose or dangling clothing.
- When lifting any object, get a secure grip with solid footing. Keep the load close to your body to minimize the strain. Lift with your legs and arms, not your back.
- Do not twist your body when carrying a load. Instead, pivot your feet to help prevent strain on the spine.
- Ask for help when moving or lifting heavy objects.
- Push a heavy object rather than pull it. (This is opposite to the way you should work with tools—never push a wrench! If you do and a bolt or nut

Figure 2–45 A group of feeler gauges (also known as thickness gauges), used to measure between two parts. The long gauges on the bottom are used to measure the piston-to-cylinder wall clearance.

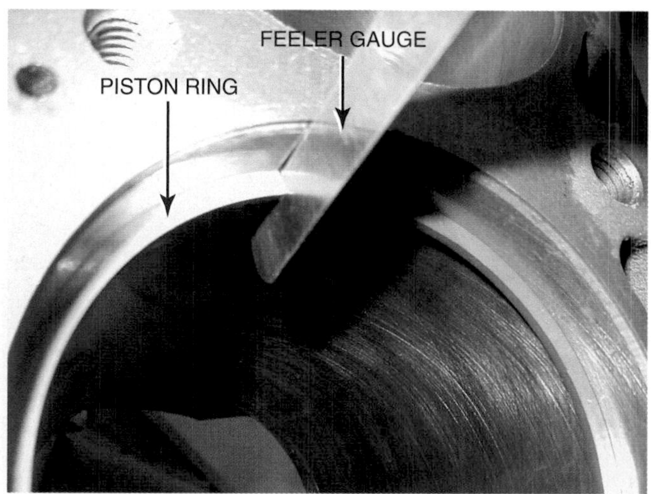

Figure 2–46 A feeler gauge, also called a thickness gauge, is used to measure the small clearances such as the end gap of a piston ring.

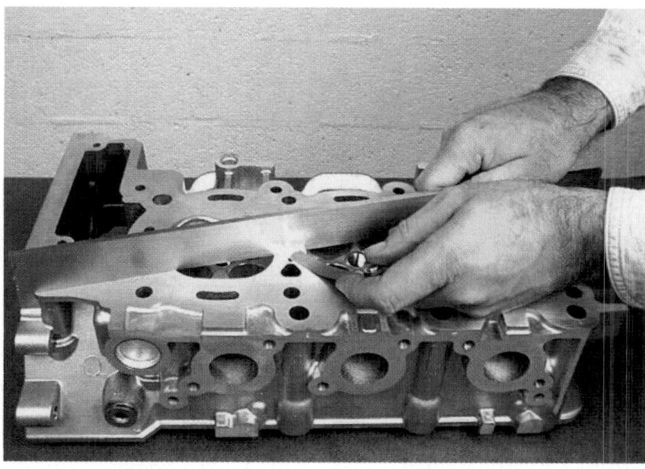

Figure 2–47 A straightedge is used with a feeler gauge to determine if a cylinder head is warped or twisted.

loosens, your entire weight is used to propel your hand(s) forward. This usually results in cuts, bruises, or other painful injury.)

- Always connect an exhaust hose to the tailpipe of any running vehicle to help prevent the build-up of carbon monoxide inside a closed garage space. See Figure 2–50.
- When standing, keep objects, parts, and tools with which you are working between chest height and waist height. If seated, work at tasks that are at elbow height.
- Store all flammable liquids in an approved fire safety cabinet. See Figure 2–51.
- Always be sure the hood is securely held open. See Figure 2–52.

Figure 2–48 A dial indicator is used to measure valve lift during flow testing of a high performance cylinder head.

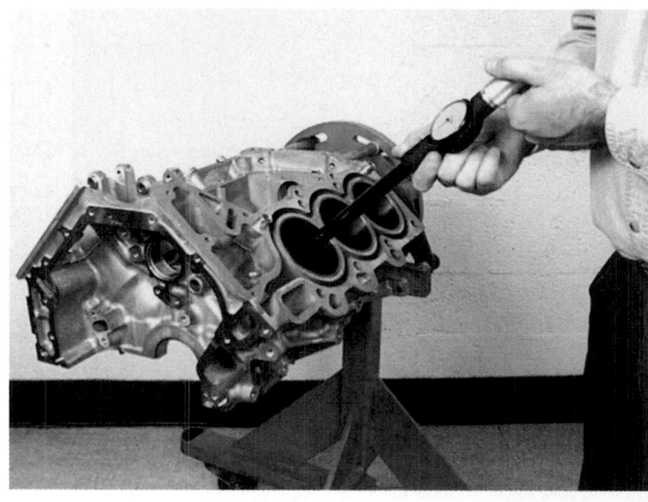

Figure 2–49 A dial bore gauge is used to check a cylinder for out-of-round and taper.

SAFETY IN LIFTING (HOISTING) A VEHICLE

Many chassis and underbody service procedures require that the vehicle be hoisted or lifted off the ground. The simplest methods involve the use of drive-on ramps or a floor jack and safety (jack) stands, whereas in-ground or surface-mounted lifts

Figure 2–50 Always connect an exhaust hose to the tailpipe of the engine of a vehicle to be run inside a building.

Figure 2–51 Typical fireproof flammable storage cabinet.

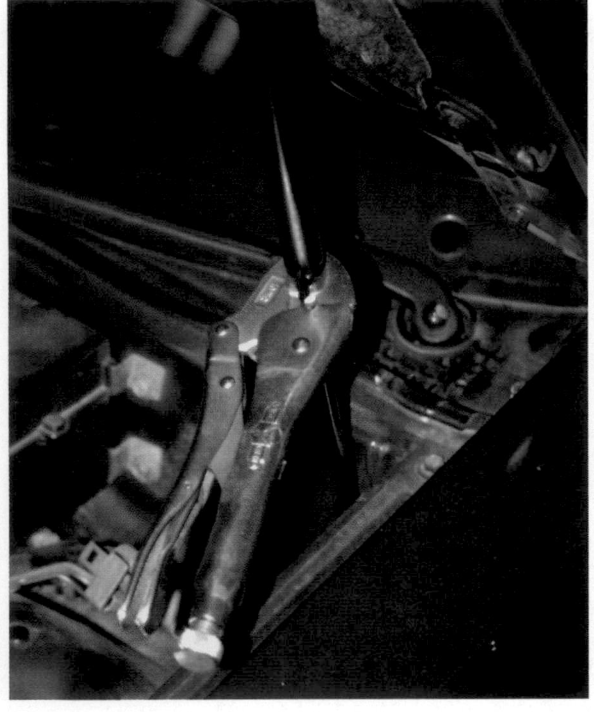

(a)

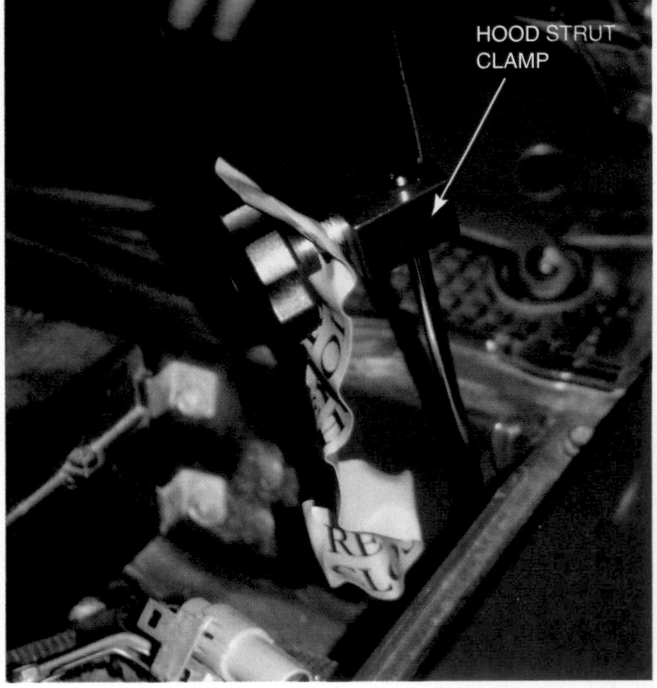

(b)

Figure 2–52 (a) A crude but effective method is to use locking pliers on the chrome-plated shaft of a hood strut. Locking pliers should only be used on defective struts because the jaws of the pliers can damage the strut shaft. (b) A commercially available hood clamp. This tool uses a bright orange tag to help remind the technician to remove the clamp before attempting to close the hood. The hood could be bent if force is used to close the hood with the clamp in place.

SAFETY TIP 

Shop Cloth Disposal

Always dispose of oily shop cloths in an enclosed container to prevent a fire. See Figure 2–53. Whenever oily cloths are thrown together on the floor or workbench, a chemical reaction can occur which can ignite the cloth even without an open flame. This process of ignition without an open flame is called spontaneous combustion.

Figure 2–53 All oily shop cloths should be stored in a metal container equipped with a lid to help prevent spontaneous combustion.

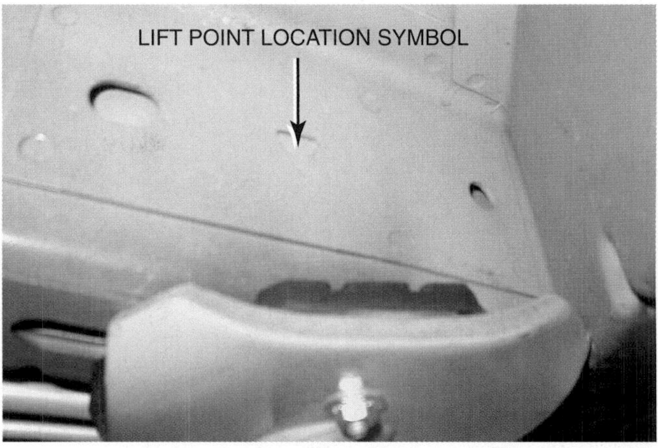

Figure 2–54 Most newer vehicles have a triangle or indent symbol indicating the recommended hoisting lift points.

provide greater access. *Setting the pads is a critical part of this procedure.* All automobile and light-truck service manuals include recommended locations to be used when hoisting (lifting) a vehicle. Newer vehicles have a triangle decal on the driver's door indicating the recommended lift points. The recommended standards for the lift points and lifting procedures are found in SAE Standard JRP-2184. See Figure 2–54. These recommendations typically include the following points:

1. The vehicle should be centred on the lift or hoist so as not to overload one side or put too much force either forward or rearward. See Figure 2–55.
2. The pads of the lift should be spread as far apart as possible to provide a stable platform.
3. Each pad should be placed under a portion of the vehicle that is strong and capable of supporting the weight of the vehicle.
   a. Pinch welds at the bottom edge of the body are generally considered to be strong.

CAUTION: Even though pinch weld seams are the recommended location for hoisting many vehicles with unitized bodies (unit-body), care should be taken not to place the pad(s) too far forward or rearward. Incorrect placement of the vehicle on the lift could cause the vehicle to be imbalanced, and the vehicle could fall. This is exactly what happened to the vehicle in Figure 2–56.

   b. Boxed areas of the body are the best places to position the pads on a vehicle without a frame. Be careful to note whether the arms of the lift might come into contact with other parts of the vehicle before the pad touches the intended location. Commonly damaged areas include the following:
      (1) Rocker panel moldings
      (2) Exhaust system (including catalytic converter)
      (3) Tires, especially if the edges of the pads or arms are sharp (See Figures 2–57 through 2–59.)
4. The vehicle should be raised about 30 cm off the floor, then stopped and shaken to check for stability. If the vehicle seems to be stable when checked at a short distance from the floor, continue raising the vehicle and continue to view the vehicle until it has reached the desired height.

(a)

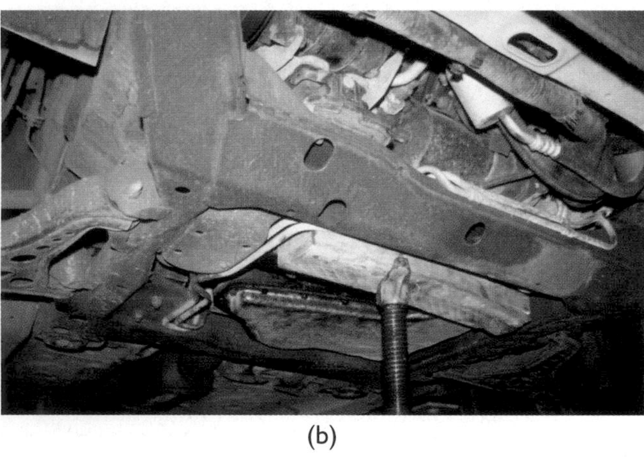

(b)

Figure 2–55 (a) Tall safety stands can be used to provide additional support for a vehicle while on a hoist. (b) A block of wood should be used to avoid the possibility of doing damage to components supported by the stand.

CAUTION: Do not look away from the vehicle while it is being raised (or lowered) on a hoist. Often one side or one end of the hoist can stop or fail, resulting in the vehicle being slanted enough to slip or fall, creating physical damage not only to the vehicle and/or hoist but also to the technician or others who may be nearby.

Figure 2–56 This vehicle fell from the hoist because the pads were not set correctly. No one was hurt, but the vehicle was a total loss.

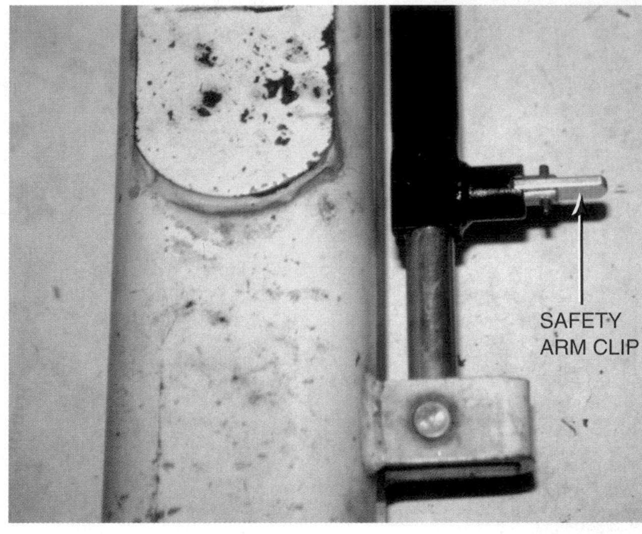

Figure 2–57 The safety arm clip should be engaged to prevent the possibility that the hoist support arms can move.

HINT: Most hoists can be safely placed at any desired height. For ease while working, the area in which you are working should be at chest level. When working on brakes or suspension components, it is not necessary to work on them down near the floor or over your head; raise the hoist so that the components are at chest level.

5. Before lowering the hoist, the safety latch(es) must be released and the direction of the controls reversed. The speed downward is often adjusted to be as slow as possible for additional safety.

(a)

(b)

Figure 2–58 (a) An assortment of hoist pad adapters that are often necessary to use to safely hoist many pickup trucks, vans, and sport utility vehicles. (b) A view from underneath a Chevrolet pickup truck showing how the pad extensions are used to attach the hoist lifting pad to contact the frame.

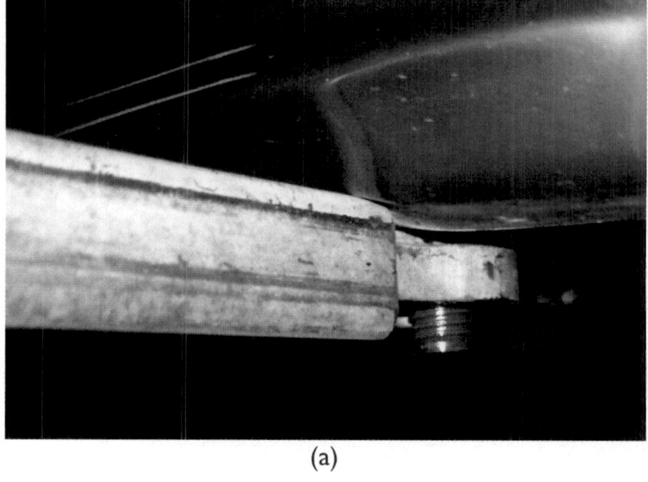

(a)

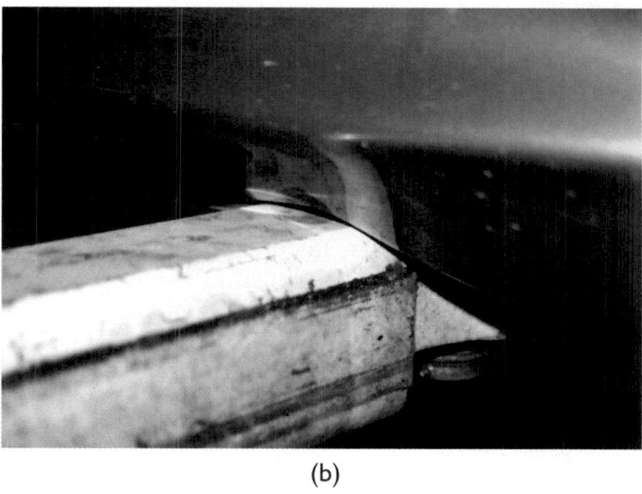

(b)

Figure 2–59 (a) In this photo the pad arm is just contacting the rocker panel of the vehicle. (b) This photo shows what can occur if the technician places the pad too far inward underneath the vehicle. The arm of the hoist has dented the rocker panel.

HAZARDOUS MATERIALS

The Workplace Hazardous Materials Information System (WHMIS) is Canada's hazard communication standard. Its regulations are coordinated by the WHMIS Division of Health Canada. A material is considered hazardous if it meets one or more of the following conditions:

- It contains over 1000 parts per million (PPM) of halogenated compounds (halogenated compounds are chemicals containing chlorine, fluorine, bromine, or iodine). Common items that contain these solvents include the following:

  Carburetor cleaner
  Silicone spray

Aerosols
Adhesives
Stoddard solvent
Trichloromethane
Gear oils
Brake cleaner
Air-conditioning (A/C) compressor oils
Floor cleaners
Anything else that contains a chlor or fluor in its ingredient name

- It has a flash point below 140°F (60°C).
- It is corrosive (has a pH level of 2 or lower or 12.5 or higher).
- It contains toxic metals or organic compounds. Volatile organic compounds (VOCs) must also be limited and controlled. This classification greatly affects the painting and finishing aspects of the automobile industry.

Always follow material safety data sheets (MSDS) procedures for the handling of any chemicals and dispose of all used engine oil and other waste products according to local, provincial, or federal laws.

To help safeguard workers and the environment, the following guidelines are recommended:

- A technician's hands should always be covered with latex gloves when touching used engine oils, transmission fluids, and greases. Dispose of all waste oil according to established standards and laws in your area. See Figure 2–60.
- Asbestos and products that contain asbestos are known cancer-causing agents. Even though most brake linings and clutch facing materials are now manufactured without asbestos, millions of vehicles are being serviced every day that *may* contain asbestos. The general procedure for handling asbestos is to put the used parts into a sealed plastic bag and return the parts as cores for rebuilding or dispose of them according to current laws and regulations.
- Eyewash stations should be readily accessible near the work area or near where solvents or other contaminants could get into the eyes. See Figure 2–61.

Figure 2–60 All solvents and other hazardous waste should be disposed of properly.

MATERIAL SAFETY DATA SHEETS

Businesses and schools in Canada are required to provide a detailed data sheet on each of the chemicals or materials to which a person may be exposed within their buildings. These sheets of information on each of the materials that *may* be harmful are called **material safety data sheets (MSDS).** See Figure 2–62.

Every item on the WHMIS list of hazardous materials must have an associated MSDS. Each MSDS must match the product precisely, including the names of the product and the supplier.

Every supplier of a hazardous material is responsible for providing its MSDS. This data sheet

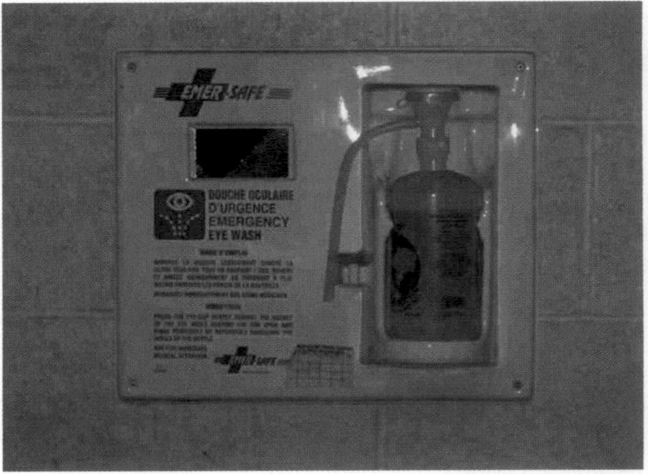

Figure 2–61 An eyewash station should be centrally located in the shop and near where solvent may be splashed. (Courtesy of Roger Davey)

must contain nine categories of information. Besides the identification details, the MSDS must provide specific data on the contents and properties of the material. In addition it must give the nature of the health effects of the product and describe measures for their prevention or alleviation (i.e., first aid treatments).

Employers are required to keep the MSDSs of all their hazardous materials in a place readily available to all employees. Before technicians use any such product they should check its MSDS. They should study it carefully to know how the material should be handled and stored. Also, they should ensure that they know what to do if an emergency occurs while using the product. Note that you may need to consult a health and safety specialist to learn more details about using the material.

ELECTRICAL CORD SAFETY

Use correctly grounded three-prong sockets and extension cords to operate power tools. Some tools use only two-prong plugs. Make sure these are double insulated. When not in use, keep electrical cords off the floor to prevent tripping over them. Tape the cords down if they are placed in high foot traffic areas.

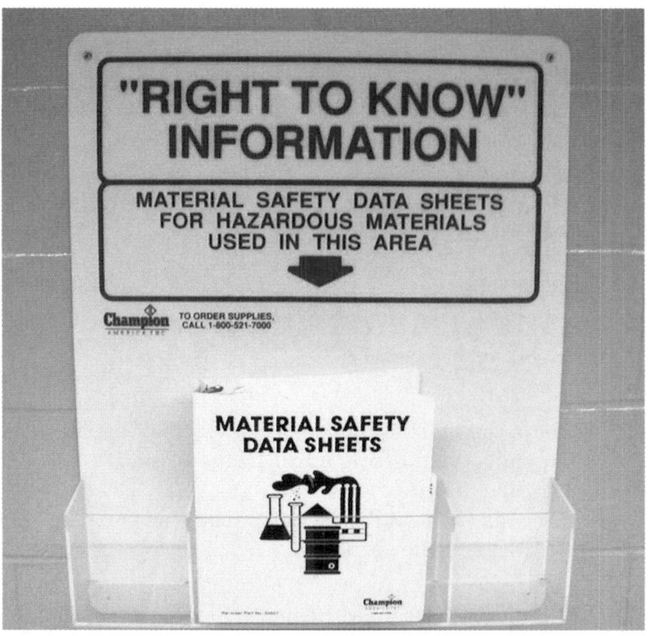

Figure 2–62 Material safety data sheets (MSDS) should be readily available for use by anyone in the area who may come into contact with hazardous materials.

FIRE EXTINGUISHERS

There are four classes of fire extinguishers. Each class should be used on specific fires only:

- **Class A** is designed for use on general combustibles, such as cloth, paper, and wood.
- **Class B** is designed for use on flammable liquids and greases, including gasoline, oil, thinners, and solvents.
- **Class C** is used only on electrical fires.
- **Class D** is effective only on combustible metals such as powdered aluminum, sodium, or magnesium.

The class rating is clearly marked on the side of every fire extinguisher. Many extinguishers are good for multiple types of fires. See Figure 2–63.

When using a fire extinguisher, remember the word "PASS."

P = Pull the safety pin.

A = Aim the nozzle of the extinguisher at the base of the fire.

S = Squeeze the lever to actuate the extinguisher.

S = Sweep the nozzle from side to side.

See Figure 2–64.

Types of Fire Extinguishers

Types of fire extinguishers include:

- **Water**—A water fire extinguisher is usually in a pressurized container and is good to use on

Pound with Something Softer

If you must pound on something, be sure to use a tool that is softer than what you are about to pound on to avoid damage. Examples are given in the following table.

The Material Being Pounded	What to Pound With
Steel or cast iron	Brass or aluminum hammer or punch
Aluminum	Plastic or rawhide mallet or plastic-covered dead-blow hammer
Plastic	Rawhide mallet or plastic dead-blow hammer

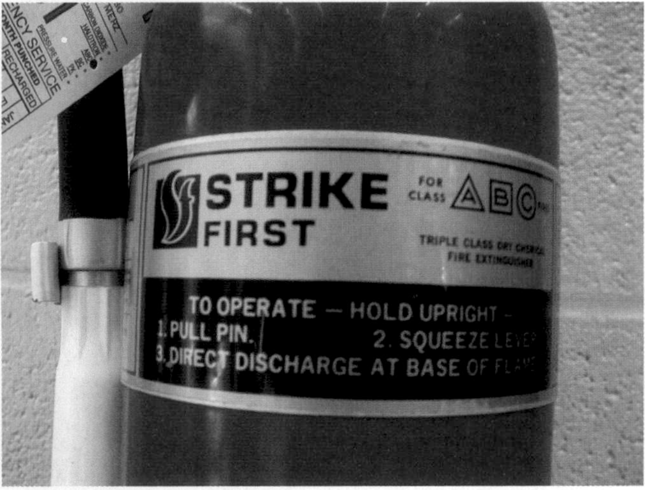

Figure 2–63 A typical fire extinguisher designed to be used on type A, B, or C fires.

SAFETY TIP

Air Hose Safety

Improper use of an air nozzle can cause blindness or deafness. If an air nozzle is used to dry and clean parts, make sure the air stream is directed away from anyone else in the immediate area. Coil and store air hoses when they are not in use.

Class A fires by reducing the temperature to the point where a fire cannot be sustained.

- **Carbon dioxide (CO_2)**—A carbon dioxide fire extinguisher is good for almost any type of fire, especially Class B or Class C materials. A CO_2 fire extinguisher works by removing the oxygen from the fire, and the cold CO_2 also helps reduce the temperature of the fire.
- **Dry chemical (yellow)**—A dry chemical fire extinguisher is good for Class A, B, or C fires by coating the flammable materials, which eliminates the oxygen from fire. A dry chemical fire extinguisher tends to be very corrosive and will cause damage to electronic devices.

SUMMARY

1. Bolts, studs, and nuts are commonly used as fasteners in the chassis. The sizes for metric and fractional threads are different and are not interchangeable. The grade is the rating of the strength of a fastener.
2. Whenever a vehicle is raised above the ground, it must be supported at a substantial section of the body or frame.

Figure 2–64 A CO_2 fire extinguisher being used on a fire set in an open steel drum during a demonstration at a fire department training centre.

3. Hazardous materials include common automotive chemicals, liquids, and lubricants, especially those whose ingredients contain *chlor* or *fluor* in their name. Asbestos fibres should be avoided and removed according to current laws and regulations.

REVIEW QUESTIONS

1. List three precautions that must be taken whenever hoisting (lifting) a vehicle.
2. List five common automotive chemicals or products that may be considered hazardous materials.
3. List five precautions to which every technician should adhere when working with automotive products and chemicals.
4. Describe how to determine the grade of a fastener, including how the markings differ between customary and metric bolts.

RED SEAL CERTIFICATION-TYPE QUESTIONS

1. What is the most stable position at which to place the hoist pads when lifting a full-frame vehicle?
   - **a.** Body welds
   - **b.** Gas tank and radiator bracket
   - **c.** Four frame corners
   - **d.** Floor pan
2. The correct location for the pads when hoisting or jacking the vehicle can often be found in the _____.
   - **a.** Service manual
   - **b.** Shop manual
   - **c.** Owner's manual
   - **d.** All of the above

3. Hazardous materials include all of the following except _____.
  a. Engine oil
  b. Asbestos
  c. Water
  d. Brake cleaner

4. To determine if a product or substance being used is hazardous, consult _____.
  a. A dictionary
  b. An MSDS
  c. SAE standards
  d. EPA guidelines

5. For the best working position, the work should be ____.
  a. At neck or head level
  b. At knee or ankle level
  c. Overhead by about 1 foot
  d. At chest or elbow level

6. When working with hand tools, always _____.
  a. Push the wrench—don't pull toward you
  b. Pull a wrench—don't push a wrench

7. A high-strength bolt is identified by _____.
  a. A UNC symbol
  b. Lines on the head
  c. Strength letter codes
  d. The coarse threads

8. A fastener that uses threads on both ends is called a _____.
  a. Cap screw
  b. Stud
  c. Machine screw
  d. Crest fastener

9. The proper term for Channel Locks is _____.
  a. Vise Grips
  b. Crescent wrench
  c. Locking pliers
  d. Multigroove adjustable pliers

10. The proper term for Vise Grips is _____.
  a. Locking pliers
  b. Slip-joint pliers
  c. Side cuts
  d. Multigroove adjustable pliers

3

Preventative Maintenance and Service Procedures

OBJECTIVES: After studying Chapter 3, you should be able to:

1. Prepare for the interprovincial Red Seal certification examination in Appendix I (Engine Repair) on the topics covered in this chapter.
2. Correctly identify a vehicle using the vehicle identification number (VIN).
3. Perform routine fluid and service checks.
4. Describe how to install wheels and tighten lug nuts using a torque wrench and the proper sequence.
5. Describe the proper procedure for changing the engine oil and performing complete chassis system lubrication and under-vehicle inspection.

Beginning automotive service technicians are often required to perform routine service operations. It is the purpose of this chapter to introduce the reader to these various service procedures.

IDENTIFYING A VEHICLE

Before service work is started, the vehicle must be properly identified to be sure that the proper replacement parts are ordered. A vehicle is first identified by make, model, and year. For example:

Make—Chevrolet
Model—Blazer
Year—1998

The year of the vehicle is often difficult to determine exactly. A model may be introduced as the next year's model as soon as January of the previous year. Typically, a new model year starts in September or October of the year prior to the actual new year, but not always. This is why the **vehicle identification number,** usually abbreviated **VIN,** is so important. See Figure 3–1. Since 1981 all vehicle manufacturers have used a VIN that is 17 characters long. Although every vehicle manufacturer assigns various letters or numbers within these seventeen characters, there are some constants, including:

- The first number or letter designates the country of origin.

1 = United States	K = Korea
2 = Canada	L = Taiwan
3 = Mexico	S = England
4 = United States	V = France
6 = Australia	W = Germany
9 = Brazil	Y = Sweden
J = Japan	Z = Italy

- The model of the vehicle is commonly the fourth or fifth character.
- The eighth character is often the engine code. (Some engines cannot be determined by the VIN number.)
- The tenth character represents the year on all vehicles. See the following chart.

VIN Year Chart

A = 1980	B = 1981	C = 1982
D = 1983	E = 1984	F = 1985
G = 1986	H = 1987	J = 1988

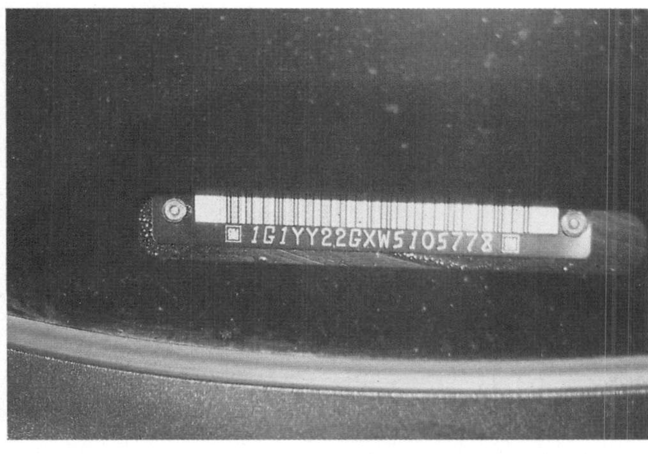

Figure 3–1 Typical vehicle identification number (VIN) as viewed through the windshield.

K = 1989	L = 1990	M = 1991
N = 1992	P = 1993	R = 1994
S = 1995	T = 1996	V = 1997
W = 1998	X = 1999	Y = 2000
1 = 2001	2 = 2002	3 = 2003
4 = 2004	5 = 2005	6 = 2006
7 = 2007	8 = 2008	9 = 2009

GETTING READY FOR SERVICE

Before most service work is done, the hood (engine compartment cover) must be opened. Often the struts that hold a hood open are weak or defective. Therefore, before starting to work under the hood, always make sure that the hood is securely held open. See Figure 3–2 for two examples of how this could be done.

(a)

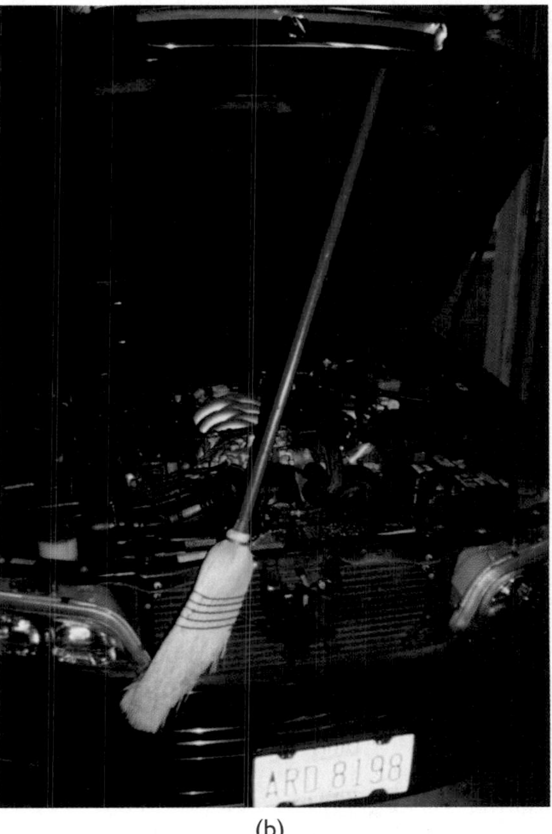

(b)

Figure 3–2 (a) To properly secure the hood in the open position, be certain that the prop rod is inserted into the designated opening in the hood. (b) If all else fails, the technician should use a stick or broom to hold the hood in the open position. The technician has to be careful to not bump the stick or the hood could cause serious injury.

Frequently Asked Question ???

What Is the Julian Date?

Often, engine designs or parts change during a production year. The point at which a change occurred is usually reported to technicians in service bulletins, service manuals, or parts books as a vehicle serial number or a certain Julian date. A Julian date is simply the number of the day of the year. For example, January 1 is the day 001 and December 31 is usually day 365. The Julian date is commonly used in industry and is named for Julius Caesar, who first used a 365-day calendar, with 366 days every four years. There are calendars available that list the number of the day of the year, making usage of the Julian date easier.

TECH TIP 

Do No Harm

As stated in the Hippocratic oath, a doctor agrees first to do no harm to the patient during treatment. Service technicians should also try to do no harm to the vehicle while it is being serviced.

Always ask, "Am I going to do any harm if I do this?" before you do it.

To protect the fenders of the vehicle from possible damage, fender covers should always be used, as shown in Figure 3–3.

WIPER BLADE INSPECTION AND REPLACEMENT

Windshield wiper blades are constructed of rubber and tend to become brittle due to age. Wiper blades should be cleaned whenever the vehicle is cleaned using water and a soft cloth. Wiper blade or wiper blade insert replacement includes the following steps:

- Turn the ignition switch to on (run).
- Turn the wiper switch on and operate the wipers.
- When the wipers are located in an easy-to-reach location, turn the ignition switch off. The wipers should stop.
- Remove the insert or the entire arm as per the instructions on the replacement windshield wiper blade package.
- After double-checking that the wiper is securely attached, turn the ignition switch on (run).

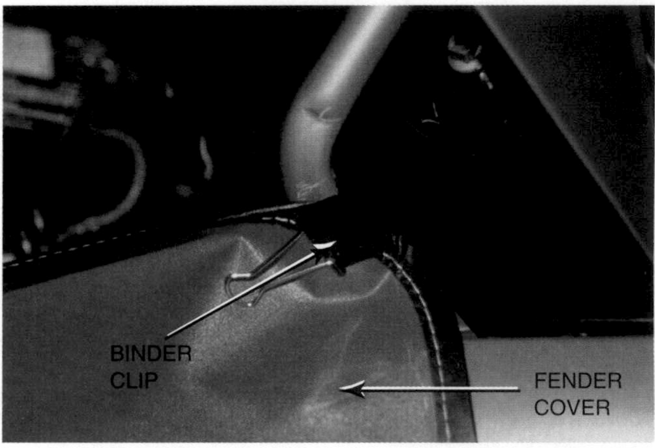

Figure 3–3 A binder clip available at most office supply stores can be used to hold a fender cover to the lip of the fender to prevent it from falling off. The clip in this photo attaches the cover to the hood hinge because this particular vehicle did not have a lip on the inside of the fender.

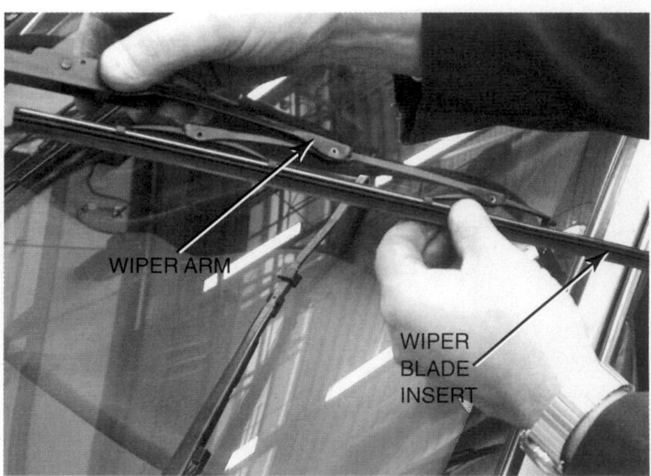

Figure 3–4 Installing a wiper blade insert into a wiper arm.

- Turn the wiper switch off and allow the wipers to reach the park position. Check for proper operation.

See Figure 3–4.

AIR FILTER INSPECTION/REPLACEMENT

The air filter should be replaced according to the vehicle manufacturer's recommendations. Many vehicle manufacturers recommend replacing the air filter every 50 000 km (30 000 miles) or more frequently under dusty conditions. Many service technicians recommend replacing the air filter every year. See Figure 3–5.

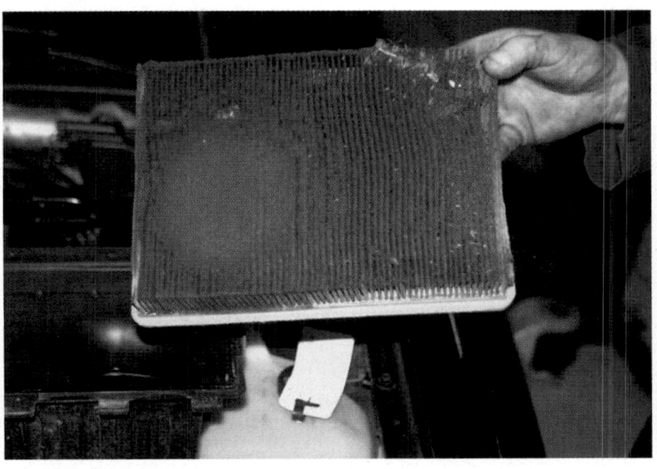

Figure 3–5 An excessively dirty air filter. This filter came from a Pontiac Bonneville that had not been serviced for over 80 000 km!

Figure 3–6 A master brake cylinder with a transparent reservoir. The brake fluid should be between the "MAX" and the "MIN" levels as indicated on the reservoir.

BRAKE FLUID LEVEL INSPECTION

The brake fluid should be checked at the same time the engine oil is changed (every 5000 km [3000 mi] or every three months, whichever occurs first). There are two types of brake master cylinders:

- *Transparent Reservoir*—This type allows viewing of the brake fluid (and hydraulic clutch master cylinder if so equipped) without having to remove the cover of the reservoir. See Figure 3–6. The proper level should be between the MIN (minimum) level indicated and the MAX (maximum) level indicated on the clear plastic reservoir.
- *Metal or Nontransparent Plastic Reservoir*—This type of reservoir requires that the cover be removed to check the level of the brake fluid. The proper level of brake fluid should be 6 mm from the top.

CAUTION: Do not overfill a brake master cylinder. The brake fluid gets hotter as the brakes are used and there must be room in the master cylinder reservoir for the brake fluid to expand.

BRAKE FLUID TYPES

Brake fluid is made from a combination of various types of glycol, a non-petroleum based fluid. Brake fluid is a polyalkylene-glycol-ether mixture called **polyglycol** for short. *All polyglycol brake fluid is clear to amber in colour.*

CAUTION: DOT 3 brake fluid is a very strong solvent and can remove paint! Care is required when working with DOT 3 brake fluid to avoid contact with the vehicle's painted surfaces. It also takes the colour out of leather shoes.

All automotive brake fluid must meet Transport Canada's Motor Vehicle Safety Standard 116. The Society of Automotive Engineers (SAE) and the Canadian Standards Association (CSA) have established brake fluid specification standards.

DOT 3

DOT 3 is the brake fluid most often used. It absorbs moisture and according to SAE, DOT 3 can absorb 2% of its volume in water per year. Moisture is absorbed by the brake fluid through microscopic seams in the brake system and around seals. Over time, the water will corrode the system and thicken the brake fluid. The moisture also can cause a spongy brake pedal action due to reduced vapor-lock temperature. See Figure 3–7. DOT 3 must be used from a sealed (capped) container. If allowed to remain open for any length of time, DOT 3 will absorb moisture from the surrounding air.

DOT 4

DOT 4 is formulated for use by all vehicles, imported or domestic. It is commonly called LMA (low

Figure 3–7 DOT 3 brake fluid. Always use brake fluid from a sealed container because the fluid absorbs moisture from the air. Such contaminated brake fluid has a lower boiling point and can cause rust to form in the brake system components.

moisture absorption) because DOT 4 does not absorb water as fast as DOT 3. It is still affected by moisture, however, and should be used only from a sealed container. The cost of DOT 4 is approximately double the cost of DOT 3. *DOT 4 can be used wherever DOT 3 is specified.*

DOT 5

DOT 5 is commonly called **silicone brake fluid** and is made from polydimethylsiloxanes. It does not absorb any water and is therefore called nonhygroscopic. DOT 5 brake fluid does not mix with and should not be used with DOT 3 or DOT 4 brake fluid. *DOT 5 brake fluid is purple (violet) in color to distinguish it from DOT 3 or DOT 4 brake fluid.*

NOTE: Even though DOT 5 does not normally absorb water, it is still tested using standardized SAE procedures in a humidity chamber. After a fixed amount of time, the brake fluid is measured for boiling point. Since it has had a *chance* to absorb moisture, the boiling point after this sequence is called the minimum wet boiling point.

DOT 5.1

DOT 5.1 is a non-silicone-based polyglycol fluid and is clear to amber in colour. This severe duty fluid has a boiling point of over 260°C (500°F) equal to the boiling point of silicone-based DOT 5 fluid. Unlike DOT 5, DOT 5.1 can be mixed with either DOT 3 or DOT 4 according to the brake fluid manufacturer's recommendations.

CAUTION: Some vehicle manufacturers such as DaimlerChrysler do not recommend the use of or the mixing of other types of polyglycol brake fluid and specify the use of DOT 3 brake fluid only. Always follow the vehicle manufacturer's recommendation.

Brake Fluid Boiling Point

	Dry	Wet
DOT 3	205°C (401°F)	140°C (284°F)
DOT 4	230°C (446°F)	155°C (311°F)
DOT 5.1	260°C (500°F)	180°C (356°F)
DOT 5*	260°C (500°F)	180°C (356°F)

*Do not use DOT 5 in vehicles with ABS.

ENGINE OIL LEVEL AND CONDITION

The oil level should be checked when the vehicle is parked on level ground and after the engine has been off for at least several minutes. Remove the oil level indicator, commonly called a **dipstick,** wipe the oil off, and reinsert it all the way down. See Figure 3–8. Once again remove the dipstick and check where the oil level touches the indicator. The "add" mark is usually at the 1 L (one litre) low point. See Figure 3–9. If oil needs to be added, use the proper oil and add to the engine through the oil fill opening. Engine oil specifications and the procedure for changing the oil are included later in this chapter.

Figure 3–8 A typical engine oil level indicator (dipstick).

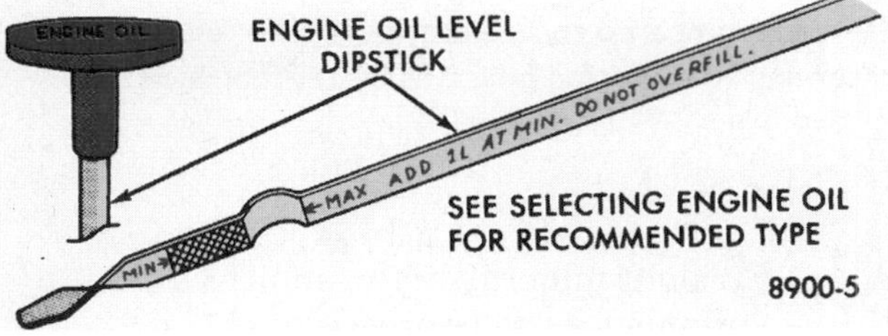

Figure 3–9 The oil level should read no higher than the "MAX" level and no lower than the "MIN" level when the vehicle is parked on a level surface and the oil has had some time to sit with the engine off. This time is necessary to allow the oil to flow from the upper region of the engine down into the oil pan. (Courtesy of Chrysler Corporation)

TECH TIP 

Follow the Seasons

Vehicle owners often forget when they last changed the oil. This is particularly true of the person who owns or is responsible for several vehicles. A helpful method for remembering when the oil should be changed is to change the oil at the start of each season of the year.

- **Fall** (September 21)
- **Winter** (December 21)
- **Spring** (March 21)
- **Summer** (June 21)

Remembering that the oil needs to be changed on these dates helps owners budget for the expense and the time needed.

ENGINE OIL CHANGES

Most automotive experts recommend that the engine oil be replaced and a new oil filter installed every 5000 km (3000 mi) or every three months, whichever occurs first. Most vehicle manufacturers recommend that the oil be changed according to a "normal" or "severe use" schedule, described below.

Most vehicles can be driven under severe conditions if all of these factors are considered. Most manufacturers use an oil life indicator to inform the driver when oil needs to be changed.

VISCOSITY OF OIL (SAE RATING)

The word **viscosity** means resistance to flow. An oil with a high viscosity has a higher resistance to flow and is thicker than a lower-viscosity oil.

Normal Use	Severe Use
Most trips over 15 km (9 mi).	Most trips less than 5 to 15 km (3–9 mi).
Operating a vehicle when the outside temperature is above freezing (0°C/32°F).	Operating the vehicle when the outside temperature is below freezing (0°C/32°F).
Most trips do not include slow or stop-and-go driving.	Most trips include slow or stop-and-go driving.
Not towing a trailer or carrying a heavy load.	Towing a trailer or hauling a heavy load.
Driving without dusty conditions.	Driving in dusty conditions.
No police, taxi, or commercial use of the vehicle.	Use by police, taxi, or commercial operation.
The oil change interval recommended by most vehicle manufacturers under normal conditions is 12 000 km (7500 miles) or six months, whichever occurs first.	The oil change interval recommended by most vehicle manufacturers operating under severe conditions is every 5000 km (3000 mi) or every three months, whichever occurs first.

Oil is tested and assigned a viscosity number according to standards established by the Society of Automotive Engineers (SAE). It is tested at two different temperatures and assigned a number based on the oil's flow characteristics at that temperature. A thin oil is assigned a lower number and a thicker oil is assigned a higher number. Oil tested at −18°C (0°F) has the letter W after its number. The W represents **winter.** For example, an SAE 10W engine oil was tested at −18°C (0°F) and assigned a thickness rating of 10. Oil tested at 100°C (212°F) has no letter after its number. Again, the higher the number assigned, the thicker the oil. For example, an SAE 30 oil is an oil tested at 100°C (212°F).

Multi-Viscosity Engine Oils

Viscosity index (VI) improvers can be added to engine oil to prevent it from becoming thin at higher temperatures. For example, SAE 5W oil with the VI improvers added can be rated as an SAE 30 when tested at 100°C (212°F). This oil is therefore rated as an SAE 5W-30 indicating that it flowed the same as an SAE 5W when tested at 0°F and flowed the same as an SAE 30 when tested at 100°C (212°F).

Because of the wide range of temperatures at which this oil can function, multi-viscosity oils such as SAE 5W-30 and SAE 10W-30 are often the only oils recommended for use.

NOTE: Some vehicle manufacturers such as Ford and Honda recommend the exclusive use of SAE 5W-20 or SAE 0W-20 engine oil. The owner's manual warns that this is the only viscosity that is acceptable to use under all temperatures and operating conditions. Always follow the vehicle manufacturer's recommended engine oil and viscosity.

QUALITY OF OIL (API RATING)

Although it is generally difficult to purchase low-quality oil today, it is possible to select the incorrect grade for the intended application. The quality rating is established by test procedures set up by the American Petroleum Institute (API), formerly the American Society for Testing and Materials (ASTM), with the cooperation of the Society of Automotive Engineers.

In gasoline engine oil ratings, the letter *S* means *service,* but it can be remembered as standing for oil to be used in *s*park ignition engines. The rating system is open-ended, so newer, improved ratings can be readily added as necessary (skipping the letter *I* to avoid confusion with the number 1).

Figure 3–10 API doughnut for an SAE 5W-30, SL engine oil. When compared to a reference oil, the "energy conserving" designation indicates better fuel economy.

SA	Straight mineral oil (no additives), not suitable for use in any engine
SB	Nondetergent oil with additives to control wear and oil oxidation
SC	Obsolete (1964)
SD	Obsolete (1968)
SE	Obsolete (1972)
SF	Obsolete (1980)
SG	Obsolete (1988)
SH	Obsolete (1993)
SJ	Obsolete (1997)
SL	Highest rating starting in 2001

See Figure 3–10.

NOTE: Older-model vehicles for which older, now obsolete ratings were specified can use the newer, higher-rated engine oil. Newly overhauled antique cars or engines can also use the newer, improved oils. The new oils give all the protection of the older oils, plus additional protection.

Diesel classifications begin with the letter *C,* which stands for *commercial,* but which can also be remembered as standing for oil to be used in *c*ompression ignition or diesel engines.

ILSAC OIL RATING

The International Lubricant Standardization and Approval Committee (ILSAC) developed an oil rating that consolidates the SAE viscosity rating and the API quality rating. If an engine oil meets the standards, a starburst symbol is displayed on the front of the oil container. If the starburst is present, the vehicle owner and technician know that the oil is suitable for use in almost any gasoline engine. See Figure 3–11. The original GF-1 (gasoline fueled) rating was updated to GF-2 in 1997 and to GF-3 in 2001.

Figure 3–11 The International Lubricant Standardization and Approval Committee (ILSAC) starburst symbol. If this symbol is on the front of the container of oil, then it is acceptable for use in almost any gasoline engine.

TECH TIP 

Wearing Rubber Gloves Saves Your Hands

Many technicians wear rubber gloves not only to help keep their hands clean but also to help protect their skin from the effects of dirty engine oil and other possibly hazardous materials. Several types of gloves and their characteristics include:

- **Latex surgical gloves**—These gloves are relatively inexpensive, but tend to stretch, swell, and weaken when exposed to gas, oil, or solvents.
- **Vinyl gloves**—These gloves are also inexpensive and are not affected by gas, oil, or solvents. See Figure 3–12.
- **Polyurethane gloves**—These gloves are more expensive, yet very strong. Even though these gloves are also not affected by gas, oil, or solvents, they do tend to be slippery.
- **Nitrile gloves**—These gloves are exactly like latex gloves, but are not affected by gas, oil, or solvents, yet they tend to be expensive.

Many service technicians prefer to use the vinyl gloves, but with an additional pair of nylon gloves worn under the vinyl. Nylon gloves look like white cotton gloves and when worn under the others help keep moisture under control. (Plastic gloves on a hot summer day can soon become wet with perspiration.) The nylon gloves provide additional protection and are washable.

Diesel Engines

Category	Status	Service
CH-4	Current	Introduced December 1, 1998. For high-speed, four-stroke engines designed to meet 1998 exhaust emission standards. Can be used in place of CD, CE, CF-4, and CG-4 oils.
CG-4	Current	Introduced in 1995. For severe duty, high-speed, four-stroke engines using fuel with less than 0.5% weight sulfur. Can be used in place of CD, CE, and CF-4 oils.
CF-4	Current	Introduced in 1990. For high-speed, four-stroke, naturally aspirated and turbocharged engines. Can be used in place of CD and CE oils.
CF-2	Current	Introduced in 1994. For severe duty, two-stroke-cycle engines. Can be used in place of CD-II oils.
CF	Current	Introduced in 1994. For off-road, indirect-injected and other diesel engines including those using fuel with over 0.5% weight sulfur. Can be used in place of CD oils.
CE	Obsolete	Introduced in 1987. For high-speed, four-stroke, naturally aspirated and turbocharged engines. Can be used in place of CC and CD oils.
CD-II	Obsolete	Introduced in 1987. For two-stroke-cycle engines.
CD	Obsolete	Introduced in 1955. For certain naturally aspirated and turbocharged engines.
CC	Obsolete	For engines introduced in 1961.
CB	Obsolete	For moderate duty engines from 1949 to 1960.
CA	Obsolete	For light duty engines (1940s and 1950s).

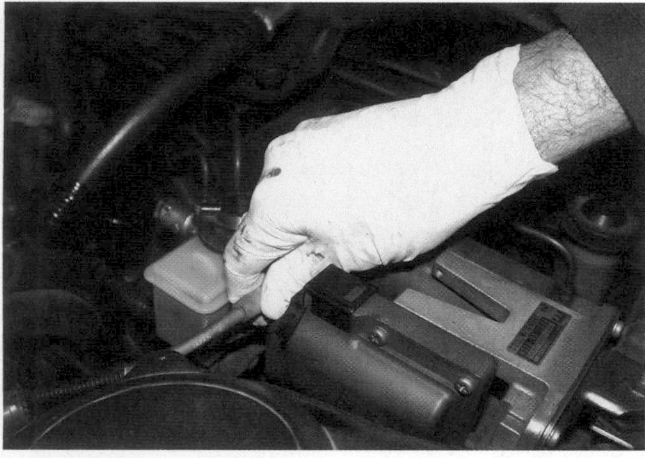

Figure 3–12 Protective gloves should be worn whenever working around grease or oil to help prevent possible skin problems. They help keep your hands clean, too!

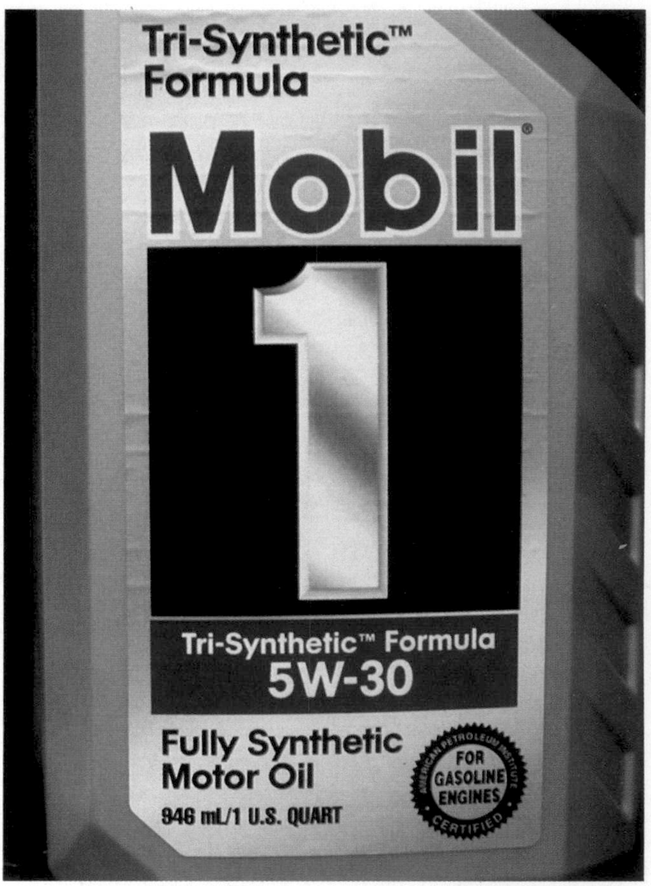

Figure 3–13 Mobil 1 synthetic engine oil is used by several vehicle manufacturers in new engines.

SYNTHETIC ENGINE OIL

According to the Society of Automotive Engineers publications, engine oil is classified into groups as follows.

Group I—Mineral, non-synthetic, base oil with few if any additives. This type of oil is suitable for light lubricating needs and rust protection and is not to be used in an engine.

Group II—Mineral oils with quality additive packages. Most of the conventional engine oils are Group II.

Group III—Hydrogenated synthetic compounds commonly referred to as hydrowaxes. This is the lowest cost synthetic engine oil. Castrol Syntec is a Group III oil.

Group IV—Synthetic oils made from mineral oil and monomolecular oil called polyalphaolefin or POA. Mobil 1 is an example of a Group IV synthetic oil as shown in Figure 3–13.

Group V—Non-mineral sources such as alcohol from corn called diesters or polyolesters. Red Line synthetic oil is an example of a Group V oil.

Groups III, IV, and V are all considered to be synthetic because the molecular structure of the finished product does not occur naturally and is man-made through chemical processes. All synthetic engine oils perform better than Group II (mineral) oils especially when tested according to the Noack Volatility Test ASTM D-5800. This test procedure measures the ability of an oil to stay in grade after it has been heated to 150°C (300°F) for one hour. The oil is then measured for percentage of weight loss. As the lighter components boil off, the oil's viscosity will increase. If you start with an SAE 5W oil, it could test as an SAE 15W or even an SAE 20W at the end of the test. It is important that the oil you buy stay in grade for the proper lubrication of your engine.

Another major advantage of using synthetic engine oil is its ability to remain fluid at very low temperatures. This characteristic of synthetic oil makes it popular in colder climates where cold-engine cranking is important.

The major disadvantage is cost. The cost of synthetic engine oils can be four or five times the cost of Group II mineral engine oils. Some synthetic engine oils are blended with Group II mineral oils and these must be labeled as *blends*.

ENGINE OIL DISPOSAL

All used engine oil should be disposed of or recycled according to federal, provincial, or local rules and regulations. Used engine oil is considered to be haz-

TECH TIP 

Use Synthetic Engine Oil in Lawn and Garden Equipment

Most 4-cycle lawn and garden equipment engines are air cooled and operate hotter than many liquid cooled engines. Lawn mowers and other small engines are often operated near or at maximum speed and power output for hours at a time. These operating conditions are hard on any engine oil. Try using a synthetic oil. The cost is not as big a factor because most small 4-cycle lawn mower engines require only about 0.5 litre (1/2 quart) of oil. The synthetic oil is able to perform under high temperatures better than conventional mineral oils.

ardous due to the dissolved metals and acids that are created in an operating engine.

OIL FILTERS

The oil within the engine is pumped from the oil pan through the filter before it goes into the engine lubricating system passages. The filter is made from either closely packed cloth fibres or a porous paper. Large particles are trapped by the filter, while microscopic particles will flow through the filter pores. These particles are so small that they can flow through the bearing oil film and not touch the surfaces, so they do no damage. See Figure 3–15.

Many oil filters are equipped with an **anti-drainback valve** that prevents oil from draining out of the filter when the engine is shut off. See Figure 3–16. This valve keeps oil in the filter and allows the engine to receive immediate lubrication as soon as the engine starts.

TECH TIP 

The Pick Trick

Removing an oil filter that is installed upside down can be a real mess. When this design filter is loosened, oil flows out from around the sealing gasket. To prevent this from happening, use a pick and poke a hole in the top of the filter, as shown in Figure 3–14. This small hole allows air to get into the filter, thereby allowing the oil to drain back into the engine rather than remain in the filter. After punching the hole in the filter, be sure to wait several minutes to allow time for the trapped oil to drain down into the engine before loosening the filter.

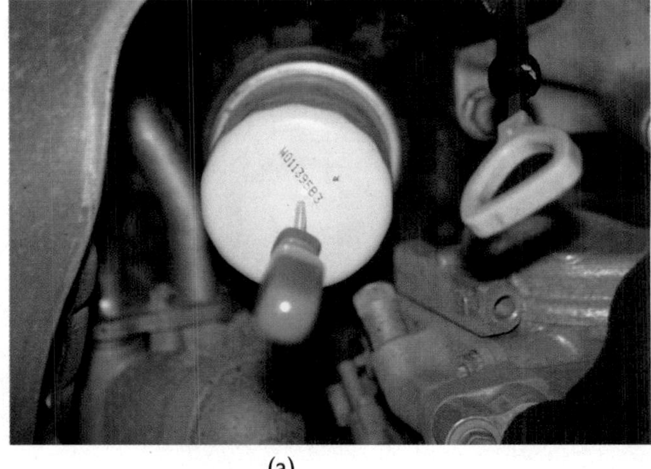

(a)

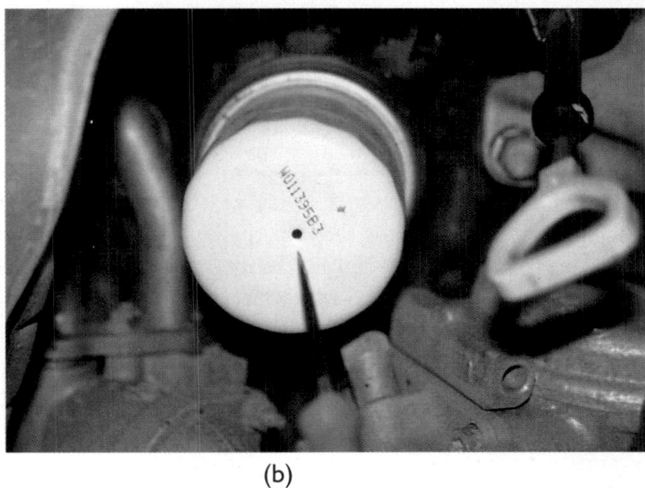

(b)

Figure 3–14 (a) A pick is pushed through the top of an oil filter that is positioned vertically. (b) When the pick is removed, a small hole allows air to get into the top of the filter which then allows the oil to drain out of the filter and back into the engine.

Either the engine or the filter has a **bypass** that will allow the oil to go around the filter element. The bypass allows the engine to be lubricated with dirty oil, rather than having no lubrication, if the filter becomes plugged. The oil also goes through the bypass when the oil is cold and thick. Most engine manufacturers recommend filter changes at every other oil change period. Correct oil filter selection includes using a filter with an internal bypass when the engine is not equipped with one.

Oil filters should be crushed and drained of oil before discarding. See Figure 3–17. After the oil has been drained, the filter can usually be disposed of as regular metal scrap. Always check and follow government oil filter disposal rules, regulations, and procedures.

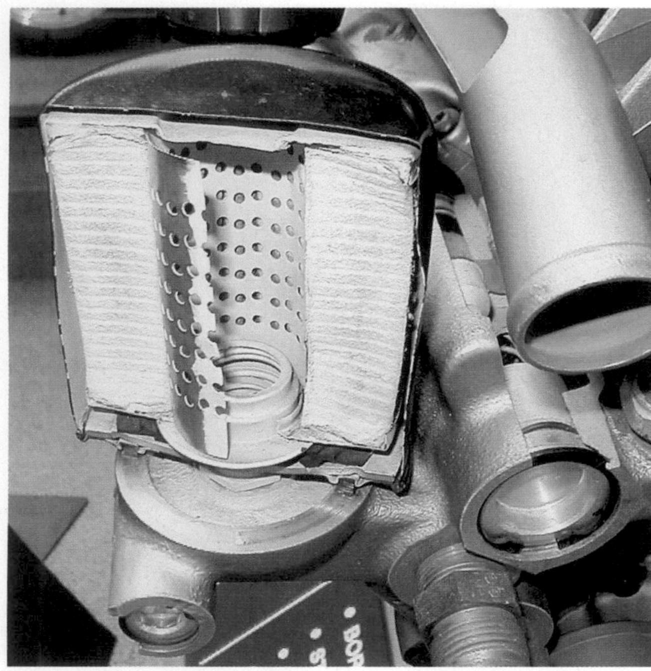

Figure 3–15 A cutaway of a typical spin-on oil filter. Engine oil enters the filter through the small holes around the centre of the filter and flows through the pleated paper filtering media and out through the large hole in the centre of the filter. The centre metal cylinder with holes is designed to keep the paper filter from collapsing under the pressure.

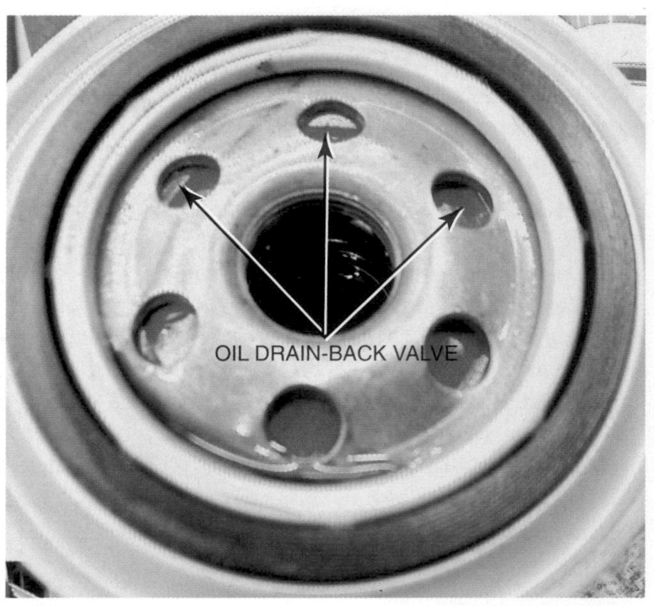

Figure 3–16 A rubber diaphragm acts as an antidrainback valve to keep the oil in the filter when the engine is stopped and the oil pressure drops to zero.

Figure 3–17 A typical oil filter crusher. The hydraulic ram forces out most of the oil from the filter. The oil is trapped underneath the crusher and is recycled.

Frequently Asked Question ???

Does the Oil Filter Remove All the Dirt?

Many persons believe that oil filters will remove all dirt from the oil being circulated through the filtering material. Most oil filters will filter particles that are about 10 to 20 μm in size. 1 μm (often called a micron) is one millionth of a metre.

Most dirt and carbon particles that turn engine oil black are less than a micron in size. In other words, it takes about three million of these carbon particles to cover a pinhead. To help visualize how small these particles are, consider that a typical human hair is 60 μm in diameter. In fact, anything smaller than 40 μm is not visible to the human eye. Dispersants are added to engine oil to prevent dirt from adhering to form sludge. It is the same dispersant additive that prevents dirt from being filtered or removed by other means. If an oil filter could filter particles down to 1 μm in size, the engine would not receive sufficient oil through the filter for lubrication. Oil recycling companies use special chemicals to break down the dispersants, which permits the dirt in the oil to combine into larger units that can be filtered or processed out of the oil.

COOLING SYSTEM SERVICE

Normal maintenance involves an occasional check on the coolant level. The front of the radiator should be carefully inspected and cleaned of bugs, dirt, or mud that can often restrict air flow. Maintenance should also include a visual inspection for signs of coolant system leaks and for the condition of the coolant hoses and accessory drive belts.

CAUTION: The coolant level should only be checked when the engine is cool. Removing the pressure cap from a hot engine will release the cooling system pressure when the coolant temperature is above its atmospheric boiling temperature. When the cap is removed, the pressure will instantly drop to atmospheric pressure level, causing the coolant to boil immediately. Vapours from the boiling liquid will blow coolant from the system. Coolant will be lost, and a person may be injured or burned by the high-temperature coolant that is blown out of the filler opening.

The coolant-antifreeze mixture is renewed at periodic intervals. There are five types of antifreeze coolant available including:

- **Ethylene glycol**—This is the type that has been used almost exclusively since the 1950s. It is sweet tasting and can harm or kill animals or pets if swallowed.
- **Propylene glycol**—Similar to ethylene glycol, this type of coolant is less harmful to pets and animals because it is not sweet tasting, although it is still harmful if swallowed. This type of coolant should not be mixed with ethylene glycol coolant.

Figure 3–18 Since the mid 1990s, many vehicle manufacturers have been using antifreeze coolant that is silicate and phosphate free. Always check the owner's manual for the specifications for the recommended engine coolant.

NOTE: Some vehicle manufacturers do not recommend the use of propylene glycol coolant. Check the recommendations in the owner's manual or service manual before using it in a vehicle.

- **Organic acid technology (OAT)** antifreeze coolant—This type does not contain silicates or phosphates. It is usually orange in color and was first developed by Havoline (called **DEX-COOL**) and used in General Motors vehicles starting in 1996. See Figure 3–18.
- **Hybrid organic acid technology (HOAT)**—This is a newer variation of this technology and is similar to the OAT-type antifreeze as it uses additives that are not abrasive to water pumps, yet provide the correct pH. The pH of the coolant is usually above 11. A pH of 7 is neutral, with lower numbers indicating an acidic solution and higher numbers indicating a caustic solution. If the pH is too high, the coolant can cause scaling and reduce the heat transfer ability of the coolant. If the pH is too low, the resulting acidic

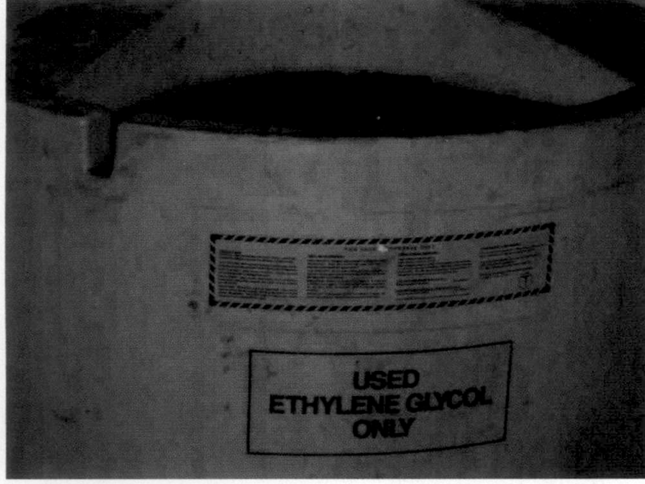

Figure 3–19 Used antifreeze coolant should be kept separate and stored in a leak-proof container until it can be recycled or disposed of according to federal, provincial, and local laws. Often the storage barrel is placed inside another container to catch any coolant that may spill out of the inside barrel. (Courtesy of Roger Davey)

solution could cause corrosion of the engine components exposed to the coolant.

- **Phosphate-free antifreeze**—Some vehicle manufacturers recommend the use of phosphate-free coolant. This coolant is ethylene-glycol based and formulated without phosphate. Some ethylene-glycol based coolant contains phosphate that could cause a white deposit to form in the cooling system if the water used to mix with the coolant is high in mineral content.

ANTIFREEZE/COOLANT DISPOSAL

Used coolant drained from the engine can be disposed of by carefully pouring it into a proper antifreeze recycling container. Most antifreeze recycling machines will separate any of the blends of antifreeze mixes. The most accurate way to determine your area's correct procedure in accordance with provincial laws is to consult a recycling company. Figure 3–19 shows a typical recycling container.

RADIATOR AND HEATER HOSES

Upper and lower radiator hoses must be pliable, yet not soft. The lower hose must have a spring inside to prevent the hose from being sucked closed, since the lower hose is attached to the suction side of the water pump. The bypass hose (if equipped) and heater hoses have a 13, 16, or 19 mm inside diameter and connect the engine cooling system to the heater core. (A heater core looks like a small radiator located inside the vehicle.) All automotive hose is constructed of rubber with reinforcing fabric weaving for strength. All hoses should be inspected for leaks (especially near hose clamps), cracks, swollen areas indicating possible broken reinforcing material, and excessively brittle, soft, and swollen sections. See Figure 3–20.

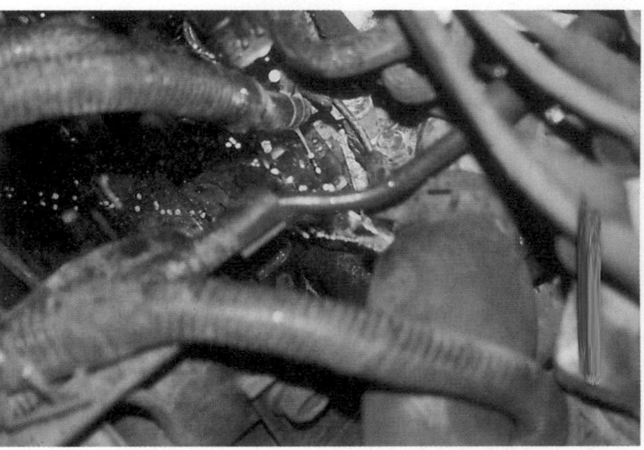

Figure 3–20 This old upper hose had a split, causing coolant to squirt out.

AUTOMATIC TRANSMISSION FLUID CHECK

The automatic transmission fluid is another vital fluid that should be checked regularly. Most automatic transmission fluid levels should be checked under the following conditions:

- The vehicle should be parked on a level surface.
- The transmission fluid should be at normal operating temperature. This may require the vehicle to be driven several miles before the level is checked.
- The engine should be running with the transmission in neutral or park as specified by the vehicle manufacturer.

> **NOTE:** Honda and Acura manufacturers usually specify that the transmission fluid be checked with the engine off. The recommended procedure is usually stamped on the transmission dipstick or written in the owner's manual and/or service manual.

TECH TIP 

The Cut-and-Peel Trick

It is often difficult to remove a radiator or heater hose from the fittings on the radiator or heater core. To avoid possible damage to expensive radiator or heater cores, do not pull or twist the hose to remove it. Simply use a utility knife and slit the hose lengthwise and then use your finger to peel the hose off of the radiator or heater core. Although this procedure will not work if the hose is to be reused, it is a real time saver when it comes to replacing old hoses.

TECH TIP 

Quick-and-Easy Cooling System Problem Diagnosis

If overheating occurs in slow stop-and-go traffic, the usual cause is low airflow through the radiator. Check for air-flow blockages or cooling fan malfunction. If overheating occurs at highway speeds, the cause is usually a radiator or coolant circulation problem. Check for a restricted or clogged radiator.

To check the automatic transmission fluid, start the engine and move the gear selector to all gear positions and return to park or neutral as specified by the vehicle manufacturer. Remove the transmission/transaxle dipstick (fluid level indicator) and wipe it off using a clean cloth. Then reinsert the dipstick until fully seated. Remove the dipstick again and note the level. See Figure 3–21.

NOTE: The "add" mark on most automatic transmission/transaxle dipsticks means that 1/2 quart (1/2 litre) of automatic transmission fluid needs to be added.

- **Do not overfill any automatic transmission/transaxle.** Even if just half a litre too much were added by mistake (for example, adding 1 L when the fluid was at the "add" line instead of the correct amount of 0.5 L) that could cause the fluid to foam. Foaming of the ATF is caused by the moving parts inside the transmission/transaxle, which stir up the fluid and introduce air into it. This foamy fluid cannot adequately lubricate or operate the hydraulic clutches that make the unit function correctly.

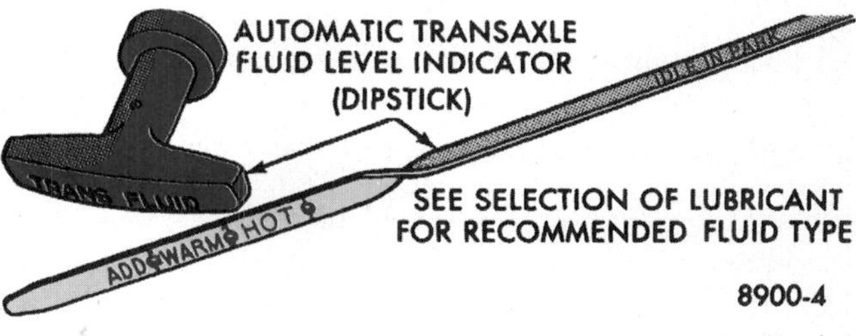

Figure 3–21 A typical automatic transmission dipstick. (Courtesy of Chrysler Corporation)

- **Smell the ATF on the dipstick.** If it seems burned or rancid, further service of the automatic transmission/transaxle will be necessary.
- **Look at the colour of the fluid.** It should be red or light brown. A dark brown or black colour indicates severe oxidation usually caused by too high an operating temperature. Further service and diagnosis of the automatic transmission/transaxle will be required. See Chapter 50.

NOTE: DaimlerChrysler warns that colour and smell should not be used to determine the condition of ATF+4 used in most Chrysler-built vehicles since the 2000 model year. The dyes and additives can change during normal use and not be an indication of fluid contamination. Always follow the vehicle manufacturer's recommendation.

TYPES OF AUTOMATIC TRANSMISSION FLUID

Automatic transmission fluid (usually abbreviated **ATF**) is a high quality oil that has additives that resist oxidation, inhibit rust formation, and allow the fluid to flow easily at all temperatures. The automatic transmission fluid is dyed red for identification. Various vehicle manufacturers recommend a particular type of ATF based mainly on its friction characteristics. Friction is needed between the bands, plates, and clutches of an automatic transmission/transaxle. There are three types of fluid:

- **Nonfriction modified**—This fluid does not contain any friction-reducing additives. Type F is an example of a nonfriction-modified ATF. It was primarily used in band-type Ford automatic transmissions until 1977.
- **Friction modified**—This fluid type has additives that reduce friction. Dexron III® and Mercon V® are examples of friction-modified ATF.

TECH TIP 

The Paper Towel Test

New ATF will penetrate a paper towel better than used oxidized ATF. To compare old fluid with new, place three drops of new fluid on a paper towel and three drops of used ATF on the paper towel about 8 cm from the first sample. Wait for 30 minutes. The new ATF will have expanded (penetrated through the paper towel) much further than the old, oxidized fluid. This test can be used to convince a customer that the ATF should be changed according to the vehicle manufacturer's recommended interval even though, to the naked eye, the fluid looks okay.

NOTE: Mercon replaced earlier Ford ATF specifications for CJ, H, and MV.

- **Highly friction modified**—This fluid type has additional friction-reducing additives beyond those specified for a friction-modified ATF. Chrysler Mopar 7176, ATF+2, ATF+3, ATF+4, Honda, and Toyota specific ATF are examples of fluids that are highly friction modified. See Figure 3–22.

Always use the exact ATF recommended by the vehicle manufacturer.

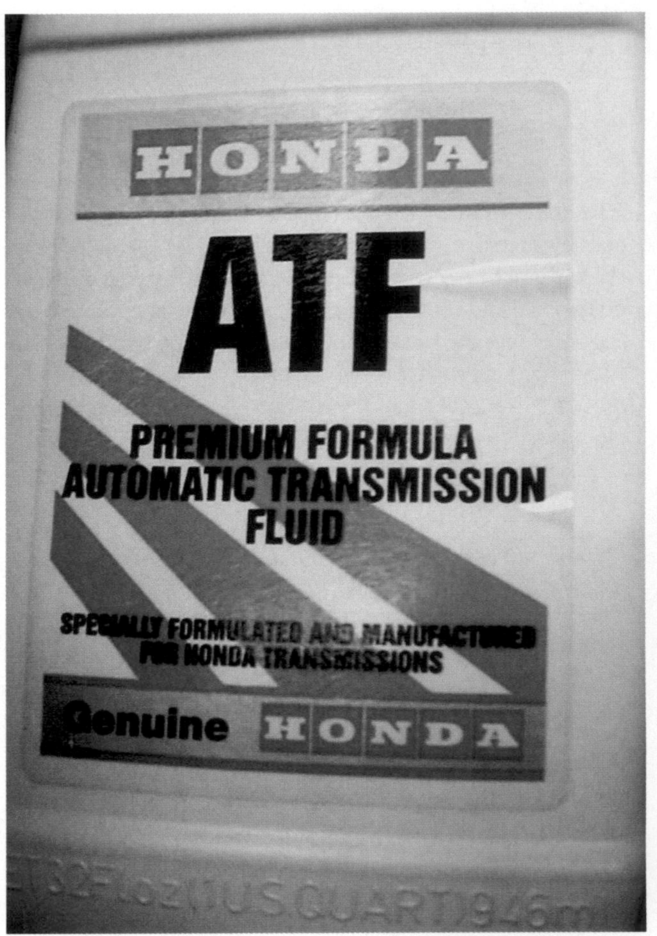

Figure 3–22 Honda ATF is highly friction modified and should be used in all Honda vehicles. Substituting another type of ATF can cause harsh shifting or shudders during acceleration.

POWER STEERING FLUID

The correct power steering fluid is *critical* to the operation and service life of the power steering system! The *exact* power steering fluid to use varies by vehicle manufacturer and sometimes between models made by the same manufacturer because of differences among various steering component manufacturers. See Figure 3–23.

NOTE: Remember, multiple-purpose power steering fluid does not mean *all*-purpose power steering fluid. Always consult the power steering reservoir cap, service manual, or owner's manual for the exact fluid to be used in the vehicle being serviced.

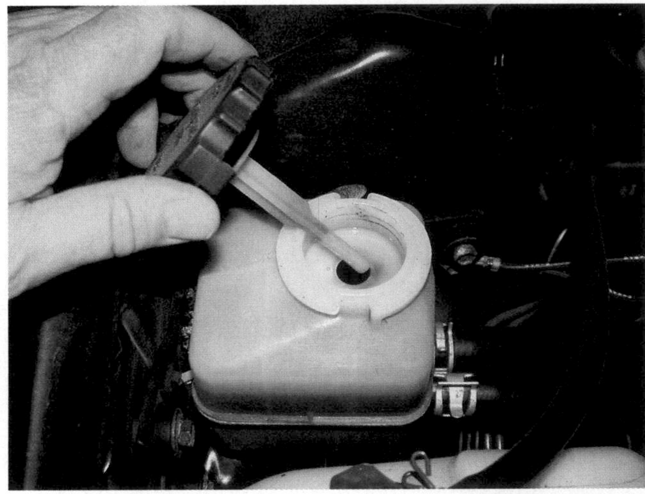

Figure 3–23 Many vehicles use a combination filler cap and level indicator (dip stick) that shows the amount of power steering fluid in the reservoir. The power steering fluid should also be checked for colour that could indicate wear in the system or contamination.

WINDSHIELD WASHER FLUID

Windshield washer fluid level should be checked regularly and refilled as necessary. Use only the fluid that is recommended for use in vehicle windshield washer systems. See Figure 3–24. Most windshield washer fluid usually looks like blue water. It

(a)

(b)

Figure 3–24 (a) Windshield washer fluid caps are usually labelled with this symbol. (b) Only use the recommended windshield washer fluid. Do not use water in climates where freezing temperatures are possible or damage to the reservoir, pump, and lines could result when the water freezes and expands.

is actually water with an alcohol (methanol) additive to prevent freezing and to help clean the windshield by dissolving bugs, etc.

CAUTION: Some mixed fluids are for summer use only and do not contain antifreeze protection. Read the label carefully! Some fluids must be mixed with water because they are in concentrated form. Follow the directions on the container *exactly*. If not enough water is used, the additives in the washer fluid could damage the paint on the roof and trunk lid. Windshield washer fluid may also be flammable because it often contains alcohol. Keep the fluid away from open flames or excessive heat.

TECH TIP 

The Hand Cleaner Trick

Lower-than-normal alternator output could be the result of a loose or slipping drive belt. All belts (V and serpentine multigroove) use an interference angle between the angle of the V's of the belt and the angle of the V's on the pulley. A belt wears this interference angle off the edges of the V of the belt. As a result, the belt may start to slip and make a squealing sound even if tensioned properly.

A common trick used to determine if the noise is belt related is to use grit-type hand cleaner or scouring powder. With the engine off, sprinkle some powder onto the pulley side of the belt. Start the engine. The excess powder will fly into the air, so get out from under the hood when the engine starts. If the belts are now quieter, you know that it was the glazed belt that made the noise.

NOTE: Often, belt noise sounds exactly like a noisy bearing. Therefore, before you start removing and replacing parts, try the hand cleaner trick.

Often, the grit from the hand cleaner will remove the glaze from the belt and the noise will not return. However, if the belt is worn or loose, the noise will return and the belt should be replaced. A fast alternative method to determine if the noise is from the belt is to spray water from a squirt bottle at the belt with the engine running. If the noise stops, the belt is the cause of the noise. The water quickly evaporates and therefore, unlike the gritty hand cleaner, water just finds the problem—it does not provide a short-term fix.

ACCESSORY DRIVE BELT INSPECTION

There should be a *maximum* of 12 mm of play when a belt is depressed midway between pulleys. Power steering (PS) and air conditioning (A/C) belts usually must be even tighter. The work these belts are required to perform is deceptive. For example, an air conditioning belt must transfer approximately 12 horsepower whenever the A/C is being used. This could not be accomplished with a belt which depended on tightness alone. Most V-belts (called this because of their shape) are 34 degrees at the V. The pulley they ride through is generally 36 degrees. This 2-degree difference results in a wedging action and makes power transmission possible, but it is also the reason why V-belts must be closely inspected.

It is generally recommended that all belts, including the **serpentine** (or **Poly V**) belts be replaced

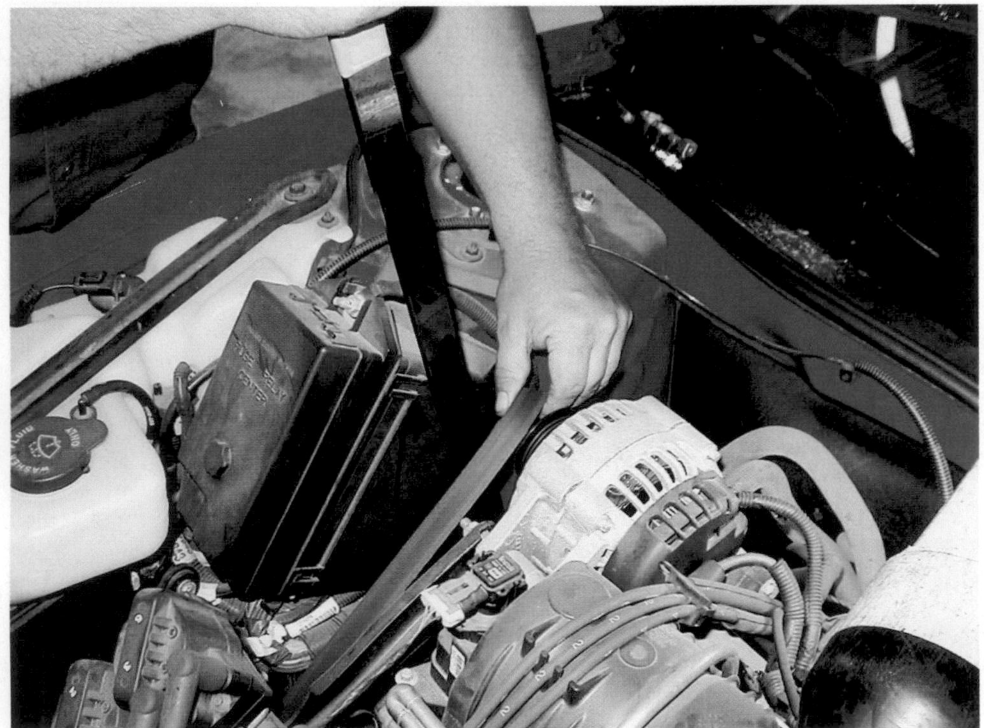

Figure 3–25 A special tool is useful when installing a new accessory drive belt. The long-handled wrench fits the hole in the belt tensioner.

Figure 3–26 Typical worn serpentine accessory drive belt. A defective or worn belt can cause a variety of noises, including squealing and severe knocking similar to a main bearing knock, if glazed or loose.

every four years. The old belts should be kept in the trunk for use in an emergency. When a belt that turns the water pump breaks, the engine could rapidly overheat, causing serious engine damage, and if one belt breaks, it often causes the other belts to become tangled, causing them to break. See Figures 3–25 through 3–27.

CHECKING TIRE PRESSURE

Tire pressures should be checked when the tires are cold. As a vehicle is driven, the flexing of the tire and friction between the tire and the road causes an increase in temperature. As the tire heats up, the air inside the tire also increases in temperature. The increased temperature of the air increases the air pressure inside the tire. The air pressure typically increases in pressure 30 to 40 kPa (4 to 6 psi) after the vehicle has been driven several kilometres. If air is then removed from the hot tire, the tire would be underinflated. The tire pressure specified is for a tire that has not been driven and is therefore cold, so the air pressure should be checked before the vehicle has been driven more than 3 km (2 miles).

NOTE: Tire pressure changes according to air temperature about 7 kPa per 5°C (1 psi per 10°F); therefore, during a change of season the tire pressure has to be adjusted. For example, when the summer temperature of 25°C (80°F) changes to 5°C (40°F) in the fall, the tire pressure will drop about 4 psi (80 − 40 = 40) or 28 kPa (25°C − 5°C = 20° C).

Use a good-quality tire pressure gauge and push it against the tire valve stem after removing the cap.

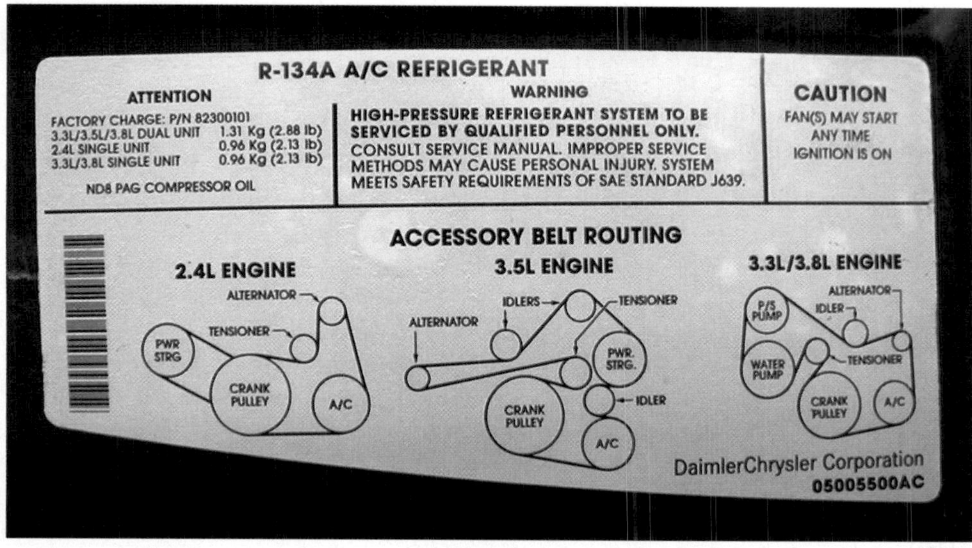

Figure 3–27 Always check the belt routing whenever replacing or checking the operation or noise in the accessory drive belts.

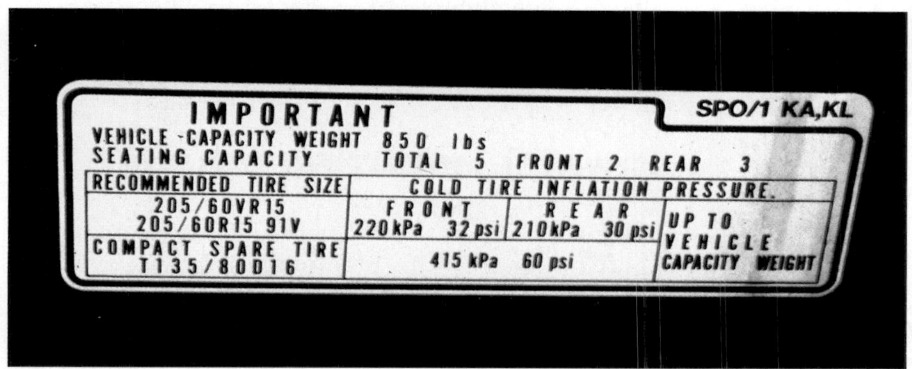

Figure 3–28 Many vehicle manufacturers print the recommended tire pressure on a placard attached to the driver's door or the door jamb.

Compare the pressure reading with the specified tire pressure. The specified pressure is located on a placard attached to the driver's door or door post or in the glove compartment. See Figure 3–28.

> **CAUTION:** Do not inflate tires to the maximum rating on the tire sidewall. Even though this pressure represents the maximum tire pressure, inflating the tires to this pressure usually results in a very hard ride and often unacceptable handling.

The recommended tire pressure often specifies a different pressure for front and rear tires. This is very important to remember especially when the tires are being rotated. Tire pressure should be checked and adjusted if necessary after a tire rotation has been completed. The recommendation often includes a statement about tire pressures to use if operating under all highway driving conditions or operating the vehicle in a fully loaded condition. Specifications for these conditions commonly include increasing the pressure (usually about 30 to 40 kPa or 4 to 6 psi).

TIRE ROTATION

To assure long life and even tire wear, it is important to rotate each tire to another location. Some rear-wheel-drive vehicles, for example, may show premature tire wear on the front tires. The wear usually starts on the outer tread row and usually appears as a front-to-back (high and low) wear pattern on individual tread blocks. These *blocks of tread* rubber are deformed during cornering, stopping, and turning, which can cause tire noise and/or tire roughness. While some shoulder wear on front tires is normal, it

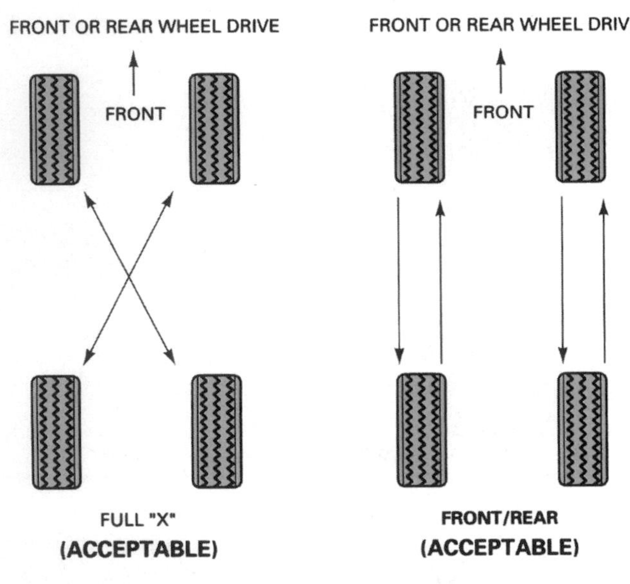

Figure 3–29 The preferred method most often recommended is the modified X method. Using this method, each tire eventually is used at each of the four wheel locations. An easy way to remember the sequence, whether front wheel drive or rear wheel drive, is to say to yourself, "Drive wheels straight, cross the nondrive wheels."

can be reduced by proper inflation, alignment, and tire rotation. For best results, tires should be rotated every 10 000 km (6000 miles) or six months. See Figure 3–29 for suggested methods of rotation.

NOTE: Radial tires can cause a radial pull due to their construction. If the wheel alignment is correct, attempt to correct a pull by rotating the tires front to rear or, if necessary, side to side.

Frequently Asked Question ???

"I Thought Radial Tires Couldn't Be Rotated!"

When radial tires were first introduced by American tire manufacturers in the 1970s, rotating tires side to side was *not* recommended because of concern over a belt or tread separation. Since the late 1980s, most tire manufacturers throughout the world including Canada use tire-building equipment specifically designed for radial ply tires. These newer radial tires are constructed so that the tires can now be rotated from one side of the vehicle to the other without fear of a separation being caused by the resulting reversal of the direction of rotation.

HINT: To help remember when to rotate the tires, just remember that it should be done at every other oil change. Most manufacturers recommend changing the engine oil every 5000 km (3000 miles) or every three months and recommend tire rotation every 10 000 km (6000 miles) or every six months.

WHEEL MOUNTING TORQUE

Make certain that the wheel studs are clean and dry and torqued to the manufacturer's specifications. Most vehicles specify a tightening torque of between 110 and 135 N·m (80 and 100 lb-ft).

CAUTION: Most manufacturers warn that the wheel studs should not be oiled or lubricated with grease because this can cause the wheel lug nuts to loosen while driving.

Always tighten lug nuts gradually tighter in the proper sequence (tighten one nut, skip one, and tighten the next nut)–a star-shaped tightening pattern. See Figure 3–30. This helps prevent warping the brake drums or rotors, or bending a wheel.

NOTE: Any time you install a brand-new set of aluminum wheels, retorque the wheels after the first 25 miles. The soft aluminum often compresses slightly, loosening the torque on the wheels. See Chapter 40 for additional information on tires and wheels.

TIRE INSPECTION

All tires should be carefully inspected for faults in the tire itself or for signs that something may be

(a)

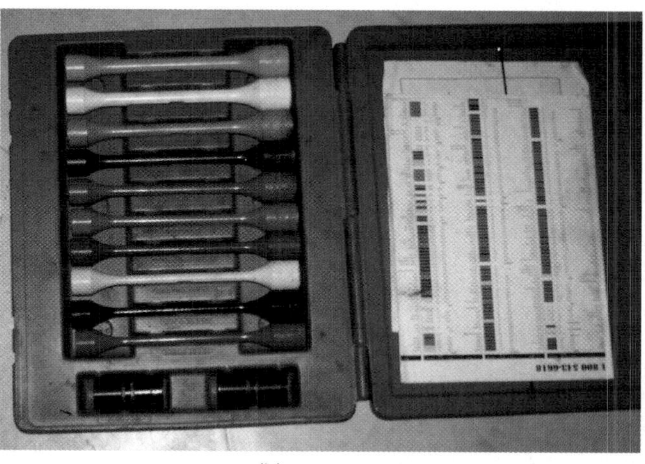

(b)

Figure 3–30 (a) A torque absorbing adapter (often called a torque stick) being used to tighten lug nuts. The adapter should not be held as it could change the torque calibration or cause personal injury if the adapter were to break. (b) An assortment of torque limiting adapters.

wrong with the steering or suspension systems of the vehicle. See Figures 3–31, 3–32, and 3–33 for examples of common problems and Chapter 40 for additional information on tire repair and tire balancing procedures.

CHASSIS LUBRICATION

Chassis lubrication refers to the greasing of parts that rub against each other or installing grease into

TECH TIP 

Two Quick Checks

If the vehicle is hoisted on a frame-contact lift, spin each tire to check that the brakes are not dragging. You should be able to turn all four wheels by hand if the parking brake is off and the transmission is in neutral. Also, when spinning the tire, look over the top of the tire to check if it is round. An improperly mounted tire or a tire that is out-of-round can be detected by watching for the outside of the tire to move up and down as it is being rotated.

DIAGNOSTIC STORY 

Waiting for the Second Click

A student service technician was observed applying a lot of force to a torque wrench attached to a wheel lug nut. When the instructor asked what he was doing, the student replied that he was turning the lug nut tighter until he heard a second click from the torque wrench.

This was confusing to the instructor until the student explained that he had heard a second click of the torque wrench during the demonstration. The instructor at once realized that the student had heard a click when the proper torque was achieved, plus another click when the force on the torque wrench was released.

No harm occurred to the vehicle because all of the lug nuts were reinstalled and properly torqued. The instructor learned that a more complete explanation for the use of click-type torque wrenches was needed.

Figure 3–31 All tires should be checked for wear by observing the wear bars. These strips cause the tire to be bald in this area when the tire tread depth is less than 1.6 mm (2/32").

a pivot (or ball joints) through a grease fitting. Grease fittings are also called **Zerk fittings** (named for Oscar U. Zerk) or **Alamite fittings** (named for the manufacturer of early grease fittings). These fittings contain a one-way check valve that prevents the grease from escaping. See Figure 3–34. Grease fittings are used on steering components, such as tie-rod ends, and in the suspension ball joints, which require lubrication to prevent wear and noise caused by the action of a ball rotating within a joint during vehicle operation.

> **CAUTION:** If too much grease is forced into a sealed grease boot, the boot itself may rupture, requiring the entire joint to be replaced.

CHASSIS GREASE

Vehicle manufacturers specify the type and consistency of grease for each application. Technicians should know what these specifications mean. Grease is an oil with a thickening agent added to allow it to be installed in places where a liquid lubricant would not stay. Greases are named for their thickening agent, such as aluminum, barium, calcium, lithium, or sodium.

Figure 3–32 This tire is worn on the outside. If both front tires are worn the same way, then excessive toe-in is most likely the cause. If just one tire shows this type of wear, then the camber is not correct and the vehicle should be inspected for a fault in the suspension system.

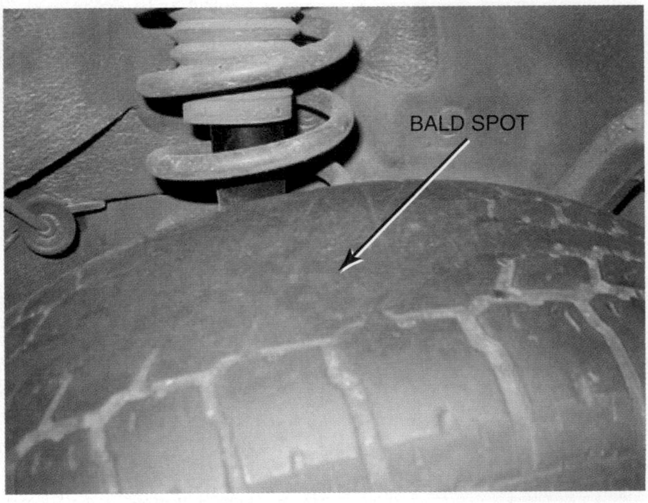

Figure 3–33 This tire should be replaced. The unusual wear pattern indicates a possible fault with the tire itself or a suspension fault that has caused the wheel/tire assembly to wear unevenly.

The **American Society for Testing Materials (ASTM)** specifies the consistency of grease using a **penetration test.** The **National Lubricating Grease Institute (NLGI)** uses the penetration test as a guide to assign the grease a number. Low num-

Figure 3–34 A hand-operated grease gun is being used to lubricate a grease fitting on a pitman arm.

bers are very fluid and higher numbers are more firm or hard. Most vehicle manufacturers specify NLGI #2 for wheel bearing and chassis lubrication. See Figure 3–35. NLGI also specifies grease by its use:

The GC designation is acceptable for wheel bearings.

The LB designation is acceptable for chassis lubrication.

Many greases are labeled with both GC and LB and are therefore acceptable for both wheel bearings and chassis use, such as in lubricating ball joints, tie-rod ends, etc.

OTHER UNDER-THE-VEHICLE LUBRICATION CHECKS

Other items underneath the vehicle that may need checking or lubricating include:

- Shock absorbers and springs (see Figure 3–36)
- The transmission/transaxle shift linkage (check the service manual for the correct lubricant to use)
- The parking brake cable guides

Figure 3–35 Most vehicle manufacturers recommend the use of grease rated NLGI #2 and GC for wheel bearings, and LB for chassis lubrication. Many greases have both designations and are therefore acceptable for use as wheel bearing grease as well as chassis grease for ball-joints and tie rod ends.

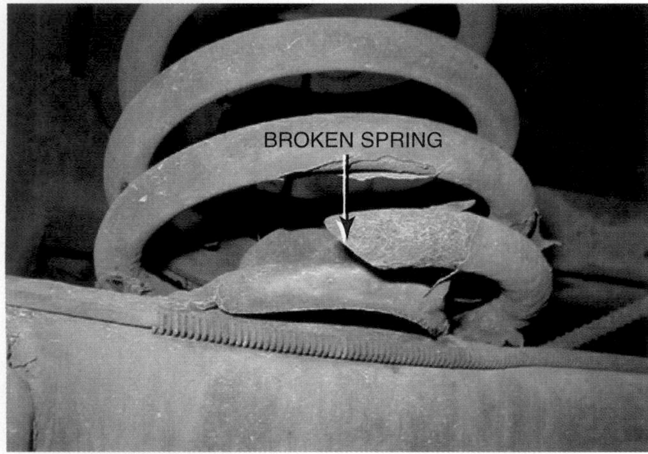

Figure 3–36 This broken coil spring was found during an under-vehicle inspection. The owner was unaware of the problem and it did not make any noise.

Figure 3–37 A visual inspection should include checking the differential fluid, especially after noting that a leak has occurred.

CAUTION: Do not lubricate plastic-coated parking brake cables. The lubricant can destroy the plastic coating.

DIFFERENTIAL FLUID CHECK

Rear-wheel drive vehicles use a differential in the rear of the vehicle to change the direction of power flow from the engine to the rear wheels. The differential also provides a gear reduction to increase engine torque applied to the drive wheels. Four-wheel drive vehicles also use a differential at the front of the vehicle in addition to the differential in the rear. To check the differential fluid level and condition, perform the following:

- Hoist the vehicle safely.
- Visually check for any signs of leakage. See Figure 3–37.
- Remove the inspection plug from the side of the differential assembly.
- Insert your small finger into the hole in the housing and then remove your finger.
  1. If the differential fluid is on your finger, then the level of the fluid is okay. Rub the fluid between your fingers. If the fluid is not gritty feeling, reinstall the inspection plug. If the fluid is gritty feeling, further service will be necessary to determine the cause and correct it. (See Chapter 47 for details.)
  2. If the differential fluid is not on your finger, then the level of the fluid is too low.

NOTE: The reason for the low fluid level should be determined. If repairs are not completed immediately, additional differential fluid should be added by pumping it into the differential through the inspection hole.

DIFFERENTIAL LUBRICANTS

All differentials use hypoid gear sets and a special lubricant is necessary because the gears both roll and slide between their meshed teeth. Gear lubes are specified by the **American Petroleum Institute (API).** Most differentials require:

1. SAE 80W-90 GL-5 *or*
2. SAE 75W-90 GL-5 *or*
3. SAE 80W GL-5

Limited slip differentials (often abbreviated LSD) usually use an additive that modifies the friction characteristics of the rear axle lubricant to prevent chattering while cornering.

MANUAL TRANSMISSION/TRANSAXLE LUBRICANT CHECK

Manual transmissions/transaxles may use any one of the following lubricants:

- Gear lube (usually SAE 80W-90)
- Automatic transmission fluid (ATF)

SAFETY TIP 

Hand Safety

Service technicians should wash their hands with soap and water after handling engine oil or differential or transmission fluids, or wear protective rubber gloves. Another safety hint is that the service technician should not wear watches or rings or other jewellery that could come in contact with electrical or moving parts of a vehicle. See Figure 3–38.

TECH TIP 

Use a Hydrocarbon Detector

One of the many items that should be inspected while underneath the vehicle is the condition of all the fuel lines. Many gasoline (fuel) leaks do not show as wet areas. A hydrocarbon detector available from automotive test equipment suppliers is an excellent tool to use to locate small gasoline leaks that may not be visible. See Figure 3–39.

Figure 3–38 Washing hands and removing jewellery are two important safety habits all service technicians should practice.

Figure 3–39 An electronic hand-held hydrocarbon tester is an excellent tool to use to check for possible gasoline leaks from lines or components.

- Engine oil (usually SAE 5W-30)
- Manual transmission fluid (sometimes called **syncromesh transmission fluid (STF)**—this type of lubricant is similar to ATF with special additives to ease shifting especially when cold)

To check manual transmissions/transaxles lubricant, perform the following:

- Hoist the vehicle safely.
- Locate the transmission/transaxle inspection (fill) plug. Consult the factory service manual for the proper plug to remove to check the fluid level.
- If the fluid drips out of the hole, then the level is correct. If the fluid runs out of the hole, the level is too full. Allow it to flow out until it stops. The correct level of fluid is at the bottom of the inspection hole.
- If low, first determine the correct fluid to use and then fill until the fluid level is at the bottom of the inspection hole or until the fluid runs out of the inspection hole.

PHOTO SEQUENCE 1 Oil Change

P1–1 Begin the oil change process by safely hoisting the vehicle.

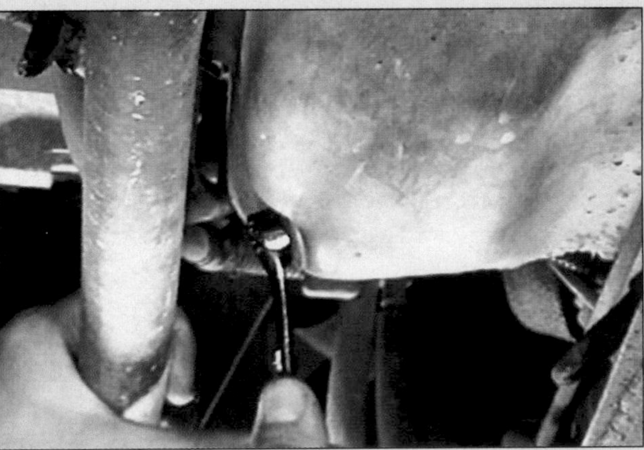

P1–2 Locate and remove the oil drain plug. On this 5.0 L, V-8 Ford Mustang, two oil drain plugs are used. This is the front drain plug.

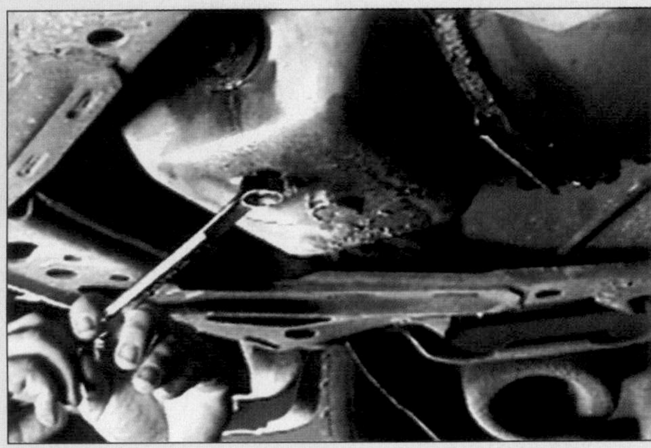

P1–3 Loosen and remove the rear oil drain plug.

P1–4 Allow the oil to drain into a suitable container. For best results, the oil drain should be close to the oil pan to help prevent the possibility of the oil splashing onto the floor or onto the service technician.

P1–5 Carefully inspect the oil drain plug and gasket. Replace the gasket as needed or specified by the vehicle manufacturer (for example, Honda specifies that the aluminum seal on the drain plug be replaced at every oil change).

Oil Change—continued

P1–6 After all of the oil has been allowed to drain from the oil pan, reinstall the plug in the rear portion of the oil pan.

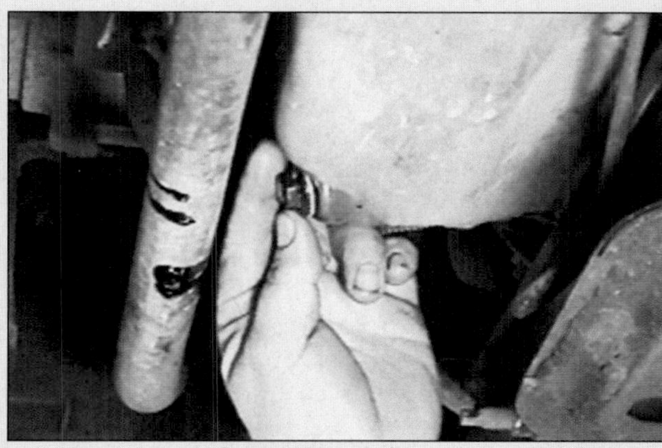

P1–7 Also replace the oil drain plug in the front portion of the oil pan.

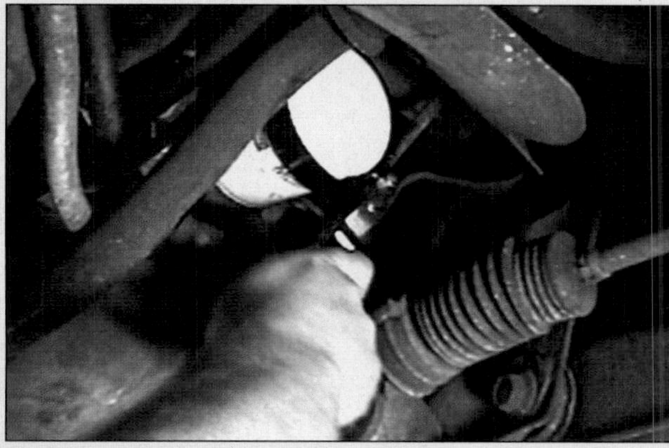

P1–8 Using an oil filter wrench, remove the oil filter. Remember, "righty, tighty and lefty, loosy." Also be sure the oil drain pan is placed under the oil filter because oil will often drain from the filter and engine passages as the oil filter is removed.

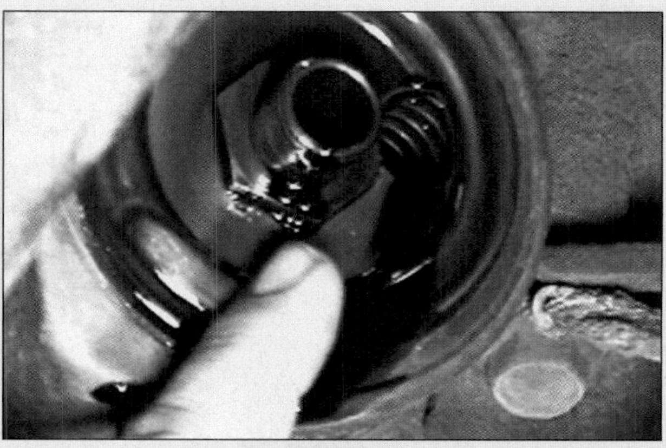

P1–9 Check the area where the oil filter gasket seats to be sure that no part of the gasket remains that could cause an oil leak if not fully removed.

P1–10 Also check the old oil filter to make sure the gasket has been removed with the oil filter. Also compare the replacement filter with the oil filter to double check that the correct filter will be installed.

Oil Change—continued

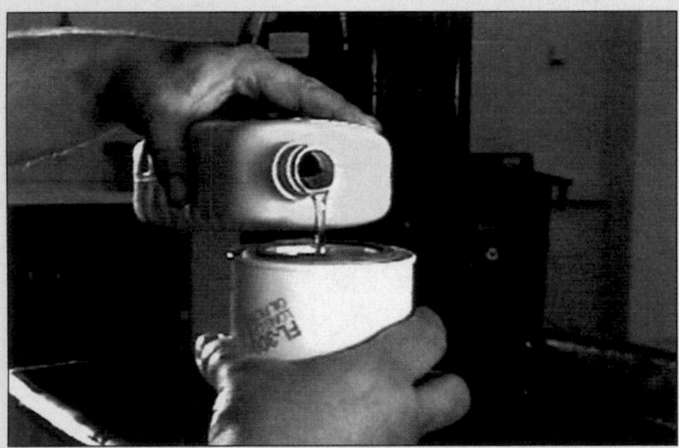

P1–11 The wise service technician adds oil to the oil filter whenever possible. This provides faster filling of the filter during start-up and a reduced amount of time that the engine does not have oil pressure.

P1–12 Apply a thin layer of clean engine oil to the gasket of the new filter. This oil film will allow the rubber gasket to slide and compress as the oil filter is being rotated on the oil filter thread.

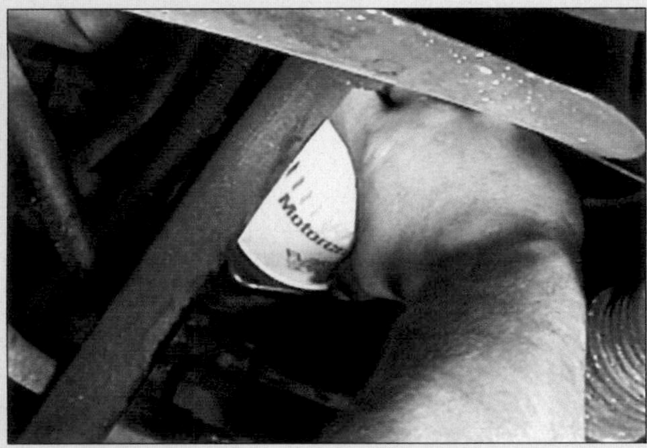

P1–13 Install the new oil filter and tighten the recommended amount—usually 3/4 of a turn after the gasket contacts the engine.

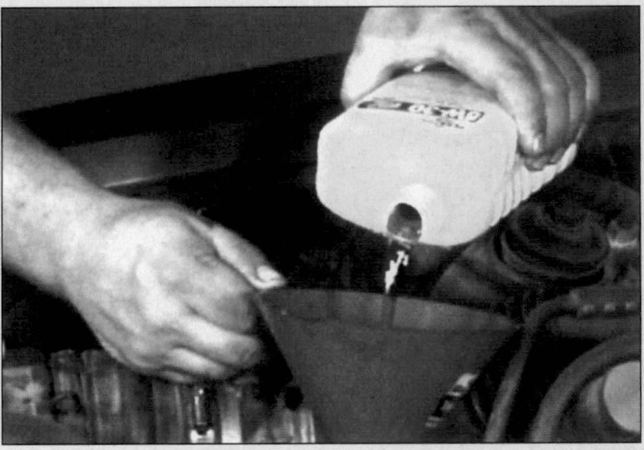

P1–14 Use a funnel to help avoid spills and add the specified amount of oil to the engine at the oil-fill opening. Oil capacity for passenger vehicles can vary from 3 L to over 7 L.

P1–15 Inspect and clean the oil-fill cap and reinstall before starting the engine.

Oil Change—continued

P1–16 Start the engine and allow it to idle while watching the oil pressure gauge and/or oil pressure warning lamp.

P1–17 The oil pressure gauge should register and the oil pressure warning lamp should go out within 15 seconds of starting the engine. If not, stop the engine and determine the cause before starting the engine again.

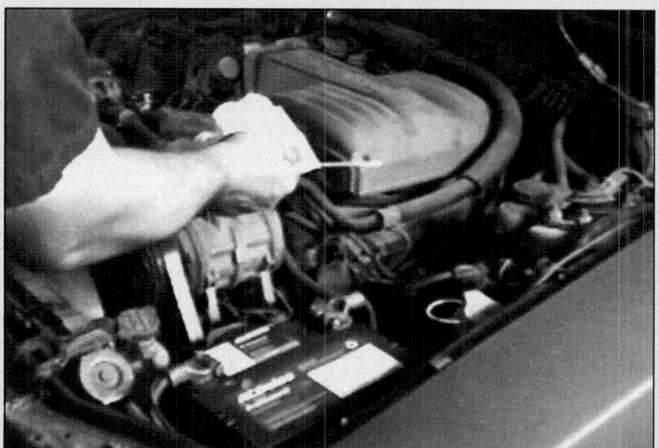

P1–18 Look underneath the vehicle to check for any oil leaks at the oil drain plug(s) or oil filter. Pull out the oil-level dipstick and wipe it clean with a shop cloth.

P1–19 Reinstall the oil-level dipstick to check the oil level.

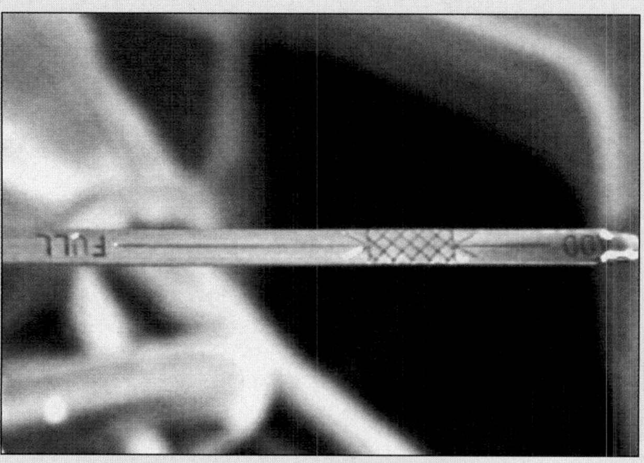

P1–20 Remove the dipstick a second time and read the oil level. The oil level should be at the full mark as shown. If overfilled, hoist the vehicle and drain some oil out. An engine that has been overfilled with oil can be damaged because the oil can be aerated (filled with air like a milkshake), reducing the lubricating properties of the engine oil. Be sure to thoroughly wash your hands with soap and water after touching used engine oil or wear protective rubber gloves.

■ SUMMARY

1. The tenth character of the vehicle identification number (VIN) represents the model year of the vehicle.
2. Brake fluid should be checked regularly and not filled above 6 mm (1/4") from the top of the reservoir or above the "maximum" line imprinted on the side of the master cylinder.
3. Most vehicle manufacturers specify DOT 3 brake fluid.
4. Most vehicle manufacturers specify SAE 5W-30 or 10W-30 engine oil with an API rating of SL and an ILSAC rating of GF-3.
5. The engine oil should be changed more frequently if the vehicle is driven under severe conditions such as stop-and-go city-type driving.
6. When replacing any radiator or heater hose, the end of the hose should be cut to prevent possible damage to the radiator or heater core.
7. Always use the specified automatic transmission fluid when topping off or when changing the fluid. Using the wrong type of ATF can cause the transmission to shift too harshly or cause a vibration when the transmission shifts.
8. The tire pressure should be checked when the tires are cold, and the tires should be inflated to the pressure specified on the door placard or in the owner's manual.
9. Tires should be rotated every 8000–11 000 km (5000–7000 miles) or at every other oil change.
10. Wheels should always be tightened with a torque wrench to the proper torque and in a star pattern.
11. All grease fittings should be cleaned before using a grease gun to lubricate any greaseable joints under the vehicle.
12. Most differentials require an SAE 80W-90 GL-5 rated lubricant.
13. Manual transmissions/transaxles may require one of several different lubricants including gear lube such as SAE 80W-90, ATF, engine oil (SAE 5W-30), or special manual transmission fluid.

■ REVIEW QUESTIONS

1. Explain why brake fluid should not be filled above the full or MAX level as indicated on the master cylinder reservoir.
2. Explain why brake fluid should be kept in an airtight container.
3. Explain the terms SAE 5W-30, API SL, and GF-3.
4. List three types of automatic transmission fluid.
5. Describe the most common sequence for tire rotation.
6. Discuss how to check differential fluid.
7. List four lubricants that a manual transmission/transaxle *may* require depending on exact year, make, and model of vehicle.

■ RED SEAL CERTIFICATION-TYPE QUESTIONS

1. The model year of the vehicle is indicated in the vehicle identification number (VIN) by which character?
   - **a.** 4th
   - **b.** 5th
   - **c.** 8th
   - **d.** 10th
2. Most vehicle manufacturers specify brake fluid that meets what specification?
   - **a.** DOT 2
   - **b.** DOT 3
   - **c.** DOT 4
   - **d.** DOT 5
3. The thicker the engine oil, the better the quality.
   - **a.** True
   - **b.** False
4. The letter *W* as in SAE 10W-30 means
   - **a.** Weight
   - **b.** Wrought
   - **c.** With
   - **d.** Winter
5. Most antifreeze coolant is
   - **a.** Phosphate
   - **b.** Propylene glycol
   - **c.** Ethylene glycol
   - **d.** Dexthylene
6. Dexron and Mercon are examples of which type of ATF?
   - **a.** Nonfriction modified
   - **b.** Friction modified
   - **c.** Highly friction modified
   - **d.** Straight-weight mineral oil
7. Using the modified X tire rotation method on a front-wheel drive vehicle would place the right front tire on the _____.
   - **a.** Left front
   - **b.** Left rear
   - **c.** Right rear
8. Most vehicle manufacturers specify a lug nut (wheel nut) tightening torque specification of about _____.
   - **a.** 110 to 135 N · m (80 to 100 lb-ft.)
   - **b.** 135 to 170 N · m (100 to 125 lb-ft.)
   - **c.** 170 to 210 N · m (125 to 150 lb-ft.)
   - **d.** 210 to 240 N · m (150 to 175 lb-ft.)
9. A grease labeled NLGI #2 GC is suitable for use on what vehicle components?
   - **a.** Wheel bearings
   - **b.** Chassis parts
   - **c.** Both wheel bearings and chassis parts
   - **d.** Door hinges only
10. What is the correct oil level for the differential of a rear-wheel drive vehicle?
    - **a.** Gearlube should run out when inspection plug is removed
    - **b.** Oil is level with bottom of the inspection plug hole
    - **c.** 25 mm below the inspection plug hole
    - **d.** 50 mm below the inspection plug hole

SECTION II

Engine Repair

Chapter 4 covers basic engine operation, parts, and specifications. Chapter 5 includes all areas of engine condition diagnosis. Chapter 6 describes proper disassembly, cleaning, and crack detection procedures. Chapter 7 explains the entire cooling and engine lubrication system including problem diagnosis and service procedures. Chapter 8 covers all areas of cylinder head and valve service and Chapter 9 describes camshafts, valve trains and intake and exhaust systems: principles, problem diagnosis and service procedures. Chapter 10 includes details on piston rings and connecting rods and Chapter 11 describes the principles and service procedures for the engine block, crankshafts, and bearings. Chapter 12 completes the section by detailing proper engine assembly and reinstallation into the vehicle.

4

Engine Operation, Parts, and Specifications

OBJECTIVES: After studying Chapter 4, you should be able to:

1. Prepare for the interprovincial Red Seal certification examination in Appendix I (Engine Repair) on the topics covered in this chapter.
2. Explain how a four-stroke cycle gasoline engine operates.
3. Explain how a four-stroke cycle diesel engine operates.
4. List the various characteristics by which vehicle engines are classified.
5. Describe how engine power is measured and calculated.
6. Discuss how a compression ratio is calculated.
7. Explain how engine size is determined.
8. Describe how turbocharging or supercharging increases engine power.

The engine converts part of the fuel energy to useful energy that moves the vehicle.

ENERGY AND POWER

The chemical energy in fuel is converted to heat by the burning of the fuel at a controlled rate. This process is called **combustion.** If engine combustion occurs within the power chamber, the engine is called an **internal combustion engine.**

NOTE: An **external combustion engine** is an engine that burns fuel outside of the engine itself, such as a steam engine.

Engines used in automobiles are internal combustion heat engines. They convert the chemical energy of the gasoline into heat within a **combustion chamber.** Heat energy released in the combustion chamber raises the temperature of the combustion gases within the chamber. The increase in gas temperature causes the pressure of the gases to increase. The pressure developed within the combustion chamber is applied to the head of a piston or to a turbine wheel to produce a usable **mechanical force,** which is then converted into useful **mechanical energy.**

FOUR-STROKE CYCLE OPERATION: GASOLINE ENGINE

Most automotive engines use the four-stroke cycle of events, begun by the starter motor which rotates the engine. The four-stroke cycle is repeated for each cylinder of the engine. See Figure 4–1.

- **Intake stroke**—The **intake valve** is open and the piston inside the cylinder travels downward, drawing a mixture of air and fuel into the cylinder.
- **Compression stroke**—As the engine continues to rotate, the intake valve closes and the piston moves upward in the cylinder, compressing the air–fuel mixture.
- **Power stroke**—When the piston gets near the top of the cylinder (called **top dead centre [TDC]**), the spark at the spark plug ignites the air–fuel mixture, which forces the piston downward.
- **Exhaust stroke**—The engine continues to rotate, and the piston again moves upward in the

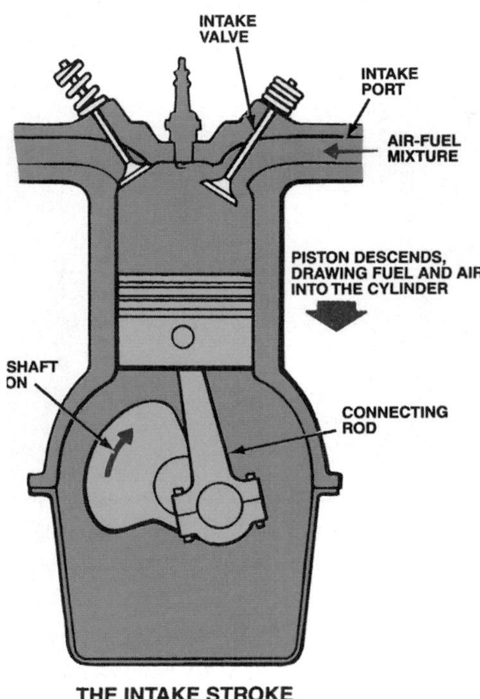

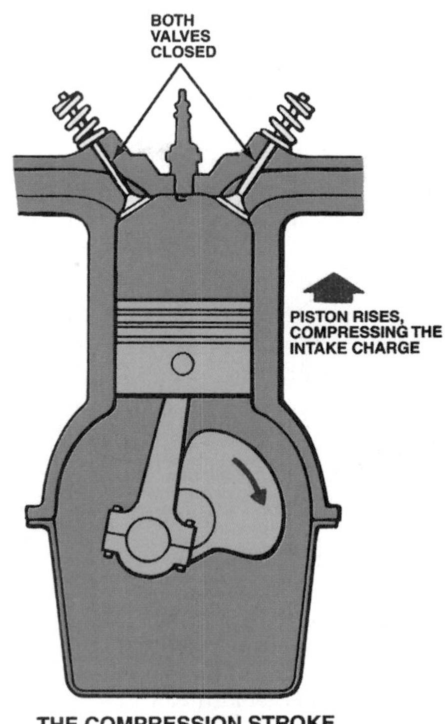

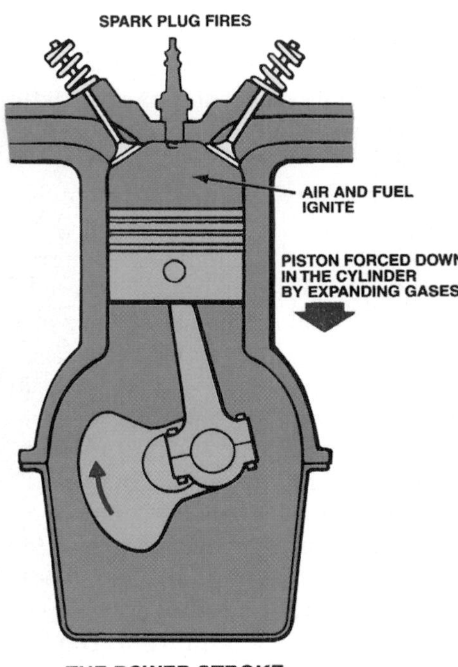

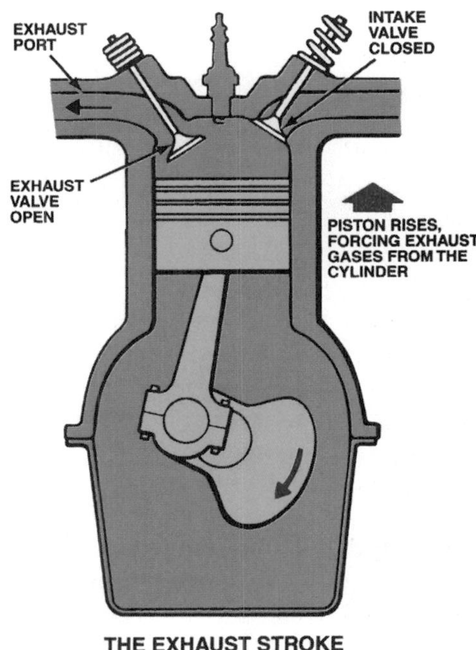

Figure 4–1 The downward movement of the piston draws the air–fuel mixture into the cylinder through the intake valve on the intake stroke. On the compression stroke, the mixture is compressed by the upward movement of the piston with both valves closed. Ignition occurs at the beginning of the power stroke, and combustion drives the piston downward to produce power. On the exhaust stroke, the upward-moving piston forces the burned gases out the open exhaust valve.

cylinder. The exhaust valve opens, and the piston forces the residual burned gases out of the **exhaust valve** and into the exhaust manifold and exhaust system.

This sequence repeats as the engine rotates. To stop the engine, the electrical current to the ignition system is shut off by the ignition switch.

A piston that moves up and down, or reciprocates, in a **cylinder** can be seen in this illustration. The piston is attached to a **crankshaft** with a **connecting rod.** This arrangement allows the piston to reciprocate (move up and down) in the cylinder as the crankshaft rotates. See Figure 4–2. The combustion pressure developed in the combustion chamber at the correct time will push the piston downward to rotate the crankshaft.

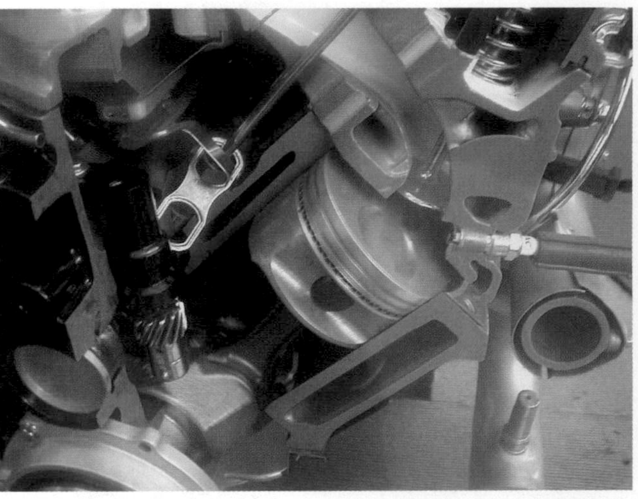

Figure 4–2 Cutaway of a Chevrolet V-8 engine showing the overhead valves, piston, connecting rod, and crankshaft.

THE 720° CYCLE

Each cycle of events requires the engine crankshaft to make two complete revolutions, or 720° (360° × 2 = 720°). The greater the number of cylinders, the closer together the power strokes occur. To find the number of crankshaft degrees between cylinder firing (power strokes), divide the number of cylinders into 720° (i.e., 720° ÷ 4 = 180°).

Four cylinder = 180°

Six cylinder = 120°

Eight cylinder = 90°

Ten cylinder = 72°

Twelve cylinder = 60°

This means that in a four-cylinder engine, a power stroke occurs at every 180° of crankshaft rotation (every half-revolution). A V-8 engine operates much more smoothly because a power stroke occurs twice as often (every 90° of crankshaft rotation). Compare this to a 12-cylinder engine where power strokes are only 60° apart. Any engine with more than four cylinders will have overlapping power strokes.

It is an easy matter to have an equal number of degrees between firings on an inline-type engine as each piston and connecting rod has its own crankshaft journal (crankpin). This can be difficult on 6-cylinder V-type engines where two connecting rods operate on the same crankpin. This leads to uneven firing and general engine roughness. Later V-6 engines reposition the crankpins so each cylinder has its own journal. This is called a splayed crank, so that equal firing V-6 engines are now common.

Engine cycles are identified by the number of **piston strokes** required to complete the cycle. A piston stroke is a one-way piston movement between the top and bottom of the cylinder. During one stroke, the crankshaft revolves 180° (a half-revolution). A **cycle** is a complete series of events that continually repeat. Most automobile and light truck engines use a **four-stroke cycle.**

ENGINE CLASSIFICATION

Engines are classified by several characteristics including:

- **Number of strokes.** Most automotive engines use the four-stroke cycle.
- **Cylinder arrangement.** An engine with more cylinders is smoother operating because the power pulses produced by the power strokes are more closely spaced. An inline engine places all cylinders in a straight line. Four- , five- , and six-cylinder engines are commonly manufactured inline engines. A V-type engine, such as a V-6 or V-8, has the number of cylinders split and built into a V-shape. See Figure 4–3.
- **Longitudinal or transverse mounting.** Engines may be mounted either parallel with the length of the vehicle (longitudinally) or crosswise (transversely). See Figures 4–4 and 4–5. The same engine may be mounted in various vehicles in either direction.

NOTE: Although it might be possible to mount an engine in different vehicles both longitudinally and transversely, the engine component parts may *not* be interchangeable. Differences can include different engine blocks and crankshafts, as well as different water pumps.

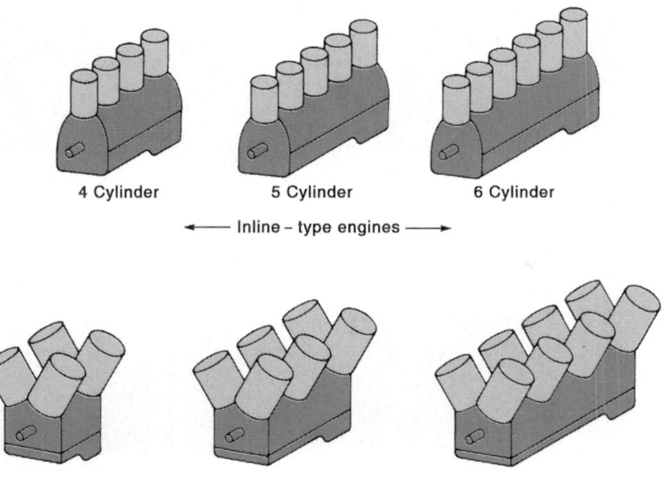

Figure 4–3 Automotive engine cylinder arrangements.

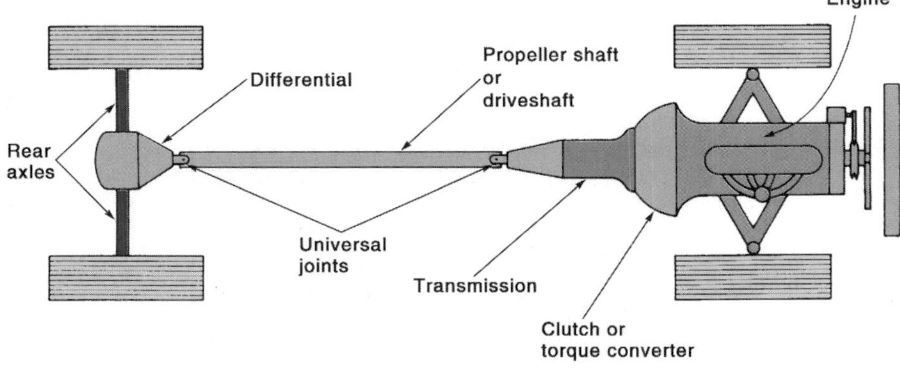

Figure 4–4 Longitudinal front engine, rear-wheel drive.

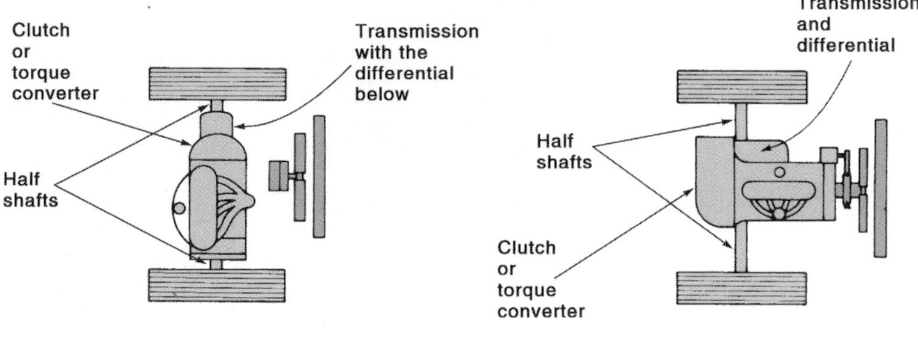

Figure 4–5 Two types of front engine, front-wheel drive.

- **Valve and camshaft number and location.** The number of valves and the number and location of camshafts are a major factor in engine operation. A typical older-model engine uses one intake valve and one exhaust valve per cylinder. Many newer engines use two or more intake and two exhaust valves per cylinder. The valves are opened by a **camshaft.** For high-speed engine operation, the camshaft should be overhead (over the valves). Some engines use one camshaft for the intake valves and a separate camshaft for the exhaust valves. When the camshaft is located in the block, the valves are operated by lifters, push rods, and rocker arms. See Figure 4–6. This type of engine is called a **push rod engine.** An overhead camshaft engine has the camshaft above the valves in the cylinder head. When one overhead camshaft is used, the design is called a **single overhead camshaft (SOHC)** design. When two overhead camshafts are used, the design is called a **double (or dual) overhead camshaft (DOHC)** design. See Figures 4–7 and 4–8.

Figure 4–6 Cutaway of a V-8 engine showing the lifters, push rods, roller rocker arms, and valves.

Figure 4–8 A double overhead camshaft V-6 engine with the cam covers and timing belt removed.

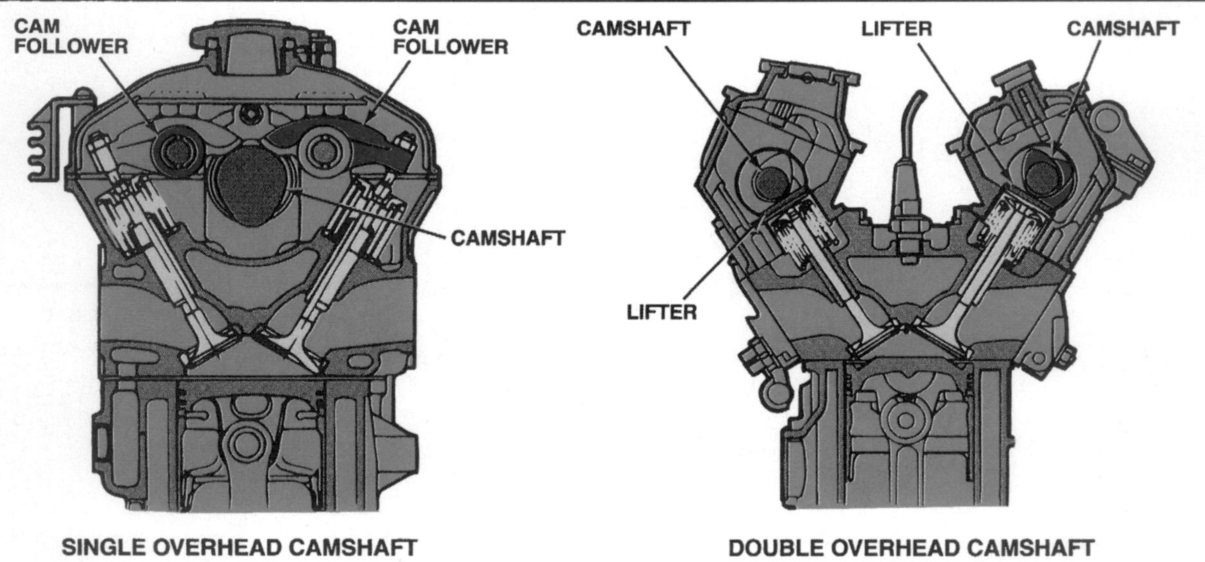

Figure 4–7 Single overhead camshaft engines usually require additional components such as a rocker arm to operate all of the valves. Double overhead camshaft engines often operate the valves directly.

> **NOTE:** A V-type engine uses two banks or rows of cylinders. An SOHC design therefore uses two camshafts, but only one camshaft per bank (row) of cylinders. A DOHC V-6 therefore has four camshafts, two for each bank.

- **Type of fuel.** Most engines operate on gasoline, whereas some engines are designed to operate on methanol, natural gas, propane, or diesel fuel.
- **Cooling method.** Most engines are liquid cooled, but some older models were air cooled.
- **Type of induction pressure.** If atmospheric air pressure is used to force the air–fuel mixture into the cylinders, the engine is called **normally aspirated.** Some engines use a **turbocharger** or **supercharger** to force the air–fuel mixture into the cylinder for even greater power.

Frequently Asked Question ???

What Is a Rotary Engine?

A successful alternative engine design is the **rotary engine,** also called the **Wankel engine** after its inventor. The Mazda RX-7 represents the only long-term use of the rotary engine. The rotating combustion chamber engine runs very smoothly, and it produces high power for its size and weight.

The basic rotating combustion chamber engine has a triangular-shaped rotor turning in a housing. The housing is in the shape of a geometric figure called a **two-lobed epitrochoid.** A seal on each corner, or apex, of the rotor is in constant contact with the housing, so the rotor must turn with an eccentric motion. This means that the centre of the rotor moves around the centre of the engine. The eccentric motion can be seen in Figure 4–9.

Each of the three rotor faces contains a combustion chamber called a **combustion recess.** This allows three power impulses (strokes) for each revolution of the rotor. A typical two-rotor passenger car engine has six power strokes while the Mazda three-rotor racing engine has nine.

In 1995, Mazda elected to discontinue sales of rotary vehicles in North America; this decision was recently reversed with the introduction of the new 2004 RX-8 sports car.

Figure 4–9 Disassembled Mazda rotary engine.

ENGINE ROTATION DIRECTION

The SAE (Society of Automotive Engineers) standard for automotive engine rotation is counterclockwise (CCW) as viewed from the flywheel end (clockwise as viewed from the front of the engine). The flywheel end of the engine is the end to which the power is applied to drive the vehicle. This is called the **principal end** of the engine. The **nonprincipal** end of the engine is opposite the principal end and is generally referred to as the *front* of the engine, where the accessory belts are used. See Figure 4–10. In most rear wheel-drive vehicles, therefore, the engine is mounted longitudinally with the principal end at the rear of the engine. Most transversely mounted engines also adhere to the same standard for direction of rotation. Honda vehicles and some marine applications may differ from this standard.

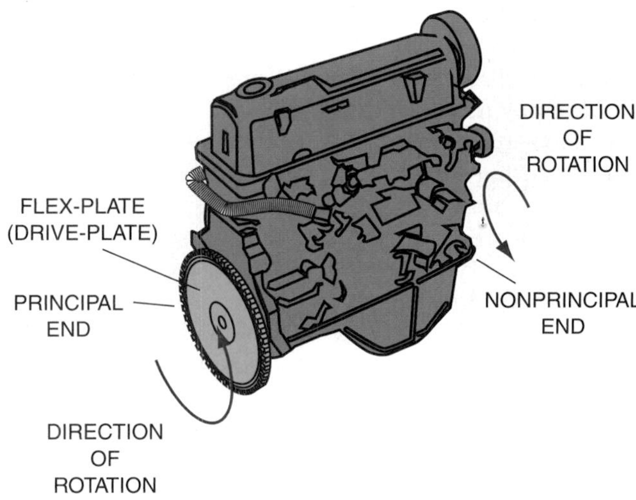

Figure 4–10 Inline four-cylinder engine showing principal and nonprincipal ends. Normal direction of rotation is clockwise (CW) as viewed from the front or accessory belt end (nonprincipal end).

BORE

The diameter of a cylinder is called the **bore.** The larger the bore, the greater the area of the piston surface on which the gases can work.

Pressure is measured in units such as kilopascals (1 kPa = 1 N/m^2) or pounds per square inch (psi). The greater the area, the higher the force exerted by the pistons to rotate the crank. See Figure 4–11.

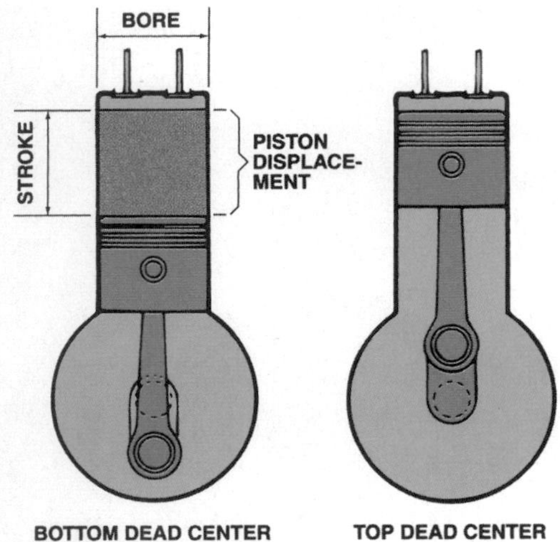

Figure 4–11 The bore and stroke of pistons are used to calculate an engine's displacement.

STROKE

The distance the piston travels down in the cylinder is called the **stroke.** The longer this distance, the greater the amount of air–fuel mixture that can be drawn into the cylinder. The more air–fuel mixture inside the cylinder, the more force will result when the mixture is ignited.

ENGINE DISPLACEMENT

As a general rule, the power output of an engine is determined by its **displacement:** a 7 L engine will produce more horsepower and torque than a 5 L engine, provided other factors such as compression, fuel delivery, intake manifold and exhaust design are the same.

Displacement is the total number of cubic centimetres (cm^3) or cubic inches (cu in.) of cylinder volume displaced by all pistons when they move from bottom dead centre (BDC) to top dead centre (TDC).

Engine displacement can only be changed by increasing or decreasing the size of the cylinder bore, lengthening or shortening the stroke of the crankshaft or changing the number of cylinders. Other factors such as connecting rod length have no influence on displacement.

Engine Displacement (cubic centimetres)

To determine engine displacement, use the formula:

$$0.7854 \times D^2 \times \text{stroke} \times \text{number of cylinders}$$

For an example, let's use a 6-cylinder engine with a bore size of 100 mm and a stroke of 50 mm. For this metric formula convert millimetres to centimetres, since metric displacements are given in cubic centimetres (cm^3) or litres (L).

$$\text{Area of piston surface} = 0.7854 \times 10 \text{ cm} \times 10 \text{ cm} = 78.54 \text{ cm}^2$$

$$\text{Displacement (one cylinder)} = \text{area} \times \text{stroke} = 78.54 \text{ cm}^2 \times 5 \text{ cm} = 382.7 \text{ cm}^3$$

$$\text{Engine displacement for 6 cylinders} = 382.7 \text{ cm}^3 \times 6 = 2296.2 \text{ cm}^3$$

2296.2 cubic centimetres would be rounded off and rated as a 2.3 L engine.

Older engines in both Canada and the United States were rated in cubic inches. Today, even though the imperial (inch) measurements are still the U.S. standard, engine displacement is rated in litres or cubic centimetres in both countries.

Engine Displacement (cubic inches)

One popular V8 engine had a cylinder bore of 4 inches (4.000") and a stroke of 2 7/8" (2.875"). Using our formula:

$$\text{Area of piston surface} = 0.7854 \times 4.000" \times 4.000" = 12.57 \text{ sq in.}$$

$$\text{Displacement (one cylinder)} = \text{area} \times \text{stroke} = 12.57 \text{ sq in.} \times 2.875 \text{ in.} = 36.14 \text{ cu in.}$$

$$\text{Engine displacement for 8 cylinders} = 36.14 \text{ in.}^3 \times 8 = 289 \text{ cu in.}$$

Moving the connecting rod journal out 1/16" (0.0625") changes the stroke by 1/8" (0.125"): 1/16" at TDC and 1/16" at BDC = 1/8".

Using our formula to determine the new displacement:

$$\text{Area of piston surface} = 0.7854 \times 4.000" \times 4.000" = 12.57 \text{ in.}^2$$

$$\text{Displacement (one cylinder)} = \text{area} \times \text{stroke} = 12.57 \text{ in.}^2 \times 3.000 \text{ in.} = 37.70 \text{ in.}^3$$

$$\text{Engine displacement for 8 cylinders} = 37.70 \text{ in.}^3 \times 8 = 301.6 \text{ cu in.}$$

This would be rounded off to 302 cu in. or 5 L. Note the increase in displacement of 13 cu in.

Note that the relations among the main units of volume are

$$1 \text{ L} = 1000 \text{ cm}^3 = 61 \text{ cu in.} \qquad 1 \text{ cu in.} = 16.4 \text{ cm}^3$$

Engine Size Versus Horsepower

The larger the engine, the more power the engine is capable of producing. Several sayings are often quoted about engine size:

"There is no replacement for displacement."

"There is no substitute for cubic inches."

Although a large engine generally uses more fuel, making an engine larger is often the easiest way to increase power.

VARIABLE CYLINDER ENGINES

Fuel efficiency and emissions reductions are gained with the new cylinder-deactivation systems where the number of operating cylinders is tailored to the load and operating conditions.

In the early 1980s, Cadillac was the first to offer the 4-6-8, a V-8 engine that would run on four, six or eight cylinders. There were a number of driveability concerns that could not be addressed by the electronics of the day and the project was discontinued.

The latest designs still disable cylinders by stopping the valves from opening. On one type, the hydraulic valve lifters are allowed to collapse within themselves; another stops the overhead camshaft rocker arm from opening the valves by deactivating the arm. In both cases, the camshaft lifts the valve lifter or rocker but the valves do not open.

The Japanese Honda Inspire, similar to the North American Accord, uses a 3.0-litre V6, which operates on only three cylinders when needed. All valves in the rear bank are closed and no fuel is injected, however the spark plugs still fire to keep them clean.

General Motors is using displacement-on-demand (DOD) with their new Generation IV V8 and High Value V6 engines.

Varying the number of cylinders changes the volume of air flowing through the intake manifold which can cause driveability and vibration problems. The latest electronic engine technology controls the throttle plate (throttle-by-wire), lockup torque converter clutch and ignition timing to smooth cylinder switching.

COMPRESSION RATIO

The compression ratio of an engine is an important consideration when rebuilding or repairing an engine. **Compression ratio (CR)** is the ratio of the volume in the cylinder above the piston when the piston is at the bottom of the stroke to the volume in the cylinder above the piston when the piston is at the top of the stroke. See Figures 4–12 and 4–13.

If Compression Is Lower	If Compression Is Higher
Lower power	Higher power possible
Poorer fuel economy	Better fuel economy
Easier engine cranking	Harder to crank engine, especially when hot
More advanced ignition timing possible without spark knock (detonation)	Less ignition timing required to prevent spark knock (detonation)

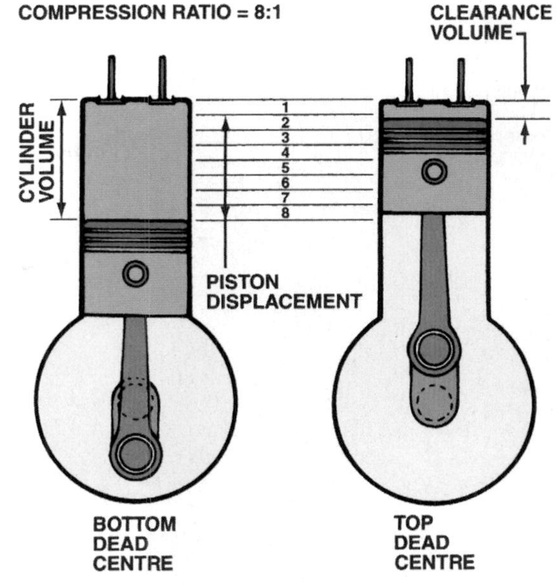

Figure 4–12 Compression ratio is the ratio of the total cylinder volume (when the piston is at the bottom of its stroke) to the clearance volume (when the piston is at the top of its stroke).

TECH TIP 

All 3.8-Litre Engines Are Not the Same!

Most engine sizes are currently identified by displacement in litres. However, not all 3.8-litre engines are the same. See, for example, the following table:

Engine	Displacement
Chevrolet-built 3.8 L, V-6	229 cu in
Buick-built 3.8 L, V-6 (also called 3800 cc)	231 cu in
Ford-built 3.8 L, V-6	232 cu in

The exact conversion from litres (or cubic centimetres) to cubic inches figures to 231.9 cu in. However, due to rounding of exact cubic-inch displacement and rounding of the exact cubic-centimetre volume, several entirely different engines can be marketed with the exact same litre designation. To reduce confusion and reduce the possibility of ordering incorrect parts, the vehicle identification number (VIN) should be noted for the vehicle being serviced. The VIN should be visible through the windshield on all vehicles. Since 1980, the *engine* identification number or letter is usually the eighth digit or letter from the left.

Smaller, four-cylinder engines can also cause confusion because many vehicle manufacturers use engines from both overseas and domestic manufacturers. Always refer to service manual information to be assured of correct engine identification.

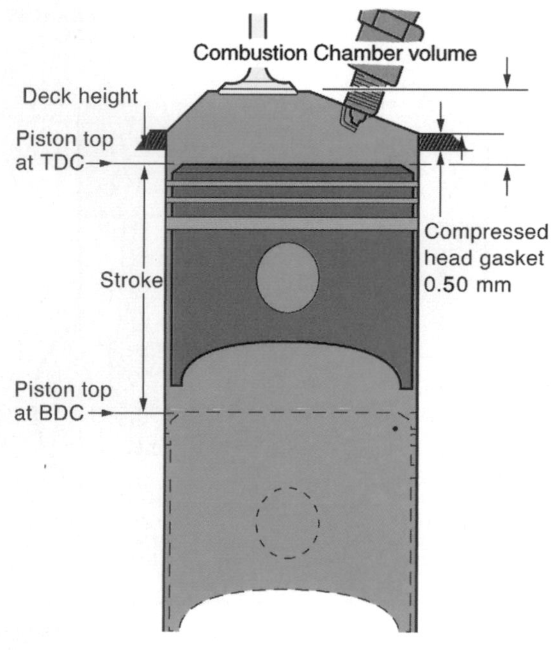

Figure 4–13 Combustion chamber volume is the volume above the piston with the piston at top dead centre.

To determine compression ratio, add the cylinder volume (displacement) and the clearance volume (combustion chamber) together and then divide by the clearance volume.

$$\text{Compression ratio} = \frac{\text{cylinder volume} + \text{clearance volume}}{\text{clearance volume}}$$

Gasoline engine compression ratios range from approximately 8:1 to 11:1. Computerized engine controls and fuel injection allow the higher ratios (11:1) to be used without engine detonation.

Diesel engines have a much higher compression ratio, in the range of 17:1 to 23:1.

COMPRESSION AFTER MACHINING

During routine engine remanufacturing, the following machining operations are performed:

1. Cylinders are bored oversize and larger-diameter pistons are installed. Boring the cylinder increases displacement and the compression ratio because the cylinder volume is increased and the combustion chamber volume remains the same, resulting in more air being squeezed into the same volume.
2. Block top surfaces are refinished. This machining operation is called *decking the block* and increases the compression ratio because it results in the cylinder heads being closer to the tops of the pistons.
3. Cylinder heads are resurfaced, which also increases the compression ratio.

NOTE: To avoid raising the compression ratio beyond stock rating, most remanufacturers use replacement pistons that are 0.35 mm to 0.50 mm (0.015 in. to 0.020 in.) shorter than usual.

THE CRANKSHAFT DETERMINES THE STROKE

The stroke of an engine is the distance the piston travels from top dead centre (TDC) to bottom dead centre (BDC). This distance is determined by the throw of the crankshaft. The throw is the distance from the centreline of the crankshaft to the centreline of the crankshaft rod journal. The throw is one-half of the stroke. See Figure 4–14 for an example of a crankshaft as installed in a General Motors V-6 engine.

If the crankshaft is replaced with one with a greater stroke, the pistons will be pushed up over the height of the top of the block (deck). The solution to this problem is to install replacement pistons with the piston pin relocated higher on the piston. Another alternative is to replace the connecting rod with a shorter one to prevent the piston from travelling too far up in the cylinder. Changing the connecting rod length does *not* change the stroke of an engine. Changing the connecting rod only changes the position of the piston in the cylinder.

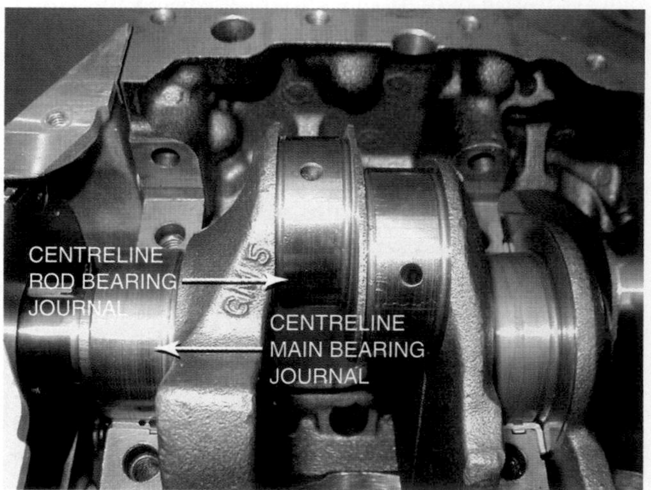

Figure 4–14 The distance between the centreline of the main bearing journal and the centreline of the connecting rod journal determines the stroke of the engine. This photo is a little unusual because this is from a V-6 with a splayed crankshaft used to even out the impulses on a 90°, V-6 engine design.

TORQUE

Torque is the term used to describe a rotating force that may or may not result in motion. Torque is measured as the amount of force multiplied by the length of the lever through which it acts. If a one metre long wrench is used to apply 10 newtons of force to the end of a wrench (turning a bolt), then you are exerting 10 N·m of torque. See Figure 4–15.

Some workshop manuals use kilograms instead of newtons. This would give torque in units of kilogram-metres (one kilogram-force = 9.8 N).

The imperial torque rating, in pound-feet, is the U.S. standard and is still commonly used in Canada.

One newton-metre (N·m) = 0.7376 lb-ft

One kilogram-metre (kg·m) = 7.23 lb-ft

One pound-foot (lb-ft) = 1.3558 N·m

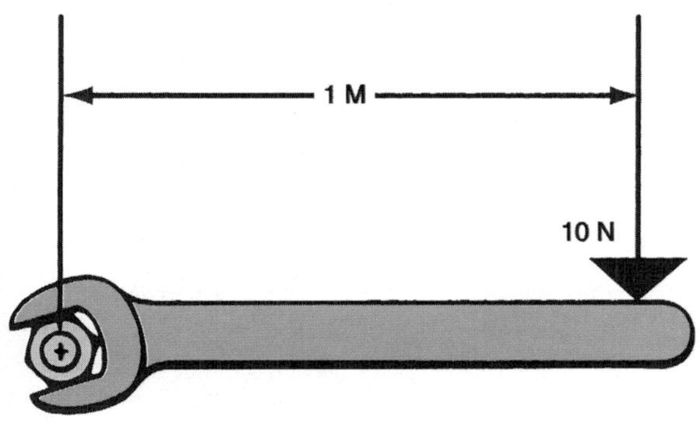

Figure 4–15 Torque is a twisting force equal to the distance from the pivot point times the force applied expressed in units called newton-metres (N·m) or pound-feet (lb-ft).

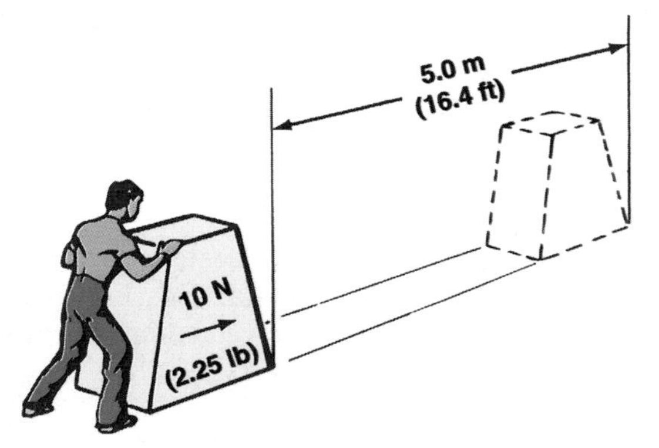

Figure 4–16 Work is calculated by multiplying force times distance. If you exert a force of 10 N (2.25 pounds) through a distance of 5 m (16.4 ft), you have done 50 J (37 ft-lb) of work.

WORK

Work is defined as actually accomplishing movement when force is applied to an object. A service technician can apply torque to a bolt in an attempt to loosen it, yet no work is done until the bolt actually moves. Work is calculated by multiplying the applied force (in newtons or pounds) by the distance the object moves (in metres or feet).

$$W = F \times D$$

If you applied a force of 10 N to move an object 5 m, then you accomplished 50 N·m of work (10 N × 5 m = 50 N·m). See Figure 4–16. The metric unit of work (and energy) is the joule.

$$1\ J = 1\ N{\cdot}m$$

Using joule for work/energy allows you to distinguish work from torque (newton-metre).

The formula W = F × D also applies with imperial calculations. If you apply 100 pounds of force to move an object 10 feet, then you accomplished 1000 foot-pounds of work.

NOTE: The imperial designations for torque and work are often confusing. Torque is expressed in pound-feet because it represents a force exerted a certain distance from the object and acts as a lever. Work on the other hand is expressed in foot-pounds because work is the movement over a certain distance (feet) multiplied by the force applied (pounds). Engines produce torque and service technicians exert torque represented by the unit pound-feet.

HORSEPOWER (KILOWATTS)

The most common engine power rating in Canada is still **horsepower** (hp), although the metric unit, kilowatts, is being used more often (746 watts is the equivalent of 1 hp). One horsepower is the power required to lift 550 pounds (force of 2450 N) a distance of 1 ft (0.305 m) in one second, or 746 J/s = 746 W. Also, 550 ft-lb/s = 45 kJ (33 000 ft-lb) per minute. See Figure 4–17.

The actual horsepower produced by an engine is measured with a **dynamometer.** A dynamometer (often abbreviated as **dyno**) places a load on the engine and measures the amount of twisting force the engine crankshaft places against the load. The load holds the engine speed, so it is called a **brake.** The horsepower derived from a dynamometer is called **brake horsepower (bhp).** The dynamometer actually measures the torque output of the engine. The horsepower is calculated from the torque readings at various engine speeds (in revolutions per minute or RPM). Torque is what the driver "feels" as the vehicle

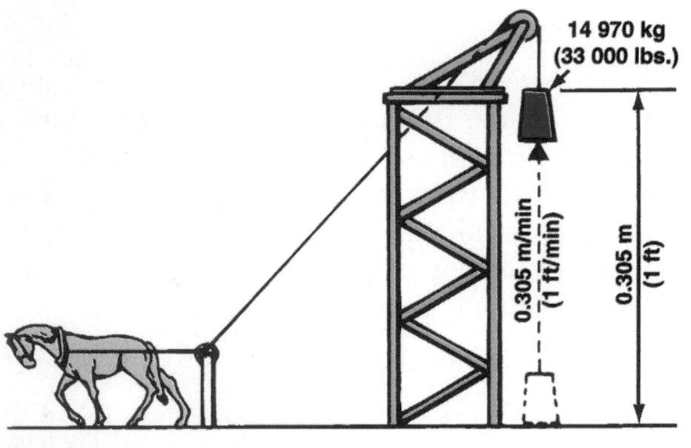

Figure 4–17 One horsepower is equal to 44 741 N·m (33 000 foot-pounds) of work per minute. Also equals 746 watts.

is being accelerated. A small engine operating at a high RPM may have the same horsepower as a large engine operating at a low RPM.

> **NOTE:** The higher the engine speed for a given amount of torque, the greater the horsepower. Many engines are high revving. To help prevent catastrophic damage due to excessive engine speed, most manufacturers limit the maximum RPM by programming fuel injectors to shut off if the engine speed increases past a certain level. Sometimes this cutoff speed can be as low as 3000 rpm if the transmission is in neutral or park. Complaints of high-speed miss or cutting out may be normal if the engine is approaching the rev limit.

SAE Gross Versus Net Horsepower

SAE standards for measuring horsepower include gross and net horsepower ratings. **SAE gross horsepower** is the maximum power an engine develops without some accessories in operation. **SAE net horsepower** is the power an engine develops as installed in the vehicle. A summary of the differences is given in the following table.

SAE Gross Horsepower	SAE Net Horsepower
No air cleaner or filter	Stock air cleaner or filter
No cooling fan	Stock cooling fan
No alternator	Stock alternator
No mufflers	Stock exhaust system
No emission controls	Full emission and noise control

Ratings are about 20% lower for the net rating method. Before 1971, most manufacturers used gross horsepower rating (the higher method) for advertising purposes. After 1971, the manufacturers started advertising only SAE net-rated horsepower.

HORSEPOWER AND ALTITUDE

Because air is less dense at high altitude, the power that a normal engine can develop is greatly reduced at higher altitudes. According to SAE conversion factors, a non-supercharged or non-turbocharged engine loses about 3% of its power for every 300 m (1000 ft) of altitude.

Therefore, an engine that develops 150 bhp in Vancouver, B.C. at sea level will only produce 115 bhp at Big White Mountain, 2345 m (7693 ft) high, near Kelowna, B.C.

Supercharged and turbocharged engines are not as greatly affected by altitude as normally aspirated engines. Normally aspirated means engines that breathe air at atmospheric pressure only.

TURBOCHARGING

A turbocharger is an exhaust-driven air compressor that is designed to provide a pressure greater than atmospheric pressure in the intake manifold. This increased pressure forces additional amounts of air into the cylinder—more than is normally forced in by atmospheric pressure. Getting fuel into an engine is simple; getting *air* into the engine is far more difficult. The turbocharger increases the *charge* (volume of air), which increases engine power. The amount of boost (pressure in the intake manifold) is measured in kilopascals (kPa) or pounds per square inch (psi); 6.9 kPa = 1 psi. As an example 69 kPa (10 psi) of positive boost is measured over and above the normal atmospheric pressure of 101 kPa (14.7 psi). The combined pressures equal 170 kPa (24.7 psi) pushing air into the engine. Boost gauges on the instrument panel indicate boost pressure only; they do not include atmospheric pressure.

The higher the level of boost (pressure), the greater the horsepower potential. See Figure 4–18. However, other factors must be considered when increasing boost pressure:

1. As boost pressure increases, the temperature of the air also increases.
2. As the temperature of the air increases, combustion temperatures also increase, which increases the possibility of detonation.

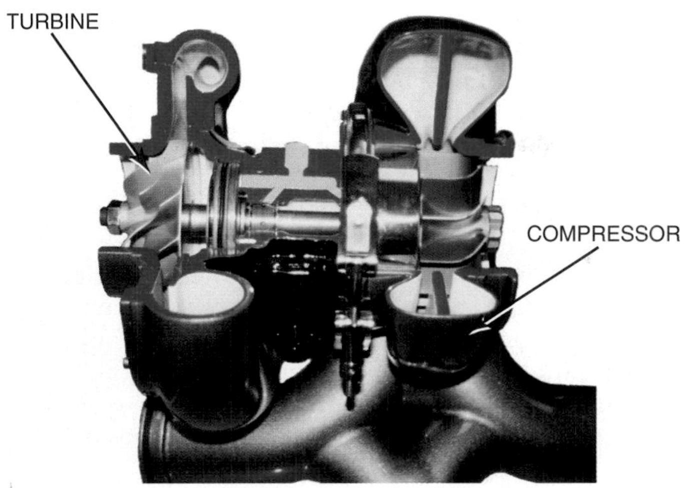

Figure 4–18 A cutaway of a typical turbocharger. The exhaust from the engine turns the turbine on the left side over 100 000 rpm. The turbine is connected by a shaft to a compressor located on the right side of the turbocharger. The compressor blades draw air from the air filter housing and force it into the intake manifold to give the engine extra power.

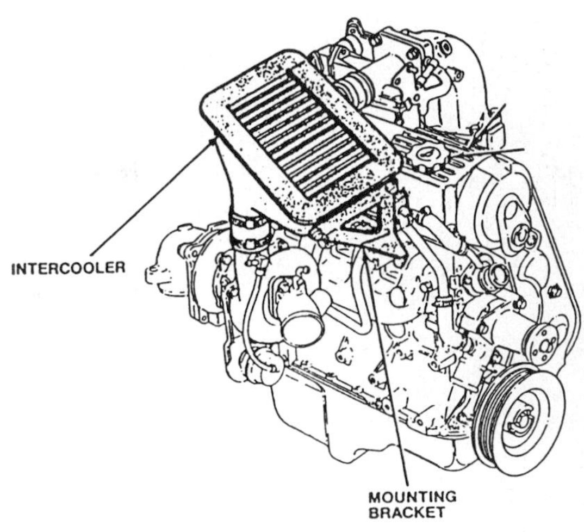

Figure 4–19 An intercooler is a radiator-like device that is used between the turbocharger and the engine to cool the air. When air is compressed, it gets hot. Cooler air is more dense than warm air and power is increased about 1% for each 5°C (9°F) drop in the temperature of air entering the engine. (Courtesy Ford)

TECH TIP

Quick-and-Easy Efficiency Check

An efficient engine is able to produce good power from little displacement. A common rule of thumb is that an engine is efficient if it can produce 61 hp/L of displacement (1 hp/in.^{3}). Many engines today are capable of this feat, such as the following:

Ford	4.6 L V-8 (281 cu. in.)—305 hp
Chevrolet	3.4 L V-6 (207 cu. in.)—210 hp
Chrysler	3.5 L V-6 (214 cu. in.)—214 hp
Acura	3.2 L V-6 (195 cu. in.)—230 hp

An engine is very powerful for its size if it can produce 100 hp/L (1.64 hp/in.^{3}). This 64% increase in efficiency is hard to achieve. Most factory stock engines with this power level are supercharged or turbocharged.

3. Power can be increased by cooling the compressed air after it leaves the turbocharger. *The power can be increased about 1% per 5°C (9°F) by which the air is cooled.* A typical cooling device is called an **intercooler** and is similar to a radiator, wherein outside air can pass through, cooling the pressurized heated air. See Figure 4–19.
4. As boost pressure increases, combustion temperature and pressures increase, which, if not limited, can do severe engine damage. The maximum exhaust gas temperature must be limited to 850°C (1560°F). Higher temperatures decrease the durability of the turbocharger *and* the engine.

Wastegate Operation

To prevent severe engine damage, most turbocharger systems use a wastegate. A wastegate is a valve similar to a door that can open and close. If the valve is closed, all of the exhaust travels to the turbocharger. When a predetermined amount of boost pressure develops in the intake manifold, the wastegate valve is opened. As the valve opens, most of the exhaust flows directly out the exhaust system, bypassing the turbocharger. With less exhaust flowing across the vanes of the turbocharger, the turbocharger decreases in speed and boost pressure is reduced. When the boost pressure drops, the wastegate valve closes to direct the exhaust over the turbocharger vanes and again allow the boost pressure to rise. Wastegate operation is a continuous process to control boost pressure.

The wastegate is the pressure control valve of a turbocharger system. The wastegate is usually controlled by the on-board computer. The **manifold absolute pressure (MAP) sensor,** which measures intake manifold vacuum (or pressure), is the most important sensor used by the computer to control the wastegate. The computer usually controls a pressure actuator, which operates the wastegate valve. See Figures 4–20 and 4–21.

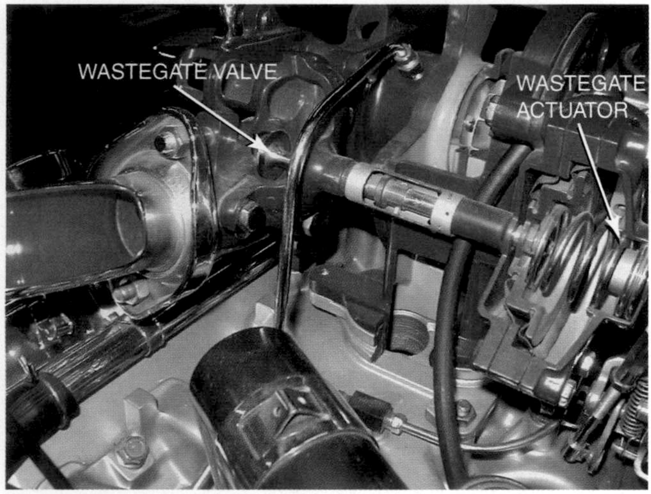

Figure 4–20 Whenever the turbocharger boost pressure exceeds a predetermined value, the wastegate actuator spring compresses, which moves the wastegate valve. When the wastegate is moved, the exhaust from the engine flows directly into the exhaust system bypassing the turbocharger, which reduces the turbocharger boost pressure.

Turbocharger Failures

When turbochargers fail to function correctly, a drop in power is noticed. To restore proper operation, the turbocharger must be rebuilt, repaired, or replaced. It is not possible to simply remove the turbocharger, seal any openings, and still maintain decent driveability. Bearing failure is a common cause of turbocharger failure, and replacement bearings are usually only available to rebuilders. Another common turbocharger problem is excessive and continuous oil consumption resulting in blue exhaust smoke. Turbochargers use small rings similar to piston rings on the shaft to prevent exhaust (combustion gases) from entering the central bearing. Because there are no seals to keep oil in, excessive oil consumption is usually caused by

1. A plugged positive crankcase ventilation (PCV) system resulting in excessive crankcase pressures forcing oil into the air inlet. This failure is not related to the turbocharger, but the turbocharger is often blamed.
2. A clogged air filter, which causes a low-pressure area in the inlet, which can draw oil past the turbo shaft rings and into the intake manifold.
3. A clogged oil return (drain) line from the turbocharger to the oil pan (sump), which can cause the engine oil pressure to force oil past the turbocharger's shaft rings and into the intake *and* exhaust manifolds. Obviously, oil being forced into both the intake and exhaust would create lots of smoke.

SUPERCHARGING

A supercharging system is an engine-driven system designed to provide pressure greater than atmospheric pressure in the intake manifold. A supercharger is used in some engines from the factory including the General Motors 3800 cc V-6, which uses an Eaton-built unit. See Figures 4–22 to 4–25.

HIGH PERFORMANCE TIP 

If One Is Good, Two Are Better

A turbocharger uses the exhaust from the engine to spin a turbine, which is connected to an impeller inside a turbocharger. This impeller then forces air into the engine under pressure higher than is normally achieved without a turbocharger. The more air that can be forced into an engine, the greater the power potential. A V-type engine has two exhaust manifolds, so two turbochargers can be used to help force greater quantities of air into an engine.

HIGH PERFORMANCE TIP 

Boost Is the Result of Restriction

The boost pressure of a turbocharger (or supercharger) is commonly measured in kilopascals or pounds per square inch. If a cylinder head is restricted because of small valves and ports, the turbocharger will quickly provide boost. Boost results when the air being forced into the cylinder heads cannot flow into the cylinders fast enough and "piles up" in the intake manifold, increasing boost pressure. If an engine had large valves and ports, the turbocharger could provide a much greater *amount* of air into the engine at the same boost pressure as an identical engine with smaller valves and ports. Therefore by increasing the size of the valves, a turbocharged or supercharged engine will be capable of producing much greater power.

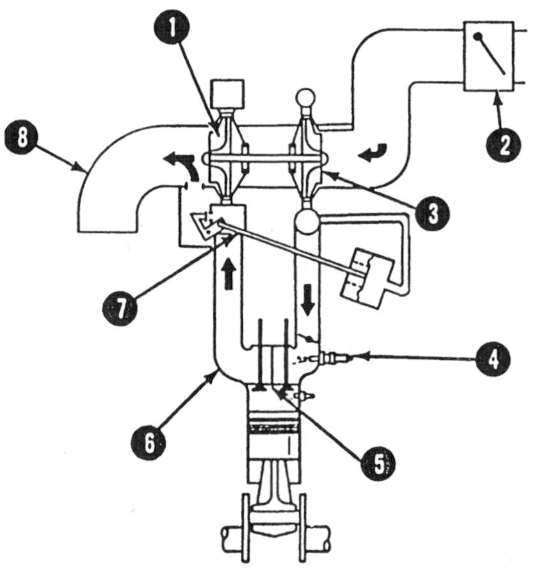

1) Exhaust gas pressure and heat energy cause the turbine wheel to rotate, which causes the compressor wheel to rotate.
2) A vane air meter measures intake airflow and temperature.
3) The rotating compressor wheel compresses the air it receives and delivers it under pressure to the intake manifold.
4) Fuel is introduced downsteam of the compressor and mixes with the air charge.
5) The denser air/fuel charge in the combustion chamber develops more horsepower during the combustion cycle.
6) Exhaust gas from the exhaust manifold flows into the turbine.
7) When the intake manifold pressure reaches a set value, the actuator opens the wastegate to bypass some exhaust gas.
8) The cooled, expanded exhaust gas is directed by the turbine housing to the exhaust system.

Figure 4–21 Turbocharger operation. (Courtesy Ford)

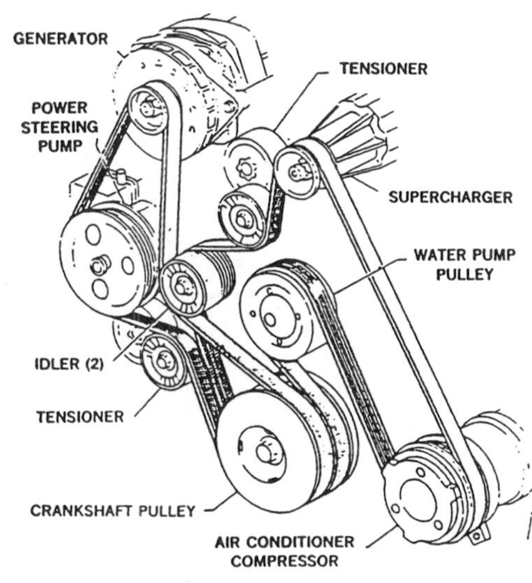

Figure 4–22 Supercharger drive arrangement: General Motors V-6. (Courtesy General Motors)

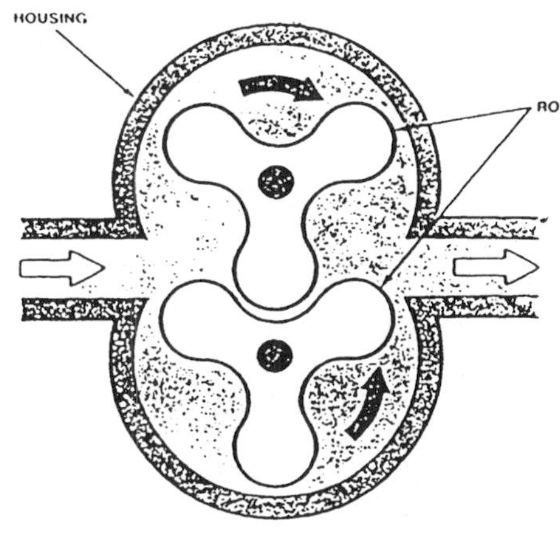

Figure 4–23 Supercharger end view. (Courtesy Ford)

Figure 4–24 A high-performance engine equipped with a belt-driven supercharger. Because a supercharger is always turning when the engine is running, a supercharger provides additional power all the time without the slight delay or lag often associated with turbocharged engines.

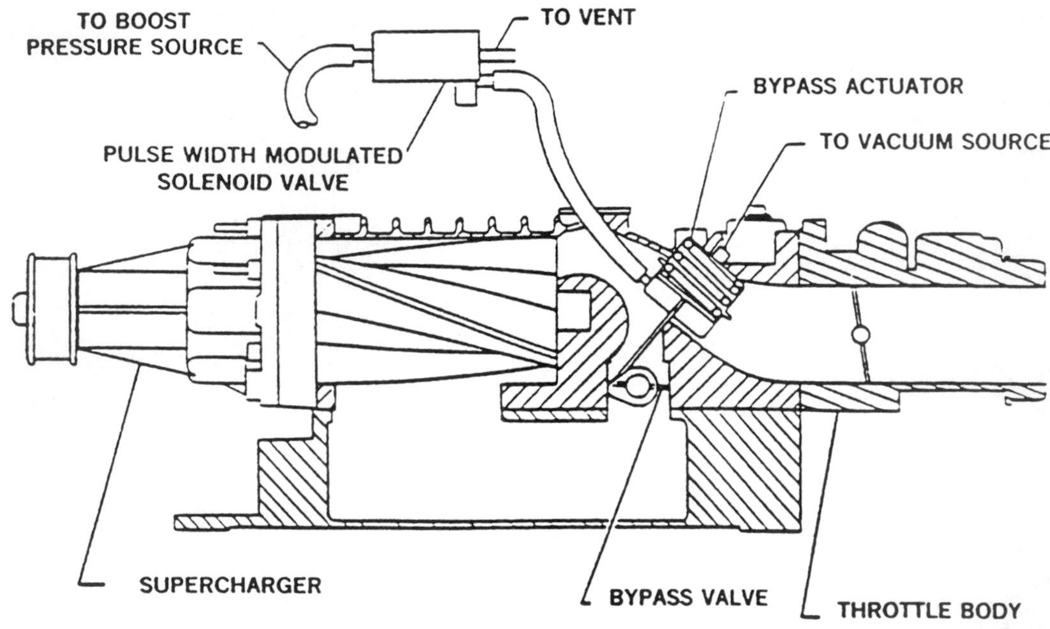

Figure 4–25 Supercharger cross-section: General Motors V-6. (Courtesy General Motors)

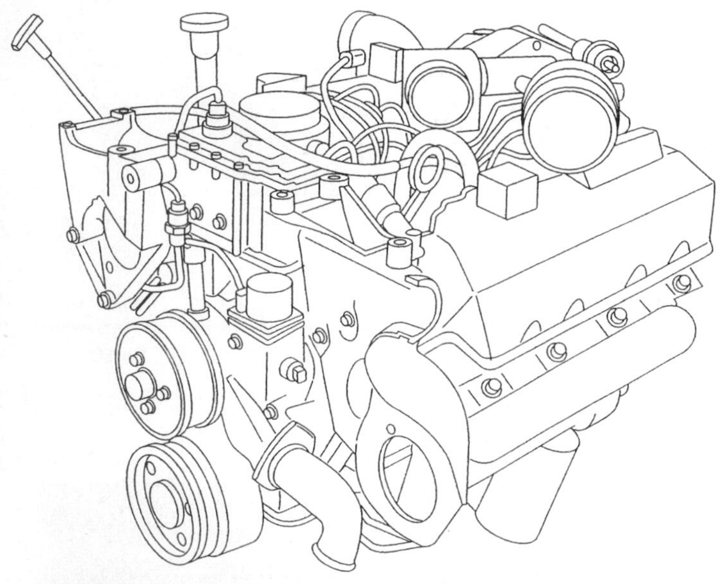

Figure 4–26 Diesel engine. (Courtesy Ford)

DIESEL ENGINES

Dr. Rudolph Diesel, a German engineer, is credited with the invention and development of the diesel engine during the 1890s.

Diesels have been gaining popularity in Canada and North America, primarily due to the large numbers of sports utility vehicles (SUVs) and pickup trucks that are now being sold. See Figure 4–26. Although gasoline shortages in the late 1970s and early 1980s caused a brief rise in diesel sales, passenger car/light truck diesel numbers have generally been low. The diesel engine penetration rate in Europe is approaching 40% as opposed to 1% in North America, though this is changing.

Advantages and Disadvantages

Diesels have a number of advantages and disadvantages compared to gasoline engines: They are very fuel-efficient, provide exceptional low-speed torque, are very reliable, and normally last for many kilometres. See Figure 4–27.

On the downside, diesels are very heavily built to withstand greater internal pressures; they are noisier and lack the acceleration and high RPMs of a comparable gasoline engine. Some passenger-car/light-truck diesels are equipped with turbochargers to increase power and performance. For many of them it is difficult to tell which engine is under the hood—gasoline or diesel. Many high-end vehicles, such as Mercedes, BMW, and Jaguar, offer turbo diesel engines.

Differences

Diesels are manufactured with both two-stroke and four-stroke cycles; however, four-stroke engines are almost always used with light vehicles. Both types are used for large truck and industrial uses.

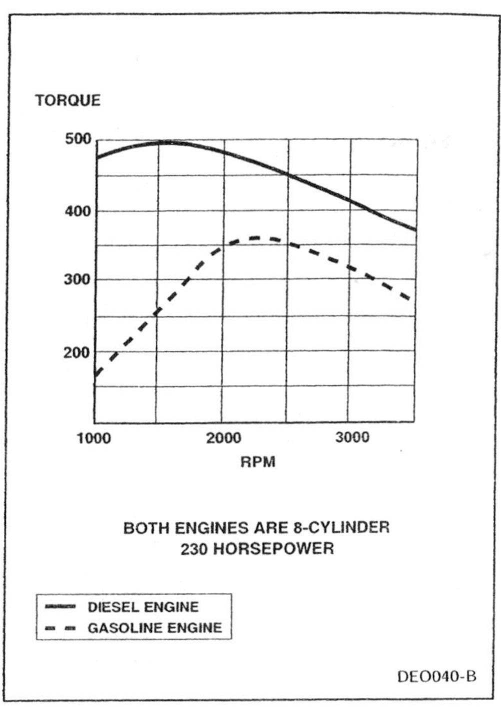

Figure 4–27 Gasoline to diesel torque comparison. (Courtesy Ford)

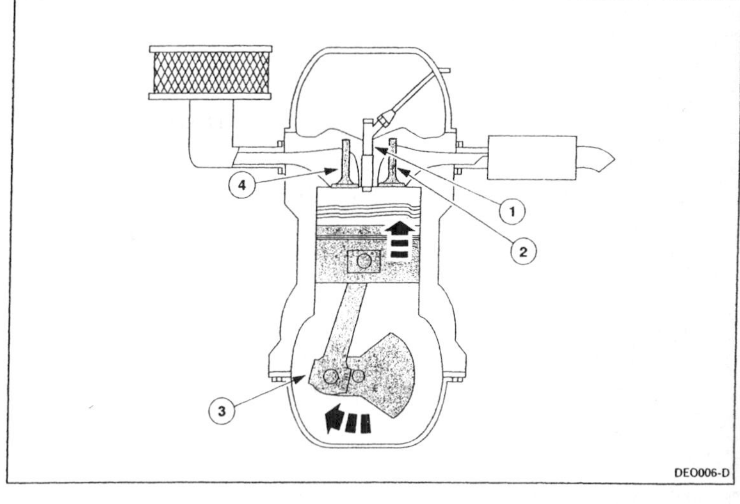

Item	Description
1	Fuel Injector
2	Exhaust Valve (Closed)

Item	Description
3	Crankshaft
4	Intake Valve (Closed)

Figure 4–28 Diesel compression stroke. (Courtesy Ford)

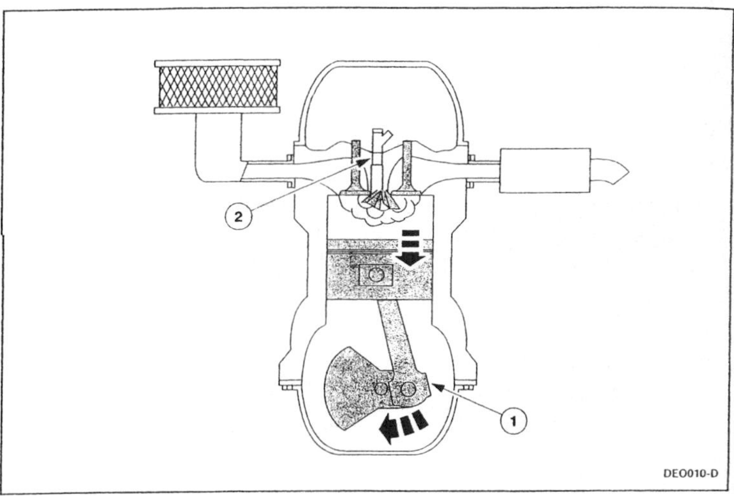

The Diesel Power Stroke

Item	Description
1	Fuel Injector
2	Crankshaft

Figure 4–29 Diesel power stroke. (Courtesy Ford)

Although a four-stroke diesel engine and a four-stroke gasoline engine share many of the same principles, there are a number of differences. Diesel engines:

- have no ignition system, no distributor or spark plugs;
- do not have a throttle plate at the intake manifold to regulate the amount of air entering the engine;
- do not develop any intake manifold vacuum: an engine driven vacuum pump may be used to operate accessories;
- have much higher compression than a gasoline engine: usually in the 17:1 to 23:1 range;
- draw in and compress air only during the intake and compression strokes. There is no fuel in the cylinder at this time.

DIESEL PRINCIPLES

During the intake stroke, the diesel allows a large volume of air to enter the cylinder because of the unrestricted (no throttle plate) intake manifold. As the piston moves up the cylinder on the compression stroke (Figure 4–28), the increasing pressure causes the temperature to rise, usually above 550°C (1020°F). At approximately top dead centre, diesel fuel is injected through the fuel injector into this hot air mass. The fuel, which ignites at a lower temperature than the compressed air, begins to burn and combustion starts. This is known as compression ignition (CI) as opposed to a gasoline engine, which uses spark ignition (SI).

Diesel fuel takes longer to burn than gasoline and as a result, combustion during the power stroke continues for a greater period of time, Figure 4–29. This allows the piston to apply higher force to the crankshaft because of the increasing connecting rod/crankshaft angles (mechanical advantage) as the crankshaft rotates. This is one of the reasons why diesels produce more torque than a similar displacement gasoline engine.

The piston reverses on the exhaust stroke, the burned exhaust gasses are pushed out of the cylinder and the process begins again on the following intake stroke.

The power output of a gasoline engine is controlled by restricting air with a throttle plate: diesel engines do not use a throttle plate, they control speed and power by metering the amount of fuel injected.

Starting Aids

Compression ignition engines, such as our diesel, may be hard to start when cold; this can be a concern in areas where low temperatures are common. The heat of compression is dissipated into the surrounding cylinder head and block. Cold weather starting aids include block heaters (an electrical heating element fitted to the side of the engine) and glow plugs (battery powered heating elements that extend into the combustion chamber area). See Figures 4–30 and 4–31.

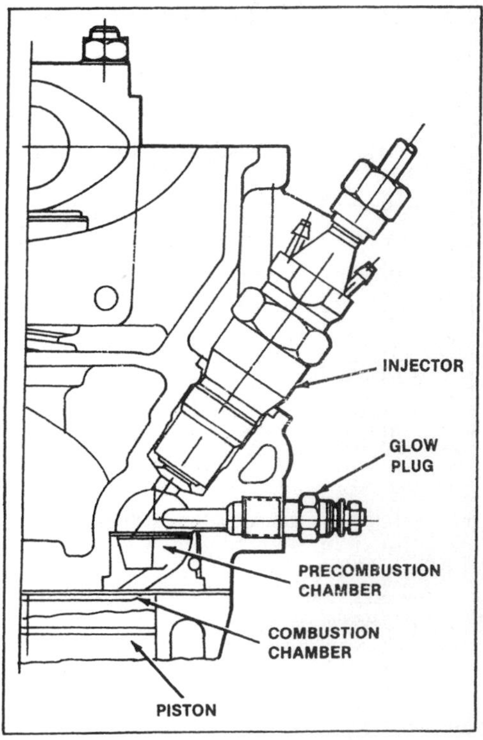

Figure 4–31 Fuel injector and glow plug. (Courtesy Ford)

SAFETY TIP

Avoid Starting Fluids with Glow Plugs

Starting fluids such as ether should never be used on any diesel equipped with glow plugs. The plugs may ignite the ether being sprayed into the intake, causing personal injury.

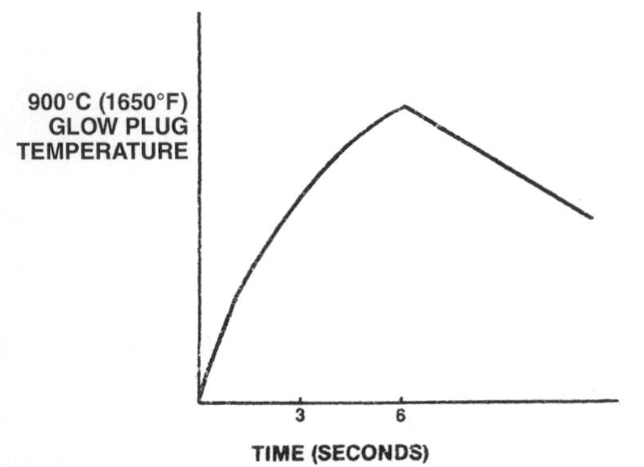

Figure 4–30 Glow plug temperature. (Courtesy Ford)

SUMMARY

1. The four strokes of the four-stroke cycle are intake, compression, power, and exhaust.
2. Engines are classified by number and arrangement of cylinders and by number and location of valves and camshafts, as well as by type of mounting, fuel used, cooling method, and induction pressure.
3. Most engines rotate clockwise as viewed from the front (accessory) end of the engine. The SAE standard is counterclockwise as viewed from the principal (flywheel) end of the engine.
4. Engine size is called displacement and represents the volume displaced or swept by all of the pistons.
5. Engine power is expressed in horsepower, which is a calculated value based on the amount of torque or twisting force the engine produces.

REVIEW QUESTIONS

1. Name the strokes of a four-stroke cycle.
2. What does a dynamometer actually measure?
3. What is the difference between SAE net and SAE gross horsepower?
4. How is the air–fuel mixture in the combustion chamber ignited in a diesel engine?

RED SEAL CERTIFICATION-TYPE QUESTIONS

1. Overhead valve engines _____.
   a. Use an overhead camshaft
   b. Have the valves in the head
   c. Operate by the two-stroke cycle
   d. Use the camshaft to close the valves
2. An SOHC V-8 engine has how many camshafts?
   a. One
   b. Two
   c. Three
   d. Four
3. On the intake stroke, a four-stroke cycle gasoline engine draws in ____________.
   a. Air only
   b. An oil and fuel mix
   c. A mixture of air and fuel
   d. Only gasoline
4. Torque is expressed in units of ______________.
   a. Newton-metres
   b. Metres per minute
   c. Torque times RPM
   d. Metres per second
5. Boost pressure from a turbocharger is controlled by ____________.
   a. A spring-loaded relief valve
   b. A wastegate
   c. A governor
   d. An ignition RPM limit
6. A normally aspirated automobile engine loses about ___________ of its power per 300 metres (1000 feet) of altitude.
   a. 1%
   b. 3%
   c. 5%
   d. 7%
7. One cylinder of an automotive four-stroke cycle engine completes a cycle every _____.
   a. 90°
   b. 180°
   c. 360°
   d. 720°
8. How many rotations of the crankshaft are required to complete each stroke of a four-stroke cycle engine?
   a. One-fourth
   b. One-half
   c. One
   d. Two
9. A rotating force is called ______.
   a. Horsepower
   b. Torque
   c. Combustion pressure
   d. Eccentric movement
10. The stroke of an engine can be increased by ___________.
    a. Changing the crankshaft throw
    b. Decking the cylinder block
    c. Lengthening the connecting rod
    d. Moving the piston pin location on the piston

5

Engine Condition Diagnosis

OBJECTIVES: After studying Chapter 5, you should be able to:

1. Prepare for the interprovincial Red Seal certification examination in Appendix I (Engine Repair) on the topics covered in this chapter.
2. List the visual checks that can be performed to determine the engine condition.
3. Describe how to perform a dry and wet compression test on a gasoline engine.
4. Describe how to perform a dry compression test on a diesel engine.
5. Explain how to perform a cylinder leakage test.
6. Describe how an oil sample analysis can be used to determine the condition of the engine.

ENGINE SMOKE DIAGNOSIS: GASOLINE ENGINE

The colour of engine exhaust smoke can indicate what engine problem might exist.

Typical Exhaust Smoke Colour	Possible Causes
Blue	Blue exhaust indicates that the engine is burning oil. Oil is getting into the combustion chamber either past the piston rings or past the valve stem seals. Blue smoke only after start-up is usually due to defective valve stem seals. See Figure 5–1.
Black	Black exhaust smoke is due to excessive fuel being burned in the combustion chamber. Typical causes include a defective or misadjusted carburetor, leaking fuel injector, or excessive fuel pump pressure.
White (steam)	White smoke or steam from the exhaust is normal during cold weather and represents condensed steam. Every engine creates about one litre of water for each litre of gasoline burned. If the steam from the exhaust is excessive, then water (coolant) is getting into the combustion chamber. Typical causes include a defective cylinder head gasket, a cracked cylinder head, or in severe cases, a cracked block. See Figure 5–2. NOTE: Exhaust smoke can also be created when automatic transmission fluid (ATF) is burned. A common source of ATF getting into the engine is through a defective vacuum modulator valve on the automatic transmission.

ENGINE NOISE DIAGNOSIS

An engine noise is often difficult to diagnose. An industrial stethoscope is a useful tool often used to help pinpoint the problem area.

Several items that can cause an engine noise include the following:

- **Valves clicking** because of lack of oil to the lifters. This noise is most noticeable at idle when the oil pressure is the lowest.
- **Torque converter** attaching bolts or nuts loose on the flex plate. This noise is most noticeable at idle or when there is no load on the engine.

Figure 5–1 Blowby gases coming out of the crankcase vent hose. Excessive amounts of combustion gases flow past the piston rings and into the crankcase.

Figure 5–2 White steam is usually an indication of a blown (defective) cylinder head gasket that allows engine coolant to flow into the combustion chamber where it is turned to steam.

- **Cracked flex plate.** The noise of a cracked flex plate is often mistaken for a rod or main bearing noise.
- **Loose or defective drive belts.** If an accessory drive belt is loose or defective, the flopping noise often sounds similar to a bearing knock.
- **Piston pin knock.** This knocking noise is usually not affected by load on the cylinder. If the clearance is too great, a double knock is heard when the engine idles. If all cylinders are grounded out one at a time and the noise does not change, a defective piston pin could be the cause.
- **Piston slap.** A piston slap is usually caused by an undersize or improperly shaped piston or oversize cylinder bore. A piston slap is most noticeable when the engine is cold and tends to decrease or stop as the piston expands during engine operation.
- **Timing chain noise.** An excessively loose timing chain can cause a severe knocking noise when the chain hits the timing chain cover. This noise often sounds like a rod-bearing knock.
- **Heat riser noise.** A loose (worn) or defective heat riser valve in the exhaust on older model vehicles can make a knocking noise similar to a bearing noise. Even a vacuum-controlled heat riser (also called an **early fuel evaporation (EFE) valve**) can make a knocking noise, especially under load, as the result of slight vacuum variations applied to the actuator diaphragm. To eliminate the heat riser as a possible cause, remove the vacuum hose to the actuator or restrain the thermostatic valve with a wire or other suitable means.
- **Rod-bearing noise.** The noise from a defective rod bearing is usually load sensitive and changes in intensity as the load on the engine increases and decreases. A rod-bearing failure can often be detected by grounding out the spark plugs one cylinder at a time. If the knocking noise decreases or is eliminated when a particular cylinder is grounded, then the grounded cylinder is the one from which the noise is originating.

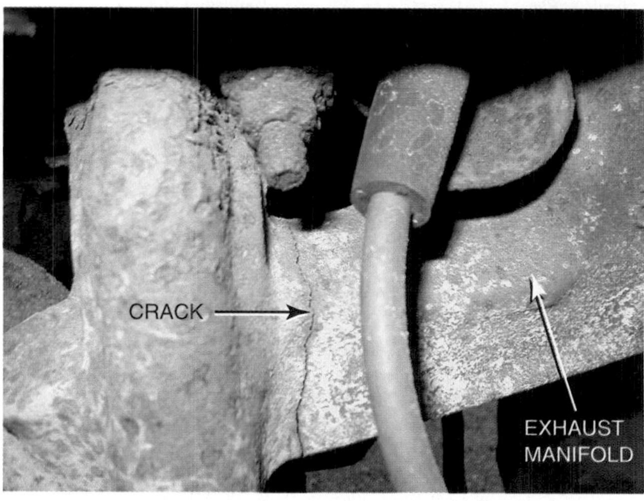

Figure 5–3 A cracked exhaust manifold on a Ford V-8.

- **Main-bearing knock.** A main-bearing knock often cannot be isolated to a particular cylinder. The sound can vary in intensity and may disappear at times depending on engine load.
- **Exhaust leak.** This noise may sound like a noisy valve because it often makes a clicking sound, especially during acceleration. See Figure 5–3.

The thickness (viscosity) of oil at lower temperatures will often mask many internal noises until the

Typical Noises	Possible Causes
Clicking noise (like the clicking of a ball-point pen)	1. Loose spark plug 2. Loose accessory mount (for air conditioning compressor, alternator, power steering pump, etc.) 3. Loose rocker arm 4. Worn rocker arm pedestal 5. Fuel pump (broken mechanical fuel pump return spring) 6. Worn camshaft 7. Exhaust leak 8. Ping (detonation)
Clacking noise (like tapping on metal)	1. Worn piston pin 2. Broken piston 3. Excessive valve clearance 4. Timing chain hitting cover
Knock (like knocking on a door)	1. Rod bearing(s) 2. Main bearing(s) 3. Thrust bearing(s) 4. Loose torque converter 5. Cracked flex plate (drive plate)
Rattle (like a baby rattle)	1. Manifold heat control valve 2. Broken harmonic balancer 3. Loose accessory mounts 4. Loose accessory drive belt or a defective tensioner. See Figure 5–4.
Clatter (like rolling marbles)	1. Rod bearings 2. Piston pin 3. Loose timing chain
Whine (like an electric motor running)	1. Generator (alternator) bearing 2. Drive belt 3. Power steering 4. Belt noise (accessory or timing)
Clunk (like a door closing)	1. Engine mount 2. Drive axle shaft U-joint or constant velocity (CV) joint

engine is warm. Engine clearances will also change with temperature; when diagnosing engine noise, test under both cold and warm operating conditions.

Colder Canadian winter temperatures often bring out sounds (e.g., piston slap) that may not be noticed in moderate climates.

Regardless of the type of loud knocking noise, after the external causes of knocking noise have been eliminated, the engine should be disassembled and carefully inspected to determine the exact cause.

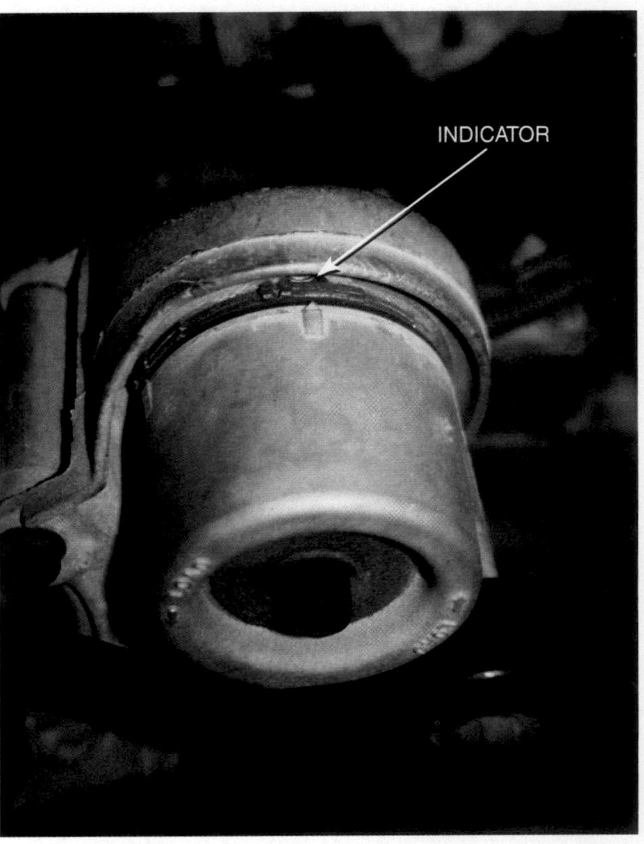

Figure 5–4 An accessory drive belt tensioner. Most tensioners have a mark that indicates normal operating location. If the belt has stretched, this indicator mark will be outside of the normal range. Anything wrong with the belt or the tensioner can cause noise.

VACUUM TEST

Vacuum is pressure below atmospheric pressure and is measured in **millimetres** (or inches) **of mercury (Hg).** An engine in good mechanical condition will run with high manifold vacuum. Manifold vacuum is developed by the pistons as they move down on the intake stroke to draw the charge from the intake manifold.

Idle Vacuum Test

An engine in proper condition should idle with a steady vacuum between 430 and 530 mm (17 and 21 inches) Hg. See Figure 5–5.

> **NOTE:** Engine vacuum readings vary with altitude. A reduction of 25 mm (1 in.) Hg per 300 m (1000 ft) of altitude should be subtracted from the expected values if testing a vehicle above 300 m (1000 ft).

Figure 5–5 A typical vacuum gauge showing about 485 mm (19 in.) Hg of vacuum at idle—well within the normal reading of 430 to 530 mm (17 to 21 in.) Hg.

Low and Steady Vacuum

If the vacuum is lower than normal, yet the gauge reading is steady, the most common causes include

- Retarded ignition timing
- Retarded cam timing (check timing chain for excessive slack or timing belt for proper installation)

Fluctuating Vacuum

If the needle drops then returns to a normal reading, then drops again and then again returns, this indicates a sticking valve. A common cause of sticking valves is lack of lubrication of the valve stems. See Figures 5–6 through 5–16 for some other examples.

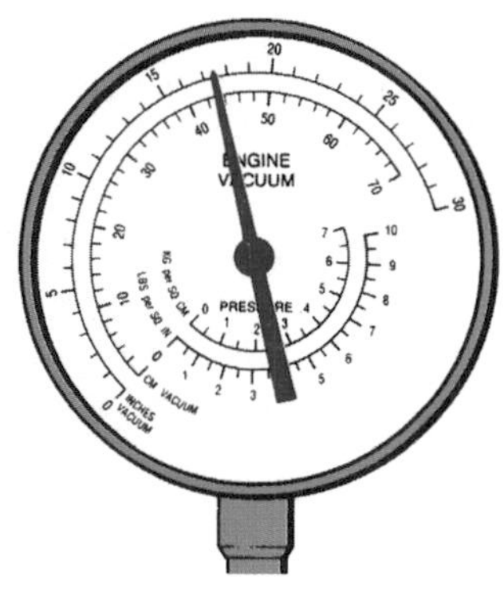

Figure 5–6 An engine in good mechanical condition should produce 430 to 530 mm (17 to 21 in.) Hg of vacuum at idle at sea level.

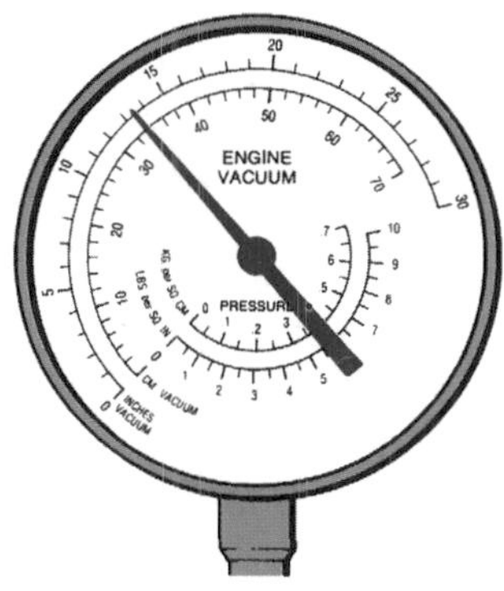

Figure 5–7 A steady but low reading could indicate retarded valve or ignition timing.

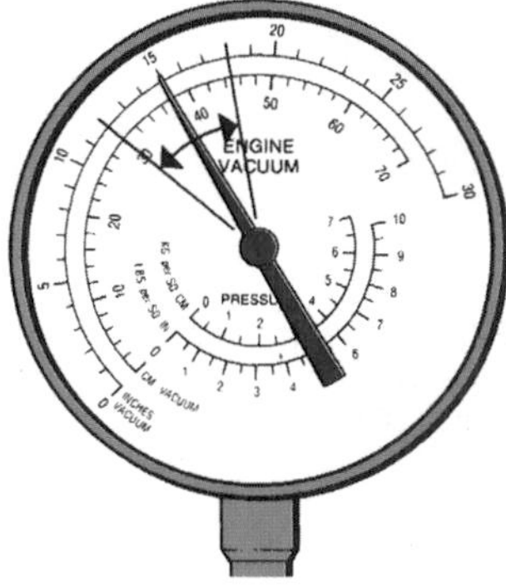

Figure 5–8 A gauge reading with the needle fluctuating 75 to 230 mm (3 to 9 in.) Hg below normal often indicates a vacuum leak in the intake system.

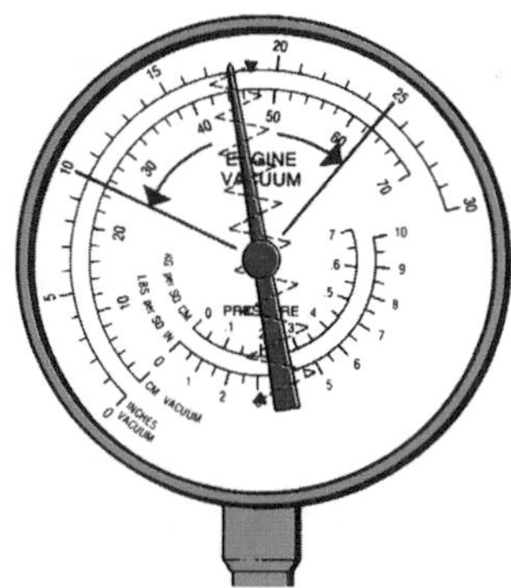

Figure 5–9 A leaking head gasket can cause the needle to vibrate as it moves through a range from below to above normal.

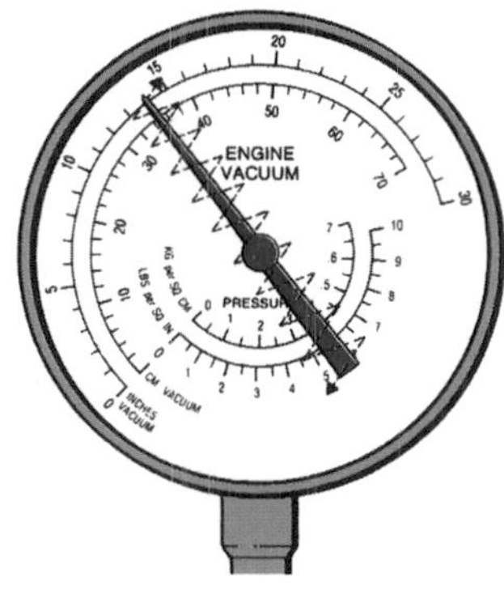

Figure 5–10 An oscillating needle 25 to 50 mm (1 to 2 in.) Hg below normal could indicate an incorrect air–fuel mixture (either too rich or too lean).

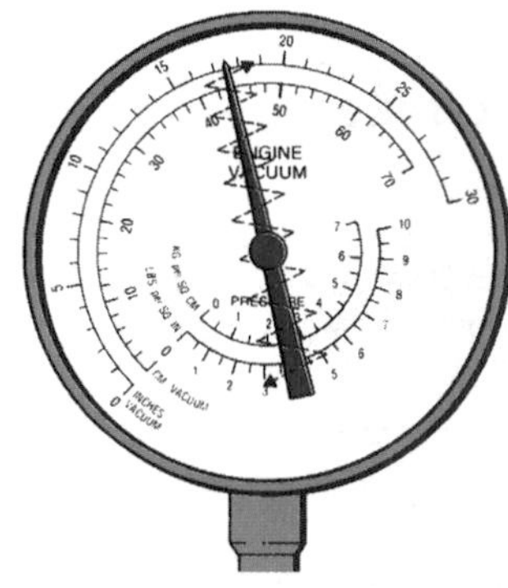

Figure 5–11 A rapidly vibrating needle at idle that becomes steady as engine speed is increased indicates worn valve guides.

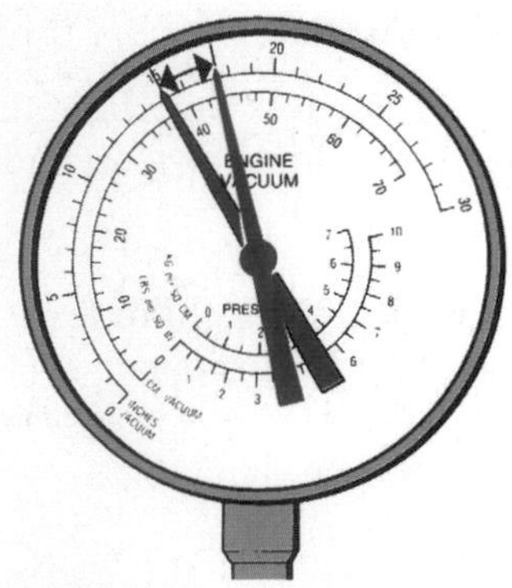

Figure 5–12 If the needle drops 25 to 50 mm (1 to 2 in.) Hg from the normal reading, one of the engine valves is burned or not seating properly.

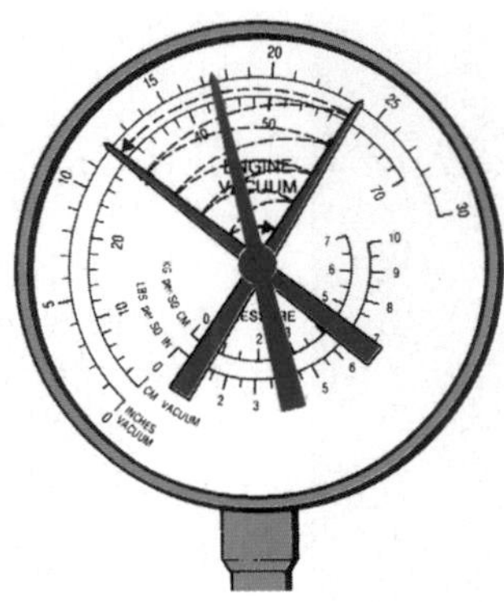

Figure 5–13 Weak valve springs will produce a normal reading at idle, but as engine speed increases, the needle will fluctuate rapidly between 300 and 600 mm (12 and 24 in.) Hg.

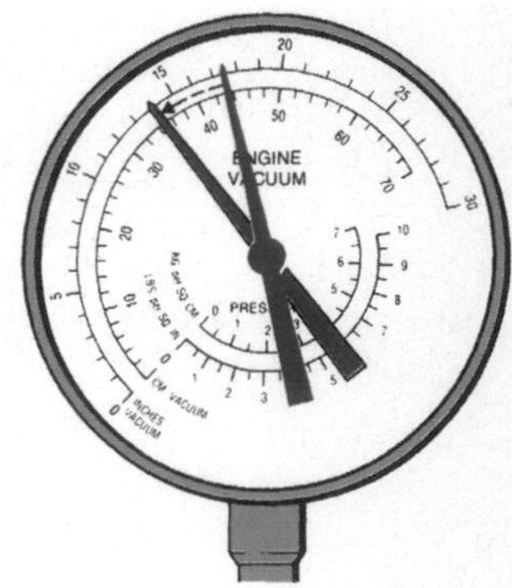

Figure 5–14 A steady needle reading that drops 50 to 75 mm (2 or 3 in.) Hg when the engine speed is increased slightly above idle indicates that the ignition timing is retarded.

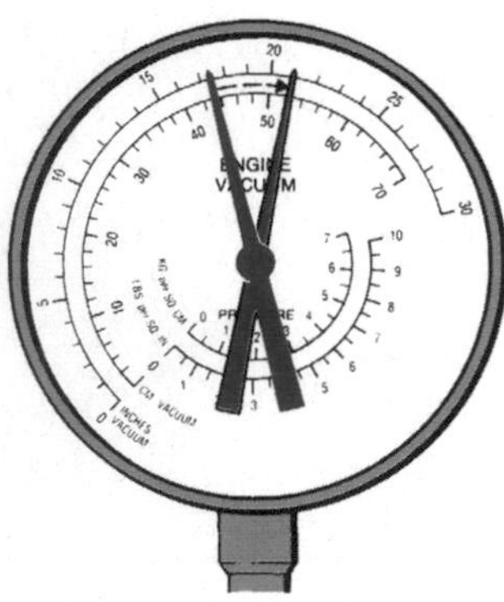

Figure 5–15 A steady needle reading that rises 50 to 75 mm (2 to 3 in.) Hg when the engine speed is increased slightly above idle indicates that the ignition timing is advanced.

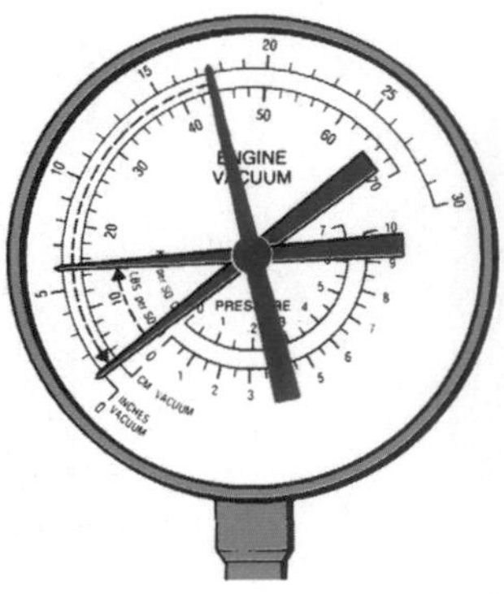

Figure 5–16 A needle that drops to near zero when the engine is accelerated rapidly and then rises slightly to a reading below normal indicates an exhaust restriction.

COMPRESSION TEST

Testing an engine for proper compression is one of the fundamental engine diagnostic tests that can be performed. For smooth engine operation, all cylinders must have equal compression. An engine can lose compression by leakage of air through one or more of only three routes:

- Intake or exhaust valve
- Piston rings (or piston, if there is a hole)
- Cylinder head gasket

For best results, the engine should be warmed to normal operating temperature before testing. An accurate compression test should be performed as follows:

1. Remove all spark plugs. This allows the engine to be cranked to an even speed. Be sure to label all spark plug wires.

> **CAUTION:** Disable the ignition system by disconnecting the primary leads from the ignition coil or module or by grounding the coil wire after removing it from the centre of the distributor cap. Also disable the fuel-injection system to prevent the squirting of fuel into the cylinder.

2. Block open the throttle and choke (if the vehicle is so equipped). This permits the maximum amount

TECH TIP

The Paper Test

A soundly running engine should produce even and steady exhaust at the tail pipe. Hold a piece of paper (even a bank note works) or a 75 mm by 125 mm (3 in. by 5 in.) card, within 25 mm (1 inch) of the tail pipe with the engine running at idle. See Figure 5–17. The paper should blow out evenly without "puffing." If the paper is drawn *toward* the tail pipe at times, the valves in one or more cylinders could be burned. Other reasons why the paper might be sucked toward the tail pipe include the following:

1. The engine could be misfiring because of a lean condition that could occur normally when the engine is cold.
2. Pulsing of the paper toward the tail pipe could also be caused by a hole in the exhaust system.

If exhaust escapes through a hole in the exhaust system, air could be drawn—in the intervals between the exhaust puffs—from the tail pipe to the hole in the exhaust, causing the paper to be drawn toward the tail pipe.

Figure 5–17 The paper test involves holding a piece of paper near the tail pipe of an idling engine. A good engine should produce even outward puffs of exhaust. If the paper is sucked in toward the tail pipe, a burned valve is a possibility.

of air to be drawn into the engine. This step also ensures consistent compression test results.

3. Thread a compression gauge into one spark plug hole and crank the engine. See Figure 5–18. Continue cranking the engine through four compression strokes. Each compression stroke makes a puffing sound.

HINT: Note the reading on the compression gauge after the first puff. This reading should be at least one-half of the final reading. For example, if the final, highest reading is 1050 kPa, 10.6 kg/cm^2 (150 psi) then the reading after the first puff should be higher than 525 kPa, 5.3 kg/cm^2 (75 psi). A low first-puff reading indicates possible weak, broken, or worn piston rings.

TECH TIP

The Hose Trick

Installing spark plugs can be made easier by using a rubber hose on the end of the spark plug. The hose can be a vacuum hose, fuel line, or even an old spark plug wire end. See Figure 5–19. The hose makes it easy to start the threads of the spark plug into the cylinder head. After starting the threads, continue to thread the spark plug for several turns. Using the hose eliminates the chance of cross-threading the plug. This is especially important when installing spark plugs in aluminum cylinder heads.

Figure 5–18 A two-piece compression gauge set. The threaded hose is screwed into the spark plug hole after removing the spark plug. The gauge part is then snapped onto the end of the hose.

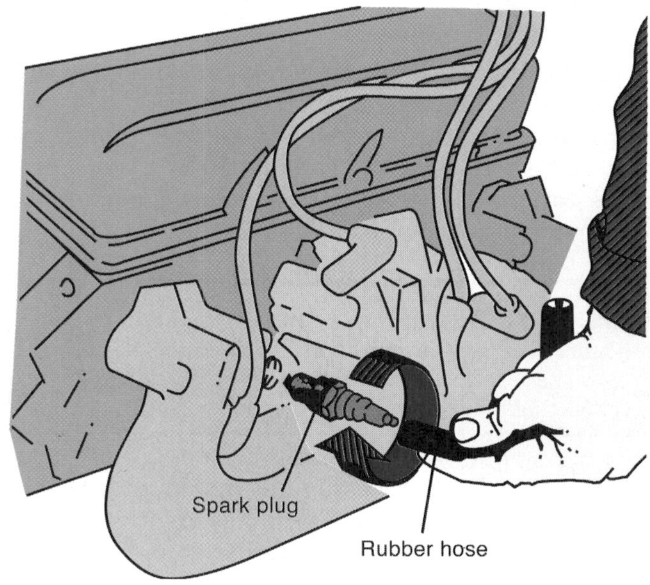

Figure 5–19 Use a vacuum or fuel line hose over the spark plug to install it without danger of cross-threading the cylinder head.

Record the highest readings and compare the results. Most vehicle manufacturers specify the minimum compression reading, the maximum allowable variation among cylinders, and a maximum difference of 20% between the highest reading and the lowest reading. Many service manuals use two metric units for compression specifications, kilopascals and kilograms per square centimetre. Imperial specifications are given in psi. For example,

If the high reading is	1050 kPa, 10.6 kg/cm^2 (150 psi)
Subtract 20%	210 kPa, 2.1 kg/cm^2 (30 psi)
Lowest allowable compression is	840 kPa, 8.5 kg/cm^2 (120 psi)

Low compression in all cylinders may be caused by incorrect valve timing or a stretched timing belt. Low compression in two adjacent cylinders often points to a blown head gasket.

NOTE: During cranking, the oil pump cannot maintain normal oil pressure. Extended engine cranking such as occurs during a compression test can cause hydraulic lifters to collapse. When the engine starts, loud valve clicking noises may be heard. This should be considered normal after performing a compression test, and the noise should stop after the vehicle has been driven a short distance.

WET COMPRESSION TEST: GASOLINE ENGINE

If the reading of the compression test indicates low compression on one or more cylinders, add two squirts of oil to the cylinder to help seal around the piston rings and retest. This is called a **wet compression test.** A wet compression test should not be done on a diesel engine.

CAUTION: Do not use more oil than three squirts from a hand-operated oil squirt can. Too much oil can cause a hydrostatic lock, which can damage or break pistons or connecting rods or even crack a cylinder head.

Perform the compression test again and observe the results. If the first-puff readings greatly improve and the readings are much higher than they were without the oil, the cause of the low compression is worn or defective piston rings. If the compression readings increase only slightly (or not at all), then the cause of the low compression is usually defective valves. See Figure 5–20.

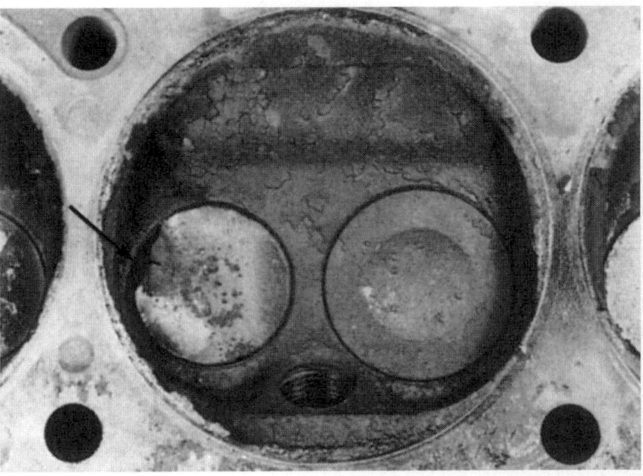

Figure 5–20 Badly burned exhaust valve. A compression test could have detected a problem, and a cylinder leakage test (leak-down test) could have been used to determine the exact problem.

Figure 5–21 A typical hand-held cylinder leakage tester.

CYLINDER LEAKAGE TEST

One of the best tests that can be used to determine engine condition is the cylinder leakage test. This test involves injecting air under pressure into the cylinders one at a time. The amount and location of any escaping air helps the technician determine the condition of the engine. The air is put into the cylinder through a cylinder leakage gauge inserted in the spark plug hole. See Figure 5–21. To perform the cylinder leakage test, take the following steps:

1. For best results, the engine should be at normal operating temperature (upper radiator hose hot and pressurized).
2. The cylinder being tested must be at top dead centre (TDC) of the compression stroke.

NOTE: The greatest amount of wear occurs at the top of the cylinder because of the heat generated near the top. The piston ring flex also adds to the wear at the top of the cylinder.

3. Calibrate the cylinder leakage unit per manufacturer's instructions.
4. Inject air into the cylinders one at a time, rotating the engine by firing order to test each cylinder at TDC on the compression stroke.
5. Evaluate the results:
   - Less than 10% leakage: good
   - Less than 20% leakage: acceptable
   - Less than 30% leakage: poor
   - More than 30% leakage: definite problem

HINT: If leakage seems unacceptably high, repeat the test, making sure that the test is being performed correctly and that the cylinder being tested is at TDC on the compression stroke.

6. Check the source of air leakage.
   - If air is heard escaping from the oil fill opening, the *piston rings* are worn or broken.
   - If air is observed bubbling out of the radiator, there is a possible blown *head gasket* or cracked *cylinder head.*
   - If air is heard coming from the carburetor or air inlet on fuel-injection equipped engines, there is a defective *intake valve(s).*
   - If air is heard coming from the tail pipe, there is a defective *exhaust valve(s).*

CYLINDER POWER BALANCE TEST

Most large engine analyzers have a cylinder power balance feature. The purpose of a cylinder power balance test is to determine if all cylinders are contributing power equally. The equipment measures this by shorting out one cylinder at a time while the engine is running. If the engine speed (RPM) does not drop as much for one cylinder as for other cylinders of the same engine, then the shorted cylinder must be weaker than the other cylinders. For example:

Cylinder Number	RPM Drop When Ignition Is Shorted
1	75
2	70
3	15
4	65
5	75
6	70

Cylinder 3 is the weak cylinder.

NOTE: Most automotive test equipment tests cylinder balance automatically. Be certain to identify the offending cylinder correctly. Cylinder 3 as identified by the equipment may be the third cylinder in the firing order instead of the actual cylinder 3.

POWER BALANCE TEST PROCEDURE: GASOLINE ENGINE

When point-type ignition was used on all vehicles, the common method for determining which, if any, cylinder was weak was to remove a spark plug wire from one spark plug at a time while watching a tachometer and a vacuum gauge. This method is not recommended on any vehicle with any type of electronic ignition. For these vehicles, if any spark plug wires are removed from a spark plug while the engine is running, the ignition coil tries to supply increasing levels of voltage in an attempt to jump the increasing gap as the plug wires are removed. This high voltage could easily damage the ignition coil or the ignition module or both. Many engine analyzers ground the primary of the ignition circuit to perform a cylinder power balance test.

The acceptable method of cancelling cylinders, which will work on all types of ignition systems including distributorless, is to *ground* the secondary current for each cylinder by using a test light and short lengths of rubber vacuum hose as shown in Figure 5–22. The cylinder with the least RPM drop is the cylinder not producing its share of power.

Some sequential electronic fuel injection systems cancel cylinders by shutting off the injectors with a scan tool. This is desirable, as catalytic converters can be damaged by excess fuel from the dead cylinder when the ignition is disabled and fuel flow continues.

Some items that could cause the engine speed to remain steady (no RPM drop) include:

- A defective spark plug wire
- A defective or excessively worn spark plug
- A faulty fuel injector (if individual injectors for each cylinder)
- Burned valve
- Broken valve spring
- Worn cam lobe affecting the opening of the valves
- Bent pushrod (if OHV engine)
- Broken rocker arm (if equipped)
- Hole in the piston or an excessively worn or damaged piston ring

Figure 5–22 Using a vacuum hose and a test light to ground one cylinder at a time on a distributorless ignition system. This works on all types of ignition systems and provides a method for grounding out one cylinder at a time without fear of damaging any component. Limit the time the cylinder is killed, because unburned fuel can damage the catalytic converter.

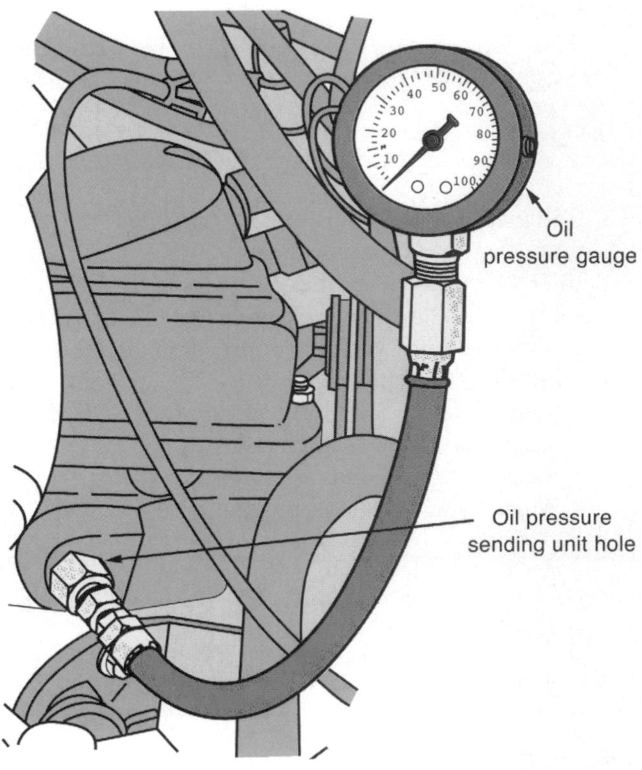

Figure 5–23 To measure engine oil pressure, remove the oil pressure sending (sender) unit usually located near the oil filter. Screw the pressure gauge into the oil pressure sending unit hole.

NOTE: Many late model gasoline and diesel powered vehicles are equipped with computers that have on-board diagnostic capabilities. The computer, called the PCM (powertrain control module), has the ability to store many engine driveability malfunctions in memory. These trouble codes can be read by a technician.

Current second generation (OBD II) diagnostics will also pinpoint which cylinder is misfiring.

OIL PRESSURE TEST

Proper oil pressure is very important for the operation of any engine. Low oil pressure can cause engine wear, and engine wear can cause low oil pressure.

If the main and rod bearings are worn, oil pressure is reduced because of oil leakage around the bearings. Oil pressure testing is usually performed according to the following steps:

1. Operate the engine until normal operating temperature is achieved.
2. With the engine off, remove the oil pressure sending unit or sender, usually located near the oil filter. Thread an oil pressure gauge into the threaded hole. See Figure 5–23.

HINT: An oil pressure gauge can be made from another gauge, such as an old air-conditioning gauge no longer used for air-conditioning work, and a flexible brake hose. The threads are often the same as those used for the oil pressure sending unit.

3. Start the engine and observe the gauge. Record the oil pressure at idle and at 2500 rpm.

Most vehicle manufacturers recommend a minimum oil pressure of 70 kPa (10 psi) per 1000 rpm. Therefore, at 2500 rpm, the oil pressure should be at least 175 kPa (25 psi). Always compare your test results with the manufacturers' recommended oil pressure.

In addition to engine bearing wear, other possible causes for low oil pressure include:

- Low oil level
- Diluted oil
- Stuck oil pressure relief valve

OIL PRESSURE WARNING LAMP

The red oil pressure warning lamp in the dash usually lights when the oil pressure is less than 30 to 50 kPa

TECH TIP

What's Leaking?

The colour of the leaks observed under a vehicle can help the technician determine and correct the cause. Some leaks such as condensate (water) from the air conditioning system are normal, whereas a brake fluid leak is very dangerous. The following are colours of common leaks:

Sooty black	Engine oil
Yellow, green, blue, or orange	Antifreeze (coolant)
Red	Automatic transmission fluid
Murky brown	Brake or power steering fluid or very neglected antifreeze (coolant)
Clear	Air conditioning condensate (water, normal)

(4 to 7 psi) depending on vehicle and engine. The oil light should not be on during driving. If the oil warning lamp is on, stop the engine immediately. Always confirm oil pressure with a good and tested mechanical gauge before performing engine repairs because the sending unit or circuit may simply be defective.

OIL LEAKS

Oil leaks can lead to severe engine damage if the resulting low oil level is not corrected. Besides causing an oily mess where the vehicle is parked, the oil leak can cause blue smoke to occur under the hood as leaking oil drips on the exhaust system. Finding the location of the oil leak can often be difficult. See Figures 5–24 and 5–25. To help find the source of oil leaks follow these steps:

1. Clean the engine or area around the suspected oil leak. Use a high-powered hot water spray to wash the engine or take it to a coin-operated car wash. Keep the engine running and spray the entire engine and the engine compartment. Avoid letting the water come into direct contact with the air inlet and ignition distributor or ignition coil(s).

HINT: If the engine starts to run rough or stalls when it gets wet, then the secondary ignition wires (spark plug wires) or distributor cap may be defective or have weak insulation. Be certain to wipe all wires and the distributor cap dry with a soft, dry cloth if the engine stalls.

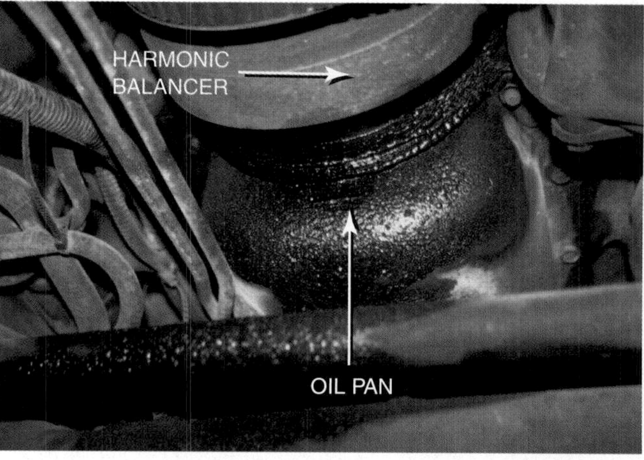

Figure 5–24 What looks like an oil pan gasket leak can be a rocker cover gasket leak. Always look up and look for the highest place you see oil leaking; that should be repaired first.

Figure 5–25 The transmission and flexplate (flywheel) were removed to check the exact location of this oil leak. The rear main seal and/or the oil pan gasket could be the cause of this leak.

HINT: Do not use steam cleaners or high-powered hot water spray equipment on vehicles with electronic engine controls. Water driven into electronic components could damage the system.

An alternative method is to spray a degreaser on the engine and then start and run the engine until warm. Engine heat helps the degreaser penetrate the grease and dirt. Use a water hose to rinse off the engine and engine compartment.

CAUTION: Be sure that the floor drains are equipped with the proper oil separator to prevent the waste from getting into the sewer system. Always follow federal, provincial, and local regulations.

2. If the oil leak is not visible or oil seems to be coming from everywhere, sprinkle a white talcum powder on the engine. The leaking oil will show up as a dark area on the white powder. See Tech Tip "The Foot Powder Spray Trick."
3. Fluorescent dye can also be added to the engine oil. Add about 15 mL (0.5 oz) of dye per 5 L of engine oil. Start the engine and allow it to run about ten minutes to thoroughly mix the dye throughout the engine. A black light then shone around every suspected oil leak area will easily locate any and every leak.

TECH TIP

The Foot Powder Spray Trick

The source of an oil or other fluid leak is often difficult to determine. A quick-and-easy method that works is the following. First, clean the entire area. This can best be done by spraying a commercially available degreaser on the entire area. Let it soak to loosen all accumulated oil and greasy dirt. Clean off the degreaser with a water hose. Let the area dry. Start the engine, and using spray foot powder or other aerosol powder product, spray the entire area. The leak will turn the white powder dark. In this way the exact location of any leak can be quickly determined.

4. Low-pressure air may be used to locate the source of some oil leaks. Block off any external openings to the crankcase and cam cover areas (PCV valves, oil filter caps, etc.); then attach a rubber hose to the dipstick tube with a hose clamp. Attach the other end to a regulated air supply, which has been set to a maximum of 10 kPa (1.5 psi). Do not start the engine. Turn on the air and listen for air escaping. Soap and water can also be sprayed over the suspected area while watching for bubbles.

PHOTO SEQUENCE 2 Performing a Compression Test: Gasoline Engine

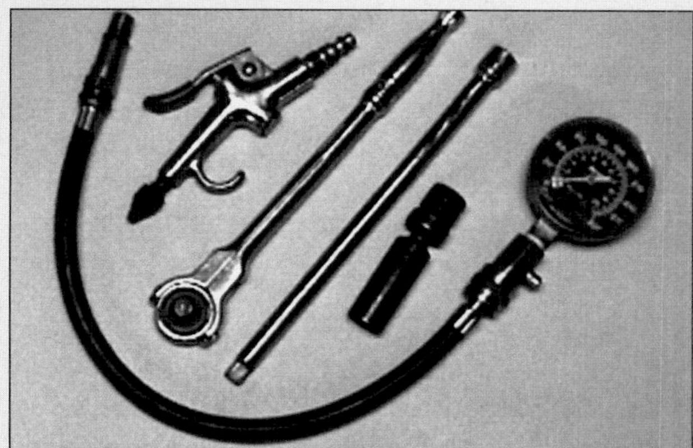

P2–1 The tools and equipment needed to perform a compression test include a compression gauge, an air nozzle, and the socket ratchets and extensions that may be necessary to remove the spark plugs from the engine.

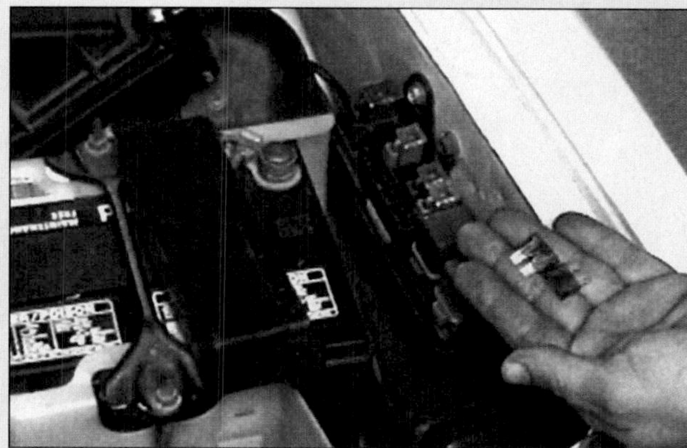

P2–2 To prevent ignition and fuel-injection operation while the engine is being cranked, remove both the fuel-injection fuse and the ignition fuse. If the fuses cannot be removed, disconnect the wiring connectors for the injectors and the ignition system.

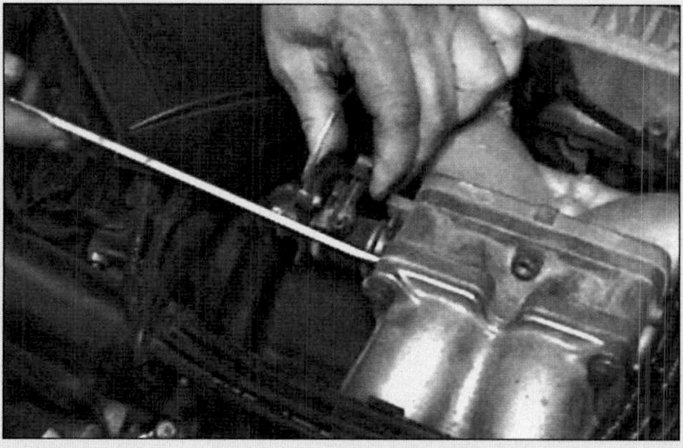

P2–3 Block open the throttle (and choke, if the engine is equipped with a carburetor). Here a screwdriver is being used to wedge the throttle linkage open. Keeping the throttle open ensures that enough air will be drawn into the engine so that the compression test results will be accurate.

P2–4 Before removing the spark plugs, use an air nozzle to blow away any dirt that may be around the spark plug. This step helps prevent debris from getting into the engine when the spark plugs are removed.

P2–5 Remove all of the spark plugs. Be sure to mark the spark plug wires so that they can be reinstalled onto the correct spark plugs after the compression test has been performed.

P2–6 Select the proper adapter for the compression gauge. The threads on the adapter should match those on the spark plug.

Performing a Compression Test: Gasoline Engine—continued

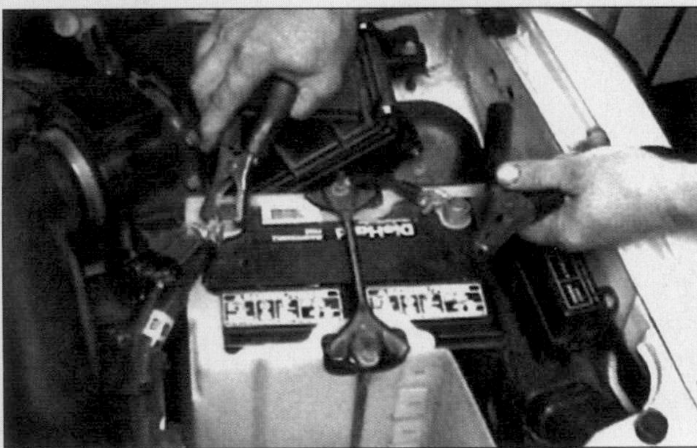

P2–7 If necessary, charge the battery before starting the compression test. It is important that consistent cranking speed be available for each cylinder being tested.

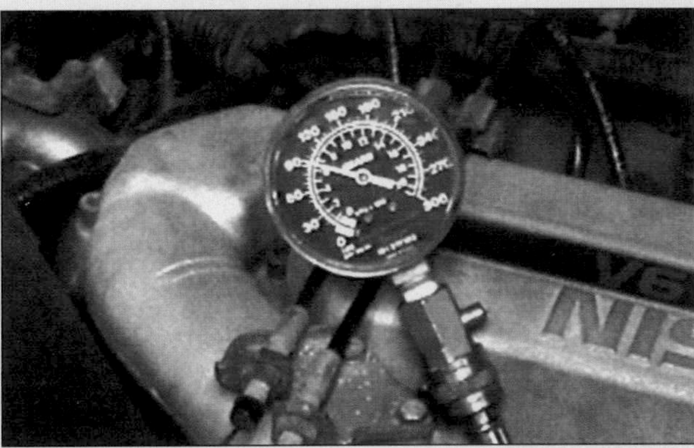

P2–8 Have an assistant use the ignition key to crank the engine while you are observing the compression gauge. Make a note of the reading on the gauge after the first puff, which indicates the first compression stroke that occurred on that cylinder as the engine was being rotated. An engine with good piston rings should indicate at least one-half the final reading on the first puff. If the first puff reading is low and the reading gradually increases with each puff, weak or worn piston rings may be indicated.

P2–9 After the engine has been cranked for four puffs, stop cranking the engine and observe the compression gauge.

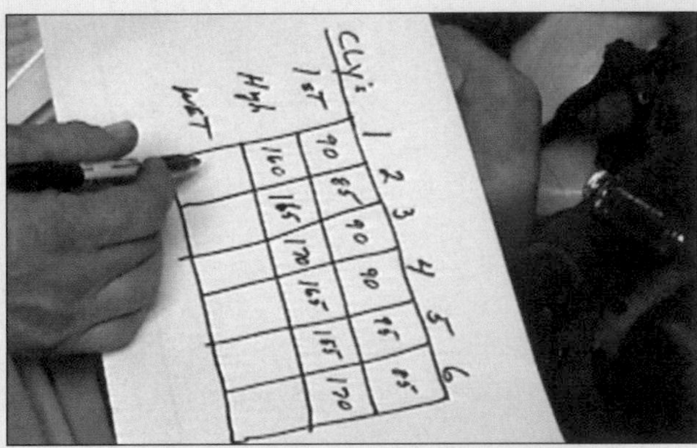

P2–10 Record the first puff and this final reading for each cylinder. The final readings should all be within 20% of each other.

P2–11 If a cylinder(s) is lower than most of the others, use an oil can and pump two squirts of engine oil into the cylinder and repeat the compression test. This is called performing a wet compression test.

P2–12 If the gauge reading is now much higher than the first test results, then the cause of the low compression is worn or defective piston rings. The oil in the cylinder temporarily seals the rings, which causes the higher reading.

DIESEL ENGINE CONDITION DIAGNOSIS

Although four-cycle diesel and gasoline engines share many of the same principles, test procedures are far different: care must be taken to follow the manufacturer's service instructions exactly as engine damage or personal injury may result.

The following tests are typical for diesel engines.

Power Balance (Cylinder Contribution) Test

The purpose of a power balance test is to compare the RPM drop between cylinders as each cylinder is disabled. A smaller RPM decrease would point to a weaker cylinder. Past practice with earlier engines was to crack open an injector line with the engine running to kill a cylinder. Not only is this procedure dangerous, it will not work with common-rail injection, sinces all injectors share the same high-pressure rails. These, and other electronic injection systems, cancel the injectors with a scan tool.

Misfire Diagnostics (OBD II)

Any misfire detected by the on-board computer will be stored in memory; these data may be accessed with a scan tool and the problem cylinder identified.

Exhaust Temperature

A hand-held pyrometer is used to measure the exhaust manifold temperatures at each cylinder; a lower temperature at one cylinder indicates a fuel or compression problem.

SAFETY TIP 

Avoid Wet Compression Test on Diesels

A wet compression test should never be carried out on a diesel engine; the oil used in the test will fill the small combustion chamber and engine damage may result.

Compression Testing

As the diesel engine has no spark plugs, access to the cylinder is gained by installing the compression-gauge test adapter (see Figure 5-26) into a glow plug hole. The gauge must be capable of reading up to 3500 kPa (500 psi).

Disable the fuel injectors by shutting off the fuel supply or removing the injector fuse. Crank the engine a minimum of five compression strokes and note the gauge reading. It should not vary by more than 350 kPa (50 psi) or internal engine problems are indicated.

Crankcase Pressure Test

Piston ring and cylinder wall condition is determined by measuring crankcase pressure while the engine is running at high RPM, under no load. If gauge readings are greater than 100 mm (4 in.) of water, mechanical concerns exist and further testing is required.

The service manual for each engine model should be consulted for exact specifications.

EXHAUST COLOUR DIAGNOSTICS

The colour of the exhaust on a diesel engine will also point to a normal condition or a problem area. Three basic colours may be seen in visible exhaust.

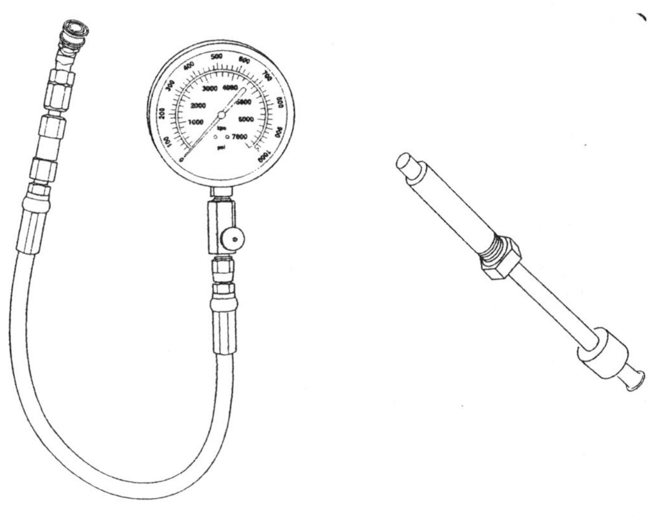

Figure 5–26 Diesel compression gauge and adapter.

DIESEL ENGINE EXHAUST SMOKE DIAGNOSTICS

Colour	Diesel Engine Exhaust Smoke Diagnostics
Black smoke	Indicates a lack of air in the cylinders, or disturbance in the air-to-fuel ratio within the cylinders (excessive fuel). May be caused by: • air inlet restriction • exhaust restriction • faulty injector(s) • faulty turbocharger • electronic engine control concern
White smoke	Indicates cold combustion chamber temperatures, low cetane rating of fuel, or coolant leak. Some white smoke on cold starts is normal until the engine warms up. May be caused by: • cold engine • inoperative glow plug • injector malfunction • low compression • coolant leaking into the cylinder(s) • electronic engine control concern • poor fuel quality The cetane level of the fuel being used can lead to white smoke concerns. A fuel that has too low of a cetane rating will take longer to heat the cylinders to operating temperatures, because a fuel with lower cetane will burn much slower and not create as much temperature rise in the cylinders.
Bluish-grey smoke	Indicates oil leaking into the engine. May be caused by: • injector leakage • worn intake/exhaust valve guide/seal • oil leak in the turbocharger on the turbine side

(Courtesy Ford)

SUMMARY

1. The first step in diagnosing engine condition is to perform a thorough visual inspection, including a check of oil and coolant levels and conditions and checking for abnormal smoke or smells.
2. Many engine-related problems make a characteristic noise.
3. A compression test can be used to test the condition of valves and piston rings.
4. A cylinder leakage test fills the cylinder with compressed air, and the gauge indicates the percentage of leakage.
5. A cylinder balance test indicates whether all cylinders are working equally.
6. Testing engine vacuum is another procedure that can help the service technician determine engine condition.
7. Oil leaks can be found by using a white powder or a fluorescent dye and a black light.
8. Compression testing on a diesel engine is done at the glow plug opening.

REVIEW QUESTIONS

1. List three simple items that could cause engine noises.
2. Describe how to perform a compression test and how to determine what is wrong with an engine based on a compression test result.
3. Describe the cylinder leakage test.
4. Explain how a technician can safely ground out one cylinder at a time without damage to the electronics of the vehicle.
5. Describe how a vacuum gauge would indicate if the valves were sticking in their guides.

RED SEAL CERTIFICATION-TYPE QUESTIONS

1. A bank note is held within 25 mm (1 in.) of the tail pipe with the engine idling. If the paper is drawn toward the pipe at times, it could indicate burned valves, or ________.
   a. Incorrect ignition timing
   b. A restricted air intake
   c. A hole in the exhaust
   d. Too high an idle speed
2. Oil leaks may be detected by adding a fluorescent dye to the oil and checking with ________.
   a. Spray powder
   b. A hand-held trouble light
   c. A black light
   d. Litmus paper strips
3. A smooth-running engine depends on ________.
   a. High compression on most cylinders
   b. Equal compression among cylinders
   c. Cylinder compression levels about 700 kPa (100 psi) and within 500 kPa (70 psi) of each other
   d. Compression levels below 700 kPa (100 psi) on most cylinders

4. A good reading for a cylinder leakage test would be _____.
   a. Within 20% among cylinders
   b. All cylinders below 20% leakage
   c. All cylinders above 20% leakage
   d. All cylinders above 70% leakage and within 7% of each other
5. During a power balance test, the cylinder that causes the least RPM change is_____.
   a. The first cylinder tested
   b. The weakest cylinder
   c. Producing the most power
   d. The strongest cylinde
6. Engine vacuum at idle speed should be _____.
   a. 65 mm (2.5 in.) Hg or higher
   b. Over 635 mm (25 in.) Hg
   c. 430 to 530 mm (17 to 21 in.) Hg
   d. Higher at higher altitudes
7. The low oil pressure warning light usually comes on when ________.
   a. An oil change is required
   b. Oil pressure drops dangerously low (30 to 50 kPa, 4 to 7 psi)
   c. The oil filter bypass valve opens
   d. The oil filter anti-drainback valve opens
8. White smoke from a diesel exhaust may be normal during ________.
   a. Full-throttle acceleration
   b. Extended idle periods
   c. Cold engine operation
   d. High-speed operation
9. Normal oil pressure should be ________.
   a. Above 70 kPa (10 psi)
   b. 70 kPa (10 psi) per 1000 rpm
   c. 210 kPa (30 psi) at idle; 420 kPa (60 psi at 2000 rpm)
   d. 350 kPa (50 psi) to 700 kPa (100 psi)
10. Diagnosing engine noises is best done ________.
   a. after a period of prolonged idle
   b. under high load conditions
   c. during both cold and warm operation
   d. with the engine at normal operating temperature

6

Engine Disassembly, Cleaning, and Crack Detection

OBJECTIVES: After studying Chapter 6, you should be able to:

1. Prepare for the interprovincial Red Seal certification examination in Appendix I (Engine Repair) on the topics covered in this chapter.
2. Describe how to remove an engine from a vehicle.
3. Discuss how to remove cylinder heads without causing warpage.
4. List the steps necessary to remove a piston from a cylinder.
5. Explain how to remove a valve from a cylinder head.
6. List the types of engine cleaning methods.
7. List the various methods that can be used to check engine parts for cracks.
8. Describe crack-repair procedures.

The decision to repair an engine should be based on all the information about the engine that is available to the service technician. In some cases, the engine might not be worth repairing. It is the responsibility of the technician to discuss the advantages and disadvantages of the different repair options with the customer.

ENGINE REMOVAL

The engine exterior and the engine compartment should be cleaned before work is begun. A clean engine is easier to work on and the cleaning not only helps to keep dirt out of the engine but also minimizes accidental damage from slipping tools. On vehicles with electronic engine controls use only low-pressure cleaning methods. The battery ground cable is disconnected to avoid the chance of electrical shorts. An even better procedure is to remove the battery from the vehicle. Follow the manufacturer's instructions exactly when working around supplemental restraint systems (air bags), so accidental deployment does not occur.

The on-board computer (if installed) will lose some adaptive memory when the battery is disconnected. To prevent this from happening, a special tool with a 9 V dry-cell battery is inserted into the lighter socket: this keeps the computer "alive" during minor repairs, e.g., seal or gasket replacement. It is not required with major service since the computer will "relearn" during an extended road test.

NOTE: Most technicians lightly scribe around the hood hinges prior to removal to make aligning the hood easier during reinstallation.

Working on the top of the engine is made easier if the hood is removed. With fender covers in place, the hood is loosened from the hinges. With a person on each side of the hood to support it, the hood is lifted off as the bolts that hold the hood are removed.

The hood is often stored on fender covers placed on the top of the vehicle, where it is least likely to be damaged.

The coolant is drained from the radiator and the engine block to minimize the chance of coolant getting into the cylinders when the head is removed. Ensure that all of the coolant is contained or wiped up. Ethylene glycol coolant is poisonous. The exhaust manifold is disconnected.

TECH TIP ✔

A Picture Is Worth a Thousand Words

Take pictures of the engine being serviced with a Polaroid, digital, or video camera. These pictures will be worth their weight in gold when it comes time to reassemble or reinstall the engine. It is very difficult for anyone to remember the *exact* location of every bracket, wire, and hose. Referring back to the photos of the engine before work was started will help you restore the vehicle to like-new condition.

HINT: On some engines, it is easier to remove the exhaust pipe from the manifold. On others, it is easier to separate the exhaust manifold from the head and leave the manifold attached to the exhaust pipe.

On V-type engines, the intake manifold must be removed before the heads can be taken off. In most cases, a number of wires, accessories, hoses, and tubing must be removed before the manifold head can be removed. If the technician is not familiar with the engine, it is a good practice to put tape on each of the items removed, marked with the proper location of each item so that all items can be easily replaced during engine assembly.

All coolant hoses are removed, and the transmission oil cooler lines are disconnected from the radiator. The radiator mounting bolts are removed, and the radiator is lifted from the engine compartment. This gets the radiator out of the way so that it will not be damaged while you are working on the engine. This is a good time to have the radiator cleaned, while it is out of the chassis.

The air-conditioning compressor can usually be separated from the engine, leaving all air-conditioning hoses securely connected to the compressor and lines. The compressor can be fastened to the side of the engine compartment, where it will not interfere with engine removal. If it is necessary to disconnect the air-conditioning lines, use a refrigerant recovery system to prevent loss of refrigerant to the atmosphere. All open air-conditioning lines should be securely plugged immediately after they are disconnected to keep dirt and moisture out of the system. They should remain plugged until immediately prior to reassembly.

There are two ways to remove the engine:

- The engine can be lifted out of the chassis with the transmission/transaxle attached.
- The transmission/transaxle can be disconnected from the engine and left in the chassis.

Under the vehicle, the drive shaft (propeller shaft) or half shafts are removed and locations marked; and the exhaust pipes disconnected. In some installations, it may be necessary to loosen the steering linkage idler arm to give clearance. The transmission controls, speedometer cable wiring, and clutch linkages are disconnected and tagged.

A sling, either a chain or lift cable, is attached to the engine. Some slings allow the engine angle to be adjusted while loaded: this makes removal and installation much easier.

HINT: For the best results, use the factory-installed lifting hooks that are attached to the engine. These hooks were used in the assembly plant to install the engine and are usually in the best location to remove the engine.

HINT: Use an old slip yoke to prevent oil leaking from the rear of the transmission.

A hoist is attached to the sling and snugged to take most of the weight. This leaves the engine resting on the mounts. (Most engines use three mounts, one on each side and one at the back of the transmission or at the front of the engine.) The rear crossmember is removed, and on rear-wheel-drive vehicles, the transmission is lowered. Transmissions that are not removed with the engine should be supported under the bell housing area. The hoist is tightened to lift the engine. The engine will have to nose up as it is removed, and the front of the engine must come almost straight up as the transmission slides from under the floor pan, as illustrated in Figure 6–1. The engine and transmission are hoisted free of the automobile, swung clear, and lowered onto an open floor area. Mount on an engine stand if possible; it will make the job easier, faster, and safer.

NOTE: The engine is lowered and removed from underneath on many front-drive vehicles. See Figures 6–2 and 6–3.

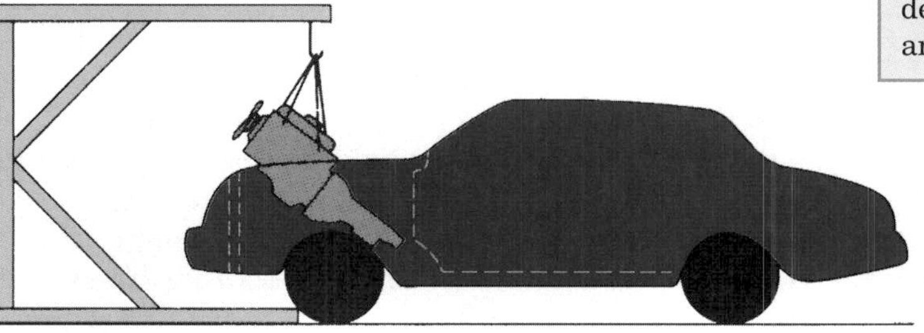

Figure 6–1 An engine must be tipped as it is pulled from the chassis.

Figure 6–2 When removing just the engine from a front-wheel-drive vehicle, the transaxle must be supported. Shown here is a typical fixture that can be used to hold the engine if the transaxle is removed or to hold the transaxle if the engine is removed.

TECH TIP 

Use the Proper Disassembly Procedure

When an engine is operated, it builds up internal stresses. Even cast iron parts such as cylinder heads can warp if the proper disassembly procedure is not followed. To disassemble any engine without causing harm, just remember these important points:

- Disassemble parts from an engine only after it has been allowed to sit for several hours. All engines should be disassembled when the engine is at room temperature.
- Always loosen retaining bolts/nuts in the reverse order of assembly. Most vehicle manufacturers recommend tightening bolts from the centre of the component such as a cylinder head toward the outside (ends). Therefore, to disassemble the engine, the outside (outer) bolts should be loosened first, followed by bolts closer to the centre. Taking these steps will help reduce the possibility of warpage occurring when the parts are removed.
- Keep the hardware (bolts, nuts, brackets, etc.) in three separate containers: one for the top of the engine, one for the front and one for the bottom. This saves time looking for the correct part when the engine is reassembled.

(a)

(b)

Figure 6–3 (a) General Motors front-wheel-drive vehicle with the drivetrain (engine and transaxle) removed. (b) The entire cradle, which included the engine, transaxle, and steering gear, was removed and placed onto a stand. The rear cylinder head has been removed to check for the root cause of a coolant leak.

ENGINE DISASSEMBLY

The following disassembly procedure applies primarily to pushrod engines. The procedure will have to be modified somewhat when working on overhead cam engines. Engines should be cold before disassembly to minimize the chance of warpage.

Remove the manifold hold-down cap screws and nuts, and lift off the manifold.

With the manifold off of the V-type engine, loosen the rocker arms, and remove the pushrods. The usual practice is to leave the lifters in place when doing

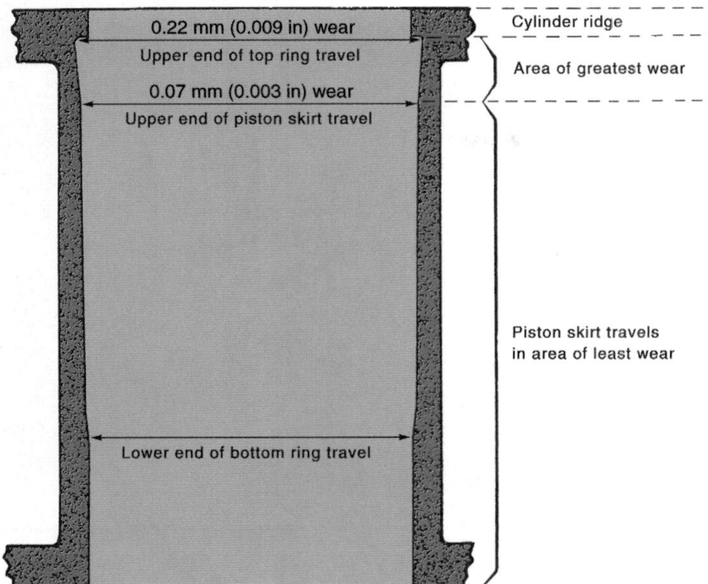

Figure 6–4 Most of the cylinder wear is on the top 25 mm (1 inch) just below the cylinder ridge. This wear is due to the heat and combustion pressures that occur when the piston is near the top of the cylinder. (Courtesy of Dana Corporation, Perfect Circle Products)

only a valve job. Remove the head cap screws and lift the head from the block deck.

CHECKING CYLINDER BORE

At this point, the cylinder taper and out-of-round of the cylinder bore should be checked, just below the ridge and just above the piston when it is at the bottom of the stroke, as shown on the cutaway cylinder in Figure 6–4. These measurements will indicate how much cylinder-wall work is required. If the cylinders are worn beyond the specified limits, they will have to be rebored to return them to a satisfactory condition.

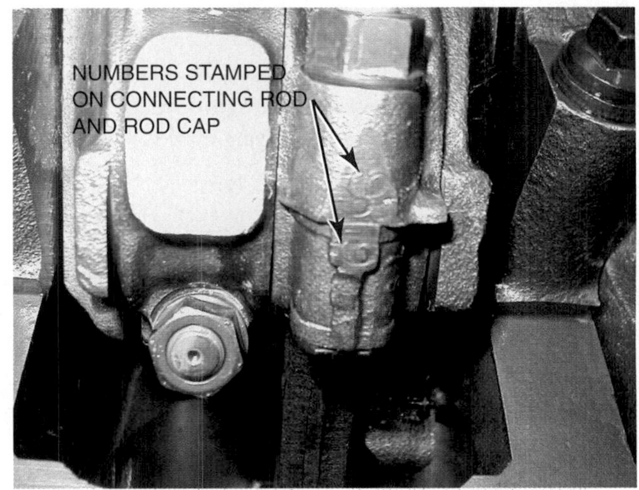

Figure 6–5 These connecting rods were numbered from the factory.

REMOVING THE OIL PAN

The oil may be drained and inspected while the engine is in the vehicle or mounted on a stand after removal. If internal damage is suspected, drain the oil through a filtering screen where any debris will be collected for inspection. Do not turn the engine upside down; remove the pan with the engine upright so metal particles and other contaminants do not fall into the engine.

The engine can be turned upside down to remove the oil pan if the drained oil did not show any signs of engine damage. The same applies if the engine is being disassembled for a major rebuild.

This will be the first opportunity to see the working parts in the bottom end of the engine. Deposits are again a good indication of the condition of the engine and the care it has had. Heavy sludge indicates infrequent oil changes; hard carbon indicates overheating. Milky oil (looks like a milkshake) is usually a sign of an internal water leak: a leaking head gasket or a crack in the head or block casting is the usual cause. The oil pump pickup screen should be checked to see how much plugging exists. The connecting rods and caps and main bearing caps should be checked to make sure that they are *numbered;* if not, they should be numbered with number stamps or a punch so that they can be reassembled in exactly the same position. See Figures 6–5 and 6–6.

Figure 6–6 If the rods and mains are not marked, it is wise to use a punch to make identifying marks *before* disassembly of the engine.

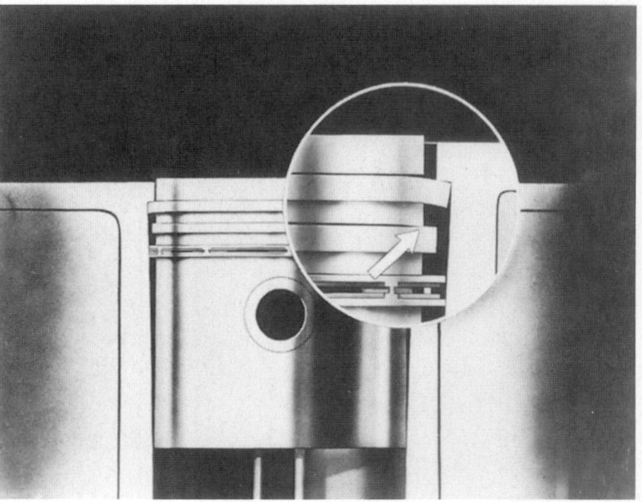

Figure 6–7 If the ridge at the top of a cylinder is not removed, the top piston ring could break the second piston ring land when the piston is pushed out of the cylinder during disassembly, or the second piston ring land could break when the engine is first run after reassembly with new rings. (Courtesy of Sealed Power Corporation)

REMOVING THE CYLINDER RIDGE

The ridge above the top ring must be removed before the piston and connecting rod assembly is removed. Cylinder wear leaves an upper ridge, and removing it is necessary to avoid catching a ring on the ridge and cracking the piston ring land. Failure to remove the ridge is likely to cause the second piston land to break when the engine is run after reassembly with new rings, as pictured in Figure 6–7. The ridge is removed with a cutting tool that is fed into the metal ridge. One type of ridge reamer is shown in Figure 6–8. A guide on the tool prevents accidental cutting below the ridge. The reaming job should be done carefully with frequent checks of the work so that no more material than necessary is removed.

Figure 6–8 Ridge being removed with one type of ridge reamer before the piston assemblies are removed from the engine.

REMOVING THE PISTONS

Before removing the pistons and rods, note the position of the connecting rod "eye" (small end) in each piston. It should be positioned approximately in the centre between the piston pin bosses. If the rod eye is touching a pin boss, it is a good indication of a bent rod.

Rotate the engine until the piston that is to be removed is at bottom dead centre (BDC). Remove connecting rod nuts from the rod so that the rod cap with its bearing half can be taken out. Fit the rod bolts with protectors to keep the bolt threads from damaging the crankshaft journals, and remove the piston

Figure 6–9 Puller being used to pull the vibration damper from the crankshaft.

Figure 6–10 Worn timing chain on a high-mileage engine. Notice that the timing chain could "jump a tooth" at the bottom of the smaller crankshaft sprocket where the chain is in contact with fewer teeth. Notice also that the technician placed all of the bolts back in the block after removal of the part. This procedure helps protect against lost or damaged bolts and nuts.

and rod assemblies. Keep the bearings with the rod, in their original location, for bench inspection.

REMOVING THE HARMONIC BALANCER

The next step in disassembly is to remove the coolant pump and the crankshaft **vibration damper** (also called a **harmonic balancer**). First, the bolt and washer that hold the damper are removed. The damper itself should be removed only with a threaded puller similar to the one in Figure 6–9. If a hook-type puller is used around the edge of the damper, it may pull the damper ring from the hub. If this happens, the damper assembly will have to be replaced with a new assembly. Check the seal area on the damper for signs of grooving (wear from the seal); press-on sleeves are available to repair front dampers and rear crankshaft flanges for many popular engines. Check the elastomer ring between the damper hub and the outer ring for signs of deterioration; if the rubber is cracked, soft, or swollen, or pieces are breaking away, replace the damper.

REMOVING THE TIMING CHAIN AND CAMSHAFT

With the damper assembly off, the timing cover can be removed, exposing the timing gear or timing chain. Examine these parts for excessive wear and looseness. A worn timing chain on a high-mileage engine is shown in Figure 6–10. Bolted cam sprockets can be removed to free the timing chain. On overhead camshaft engines, do not rotate the crankshaft (cylinder head on) with the timing belt or chain removed. The pistons may hit any valve that is held open and engine damage will result. This does not apply to "non-interference" engines where the valves are well away from the pistons. If camshaft thrust plate retaining screws are used, it will be necessary to remove them.

The camshaft can be removed at this time, or it can be removed after the crankshaft is out. It must be carefully eased from the engine to avoid damaging the cam bearings or cam lobes. This is done most easily with the front of the engine pointing up. Bearing surfaces are soft and scratch easily, and the cam lobes are hard and chip easily. A long, tapered punch inserted into the camshaft sprocket bolt hole will help support the camshaft during removal and installation.

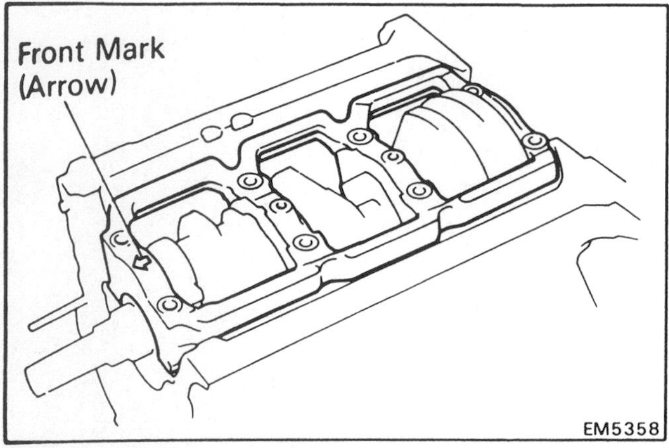

Figure 6-11 This V-6 engine uses a one-piece main bearing cap bedplate for additional block support. (Courtesy Toyota)

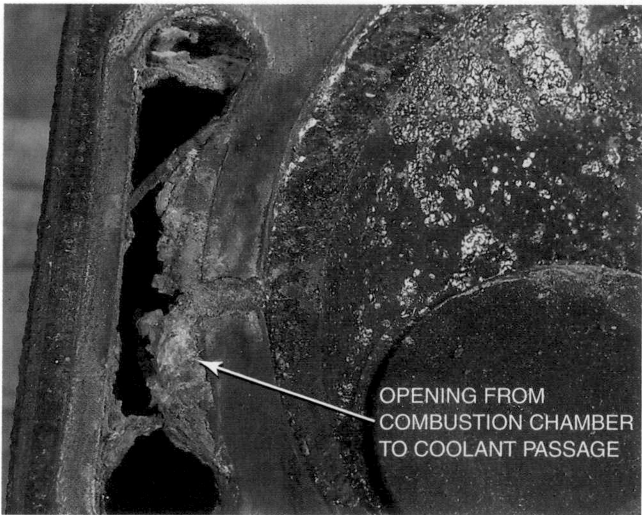

Figure 6–12 This defective cylinder head gasket was discovered as soon as the head was removed. This cylinder head will require machining or replacement.

Figure 6–13 A valve spring compressor being used to remove the valve keepers (locks).

REMOVING THE MAIN BEARING AND CRANKSHAFT

The crankshaft end-play and rear flange runout should be measured with a dial indicator before the crankshaft is removed. Any out-of-tolerance readings can be addressed when the crankshaft is out of the engine. The main bearing caps should be checked for position markings before they are removed. They have been machined in place and will not fit perfectly in any other location. Many engines use arrows on the main caps, which point to the front of the engine. If there are no arrows, note that the bearing tang in the cap should be on the same side as the tang in the block. After marking, they can be removed to free the crankshaft. When the crankshaft is removed, the main bearing caps and bearings are reinstalled on the block to reduce the chance of damage to the caps. Inspect the main bearings for signs of unusual wear when the crankshaft is out. A warped block or a bent crankshaft will cause excessive wear on one or more bearings. Check the back of the bearing inserts for signs of movement in the block.

All, or some, of the main bearing caps may be joined together in one piece to add rigidity at the lower block. These units, called *bed plates,* are often made of powdered (sintered) metal. See Figure 6-11.

REMOVE AND DISASSEMBLE THE CYLINDER HEAD

Remove the cylinder head retaining bolts by loosening them from the outside toward the centre to help prevent the possibility of warpage of the head. Remove the cylinder head(s) and check the head gasket for signs of failure. See Figure 6–12.

After the heads are removed and placed on the bench, the valves are removed. A C-type valve spring compressor, similar to the one in Figure 6–13, is used to free the **valve locks** or **keepers.** The valve spring compressor is air powered in production shops where valve jobs are done on a regular basis. Mechanical valve spring compressors are used where valve work is done only occasionally. After the valve lock is removed, the compressor is released to free the valve retainer and spring. The spring assemblies are lifted from the

Figure 6–14 After removing this intake valve, it became obvious why this engine had been running so poorly.

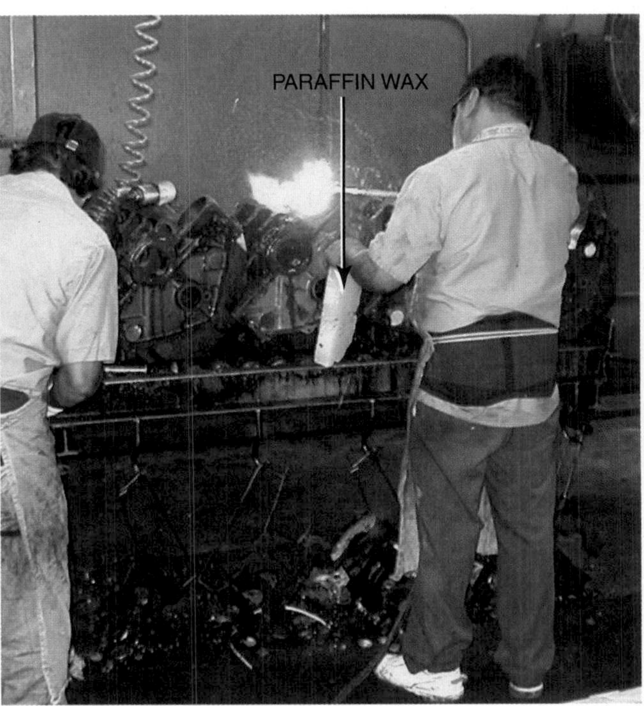

Figure 6–15 A torch is used to heat gallery plugs. Paraffin wax is then applied and allowed to flow around the threads. This procedure results in easier removal of the plugs and other threaded fasteners that cannot otherwise be loosened.

head together with any spacers used under them. The parts should be removed in order to aid in diagnosing the exact cause of any malfunction that shows up. The valve tip edge and lock area should be lightly filed to remove any burrs *before* sliding the valve from the head. Burrs will scratch the valve guide.

When all valves have been removed following this procedure for each one, the valve springs, retainers, locks, guides, and seats should be given another visual examination. See Figure 6–14. Inspect the valves and piston heads for damage if the timing belt or chain has jumped. Contact between pistons and valve heads may occur when the valve timing changes.

CAUTION: Many engines have spark-plug replacement intervals of 160 000 kilometres (100 000 miles). It is not unusual to find spark plugs that are seized in aluminum cylinder heads. Follow the vehicle maker's recommendations for removing seized plugs, otherwise damaged cylinder head threads may result. It is now industry practice for the technician to brush a very light coat of never-seize compound on spark plug threads before installation.

READ THE CARBON COLOUR

Inspect the carbon colour and build-up on the intake and exhaust ports, combustion chambers, and piston tops. Excessive and oily carbon in the intake ports could indicate worn valve guides or seals. Combustion-chamber carbon colour relates to good or poor combustion, burned valves or weak piston rings. Piston crowns (tops) that show no carbon along one edge may point to a piston ring concern. No carbon at all in one or two cylinders usually points to water entering the cylinder through a leaking head gasket or casting crack.

Oily carbon in the exhaust ports, while the combustion chambers are normal, is an indicator of worn exhaust valve guides or seals.

Diagnose as much as possible during disassembly; be aware of anything unusual.

TECH TIP 

The Wax Trick

Before the engine block can be thoroughly cleaned, all oil gallery plugs must be removed. A popular trick of the trade for plug removal involves heating the plug (not the surrounding metal) with an oxyacetylene torch. The heat tends to expand the plug and make it tighter in the block. Do not overheat.

As the plug is cooling, touch the plug with paraffin wax (beeswax or candle wax may be used). See Figure 6–15. The wax will be drawn down around the threads of the plug by capillary attraction as the plug cools and contracts. After being allowed to cool, the plug is easily removed.

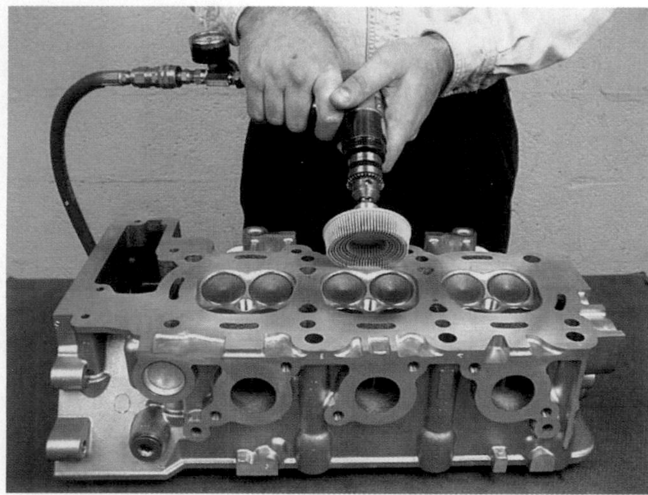

Figure 6–16 An air-powered grinder attached to a bristle pad being used to clean the gasket surface of a cylinder head. The colour of the bristles indicates the grit number. The white is the finest and should be used on aluminum. Yellow is coarse and must be used carefully on aluminum. Green is designed for cast-iron parts only. This type of cleaning pad should not be used on the engine block where the grit could get into the engine oil and cause harm when the engine is started and run after the repair.

MECHANICAL CLEANING

Heavy deposits that remain after chemical cleaning will have to be removed by mechanical cleaning. Mechanical cleaning involves scraping, brushing, and abrasive blasting. It should, therefore, be done very carefully on soft metals.

The scraper most frequently used is a **putty knife** or a plastic card. The broad blade of the putty knife helps avoid scratching the surface as it is used to clean the parts. A rotary disc can be used on disassembled parts that will be thoroughly cleaned to remove the fine abrasive that is part of the plastic bristles. See Figure 6–16.

> **CAUTION:** Do not use a steel wire brush on aluminum parts! Steel is harder than aluminum and will remove some of the aluminum from the surface during cleaning.

CHEMICAL CLEANERS

Cleaning chemicals applied to engine parts will mix with and dissolve deposits. The chemicals loosen the deposits so that they can be brushed or rinsed from the surface. A deposit is said to be **soluble** when it can be dissolved with a chemical or solvent.

Most chemical cleaners used for cleaning carbon-type deposits are strong soaps called **caustic materials.** A **pH** value, measured on a scale from 1 to 14, indicates the amount of chemical activity in the soap. The term *pH* is from the French *pouvoir hydrogine,* meaning "hydrogen power." Pure water is neutral; on the pH scale, water is pH 7. Caustic materials have pH numbers from 8 through 14. The higher the number, the stronger the caustic action will be. **Acid materials** have pH numbers from 1 through 6. The lower the number, the stronger the acid action will be. Caustic materials and acid materials neutralize each other. This is what happens when baking soda (a caustic) is used to clean the outside of the battery (an acid surface). The caustic baking soda neutralizes any sulfuric acid that has been spilled or splashed on the outside of the battery.

> **CAUTION:** Safety glasses and elbow-high rubber gloves are required for any cleaning operation that involves chemicals, steam cleaning, or high-pressure washing.

SOLVENT-BASED CLEANING

Chemical cleaning can involve a spray washer or a soak in a cold or hot tank. The cleaning solution is usually solvent based, with a medium pH rating of between 10 and 12. Most chemical solutions also contain silicates to protect the metal (aluminum) against corrosion. Stronger caustics do an excellent job on cast-iron items but are often too corrosive for aluminum parts. Aluminum cleaners include mineral spirit solvents as well as alkaline detergents.

> **CAUTION:** When cleaning aluminum cylinder heads, blocks, or other engine components, make sure that the chemicals used are aluminum safe. Many chemicals that are not aluminum safe may turn the aluminum metal black. Try to explain that to a customer!

WATER-BASED CHEMICAL CLEANING

Because of environmental concerns, most chemical cleaning is now performed using water-based solutions (called **aqueous-based**). Most aqueous-based

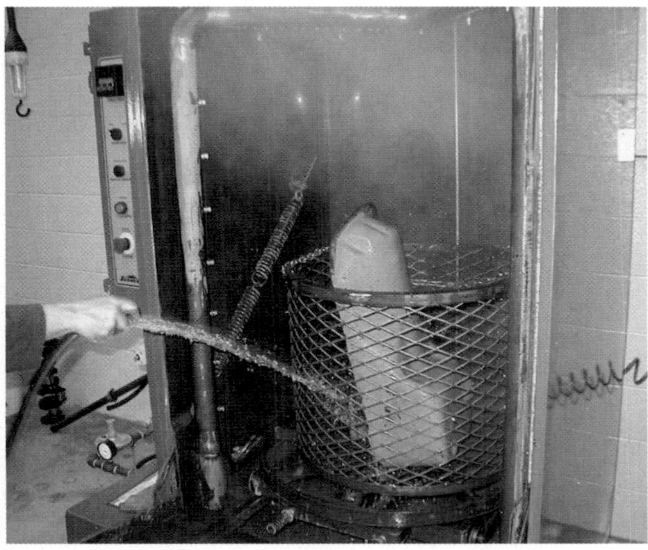

Figure 6–17 A pressure jet washer is similar to a large industrial-sized dishwasher. The part(s) is then rinsed with water to remove chemicals or debris that may remain on the part while it is still in the tank.

chemicals are silicate based and are mixed with water. Aqueous-based solutions can be sprayed on or used in a tank for soaking parts. Aluminum heads and blocks usually require overnight soaking in a solution kept at about 90°C (190°F). For best results, the cleaning solution should be agitated.

SPRAY WASHING

A spray washer directs streams of liquid through numerous high-pressure nozzles to dislodge dirt and grime on an engine surface. The force of the liquid hitting the surface, combined with the chemical action of the cleaning solution, produces a clean surface. Spray washing is typically performed in an enclosed washer (like a dishwasher), where parts are rotated on a washer turntable. See Figure 6–17.

Spray washing is faster than soaking. A typical washer cycle is less than thirty minutes per load, compared to eight or more hours for soaking. Most spray washers use an aqueous-based cleaning solution heated to 70° to 80°C (160° to 180°F) with foam suppressants. High-volume remanufacturers use industrial dishwashing machines to clean the disassembled engines' component parts.

STEAM CLEANING

Steam cleaners are a special class of sprayers. Steam vapour is mixed with high-pressure water and sprayed on the parts. The heat of the steam and the propellant force of the high-pressure water combine to do the cleaning. Steam cleaning must be used with extreme care. Usually, a caustic cleaner is added to the steam and water to aid in the cleaning. This mixture is so active that it will damage and even remove paint, so painted surfaces must be protected from the spray. Engines are often steam cleaned before they are removed from the chassis.

THERMAL CLEANING

Thermal cleaning uses heat to vaporize and char dirt into a dry, powdery ash. Thermal cleaning is best suited for cleaning cast iron, where temperatures as high as 425°C (800°F) are used, whereas aluminum should not be heated to over 310°C (590°F).

The major advantages of thermal cleaning include the following:

1. This process cleans the inside as well as the outside of the casting or part.
2. The waste generated is nonhazardous and is easy to dispose of. However, the heat in the oven usually discolours the metal, leaving it looking dull.

A **pyrolytic** (high-temperature) oven cleans engine parts by decomposing dirt, grease, and gaskets with heat in a manner similar to that of a self-cleaning oven. This method of engine-part cleaning is becoming the most popular because there is no hazardous waste associated with it. Labour costs are also reduced because the operator does not need to be present during the actual cleaning operation. See Figure 6–18.

COLD TANK CLEANING

The cold soak tank is used to remove grease and carbon. The disassembled parts are placed in the tank so that they are *completely* covered with the chemical cleaning solution. After a soaking period, the parts are removed and rinsed until the milky appearance of the emulsion is gone. The parts are then dried with compressed air. The clean, dry parts are then usually given a very light coating of clean oil to prevent rusting. Carburetor cleaner, purchased with a basket in a bucket, is one of the most common types of cold soak agents in the automotive shop. Usually, there will be a layer of water over the chemical to prevent evaporation of the chemical. This water layer is called a **hydroseal.**

Parts washers are often used in place of soaking tanks. This equipment can move parts back and forth

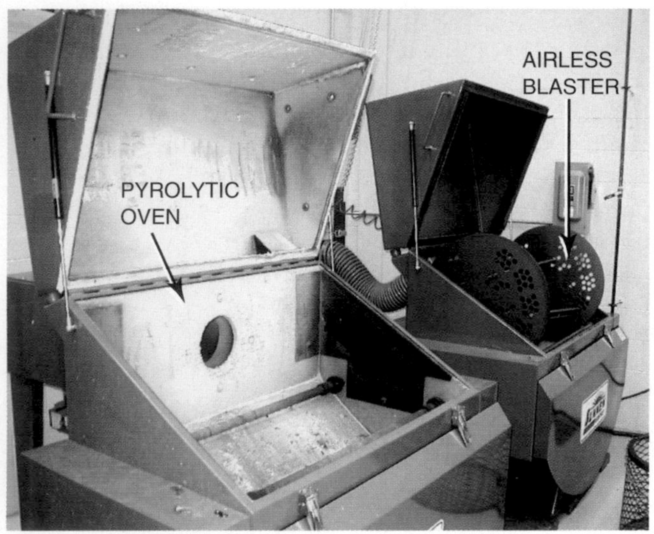

(a)

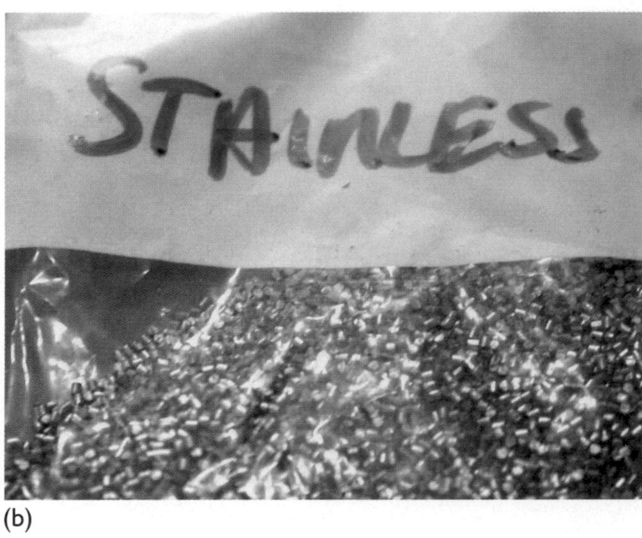

(b)

Figure 6–18 (a) A pyrolytic (high temperature) oven cleans by baking the engine parts. After the parts have been cleaned, they are then placed into an airless blaster. This unit uses a paddle to scoop stainless steel shot from a reservoir and forces it against the engine part. The parts must be free of grease and oil to function correctly. (b) Stainless steel shot used in an airless blaster.

through the cleaning solution or pump the cleaning solution over the parts. This movement, called **agitation,** keeps fresh cleaning solution moving past the soil to help it loosen. The parts washer is usually equipped with a safety cover held open by a low-temperature **fusible link.** If a fire occurs, the fusible link will melt and the cover will drop closed to snuff the fire out.

HOT TANK CLEANING

The hot soak tank is used for cleaning heavy organic deposits and rust from iron and steel parts. Camshaft bearings and other soft materials should be removed from the block before soaking. Many hot tank solutions will dissolve the bearings, which contaminates both the chemicals and the block.

Some oil pans are made from a sandwich of two sheets of steel surrounding a layer of sound-deadening mastic; ensure that the cleaning chemicals will not damage the mastic. The caustic cleaning solution used in the hot soak tank is heated to near 90°C (195°F) for rapid cleaning action. The solution must be inhibited when aluminum is to be cleaned. After the deposits have been loosened, the parts are removed from the tank and rinsed with hot water or steam cleaned, which dries them rapidly. They must then be given a light coating of oil to prevent rusting.

> **HINT: Fogging oil** from a spray can does an excellent job of coating metal parts to keep them from rusting.

VAPOUR CLEANING

Vapour cleaning is popular in some automotive service shops. The parts to be cleaned are suspended in hot vapours above a perchloroethylene solution. The vapours of the solution loosen the soil from the metal so that it can be blown, wiped, or rinsed from the surface.

ULTRASONIC CLEANING

Ultrasonic cleaning is used to clean small parts that must be absolutely clean; for example, hydraulic lifters and gasoline or diesel fuel injectors. The disassembled parts are placed in a tank of cleaning solution which is then vibrated at ultrasonic speeds to loosen all the soil from the parts. The soil goes into the solution or falls to the bottom of the tank.

VIBRATORY CLEANING

The vibratory method of cleaning is best suited for small parts. Parts are loaded into a vibrating bin with small odd-shaped ceramic or steel pieces, called media, with a cleaning solution of mineral spirits or water-based detergents that usually contain a lubricant additive to help the media pieces slide around more freely. The movement of the vibrating solution and the scrubbing action of the media do an excellent job of cleaning metal.

BLASTERS

Cleaning cast-iron or aluminum engine parts with solvents or heat usually requires another operation to achieve a uniform surface finish. Blasting the parts with steel, cast-iron, aluminum, or stainless-steel shot or glass beads is a simple way to achieve a matte or satin surface finish on the engine parts. To keep the shot or beads from sticking to the parts, they must be dry, without a trace of oil or grease, prior to blasting. This means that blasting is the second cleaning method, after the part has been precleaned in a tank, spray washer, or oven. Some blasting is done automatically in an airless shot-blasting machine. Another method is to hard-blast parts in a sealed cabinet. See Figure 6–19.

CAUTION: Glass beads often remain in internal passages of engine parts, where they can come loose and travel through the cylinders when the engine is started. Among other places, these small but destructive beads can easily be trapped under the oil baffles of rocker covers and in oil pans and piston-ring grooves. To help prevent the glass beads from sticking, make sure that the parts being cleaned are free of grease and dirt and completely dry. Walnut shells are often used as blasting media when cleaning soft materials: they are also used in areas where it is difficult to remove all of the abrasive. The shells break up very quickly and cause no damage.

Figure 6–19 Small engine parts can be blasted clean in a sealed cabinet.

VISUAL INSPECTION

After the parts have been thoroughly cleaned, they should be re-examined for defects. A magnifying glass is helpful in finding defects. Late-model cast iron cylinder heads and blocks are made thinner to reduce vehicle weight. Watch for cracks at the exhaust valve seats and the cylinder walls in these light-weight castings. Critical parts of a performance engine should be checked for cracks using specialized magnetic or penetration inspection equipment. Internal parts such as pistons, connecting rods, and crankshafts that have cracks should be replaced. Cracks in the block and heads, however, can often be repaired, and these repair procedures are described in a later section.

MAGNETIC CRACK INSPECTION

Checking for cracks using a magnetic field is commonly called Magnafluxing, a brand name. Cracks in engine blocks, cylinder heads, crankshafts, and other engine components are sometimes difficult to find during a normal visual inspection, which is why all remanufacturers and most engine builders use a crack detection procedure on all critical engine parts.

Magnetic flux testing is the method most often used on steel and iron components. A metal engine part (such as a cast-iron cylinder head) is connected to a large electromagnet. Magnetic lines of force are easily conducted through the iron part and concentrate on the edges of a crack. A fine iron powder is then applied to the part being tested, and the powder will be attracted to the strong magnetic concentration around the crack. See Figures 6–20 and 6–21.

Figure 6–20 The top deck surface of a block being tested using magnetic crack inspection equipment.

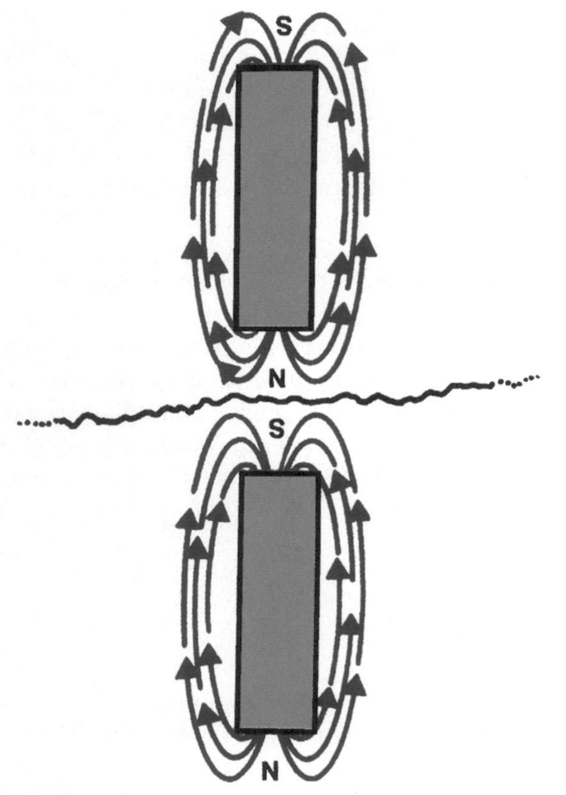

Figure 6–21 If the lines of force are interrupted by a break (crack) in the casting, two magnetic fields are created and the powder will lodge in the crack.

DYE-PENETRANT TESTING

Dye-penetrant testing is usually used on pistons and other parts constructed of aluminum or other nonmagnetic material. A dark-red penetrating chemical is first sprayed on the component being tested. After cleaning, a white powder is sprayed over the test area. If a crack is present, the red dye will stain the white powder. Even though this method will also work on iron and steel (magnetic) parts, it is usually used only on nonmagnetic parts because magnetic methods do not work on these parts.

FLUORESCENT-PENETRANT TESTING

To be seen, fluorescent penetrant requires a black light. It can be used on iron, steel, or aluminum parts. Cracks show up as bright lines when viewed with a black light. The method is commonly called **Zyglo,** a trademark of the Magnaflux Corporation.

PRESSURE TESTING

Cylinder heads and blocks are often pressure tested with air and checked for leaks. All coolant passages are blocked with rubber plugs or gaskets, and compressed air is applied to the water jacket(s). The head or block is then lowered into water, where air bubbles indicate a leak. For more accurate results, the water should be heated because the hot water expands the casting by about the same amount as an operating engine would. An alternative method

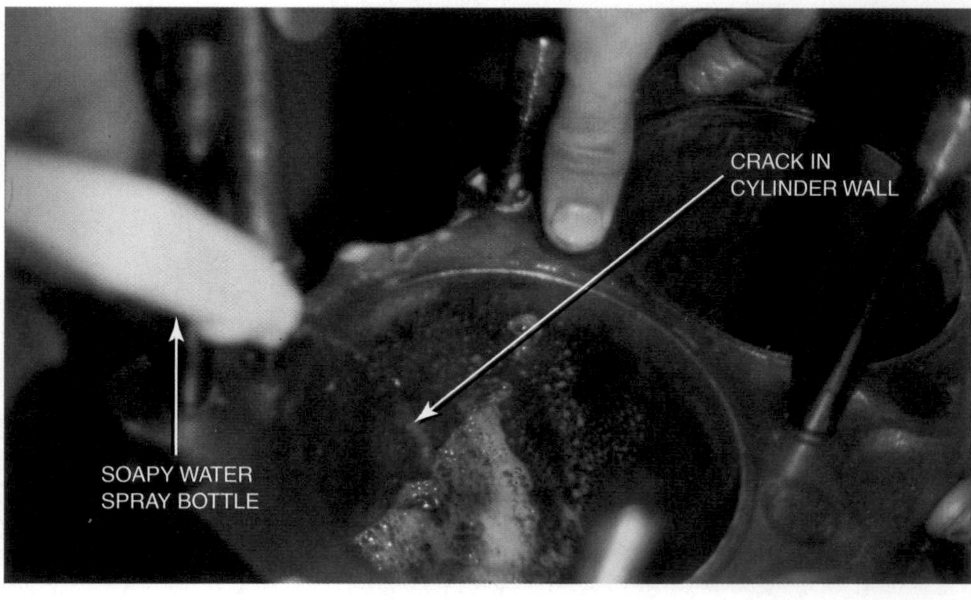

Figure 6–22 To make sure that the mark observed in the cylinder wall was a crack, compressed air was forced into the water jacket while soapy water was sprayed on the cylinder wall. Bubbles confirmed that the mark was indeed a crack.

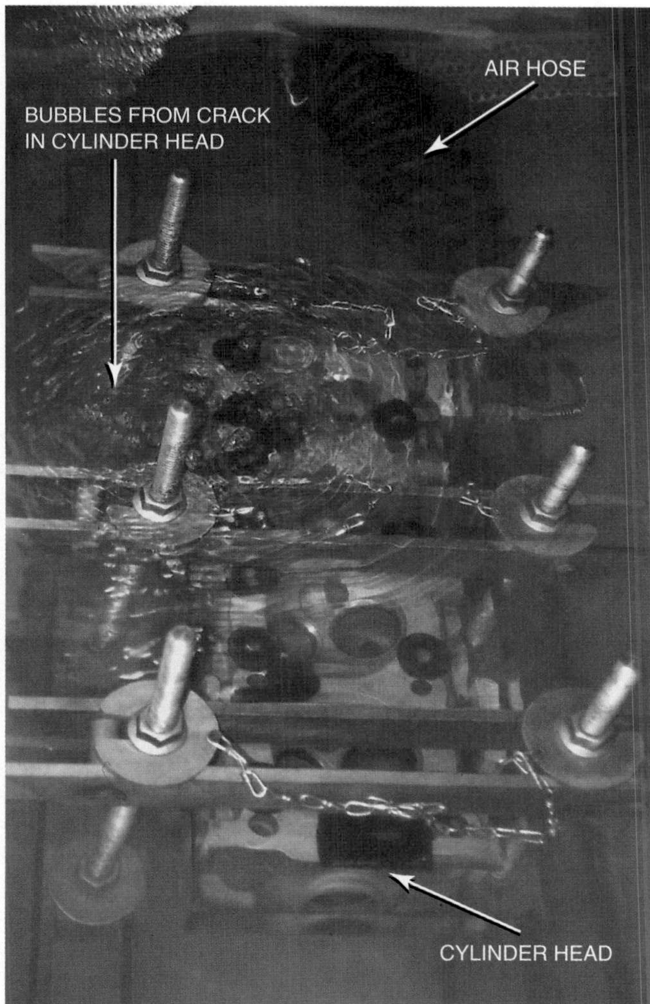

Figure 6–23 A cylinder head is under water and being pressure tested using compressed air. Note that the air bubbles indicate a crack.

involves running heated water with a dye through the cylinder or block. Any leaks revealed by the dyed water indicate a crack. See Figures 6–22 and 6–23.

CRACK REPAIR

Cracks in the engine block can cause coolant to flow into the oil or oil into the coolant. A cracked block can also cause coolant to leak externally from a crack that goes through to a coolant passage. Cracks in the head will allow coolant to leak into the engine, or they will allow combustion gases to leak into the coolant. Cracks across the valve seat cause hot spots on the valve, which will burn the valve face. A head with a crack will either have to be replaced or the crack will have to be repaired. Two common methods of crack repair are welding and plugging.

NOTE: A hole can be drilled at each end of the crack to keep it from extending further, a step sometimes called **stop drilling.** Cracks that do not cross oil passages, bolt holes, or seal surfaces can sometimes be left alone if stopped.

CRACK-WELDING CAST IRON

It takes a great deal of skill to weld cast iron. The cast iron does not puddle or flow as steel does when it is heated. Heavy cast parts, such as the head and block, conduct heat away from the weld so fast that it is difficult to get the part hot enough to melt the iron for welding. When it does melt, a crack will often develop next to the edge of the weld bead. Welding can be done satisfactorily when the entire cast part is heated red hot.

A new technique involves flame welding using a special torch. See Figure 6–24.

CRACK-WELDING ALUMINUM

Cracks in aluminum can be welded using a Heli-arc® or similar welder that is specially designed to weld aluminum. The crack should be cut or burned out before welding begins. The old valve-seat insert should be removed if the crack is in or near the combustion chamber.

CRACK PLUGGING

In the process of crack plugging, a crack is closed using interlocking tapered plugs. This procedure can be performed to repair cracks in both aluminum and cast-iron engine components. The ends of the crack are centre punched and drilled with the proper size of tap drill for the plugs. The hole is reamed with a tapered reamer (Figure 6–25) and is then tapped to give full threads (Figure 6–26). The plug is coated with sealer; then it is tightened into the hole (Figure 6–27), sawed about one-fourth of the way through, and broken off. The saw slot controls the breaking point (Figure 6–28). If the plug should break below the surface, it will have to be drilled out and a new plug installed. The plug should go to the full depth or thickness of the cast metal. After the first plug is installed on each end, a new hole is drilled with the tap drill so that it cuts into the edge of the first plug. This new hole is reamed and tapped, and a plug is inserted as before. The plug should fit about one-fourth of the way into the first plug to lock it into place (Figure 6–29). Interlocking plugs are placed along the entire crack,

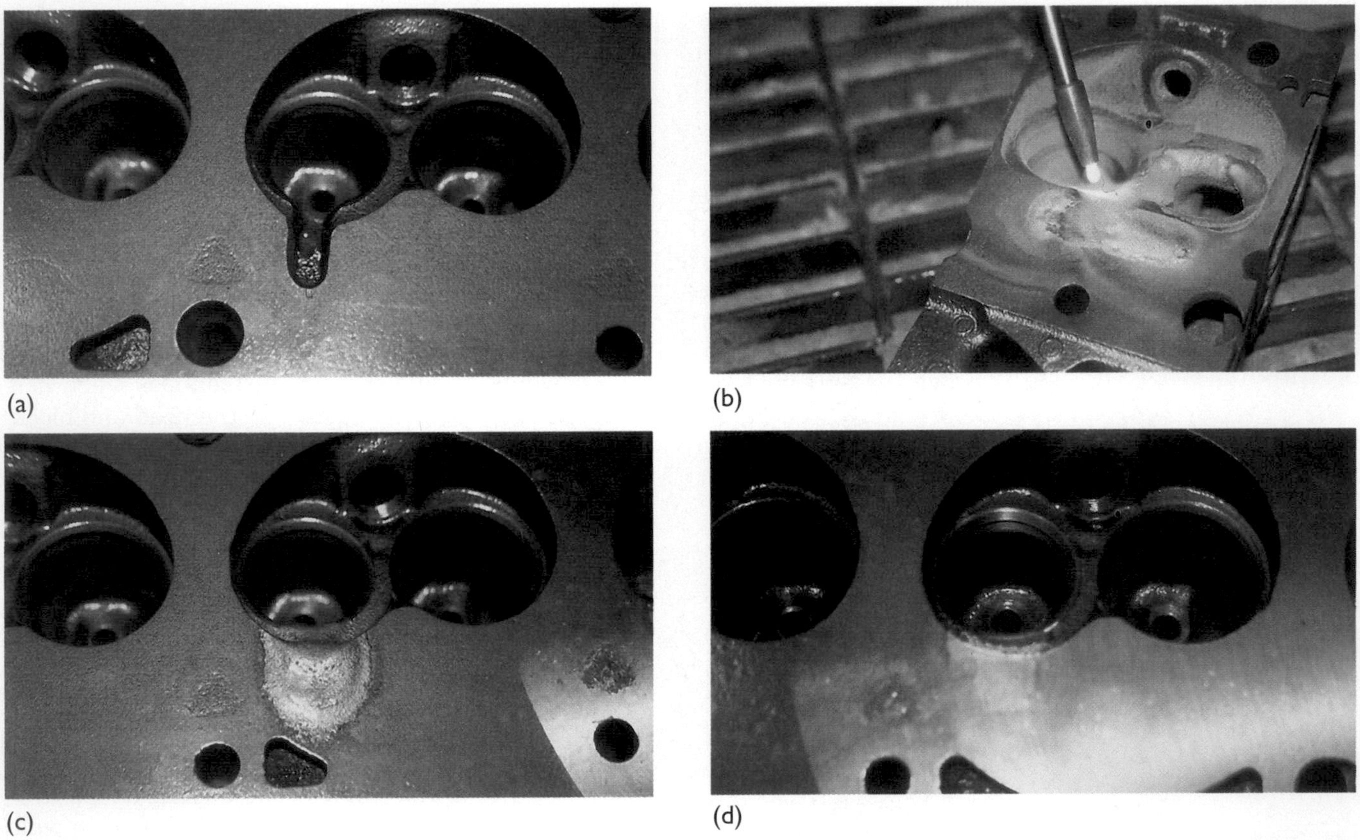

(a)

(b)

(c)

(d)

Figure 6–24 (a) Before welding, the crack is ground out using a carbide grinder. (b) Here the technician is practising using the special cast-iron welding torch before welding the cracked cylinder head. (c) The finished welded crack before final machining. (d) The finished cylinder head after the crack has been repaired using welding.

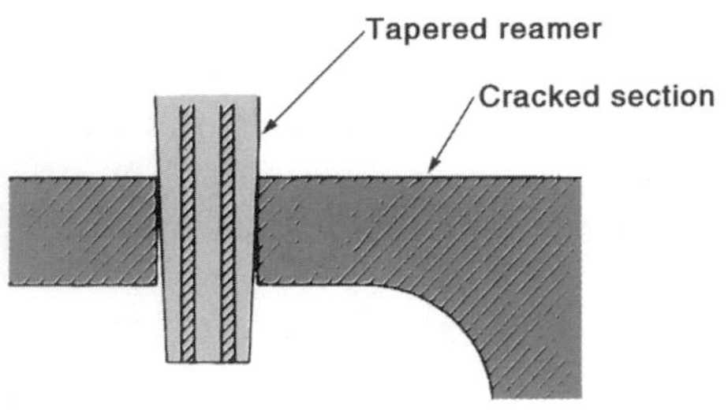

Figure 6–25 Reaming a hole for a tapered plug.

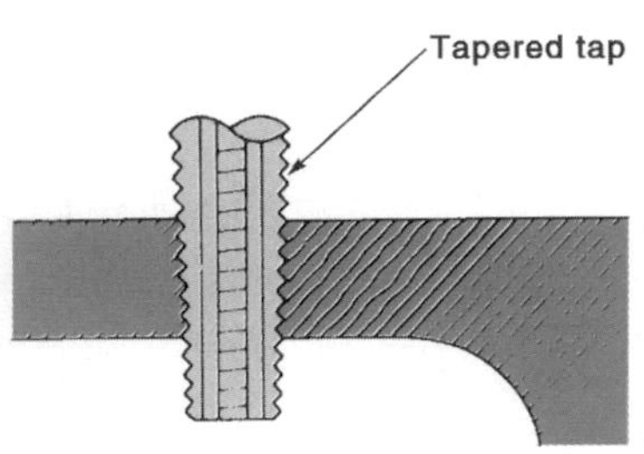

Figure 6–26 Tapping a tapered hole for a plug.

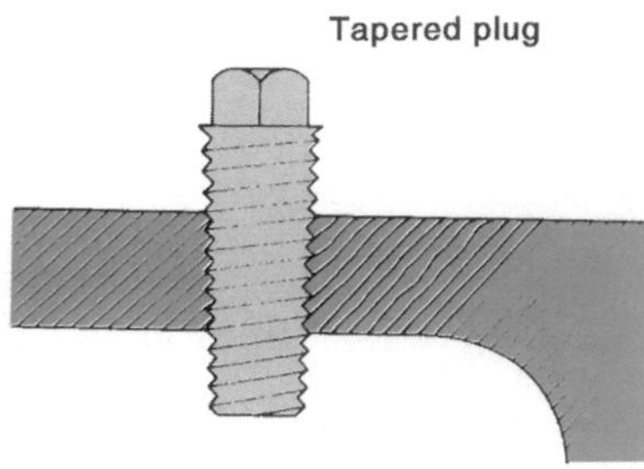

Figure 6–27 Screwing a tapered plug in the hole.

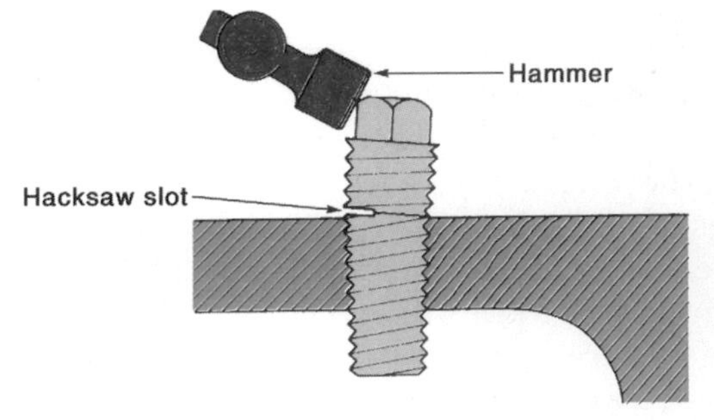

Figure 6–28 Cutting the plug with a hacksaw.

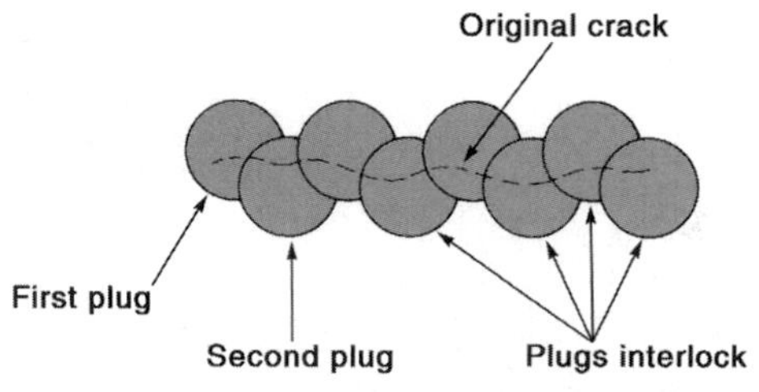

Figure 6–29 Interlocking plugs.

alternating slightly from side to side. The exposed ends of the plugs are peened over with a hammer to help secure them in place. The surface of the plugs is then ground or filed down nearly to the gasket surface. The gasket surface of the head must be resurfaced after the crack has been repaired. In the combustion chamber and at the ports, the plugs are ground down to the original surface using a hand grinder.

CHEMICAL SEALANTS

Pin-hole leaks in cylinder heads and blocks are often caused by casting porosity. This type of leak may be repaired with an epoxy-based sealant which is spread over the porous area. Most of these sealants are not approved for use where high temperatures or pressures may be found.

PHOTO SEQUENCE 3 Checking a Cylinder Head for Cracks

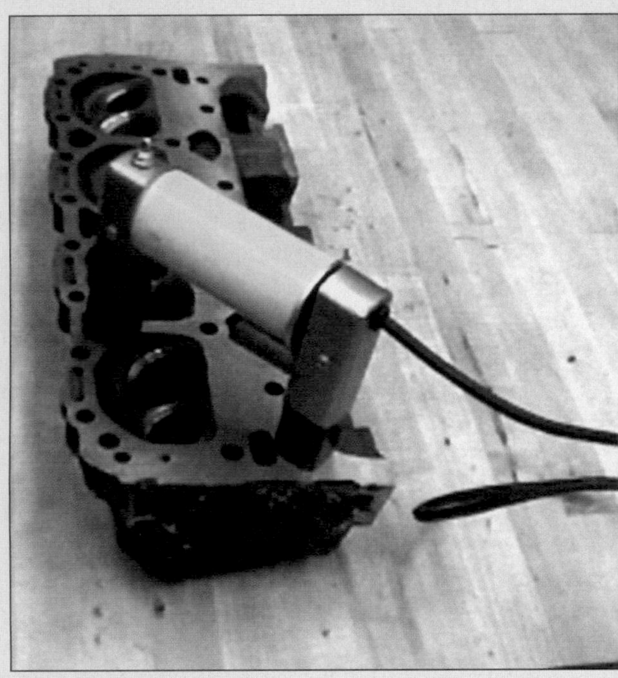

P3–1 A strong electromagnet can be used to check a cast-iron cylinder head for cracks. The cylinder head should be thoroughly cleaned and placed on a work surface that gives good visibility.

P3–2 Turn the electromagnet on using the switch at the top and spray a fine iron powder between the poles of the magnet. The magnetic lines of force are more concentrated on the edges of a crack, and the iron powder will be attracted to the strong magnetic concentration around the crack.

P3–3 Pay particular attention to the area around and between the valve seats.

P3–4 This cylinder head has cracks running from two valve seats. The head will either have to be replaced or repaired.

SUMMARY

1. The factory-installed lifting hooks should be used when hoisting an engine.
2. Engine component parts should only be removed when the engine is cold. Also, the torque table should always be followed backward, starting with the highest-number head bolt and working toward the lowest-number. This procedure helps prevent warpage.
3. The ridge at the top of the cylinder should be removed before removing the piston(s) from the cylinder.
4. The connecting rod and main bearing caps should be marked before removing to ensure that they can be reinstalled in the exact same location when the engine is reassembled.
5. The tip of the valve stem should be filed before removing valves from the cylinder head to help prevent damage to the valve guide.
6. Mechanical cleaning with scrapers or wire brushes is used to remove deposits.
7. Steel wire brushes should never be used to clean aluminum parts.
8. Most chemical cleaners are strong soaps called caustic materials.
9. Always use aluminum-safe chemicals when cleaning aluminum parts or components.
10. Thermal cleaning is done in a pyrolytic oven in temperatures as high as 425°C (800°F) to turn grease and dirt into harmless ash deposits.
11. Blasters use metal shot or glass beads to clean parts. All of the metal shot or glass beads must be cleaned from the part so as not to cause engine problems.
12. All parts should be checked for cracks using magnetic, dye-penetrant, fluorescent-penetrant, or pressure testing methods.
13. Cracks can be repaired by welding or by plugging.

REVIEW QUESTIONS

1. When should the factory-installed lifting hooks be used?
2. Explain why the cylinder bore should be measured for taper and out-of-round before continuing with an engine disassembly.
3. State two reasons for the removal of the ridge at the top of the cylinder.
4. Explain why the burrs must be removed from valves before removing the valves from the cylinder head.
5. Describe five methods that could be used to clean engines or engine parts.
6. Explain magnetic crack inspection, dye-penetrant testing, and fluorescent-penetrant testing methods and where each can be used.

RED SEAL CERTIFICATION-TYPE QUESTIONS

1. When removing an engine, the air conditioning compressor, if equipped, should be
   - **a.** Left with the engine
   - **b.** Unbolted from the engine and left with all hoses attached
   - **c.** Removed from the engine and discharged to the atmosphere
   - **d.** Rotated by hand to circulate the refrigerant oil
2. Lifting hooks are often installed at the factory because _____.
   - **a.** They make removing the engine easier for the technician
   - **b.** They are used to install the engine at the factory
   - **c.** They are part of the engine and should not be removed
   - **d.** They make servicing the top of the engine easier for the technician
3. The ridge at the top of the cylinder _____.
   - **a.** Is caused by wear at the top of the cylinder by the rings
   - **b.** Represents a failure of the top piston ring to correctly seal against the cylinder wall
   - **c.** Should not be removed before removing pistons except when reboring the cylinders
   - **d.** Means that a crankshaft with an incorrect stroke was installed in the engine
4. A loose timing chain or belt that jumps teeth on the crankshaft sprocket may allow contact between the
   - **a.** Pistons and cylinder head
   - **b.** Valve heads and pistons
   - **c.** Valves and cylinder head
   - **d.** Pistons in adjacent cylinders
5. Before the valves are removed from the cylinder head, what operations need to be completed?
   - **a.** Remove valve locks (keepers)
   - **b.** Remove cylinder head(s) from the engine
   - **c.** Remove burrs from the stem of the valve(s)
   - **d.** All of the above
6. Cleaning chemicals are usually either a caustic material or an acid material. Which of the following statements is true?
   - **a.** Both caustics and acids have a pH of 7 if rated according to distilled water.
   - **b.** An acid is lower than 7 and a caustic is higher than 7 on the pH scale.
   - **c.** An acid is higher than 7 and a caustic is lower than 7 on the pH scale.
   - **d.** Pure water is a 1 and a strong acid is a 14 on the pH scale.
7. Many cleaning methods involve chemicals that are hazardous to use and expensive to dispose of after use. The least hazardous method is generally considered to be the _____.
   - **a.** Pyrolytic oven
   - **b.** Hot vapour tank
   - **c.** Hot soak tank
   - **d.** Cold soak tank

8. Magnetic crack inspection _____.
   a. Uses a red dye to detect cracks in aluminum
   b. Uses a black light to detect cracks in iron parts
   c. Uses a fine iron powder to detect cracks in iron parts
   d. Uses a magnet to remove cracks from iron parts

9. Epoxy-based sealants are used to seal porous castings in
   a. Combustion chambers
   b. Exhaust ports
   c. Low-temperature/pressure areas
   d. Cylinder heads only

10. Plugging can be used to repair cracks_____.
    a. In cast-iron cylinder heads
    b. In aluminum cylinder heads
    c. In both cast-iron and aluminum cylinder heads
    d. Only in cast-iron blocks

7

Cooling and Lubrication Systems

OBJECTIVES: After studying Chapter 7, you should be able to:

1. Prepare for the interprovincial Red Seal certification examination in Appendix I (Engine Repair) on the topics covered in this chapter.
2. Describe how coolant flows through an engine.
3. Discuss the operation of the thermostat.
4. Explain the purpose and function of the radiator pressure cap.
5. Describe the various types of antifreeze and how to recycle and discard used coolant.
6. Discuss how to diagnose cooling system problems.
7. Describe how oil pumps and engine lubrication work.
8. Explain how to inspect an oil pump for wear.

Satisfactory cooling system operation depends on the design and operating conditions of the system. Unfortunately, the cooling system is usually neglected until there is a problem. Proper routine maintenance can prevent problems.

PURPOSE AND FUNCTION OF THE COOLING SYSTEM

The cooling system must allow the engine to warm up to the required operating temperature as rapidly as possible and then maintain that temperature. It must be able to do this when the outside air temperature is as low as −35°C (−30°F) and as high as 45°C (110°F) or more.

Peak combustion temperatures in the engine cycle run from 2200°C to 3300°C (4000°F to 6000°F). The combustion temperatures will *average* between 650° and 925°C (1200°F and 1700°F). Continued temperatures as high as these would weaken engine parts, so heat must be removed from the engine. Oxides of nitrogen (NO_x), a major exhaust pollutant, are formed at high combustion temperatures of 1400°C (2550°F) and above. The cooling system keeps the head and cylinder walls at a temperature that is within the range for maximum efficiency. See Figure 7–1.

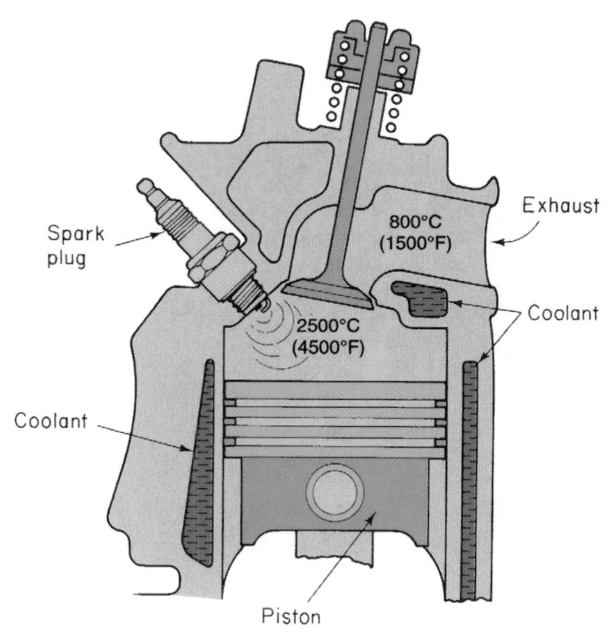

Figure 7–1 Typical peak combustion and exhaust temperatures.

TECH TIP 

Overheating Can Be Expensive

A faulty cooling system seems to be a major cause of engine failure. Engine rebuilders often have nightmares about seeing their rebuilt engine placed back in service in a vehicle with a clogged radiator. Most engine technicians routinely replace the water pump and all hoses after an engine overhaul or repair. The radiator should also be checked for leaks and proper flow whenever the engine is repaired or replaced. Overheating is one of the most common causes of engine failure. Some engine rebuilders place a temperature-sensitive tag on the engine. If a failure occurs and the tag indicates excessive temperature, often the engine warranty will be void.

AIR-COOLED ENGINES

Some earlier engine designs, usually European, were air-cooled and did not use liquid. The cylinder heads and cylinder walls were surrounded by cast-in fins, which increased the surface area. A large fan, driven by the engine, forced air around the fins, which kept the cylinders cool. The majority of today's vehicles use liquid cooling.

COOLING SYSTEM DESIGN

Coolant flows through the engine, where it picks up heat. It then flows to the radiator, where the heat is given up to the outside air. The coolant continually recirculates through the cooling system, as illustrated in Figures 7–2 and 7–3. Its temperature rises as much as 8°C (15°F) as it goes through the engine; then it cools back down as it goes through the radiator. *The coolant flow rate may be as high as four litres (one gallon) per minute for each horsepower the engine produces.*

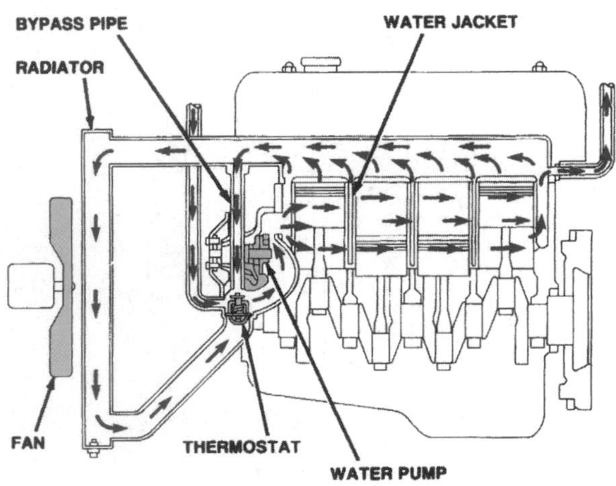

Figure 7–2 A typical cooling system showing how the coolant flows through the block first, then through the cylinder head, and finally through the radiator after the thermostat opens. Notice that coolant flows through the heater core even when the thermostat is closed.

Figure 7–3 A Northstar V-8 with the cylinder head removed shows the coolant passages around the cylinder. This engine has additional overheating protection built into the on-board computer program. If the engine temperature exceeds safe limits, the computer will cancel fuel delivery to every second cylinder. Cool air, which is still passing through the dead cylinders, absorbs engine heat and holds the temperature to an acceptable level.

Hot coolant comes out of the thermostat housing on the top of the engine. The engine coolant outlet is connected to the top of the radiator by the upper hose and clamps. The coolant in the radiator is cooled by air flowing through the radiator. Cool coolant leaves the radiator through an outlet and lower hose, going into the inlet side of the water pump, where it is recirculated through the engine. The flow of cool air through the radiator is aided by a belt- or electric motor-driven cooling fan.

THERMOSTAT TEMPERATURE CONTROL

There is a normal operating temperature range between low-temperature and high-temperature extremes. The thermostat controls the minimum normal temperature. The thermostat is a temperature-controlled valve placed at the engine coolant outlet. See Figure 7–4.

NOTE: Some engine designs place the thermostat at the inlet side of the water pump.

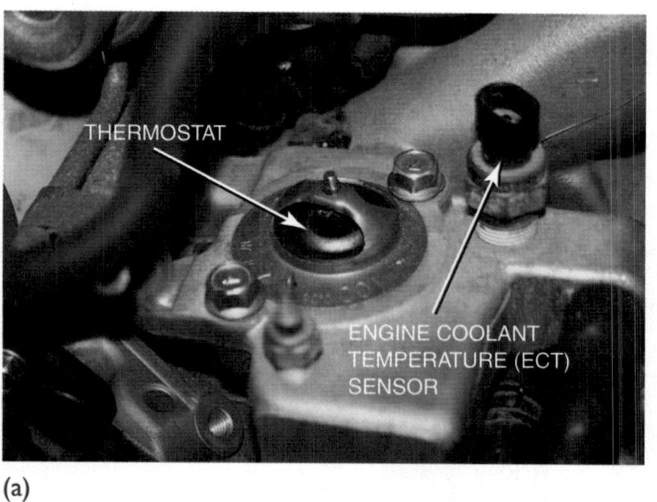

(a)

(b)

Figure 7–4 (a) Typical thermostat located in the intake manifold with the thermostat housing removed. (b) A thermostat that is stuck in the open position. This caused the engine to operate too cold and the vehicle failed an exhaust emission test because of this defect.

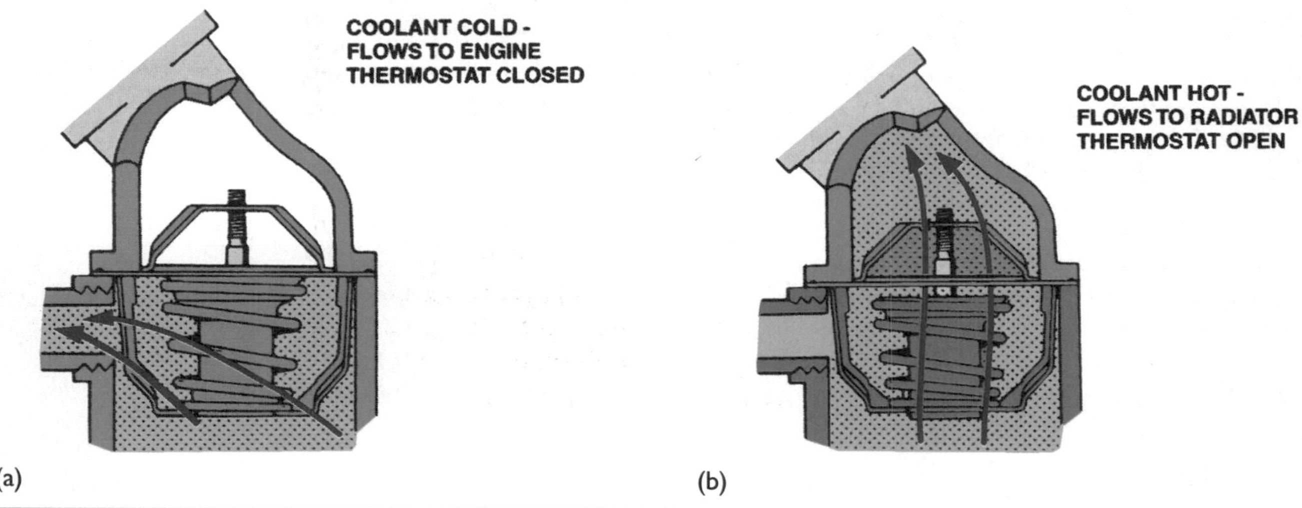

Figure 7–5 (a) The thermostat is closed when the engine is cold, and the coolant flows through the bypass passage thereby bypassing the thermostat. (b) When the thermostat opens, most of the coolant flows through the thermostat to the radiator. Some cooling systems use a double-ended thermostat: one end controls flow through the bypass circuit and the other end controls flow to the radiator.

- Cold—bypass circuit open, radiator closed.
- Hot—bypass closed, flow to radiator open.

An encapsulated, wax-based, plastic-pellet heat sensor is located on the engine side of the thermostatic valve. As the engine warms, heat swells the heat sensor and a mechanical link connected to the heat sensor opens the thermostat valve. As the thermostat begins to open, it allows some coolant to flow to the radiator, where it is cooled. The remaining part of the coolant continues to flow through the **bypass,** thereby bypassing the thermostat and flowing back through the engine. See Figure 7–5. The rated temperature of the thermostat indicates the temperature at which the thermostat starts to open. The thermostat is fully open at about 11°C (20°F) higher than its opening temperature. See the following examples.

Thermostat Opening Temperature	Starts to Open	Fully Open
82°C(180°F)	82°C (180°F)	93°C (200°F)
91°C (195°F)	91°C (195°F)	102°C (215°F)

Figure 7–6 Is this engine operating at the correct temperature? This is a Pontiac Grand Prix. This gauge shows about 90°C or (195°F), which is about the opening temperature of the thermostat.

If the radiator, water pump, and coolant passages are functioning correctly, the engine should always be operating within the opening and fully open temperature range of the thermostat. See Figure 7–6.

HINT: Many electronic automatic transmissions will not shift into the highest gear until the engine is close to operating temperature. A customer's complaint of a transmission shift problem may be as simple as a malfunctioning thermostat.

An infrared pyrometer can be used to measure the temperature of the coolant near the thermostat. The area on the engine side of the thermostat should be at the highest temperature that exists in the engine.

HINT: For a more accurate reading while using an infrared temperature probe, place some black electrical tape on the area to be tested. Because the infrared depends on a reflective surface to determine the temperature, the black surface makes the readings more accurate.

A properly operating cooling system should cause the pyrometer to read as follows:

1. As the engine warms up, the temperature reaches near thermostat-opening temperature.

TECH TIP 

Engine Temperature and Exhaust Emissions

Many areas of Canada and the United States have exhaust emission testing. Hydrocarbon (HC) emissions are simply unburned gasoline. To help reduce HC emissions and to pass emission tests, be sure that the engine is at normal operating temperature. Vehicle manufacturers' definition of "normal operating temperature" includes the following:

- Upper radiator hose is hot and pressurized
- Electric cooling fan(s) cycles twice

For best results, the vehicle should be driven about 31 km (20 mi.) to be certain that the catalytic converter and engine oil, as well as the coolant, are at normal temperature.

2. As the thermostat opens, the temperature drops just as the thermostat opens, sending coolant to the radiator.
3. As the thermostat cycles, the temperature should range between the opening temperature of the thermostat and 11°C (20°F) above the opening temperature. See Figures 7–7 and 7–8.

Figure 7–7 A cutaway of a small block Chevrolet V-8 showing the passage from the cylinder head through the front of the intake manifold to the thermostat.

Figure 7–8 Some thermostats are an integral part of the housing and are replaced as an assembly.

NOTE: If the temperature rises higher than 11°C (20°F) above the opening temperature of the thermostat, inspect the cooling system for a restriction or low coolant flow. A clogged radiator could also cause the excessive temperature rise.

A scan tool can be used on many vehicles to read the actual temperature of the coolant as detected by the engine coolant temperature (ECT) sensor. Although the sensor or the wiring to and from the sensor may be defective, at least the scan tool can indicate what the computer "thinks" the coolant temperature is.

HINT: Although an engine that does not come up to temperature usually indicates a faulty thermostat, there are exceptions. The engine in a vehicle travelling at 80 km/h (50 mph) on a flat highway in Manitoba, during the winter, may never warm up enough for the thermostat to open. Shutters, or even cardboard restrictors, are often used to limit airflow through the radiator.

TECH TIP 

Ignore the Windchill Factor

Windchill is a factor that combines the actual temperature and the wind speed to determine the overall heat loss effect on bare skin. Because it is the heat loss factor for bare skin, the windchill temperature is *not* to be considered when determining antifreeze protection levels.

Although moving air does make it feel colder, the actual temperature is not changed by the wind and the engine coolant will not be affected by the windchill. Not convinced? Try this. Place a thermometer in a room and wait until a stable reading is obtained. Then turn on a fan and have the air blow across the thermometer. The temperature will not change.

COOLANT

Organic acid technology (OAT) antifreeze coolant does not contain silicates or phosphates. This type of coolant is usually orange in colour and was first developed by Havoline (called **DEX-COOL**) and used in General Motors vehicles starting in 1996.

Hybrid organic acid technology (HOAT) is a newer variation of this technology and is similar to the OAT-type antifreeze as it uses additives that are not abrasive to water pumps, yet provide the correct pH. The pH of the coolant is usually above 11. A pH of 7 is neutral, with lower numbers indicating an acidic solution and higher numbers indicating a caustic solution. If the pH is too high, the coolant can cause scaling and reduce the heat transfer ability of the coolant. If the pH is too low, the resulting acidic solution could cause corrosion of the engine components exposed to the coolant.

Testing the Coolant with a Hydrometer

Coolant can be checked using a coolant hydrometer, which measures the density of the coolant. The higher the density, the more concentration of antifreeze in the water. Most coolant hydrometers read the freezing point and boiling point of the coolant.

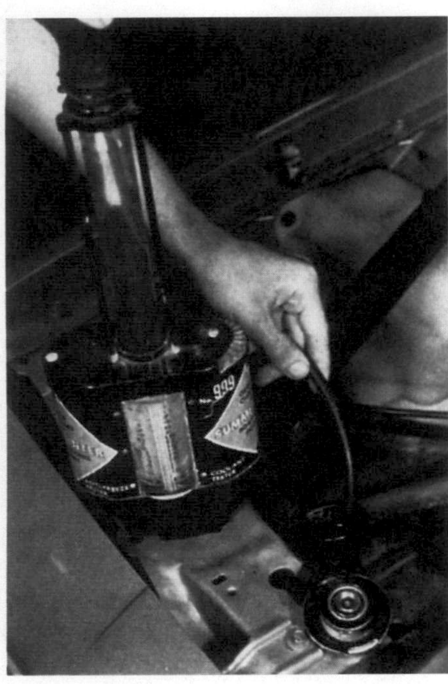

Figure 7–9 Checking the freezing and boiling protection levels of the coolant using a hydrometer.

See Figure 7–9. For best results, the coolant should have a freezing point lower than −37°C (−35°F) and a boiling point above 112°C (235°F).

Testing the Coolant with a DC Voltmeter

Coolant that becomes acidic will cause erosion of aluminum engine components. The acidity level may be checked by placing the positive probe of a digital DC voltmeter into the coolant and the meter's ground probe on the negative battery terminal.

Readings of 0.5 V, or less, are acceptable; readings of 0.7 V, or more, indicate that flushing of the system and coolant replacement are required.

Coolant Replacement

Many vehicle manufacturers recommend coolant replacement every two to three years or every 40 000 to 60 000 km (24 000 to 36 000 mi) depending on make and model. The trend to use long-life coolant has extended the change interval to 160 000 km (100 000 mi) or longer. Several European car-makers are using coolant that lasts for the service life of the engine.

Recycling and Disposing of Used Coolant

Coolant (antifreeze and water) should be recycled. Used coolant may contain heavy metals, such as lead, aluminum, and iron, that are absorbed by the coolant during its use in the engine.

Recycle machines filter out these metals and dirt and reinstall the depleted additives. The recycled coolant, restored to be like new, can be reinstalled into the vehicle.

CAUTION: Most vehicle manufacturers warn that antifreeze coolant should not be reused unless it is recycled and the additives restored.

Used coolant drained from vehicles should be disposed of according to federal, provincial, and local laws. Check with recycling companies authorized by local or provincial government for the exact method recommended for disposal in your area.

NOTE: Each year thousands of small animals are poisoned in Canada and the U.S. by ethylene-glycol based coolant. Many die. U.S. states California and Oregon require antifreeze manufacturers to add a bittering agent to any coolant sold in their states. This counteracts the sweet taste that attracts animals. Animal protection groups are lobbying for the use of this product throughout Canada and the U.S.

THE DESIGN AND FUNCTION OF THE RADIATOR

Two types of radiator cores are in common use in domestic vehicles—the serpentine fin core and the plate fin core. In each of these types the coolant flows through oval-shaped **core tubes.** Heat is transferred through the tube wall and soldered joint to **fins.** The fins are exposed to airflow, which removes heat from the radiator and carries it away. See Figures 7–10 and 7–11. Radiators are also classified either as *down-flow,* where the tanks are placed on the top and bottom of the radiator, or *cross-flow,* where the tanks are located on the radiator sides. Both types are equally efficient, but the cross-flow allows a lower hood line.

Most automobile radiators are made from yellow brass or aluminum. These materials are corrosion resistant, have good heat-transferring ability, and are easily formed.

Core tubes are made from 0.1 to 0.3 mm (0.0045 to 0.012 in.) sheet brass or aluminum. The metal is rolled into round tubes and the joints are sealed with a locking seam.

The thickness of the radiator core may vary with the engine size, even in the same vehicles. Whether the engine is 4-cylinder, 6-cylinder, V-8 or has an optional air conditioner—all have an influence on the radiator cooling capacity.

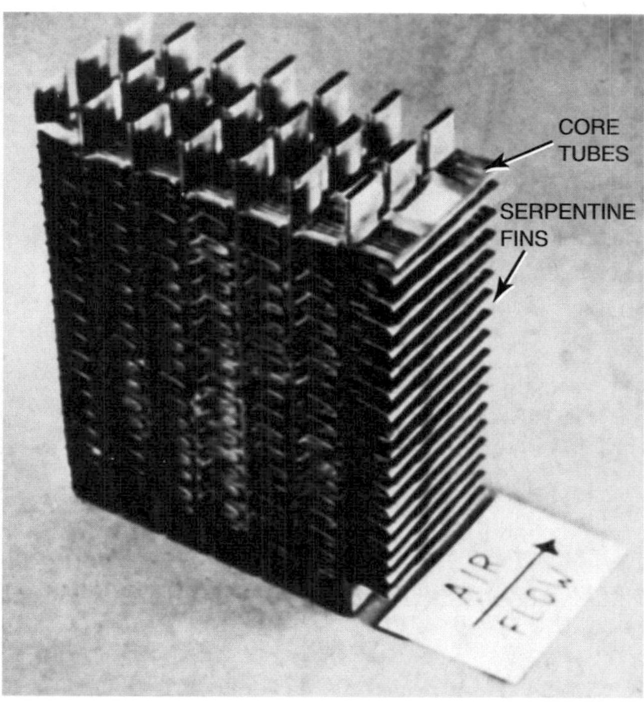

Figure 7–10 Section from a serpentine core radiator. (Courtesy of Modine Manufacturing Company)

Figure 7–11 Cutaway of a typical radiator showing restriction of tubes. Changing antifreeze frequently helps prevent this type of problem.

The radiator must be capable of removing an amount of heat energy approximately equal to the heat energy of the power produced by the engine. *Each horsepower is equivalent to 10.8 kcal (42 BTU) per minute.*

Radiator headers and tanks that close off the ends of the core are made of sheet brass 0.5 to 1.25 mm (0.020 to 0.050 in.) thick or of molded plastic. When a transmission oil cooler is used in the radiator, it is placed in the outlet tank, where the coolant has the lowest temperature (Figure 7–12).

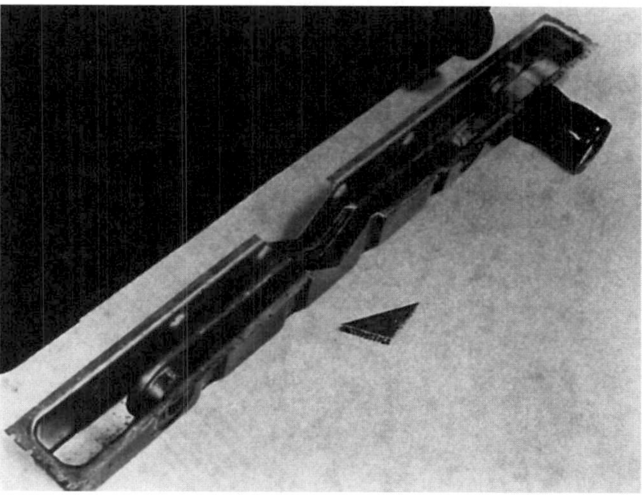

Figure 7–12 Cutaway showing an automatic transmission cooler passage inside the radiator. Air cools the coolant, which then cools the automatic transmission fluid that flows through the radiator. (Courtesy of The Dow Chemical Company)

The Cooling System Pressure Cap

The filler neck or reservoir of the radiator is fitted with a pressure cap. The cap has a spring-loaded valve that closes the cooling system vent, which causes cooling pressure to build up to the pressure setting of the cap. At this point, the valve will release the excess pressure to prevent system damage. See Figure 7–13.

Engine cooling systems are pressurized to raise the boiling temperature of the coolant. *The boiling temperature will increase with pressure by approximately 0.25°C/kPa (3°F/psi).* At standard atmosphere pressure (sea level), water will boil at 100°C (212°F). With a 103 kPa (15 psi) pressure cap, water will boil at 125°C (257°F), which is a maximum operating range for the engine. With the correct antifreeze/water mixture, the boiling point should exceed 132°C (270°F) when under 103 kPa (15 psi) of pressure.

Never remove the pressure cap from a radiator that is at operating temperature. The sudden drop in pressure will lower the boiling point and an eruption of steam and boiling coolant will occur. It is far safer to let the engine cool before loosening the cap.

NOTE: The proper operation of the pressure cap is especially important at higher altitudes. The boiling point of water is lowered by about 1°C (1.8°F) for every 300 m (1000 ft) increase in altitude. Therefore in Toronto, Ontario, altitude 172 metres (565 feet), the boiling point of water is about 99.5°C (211°F). In Saskatoon, Saskatchewan, altitude 503 m (1653 ft), water boils at approximately 98.5°C (209°F).

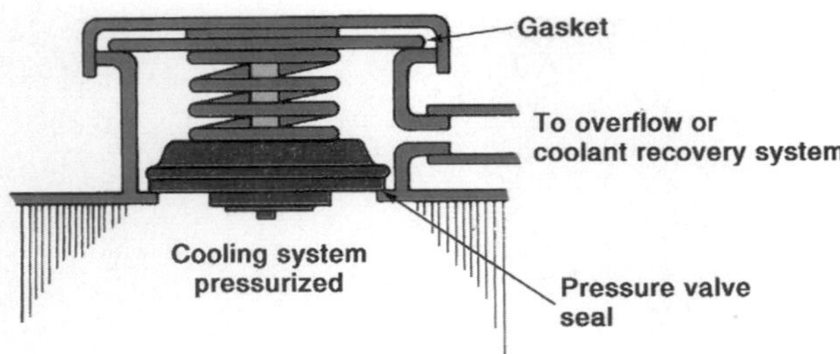

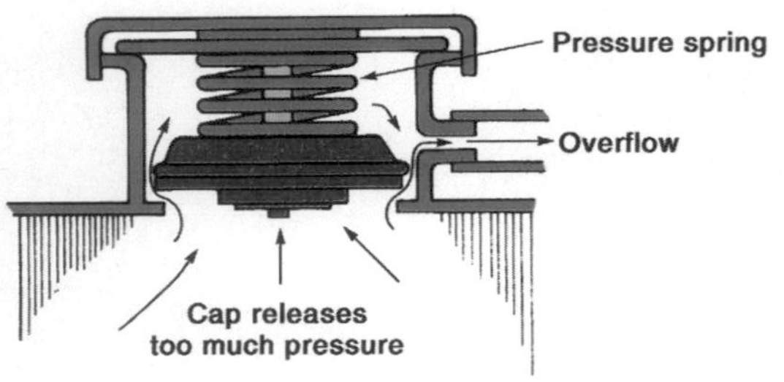

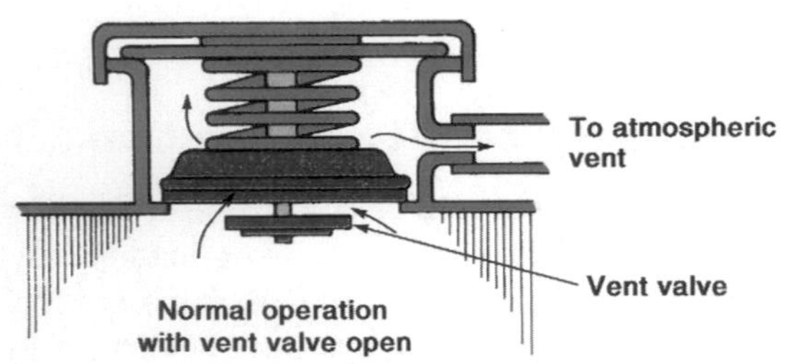

Figure 7–13 The operation of a typical pressure cap.

Figure 7–14 A radiator cap from a truck that operated with a low coolant level.

NOTE: If you notice a radiator hose has collapsed when the engine cools, do not assume it is a bad hose. This collapse of the hose is a result of a defective radiator cap. A properly operating cap should draw coolant from the radiator overflow container back into the radiator and not form a vacuum in the system.

DIAGNOSTIC STORY

The Case of the Rusting Radiator Cap

During a routine service on a General Motors pickup truck, a service technician discovered that the entire cooling system was full of rust. See Figure 7–14. A search of technical service bulletins (TSBs) indicated that the rust is often caused by a lower level of coolant caused by a leak. When cast-iron parts of the engine are exposed to the oxygen in the air, they rust. This rust will then travel through the cooling system causing clogs or preventing the proper operation of the thermostat and radiator cap. The repair, according to the TSB, was to flush the system and refill with coolant. A careful analysis of this particular case indicated that the radiator cap seal had failed, allowing a loss of coolant, which then led to the rust problem.

COOLANT RECOVERY SYSTEM

Excess pressure usually forces some coolant from the system through an overflow. Most cooling systems connect the overflow to a plastic reservoir to hold excess coolant while the system is hot. See Figure 7–15. When the system cools, the pressure in the cooling system is reduced and a partial vacuum forms. This pulls the coolant from the plastic container back into the cooling system, keeping the system full. Because of this action, this system is called a **coolant recovery system.**

Frequently Asked Question ???

How Does the Pressure Cap Make the Water Pump More Efficient?

A problem that sometimes occurs with a high-pressure cooling system involves the water pump. For the pump to function, the inlet side of the pump must have a lower pressure than its outlet side. If inlet pressure is lowered too much, the coolant at the pump inlet can boil, producing vapour. The pump will then spin the coolant vapours and not pump coolant. This condition is called **pump cavitation.** Therefore, a radiator cap could be the cause of an overheating problem. A pump will not pump enough coolant if not kept under the proper pressure for preventing vaporization of the coolant.

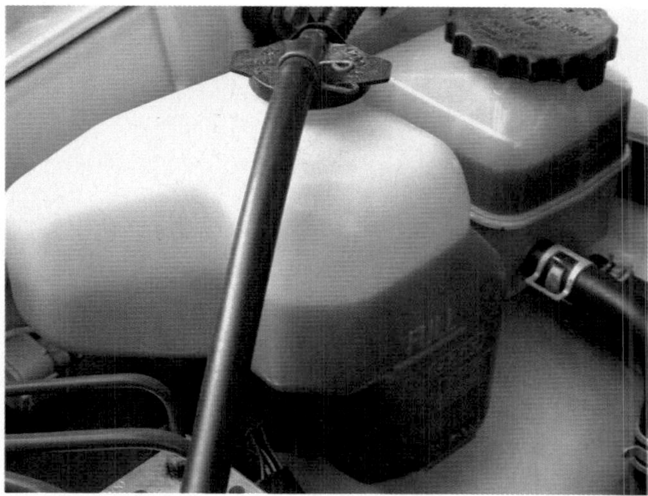

Figure 7–15 A typical coolant recovery container.

TECH TIP 

Check the Radiator, Not the Overflow Container

If an engine is overheating or if the heater produces heat only once in a while, the coolant level should be checked. Many people check the level of coolant in the overflow container and believe that if the radiator were low, the coolant would be drawn from the overflow container into the radiator. However, if there is a leak from a defective water pump, for example, the cooling system will not be airtight and a vacuum will not be formed to draw coolant from the overflow back into the radiator.

Therefore, if there is a cooling system problem, always check the level of the coolant at the radiator itself. See Figure 7–16. Always check the coolant when the engine is cold or before the engine is started to avoid getting burned by hot coolant, which will gush from the radiator if the pressure cap is removed when the coolant is hot.

TESTING THE COOLING SYSTEM

Pressure Testing

Pressure testing using a hand-operated pressure tester is a quick and easy cooling system test. The radiator cap is removed (engine cold!) and the tester attached in the place of the radiator cap. By operating the plunger on the pump, the entire cooling system is pressurized. See Figures 7–17 and 7–18.

CAUTION: Do not pump up the pressure beyond that specified by the vehicle manufacturer. Most systems should not be pressurized beyond 100 kPa (14 psi). If a greater pressure is used, it may cause the water pump, radiator, heater core, or hoses to fail.

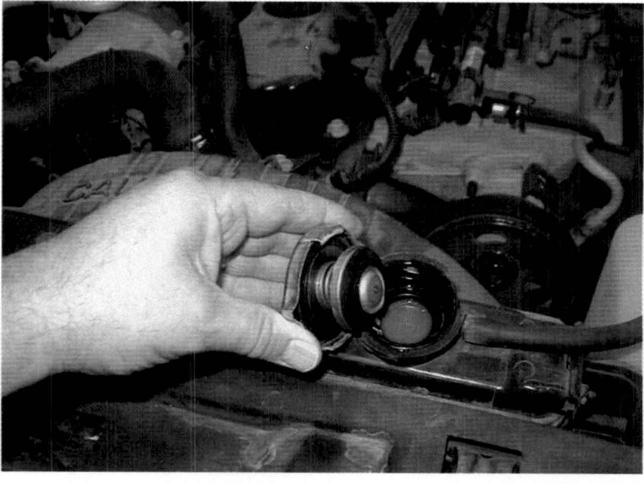

Figure 7–16 When checking the cooling system, always inspect the coolant level in the radiator itself, but never when the engine is warm. Always allow the engine to cool to room temperature before removing the radiator pressure cap.

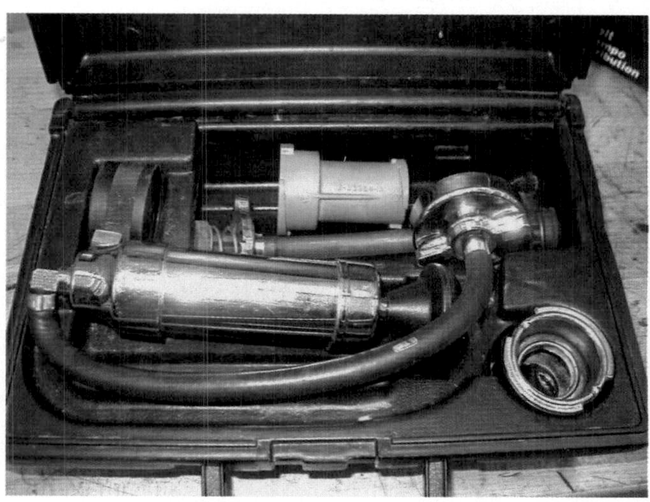

Figure 7–17 A typical radiator pressure tester set showing the various adapters needed to test different sizes of radiator cap openings.

TECH TIP 

Use Distilled Water in the Cooling System

Two technicians are discussing refilling the radiator after changing antifreeze. One technician says that distilled water is best to use because it does not contain minerals that can coat the passages of the cooling system. The other technician says that any water suitable to drink can be used in a cooling system. Both technicians are correct. If water contains minerals, however, it can leave deposits in the cooling system that could prevent proper heat transfer. Distilled water should be used in areas where the water has a high mineral content.

Figure 7–18 Pressure testing the cooling system. A typical hand-operated pressure tester applies pressure equal to the radiator cap pressure. The pressure should hold; if it drops, this indicates a leak somewhere in the cooling system. An adapter is used to attach the pump to the cap to determine if the radiator can hold pressure, and release it when pressure rises above its maximum rated pressure setting.

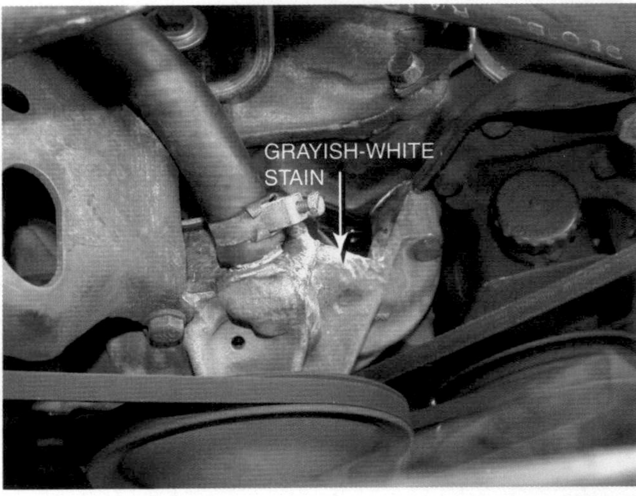

Figure 7–19 A coolant leak usually leaves a grayish-white stain.

If the cooling system is free of leaks, the pressure should stay and not drop. If the pressure drops, look for evidence of leaks anywhere in the cooling system including:

- Heater hoses
- Radiator hoses
- Radiator
- Heat core
- Cylinder head
- Core plugs in the side of the block or cylinder head

Pressure testing should be performed whenever there is a leak or suspected leak. The pressure tester can also be used to test the radiator cap by using an adapter to connect the pressure tester to the radiator cap. Replace any cap that will not hold pressure.

Coolant Dye Leak Testing

A coolant leak is normally identified as a grayish-white stain as shown in Figure 7–19. One of the best methods for checking for a coolant leak is to use a fluorescent dye in the coolant. Use a dye designed for coolant. See Figure 7–20. Operate the vehicle with the dye in the coolant until the engine reaches normal operating temperature. Use a black light to inspect all areas of the cooling system. When there is a leak, it will be easy to spot because the dye in the coolant will be seen as a bright green.

Figure 7–20 Use dye specifically made for coolant when checking for leaks using a black light.

THE WATER PUMP

Operation

The water pump is driven by a belt from the crankshaft or driven by the camshaft.

NOTE: A water pump is also called a coolant pump.

Coolant recirculates from the radiator to the engine and back to the radiator. Low-temperature coolant leaves the radiator by the bottom outlet. It is pumped into the warm engine block, where it picks up some heat. From the block, the warm coolant flows to the hot cylinder head, where it picks up more heat.

Water pumps are not positive displacement pumps. The water pump is a **centrifugal pump** that can move a large volume of coolant without increasing the pressure of the coolant. The pump pulls coolant in at the centre of the **impeller.** Centrifugal force then throws the coolant outward so that it is discharged at the impeller tips. This can be seen in Figure 7–21.

As engine speeds increase, more heat is produced by the engine and more cooling capacity is required. The pump impeller speed increases as the engine speed increases to provide extra coolant flow at the very time it is needed.

NOTE: Many early engines did not use a water pump to circulate coolant. As coolant temperature increases, it becomes lighter and rises. The rising coolant, absorbing engine heat, pushes the hotter liquid out of the cylinder head and into the radiator where the temperature drops and the heavier coolant falls to the bottom. It then pushes into the cylinder block and the cycle begins again. This is known as thermo-siphon cooling. The direction of coolant flow was set using this principle.

Light-weight cast iron and aluminum cylinder blocks suffered from unequal expansion rates as the lowest temperature coolant from the radiator was pumped into the coldest area of the block. Many vehicles are now using **reverse cooling** where the water pump forces coolant into the cylinder head first, and the return path is from the block. This helps to equalize thermal expansion. See Figure 7–22.

Service

A worn impeller on a water pump can reduce the amount of coolant flow through the engine. If the seal of the water pump fails, coolant will leak out of the hole, often called a *weep* hole. The hole allows coolant to escape without getting trapped and forced into the water pump bearing assembly. See Figure 7–23.

Figure 7–21 Coolant flow through the impeller and scroll of a coolant pump for a V-type engine.

If the bearing is defective, the pump will usually be noisy and will have to be replaced. Before replacing a water pump that has failed because of a loose or noisy bearing, be sure to do all of the following:

- Check the belt tension with a belt tension gauge.
- Check for a bent fan.
- Check the fan for balance.

If the water pump drive belt is too tight, excessive force may be exerted against the pump bearing. If the cooling fan is bent or out of balance, the resulting vibration can damage the water pump bearing.

RADIATOR COOLING FANS

Air is forced across the radiator core by a cooling fan. On older engines used in rear-wheel-drive vehicles, the fan is attached to a fan hub that is pressed on the water pump shaft. See Figure 7–24. In most installations in rear-wheel-drive and transverse engines, the fan is driven by an electric motor. See Figure 7–25.

NOTE: Most electric cooling fans are computer controlled. To save energy, most cooling fans are turned off whenever the vehicle is travelling faster than 55 km/h (35 mph). The ram air at that speed should be enough to keep the radiator cool. Of course, if the computer senses that the temperature is still too high, it will turn the cooling fan on, to "high," if possible, in an attempt to cool the engine and avoid severe engine damage.

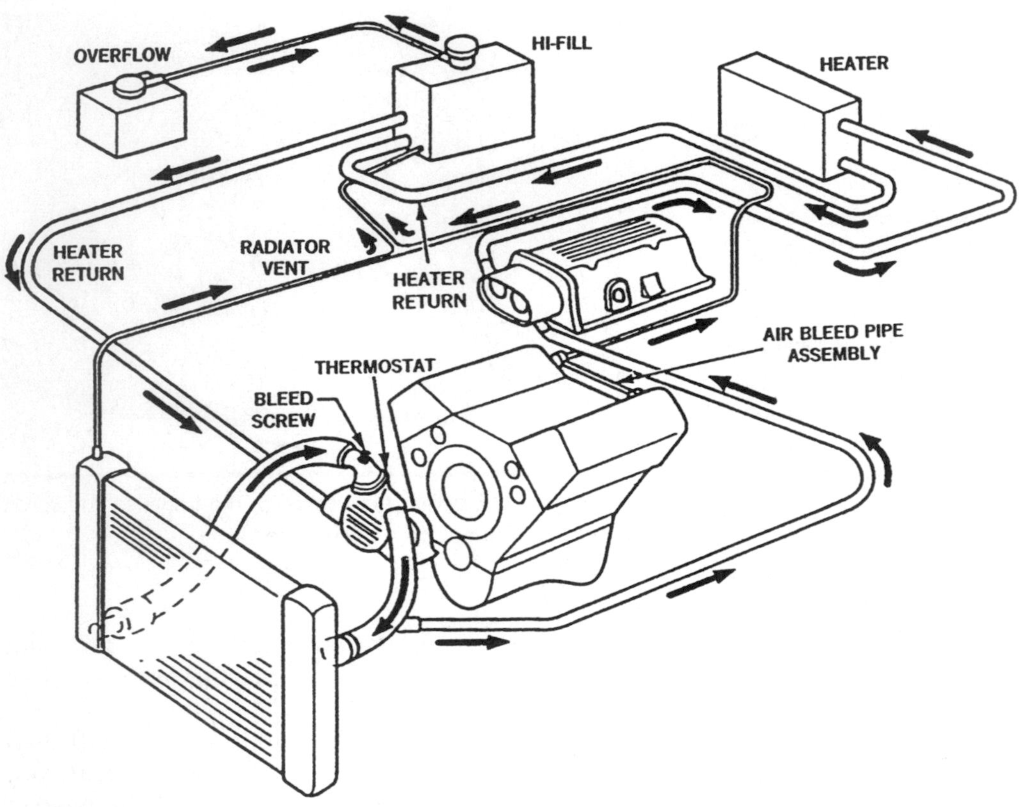

Figure 7–22 Reverse flow cooling system (Corvette). (Courtesy General Motors)

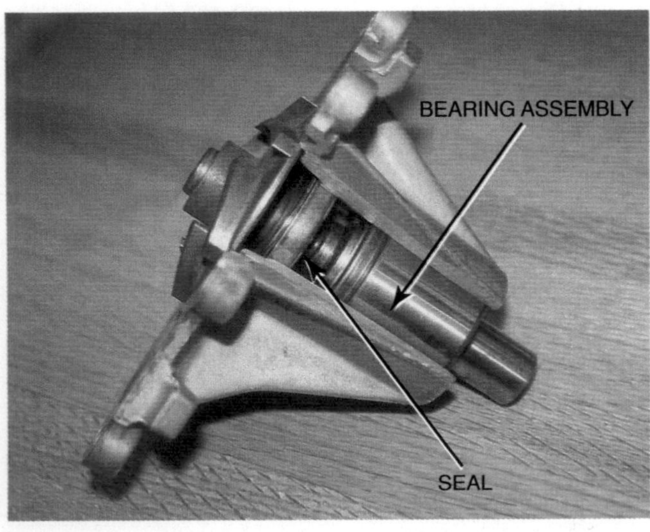

Figure 7–23 Cutaway of a typical water pump showing the long bearing assembly and seal. The weep hole is located between the seal and the bearing. If the seal fails, then coolant flows out of the weep hole to prevent the coolant from damaging the bearing.

CAUTION: Be aware that an electric fan may come on even when the engine is shut off and the ignition key removed. The "heat soak" from the hot metal to the coolant may cause the fan switch to activate the fan. Keep your hands away from that area.

The fan is designed to move enough air at the lowest fan speed to cool the engine when it is at its highest coolant temperature. The **fan shroud** is used to increase cooling system efficiency by drawing all of the air through the radiator rather than under or over it.

NOTE: Never stand in line with the blades of a belt driven fan. Blades that have fatigued or sheared their retaining rivets have gone through hoods, flattened tires and caused major damage. If you are in the way, they could kill you!

Figure 7–24 A typical engine-driven cooling fan.

Figure 7–25 A typical electric cooling fan assembly.

THERMOSTATIC FANS

Since the early 1980s, most cooling fans have been computer-controlled electric motor units. On some rear-wheel-drive vehicles, the thermostatic cooling fan is driven by a belt from the crankshaft, so it turns faster as the engine turns faster. Generally, since the engine is required to produce more power at higher speeds, the cooling system must also transfer more heat at those speeds, which aids in the required cooling. Reducing engine heat becomes critical at low engine speeds in traffic when the vehicle is moving slowly.

The thermal fan is designed to use little power at high engine speeds and to minimize noise. It has a

Figure 7–26 Cutaway of a viscous fan clutch showing the many grooves that are filled with viscous silicone fluid during operation.

silicone coupling fan drive mounted between the drive pulley and the fan. This coupling slips at higher engine speeds provided engine temperature is in the normal range.

> **HINT:** Whenever diagnosing an overheating problem, look carefully at the cooling fan. If silicone is leaking, then the fan may not be able to function correctly and should be replaced.

A second type of thermal fan has a **thermostatic spring** added to the silicone coupling fan drive. The thermostatic spring operates a valve that allows the fan to freewheel when the radiator is cold. As the radiator warms to about 65°C (150°F), the air hitting the thermostatic spring will cause the spring to change its shape. The new shape of the spring opens a valve that allows the drive to operate like the silicone coupling drive. When the engine is very cold, the fan may operate at high speeds for a short time until the drive fluid warms slightly. The silicone fluid will then flow into a reservoir to let the fan speed drop to idle. See Figure 7–26.

HEATER CORE

Most of the heat absorbed from the engine by the cooling system is wasted, but some is recovered by the vehicle heater. Heated coolant is passed through tubes in the small core of the heater. Air is passed across the heater fins and then is sent to the passenger compartment. In some vehicles, the heater and air conditioner work in series to maintain vehicle compartment temperature.

HEATER PROBLEM DIAGNOSIS

When the vehicle's heater does not produce the desired amount of heat, many owners and technicians replace the thermostat before doing any other troubleshooting. It is true that a defective thermostat is the reason for the *engine* not reaching normal operating temperature. But many other causes besides a defective thermostat can result in lack of heat from the heater. To determine the exact cause, follow the procedure described below.

With the engine running, feel both heater hoses. (The heater should be set to the maximum heat position.) Both hoses should be too hot to hold. If both hoses are warm (not hot) or cool, check the heater control valve for proper operation. If one hose is hot and the other (return) is just warm or cool, remove both hoses from the heater core or engine and flush the heater core with water from a garden hose. See Figure 7–27.

HINT: Heat from the heater that "comes and goes" is most likely the result of low coolant level. Usually with the engine at idle, there is enough coolant flow through the heater, but at higher engine speeds the circulation of coolant through the head(s) and block prevents sufficient flow through the heater.

COOLANT TEMPERATURE WARNING LIGHT

Most vehicles are equipped with a heat sensor for the engine operating temperature. If the "hot" light comes on during driving (or the temperature gauge goes into the red danger zone), the coolant temperature is about 120° to 125°C (250° to 260°F), which is still *below* the boiling point of the coolant (assuming a properly operating pressure cap and system). If this happens, follow these steps:

Step 1. Shut off the air conditioning and turn on the heater. The heater will help get rid of extra heat from the engine. Set the blower speed to high. If this fails to reduce engine temperature, proceed to Step 2.

Step 2. If possible, shut the engine off and let it cool. (This may take over an hour.)

Step 3. Never remove the radiator cap when the engine is hot.

Step 4. Do *not* continue to drive with the hot light on, or serious damage to your engine could result.

(a)

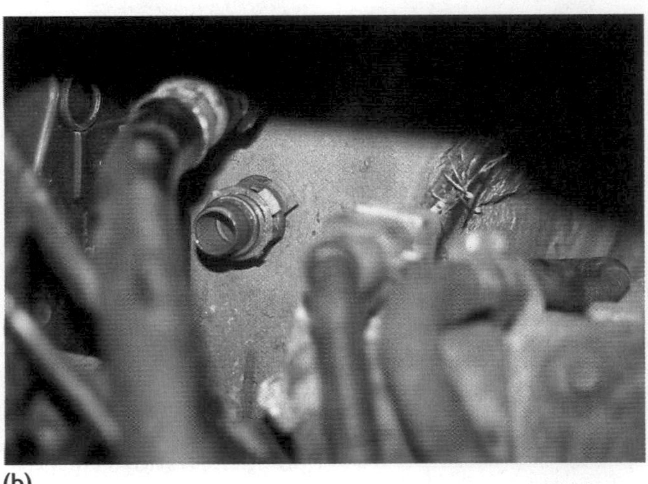

(b)

Figure 7–27 (a) Many vehicles today use quick connect-type fittings on the heater hose. (b) The outside of the heater core housing showing one hose removed. Carefully inspect and clean these connections to prevent a leak.

Step 5. If the engine does not feel or smell hot, it is possible that the problem is a faulty hot light sensor or gauge. Continue to drive, but to be safe, stop occasionally and check for any evidence of overheating or coolant loss.

DIAGNOSTIC STORY

Highway Overheating

A vehicle owner complained of an overheating vehicle, but the problem occurred only while driving at highway speeds. The vehicle, equipped with a General Motors Quad 4, would run in a perfectly normal manner in city-driving situations. See Figure 7–28.

The technician flushed the cooling system and replaced the radiator cap and the water pump, thinking that restricted coolant flow was the cause of the problem. Further testing revealed coolant spraying out of one cylinder when the engine was turned over by the starter with the spark plugs removed.

A new head gasket solved the problem. Obviously, the head gasket leak was not great enough to cause any problems until the engine speed and load created enough flow and heat to cause the coolant temperature to soar.

The technician also replaced the oxygen (O_2) sensor because coolant contains silicone and silicates that often contaminate the sensor. The deteriorated oxygen sensor could have contributed to the problem.

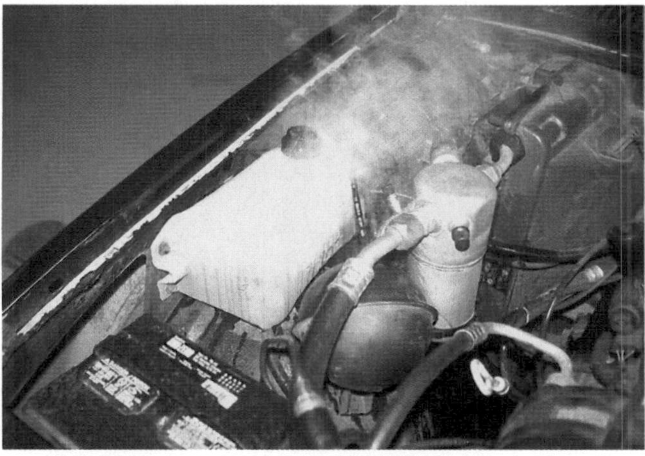

Figure 7–28 When an engine overheats, often the coolant in the overflow container boils.

BURPING THE SYSTEM

In most systems, small air pockets can occur. The engine must be thoroughly warmed to open the thermostat. This allows full coolant flow to remove the air pockets. The heater must also be turned to full heat. Some engines are equipped with a bleeder valve to allow air to escape when filling the cooling system with coolant. See Figure 7–29.

TECH TIP

Quick-and-Easy Cooling System Problem Diagnosis

If overheating occurs in slow, stop-and-go traffic, the usual cause is low airflow through the radiator. Check for airflow blockages or cooling fan malfunctioning. If overheating occurs at highway speeds, the cause is usually a radiator or coolant circulation problem. Check for a restricted or clogged radiator.

HINT: The cooling system will not function correctly if air is not released (burped) from the system after a refill. An easy method of doing this involves replacing the radiator cap after the refill, but only to the first locked position, and driving the vehicle for several minutes. With the radiator cap loosely sealed, no pressure can build up in the cooling system, and driving the vehicle helps circulate the coolant enough to force all air pockets up and out of the radiator filler. Top off the radiator after burping and replace the radiator cap to the fully locked position. Failure to burp the cooling system to remove all the air will often result in lack of heat from the heater and may result in engine overheating.

THE LUBRICATION SYSTEM

Oil Pumps

All production automobile engines have a full-pressure oil system in which oil is forced into the lubrication system under pressure. The pressure is maintained by an oil pump. See Figures 7–30 and 7–31.

In many engines, the distributor drive gear meshes with a gear on the camshaft, as shown in Figures 7–32 and 7–33. The oil pump is driven from the end of the distributor shaft, often by a hexagon-shaped shaft. Some engines have a short shaft gear that meshes with the cam gear to drive both the distributor and oil pump. In other engines, the oil pump is driven by the front of the crankshaft, in a setup similar to that of an automatic transmission pump, so that it turns at the same speed as the crankshaft. Examples of a crankshaft-driven oil pump are shown in Figures 7–34 and 7–35. Crankshaft-driven oil pumps are common with overhead cam and distributorless engines.

Most automotive engines use one of two types of oil pump: **gear** or **rotor.** All oil pumps are called

(a)

(b)

Figure 7–29 (a) DaimlerChrysler recommends that the bleeder valve be opened whenever refilling the cooling system. (b) DaimlerChrysler also recommends that a clear plastic hose 6 mm (1/4 in.) ID be attached to the bleeder valve and directed into a suitable container to keep from spilling coolant onto the ground and the engine. This also allows the technician to observe the flow of coolant for any remaining air bubbles.

Figure 7–30 Cutaway of a Chevrolet V-8 engine showing the location of the oil pump.

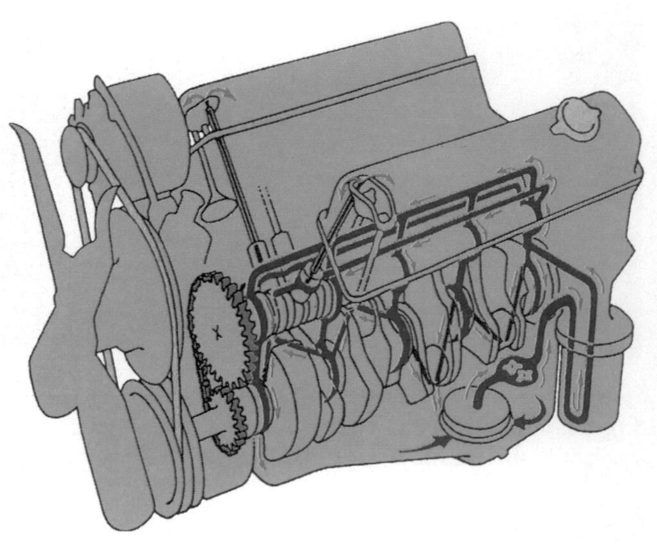

Figure 7–31 Typical V-8 engine lubrication system. Oil is stored in the oil pan (sump) and drawn into the oil pump and through the oil filter and on through the oil passages (oil galleries).

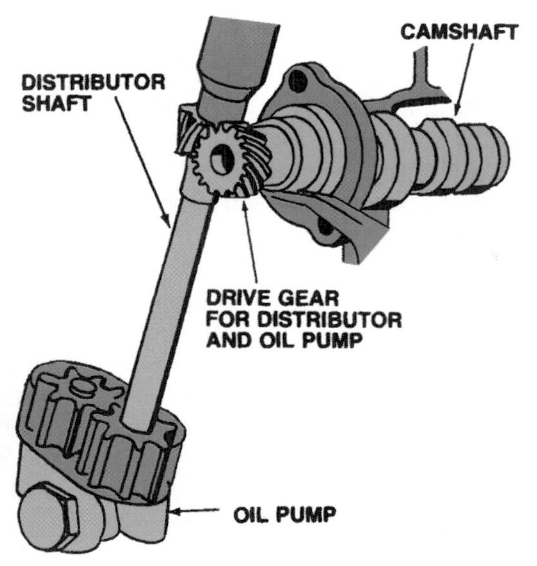
CAMSHAFT
DISTRIBUTOR SHAFT
DRIVE GEAR FOR DISTRIBUTOR AND OIL PUMP
OIL PUMP

Figure 7–32 An oil pump driven by the camshaft.

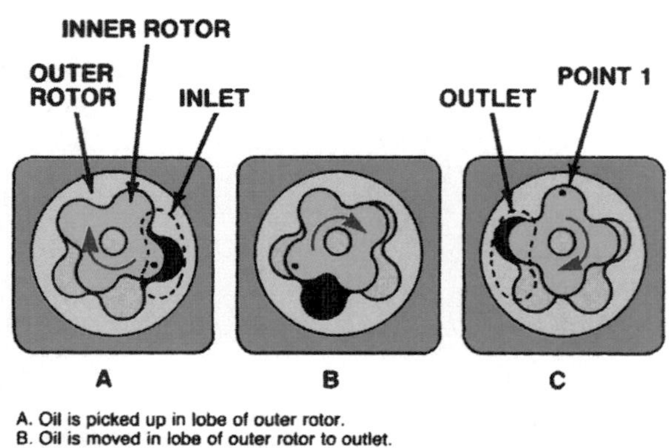
INNER ROTOR
OUTER ROTOR
INLET
OUTLET
POINT 1
A
B
C
A. Oil is picked up in lobe of outer rotor.
B. Oil is moved in lobe of outer rotor to outlet.
C. Oil is forced out of outlet because the inner and outer rotors mesh too tightly at point 1 and the oil cannot pass through.

Figure 7–33 The operation of a rotor-type oil pump.

positive displacement pumps; each rotation of the pump delivers the same volume of oil. This means that everything that enters must exit. The gear-type oil pump consists of two spur gears in a close-fitting housing. One gear is driven and the other idles. As the gear teeth come out of mesh, they tend to leave a space, which is filled by oil drawn through the pump inlet. When the pump is pumping, oil is carried around the *outside* of each gear in the space between the gear teeth and the housing, as shown in Figure 7–36. The rotor-type oil pump consists essentially of a special lobe-shaped gear meshing with the inside of a lobed rotor. The centre lobed section is driven and the outer section idles. As the lobes separate, oil is drawn in just as it is drawn into gear-type pumps. As the pump rotates, it carries oil around and between the lobes. As the lobes mesh, they force the oil out from between them into an oil

Figure 7–34 A typical oil pump mounted in the front cover of the engine that is driven by the crankshaft.

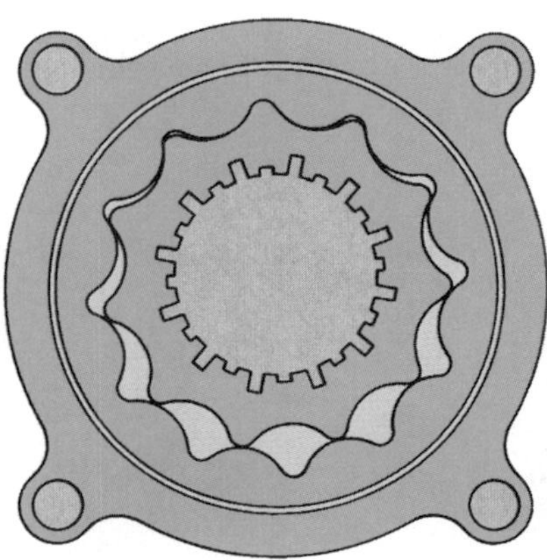

Figure 7–35 Geroter type oil pump driven by the crankshaft.

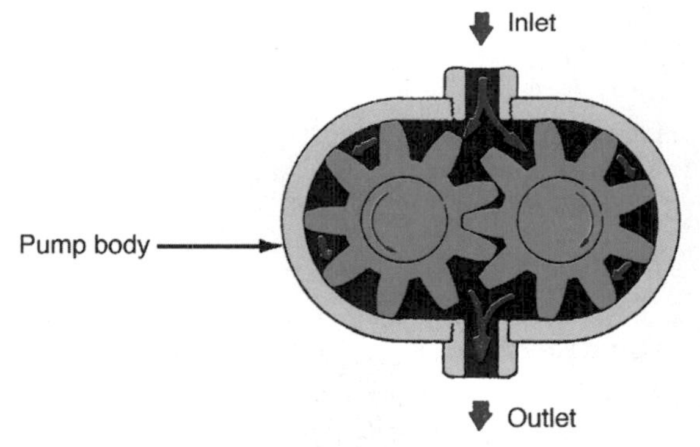
Inlet
Pump body
Outlet

Figure 7–36 In a gear-type oil pump, the oil flows through the pump around the outside of each gear. This is an example of a positive displacement pump, wherein everything entering the pump must leave the pump.

passage (gallery) and produce pressure in the same manner as the gear-type pump does. The pump is designed so that it will maintain a pressure of at least 70 kPa (10 psi) in the oil gallery when the engine is hot and idling. Pressure will increase by about 70 kPa (10 psi) for each 1000 rpm as the engine speed increases and the engine-driven pump rotates faster.

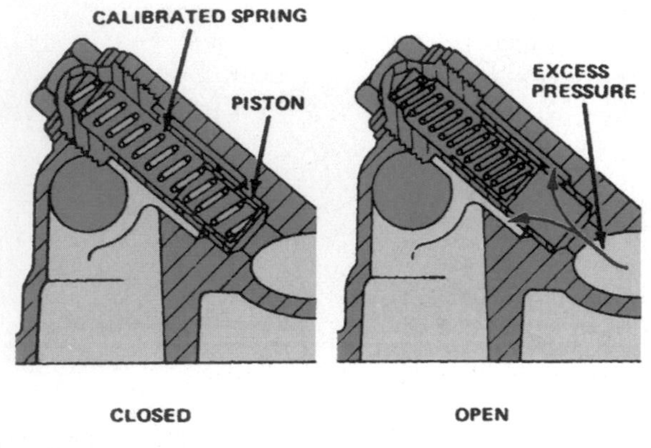

Figure 7–37 Oil pressure relief valves are spring loaded. The stronger the spring tension, the higher the oil pressure.

Oil Pressure Regulation

In engines with a full-pressure lubricating system, the maximum pressure is limited by a pressure relief valve. The **relief valve** (sometimes called the **pressure regulating valve**) is located at the outlet of the pump. The relief valve controls maximum pressure by bleeding off oil to the inlet side of the pump. See Figure 7–37. *The relief valve spring tension determines the maximum oil pressure.* If a pressure relief valve was not used, the engine oil pressure would continue to increase as the engine speed increased. Maximum pressure is usually limited to the lowest pressure that will deliver enough lubricating oil to all engine parts that need to be lubricated. *Lubrication of the engine requires 12 to 24 L (3 to 6 gal) per minute.* See Figure 7–38.

Oil Pump Checks

The cover must be removed to check the condition of the oil pump. Gears and housing should be examined for scoring. If the gears and housing are heavily scored, the entire pump should be replaced. If they are lightly scored, the clearances in the pump

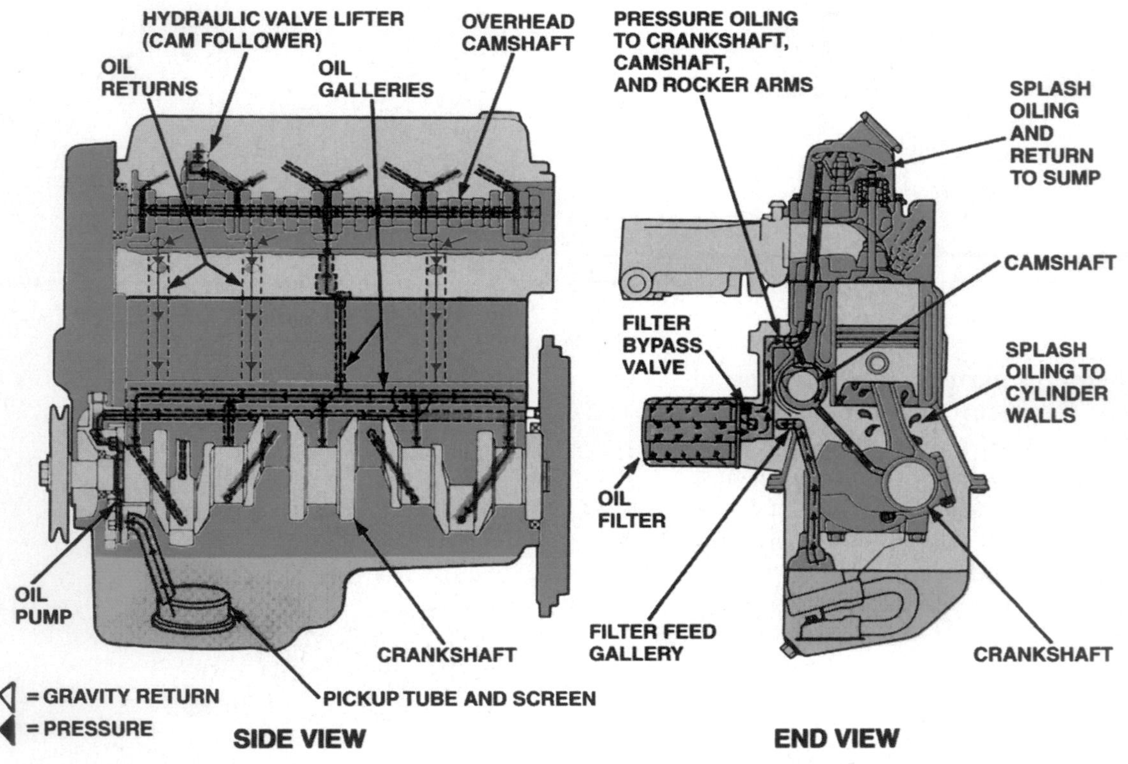

Figure 7–38 A typical engine design that uses both pressure and splash lubrication. Oil travels under pressure through the galleries (passages) to reach the top of the engine. Other parts are lubricated as the oil flows back down into the oil pan or is splashed onto parts.

should be measured. These clearances include the space between the gears and housing, the space between the teeth of the two gears, and the space between the side of the gear and the pump cover. A feeler gauge is usually used to make these measurements. Gauging plastic can be used to measure the space between the side of the gears and the cover. The oil pump should be replaced when excessive clearance or scoring is found. See Figure 7–39.

On most engines, the oil pump should be replaced as part of any engine work, especially if the cause for the repair is lack of lubrication.

> **NOTE:** The oil pump is the "garbage pit" of the entire engine. The oil pump is the only engine part lubricated with unfiltered oil and any and all debris is often forced through its gears and housing. The oil pump pickup filter screen should be cleaned whenever the oil pan is removed. See Figure 7–40.

Always refer to the manufacturer's specifications when checking the oil pump for wear. Typical oil pump clearances include the following:

1. End plate clearance: 0.04 mm (0.0015 in.)
2. Side (rotor) clearance: 0.30 mm (0.012 in.)
3. Rotor tip clearance: 0.25 mm (0.010 in.)
4. Gear end play clearance: 0.10 mm (0.004 in.)

All parts should also be inspected closely for wear. Check the relief valve for scoring and check the condition of the spring. When installing the oil pump, coat the sealing surfaces with engine assembly lubricant. This lubricant helps draw oil from the oil pan on initial start-up. The oil filter, usually made of pleated paper, is located directly after the oil pump: it filters all of the oil (full-flow) before it enters the engine.

Most oil filters have a built-in bypass valve, which will allow unfiltered oil to pass around the filter if the filter plugs. Certain high RPM and cold operating conditions will also allow unfiltered oil to flow into the engine.

Oil Passages in the Block

From the filter, oil goes through a drilled hole that intersects with a drilled main oil **gallery,** a long hole drilled from the front of the block to the back. Inline engines use one oil gallery. See Figure 7–41. V-type engines may use two or three galleries. One of the main galleries and two hydraulic valve lifter galleries are used on V-type engines. Passages drilled through the block bulkheads allow the oil to go from the main oil gallery to the main and cam bearings. In some engines, oil goes to the cam bearings first, and then to the main bearings. Whenever

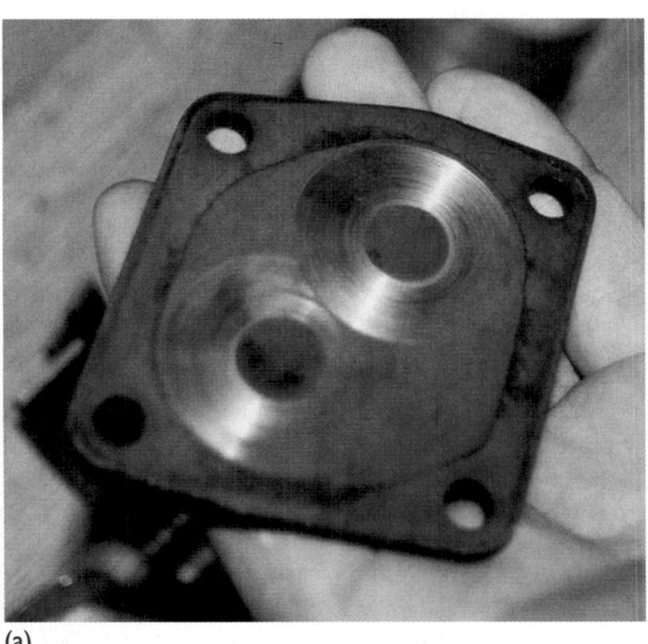

(a)

(b)

Figure 7–39 (a) A visual inspection indicated that this pump cover was worn. (b) An embedded particle of something was found on one of the gears, making this pump worthless except for scrap metal.

(a)

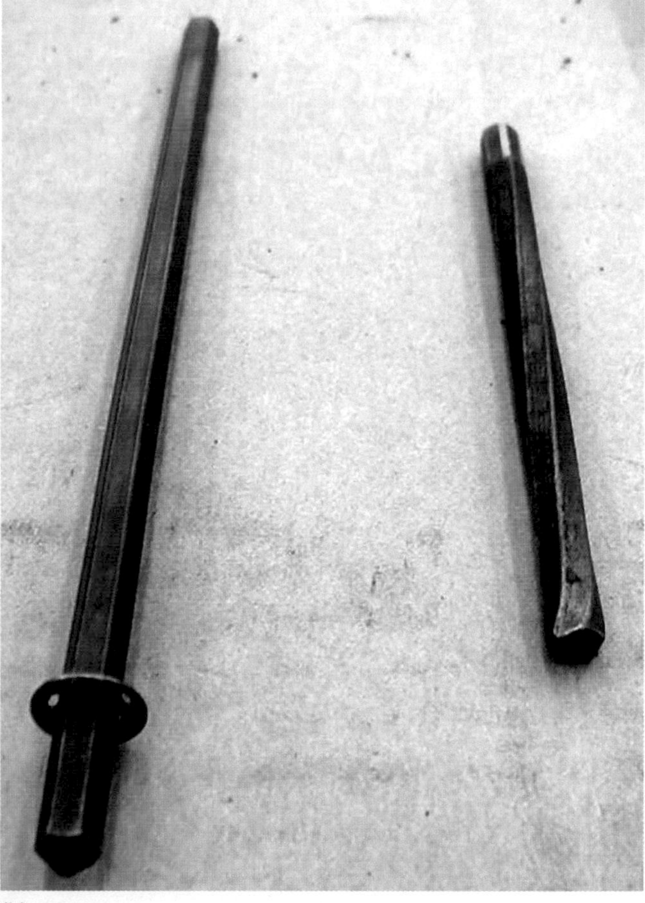
(b)

Figure 7–40 (a) The oil pump is the only part in an engine that gets unfiltered engine oil. The oil is drawn up from the bottom of the oil pan and is pressurized before flowing to the oil filter. (b) If debris gets into an oil pump, the drive or distributor shaft can twist and/or break. When this occurs, the engine will lose all oil pressure.

an engine has suffered extensive damage, the oil galleries must be cleaned with a long gallery brush. If this is not done, any contaminant left in the galleries will be carried to the new bearings.

Valve Train Lubrication

The oil gallery may intersect with or have drilled passages to the valve lifter bores to lubricate the lifters. When hydraulic lifters are used, the oil pressure in the gallery keeps refilling them. On some engines, oil from the lifters goes up the centre of a hollow pushrod to lubricate the pushrod ends, the rocker arm pivot, and the valve stem tip. See Figure 7–42. In other engines, an oil passage is drilled from the gallery or from a cam bearing to the block deck, where it matches with a gasket hole and a hole drilled in the head to carry the oil to a rocker arm shaft. Often, holes are drilled in cast rocker arms to carry oil to the pushrod end and to the valve tip. Rocker arm assemblies need only a surface coating of oil, so the oil flow to the rocker assembly is minimized by restrictions or metered openings. The restriction or metering disk is in the lifter when the rocker assembly is lubricated through the pushrod. Cam journal holes that line up with oil passages are often used to meter oil to the rocker shafts.

Oil that seeps from the rocker assemblies is returned to the oil pan through drain holes. These oil drain holes are often placed so that the oil drains on to the camshaft or cam drive gears to lubricate them.

Some engines are designed to direct a positive oil flow to the cam drive gears or chain. This may be a nozzle or a chamfer on a bearing parting surface that allows oil to spray on the loaded portion of the cam drive mechanism.

Oil Pans

As the vehicle accelerates, brakes, or is turned rapidly, the oil tends to move around in the oil pan. Baffles and overall design of the pan are often used to keep the oil inlet under the oil at all times. As the crankshaft rotates, it acts like a fan and causes air within the crankcase to rotate with it. This can cause a strong draft on the oil, churning it so that air bubbles enter the oil. This causes oil foaming. Oil with air will not lubricate like liquid oil, so oil foaming can cause bearings to fail. A baffle or **windage tray** is sometimes installed or built into the oil pan to eliminate the oil churning problem. See Figure 7–43. Windage trays have the positive side effect of reducing the amount of air disturbed by the crankshaft, so that less power is drained from the engine at high crankshaft speeds. Oil pans

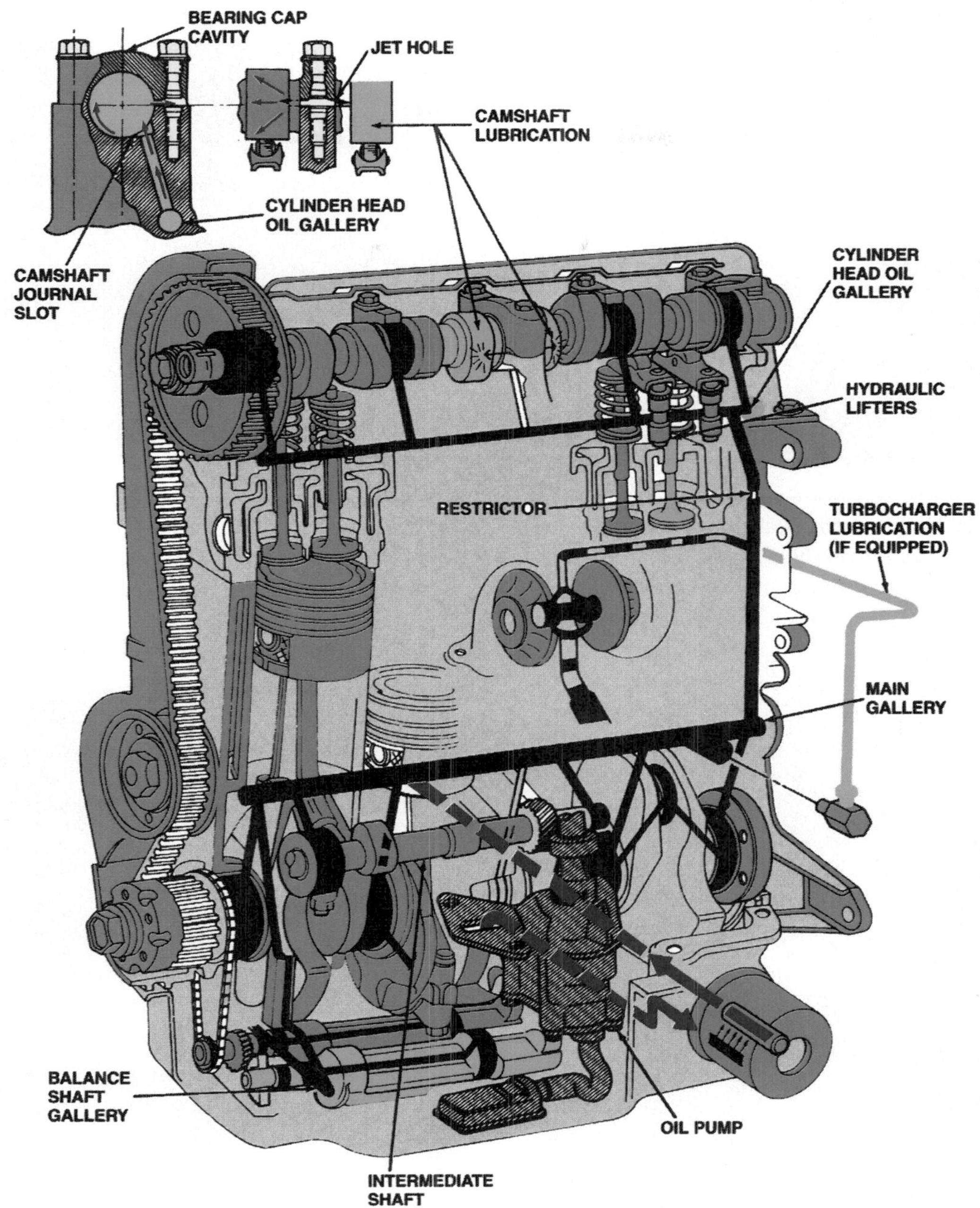

Figure 7–41 An intermediate shaft drives the oil pump on this overhead camshaft engine. Note the main gallery and other drilled passages in the block and cylinder head.

on many engines are part of the structure of the engine itself. See Figure 7–44.

Oil Coolers

Oil temperature must also be controlled on many high-performance or turbocharged engines. Figure 7–45 shows an engine oil cooler used on a production high-performance engine. A larger-capacity oil pan also helps to control oil temperature. Coolant flows through the oil cooler to help warm the oil when the engine is cold and cool the oil when the oil is hot. Oil temperature should be above 100°C (212°F) to boil off any accumulated moisture, but it should not exceed about 140° to 150°C (285° to 300°F). One of the advantages of synthetic oil is reduction of viscosity (thickness) changes compared to conventional oil. Synthetics do not thicken as much in cold climates or thin out as much under high temperatures. Synthetics are often a good choice when the vehicle operates in the extreme temperatures found in certain parts of Canada and the U.S.

Figure 7–42 Oil is sent to the rocker arms on this Chevrolet V-8 engine through the hollow pushrods. The oil returns to the oil pan through the oil drain back holes in the cylinder head.

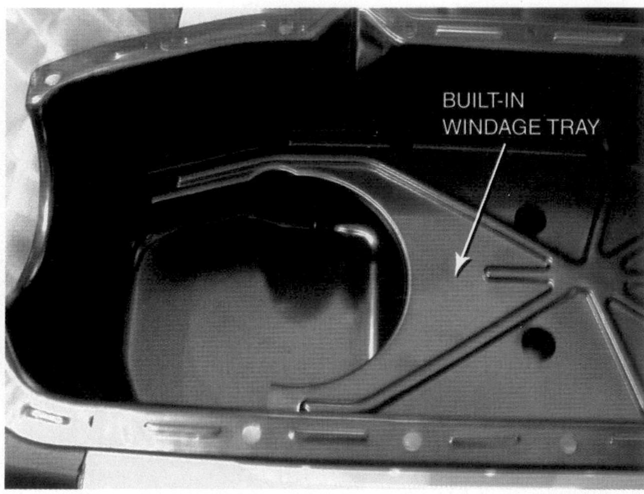

Figure 7–43 A typical oil pan with a built-in windage tray used to keep oil from being churned up by the rotating crankshaft.

Figure 7–44 A straightedge and a feeler gauge are being used to check that the oil pan has been correctly installed on this 5.7 L Chevrolet V-8 engine. The oil pan is part of the engine itself and must be properly installed to ensure that other parts attached to the engine are not being placed in a bind.

Figure 7–45 A typical engine oil cooler. Engine coolant flows through the cooler that fits between the engine block and the oil filter.

OIL PRESSURE WARNING LAMP

All vehicles are equipped with an oil pressure gauge or a warning lamp. The warning lamp comes on whenever the engine oil pressure has dropped to 20 to 50 kPa (3 to 7 psi). Normal oil pressure is considered to be 70 kPa (10 psi) per 1000 rpm. An electrical switch is used to convert the ground circuit of the oil pressure warning lamp if the oil pressure is below the rating of the sending unit. See Figures 7–46 and 7–47. Low oil pressure, especially at idle, is often caused by excessive main, rod, or cam bearing clearances. The oil pressure bleeds away through the larger openings.

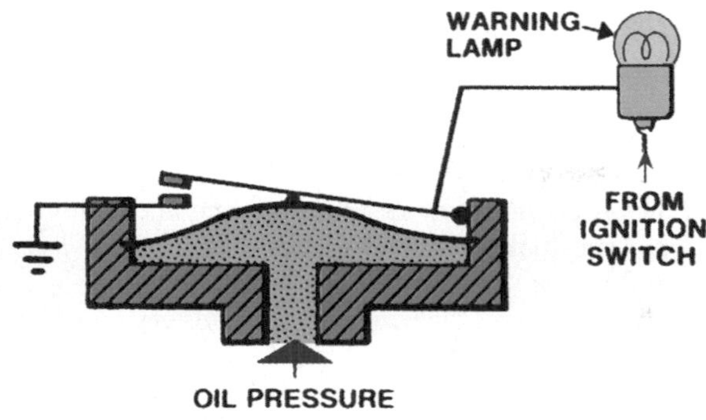

Figure 7–46 The oil pressure switch is connected to a warning lamp that alerts the driver to low oil pressure.

Figure 7–47 A typical oil pressure sending unit on a Ford V-8.

SUMMARY

1. The purpose and function of the cooling system is to maintain proper engine operating temperature.
2. The thermostat controls engine coolant temperature by opening at its rated opening temperature to allow coolant to flow through the radiator.
3. Used coolant should be recycled whenever possible.
4. Coolant fans are designed to draw air through the radiator to aid in the heat transfer process, drawing the heat from the coolant and transferring it to the outside air through the radiator.
5. The cooling system should be tested for leaks using a hand-operated pressure pump.
6. The freezing and boiling temperature of the coolant can be tested using a hydrometer.
7. Proper cooling system maintenance may call for replacing the antifreeze coolant every two years or every 36 000 km (24 000 miles).
8. Normal engine oil pump pressure ranges from 70 to 420 kPa (10 to 60 psi), or 70 kPa (10 psi) for every 1000 engine RPM.
9. The oil pump is driven directly by the crankshaft or by a gear or shaft from the camshaft.

REVIEW QUESTIONS

1. Explain why internal engine leakage affects oil pressure.
2. Describe how the oil flows from the oil pump through the filter and main engine bearings to the valve train.
3. Explain why the normal operating coolant temperature is about 95° to 105°C (200° to 220°F).
4. Explain the flow of coolant through the engine and radiator.
5. Why is a cooling system pressurized?
6. Explain the operation of a thermostatic cooling fan.
7. Describe how to diagnose a heater problem.

RED SEAL CERTIFICATION-TYPE QUESTIONS

1. Normal oil pump pressure in an engine is _____.
   a. 20 kPa (3 psi)
   b. 70 to 420 kPa (10 to 60 psi)
   c. 700 to 1050 kPa (100 to 150 psi)
   d. 1240 to 1450 kPa (180 to 210 psi)
2. A typical oil pump can pump how many litres (gallons) per minute?
   a. 12 to 24 (3 to 6)
   b. 24 to 40 (6 to 10)
   c. 40 to 240 (10 to 60)
   d. 200 to 400 (50 to 100)
3. In typical engine lubrication systems, what components are the last to receive oil and the first to suffer from a lack of oil or oil pressure?
   a. Main bearings
   b. Rod bearings
   c. Valve trains
   d. Oil filters
4. As the percentage of antifreeze in the coolant increases, _____.
   a. The freezing point decreases (up to a point)
   b. The boiling point decreases
   c. The heat transfer increases
   d. Antifreeze replacement is not required as often
5. Heat transfer is improved from the coolant to the air when
   a. The temperature difference is great
   b. The temperature difference is small
   c. The coolant is 95% antifreeze
   d. Ambient temperatures are very warm

6. Water pumps _____.
   a. Only work at idle and low speeds; the pump is disengaged at higher speeds
   b. Use engine oil as a lubricant and coolant
   c. Rotate at about the same speed as the engine
   d. Disengage during freezing weather to prevent radiator failure
7. The procedure that should be used when refilling an empty cooling system includes the following: _____.
   a. Determine capacity, then fill the cooling system halfway with antifreeze and the rest of the way with water
   b. Fill completely with antifreeze, but mix a 50/50 solution for the overflow bottle
   c. Fill the block and one-half of the radiator with 100% pure antifreeze and fill the rest of the radiator with water
   d. Fill the radiator with antifreeze, start the engine, drain the radiator, and refill with a 50/50 mixture of antifreeze and water
8. Which statement is true about thermostats?
   a. The temperature marked on the thermostat is the temperature at which the thermostat should be fully open.
   b. Thermostats often cause overheating.
   c. The temperature marked on the thermostat is the temperature at which the thermostat should start to open.
   d. A hotter thermostat should be installed in warmer climates.
9. Low oil pressure on an idling engine is causing noise from the hydraulic valve lifters. One of the reasons could be:
   a. Excessive clearance in the connecting rod or main bearings
   b. Too heavy an oil used for that particular temperature
   c. The idle speed is too fast
   d. The cooling system thermostat is sticking open
10. Which engine part is lubricated with unfiltered engine oil?
   a. Oil pump
   b. Rocker arms
   c. Main bearings
   d. Pistons

8

Cylinder Heads and Valves

OBJECTIVES: After studying Chapter 8, you should be able to:

1. Prepare for the interprovincial Red Seal certification examination in Appendix I (Engine Repair) on the topics covered in this chapter.
2. Identify combustion chamber types.
3. List the steps necessary to recondition a cylinder head.
4. Describe how to inspect and measure valve guides.
5. Discuss valve-guide repair options.
6. Discuss various engine-valve types and materials.
7. Describe how to test valve springs.
8. Explain the purpose, function, and operation of valve rotators.
9. List the steps necessary to reface a valve.
10. Describe how to grind valve seats.
11. Discuss how to measure and correct installed height and valve-stem height.

Cylinder heads are the most frequently serviced engine components. The highest temperatures and pressures in the entire engine are located in the combustion chamber. The valves in the cylinder head(s) must open and close thousands of times each time the engine is operated.

Combustion chambers of modern automotive overhead-valve engines are of two basic types: the nonturbulent hemispherical chamber and the turbulent wedge chamber.

THE HEMISPHERICAL COMBUSTION CHAMBER

In nonturbulent hemispherical combustion chambers, the charge is inducted through widely slanted valves. The charge is compressed and then ignited from a centrally located spark plug (Figure 8–1). The spark plug is as close as possible to all edges of the combustion chamber. Combustion radiates out from it, completely burning the fuel in the shortest possible time.

Hemispherical combustion chambers are usually fully machined to form the hemispherical shape. This is an expensive operation that increases the cost of the engine.

Figure 8–1 Hemispherical combustion chamber with a two-valve head.

THE WEDGE COMBUSTION CHAMBER

The wedge-shaped combustion chamber is designed to produce smooth, uniform burning by controlling the rate of combustion. A sectional view of a wedge-shaped combustion chamber is shown in Figure 8–2. In wedge-shaped combustion chambers, the charge is inducted through valves that are side by side. As the piston nears the top of the compression stroke, it moves to a position that is close to a low or flat portion of the head. The gases are squeezed between the piston and this head surface area, called a **squish** or **quench area.** The gases squeezed from the squish area produce turbulence within the charge. This is important, as variations in the air/fuel mix will cause a change in the burning rate. Slightly lean mixtures (more air) burn slower, slightly richer mixtures (more fuel) burn faster. The turbulence thoroughly mixes the air and fuel in the charge and a fast, but controlled, burn takes place. Lack of turbulence leads to pockets of lean or rich mixtures that can cause engine detonation and increased emissions. The spark plug is positioned so as to be in the highly turbulent part of the charge. Ignition is followed by smooth and rapid burning of the turbulent charge. The combustion flame front radiates out from the spark plug.

New designs use cast combustion chambers rather than expensive machined chambers. These chambers are called by such names as **polyspherical, hemi-wedge, kidney-shaped,** and **pentroof.** All cylinder head designs try to place the spark plug in an ideal location for best combustion as shown in Figure 8–3.

Figure 8–2 Cutaway of a Chevrolet V-8 cylinder head showing a wedge-shaped combustion chamber.

MULTIPLE-VALVE COMBUSTION CHAMBER

The power that any engine produces is directly related to the amount of air–fuel mixture that is ignited in the cylinder. Increasing cylinder displacement is a common method of increasing engine power. Turbocharging and supercharging also increase engine power, but these increase engine cost as well.

Adding more than two valves per cylinder permits more gas to flow into and out of the engine with greater velocity without excessive valve duration. The maximum amount of gas moving through the opening area of a valve depends on the distance around the valve and the degree to which it lifts open.

More total area under the valve is possible when two smaller valves are used rather than one larger valve at the same valve lift. The smaller valves allow smooth low-speed operation (because of the increased velocity of the mixture as it enters the cylinder as a result of smaller intake ports). Good high-speed performance with smaller valves is also possible because

Figure 8–3 A General Motors Quad-4 engine with a combustion chamber shape called a modified pentroof. Note the central location of the spark plug.

DISTANCE AROUND
36.5 MM (1 7/16") INTAKE
VALVE = 115 MM (4.52")

DISTANCE AROUND
30 MM (1 3/16") EXHAUST
VALVE = 95 MM (3.73")

DISTANCE AROUND
32 MM (1 1/4") EXHAUST
VALVE = 99 MM (3.927")

DISTANCE AROUND
EACH 29 MM (1 1/8") INTAKE
VALVES = 90 MM (3.54")

TOTAL DISTANCE
AROUND BOTH
VALVES = 180 MM (7.08")

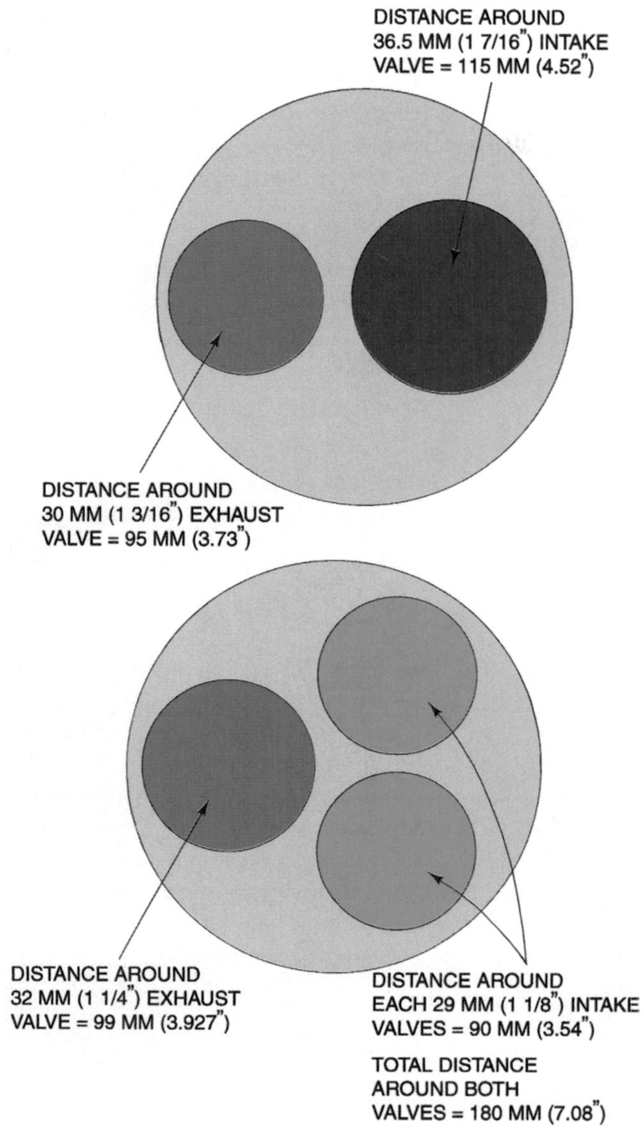

Figure 8–4 Comparing the valve opening areas between two- and three-valve combustion chambers when the valves are open.

of the increased valve area and lighter-weight valves. See Figures 8–4 and 8–5.

Engine valves shed their heat through the valve guide and valve seat. The total valve seat area of two small valves is greater than that of one single valve and the valves run cooler.

INTAKE AND EXHAUST PORTS

The part of the intake or exhaust system passage that is cast in the cylinder head is called a **port.** Ports lead from the manifolds to the valves. Engines that have the intake port on one side of the head and the exhaust port on the opposite side are said to have a **cross-flow** head design. The cross-flow head shown in Figure 8–6 allows the valve to be located

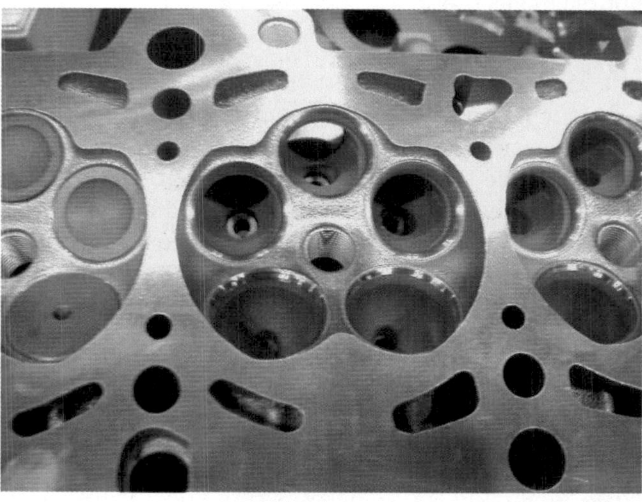

Figure 8–5 Audi five-valve cylinder head. This design uses three intake valves (top) and two exhaust valves (bottom).

Figure 8–6 A typical two-valve cross flow cylinder head. The intake is on the top and the exhaust is on the bottom.

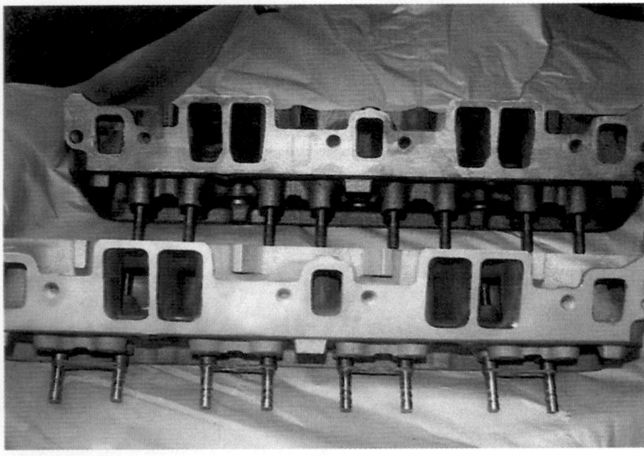

Figure 8–7 The top cylinder head is stock and the bottom cylinder head has been ported.

and angled so as to permit the most efficient engine breathing. It also allows the spark plug to be placed near the centre of the combustion chamber. All V-type engines have the cross-flow head design.

Designing a cylinder head that produces power at both high and low RPM is very often a compromise. In general, small ports increase the speed of the incoming charge, which enhances cylinder filling at low RPM. The engine feels very crisp and responsive. As the RPM increases, the smaller ports restrict the amount of air that is required and high RPM power suffers.

On the other hand, if large ports are used, low-end power is reduced because the incoming charge slows down and the velocity or ram effect is lost. Top-end power is increased as there is little restriction to the amount of air entering the cylinder.

The flow of gases is often different than one might expect. At times, a restricting hump within a port may actually increase the airflow capacity of the port. It does this by redirecting the flow to an area of the port that is large enough to handle the flow. Modifications in the field, such as **porting,** may result in restricting the flow of such a carefully designed port. See Figures 8–7 and 8–8.

The intake port in the head is relatively long, whereas the exhaust port is short. The long intake port wall is heated by coolant flowing through the head. The heat aids in vaporizing the fuel in the intake charge. The exhaust port is short so that the least amount of exhaust heat is transferred to the engine coolant.

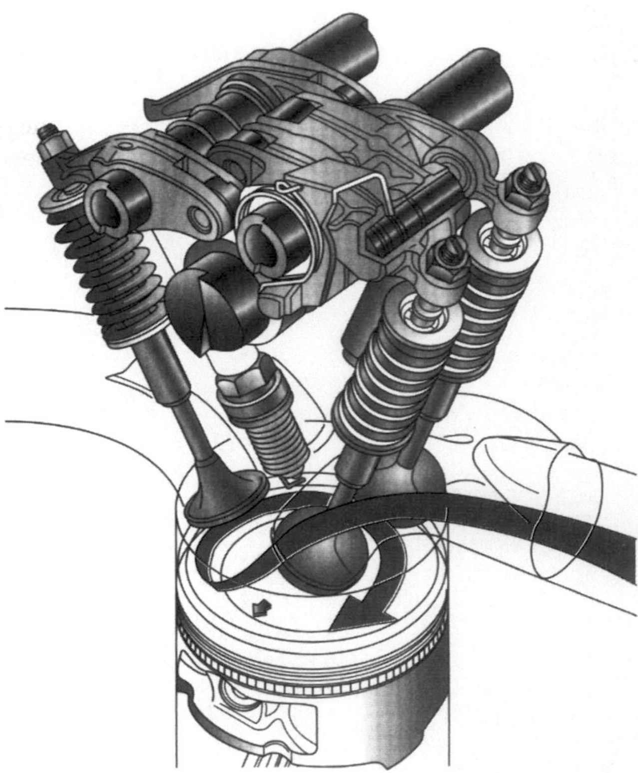

Figure 8–8 The intake manifold design and combustion chamber design work together to cause the air–fuel mixture to swirl as it enters the combustion chamber.

Figure 8–9 A high-performance racing engine that uses a rocker arm shaft. When disassembling this style of engine, it is important to loosen the rocker arm shaft bearing caps a little at a time along the entire length of the shaft to prevent binding.

REMOVING THE OVERHEAD CAMSHAFT

The overhead camshaft will have either one-piece bearings in a solid bearing support or split bearings and a bearing cap. When one-piece bearings are used, the valve springs will have to be compressed with a fixture or the finger follower will have to be removed before the camshaft can be pulled out endwise. When bearing caps are used, they should be loosened alternately so that bending loads are not placed on either the cam or bearing caps (Figure 8–9).

CYLINDER HEAD RECONDITIONING SEQUENCE

Although not all cylinder heads require all service operations, cylinder heads should be reconditioned using the following sequence:

1. Disassemble and thoroughly clean the heads. (See Chapter 6.)
2. Check for cracks and repair as necessary. (See Chapter 6.)
3. Check the surface that contacts the engine block and machine if necessary.
4. Check valve guides and replace or service as necessary.
5. Grind or machine valve seats; replace seats if required.
6. Grind valves and reinstall the valves in the cylinder head with new valve-stem seals.
7. Check valve spring force and installed height.

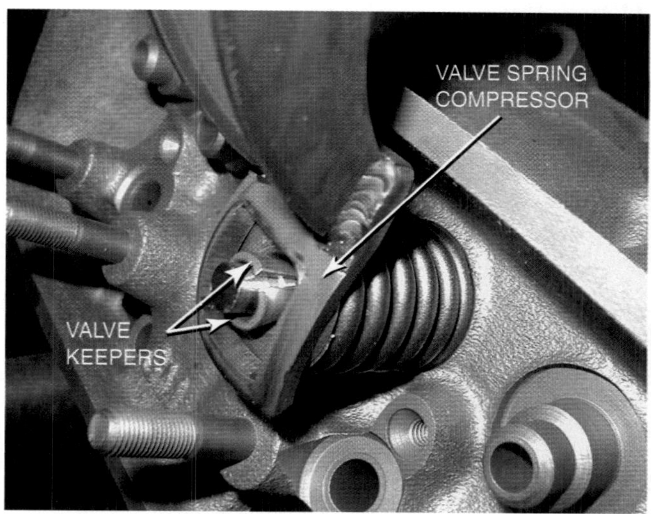

Figure 8–10 A valve spring compressor is used to compress the valve spring before removing the keepers (locks).

SAFETY TIP

Boing!

When disassembling or reassembling a cylinder head, always wear safety glasses. Valve springs, when compressed, represent stored energy. Valve keepers can be sent flying through the air by the force of an expanding valve spring, which could put out an eye or cause other physical harm.

Disassembling the Cylinder Head

The engine should be cool (room temperature) before the cylinder heads are removed. As mentioned in Chapter 6, the head bolts should be loosened in the reverse of the order used for tightening to avoid the possibility of warping. In other words, the head bolts should be loosened from the outside and you should work your way toward the centre of the head. Remove the valves from the cylinder head as illustrated in Figure 8–10. Any "mushrooming" at the valve tip should be removed with a fine file before pulling the valve through the guide: this prevents guide damage.

CAUTION: All valve train components that are to be reused must be kept together. As wear occurs, parts become worn together. Pushrods can be labelled and kept in order if stuck through a cardboard box as shown in Figure 8–11. Be sure to keep the top part of the push rod at the top. Intake and exhaust valve springs may be different and must be kept with the correct valve.

Figure 8–11 Sticking pushrods through a cardboard box is a method used to keep the valve train parts in proper order.

The surface of the head must be thoroughly cleaned and inspected as follows:

- The surface is first scraped and then draw-filed to remove any small burrs.
- The head should be checked in five planes as shown in Figures 8–12 and 8–13 for **warpage, distortion, bend,** and **twist.**

Trying to slide a 0.10-mm (0.004-in.) feeler gauge under a straightedge held against the head surface will reveal these defects.

The head should not vary by over 0.05 mm (0.002 in.) in any 150 mm (6 in.) length, or by more than 0.010 mm (0.004 in.) overall. Always check the manufacturer's recommended specifications.

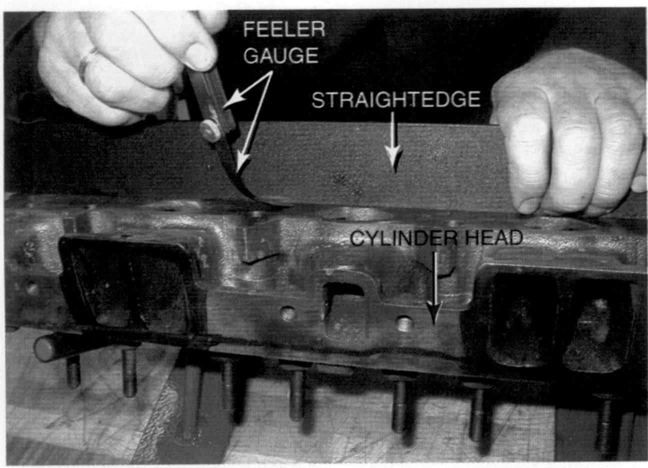

Figure 8–12 A precision ground straightedge and a feeler gauge are used to check the cylinder head for flatness.

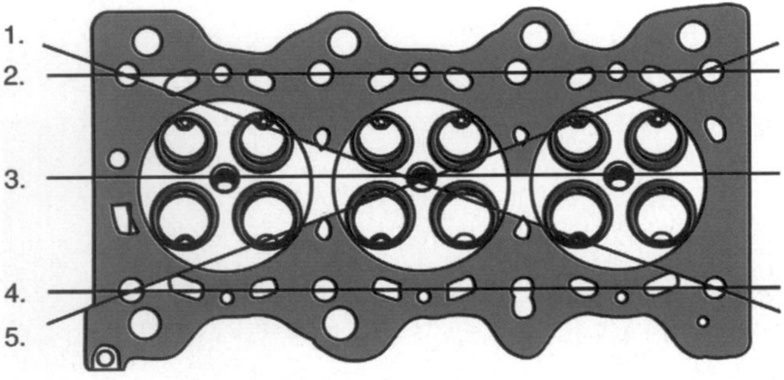

Figure 8–13 Cylinder heads should be checked in five planes for warpage, distortion, bend, or twist.

Cylinder Head Resurfacing

The head should be resurfaced if there is any roughness caused by corrosion of the head gasket. This roughness can be felt on the head surface when you rub your fingernail across it. In precision engine rebuilding, *both* the head and the block deck are resurfaced as a standard practice. See Figure 8–14. On "V" type engines, the intake manifold surface of the cylinder head should also be resurfaced if the head is machined more than 0.025 mm (0.010 in.).

> **NOTE:** Always check the cylinder head thickness and specifications to be sure that material can be safely removed from the surface. Some manufacturers do not recommend *any* machining, but rather require cylinder head replacement if cylinder head surface flatness is not within specifications.

The head will usually have some warpage when the engine is disassembled. Aluminum heads, especially if the engine has overheated, warp more often than cast-iron ones. Because of the length of inline 6-cylinder heads, they are more susceptible to warping than shorter V-6 heads.

Figure 8–14 A cylinder head being resurfaced.

> **NOTE:** Aluminum cylinder heads are usually straightened before being resurfaced.

> **NOTE:** Valve timing is usually altered on overhead camshaft engines when the cylinder head is resurfaced: timing retards about 1° for each 0.50 millimetre (0.020 inch) of material removed.

Surface Finish

The surface finish of a reconditioned part is as important as the size of the part. Surface finish is measured in units called *micrometres* (abbreviated μm) or *microinches* (abbreviated μin.). One μm is one-millionth of a metre (0.000 001 m) and 1 μin. is one millionth of an inch (0.000 001 in.): 0.025 μm equals 1.0 μin.

The finish classification in micrometres, or microinches, gives the distance between the highest peak and the deepest valley. The usual method of expressing surface finish is by the **arithmetic average roughness height,** abbreviated **RA,** which is the average of the distances of all peaks and valleys from the mean (average) line. See Figure 8-15. The majority of RA specifications are still given in microinches, rather than micrometres.

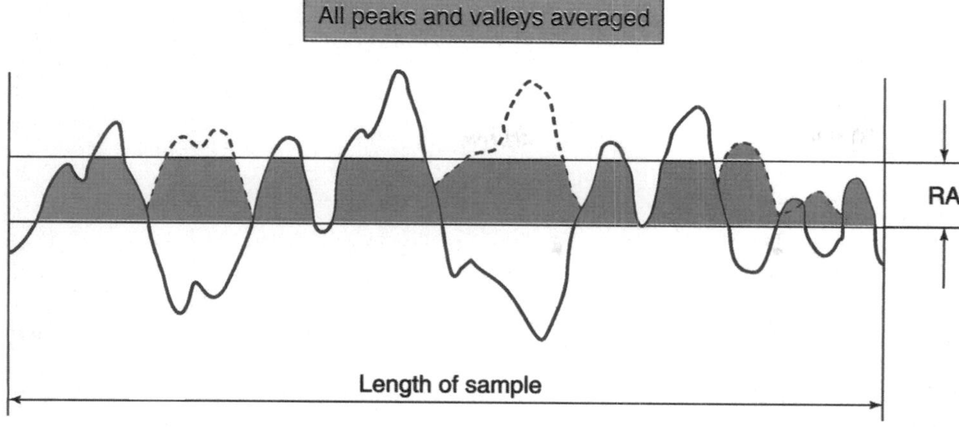

Figure 8–15 A graph showing a typical rough surface as would be viewed through a magnifying glass. RA is an abbreviation indicating the average height of all peaks and valleys.

Typical surface finish roughness recommendations for cast-iron and aluminum cylinder heads and blocks include the following:

- **Cast Iron.** Recommended range: 60 to 100 RA
- **Aluminum.** Recommended range: 50 to 60 RA

The rougher the surface is, the higher the microinch finish measurement will be.

VALVE GUIDES

The valve guide supports the valve stem so that the valve face will remain perfectly centred or **concentric** with the valve seat. The valve guide in cast-iron heads is generally **integral** with the head casting for better heat transfer and for lower manufacturing costs. See Figure 8–16. **Valve guide inserts** are always used where the valve stem and head materials are not compatible. See Figure 8–17.

A valve guide must be reconditioned to match the valve that is to be used with it.

Engine manufacturers usually recommend the following valve stem-to-valve guide clearances.

Intake valve: 0.025 to 0.075 mm (0.001 to 0.003 in.)
Exhaust valve: 0.05 to 0.10 mm (0.002 to 0.004 in.)

Be sure to check the exact specifications for the engine being serviced. The exhaust valve clearance is greater than the intake valve clearance because the exhaust valve runs hotter and therefore expands more than the intake valve. Some aftermarket manufacturers taper the valve stem on exhaust valves, about 0.025 mm (0.001 in.) smaller near the head, to compensate for expansion.

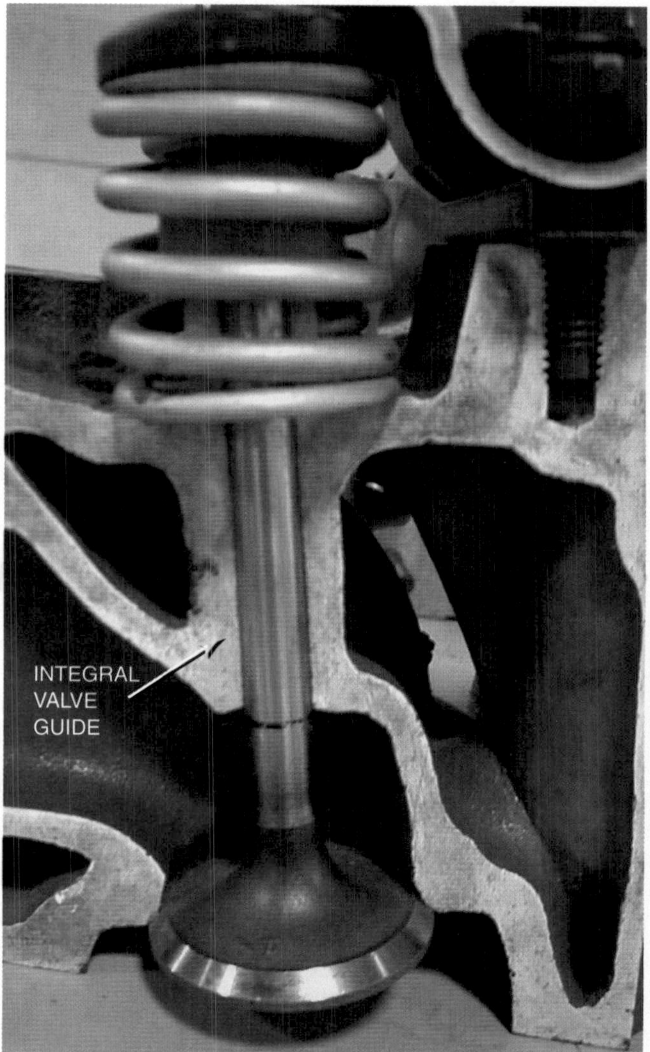

Figure 8–16 An integral valve guide is simply a guide that has been drilled into the cast iron cylinder head.

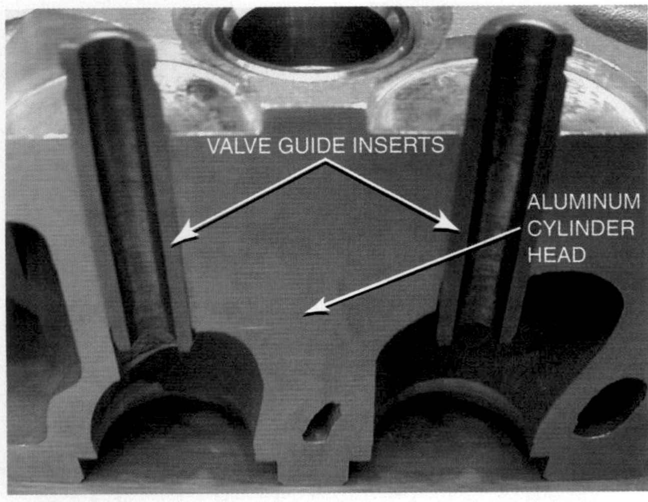

Figure 8–17 All aluminum cylinder heads use valve guide inserts.

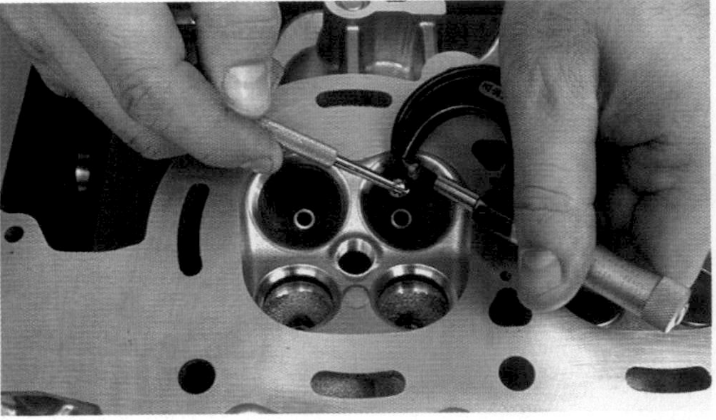

Figure 8–18 A small hole gauge and a micrometer are being used to measure the valve guide. The guide should be measured in three places: at the top, middle, and bottom.

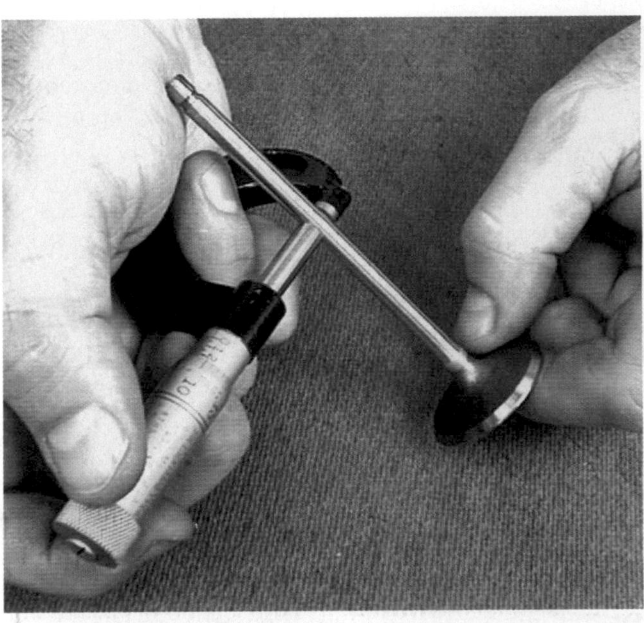

Figure 8–19 The diameter of the valve stem is being measured using a micrometer. The difference between the inside diameter of the valve guide and the diameter of the valve stem is the valve guide-to-valve stem clearance.

Excessive valve stem-to-valve guide clearance can cause excessive oil consumption. The intake valve guide is exposed to manifold vacuum that can draw oil from the top of the cylinder head down into the combustion chamber. The exhaust valve guide is subject to vacuum as well, caused by the exiting exhaust gases. Worn guides or seals will lead to a smoking exhaust and increased oil consumption.

> **HINT:** A human hair is about 0.05 mm (0.002 in.) in diameter. Therefore, the typical clearance between a valve stem and the valve guide is only the thickness of a human hair.

Measuring Valve Guides for Wear

Valves should be measured for stem wear before valve guides are measured. The valve guide is measured in three places with a small hole gauge. The gauge size is then checked with a micrometer. The dimension of the valve stem diameter is subtracted from the dimension of the valve guide diameter. If the clearance between the stem and the guide exceeds the specified clearance, the valve guide will have to be reconditioned. See Figures 8–18 and 8–19.

Valve stem-to-valve guide clearance can also be checked using a dial indicator (gauge) to measure how much the valve moves when it is lifted off the valve seat. See Figure 8–20. The dial indicator should be positioned across the head when checking clearance. Rocker arm action usually causes guide wear in line with the rocker because of side thrust. Overhead camshaft engines that do not use rockers may be checked in any direction. Larger engine shops often use a special guide tool that is quick and accurate. A long mandrel, with built-in dial indicator, is adjusted to the size of the valve stem; inserting the mandrel into the valve guide gives the exact valve-to-guide clearance.

Valve guides must be checked for wear and reconditioned, if needed, before the valve seats are refinished: this ensures that the valve seat is concentric with the valve guide.

Oversize Stem Valves

Most domestic automobile manufacturers recommend reaming worn valve guides and installing new valves with **oversize** stems in engines that have in-

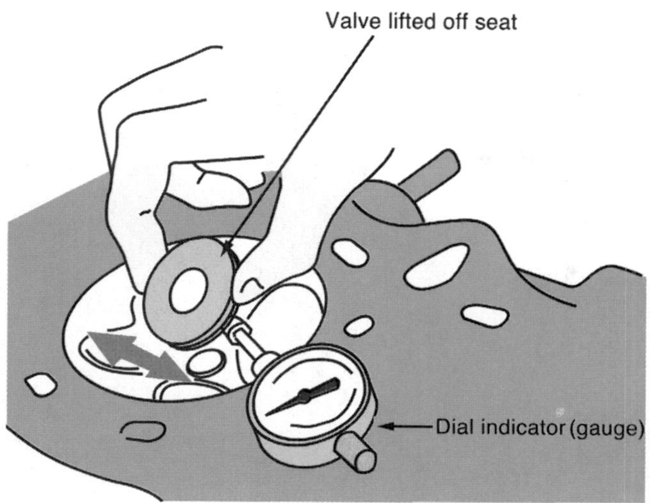

Figure 8–20 Measuring valve guide-to-stem clearance with a dial indicator while rocking the stem in the direction of normal thrust. The reading on the dial indicator should be compared to specifications because it does not give the guide-to-stem clearance directly. The valve is usually limited to its maximum operating lift.

tegral valve guides. When a valve guide is worn, the valve stem is also likely to be worn. In this case, new valves are required. New valves can just as well have oversize stems as standard stems. Typically, available sizes include 0.08, 0.13, 0.20, 0.38, and 0.75 mm (0.003, 0.005, 0.008, 0.015, and 0.030 in.) oversize (often abbreviated **OS**). The valve guide is reamed or honed to the correct size to fit the oversize stem of the new valve.

> **NOTE:** Many remanufacturers of cylinder heads use oversize valve stems to simplify production.

Valve Guide Knurling

In the process known as valve guide knurling, a tool is rotated as it is driven into the guide. The tool **displaces** the metal to reduce the hole diameter of the guide. Knurling is ideally suited to engines with integral valve guides (guides that are part of the cylinder head and are nonremovable). It is recommended that knurling not be used to correct wear exceeding 0.15 mm (0.006 in.). In the displacing process, the knurling tool pushes a small tapered wheel or dull threading tool into the wall of the guide hole. This makes a groove in the wall of the guide without removing any metal, as pictured in Figure 8–21. Knurling is normally used on engines that are being repaired, e.g., a valve grind or a re-ring. Major engine rebuilds use oversize valves, new valve guides, or guide inserts.

Figure 8–21 Sectional view of a knurled valve guide.

VALVE GUIDE REPLACEMENT

When an engine is designed with replaceable valve guides, their replacement is often recommended when the valve assembly is being reconditioned. The original valve guide height should be measured before the guide is removed so that the new guide can be properly positioned.

Replacement valve guides can also be installed to repair worn integral guides. Both **cast-iron** and **bronze** guides are available. See Figure 8–22.

Valve Guide Inserts

A badly worn integral valve guide can be reconditioned using an insert. Two types of guide inserts are commonly used for guide repair: a thin-walled bronze alloy sleeve bushing or a spiral bronze alloy bushing. The thin-walled bronze sleeve bushings are also called **bronze guide liners.** The valve guide rebuilding kit used to install each of these bushings includes all of the reamers, installing sleeves, broaches, burnishing tools, and cutoff tools that are

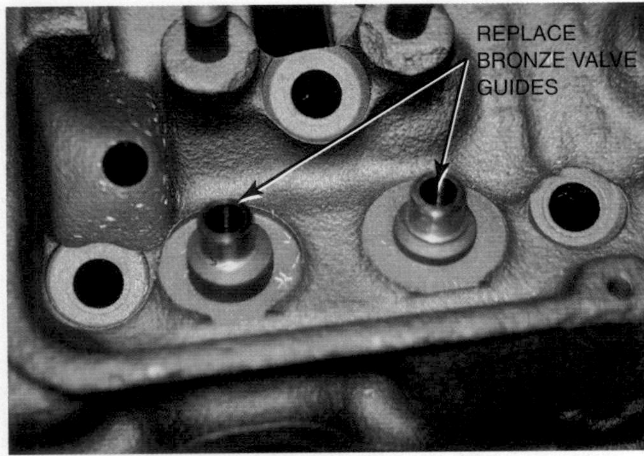

Figure 8–22 This cylinder head has been restored to service by replacing original valve guides with bronze valve guides.

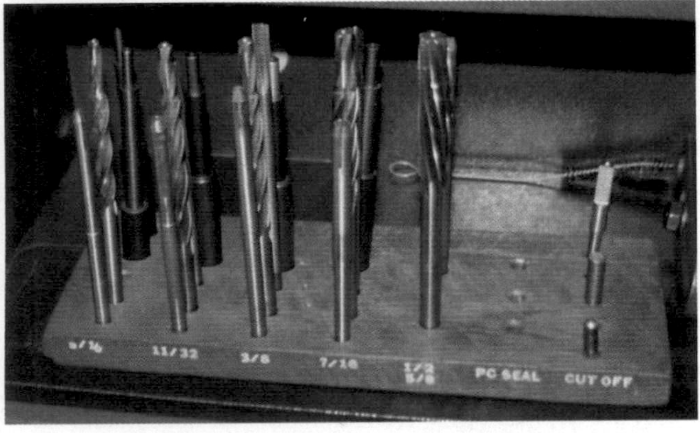

Figure 8–23 A typical assortment of valve guide reamers as found in an engine rebuilding shop.

needed to install and properly size the bushings. See Figure 8–23. Valve guide inserts are a very common method of reconditioning integral valve guides.

INTAKE AND EXHAUST VALVES

Valves need to be reconditioned more often than any other engine part. Automotive engine valves are of a **poppet valve** design. The valve is opened by means of a valve train that is operated by a cam. The cam is timed to the piston position and crankshaft cycle. The valve is closed by one or more springs.

The valve guide is centred over the **valve seat** so that the **valve face** and seat make a gas-tight fit. The face and seat will have an angle of 30° or 45°. Actual service angles might be a degree or two different from these. Most engines use a nominal 45° valve

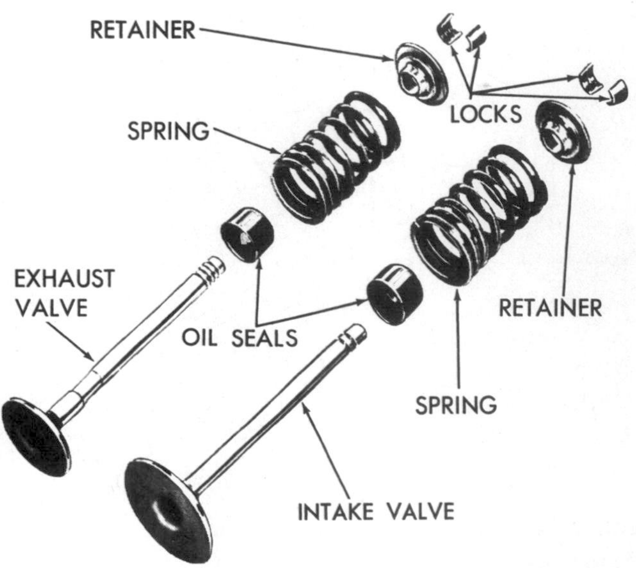

Figure 8–24 Identification and relationship of valve components. Note the different valve locks (keepers) used on the exhaust valve as compared to the intake valve. The multi-groove exhaust keepers allow the valve to rotate. The oil seals shown are also called umbrella-type valve stem seals. (Courtesy of Chrysler Corporation)

and seat angle. A typical valve assembly is shown in Figure 8–24.

Valve Materials

Alloys used in exhaust valve materials are largely of chromium for oxidation resistance, with small amounts of nickel, manganese, and nitrogen added. Many vehicle manufacturers use valves that have chrome-plated stems. Because chrome provides a hard, smooth surface, this design feature helps prevent valve scuffing and galling, especially when the engine is first started. In severe applications, facing alloys such as stellite are welded to the valve face and valve tip. **Stellite** is an alloy of nickel, chromium, and tungsten and is nonmagnetic. Some heavy-duty applications use hollow stem exhaust valves that are partially filled with metallic sodium. An unfilled hollow valve stem is shown in Figure 8–25. The sodium in the valve becomes a liquid at operating temperatures. As it splashes back and forth in the valve stem, the sodium transfers heat from the valve head to the valve stem. The heat goes through the valve guide into the coolant.

HINT: Combustion chamber temperatures in gaseous fuel engines (propane or natural gas) are higher than in gasoline powered engines. For this reason, only premium quality exhaust valves and seats must be used.

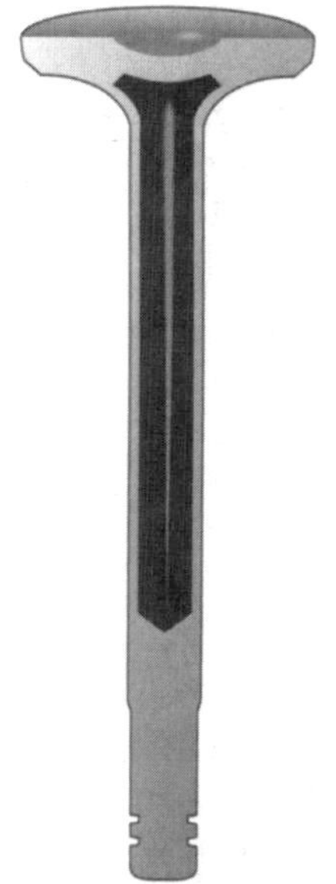

Figure 8–25 Hollow valve stem.

Figure 8–26 A valve assembly after being removed from the cylinder head. Note how the technician tried to keep the valve spring, retainer, and locks (keepers) together as a set. The typical valve spring is commonly called a **beehive** spring.

> **HINT:** Tetraethyl lead, previously used as a gasoline additive, had a lubricating quality that reduced valve face and seat wear. This was lost with the introduction of no-lead fuels. When valve service is required, older engines that were designed for leaded gasoline should have their valves and seats upgraded to match current fuels.

Valve Springs

A valve spring holds the valve tightly against the seat when the valve is closed. One end of the valve spring is seated against the head. The other end of the spring is attached under compression to the valve stem through a **valve spring retainer** and a **valve spring lock (keeper),** as shown in Figure 8–26.

Variable-rate springs add spring force when the valve is in its open position by using closely spaced coils on the cylinder head end of the spring. The closely spaced coils also tend to dampen vibrations that may be created by an equally wound coil spring. Some valve springs use a flat coiled damper inside the spring. This eliminates spring surge and adds some valve spring tension. The damper also helps to reduce valve seat wear.

Multiple valve springs are used where large lifts are required and a single spring does not have enough strength to control the valve. Multiple valve springs generally have their coils wound in opposite directions.

Valve Spring Inspection

Valve springs close the valves after they have been opened by the cam. Valve springs must close the valve squarely to form a tight seal. The valve springs are checked for squareness by rotating them on a flat surface with a square held against the side. They should be within 1.6 mm or 1/16 in. of being square. This is shown in Figure 8–27. A valve spring scale is used to measure the valve spring force. One popular type of scale, shown in Figure 8–28, measures the spring force directly. Valve springs are checked for the following:

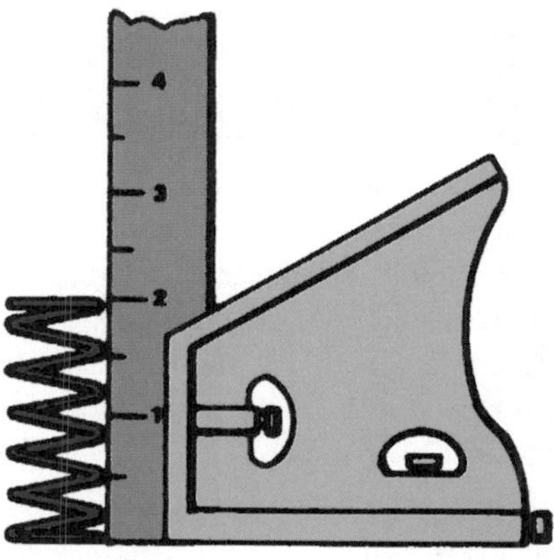

Figure 8–27 All valve springs should be checked for squareness by using a square on a flat surface. The spring should be replaced if more than 1.6 mm (1/16 in.) is measured between the top of the spring and the square.

1. Free height (without being compressed) should be within 1.6 mm (0.060 in.)

2. Force with valve closed and height as per specifications (with damper spring removed)
3. Force with valve open and height as per specifications (with damper spring removed)

Figure 8–28 One popular type of valve spring tester used to measure the compressed force of valve springs. Specifications usually include (1) free height (height without being compressed), (2) pressure at installed height with the valve closed, and (3) pressure with the valve open to the height specified.

Most specifications allow for variations of plus or minus 10% from the published figures.

Many engine builders recommend replacing the valve springs if the engine has suffered a blown head gasket and coolant has mixed with the oil. The water in the coolant may cause hairline cracks on the springs.

Valve Rotators

Some retainers have built-in devices called **valve rotators.** They cause the valve to rotate in a controlled manner as it is opened. The purposes and functions of valve rotators include the following:

- Preventing carbon build-up from forming
- Reducing hot spots on the valves by constantly turning them
- Evening out the wear on the valve face and seat
- Improving valve guide lubrication

There are two types of valve rotators: free and positive.

Free Rotators The free rotators simply take the pressure off the valve to allow engine vibration to rotate the valve.

Positive Rotators The opening of the valve forces the valve to rotate. See Figure 8–29.

> **NOTE:** Some engines have the rockers offset slightly where they contact the valve tip. This causes the valve to rotate as it is being lifted.

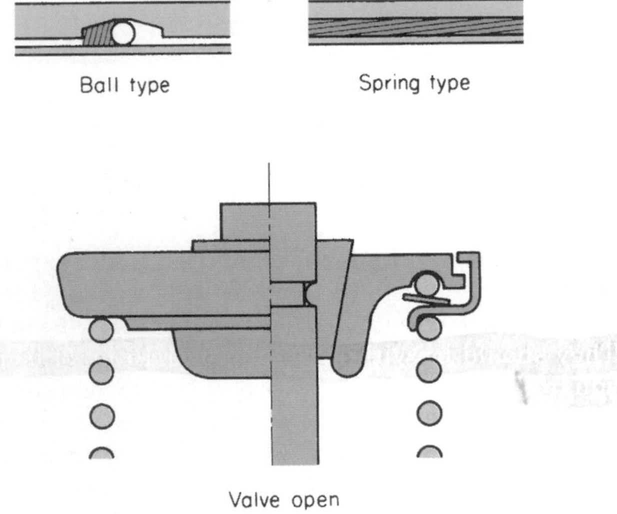

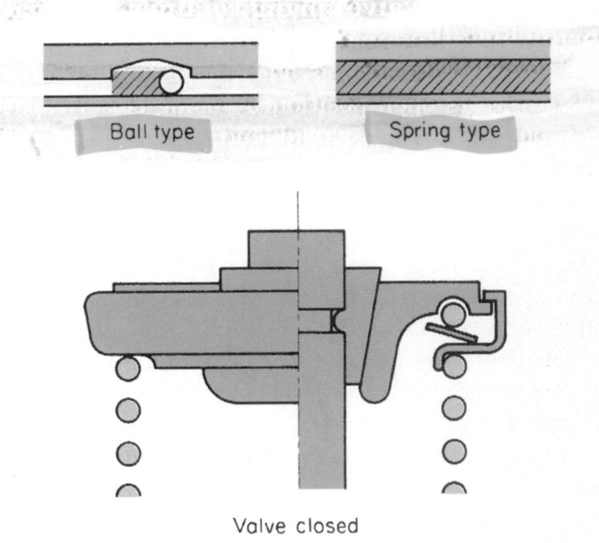

Figure 8–29 Types of valve rotator operation. Ball-type operation is on the left and spring-type operation is on the right.

VALVE RECONDITIONING PROCEDURE

Valve reconditioning is usually performed using the following sequence:

- The tip of the valve stem is lightly ground and chamfered. This step helps to ensure that the valve will rest in the **collet** (holder of the valve stem during valve grinding) of the valve grinder correctly. This process is often called **truing the valve tip.**
- The face of the valve is ground using a valve grinder. See Figure 8–30.
- The valve seat is ground or machined in the head (the seat must be matched to the valve that will be used in that position). See Figures 8–31 through 8–34.
- Many manufacturers recommend that the angle ground on the valve seat and valve face be 1° different to provide a wedging force that results in a better initial seal. This 1° difference is called the **interference angle.** The lower angle, i.e. 44°, is always on the valve.

> **NOTE:** Some experts recommend using lapping compound on the valve seat and valve face and rotating the valve to improve the valve seating. See Figure 8–35.

Figure 8–30 Resurfacing the face of a valve. Both the valve and the grinder stone are turned to ensure a smooth surface finish on the face of the valve.

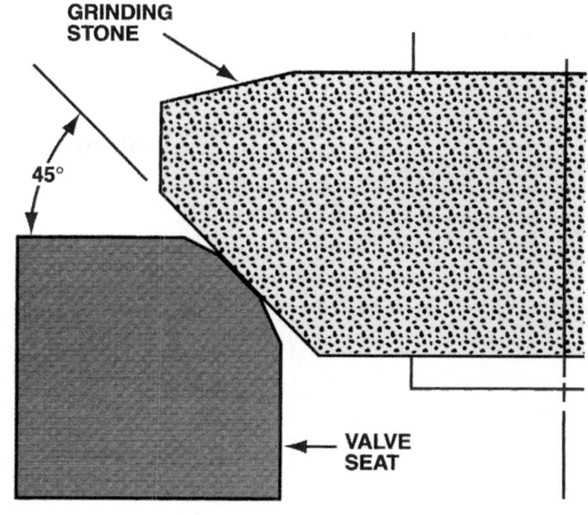

Figure 8–31 Grinding a 45° angle establishes the valve seat in the combustion chamber.

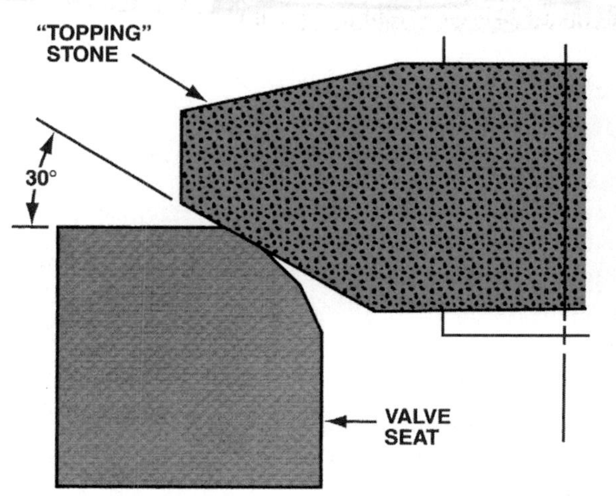

Figure 8–32 Grinding a 30° angle removes metal from the top to lower and narrow the seat.

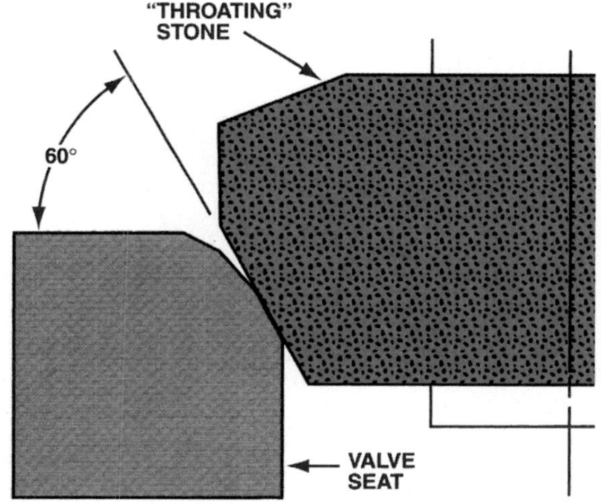

Figure 8–33 Grinding a 60° angle removes metal from the bottom to raise and narrow the seat.

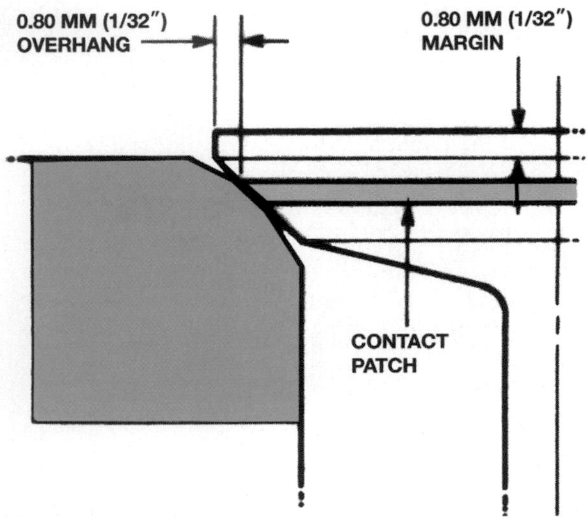

Figure 8–34 The seat must contact evenly around the valve face. For good service life, both margin and overhang should be at least 0.8 mm (1/32 in.).

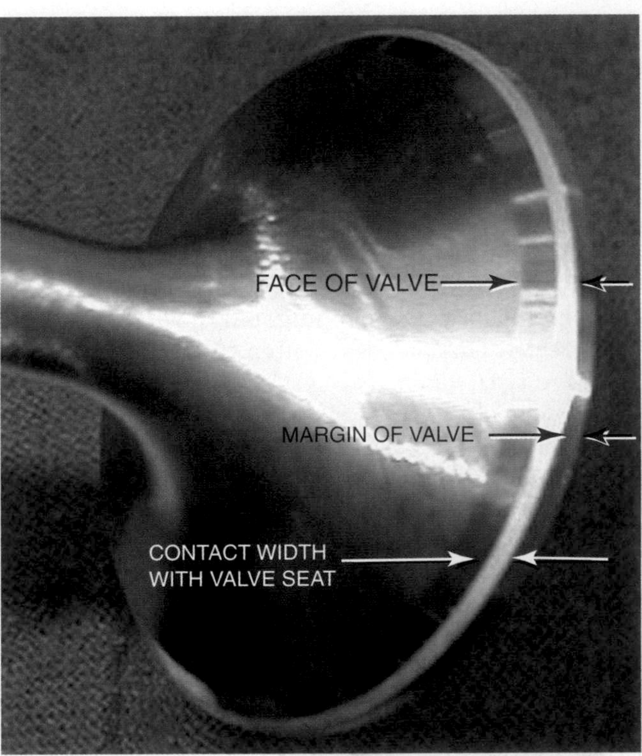

Figure 8–35 After the valve face and the valve seat are ground (reconditioned), lapping compound is used to smooth the contact area between the two mating surfaces. Notice that the contact is toward the top of the face. For maximum life, the contact should be in the middle of the face. Lapping is usually not recommended with interference angles.

NOTE: North American manufacturers have been recommending that valve seats be reconditioned by grinding; European and Asian car makers usually recommend valve seat machining with cutters. Both methods work well. Some very hard seat inserts do not machine well and require grinding.

Many larger machine shops use a head bench where both valve guide and valve seat repairs are performed. Some head benches incorporate a three-angle valve seat cutter that machines the seat, plus the top and bottom angles, all at the same time.

HIGH PERFORMANCE TIP

Grinding the Valves for More Power

A normal valve job includes grinding the face of the valve to clean up any pits and grinding the valve stems to restore the proper stem height. However, a little more airflow in and out of the cylinder head can be accomplished by performing two more simple grinding operations.

- Use the valve grinder and adjust to 30° (for a 45° valve) and grind a transition between the valve face and the valve stem area of the valve. While this step may reduce some desirable swirling of the air–fuel mixture at lower engine speeds, it also helps increase cylinder filling, especially at times when the valve is not fully open.
- Chamfer or round the head of the valve between the top of the valve and the margin on the side. By rounding this surface, additional airflow into the cylinder is achieved. See Figure 8–36.

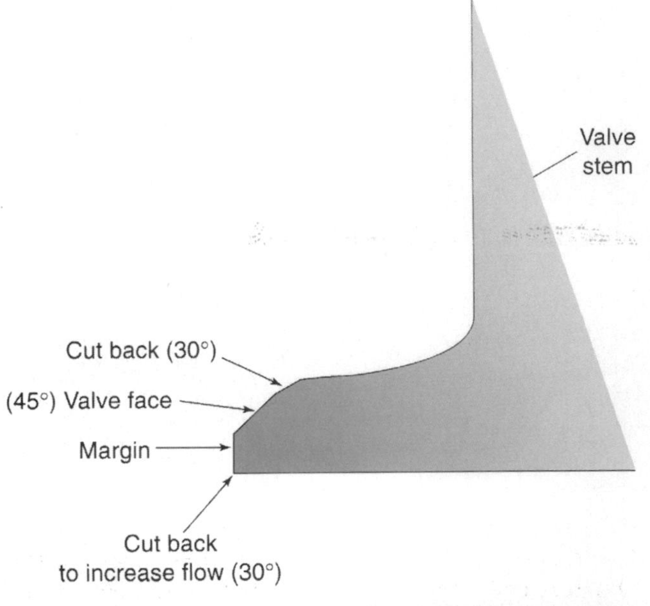

Figure 8–36 After grinding the 45°face angle, additional airflow into the engine can be accomplished by grinding a transition between the face angle and the stem, and by angling or rounding the transition between the margin and the top of the valve.

- Installed height and valve stem height are checked and corrected as necessary.
- After a thorough cleaning, the cylinder head is assembled with new valve stem seals installed. See the photo sequence at chapter's end for details on valve reconditioning.

VALVE SEAT REPLACEMENT

Valve seats need to be replaced if they are cracked or if they are burned or eroded too much to be resurfaced. Damaged integral valve seats must be counterbored to make a place for the new insert seat.

Manufacturers of replacement valve seats supply tables that specify the proper seat insert to be used. Because of reduced heat transfer, insert exhaust valve seats operate at temperatures that are 40° to 65°C (100° to 150°F) hotter than those of integral seats, up to 480°C (900°F). Removable valve seats are available in **cast iron, stainless steel, nickel cobalt,** or **powdered metal (PM).** See Figure 8–37.

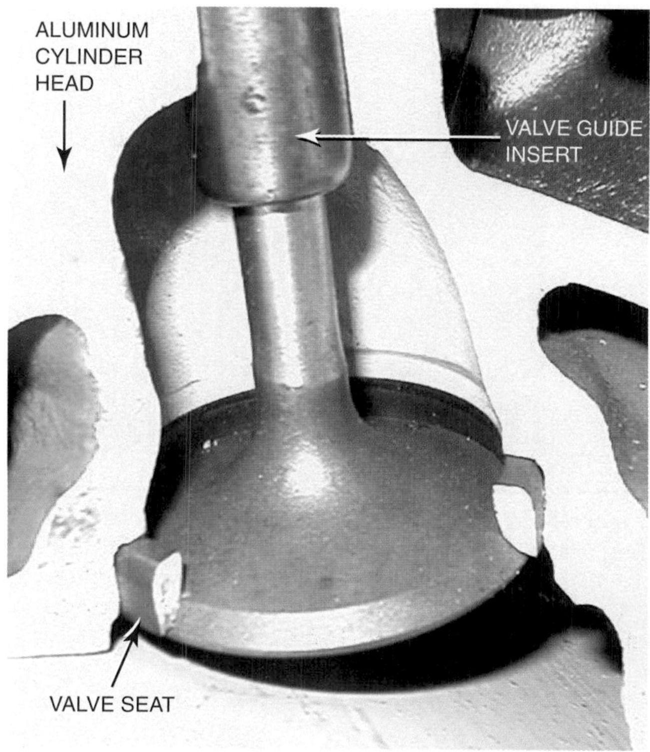

Figure 8–37 All aluminum cylinder heads use valve seat inserts. If an integral valve seat (cast-iron head) is worn, it can be replaced with a replacement valve seat by machining a pocket (counterbore) to make a place for the new insert seat.

NOTE: Some lightweight cast-iron cylinder heads may not have enough material under the valve seats to machine for valve seat inserts.

NOTE: Chrysler Canada, supported by Energy, Mines and Resources Canada and the Ontario Ministry of Energy, made significant advancements in the development of valve seat materials. They produced a sintered metal tool steel alloy seat that is superior to nickel-based or Stellite inserts.

VALVE STEM HEIGHT

Valve stem height is different from installed spring height. See Figure 8–38. Valve stem height is important to maintain for all engines, but especially for overhead camshaft engines. When the valve seat and the valve face are ground, the valve moves deeper into the combustion chamber. This causes the valve stem and tip to extend further out of the cylinder head.

The valve is put in the head, and the length of the valve tip is measured. The tip is ground to shorten the valve stem length to compensate for the valve face and seat grinding. The valve will not close if the valve tip extends too far from the valve guide in engines that have hydraulic lifters and nonadjustable rocker arms. The tip (most engines) may be ground by as much as 0.50 mm (0.020 in.) to reduce its length.

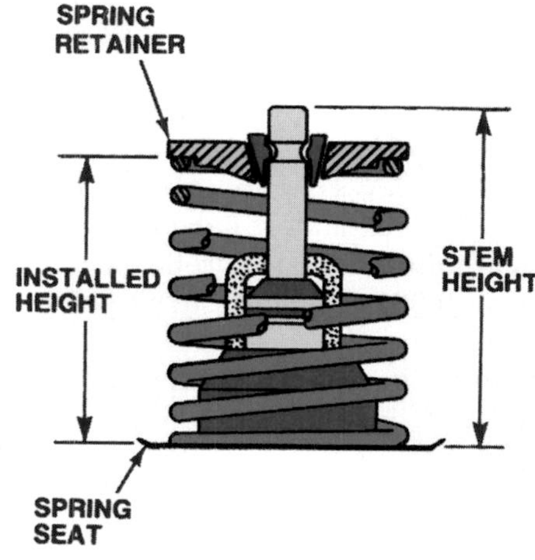

Figure 8–38 Installed height is determined by measuring the distance from the spring seat to the bottom of the valve spring retainer.

Checking Installed Height

When the valves and/or valve seats have been ground or machined, the valve projects farther than before on the rocker arm side of the head. (The valve face is slightly recessed into the combustion chamber side of

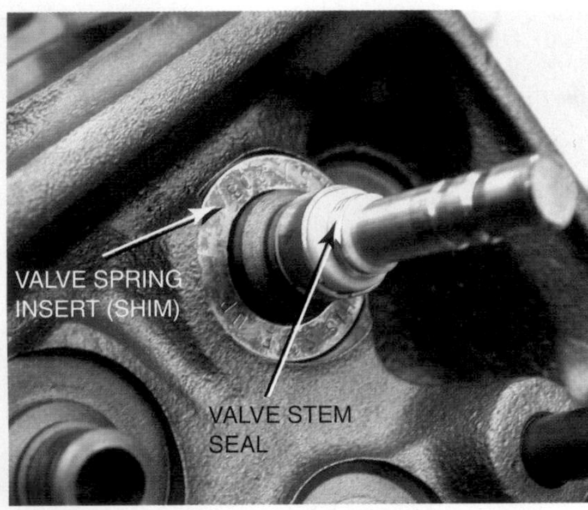

Figure 8–39 Valve spring inserts are used to restore proper installed height.

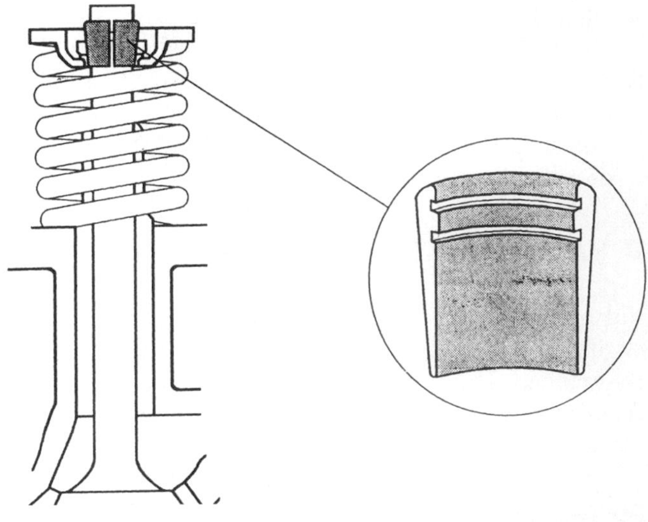

Figure 8-40 The "bead" location has been moved to compress the spring more. CLASSIC Keepers automatically give more valve tip protrusion out of the retainer. (Courtesy Classic Engine Supplies Inc.)

the head.) The valve spring tension is, therefore, reduced because the spring is not as compressed as it was originally. To restore original valve spring tension, special valve spring spacers or inserts are installed under the valve springs. These shims are usually called **valve spring inserts** (VSI). Valve spring inserts are generally available in three different thicknesses:

1. 0.38 mm (0.015 in.) for balancing valve spring pressure
2. 0.75 mm (0.030 in.) generally for new springs on cylinder heads that have had the valve seats ground and valves refaced
3. 1.5 mm (0.060 in.) necessary to bring assembled height to specifications, especially if the seats have been resurfaced more than one time

- To determine the exact thickness of the insert to install, measure the valve spring height (as installed in the head).
- If the installed height is greater than specifications, select the insert (shim) that brings the installed height to within specifications. See Figure 8–39.
- Valve keepers with a relocated bead (shoulder) are another method of adjusting spring height. The bead has been moved up 0.75 millimetre (0.030 inch) or 1.5 millimetres (0.060 inch), which in turn compresses the valve spring by the same amount. See Figure 8-40.

VALVE STEM SEALS

Leakage past the valve guides is a major oil consumption problem in any overhead valve (or overhead cam) engine. A high vacuum exists in the intake port, and a lower vacuum, caused by the exiting exhaust, exists in the exhaust ports. Most engine manufacturers use valve stem seals on both the intake and the exhaust valve.

Two basic types of valve stem seals are used. The **umbrella valve stem seal** holds tightly to the valve stem and moves up and down with the valve. Any oil that spills off the rocker arms is deflected out over the valve guide, much as water is deflected away from an umbrella. As a result, umbrella valve stem seals are often called **deflector valve stem seals.**

Positive valve stem seals hold tightly around the valve guide, and the valve stem moves through the seal. The seal wipes the excess oil from the valve stem (Figures 8–41 through 8–43).

The **O-ring type of valve stem seal** keeps oil from leaking between the valve stem and valve spring retainer. The oil is deflected over the retainer and shield. The assembly controls oil like an umbrella-type oil seal.

Be aware that some manufacturers, such as Chrysler, supply oversize valve seals for the largest 0.75 millimetre (0.030 inch) oversize valve systems.

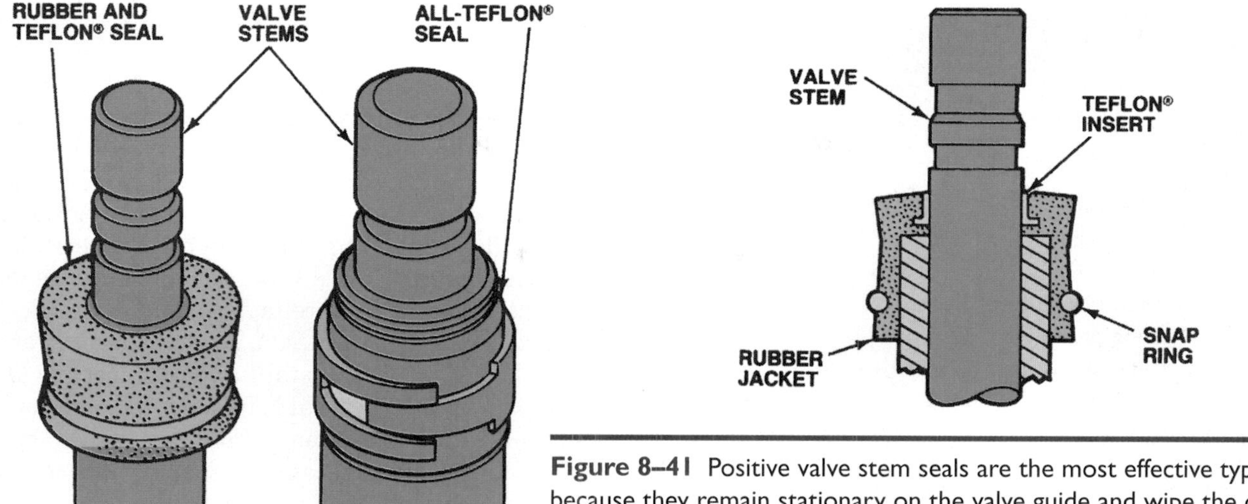

Figure 8–41 Positive valve stem seals are the most effective type because they remain stationary on the valve guide and wipe the oil from the stem as the valve moves up and down.

Figure 8–42 An assortment of shapes, colours, and materials of positive valve stem seals.

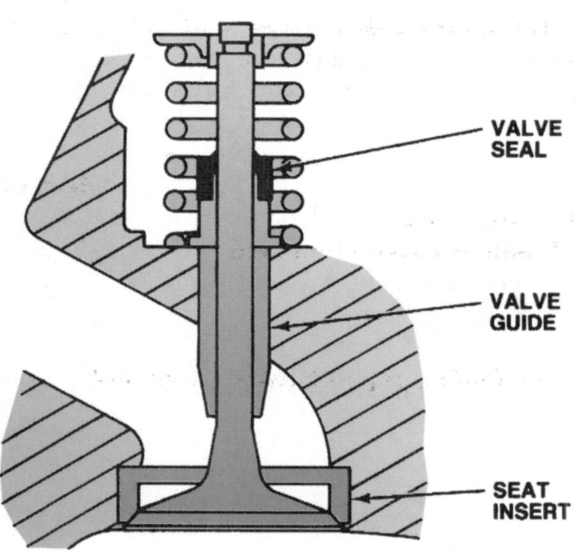

Figure 8–43 The positive valve stem seal is installed on the valve.

TECH TIP 

Do Not Simply Bolt on New Cylinder Heads

New, assembled cylinder heads, whether aluminum or cast iron, are a popular engine build-up option. However, experience has shown that metal shavings and casting sand are often found inside the passages.

Before bolting on these "ready-to-install" heads, check for debris (metal shavings, etc.) and clean all passages. If this debris were to get into the engine, the result would be extreme wear or damage to the pistons, rings, block, and bearings.

INSTALLING THE VALVES

The cylinder head can be assembled after the head is thoroughly cleaned with soap and water to wash away any remaining grit and metal shavings from the valve grinding operation. Valves are assembled in the head one at a time. Give the valve guide and stem a liberal coating of engine oil, and install the valve in its guide. Install umbrella or positive valve stem seals. Push umbrella seals down until they touch the valve guide. Use a plastic sleeve over the tip of the valve when installing positive seals. Make sure that the positive seal is fully seated on the valve guide and that it is square. Hold the valve against the seat as the valve spring seat or insert, valve spring, valve seals, and retainer are placed over the valve stem. Install the valve spring seat if assembling an aluminum head. See Figure 8–44. One end of the valve spring compressor pushes on the retainer to compress the spring. The O-ring type of valve stem seal is installed in the lower groove on the valve. The valve locks are installed while the valve spring is compressed. See Figure 8–45. To test the seal, attach the hose from a vacuum pump to the top of the assembled valve. *A vacuum will hold if the O-ring type of valve stem seal is correctly installed.*

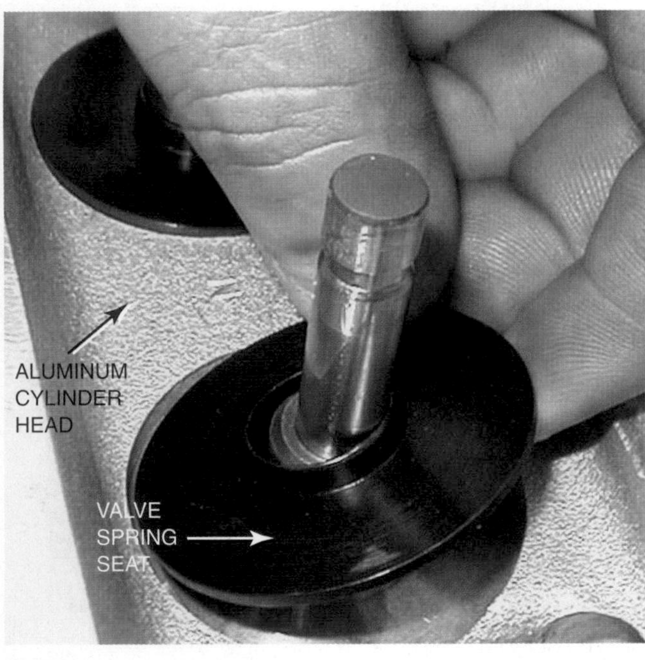

Figure 8–44 A metal valve spring seat must be used between the valve spring and the aluminum head. Many DaimlerChrysler aluminum cylinder heads use a combination valve spring seat and valve stem seal.

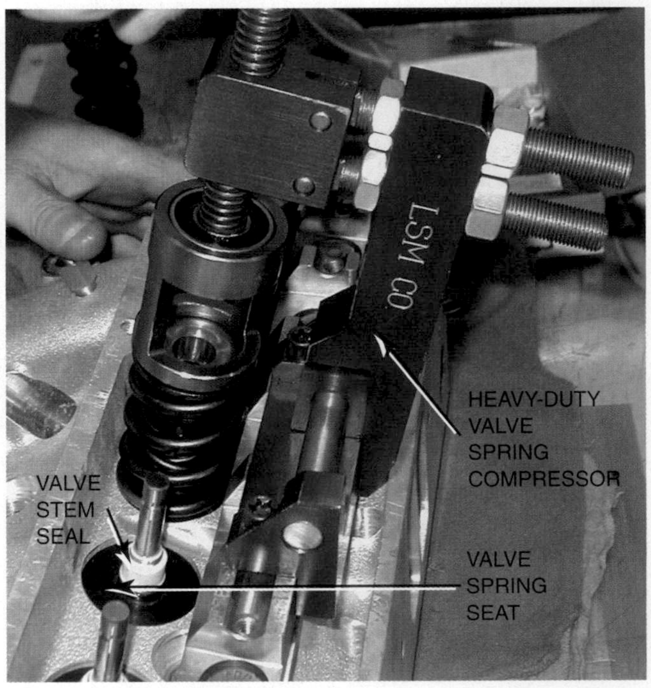

Figure 8–45 Assembling a race engine using a heavy-duty valve spring compressor.

PHOTO SEQUENCE 4 Grinding a Valve

P4–1 A typical valve grinding machine.

P4–2 Before grinding the face of a valve, the tip of the stem should be chamfered so that the valve will seat properly in the collet during the grinding operation, especially if using a Sioux valve grinder where the valve tip is used to centre the valve stem.

P4–3 Insert the valve into the collet. Try to keep the distance that the valve extends out to a minimum. Start the valve grinder and observe the valve face. If it wobbles, the stem is bent and the valve must be replaced.

P4–4 Remove as little material as possible when grinding a valve. Check the face of the valve for a smooth surface. Also check that the margin is greater than the minimum specification.

PHOTO SEQUENCE 5 Valve Seat Grinding

P5–1 To grind the valve seats in a cylinder head, the proper equipment and grinding stones must be available. On the left is a 45° stone for the valve seat angle. In the centre is a 60° stone used to raise and narrow the valve seat. The 30° stone on the right is used to narrow and lower the valve seat as necessary.

P5–2 A pilot of the correct size is inserted into the valve guide. The pilot will keep the grinding stone in the centre of the valve pocket so that a concentric valve seat will be ground.

P5–3 The grinding stone is turned by the high-speed air-powered grinder. Use short bursts and avoid pressing down on the grinder.

P5–4 A light coating of layout dye or Prussian blue is spread evenly over the valve face. The valve is installed into the guide, rotated by hand, and removed for examination. Notice that the seat is contacting the valve is approximately the centre of the face.

SUMMARY

1. The most commonly used combustion chamber types include hemispherical, wedge, and pentroof.
2. Cylinder head reconditioning should start with head cleaning and repairing, if needed, followed by resurfacing of valves and, finally, grinding of valves and seats.
3. Valve guides should be checked for wear using a ball gauge or a dial indicator. Typical valve stem-to-guide clearance is 0.025 to 0.075 mm (0.001 to 0.003 in.) for intake valves and 0.05 to 0.10 mm (0.002 to 0.004 in.) for exhaust valves.
4. Valve guide repair options include using oversize stem valves, replacement valve guides, valve guide inserts, and knurling of the original valve guide.
5. Valve springs should be kept with the valve at the time of disassembly and tested for squareness and proper spring force.
6. Free and positive are two types of valve rotators.
7. Valve grinding should start with truing the valve tip; then the face should be refinished. A pilot is placed into the valve guide to position the stone or cutter correctly for resurfacing the valve seat.
8. The installed spring height should be checked and corrected with valve spring inserts if needed.
9. Valve stem height should be checked and the tip of the valve ground if necessary.
10. After a thorough cleaning, the cylinder head should be assembled using new valve stem seals.

REVIEW QUESTIONS

1. What is meant by the term *cross-flow head?*
2. What are the advantages of using four valves per cylinder?
3. Why is valve guide reconditioning the first cylinder head servicing operation?
4. When is the valve tip ground? How do you know how much to remove from the tip?
5. What is an interference angle between the valve and the seat?
6. How is a valve seat insert installed?
7. How is the correct valve spring insert (shim) selected and why are shims used?

RED SEAL CERTIFICATION-TYPE QUESTIONS

1. The gasket surface of a cylinder head, as measured with a straightedge, should have a maximum variation of no more than _____.
   - **a.** 0.05 mm (0.002 in.) in any 150 mm (6-in.) length or 0.10 mm (0.004 in.) overall
   - **b.** 0.02 mm (0.001 in.) in any 150 mm (6-in.) length or 0.10 mm (0.004 in.) overall
   - **c.** 0.50 mm (0.020 in.) in any 250 mm (10-in.) length or 0.50 mm (0.020 in.) overall
   - **d.** 0.10 mm (0.004 in.) in any 250 mm (10-in.) length or 0.20 mm (0.008 in.) overall
2. Most vehicle manufacturers recommend repairing integral guides using _____.
   - **a.** OS stem valves
   - **b.** Knurling
   - **c.** Replacement valve guides
   - **d.** Valve guide inserts
3. The typical valve stem-to-valve guide clearance is _____.
   - **a.** 0.8 to 0.10 mm (0.030 to 0.045 in.)
   - **b.** 0.4 to 0.5 mm (0.015 to 0.020 in.)
   - **c.** 0.13 to 0.25 mm (0.005 to 0.010 in.)
   - **d.** 0.03 to 0.01 mm (0.001 to 0.004 in.)
4. Which statement is true about surface finish?
   - **a.** Cast-iron surfaces should be smoother than aluminum surfaces.
   - **b.** The rougher the surface, the higher the microinch finish measurement.
   - **c.** The smoother the surface, the higher the microinch finish measurement.
   - **d.** A cylinder head should be smoother than a crankshaft journal.
5. In a normally operating engine, intake and exhaust valves are opened by a cam and closed by the _____.
   - **a.** Rocker arms or cam follower
   - **b.** Valve spring
   - **c.** Lifters (tappets)
   - **d.** Valve guide and/or pushrod
6. If an interference angle is machined on a valve or seat, this angle is usually _____.
   - **a.** 1°
   - **b.** 0.005°
   - **c.** 1° to 3°
   - **d.** 0.5° to 0.75°
7. A valve should be discarded if the margin is less than _____ after refacing.
   - **a.** 0.02 mm (0.001 in.)
   - **b.** 0.15 mm (0.006 in.)
   - **c.** 0.80 mm (0.030 in.)
   - **d.** 1.50 mm (0.060 in.)
8. To lower and narrow a valve seat that has been cut at a 45° angle, use a cutter or stone of what angle?
   - **a.** 60°
   - **b.** 45°
   - **c.** 30°
   - **d.** 15°
9. Valve spring inserts (shims) are designed to
   - **a.** Increase installed height of the valve spring
   - **b.** Decrease installed height of the valve spring
   - **c.** Adjust the correct installed height of the valve
   - **d.** Decrease valve spring pressure to compensate for decreased installed height
10. Umbrella-type valve stem seals _____.
    - **a.** Fit tightly onto the valve guide
    - **b.** Fit on the valve face to prevent combustion leaks
    - **c.** Fit tightly onto the valve stem
    - **d.** Lock under the valve retainer

9

Camshafts, Valve Trains, Intake and Exhaust Systems

OBJECTIVES: After studying Chapter 9, you should be able to:

1. Prepare for the interprovincial Red Seal certification examination in Appendix I (Engine Repair) on the topics covered in this chapter.
2. Describe how camshafts and valve trains function.
3. Discuss valve train noise and its causes.
4. Explain how a hydraulic lifter works.
5. Discuss the operation of variable-length intake manifolds.
6. Explain the differences between air cleaners for "wet" and "dry" manifolds.
7. Explain the relationship of valve timing to intake runner length.

The cam is driven by timing gears, chains, or belts located at the front of the engine. The gear or sprocket on the camshaft has twice as many teeth, or notches, as the one on the crankshaft. This results in two crankshaft revolutions for each revolution of the camshaft. *The camshaft turns at one-half the crankshaft speed in all four-stroke-cycle engines.*

CAMSHAFT FUNCTION

The camshaft's major function is to operate the valve train. Cam shape or **contour** is the major factor in determining the operating characteristics of the engine. The lobes on the camshaft open the valves against the force of the valve springs. The camshaft lobe changes rotary motion (camshaft) to linear motion (valves).

Cam lobe shape has more control over engine performance characteristics than does any other single engine part. Engines identical in every way except cam lobe shape may have completely different operating characteristics and performance. See Figure 9–1. The camshaft may also operate the following:

- Mechanical fuel pump
- Oil pump
- Distributor

See Figures 9–2 and 9–3.

CAMSHAFT LOCATION

Pushrod engines have the cam located in the block. The camshaft is supported in the block by **camshaft bearings** and driven by the crankshaft with a gear or sprocket and chain drive. See Figure 9–4. Many over-

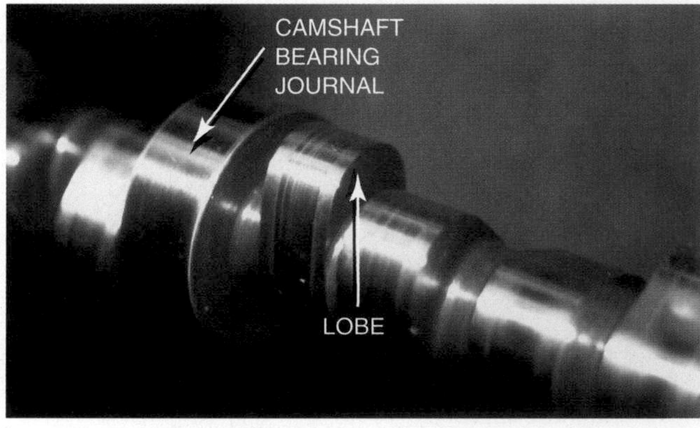

Figure 9–1 This high-performance camshaft has a lobe that opens the valve quickly and keeps it open for a long time.

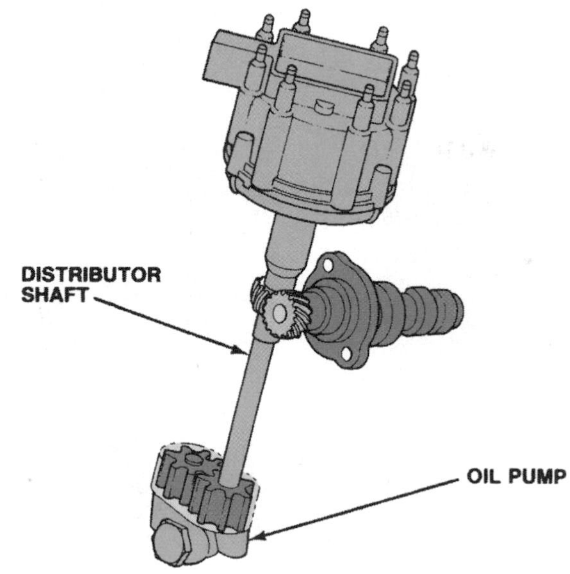

Figure 9–2 In many engines, the camshaft drives the distributor and the oil pump through a shaft from the end of the distributor.

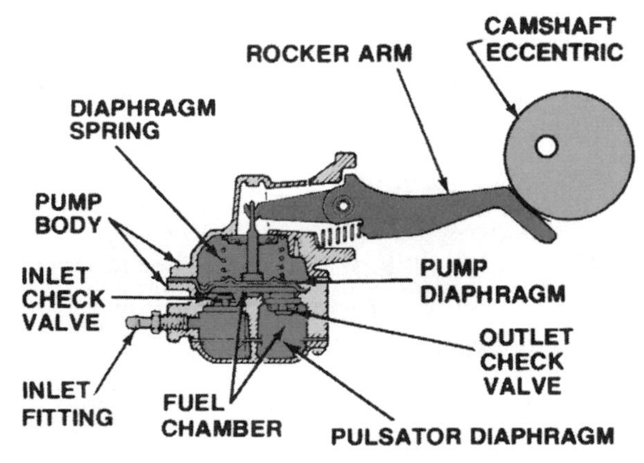

Figure 9–3 The fuel pump plunger rides on the camshaft eccentric.

head camshaft (OHC) engines do not use cam bearings; the camshaft runs directly on the aluminum cylinder head. In order to salvage heads with a worn camshaft bore, the aftermarket suppliers often provide camshafts with larger bearing journals. The head is bored (machined) to match the new, larger cam. Another repair method is to bore out the head and install bearings that allow the use of the original camshaft.

CAMSHAFT PROBLEM DIAGNOSIS

A partially worn lobe on the camshaft is often difficult to diagnose. Sometimes a valve "tick tick tick" noise is heard if the cam lobe is worn. The ticking noise can be intermittent, which makes it harder to determine the cause. If the engine has an overhead camshaft (OHC), it is usually relatively easy to remove the cam cover and make a visual inspection of all cam lobes and the rest of the valve train. In an overhead valve (OHV) engine, the camshaft is in the block, where easy visual inspection is not possible. See Figure 9–5 and Tech Tip "The Rotating Pushrod Test."

Push rod engines with flat tappets often use the cam lobe taper and lifter offset to push the camshaft in toward the block. No cam thrust plate (retainer) is required. Camshafts designed for roller lifters have no taper and must use a retainer to keep the camshaft from "walking" back and forth in the block.

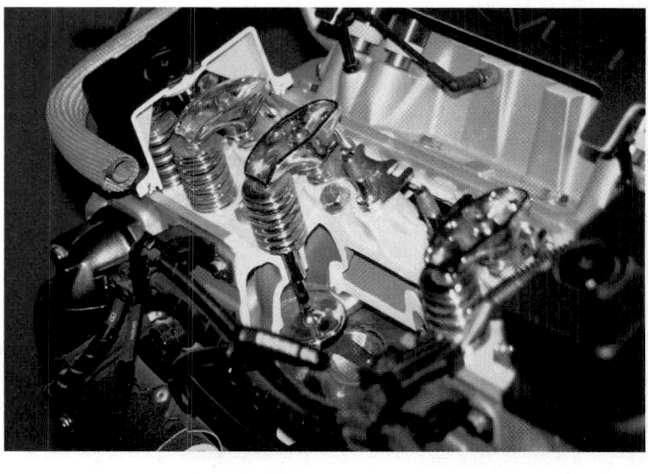

Figure 9–4 Cutaway of a Chevrolet V-8 showing the valve train components.

TECH TIP 

The Rotating Pushrod Test

To quickly and easily test whether or not the camshaft is okay, observe if the pushrods are rotating when the engine is running. This test will work on any overhead valve pushrod engine that uses a flat-bottom lifter. Due to the slight angle on the cam lobe and lifter offset, the lifter (and pushrod) should rotate whenever the engine is running. To check, simply remove the rocker arm cover and observe the pushrods when the engine is running. If one or more pushrods is *not* rotating, the camshaft and/or the lifter for that particular valve is worn and needs to be replaced.

CAMSHAFT REMOVAL (PUSHROD ENGINE)

If the engine has an overhead valve design, the camshaft is usually located in the block above the

(a)

(b)

Figure 9–5 (a) Here is what can happen if a roller lifter breaks loose from its retainer. The customer complained of "a little noise from the engine." (b) All engines equipped with roller lifters have some type of retainer for keeping the lifters from rotating.

crankshaft. The timing chain and gears (if the vehicle is so equipped) should be removed after the timing chain (gear) cover is removed. Loosen the rocker arms (or rocker arm shaft) and remove the pushrods. Remove or lift up the lifters before carefully removing the camshaft. See Tech Tip "The Tube Trick."

> **NOTE:** Be sure to keep the pushrods and rocker arms together if they are to be reused.

CAMSHAFT DRIVES

The crankshaft gear or sprocket that drives the camshaft is usually made of sintered iron. When gears are used, the camshaft gear teeth must be made from a soft material to reduce noise. Usually, the whole gear is made of aluminum or fibre. See Figure 9–6. When a chain and sprocket are used, the

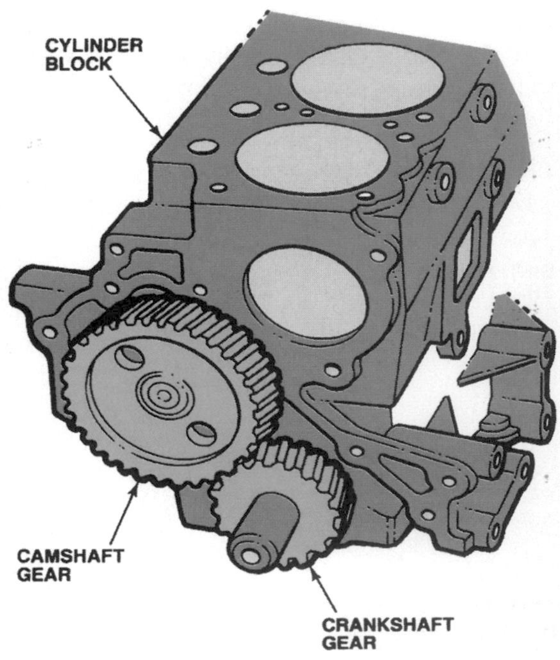

Figure 9–6 The larger camshaft gear is usually made from fibre and given a helical cut to help reduce noise. By making the camshaft gear twice as large as the crankshaft gear, the camshaft rotates one revolution for every two of the crankshaft.

TECH TIP

The Tube Trick

Valve lifters are often difficult to remove because the ends of the lifters become mushroomed (enlarged) where they have contacted the camshaft. Varnish buildup can also prevent the lifters from being removed. Try this method:

Step 1. Raise the lifters upward as far away from the camshaft as possible.

Step 2. Slide in a thin plastic or cardboard tube with slots in place of the camshaft.

Step 3. Push the lifters downward into the tube. Use a long magnet to retrieve the lifters from the end of the tube.

This trick will work on almost every engine that has the camshaft in the block. If the tube is made from plastic, it has to be thin plastic to allow it to flex slightly. The length of the lifters is greater than the diameter of the cam bearings. Therefore, the lifter has to be pushed downward into the tube slightly to allow the lifter room to fall over into the tube.

camshaft sprocket may be made of iron or it may have an aluminum hub with nylon teeth for noise reduction. Two types of timing chains are used.

1. **Silent chain type** (also known as a **flat-link type,** or **Morse** type for its original manufacturer). This type operates quietly but tends to stretch with use. See Figures 9–7 and 9–8.

> **NOTE:** When the timing chain stretches, the valve timing will be retarded and the engine will lack low-speed power. In some instances, the chain can wear through the timing-chain cover and create an oil leak.

2. **Roller chain type.** This type is noisier but operates with less friction and stretches less than the silent type of chain. See Figure 9–9. Roller chains are superior to the silent (flat link) type and last longer. Often, the engine for a passenger car may use a silent chain; the same engine for a truck may come equipped with a roller chain.

Some four-cam "V" type engines use a two-stage camshaft drive system. See Figure 9–10. Some four cylinder, two cam engines use two chains; the primary chain drives one camshaft and the secondary chain connects the two camshafts.

> **NOTE:** Beware of low cost roller chains. They often use inferior materials and poor hardening. Saving money with minimum quality parts will end up costing more when the vehicle returns with a problem.

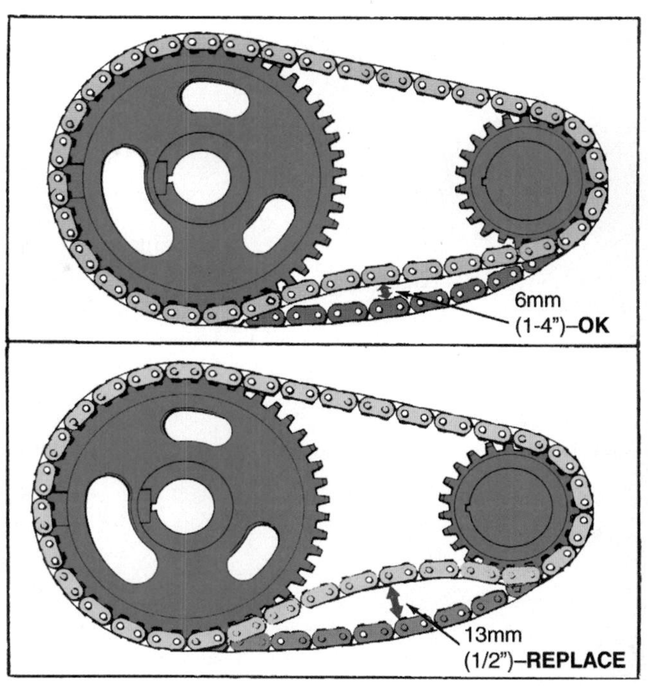

Figure 9–8 The industry standard is to replace a timing chain and sprockets when 13 mm (1/2 in.) or more of slack is measured in the sprockets. However, it is best to replace the timing chain and sprockets anytime the camshaft is replaced or the engine is disassembled for repair or overhaul. (Courtesy of Sealed Power Corporation)

Figure 9–7 A replacement silent chain and sprockets. The original camshaft sprocket was aluminum with nylon teeth to help control noise. This replacement set will not be noticeably louder than the original and should give the owner many thousands of kilometres of useful service.

Figure 9–9 A replacement high-performance double roller chain. Even though a bit noisier than a flat-link chain, a roller chain does not stretch as much and will therefore be able to maintain accurate valve timing for a longer time.

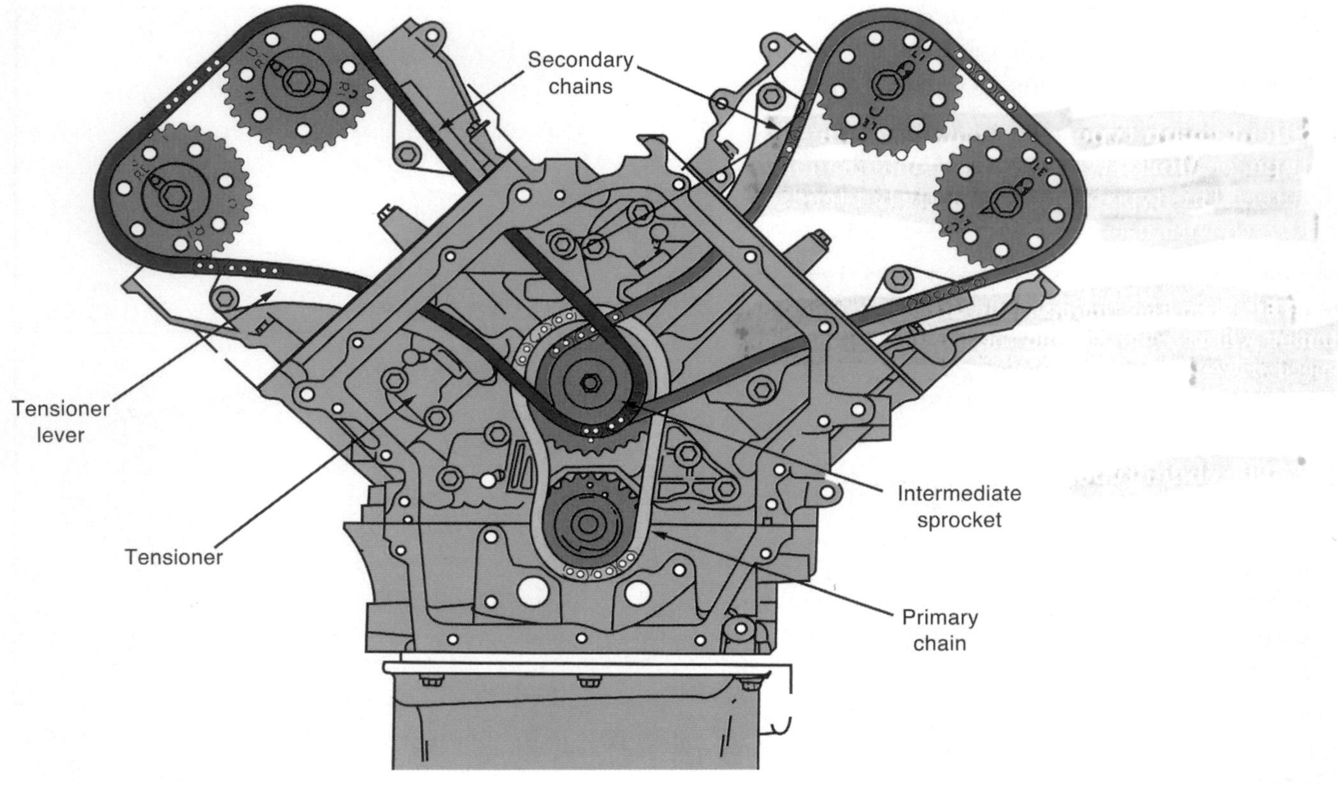

Figure 9–10 Typical dual overhead camshaft V-type engine that uses one primary timing chain and two secondary chains.

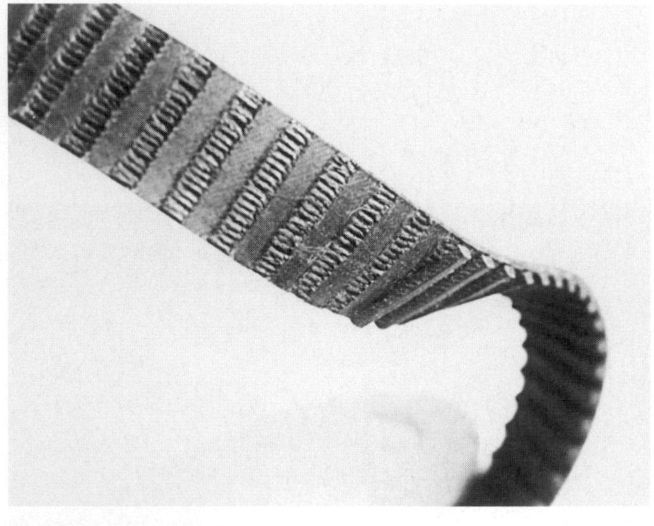

Figure 9–11 Broken timing belt. Also notice the missing teeth. This belt broke at 142 000 km (88 000 mi) because the owner failed to replace it at the recommended interval of 96 000 km (60 000 mi).

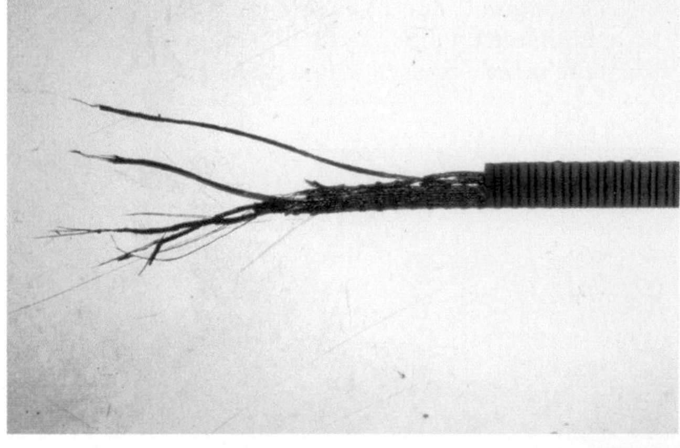

Figure 9–12 This timing belt broke because an oil leak from one of the camshaft seals caused oil to get into and weaken the belt. Many experts recommend replacing all engine seals in the front of the engine when a timing belt is replaced. If the timing belt travels over the water pump, the water pump should also be replaced as a precaution.

CAMSHAFT BELT DRIVES

Many overhead camshaft engines use a timing belt rather than a chain. The belt is generally considered to be quieter, but it requires periodic replacement, usually every 100 000 km (60 000 mi). Unless the engine is **free wheeling,** the piston can hit the valves if the belt breaks. See Figures 9–11 through 9–13.

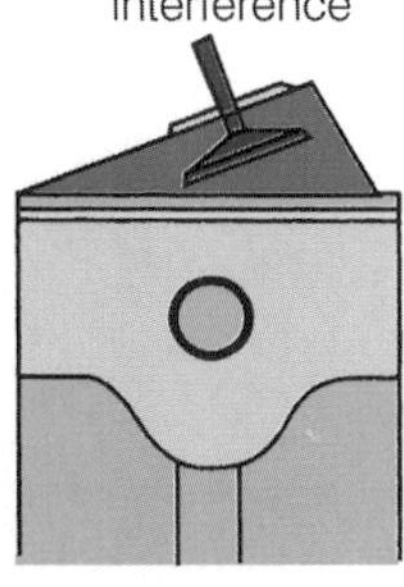

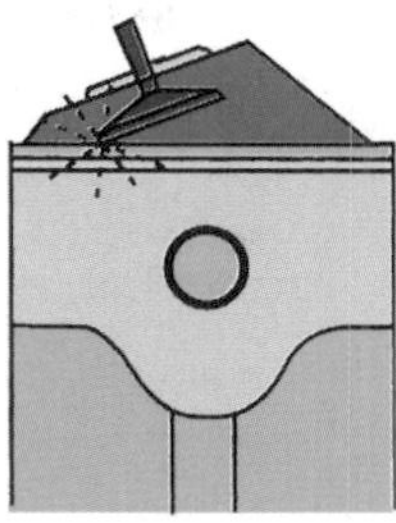

Figure 9–13 Many engines are of the interference design. If the timing belt (or chain) breaks, the piston still moves up and down in the cylinder while the valves remain stationary. With a freewheeling design, nothing is damaged, but in an interference engine, the valves are often bent.

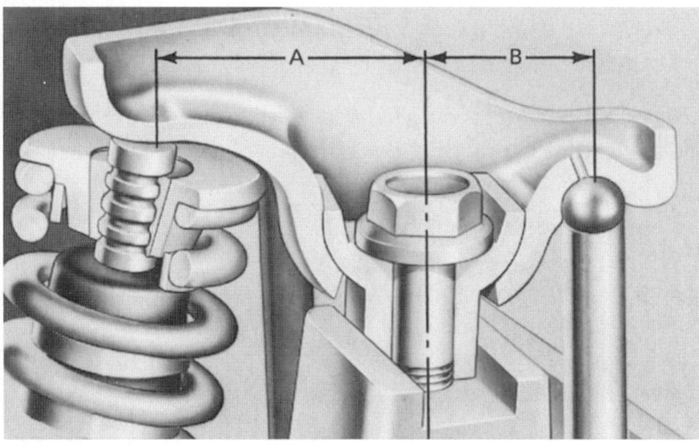

Figure 9–14 A 1.5:1 ratio rocker arm means that dimension A is 1.5 times the length of B. Therefore, if the pushrod is moved up 10 mm (0.400 in.) by the camshaft lobe, the valve will be pushed down (opened) 10 mm (0.400 in.) × 1.5, or 15 mm (0.600 in.).

ROCKER ARMS

Rocker arms reverse the upward movement of the pushrod to produce a downward movement on the tip of the valve. They are designed to reduce the travel of the cam follower or lifter and pushrod while maintaining the required valve lift. This is done by using a rocker arm ratio of approximately 1.5:1, as shown in Figure 9–14. For a given amount of lift on the pushrod, the valve will open up to 1.5 times the pushrod lift distance. This ratio allows the camshaft to be small, so the engine can be smaller. It also results in higher lobe-to-lifter rubbing pressure.

CAUTION: Using rocker arms with a higher ratio than stock can also cause the valve spring to compress too much and actually bind. Valve spring bind occurs when the valve spring is compressed to the point where there is no clearance at all in the spring. (It is completely compressed.) When coil bind occurs in a running engine, bent pushrods, broken rocker arms, or other valve train damage can result.

Rocker arms may be cast, forged, or stamped. See Figure 9–15.

DIAGNOSTIC STORY

Best to Warn the Customer

A technician replaced a timing chain and sprockets. The repair was accomplished correctly, yet, after starting, the engine burned an excessive amount of oil. Before the timing chain replacement, oil consumption was minimal. The replacement timing chain restored proper operation of the engine and increased engine vacuum. Increased vacuum can draw oil from the crankcase past worn piston rings and through worn valve guides during the intake stroke. Similar increased oil consumption problems occur if a valve regrind is performed on a high-mileage engine with worn piston rings and/or cylinders.

To satisfy the owner of the vehicle, the technician had to disassemble and refinish the cylinders and replace the piston rings. Therefore, all technicians should warn customers that increased oil usage may result from almost any repair to a high-mileage engine.

DIAGNOSTIC STORY

The Noisy Camshaft

The owner of an overhead cam four-cylinder engine complained of a noisy engine. After taking the vehicle to several technicians and getting high estimates to replace the camshaft and followers, the owner tried to find a less expensive solution. Finally, another technician replaced the serpentine drive belt on the front of the engine and cured the "camshaft" noise for a fraction of the previous estimates.

Remember, accessory drive belts can often make noises similar to valve or worn-bearing types of noises. Many engines have been disassembled and/or overhauled because of a noise that was later determined to be from one of the following:

- Loose or defective accessory drive belt(s)
- Cracks in the torque converter flex plate (drive plate)
- Defective mechanical fuel pump

Figure 9–15 A high-performance aluminum roller arm. Both the pivot and the tip that contacts the stem of the valve are equipped with rollers to help reduce friction for more power and better fuel economy.

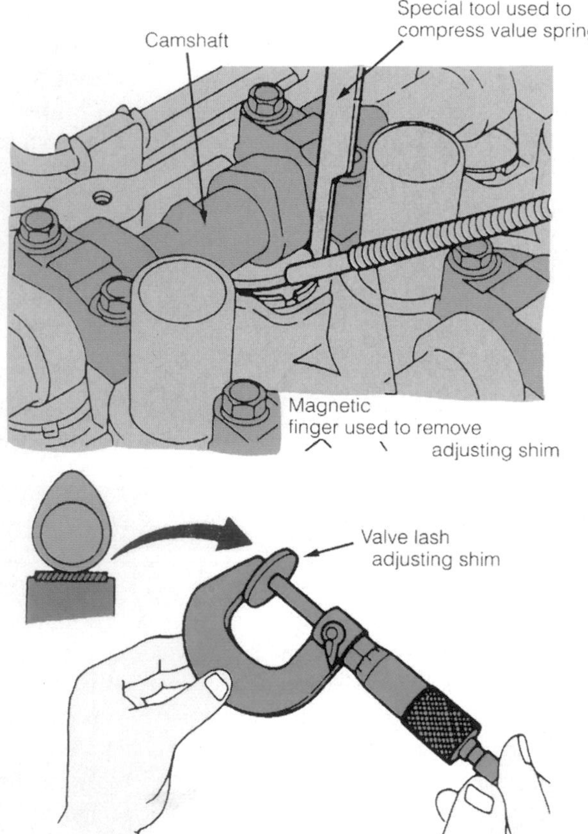

Figure 9–16 Some overhead camshaft engines use a bucket-type cam follower which uses valve lash adjusting shims to adjust the valve lash. A special tool is usually required to compress the valve spring so that a magnet can remove the shim.

1. One type of valve mechanism opens the valves directly with a **cam follower** or **bucket.** See Figure 9–16.
2. The second type uses a **finger follower** that provides an opening ratio similar to that of a rocker arm. Finger followers open the valves by approximately 1 1/2 times the cam lift. The pivot point of the finger follower may have a mechanical or automatic hydraulic adjustment.
3. A third type moves the rocker arm directly through a hydraulic lifter.

NOTE: Some newer engines have the hydraulic adjustment in the rocker arm and are called hydraulic lash adjusters (HLA). See Figure 9–17.

TECH TIP

Varnish on Valve Stems Can Cause Sticking Valves

As oil oxidizes, it forms a varnish. Varnish build-up is particularly common on hot upper portions of the engine, such as valve stems. The varnish restricts clean oil from getting into and lubricating the valve guides. The cam lobe can easily *force* the valves open, but the valve springs often do not exert enough force to fully close the valves. The result is an engine miss, which may be intermittent. Worn valve guides and/or weak valve springs can also cause occasional rough idle, uneven running, or missing. See Figure 9–18.

Figure 9–17 This single overhead camshaft engine has four valves per cylinder because each pivot arm opens two valves and each contains a small hydraulic lash adjuster (hydraulic lifter).

CAUTION: Some rockers are offset to the right, or left, for correct rocker tip to valve alignment. Installing a rocker in the wrong position could cause the rocker to slip off the valve. Always check for correct location.

PUSHRODS

Pushrods are designed to be as light as possible and still maintain their strength. They may be either solid or hollow. If they are to be used as passages for oil to lubricate rocker arms, they *must* be hollow. Pushrods have a convex ball on the lower end that seats in the lifter. The rocker arm end is also a convex ball unless there is an adjustment screw in the pushrod end of the rocker arm. In this case, the rocker arm end of the pushrod has a concave socket. It mates with the convex ball on the adjustment screw in the rocker arm. All pushrods should be rolled on a flat surface to check if they are bent. See Figure 9–19.

Some pushrods are hardened at the upper end to reduce wear at the point where they pass through the cylinder head. The hardened end faces up.

Figure 9–18 Some engines today use rocker shafts to support rocker arms such as the V-6 engine with a single overhead camshaft located in the centre of the cylinder head. This engine uses a roller on the rocker arm.

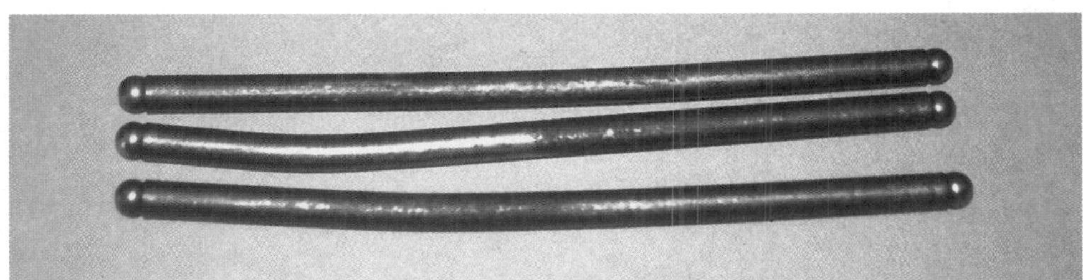

Figure 9–19 When the timing chain broke, it caused the camshaft to go out-of-time, which allowed the pistons and valves to collide on this interference engine. This may also bend the pushrods. Valve-to-piston contact will not occur on freewheeling engines.

CAMSHAFT DURATION, TIMING AND OVERLAP

1. Camshaft duration is the number of degrees of crankshaft rotation during the time the valve is lifted off the valve seat. See Figures 9–20 and 9–21.

   If we follow the cam timing diagram (Figure 9–24, p. 179), we find that the intake valve opens at 15° before top dead centre (TDC), stays open from top dead centre to bottom dead centre (BDC), which is a further 180°, and closes 59° after BDC.

   Adding the three, 15° + 180° + 59° = 254°, gives the duration. The intake valve is open for 254° of crankshaft rotation.

   The exhaust valve opens at 59° before BDC, stays open from BDC to TDC (a further 180°) and closes at 15° after TDC.

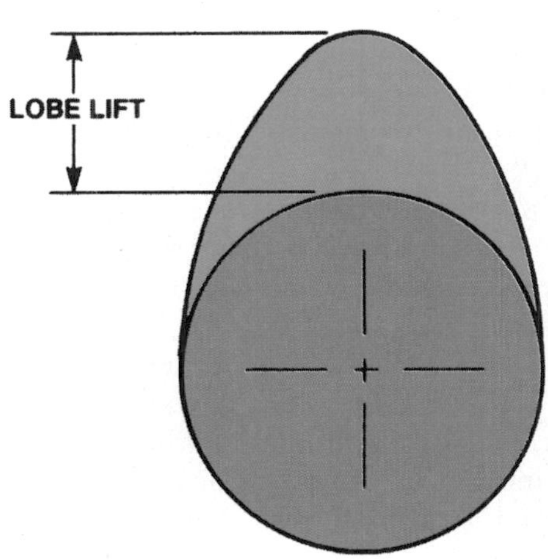

Figure 9–20 The lobe lift is the amount the cam lobe lifts the lifter. Because the rocker arm adds to this amount, the entire valve train has to be considered when selecting a camshaft that has the desired lift and duration.

TECH TIP 

Hollow Pushrod Dirt

Many engine rebuilders and remanufacturers do not reuse old hollow pushrods. Dirt, carbon, and other debris are difficult to thoroughly clean from inside a hollow pushrod. When an engine is run with used pushrods, the trapped particles can be dislodged and ruin new bearings and other new engine parts.

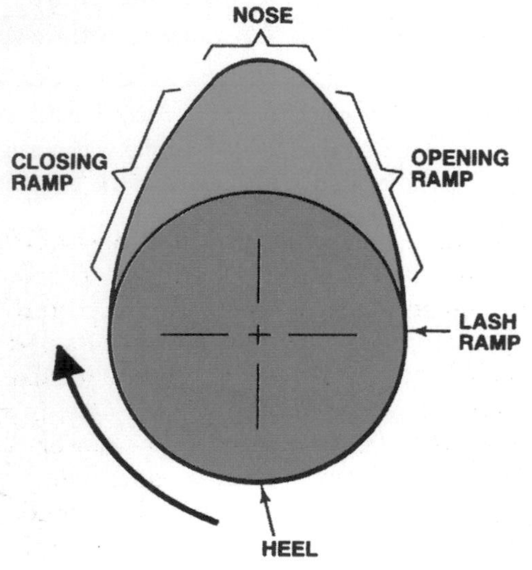

Figure 9–21 The ramps on the cam lobe allow the valves to be opened and closed quickly yet under control to avoid damaging valve train components, especially at high engine speeds.

Adding the three, 59° + 180° + 15° = 254°, gives the duration of the exhaust valve. In this case, both the intake and exhaust have the same duration. This is not always the case as different durations are often used for intake and exhaust valves.

If a hydraulic lifter is used, the valve lash is zero. If a solid lifter is used, duration begins after the specified clearance (lash) has been closed.

Overlap is the time, in crankshaft degrees, that both valves are open at the same time. Overlap on our example would be 15° + 15° = 30°.

2. Advancing the camshaft: the camshaft is moved ahead in relation to the crankshaft. The valve now opens earlier and also closes earlier. The duration does not change.
3. Retarding the camshaft: the camshaft is moved back (behind) in relation to the crankshaft. The valve now opens later and closes later. The duration does not change.

Figure 9–22 A camshaft can be checked for straightness as well as for lift and duration using a dial indicator on a fixture that allows the camshaft to be rotated. This same equipment can be used to check crankshafts.

CAMSHAFT TESTING

The camshaft should be inspected visually for wear and measured with a dial indicator as shown in Figures 9–22 and 9–23.

CAM TIMING CHART

Four Strokes

During the four strokes of a four-cycle gasoline engine, the crankshaft rotates two complete revolutions or 720° (2 × 360° = 720°). The four strokes, of 180° each, are:

- Intake—an air/fuel mixture is drawn into the cylinder.
- Compression—the piston compresses the air into a high temperature mass.
- Power—the compressed air/fuel mass is ignited and the expanding gases push the piston down the cylinder.
- Exhaust—the burned gases are pushed out of the cylinder by the piston.

VALVE TIMING

The timing for these four events is expressed in degrees of crankshaft rotation; camshaft specifications are also given in crankshaft degrees. The usual method of drawing a camshaft timing diagram is a circle illustrating two revolutions (720°) of the crankshaft. See Figure 9–24. We'll use this again as an example.

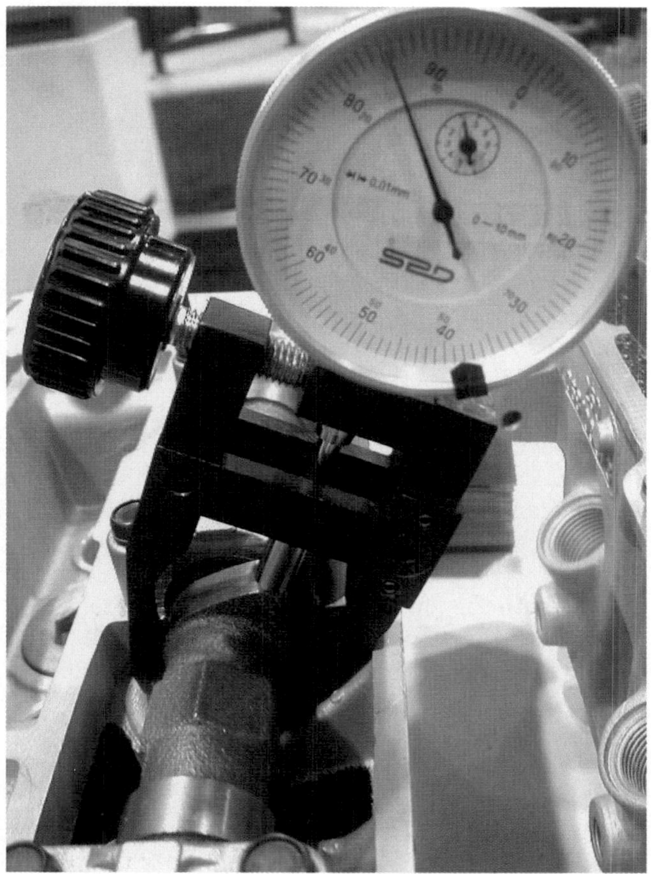

Figure 9–23 The lift of a camshaft lobe can be quickly determined by using this dial indicator that attaches directly to the camshaft.

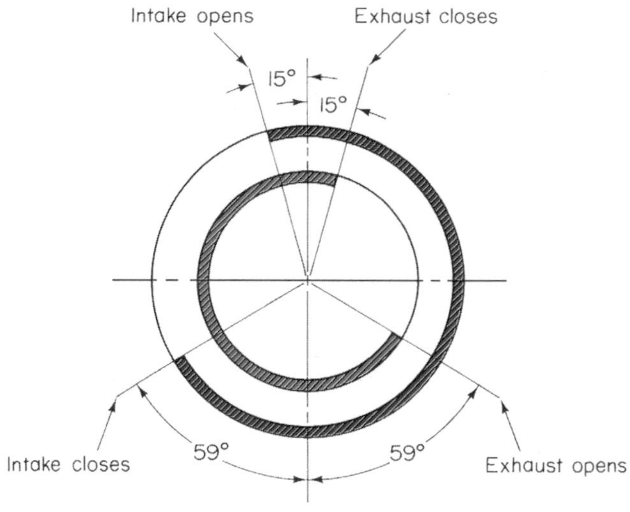

Figure 9–24 Typical cam timing diagram.

Let's begin at TDC. At the beginning of the intake stroke, the intake valve has already started to open and the piston is moving down the cylinder. Air and fuel rush into the low-pressure void (vacuum) caused by the piston movement. When the piston reaches BDC, it reverses direction and starts to move up the cylinder on the compression stroke.

When do we close the intake valve? It depends. The air rushing into the cylinder has both speed and inertia, it doesn't want to stop. The intake valve should close just before the pressure in the cylinder overcomes the velocity of the air. This prevents the air from being pushed back into the intake manifold. We know that air speed varies with engine RPM. The air flow at higher RPM has greater speed and force, therefore the intake valve can be held open longer (later) and use more duration.

Using a camshaft with more duration increases high RPM power, but low RPM power suffers as part of the air/fuel charge is pushed back into the intake manifold. Engine vacuum also suffers. In general, long duration camshafts work well at higher engine speeds and short duration camshafts work well at lower speeds.

Advancing the camshaft will help at low RPM because the intake valve opens earlier, but also closes earlier. Retarding the camshaft helps at high RPM as the intake valve opens later, but also closes later, allowing more of the high velocity charge to enter.

Stretched timing chains and belts allow the valve timing to retard, which affects low-end power. Replacing the belt or chain restores the original valve timing and the engine is much smoother at low speeds.

As the piston moves up the cylinder on the compression stroke, both valves are closed, the air is being compressed, and just before TDC the mixture is ignited. The combustion pressure forces the piston down the cylinder on the power stroke. When do we open and close the exhaust valve? Again, it depends on RPM.

The greatest mechanical leverage between the connecting rod and crankshaft (90°) occurs approximately half way down the cylinder. As the piston gets closer to BDC, we begin to lose this mechanical advantage. Rather than using the remaining pressure in the cylinder to push on the piston, we're going to open the exhaust valve before BDC, which lets the cylinder pressure push the exhaust gases out into the exhaust system. At BDC as the piston reverses direction, it continues to force the spent exhaust gases out of the cylinder. When do we close the exhaust valve?

Our chart shows the valve closing at 15° after TDC, as the piston begins the intake stroke. The exiting exhaust gas also has inertia that creates a vacuum behind it. This vacuum draws out (scavenges) the last of the exhaust from the combustion chamber. We also note that the intake valve started to open before the exhaust valve closed. The period of time that both valves are open together is called the overlap period. During the overlap period (in our example 15° + 15° = 30°), the vacuum created by the exiting exhaust is used to draw in some of the new intake charge.

In general, long (high) overlap camshafts produce good top end power, but kill the low end because the incoming air/fuel charge flows right out the exhaust at low RPM. Reducing the overlap increases low speed power and compression, but top end power suffers.

The camshaft characteristics must match the operating range of the engine; so one engine may list three or more different camshafts, each designed for specific conditions.

Using the correct camshaft is a must!

VARIABLE VALVE TIMING

Variable valve timing was developed to improve engine performance at both low and high speeds. This is achieved in a number of ways.

- A moveable sprocket on the front of the camshaft allows the shaft to rotate in relation to the sprocket. Allowing oil pressure into the sprocket body moves the drive along a helical gear, which changes the timing. Oil volume is set by an electrical solenoid which is computer controlled. See Figure 9–25(a).
- Engines with a single camshaft advance the timing at low RPM and retard the timing at higher speeds.
- Dual overhead camshaft engines usually control the intake cam only. This allows the overlap to be adjusted for operating conditions. Low speeds requires short overlap, increasing the speed requires longer overlap. See Figures 9–25(b) and 9–25(c).
- The Honda VTEC variable valve timing uses a different principle. Both short duration low lift cam lobes and a long duration high lift lobe are used. At low speeds, the rocker for the mild lobe is active and the high lift rocker is inactive. Around 4800 rpm, a piston located in the high lift rocker is moved by oil pressure (computer activated) which locks both the low and high speed rockers together. The long duration, high lift cam lobe now controls the valve action. See Figures 9–25(d) and 9–25(e).

INSTALLING THE CAMSHAFT

When the camshaft is installed, the lobes must be coated with a special lubricant containing molydisulfide. This special lube helps to ensure proper initial lubrication to the critical cam lobe sections of the camshaft. Many manufacturers recommend multi-viscosity engine oil such as SAE 5W-30 or SAE 10W-30. Some camshaft manufacturers recommend using

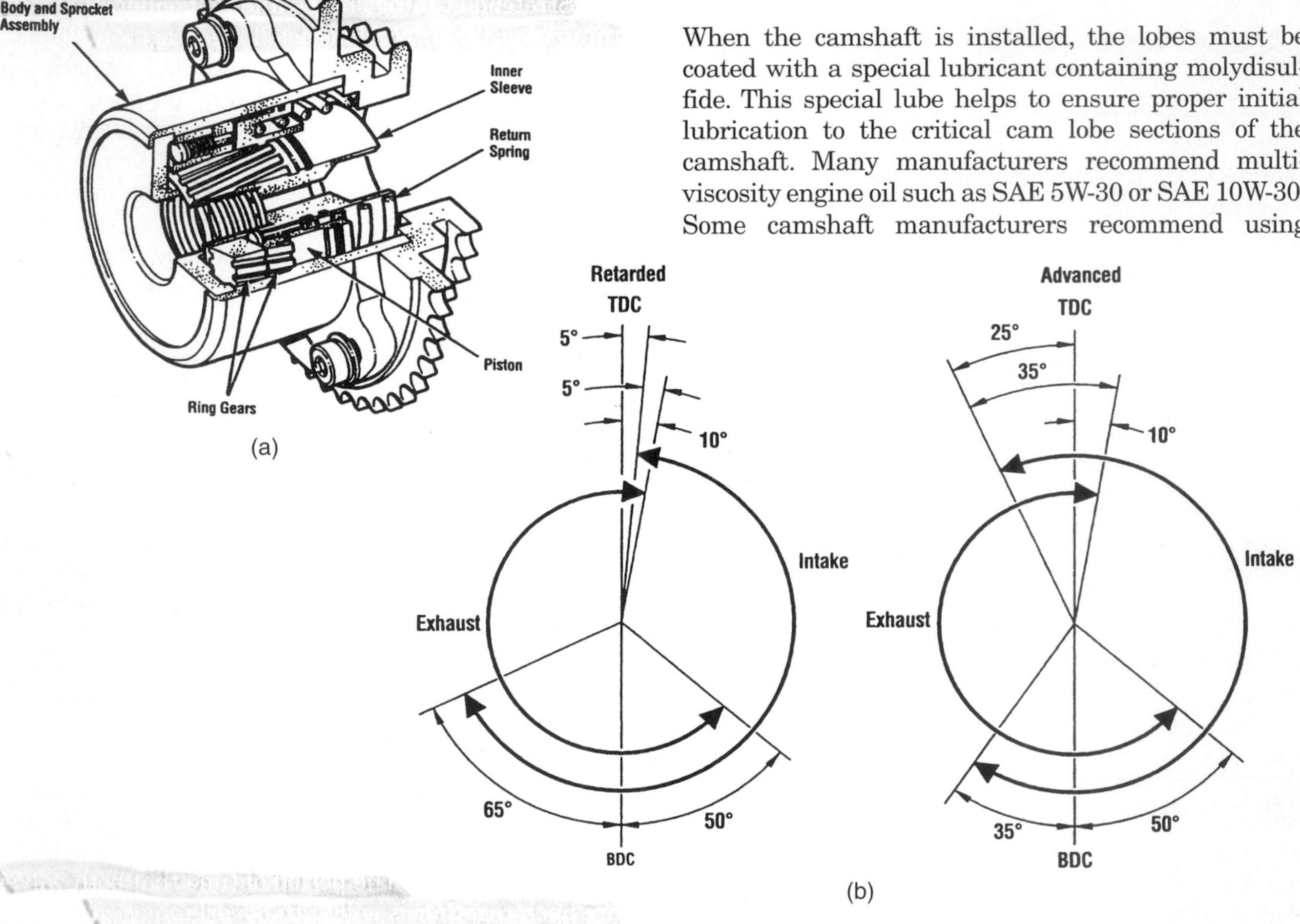

Figure 9–25 Variable valve timing components. (a) Cross-section of a moveable camshaft drive sprocket. (b) Valve timing chart for intake camshaft control. Advancing one cam only increases valve overlap. (Jaguar Canada and Ford Motor Company trademarks and Jaguar branded products used with permission)

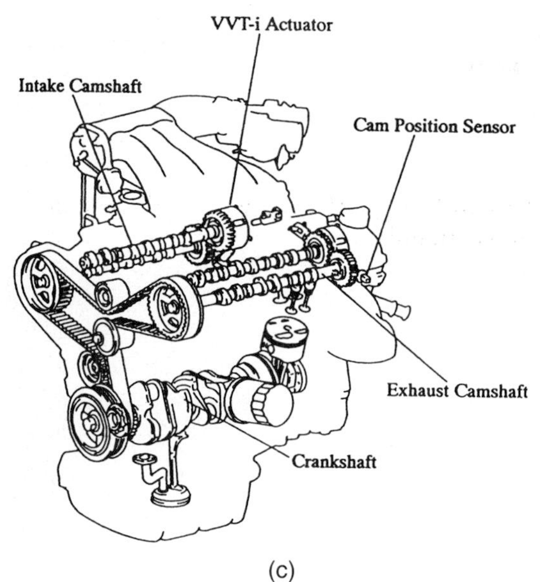

Figure 9–25 Continued (c) A dual overhead camshaft engine with the moveable camshaft drive sprocket (VVT-iActuator) mounted on the intake camshaft. (Courtesy Toyota Motor Co.) (d) The Honda V-TEC engine uses both outer short-duration cam lobes at low speed. The centre cam and rocker are not connected to the valves. (Courtesy Honda Motor Co.) (e) At higher speeds, a piston, controlled with oil pressure, locks all three rockers together. The centre long-duration cam lobe now overrides the short-duration lobes. (Courtesy Honda Motor Co.)

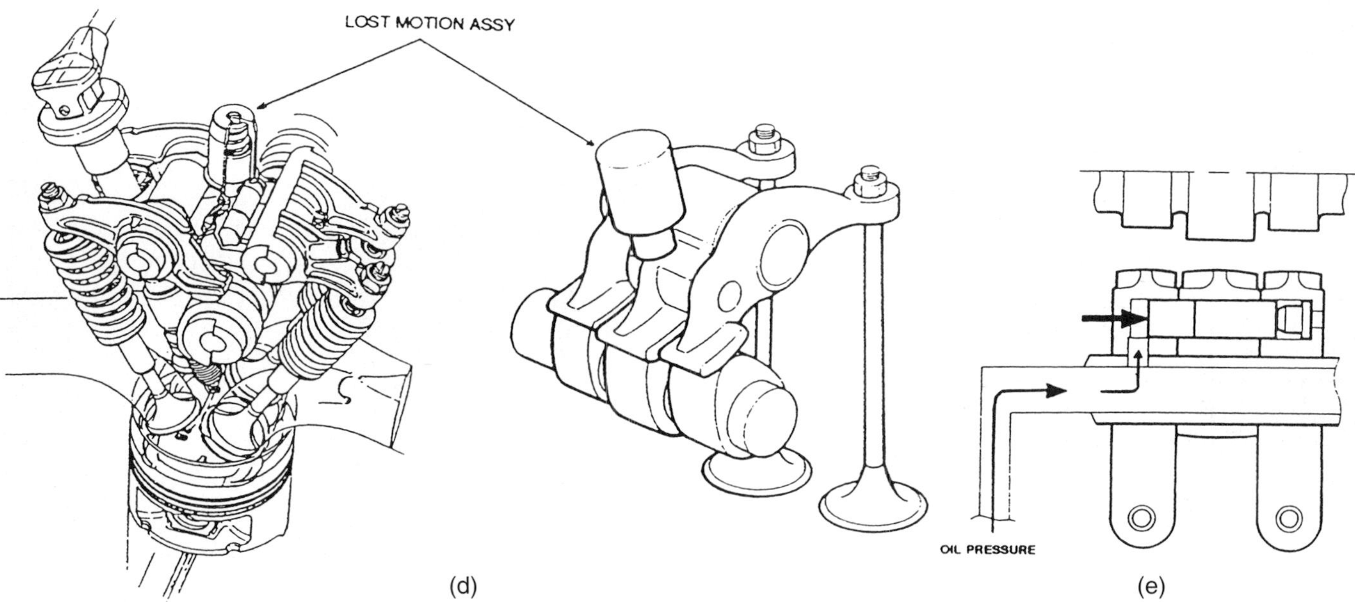

straight SAE 30 or SAE 40 engine oil and not a multi-viscosity oil for the first oil fill. Some manufacturers also recommend the use of an antiwear additive such as zinc dithiophosphate (ZDP). See Figures 9–26 and 9–27.

The camshaft must be broken in by maintaining engine speed above 1500 rpm for the first 10 minutes of engine operation. If the engine speed is decreased to idle (about 600 rpm), the lifter (tappet) or rocker arm will be in contact with and exerting force on the lobe of the cam for a longer period of time than occurs at higher engine speeds. The pressure and volume of oil supplied to the camshaft area are also increased at the higher engine speeds. Therefore, to ensure long camshaft and lifter/rocker life, make certain that the engine will start quickly after a new camshaft and lifters have been installed to prevent long cranking periods and subsequent low engine speeds. When repairing an engine, follow these rules regarding the camshaft and lifters:

1. When installing a new camshaft, always install new valve lifters (tappets).
2. When installing new lifters, if the original cam is not excessively worn and if the pushrods all rotate with the original camshaft, the camshaft may be reused.
3. *Never* use a hydraulic camshaft with solid lifters or hydraulic lifters with a solid lifter camshaft.

NOTE: Some manufacturers recommend that a new camshaft always be installed when replacing valve lifters.

NOTE: Some performance engine builders use a degree wheel (Figure 9–28) to ensure that valve timing is correct.

Figure 9–26 Special lubricant such as this one from General Motors is required to be used on the the lobes of the camshaft and the bottom of the flat-bottomed lifters.

Figure 9–27 Care should be taken when installing a camshaft not to nick or scrape the cam bearings.

(a)

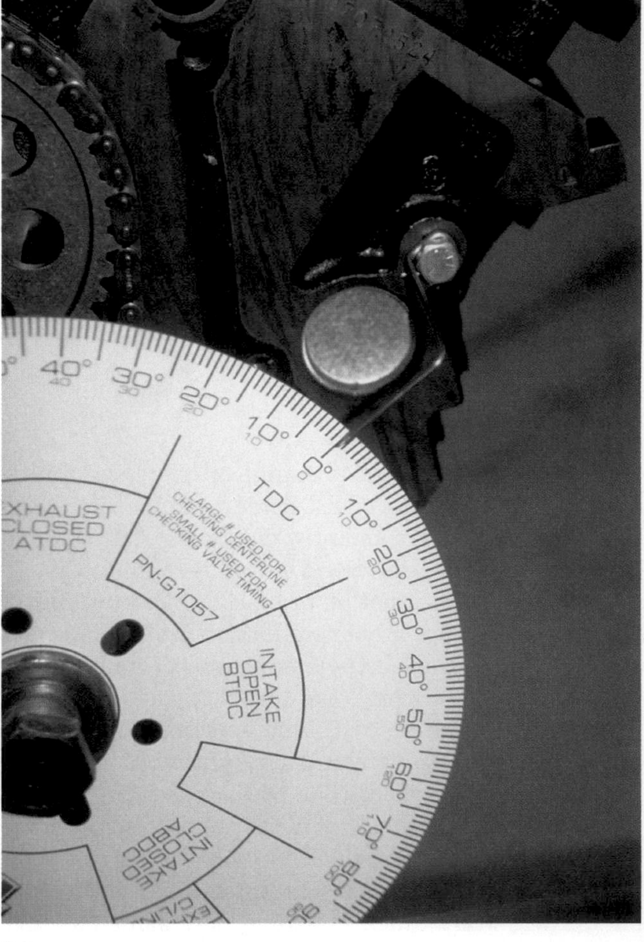

(b)

Figure 9–28 (a) The set-up required to degree a camshaft. (b) Closeup of the pointer and the degree wheel.

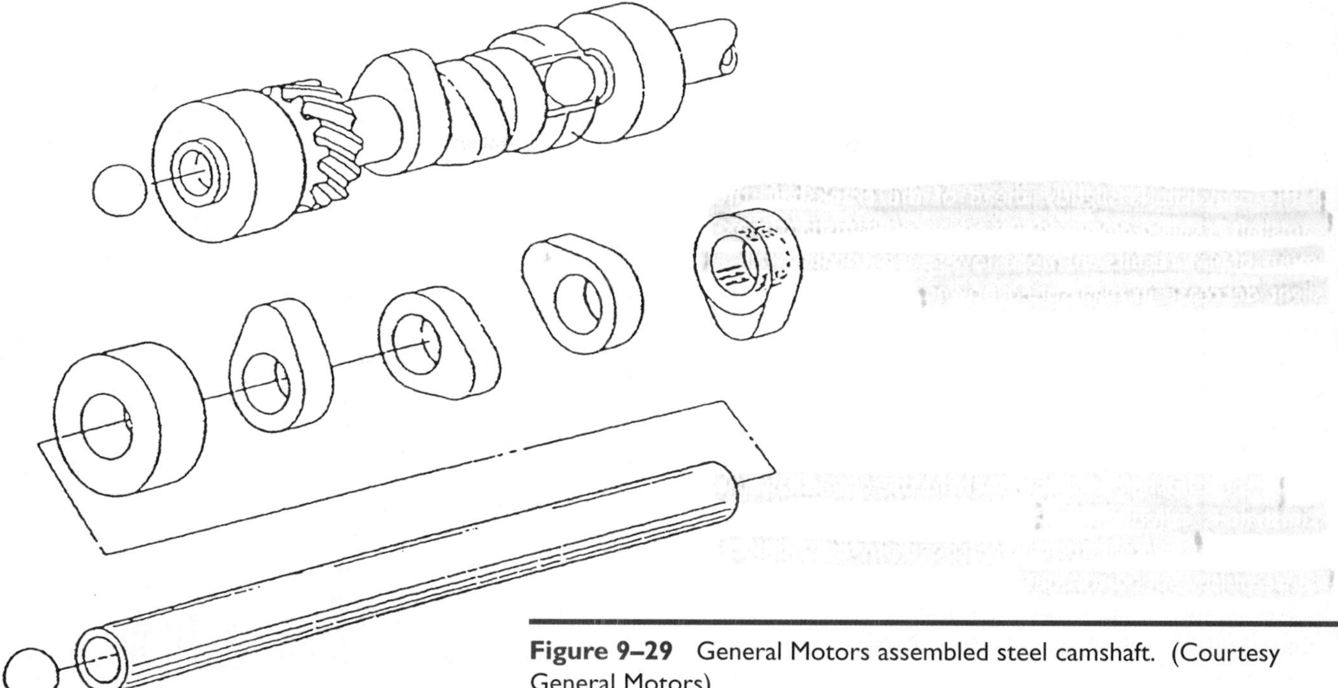

Figure 9–29 General Motors assembled steel camshaft. (Courtesy General Motors)

ASSEMBLED CAMSHAFTS

Camshafts are normally cast or machined in one piece. Several manufacturers are now using assembled camshafts which allows different materials to be combined on a single shaft. General Motors uses three different steel alloys and a cast-iron gear to increase durability.

The manufacturing process starts with individual cam lobes being positioned on a hollow steel shaft. A steel ball, larger than the inside diameter, is forced through the hollow shaft which expands and locks the lobes. See Figure 9–29.

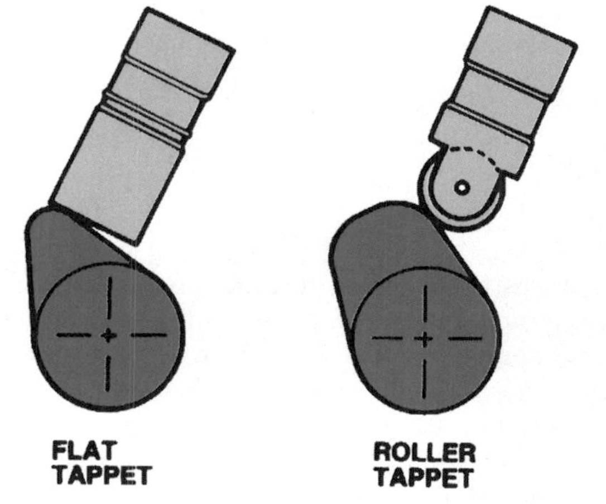

Figure 9–30 Lifters or tappets are made in two styles: flat bottom and roller.

LIFTERS

Valve lifters (also called **tappets**) follow the contour or shape of the camshaft lobe. This arrangement changes the cam motion to a reciprocating motion in the valve train. Most older-style lifters have a slightly convex surface that slides on the cam. See Figure 9–30. Some lifters, however, are designed with a roller to follow the cam contour. Roller lifters are used in production engines to reduce valve train friction (by up to 8%). This friction reduction can increase fuel economy and help to offset the greater manufacturing cost. All roller lifters must use a retainer to prevent lifter rotation.

Camshaft lobes designed for roller lifters must have a very hard surface to match the steel rollers. Some cams are made of steel and others use heat-treated iron. In some cases, the distributor gear material is matched for compatibility with the camshaft gear. Using the incorrect distributor gear will ruin both the camshaft and distributor gear.

Valve train clearance is also called **valve lash.** Valve train clearance must not be excessive, or it will cause noise or result in premature failure. Two methods are commonly used to make the necessary valve clearance adjustments. One involves a **solid valve lifter** with a mechanical adjustment, and the other involves a lifter with an automatic hydraulic adjustment built into the lifter body, called a **hydraulic valve lifter.**

A hydraulic lifter consists primarily of a hollow cylinder body enclosing a closely fitted hollow plunger, a check valve, and a pushrod cup. Lifters that feed oil up through the pushrod have a metering

HIGH PERFORMANCE TIP

Varying the Valve Timing to Vary Engine Performance

If the camshaft is slightly ahead of the crankshaft, the camshaft is called *advanced.* An advanced camshaft (maximum of 4°) results in more low-speed torque with a slight decrease in high-speed power. Some aftermarket camshaft manufacturers design about a 4° advance into their timing gears or camshaft. This permits the use of a camshaft with more lift and duration, yet still provides the smooth idle and low-speed responses of a milder camshaft.

If the camshaft is slightly behind the crankshaft, the camshaft is called *retarded.* A retarded camshaft (maximum of 4°) results in more high-speed power at the expense of low-speed torque.

If the measured values are different from specifications, special offset pins or keys are available to relocate the cam gear by the proper amount. Some manufacturers provide adjustable cam timing sprockets for overhead cam engines.

Be aware that changing cam timing may cause a rise in emissions.

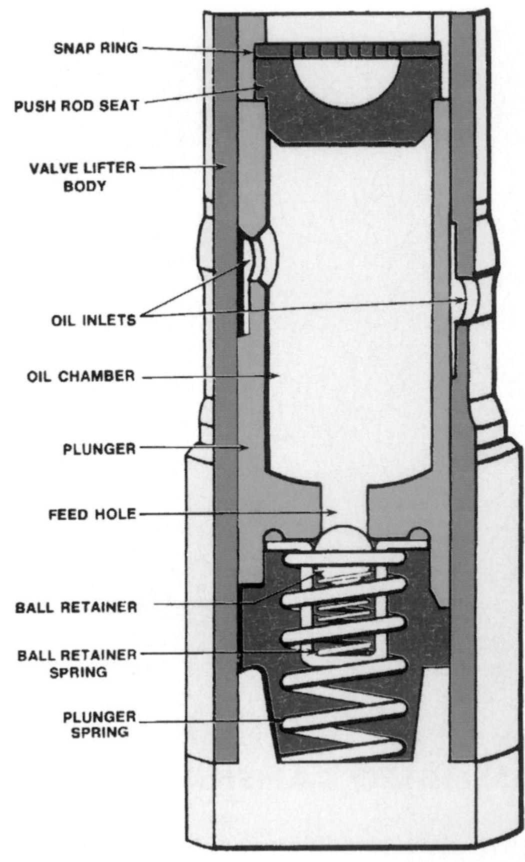

Figure 9–31 A cross-sectional view of a typical flat-bottomed hydraulic lifter.

disk or restrictor valve located under the pushrod cup. Engine oil under pressure is fed through an engine passage to the exterior lifter body. An undercut portion allows the oil under pressure to surround the lifter body. Oil under pressure goes through holes in the undercut section into the centre of the plunger. From there, it goes down through the check valve to a clearance space between the bottom of the plunger and the interior bottom of the lifter body. It fills this space with oil at engine pressure. Slight leakage allowance is designed into the lifter so that the air can bleed out and the lifter can leak down if it should become overfilled. See Figures 9–31 through 9–34.

CAUTION: Using too thick (high viscosity) an engine oil can cause the hydraulic lifters or hydraulic lash adjusters to not bleed down as fast as they should. This slow bleed-down can cause a valve(s) to remain open, which results in an engine miss. Using an SAE 10W-40 instead of the specified SAE 5W-20 could cause the lifters to bleed down more slowly than normal and cause a driveability problem, especially if the oil is not changed at specified intervals.

INTAKE MANIFOLDS

The intake manifold is designed to deliver equal amounts of air (or air and fuel) to each intake port in the cylinder head. Older intake manifolds were made of cast iron or aluminum; newer V-type manifolds are usually made of aluminum (bottom) and the top from a plastic composite. The latest manifolds are often all plastic, although aluminum tubing is still found on some imports. See Figure 9–35.

Manifolds are classified as wet when a carburetor, or throttle-body type of fuel injection (TBI), delivers fuel to the *plenum* (the open area under the carburetor) and both air and fuel pass through the intake manifold. The combination of the manifold passage and the cylinder head intake port is known as the *runner.*

Dry manifolds pass air only through the intake runners. Fuel is injected into the cylinder head intake port or directly into the combustion chamber. See Figure 9–36. Dry manifolds are more efficient than wet because:

1. Intake air does not require heating to vaporize the fuel.

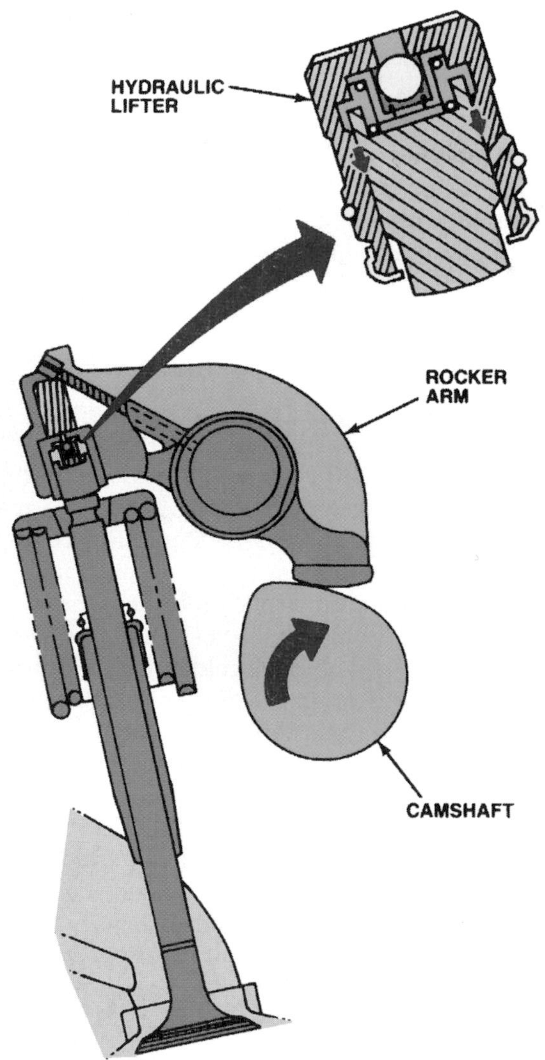

Figure 9–32 Hydraulic lash adjusters (HLA) are built into the rocker arm on some OHC engines.

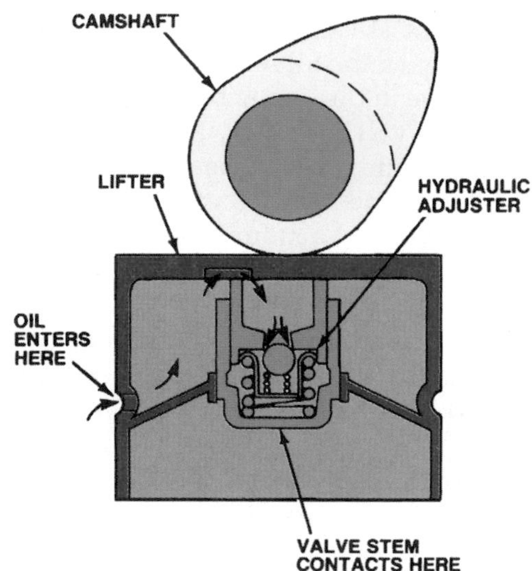

Figure 9–33 Hydraulic lifters are also built into bucket-type lifters on many OHC engines.

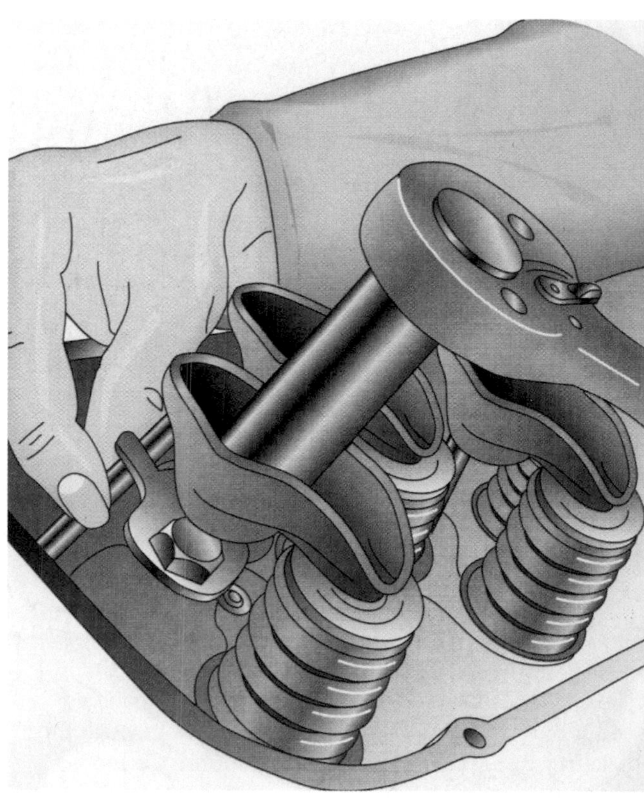

Figure 9–34 To correctly adjust hydraulic valve lifters, position the camshaft on the base circle of the camshaft lobe for the valve being adjusted. Remove all clearance by spinning the pushrod and tightening the nut until all clearance is removed. The adjusting nut is then tightened one complete revolution. This is what is meant by the term "zero lash plus 1 turn."

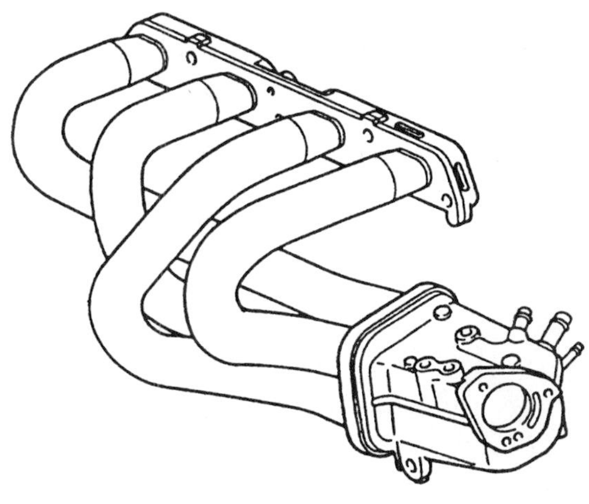

Figure 9–35 This four cylinder all-aluminum tubular intake manifold uses long runners to improve low and mid-range torque. (Courtesy Toyota Canada Inc.)

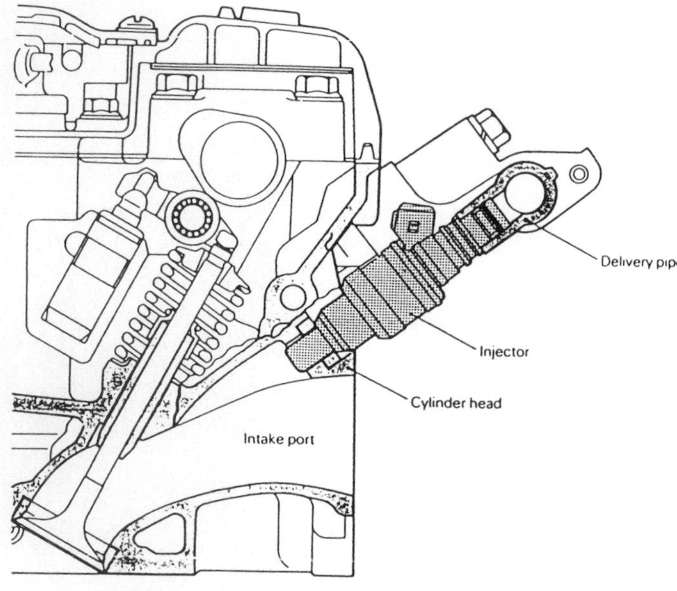

Figure 9–36 Port fuel injection sprays fuel into the cylinder head intake port. This type of intake manifold used is classified as dry since air only passes through the intake runners. (Courtesy Mitsubishi Motor Co.)

2. Fuel does not drop out of suspension in the air and stick to the walls of the intake runner.
3. Equal amounts of fuel are supplied to each cylinder by the fuel injectors.

Dual-Plane Manifolds

Older carburetted (and some TBI) V-8 engines have a concern with unequal air-fuel distribution; cylinders that are side by side and follow each other in firing order often draw mixture from the same corner of the manifold. Dual-plane manifolds are essentially two four-cylinder manifolds joined together at the plenum area. See Figure 9–37. Cylinders close to one another in firing order now draw mixture from opposite sides of the engine correcting the problem.

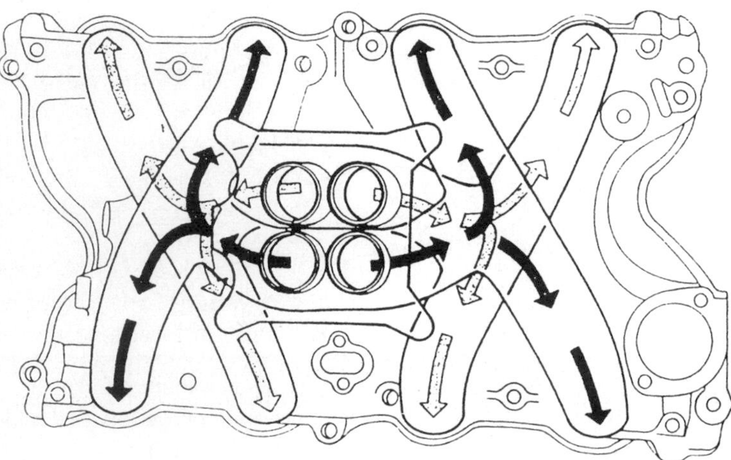

Figure 9–37 Dual plane manifold. Notice that each side of the carburetor feeds two cylinders on the right bank and two on the left bank, *not* all four on the left and all four on the right. (Courtesy Ford Motor Co. of Canada Ltd.)

It is important to understand the manifold layout when diagnosing carburetion problems.

Intake Manifold Heat Control

The air–fuel mixture passing through the intake runners requires engine heat to assist in vaporizing the fuel, making it easier to ignite. When the engine is cold, much of the fuel still remains in liquid form, which makes driveability problems, such as stalling and hesitation, common.

Warming the Mixture

Many engines heat the floor (bottom) of the intake manifold plenum area to vaporize the fuel. V-type engines have an exhaust crossover passage connected to one cylinder head exhaust port in each bank. See Figure 9–38. An exhaust manifold heat riser valve, usually vacuum controlled, closes off one exhaust manifold when the engine is cold. Exhaust from that bank must pass through the crossover passage in order to leave the engine: This heats the intake manifold. As the engine comes up to temperature, a vacuum switching valve cuts off manifold vacuum to the heat riser valve and the valve opens, allowing the exhaust to leave from both exhaust manifolds. A very small amount of exhaust now passes under the plenum and the intake manifold cools.

Heat riser valves that stick in the open position cause cold driveability problems; engine operation is normal after warm-up. Valves that stay closed cause problems with a warm engine, such as carburetor percolation (fuel overheating), hard starting, and loss of power from the restricted exhaust.

The system is simple to test—applying vacuum to the heat riser diaphragm should cause the valve to close without sticking. The vacuum should hold. Releasing the vacuum allows the valve to open. Place a vacuum gauge in the line at the heat riser. The vacuum switching valve (VSV), which is threaded into the cooling system, should pass manifold vacuum when cold and restrict vacuum when the engine is warm. Vacuum lines to the VSV and heat riser should be inspected for cracks or blockage.

The crossover passage in the manifold may plug with carbon, usually on high-kilometre oil-burning engines. If the manifold below the

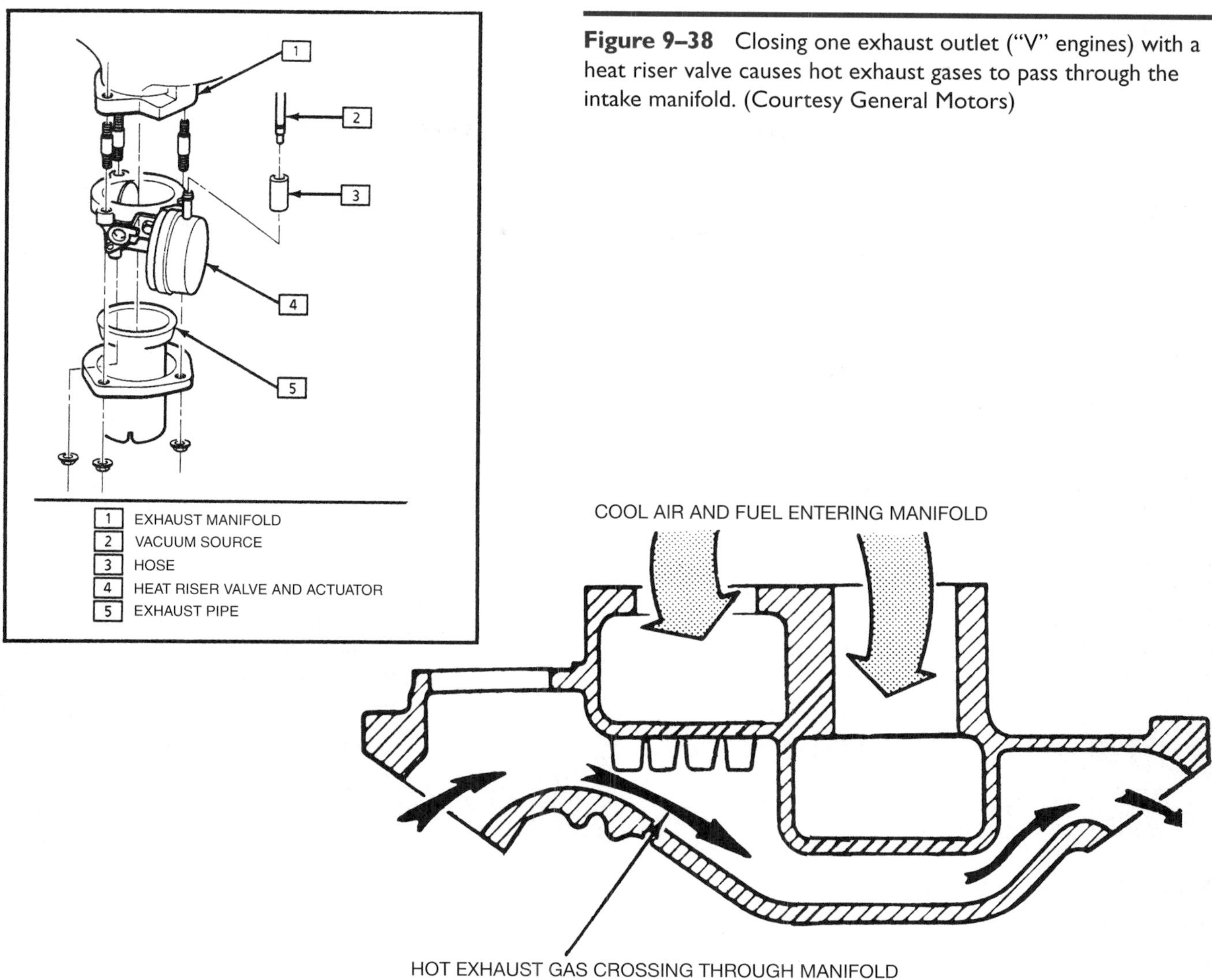

Figure 9–38 Closing one exhaust outlet ("V" engines) with a heat riser valve causes hot exhaust gases to pass through the intake manifold. (Courtesy General Motors)

carburetor base does not warm up quickly on a cold engine, suspect a plugged manifold (if the heat riser valve is closing). Lack of power and stalling, cold, is another indication. The manifold must be removed for cleaning.

Older in-line engines (and some V-8s) use a spring-loaded damper as a heat riser valve. Exhaust heat causes the spring to unwind and the damper opens. The damper shaft should be lubricated with a special heat-riser penetrating oil at every tune-up to prevent sticking.

Tuned Intake Manifolds

The section on valve timing stated that the intake valve should close just before cylinder pressure (piston coming up on the compression stroke) overcomes the speed and pressure of the air rushing into the cylinder. Engines running at high RPM could keep the valve open later because of the increased air speed in the intake runner.

Tuning the intake manifold runner length to the normal operating range of the engine will improve cylinder filling (volumetric efficiency). In general, long, small diameter runners increase air speed (ram effect) at lower RPM for good low and mid-range torque. This type of manifold limits air flow at higher RPM and top-end power suffers. See Figure 9–39.

Long, narrow runners increase intake air speed at lower RPM, good for low-medium RPM power. Short, wide runners do not restrict the incoming air and rely on high RPM for increasing the air speed: good for mid-range and top-end power.

Shorter, larger diameter runners work well at higher RPM; however, at low speeds the air mass slows down and low-end power suffers.

Many larger V engines run at lower RPM and utilize long, narrow runners. Four-cylinder engines usually operate at higher RPM and require short, wide runners. It is important to match the camshaft and the intake manifold to the usual operating range of the engine.

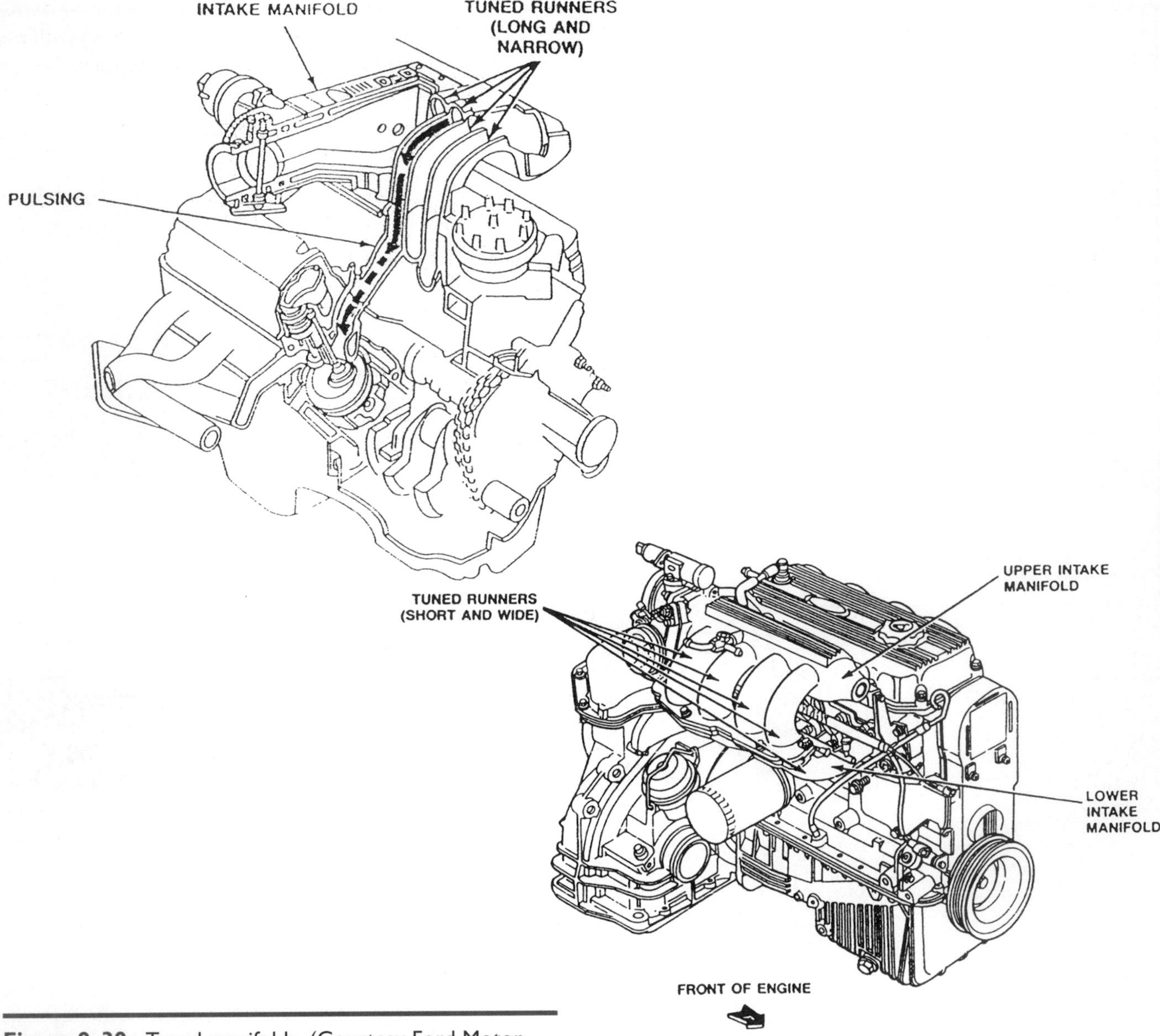

Figure 9–39 Tuned manifolds. (Courtesy Ford Motor Company of Canada Ltd.)

Variable Induction Systems

Variable induction systems have the advantage of changing the runner size or length, to match the operating RPM of the engine.

The Toyota manifold in Figure 9–40 fits a four-cylinder engine with a four-valve (two intake, two exhaust) cylinder head. Each intake valve has its own runner. At lower RPM, the four intake air control valves (not to be confused with the throttle plate) are closed. All of the air must pass through a single runner for each cylinder. This increases air speed providing a ram effect for improved cylinder filling. At higher RPM, the air control valves open, intake air now flows through all runners, and top end power increases.

Closing the four intake air control valves causes the air speed to increase in the four open runners. Although two intake valves are open (four-valve head), only one is functional until the second runner is opened.

At higher speeds, about 4000 to 5500 rpm, the powertrain control module (PCM) energizes an electrical vacuum switching valve (VSV), which allows vacuum to reach the actuator. This opens the air control valves and all eight runners now function.

Another type of variable manifold is on the Ford high-output V-6. See Figure 9–41. The short runners are closed at low speed with a throttling valve—air enters through the long runners only. At higher speeds (RPM), the valve opens and air now passes via the short runners.

V-6 engines often use a variable tuning control valve to change the runner length. See Figure 9–42(a). This General Motors intake manifold has a normally closed tuning valve (IMTV), which splits the manifold into two separate plenums. See Figure

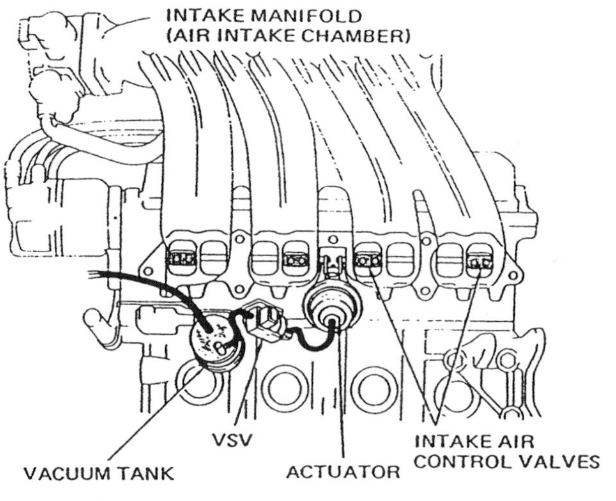

Figure 9–40 Toyota four-cylinder variable induction system. (Courtesy Toyota Canada Inc.)

9–42(b). This effectively increases the runner length. At higher RPM the IMTV opens and the operating length shortens as it now begins at the common plenum.

AIR INTAKE SYSTEMS

The air intake system has a number of functions, including

- Filtering the incoming air
- Heating the air to prevent throttle-plate icing
- Reducing noise levels
- Holding positive crankcase ventilation (PCV) filters
- Providing a mounting for the electronic engine sensors on some models, such as mass airflow sensors or intake air temperature sensors

Throttle-Plate Icing

Throttle-plate icing, also known as carburetor icing, happens when moisture from the incoming air freezes on the throttle plate (and venturi area with carburetors), blocking airflow and causing the engine to stall. It does not usually occur when temperatures are very low, below freezing, or above 10°C (50°F). It is a major problem in areas with high humidity—such as Vancouver, Toronto, and Halifax—when ambient temperatures are in the range of 1° to 10°C (34° to 50°F). Heating the air before it reaches the low-pressure, low-temperature area around the throttle prevents freezing. This is one function of the air cleaner.

Air Temperature Control

The air intake system supplies heated air from around the exhaust manifold during cold weather operation. See Figure 9–43. As the engine comes up to temperature, the damper valve gradually shuts off heated air and opens to cool air. See Figure 9–44.

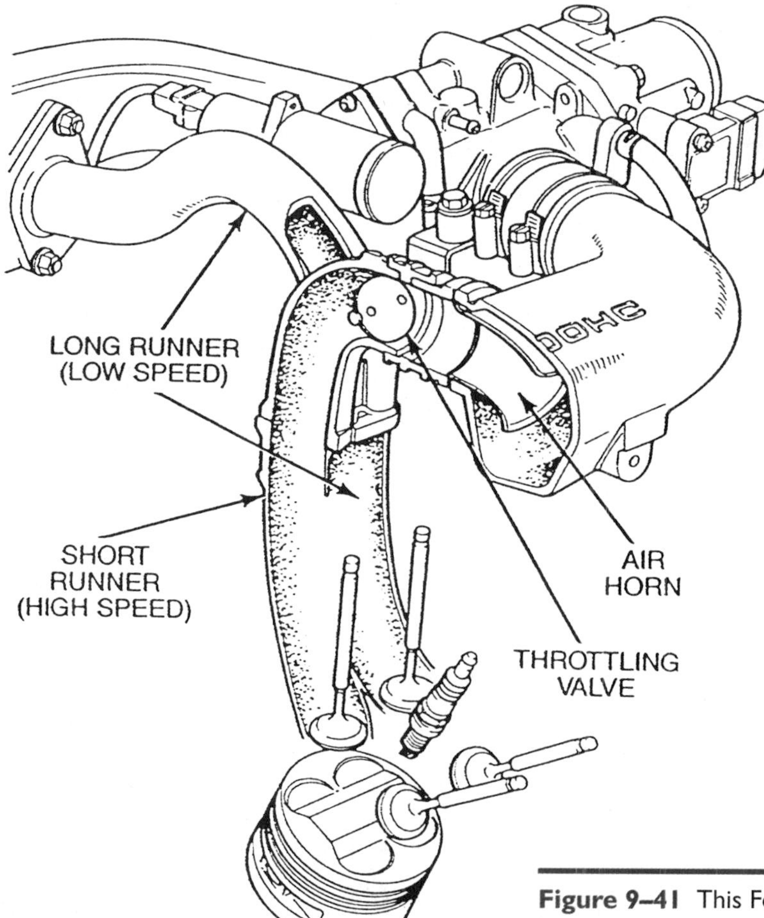

Figure 9–41 This Ford V-6 manifold uses long runners for improved low-speed power and short runners for enhanced high-speed performance. (Courtesy Ford Motor Co. of Canada)

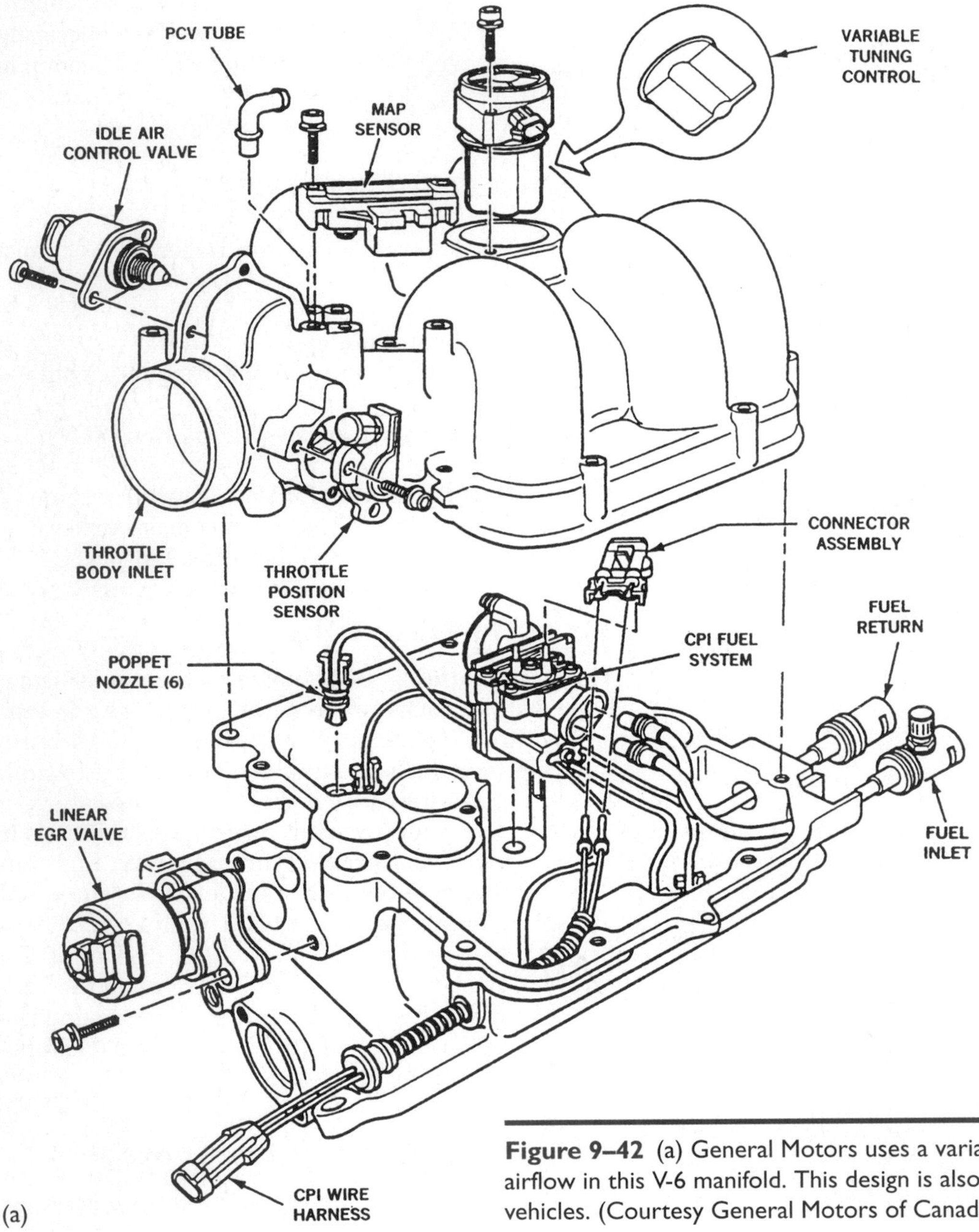

PCV TUBE
VARIABLE TUNING CONTROL
MAP SENSOR
IDLE AIR CONTROL VALVE
THROTTLE BODY INLET
THROTTLE POSITION SENSOR
CONNECTOR ASSEMBLY
FUEL RETURN
CPI FUEL SYSTEM
POPPET NOZZLE (6)
LINEAR EGR VALVE
FUEL INLET
CPI WIRE HARNESS

(a)

Figure 9–42 (a) General Motors uses a variable tuning valve to control airflow in this V-6 manifold. This design is also found on some Asian vehicles. (Courtesy General Motors of Canada Ltd.)

INTAKE AIR FLOW
ZIP TUBES
IMTV CLOSED (OFF)
INTAKE AIR FLOW
ZIP TUBES
IMTV OPEN (ON)

(b)

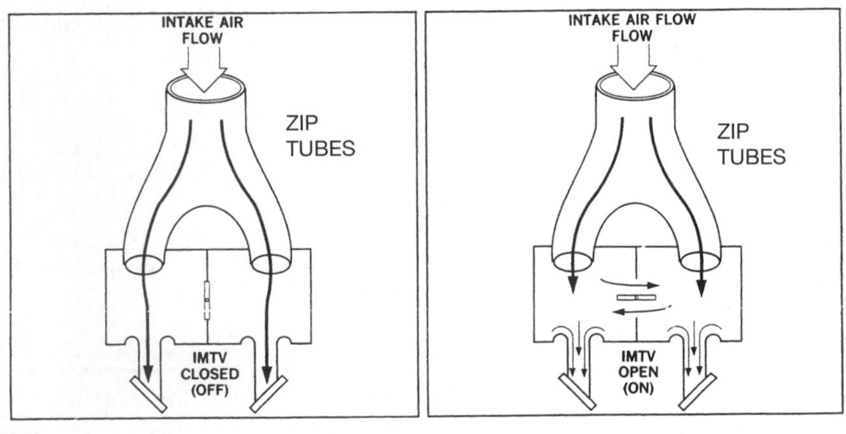

Figure 9–42 (b) Runner length (long) includes the "zip" tubes when the intake manifold tuning valve (IMTV) is closed. Opening the IMTV effectively shortens the runner length, which now begins at the plenum area. (Courtesy General Motors of Canada Ltd.)

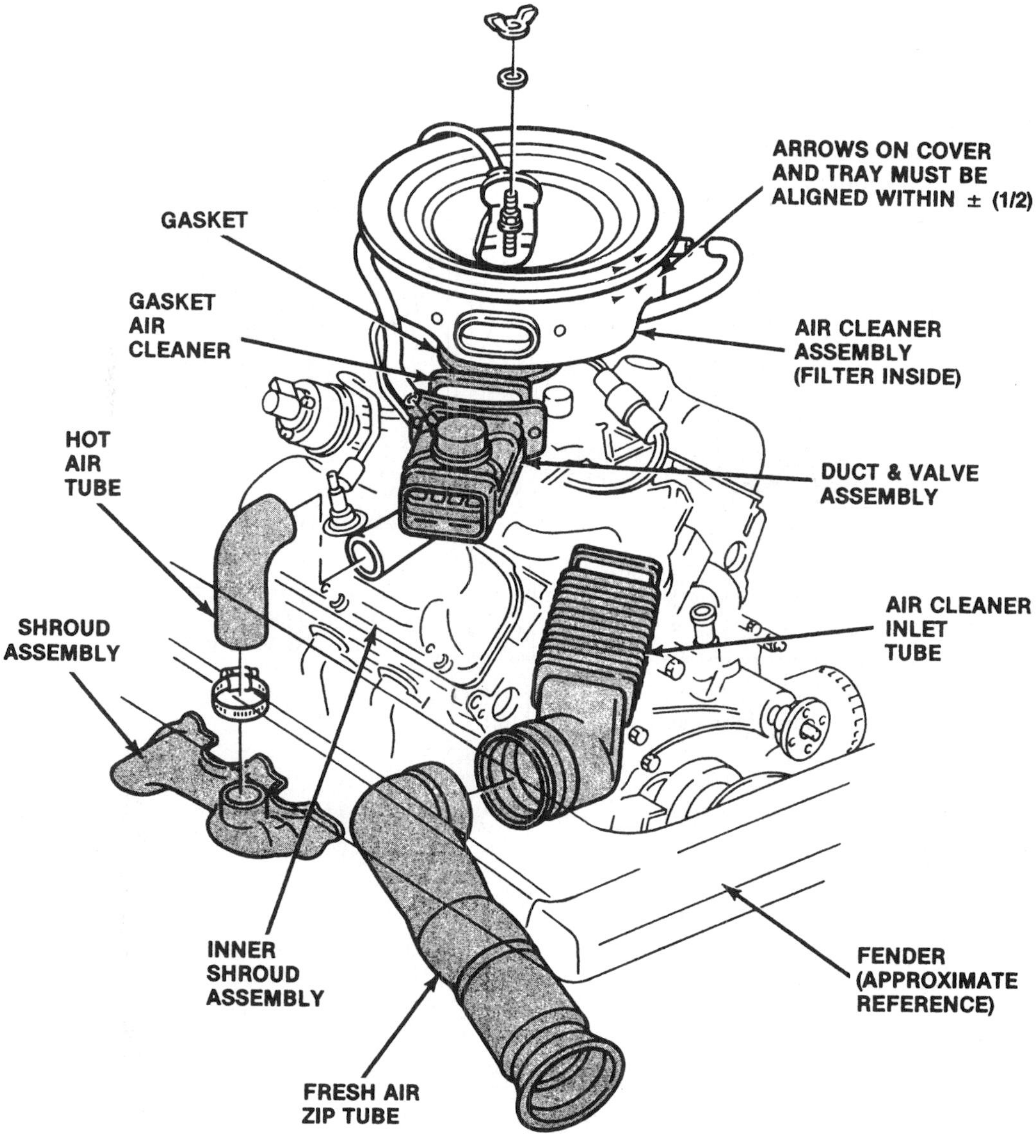

Figure 9–43 This air cleaner, found on carbureted engines, has both hot and cold air pickups. During cold engine operation, hot air from around the exhaust manifold mixes with fuel at the carburetor. This provides better fuel vaporization and reduces, or eliminates throttle-plate icing. As the engine warms up, the damper door closes the hot air pickup and opens to cold air delivery. (Courtesy Ford Motor Co. of Canada Ltd.)

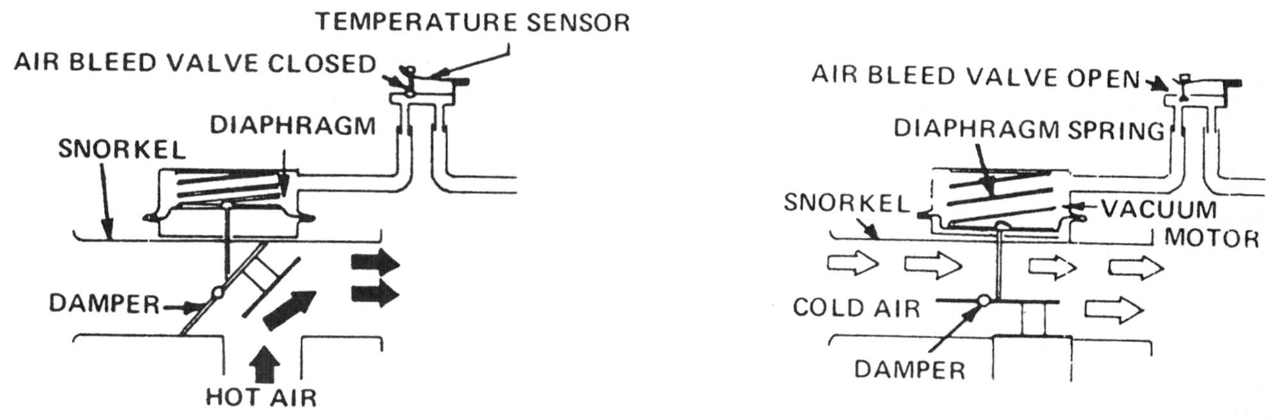

Figure 9–44 Intake manifold vacuum passes through the temperature sensor (mounted inside the air cleaner) to the vacuum motor at the snorkel. This raises the damper, allowing hot air into the engine. (Courtesy Ignition Manufacturers Institute, *Automotive Emission Controls and Tune-Up Procedures* [Prentice Hall, 1980])

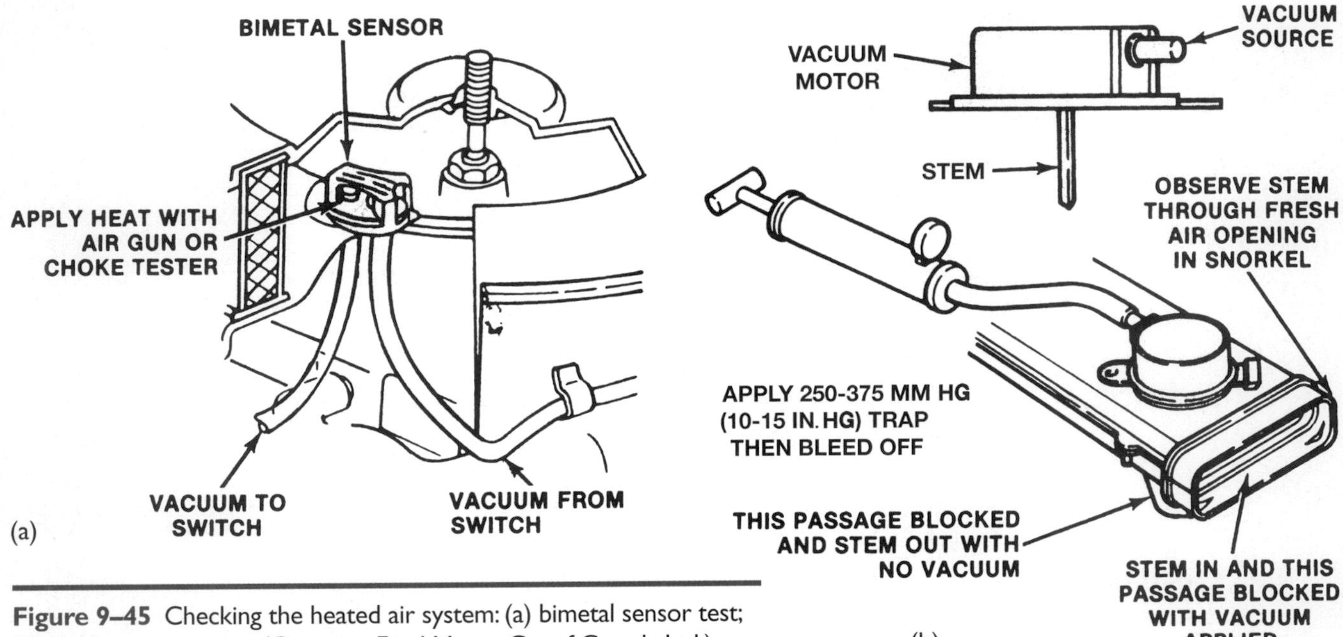

Figure 9–45 Checking the heated air system: (a) bimetal sensor test; (b) vacuum motor test. (Courtesy Ford Motor Co. of Canada Ltd.)

The bimetal spring in the temperature sensor bends from the incoming warm air; this creates an air leak at the bleed valve; vacuum is lost and the diaphragm spring forces the damper to gradually close the hot air duct. Cold air now enters.

Wet versus Dry Manifolds

Heated air cleaners also play a large part in cold engine driveability. Warm incoming air helps the liquid fuel to vaporize and ignite easily until the engine temperature rises. This is not a problem with dry manifolds, as air only passes through the manifold. Fuel is injected, usually, at the intake valve.

Throttle-plate icing is still a concern with dry manifolds; the moisture in the air freezes, not the fuel. These engines often have a heated grid or a hot water pocket at the throttle body to prevent icing.

Testing the Heated Air System

These systems are also simple to test.

- Place a thermometer inside the air cleaner.
- Start the engine and observe the damper; it should be closed to cold air.
- As the engine warms up, note when the damper begins to open. Remove the thermometer from inside the air cleaner and record the temperature. Compare the reading to the service manual specification. An incorrect opening temperature indicates a faulty bimetal sensor, provided there are no leaks in the hoses or vacuum motor.
- The bimetal sensor can also be tested by applying heat to the sensor with a heat gun (normally used to collapse shrink tubing), and checking the vacuum signal at the vacuum motor hose. See Figure 9–45(a).
- The vacuum motor is tested by applying vacuum from a hand-held vacuum pump to the motor. Vacuum should hold and the damper should close. Releasing vacuum will allow the damper to open with no signs of dragging on the snorkel. See Figure 9–45(b).

Air Cleaner Filter Element

These filters are usually made of pleated paper and are replaced at a given number of kilometres or elapsed time. Vehicles driven on dusty roads will need more frequent replacement. If the filter looks clean on a visual inspection and light from a trouble lamp can be seen through the filter, it may be reinstalled after being blown out with compressed air. See Figure 9–46. If in doubt, replace the filter element.

Air Filter Restriction Indicators

Some vehicles are equipped with filter indicators (sometimes called filter minders) that change colour when the filter becomes restricted. See Figure 9–47.

EXHAUST SYSTEMS

The original purpose of the exhaust system was to route spent gases to the rear of the vehicle and lower exhaust noise.

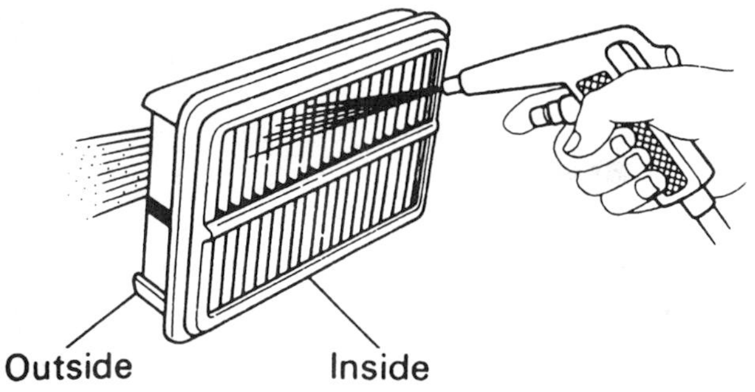

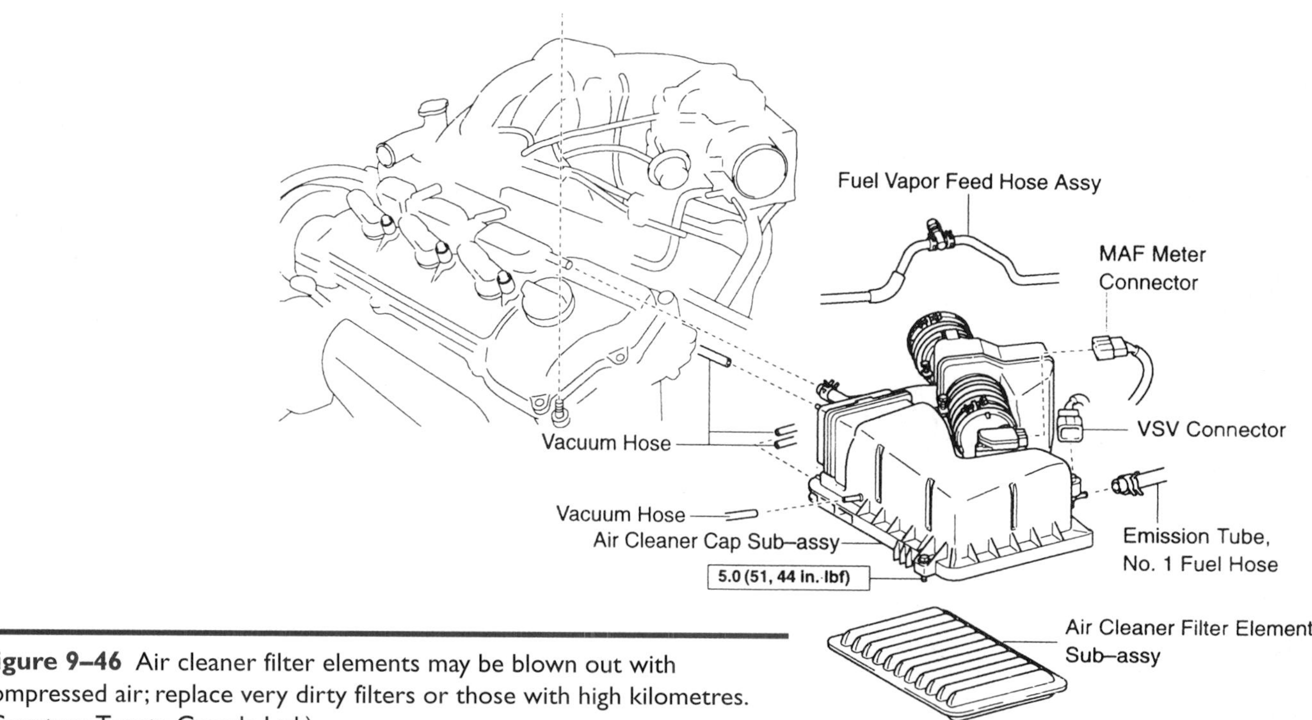

Figure 9–46 Air cleaner filter elements may be blown out with compressed air; replace very dirty filters or those with high kilometres. (Courtesy Toyota Canada Ltd.)

Since the introduction of emission controls, the exhaust system also

- Provides air injection mountings in the manifold
- May contain one to six oxygen sensors that monitor engine air-fuel ratios and catalytic converter(s) condition
- Includes three-way (hydrocarbon, carbon monoxide and oxides of nitrogen) converters in the exhaust manifold or front pipes
- May contain an adsorber to store hydrocarbons or oxides of nitrogen. See Figure 9–48.

This section will cover the standard exhaust items found on passenger cars and light trucks. Catalytic converters and other emission related components are found in Chapter 30: "Emission Control Device Operation, Diagnosis and Service."

Exhaust Manifolds

Exhaust manifolds are usually made of lightweight stainless steel tubing. Individual tubes for each cylinder are tuned for maximum power at the normal operating range. See Figure 9–49. Cast-iron manifolds are still used on some heavy vehicles where weight is not a major concern, or on passenger cars that require a lower noise level. Tubular "header" style manifolds are generally noisier than cast iron—iron dampens exhaust pulse noises.

Iron manifolds are prone to crack when mounted on inline four- and six-cylinder aluminum cylinder heads because of differing expansion rates. Only high quality exhaust gaskets should be used and torquing is a must. Over-torquing stops the manifold from "sliding" on the head and a crack often develops.

The Honda Insight casts the exhaust manifold and cylinder head in one unit. This reduces weight

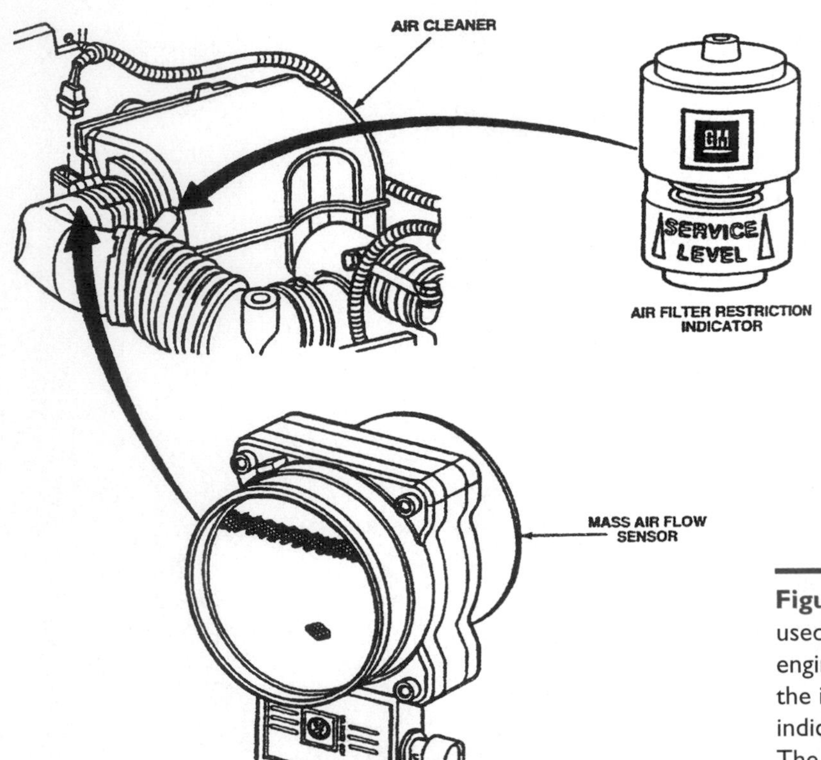

Figure 9–47 Air filter restriction indicators (if used) are located between the air cleaner and the engine. If the air filter becomes clogged or restricted, the increase in intake hose vacuum will cause this indicator to change colour, from green to orange. The indicator must be reset when a new filter is installed. (Courtesy General Motors of Canada Ltd.)

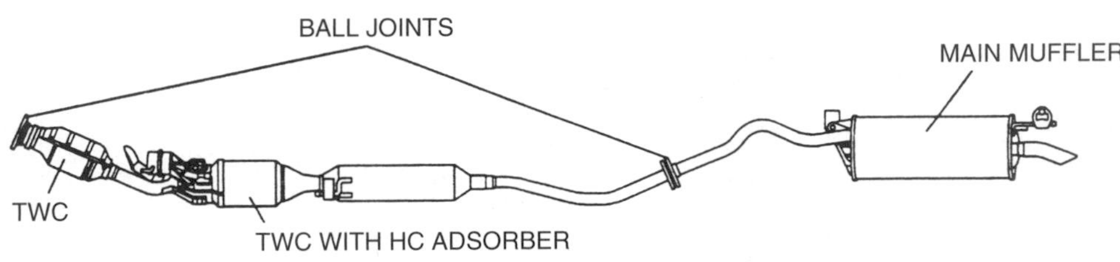

Figure 9–48 A typical exhaust system with three-way catalytic converters, a hydrocarbon adsorber, and a main muffler. (Courtesy Toyota Canada Inc.)

and allows the catalytic converter to heat up more quickly. See Figure 9–50.

Catalyst Location

Catalytic converters require a great deal of engine exhaust heat in order to function. The closer to the engine, the better. Some vehicles have the converter bolted directly to the exhaust manifold (see Figure 9–51); others build the converter and manifold as one unit. One-piece converter-manifolds are replaced as an assembly. Bolt-on or weld-on converters are also located in the front exhaust pipe(s).

Mufflers and Resonators

The most common original equipment muffler is the reverse-flow type. See Figure 9–52. These mufflers are very quiet; however, they limit power at higher speeds because of the restrictive design (back pressure).

Straight-through mufflers reduce back pressure. They are usually found on some factory high-performance vehicles and many aftermarket sports exhausts. Straight-through mufflers use fibreglass or steel-wool packing for noise control; this often burns out or compacts with carbon, increasing noise levels.

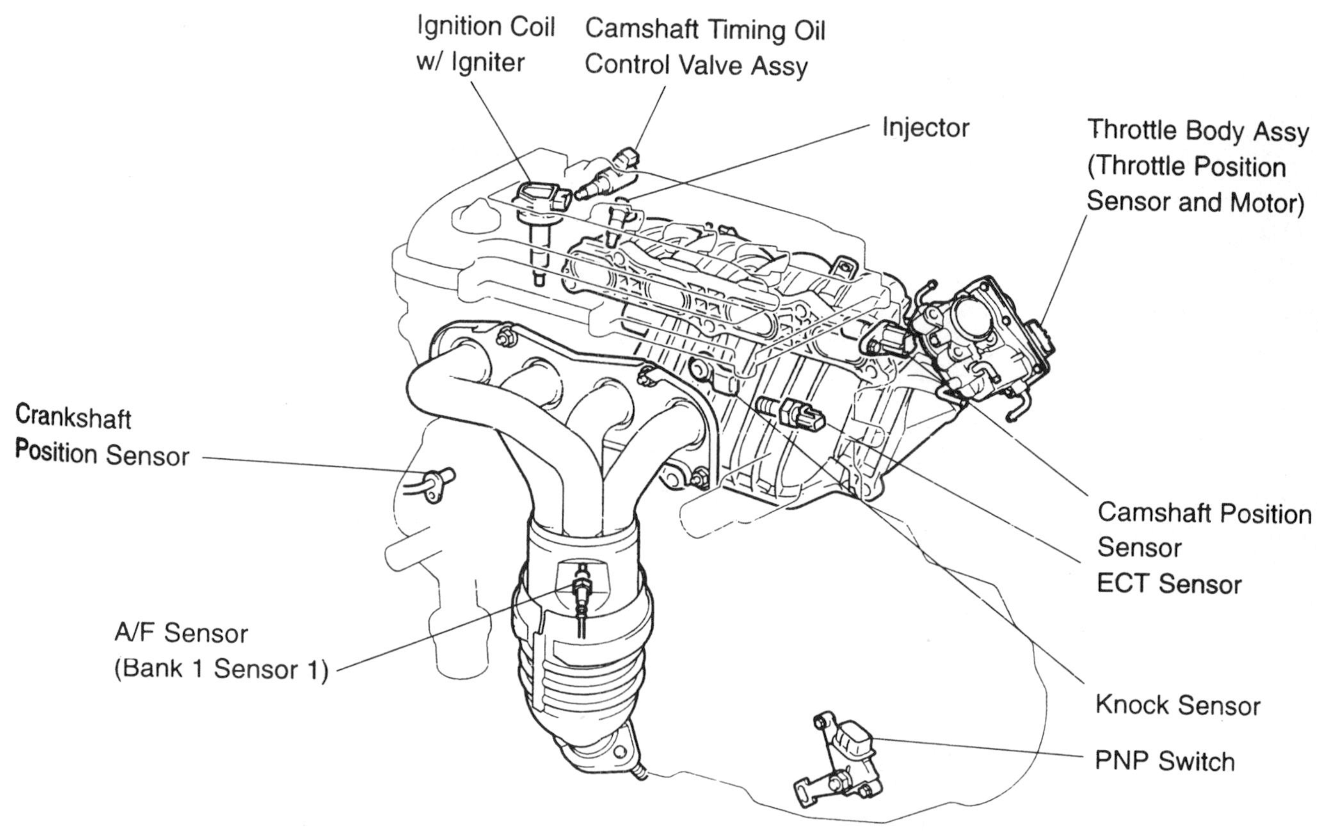

Figure 9–49 Stainless steel tubular exhaust manifolds are lighter and usually more efficient than cast-iron manifolds. Note the air–fuel (oxygen) sensor mounted very close to the engine. (Courtesy Toyota Motor Co.)

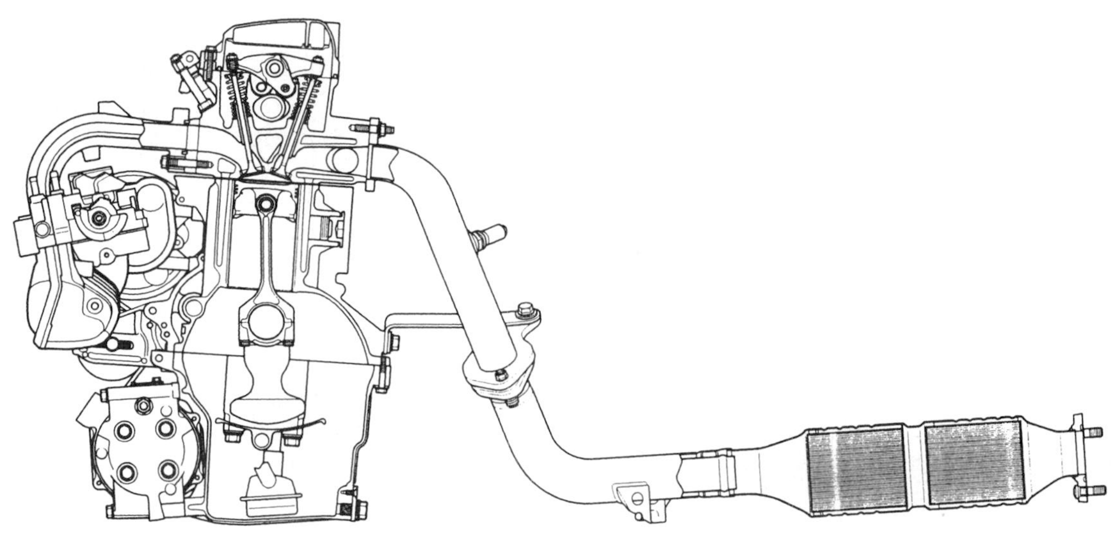

Figure 9–50 The Honda Insight combines the exhaust manifold and cylinder head into one unit. (Courtesy Honda Motor Co.)

A newer design reverse-flow muffler uses a spring-loaded damper that opens at high exhaust pressure. This decreases back pressure. See Figure 9–53.

Resonators are smaller secondary mufflers installed to further reduce exhaust noise and resonance. They can be straight-through or reverse-flow; both designs are used. They mount after the muffler (most common) or before, depending on space limitations.

Exhaust Mounting

Transverse mounted engines rock front-to-rear and longitudinal engines rock side-to-side. Each creates

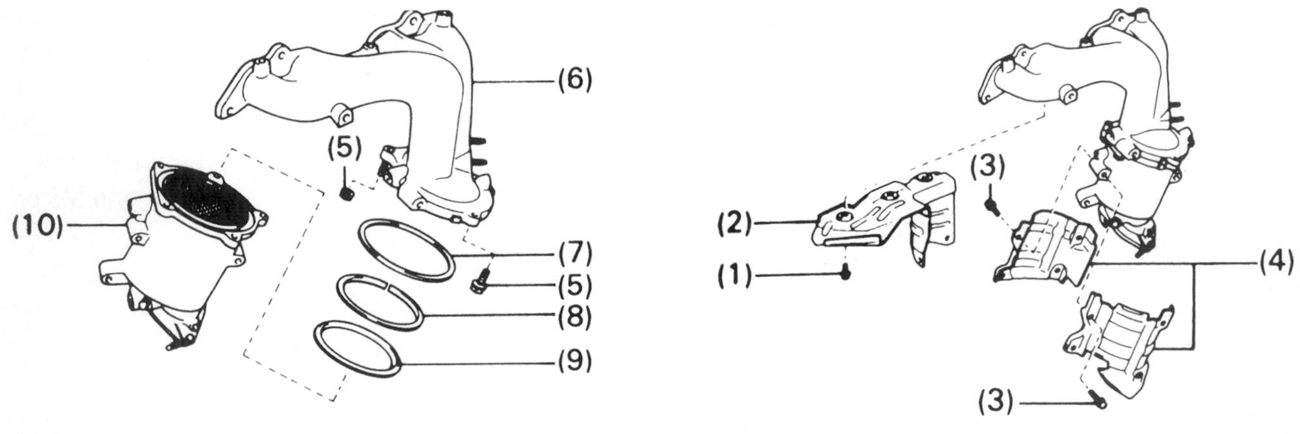

Figure 9–51 A cast-iron exhaust manifold (#6) and bolt-on catalytic converter (#10) use heat shields (#2, 3, 4) to protect adjoining components from high temperatures. The shields also allow the converter to retain much of its internal heat needed for proper operation. (Courtesy Toyota Canada Inc.)

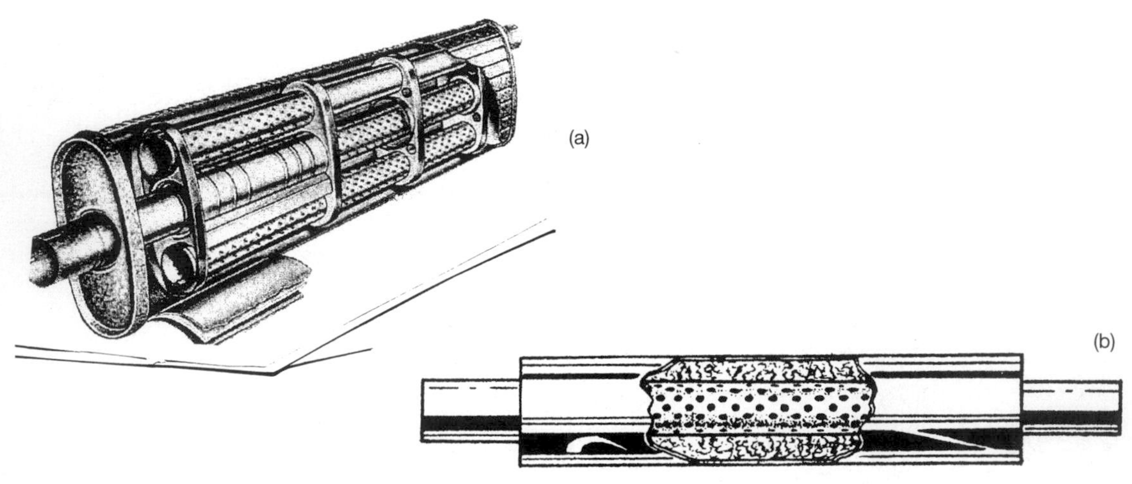

Figure 9–52 Muffler designs: (a) reverse-flow (b) straight-through. (McCord Manufacturing)

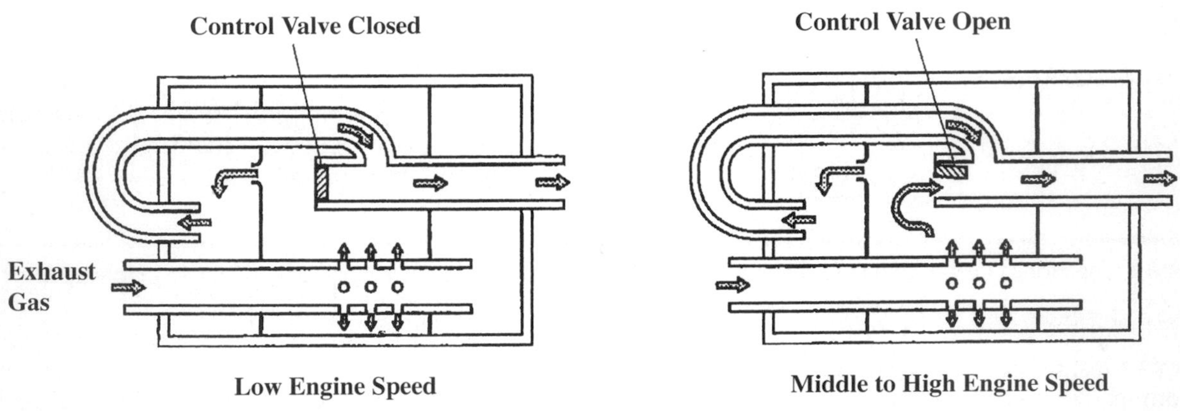

Figure 9–53 Schematic of a Toyota muffler with two-way exhaust control. The control valve, a spring-loaded damper, is closed at low engine speeds: exhaust noise is decreased. At higher engine speeds, the exhaust pressure overcomes spring pressure and the control valve opens, reducing system back pressure. (Courtesy Toyota Canada Inc.)

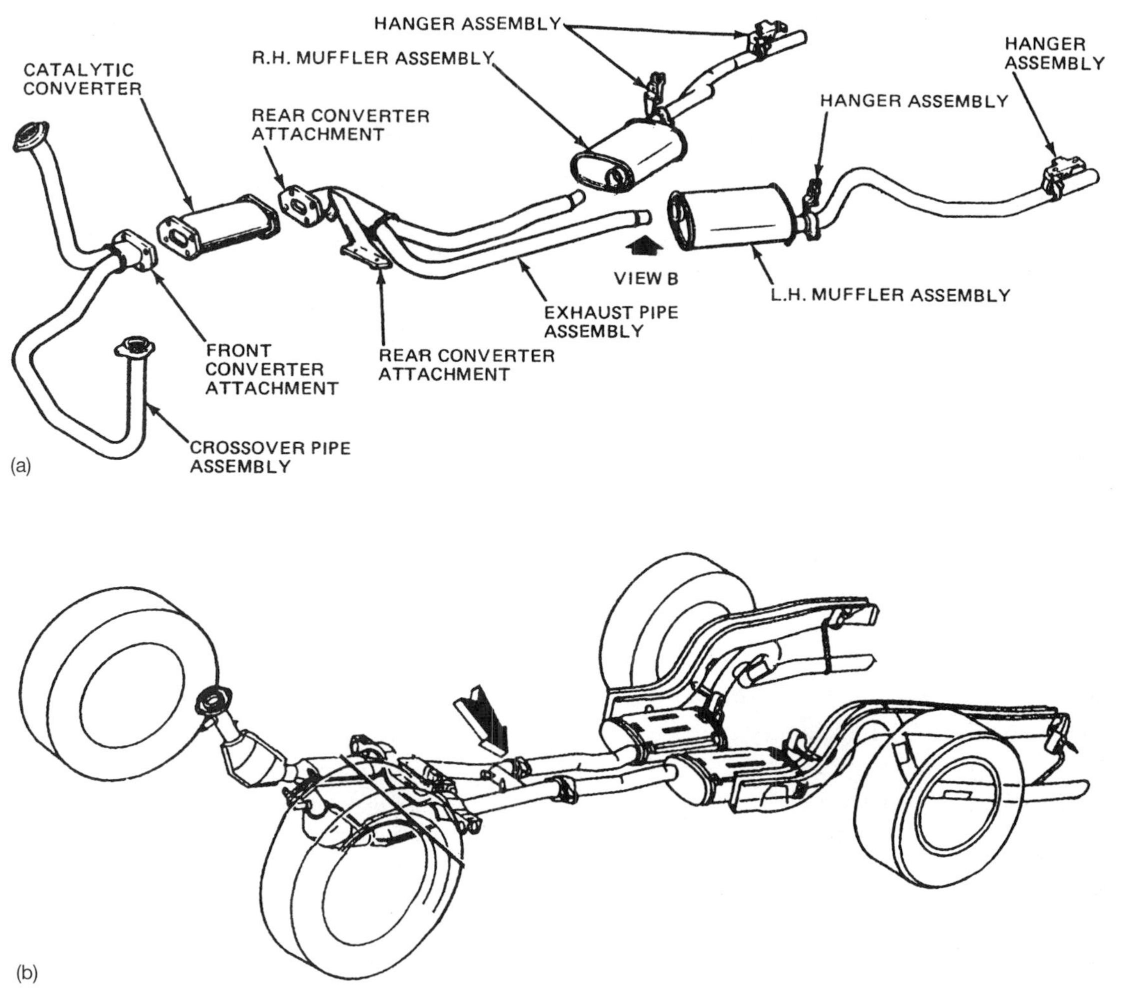

Figure 9–54 Two examples of a dual exhaust: (a) "cat" back system; (b) full length dual exhaust—note the equalizer tube between the front pipes. (Courtesy General Motors of Canada Ltd.; Ford Motor Co. of Canada Ltd.)

different stresses on the exhaust system. Transverse engines require ball-type joints, often spring loaded, or a flexible pipe to relieve pipe loading. Longitudinal engines absorb the twisting over a greater length and usually do not need flexible joints.

Exhaust systems are suspended from the chassis by high-temperature rubber straps, O-rings or "doughnuts" that insulate exhaust vibrations from the body. These mounts should be inspected for cracks or hardening whenever the vehicle is raised for service.

Exhaust Pipes

Most pipes are made of aluminized steel (a coating of aluminum on the inside and outside of the pipe) to resist corrosion. Pipes and mufflers do not burn out, they rust out internally from acids, water and contaminants created by engine combustion. These items last much longer when the system is equipped with a catalytic converter; the heat from the converter keeps moisture to a minimum.

Early vehicles joined the exhaust pipes and muffler with slip-joints and clamps. These are difficult to remove and usually require heat from a welding torch. Many recent vehicles use flanges that bolt together (with a gasket), making removal and replacement much easier.

Single and Dual Exhausts

Single exhaust systems are standard with most inline and V-type engines. Dual exhausts are usually found on longitudinally mounted V-8s, either factory high-performance or installed aftermarket. Factory installed duals often have an equalizer pipe (joining the two head pipes) balancing the pressure between the two sides. See Figure 9–54.

SUMMARY

1. The camshaft rotates at one-half the crankshaft speed.
2. The pushrods should be rotating while the engine is running if the camshaft and lifters are okay.
3. On overhead valve pushrod engines, the camshaft is usually placed in the block above the crankshaft. The lobes of the camshaft are usually lubricated by splash lubrication.
4. Silent chains are quieter than roller chains but tend to stretch with use.
5. The lift of a cam is usually expressed in decimal inches and represents the distance that the valve is lifted off the valve seat.
6. In many engines, camshaft lift is transferred to the tip of the valve stem to open the valve by the use of a rocker arm or follower.
7. Pushrods transfer camshaft motion upward from the camshaft to the rocker arm.
8. Camshaft duration is the number of degrees of crankshaft rotation for which the valve is lifted off the seat.
9. Valve overlap is the number of crankshaft degrees for which both valves are open.
10. Camshafts should be installed according to the manufacturer's recommended procedures. Flat lifter camshafts should be thoroughly lubricated with extreme pressure lubricant.
11. If a new camshaft is installed, new lifters should also be installed.
12. Wet intake manifolds require heating (during cold operation) to vaporize the fuel.
13. Long intake runners improve low RPM cylinder filling.
14. Tubular stainless steel exhaust manifolds improve exhaust flow and decrease weight.
15. Some vehicles use a one-piece exhaust manifold-catalytic converter; being close to the engine heats the converter quickly and keeps it at a high temperature.

REVIEW QUESTIONS

1. Explain why the lift and duration of the camshaft determines the power characteristics of the engine.
2. Describe the operation of a hydraulic lifter.
3. Describe how to adjust hydraulic lifters.

RED SEAL CERTIFICATION-TYPE QUESTIONS

1. The camshaft makes _____ for every revolution of the crankshaft.
   - **a.** One-quarter revolution
   - **b.** One-half revolution
   - **c.** One revolution
   - **d.** Two revolutions
2. Valve lifters rotate during operation because of the _____ of the camshaft.
   - **a.** Taper of the lobe
   - **b.** Thrust plate
   - **c.** Chain tensioner
   - **d.** Bearings
3. Advancing the camshaft (SOHC) will result in _______________.
   - **a.** A rougher idle
   - **b.** Less low-speed torque
   - **c.** Better high-speed performance
   - **d.** More low-speed torque
4. Which timing chain type is also called a "silent chain"?
   - **a.** Roller
   - **b.** Double roller
   - **c.** Double belt
   - **d.** Morse
5. On an engine equipped with a timing belt, engine damage can occur if the engine is which design?
   - **a.** Freewheeling
   - **b.** Interference
6. Many technicians always use new pushrods because _______________.
   - **a.** It is less expensive to buy than clean
   - **b.** All of the dirt cannot be cleaned out from the hollow centre
   - **c.** Pushrods wear at both ends
   - **d.** Pushrods shrink in length if removed from an engine
7. A DOHC V-6 has how many camshafts?
   - **a.** 4
   - **b.** 3
   - **c.** 2
   - **d.** 1
8. The intake valve opens at 39° BTDC and closes at 71° ABDC. The exhaust valve opens at 78° BBDC and closes at 47° ATDC. Which answer is correct?
   - **a.** Intake valve duration is 110°
   - **b.** Exhaust valve duration is 125°
   - **c.** Overlap is 86°
   - **d.** Overlap is 149°
9. Fuel injection systems that inject fuel into the cylinder head intake port may require heat at the throttle body to
   - **a.** Vaporize the incoming fuel
   - **b.** Stop throttle-plate icing
   - **c.** Cause turbulence in the intake runner
   - **d.** Stop the fuel from freezing at low temperatures
10. Mufflers on catalytic converter equipped vehicles last longer because
    - **a.** The converter reduces the exhaust volume
    - **b.** Converters require water to function
    - **c.** The heat from the converter reduces water in the muffler
    - **d.** They are made of high temperature steel compatible with the converter

10

Pistons, Rings, and Connecting Rods

OBJECTIVES: After studying Chapter 10, you should be able to:

1. Prepare for the interprovincial Red Seal certification examination in Appendix I (Engine Repair) on the topics covered in this chapter.
2. Describe the purpose and function of pistons, rings, and connecting rods.
3. Explain how pistons and rods are serviced and inspected.
4. Discuss connecting rod reconditioning procedures.
5. Explain how piston rings operate and how to install them.

All engine power is developed by burning fuel in the presence of air in the combustion chamber. Heat from the combustion causes the pressure of the burned gas to increase. The force of this pressure is converted into useful work through the piston, connecting rod, and crankshaft.

PURPOSE AND FUNCTION OF PISTONS, RINGS, AND CONNECTING RODS

The **piston** forms a movable bottom to the combustion chamber. It is attached to the connecting rod with a **piston pin** or **wrist pin.** The connecting rod is connected to a part of the crankshaft called a **crank throw, crankpin,** or **connecting rod bearing journal.** The centre of the crank throw determines the amount by which the large end of the connecting rod is offset from the crankshaft main bearing centreline. This dimension of the crankshaft determines the stroke of the engine.

NOTE: The crankshaft *throw* is the distance from the centre of the main bearing journal to the centre of the connecting rod journal. The throw, times two, equals the *stroke.*

PISTON AND ROD REMOVAL

The rod and caps should be checked for markings that identify their location. If the rod and caps are not marked, they should be marked before disassembly. If number stamps are not available, centre punch marks can be used. The best location is the big end of the connecting rod on both sides of the parting line. The beam of the rod should never be marked as cracks may form from the stamping.

CAUTION: If powdered-metal connecting rods are being disassembled, do not use a number punch to mark the rods (see Figure 10–1). The distortion caused by the hammer blow can ruin the connecting rod. Most vehicle manufacturers say that an electric engraving tool can be used to identify the location of the rods in an engine. Always follow the method recommended by the vehicle manufacturer.

The crankshaft is rotated until the piston is at the bottom of its stroke. Remove the connecting rod nuts or cap screws and remove the connecting rod cap. Place

Figure 10–1 Powdered metal connecting rods can be identified by their smooth appearance.

protective covers over the connecting rod bolt threads before pushing the piston/rod assembly out of the engine through the top of the cylinder. The protectors help protect the crankshaft journal from possible damage. Keep the connecting rod bearings with the rod for inspection after the piston/rod assembly is removed.

PISTONS

Recesses machined or cast into the tops of the pistons for valve clearance are commonly called **eyebrows.** These recesses are also called **valve reliefs** or **valve pockets.** The depth of the eyebrows has a major effect on the compression ratio and is necessary to provide clearance for the valves. It is still possible on some engines for the valves and pistons to collide, even with valve reliefs, if the timing belt or chain should break. See Figures 10–2 and 10–3.

Piston ring **grooves** are located between the piston head and skirt. The width of the grooves, the width of the **lands** between the ring grooves, and the number of rings are major factors in determining minimum piston height. The outside diameter of the ring land area is about 0.5 to 1.0 mm (0.020 to 0.040 in.) smaller than the **skirt** diameter. See Figure 10–4.

Figure 10–2 A high-performance piston with valve reliefs machined into the head of the piston to provide for valve clearance. The valve relief is usually larger for the intake valve and smaller for the exhaust. These pistons must be matched to the valve location in the cylinder head (e.g., of a small-block Chevrolet) or valve/piston contact will occur.

Figure 10–3 Another style of piston with a recessed head to not only provide valve clearance but also control compression ratio.

Ring grooves have been moved higher on the piston (on some emission control engines) to reduce the amount of air and unburned fuel (hydrocarbons) trapped between the piston and cylinder wall. Although this is harder on the top ring, being closer to

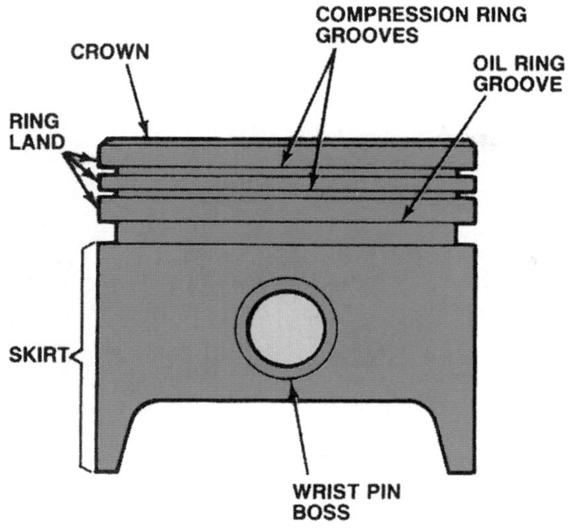

Figure 10–4 A typical piston illustrating the various parts and the names.

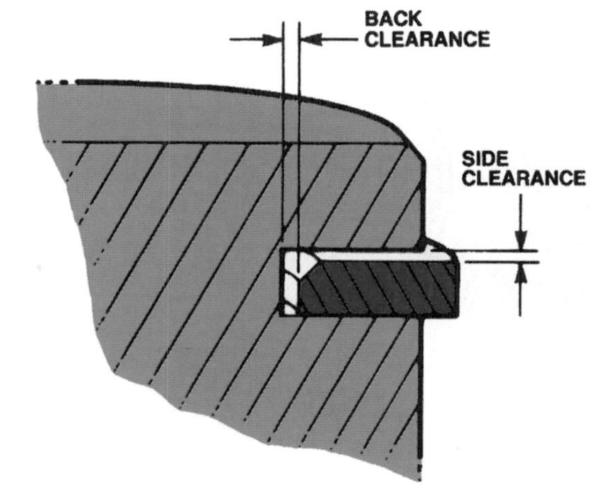

Figure 10–6 The piston rings must have the specified side and back clearance.

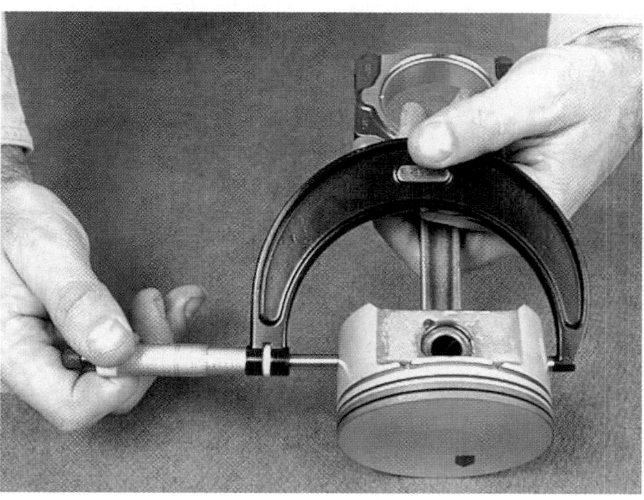

Figure 10–5 All pistons are measured across the skirt. Most are measured in line with the piston pin bore; however, a few are measured at the bottom of the skirt. Always check the shop manual or the installation instructions supplied with a replacement set of pistons.

the combustion, emissions are lower. Several automakers have switched the top ring material from cast iron to steel for improved durability.

See Figure 10–5 for an example of piston diameter being measured. Always check the service manual for the exact location and specifications for the piston being checked.

> **NOTE:** Some engines, such as the Honda high-fuel-economy engine, use pistons with two rings: one compression ring and one oil ring.

The piston ring groove must be deep enough to prevent the ring from hitting the base of the groove when the ring is pressed in so that it is flat with the land face. This is called **back spacing.** See Figure 10–6.

> **NOTE:** High-performance engines often use pistons with a "pop-up" (domed) head, which extends into the combustion chamber and raises the compression.
>
> The same type of piston is also used when modifying engines to run on propane or natural gas.

Cam Ground Pistons

Aluminum pistons expand when hot. To control the expansion of the piston, the skirt of the piston is **cam ground.** With this design, the piston is ground to an elliptical (oval) shape. The widest part is across the skirt, 90° from the piston pin. The piston is then fitted to the cylinder with a minimum of clearance. As the engine warms up, the expansion takes place along the pin boss area; the piston becomes nearly round at operating temperature. A cam-ground piston skirt is illustrated in Figure 10–7.

Hypereutectic Cast Pistons

A standard cast-aluminum piston contains about 9% to 12% silicon and is called a *eutectic piston.* To add strength, the silicon content is increased to about 16%, and the resulting piston is called a **hypereutectic** piston. Other advantages of a hypereutectic piston are its 25% weight reduction and lower expansion rate. The disadvantage of hypereutectic pistons is their higher cost, because they are more difficult to cast and machine.

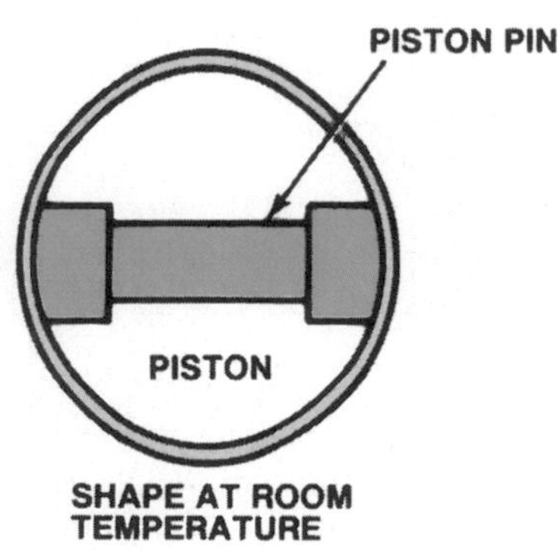

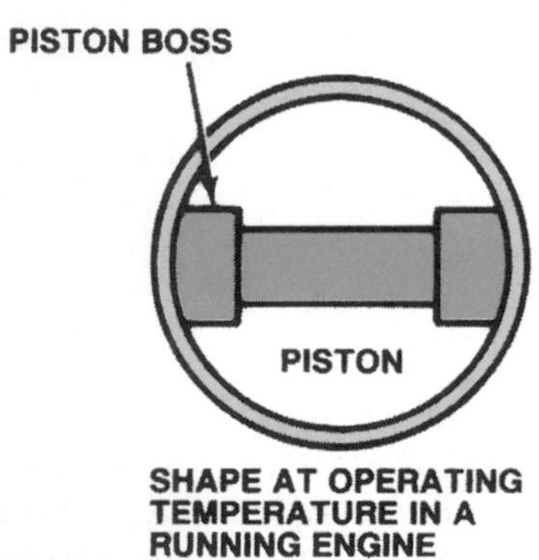

Figure 10–7 Pistons are often cam-ground to produce the elliptical shape when the piston is at room temperature.

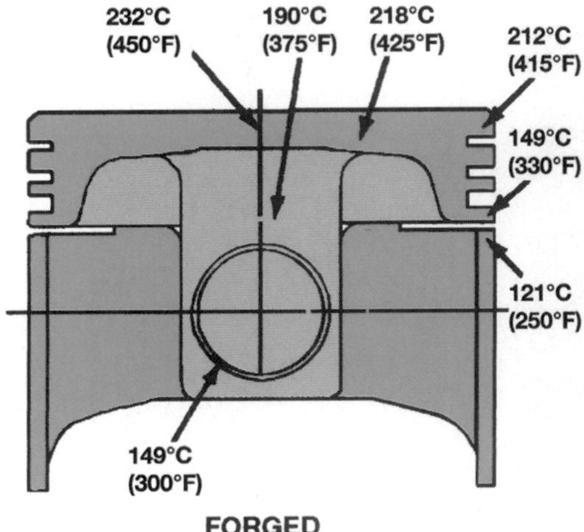

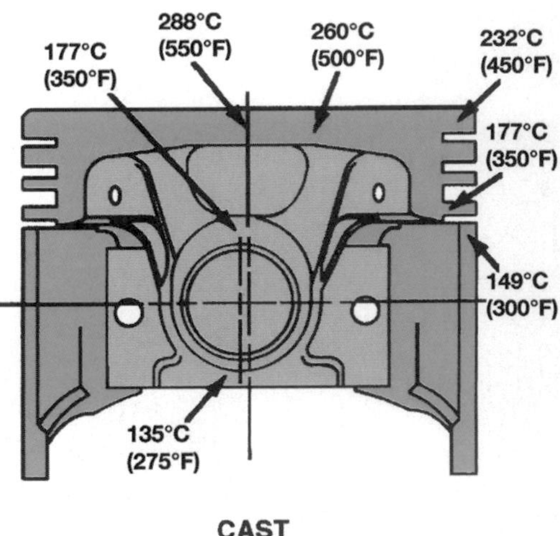

Figure 10–8 Notice the temperature difference between a forged piston and a cast piston.

TECH TIP ✔

Piston Weight Is Important!

All pistons in an engine should weigh the same to help ensure a balanced engine. Piston weight becomes a factor whenever changing pistons. Most aluminum pistons range in weight from 280 to 850 g (10 to 30 ounces) (100 g = 3.527 oz). *A typical paper clip weighs one gram.* If the cylinder has been bored, larger replacement pistons are obviously required.

If quality engine parts are used, the oversize replacement pistons should weigh the same as the original standard size. This ensures that the engine remains balanced. Oversize pistons often have the piston tops (crowns) reduced in height so the original compression ratio is retained.

CAUTION: Some less expensive replacement pistons are a great deal heavier than the stock pistons, even in the same stock bore size. If these heavy pistons are used, engine vibration and connecting rod bearing failure can occur.

For the same reason, if one piston is being replaced, it should be checked to ensure it is the same weight as the old piston.

Hypereutectic pistons are commonly used in the aftermarket and as original equipment in many turbocharged and supercharged engines.

Forged Pistons

High-performance engines need pistons with added strength. They use impact-extruded forged pistons whose design allows for great strength. They are often used whenever the engine is going to be exposed to extreme operation conditions such as racing or turbocharging. A forged piston is denser than a cast piston and conducts heat faster so it operates cooler. See Figure 10–8.

Piston Skirt Finish

For maximum life, the piston skirt surface finish is important. Turned grooves or waves 0.0125 mm (0.0005 in.) deep on the surface of some piston skirts produce

Figure 10–9 A low-friction moly coating on the skirt of this piston helps prevent piston scuffing when the engine is cold.

Frequently Asked Question ???

How Can a Piston Have a Negative Clearance?

The specification for some DaimlerChrysler engines includes a piston-to-cylinder wall clearance as small as 0.0125 mm (0.0005 in.) *negative*. This means that the piston is larger than the bore! How is that possible? According to DaimlerChrysler, a service technician cannot accurately measure the diameter of the piston and determine the piston-to-cylinder clearance due to the application of the antifriction coating on the skirts of the piston. The coating is about 0.0125 mm (0.0005 in.) and it is applied to both sides of the piston, so the coating alone means that the piston skirt would measure 0.025 mm (0.001 in.) larger in diameter if the coating could be accurately measured. Always follow the vehicle manufacturer's recommended service procedures.

a finish that will carry oil for lubrication. Other piston skirts are relatively smooth. A thin tin-plated surface, approximately 0.001 25 mm (0.000 05 in.) thick, is also used on some aluminum pistons to help reduce scuffing and scoring during occasional periods of minimum lubrication. Some pistons have a moly coating on the skirt to prevent scuffing, as shown in Figure 10–9.

Piston Pins

Piston pins are used to attach the piston to the connecting rod. Piston pins are also known as wrist pins. The piston pin transfers the force produced by combustion chamber pressures and piston inertia to the connecting rod. The piston pin is made from high-quality steel in the shape of a tube to make it both strong and light. See Figure 10–10.

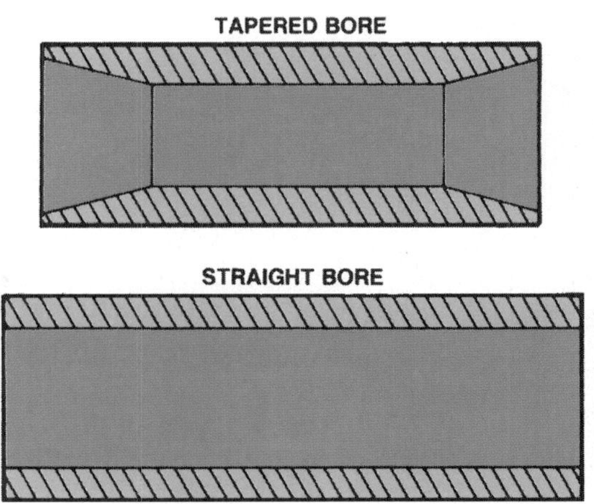

Figure 10–10 Cross-sectional piston pins. Most piston pins are hollow to reduce weight and have a straight bore. Some pins use a tapered bore to add strength.

Piston Pin Offset

The piston pin holes are not centred in the piston. They are located toward the **major thrust surface,** approximately 1.5 mm (0.062 in.) from the piston centreline, as shown in Figure 10–11.

> **NOTE:** The major thrust side is the side of the cylinder to which the rod points during the power stroke.

Pin offset is designed to reduce piston slap and the noise that can result as the piston crosses over top dead centre.

The minor thrust side of the piston head has a greater area than does the major side. This is caused by the pin offset. As the piston moves up in the cylinder on the compression stroke, it is riding against the minor thrust surface. When compression pressure becomes high enough, the greater head area on the minor side causes the piston to cock slightly in the cylinder. This keeps the *top* of the minor thrust surface on the cylinder. It forces the *bottom* of the major thrust surface to contact the cylinder wall. As the piston approaches top centre, both thrust surfaces are in contact with the cylinder wall. When the crankshaft crosses over top centre, the force on the connecting rod moves the entire piston toward the major thrust surface. The lower portion of the major thrust surface has already been in contact with the cylinder wall.

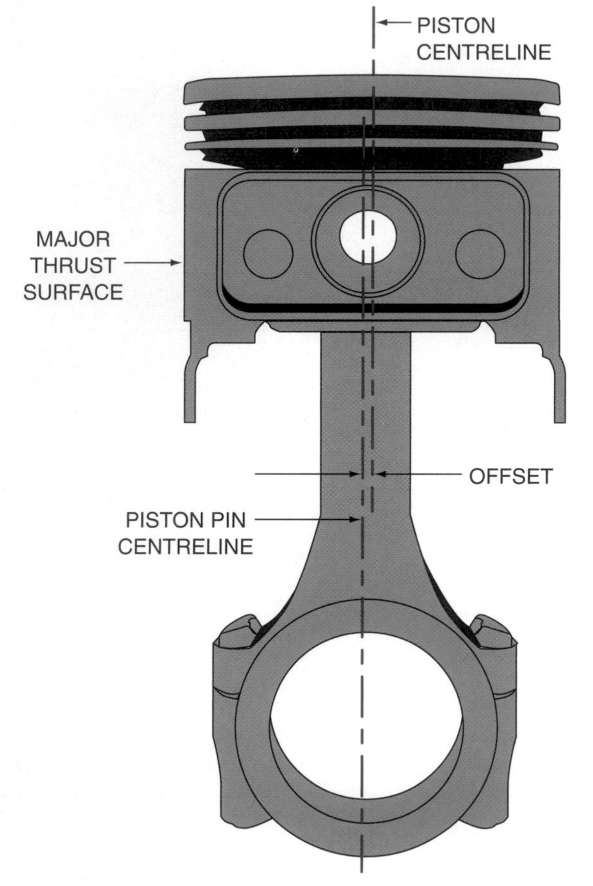

Figure 10–11 Piston pin is offset toward the major thrust surface.

The rest of the piston skirt wipes into full contact just after the crossover point, thereby controlling piston slap. This action is illustrated in Figure 10–12.

NOTE: Not all piston pins are offset. In fact, many engines operate without the offset to help reduce friction and improve power and fuel economy.

NOTE: When the crankshaft stroke is lengthened (connecting rod journal moved out) to increase engine displacement and power, the piston is now located higher in the cylinder. Rather than using shorter connecting rods, it is common practice for the manufacturer to move the piston pin hole up, closer to the top. This positions the piston back to its original location.

Always measure the distance from the pin hole to the top of the new piston and compare it to the piston being replaced. This helps ensure that the correct part is being installed.

Piston Pin Retaining Methods

It is necessary to retain or hold piston pins so that they stay centred in the piston. If piston pins were not retained, they would move endwise and groove the cylinder wall. Piston pins are retained in one of two common ways. The piston pin may be **full floating,** with some type of stop located at each end. Full-floating piston pins in automotive engines are retained by lock rings located in grooves in the piston pin hole at the ends of the piston pin. See Figures 10–13 and 10–14.

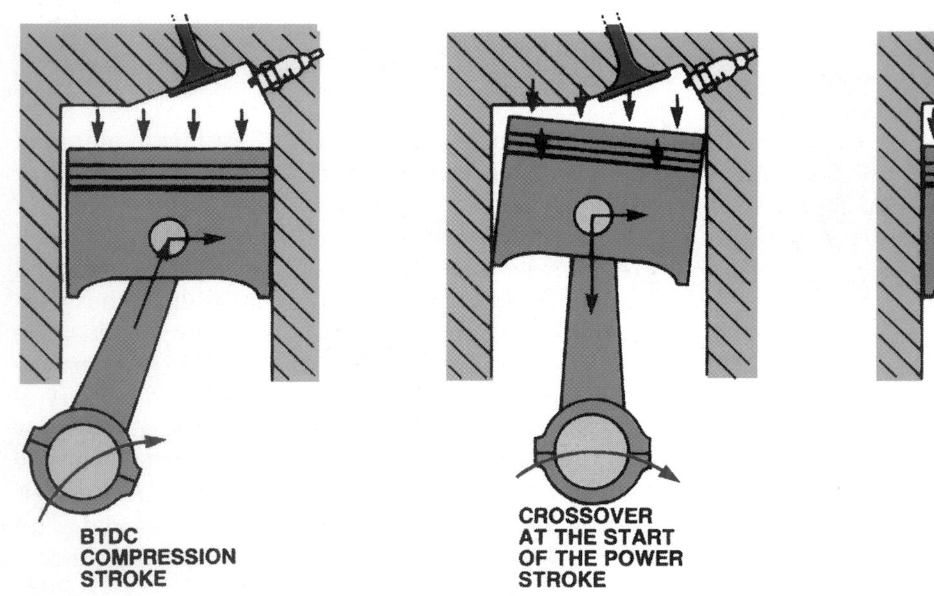

Figure 10–12 Engine rotation and rod angle during the power stroke causes the engine to press harder against one side of the cylinder, creating a major thrust surface. In this clockwise-rotating engine, as viewed from the front of the engine, the major thrust surface is on the left side.

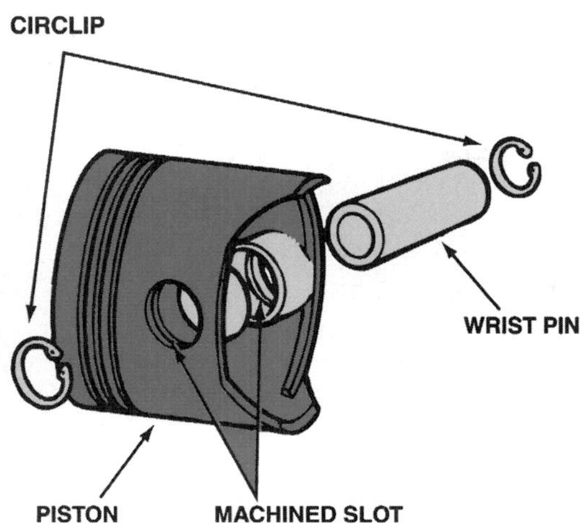

Figure 10–13 Circlips or snap rings hold full-floating piston pins in place.

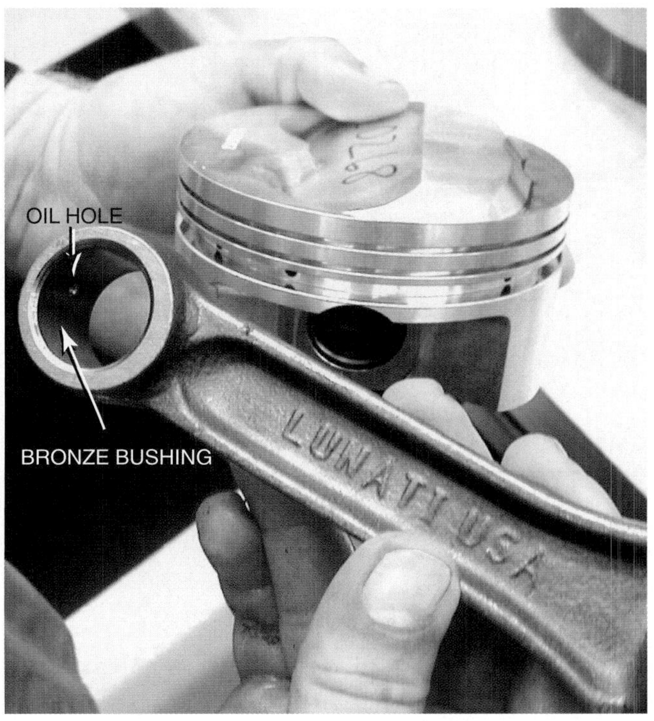

Figure 10–14 This high-performance connecting rod uses a bronze bushing in the small end of the rod and an oil hole to allow oil to reach the full-floating pin.

The most common method of retaining the piston pin in the connecting rod is to make the connecting rod hole slightly smaller than the piston pin. The pin is installed by heating the rod to expand the hole or by pressing the pin into the rod. This press or shrink fit is called an **interference fit.**

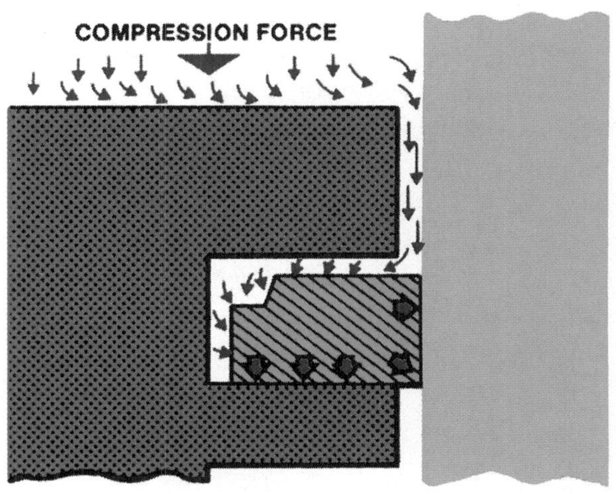

Figure 10–15 Combustion chamber pressure forces the ring against the cylinder wall and the bottom of the ring groove. These are the two sealing surfaces that the top ring must be able to seal for maximum engine power.

TECH TIP 

What's That Knocking Noise?

A worn piston pin or an enlarged piston pin hole in the piston causes a double knock sound when the engine is running. Unlike other knocking sounds, the sound of a worn piston pin will not disappear when the cylinder is grounded out and prevented from firing. Obviously, the engine will have to be disassembled and replacement piston(s) installed to correct the knocking noise. Piston pin noise usually increases as the aluminum piston heats up and expands. It may be gone when the engine is cold.

COMPRESSION RINGS

A compression ring is designed to form a seal between the moving piston and the cylinder wall. Combustion chamber pressure during the compression, power, and exhaust strokes is applied to the top and back of the ring. This pressure will add the force to the ring that is required to seal the combustion chamber during these strokes. Figure 10–15 illustrates how the combustion chamber pressure adds force to the ring.

Top compression rings are usually rectangular or **barrel shaped.** See Figure 10–16. A piston ring with a **taper face** would contact the cylinder wall at the lower edge of the piston ring. See Figure 10–17. **Positive twist** will give the same wall

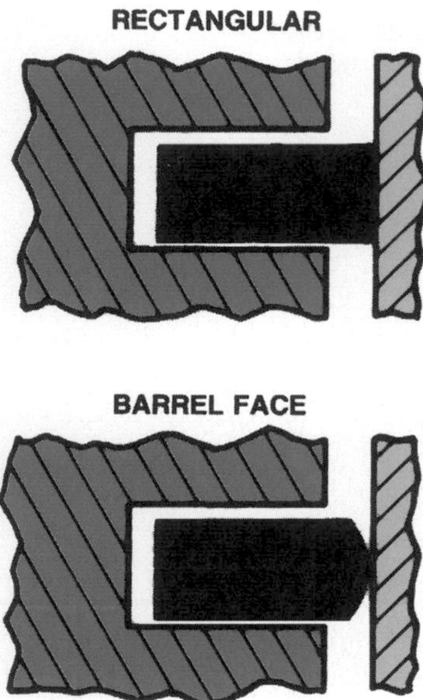

Figure 10–16 The rectangular and the barrel face are the most commonly used top compression rings because they provide the best seal.

DIAGNOSTIC STORY 

Big Problem, No Noise

Sometimes the piston pin can "walk" off the centre of the piston and score the cylinder wall. This scoring is often not noticed because this type of wear does not create noise. As the piston rings pass over the cylinder score, both combustion and compression pressures will be reduced. Blow-by gases and oil consumption also increase.

Troubleshooting the exact cause of the increased oil consumption is difficult because the damage done to the oil control rings by the groove usually affects only one cylinder.

Often, compression tests indicate good compression because the cylinder seals, especially at the top. More than one technician has been surprised to see the cylinder gouged by a piston pin when the cylinder head is removed for service. In such a case, the cost of the engine repair immediately increases far beyond that of normal cylinder head service.

contact as the taper-faced ring and will also provide a line contact seal on the bottom side of the groove. By chamfering the ring's *lower inner* corner, a **reverse twist** is produced. This seals the lower, outer section of the ring and piston ring groove, thus improving oil control. Reverse twist rings require a greater taper face or barrel face to maintain the desired ring-face-to-cylinder-wall contact. See Figure 10–18.

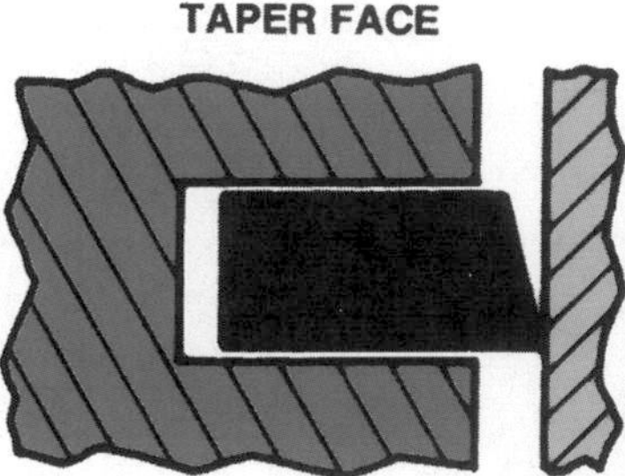

Figure 10–17 The taper face ring provides good oil control by scraping the cylinder wall. If this design ring were accidentally installed upside down, the tapered face would pump oil into the combustion chamber.

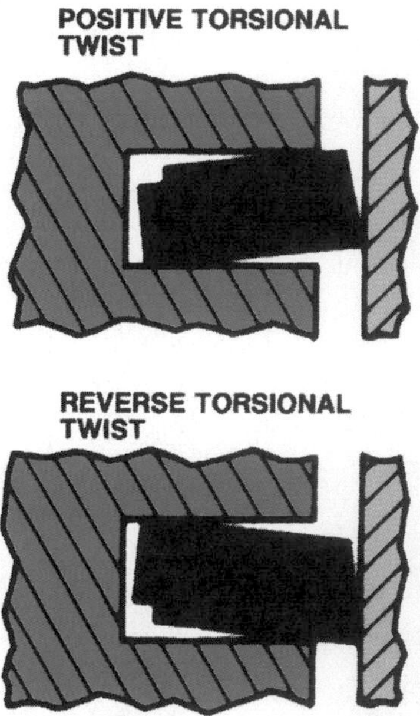

Figure 10–18 Torsional twist rings provide better compression sealing and oil control than regular taper face rings.

Ring End Gap

The piston **ring end gap** will allow some leakage of gases past the top compression ring. This leakage is useful in providing pressure on the second ring to develop a dynamic sealing force. The amount of piston ring gap is critical. Too much gap will allow excessive **blowby,** the leakage of combustion gases past the rings. Too little gap, on the other hand, will allow the piston ring ends to butt when the engine is hot. Ring end butting increases the mechanical force against the cylinder wall, causing excessive wear and possible engine failure.

Chromium Piston Rings

A chromium facing on cast-iron rings greatly increases piston ring life, especially where abrasive materials are present in the air. During manufacture, the chromium-plated ring is slightly chamfered at the outer corners. About 0.010 mm (0.0004 in.) of chrome is then plated on the ring face. Chromium-faced rings are prelapped or honed before they are packaged and shipped to the customer. The finished chromium facing is shown in a sectional view in Figure 10–19.

Molybdenum Piston Rings

Early in the 1960s, molybdenum piston ring faces were introduced. These rings proved to have good service life, especially under scuffing conditions. Most molybdenum-faced piston rings have a groove that is 0.1 to 0.2 mm (0.004 to 0.008 in.) deep cut into the ring face. This groove is filled with molybdenum, using a metallic (or plasma) spray method, so that there is a cast-iron edge above and below the molybdenum. A sectional view of a molybdenum-faced ring is shown in Figure 10–20.

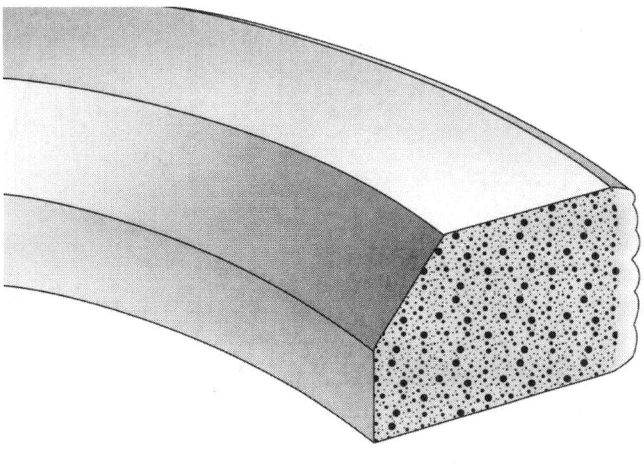

Figure 10–19 Chromium facing can be seen on the right side of the sectional view of the piston ring.

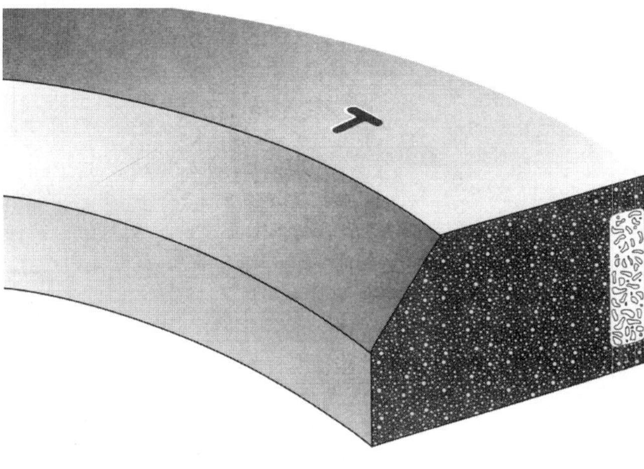

Figure 10–20 Molybdenum facing can be seen on the right side of the sectional view of the piston ring.

TECH TIP 

Gap the Second Ring Wider Than the Top Ring

In the past, it was standard operating procedure that vehicle and piston ring manufacturers specified a wider piston ring gap on the top ring and a narrower gap for the second compression ring. The reason given was the top ring was exposed to greater heat and, therefore, would expand more than the second ring.

Today many vehicle manufacturers, as well as piston ring manufacturers, are specifying that the second ring gap should be greater than the top ring gap. The reason given is that the larger second ring gap prevents combustion pressure between the rings that can cause the top ring to be lifted up off the bottom of the ring groove. If the top ring is raised up, it cannot properly seal the combustion gases. With this in mind, many high-performance engine builders are specifying a standard ring gap for the top ring and a ring gap of 0.05 to 0.100 mm (0.002 to 0.004 in.) greater for the second ring.

Piston-ring end gap must always be checked below the ring-travelled area as cylinder taper will change the readings. The exception is a cylinder that has just been rebored.

A molybdenum-faced ring, when used, will be found in the top groove, and a plain cast-iron or chromium-faced ring will be found in the second groove.

Moly-Chrome-Carbide Rings

Rings with a moly-chrome-carbide coating are also used in some original equipment (OE) and replacement applications. The coating has properties that include the hardness of the chrome and carbide combined with the heat resistance of molybdenum. Ceramic-coated rings are also used when additional heat resistance is needed, such as in some heavy-duty, turbocharged, or supercharged engines.

Oil Control Rings

Steel **rails** with chromium or other types of facings are used on most oil control rings. The rails are backed with **expanders** and separated with a **spacer,** seen in Figure 10–21.

Piston Ring Materials

The majority of top compression rings are made of cast iron with some type of coating, usually chrome. Steel top rings are also becoming common.

The second compression ring is often unplated cast iron with a steel expander spring used to push the ring against the cylinder wall.

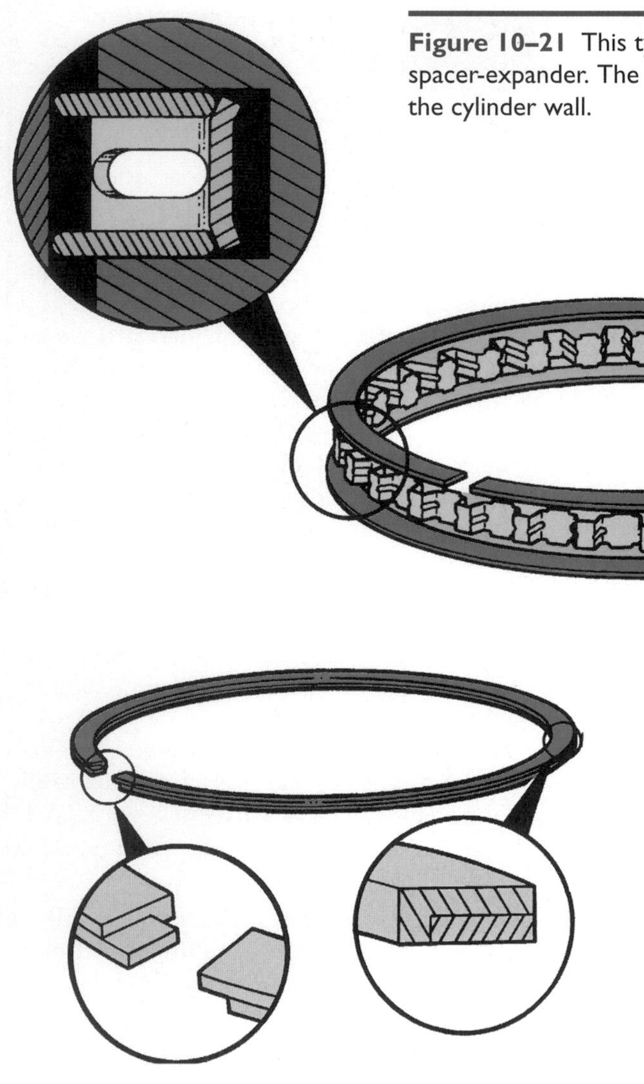

Figure 10–21 This typical three-piece oil control ring uses a hump-type stainless steel spacer-expander. The expander separates the two steel rails and presses them against the cylinder wall.

Figure 10–22 The gapless ring overlaps, while the conventional ring design uses a gap.

Frequently Asked Question ???

What Is a Gapless Piston Ring?

A gapless piston ring is a type of piston ring that overlaps and therefore, can compensate for temperature changes without a gap between the ends of the ring. See Figure 10–22.

Oil control rings are almost always stainless or chrome-plated steel rails.

CONNECTING RODS

The connecting rod transfers the force and reciprocating motion of the piston to the crankshaft. The small end of the connecting rod reciprocates with the piston. The large end rotates with the crankpin. See Figure 10–23. These dynamic motions make it desirable to keep the connecting rod as light as possible while still having a rigid beam section. Lightweight rods also reduce the total connecting rod material cost.

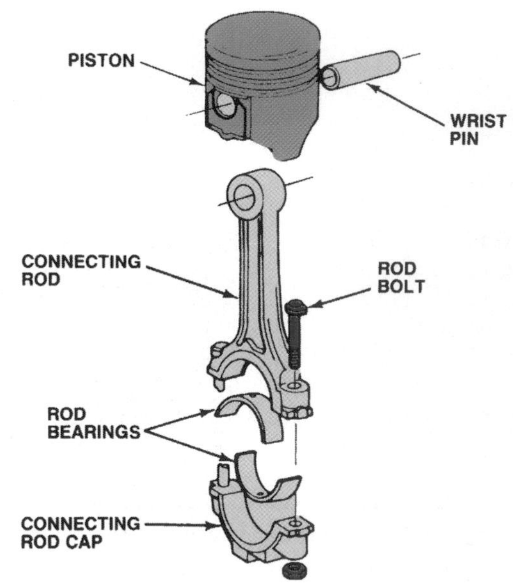

Figure 10–23 A typical connecting rod and related engine parts. The connecting rod is probably the most highly stressed part in the engine. Combustion forces try to compress it and when the piston stops at the top of the cylinder, inertial forces try to pull it apart.

Connecting rods are manufactured by casting, forging, and powdered (sintered) metal processes. Forged connecting rods have been used for years and have a thick parting line along the length of the rod. They are always used in high-performance engines and are generally used in heavy-duty engines. The cost of cast rods is lower than that of forged rods, both in the initial casting and in the machining. Cast rods can be identified by a thin parting line along the

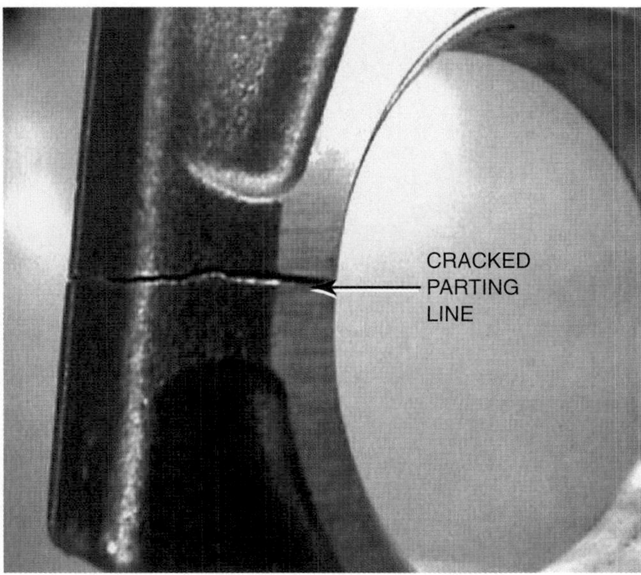

Figure 10–24 Most powdered metal cast connecting rods are broken at the parting line.

length of the rod. Generally, the forging method produces lighter weight and stronger, but more expensive, connecting rods.

Powdered Metal Connecting Rods

Many automakers, domestic and import, have been switching from forged steel to powdered metal (PM) connecting rods for their engines. These rods are easier to balance, less machining is required and they are often stronger. Each of the rods is blended into a tapered I-beam section. The large split-ring form for the crankshaft end is machined *after* the cap is assembled on the rod.

> **NOTE:** Most powdered (sintered) metal connecting rods are broken at the parting end of the big end of the connecting rod. This rough, broken surface helps ensure a perfect match when the pieces are bolted together. See Figure 10–24.

The hole will be a perfect circle. Therefore, the rod caps must not be interchanged. Assembly bolt holes are closely reamed in both the cap and connecting rod to ensure alignment. The connecting rod bolts have **piloting surfaces** that closely fit these reamed holes.

Connecting Rod Design

In some engines, offset connecting rods provide the most economical distribution of main bearing space and crankshaft cheek clearance. Some V-6 engines have the connecting rods offset by approximately 2.50 mm (0.100 in.).

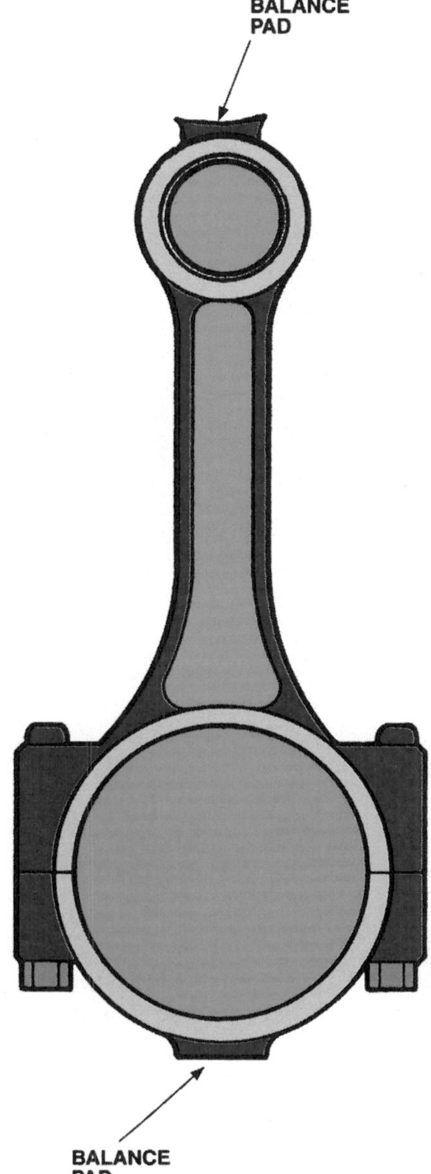

Figure 10–25 Some connecting rods have balancing bosses (pads) on each end of the rod.

Connecting rods are made with balancing bosses so that their weight can be adjusted to specifications. Some have balancing bosses only on the rod cap. Others have a balancing pad on the small end of the rod as well. Some manufacturers put balancing bosses on the side of the rod, near the centre of gravity of the connecting rod. Typical balancing bosses can be seen in Figure 10–25. Balancing is done on automatic balancing machines as the final machining operation before the rod is installed in an engine.

Connecting Rod Service

As an engine operates, the forces go through the large end of the connecting rod. This causes the crankshaft end opening of the rod (eye) to gradually

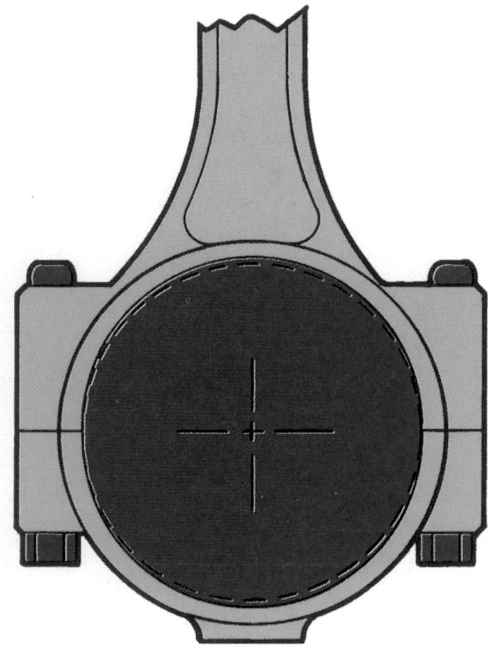

Figure 10–26 The rod bearing bores normally stretch from top to bottom causing the rod bearing to wear most near the parting line.

TECH TIP 

The Might-As-Wells

One of the hardest questions a technician or vehicle owner faces is, "How much work should be done to make a proper repair without incurring too much cost?" The technician wants to make a proper repair to prevent an early failure (and a customer comeback). The vehicle owner does not want to spend any more than is necessary for the repair service.

When the engine is disassembled, many small procedures, such as connecting rod reconditioning, are often left unperformed because of additional effort and cost. Connecting rod reconditioning is one of many operations considered important enough to be included in a proper engine repair or overhaul. Many engine rebuilders also recommend replacing all connecting rod bolts whenever the engine is disassembled. The major expense is removing the engine from the vehicle; therefore, the technician "might as well" do a complete and thorough engine service job and convince the customer that the added expense of "doing it right" is money well spent.

deform. The big end of the connecting rod is resized during precision engine service. See Figure 10–26.

Step 1 The parting surfaces of the rod and cap are smoothed to remove all high spots before resizing. About 0.05 mm (0.002 in.) of metal is removed from the rod cap parting surface. The

Figure 10–27 A connecting rod being reconditioned.

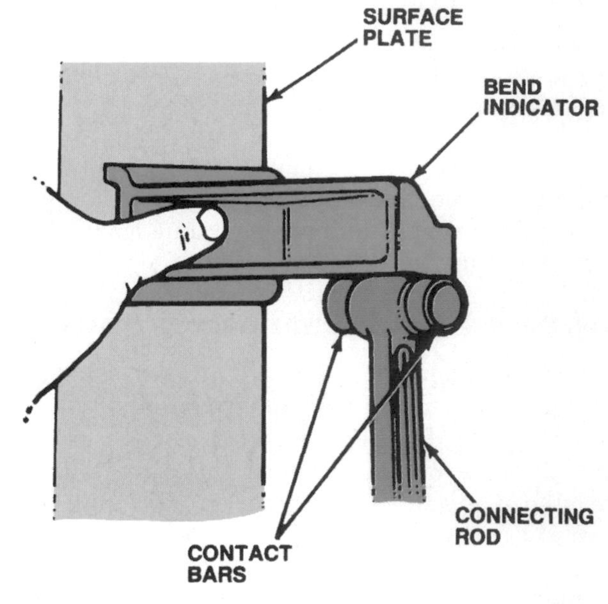

Figure 10–28 A rod alignment fixture being used to check a connecting rod to see if it is bent or twisted.

amount removed from the rod and rod cap only reduces the bore size 0.08 to 0.15 mm (0.003 to 0.006 in.).

> **NOTE:** Powdered metal connecting rods cannot be reconditioned using this method. Most manufacturers recommend replacing worn powdered metal connecting rods.

Step 2 The cap is installed on the rod, and the nuts or cap screws are properly torqued.

Step 3 The hole is then bored or honed back to standard, as shown in Figure 10–27.

Step 4 The connecting rod is checked for bend and twist (misalignment). See Figure 10–28.

PISTON AND ROD ASSEMBLY

To assemble the piston and rod, the piston pin is put in one side of the piston. The piston and rod are placed on a press, using adapters and supports. This setup is shown in Figure 10–29. The pin is pressed into the rod until it is centred. The press-fit of the pin in the small eye of the rod will hold the pin securely in place during engine operation. In precision engine shops, the small eye of the connecting rod is heated before the pin is installed. This causes the rod eye to expand so that the pin can be pushed into place with little force. The pin must be rapidly pushed into the correct centre position.

NOTE: Connecting rod big end bores go oval (elongate) during the intake stroke, especially while decelerating from high RPM. Many connecting rod bearings are made thinner at the parting line to compensate for this.

Full-floating piston pins operate in a bushing in the small eye of the connecting rod. The full-floating piston pin is held in place with a lock ring at each end. The lock rings should always be replaced with new rings if they are removed. Full-floating piston pins should be installed using thumb pressure only: a press is not required.

There is usually a **notch** on the piston head indicating the *front*. Using this will correctly position the piston pin offset toward the right side of the engine. The connecting rod **identification marks** on pushrod inline engines are normally placed on the camshaft side.

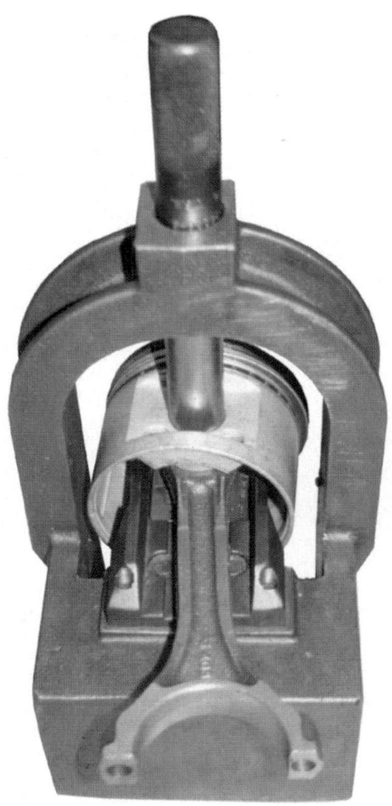

Figure 10–29 A press used to remove and install connecting rods to the pistons.

HIGH PERFORMANCE TIP

Use a Rod Bolt Stretch Gauge

When a fastener is torqued to specification, it may or may not be applying the clamping force that is necessary. Many high-performance engine builders use a connecting rod bolt stretch gauge to measure the actual amount the rod bolt is being stretched. This process results in uniform clamping force on all connecting rod cap bolts. See Figure 10–30.

HINT: Always refer to the shop manual before installing connecting rods; many have directional requirements. As an example, they may have oil squirt holes for cylinder or camshaft lubrication; the big end may have a larger chamfer on one side to clear the crankshaft fillet area. There are many reasons.

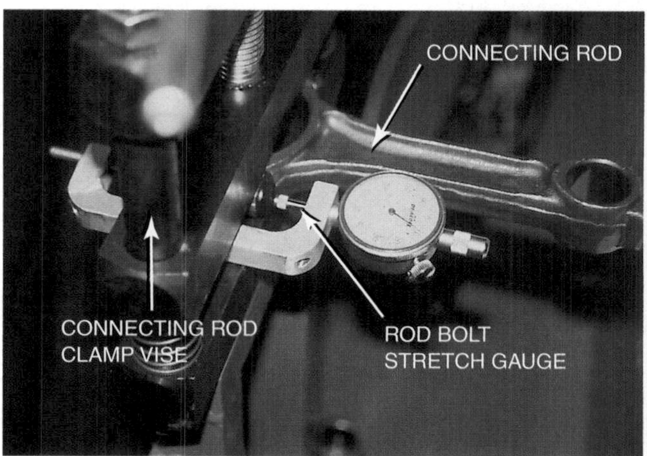

Figure 10–30 Using a connecting rod bolt stretch gauge to measure the amount the rod bolt stretches to tighten the fastener to its ultimate strength.

PHOTO SEQUENCE 6 Piston Ring Fitting

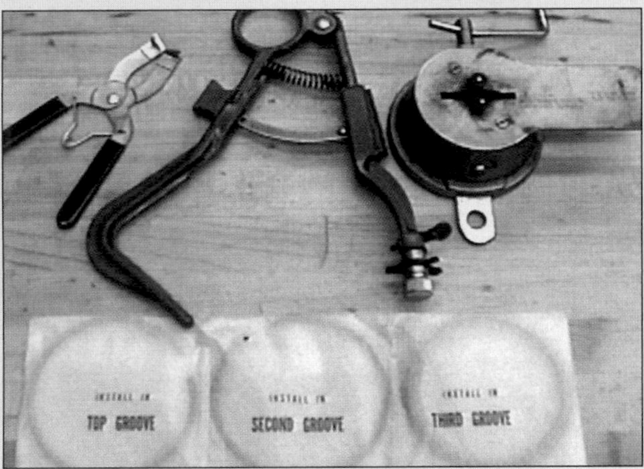

P6–1 New piston rings, piston ring expanders, piston groove cleaner, and a piston ring grinder are all necessary items to fit piston rings to a particular cylinder.

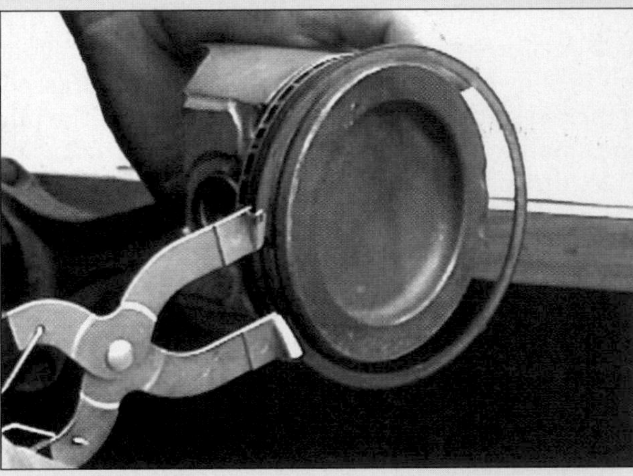

P6–2 Remove the old piston rings from the piston using a piston ring expander tool.

P6–3 Carefully clean the piston ring grooves using a piston ring groove-cleaning tool.

P6–4 The oil drain holes behind the oil control rings should be cleaned.

P6–5 Always be certain to properly assemble the piston on the connecting rod. The rod should be marked with its cylinder position in the engine.

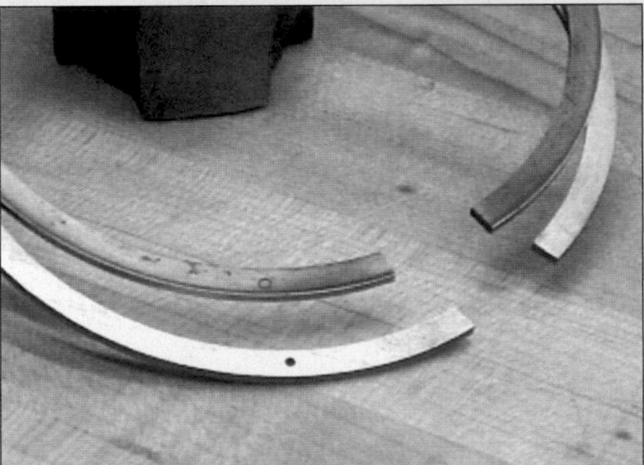

P6–6 Piston rings should be checked for proper size and application. Consult the instructions in the ring package for the meaning of the marks (data) on the rings.

Piston Ring Fitting—continued

P6–7 Measure the side clearance between the piston ring and the piston ring groove using a feeler (thickness) gauge. Compare the readings to factory specifications, usually between 0.025 and 0.075 mm (0.001 in.–0.003 in.).

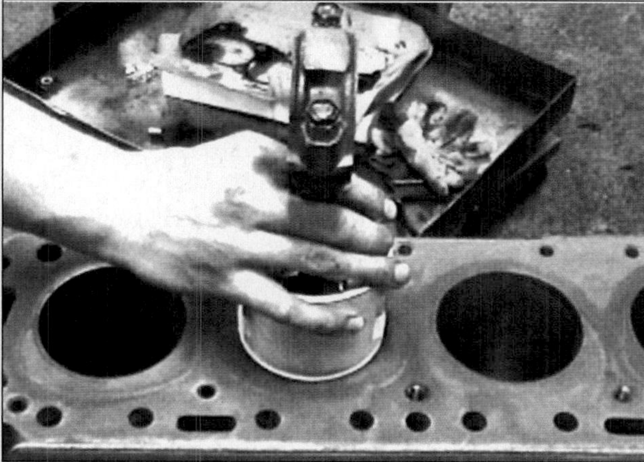

P6–8 Insert a piston ring into the proper cylinder and use a piston upside down to help position the ring squarely in the cylinder bore. Push the piston ring down, below the ring-travelled area.

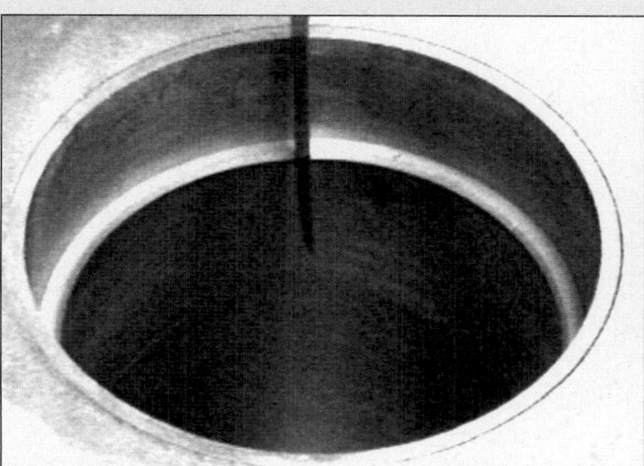

P6–9 Use a feeler gauge to measure the piston ring end gap and compare to the factory specifications, usually 0.04 mm per 10 mm (0.004 in. per inch) of bore.

P6–10 If the piston ring end gap is too close, use a grinder to remove material from the ends of the piston rings until the proper end gap has been achieved.

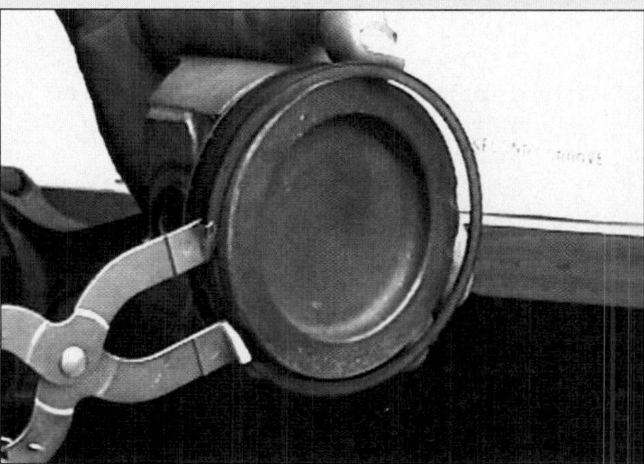

P6–11 Carefully install the piston rings onto the piston using a piston ring expander.

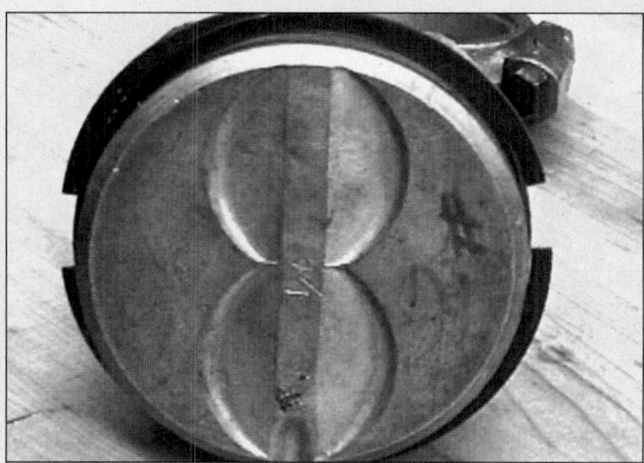

P6–12 Be sure to position the gap of the rings according to factory recommendations. Lubricate both the piston rings and cylinder walls with engine oil before installing the piston in the cylinder.

SUMMARY

1. The connecting rods should be marked before disassembly.
2. Pistons are cam ground so that when operating temperature is reached, the piston will have expanded enough across the piston pin area to become round.
3. Replacement pistons should weigh the same as the original pistons to maintain proper engine balance.
4. Some engines have an offset piston pin to help reduce piston slap when the engine is cold.
5. Piston rings usually include two compression rings at the top of the piston and an oil control ring below the compression rings.
6. If the ring end gap is excessive, blowby gases can travel past the rings and into the crankcase.
7. Many piston rings are made of coated cast iron to provide proper sealing.
8. If the connecting rod is twisted, diagonal wear will be noticed on the piston skirt.
9. Powdered metal connecting rods are usually broken at the big end parting line. Because of this rough junction, powdered metal connecting rods cannot be reconditioned—they must be replaced if damaged or worn.
10. The piston and the connecting rod must be correctly assembled according to identifying notches or marks.

REVIEW QUESTIONS

1. Describe the procedure for correctly removing the piston and rod assembly from the engine.
2. Why are some piston skirts plated or coated?
3. Describe the effect of the piston pin offset as it controls piston slap.
4. Why is it important to keep the connecting rod cap with the rod on which it was originally used and to install it in the correct way?
5. Describe how connecting rods are reconditioned.
6. How is the piston pin installed in the piston and rod assembly?

RED SEAL CERTIFICATION-TYPE QUESTIONS

1. Connecting rod caps should be marked (if they were not marked at the factory) before the piston and connecting rod assembly is removed from the engine _____.
   a. Because they are balanced together
   b. Because they are machined together
   c. To make certain that the heavier rod is matched to the heavier piston
   d. To make certain that the lighter rod is matched to the lighter piston
2. Many aluminum pistons skirts are plated with _____.
   a. Tin
   b. Lead
   c. Antimony
   d. Terneplate
3. A hypereutectic piston has _____.
   a. A higher weight than a eutectic piston
   b. A higher silicon content
   c. A higher tin content
   d. A higher nickel content
4. Protective covers should be placed over the connecting rod threads to help prevent damage to the _____.
   a. Connecting rod
   b. Crankshaft
   c. Cylinder wall
   d. Camshaft
5. Full-floating piston pins are retained by _____.
   a. Lock rings
   b. A drilled hole with roll pin
   c. An interference fit between rod and piston pin
   d. An interference fit between piston and piston pin
6. A misaligned connecting rod causes what type of engine wear?
   a. Cylinder taper
   b. Barrel-shaped cylinders
   c. Ridge wear
   d. Angle wear on the piston skirt
7. Piston damage is most likely to be caused by _____.
   a. Valves hitting the piston head
   b. Abnormal combustion
   c. Lugging the engine during operation
   d. High engine speeds that can break piston heads
8. The diameter of the piston is measured _____.
   a. Across the top (head) of the piston
   b. Across the piston pin
   c. Across the thrust surfaces
   d. Between the top and second piston ring
9. Full-floating piston pins use an interference fit between the piston and the piston pin.
   a. True
   b. False
10. A worn piston pin causes what type of problem?
    a. Engine burns an excessive amount of oil (blue smoke)
    b. Engine produces a knocking noise that will disappear if the cylinder is grounded out
    c. Engine produces a double knocking noise that will not disappear if the cylinder is grounded out
    d. Engine knock when cold only

11

Engine Blocks, Crankshafts, and Bearings

OBJECTIVES: After studying Chapter 11, you should be able to:

1. Prepare for the interprovincial Red Seal certification examination in Appendix I (Engine Repair) on the topics covered in this chapter.
2. List the machining operations required on most engine blocks.
3. Explain how the surface finish is achieved inside a cylinder bore.
4. Distinguish a cast crankshaft from a forged crankshaft.
5. Describe the purpose and function of a vibration damper.
6. Explain how crankshafts are reground and polished.
7. Discuss engine balance shafts and how they function.

The engine block, which is the supporting structure for the entire engine, is made from gray cast iron or from cast or die-cast aluminum alloy. Cast iron is strong for its weight and usually is magnetic. Blocks are often of the **monoblock** design, which means that the cylinders, cooling passages (water jacket), main bearing supports (**saddles**), and oil passages are all cast as one structure. The cylinder holes are called **bores.** A large mounting surface at the rear of the engine block is used for fastening a bell housing or transmission.

The cylinder head(s) attach to the block. The attaching joints are sealed so that they do not leak. Gaskets are used in the joints to correct irregularities that are created by machining and that result from different pressures and temperatures. See Figure 11–1.

BLOCK MANUFACTURING

Oil-sand cores are forms that shape the internal openings and passages in the engine block. Before casting, the cores are supported within a core box.

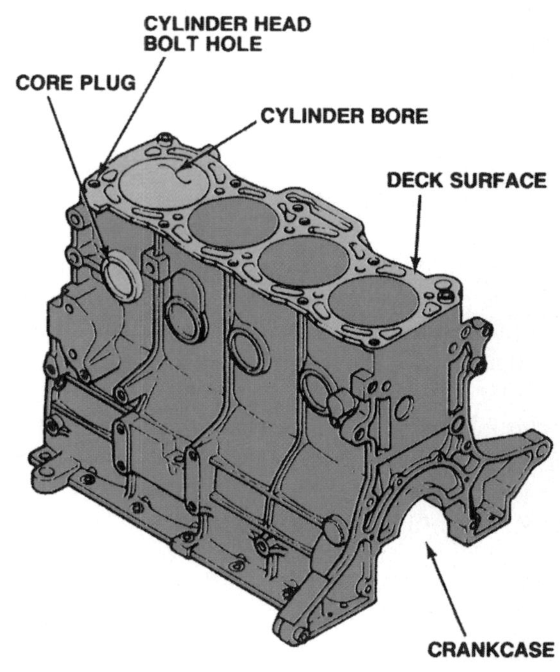

Figure 11–1 The cylinder block usually extends from the oil pan rails at the bottom to the deck surface at the top.

TECH TIP 

How to Tell If the Block Is Cast Iron or Aluminum

Many engines are manufactured using either aluminum or cast iron. Engine components such as water pumps may be available made either of cast iron or aluminum. A quick and easy test is to use a magnet. A magnet will stick to cast iron, but not to aluminum.

The core box also has a liner to shape the outside of the block. Special-alloy cast iron or aluminum is poured into the box. See Figure 11–2.

NOTE: Many aluminum blocks are cast using the die-cast method rather than the sand-cast method.

As the cast iron cools, the core breaks up. When the cast iron has hardened, it is removed from the core box, and the pieces of sand core are removed through the openings in the block by vigorously shaking the casting. These openings in the block are plugged with **core plugs,** also called **expansion plugs, Welsh plugs, freeze plugs,** or **frost plugs.** See Figure 11–3. Although the name implies that the plugs would be pushed outward if the coolant in the passages were to freeze, seldom do they work in this way. Oil passages, called **oil galleries,** are drilled in the block. Plugs are used to cap these galleries and are called gallery plugs. See Figure 11–4.

ENGINE CASTING AND SERIAL NUMBERS

Whenever an engine part such as a block is cast, a number is put into the mould to identify the casting. These casting numbers can be used to check dimensions such as the displacement (in L, cm^3, or $in.^3$) and other information such as the year of manufacture.

The factory also stamps the engine serial number on a machined area of the block, since only the casting number may not provide enough information required to obtain the correct parts or service specifications. The same block and casting number is often used for many different vehicle models; internal changes such as crankshaft stroke, compression ratio, piston design, and camshaft duration are a few of the variables. Provided that the original engine is in the car (this can be a challenge with older vehicles that may have had an engine replaced), both the serial number and casting number should be noted.

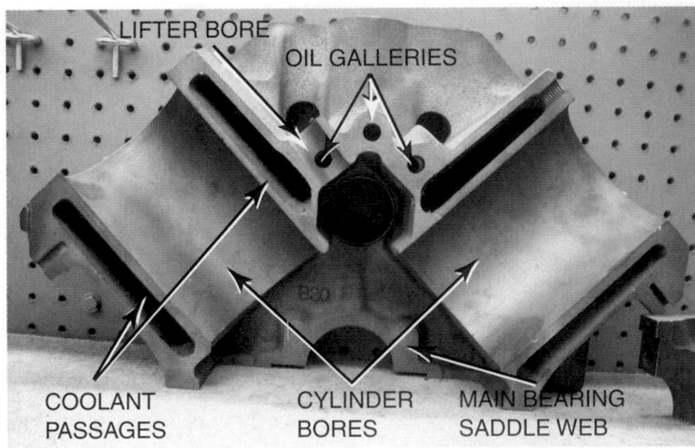

Figure 11–2 Cutaway of a Chevrolet V-8 block showing all of the internal passages.

Figure 11–3 An expansion plug is used to block the opening in the cylinder head or block where the core sand is removed after the part is cast.

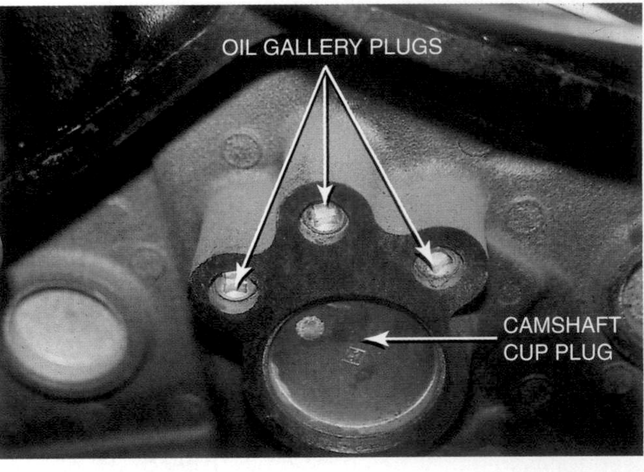

Figure 11–4 Oil gallery plugs are usually threaded plugs used to cap the ends of drilled oil passages in the block.

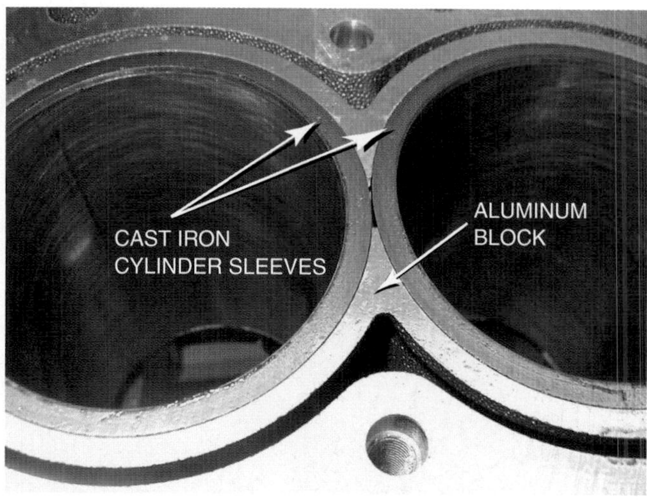

Figure 11–5 Cast-iron dry sleeves are commonly used in aluminum block engines.

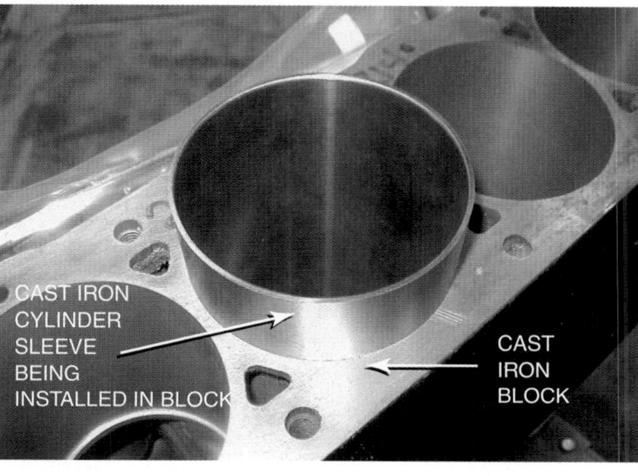

Figure 11–6 A dry cylinder sleeve can also be installed in a cast-iron block to repair a worn or cracked block.

ALUMINUM BLOCKS

Aluminum is used for some cylinder blocks and is nonmagnetic and light in weight. Aluminum blocks may have one of several different types of cylinder walls:

- Cast-aluminum blocks may have iron cylinder liners (Saturn, Northstar, and Ford modular V-8s and V-6s). The cast-iron cylinder sleeves are either cast into the aluminum block during manufacturing or pressed into the aluminum block. These sleeves are not in contact with the coolant passages and are called **dry cylinder sleeves.** See Figure 11–5. A dry sleeve may also be used as a repair in cast-iron blocks as shown in Figure 11–6.

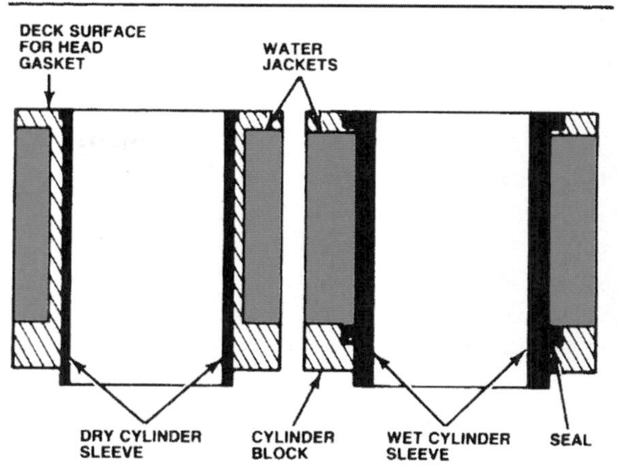

Figure 11–7 A dry sleeve is supported by the surrounding cylinder block. A wet sleeve must be thicker to withstand combustion pressures without total support from the block.

TECH TIP 

The Most Forward

Cylinder #1 is usually the cylinder that is most forward in the engine block. Most forward means closest to the accessory drive belts. This is helpful to remember when attempting to find cylinder #1, especially with transversely mounted V-type engines.

- Another aluminum block design has the block die cast from silicon-aluminum alloy with no cylinder liners. Mixing a high-strength material such as carbon fibre with the aluminum adds additional strength to the block (Honda).
- Some engines have die-cast aluminum blocks with replaceable cast-iron cylinder sleeves. The sleeves are sealed at the block deck and at their base. Coolant flows around the cylinder sleeve, so this type of sleeve is called a **wet cylinder sleeve** (Cadillac 4.1-, 4.5-, and 4.9-L V-8 engines). See Figure 11–7.

Main bearing caps used with aluminum blocks can be either aluminum or cast iron.

THE BLOCK DECK AND PASSAGES

The cylinder head is fastened to the top surface of the block. This surface is called the **block deck.** The deck

Frequently Asked Question ???

What Does LHD Mean?

LHD means **left-hand dipstick.** This abbreviation is commonly used by rebuilders and remanufacturers in their literature describing Chevrolet small-block V-8 engines. Older small-block Chevrolet V-8s used an oil dipstick pad on the left side (driver's side) of the engine block. When oxygen sensors were first used on this engine, the dipstick was relocated to the right side of the block. Engine blocks with the dipstick pad cast on the right side are coded as right-hand dipstick (RHD) engines.

Therefore, to be assured of ordering or delivering the correct engine, knowing the dipstick location is critical. An LHD block cannot be used with an exhaust manifold setup that includes the oxygen sensor without major refitting or the installing of a different style of oil pan that includes a provision for an oil dipstick.

has a smooth surface to seal *against* the head gasket. Bolt holes are positioned around the cylinders to form an even holding pattern. Four, five, or six head bolts are used around each cylinder in automobile engines. These bolt holes go into reinforced areas within the block that carry the combustion pressure load to the main bearing bulkheads. Additional holes in the block are used to transfer coolant and oil.

HINT: Cylinder blocks may appear to be the same at first glance; however, closer inspection dictates that the block cannot be used. As an example, certain V-6 engines are used in both General Motors and Jeep vehicles—the castings appear the same, but the starter mounts are on opposite sides. Some Ford V-6 engines use a different block for front-wheel and rear-wheel drive vehicles.

Cross-checking the block casting numbers before the block is replaced will save not only time, but some expensive machine work as well.

MAIN BEARING CAPS

The main bearing caps are cast separately. They are machined and then installed on the block for a final bore finishing operation. Main bearing caps are not interchangeable or reversible because they are individually finished in place. Main bearing caps may have cast numbers indicating their position on the block. If not, they should be marked.

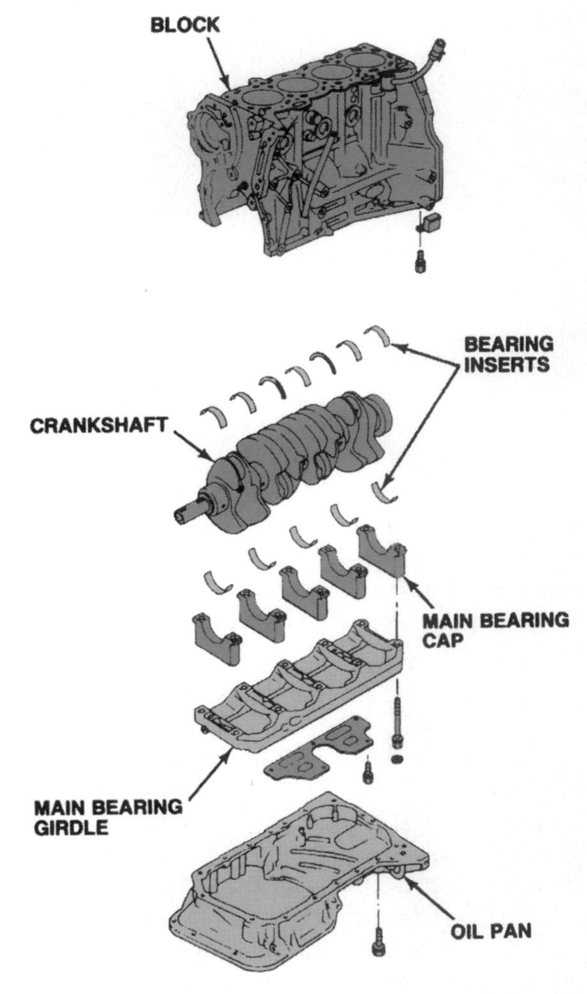

Figure 11–8 Notice that this four-cylinder engine uses a girdle that, when bolted in place, ties the main bearing caps together, increasing block strength.

Aluminum caps often have cast-iron liners moulded into the cap (or bed plate). This not only adds strength to the cap, it limits the amount of cap expansion. The growth rate of aluminum is greater than for cast iron; this allows the bearing crush to relax, reducing the ability of the cap to grip the main bearing insert. Many aftermarket aluminum connecting rods and some factory aluminum main caps are drilled for a pin that is pressed into the cap. This pin fits into an opening in the bearing shell that prevents the bearing from moving.

Main bearing cap design has also been changing. The use of aluminum and light-weight iron cylinder blocks, combined with turbochargers and increased horsepower, all demand greater rigidity at the lower end of the block. For example,

1. Main bearing girdles that bolt all of the caps together for additional strength. See Figure 11–8.
2. The caps and girdle are cast together as one unit called a main bearing cap, or bed-plate. Pressed

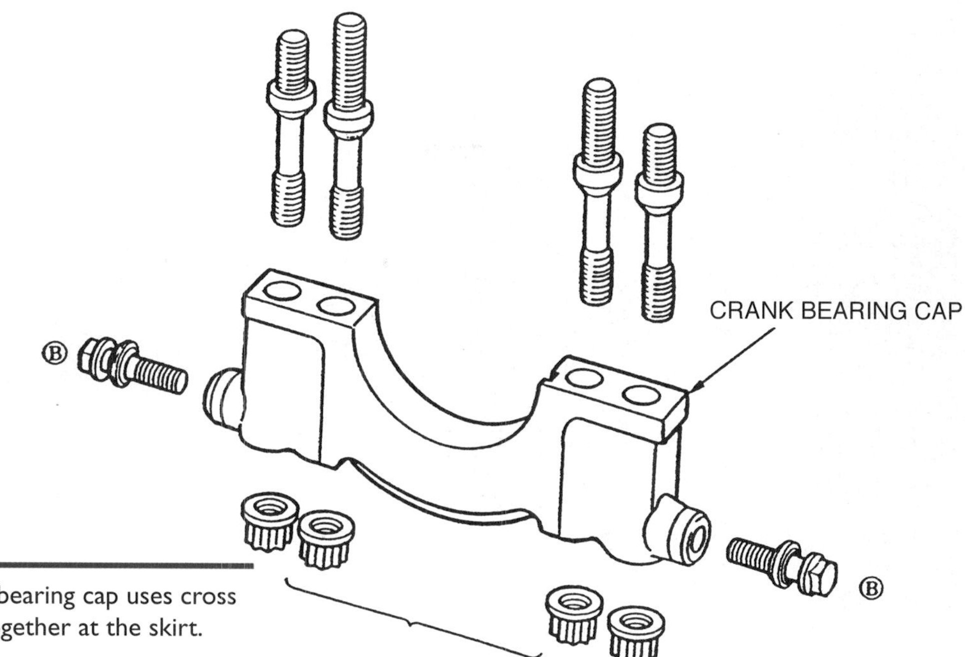

Figure 11–9 This Lexus V-8 main bearing cap uses cross bolts (B) to tie the block and cap together at the skirt. (Courtesy Toyota Motor Co.)

powder (sintered metal) is often used to form this unit.

3. Four-bolt main caps cross-bolted. Two bolts hold the cap in the conventional position; the other two reach through the sides of a deep-skirted block and fasten the caps to the block.
4. Four-bolt main caps. All four bolts, in a row, fasten a wider main cap to a shallow skirt block. The outer two bolts, which are smaller, may go straight into the block, or be angled (splayed) for additional strength.
5. Six-bolt main caps. Some high-end engines (Toyota Lexus V-8) use a combination of four studs and two bolts. See Figure 11–9.

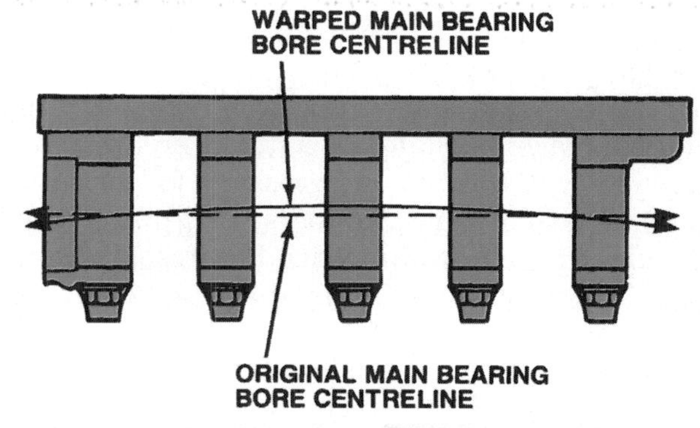

Figure 11–10 The main bearing bores of a warped block usually bend into a bowed shape. The greatest distortion usually occurs in the centre bores.

ENGINE BLOCK SERVICE

After a thorough cleaning, the block should be inspected for cracks or other flaws before machine work begins. If the block is in serviceable condition, the block should be prepared in the following sequence:

Operation 1. Align boring or honing main bearing saddles and caps, if needed

Operation 2. Machining the block deck surface parallel to the crankshaft

Operation 3. Boring and honing cylinders

Main Bearing Bore Alignment

The main bearing journals of a straight crankshaft are in alignment. If the main bearing bores in the block are not in alignment, the crankshaft will bend as it rotates. This will lead to premature bearing failure, and it could lead to a broken crankshaft. See Figures 11–10 and 11–11. Realigning and resizing the main bearing bores in the block is a procedure called **align boring** or **align honing.**

The main bearing bores are resized in the same manner as connecting rods. The flat area of the caps are ground, which reduces the bore diameters. The bores are now machined (align bored) or ground (align honed) to re-establish the original size.

> **NOTE:** Align boring moves the crankshaft deeper into the block. Excess machining causes less backlash on gear drives and more slack with chain drives.

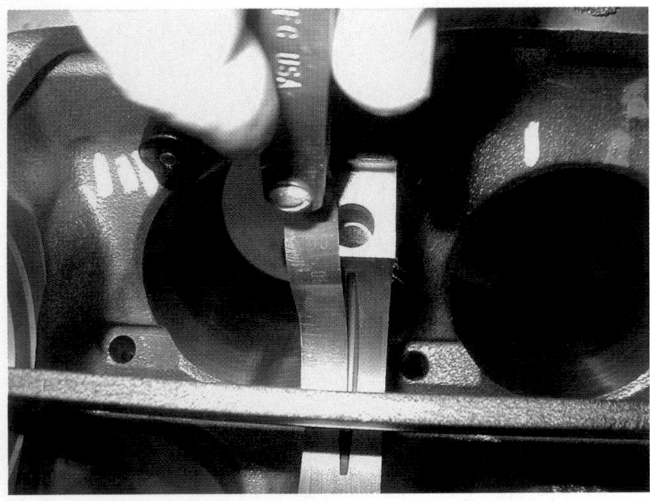

Figure 11–11 The main bearing bores can be checked using a precision straightedge and a feeler gauge.

Machining the Deck Surface of the Block

An engine should have the same combustion chamber size in each cylinder. For this to occur, each piston must come up to an equal distance from the block deck. The block deck must be resurfaced in a surfacing machine that can control the amount of metal removal when it is necessary to match the size of the combustion chambers. This procedure is called **decking the block.** See Figures 11–12 and 11–13. This procedure is also used to repair any damage or warping at the top of the block. The amount of stock removed is limited, or not allowed, with some engines.

Maximum warpage limits are usually about 0.075 mm (0.003 in.) within a 250 mm (10 in.) length, or 0.100 mm (0.004 in.) over the full length. The specifications will vary between shorter blocks (V-6) or longer blocks (inline 6); so always check.

Cylinder Boring

Cylinders should be measured across the engine (perpendicular to the crankshaft) where the greatest wear occurs. Most wear will be found just below the ridge, and the least amount of wear will occur below the lowest ring travel. See Figure 11–14. A dial bore gauge is the best measuring tool to use to determine out-of-round and taper of the cylinders. See Figure 11–15. Most cylinders are serviceable if they are no more than 0.075 mm (0.003 in.) out of round, if they have no more than 0.125 mm (0.005 in.) taper, and if they have no deep scratches in the cylinder wall. The most effective way to correct excessive cylinder out-of-round, taper, or scoring is to **rebore** the cylinder. The rebored cylinder requires the use of a new, oversize piston. See Figure 11–16.

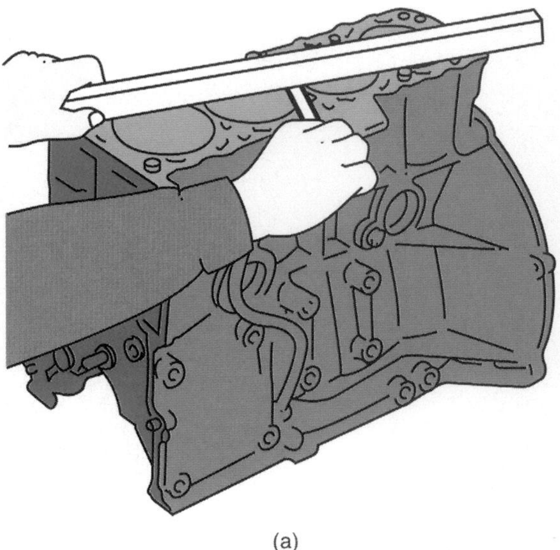

(a)

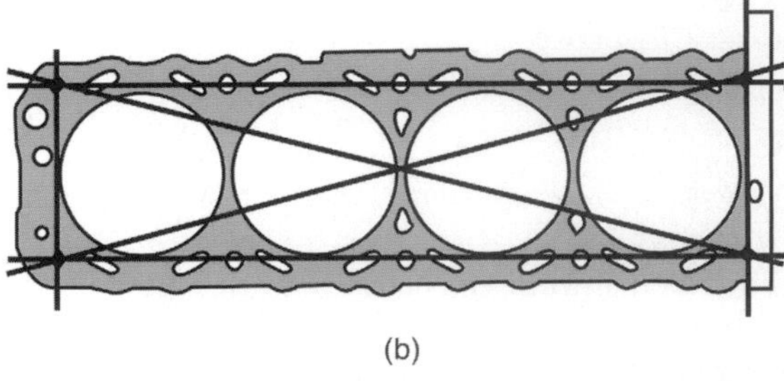

(b)

Figure 11–12 (a) Checking the flatness of the block deck surface using a straightedge and a feeler (thickness) gauge. (b) To be sure that the top of the block is flat, check the block in six places as shown.

Figure 11–13 Grinding the deck surface of the block.

Older cast-iron cylinder blocks were heavy, thick and allowed oversize bores of 1.50 mm (0.060 in.) or more. As iron blocks became thinner to reduce weight, the maximum overbore was limited to about 1.00 mm (0.040 in.). Some very late iron and alu-

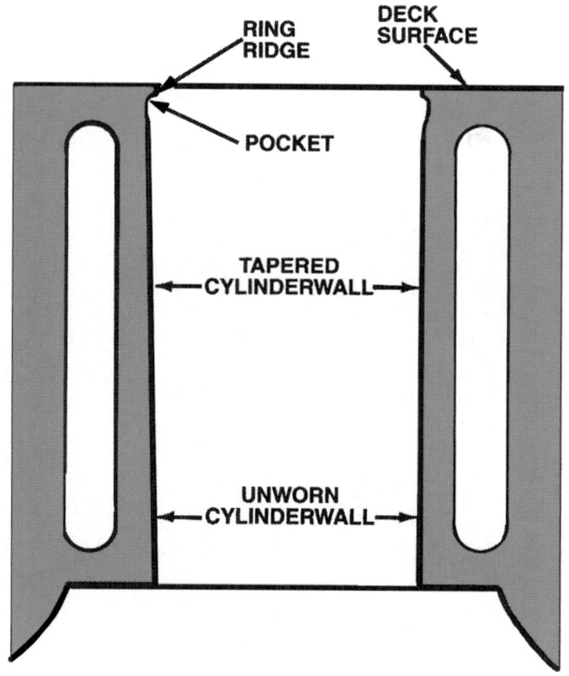

Figure 11–14 Cylinders wear in a taper, with most of the wear occurring at the top where the greatest amount of heat is created under the ridge that is not worn by the rings.

Figure 11–15 Measure the bore diameter at the top just below the ridge and at the bottom below the ring travel. Take measurements in line with the crankshaft and then repeat the measurements at right angles to the centreline of the block in each cylinder.

Figure 11–16 A cylinder boring machine (boring bar) is usually used to enlarge cylinder bore diameter so a replacement oversize piston can be used to restore a worn engine to useful service or to increase the displacement of an engine in an attempt to increase power output.

minum blocks are limited to one rebore only: 0.25 mm (0.010 in.) maximum oversize.

HINT: An easy way to calculate oversize piston size is to determine the amount of taper, double it, and add 0.25 mm (0.010 in.); taper × 2 + 0.25 mm = OS piston. Common oversize measurements include 0.50, 0.75, 1.00, and 1.50 mm (0.020, 0.030, 0.040, 0.060 in.). Use caution when boring for an oversize measurement larger than 0.75 mm (0.030 in.).

HINT: Don't confuse metric and imperial specifications. More than one technician has read 1.00 mm and has ordered pistons 0.100 in. oversize. Obviously they didn't arrive.

CYLINDER HONING

It is important to have the proper surface finish on the cylinder wall for the rings to seat against. Some ring manufacturers recommend breaking the hard surface glaze on the cylinder wall with a hone before installing new piston rings.

Two types of hones are used for cylinder service. A **deglazing hone** removes the hard surface glaze remaining in the cylinder. It is a flexible hone that follows the shape of the cylinder wall, even when the wall is wavy. It cannot be used to straighten the cylinder. Several brush-type (ball-type) deglazing hones are shown in Figure 11–17. A **sizing hone** can be used to straighten the cylinder. Its honing stones are held in a rigid fixture with an expanding mechanism to control the size of the hone. The sizing hone can be used to straighten the cylinder taper by honing the

Figure 11–17 An assortment of ball-type deglazing hones. This type of hone does not straighten wavy cylinder walls.

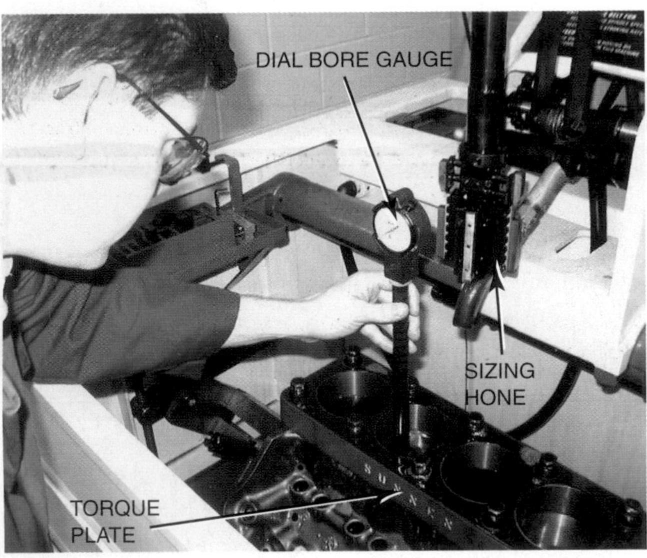

Figure 11–18 An engine being honed. The block is equipped with a torque plate to stress the block the same as if the cylinder head was attached. The machinist is checking the cylinder using a dial bore gauge.

lower cylinder diameter more than the upper diameter. As it rotates, the sizing hone only cuts the high spots so that cylinder out-of-round is also reduced. The cylinder wall surface finish is about the same when the cylinder is refinished with either type of hone. See Figures 11–18 through 11–20.

The hone is stroked up and down in the cylinder as the hone rotates. This produces a **crosshatch finish** on the cylinder wall. A typical honed cylinder is pictured in Figure 11–21. The angle of the crosshatch should be between 20° and 60°. Higher angles are produced when the hone is stroked more rapidly in the cylinder.

The finished cylinder should be within 0.013 mm (0.0005 in.) on both out-of-round and taper measurements. After honing, the top edge of the cylinder is given a slight chamfer to allow the rings to enter the cylinder during assembly.

It is not unusual to remove the cylinder head of an engine with over 160 000 km (100 000 mi.) on it and observe the hone marks still on the cylinder

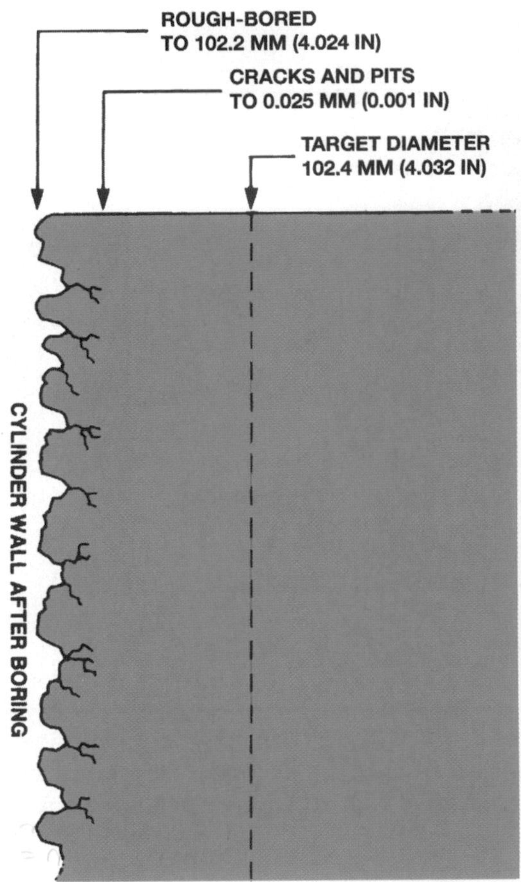

Figure 11–19 After boring, the cylinder surface is rough and fractured to a depth of about 0.025 mm (0.001 in.).

TECH TIP

Always Use Torque Plates

Torque plates are thick metal plates that are bolted to the cylinder block to duplicate the forces on the block that occur when the cylinder head is installed. Even though not all machine shops use torque plates during the boring operation, the use of torque plates during the final dimensional honing operation is very beneficial. Without torque plates, cylinders can become out of round—up to 0.075 mm (0.003 in.)—and distorted when the cylinder heads are installed and torqued down. Even though torque plates do not eliminate all distortion, their use helps to ensure a truer cylinder dimension.

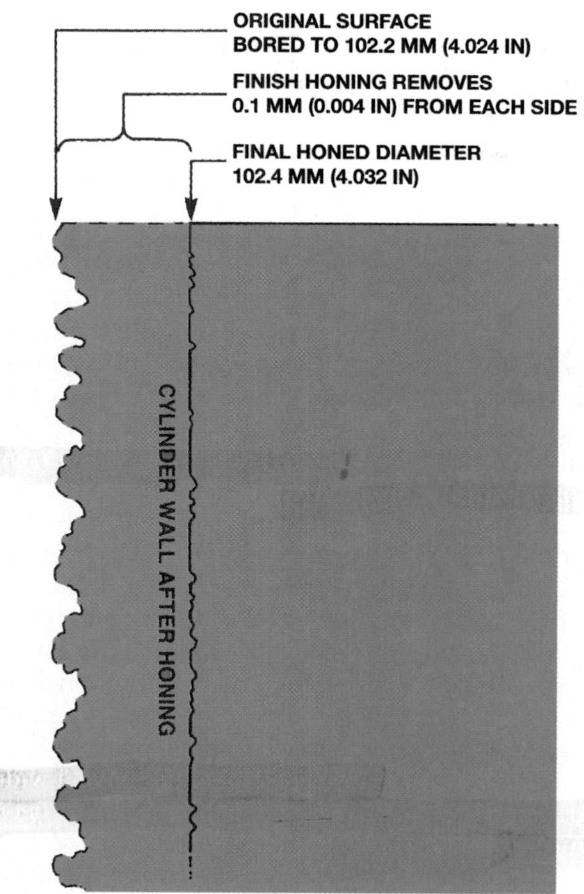

Figure 11–20 Honing enlarges the cylinder to final size and leaves a crosshatch surface that retains oil.

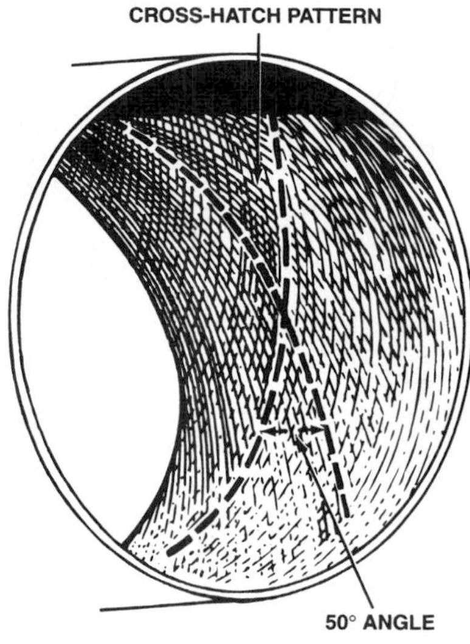

Figure 11–21 The crosshatch pattern holds oil and keeps the rings from wearing excessively.

TECH TIP 

Bore to Size, Hone for Clearance

Many engine rebuilders and remanufacturers bore the cylinders to the exact size of the oversize pistons that are to be used. After the block is bored to a standard oversize measurement, the cylinder is honed. The rigid hone stones in the hands of an experienced operator can increase the bore size by 0.025 to 0.075 mm (0.001 to 0.003 in.) for the typical clearance needed between the piston and the cylinder walls.

For example:

Actual piston diameter	= 102.30 mm (4.028 in.)
Bore diameter	= 102.30 mm (4.028 in.)
Diameter after honing	= 102.35 mm (4.030 in.)
Amount removed by honing	= 0.05 mm (0.002 in.)

NOTE: The minimum recommended amount to be removed by honing is 0.05mm (0.002 in.) to remove the fractured metal in the cylinder wall caused by boring.

walls. Wet and dry sleeves are also plateau honed in some engines. Plateau honing is a two-stage (coarse and fine) honing operation that leaves a few deep scratches to improve cylinder lubrication.

Cylinder Cleaning after Machining

Cleaning the honed cylinder wall is an important part of the honing process. If any grit remains on the cylinder wall, it will rapidly wear the piston rings. The *best* way to clean the honed cylinders is to scrub the cylinder walls with a brush using a mixture of *soap* or *detergent* and *water.* The block is scrubbed until it is absolutely clean. This can be determined by wiping the cylinder wall with a clean cloth. The clean cylinder wall should be given a light coat of oil to protect it from rust until the block is recleaned for assembly.

Block Detailing

Before the engine block can be assembled, a final detailed cleaning should be performed.

1. All tapped holes should be chamfered and cleaned with the correct size of tap or thread chasing tool to remove any dirt and burrs. See Figure 11–22.
2. All bolt holes should be chamfered as shown in Figure 11–23.
3. Oil passages (galleries) should be cleaned by running a long bottle-type brush through all holes in the block.

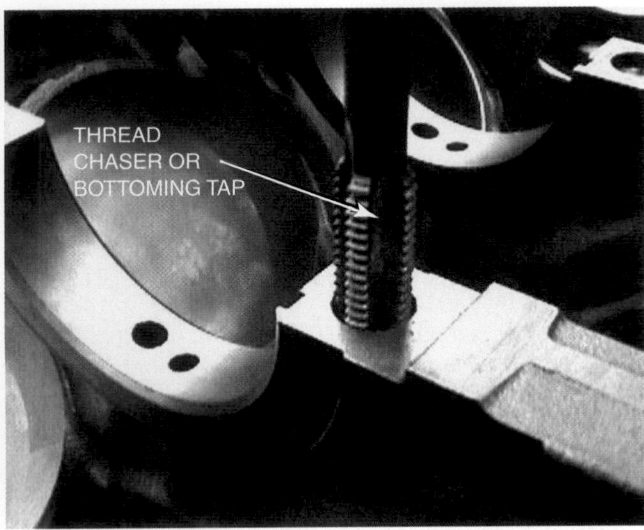

Figure 11–22 A thread chaser or a bottoming tap should be used in all threads before assembling the engine.

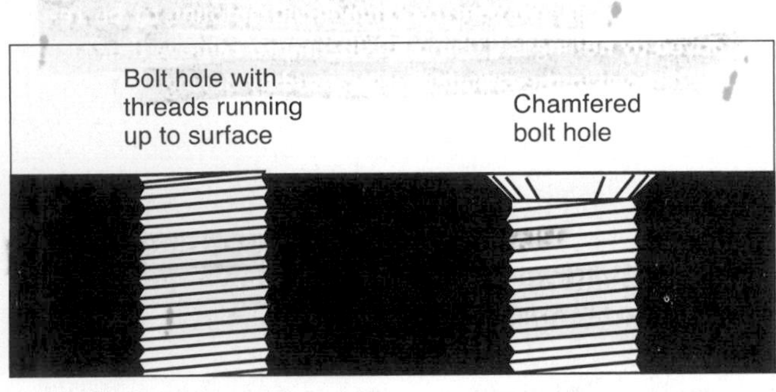

Figure 11–23 All bolt holes should be chamfered at the top to prevent the attaching bolts from pulling threads at the top surface.

4. Coat the newly cleaned block with fogging oil to prevent rust. Cover the block with a large plastic bag to keep out dirt until it is time to assemble the engine.

CRANKSHAFT PURPOSE AND FUNCTION

All the engine power is delivered through the crankshaft. Power from expanding gases in the combustion chamber is delivered to the crankshaft through the piston, piston pin, and connecting rod. The connecting rods and their bearings are attached to a bearing journal on the crank throw. The crank throw is offset from the **crankshaft centreline.** The crankshaft rotates on main bearings. These bearings are split in half so that they can be assembled around the crankshaft main bearing journals. The bearing journal is the surface of the crankshaft that operates on a bearing. Parts of a typical crankshaft are illustrated in Figure 11–24.

Crankshafts used in production automotive engines may be either **forged** or **cast.** Forged crankshafts are stronger than cast crankshafts, but they are more expensive. Forged crankshafts have a wide separation line where the flashings have been ground off. Cast crankshafts are used in most production automotive engines. Automotive crankshafts may be cast in steel, nodular iron, or malleable iron. Steel crankshafts are often found in high-performance engines or truck applications.

The crankshaft is drilled, as shown in Figure 11–25, to allow oil from the main bearing oil groove to be directed to the connecting rod bearings. The hole in the crankshaft counterweight is there for balancing, which is controlled by the depth of the hole (Figure 11–26).

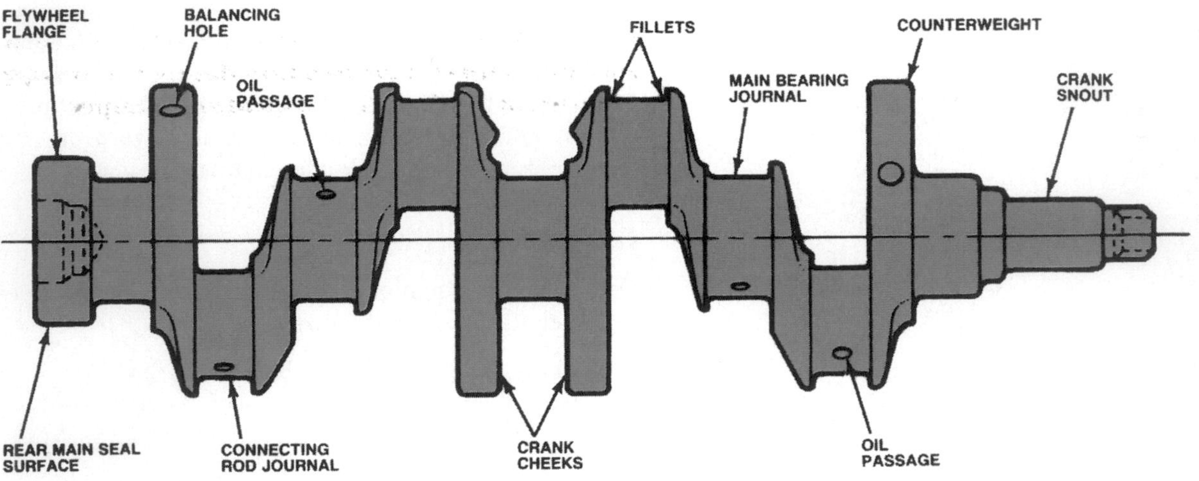

Figure 11–24 Typical crankshaft with main journals that support the crankshaft in the block. Rod journals are offset from the crankshaft centreline.

Figure 11–25 Holes are drilled at an angle from the main bearing journal to the rod bearing journal to provide a direct path for pressurized oil to flow between the crankshaft journal and the bearing.

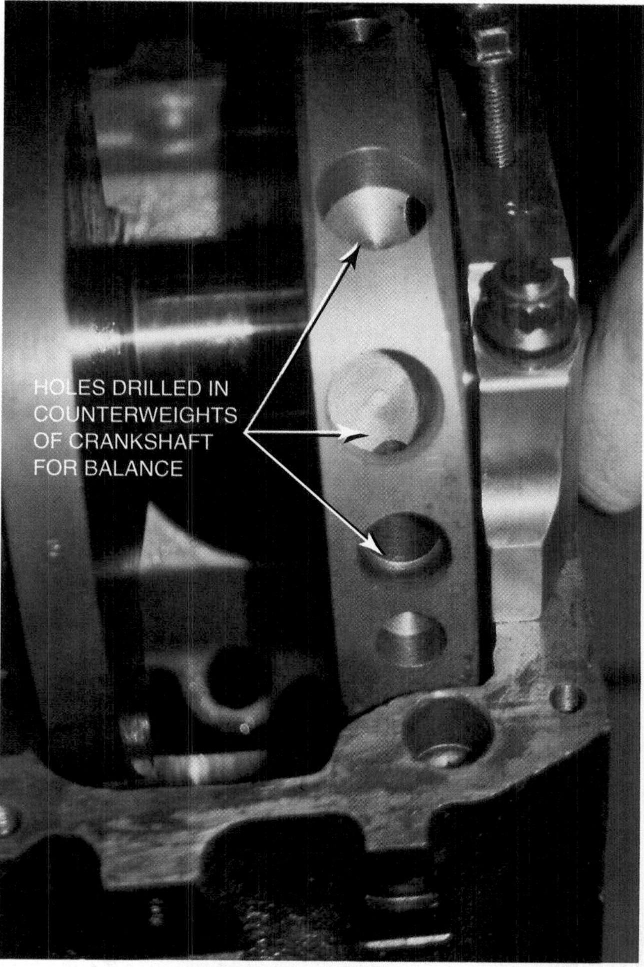

Figure 11–26 Crankshaft balance is accomplished by drilling holes in the counterweights. The deeper and larger the hole, the more weight that is removed.

DIAGNOSTIC STORY

The Mysterious Engine Vibration

A Buick-built 3.8-liter V-6 engine vibrated the whole car after a new short block had been installed. The technician who had installed the replacement engine did all of the following:

1. Checked the spark plugs
2. Checked the spark plug wires
3. Checked the distributor cap and rotor
4. Disconnected the torque converter from the flex plate (drive plate) to eliminate the possibility of a torque converter or automatic transmission pump problem
5. Removed all accessory drive belts one at a time

Yet the vibration still existed.

Another technician checked the engine mounts and found that the left (driver's side) engine mount was out of location, ripped, and cocked. The transmission mount was also defective. After the technician replaced both mounts and made certain that all mounts were properly set, the vibration was eliminated. The design and location of the engine mounts are critical to the elimination of vibration, especially on 90° V-6 engines.

HARMONIC BALANCER

Harmful crankshaft twisting vibrations are dampened with a **torsional vibration damper,** also called a **harmonic balancer** or **vibration damper.** This damper or balancer usually consists of a cast-iron **inertia ring** mounted to a cast-iron **hub** with an **elastomer** (rubber) sleeve. See Figures 11–27 and 11–28.

HINT: Push on the rubber (elastomer sleeve) of the vibration damper with your fingers or a pencil. *If the rubber does not spring back, replace the damper.*

HINT: The inertia ring on the damper will sometimes break loose from the elastomer (rubber) and rotate. This may lead to engine vibration. The timing marks stamped on the inertia ring are now in the wrong location, which makes ignition timing adjustments incorrect. Many current engines have non-adjustable timing and the dampers are not marked.

Figure 11–27 This Chevrolet V-8 harmonic balancer also has a line cut into the outer ring that is used to indicate top dead centre to set the ignition timing on engines that are equipped with a distributor ignition.

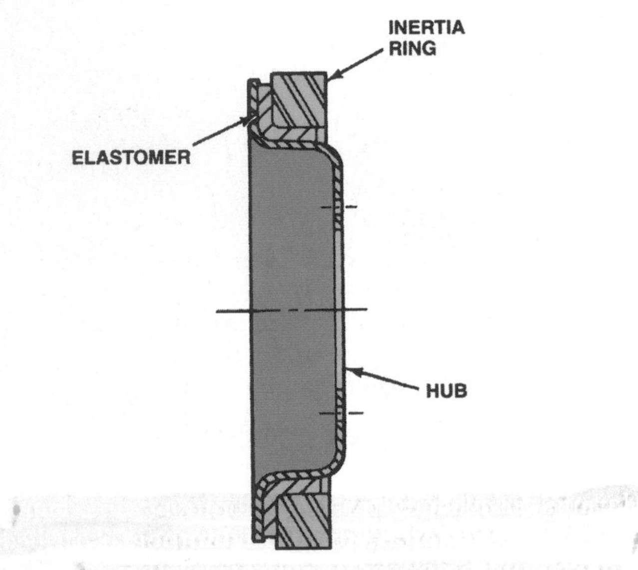

Figure 11–28 The hub of the harmonic balancer is attached to the front of the crankshaft. The elastomer (rubber) between the inertia ring and the centre hub allows the absorption of crankshaft firing impulses.

CRANKSHAFT THRUST SURFACE

Automatic transmission pressure in the torque converter or clutch pressure plate release springs tends to push the crankshaft toward the front of the engine. Thrust bearings in the engine will support thrust loads, as well as maintaining the crankshaft position. Smooth, thrust-bearing journal surfaces are machined on a small boss located on the crankshaft cheek next

Figure 11–29 One bearing journal has a thrust surface to limit the amount of crankshaft endplay movement.

to one of the main bearing journals (Figure 11–29). One main bearing has thrust-bearing flanges that ride against these thrust bearings. Thrust bearings may be located on any one of the main bearing journals.

> **NOTE:** Earlier clutch pressure plates used coil springs to apply pressure. This imparted a very high load to the crankshaft and thrust bearings while the clutch was released. Late model clutches now use diaphragm springs in place of coils, which reduces the load on the crankshaft so that thrust-bearing wear is no longer a problem.

CRANKSHAFT GRINDING

Crankshaft journals that have excessive out-of-round or excessive taper should be reground. See Figures 11–30 through 11–32. The crankshaft will also have to be reground if the journals are badly scored. Crankshafts are usually ground to be 0.250, 0.500, or 0.750 mm (0.010, 0.020, or 0.030 in.) undersize. See Figures 11–33 and 11–34. The journal is polished, using a #320 grit polishing cloth and oil, to remove the fine metal fuzz remaining on the journal from grinding. Finally, the crankshaft oil passages are thoroughly cleaned. Thicker bearings are now used to compensate for the smaller journal.

BALANCE SHAFTS

Some engines use balance shafts to dampen normal engine vibrations. Balance shafts are commonly found on the larger-displacement (over 2.0-litre) four-cylinder automotive engines, as shown in Figure 11–35. Both Ford and General Motors have used

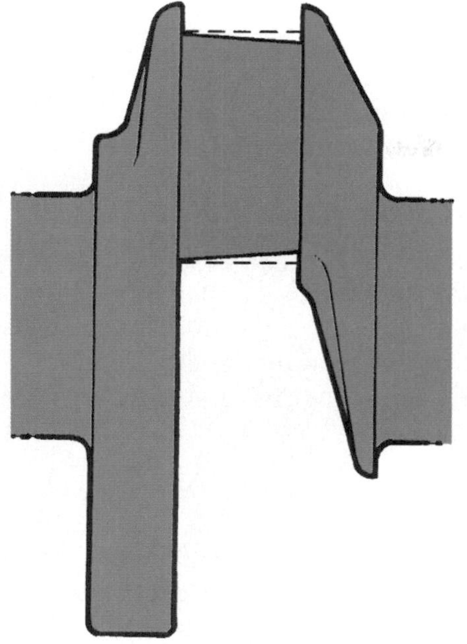

Figure 11–30 Crankshaft journal wear with end-to-end taper.

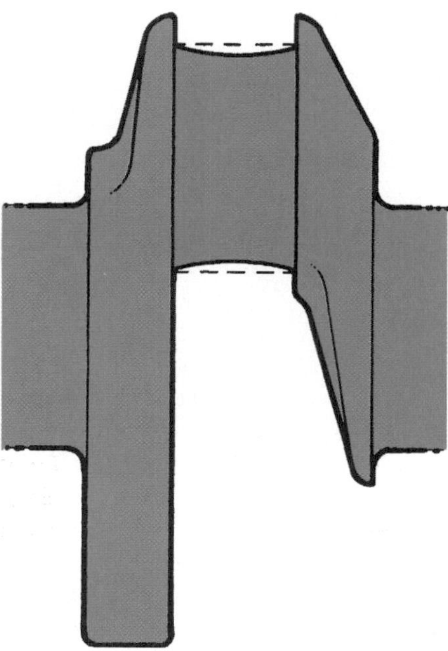

Figure 11–31 Crankshaft journal wear with hourglass taper.

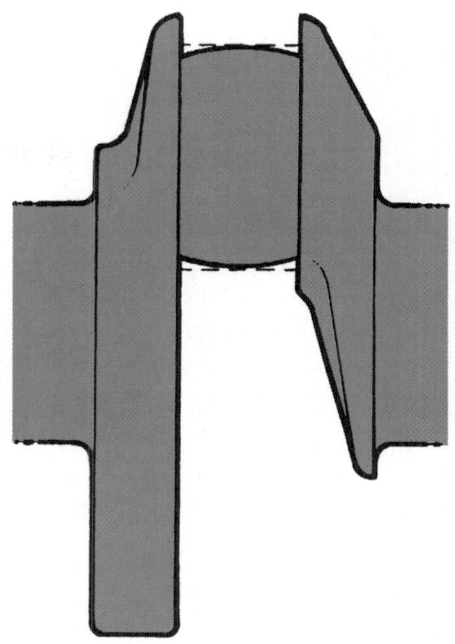

Figure 11–32 Crankshaft journal wear with barrel taper.

Figure 11–33 Crankshaft being ground on a precision crankshaft grinding machine.

a balance shaft on some of their 3.8-litre V-6 engines. The addition of a balance shaft makes a big improvement in the smoothness of the engine. In V-6 engines, the improvement is most evident during idling and low-speed operation, whereas in the four-cylinder engines, balance shafts are especially helpful at higher engine speeds. Balance shafts require correct phasing (timing) with the crankshaft to decrease vibration. Installing the shaft out of time will create major vibrations.

TECH TIP

The Knock of a Flex Plate

The source of a knocking noise in an engine is often difficult to determine without disassembling the engine. Generally, a deep engine knocking noise means that serious damage has occurred to the rods or main bearings and related parts. One source of the noise may be a damaged flex plate. A flex plate (drive plate) is used on automatic-transmission equipped engines to drive the torque converter and provide a ring gear for the starter motor to crank the engine. Two common flex plate-related noises and their causes are as follows:

- Torque converter attaching bolts or nuts can loosen (this is most common in four-cylinder engines, where vibration is more severe than in six- or eight-cylinder engines). The torque converter can then pound on the holes of the flex plate, causing a loud knocking sound. However, if there is a load on the engine, as when the transmission is in drive or while driving under load, the sound should stop. At idle in park or neutral, the noise will be loudest, because the torque converter can float and will hit the sides of the holes in the flex plate.
- If the flex plate is cracked, the resulting noise is very similar to a connecting rod or main bearing knock.

The noise also seems to change at times, leading many technicians to believe that it involves a moving internal part that is lubricated, such as a rod or main bearing. The drive belts can also make a similar noise when they are loose, and belt-driven accessories can also produce similar noises.

Diagnosis should proceed as follows: During the diagnostic procedure, the technician should disconnect one drive belt at a time (if there is more than one) and then start the engine in an attempt to isolate the noise. Noises can be transmitted throughout the entire length of the engine through the crankshaft, making the source of the noise more difficult to isolate. If the flex plate is cracked, the noise is most noticeable when there is a change in engine speed or load. To help diagnose a cracked flex plate, raise engine speed to a high idle (1500 to 2000 rpm), then turn the ignition switch off. Before the engine stops, turn the ignition back on. If a knocking noise is heard when the engine restarts, the flex plate may be cracked. Shifting the gear lever between *neutral* and *drive* (slow idle) while listening for changes in the noise level may also help. Using an automotive stethoscope will often amplify noises for easier diagnosis.

Figure 11–34 If a crankshaft is too worn to be ground, it can be welded to add material to the journals and then precision ground to size.

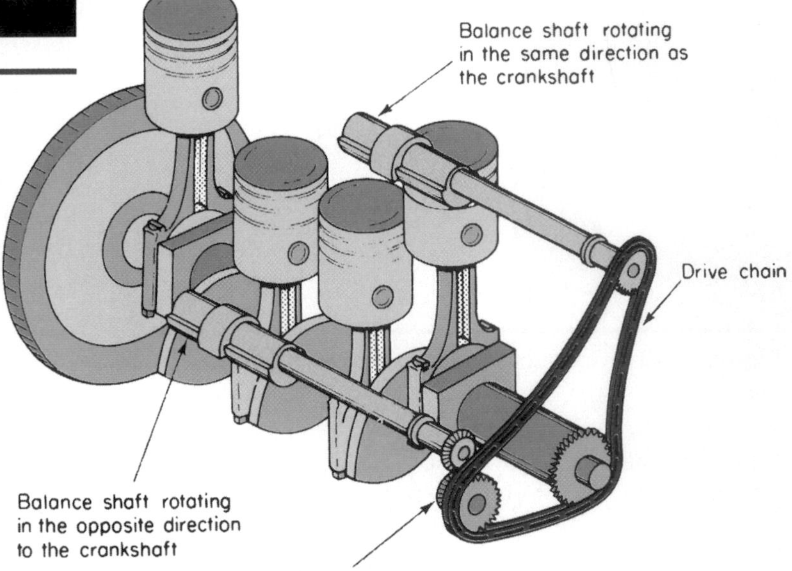

Figure 11–35 Two counter-rotating balance shafts used to counterbalance the vibrations of a four-cylinder engine.

ENGINE BEARINGS

Engine bearings are the main supports for the major moving parts of any engine. The clearance between the bearings and the crankshaft is a major factor in maintaining the proper oil pressure throughout the entire engine.

Most engine bearings are of the **plain** or **sleeve-bearing** type. See Figures 11–36 and 11–37. They need a constant flow of lubricating oil. The crankshaft is actually rolling on a film of oil.

Three materials are used for automobile engine bearings: **babbitt, copper-lead alloy,** and **aluminum.** A layer of the bearing materials 0.250 to 0.500 mm (0.010 to 0.020 in.) thick is applied over a low-carbon steel backing. The steel backing with a surface coating of bearing material formed as an engine bearing is called a bearing **shell.** The steel provides support needed for the shaft load. See Figure 11–38.

Automotive engines use **precision insert-type** bearing shells sometimes called **half-shell** bearings. **Babbitt** is the oldest automotive bearing material. Babbitt is the name given to an excellent bearing material made originally from a combination of lead, tin, and antimony. Isaac Babbitt (1799–1862) first formulated this material in 1839.

Some properties of a good bearing are:

- Embedability — Foreign material on the surface of the bearing may score the shaft. To fully embed the particle, the bearing material gradually works across the particle, completely covering it.
- Conformation — The bearing must be soft enough to conform to a less than perfect crankshaft journal.
- Load strength — A soft bearing may not have sufficient strength to support heavy loads. A harder bearing is required.
- Anti-scuffing — The bearing must resist scuffing during periods of limited lubrication.

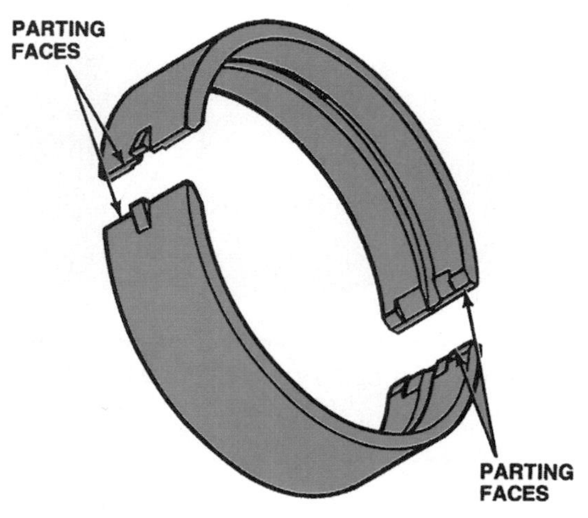

Figure 11–36 A plain insert-type bearing is designed to fit around the journal of the crankshaft. The two halves meet at the parting faces.

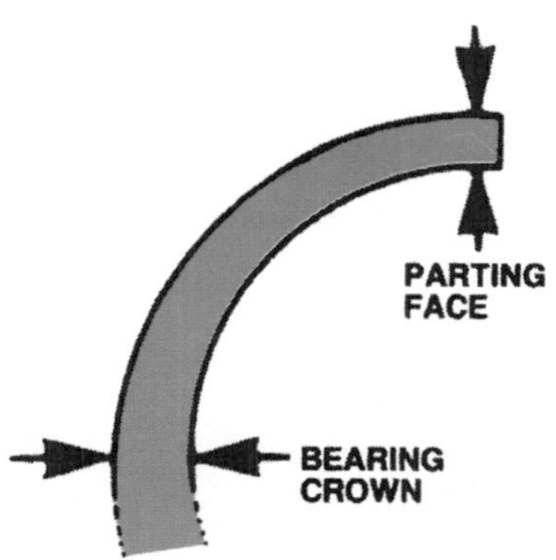

Figure 11–37 A typical plain bearing insert is not the same thickness. Bearing manufacturers refer to this bearing wall shape as an eccentric wall.

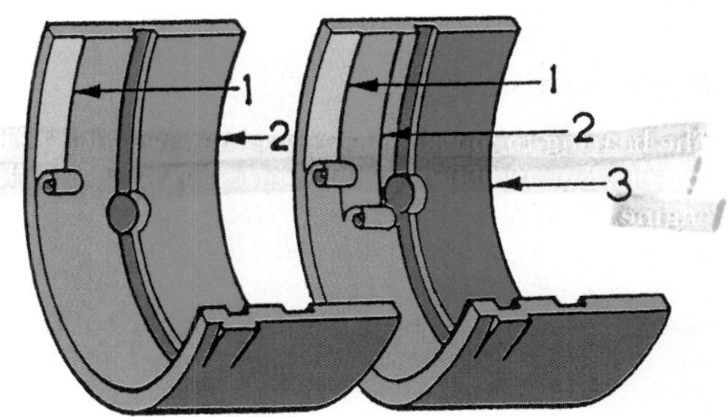

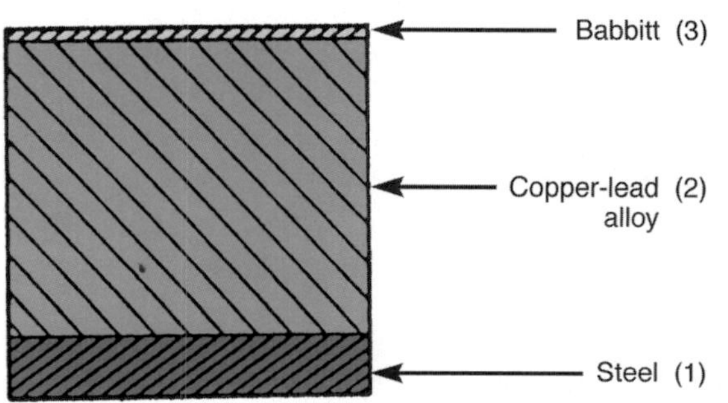

Figure 11–38 Typical two-layer and three-layer engine bearing insert showing the relative thickness of the various materials.

Bearing manufacturers supply a variety of bearings to cover the majority of operating conditions. Refer to the recommendations listed in the parts manual for the correct bearing selection.

NOTE: Many new bearings are damaged after installation because the technician failed to pre-oil (prime) the lubrication system.

NOTE: Cast-iron crankshafts and cylinder walls have a higher level of porosity compared to steel. Thus, the oil retained in the porous iron surfaces provides some residual lubrication when the engine is first started.

Bearing Sizes

Bearings are usually available in standard (std) size and in measurements of 0.250, 0.500 and 0.750 mm (0.010, 0.020, and 0.030 in.) *undersize.* Even though the bearing itself is thicker for use on a machined crankshaft, the bearing is referred to as **undersize** because the crankshaft journals are undersize. Factory bearings may be available in 0.012 to 0.025 mm (0.0005 or 0.001 in.) undersize for precision fitting of a production crankshaft.

Before purchasing bearings, be sure to use a micrometer to measure *all* main and connecting rod journals.

Bearing Clearance

The bearing-to-journal clearance may be from 0.012 to 0.063 mm (0.0005 to 0.0025 in.), depending on the engine. *Doubling the journal clearance will allow more than four times as much oil to flow from the edges of the bearing.* The oil clearance must be large enough to allow an oil film to build up, but small enough to prevent excess oil leakage, which would cause loss of oil pressure. A large amount of oil leakage at one of the bearings would starve other bearings farther along in the oil system. This would result in the failure of the oil-starved bearings. See Figure 11–39. The excess oil leakage also sprays a greater volume of oil onto the cylinder walls. This is difficult for the piston rings to control and higher oil consumption will result.

Bearing Spread and Crush

The bearing design also includes bearing **spread,** which is illustrated in Figure 11–40, and bearing **crush,** shown in Figure 11–41. The bearing shell has a slightly larger arc than does the bearing housing. This difference is called *bearing spread,* and it makes the shell 0.125 to 0.500 mm (0.005 to 0.020 in.) wider than the housing bore. Spread holds the bearing shell in the housing while the engine is being assembled. When the bearing is installed, each end of the bearing shell is slightly above the parting surface. When

Figure 11–39 A lack of lubrication caused these bearings to actually touch the crankshaft journal surface rather than ride on a film of oil.

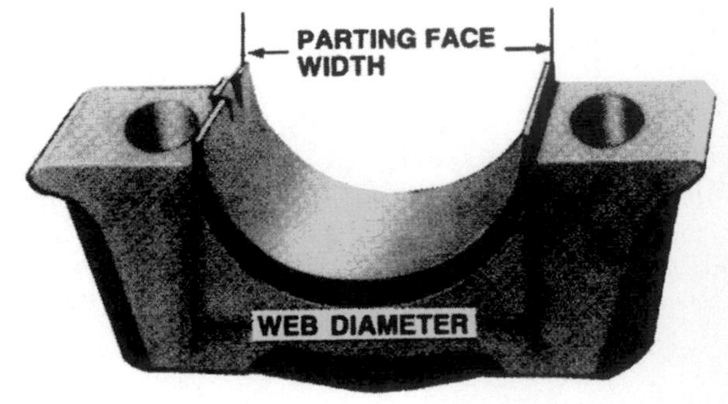

Figure 11–40 Bearing spread allows the bearing to snap into place.

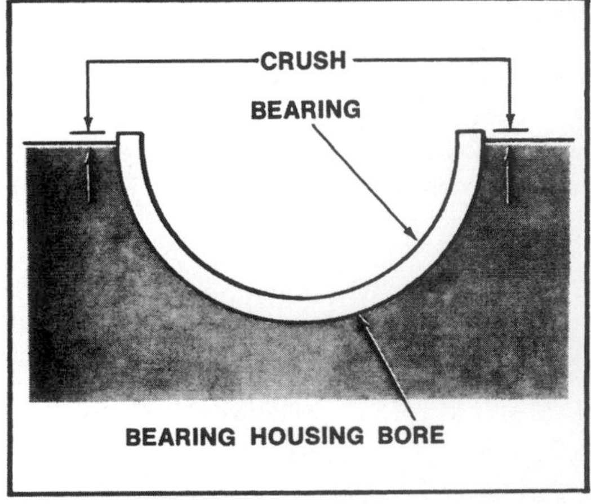

Figure 11–41 Bearing crush holds the bearing tightly in the bore and keeps it from spinning with the crankshaft, which helps prevent a spun bearing.

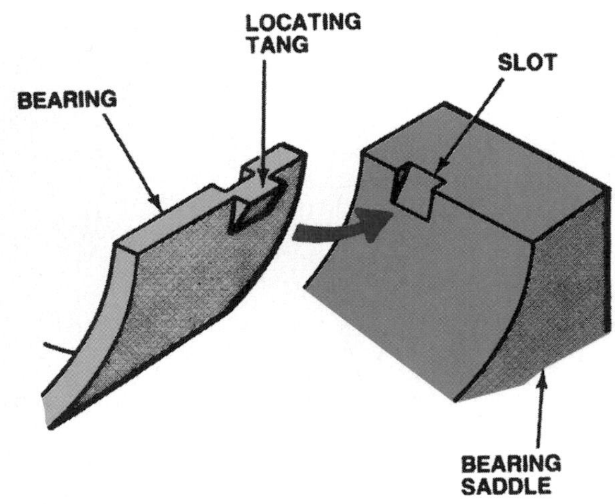

Figure 11–42 The tang and slot help index the bearing in the bore.

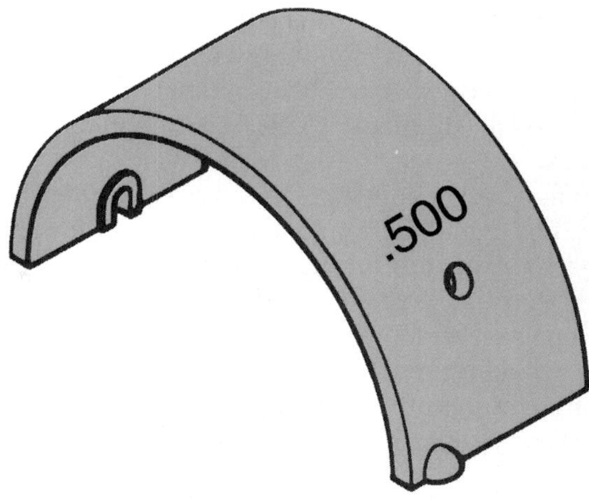

Figure 11–43 Many bearings are marked with their size. This mark means that it is a 0.50 mm (0.020 in.) undersize bearing designed to fit a crankshaft that has been ground 0.50 mm (0.020 in.) undersize.

the bearing cap is tightened, the ends of the two bearing shells touch and are forced together. This force is called **bearing crush.** Crush holds the bearing in place and keeps the bearing from turning when the engine runs. Bearing shells that do not have enough crush may rotate with the shaft. The result is called a **spun bearing.** A lip or **tang** locates the bearing endwise in the housing. The tang can be identified in Figure 11–42.

The replacement bearings must have the same oil holes and grooves and match the journal diameter if the crankshaft has been ground. See Figure 11–43.

CAUTION: Some main bearings may have oil holes in the top shell only. If these are incorrectly installed (top shell in main cap), no oil will flow through the main bearing to the connecting rod; this results in instant engine failure.

Some main bearings and main caps have the locating tangs in different positions, top and bottom, to prevent the bearings from being reversed.

Main bearings that have insufficient crush may move (spin) in the block. This also cuts off the oil supply and the same damage results: instant failure.

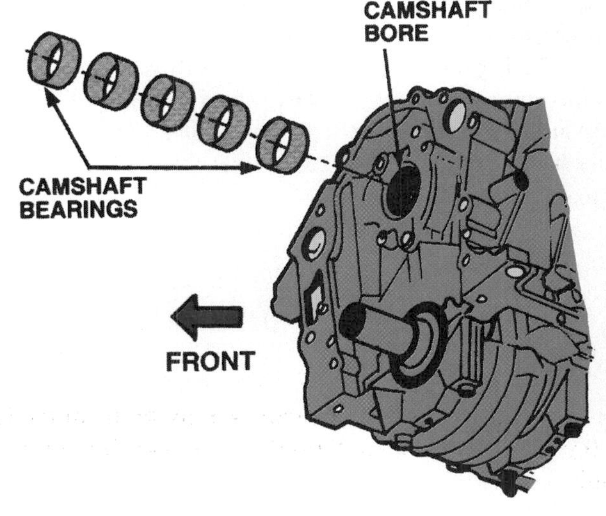

Figure 11–44 Most overhead valve (cam in the block) engines use sleeve-type camshaft bearings.

Camshaft Bearings

The camshaft in pushrod engines rotates in **sleeve** bearings that are pressed into bearing bores within the engine block. See Figure 11–44. Overhead camshaft bearings may be either sleeve-type bushings, called **full round** bearings, or split-type (half-shell) bearings, depending on the design of the bearing supports. In pushrod engines, the cam bearings are installed in the block. The best rule of thumb to follow is to replace the cam bearings whenever the engine is disassembled for major repairs. The replacement cam bearings must have the correct outside diameter to fit

TECH TIP 

Count Your Blessings and Your Pan Bolts!

Replacing cam bearings can be relatively straightforward or can involve keeping count of the number of oil pan bolts! For example, Buick-built V-6s have different cam bearings depending on the number of bolts used to hold the oil pan to the block.

- Fourteen bolts in the oil pan: The front bearing is special, but the rest of the bearings are the same.
- Twenty bolts in the oil pan: Bearings #1 and #4 use two oil feed holes. Bearings #2 and #3 use single oil feed holes.

snugly in the cam bearing bores of the block. They must have the correct number of oil holes and be positioned correctly. Cam bearings must also have the proper inside diameter to fit the camshaft bearing journals.

Some overhead-cam aluminum cylinder heads do not use camshaft bearings; the camshaft runs directly on the aluminum. Although the factory recommends that the head be replaced when the cam bores are worn excessively or scored, the aftermarket suppliers provide camshafts with larger journals or cam bearings that can be installed in the head. Machining of the cylinder head is required in both cases.

Figure 11–45 Crankshafts should be stored vertically to prevent possible damage or warpage. This clever bench-mounted tray for crankshafts not only provides a safe place to store crankshafts but it is out of the way and cannot be accidentally tipped.

TECH TIP 

Do No Harm

All engine parts should be stored in a safe location to help avoid damage prior to being installed in an engine. All camshafts and crankshafts should be stored vertically to avoid causing bending or warpage of these parts that could cause difficulty when the engine is being assembled. See Figure 11–45 for one method of safely storing crankshafts.

TECH TIP 

Check Main Bearing Clearance: The Right Way!

If the engine is in the vehicle when the main bearing clearances are being checked with Plastigage, the crankshaft must be pushed up into the block to obtain accurate readings.

Place a piece of thin cardboard on the two outside lower main bearings and bolt the caps back to the block. This will push the crank up. Check all other mains for clearance. Move the cardboard to the second two mains when it is time to measure the outer pair.

PHOTO SEQUENCE 7 Measuring Main Bearing Oil Clearance Using Plastigage

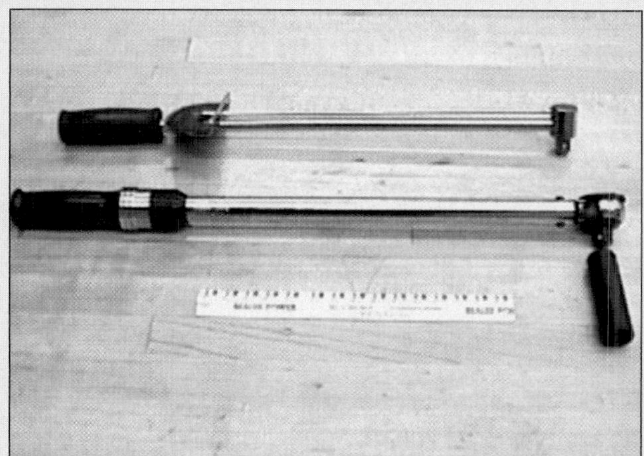

P7–1 The tools required to measure the main bearing oil clearance include a torque wrench, appropriate size socket(s), and Plastigage material.

P7–2 Start the measuring process by thoroughly cleaning the main bearing journal.

P7–3 Place a strip of Plastigage onto the main bearing journal.

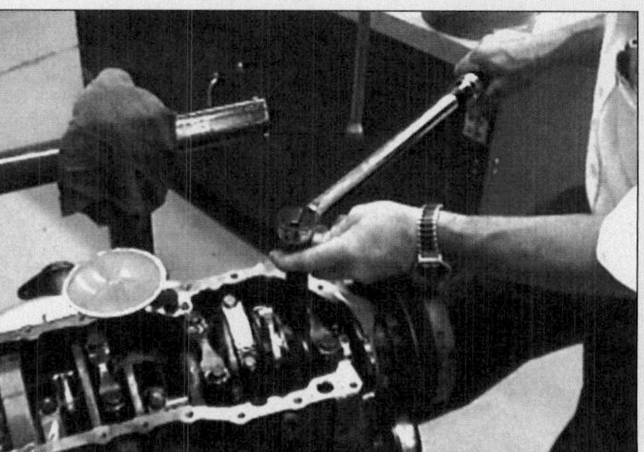

P7–4 Carefully install the main bearing cap and torque the retaining bolts to factory specifications. Do not rotate the crankshaft.

P7–5 After torquing the main bearing cap to specifications, loosen the bolts and carefully remove the bearing cap.

Measuring Main Bearing Oil Clearance Using Plastigage—continued

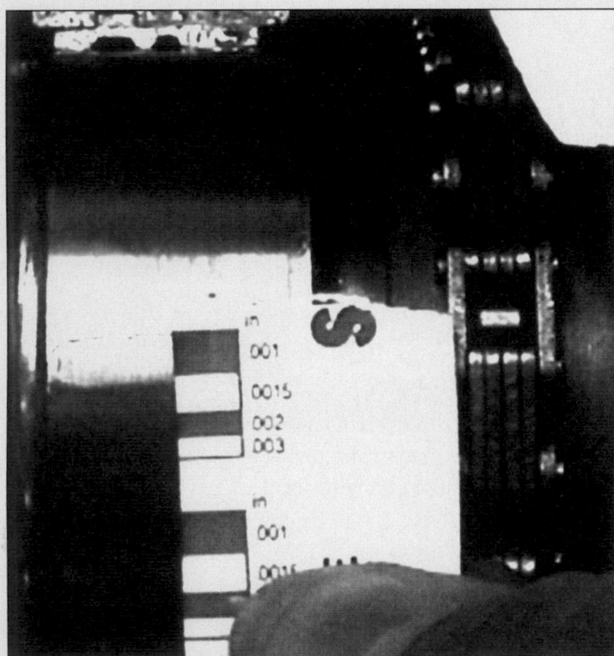

P7–6 Using the scale on the package of Plastigage, determine the main bearing oil clearance by comparing the width of the squeezed plastic gauging strip. In this case, the width is about equal to the green 0.025 mm (0.001″) strip. The wider the strip of Plastigage, the narrower the bearing oil clearance.

P7–7 After comparing the width of the Plastigage to the scale on the package, all of the squeezed Plastigage material must be removed from the crankshaft journal. Removal often requires using your fingernail to get all of the material removed.

P7–8 After measuring all main rod bearing oil clearances, the main bearing caps can be reinstalled, this time using assembly lube on the crankshaft journal before installing the main bearing cap.

P7–9 After replacing the main bearing cap, torque the bolts to factory specifications.

SUMMARY

1. Engine blocks are either cast iron or aluminum.
2. Cores are used inside a mould to form water jackets and cylinder bores. After the cast iron has cooled, the block is shaken, which breaks up the cores so that they fall out of openings in the side of the block. Core plugs are used to fill the holes.
3. Aluminum blocks usually use cast-iron cylinder liners. Some engines use cylinder sleeves that are in contact with the coolant; these are called *wet* cylinder sleeves.
4. The block deck is the surface to which the cylinder head attaches. This surface must be flat and true for proper engine operation.
5. Main bearing caps should be installed and torqued to specification before any machining is performed on the block.
6. The first machining operation is align boring or honing, followed by machining the block deck surface, followed by cylinder boring and honing.
7. The cylinder should be bored to the same size as the piston diameter and then honed to the specified amount of cylinder bore-to-piston clearance.
8. Forged crankshafts have a wide separation line.
9. Cast crankshafts have a narrow mould parting line.
10. Lubrication for the main bearings is fed through the main oil gallery in the block. Oil for the rod bearings comes from holes in the crankshaft drilled between the main journal and the rod journal.
11. A vibration damper, also known as a *harmonic balancer,* is used to dampen harmful twisting vibrations of the crankshaft.
12. Many crankshafts can be reground to be 0.250, 0.500 or 0.750 mm (0.010, 0.020, or 0.030 in.) undersize.
13. Most engine bearings are constructed with a steel shell for strength and are covered with a copper-lead alloy. Many bearings also have a thin overlay of babbitt.
14. Bearings should have spread to hold them in place during installation and crush to keep them from spinning when the crankshaft rotates.

REVIEW QUESTIONS

1. Describe the difference between a forged and a cast crankshaft.
2. Describe bearing crush and bearing spread.
3. Explain why core plugs are called by that name.
4. What does "decking the block" mean?
5. What is the best method to use to clean an engine block after honing?

RED SEAL CERTIFICATION-TYPE QUESTIONS

1. A forged crankshaft ________.
   - **a.** Has a wide parting line
   - **b.** Has a thin parting line
   - **c.** Has a parting line in one plane
   - **d.** Does not have a parting line
2. A typical V-8 engine crankshaft has _____ main bearings.
   - **a.** Three
   - **b.** Four
   - **c.** Five
   - **d.** Seven
3. The thrust bearing surface is located on one of the main bearings to control thrust loads caused by ________.
   - **a.** Lugging the engine
   - **b.** Torque converter or clutch release forces
   - **c.** Rapid deceleration forces
   - **d.** Torsional vibration
4. The typical journal-to-bearing clearance is ________.
   - **a.** 0.004 to 0.005 mm (0.00015 to 0.00018 in.)
   - **b.** 0.012 to 0.063 mm (0.0005 to 0.0025 in.)
   - **c.** 3.810 to 6.350 mm (0.150 to 0.250 in.)
   - **d.** 0.500 to 0.890 mm (0.020 to 0.35 in.)
5. A bearing shell has a slightly larger arc than the bearing housing. This difference is called ________.
   - **a.** Bearing crush
   - **b.** Bearing tang
   - **c.** Bearing spread
   - **d.** Bearing saddle
6. Bearing _____ occurs when a bearing shell is slightly above the parting surface of the bearing cap.
   - **a.** Overlap
   - **b.** Crush
   - **c.** Cap lock
   - **d.** Interference fit
7. The block deck is the ________.
   - **a.** Bottom (pan rail) of the block
   - **b.** Top surface of the block
   - **c.** Valley surface of a V-type engine
   - **d.** Area where the engine mounts are attached to the block
8. Which engine block machining process should be done first when reconditioning?
   - **a.** Cylinder boring
   - **b.** Decking the block
   - **c.** Honing the cylinders
   - **d.** Align boring (honing)
9. An engine vibration could be caused by a defective engine (motor) mount.
   - **a.** True
   - **b.** False
10. Sleeving a cylinder means _________.
    - **a.** Plating the inner walls of the cylinder with a different metal, such as nickel
    - **b.** Boring the cylinder to be oversize and installing a cast-iron sleeve to restore the cylinder to the original diameter
    - **c.** Boring the cylinder to be 0.500 to 1.500 mm (0.020 to 0.060 in.) oversize to accept oversize pistons
    - **d.** Using a hone to finish the cylinder after boring

12

Engine Assembly and Installation

OBJECTIVES: After studying Chapter 12, you should be able to:

1. Prepare for the interprovincial Red Seal certification examination in Appendix I (Engine Repair) on the topics covered in this chapter.
2. List the steps for assembling an engine.
3. Explain how to check for crankshaft end play and connecting rod side clearance.
4. Discuss how to fit pistons to individual cylinder bores.
5. Describe how to test for proper oil pressure before starting the engine.
6. List the steps necessary to install and start up a rebuilt engine.
7. Discuss the importance of torquing all bolts or fasteners that connect accessories to the engine block.
8. Describe what precautions must be taken to prevent damage to the engine when it is first started.
9. Explain how to break in a newly rebuilt engine.

All parts of an engine are attached to the engine block. The block, therefore, must be prepared before assembly can begin. The key to proper assembly of any engine is cleanliness. The work area must be spotless, as well as the workbench space, to prevent dirt or other engine-damaging particles from being picked up and causing possible serious engine damage later.

CLEANING OIL GALLERIES IN THE BLOCK

As mentioned in Chapter 11, the block should be cleaned using soap and water after it has been machined to clean all remaining grinding residue. The block should then be coated lightly with oil to prevent it from rusting.

Most experts suggest using long-handled oil gallery brushes, commonly called *bottle brushes,* to clean out all of the varnish and debris from the small oil passages by dipping them in solvent and running them through the oil galleries by hand. See Figures 12–1 and 12–2.

BLOCK PREPARATION

All surfaces of the block should also be checked for damage resulting from the machining processes. Other steps that should be taken before assembly begins include the following:

1. All threaded bolt holes should be chamfered.
2. All threaded holes should be cleaned with a tap. See Figure 12–3.
3. Core plugs should be installed.
4. Oil gallery plugs should be installed using sealant on the threads.

CAUTION: Avoid using Teflon tape on the threads of oil gallery plugs. The tape is often cut by the threads, and thin strips of the tape are then free to flow through the oil galleries where they can cause a clog, thereby limiting lubricating engine oil to important parts of the engine.

Figure 12–1 The best way to clean cylinders that have been machined is to use soap (detergent) and water and thoroughly clean with a large washing brush.

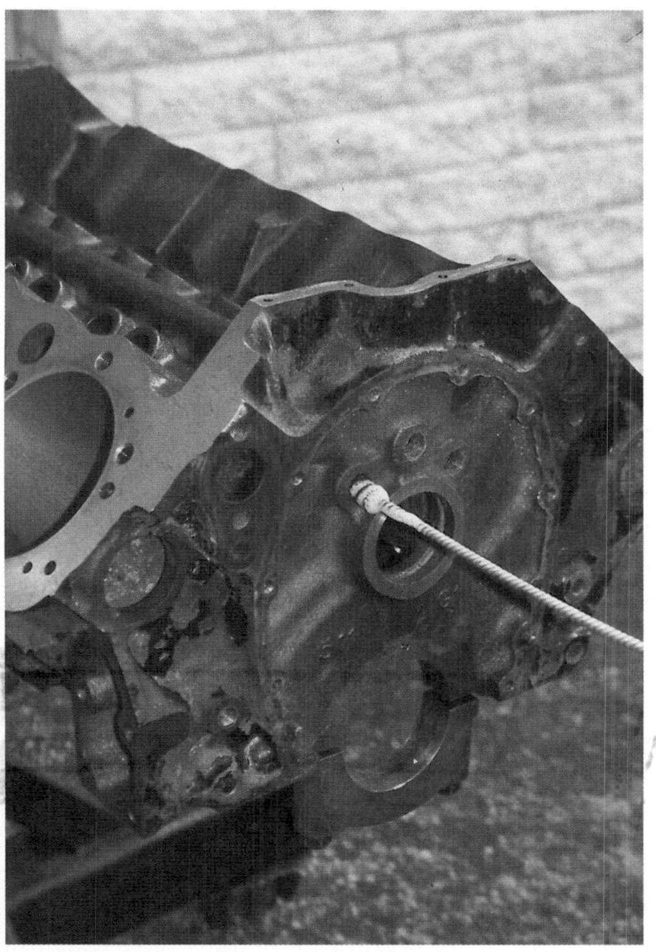

Figure 12–2 All oil galleries should be cleaned with soap (detergent) and water and a long oil gallery cleaning brush.

Figure 12–3 All threaded holes should be cleaned using a thread chaser or a bottoming tap.

INSTALLING CUPS AND PLUGS

Core holes left in the external block wall are machined and sealed with soft core plugs or expansion plugs (also called freeze plugs or Welsh plugs).

Soft plugs are of two designs. One type is a **convex type.** The convex soft plug is placed in the counter bore, convex side out. It is driven in until it reaches the counter bore of the core plug hole and upset (driven flat) with a fitted seating tool. The second and the most common type of hole plug is a **cup type.** An installed cup-type soft plug is shown in Figures 12–4 and 12–5. A cup plug is installed about 0.500 to 1.25 mm (0.020 to 0.050 in.) below the surface of the block, using sealant to prevent leaks.

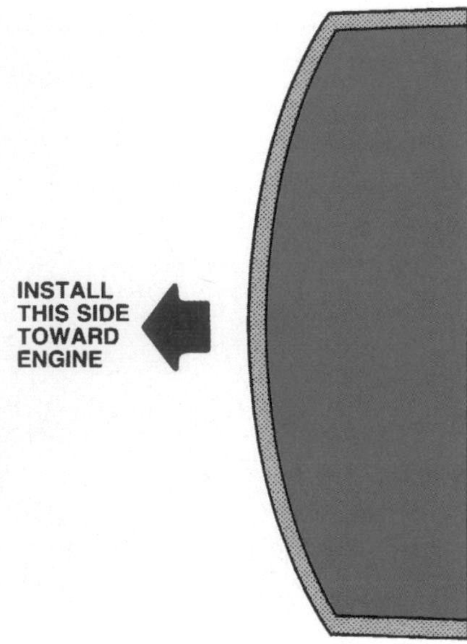

Figure 12–4 Cup plugs have a deep tapered flange. The flange should be coated with water-resistant sealer before being driven into the block.

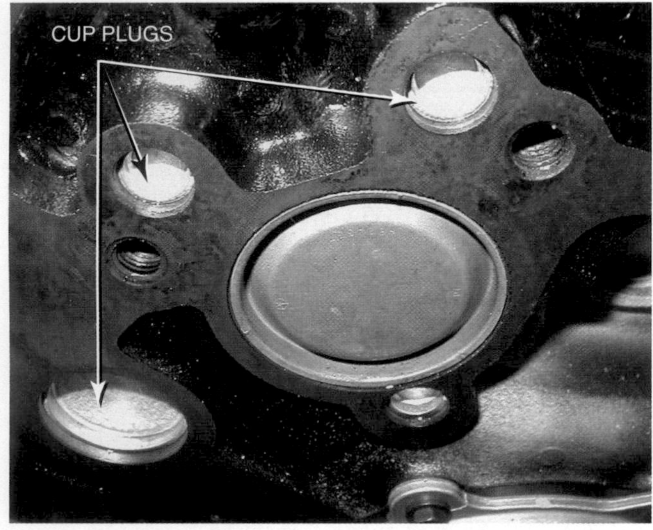

Figure 12–5 This engine uses many cup plugs to block off coolant and oil passages as well as a large plug over the end of the camshaft bore.

ENGINE ASSEMBLY

Measuring Main Bearing Clearance

The engine is assembled from the inside out. This method allows the technician to support the inner parts as they are assembled. Checks are made during assembly to ensure correct fits and proper assembly of the parts.

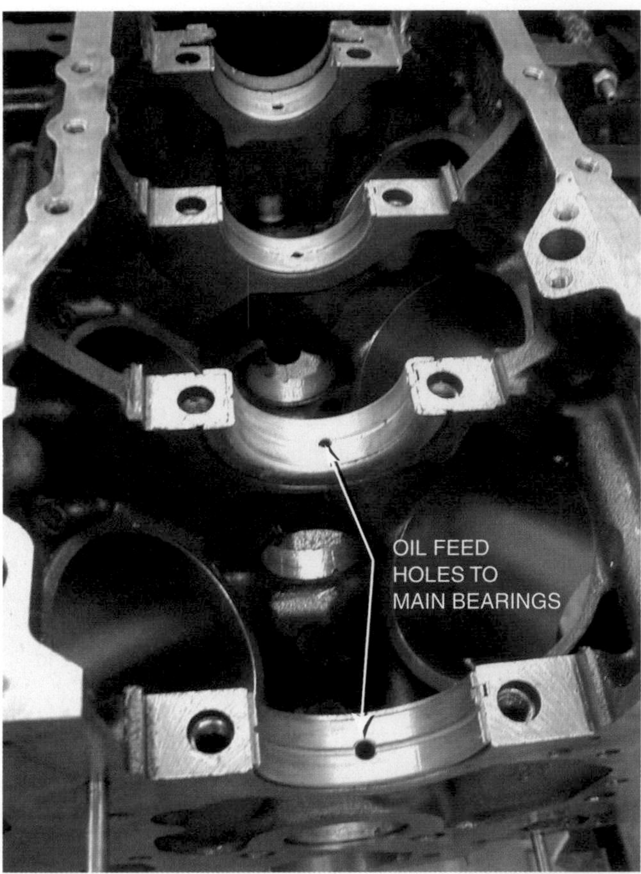

Figure 12–6 Note the upper bearing shells have an oil feed hole. (This block is upside down.) Often the mating bearing does not have an oil hole and an engine can be ruined if the plain bearing shell is installed in the wrong location.

The main bearings are properly fit *before* the crankshaft is installed.

> **CAUTION:** Avoid touching bearings with bare hands. The oils on your fingers can start corrosion of the bearing materials. Always wear protective cloth or rubber gloves to avoid the possibility of damage to the bearing surface.

Standard bearings are often available in measurements of 0.025, 0.050 and 0.075 mm (0.001, 0.002, and 0.003 in.) undersize to compensate for worn bearing journals. Bearings are also made in 0.250, 0.500 and 0.750 mm (0.010, 0.020, and 0.030 in.) undersize for use on reground journals.

The crankshaft bearing journals should be measured with a micrometer to determine the required bearing size. The correct-size bearings should be placed in the block and cap, making sure that the bearing tang locks into its slot. The upper main bearing has an oil feed hole. See Figure 12–6. Carefully rest the clean crankshaft in the block on the upper main bearings. Lower it squarely so that it does not

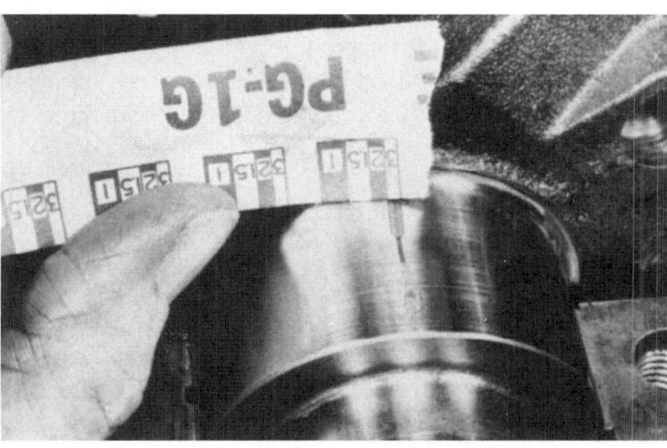

Figure 12–7 Checking the width of the plastic gauging strip to determine the oil clearance of the main bearing. An alternate method of determining oil clearance includes careful measurement of crankshaft journal and bearings.

damage the thrust bearing. Place a strip of Plastigage (gauging plastic) on each main bearing journal. Install the main bearing caps and tighten the bolts to specifications. Remove each cap and check the width of the Plastigage with the markings on the gauge envelope, as shown in Figure 12–7.

> **CAUTION:** Do not rotate the crankshaft when checking for bearing clearance using Plastigage.

Compare the width of the Plastigage to the width printed on the edge of the package.

- The wider the Plastigage, the narrower the oil clearance
- The narrower the Plastigage, the greater the oil clearance

Compare the oil clearance to specifications. If the clearance is not within factory specifications, reexamine the journal diameter and bearing bore as well as the bearings.

Instead of using Plastigage to measure the bearing oil clearance, the crankshaft can be measured with a micrometer along with the inside diameter of the assembled bearing cap with bearings installed. The difference in the measurements is the bearing oil clearance.

Of the two methods, Plastigage provides the most accurate readings.

> **HINT:** Most engine bearing clearance specifications fall within 0.025 to 0.075 mm (0.001 to 0.003 in.). The written specification could be a misprint; therefore, if the specification does not fall within this general range, double-check the clearance value using a different source.

Crankshaft Seal Installation

Seals are always used at the front and rear of the crankshaft. The front uses a one-piece lip seal pressed into the timing cover; a rope-type seal or a one- or two-piece lip seal is used at the rear.

Rope seals must be left out during the Plastigage operation as they "lift" the crank; lip seals can be left in place.

Rope-type oil seals must be compressed tightly into the groove so that no oil can leak behind them. With the crankshaft removed, the upper half of the rope seal is put in a clean groove and compressed by rolling a round object against it to force it tightly into the groove. See Figure 12–8. When the seal is fully seated in the groove, the ends that extend above the parting surface are cut to be flush with the surface using a sharp single-edge razor blade or a sharp tool specially designed to cut the seal.

One- and two-piece lip seals have different installation procedures. One half of the two-piece split seal is placed in the block before the crankshaft is installed; the other half is put into the main cap. See Figure 12–9. The one-piece full round lip seal fits into a recess machined into the back of the block or in a separate bolt-on retainer. One-piece seals may be installed before or after the oil pan is bolted to the engine.

> **NOTE:** Seal pressure often wears a groove into the rear crankshaft flange or the front harmonic balancer hub; repair sleeves (thin wall tubes) are pressed over the worn area to salvage the crank or balancer.

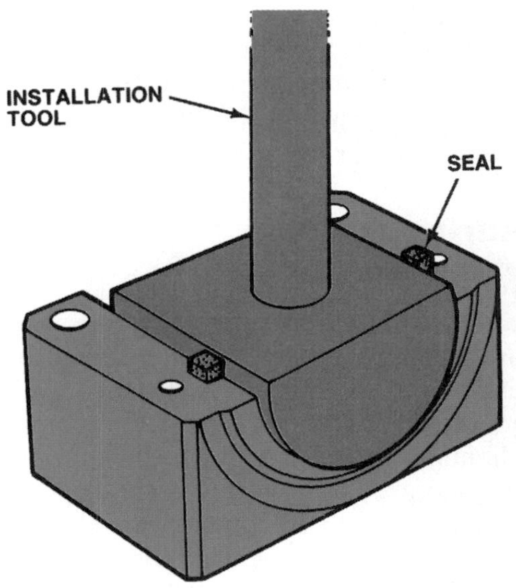

Figure 12–8 Use a special tool or other round object such as a hammer handle to roll the seal to the bottom of the groove.

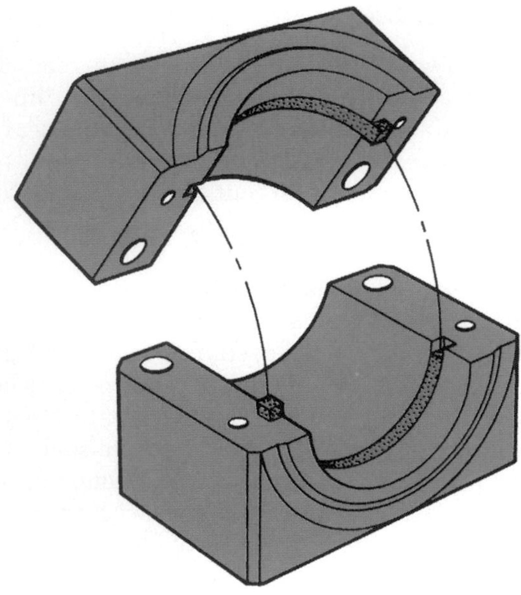

Figure 12–9 Many engine builders prefer to stagger the parting lines of a split seal.

Installing the Crankshaft

The main bearing saddles, the caps, and the back of all the main bearing shells should be wiped clean; then the bearing shells can be put in place. It is important that each bearing tang line up with the slot in the bearing support. The bearing shells must have some spread to hold them in the bearing saddles and caps during assembly. The surface of the bearings is then given a thin coating of assembly lubricant to provide initial lubrication for engine start-up. See Figure 12–10.

The crankshaft with lubricant on the journals is carefully placed in the bearings to avoid damage to the thrust bearing surfaces. The bearing caps are installed with their identification numbers correctly positioned. The bearing tang slots in the cap are usually on the same side as the block – remember "tang to tang."

Measuring Thrust Bearing Clearance

All main caps should be tight, with the exception of the cap which holds the thrust bearing or thrust washers. The crankshaft is first pushed to the front with a large screwdriver; the cap is then tapped with a soft hammer or brass drift, in the opposite direction (to the rear) and then tightened. This will align the cap half of the thrust bearing with the block saddle half. Most engine specifications call for a range of from 0.050 to 0.300 mm (0.002 to 0.012 in.) of clearance. A dial indicator or a thickness (feeler) gauge can be used to determine the end thrust of the crankshaft (also called **crankshaft end play**). See Figure 12–11.

Figure 12–10 Engine assembly lubricant should be used because it contains additives that provide protection to engine parts during the critical engine start-up phase.

Figure 12–11 A dial indicator is being used to check the crankshaft end play (also known as thrust bearing clearance).

> **NOTE:** Many late engines have thrust washers in the block only, none in the cap. There is no need to align the cap for crank end-play.

Tightening Procedure for the Main Bearing

Tighten the main bearing caps to the specified assembly torque, and in the specified sequence. Most vehicle manufacturers specify that the centre fastener be tightened, then tighten others out from the centre. See Figure 12–12. The crankshaft should be rotated one complete revolution after each cap is torqued. Any sudden increase in the effort required to turn the crank could indicate a problem with that particular bearing or journal.

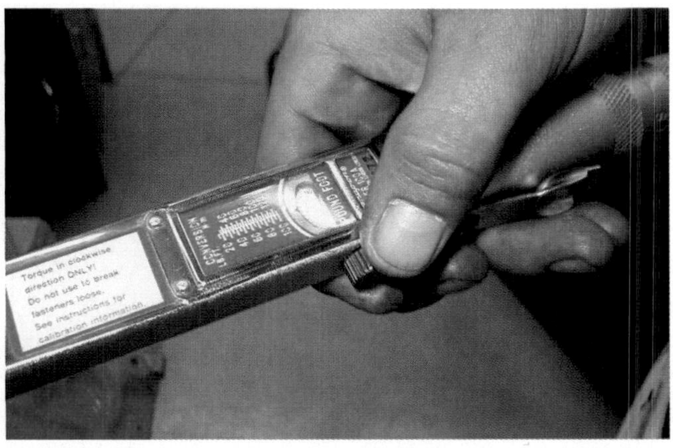

Figure 12–12 Do not jerk a torque wrench and always use a quality torque wrench that has been recently calibrated to be assured that all engine fasteners are properly torqued to factory specifications.

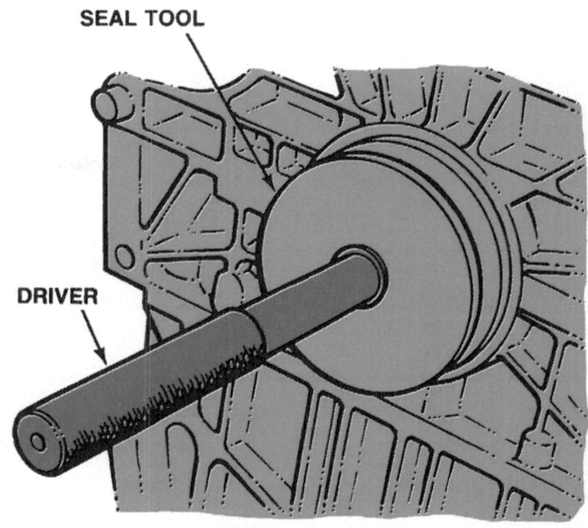

Figure 12–13 Always use the proper driver to install a main seal. Never pound directly on the seal.

The shaft should turn *freely* after all of the main bearing cap bolts are fully torqued. It should never require over 7 N·m (5.2 lb-ft) of torque to rotate the crankshaft. An increase in the torque needed to rotate the crankshaft is often caused by a foreign particle that was not removed during cleanup. It may be on the bearing surface, on the crankshaft journal, or between the bearing and saddle.

Rope seals initially apply more pressure, which increases the torque required to turn the crank. This makes a rotational check difficult. Some engine builders test for freedom of rotation after bearing clearances are measured with Plastigage (rope seal out). The crank is then removed, the seal is pushed into place and the crankshaft is reinstalled.

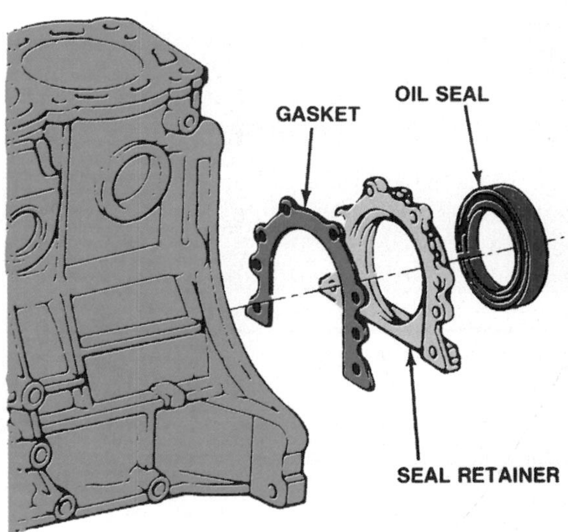

Figure 12–14 The rear main seal for this engine mounts in a retainer plate. The retainer is then bolted to the engine block.

INSTALLING ONE-PIECE MAIN SEALS

NOTE: A very light coat of non-hardening sealer should be brushed on the block at the rear main-cap machined surface. This prevents an oil leak between the block and main cap. This will not apply to engines that mount the seal in a retainer plate.

After the crankshaft has been carefully installed and the main bearing caps torqued to factory specifications, the one-piece main seal can be installed. The seal must go in straight or it could leak. Some engines have a groove machined directly into the engine block for the seal. Half of the groove is cut into the main bearing cap, and the other half is in the block. This type of seal should be installed using a seal driver. Inspect the seating groove for dirt or debris and lubricate the seal lip with engine oil if specified by the vehicle manufacturer.

CAUTION: Do not apply engine oil to a Teflon oil seal. A Teflon seal will leak if oil is applied during installation. A Teflon seal is designed to be installed clean and dry so that as the crankshaft rotates, some of the Teflon will transfer to the surface of the crankshaft thereby creating a Teflon-to-Teflon sealing surface.

Fit the seal driver over the seal and then seat it by striking the driver with a hammer. See Figure 12–13.

Some engines have the rear main seal mounted to a retainer plate which is bolted to the engine block as shown in Figure 12–14.

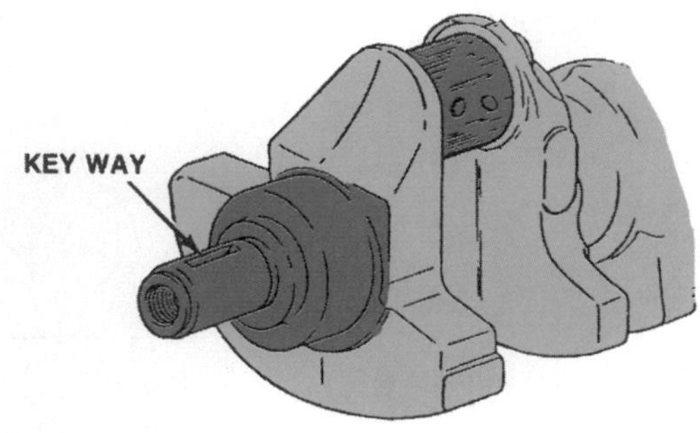

Figure 12–15 A key in the keyway locks the timing gear or sprocket to the snout so that the crankshaft can drive the camshaft.

Figure 12–16 Timing chain and sprockets can be installed after the crankshaft and camshaft have been installed. The service technician is rotating the engine using the harmonic balancer bolt to check for proper rotating torque.

INSTALLING TIMING DRIVES FOR PUSHROD ENGINES

For pushrod engines, the timing chain and sprockets or timing gears should be installed next. Some crankshaft timing gears are a press fit and require a special installation tool to prevent crankshaft or bearing damage. Press fit camshaft gears are usually fitted while the camshaft is out of the engine. See Figures 12–15 and 12–16. The timing marks on the gears must line up with each other. Timing chains and sprockets are usually positioned with the timing marks in line, similar to timing gears, but this is not always the case. Check the shop manual for specifications first. A camshaft "out of time" may allow the valves and pistons to contact each other the first time the engine is rotated with the cylinder head(s) in place. Expensive mistake!

PISTON FITTING

All pistons should be rechecked for clearance in all cylinder bores. Even though all of the cylinders were honed to the exact same dimension and all pistons were machined to the same diameter, some variation in dimensions will occur. *Each piston should have been selectively fitted to each cylinder at the time the block was rebored.*

TECH TIP 

Hot Water to the Rescue

Some timing chain sprockets are an interference fit on the end of the crankshaft. If the proper installation tool is not available, try heating the sprocket on the stove in a metal container filled with very hot water: 95°C (200°F).

After a few minutes of "cooking" on the stove, the timing gear sprocket should easily slide onto the end of the crankshaft.

Ring End Gap

The bottom of the combustion chamber is sealed by the piston rings. They have to fit correctly in order to seal properly. The piston ring end gap is determined by placing the piston ring into the cylinder and using a feeler gauge to determine the end gap. To fit a ring into the cylinder, invert a piston and use it to squarely push the ring down into the cylinder. See Figure 12–17. Because of cylinder taper with used engines, the ring end gap must be measured at the bottom of the ring-travelled area. Cylinders that have just been rebored are straight; the ring gap can be checked near the top of the cylinder. Typical ring gap clearances are about 0.10 mm per 25 mm (0.004 inch per inch) of cylinder bore or as follows:

Piston Diameter	Ring Gap Clearance
50 to 75 mm (2 to 3 in.)	0.18 to 0.46 mm (0.007 to 0.018 in.)
76 to 100 mm (3 to 4 in.)	0.25 to 0.50 mm (0.010 to 0.020 in.)
101 to 125 mm (4 to 5 in.)	0.33 to 0.58 mm (0.013 to 0.023 in)

NOTE: If the gap is greater than recommended, some engine performance is lost. However, too small a gap will result in scuffing because of ring butting during operation, which forces the rings to scrape the cylinders.

If the ring gap is too small, the ring should be removed and filed to make the gap larger. A special hand-operated rotary grinder is usually used to remove material from the ends of piston rings. See Figure 12–18.

Figure 12–17 Using a feeler gauge to determine piston ring end gap.

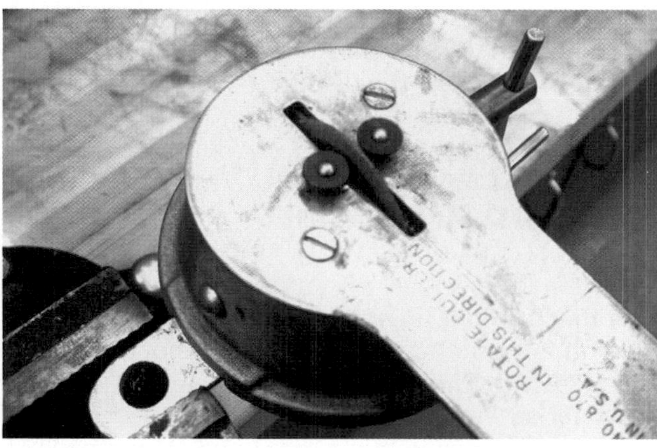

Figure 12–18 A hand-operated piston ring end gap grinder. The ring gap is placed over the cutter and pressed against the grinding stone while it is being rotated by hand. Stop and check your work often to avoid enlarging the piston ring end gap too much.

INSTALLING PISTON RINGS ONTO PISTONS

Piston rings must be installed in the specified groove (top or second) and with the correct side up. The ring installation instructions are found on, or in, the ring box or package. Never reuse old rings. Most piston rings are marked or stamped with "top," "T," a dot, a notch, or some other symbol. See Figure 12–19. If there are no installation instructions and the rings are not marked, follow this guideline:

- Install rings with a groove on the inside with the groove facing toward the piston top and install the rings with a groove on the outside with the groove facing down toward the piston skirt. See Figure 12–20.
- Install tapered face rings with the taper up and the widest side of the ring toward the skirt as shown in Figure 12–21.

Use a piston ring expander to install the rings into the correct piston ring groove as shown in Figure 12–22. The piston and rod assembly should be clamped in a vise (grip the I-beam of the rod, using "soft jaws") during ring installation. The extra stability helps to

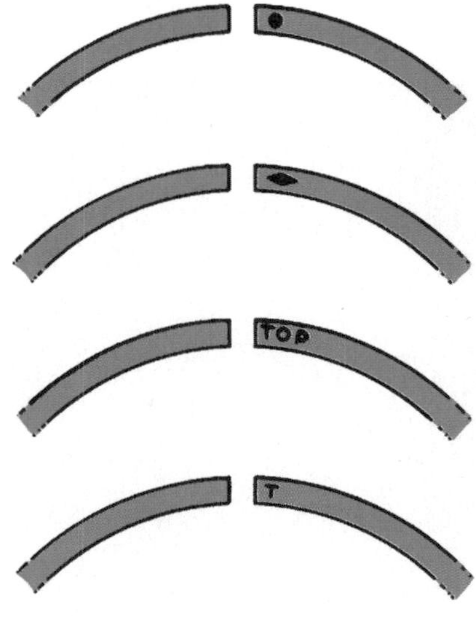

Figure 12–19 Piston ring manufacturers use a variety of different markings to show proper installation position.

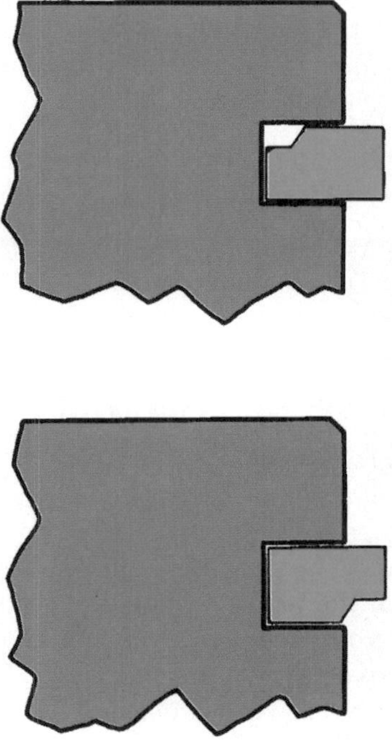

Figure 12–20 An undercut on the inside of the ring should face up and a groove on the outside faces down.

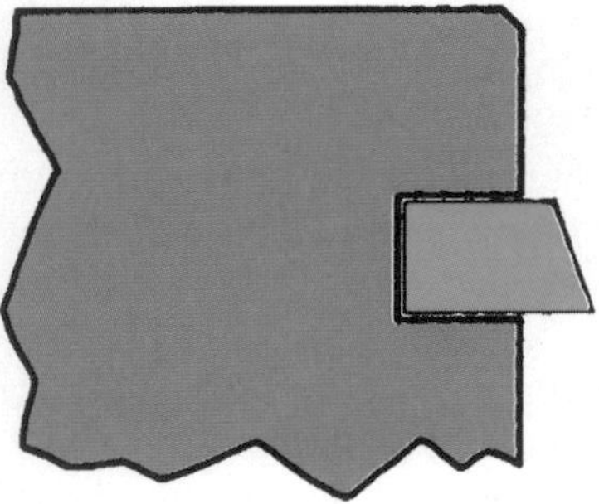

Figure 12–21 Piston rings with a tapered face are installed with the taper toward the top of the cylinder.

Figure 12–22 Using a piston ring expander to install a piston ring.

prevent ring breakage. This procedure should also be used when installing the ring compressor.

CAUTION: Do not overexpand the ring or it can break.

CHECKING PISTON RING SIDE CLEARANCE

After the rings have been installed in the grooves, check the side clearance. Side clearance is the difference between the width of ring and the width of the piston ring groove. Side clearance is measured with a feeler gauge as shown in Figure 12–23. Side clearance is usually between 0.04 and 0.15 mm (0.0015 and 0.006 in.). Too much side clearance can allow the ring to flutter or twist past its limit, causing compression leakage and possible piston ring breakage.

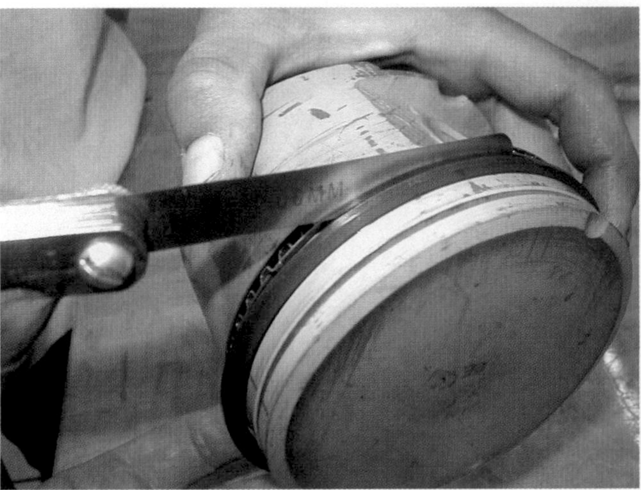

Figure 12–23 Side clearance is checked using a feeler gauge inserted between the piston ring and the piston ring groove.

Too little gap can cause the ring to expand in the groove, seizing it to the piston.

INSTALLING PISTON AND ROD ASSEMBLIES

The cylinder is wiped with a lintless cleaning cloth. It is then given a liberal coating of clean engine oil. This oil is spread over the entire cylinder wall surface by hand. The connecting rod bearings are prepared for assembly in the same way as are the main bearings. The piston is air dried and then dipped in a bath of clean engine oil.

NOTE: Some overlapping (gapless) piston rings are installed dry, without oil. Some manufacturers recommend oiling only the oil control ring. Always check the piston ring instruction sheet for the exact procedure.

When the piston is lifted from the oil, it is allowed to drip for a few seconds. This allows the largest part of the oil to run out of the piston and ring grooves. Double check that the piston ring gaps are arranged according to the factory specifications. See Figure 12–24 for one example of how the ring gaps should be installed. The **piston ring compressor** is then put on the piston to hold the rings in their grooves. See Figures 12–25 and 12–26.

The bearing cap is removed from the rod, and protectors are placed over the rod bolts. This prevents the rod bolts from nicking or scratching the crank journal. See Figures 12–27 and 12–28. The crankshaft is rotated so that the crankpin is at bottom dead

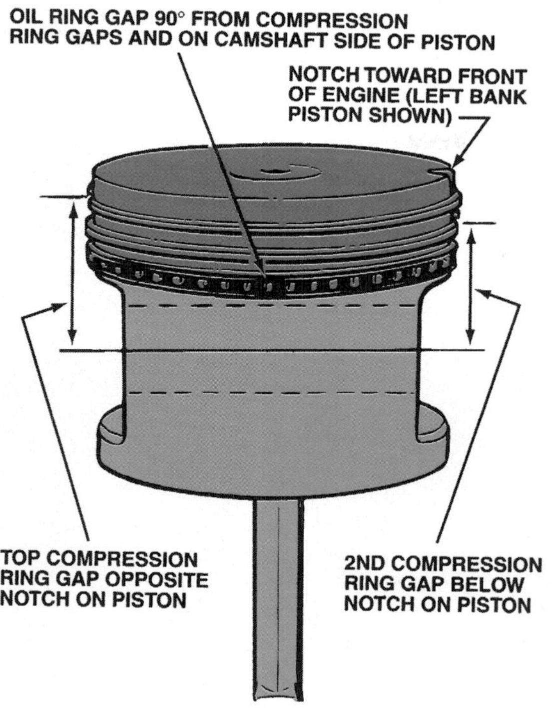

Figure 12–24 Be sure the piston ring end gaps are in the specified position before being installed in the engine.

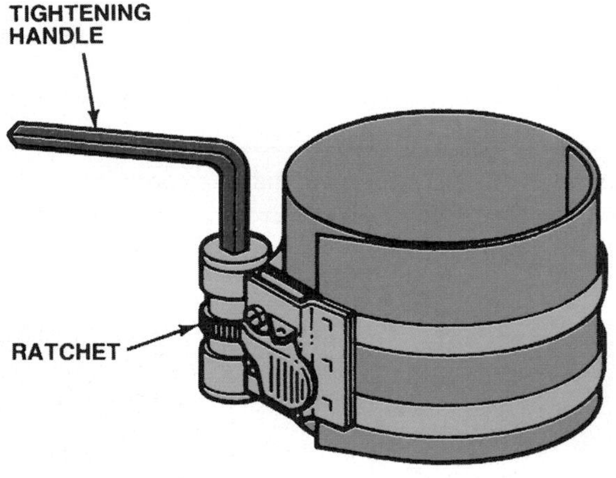

Figure 12–25 This style of ring compressor uses a ratchet to contract the spring band and compress the rings into their grooves.

centre. The upper rod bearing should be in the rod, and the piston should be turned so that the notch on the piston head is facing the front of the engine.

> **NOTE:** If the piston does not have a notch or a front stamp, install the piston so that the valve reliefs end up being closest to the lifter valley on a V-type OHV engine. Also, be sure to install the piston in the correct bore and check to make sure that the larger valve relief aligns with the intake valve location.

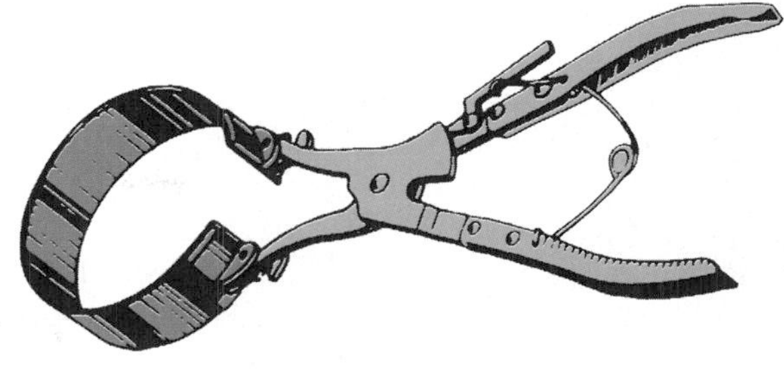

Figure 12–26 This pliers-like tool is used to close the metal band around the piston to compress the rings. An assortment of bands are available to service different size pistons.

Figure 12–27 When threaded onto the rod bolts, these guides not only help align the rod but they also protect the threads and hood the bearing shell in place. The soft ends also will not damage the crankshaft journals.

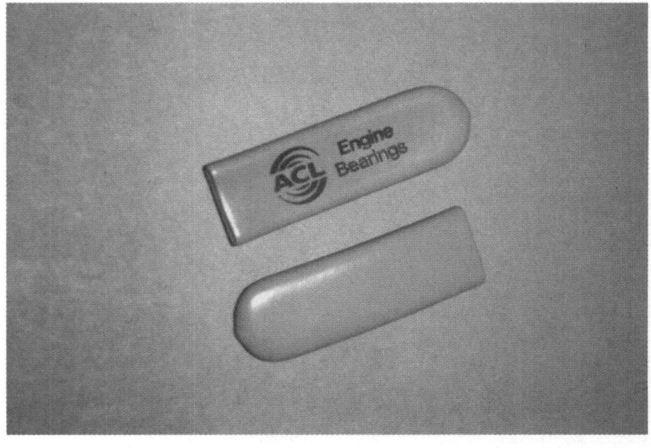

Figure 12–28 These rod bolt protective covers were given away free at a trade show for automotive engine rebuilders.

The piston and rod assembly is placed in the cylinder through the block deck. Tap the ring compressor lightly with a hammer to square it on the block. The ring compressor must be held tightly against the block deck as the piston is pushed into the cylinder. The piston is pushed into the cylinder until the rod bearing is fully seated on the journal. See Figure 12–29. The rod cap, with the bearing in place, is put on the rod. Check for proper connecting rod clearance using Plastigage. If the clearance is correct, lubricate the upper and lower bearings and torque the rod cap to factory specifications (see Figure 12–30). Rotate the crankshaft one full turn while feeling for any unusual drag or stiffness. Repeat for all other cylinders.

Measuring Connecting Rod Side Clearance

The connecting rods should be checked to make sure that they still have the correct side clearance. This is measured by fitting a feeler gauge of the correct thickness between the connecting rod and the crankshaft cheek of the bearing journal (Figure 12–31). A typical connecting rod side clearance is 0.10 to 0.35 mm (0.004 to 0.014 in.).

If the side clearance is too great, excessive amounts of oil may escape that can cause lower-than-normal oil pressure. To correct excessive clearance:

- Weld and regrind or replace the crankshaft
- Carefully measure all connecting rods and replace those that are too thin or mismatched.

If the side clearance is too small, there may not be enough room for heat expansion. To correct a side clearance that is too small:

- Regrind the crankshaft
- Replace the rods (see Hint on page 247).

Figure 12–30 After checking that the connecting rod bearing oil clearance is within factory specifications, the connecting rods are tightened using a torque wrench.

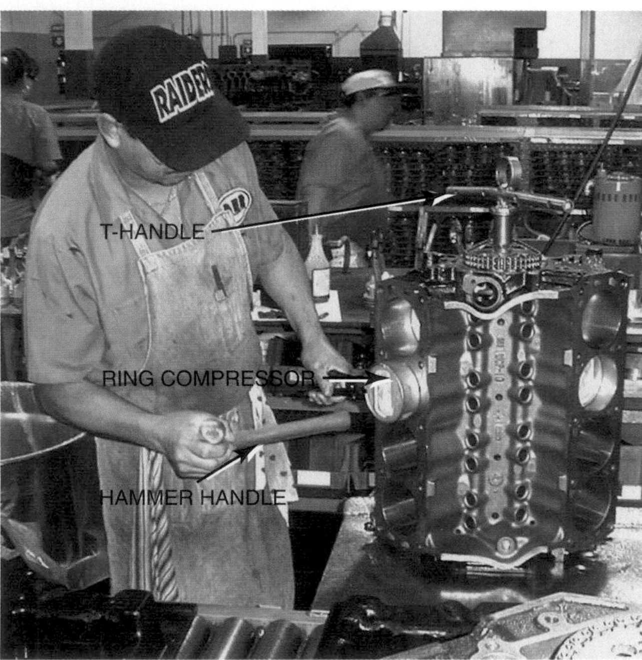

Figure 12–29 Piston being installed at an engine rebuilding company. Notice the T-handle used to rotate the engine. This technician is using the plastic handle of a hammer to drive the piston into the bore.

Figure 12–31 Check the connecting rod side clearance using a feeler gauge.

DIAGNOSTIC STORY

The New Oil Pump That Failed

A technician replaced the oil pump and screen on a V-8 with low oil pressure. After the repair, the oil pressure returned to normal for two weeks, but then the oil pressure light came on and the valve train started making noise. The vehicle owner returned to the service garage where the oil pump had been replaced. The technician removed the oil pan and pump. The screen was almost completely clogged with the RTV sealant that the technician had used to seal the oil pan gasket. The technician had failed to read the instructions that came with the oil pan gasket. Failure to follow directions and using too much of the wrong sealer cost the repair shop an expensive comeback repair.

HINT: Place a piece of medium grit abrasive paper on a flat surface i.e., a machined sanding block or a piece of heavy glass. Position the connecting rod, complete with tightened cap, on the paper; using a circular motion, remove material from both sides of the rod. Measure the rod width with a micrometer before and during the sanding process. After the desired clearance is achieved, the rod can be cleaned and reinstalled. If a large amount of material has to be removed, check the crankshaft; rods are usually very consistent with their width.

HEAD GASKETS

The head gasket is under the highest clamping loads. The most demanding job of the head gasket is to seal the combustion chamber. As a rule of thumb, about 75% of the head bolt clamping force is used to seal the combustion chamber. The remaining 25% seals the coolant and oil passages.

The first no-retorque gasket was the **embossed steel shim** gasket (see Figure 12–32), made from steel 0.038 to 0.53 mm (0.015 to 0.021 in.) thick.

NOTE: Older-style head gaskets required that the technician retorque the cylinder head bolts after the engine had been operated for a short time. Modern gaskets do not require this extra step and are often called *no-retorque gaskets.*

Shim gaskets require smooth sealing surfaces because they have no fibres to conform to sealing surface roughness. Shim gaskets also require a flat sealing surface because the steel cannot compensate for slight warpage of the head and block deck.

Perforated steel-core gaskets often use aramid fibres with clay and synthetic bonders or **expanded graphite.** See Figure 12–33. The fibre facing is protected around the combustion chamber with a metal **fire ring** or **armour.** See Figure 12–34.

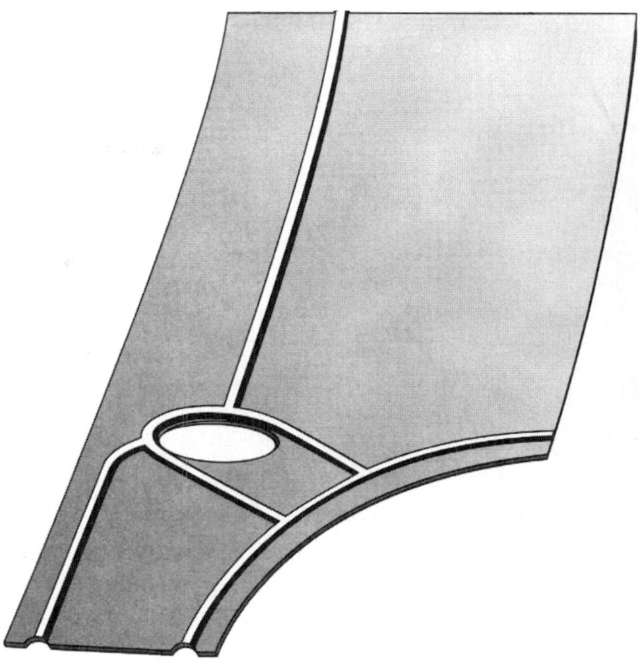

Figure 12–32 Embossed steel head gasket.

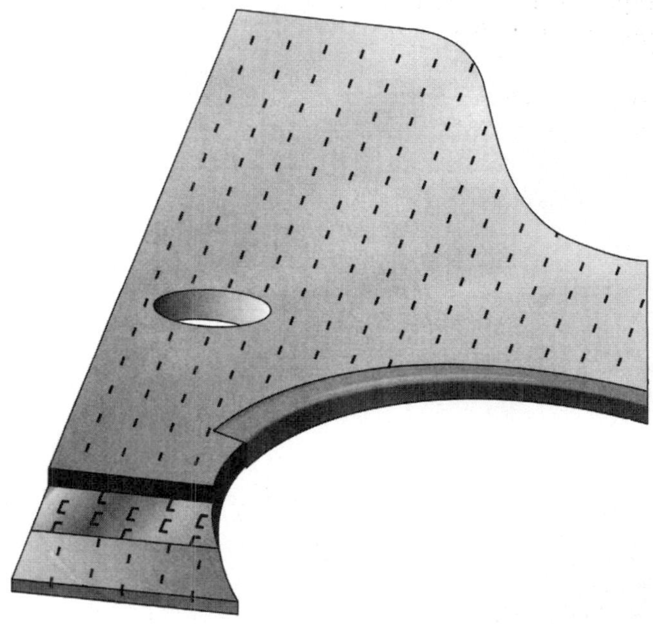

Figure 12–33 Perforated steel core head gasket.

Multilayered steel (MLS) gaskets are being installed in the factory on many newer engine designs, such as the overhead camshaft Ford V-8. The many layers of thin steel reduce bore and overhead camshaft distortion with less clamping force loss than previous designs. The use of multilayered steel gaskets also reduces the torque requirement and, therefore, reduces the stresses on the fastener and engine block. See Figure 12–35.

NOTE: Engines that use dissimilar metals for cylinder heads (aluminum) and cylinder blocks (cast iron) are the most difficult to seal because of differing expansion rates. The greater expansion of aluminum, compared to cast iron, creates a shearing effect on the head gasket; this can lead to early failure. The introduction of MLS gaskets has reduced the number of leaking gaskets on these models.

Installing the Head Gasket

First, the block deck and head surfaces should be rechecked for any handling nicks that could cause a gasket leak. All tapped holes should be cleaned with the correct-size bottoming tap to remove any dirt or burrs. There are usually alignment pins or dowels at the front and rear of the block deck to position the gasket and head. Care should be taken to properly align any head gasket with markings (up, top, front, and so forth). See Figure 12–36. Watch for the oil hole location in the head gasket; some gaskets are identical end to end, with the exception of the oil transfer hole which feeds lubricant to the overhead cam and valve train. The engine may run well with the gasket reversed, but not for long! The gasket and head are placed on the block deck and all the head bolts are loosely installed. Very often, the head bolts have different lengths, so make sure that a bolt of the correct length is put into each location.

Put sealer on the threads of the assembly bolts that go into the cooling system. Lightly oil the threads of bolts that go into blind holes. See the Tech Tip "Watch Out for Wet and Dry Holes!"

Figure 12–34 Head gasket with a fire ring.

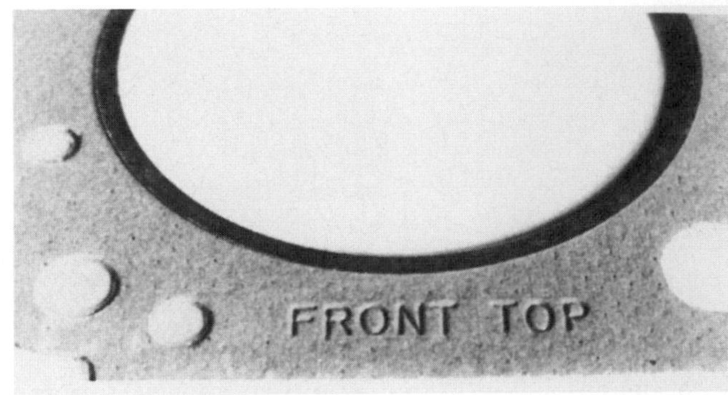

Figure 12–36 Typical head gasket markings.

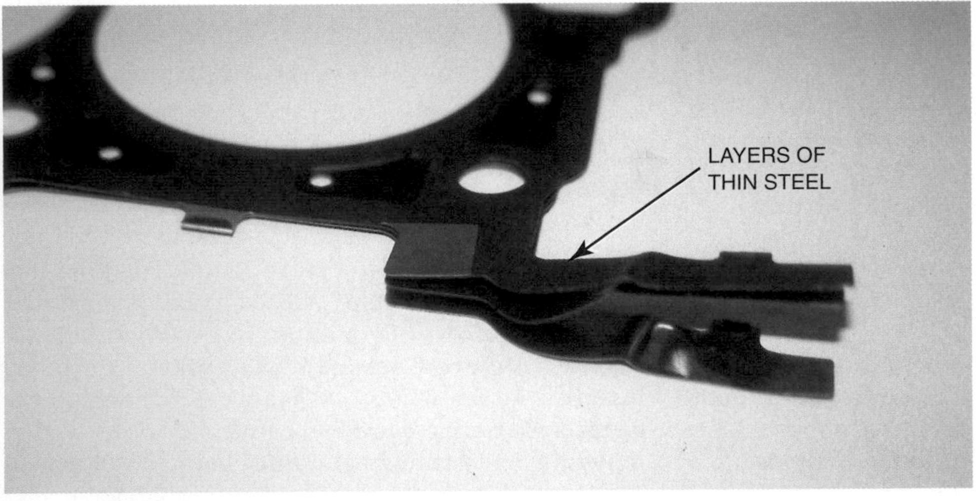

Figure 12–35 Multilayered steel (MLS) head gaskets are commonly used on engines with aluminum cylinder heads and cast iron blocks.

NOTE: Most manufacturers recommend putting engine oil on the threads of bolts during reassembly. Lubricated threads will give as much as 50% more clamping force at the same bolt torque than threads that are tightened dry.

A few drops of oil should also be applied to the underside of the bolt head.

TECH TIP 

Watch Out for Wet and Dry Holes!

Many engines, such as the small-block Chevrolet V-8, use head bolts that extend through the top deck of the block and end in a coolant passage. These bolt holes are called **wet holes.** Whenever head bolts that end up in the coolant passage are being installed, non-hardening sealer must be used on the threads of the head bolt. Some engines have head bolts that are "wet," whereas others are "dry" because they end in solid cast-iron material. Dry hole bolts do not require sealant, but they still require some oil on the threads of the bolts for lubrication. To lubricate the bolts going into a dry hole, simply place some oil on a shop cloth and rotate the threaded portion of the bolt on the oily cloth. Do not put oil into a dry hole because the bolt may bottom out in the oil. The liquid oil cannot compress, so the force of the bolt being tightened is transferred to the block by hydraulic force, which can crack the block.

Head Bolt Torque Sequence

The torque put on the head bolts is used to control the clamping force. The clamping force is correct only when the threads are clean and properly lubricated. In general, the head bolts are tightened in a specified torque sequence in three steps. By tightening the head bolts in three steps, the head gasket has time to compress and conform to the block deck and cylinder head gasket surfaces. Follow that sequence and tighten the bolts to *one-third* the specified torque. Tighten them a second time following the torque sequence to *two-thirds* the specified torque. Follow the sequence with a final tightening to the specified torque. See Figure 12–37.

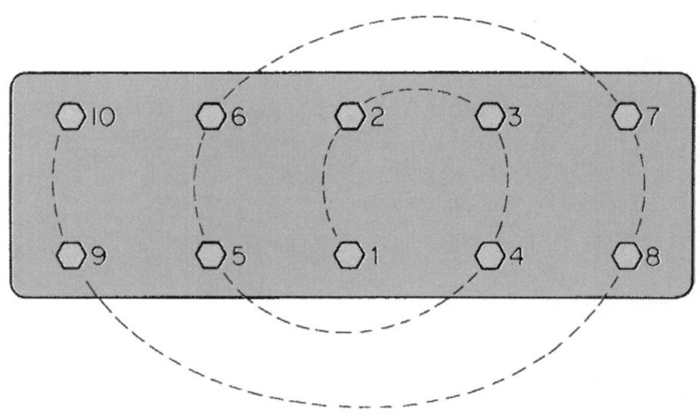

Figure 12–37 Typical cylinder head tightening sequence.

Torque-to-Yield Bolts

For years many diesel engines used a tightening procedure called the **torque-to-yield** or **torque-angle** method. The purpose of the torque-to-yield procedure is to have a more constant clamping load from bolt to bolt. Torque-to-yield head bolts will not become any tighter once they reach this elastic limit, as you can see from the graph in Figure 12–38.

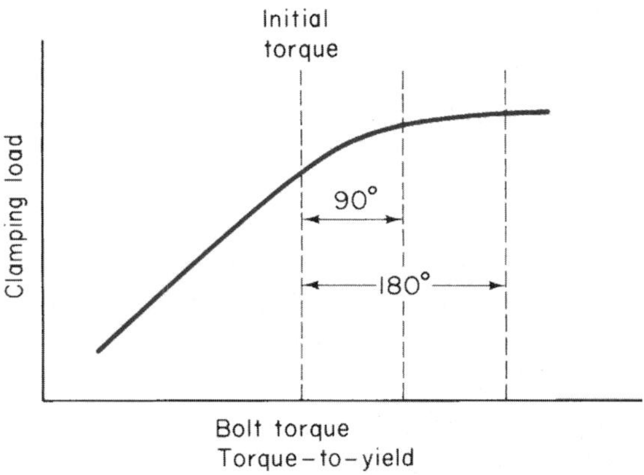

Figure 12–38 Due to variations in clamping force with turning force (torque) of head bolts, some engines are specifying the torque-to-yield procedure. The first step is to torque the bolts by an even amount called the initial torque. Final clamping load is achieved by turning the bolt a specified number of degrees. Bolt stretch provides the proper clamping force.

As a result, many gasoline engine manufacturers now specify *new* head bolts each time the head is installed. Used bolts that have been stretched to their elastic limit no longer have the elasticity to apply the clamping loads that are required when the head expands and contracts. If there are any doubts about the bolts, replace them. Many cylinder head gasket sets also include new bolts.

Torque-to-yield bolts are tightened to a specific initial torque, from 25 to 68 N·m (18 to 50 lb-ft). The bolts are then tightened a specified number of degrees, following the tightening sequence. The torque-to-yield method is also called the **torque-turn** method because it involves torquing the bolt and then turning it a specified number of degrees. Torque tables in a service manual will show how much initial torque should be applied to the bolt and how many degrees the bolt should be rotated after torquing. See Figures 12–39 and 12–40.

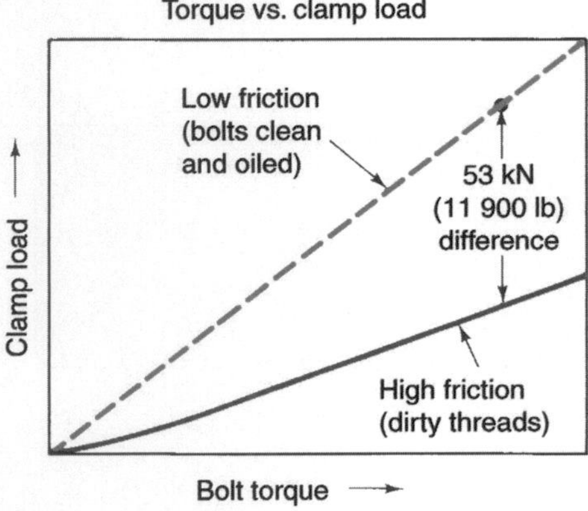

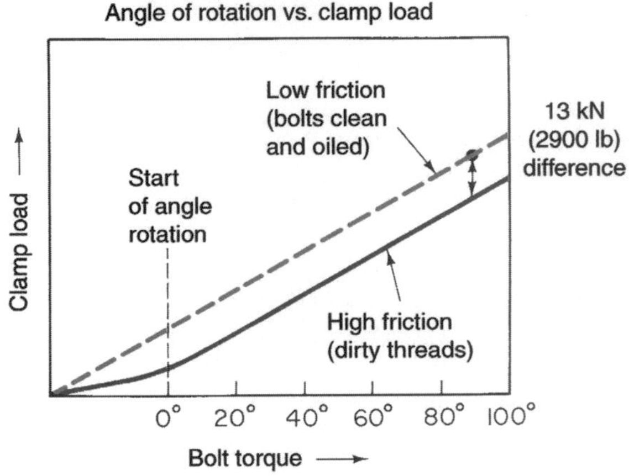

Figure 12–39 To ensure consistent clamp force (load), many manufacturers are recommending the torque-angle or torque-to-yield method of tightening head bolts. The torque-angle method specifies tightening fasteners to a low torque setting and then giving an additional angle of rotation. Notice that the difference in clamping force is much smaller than it would be if just a torque wrench with dirty threads were used.

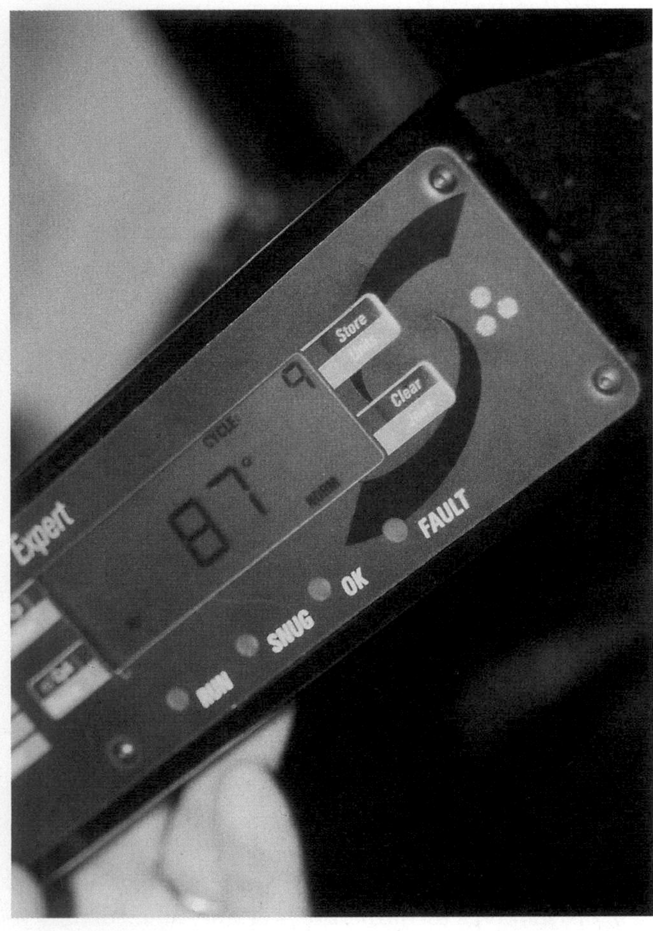

Figure 12–40 An expensive electronic torque wrench is the best tool to use whenever assembling an engine. This torque wrench can display angle (degrees) and total torque at the same time.

NOTE: As a bolt or stud is tightened, it stretches and becomes longer; the centre of the bolt (shank) now becomes thinner. Some automakers (e.g., Toyota) list both the original dimension and a minimum thickness. If the stud (main bearing, cylinder head) measures above the minimum thickness, it may be reused.

HINT: Head bolts are tightened following a sequence specified in the service manual or torque tables. In general, the tightening sequence starts at the centre of the head and moves outward, alternating front to rear and side to side.

Assembly Sealants

RTV silicone is used by most technicians to seal engines. RTV, or room-temperature vulcanization, means that the silicone rubber material in the sealant will cure at room temperature. It is not really the temperature that causes RTV silicone to cure, but the moisture in the air. RTV silicone cures to a tack-free state in about 45 minutes. It takes 24 hours to fully cure.

RTV silicone is available in a number of different colours. The colour identifies the special blend within a manufacturer's product line. Equal grades of silicone made by different manufacturers may have different colours. RTV silicone can be used in two ways in engine sealing:

1. It can be used as a gasket substitute between a stamped cover and a cast surface.
2. It is used to fill gaps or potential gaps. A joint between gaskets or between a gasket and a seal is a potential gap.

NOTE: RTV silicone should never be used around fuel because the fuel will cut right through it. Silicone should not be used as a sealer on gaskets. It will squeeze out to leave a bead inside and a bead outside the flange. The inside bead might fall into the engine, plugging passages and causing engine damage. The thin film still remaining on the gasket stays uncured, just as it would be in the original tube. The uncured silicone is likely to let the gasket or seal slip out of place.

Anaerobic sealers are sealers that cure in the absence of air. They are used as thread lockers (such as Loctite) and to seal rigid machined joints between cast parts. Anaerobic sealers lose their sealing ability at temperatures above 150°C (300°F). On production lines, the curing process is speeded up by using ultraviolet light.

When the anaerobic sealer is used on threads, air does not get to it so it hardens to form a seal to prevent the fastener from loosening. Teflon is added to some anaerobic sealers to seal fluids better. Anaerobic sealers can be used to seal machined surfaces without a gasket. The surfaces *must* be thoroughly clean to get a good seal. Special primers are recommended for use on the sealing surface to get a better bond with anaerobic sealers.

TECH TIP

Hints for Gasket Usage

- Never reuse an old gasket. A used gasket or seal has already been compressed, lost some of its resilience, and taken a set. If a used gasket does reseal, it will not seal as well as a new gasket or seal.
- A gasket should be checked to make sure it is the correct one. Check the list on the outside of the gasket set to make sure that the set has all of the gaskets that may be needed *before* the package is opened.
- Read the instruction sheet that is included with most gaskets. It includes a review of the things the technician should do to prepare and install the gaskets to give the best chance of a good seal. The instruction sheet also includes special tips on how to seal spots that are difficult to seal or that require special care to seal on a particular engine.
- Reusable "spaghetti seals" are common on many late engines. A bead of flexible silicone rubber is cured onto both sides of a metal gasket. They are often found on items (such as camshaft covers) that are removed for normal service.

INSTALLING MANIFOLDS

The intake manifold gasket for a V-type engine may be a one-piece gasket, or it may have several pieces. Use a contact adhesive to hold the gasket and end seal if there is a chance they might slip out of place. Just before the manifold is installed, put a spot of RTV silicone on each of the four joints between the intake manifold gasket and end seals. Then manifold bolts of the correct length are tightened to the specified torque following the tightening sequence given in the applicable service manual.

NOTE: When the exhaust manifold gasket has a facing on one side, put the facing toward the head and let the manifold rest against the metal side of the gasket.

INSTALLING THE VIBRATION DAMPER

Vibration dampers are seated in place by one of three methods. First, the damper hub of some engines is pulled into place using the hub attaching bolt. For other engines a special installing tool that screws into the attaching bolt hole may be used to pull the hub into place. The tool is then removed and the attaching bolt installed and torqued. The last method is used on engines that have no attaching bolt. These hubs depend on a press-fit to hold the hub on the crankshaft. The hub is seated using a hammer and a special tube-type driver. Some engine builders apply a very light coat of non-hardening sealer to the back of the damper hub. This prevents oil from leaking through the damper keyway.

INSTALLING THE OIL PUMP

When an engine is rebuilt, the oil pump is replaced with a new one, which ensures positive lubrication and long pump life. The space between the new oil pump gears is filled with assembly lubricant before the cover is put on the pump. This provides initial lubrication and primes the pump so that it will draw the oil from the pan when the lubrication system is first operated.

TECH TIP 

Oil Pump Precautions

The oil pump is the heart of any engine, and any failure of the oil circulation system often results in severe and major engine damage. To help prevent possible serious oil pump-related failures, many engine builders recommend the following precautions:

1. Always be sure that the oil pump pickup tube (screen) is securely attached to the oil pump to prevent the pickup tube from vibrating out of the pump.
2. Measure from the pan rail on the block to the bottom of the oil pump pickup. Note the reading. Measure from the pan flange to the bottom (floor) of the oil pan. The difference is the pickup to oil pan clearance, which should be about 6 to 10 mm (1/4 to 3/8 in.). Remember to add in the thickness of the oil pan gasket.

THE OIL PAN

The oil pan should be checked and straightened as necessary. See Figure 12–41. With the oil pump in place, the oil pan gaskets are properly positioned. A spot of RTV silicone is placed at each gasket joint just before the pan is installed. The oil pan is carefully placed over the gaskets. All of the oil pan bolts should be started into their holes before any are tightened. The bolts should be alternately snugged up, then they should be properly torqued.

HINT: Gasket manufacturers have developed one-piece oil pan gaskets not only for newer engines but also for older engines. These one-piece oil pan gaskets are easy to install and include spacers around the bolt holes to prevent overtightening. Check with your local parts supplier regarding new gasket designs.

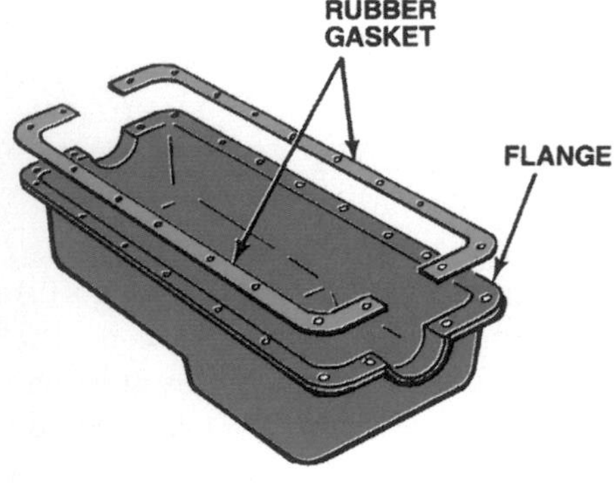

Figure 12–41 An oil pan gasket seals against fluid leaks. A flange on the pan positions the gasket.

Figure 12–42 An aerosol can with engine oil can be used to pre-oil an engine.

Checking for Proper Oil Pressure

With oil in the engine and the distributor out of the engine, oil pressure should be established before the newly assembled engine is started. This can be done on many engines by turning the oil pump with a speed handle or variable speed drill. This ensures that oil is delivered to all parts of the engine before the engine is started. See Figures 12–42 and 12–43. Also see the photo sequence at the end of this chapter that illustrates how to pre-oil an engine.

Aerosol pre-oilers or compressed air driven pressurizer tanks are also used to feed oil in through the oil pressure gauge opening in the block.

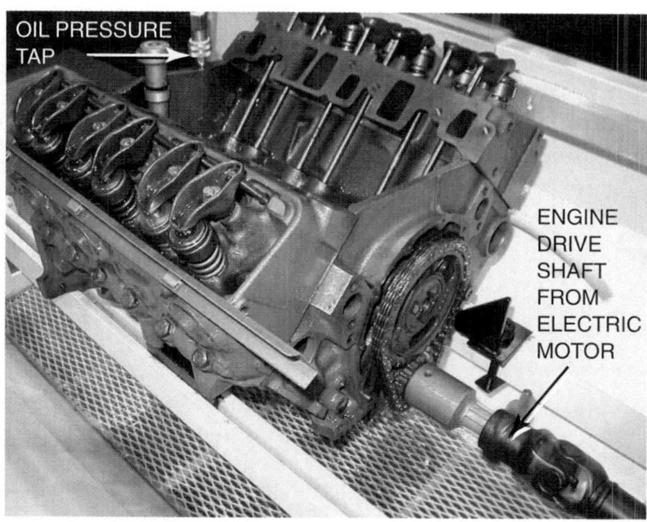

Figure 12–43 Most engine rebuilders spin test the engine to be sure that it has proper oil pressure and compression. As an electric motor spins the engine, a technician can observe the oil flowing to the rocker arms as well as past the main and rod bearings. Too much oil flowing from the bearing means too great a bearing clearance. Many engine builders that use this method also measure the electrical amperage needed to turn the engine. Any binding or excessive drag will increase the amperage required to rotate the engine.

If none of the above are applicable, remove the spark plugs and crank the engine for 30 seconds—do this again after letting the starter cool for one minute. Electronic fuel injection engines should have either the injection wiring harness or the fuel pump wire disconnected before cranking.

ENGINE INSTALLATION

When reinstalling the repaired engine in the chassis, a sling, either a chain or lift cable, is attached to the factory lifting hooks on the top of the engine. A hoist is attached to the sling and snugged up to take the weight and to make sure that the engine is supported and balanced properly.

NOTE: Many engines for front-wheel-drive vehicles are installed from underneath the vehicle. Often, the entire drivetrain package is placed back in the vehicle while it is attached to the cradle. Always check the recommended procedure for the vehicle being serviced.

The engine must be tipped as it was during removal to let the transmission go into the engine compartment first. The transmission is worked under the floor pan on rear-wheel-drive vehicles as the engine is lowered into the engine compartment. The front engine mounts are aligned; then the rear cross-member and rear engine mount are installed. The engine mount bolts are installed, and the nuts are torqued. Then the hoist is removed. After the engine is in place, the front engine accessories can all be installed if they were not installed before the engine was put in the chassis.

NOTE: Many experts recommend that the oxygen sensor(s) (O2S) be replaced to ensure that the engine operation will be within acceptable limits. Be aware that any RTV silicone sealant used during assembly must be oxygen-sensor compatible. The solvents used in some sealants will damage the sensor.

Break-in Engine Oil

Many years ago vehicle manufacturers used straight-weight nondetergent engine oil as break-in oil. Today the engine oil recommended for break-in (running in) is the same type of oil recommended for use in the engine. No special break-in oil is recommended or used by the factory in new vehicles. Good quality SAE 5W-30 or

DIAGNOSTIC STORY 

"Oops"

After overhauling a big-block Ford V-8 engine, a technician used an electric drill to rotate the oil pump with a pressure gauge connected to the oil pressure sending unit hole. When the electric drill was turned on, oil pressure would start to increase to about 70 kPa (10 psi) then drop to zero. Also the oil was very aerated (full of air). Replacing the oil pump did not solve the problem. After hours of troubleshooting and disassembly, it was discovered that an oil gallery plug had been left out underneath the intake manifold. The oil pump was working correctly and pumped oil throughout the engine and out through the end of the unplugged oil gallery. It did not take long for the oil pan to empty; therefore, the oil pump began drawing in air that aerated the oil and the oil pressure dropped. Installing the gallery plug solved the problem. It was smart of the technician to check the oil pressure before starting the engine. The oversight of leaving out one gallery plug could have resulted in a ruined engine shortly after the engine was started.

NOTE: Many overhead camshaft engines have an oil passage check valve in the block near the deck. The purpose of this valve is to hold oil in the cylinder head around the camshaft and lifters when the engine is stopped. Failure to reinstall this check valve can cause the valve train to be noisy after engine start-up.

DIAGNOSTIC STORY 

Check for Oil Leaks with the Engine Off

The owner of an older vehicle equipped with a V-6 engine complained to his technician that he smelled burning oil, but only *after* shutting off the engine. The technician found that the rocker cover gaskets were leaking. But why did the owner only notice the smell of hot oil when the engine was shut off? Because of the positive crankcase ventilation (PCV) system, engine vacuum tends to draw oil away from gasket surfaces. But when the engine stops, engine vacuum disappears and the oil remaining in the upper regions of the engine will tend to flow down and out through any opening. Therefore, a good technician should check an engine for oil leaks not only with the engine running but also shortly after shut-down.

SAE 10W-30 engine oil is usually the viscosity recommended by most vehicle manufacturers.

Engine Break-in

Before starting the engine, the oil and coolant levels should be checked. Both oil and coolant should be brought up to the normal full level. The level of the oil in the manual transmission should also be checked.

The engine installation should be given one last inspection to make sure that everything has been put together correctly before the engine is started. Fuel-injected engines should have the electric fuel pump activated to prime the system; carbureted engines should have the float bowl filled. If the engine overhaul and installation have been done properly, the engine should crank and start on its own fully charged battery without the use of a fast charger or jumper battery. As soon as the engine starts and shows oil pressure, it should be brought up to a fast idle speed and *kept there* for 15 minutes. This is necessary to make sure that the engine gets proper lubrication. The fast-running oil pump develops full pressure, and the fast-turning crankshaft throws plenty of oil on the cam and cylinder walls. Automatic transmission oil levels are checked at this time.

NOTE: In camshaft-in-block engines, the only lubrication sent to the contact point between the camshaft lobes and the lifters (tappets) is from the splash off the crankshaft and connecting rods. At idle, engine oil does not splash enough for proper break-in lubrication of the camshaft. This is especially necessary if the engine is equipped with flat-bottom lifters.

Just as soon as you can tell that there are no serious leaks and the engine is running reasonably well, the vehicle should be driven to a road having minimum traffic. Here, the vehicle should be accelerated, full throttle, from 50 to 80 km/h (30 to 50 mph). Then the throttle is fully closed while the vehicle is allowed to return to 50 km/h (30 mph). This procedure is repeated ten to twelve times. The acceleration sequence puts a high load on the piston rings in order to properly seat them against the cylinder walls. The piston rings are the only part of the modern engine that needs to be broken in.

The customer should be instructed to drive the vehicle in a normal fashion, neither babying it at slow speeds nor beating it at high speeds, for the first 160 km (100 mi). The oil and filter should be changed at 800 km (500 mi) to remove any dirt that may have been trapped in the engine during assembly and to remove the material that has worn from the surfaces during the break-in period.

PHOTO SEQUENCE 8 Preoiling an Engine

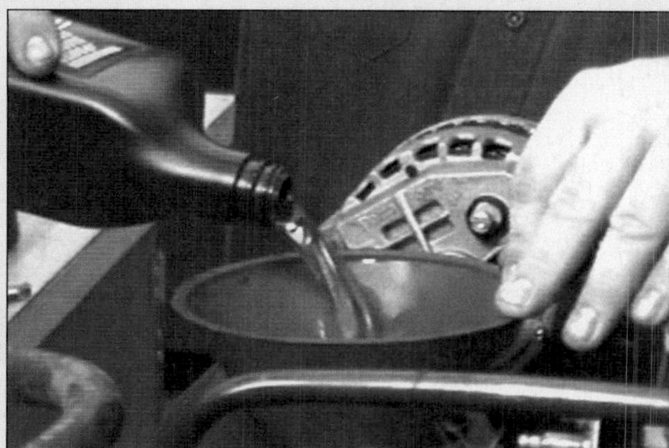

P8–1 Whenever an engine has been disassembled and then reassembled, it is important to make sure that all internal parts are preoiled before starting the engine. Start by filling the crankcase with the specified amount of oil.

P8–2 Attach an oil pressure gauge to the engine. On this small-block Chevrolet V-8, the oil pressure tap is located near the distributor at the top of the block.

P8–3 To rotate the oil pump, an old distributor was cut down and the shaft installed in the chuck of an electric drill.

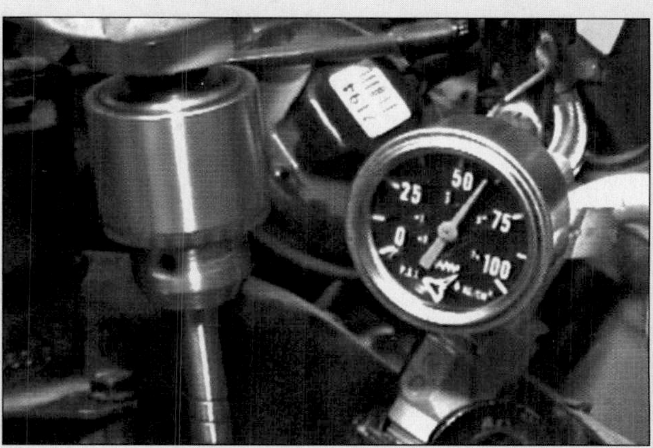

P8–4 Rotating the oil pump using an electric drill results in the oil pressure increasing to over 350 kPa (50 psi).

P8–5 The drill should continue being used to prime the engine until oil is observed coming from the rocker arms, indicating that oil has reached the highest part of the engine.

P8–6 An overall view of the oil pump drive adapter made from an old distributor and the oil pressure gauge. After the engine has been primed, the distributor can be installed and the engine can be installed in the vehicle.

PHOTO SEQUENCE 9 Valve Adjustment

P9–1 Before starting the process of adjusting the valves, look up the specifications and exact procedures. The technician is checking this information from a computer CD-ROM-based information system.

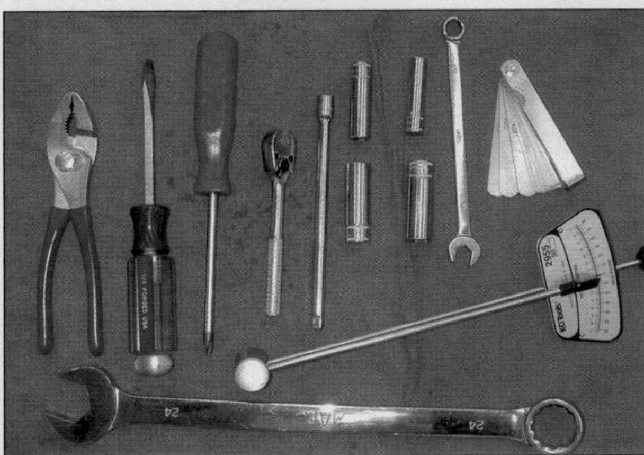

P9–2 The tools necessary to adjust the valves on an engine with adjustable rocker arms include basic hand tools, feeler gauge, and a torque wrench.

P9–3 With all vacuum lines and the intake tube removed, the valve cover can be removed after removing all retaining bolts.

P9–4 To help locate how far the engine is being rotated, the technician is removing the distributor cap to be able to observe the position of the rotor.

P9–5 The engine is rotated until the timing marks on the front of the crankshaft line up with zero degrees—top dead centre (TDC)—with both valves closed on #1 cylinder.

P9–6 With the rocker arms contacting the base circle of the cam, insert a feeler gauge of the specified thickness between the camshaft and the rocker arm. There should be a slight drag on the feeler gauge if the clearance is the same as the thickness of the feeler gauge.

Valve Adjustment—continued

P9–7 If the valve clearance (lash) is not correct, loosen the retaining nut and turn the valve adjusting screw with a screwdriver to achieve the proper clearance.

P9–8 On some engines, it is necessary to watch the direction the rotor is pointing to help determine how far to rotate the engine. Always follow the vehicle manufacturer's recommended procedure.

P9–9 The exhaust valves often have a greater clearance (lash) than the intake valves. Here the service technician is using a feeler gauge that is 0.025 mm (0.001 in.) thinner and another 0.025 mm thicker than the specified clearance as a double-check that the clearance is correct. Stepped feeler gauges (go-no-go) are also used for this purpose.

P9–10 Adjusting a valve takes both hands—one to hold the wrench to loosen and tighten the lock nut and one to turn the adjusting screw. Always double-check the clearance after an adjustment is made.

P9–11 After all valves have been properly measured and adjusted as necessary, start the reassembly process by replacing all gaskets and seals as specified by the vehicle manufacturer.

P9–12 Reinstall the valve cover being careful to not pinch a wire or vacuum hose between the cover and the cylinder head.

SUMMARY

1. All oil galleries must be thoroughly cleaned before engine assembly can begin.
2. All expansion cups and plugs should be installed with a sealer to prevent leaks. Avoid the use of Teflon tape on threaded plugs.
3. The cam bearings should be installed using a cam bearing installation tool.
4. Main bearings and rod bearings should be checked for proper oil clearance by precision measuring the crankshaft journals and inside diameter of bearings or by using plastic gauging material.
5. The piston and rod assembly should be installed in the cylinder after being carefully fitted for each bore.
6. Connecting rod side clearance should be checked with a feeler (thickness) gauge.
7. Double-check the flatness of the block deck and cylinder head before installing the cylinder head.
8. Torque the cylinder head bolts according to the proper sequence and procedures.
9. Many cylinder heads use the torque-to-yield method, wherein the head bolts are tightened to a specified torque and then rotated a specified number of degrees.
10. The oil pressure should be tested before installation of the engine in the vehicle.
11. When installing the transmission and other components on the engine block, be sure to use a torque wrench and tighten all fasteners to factory specifications.
12. Change the engine oil after 800 km (500 mi.) or sooner, and use SAE 5W-30 or SAE 10W-30 engine oil.

REVIEW QUESTIONS

1. Describe the procedure for fitting pistons to a cylinder.
2. Explain how main bearings should be checked and fitted to the crankshaft.
3. How is plastic gauging material used to determine oil clearance?
4. What is the procedure for checking thrust bearing clearance?
5. How should the connecting rod side clearance be measured and corrected?
6. How is the piston and connecting rod assembly installed in the engine?
7. What procedures should be followed for installing and torquing the cylinder head?
8. Describe the torque-to-yield head bolt tightening procedure.
9. What should be done to help prevent rear cylinder distortion when the bell housing is being installed on the engine?
10. Describe the engine break-in procedure.

RED SEAL CERTIFICATION-TYPE QUESTIONS

1. Typical piston-to-cylinder clearance is _________.
   - **a.** 0.025 to 0.075 mm (0.001 to 0.003 in.)
   - **b.** 0.250 to 0.584 mm (0.010 to 0.023 in.)
   - **c.** 2.540 to 3.810 mm (0.100 to 0.230 in.)
   - **d.** 4.572 to 5.842 mm (0.180 to 0.230 in.)
2. If the gauging plastic strip is wide after the bearings are tightened, this indicates _____.
   - **a.** A large oil clearance
   - **b.** An old, dried strip of plastic gauging material
   - **c.** A small oil clearance
   - **d.** A small side (thrust) clearance
3. Typical thrust bearing clearance is:
   - **a.** 0.025 to 0.075 mm (0.001 to 0.0003 in.)
   - **b.** 0.050 to 0.305 mm (0.002 to 0.012 in.)
   - **c.** 0.633 to 0.889 mm (0.025 to 0.035 in.)
   - **d.** 1.270 to 2.540 mm (0.050 to 0.100 in.)
4. The cylinder head should be tightened (torqued) in what general sequence?
   - **a.** The four outside bolts first, then from the centre out
   - **b.** From the outside bolts to the inside bolts
   - **c.** From the inside bolts to the outside bolts
   - **d.** From the front of the engine and torquing bolts from front to rear
5. The torque-angle method involves _____.
   - **a.** Turning all bolts the same number of turns
   - **b.** Torquing to specifications and loosening by a specified number of degrees
   - **c.** Torquing to one-half specifications, then to three-quarter torque, then to full torque
   - **d.** Turning bolts a specified number of degrees after initial torque
6. Turning the oil pump before starting the engine should be done _____.
   - **a.** To test for leaks
   - **b.** For at least 10 seconds
   - **c.** To fill the oil filter
   - **d.** To lubricate the bearings and valve train
7. Most bolt torque specifications are for _____.
   - **a.** Clean threads only
   - **b.** Clean and lubricated threads
   - **c.** Dirty threads
   - **d.** Dirty threads, but 50% can be added for clean threads
8. Engines with cast iron blocks and aluminum cylinder heads (dissimilar metals) should use a _____________ head gasket.
   - **a.** embossed steel shim
   - **b.** expanded graphite
   - **c.** multilayered steel
   - **d.** perforated steel
9. Break-in engine oil is _____.
   - **a.** Of the same viscosity and grade as that specified for normal engine operation
   - **b.** SAE 40
   - **c.** SAE 30
   - **d.** SAE 20W-50
10. As soon as a rebuilt engine is started, it should be operated at what speed for 15 minutes?
    - **a.** Idle speed
    - **b.** Fast idle (1500 to 1500 rpm)
    - **c.** Varying speeds
    - **d.** 3000 to 5000 rpm

SECTION III

Electrical/Electronic Systems

Electrical and electronic systems represent one of the most serviced areas of any vehicle. Chapter 13 introduces the terms and principles involved including how basic circuits work. Chapter 14 includes how to read wiring schematics and interpret meter readings. Chapter 15 covers battery construction, testing, and servicing procedures. Chapter 16 includes how to diagnose starting (engine cranking) problems and includes information on the entire cranking circuit including the operation and servicing of starters. Generators (alternators) and the charging circuit are thoroughly covered in Chapter 17, and Chapter 18 includes necessary information on the operation, diagnosis, and service of lighting and signalling circuits. Chapter 19 covers dash instruments, and Chapter 20 covers electrical accessories such as cruise control, power door locks, power windows, and electric rear window defoggers. Chapter 21 discusses operation and diagnosis of the audio system.

13

Electrical and Electronic Principles and Circuits

OBJECTIVES: After studying Chapter 13, you should be able to:

1. Prepare for the interprovincial Red Seal certification examination in Appendix III (Electrical/Electronic Systems) on the topics covered in this chapter.
2. Define electricity.
3. Explain the units of electrical measurement.
4. Discuss the relationship among volts, amperes, and ohms.
5. Explain how magnetism is used in automotive applications.
6. State Ohm's law.
7. Identify a series and a parallel circuit.
8. Explain voltage drops.
9. Discuss electrical power measured in watts.
10. Identify semiconductor components.
11. Explain the precautions necessary when working around semiconductor circuits.
12. Discuss where various electronic and semiconductor devices are used in vehicles.

The electrical system is one of the most important systems in a vehicle today. Every year more and more components and systems use electricity. Technicians who know and understand automotive electrical and electronic systems will be in great demand.

ELECTRICITY

Electricity is the movement of electrons from one atom to another. An atom is the smallest unit of all matter in the universe. Our universe is composed of matter, which is *anything* that has mass and occupies space, and all matter is made from slightly over 100 individual components called *elements.*

If an element is cut down or reduced in size, the smallest remaining part that can still be identified as that particular element is called an *atom.* See Figure 13–1. The dense centre of each atom is called the *nucleus.* The nucleus contains *protons,* which have a positive charge, and *neutrons,* which are electrically neutral (have no charge). In orbits surrounding the nucleus are the *electrons* which have a negative charge. Each atom contains an equal number of electrons and protons. Because the number of negative-charged electrons is balanced with the same number of positive-charged protons, an atom has a **neutral charge** (no charge).

NOTE: As an example of the relative sizes of the parts of an atom, consider that if an atom were magnified so that the nucleus were the size of the period at the end of this sentence, the whole atom would be bigger than a house.

Positive and Negative Charges

The parts of the atom have different charges. The orbiting electrons are negatively charged, while the protons are positively charged. Positive charges are indicated by the plus sign (+), negative charges by the minus sign (−) as shown in Figure 13–2. These same + and − signs are used to identify parts of an electrical circuit. Neutrons have no charge at all. They are neutral. In a normal, or balanced, atom, the

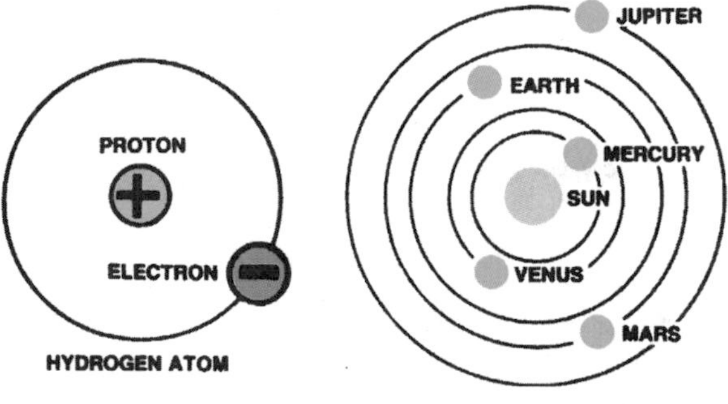

Figure 13–1 In an atom (left), electrons orbit protons in the nucleus just as planets orbit the sun in our solar system (right).

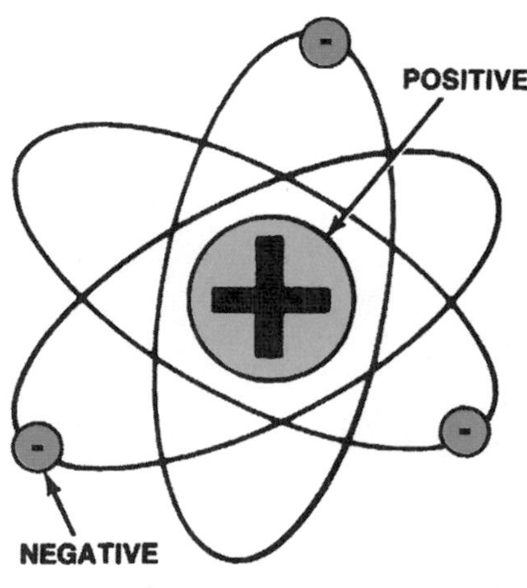

Figure 13–2 The nucleus of an atom has a positive (+) charge and the surrounding electrons have a negative (−) charge.

number of negative particles equals the number of positive particles. That is, there are as many electrons as there are protons. See Figure 13–3. The number of neutrons varies according to the type of atom.

The charges within an atom behave like the poles of a magnet. An ordinary magnet has two ends, or poles. One end is called the south pole, and the other is called the north pole. If two magnets are brought close to each other with like poles together (south to south or north to north), the magnets will push each other apart. This is because like poles repel each other. If the opposite poles of the magnets are brought close to each other, south to north, the magnets will snap together. This is because unlike poles attract each other.

The positive and negative charges within an atom are like the north and south poles of a magnet. Charges that are alike will repel each other, similar to the poles of a magnet. See Figure 13–4. That is why the negative electrons continue to orbit around the positive protons. They are attracted and held by the opposite charge of the protons. The electrons keep moving in orbit because they repel each other.

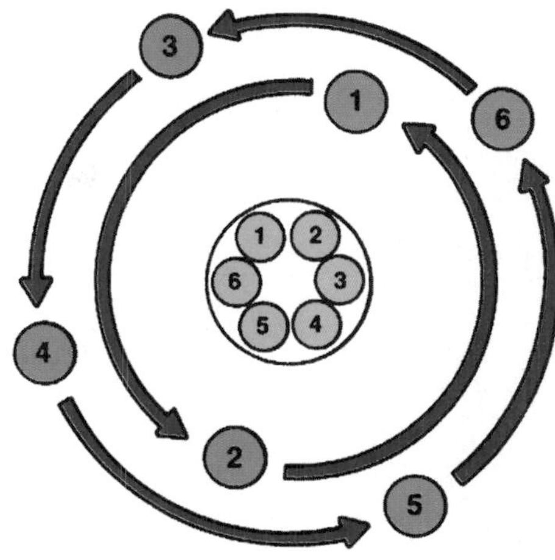

Figure 13–3 A balanced atom.

Figure 13–4 Unlike charges attract and like charges repel.

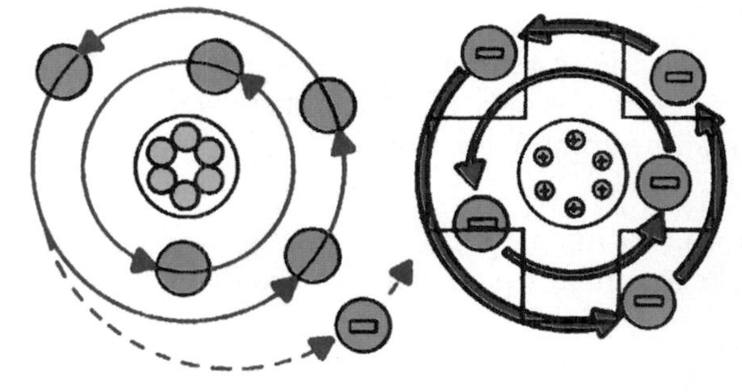

Figure 13–5 An unbalanced, positively charged atom (ion) will attract electrons from neighboring atoms.

When an atom loses any electrons, it becomes unbalanced. It will have more protons than electrons, and therefore, will have a positive charge. If it gains more electrons than protons, the atom will be negatively charged. When an atom is not balanced, it becomes a charged particle called an **ion.** Ions try to regain their balance of equal protons and electrons. They do this by exchanging electrons with neighbouring atoms. See Figure 13–5. This is the flow of electric current or electricity.

Electron Shells

Electrons orbit around the nucleus in definite paths. These paths form **shells,** like concentric rings, around the nucleus. Only a specific number of electrons can orbit within each shell. If there are too many electrons for the first and closest shell to the nucleus, the others will orbit in additional shells until all electrons have

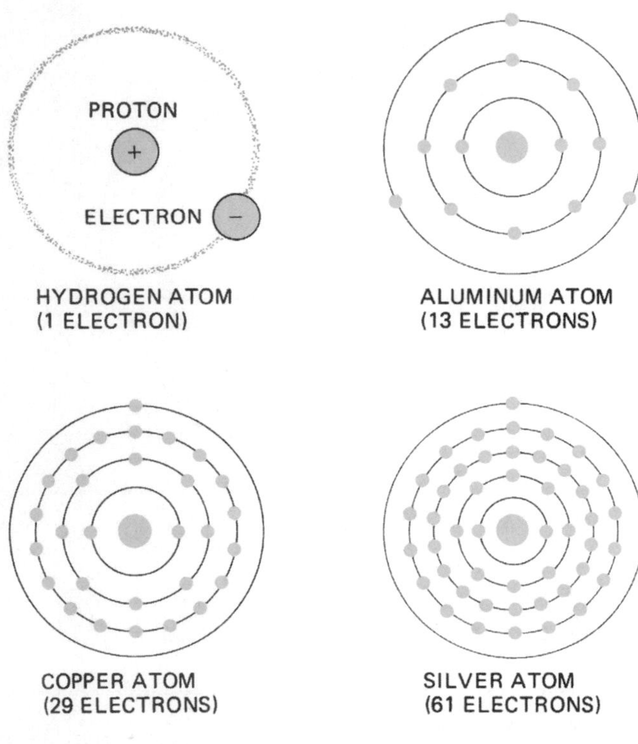

Figure 13–6 The hydrogen atom is the simplest atom, with only one proton, one neutron, and one electron. More complex elements contain higher numbers of protons, neutrons, and electrons.

an orbit within a shell. There can be as many as seven shells around a single nucleus. See Figure 13–6.

Free and Bound Electrons

The outermost electron shell, or ring, is the most important to our study of electricity. It is called the **valence ring.** The number of electrons in this ring determines the valence of the atom, and indicates its capacity to combine with other atoms.

If the valence ring of an atom has three or fewer electrons in it, the ring has room for more. The electrons there are held very loosely, and it is easy for a drifting electron to join the valence ring and push another electron away. These loosely held electrons are called **free electrons.** When the valence ring has five or more electrons in it, it is fairly full. The electrons are held tightly, and it is hard for a drifting electron to push its way into the valence ring. These tightly held electrons are called **bound electrons.** See Figures 13–7 and 13–8.

The movement of these drifting electrons is called current. Current can be small, with only a few electrons moving, or it can be large, with a tremendous number of electrons moving. However, current only flows in a conductor. Electric current is the controlled, directed movement of electrons from atom to atom within a conductor.

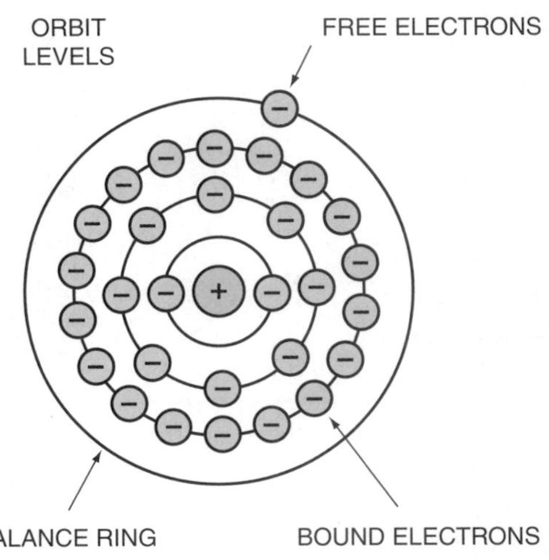

Figure 13–7 As the number of electrons increases, they occupy increasing energy levels that are further from the centre of the atom.

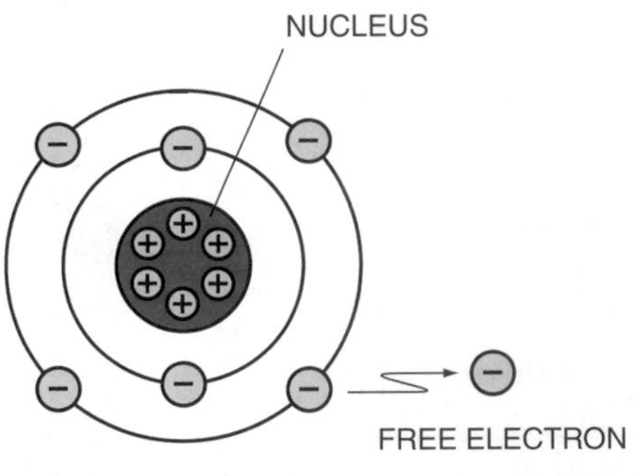

Figure 13–8 Electrons in the outer orbit, or shell, can often be drawn away from the atom and become free electrons.

Conductors

Conductors are materials with fewer than four electrons in their atom's outer orbit. See Figure 13–9. Copper is an excellent conductor because it has only one electron in its outer orbit. This orbit is far enough away from the nucleus of the copper atom that the pull or force holding the outermost electron in orbit is relatively weak. See Figure 13–10. Copper is the conductor most used in vehicles because the price of copper is reasonable compared to the relative cost of other conductors with similar properties.

Insulators

Insulators are materials with more than four electrons in their atom's outer orbit. Because they have more than four electrons in their outer orbit, it becomes easier for these materials to acquire (gain) electrons than to release electrons. See Figure 13–11. Examples of insulators include plastics, wood, glass, rubber, ceramics (spark plugs), and var-

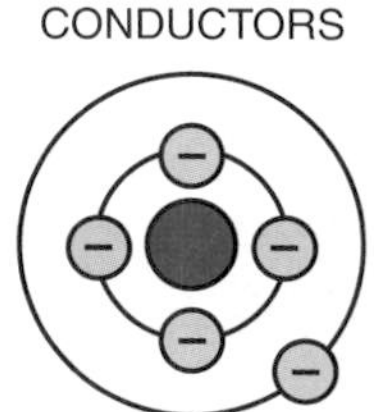

Figure 13–9 A conductor is any element that has one to three electrons in its outer orbit.

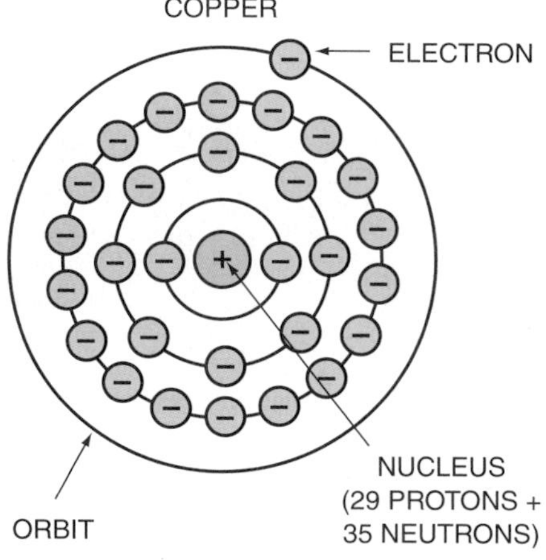

Figure 13–10 Copper is an excellent conductor of electricity because it has just one electron in its outer orbit, making it easy to be knocked out of its orbit and flow to other nearby atoms causing electron flow, which is the definition of electricity.

nish for covering (insulating) copper wires in alternators and starters.

Semiconductors

Materials with exactly four electrons in their outer orbit are neither conductors nor insulators and are called *semiconductor* materials. See Figure 13–12.

How Electrons Move Through a Conductor

If an outside source of power, such as a battery, is connected to the ends of a conductor, a positive charge (lack of electrons) is placed on one end of the conductor and a negative charge is placed on the opposite end of the conductor. The negative charge will repel the free electrons from the atoms of the conductor, whereas the positive charge on the opposite end of the conductor will attract electrons. As a result of this attraction of opposite charges and repulsion of like charges, electrons will flow through the conductor. See Figure 13–13.

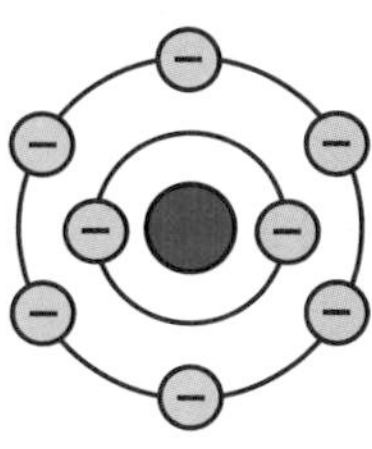

Figure 13–11 Insulators are elements with five to eight electrons in the outer orbit.

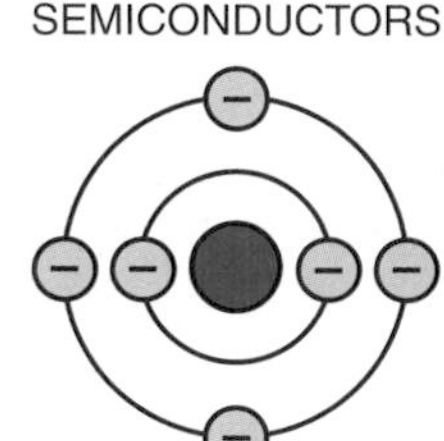

Figure 13–12 Semiconductor elements contain exactly four electrons in the outer orbit.

Figure 13–13 Current electricity is the movement of electrons through a conductor.

Conventional Theory versus Electron Theory

It was once thought that electricity had only one charge and moved from positive to negative. This theory of the flow of electricity through a conductor is called the **conventional theory** of current flow. See Figure 13–14. After the discovery of the electron and its negative charge came the **electron theory,** which states that there is electron flow from negative to positive. Most automotive applications use the conventional theory. This book will use the conventional theory unless stated otherwise.

Amperes

The **ampere** is the unit used throughout the world as a measure of the amount of current flow. When 6.28 billion billion electrons (the name for this large number of electrons is a **coulomb**) move past a certain point in 1 second, this represents 1 ampere of current. See Figure 13–15. The ampere is the electrical unit for

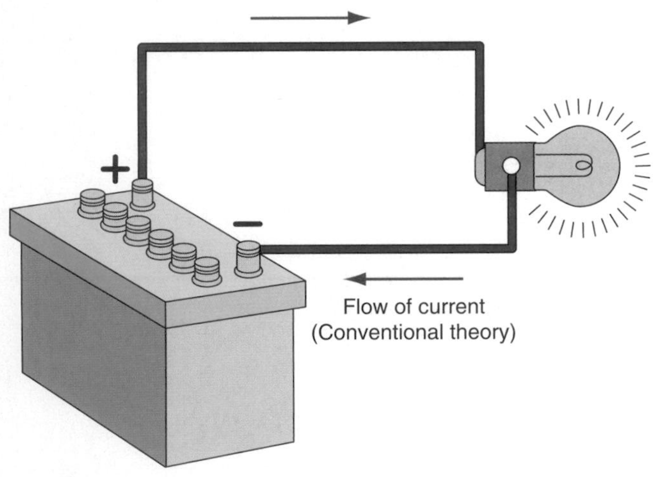

Figure 13–14 Conventional theory states that current flows through a circuit from positive (+) to negative (−). Automotive electricity uses the conventional theory in all electrical diagrams and schematics.

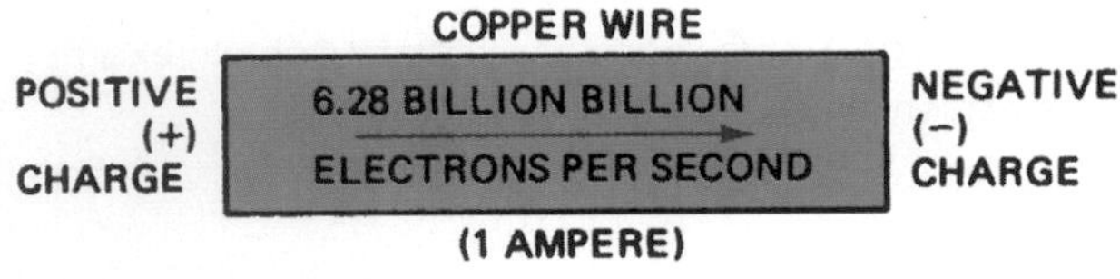

Figure 13–15 One ampere is the movement of 1 coulomb (6.28 billion billion electrons) past a point in 1 second.

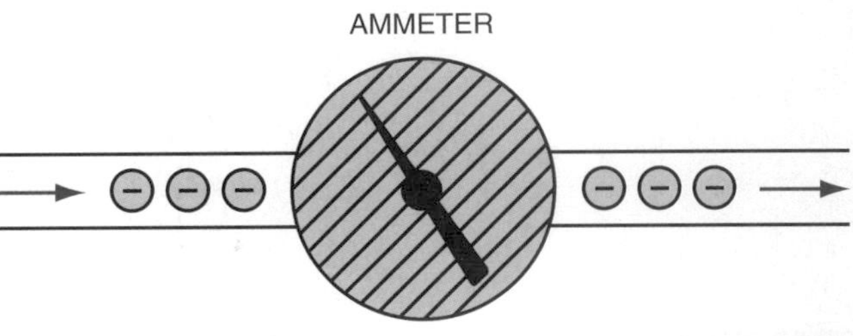

Figure 13–16 An ammeter is installed in the path of the electrons similar to a water meter used to measure the flow of water in litres per second or gallons per minute. The ammeter displays current flow in amperes.

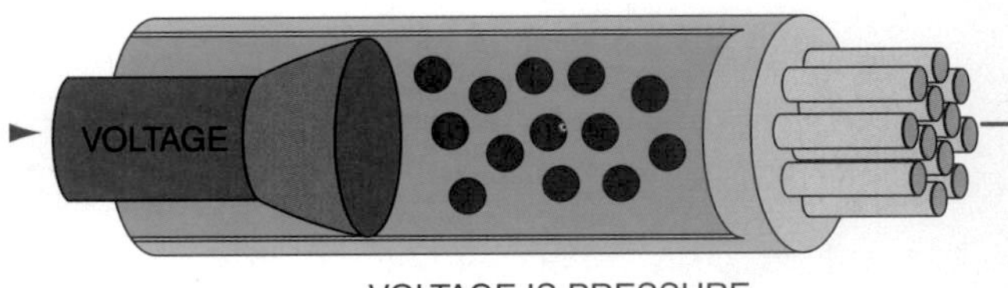

Figure 13–17 Voltage is the electrical pressure that causes the electrons to flow through a conductor.

the amount of electron flow just as litres per second or gallons per minute are units that can be used to measure the rate of water flow. It was named for the French electrician André Marie Ampère (1775–1836). The conventions and measurements for amperes are summarized as follows:

1. The ampere is the unit of measurement for the amount of current flow.
2. The symbol for the unit *ampere* is A (one ampere = 1 A).
3. The capital letter *I*, for *intensity*, is used in mathematical calculations to represent amperes.
4. Amperes are measured by an **ammeter** (not ampmeter). See Figure 13–16.

Volts

The **volt** is the unit of measurement for electrical pressure. It is named for Alessandro Volta (1745–1827), an Italian physicist. The comparable units using water as an example would be kPa or psi. It is possible to have very high pressures (volts) and low water flow (amperes). It is also possible to have high water flow (amperes) and low pressure (volts). Voltage is also called **electrical potential,** because if there is voltage present in a conductor, there is a potential (possibility) for current flow. Voltage does *not* flow through conductors, but voltage does cause current (in amperes) to flow through conductors. See Figure 13–17. The conventions and measurements for voltage are as follows:

1. The volt is the unit of measurement for the amount of electrical pressure.
2. **Electromotive force,** abbreviated **EMF,** is another way of indicating voltage.
3. The symbol for the unit *volt* is V (one volt = 1 V).
4. The symbol used in calculations is *E,* for *electromotive force.*
5. Volts are measured by a **voltmeter.** See Figure 13–18.

Ohms

Resistance to the flow of current through a conductor is measured in units called **ohms,** named after the German physicist Georg Simon Ohm (1787–1854). The resistance to the flow of free electrons through a conductor results from the countless collisions the electrons cause within the atoms of the conductor. See Figure 13–19. The conventions and measurements for resistance are as follows:

1. The ohm is the unit of measurement for electrical resistance.
2. The symbol for ohms is Ω (Greek capital letter omega), the last letter of the Greek alphabet.

Figure 13–18 A digital multimeter set to read DC volts and being used to test the voltage of a vehicle battery. Most multimeters can also measure resistance (ohms) and current flow (amperes).

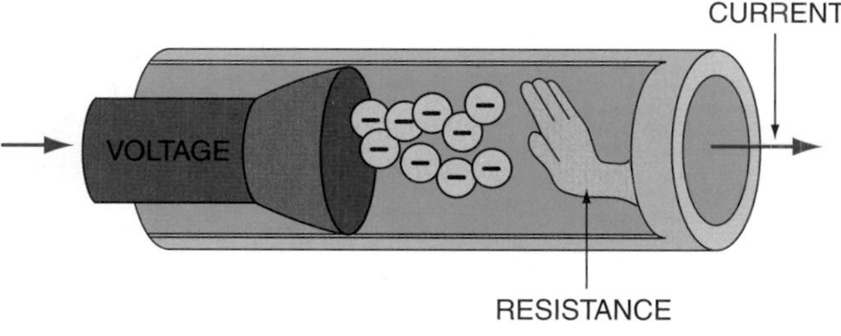

Figure 13–19 Resistance to the flow of electrons through a conductor is measured in ohms.

3. The symbol used in calculations is *R,* for *resistance.*
4. Ohms are measured by an **ohmmeter.**

HINT: It may help to think of the *ampere,* which does all of the work, as "volume." The greater the volume (number of amperes flowing), the more work that can be done, i.e., lights are brighter, motors turn faster, magnetic fields are stronger.

Voltage, which is electrical pressure, pushes the ampere (current) through a conductor. The higher the voltage, the greater the amperage. There must be voltage for current to flow.

An *ohm* is a unit of electrical resistance. The greater the resistance, the less current that flows. Controlled resistance could be a variable resistor used to increase or decrease the amount of current flowing, e.g., dimming a dash light or changing the speed of a heater motor. Unwanted resistance, such as a dirty wiring connection, may cause a starter to turn slowly or an ignition spark to be weak.

Figure 13–20 A display at the Henry Ford Museum in Dearborn, Michigan, that includes a hand-cranked generator and a series of light bulbs. Shown is a young man attempting to light as many bulbs as possible. The crank gets harder to turn as more bulbs light because it requires more power to produce the necessary watts of electricity.

Watts

A **watt** is the electrical unit for *power,* the capacity to do work. It is named after a Scottish inventor, James Watt (1736–1819). The symbol for the unit *watt* is W (one watt = 1 W). The symbol for power is *P.* Electrical power is calculated as amperes times volts:

$$P \text{ (power)} = I \text{ (amperes)} \times E \text{ (volts)}$$

This can easily be remembered by thinking of lowercase letters and what the formula spells: pie. For example, how many watts are used to run an electric motor on 110 V using 2 A?

$$P = I \times E = 2\text{ A} \times 110\text{ V}$$

P is, therefore, 220 W. This could also be expressed in kilowatts (kW). One thousand watts equals 1 kilowatt (kW); therefore, 220 W equals 0.22 kW. A watt is also the metric standard for engine power. One horsepower (hp) equals 746 W. See Figure 13–20.

Conductors and Resistance

All conductors have some resistance to current flow. Several principles of conductors and their resistance include the following:

- *If the conductor length is doubled, its resistance doubles.* This is the reason battery cables are designed to be as short as possible.
- *If the conductor diameter is increased, its resistance is reduced.* This is the reason starter

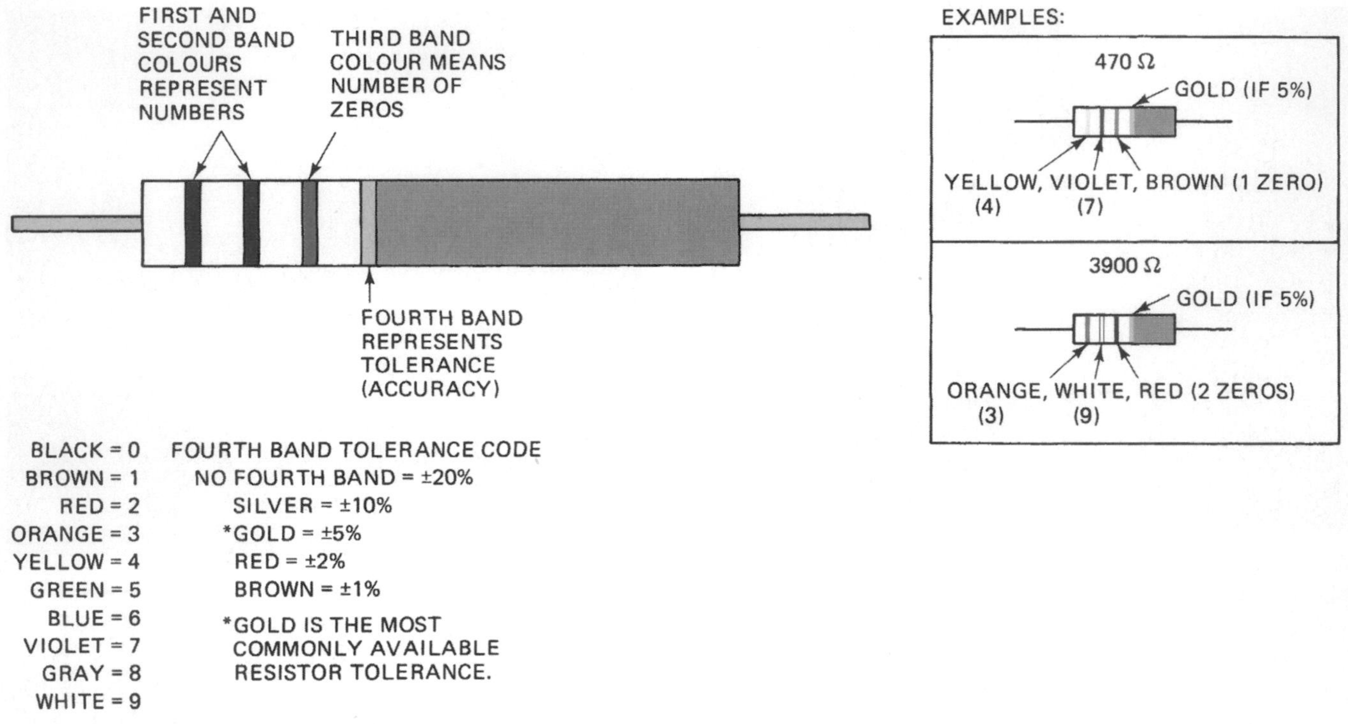

Figure 13–21 Resistor colour code interpretation.

motor cables are larger in diameter than other wiring in the vehicle. See Chapter 14 for further details on wiring sizes.

- *As the temperature increases, the resistance of the conductor also increases.* This is the reason for installing heat shields on some starter motors. The heat shield helps to protect the conductors (copper wiring inside the starter) from excessive engine heat and so reduces the resistance of starter circuits. Because a conductor increases in resistance with increased temperature, the conductor is called a **positive temperature coefficient (PTC)** resistor.

Resistors

Resistance is the opposition to current flow. **Resistors** represent an electrical load, or resistance, to current flow. Electrical and electronic circuits use resistors of specific values to limit and control the flow of current. Resistors can be made from carbon or from other materials that restrict the flow of electricity and are available in various sizes and resistance values. Most resistors have a series of painted colour bands around them. These colour bands are coded to indicate the degree of resistance. See Figures 13–21 and 13–22.

Variable Resistors

Two basic types of mechanically operated variable resistors are used in automotive applications. A **potentiometer** is a three-terminal variable resistor where the majority of the current flow travels through the resistance of the unit and a wiper contact provides a variable voltage output. See Figure 13–23.

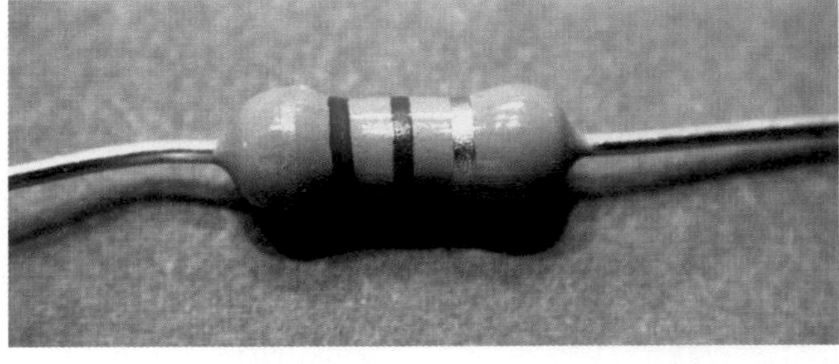

Figure 13–22 A typical carbon resistor.

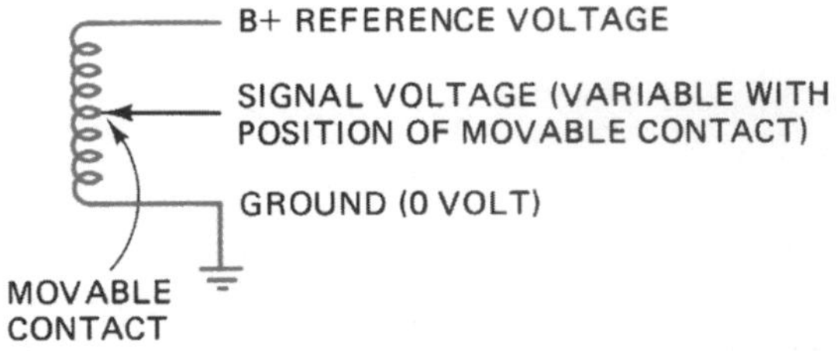

Figure 13–23 A three-wire variable resistor is called a potentiometer.

Potentiometers are most commonly used as throttle position (TP) sensors on computer-equipped engines. See Chapter 25 for general specifications and testing procedures.

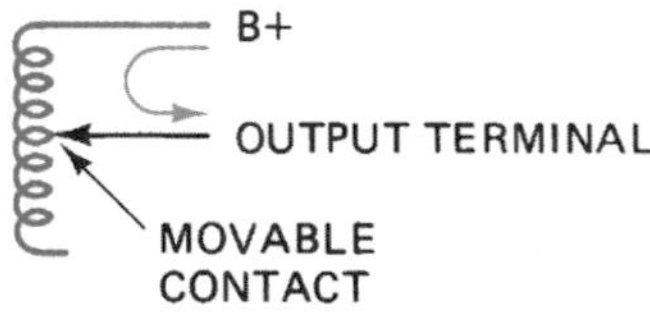

Figure 13–24 A two-wire variable resistor is called a rheostat.

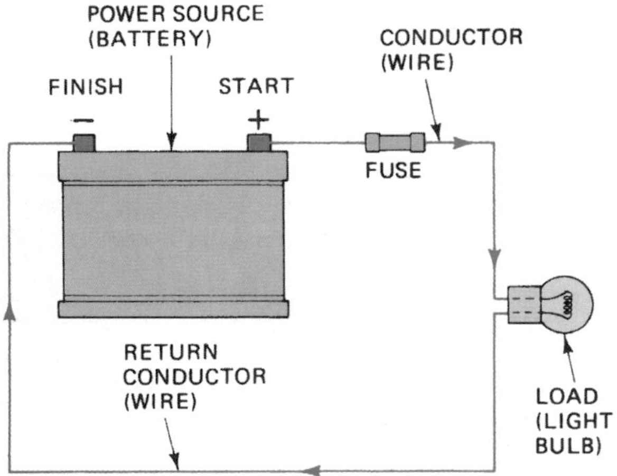

Figure 13–25 All complete circuits must have a power source, a power path, protection (fuse), an electrical load (light bulb in this case), and a return path back to the power source.

Another type of mechanically operated variable resistor is the **rheostat.** A rheostat is a *two*-terminal unit in which all of the current flows through the movable arm. See Figure 13–24. A rheostat is commonly used for a dash light dimmer control.

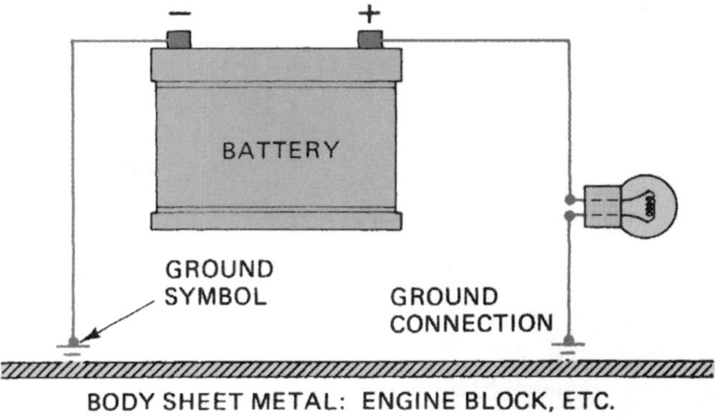

Figure 13–26 The return path back to the battery can be any electrical conductor, such as the metal frame or body of the vehicle.

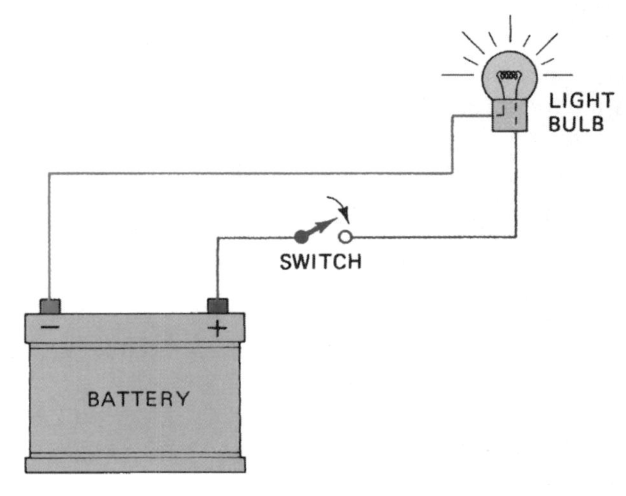

Figure 13–27 An electrical switch opens the circuit and no current flows. The switch could also be on the return (ground) path wire.

CIRCUITS

A **circuit** is a path where electrons travel from a power source (such as a battery) through a resistance (such as a light bulb) and back to the power source. It is called a *circuit* because the current must start and finish at the same place (power source). See Figure 13–25.

For *any* electrical circuit to work at all, it must be continuous from the battery (power), through all the wires and components, and back to the battery (ground). A circuit that is continuous throughout is said to have **continuity.**

Parts of a Complete Circuit

Every **complete circuit** contains the following parts:

1. A **power source,** such as a vehicle's battery.
2. **Protection** from harmful overloads (excessive current flow). Fuses, circuit breakers, and fusible links are examples of electrical circuit protection devices.
3. A **path** for the current to flow through from the power source to the resistance. This path from a power source to the resistance (a light bulb in this example) is usually an insulated copper wire.
4. The **electrical load** or resistance—the object the electrical current is operating or lighting.
5. A **return path** for the electrical current from the load back to the power source so that there is a *complete* circuit. This return path is usually the metal body, frame, and engine block of the vehicle. This is called the **ground return path.** See Figure 13–26.
6. Switches and controls to turn the circuit on and off. See Figure 13–27.

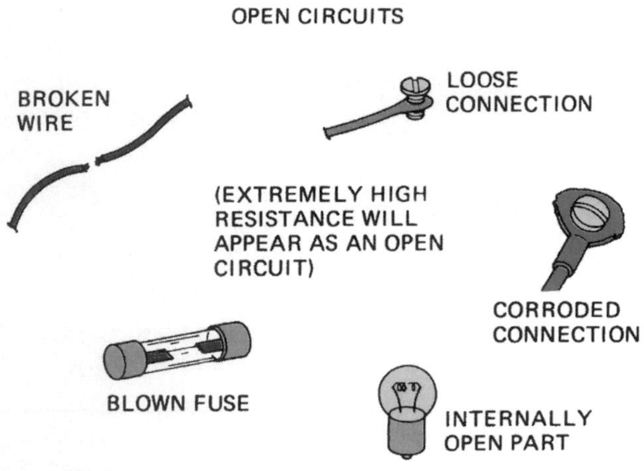

Figure 13–28 Examples of common causes of open circuits. Some of these causes are often difficult to find.

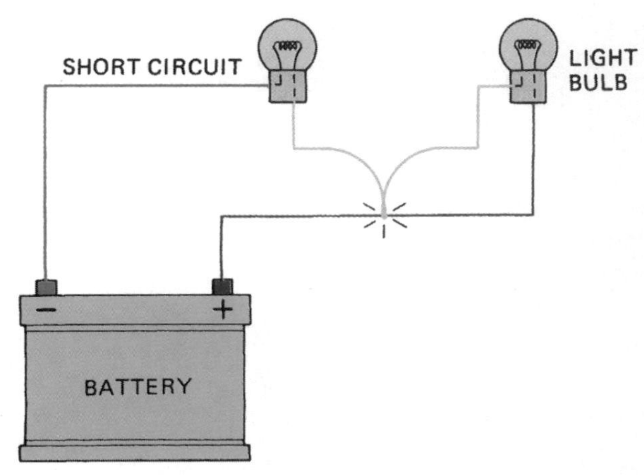

Figure 13–29 A short circuit permits electrical current to bypass some or all of the resistance in the circuit.

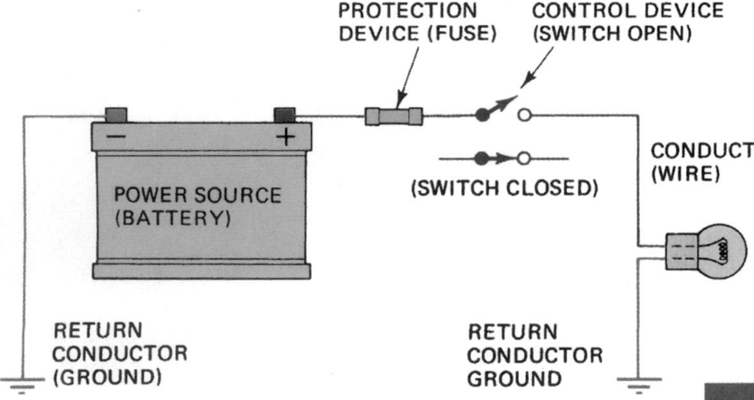

Figure 13–30 A fuse or circuit breaker opens the circuit to prevent possible overheating damage in the event of a short circuit.

Open Circuits

An **open circuit** is any circuit that is *not* complete, or that lacks continuity. See Figure 13–28. *No current at all* will flow through an incomplete circuit. An open circuit may be created by a break in the circuit or by a switch that opens (turns off) the circuit and prevents the flow of current. In any circuit containing a power load and ground, an opening anywhere in the circuit will cause the circuit not to work. A light switch in a home and the headlight switch in a vehicle are examples of devices that open a circuit to control its operation.

Short-to-Voltage

If a wire (conductor) or component is shorted to voltage, it is commonly called **shorted.** See Figure 13–29. A short circuit:

1. Is a complete circuit in which the current bypasses *some* or *all* of the resistance in the circuit
2. Involves the power side of the circuit
3. Involves a copper-to-copper connection
4. Is also called a *short-to-voltage*
5. Usually affects more than one circuit
6. *May* or *may not* blow a fuse See Figure 13–30. See Chapter 14 for additional information about fuses and fuse ratings.

See the Diagnostic Story "The Short-to-Voltage Story" for an example.

TECH TIP 

Open Is a Four-Letter Word

An open in a circuit breaks the path of current flow. The open can be any break in the power side, load, or ground side of a circuit. A switch is often used to close and open a circuit to turn it on and off. Just remember,

open = no current flow
closed = current flow

Trying to locate an open circuit in a vehicle is often difficult and may cause the technician to use other four-letter words such as "HELP"!

Short-to-Ground

A **short-to-ground** is a type of short circuit wherein the current bypasses part of the normal circuit and

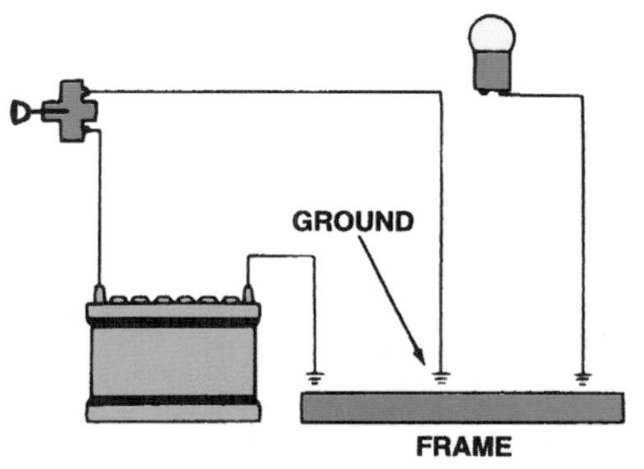

Figure 13–31 A short-to-ground affects the power side of the circuit. Current flows directly to the ground return bypassing some or all of the electrical loads in the circuit. There is no current in the circuit past the short.

flows directly to ground. Because the ground return circuit is metal (vehicle frame, engine, or body), this type of circuit is identified as having current flowing from copper to steel. A defective component or circuit that is shorted to ground is commonly called **grounded.** For example, if a penny were accidentally inserted into a cigarette lighter socket, the current would flow through the penny to ground. Because the penny has little resistance, an excessive amount of current flow causes the fuse to blow. See Figure 13–31.

SERIES CIRCUITS

A simple circuit consists of a power source, power side (wire), an electrical load or resistance such as a bulb, and a return path as shown in Figure 13–32. A **series circuit** is a complete circuit with two or more resistances connected so that the current has to go through one resistance to go through the next. See Figure 13–33.

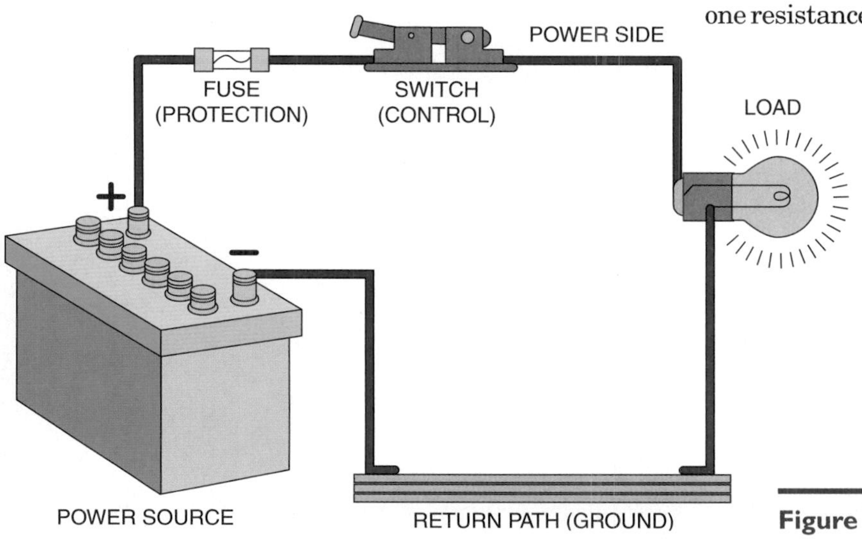

Figure 13–32 A simple electrical circuit.

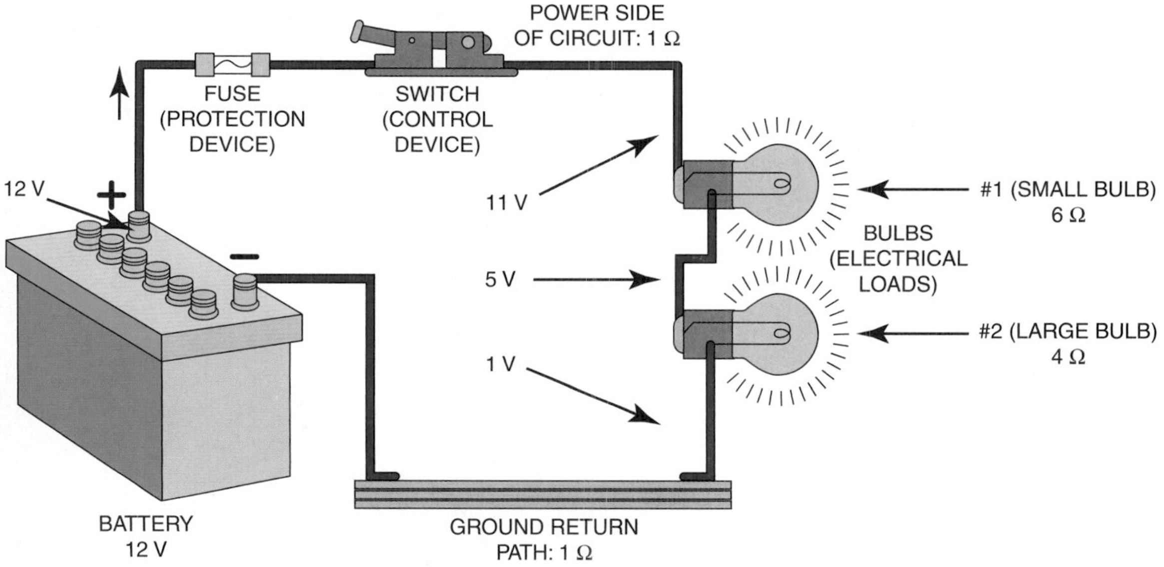

Figure 13–33 A series circuit with two electrical loads (bulbs). All electrical current must flow through both bulbs. Because each bulb offers resistance, the bulbs will be dim as a result of the reduced current flow compared to the brightness of either one if connected to the battery directly.

A series circuit can have any number of resistances in the circuit. The resistances can be any of the following:

1. Resistors
2. Light bulbs
3. Horn
4. Electric motors
5. Coils
6. Relays
7. Solenoids
8. Heating elements (cigarette lighter)
9. Connectors or junctions
10. Lengths of wire or conductors

In a series circuit, the voltage varies across each resistance, but the current flow in amperes is constant throughout the entire circuit.

HINT: The voltage is always used up in pushing current (amperage) through a circuit. The amount of voltage used (voltage drop) is determined by the resistance in each part of the circuit. High resistance uses more voltage and low resistance uses less.

If we follow the circuit in Figure 13-33, we note that 12 V of pressure is available at the battery positive post. If we now measure the voltage available at the small bulb (#1), it has dropped to 11 V. It took 1 V of pressure to push current through the low resistance of the fuse and switch. Checking the voltage again after the first bulb (#1), we find the voltage has dropped to 5 V. It took 6 V of pressure to continue pushing current through the high resistance of this bulb.

If we measure the voltage again after the large bulb (#2), we find the voltage has dropped further to only 1 V, a loss of 4 V. Less voltage was used to push through the low resistance of the large bulb (#2) and more voltage was used at the high resistance of the small bulb (#1).

One volt is left to push the current back to the battery. Even though the current flow is exactly the same everywhere in this series circuit, the voltage is always completely used up.

Note again that it took more voltage to push through the high resistance of bulb #1 and less voltage to push through the lower resistance of bulb #2.

If we found the voltage available at bulb #1 was less than 11 V, what would this indicate? Right; more than 1 V of lost pressure tells us there is high resistance somewhere between the battery and bulb #1.

Voltage available and voltage drop testing are very common methods of checking resistance in a circuit.

DIAGNOSTIC STORY

The Short-to-Voltage Story

A technician was working on a pickup truck with unusual electrical problems including the following:

1. Whenever the brake pedal was depressed, the dash light and the side marker lights would light.
2. The turn signals caused all lights to blink and the fuel gauge needle to bounce up and down.
3. When the brake lights were on, the front parking lights also came on.

The technician tested all fuses using a conventional test light (not a low-current test light) and found them to be okay. All body-to-engine block ground wires were clean and tight. All bulbs were of the correct trade number as specified in the owner's manual.

NOTE: Using a single-filament bulb (such as a #1156) in the place of a dual-filament bulb (such as a #1157) could also cause many of these same problems.

Because most of the trouble occurred when the brake pedal was depressed, the technician decided to trace all the wires in the brake light circuit. The problem was found near the exhaust system. A small hole in the tail pipe (after the muffler) directed hot exhaust gases to the wiring harness containing all of the wires for circuits at the rear of the truck. The heat had melted the insulation and caused most of the wires to touch. Whenever one circuit was activated (such as when the brake pedal was applied), the current had a complete path to several other circuits. A fuse did not blow because there was enough resistance in the circuits being energized so that the current (in amperes) was too low to blow any fuses.

TECH TIP

Think of a Waterwheel

A beginner technician cleaned the positive terminal of the battery because the starter had been cranking the engine slowly. When questioned by the shop foreman as to why only the positive post had been cleaned, the technician responded that the negative terminal was "only a ground." The foreman reminded the technician that the current, in amperes, is constant throughout a series circuit (such as the cranking motor circuit). If 200 A leaves the positive post of the battery, then 200 A must return to the battery through the negative post.

The technician just could not understand how electricity can do work (crank an engine), yet return the same amount of current, in amperes, as left the battery. The shop foreman explained that even though the current is constant throughout the circuit, the voltage (electrical pressure or potential) is dropped to zero in the circuit. To explain further, the shop foreman drew a waterwheel. See Figure 13–34.

As water drops from a higher level to a lower level, high potential energy (or voltage) is used to turn the waterwheel and results in low potential energy (or lower voltage). The same amount of water (or amperes) reaches the pond under the waterwheel as started the fall above the waterwheel. As current (amperes) flows through a conductor, it performs work in the circuit (turns the waterwheel) while its voltage (potential) is dropped.

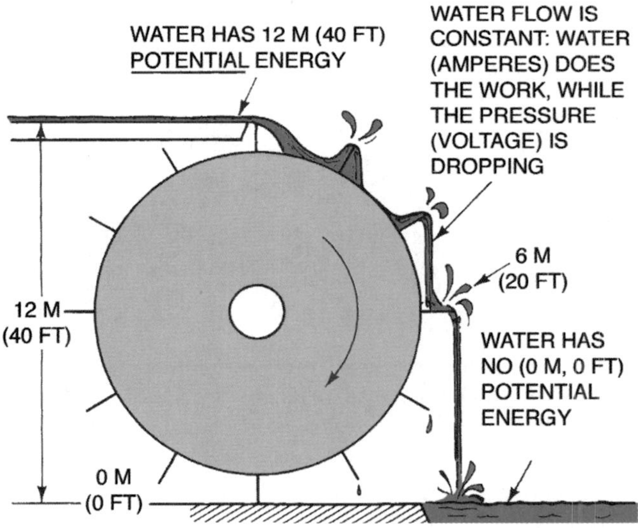

Figure 13–34 Electrical flow through a circuit is similar to water flowing over a waterwheel. The more water flowing (amperes in electricity), the greater the amount of work (waterwheel). The amount of water remains constant, yet the pressure (voltage in electricity) drops as the current flows through the circuit.

PARALLEL CIRCUITS

A **parallel circuit** is a type of complete circuit in which the current flows through the circuit by more than one path. The concept is similar to that of traffic going through a city. A driver can travel straight through the city, fighting heavy traffic (high resistance), or go around the city using a long bypass. Since both paths are available to all traffic, each road carries fewer vehicles.

In picture form, a parallel circuit appears as shown in Figure 13–35. In a parallel circuit, the voltage in each leg of the circuit is the same, but the current flow in amperes varies according to the resistance in each leg.

Parallel circuits are used in almost every automotive electrical circuit. The exterior lights are all controlled by the headlight switch and are wired in parallel. See Figure 13–36. If they were wired in series and one bulb burned out, *all* lights would go out because of the open circuit caused by the one defective bulb. This does not occur with a parallel circuit. If any bulb is defective, current can still flow through the other resistances (bulbs) as if nothing has happened.

TECH TIP

How to Determine a Parallel Circuit

To test whether a circuit is truly a parallel circuit, assume that one wire going to one of the light bulbs is cut. See Figure 13–37. If the other bulbs are still connected to both a power source and a ground, the circuit is still complete and current can still flow. The circuit is therefore a parallel circuit.

SERIES-PARALLEL CIRCUITS

A **series-parallel circuit** is any type of circuit containing resistances in both series and parallel in one circuit. Series-parallel circuits are also called **combination,** or **compound, circuits.** A series-parallel circuit is the most commonly used type of automotive circuit. See Figure 13–38.

OHM'S LAW

The German physicist, Georg Simon Ohm, established that electric pressure (EMF) in volts, electrical resistance in ohms, and the amount of current in

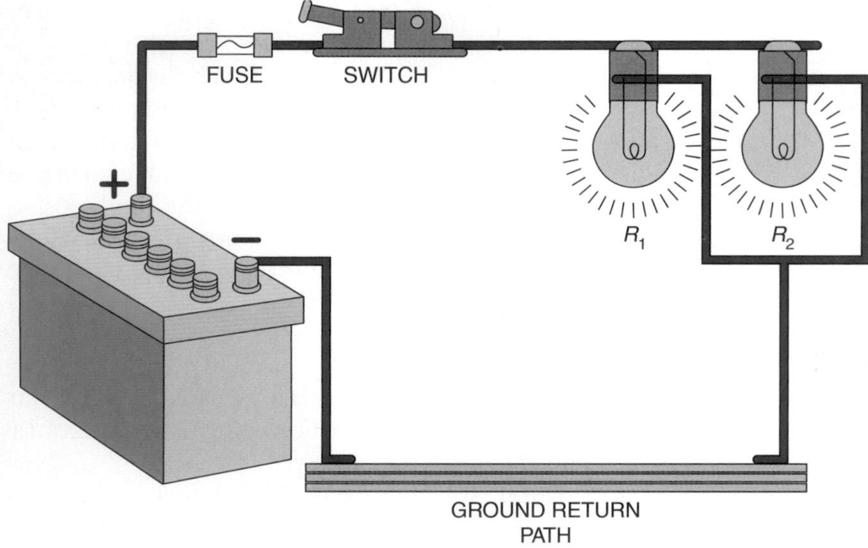

Figure 13–35 Parallel circuits are the most commonly used circuit in the vehicle. Most items and exteriors lights are connected in parallel. If one bulb burns out, the other will light because each bulb has its own power and ground connections.

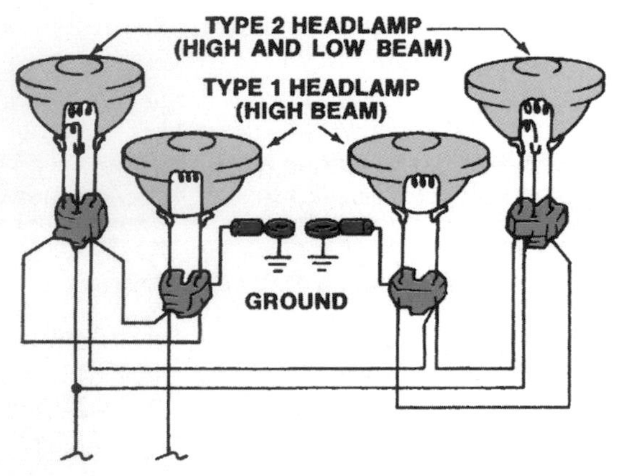

Figure 13–36 A typical headlight circuit showing that all of the headlights are wired in parallel.

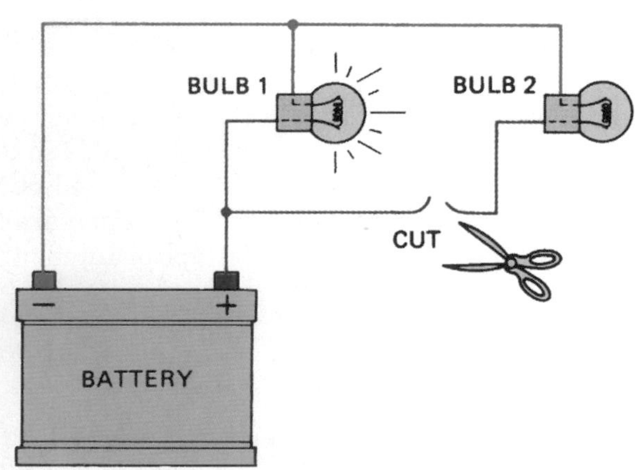

Figure 13–37 If the wire going to bulb 2 is cut, the bulb will not light because of the open circuit created. Bulb 1 is still connected to a complete circuit and will operate normally.

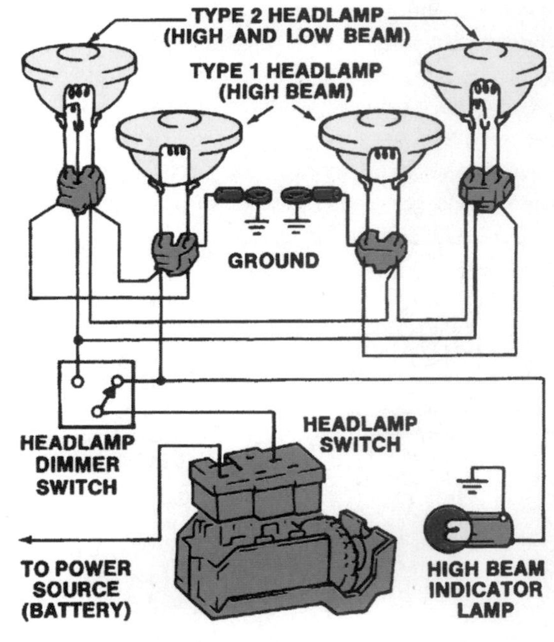

Figure 13–38 A complete headlight circuit with all bulbs and switches is a series–parallel circuit because some components are connected in series and others such as the headlights are connected in parallel.

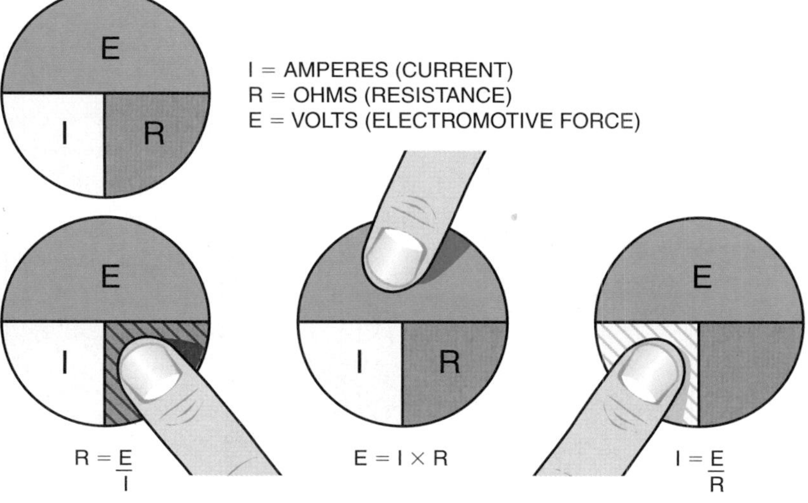

Figure 13–39 To calculate one unit of electricity when the other two are known, simply use your finger and cover the unit you do not know. For example, if both voltage (*E*) and resistance (*R*) are known, cover the letter *I* (amperes). Notice that the letter *E* is above the letter *R*, so divide the resistor's value into the voltage to determine the current in the circuit.

amperes flowing through any circuit are all related. See Figure 13–39. According to **Ohm's law,** it requires 1 volt to push 1 ampere through 1 ohm of resistance. This means that if the voltage is doubled, then the number of amperes of current flowing through a circuit will also double if the resistance of the circuit remains the same.

Ohm's law can also be stated as a simple formula used to calculate one value of an electrical circuit if the other two are known:

$$I = \frac{E}{R}$$

where

I = Current in amperes (A)

E = Electromotive force (EMF) in volts (V)

R = Resistance in ohms (Ω)

1. Ohm's law can determine the *resistance* if the voltage and current are known: $R = E/I$.
2. Ohm's law can determine the *voltage* if the resistance (ohms) and current are known: $E = I \times R$.
3. Ohm's law can determine the *current* if the resistance and voltage are known: $I = E/R$.

See the following table for a quick summary of relationships under Ohm's law.

Ohm's Law Relationships

Voltage	Resistance	Amperage
Up	Down	Up
Up	Same	Up
Up	Up	Same
Same	Down	Up
Same	Same	Same
Same	Up	Down
Down	Up	Down
Down	Same	Down

Ohm's Law Applied to Simple Circuits

If a battery with 12 volts is connected to a light bulb with a resistance of 4 ohms as shown in Figure 13–40, how many amperes will flow through the circuit? Using Ohm's law, we can calculate the number of amperes that will flow through the wires and the bulb. Remember, if two factors are known (volts and ohms in this example), the remaining factor (amperes) can be calculated using Ohm's law.

$$I = E/R = 12\text{ V}/4\ \Omega$$

The values for the voltage (12) and the resistance (4) were substituted for the variables *E* and *R,* and *I* is thus 3 amperes (12/4 = 3).

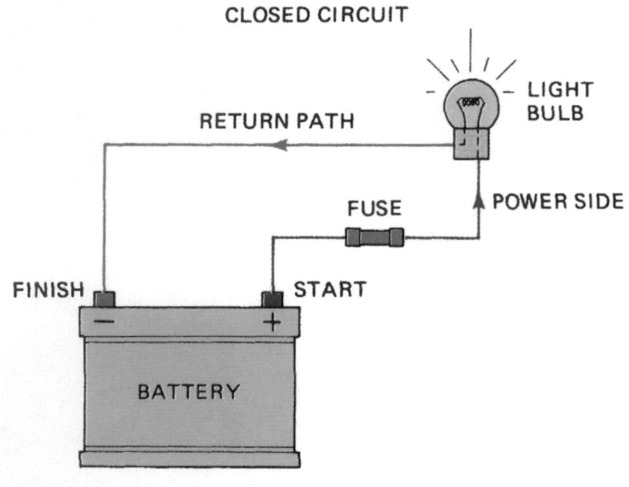

Figure 13–40 Closed circuit, including a power source, power-side wire, circuit protection (fuse), resistance (bulb), and return path wire.

If we want to connect a light bulb to a 12 volts battery, we now know that this simple circuit requires 3 amperes to operate. This may help us for two reasons:

1. We can now determine the wire diameter that we will need based on the number of amperes flowing through the circuit.
2. The correct fuse rating can be selected to protect the circuit.

Ohm's Law and Series Circuits

A series circuit is a circuit containing more than one resistance in which all current must flow through all resistances in the circuit. Ohm's law can be used to calculate the value of one unknown (voltage, resistance, or amperes), if the other two values are known.

Because *all* current flows through all resistances, the total resistance is the sum (addition) of all resistances. See Figure 13–41. The total resistance of the circuit shown here is 6 ohms (1 ohm + 2 ohms + 3 ohms). The formula for total resistance (R_T) for a series circuit is

$$R_T = R_1 + R_2 + R_3 + \ldots$$

Using Ohm's law to find the current flow, we have

$$I = E/R = 12\ \text{V}/6\ \Omega = 2\ \text{A}$$

Therefore, with a total resistance of 6 ohms using a 12 volt battery in the series circuit shown, 2 amperes of current will flow through the entire circuit. If the amount of resistance of a circuit is reduced, more current will flow.

In Figure 13–42, one resistance has been eliminated and now the total resistance is 3 ohms (1 ohm + 2 ohms). Using Ohm's law to calculate current flow yields 4 amperes.

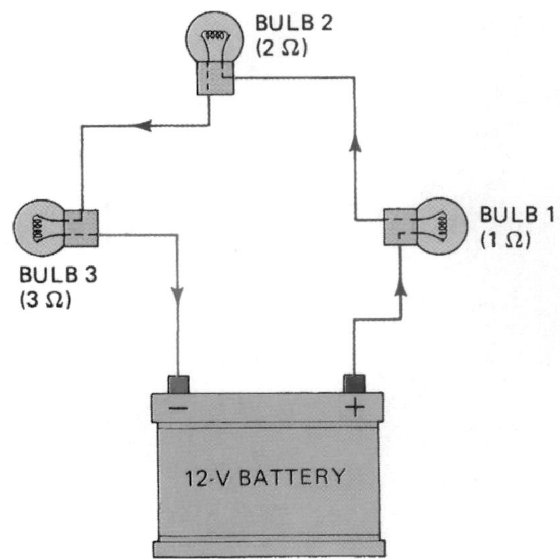

Figure 13–41 Series circuit with three bulbs. All current flows through all resistances (bulbs). The total resistance of the circuit is the sum of the total resistance of the bulbs, and the bulbs will light dimly because of the increased resistance and the reduction of current flow (amperes) through the circuit.

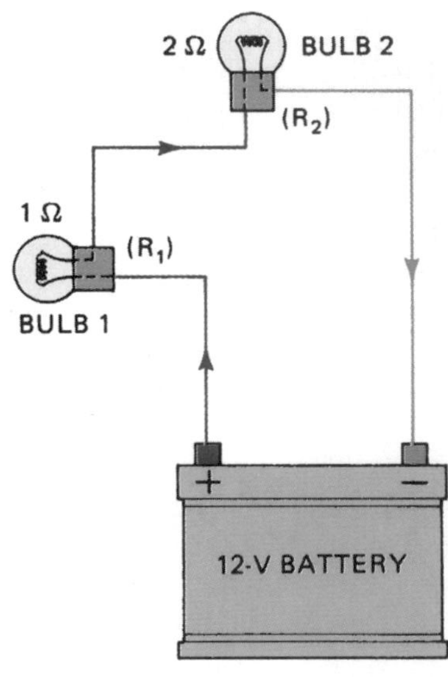

Figure 13–42 Series circuit with two bulbs.

$$I = E/R = 12\ \text{V}/3\ \Omega = 4\ \text{A}$$

Notice that the current flow was doubled (4 amperes instead of 2 amperes) when the resistance was cut in half (from 6 ohms to 3 ohms).

KIRCHHOFF'S VOLTAGE LAW

The source voltage applied to a series circuit drops with each resistor in a manner similar to that in

Frequently Asked Question ???

What Are the Series Circuit Laws?

1. The total resistance in a series circuit is the sum total of the individual resistances.
2. The current is constant throughout the entire circuit. If 2 amperes of current leave the battery, 2 amperes of current return to the battery.
3. Although the current (in amperes) is constant, the voltage drops across each resistance in the circuit. The sum total of all individual voltage drops equals the applied source voltage.

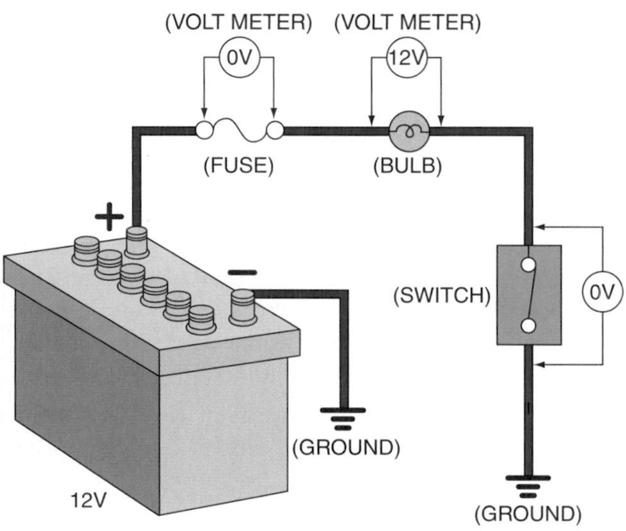

Figure 13–43 As current flows through a circuit, the voltage drops in proportion to the amount of resistance in the circuit. Most, if not all, of the resistance should occur across the load such as the bulb in this circuit. All of the other components and wiring should produce little, if any, voltage drop. If a wire or connection did cause a voltage drop, less voltage would be available to light the bulb and the bulb would be dimmer than normal.

which the strength of an athlete drops each time a strenuous physical feat is performed. The greater the resistance, the greater the drop in voltage.

A German physicist, Gustav Robert Kirchhoff (1824–1887), developed laws about electrical circuits. His second law, **Kirchhoff's voltage law,** concerns voltage drops. It states: *The voltage around any closed circuit is equal to the sum (total) of the voltage drops across the resistances.*

Applying Kirchhoff's Voltage Law

Kirchhoff states in his second law that the voltage will drop in proportion to the resistance and that the

TECH TIP 

Farsighted Quality of Electricity

Electricity seems to act as if it knows what resistances are ahead on the long trip through a circuit. If the trip through the circuit has many high-resistance components, very few electrons (amperes) will choose to attempt to make the trip. If a circuit has little or no resistance (for example, a short circuit), then as many electrons (amperes) as possible attempt to flow through the complete circuit. If the flow exceeds the capacity of the fuse or the circuit breaker, then the circuit is opened and all current flow stops.

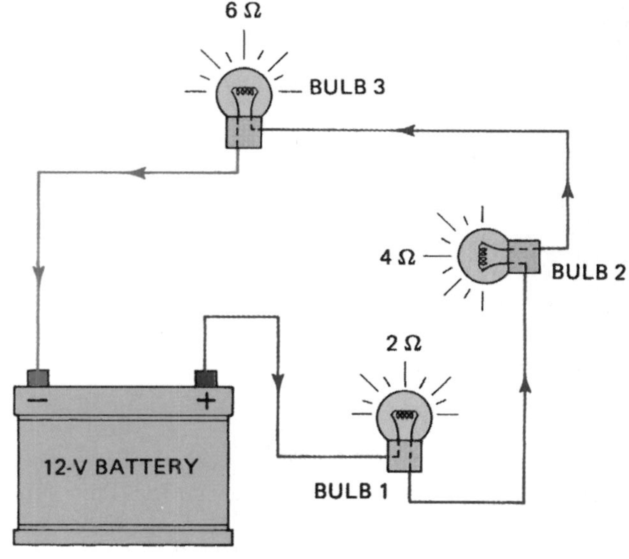

Figure 13–44 In a series circuit, the voltage is dropped or lowered by each resistance in the circuit. The higher the resistance, the greater the drop in voltage.

total of all voltage drops will equal the applied voltage. See Figure 13–43. Using Figure 13–44, the total resistance of the circuit can be determined by adding the individual resistances ($2\ \Omega + 4\ \Omega + 6\ \Omega = 12\ \Omega$). The current through the circuit is determined by using Ohm's law, $I = E/R = 12\ \text{V}/12\ \Omega = 1\ \text{A}$. Therefore, in the circuit shown, the following values are known:

Resistance = 12 Ω
Voltage = 12 V
Current = 1 A

Everything is known *except* the voltage drop caused by each resistance. The **voltage drop** can be determined by using Ohm's law and calculating for voltage (E) using the value of each resistance individually:

$$E = I \times R$$

where

E = Voltage

I = Current in the circuit (remember, the current is constant in a series circuit; only the voltage varies)

R = Resistance of only one of the resistances

The voltage drops are as follows:

Voltage drop for bulb 1: $E = I \times R = 1\text{ A} \times 2\ \Omega = 2\text{ V}$
Voltage drop for bulb 2: $E = I \times R = 1\text{ A} \times 4\ \Omega = 4\text{ V}$
Voltage drop for bulb 3: $E = I \times R = 1\text{ A} \times 6\ \Omega = 6\text{ V}$

According to Kirchhoff, the sum (addition) of the voltage drops should equal the applied voltage (battery voltage):

$$\text{Total of voltage drops} = 2\text{ V} + 4\text{ V} + 6\text{ V} = 12\text{ V} = \text{Battery voltage}$$

This proves Kirchhoff's second (voltage) law. Another example is illustrated in Figure 13–45.

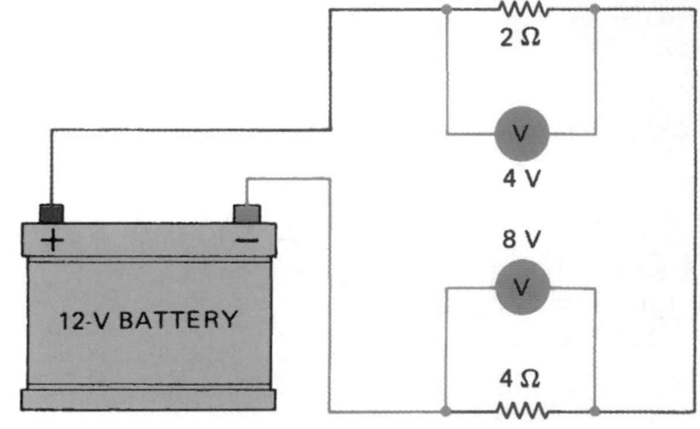

A. I = E/R (TOTAL R = 6 Ω)
= 12/6 = 2 A

B. E = IR (VOLTAGE DROP)
AT 2 Ω RESISTANCE =
E = 2 X 2 = 4 V
AT 4 Ω RESISTANCE =
E = 2 X 4 = 8 V

C. 4 + 8 = 12 V
SUM OF VOLTAGE DROP
EQUALS APPLIED VOLTAGE

Figure 13–45 A voltmeter reads the differences of voltage between the test leads. The voltage read across a resistance is the voltage drop that occurs when current flows through a resistance. A voltage drop is also called an *IR* drop because it is calculated by multiplying the current (*I*) through the resistance (electrical load) by the value of the resistance (*R*).

Use of Voltage Drops

Voltage drops, due to built-in resistance, are used in automotive electrical systems to drop the voltage in the following examples:

1. *Dash lights.* Most vehicles are equipped with a method of dimming the brightness of the dash lights by turning a variable resistor. This type of resistor allows resistance to be changed, which varies the voltage to the dash light bulbs. A high voltage to the bulbs causes them to be bright, and a lower voltage results in a dimmer light.
2. *Blower motor* (heater or air-conditioning fan). Speeds are usually controlled by a fan switch sending current through high-, medium-, or low-resistance wire resistors. The highest resistance will drop the voltage the most, causing the motor to run at the lowest speed. The highest speed of the motor will occur when *no* resistance is in the circuit and full battery voltage is switched to the blower motor.

Voltage Drops as a Testing Method

Any resistance in a circuit causes the voltage to drop in proportion to the amount of the resistance. Because a high resistance will drop the voltage more than a lower resistance, we can use a voltmeter to measure resistance. Voltage-drop testing for determining high resistance in wiring or connections is discussed in detail in Chapters 16 and 17.

KIRCHHOFF'S CURRENT LAW

A parallel circuit is a complete circuit in which the current has more than one path to travel to complete the circuit. A break or open in one leg or section of a parallel circuit does not stop the current flow through the remaining legs of the parallel circuit.

Kirchhoff's current law (his first law) states: *The current flowing into any junction of an electrical circuit is equal to the current flowing out of that junction.* This first law can be illustrated using Ohm's law as seen in Figure 13–46. Kirchhoff's law states that the amount of current flowing into junction A will equal the current flowing out of junction A.

Because the 6 ohm leg requires 2 amperes and the 3 ohm resistance leg requires 4 amperes, it is necessary that the wire from the battery to junction A be capable of handling 6 amperes. Also notice that the sum of the current flowing *out* of a junction (2 + 4 = 6 amperes) is equal to the current flowing *into* the junction (6 amperes), proving Kirchhoff's current law.

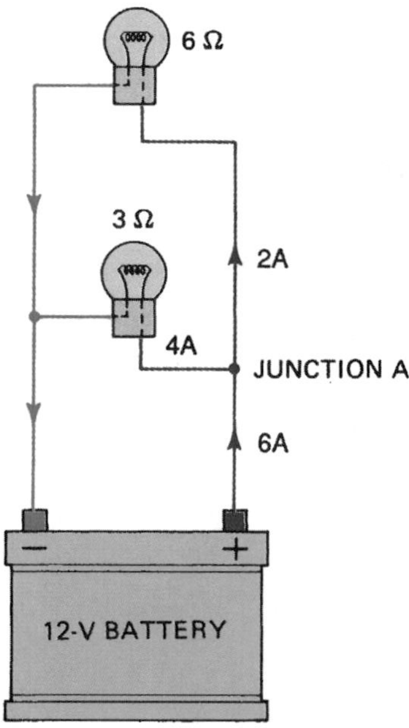

Figure 13–46 The amount of current flowing into junction point A equals the total amount of current flowing out of the junction.

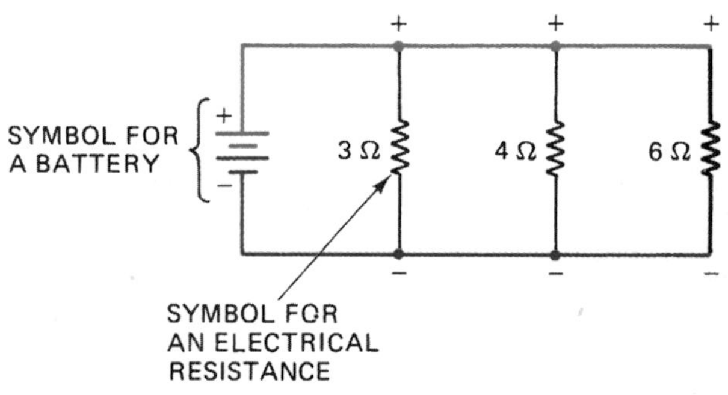

Figure 13–47 Typical parallel circuit. Each resistance has power and ground and each leg operates independently of the other legs of the circuit.

Frequently Asked Question ???

What Are the Parallel Circuit Laws?

1. The total resistance of a parallel circuit is always less than that of the smallest-resistance leg.
2. The voltage is the same for each leg of a parallel circuit.
3. The amount of current flow through a parallel circuit may vary for each leg depending on the resistance of that leg. The current flowing through each leg results in the same voltage drop (from the power side to the ground side) as for every other leg of the circuit.

NOTE: A parallel circuit drops the voltage from source voltage to zero (ground) across the resistance in each leg of the circuit.

DETERMINING TOTAL RESISTANCE IN A PARALLEL CIRCUIT

There are five methods commonly used to determine total resistance in a parallel circuit.

NOTE: Determining the total *resistance* of a parallel circuit is very important in automotive service. Electronic fuel-injector and diesel engine glow-plug circuits are two of the most commonly tested circuits where parallel circuit knowledge is required. Also, when installing extra lighting, the technician must determine the proper gauge wire and protection device.

Method 1

The total *current* (in amperes) can be calculated first by treating each leg of the parallel circuit as a simple circuit. See Figure 13–47. Each leg has its own power and ground (−), and therefore, the current through each leg is independent of the current through any other leg.

Current through the 3 Ω resistance $= I = E/R = 12\ \text{V}/3\ \Omega = 4\ \text{A}$
Current through the 4 Ω resistance $= I = E/R = 12\ \text{V}/4\ \Omega = 3\ \text{A}$
Current through the 6 Ω resistance $= I = E/R = 12\ \text{V}/6\ \Omega = 2\ \text{A}$

The total current flowing from the battery is the sum total of the individual currents for each leg. Total current from the battery is, therefore, 9 amperes ($4\ \text{A} + 3\ \text{A} + 2\ \text{A} = 9\ \text{A}$).

If **total circuit resistance** (R_T) is needed, Ohm's law can be used to calculate it because voltage (E) and current (I) are now known.

$$R_T = E/I = 12\ \text{V}/9\ \text{A} = 1.33\ \Omega$$

Note that the total resistance (1.33 Ω) is smaller than that of the smallest-resistance leg of the parallel circuit. This characteristic of a parallel circuit holds true because not all current flows through all resistances as in a series circuit.

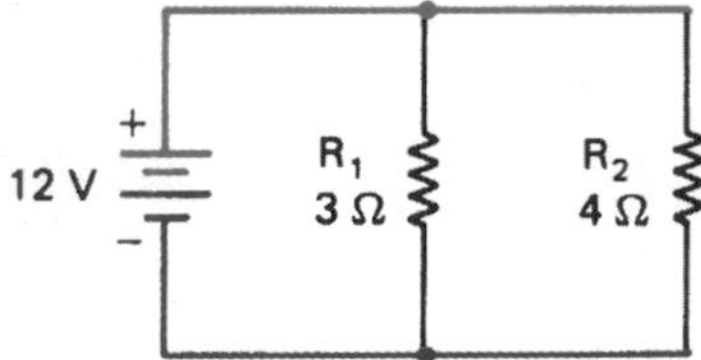

Figure 13–48 A schematic showing two resistors in parallel connected to a 12 V battery.

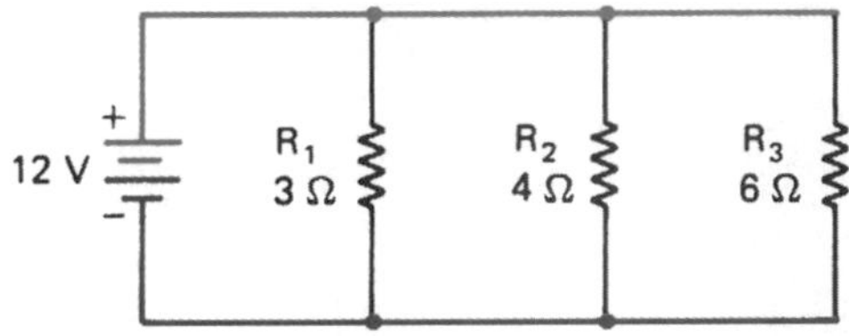

Figure 13–49 A parallel circuit with three resistors connected to a 12 V battery.

Because the current has alternative paths to ground through the various legs of a parallel circuit, as additional resistances (legs) are added to a parallel circuit, the total current from the battery (power source) *increases.*

Additional current can flow when resistances are added in parallel, because each leg of a parallel circuit has its own power and ground and the current flowing through each leg is strictly dependent on the resistance of *that* leg.

Method 2

If only two resistors are connected in parallel, the total resistance (R_T) can be found using the formula $R_T = (R_1 \times R_2)/(R_1 + R_2)$. For example, using the circuit in Figure 13–48 and substituting 3 ohms for R_1 and 4 ohms for R_2,

$$R_T = (3 \times 4)/(3 + 4) = 12/7 = 1.7\ \Omega.$$

Note that the total resistance (1.7 Ω) is smaller than that of the smallest-resistance leg of the circuit.

> **NOTE:** Which resistor is R_1 and which is R_2 is not important. The position in the formula makes no difference in the multiplication and addition of the resistor values.

This formula can be used for more than two resistances in parallel, but only two resistances can be calculated at a time. After solving for R_T for two resistors, use the value of R_T as R_1 and the additional resistance in parallel as R_2 and solve for another R_T. Continue the process for all resistance legs of the parallel circuit. However, note that it might be easier to solve for R_T when there are more than two resistances in parallel by using method 3 or 4.

Method 3

A formula that can be used to find the total resistance for any number of resistances in parallel is

$$1/R_T = 1/R_1 + 1/R_2 + 1/R_3 + \dots$$

To solve for R_T for the three resistance legs in Figure 13–49, substitute the values of the resistances for R_1, R_2, and R_3:

$$1/R_T = 1/3 + 1/4 + 1/6$$

The fractions cannot be added together unless they all have the same denominator. The lowest common denominator in this example is 12. Therefore, 1/3 becomes 4/12, 1/4 becomes 3/12, and 1/6 becomes 2/12.

$$1/R_T = 4/12 + 3/12 + 2/12 = 9/12$$

Cross multiplying $R_T = 12/9 = 1.33\ \Omega$. Note that the result (1.33 Ω) is the same regardless of the method used (see method 1). The most difficult part of using this method (besides using fractions) is determining the lowest common denominator, especially for circuits containing a wide range of ohmic values for the various legs. For an easier method using a calculator, see method 4.

Method 4

This method uses an electronic calculator, commonly available at very low cost. Instead of determining the lowest common denominator as in method 3, one can use the electronic calculator to convert the fractions to decimal equivalents. The memory buttons on most calculators can be used to keep a running total of the fractional values. Use Figure 13–50 and calculate the total resistance (R_T) by pushing the indicated buttons on the calculator. Also see Figure 13–51. Be sure MRC = 0 before starting each new problem.

> **NOTE:** This method can be used to find the total resistance of *any number* of resistances in parallel.

The memory recall (MRC) and equals (=) buttons invert the answer to give the correct value for total resistance (1.33 Ω). The inverse (1/X) button can be used with the sum (SUM) button on scientific calculators without using the memory button.

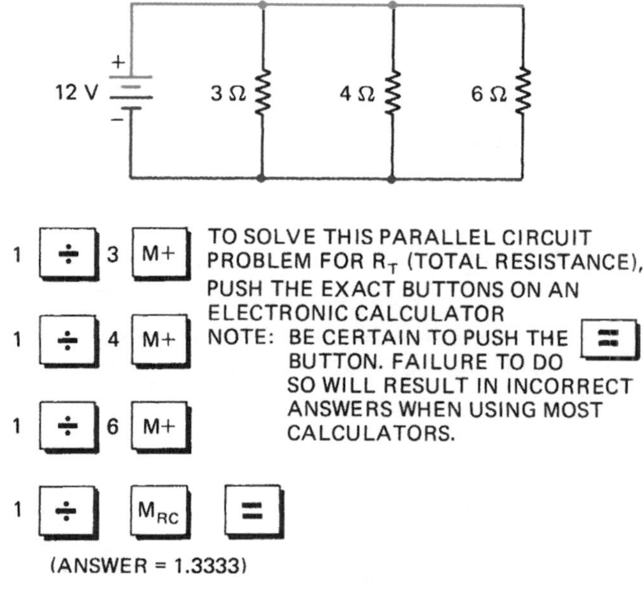

Figure 13–50 Using an electronic calculator to determine the total resistance of a parallel circuit.

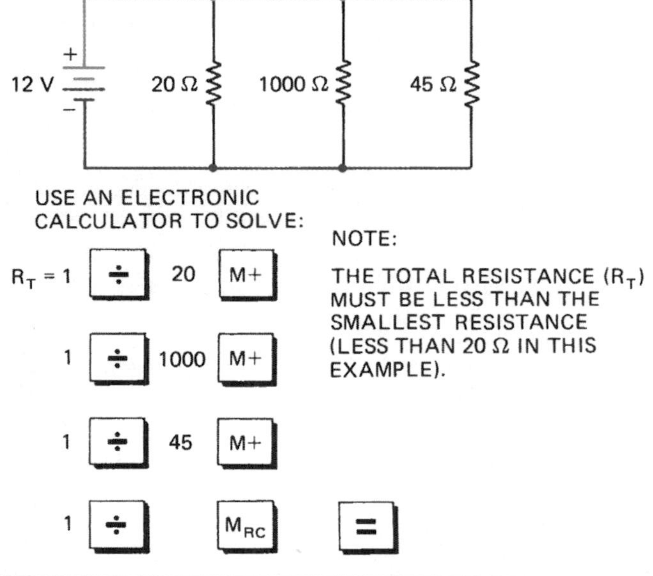

Figure 13–51 Another example of how to use an electronic calculator to determine the total resistance of a parallel circuit. The answer is 13.66 Ω. Notice that the effective resistance of this circuit is less than the resistance of the lowest branch (20 Ω).

Method 5

This method can be easily used whenever two or more resistances connected in parallel are of the same value. See Figure 13–52.

To calculate the total resistance (R_T) of equal-value resistors, divide the number of equal resistors into the value of the resistance.

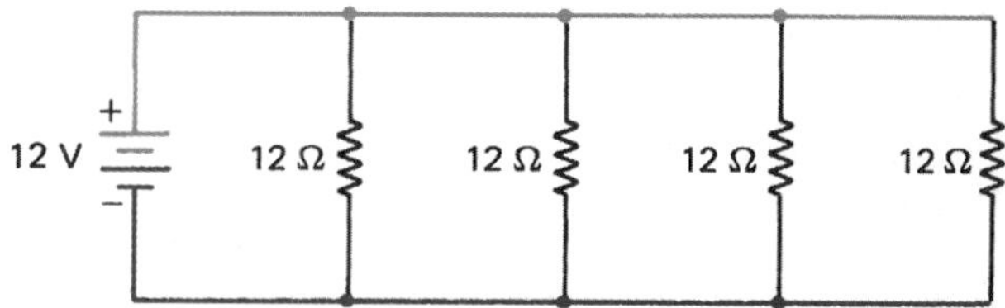

Figure 13–52 A parallel circuit containing four 12 Ω resistors. When a circuit has more than one resistor of equal value, the total resistance can be determined by simply dividing the value of the resistance (12 Ω in this example) by the number of equal-value resistors (4 Ω in this example) to get 3 Ω.

$$R_T = \frac{\text{Value of equal resistance}}{\text{Number of equal resistances}}$$

$$= \frac{12\ \Omega}{4} = 3\ \Omega$$

> **NOTE:** Since most automotive and light-truck electrical circuits involve multiple use of the same resistance, this method is the most useful. For example, if six additional 12 Ω lights were added to a vehicle, the additional lights would represent just 2 Ω of resistance (12 Ω/6 lights = 2 Ω). Therefore, 6 A of additional current would be drawn by the additional lights ($I = E/R$ = 12 V/2 Ω = 6 A).

Determining Total Resistance in a Series-Parallel Circuit

A series-parallel circuit is a combination of a series circuit and a parallel circuit. To determine the total resistance, first work out the resistance of the parallel circuits. Add this value to the resistance(s) of the series circuit to determine the total resistance. Divide the applied voltage by the total resistance to determine the current flow.

Magic Circle

The formulas for calculating any combination of electrical units are shown in Figure 13–53.

CAPACITORS OR CONDENSERS

Capacitors (also called **condensers**) are electrical components that can be used to perform a variety of functions. Electrons can be stored on the inside of a capacitor on two or more conductor plates separated by an insulator called a **dielectric.**

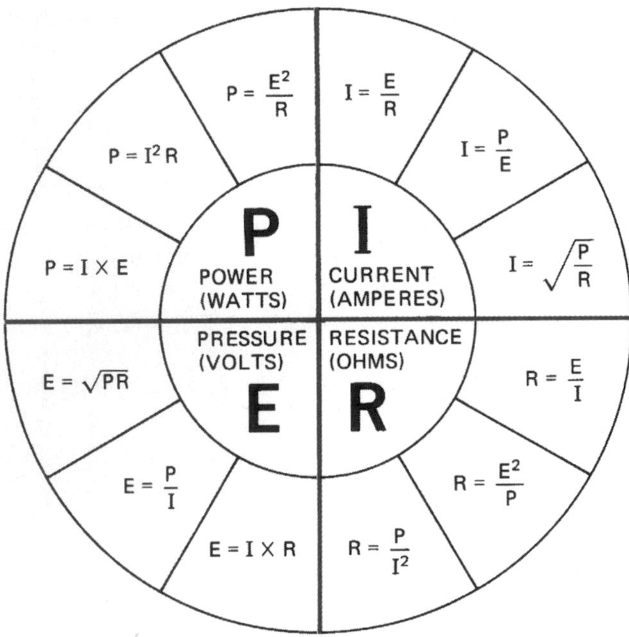

Figure 13–53 "Magic circle" of most of the formulas for problems involving Ohm's law. Each quarter of the "pie" has formulas used to solve for a particular unknown value: current (amperes), in the upper right segment; resistance (ohms), in the lower right; voltage (*E*), in the lower left; and power (watts), in the upper left.

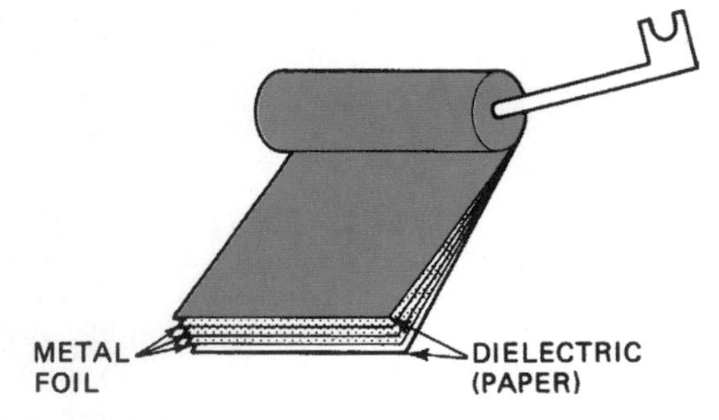

Figure 13–54 A foil and paper condenser (capacitor) can store electrons on the surface of the foil.

If a capacitor is connected to a battery or another electrical power source, it is capable of storing the electrons from the power source. See Figures 13–54 and 13–55. This storing capacity is called **capacitance,** and it is measured in the unit called a **farad,** named for Michael Faraday (1791–1867), an English physicist. A farad is the capacity to store 1 coulomb of electrons at 1 V of potential difference between the plates of the capacitor. This is a very large quantity, so most capacitors for automotive use list values measured in microfarads (one millionth of a farad). A capacitor can pass current that is constantly changing its direction of flow (alternating current, or AC), but blocks the flow of direct current (DC). See Figure 13–56.

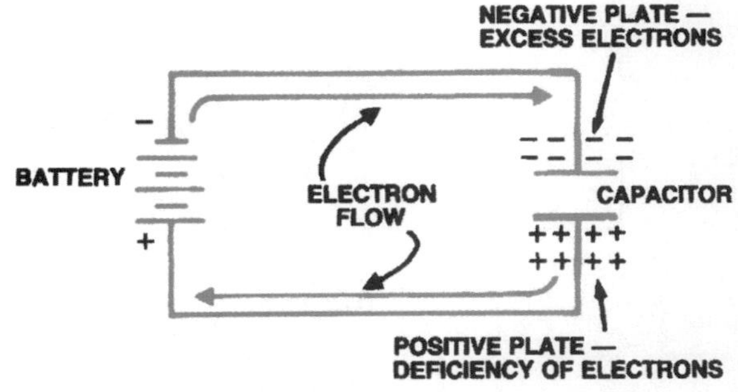

Figure 13–55 As the capacitor is charging, the battery forces electricity through the circuit.

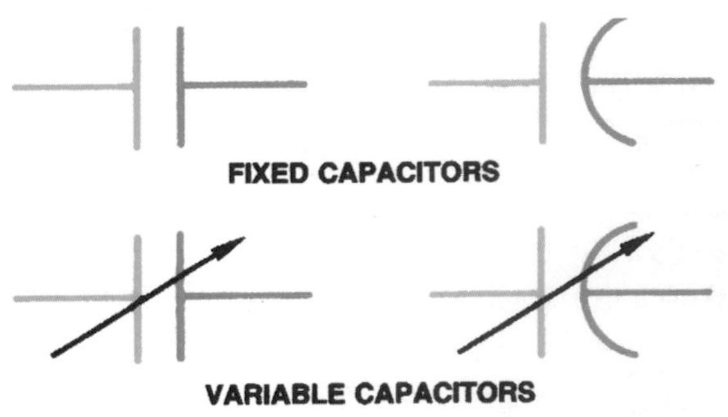

Figure 13–56 Capacitor symbols are shown in electrical diagrams. The negative plate is often shown curved.

TECH TIP

A Capacitor Makes an Excellent Sound System Noise Filter

Interference in a sound system or radio is usually due to alternating current (AC) voltage created somewhere in the vehicle, such as in the AC generator (alternator). By connecting a capacitor (also known as a condenser) to the power lead of the radio or sound system amplifier, the AC voltage passes through the capacitor to the ground where the other end of the capacitor is connected. Therefore, the capacitor provides a path for the AC without affecting the DC power circuit. See Figure 13–57.

MAGNETISM

Like electricity, magnetism is sometimes difficult to visualize. Although electricity and magnetism cannot be seen, the *effects* of both can be seen and felt.

NOTE: Magnetism is extremely important to automotive applications because everything electrical in the automobile, except the lights and the cigarette lighter, works as a result of magnetism.

TECH TIP

Wattage Increases by the Square of the Voltage

The brightness of a light bulb, such as an automotive headlight or courtesy light, depends on the number of watts available. The watt is the unit by which electrical power is measured. If the battery voltage drops, even slightly, the light becomes noticeably dimmer. The formula for calculating power (P) in watts is $P = I \times E$. This can also be expressed as watts = amps × volts.

According to Ohm's law, $I = E/R$. Therefore, E/R can be substituted for I in the previous formula resulting in $P = E/R \times E$ or $P = E^2/R$.

E^2 means E multiplied by itself. A small change in the voltage (E) has a big effect on the total brightness of the bulb. (Remember, household light bulbs are sold according to their wattage.) Therefore, if the voltage to an automotive bulb is reduced, such as by a poor electrical connection, the brightness of the bulb is *greatly* affected. A poor electrical ground causes a voltage drop, and because the sum of the voltage drops must equal the applied voltage (Kirchhoff's law), the voltage at the bulb is reduced and the bulb's brightness is reduced.

Frequently Asked Question ???

How Do You Calculate Current or Voltage If Watts Are Known?

Watts is the unit of electrical power represented by the capital letter P. Watts is calculated by multiplying the volts (E) in the current by the amperes (I), or $P = I \times E$. If watts are known but the voltage is not known, use $E = P / I$.

Because a magnet shows attraction for metal objects such as tacks, nails, and iron filings, it is clear that a force surrounds the magnetic material. Magnetic lines of force are invisible, but when iron filings are placed on a piece of paper held above a magnet, the filings move and then become stationary along a definite pattern formed between and around both the north and south poles. See Figures 13–58 and 13–59. The poles of a magnetic substance act similarly to electrostatic charges: Like poles repel each other, whereas opposite poles are attracted. See Figure 13–60.

TECH TIP

A Cracked Magnet Becomes Two Magnets

Magnets are commonly used in vehicle crankshaft, camshaft, and wheel speed sensors. If a magnet is struck and cracks or breaks, the result is two smaller-strength magnets. Because the strength of the magnetic field is reduced, the sensor output voltage is also reduced. A typical problem occurs when a magnetic crankshaft sensor becomes cracked, resulting in a no-start condition. Sometimes the cracked sensor works well enough to start an engine that is cranking at normal speeds but will not work when the engine is cold. See Figure 13–61.

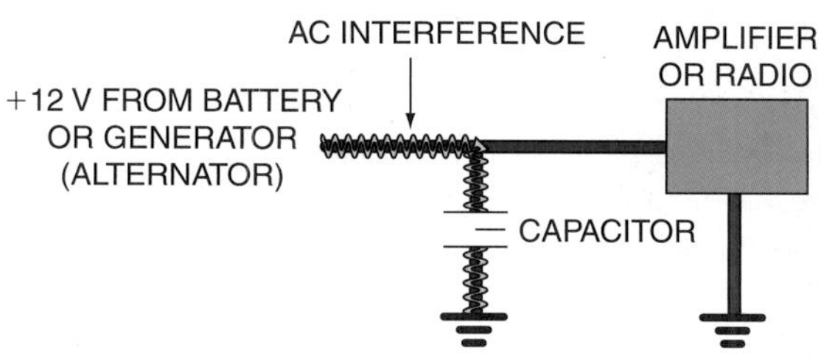

Figure 13–57 A capacitor blocks direct current (DC) but passes alternating current (AC). A capacitor makes a very good noise suppressor because most of the interference is AC and the capacitor will conduct this AC to ground before it can reach the radio or amplifier.

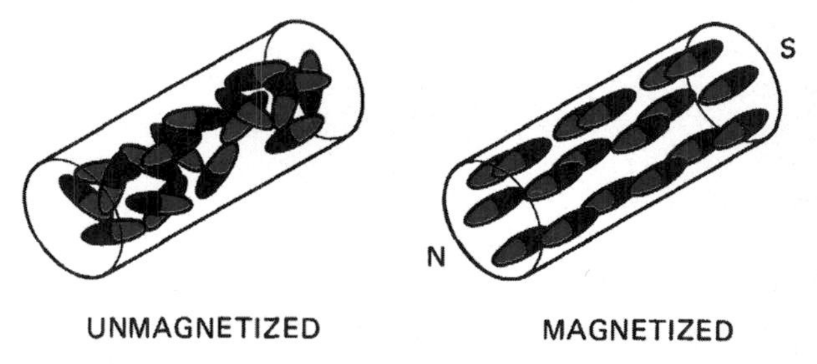

Figure 13–58 When a material is magnetized, the atoms all align in one direction.

Electromagnetism

It was not until about 1820 that it was discovered that a wire carrying an electrical current had an effect on a compass. See Figure 13–62. Until that time,

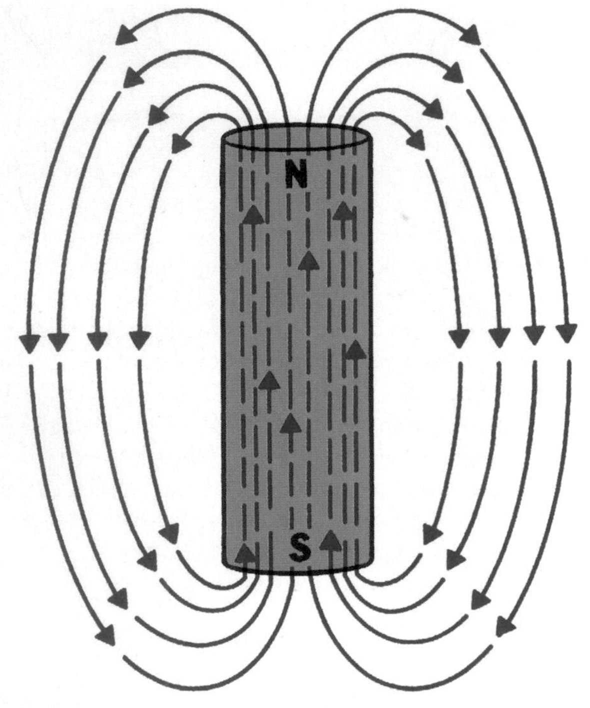

Figure 13–59 Magnetic lines of force leave the north pole and return to the south pole of a bar magnet.

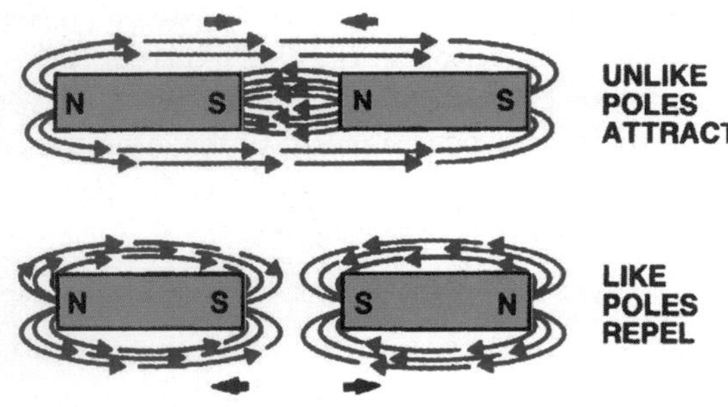

Figure 13–60 Magnetic poles behave like electrically charged particles—unlike poles attract and like poles repel.

the only thing known to affect a compass was a magnetic field. Further study revealed that a magnetic field surrounds any conductor (wire) that carries an electrical current. A magnetic field created by current flow is called **electromagnetism.**

Whenever there is electricity flowing through a conductor, magnetic lines of force are produced around the conductor. If a wire (conductor) is coiled and current is sent through the wire, the same magnetic fields that would surround straight wires combine to form one larger magnetic field with true north and south poles. The strength of a magnetic field can be changed by increasing or decreasing the current flowing through the conductor.

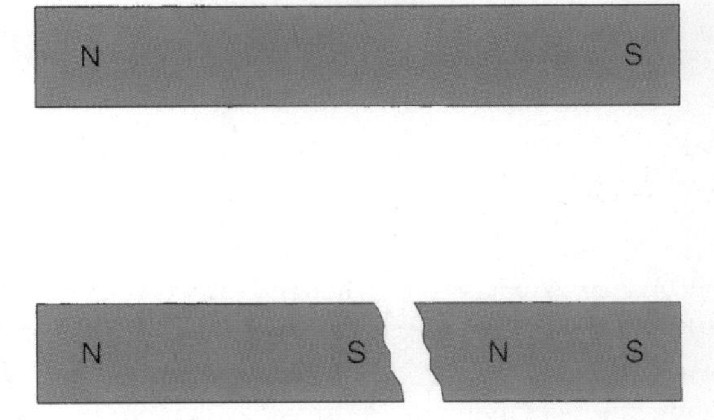

Figure 13–61 If a magnet breaks or is cracked, it becomes two weaker magnets.

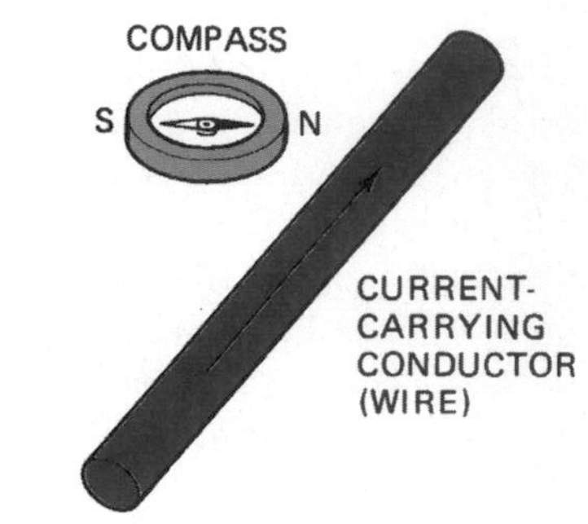

Figure 13–62 Surrounding any conductor carrying an electrical current is a magnetic field.

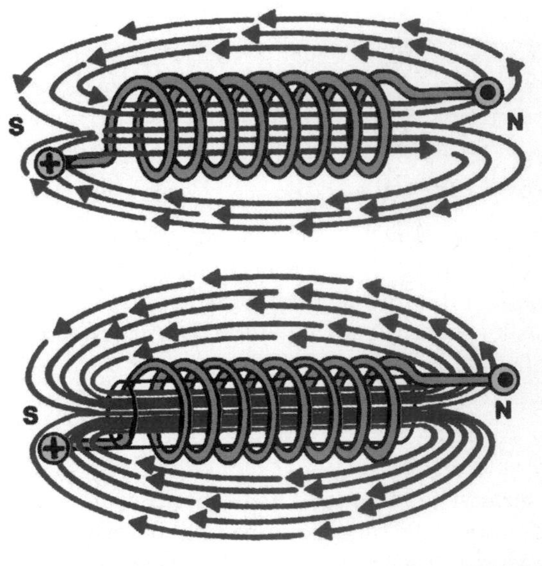

Figure 13–63 An iron core concentrates the magnetic lines of force surrounding a coil.

The iron in the centre of the coil provides an excellent conductor for the magnetic field that travels through the centre of the wire coil. This is the reason all ignition coils use laminated iron cores in their construction. See Figure 13–63.

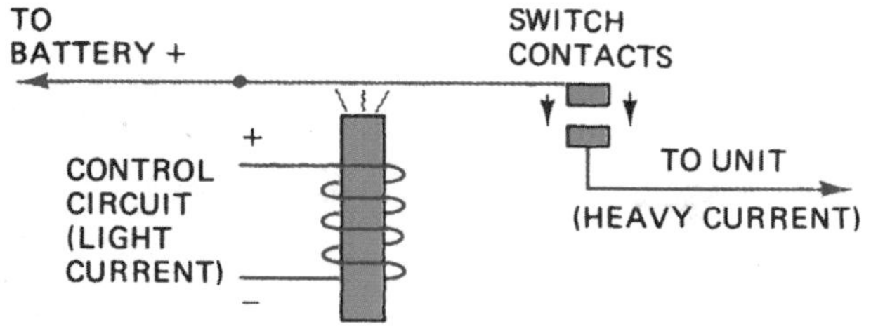

Figure 13–64 Electromagnetic switch. A light current (low amperes) produces an electromagnet and causes the contact points to close. The contact points then conduct a heavy current (high amperes) to an electrical unit.

Figure 13–65 An automotive relay with the cover removed. Note the coil of wire used to create an electromagnet. The electromagnet pulls the movable arm of the relay down when it makes contact and completes the circuit being controlled by the relay.

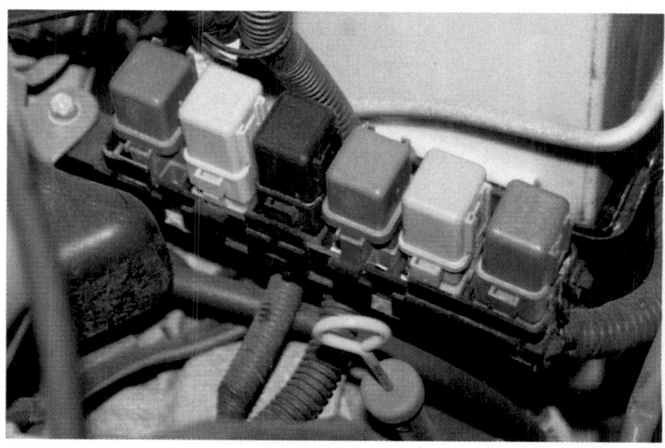

Figure 13–66 A row of relays as found in a vehicle. The different colours represent different ratings and therefore different applications for each colour of relay.

Figure 13–67 Cutaway of a typical automotive solenoid. A solenoid uses a movable core to force a disc into contact with the two terminals of the solenoid.

Electromagnetic Switches

Electromagnets are widely used in automotive electrical systems in the form of electromagnetic switches. An electromagnetic switch is one that opens or closes electrical contacts using an electromagnet. See Figure 13–64.

A low-current electromagnetic switch is usually used to control (open or close) a high-current circuit. For example, an ignition switch circuit (low current) can control a high-current starter motor circuit by using an electromagnetic switch. When the electromagnetic wires are connected to a power source, the resulting magnetic pull on the upper movable contact point forces the switch into contact with the lower contact point. These contact points complete (close) another circuit. Because the electromagnetic switch controls a higher current than the control current, it is often called a **relay:** it relays the control-circuit signal (e.g., "on") to the heavy current in the main circuit.

If an electromagnetic switch has a movable arm (armature), it is called a relay. See Figures 13–65 and 13–66. If an electromagnetic switch uses a movable iron core, it is called a **solenoid.** A solenoid, besides operating as a switch, can also use a movable core to perform mechanical work, such as engaging a starter gear. Solenoids are usually constructed to transfer heavier current than a movable-arm relay. See Figure 13–67. See Chapter 14 for additional information on relays and relay circuits.

Electromagnetic Induction

In 1831, Michael Faraday discovered that electrical energy can be induced from one circuit to another by using magnetic lines of force. When a conductor is moved through a magnetic field, a difference of

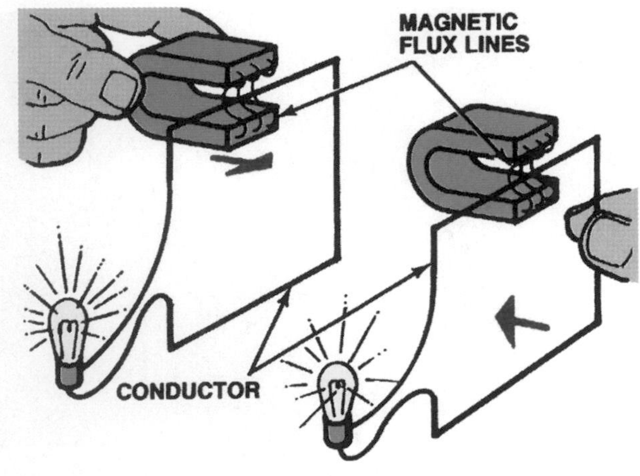

Figure 13–68 Voltage can be induced by the relative motion between a conductor and magnetic lines of force.

potential is set up between the ends of the conductor, and a voltage is induced. This action is called **electromagnetic induction.** See Figure 13–68. This voltage exists only when the magnetic field *or* the conductor is in motion.

The induced voltage can be increased by increasing the *speed* with which the magnetic lines of force cut the conductor, or by increasing *the number of conductors* that are cut. Electromagnetic induction is the principle behind the operation of all ignition systems, coils, starter motors, generators, alternators, and relays. See Figure 13–69.

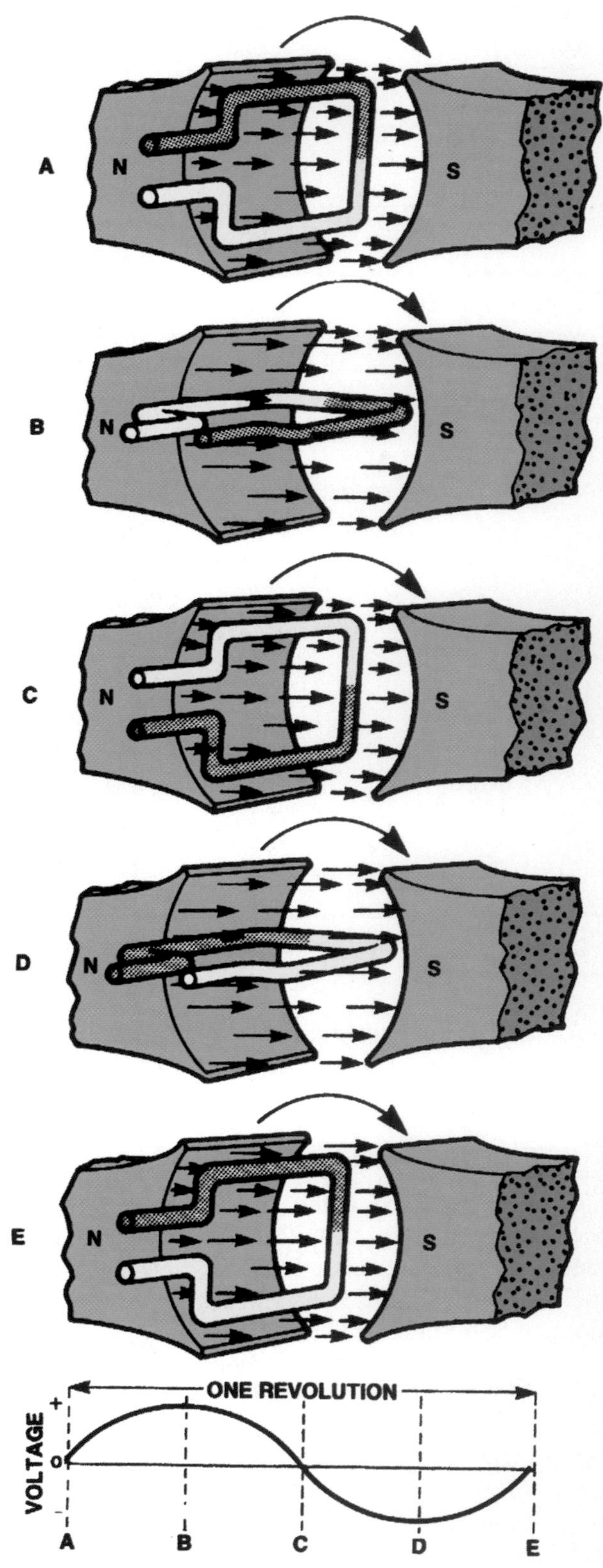

Figure 13–69 Alternating current (AC) voltage can be generated by rotating a loop conductor in a magnetic field. This is the principle of operation of generators (alternators).

ELECTRONIC PRINCIPLES

Electronics is the movement of electrons through solid-state components. The basis of all solid-state components is the semiconductor. **Semiconductors** are materials that contain exactly four electrons in the outer orbit of their atomic structure and are, therefore, neither good conductors nor good insulators. Two examples of semiconductor materials are **germanium** and **silicon,** which have no free electrons to provide current flow.

N-Type Material

N-type material is silicon or germanium that is doped with an element such as *phosphorus, arsenic,* or *antimony,* each having five electrons in its outer orbit. These five electrons are combined with the four electrons of the silicon or germanium to total nine electrons. There is room for only eight electrons in the bonds between the semiconductor atom and the doping atom. This leaves an extra electron per N-atom, and, even though the material is still electrically neutral, the extra electrons tend to repel other electrons outside the material. See Figure 13–70.

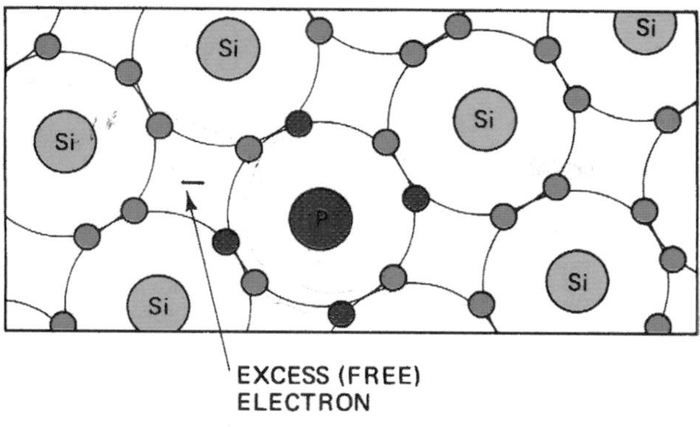

Figure 13–70 N-type material. Silicon (Si) doped with a material such as phosphorus (P) with five electrons in the outer orbit results in an extra free electron.

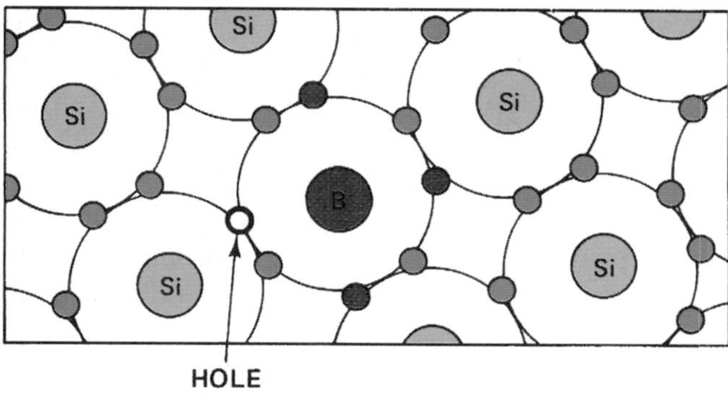

Figure 13–71 P-type material. Silicon (Si) doped with a material such as boron (B) with three electrons in the outer orbit results in a hole capable of attracting an electron.

P-Type Material

P-type material is produced by doping silicon or germanium with the element *boron* or the element *indium.* These impurities have only three electrons in their outer shell and, when combined with the semiconductor material, result in a material with seven electrons, one electron *less* than is required for atomic bonding. This lack of one electron gives the material the ability to attract electrons, even though it still has a neutral charge. The material tends to attract electrons to fill the **holes** for the missing eighth electron in the bond. See Figure 13–71.

Current Carriers

Current flow is expressed as the movement of electrons from one atom to another. In semiconductor and electronic terms, the movement of electrons fills the holes of the P-type material. Therefore, as the holes are filled with electrons, the unfilled holes

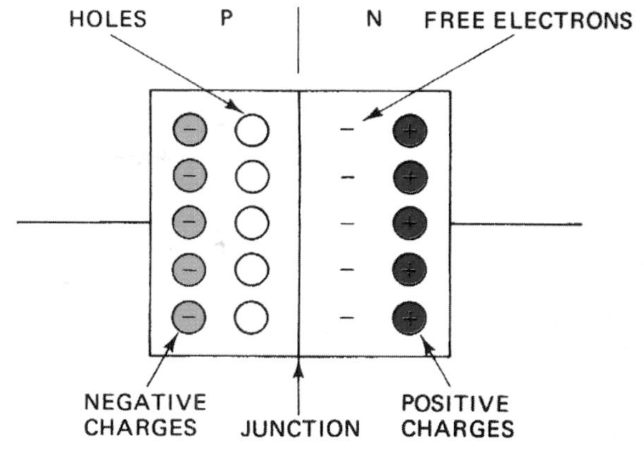

Figure 13–72 Unlike charges attract and the current carriers (electrons and holes) move toward the junction.

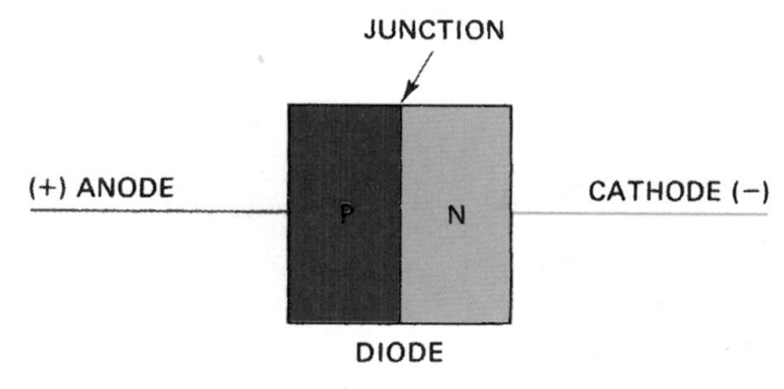

Figure 13–73 A diode is a component with P- and N-type material together. The negative electrode is called the cathode and the positive electrode is called the anode.

move in the opposite direction to the flow of the electrons. See Figure 13–72.

Diodes

A **diode** is an electrical one-way check valve made by combining a P-type material and an N-type material. The region where the two types of material join is called the **junction.** The word *diode* means "having two electrodes." Electrodes are electrical connections. The positive electrode is called the **anode** and the negative electrode is called the **cathode.** See Figure 13–73.

The N-type material has one extra electron, and that can flow into the P-type material, which has a need for electrons to fill its holes. If a battery were connected to the diode positive (+) to P-type material and negative (−) to N-type material, as illustrated in Figure 13–74, current would flow through the diode with low resistance. This condition is called **forward bias.** If the battery connections were reversed, the diode offers very high resistance to current flow, and this condition is called **reverse bias.** See Figure 13–75.

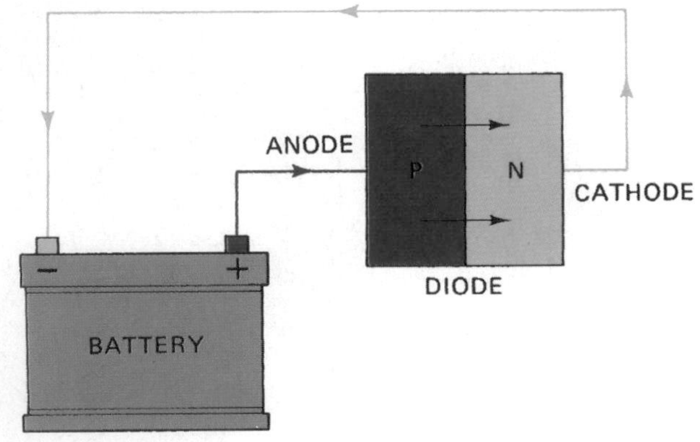

Figure 13–74 Diode connected to a battery with correct polarity (+ to + and − to −). Current flows through the diode. This condition is called forward bias.

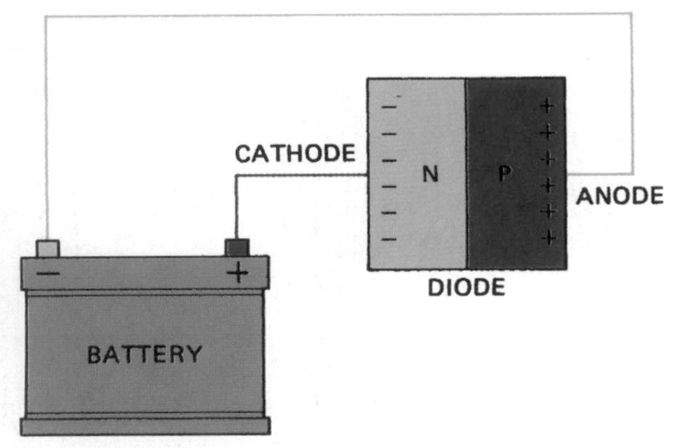

Figure 13–75 Diode connected with reversed polarity. No current flows across the junction between the P-type and N-type material. This connection is called reverse bias.

Frequently Asked Question ???

Which End of a Diode Is Which?

Diodes allow current flow in just one direction. A line is painted around one end of a diode that indicates the cathode (−). See Figure 13–76 for a line drawing of the symbol and the marking on a diode. See Figure 13–77 for a photo of two actual diodes.

Clamping Diodes

Diodes therefore allow current flow only when current of the correct polarity is connected to the circuit. Diodes are used in alternators to rectify AC voltage into DC voltage. Diodes are also used in computer controls, air-conditioning circuits, and many other circuits to prevent possible damage due to reverse current flows that may be generated within the circuit. See Figure 13–78.

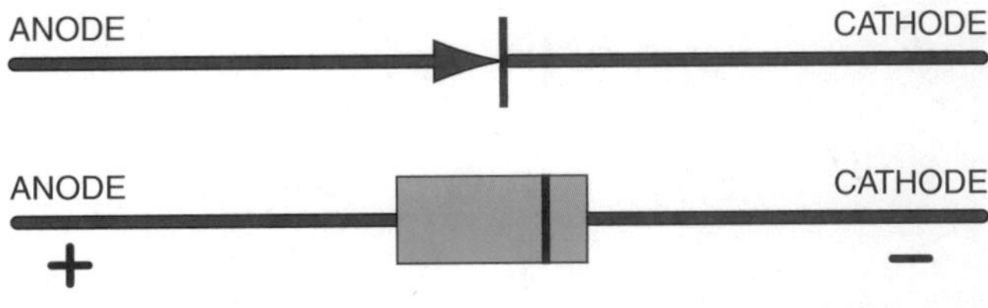

Figure 13–76 A symbol of a diode (top) and the markings on a typical diode (bottom).

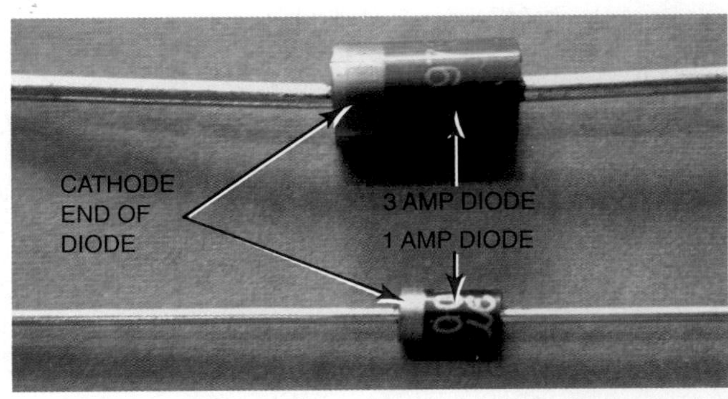

Figure 13–77 Two diodes. The size of a diode is one of the factors that determines how much current in amperes it is designed to control.

Diodes can be used as high-voltage clamping devices when the power is connected to the cathode (−) of the diode. If a coil is pulsed on and off, a high-voltage spike is produced whenever the coil is turned off. To control and direct this possibly damaging high-voltage spike, a diode can be installed across the leads to the coil to redirect the high-voltage spike back through the coil windings to prevent possible damage to the rest of the vehicle's electrical or electronic circuits. See Figure 13–79. Clamping diodes can also be called **de-spiking** or **suppression diodes.**

Zener Diodes

A **zener diode** is a specially constructed diode designed to operate with a reverse-bias current. Zener diodes were named in 1934 for their inventor, Clarence Melvin Zener, an American professor of physics. A zener diode acts like any diode in that it blocks reverse-bias current but only up to a certain voltage. Above this certain voltage (called the **breakdown voltage** or the **zener region**), a zener diode will conduct current without damage to the diode. A zener diode is perfect for voltage regulation. Zener diodes can be constructed for various breakdown voltages and can be used in a variety of automotive and electronic applications, especially for electronic voltage regulators. See Figure 13–80.

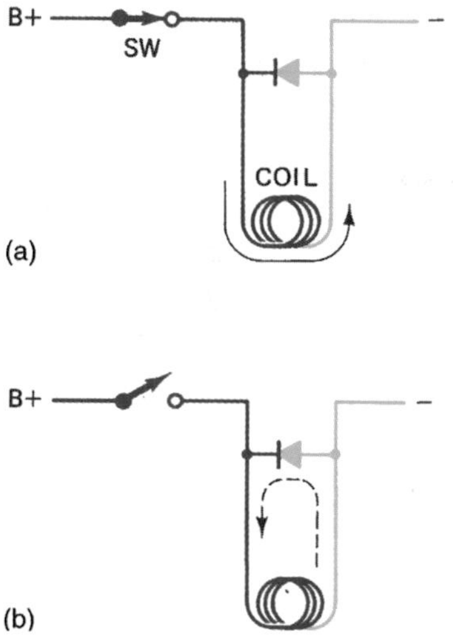

Figure 13–78 (a) Notice that when the coil is being energized, the diode is reverse biased and the current is blocked from passing through the diode. The current flows through the coil in the normal direction.
(b) When the switch is opened, the magnetic field surrounding the coil collapses, producing a high-voltage surge in the reverse polarity of the applied voltage. This voltage surge forward biases the diode, and the surge is dissipated harmlessly back through the windings of the coil.

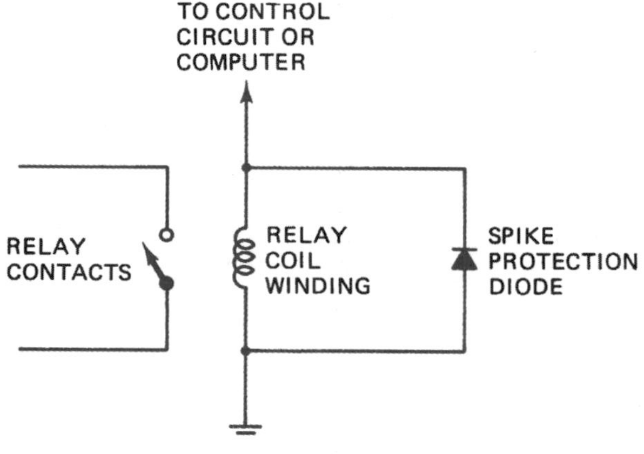

Figure 13–79 Spike protection diodes are commonly used in computer-controlled circuits to prevent damaging high-voltage surges that occur any time current flowing through a coil is stopped.

NOTE: The circuits most likely to be affected by the high-voltage surge, if the diode fails, are the circuits controlling the operation of the AC compressor clutch and related circuits such as those of the blower motor and climate control units.

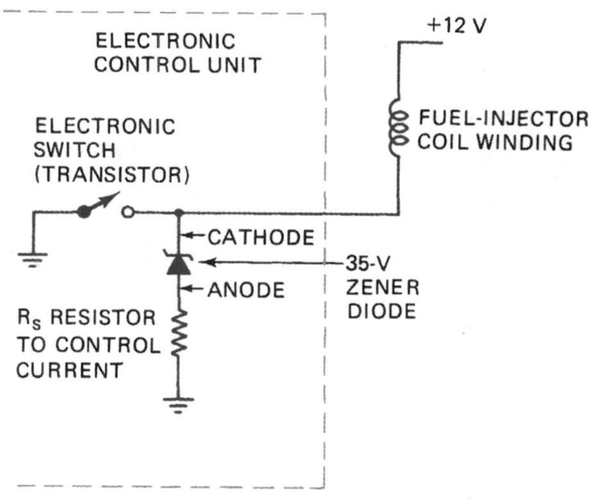

Figure 13–80 A zener diode is commonly used inside automotive computers to protect delicate electronic circuits from high-voltage spikes. A 35-volt zener diode will conduct any voltage spike resulting from the discharge of a coil safely to ground through a current-limiting resistor in series with the zener diode.

TECH TIP

Burn in to Be Sure

A common term heard in the electronic and computer industry is the term **burn in.** "Burn in" means to operate an electronic device, such as a computer, for a period of from several hours to several days.

Most electronic devices fail in infancy, or during the first few hours of operation. This early failure occurs if there is a manufacturing defect, especially at the P-N junction of any semiconductor device. The junction will usually fail after only a few operating cycles.

What does this information mean to the average person? If purchasing a personal or business computer, have the computer burned in before delivery. This step helps ensure that all of the circuits have survived infancy and that the chances of a chip failing are greatly reduced. Display model sound or television equipment may be a good value, because during its operation as a display model, it has been burned in. The automotive service technician should be aware that if a replacement electronic device fails shortly after installation, the problem may be a case of early electronic failure.

NOTE: Whenever there is a failure of a replacement part, the technician should always check for excessive voltage, current flow, or heat to and around the problem component.

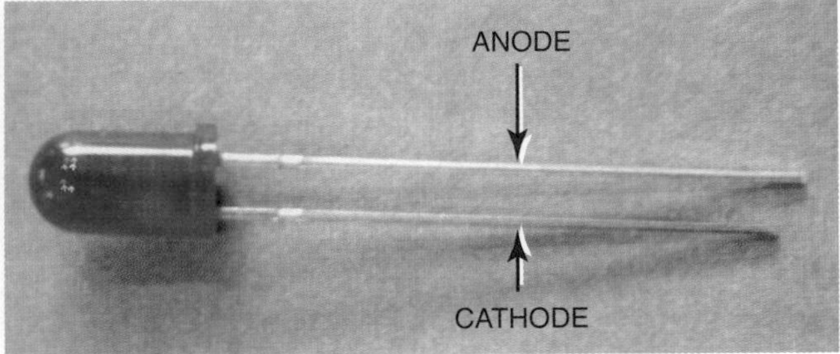

Figure 13–81 A typical light emitting diode (LED). This particular LED is designed with a built-in resistor so that 12 volts DC may be applied directly to the leads without an external resistor. Normally a 300 to 500 Ω 1/2 W resistor is required to be attached in series with the LED to control current flow to about 0.020 A (20 mA) or damage to the P-N junction can occur.

Figure 13–82 A seven-segment LED can be used to display a number or letter.

Light-Emitting Diodes (LED)

All diodes radiate some energy during normal operation. Most diodes radiate heat because of the junction barrier voltage drop (typically 0.6 volt for silicon diodes). **Light-emitting diodes (LEDs)** radiate light when current flows through the diode in the forward-bias direction. See Figure 13–81.

Frequently Asked Question ???

What Is a Seven-Segment LED?

A seven-segment LED is an electric display made from seven long narrow light emitting diodes (LEDs). See Figure 13–82. By lighting various combinations of the seven LEDs, all the numbers from zero to nine and all the letters of the alphabet can be displayed. LED displays require very little electrical power and are durable, which makes them perfect for automotive use.

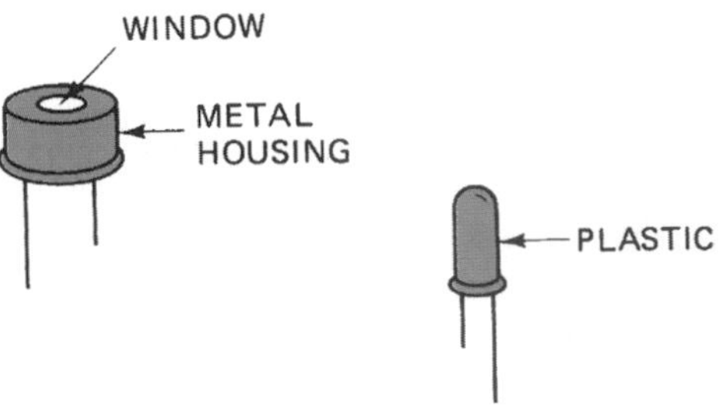

Figure 13–83 Typical photodiodes.

An LED will light only if the voltage at the anode (positive electrode) is at least 1.5 to 2.2 V higher than the voltage at the cathode (negative electrode). LCDs are often used for high-mounted stop lights (the third brake light).

Photodiodes

A **photodiode** is a diode that is sensitive to light. When light energy strikes the diode, electrons are released and the diode will conduct in the forward-bias direction. (The light energy is used to overcome the barrier voltage.)

All P-N junctions emit energy, mostly in the form of heat or light as with an LED. In fact, if an LED is exposed to bright light, a voltage potential is established between the anode and the cathode. Photodiodes are specially constructed to respond to various wavelengths of light with a "window" built into the housing. See Figure 13–83.

Photodiodes are frequently used in steering wheel controls. If several photodiodes are placed on the steering column end and LEDs or photo transistors are placed on the steering wheel side, data can be transmitted between the two moving points without the interference that could be caused by physical-contact types of units.

The resistance across the photodiode decreases as the intensity of the light increases. This characteristic makes the photodiode a useful electronic device for controlling some automotive lighting

Figure 13–84 Symbol for a photodiode. The arrows represent light striking the P-N junction of the photodiode.

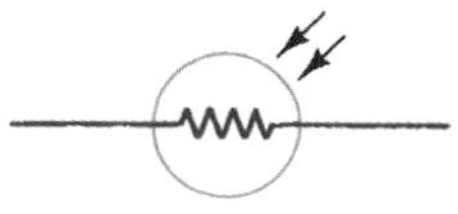

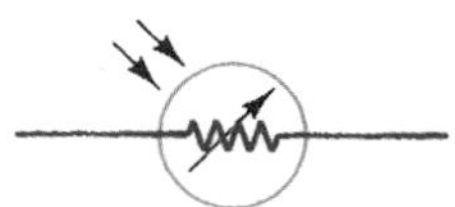

Figure 13–85 Either symbol may be used to represent a photoresistor.

systems. The symbol for a photodiode is shown in Figure 13–84.

Photoresistors

A **photoresistor** is a semiconductor material (usually cadmium sulfide) that changes resistance with the presence or absence of light.

DARK = high resistance
LIGHT = low resistance

Because resistance is reduced when the photoresistor is exposed to light, the photoresistor can be used to control headlight dimmer relays, plus many other nonautomotive applications. See Figure 13–85 for the symbols for a photoresistor.

Thermistors

A **thermistor** is a semiconductor material such as silicon that has been doped to provide a given resistance. When the thermistor is heated, the electrons within the crystal gain energy and electrons are released. This means that a thermistor actually produces a small voltage when heated. If voltage is applied to a thermistor, its resistance decreases because the thermistor itself is acting as a current carrier rather than as a resistor at higher temperatures.

A thermistor is commonly used as a temperature-sensing device for coolant temperature and intake manifold air temperature. Because thermistors operate in a manner opposite to that of a typical conductor, they are called **negative coefficient thermistors (NCT);** their resistance decreases as the temperature increases. Thermistor symbols are shown in Figure 13–86.

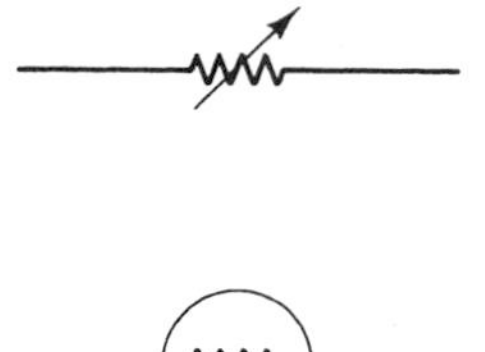

Figure 13–86 Symbols used to represent a thermistor.

Sparks Can Hurt

Never disconnect any electrical device when the ignition key is on and/or current is flowing through the circuit. Surrounding a wire or coil carrying a current is a magnetic field. Whenever the current flow stops, a voltage spike is produced as the magnetic field collapses into the wire or coil. This very high voltage (up to several thousands of volts) can damage delicate electronic devices. Never disconnect any electrical circuit when the ignition switch is in the "on" or "run" position.

TRANSISTORS

A **transistor** is a semiconductor device that can perform the following electrical functions:

1. An electrical switch in a circuit
2. An amplifier of current in a circuit
3. A regulator of current in a circuit

The word *transistor,* derived from the words *transfer* and *resistor,* is used to describe the transfer of current across a resistor.

A transistor is made of three alternating sections or layers of P- and N-type material. See Figure 13–87. A transistor that has P-type material on each end, with N-type material in the centre, is called a **PNP transistor.** Another type, with an arrangement exactly opposite, is an **NPN transistor.**

The centre section of a transistor is called the **base,** and it controls current flow through the transistor. The material at one end of a transistor is called the **emitter,** and the material at the other end is called the **collector.** On all symbols for a transistor, there is an arrow indicating the emitter part of the transistor. The arrow points in the direction of current flow (conventional theory).

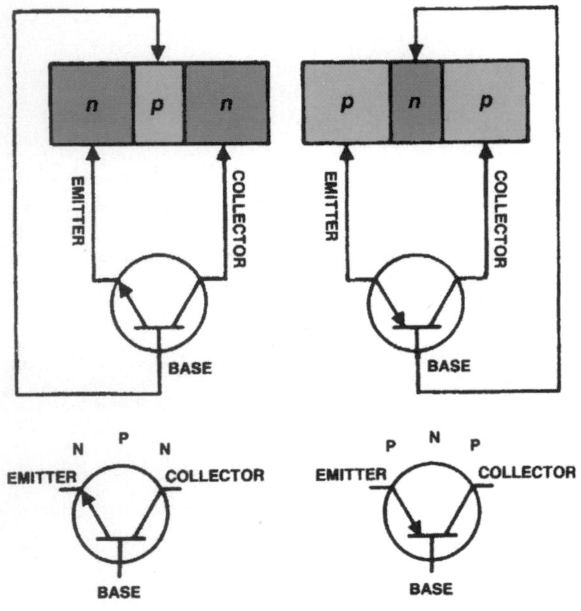

Figure 13–87 Transistor symbols and construction.

> **NOTE:** When an arrowhead appears in any semiconductor symbol, it stands for a P-N junction and it points from the P-type material toward the N-type material. The arrow on a transistor is always attached to the *emitter* side of the transistor.

A transistor will allow current flow if the electrical conditions allow it to switch on, in a manner similar to the working of an electromagnetic relay. If the base current is turned off or on, the current flow from collector to emitter is turned off or on. Think of the emitter/collector path as a heavy current-carrying circuit being controlled by a small current flow in the base. Depending on the type of transistor, grounding the base (PNP) or powering the base (NPN) will turn the transistor on.

Current through the collector and emitter must be limited by the resistance of the device (e.g., fuel injector, solenoid coil) in the circuit or damage to the transistor will occur. A short-circuit in the fuel injector or solenoid coil will cause high current flow through the transistor, which could be destroyed.

The current flowing through a transistor can also be regulated or controlled just as a valve on a water faucet controls the flow of water—by varying the current to the base, the current flowing through the collector and emitter is also controlled. See Figure 13–88.

Phototransistors

Similar in operation to a photodiode, a phototransistor uses light energy to turn on the base of a transistor. A phototransistor is an NPN transistor that has a large exposed base area to permit light to act as the

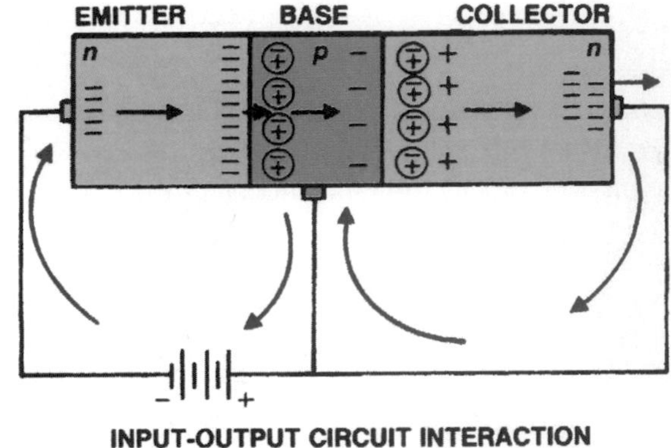

Figure 13–88 When a transistor is forward biased (+ to base of an NPN transistor), electrons from the emitter pass through the base to the collector and greater overall forward current flows. Note that greater reverse current flows in the output circuit because more holes in the collector are filled by free electrons.

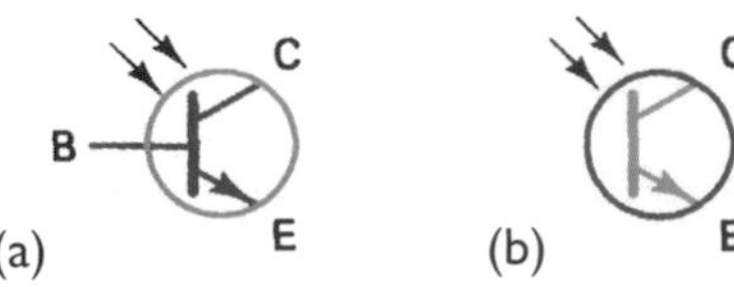

Figure 13–89 Symbols for a phototransistor: (a) uses the line for the base, whereas (b) does not.

control for the transistor. Therefore, a phototransistor may or may not have a base lead. Many phototransistors do not have a base lead; they have only a collector and emitter lead. When the phototransistor is connected to a powered circuit, the light intensity is amplified by the gain of the transistor. Phototransistors are frequently used in steering wheel controls. Figure 13–89 shows phototransistor symbols.

SOLAR CELLS

Solar cells are another type of semiconductor device. In a solar cell, light energy is used to produce a small current flow by dislodging electrons within the structure. Solar cells are stacked and/or grouped in large sections to enable them to supply useful amounts of current.

INTEGRATED CIRCUITS

Integrated circuits are tiny combinations of many transistors, diodes, and capacitors on one plastic-encased **chip.** Today's computers are made up of many integrated circuits (abbreviated IC). These integrated circuits (chips) are not serviceable as individual components. See Figure 13–90. This means that if just one circuit fails, the entire computer has to be replaced. This is why it is so important that

TECH TIP

Electronic Components Do Not Like Three Things

Computers are sensitive electronic devices that can be damaged if subjected to

- **High voltage**—especially static electricity
- **High current (amperes)**—current through a computer circuit is usually limited to one ampere or less
- **High heat**—electronic devices work best when isolated from extreme heat

There is another item that may be of interest. While troubleshooting a computer-related problem, this author found the vehicle computer full of water because of a leaky windshield. So add another item to the list—computers can't swim!

DIAGNOSTIC STORY

The Grand Prix Radio Problem

The owner of a Pontiac Grand Prix complained that the radio would stop working at times. No problem could be found because it occurred just occasionally. Finally, a technician noticed that the seats were covered with wool seat covers. The technician then asked the owner if the problem occurred most often in the winter months when the air is dry. The customer confirmed that the problem only occurred in cold weather and when the seat covers were used. The service technician sprayed anti-static spray on the seat covers and the problem never reoccurred. Obviously, static electricity was created by the driver while sliding in and out of the vehicle across the seat covers. The radio malfunctioned because the static charge caused the internal circuitry to lock up or shut down.

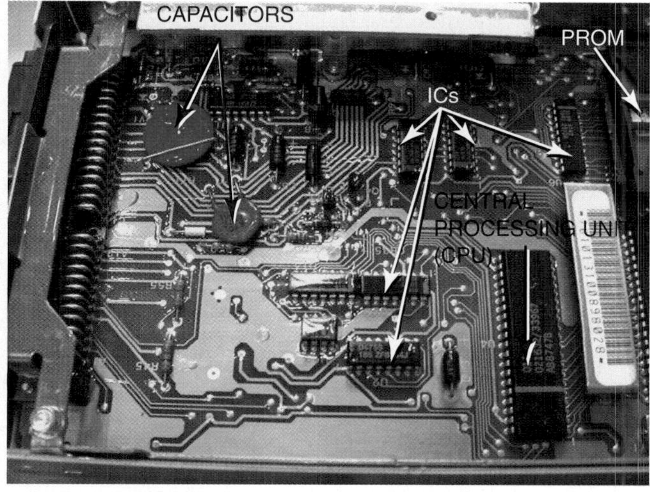

Figure 13–90 A typical automotive computer with the case removed to show all of the various electronic devices and integrated circuits (ICs). The large red and orange devices are ceramic capacitors.

proper procedures be followed to avoid damaging delicate electronic circuits. See the Tech Tip "Electronic Components Do Not Like Three Things."

ELECTROSTATIC DISCHARGE (ESD)

Static charges can build up on the human body whenever we move. The friction of clothing and the movement of shoes against carpet or vinyl floors cause a high voltage to build. Then, when we touch a conductive material, such as a doorknob, the static charge is rapidly discharged. These charges, although just slightly painful to us, can cause severe damage to delicate electronic components. The following are typical static voltages:

If you can feel it, it is at least 3000 volts.
If you can hear it, it is at least 5000 volts.
If you can see it, it is at least 10 000 volts.

Although these voltages seem high, the current, in amperes, is extremely low. However, sensitive electronic components such as vehicle computers, radios, and instrument panel clusters can be ruined if exposed to as little as 30 volts. This is a problem, because harm can be done to components by voltages lower than we can feel. To help prevent damage to components, follow these easy steps:

1. Keep the replacement electronic component in the protective wrapping until just before installation.
2. Before handling any electronic component, ground yourself to a good conductor to drain away any static charge. Use a wrist strap. This fastens around the wrist, similar to a watchband; the strap is attached to a length of wire, which in turn is connected with an alligator clip to a good ground.
3. Do not touch the terminals of electronic components.

If these precautions are observed, ESD damage can be eliminated or reduced. Remember, just because

DIAGNOSTIC STORY

Road salt used in many areas of Canada and the U.S. causes electrical problems when salt water enters wiring connections. Because of this, the connectors used with computer circuit wiring have additional rubber seals to reduce the entrance of foreign substances.

The owner of a full-size domestic vehicle arrived with two concerns: the car did not run well and the windshield kept fogging. When the vehicle was inspected, the technician found the front floor mat saturated with antifreeze. The heater core and hoses are the only items in the cabin supplied with coolant; further inspection at the heater showed no leaks in that area.

The technician then referred to the TSBs (Technical Service Bulletins) for additional information. A bulletin from the manufacturer advised that a number of faulty coolant temperature sensors were leaking internally, allowing antifreeze to pass through the sensor and into the wiring connector. The coolant then continued flowing inside the wire until it reached the computer, flooded the processor and ran onto the floor.

Replacement of the sensor, computer, and some wiring corrected both the rough running and the fogged windshield. When a problem does not appear obvious, TSBs are another avenue for help.

the component works after being touched does not mean that damage has not occurred. Often, a section of the electronic component may be damaged yet will not fail until several days or weeks later.

SUMMARY

1. Electricity is the movement of electrons from one atom to another.
2. Automotive electricity uses the conventional theory that electricity flows from positive to negative.
3. The ampere is the measure of the amount of current flow.
4. Voltage is the unit of electrical pressure.
5. The ohm is the unit of electrical resistance.
6. All complete electrical circuits have a power source (such as a battery), a circuit protection device (such as a fuse), a power-side wire or path, an electrical load, a ground return path, and a switch or a control device.
7. A short-to-voltage involves a copper-to-copper connection and usually affects more than one circuit.
8. A short-to-ground involves a copper-to-steel connection and usually causes the fuse to blow.
9. An open is a break in the circuit resulting in no current flow at all through the circuit.
10. The greater the resistance, the greater the voltage drop.
11. In a series circuit, the current is constant throughout but the voltage varies.
12. Most automotive electrical circuits are connected in parallel.
13. Ohm's law states: "It requires 1 volt to push 1 ampere through 1 ohm of resistance."
14. Capacitors can store electrons, and this storage capacity is measured in farads.
15. Magnetism and electricity are related. Electricity creates magnetism and magnetism creates electricity.
16. Diodes can be used to direct and control current flow in circuits and to provide despiking protection.
17. Transistors are electronic relays that can also amplify.
18. Never touch the terminals of a computer or electronic device; static electricity can damage electronic components.

REVIEW QUESTIONS

1. List the parts of a complete electrical circuit.
2. Describe the difference between a short-to-voltage and a short-to-ground.
3. Describe the difference between an open and a short.
4. State Ohm's law.
5. Explain what happens to current flow (amperes) and wattage if the resistance of a circuit is increased because of a corroded connection.
6. Define electricity.
7. Define ampere, volt, and ohm.
8. List three functions that a capacitor (condenser) can perform.
9. Explain the difference between P-type material and N-type material.
10. Describe how a diode can be used to suppress high-voltage surges in automotive components or circuits containing a coil.
11. Explain how a transistor works.
12. List the precautions that all service technicians should take in order to avoid damage to electronic and computer circuits.

RED SEAL CERTIFICATION-TYPE QUESTIONS

1. If an insulated wire rubbed through a part of the insulation and the wire conductor touched the steel body of a vehicle, the type of failure would be called ________.
   - **a.** A short-to-voltage
   - **b.** A short-to-ground
   - **c.** An open
   - **d.** A chassis ground

2. If two insulated wires were to melt together where the copper conductors touched each other, the type of failure would be called
   a. A short-to-voltage
   b. A short-to-ground
   c. An open
   d. A floating ground
3. If 12 V are being applied to a resistance of 3 Ω, _______ A will flow.
   a. 12
   b. 3
   c. 4
   d. 36
4. Like charges _______.
   a. Attract
   b. Repel
   c. Neutralize each other
   d. Add
5. If an accessory such as an additional light is spliced into an existing circuit in parallel, what happens?
   a. The current increases in the circuit.
   b. The current decreases in the circuit.
   c. The voltage drops in the circuit.
   d. The resistance of the circuit increases.
6. Which unit of electricity does the work in a circuit?
   a. A volt
   b. An ampere
   c. An ohm
   d. A coulomb
7. As temperature increases, _______.
   a. The resistance of a conductor decreases
   b. The resistance of a conductor increases
   c. The resistance of a conductor remains the same
   d. The voltage of the conductor decreases
8. The _______ is a unit of electrical pressure.
   a. Coulomb
   b. Volt
   c. Ampere
   d. Ohm
9. Capacitors are measured in units called _______.
   a. Watts
   b. Farads
   c. Coulombs
   d. Dielectrics
10. A transistor is a(n):
   a. One-way electrical check valve
   b. Form of light-emitting diode
   c. NTC thermistor
   d. Electronic switch in a circuit

14

Meters, Scopes, Wiring, and Schematics

OBJECTIVES: After studying Chapter 14, you should be able to:

1. Prepare for the interprovincial Red Seal certification examination in Appendix III (Electrical/Electronic Systems) on the topics covered in this chapter.
2. Use a digital meter to measure voltage, resistance, and current in a circuit.
3. Explain the wire gauge number system.
4. Describe how fusible links protect electrical circuits.
5. Discuss wiring schematics.
6. List the steps for performing a proper wire repair.

Today's vehicles contain kilometres of wire and hundreds of connections. The service technician has to be able to read and understand wiring diagrams to be able to diagnose and repair electrical problems.

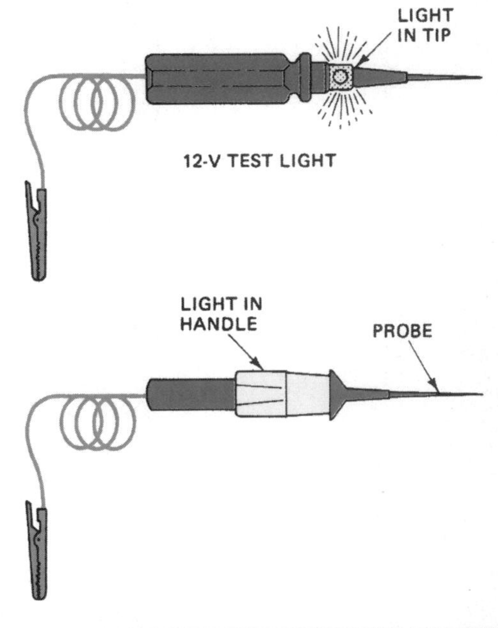

Figure 14–1 Examples of probe-type test lights.

TEST LIGHTS

A test light is simply a light bulb with a probe and a ground wire attached. See Figure 14–1. It is used to detect voltage potential (6 to 12 volts) at various test points. Battery voltage cannot be seen or felt and can be detected only with test equipment.

A test light can be purchased or homemade. See Figure 14–2. A purchased test light could be labelled as a "6- to 12-volt test light." Do not purchase a test light designed for household current (110 or 220 volts). It will not light with 12 volts.

Continuity Test Lights

A continuity light is similar to a test light but includes a battery for self-power. A continuity light lights whenever it is connected to both ends of a wire that has continuity or that is not broken. See Figure 14–3.

CAUTION: The use of a continuity test light is not recommended on any electronic circuit, because a continuity light contains a battery and applies voltage, and so it may harm delicate electronic components.

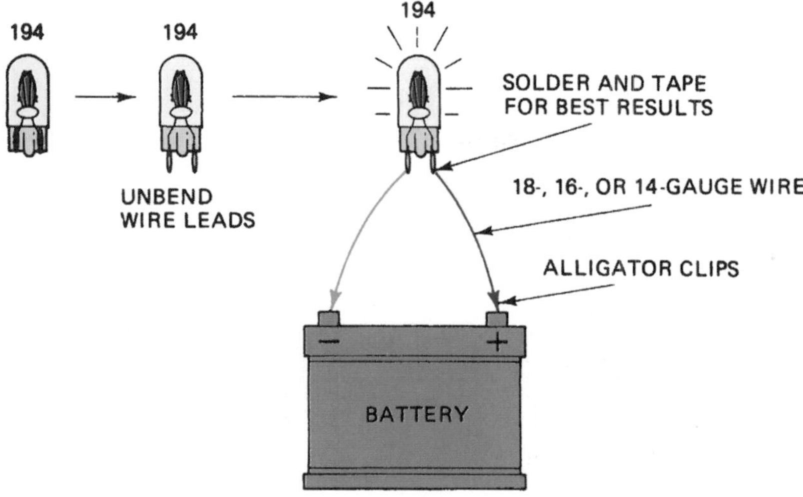

Figure 14–2 Homemade test light. A #194 bulb is the type normally used for side marker lights and is readily available at most automotive supply stores.

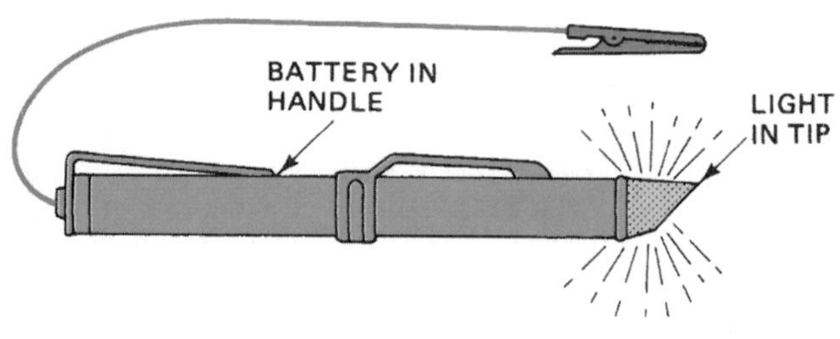

Figure 14–3 A continuity light should not be used on computer circuits because the applied voltage can damage delicate electronic components or circuits.

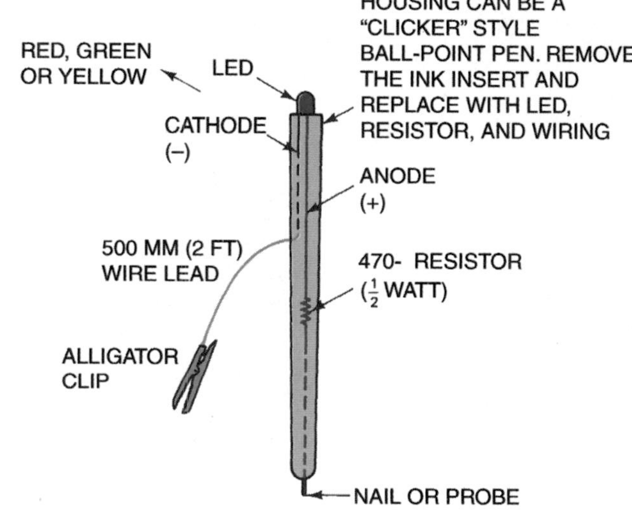

Figure 14–4 High-impedance test light. An LED test light can be easily made using low-cost components and an old ink pen. With the 470 ohm resistor in series with the LED, this tester only draws 0.025 amperes (25 milliamperes) from the circuit being tested. This low current draw helps assure the technician that the circuit or component being tested will not be damaged by excessive current flow.

LED Test Light

Another type of test light uses an LED instead of a standard automotive bulb for a visual indication of voltage. An LED test light requires only about 25 milliamperes (0.025 amperes) to light, and therefore it can be used on electronic circuits as well as on standard circuits. See Figure 14–4 for construction details.

DIGITAL MULTIMETERS

Digital multimeter (DMM) and *digital volt-ohm-milliammeter (DVOM)* are terms commonly used for electronic high-impedance test meters. High-impedance meters, required for measuring computer circuits, are digital meters; however, not all digital meters have the required 10 MΩ (10 million ohms) of internal resistance. *Analog (needle-type) meters are almost always lower than* 10 MΩ *and should not be used to measure any computer circuit* unless recommended by the vehicle manufacturer. A high-impedance meter can be used to measure any automotive circuit within the ranges of the meter. See Figures 14–5 through 14–7.

Measuring Voltage

A **voltmeter** measures the *pressure* or potential of electricity in units of volts. A voltmeter is connected to a circuit in parallel. All voltmeters have a large built-in resistance so that the current flow through the meter will not affect the circuit being tested or the meter.

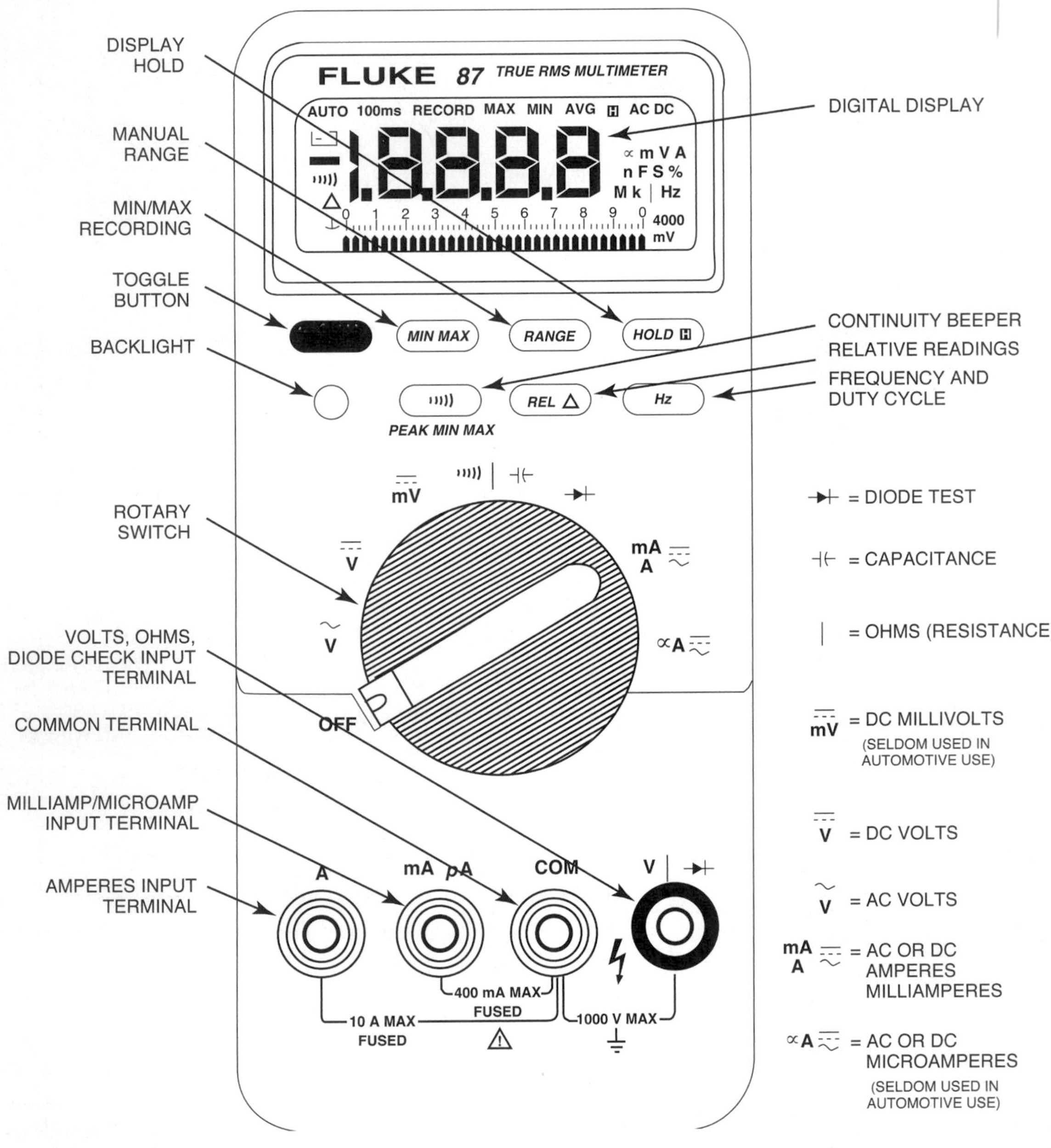

Figure 14–5 Typical digital multimeter. The black meter lead always is placed in the COM terminal. Except when measuring the current in amperes, the red meter test lead remains in the VΩ terminal.

SYMBOL	MEANING
AC	Alternating current or voltage
DC	Direct current or voltage
V	Volts
mV	Millivolts (1/1000 volts)
A	Ampere (amps). Current
mA	Milliampere (1/1000 amps)
%	Percent (for duty cycle readings only)
Ω	Ohms. Resistance
kΩ	Kilohm (1000 ohms). Resistance
MΩ	Megohm (1,000,000 ohms). Resistance
Hz	Hertz (1 cycle/sec). Frequency
kHz	Kilohertz (1000 cycles/sec). Frequency
RPM 1	Revolutions/minute. Counting one cycle per spark
RPM 2	Revolutions/minute. Counting 2 cycles per spark
ms	Milliseconds (1/1000 sec) for Pulse Width measurements.

Figure 14–6 Common abbreviations used on the display face of many digital multimeters. (Courtesy of Fluke Corporation)

SYSTEM & COMPONENTS	MEASUREMENT TYPES				
	Voltage Presence & Level	Voltage Drop	Current (Amps)	Resistance (Ohms)	Frequency (Hz)
Charging System					
AC Generators	•		•		•
Connectors	•	•		•	
Diodes		•		•	
Regulators	•				•
Cooling System					
Connectors	•	•		•	
Fan Motors	•		•	•	
Relays	•	•		•	
Temperature Switches	•	•		•	
Ignition System					
Coils	•			•	
Condensors	•			•	
Connectors	•	•		•	
Contact Set (points)	•			•	
MAF Sensors	•			•	
Magnetic Pick-up	•		•	•	
MAP/BP Sensors	•			•	•
O_2 Sensors	•			•	
Starting System					
Batteries	•	•			
Connectors		•	•		
Interlocks			•		
Solenoids	•	•		•	
Starters	•	•	•		

Figure 14–7 A summary chart indicating what measurement type may be used to test which vehicle system. (Courtesy of Fluke Corporation)

Most digital meters have an internal resistance of 10 MΩ or more on the voltmeter scale only. This is called the **impedance** of the meter and represents the total internal resistance of the meter circuit due to internal coils, capacitors, and resistors. See Figure 14–8. Digital multimeters are usually the best choice for testing electrical and electronic circuits; however, an analog meter may still be specified for some tests.

> **NOTE:** Analog (needle-type) voltmeters are used to access diagnostic trouble codes on certain models of Ford, Mitsubishi, DaimlerChrysler imports, and others. When the voltmeter is connected to the appropriate circuit, the needle begins to sweep across the dial. Counting the needle sweeps identifies the code.

Measuring Resistance

An **ohmmeter** measures the resistance in ohms of a component or circuit section when no current is flowing through the circuit. An ohmmeter contains a battery (or other power source). When the leads are connected to a component, current flows through the test leads and the difference in voltage (voltage drop) between the leads is measured as resistance. Zero ohms on the scale means no resistance between the test leads, indicating that there is continuity or a continuous path for the current to flow in a closed circuit. Infinity means no connection, as in an open circuit.

With a closed circuit (low ohms), maximum current from the built-in battery of the meter causes a low reading, whereas an open circuit prevents any current from flowing. Different meters have different ways of indicating infinity resistance, or a reading higher than the scale allows. For example, most meters read "OL," meaning "over limit," whereas others may show a number 1 or 3 on the left side of the display. See Figures 14–9 through 14–11. To summarize, open and zero readings are as follows:

0.00 Ω = zero resistance
OL = an open circuit (no current flows)

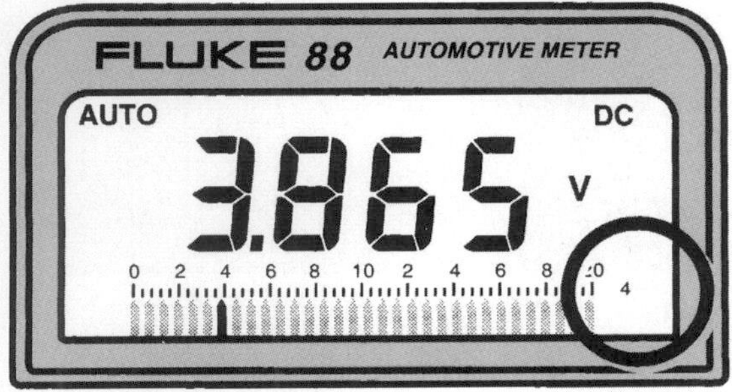

Since the signal your meter's reading is below 4 volts, the meter autoranges to the 4-volt scale. In this scale, the meter provides you with three decimal places.

(a)

When the voltage exceeded 4 volts, the meter autoranges into the 40-volt scale. The decimal point moves one place to the right, leaving you with only two decimal places.

(b)

Figure 14–8 A typical auto ranging digital multimeter automatically selects the proper scale to read the voltage being tested. The scale selected is usually displayed on the meter face. (a) Note that the display indicates "4," meaning that this range can read up to 4 volts. (b) The range is now set to the 40-volt scale, meaning that the meter can read up to 40 volts on the scale. Any reading above this level will cause the meter to reset to a higher scale. If not set on auto ranging, the meter display would indicate OL if a reading exceeds the limit of the scale selected. (Courtesy of Fluke Corporation)

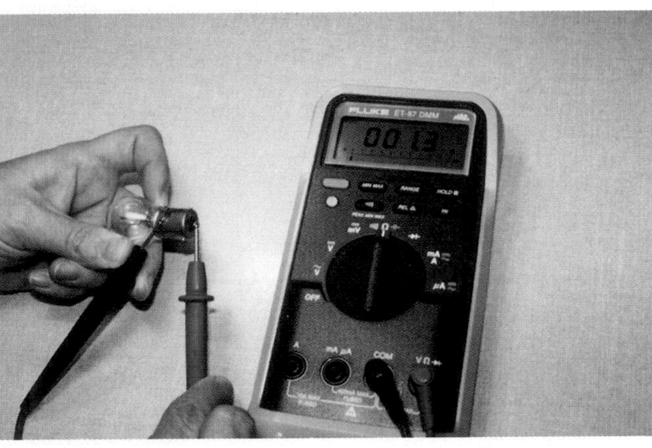

Figure 14–9 Using a digital multimeter set to read ohms (Ω) to test this light bulb. The meter reads the resistance of the filament.

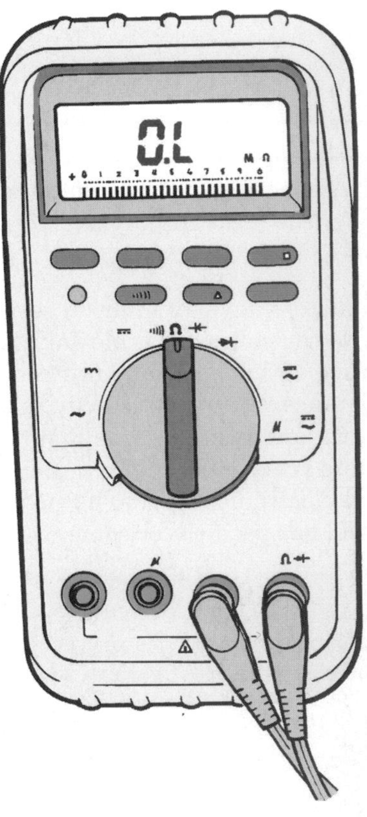

Figure 14–10 Typical digital multimeter showing OL (over limit) on the readout with the ohms (Ω) unit selected. This usually means that the unit being measured is open (infinite resistance) and has no continuity.

HINT: Although ohmmeters are excellent instruments for checking component or circuit resistance, they are of little value when testing a high current circuit. As an example, the large battery cables used with cranking systems would indicate almost no resistance when tested with an ohmmeter, even if the cable was badly frayed. The few remaining strands would carry the small current required to operate the ohmmeter, but not the high current needed to operate the starter.

Voltage drop testing with a voltmeter is a better choice; remember—higher resistance causes a greater voltage drop.

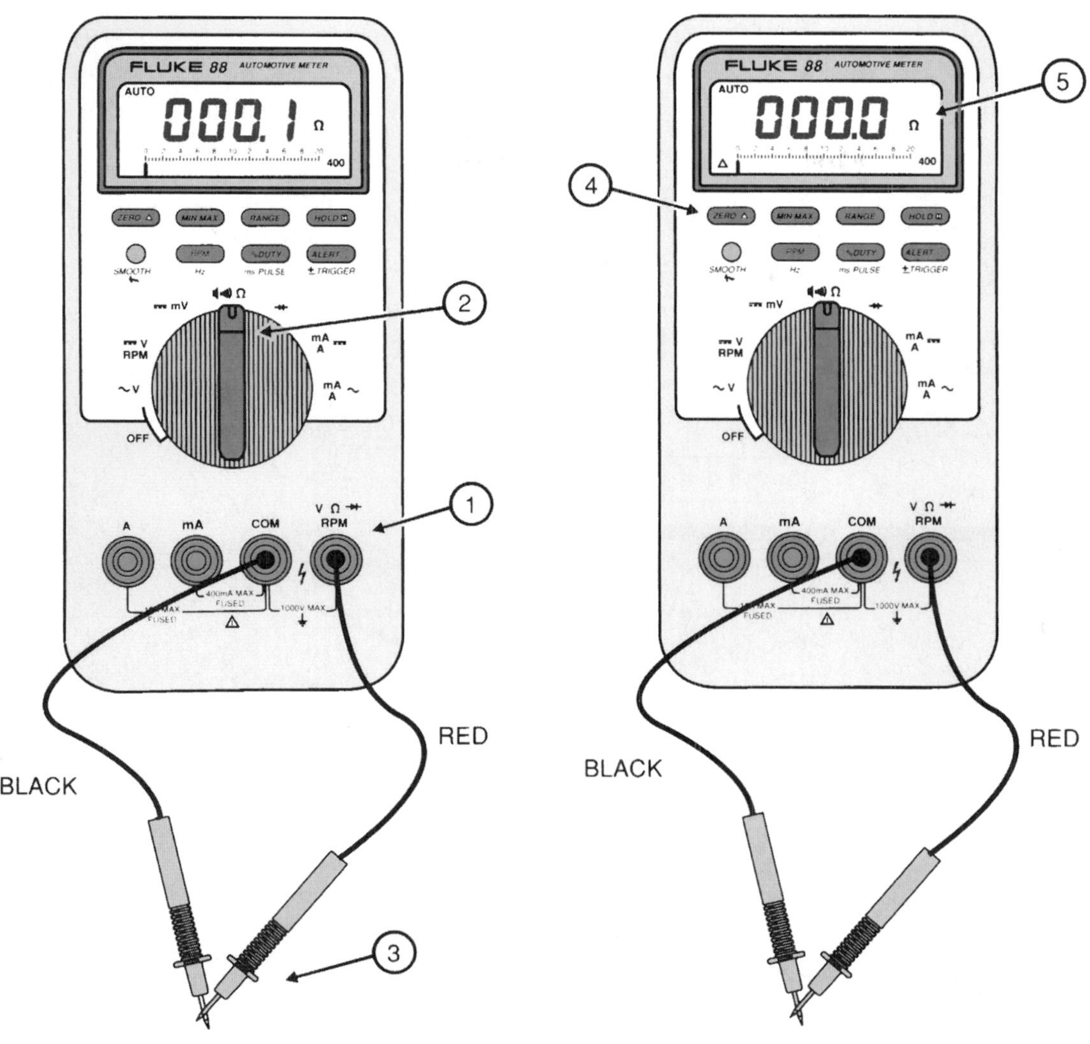

Figure 14–11 Many digital multimeters can have the display indicate zero to compensate for test lead resistance. (1) Connect leads in the VΩ and COM meter terminals. (2) Select the Ω scale. (3) Touch the two meter leads together. (4) Push the "zero" or "relative" button on the meter. (5) The meter display will now indicate zero ohms of resistance. (Courtesy of Fluke Corporation)

Frequently Asked Question ???

How Much Voltage Does an Ohmmeter Apply?

Most digital meters that are set to measure ohms (resistance) apply a voltage of from 0.3 volt to 1.0 volt to the component being measured. The voltage comes from the meter itself to measure the resistance. Two things are important to remember about an ohmmeter.

1. The component or circuit must be disconnected from any electrical circuit while the resistance is being measured.
2. Because the meter itself applies a voltage (even though it is relatively low), a meter set to measure ohms can damage electronic circuits. Computer or electronic chips can be easily damaged if subjected to only a few milliamperes of current similar to the amount an ohmmeter applies when a resistance measurement is being performed.

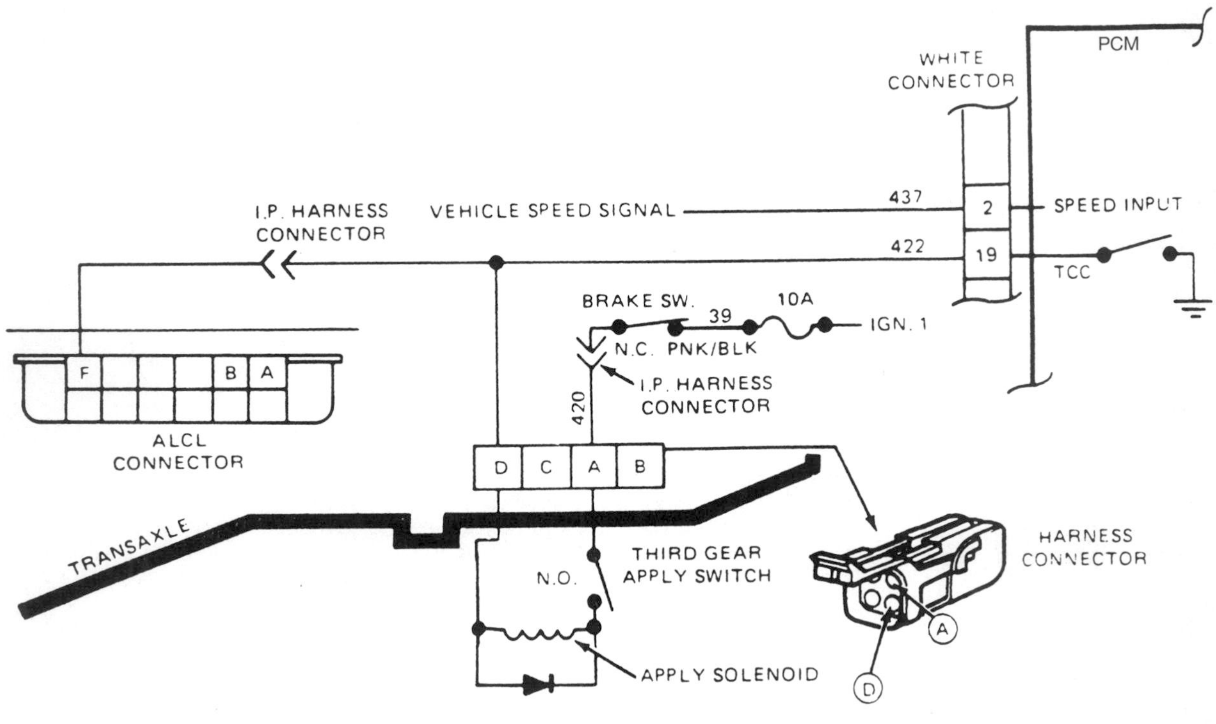

Figure 14–12 This wiring diagram for a computer controlled lock-up torque converter uses electrical and electronic symbols to identify circuit components. (Courtesy General Motors)

TECH TIP

Why Reverse Meter Leads?

The schematic of a lock-up torque-converter clutch circuit is identified in Figure 14–12. We begin at the ignition switch.

Fused battery power from the ignition switch is supplied to the converter clutch-apply solenoid after going through the brake (pedal) switch and the third gear-apply switch (closes in third gear). After the apply solenoid, the current continues on to the PCM (Powertrain Control Module), where it flows to ground when the TCC transistor, shown as a single-pole switch, is turned on.

When the transistor turns off to deactivate the converter, the magnetic field around the apply solenoid coil collapses, which induces a very high voltage into the coil. This high voltage, if allowed to reach the PCM, could damage the TCC transistor.

Note the clamping (spike) diode built into the apply solenoid. When the induced voltage exceeds the 12 volts apply voltage, current now flows back through the clamping diode; this relieves the high voltage and the transistor is protected.

We know that a short circuit inside the apply solenoid coil will lower the coil resistance, which allows higher current flow. Excess current will also damage the TCC transistor. The shop manual tells us that the apply solenoid coil must be tested for low resistance if the PCM has failed. It must measure 20 ohms or more to limit current flow. But how do we check the clamping diode? We could use the diode function found on some digital multimeters, but here's a simpler way.

Most DMMs will read the same resistance of the coil (solenoid out of the vehicle), even if the test leads are reversed. In our example, both readings are 22 ohms.

When we perform the same test with a larger analog ohmmeter, we find a reading, again, of 22 ohms; reverse the leads and the reading drops to 16 ohms. What happened?

The higher voltage from the analog meter turned "on" the clamping diode. The lower voltage of the DMM was not high enough to activate the diode. Germanium diodes require about 0.3 volt to turn on and silicon diodes about 0.7 volt. The difference in the readings indicates that both the solenoid coil and the clamping diode are fine; the same reading in both directions tells us the diode is bad.

CAUTION: Be extremely careful of ohmmeters around air-bag (supplemental restraint system) circuits; it is possible to activate the air bag with an ohmmeter. The bag could cause major injuries, or even kill you, if it deploys. Follow the service manual instructions in detail before diagnosing these systems.

CAUTION: An ammeter must be installed in the circuit to measure the current flow in the circuit. If a meter set to read amperes is connected in parallel, such as across a battery, the meter or the leads may be destroyed by the current available across the battery. Some digital multimeters (DMM) beep if the unit selection does not match the test lead connection on the meter. However, in a noisy shop, this beep sound may not be heard.

Measuring Amperes

An **ammeter** measures the flow of current through a complete circuit in units of amperes. The ammeter has to be installed in the circuit (in series) so that it can measure all the current flow in that circuit, just as a water flow meter would measure the amount of water flow (cubic feet per minute, for example).

Digital meters require that the meter leads be moved to the ammeter terminals. Most digital meters have an ampere scale that can accommodate a maximum of 10 amperes. See Figure 14–13 and the Tech Tip "Fuse Your Meter Leads!"

Many ammeters are the **inductive** type, as shown in Figure 14–14. This means that the meter probe surrounds the wire(s) carrying the current and measures the strength of the magnetic field that surrounds any conductor carrying a current.

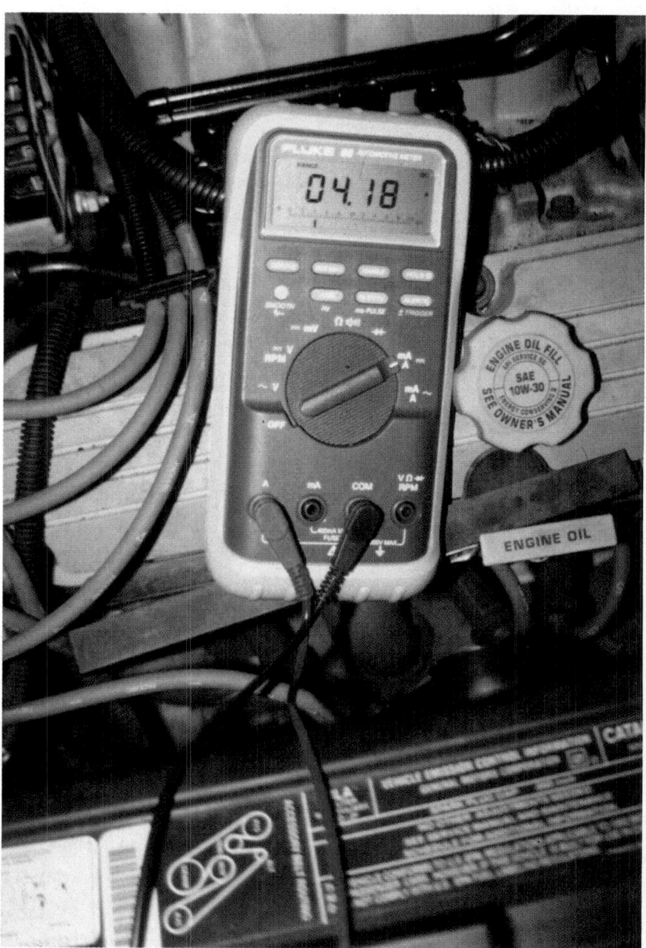

Figure 14–13 A digital multimeter set to read DC amperes. Note that the red lead is placed in the far left-hand socket of the meter. The meter is displaying the current flow (4.18 A) through the electric fuel pump on this General Motors 3800 V-6 engine.

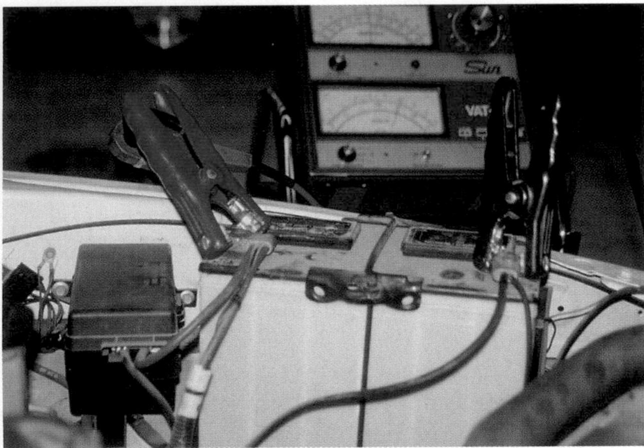

Figure 14–14 An inductive ammeter such as this SUN VAT-40 is commonly used to measure current in the starting (cranking) and charging circuits.

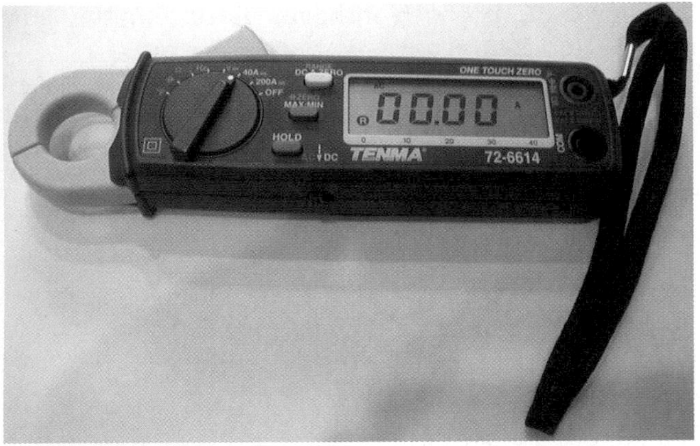

Figure 14–15 A typical mini clamp-on-type digital multimeter. This meter is capable of measuring alternating current (AC) and direct current (DC) without requiring that the circuit be disconnected to install the meter in series. The jaws are simply placed over the wire and current flow through the circuit is displayed.

AC/DC CLAMP-ON DIGITAL MULTIMETER

An AC/DC clamp-on digital multimeter (DMM) is a very useful meter to use for automotive diagnostic work. See Figures 14–15 and 14–16.

The major advantage of the clamp-on type meter is that there is no need to break the circuit to measure current (amperes). Simply clamp the jaws of the meter around the power lead(s) or ground lead(s) of the component being measured and read the display. Most clamp-on meters can also measure AC current, which is helpful in the diagnosis of a generator (alternator) problem. See Chapter 17 for details on generators and charging circuit diagnosis. Volts, ohms, frequency, and temperature can also be measured with the typical clamp-on DMM.

HINT: Many clamp-on ammeters are not capable of measuring small amounts of current, such as the milliampere drain from a battery that goes dead in one or two weeks. Try this:

Take a coil of wire (or make your own) and count 50 turns. Solder a wire and alligator clip to each end of the coil. Place the coil, in series, into the circuit you are testing. Position the inductive clamp of the ammeter around all 50 loops; the ammeter will now read the current flow, times 50, i.e., 50 mA actual current flow will now read 2.5 A.

Any number of loops, 5, 10, 25, 50, 100 may be used; always remember to divide your reading by the number of loops to determine the actual amperage.

Obviously, adding the additional resistance for the coil into the circuit will reduce current flow; this does not make a major change when measuring milliamperes, but higher current readings will be skewed.

TECH TIP

Fuse Your Meter Leads!

Most digital meters include an ammeter capability. When reading amperes, the leads of the meter must be changed from volts or ohms (V or Ω) to amperes (A), milliamperes (mA), or microamperes (μA).

A common problem may then occur the next time voltage is measured. Although the technician may switch the selector to read volts, often the leads are not switched back to the volt or ohm position. Because the ammeter lead position results in zero ohms of resistance to current flow through the meter, the meter or the fuse inside the meter will be destroyed if the meter is connected to a battery. Many meter fuses are expensive and difficult to find. See Figure 14–17.

To avoid this problem, simply solder an inline blade-fuse holder into one meter lead. Do not think that this technique is necessary only for beginners. Experienced technicians often get in a hurry and forget to switch the lead. A blade fuse is faster, easier, and less expensive to replace than a meter fuse or the meter itself. Also, if the soldering is done properly, the addition of an inline fuse holder and fuse does not increase the resistance of the meter leads. All meter leads have some resistance. If the meter is measuring very low resistance, touch the two leads together and read the resistance (usually only a couple of tenths of an ohm). Simply subtract the resistance of the leads from the resistance of the component being measured.

Figure 14–16 An AC and DC current clamp such as the one shown can be used with a regular digital multimeter. The ampere probe contains a separate battery and electronic circuit that converts the amperage reading into a millivolt (mV) signal.

Figure 14–17 Note the blade-type fuse holder soldered in series with one of the meter leads. A 10 ampere fuse helps protect the internal meter fuse (if equipped) and the meter itself from damage that might result from excessive current flow if accidentally used incorrectly.

TECH TIP

"OL" Does Not Mean the Meter Is Reading "Nothing"

Beginning technicians are often confused by the meaning of the display on a digital meter. When asked what the meter is reading when OL is displayed on the meter face, the response is often "nothing." Many meters indicate OL on the display to indicate *over limit* or *over load.* "Over limit" simply means that the reading is over the maximum that can be displayed for the selected range. For example, the meter will display OL if 12 volts are being measured but the meter has been set to read a maximum of 4 volts.

Autoranging meters adjust the range to match what is being measured. Here OL means a value higher than the meter can read (unlikely on the voltage scale for automobile usage), or infinity when measuring resistance (ohms). Therefore, OL means infinity when measuring resistance, or an open circuit is being indicated. The meter will read 00.0 if the resistance is zero, so "nothing" in this case indicates continuity (zero resistance), whereas OL indicates infinite resistance. Therefore, when talking with another technician about a meter reading, make sure you know exactly what the reading on the face of the meter means. Also be sure that you are connecting the meter leads correctly. See Figure 14–18.

ELECTRICAL UNIT PREFIXES

Electrical units are measured in numbers such as 12 V, 150 A, and 470 Ω. Large units over 1000 may be expressed in kilo units. **Kilo (k)** means 1000. See Figure 14–19.

1100 volts = 1.1 kV
4700 ohms = 4.7 kΩ

If the value is over 1 million (1 000 000), then the prefix **mega (M)** is often used. For example,

1 100 000 volts = 1.1 MV
4 700 000 ohms = 4.7 MΩ

Sometimes a circuit conducts so little current that a smaller unit of measure is required. Small units of measure expressed in 1/1000 are prefixed by **milli (m).** The **micro** unit is represented by the Greek letter *mu* (μ). One microampere is one millionth (1/1 000 000) of an ampere. To summarize:

mega (M) = 1 000 000 (decimal point 6 places to the right = 1 000 000)

kilo (k) = 1,000 (decimal point 3 places to the right = 1000)

milli (m) = 1/1000 (decimal point 3 places to the left = 0.001)

micro (μ) = 1/1 000 000 (decimal point 6 places to the left = 0.000 001)

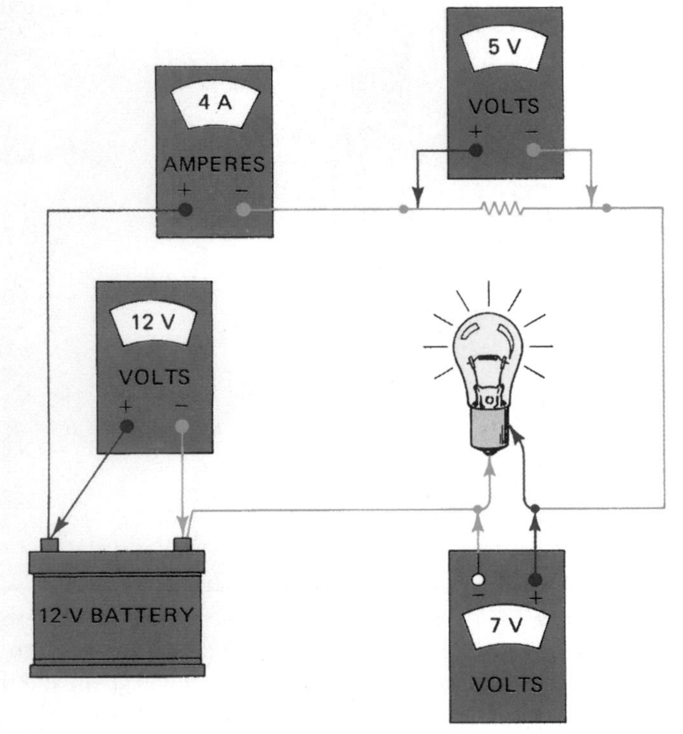

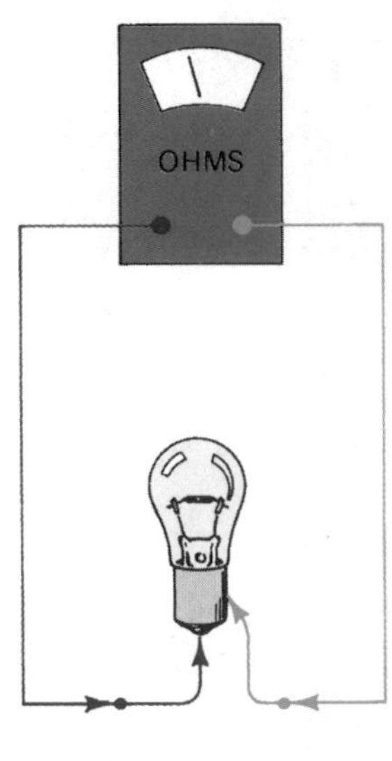

AMMETER

1. Connected in series IN a circuit according to polarity.
2. Measures current flow.
3. Used in a closed circuit.

VOLTMETER

1. Connected in parallel to a circuit or part of a circuit according to polarity.
2. Measures voltage drop:
   This is the difference between voltage at its two leads.
3. Used in a closed circuit.

OHMMETER

1. Has its own supply of power.
2. USED ONLY WHEN UNIT IS DISCONNECTED from its original circuit.
3. Measures resistance directly on meter.
4. Low ohms means continuity.
5. Infinity reading means open circuit.

Figure 14–18 Summary of test meter hookup.

> **HINT:** Lowercase m equals a small unit (milli), whereas a capital M represents a large unit (mega).

These prefixes can be confusing because most digital meters can express values in more than one unit, especially if the meter is autoranging. For example, an ammeter reading may show 36.7 mA on autoranging. When the scale is changed to amperes ("A" in the window of the display), the number displayed will be 0.037 A. Note that the resolution (precision) of the value is reduced.

To From	Mega	Kilo	Base	Milli	Micro
Mega	0 places	3 places to the right	6 places to the right	9 places to the right	12 places to the right
Kilo	3 places to the left	0 places	3 places to the right	6 places to the right	9 places to the right
Base	6 places to the left	3 places to the left	0 places	3 places to the right	6 places to the right
Milli	9 places to the left	6 places to the left	3 places to the left	0 places	3 places to the right
Micro	12 places to the left	9 places to the left	6 places to the left	3 places to the left	0 places

The symbol on the right side of the display tells you what range your meter's in. Ω means the display is the resistance in ohms; kΩ means ohms times 1000, and MΩ is ohms times 1 000 000.

Ω = ohms

If the only symbol on the display is the ohms symbol, the reading on the display is exactly the resistance in ohms.

kΩ = kilohms = ohms times 1000

A "k" in front of the ohms symbol means "kilohms"; the reading on the display is in kilohms. You have to multiply the reading on the display by 1000 to get the resistance in ohms.

MΩ = megohms = ohms times 1 000 000

An "M" in front of the ohms symbol means "megohms"; the reading on the display is in megohms. You have to multiply by one million (1 000 000) to get the resistance in ohms.

Figure 14–19 Always look at the meter display when a measurement is being made, especially if using an autoranging meter. (Courtesy of Fluke Corporation)

HINT: Always check the face of the meter display for the unit being measured. To best understand what is being displayed on the face of a digital meter, select a manual scale and move the selector until *whole units appear,* such as "A" for amperes instead of "mA" for milliamperes.

HOW TO READ DIGITAL METERS

Getting to know and use a digital meter takes time and practice. The first step is to read, understand, and follow all safety and operational instructions that come with the meter. Use of the meter usually involves the following steps.

1. *Select the proper unit of electricity for what is being measured:* volts, ohms (resistance), or amperes (amount of current flow). If the meter is not autoranging, select the proper scale for the anticipated reading. For example, if a 12 V battery is being measured, select a meter reading

TECH TIP

Think of Money

Digital meter displays can often be confusing. The display for a battery measured as 12 1/2 volts would be 12.50 volts, just as $12.50 is 12 dollars and 50 cents. A 1/2 volt reading on a digital meter will be displayed as 0.50 volt, just as $.50 is half of a dollar.

It is more confusing when low values are displayed. For example, if a voltage reading is 0.063 volts, an autoranging meter will display 63 millivolts (63 mV) or 63/1000 of a volt, or $63 out of $1000. (It takes 1000 mV to equal 1 V.) Or think of millivolts as one-tenth of a cent, with one volt being $1.00. Therefore, 630 mV are equal to $0.63 out of a dollar (630 tenths of a cent, or 63 cents).

To avoid confusion, try to manually range the meter to read base units (whole volts). If the meter is ranged to base unit volts, 63 mV would be displayed as 0.063 or maybe just 0.06, depending on the display capabilities of the meter.

range that is higher than the voltage but not too high. A 20 or 30 volt range will accurately show the voltage of a 12 volt battery. If a 1000 volt scale is selected, a 12 volt reading may not be accurate.

2. *Place the meter leads into the proper input terminals.*
   - The black lead usually is inserted into the common (COM) terminal. This meter lead usually stays in this location for all meter functions.
   - The red lead is inserted into the volt, ohm, or diode check terminal usually labeled "V Ω," when voltage, resistance, or diodes are being measured.
   - When current flow in amperes is being measured, most digital meters require that the red test lead be inserted in the ammeter terminal, usually labeled "A" or "mA."

CAUTION: If the meter leads are inserted into ammeter terminals, even though the selector is set to volts, the meter may be damaged or an internal fuse may blow if the test leads touch both terminals of a battery.

3. *Measure the component being tested.* Carefully note the decimal point and the unit on the face of the meter.
   - *Correct scale.* A 12 volt battery is measured with a low voltage scale selected. The proper reading of 12.0 is given.
   - *Incorrect scale.* A 12 volt battery is measured with a high voltage scale selected. Use of the incorrect scale results in a reading of 0.012.

   If a 12 volt battery is measured with an autoranging meter, the correct reading of 12.0 is given. "AUTO" and "V" should show on the face of the meter.

4. *Interpret the reading.* This is especially difficult on auto ranging meters, where the meter itself selects the proper scale. The following are two examples of different readings.
   - A voltage drop is being measured. The specifications indicate a maximum voltage drop of 0.2 volt. The meter reads "AUTO" and "43.6 mV." This reading means that the voltage drop is 0.0436 volt, or 43.6 mV, which is far lower than the 0.2 volt (200 mV). Because the number showing on the meter face is much larger than the specifications, however, many beginner technicians are led to believe that the voltage drop is excessive.

HINT: Pay attention to the units displayed on the meter face and convert to whole units.

   - The resistance of a spark plug wire is being measured. If the wire is okay, its resistance should be less than 330 Ω per 10 mm of length (10 kΩ/ft). The wire being tested is 900 mm (3 ft) long, making a maximum allowable resistance of 30 kΩ. The meter reads "AUTO" and "14.85 kΩ." This reading is equivalent to 14 850 Ω.

Because this reading is well below the specified maximum allowable, the spark plug wire is okay.

Resolution, Digits, and Counts

Resolution refers to how small or fine a measurement the meter can make. By knowing the resolution of a DMM you can determine whether the meter could measure down to only 1 volt or down to 1 millivolt (1/1000 of a volt).

You would not buy a ruler marked in centimetre or inch segments if you had to measure down to 1 millimetre or 1/16 in. A thermometer that only measures in whole degrees is not much use when your normal temperature is 37.0°C (98.6°F). You need a thermometer with 0.1° resolution.

The terms *digits* and *counts* are used to describe a meter's resolution. DMMs are grouped by the number of counts or digits they display. A 3 1/2-digit meter can display three full digits ranging from 0 to 9, and one "half" digit which displays only a 1 or is left

TECH TIP 

Purchase a Digital Meter That Will Work for Automotive Use

Try to purchase a digital meter that is capable of reading the following:

- DC volts
- AC volts
- DC amperes (up to 10 A or more is helpful)
- Ohms (Ω) up to 40 MΩ (40 million ohms)
- Diode check

Additional features for advanced automotive diagnosis include:

- Frequency [hertz (Hz)]
- Temperature probe (F° and/or C°)
- Pulse width [millisecond (ms)]
- Duty cycle (%)
- 10 MΩ impedance

If working on older model vehicles, select a meter that includes:

- RPM (engine speed)
- Dwell (degrees)

blank. A 3 1/2-digit meter will display up to 1999 counts of resolution. A 4 1/2-digit meter can display up to 19 000 counts of resolution.

It is more precise to describe a meter by counts of resolution rather than by 3 1/2 or 4 1/2 digits. Some 3 1/2-digit meters have enhanced resolution of up to 3200 or 4000 counts.

Meters with more counts offer better resolution for certain measurements. For example, a 1999 count meter will not be able to measure down to a tenth of a volt when measuring 200 volts or more. See Figure 14–20. However, a 3200 count meter will display a tenth of a volt up to 320 volts. Digits displayed to the far right of the display may at times flicker or constantly change. This is called *digit rattle* and represents a changing voltage being measured on the ground (COM terminal of the meter lead). High-quality meters are designed to reject this unwanted voltage.

Accuracy

Accuracy is the largest allowable error that will occur under specific operating conditions. In other words, it is an indication of how close the DMM's displayed measurement is to the actual value of the signal being measured.

Figure 14–20 This meter display shows 052.2 volts (AC). Notice that the zero beside the 5 indicates that the meter can read over 100 volts AC with a resolution of 0.1 volt.

Accuracy for a DMM is usually expressed as a percent of reading. An accuracy of ±1 percent of reading means that for a displayed reading of 100.0 V, the actual value of the voltage could be anywhere between 99.0 V to 101.0 V. Thus, a lower percent of accuracy is better.

- Unacceptable = 1.00%
- Okay = 0.50% (1/2%)
- Good = 0.25% (1/4%)
- Excellent = 0.10% (1/10%)

For example, if a battery had 12.6 volts, a meter could read between the following, based on its accuracy.

±0.1%:	high	=	12.61
	low	=	12.59
±0.25%:	high	=	12.63
	low	=	12.57
±0.50%:	high	=	12.66
	low	=	12.54
±1.00%:	high	=	12.73
	low	=	12.47

Before you purchase a meter, check the accuracy. Accuracy is usually indicated on the specifications sheet for the meter.

ANALOG VERSUS DIGITAL STORAGE OSCILLOSCOPE

An **oscilloscope** (usually called a **scope**) is a visual voltmeter with a timer (clock) that shows when a voltage changes. An *analog scope* uses a **cathode ray tube (CRT)** similar to a television screen to display voltage patterns. The scope screen displays the electrical signal constantly. A *digital scope* commonly uses a liquid crystal display (LCD), but a CRT may also be used on some digital scopes. A digital scope takes samples of the signals that can be stopped or stored; hence the term **digital storage oscilloscope** or **DSO.** Because an analog scope displays all voltage signals and does not take samples, it cannot miss something that occurs. A digital storage scope can miss glitches that may occur between samples. This is why a DSO with a high "sampling rate" is preferred.

NOTE: Some digital storage scopes such as the Fluke 98 increase the capture rate to 25 million (25 000 000) samples per second. This means that the scope can capture a glitch (fault) that lasts for just 40 nano (0.000 000 040) seconds.

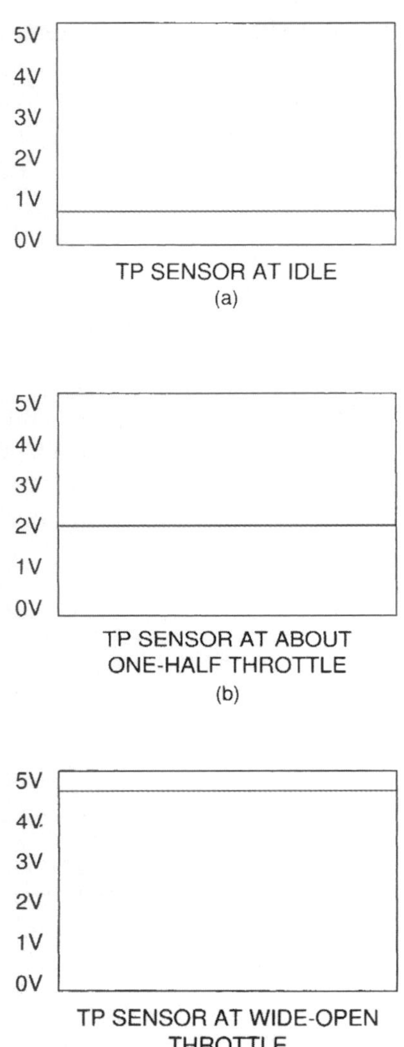

Figure 14–21 (a) On an analog scope, the voltage measured at the throttle position signal wire is displayed on a horizontal line at about 0.5 volts. (b) As the throttle is opened, the horizontal line representing the voltage increases. (c) At wide-open throttle (WOT), the horizontal line indicates about 4.5 volts.

For example, if a throttle position sensor was to be tested on an analog scope and a DSO, the results would be as shown in Figure 14–21 and Figure 14–22.

OSCILLOSCOPE DISPLAY GRID

Bench scopes have a grid face. Each square is called a **graticule.** A typical scope face has 8 graticules vertically (up and down) and 10 graticules horizontally. This arrangement is commonly called an **8 × 10 display.**

> **NOTE:** These numbers represent the metric dimensions of the graticule in centimetres. Therefore, the display would be 80 mm (3.14 in.) high and 100 mm (3.90 in.) wide.

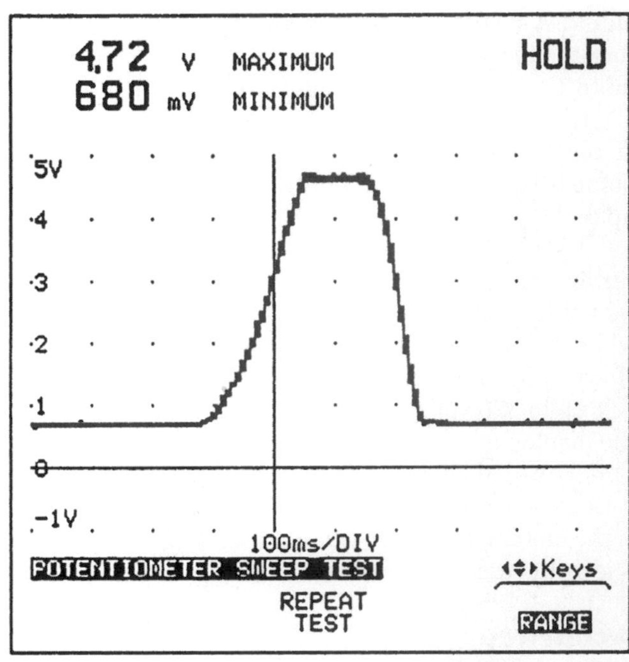

Figure 14–22 The display on a digital storage oscilloscope (DSO) displays the entire waveform from idle to wide-open throttle and then returns to idle. The display also indicates the maximum reading (4.72 V) and the minimum (680 mV or 0.68 V). The display does not show anything until the throttle is opened, because the scope has been set up to start displaying a waveform only after a certain voltage level has been reached. This voltage is called the trigger. (Courtesy of Fluke Corporation)

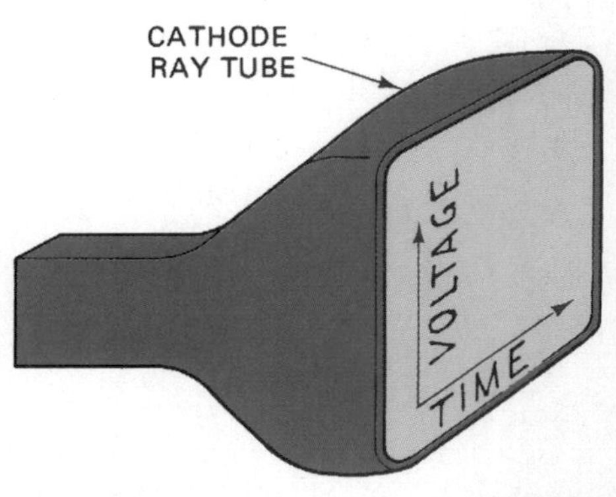

Figure 14–23 An automotive oscilloscope (scope) is of the same construction as a cathode ray tube (CRT) or television screen. An automotive oscilloscope is a visual voltmeter. The higher up a trace (line) is on the scope, the higher the voltage. The scope illustrates time from left to right. The longer the horizontal line, the longer the amount of time.

Voltage is displayed on a scope as a line vertically from the bottom. The scope illustrates time left to right as shown in Figure 14–23.

Setting the Time Base

Most scopes use 10 graticules from left to right on the display. Setting the **time base** means setting how much time will be displayed in each graticule. A graticule is commonly referred to as a **division.** For example, if the scope is set to read 200 ms (0.200 s) per division, then the total displayed would be 2 s (0.200 × 10 divisions = 2 s). The time base should be set to an amount of time that allows two to four events to be displayed. Sample time is milliseconds per division (indicated as ms/div) and total time includes:

ms/Division	Total Time
1 ms	10 ms (0.010 s)
10 ms	100 ms (0.100 s)
50 ms	500 ms (0.500 s)
100 ms	1 s (1.000 s)
500 ms	5 s (5.0 s)
1 s	10 s (10.0 s)

NOTE: Increasing the time base reduces the number of samples per second.

The horizontal scale is divided into 10 divisions (grats). If each division represented 1 second of time, then the total time period displayed on the screen would be 10 seconds. Time per division can vary greatly in automotive use, including:

Fuel injector: 2 ms per division (20 ms total)

Throttle position (TP) sensor: 100 ms per division (1 s total)

Oxygen sensor: 1 s per division (10 s total)

The time per division is selected so that several events of the waveform are displayed. This allows comparisons to see if the waveform is consistent or is changing. Multiple waveforms shown on the display at the same time also allow for measurements to be seen more easily.

Commonly used time per division for various component tests include:

- Oxygen sensor: 1 s/div
- TP sensor: 100 ms/div
- MAP/MAF: 2 ms/div
- Fuel injector: 2 ms/div
- Primary ignition: 10 ms/div
- Secondary ignition: 10 ms/div
- Voltage measurements: 5 ms/div

Setting the Volts per Division

The vertical scale has eight divisions (grats). If each division is set to equal 1 volt, the display will show 0 to 8 volts. This is okay in a 0 to 5 volts variable sensor such as a throttle position (TP) sensor. The volts per division (V/div) should be set so that the entire anticipated waveform can be viewed. Examples include:

Throttle position (TP) sensor: 1 V/div (8 V total)

Battery, starting and charging: 2 V/div (16 V total)

Oxygen sensor: 200 mV/div (1.6 V total)

Notice from the examples that the total voltage to be displayed exceeds the voltage range of the component being tested. This ensures that all the waveform will be displayed. It also allows for some unanticipated voltage readings. For example, an oxygen sensor should read between 0 V and 1 V (1000 mV). By setting the V/div to 200 mV, up to 1.6 V (1600 mV) will be displayed.

AC Coupling

AC coupling allows the scope to read alternating current (AC) voltage signals and ignore any direct current (DC) voltage present in the circuit. For example, this setting allows the technician to view the ripple voltage of the charging circuit without seeing the 14 volts DC signal. For example, connect the scope probes to display 120 volts AC household voltage at an outlet.

CAUTION: 110 V AC can cause bodily injury. Always touch the rubber or plastic portions of the scope probes when making measurements of any circuit that exceed 30 volts (AC or DC).

An AC voltage rises and falls above and below the zero level. To display several repeating continuously variable voltage signals, the proper time per division must be selected. Household electricity is 60 Hz (60 cycles per second), where one cycle requires just 18 ms (0.018 second). To see one cycle on the display, 0.2 ms/div would display one complete cycle (10 divisions × 2 ms/div = 20 ms). Because it is best to be able to view two or three cycles, set the time base to 4 ms or 6 ms per division.

Setting the volts per division is a little tricky. A 120 V AC signal actually goes over 120 volts positive and down more than 120 volts negative. Therefore, to view the entire waveform, the total voltage range on the display would have to be greater than 240 volts. Because there are eight vertical grids, a setting of 50 volts per division would allow the scope to display a total of 400 volts (50 volts × 8 = 400 volts), with 200 volts positive and 200 volts negative.

DC Coupling

DC coupling allows the scope to display only the DC voltage signal and to ignore (block) any AC voltage signal. An example of a DC voltage signal is the starting and charging voltage measured at the battery.

A flat horizontal line across the display at a level of 12 volts indicates the DC voltage signal. When the starter motor is energized, a load is applied to the battery and the battery voltage drops to about 10.5 volts. This is displayed again as a horizontal line, but now at a level lower than previously seen. When the engine starts, the AC generator starts to charge the battery and the voltage increases to about 14.5 volts. Again, the display is a horizontal line, but with a higher level than before that shows the charging voltage.

Pulse Trains

A DC voltage that turns on and off in a series of pulses is called a **pulse train.** See Figure 14–24. Pulse train signals can vary in several ways.

Frequency

Frequency is the number of cycles per second measured in hertz. Engine RPM signal is an example of a signal that can occur at various frequencies. At low engine speed, the ignition pulses occur fewer times per second (lower frequency) than when the engine is operated at higher engine speeds (RPM).

1. **Frequency** — Frequency is the number of cycles that take place per second. The more cycles that take place in one second, the higher the frequency reading. Frequencies are measured in hertz, which is the number of cycles per second. An **8 Hz** signal cycles eight times per second.

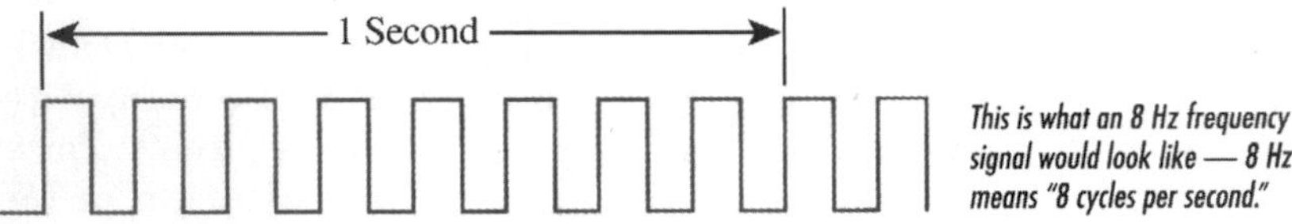

1 Second
This is what an 8 Hz frequency signal would look like — 8 Hz means "8 cycles per second."

2. **Duty Cycle** — Duty cycle is a measurement comparing the signal on-time to the length of one complete cycle. As on-time increases, off-time decreases. Duty cycle is measured in percentage of on-time: A 60% duty cycle is a signal that's on 60% of the time, and off 40% of the time. Another way to measure duty cycle is dwell, which is measured in degrees instead of percent.

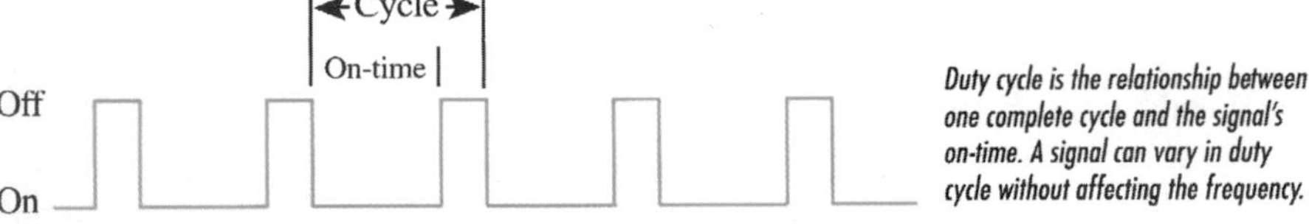

3. **Pulse Width** — Pulse width is the actual on-time of a signal, measured in milliseconds. With pulse width measurements, off-time doesn't really matter — the only real concern is how long the signal's on. This is a useful test for measuring conventional injector on-time, to see that the signal varies with load changes.

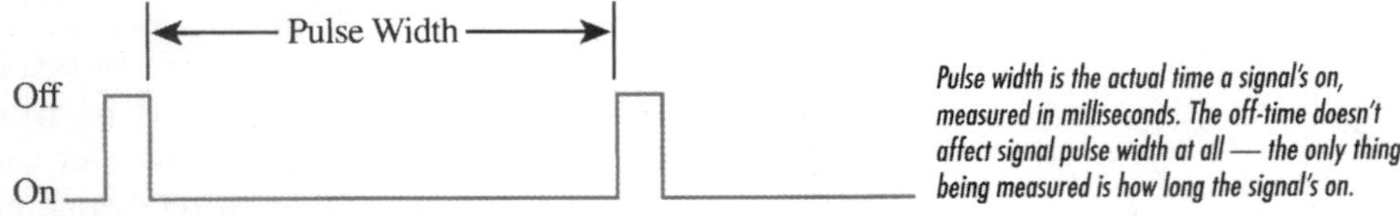

Pulse Width
Off
On
Pulse width is the actual time a signal's on, measured in milliseconds. The off-time doesn't affect signal pulse width at all — the only thing being measured is how long the signal's on.

Figure 14–24 A pulse train is any electrical signal that turns on and off, or goes high and low in a series of pulses. Ignition primary and fuel-injector pulses are examples of a pulse train signal. (Courtesy of Fluke Corporation)

Duty Cycle

Duty cycle refers to the percentage of on-time of the signal during one complete cycle. As on-time increases, the amount of time the signal is off decreases. Duty cycle is also called **pulse width modulation (PWM)** and also can be measured in degrees. The General Motors computer-controlled carburetors are an example in which the carburetor mixture-control solenoid is pulsed on and off with a variable duty cycle. The solenoid activation is constantly changing at 10 times per second (10 Hz), but the on-time varies. In this example, the duty cycle is measured in degrees. See Figure 14–25.

NOTE: At this point, we know changes with either voltage or resistance will have an effect on current flow. There is a third: duty cycle.

As an example, if a pressure of 12 V is pushing current through a resistance of 1.5 Ω, the current would be 8 A. If we have a duty cycle of 50% (switch closed for 50% . . . 8 A flow, switch open for 50% . . . 0 A flow), the *average* current is only 4 A. The higher the duty cycle, the greater the current flow. We also call the "on" (switch closed) duty cycle "dwell"; the greater the dwell, the higher the average current flow.

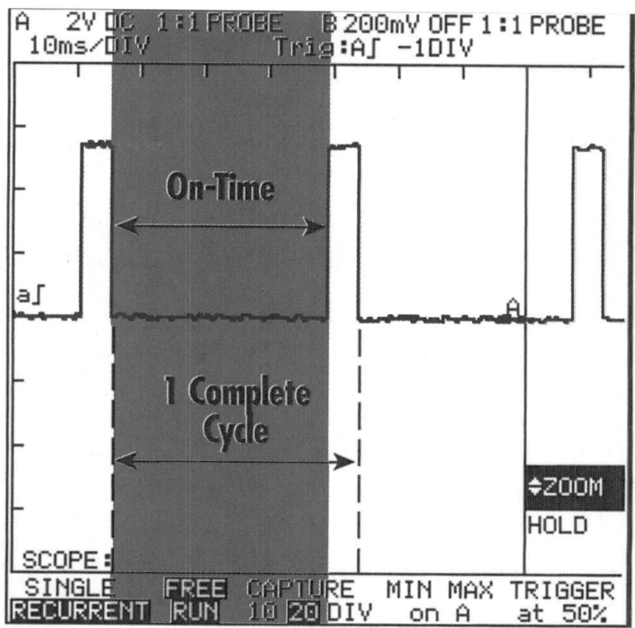

(a)

FLUKE 88 AUTOMOTIVE METER
AUTO
082.4 %
TRIG
40

The "%" symbol in the upper right corner of the display tells you your meter's reading a duty cycle signal.

(b)

Figure 14–25 (a) A scope representation of a complete cycle showing both on-time and off-time. (b) A meter display indicating the on-time duty cycle in percent (%). Note the trigger and negative (−) symbol. This indicates that the meter started to record the percentage of on-time when the voltage dropped (start of on-time). (Courtesy of Fluke Corporation)

Pulse Width

The **pulse width** is a measure of the actual on-time measured in milliseconds. Fuel injectors are usually controlled by varying the pulse width. See Figure 14–26.

External Trigger

An **external trigger** occurs when the trace starts as a signal received from another (external) source. A common example of an external trigger comes from the probe clamp around cylinder #1 spark plug wire to trigger the start of an ignition pattern.

Trigger Level

A scope will not start displaying a voltage signal until it is triggered or told to start. The **trigger level** must be set to start the display. If, for example, we want the pattern to start at 1 volt, then the trace will begin displaying on the left side of the screen *after* the trace has reached 1 volt.

Trigger Slope

The **trigger slope** is the voltage direction that a waveform must have in order to start the display. Most often, the trigger to start a waveform display is taken from the signal itself. Besides trigger voltage level, most scopes can be adjusted to trigger only when the voltage rises past the trigger-level voltage. This is called a *positive slope.* When the trigger is activated by the voltage falling past the higher level, it is called a *negative slope.* The scope display indicates both a positive and a negative slope symbol. See Figure 14–27.

For example, if a waveform such as a magnetic sensor used for crankshaft position or wheel speed starts moving upward, a positive slope should be selected. If a negative slope is selected, the waveform will not start showing until the voltage reaches the trigger level in a downward direction. A negative slope should be used when a fuel-injector circuit is being analyzed. In this circuit, the computer provides the ground and the voltage level drops when the computer commands the injector on. See the remaining chapters for examples of scope usage.

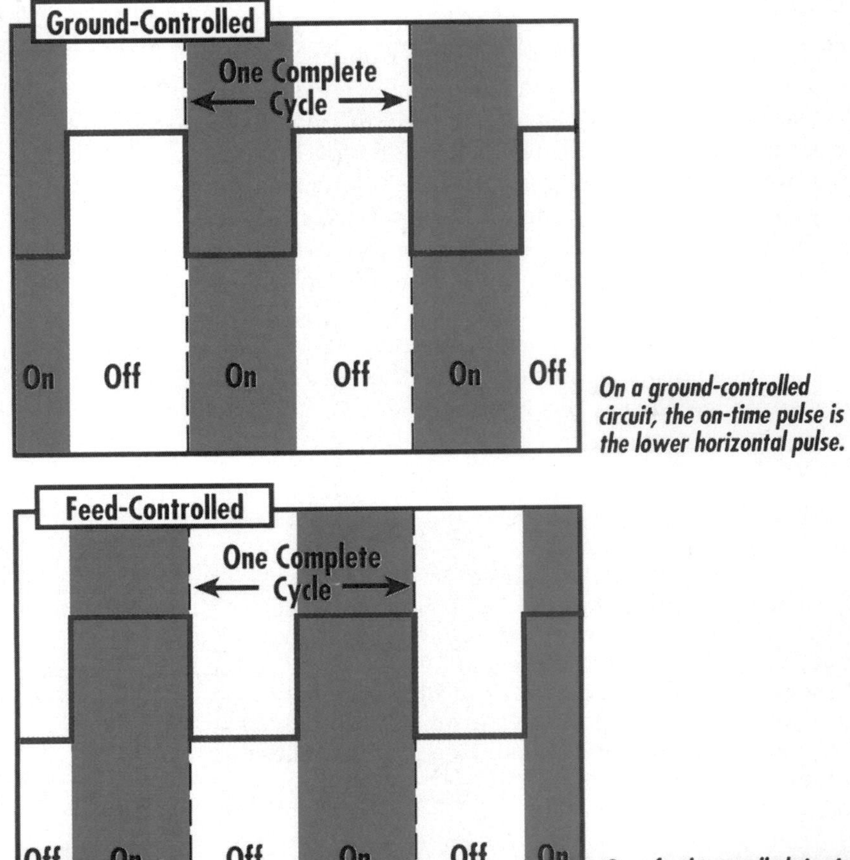
Ground-Controlled
One Complete Cycle
On Off On Off On Off
On a ground-controlled circuit, the on-time pulse is the lower horizontal pulse.
Feed-Controlled
One Complete Cycle
Off On Off On Off On
On a feed-controlled circuit, the on-time pulse is the upper horizontal pulse.

Figure 14–26 Most automotive computer systems control the device by opening and closing the ground to the component. (Courtesy of Fluke Corporation)

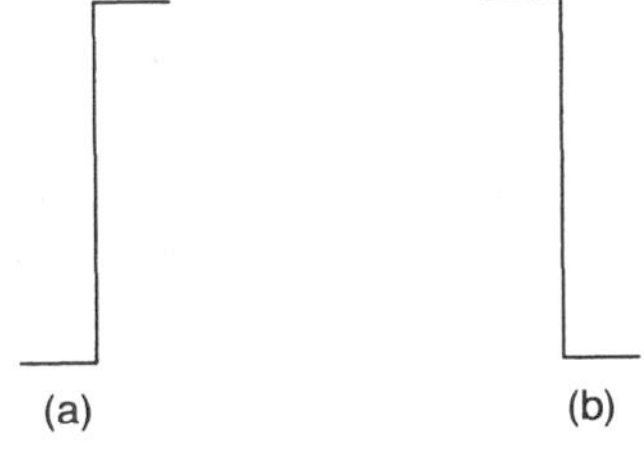
(a)
(b)

Figure 14–27 (a) A symbol for a positive trigger—a trigger occurs at a rising (positive) edge of the signal (waveform). (b) A symbol for a negative trigger—trigger occurs at a falling (negative) edge of the signal (waveform).

Using Scope Leads

Most scopes, both analog and digital, normally use the same test leads. These leads usually attach to the scope through a **BNC connector,** a miniature standard coaxial cable connector named after its inventor, Baby Neil Councilman. BNC is an international standard that is used in the electronics industry. Each scope lead has an attached ground lead that should be connected to a good clean, metal engine ground. The probe of the scope lead attaches to the circuit or component being tested.

Measuring Battery Voltage with a Scope

One of the easiest things to measure and observe on a scope is battery voltage. A lower voltage can be observed on the scope display as the engine is started, and a higher voltage should be displayed after the engine starts. See Figure 14–28. See other chapters for applications to specific components and systems when a scope is used.

An analog scope displays rapidly and cannot be set to show or freeze a display. Therefore, even though an analog scope shows all voltage signals, it is easy to miss a momentary glitch on an analog scope.

AUTOMOTIVE WIRING

Most automotive wire is made from strands of copper covered by insulating plastic. Copper is an excellent conductor of electricity, reasonably priced, and very flexible. Even copper can break when moved repeatedly; therefore, most copper wiring is constructed of multiple small strands that allow for repeated bending and moving without breaking. Solid copper wire

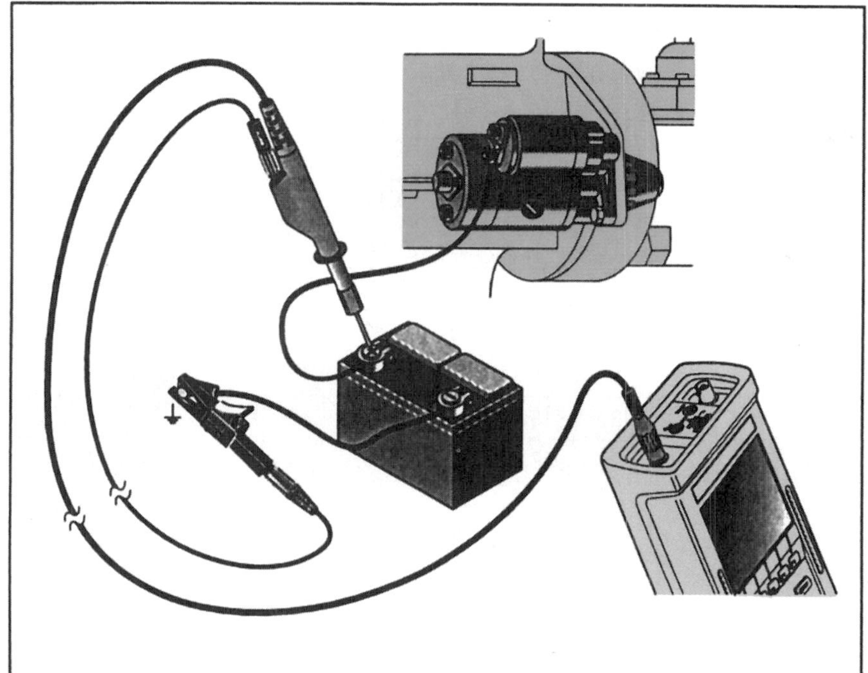

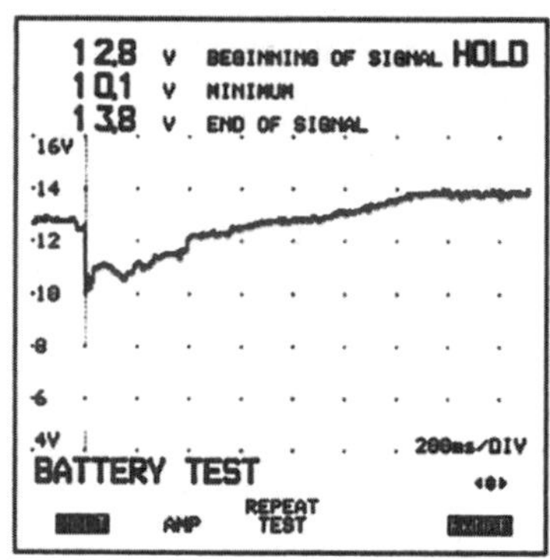

Figure 14–28 Battery voltage is represented by a flat horizontal line. In this example, the engine was started and the battery voltage dropped to about 10 V as shown on the left side of the scope display. After the engine started, the AC generator (alternator) started to charge the battery and the voltage is shown as climbing. (Courtesy of Fluke Corporation)

Conductor Rating (Starting with the Best)
1 silver
2 copper
3 gold
4 aluminum
5 tungsten
6 zinc
7 brass (copper and zinc)
8 platinum
9 iron
10 nickel
11 tin
12 steel
13 lead

is generally used for components such as starter armature and AC generator stator windings that do not bend or move during normal operation. Copper is the best electrical conductor besides silver, which is a great deal more expensive. See the chart that ranks the conductivity of various metals.

American Wire Gauge

Wiring is sized and purchased according to gauge size as assigned by the **American Wire Gauge (AWG)** system. AWG is the most common system for sizing wiring in Canada and the U.S. AWG numbers can be confusing because as the gauge number *increases,* the size of the conductor wire *decreases.* Therefore, a 14-gauge wire is smaller than a 10-gauge wire. The *greater* the amount of current (in amperes), the *larger* the conducting wire (the smaller the gauge number) required. See the chart that compares the AWG number to the actual wire diameter in inches.

The following are general applications for the most commonly used wire gauge sizes. Always check installation instructions or the manufacturer's specifications for wire gauge size before replacing any automotive wiring.

20–22 gauge: radio speaker wires

18 gauge: small bulbs and short leads

16 gauge: taillights, gas gauge, turn signals, windshield wipers

14 gauge: horn, radio power lead, headlights, cigarette lighter, brake lights

12 gauge: headlight switch-to-fuse box, rear window defogger, power windows and locks

10 gauge: ammeter, generator, or alternator-to-battery

Wire Gauge Diameter Chart	
American Wire Gauge	**Wire Diameter in Inches**
20	0.03196118
18	0.040303
16	0.0508214
14	0.064084
12	0.08080810
10	0.10189
8	0.128496
6	0.16202
5	0.18194
4	0.20431
3	0.22942
2	0.25763
1	0.2893
0	0.32486
00	0.3648

Metric Wire Gauge

Most manufacturers indicate on the wiring diagrams the wire sizes measured in square millimetres (mm^2) of cross-sectional area. The following chart gives conversions or comparisons between metric and AWG gauge sizes. Notice that the metric wire size increases with size (area), whereas the AWG gauge size gets smaller with larger-size wire.

Metric-to-AWG Conversion Table	
Metric Size mm^2	**AWG Size**
0.5	20
0.8	18
1.0	16
2.0	14
3.0	12
5.0	10
8.0	8
13.0	6
19.0	4
32.0	2
52.0	0

The AWG gauge number should be decreased (wire size increased) with increased lengths of wire. See the chart.

12 V	Wire Gauge for Length in Metres (Feet)*						
Amps	**1 (3′)**	**1.5 (5′)**	**2 (7′)**	**3 (10′)**	**5 (15′)**	**6 (20′)**	**8 (25′)**
5	18	18	18	18	18	18	18
7	18	18	18	18	18	18	16
10	18	18	18	18	16	16	16
12	18	18	18	18	16	16	14
15	18	18	18	18	14	14	12
18	18	18	16	16	14	14	12
20	18	18	16	16	14	12	10
22	18	18	16	16	12	12	10
24	18	18	16	16	12	12	10
30	18	16	16	14	10	10	10
40	18	16	14	12	10	10	8
50	16	14	12	12	10	10	8
100	12	12	10	10	6	6	4
150	10	10	8	8	4	4	2
200	10	8	8	6	4	4	2

*When mechanical strength is a factor, use the next larger wire gauge.

For example, a trailer may require 14-gauge wire to light all the trailer lights, but if the wire required is over 8 m (25 ft) long, 12-gauge wire should be used. Most automotive wire, except for spark plug wire, is often called **primary wire** (named for the voltage range used in the primary ignition circuit) because it is designed to operate at or near battery voltage.

BRAIDED GROUND STRAPS

All vehicles use ground straps between the engine and body and/or between the body and the negative terminal of the battery. Many of the engine-to-body straps are braided and uninsulated, as shown in Figure 14–29. It is not necessary to insulate a ground strap because it does not matter if it touches metal; it already attaches to ground. Braided ground straps are more flexible than stranded wire. Because the braided ground strap is able to flex without breaking, the engine is free to move slightly on its mounts. The braided strap also dampens out some radio-frequency interference that otherwise might be transmitted through standard stranded wiring.

NOTE: Body ground wires (lights and accessory circuits) provide a ground to the body and allow current flow to the negative battery terminal.

Figure 14–29 A braided ground strap used to reduce radio interference by electrically connecting the hood to the rest of the body.

BATTERY CABLES

Battery cables are the largest wires used in the automotive electrical system. The cables are usually 4-gauge, 2-gauge, or 1-gauge wires (19 mm^2 or larger). See Figure 14–30. Wires larger than 1-gauge are called 0-gauge (pronounced "ought"). Larger cables are labeled 2/0 or 00 (double ought) and 3/0 or 000 (triple ought). Six-volt electrical systems require battery cables two sizes larger than those for 12 volt electrical systems.

The power required to operate a circuit is measured in watts (1 volt × 1 ampere = 1 watt); thus a 12 volt circuit requires only 50% of the current that a 6 volt system uses to achieve the same power level. As the voltage climbs, current is reduced and the conductors are made smaller.

Power demands are so high with many late model vehicles that the AC generators (alternators) are having difficulty keeping up with demand. The automobile industry is considering a switch to 36 volt batteries and 42 volt charging systems. Tripling the voltage increases the power by 3, for the same current. A limited number of vehicles currently use 42 volt systems.

Figure 14–30 Battery cables are designed to carry the heavy starter current and are therefore usually 4-gauge or larger wire. Auxiliary wiring for accessories and other electrical components is also connected to the positive battery cable on this vehicle. The plastic conduit (also called split-loom tubing) reduces the risk of damage.

JUMPER CABLES

Jumper cables are 4- to 2/0-gauge electrical cables with large clamps attached and are used to connect a vehicle with a discharged battery to a vehicle that has a good battery. Good-quality jumper cables are necessary to prevent excessive voltage drops caused by the cables' resistance. Aluminum wire jumper cables should not be used, because even though aluminum is a good electrical conductor (although not as good as copper), it is less flexible and can crack and break when bent or moved repeatedly. The size should be 4-gauge or larger. Ought-gauge welding cable can be used to construct an excellent set of jumper cables using welding clamps on both ends. Welding cable is usually constructed of many very fine strands of wire, which allows for easier bending of the cable as the strands of fine wire slide against each other inside the cable.

FUSES AND CIRCUIT PROTECTION DEVICES

Fuses should be used in every circuit to protect the wiring from overheating and damage caused by excessive current flow as a result of a short circuit or other malfunction. The symbol for a fuse is a wavy line between two points: ∽

A fuse is constructed of a fine tin conductor inside a glass, plastic, or ceramic housing. The tin is designed to melt and open the circuit if excessive current flows through the fuse. Each

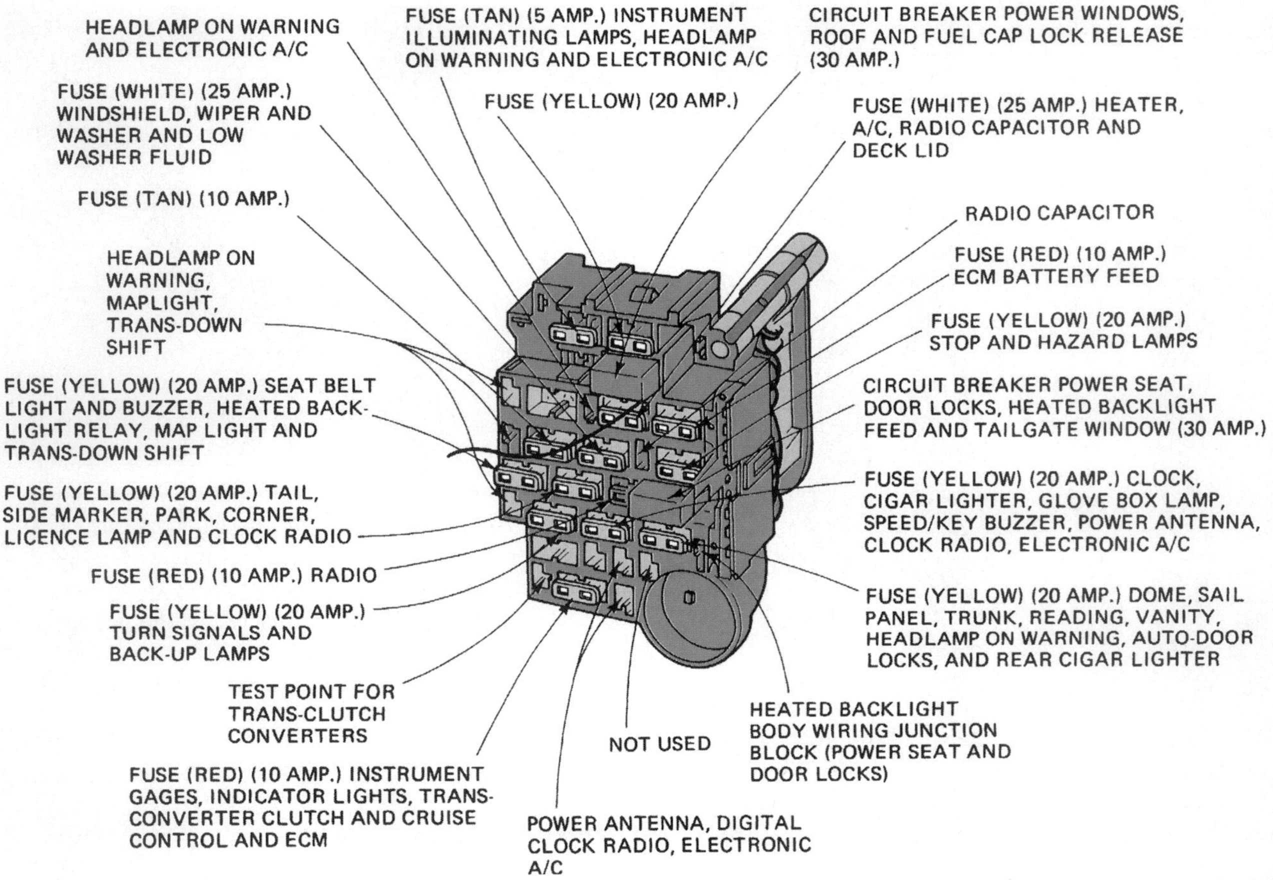

HEADLAMP ON WARNING AND ELECTRONIC A/C
FUSE (TAN) (5 AMP.) INSTRUMENT ILLUMINATING LAMPS, HEADLAMP ON WARNING AND ELECTRONIC A/C
CIRCUIT BREAKER POWER WINDOWS, ROOF AND FUEL CAP LOCK RELEASE (30 AMP.)
FUSE (WHITE) (25 AMP.) WINDSHIELD, WIPER AND WASHER AND LOW WASHER FLUID
FUSE (YELLOW) (20 AMP.)
FUSE (WHITE) (25 AMP.) HEATER, A/C, RADIO CAPACITOR AND DECK LID
FUSE (TAN) (10 AMP.)
RADIO CAPACITOR
HEADLAMP ON WARNING, MAPLIGHT, TRANS-DOWN SHIFT
FUSE (RED) (10 AMP.) ECM BATTERY FEED
FUSE (YELLOW) (20 AMP.) STOP AND HAZARD LAMPS
FUSE (YELLOW) (20 AMP.) SEAT BELT LIGHT AND BUZZER, HEATED BACK-LIGHT RELAY, MAP LIGHT AND TRANS-DOWN SHIFT
CIRCUIT BREAKER POWER SEAT, DOOR LOCKS, HEATED BACKLIGHT FEED AND TAILGATE WINDOW (30 AMP.)
FUSE (YELLOW) (20 AMP.) TAIL, SIDE MARKER, PARK, CORNER, LICENCE LAMP AND CLOCK RADIO
FUSE (YELLOW) (20 AMP.) CLOCK, CIGAR LIGHTER, GLOVE BOX LAMP, SPEED/KEY BUZZER, POWER ANTENNA, CLOCK RADIO, ELECTRONIC A/C
FUSE (RED) (10 AMP.) RADIO
FUSE (YELLOW) (20 AMP.) TURN SIGNALS AND BACK-UP LAMPS
FUSE (YELLOW) (20 AMP.) DOME, SAIL PANEL, TRUNK, READING, VANITY, HEADLAMP ON WARNING, AUTO-DOOR LOCKS, AND REAR CIGAR LIGHTER
TEST POINT FOR TRANS-CLUTCH CONVERTERS
HEATED BACKLIGHT BODY WIRING JUNCTION BLOCK (POWER SEAT AND DOOR LOCKS)
NOT USED
FUSE (RED) (10 AMP.) INSTRUMENT GAGES, INDICATOR LIGHTS, TRANS-CONVERTER CLUTCH AND CRUISE CONTROL AND ECM
POWER ANTENNA, DIGITAL CLOCK RADIO, ELECTRONIC A/C

Figure 14–31 Typical automotive fuse panel.

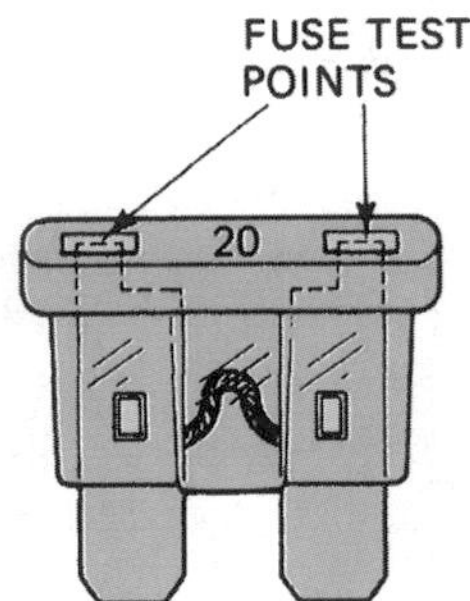

Figure 14–32 Blade-type fuses can be tested through openings in the plastic at the top of the fuse.

fuse is rated according to its maximum current-carrying capacity.

Many fuses are used to protect more than one circuit of the automobile. See Figure 14–31. A typical example is the fuse for the cigarette lighter that also protects many other circuits such as those for the courtesy lights, clock, and other circuits. A fault in one of these circuits can cause this fuse to melt, which will prevent the operation of all other circuits that are protected by the fuse.

Blade Fuses

Coloured blade-type fuses are also referred to as ATO fuses and have been used since 1977. The colour of the plastic of blade fuses indicates the maximum current flow, measured in amperes. Each fuse has an opening in the top of the plastic portion of the fuse to allow access to the metal contacts of the fuse for testing purposes. See Figure 14–32. The following table lists the colour and the amperage rating of blade fuses:

Amperage Rating	Colour
1	Dark green
2	Gray
2.5	Purple
3	Violet
4	Pink
5	Tan
6	Gold
7.5	Brown
9	Orange
10	Red
14	Black
15	Blue
20	Yellow
25	White
30	Green

Mini Fuses

To save space, many vehicles use mini (small) blade fuses. Not only do they save space but they allow the vehicle design engineer to fuse individual circuits instead of grouping many different components on one fuse. This improves customer satisfaction because if one component fails, it only affects that one circuit without stopping electrical power to several other circuits as well. This also makes troubleshooting easier because each circuit is separate. The amperage rating and corresponding fuse colour for mini fuses include:

Amperage Rating	Colour
5	Tan
7.5	Brown
10	Red
15	Blue
20	Yellow
25	Natural
30	Green

See Figure 14–33.

Maxi Fuses

Maxi fuses are a large version of blade fuses and are used to replace fusible links in many vehicles. Maxi fuses are rated up to 80 amperes or more. The amperage rating and corresponding colour for maxi fuses include:

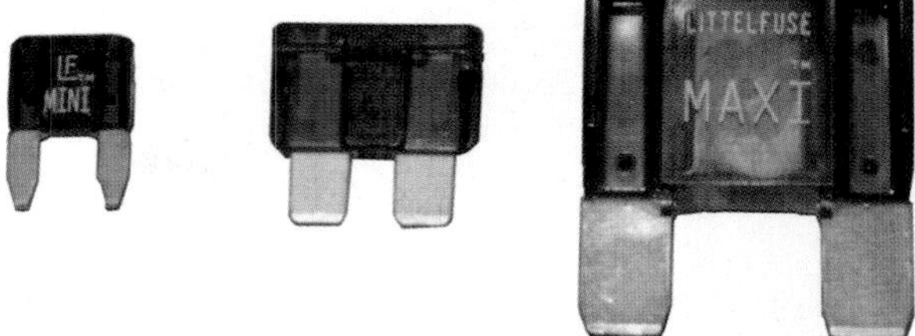

Figure 14–33 Three sizes of blade-type fuses. Mini on the left, standard or ATO type in the centre, and maxi on the right.

Amperage Rating	Colour
20	Yellow
30	Green
40	Amber
50	Red
60	Blue
70	Brown
80	Natural

Pacific Fuse Element

First used in the late 1980s, Pacific fuse elements (also called a **fuse link** or **auto link**) are used to protect wiring from a direct short-to-ground. The housing contains a short link of wire sized for the rated current load. The transparent top allows inspection of the link inside. See Figure 14–34.

Testing Fuses

It is important to test the condition of a fuse if the circuit being protected by the fuse does not operate. Most blown fuses can be detected quickly because the centre conductor is melted. Fuses can also fail and open the circuit because of a poor connection in the fuse itself or in the fuse holder. Therefore, just because a fuse "looks okay" does not mean that it *is* okay. All fuses should be tested with a test light. The test light should be connected to first one side of the fuse and then the other. A test light should light on both sides. If the test light only lights on one side, the fuse is blown or open. If the test light does not light on either side of the fuse, then that circuit is not being supplied power.

Circuit Breakers

Circuit breakers are used to prevent harmful overload (excessive current flow) in a circuit by opening the circuit and stopping the current flow, preventing overheating and possible fire caused by hot wires or

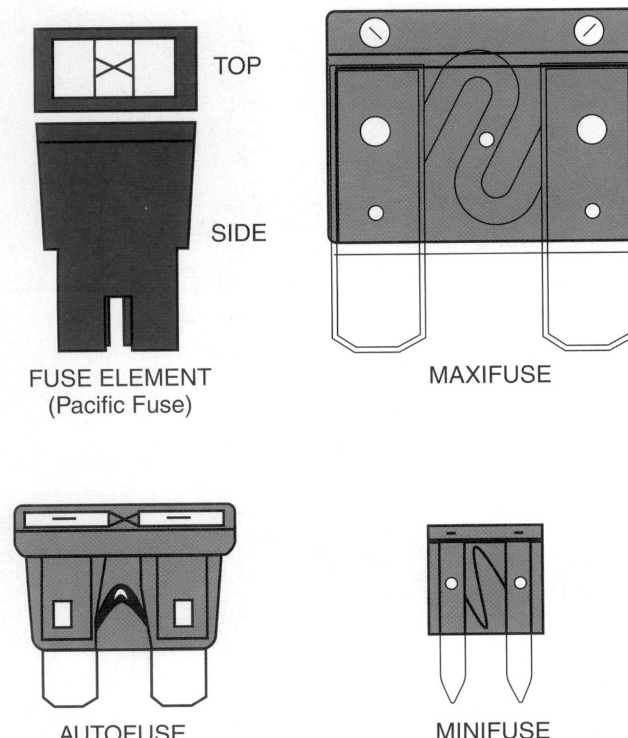

Figure 14–34 A comparison of the various types of protective devices used in most vehicles.

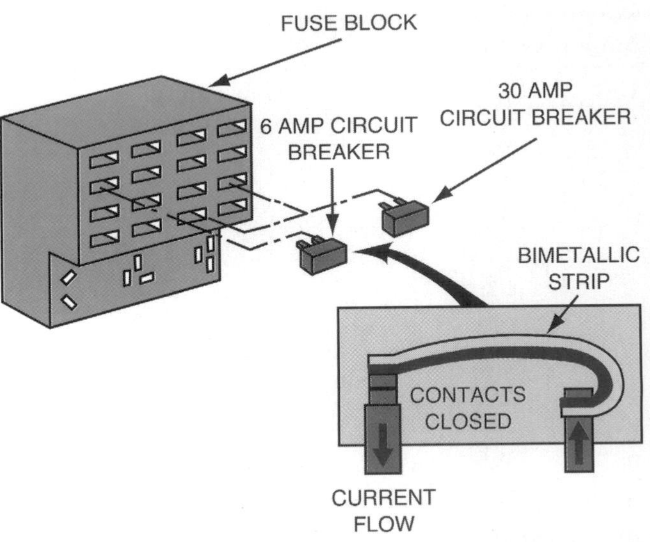

Figure 14–35 Typical blade circuit breaker fits into the same space as a blade fuse. If excessive current flows through the bimetallic strip, the strip bends and opens the contacts and stops current flow. When the circuit breaker cools, the contacts close again, completing the electrical circuit.

electrical components. Circuit breakers are mechanical units made of two different metals (bimetallic) that deform when heated and open a set of contact points that work in the same manner as an off switch. See Figure 14–35.

Circuit breakers, therefore, are reset when the current stops flowing, which causes the bimetallic strip to cool and the circuit to close again. A circuit breaker is used in circuits that could affect the safety of passengers if a conventional nonresetting fuse were used. The headlight circuit is an excellent example of the use of a circuit breaker rather than a fuse. A short or grounded circuit anywhere in the headlight circuit could cause excessive current flow and, therefore, the opening of the circuit. A sudden loss of headlights at night could have disastrous results. A circuit breaker opens and closes the circuit rapidly, thereby protecting the circuit from overheating and also providing sufficient current flow to maintain at least partial headlight operation.

Circuit breakers are also used in other circuits where conventional fuses could not provide for the surges of high current commonly found in those circuits. Examples are the circuits for the following accessories:

1. Power seats
2. Power door locks
3. Power windows

PTC Circuit Protectors

Positive temperature coefficient (PTC) circuit protectors are solid state (without moving parts). Like all other circuit protection devices, PTCs are installed in series in the circuit being protected. If excessive current flows, the temperature and resistance of the PTC increase.

This increased resistance reduces current flow (amperes) in the circuit and may cause the electrical component in the circuit not to function correctly. For example, when a PTC circuit protector is used in a power window circuit, the increased resistance causes the operation of the power window to be much slower than normal.

Unlike circuit breakers or fuses, PTC circuit protection devices do *not* open the circuit, but rather provide a very high resistance between the protector and the component. See Figure 14–36. In other words, voltage will be available to the component. This fact has led to a lot of misunderstanding about how these circuit protection devices actually work. It is even more confusing when the circuit is opened and the PTC circuit protector cools down. When the circuit is turned back on, the component may operate normally for a short time until the PTC circuit protector again gets hot because of too much current flow, and then its resistance again increases to limit current flow.

The electronic control unit (computer) used in most vehicles today incorporates thermal overload protection devices. See Figure 14–37. Therefore, whenever a component fails to operate, do not blame

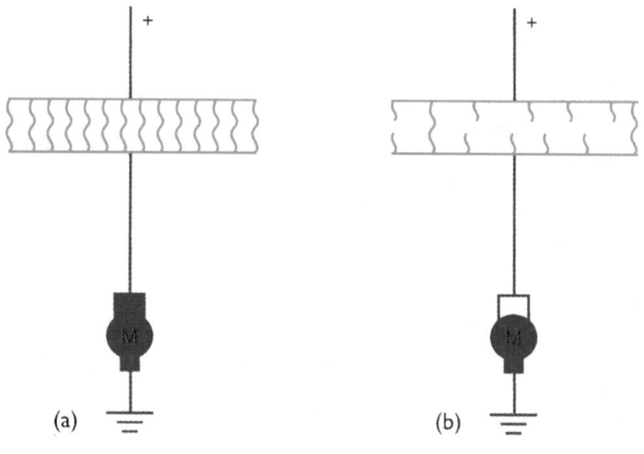

Figure 14–36 (a) Normal operation of a PTC circuit protector in a power window motor circuit. Note the many conducting paths. With normal current flow, temperature of the PTC circuit protector remains normal. (b) When current exceeds the amperage rating of the PTC circuit protector, the polymer material that makes up the electronic circuit protector increases in resistance. As shown here, a high-resistance electrical path still exists even though the motor will stop operating as a result of the very low current flow through the very high resistance. The circuit protector will not reset or cool down until voltage is removed from the circuit.

Figure 14–37 The yellow ceramic-like units are called electronic circuit breakers or PTC circuit protector devices. This under-hood circuit control panel shows that many circuits in this vehicle are being protected from excessive current flow through the use of PTC circuit protectors.

the computer. The current control device is controlling current flow to protect the computer. Components that do not operate correctly should be checked for proper resistance and current draw.

TECH TIP 

Look for the "Green Crud"

Corroded connections are a major cause of intermittent electrical problems and open circuits. The usual sequence of conditions is as follows:

1. Heat causes expansion. This heat can be from external sources such as connectors being too close to the exhaust system. Another possible source of heat is a poor connection at the terminal, causing a voltage drop and heat due to the electrical resistance.
2. Condensation is created when a connector cools. The moisture in the condensation causes rust and corrosion.

If corroded connectors are noticed, the terminal should be cleaned and the condition of the electrical connection to the wire terminal end(s) confirmed. Many automobile manufacturers recommend using a dielectric silicone or lithium-based grease inside connectors to prevent moisture from getting into and attacking the connector.

TECH TIP 

Do We Grease the Connector?

Although silicone dielectric grease is an inert material that adds almost no additional resistance to a circuit, it is usually approved for use where higher amperage (1 or more amps) is found.

Some automakers do not recommend dielectric grease in computer circuit connectors where only milliamperes flow. Excellent connections are so important with these systems that some manufacturers gold plate the connector pins.

Exceptions to the rule are regions of Canada and the U.S. where road salt is used. Dielectric grease provides additional protection against the entrance of salt water and should be used inside underbody and underhood connectors that may contact water.

Fusible Links

A fusible link is a type of fuse that consists of a short length of standard copper-strand wire covered with a special nonflammable insulation. This wire is usually four wire sizes smaller than the wire of the circuits it protects. The special thick insulation over the wire may make it look larger than other wires of the same gauge number. See Figure 14–38.

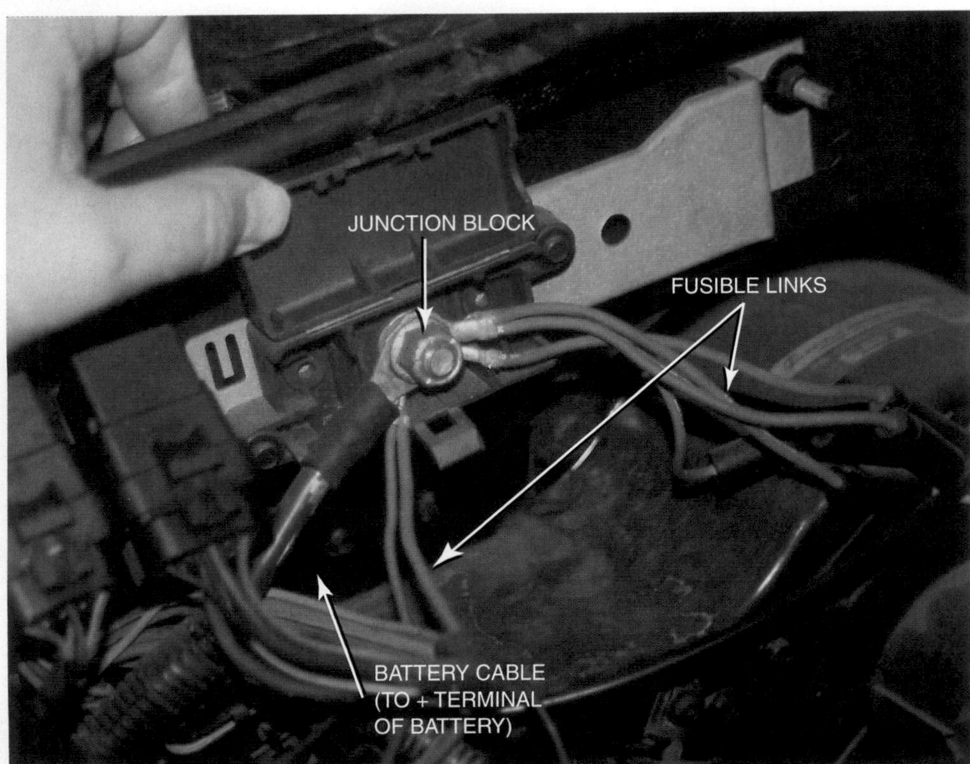

Figure 14–38 Fusible links are usually located close to the battery and are usually attached to a junction block. Notice that they are only 150 to 200 mm (6 to 8 in.) long and feed more than one fuse from each fusible link.

If excessive current flow (caused by a short to ground or a defective component) occurs, the fusible link will melt in half and open the circuit to prevent a fire hazard. Some fusible links are identified with "fusible link" tags at the junction between the fusible link and the standard chassis wiring, which represent only the junction. Fusible links are the backup system for circuit protection. All current except the current used by the starter motor flows through fusible links and then through individual circuit fuses. It is possible that a fusible link will melt and not blow a fuse. Fusible links are installed as close to the battery as possible so that they can protect the wiring and circuits coming directly from the battery.

TERMINALS AND CONNECTORS

A **terminal** is a metal fastener attached to the end of a wire. The term **connector** usually refers to the plastic portion that snaps or connects together. Wire terminal ends usually snap into and are held by a connector. Male and female connectors can then be snapped together, thereby completing an electrical connection. Connectors exposed to the environment are also equipped with a weather-tight seal.

A typical repair often involves removing a wire's terminal from a connector and replacing that terminal on the end of the lead (wire). A terminal may be corroded or has lost its tension or grip on the mating terminal. Terminals are usually retained in a connector by a locking tang or tab that must be depressed to release the terminal end from the plastic connector. See Figures 14–39 through 14–41.

WIRE REPAIR

Many manufacturers recommend that all wiring repairs be soldered.

Solder

Solder is used to make a good electrical contact between two wires or connections in an electrical circuit. The solder itself is made from an alloy of tin and lead. However, a flux must be used to help clean the area and to help make the solder flow. Therefore, solder is made with a resin (rosin) contained in the centre, and is called **rosin-core solder.** See Figure 14–42. An acid-core solder is also available but should only be used for soldering sheet metal. The acid used with this type of solder will continue to attack the copper wire at the splice. Solder is available with various percentages of tin and lead in the alloy. Ratios are used to identify these various types of solder, with the first number denoting the percentage of tin in the alloy and the second number giving the percentage of lead. The most commonly used solder is 50/50, which means that 50% of the solder is tin

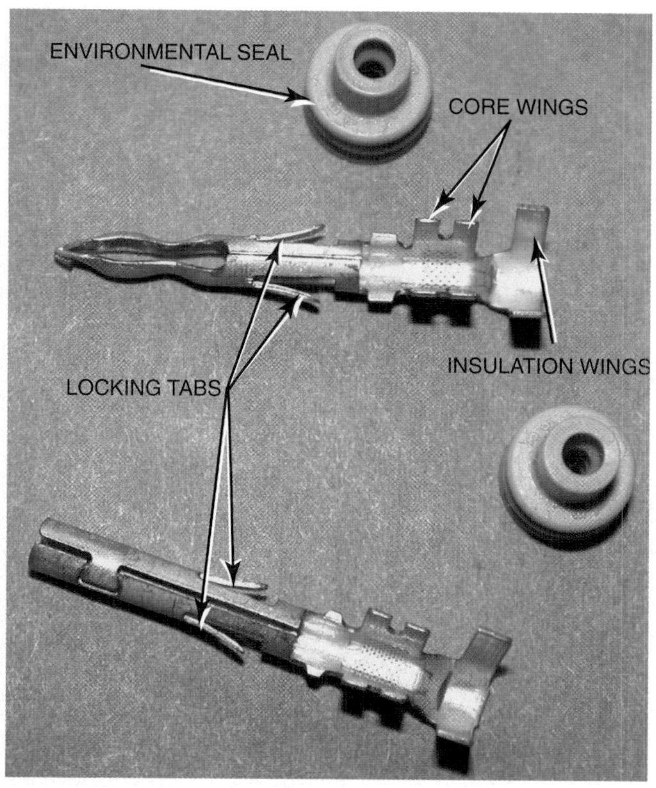

Figure 14–39 Male (top) and female (bottom) weather-pack terminals. The insulation is stripped from the end of the wire (core), which is crimped under the core wings. The insulation wings are then crimped over the insulation to help prevent the wire from being pulled out of the terminal.

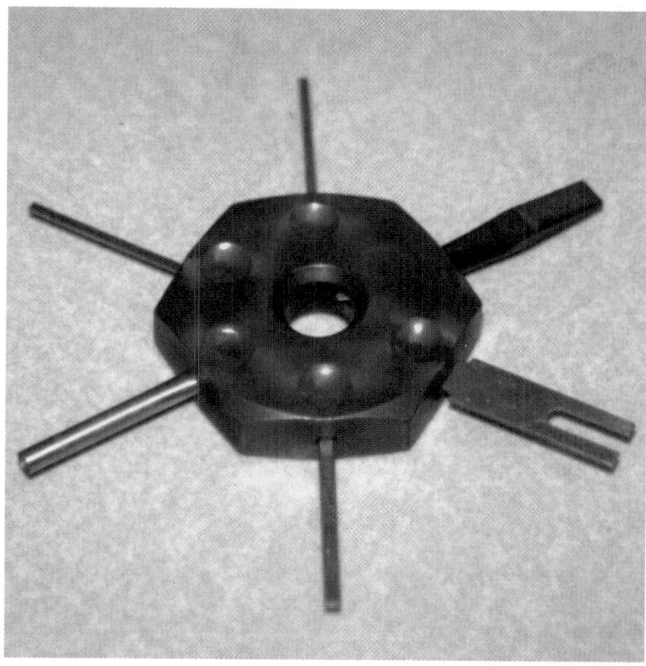

Figure 14–41 An example of a universal pick. This one tool combines various sizes of picks that can be used to remove terminals from connectors.

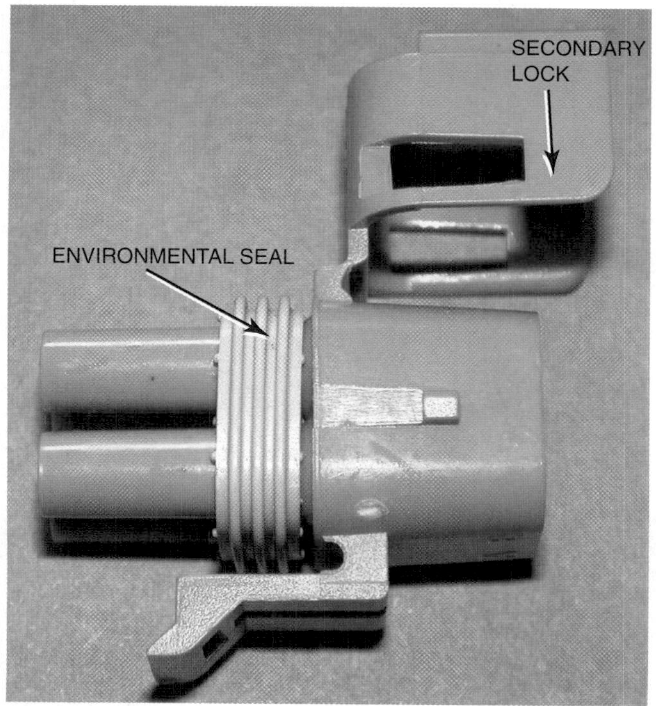

Figure 14–40 A male weather-pack connector. The plastic connector holds the metal terminals in position and locks to the female connector to make a good tight connection.

Figure 14–42 Always use rosin-core solder for electrical or electronic soldering. Also, use small-diameter solder for small soldering irons. Use large-diameter solder only for large-diameter (large-gauge) wire and higher-wattage soldering irons (guns).

and the other 50% is lead. The percentages of each alloy primarily determine the melting point of the solder:

60/40 solder (60% tin/40% lead) melts at 183°C (361°F).

50/50 solder (50% tin/50% lead) melts at 216°C (421°F).

40/60 solder (40% tin/60% lead) melts at 238°C (460°F).

NOTE: The melting points stated here can vary depending on the purity of the metals used.

Because of the lower melting point, 60/40 solder is the most highly recommended solder to use, followed by 50/50. When soldering wires, be sure to heat the wires (not the solder) using a soldering gun or butane tool such as shown in Figure 14–43. While touching the soldering gun to the splice, apply solder to the junction of the gun and the wire. The solder will start to flow. Do not move the soldering gun. Just keep feeding more solder into the splice as it flows into and around the strands of the wire. After the solder has flowed throughout the splice, remove the soldering gun from the splice and allow the solder to cool slowly. The solder should have a shiny appearance. Dull looking solder may be caused by not reaching a high enough temperature, which results in a **cold solder joint.** Reheating the splice and allowing it to cool often restores the shiny appearance.

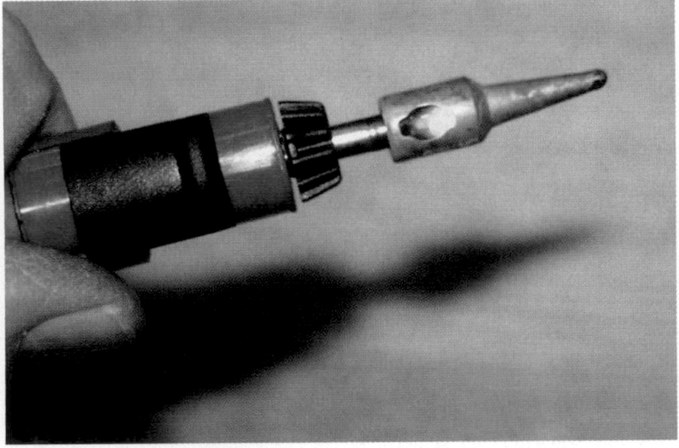

Figure 14–43 A butane soldering tool. The cap has a built-in striker to light a converter in the tip of the tool. This handy soldering tool produces the equivalent of 60 watts of heat. It operates for about 1/2 hour on one charge from a commonly available butane refill dispenser.

Heat Shrink

Heat shrink tubing is usually made from polyvinylchloride (PVC) or polyolefin and shrinks to about half of its original diameter when heated. This is usually called a 2:1 shrink ratio. Heat shrink by itself does not provide protection against corrosion, because the ends of the tubing are not sealed against moisture. DaimlerChrysler Corporation recommends that all wire repairs that may be exposed to the elements be repaired and sealed using **adhesive-lined** heat shrink tubing. The tubing is usually made from flame-retardant flexible polyolefin with an internal layer of special thermoplastic adhesive. When heated, this tubing shrinks to one-third of its original diameter (3:1 shrink ratio) and the adhesive melts and seals the ends of the tubing. See Figure 14–44.

Crimp-and-Seal Connectors

General Motors Corporation recommends the use of crimp-and-seal connectors as the method for wire repair. Crimp-and-seal connectors are *not* simply butt connectors. Crimp-and-seal connectors contain a sealant and shrink tubing in one piece. See Figure 14–45.

The usual procedure specified for making a wire repair using a crimp-and-seal connector is as follows:

Step 1 Strip the insulation from the ends of the wire: about 8 mm (5/16 in.).

Step 2 Select the proper size of crimp-and-seal connector for the gauge of wire being repaired. Insert the wires into the splice sleeve and crimp.

Step 3 Apply heat to the connector until the sleeve shrinks down around the wire and a small

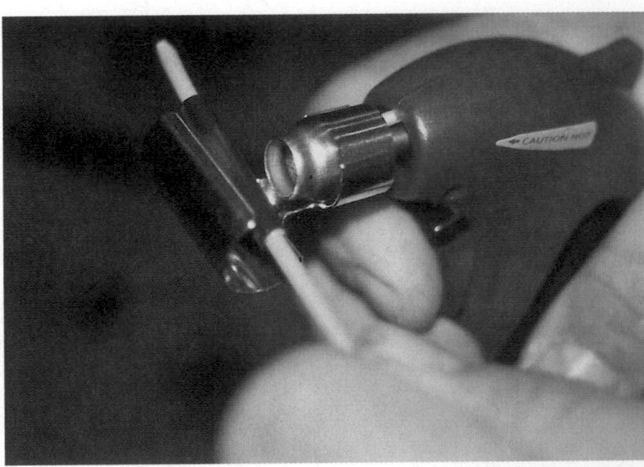

Figure 14–44 A butane torch especially designed for use on heat shrink applies heat without an open flame which could cause damage.

amount of sealant is observed around the ends of the sleeve as shown in Figure 14–46.

Aluminum Wire Repair

Since the mid-1970s, many automobile manufacturers have used plastic-coated solid aluminum wire for some body wiring. Because aluminum wire is brittle and can break as a result of vibration, it is only used where there is no possible movement of the wire, such as along the floor or sill area. This section of wire is stationary, and the wire changes back to copper at a junction terminal after the trunk or rear section of the vehicle, where movement of the wiring may be possible.

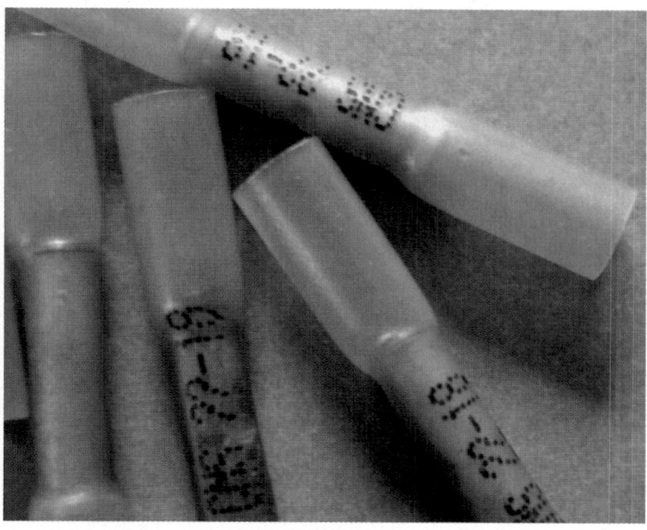

Figure 14–45 A typical crimp-and-seal connector. This type of connector is first lightly crimped to retain the ends of the wires and then it is heated. The tubing shrinks around the wire splice and a thermoplastic glue melts on the inside to provide an effective weather-resistant seal.

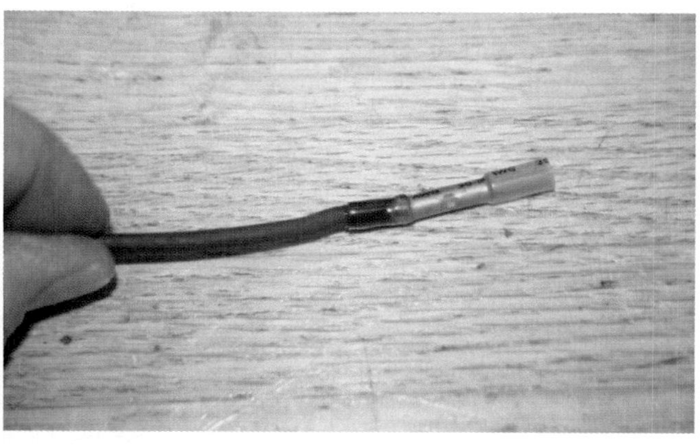

Figure 14–46 The left side of this crimp-and-seal connector has been gently crimped and heated. Note how the connector has shrunk down around the wire. The heat has also released a thermal sealant that forms an effective environmental seal around the wire.

If any aluminum wire must be repaired or replaced, the following procedure should be used to be assured of a proper repair. The aluminum wire is usually found protected in a plastic conduit. This conduit is then normally slit, after which the wires can easily be removed for repair.

Step 1 Carefully strip only about 6 mm (1/4 inch) of insulation from the aluminum wire, being careful not to nick or damage the aluminum wire case.

Step 2 Use a crimp connector to join two wires together. Do *not* solder an aluminum wire repair. Solder will not readily adhere to aluminum because the heat causes an oxide coating on the surface of the aluminum.

Step 3 The spliced, crimped connection must be coated with petroleum jelly to prevent corrosion.

Step 4 The coated connection should be covered with shrinkable plastic tubing or wrapped with electrical tape to seal out moisture.

WIRING DIAGRAMS

Automotive manufacturers' service manuals include wiring diagrams of all the electrical circuits. These wiring diagrams may include all of the circuits combined on several large fold-out sheets, or they may be broken down to show individual circuits. All circuit diagrams include the power-side wiring of the circuit and all splices, connectors, electrical components, and ground return paths. The gauge and colour of the wiring are also included on most wiring diagrams.

SAFETY TIP

Orange Alert!

Use caution when servicing hybrids; 144 volt and 274 volt batteries are common on these vehicles. Because operating voltages are approaching 500 volts on the latest models, high voltage wiring is bright orange in colour as a warning to the technician.

Never work on these high voltage components without training or personal injury could result.

Circuit Information

Many wiring diagrams include numbers and letters near components and wires that may confuse readers of the diagram. Most letters used near or on a wire identify the colour or colours of the wire. The first colour or colour abbreviation is the colour of the wire insulation, and the second colour (if mentioned) is the colour of the strip or tracer on the base colour. See Figure 14–47.

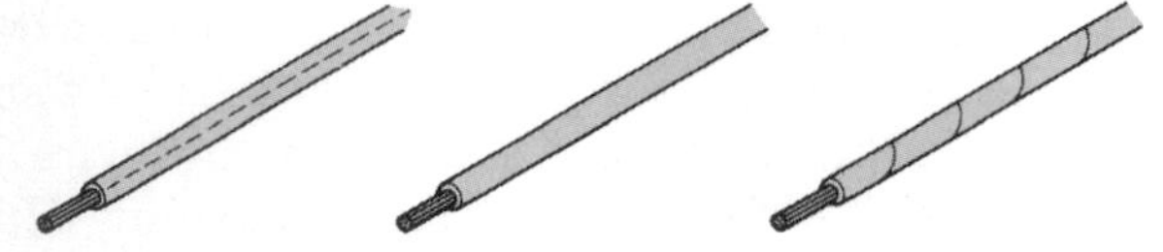

Figure 14–47 The centre wire is a solid colour wire, meaning that the wire has no other identifying tracer or stripe colour. The two end wires could be labeled "BRN/WHT," indicating a brown wire with a white tracer or stripe.

Wires with different-colour tracers are indicated by both colours with a slash (/) between them. For example, BRN/WHT means a brown wire with a white stripe or tracer.

Abbreviation	Colour
BRN	Brown
BLK	Black
GRN	Green
WHT	White
PPL	Purple
PNK	Pink
TAN	Tan
BLU	Blue
YEL	Yellow
ORN	Orange
DK BLU	Dark blue
LT BLU	Light blue
DK GRN	Dark green
LT GRN	Light green
RED	Red
GRY	Gray

Figure 14–48 illustrates a rear side-marker bulb circuit diagram where ".8" indicates the metric wire gauge size in square millimetres (mm^2) and "PPL" indicates a solid purple wire.

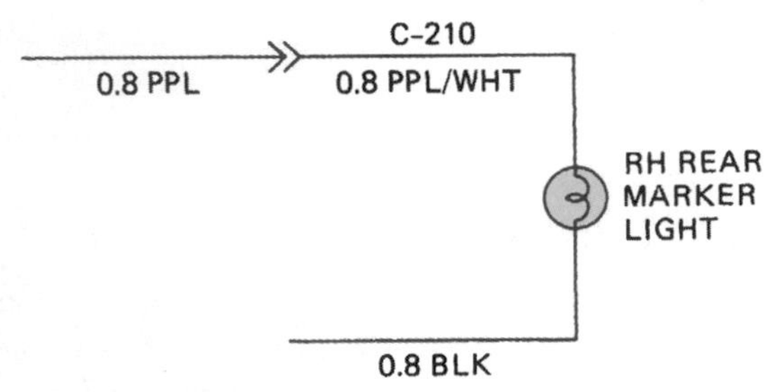

Figure 14–48 Typical section of a wiring diagram. Notice that the wire colour changes at connection C210. The ".8" represents the metric wire size in square millimetres.

The wire diagram also shows that the colour of the wire changes at the number C210. This stands for "connector #210" and is used for reference purposes. The symbol for the connection can vary depending on the manufacturer. The colour change from purple (PPL) to purple with a white tracer (PPL/WHT) is not important except for knowing where the wire changes colour in the circuit. The wire gauge has remained the same on both sides of the connection (0.8 square millimeters or 18-gauge). The ground circuit is the "0.8 BLK" wire. Figure 14–49 shows electrical and electronic symbols that are used in wiring and circuit diagrams.

Many other wiring diagrams use three-digit numbers for grounds (*G*), splices (*S*), and connectors (*C*). These numbers are arranged so that 100 through 199 indicate locations under the hood; 200 through 299 indicate locations under the dash; 300 through 399 indicate locations in the passenger compartment; and 400 through 499 indicate locations in the trunk area. See Figure 14–50.

SWITCHES

Electrical switches are drawn on a wiring diagram in their normal position. This can be one of two possible positions:

- **Normally open**—the switch is not connected to a terminal and no current flows in this position. This type of switch is labeled **N.O.**
- **Normally closed**—the switch is electrically connected to a contact and current will flow through the switch. This type of switch is labeled **N.C.**

Other switches can use more than two contacts.

The **poles** refer to the number of circuits completed by the switch, and the **throws** refer to the number of output circuits. A single-pole, single-throw

TECH TIP 

Read the Arrows

Wiring diagrams indicate connections by symbols that look like arrows. See Figure 14–51. Do *not* read these "arrows" as pointers showing the direction of current flow. Also observe that the power side (positive side) of the circuit is usually the female end of the connector. If a connector becomes disconnected, it will be difficult for the circuit to become shorted to ground or to another circuit because the wire is recessed inside the connector.

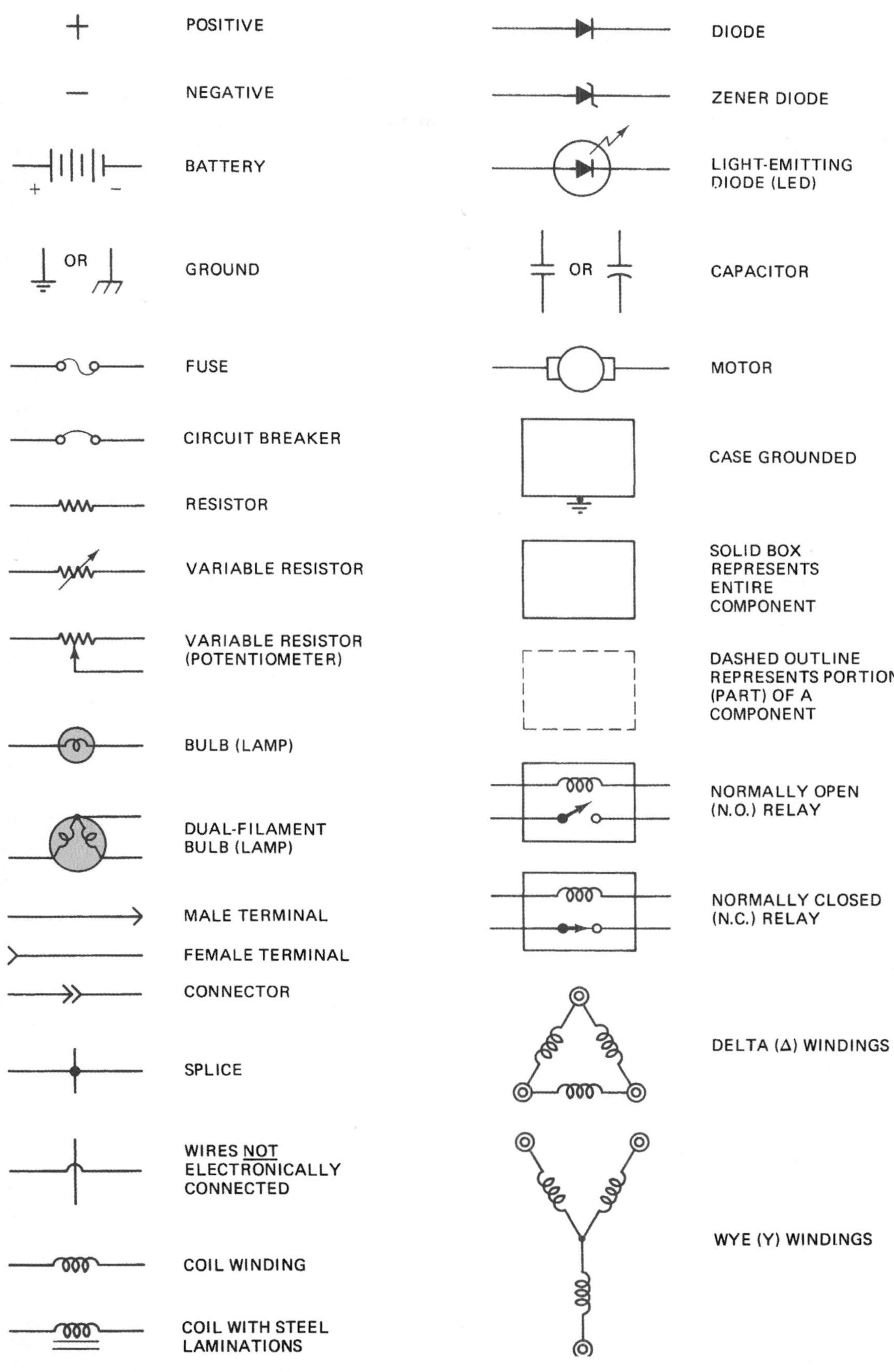

Figure 14–49 Typical electrical and electronic symbols used in automotive wiring and circuit diagrams.

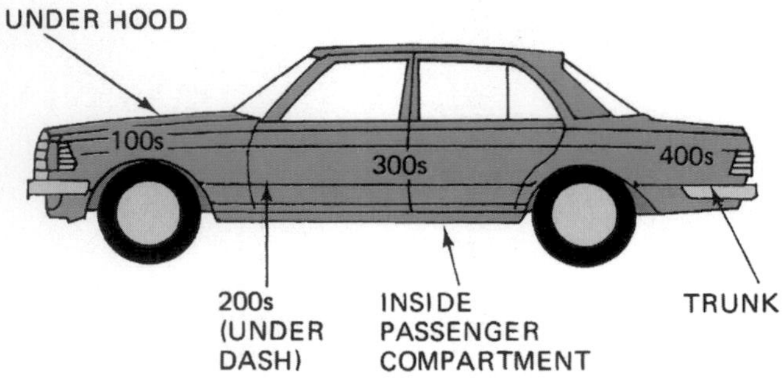

Figure 14–50 Connectors (*C*), grounds (*G*), and splices (*S*) are followed by a number generally indicating the location in the vehicle. For example, G209 is a ground connection located under the dash.

Figure 14–51 Typical connector. Note that the positive terminal is usually a female connector.

(SPST) switch has only two positions—on or off. A single-pole, double-throw (SPDT) switch has three terminals—one wire in and two wires out. A headlight dimmer switch is an example of a typical SPDT switch. In one position, the current flows to the low-filament headlight and in the other, the current flows to the high-filament headlight. There are also double-pole, single-throw (DPST) switches and double-pole, double-throw (DPDT) switches. See Figure 14–52.

RELAY TERMINAL IDENTIFICATION

Most automotive relays adhere to common terminal identification. Knowing this terminal information will help in the correct diagnosis and troubleshooting of any circuit containing a relay. See Figures 14–53 and 14–54.

The schematic is often printed or embossed on the side of the relay. The terminals are labelled to help the technician test and check for proper operation as shown in Figure 14–55. The identification of relay terminals also helps when trying to diagnose a circuit that contains a relay such as the horn circuit as shown in Figure 14–56.

De-spiking diodes or resistors are connected in parallel across the coil of most automotive relays (terminals 85 and 86).

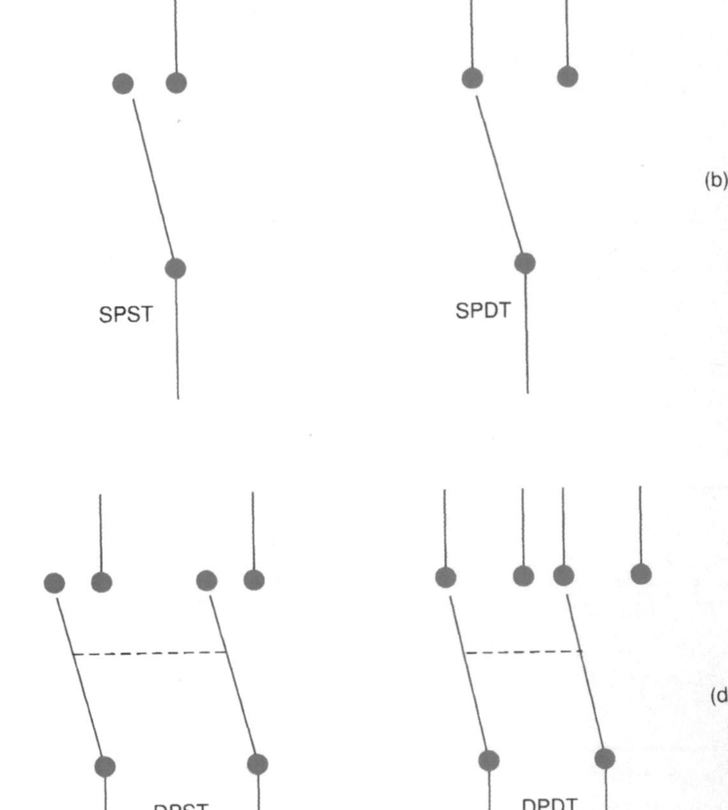

Figure 14–52 (a) A symbol for a single-pole, single-throw (SPST) switch. This type of switch is normally open (N.O.) because nothing is connected to the terminal that the switch is contacting in its normal position. (b) A single-pole, double-throw (SPDT) switch has three terminals. (c) A double-pole, single-throw (DPST) switch has two positions (off and on) and can control two separate circuits. (d) A double-pole, double-throw (DPDT) switch has six terminals—three for each pole.

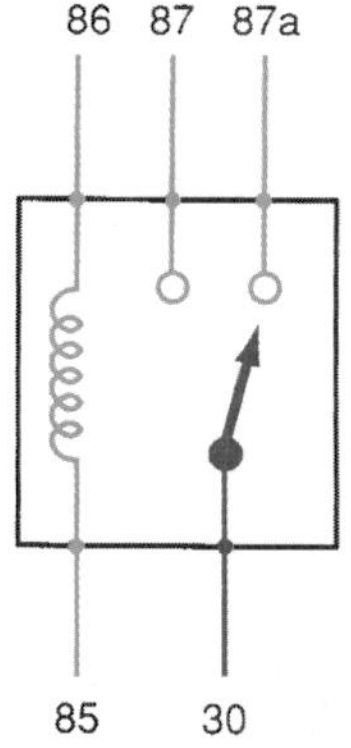

Figure 14–53 A relay uses a movable arm to complete a circuit whenever there is a power at terminal 86 and a ground at terminal 85. A typical relay only requires about 1/10 A through the relay coil. The movable arm then closes the contacts (#30 to #87) and can relay 30 A or more.

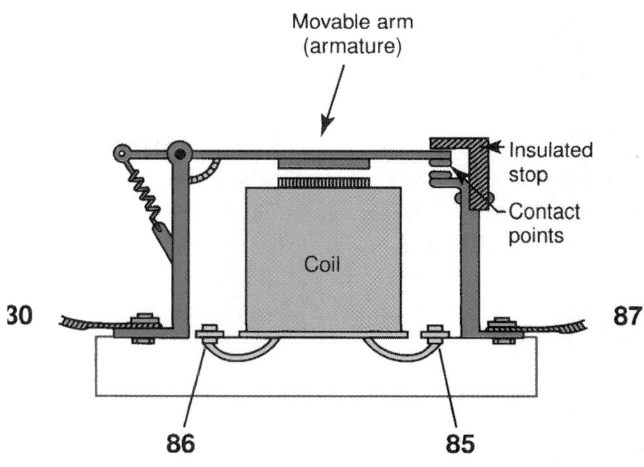

Figure 14–54 A cross-sectional view of a typical four-terminal relay. Current flowing through the coil (terminals 86 and 85) causes the movable arm (called the armature) to be drawn toward the coil magnet. The contact points complete the electrical circuit connected to terminals 30 and 87.

Figure 14–55 A typical relay showing the schematic of the wiring in the relay. Terminals #30 and #87 are electrically connected when the relay is energized.

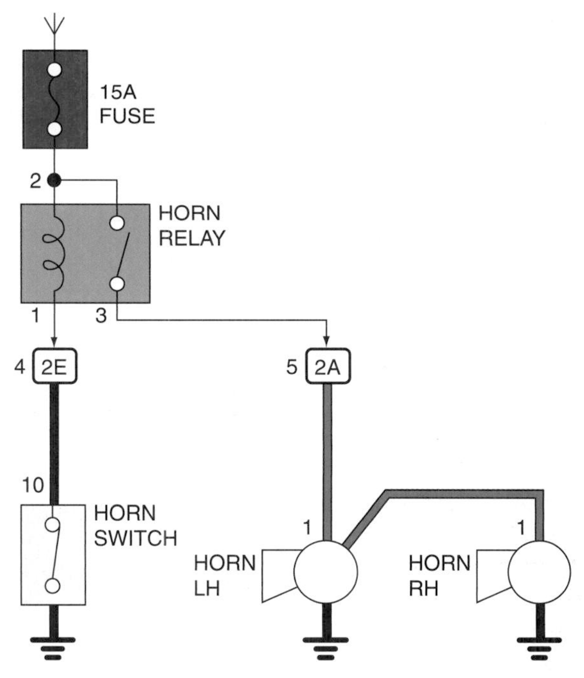

Figure 14–56 A typical horn circuit. Note that the relay contacts supply the heavy current to operate the horn when the horn switch simply completes a low current circuit to ground to cause the relay contacts to close.

TECH TIP 

Do It Right—Install a Relay

Often owners of vehicles, especially owners of pickup trucks and sport utility vehicles (SUVs), want to add additional electrical accessories or lighting. It is tempting to simply splice into an existing circuit. However, whenever another circuit or component is added, the current that flows through the newly added component is also added to the current for the original component. This additional current can easily overload the fuse and wiring. Do not simply install a larger-amperage fuse. The wire gauge size was not engineered for the additional current and could overheat.

The solution is to install a relay. A relay uses a small coil to create a magnetic field that causes a movable arm to switch on a higher-current circuit. The typical relay has from 50 to 150 ohms (usually 60 to 100 ohms) of resistance and requires just 0.24 to 0.08 ampere when connected to a 12 volt source. This small additional current will not be enough to overload the existing circuit. See Figure 14–57 for an example of how additional lighting can be added.

MULTIPLEXING

Multiplexing is a system that allows a number of on-board computers to share information. The signals are exchanged on a single, or two-wire, bus link that interconnects the computers, sensors, and actuators. The bus data link sends many signals over the same wire at almost the same time. If one computer is transmitting, the transfer of data from another computer (overlapping) is stopped until the bus data link is clear.

Digital signals are assigned identification codes that identify their priority. When two or more signals are sent at the same time, the signal with the highest priority is sent first.

Multiplexing also reduces the size of the wiring harnesses. Bulky harnesses that contained over 100 individual wires are now replaced by only one or two wires. Magnetic interference among the many wires in a conventional harness is virtually eliminated. The remaining two wires are often twisted to reduce electromagnetic induction.

Engines and transaxle/transmissions communicate through a local interconnect network (LIN), which reduces the number of sensors. As an example, one vehicle previously used a six-wire double TPS, one three-wire TPS for the transmission, and another three-wire TPS for the engine management; only one sensor is now needed to provide information for both.

Engine control, climate control (air conditioning), cruise control, and electronic speedometers often share the same LIN. Smaller systems such as door modules, mirrors, vehicle theft devices, horns, and locks will operate on small local area networks (LAN). These body control modules also share data with the PCM. See Figures 14–58 and 14–59.

Some bus data links are using fibre-optic cables and light signals in place of bus wiring.

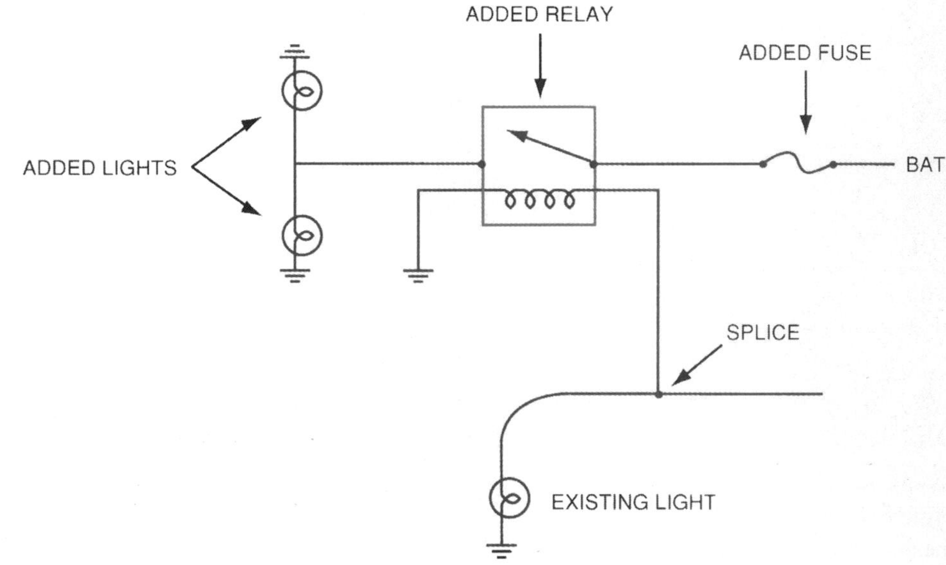

Figure 14–57 To add additional lighting, simply tap into an existing light wire and connect a relay. Whenever the existing light is turned on, the coil of the relay is energized. The arm of the relay then connects power from another circuit (fuse) to the auxiliary lights without overloading the existing light circuit.

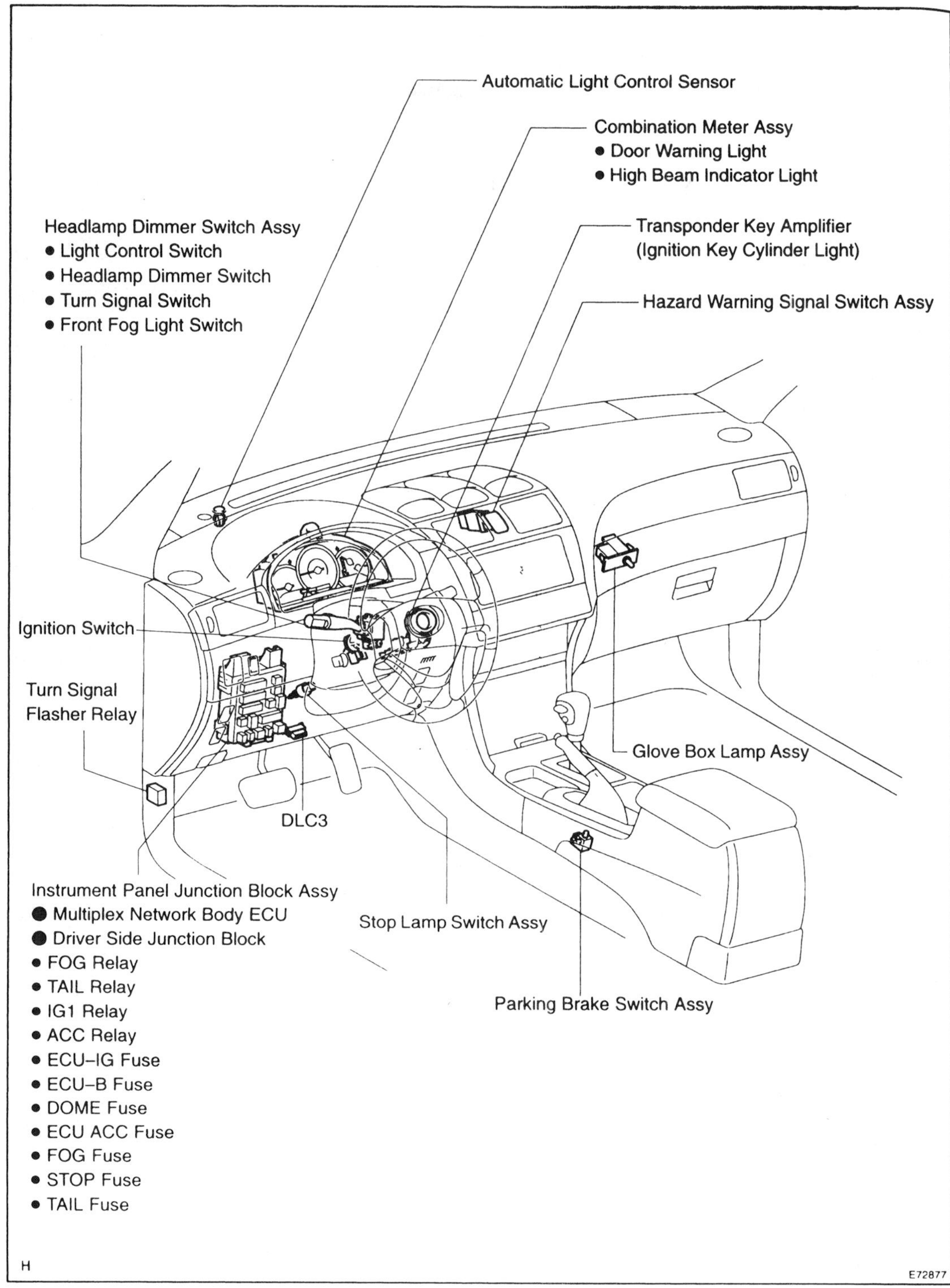

Figure 14–58 The multiplex network body ECU is located in the driver side junction block. (Courtesy Toyota Canada Inc.)

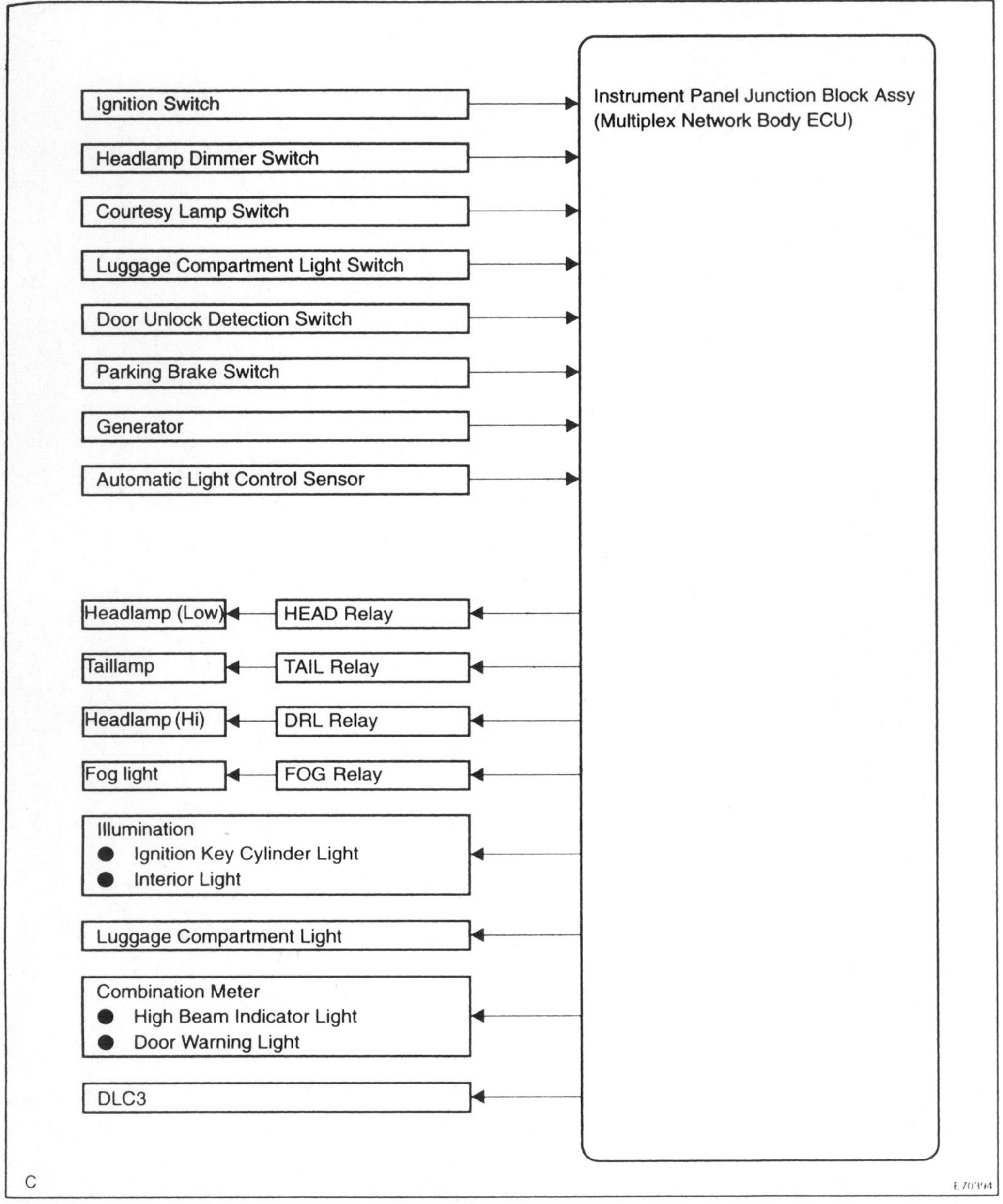

Figure 14–59 Lighting, illumination, generator, door locks, and brake switch all share information and control with the multiplex network body ECU. (Courtesy Toyota Canada Inc.)

USING WIRING DIAGRAMS FOR TROUBLESHOOTING

Follow these steps when troubleshooting wiring problems:

Step 1 Verify the malfunction. If, for example, the backup lights do not operate, make certain that the ignition is on (run position/engine off), with the gear selector in reverse, and check for operation of the backup lights.

Step 2 Check everything else that does or does not operate correctly. For example, if the taillights are also failing to operate, the problem could be a loose or broken ground connection in the trunk area that is shared by both the backup lights and the taillights.

Step 3 Check the fuse for the backup lights. See Figure 14–60.

Step 4 Check for voltage at the backup light socket. This can be done using a test light or a voltmeter.

If voltage is available at the socket, the problem is either a defective bulb or a poor ground at the socket or a ground wire connection to the body

Figure 14–60 Always check the simple things first. Check the fuse for the circuit you are testing. Maybe a fault in another circuit controlled by the same fuse could have caused the fuse to blow. Use a test light to check that both sides of the fuse have voltage.

or frame. If no voltage is available at the socket, consult a wiring diagram for the type of vehicle being tested. The wiring diagram should show all of the wiring and components included in the circuit. For example, the backup light current must flow through the fuse and ignition switch to the gear selector switch before travelling to the rear backup light socket. As stated in the second step, the fuse used for the backup lights may also be used for other circuits in the vehicle.

The wiring diagram can be used to determine all other components that share the same fuse. If the fuse is blown (open circuit), the cause can be a short in any of the circuits sharing the same fuse. Because the backup light circuit current must be switched on and off by the gear selector switch, an open in the switch can also prevent the backup lights from functioning.

HINT: Bad grounds in headlight circuits often cause dim lighting because of added resistance. Although the total current is reduced, current flow actually "speeds up" getting through the smaller conductor area at the bad connection. This creates heat that may be felt by running your hand over the suspected area.

Frequently Asked Question ???

Where to Start?

The common question is, where does a technician start the troubleshooting when using a wiring diagram (schematic)?

Hint 1 If the circuit contains a relay, start your diagnosis at the relay. The entire circuit can be tested at the terminals of the relay.

Hint 2 The easiest first step is to locate the unit on the schematic that is not working at all or not working correctly.
(a) Trace where the unit gets its ground connection.
(b) Trace where the unit gets its power connection.
Often a ground is used by more than one component. Therefore, ensure that everything else is working correctly. If not, then the fault may lie at the common ground (or power) connection.

Hint 3 Divide the circuit in half by locating a connector or a part of the circuit that can be accessed easily. Then check for power and ground at this midpoint. This step could save you much time.

LOCATING A SHORT CIRCUIT

A short circuit usually blows a fuse and a replacement fuse often also blows in the attempt to locate the source of the short circuit. Several methods can be used to locate the short.

Fuse Replacement Method

Disconnect one component at a time and then replace the fuse. If the new fuse blows, continue the process until the location of the short is determined. This method uses many fuses and is *not* a preferred method for finding a short circuit.

Circuit Breaker Method

Another method is to connect an automotive circuit breaker to the contacts of the fuse holder with alligator clips. Circuit breakers are available that plug directly into the fuse panel, replacing a blade-type fuse. The circuit breaker will alternately open and close the circuit, protecting the wiring from possible overheating damage while still providing current flow through the circuit.

NOTE: A heavy-duty (HD) flasher can also be used in place of a circuit breaker to open and close the circuit. Wires and terminals must be made to connect the flasher unit where the fuse normally plugs in.

All components included in the defective circuit should be disconnected one at a time until the circuit breaker stops clicking. The last unit disconnected is the unit causing the short circuit. If the circuit breaker continues to click with all circuit components unplugged, the problem is in the wiring *from* the fuse panel *to* any one of the units in the circuit. Visual inspection of all the wiring or further disconnecting will be necessary to locate the problem.

NOTE: A buzzer or 12 V test light may be substituted for the circuit breaker.

Ohmmeter Method

The third method uses an ohmmeter connected to the fuse holder and ground. This is the recommended method of finding a short circuit. What is a short circuit? It is an electrical connection to another wire or to ground before the current flows through some or all of the resistance in the circuit. An ohmmeter will indicate low ohms when connected to a short circuit. An ohmmeter should never be connected to an operating circuit. The correct procedure for locating a short using an ohmmeter is as follows:

1. Connect one lead of an ohmmeter (set to a low scale) to a good clean metal ground and the other lead to the *circuit side* of the fuse holder.

CAUTION: Connecting the lead to the power side of the fuse holder will cause current flow through and damage to the ohmmeter.

2. The ohmmeter will read zero or almost zero ohms if the circuit is shorted.
3. Disconnect one component in the circuit at a time and watch the ohmmeter. If the ohmmeter reading goes to high ohms or infinity, the component just unplugged was the source of the short circuit.

Gauss Gauge Method

If a short circuit blows a fuse, a special pulsing circuit breaker (similar to a flasher unit) can be installed in the circuit in place of the fuse. Current will flow through the circuit until the circuit breaker opens the circuit. As soon as the circuit breaker opens the circuit, it closes again. This on-and-off current flow creates a pulsing magnetic field around the wire carrying the current. Use a small handheld Gauss gauge to observe this pulsing magnetic field, which is indicated on the gauge as needle movement to the left, then to the right of centre. This pulsing magnetic field will register on the Gauss gauge even through the metal body of the vehicle. A needle-type compass can also be used to observe the pulsing magnetic field. See Figures 14–61 and 14–62.

Electronic Tone Generator Tester

An electronic tone generator tester can be used to locate a short-to-ground or an open circuit. Similar to test equipment used to test telephone and cable television lines, this tester generates a tone that can be heard through a receiver (probe). See Figure 14–63. The tone will be heard as long as there is a continuous electrical path along the circuit. The signal will stop if there is an open (break) or short-to-ground in the circuit. See Figures 14–64 and 14–65. The windings in solenoids and relays will increase the strength of the signal in these locations.

(a)

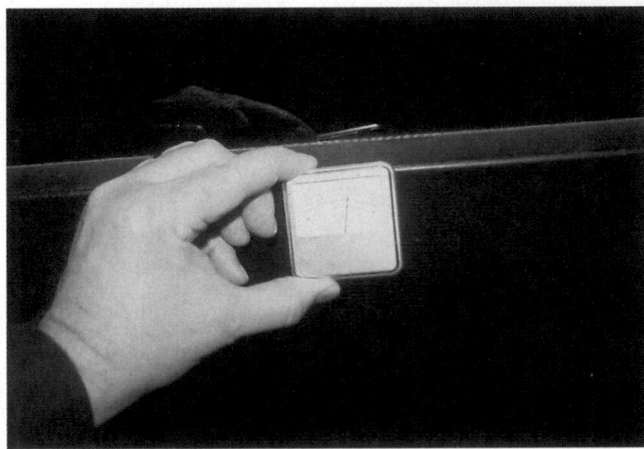

(b)

Figure 14–61 (a) After removing the blown fuse, a pulsing circuit breaker is connected to the terminals of the fuse. (b) The circuit breaker causes current to flow, then stop, then flow again, through the circuit up to the point of the short-to-ground. By observing the Gauss gauge, the location of the short is indicated near where the needle stops moving due to the magnetic field created by the flow of current through the wire.

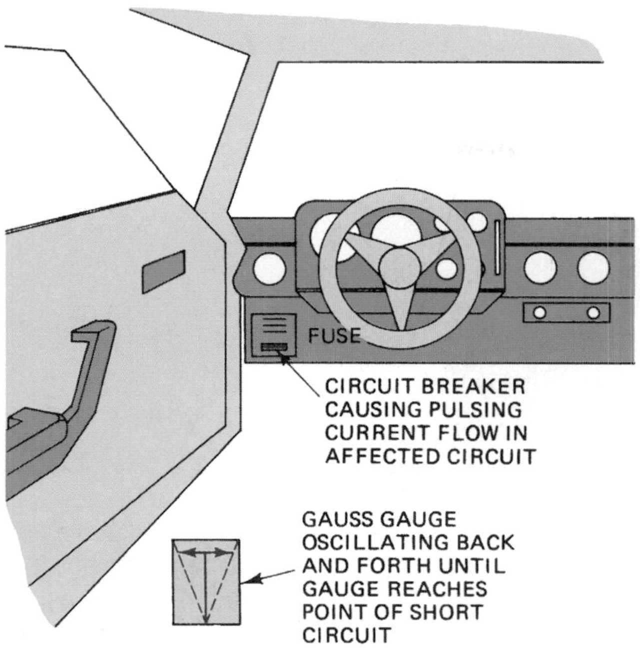

Figure 14–62 A Gauss gauge can be used to determine the location of a short circuit even behind a metal panel.

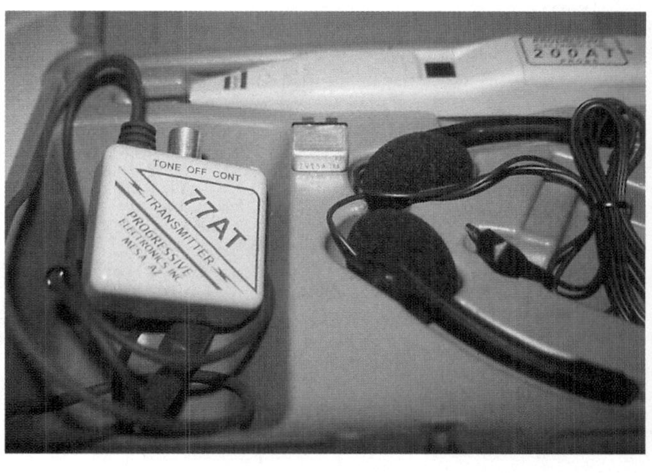

Figure 14–63 A tone-generator-type tester used to locate open circuits and circuits that are shorted-to-ground. Included with this tester is a transmitter (tone generator), receiver (probe), and headphones for use in noisy shops.

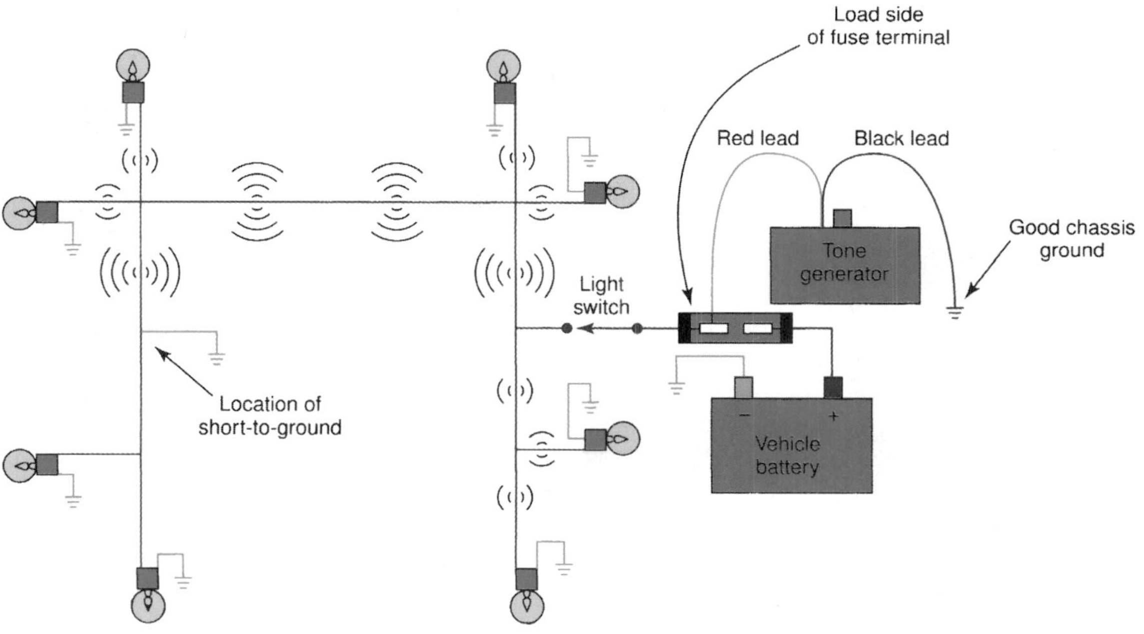

Figure 14–64 To check for a short-to-ground using a tone generator, connect the black transmitter lead to a good chassis ground and the red lead to the load side of the fuse terminal. Turn the transmitter on and check for tone signal with the receiver. Using a wiring diagram, follow the strongest signal to the location of the short-to-ground. There will be no signal beyond the fault.

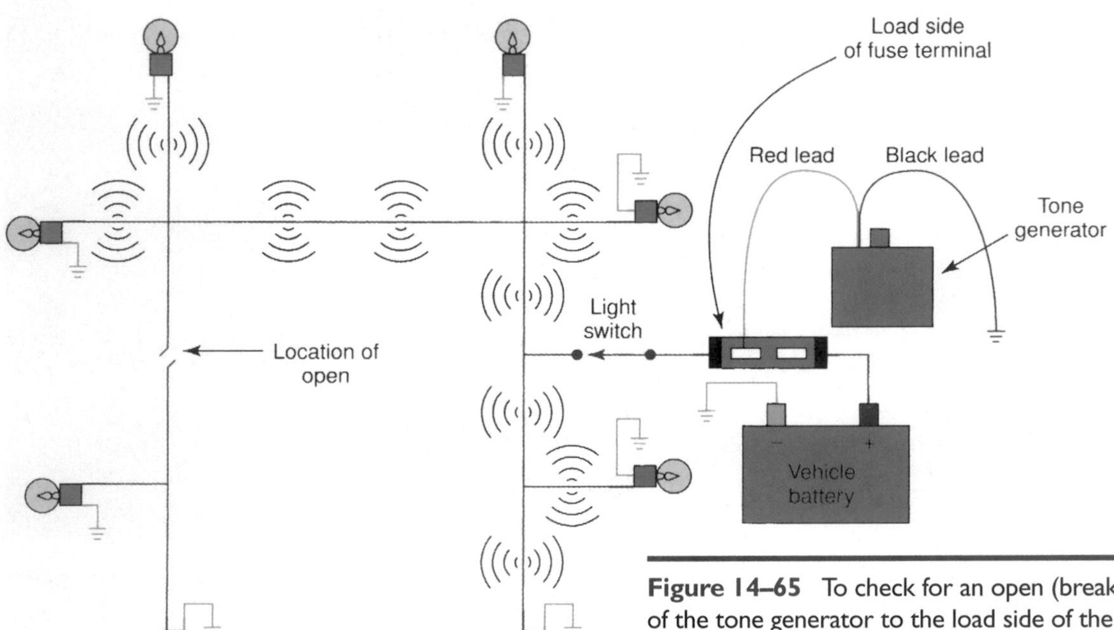

Figure 14–65 To check for an open (break), connect the red lead of the tone generator to the load side of the fuse terminal and the black lead to a good chassis ground. Turn on the transmitter and then listen for the tone signal with the receiver set in the open position. Using a wiring diagram, follow the signal along the circuit until the tone stops, indicating the location of the open.

TECH TIP

Heat or Movement

Electrical shorts are commonly caused either by movement, which causes the insulation around wiring to be worn away, or by heat melting the insulation. When checking for a short circuit, first check the wiring that is susceptible to heat, movement, and damage:

1. Heat: wiring near heat sources, such as the exhaust system, cigarette lighter, or generator
2. Wire movement: wiring that moves, such as in areas near the doors, trunk, or hood
3. Damage: wiring subject to mechanical injury, such as in the trunk, where heavy objects can move around and smash or damage wiring

TECH TIP

Wiggle Test

Intermittent electrical problems are common yet difficult to locate. To help locate these hard-to-find problems, try operating the circuit and then start wiggling the wires and connections that control the circuit. If in doubt where the wiring goes, try moving all the wiring starting at the battery. Pay particular attention to wiring running near the battery or the windshield washer container. Corrosion can cause wiring to fail, and battery acid fumes and alcohol-based windshield washer fluid can start or contribute to the problem. If you notice any change in the operation of the device being tested while wiggling the wiring, look closer in the area you were wiggling until the actual problem is located and corrected

Ford vehicles have a built-in "wiggle test" programmed into the on-board computer. A handheld scan tool is used to activate this program when a wiring problem is indicated with any of the computer-controlled circuits.

During this test, the wiring harness and connectors are manipulated – tapped lightly and wiggled. The scan tool will emit an audible "buzz" when the bad connection is disturbed.

ELECTRICAL TROUBLESHOOTING GUIDE

When troubleshooting any electrical component, remember the following hints to find the problem faster and more easily:

- For a device to work, it must have two things: power and ground.
- If there is no power to a device, an open power side (blown fuse, etc.) is indicated.
- If there is power on both sides of a device, an open ground is indicated.
- If a fuse blows immediately, a grounded power-side wire is indicated.
- Most electrical faults result from heat, movement or corrosion.
- Most noncomputer-controlled devices operate by opening and closing the power side of the circuit.
- Most computer-controlled devices operate by opening and closing the ground side of the circuit.

PHOTO SEQUENCE 10 Meter Usage

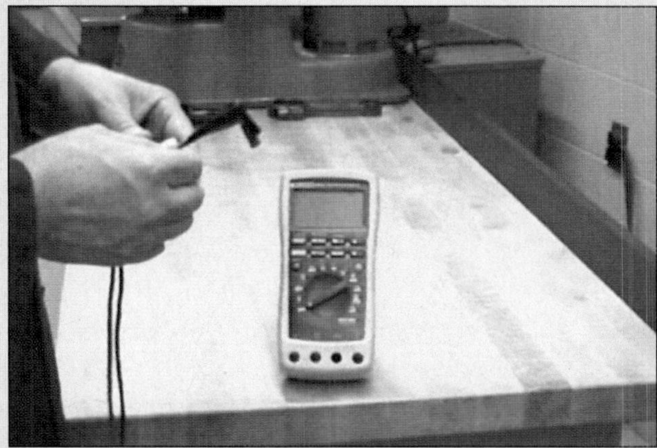

P10–1 Meter leads often become tangled. Start work with a digital meter by straightening the meter leads.

P10–2 To help prevent the leads from becoming tangled, tie a loose knot at the meter end of the leads.

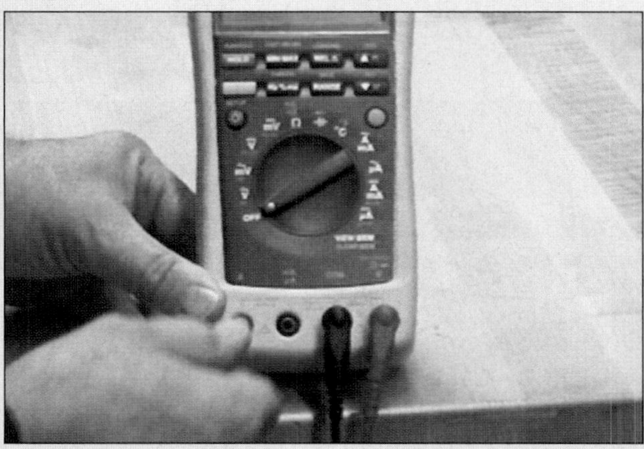

P10–3 For most electrical measurements, the black meter lead is inserted in the terminal labeled COM and the red meter lead is inserted into the terminal labeled V.

P10–4 To use a digital meter, turn the power switch on and select the unit of electricity to be measured. In this case, the rotary switch is turned to select DC volts indicated by the letter V with a straight line and a straight dotted line over the V.

P10–5 If AC volts are selected (a V with a wavy line on top)—AC millivolts in this case—a reading usually appears on the display indicating an AC voltage is being induced in the meter leads from the fluorescent lights in the room.

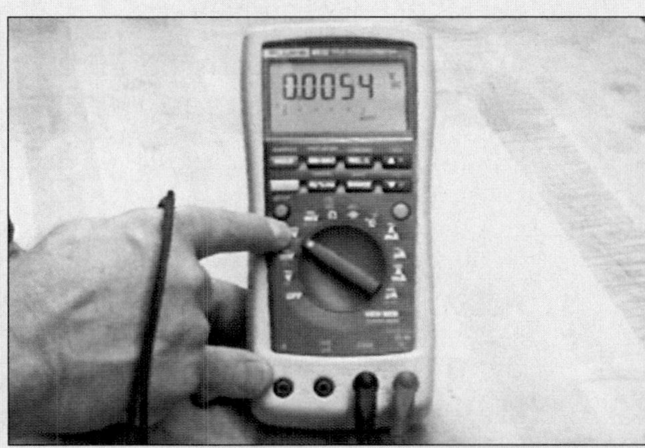

P10–6 For most automotive electrical use, select DC volts.

Meter Usage—continued

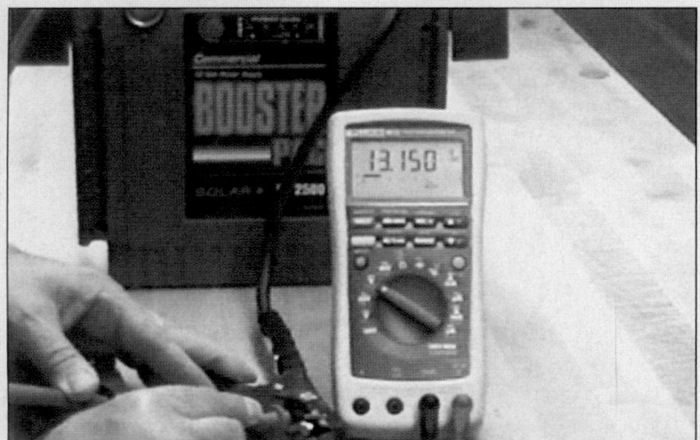

P10–7 Connect the red meter lead to the positive (+) terminal of a battery and the black meter lead to the negative (−) terminal. The meter reads the voltage difference between the leads.

P10–8 This jump-start battery unit measures 13.151 volts with the meter set on auto ranging on the DC voltage scale. The accuracy of this meter (Fluke 89 IV) is greater than necessary for most automotive service work so the reading could be rounded to 13.2 V.

P10–9 Another meter (Fluke 87 III) displays four digits when measuring the voltage of the battery jumper start unit.

P10–10 Both meters are displayed side by side to show the readings of both. The Fluke 89 IV (right) is capable of measuring down to 1/1000 of a volt.

P10–11 Meters can also be set to read different ranges. The "range" button was pressed once on the meter on the left and notice that the meter is now set to read higher voltages. Note the added zero on the left of the display. The meter in this range setting cannot display any more accurately than 1/10 of a volt (13.1).

P10–12 Pressing the range button a second time on the meter results in the loss of 1/10 of a volt reading and the addition of another zero on the left of the display.

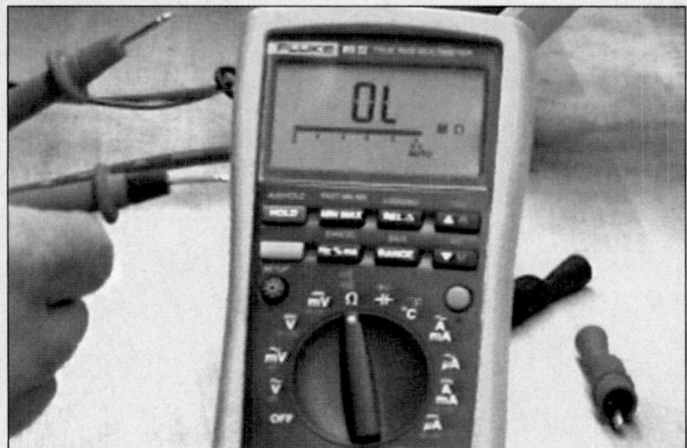

P10–13 To measure resistance, turn the rotary dial to the ohm (Ω) symbol. With the meter leads separated, the meter display reads OL (over limit), meaning that the resistance between the meter leads is higher than is being read by the meter.

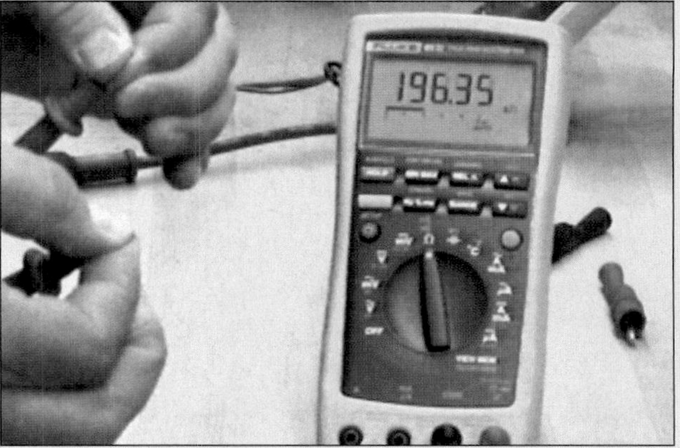

P10–14 The meter can read your own body resistance if you grasp the meter lead terminals with your fingers. The reading on the display indicates 196.35 kΩ or 196 350 Ω. Typical body resistance constantly changes and is usually between 100 000 and 300 000 Ω (100 kΩ to 300 kΩ).

P10–15 When measuring anything, be sure to read the meter face. In this case, the meter is reading 291.10 kΩ. The letter k represents 1000 Ω so the reading displayed is 291.10 thousand ohms or 291 100 Ω.

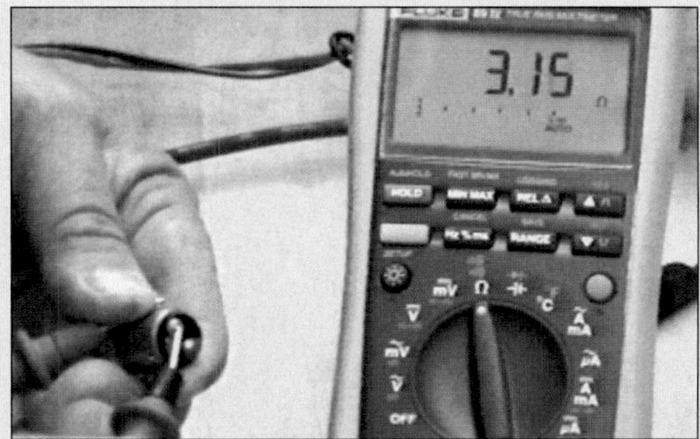

P10–16 A meter set on ohms can be used to check the resistance of a light bulb filament. In this case, the meter reads 3.15 Ω. If the bulb were bad (filament open), the meter would display OL.

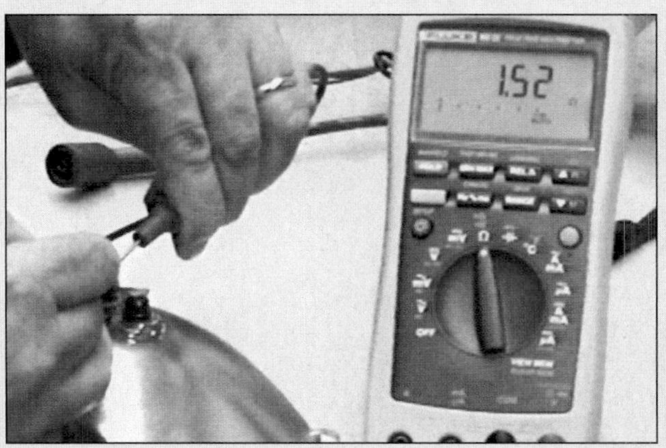

P10–17 A sealed beam headlight bulb is being measured. The filament being measured has 1.52 Ω. The only symbol in the window is the Ω symbol, which means that the display is showing the actual resistance in ohms (and not kΩ or MΩ).

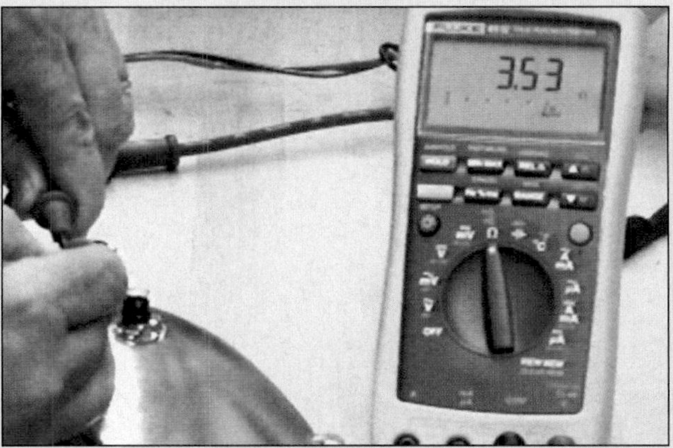

P10–18 The other filament reads 3.53 Ω. Obviously, this filament is the low beam (high resistance means less current flow and a dimmer light).

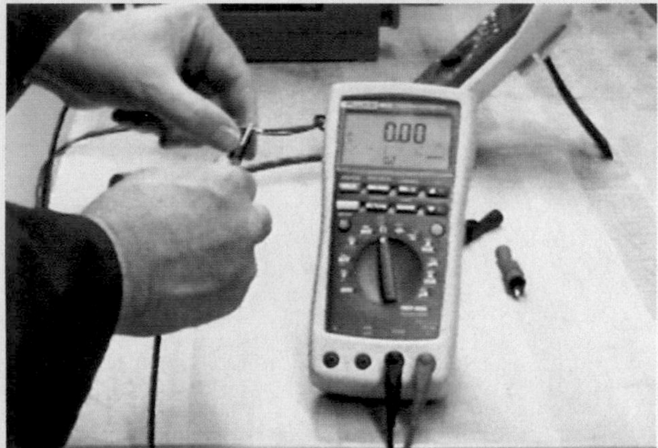

P10–19 A digital meter set to read ohms should measure 0.00 as shown when the meter leads are touched together. Some meters, such as this Fluke, have a relative button that can be pushed in order to zero the reading if necessary to compensate for the resistance of the meter leads.

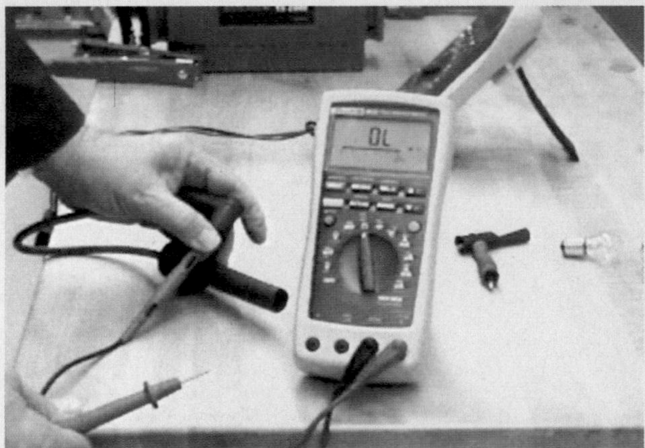

P10–20 To measure the resistance of a spark plug wire, attach one end of the meter to one end and the other meter lead to the other end. The polarity (which meter lead is attached to which part of the component being measured) is not important when measuring resistance.

P10–21 The spark plug wire measures 5.900 kΩ. With length of 300 mm (1ft) the wire is okay because its resistance is less than 33 Ω/mm × 300 mm = 10 kΩ (10 kΩ/ft).

P10–22 A digital multimeter can also be used to check the voltage of an electrical outlet. Set the meter to read AC volts. When measuring AC volts, either meter lead can be inserted in either outlet terminal. Just be careful not to touch either of the metal tips of the meter leads.

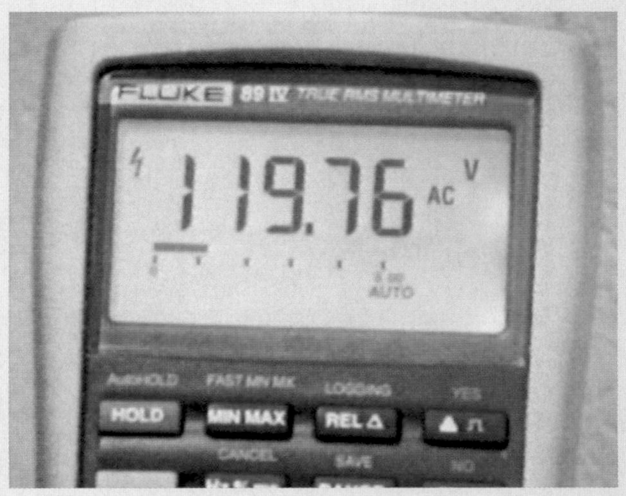

P10–23 The outlet voltage is 119.76 V AC. Note the AC and V in the window display.

■ SUMMARY

1. The higher the AWG size number, the smaller the wire.
2. Metric wire is sized in square millimeters (mm^2).
3. All circuits should be protected by a fuse. The current in the circuit should be about 80% of the fuse rating.
4. Circuit breakers and fusible links are other circuit protection devices.
5. A terminal is the metal end of a wire, whereas a connector is the plastic connection.
6. All wire repair should use either soldering or a crimp-and-seal connector.
7. Most wiring diagrams include the wire colour, circuit number, and wire gauge.

■ REVIEW QUESTIONS

1. Describe the AWG wire gauge system and compare it to the metric system.
2. Explain the difference between a terminal and a connector.
3. Discuss how fuses, PTC circuit protectors, circuit breakers, and fusible links protect a circuit.
4. Describe how to perform a wire repair.
5. Describe how to locate a short circuit using a Gauss gauge.

■ RED SEAL CERTIFICATION-TYPE QUESTIONS

1. The higher the AWG number, ________.
   - **a.** The smaller the wire
   - **b.** The larger the wire
   - **c.** The thicker the insulation
   - **d.** The more strands in the conductor core
2. Metric wire size is measured in units of ________.
   - **a.** Metres
   - **b.** Cubic centimetres
   - **c.** Square millimetres
   - **d.** Cubic millimetres
3. Which statement is true about fuse ratings?
   - **a.** The fuse rating should be 80% of the maximum current for the circuit.
   - **b.** The lead strip in a fuse melts with excessive current.
   - **c.** The current in the circuit should equal 50% of the fuse rating.
   - **d.** The fuse rating should be higher than the normal current for the circuit.
4. Which statements are true about wire, terminals, and connectors?
   - **a.** Wire is called a *lead,* and the metal end is a *connector.*
   - **b.** A connector is usually a plastic piece where terminals lock in.
   - **c.** A lead and a terminal are the same thing.
   - **d.** A lead and a connector are the same thing.
5. The type of solder that should be used for electrical work is ________.
   - **a.** Rosin core
   - **b.** Acid core
   - **c.** 60/40 with no flux
   - **d.** 50/50 with acid paste flux
6. On a wiring diagram, S-110 with a ".8 BRN/BLK" means ______.
   - **a.** Circuit #.8 is spliced under the hood
   - **b.** A connector with 0.8 square millimeter wire
   - **c.** A splice of a brown with black stripe, wire size being 0.8 square millimetres (18 gauge AWG)
   - **d.** A black and brown 8 gauge AWG wire
7. A high-impedance digital meter is necessary to measure electronic circuits because it _____.
   - **a.** Is very accurate
   - **b.** Can measure high resistances
   - **c.** Will not interfere with the electronic circuit due to its high internal resistance
   - **d.** Interfaces with the electronics on the proper scale
8. A voltmeter ______________.
   - **a.** Is connected to a circuit in parallel
   - **b.** Is connected to a circuit in series
   - **c.** Requires that the circuit be disconnected from a power source before being connected
   - **d.** Must be used on a circuit with no current flowing
9. An ohmmeter ______________.
   - **a.** Is connected to a circuit in parallel
   - **b.** Is connected to a circuit in series
   - **c.** Requires that the circuit be disconnected from a power source before being connected
   - **d.** Both a and c
10. An ammeter ________________.
    - **a.** Is connected to a circuit in parallel
    - **b.** Is connected to a circuit in series
    - **c.** Requires that the circuit be disconnected from a power source before being connected
    - **d.** Can only be used in a circuit with no current flowing

15

Batteries and Battery Testing

OBJECTIVES: After studying Chapter 15, you should be able to:

1. Prepare for the interprovincial Red Seal certification examination in Appendix III (Electrical/Electronic Systems) on the topics covered in this chapter.
2. Describe how a battery works.
3. List the precautions necessary whenever working with batteries.
4. Explain how to safely charge a battery.
5. Discuss how to perform a battery drain test.
6. Explain the construction of an absorbent glass mat (AGM) battery.
7. Describe the difference between a spiral wound and a flat plate battery.
8. Describe the advantages and disadvantages of a 42 volt electrical system.

Everything electrical in a vehicle is supplied with current from the battery. The battery is one of the most important parts of a vehicle.

PURPOSE OF A BATTERY

The primary purpose of an automotive battery is to provide a source of electrical power for starting and for electrical demands that exceed generator output. The battery also acts as a stabilizer to the voltage for the entire electrical system. The battery is a voltage stabilizer because it acts as a reservoir where large amounts of current (amperes) can be removed quickly during starting and replaced gradually by the generator during charging. The battery *must* be in good (serviceable) condition before the charging system and the cranking system can be tested.

BATTERY CONSTRUCTION

Most automotive battery cases (container or covers) are constructed of polypropylene, a thin, strong, and lightweight plastic. Inside the case there are six cells of 2.1 volts each connected in series (for a 12 volt battery). Each cell has positive and negative plates. See Figures 15–1 and 15–2. Built into the bottom of many batteries are ribs that support the lead-alloy plates and provide a space for sediment to settle, called the **sediment chamber.** Some maintenance-free batteries do not have a sediment chamber but enclose the plates in an envelope-type separator that prevents material from settling to the bottom of the battery case. See Figure 15–3.

Maintenance-free is a term used to describe batteries that use little water during normal service because of the alloy material used to construct the battery plate grids. Maintenance-free batteries are also called **low-water-loss** batteries.

Grids

Each positive and negative plate in a battery is constructed on a framework or **grid** made primarily of lead. Lead is a soft material and must be strengthened for use in an automotive battery grid. Adding antimony or calcium to the pure lead adds strength to the lead grids. See Figure 15–4. Battery grids hold the active material and provide the electrical pathways for the current created in the plate.

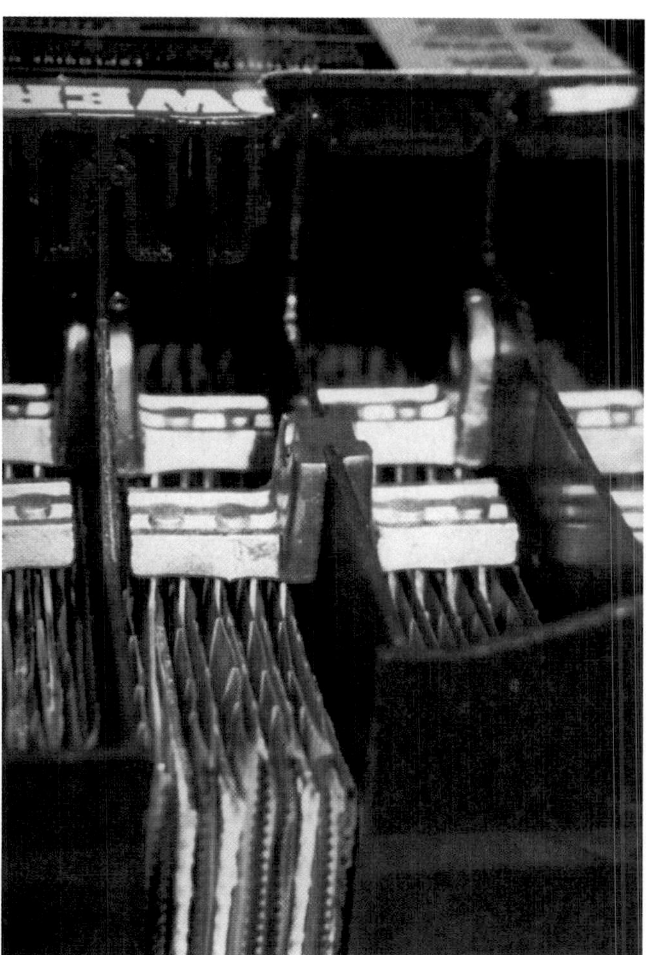

Figure 15–1 Photo of a cutaway battery showing the connection of the cells to each other through the partition.

Figure 15–2 Take a metal-cased 9 volt battery apart and you will discover six individual 1.5 volt AAAA dry-cell batteries electrically connected in series to provide 9 volts ($1.5 \times 6 = 9$). An automotive battery uses individual cells (2.1 volts each) that are connected in series to provide a battery with 12.6 volts fully charged.

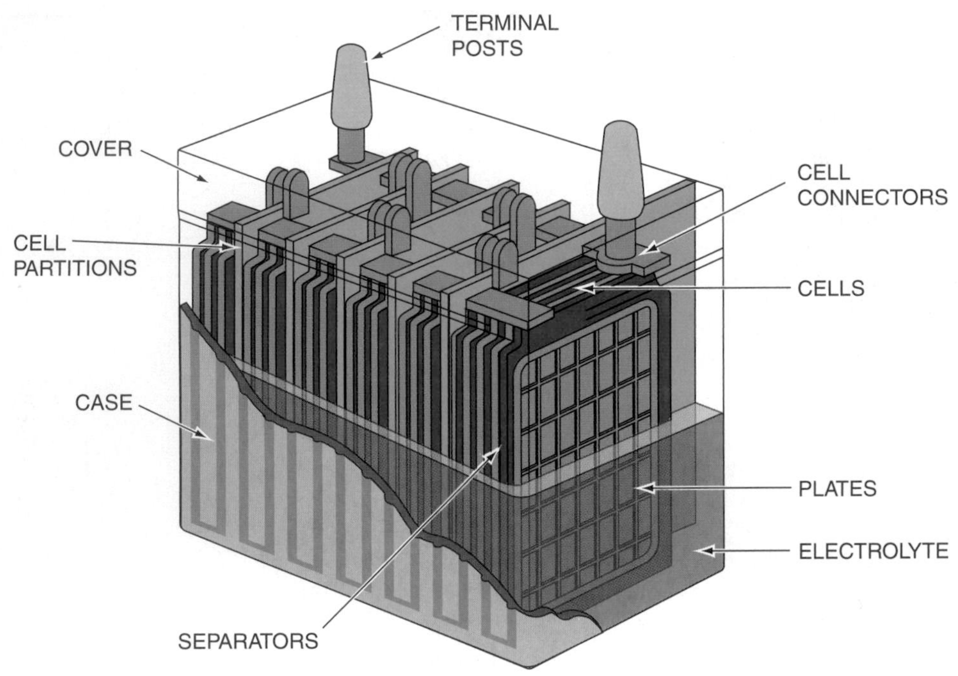

Figure 15–3 A typical battery showing all of its component parts.

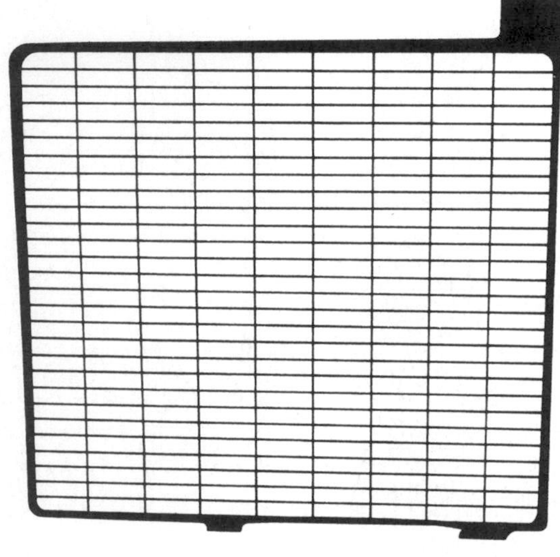

Figure 15–4 Lead-alloy grid. The active battery materials are "pasted" onto these grids.

Maintenance-Free Battery Grids Older batteries used up to 5% **antimony** in the construction of the plate grids to add strength. However, the greater the amount of antimony, the greater the amount of gassing (releasing of hydrogen gas and oxygen gas), and therefore the amount of water used. Newer low-maintenance batteries use **calcium** instead of antimony.

Low-maintenance batteries use a low percentage of antimony (about 2% to 3%) or use antimony only in the positive plates and use calcium for the negative plates. The chemical reactions that occur inside each battery are identical regardless of the type of material used to construct the grid plates.

Positive Plates The positive plates have *lead dioxide (peroxide)* placed onto the grid framework, a process called **pasting.** This active material can react with the sulphuric acid of the battery and is dark brown in colour.

Negative Plates The negative plates are pasted with a pure **porous lead,** called **sponge lead,** and are gray in colour.

Separators The positive and the negative plates must be installed alternately next to each other without touching. Nonconducting **separators** are used, which allow room for the reaction of the acid with both plate materials yet insulate the plates to prevent shorts. These separators are porous (with many small holes) and have ribs facing the positive plate. Separators can be made from resin-coated paper, porous rubber, fibreglass, or expanded plastic. Many batteries use envelope-type separators that encase the entire plate and help prevent any material that may shed from the plates from causing a short circuit between the plates at the bottom of the battery.

Cells **Cells,** also called **elements,** are constructed of positive and negative plates with insulating separators between each plate. Most batteries use one more negative plate than positive plate in each cell, but many newer batteries use the same number of positive and negative plates. Each cell is actually a 2.1 V battery, regardless of the number of positive or negative plates used. The greater the number of plates used in each cell, the greater the amount of *current* that can be produced. The capacity of a battery is determined by the amount of active plate material in the battery and the area of the plate material exposed to the liquid, called *electrolyte,* in the battery.

Electrolyte The electrolyte used in automotive batteries is a solution (liquid combination) of 36% sulphuric acid and 64% water. This electrolyte is used for both lead-antimony and lead-calcium (maintenance-free) batteries. The chemical symbol for this sulphuric acid solution is H_2SO_4.

H = Symbol for hydrogen (the subscript 2 means that there are two atoms of hydrogen)

S = Symbol for sulphur

O = Symbol for oxygen (the subscript 4 indicates that there are four atoms of oxygen)

This electrolyte is sold premixed in the proper proportion and is factory installed or added to the battery when the battery is sold. Additional electrolyte must *never* be added to any battery after the original electrolyte fill. It is normal for some water (H_2O) to escape during charging as a result of the **gassing** that is produced by the chemical reactions. Only pure distilled water should be added to a battery. If distilled water is not available, clean drinking water can be used.

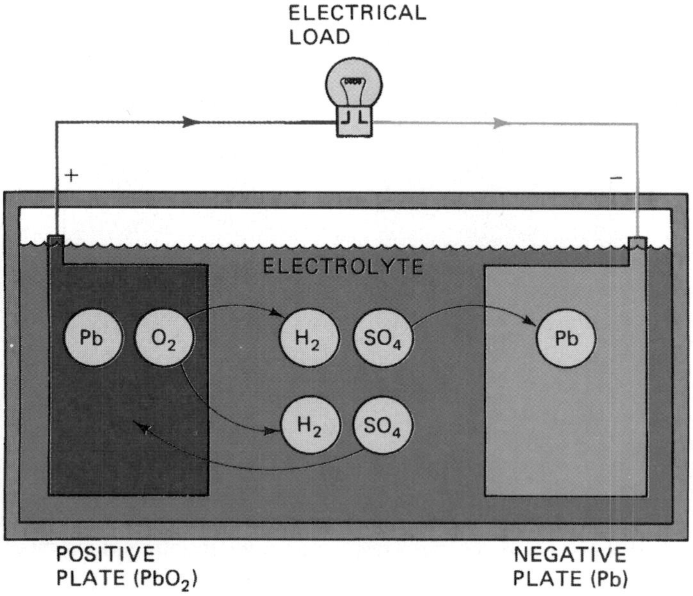

Figure 15–5 Chemical reaction for a lead-acid battery that is fully *charged* being discharged by the attached electrical load.

HOW A BATTERY WORKS

A fully charged lead-acid battery has a positive plate of lead dioxide (peroxide) and a negative plate of lead surrounded by a sulphuric acid solution (electrolyte). The difference in potential (voltage) between lead peroxide and lead in acid is approximately 2.1 V.

During Discharging

The positive-plate lead dioxide (PbO_2) combines with the SO_4 from the electrolyte and releases its O_2 into the electrolyte, forming H_2O. The negative plate also combines with the SO_4 from the electrolyte and becomes lead sulphate ($PbSO_4$). See Figure 15–5.

The Fully Discharged State

When the battery is fully discharged, both the positive and the negative plates are $PbSO_4$ (**lead sulphate**) and the electrolyte has become mostly water (H_2O). It is usually not possible for a battery to become 100% discharged. However, as the battery is being discharged, the plates and electrolyte approach the completely dead situation. There is also the danger of freezing when a battery is discharged, because the electrolyte is mostly water.

During Charging

During charging, the sulphate (acid) leaves both the positive and the negative plates and returns to the electrolyte, where it becomes normal-strength sulphuric acid solution. The positive plate returns to lead dioxide (PbO_2) and the negative plate is again pure lead (Pb). See Figure 15–6.

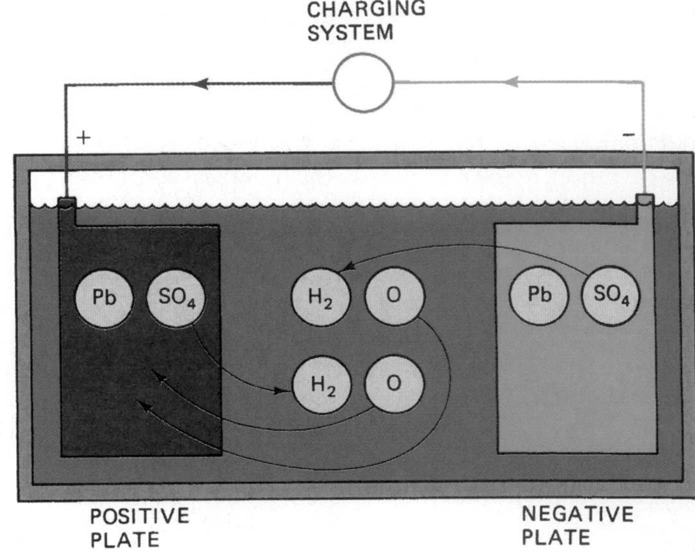

Figure 15–6 Chemical reaction for a lead-acid battery that is fully *discharged* being charged by the attached generator.

SPECIFIC GRAVITY

The amount of sulphate in the electrolyte is determined by the electrolyte's **specific gravity.** Specific gravity is the ratio of the weight of a given volume of a liquid to the weight of an equal volume of water. In other words, the more dense the material (liquid), the higher its specific gravity. Pure water is the basis for this measurement and has a specific gravity of 1.000 at 27°C (80°F). Pure sulphuric acid has a specific gravity of 1.835. The *correct* concentration of water and sulphuric acid (called *electrolyte*—64% water, 36% acid) is 1.260 to 1.280 at 27°C (80°F). The higher the battery's specific gravity, the more fully it is charged. See Figure 15–7. The majority of original-equipment batteries found in new vehicles are sealed and the specific gravity cannot be tested. A few over-the-counter aftermarket batteries still have open tops, but they are a minority.

Charge Indicators

Some batteries are equipped with a built-in state-of-charge indicator. This indicator is simply a small ball-type hydrometer that is installed in one cell. This hydrometer uses a plastic ball that floats if the electrolyte is dense enough (which it is when the battery is about 65% charged). When the ball floats, it appears in the hydrometer's sight glass, changing its colour. The ball expands and contracts for temperature compensation in some brands. See Figures 15–8 and 15–9. Because the hydrometer is only testing one cell (out of six on a 12 volt battery), and because the hydrometer ball can easily stick in one position, it should not be trusted to give accurate information about a battery's state of charge.

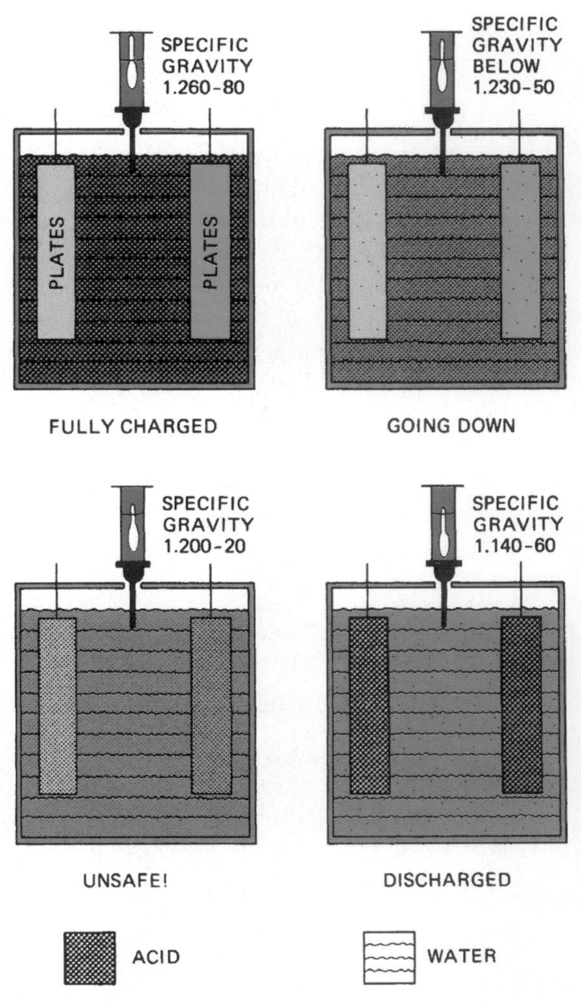

Figure 15–7 As the battery becomes discharged, the specific gravity of the battery acid decreases.

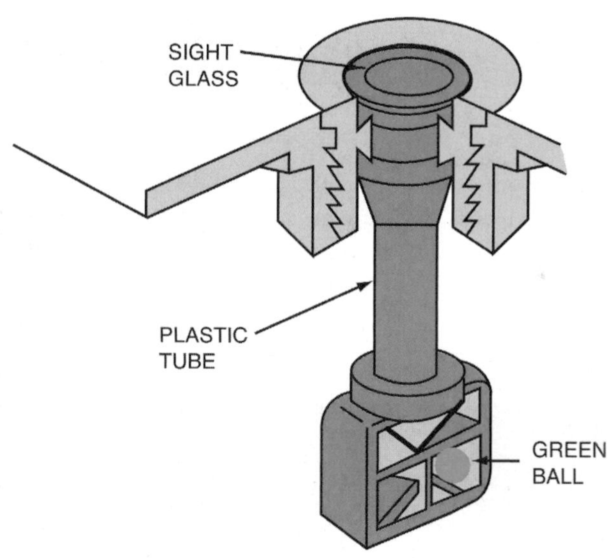

Figure 15–8 Typical battery charge indicator. If the specific gravity is low (battery discharged), the ball drops away from the reflective prism. When the battery is charged enough, the ball floats and reflects the colour of the ball (usually green) back up through the sight glass and the sight glass is dark.

Figure 15–9 Cutaway of the battery showing the charge indicator. If the electrolyte level drops below the bottom of the prism, the sight glass shows clear (light). Most battery manufacturers warn that if the electrolyte level is low on a sealed battery, the battery must be replaced. Attempting to charge a battery that has a low electrolyte level can cause a buildup of gases and possibly an explosion.

Specific Gravity versus State of Charge and Battery Voltage

Values for specific gravity, state of charge, and battery voltage at 27°C (80°F) are given in the following table:

Specific Gravity	State of Charge	Battery Voltage (V)
1.265	Fully charged	12.6 or higher
1.225	75% charged	12.4
1.190	50% charged	12.2
1.155	25% charged	12.0
Lower than 1.120	Discharged	11.9 or lower

Battery Hold-Downs

All batteries must be attached securely to the vehicle to prevent battery damage. Normal vehicle vibrations can cause the active materials inside the battery to shed. Battery hold-down clamps or brackets help reduce vibration, which can greatly reduce the capacity and life of any battery.

BATTERY RATINGS

Batteries are rated according to the amount of current they can produce under specific conditions.

Cold-Cranking Amperes

Every automotive battery must be able to supply electrical power to crank the engine in cold weather and still provide voltage high enough to operate the ignition system for starting. The cold-cranking power of a battery is the number of amperes that can be supplied by a battery at −18°C (0°F) for 30 seconds while the battery still maintains a voltage of 1.2 volts per cell or higher. This means that the battery voltage would be 7.2 volts for a 12 volt battery and 3.6 volts for a 6 volt battery. The cold-cranking performance rating is called **cold-cranking amperes (CCA).** See vehicle manufacturers' specifications for recommended battery capacity.

Reserve Capacity

The **reserve capacity** rating for batteries is *the number of minutes* for which the battery can produce 25 A and still have a battery voltage of 1.75 volts per cell (10.5 volts for a 12 volt battery). This rating is actually a measurement of the time for which a vehicle can be driven at night in the event of a charging system failure.

Cranking Amperes

Cranking amperes, abbreviated CA, are not the same as CCA, but are often advertised and labelled on batteries. The designation of CA refers to the

Figure 15–10 This battery has a cranking amperes (CA) rating of 1000. This means that this battery is capable of cranking an engine for 30 seconds at a temperature of 0°C (32°F) at a minimum of 1.2 V per cell (7.2 volts for a 12 volt battery).

number of amperes that can be supplied by the battery at 0°C (32°F). This rating results in a higher number than the more stringent rating of CCA. See Figure 15–10.

Battery Capacity

Capacity is a term used to describe the power supplied by the battery. In some instances, the automaker will install a low capacity battery as original equipment and offer a higher capacity battery as an option. Vehicles with greater power demands, such as factory-installed air conditioning, usually have high-output charging systems and batteries.

Lead-acid batteries do not function well in cold weather; they are only 65% efficient at 0°C (32°F). The highest CCA rated battery that fits should be installed in any vehicle that operates during the winter.

DEEP CYCLING

Deep cycling is the process of almost fully discharging a battery and then completely recharging it. Golf cart batteries are an example of lead-acid batteries that must be designed to be deep cycled. A golf cart must be able to cover two 18-hole rounds of golf and then be fully recharged overnight. Because charging is hard on batteries (the internal heat generated can cause plate warpage), these specially designed batteries use thicker plate grids, which resist warpage. Normal automotive batteries are not designed for repeated deep cycling. Each time a conventional battery is deep cycled, it loses capacity.

SAFETY TIP 

Be Prepared for the Unexpected

A battery that was being charged exploded and battery acid was blown in a wide area. Always expect the unexpected and keep batteries away from flammable liquids. Always wear safety glasses when changing or servicing any battery. See Figure 15–11.

(a)

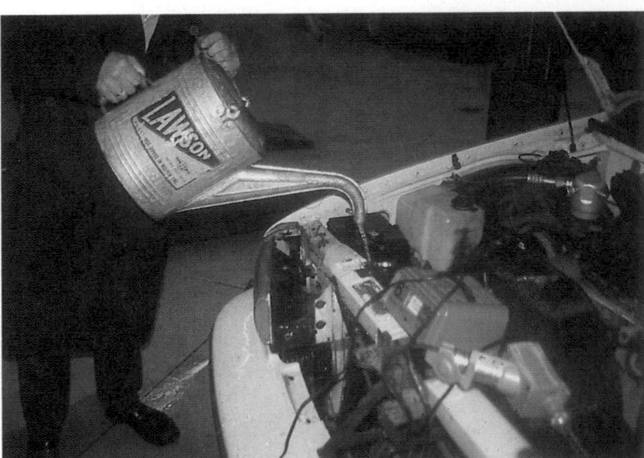

(b)

Figure 15–11 (a) A small spark inside the battery was the most likely cause of this battery explosion. Parts of the battery were thrown 10 m (30 ft), and luckily no one was around the vehicle at the time. (b) Because battery acid was spilled and sprayed around the battery, the entire area was rinsed with water after unplugging the battery charger.

DUAL BATTERIES

Dual batteries are found with some older diesel-powered light vehicles and in many light trucks with campers.

The diesel batteries are usually mounted in parallel and are both charged with the 12 volt AC generator. When the engine is cranked, a special series-parallel switch connects the batteries in series and isolates the 12 volt circuits. Two 12 volt batteries in series equals 24 volts, which is used to operate the 24 volt diesel starter.

Dual 12 V batteries used with campers are also mounted in parallel and are charged with the 12 volt AC generator. When the ignition switch is turned off, an isolation solenoid disconnects the camper battery from the vehicle battery. The camper battery supplies power for the appliances, lights, etc. needed for the camper. If this battery becomes discharged, the vehicle battery will still start and run the truck.

Dual battery installations must use two identical batteries or shorter battery life may occur.

VALVE-REGULATED LEAD-ACID (VRLA) OXYGEN RECOMBINANT BATTERIES

In a conventional battery, water in the electrolyte is broken down by electrolysis during charging. The resulting explosive gases, hydrogen and oxygen, reduce the electrolyte level when they are vented to the atmosphere. Periodic replenishment of the water is required.

One type of recombinant battery (reclaims water) is the absorbent glass mat type (AGM), which uses paper and fibrous glass as separator material. These separators act like a sponge to absorb and hold the electrolyte; there is no free electrolyte. AGM separators allow a transfer of oxygen between the plates, rather than allowing it to vent. A special one-way valve, which replaces the open vent, holds a small pressure inside the battery; this helps the internal gases to recombine back into water. This pressure also keeps outside air from drying out the AGM separators.

AGM separators are used in both flat-plate and spiral-wound construction. They provide higher output because of low internal resistance and higher gravity electrolyte. General Motors began using AGM batteries as original equipment in selected models beginning in 2004.

GEL-CELL BATTERIES

Gel-cell batteries are similar to conventional "flooded" lead-acid batteries. A gelling agent such as pure silica is added to the electrolyte, which reduces movement in the case.

SPIRAL-WOUND BATTERIES

Spiral-wound (spiral cell) batteries, such as the Exide Orbital and the Johnson Controls Optima, are lead-acid batteries that wind the plates into a cylindrical cell. Plate material and electrolyte are similar to a conventional battery. See Figure 15–12.

Cylindrical cells allow more plate surface, closer plate spacing and higher purity lead; this results in low internal resistance.

AGM separators are often used to provide full electrolyte contact with the spiral plates. Stronger electrolyte may also be used. These batteries provide a higher power level for starting than conventional batteries.

Although VRLA valving is used, hydrogen gassing usually does not occur unless high voltage charging rates (over 15 V) or extremely high temperatures are found.

The recommended charging rate, off vehicle, is 10 amperes; a fast charge of up to 100 amperes may be allowed provided the charging voltage does not exceed 15.6 volts and the battery temperature does

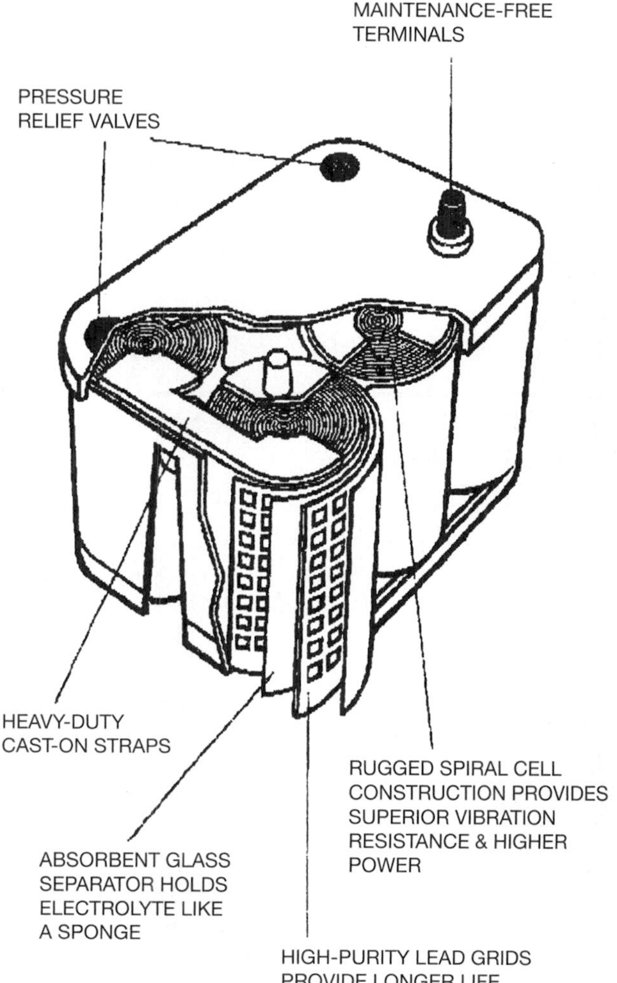

Figure 15–12 Cutaway view of a spiral-wound battery. Note the cells are wound in a rolled-cell construction. (Courtesy Optima Batteries [a Division of Johnson Controls Inc.])

not exceed 50°C (125°F). Always refer to the manufacturers' guidelines before charging any battery.

NICKEL METAL HYDRIDE (NIMH) BATTERIES

NiMH batteries are made in both flat grid and spiral grid designs. The negative electrodes use a metal-hydride alloy and the positive electrode uses nickel hydroxide. Potassium hydroxide is used as electrolyte. See Figure 15–13.

Only hydrogen is exchanged at the positive and negative electrodes; this results in very slight plate deterioration, which gives the battery a very long service life.

NiMH batteries are found in hybrid vehicles, such as the 144 volt Honda Insight and Civic, the 274 volt Toyota Prius and the 300 volt Ford electric Ranger. See Figure 15–14.

NiMH batteries have excellent energy density and specific power; they function well in cold weather and are expected to last in excess of 10 years. The downside of NiMH batteries is the high initial cost, which can run into many thousands of dollars. Toyota Motor Co. has built a dedicated battery rebuild facility that should be in operation as these batteries approach the end of their service life. This should provide a viable alternate to new battery replacement.

Use extreme care and follow all the manufacturers' cautions when working near these batteries; special insulated tools may be required.

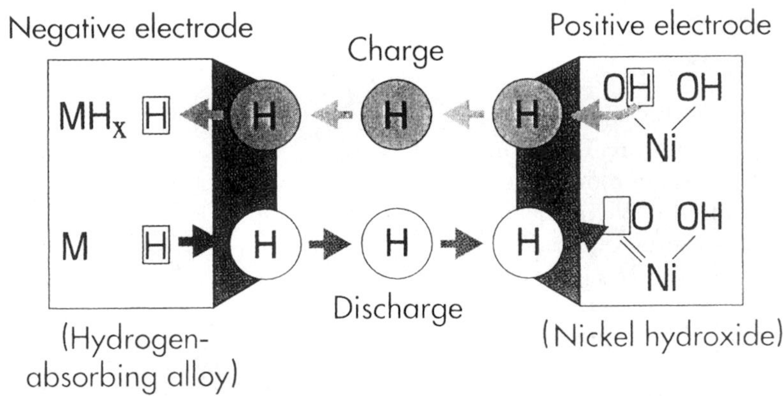

Figure 15–13 Nickel metal hydroxide batteries exchange only hydrogen between the positive and negative electrodes. (Courtesy Panasonic Energy Co.)

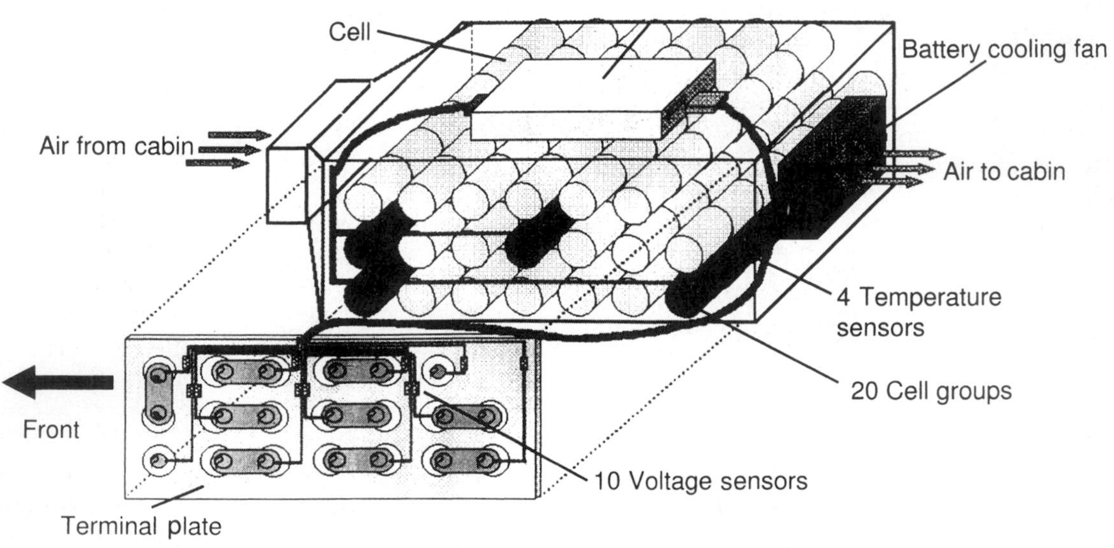

Figure 15–14a Rolled-cell construction of a 144 volt nickel metal hydride battery. (Courtesy Honda Motor Co.)

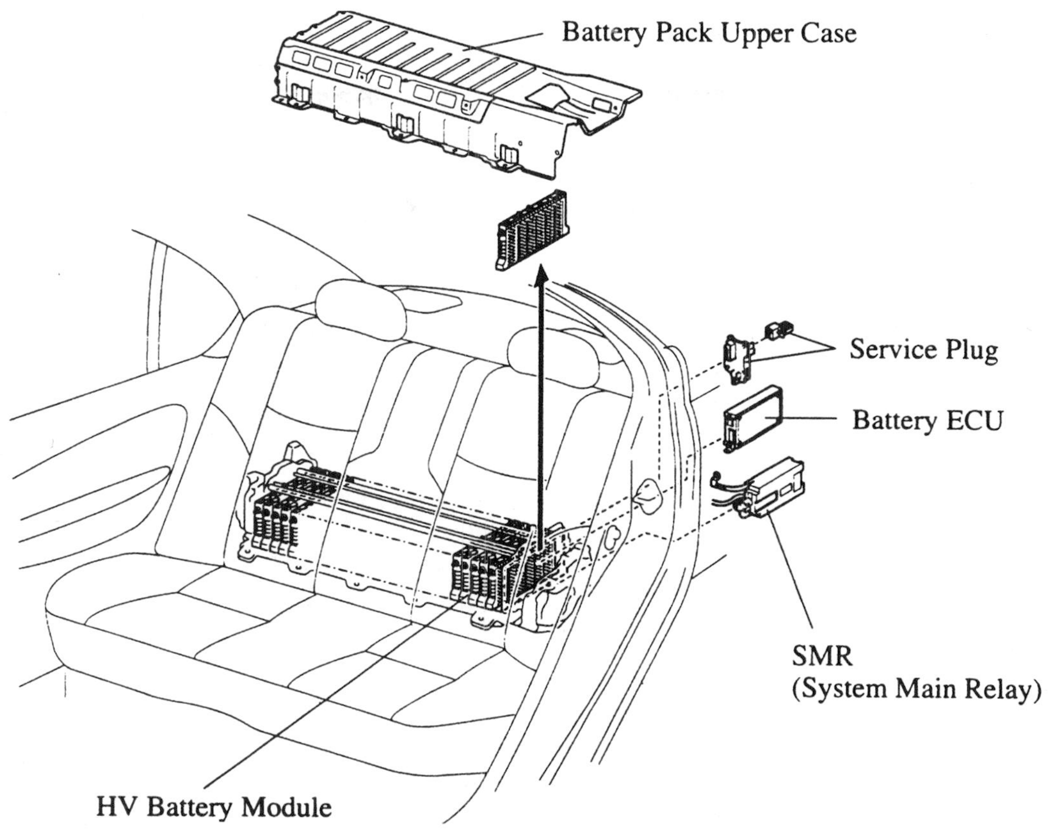

Figure 15–14b Location and mounting of a 274 volt battery in a hybrid vehicle. (Courtesy Toyota Motor Co.)

42 VOLT AUTOMOTIVE ELECTRICAL SYSTEMS

14 volt electrical systems (12 volt battery) have been the automotive standard for almost 50 years; however, the increasing use of electronics and electrical components since the mid 1980s has stretched 14 volt power demands to the limit. In the near future, additional electrical power will be needed to drive air conditioning compressors, to operate electric steering, and to heat catalytic converters, as a few examples.

One approach currently being considered is a switch to 42 volts (36 volt battery). Theoretically, three times the voltage will supply three times the power at the same current.

The use of 42 volts creates a number of concerns: higher costs associated with charging systems, arcing at switch contacts, use of 12 volt lighting and accessories are only a few. Some of these problems are addressed with dual 14 volt /42 volt circuits, which can be costly.

Some companies are testing super high-output, 300 ampere AC generators while others believe that 42 volts will be the operating voltage of the future. The Toyota Crown and the G.M. Silverado are expected to use 36 volt batteries in a few select models.

BATTERY SERVICE

Safety Considerations

Batteries contain acid and release explosive gases (hydrogen and oxygen) during normal charging and discharging cycles. To help prevent physical injury or damage to the vehicle, always adhere to the following safety procedures:

1. Whenever working on any electrical component of a vehicle, disconnect the negative battery cable from the battery. When the negative cable is disconnected, all electrical circuits in the vehicle will be open, which will prevent accidental electrical contact between an electrical component and ground. Any electrical spark has the potential to cause explosion and personal injury.
2. Wear eye protection whenever working around any battery.
3. Wear protective clothing to avoid skin contact with battery acid.
4. Always adhere to all safety precautions as stated in the service procedures for the equipment used in battery service and testing.
5. Never smoke or use an open flame around any battery.

Battery Maintenance

Most new-style batteries are of a maintenance-free design that uses lead-calcium instead of lead-antimony plate-grid construction. Because lead-calcium batteries do not release as much gas as do the older-style lead-antimony batteries, there is less consumption of water during normal service. Also, with less gassing, less corrosion is observed on the battery terminals, wiring, and support trays.

Battery maintenance includes making certain that the battery case is clean and adding clean water, if necessary. Distilled water is recommended by all battery manufacturers, but if distilled water is not available, clean ordinary drinking water, low in mineral content, can be used. Because water is the only thing in a battery that is consumed, acid should never be added to a battery. Some of the water in the electrolyte escapes during the normal operation of charging and discharging, but the acid content of the electrolyte remains in the battery. Do not overfill a battery, because normal bubbling (gassing) of the electrolyte will cause the electrolyte to escape and start corrosion on the battery terminals, hold-down brackets, and battery tray. Fill batteries to the indicator that is approximately 40 mm (1 1/2 in.) from the top of the filler tube. The battery should also be secured with a hold-down bracket to prevent vibration from damaging the plates inside the battery. The hold-down bracket should be snug enough to prevent battery movement, yet not so tight as to cause the case to crack. Factory-original hold-down brackets are often available through local automobile dealers, and universal hold-down units are available through local automotive parts stores.

Battery cable connections should be checked and cleaned to prevent voltage drop at the connections. One of the most common reasons for an engine not starting is loose or corroded battery cable connections. See Figure 15–15.

Figure 15–15 This battery cable was found to be corroded underneath. The corrosion had eaten through the insulation yet was not noticeable until it was carefully inspected. This cable should be replaced.

Battery Voltage Testing

Testing the battery voltage with a voltmeter is a simple method for determining the state of charge of any battery. The voltage of a battery does not necessarily indicate whether the battery can perform satisfactorily, but it does indicate to the technician more about the battery's condition than a simple visual inspection. A battery that looks good may not be good. This test is commonly called an **open-circuit battery voltage test** because it is conducted with an open circuit—with no current flowing and no load applied to the battery.

1. If the battery has just been charged or the vehicle has recently been driven, it is necessary to remove the surface charge from the battery before testing. A surface charge is a charge of higher-than-normal voltage that is just on the surface of the battery plates. The surface charge is quickly removed whenever the battery is loaded and therefore does not accurately represent the true state of charge of the battery.
2. To remove the surface charge, turn the headlights on high beam (brights) for 1 minute, then turn the headlights off and wait 2 minutes.
3. With the engine and all electrical accessories off, and the doors shut (to turn off the interior lights), connect a voltmeter to the battery posts. Connect the red positive lead to the positive post and the black negative lead to the negative post.

NOTE: If the meter reads negative, the battery has been reverse charged (has reversed polarity) and should be replaced, or the meter has been connected incorrectly.

4. Read the voltmeter and compare the results with the state-of-charge table below. The voltages shown are for a battery at or near room temperature 20° to 25°C (68° to 77°F). See Figure 15–16.

Battery Voltage (V)	State of Charge
12.6 or higher	100% charged
12.4	75% charged
12.2	50% charged
12.0	25% charged
11.9 or lower	Discharged

Hydrometer Testing

If the battery has removable filler caps, the specific gravity of the electrolyte can also be checked. This test can be performed on some maintenance-free

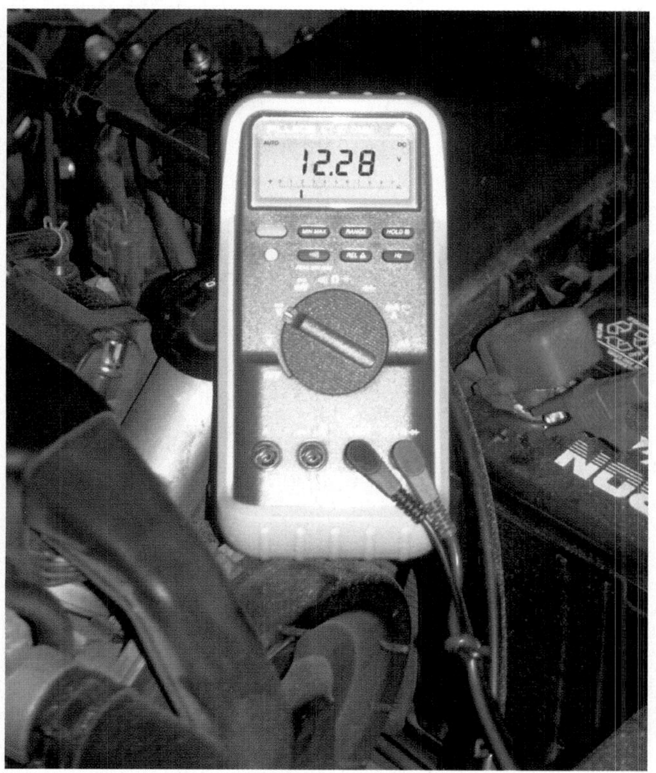

(a)

(b)

Figure 15–16 (a) Voltmeter showing the battery voltage after the headlights were on (engine off) for 1 minute. (b) Headlights were turned off and the battery voltage quickly recovered to indicate 12.6 volts.

batteries because the filler caps may be removable. The specific gravity test indicates the state of charge of the battery and can indicate a defective battery if the specific gravity of one or more cells varies by more than 0.050 from the value of the highest-reading cell.

Specific Gravity	State of Charge
1.265	100% charged
1.225	75% charged
1.190	50% charged
1.155	25% charged
Lower than 1.120	Discharged

The hydrometer reading must also be corrected for temperature because if the battery is colder than 27°C (80°F), the specific gravity reading on the hydrometer will be inaccurate. See Figure 15–17. While a specific gravity reading of 1.190 at –1°C (30°F) suggests 50% charged, the actual specific gravity is only 1.170, meaning that the charge is much lower than that. Hydrometers sold in Canada and the U.S. often have correction scales printed on their face.

Battery Load Testing

One of the most accurate tests to determine the condition of any battery is the **load test.** Most automotive starting and charging testers use a carbon pile to create an electrical load on the battery. The amount of the load is determined by the original capacity of the battery being tested. The capacity is measured in cold-cranking amperes, which is the number of amperes that a battery can supply at −18°C (0°F) for 30 seconds. An older type of battery rating is called the **ampere-hour rating.** *The proper electrical load to be used to test a battery is one-half of the CCA rating or three times the ampere-hour rating, with a minimum of a 250 ampere load.* After the battery has been tested to be at least 75% charged by observing the built-in hydrometer or by performing an open circuit voltage test, a load test can be performed. Apply the load for a full 15 seconds and observe the voltmeter at the end of the 15-second period while the battery is still under load. A good battery should indicate above 9.6 volts. Many battery manufacturers recommend performing the load test twice, using the first load period to remove the surface charge on the battery and the second test to provide a truer indication of the condition of

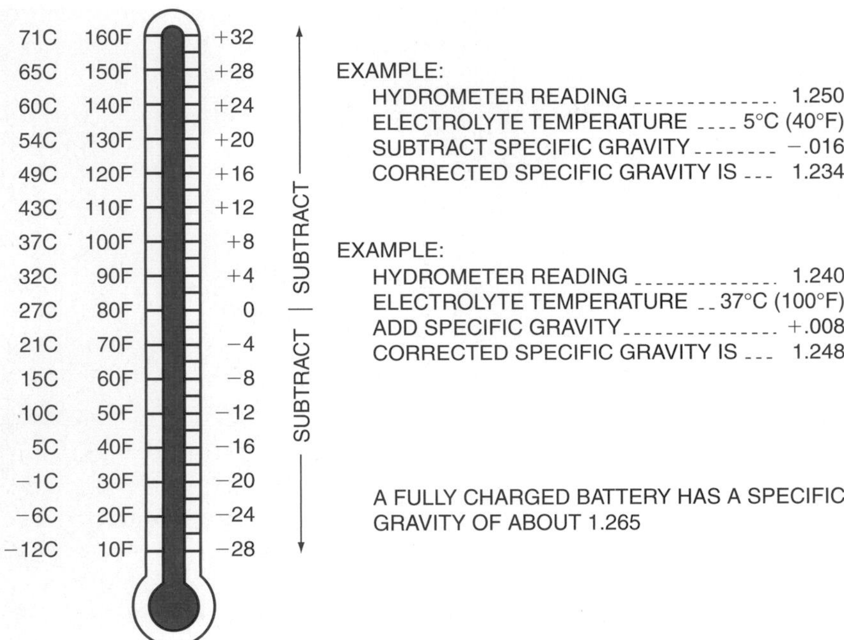

Figure 15–17 When testing a battery using a hydrometer, the reading must be corrected if the temperature is above or below 27°C (80°F).

Figure 15–18 A Bear Automotive starting and charging tester. This tester automatically loads the battery for 15 seconds to remove the surface charge, then waits 30 seconds to allow the battery to recover, then again loads the battery. The LCD indicates the status of the battery.

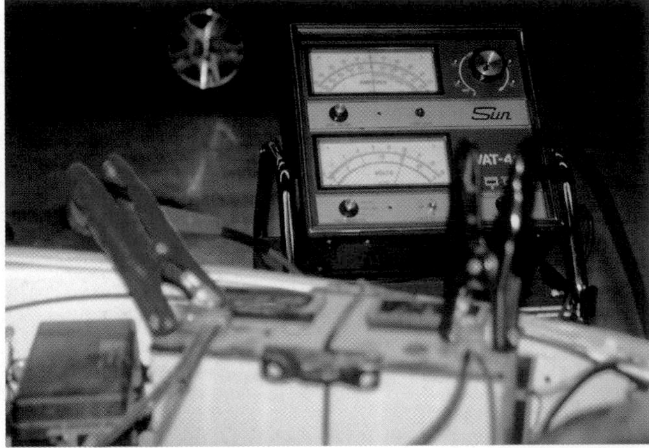

Figure 15–19 A Sun Electric VAT-40 (volt-amp tester, model 40) connected to a battery for load testing. The technician turns the load knob until the ammeter registers an amperage reading equal to one-half the battery's CCA rating. The load is maintained for 15 seconds, and the voltage of the battery should be higher than 9.6 volts at the end of the time period *with the load still applied.* Remember to temperature compensate in cold weather.

the battery. Wait 30 seconds between tests to allow time for the battery to recover. See Figures 15–18 and 15–19.

If the battery fails the load test, recharge the battery and retest. If the load test is failed again, replacement of the battery is required.

Load-test values are also affected by lower temperatures. 9.6 volts is the minimum voltage of a serviceable battery at 21°C (70°F); at –1°C (30°F), the acceptable voltage drops to 9.1 volts. Always check the charts for voltage compensation. Remember that the temperature listed is the battery temperature, not ambient; pushing the vehicle into a heated shop will not warm the battery for a number of hours.

NOTE: Some battery testers measure the capacitance of the battery to determine the state of charge and battery condition. Always follow the test equipment manufacturer's recommended test procedure.

Capacitance Testing

General Motors Corporation and DaimlerChrysler Corporation specify that a capacitance tester be used to test batteries in vehicles still under factory warranty. See Figure 15–20. Connect the unit to the positive and negative terminals of the battery and after entering the CCA rating (if known), push the arrow keys and the tester determines one of the following:

- **Good battery:** the battery can return to service
- **Charge and retest:** fully recharge the battery and return it to service
- **Replace the battery:** the battery is not serviceable and should be replaced
- **Bad cell—replace:** the battery is not serviceable and should be replaced

CAUTION: Test results can be incorrectly reported on the display if proper, clean connections to the battery are not made. Also be sure that all accessories and the ignition switch are in the off position.

Battery Charging

If the state of charge of a battery is low, it must be recharged. See the battery charging guide in Figure 15–21. It is best to slow-charge any battery to prevent possible overheating damage to the battery. See Figure 15–22 for the recommended charging rate. *Remember, it may take 8 hours or more to charge a fully discharged battery.* See

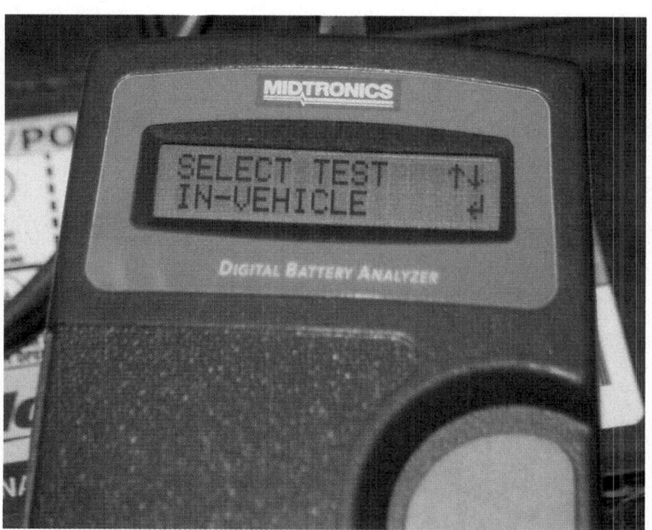

(a)

(b)

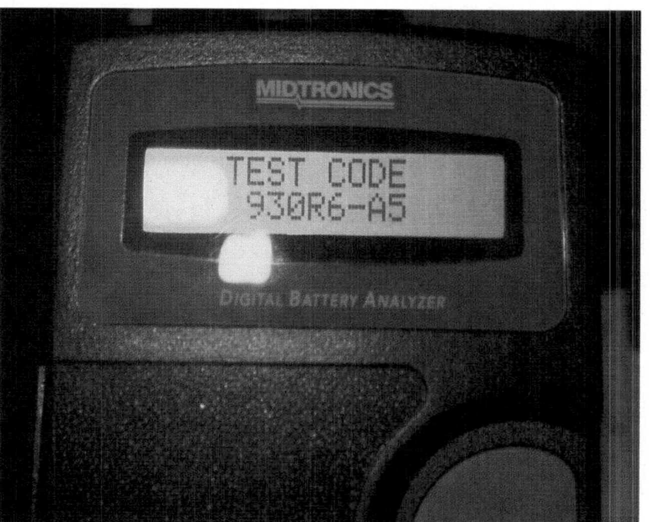

(c)

Figure 15–20 A capacitance-type battery tester. (a) The up and down arrow keys are used to answer questions about the battery before it is tested. (b) This battery shows a calculated CCA of 729 amperes and a voltage of 12.37 volts. The display indicates that the battery is good, but should be charged before returning the vehicle to service. (c) A test code is displayed for warranty record-keeping purposes.

Figure 15–21 Battery-charging guide (6 volt and 12 volt batteries).

BATTERY CHARGING GUIDE
(6 V and 12 V Batteries)
Caution:Do Not Use for Low Water Loss Batteries
Recommended Rate and Time for Fully Discharged Condition

Rated Battery Capacity (Reserve Minutes)	Slow Charge	Fast Charge
80 Minutes or Less	10 h @ 5 A 5 h @ 10 A	2.5 h @ 20 A 1.5 h @ 30 A
Above 80 to 125 Minutes	15 h @ 5 A 7.5 h @ 10 A	3.75 h @ 20 A 1.5 h @ 50 A
Above 125 to 170 Minutes	20 h @ 5 A 10 h @ 10 A	5 h @ 20 A 2 h @ 50 A
Above 170 to 250 Minutes	30 h @ 5 A 15 h @ 10 A	2.5 h @ 20 A 3 h @ 50 A
Above 250 Minutes	24 h @ 10 A	6 h @ 40 A 4 h @ 60 A

Figure 15–22 This battery charger is charging the battery at a 10 A rate. A slow rate such as this is easier on the battery than a fast charge that may overheat the battery and cause warpage of the plates inside the battery.

Figure 15–23. The initial charge rate should be about 35 amperes for 30 minutes to help start the charging process. Fast-charging a battery increases the temperature of the battery and can cause warping of the plates inside the battery. Fast-charging also increases the amount of gassing (release of hydrogen and oxygen), which can create a health and fire hazard. The battery temperature should not exceed 50°C (125°F) (hot to the touch). *Most batteries should be charged at a rate equal to 1% of the battery's CCA rating.*

Fast charge: 15 amperes maximum

Slow charge: 5 amperes maximum

Some battery chargers are polarity protected to prevent the charger from being hooked up backwards.

TECH TIP 

It Could Happen to You!

The owner of a Toyota replaced the battery. After replacing the battery, the owner noted that the "airbag" amber warning lamp was lit and the radio was locked out. The owner had purchased the vehicle used from a dealer and did not know the four-digit security code needed to unlock the radio. Determined to fix it, the owner tried three four-digit numbers, hoping that one of them would work. However, after three tries, the radio became permanently disabled.

Frustrated, the owner went to a dealer. It cost over $300 to fix the problem. A special tool was required to reset the airbag lamp. The radio had to be removed and sent to an authorized radio service centre and then reinstalled into the vehicle.

Therefore, before disconnecting the battery, please check with the owner to be certain that the owner has the security code for a security-type radio. A memory saver may be needed to keep the radio powered up when the battery is being disconnected. See Figure 15–24.

NOTE: Some vehicles have battery-rundown protection in the event of extended parking or storage. After 24 days the control module shuts down the radio, ABS, dash cluster, and keyless entry; it maintains only the PCM and itself. Radio presets will require resetting.

JUMP-STARTING

To jump-start another vehicle with a dead battery, connect good-quality copper jumper cables as indicated in Figure 15–25. The last connection made should always be on the engine block or an engine bracket as far from

Figure 15–23 A typical industrial battery charger. Be sure that the ignition switch is in the off position before connecting any battery charger. Connect the cables of the charger to the battery before plugging the charger into the outlet. This helps prevent a voltage spike that could occur if the charger happened to be accidentally left on. Always follow the battery charger manufacturer's instructions.

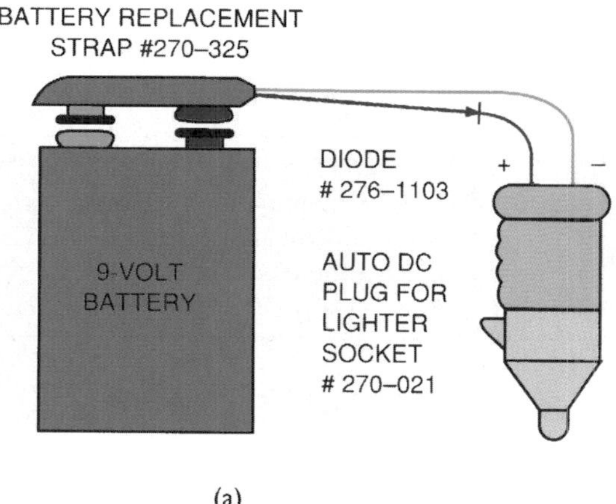

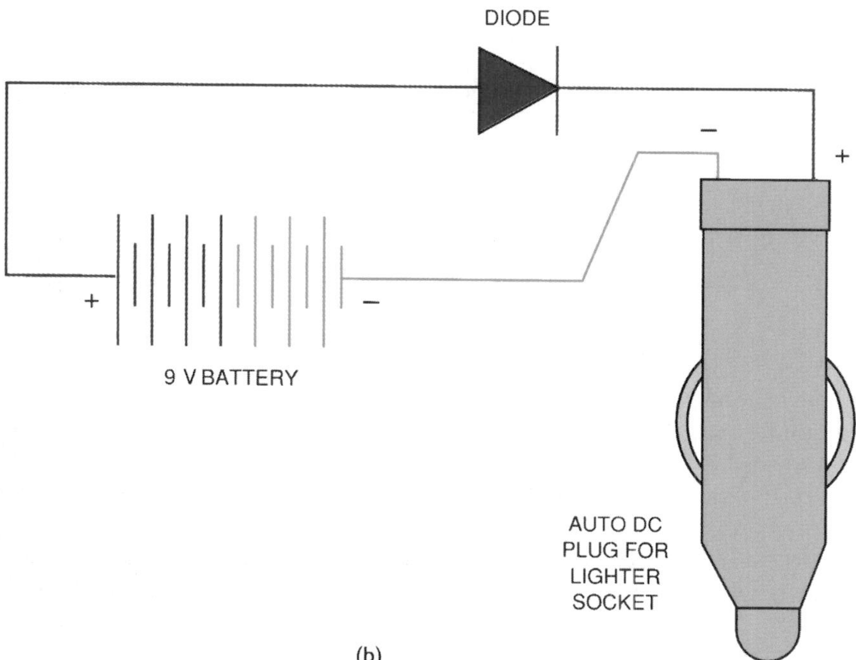

Figure 15–24 (a) Memory saver. The part numbers represent components from Radio Shack. (b) A schematic drawing of the same memory saver. Some experts recommend using a 12 volt lantern battery instead of a small 9 volt battery to help ensure that there will be enough voltage in the event that a door is opened while the vehicle battery is disconnected. Interior lights could quickly drain a small 9 volt battery.

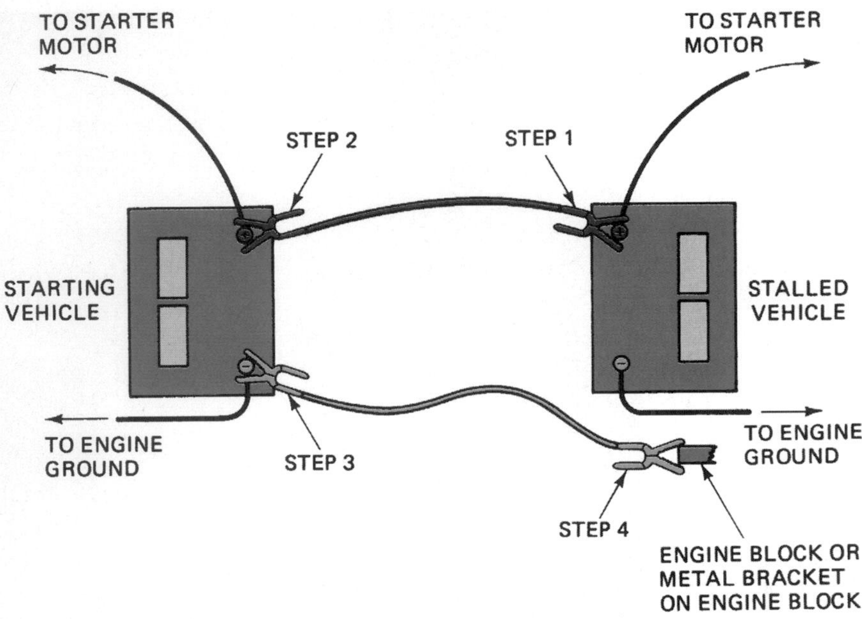

Figure 15–25 Jumper cable usage guide. Notice that the last connection should be the engine block of the disabled vehicle to help prevent the spark that normally occurs from igniting the gases from the battery.

Figure 15–26 A typical battery jump box used to jump-start vehicles. These hand-portable units have almost made jumper cables obsolete.

the battery as possible. It is normal for a spark to be created when the jumper cables finally complete the jumping circuit, and this spark could cause an explosion of the gases around the battery. See Figure 15–26. Many newer vehicles have special ground connections built away from the battery just for the purpose of jump-starting. Check the owner's manual or service manual for the exact location.

CAUTION: When replacing a battery, always remove the battery ground cable first, and reinstall it last. This prevents a spark (and possible explosion) if your wrench touches any metal while on the positive cable clamp.

BATTERY DATE CODES

All major battery manufacturers stamp codes on the battery case that give the date of manufacture and other information. Most battery manufacturers use a number to indicate the year of manufacture and a letter to indicate the month of manufacture, skipping the letter I, because it can be confused with the number 1. For example:

A = January	G = July
B = February	H = August
C = March	J = September
D = April	K = October
E = May	L = November
F = June	M = December

The shipping date from the manufacturing plant is usually indicated by a *sticker* on the end of the battery. Almost every battery manufacturer uses just one letter and one number to indicate the month and year. For example, a shipping sticker with an "A3" indicates that the battery was shipped in January, 2003. See Figure 15–27.

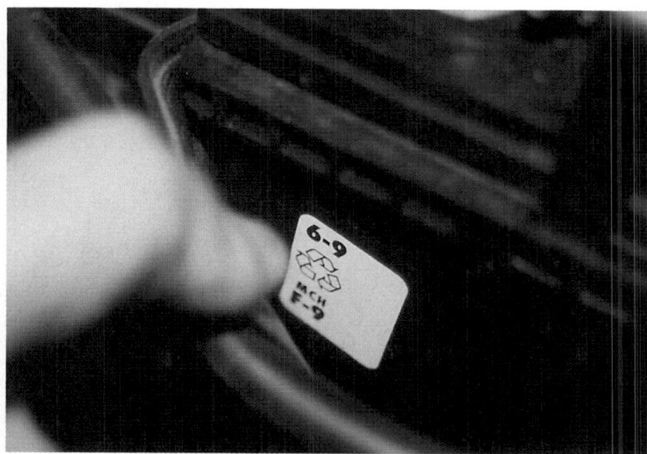

Figure 15–27 The (F9) indicates that this battery was shipped from the manufacturing plant in June, 1999.

BATTERY DRAIN TEST

The **battery drain test** determines if some component or circuit in a vehicle is causing a drain on the battery when everything is off. This test is also called the **ignition off draw (IOD)** or **parasitic load** test. This test should be performed whenever one of the following conditions exists:

1. Whenever a battery is being charged or replaced (a battery drain could have been the cause for charging or replacing the battery)
2. Whenever the battery is suspected of being drained

Battery Drain Test Using an Ammeter

The ammeter method is the most accurate way to test for a possible battery drain. The use of a clamp-on ammeter designed to read DC amperes to within 10 milliamperes (0.01) is a fast and easy method. See Figure 15–28. Connect an ammeter in series between the terminal of the battery and the disconnected cable. See Figure 15–29. (Normal battery drain is 0.020 to 0.030 ampere and any drain greater than 0.050 ampere should be found and corrected.)

NOTE: Some inductive ammeters are sensitive enough to measure battery electrical drain without having to disconnect the battery to connect the meter leads.

Many digital multimeters have an ammeter scale that can be used to safely and accurately test for an abnormal parasitic electrical drain. See Figure 15–30.

DIAGNOSTIC STORY 

Park on the North or Park on the South?

A vehicle owner complained to a dealer service department that every time he parked his vehicle on the north side of the street, his vehicle would fail to start the next morning because of a dead battery. Whenever he parked on the south side of the street, the battery would not be drained and the vehicle always started. The service technician learned that the owner lived on a steep hill and that whenever he parked with the vehicle facing downhill, the battery was drained. The cause of the battery drain was discovered to be a trunk light switch that was operated by a mercury (liquid metal) switch. The switch had to be level, or current would flow through the switch to the bulb. The technician rewired the trunk light and used a contact-type switch instead of the mercury switch to prevent future problems.

CAUTION: Be certain to use an ammeter that is rated to read the anticipated current and be sure you have the radio security code from the vehicle owner before disconnecting the battery. See Figure 15–31.

Finding the Source of the Drain

If there is a drain, check and temporarily disconnect the following components:

1. Light under the hood—some lights under the hood are hot all the time and light by means of a mercury switch whenever the hood is opened
2. Glove compartment light
3. Trunk light

If after disconnecting all three of these components, the battery drain can still light the test light or draws more than 50 milliamperes, disconnect one fuse at a time from the fuse box until the test light goes out. If the test light goes out after one fuse is disconnected, the source of the drain is located in that particular circuit, as labelled on the fuse box. Continue to disconnect the *power-side* wire connectors from each component included in that particular circuit until the test light goes off. The source of the battery drain can then be traced to an individual component or part of one circuit.

Figure 15–28 This mini clamp-on digital multimeter is being used to measure the amount of battery electrical drain that is present. In this case, a reading of 20 mA (displayed on the meter as 00.02 ampere) is within the normal range of 20 to 30 mA. Be sure to clamp around all of the positive battery cable or all of the negative battery cable, whichever is easiest to get the clamp around.

Frequently Asked Question ???

Why Should a Discharged Battery Be Recharged or Replaced Before Further Testing?

A discharged or defective battery has lower voltage potential than a good battery that is at least 75% charged. This lower battery voltage cannot properly power the starter motor without causing excessive current flow (in amperes) to the starter. This excessive current flow through the starter can damage the starter *and* cause starter tests to indicate a defective starter when the real problem is a weak battery. A weak battery could also prevent the charging voltage from reaching the voltage regulator cutoff point. This lower voltage could be interpreted as indicating a defective generator and/or voltage regulator. If the vehicle continues to operate with low system voltage, the stator winding in the generator can be overheated, causing generator failure.

Frequently Asked Question ???

Should Batteries Be Kept off Concrete Floors?

All batteries should be stored in a cool, dry place when not in use. Many technicians have been warned not to store or place a battery on concrete. According to battery experts, it is the temperature difference between the top and the bottom of the battery that causes a difference in the voltage potential between the top (warmer section) and the bottom (colder section). It is this difference in temperature that causes self-discharge to occur. In fact, submarines cycle sea water around their batteries to keep all sections of the battery at the same temperature to help prevent self-discharge.

Therefore, always store or place batteries up off the floor and in a location where the entire battery can be kept at the same temperature, avoiding extreme heat and freezing temperatures. Concrete cannot drain the battery directly, because the case of the battery is a very good electrical insulator.

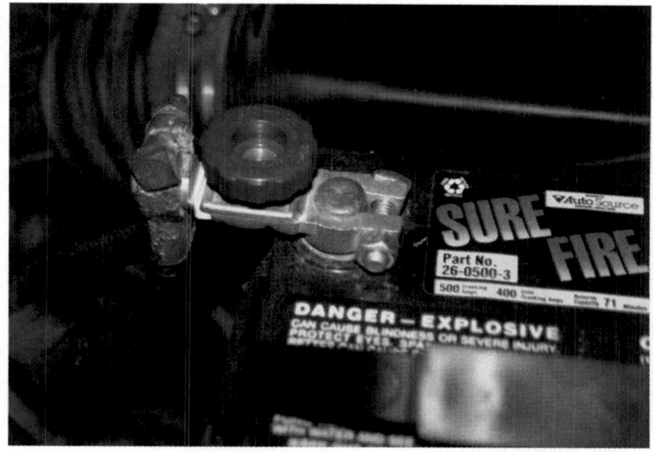

Figure 15–29 After connecting the shutoff tool, start the engine and operate all accessories. Stop the engine and turn off everything. Connect the ammeter across the shutoff switch in parallel. Wait 20 minutes. This time allows all electronic circuits to time out or shut down. Open the switch—all current now will flow through the ammeter. A reading greater than specified (usually greater than 50 milliamperes [0.05 ampere]) indicates a problem that should be corrected.

SURE FIRE
Part No. 26-0500-3
DANGER – EXPLOSIVE

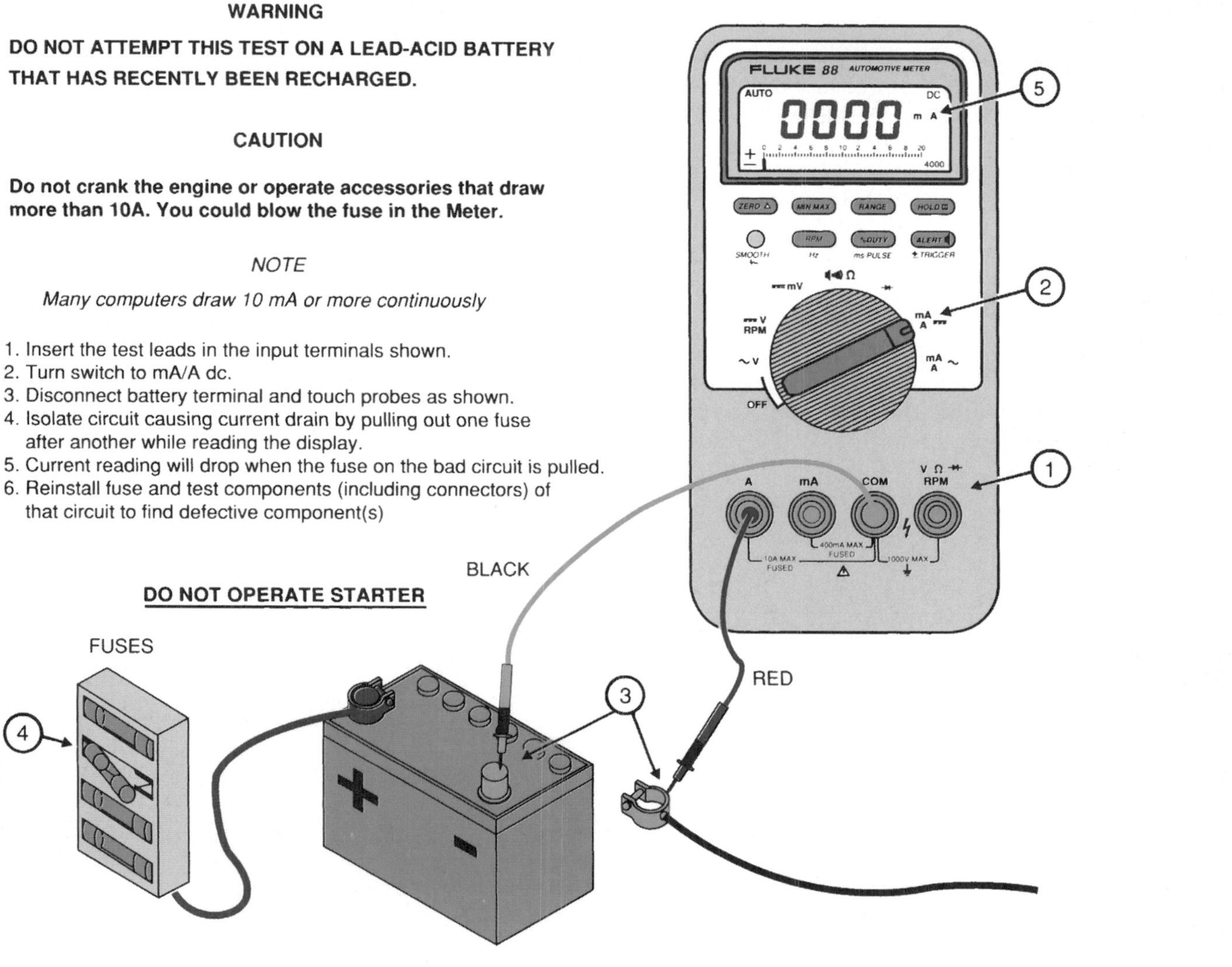

WARNING
DO NOT ATTEMPT THIS TEST ON A LEAD-ACID BATTERY THAT HAS RECENTLY BEEN RECHARGED.
CAUTION
Do not crank the engine or operate accessories that draw more than 10A. You could blow the fuse in the Meter.
NOTE
Many computers draw 10 mA or more continuously
1. Insert the test leads in the input terminals shown.
2. Turn switch to mA/A dc.
3. Disconnect battery terminal and touch probes as shown.
4. Isolate circuit causing current drain by pulling out one fuse after another while reading the display.
5. Current reading will drop when the fuse on the bad circuit is pulled.
6. Reinstall fuse and test components (including connectors) of that circuit to find defective component(s)
DO NOT OPERATE STARTER
FUSES
BLACK
RED
FLUKE 88 AUTOMOTIVE METER
AUTO
DC
0000
m A
4000
ZERO
MIN MAX
RANGE
HOLD
RPM
%DUTY
ALERT
SMOOTH
Hz
ms PULSE
TRIGGER
mV
V
RPM
~V
OFF
mA A
mA A ~
A
mA
COM
V Ω RPM
10A MAX FUSED
400mA MAX FUSED
1000V MAX
1
2
3
4
5

Figure 15–30 Measuring battery electrical drain using a multimeter set to read DC amperes. (Courtesy of Fluke Corporation)

Figure 15–31 The battery was disconnected in this Acura and the radio displayed "code" when it was reconnected. Thankfully, the owner had the five-digit code required to unlock the radio.

What to Do If a Battery Drain Still Exists After All the Fuses Are Disconnected

If all the fuses have been disconnected and the drain still exists, the source of the drain has to be between the battery and the fuse box. The most common sources of drain under the hood include the following:

1. The generator (alternator)—disconnect the generator wires and retest; if the test light is now off, the problem is a defective diode(s) in the generator (see Chapter 17 for details)
2. The starter solenoid (relay) or wiring near its components—these are also a common source of battery drain, due to high current flows and heat, which can damage the wires or insulation

BATTERY TROUBLESHOOTING GUIDE

Problem	Possible Causes and/or Solutions
Headlights are dim	• Discharged battery or poor connections on the battery, engine, or body.
Solenoid clicks	• Discharged battery or poor connections on the battery or the engine.
Engine is slow in cranking	• Discharged battery, high-resistance battery cables, or defective starter or solenoid.
Battery will not accept a charge	• If the battery is a maintenance-free type, attempt to fast-charge the battery for several hours. If the battery still will not accept a charge, replace the battery.
Battery is using water	• Check the charging system for too high a voltage. If the voltage is normal, the battery is showing signs of gradual failure. • Load-test and replace the battery if necessary.

PHOTO SEQUENCE 11 Battery Load Testing

P11–1 A typical Sun VAT-40 used to perform a battery load test. This type of tester uses a carbon pile to provide a connective path to load the battery, and therefore, is often called a carbon-pile tester.

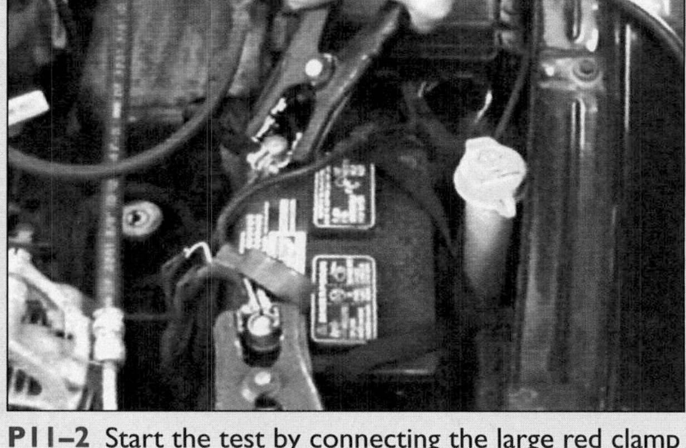

P11–2 Start the test by connecting the large red clamp from the tester to the positive (+) terminal of the battery and the large black clamp to the negative (−) terminal of the battery.

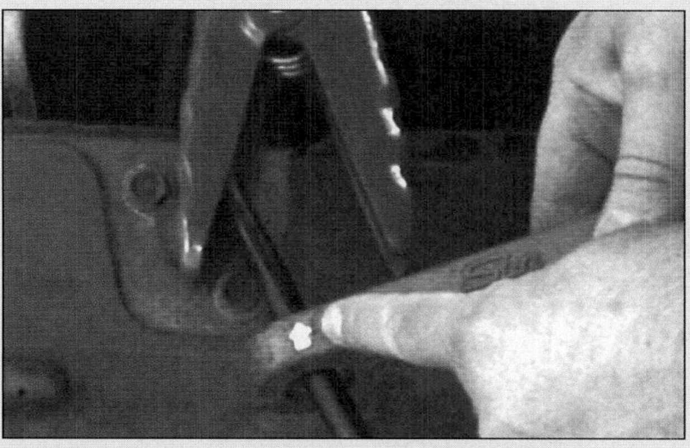

P11–3 Attach the inductive amp probe over the meter red tester lead wire. According to Sun Electric, the arrow on the probe should point toward the battery.

P11–4 Zero the ammeter by turning the zero adjust knob until the needle on the meter indicates zero.

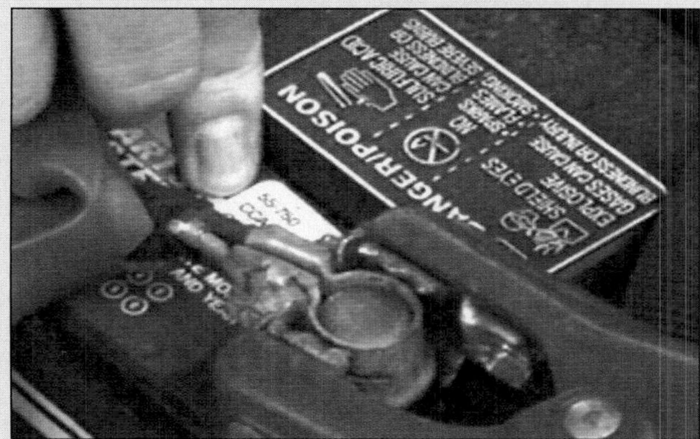

P11–5 Determine the cold cranking amperes (CCA) of the battery. This rating is usually on a sticker on the battery case.

P11–6 Turn the load knob until the ammeter reading is one-half of the CCA rating of the battery. Maintain applying this load for 15 seconds. With the load still applied, observe the voltmeter reading at the end of the 15-second test. The battery voltage should be above 9.6 volts. Most vehicle manufacturers recommend that the test be repeated, often waiting a few minutes to allow the battery time to recover. The first load test is used to remove the surface charge.

SUMMARY

1. Maintenance-free batteries use lead-calcium grids instead of lead-antimony grids to reduce gassing.
2. When a battery is being discharged, the acid (SO_4) is leaving the electrolyte and being deposited on the plates. When the battery is being charged, the acid (SO_4) is forced off the plates and back into the electrolyte.
3. Batteries are rated according to CCA and reserve capacity.
4. All batteries should be securely attached to the vehicle with hold-down brackets to prevent vibration damage.
5. Batteries can be tested with a voltmeter to determine the state of charge. A battery load test (also called a high rate discharge test or a capacity test) loads the battery to one-half of its CCA rating. A good battery should be able to maintain higher than 9.6 volts for the entire 15-second test period.
6. A battery drain test should be performed if the battery runs down.

REVIEW QUESTIONS

1. Explain why discharged batteries can freeze.
2. Identify the two most commonly used battery rating methods.
3. Describe the results of a voltmeter test of a battery and its state of charge.
4. List the steps for performing a battery load test.
5. Explain how to perform a battery drain test.

RED SEAL CERTIFICATION-TYPE QUESTIONS

1. When a battery becomes completely discharged, both positive and negative plates become _____ and the electrolyte becomes _____.
   - **a.** H_2SO_4; Pb
   - **b.** $PbSO_4$; H_2O
   - **c.** PbO_2; H_2SO_4
   - **d.** $PbSO_4$, H_2SO_4
2. A fully charged 12 volt battery should indicate _____.
   - **a.** 12.0 volts or higher
   - **b.** Specific gravity of 1.200 or higher
   - **c.** 1.1 volts per cell
   - **d.** 12.6 volts or higher
3. Deep cycling means _____.
   - **a.** Overcharging the battery
   - **b.** Overfilling or underfilling the battery with water
   - **c.** Fully discharging and then recharging the battery
   - **d.** Overfilling the battery with acid (H_2SO_4)
4. Many vehicle manufacturers recommend that a special electrical connector be installed between the battery and the battery cable when testing for _____.
   - **a.** Battery drain (parasitic drain)
   - **b.** Specific gravity
   - **c.** Battery voltage
   - **d.** Battery charge rate
5. A battery measures 12.4 volts after removing the surface charge. This battery is charged at what percent?
   - **a.** 100%
   - **b.** 75%
   - **c.** 50%
   - **d.** 25%
6. Reserve capacity for batteries means _____.
   - **a.** The number of *hours* the battery can supply 25 amperes and remain higher than 10.5 volts
   - **b.** The number of *minutes* the battery can supply 25 amperes and remain higher than 10.5 volts
   - **c.** The number of *minutes* the battery can supply 20 amperes and remain higher than 9.6 volts
   - **d.** The number of *minutes* the battery can supply 10 amperes and remain higher than 9.6 volts
7. A battery high rate discharge test (capacity test, load test) is being performed on a 12 volt battery. While at 50% of its CCA rating for 15 seconds, a good battery should have a voltage reading of
   - **a.** 9.6 volts or higher
   - **b.** 6.3 volts or above
   - **c.** 9.6 volts or lower
   - **d.** 50% of its rated voltage
8. When charging a maintenance-free (lead-calcium) battery, _____________________.
   - **a.** The initial charging rate should be 5 amperes for 30 minutes
   - **b.** If the battery does not accept a charge for several hours, it should be replaced
   - **c.** The battery temperature should not exceed 38°C (100°F)
   - **d.** The battery may not accept a charge for several hours, yet may still be a good (serviceable) battery
9. Normal battery drain (parasitic drain) on a vehicle with many computer and electronic circuits is _____.
   - **a.** 20–30 milliamperes
   - **b.** 2–3 amperes
   - **c.** 150–300 milliamperes
   - **d.** None of the above
10. Whenever jump-starting, _____.
    - **a.** The last connection should be the positive post of the dead battery
    - **b.** The last connection should be the engine block of the dead vehicle
    - **c.** The generator must be disconnected on both vehicles
    - **d.** The last connection should be to the negative post of the dead battery

16

Cranking System Operation, Diagnosis, and Service

OBJECTIVES: After studying Chapter 16, you should be able to:

1. Prepare for the interprovincial Red Seal certification examination in Appendix III (Electrical/Electronic Systems) on the topics covered in this chapter.
2. Describe how the cranking circuit works.
3. Describe the operation of an integrated starter-generator.
4. Explain how to disassemble and reassemble a starter motor and solenoid.
5. Discuss how to test the cranking circuit.
6. Describe how to perform cranking system testing procedures.

For any engine to start, it must be rotated. It is the purpose and function of the cranking circuit to create the necessary power and transfer it from the battery to the starter motor that rotates the engine.

CRANKING CIRCUIT

The cranking circuit includes those mechanical and electrical components required to crank the engine for starting. The cranking force in the early 1900s was the driver's arm. Modern cranking circuits include the following:

1. *Starter motor.* The starter is normally a 0.5 to 2.6 hp (0.4 to 2.0 kW) electric motor that can develop nearly 8 hp (6 kW) for a very short time when first cranking a cold engine. See Figure 16–1.
2. *Battery.* The battery must be of the correct capacity and be at least 75% charged to provide the necessary current and voltage for correct operation of the starter.
3. *Starter solenoid or relay.* The high current required by the starter must be able to be turned on and off. A large switch would be required if the current were controlled by the driver directly. Instead, a small current switch (ignition

Figure 16–1 Typical solenoid-operated starter.

switch) operates a solenoid or relay that controls the high starter current.

4. *Starter drive.* The starter drive uses a small gear that contacts the engine flywheel gear and transmits starter motor power to rotate the engine.
5. *Ignition switch.* The ignition switch and safety control switches control the starter motor operation. See Figure 16–2.

The engine is cranked by an electric motor that is controlled by a key-operated ignition switch. The ignition switch will not operate the starter unless the automatic transmission is in neutral or park. This is to prevent an accident that might result from the vehicle moving forward or rearward when the engine is started. Many automobile manufacturers use an electric switch called a **neutral safety switch** that opens the circuit between the ignition switch and the starter to prevent starter motor operation unless the gear selector is in neutral or park. See Figure 16–3. The safety switch can either be attached to the steering column inside the vehicle near the floor or on the side of the transmission.

Many neutral safety switches can be adjusted by loosening the hold-down screws and moving the switch slightly to be certain that the engine will crank only with the transmission in the neutral and park positions. Many manufacturers use a mechanical blocking device in the steering column to prevent the driver from turning the key switch to the start position unless the gear selector is in neutral or park. Many manual transmission vehicles also use a safety switch to permit cranking only if the clutch is depressed.

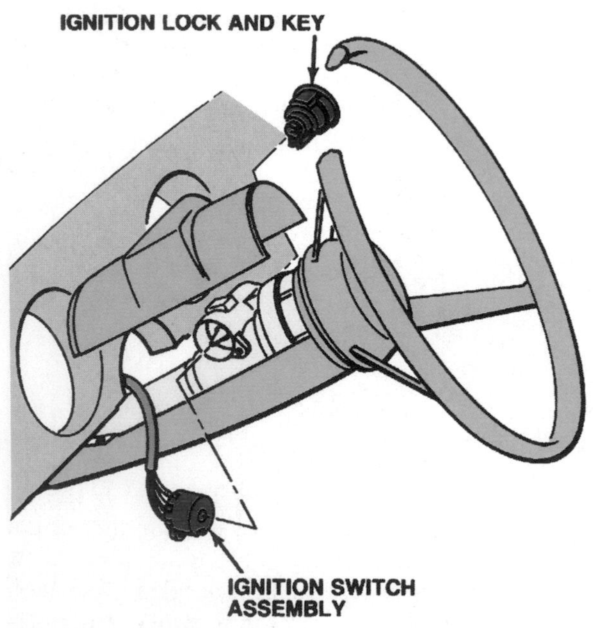

Figure 16–2 Some column-mounted ignition switches act directly on the contact points, whereas others use a link from the lock cylinder to the ignition switch.

HOW THE STARTER MOTOR WORKS

A starter consists of a **main field housing,** one end of which is called a **commutator-end** (or **brush-end**) **housing** and the other end a **drive-end housing.** The drive-end housing contains the drive pinion gear, which meshes with the engine flywheel gear teeth to start the engine. The commutator-end plate supports the end containing the starter brushes. **Through bolts** hold the three components together. See Figure 16–4.

A starter motor uses electromagnetic principles to convert electrical energy from the battery (up to

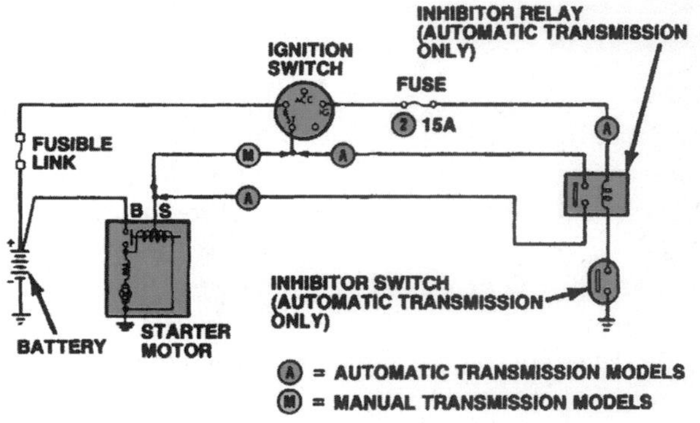

Figure 16–3 A typical wiring diagram of a starter circuit.

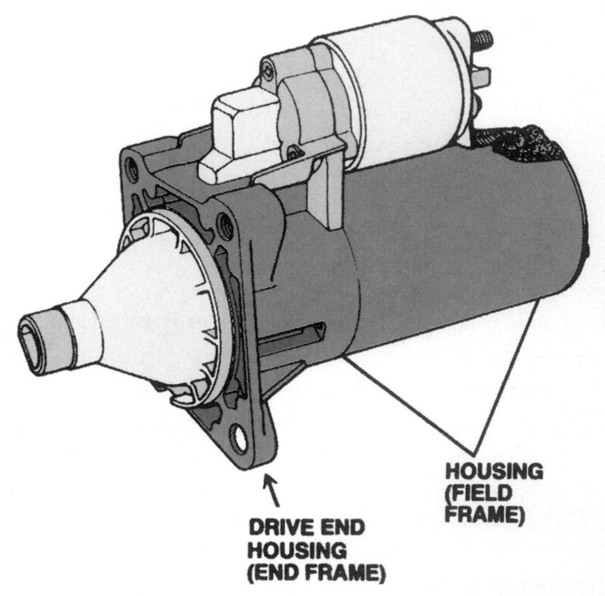

Figure 16–4 A typical starter motor.

TECH TIP 

Watch the Dome Light

Whenever diagnosing any starter-related problem, open the door of the vehicle and observe the brightness of the dome or interior light(s).

- The brightness of any electrical lamp is proportional to the voltage.
- Normal operation of the starter results in a slight dimming of the dome light.
- If the light remains bright, the problem is usually an open circuit in the control circuit.
- If the light goes out or almost goes out, the problem is usually a shorted or grounded armature or field coils inside the starter.

500 A) to mechanical power (up to 8 hp [6 kW]) to crank the engine. The steel housing of the starter motor contains four electromagnets that are connected directly to the positive post of the battery to provide a strong magnetic field inside the starter. Current for the starter is controlled by a solenoid or relay that is controlled by the driver-operated ignition switch. The four electromagnets use heavy copper or aluminum wire wrapped around a soft-iron core. The core is contoured to fit against the rounded internal surface of the starter frame. The soft-iron cores are called **pole shoes.** Two of the four pole shoes are wrapped with copper wire in one direction to create a north pole magnet, and the other two pole shoes are wrapped in the opposite direction to create a south pole magnet. These magnets, when energized, create strong magnetic fields inside the starter housing and therefore are called **field coils.** The soft-iron cores (pole shoes) are often called **field poles.**

Inside the field coils is an **armature** that is supported with bushings at both ends, which permit it to rotate. The armature is constructed of thin, circular disks of steel laminated together and wound lengthwise with heavy-gauge insulated copper wire. The laminated iron core supports the copper loops of wire and helps concentrate the magnetic field produced by the coils. The ends of the copper armature windings are soldered to **commutator segments.** The electrical current that passes through the field coils is then connected to the commutator of the armature by brushes that can move over the segments of the rotating armature. These **brushes** are made of a combination of copper and carbon. The copper is a good conductor material, and the carbon added to the starter brushes helps provide the graphite-type lubrication needed to reduce wear of the brushes and the commutator segments.

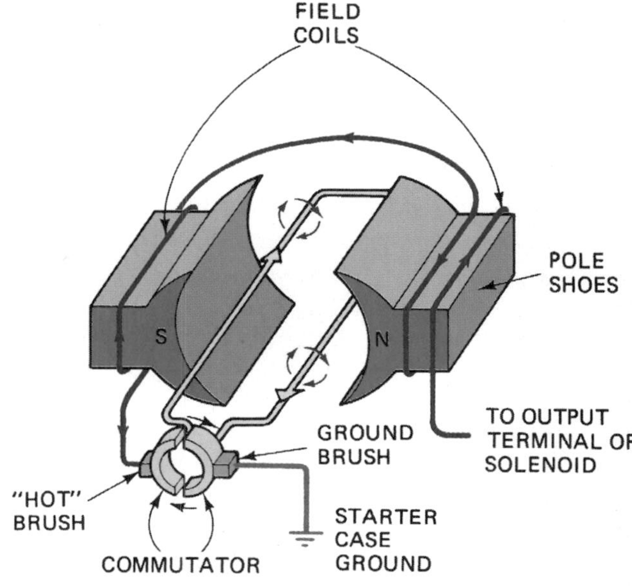

Figure 16–5 Series-wound electric motor showing the basic operation with only two brushes: one hot brush and one ground brush. The current flows through both field coils, then through the hot brush and through the loop winding of the armature before reaching ground through the ground brush.

The starter uses four brushes—two brushes to transfer the current from the field coils to the armature, and two brushes to provide the ground return path for the current that flows through the armature. See Figure 16–5. Therefore, two **hot brushes** are in holders, which are insulated from the housing, and two **ground brushes** primarily use bare, stranded copper wire connections to the brushes. The ground brush holders are not insulated and attach directly to the field housing.

The current travels through the brushes and into the armature windings, where other magnetic fields are created around each copper wire loop in the armature. The two strong magnetic fields created inside the starter housing create the force that rotates the armature.

How Magnetic Fields Turn an Armature

One basic principle of electromagnetism is that a magnetic field surrounds every conductor carrying a current. The strength of the magnetic field is increased as the current flow (in amperes) is increased.

Inside the starter housing is a strong magnetic field created by the field coil magnets. The armature, a conductor, is installed inside this strong magnetic field, with very little clearance between the armature and the field coils.

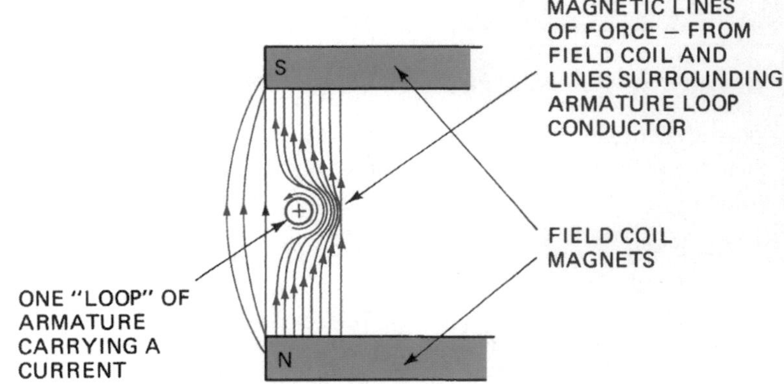

Figure 16–6 The interaction of the magnetic fields of the armature loops and field coils creates a stronger magnetic field on the right side of the conductor, causing the armature loop to move toward the left.

The two magnetic fields act together, and their lines of force "bunch up" or are strong on one side of the armature loop wire and become weak on the other side of the conductor. This causes the conductor (armature) to move from the area of strong magnetic field strength toward the area of weak magnetic field strength. See Figures 16–6 and 16–7. This causes the armature to rotate. This rotation force (torque) is increased as the current flowing through the starter motor increases. The torque of a starter is determined by the strength of the magnetic fields inside the starter. Magnetic field strength is measured in ampere-turns. If the current or the number of turns of wire are increased, the magnetic field strength is increased.

The magnetic field of the starter motor is provided by two or more pole shoes and field windings. The pole shoes are made of iron and are attached to the frame with large screws. See Figure 16–8. Some pole shoes are welded to the starter frame and are not removable. Figure 16–9 shows the paths of magnetic flux lines within a four-pole motor. The field windings are usually made of a heavy copper ribbon (see Figure 16–10, p. 368) to increase their current-carrying capacity and electromagnetic field strength. Automotive starter motors usually have four pole shoes and two to four field windings to provide a strong magnetic field within the motor. Pole shoes that do not have field windings are magnetized by flux lines from the wound poles.

TYPES OF STARTER MOTORS

Starter motors must provide high power at low starter motor speeds to crank an automotive engine at all temperatures and at the cranking speed required for the engine to start (60 to 250 engine rpm). Electric motors are classified according to the internal electrical motor connections. The method used determines the power-producing characteristics of the electric motor. Many starter motors are series wound, which means that the current flows first through the field coils, then in series through the armature, and finally to a ground through the ground brushes. See Figure 16–11.

Series Motors

A series motor develops its maximum torque at the initial start (0 rpm) and develops less torque as the speed increases. A series motor is commonly used for an automotive starter motor because of its high starting power characteristics. A series starter motor develops less torque at high RPM, because a current is produced in the starter itself that acts against the current from the battery. Because this current works against battery voltage, it is called **counter electromotive force** or **CEMF.** This counter EMF is produced by electromagnetic induction in the armature conductors, which are cutting across the magnetic lines of force formed by the field coils. This induced voltage operates against the applied voltage supplied by the battery, which reduces the strength of the magnetic field in the starter.

Because the power (torque) of the starter depends on the strength of the magnetic fields, the torque of the starter decreases as the starter speed increases. It is also characteristic of series-wound motors to keep increasing in speed under light loads. This could lead to the destruction of the starter motor unless controlled or prevented.

Shunt Motors

Shunt-type electric motors have the field coils in parallel (or shunt) across the armature as shown in Figure 16–12. A shunt motor does not decrease in torque at higher motor RPM, because the CEMF produced in the armature does not decrease the field coil strength. A shunt motor, however, does not produce as high a starting torque as that of a series-wound motor, and is not used for starters. Many small electric motors used in automotive blower motors, windshield wipers, power windows,

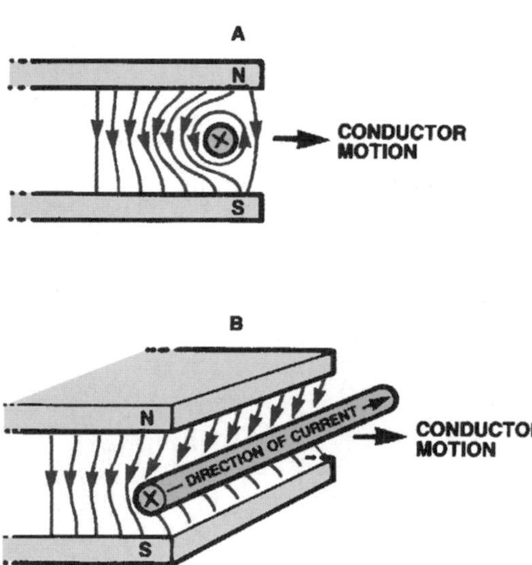

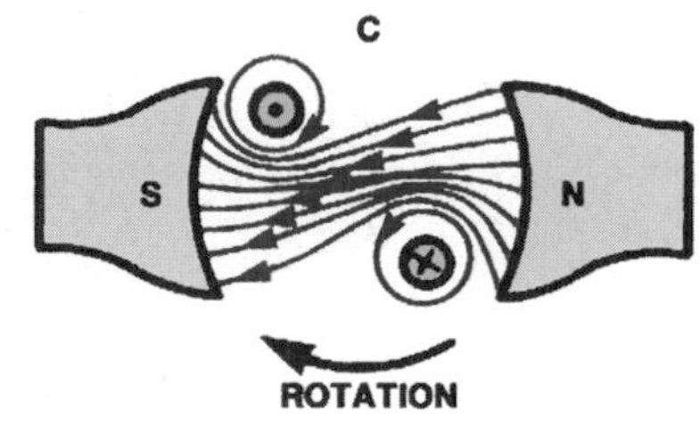

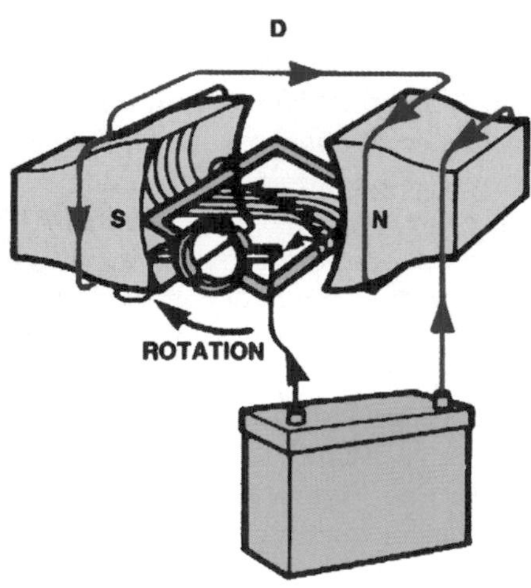

Figure 16–7 The armature loops rotate due to the difference in the strength of the magnetic field. The loops move from a strong magnetic field strength toward a weaker magnetic field strength.

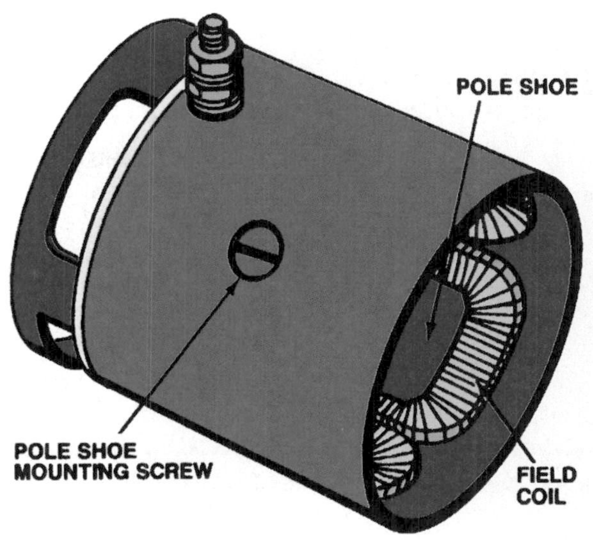

Figure 16–8 Pole shoes and field windings installed in the housing.

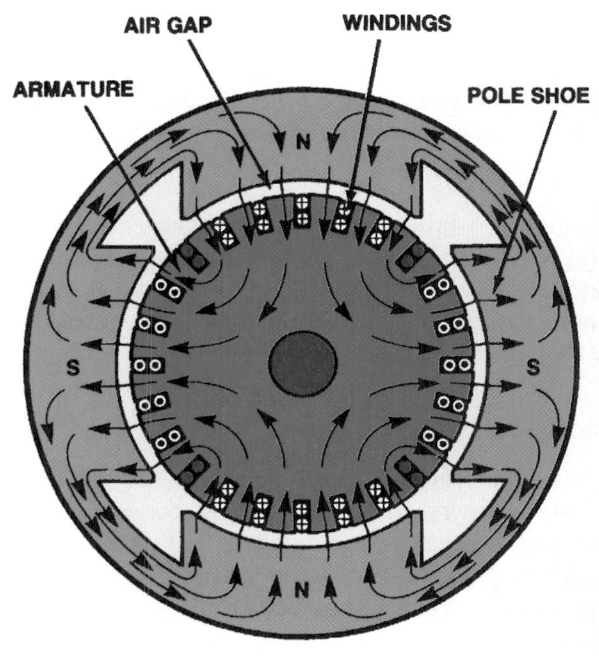

Figure 16–9 Magnetic lines of force in a four-pole motor.

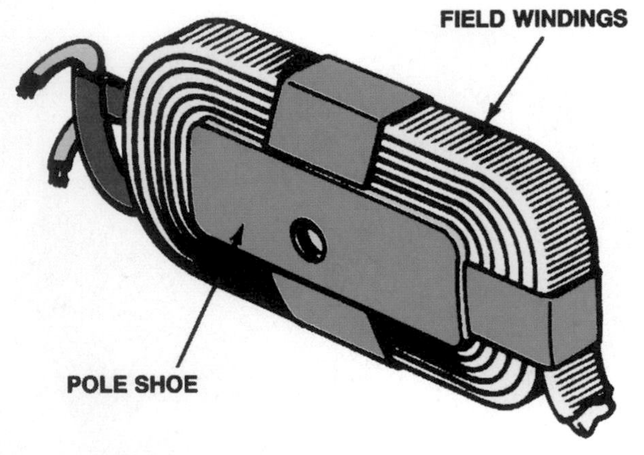

Figure 16–10 A pole shoe and field winding.

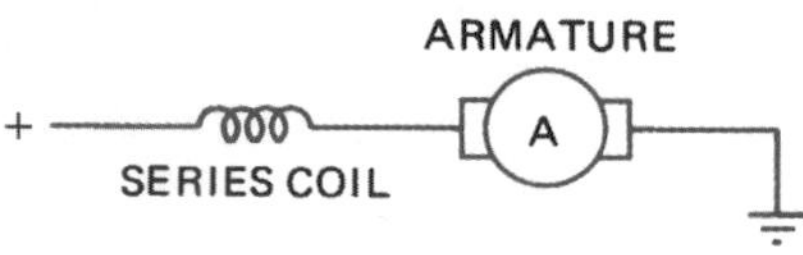

Figure 16–11 Wiring diagram illustrating the construction of a series-wound electric motor. Notice that all current flows through the field coils, then through the armature (in series) before reaching ground.

and power seats use permanent magnets rather than electromagnets. Because these permanent magnets maintain a constant field strength, the same as a shunt-type motor, they have similar operating characteristics.

Compound Motors

A compound-wound, or compound, motor has the operating characteristics of a series motor *and* a shunt-type motor, because some of the field coils are connected to the armature in series and some (usually only one) are connected directly to the battery in parallel (shunt) with the armature. See Figure 16–13.

Compound-wound starter motors are often used in both domestic and import starters. The shunt-wound field coil is called a shunt coil and is used to limit the maximum speed of the starter. Because the shunt coil is energized as soon as the battery current is sent to the starter, it is used to engage the starter drive on Ford positive-engagement starters.

ARMATURE AND COMMUTATOR ASSEMBLY

The motor armature, Figure 16–14, has a laminated core. Insulation between the laminations helps to reduce eddy currents in the core. For reduced resistance, the armature conductors are made of a thick copper wire. Motor armatures are connected to the commutator in one of two ways. In a **lap winding,** the two ends of each conductor are attached to two adjacent commutator bars. See Figure 16–15. In a **wave winding,** the two ends of a conductor are attached to commutator bars that are 180 degrees apart (on opposite sides of the commutator). A lap-wound armature is more commonly used because it offers less resistance.

The commutator is made of copper bars insulated from each other by mica or some other insulating material. The armature core, windings, and commutator are assembled on a long armature shaft. This shaft also carries the pinion gear that meshes with the engine flywheel ring gear. See Figure 16–16. The shaft is supported by bearings or bushings in the end housings.

To supply the proper current to the armature, a four-pole motor must have four brushes riding on the commutator. Most automotive starters have two grounded and two insulated brushes. The brushes are held against the commutator by spring force. See Figure 16–17.

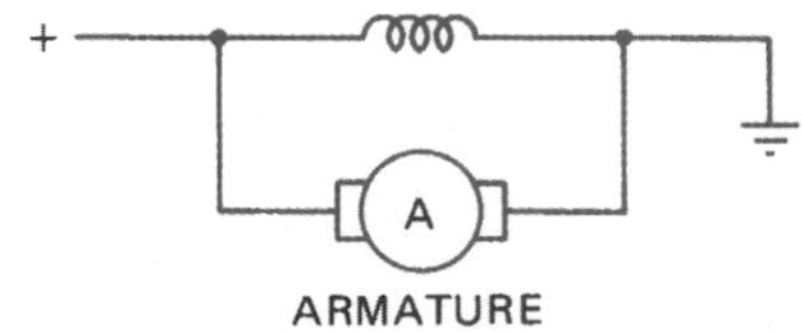

Figure 16–12 Wiring diagram illustrating the construction of a shunt-type electric motor. Shunt-type electric motors have the field coils in parallel (or shunt) across the armature as shown.

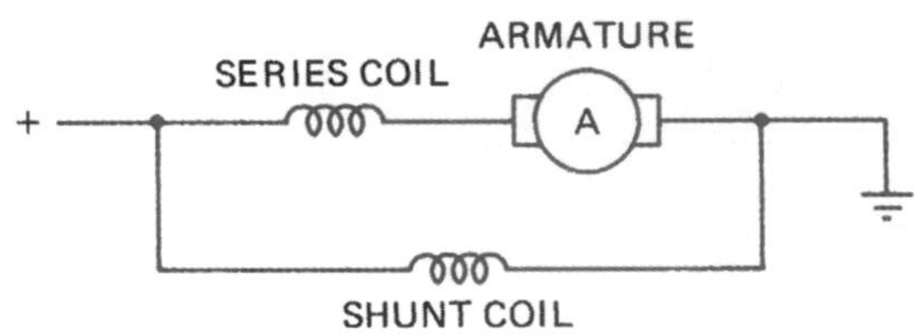

Figure 16–13 A compound motor is a combination of series and shunt types, using part of the field coils connected electrically in series with the armature and some in parallel (shunt).

PERMANENT-MAGNET FIELDS

The permanent magnet, planetary drive starter motor was first introduced on some 1986 DaimlerChrysler and General Motors cars and light trucks. The electromagnetic field coils and pole shoes have been replaced by permanent magnets. General

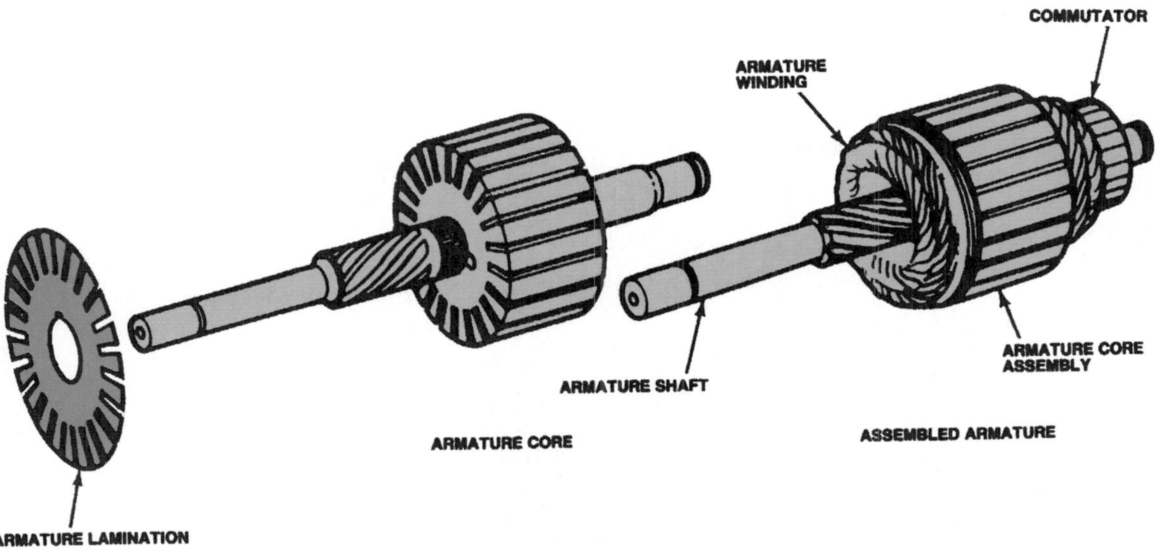

Figure 16–14 A typical starter motor armature.

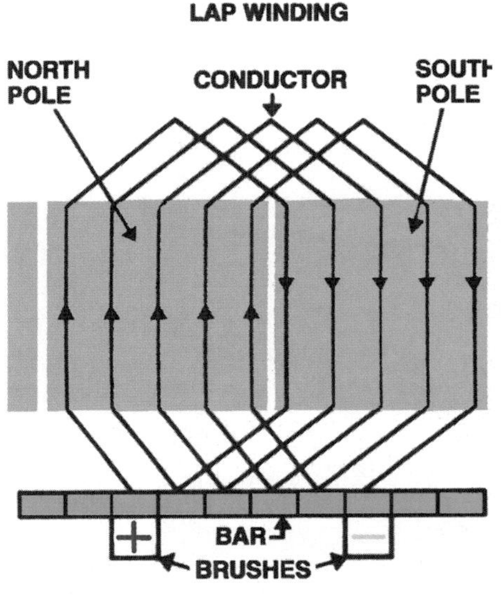

Figure 16–15 Armature lap winding.

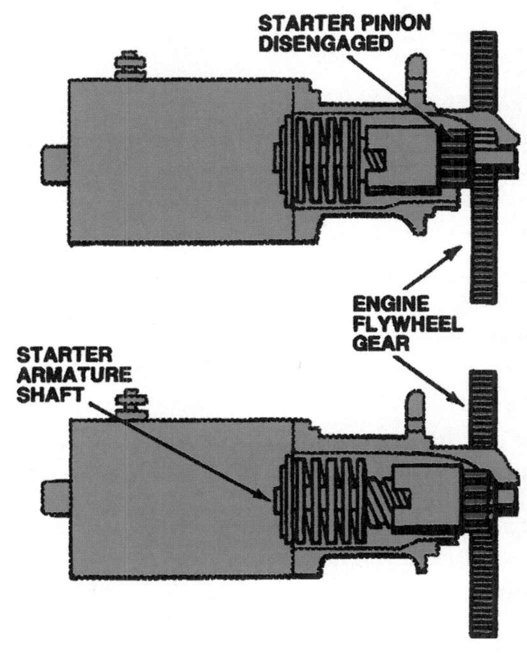

Figure 16–16 The pinion gear meshes with the flywheel ring gear.

Motors uses iron alloy, boron and a rare earth element, neodymium, to produce permanent magnets ten times stronger than ferrite magnets. These starters are almost 50% lighter and much smaller than conventional starter motors.

The elimination of the field circuit eliminates the potential for field wire-to-frame shorts, field coil welding, and other electrical problems. The motor has only an armature circuit. See Figure 16–18. Permanent magnet starters are now the industry standard.

GEAR-REDUCTION STARTERS

Gear-reduction starters are used by many automotive manufacturers. The purpose of the gear reduction (typically 2:1 to 4:1) is to increase starter motor speed and provide the torque multiplication necessary to crank an engine. See Figures 16–19 and 16–20. As a series-wound motor increases in rotational speed, the starter produces less power, and less current is drawn from the battery because the armature generates greater CEMF as the starter speed increases. However, a starter motor's maximum torque occurs at 0 rpm and torque decreases with increasing RPM. A smaller starter using a gear-reduction design can produce the necessary

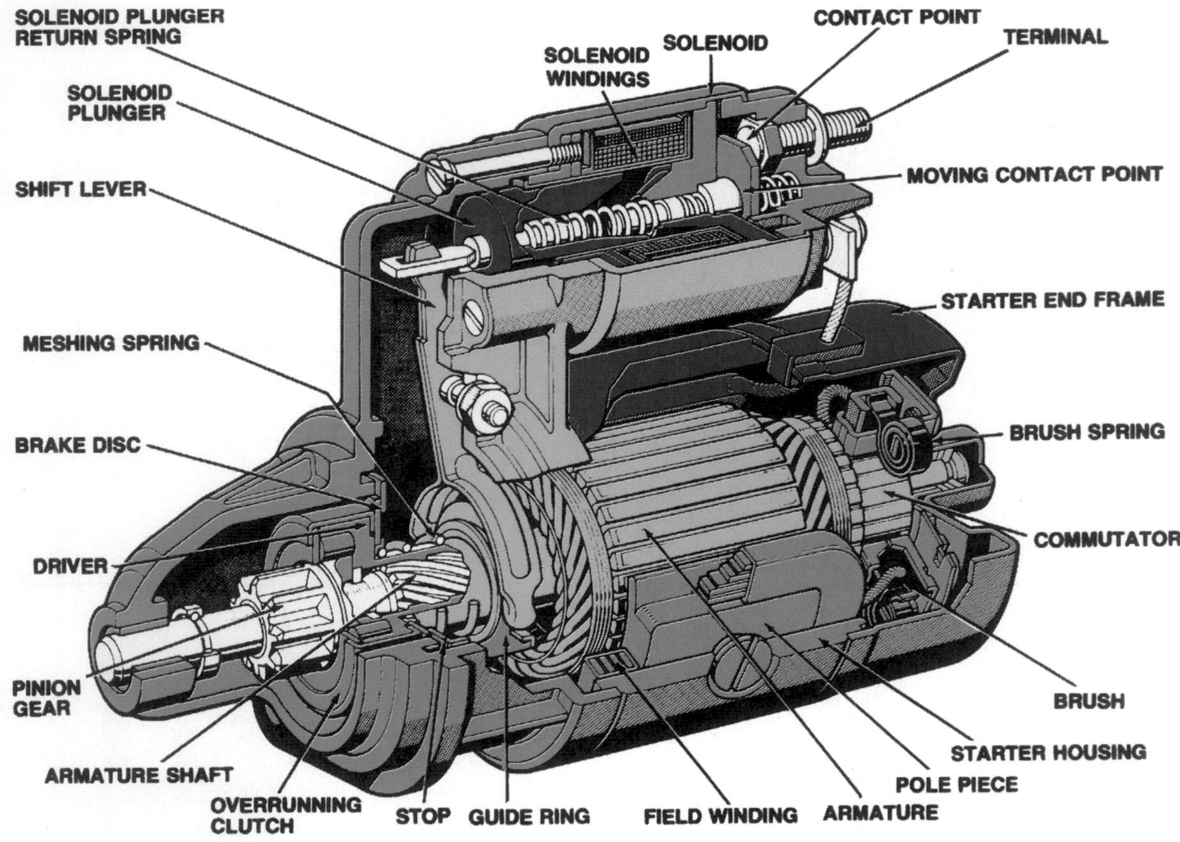

Figure 16–17 A cutaway of a typical starter motor.

TECH TIP 

Don't Hit That Starter!

In the past, it was common to see service technicians hitting a starter in their effort to diagnose a no-crank condition. Often the shock of the blow to the starter aligned or moved the brushes, armature, and bushings. Many times, the starter functioned after being hit—even if only for a short time.

However, most of today's starters use permanent-magnet fields, and the magnets can be easily broken if hit. A magnet that is broken becomes two weaker magnets. Some early GM starters used magnets that were glued or bonded to the field housing. If struck with a heavy tool, the magnets could be broken, with parts of the magnet falling onto the armature and into the bearing pockets, making the starter impossible to repair or rebuild.

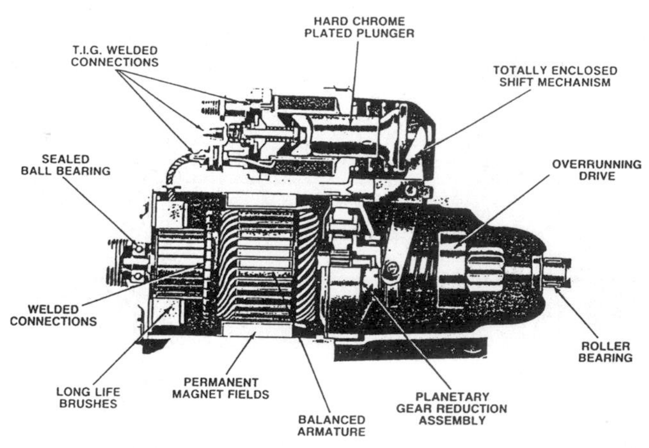

Figure 16–18 Permanent magnet gear reduction (PM/GR) starters use permanent magnets to eliminate the field coils, and a planetary gear reduction assembly. (Courtesy General Motors of Canada Ltd.)

cranking power with reduced starter amperage requirements. Lower current requirements mean that smaller battery cables can be used. Permanent-magnet starters use a planetary gear set (a type of gear reduction) to provide the necessary torque for starting. See Figure 16–20.

STARTER DRIVES

A starter drive includes a small pinion gear that meshes with and rotates the larger gear on the engine for starting. The pinion gear must engage with the engine gear slightly *before* the starter motor ro-

Figure 16–19 A Chrysler starter motor showing the starter drive and gear-reduction gear.

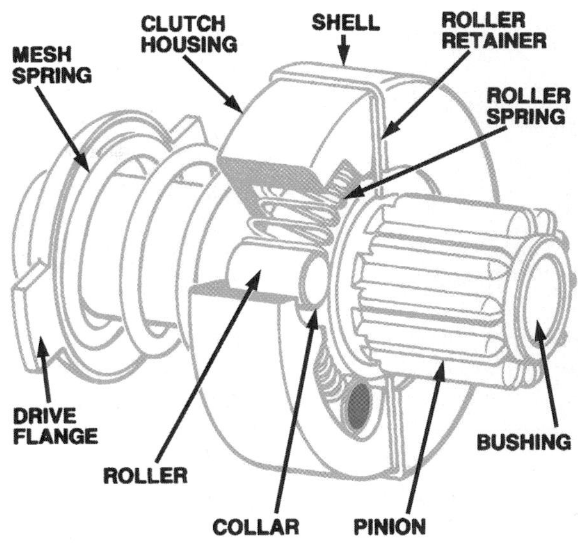

Figure 16–21 A cutaway of a typical starter drive.

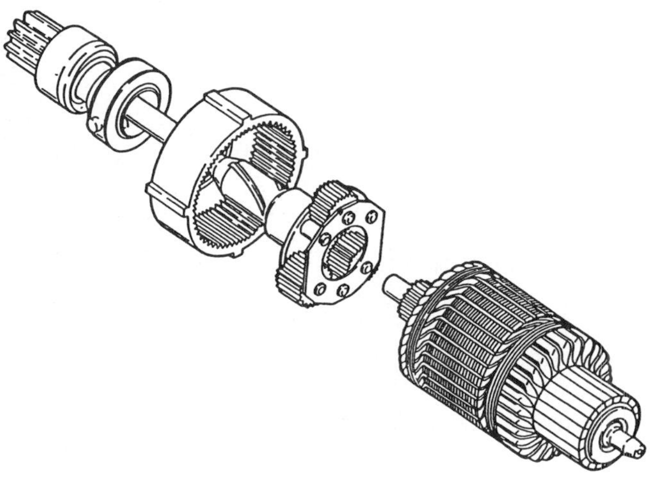

Figure 16–20 Many gear-reduction starters use a planetary gear-reduction assembly similar to that used in an automatic transmission. (Courtesy General Motors of Canada Ltd.)

tates, to prevent serious damage to either the starter gear or the engine, but must be disengaged after the engine starts. The ends of the starter pinion gear are tapered to help the teeth mesh more easily without damaging the flywheel ring gear teeth. See Figure 16–21. The ratio of the number of teeth on the engine gear to the number on the starter pinion is between 15:1 and 20:1. A typical small starter pinion gear has 9 teeth that turn an engine gear with 166 teeth. This provides an 18:1 gear reduction; thus, the starter motor is rotating approximately 18 times faster than the engine. Normal cranking speed for the engine is 200 rpm. This means that the starter motor speed is 18 times faster, or 3600 starter rpm ($200 \times 18 = 3600$). If the engine started and was accelerated to 2000 rpm (normal cold engine speed), the starter would be destroyed by the high speed (36 000 rpm) if the starter were not disengaged from the engine.

Older-model starters (made before the early 1960s) often used a Bendix drive mechanism, which used inertia to engage the starter pinion with the engine flywheel gear. Inertia is the tendency of a stationary object to remain stationary, because of its weight, unless forced to move. On these older-model starters the small starter pinion gear was attached to a threaded shaft. Rotation of the armature and threaded shaft caused the pinion gear to be spun along the threaded shaft and mesh with the flywheel whenever the starter motor spun. If the engine speed was greater than the starter speed, the pinion gear was forced back along the threaded shaft and out of mesh with the flywheel gear. The Bendix drive mechanism has generally not been used since the early 1960s.

All current starter drive mechanisms use a type of one-way clutch that allows the starter to rotate the engine, but freewheel if the engine speed is greater than the starter motor speed. This clutch is called an **overrunning clutch,** and it protects the starter motor from damage if the ignition switch is held in the start position after the engine starts. The overrunning clutch, which is built in as part of the starter drive unit, uses steel balls or rollers installed in tapered notches. See Figure 16–22. This taper forces the balls or rollers tightly into the notch when rotating in the direction necessary to start the engine. Whenever the engine rotates faster than the starter pinion, the balls or rollers are forced out of the narrow tapered notch, allowing the pinion gear to turn freely (overrun).

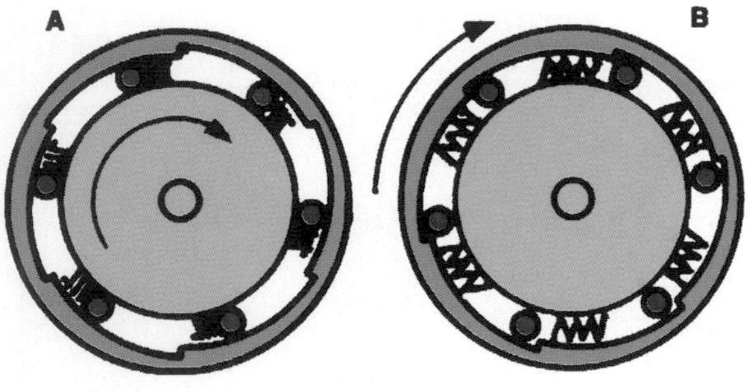

Figure 16–22 Operation of the overrunning clutch. (a) Starter motor is driving the starter pinion and cranking the engine. The rollers are wedged against spring force into their slots. (b) The engine has started and is rotating faster than the starter armature. Spring force pushes the rollers so they can rotate freely.

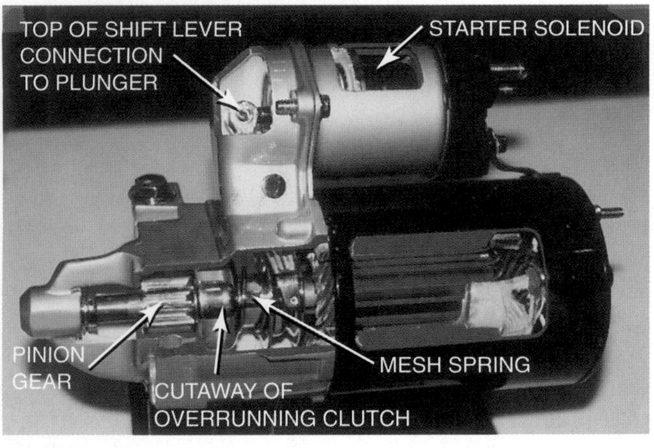

Figure 16–23 Cutaway of a solenoid-activated starter showing the solenoid, shift lever, and starter drive assembly that includes the starter pinion and overrunning clutch with a mesh spring in one unit.

The spring between the drive tang or pulley and the overrunning clutch and pinion is called a **mesh spring.** It helps to cushion and control the engagement of the starter drive pinion with the engine flywheel gear. This spring is also called a **compression spring** because the starter solenoid or starter yoke compresses the spring and the spring tension causes the starter pinion to engage the engine flywheel. See Figure 16–23.

Symptoms of a Defective Starter Drive

A starter drive is generally a dependable unit and does not require replacement unless defective or worn. The major wear occurs in the overrunning clutch section of the starter drive unit. The steel balls or rollers wear and often do not wedge tightly into the tapered notches, as is necessary for engine cranking. A worn starter drive can cause the starter motor to operate freely and not rotate the engine. Therefore, the starter makes a whining noise. The whine indicates that the starter motor is operating and that the starter drive is not rotating the engine flywheel. The entire starter drive is replaced as a unit. The overrunning clutch section of the starter drive cannot be serviced or repaired separately because the drive is a sealed unit. Starter drives are most likely to fail intermittently at first and then gradually more frequently, until replacement becomes necessary to start the engine. Intermittent starter drive failure (starter whine) is often most noticeable during cold weather.

Starter Drive Operation

The starter drive (pinion gear) must be moved into mesh with the engine ring gear before the starter motor starts to spin. Most automotive starters use a solenoid or the magnetic pull of the shunt coil in the starter to engage the starter pinion.

POSITIVE-ENGAGEMENT STARTERS

Positive-engagement starters, used on many Ford engines, utilize the shunt coil winding of the starter to engage the starter drive. The high starting current is controlled by an ignition switch–operated starter solenoid, usually mounted near the positive post of the battery. When this control circuit is closed, current flows through a hollow field coil (called a drive coil) directly to ground at the grounding contacts. This creates a very strong magnetic field, which attracts, and pulls down, a movable pole shoe. See Figure 16–24. The metal movable pole shoe is attached to a lever (called the plunger lever); it pushes the starter drive into the flywheel as the pole shoe is being pulled down.

As soon as the starter drive has engaged the flywheel, a tang on the movable pole shoe opens the contact points. The starter current now flows through all four field coils and on through the brushes to the armature. This causes the armature to rotate.

The movable pole shoe is held down (which keeps the starter drive engaged) by a smaller coil on the inside of the main drive coil. This coil is called the **holding** (or **hold-in**) **coil,** and it is strong enough to hold the starter drive engaged while permitting the flow of the maximum possible current to operate the starter. See Figure 16–25. If the grounding contact points are severely pitted, the starter may not operate the starter drive or the starter motor because of the resulting poor ground for the drive coil. If the contact points are

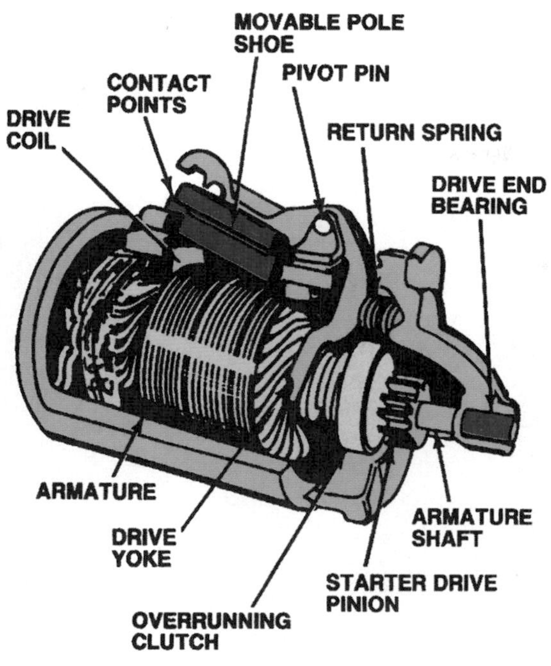

Figure 16–24 A Ford movable-pole-shoe starter.

bent or damaged enough to prevent them from opening, the starter will clunk the starter drive into engagement but will not allow the starter motor to operate.

SOLENOID-OPERATED STARTERS

A starter solenoid is an **electromagnetic switch** containing two separate, but connected, electromagnetic windings. This switch is used to engage the starter drive and control the current from the battery to the starter motor. See Figure 16–26.

The two internal windings contain approximately the same number of turns but are made from different-gauge wire. Both windings together produce a strong magnetic field that pulls a metal plunger into the solenoid. The plunger is attached to the starter drive through a **shift fork lever.** When the ignition switch is turned to the start position, the motion of the plunger into the solenoid causes the starter drive to move into mesh with the flywheel ring gear. The heavier-gauge winding (called the **pull-in winding**) is needed to draw the plunger into the solenoid. The lighter-gauge winding (called the **hold-in winding**) produces enough magnetic force to keep the plunger in position. The main purpose of using two separate windings is to permit as much current as possible to operate the starter and yet provide the strong magnetic field required to move the starter drive into engagement. The instant the plunger is drawn into the solenoid enough to engage the starter drive, the plunger makes contact with a metal disk that connects the battery terminal post of the solenoid to the motor terminal. This permits full battery current to flow through the solenoid to operate the starter motor. The contact disk also electrically disconnects the pull-in winding. The solenoid *has* to work to supply current to the starter. Therefore, if the starter motor operates at all, the solenoid is working, even though it may have high external resistance that could cause slow starter motor operation.

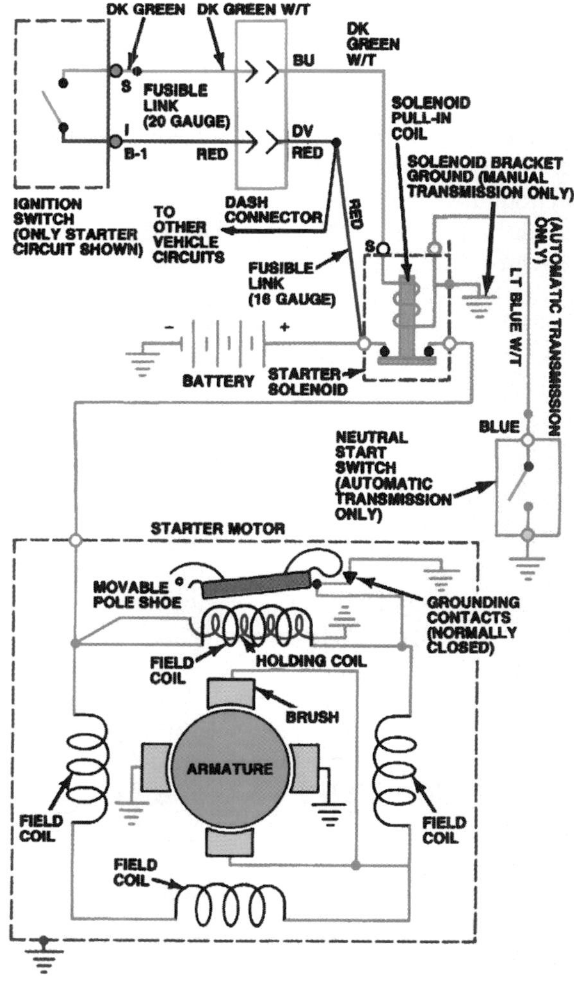

Figure 16–25 A circuit diagram of a Ford system using a movable-pole-shoe starter.

NOTE: Induced voltage from the collapsing magnetic field in the starter solenoid may backfeed through the circuit and damage the on-board computer. A clamping diode connected across the hold-in winding will suppress the voltage spike.

Many Ford, DaimlerChrysler, Mazda, and others, use diode-protected starter solenoids. Do not substitute an earlier non-protected solenoid or electronic damage may result.

Some cheaper aftermarket parts also have no protection—always use quality replacements.

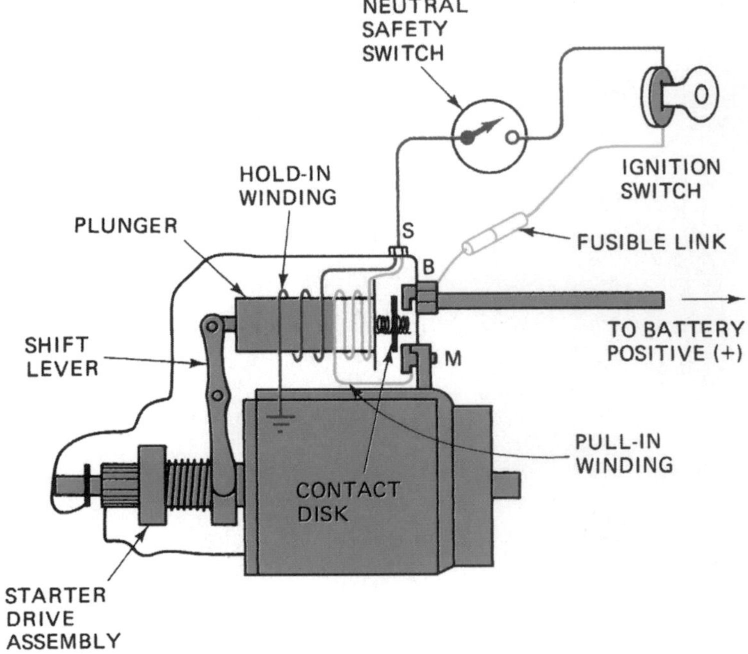

Figure 16–26 Wiring diagram of a typical starter solenoid. Notice that both the pull-in winding and the hold-in winding are energized when the ignition switch is first turned to the "start" position. As soon as the solenoid contact disk makes electrical contact with both the B and M terminals, the battery current is conducted to the starter motor and electrically neutralizes the pull-in winding.

COMBINATION STARTER-GENERATORS

Hybrid vehicles typically use a high voltage electric motor operating in parallel with the gasoline engine; this supplies additional torque when required. The electric motor also functions as a generator to charge the batteries and as a high RPM starter. See Figure 16–27.

Many hybrid vehicles allow the gasoline engine to stop during idle periods to preserve fuel; the engine cranks and restarts when the accelerator pedal is depressed.

Honda integrates the starter-generator into the bell housing of the gasoline engine. If the outside temperature is very low, the high voltage battery is discharged or a problem exists with the integrated starter-generator, a conventional 12 V starter is used to start the engine.

STARTING SYSTEM TROUBLESHOOTING

The proper operation of the starting system depends on a good battery, good cables and connections, and a good starter motor. Because a starting problem can be caused by a defective component anywhere in the starting circuit, it is important to check for the proper operation of each part of the circuit to diagnose and repair the problem quickly.

TECH TIP 

Voltage Drop Is Resistance

Many technicians have asked, why measure voltage drop when the resistance can be easily measured using an ohmmeter? Think of a battery cable with all the strands of the cable broken, except for one strand. If an ohmmeter were used to measure the resistance of the cable, the reading would be very low, probably less than 1 ohm. However, the cable is not capable of conducting the amount of current necessary to crank the engine. In less severe cases, several strands can be broken, and affect the operation of the starter motor. While the resistance of the battery cable will not indicate any increased resistance, the restriction to current flow will cause heat and a drop of voltage available at the starter. Since resistance is not effective until current flows, measuring the voltage drop (differences in voltage between two points) is the most accurate method of determining the true resistance in a circuit.

How much is too much? According to Bosch Corporation, all electrical circuits should have a maximum of 3% loss of the voltage of the circuit to resistance. Therefore, in a 12 V circuit, the maximum loss of voltage in cables and connections should be 0.36 volt ($12 \times 0.03 = 0.36$ volt). The remaining 97% of the circuit voltage (11.64 volts) is available to operate the electrical device (load). Just remember:

Low-voltage drop = Low resistance

High-voltage drop = High resistance

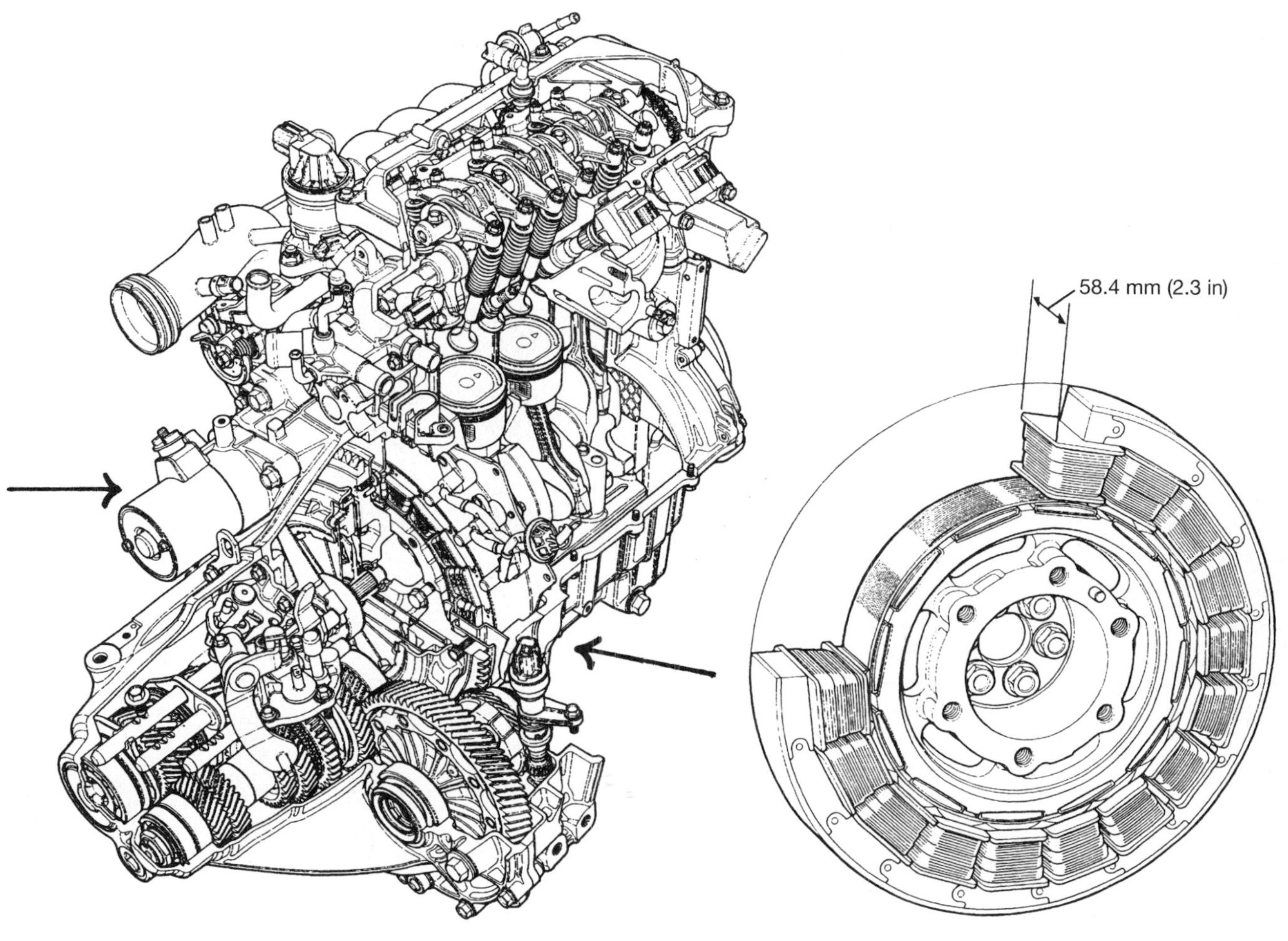

Figure 16–27 Cutaway view of the Honda Integrated Motor Assist (IMA) system. Note the 144 volt integrated motor located in the bell housing and the conventional 12 volt starter. (Courtesy Honda Motor Co.)

> **NOTE:** Starter remanufacturers state that the single most common cause of starter motor failure is **low battery voltage.** When battery voltage drops, additional current (amperes) must flow through the starter to maintain the balance of electrical power. Since electrical power is amperes times volts, a drop in battery voltage causes the increase in starter current draw.

VOLTAGE-DROP TESTING

Voltage drop is the drop in voltage that occurs when current is flowing through a resistance. For example, a voltage drop is the difference between voltage at the source and the voltage at the electrical device to which it is flowing. The higher the voltage drop, the greater the resistance to that point. Even though voltage-drop testing can be performed on any electrical circuit, the most common areas of testing include the cranking circuit and the charging circuit wiring and connections.

A high-voltage drop (high resistance) in the cranking circuit wiring can cause slow engine cranking with less than normal starter current draw as a result of the excessive circuit resistance. If the voltage drop is high enough, such as could be caused by dirty battery terminals, the starter may not operate. A typical symptom of high resistance in the cranking circuit is a clicking of the starter solenoid.

Voltage-drop testing of the wire involves connecting any voltmeter (on the low scale, while cranking) to the suspected high-resistance cable ends and cranking the engine. See Figures 16–28 and 16–29.

> **NOTE:** Before a difference in voltage (voltage drop) can be measured between the ends of a battery cable, current must be flowing through the cable. *Resistance is not effective unless current is flowing.* If the engine is not being cranked, current is not flowing through the battery cables and the voltage drop cannot be measured.

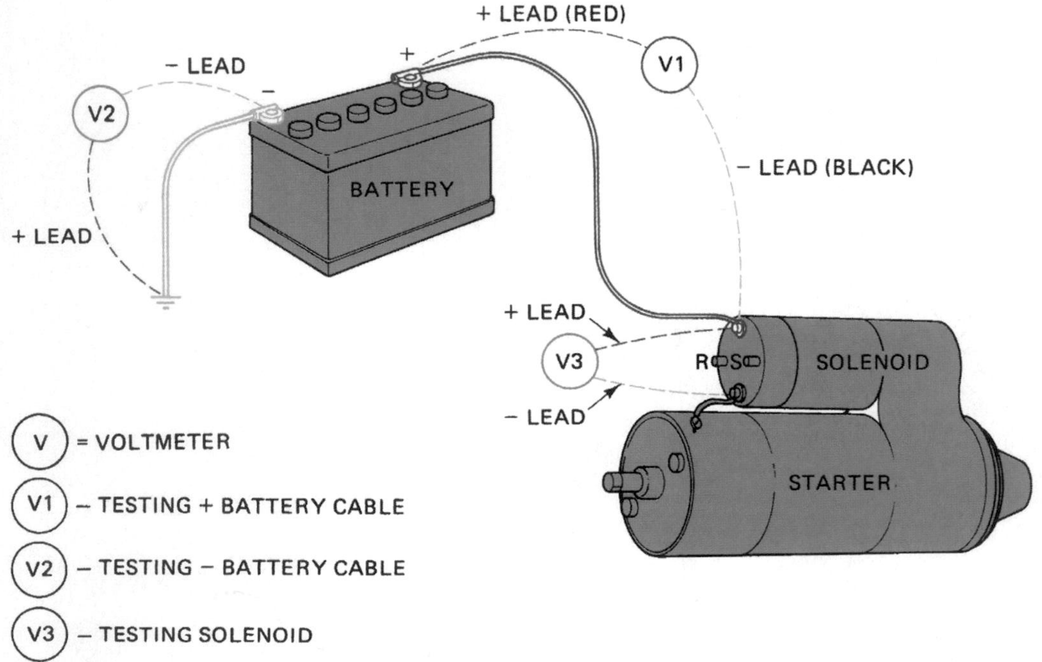

Figure 16–28 Voltmeter hookups for voltage-drop testing of a GM-type cranking circuit.

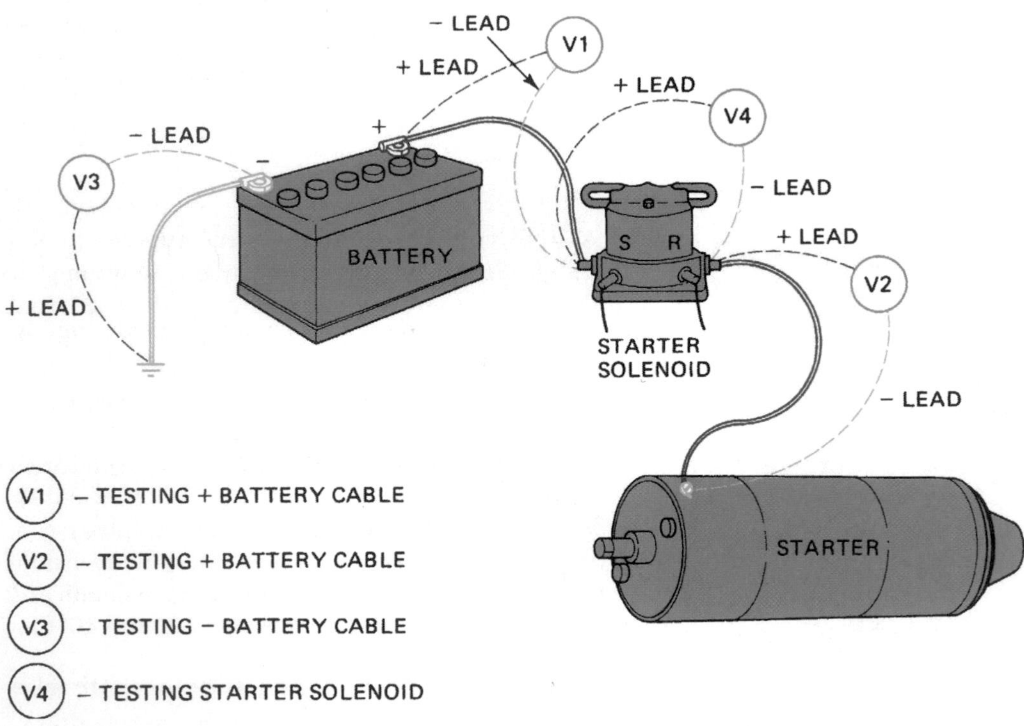

Figure 16–29 Voltmeter hookups for voltage-drop testing of a Ford-type cranking circuit.

Crank the engine with the voltmeter positive lead connected to the battery positive terminal and the voltmeter negative lead connected to the starter terminal and record the reading. Crank the engine and record the reading. If the difference in the two readings exceeds 0.5 V, perform the following steps to determine the exact location of the voltage drop.

Step 1 Connect the positive voltmeter test lead to the most-positive end of the cable being tested. The most-positive end of a cable is the end closest to the positive terminal of the battery.

Step 2 Connect the negative voltmeter test lead to the other end of the cable being tested. With no current flowing through the cable, the voltmeter should read zero because both ends of the cable have the same voltage.

Step 3 Crank the engine. The voltmeter should read less than 0.2 volt.

Step 4 Evaluate the results. If the voltmeter reads zero, the cable being tested has no resistance and is good. If the voltmeter reads higher than 0.2 volt, the cable has excessive resistance and should be replaced. However, before replacing the cable, make certain that the connections at both ends of the cable being tested are clean and tight.

Step 5 Test the ground circuit; any current flowing to the starter must also return to the battery. This procedure is similar to the insulated circuit test. Connect the negative voltmeter lead to the negative terminal of the battery and the positive voltmeter lead to the starter field frame. Crank the engine. Typical voltage drop is about 0.2 volt; higher than 0.5 volt indicates a poor ground at the starter-to-engine mounting or a corroded or loose ground cable.

CONTROL CIRCUIT TESTING

The control circuit for the starting circuit includes the battery, ignition switch, neutral or clutch safety switch, and starter solenoid. Whenever the ignition switch is rotated to the start position, current flows through the ignition switch and the neutral safety switch and activates the solenoid. High current then flows directly from the battery through the solenoid and to the starter motor. Therefore, an open or break anywhere in the control circuit will prevent the operation of the starter motor. See Figure 16–30. If a starter is inoperative, first check for voltage at the S (start) terminal of the starter solenoid. See Figure 16–31. Some newer models with antitheft controls use a relay to open this control circuit to prevent starter operation.

TECH TIP 

Too Hot!

If a cable or connection is hot to the touch, there is electrical resistance in the cable or connection. The resistance changes electrical energy into heat energy. Therefore, if a voltmeter is not available, touch the battery cables and connections while cranking the engine. If any cable or connection is hot to the touch, it should be cleaned or replaced.

SPECIFICATIONS FOR A STARTER AMPERAGE TEST

Before performing a starter amperage test, be certain that the battery is sufficiently charged (75% or more) and capable of supplying adequate starting current.

A starter amperage test should be performed whenever the starter fails to operate normally (is slow in cranking) or as part of a routine electrical system inspection. Some service manuals specify normal starter amperage for starter motors being tested on the vehicle; however, most service manuals only give the specifications for bench testing a starter without a load applied. These specifications are helpful in making certain that a repaired starter meets exact specifications, but they do not apply to starter testing on the vehicle. If exact specifications are not available, the following can be used as general specifications for testing a starter on the vehicle:

- **Four-cylinder engines:** 150–185 amperes
- **Six-cylinder engines:** 160–200 amperes
- **Eight-cylinder engines:** 185–250 amperes

Excessive current draw may indicate one or more of the following:

1. Low battery voltage (discharged or defective battery)
2. Binding of starter armature as a result of worn bushings
3. Oil too thick (viscosity too high) for weather conditions
4. Shorted or grounded starter windings or cables
5. Tight or seized engine

Lower than normal current draw (with slow cranking) may indicate:

1. High-resistance battery cables or connections (caused by loose or corroded terminals, for example)
2. High resistance inside the starter solenoid
3. High resistance in the starter motor (usually caused by excessively worn brushes)

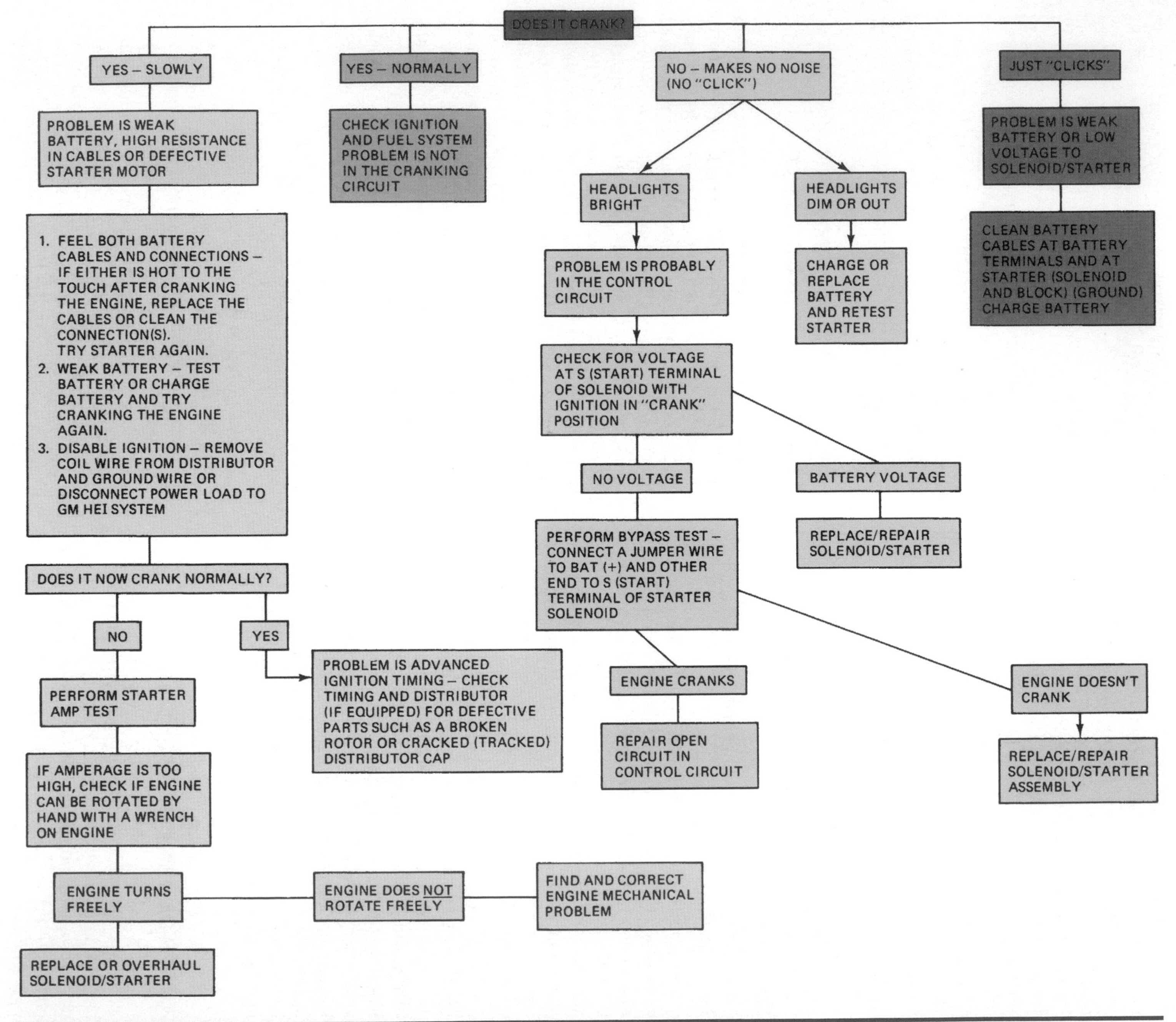

Figure 16–30 Starter trouble diagnostic chart.

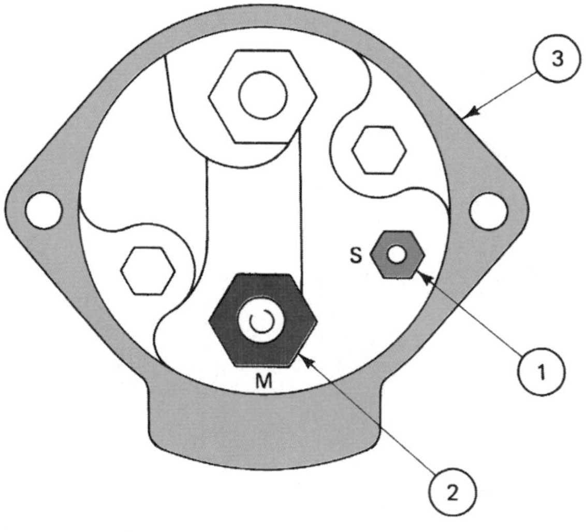

Figure 16–31 GM solenoid ohmmeter check. (See also Figure 16–26 for wiring schematic.) The reading between 1 and 3 (S terminal and ground) should be 0.4 to 0.6 ohm (hold-in winding). The reading between 1 and 2 (S terminal and M terminal) should be 0.2 to 0.4 ohm (pull-in winding).

Frequently Asked Question ???

Why Does a Weak Battery Cause an Increase in the Starter Current?

A starter motor requires a certain amount of *power* to start an engine. Power expressed in electrical terms is amperes times volts (Power = $I \times E$). The power required to start an engine remains the same even if the battery voltage decreases. For example:

Good Battery	Weak Battery
11.0 V during cranking	9.8 V during cranking
190 A	213 A
Power = 11.0 × 190	Power = 9.8 × 213
= 2090 W	= 2090 W

Notice that the power required for the starter motor to crank the engine is the same (2090 W). However, the good battery can maintain 11.0 V while supplying the necessary current for starter operation (190 A). A weak battery decreases in voltage while supplying the high current required for cranking. The *power* required by the starter to crank an engine is constant. If the battery voltage decreases, the amount of current must *increase* to compensate for the drop in voltage. Notice that the required current is increased from 190 A (good battery) to 213 A for the weak battery. Therefore, to get accurate test results, a battery that is known to be good and that is at least 75% charged should be used during starter testing.

DIAGNOSTIC STORY

Battery Cable Heat and Counter EMF

Battery cables can overheat when there is excessive current flow through the cable. The amount of current (in amperes) is determined by the power required to operate the starter motor. A typical problem involved a vehicle driven to Montreal from Toronto. The battery cables overheated when the driver tried to start the vehicle. At a service centre, some technicians believed that the cause of the overheated cables was an oversize battery, which is often used in vehicles from northern climates. Although it is true that a smaller battery can be used in warmer climates, a large battery does absolutely no harm and, in fact, generally lasts longer than a smaller battery. The cause of the problem was discovered (by testing) to be a defective starter motor that rotated too slowly. The too-slow rotation of the starter meant that the starter was not producing the normal amount of counter EMF, or CEMF. The overall result was a tremendous increase in current being drawn from the battery, and it was this extra current flow that overheated the battery cables.

NOTE: Counter-EMF (CEMF) must be taken into consideration when testing starter circuits for current draw.

As the armature loop passes through the magnetic field (created by the field coils or permanent magnets), voltage is induced into the loop. This induced voltage acts against battery voltage; the faster the armature turns, the stronger the counter-voltage (CEMF).

Amperage flow determines the power of the starter; high current-high power, low current-reduced power.

Amperage flow is greatest at zero armature speed; battery voltage pushes current through the very low resistance of the battery cables, field coils (if used) and the armature.

As the armature begins to rotate induced counter-voltage in the armature loops act against battery voltage and current flow is reduced, the faster the armature spins, the greater the counter-voltage and current flow is further reduced.

Amperage-draw specifications are given for a starter that rotates at a normal speed. Stiff engines (increased compression, mechanical drag) will not turn over as fast and amperage flow will increase.

Engines with high kilometres have less internal friction; they crank faster and current flow decreases.

Engine speed, while cranking, must be considered when evaluating starter current draw readings.

DIAGNOSTIC STORY

The Starter That Croaked and the Jumping Battery Cables

Once upon a time a vehicle would not start (crank). A technician at first hoped that the problem was a simple case of loose or corroded battery terminal connections; but after the technician cleaned the cables, the starter still made no noise when the ignition switch was turned to the start position. The technician opened the vehicle door and observed the dome (interior) light. The light was bright, indicating that the battery voltage was relatively high and that the battery should be adequately charged to crank the engine. However, when the technician turned the ignition switch to the start position, the dome light went out completely! This indicated that the battery voltage went down considerably.

NOTE: It is normal for the dome light to dim during cranking as a result of the lowered battery voltage during cranking. However, the voltage should not drop below 9.6 volts, which normally will still provide adequate voltage to light the dome light dimly.

The technician then arranged the two battery cables so that they were parallel for a short distance and repeated the test. As soon as the ignition switch was turned to the start position, the battery cables jumped toward each other. The technician knew that the starter had a shorted or grounded field coil or armature. This provided a direct path to ground for the starter current, which resulted in a substantially greater amount of current (in amperes) leaving the battery than would normally occur with a good starter. This amount of current drain lowered the battery voltage so much that the dome light did not light.

Why did the battery cables jump? The battery cables jumped because the high current flow created a strong magnetic field around each cable. Because one cable is positive and the other cable is negative, the magnetic fields were of opposite polarity and were attracted toward each other.

STARTER OVERHAUL

To remove the starter motor from the vehicle, first remove the negative (or ground) battery cable from the battery to prevent any possible shorts from causing personal injury or property damage. Because most starter motors must be removed from underneath, the vehicle must be safely raised and supported. Remove attaching bolts, nuts, and braces. Before disconnecting the wiring, mark or tag the location of all wiring connections. See Figures 16–32 through 16–37.

Figure 16–32 Before disassembly of any starter, mark the location of the through-bolts on the field housing. This makes reassembly easier.

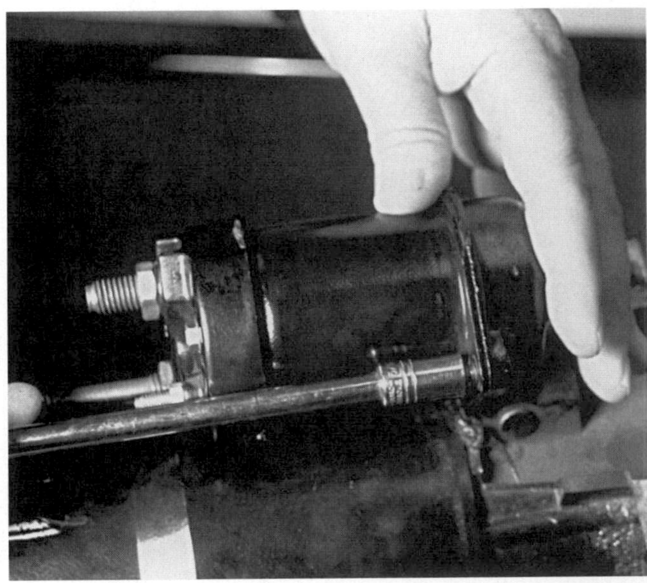

Figure 16–33 Removing the solenoid from the starter on a GM-type starter assembly.

Testing Starter Armatures

After the starter drive has been removed from the armature, it can be checked for runout using a dial indicator and V blocks as shown in Figure 16–38. Because the loops of copper wire are interconnected in the armature of a starter, an armature can be accurately tested only by use of a **growler.** A growler is a 110 volt AC test unit that generates an alternating (60 Hz) magnetic field around an armature. A starter armature is placed into the V-shaped top portion of a laminated soft-iron

Figure 16–34 Rotate the solenoid to remove it from the starter housing. (*Caution:* The plunger return spring exerts a force on the solenoid and may cause personal injury if not carefully released.)

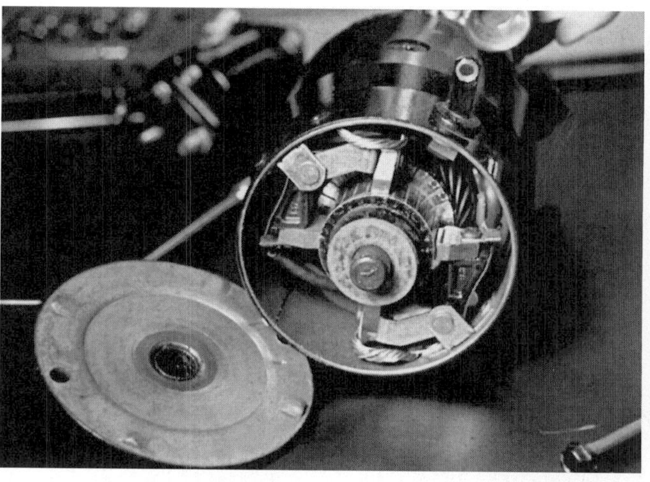

Figure 16–35 The brushes should be replaced if worn to less than 50% of their original length. Replace if less than 13 mm (1/2 in.) long.

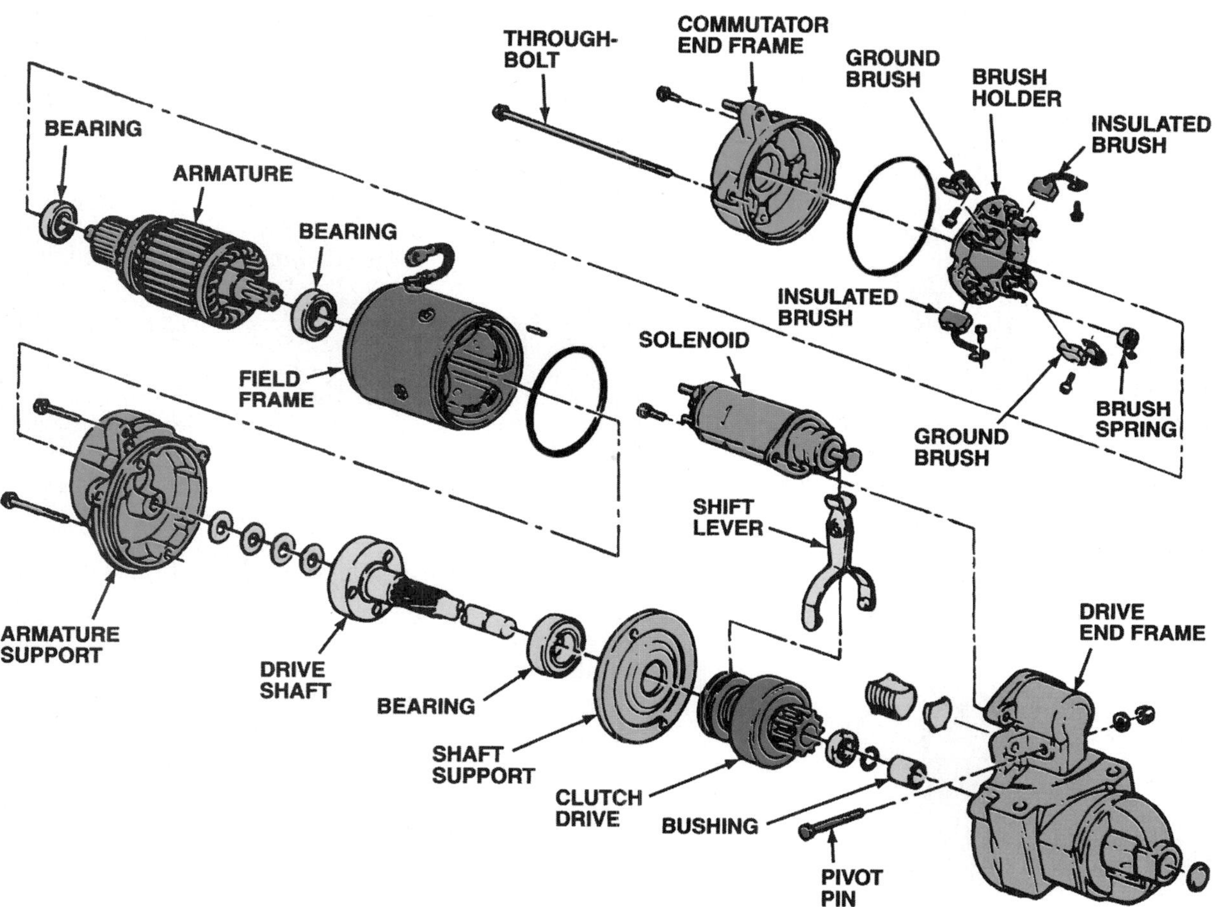

Figure 16–36 An exploded view of a General Motors starter.

core surrounded by a coil of copper wire. When the growler is plugged into a 110 V outlet and switched on, the moving magnetic field creates an alternating current in the windings of the armature.

Growler Test for Shorted Armature Windings

Place the armature on the growler and turn the growler on. While rotating the armature by hand, gently place

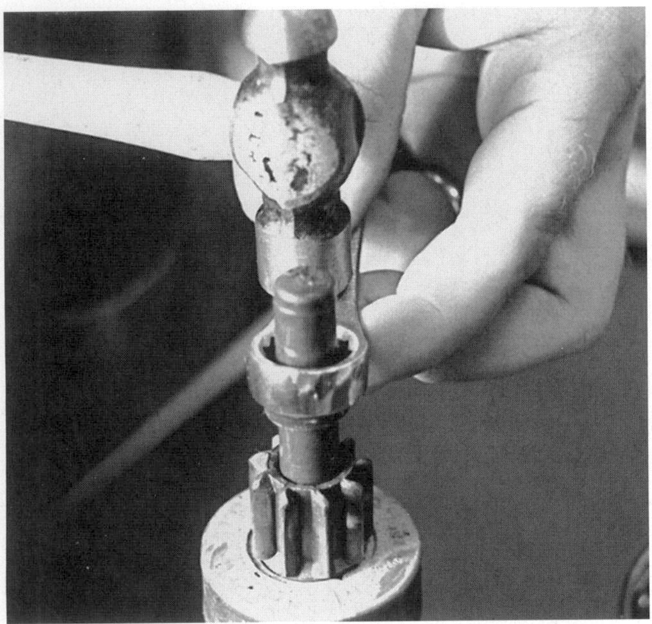

Figure 16–37 To replace the starter drive unit, the retainer and clip must be removed from the armature shaft. A box-end wrench and a hammer can be used to pop the retainer off of the spring clip.

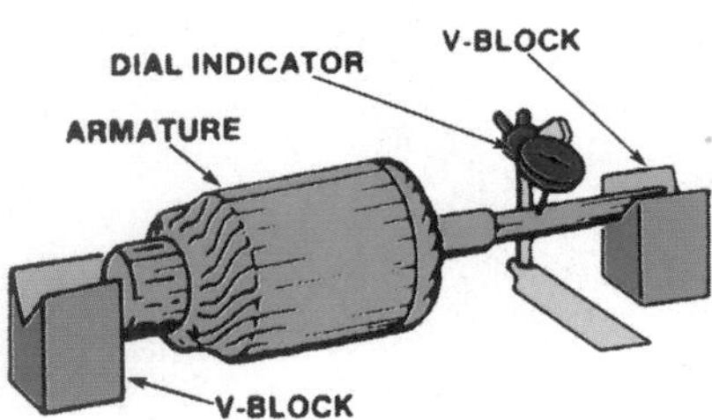

Figure 16–38 Measuring an armature shaft for runout using a dial indicator and V blocks.

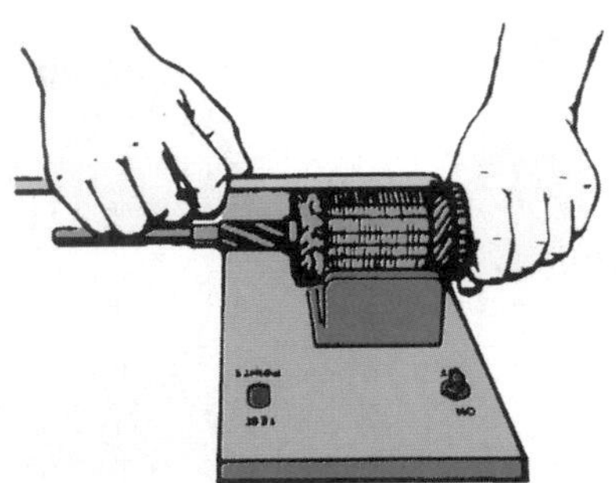

Figure 16–39 Using a growler to check for shorted armature windings.

a hacksaw blade along the top of the armature. If any loop of the armature is **shorted,** the hacksaw blade will vibrate. If an armature is shorted (copper-to-copper connection), it must be replaced or rewound by a specialist. The hacksaw vibrates because the alternating current creates an alternating electromagnet in the armature. If only one loop is shorted, it does not create the magnetic pull on the hacksaw blade in one direction and the blade vibrates. See Figure 16–39.

CAUTION: Do not turn the growler on without an armature, or the growler could be damaged.

Testing the Armature for Grounds

Built into growlers is a 110 volt test light with two test leads. Touch one lead to all segments (copper strips separated by mica insulation) of the commutator and touch the other test lead to the steel armature shaft or armature steel core. The test light should *not* light. If the test light is on, the armature is *grounded* (shorted to ground) and must be replaced.

Testing the Armature for Opens

An *open* in an armature is usually observed visually as a loop that is broken or unsoldered where it connects to the commutator segments. An open is usually caused by overheating of the starter due to excessive cranking time, or by a shorted or grounded armature. A loose or broken solder connection can often be repaired by resoldering the broken connection using rosin-core solder.

NOTE: If the armature is open, shorted (copper to copper), or grounded (copper to steel), the armature must be repaired or replaced. The cost of a replacement armature often exceeds the cost of a replacement starter.

Armature Service

If the armature tests okay, the commutator should be measured and machined on a lathe, if necessary, to be certain that the surface is smooth and round. Some manufacturers recommend that the insulation between the segments of the armature (mica or hard plastic) be **undercut,** as shown in Figure 16–40. Mica is harder than copper and will form raised bumps as the copper segments of the commutator wear. Undercutting the mica permits a longer service life for this type of starter armature.

Many late-model armatures are very thin at the commutator segments and cannot be machined. If the surface is worn or damaged, the armature must be replaced.

Testing Starter Motor Field Coils

With the armature removed from the starter motor, the field coils should be tested for opens and grounds. A powered test light or an ohmmeter can be used. To

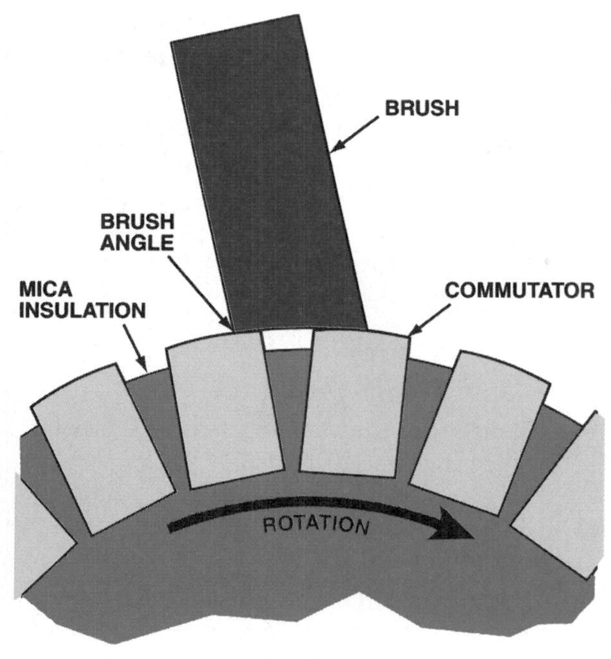

Figure 16–40 Replacement starter brushes should be installed so the beveled edge matches the rotation of the commutator.

test for a grounded field coil, touch one lead of the tester to a field brush (insulated or hot) and the other end to the starter field housing. The ohmmeter should indicate infinity (no continuity), and the test light should *not* light. If there is continuity, replace the field coil housing assembly. The ground brushes should show continuity to the starter housing.

Some Ford and G.M. starters connect one field winding directly to ground. This provides a very strong magnetic field around the winding, which is used to enhance torque or to pull a movable pole shoe into place. The grounding wire must be disabled or the field coils will not pass a ground test.

NOTE: Many older starters use removable field coils, and these coils must be rewound using the proper equipment and insulating materials. Usually, the cost involved in replacing defective field coils exceeds the cost of a replacement starter.

Starter Brush Inspection

Starter brushes should be replaced if the brush length is less than one-half of its original length (less than 13 mm [1/2 in.]). On some models of starter motors, the field brushes are serviced with the field coil assembly and the ground brushes with the brush holder. Many starters use brushes that are held in with screws and are easily replaced, whereas other starters may require soldering to remove and replace the brushes.

Bench Testing

Every starter should be tested before installation in a vehicle. The usual method includes clamping the starter in a vise to prevent rotation during operation and connecting heavy-gauge jumper wires (minimum 4 gauge) to a battery known to be good and the starter. The starter motor should rotate as fast as specifications indicate and not draw more than the free-spinning amperage permitted. A typical amperage specification for a starter being tested on a bench (not installed in a vehicle) usually ranges from 60 to 100 amperes.

Starter Drive-to-Flywheel Clearance

For the proper operation of the starter and absence of abnormal starter noise, there must be a slight clearance between the starter pinion and the engine flywheel ring gear. Many starters use shims (thin metal strips) between the flywheel and the engine block mounting pad to provide the proper clearance. See Figure 16–41.

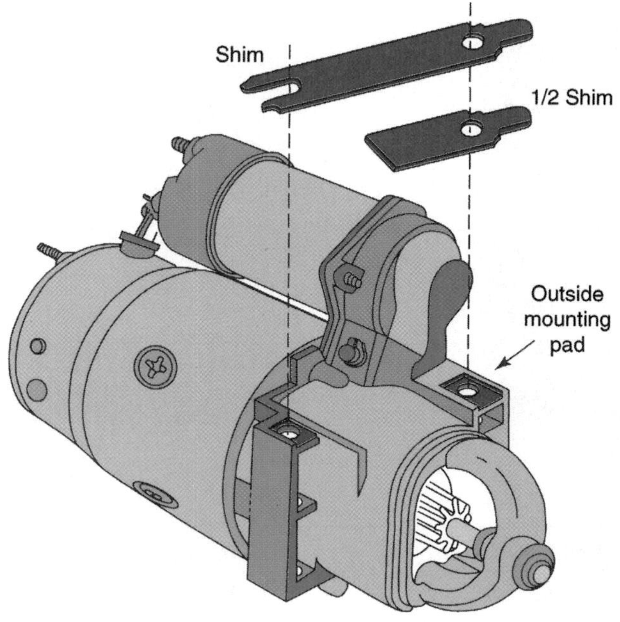

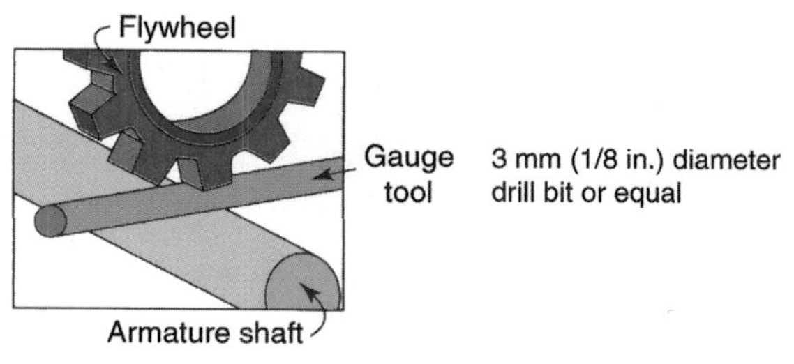

Figure 16–41 A shim (or half shim) may be needed to provide the proper clearance between the flywheel teeth of the engine and the pinion teeth of the starter.

TECH TIP 

Reuse Drive-End Housing to Be Sure

Most General Motors starter motors use a pad mount and attach to the engine with bolts through the drive-end (nose) housing. Many times when a starter is replaced on a GM vehicle, the starter makes noise because of improper starter pinion-to-engine flywheel ring gear clearance. Instead of spending a lot of time shimming the new starter, some technicians simply remove the drive-end housing from the original starter and install it on the replacement starter. Because the original starter did not produce excessive gear engagement noise, the replacement starter will also be okay. Reuse any shims that were used with the original starter.

NOTE: Some manufacturers use shims under the starter drive end housings during production for pinion clearance. If *any* GM starter is replaced, the starter pinion *must* be checked and corrected as necessary to prevent starter damage and excessive noise.

If the clearance is too great, the starter will produce a high-pitched whine *during* cranking. If the clearance is too small, the starter will produce a high-pitched whine *after* the engine starts, just as the ignition key is released.

NOTE: The major cause of broken drive-end housings on starters is too small a clearance. If the clearance cannot be measured, it is better to put a shim between the engine block and the starter than to leave one out and chance breaking a drive-end housing.

To be sure that the starter is shimmed correctly, use the following procedure:

Step 1 Place the starter in position and finger tighten the mounting bolts.

Step 2 Use a 3 mm (1/8 in.) diameter drill bit (or gauge tool) and insert between the armature shaft and a tooth of the engine flywheel.

Step 3 If the gauge tool cannot be inserted, use a full-length shim across both mounting holes, which moves the starter away from the flywheel.

Step 4 Remove a shim or shims if the gauge tool is loose between the shaft and the tooth of the engine flywheel.

Step 5 If no shims have been used and the fit of the gauge tool is too loose, add a half shim to the outside pad only. This moves the starter closer to the teeth of the engine flywheel.

STARTING SYSTEM TROUBLESHOOTING GUIDE

Problem	Possible Causes
Starter motor whines	• Defective starter drive • Worn starter drive engagement yoke • Defective flywheel
Starter rotates slowly	• High resistance in the battery cables or connections • Defective or discharged battery • Worn starter bushings, causing the starter armature to drag on the field coils • Worn starter brushes or weak brush springs • Defective (open or shorted) field coil
Starter fails to rotate	• Defective ignition switch or neutral safety switch, or open in the starter motor control circuit • Shorted field coils • Defective starter armature • Open in the power circuit between the battery and the starter • Defective starter solenoid
Starter produces grinding noise	• Defective starter drive unit • Defective flywheel • Incorrect distance between the starter pinion and the flywheel • Cracked or broken starter drive-end housing

PHOTO SEQUENCE 12 Starter Amperage Draw Test

P12–1 A Sun Electric VAT-40 is being used to measure the amount of current, in amperes, required to crank the engine.

P12–2 Attach the red clamp from the tester to the positive terminal of the battery and the black clamp to the negative terminal of the battery. Clamp the inductive ampere probe around either all of the wires from the positive terminal or over all of the wires from the negative terminal as shown.

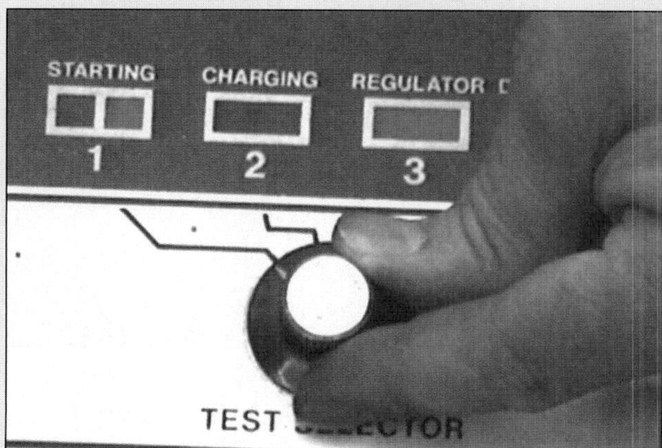

P12–3 Select "starting" with the test selector knob. This position indicates that the amperage should be read on the red-lettered scale and the voltage read on the green-lettered scale.

P12–4 Disable the ignition or the fuel system to prevent the engine from starting when the engine is being cranked. The "computer" fuse is being removed on this Chrysler vehicle to disable the fuel delivery system.

P12–5 Crank the engine and observe the ammeter reading.

P12–6 The starter on this vehicle equipped with a V-6 engine requires 120 amperes as displayed on the VAT-40 display. Disregard the first initial higher amperage reading. This starter motor is okay because the allowable starter amperage draw for most six-cylinder engines is 150 amperes or less.

PHOTO SEQUENCE 13 Voltage-Drop Testing

P13–1 To perform a voltage drop test of the battery cables, select DC volts on the digital multimeter (DMM).

P13–2 Disable the ignition system or fuel injector system to keep the engine from starting. On this Chrysler vehicle, the fuse for the computer was removed.

P13–3 To test the resistance (voltage drop) of the negative (ground) battery cable, attach the black meter lead to the negative terminal of the battery and the red lead to a good engine ground.

P13–4 Crank the engine while an assistant observes the meter display.

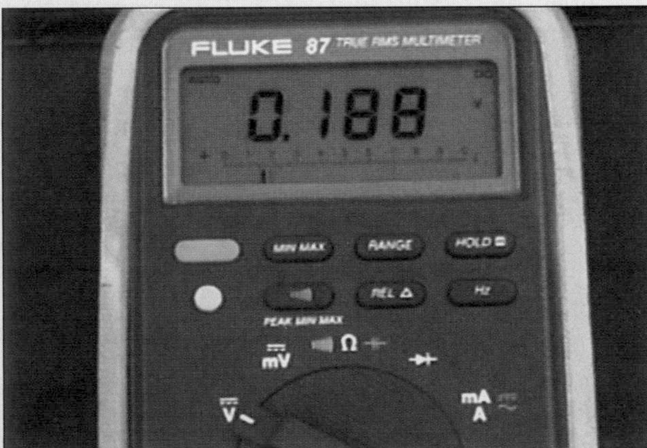

P13–5 The meter display indicates less than 0.2 volt drop (0.2 volt is equal to 0.200 volt and the display shows 0.188 V). Repeat the test for the positive battery cable by connecting the red meter lead to the positive terminal of the battery and the black meter lead to the battery terminal of the starter motor and crank the engine.

P13–6 Reinstall the fuse and the test is complete. If the results indicate excessive voltage drop, carefully inspect and clean all battery cable connections and retest. If the voltage drop is still higher than factory specifications, replace the battery cable(s).

SUMMARY

1. All starter motors use the principle of magnetic interaction between the field coils attached to the housing and the magnetic field of the armature.
2. Proper operation of the starter motor depends on the battery being at least 75% charged and the battery cables being of the correct size (gauge) and having no more than 0.2 V drop.
3. Voltage-drop testing includes cranking the engine, measuring the drop in voltage from the battery to the starter, and measuring the drop in voltage from the negative terminal of the battery to the engine block.
4. The cranking circuit should be tested for proper amperage draw.
5. An open in the control circuit can prevent starter motor operation.

REVIEW QUESTIONS

1. List the parts of the cranking circuit.
2. Describe the difference between the control circuit and the power circuit sections of a typical cranking circuit.
3. Explain how to perform a voltage-drop test of the cranking circuit.
4. List the steps necessary to overhaul a starter.

RED SEAL CERTIFICATION-TYPE QUESTIONS

1. Starter motors operate on the principle that _____.
   - **a.** The field coils rotate in the opposite direction from the armature
   - **b.** Opposite magnetic poles repel
   - **c.** Like magnetic poles repel
   - **d.** The armature rotates from a strong magnetic field toward a weaker magnetic field
2. Series-wound electric motors _____.
   - **a.** Produce electrical power
   - **b.** Produce maximum power at 0 rpm
   - **c.** Produce maximum power at high RPM
   - **d.** Use a shunt coil
3. A high-pitched whine is noted after the engine starts; this could indicate
   - **a.** Low battery voltage
   - **b.** Insufficient pinion to ring gear clearance
   - **c.** A short in the armature windings
   - **d.** Excessive pinion to ring gear clearance
4. The instant the ignition switch is turned to the start position, _____.
   - **a.** Both the pull-in winding and the hold-in winding are energized
   - **b.** The hold-in winding is energized
   - **c.** The pull-in winding is energized
   - **d.** The starter motor starts to rotate before energizing the starter pinion gear
5. A hybrid vehicle has a discharged high voltage battery pack. How is the engine started?
   - **a.** The battery pack must be slow charged
   - **b.** It must be push started
   - **c.** It has a secondary 12 volt starter (if equipped)
   - **d.** The engine is jump-started from another high-voltage battery
6. Slow cranking by the starter can be caused by all *except* the following: _____.
   - **a.** A low or discharged battery
   - **b.** Corroded or dirty battery cables
   - **c.** Engine mechanical problems
   - **d.** An open neutral safety switch
7. If the starter "whines" when engaged, a possible cause is _____.
   - **a.** A worn or defective starter drive
   - **b.** A defective solenoid
   - **c.** An "open" pull-in winding
   - **d.** A worn leather armature brake
8. If the clearance between the starter pinion and the engine flywheel is too great, _____.
   - **a.** The starter will produce a high-pitched whine during cranking
   - **b.** The starter will produce a high-pitched whine after the engine starts
   - **c.** The starter drive will not rotate at all
   - **d.** The solenoid will not engage the starter drive unit
9. To voltage drop the (negative) ground circuit, the meter leads are connected to
   - **a.** Battery positive and starter field frame
   - **b.** Battery positive and starter solenoid
   - **c.** Battery negative and starter field frame
   - **d.** Starter solenoid B terminal and battery negative
10. Sparks are observed at the negative terminal of the battery while cranking. This could be caused by:
    - **a.** High-resistance in the ground circuit
    - **b.** A loose ground cable
    - **c.** A discharged battery
    - **d.** An internal starter problem

17

Charging System Operation, Diagnosis, and Service

OBJECTIVES: After studying Chapter 17, you should be able to:

1. Prepare for the interprovincial Red Seal certification examination in Appendix III (Electrical/Electronic Systems) on the topics covered in this chapter.
2. Describe how a generator works.
3. Discuss the various generator test procedures.
4. Explain how to disassemble a generator and test its component parts.
5. Discuss how to check the wiring from the generator to the battery.

All vehicles operate electrical components by taking current from the battery. It is the purpose and function of the charging system to keep the battery fully charged. The Society of Automotive Engineers (SAE) term for the unit that generates electricity is the **generator.** The term **alternator** is also commonly used, especially in service manuals before 1993 when the SAE term was adopted by most vehicle manufacturers.

PRINCIPLES OF GENERATOR OPERATION

All electrical generators use the principle of electromagnetic induction to generate electrical energy from mechanical energy. Electromagnetic induction involves the generation of an electrical current in a conductor when the conductor is moved through a magnetic field. The amount of current generated can be increased by the following factors:

1. Increasing the *speed* of the conductor through the magnetic field
2. Increasing the *number* of conductors passing through the magnetic field
3. Increasing the *strength* of the magnetic field

ALTERNATING-CURRENT GENERATORS (ALTERNATORS)

An AC generator generates an alternating current when the current changes polarity during the generator's rotation. However, a battery cannot store alternating current; therefore, this alternating current is changed to direct current (DC) by diodes inside the generator. Diodes are one-way electrical check valves that permit current to flow in only one direction. Most manufacturers call an AC generator a generator.

GENERATOR CONSTRUCTION

A generator is constructed of a two-piece cast-aluminum housing. Aluminum is used because of its lightweight, nonmagnetic properties, and heat transfer properties needed to help keep the generator cool. A front ball bearing is pressed into the front housing (called the **drive-end [DE]** housing) to provide the support and friction reduction necessary for the belt-driven rotor assembly. The rear housing, or the **slip ring end (SRE),** usually contains a roller-bearing support for the rotor and mounting for the brushes, diodes, and internal voltage regulator (if the generator is so equipped). See Figures 17–1 and 17–2.

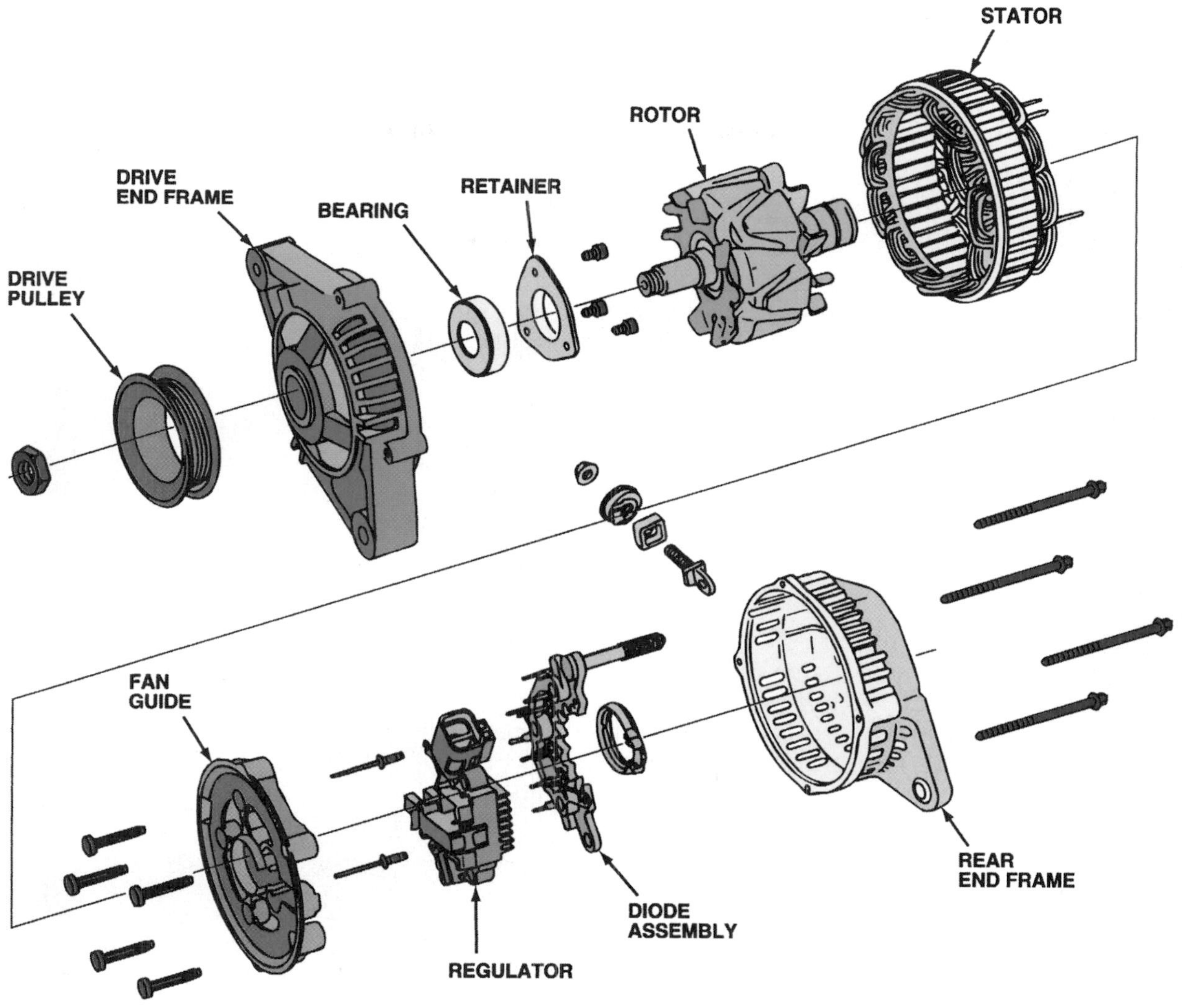

Figure 17–1 An exploded view of a typical generator (alternator) showing all of its internal parts.

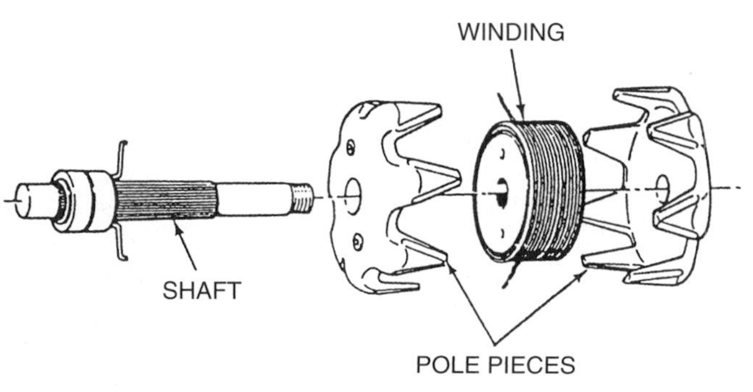

Figure 17–2 Exploded view of an AC generator rotor. Note the coil winding between the two pole pieces. (Courtesy General Motors)

Rotors

The rotor creates the magnetic field of the generator and produces a current by electromagnetic induction in the stationary stator windings. This differs from a DC generator, where the field current is created in the stationary field windings and the current is generated in the rotating armature. The generator rotor is constructed of many turns of copper wire coated with a varnish insulation wound over an iron core. The iron core is attached to the rotor shaft.

The maximum-rated generator output in amperes is largely dependent on the number and gauge of the windings of the rotor. Substituting rotors from one generator into another can greatly affect maximum output. Many commercially rebuilt generators are tested and have a sticker put on them indicating their tested output. The original rating stamped on the housing is then ground off. The current for the field is

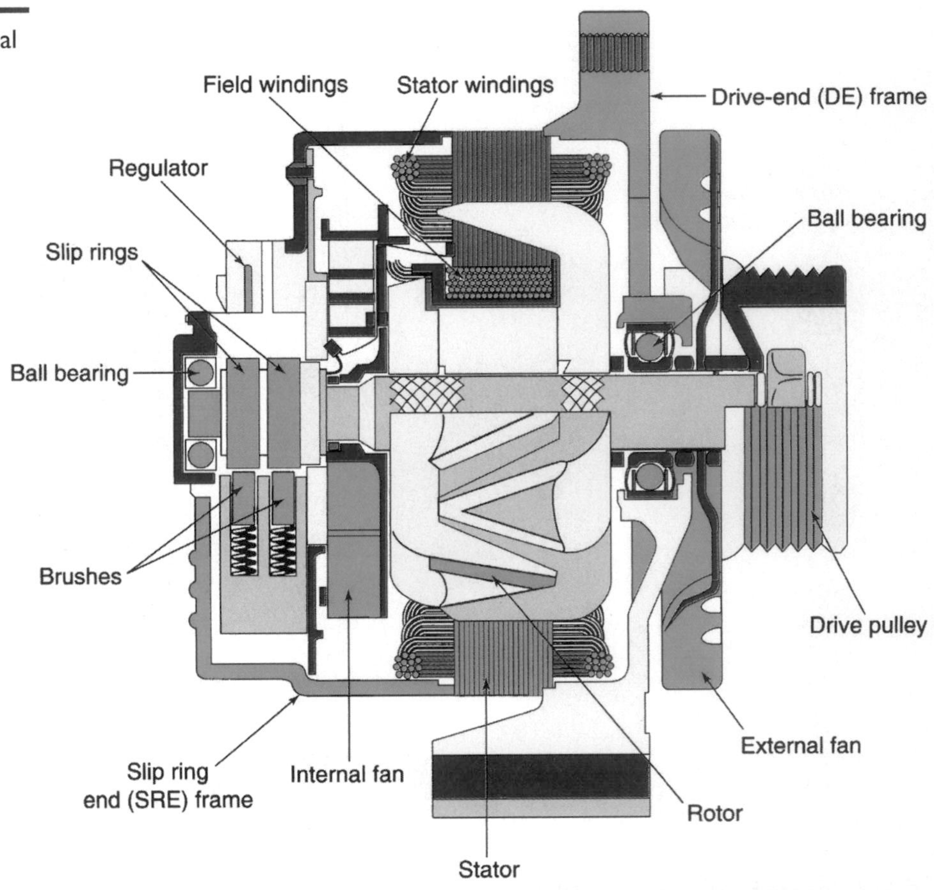

Figure 17–3 Cutaway view of a typical AC generator (alternator).

Figure 17–4 Diode symbol.

controlled by the voltage regulator and is conducted to the slip rings through carbon brushes. The brushes conduct only the field current (approximately 2 to 5 amperes).

Stators

Supported between the two halves of the generator housing are three copper wire windings wound on a laminated metal core. See Figure 17–3. As the rotor revolves, its moving magnetic field induces a current in the windings of the stator.

Diodes

Diodes are constructed of a semiconductor material (usually silicon) and operate as a one-way electrical check valve that permits the current to flow in only one direction. Most AC generators use six diodes (one positive and one negative set for each of the three stator windings) to convert alternating current to direct current. The symbol for a diode is shown in Figure 17–4.

TECH TIP 

Generator Horsepower and Engine Operation

Many technicians are asked how much power certain accessories require. A 100 ampere generator requires about 2 hp from the engine. One horsepower is equal to 746 W. Watts are calculated by multiplying amperes times volts.

$$\text{Power} = 100 \text{ A} \times 14.5 \text{ V} = 1450 \text{ W}$$
$$1 \text{ hp} = 746 \text{ W}$$

Therefore, 1450 W is about 2 hp.

Allowing about 20% for mechanical and electrical losses adds another 0.4 hp. Therefore, whenever anybody asks how much power it takes to produce 100 amperes from a generator, the answer is 2.4 hp.

Many generators delay the electrical load to prevent the engine from stumbling whenever a heavy electrical load is applied. The voltage regulator or vehicle computer is capable of gradually increasing the output of the generator over a period of up to several minutes. Even though 2 hp does not sound like much, a sudden demand for 2 hp from an idling engine can cause the engine to run rough or stall. The difference in part numbers of various generators is often an indication of the time interval over which the load is applied. Therefore, the use of the wrong replacement generator could cause the engine to stall!

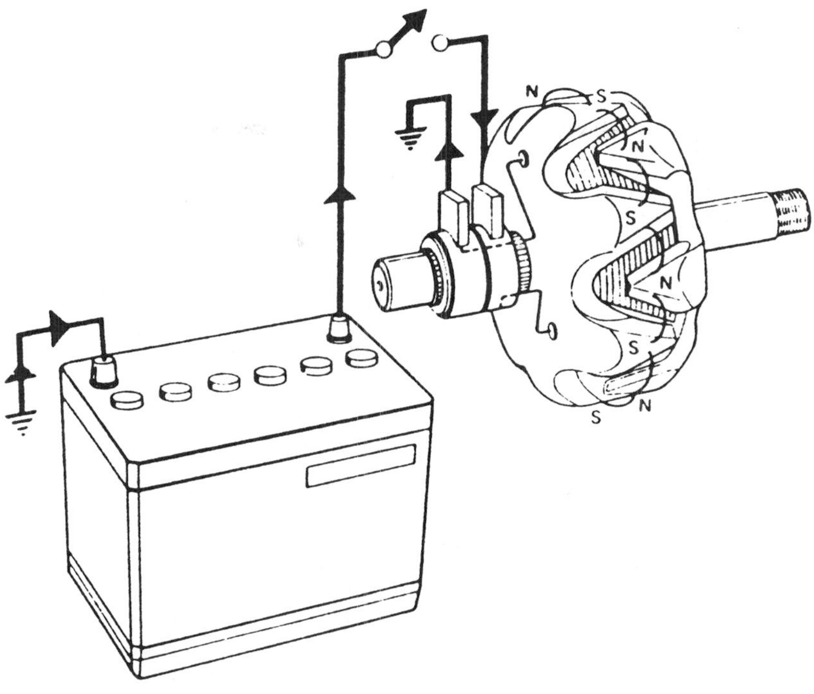

Figure 17–5 An AC generator basic field circuit. (Courtesy General Motors)

TECH TIP 

The Sniff Test

Whenever checking for the root cause of a generator failure, one of the first things that a technician should do is to sniff (smell) the generator! If the generator smells like a dead rat (rancid), the stator windings have been overheated by trying to charge a discharged or defective battery. If the battery voltage is continuously low, the voltage regulator will continue supplying full field current to the generator. The voltage regulator is designed to cycle on and off to maintain a narrow charging system voltage range.

If the battery voltage is continually below the cutoff point of the voltage regulator, the generator is continually producing current in the stator windings. This constant charging can often overheat the stator and burn the insulating varnish covering the stator windings. If the generator fails the sniff test, the technician should replace the stator and other generator components that are found to be defective *and* replace or recharge and test the battery.

HOW A GENERATOR WORKS

A rotor inside the generator is turned by a belt and drive pulley rotated by the engine. The magnetic field of the rotor generates a current in the windings of the stator by electromagnetic induction.

Field Circuit

When the ignition switch is turned on, current flows from the battery, through the ignition switch to the generator field terminal, in through the "hot" brush and slip ring to the rotor coil. This coil of wire, sometimes called a field winding, is wound around a soft iron core; a full-strength magnetic field is now formed around the rotor coil. The current continues flowing out of the rotor by way of the second slip ring and ground brush and on to ground. See Figure 17–5.

Magnetic Field

The magnetic field surrounding this current-carrying conductor has polarity—one end of the coil is the north pole and the other end is the south pole. The electrons in the magnetic field flow from the north pole to the south pole; they have direction. The rotor is a rotating magnetic field. See Figure 17–6.

Air, in itself, is a very poor conductor. Placing a core of soft iron in the centre of the coil reduces the resistance (iron is a good conductor) and the magnetic field strength is increased many times. Placing an iron pole piece on each end of the rotor coil further increases the strength of the field; the only open-air gap is between the fingers of the north and south pole pieces.

Note that the magnetic field flows in two directions when it leaves the north rotor pole piece fingers and jumps to the south pole piece fingers. See Figure 17–7.

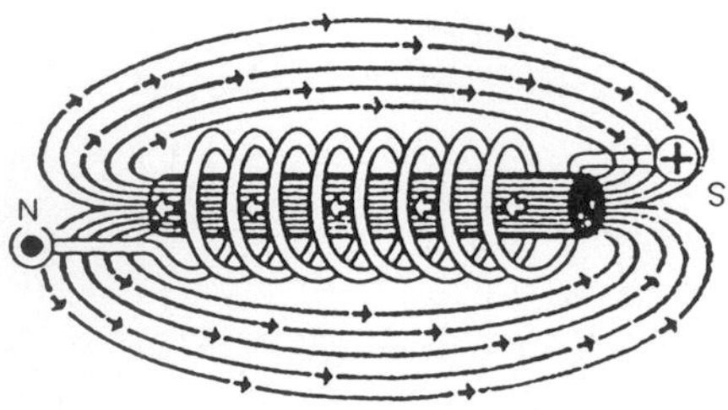

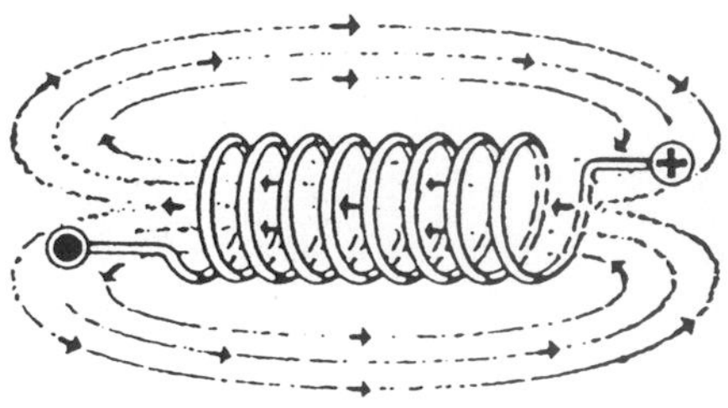

Figure 17–6 The magnetic field is stronger when the coil is wrapped around a soft iron core. Coils also have polarity, a north and a south pole. (Courtesy General Motors)

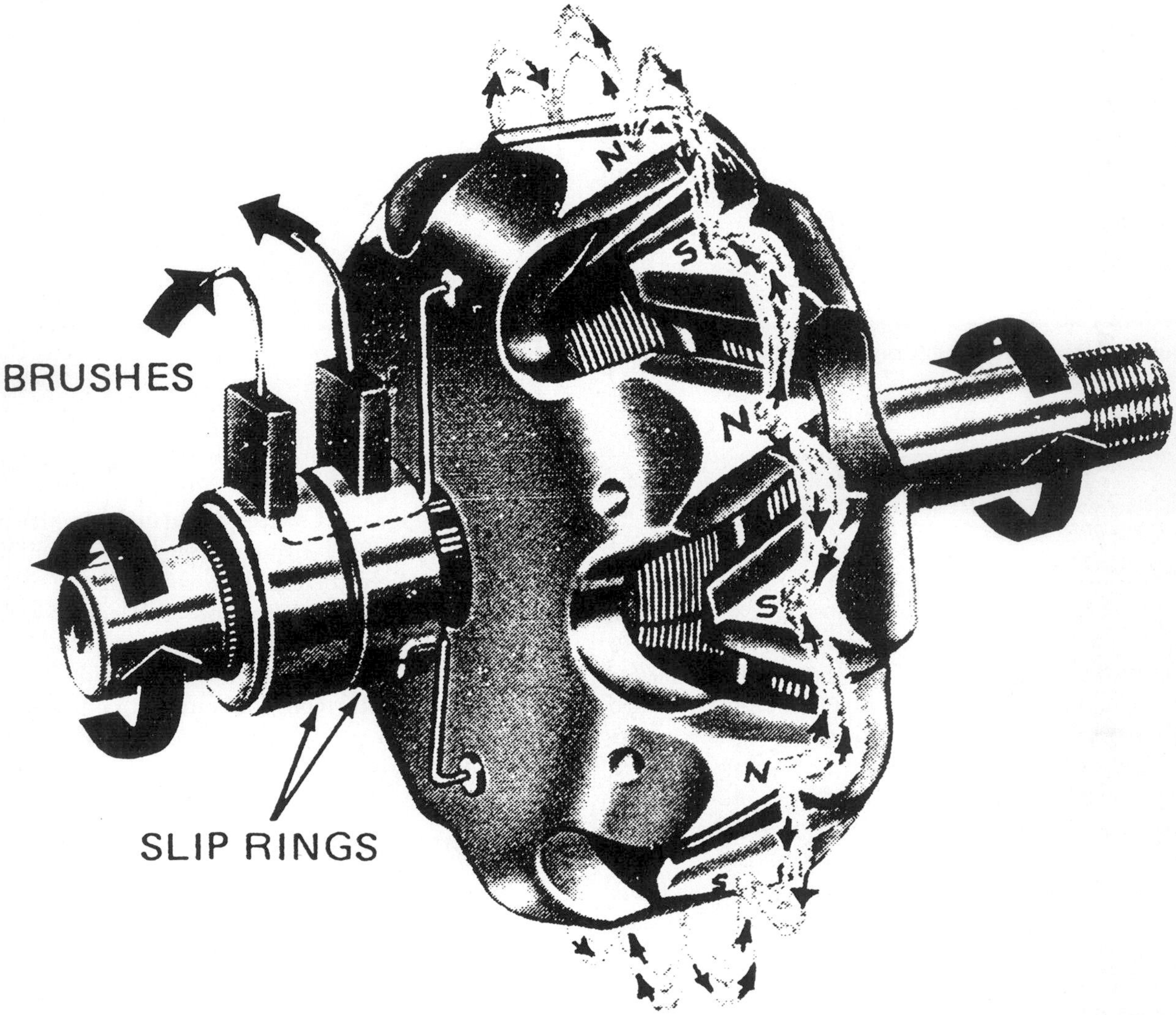

Figure 17–7 The rotor pole pieces that surround the coil help to produce a stronger magnetic field. Note the direction of the field: it flows from the north pole fingers to the south pole fingers. (Courtesy General Motors)

Stator Operation

The stator is a stationary conductor. When the rotor is placed inside the stator windings and rotated, the magnetic fields of the rotor cut across the stator windings, inducing current in the stator. See Figure 17–8.

Because the magnetic fields at the rotor flow in two directions, the induced current in the stator windings also changes direction; this is called alternating current (AC). AC cannot be used to charge a battery.

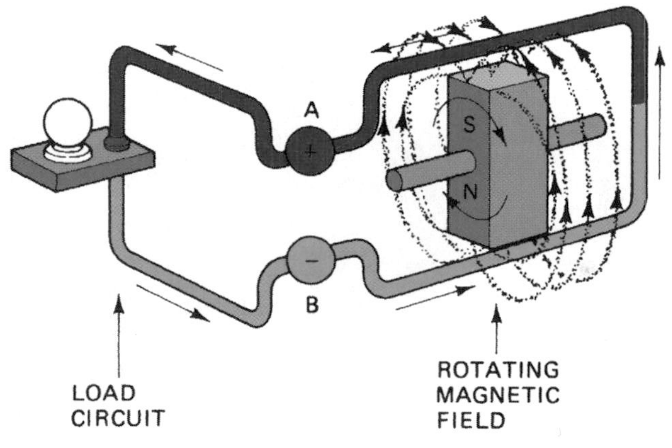

Figure 17–8 Magnetic lines of force cutting across a conductor induce a voltage and current in the conductor.

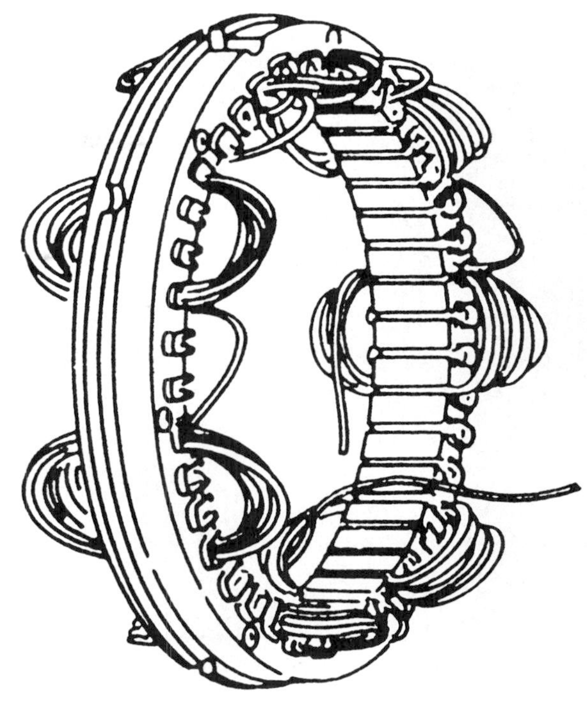

Figure 17–9 Stator with the coils making up one winding only—single- (one-) phase output. (Courtesy General Motors)

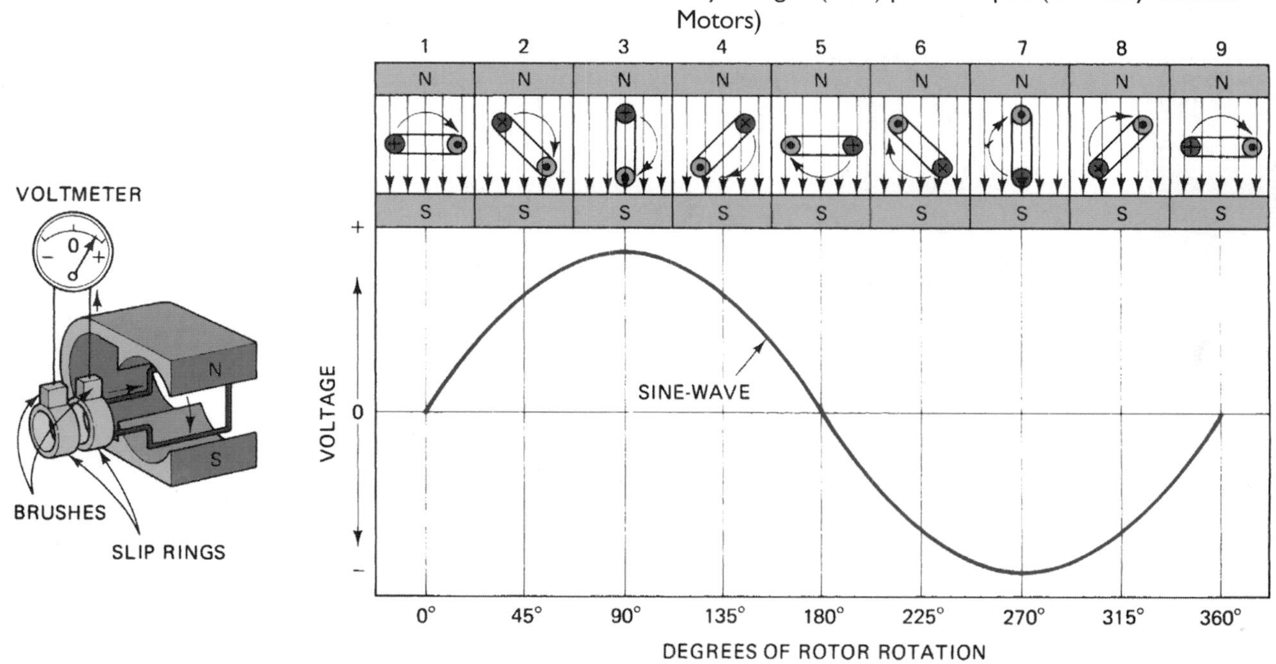

Figure 17–10 Sine wave voltage curve created by one revolution of a winding rotating in a magnetic field: single phase output.

Three Phase Output

A stator with only one set of coils (single phase) produces a lumpy or pulsating flow. By adding two more sets of coils, each offset 120° from the first group, all three sets work to produce a smoother, higher current three-phase output. See Figures 17–9, 17–10, 17–11 and 17–12.

AC to DC

The three-stator output wires, called phase leads, supply alternating current. Each phase lead is connected to a pair of diodes (one-way electrical check valves) that permit the generator output current to flow in only one direction. Most AC generators contain six

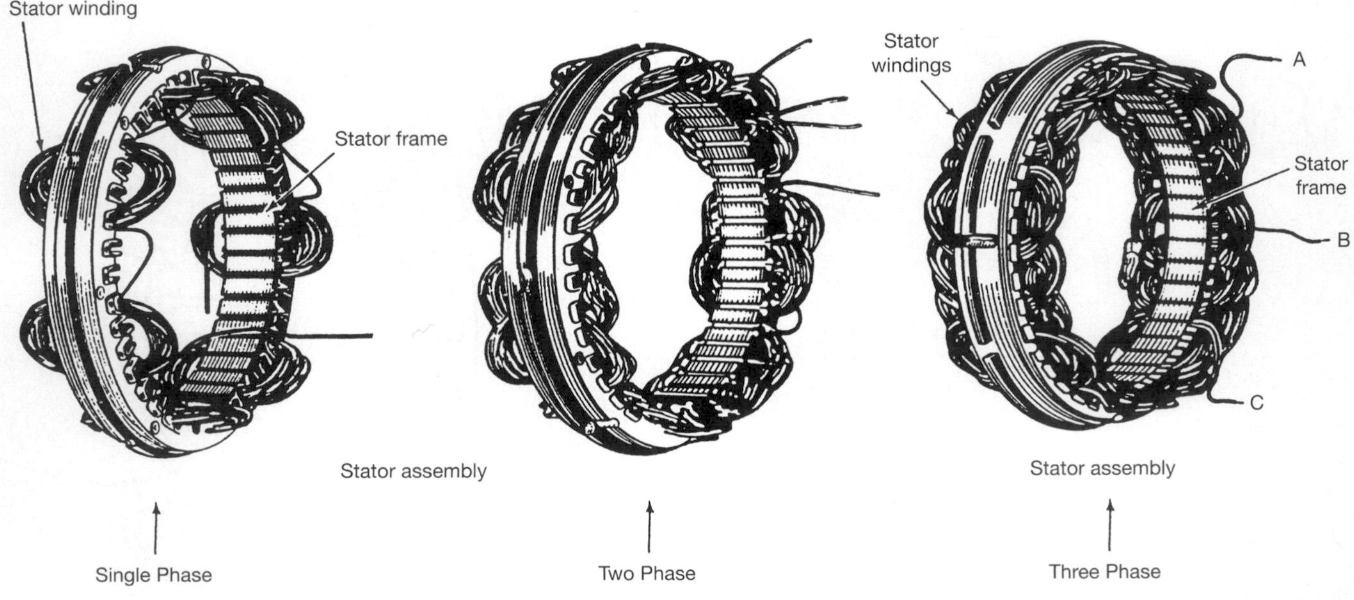

Figure 17–11 Stator construction. Note three complete sets of coils (windings) in a three-phase stator. (Courtesy General Motors)

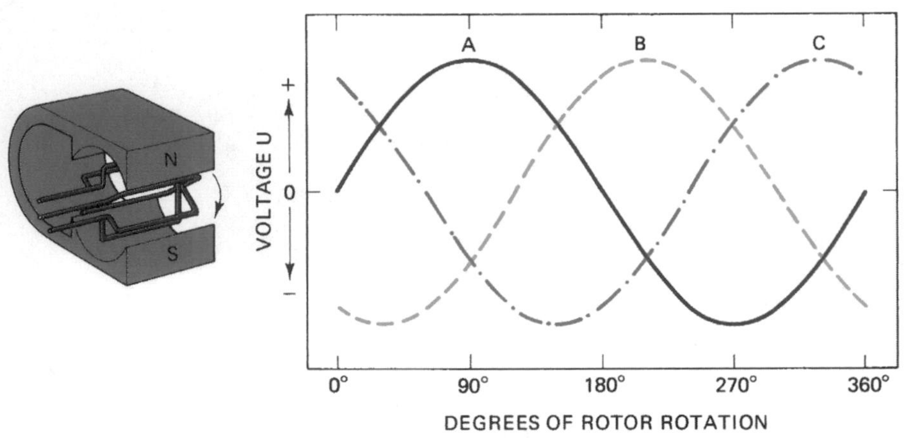

Figure 17–12 When three windings (A, B, and C) are present in a stator, the resulting current generation is represented by the three sine waves. The voltages are 120° out of phase. The connection of the individual phases produces a three-phase alternating voltage.

diodes, one pair of a positive and negative diode for each of the three-stator windings. The AC current from the stator is rectified to DC current by the action of the diodes. DC current is used to charge the battery and supply electrical power for all circuits and accessories on the vehicle. See Figure 17–13.

Wye-Connected Stators

The **Y** (pronounced **"wye"** and generally so written) type or star pattern is the most commonly used generator stator winding connection. See Figure 17–14. The output current with a wye-type stator connection is constant over a broad generator speed range.

Current is induced in each winding by electromagnetic induction from the rotating magnetic fields of the rotor. In a wye-type stator connection the currents must combine because two windings are always connected in series. The current produced in each winding is added to the other windings' current and then flows through the diodes to the generator output terminal. One-half of the cur-

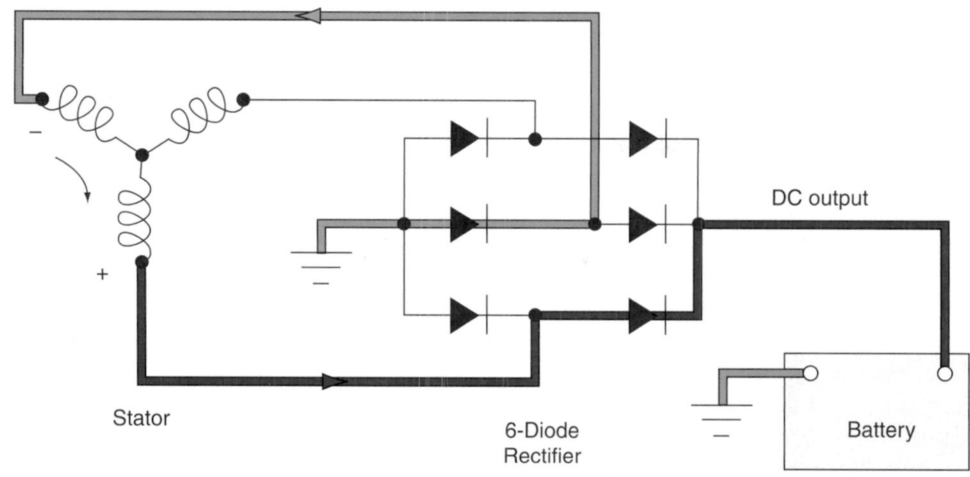

Figure 17–13 As the magnetic field, created in the rotor, cuts across the windings of the stator, a current is induced. Notice that the current path includes passing through one positive (+) diode on the way to the battery and one negative (−) diode as a complete circuit is completed through the rectifier and stator.

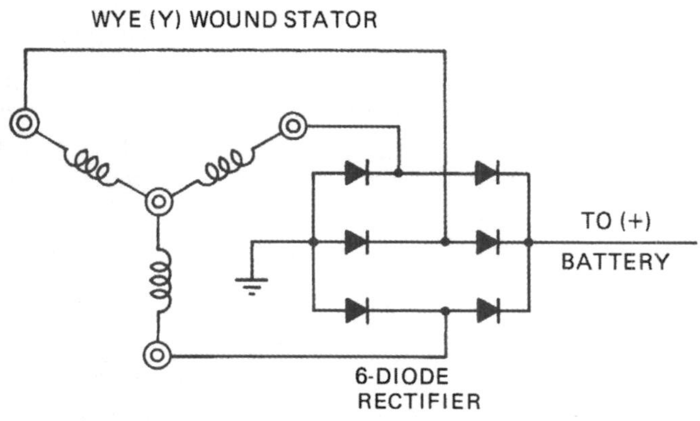

Figure 17–14 Wye-connected stator winding.

DELTA (Δ) WOUND STATOR
TO (+)
BATTERY
6-DIODE
RECTIFIER

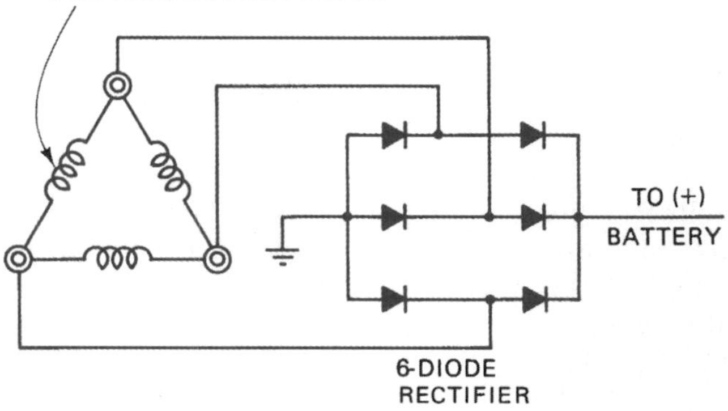

Figure 17–15 Delta-connected stator winding.

rent produced is available at the neutral junction (usually labelled STA for stator). The voltage at this centre point is used by some generator manufacturers (especially Ford) to control the charge indicator light or is used by the voltage regulator to control the rotor field current.

Delta-Connected Stators

The **delta winding** is connected in a triangular shape, as shown in Figure 17–15. (Delta is a Greek letter shaped like a triangle.) Current induced in each winding flows to the diodes in a parallel circuit. More current can flow through two parallel circuits than can flow through a series circuit (as in a wye-type stator connection).

Delta-connected stators are used on generators where high output at high-generator RPM is required. The delta-connected generator can produce 73% more current than the same generator with wye-type stator connections. For example, if a generator with a wye-connected stator can produce 55 amperes, the *same* generator with delta-connected stator windings can produce 73% more current, or 95 amperes ($55 \times 1.73 = 95$). The delta-connected generator, however, produces lower current at low speed and must be operated at high speed to produce its maximum output.

Generator Output Factors

The output voltage and current of a generator depend on several factors:

1. *Speed of rotation.* Generator output is increased with generator rotational speed up to the generator's maximum possible ampere output. Generators normally rotate at a speed two to three times faster than engine speed, depending on the relative pulley sizes used for the belt drive.

2. *Number of conductors.* A high-output generator contains more turns of wire in the stator windings. Stator winding connections (whether wye or delta) also affect the maximum generator output.
3. *Strength of the magnetic field.* If the magnetic field is strong, a high output is possible because the current generated by electromagnetic induction is dependent on the number of magnetic lines of force that are cut.
   a. The strength of the magnetic field can be increased by increasing the number of turns of conductor wire wound on the rotor. A higher-output generator has more turns of wire than a generator with a low-rated output.
   b. The strength of the magnetic field also depends on the current through the field coil (rotor). Because magnetic field strength is measured in ampere-turns, the greater the current or the number of turns, or both, the greater the generator output.

Generator Voltage Regulation

An automotive generator must be able to produce electrical pressure (voltage) higher than battery voltage to charge the battery. Excessively high voltage can damage the battery, electrical components, and the lights of a vehicle. If no current (0 A) existed throughout the field coil of the generator (rotor), generator output would be zero because without field current a magnetic field does not exist. The field current required by most automotive generators is less than 3 A. It is the *control* of the *field* current that controls the output of the generator. Current for the rotor flows from the battery through the brushes to the slip rings. After generator output begins, the voltage regulator controls the current flow through the rotor. See Figure 17–16. The voltage regulator simply opens the field circuit if the voltage reaches a predetermined level, then closes the field circuit again as necessary to maintain the correct charging voltage.

Battery Condition and Charging Voltage

If the automotive battery is discharged, its voltage will be lower than the voltage of a fully charged battery. The generator will supply charging current, but it may not reach the maximum charging voltage. For example, if a vehicle is jump-started and run at a fast idle (2000 rpm), the charging voltage may be only 12 volts. As the battery becomes charged and the battery voltage increases, the charging voltage will also increase, until the voltage regulator limit is

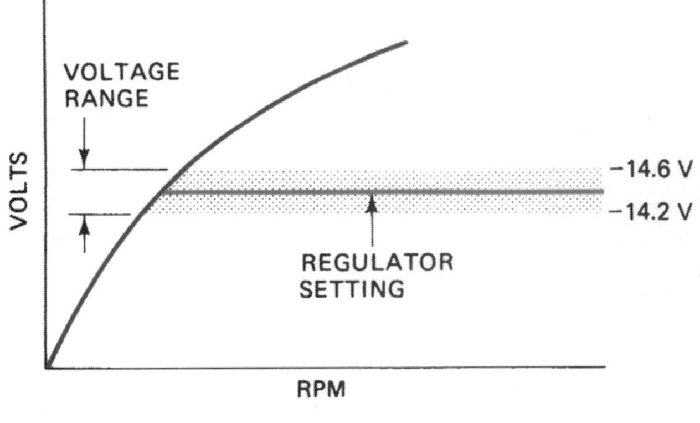

Figure 17–16 Typical voltage regulator voltage range.

reached; then the voltage regulator will start to control the charging voltage. A good, but discharged, battery should be able to convert into chemical energy all the electrical energy the generator can produce. As long as generator voltage is higher than battery voltage, current will flow from the generator (high pressure, high voltage) to the battery (lower pressure, lower voltage). Therefore, if a voltmeter is connected to a discharged battery with the engine running, it may indicate charging voltage that is lower than normally acceptable.

In other words, the condition and voltage of the battery *do* determine the charging rate of the generator. It is often stated that the battery is the true "voltage regulator" and that the voltage regulator simply acts as the upper-limit voltage control. This is the reason that all charging system testing *must* be performed with a reliable (known to be good) battery, at least 75% charged, to be assured of accurate test results. If a discharged battery is used during charging-system testing, tests could mistakenly indicate a defective generator and/or voltage regulator.

Temperature Compensation

All voltage regulators (mechanical or electronic) provide a method for increasing the charging voltage slightly at low temperatures and for lowering the charging voltage at high temperatures. A higher charging voltage is needed at low temperatures, when chemical reactions require more energy. On the other hand, the battery would be overcharged if the charging voltage were not reduced during warm weather. Electronic voltage regulators use a temperature-sensitive resistor in the regulator circuit. This resistor is called a **thermistor,** and it provides lower resistance as the temperature increases. A thermistor is used in the electronic circuits of the voltage regulator to control charging voltage over a wide range of under-the-hood temperatures.

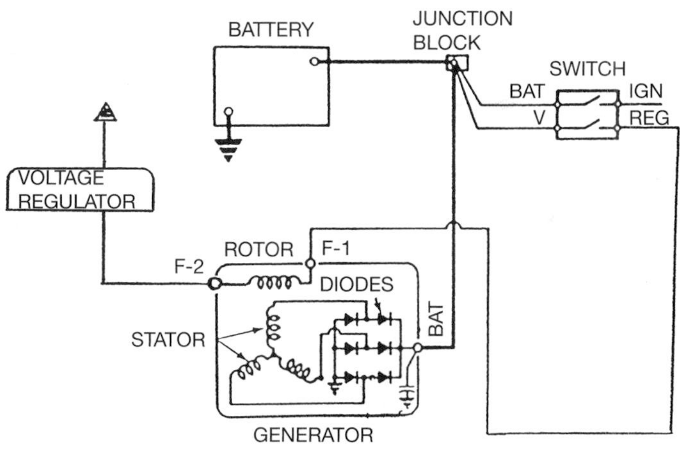

Figure 17–17 Diagram of an external A-type field circuit. Note the regulator is *after* the rotor and grounds the circuit.

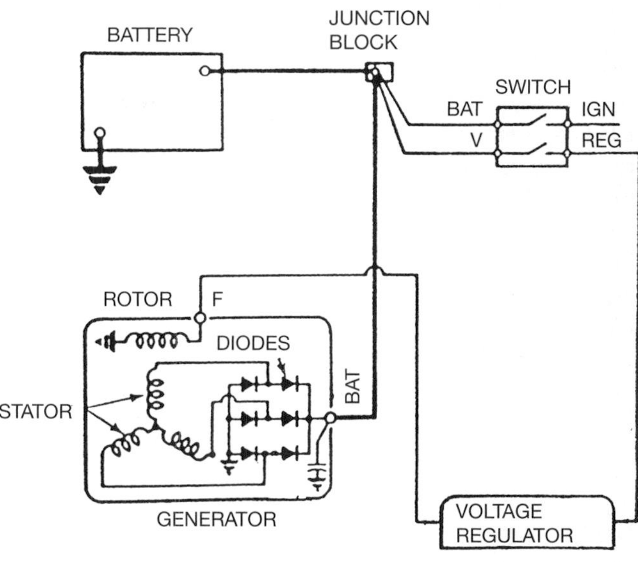

Figure 17–18 Diagram of a B-type field circuit. Note the regulator is *before* the rotor and supplies power to the field circuit.

NOTE: Voltmeter test results may vary according to temperature. Charging voltage tested at 0°C (32°F) will be higher than for the same vehicle tested at 27°C (80°F) because of the temperature-compensation factors built into voltage regulators.

A and B Field Circuits

When testing the charging circuit, most test equipment requires the technician to select either A or B field type. An A circuit is the most commonly used. This type of circuit controls the ground. It may use a remote voltage regulator (external A) or the regulater may be part of the generator (internal A). The function is the same. All electronic voltage regulators use A circuits because the controlling transistor(s) control the opening and closing of the ground return path. See Figure 17–17.

In a B-circuit field, the voltage regulator controls (opens and closes) the power side of the field circuit, and the circuit is grounded inside the generator. See Figure 17–18.

Electronic Voltage Regulators

Electronic voltage regulators have been used since the early 1970s. The electronic circuit of the voltage regulator cycles between 10 and 7000 times per *second* as needed to accurately control the field current through the rotor, and therefore control the generator output. The control of the field current is accomplished by opening and closing the *ground* side of the field circuit through the rotor of the generator (A circuit). Electronic voltage regulators also use many resistors to help reduce the current through the regulator, and the resulting heat must be dissipated into the air to prevent damage to the diodes and transistors. Whether mounted inside the generator or externally under the hood, electronic voltage regulators are mounted where normal airflow can keep the electronic components cool.

The **zener diode** is a major electronic component that makes voltage regulation possible. A zener diode blocks current flow until a specific voltage is reached, then it permits current to flow. Generator voltage from the stator and diodes is first sent through a thermistor, which changes resistance with temperature, and then to a zener diode. Whenever the upper-limit voltage is reached, the zener diode conducts current to a transistor, which then opens the field (rotor) circuit. All the current stops flowing through the generator's brushes, slip rings, and rotor, and no magnetic field is formed. Without a magnetic field, a generator does not produce current in the stator windings. When no voltage is applied to the zener diode, current flow from the zener stops and the base of the transistor is turned off, closing the field circuit. The magnetic field is thus restored in the rotor. The rotating magnetic fields of the rotor induce a current in the stator, which is again controlled if the output voltage exceeds the designed limit as determined by the zener diode breakdown voltage. Depending on the generator RPM, vehicle electrical load, and state of charge of the battery, this controlled switching on and off can occur between 10 and 7000 times per second. See Figure 17–19.

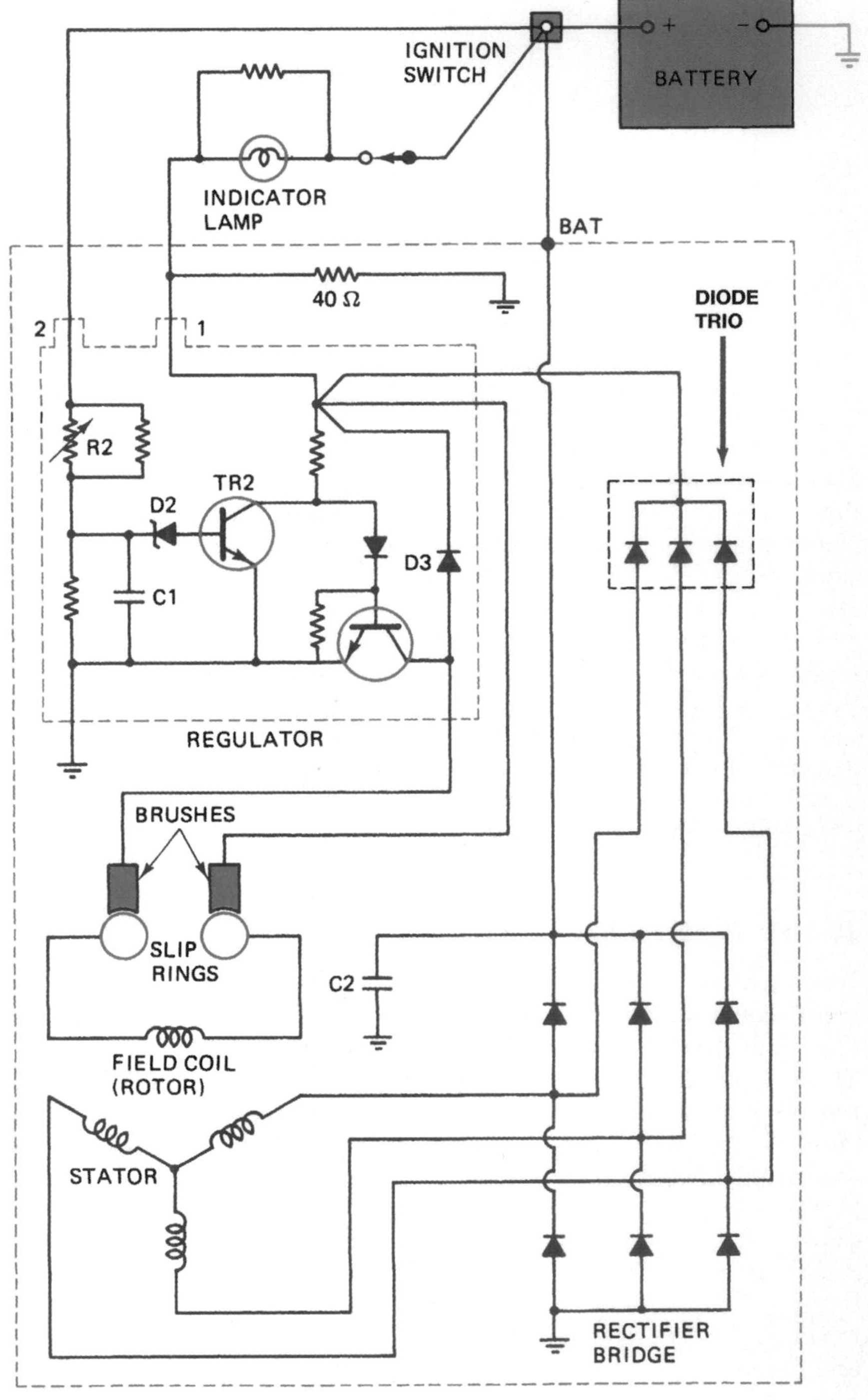

Figure 17–19 Typical General Motors SI-style AC generator with an integral voltage regulator. Voltage present at terminal 2 is used to reverse bias the zener diode (D2) that controls TR2. The hot brush is fed by the ignition current (terminal 1) plus current from the diode trio. This is an internal A field circuit. The regulator is inside the generator and completes the circuit to ground when it is turned on.

COMPUTER-CONTROLLED GENERATORS

Beginning in the mid-1980s, General Motors introduced a smaller, yet high-output series of generators. These generators are called the CS (charging system) series. See Figure 17–20. Following the *CS* are numbers indicating the *outside diameter* (in millimetres) of the stator laminations. Typical sizes, designations, and outputs include the following:

CS-121, 5-SI 74 A
CS-130, 9-SI 105 A
CS-144, 17–SI 120 A

These generators feature two cooling fans (one internal) and terminals designed to permit connections to an on-board body computer through terminals L and F.

The reduced-size generators also feature ball bearings front and rear, and totally soldered internal electrical connections. The voltage is controlled ei-

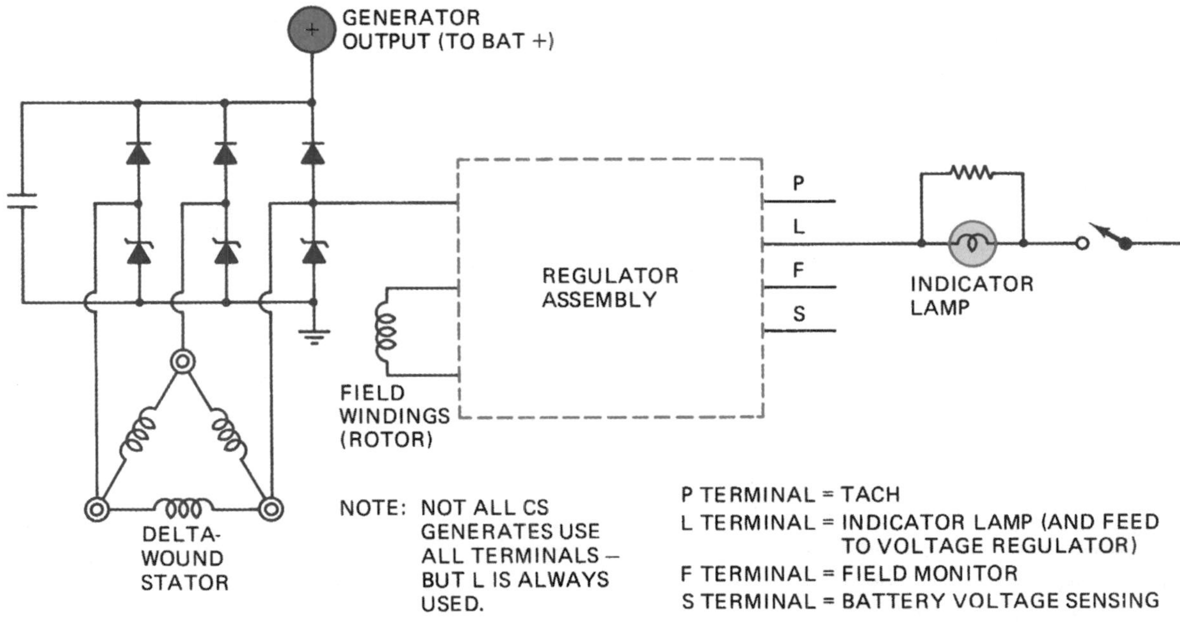

Figure 17–20 General Motors CS generator. Notice the use of zener diodes in the rectifier to help control any high-voltage surges that could affect delicate computer circuits. If a high-voltage surge does occur, the zener diode(s) will be reverse biased and the potentially harmful voltage will be safely conducted to ground. Voltage must be preset at the L terminal to allow the generator to start producing current.

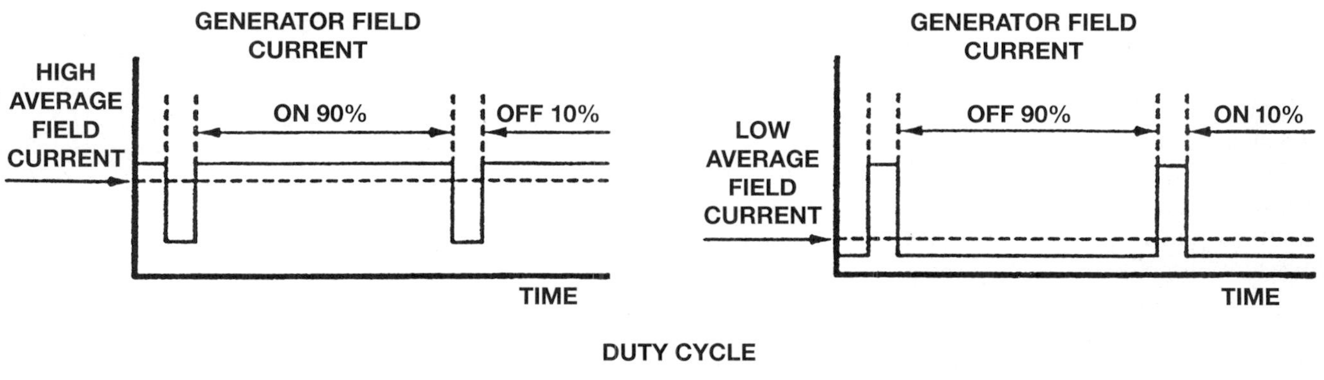

Figure 17–21 Frequency vs. duty cycle. (Courtesy General Motors)

- Frequency is the number of times, per second, that a circuit is opened and closed.
- Duty cycle has a fixed rate, per second, but the on-off time will vary.

ther by the body computer (if the vehicle is so equipped) or by the built-in voltage regulator. The voltage regulator switches the field voltage on and off at a fixed frequency of about 400 times per second. Voltage is controlled by varying the on and off time (duty cycle) of the field current. See Figure 17–21.

DaimlerChrysler Charging Systems

These systems incorporate the regulator as part of the on-board computer. See Figure 17–22. The computer (SMEC) acts as a regulator by completing the ground circuit. External A type circuits such as this usually have two field terminals. Many computer-controlled charging systems have built-in diagnostics; problems are recorded in the computer memory and may be accessed by the technician.

Generator Cooling

The AC generator produces a great deal of heat, especially as the current output rises. It is important that the generator is located in an area where air passing

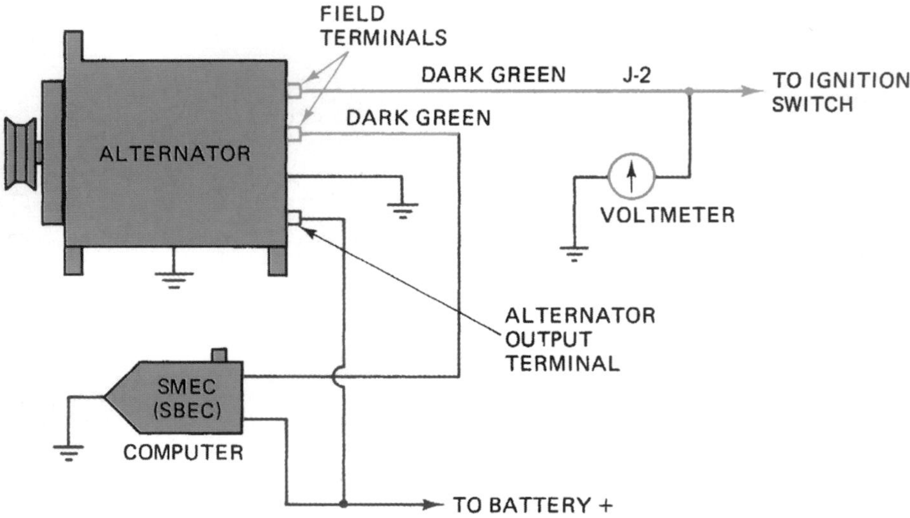

Figure 17–22 The alternator field (rotor) current is controlled by the computer. SMEC stands for *single module engine controller.*

through the engine will help to cool the housing and stator; the built-in fan also draws this air inside, past the rotor, stator, and diode heat sink. AC generators will charge, regardless of rotation, either clockwise or counter-clockwise; the only difference may be the fan at the front of the rotor. Mixing the fan from a marine application with a passenger-car generator will shorten generator life if the rotation rates differ.

Liquid-cooled generators, which have been used on trucks, are now finding their way onto some automobiles with high-output charging systems. The generator bolts directly to the engine where the coolant circulates through the aluminum housing, which doubles as a water jacket.

There is some industry resistance against the 12 volt to 42 volt switchover because of the higher costs involved. Super-high-output 12 volt generators, up to 350 amperes, are now being tested and may find their way into use. Obviously, cooling will be a major consideration.

CHARGING SYSTEM TESTING AND SERVICE

The charging system can be tested as part of a routine vehicle inspection or to determine the reason for a no-charge or reduced-charging circuit performance.

Charging Voltage Test

The first and easiest test to perform to check if the generator is working correctly is to check the charging system voltage at the battery. Use a digital multimeter to check using the following steps:

Step 1 Select DC volts.

Step 2 Connect the red meter lead to the positive (+) terminal of the battery and the black meter lead to the negative (−) terminal of the battery.

> **NOTE:** The polarity of the meter leads is not really important when using a digital multimeter. If the meter leads are connected backward on the battery, the resulting readout will simply have a negative (−) sign in front of the voltage reading.

Step 3 Start the engine and increase the engine speed to about 2000 rpm (fast idle) and record the charging voltage. See Figure 17–23. Specifications for charging voltage, 13.5 – 15.0 volts.

If the voltage is too high, check that the charging system components such as the generator and voltage regulator (if separate) are properly grounded. If the battery voltage is still higher than specified, then there is a likely fault with the electrical connections at the voltage regulator or generator. If the voltage is lower than specifications, there is a fault with the wiring, generator, or regulator (if external). Additional testing is required to help pinpoint the root cause.

Magnetized Rear Bearing Test

All 12 V automotive generator systems use the voltage regulator to control the current through the rotor of the generator. The rotor creates a magnetic field whenever there is a complete circuit through

Figure 17–23 The digital multimeter should be set to read DC volts and the red lead connected to the battery positive (+) terminal and the black meter lead connected to the negative (−) battery terminal.

the brushes and slip rings of the rotor. If there is no current through the rotor, there is no generator output. Whenever the rotor is energized, the entire rotor shaft and the generator bearings become magnetized. Technicians often use this information to help diagnose a no-charging problem. With the engine running, use a screwdriver or other metallic object to test for magnetism at the rear bearing of the generator.

NOTE: The front bearing is also magnetized, but testing for magnetism of the front bearing with the engine running can be dangerous.

If the rear bearing *is* magnetized, then the following facts are known:

1. The voltage regulator is working.
2. The generator brushes are working.
3. The rotor in the generator is producing a magnetic field.

If the rear bearing is *not* magnetized, then one or more of the following problems exist:

1. The voltage regulator is not working.
2. The generator brushes are worn or stuck, and they are not making good electrical contact with the rotor slip rings.
3. The generator rotor could be defective.

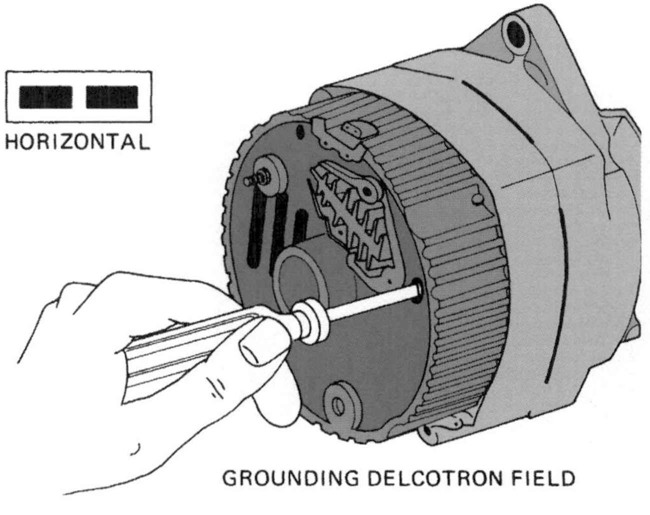

Figure 17–24 A GM generator with an internal voltage regulator can be identified by the horizontal plug-in connector.

No automotive generator can produce charging current if the rotor is not producing a magnetic field. It is this rotating magnetic field created in the rotor that induces current in the stator windings. Therefore, by checking for a magnetized rear bearing, the technician can better determine where the charging system problem is located. If, for example, the rear bearing is magnetized, yet the "charge" (GEN) light is on and the generator is not charging, the problem has to be inside the generator (diodes, stator, etc.).

Full-Fielding Test

If the rear bearing is not magnetized, then a procedure for bypassing the voltage regulator should be used to determine if the generator is capable of producing its designed output. This procedure is called *full fielding* the generator. See Figures 17–24 through 17–30 for examples of procedures and connections necessary to full-field various charging systems. B circuits are powered and A circuits are grounded to full-field the generator. Bypassing the regulator removes the regulator from the circuit and provides full battery voltage to the rotor; the system is now unregulated and charging voltage rises quickly. Even with zener diode protection (see Figure 17–20), delicate electronic components could be damaged; follow the service instructions exactly.

Many recent charging systems do not have provisions for full-fielding the generator; if a bad regulator is suspected, it must be replaced and the system rechecked. Often a completely rebuilt generator, with regulator, is installed, being less expensive.

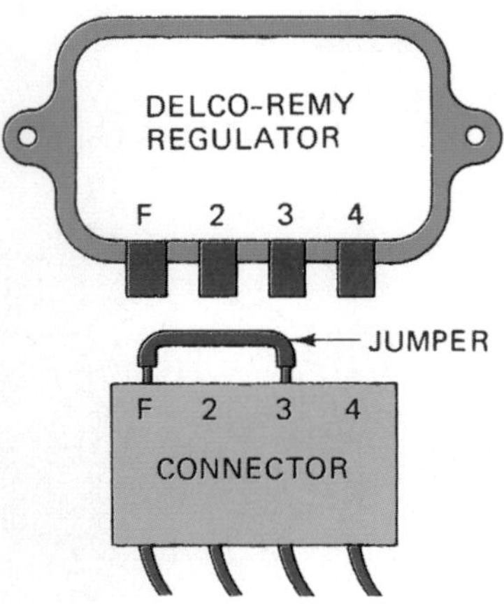

Figure 17–25 Connections required to full-field a GM B circuit generator with an external voltage regulator. Terminal 3 (battery power) is jumped to terminal F (field wire to rotor).

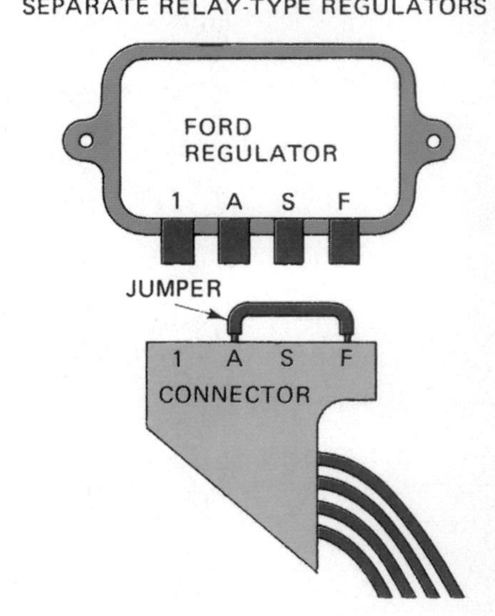

Figure 17–26 Connections required to full-field a Ford B circuit generator with an external voltage regulator. The A terminal (battery power) is jumped to terminal F (field wire to rotor).

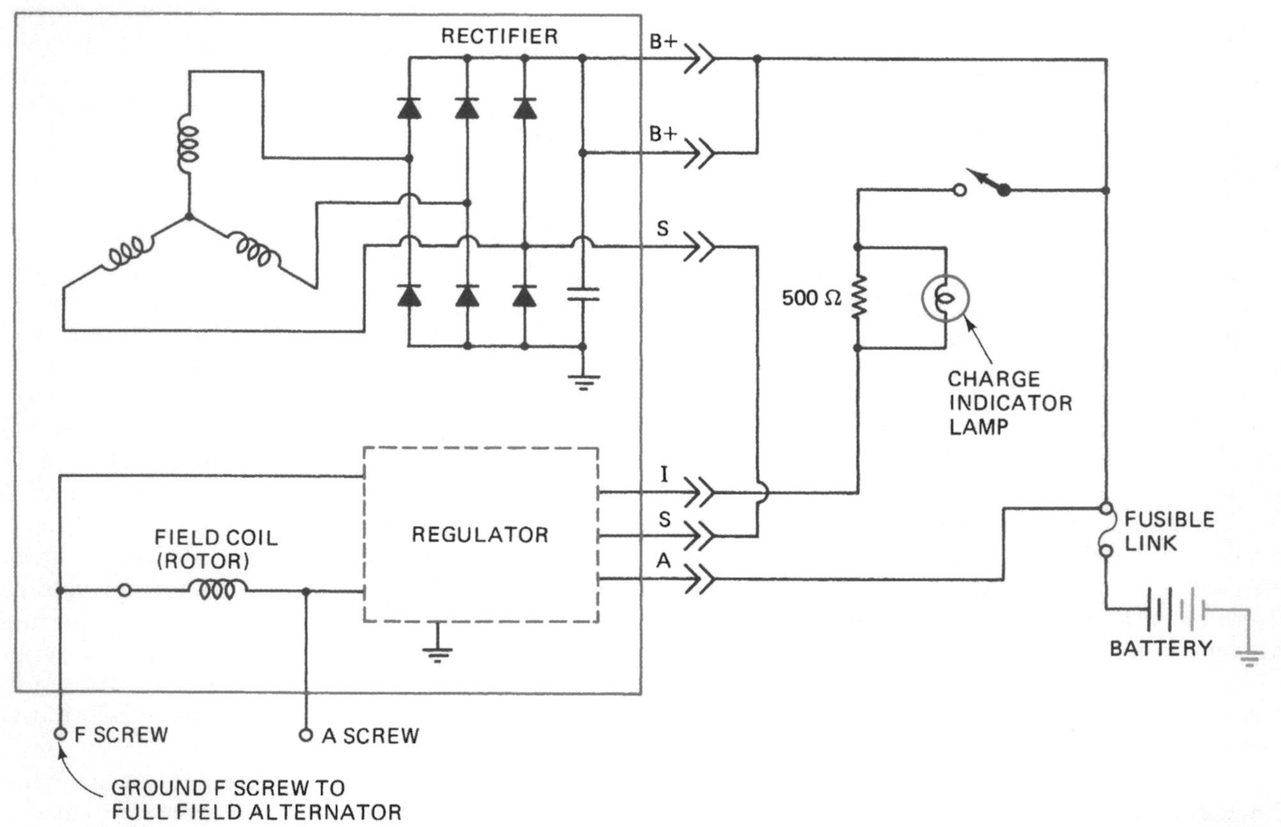

Figure 17–27 Wiring diagram of a Ford A circuit generator and integral regulator. Note the test circuit screws that allow access to the system; the A screw is used to check for battery power and the F screw is used to full-field the generator.

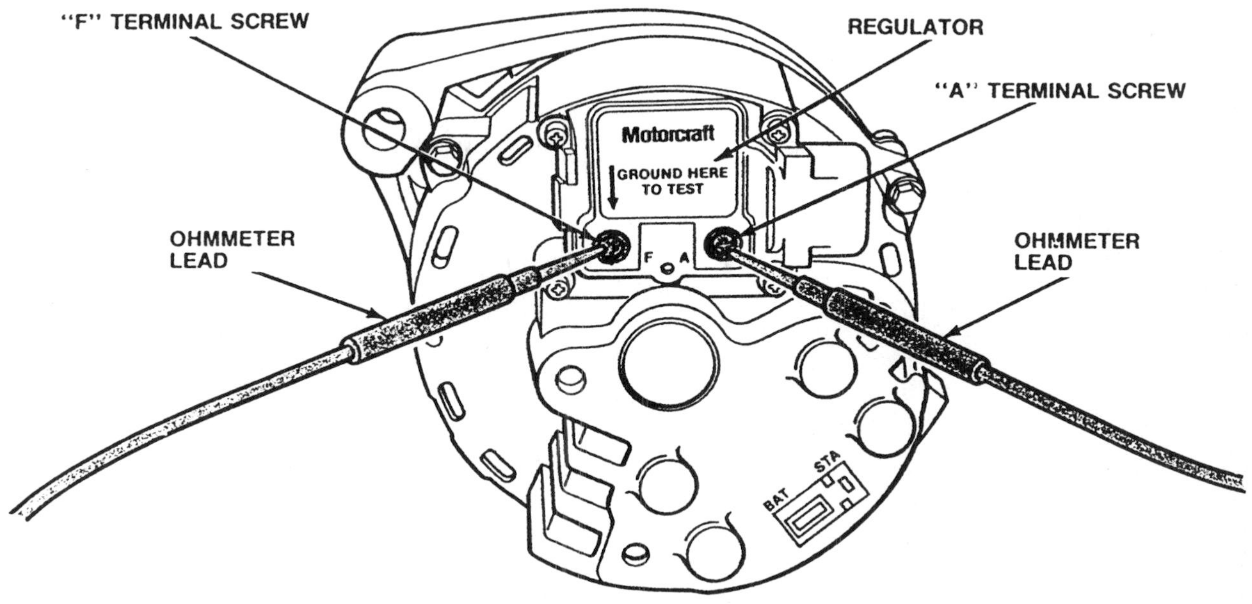

Figure 17–28 Ford IAR Generator. Testing rotor resistance with an ohmmeter (the battery must be disconnected from the generator). See Figure 17–27 for the circuit schematic. The F screw is also used for a full-field test. (Courtesy Ford Motor Co.)

TECH TIP 

The Lighter Plug Trick

Battery voltage measurements can be read through the lighter socket. Simply construct a test tool using a lighter plug at one end of a length of two-conductor wire and the other end connected to a double banana plug. The double banana plug will fit most meters in the common (COM) terminal and the volt terminal of the meter.

CURRENT OUTPUT AND FULL-FIELD TEST—EXTERNAL A CIRCUIT

1. Connect an ammeter to the generator (alternator) output wire. See Figure 17–30. Note: an inductive ammeter placed around the output wire is a better choice.
2. Connect a voltmeter to the output terminal.
3. Install a carbon pile rheostat across the battery terminals.
4. Run the engine at 2000 rpm.
5. Turn the carbon pile rheostat knob to load the battery.
6. Do not let the battery voltage drop below 12 V.
7. Note the maximum current output.
8. If the output is low, full-field the generator by disconnecting and grounding the field wire at the regulator. See Figure 17–30. This bypasses the regulator.
9. If the current output is now within specifications, the regulator, or ground, is at fault; if the output is still low, the generator, or wiring, is at fault.

TECH TIP 

Use a Test Light to Check for a Defective Fusible Link

Most AC generators (alternators) use a fusible link between the output terminal located on the slip-ring-end frame and the positive (+) terminal of the battery. If this fusible link is defective (blown), then the charging system will not operate at all. Many AC generators have been replaced repeatedly because of a blown fusible link that was not discovered until later. A quick-and-easy test to check if the fusible link is okay is to touch a test light to the output terminal. With the other end of the test light attached to a good ground, the fusible link is okay if the light lights. This test confirms that the circuit between the AC generator and the battery has continuity.

AC Voltage Check

A good generator should *not* produce any AC voltage. It is the purpose of the diodes in the generator to rectify all AC voltage into DC voltage. The procedure to check for AC voltage includes the following steps:

Step 1 Set the digital meter to read AC volts.

Step 2 Start the engine and operate it at 2000 rpm (fast idle).

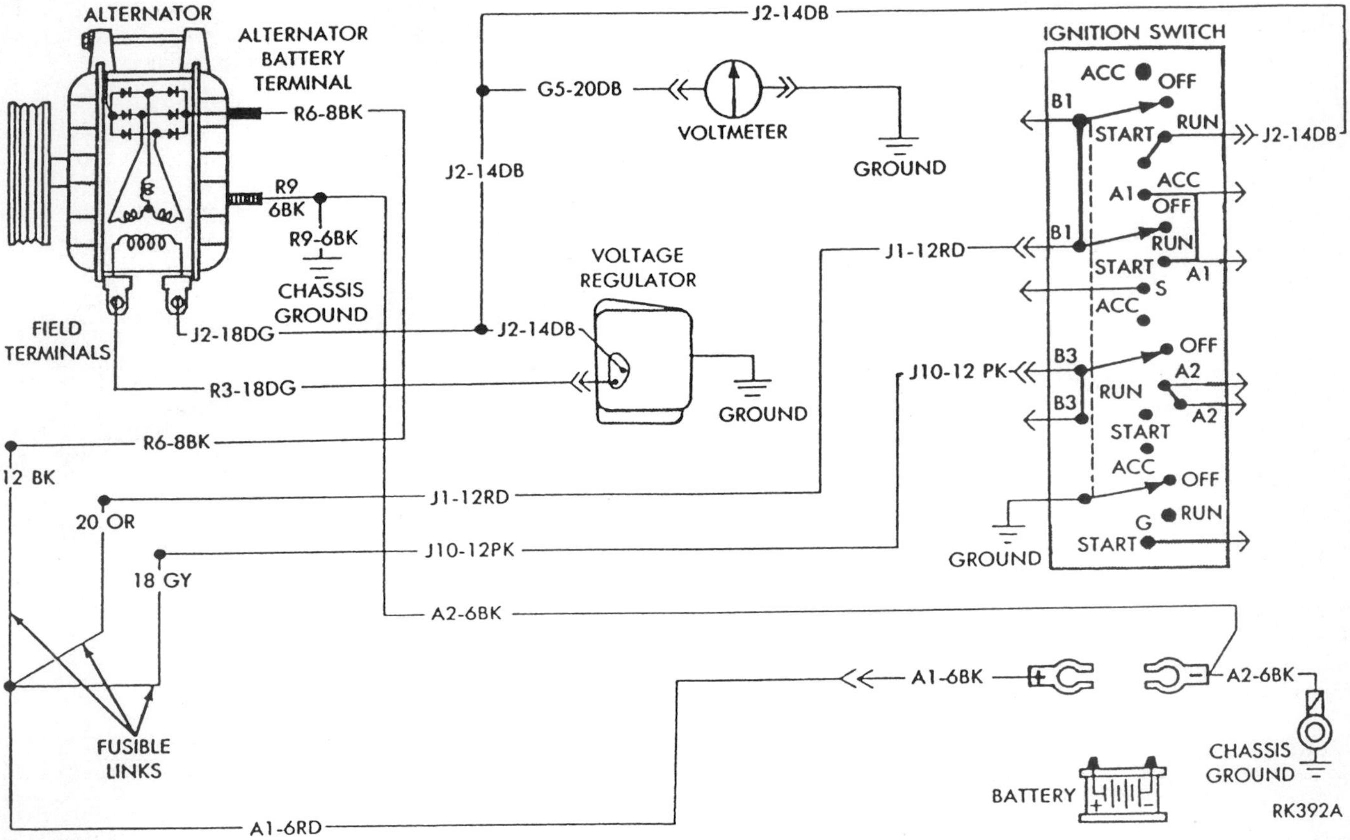

Figure 17–29 Wiring schematic of a Chrysler external A charging system. An electronic voltage regulator is used. Note the use of a dash-mounted voltmeter as a charge indicator. Ammeters are seldom used. (Courtesy DaimlerChrysler)

Step 3 Connect the voltmeter leads to the positive and negative battery terminals.

Step 4 Turn on the headlights to provide an electrical load on the generator.

> **NOTE:** A higher, more accurate reading can be obtained by touching the meter lead to the output terminal of the generator. See Figure 17–31.

The results should be interpreted as follows: If the diodes are good, the voltmeter should read *less* than 0.4 volt AC. If the reading is over 0.5 volt AC, the rectifier diodes are defective.

> **NOTE:** This test will *not* test for a defective diode trio.

Charging System Voltage-Drop Testing

For the proper operation of any charging system, there must be good electrical connections between the battery positive terminal and the generator output terminal. The generator must also be properly grounded to the engine block.

Many manufacturers of vehicles run the lead from the output terminal of the generator to other connectors or junction blocks that are electrically connected to the positive terminal of the battery. If there is high resistance (a high voltage drop) in these connections or in the wiring itself, the battery will not be properly charged.

TECH TIP 

"2 to 4"

Most voltage-drop specifications range between 0.2 and 0.4 volt. Generally, if the voltage loss (voltage drop) in a circuit exceeds 0.5 volt, the wiring in that circuit should be repaired or replaced. During automotive testing, it is sometimes difficult to remember the exact specification for each test; therefore, the technician can simply remember "2 to 4" and that any voltage drop over this amount indicates a problem.

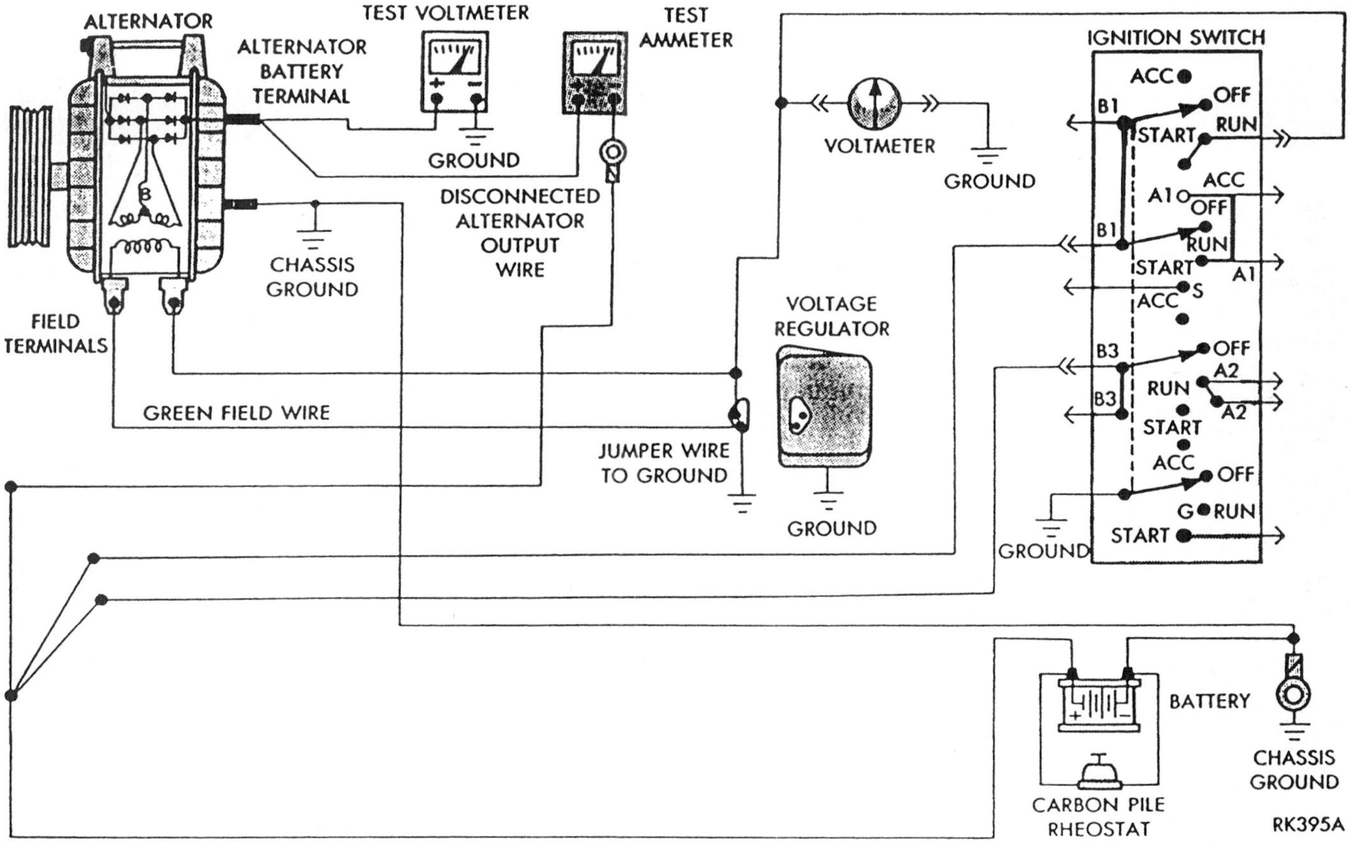

ALTERNATOR
TEST VOLTMETER
TEST AMMETER
ALTERNATOR BATTERY TERMINAL
GROUND
DISCONNECTED ALTERNATOR OUTPUT WIRE
CHASSIS GROUND
FIELD TERMINALS
GREEN FIELD WIRE
VOLTMETER
GROUND
IGNITION SWITCH
VOLTAGE REGULATOR
JUMPER WIRE TO GROUND
GROUND
GROUND
BATTERY
CHASSIS GROUND
CARBON PILE RHEOSTAT
RK395A

Figure 17–30 Full field test hook-up for a Chrysler external A charging system. Note the voltmeter, ammeter, and carbon pile rheostat. (Courtesy DaimlerChrysler)

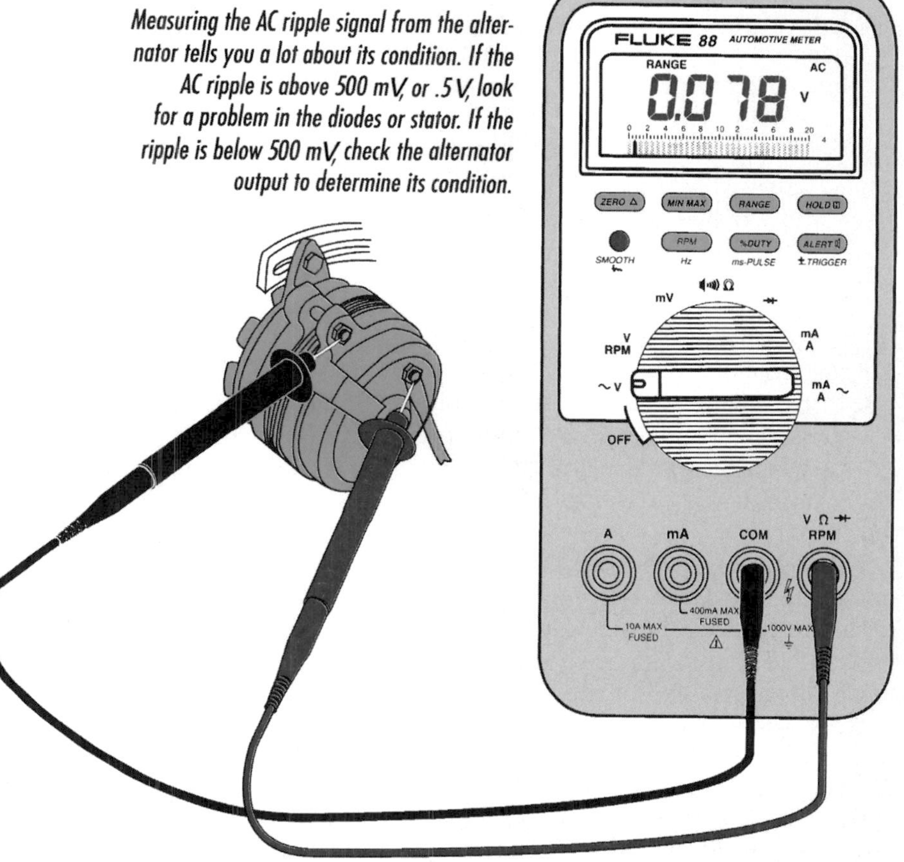

Measuring the AC ripple signal from the alternator tells you a lot about its condition. If the AC ripple is above 500 mV, or .5 V, look for a problem in the diodes or stator. If the ripple is below 500 mV, check the alternator output to determine its condition.
FLUKE 88 AUTOMOTIVE METER
RANGE
AC
0.078
V
OFF
A
mA
COM
V Ω RPM

Figure 17–31 AC ripple at the output terminal of the generator is more accurate than testing at the battery due to the resistance of the wiring between the generator and the battery. The reading shown on the meter is only 78 mV (0.078 volt), far below what the reading would be if a diode were defective. (Courtesy of Fluke Corporation)

TECH TIP 

Use Jumper Cables as a Diagnostic Tool

Whenever diagnosing a generator charging problem, try using jumper cables to connect the positive and negative terminals of the generator directly to the positive and negative terminals of the battery. If a definite improvement is noticed, the problem is in the wiring of the vehicle. High resistance, due to corroded connections or loose grounds, can cause low generator output, repeated regulator failures, slow cranking, and discharged batteries. A voltage-drop test of the charging system can also be used to locate excessive resistance (high-voltage drop) in the charging circuit, but using jumper wires (cables) is often faster and easier.

Whenever there is a suspected charging system problem (with or without a charge indicator light on), simply follow these steps to measure the voltage drop of the insulated (power side) charging circuit:

Step 1 Start the engine and run it at a fast idle (about 2000 engine rpm).

Step 2 Turn on the headlights to ensure an electrical load on the charging system: about 20 A.

Step 3 Using any voltmeter, connect the positive test lead (usually red) to the output terminal of the generator. Attach the negative test lead (usually black) to the positive post of the battery.

The results should be interpreted as follows:

1. If there is less than a 0.4 volt reading, then all wiring and connections are satisfactory.
2. If the voltmeter reads higher than 0.4 volt, there is excessive resistance (voltage drop) between the generator output terminal and the positive terminal of the battery.
3. If the voltmeter reads battery voltage (or close to battery voltage), there is an open circuit between the battery and the generator output terminal.

To determine whether the generator is correctly grounded, maintain the engine speed at 2000 rpm with the headlights on. Connect the positive voltmeter lead to the case of the generator and the negative voltmeter lead to the negative terminal of the battery. The voltmeter should read less than 0.2 volt if the generator is properly grounded. If the reading is over 0.2 volt, connect one end of an auxiliary ground wire to the case of the generator and the other end to a good engine ground. See Figure 17–32.

TECH TIP 

The Mini Clamp-On DMM Test

The generator output can be easily measured using a digital mini clamp-on-type digital multimeter. A typical clamp-on meter is capable of reading from as low as 10 mA (0.01 amperes) to 200 amperes or more. See Figure 17–33. To set up for the test, clamp the meter around the generator output wire and select DC amperes and the correct scale. Start the engine, run at 2000 rpm, turn all lights and accessories on and then observe the meter display. The results should be within 10% of the specified generator rating. An AC/DC current clamp adapter can also be used along with a conventional digital multimeter set on the DC millivolt scale. To check for AC current ripple, switch the meter to read AC amperes and record the reading. A reading of greater than 10 amperes AC indicates defective generator diodes.

Generator Output Test

A charging circuit may be able to produce correct charging circuit voltage, but not be able to produce adequate current output. If in doubt about charging system output, first check the condition of the generator drive belt. See Figure 17–34. With the engine off, attempt to rotate the fan of the generator by hand. Replace or tighten the drive belt if the generator fan can be rotated this way. See Figure 17–35 for typical test equipment hookup.

The testing procedure for generator output is as follows:

Step 1 Connect the starting and charging test leads according to the manufacturer's instructions.

Step 2 Turn the ignition switch on (engine off) and observe the ammeter. This is the ignition circuit current, and it should be about 2 to 8 A.

HINT: Step 2 can be skipped if the ammeter current clamp can be connected around the generator output wire instead of around the battery cable(s) as shown in Figure 17–36.

Step 3 Start the engine and operate it at 2000 rpm (fast idle). Turn the load increase control slowly to obtain the highest reading on the ammeter scale. Note the ampere reading.

Step 4 Total the amperes from step 2 and step 3. Results should be within 10% (or 15 A) of the rated output. Rated output may be stamped or printed on the generator as shown in Figures 17–37 and 17–38.

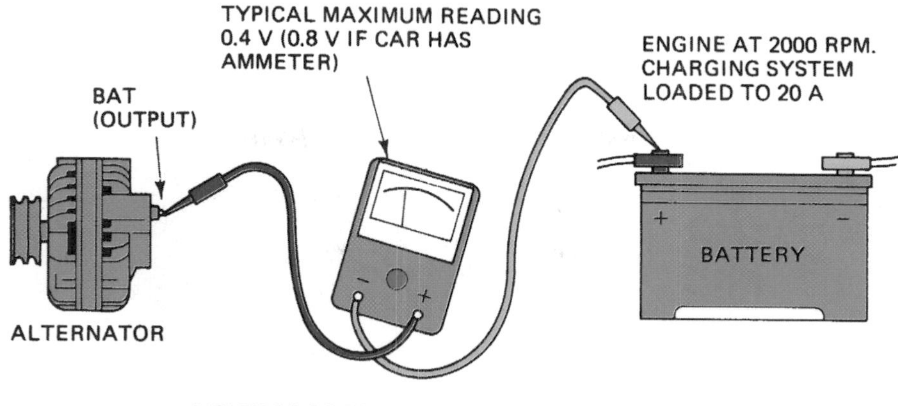

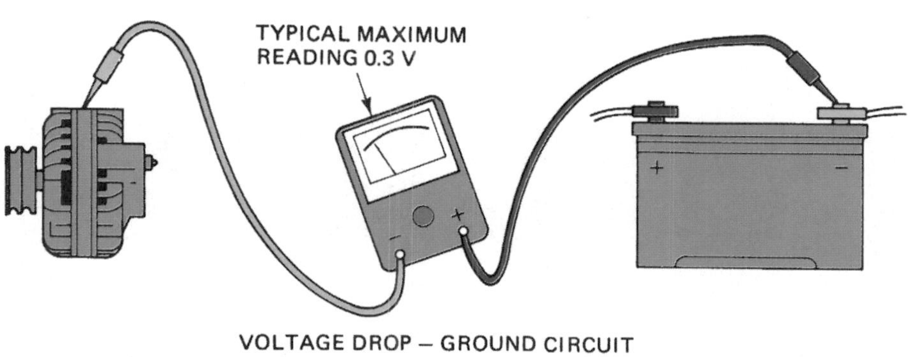

Figure 17–32 Voltage hookup to test the voltage drop of the charging circuit. Voltage drop specifications are usually rated with 20 amperes flowing in the circuit; higher amperage will show a greater drop, less amperage a lower drop.

Figure 17–33 A mini clamp-on digital multimeter can be used to measure generator output. This meter was set on the 200-ampere DC scale. With the engine running and all lights and accessories on, the generator was able to produce almost exactly its specified rating of 105 amperes.

Figure 17–34 This accessory drive belt should be replaced because it has many cracks. The usual specification for a serpentine belt replacement is when there are 3 or more cracks in any one rib in any 75 mm (3 in.) length. Many serpentine drive belts have automatic spring-loaded tensioners that require no adjustment. Some have pointers that indicate the belt has stretched and needs replacing.

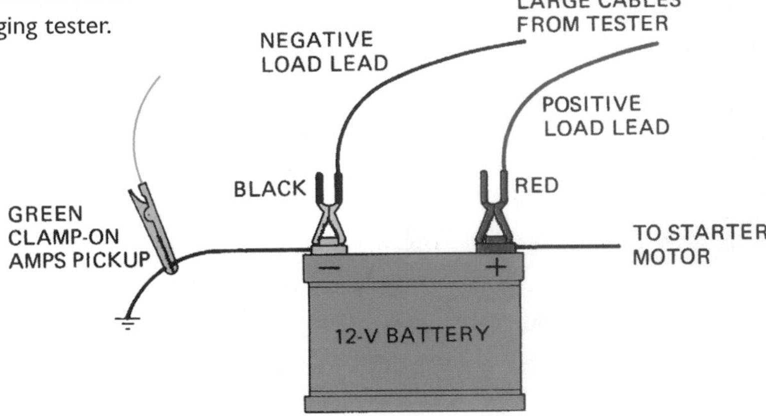

Figure 17–35 Typical hookup of a starting and charging tester.

Figure 17–36 The best place to install a charging system tester amp probe is around the generator output terminal wire as shown.

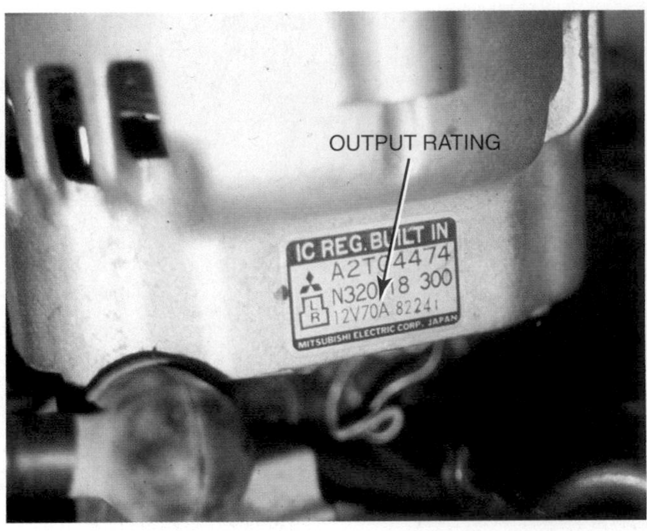

Figure 17–38 The output on this generator is printed on a label.

Figure 17–37 The output rating on the General Motors generator (alternator) is stamped into the case.

If the generator output is not within 10% of its rated output, perform the same test as just described, but this time bypass the voltage regulator (if possible) and provide a full-field current to the rotor (field) of the generator.

> **NOTE:** When applying a load to the battery with a carbon pile tester during a generator output test, do not permit the battery voltage to drop below 12 volts. Most generators will produce their maximum output (in amperes) above 13 volts.

DIAGNOSTIC STORY

Guitar Player Wanted

Adjusting the generator drive belt on some models of the PT Cruiser may be difficult because of limited space at the front of the engine.

DaimlerChrysler has a unique procedure for testing belt tension; a special pick-up is attached to a scan tool (normally used to access the on-board computer) and positioned about 25 mm (1 in.) away from the centre of the belt span. The belt is plucked three times and the resulting frequency is noted on the scan tool. The reading is compared to factory specifications and the belt is adjusted if required.

TECH TIP

Bigger Is Not Always Better

Many technicians are asked to install a higher-output generator to allow the use of emergency equipment or other high-current equipment such as a high-power sound system.

Although many higher-output units can be physically installed, it is important not to forget to upgrade the wiring and the fusible link(s) in the generator circuit. Failure to upgrade the wiring could lead to overheating. The usual failure locations are at junctions or electrical connectors.

NOTE: Some generators of different-colour tags or insulators have the same rated output for different-colour codes used in different years of production or for different vehicle applications. Not every generator is marked to indicate its output rating. When load testing any generator, always check the manufacturer's specification for the vehicle being tested.

How to Determine Minimum Required Generator Output

All charging systems must be able to supply the electrical demands of the electrical system. If lights and accessories are used constantly and the generator cannot supply the necessary ampere output, the battery will be drained. To determine the minimum electrical load requirements, connect an ammeter in series with either battery cable.

NOTE: If using an inductive-pickup ammeter, be certain that the pickup is over *all* the wires leaving the battery terminal. See Figure 17–39. Failure to include the small body ground wire from the negative battery terminal to the body or the small positive wire (if testing from the positive side) will *greatly decrease* the current flow readings.

Frequently Asked Question ???

What Is a Clock Position?

Most generators of a particular manufacturer can be used on a variety of vehicles, which may require wiring connections placed in various locations. For example, a Chevrolet and an Oldsmobile generator may be identical except for the position of the rear section containing the electrical connections. The four through-bolts that hold the two halves together are equally spaced; therefore, the rear generator housing *can* be installed in any one of four positions to match the wiring needs of various models. See Figure 17–40. These positions are referred to as the clock positions.

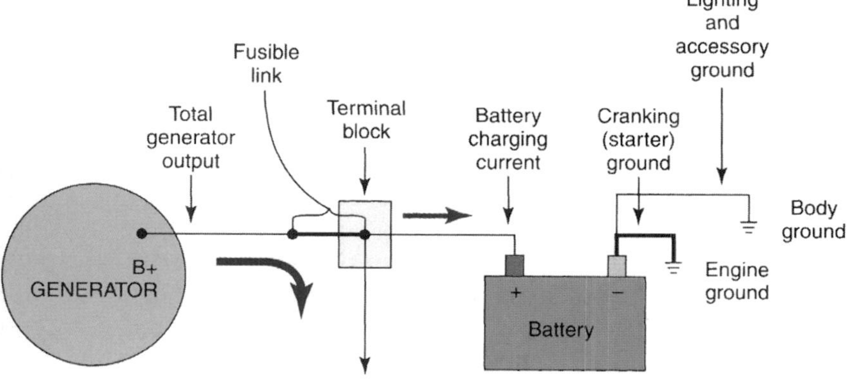

Figure 17–39 A diagram showing the location of the charging system wiring of a typical vehicle. The best location to use to check for the generator (alternator) output is at the output wire from the B+ (BAT) terminal. Notice that the generator supplies all electrical needs of the vehicle first, then charges the battery if needed.

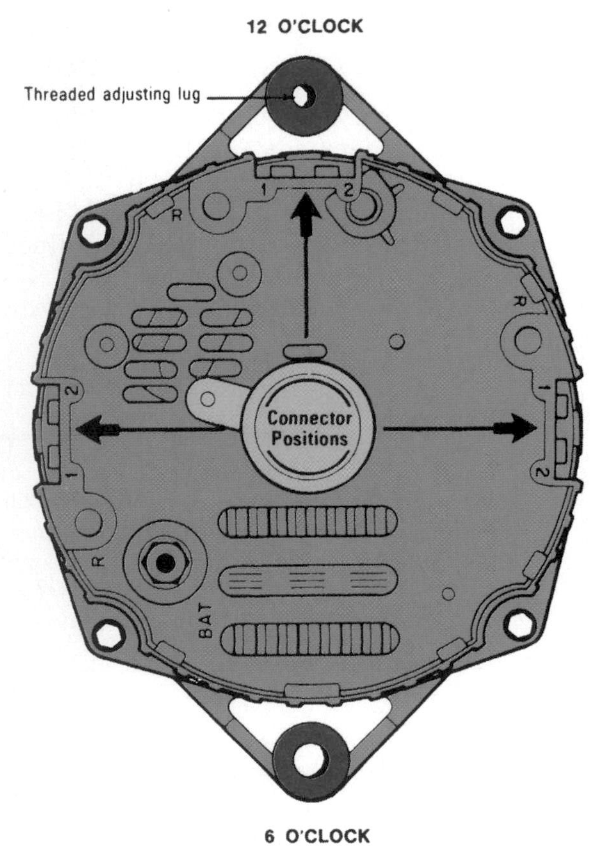

Figure 17–40 Explanation of Delco clock positions. Because the four through-bolts are equally spaced, it is possible for a generator to be installed in one of four different clock positions. The connector position is determined by viewing the generator from the diode end with the threaded adjusting lug in the up or 12 o'clock position. Select the 3 o'clock, 6 o'clock, 9 o'clock, or 12 o'clock position to match the unit being replaced.

After connecting an ammeter in the battery circuit, continue as follows:

1. Start the engine and operate to about 2000 rpm (fast idle).
2. Turn the heat selector to air conditioning (if the vehicle is so equipped).
3. Turn the blower motor to high speed.
4. Turn the headlights on bright.
5. Turn on the radio.
6. Turn on the windshield wipers.
7. Turn on any other accessories that may be used continuously (do not operate the horn, power door locks, or other units that are not used for more than a few seconds).

Observe the ammeter. The current indicated is the electrical load that the generator is able to exceed to keep the battery fully charged. The minimum acceptable generator output is 5 amperes greater than the accessory load. A negative (discharge) reading indicates that the generator is not capable of supplying the current (amperes) that may be needed.

GENERATOR DISASSEMBLY

If testing has confirmed that there are generator problems, remove the generator from the vehicle *after* disconnecting the *negative* battery cable. This will prevent the occurrence of damaging short circuits. Mark the case with a scratch or with a paint pen to ensure proper reassembly of the generator case.

After the through-bolts have been removed, carefully separate the two halves; the stator windings stay with the rear case. The rotor can be inspected and tested while attached to the front housing.

Testing the Rotor

The slip rings on the rotor should be smooth and round within 0.05 mm (0.002 in.) of being perfectly round. If grooved, some slip rings can be machined to provide a suitable surface for the brushes. Do not machine beyond the minimum slip ring dimension as specified by the manufacturer. Rotor slip rings are usually made of copper; however, some import vehicles use steel for the rings.

If the slip rings are discoloured or dirty, they can be cleaned with 400-grit or fine emery (polishing) cloth. The rotor must be turned while being cleaned to prevent flat spots on the slip rings.

The field coil continuity in the rotor can be checked by touching one test lead of a 110 volt (15 watt bulb) tester on each slip ring. The test light should light. A more accurate method is to measure the resistance between the slip rings using an ohmmeter. Typical values of resistance and

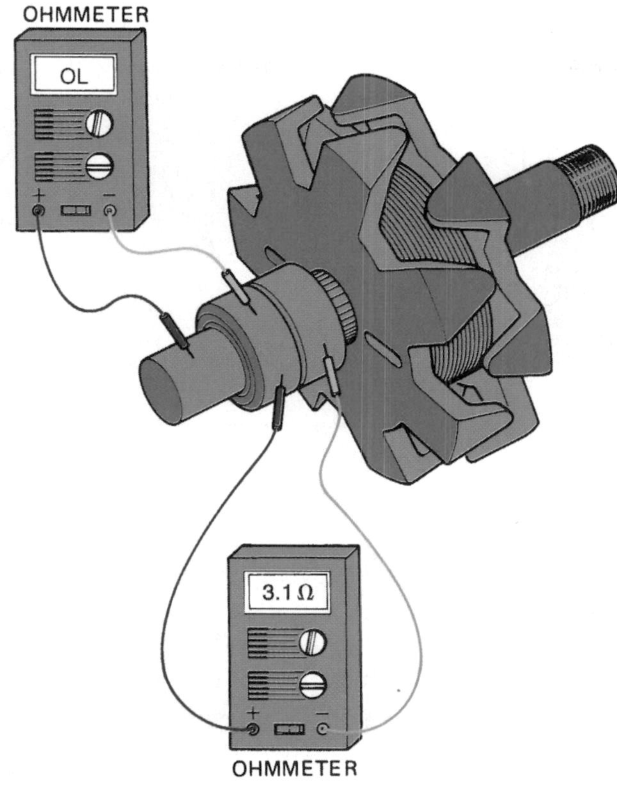

Figure 17–41 Testing a generator rotor using an ohmmeter.

current depend on the duty (load requirements) the rotor is designed for.

Field Coil Resistance and Current

Duty	Resistance Ohms	Current Amperes
Light	4 to 6	3 to 2
Medium	3 to 4	4 to 3
Heavy	2 to 3	6 to 4

Compare the decrease in resistance to the increase in current. The resistance values listed here are typical only; exact specifications for the generator being tested should be consulted before condemning a rotor. Ohmmeters can also vary in accuracy. See Figure 17–41.

1. If the resistance is below specification, the rotor is shorted.
2. If the resistance is above specification, the rotor connections are corroded or open.

Rotor inspection specifications often include amperage. With an ammeter connected in series with the battery, connect one test lead directly to the positive post of the battery and one slip ring. Connect the other test lead between the negative post of the battery and the other slip ring. Current will flow through the field windings of the rotor and create a magnetic field. Compare the ammeter reading with the manufacturer's specifications. If the current draw is above specification, the rotor is shorted. If the current draw is below specification, the rotor has high resistance, corroded connections, or an open rotor winding.

If the rotor is found to be open, shorted (copper to copper), or grounded (copper to steel), the rotor must be replaced or repaired at a specialized shop. Loose connections at the rotor slip rings may be repaired by resoldering.

NOTE: The cost of a replacement rotor may exceed the cost of an entire rebuilt generator. Be certain, however, that the rebuilt generator is rated at the same output as the original or higher.

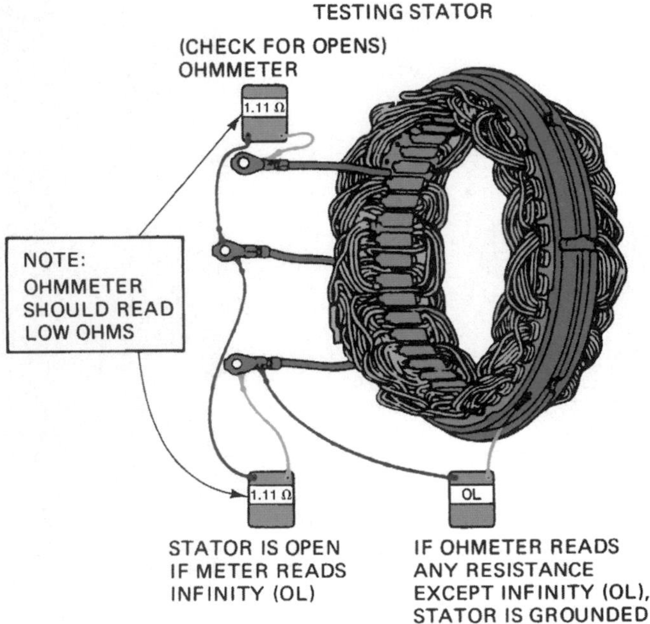

Figure 17–42 If the ohmmeter reads infinity between any two of the three stator windings, the stator is open and, therefore, defective. The ohmmeter should read infinity between any stator lead and the steel laminations. If the reading is less than infinity, the stator is grounded. Stator windings cannot be tested if shorted because the normal resistance is very low.

Testing the Stator (Wye Wound)

The stator must be disconnected from the diodes (rectifiers) before testing. Because all three windings of the stator are electrically connected, a powered (110 or 12 volt) test light or an ohmmeter can be used to check a stator. There should be low resistance at all three stator leads (continuity), and the test light *should* light. There should *not* be continuity (in other words, there should be infinite ohms, or the test light should *not* light) when the stator is tested between any stator lead and the metal stator core. If there is continuity, the stator is *grounded* (short to ground) and must be repaired or replaced. See Figure 17–42. Because the resistance is very low for a normal stator, it is generally *not* possible to test for a *shorted* (copper to copper) stator. A shorted stator will, however, greatly reduce generator output.

If all generator components test okay and the output is still low, substitute a reliable stator and retest. If the stator is black or smells burned, check the vehicle for a discharged or defective battery. If battery voltage never reaches the voltage regulator cutoff point, the generator will be continuously producing current in the stator windings. This continuous charging often overheats the stator.

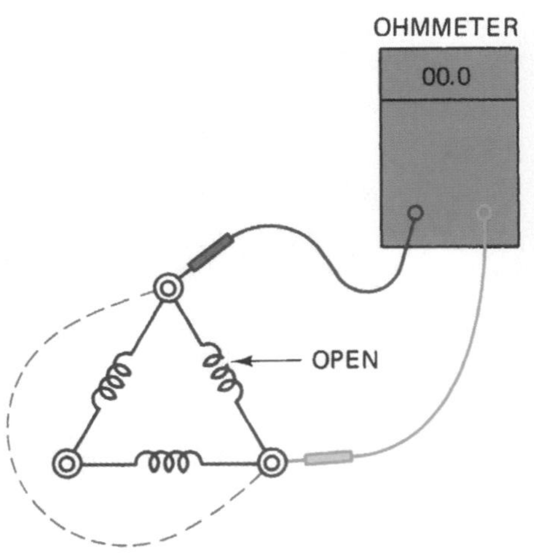

Figure 17–43 An open in a delta-wound stator cannot be detected using an ohmmeter.

Testing the Stator (Delta Wound)

Delta wound stators can be tested for grounds in the same manner as wye wound; however, a test light or an ohmmeter cannot detect an open stator if the stator is delta wound. The ohmmeter will still indicate low resistance because all three windings are electrically connected and the test light will still light. See Figure 17–43.

Testing the Diode Trio

Many generators are equipped with a diode trio. A diode is an electrical one-way check valve that permits current to flow in only one direction. Because *trio* means three, a diode trio is three diodes connected together. The diode trio is connected to all three stator windings. See Figure 17–19. The current generated in the stator flows through the diode trio to the internal voltage regulator. The diode trio is designed to supply current for the field (rotor) and turns off the charge indicator light whenever the generator voltage equals or exceeds the battery voltage. If one of the three diodes in the diode trio is defective (usually open), the generator may produce close-to-normal output; however, the charge indicator light will be on dimly.

A diode trio should be tested with a digital multimeter. The meter should be set to the diode-check position. The multimeter should indicate 0.5 to 0.7 volt one way and OL (over limit) after reversing the test leads and touching all three connectors of the diode trio.

Testing the Rectifier Bridge (Diodes)

Generators are equipped with six diodes to convert the alternating current (AC) generated in the stator windings into direct current (DC) for use by the vehicle's battery and electrical components. The six

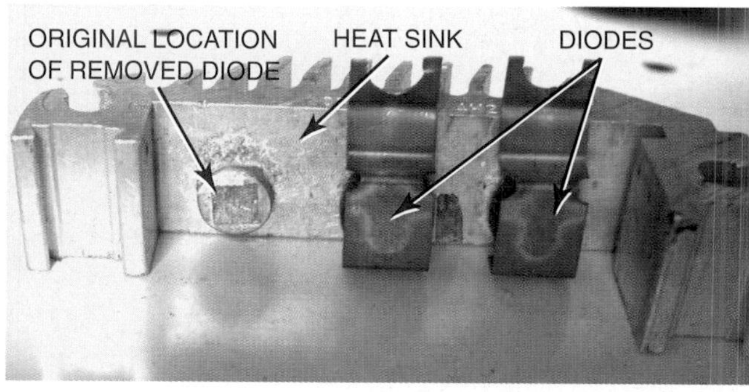

Figure 17–44 A GM rectifier bridge that has been disassembled to show the individual diodes.

diodes include three positive diodes and three negative diodes (one positive and one negative for each winding of the stator). These diodes can be individual diodes or grouped into a positive and a negative rectifier that each contain three diodes. All six diodes can be combined into one replaceable unit called a **rectifier bridge.** The rectifier(s) (diodes) should be tested using a multimeter that is set to "diode check."

Because a diode (rectifier) should allow current to flow in only one direction, each diode should be tested to determine if the diode allows current flow in one direction and blocks current flow in the opposite direction. To test many generator diodes, it may be necessary to unsolder the stator connections. See Figure 17–44. Accurate testing is not possible unless the diodes are separated electrically from other generator components. Connect the leads to the leads of the diode (pigtail and housing of the rectifier bridge). Read the meter. Reverse the test leads. A good diode should show OL (over limit) one way (reverse bias) and low-voltage drop (0.5 to 0.7 volt) the other way (forward bias).

Open or shorted diodes must be replaced. Most generators group or combine all positive and all negative diodes in the one replaceable rectifier component. General Motors Delcotron generators use a replaceable rectifier bridge containing all six diodes in one unit combined with a finned heat sink. Some Ford and other generators also use six diodes in a single replaceable bridge.

Heavy-duty AC generators often double the diodes (two positive and two negative) at each phase lead. Sharing the output current allows the diodes to run cooler. A total of 12 diodes are used.

Testing the Internal Voltage Regulator

Even though the voltage regulator can be tested on the vehicle with the engine running, the internal voltage regulator can also be tested using a special tester. See Figure 17–45.

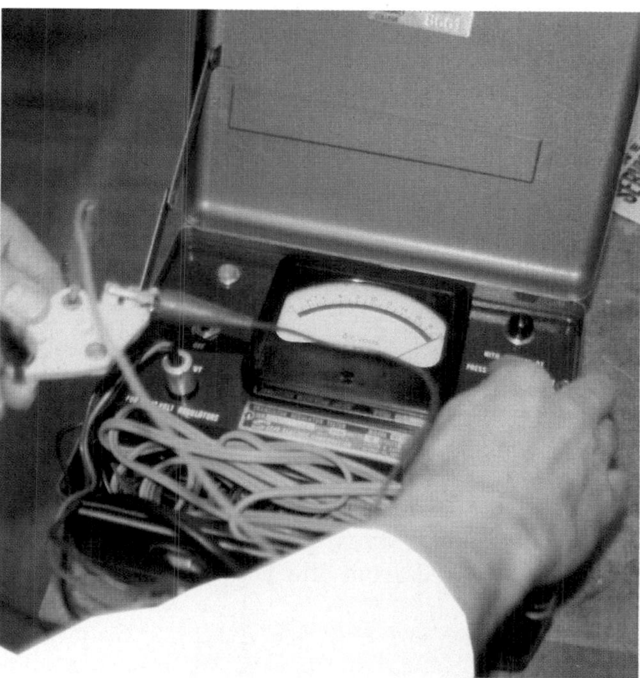

Figure 17–45 Testing an internal voltage regulator (off the vehicle) using a voltage regulator tester. This tester can be used to test most internal and external electronic voltage regulators by using the appropriate adapter harness and test leads.

Brush Holder Replacement

Generator carbon brushes often last for many years and require no scheduled maintenance. The life of the generator brushes is extended because they conduct only the field (rotor) current, which is normally only 2 to 5 amperes. The generator brushes should be inspected whenever the generator is disassembled and should be replaced when worn to less than 13 mm (1/2 in.) in length. Generator brushes are spring loaded, and if the springs are corroded or damaged, the brushes will not be able to keep constant contact with the slip rings of the rotor. If the brushes do not contact the slip rings, field current cannot create the magnetic field in the rotor that is necessary for current generation. Brushes are commonly purchased assembled together in a brush holder. After the brushes are installed (usually retained by two or three screws) and the rotor is installed in the generator housing, a brush retainer pin can be pulled out through an access hole in the rear of the generator, allowing the brushes to be pressed against the slip rings by the brush springs.

Bearing Service and Replacement

The bearings of a generator must be able to support the rotor, reduce friction, and withstand the forces created by the drive belt. The crankshaft pulley is much larger than the generator pulley; this difference in ratio causes the generator to rotate at up to 15 000 rpm. The front bearing is usually a ball bearing type, and the rear is a smaller roller bearing. The front bearing is located under a retainer and pressed into the front generator case. The pulley must be removed before the rotor can be separated from the case. Generator pulleys are either (a) pressed on the rotor and require a puller for removal, or (b) held in place with a large nut.

The old or defective bearing can sometimes be pushed out of the front housing and the replacement pushed in by applying pressure with a socket or pipe against the outer edge of the bearing (outer race). Replacement bearings are usually prelubricated and sealed. Many generator front bearings must be removed from the rotor using a special puller.

GENERATOR ASSEMBLY

After testing or servicing, the generator rectifier(s), regulator, stator, and brush holder must be reassembled. If the brushes are internally mounted, insert a wire through the holes in the brush holder and in the generator rear frame to retain the brushes for reassembly. Install the rotor and front-end frame in proper alignment with the mark made on the outside of the generator housing. Install the through-bolts. Before removing the wire pin holding the brushes, spin the generator pulley. If the generator is noisy or not rotating freely, the generator can easily be disassembled again to check for the cause. After making certain the generator is free to rotate, remove the brush holder pin and spin the generator again by hand. The noise level may be slightly higher with the brushes released onto the slip rings.

Generators should be tested on a bench tester, if available, before they are reinstalled on a vehicle. When installing the generator on the vehicle, be certain that all mounting bolts and nuts are tight. The battery terminal should be covered with a plastic or rubber protective cap to help prevent accidental shorting to ground, which could seriously damage the generator.

Remanufactured Generators

Remanufactured or rebuilt generators are totally disassembled and rebuilt. Even though there are many smaller rebuilders who may not replace all worn parts, the major national remanufacturers *totally* remanufacture the generator. Old generators (called cores) are totally disassembled and cleaned. Both bearings are replaced and all components tested. Rotors are rewound to original specifications if required. The rotor windings are not counted but are rewound on the rotor spool, using the correct-gauge copper wire, to the *weight* specified by the original manufacturer. New slip rings are replaced as required and soldered to the rotor spool windings and machined. The rotors are also balanced and measured to ensure that the outside diameter of the rotor meets specifications. An undersized rotor will produce less generator output because the field must be close to the stator windings for maximum output. *Individual* diodes (within the rectifiers) are replaced if required. Every generator is then assembled and tested for proper output, boxed, and shipped to a warehouse. Individual parts stores (called jobbers) purchase these parts from various regional or local warehouses. See Figure 17–46.

DIAGNOSTIC STORY 

The 2-Minute Generator Repair

A Chevrolet pickup truck was brought to a dealer for routine service. The owner stated that the battery required a jump-start after a weekend of sitting. Almost immediately, the technician who was assigned to service the truck found a slightly loose generator belt. The belt felt tight (less than 13 mm [½ in.] of deflection), yet the generator cooling fan blade could be turned by hand. After retensioning the generator drive belt, the technician tested the battery and charging system voltage using a small handheld digital multimeter. The battery voltage was 12.4 volts (about 75% charged), but the charging voltage was also 12.4 volts at 2000 rpm. Because normal charging voltage should be 13.5 to 15.0 volts, it was obvious that the charging system was not operating correctly.

The technician checked the dash and found that the "charge" light was *not* on, even though the rear bearing was *not* magnetized, indicating that the voltage regulator was not working. Before removing the generator for service, the technician checked the wiring connection on the generator. When the two-lead regulator connector was removed, the connector was discovered to be rusty. After the contacts were cleaned, the charging system was restored to normal operation. The technician had learned that the simple things should always be checked first before tearing into a big (or expensive) repair.

(a)

(b)

Figure 17–46 (a) A generator for a GEO Prizm looks like a typical General Motors CS-130 except for this adapter that converted the Toyota wiring harness to the GM generator. (b) After removing the adapter, the original generator connection is visible.

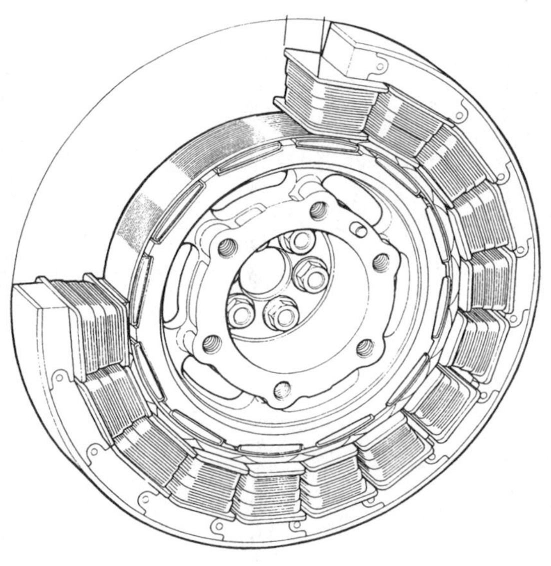

The electric-motor component of the integrated motor assist system consists of an ultra-thin 58.4 mm (2.3-inch-wide) permanent-magnet electric motor with a maximum output of 10 kW, which provides power assistance to the gasoline engine. It also functions as a starter motor for the idle-stop feature, and as a generator for the IMA system and batteries.

Figure 17–47 Honda Integrated Motor Assist (IMA) system. (Courtesy Honda Motor Co.)

COMBINATION STARTER-GENERATORS

Hybrid vehicles often combine the charging system and the starting motor in one single assembly. This unit may be enclosed in the bell housing or mounted with the transaxle. No belts are required as the starter-generator has a direct drive from the engine or drive train. See Figure 17–47. The European Peugeot Citroen uses an external 14 volt belt-driven starter-generator. A limited number of domestic vehicles began using starter-generators in 2005.

PHOTO SEQUENCE 14 Generator Overhaul

P14–1 The first step is to remove the drive pulley and spacers. This rebuilder is using an electric impact wrench to accomplish the task. Inspect the pulley for damage or embedded rubber.

P14–2 Next pop off the plastic cover (shield) covering the stator/rectifier connection.

P14–3 Using a diagonal cutter, cut the weld to separate the stator from the rectifier.

P14–4 The drive-end housing and the stator are being separated from the rear (slip-ring end) housing. Both halves should be marked for location before disassembly.

P14–5 After removing the stator from the drive-end housing, it is checked by visual inspection for discolouration or other physical damage, and then checked with an ohmmeter to see if the windings are shorted to ground.

P14–6 After the plastic shield has been removed, the rectifier, regulator, and brush holder assembly can be removed by removing the retaining screws.

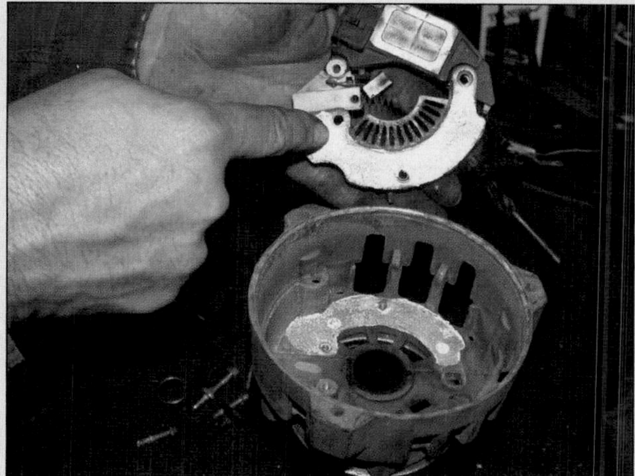

P14–7 The heat transfer grease is visible when the rectifier assembly is lifted out of the rear housing.

P14–8 The slip rings on the rotor are being machined on a lathe.

P14–9 The rotor is being tested using an ohmmeter. The specifications for the resistance between the slip rings on this CS-130 is 2.2 to 3.5 Ω.

P14–10 The rotor is also tested between the slip ring and the rotor shaft. This reading should be infinity. If there was continuity between the slip ring and the shaft, the rotor windings are shorted to ground and the rotor should be replaced.

P14–11 A new rectifier. This replacement unit is significantly different than the original but is designed to replace the original unit and meets the original factory specifications.

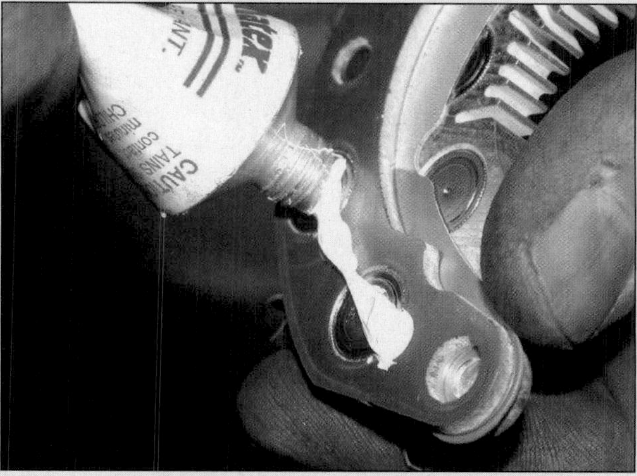

P14–12 Silicone heat transfer compound is applied to the heat sink of the new rectifier.

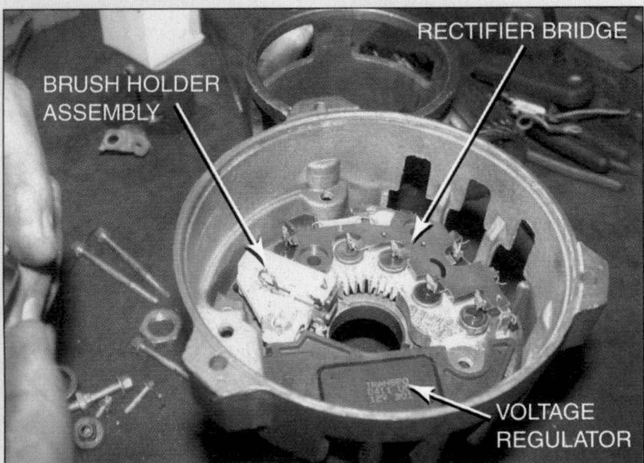

P14–13 Here is what the CS generator looks like after installing the new brush holder assembly, rectifier bridge, and voltage regulator.

P14–14 The junction between the rectifier bridge and the voltage regulator is soldered.

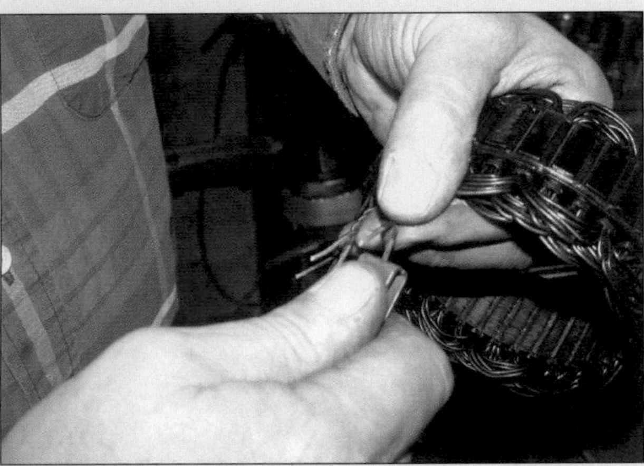

P14–15 Before the stator windings can be soldered to the rectifier bridge, the varnish insulation is removed from the ends of the leads.

P14–16 After the stator has been inserted into the rear housing, the stator leads are soldered to the copper lugs of the rectifier bridge.

P14–17 The slip ring end (SRE) housing is aligned with the marks made during disassembly and is pressed into the drive end (DE) housing.

P14–18 The external fan and drive pulley are installed and the retaining nut is tightened on the rotor shaft. A final bench test is performed with a generator tester.

SUMMARY

1. Charging system testing requires that the battery be at least 75% charged to be assured of accurate test results. The charge indicator light should be on with the ignition switch on, but should go out whenever the engine is running. Normal charging voltage (at 2000 engine rpm) is 13.5 to 15.0 volts.
2. If the charging system is not charging properly, the rear bearing of the generator should be checked for magnetism. If the rear bearing is magnetized, the voltage regulator, brushes, and generator rotor are functioning correctly. If the rear bearing is not magnetized, the voltage regulator, generator brushes, or rotor is not functioning. Bypass the voltage regulator. If the rear bearing is now magnetized and the charging system output is normal, the voltage regulator is at fault.
3. To check for excessive resistance in the wiring between the generator and the battery, a voltage-drop test should be performed.
4. Electricity is lazy, because it always travels the path of least resistance. Generators are also lazy, because they do not produce their maximum-rated output unless required by circuit demands. Therefore, to test for maximum generator output, the battery must be loaded to force the generator to produce its maximum output.
5. Each generator should be marked across its case before disassembly to ensure proper clock position during reassembly. After disassembly, all generator internal components should be tested using a continuity light or an ohmmeter. The following components should be tested:
    a. Stator
    b. Rotor
    c. Diodes
    d. Diode trio (if the generator is so equipped)
    e. Bearings
    f. Brushes (should be more than 13 mm (½ in.) in length)
6. Electronic voltage regulators can be tested either off the vehicle using a special tester or on the vehicle using the full-field bypass procedure.
7. Automotive engineers are considering using the hybrid bell housing mounted starter-generator on conventional vehicles. This would eliminate all drive belts if combined with electric air conditioning compressors and power steering.

REVIEW QUESTIONS

1. Describe how a small electronic voltage regulator can control the output of a typical 100 ampere generator.
2. Describe how to test the voltage drop of the charging circuit.
3. Discuss how to measure the current output of a generator.
4. Explain how testing can be used to determine whether a diode or stator is defective before removing the generator from the vehicle.

RED SEAL CERTIFICATION-TYPE QUESTIONS

1. AC generators control output voltage by
    a. The design of the stator coils
    b. Regulating the field current
    c. Limiting the maximum rotor RPM
    d. Full-fielding the rotor
2. A magnetic field is created in the _____ in a generator (AC generator).
    a. Stator
    b. Diodes
    c. Rotor
    d. Drive-end frame
3. The voltage regulator controls the current _____.
    a. To the generator stator terminal
    b. At the diode trio
    c. To the stator windings
    d. Through the brushes and rotor
4. Four diodes are used for each stator phase lead on a heavy-duty wye-connected generator. The total number of diodes would be
    a. 6
    b. 8
    c. 12
    d. 16
5. An acceptable charging circuit voltage on a 12 volt system is _____.
    a. 13.5 to 15.0 volts
    b. 12.6 to 15.6 volts
    c. 12 to 14 volts
    d. 14.9 to 16.1 volts
6. Full-fielding an A circuit generator requires
    a. Grounding the field lead before the rotor
    b. Powering the field lead after the rotor
    c. Grounding the field lead after the rotor
    d. Applying battery voltage to the field terminal
7. Voltage-drop testing of the charging circuit must be performed when _________ amperes are flowing through the circuit.
    a. 20
    b. 0
    c. 40
    d. Maximum
8. When a generator rotor is checked, if an ohmmeter shows zero ohms between the slip rings and the rotor shaft, the rotor is _____.
    a. Okay (normal)
    b. Defective (shorted to ground)
    c. Defective (shorted to voltage)
    d. Okay (rotor windings are open)

9. A generator diode is being tested using a digital multimeter set to the diode check position. A good diode will read _____ if the leads are connected one way across the diode and _____ if the leads are reversed.
   a. 300; 300
   b. 0.575; 0.575
   c. OL; OL
   d. 0.651; OL

10. A generator (AC generator) could test as producing lower-than-normal output, yet be okay, if _____.
   a. A delta-wound stator is used
   b. A high-output generator is installed
   c. The regulator full-fields the rotor
   d. The engine speed is not high enough during testing

18

Lighting and Signalling Circuit Operation and Diagnosis

OBJECTIVES: After studying Chapter 18, you should be able to:

1. Prepare for the interprovincial Red Seal certification examination in Appendix III (Electrical/Electronic Systems) on the topics covered in this chapter.
2. Determine which replacement bulb to use on a given vehicle.
3. Describe how turn signals work.
4. Use a bulb chart.
5. Discuss troubleshooting procedures for lighting and signalling circuits.

The lighting and signalling circuits represent two of the most frequently serviced automotive electrical areas.

LIGHTING

Exterior lighting is controlled by the headlight switch, which is connected directly to the battery on most vehicles. Therefore, if lights are left on, it can drain the battery. Many headlight switches contain a built-in circuit breaker. If excessive current flows through the headlight circuit, the circuit breaker will momentarily open the circuit, then close it again. The result is headlights that flicker on and off rapidly.

Some imported vehicles do not use circuit breakers; there are separate fused circuits for the left and right headlights. A short circuit will blow one fuse and the headlight will go out; however, the opposite side will still remain functional.

NOTE: Headlights flickering on and off is misunderstood by many drivers and technicians. Because the flickering is rapid, many people believe that the problem is caused by a loose headlight or by a defective voltage regulator.

These features allow the headlights to function, as a safety measure, in spite of current overload. The headlight switch controls the following lights on most vehicles:

1. Headlights
2. Taillights
3. Side marker lights
4. Front parking lights
5. Dash lights
6. Interior (dome) light(s)

NOTE: Because these lights can easily drain the battery if accidentally left on, many newer vehicles control these lights through the vehicle's computer. The computer keeps track of the time the lights are on (ignition switch off) and can turn them off if the time is excessive. The computer can control either the power side or the ground side of the circuit.

BULB NUMBERS

The number used on automotive bulbs is called the bulb **trade number,** as recorded with the American National Standards Institute (ANSI), and the number is the same regardless of the manufacturer. Amber-colour bulbs that use natural amber glass are indicated with an NA for *natural amber* at the end of the number (for example, #1157NA). A less expensive amber bulb that uses painted glass is labelled A for *amber* (for example, #1157A). See Figure 18–1.

Figure 18–1 Bulbs that have the same trade number have the same operating voltage and wattage. The NA means that the bulb uses a natural amber glass ampoule for use with clear turn signal lenses.

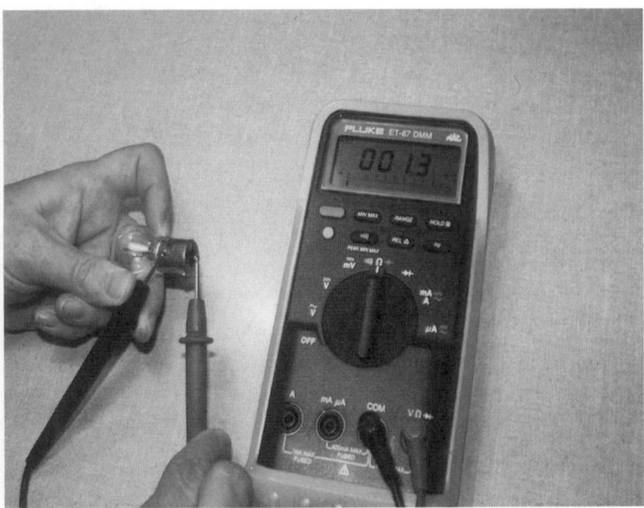

Figure 18–2 This single-filament bulb is being tested with a digital multimeter set to read resistance in ohms. The reading of 1.3 ohms is the resistance of the bulb when cold. As soon as current flows through the filament, the resistance increases about 10 times. It is the initial surge of current flowing through the filament when the bulb is cool that causes many bulbs to fail in cold weather as a result of the reduced resistance. As the temperature increases, the resistance increases.

The trade number also identifies the size, shape, number of filaments, and amount of light produced. The amount of light produced is measured in **candlepower.** For example, the candlepower of a #1156 bulb, commonly used for backup lights, is 32. A #194 bulb, commonly used for dash or side marker lights, is rated at only 2 candlepower. The amount of light produced by a bulb is determined by the resistance of the filament wire, which also affects the amount of current (in amperes) required by the bulb. See Figures 18–2 and 18–3.

It is important that the correct trade number of bulb always be used for replacement to prevent circuit or component damage. It is common practice to apply a very light coating of silicone dielectric grease to the bottom of metal-based bulbs; this retards corrosion. The correct replacement bulb for your vehicle is usually listed in the owner's manual or service manual. See Figure 18–4 and the bulb chart.

Typical Automotive Light Bulbs

Trade Number	Design Volts	Design Amperes	Watts: $P = I \times E$
37	14.0	0.09	1.3
37E	14.0	0.09	1.3
51	7.5	0.22	1.7
53	14.4	0.12	1.7
55	7.0	0.41	2.9
57	14.0	0.24	3.4
57X	14.0	0.24	3.4

(continued)

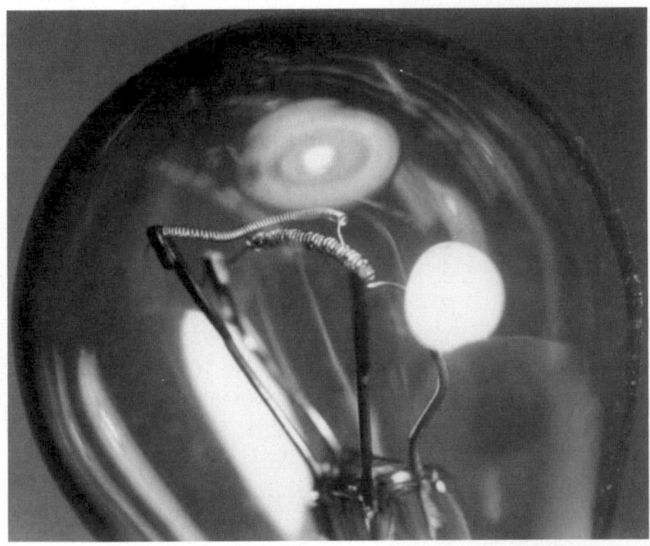

Figure 18–3 Close-up of a dual-filament (double filament) bulb (#1157) that failed. Notice that one filament (top) broke from its mounting and melted onto the lower filament. This bulb caused the dash lights to come on whenever the brakes were applied.

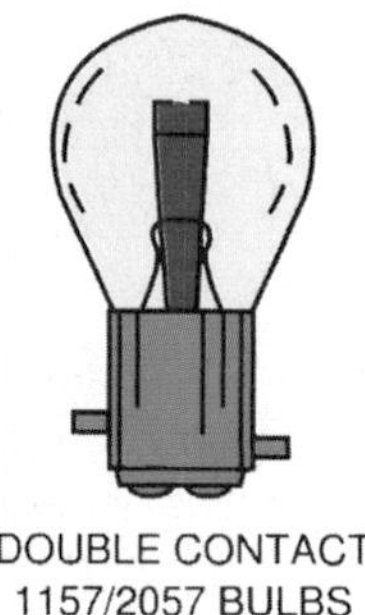

Figure 18–4 Bulbs #1157 or #2057 are typically used for taillight and front parking lights. These bulbs contain both a low-intensity filament for taillights or parking lights and a high-intensity filament for brake lights and turn signals.

Trade Number	Design Volts	Design Amperes	Watts: P = I × E
63	7.0	0.63	4.4
67	13.5	0.59	8.0
68	13.5	0.59	8.0
70	14.0	0.15	2.1
73	14.0	0.08	1.1
74	14.0	0.10	1.4
81	6.5	1.02	6.6
88	13.0	0.58	7.5
89	13.0	0.58	7.5
90	13.0	0.58	7.5
93	12.8	1.04	13.3
94	12.8	1.04	13.3
158	14.0	0.24	3.4
161	14.0	0.19	2.7
168	14.0	0.35	4.9
192	13.0	0.33	4.3
194	14.0	0.27	3.8
194E-1	14.0	0.27	3.8
194NA	14.0	0.27	3.8
209	6.5	1.78	11.6
211-2	12.8	0.97	12.4
212-2	13.5	0.74	10.0
214-2	13.5	0.52	7.0

Trade Number	Design Volts	Design Amperes	Watts: P = I × E
561	12.8	0.97	12.4
562	13.5	0.74	10.0
563	13.5	0.52	7.0
631	14.0	0.63	8.8
880	12.8	2.10	27.0
881	12.8	2.10	27.0
906	13.0	0.69	9.0
912	12.8	1.00	12.8
1003	12.8	0.94	12.0
1004	12.8	0.94	12.0
1034	12.8	1.80/0.59	23.0/7.6
1073	12.8	1.80	23.0
1076	12.8	1.80	23.0
1129	6.4	2.63	16.8
1133	6.2	3.91	24.2
1141	12.8	1.44	18.4
1142	12.8	1.44	18.4
1154	6.4	2.63/0.75	16.8/4.5
1156	12.8	2.10	26.9
1157	12.8	2.10/0.59	26.9/7.6
1157A	12.8	2.10/0.59	26.9/7.6
1157NA	12.8	2.10/0.59	26.9/7.6
1176	12.8	1.34/0.59	17.2/7.6
1195	12.5	3.00	37.5
1196	12.5	3.00	37.5
1445	14.4	0.13	1.9
1816	13.0	0.33	4.3
1889	14.0	0.27	3.8
1891	14.0	0.24	3.4
1892	14.4	0.12	1.7
1893	14.0	0.33	4.6
1895	14.0	0.27	3.8
2033	13.5	0.22	3.0
2057	12.8	2.10/0.48	26.9/6.1
2057NA	12.8	2.10/0.48	26.9/6.1
2322-1	12.0	0.16	2.0
2721	12.0	0.10	1.2
2821	12.0	4.00	3.0
2825	12.0	0.42	5.0
3057	12.8	0.16	2.1
3157	12.0	1.10	12.8

(continued)

Trade Number	Design Volts	Design Amperes	Watts: $P = I \times E$
3796	12.0	6.00	2.0
3893	12.0	3.00	4.0
3894	12.0	4.00	3.0
3898	12.0	6.00	2.0
3966	12.0	4.00	3.0
5004	12.0	4.00	3.0
5006	6.0	1.20	5.0
5007	12.0	2.40	5.0
5008	12.0	1.20	10.0
6418	12.0	0.42	5.0
6428	12.0	0.25	3.0
6461	12.0	0.83	10.0
7230	12.0	2.40	5.0
7301	12.0	3.75	45.0
7309	12.0	2.92	35.0
7506	12.0	0.60	21.0
7527	12.0	0.69	18.0
7528	12.0	2.40	5.0
7533	12.0	0.80	15.0
9004 H*	12.8	5.00/35.00	65.0/45.0
9005 H^+	12.8	5.00	65.0
9006 H^	12.8	4.30	55.0
26736	12.0	0.83	10.0
64150 H1	12.0	4.50	55.0
64151 H3	12.0	4.50	55.0
64152 H1	12.0	8.30	100.0
64153 H3	12.0	8.30	100.0
64173 H2	12.0	4.50	55.0
64174 H2	12.0	8.30	100.0
64185 H4	12.0	2.90	35.0
64193 H4	12.0	5.00	60.0
P25-1	13.5	1.86	25.1
P25-2	13.5	1.86	25.1
R19/5	13.5	0.37	5.1
R19/10	13.5	0.74	10.0
W10/3	13.5	0.25	3.4

DIAGNOSTIC STORY

Weird Problem—Easy Solution

A minivan had the following electrical problems:

- The turn signals flash rapidly on the left side.
- With the ignition key off, the lights-on warning chime sounds if the brake pedal is depressed.
- When the brake pedal is depressed, the dome light comes on.

All of these problems were caused by just one defective 2057 dual-filament bulb shown in Figure 18–5. Apparently, the two filaments were electrically connected through the corrosion observed between the terminals of the bulb. This caused the electrical current to feed back from the brake light filament into the taillight circuit causing all the problems. See Figure 18–6 for another example of a weird bulb problem.

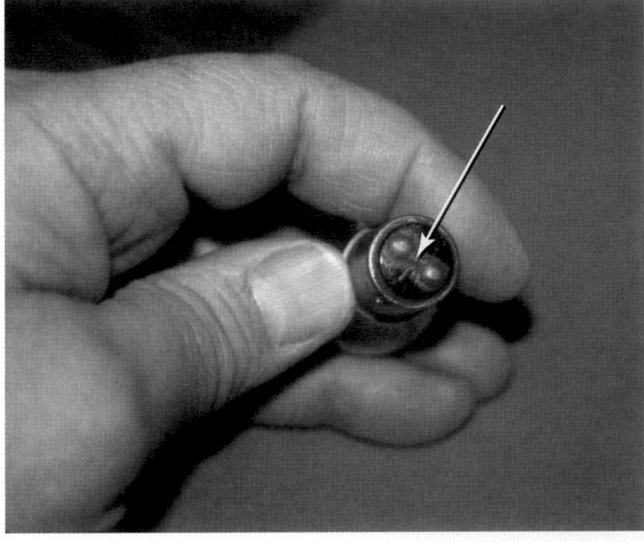

Figure 18–5 Corrosion caused the two terminals of this dual-filament bulb to be electrically connected.

BRAKE LIGHTS

Brake lights use the high-intensity filament of a double-filament bulb. (The lower intensity filament is for the taillights.) The brake light switch is a normally open (N.O.) switch but is closed when the driver depresses the brake pedal. All vehicles now sold in Canada and the U.S. have a third brake light commonly referred to as the **centre high-mounted**

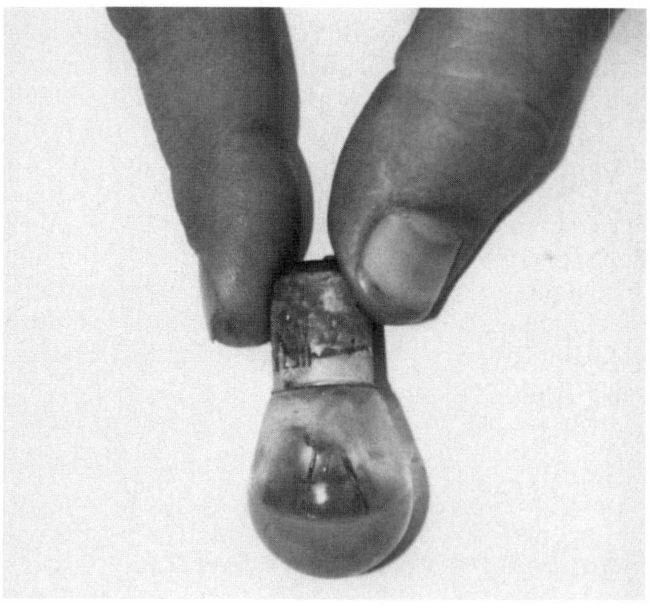

Figure 18–6 Often the best diagnosis is a thorough visual inspection. This bulb was found to be filled with water, causing weird problems.

TECH TIP 

No Cruise Control? Check the Third Brake Light

A common cause of an inoperative cruise control, especially on General Motors vehicles, is a burned-out bulb in the third stop light. The cruise control uses the filaments of the third brake bulb as a ground and shuts off the cruise if the bulbs are burned out (open). See Figure 18–7.

stop light (CHMSL). The brake switch is also used as an input switch (signal) for the following:

1. Cruise control (deactivates when the brake pedal is depressed)
2. Antilock brakes (ABS)
3. Brake shift interlock (prevents shifting from "park" position unless the brake pedal is depressed)

HOT IN RUN, BULB TEST OR START
SEE POWER DISTRIBUTION
TURN B/U FUSE 20 AMP
FUSE BLOCK
1 DK BLK
75
BACK UP LIGHTS
1 DK BLU 75
H3 C205 (NOT USED)
TURN FLASHER
.8 PPL 16
L
PPL 16
HOT AT ALL TIMES
SEE POWER DISTRUBUTION
STOP HAZ FUSE 20 AMP
FUSE BLOCK
.8 ORN 140
.5 ORN 140
CONVENIENCE CENTER
HAZARD FLASHER
W
V
.8 BRN 27
K C201
BRN 27
BRAKE SWITCH CLOSED WITH BRAKE PEDAL DEPRESSED
.8 LT BLU/BLK 820
M C204
.8 LT BLU/BLK 820
A C324
.8 LT BLU 820
A C318
HIGH LEVEL STOP LIGHT
B C318
.8 BLK 150
B C324
1 BLK 150
S317
1 WHT 17
HAZARD SWITCH
NORMAL
HAZARD
TURN/HAZARD SWITCH
WHT P
17 C201
H LT BLU
C201 14
.8 LT BLU 14
DK GRN 19
M N C201
.8 YEL 18
.8 DK GRN 19
D E C204
1 YEL 18
1 DK GRN 19
A C325
1 YEL 18
1 DK GRN 19
1 YEL 18
1 DK GRN 19
DK BLU 15
J C201
.8 DK BLU 15
LH LH RH RH
TAIL/STOP-TURN LIGHTS
STOP-TURN TAIL
.8 BLK 150
.8 BLK
S403 S404
.3 BLK 150
C C325
150 SEE GROUND DISTRIBUTION
SEE GROUND DISTRIBUTION
G200
A
B

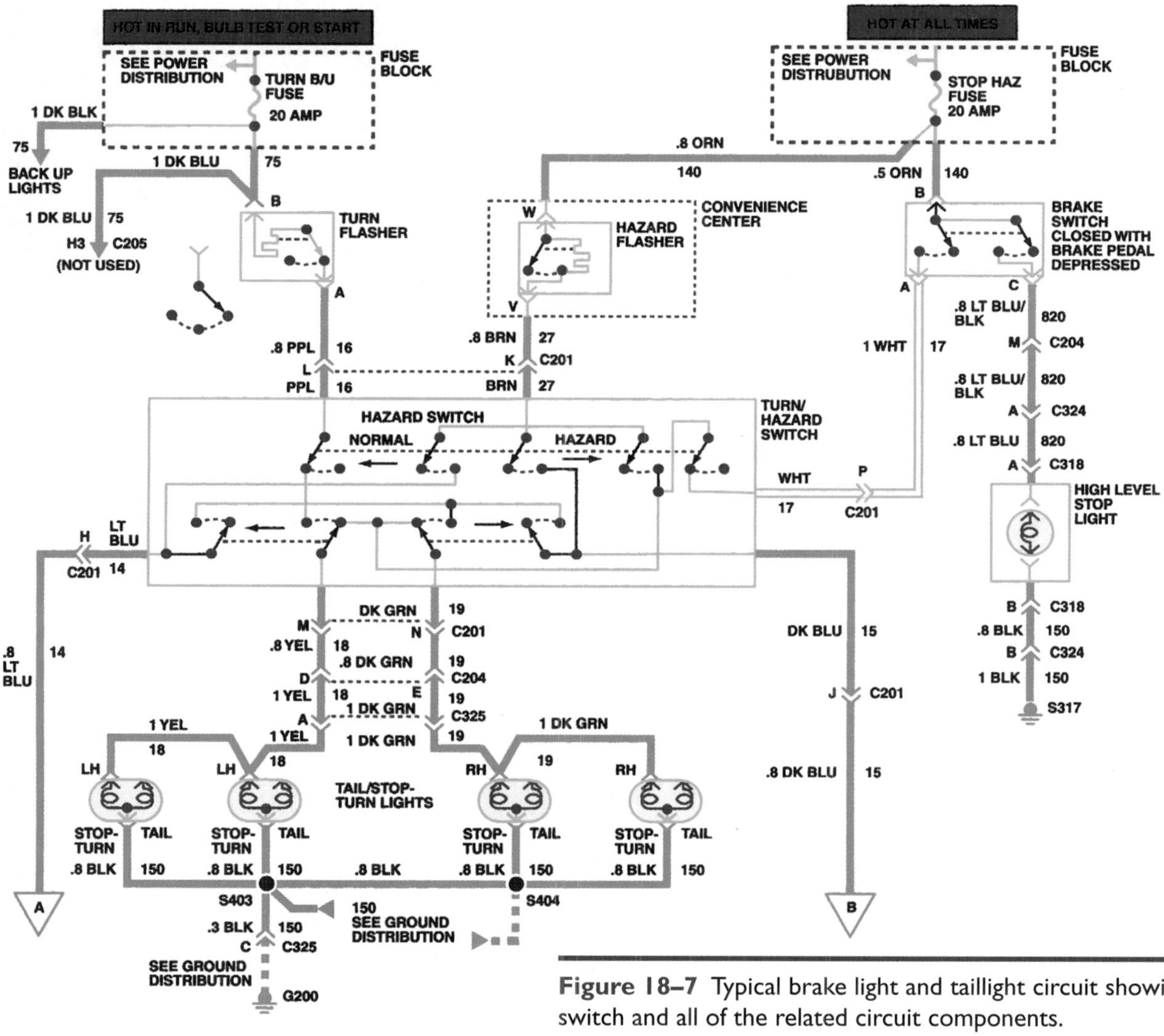

Figure 18–7 Typical brake light and taillight circuit showing the brake switch and all of the related circuit components.

HEADLIGHT SWITCHES

The headlight switch operates the exterior and interior lights of most vehicles. The headlight switch is connected directly to the battery through a fusible link and has continuous power or is "hot" all the time. A circuit breaker is built into many headlight switches to protect the headlight circuit. See Figure 18–8. The interior dash lights can be dimmed manually by rotating the headlight switch knob, which controls a variable resistor (called a **rheostat**) built into the headlight switch.

The rheostat drops the voltage sent to the dash lights. Whenever there is a voltage drop (increased resistance), there is heat. A coiled resistance wire is built into a ceramic holder that is designed to insulate the rest of the switch from the heat and allow heat to escape. Continual driving with the dash lights dimmed can result in the headlight switch knob getting hot to the touch. This is normal, and the best prevention is to increase the brightness of the dash lights to reduce the amount of heat generated in the switch. The headlight switch also contains a built-in circuit breaker that will rapidly turn the headlights on and off in the event of a short circuit. This prevents a total loss of headlights. If the headlights are rapidly flashing on and off, check the entire headlight circuit for possible shorts. The circuit breaker controls only the headlights. The other lights controlled by the headlight switch (taillights, dash lights, and parking lights) are fused separately. Flashing headlights may also be caused by a failure in the built-in circuit breaker, requiring replacement of the switch assembly.

Headlights on imported vehicles with separate fused circuits do not flash; when a fuse blows, one headlight will go out.

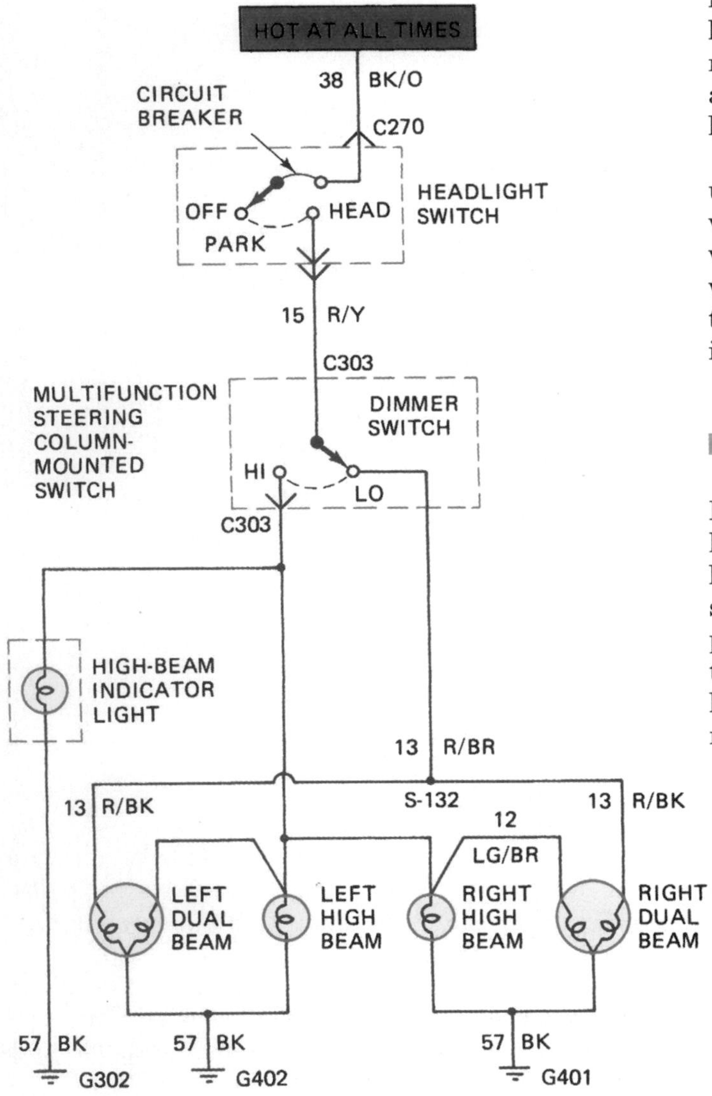

Figure 18–8 Typical headlight circuit diagram. Note that the headlight switch is represented by a dotted outline indicating that other circuits (such as dash lights) also operate from the switch.

Removing a Headlight Switch

Most dash-mounted headlight switches can be removed by first removing the dash panel. However, to get the dash panel off, the headlight switch knob usually has to be removed. Some knobs can be removed by depressing a small clip in a notch in the knob itself. Other headlight switch knobs are removed by depressing a spring-loaded release, which allows for removal of the entire headlight switch knob and shaft as shown in Figure 18–9.

Headlight switches mounted on the steering column are removed as part of the turn signal and wiper switch assembly. Many can be easily removed, whereas others require the removal of the steering wheel and so forth. See the service information for the exact year and model on which you are working in order to be assured of the correct procedure.

SEALED-BEAM HEADLIGHTS

Low-beam headlights contain two filaments: one for low beam and the other for high beam. High-beam headlights contain only one filament. Headlights are standardized so that sealed-beam units that can be purchased at most auto parts stores can replace them. Because low-beam headlights also contain a high-beam filament, the entire headlight assembly must be replaced if either filament is defective.

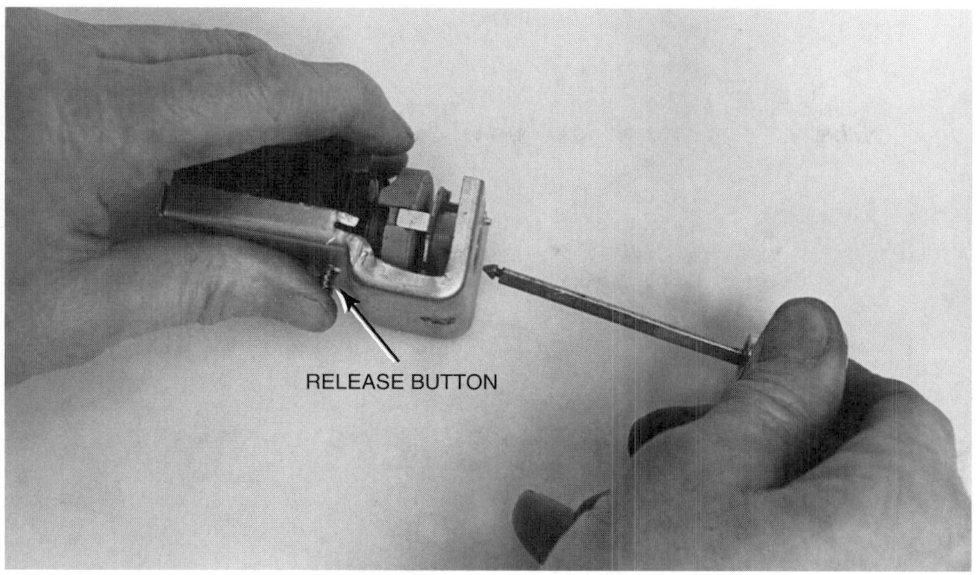

Figure 18–9 To remove the headlight switch from an older vehicle that uses a knob and shaft, a release button has to be pushed to release the shaft. After the knob and shaft assembly has been removed, then the retaining nut can be removed from the headlight switch so it can be removed from the dash.

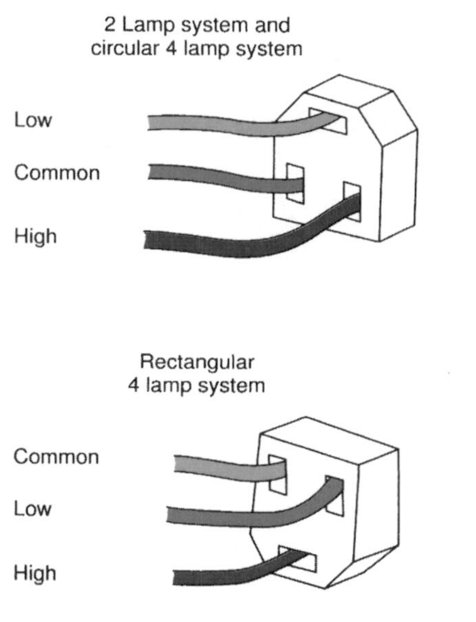

Figure 18–10 Typical headlight socket connections. Some vehicles may be different. The high- and low-beam connections must be determined by visual inspection.

A sealed-beam headlight can be tested with an ohmmeter. A good bulb should indicate low ohms between the ground terminal and both power-side (hot) terminals. If either the high-beam or the low-beam filament is burned out, the ohmmeter will indicate infinity (OL). See Figure 18–10.

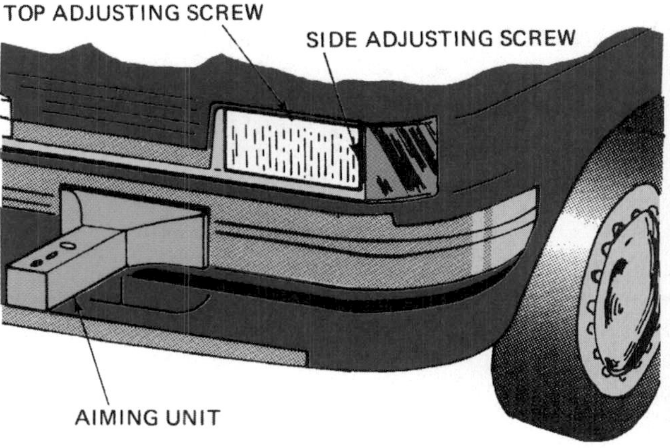

Figure 18–11 All vehicles sold in Canada and the U.S. must have provision for the use of mechanical aiming devices. Even the halogen bulb units with plastic or glass lenses have locating points and adjustment screws.

HEADLIGHT AIMING

According to Canadian and U.S. federal law, all headlights, regardless of shape, must be able to be aimed using headlight-aiming equipment. See Figures 18–11 through 18–13.

Moveable headlights that turn while cornering are being used on a few high-end vehicles. They improve road surface illumination while turning and allow the driver to "see around the corner."

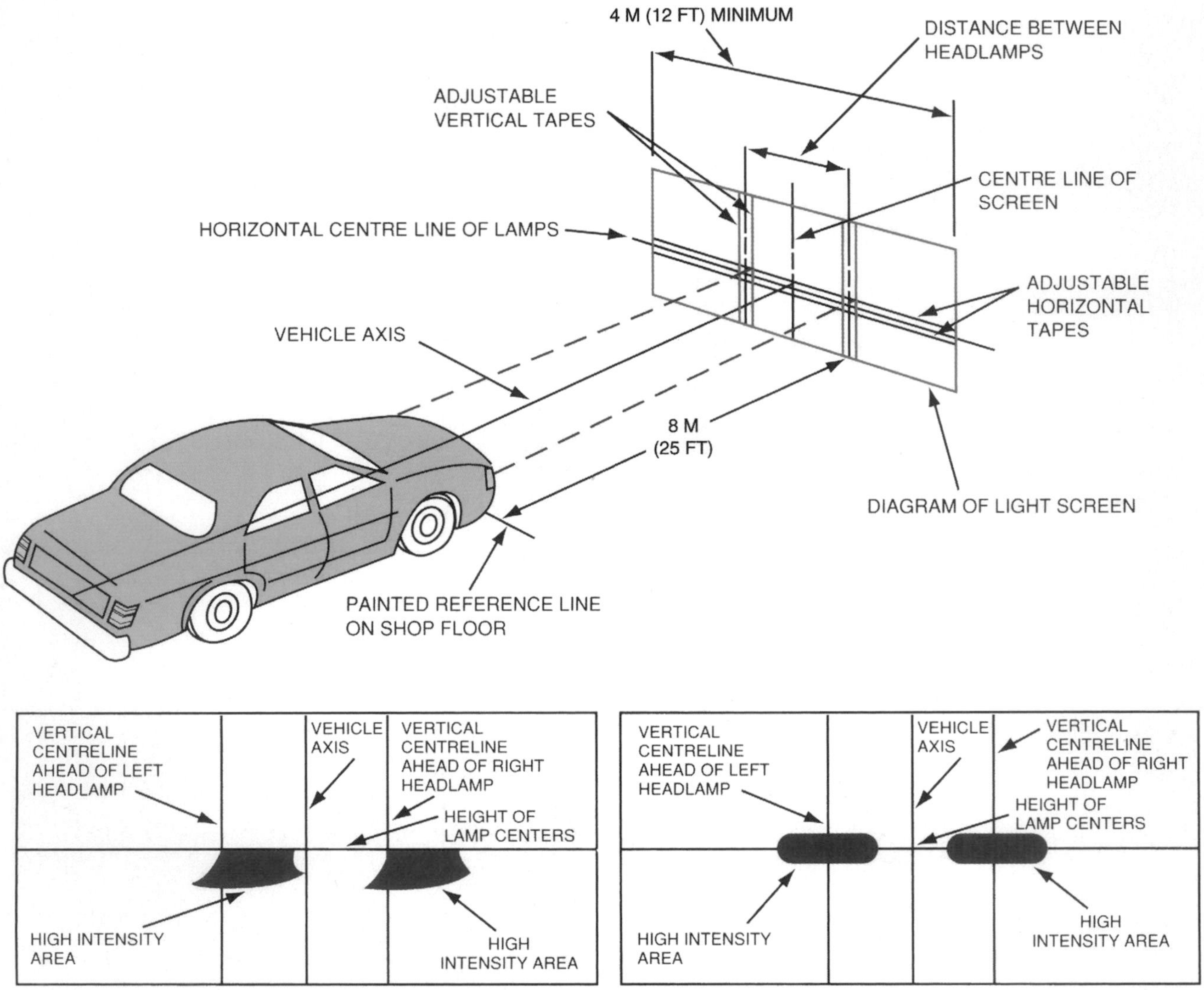

Figure 18–12 Typical headlight-aiming diagram as found in a service manual.

Figure 18–13 Many composite headlights have a built-in bubble level to make aiming easy and accurate.

COMPOSITE HEADLIGHTS

Composite headlights are constructed using a replaceable bulb and a fixed lens cover that is part of the vehicle. See Figure 18–14. The replaceable bulbs are usually bright halogen bulbs. Halogen bulbs get very hot during operation (between 260° and 700°C [500° and 1300°F]). It is important never to touch the glass of any halogen bulb with bare fingers because the natural oils of the skin on the glass bulb can cause the bulb to break when it heats during normal operation.

HALOGEN SEALED-BEAM HEADLIGHTS

Halogen sealed-beam headlights are brighter and more expensive than normal headlights. Because of their extra brightness, it is common practice to have

TECH TIP

Diagnose Bulb Failure

Halogen bulbs can fail for various reasons. Some causes for halogen bulb failure and their indications are as follows:

- Gray colour—low voltage to bulb (check for corroded socket or connector)
- White (cloudy) colour—indication of an air leak
- Broken filament—usually caused by excessive vibration (see Figure 18–15)
- Blistered glass—indication that someone has touched the glass

NOTE: *Never touch the glass ampoule of any halogen bulb.* The oils from your fingers can cause unequal heating of the glass during operation, leading to a shorter-than-normal service life.

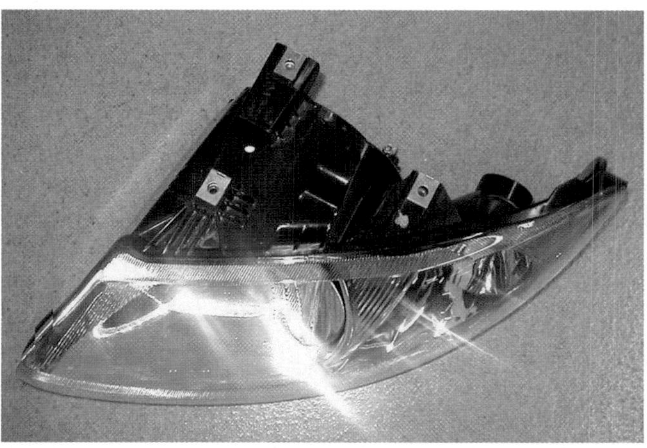

Figure 18–14 A typical composite headlamp assembly. The lens, housing, and bulb sockets are usually included as a complete assembly.

only two headlights on at any one time because the candlepower output would exceed the maximum Canadian and U.S. federal standards if all four halogen headlights were on. Therefore, before trying to repair the problem that only two of the four lamps are on, check with the owner's manual or the shop manual for proper operation.

CAUTION: Do not attempt to wire all headlights together. The extra current flow could overheat the wiring from the headlight switch through the dimmer switch and to the headlights. The overloaded circuit could cause a fire.

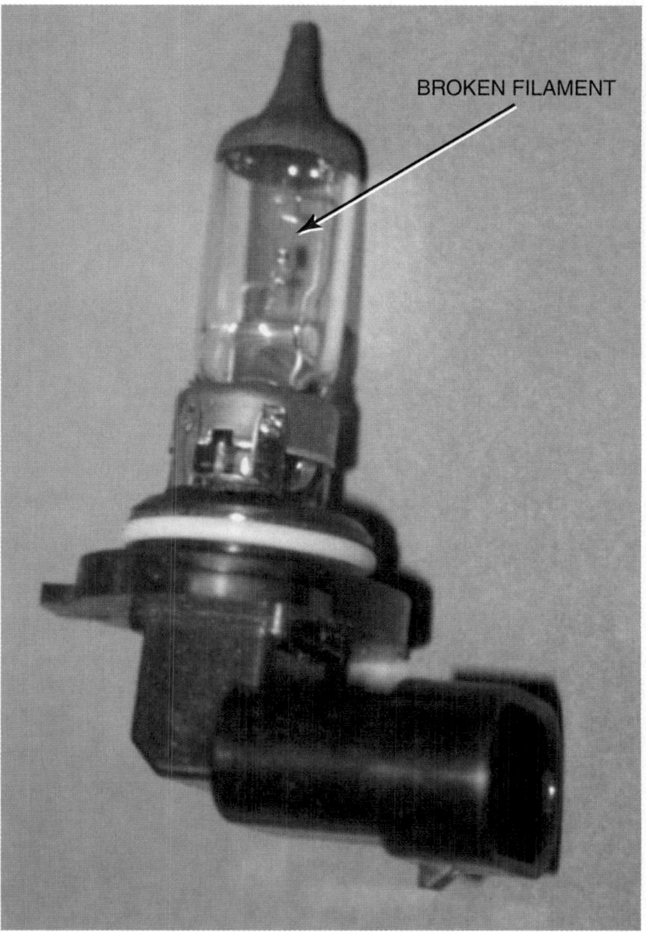

Figure 18–15 Notice the broken filament in this halogen headlight bulb.

HIGH-INTENSITY DISCHARGE HEADLIGHTS

High-intensity discharge (HID) headlights produce a distinctive blue-white light that is crisper, clearer, and brighter than light produced by a halogen headlight. Unlike a halogen bulb, the HID bulb has no filament. It creates light from an electrical discharge between two electrodes in a gas-filled arc tube. It produces twice the light with less electrical input than conventional halogen bulbs. The HID white light provides better illumination than conventional incandescent or halogen headlights; it also enhances the phosphorous printing on road signs, making them easier to read.

The HID lighting system consists of the discharge arc source, igniter, ballast, and headlight assembly. The two electrodes are contained in a tiny quartz capsule filled with xenon gas, mercury, and metal halide salts. The lights and support electronics are expensive, but they should have twice the bulb life because of filament elimination. See Figure 18–16.

Figure 18–16 HID (Xenon) headlights emit a whiter light than halogen headlights and usually look blue.

DAYTIME RUNNING LIGHTS

Daytime running lights (DRLs) involve operating front parking lights or the headlights (usually at reduced current and voltage) whenever the vehicle is running. Canada has required daytime running lights on all new vehicles since 1990. DRLs have reduced accidents where used.

Daytime running lights primarily use a control module that turns on either the low- or high-beam lamps. The lights on some vehicles come on whenever the engine starts. Some vehicles will turn on the lamps when the engine is running, but delay their operation until a signal from the vehicle speed sensor indicates that the vehicle is moving.

To avoid having the lights on during servicing, some systems will turn off the headlights whenever the parking brake is applied. Others will only light the headlights when the vehicle is in a drive gear. See Figure 18–17.

> **CAUTION:** Most factory daytime running lights operate the headlights at reduced intensity. These are *not* designed to be used at night. Normal intensity of the headlights (and operation of the other external lamps) is actuated by turning on the headlights as usual.

DIMMER SWITCHES

The headlight switch controls the power or hot side of the headlight circuit. The current is then sent to the dimmer switch, which allows current to flow to either the high-beam or the low-beam filament of the headlight bulb as shown in Figure 18–18. An indicator light lights on the dash whenever the bright lights are selected.

The dimmer switch is usually on the steering column. The steering column switches are actually attached to the *outside* of the steering column on most vehicles and are spring loaded. To replace most of these types of dimmer switches, the steering column needs to be lowered slightly to gain access to the switch itself, which is also adjustable for proper lever operation.

TURN (DIRECTIONAL) SIGNALS

A turn signal flasher unit is a metal or plastic can containing a switch that opens and closes the turn signal circuit. See Figure 18–19. This turn signal flasher unit is usually installed in a metal clip attached to the dash panel to allow the clicking noise of the flasher to be heard by the driver. The turn signal flasher is designed to transmit the current to light the front and rear bulbs on only one side at a time. Canadian and U.S. regulations require that the driver be alerted when a turn signal bulb is not working. This is achieved by using a series-type flasher unit. The flasher unit requires current flow through two bulbs (one in the front and one in the rear) in order to flash. If one bulb burns out, the current flow through only one bulb is not sufficient to make the unit flash; it will be a steady light. When the turn signal flasher unit is old, the lights will flash more slowly (both sides affected equally). The contact points inside the flasher unit may become corroded and pitted, requiring higher voltage to operate. To restore normal operation, replace the turn signal flasher unit. Other common turn signal problems and possible solutions include the following:

Problem	**Possible Causes and/ or Solutions**
1. Slow flashing on both sides equally	**1.** Replace the worn flasher unit. Check the battery and the charging voltage to be certain that the charging circuit and battery are supplying high enough voltage for proper operation of the turn signals.
2. Slow or no flashing on one side only	**2.** Replace the defective bulb, or clean poor connections on the front or rear bulbs on the side that does not work.
3. Turn signals not flashing on either side	**3.** The most likely cause is a defective flasher unit, in which case replacement will be necessary. However, defective bulbs or connections on *both* sides could also be the cause.

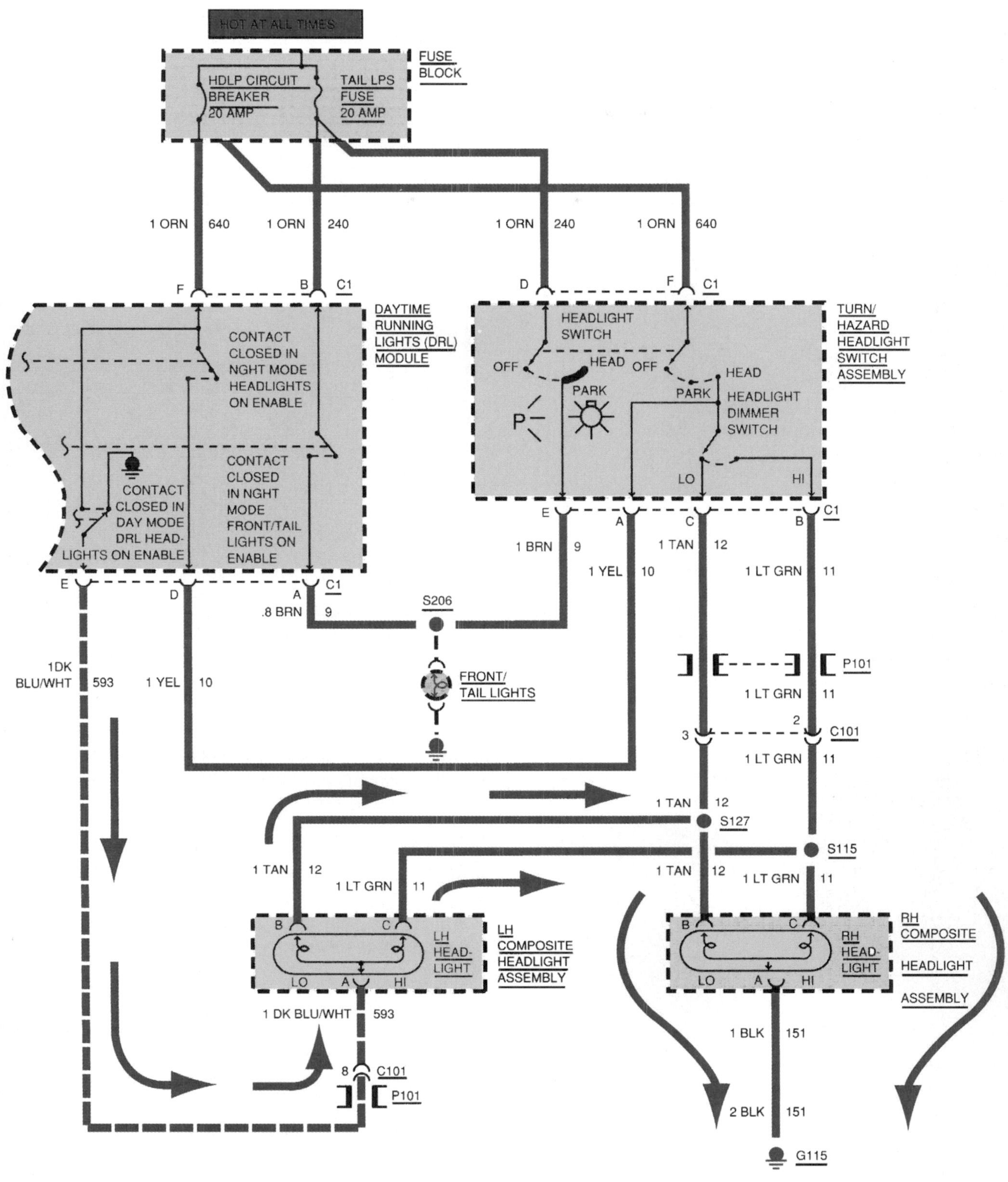

Figure 18–17 Typical daytime running light (DRL) circuit. Follow the arrows from the DRL module through both headlights. Notice that the left and right headlights are connected in series, resulting in increased resistance, less current flow, and dimmer than normal lighting. When the normal headlights are turned on, both headlights receive full battery voltage, with the left headlight grounding through the DRL module.

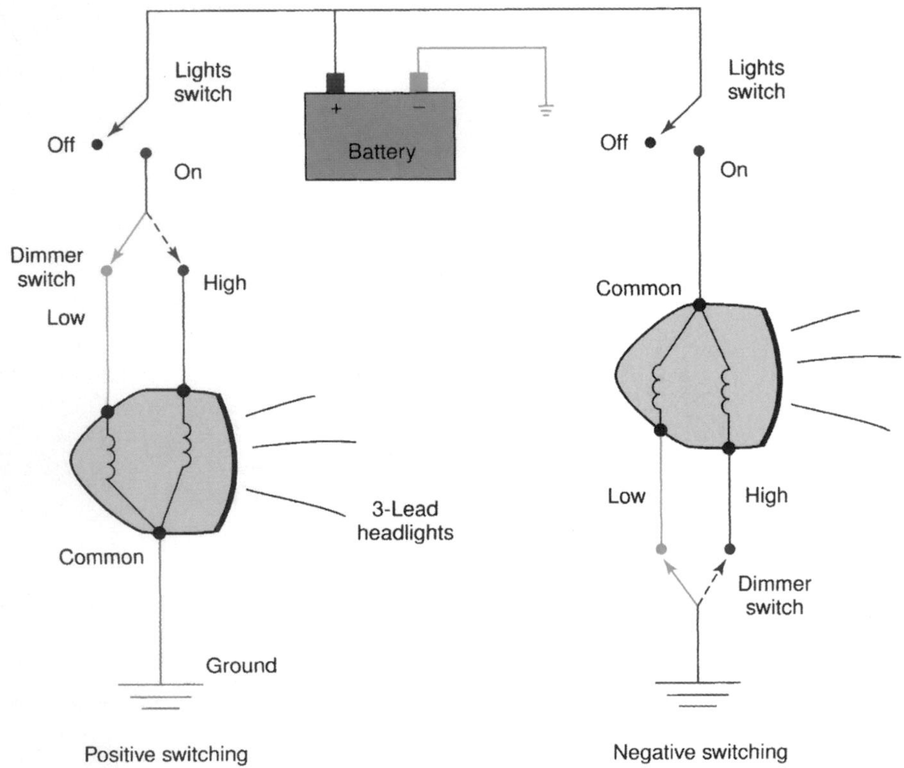

Figure 18–18 Most vehicles use positive switching of the high- and low-beam headlights. Notice that both filaments share the same ground connection. Some vehicles use negative switching and place the dimmer switch between the filaments and the ground.

Figure 18–19 Two styles of two-prong flashers.

Most turn signal flasher units are mounted in a metal clip that is attached to the dash. The dash panel acts as a sounding board, increasing the sound of the flasher unit. Most four-way hazard flasher units are plugged into the fuse panel. Some two-way turn signal flasher units are also plugged into the fuse panel. How do you know for sure where the flasher unit is located? With both the turn signal and the ignition on, listen and/or feel for the clicking of the flasher unit. Some service manuals also give general locations for the placement of flasher units.

NOTE: Some vehicles use heavy duty flashers that flash rapidly if one bulb is not working.

Frequently Asked Question ???

Why Does the Side Marker Light Alternately Flash?

A question that service technicians are asked frequently is why the side marker light alternately goes out when the turn signal is on and is on when the turn signal is off. Some vehicle owners think that there is a fault with their vehicle while actually it is normal operation. The side marker light goes out whenever the lights are on and the turn signal is flashing because there are 12 volts on both sides of the bulb (see points X and Y in Figure 18–20). Normally, the side marker light gets its ground through the turn-signal bulb.

HAZARD FLASHERS

Hazard flasher units are usually plugged into the fuse panel and are designed to flash four or more bulbs safely and at the same flashing speed regardless of the number of bulbs used in the lighting circuit.

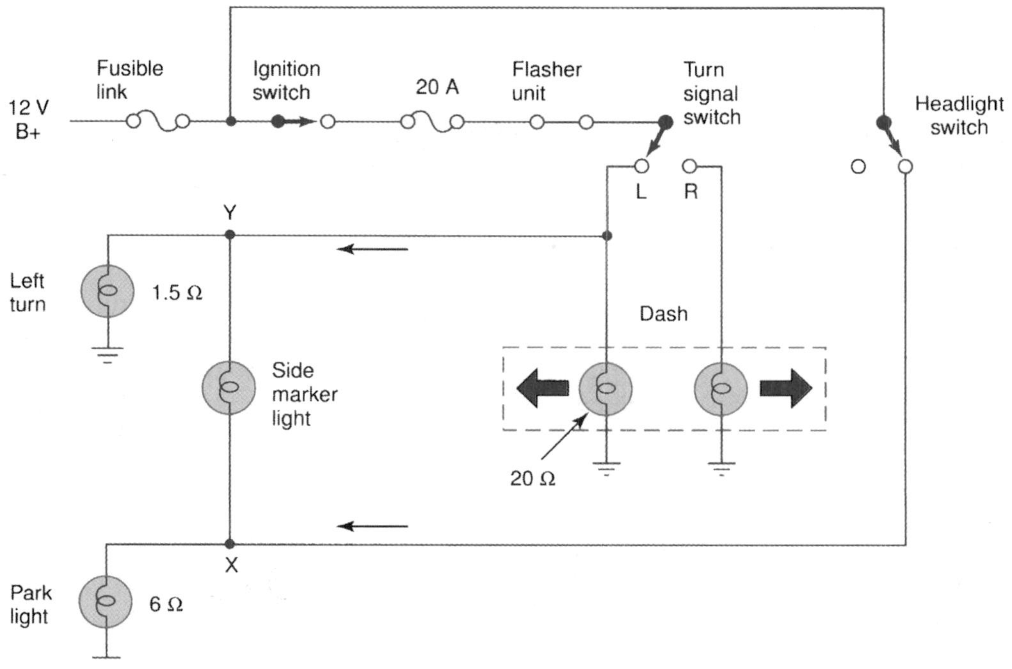

Figure 18–20 The side marker light goes out whenever there is voltage at both point X and Y. These opposing voltages stop current flow through the side marker light. The left turn light and left park light are actually the same bulb (usually a #2057) and are shown separately to help explain how the side marker light works on many vehicles.

Therefore, if trailer lights are connected to the taillights, the flasher unit for the four-way hazard flasher should be used in place of the standard turn signal flasher. However, the regular turn signal flasher *cannot* be used for the four-way hazard flashers. The result would be the very rapid flashing of the hazard flasher and damage to the flasher itself.

COURTESY LIGHTS

Courtesy lights is a generic term primarily used for interior lights, including overhead (dome) and under-the-dash (courtesy) lights. These interior lights can be operated by rotating the headlight switch knob fully counterclockwise (left) or by operating switches located in the door jambs of the vehicle doors and/or near the dome light. There are two types of circuits commonly used for these interior lights. Most manufacturers, except Ford, use the door switches to ground the courtesy light circuit. See Figure 18–21. Many Ford vehicles use the door switches to open and close the power side of the circuit.

Many newer vehicles operate the interior lights through the vehicle computer or through an electronic module. Because the exact wiring and operation of these units differ, consult the service literature for the exact model on which you are working.

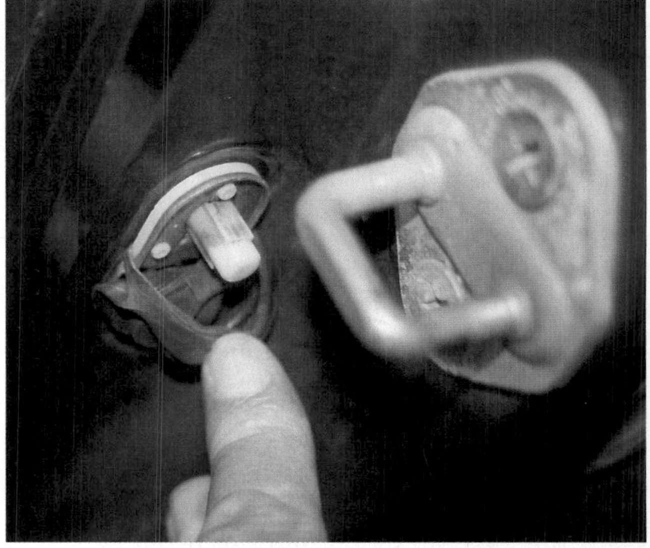

Figure 18–21 A typical courtesy light door jamb switch. Newer vehicles use the door switch as an input to the vehicle computer and the computer turns on or off the interior lights. By placing the lights under the control of the computer, the vehicle engineers have the opportunity to delay the lights after the door is closed and to shut them off after a period of time to avoid draining the battery.

TECH TIP 

Service Manual Diagnosis

It used to be that if a technician could see the schematic of the circuit being diagnosed, then the problem could be corrected. From the schematic or wiring diagram, the technician could see where voltage should be at various parts of the circuit. Not any more! Many of today's vehicles use a computer to control almost everything, including interior lights. The switches in the door jamb simply signal the computer that a door has been opened. The computer controls the lighting to help control against accidental battery drain. For example, in the event that the vehicle door has been left open, the computer can open the circuit and prevent a dead battery.

The schematic rarely shows exactly how the circuit works. However, most service manuals walk you through the diagnosis. With a service manual, or service disk if on compact disk with read-only memory (CD-ROM), the technician is not lost. Always follow the procedures exactly! Even if the service procedure sounds long and involved, the procedure will lead you to the correct diagnosis.

Wiring schematics available on disk are often expanded on the screen and printed. A yellow highlighter is then used to trace the circuit, making diagnosis much easier.

ILLUMINATED ENTRY

Some vehicles are equipped with illuminated entry, whereby the interior lights are turned on for a given amount of time whenever the outside door handle is operated while the doors are locked. Most vehicles equipped with illuminated entry also light the exterior door keyhole. Some vehicles equipped with body computers use the door handle electrical switch of the illuminated entry circuit to "wake up" the power supply for the body computer.

FIBRE OPTICS

Fibre optics is the transmission of light through special plastic (polymethyl methacrylate) that keeps the light rays parallel even if the plastic is tied in a knot. These strands of plastic are commonly used in automotive applications as indicators for the driver that certain lights are functioning. For example, some vehicles are equipped with fender-mounted units that light whenever the lights or turn signals are operating. Plastic fibre-optic strands, which often look like standard electrical wire, transmit the light at the bulb to the indicator on top of the fender so that the driver can determine if a certain light is operating. Fibre-optic strands can also be run like wires to indicate the operation of all lights on the dash or console. Fibre-optic strands are also commonly used to light ashtrays, outside door locks, and other areas where a small amount of light is required. The source of the light can be any normally operating light bulb. A special bulb clip is usually used to retain the fibre-optic plastic tube near the bulb.

FEEDBACK

When current that lacks a good ground goes backward along the power side of the circuit in search of a return path (ground) to the battery, this reverse flow is called **feedback** or **reverse-bias** current flow. Feedback can cause other lights or gauges to work that should not be working.

Feedback Example

A customer complained that when the headlights were on, the left turn signal indicator light on the dash remained on. The cause was found to be a poor ground connection for the left front parking light socket. The front parking light bulb is a dual filament: one filament for the parking light (dim) and one filament for the turn signal operation (bright). A corroded socket did not provide a good enough ground to conduct all current required to light the dim filament of the bulb.

The two filaments of the bulb share the same ground connection and are electrically connected. When all the current could not flow through the bulb's ground in the socket, it caused a feedback or reversed its flow through the other filament, looking for ground. The turn signal filament is electrically connected to the dash indicator light; therefore, the reversed current on its path toward ground could light the turn signal indicator light. Cleaning or replacing the socket usually solves the problem if the ground wire for the socket is making a secure chassis ground connection.

LIGHTING SYSTEM TROUBLESHOOTING GUIDE	
Problem	**Possible Causes and/or Solutions**
One headlight out (low or high beam)	• Burned-out headlight filament. Check the headlight with an ohmmeter. There should be a low-ohm reading between the power-side connection and the ground terminal of the bulb.
Both high- and low-beam headlights out	• Burned-out bulbs. Check for voltage at the wiring connector to the headlights (possible open circuit to the headlights or open [defective] dimmer switch).
All headlights inoperative	• Burned-out filaments in all headlights. Check for proper charging system voltage • Defective dimmer switch • Defective headlight switch
Slow turn signal operation	• Defective flasher unit • High resistance in sockets or ground wire connections • Incorrect bulb numbers
Turn signals operating on one side only	• Burned-out bulb on affected side • Poor ground connection or defective socket on affected side • Incorrect bulb number on affected side
Interior light(s) inoperative	• Burned-out bulb(s) • Open in the power-side circuit (blown fuse) • Open in door jamb switch(es)
Interior lights on all the time	• Shorted door jamb switch • Headlight switch turned fully counterclockwise
Brake lights inoperative	• Defective brake switch • Defective turn signal switch • Burned-out brake light bulbs • Open circuit or poor ground connection
Hazard warning lights inoperative	• Defective hazard flasher unit • Open in hazard circuit
Hazard warning lights blinking too rapidly	• Incorrect flasher unit • Shorted wiring to front or rear lights • Incorrect bulb numbers

SUMMARY

1. Automotive bulbs are identified by trade numbers.
2. The trade number is the same regardless of manufacturer for the exact same bulb specification.
3. Daytime running lights (DRLs) light the headlights, usually at reduced intensity, whenever the engine is running or the vehicle is moving.
4. High-intensity discharge (HID) headlights are brighter and have a blue tint.
5. One defective turn signal bulb causes the turn signal on the affected side to stop blinking (flashing).

REVIEW QUESTIONS

1. Explain why the exact same trade number of bulb should be used as a replacement.
2. Explain why you should not touch a halogen bulb with your fingers.
3. Describe how to diagnose a turn signal operating problem.
4. Discuss how to aim headlights on a vehicle equipped with aerodynamic-style headlights.

RED SEAL CERTIFICATION-TYPE QUESTIONS

1. High-intensity discharge (HID) headlights produce a ______________ light.
   - **a.** Pale amber
   - **b.** Red tinted
   - **c.** Blue-white
   - **d.** Pale green
2. Factory daytime running lights, introduced by Canada in 1990, should not be used for night driving because
   - **a.** They will blind oncoming traffic
   - **b.** They cannot be aimed
   - **c.** They have reduced intensity
   - **d.** The bulb life will be shortened
3. Interior overhead lights (dome lights) are operated by door jamb switches that ________.
   - **a.** Move the bulbs into contact with the switch
   - **b.** Control a mechanical relay
   - **c.** Signal the headlight switch
   - **d.** Complete either the power or ground side of the circuit, depending on application
4. Electrical feedback is usually a result of ________.
   - **a.** Too high a voltage in a circuit
   - **b.** Too much current (in amperes) in a circuit
   - **c.** Lack of a proper ground
   - **d.** Insufficient resistance
5. Which bulb is brightest (see the bulb table)?
   - **a.** #194
   - **b.** #168
   - **c.** #194NA
   - **d.** #57
6. If a #1157 bulb were to be installed in a left front parking brake socket instead of a #2057 bulb, what would be the most likely result?
   - **a.** The left turn signal would flash faster.
   - **b.** The left turn signal would flash slower.
   - **c.** The left parking light would be slightly brighter.
   - **d.** The left parking light would be slightly dimmer.
7. A technician replaced a #1157NA with a #1157A bulb. Which is the most likely result?
   - **a.** The bulb is brighter because the #1157A candlepower is higher.
   - **b.** The amber colour of the bulb is a different shade.
   - **c.** The bulb is dimmer because the #1157A candlepower is lower.
   - **d.** The #1157A bulb will last longer.
8. A customer complained that every time he turned on his vehicle's lights, the left-side turn signal indicator light on the dash remained on. The most likely cause is ________.
   - **a.** A poor ground to the parking light (or taillight) bulb on the *left* side
   - **b.** A poor ground to the parking light (or taillight) bulb on the *right* side causing current to flow to the left-side lights
   - **c.** A defective (open) parking light (or taillight) bulb on the left side
   - **d.** A defective (open) parking light (or taillight) bulb on the right side
9. A defective taillight or front park light bulb could cause
   - **a.** The turn signal indicator on the dash to light when the lights are turned on
   - **b.** The dash lights to come on when the brake lights are on
   - **c.** The lights-on warning chime to sound if the brake pedal is depressed
   - **d.** All four turn signal bulbs to flash
10. A defective brake switch could prevent proper operation of the ____________.
    - **a.** Interior lights
    - **b.** Hazard flashers
    - **c.** Headlight relay
    - **d.** Cruise control

19

Dash Instruments Operation and Diagnosis

OBJECTIVES: After studying Chapter 19, you should be able to:

1. Prepare for the interprovincial Red Seal certification examination in Appendix III (Electrical/Electronic Systems) on the topics covered in this chapter.
2. Discuss how a fuel gauge works.
3. Explain how to use a service manual to troubleshoot a malfunctioning dash instrument.
4. Describe how to use the bulb test position to help diagnose problems.
5. List the various types of dash instrument displays.

Dash instruments are the main communication with the driver regarding vehicle operation.

ANALOG DASH INSTRUMENTS

Dash instruments are either analog or digital. This section describes only the operation and testing of **analog** (also called **needle**) **dash instruments.** (The next section will discuss digital instruments.) The two basic types of gauges used are the **electromagnetic** and the **thermoelectric gauges.** The type used, if unknown, can normally be determined by looking at the fuel gauge with the ignition off.

If the gauge reads the fuel level with the ignition off, it is an electromagnetic gauge. If the gauge falls to empty with the ignition off, the gauge is thermoelectric. All dash instruments on a vehicle work the same way as the fuel gauge; only the function being measured is different.

Thermoelectric Gauges

A thermoelectric gauge uses electrical current flow through the meter, controlled by a **sending unit** or **sensor,** to heat a curved bimetallic strip. As the current flow increases, the heat generated inside the gauge causes the indicator needle to swing toward the right.

This type of gauge moves very slowly, which is an advantage because turns and hills do not affect the readings of the fuel gauge, for example, and the needle tends to remain steady. However, a thermoelectric gauge is sensitive to battery voltage variations. Therefore, to maintain accuracy, thermoelectric-type gauges use an **instrument voltage regulator (IVR).** An IVR maintains instrument voltage at an average of 5 volts. See Figure 19–1.

The regulator uses a bimetallic strip and an electric heating coil, which will alternately open and close (pulse) a contact that produces the average 5 volts for all instrument gauges. To prevent radio interference caused by the pulsation from the regulator, a small coil of wire called a **radio choke** is installed in the power lead going to the IVR. If *all* dash instruments are functioning incorrectly, as when all are reading high or low, the usual cause is the instrument voltage regulator located on the back of the instrument panel. See Figure 19–2.

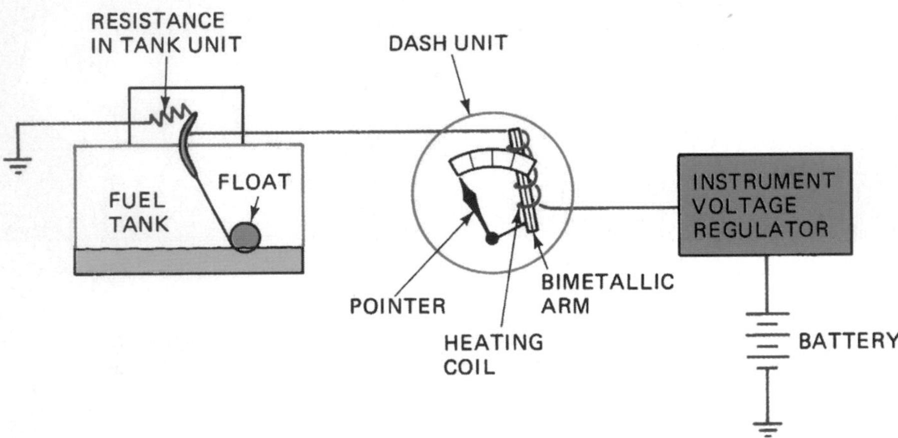

Figure 19–1 A thermoelectric fuel gauge has 5 volts coming from the instrument voltage regulator (IVR). The IVR is shared by all other dash instruments. Electronic gauges use the same sensor (sending unit), but use electronic circuits to control needle movement or digital display.

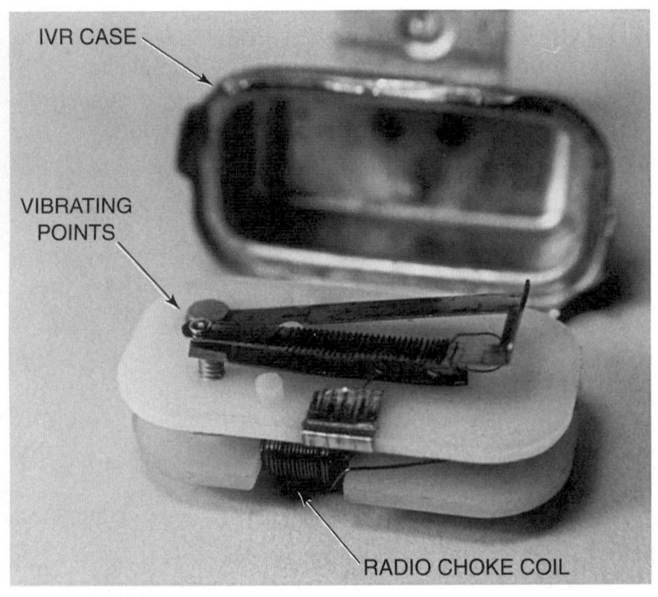

Figure 19–2 Instrument voltage regulator. Vibrating points maintain current through the instruments at 5 volts. The radio choke prevents radio interference created by the pulsing current flow.

Electromagnetic Gauges

Electromagnetic dash instruments use small electromagnetic coils that are connected to a sending unit for such things as fuel level, water temperature, and oil pressure. The resistance of the sensor varies with what is being measured. See Figure 19–3 for typical electromagnetic fuel gauge operation.

Many fuel gauges also incorporate a low-level warning light which illuminates when the fuel in the tank drops to a given level, usually enough to continue driving for 20 to 30 km (12 to 19 mi).

COMPUTER-CONTROLLED INSTRUMENT PANELS

Many instrument panels are operated by electronic control units that communicate with the engine control computer for engine data such as revolutions per minute (RPM) and engine temperature. These electronic instrument panels (IPs) use the voltage change from varying-resistance sensors, such as that of the fuel gauge to determine fuel level. Therefore, even though the sensor in the fuel tank is the same, the display itself may be computer controlled. Because all sensor inputs are interconnected, the technician should always follow the factory-recommended diagnostic procedures. See Figure 19–4.

TECH TIP 

Get a Service Manual and Use It

Today's electronic circuits are often too complex to show on a wiring diagram. Instead, all electronics are simply indicated as a solid box with "electronic module" printed on the diagram. Even if all electronic circuitry was shown on the wiring diagram, it would require the skill of an electronic engineer to determine exactly how the circuit was designed to work. Study Figure 19–5 (p. 441). Note that the grounding for the "check oil" dash indicator lamp is accomplished through an electronic buffer. The exact conditions, such as amount of time since the ignition was shut off, are unknown to the technician. To correctly diagnose problems with this type of circuit *requires* that the technicians read, understand, and follow the written diagnostic procedures specified by the vehicle manufacturer.

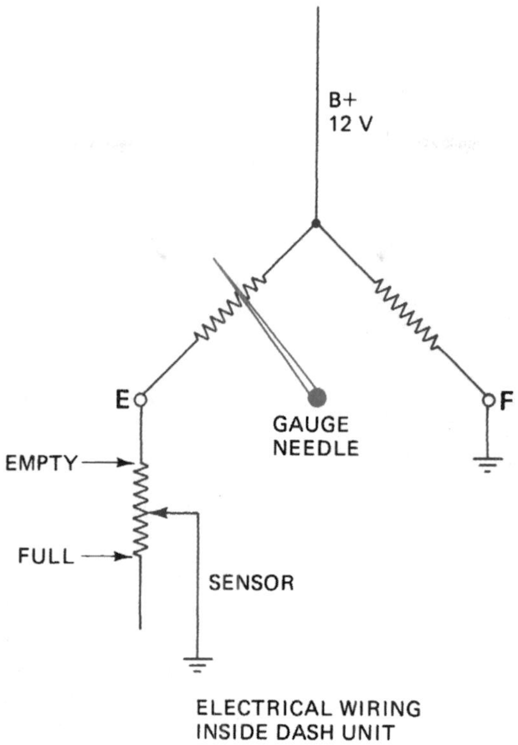

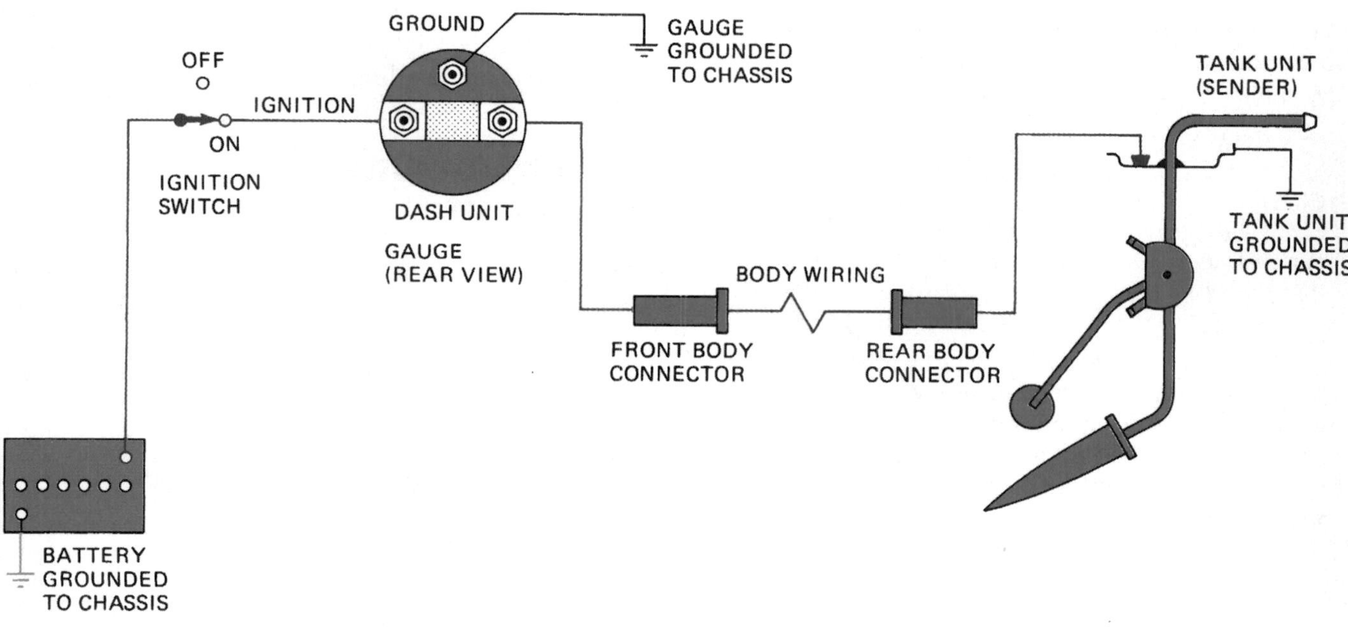

Figure 19–3 Electromagnetic fuel gauge wiring. If the sensor wire is unplugged and grounded, the needle should point to E (empty). If the sensor wire is unplugged and held away from ground, the needle should point to F (full).

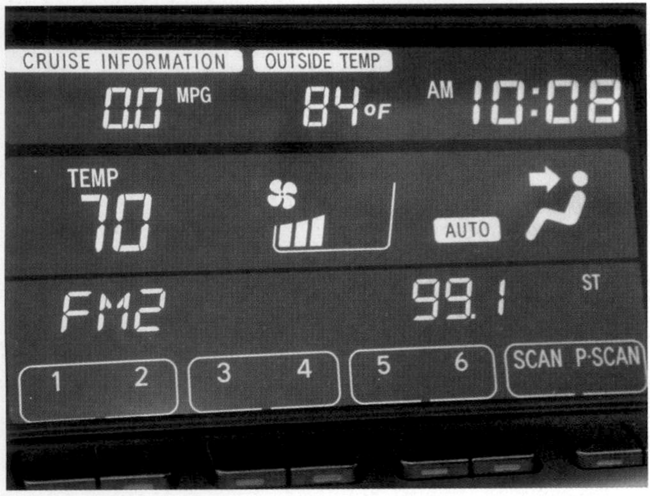

Figure 19–4 Many vehicles use a computer display for many functions, including trip computers, radio, clock, and air conditioning. This vehicle is not moving and yet the engine is running so the fuel economy is zero.

DASH INSTRUMENT DIAGNOSIS

With electromagnetic gauges, if the resistance of the sensor is low, the meter reads low. If the resistance of the sensor is high, the meter reads high.

NOTE: Thermoelectric gauges are opposite from electromagnetic gauges and read low when resistance is high. The following procedures are given for electromagnetic gauges and should be reversed for working on thermoelectric gauges.

When a technician is troubleshooting a fuel gauge, if the power wire is unplugged from the tank unit with the ignition on, the dash unit should move toward full (high resistance). If the power lead is touched to a ground (low resistance), the fuel gauge should register empty. The same operation can be used with oil pressure and water temperature gauges.

TELLTALE LAMPS

Telltale lamps (often called **idiot lights**) warn the driver of system failure. Whenever the ignition is turned on, all warning lamps come on as a bulb check.

The charging-system warning lamp may be labelled CHARGE, GEN, or ALT and will light if the charging system voltage is lower than battery voltage. Complete operation of the charging system and the warning lamp circuit is discussed in Chapter 17.

OIL PRESSURE WARNING DEVICES

The oil pressure lamp operates through use of an oil pressure sensor unit, which is threaded into the engine block, and which grounds the electrical circuit and lights the dash warning lamp in the event of low oil pressure (20 to 50 kPa [3 to 7 psi]). See Figure 19–6. Normal oil pressure is generally between 70 and 400 kPa (10 and 60 psi). See Figure 19–7.

Oil Pressure Lamp Diagnosis

To test the operation of the oil pressure warning circuit, unplug the wire from the oil pressure sending unit, usually located near the oil filter, with the ignition switch on. With the wire disconnected from the sending unit, the warning lamp should be off. If the wire is touched to a ground, the warning lamp should be on. If there is *any* doubt of the operation of the oil pressure warning lamp, always check actual engine oil pressure using a gauge that can be screwed into the opening that is left after unscrewing the oil pressure sending unit. For removing the sending unit, special sockets are available at most auto parts stores, or a large six-point socket may be used for most units. See Figure 19–8 for the location of typical oil pressure sending units.

TEMPERATURE LAMP DIAGNOSIS

The hot lamp or engine coolant overheat warning lamp warns the driver whenever the engine coolant temperature is between 120° and 125°C (248° and 258°F). This temperature is just slightly below the

TECH TIP 

Oops!

After replacing valve cover gaskets, the technician discovered that the oil pressure warning lamp was on. After checking the oil level and finding everything else okay, the technician discovered a wire pinched under the valve cover.

The wire went to the oil pressure sending unit. The edge of the valve cover had cut through the insulation and caused the current from the oil lamp to go to ground through the engine. Normally the oil lamp comes on when the sending unit grounds the wire from the lamp.

The technician freed the pinched wire and covered the cut with silicone sealant to prevent corrosion damage.

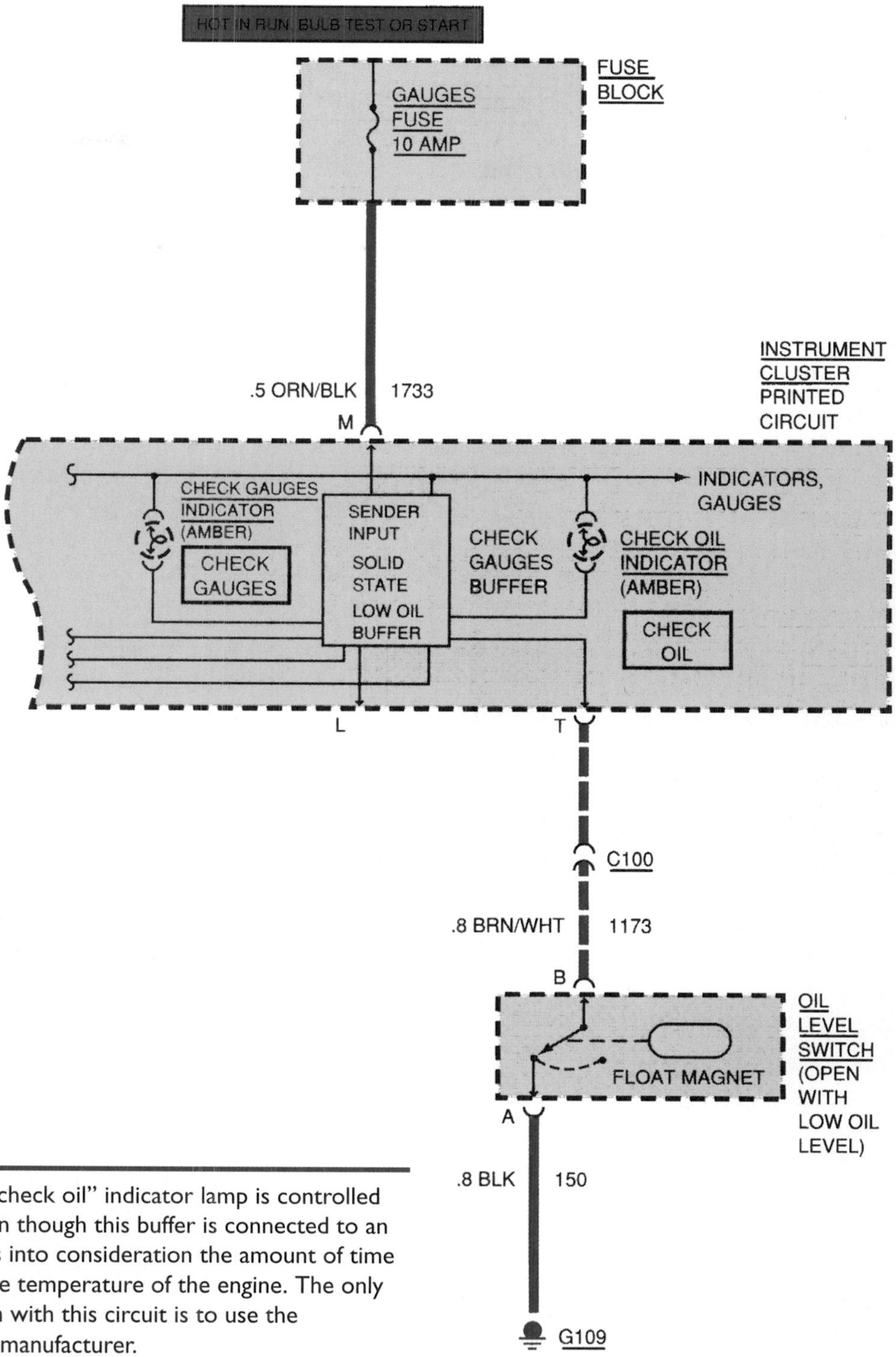

HOT IN RUN, BULB TEST OR START
GAUGES FUSE 10 AMP
FUSE BLOCK
.5 ORN/BLK
1733
M
INSTRUMENT CLUSTER PRINTED CIRCUIT
INDICATORS, GAUGES
CHECK GAUGES INDICATOR (AMBER)
CHECK GAUGES
SENDER INPUT
SOLID STATE
LOW OIL BUFFER
CHECK GAUGES BUFFER
CHECK OIL INDICATOR (AMBER)
CHECK OIL
L
T
C100
.8 BRN/WHT
1173
B
OIL LEVEL SWITCH (OPEN WITH LOW OIL LEVEL)
FLOAT MAGNET
A
.8 BLK
150
G109

Figure 19–5 The ground for the "check oil" indicator lamp is controlled by the electronic low-oil buffer. Even though this buffer is connected to an oil level sensor, the buffer also takes into consideration the amount of time the engine has been stopped and the temperature of the engine. The only way to properly diagnose a problem with this circuit is to use the procedures specified by the vehicle manufacturer.

WARNING LAMP
FROM IGNITION SWITCH
OIL PRESSURE

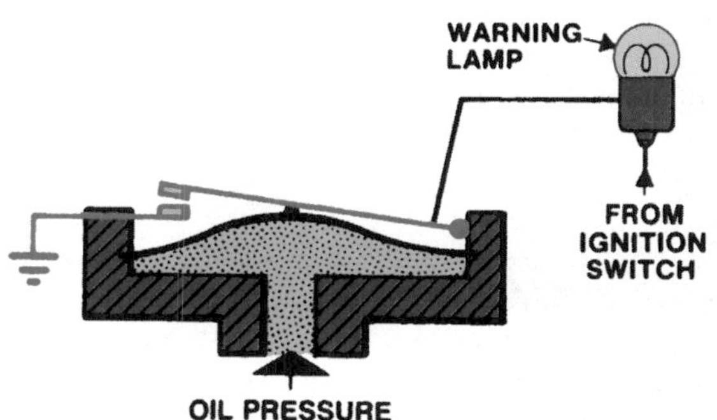

Figure 19–6 This oil pressure grounding switch (sending unit) has a fixed contact connected to ground and a contact that is moved by the pressure-sensitive diaphragm.

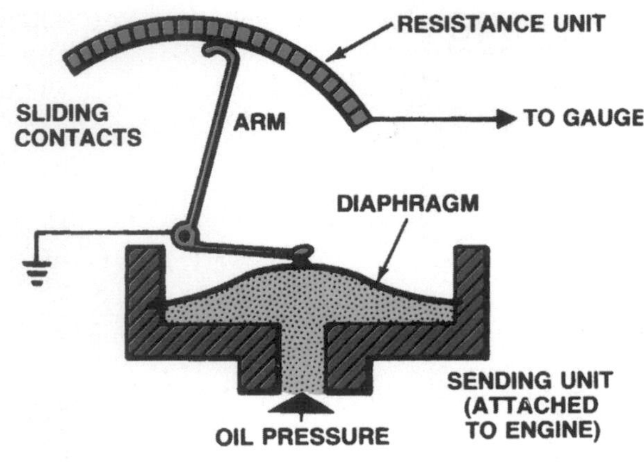

Figure 19–7 A typical oil pressure sending unit provides a varying amount of resistance as engine oil pressure changes.

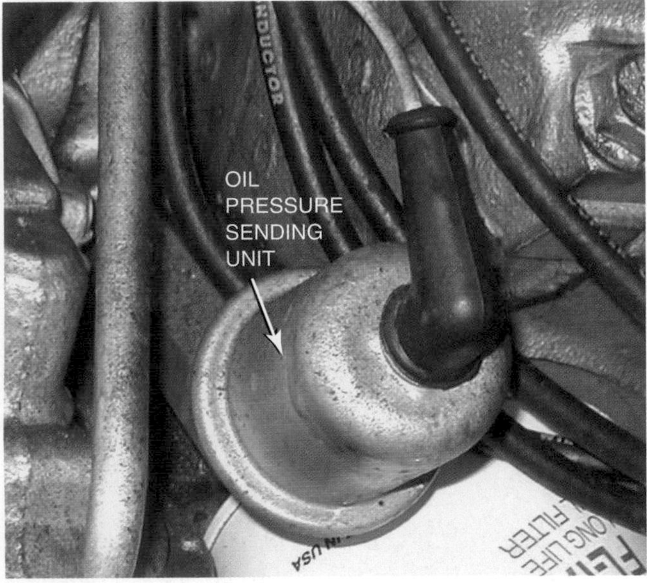

Figure 19–8 An oil pressure sending unit. Most oil pressure sending units are located near the oil filter and are threaded into an oil gallery.

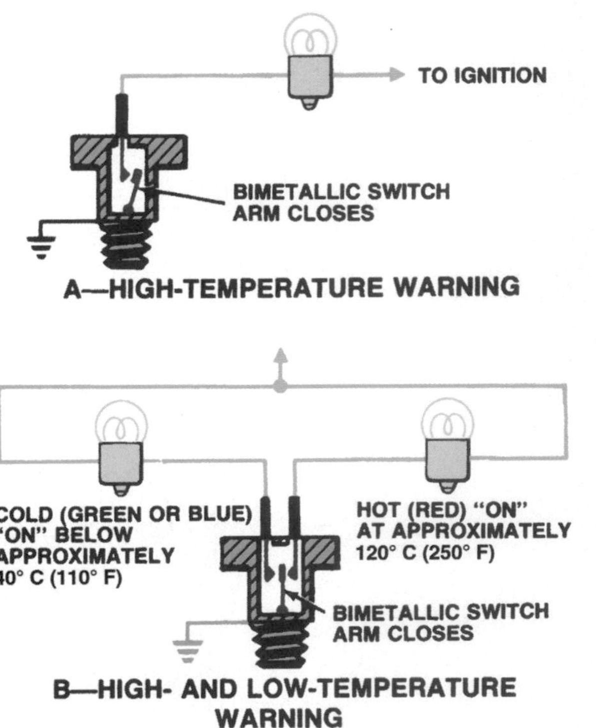

Figure 19–9 Temperature grounding switches expose a bimetallic strip to engine coolant temperature to light a high-temperature lamp or both high- and low-temperature warning lamps.

Figure 19–10 Typical red brake warning lamp.

boiling point of the coolant in a properly operating cooling system. To test the hot lamp, disconnect and ground the wire from the water temperature sending unit. The hot lamp should come on. The sensor is located in the engine block, usually near the thermostat. Always check the cooling system operation and the operation of the warning lamp circuit whenever the hot lamp comes on during normal driving. See Figure 19–9.

BRAKE WARNING LAMP

All vehicles sold in Canada and the U.S. after 1967 must be equipped with a dual braking system and a dash-mounted warning lamp to signal the driver of a failure in one part of the hydraulic brake system. See Figure 19–10. The switch that operates the warning lamp is called a **pressure differential switch.** This switch is usually the centre portion of a multiple-purpose brake part called a **combination valve.** If there is unequal hydraulic pressure in the braking system, the switch usually grounds the 12 V lead at the switch and the lamp comes on. See Figure 19–11.

Unfortunately, the dash warning lamp is often the same lamp as that used to warn the driver that the parking brake is on. The warning lamp is usually operated by using the parking brake lever or brake hydraulic pressure switch to complete the ground for the warning lamp circuit. If the warning lamp is on, first check if the parking brake is fully released. If the parking brake is fully released, the problem could be a defective parking brake switch or a hydraulic brake problem. To test for which system is causing the lamp to remain on, simply unplug the wire from the valve or switch. If the wire on the pressure differential switch is disconnected and the warning lamp remains on, then the problem is from a defective or misadjusted parking brake switch. If, however, the warning lamp goes out when the wire is removed from the brake switch, then the problem is a hydraulic brake fault that caused the pressure differential switch to complete the warning lamp circuit. The red brake warning lamp can also be turned on if the brake fluid is low. See Figure 19–12 for an example of a brake fluid level sensor.

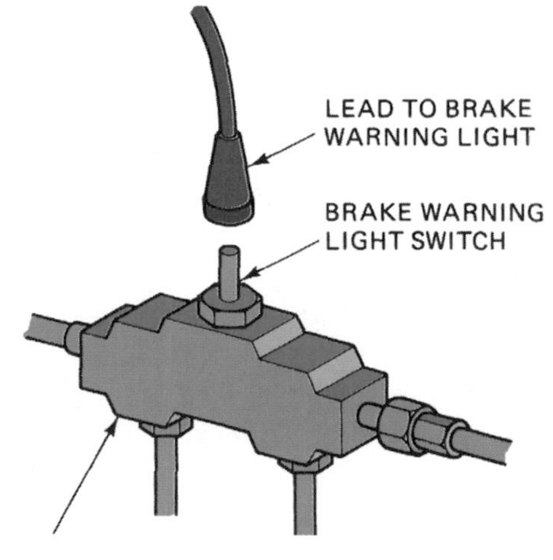

Figure 19–11 Typical brake warning light switch located on or near the master brake cylinder.

DIGITAL ELECTRONIC DASH OPERATION

Mechanical or electromechanical dash instruments use cables, mechanical transducers, and sensors to operate a particular dash instrument. Digital dash instruments use various electric and electronic sensors that activate segments or sections of an electronic display. Most electronic dash clusters use a computer chip and various electronic circuits to operate and control the internal power supply, sensor voltages, and display voltages. Electronic dash display systems may use one or more of the several types of displays: LED, liquid crystal display (LCD), vacuum tube fluorescent (VTF), and cathode ray tube (CRT).

LED Digital Displays

All diodes emit some form of energy during operation; the **light-emitting diode (LED)** is a semiconductor that is constructed to release energy in the form of light. Many colours of LEDs can be constructed, but the most popular are red, green, and yellow. Red is

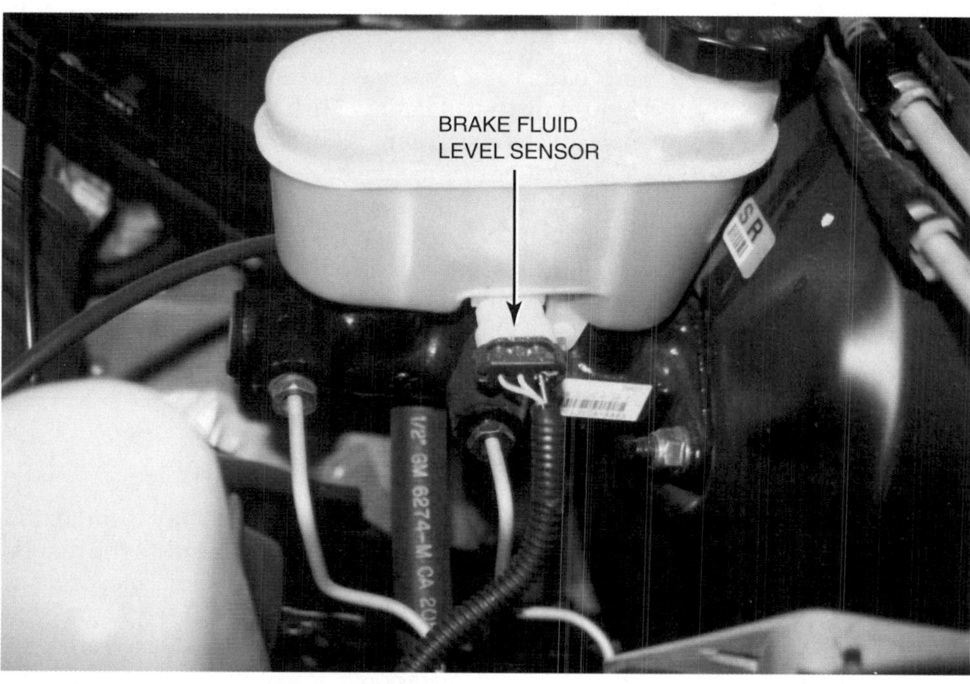

Figure 19–12 The red brake warning lamp can be turned on if the brake fluid level is low.

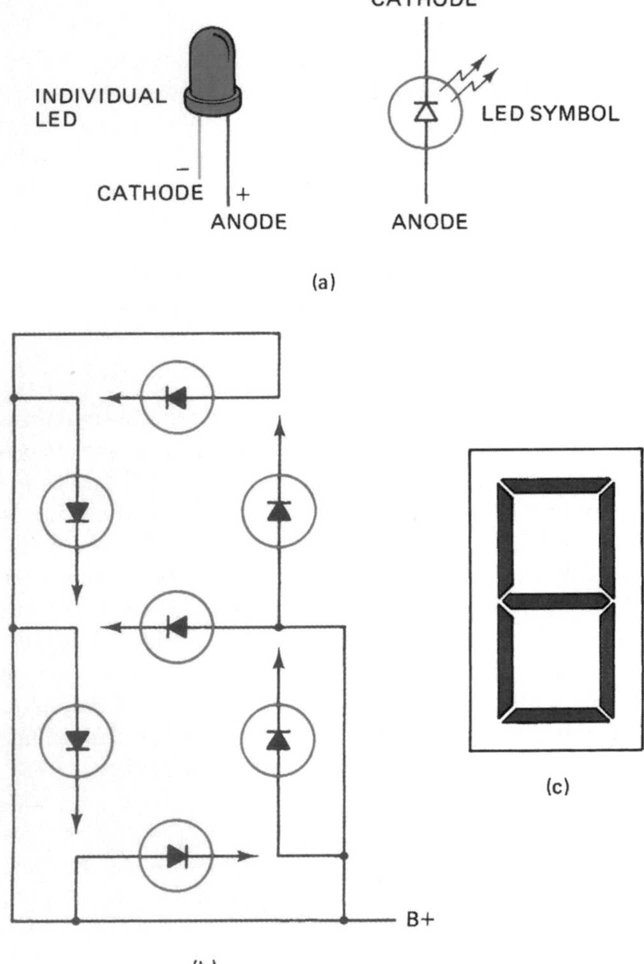

Figure 19–13 (a) Symbol and line drawing of a typical light-emitting diode (LED). (b) Grouped in seven segments, this array is called a seven-segment LED display with a common anode (positive connection). The dash computer toggles the cathode (negative) side of each individual segment to display numbers and letters. (c) When all segments are turned on, the number 8 is displayed.

difficult to see in direct sunlight; therefore, if an LED is used, most vehicle manufacturers use yellow. Light-emitting diodes can be arranged in a group of seven. Seven-segment LEDs can be used to display both numbers and letters. See Figure 19–13.

An LED display requires more electrical power than other types of electronic displays. A typical LED display requires 30 mA for each *segment;* therefore, each number or letter displayed could require 210 mA (0.210 ampere).

Liquid Crystal Displays

Liquid crystal displays (LCDs) can be arranged into a variety of forms, letters, numbers, and bar graph displays. LCD construction consists of a special fluid sandwiched between two sheets of polarized glass. The special fluid between the glass plates will permit light to pass if a small voltage is applied to the fluid through a conductive film laminated to the glass plates.

The light from a very bright halogen bulb behind the LCD shines through those segments of the LCD that have been polarized to let the light through, which then show numbers or letters. Colour filters can be placed in front of the display to change the colour of certain segments of the display, such as the maximum engine speed on a digital tachometer. LCDs are used on newer-model Chevrolet Corvettes and several other makes and models.

NOTE: Be careful, when cleaning an LCD, not to push on the glass plate covering the special fluid. If excessive pressure is exerted on the glass, the display may be permanently distorted. If the glass breaks, the fluid will escape and could damage other components in the vehicle as a result of its strong alkaline nature. Use only a soft, damp cloth to clean these displays.

The major disadvantage of an LCD digital dash is that the numbers or letters are slow to react or change at low temperatures.

Vacuum Tube Fluorescent Displays

The vacuum tube fluorescent (VTF) display is a popular automotive and household appliance display because it is very bright and can easily be viewed in strong sunlight. The usual VTF display is green, but white is often used for home appliances. The VTF display generates its bright light in a manner similar to that of a TV screen, whereby a chemical-coated light-emitting element called a **phosphor** is hit with high-speed electrons. VTF displays are very bright and must be dimmed by use of dense filters or by controlling the voltage applied to the display. A typical VTF dash is dimmed to 75% brightness whenever the parking lights or headlights are turned on. Some displays use a photocell to monitor and adjust the intensity of the display during daylight viewing. Most VTF displays are green for best viewing under most lighting conditions.

Navigation System Display

A cathode ray tube (CRT) dash display, similar to a television tube or similar display, permits the display of hundreds of controls and diagnostic messages in one convenient location. See Figure 19–14.

Using the touch-sensitive cathode ray tube, the driver or technician can select from many different displays, including those of radio, climate, trip, and dash instrument information. All of these functions

Figure 19–14 A typical navigation system. This Acura system incorporates some of the climate control functions as well as the trip information on the display. This particular unit uses a DVD unit in the trunk along with a global positioning satellite (GPS) to display a map and your exact location for the entire country.

can be accessed readily by the driver. Further diagnostic information can be displayed on the CRT if the proper combination of air-conditioning controls is touched. The diagnostic procedures for these displays involve pushing two or more buttons at the same time to get into the diagnostic menu. Always follow the factory service manual recommendations.

Portable mobile navigation systems (MNS) are also available from companies such as Cobra Electronics. The plug-and-go functionality allows the unit to be moved from car to car. It provides turn-by-turn directions to a specific address as well as points of interest, hotels, restaurants and gas stations.

Cold Cathode Fluorescent Displays

Cold cathode fluorescent (CFL) lighting models are used by many vehicle manufacturers for backlighting. Current consumption ranges from 3 to 5 mA (0.003 to 0.005 ampere) with an average life of 40 000 hours. CFL is replacing conventional incandescent light bulbs.

Electronic Analog Displays

Most analog dash displays since the early 1990s are electronically or computer controlled. The sensors may be the same, but the sensor information is sent to the body or vehicle computer and then the computer controls current through small electromagnets that move the needle of the gauge. A scan tool is often needed to diagnose the operation of a computer-

(a)

(b)

(c)

Figure 19–15 (a) View of the vehicle dash with the instrument cluster removed. Sometimes the dash instruments can be serviced by removing the padded dash cover (crash pad) to gain access to the rear of the dash. (b) The front view of the electronic analog dash display. (c) The rear view of the dash display showing that there are a few bulbs that can be serviced; otherwise the unit is serviced as an assembly.

controlled analog dash instrument display. See Figure 19–15.

Other Electronic Gauge Displays

Oil pressure, water temperature, and voltmeter readings are other commonly used electronic dash displays. Oil pressure is monitored by a variable-resistance sending unit threaded into an oil passage, usually near the oil filter. A typical oil pressure sending unit will have low resistance when the oil pressure is zero and higher resistance when the oil pressure is high.

Water temperature is also sensed by a variable-resistance sending unit, usually located near the engine's thermostat. Similar to the case with oil pressure, the higher the coolant temperature, the

TECH TIP 

The Bulb Test

Many ignition switches have six positions. See Figure 19–16.

Notice the **bulb test** position—the position between "on" and "start." When the ignition is turned to "on" (run), some dash warning lamps are illuminated. When the bulb test position is reached, additional dash warning lamps are often lighted. Technicians often use this ignition switch position to check the operation of fuses that protect various circuits. Dash warning lamps are not all powered by the same fuses. If an electrical component or circuit does not work, the power side (fuse) can be quickly checked by observing the operation of the dash lamps that share a common fuse with the problem circuit. Consult a wiring diagram for fuse information on the exact circuit being tested.

greater the number of segments that will be indicated, based on the resistance of the coolant temperature sensor.

NOTE: The coolant temperature sensor for the dash display is usually a separate sensor from the engine coolant temperature (ECT) sensor used by the engine computer.

A voltmeter is often included in a digital display, and each segment of the display represents a particular voltage range. A warning lamp is often part of the electronic circuits in the electronic display to warn the driver of high or low battery voltage. Additional displays for kilometres (miles) to zero, outside temperature, and a directional compass are a few of other read-outs found on some vehicles.

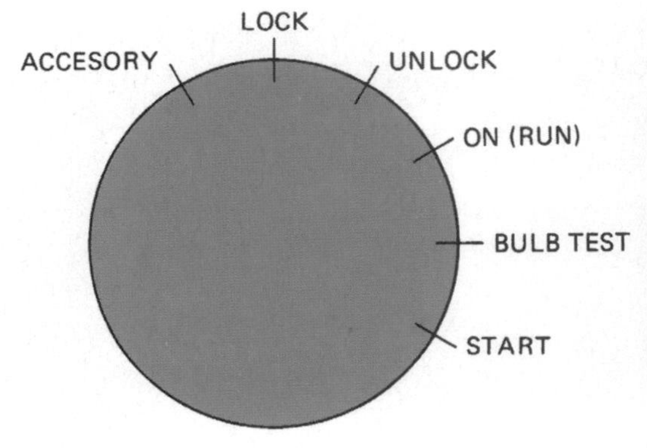

Figure 19–16 Typical ignition switch positions. Notice the bulb check position between ON (RUN) and START.

Warning lights may include the malfunction indicator lamp (MIL), formerly called the service-engine light, open-door lights, seat belt reminders and many others. See Figures 19–17 and 19–18.

The Wow Display

When a vehicle equipped with a digital dash is started, all segments of the electronic display are turned on at

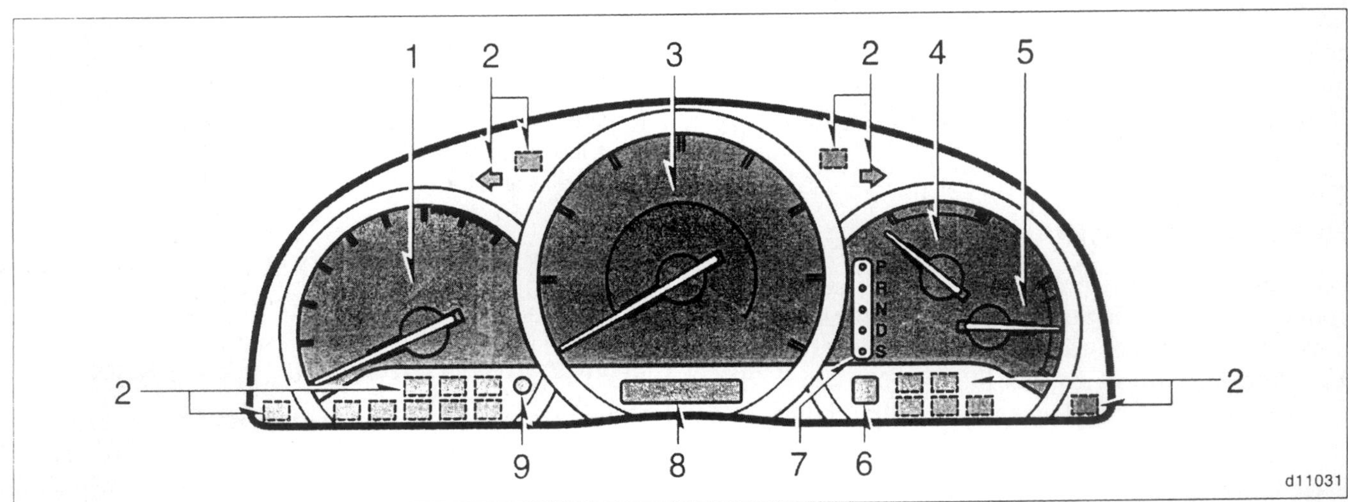

1. Tachometer
2. Service reminder indicators and indicator lights
3. Speedometer
4. Engine coolant temperature gauge
5. Fuel gauge
6. Automatic transmission shift range position display
7. Automatic transmission shift position indicator lights
8. Odometer and two trip meters
9. Trip meter reset knob/instrument panel light control knob

Figure 19–17 Typical instrument cluster. (Courtesy Toyota Canada Inc.)

BRAKE or (!)	Brake system warning light
	Driver's seat belt reminder light
PASSENGER	Front passenger's seat belt reminder light
− +	Discharge warning light
CHECK	Malfunction indicator lamp
	Low engine oil pressure warning light
MAINT	Engine oil replacement reminder light
PASSENGER AIRBAG ON OFF	Front passenger occupant classification indicator light
	Turn signal indicator lights
	Low fuel level warning light
ABS or (ABS)	Anti-lock brake system warning light
	Open door warning light
	SRS warning light
(!)	Low tire pressure warning light
VSC	Vehicle stability control system/traction control system warning light
	Low windshield washer fluid level warning light
	Headlight high beam indicator light
	Slip indicator light
TRAC OFF	Traction control system off indicator light
CRUISE	Cruise control indicator light

Figure 19–18 Typical dash indicator symbols. (Courtesy Toyota Canada Inc.)

DIAGNOSTIC STORY

The Speedometer Works As If It Is a Tachometer

The owner of a Lincoln Town Car complained that all of a sudden the speedometer needle goes up and down with engine speed rather than vehicle speed. In fact, the speedometer needle goes up and down with engine speed even though the gear selector is in "park" and the vehicle is not moving. After hours of troubleshooting, the service technician went back and started checking the basics and discovered that the generator (alternator) had a bad diode. The technician measured over 1 volt AC and over 10 amperes of AC current using a clamp-on AC/DC ammeter. Replacing the generator restored the proper operation of the speedometer.

full brilliance for 1 or 2 seconds. This is commonly called the WOW and is used to show off the brilliance of the display. If numbers are part of the display, the number 8 is displayed, because this number uses all segments of a number display. Technicians can also use the WOW display to determine if all segments of the electronic display are functioning correctly.

ELECTRONIC SPEEDOMETERS

Electronic dash displays ordinarily use an electric vehicle-speed sensor driven by a small gear on the output shaft of the transmission. These speed sensors contain a permanent magnet and generate a voltage in proportion to the vehicle speed. These speed sensors are commonly called **permanent-magnet (PM) generators.** See Figure 19–19.

The output of a PM generator speed sensor is an AC voltage that varies in frequency and intensity

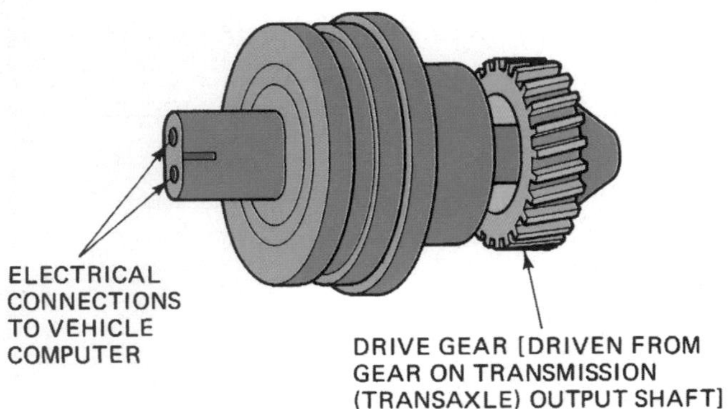

Figure 19–19 Permanent-magnet (PM) generator vehicle speed sensor. The unit is usually driven by a gear on the output section of the transmission or transaxle. Some older vehicle speed sensors are driven by a speedometer cable and are used by the vehicle computer (the cable still drives the speedometer).

with increasing vehicle speed. The PM generator speed signal is sent to the instrument cluster electronic circuits. These specialized electronic circuits include a buffer amplifier circuit that converts the variable sine wave voltage from the speed sensor to an on–off signal that can be used by other electronic circuits to indicate a vehicle's speed. The vehicle speed is then displayed by either an electronic needle-type speedometer or by numbers on a digital display.

Electronic speedometers on some vehicles will read in either kilometres or miles. A driver travelling from Canada (kilometres) to the U.S. (miles) and back may find it convenient to reset the dash display. The English/Metric switch may be located on the dashboard or the centre console. Fuel readings may also change: select "Metric," read "kilometres to zero," select "English," read "miles to zero."

ELECTRONIC ODOMETERS

An odometer is a dash display that indicates the total kilometres travelled by the vehicle. Some dash displays also include a trip odometer that can be reset and used to record total kilometres travelled on a trip or the distance travelled between fuel stops. Electronic dash displays can use either an electrically driven mechanical odometer or a digital display odometer to indicate kilometres travelled. A small electric motor called a **stepper motor** is used to turn the number wheels of a mechanical-style odometer. A pulsed voltage is fed to this stepper motor, which moves in relation to the kilometres travelled. See Figure 19–20.

Digital odometers use LED, LCD, or VTF displays to indicate kilometres travelled. Because total kilometres must be retained when the ignition is turned off or the battery is disconnected, a special electronic chip must be used that will retain the kilometres travelled.

TECH TIP 

The Soldering Gun Trick

Diagnosing problems with digital or electronic dash instruments can be difficult. Replacement parts are generally expensive and usually not returnable if installed in the vehicle. A popular trick that helps pin down the problem is to use a soldering gun near the PM generator.

A PM generator contains a coil of wire. As the magnet inside revolves, a voltage is produced. It is the *frequency* of this voltage that the dash (or engine) computer uses to calculate vehicle speed.

A soldering gun plugged into 110 volts AC will provide a strong *varying* magnetic field around the soldering gun. This magnetic field is constantly changing at the rate of 60 times per second. This frequency of the magnetic field induces a voltage in the windings of the PM generator. This induced voltage at 60 Hz is converted by the computer circuits to a kilometres-per-hour (km/h) reading on the dash.

To test the electronic speedometer, turn the ignition to "on" (engine off) and hold a soldering gun near the PM generator.

CAUTION: The soldering gun tip can get hot, so hold the soldering gun tip away from wiring or other components that may be damaged by the hot tip.

If the PM generator, wiring, computer, and dash are okay, the speedometer should register a speed, usually 87 km/h (54 mph). If the speedometer does not work when the vehicle is driven, then the problem is in the PM generator drive.

If the speedometer does not register a speed when the soldering gun is used, the problem could be caused by:

1. A defective PM generator (check the windings with an ohmmeter)
2. Defective (open or shorted) wiring from the PM generator to the computer
3. Defective computer or dash circuit

HINT: Use a pulsing logic probe and apply a pulse to the wiring after unplugging from the PM generator. If the speedometer now registers a speed, the wiring, computer, and dash are okay and therefore, the PM generator must be defective.

These special chips are called **nonvolatile random access memory (NVRAM).** Nonvolatile means that the information stored in the electronic chip is not lost when electrical power is removed. Some vehicles use a chip called **electronically**

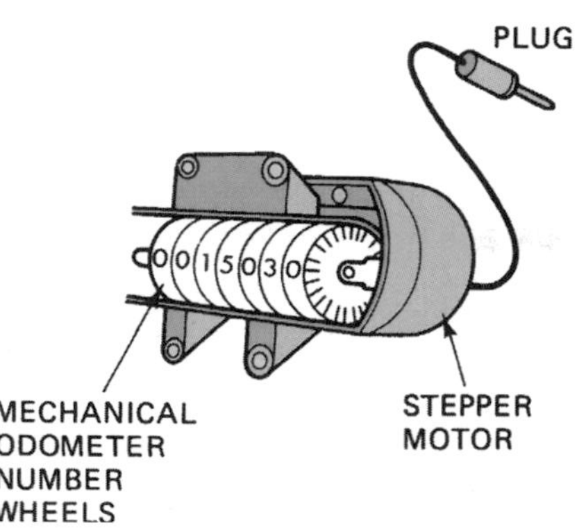

Figure 19–20 Some vehicles that use a PM generator for a vehicle speed sensor use a stepper motor to drive a mechanical odometer. The stepper motor receives a signal (pulses) from the vehicle computer and rotates in steps corresponding to the distance travelled.

DIAGNOSTIC STORY

Look for Previous Repairs

A technician was asked to fix the speedometer on a Pontiac Grand Am that showed approximately double the actual speed. Previous repairs had included a new vehicle speed sensor (VSS) and computer. Nothing made any difference. The customer stated that the problem happened all of a sudden. After hours of troubleshooting, the customer just happened to mention that the automatic transaxle had been repaired shortly before the speedometer problem. The root of the problem was discovered when the technician learned that a final drive assembly from a TH-440 transaxle had been installed on the TH-125C transaxle. The 440 final drive assembly has 13 reluctor teeth, whereas the 125C has 7 teeth. This difference in the number of teeth caused the speedometer to read almost double the actual vehicle speed. After the correct part was installed, the speedometer worked correctly. The technician now always asks if there has been any recent work performed on the vehicle before diagnosis is started.

erasable programmable read-only memory (EEPROM). Most digital odometers can read up to 999 999.9 km; after that the display indicates error. If the chip is damaged or exposed to static electricity, it may fail to operate and "error" may appear.

ELECTRONIC SPEEDOMETER AND ODOMETER SERVICE

If the speedometer and odometer fail to operate, the speed sensor should be the first item checked. With the vehicle safely raised off the ground and supported, disconnect the wires from the speed sensor near the output shaft of the transmission. Connect a multitester, set on AC volts, or a lab scope, to the terminals of the speed sensor, and rotate the drive wheels with the transmission in neutral. A good speed sensor should indicate approximately 2 V AC if the drive wheels are rotated by hand. If the speed sensor is working, check the wiring from the speed sensor to the dash cluster. If the wiring is good, the dash should be sent to a specialty repair facility. Consult your local dealer for the nearest authorized repair facility.

If the speedometer operates correctly but the mechanical odometer does not work, the odometer stepper motor, the number wheel assembly, or the circuit controlling the stepper motor is defective. If the digital odometer does not operate but the speedometer operates correctly, then the dash cluster must be removed and sent to a specialized repair facility. A replacement chip is available only through authorized sources and if the odometer chip is defective, the original number of kilometres must be programmed into the replacement chip.

NOTE: Some digital odometers only change (update) every 24 km (15 mi) or whenever the ignition is turned off. Be certain to check for normal operation before attempting to repair the odometer. Digital dash displays that use EEPROM odometer chips are the type most likely to update odometer readings periodically rather than continuously.

DIAGNOSTIC STORY

How Can We Be Moving When the Van is Stopped?

A number of domestic minivans were experiencing automatic transaxle shifting problems; the transmission would shift normally during one road test and far too early on another test.

The factory technical service bulletin (TSB) asked the technician to monitor vehicle speed with a scan tool while the van was stationary and to rev the engine while noting the vehicle speed on the scan tool display.

If the scan tool readout showed any speed above zero kilometres per hour, the technician was instructed to move the transaxle speed sensor wiring away from the spark plug high tension leads. The magnetic field around the spark plug wires was being picked up by the speed sensor wiring. Relocating the harness corrected the transmission malfunction.

■ ELECTRONIC FUEL-LEVEL GAUGES

Electronic fuel-level gauges ordinarily use the same fuel tank sending unit as that used on conventional fuel gauges. The tank unit consists of a float attached to a variable resistor. As the fuel level changes, the resistance of the sending unit changes. As the resistance of the tank unit changes, the dash-mounted gauge also changes. The only difference between a digital fuel level gauge and a conventional needle type is in the display. Digital fuel-level gauges can be either numerical (indicating litres or gallons remaining in the tank) or a bar graph display. A bar graph consists of light segments, often with each segment corresponding to 5 L of fuel. The electronic circuits inside the cluster light the correct number of litres remaining or the number of segments, depending on the resistance of the tank sending unit. For example, a typical General Motors tank unit has 90 ohms when the fuel tank is full and zero ohms when the tank is empty. See Figure 19–21. Therefore, every decrease of 6 ohms will decrease the display by a segment if it is a 16-segment bar graph fuel gauge.

NOTE: Many General Motors vehicles built since 1996 and equipped with enhanced evaporation control systems use a fuel-level sensing unit that varies between 40 ohms empty and 250 ohms full.

Frequently Asked Question ???

Why Does the Oil Pressure Gauge on My Ford Always Read in the Middle?

Some Ford Motor Company vehicles use an analog oil pressure display that is set to read in the middle of the scale as long as there is a minimum oil pressure. Think of the gauge as an oil pressure switch (on or off) rather than an analog (variable) display of the actual oil pressure. See Figure 19–22. The older-style gauge (before 1986) used a variable resistance oil pressure sending unit. See Figure 19–23.

After 1986 on some models, Ford started using an oil pressure switch that electrically grounded the oil pressure gauge through a 20 Ω resistor whenever the oil pressure is above 30 to 50 kPa (4.5 to 7.5 psi). See Figure 19–24.

To determine which type of gauge you have, simply ground the sending unit with the key on (engine off) and observe the gauge. If the gauge reads exactly one-half, then the vehicle has a switch-type oil pressure sending unit.

The diagnosis of a problem is the same as that described earlier for conventional fuel gauges. If the tests indicate that the dash unit is defective, usually the *entire* dash gauge assembly must be replaced.

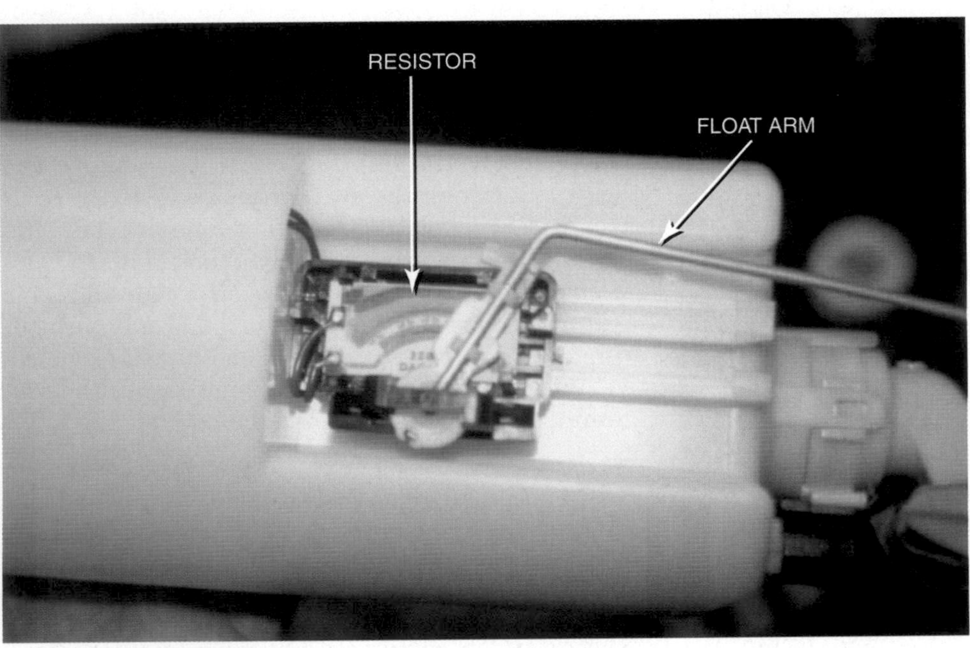

Figure 19–21 A typical fuel pump and fuel-level gauge module. The float moves against a resistor and changes the resistance of the circuit with the fuel level.

(a)

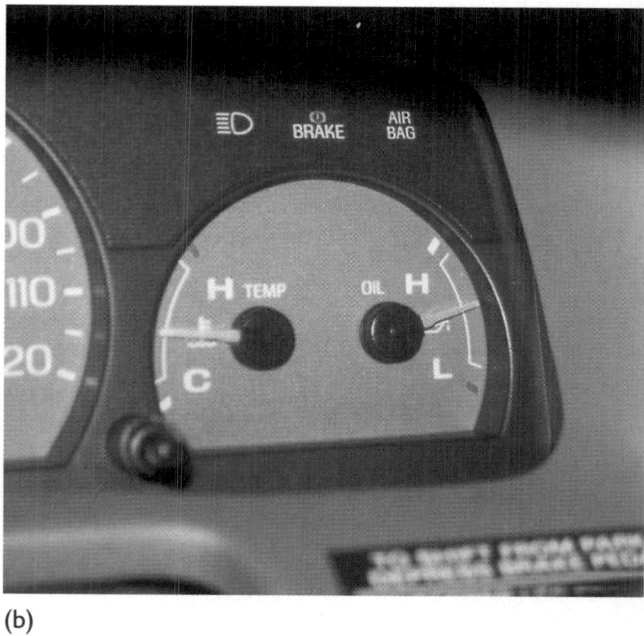

(b)

Figure 19–22 (a) A Ford dash display with the key on, engine off. (b) As soon as the engine starts, the oil pressure gauge goes immediately to the midpoint on the gauge. This seems strange to some vehicle owners.

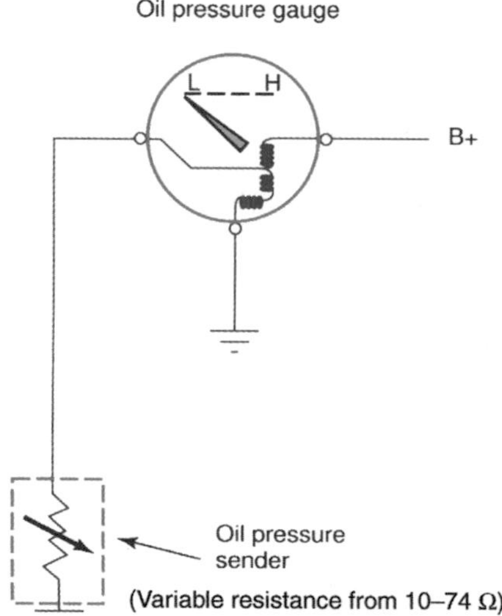

Figure 19–23 A typical magnetic and pressure gauge circuit. Notice that the oil pressure gauge reading depends on the resistance of the sensor. The lower the resistance, the higher the oil pressure on most Ford vehicles.

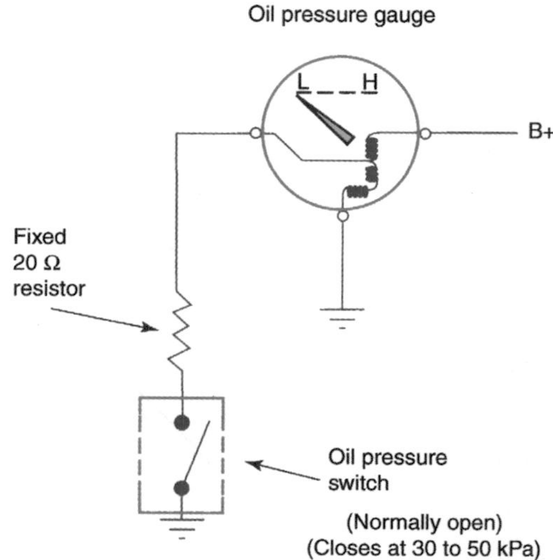

Figure 19–24 Whenever the oil pressure exceeds 30 to 50 kPa (4.5 to 7.5 psi), the oil pressure switch closes and the meter reads in about the middle of its range due to the fixed 20 ohm resistor in the meter circuit.

ELECTRONIC DASH INSTRUMENT DIAGNOSIS AND TROUBLESHOOTING

If one or more electronic dash gauges do not work correctly, first check the WOW display that lights all segments to full brilliance whenever the ignition switch is first switched on. If *all* segments of the display do *not* operate, then the entire electronic cluster must be replaced in most cases. If all segments operate during the WOW display but do not function correctly afterwards, the problem is most often a defective sensor or defective wiring to the sensor.

All dash instruments except the voltmeter use a variable-resistance unit as a sensor for the system being monitored. Most new-vehicle dealers are required to purchase essential test equipment, including a test unit that permits the technician to insert various fixed-resistance values in the suspected circuit. For example, if a 45 Ω resistance is put into the fuel gauge circuit that reads from 0 to 90 Ω, a properly operating dash unit should indicate one-half tank. The same tester can produce a fixed signal to test the operation of the speedometer and tachometer. If this type of special test equipment is not available, the electronic dash instruments can be tested using the following procedure:

1. With the ignition switched off, unplug the wire(s) from the sensor for the function being tested. For example, if the oil pressure gauge is not functioning correctly, unplug the wire connector at the oil pressure sending unit.
2. With the sensor wire unplugged, turn the ignition switch on and wait until the WOW display stops. The display for the affected unit should show either fully lighted segments or no lighted segments, depending on the make of the vehicle and the type of sensor.
3. Turn the ignition switch off. Connect the sensor wire lead to ground and turn the ignition switch on. After the WOW display, the display should be the opposite (either fully on or fully off) of the results in step 2.

Testing Results

If the electronic display does function fully on and fully off with the sensor unplugged and then grounded, the problem is a defective sensor. If the electronic display fails to function fully on and fully off when the sensor wire(s) are opened and grounded, the problem is usually in the wiring from the sensor to the electronic dash or is a defective electronic cluster.

CAUTION: Whenever working on or *near* any type of electronic dash display, always wear a wire attached to your wrist (wrist strap) connected to a good body ground, to prevent damaging the electronic dash with static electricity.

MAINTENANCE REMINDER LAMPS

Maintenance reminder lamps indicate that the oil should be changed or that other service is required. There are numerous ways to extinguish a maintenance reminder lamp. Some require the use of a special tool. Consult service literature or dealership personnel for the exact procedure for the vehicle being serviced. For example, to reset the oil service reminder light on one domestic vehicle, you have to perform the following:

TECH TIP 

KISS—Keep It Stock, Stupid!

Whenever larger (or smaller) wheels or tires are installed, the speedometer and odometer calibration are also thrown off. This can be summarized as follows:

- **Larger-diameter tires**—The speed showing on the speedometer is slower than actual speed. The odometer reading will show fewer kilometres than actual.
- **Smaller-diameter tires**—The speed showing on the speedometer is faster than actual speed. The odometer reading will show more kilometres than actual.

General Motors trucks can be recalibrated with a recalibration kit (1988–1991) or with a replacement controller assembly called a digital ratio adapter controller (DRAC) located under the dash. It may be possible to recalibrate the speedometer and odometer on earlier models, before 1988, or vehicles that use speedometer cables by replacing the drive gear in the transmission. Check with a speedometer repair company or vehicle dealer for details.

Step 1 Turn the ignition key on (engine off).

Step 2 Depress the accelerator pedal three times and hold it down on the fourth.

Step 3 When the reminder light flashes, release the accelerator pedal.

Step 4 Turn the ignition key to the off position.

Step 5 Start the engine and the light should be off.

LOW TIRE PRESSURE WARNING SYSTEM

The tire pressure warning system alerts the driver if it detects a low tire, which could affect safe driving. Some systems use a wheel-mounted pressure sensor inside the tire, while others use the signals generated by the anti-lock braking system (ABS) wheel speed sensors. See Figure 19–25. A low tire will rotate faster than one with the correct pressure; this increase in speed is noted by the wheel speed sensor and sent to the ABS electronic control unit (ECU). The ECU, which constantly monitors wheel speeds, will illuminate the instrument panel warning light. A hand-held scan tool is used to access diagnostic trouble codes (DTC), which are stored in computer memory. Service repair procedures for that code are now followed in the shop manual.

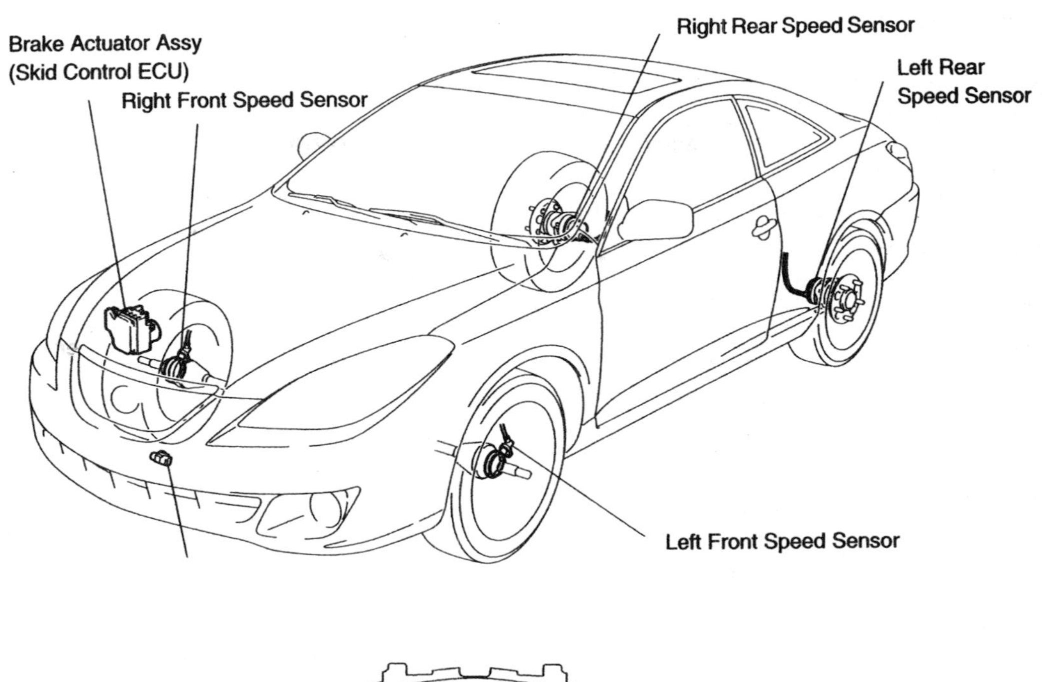

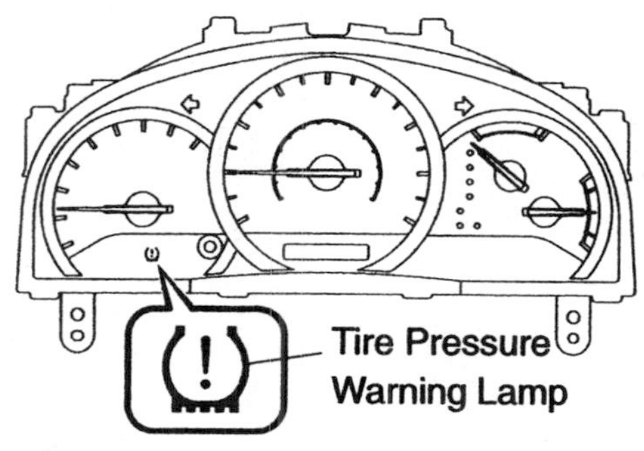

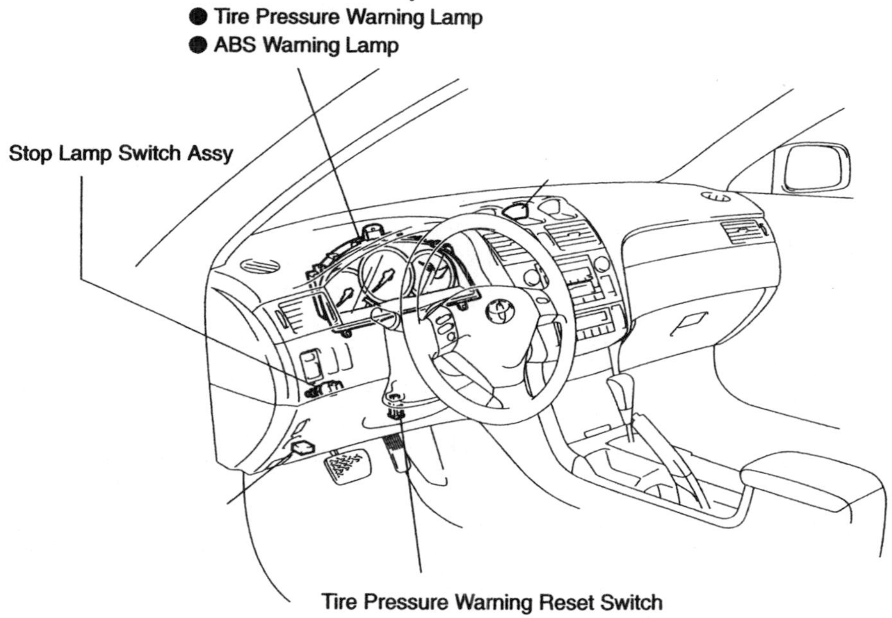

Figure 19–25 A typical tire pressure warning system. Notice the four speed sensors and the reset switch. (Courtesy Toyota Canada Inc.)

PHOTO SEQUENCE 15 Fuel Gauge Diagnosis (Typical)

P15–1 Observe the fuel gauge. This vehicle shows an indicated reading of slightly above one-half tank.

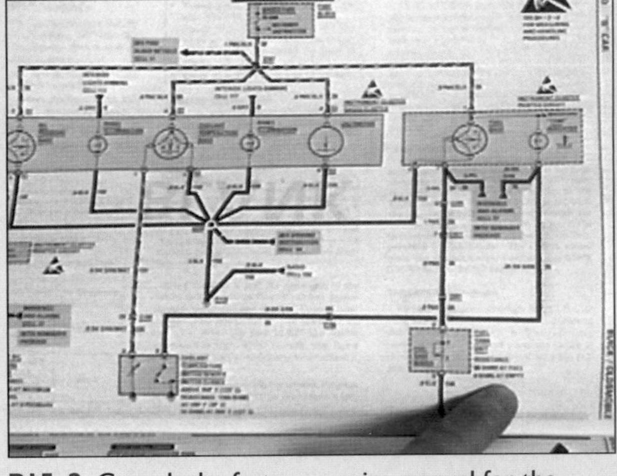

P15–2 Consult the factory service manual for the specifications, wire colour, and recommended test procedure.

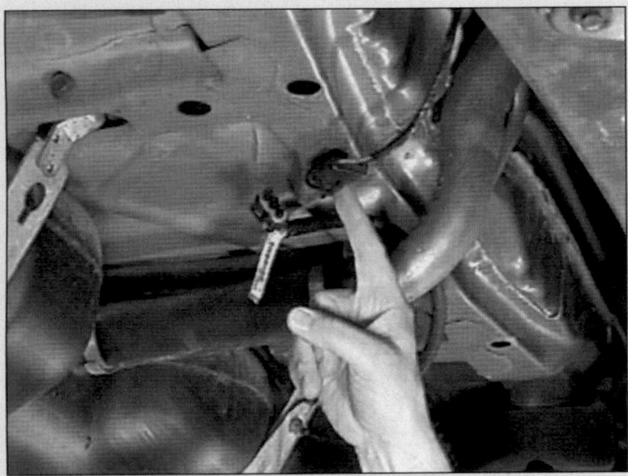

P15–3 From the service manual, the connector for the fuel gauge sending unit was located under the vehicle near the rear. A visual inspection indicated that the electrical wiring and connector were not damaged or corroded.

P15–4 To test the resistance of the sending unit (tank unit), use a digital multimeter and select ohms (Ω).

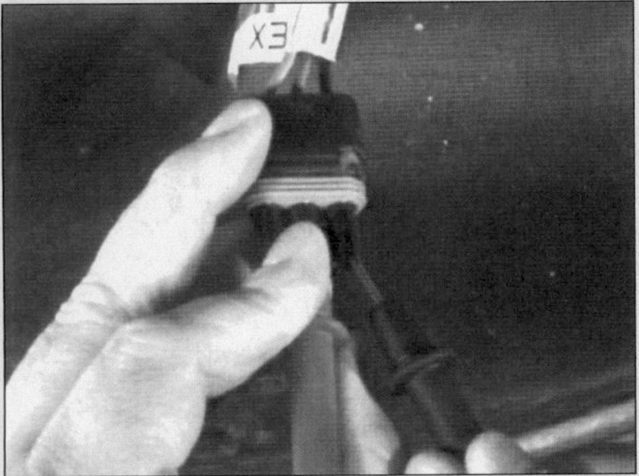

P15–5 Following the schematic in the service manual, the sending unit resistance can be measured between the pink and the black wires in the connector.

P15–6 The meter displays 50 Ω or slightly above the middle of the normal resistance value for the vehicle of 0 ohms (empty) to 90 ohms (full).

Fuel Gauge Diagnosis—continued

P15–7 To check if the dash unit can move, the connector is unplugged with the ignition key on (engine off).

P15–9 After a few seconds, the needle disappears above the full reading. The open connector represented infinite ohms and normal maximum reading occurs when the tank unit reads 90 ohms. If the technician does not realize that the needle could disappear, an incorrect diagnosis could be made.

P15–11 A check of the dash unit indicates that the needle does accurately read empty.

P15–8 As the connector is disconnected, the needle of the dash unit moves toward full.

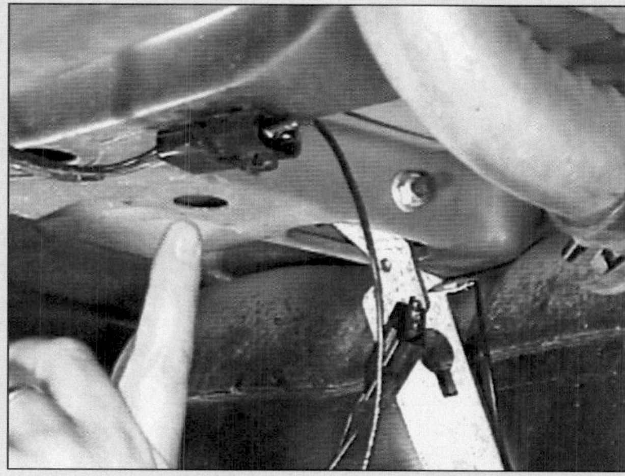

P15–10 To check if the dash unit is capable of reading empty, a fuse jumper wire is connected between the signal wire at the dash end of the connector and a good chassis ground.

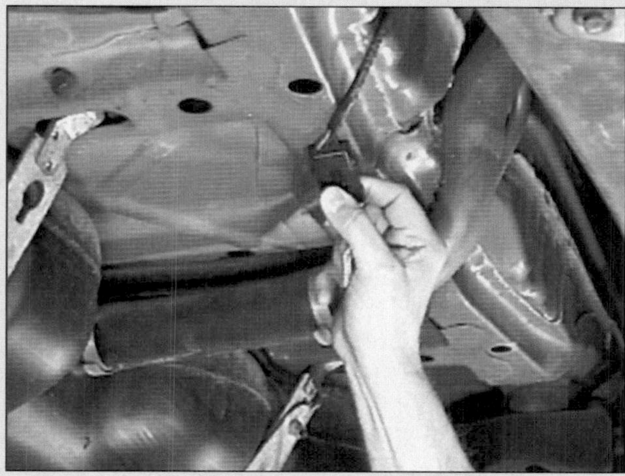

P15–12 After testing, reconnect the electrical connectors and verify for proper operation of the fuel-level gauge.

SUMMARY

1. Most digital and analog (needle-type) dash gauges use variable resistance sensors.
2. Dash warning lamps are called idiot lights or telltale lamps.
3. Many electronically operated or computer-operated dash indicators require that a service manual be used to perform accurate diagnosis.
4. Permanent-magnet (PM) generators produce an AC signal and are used for vehicle speed and wheel speed sensors.

REVIEW QUESTIONS

1. Explain the difference between thermoelectric and electromagnetic dash instruments.
2. Describe LED, LCD, VTF, and CRT dash displays.
3. Discuss how to diagnose a problem with a red brake warning lamp.
4. Explain how to test the dash unit of a fuel gauge.

RED SEAL CERTIFICATION-TYPE QUESTIONS

1. A General Motors vehicle has the power lead to the fuel tank sending unit disconnected from the tank unit and reconnected to ground (ignition switch on); the instrument panel fuel gauge reading will
   - **a.** Not change
   - **b.** Go to empty
   - **c.** Go to full
   - **d.** Move to the centre position
2. If an oil pressure warning lamp on a General Motors vehicle is on all the time, yet the engine oil pressure is normal, the problem could be ______.
   - **a.** A defective (shorted) oil pressure sending unit (sensor)
   - **b.** A defective (open) oil pressure sending unit (sensor)
   - **c.** An open wire between the sending unit (sensor) and the dash warning lamp
   - **d.** An open circuit between the ignition switch and the dash warning lamp
3. When the oil pressure drops below 20 to 50 kPa (3 to 7 psi), the oil pressure lamp lights by ____________.
   - **a.** Opening the circuit
   - **b.** Shorting the circuit
   - **c.** Grounding the circuit
   - **d.** Conducting current to the dash lamp by oil
4. The brake warning light on the instrument panel remains on when the ignition is on. When the wire to the pressure differential switch (either a part of the combination valve or built into the master cylinder) is unplugged, the light goes out. This is an indication of a/an
   - **a.** Hydraulic brake fault
   - **b.** Stuck parking brake switch
   - **c.** Wiring problem at the dash connector
   - **d.** Open circuit in the warning light wiring harness
5. A customer complains that every time the lights are turned on in the vehicle, the dash display dims. What is the most probable explanation?
   - **a.** Normal behavior for LED dash displays
   - **b.** Normal behavior for VTF dash displays
   - **c.** Poor ground in lighting circuit causing a voltage drop to the dash lamps
   - **d.** Feedback problem most likely caused by a short to voltage between the headlights and dash display
6. An LCD dash display can be damaged by
   - **a.** Arc welding on the chassis
   - **b.** Applying 12 volts when testing
   - **c.** Exerting pressure on the display when cleaning
   - **d.** An overheated dashboard (instrument panel)
7. Some low tire warning systems monitor tire pressures with information from
   - **a.** Vehicle height sensors
   - **b.** Vehicle speed versus engine speed sensors
   - **c.** ABS wheel speed sensors
   - **d.** A transaxle speed sensor
8. To repair a single defective gauge (dash unit) in many electronic dash gauge assemblies
   - **a.** The entire dash gauge assembly must be replaced
   - **b.** An exchange dash gauge assembly is installed
   - **c.** The defective gauge is recalibrated
   - **d.** The gauge must be diagnosed with a digital ohmmeter
9. Some electronic speedometers will read in kilometres or miles, depending on the position of the
   - **a.** Radio calibration
   - **b.** Navigation panel selection
   - **c.** English/Metric switch
   - **d.** Border updating satellite signal
10. How does changing the size of the tires affect the speedometer reading?
    - **a.** A smaller-diameter tire causes the speedometer to read faster than actual speed and more than the actual reading on the odometer.
    - **b.** A smaller-diameter tire causes the speedometer to read slower than the actual speed and less than the actual reading on the odometer.
    - **c.** A larger-diameter tire causes the speedometer to read faster than the actual speed and more than the actual reading on the odometer.
    - **d.** A larger-diameter tire causes the speedometer to read slower than the actual speed and more than the actual reading on the odometer.

20

Accessory Circuits Operation and Diagnosis

OBJECTIVES: After studying Chapter 20, you should be able to:

1. Prepare for the interprovincial Red Seal certification examination in Appendix III (Electrical/Electronic Systems) on the topics covered in this chapter.
2. Explain how different speeds of a blower motor can be achieved.
3. Describe how power door locks and windows operate.
4. Discuss steps to take to eliminate sound system interference.
5. List the safety precautions for working around an airbag.
6. Describe the operation of a remote security system.
7. Explain how satellite technology is used to locate a vehicle.

Electrical accessories provide comfort and assistance to the driver and passengers. The growing list of electrical accessories makes this an area of much concern to vehicle owners and service technicians.

BLOWER MOTOR OPERATION

The same blower motor moves air inside the vehicle for air conditioning, heat, and defrosting or defogging. The fan switch controls the path that the current follows to the blower motor. The motor is usually a permanent-magnet, one-speed motor that operates at its maximum speed with full battery voltage. The switch is fed from the fuse panel with the ignition switch on. The switch applies full battery voltage to the blower motor for high speed and reduces voltage to the blower motor through resistors for lower speeds. See Figures 20–1 and 20–2. Some vehicles locate the controls and resistor block in the ground side (after the blower motor), but the function is the same.

BLOWER MOTOR DIAGNOSIS

If the blower motor does not operate at any speed, the problem could be any of the following:

1. A defective ground wire or ground wire connection
2. A defective blower motor (not repairable; must be replaced)
3. An open circuit in the power-side circuit, including fuse, wiring, or fan switch

If the blower works on lower speeds but not on high speed, the problem is usually an inline fuse or high-speed relay that controls the heavy current flow for high-speed operation. The high-speed fuse or relay usually fails as a result of internal blower-motor bushing wear, which causes excessive resistance to motor rotation. At slow blower speeds, the resistance is not as noticeable and the blower operates normally. The blower motor is a sealed unit, and if defective, must be replaced as a unit. If the blower motor operates normally at high speed but not at any of the lower speeds, the problem could be melted wire

Figure 20–1 A typical squirrel cage blower motor. A replacement blower motor usually does not come equipped with the squirrel cage blower, so it has to be switched from the old motor.

Figure 20–2 Blower motor resistors. If they are defective, replacement resistors are purchased as a unit, as shown.

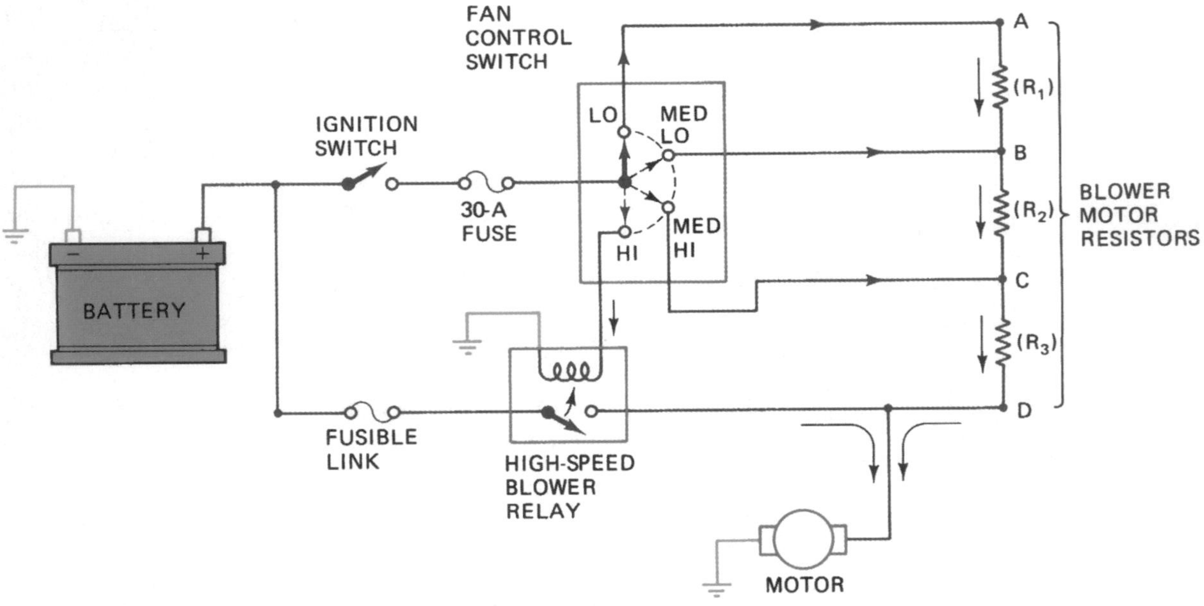

Figure 20–3 Typical blower motor circuit with four speeds. The three lowest fan speeds (low, medium low, and medium high) use the blower motor resistors to drop the voltage to the motor and reduce current to the motor. On high, the resistors are bypassed. The "hi" position on the fan switch often energizes a relay. This relay supplies the current for the blower on high through a fusible link.

resistors or a defective switch. See Figure 20–3. The blower motor can be tested using a clamp-on DC ammeter as shown in Figure 20–4. Most blower motors do not draw more than 15 amperes on high speed. A worn or defective motor usually draws more current than normal and could damage the blower motor resistors or blow a fuse if not replaced.

WINDSHIELD WIPERS

The windshield wipers ordinarily use a special two-speed electric motor. Most are compound-wound motors, which are a type of motor with both a **series-wound field** and a **shunt field,** which provides for two different speeds. The wiper switch pro-

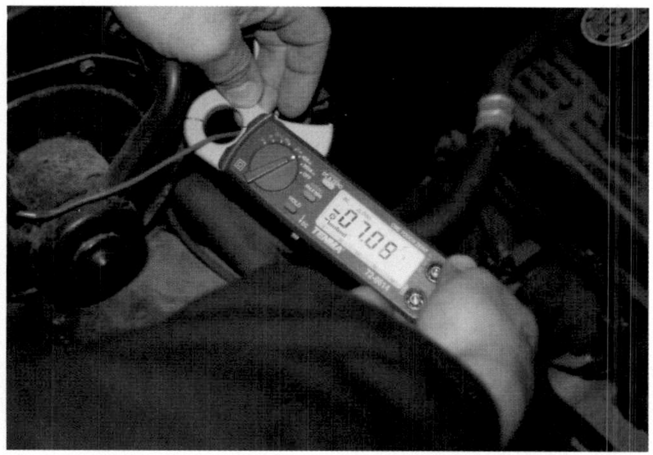

Figure 20–4 Using a mini AC/DC clamp-on multimeter to measure the current draw of a blower motor.

The 20-Ampere Fuse Trick

Most blower motors operate at about 12 amperes on high speed. If the bushings (bearings) on the armature of the motor become worn or dry, the motor turns more slowly. Because a motor also produces **counter EMF,** or **CEMF,** as it spins, a slower-turning motor will actually draw more amperes than a fast-spinning motor.

If a blower motor draws too many amperes, the resistors or the electronic circuit controlling the blower motor can fail. Testing the actual current draw of the motor is sometimes difficult because the current often exceeds the permissible amount for most digital meters.

A commonly used trick is to unplug the power lead to the motor (retain the ground on the motor) and use a fused jumper lead with one end connected to the battery's positive terminal and the other end to the motor terminal. Use a 20 ampere fuse in the test lead. Operate the motor for several minutes. If the blower motor is drawing more than 20 amperes, the fuse will blow. Some experts recommend using a 15 ampere fuse. If the 15 ampere fuse blows and the 20 ampere fuse does not, then you know the approximate blower motor current draw.

(a)

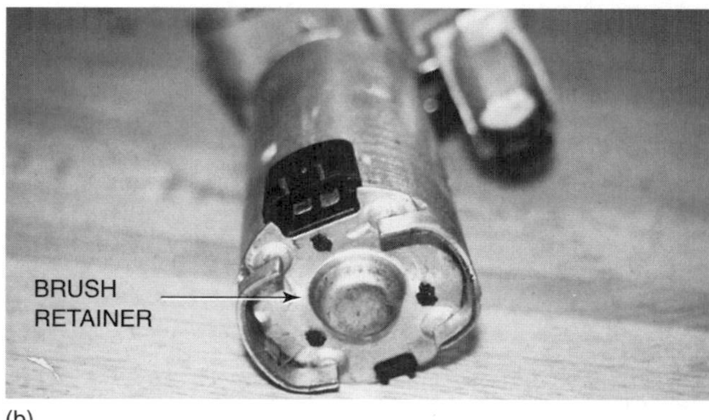

(b)

Figure 20–5 (a) A typical wiper motor with the housing cover removed. The motor itself has a worm gear on the shaft that turns the small intermediate gear which then rotates the gear and tube assembly, which rotates the crank arm (not shown) that connects to the wiper linkage. (b) If the brush retainer becomes loose, the wiper motor will stop because the brushes get their ground connection through the retainer and housing.

vides the necessary electrical connections for either speed. Switches in the mechanical wiper motor assembly provide the necessary operation for parking and concealing of the wipers. See Figure 20–5 for a typical wiper motor assembly.

Other wiper motors normally use a permanent-magnet motor with a low-speed brush and a high-speed brush. The brush connects the battery to the internal windings of the motor, and the two brushes provide for two different motor speeds.

The ground brush is directly opposite the low-speed brush. Off to the side of the low-speed brush is the high-speed brush. When current flows through the high-speed brush, there are fewer turns on the armature between the hot and ground brushes, and therefore the resistance is less. With less resistance, more current flows and the armature revolves faster. See Figures 20–6 through 20–8.

Variable-delay wipers (also called **pulse wipers**) use an electronic circuit with a variable resistor that controls the time of the charge and discharge of a capacitor. This charging and discharging

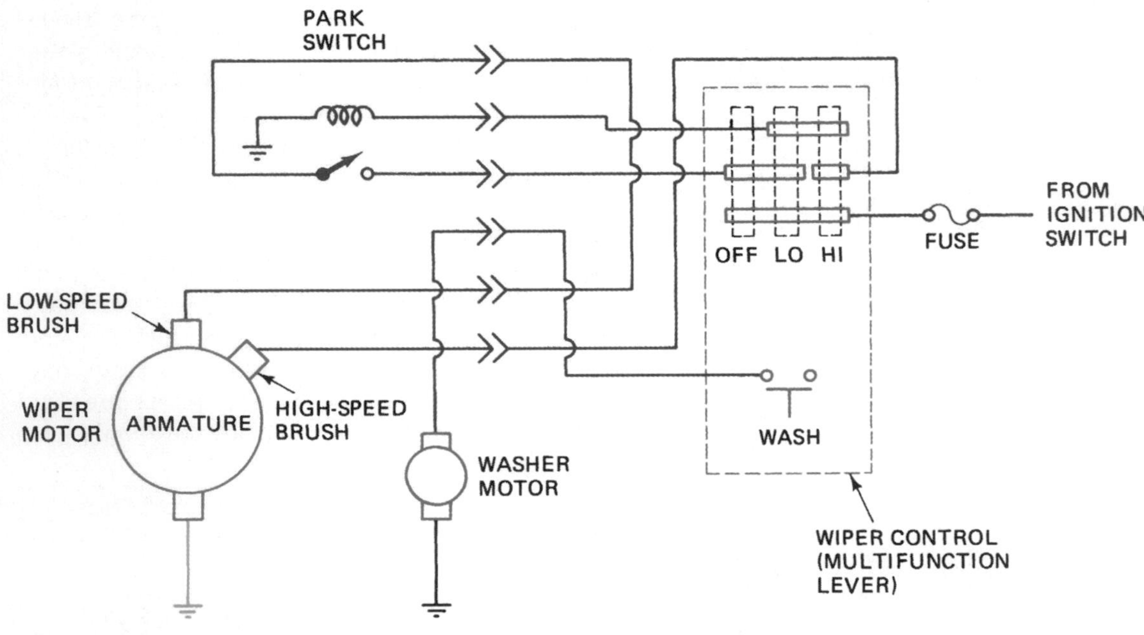

Figure 20–6 Typical wiring diagram of a two-speed windshield wiper circuit using a three-brush, two-speed motor. The dashed line for the multifunction lever indicates that the circuit shown is only a part of the total function of the steering column lever.

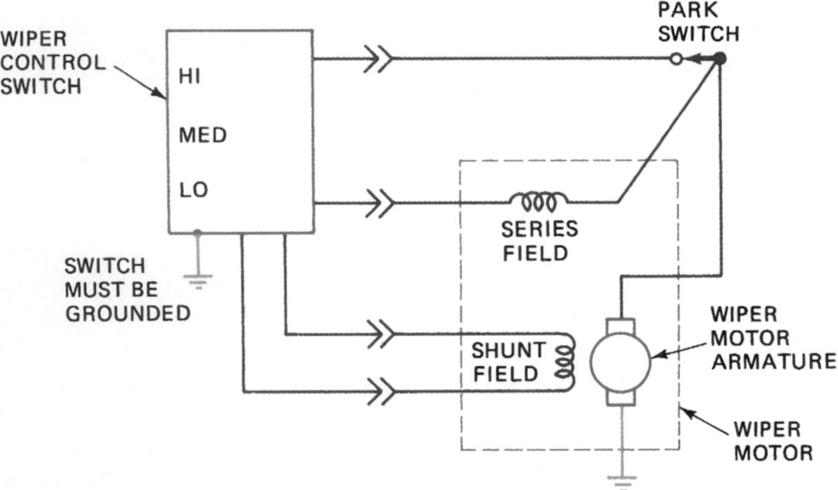

Figure 20–7 Typical wiring diagram of a three-speed windshield wiper circuit using a two-brush motor, but both a series and a shunt field coil.

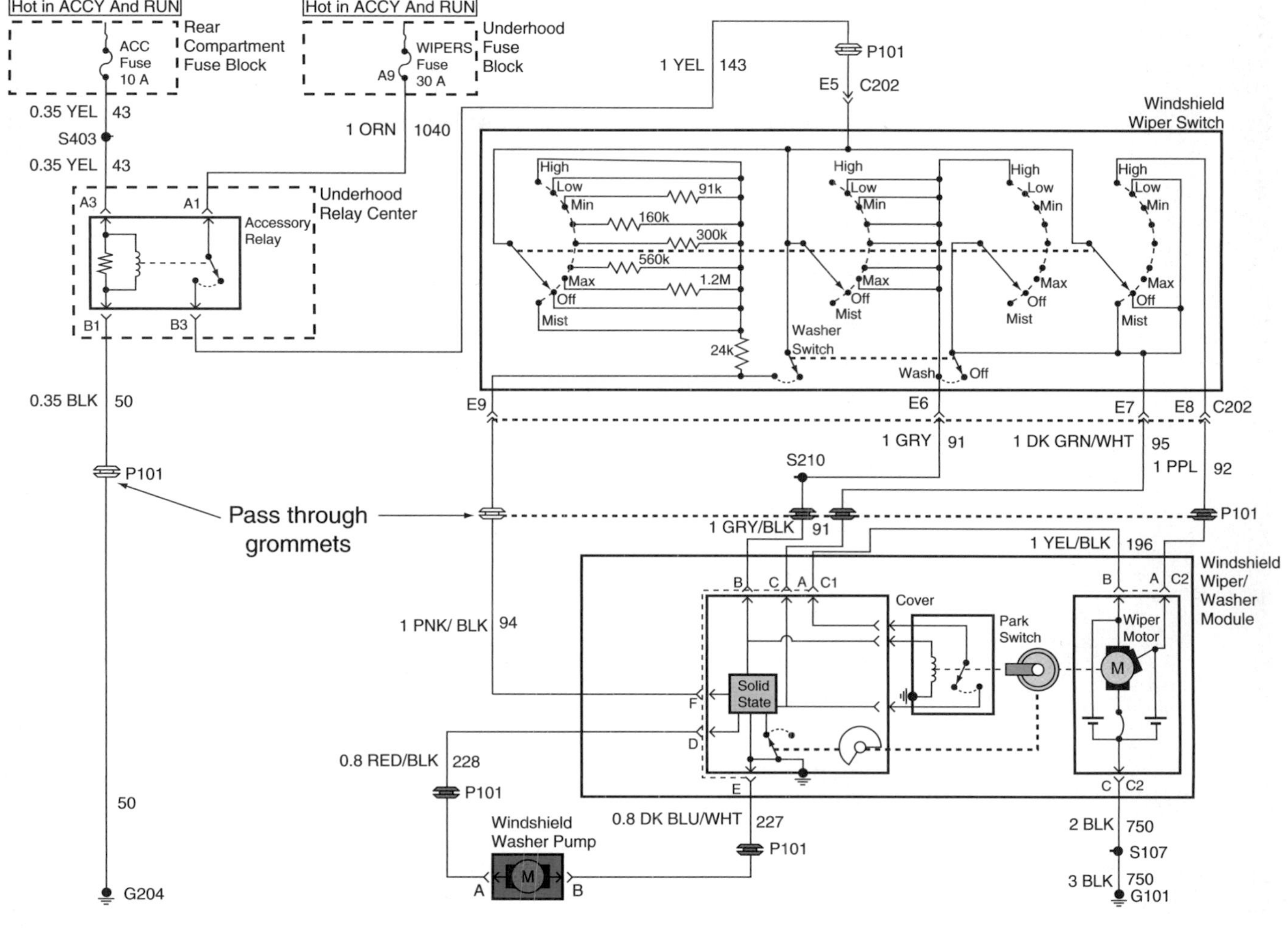

Figure 20–8 A variable pulse rate windshield wiper circuit. Notice that the wiring travels from the passenger compartment to underhood through rubber grommets called pass-throughs.

of the capacitor controls the circuit for the operation of the wiper motor.

HORNS

Vehicles have one or two horns. See Figure 20–9. When two horns are used, each has a different tone when operated separately, yet the sound combines when both are operated. Automotive horns, or horn relays, are usually wired directly to battery voltage from the fuse panel; they are hot at all times. The majority of automobiles, except for most Fords, utilize a horn relay. With a relay, the horn button on the steering wheel or column completes a circuit to ground that closes a relay, and the heavy current flow required by the horn then travels from the relay to the horn. See Figure 20–10.

Horns are manufactured in several different tones or frequencies ranging between 1800 and 3550 Hz. Vehicle manufacturers can select from various horn tones for a particular vehicle sound.

Horn Diagnosis

To help determine the cause of an inoperative horn, use a jumper wire and connect one end to the positive post of the battery and the other end to the wire terminal of the horn itself. If the horn works, the problem is in the circuit supplying current to the horn. If the horn does not work, the horn itself could be defective or the mounting bracket may not be providing a good ground.

If a replacement horn is required, attempt to use a horn of the same tone as the original. The tone is usually indicated by a number or letter stamped on the body of the horn.

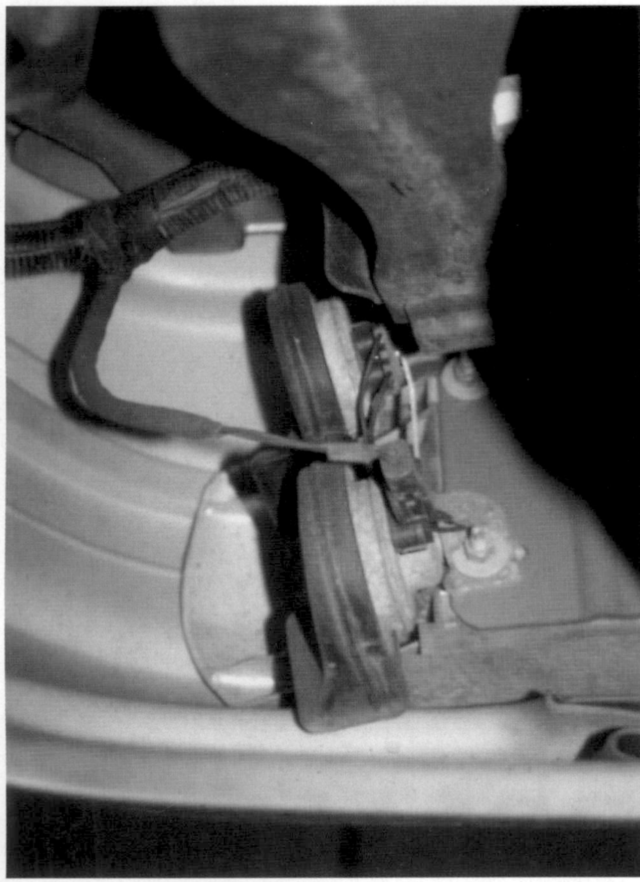

Figure 20–9 The two horns on this vehicle were finally located under the front bumper. They were not visible until the vehicle was hoisted.

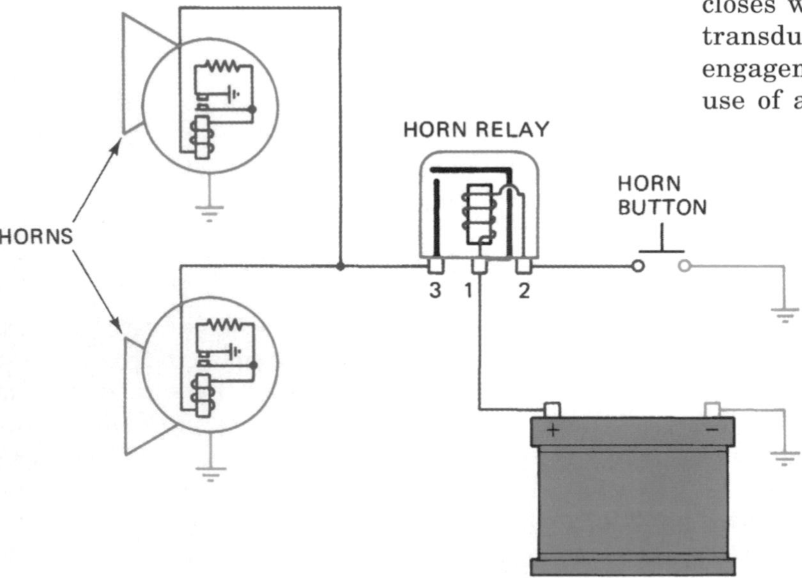

Figure 20–10 Typical horn circuit. Note that the horn button completes the ground circuit for the relay.

CRUISE CONTROL

Cruise (speed) control is a combination of electrical and mechanical components designed to maintain a constant, set vehicle speed without driver pressure on the accelerator pedal. Major components of a typical cruise control system include the following:

1. **Servo unit.** The servo unit attaches to the throttle linkage through a cable or chain. The servo unit controls the movement of the throttle by receiving a controlled amount of vacuum from a control unit. See Figure 20–11.
2. **Transducer.** A transducer is an electrical and mechanical speed-sensing and control unit.
3. **Speed set control.** A speed set control is a switch or control located on the steering column, steering wheel, dash, or console. Many cruise control units feature coast, accelerate, and resume functions. See Figure 20–12.
4. **Safety release switches.** Whenever the brake pedal is depressed, the cruise control system is disengaged through use of an electrical and vacuum switch, usually located on the brake pedal bracket. Both electrical and vacuum releases are used to be certain that the cruise control system is released, even in the event of failure of one of the release switches.

Basic Cruise Control Operation

A typical cruise control system can be set only if the vehicle speed is 50 km/h (30 mph) or more. In older noncomputer-operated systems, the transducer contains a low-speed electrical switch that closes whenever the speed-sensing section of the transducer senses a speed exceeding the minimum engagement speed. Most transducers operate by use of a speedometer cable driven off the trans-

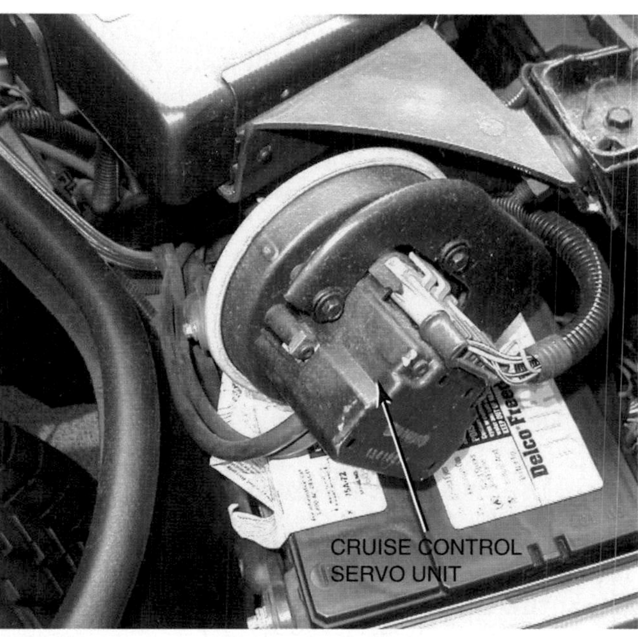

Figure 20–11 This cruise control servo unit has an electrical connection with wires that go to the cruise control module or the vehicle computer, depending on the vehicle. The vacuum hoses supply engine manifold vacuum to the rubber diaphragm that moves the throttle linkage to maintain the preset speed.

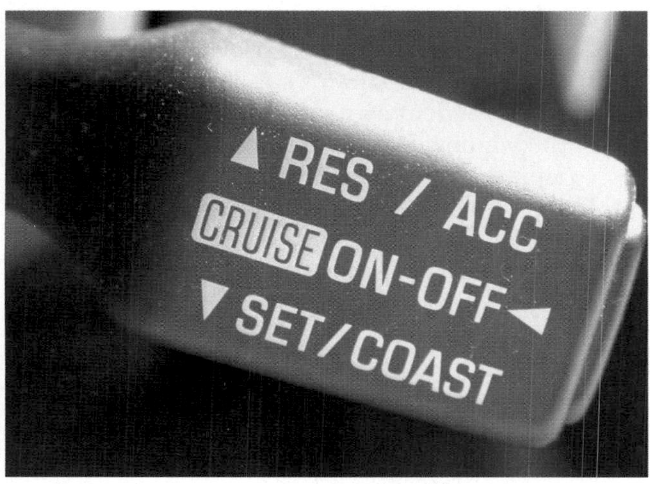

Figure 20–12 A cruise control used on a Toyota/Lexus.

mission. The speedometer cable rotates a magnetic disk that applies a rotary force to a rubber clutch. As the rubber clutch tends to rotate, a tang on the clutch closes the low-speed switch whenever the road speed exceeds the minimum engagement speed.

An electric solenoid operates a clutch spring wrapped around the rubber clutch and squeezes the rubber clutch whenever the driver-operated engagement switch is activated. The clutch spring is held tight around the rubber clutch and opens and closes vacuum ports that control the amount of vacuum for the vacuum servo attached to the throttle linkage. If the vehicle speed increases, a greater rotary force is exerted on the rubber clutch, which rotates slightly, uncovering vent slots in the vacuum control for the servo, reducing its pull on the throttle linkage. If the vehicle speed is reduced, the force on the rubber clutch is reduced, which closes the vacuum vent for the servo, resulting in a greater vacuum in the servo. This high vacuum exerts a greater opening force on the throttle, and the engine speed is increased. In actual operation, the throttle is moved only enough to maintain a constant road speed regardless of terrain.

TECH TIP 

Bump Problems

Cruise-control problem diagnosis can involve a complex series of checks and tests. The troubleshooting procedures vary from manufacturer to manufacturer (and year to year), so a technician should always consult a service manual for the exact vehicle being serviced. However, every cruise-control system uses a brake safety switch and, if the vehicle has manual transmission, a clutch safety switch. The purpose of these safety switches is to ensure that the cruise-control system is disabled if the brakes are applied. Some systems use two brake pedal safety switches, one electrical to cut off power to the system and the other vacuum to bleed vacuum away from the actuating unit.

If the cruise control "cuts out" or disengages itself while travelling over bumpy roads, the most common cause is a misadjusted brake (and/or clutch) safety switch(es). Often, a simple readjustment of these safety switches will cure the intermittent cruise-control disengagement problems.

CAUTION: Always follow manufacturers' recommended safety switch adjustment procedures. If the brake safety switch(es) is misadjusted, it could keep pressure applied to the master brake cylinder, resulting in severe damage to the braking system.

Noncomputer-Controlled Resume-Type Cruise Control

Most resume-style noncomputer-controlled cruise control systems use a two-piece rubber clutch to retain a "mechanical memory" of the vehicle road speed. Depressing the brake pedal causes a vacuum-release solenoid to release vacuum from the servo unit, and the cruise control stops maintaining vehicle speed. When "resume" is pushed, the vacuum solenoid closes and vacuum is again applied to the servo unit. The speed is "remembered" by the position of the split rubber clutch.

Computer-Controlled Cruise Control

Most computer-controlled cruise-control systems use the vehicle's speed sensor input to the engine-control computer for speed reference. Computer-controlled cruise-control units use servo units or electric drive motors for throttle control, control switches for driver control of cruise control functions, and electrical brake pedal release switches.

Troubleshooting Cruise Control

Cruise-control system troubleshooting is usually performed using the step-by-step procedure as specified by the vehicle manufacturer. A quick method used by many dealers is to use known good components (usually from a demonstrator vehicle) that can be quickly plugged in to check for proper operation.

POWER WINDOWS

Power windows use electric motors to raise and lower door glass. They can be operated by both a **master control switch** located beside the driver and additional **independent switches** for each electric window. Some power window systems use a **lockout switch** located on the driver's controls to prevent operation of the power windows from the independent switches. Power windows are designed to operate only with the ignition switch in the "on" (run) position. This safety feature of power windows should never be defeated. Some manufacturers use a time delay for accessory power after the ignition switch is turned off. This feature permits the driver and passengers an opportunity to close all windows or operate other accessories for about 10 minutes or until a vehicle door is opened after the ignition has been turned off.

Most power window systems use permanent-magnet electric motors. It is possible to run a PM motor in the reverse direction simply by reversing the polarity of the two wires going to the motor. Most power window motors do not require that the motor be grounded to the body (door) of the vehicle. The ground for all the power windows is most often centralized near the driver's master control switch. The up-and-down motion of the individual window motors is controlled by double-pole, double-throw (DPDT) switches. These DPDT switches have five contacts and permit battery voltage to be applied to the power window motor and to reverse the polarity and direction of the motor. See Figures 20–13 and 20–14.

The power window motors rotate a mechanism called a window **regulator.** The window regulator is attached to the door glass and controls opening and closing of the glass. Door glass adjustments such as glass tilt and upper and lower stops are usually the same for both power and manual windows.

Troubleshooting Power Windows

Before troubleshooting a power window problem, check for proper operation of all power windows. If one of the **control** wires that run from the independent switch to the master switch is cut (open), the power window may operate in just one direction. The window may go down but not up, or vice versa. However, if one of the **direction** wires that run from the independent switch to the motor is cut (open), the window will not operate in either direction. The direction wires and the motor must be electrically connected to permit operation and change of direction of the electric lift motor in the door.

1. If *both* rear door windows fail to operate from the independent switches, check the operation of the window lockout (if the vehicle is so equipped) and the master control switch.
2. If one window can move in one direction only, check for continuity in the control wires (wires between the independent control switch and the master control switch).
3. If *all* windows fail to work or fail to work occasionally, check, clean, and tighten the ground wire(s) located either behind the driver's interior door panel or under the dash on the driver's side. A defective fuse or circuit breaker could also cause all the windows to fail to operate.
4. If one window fails to operate in both directions, the problem could be a defective window lift motor. The window could be stuck in the track of the door, which could cause the circuit breaker built into the motor to open the circuit to protect the wiring, switches, and motor from damage. To check for a stuck door glass, attempt to move (even slightly) the door glass up and down, forward and back, and side to side. If the window glass can move slightly in all directions, the power window motor should be able to at least move the glass.

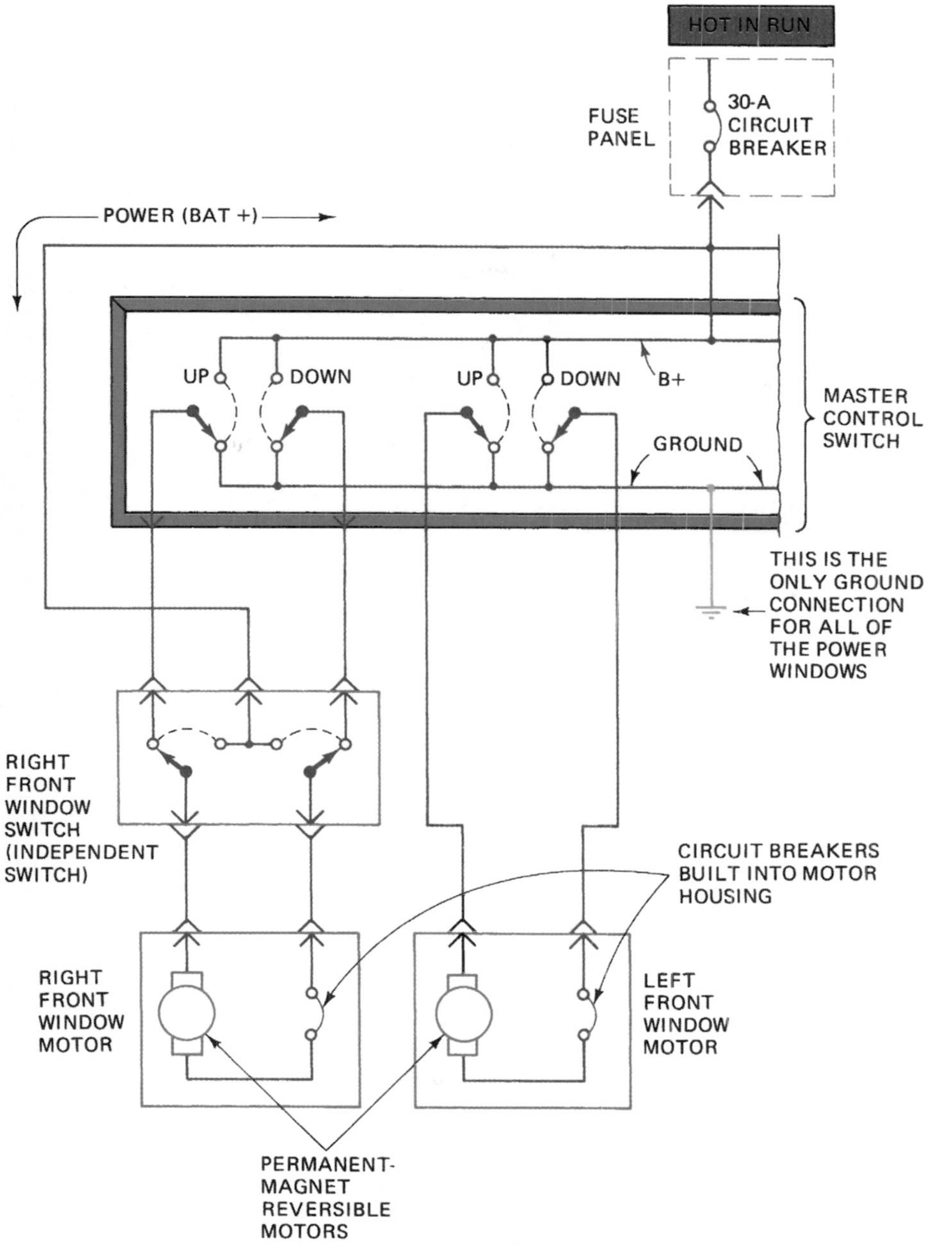

HOT IN RUN
FUSE PANEL
30-A CIRCUIT BREAKER
POWER (BAT +)
UP
DOWN
UP
DOWN
B+
GROUND
MASTER CONTROL SWITCH
THIS IS THE ONLY GROUND CONNECTION FOR ALL OF THE POWER WINDOWS
RIGHT FRONT WINDOW SWITCH (INDEPENDENT SWITCH)
CIRCUIT BREAKERS BUILT INTO MOTOR HOUSING
RIGHT FRONT WINDOW MOTOR
LEFT FRONT WINDOW MOTOR
PERMANENT-MAGNET REVERSIBLE MOTORS

Figure 20–13 Typical power window circuit using PM motors. Control of the direction of window operation is achieved by directing the polarity of the current through the nongrounded motors. The *only* ground for the entire system is located at the master control (driver's side) switch assembly.

(a)

(b)

Figure 20–14 (a) The independent (driver's door) power window switch plate looks like a normal simple switch until you turn it over. (b) Notice that this power window contains a large integrated circuit with a number of other electronic components to operate the express up and express down.

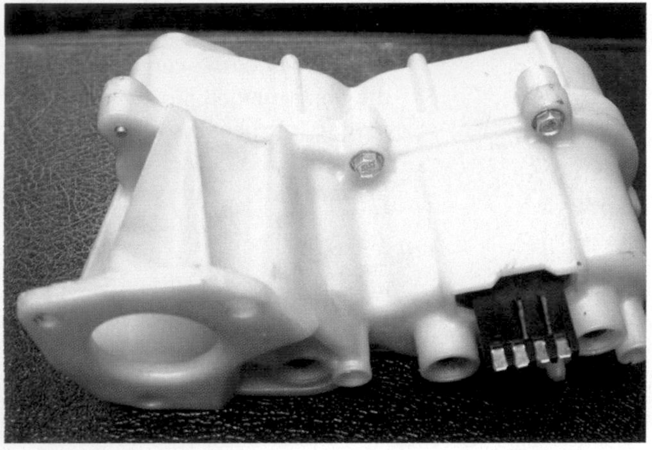

Figure 20–15 A typical power seat transmission assembly. Even though many of these units can be disassembled, they are designed to be replaced as an assembly if any part inside is defective.

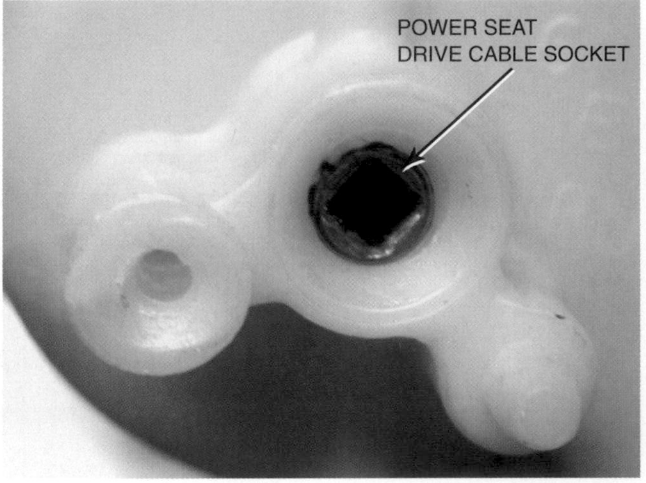

Figure 20–16 A close-up of the socket where the drive cable is inserted into the power seat transmission assembly.

POWER SEATS

A typical power-operated seat includes a reversible electric motor and a transmission assembly that has three solenoids and six **drive cables** that turn the six seat adjusters. See Figure 20–15. A six-way power seat offers seat movement forward and backward, plus seat cushion movement up and down at the front and the rear. The drive cables are very similar to speedometer cables because they rotate inside a cable housing and connect the power output of the seat transmission to a gear or screw jack assembly that moves the seat. See Figure 20–16. A **screw jack assembly,** often called a **gear nut,** is used to move the front or back of the seat cushion up and down. Between the electric motor and the transmission is usually a **rubber coupling** that could permit the electric motor to continue to rotate in the event of a jammed seat. This coupling is designed to prevent motor damage.

Most power seats use a permanent-magnet motor that can be reversed by simply reversing the polarity of the current sent to the motor by the seat switch. See Figure 20–17. Most PM motors have a built-in circuit breaker to protect the motor from overheating. Many Ford power seat motors use three separate armatures inside one large permanent-magnet field housing. Some power seats use a series-wound electric motor with two separate field coils, one field coil for each direction of rotation. This type of power seat motor typically uses a relay to control the direction of current from the seat switch to the corresponding field coil of the seat motor. This type of power seat can be identified by the click heard whenever the seat switch is changed from up to down or front to back, or vice versa. The click is the sound of the relay switching the field coil current. Some power seats use as many as eight separate PM motors that operate all functions of the seat, including headrest height, seat length, and side bolsters, in addition to the usual six-way power seat functions. Some power seats use a small air pump to inflate a bag or bags in the lower part of the back of the seat, called the **lumbar** because it supports the lumbar section of the spine.

Troubleshooting Power Seats

Power seats are usually wired from the fuse panel to operate continuously without having to turn the ignition switch to "on" (run). If a power seat does not operate or make any noise, the circuit breaker (or fuse, if the vehicle is so equipped) should be checked first.

Step 1 Check the circuit breaker, usually located on the fuse panel, using a test light. The test light should light on both sides of the circuit breaker even with the ignition off. If the seat relay clicks, the circuit breaker is functioning, but the relay or electric motor may be defective.

Step 2 Remove the screws or clips that retain the controls to the inner door panel or seat and check for voltage at the seat control.

Step 3 Also check the ground connection(s) at the transmission and clutch control solenoids (if equipped). The solenoids must be properly grounded to the vehicle body for the power seat circuit to operate.

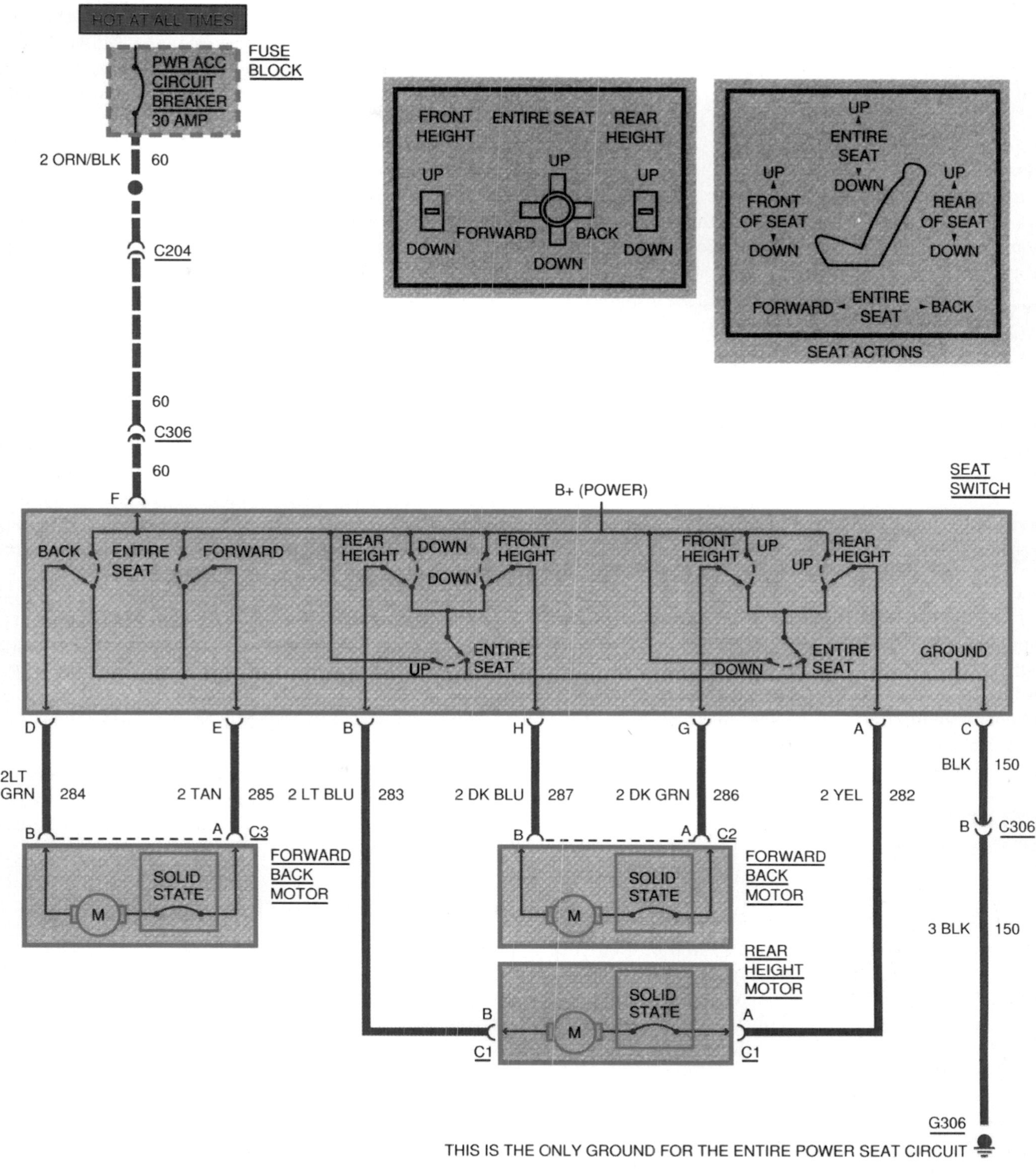

Figure 20–17 Typical power seat circuit diagram. Notice that each motor has a built-in electronic (solid state) PTC circuit protector. The seat control switch can change the direction in which the motor(s) run by reversing the direction in which the current flows through the motor.

If the power seat motor runs but does not move the seat, the most likely fault is a worn or defective rubber clutch sleeve between the electric seat motor and the transmission.

If the seat relay clicks but the seat motor does not operate, the problem is usually a defective seat motor or defective wiring between the motor and the relay. If the power seat uses a motor relay, the motor has a double reverse-wound field for reversing the motor direction. This type of electric motor must be properly grounded.

HINT: Power seats are often difficult to service because of restricted working room. If the entire seat cannot be removed from the vehicle because the track bolts are covered, attempt to remove the seat from the top of the power seat assembly. These bolts are almost always accessible regardless of seat position.

What Every Driver Should Know About Power Seats

Power seats use an electric motor or motors to move the position of the seat. These electric motors turn small cables that operate mechanisms that move the seat. *Never* place rags, newspapers, or any other object under a power seat. Even ice scrapers can get caught between moving parts of the seat and can often cause serious damage or jamming of the power seat.

ELECTRIC POWER DOOR LOCKS

Electric power door locks use either a solenoid or a permanent-magnet (PM) motor to lock or unlock all vehicle door locks from a control switch or switches. Large (heavy) solenoids were typically used before the mid-1970s. These solenoids normally used two-wire connections that carried a high current through a relay controlled by a door lock switch. With a solenoid-style door lock, only one of the two wires is used at any one time. If current flows through one wire to the solenoid, the door locks; the door unlocks when current flows through the other wire to the solenoid. The solenoids must be grounded to the metal of the door to complete the electrical circuit. Because of constant opening and closing of a typical vehicle door, a solenoid-style power door lock frequently vibrates loose from the mounting inside the door and fails to operate because of the poor ground connection with the metal door.

Most electric door locks use a permanent-magnet (PM) reversible electric motor that operates the lock-activating rod. PM reversible motors do not require grounding because, as with power windows, the motor control is determined by the polarity of the current through the two motor wires. See Figure 20–18. Some two-door vehicles do *not* use a power door lock relay because the current flow for only two PM motors can be handled through the door lock switches. However, most four-door vehicles and vans with power locks on rear and side doors use a relay to control the current flow necessary to operate four or more power door lock motors. The door lock relay is controlled by the door lock switch and is commonly the location of the one and only *ground* connection for the entire door lock circuit.

SECURITY SYSTEMS

Canada is no stranger to auto theft; in fact one Canadian city holds the distinction of having the highest auto theft rate in North America. While older vehicles are very vulnerable, easy to break into and start, late model passenger cars have a number of factory installed security systems that make theft not impossible, but much more difficult.

The Insurance Corporation of British Columbia (ICBC) tests many factory and after-market anti-theft devices, rates their effectiveness and provides this information to companies in Canada, the U.S., and many other countries around the world.

Although add-ons such as steering wheel locking bars, brake pedal and shifter lever locks are worthwhile, police officers from the Integrated Municipal Provincial Auto Crime Team (IMPACT) and ICBC both rate electronic security, such as vehicle immobilizers, the most effective auto-theft deterrent.

Perimeter Anti-Theft Alarms

This is a fairly simple system that uses the factory "door open" warning light switches to communicate with the anti-theft module (computer). If any of the doors, trunk or hood are forcibly unlocked, the horn will blow, the headlights, taillights and turn signals will flash, and the interior lights will turn on (see Figure 20–19).

Factory systems are usually set with the keyless-entry remote transmitter. An anti-theft indicator lamp on the dashboard will illuminate or flash when the system is armed.

Remote Keyless Entry

The wireless remote-control system is used to lock and unlock doors, open the trunk, provide interior illumination with the "unlock" command and activate the alarm system, all from a distance. The number of functions and the operating range, 1 to 10 m (3 to 30 ft), will vary among makes. See Figure 20–20.

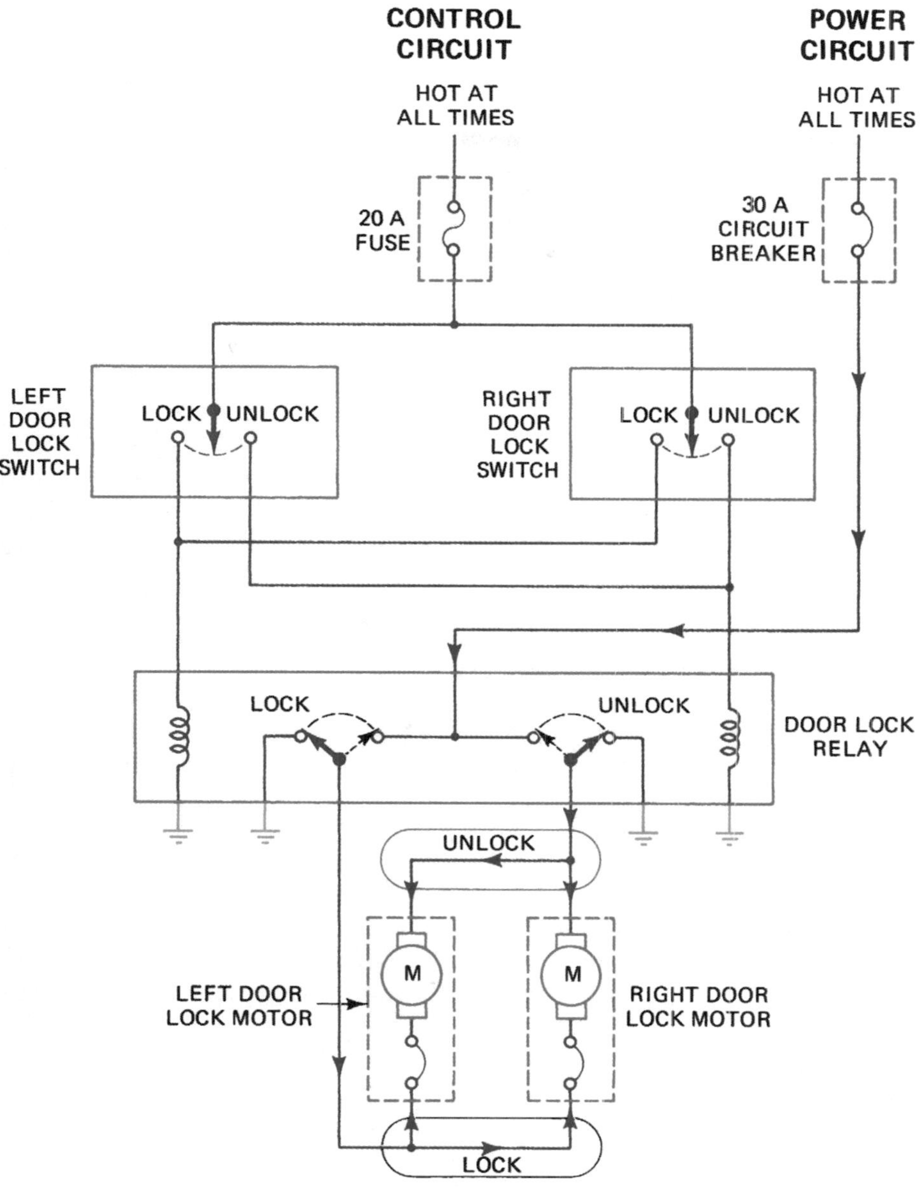

Figure 20–18 Typical electric power door lock circuit diagram. Note that the control circuit is protected by a fuse, whereas the power circuit is protected by a circuit breaker. As with the operation of power windows, power door locks typically use reversible PM nongrounded electric motors. These motors are geared mechanically to the lock-unlock mechanism.

The hand-held transmitter is powered by one, or two, lithium batteries, which require periodic replacement. The transmitter sends out a signal frequency that is received by a lock control module mounted in the vehicle. See Figure 20–21. The lock module activates relays, which operate the door and trunk lock mechanisms, lights and alarm.

On a typical four-button transmitter, pushing the "unlock" button once will unlock the driver's door, twice unlocks all the doors; pushing the "lock" button locks all the doors. A light flash and an audible beep confirms the command has been completed. A third button opens the trunk and the fourth button operates the alarm.

Diagnosis

If the system is intermittent or not operating, perform the following:

1. Try the second transmitter (if available).
2. If the system now operates, the first transmitter requires batteries or replacement. The replacement will require programming to match the vehicle receiver.

(a)

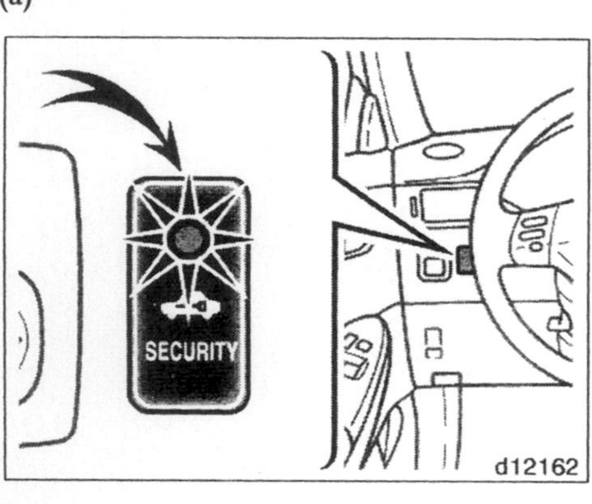

(b)

Figure 20–19 Perimeter anti-theft alarm. (a) The horns blow, lights flash, and the interior lights come on. (b) The security indicator light flashes when the system is armed. (Courtesy Toyota Canada Inc.)

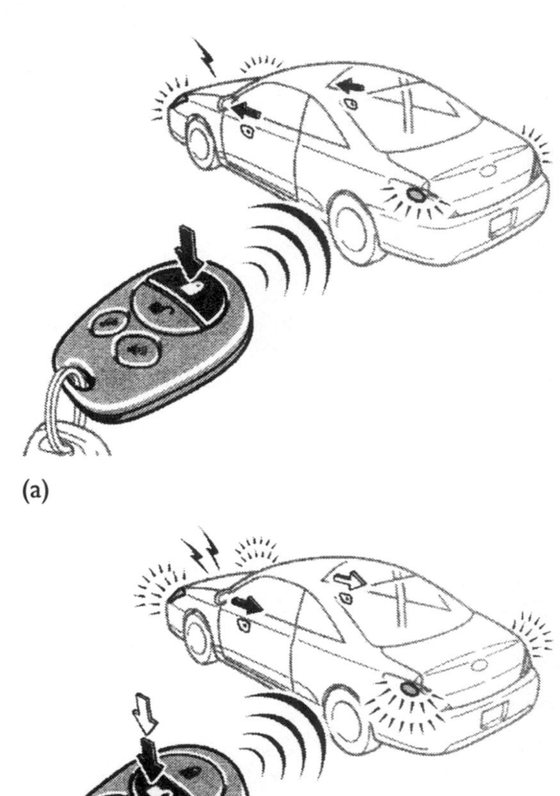

(a)

(b)

Figure 20–20 This four-button transmitter controls locks, interior lights, and the alarm system. (a) Locking operation. (b) Unlocking operation. (Courtesy Toyota Canada Inc.)

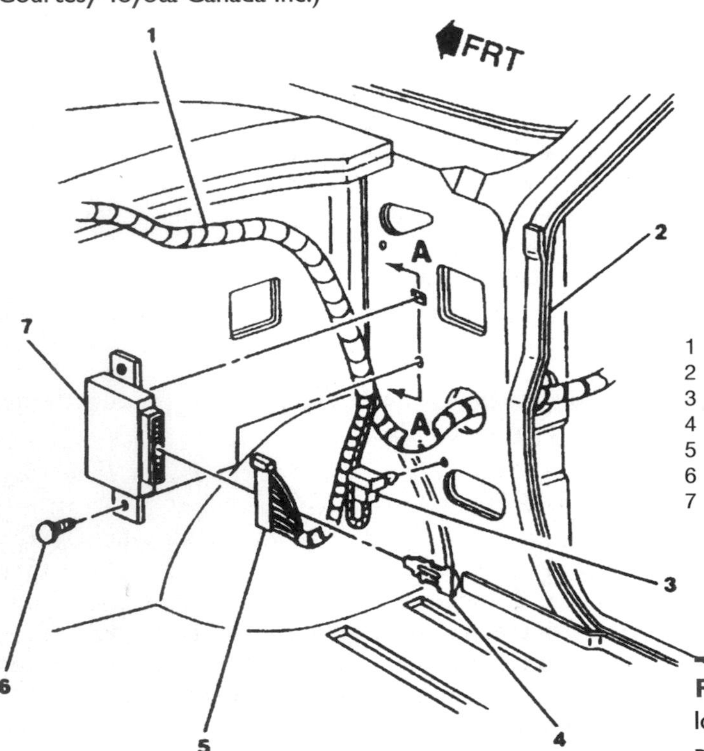

Figure 20–21 The lock control module (receiver) can be located behind the kick panels, glove box, or rear quarter panels. (Courtesy General Motors of Canada Ltd.)

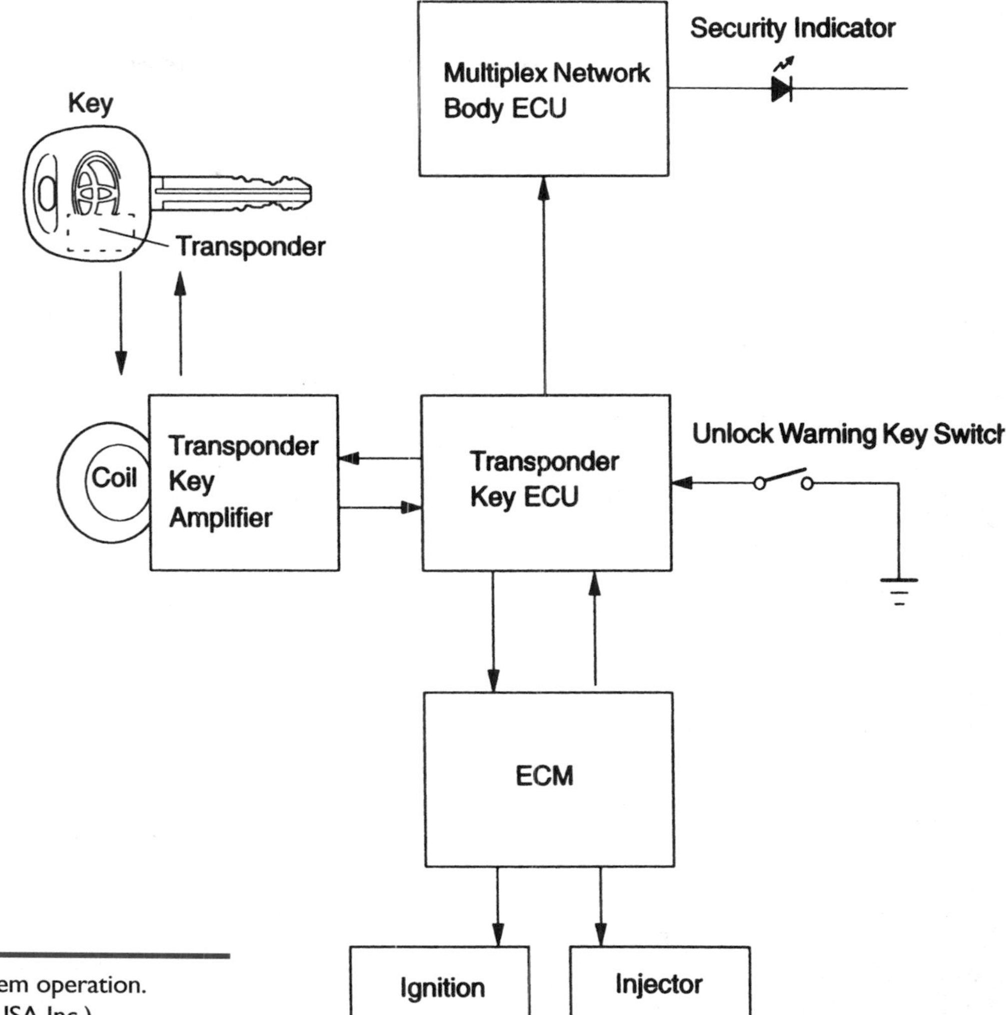

Figure 20–22 Immobilizer system operation. (Courtesy Toyota Motor Sales, USA Inc.)

3. The batteries should be replaced first when only one transmitter is available.
4. Confirm the operation of other system components by using the vehicle key, rather than the remote.
5. Cold temperatures will reduce range; one maker reports a loss of 3 m (10 ft) when the temperature drops from 20°C (70°F) to 0°C (32°F).
6. If the above steps have not isolated the problem, consult the shop manual for symptom-driven electrical diagnostics.

Immobilizer Systems

High-tech immobilizers are difficult to defeat and are the most effective theft deterrent. They first became original equipment on mid-1990s Ford Mustangs. They are expected to be an industry standard by 2006. Although many passenger cars are now factory equipped, the majority of light trucks are not. Insurance statistics indicate a reduction of stolen late-model passenger cars, but an increase in light truck and older vehicle thefts.

There are a number of after-market immobilizers that can be retrofitted to almost any vehicle. Good ones can be expensive, up to $500 or more, but worth it for the added security.

Operation

The immobilizer anti-theft system uses radio frequency identification that adds an additional level of theft deterrence.

Embedded in the ignition key is an electrical transponder that communicates with a transceiver module mounted near, or around, the ignition switch. The transponder contains an electronic identification code with billions of possible combinations. The transceiver module must receive the correct key code from the transponder before it will allow the powertrain control module (PCM) to start the engine. If the PCM does not receive the correct password from the transceiver, it will disable the starter and fuel injectors. See Figures 20–22 and 20–23.

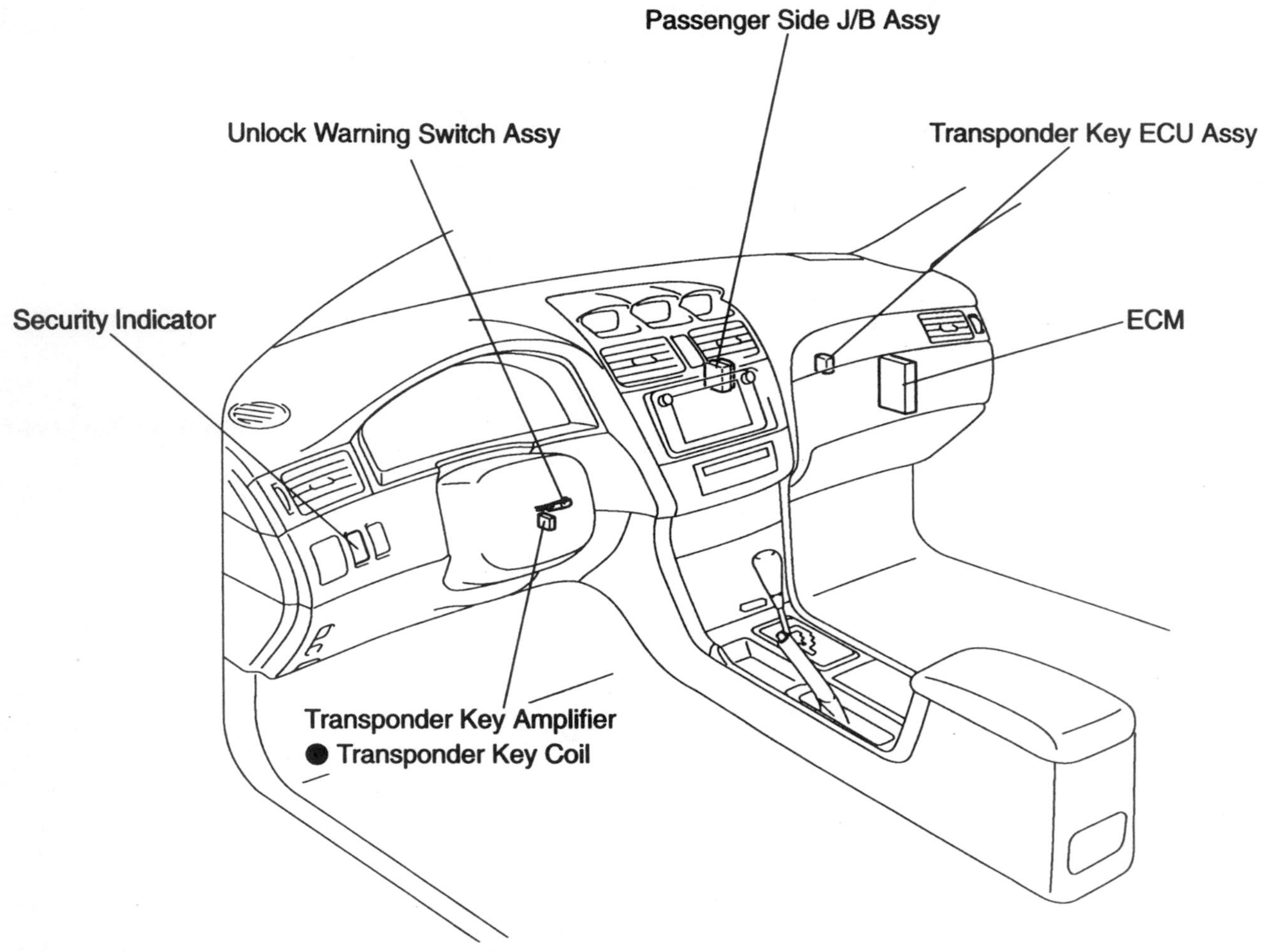

Figure 20–23 Immobilizer system components. (Courtesy Toyota Motor Sales, USA Inc.)

Even though a recut key will turn the ignition lock, the vehicle will not start. Replacement keys can be purchased from the dealer and must be programmed to match the transceiver module.

Satellite Tracking

The global positioning system (GPS), which originated with the military, allows vehicle tracking to within 100 m (300 ft). The systems range from a simple after-market retrofit to a sophisticated factory supplied installation that includes driver assistance, remote door opening, and vehicle location. See Figure 20–24.

General Motors OnStar System

This system links the customer to the GM OnStar centre with cellular technology. Centre advisors will assist OnStar subscribers by summoning emergency service, roadside assistance, vehicle location, and a number of other services. Deployment of the air bags automatically sends a signal to the centre.

Satellite signals are received by the vehicle's GPS antenna. The receiver uses this information to calculate the position of the vehicle. The driver sends this information to the OnStar centre via the on-board cellular telephone; the OnStar advisor will then send assistance or guide the customer to their destination.

The OnStar system is made up of several components:

- Vehicle communication unit (VCU)—contains the cellular phone transceiver.
- Vehicle interface unit (VIU)—contains the GPS receiver and exchanges data with other electronic modules.
- Phone hand-set—usually located on the console.
- Cellular antenna.
- GPS antenna.

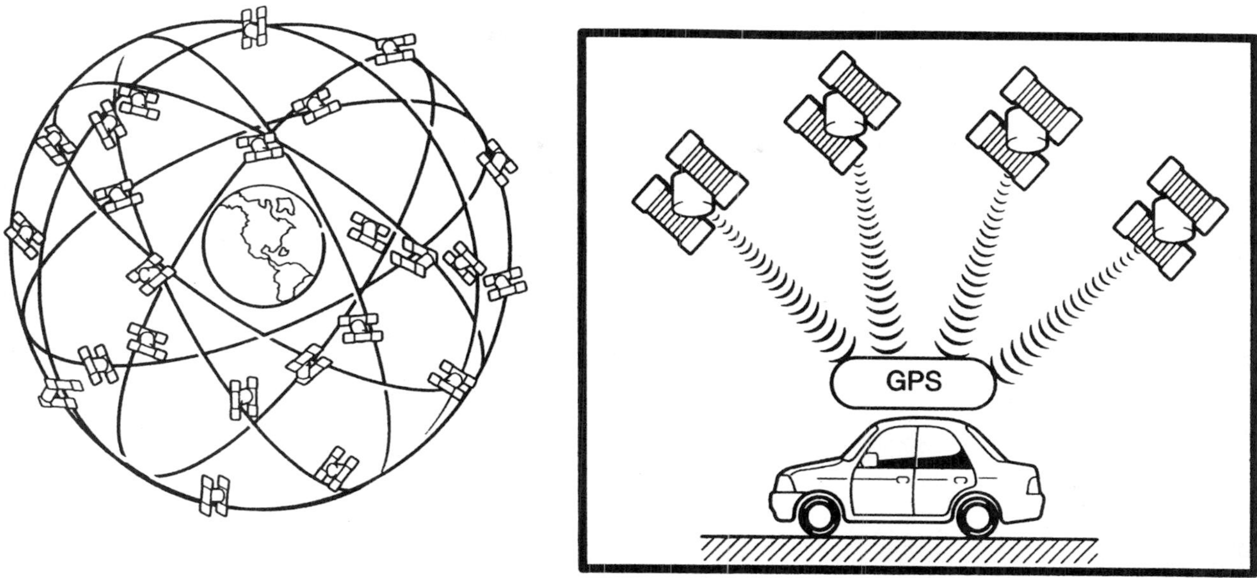
Current longitude/latitude/altitude is determined using the radio wave arrival time from four satellites.
GPS

Figure 20–24 GPS satellite tracking. (Courtesy Toyota Motor Sales, USA Inc.)

- Hands-free microphone—mounted in the headliner.

The OnStar centre can also be contacted from an outside telephone for remote door unlocking, provided the customer gives the OnStar advisor the correct unlock code for that vehicle.

Service and repair of this system is usually performed at the dealership level by factory trained technicians. After-market systems are serviced by independent technicians who specialize in this type of repair.

HEATED REAR WINDOW DEFOGGERS

An electrically heated rear window defogger system uses an electrical grid baked on the glass that warms the glass to about 30°C (85°F) and clears it of fog or frost. The rear window is also called a **backlight.** The rear window defogger system is controlled by a driver-operated switch and a timer relay. The timer relay is necessary because the window grid can draw up to 30 A, and continued operation would put a strain on the battery and the charging system. Generally, the timer relay permits current to flow through the rear window grid for only 10 minutes. If the window is still not clear of fog after 10 minutes, the driver can turn the defogger on again, but after the first 10 minutes any additional defogger operation is limited to 5 minutes.

Electric grid-type rear window defoggers can be damaged easily by careless cleaning or scraping of the inside of the rear window glass. Short broken sections of the rear window grid can be repaired using a special epoxy-based electrically conductive material. If more than one section is damaged or if the damaged grid length is greater than approximately 50 mm (2 in.), a replacement rear-window glass may be required to restore proper defogger operation.

The electrical current through the grids depends, in part, on the temperature of the conductor grids. As the temperature decreases, the resistance of the grids decreases and the current flow increases, helping to warm the rear glass. As the temperature of the glass increases, the resistance of the conductor grids increases and the current flow decreases. Therefore, the defogger system tends to self-regulate the electrical current requirements to match the need for defogging.

Troubleshooting a Heated Rear Window Defogger

Troubleshooting a nonfunctioning rear-window defogger unit involves using a test light or a voltmeter to check for voltage to the grid. If no voltage is present at the rear window, check for voltage at the switch and relay timer assembly. A poor ground

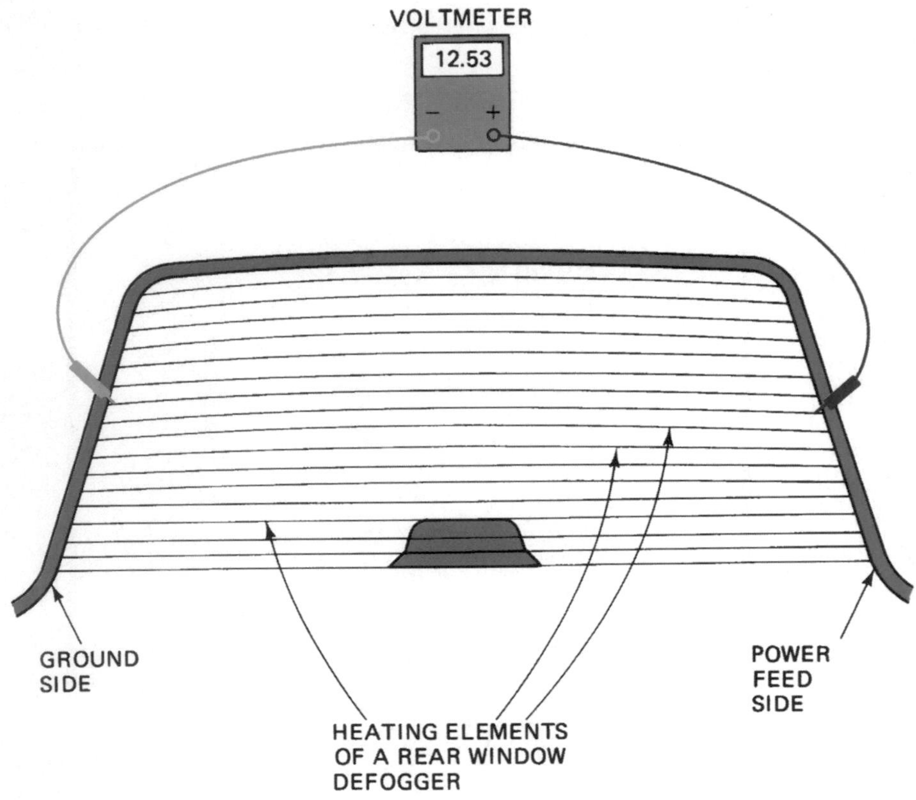

Figure 20–25 Checking a rear-window defogger grid with a voltmeter. As the voltmeter positive lead is moved along the grid (on the inside of the vehicle), the voltmeter reading should steadily decrease as the meter approaches the ground side of the grid.

connection on the opposite side of the grid from the power side can also cause the rear defogger not to operate. Because most defogger circuits use an indicator light switch and a relay timer, it is possible to have the indicator light on, even if the wires are disconnected at the rear-window grid. A voltmeter can be used to test the operation of the rear-window defogger grid. See Figure 20–25. With the negative test terminal attached to a good body ground, carefully probe the grid conductors. There should be a decreasing voltage reading as the probe is moved from the power ("hot") side of the grid toward the ground side of the grid. If there is a broken grid wire, it can be repaired using an electrically conductive substance available in a repair kit. See Figure 20–26. Most vehicle manufacturers recommend that grid wire less than 50 mm (2 in.) long be repaired; otherwise the entire rear window will need to be replaced.

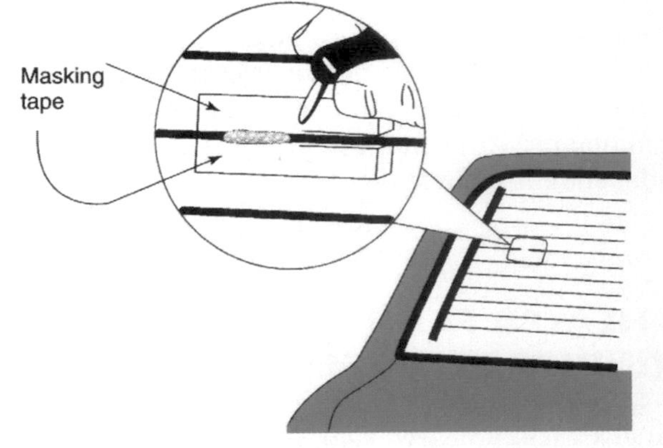

Figure 20–26 The typical repair material contains conductive silver-filled polymer, which dries in about 10 minutes and is usable in about 30 minutes.

AIRBAGS

Airbag-type passive restraints are designed to cushion the driver (or passenger, if the passenger side is so equipped) during a frontal collision. Airbags may be known by many different names including the following:

1. Supplemental restraint system (SRS)
2. Supplemental inflatable restraints (SIR)
3. Supplemental air restraints (SAR)
4. Supplemental air bag system

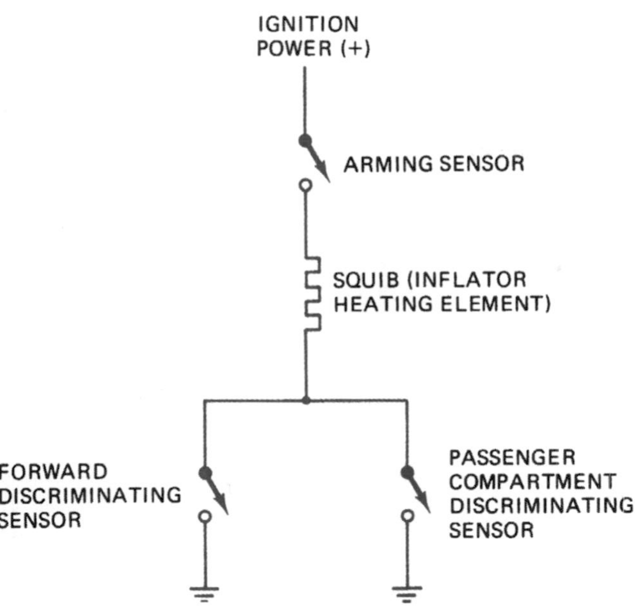

Figure 20–27 Typical airbag deployment circuit. Note that both the arming sensor and at least one of the discriminating sensors must be activated at the same time.

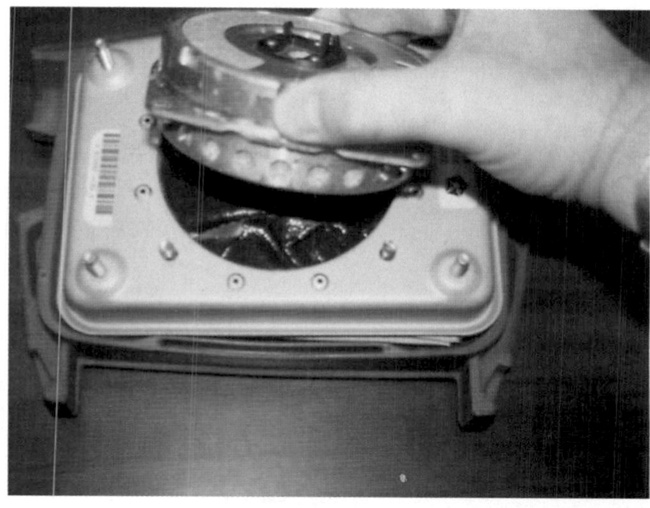

Figure 20–28 Lifting the squib from the air bag housing. The squib is the heating element that ignites the pyrotechnic gas generator that rapidly produces nitrogen gas to fill the airbag.

Airbags are designed to supplement the safety belts in the event of a collision. Most airbags are designed to be deployed only in the event of a frontal impact within 30 degrees of centre. Most airbag systems are *not* designed to inflate during side or rear impact. The force required to deploy a typical airbag is approximately equal to the force of a vehicle hitting a parked car of similar size and weight, head-on, at about 45 km/h (28 mph). The air bag system senses the severity of the crash, rather than the speed of the vehicle.

The force required to trigger the sensors within the system prevents accidental deployment if curbs are hit or the brakes are rapidly applied. The system requires a substantial force to deploy the airbag as a measure to help prevent accidental inflation.

Many recent systems incorporate air bags in the door panels or the upper sides of the front seats that will deploy if the vehicle is hit in the side with sufficient force. Some vans are also using side curtains that roll down from the roof line; these require a high roll angle before they will deploy. These side-curtain air bags are now being offered, either as an option or as original equipment, on a number of passenger cars.

Operation

A typical airbag system includes three sensors. See Figure 20–27 for the electrical operation. The **squib** is the heating element used to ignite the gas-generating material, usually sodium azide. It requires about 2 amperes of current to heat the element to ignite the inflator. See Figure 20–28. Once the inflator is ignited, the nylon bag quickly inflates (in about 30 ms, or 0.030 s) with nitrogen gas generated by the inflator. During an accident, the driver is thrown forward by the driver's own momentum toward the steering wheel. The strong nylon bag inflates at the same time. Personal injury is reduced by the spreading of the stopping force over the entire upper-body region. The normal collapsible steering column remains in operation and collapses in a collision when equipped with an airbag system. The bag is equipped with two large side vents that allow the bag to deflate immediately after inflation, once the bag has cushioned the occupant in a collision. See Figure 20–29. To cause inflation, the closing of the **arming sensor** is required to provide the power-side voltage to the inflator module. Before the airbag can inflate, however, the squib circuit must also have a ground. The ground is provided through the actuation of either the **forward** or the **passenger discriminating sensor.** Discriminating sensors are also known as crash sensors. In other words, two sensors *must* be triggered *at the same time* before the airbag will be deployed.

Sensors

All three sensors are basically switches that complete an electrical circuit when activated. The sensors are similar in construction and operation, and the *location* of the sensor determines its name. All airbag sensors are rigidly mounted to the vehicle and *must* be mounted with the arrow pointing toward the front of the vehicle to ensure that the sensor can detect rapid forward deceleration.

There are three basic styles (designs) of airbag sensors:

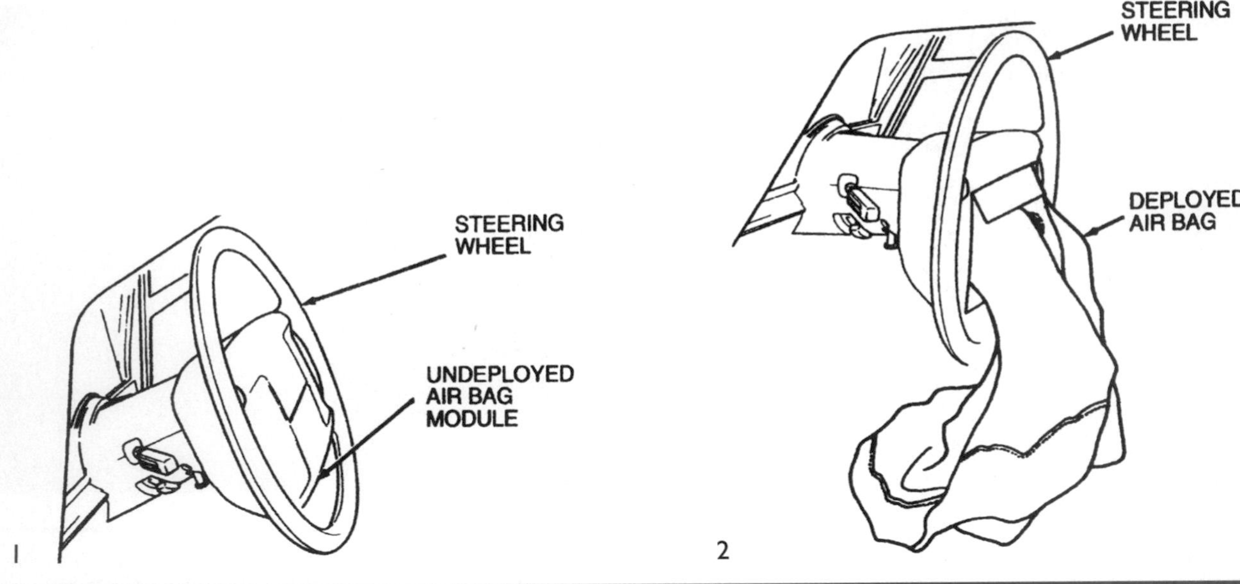

Figure 20–29 Airbag operation.
1. Undeployed. (Courtesy Ford Motor Co. of Canada Ltd.)
2. Deployed (deflated) (Courtesy Ford Motor Co. of Canada Ltd.)

1. *Magnetically retained gold-plated ball sensor.* This sensor uses a permanent magnet to hold a gold-plated steel ball away from two gold-plated electrical contacts. See Figure 20–30(a). If the vehicle (and the sensor) stop rapidly enough, the steel ball is released from the magnet and makes contact with the two gold-plated electrodes. The steel ball only remains in contact with the electrodes for a relatively short time because the steel ball is drawn back into contact with the magnet.
2. *Rolled up stainless-steel ribbon-type sensor.* This sensor is housed in an airtight package with nitrogen gas inside to prevent harmful corrosion of the sensor parts. See Figure 20–30(b). If the vehicle (and the sensor) stop rapidly, the stainless-steel roll unrolls and contacts the two gold-plated contacts. Once the force is stopped, the stainless-steel roll rolls back into its original shape.
3. *Integral sensor.* Some vehicles use electronic **deceleration sensors** built into the inflator module. These sensors measure the rate of deceleration and, through the computer logic, determine if the airbags should be deployed. See Figure 20–31 for a time line that illustrates how quickly a typical airbag system can react and inflate.

CAUTION: In the event of a collision that causes the airbag to deploy, some vehicle manufacturers require that all sensors be replaced along with the airbag assembly. The force of impact can cause unseen damage inside the sensor and the sensor may not work correctly if used again.

Pretensioners

A pretensioner is an explosive device that tightens the seat belt as the air bag is being deployed. The purpose of the pretensioning device is to force the occupant back into position against the seat back and to remove any slack in the seat belt. See Figure 20–32.

CAUTION: The seat belt pretensioner assemblies must be replaced in the event of an airbag deployment. Always follow the vehicle manufacturer's recommended service procedure. Pretensioners are explosive devices that could be ignited if voltage is applied to the terminals. Do not use a jumper wire or powered test light around the wiring near the seat belt latch wiring. Always follow the vehicle manufacturer's recommended test procedures.

Figure 20–30 (a) Airbag magnetic sensor. (b) Airbag ribbon-type sensor.

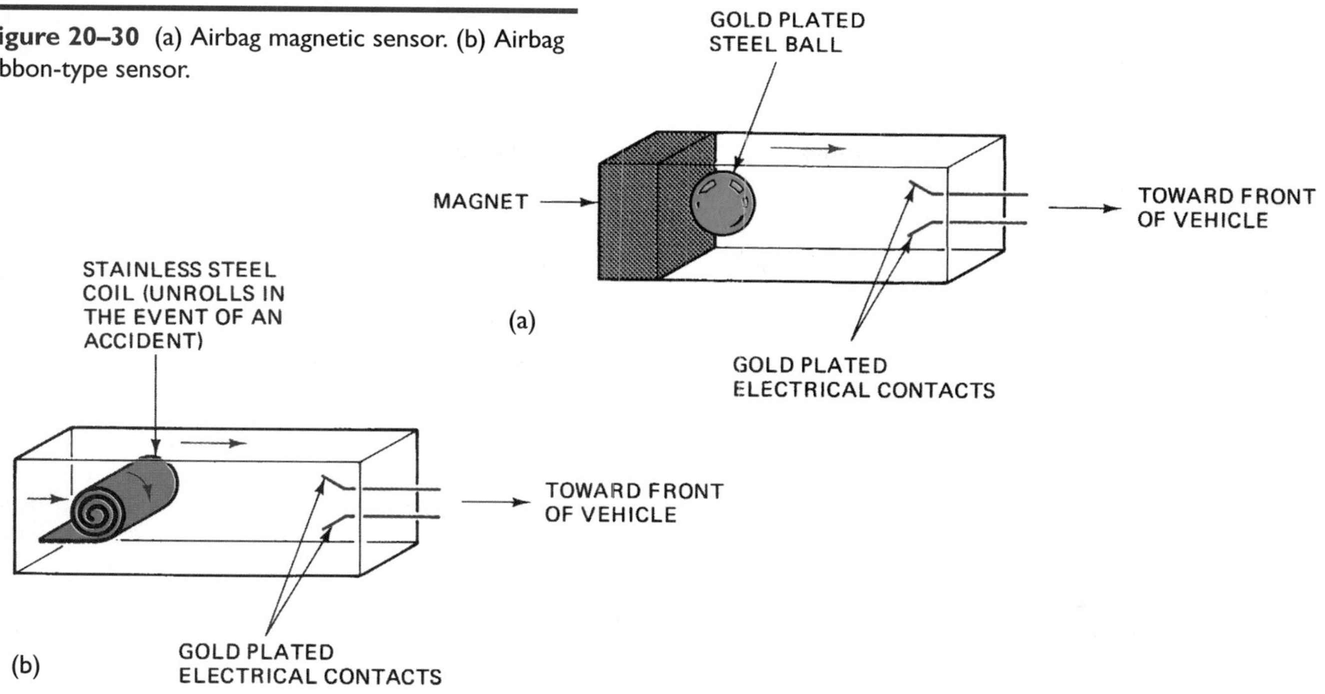

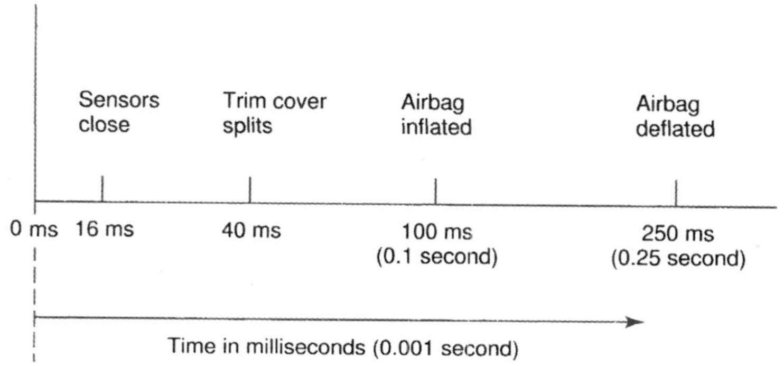

Figure 20–31 Notice that within 1/4 second of a collision, the sensors have closed, the airbag has deployed, and the airbag has deflated.

TECH TIP 

Pocket the Ignition Key to Be Safe

When replacing any steering gear such as a rack-and-pinion steering unit, be sure that no one accidentally turns the steering wheel! If the steering wheel is turned without being connected to the steering gear, the airbag wire coil (clock spring) can become off centre. This can cause the wiring to break when the steering wheel is rotated after the steering gear has been replaced. To help prevent this from occurring, simply remove the ignition key from the ignition and put it in your pocket while servicing the steering gear.

Wiring

By worldwide agreement, all electrical wiring for airbags is yellow. See Figure 20–33. To ensure proper electrical connection to the inflator module in the steering wheel, a coil assembly, often called a "clock spring," is used in the steering column. This coil is a copper wire ribbon conductor that operates much like a window shade when the steering wheel is rotated. This coil prevents the lack of continuity between the sensors and the inflator assembly that might result from a horn-ring type of sliding conductor. Most airbag systems also contain a diagnostic unit that often includes an auxiliary power supply. This supply is used to provide the current to inflate the airbag if the

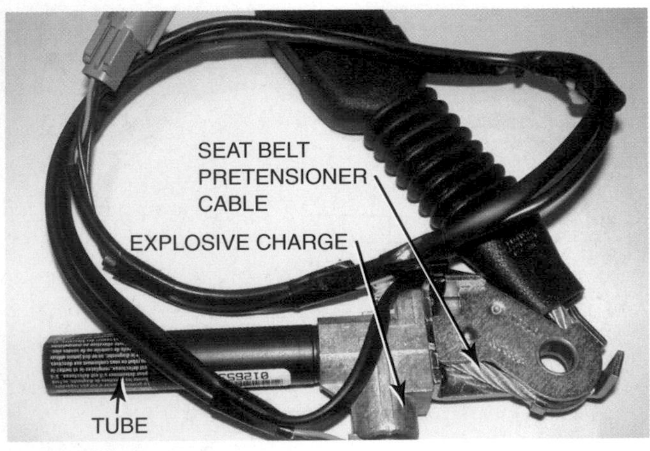

Figure 20–32 A small explosive charge forces the end of the seat belt down the tube, which removes any slack in the seat belt.

battery is disconnected from the vehicle during a collision. This auxiliary power supply usually involves capacitors that are discharged through the squib of the inflation module. See Figure 20–34.

Troubleshooting

The electrical portion of most airbag systems is constantly checked by the circuits within the airbag-energizing power unit or through the vehicle's computer system. The electrical system is monitored by the electronic system by the application of a small-signal voltage through the various sensors and components. If continuity exists, a small voltage drop will be measured by the testing circuits. If an open or short circuit occurs, a dash warning light is lighted. Follow exact manufacturer's recommended procedures for accessing and erasing airbag diagnostic trouble codes. Some manufacturers provide air bag simulators for diagnostic purposes; the air bag is removed and the simulator, which matches the air bag for continuity and resistance, is installed. See Figure 20–35. This pro-

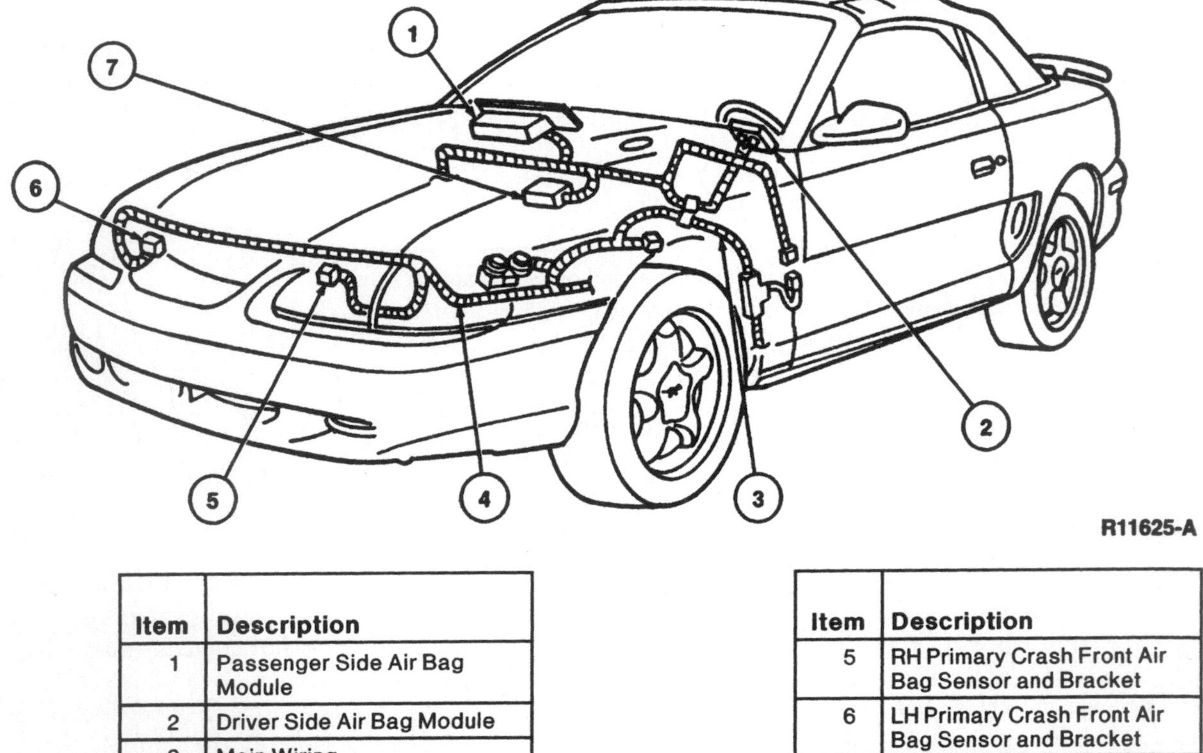

Item	Description
1	Passenger Side Air Bag Module
2	Driver Side Air Bag Module
3	Main Wiring
4	Headlamp Dash Panel Junction Wire

Item	Description
5	RH Primary Crash Front Air Bag Sensor and Bracket
6	LH Primary Crash Front Air Bag Sensor and Bracket
7	Air Bag Diagnostic Monitor

Figure 20–33 Component location.
Note the larger dash-mounted passenger air bag (#1) compared to the steering-wheel-mounted driver-side air bag (#2). The larger bag has more area to fill and a greater distance to travel. (Courtesy Ford Motor Company of Canada Ltd.)

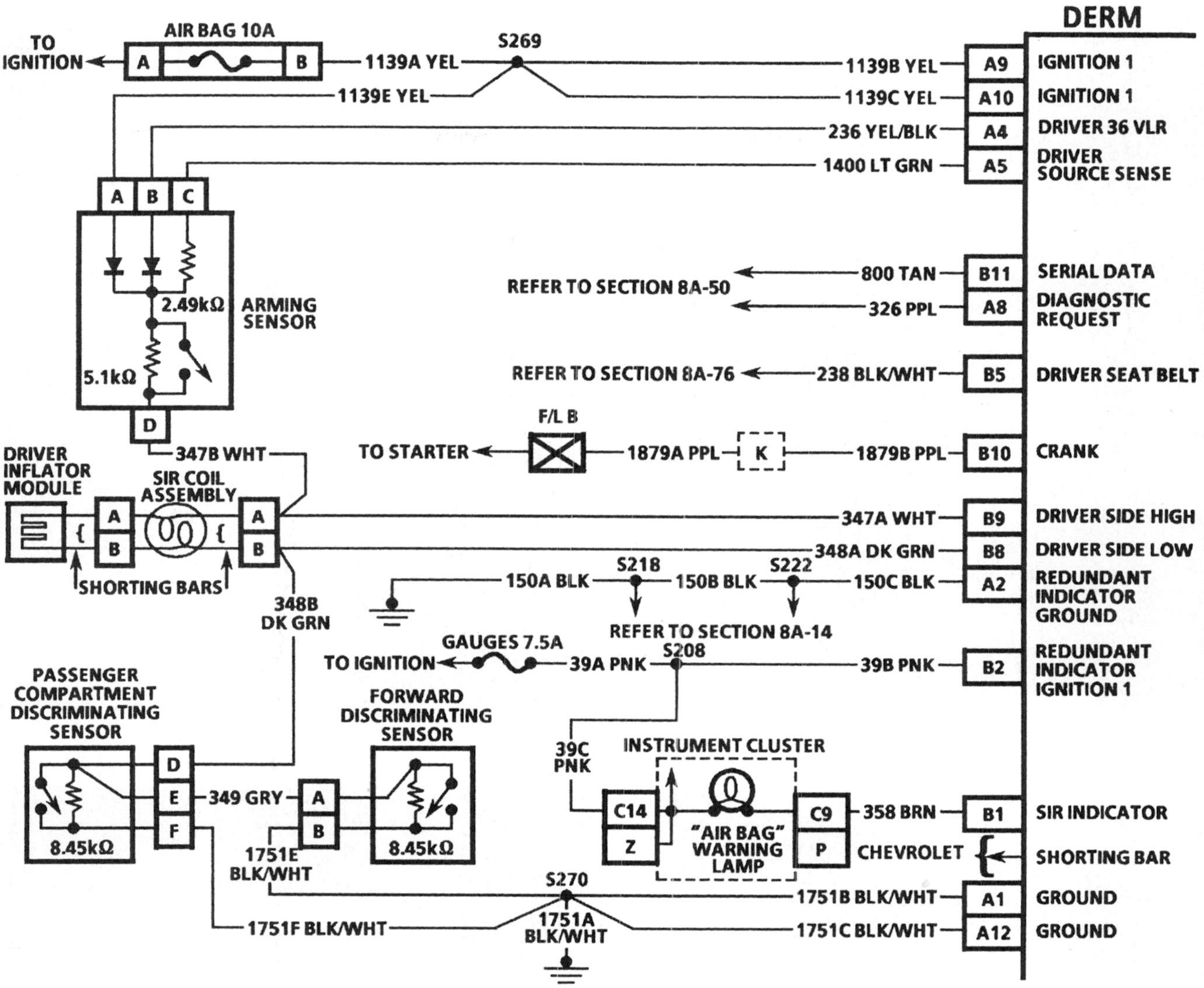

Figure 20–34 Airbag wiring schematic.
The diagnostic energy reserve model (DERM) monitors the system, provides diagnostics and supplies 36 V loop reserve (36 VLR) power if the ignition feed is lost during a frontal crash. Both the arming sensor and at least one discriminating (crash) sensor must close simultaneously before the air bags will deploy. (Courtesy General Motors of Canada Ltd.)

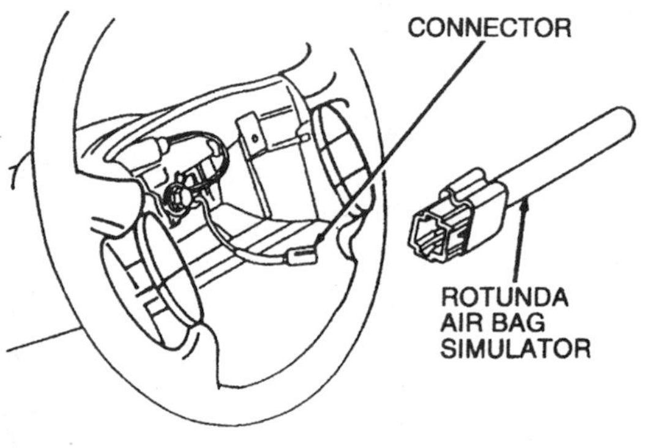

Figure 20–35 Airbag simulators are used in place of the air bags for testing purposes. (Courtesy Ford Motor Co. of Canada Ltd.)

tects against accidental deployment. See Figures 20–36 through 20–38.

Airbag Monitoring

On-board computer chips in many late-model vehicles are used to record the airbag performance and vehicle status during an accident. Vehicle speed, engine speed, brake and throttle position, seat belt use and deployment time are monitored and recorded during the 5 seconds prior to air bag deployment.

Insurance companies, in some cases, have been using this data to confirm witness statements regarding the accident.

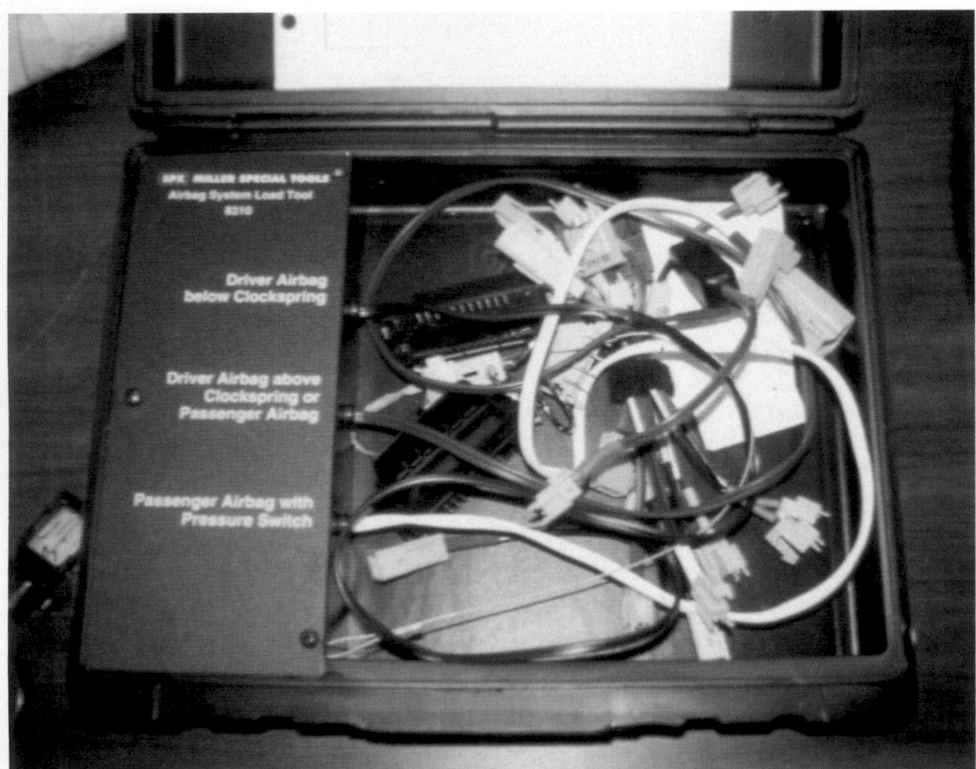

Figure 20–36 An airbag diagnostic tester. Included in the plastic box are electrical connectors and a load tool that substitutes for the inflator module during troubleshooting.

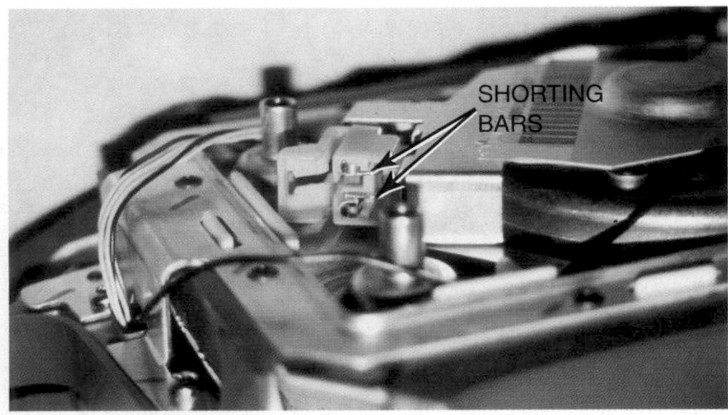

Figure 20–37 Shorting bars are used in most airbag connectors. These spring-loaded clips short across both terminals of an airbag connector to help prevent accidental deployment of the airbag. If electrical power was applied to the terminals, the shorting bars would simply provide a low-resistance path to the other terminal and not allow current to flow past the connector. The mating part of the connector has a tapered piece that spreads the shorting bars apart.

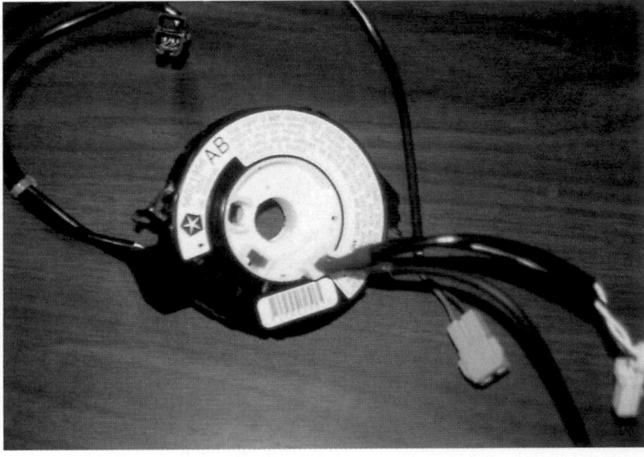

Figure 20–38 A typical coil assembly (often called a clock spring) is used to electrically connect the inflation module with the airbag module that actually supplies the voltage at the time of a collision to deploy the airbag. It is critical that the column-mounted coil assembly be installed correctly.

Canadian courts have ruled that the on-board computer information belongs to the vehicle owner and cannot be downloaded; however if the car is written off, the data now belong to the insurance company. Ontario Provincial Police, who were the first in Canada to develop a downloading program, use a search warrant before proceeding.

Precautions

Take the following precautions when working with or around airbags.

1. Always follow all precautions and warning stickers on vehicles equipped with airbags.

2. In the event of a collision in which the bag(s) were deployed, the inflator module *and* all sensors usually must be replaced to ensure proper future operation of the system.
3. Avoid using a self-powered test light around the yellow airbag wiring. Even though it is highly unlikely, a self-powered test light could provide the necessary current to accidentally set off the inflator module and create an airbag deployment.
4. Never use an ohmmeter to test an air bag or pretensioner. The battery in the ohmmeter could set them off. See Figure 20–39.
5. Use care when handling the inflator module section when it is removed from the steering wheel. Always hold the inflator away from your body.
6. Always place the airbag module on the bench with the trim cover facing up. See Figure 20–40.
7. If handling a deployed inflator module, always wear gloves and safety glasses to avoid the possibility of skin irritation from the sodium hydroxide dust that remains after deployment.
8. Never jar, drop, or strike a sensor. The contacts inside of the sensor may be damaged, preventing the proper operation of the airbag system in the event of a collision.
9. When mounting a sensor in a vehicle, make certain that the arrow on the sensor is pointing toward the front of the vehicle. Also be certain that the sensor is securely mounted.
10. Pay particular attention to the service instructions when dealing with dual stage airbags. A deployed airbag may still be "live."
11. Some systems require the built-in reserve power supply module to be removed, or given time (10 to 30 minutes) to discharge, before service.
12. Damaged vehicles that are to be scrapped should have their airbags deployed. A 12-volt battery and two wires, each a minimum of 10 m (33 ft) long, are used to deploy the bags. See Figure 20–41. After activation, allow 10 minutes for cooling before handling the module.

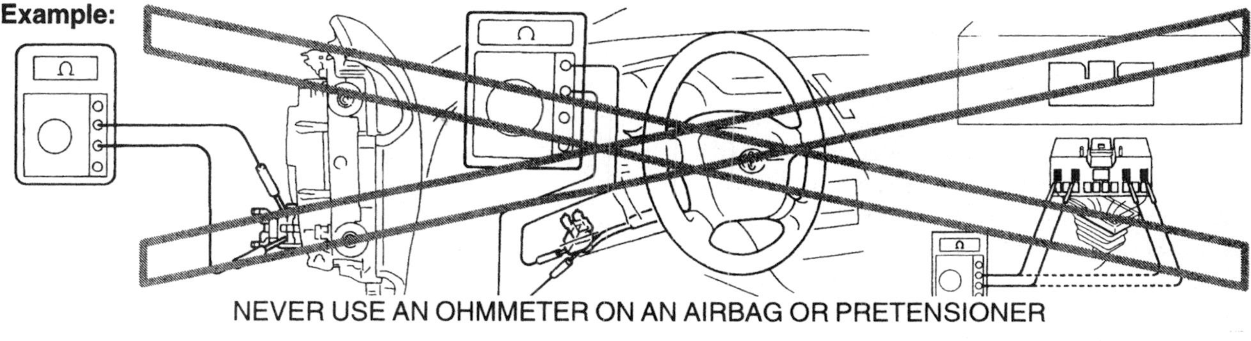
Example:
NEVER USE AN OHMMETER ON AN AIRBAG OR PRETENSIONER

Figure 20–39 The battery in the ohmmeter could cause the airbag or pretensioner to deploy. (Courtesy Toyota Canada Inc.)

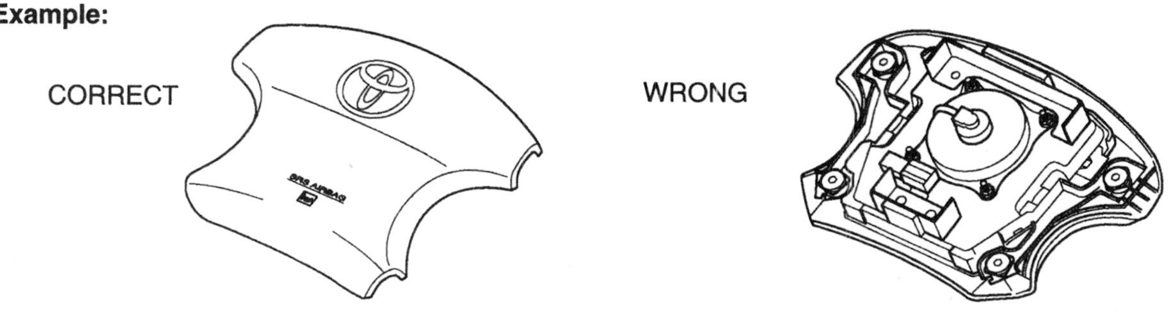
Example:
CORRECT
WRONG

Figure 20–40 Airbag modules must be placed on the bench with the trim pad facing up. (Courtesy Toyota Canada Inc.)

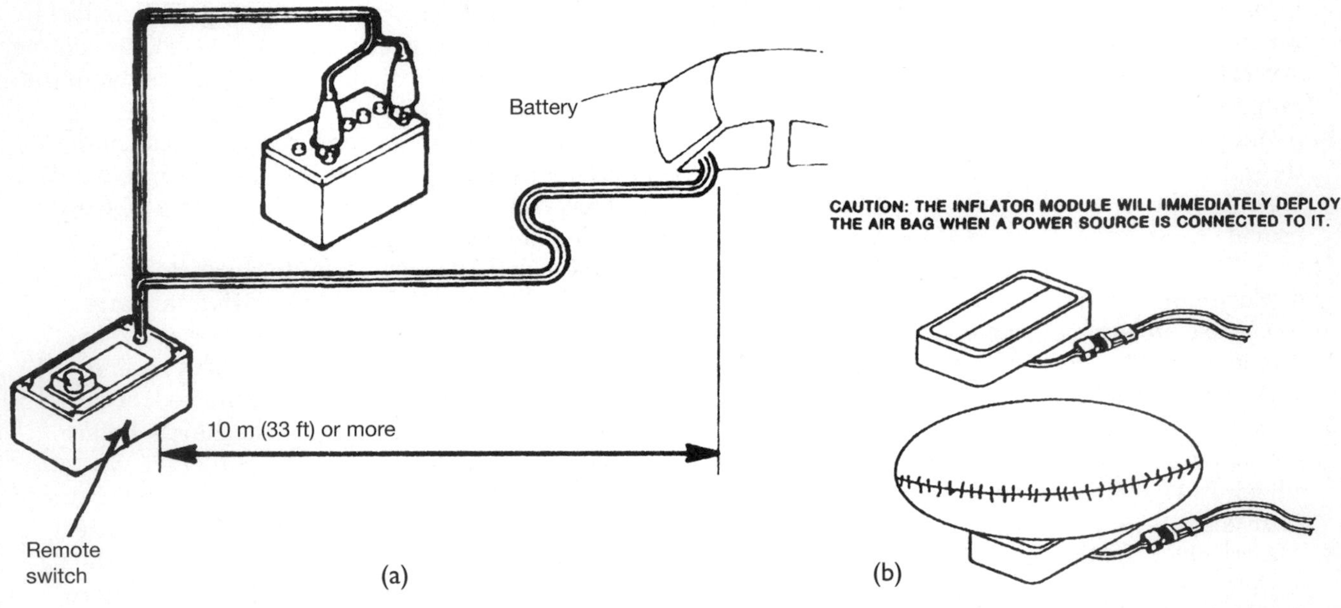
Battery
CAUTION: THE INFLATOR MODULE WILL IMMEDIATELY DEPLOY THE AIR BAG WHEN A POWER SOURCE IS CONNECTED TO IT.
10 m (33 ft) or more
Remote switch
(a)
(b)

Figure 20–41 Remote airbag deployment.
Air bags may be deployed remotely; either in the vehicle (a) or after removal (b). All personnel must be at least 10 m (33 ft) away for both safety and noise concerns. (Courtesy Toyota Canada Inc.; General Motors of Canada Ltd.)

SAFETY TIP

Dual-stage Airbag Warning

Many late-model air bag systems use dual-stage (dual squib) control of deployment. Low-speed, low-impact crashes may activate the bag with less force to reduce bag-to-body injuries. Higher-speed, high-impact crashes deploy the bag with greater speed and force.

The vehicle you are working on may have a deflated bag, outside of the steering wheel or dashboard, that could still go off in your face! Follow the service instructions exactly. One company recommends that a scan tool should be used first, to determine if one, or both, stages have been activated. Be careful!

ELECTRICAL ACCESSORY TROUBLESHOOTING GUIDE	
Problem	**Possible Causes and/or Solutions**
Blower Motor	
Blower motor does not operate	• Blown fuse • Poor ground connection on blower motor • Defective motor (use a jumper wire connected between the positive terminal of the battery and the blower motor power lead connection [lead disconnected] to check for blower motor operation)
Blower motor operates only on high speed.	• Open in the cruise control resistors located in the air box near the blower motor • Stuck or defective high-speed relay • Defective blower motor control switch
Blower motor operates in lower speed(s) only—no high speed	• Defective high-speed relay or blown high-speed fuse
Windshield Wiper or Washer	
Windshield wipers are inoperative	• Blown fuse • Poor ground on the wiper motor or the control switch • Defective motor
Windshield wipers operate on high speed or low speed only	• Defective switch • Defective motor assembly • Poor ground on the wiper control switch
Windshield washers are inoperative	• Defective switch • Empty reservoir or clogged lines or discharge nozzles • Poor ground on the washer pump motor.
Horn	
Horn(s) are inoperative	• Poor ground on horn(s) • Defective relay (if used) • Open circuit in the steering column • Defective horn (use a jumper wire connected between the positive terminal of the battery and the horn [horn wire disconnected] to check for proper operation of the horn).
Horn(s) produce low volume or wrong sound	• Poor ground at horn • Incorrect frequency of horn
Horn blows all the time	• Stuck horn relay (if used) • Short to ground in the wire to the horn button
Cruise Control	
Cruise (speed) control is inoperative	• Broken speedometer cable • Blown fuse • Defective or misadjusted electrical or vacuum safety switch near the brake pedal arm • Lack of engine vacuum to servo or transducer • Defective transducer • Defective speed control switch
Cruise (speed) control speed is incorrect or variable	• Misadjusted activation cable or chain • Defective or pinched vacuum hose • Binding of speedometer cable (remove and lubricate) • Misadjustment of transducer
Power Windows	
Power windows are inoperative	• Defective (blown) blower fuse (circuit breaker) • Defective relay (if used) • Poor ground for master control switch • Poor connections at switch(es) or motor(s) • Open circuit (usually near the master control switch) • Defective lockout switch

ELECTRICAL ACCESSORY TROUBLESHOOTING GUIDE	
Problem	**Possible Causes and/or Solutions**
Power Windows (continued)	
One power window is inoperative	• Defective motor • Defective or open control switch • Open or loose wiring to the switch or the motor
Only one power window can be operated from the master switch	• Poor connection or open circuit in the control wire(s)
Power Seats	
Power seats are inoperative—no click or noise	• Defective circuit breaker • Poor ground at the switch or relay (if used) • Open in the wiring between the switch and relay (if used) • Defective switch • Defective solenoid(s) or wiring • Defective door switch
Power seats are inoperative—click is heard	• Check for "flex" in the cables from the motor(s) to check for motor operation. If flex is felt, the motor is trying to operate the gear nut or the screw jack • Check for binding or obstruction • Defective motor (the click is generally the relay sound) • Defective solenoid(s) or wiring to the solenoid(s)
All power seat functions are operative except one	• Defective motor. • Defective solenoid or wiring to the solenoid
Electric Power Door Lock Problem	
Power door locks are inoperative	• Defective circuit breaker, fuse, or wiring to the switch or relay (if used) • Defective relay (if used) • Defective switch • Defective door lock solenoid or ground for solenoid (if solenoid operated) • Open in the wiring to the door lock solenoid or the motor • Mechanical obstruction of the door lock mechanism
Only one door lock is inoperative	• Defective switch • Poor ground on the solenoid (if solenoid operated) • Defective door lock solenoid or motor • Poor electrical connection at the motor or solenoid
Rear-Window Defogger	
Rear-window defogger is inoperative	• Check for proper operation by performing a voltmeter check at the power side of the rear window grid • Defective relay or timer assembly • Defective switch • Open ground connection at the rear-window grid
Rear-window defogger cleans only a portion of the rear window	• Broken grid wire(s) or poor electrical connections at either the power side or the ground side of the wire grid

NOTE: If the high-speed fuse blows a second time, check the current draw of the motor and replace the blower motor if the current draw is above specifications. Check for possible normal operation if the rear-window defogger is not in operation; some vehicles electrically prevent simultaneous operation of the high-speed blower and rear-window defogger to help reduce the electrical loads.

NOTE: If there is an open circuit (power side or ground side), the dash indicator light will still operate in most cases.

PHOTO SEQUENCE 16 Temporary Disconnection of Airbags

P16–1 Before working around the dash or steering column of a vehicle equipped with airbags, always consult the factory information regarding how to safely and temporarily disconnect the airbags. Procedures vary.

P16–2 The service information specifies that the front wheels should be in the straight ahead position for this vehicle.

P16–3 The ignition switch should be in the off or locked position and the key removed.

P16–4 Locate the fuse panel. The fuses are located on the passenger side of the dash on this vehicle.

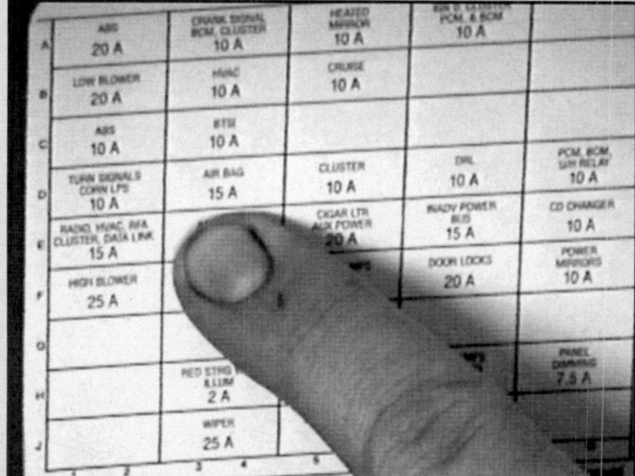

P16–5 The fuse panel cover shows the location of the airbag fuse.

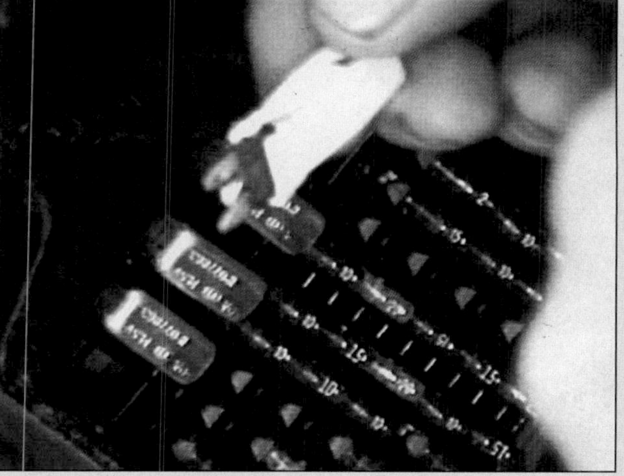

P16–6 Locate and remove the 15 A airbag fuse.

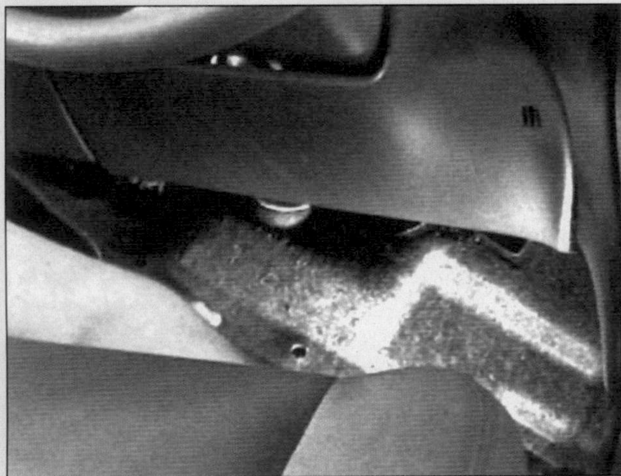

P16–7 Remove the panel under the steering column to gain access to the driver-side airbag connector.

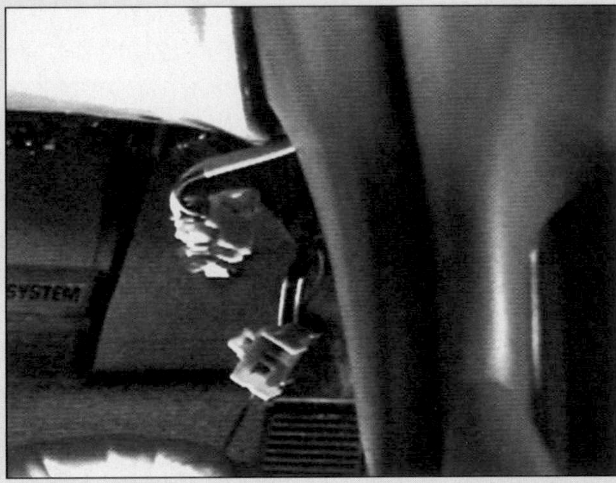

P16–8 Locate and disconnect the yellow driver-side airbag wiring located under the dash below the steering column.

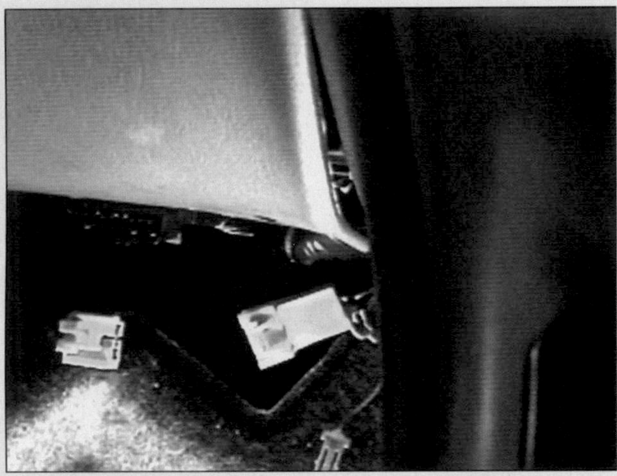

P16–9 Locate the passenger-side airbag connector either under the dash in this case or behind the glove box (instrument panel compartment) and then disconnect the passenger-side airbag connector.

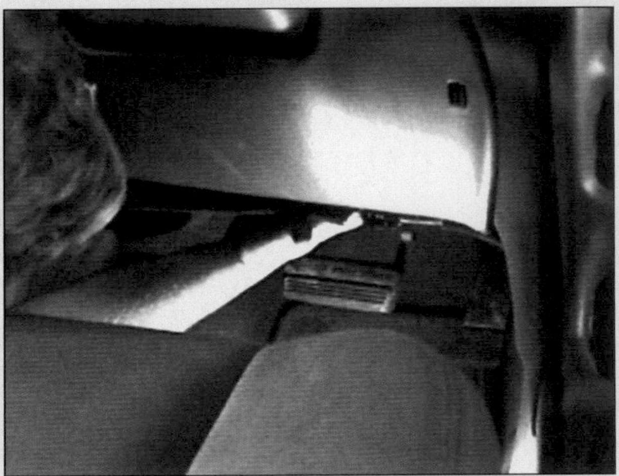

P16–10 After all service work has been completed, reconnect the electrical connectors and reinstall the panel under the dash.

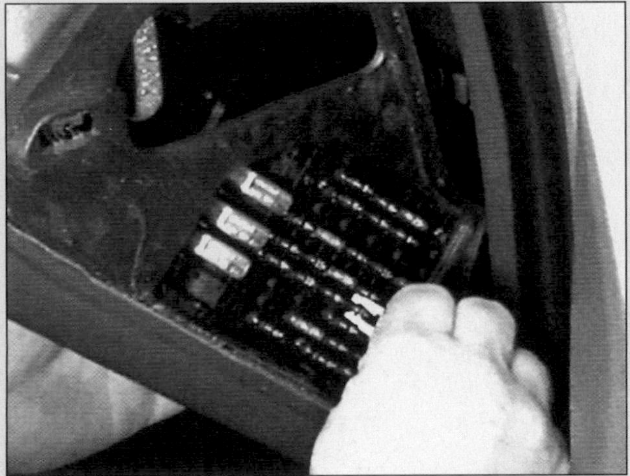

P16–11 Reinstall the airbag fuse.

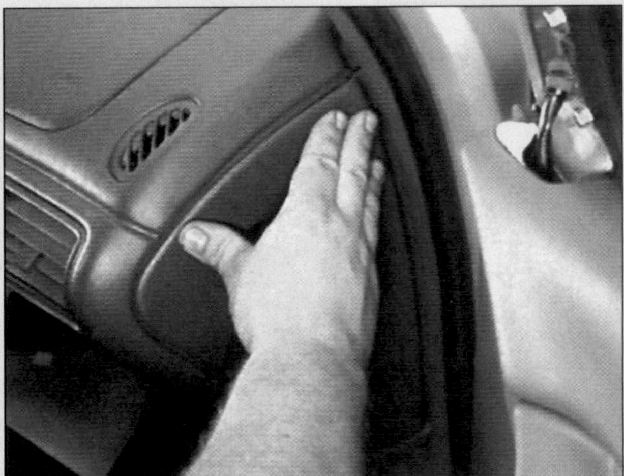

P16–12 Complete the airbag reconnecting process by reinstalling the fuse panel cover.

SUMMARY

1. Most blower motors use resistors to control blower motor speed.
2. Most windshield wipers use a three-brush two-speed motor.
3. Most power windows and power door locks use a permanent-magnet motor that has a built-in circuit breaker and is reversible. The control switches and relays direct the current through the motors.
4. The current flow through a rear-window defogger is often self-regulating. As the temperature of the grid increases, its resistance increases, reducing current flow. Some rear-window defoggers are also used as radio antennas.
5. Airbags use a sensor(s) to determine if the rate of deceleration is enough to cause bodily harm. All airbag wiring is yellow. When working around an airbag, disconnect the wiring connectors to help prevent accidental deployment. Follow the factory procedure exactly.

REVIEW QUESTIONS

1. Explain why a defective blower motor draws more current (amperes) than a good motor.
2. Describe how power door locks on a four-door vehicle can function with only one ground wire connection.
3. Explain how a rear-window defogger can regulate how much current flows through the grids based on temperature.
4. List the safety precautions to follow whenever working around an airbag.

RED SEAL CERTIFICATION-TYPE QUESTIONS

1. The blower motor operates on high speed only; there is no low-speed operation. The most common problem would be
   - **a.** A shorted blower motor
   - **b.** An open blower motor resistor
   - **c.** A defective blower motor
   - **d.** Grounded blower power wiring
2. With most windshield wiper systems, ________.
   - **a.** Both the motor and the control switch must be grounded
   - **b.** No ground is necessary if PM motors are used
   - **c.** Only the motor unit itself must be properly grounded
   - **d.** The only ground is located at the control unit (switch) if PM motors are used
3. The General Motors OnStar centre is contacted automatically when the
   - **a.** Keys are locked in the vehicle
   - **b.** Vehicle is stolen
   - **c.** Air bags deploy
   - **d.** Driver becomes lost
4. Why is the use of an ohmmeter not recommended for testing air bags?
   - **a.** An open circuit cannot be tested
   - **b.** The backup power supply may damage the ohmmeter
   - **c.** The ohmmeter battery could set off the air bag
   - **d.** Resistance is too low to measure
5. A typical six-way power seat ________.
   - **a.** Uses six separate PM nongrounded electric motors
   - **b.** Uses one or three motors (depending on manufacturer)
   - **c.** Uses six separate grounded electric motors only
   - **d.** Uses two electric motors and a three-way direct-acting solenoid-controlled transmission device
6. When checking the operation of a rear-window defogger with a voltmeter, ________.
   - **a.** The voltmeter should be set to read AC volts
   - **b.** The voltmeter should read close to battery voltage anywhere along the grid
   - **c.** Voltage should be available anytime at the power side of the grid because the control circuit just completes the ground side of the heater grid circuit
   - **d.** The voltmeter should indicate decreasing voltage when the grid is tested across the width of the glass
7. PM motors used in power windows, mirrors, and seats can be reversed by ________.
   - **a.** Sending current to a reversed field coil
   - **b.** Reversing the polarity of the current to the motor
   - **c.** Using a reverse relay circuit
   - **d.** Using a relay and a two-way clutch
8. A remote keyless entry (wireless remote control) transmitter will not open any door. All opening functions are normal when operated with the vehicle key. The first diagnostic step would be
   - **a.** Replace the transmitter
   - **b.** Hook a scan tool into the system
   - **c.** Try the second transmitter
   - **d.** Charge the vehicle battery
9. By worldwide agreement, the colour of all electrical wiring for airbags is ____________.
   - **a.** Green
   - **b.** Red
   - **c.** Yellow
   - **d.** Orange
10. If only one power door lock is inoperative, a possible cause is ________.
    - **a.** A poor ground connection at the power door lock relay
    - **b.** A defective motor (or solenoid)
    - **c.** A defective (open) circuit breaker for the power circuit
    - **d.** A defective (open) fuse for the control circuit

21

Audio System Operation and Diagnosis

OBJECTIVES: After studying Chapter 21, you should be able to:

1. Prepare for the interprovincial Red Seal certification examination in Appendix III (Electrical/Electronic Systems) on the topics covered in this chapter.
2. Describe how AM and FM radio works.
3. Explain how to test speaker polarity.
4. Explain how to match speaker impedance.
5. Explain how crossovers and powerline capacitors work.
6. List causes and corrections of radio noise and interference.

The audio system of today's vehicles is a complex combination of antenna system, receiver, amplifier, and speakers all designed to provide living room-type music reproduction while the vehicle is travelling in city traffic or at highway speed.

RADIOS

The power feed for automobile radios should be fused to an ignition switch-controlled circuit that permits radio operation only when the ignition switch is in the "on" (run) or "accessory" position. All radios also use electrical connections for an antenna and for one or more speakers. Most newer radios are called **electronically tuned receivers (ETRs).** They play both AM and FM and usually contain a built-in cassette or compact disc player. Secondary radio controls may be mounted in the steering wheel for safety and convenience.

AM Reception

Amplitude modulation (AM) is a method of varying the carrier signal in such a way as to vary the amplitude or strength of the signal. Frequencies range from 550 to 1600 kHz and may be received a long distance from the transmitting station because the signal waves can be reflected by the ionosphere. The AM method of transmitting is subject to noise and is therefore more sensitive to interferences when tuned to weak stations or lacking a properly functioning radio antenna.

FM Reception

Frequency modulation (FM) is a method of varying the frequency of the carrier wave to represent the audio broadcast signal. An FM signal is broadcast between 88 and 108 MHz, and because the frequency is so high, the signal is *not* reflected by the ionosphere and the range is limited to line-of-sight distances. Because the radio antenna must be "seen" by the transmitting antenna, the signal can easily be blocked by a building or a hill. In cities where the radio signals are strong, the waves can bounce off tall buildings, which can provide reception to areas that are not in sight of the transmitting antenna. FM reception is usually noise free, due to the fact that the radio receives changes in frequency rather than amplitude changes, which often contain noise.

AM versus FM

AM stations are becoming less common for a number of reasons, including high costs and sound quality. AM transmitters require expensive towers to operate; FM does not. Often an entire FM station will cost less than the price of one AM tower. FM (stereo) also has superior signal quality compared to AM (mono); this is particularly noticeable with music.

Radio and television stations are closely monitored and regulated by the Canadian Radio-Television and Telecommunications Commission (CRTC). Licenses are difficult to obtain.

In the late 1990s the CRTC expanded the market and allowed each broadcaster to operate up to four stations in any one broadcast area, two AM and two FM. Although a number of stations switched from AM to FM, the remaining AM, stations have elected to wait for digital AM, which promises excellent sound quality. There is no clear winner yet; however, FM seems to have the edge.

ANTENNAS

The antenna collects all radio frequency signals. The typical radio electromagnetic energy from the broadcast antenna induces a signal in the antenna that is very small—only about 25 μV (0.000 025 volt) in strength. AM radios operate best with as long an antenna as possible, but FM reception is best when the antenna height is approximately 800 mm (31 in.). Most fixed-length antennas are, therefore, exactly this height. Many late model vehicles incorporate the antenna into the windshield or rear window; installing sunscreen film over these antenna lines will reduce radio sensitivity.

A defective antenna will be most noticeable on AM radio reception.

Antenna Testing

If the antenna or lead-in cable is broken (open), FM reception will be heard, but may be weak, and there will be *no* AM reception. An ohmmeter should read infinity between the centre antenna lead and the antenna case. For proper reception and lack of noise, the case of the antenna must be properly grounded to the vehicle body. See Figure 21–1.

TECH TIP

The Hole in the Fender Cover Trick

A common repair is to replace the mast of a power antenna. To help prevent the possibility of causing damage to the body or paint of the vehicle, cut a hole in a fender cover and place it over the antenna. See Figure 21–2. If a wrench or tool slips during the removal or installation process, the body of the vehicle will be protected.

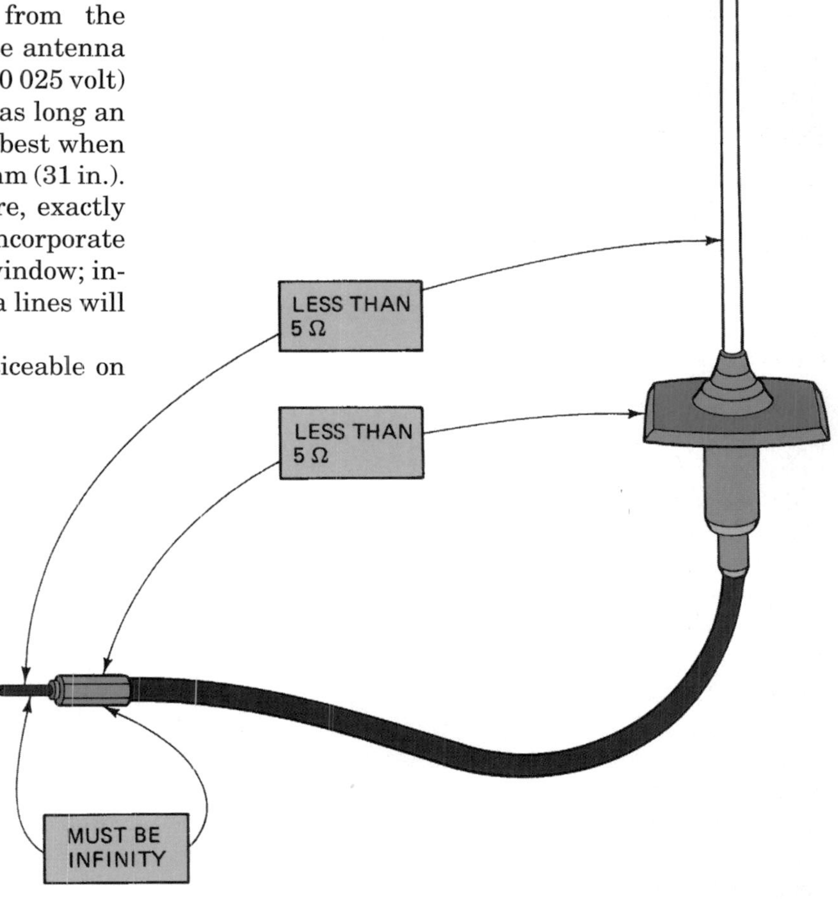

Figure 21–1 If all ohmmeter readings are satisfactory, the antenna is good.

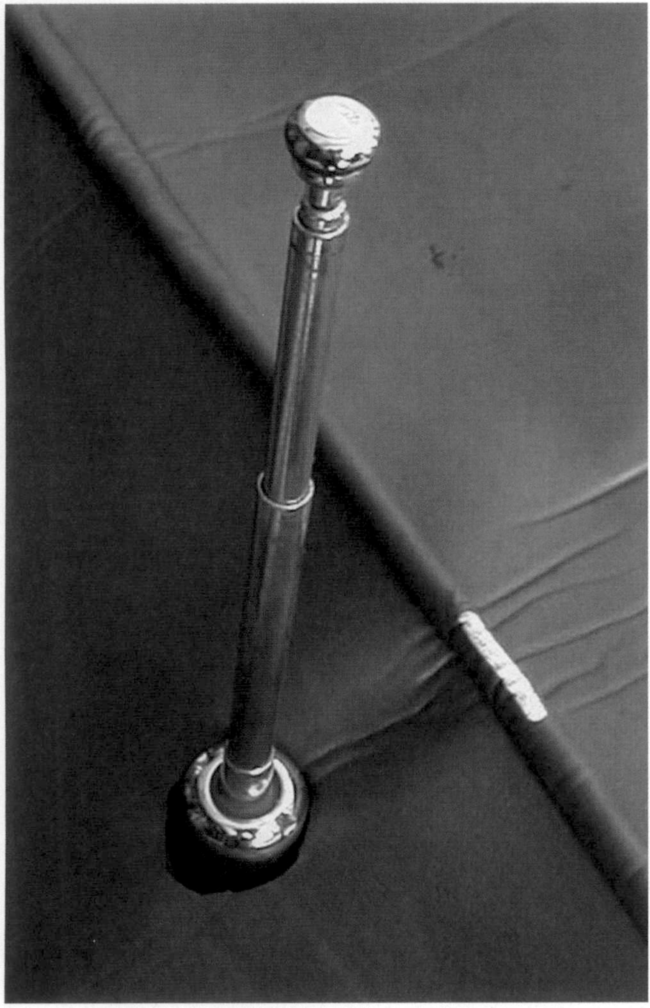

Figure 21–2 Cutting a small hole in a fender cover helps to protect the vehicle when replacing or servicing an antenna.

Figure 21–3 A typical power antenna assembly. Note the braided ground wire used to make sure that the antenna has a good ground plane.

Frequently Asked Question ???

What Is a Ground Plane?

Antennas designed to pick up the electromagnetic energy that is broadcast through the air to the transmitting antenna are usually one-half wavelength high, and the other half of the wavelength is the **ground plane.** This one-half wavelength in the ground plane is literally underground.

For ideal reception, the receiving antenna should also be the same as the wavelength of the signal. Because this length is not practical, a design compromise uses the length of the antenna as one-fourth of the wavelength; and the body of the vehicle itself is one-fourth of the wavelength. The body of the vehicle, therefore, becomes the ground plane. See Figure 21–4.

Power Antennas

Most power antennas use a circuit breaker and a relay to power a reversible electric motor that moves a nylon cord attached to the antenna mast. Some vehicles have a dash-mounted control that can regulate antenna mast height and/or operation, whereas many operate automatically when the radio is turned on and off. The power antenna assembly is usually mounted between the outer and inner front fender or in the rear quarter panel. The unit contains the motor, a spool for the cord, and upper- and lower-limit switches. The power antenna mast is tested in the same way as a fixed-mast antenna. (An infinite reading should be noted on an ohmmeter when the antenna is tested between the centre antenna terminal and the housing or ground.) Except in the case of cleaning or mast replacement, most power antennas are either replaced as a unit or repaired by specialty shops. See Figure 21–3.

Many power antenna problems can be prevented by making certain that the drain holes in the motor housing are not plugged with undercoating, leaves, or dirt. All power antennas should be kept clean by wiping the mast with a soft cloth and lubricating with a light oil.

SPEAKERS

The purpose of any speaker is to reproduce the original sound as accurately as possible. Speakers are also called *loudspeakers.* The human ear is capable of hearing sounds from a very low frequency of 20 Hz (cycles per seconds) to as high as 20 kHz. No one speaker is capable of reproducing sound over such a wide frequency range.

Good-quality speakers are the key to a proper-sounding radio or sound system. Replacement speak-

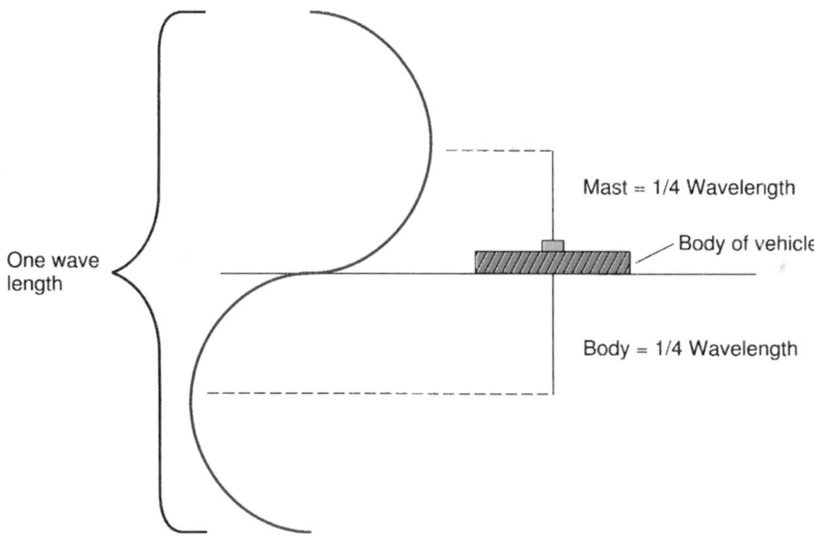

Figure 21–4 The ground plane is actually one-half of the antenna.

Figure 21–5 A typical automotive speaker with two terminals. The polarity of the speakers can be identified by looking at the wiring diagram in the service manual or by using a 1 1/2 V battery to check.

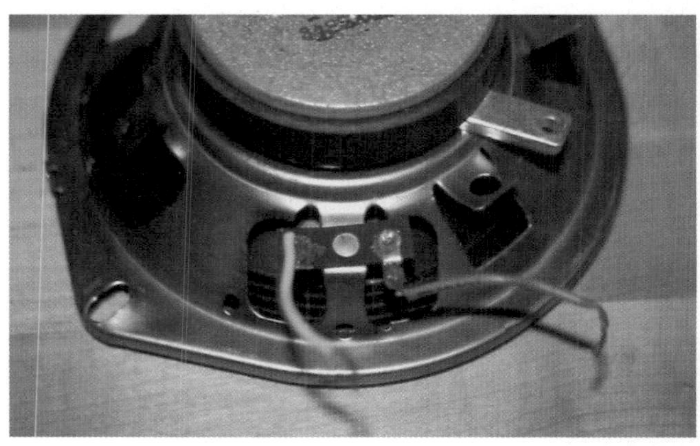

Figure 21–6 A speaker polarity tester can be easily constructed using a 1 1/2 V battery. To test a speaker, connect the positive (+) lead of the battery to one speaker terminal and the negative (−) lead to the other speaker terminal for just a second and observe the direction the speaker cone moves. The positive (+) terminal of the speaker is the terminal that causes the speaker cone to move away from the magnet when touched with the positive (+) battery lead.

Aligator clips (2)
P.N. 270-374

Fuse holder with
Fuse holder P.N. 270-1213
Fuse P.N. 270-1215

Battery holder "D"
Type P.N. 270-403
or 270-402 for a
"C" Type battery holder

All part numbers are from Radio Shack

ers should be securely mounted and wired according to the correct **polarity.** See Figures 21–5 and 21–6. All speakers used on the same radio or amplifier should have the same internal coil resistance, called **impedance.** If unequal-impedance speakers are used, sound quality may be reduced and serious damage to the radio may result.

Impedance Matching

All speakers should have the same impedance. For example, if two 4 ohm speakers are being used for the rear and they are connected in parallel, the total impedance is 2 ohms.

$$R_T = \frac{4\text{ ohms (impedance of each speaker)}}{2\text{ (number of speakers in parallel)}} = 2\text{ ohms}$$

DIAGNOSTIC STORY

The Ford Truck Radio Story

The owner of a 1998 Ford pickup truck complained that occasionally no sound came from the right speaker. The technician discovered that the radio has a self-test mode. By pressing #3 and #6 buttons at the same time, the radio is put into a speaker test mode. The radio then sends a sound to each speaker while displaying from which speaker the sound should be heard. The self-test led the technician to a poor connection at a connector in the right door, which fixed the radio problem.

Frequently Asked Question ???

What Is a "Floating Ground"?

A floating ground means that all audio components such as the receiver head, amplifier, and speakers share a common ground that is above and not connected to the chassis ground. This arrangement helps prevent interference and static that could occur if these components were connected to a chassis (vehicle) ground. If the components are chassis grounded, there may be a difference in the voltage potential (voltage), and this condition is called a **ground loop.**

The front speakers should also represent a 2 ohm load from the radio or amplifier. If, for example, you had the following equipment:

Two front speakers—each 2 ohms
Two rear speakers—each 8 ohms

the solution would be to connect the front speakers in series (connect the positive [+] of one speaker to the negative [−] of the other) for a total impedance of 4 ohms (2 ohms + 2 ohms = 4 ohms). Connect the two rear speakers in parallel (connect the positive [+] of each speaker together and the negative [−] of each speaker together) for a total impedance of 4 ohms (8 ohms ÷ 2 = 4 ohms).

Speaker Wiring

The wire used for speakers should be as large a wire (as low a gauge number) as is practical in order to be assured that full power is reaching the speakers. Typical speaker wire is about 22 gauge (0.35 mm^2), yet tests conducted by audio engineers have concluded that increasing the wire size to 14 gauge (2.0 mm^2) or larger greatly increases sound quality. All wiring connections should be soldered after making certain that all speaker connections have the correct polarity.

CAUTION: Regardless of radio speaker connections used, *never* operate any radio without the speakers connected, or a transistor in the radio may be damaged as a result of the open speaker circuit.

SPEAKER TYPES

Tweeter

A *tweeter* is a speaker designed to reproduce high-frequency sounds, usually between 4 kHz and 20 kHz. Tweeters are very directional. This means that the human ear is most likely to be able to detect the location of the speaker while listening to music. This also means that a tweeter should be mounted in the vehicle where the sound can be directed line-of-sight to the listener. Tweeters are usually mounted on the inside door near the top, windshield A pillar, or similar locations.

Midrange

A *midrange speaker* is designed and manufactured to be able to best reproduce sounds in the middle of the human hearing range from 400 Hz to 5000 Hz. Most people are sensitive to the sound produced by these midrange speakers. These speakers are also directional in that the listener can usually locate the source of the sound.

Subwoofer

A *subwoofer,* sometimes called a *woofer,* produces the lowest frequency of sounds, usually 125 Hz and lower. A *midbass* speaker may also be used to reproduce those frequencies between 100 Hz and 500 Hz. Low-frequency sounds from these speakers are *not* directional. This means that the source of the sound from these speakers usually cannot be detected by the listener. The low-frequency sounds seem to be everywhere in the vehicle so the location of the speakers are not as critical as with the higher-frequency speakers.

The subwoofer can be placed almost anywhere in the vehicle. Most subwoofers are mounted in the rear of the vehicle where there is more room for the larger subwoofer speakers.

Speaker Frequency Response

Frequency response is how a speaker responds to a range of frequencies. A typical frequency response for a midrange speaker may be 500 Hz to 4000 Hz with a tolerance of 3 **decibels (dB).** A decibel is a measure of sound power, and is the faintest sound a human can hear in the midband frequencies. The dB scale is not linear (straight line), but rather logarithmic, meaning that a small change in the dB reading results in a large change in volume of noise. An increase of 10 dB in sound pressure is equal to doubling the perceived volume. Therefore, a small difference in dB rating means a big difference in the sound volume of the speaker.

CROSSOVERS

A crossover is designed to separate the frequency of a sound and send certain frequency range such as low base sounds to a woofer designed to reproduce these low-frequency sounds. There are two types of crossovers: passive and active.

Passive Crossover

A passive crossover does not use an external power source. Rather it uses a coil and a capacitor to block certain frequencies that a particular type of speaker cannot handle and allow those frequencies that can be handled to be applied to the speaker. For example, a 6.6 mH (millihenry) coil and a 200 μF (microfarad) capacitor can effectively pass 100 Hz frequency sound to a large 250 mm (10 in.) subwoofer. This type of passive crossover is called a **low-pass filter,** because it passes (transfers) only the low-frequency sounds to the speaker and blocks all other frequencies. A **high-pass filter** is used to transfer higher frequency (over 100 Hz) to smaller speakers.

Active Crossover

Active crossovers use an external power source and produce superior performance. An active crossover is also called an *electronic crossover.* These units include many powered filters and are considerably more expensive than passive crossovers. Two amplifiers are necessary to fully benefit from an active crossover. One amplifier is for the higher frequencies and midrange and the other amplifier is for the subwoofers. If you are on a budget and plan to use just one amplifier, then use passive crossover. If you can afford to use two or more amplifiers, then consider using the electronic (active) passover.

Frequently Asked Question ???

What Is a Bass Blocker?

A bass blocker is a capacitor and coil assembly that effectively blocks low frequencies. A bass blocker is normally used to block low frequencies being sent to the front smaller speakers. Using a bass blocker allows the smaller front speakers to more efficiently reproduce the midrange and high-range frequency sound.

POWERLINE CAPACITORS

A powerline capacitor, also called a **stiffening capacitor,** refers to a large capacitor (often abbreviated CAP) of 0.25 F or larger connected to an amplifier power wire. The purpose and function of this capacitor is to provide the electrical reserve energy needed by the amplifier to provide deep bass notes. See Figure 21–7. Battery power is often slow to respond and when the amplifier attempts to draw a large amount of current, the capacitor will try to stabilize the voltage level at the amplifier and discharge stored current as needed.

A rule of thumb is to connect a capacitor with a capacity of 1 F for each 1000 W of amplifier power. See the following chart.

Powerline Capacitor Usage Guide

Watts (Amplifier)	Recommended Capacitor in Farads (Microfarads)
100 W	0.10 F (100 000 μF)
200 W	0.20 F (200 000 μF)
250 W	0.25 F (250 000 μF)
500 W	0.50 F (500 000 μF)
750 W	0.75 F (750 000 μF)
1000 W	1.00 F (1 000 000 μF)

Capacitor Installation

A powerline capacitor connects to the power leads between the inline fuse and the amplifier. See Figure 21–8.

If the capacitor were connected to the circuit as shown, the capacitor would draw so much current that it would blow the inline fuse. To safely connect a large capacitor, it must be *precharged.* To precharge the capacitor, follow these steps:

Step 1 Connect the negative (−) terminal of the capacitor to a good chassis ground.

Step 2 Insert an automotive 12 V light bulb such as a headlight or parking light between the positive (+) terminal of the capacitor and the positive terminal of the battery. The light will light as the capacitor is being charged and then go out when the capacitor is fully charged.

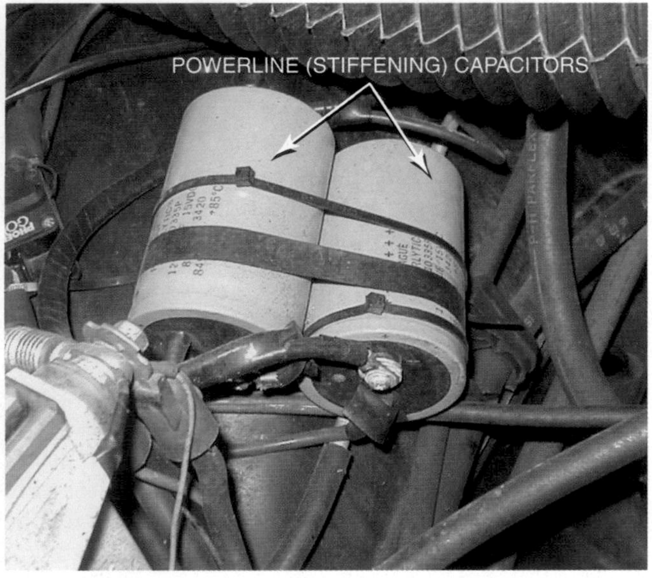

Figure 21–7 Two capacitors connected in parallel to provide the necessary current flow to power large subwoofer speakers.

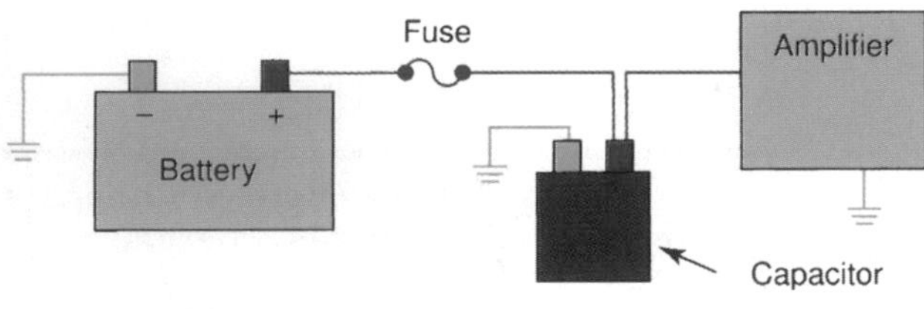

Figure 21–8 A powerline capacitor should be connected to the power wire to the amplifier as shown. When the amplifier requires more electrical power (watts) than the battery can supply, the capacitor will discharge into the amplifier and supply the necessary current for the fraction of a second it is needed by the amplifier. At other times when the capacitor is not needed, it draws current from the battery to keep it charged.

Step 3 Disconnect the light from the capacitor, then connect the power lead to the capacitor. The capacitor is now fully charged and ready to provide the extra power necessary to supplement battery power to the amplifier.

RADIO INTERFERENCE

Radio interference is caused by variations in voltage in the powerline or picked up by the antenna. A whine that increases in frequency with increasing engine speed is usually referred to as **alternator (generator) whine** and is eliminated by installing a radio choke or a filter capacitor in the power feed wire to the radio. See Figure 21–9.

Frequently Asked Question ???

What Do the Amplifier Specifications Mean?

RMS power RMS means root-mean-square and is the rating that indicates how much power the amplifier is capable of producing continuously.

RMS power at 2 ohms This specification in watts indicates how much power the amplifier delivers into a 2 ohm speaker load. This 2 ohm load is achieved by wiring two 4 ohm speakers in parallel or by using 2 ohm speakers.

Peak power Peak power is the maximum wattage an amplifier can deliver in a short burst during a musical peak.

THD **Total harmonic distortion (THD)** represents the amount of change of the signal as it is being amplified. The lower the number, the better the amplifier (for example, a 0.01% is better than a 0.07% rating).

Signal-to-noise ratio This specification is measured in decibels (dB) and compares the strength of the signal with the level of the background noise (hiss). A higher volume indicates less background noise (for example, a 105-dB rating is better than a 100-dB rating).

Ignition noise is usually a raspy sound that varies with the speed of the engine. This noise is usually eliminated by the installation of a capacitor on the positive side of the ignition coil. The capacitor should be connected to the power feed wire to either the radio or the amplifier or both. The capacitor *has* to be grounded. If a standard automotive condenser is not available, use a 470 μF 50 volt electrolytic capacitor, which is readily available from most radio supply stores. Refer to factory information if the vehicle is equipped with a coil-on-plug or a direct ignition system. A special coaxial capacitor can also be used in the powerline. See Figure 21–10.

A **radio choke** is a coil and can also be used to reduce or eliminate radio interference. Again, the radio choke is installed in the powerline to the radio equipment. Radio interference being picked up by the antenna can best be eliminated by stopping the source of the interference by making certain that all units containing a coil, such as electric motors, have a capacitor or diode attached to the power-side wire.

Most radio interference complaints come when someone installs an amplifier, power booster, equalizer, or other radio accessory. *A major cause of this interfer-*

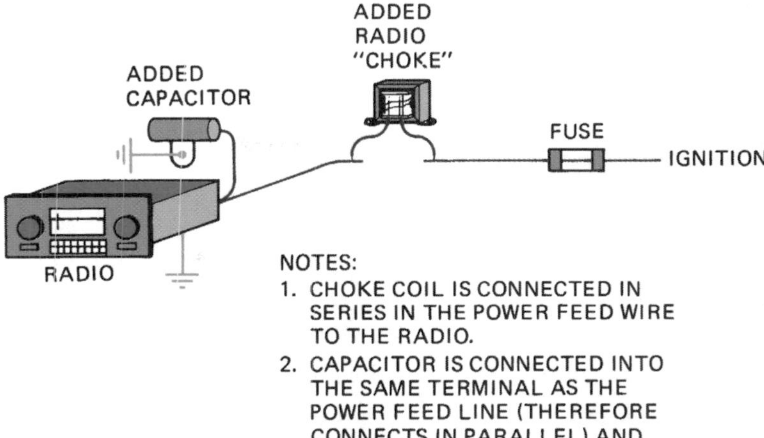
ADDED
RADIO
"CHOKE"
ADDED
CAPACITOR
FUSE
IGNITION
RADIO
NOTES:
1. CHOKE COIL IS CONNECTED IN SERIES IN THE POWER FEED WIRE TO THE RADIO.
2. CAPACITOR IS CONNECTED INTO THE SAME TERMINAL AS THE POWER FEED LINE (THEREFORE CONNECTS IN PARALLEL) AND THE CASE OF THE CAPACITOR (CONDENSER) IS GROUNDED.

Figure 21–9 A radio choke and/or a capacitor can be installed in the power feed lead to any radio, amplifier, or equalizer.

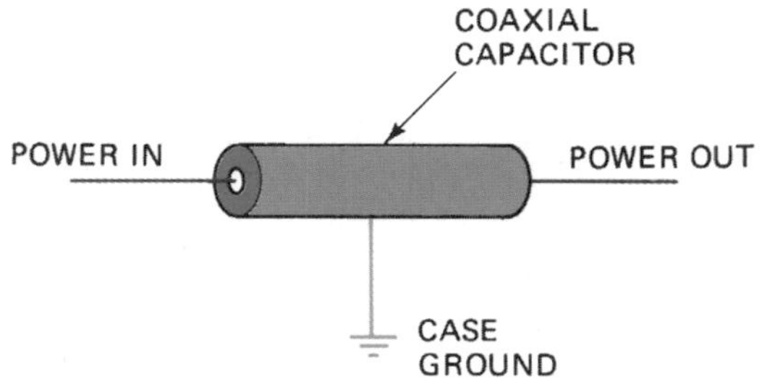
COAXIAL
CAPACITOR
POWER IN
POWER OUT
CASE
GROUND

Figure 21–10 A coaxial capacitor. Many automobile manufacturers install a coaxial capacitor in the power feed wire to the blower motor to eliminate interference caused by the blower motor.

ence is the variation in voltage through the ground circuit wires. To prevent or reduce this interference, make sure all ground connections are clean and tight. Placing a capacitor in the ground circuit may also be beneficial.

> **CAUTION:** Amplifiers sold to boost the range or power of an antenna often increase the level of interference and radio noise to a level that disturbs the driver.

In summary, radio noise can be broadcast or caused by noise (voltage variations) in the power circuit to the radio. A capacitor and/or a radio choke are the most commonly used components in servicing the problem. Two or more capacitors can be connected in parallel to increase the capacity of the original capacitor. See Figure 21–11.

Mobile Two-Way Radio Systems

The installation of a mobile two-way radio could affect engine management, emissions, cruise control, ABS and a number of other electronic systems. Follow the special instructions exactly regarding installation.

Figure 21–11 A sniffer can be made from an old antenna lead-in cable by removing about 75 mm (3 in.) of the outer shielding from the end. Plug the lead-in cable into the antenna input of the radio and tune the radio to a weak station. Move the end of the antenna wire around the vehicle dash area. The sniffer is used to locate components that may not be properly shielded or grounded and can cause radio interference through the case (housing) of the radio itself.

TECH TIP 

The Separate Battery Trick

Whenever diagnosing sound system interference, try running separate 2.0 mm^2 (14-gauge) wire(s) from the sound system power lead and ground to a separate battery outside of the vehicle. If the noise is still heard, the interference is *not* due to a generator diode or other source in the wiring of the vehicle.

Audio Noise Control Diagnostic Chart		
Noise Source	**What It Sounds Like**	**What to Try**
Generator (alternator)	A whine whose pitch changes with engine speed	Install a capacitor to a ground at the generator (alternator) output
Ignition	Ticking that changes with engine speed	Use a sniffer to further localize the source of the problem
Turn signals	Popping in time with the turn signals	Install a capacitor across the turn signal flasher
Brake lights	Popping whenever the brake pedal is depressed	Install a capacitor across the brake light switch contacts
Blower motor	Ticking in time with the blower motor	Install a capacitor to ground at the motor hot lead
Dash lamp dimmer	A buzzy whine whose pitch changes with the dimmer setting	Install a capacitor to ground at the dimmer hot lead
Horn switch	Popping when the horn is sounded	Install a capacitor between the hot lead and horn lead at the horn relay
Horn	Buzzing synchronized with the horn	Install a capacitor to ground at each horn hot lead
Amplifier power supply	A buzz, not affected by engine speed	Ground the amplifier chassis using a braided ground strap

DIAGNOSTIC STORY

The General Motors Security Radio Problem

A customer replaced the battery in a General Motors vehicle and now the radio display shows "**LOC.**" This means that the radio is locked and there is a customer code stored in the radio.

Other displays and their meaning include:

"InOP" This display indicates that too many incorrect codes have been entered and the radio must be kept powered for one hour and the ignition turned on before any more attempts can be made.

"SEC" This display means there is a customer's code stored but the radio is unlocked.

"—" This means there is no customer code stored and the radio is unlocked.

"REP" This means the customer's code has been entered once and the radio now is asking that the code be repeated to verify it was entered correctly the first time.

To unlock the radio, the technician used the following steps (the code number being used is 4321).

Step 1 Press the "HR" (hour) button—"000" is displayed.

Step 2 Set the first two digits using the hour button—"4300" is displayed.

Step 3 Set the last two digits of the code using the "MIN" (minutes) button—"4321" is displayed.

Step 4 Press the AM-FM button to enter the code. The radio is unlocked and the clock displays "1:00."

Thankfully, the owner had the security code. If the owner had lost the code, the technician would have to secure a scrambled factory backup code from the radio and then call an 800 toll-free number to obtain another code for the customer. The code will only be given to authorized dealers or repair facilities.

SUMMARY

1. Radios receive AM (amplitude modulation) and FM (frequency modulation) signals that are broadcast through the air.
2. The radio antenna is used to induce a very small voltage signal as an input into the radio from the electromagnetic energy from the broadcast station.
3. AM requires an antenna whereas FM may be heard from a radio without an antenna.
4. Speakers reproduce the original sound, and the impedance of all speakers should be equally matched.
5. Crossovers are used to block certain frequencies to allow each type of speaker to perform its job better. A low-pass filter is used to block high-frequency sounds being sent to large woofer speakers, and a high-pass filter blocks low-frequency sounds being sent to tweeters.
6. Radio interference can be caused by many different things such as a defective generator (alternator), a fault in the ignition system, or a fault in a relay or solenoid.

REVIEW QUESTIONS

1. Explain why AM signals travel farther than FM signals.
2. Explain the purpose and function of the ground plane.
3. Describe how to match the impedance of speakers.
4. List two items that may need to be added to the wiring of a vehicle to control or reduce radio noise.

RED SEAL CERTIFICATION-TYPE QUESTIONS

1. AM radios operate best with a long antenna. FM reception is best when the antenna height is
   - **a.** Also very long
   - **b.** Exactly 500 mm (20 in.)
   - **c.** Variable
   - **d.** Approximately 800 mm (31 in.)
2. An antenna lead-in wire should have how many ohms of resistance between the centre terminal and the grounded outer covering?
   - **a.** Less than 5 ohms
   - **b.** 5 to 50 ohms
   - **c.** 300 to 500 ohms
   - **d.** Infinity (OL)
3. Ignition noise is usually eliminated by installing a capacitor on the
   - **a.** Negative side of the ignition coil
   - **b.** Distributor side of the ignition module
   - **c.** Positive side of the ignition coil
   - **d.** Ground side of the ignition module
4. What maintenance should be performed to a power antenna to help keep it working correctly?
   - **a.** Remove it from the vehicle and lubricate the gears and cable
   - **b.** Clean the mast with a soft cloth
   - **c.** Disassemble the mast and pack the mast with silicone grease (or equal)
   - **d.** Loosen and then retighten the retaining nut
5. If two 4-ohm speakers are connected in parallel (positive [+] to positive [+] and negative [−] to negative [−]), the total impedance will be
   - **a.** 8 ohms
   - **b.** 4 ohms
   - **c.** 2 ohms
   - **d.** 1 ohms
6. If two 4 Ω speakers are connected in series (positive [+] of one speaker connected to the negative [−] of the other speaker), the total impedance will be
   - **a.** 8 ohms
   - **b.** 4 ohms
   - **c.** 2 ohms
   - **d.** 1 ohms
7. A low-pass filter blocks the
   - **a.** High-frequency signals
   - **b.** Low-frequency signals
8. 100 000 μF means
   - **a.** 0.10 F
   - **b.** 0.01 F
   - **c.** 0.001 F
   - **d.** 0.0001 F
9. A radio choke is actually a
   - **a.** Resistor
   - **b.** Capacitor
   - **c.** Coil (inductor)
   - **d.** Transistor
10. What device passes AC interference to ground and blocks DC voltage, and is used to control radio interference?
    - **a.** Resistor
    - **b.** Capacitor
    - **c.** Coil (inductor)
    - **d.** Transistor

SECTION **IV**

Heating and Air Conditioning

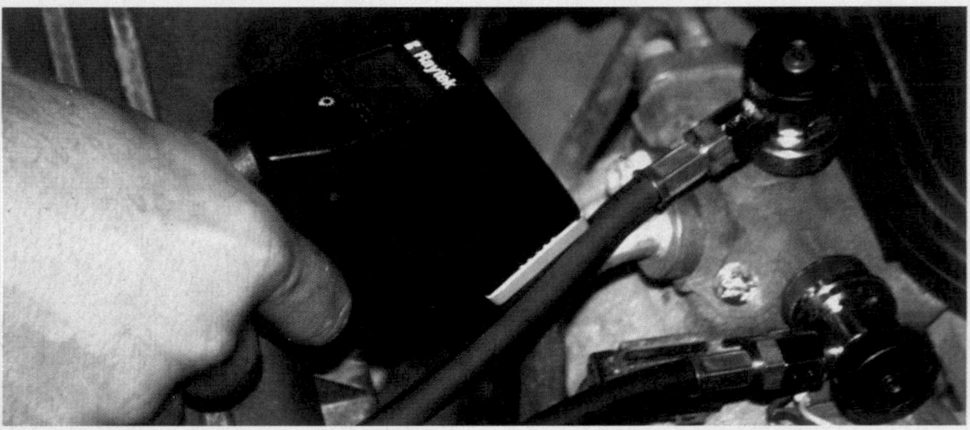

22 Heating, Ventilation, and Air-Conditioning Principles

23 Heating and Air-Conditioning Diagnosis and Service

Chapter 22 describes the operation of the heating and air-conditioning systems. Both CFC-12 and HFC-134a refrigerant systems are included. Diagnostic and service procedures are included in Chapter 23 along with how to retrofit an older air-conditioning system from CFC-12 to CFC-134a refrigerant.

22

Heating, Ventilation, and Air-Conditioning Principles

OBJECTIVES: After studying Chapter 22, you should be able to:

1. Prepare for the interprovincial Red Seal certification examination in Appendix VII (Heating and Air-Conditioning) on the topics covered in this chapter.
2. Describe how the heater functions.
3. Describe how the refrigeration cycle functions.
4. List the parts of a typical air-conditioning system.
5. Explain how the air-conditioning system removes heat from the passenger compartment.
6. Explain the four Rs of the Environment Canada Code of Practice.

Driver and passenger comfort is the primary purpose of the heating, ventilation, and air-conditioning system, often abbreviated **HVAC.** The heater is also needed in cold climates to prevent freezing or death.

PRINCIPLES OF HEATING AND REFRIGERATION

On earth, matter is found in one of three different phases or states: solid, liquid, or vapour (gas). The state depends upon the nature of the substance, the temperature, and the pressure or force exerted on it. Water occurs naturally in all three states: solid ice, liquid water, and water vapour, depending upon the temperature and pressure of the location. See Figure 22–1.

Figure 22–1 Water is a substance that can be found naturally in solid, liquid, and vapour states.

Changes of State

A **solid** is a substance that cannot be compressed and has strong resistance to flow. The molecules of a solid attract each other strongly, and resist changes in volume and shape.

A substance is solid at any temperature below its melting point. A melting point is a characteristic of a substance, and is related to the temperature at which a solid turns to a liquid. For water, the melting point is 0°C (32°F), which means that we can observe changes between liquid water and ice under normal weather conditions.

A **liquid** is a substance that cannot be compressed. A substance in a liquid state has a fixed volume, but no definite shape.

The **boiling point** is the temperature at which a liquid substance turns to a vapour. For water at normal sea level conditions, the boiling point is 100°C (212°F).

A **vapour** is a substance that can be easily compressed, has no resistance to flow, and no fixed volume. Since a vapour flows, it is considered a fluid just like a liquid.

A substance changes to a vapour if the temperature rises above its boiling point. A vapour condenses to liquid if the temperature falls below the boiling point. Just like melting and freezing, the boiling point and **condensation point** are the same temperature. Again, the difference is simply whether heat is being added or taken away. Boiling point and condensation point temperatures are not fixed; they vary with pressure.

Heat and Temperature

Molecules in a substance tend to vibrate rapidly in all directions, and this disorganized energy is called **heat.** The intensity of vibration depends on how much **kinetic energy,** or energy of motion, the atom or molecule contains. We measure the level of this energy as temperature.

Heat and temperature are not the same. Heat is measured in **calories (c).** The calorie is a metric unit that expresses the amount of heat needed to raise the temperature of one gram of water one degree Celsius.

Heat is also measured in **British Thermal Units (BTU).** One BTU is the heat required to raise the temperature of one pound of water 1°F at sea level. One BTU equals 252 calories.

Latent Heat

Latent heat is the extra heat that is needed to transform a substance from one state to another. Imagine that a solid or a liquid is being heated on a stove. When the solid reaches its melting point, or the liquid reaches its boiling point, their temperatures stop rising. The solid begins to melt, and the liquid begins to boil. This occurs without any change in temperature, even though heat is still being poured in from the burner.

The water in the container on the stove boils at a temperature of 100°C (212°F) at sea level, for as long as any liquid water remains. As you continue to add heat with the burner, it will all be absorbed in changing the state of the liquid to a vapour. This extra, hidden amount of energy necessary to change the state of a substance is called latent (or hidden) heat. See Figures 22–2 and 22–3.

Latent heat is important in air-conditioning system operation because the cooling effect is derived from changing the state of liquid refrigerant to a vapour. The refrigerant absorbs latent heat of vaporization, cooling the air blown into the passenger compartment. You take away the heat to cool the air.

Frequently Asked Question ???

Why Is Liquid Sprayed from a Can Cold?

If you spray a can of liquid continuously, the can becomes cold, and the liquid being sprayed becomes cold. The can becomes cold because the pressure in the can is reduced while spraying, allowing the liquid propellant inside the can to boil and absorb heat. The liquid being sprayed has also been cooled by the liquid propellant. The propellant vapour is further cooled as it decompresses when it hits the open air. Rapid decompression results in a rapid temperature drop.

Figure 22–2 The extra heat required to change a standard amount of water at its boiling point to a vapour is called **latent heat of vaporization.**

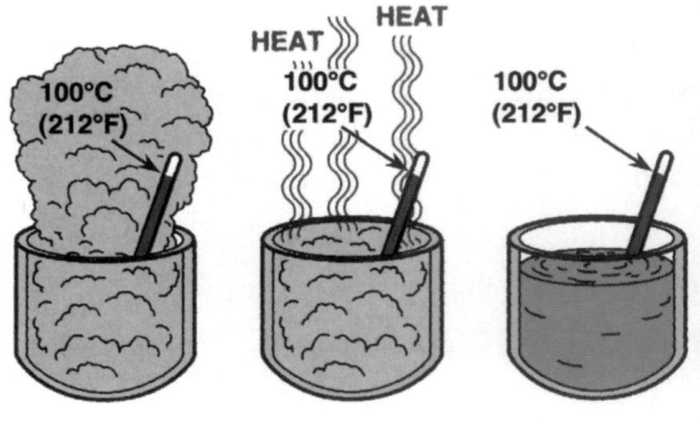

Figure 22–3 The latent heat of vaporization that water vapour stores is given off when the vapour condenses to a liquid. The temperature stays the same.

Temperature, Volume, and Pressure of a Vapour

Unlike a solid, a vapour has no fixed volume. Increasing the temperature of a vapour, while keeping the volume confined in the same space, increases the pressure. This happens as the vibrating vapour molecules collide more and more energetically with the walls of the container. Conversely, decreasing the temperature decreases the pressure. This relationship between temperature and pressure in vapour explains why a can of nonflammable refrigerant can explode when heated by a flame—the pressure buildup inside the can will eventually exceed the can's ability to contain the pressure.

Increasing the pressure by compressing a vapour also increases the temperature. Decreasing the pressure by permitting the vapour to expand decreases the temperature.

Pressure–Temperature Relationships

There are two aspects of the relationship between pressure and temperature that are important to understanding the operating of an HVAC system:

- The temperature at which a liquid boils (and vapour condenses) rises and falls with the pressure.
- Pressure in a sealed system that contains both liquid and vapour rises and falls with the temperature.

Humidity

Water vapour is in the air in varying concentrations. **Humidity** refers to water vapour present in the air. The level of humidity depends upon the amount of water vapour present and the temperature of the air.

The amount of water vapour in the air tends to be higher near lakes or the ocean, because more water is available to evaporate from their surfaces. In desert areas with little open water, the amount of water vapour in the air tends to be low.

Absolute humidity is the measurement of the weight of the water vapour in a given volume of air. **Relative humidity** is the percentage of how much moisture is present in the air compared to how much moisture the air is capable of holding at that temperature.

Relative humidity is commonly measured with a **hygrometer** or a **psychrometer.** A hygrometer depends on a sensitive element that expands and contracts, based on the humidity. Hygrometers typically resemble a clock, with the scale reading from 0 to 100% relative humidity.

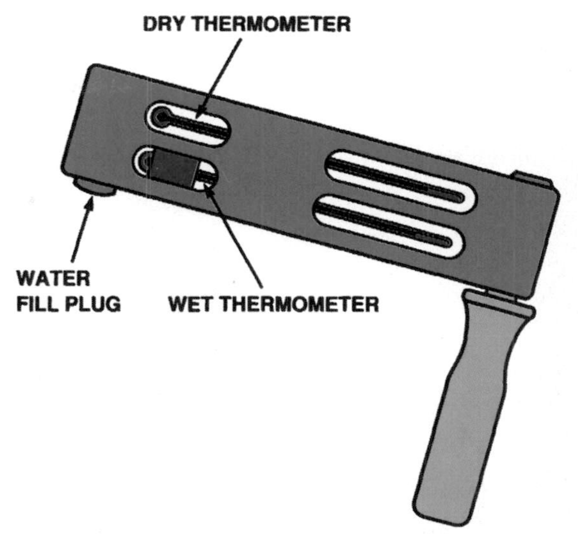

Figure 22–4 A sling psychrometer is used to measure relative humidity.

A psychrometer uses two thermometers, one of which has the bulb covered in a cotton wick soaked in distilled water from a built-in reservoir. See Figure 22–4. The wick keeps the bulb of the "wet thermometer" wet so that it can be cooled by evaporation. To take a relative humidity reading, the psychrometer is placed in the airflow for a certain time. As the evaporator blows air, the wet bulb's temperature drops, and the dry bulb reads the temperature of the airflow. Sling psychrometers are spun round in the air a certain number of times. Water evaporates from the cotton wick at a rate inversely proportional to the relative humidity of the air; faster if the humidity is low, and slower if the humidity is high.

The "dry thermometer" registers ordinary air temperature. The higher the relative humidity, the closer the readings of the two thermometers, and the lower the humidity, the greater the difference. The different temperatures indicated by the wet and dry thermometers are compared to a chart, which gives the relative humidity.

HEATING SYSTEM

All automotive and light-truck heater systems use the hot coolant from the engine to produce heat. The engine coolant (antifreeze and water) flows through **heater hoses** and a **heater core.** The engine water pump supplies the force necessary to circulate the engine coolant through the heater core. The heater core is a small radiator with tubes and fins that help transfer the heat from the coolant to the air flowing through the heater core. See Figure 22–5. A **blower motor** with a squirrel cage-type fan is usually used

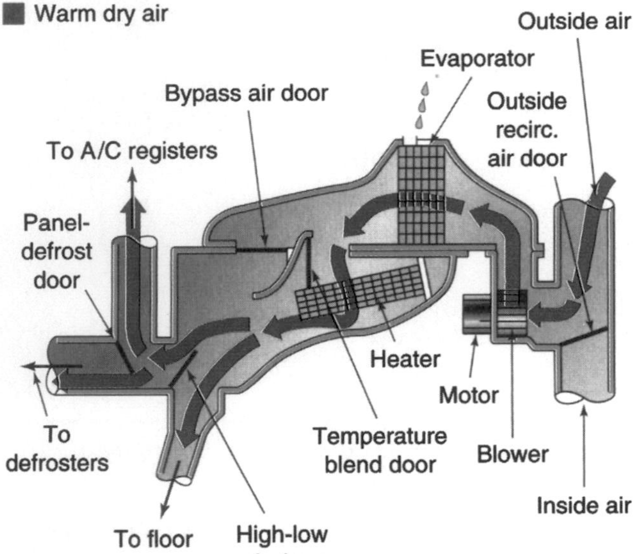

Figure 22–5 Typical flow of air through an automotive heat, ventilation, and air-conditioning system when placed in the heat position.

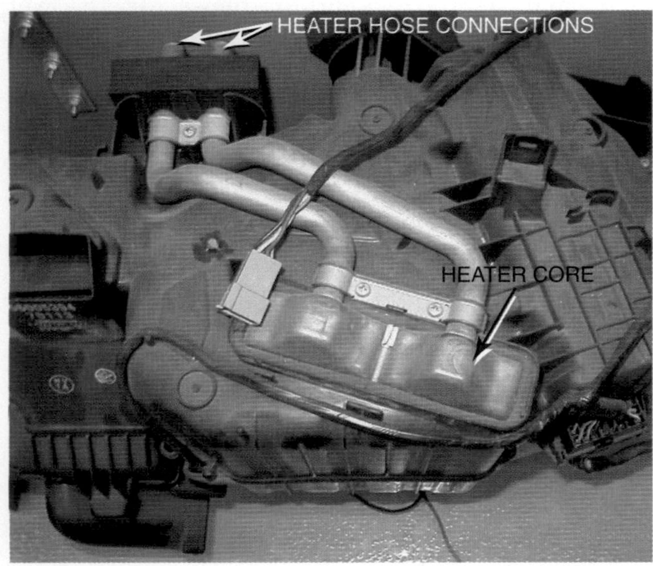

Figure 22–6 A typical heater core as installed in an HVAC housing.

to force air through the heater core and into the passenger compartment. See Figure 22–6. Before the heater can function correctly, the cooling system has to be functioning correctly. See Chapter 7 for cooling system operation, testing, and diagnosis. See Chapter 23 for heater system problem diagnosis.

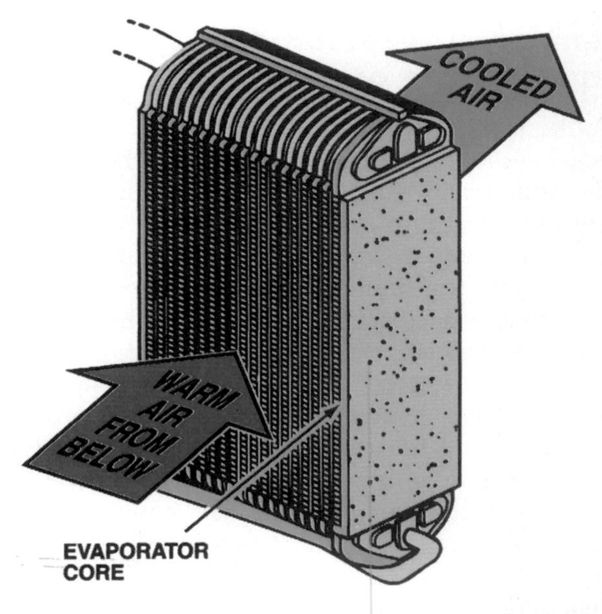

Figure 22–7 The evaporator removes heat from the air that enters a vehicle by transferring it to the vaporizing refrigerant.

AIR-CONDITIONING REFRIGERATION CYCLE

All automotive air-conditioning systems are closed and sealed. A refrigerant is circulated through the system by a **compressor** that is powered by the engine through an accessory drive belt. Older systems used a refrigerant, CFC-12, commonly referred to by its Dupont trade name of Freon or R-12. Starting in the early 1990s, vehicle manufacturers now all use HFC-134a, a refrigerant that is less harmful to the atmosphere. The basic principle of the refrigeration cycle is that as a liquid changes into a gas, heat is absorbed. The heat that is absorbed by an automotive air-conditioning system is the heat from inside the vehicle. This is how the system works:

1. The liquid refrigerant evaporates in a small radiator-type unit called the **evaporator.** As the refrigerant evaporates, it absorbs heat as it changes from a liquid to a gas. As the heat is absorbed by the refrigerant, the evaporator becomes cold. See Figure 22–7.
2. After the refrigerant has evaporated into a *low pressure gas* in the evaporator, the refrigerant flows into the engine-driven compressor. The compressor compresses the low-pressure refrigerant gas into a high-pressure gas and forces the refrigerant through the system. See Figure 22–8.
3. This high-pressure gas flows into the condenser located in front of the cooling system radiator.

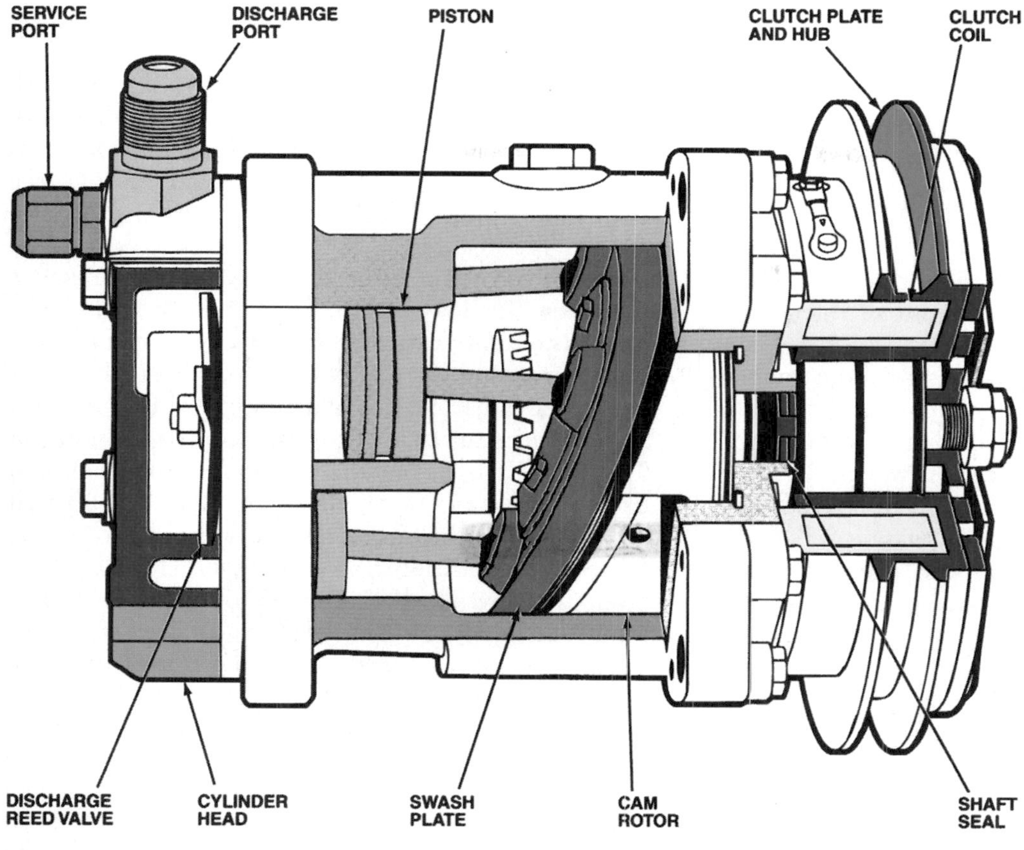

Figure 22–8 The compressor provides the mechanical force needed to pressurize the refrigerant.

Frequently Asked Question ???

How Does the Inside of the Vehicle Get Cooled?

The underlying principle involved in air-conditioning or refrigeration is that "cold attracts heat." Therefore, a cool evaporator attracts the hot air inside the vehicle. Heat always travels toward cold and when the hot air passes through the cold evaporator, the heat is absorbed by the cold evaporator, which lowers the temperature of the air. The cooled air is then forced into the passenger compartment by the blower through the air-conditioning vents.

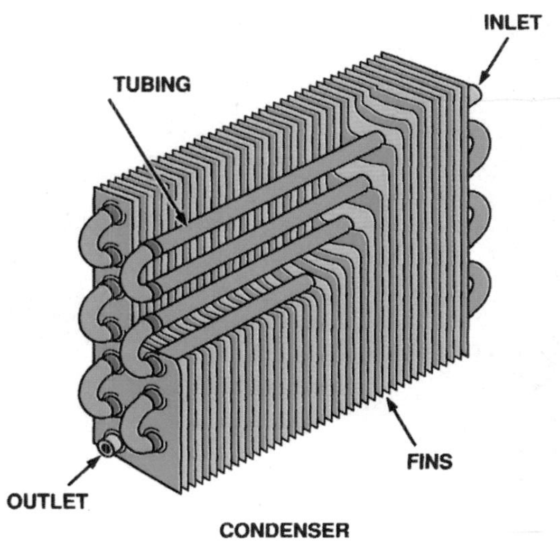

Figure 22–9 The condenser changes the refrigerant vapour into a liquid by transferring heat from the refrigerant to the air stream that flows between the condenser fins.

The **condenser** looks like another radiator, and its purpose and function is the same as the cooling system radiator, to remove heat from the high-pressure gas. In the condenser, the high-pressure gas changes (condenses) to form a high-pressure liquid as the heat from the refrigerant is released to the air. See Figure 22–9.

4. The high-pressure liquid then flows through a device that meters the flow into the evaporator. When the high pressure of the liquid drops, it causes the refrigerant to vaporize.
5. Air is blown through the evaporator by the blower motor. The air is cooled as heat is

removed from the air and transferred to the refrigerant in the evaporator. This cooled air is then directed inside the passenger compartment through vents.

EXPANSION VALVE SYSTEMS

An expansion valve is attached to the inlet to the evaporator and controls the amount of refrigerant flow into the evaporator. The expansion valve controls the flow of the refrigerant based on the temperature at the outlet of the evaporator, which is measured by a temperature-sensing bulb and tube. When the outlet of the evaporator is warm, the opening of the expansion valve is increased. This opening allows refrigerant to flow into the evaporator. As the temperature at the outlet of the evaporator decreases, the sensing bulb and tube cause the expansion valve to restrict the flow of refrigerant into the evaporator. This type of system is called the **thermostatic expansion valve** system—usually abbreviated **TEV** or **TXV.** See Figure 22–10.

ORIFICE TUBE SYSTEMS

Many air-conditioning systems today use a fixed-orifice tube at the inlet to the evaporator. As refrigerant flows through this orifice (small hole), it expands inside the evaporator, where it absorbs heat and expands into a low-pressure gas. A pressure switch located in the low-pressure line at the outlet of the evaporator senses when the pressure is too low. Too low a pressure in the evaporator can cause the temperature of the evaporator to drop to below freezing. A cold evaporator can therefore cause the moisture in the air to freeze into ice, creating a blockage to air flow through the evaporator. Therefore, whenever the pressure drops below a certain pressure (typically about 215 to 230 kPa [31 to 33 psi]), a pressure switch opens the circuit to the air-conditioning compressor clutch, which stops the flow of refrigerant through the evaporator. Then, when the temperature (and pressure) increases in the evaporator, the pressure switch closes, restoring the electrical current flow to the compressor clutch and causing the compressor to

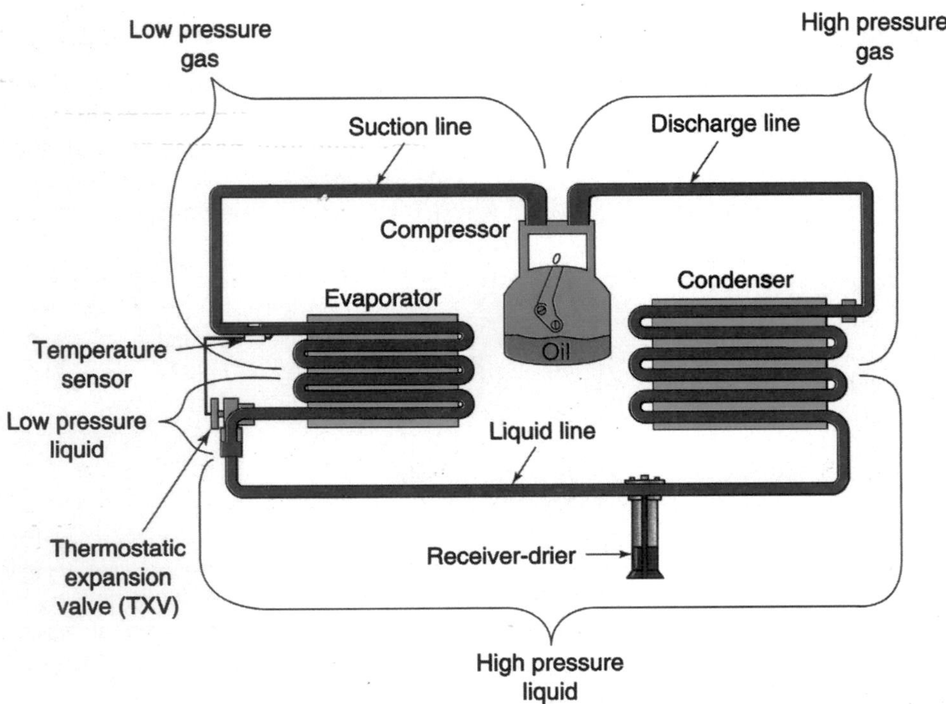

Figure 22–10 A typical air-conditioning system that uses an expansion valve. A temperature sensor bulb is attached to the outlet of the evaporator to control the amount of refrigerant allowed to flow into the evaporator.

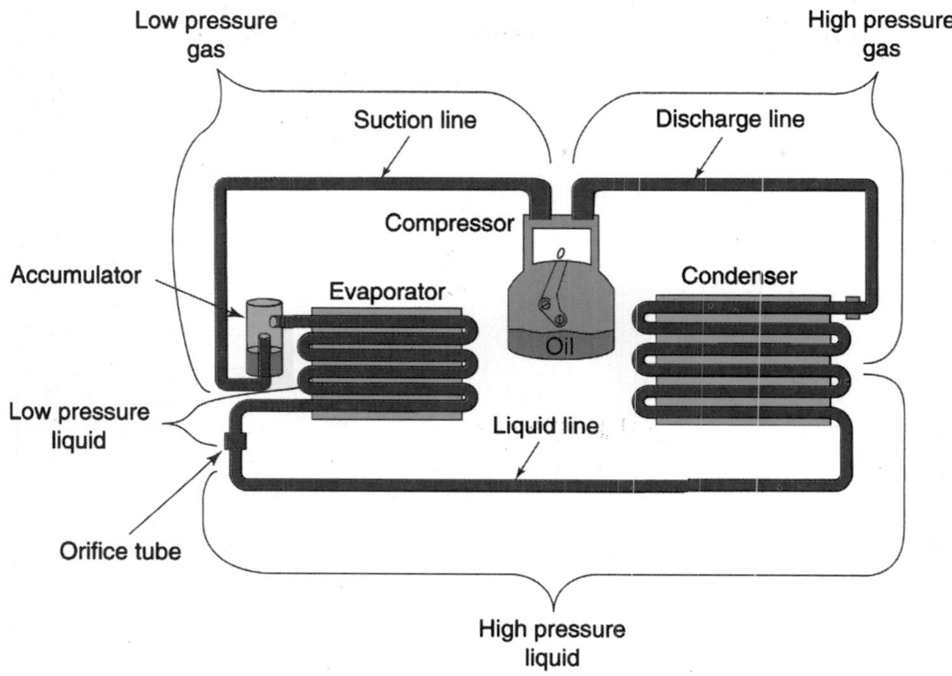

Figure 22–11 A typical automotive air-conditioning system that uses a cycling clutch and an orifice tube.

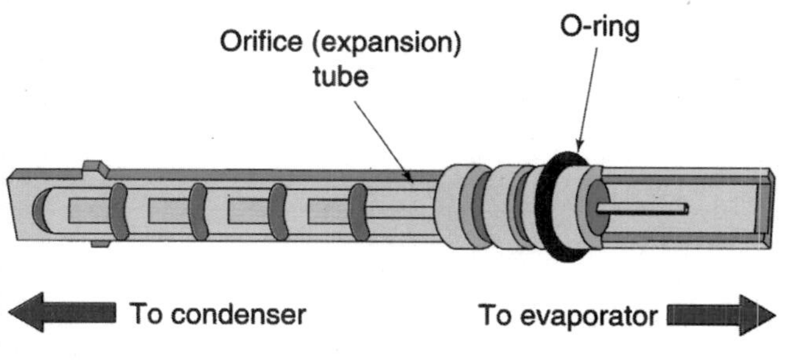

Figure 22–12 Typical orifice tube.

start forcing refrigerant through the evaporator again. This type of system is commonly called a **cycling clutch orifice tube** (or **CCOT**) system. See Figures 22–11 and 22–12.

THERMOSTATIC CONTROL

The lower the pressure of the refrigerant, the lower the temperature. If the pressure in the evaporator is above 205 kPa (30 psi) for R-12 or 190 kPa (28 psi) for an R-134a system, the temperature of the evaporator will remain about freezing, 0°C (32°F). Temperature control must be used to prevent the temperature of the evaporator from dropping below 0°C (32°F). At this temperature, the moisture in the air freezes. The resulting ice would clog the air flow through the evaporator. If air cannot flow through the evaporator, the air-conditioning system stops functioning, which would be immediately noticed by the driver and any passengers. If the A/C is turned off, heat from the surrounding air will melt the ice and the air-conditioning system will again function until it ices up again.

A commonly used method to control evaporator temperature is to use a thermostat to control the compressor. air-conditioning compressors use an **electromagnetic clutch.** See Figure 22–13. When the thermostat senses that the temperature is near freezing, 0°C (32°F), the switch opens the electrical circuit to the compressor and the compressor stops circulating refrigerant. This thermostat switch is also called a **thermo switch, icing switch,** or **defrost switch.**

NOTE: Older vehicles used a system to control evaporator pressure when used with a continuously-operating compressor, including:

STV valve—a suction throttling valve.

EPR valve—an evaporator pressure regulator. These valves maintain at least 205 kPa (30 psi) in the evaporator to prevent evaporator freeze-up.

Figure 22–13 A cutaway of an air-conditioning compressor electromagnetic clutch.

REFRIGERANTS

Air-conditioning refrigerant is used to transfer heat from the inside of the vehicle to the condenser located in the front of the vehicle. A refrigerant absorbs heat when it changes state from a liquid to a gas. One of the first refrigerants was **CFC-12,** commonly referred to as **R-12** or by its brand name **Freon,** a registered trade name of the DuPont Corporation. CFC-12 consists of one carbon atom surrounded by two chlorine (CL) and two fluorine (F) atoms and is therefore called a chlorofluorocarbon (CFC) compound. Its chemical name is dichlorodifluoromethane. It is the chlorine atoms that are believed to contribute to the destroying of the ozone layer in our upper atmosphere. Since 1995, sales of new motor vehicles whose air-conditioners contain ozone-depleting substances (ODS) are prohibited by Canadian and U.S. federal laws.

Another refrigerant, **HFC-134a,** also called **R-134a,** has been selected by vehicle manufacturers to replace the ozone-harming CFC. HFC-134a compound contains two carbon atoms and four fluorine atoms plus two hydrogen atoms and is therefore called a hydrofluorocarbon. Its chemical name is tetrafluorolthene, and DuPont calls it Suva®. See Figure 22–14.

CFC-12 and HFC-134a Boiling Temperatures at Various Pressures		
Temperature °C (°F)	CFC-12 Pressure kPa (psi)	HFC-134a Pressure kPa (psi)
−22 (0)	62 (9)	41 (6)
−15 (5)	83 (12)	62 (9)
−12 (10)	103 (15)	83 (12)
−9 (15)	124 (18)	103 (15)
−7 (20)	145 (21)	124 (18)
−4 (25)	172 (25)	152 (22)
−1 (30)	200 (29)	179 (26)
2 (32)	228 (33)	214 (31)
4 (40)	255 (37)	241 (35)
7 (45)	290 (42)	276 (40)
10 (50)	324 (47)	310 (45)
13 (55)	359 (52)	352 (51)
16 (60)	324 (47)	393 (57)
18 (65)	441 (64)	441 (64)
21 (70)	483 (70)	490 (71)
24 (75)	531 (77)	544 (79)
27 (80)	579 (84)	600 (87)
29 (85)	634 (92)	655 (95)
32 (90)	690 (100)	717 (104)
35 (95)	745 (108)	786 (114)
38 (100)	807 (117)	855 (124)
41 (105)	876 (127)	1013 (147)
43 (110)	938 (136)	1089 (158)

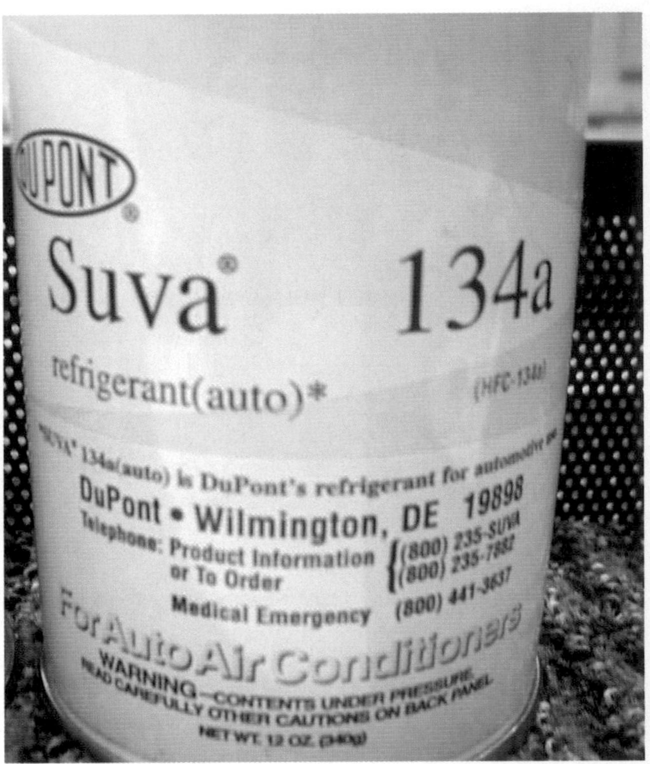

Figure 22–14 R-134a is available in 13.6 kg (30-lb) containers.

The boiling points and therefore the operation characteristics of CFC-12 and HFC-134a are similar at lower temperatures; however, HFC-134a pressures are higher at higher temperatures.

HFC-134a, a smaller molecule than CFC-12, can more easily leak out through small holes or openings in the system. HFC-134a systems require that the inside layer of the rubber refrigerant hoses contain a barrier to prevent penetration through the microscopic holes in standard rubber hoses.

NOTE: Look at the size of a blue HFC-134a 13.6 kg (30 lb) container compared to a white CFC-12 13.6 kg (30 lb) container. The blue R-134a container is larger because it requires more HFC-134a to achieve 13.6 kg (30 lb).

NOTE: Many vehicle manufacturers started using barrier-type refrigerant hoses on their vehicles in the late 1980s in anticipation of the conversion from CFC-12 to HFC-134a in future models.

Ozone Depletion

Chlorofluorocarbons (CFCs) released into the atmosphere gradually drift into the upper atmosphere where ultraviolet light breaks down the CFC molecules. Chlorine is one product of the process: the chlorine atoms destroy ozone molecules in the ozone layer.

The ozone layer is important, as it screens out the sun's ultraviolet radiation, which can cause health and skin cancer problems.

The Montreal Protocol

In 1987, representatives of 76 nations met in Montreal, QC where they signed an international accord to halt production and import of new CFCs and other ozone-depleting substances.

Training Requirements

Canadian regulations require completion of a one-day environmental awareness certification course for ODS control. The course "CFC/HCFC/HFC Control in the Refrigeration and Air-Conditioning Industry" is designed and administered by the Heating, Refrigerating, and Air-Conditioning Institute of Canada (HRAI) and Environment Canada.

The course stresses Environment Canada's Code of Practice: Recover, Recycle, Reuse and Reclaim refrigerants. HFC, while not an ODS, is considered a "greenhouse" gas (which contributes to global warming) and is also included. The course is mandatory for technicians who service air-conditioning equipment.

REFRIGERANT OILS

The oil, absorbed and carried by the refrigerant through the various components, is often the only source of lubrication for the compressor. The oil used must be able to be mixed without separating in the refrigerant. This characteristic of being able to be mixed is called **miscible.** CFC-12 systems use mineral oil. Mineral oil is not miscible in HFC-134a, and so such systems must use synthetic polyalkeline glycol, usually referred to as PAG oil. There are numerous different PAG oils, and each vehicle manufacturer (or air-conditioning compressor manufacturer) recommends which PAG to use. See Figure 22–15.

Another type of refrigerant oil is called **ester oil.** Ester is a classification of hydrocarbons and is specified for use in air-conditioning systems that have been charged (retrofitted) from CFC-12 to HFC-134a. Ester oil will mix with any remaining mineral oil and will work to lubricate the system even if some CFC-12 is still in the system. See Figure 22–16.

All refrigerant oils have a viscosity rating. Viscosity is the measure of the oil's thickness or resistance to flow. Always use the type and viscosity of oil specified by the manufacturer.

CAUTION: Failure to use the correct refrigerant oil in an air-conditioning system can cause serious (and expensive) damage to the air-conditioning compressor. Always use the refrigerant oil specified by the manufacturer.

Figure 22–15 PAG oil used in Chrysler vehicles equipped with HFC-134a refrigerant. Notice that different oils are used for different systems, depending primarily on the manufacturer of the compressor. Also notice that both PAG oils are in metal cans. PAG oil absorbs moisture so readily that it can even absorb moisture in the air through plastic—that is why metal containers are used.

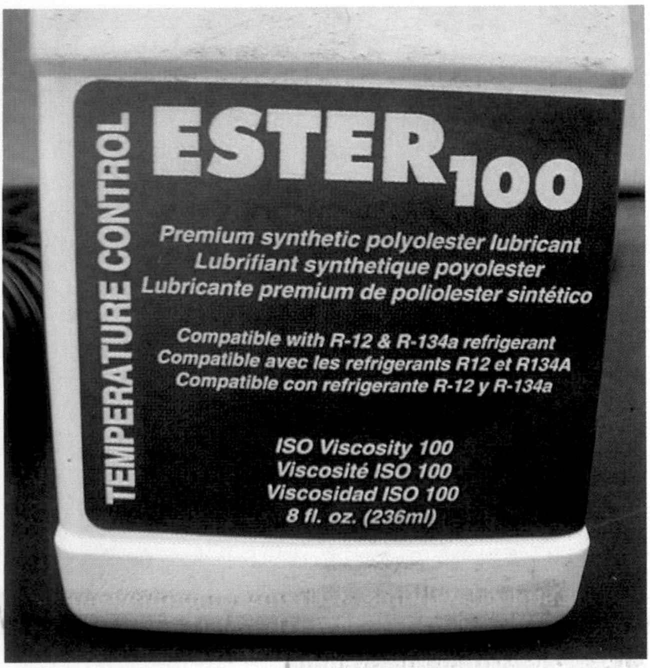

Figure 22–16 Ester refrigerant oils are often specified for use when retrofitting an R-12 system to R-134a by companies who supply refit kits. Ester refrigerant oil is not recommended by many vehicle or air-conditioning compressor manufacturers. Always use the recommended refrigerant oil for the vehicle and system being serviced.

CONDENSER

The condenser looks like a cooling system radiator. In fact, a condenser is a radiator because it is designed to radiate heat from the refrigerant to the outside air.

When the refrigerant leaves the compressor it is over 150°C (300°F) as it enters the condenser. Even on a hot 40°C (104°F) day, there is a difference in temperature between the outside air around the condenser and the temperature of the refrigerant inside the condenser. Heat always travels from hot to cold. Therefore, the heat in the hot refrigerant has a natural tendency to radiate into the outside air. As the heat travels into the air, the high-pressure gas refrigerant changes state and becomes a high-pressure liquid. This is the reason the condenser is called by that name; as the heat leaves the refrigerant, it **condenses** from a gas (vapour) to a liquid. The latent (hidden) heat in the vapour is also given off when the vapour condenses back into a liquid. See Figure 22–17.

To help in the heat transfer, most vehicles are equipped with cooling fans driven either electrically or by the engine through an accessory drive belt. The fan draws air through the condenser and increases the heat transfer rate. See Chapter 7 for details on cooling fans.

Figure 22–17 The condenser serves the same function for both the orifice-tube and the expansion valve–type air-conditioning system, and that is to remove the heat from the refrigerant and cause the hot refrigerant vapours to condense into a hot liquid.

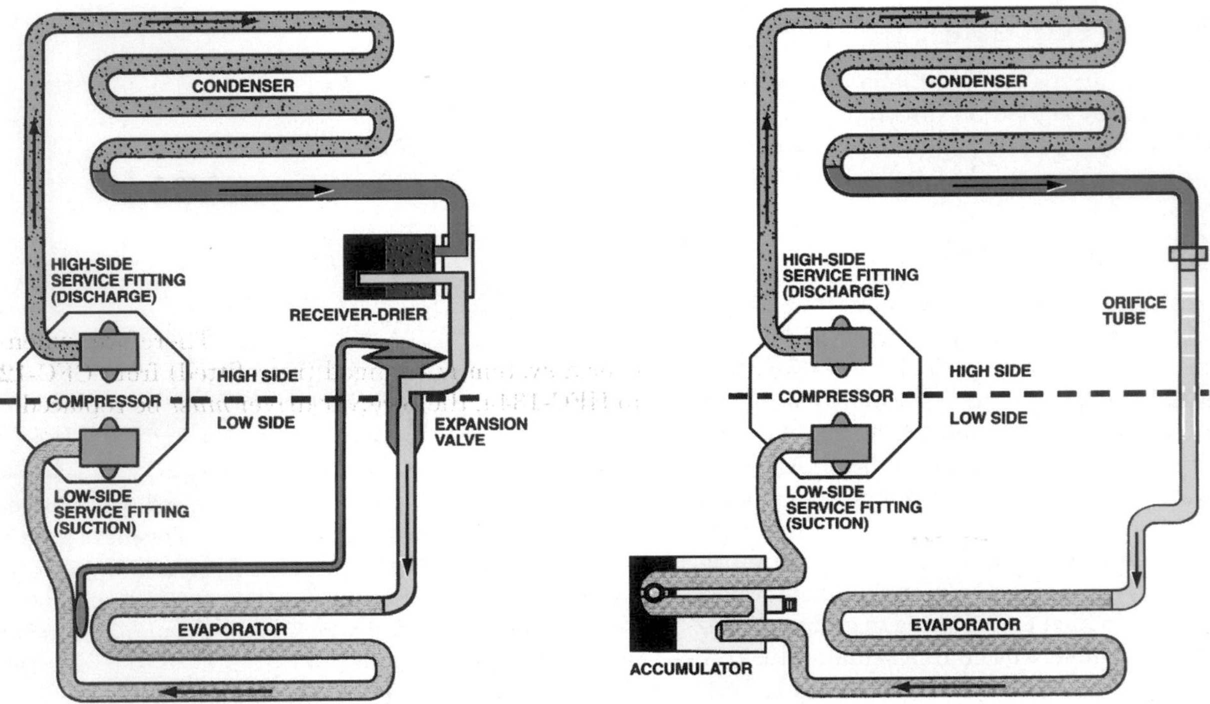

TECH TIP 

Broken Condenser Line—
Check the Engine Mounts!

Most air-conditioning systems use aluminum and flexible rubber lines between the compressor and the condenser. Because the compressor is mounted on and driven by the engine and the condenser is mounted to the body, these lines can break if the engine mounts are defective. The rubber hoses attached between the aluminum fittings of the compressor and condenser are designed to absorb normal engine movement. Worn engine mounts allow the engine to move too much. Aluminum lines cannot stand to be flexed without cracking and breaking.

Therefore, the wise technician will carefully inspect and replace any and all worn engine mounts if a broken aluminum condenser line is discovered to prevent a premature failure of a replacement condenser. See Figure 22–18.

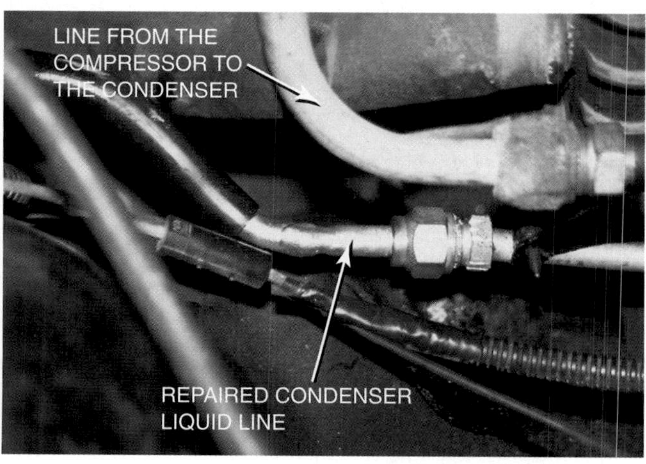

Figure 22–18 A repaired condenser refrigerant line.

EVAPORATOR

The evaporator looks like a small radiator that is located in the evaporator housing on the passenger side of the bulkhead (firewall). The purpose of the evaporator is to transfer heat from the air to the refrigerant flowing through it. Reduced pressure after the thermostatic expansion valve (or orifice tube) and heat from the air causes the low-pressure liquid inside the evaporator to evaporate into a low-pressure gas. As the refrigerant changes state from a liquid to a gas, it absorbs heat. A blower motor equipped with a squirrel cage–type fan circulates air through the evaporator and forces the cooler air into the passenger compartment.

Another benefit of the cooling of the air is a result of what happens to any moisture that may be in the air passing through the evaporator. Moisture in the air is called relative humidity and represents the percentage of water vapour that could be in the air to the actual amount in the air. High humidity feels uncomfortable. Because the evaporator is cold (usually just above the freezing point of 0°C [32°F]), any moisture in the air condenses on its cool surface. This removes the moisture from the air and lowers the relative humidity. The moisture that condenses out of the air then becomes water that is allowed to flow out of the evaporator housing and onto the ground. See Figure 22–19.

NOTE: If the carpet (or floor) of the vehicle is wet on the passenger side, the cause is often a clogged evaporator drain hose. The opening, called the **condensate line,** is frequently clogged with mud, road debris, or leaves. To check the drain opening, hoist the vehicle and insert a wire or screwdriver into the end of the hose opening at the bottom of the evaporator housing.

RECEIVER-DRIER

A receiver-drier is used on an air-conditioning system that uses an expansion valve. The receiver-drier is located between the condenser and the evaporator. This section of the air-conditioning system contains *high-pressure liquid refrigerant.* The purpose of the receiver is to provide temporary storage for the liquid refrigerant and it usually includes a filter to trap debris and a desiccant to remove moisture. Many receiver-driers contain a sight glass that provides a view of the liquid refrigerant in the system.

A drier is needed to remove moisture from the system. The drier contains a **desiccant** (usually silica alumina or silica gel). A desiccant is a drying agent that absorbs any moisture (water) that gets into the air-conditioning refrigerant system. Moisture can combine with refrigerant to form an acid. Water can also freeze and form ice in the system.

The desiccant is classified as XH-5 for CFC-12 systems and XH-7 or XH-9 for HFC-134a systems. The desiccant used on a CFC-12 system is not compatible with HFC-134a systems. Therefore, whenever a system is changed (retrofitted) from CFC-12 to HFC-134a, the receiver-driver *must* be replaced.

The desiccant (accumulator or receiver-drier) should also be replaced on any air-conditioning system that has been left open to the atmosphere for any length of time (over 24 hours) or whenever the system has been left in a discharged condition. Many technicians will automatically replace the receiver-drier or accumulator if the air-conditioning system is opened for any major repair. See Figure 22–20.

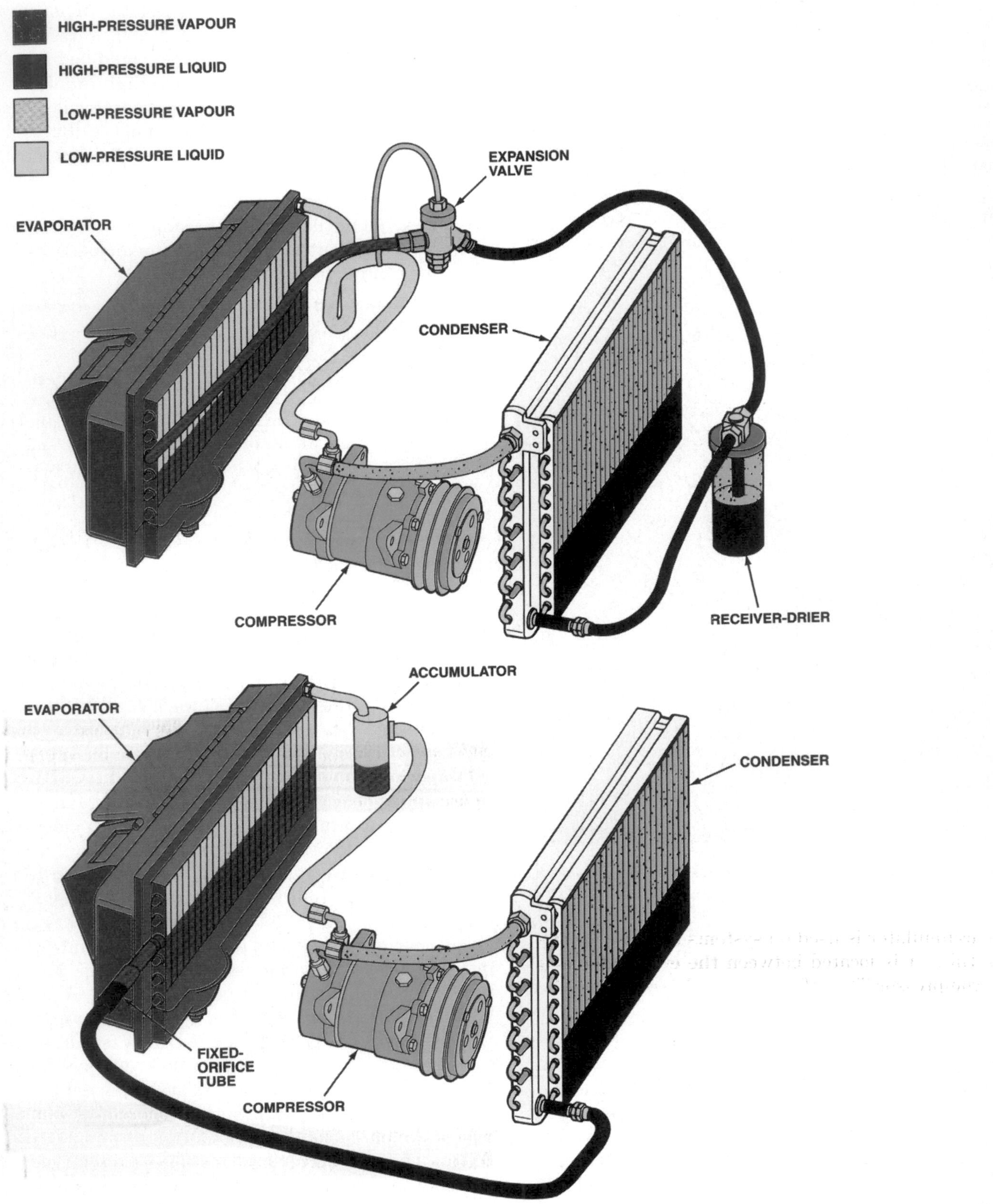

Figure 22–19 The evaporator serves the same function for both the orifice-tube and the expansion valve–type air-conditioning system, and that is to allow the liquid refrigerant to evaporate and absorb heat from the passenger compartment.

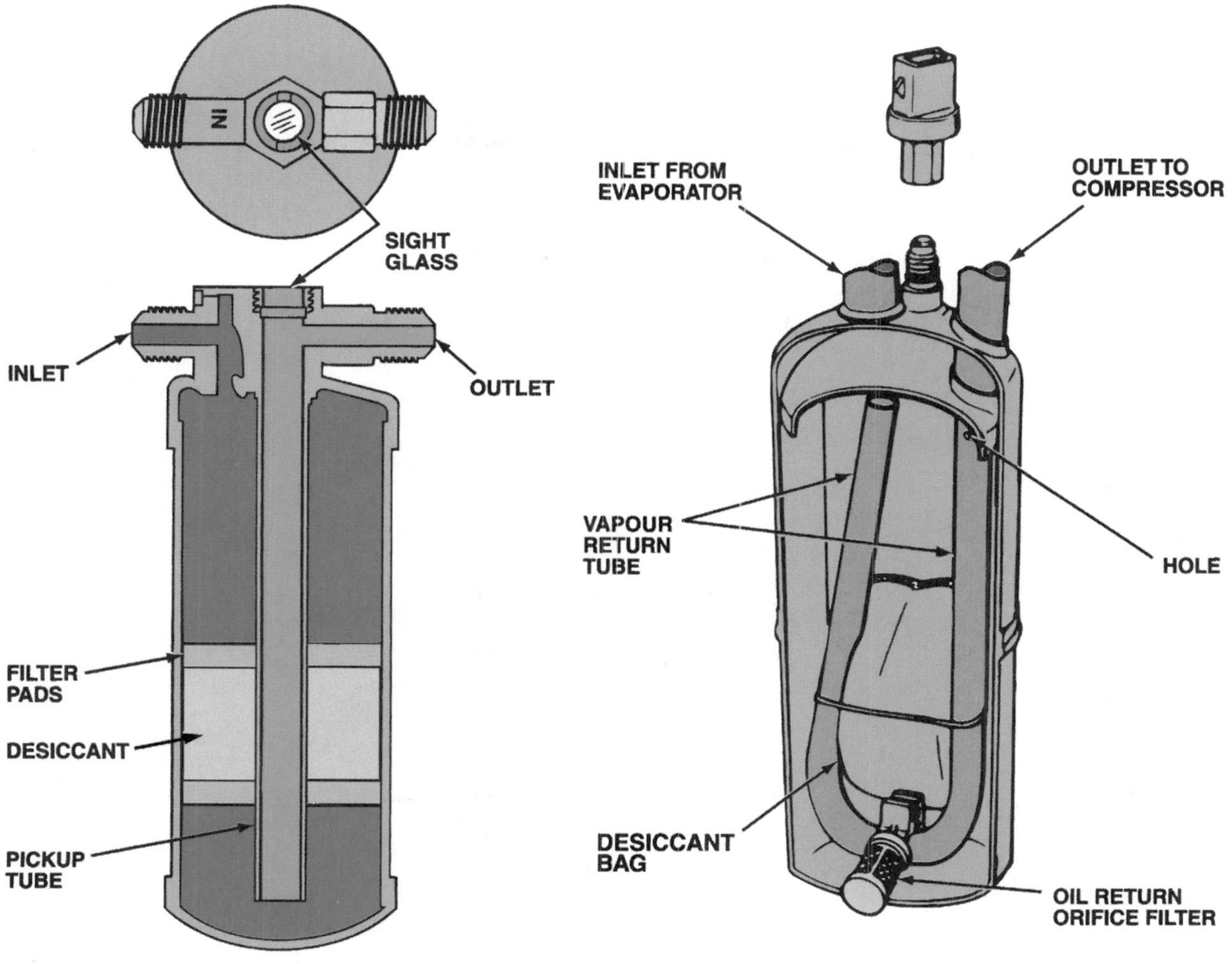

SIGHT GLASS
INLET
OUTLET
FILTER PADS
DESICCANT
PICKUP TUBE
INLET FROM EVAPORATOR
OUTLET TO COMPRESSOR
VAPOUR RETURN TUBE
HOLE
DESICCANT BAG
OIL RETURN ORIFICE FILTER

Figure 22–20 Expansion-valve systems store excess refrigerant in a receiver-drier, which is located in the high-side liquid section of the system, whereas orifice-tube systems store excess refrigerant in an accumulator located in the low-side vapour section of the system.

ACCUMULATOR

An accumulator is used on systems that use an orifice tube. It is located between the evaporator and the compressor. The refrigerant in this section of the refrigerant cycle is a *low-pressure gas*. The purposes of the accumulator include:

- Preventing liquid refrigerant from reaching the compressor

> **NOTE:** A liquid cannot be compressed. If liquid refrigerant were to enter the compressor, the compressor would lock up and be damaged.

- Holding a reserve of refrigerant
- Holding the desiccant (helping to remove moisture from the system)

See Figure 22–21.

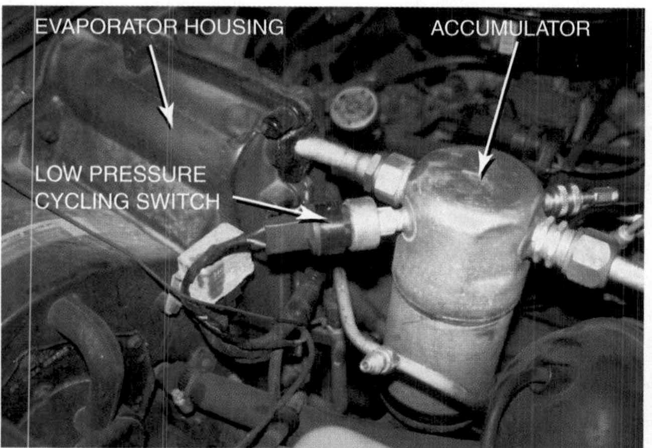

Figure 22–21 A typical accumulator used on a cycling clutch orifice-tube (CCOT) system.

REFRIGERANT LINES AND HOSES

Aluminum tubing is used to connect many stationary items together like the condenser to the receiver-drier and the receiver-drier to the evaporator. Rubber lines are usually used to and from the compressor. Because the compressor is attached to the engine and the engine is mounted on flexible rubber mounts, there is movement between the compressor and the other air-conditioning components that are attached to the body of the vehicle. These flexible refrigerant hoses are constructed from many layers of rubber and fabric. See Figure 22–22. Most hoses used on vehicles since the early 1990s use a nonpermeable inside layer of material that prevents the loss of refrigerant through the hose itself. These hoses, called **barrier hoses,** are required for use with HFC-134a refrigerant.

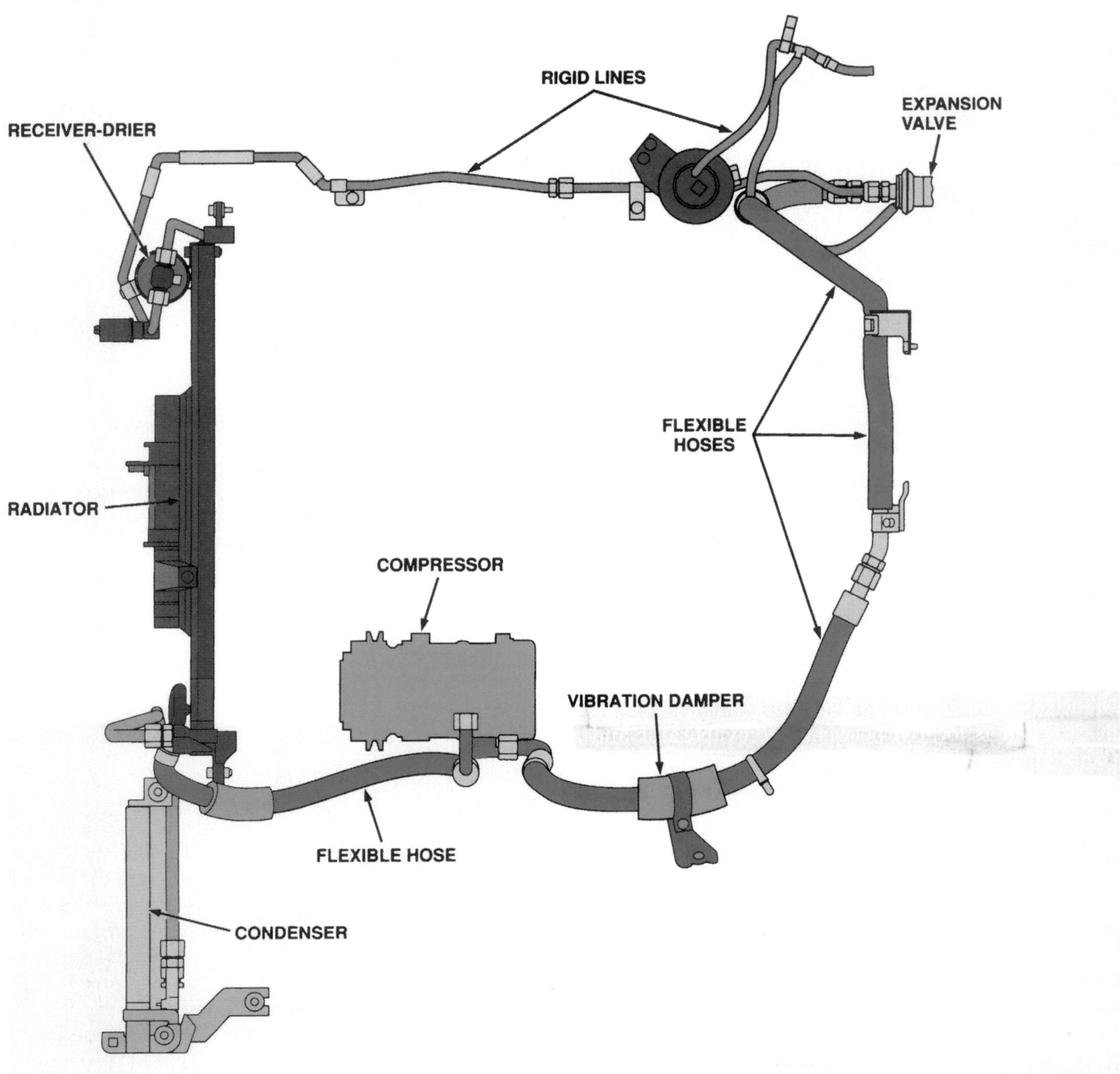

Figure 22–22 Rigid lines and flexible hoses are used throughout the air-conditioning system. The line to and from the compressor must be flexible because it is attached to the engine, which moves on its mounts during normal vehicle operation.

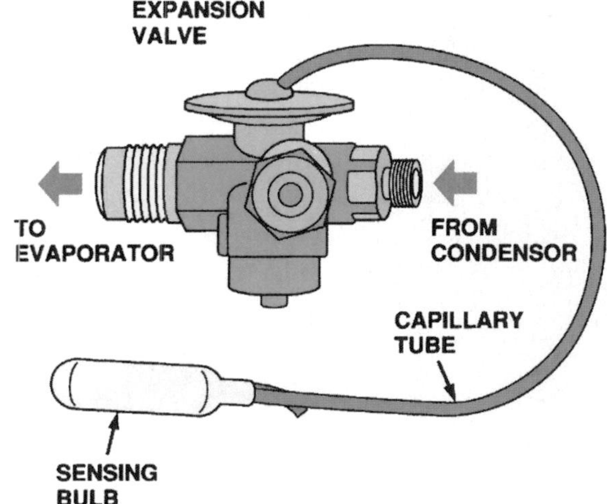

Figure 22–23 A typical thermostatic expansion valve which uses an inlet and outlet attachment for the evaporator, and a temperature-sensing bulb that is attached to the evaporator outlet tube.

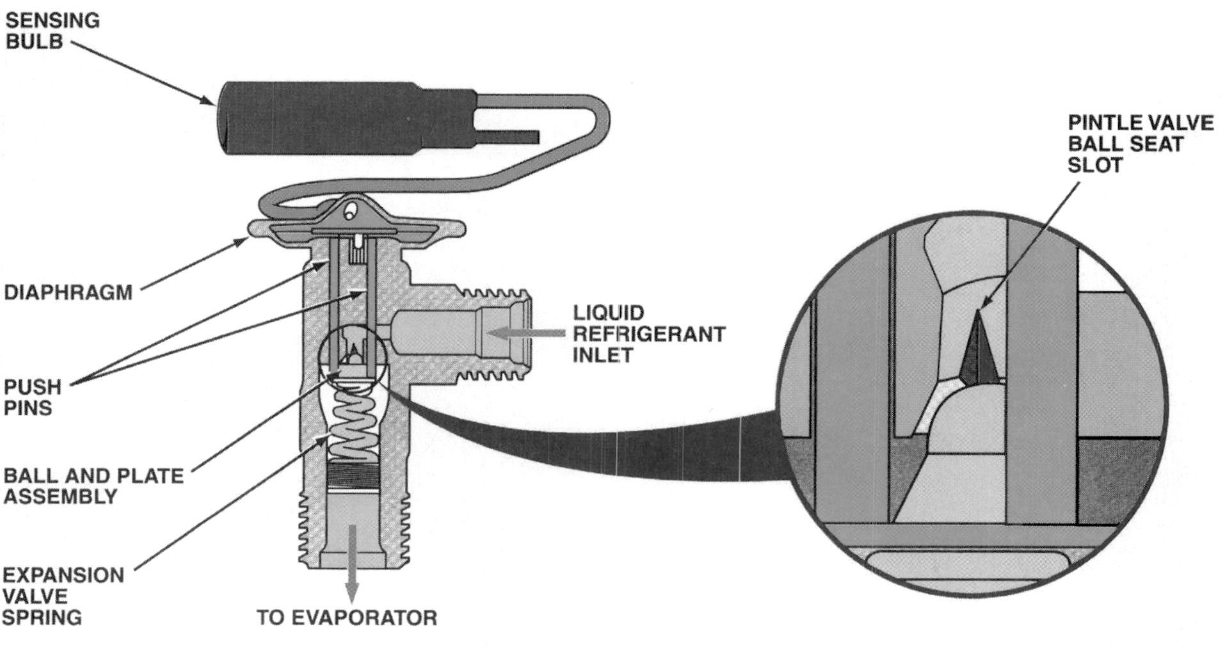

Figure 22–24 A slot cut in the ball seat inside the expansion valve permits a small amount of refrigerant and oil to pass through at all times, even when the valve is closed. This flow of oil through the system is necessary to make sure that the compressor receives the oil it needs for lubrication.

THERMOSTATIC EXPANSION VALVES

Thermostatic expansion valve (TXV) systems, as shown in Figure 22–23, use a temperature-sensitive bulb located on the evaporator outlet tube. The sensing bulb is insulated with a special tape, so it reacts only to temperature changes it senses from the outlet tube. The sensing bulb works in combination with a pressure-sensitive diaphragm inside the TXV body to control the size of the variable orifice. This regulates the rate at which liquid refrigerant flows into the evaporator.

The key to the operation of the expansion valve is the variable orifice. In these systems, the outlet from the high-pressure side to the low-pressure side is a variable-diameter hole. A **pintle valve** is a ball-and-seat valve used to increase or decrease the size of the opening. See Figure 22–24. The expansion valve uses the pintle valve to control how rapidly refrigerant enters the evaporator. The expansion valve controls the refrigerant flow in response to the temperature of the evaporator outlet, measured by the remotely mounted sensing bulb and **capillary tube.** See Figure 22–25. The sensing bulb may be clamped to the outlet pipe or mounted inside a passage near

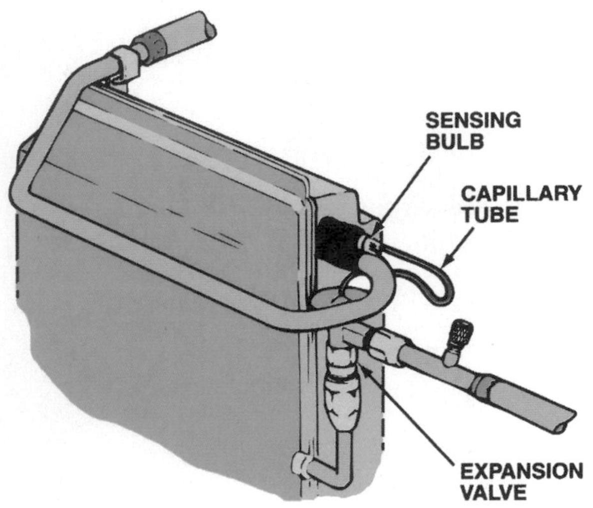

Figure 22–25 The sensing bulb is attached to the evaporator outlet tube. Refrigerant inside the bulb expands or contracts in response to the evaporator temperature.

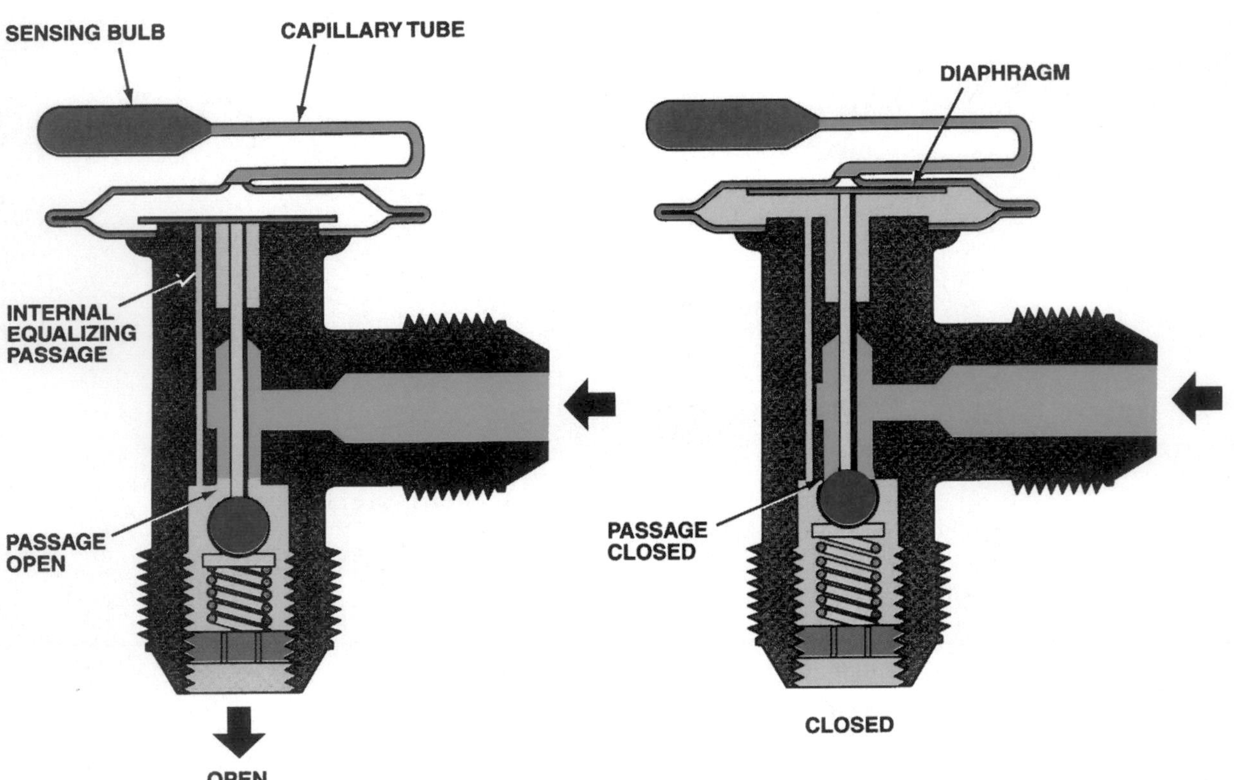

Figure 22–26 Pressure from the capillary tube pushes on the spring-loaded diaphragm to open the expansion valve. As the pressure in the capillary tube contracts, the reduced pressure on the diaphragm allows the valve to close.

the outlet of the evaporator. The bulb and tube contain refrigerant. The rise or fall of the evaporator outlet temperature causes the refrigerant in the bulb to expand or contract, resulting in a rise or fall of pressure inside the capillary.

This outlet-temperature-sensitive pressure is applied to one side of the spring-loaded diaphragm inside the expansion valve. See Figure 22–26. As the capillary tube warms, the refrigerant inside expands, forcing the diaphragm downward. The diaphragm magnifies this pressure and uses it to open the valve by pushing the pintle and ball away from its seat. This increases the size of the orifice and allows more refrigerant into the evaporator, increasing the cooling capacity.

When the evaporator cools in response to the boiling of the added refrigerant, the refrigerant in

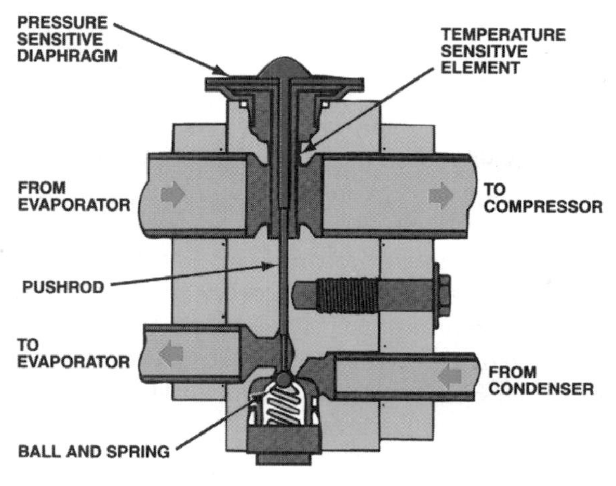

Figure 22–27 An H-valve (H-block) combines the temperature-sensing and pressure-regulating functions into a single assembly.

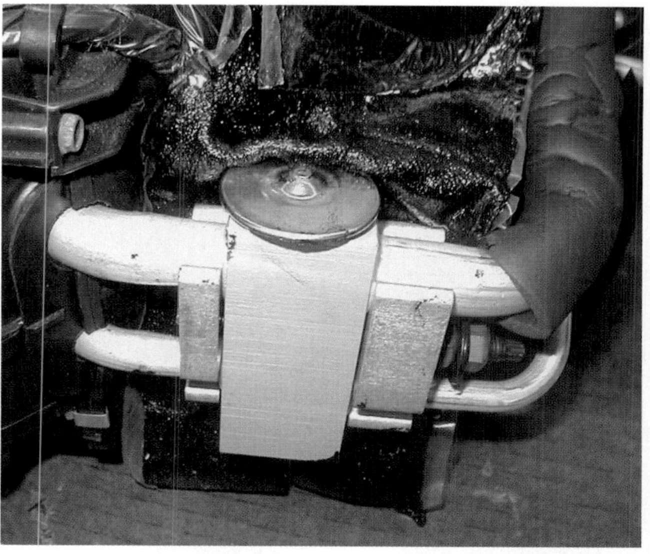

Figure 22–28 An H-valve as used on a Chrysler minivan.

the capillary contracts. This relieves the pressure on the expansion valve diaphragm, which closes the pintle and ball, and reduces refrigerant flow.

Pressure on the top of the diaphragm is applied through the capillary tube. The equalizing pressure on the underside of the diaphragm can be internal (from the evaporator inlet) or external (from the evaporator outlet):

- An internally equalized expansion valve has a passage that permits evaporator inlet pressure to reach the underside of the diaphragm.
- An externally equalized expansion valve has an extra line mounted to the underside of the diaphragm housing. This line monitors the outlet pressure of the evaporator. The connection can be either at the outlet of the evaporator or at the outlet of the evaporator pressure control device.

In an expansion-valve system, the refrigerant vapour that leaves the evaporator is warmer than the liquid refrigerant that entered it. The heat that warms the refrigerant is referred to as **superheat.** Superheat is usually measured as the actual temperature difference between the boiling point of the refrigerant at the inlet and at the outlet of the evaporator. Typical values for superheat in an evaporator are between 3° and 10°C (5° and 18°F).

Superheat is important because it ensures that all (or almost all) of the refrigerant vaporizes before leaving the evaporator.

DaimlerChrysler uses a valve called an **H-valve.** It includes both the temperature-sensing and the pressure-sensing functions of the expansion valve, but does not have any external tubes.

The H-valve has two refrigerant passages that form the legs of the "H" as shown in Figures 22–27 and 22–28. The lower passage is the refrigerant line

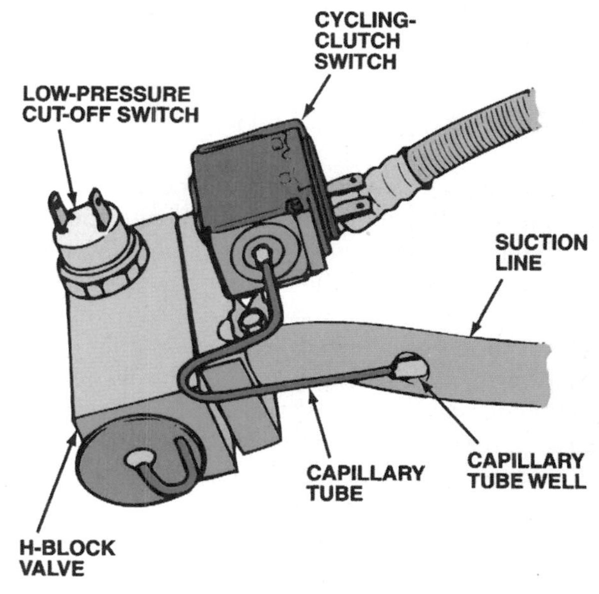

Figure 22–29 In this Chrysler system, a low-pressure cutoff switch and a cycling-clutch switch are mounted on the H-valve.

from the condenser to the evaporator, and contains the ball and spring valve. The upper passage is the refrigerant line from the evaporator to the compressor, and contains the temperature-sensing element. A push rod connects the diaphragm of the temperature sensor located at the top of the block to the valve ball at the bottom.

The cycling-clutch switch, which senses the suction line, detects the evaporator outlet temperature and cycles the compressor clutch to control system cooling. This capillary device does not directly control the metering orifice. See Figure 22–29.

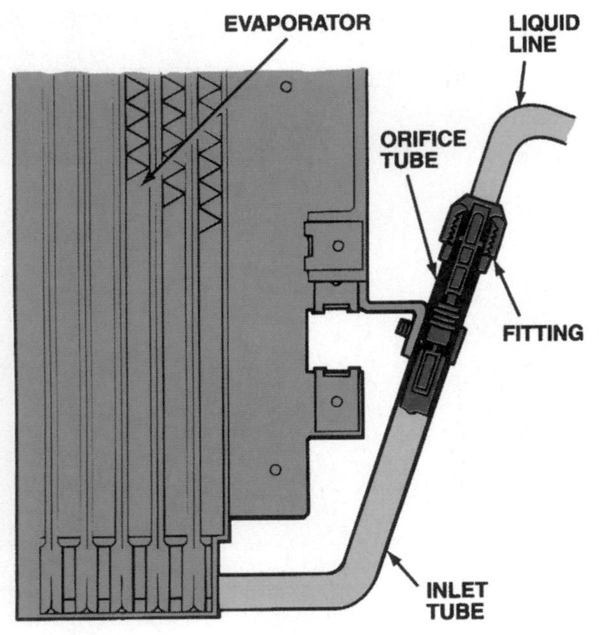

Figure 22–30 The orifice tube is usually located at the inlet tube to the evaporator.

FIXED-ORIFICE TUBES

Liquid refrigerant flows from the condenser to the orifice tube. As with expansion valves, fixed-orifice tubes provide a restriction that separates the high-pressure from the low-pressure side of the system. See Figure 22–30. When it reaches the fixed-orifice tube, the refrigerant undergoes rapid expansion and changes from a warm, high-pressure liquid to a cold, low-pressure liquid and vapour mixture. The major purpose of a fixed-orifice tube (or a thermostatic expansion valve) is to create a restriction in the high-pressure side of the system, which allows the refrigerant pressure to drop as the refrigerant flows through the restriction.

As it passes through the restriction to the low side, the refrigerant changes state from a liquid to a vapour because the pressure in the evaporator is so much lower than in the refrigerant line upstream from the orifice tube. The refrigerant begins to vaporize quickly as it absorbs the heat from the evaporator.

The orifice tube, located between the condenser and the evaporator inlet, may be inserted in the refrigerant line or may be part of the inlet refrigerant line assembly.

COMPRESSORS

The air-conditioning compressor is driven by the engine with an accessory drive belt. A magnetic clutch is usually used to connect and disconnect the drive pulley to the compressor as needed for cooling or defrosting. The oil in the refrigerant lubricates the moving parts of the compressor. The compressor performs the following functions:

- Compresses the low-pressure gas refrigerant from the evaporator into a high-pressure gas that is then sent to the condenser
- Raises the temperature of the gas so that there is a difference in temperature between the outside (ambient) air and the refrigerant in the condenser
- Acts as the pump used to circulate the refrigerant throughout the system
- Often switches on and off (cycles) to control evaporator temperatures

Positive-Displacement Piston Compressors

A **positive-displacement compressor** displaces a constant, uniform volume of refrigerant for each revolution or operating cycle. Most automotive air-conditioner compressors are positive-displacement piston designs. These compressors have from one to ten cylinders, depending on manufacturer and application. Most of these compressors use a piston-in-cylinder arrangement with intake and discharge strokes to draw in, compress, and discharge refrigerant. See Figure 22–31.

The compressor intake stroke is also known as the suction stroke. The suction stroke of a positive-displacement compressor is like that of a two-stroke gasoline engine. Just as the intake stroke of an engine's piston creates a low-pressure area that draws the air–fuel mixture in through the cylinder head, the suction stroke of the compressor piston creates a low-pressure area to draw refrigerant vapour into the cylinder. However, the similarity ends here. In a two-stroke engine, the compression stroke compresses the air–fuel mixture inside a sealed cylinder, with both the intake and exhaust valves closed. In the two-stroke piston AC compressor, the discharge valve does not resist the refrigerant flow during the upward piston stroke. As the compressor operates, the maximum possible charge of refrigerant vapour has been drawn in at bottom dead centre of the compressor piston's suction stroke. When the piston begins its discharge stroke, the pressure increases, shutting the suction valve and opening the discharge valve at the same time. The charge of refrigerant vapour is pushed out of the compressor into the high-side refrigerant line and travels toward the condenser. Therefore, the refrigerant vapour is compressed simultaneously throughout the entire high side of the air-conditioning system.

All piston compressors use one suction valve and one discharge valve for each piston. The typical valve used in compressors is the **reed valve:** a one-way, flap-type check valve that is built into the valve plate which seals one or more cylinders. See Figure 22–32. A reed valve flaps away from the valve plate to open, and to-

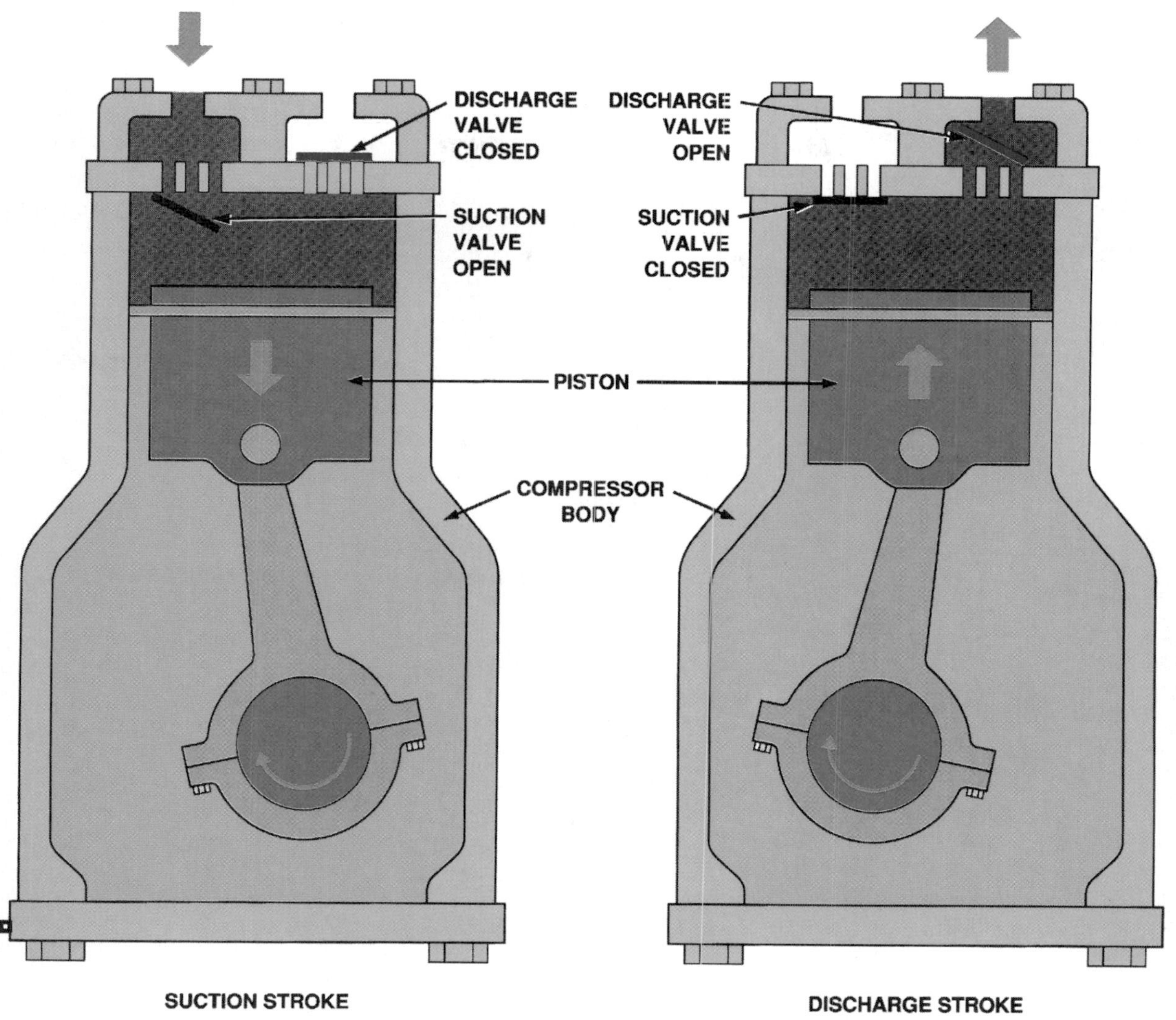

Figure 22–31 In a positive-displacement compressor, the descending piston creates a drop in pressure inside the cylinder. The resulting pressure differential allows low-side pressure to force the suction valve open. Refrigerant then flows into the cylinder. On the piston's discharge stroke, the pressure caused by the ascending piston closes the intake valve and forces the refrigerant out the discharge valve.

ward the valve plate to close. Pressure pushes the valve in one direction or the other. The suction reed valve is located on the underside of the valve plate. When the suction created by the piston's downward stroke becomes strong enough, the suction reed valve bends, or flaps, off its seat. Low-pressure refrigerant vapour then flows into the compressor. The refrigerant vapour fills the partial vacuum created by the moving piston.

The discharge reed valve is on the top side of the valve plate. The partial vacuum in the cylinder also pulls the discharge valve tightly against its seat, sealing off the system's high side from the cylinder during the suction stroke.

The reeds behave in exactly the opposite way during the piston's discharge stroke. The increasing cylinder pressure pushes the suction valve tightly against its seat, sealing off the system's low side. The discharge valve on the opposite side of the valve plate is unseated as the pressure in the cylinder increases as a result of the upward moving piston. The piston pushes the refrigerant through the discharge valve, out of the compressor, and into the air-conditioning system high side.

Pistons and Rings

The basic two-stroke cycle depends upon the pistons and their sealing rings to provide an adequate seal against the high-side refrigerant pressure. Most piston compressors have from two to six cylinders.

Some compressors use a **swash plate,** or axial plate. This plate is rigidly mounted to the belt-driven

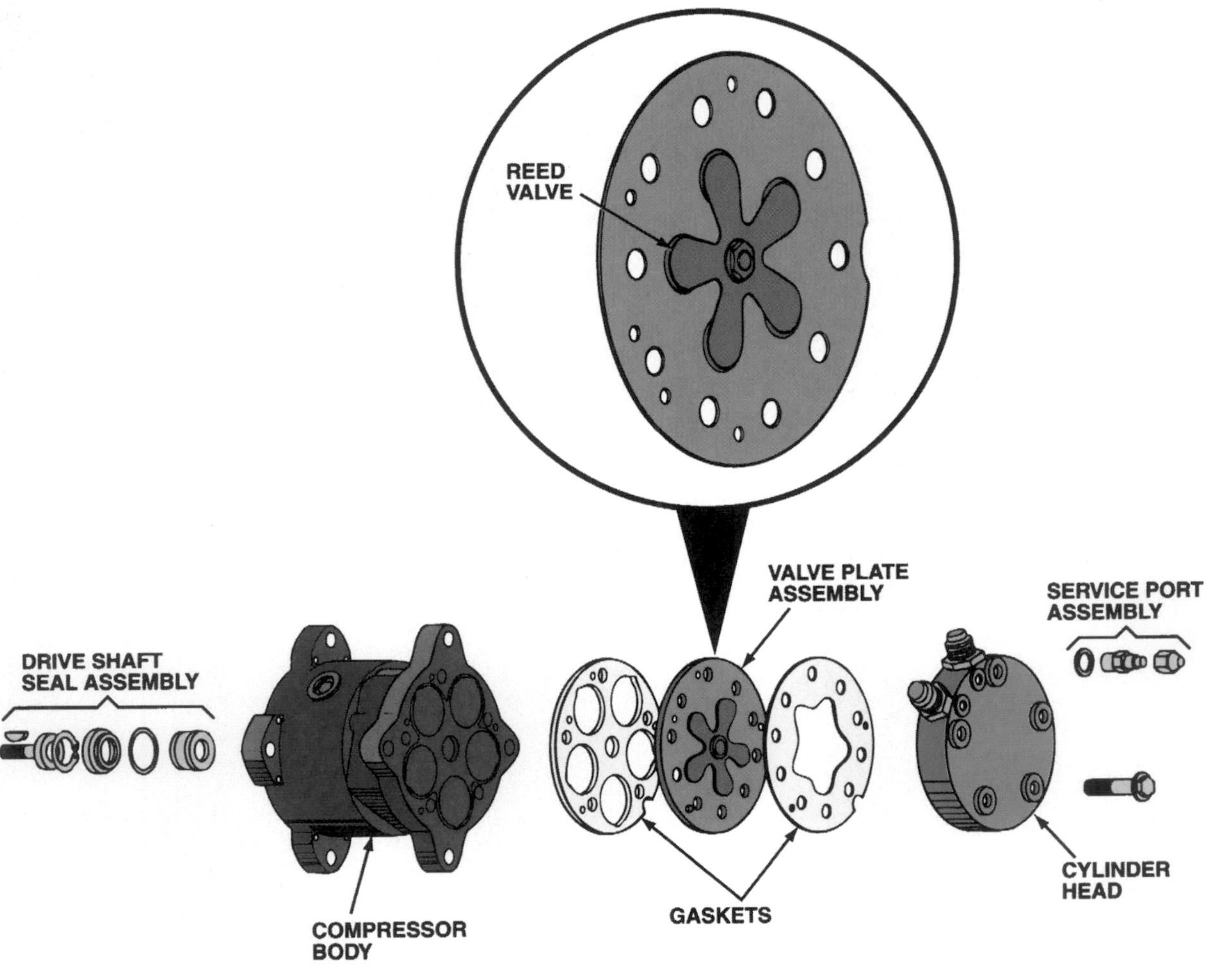

Figure 22–32 A reed valve is a one-way check valve that flaps away from the valve plate to open, and toward the valve plate to close.

shaft at an angle. See Figure 22–33. The pistons may be on one or both sides of the plate. The pistons are connected to the swash plate by means of a large ball bearing. As the pulley turns, the shaft and angled swash plate assembly rotate. This forces the pistons back and forth in their bores. In this way, the swash plate changes the rotating action of the shaft to a **reciprocating** action that provides driving force for each piston. Compressors that use a swash plate are often called **axial compressors.**

Variable Displacement Compressor

Some air-conditioning systems use variable displacement to control the amount of refrigerant flowing through the evaporator. The pressure difference between the high side and the low side causes the swash plate to move inside the compressor. As the swash plate changes its angle, the stroke of the piston is increased for more cooling or decreased to reduce the amount of cooling. See Figure 22–34.

ELECTRIC COMPRESSOR

Denso Corp. recently developed a new electric compressor that incorporates the electric motor and the compressor in one unit. It was designed for the Toyota Prius hybrid to allow the air-conditioning to function even when the vehicle is stopped and the engine shuts off.

COMPRESSOR CONTROLS

Most air-conditioning compressors use an electromagnetic clutch. A coil of wire inside the clutch creates a strong magnetic field that when activated connects the input shaft of the compressor to the drive pulley. Most electromagnetic coil assemblies have between 3 and 4 ohms of resistance. According to Ohm's law, about 3 to 4 amperes of current are required to energize the air-conditioning compressor clutch (see Chapter 13 for additional information on Ohm's law and current flow measurements).

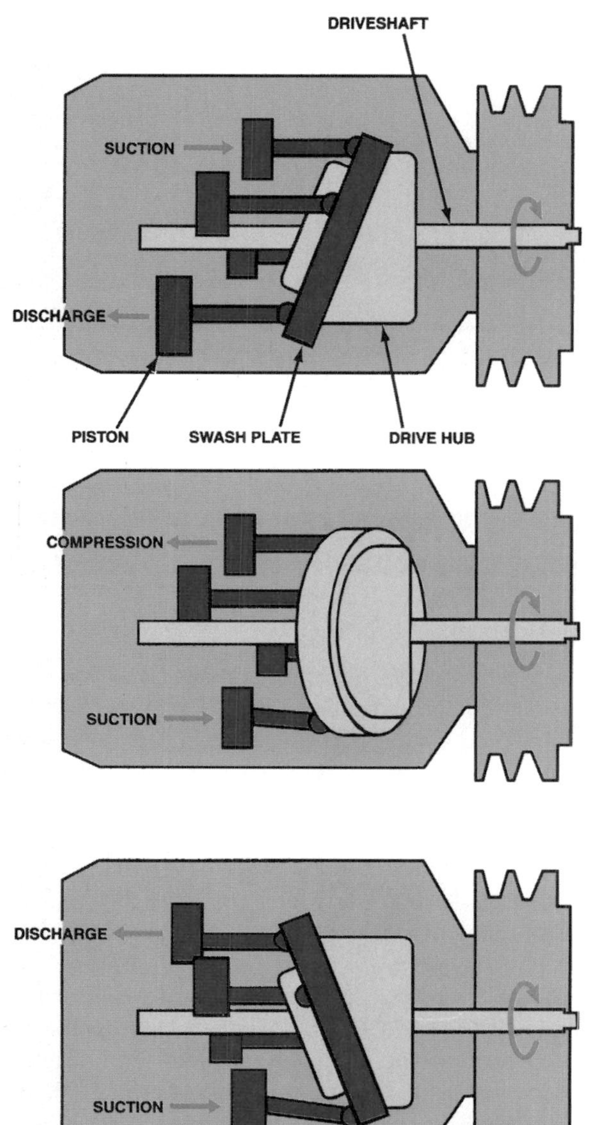

Figure 22–33 The swash plate, attached to the crankshaft at an angle, converts the pulley's rotary motion to axial motion, which drives the pistons in a reciprocating motion.

TECH TIP

The Radio "Pop" Trick

Most air-conditioning compressor clutch circuits contain a diode that is used to suppress the high-voltage spike that is generated whenever the compressor clutch coil is disengaged (turned off). If this diode were to fail, a high voltage (up to 400 V!) could damage sensitive electronic components in the vehicle including the electronic air-conditioning compressor clutch control unit (if equipped).

Another thing that can occur is that the radio will often turn off and then back on whenever the electronics inside the radio detect a high-voltage spike. This can create a pop in the radio that is very intermittent because it only occurs when the air-conditioning compressor clutch cycles off. To check this diode, simply tune the radio to a weak AM station near 1400 kHz and cycle the air-conditioning compressor on and off. If a pop is heard from the radio speaker(s), then the diode is defective and must be replaced.

NOTE: While some A/C compressor diodes can be replaced separately, some of these air-conditioning compressor clutch diodes are part of an entire wiring harness assembly.

Figure 22–34 A V-5 (five-cylinder) variable displacement compressor. Internal pressures act on the swash plate, which changes the stroke of the piston and then the displacement based on the pressures in the system.

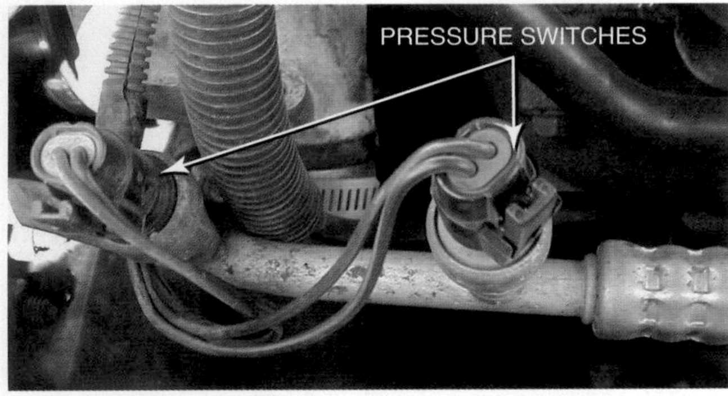

Figure 22–35 Typical air-conditioning pressure switches. A service manual would be needed to determine the function of each switch. One switch could be the low-pressure switch and the other a high-pressure switch.

All electrical circuits require three things to operate:

1. A voltage source
2. An electrical load (the air-conditioning compressor clutch)
3. A ground connection

All three of these must be in sync before current (amperes) can flow, causing the compressor clutch to engage. Most vehicle manufacturers connect several components in series with the compressor clutch so that all have to be functioning before the compressor clutch can be engaged. The most commonly used switches include:

- **Low-pressure switch:** This pressure switch is electrically closed only if there is at least 175 kPa (25 psi) of refrigerant pressure. This amount of pressure means that the system is sufficiently charged to provide lubrication for the compressor. This switch also prevents the air-conditioning compressor from being engaged when the temperature is low (low temperature means low refrigerant pressures). See Figure 22–35.
- **High-pressure switch:** This pressure switch is located in the high-pressure side of the air-conditioning system. If the pressure exceeds a certain level (typically 2600 kPa [375 psi]), the pressure switch opens, thereby preventing possible damage to the air-conditioning system due to excessively high pressure.
- **Power steering pressure switch:** This switch is used on many vehicles, especially those with four-cylinder engines. It opens the circuit to the air-conditioning compressor clutch when the driver turns the steering wheel and power steering is needed. This reduces the load on the engine at the same time power is needed by the power steering pump. Because the wheel is seldom held in a turning maneuver for a long period of time, this stoppage of the air-conditioning compressor has little, if any, effect on passenger cooling.

Figure 22–36 A climate control panel showing the controls for a dual-climate control system. Each side can be adjusted so that there could be up to an 8°C (15°F) difference between the driver side and the passenger side.

DIAGNOSTIC STORY

What Throttle Switch?

A service technician was tracing the cause of an inoperative air compressor on a Saab. The service manual showed a schematic of the air-conditioning compressor that indicated a number of switches that had to be closed for the compressor clutch to be supplied with battery voltage. Besides the low pressure switch (to assure that the system is charged so as not to damage the compressor), a throttle switch was shown on the schematic. Obviously, someone else had worked on the vehicle because the throttle switch was missing entirely—just two wires remained to indicate that anything had been installed. Connecting the two wires together provided voltage to the air-conditioning compressor clutch. The customer decided not to replace the throttle switch after learning that its purpose was to disconnect (open circuit) the air-conditioning compressor when the throttle was at wide open position to allow the maximum power for passing.

HVAC CONTROLS

All air-conditioning systems used in vehicles have controls that direct the air flow and regulate the temperature. See Figure 22–36 for a typical dual zone climate control panel. The various vacuum diaphragms are operated by a control unit like the one shown in Figure 22–37. The controls and their purpose and function include:

- Defrost (see Figure 22–38)
- Normal A/C (see Figure 22–39)
- Max A/C (see Figure 22–40)

Most air-conditioning systems also provide for outside air or recirculation, as shown in Figure 22–41.

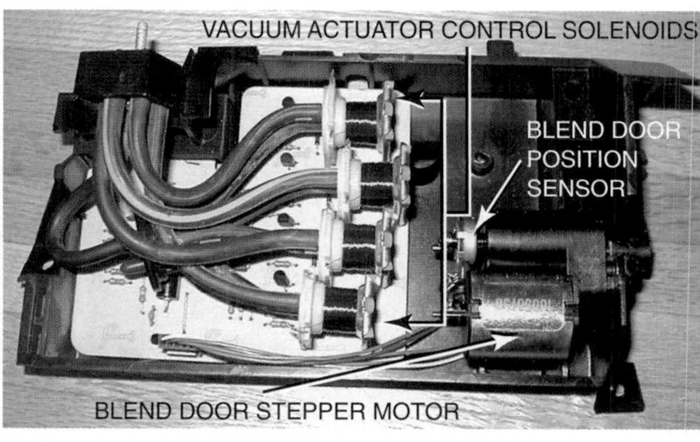

Figure 22–37 A typical HVAC control unit.

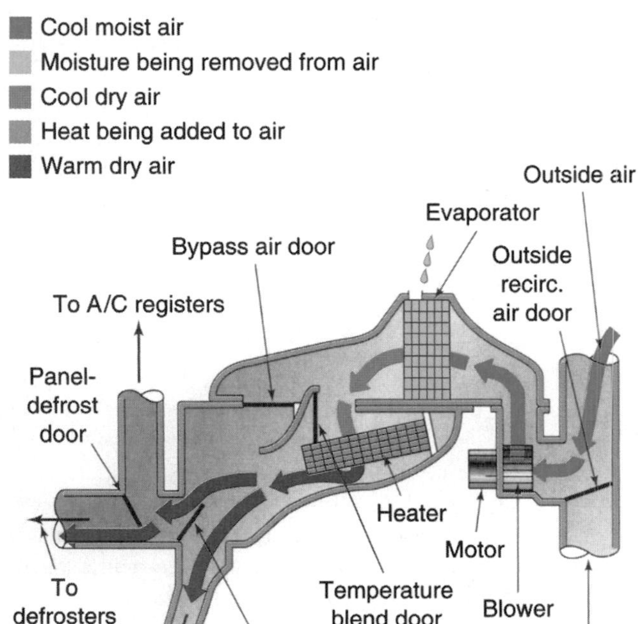

Figure 22–38 When the controls are set to defrost, air is directed first through the evaporator where any moisture in the air is condensed and removed from the air. The air-conditioning compressor is therefore operating when the controls are set to the defrost setting. The air flows through the heater core to heat the air before being directed to the defroster vents and floor.

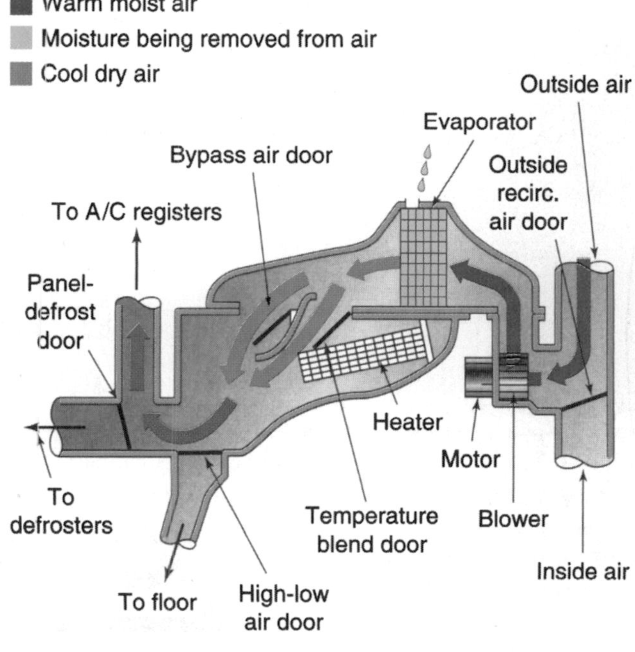

Figure 22–39 Controls set to normal air-conditioning. Note how most of the air (80% to 90%) is drawn from the outside. This means that fresh outside air is being cooled and blown into the interior through the air-conditioning vents.

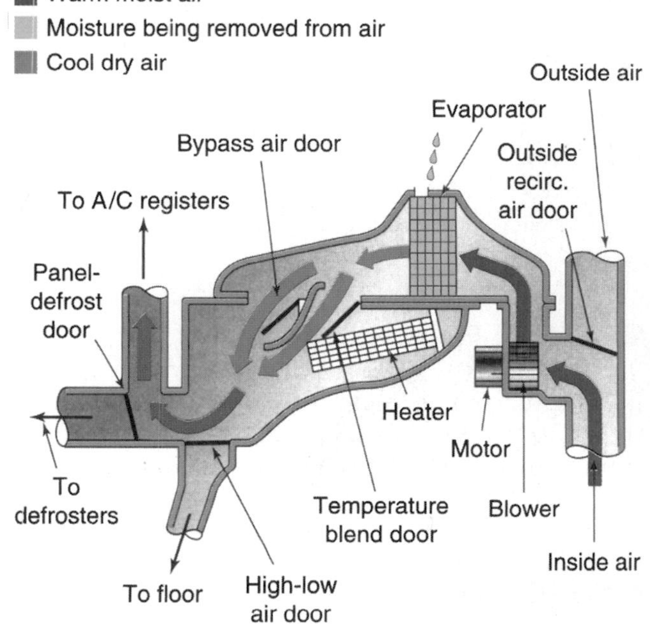

Figure 22–40 Controls set to MAX air-conditioning. Note that most of the air (80% to 90%) is drawn from inside the vehicle. Drawing the air from the inside allows the interior to cool quickly because cooler inside air is constantly being forced through the evaporator rather than hotter outside air.

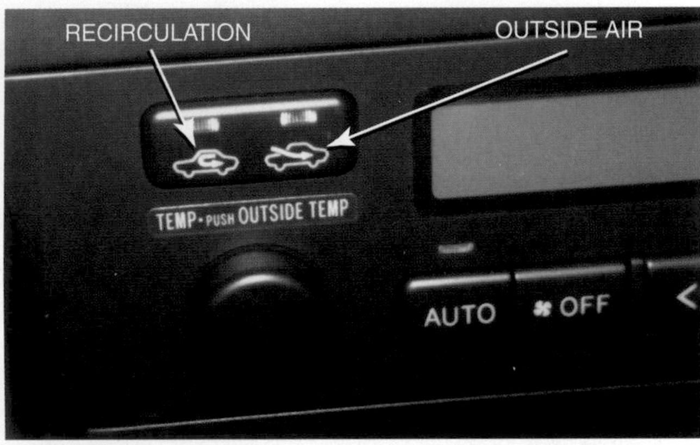

Figure 22–41 Most vehicles have controls that allow outside air or recirculated air to be used. Set the controls to recirculate when driving in dusty conditions to help prevent the dust from entering the passenger compartment.

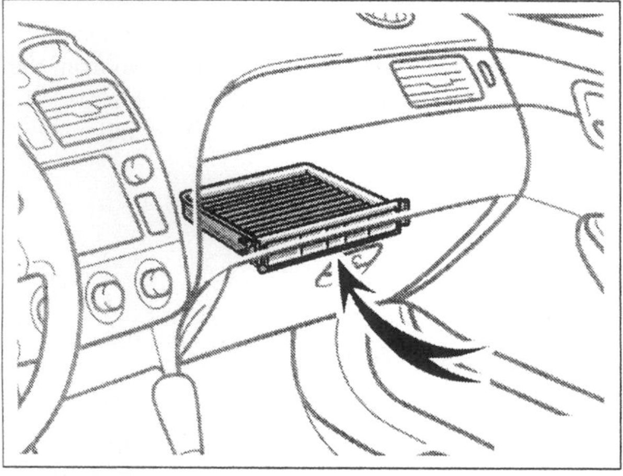

Figure 22–42 Heater/air-conditioning filters are located in the air intake area. (Courtesy Toyota Canada Inc.)

CABIN FILTERS

Many late vehicles use a filter on the air intake for the HVAC system. See Figure 22-42. The filter element is replaced about every two years.

SUMMARY

1. Engine coolant flows through heater hoses and through a heater core to provide heat to the inside of the vehicle.
2. The refrigeration cycle uses a compressor to circulate a refrigerant through a closed system.
3. Refrigerant vaporizes and expands in the evaporator. When the refrigerant expands, both its pressure and its temperature drop. The air from inside the vehicle is cooled as it passes through the evaporator.
4. The compressor forces the refrigerant through the closed system and raises the temperature of the refrigerant so that the refrigerant will condense back into a liquid in the condenser.
5. Air flow through the condenser removes heat from the hot refrigerant, which condenses back into a liquid.
6. The expansion valve (or orifice tube) restriction reduces the refrigerant pressure, which allows the refrigerant to expand. When the refrigerant expands, its pressure and temperature both drop, thereby cooling the evaporator.
7. Temperature (thermostatic) or pressure controls (EPR, POA, or VIR) prevent the freezing of the evaporator by keeping the temperature of the evaporator above freezing 0°C (32°F).
8. CFC-12 is commonly called Freon and is a chlorofluocarbon (CFC).
9. HFC-134a is less harmful to the environment because it does not contain any CFCs.
10. A desiccant is used either in the receiver-drier or accumulator to remove any moisture that may get into the system. Moisture and refrigerant combine to form harmful acid.
11. The air flow through the evaporator and heater core helps condition the air by removing moisture and directing the air flow where needed.

REVIEW QUESTIONS

1. Discuss how the air-conditioning system removes moisture from the air.
2. Describe the operation of the typical automotive air-conditioning system.
3. Explain why a desiccant is needed in automotive air-conditioning systems.
4. List three methods used to prevent the evaporator from becoming too cold and freezing.

RED SEAL CERTIFICATION-TYPE QUESTIONS

1. The colour of the R-134A refrigerant container is ________________.
   - **a.** White
   - **b.** Blue
   - **c.** Black
   - **d.** Red
2. When the defrost setting is selected, the air-conditioning compressor operates (most vehicles).
   - **a.** True
   - **b.** False

3. Where in the air-conditioning system is the refrigerant a low-pressure gas?
  a. Condenser outlet
  b. Evaporation outlet
  c. Evaporation inlet
  d. Condenser inlet

4. Where in the air-conditioning system is the refrigerant a high-pressure liquid?
  a. Condenser outlet
  b. Evaporation outlet
  c. Evaporation inlet
  d. Condenser inlet

5. The compressor operates continuously with which type of system controls?
  a. Orifice tube
  b. STV/EPR

6. PAG oil containers must be kept sealed because the oil ________________.
  a. Evaporates
  b. Absorbs moisture
  c. Loses lubricity
  d. Thickens in open air

7. A front-wheel drive vehicle has a broken condenser line. What other vehicle component may also be defective that could have caused the condenser line to break?
  a. Shock absorbers
  b. Engine mounts
  c. Cooling fan
  d. Air-conditioning compressor drive belt

8. The air-conditioning compressor is lubricated by ________.
  a. Oil that mixed with the moving refrigerant
  b. An oil pump in the compressor
  c. Splash from the crankshaft
  d. Oil mist from the compressor base

9. The material used to absorb moisture from inside the air-conditioning system is called
  a. Drier
  b. Desiccant
  c. Ester
  d. PAG

10. Which position on the climate control panel should the driver select to avoid having the air-conditioning compressor turn on?
  a. Heat
  b. Defrost
  c. A/C
  d. Panel

23

Heating and Air-Conditioning Diagnosis and Service

OBJECTIVES: After studying Chapter 23, you should be able to:

1. Prepare for the interprovincial Red Seal certification examination in Appendix VII (Heating and Air-Conditioning) on the topics covered in this chapter.
2. Diagnose lack of heat problems.
3. List the air-conditioning system performance check procedures.
4. Discuss methods used to locate the source of an air-conditioning system leak.
5. Describe how to recover, evacuate, and recharge an air-conditioning system.
6. Discuss what is necessary to retrofit a CFC-12 system to use HFC-134a refrigerant.

HEATER TROUBLE DIAGNOSIS

A lack of heat from the heater or having heat coming out of the incorrect vents can be a dangerous and uncomfortable problem. The first step in the diagnostic process is to perform a thorough visual inspection and perform simple tests. This includes the following:

- **Check the coolant level.** Low coolant level can cause a lack of heat from the heater. Low coolant level can also cause occasional loss of heat.

CAUTION: Do not remove the radiator cap when the engine is hot. Allow the vehicle to sit several hours before removing the pressure cap to check the radiator coolant level.

- **Carefully touch the upper radiator hose with the engine running.** On most vehicles, the temperature of the hose should be so hot that you cannot keep your hand on it: between 90° to 105° C (190° to 220°F).

NOTE: An infrared pyrometer can be used to measure the temperature of the upper radiator hose and the area around the thermostat housing.

  Results: If the upper radiator hose is not too hot to hold, then the engine thermostat is defective. If the radiator hose is too hot to handle, then the lack of heat from the heater is not due to a lack of hot water in the engine.
- **Carefully touch the heater hoses.** Both heater hoses should also be too hot to keep your hands on the hoses. This test confirms that engine coolant is able to flow from the engine to and through the heater core and return to the engine. See Figure 23–1.
  Results: (a) If neither heater hose is hot to the touch, it is likely there is an air pocket in the heater that is preventing the flow of coolant into the heater core. (b) If only one heater hose is hot to the touch, then the heater core is likely to be clogged or partially clogged. A clogged heater core would prevent enough hot coolant from circulating through the heater core to provide adequate heat to the passenger compartment.

Visual Inspection

The diagnosis of a heater problem or concern should start with a visual inspection. The following items should be checked or tested:

Figure 23–1 A heater control valve. This valve is normally open, allowing engine coolant to flow through the heater core. When the air-conditioning is switched to maximum cooling, the valve shuts off the flow of coolant to the heater.

TECH TIP 

Defrost All the Time? Check the Vacuum

A common problem involves airflow from the defroster ducts even though the selector lever is in other positions. The defrost setting is the default position in the event of a failure with the vacuum supply. The defrost position is used because it is the *safest* position. For safety, the windshield must remain free from frost. Heat is also supplied to the passenger compartments not only through defrost ducts but also through the heater vents at floor level.

If the airflow is mostly directed to the windshield, check under the hood for a broken, disconnected, or missing vacuum hose. Check the vacuum reserve container for cracks or rust (if metal) that could prevent the container from holding vacuum. Check all vacuum hose connections at the intake manifold and trace each carefully, inspecting for cracks, splits, or softened areas that may indicate a problem.

HINT: This problem of incorrect airflow inside the vehicle often occurs after another service procedure has been performed, such as spark plug replacement. The movement of the technician's body and arms can cause a hose to be pulled loose or a vacuum fitting to break without the service technician being aware that anything wrong has occurred.

- Verify that the upper radiator hose is hot and pressurized. The upper radiator hose should be too hot to let you keep your hand tightly around the hose due to the high temperature. If the radiator hose is not too hot to hold, the thermostat may be defective. See Chapter 7 for details on thermostat testing and installation.

TECH TIP 

The Hand Test

To check a radiator or condenser for possible clogged or restricted areas, simply touch the outside of the unit with your hand. Any cool spots indicate that the radiator or condenser is clogged in that cool area.

Frequently Asked Question ???

How Can You Easily Burp Air from the Cooling System?

The first step in being certain there is no air in the cooling system is to try to avoid getting air into the system in the first place during cooling system service. If the engine is equipped with **bleeder valves** near the high spots of the cooling system, these valves should be open when refilling the radiator. See Figure 23–2. Any trapped air will always travel to the highest portion of the cooling system and escape out of these bleeder openings. Close the valves as soon as coolant is observed coming out of the valve opening.

If the cooling system is not equipped with bleeder valves, fill the cooling system as full as possible and then start the engine. With the radiator cap removed, the coolant level will often rise as the trapped air is expanding, then drop down as the trapped air escapes out of the radiator neck opening. Air can still remain trapped. To help speed up the process, try installing the radiator cap just to the first notch. (In this position the radiator cap is closed, but will not seal enough to allow pressure to build in the cooling system.) To help force any trapped air from the cooling system, simply drive the vehicle normally for several kilometres. By driving the vehicle under load, the engine will warm up faster and the thermostat will open, allowing the coolant to flow from the engine and through the radiator. Any trapped air is then released into the radiator, where it can easily escape through the unsealed radiator cap. After filling the radiator, securely tighten the radiator cap and test drive the vehicle to verify proper operation.

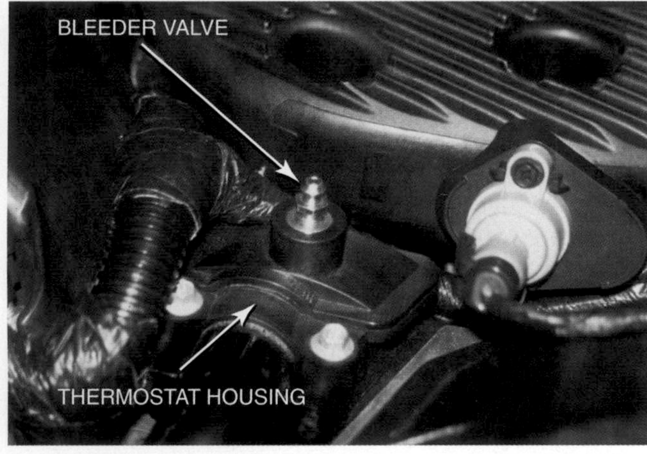

Figure 23–2 Many engines are equipped with a bleeder valve to permit the technician to bleed any trapped air from the cooling system. The valve is loosened as coolant is poured into the system. Because air is lighter than coolant, the air tends to float toward the highest part of the cooling system.

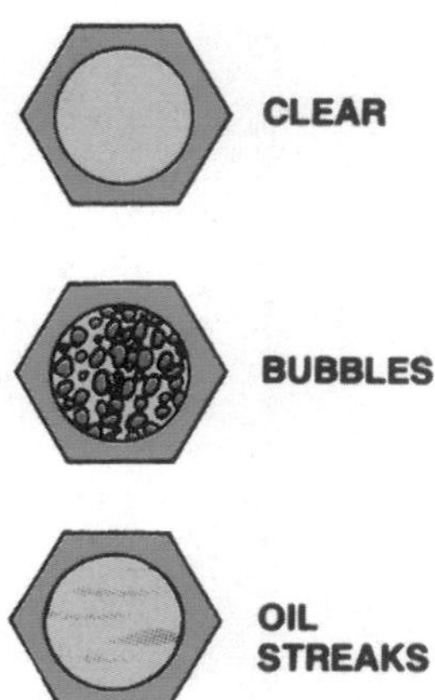

Figure 23–3 Many older CFC-12 systems are equipped with a sight glass either on or near the receiver-drier. A fully-charged (or completely empty) system is indicated by a clear sight glass. Bubbles or foam indicate that the system is not fully charged. An empty system may have oil streaks on the sight glass being moved by the vapour remaining in the system.

- Grasp the two heater hoses. Both heater hoses should be hot to the touch. If the return hose is cold or much cooler than the heater inlet hose, the heater core may be clogged or restricted.

NOTE: An air bubble could be lodged in the heater core. This is a common occurrence especially if the coolant (antifreeze) has been recently replaced. Failure to properly "burp" the air from the cooling system can cause a pocket of air to remain trapped in the heater core, preventing coolant from flowing through. See Frequently Asked Question "How Can You Easily Burp Air from the Cooling System?"

TECH TIP 

Hot/Cold/Hot/Cold Heater Diagnosis

A common customer complaint is a lack of heat from the heater but only while driving, even though there seems to be plenty of heat when the engine is at idle speed and the vehicle is stopped. This is a classic symptom of *low coolant level.* The lower than normal coolant level in the radiator prevents enough flow to supply the heater core. When the engine speed is reduced, the water pump turns slower and coolant can more easily flow through the heater core resulting in heat from the heater. As the engine speed increases, the water pump speed also increases. Because there is less than the proper amount of coolant in the system, the water pump will only be able to supply coolant through the engine (a path of lower resistance).

CHECKING A/C SYSTEM PERFORMANCE

The first step in the diagnosis of any cooling system problem is to verify the complaint (concern).

Step 1. Start the engine and turn the A/C system to maximum with the engine operating between 1500 and 2000 rpm with the doors open. Operate the system for 5 to 10 minutes.

Step 2. Verify by visual inspection that the A/C compressor clutch is engaged. Check the sight glass if the vehicle is so equipped, as shown in Figure 23–3.

HINT: If the A/C compressor clutch cannot be observed, have an assistant turn the air-conditioning on and then off and listen for the click of the A/C compressor clutch.

Step 3. Place an air-conditioning thermometer in the A/C vent near the centre of the vehicle. Wait several minutes to allow the system to reach maximum output and observe the thermometer.

- *If 2° to 7°C (35° to 45°F),* the system is functioning okay. Continue a thorough visual

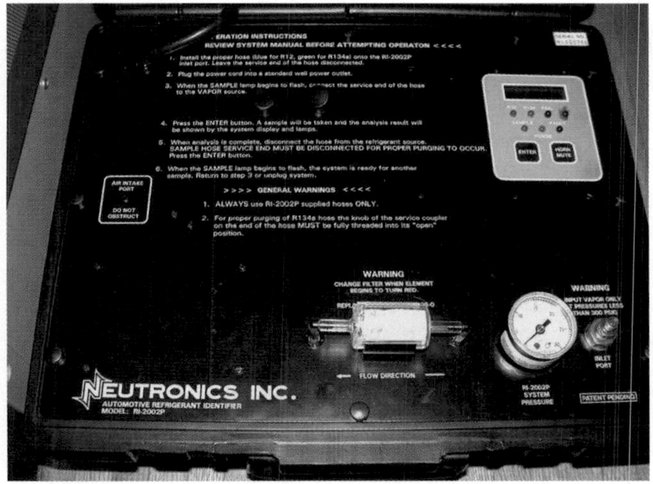

Figure 23–4 A typical refrigerant identification machine. The readout indicates what kind of refrigerant is in the system. If a blend or some other contaminated refrigerant is discovered, it should be recovered and stored in a separate container to keep it from contaminating fresh refrigerant.

inspection looking for any faults that may cause an intermittent problem.

- *If over 7°C (45°F),* continue with pressure gauge testing (Step 4). Be aware that high ambient (outside) temperatures or high humidity will reduce cooling efficiency and change system pressures.

Step 4. *Identify the refrigerant.* Before connecting the pressure gauges or performing any other service to an automotive air-conditioning system, verify the refrigerant that is presently in the system. Connect a refrigerant identification machine to the system. See Figure 23–4.

Step 5. *Connect both high-pressure and low-pressure gauges to the service ports.* The low-side pressure should be about 170 to 240 kPa (25 to 35 psi). The high-side pressure should be about 1000 to 1400 kPa (150 to 200 psi). Compare your readings to the normal and abnormal readings in the following chart. See Figure 23–5.

A/C Pressure Gauge Chart

Low Side	High Side	Condition (Possible Cause)
170 to 240 kPa (25–35 psi)	1000 to 1400 kPa (150–200 psi)	Normal
Low	Low	Low refrigerant charge level
Low	High	Defective compressor
High	High	System is overcharged Expansion valve stuck open
High	Low	Restriction in the low-side line

(a)

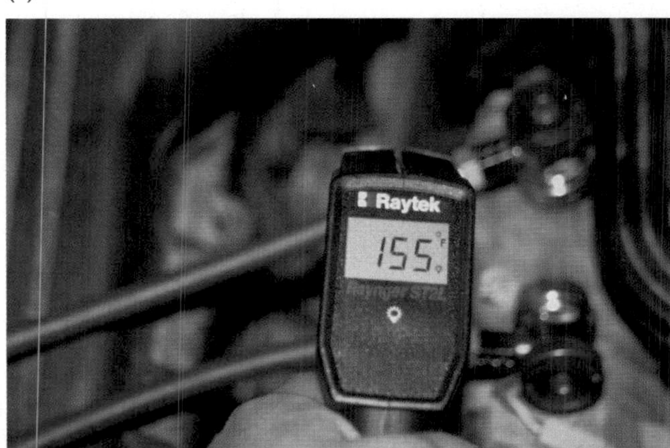

(b)

Figure 23–5 (a) Both high-pressure (red) and low-pressure (blue) hoses have been attached to the vehicle. (b) High side pressure can be compared to the temperature of the outlet from the compressor. Here a service technician is using an infrared pyrometer to measure the temperature.

IMPERIAL VERSUS METRIC READINGS

Pressure readings in psi (and refrigerant measured and sold in pounds and ounces) are still the most common units used by air-conditioning technicians and HVAC shops in Canada. Service information is often written only in imperial; older charging equipment and gauge sets are also imperial only. While the international metric unit for pressure is kilopascals (kPa), import specifications are usually listed in both kPa and psi.

TEMPERATURE AND PRESSURE MEASUREMENTS

Temperature and pressure are directly related in A/C systems. As the ambient temperature increases, the high-side pressure must also increase to have a heat transfer at the condenser. The temperature of the vapour must be higher than the ambient temperature to allow enough heat to be removed for condensation. Also, higher ambient temperatures, and high humidity, usually mean a higher heat load on the evaporator. This means a larger quantity of heat has to be removed at the condenser.

The high-side pressure is directly related to the amount of heat that needs to be removed, and the heat transfer at the condenser. Low-side pressure indicates the boiling point, or temperature of the evaporator. If the pressure is too high, the boiling point and temperature of the evaporator are too high. Low-side pressure that is too low indicates the evaporator is too cold and may ice, or that there is not enough boiling refrigerant in the evaporator to remove an adequate amount of heat. See Figure 23–6.

The heat transfer at the condenser is usually the cause of high-side pressure that is too high. The number one cause of poor heat transfer is lack of airflow across the condenser. The vehicle is dependent upon fans to move enough air when you are testing in a stall. It may be necessary to drive the vehicle at 50 km/h (30 mph) to get the ram air necessary to determine if lack of airflow is the reason for the poor heat transfer.

Another cause of excessive high-side pressure is contamination with a different refrigerant. Mixing R-12 and R-134a raises the condensing pressure of the mixture. At 65°C (150°F) the pressure of R-12 is 1620 kPa (235 psi) and R-134a is 1810 kPa (263 psi). See Figure 23–7. This is an important reason to use a refrigerant identifier.

As compressor efficiency is reduced, the high side decreases, and the low side increases. The function of the compressor is to pull down the low side and push up the high side. When the compressor is failing, it does not do either job well. Always look at both the high- and low-side pressures when diagnosing a problem. See Figures 23–8 through 23–10.

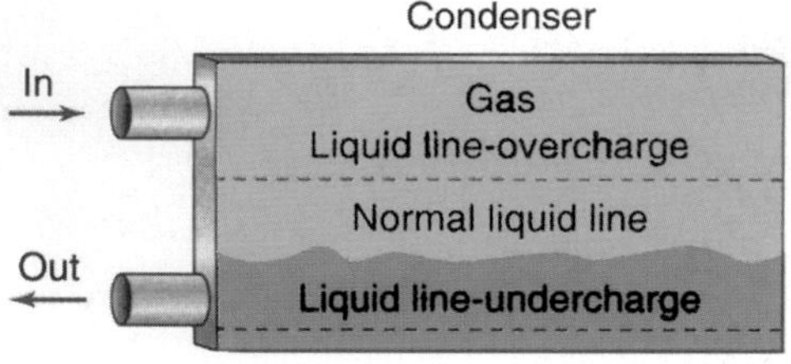

Figure 23–6 Hot refrigerant condenses in the condenser when it loses its heat to the outside air. Note how the level of the liquid line changes when undercharged or overcharged.

Frequently Asked Question ???

What's Wrong When the A/C Compressor Clutch Cycles On and Off Rapidly?

This is a common occurrence on a vehicle equipped with a cycling clutch orifice tube (CCOT) system that is low on refrigerant charge. With a normal charge, the low-side pressure should be 105 to 240 kPa (15 to 35 psi) and the clutch should be on for 45 to 90 seconds and be off for only about 15 to 30 seconds.

R-134a PRESSURE-TEMPERATURE CHART

Ambient Air Temperature		Humidity	Low-Side Pressure		High-Side Pressure	
°C	°F		kPa	psi	kPa	psi
21	70	Low	170 to 210	25 to 30	965 to 1310	140 to 190
		High	195 to 240	28 to 35	1140 to 1520	165 to 230
27	80	Low	180 to 225	26 to 33	1035 to 1380	150 to 200
		High	210 to 250	30 to 36	1310 to 1790	190 to 260
32	90	Low	215 to 255	31 to 37	1175 to 1520	170 to 220
		High	255 to 310	37 to 45	1450 to 2000	210 to 290
38	100	Low	240 to 300	35 to 44	1345 to 1690	195 to 245
		High	260 to 330	38 to 48	1590 to 2210	230 to 320
43	110	Low	275 to 350	40 to 50	1620 to 1965	235 to 285
		High	290 to 360	42 to 52	1795 to 2415	260 to 350

Figure 23–7 The average R-134a pressure–temperature readings during a performance test. The high-side pressure of R-12 systems will be lower at higher temperatures.

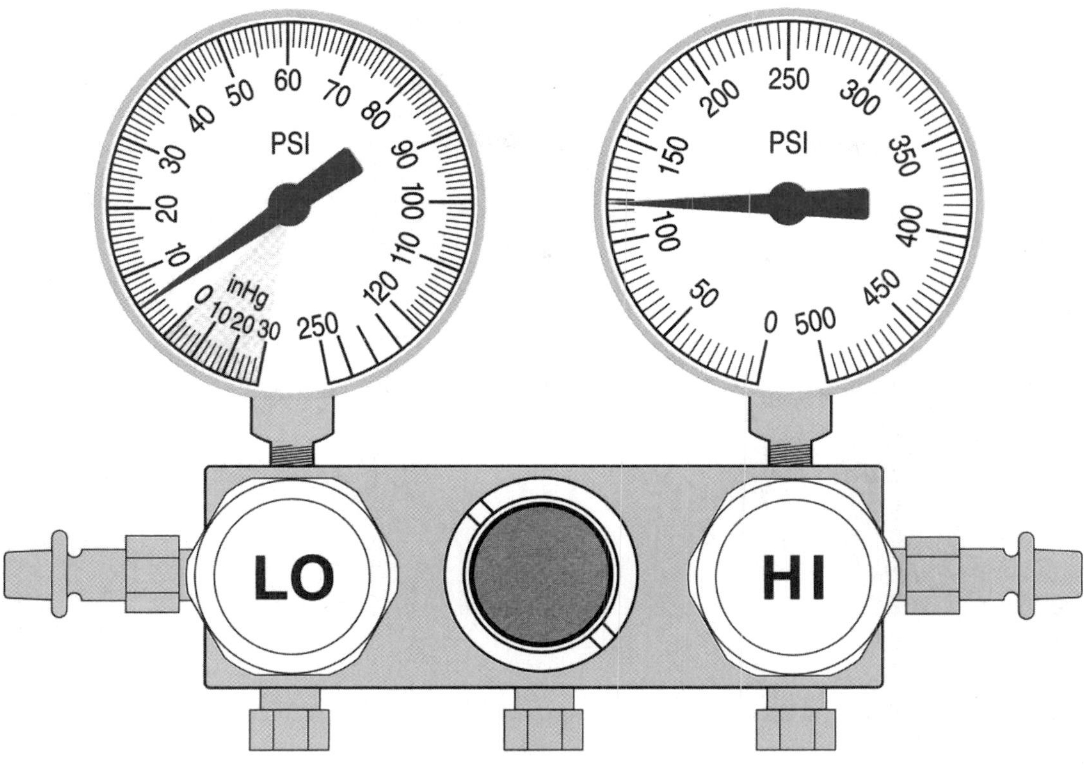

Figure 23–8 When both low- and high-side pressures are low, the system is undercharged with refrigerant.

Figure 23–9 Both low- and high-side pressures higher than normal indicate that the system is overcharged with refrigerant.

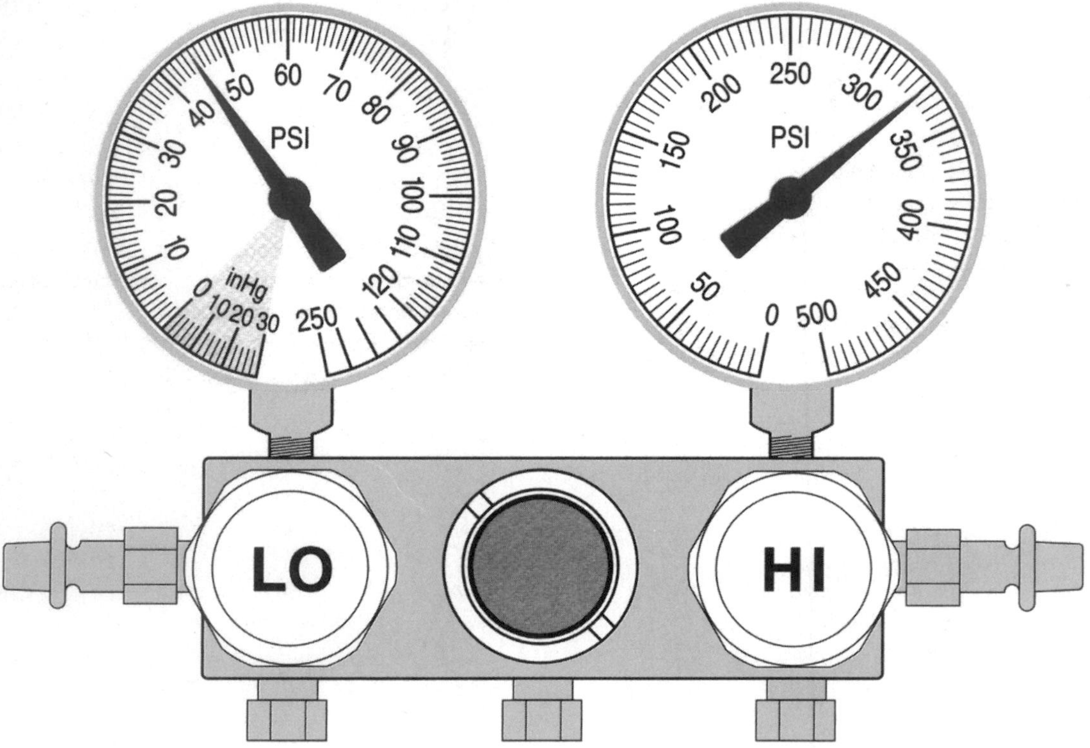

Figure 23–10 Lack of proper airflow across the condenser is usually the cause of this condition.

Figure 23–11 A clogged orifice tube.

Clogged Orifice Tube Test

A clogged orifice tube is a common air-conditioning system failure. When the orifice tube becomes clogged, it blocks the flow of refrigerant through the evaporator, which causes a reduced cooling of the passenger compartment. To check for a possible restriction in the system, follow these easy steps:

Step 1. Connect the A/C pressure gauge to both low- and high-side pressure fittings.

Step 2. Operate the A/C system for 5 to 10 minutes.

Step 3. Shut off the A/C system and watch the pressure gauges. If the pressures do not equalize quickly, then there is a restriction in the system. See Figures 23–11 and 23–12.

NOTE: To locate a restriction anywhere in the system, feel along the system lines. The restriction exists at the point of greatest temperature difference.

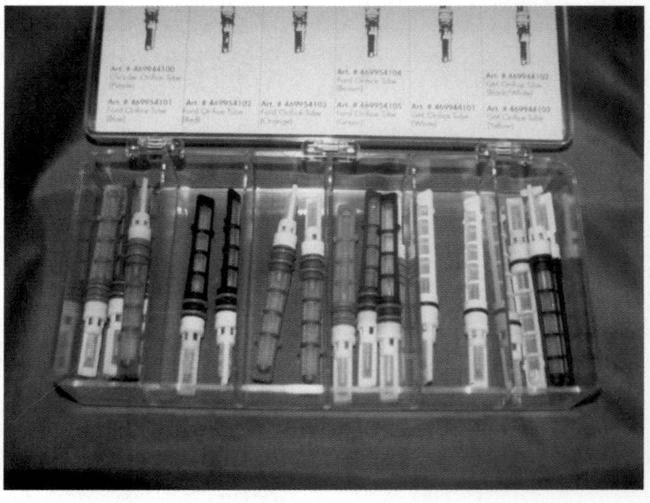

Figure 23–12 Assortment of orifice tubes. Note that each is colour coded and identified on the lid of the assortment. Even though some technicians have purposely installed an orifice tube with a larger opening in an attempt to increase cooling, it is always safe to use the exact orifice tube specified for the vehicle being serviced.

TECH TIP

The Fire Extinguisher Test

To test the expansion valve, start the engine and allow the A/C system to function with the control set to "recirculate." Using a CO_2 fire extinguisher, blast the expansion valve with CO_2. The valve should close and the low-side pressure should go into a vacuum. If the low-side pressure does not go into a vacuum, the expansion valve is faulty and should be replaced. See Figure 23–13.

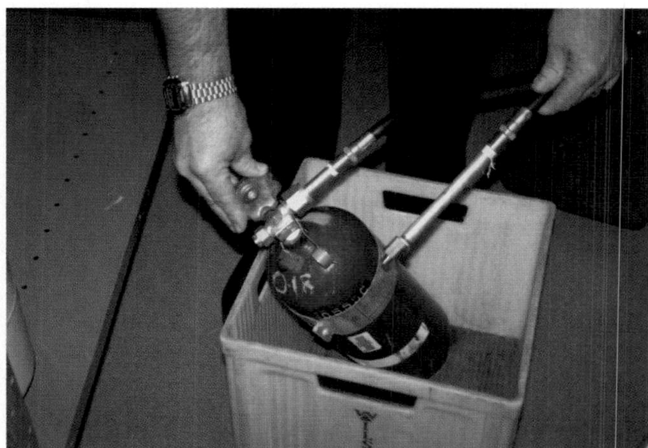

(a)

(b)

Figure 23–13 (a) A CO_2 fire extinguisher equipped with the fittings necessary to test the operation of an expansion valve. (b) The size of the opening at the end of the hose determines how much CO_2 is released to cool the expansion valve temperature sensor bulb.

TECH TIP

The Touch, Feel Test

A quick-and-easy test to check the state of charge of an orifice tube system is to use one hand and touch the evaporator side of the orifice tube. Touch your other hand to the inlet to the accumulator. The following conditions can be determined by noticing the temperature of these two locations. See Figure 23–14.

- **Normal operation**—both temperatures about the same
- **Undercharged condition**—accumulator temperature higher (warmer) than the orifice tube temperature

Just remember: High pressure means that the temperature of the component or line will also be high (hot). Low pressure means that the temperature of the component or line will also be low (cold).

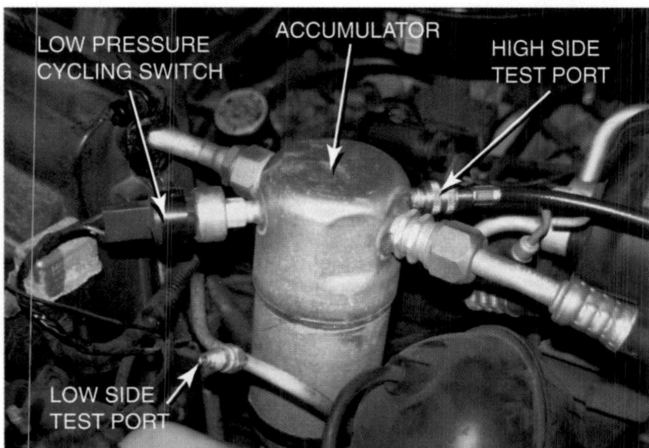

Figure 23–14 If the system is fully charged, the outlet temperature of the line leaving the evaporator should be about the same as the temperature of the line entering the evaporator after the orifice tube. The low pressure cycling switch usually has to be disconnected and a jumper wire used to connect the two electrical terminals allowing the compressor to run if the system is low on charge.

Leak Detection

If the A/C system is low on a charge of refrigerant, the sources of the leak should be found and corrected. Several different methods of leak detection are available, including:

- **Visual inspection.** Look for oily areas that are formed when refrigerant leaks and some refrigerant oil is lost. It is this oil that indicates a refrigerant leak.

- **Electronic leak detector.** Many of these units can detect both CFC-12 and HFC-134a. The detector will sound a tone if a leak is detected. See Figure 23–15. Be sure to check under the suspected component or fitting: refrigerant is heavier than air and moves down.
- **Dye in the refrigerant.** A dye is added to some refrigerant to help the technician visually spot a leak in the refrigerant system. A "black light" is often used with the dye. This method works well except for leaks in the evaporator, which are usually not visible.
- **Soap solution.** Mix a few drops of liquid soap or detergent into a small glass of water. Using a small brush or a small spray bottle, apply the soapy solution to all fittings and other areas such as the condenser and compressor, which often are sources of leaks. If the system is empty, pressurize the system with dry nitrogen.

Leak Repair Procedures

After a leak has been found, the refrigerant should be recovered and the faulty part repaired or replaced. Leaks at joints may need a replacement O-ring. Often, the leak is at a component such as the evaporator, condenser, or refrigerant line. Leaking components are usually replaced rather than repaired.

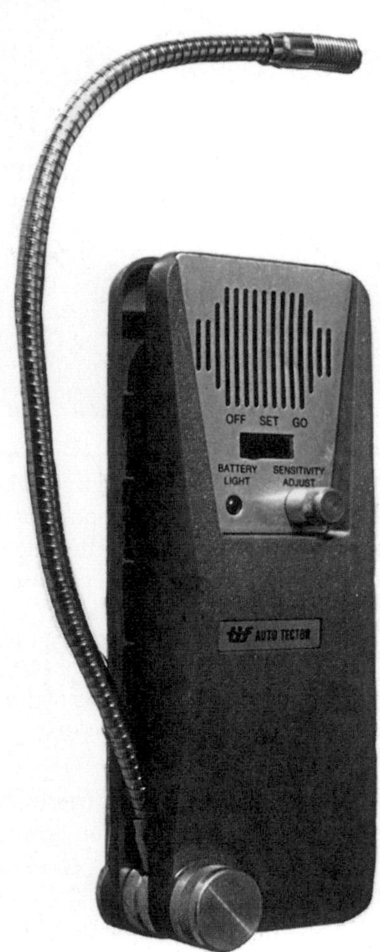

Figure 23–15 Typical electronic refrigerant leak detector. Many are capable of detecting either CFC-12 or HFC-134a.

DIAGNOSTIC STORY

The Clogged Evaporator Problem

The owner of an older vehicle complained that the blower motor must be defective because the air no longer flowed from the air-conditioning vents as it should. A check of the blower motor circuit revealed that the blower motor was working. Then the technician discovered the cause of the lack of airflow—the evaporator was covered with an oily dirt. The technician recovered the refrigerant and removed the evaporator. Apparently, the evaporator had a small refrigerant leak that allowed the refrigerant oil to coat the fins of the evaporator. Any dirt in the air stuck to the evaporator until the dirt almost completely blocked the airflow. Replacing the evaporator and recharging the system fixed the blower motor problem. See Figure 23–16.

Refrigerant Recovery Procedures

Refrigerant should be recovered and not allowed to be discharged into the atmosphere. A refrigerant recovery unit should be used to remove the refrigerant from the vehicle, and it should be stored in a container until it can be recycled. See Figures 23–17 and 23–18.

Most recovery units are capable of drawing a slight vacuum on the system of about 13 mm (5 in.) Hg to assure that all of the refrigerant is removed from

Figure 23–16 A partially clogged evaporator.

(a)

(b)

Figure 23–17 (a) A typical automotive air-conditioning service machine that is capable of handling both CFC-12 and HFC-134a systems. (b) HFC-134a systems use quick-disconnect fittings that are larger than those used for CFC-12 systems.

(a)

(b)

Figure 23–18 (a) Refrigerant oil must be retrieved and measured when the refrigerant is recovered from the system. (b) A rubber O-ring is used to indicate the level of refrigerant oil already in the container. The exact same amount of new refrigerant oil must be installed as was removed when the system is recharged.

the system. During the recovery process, any refrigerant oil removed is separated from the refrigerant and allowed to flow into a container where it can be measured. This is important because the correct total amount of lubricating refrigerant oil must be added to the system when recharged to protect the compressor.

It is important to ensure that as much CFC-12 refrigerant as possible is removed before retrofitting to HFC-134a. The two are not compatible. If more than 2% of CFC-12 is left in the system, the HFC-134a may turn black, thicken or gel.

Repairs or Replacement of Components

After all of the refrigerant has been removed from the system, repairs can be accomplished. For example, the evaporator can now be removed from the vehicle and replaced. If the system is opened for major repairs or left open to the atmosphere for a length of time (12 to 24 hours, depending on the humidity), most technicians will replace the receiver-drier, or accumulator, to help prevent damaging moisture from being trapped in the system. Driers (or accumulators) should be the last item installed. After all repairs are completed, the system should be evacuated.

NOTE: Be sure to follow all instructions regarding the amount of oil that needs to be added to the system if components have been replaced.

REFRIGERANT LINE CONNECTIONS

Refrigerant lines have connections at each end so they can be removed during system repair. Refrigerant line connections must meet three requirements:

- The connection must be vapour tight.
- The connection must be easy to disconnect and reconnect.
- The seals must withstand rapid and extreme temperature changes.

The O-ring seal, Figure 23–19, is part of a fitting that holds the ends of two refrigerant lines or hoses together inside a connector. The O-ring forms the seal between the lines or hoses and the connector. The O-rings usually are made of highly saturated nitriles (HSN) or neoprene rubber and remain flexible over a wide range of temperatures. O-rings should be lubricated with clean refrigerant oil (mineral or ester) before assembly to ensure a good seal. PAG oil is hygroscopic and will attract moisture to the connection. Replace the O-ring seals at all connections opened when you retrofit a system to R-134a.

A variation on the O-ring seal is Ford's spring-lock coupling. See Figure 23–20. It uses two O-rings mounted on the small end of the refrigeration line. The end of the joining refrigeration line is flared to slide over the two O-rings. A circular garter spring holds the connection together. You need a special tool to disconnect the coupling. See Figure 23–21.

SAFETY TIP 

Refrigerant Can Be Hazardous

Always wear safety glasses and protection gloves when servicing any automotive air-conditioning system. If any refrigerant escapes, it can cause skin to freeze or cause blindness if liquid refrigerant were to get into the eyes.

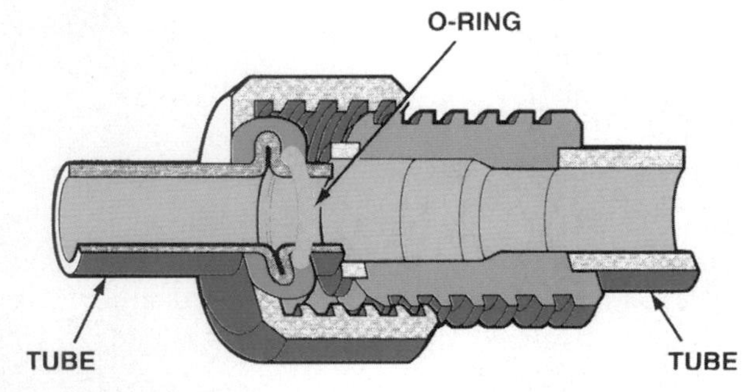

Figure 23–19 O-rings are usually made of neoprene rubber or highly saturated nitriles (HSN) to withstand high temperatures and flexing. O-rings should be changed on any component removed during a retrofit procedure.

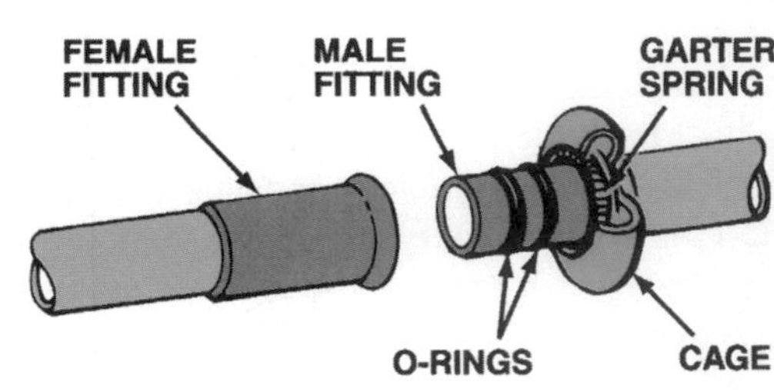

Figure 23–20 A Ford spring-lock coupling.

Figure 23–21 A special tool is needed to remove and install the Ford spring-lock coupling.

Service Valves

Service valves provide entry to the system when it is necessary to add or discharge refrigerant. The Schrader valve is used on R-12 systems. Quick-disconnect valves are used on R-134a systems. Each type of refrigerant has its own unique fitting. This prevents accidental use of the wrong service equipment and/or the introduction of the wrong refrigerant. Service valves are found almost anywhere on the system. They may be located on the receiver-drier, accumulator, compressor, muffler, or in the lines themselves.

All service valves have plastic coverings called service caps. See Figure 23–22. Along with preventing dirt from entering the system, service valve caps have O-rings which become the primary seal if a valve leaks. Always reattach the caps after any service has been performed, and replace them if you come across a system with missing service caps. Another built-in precaution is the refrigerant cut-off valve, which keeps the refrigerant in the service hose instead of allowing it to vent to the atmosphere when the hose is removed from the service valve after service.

Schrader Valves

For years, R-12 systems have used the Schrader valve. A Schrader valve is similar to a tire valve. Internal pressure holds Schrader valves closed. There is also a small spring to keep the valve seated if the internal pressure becomes insufficient. When the service connection is made, the depressor in the end of the service hose or service coupling presses on a small pin inside the valve, forcing the valve open. See Figure 23–23 (p. 537). The valve opens only when the service line connection is nearly complete, preventing contamination of the system or the unnecessary release of refrigerant.

The high-side service valve on R-12 systems is smaller and has different threads than the low-side service valve. This is the opposite of R-134A systems. This prevents incorrect connections that may result in damage to the system and to your service equipment. Some Ford systems use different sizes of quick-disconnect fittings, similar to an air-hose coupling. Adapters are available for use with standard manifold gauge sets.

Evacuation Procedures

Evacuation means that a vacuum will be applied to the system to vaporize any moisture that may be in the system. Although water boils at 100°C (212°F) at sea level, it can boil at much lower temperatures when the pressure is reduced. In other words, if a vacuum is applied to the air-conditioning system, the low pressure will cause any trapped moisture in the system to vaporize (boil). This water vapour is then removed from the system through the vacuum pump and released into the atmosphere. It is important to evacuate the system to at least 660 mm (26 in.) Hg of vacuum for at least 45 minutes to be assured that all of the moisture has been removed. For best results, the vacuum should be higher than 735 mm (29 in.) Hg. Just remember, the higher the vacuum and the longer that it is allowed to evacuate, the better.

Recharging a System

After the system has been evacuated, it can be recharged with refrigerant. Most vehicles have a placard or sticker that indicates the correct amount of refrigerant to use. See Figure 23–24. Follow the operating instructions for the equipment you are using.

> **NOTE:** Always use the specified amount of refrigerant. Reduced cooling can occur if the system is either undercharged or overcharged. Air-conditioning service is definitely not a situation where "more is better."

Some automakers recommend that the system be liquid charged, after evacuation, usually on the side with the drier or accumulator. The engine must not be running.

Others recommend that the low side be charged (VAPOUR ONLY) with the engine running. The high side should NEVER be opened with the engine running, as equipment damage or personal injury may result. About 115 g (4 oz) of refrigerant is usually put in the system (before starting the engine) to ensure the compressor is being lubricated.

Always follow the manufacturer's instructions for charging, since locations of fittings and procedures will vary.

RETROFITTING A CFC-12 SYSTEM TO AN HFC-134A SYSTEM

Older CFC-12 air-conditioning systems that require service are prohibited by federal law from being recharged with CFC-12. The system must be retrofitted (adapted) to use HFC-134a. Whenever making the change, several tasks have to be performed, including:

- Specific service fittings must be installed.
- Retrofit labels must be attached to the vehicle in a visible location.
- PAG or ester oil must be used instead of the mineral oil in a CFC-12 system.

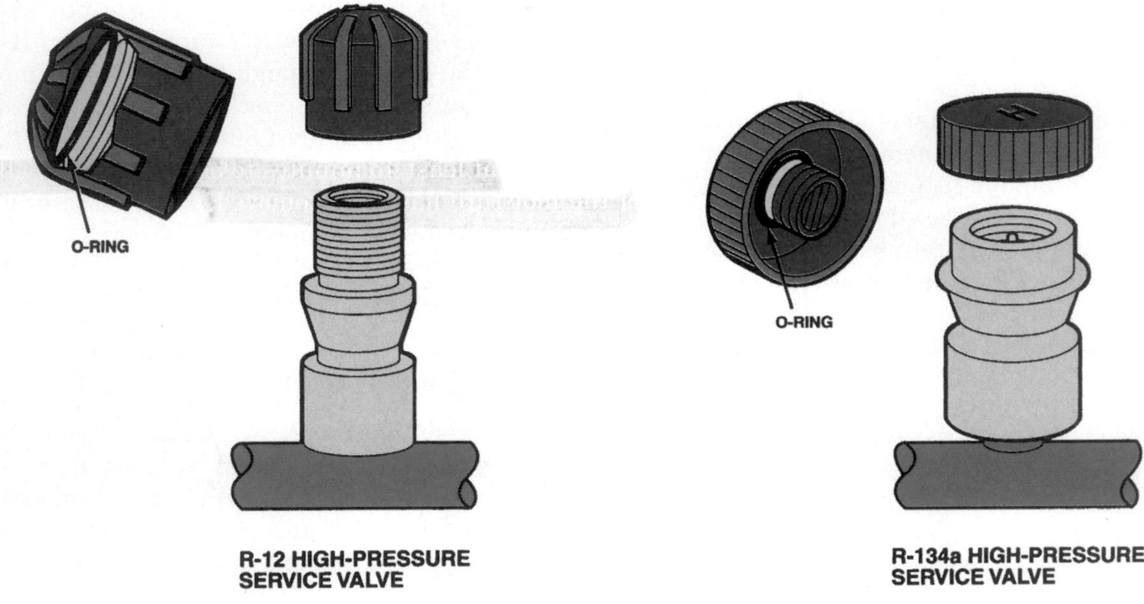

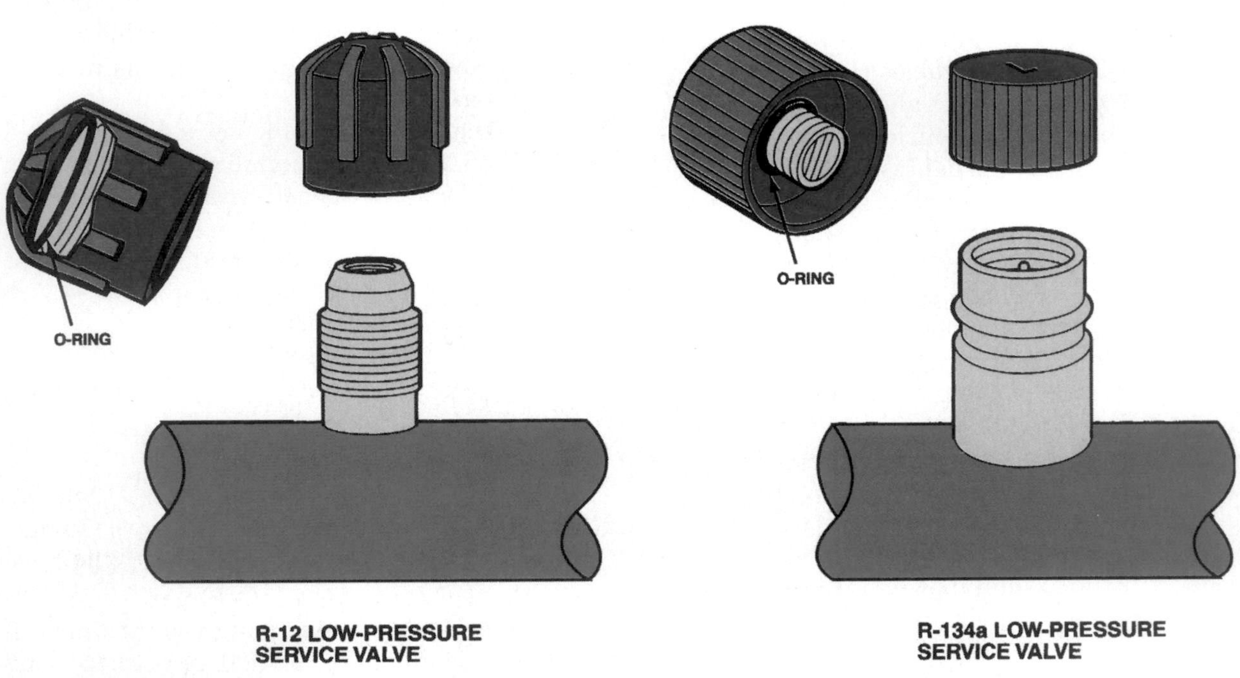

Figure 23–22 The service cap O-ring becomes the primary seal if the service valve leaks.

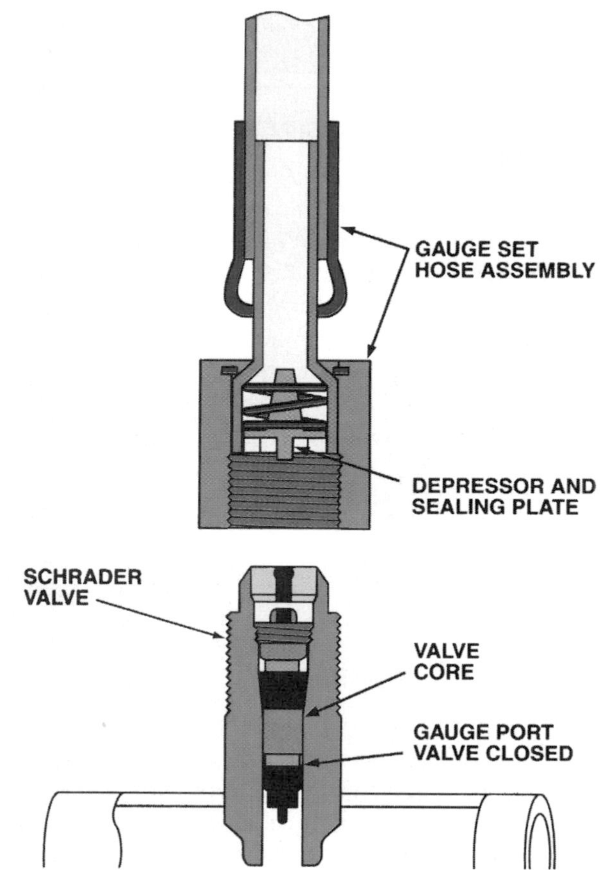

Figure 23–23 A depressor pin on the gauge set opens the Schrader valve when the connection is almost completely tightened. This prevents accidental refrigerant discharge.

Because It Fits, Does Not Mean It Is Correct!

Many air-conditioning systems use orifice tubes that look similar if not identical. They are usually colour coded for identification. Always use the recommended orifice tube for the vehicle you are servicing.

- A high-pressure shutoff switch must be installed that opens the compressor clutch circuit if the pressure exceeds 2830 kPa (410 psi.)
- Remove as much of the old CFC-12 mineral oil as possible. This oil will not damage the new PAG oil or refrigerant, but it does take up space. Some manufacturers recommend draining the compressor and replacing the drier/accumulator, as both contain a large amount of oil.

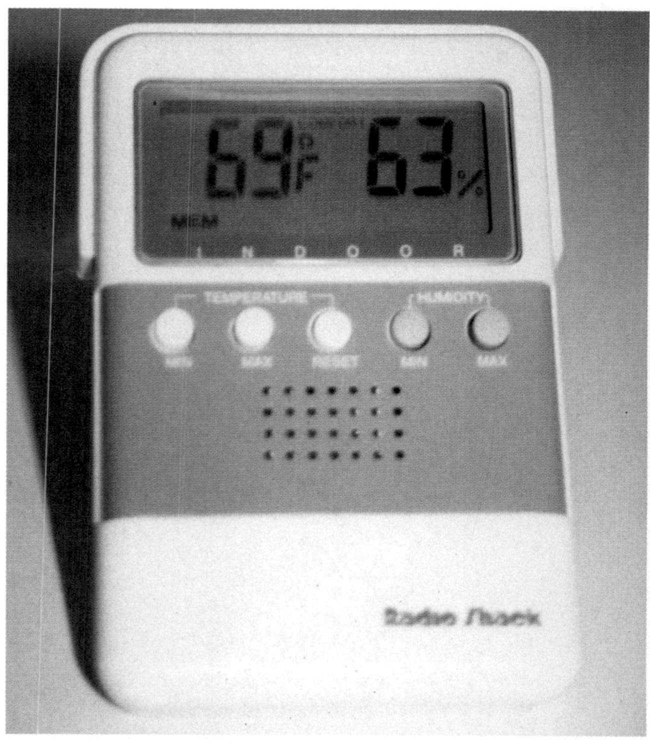

Figure 23–24 A temperature and humidity gauge is a useful tool for air-conditioning work. The higher the relative humidity, the more difficult it is for the air-conditioning system to lower the temperature inside the vehicle.

Other changes that may or may not be necessary include:

- Replacing hoses
- Replacing O-rings with HFC-134A compatible O-rings
- Replacing the receiver-drier or accumulator
- Replacing pressure switches and calibrating them for use with an HFC-134a system
- Replacing the condenser or compressor as required by some vehicle manufacturers

All of the necessary parts necessary to retrofit a particular vehicle are often included in a kit for easy use. See Figure 23–25. When the system is recharged, the amount of HFC-134a is usually 90% of the CFC-12 amount minus 115 grams (4 oz). In other words, if 850 grams (30 oz) is the normal charge of CFC-12, then 650 grams (23 oz) of HFC-134a should be used. 850 grams (30 oz) × 90% = 765 grams (27 oz) minus 115 grams (4 oz) = 650 grams (23 oz).

Later vehicles with factory HFC-134a systems generally have larger condensers and evaporators than previous CFC-12 systems because of a slight variation in efficiency between the two refrigerants. There may be a small reduction in cooling when changing from CFC-12 to HFC-134a.

(a)

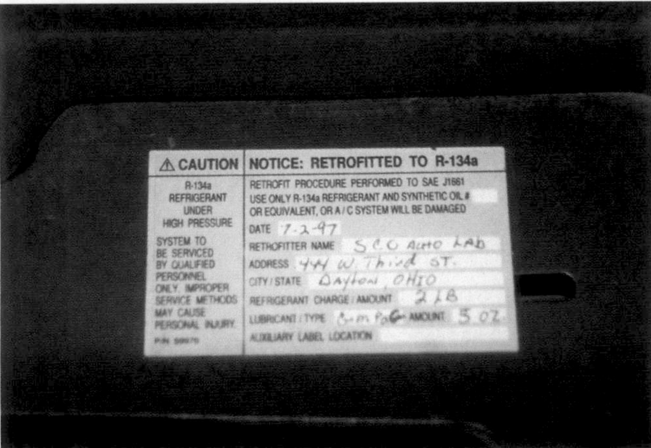

(b)

Figure 23–25 (a) When a system is retrofitted from CFC-12 to HFC-134a, the proper service fittings have to be used to help assure that cross-contamination does not occur. (b) An underhood sticker is also installed indicating that the system was retrofitted to HFC-134a and when it was done and by whom.

TECH TIP 

Leak-Testing the Evaporator

A quick-and-easy test to check whether the evaporator is leaking refrigerant is to remove the blower motor resistor pack. The blower motor resistor pack is located directly downstream and near the blower motor on many vehicles. Removing the blower motor resistor pack gives access to the area near the evaporator. Inserting the probe of a leak detector into this open area allows the detector to test the air close to the evaporator.

TECH TIP 

Might As Well Do It Now

Whenever an evaporator is being replaced, many service technicians also recommend that the heater core also be replaced. This is especially true if the vehicle had a neglected cooling system. Most heater cores are close to or even have to be removed to replace an evaporator. The only additional cost to the vehicle owner is the cost of the heater core itself. See Figure 23–26.

Figure 23–26 The entire dash had to be removed from this vehicle to replace a leaking evaporator.

PHOTO SEQUENCE 17 Air-Conditioning Service

P17–1 A typical HFC-134a reclaiming/recycling unit.

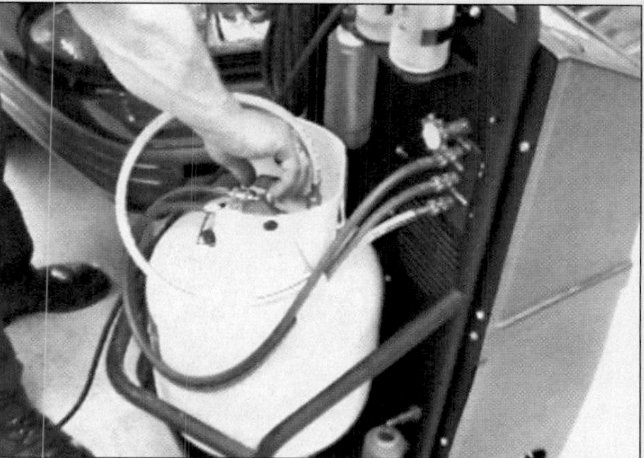

P17–2 Opening the valves to the 13.6 kg (30 lb.) storage container.

P17–3 Connecting the HFC-134a service lines from the machine to the high-side pressure and low-side pressure fittings on the vehicle. (Note—the refrigerant should have already been analyzed by a refrigerant analyzer to determine the identity of the type of refrigerant in the system and its purity.)

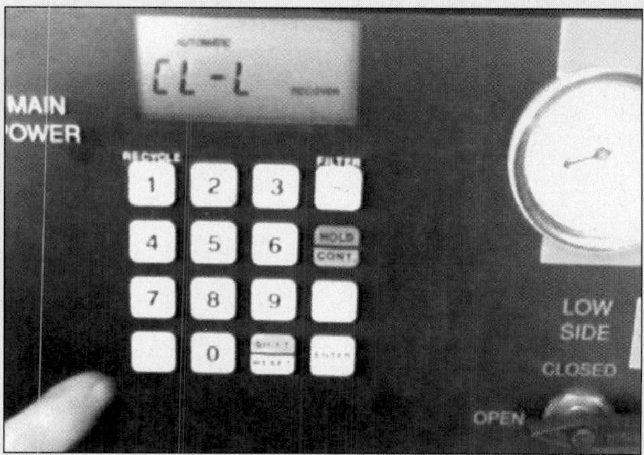

P17–4 Turning the reclaiming unit on. At this stage, the refrigerant is being drawn out of the vehicle and into the machine for recycling and eventual reuse.

P17–5 At the end of the reclaiming process, watch for a pressure gauge reading below zero, indicating that all of the refrigerant has been drawn from the system. Any remaining refrigerant would cause the pressure gauge to read a pressure above zero.

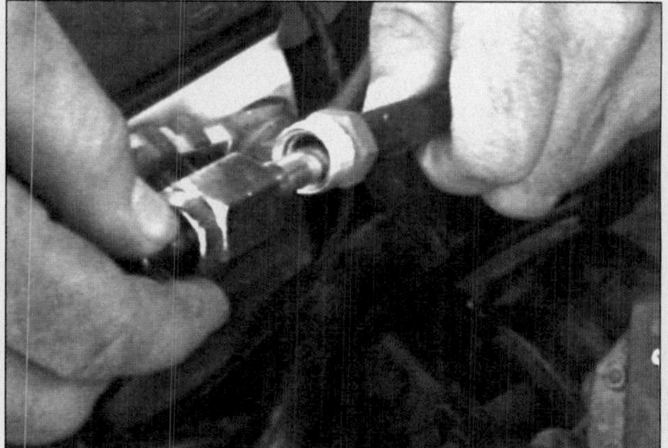

P17–6 Use two wrenches to disconnect the refrigerant lines to gain access to the orifice tube. A special tool is being used to remove the orifice tube from the refrigerant line.

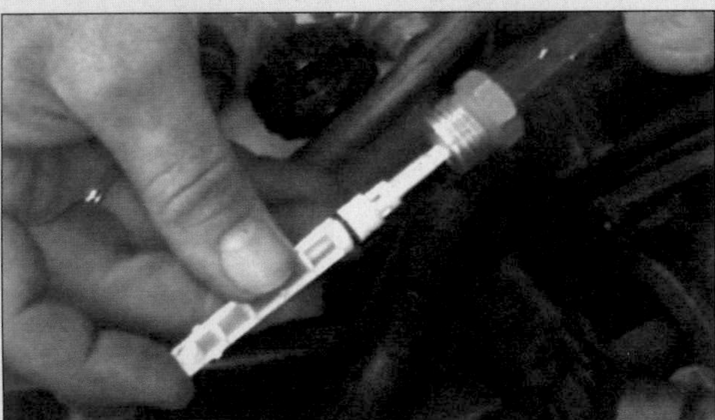

P17–7 Installing a new orifice tube. Reattach the refrigerant line fittings using two wrenches to help prevent damaging or twisting the metal refrigerant lines. The accumulator (or receiver/drier) is often replaced during major service.

P17–8 Setting the timer on the air-conditioning unit to evacuate (pull a vacuum on the system) for at least 30 minutes. Many vehicle manufacturers recommend evacuating for 45 minutes or longer—the longer, the better. The evacuation process removes any moisture from the system.

P17–9 During the evacuation, the gauge should read at least 735 mm (29 in.) Hg. When the unit is turned off, the vacuum reading should hold. If the vacuum reading decreases, there is a leak in the system that should be found and corrected before adding refrigerant to the system.

P17–10 During the reclaiming and evacuation process, the amount of refrigerant oil should be measured. This photo shows the oil being discharged into a plastic container. The same amount of fresh refrigerant oil should be added to the system as was lost during the reclaiming and evacuation process before adding refrigerant.

P17–11 Setting the unit to add 1000 grams (2.2 lb) of refrigerant to the system.

P17–12 After the recharging of the system, check the outlet temperature. The outlet temperature should be 2° to 7°C (35° to 45°F). The temperature on this vehicle is slightly higher, but the air temperature was over 32°C (90°F) with high humidity, which would tend to cause the system to discharge slightly higher than normal air temperature.

SUMMARY

1. The upper radiator hose and both heater hoses should be hot to the touch on a warm engine.
2. Failure to properly "burp" air from the cooling system after servicing can cause a lack of heat from the heater.
3. A sight glass is found on many older model vehicles equipped with CFC-12. If the sight glass is cloudy, then the system charge is low.
4. Normal air-vent temperature for a properly operating air-conditioning system is 2° to 7°C (35° to 45°F).
5. An expansion valve or orifice tube is used to allow the liquid refrigerant to expand into a gas inside the evaporator. Heat is absorbed by the refrigerant as it changes state from a liquid to a gas and the evaporator becomes cold. The outlet of the evaporator should be about the same temperature as the evaporator side of the orifice tube if the system is operating properly.
6. Refrigerant leaks can be detected by visual inspection, an electronic leak detector, dye, or a soap solution.
7. Before refrigerant is recovered from the system, it should be tested to check whether it is contaminated.
8. When the refrigerant is recovered, the refrigerant oil should be measured to be certain that the correct amount of lubricating refrigerant oil will be returned to the system.
9. All air-conditioning systems must be evacuated to a vacuum of at least 660 mm (26 in.) Hg for at least 45 minutes to be assured that all of the moisture trapped in the system has been boiled out and removed by the vacuum pump.
10. The system should be recharged with the exact amount of refrigerant specified by the vehicle manufacturer.
11. If a system is to be retrofitted from CFC-12 to HFC-134a, then change the system to 90% of the specified CFC-12 charge minus 115 grams (4 oz).

REVIEW QUESTIONS

1. Discuss how to diagnose the lack of heat from the heater.
2. Explain how the sight glass can be used to determine the state of charge.
3. List the various methods that can be used to detect refrigerant leaks.
4. Describe how to recover refrigerant from and evacuate an air-conditioning system.
5. List the components that may have to be replaced when retrofitting an air-conditioning system from CFC-12 to HFC-134a.

RED SEAL CERTIFICATION-TYPE QUESTIONS

1. Both heater hoses should be _________ to the touch when performing a heater diagnosis.
   - **a.** Hot
   - **b.** Warm
   - **c.** Cold
   - **d.** One hot and one cold
2. The engine is warm, running at 2000 rpm and the controls are set at "max air." The sight glass in the receiver-drier shows foam in the refrigerant. This would indicate the system is
   - **a.** Empty
   - **b.** Overcharged
   - **c.** Low on charge
   - **d.** Operating normally
3. Refrigerant should be checked for contaminates
   - **a.** After recovery, but before recycling
   - **b.** Before recovery
   - **c.** Before charging the system
   - **d.** After charging the system, but before releasing the vehicle to the customer
4. Fittings and O-rings should be lubricated with mineral refrigeration oil, as PAG oil
   - **a.** Thickens in open air
   - **b.** Attracts moisture
   - **c.** Will cause "galling" at the fitting
   - **d.** Attracts dirt
5. When recovering refrigerant, the oil recovered should be measured so that the proper amount of oil can be installed with the refrigerant.
   - **a.** True
   - **b.** False
6. To be sure that all of the moisture in an air-conditioning system has been boiled and removed, a vacuum of at least 660 mm (26 in.) Hg should be drawn on the system for at least _____ minutes.
   - **a.** 45
   - **b.** 60
   - **c.** 90
   - **d.** 120
7. With a properly operating air-conditioning system, the inlet hose to the compressor should be cold and the outlet hose should be _______________.
   - **a.** Cool
   - **b.** Warm
   - **c.** Hot
   - **d.** Very cold
8. Many late-model electronic refrigerant leak detectors are capable of detecting
   - **a.** HFC-134a only
   - **b.** Ethylene glycol leaks as well
   - **c.** Either CFC-12 or HFC-134a
   - **d.** CFC-12 only
9. A clogged orifice tube can cause a lack of cooling.
   - **a.** True
   - **b.** False
10. The two items that have to be replaced when retrofitting a CFC-12 system to an HFC-134a system include
    - **a.** Fittings and a sticker
    - **b.** Fittings and O-rings
    - **c.** O-rings and the condenser
    - **d.** Fittings and all rubber parts

SECTION **V**

Engine Performance

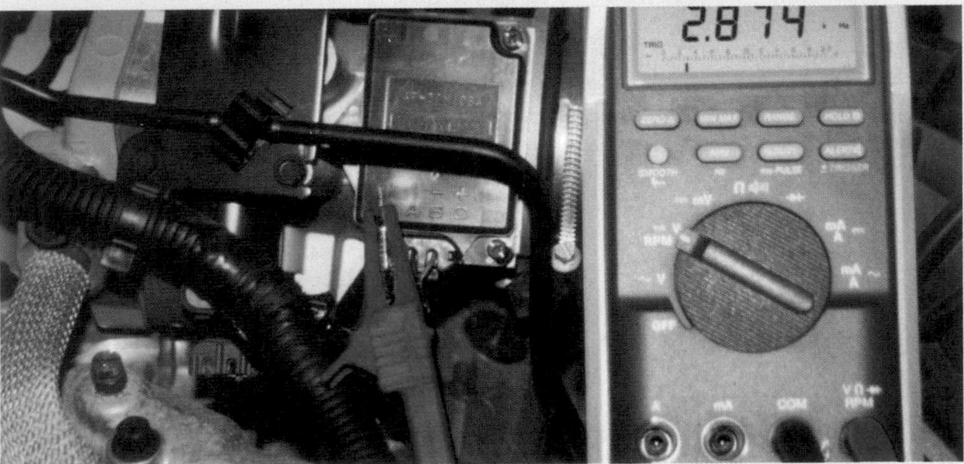

24 Ignition System Operation, Diagnosis, and Service

25 Computers and Sensors—Operation, Diagnosis, and Service

26 Computers and On-Board Diagnostics

27 Engine Fuels and Combustion

28 Computerized Carburetor Operation, Diagnosis, and Service

29 Gasoline and Diesel Fuel-Injection Operation, Diagnosis, and Service

30 Emission Control Device Operation, Diagnosis, and Service

31 Engine Performance Diagnosis and Testing

Chapter 24 includes all topics in the ignition system. Chapter 25 covers the theory of computer operation and the purpose, function, operation, and problem diagnosis of all computer sensors. Chapter 26 includes the principles and repair procedures for computerized engine management and the function of on-board diagnosis. Chapter 27 covers gasoline fundamentals and the combustion process. Chapter 28 includes computer-controlled carburetor operation, with an emphasis on diagnosis. Chapter 29 includes how the fuel injection systems work and how to test and troubleshoot fuel injection faults. Chapter 30 describes how each of the emission control devices works, plus how each affects engine operation if there is a fault. Chapter 31 contains information on how to systematically diagnose an engine performance problem.

24

Ignition System Operation, Diagnosis, and Service

OBJECTIVES: After studying Chapter 24, you should be able to:

1. Prepare for the interprovincial Red Seal certification examination in Appendix VIII (Engine Performance) on the topics covered in this chapter.
2. Describe how to check for spark using a spark tester.
3. Discuss how to test a pickup coil, Hall-effect switch, crankshaft position sensor, or optical distributor for proper operation.
4. Discuss the operation of no-distributor ignition systems.
5. Explain the difference between a waste-spark versus a coil-on-plug ignition.
6. Explain how to diagnose a no-start condition.
7. Describe how to test the ignition system using an analog and a digital oscilloscope.

The ignition system includes those parts and wiring required to generate and distribute a high voltage to the spark plugs. A fault anywhere in the primary (low-voltage) ignition circuit can cause a no-start condition. A fault anywhere in the secondary (high-voltage) ignition circuit can cause engine missing, hesitation, stalling, or excessive exhaust emissions.

IGNITION SYSTEM OPERATION

The ignition system includes components and wiring necessary to create and distribute a high voltage (up to 40 000 volts or more). All current ignition systems apply low voltage (close to battery voltage) to the positive side of the ignition coil and pulse the negative side to ground. When the coil negative lead is grounded, the primary (low-voltage) circuit of the coil is complete and a magnetic field is created by the coil windings. When the circuit is opened, the magnetic field collapses and induces a high-voltage spark from the secondary winding of the ignition coil. Early ignition systems used a mechanically opened set of contact points to make and break the electrical connection to ground. Electronic ignition uses a sensor such as a pickup coil or trigger to signal an electronic module that makes and breaks the primary connection of the ignition coil.

IGNITION COILS

The heart of any ignition system is the **ignition coil.** The coil creates a high-voltage spark by electromagnetic induction. Many ignition coils contain two separate but electrically connected windings of copper wire. Other coils are true transformers in which the primary and secondary windings are not electrically connected. See Figure 24–1.

The centre of an ignition coil contains a core of laminated soft iron (thin strips of soft iron). This core increases the magnetic strength of the coil. Surrounding the laminated core are approximately 20 000 turns of fine wire called the **secondary** coil windings. Surrounding the secondary windings are approximately 150 turns of heavy wire called the **primary** coil windings. In many coils, these windings are surrounded with a thin metal shield and insulating paper and placed into a metal container. The metal container and shield help retain the magnetic field within the coil windings. The primary and

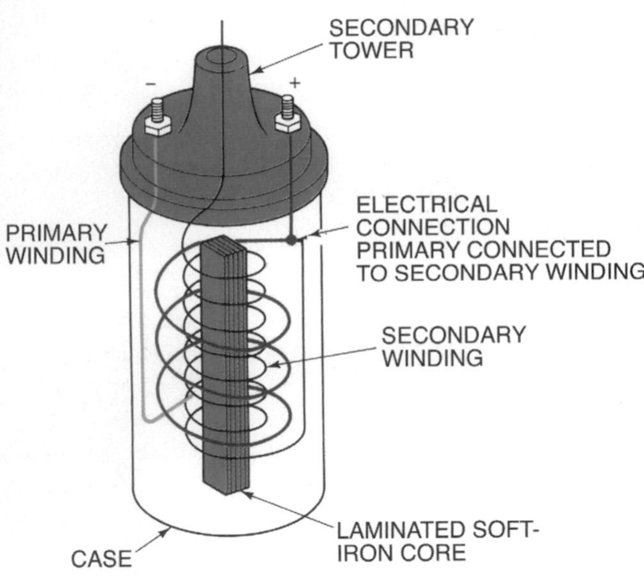

Figure 24–1 Internal construction of an oil-cooled ignition coil. Notice that the primary winding is electrically connected to the secondary winding. The polarity (positive or negative) of a coil is determined by the direction in which the coil is wound.

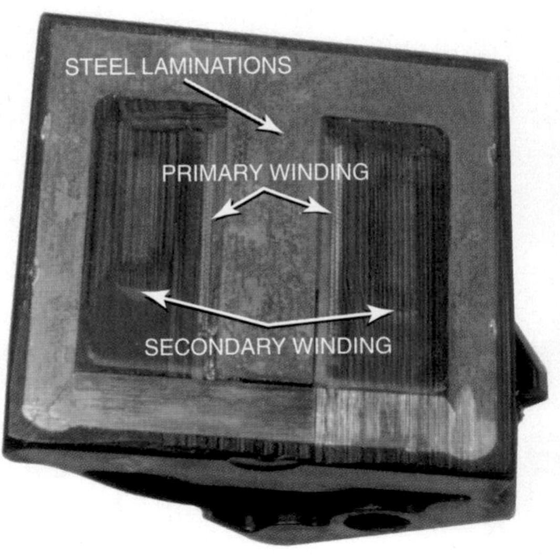

Figure 24–2 Cutaway of a General Motors Type II distributorless ignition coil. Note that the primary windings are outside of the secondary windings.

secondary windings also produce heat because of the electrical resistance in the turns of wire. Many coils contain oil to help cool the ignition coil. Other coil designs, such as those used on GM's **high energy ignition (HEI)** systems, use an air-cooled, epoxy-sealed **E coil.** It is called that because the laminated, soft iron core is E-shaped, with the coil wire turns wrapped around the centre "finger" of the E and the primary winding wrapped inside the secondary winding. See Figure 24–2.

The primary windings of the coil extend through the case of the coil and are labelled as positive and negative. The positive terminal of the coil attaches to the ignition switch, which supplies current from the positive battery terminal. The negative terminal is attached to a set of distributor contact points or an **electronic ignition module**, which opens and closes the primary ignition circuit by opening or closing the ground return path of the circuit. With the ignition switch on, current should be available at *both* the positive terminal and the negative terminal of the coil if the primary windings of the coil have continuity. The labelling of positive (+) and negative (−) of the coil indicates that the positive terminal is *more* positive (closer to the positive terminal of the battery) than the negative terminal of the coil. This condition is called the coil **polarity.** The polarity of the coil must be correct to ensure that electrons will flow from the hot centre electrode of the spark plug. *The polarity of an ignition coil is determined by the direction in which the coil is wound.* The correct polarity is then indicated on the primary terminals of the coil. If the coil primary leads are reversed, the voltage required to fire the spark plugs is increased by 40%. The coil output voltage is directly proportional to the ratio of primary to secondary turns of wire used in the coil and the amount of current flowing in the primary circuit. High current flow in the primary creates a very strong magnetic field, which in turn produces greater secondary voltage and a strong spark. Since less current flowing in the primary generates a weaker magnetic field, the spark at the plug will be weaker.

Self-Induction

When current starts to flow into a coil, an opposing current is created in the windings of the coil. This opposing current generation is caused by **self-induction** and is called **inductive reactance.** Inductive reactance is similar to resistance because it opposes any increase in current flow in a coil. Therefore, when an ignition coil is first energized, there is a slight delay of approximately 0.01 second before the ignition coil reaches its maximum magnetic field strength. The point at which a coil's maximum magnetic field strength is reached is called **saturation.**

Mutual Induction

In an ignition coil there are two windings, a primary and a secondary winding. When a *change* occurs in the magnetic field of one coil winding, that change also occurs in the other coil winding. Therefore, if the primary current is stopped from flowing (circuit is opened), the collapsing magnetic field cuts across the turns of the secondary winding and creates a high voltage in the secondary winding. This generation of an electric current in both coil windings is called **mutual induction.** The collapsing magnetic field also creates a voltage of up to 250 volts in the primary winding.

How Ignition Coils Create 40 000 Volts

All ignition systems use electromagnetic induction to produce a high-voltage spark from the ignition coil. Electromagnetic induction means that a current can be created in a conductor (coil winding) by a moving magnetic field. The magnetic field in an ignition coil is produced by current flowing through the primary windings of the coil. The current for the primary winding is supplied through the ignition switch to the positive terminal of the ignition coil. The negative terminal is connected to the ground return through a set of ignition points or a transistor mounted inside an electronic ignition module.

All ignition systems using a distributor are essentially the same, except in how the primary circuit is opened and closed. Older vehicles used contact points, while later systems replaced the points with a transistor.

Let's begin with an old-style distributor contact-point ignition. See Figure 24–3. Closing the ignition switch allows current (approximately 2 to 3 amperes) to flow from the switch, through the ignition resistor and coil primary windings to the distributor; the current then flows to ground through closed contact points. A full-strength magnetic field is formed around both the primary and secondary windings in the coil.

When the contact points open, the magnetic field collapses, inducing voltage in both the primary and secondary windings. Because the 20 000 turns of the secondary are much greater than the 150 turns of the primary, the majority of free electrons from the magnetic field are induced into the secondary. High voltage (20 000 to 25 000 volts), low current (20 to 50 milliamperes) now flows through the coil wire, distributor cap, rotor, and spark plug wires to the spark plugs. For each spark that occurs, the coil must be charged with a magnetic field and then discharged.

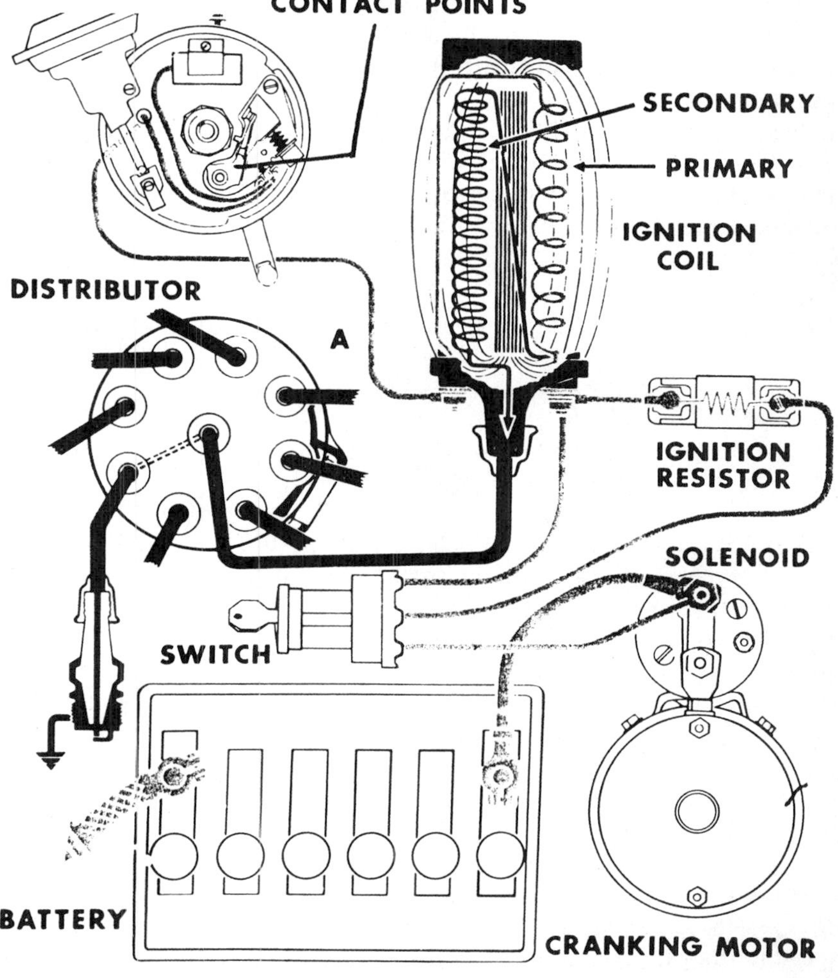

Figure 24–3 Typical contact-point ignition system (also called breaker-point ignition). Note the ignition (ballast) resistor and the bypass circuit at the ignition switch. (Courtesy Ignition Manufacturer's Institute, *Automotive Emission Controls and Tune-Up Procedures,* Prentice Hall, 1980.)

How many volts are in the secondary circuit to the plugs? It depends; if the spark plug electrodes are close together, less voltage would be needed to jump this small gap compared to the higher voltage required to jump a very wide plug gap. As an example, if the spark plug wire was removed and held away from the plug, voltage would continue building in the coil secondary because the voltage would not be high enough to jump the infinite resistance of this open circuit. Voltage would climb until it reached the maximum the coil was capable of producing. If the spark plug wire is held to ground instead, the voltage required would be very low because the resistance of the plug and plug gap are now out of the circuit.

The coil produces whatever voltage it has to, in order to fire the plug. Variations in engine compression and air-fuel ratios all have a bearing on required voltage. The energy from the collapsing magnetic field can be used in one of two ways; if high voltage is needed to fire the plug, the voltage is depleted quickly and very little is left to continue the spark (short duration). If lower voltage is needed, the spark continues to jump the gap for a longer period of time (long duration). The ignition components that regulate the current in the coil primary winding by turning it on and off are known collectively as the **primary ignition circuit.** The components necessary to create and distribute the high voltage produced in the secondary windings of the coil are called the **secondary ignition circuit.**

Spark Advance

The combustion process must start early enough so that maximum cylinder pressure is reached just after top dead centre; combustion should be complete by approximately 23° after TDC.

Igniting the air-fuel mixture too early (advanced timing) creates very high combustion temperatures and pressures as the piston continues to compress the burning charge. This may lead to engine detonation and damage.

Igniting the mixture too late (retarded timing) reduces power because the piston is moving down the cylinder during the combustion process. This increasing volume reduces maximum cylinder pressures that push down on the piston. Retarded timing also raises exhaust temperatures as combustion is still occurring later in the power stroke; this may lead to burned exhaust valves and cracked exhaust manifolds. Data from emissions testing shows exhaust temperatures rising as much as 32°C (90°F) at 1000 rpm with only a 10° timing retard. Obviously correct timing is critical.

At low engine RPM, the crankshaft travels 41° during the time it takes to complete the combustion process. In order to complete combustion by 23° ATDC, ignition must begin at 18° BTDC, a total of 41°. See Figure 24–4.

At 3600 rpm, the crankshaft is rotating much faster, but the burning rate of the fuel mixture stays approximately the same. The crankshaft travels 63° during combustion, which still must be completed by 23° ATDC. Ignition now begins at 40° BTDC, a total of 63°.

Ignition distributors usually contain a pair of advance weights that are thrown out by centrifugal force. As the weights move out against return springs, the timing advances. Changing return spring tension and length will alter the advance rate.

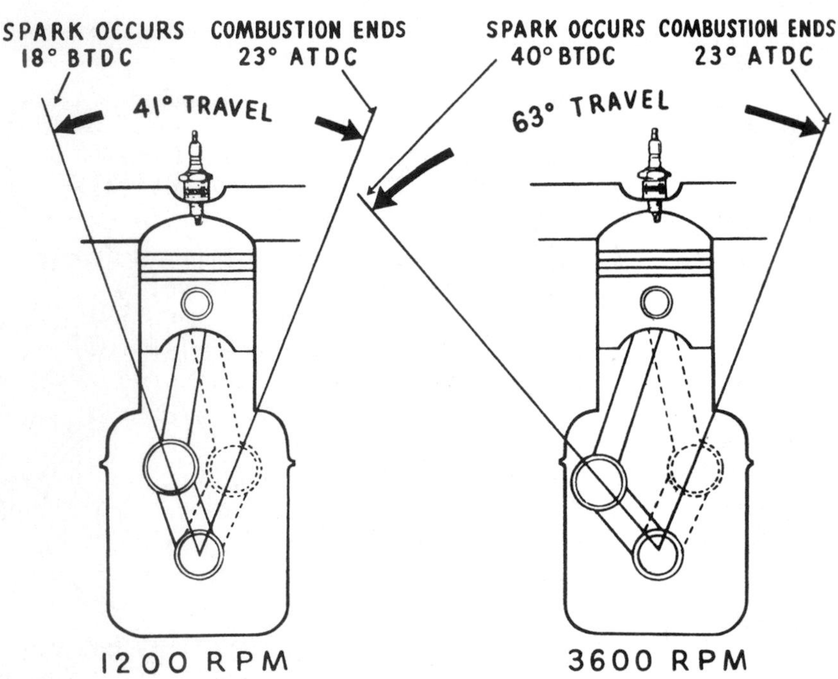

Figure 24–4 The ignition spark must be advanced as engine speed increases. (Courtesy Ignition Manufacturer's Institute, *Automotive Emission Controls and Tune-Up Procedures,* Prentice Hall, 1980.)

Air-fuel mixtures also affect ignition timing. Lean mixtures (less fuel) burn slower and timing must be advanced, rich mixtures (more fuel) burn faster, less advance is needed.

Vacuum advance mechanisms control both mixture and load related timing changes. High engine vacuum (light load, lean mixture) pulls on a distributor-mounted vacuum diaphragm, which advances the timing. Low vacuum (heavy load, rich mixture) allows the diaphragm to retract and retard the timing.

Computer-controlled ignition systems, both with and without distributors, do not use advance mechanisms. The computer regulates timing in response to signals from engine sensors.

Base timing must be set correctly, regardless of the type of ignition. As an example, if the base timing specifications call for the timing to be set at TDC, and the technician sets it at 10° BTDC, the timing will be advanced 10° too much at any RPM and load.

Dwell Angle

The strength of an ignition coil is determined by the amount of current (amperes) flowing through the coil and the number of windings (turns ratio) inside the coil. Obviously a large amount of current will produce a strong spark; the downside, of course, is high current flow creates excessive heat in the coil.

Current flow through the coil (ignition primary circuit) is a function of three factors:

- The applied voltage
- Resistance of the circuit, including the coil
- Duty cycle ("on" time)

As an example, if a pressure of 12 volts is pushing current through a circuit resistance of 1.5 ohms, the current flow would be 8 amperes. If we have a duty cycle of 50% (points closed for 50% ... 8 amperes flow, points open for 50% ... 0 amperes flow), the ***average*** current flow is now 4 amperes. We call the "on" duty cycle *dwell;* the greater the dwell, the higher the average current flow. Typical ignition dwell (duty cycle) is 60% ... current flows for 60%, no current flows for 40%.

Ignition (Ballast) Resistor

Ignition demands vary with operating conditions. Although a strong spark is needed while cranking, unfortunately the reverse occurs—the starter draw reduces battery voltage, which creates a very weak spark at this time. Full throttle opening at lower speeds allows maximum cylinder filling (high volumetric efficiency) and a stronger spark is also required to fire through the extra compression. At high speeds everything is happening so quickly that the coil does not have sufficient time to build up a strong magnetic field (fully saturated) and a weak spark develops.

An external ignition resistor made of nickel-chrome wire changes resistance with temperature. At low speeds, current flowing for a longer time causes the wire to heat, increasing the resistance and reducing the current flow—the coil now runs cooler. At higher speeds, the duration of current flow decreases, as the on/off time is much quicker. The resistor cools, lowering the resistance and increasing the current flow; this extra current then compensates for the reduced coil saturation time and a stronger spark is achieved. These resistors are also known as current compensating resistors. See Figure 24–3.

During cranking, an extra wire to the coil bypasses the ignition resistor. The reduced resistance (no ignition resistor) compensates for the starter draw by allowing increased current flow and a strong spark is generated. In many instances, the strongest spark is created during cranking because of this bypass circuit.

Primary Circuit Operation: Electronic Ignition

To get a spark from an ignition coil, the primary coil circuit must be turned on and off. This primary circuit current is controlled by a **transistor** (electronic switch) inside the ignition module (see Figure 24–5) that in turn is controlled by one of several devices, including:

- **Pickup coil (pulse generator)**—A simple and very common electronic ignition switching device is the magnetic pulse generator system. Most manufacturers use the rotation of the distributor shaft to time the voltage pulses. The **magnetic pulse generator** is installed in the distributor housing. The pulse generator consists of a wire coil wrapped around the "finger" at one end of the pole piece; a permanent magnet is attached to the opposite end. See Figure 24–6. A rotating iron reluctor is positioned inside the magnetic field created by the permanent magnet. The magnetic field starts at the magnet, jumps to the reluctor and then back to the pole piece.

  The strength of the magnetic field is determined by the air gap between the pole piece finger and the reluctor tooth. A wide gap produces a weak field; a narrow gap (when the pole piece finger and reluctor tooth align) results in a strong magnetic field.

  The magnetic field passing through the pickup coil induces a rising voltage in the coil; this voltage peaks when the reluctor tooth is closest (strong magnetic field) and falls as the tooth moves away. The polarity changes from positive to negative.

  The pickup coil signal triggers the base circuit of the transistor inside the module. This signal is

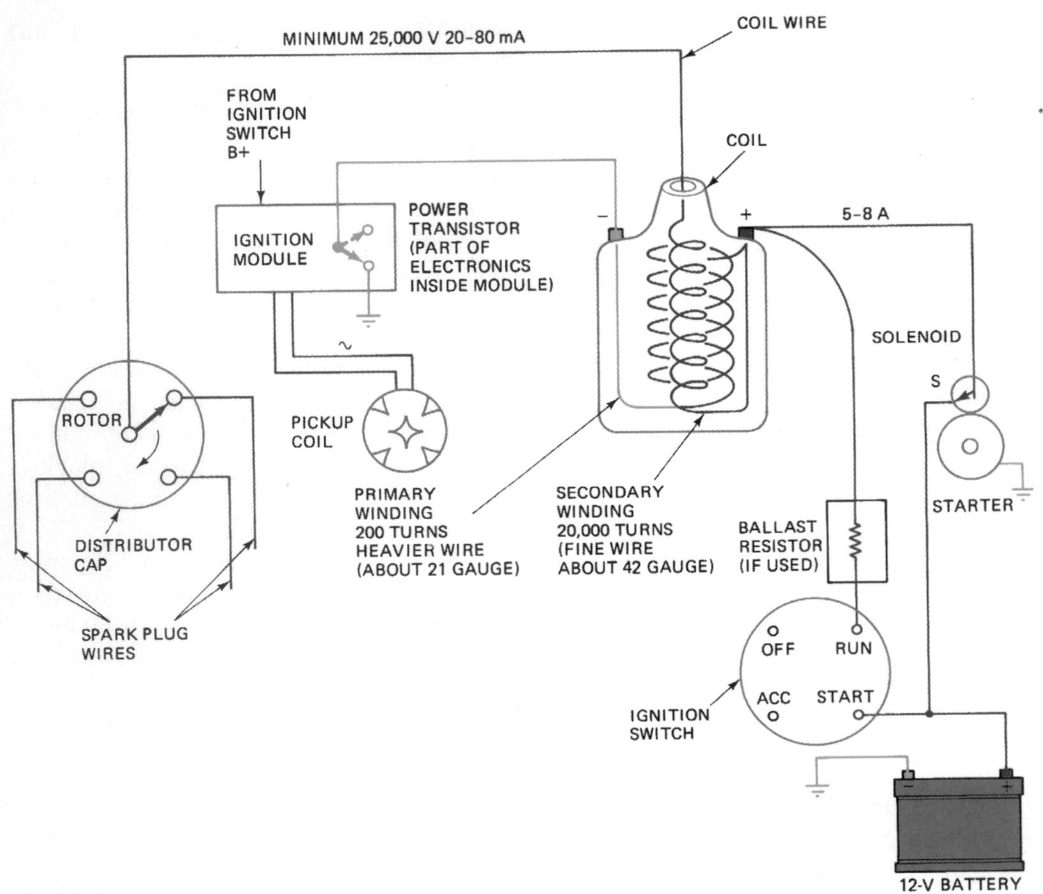

Figure 24–5 Typical primary and secondary electronic ignition using a ballast resistor and a distributor. To protect the ignition coil from overheating at lower engine speeds, many electronic ignitions do not use a ballast resistor, but rather use electronic circuits within the module.

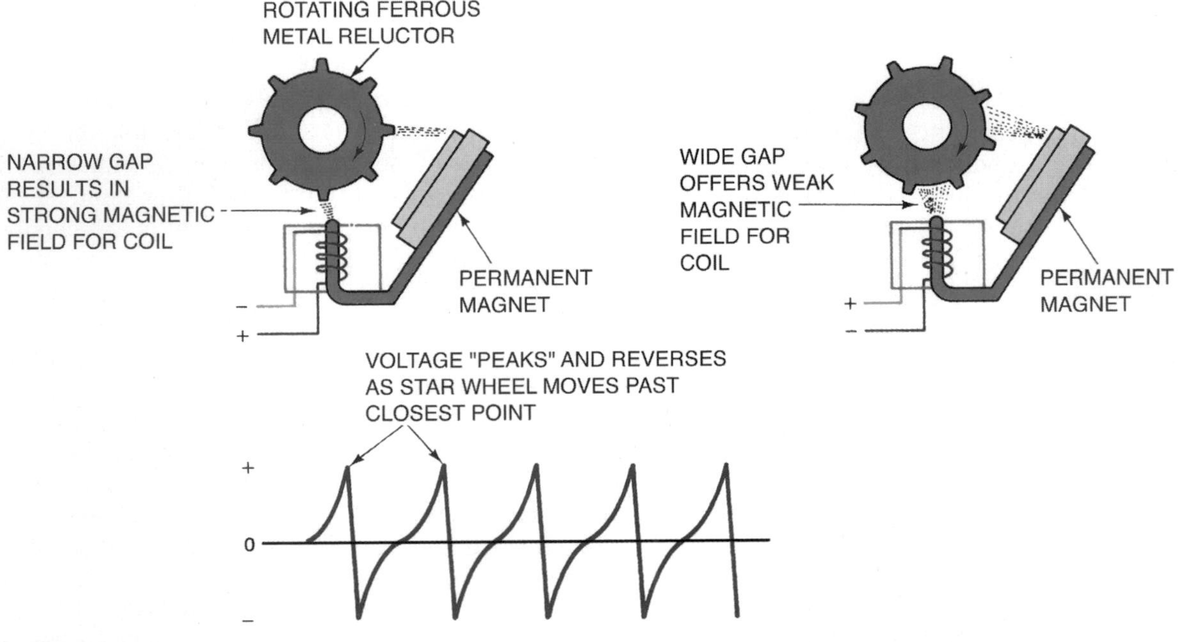

Figure 24–6 Operation of a typical pulse generator (pickup coil). At the bottom is a line drawing of a typical scope pattern of the output voltage of a pickup coil. The module receives this voltage from the pickup coil and opens the ground circuit to the ignition coil when the voltage starts down from its peak (just as the reluctor teeth start moving away from the pickup coil).

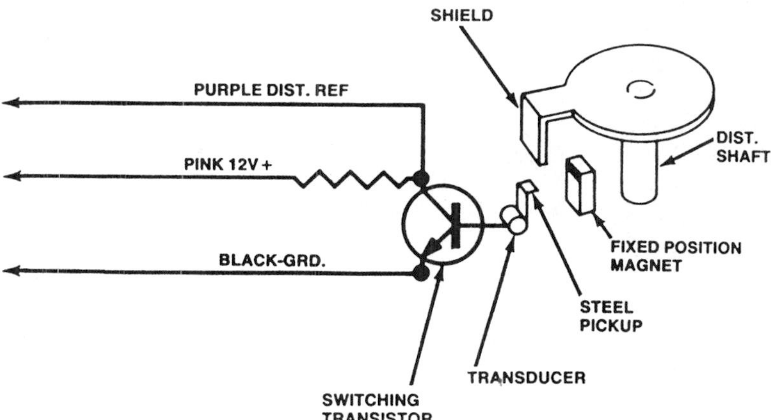

Figure 24–7 Hall-effect switches require an input voltage to function. The output signal on the distributor reference wire is digital (either on or off), compared to the analog (rising and falling) signal from a pickup coil. (Courtesy General Motors)

also used by the computer for piston position information and engine speed (RPM). Magnetic pulse generators may differ in appearance, but they all function in a similar manner.

- **Hall-effect switch**—A Hall-effect switch uses a permanent magnet, a transducer and a switching transistor. See Figure 24–7. In our example, battery voltage is applied to the (pink) 12 volt wire and resistor; voltage remains high in the (purple) distributor reference wire. A switching transistor connects the 12 volt wire to (black) ground. When the transistor is off, battery voltage is high in the distributor reference wire. Turning the transistor on shunts the voltage to ground and the voltage drops in the reference wire.

  The magnetic field from a fixed permanent magnet acts on a transducer, which sends a voltage signal to the base circuit of the switching transistor. The transistor turns on. A metal shutter (armature), driven by the distributor shaft, has a series of windows and tabs that rotate through the magnetic field. See Figure 24–8. When a tab is between the magnet and the transducer, the magnetic field is shunted into the tab—the transistor is off. When a window appears, the magnetic field acts on the transducer, the base circuit is activated and the transistor is turned on. One tab is often made narrower to identify the #1 cylinder.
- **Magnetic crankshaft position sensor**—This component uses the changing strength of the magnetic field surrounding a coil of wire to signal the module and computer. This signal is used by the electronics in the module and computer to provide piston position and engine speed (RPM). See Figure 24–9.
- **Optical sensors**—These use light from a **light emitting diode (LED)** and a phototransistor to signal the computer. An interrupter disc between the LED and the phototransistor has slits that allow the light from the LED to trigger the phototransistor on the other side of the disc. Most optical sensors (usually located inside the distributor) use two rows of slits to provide individual cylinder recognition (low-resolution) and precise distributor angle recognition (high-resolution) signals. See Figure 24–10.

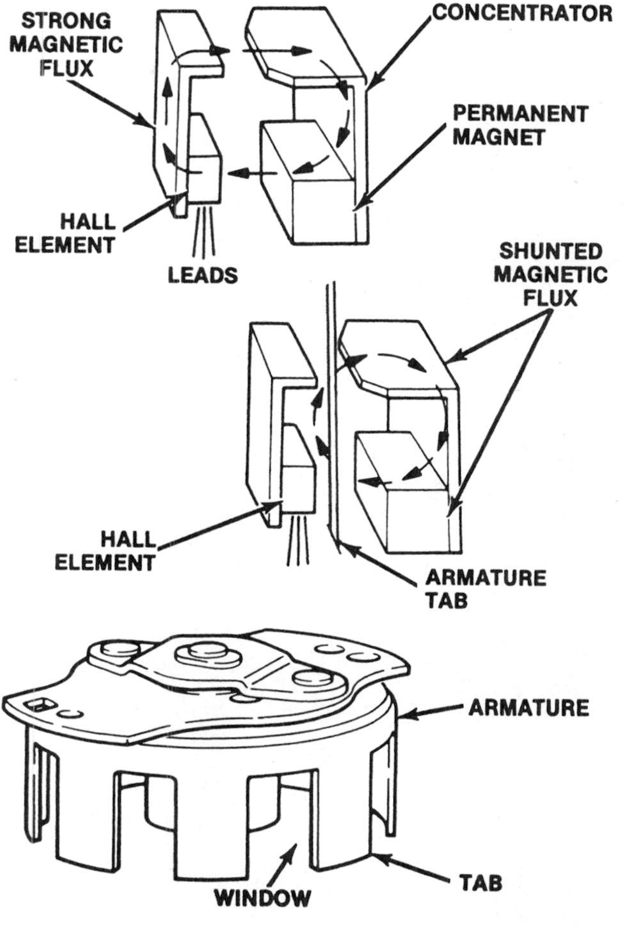

Figure 24–8 Hall-effect switches use metallic shutters to shunt magnetic lines of force away from the transducer and switching transistor. The digital (square wave) output provides a very accurate triggering signal. (Courtesy Ford Motor Co.)

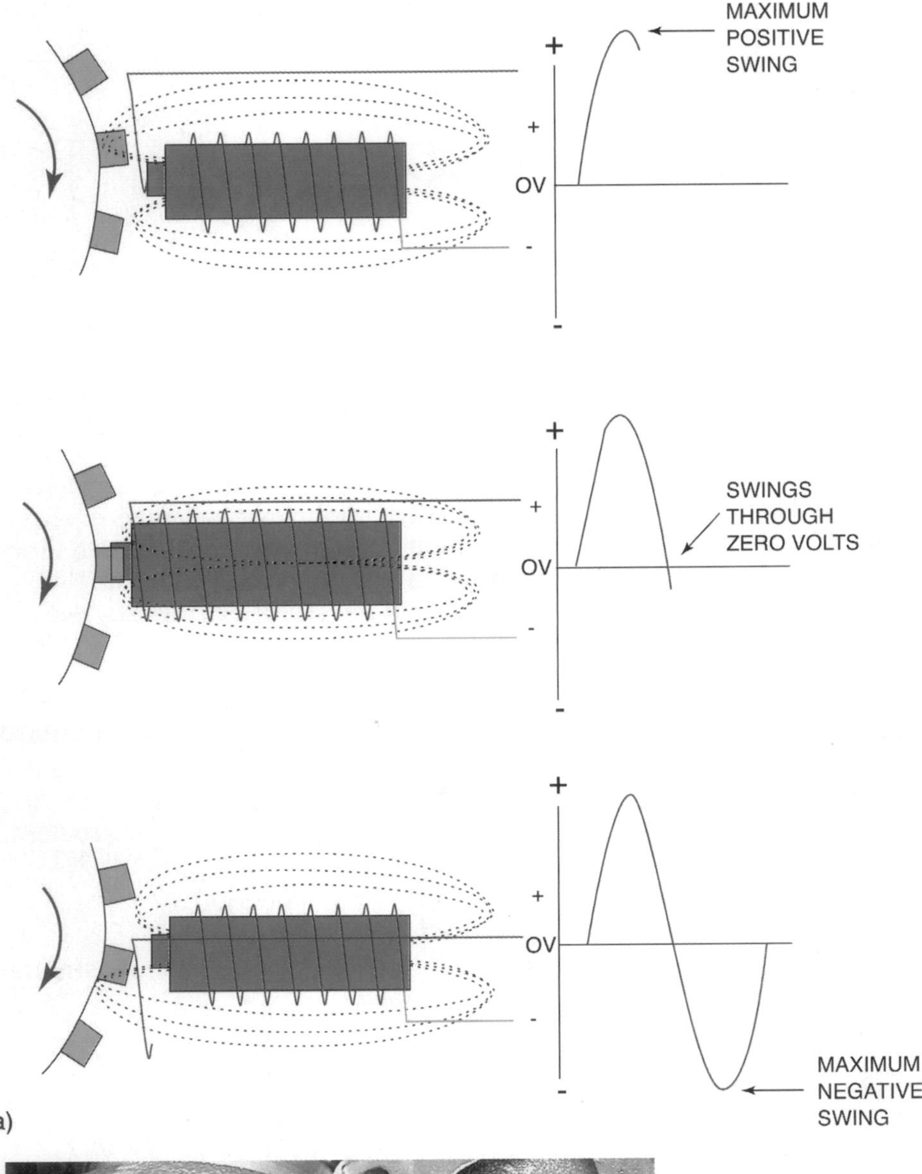

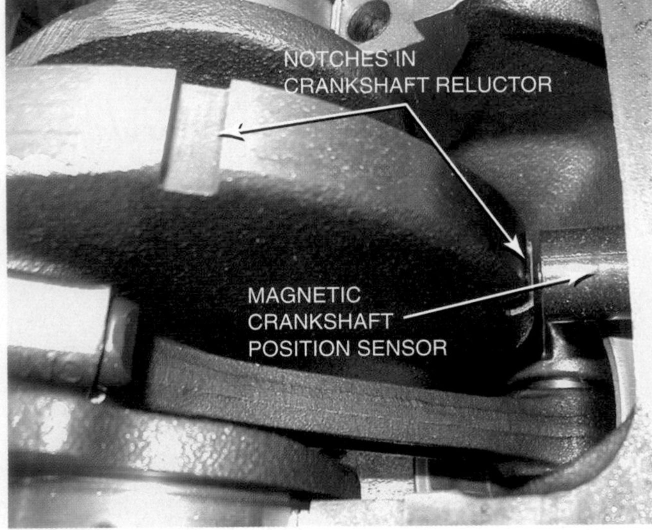

Figure 24–9 (a) A magnetic sensor uses a permanent magnet surrounded by a coil of wire. The notches of the crankshaft (or camshaft) create a variable magnetic field strength around the coil. When a metallic section is close to the sensor, the magnetic field is stronger because metal is a better conductor of magnetic lines of force than air. (b) A typical magnetic crankshaft position sensor.

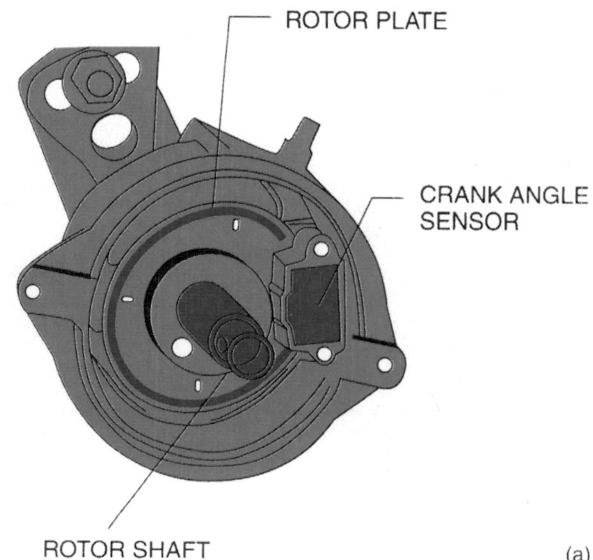

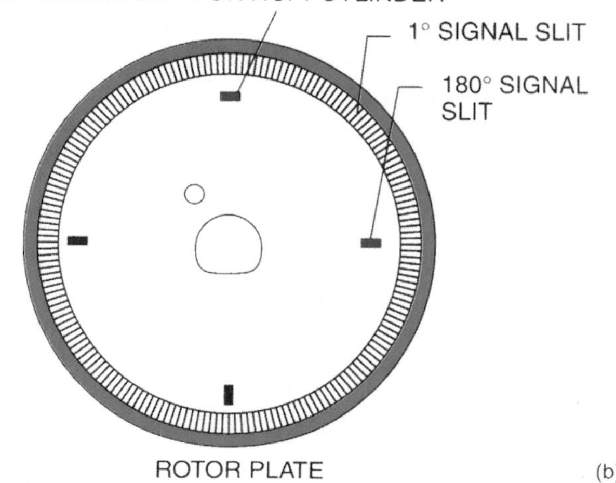

Figure 24–10 (a) Typical optical distributor. (b) The #1 cylinder slit signals the computer the piston position for cylinder #1. The 1° slits provide accurate engine speed information to the computer.

(a)

(b)

Figure 24–11 (a) An optical distributor on a Nissan 3.0 liter V-6 shown with the light shield removed. (b) A light shield being installed before the rotor is attached.

TECH TIP 

Optical Distributors Do Not Like Light

Optical distributors use the light emitted from LEDs to trigger phototransistors. Most optical distributors use a shield between the distributor rotor and the optical interrupter ring. Sparks jump the gap from the rotor tip to the distributor cap inserts. This shield blocks the light of the electrical arc from interfering with the detection of the light from the LEDs.

If this shield is not replaced during service, the light signals are reduced and the engine may not operate correctly. See Figure 24–11. This can be difficult to detect because nothing looks wrong during a visual inspection. Just remember that all optical distributors must be shielded between the rotor and the interrupter ring.

Primary Current Switching (Ignition Module)

This basic ignition circuit (see Figure 24–12) uses a single transistor to open and close the primary circuit. Positive polarity voltage from the pickup coil (or Hall switch) acts on the transistor base circuit; the transistor turns on allowing current to flow from the battery to the ignition coil primary, on through the transistor collector-emitter circuit to ground. A magnetic field forms around the coil primary.

When the pickup coil switches polarity from positive to negative, the transistor turns off, the magnetic field collapses, high voltage is induced in the coil secondary and the spark plug is fired.

Ignition modules also contain many other electronic components used to control amperage, ignition advance and dwell.

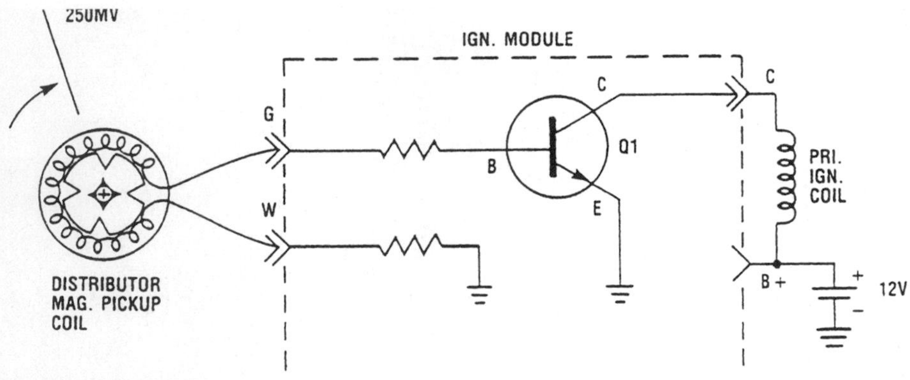

Figure 24–12 Primary circuit switching: positive polarity voltage from the pickup coil (G wire) triggers the base circuit of the transistor, which turns on. When the polarity reverses, the transistor switches off. Hall-effect switches work in a similar way; voltage from the transducer turns the transistor on; no voltage turns it off. (Courtesy General Motors)

Variable Dwell

When contact points were replaced with a transistor (located in/on the ignition module) in early electronic ignitions, dwell was fixed and non-adjustable. Primary current flow was still regulated by a ballast resistor on many systems.

Later ignition modules use variable dwell to regulate primary current, not resistance. Dwell may now vary from a low of 20% at idle, to a maximum of 85% at high RPM. Goodbye ballast resistor!

Contact points have a very short life when more than 2 or 3 amperes flow in the primary; the ignition module transistor allows 6 amperes or more, which increases available secondary voltage to about 40 000 volts.

Late-model variable-dwell ignition systems, such as the DaimlerChrysler Coil-On-Plug, permit up to 10 amperes to flow through the coil primary windings at lower engine temperatures. This reduces emissions and improves driveability.

Secondary Circuit Operation

High voltage current flows from the coil tower to the distributor cap and rotor where it is routed to the correct spark plug.

High tension spark plug leads are usually made with an internal core resistance of about 200 ohms per 300 mm (1 foot). Adding resistance increases the voltage required to fire the plug which, in turn, reduces the length of time (shortens the duration) that current flows across the plug gap. Shortened duration decreases radio/TV interference and improves spark plug life. Plug leads should be twisted at the boot and pulled gently to avoid breaking the core.

There are a number of variations with distributor caps and leads; some wires pull straight out of the cap, others have “fish hook” ends that must be released from inside, still others mould the cap and wires in one unit; preventing individual wire replacement. Often the cylinder number is printed on the plug wire; a different wire colour for the #1 cylinder is another method of identification.

Spark Plugs

The heat range of a spark plug refers to the temperature at the tip of the plug. Too cold a plug, under 370°C (700° F), will allow carbon and soot to build up on the plug causing fouling, misfire and hard starting.

Too hot a plug, over 925°C (1700°F), leads to engine detonation and a short spark plug life. See Figure 24–13(a).

Plug heat range should never be changed in the field except under unusual operating conditions: a delivery vehicle that idles for long periods and never runs at high speeds may require a hotter plug. A heavily loaded (e.g., pulling a trailer) highway vehicle may justify a cooler plug. The owner should always be informed of this change.

Tip design and electrode materials have improved with advances in ignition technology and more stringent emissions requirements. Conventional spark plugs require replacement around 32 000 km (20 000 mi) on average; the latest platinum and iridium tipped plugs have extended this interval to 160 000 to 180 000 km (100 000 to 112 000 mi). Platinum and iridium plugs also perform well during both city and highway driving; a heat range change is seldom required.

Some import vehicles are using twin ground electrodes with DIS (direct ignition system) to improve spark plug durability. See Figure 24–13(b).

It takes less voltage to fire from a hot centre electrode to a colder side (ground) electrode. Wiring the

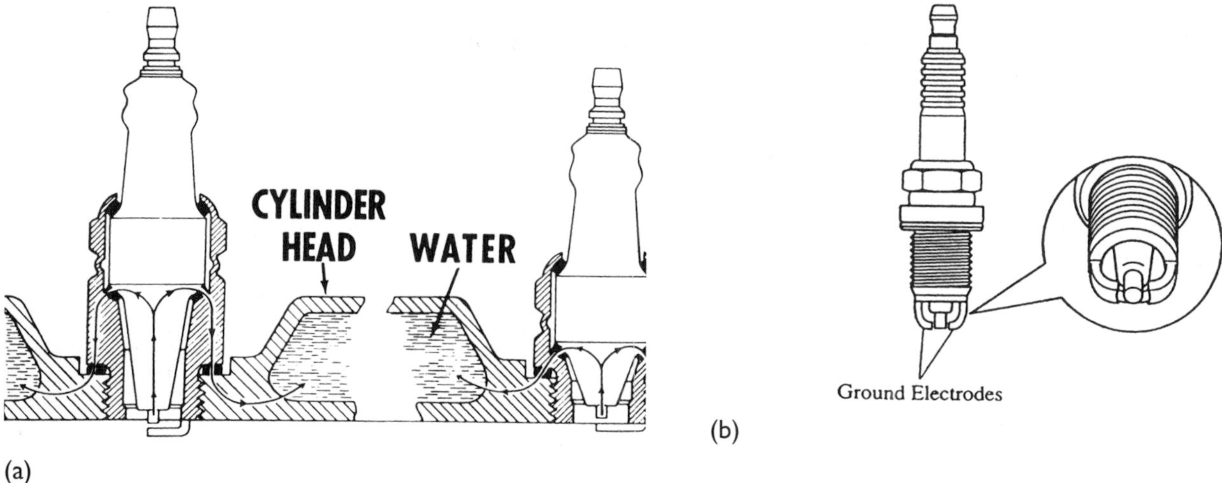

Figure 24–13 (a) Spark plug heat range; plugs with long insulators run hotter because tip heat has to travel further. (b) Twin ground electrode spark plugs are used on some DIS ignition systems to maintain plug durability. Toyota recommends a 48 000 kilometre (30 000 mile) replacement of these plugs. (Courtesy Ignition Manufacturer's Institute, *Automotive Emission Controls and Tune-Up Procedures,* Prentice Hall, 1980.)

coil primary backwards reverses the spark direction (reverse polarity) and the spark now jumps from the cold side electrode to the hot centre electrode. This increases the voltage required to bridge the gap by as much as 40%.

DISTRIBUTOR IGNITION

General Motors HEI Electronic Ignition

High energy ignition (HEI) has been the standard-equipment distributor ignition (DI) system on General Motors vehicles since the 1975 model year. Most V-6 and V-8 models use an ignition coil inside the distributor cap. Some V-6, inline 6-cylinder, and 4-cylinder models use an externally mounted ignition coil. See Figure 24–14. The operation of both styles is similar. The large-diameter distributor cap provides additional space between the spark plug connections to help prevent crossfire. Most HEI distributors also have 8 mm diameter spark plug wires that use female connections to the distributor cap towers. HEI coils must be replaced (if defective) with the exact replacement style. HEI coils differ and are identified by the colours of the primary leads. See Figures 24–15 and 24–16.

Ford Electronic Ignition

Ford electronic ignition systems all operate similarly, even though the name for the Ford electronic ignition system has changed many times since 1974.

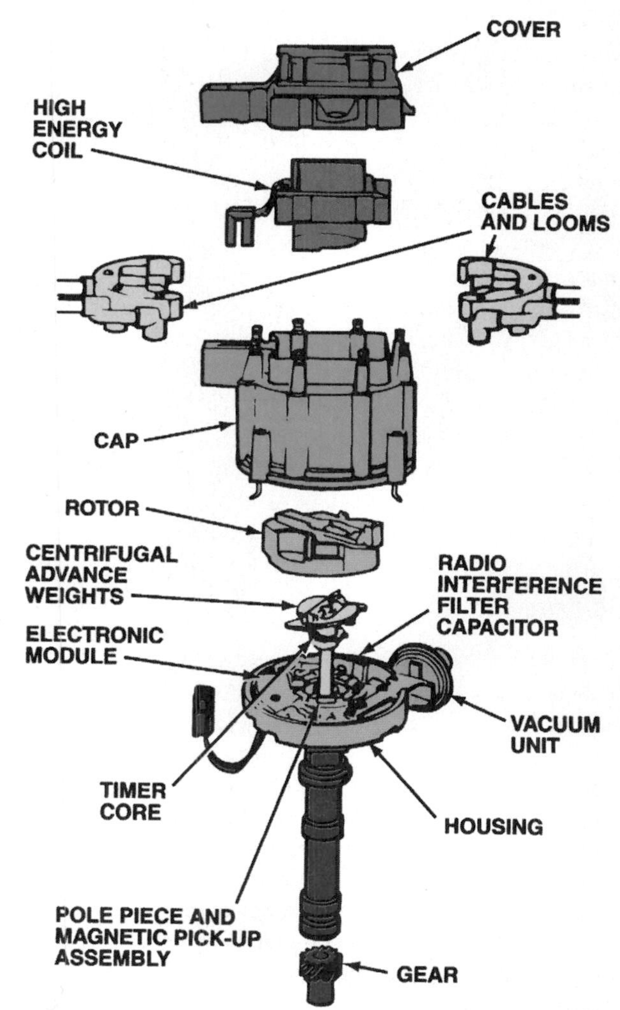

Figure 24–14 An HEI distributor equipped with centrifugal advance weights and a vacuum advance unit.

TECH TIP

The Tachometer Trick

When diagnosing a no-start or intermediate missing condition, check the operation of the tachometer. If the tachometer does not indicate engine speed (no-start condition) or drops toward zero (engine missing), then the problem is due to a defect in the **primary** ignition circuit. The tachometer gets its signal from the pulsing of the primary winding of the ignition coil. Components that are included in the primary circuit that could cause the tachometer not to work when the engine is cranking include:

- Pickup coil
- Crankshaft position sensor
- Ignition module (igniter)
- Coil primary wiring

If the vehicle is not equipped with a tachometer, connect a hand-held tachometer to the negative terminal of the coil. Just remember,

No tachometer reading = problem is in the primary ignition circuit

Tachometer reads OK = problem is in the secondary ignition circuit or is a fuel-related problem

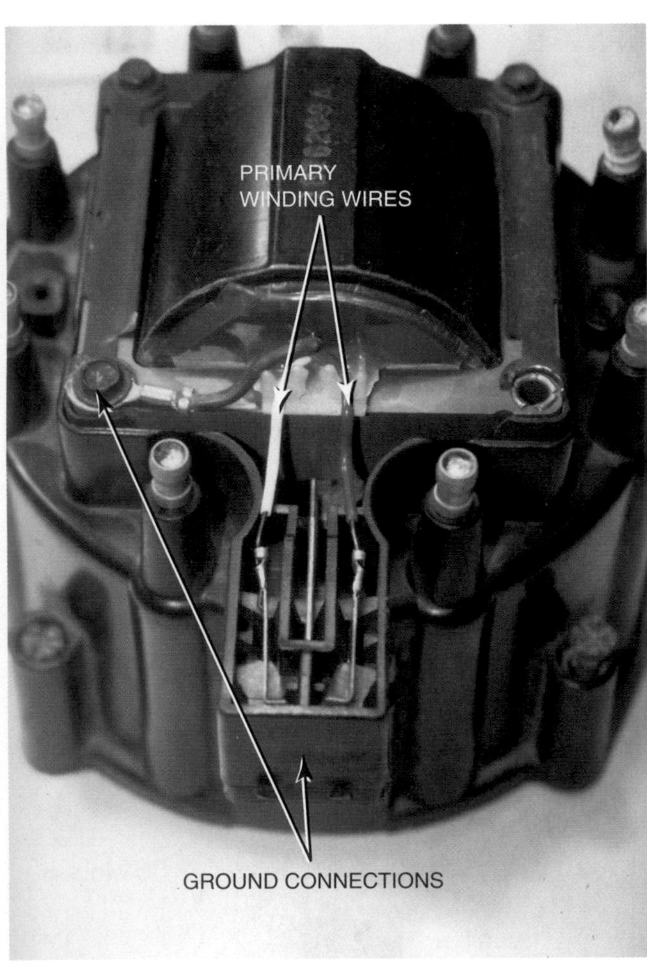

Figure 24–15 A typical General Motors HEI coil installed in the distributor cap. When the coil and/or distributor cap are replaced, always check that the ground clip is transferred from the old distributor cap to the new. Without proper grounding, coil damage is likely. There are two designs of HEI coils. One uses red and white wire as shown and the other design, which has reversed polarity, uses red and yellow wire for the coil primary.

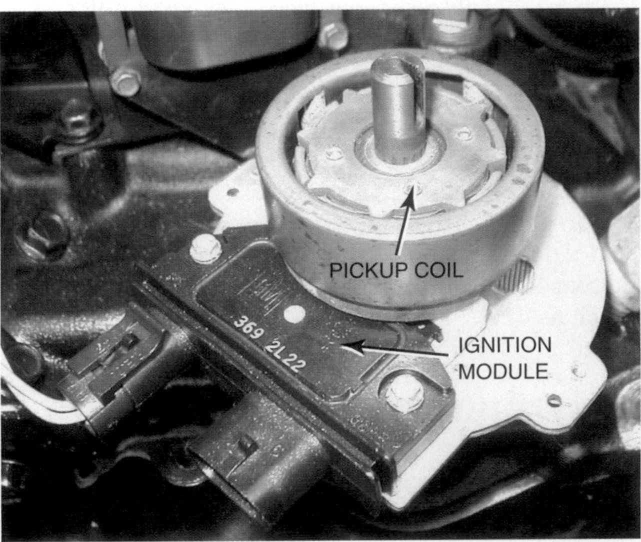

Figure 24–16 This unit uses a remotely mounted ignition coil.

Operation of Ford Electronic Ignition

Ford electronic ignition systems function in basically the same way regardless of year and name (Duraspark, EEC, etc.). See Figure 24–17. Under the distributor cap and rotor is a magnetic pickup assembly. This assembly produces a small alternating electrical pulse (approximately 1.5 volts) whenever the distributor armature rotates past the pickup assembly (stator). This low-voltage pulse is sent to the ignition module. The ignition module then switches (through transistors) off the primary ignition coil current. When the ignition coil primary current is stopped quickly, a high-voltage spike discharges from the coil secondary winding. Some Ford electronic ignition systems use a ballast resistor to help control the primary current through the ignition coil in the run mode (position); other Ford sys-

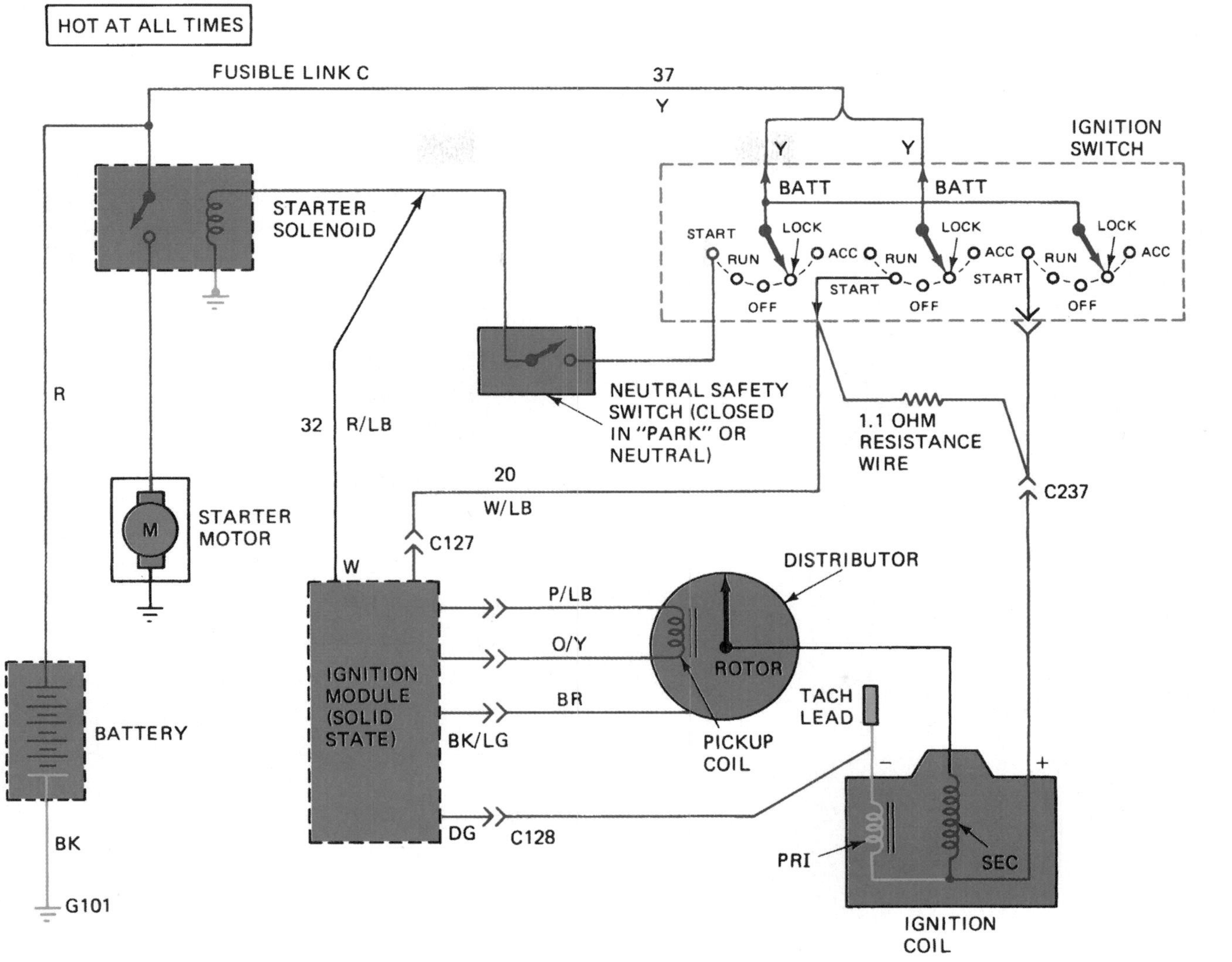

Figure 24–17 Wiring diagram of a typical Ford electronic ignition. Notice the ignition module (wire BR) grounds at the distributor.

tems do not use a ballast resistor. The coil current is controlled in the module circuits by decreasing dwell (coil-charging time) depending on various factors determined by operating conditions.

Ford Thick-Film-Integrated Ignition

The EEC IV system uses the **thick-film-integrated (TFI)** ignition system. TFI ignition systems were first used on the Escort and Lynx and similar models. This system uses a smaller control module attached to the distributor and uses an air-cooled epoxy E coil. See Figure 24–18. Thick-film ignition means that all electronics are manufactured on small layers built up to form a thick film. Construction includes using pastes of different electrical resistances that are deposited on a thin, flat ceramic material by a process similar to silk-screen printing. These resistors are

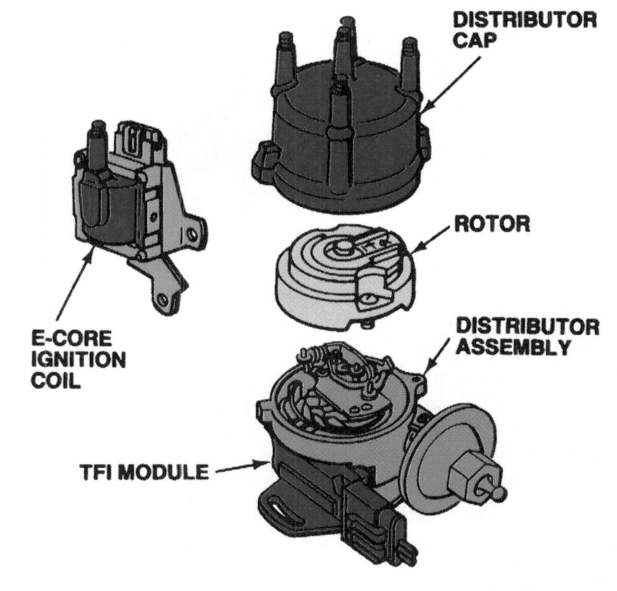

Figure 24–18 Ford TFI ignition system components.

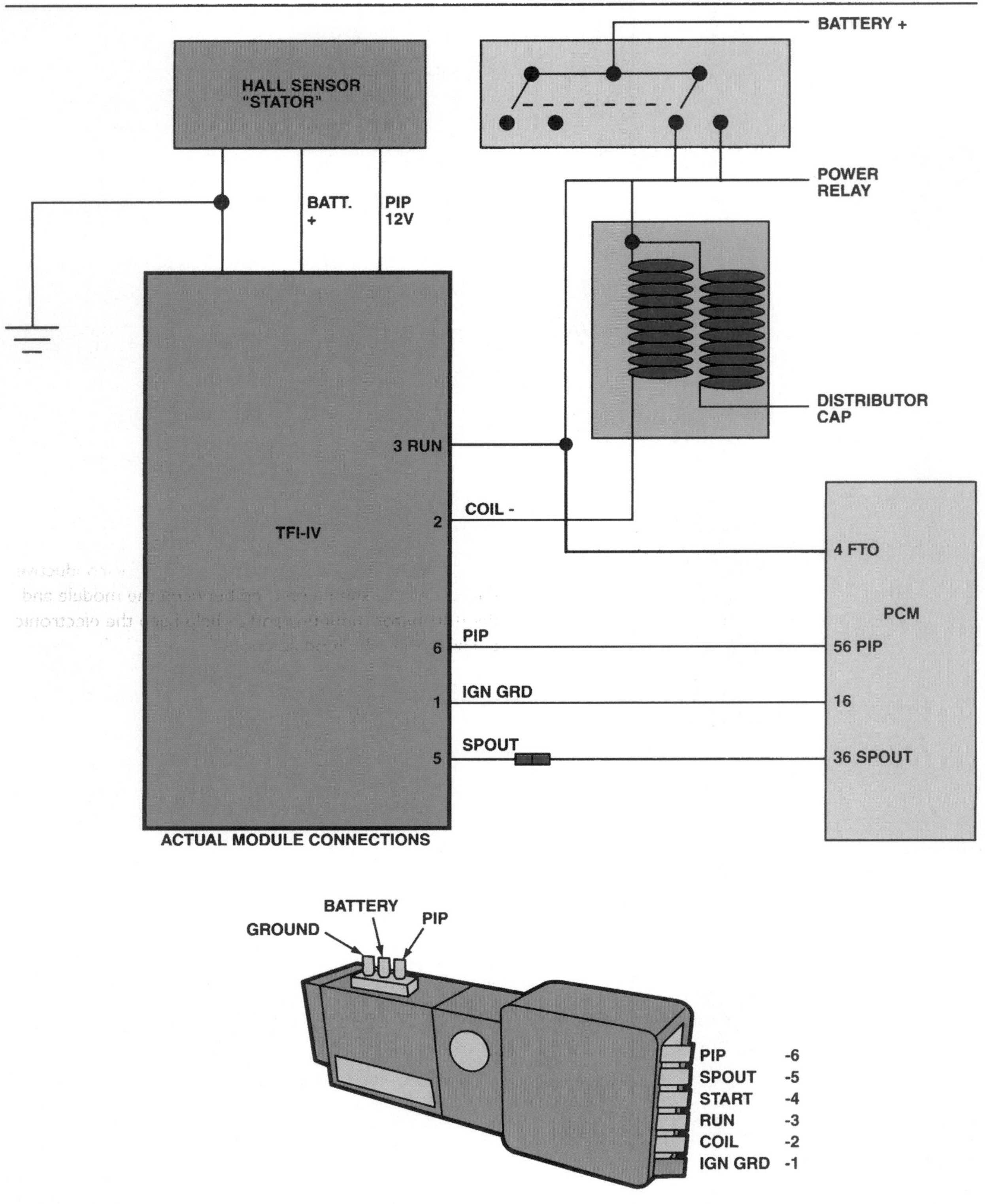

Figure 24–19 Schematic of a Ford TFI-IV ignition system. The SPOUT (spark-output) connector is unplugged when ignition timing is being set.

TECH TIP 

If It's Soft, Throw It Away

Ford uses a Hall-effect sensor in the distributor on most TFI module-equipped engines. The sensors were originally coated in a black plastic that would often become soft with age and break down electrically. The soft plastic sensor would also prevent proper connection to the TFI module as shown in Figure 24–20. If a no start or rough engine operation occurs, always check the Hall-effect sensor and the connections to the module. The original Hall-effect units were black plastic and more prone to failure. Ozone formed by the high-voltage arcing in the distributor cap is very corrosive, and it chemically attacked the plastic. When this occurred, the plastic would become soft and pliable and similar to tar in feel and texture. If the sensor is soft like tar, replace the Hall-effect switch assembly. Later production units were changed to a more chemically stable white plastic material that is soft enough to get a fingernail into, yet is not sticky.

connected by tracks of palladium silver paste. Then the chips that form the capacitors, diodes, and integrated circuits are soldered directly to the palladium silver tracks. The thick-film manufacturing process is highly automated. See Figure 24–19.

Chrysler Electronic Ignition

Chrysler was the first domestic manufacturer to produce electronic ignition as standard equipment. The Chrysler system consists of a pulse generator unit in the distributor (pickup coil and reluctor). Chrysler's name for their electronic ignition is **electronic ignition system (EIS),** and the control unit (module) is called the **electronic control unit (ECU).**

The pickup coil in the distributor (pulse generator) generates the signal to open and close the primary coil circuit. See Figure 24–21. Some engines used two (dual) pickup coils. One pickup coil is called the **starting pickup** and provides slightly retarded ignition timing to aid in starting. The other pickup is called the **run pickup.**

Import Ignition Systems

Import vehicles use essentially the same ignitions as domestic vehicles; early models used contact points, later models advanced to pickup-coil or Hall-effect electronic ignition including coil-in-cap (similar to HEI). Distributorless ignition systems (DIS) were introduced in the 1980s. Current models use coil-on-plug.

Although there are a few ignition variations between makes, there are far more similarities. The shop manual must be consulted for service procedures and specifications regardless of where the vehicle was manufactured.

Figure 24–20 Thick-film-integrated type of Ford electronic ignition. Note how the module plugs into the Hall-effect switch inside the distributor. Heat-conductive silicone grease should be used between the module and the distributor mounting pad to help keep the electronic circuits inside the module cool. Vehicles sold for use in high temperature areas have a factory-installed wiring harness that relocates the TFI module away from the distributor and into an air-cooled heat sink.

WASTE SPARK IGNITION SYSTEMS

Waste spark ignition is also called **distributorless ignition system (DIS)** or simply **electronic ignition (EI).** Waste spark ignition uses the on-board computer to fire the ignition coils. These systems were first used on some Saabs and some General Motors engines. Some four-cylinder engines use four coils, but usually a four-cylinder engine uses two ignition coils and a six-cylinder engine uses three ignition coils. Each coil is a true transformer in which the primary winding and secondary winding are not electrically connected. Each end of the secondary winding is connected to a cylinder exactly opposite the other in the firing order. See Figure 24–22. This means that *both* spark plugs fire at the same time! When one cylinder (for example, 6) is on the compression stroke, the other cylinder (3) is on the exhaust stroke. This spark that occurs on the exhaust stroke is called the **waste spark** because it does no useful work and is only used

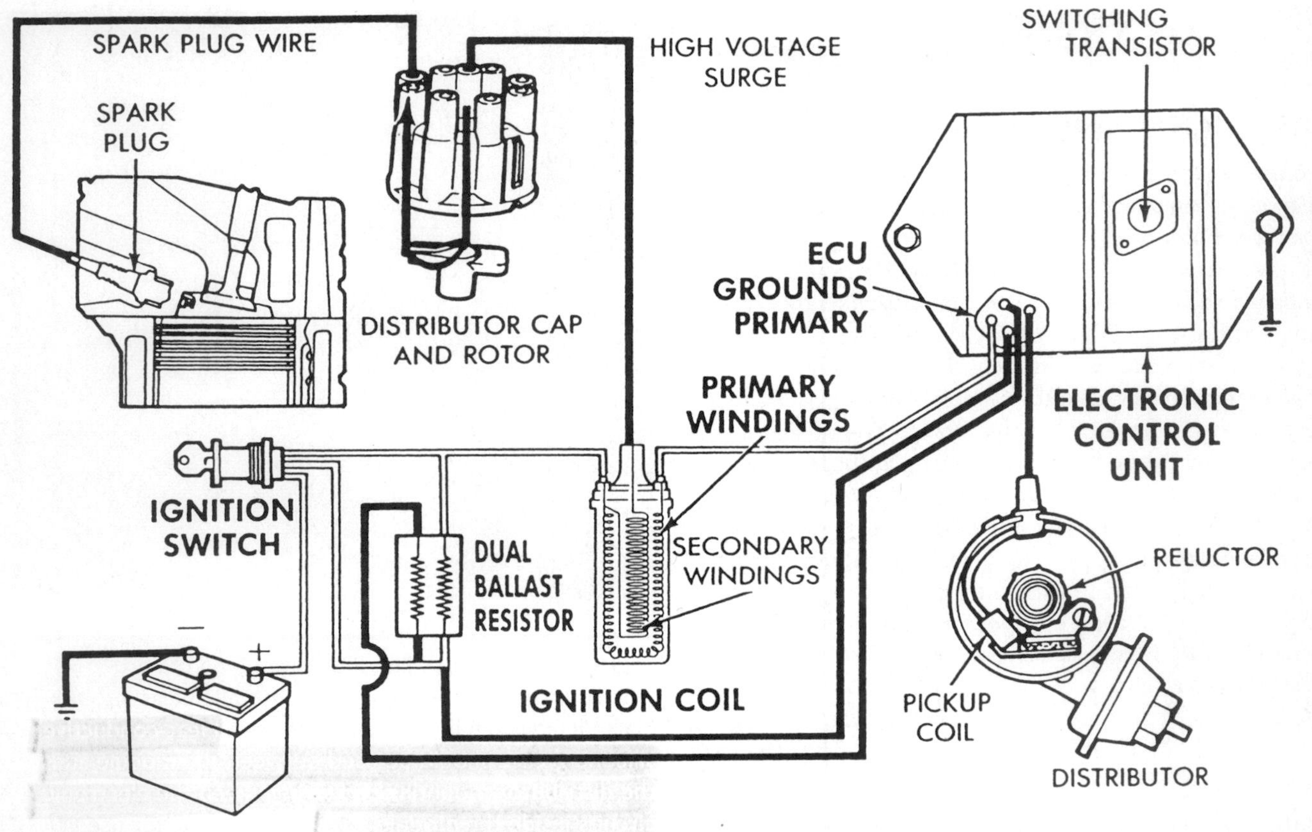

Figure 24–21 Schematic of a Chrysler electronic ignition. This system uses distributor mechanical weights to increase timing with RPM and a vacuum advance unit to further advance timing under light engine load conditions. The switching transistor is mounted outside the Electronic Control Unit (ECU) to improve cooling. (Courtesy DaimlerChrysler Corporation)

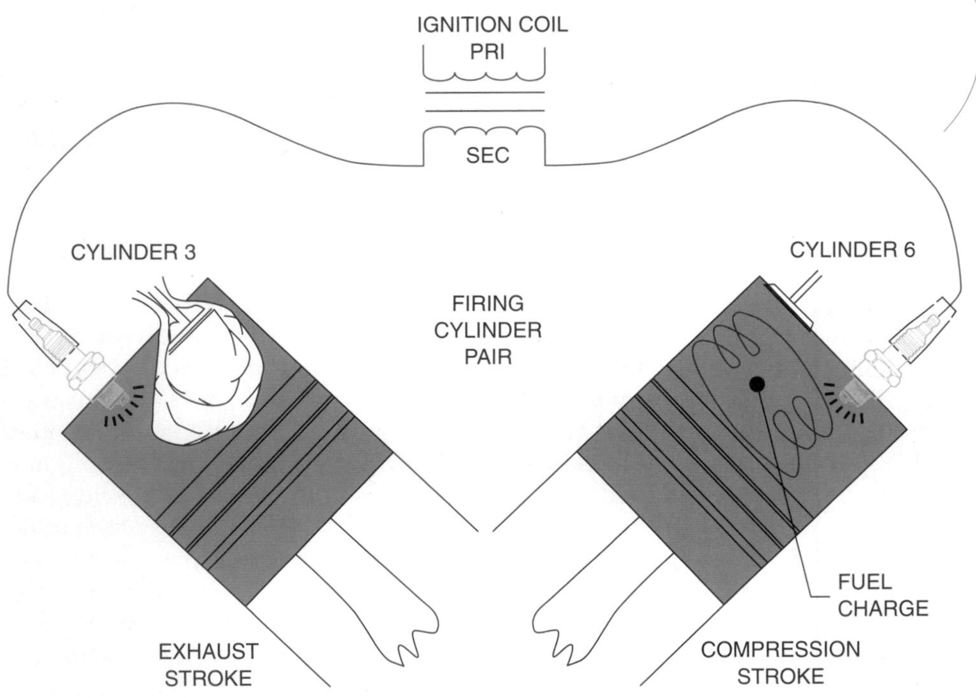

Figure 24–22 A waste spark system fires one cylinder while its piston is on the compression stroke and into the paired or companion cylinder while it is on the exhaust stroke: both spark plugs fire at the same time. In a typical engine, it requires only about 2 to 3 kilovolts to fire the cylinder on the exhaust strokes. The remaining coil energy is available to fire the spark plug under compression (typically about 8 to 12 kilovolts).

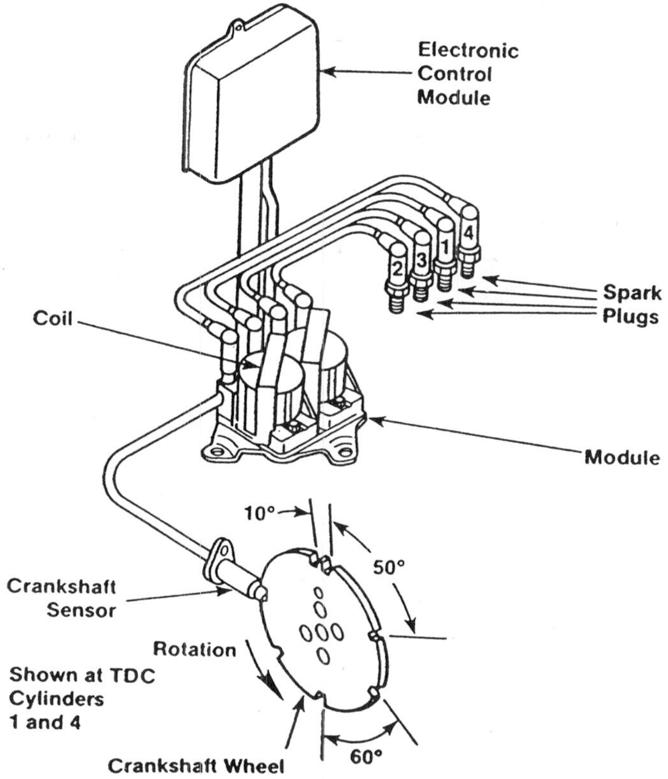

Figure 24–23 Schematic of a General Motors 4-cylinder DIS waste-spark ignition. The crank sensor is triggered by a reluctor ring, machined into the crankshaft on many 4-cylinder engines, or mounted behind the harmonic balancer on V-6 engines. (Courtesy General Motors)

as a ground path for the secondary winding of the ignition coil. The voltage required to jump the spark plug gap on cylinder 3 (the exhaust stroke) is only 2 to 3 kilovolts and provides the *ground circuit* for the secondary coil circuit. The remaining coil energy is used by the cylinder on the compression stroke. One spark plug of each pair fires straight polarity and the other cylinder fires reverse polarity. Spark plug life is not greatly affected by the reverse polarity. However, a single defective spark plug or spark-plug wire may affect the operation of *two* cylinders.

NOTE: With a distributor-type ignition system, the coil has two air gaps to fire: one between the rotor tip and the distributor insert (not under compression forces) and the other in the gap at the firing tip of the spark plug (under compression forces). A DIS system also fires two gaps: one under compression (compression stroke plug) and one not under compression (exhaust stroke plug).

Waste spark ignitions require a sensor (usually a crankshaft sensor) to trigger the coils at the correct time. See Figure 24–23. The crankshaft sensor cannot be moved to adjust ignition timing: ignition timing is not adjustable. The slight adjustment of the crankshaft sensor is designed to position the sensor exactly in the middle of the rotating metal disc for maximum clearance. A crankshaft position sensor is all that is required on a waste-spark ignition because each spark plug is fired once every revolution. See Figure 24–24. As long as the ECM receives data regarding cylinder numbers and piston location, it doesn't matter if the piston is coming up on the compression stroke or the exhaust stroke.

This changes when timed fuel injection is used. The ECM must recognize the exact stroke in order to inject fuel at the correct time. A camshaft position sensor provides this information.

COIL-ON-PLUG IGNITION

Coil-on-plug ignition (COP) uses one ignition coil for each spark plug. This system is also called **coil-by-plug, coil-near-plug,** or **coil-over-plug** and is the most popular ignition system today. See Figures 24–25 and 24–26. The coil-on-plug system eliminates the spark plug wires, which are often sources of **electromagnetic interference (EMI)** that can cause problems to some computer signals. The vehicle computer pulses the ground terminal of each coil at the proper time. **Ignition timing** can also be changed by the computer (retarded or advanced) on a cylinder-by-cylinder basis for maximum performance and to respond to knock sensor signals.

General Motors vehicles use a variety of coil-on-plug-type ignition systems. Many V-8 engines use a coil-near-plug system with individual coils and modules that are placed on the valve covers for each individual cylinder. Short secondary ignition spark

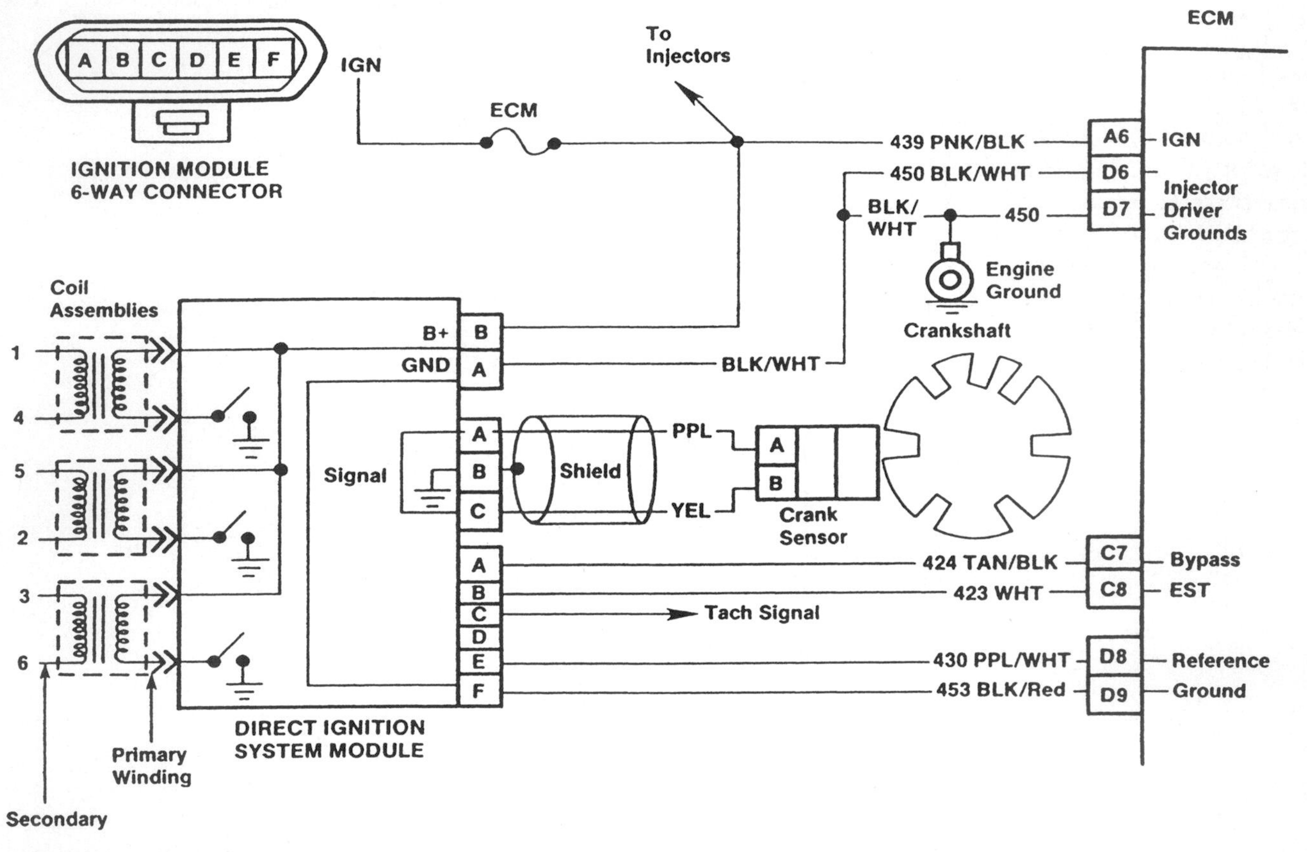

Figure 24–24 Typical wiring diagram of a V-6 distributorless (direct fire) ignition system. The switching transistors in the DIS module are shown as single-pole switches for clarity. (Courtesy General Motors)

(a)

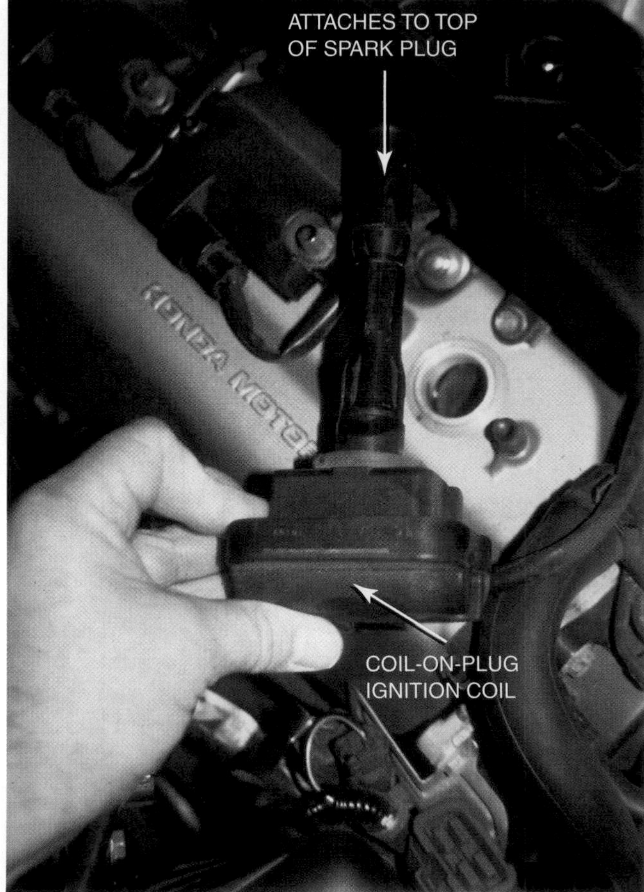

(b)

Figure 24–25 A coil-on-plug ignition system.

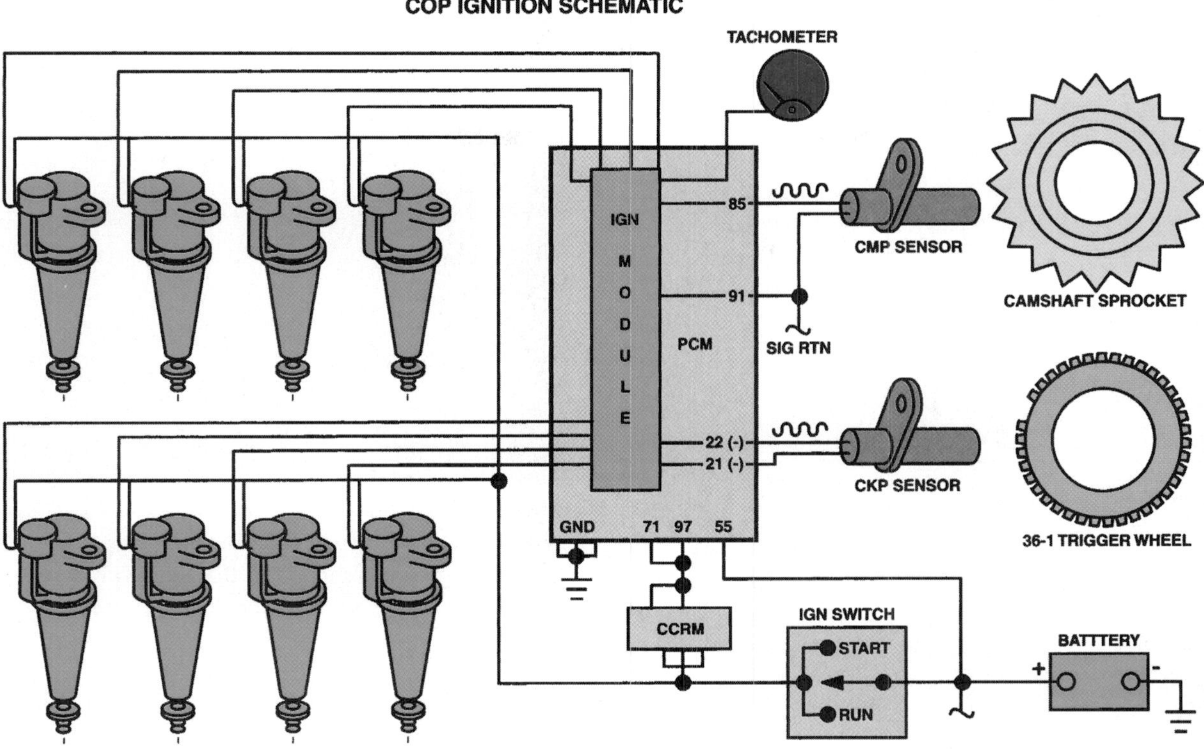

Figure 24–26 A typical coil-on-plug (COP) ignition system on a V-8 with a separate coil for each cylinder.

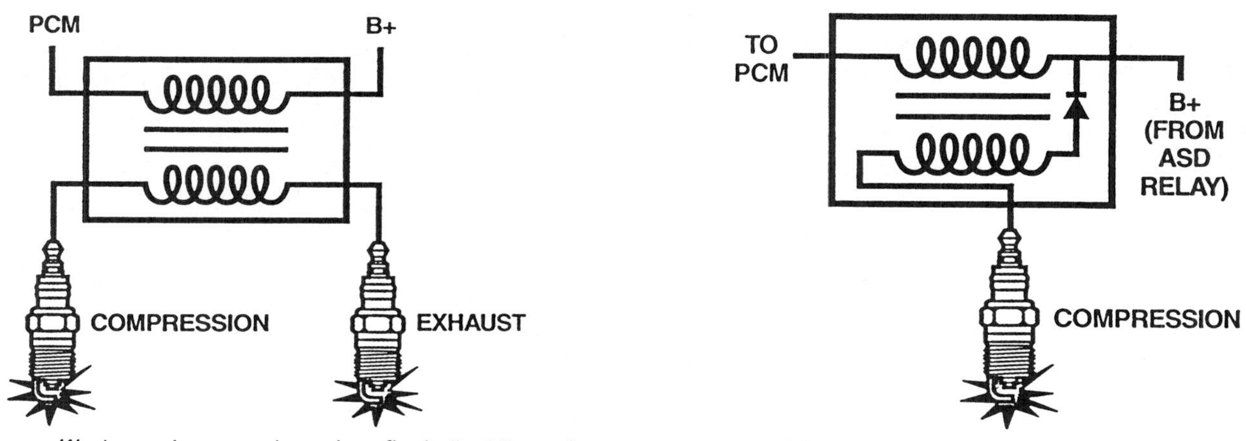

Figure 24–27 Coil-on-plug ignitions provide a stronger spark and longer plug life. (Courtesy DaimlerChrysler Corporation)

plug wires are used to connect the output terminal of the ignition coil to the spark plug.

Most newer DaimlerChrysler engines use coil-over-plug-type ignition systems. Each coil is controlled by the PCM, which can vary the ignition timing separately for each cylinder based on signals the PCM receives from the knock sensor(s). For example, if the knock sensor detects that a spark knock has occurred after firing cylinder #3, then the PCM will continue to monitor cylinder #3 and retard timing on just this one cylinder if necessary to prevent engine-damaging detonation.

DIS (waste spark) systems fire the spark plug every revolution while coil-on-plug ignitions fire the plug once every second revolution. This gives COP coils twice the time to build a magnetic field, which improves saturation. Spark plug electrode wear is also reduced, as the plugs fire half as often. See Figure 24–27.

SAFETY TIP

Never Disconnect a Spark Plug Wire When the Engine Is Running!

Ignition systems produce a high-voltage pulse necessary to ignite a lean air-fuel mixture. If you disconnect a spark plug wire when the engine is running, this high-voltage spark could cause personal injury or damage to the ignition, the ignition coil, and/or ignition module.

TECH TIP

Always Use a Spark Tester

A spark tester looks like a spark plug without a side electrode, with a gap between the centre electrode and the grounded shell. The tester commonly has an alligator clip attached to the shell so that it can be clamped on a good ground connection on the engine. A good ignition system should be able to cause a spark to jump this wide gap at atmospheric pressure. Without a spark tester, a technician might assume that the ignition system is okay because it can spark across a normal, grounded spark plug. The voltage required to fire a standard spark plug when it is out of the engine and not under pressure is about 3000 volts or less. An electronic ignition spark tester requires a minimum of 25 000 volts to jump the 18 mm (3/4 in.) gap. Therefore, never assume that the ignition system is okay because it fires a spark plug—always use a spark tester. *Remember that an intermittent spark across a spark tester should be interpreted as a no-spark condition.*

CHECKING FOR SPARK

In the event of a no-start condition, the first step should be to check for secondary voltage out of the ignition coil or to the spark plugs. If the engine is equipped with a separate ignition coil, remove the coil wire from the centre of the distributor cap, install a **spark tester,** and crank the engine. See the Tech Tip "Always Use a Spark Tester." A good coil and ignition system should produce a blue spark at the spark tester. See Figures 24–28 and 24–29.

If the ignition system being tested does not have a separate ignition coil, disconnect any spark plug wire from a spark plug and, while cranking the engine, test for spark available at the spark plug wire, again using a spark tester.

NOTE: An intermittent spark should be considered a no-spark condition.

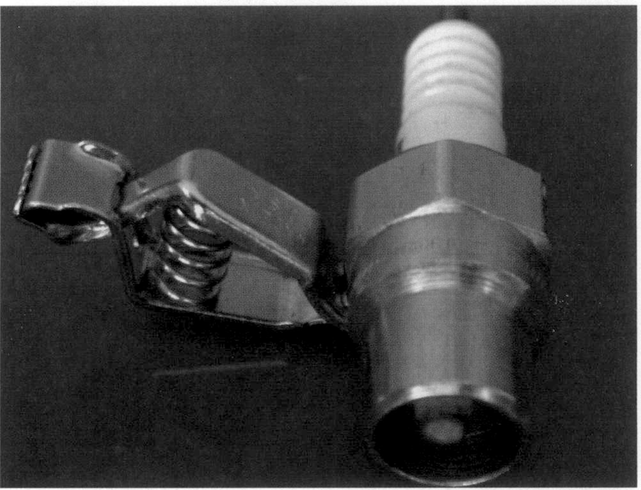

Figure 24–28 A spark tester looks like a regular spark plug with an alligator clip attached to the shell. This tester has a specified gap that requires at least 25 000 volts (25kV) to fire.

Figure 24–29 A close-up showing the recessed centre electrode on a spark tester. It is recessed 9 mm (3/8 in.) into the shell and the spark must then jump another 9 mm (3/8 in.) to the shell for a total gap of 18 mm (3/4 in.).

Typical causes of a no-spark (intermittent spark) condition include the following:

1. Weak ignition coil
2. Low or no voltage to the primary (positive) side of the coil
3. High resistance or open coil wire, or spark plug wire
4. Negative side of the coil not being pulsed by the ignition module
5. Defective pickup coil
6. Defective module

ELECTRONIC IGNITION TROUBLESHOOTING PROCEDURE

When troubleshooting any electronic ignition system for no-spark, follow these steps to help pinpoint the exact cause of the problem:

1. Turn the ignition on (engine off) and, using either a voltmeter or a test light, test for battery voltage available at the positive terminal of the ignition coil. If the voltage is not available, check for an open circuit at the ignition switch or wiring. Also check the condition of the ignition fuse (if used).

> **NOTE:** Many Chrysler products use an **automatic shutdown (ASD)** relay to power the ignition coil. The ASD relay will not supply voltage to the coil unless the engine is cranking and the computer senses a crankshaft sensor signal. This little fact has fooled a lot of technicians.

2. Connect the voltmeter or test light to the negative side of the coil and crank the engine. The voltmeter should fluctuate or the test light should blink, indicating that the primary coil current is being turned on and off. If there is no pulsing of the negative side of the coil, the problem is a defective pickup coil, electronic control module, or wiring.

IGNITION COIL TESTING USING AN OHMMETER

If an ignition coil is suspected of being defective, a simple ohmmeter check can be performed to test the resistance of the primary and secondary winding inside the coil. For accurate resistance measurements, the wiring to the coil should be removed before testing. To test the primary coil winding resistance, follow these steps (Figure 24–30):

NOTES: 1. When measuring resistance, be sure that the contact between the probes and the circuit is clean. Dirt, oil, paint, rust or other foreign matter seriously affect resistance.
2. Measure resistance in the primary and secondary coils when the coil is hot and cold.

1. Insert test leads in the input terminals shown.
2. Turn rotary switch to Ω.
3. Touch the probes as shown to measure resistance in primary windings.
4. Observe display. Resistance should be less than a few ohms.
5. Touch probes as shown to measure resistance in secondary windings.
6. Observe display. Resistance should typically be in the 10k Ω range.

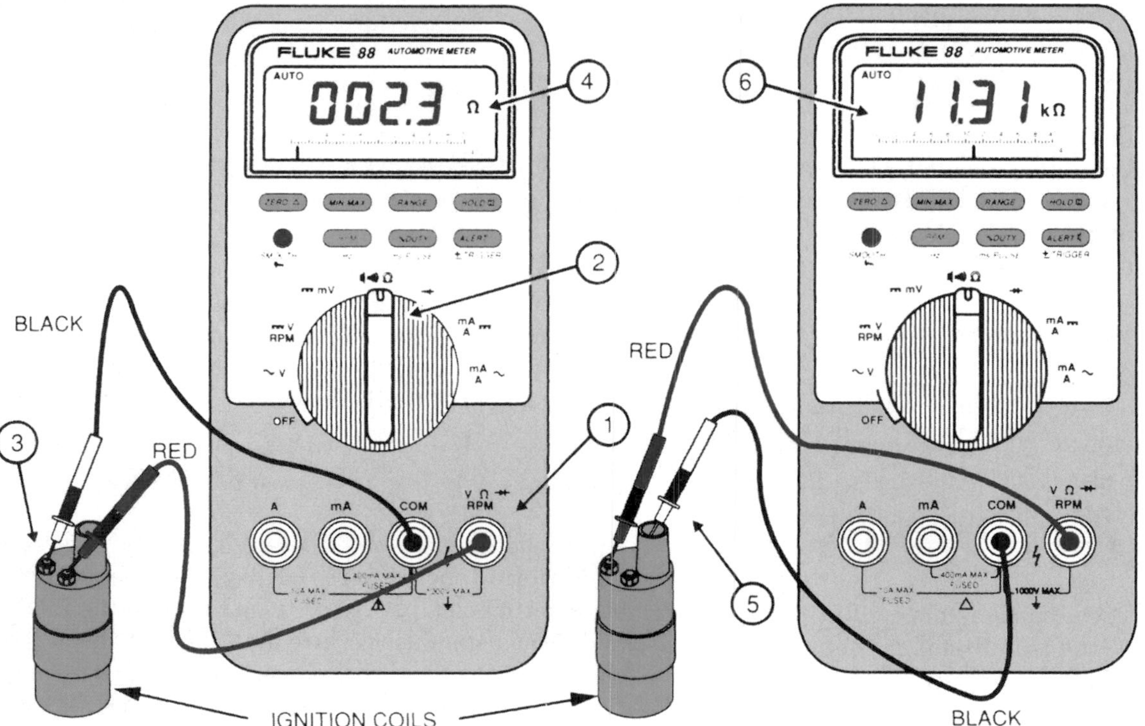

Figure 24–30 Checking an ignition coil using a multimeter set to read ohms. (Courtesy of Fluke Corporation)

1. Set the meter to read low ohms.
2. Measure the resistance between the positive terminal and the negative terminal of the ignition coil. Most coils will give a reading between 1 and 3 ohms; however, some coils should indicate less than 1 ohm. Check the manufacturer's specifications for the exact resistance values.

To test the secondary coil winding resistance, follow these steps:

1. Set the meter to read kilohms (kΩ).
2. Measure the resistance between either primary terminal and the secondary coil tower. The normal resistance of most coils ranges between 6000 and 30 000 ohms (6 and 30 kΩ). Check the manufacturer's specifications for the exact resistance values.

NOTE: Many ignition coils use a screw that is inside the secondary tower of the ignition coil. If this screw is loose, an intermittent engine miss could occur. The secondary coil would also indicate high resistance if this screw was loose.

PICKUP COIL TESTING

The pickup coil, located under the distributor cap on many electronic ignition engines, can cause a no-spark condition if defective. The pickup coil must generate an AC voltage pulse to the ignition module so that the module can pulse the ignition coil.

A pickup coil contains a coil of wire, and the resistance of this coil should be within the range specified by the manufacturer. See Figure 24–31. Some common specifications include the following:

Manufacturer	Pickup Coil Resistance (Ohms)
Chrysler	150 to 900 (orange and black leads)
Ford	400 to 1000 (orange and purple leads)
General Motors	500 to 1500 (white and green leads)
Toyota	140 to 180 (brown and yellow leads)

If the pickup coil resistance is not within the specified range, replace the pickup coil assembly.

The pickup coil can also be tested for proper voltage output. During cranking, most pickup coils should produce a minimum of 0.25 volt AC. This can be tested with the distributor out of the vehicle by rotating the distributor drive gear by hand.

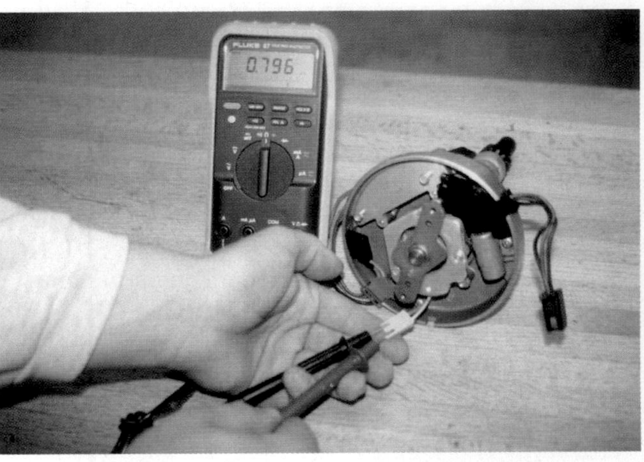

Figure 24–31 Measuring the resistance of an HEI pickup coil using a digital multimeter set to the ohms position. Always bend the pickup coil leads gently while testing; watch for major fluctuations in the ohmmeter reading. The reading on the face of the meter is 0.796 kΩ right in the middle of the 500 to 1500 Ω specifications.

TESTING MAGNETIC SENSORS

First of all, magnetic sensors have to be magnetic. If the permanent magnet inside the sensor has cracked, the result is two weak magnets.

If the sensor is removed from the engine, hold a metal (steel) object against the end of the sensor. It should exert a strong magnetic pull on the steel object. If not, replace the sensor. Second, the sensor can be tested using a digital meter set to read AC volts. See Figure 24–32.

TESTING HALL-EFFECT SENSORS

As with any other sensor, the output of the Hall-effect sensor should be tested first. Using a digital voltmeter, check for the presence of an AC voltage when the engine is being cranked. The best test is to use an oscilloscope and observe the waveform. See Figure 24–33.

TESTING OPTICAL SENSORS

Optical sensors will not operate if dirty or covered in oil. Perform a thorough visual inspection looking for an oil leak that could cause dirty oil to get on the LED or phototransistor. Also be sure that the light shield is securely fastened and that the seal is lightproof. An optical sensor can also be checked using an oscilloscope. See Figure 24–34. Because of the speed of the engine and the number of slits in the optical sensor disk, a scope is about the only tool that could capture useful

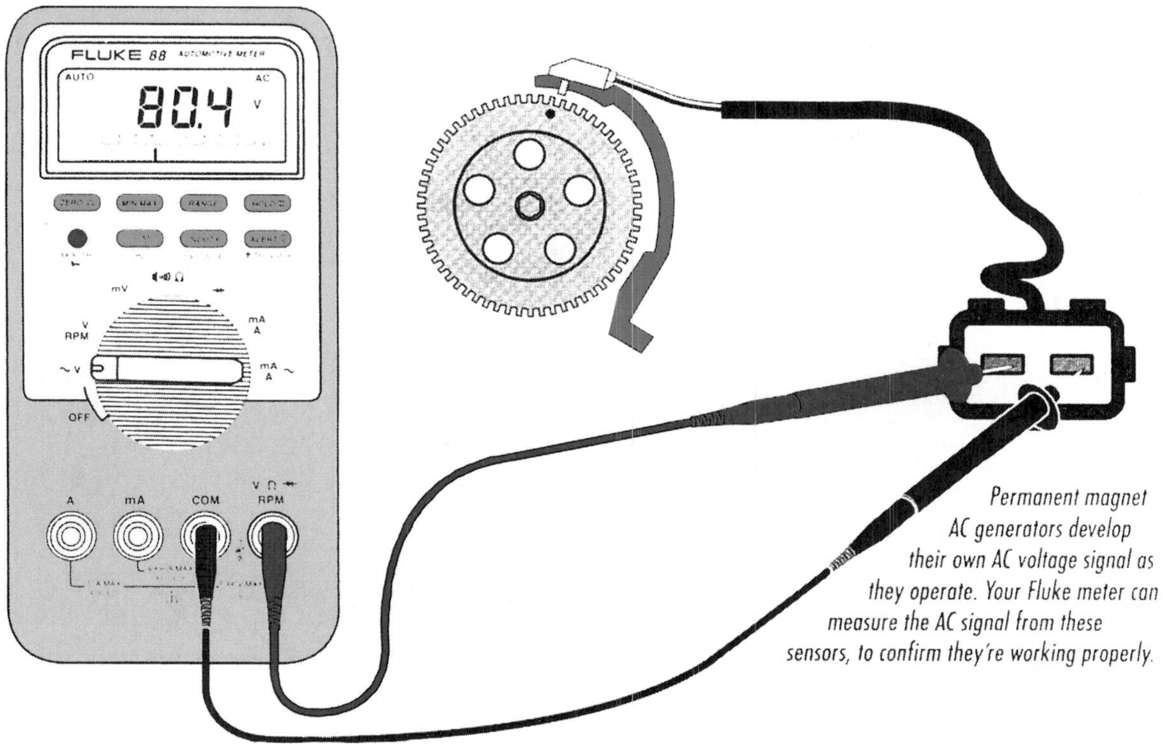

Figure 24–32 An AC voltage is produced by a magnetic sensor. Most sensors should produce at least 0.1 volt AC while the engine is cranking if the pickup wheel has many teeth. If the pickup wheel has only a few teeth, you may need to switch the meter to read DC volts and watch the display for a jump in voltage as the teeth pass the magnetic sensor. (Courtesy of Fluke Corporation)

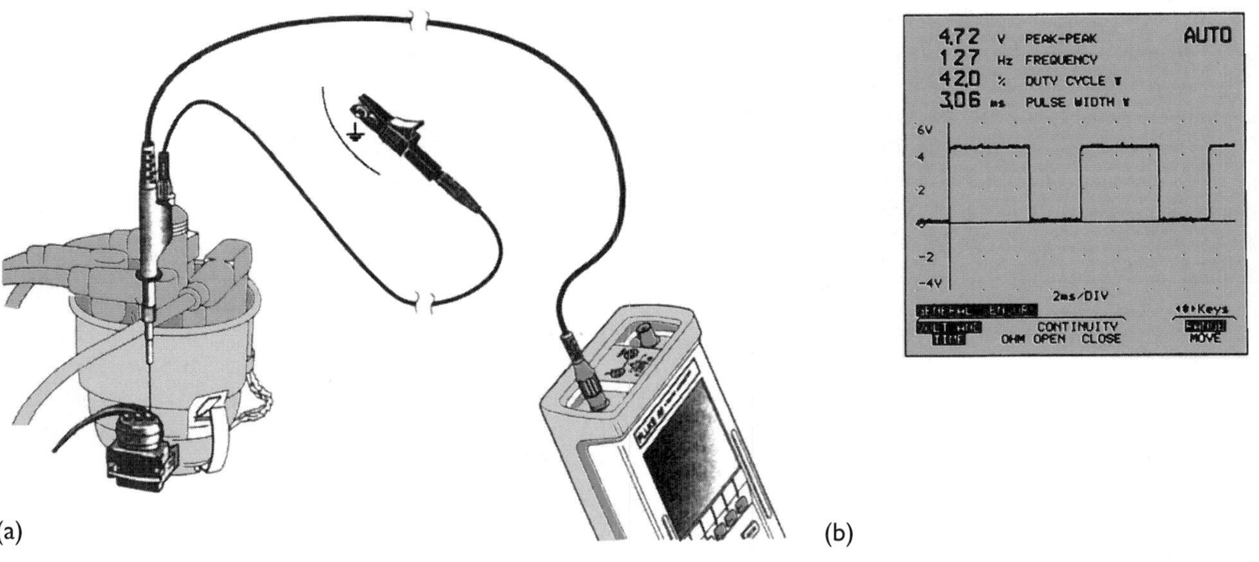

Figure 24–33 (a) The connection required to test a Hall-effect sensor. (b) A typical waveform from a Hall-effect sensor. (Courtesy of Fluke Corporation)

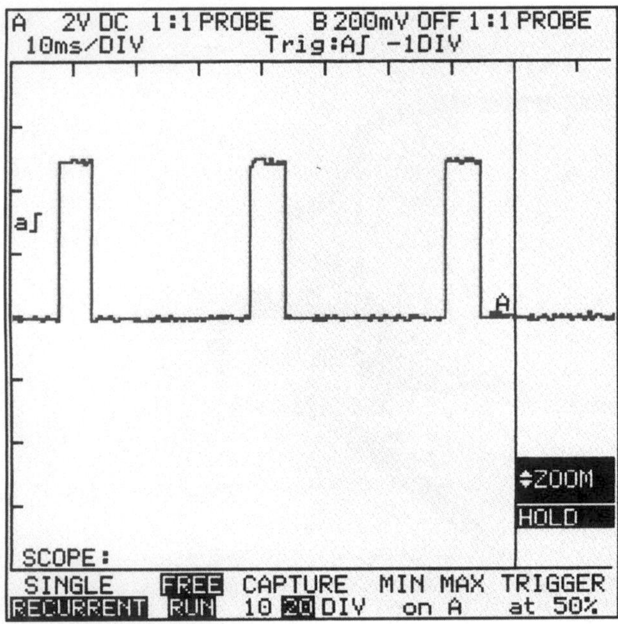

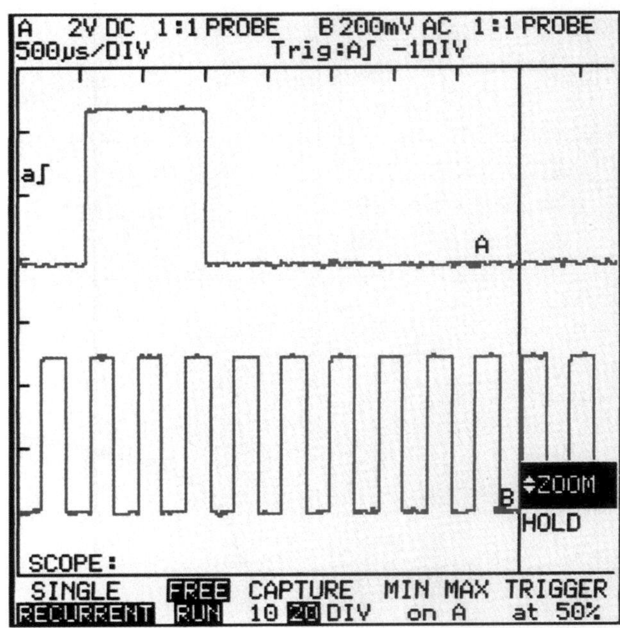

Figure 24–34 (a) The low-resolution signal has the same number of pulses as the engine has cylinders. (b) A dual trace pattern showing both the low-resolution signal and the high-resolution signals that usually represent 1 degree of rotation. (Courtesy of Fluke Corporation)

TECH TIP 

Bad Wire? Replace the Coil!

When performing engine testing (such as a compression test), always ground the coil wire. Never allow the coil to discharge without a path to ground for the spark. High-energy electronic ignition systems can produce 40 000 volts, or more, of electrical pressure. If the spark cannot spark to ground, the coil energy can (and usually does) arc inside the coil itself, creating a low-resistance path to the primary windings or the steel laminations of the coil. See Figure 24–35. This low-resistance path is called a **carbon track** and could cause an engine miss under load even though all of the remaining component parts of the ignition system are functioning correctly. Often these tracks do not show up on any coil test, including most scopes. Because the track is a lower-resistance path to ground than normal, it requires that the ignition system be put under a load for it to be detected, and even then, the problem (engine missing) may be intermittent.

Therefore, when disabling an ignition system, follow one of the following procedures to prevent possible ignition coil damage:

1. Remove the power source wire from the ignition system to prevent any ignition operation.
2. On distributor-equipped engines, remove the secondary coil wire from the centre of the distributor cap and connect a jumper wire between the disconnected coil wire and a good engine ground. (This ensures that the secondary coil energy will be safely grounded and prevents high-voltage coil damage.)

information. For example, a Nissan has 360 slits, and if it is running at 2000 rpm, a signal is generated 720 000 times per minute or 12 000 times per second.

IGNITION SYSTEM DIAGNOSIS USING VISUAL INSPECTION

One of the first steps in the diagnosis process is to perform a thorough visual inspection. A thorough visual inspection of the ignition system includes the following items:

- Check all spark plug wires for proper routing. All plug wires should be in the factory wiring separator and be clear of any metallic object that could cause damage to the insulation and cause a short-to-ground fault.
- Check that all spark plug wires are securely attached to the spark plugs and to the distributor cap or ignition coil(s).
- Check that all spark plug wires are clean and free from excessive dirt or oil. Check that all protective covers normally covering the coil and/or distributor cap are in place and not damaged.

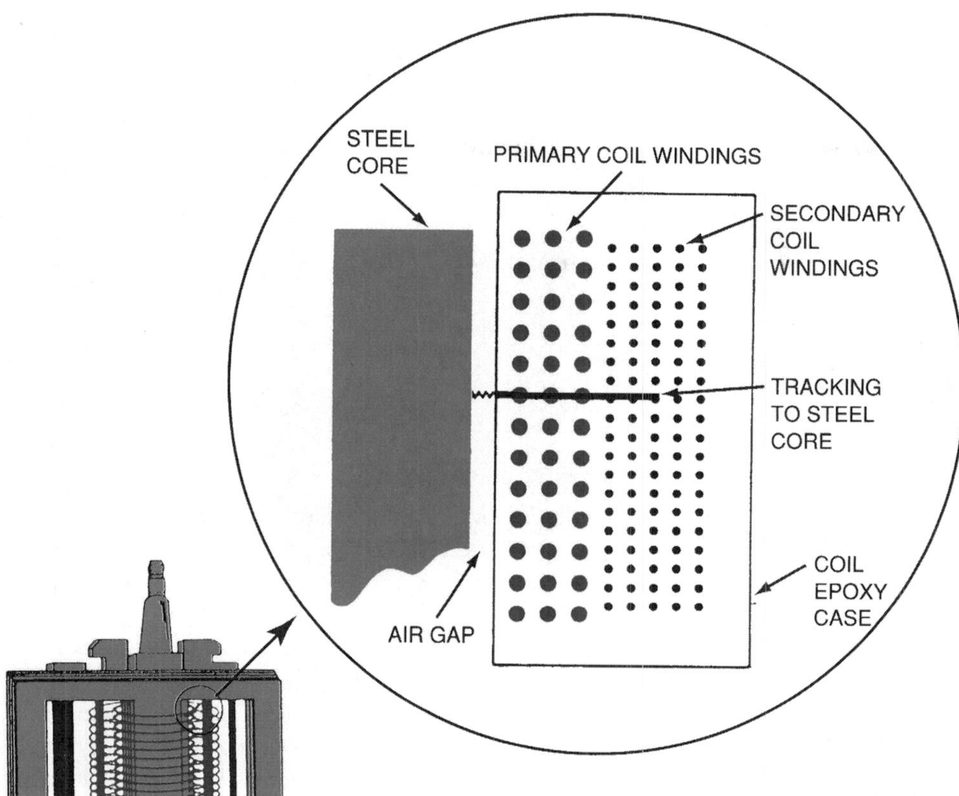

Figure 24–35 A track inside an ignition coil is not a short, but rather a low-resistance path or hole that has been burned through from the secondary wiring to the steel core.

- Remove the distributor cap and carefully check the cap and distributor rotor for faults.
- Remove the spark plugs and check for excessive wear or other visible faults. Replace if needed.

NOTE: According to research conducted by General Motors, about one-fifth (20%) of all faults are detected during a *thorough visual inspection!*

TESTING FOR POOR PERFORMANCE

Many diagnostic equipment manufacturers offer methods for testing distributorless ignition systems on an oscilloscope. When using this type of equipment, follow the manufacturers' recommended procedures and interpretation of their test results.

A simple method of testing distributorless (waste spark systems) ignition with the engine off involves removing the spark plug wires (or connectors) from the spark plugs (or coils or distributor cap) and installing short lengths 50 mm (2 in.) of rubber vacuum hose in series.

NOTE: For best results, use rubber hose that is electrically conductive. Measure the vacuum hose with an ohmmeter. Suitable vacuum hose should give a reading of less than 10 000 ohms (10 kΩ) for a length of about 50 mm (2 in.). See Figures 24–36 through 24–38.

1. Start the engine and ground out each cylinder one at a time by touching the tip of a grounded test light to the rubber vacuum hose. Even though the computer will increase idle speed and increase fuel delivery to compensate for the grounded spark plug wire, a technician should watch for a change in the operation of the engine. If no change is observed or heard, the cylinder being grounded is obviously weak or defective. Check the spark plug wire or connector with an ohmmeter to be certain of continuity.
2. Check every cylinder by grounding out the cylinders one at a time. If one weak cylinder is found, check the other cylinder using the same ignition coil (except on engines that use an individual coil for each cylinder). If both cylinders are affected, the problem could be an open spark plug wire, defective spark plug, or defective ignition coil.

Figure 24–36 A length of vacuum hose being used for a coil wire. The vacuum hose is conductive because of the carbon content of the rubber in the hose. This hose measures only 1000 ohms and is 300 mm (1 ft) long. (This is lower resistance than most spark plug wires.) Notice the spark from the hose's surface to the tip of a grounded screwdriver.

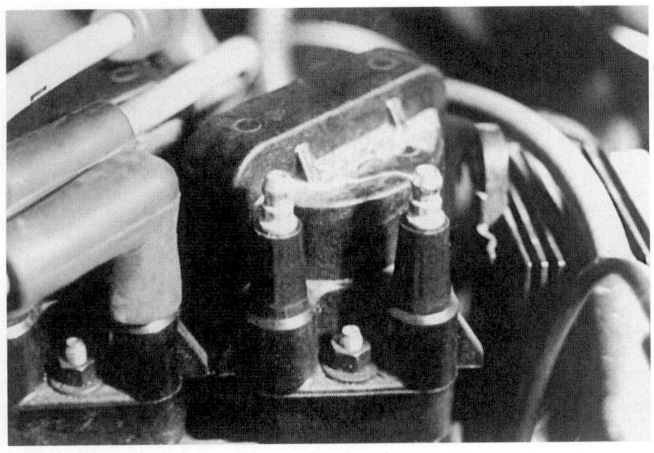

Figure 24–37 A distributorless ignition system (DIS) can be checked by unplugging *both* spark plug wires from one ignition coil and starting the engine. The spark should be able to jump the 25 mm (1 in.) distance between the terminals of the coil. No damage to the coil (or module) results because a spark occurs and does not find ground somewhere else.

3. To help eliminate other possible problems to determine exactly what is wrong, switch the suspected ignition coil to another position (if possible).
   - If the problem now affects the other cylinders, the ignition coil is defective and must be replaced.
   - If the problem does not change positions, the control module affecting the suspected coil or either cylinder's spark plug or spark plug wire could be defective.

Figure 24–38 Using a vacuum hose and a grounded test light to ground one cylinder at a time on a distributorless ignition system. This works on all types of ignition systems and provides a method for grounding out one cylinder at a time without fear of damaging any component.

TESTING FOR A NO-START CONDITION

A no-start condition (with normal engine cranking speed) can be the result of either no spark or no fuel delivery.

Computerized engine control systems use the ignition primary pulses as a signal to inject fuel (port or throttle-body injection [TBI] style of fuel-injection system). If there is no pulse, then there is no squirt of fuel. To determine exactly what is wrong, follow these steps:

1. Test the output signal from the crankshaft sensor. Most computerized engines with distributorless ignitions use a crankshaft position sensor. These sensors are either the Hall-effect type or the magnetic type. The sensors must be able to produce a variable (either sine or digital) signal. A meter set on AC volts should read a voltage across the sensor leads when the engine is being cranked. If there is no AC voltage output, replace the sensor.
2. If the sensor tests okay in step 1, check for a changing AC voltage signal at the ignition module.

> **NOTE:** Step 2 checks the wiring between the crankshaft position sensor and the ignition control module.

3. If the ignition control module is receiving a changing signal from the crankshaft position sensor, it must be capable of switching the power to the ignition coils on and off. Remove a coil or coil package, and with the ignition switched to on (run), check for voltage at the positive terminal of the coil(s).

> **NOTE:** Several manufacturers program the current to the coils to be turned off within several seconds of the ignition being switched to on if no pulse is received by the computer. This circuit design helps prevent ignition coil damage in the event of a failure in the control circuit or driver error, by keeping the ignition switch on (run) without operating the starter (start position). Some Chrysler engines do not supply power to the positive (+) side of the coil until a crank pulse is received by the computer.

If the module is not pulsing the negative side of the coil or not supplying battery voltage to the positive side of the coil, replace the ignition control module.

> **NOTE:** Before replacing the ignition control module, be certain that it is properly grounded (where applicable) and that the module is receiving ignition power from the ignition circuit.

> **CAUTION:** Most distributorless (waste spark) ignition systems can produce 40 000 volts or more, with energy levels high enough to cause personal injury. Do not open the circuit of an electronic ignition secondary wire, because damage to the system (or to you) can occur.

4. Late-model vehicles from 1998 (1996 U.S.) to date have enhanced diagnostics built into the PCM (on-board computer). This is a great help to the technician; data such as diagnostic trouble codes, primary circuit triggering, engine misfire and cylinder location of the misfire are retained in computer memory. A scan tool is used to access this information.

IGNITION SYSTEM SERVICE

At one time the term **tune-up** referred to the replacement of worn ignition parts, but now it is redefined as the diagnosis of engine performance and the replacement of parts found to be in need of replacement. Most tune-up specifications are now commonly called *performance specifications.* Even though many electronic engine analyzers can help pinpoint suspected problem areas, close visual inspection of the distributor cap, rotor, spark plugs, and spark plug wires is still important.

FIRING ORDER

Firing order means the order in which the spark is distributed to the correct spark plug at the right time. The firing order of an engine is determined by crankshaft and camshaft design. The firing order is determined by the location of the spark plug wires in the distributor cap of an engine equipped with a distributor. The firing order is often cast into the intake manifold for easy reference, as shown in Figure 24–39. Most service manuals also show the firing order and the direction of the distributor rotor rotation as well as the location of the spark plug wires on the distributor cap.

> **CAUTION:** Older Ford V-8s use two different firing orders depending on whether the engine is high output (HO) or standard. Using the incorrect firing order can cause the engine to backfire and could cause engine damage or personal injury. General Motors V-6s use different firing orders and different locations for the #1 cylinder between the 60-degree V-6 and the 90-degree V-6. Using the incorrect firing order or cylinder number location chart could result in very poor engine operation if in fact it will start at all.

Firing order is also important for waste spark-type distributorless (direct fire) ignition systems. The spark plug wire can often be installed on the wrong coil pack; that can create a no-start condition or very poor engine operation.

Figure 24–39 The firing order is cast or stamped on the intake manifold on many engines that have a distributor ignition.

DISTRIBUTOR CAP AND ROTOR INSPECTION

Inspect a distributor cap for a worn or cracked centre carbon insert, excessive side insert wear or corrosion, cracks, or carbon tracks, and check the towers for burning or corrosion by removing spark plug wires from the distributor cap one at a time. Remember, a defective distributor cap affects starting and engine performance, especially in high-moisture conditions. If a carbon track is detected, it is most likely the result of a high-resistance or open spark plug wire. Replacement of a distributor cap because of a carbon track without checking and replacing the defective spark plug wire(s) will often result in the new distributor cap failing in a short time. It is recommended that the distributor cap and rotor be inspected every year and replaced if defective. The rotor should be replaced every time the spark plugs are replaced because all ignition current flows through the rotor. Generally, distributor caps should only need replacement after every 3 or 4 years of normal service. See Figures 24–40 through 24–43.

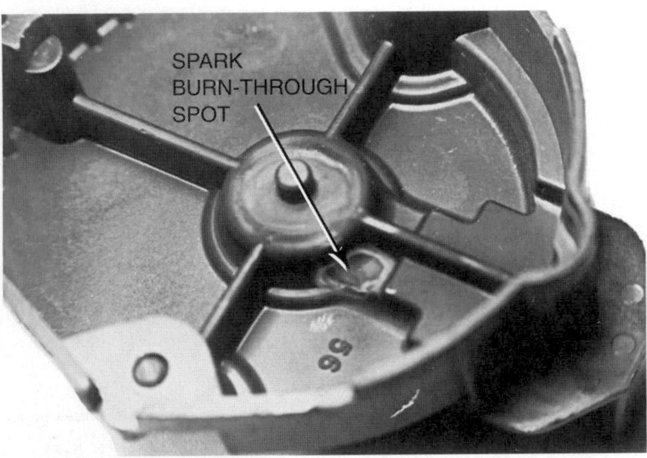

Figure 24–40 You can see where the high-voltage spark jumped through the plastic rotor to arc into the distributor shaft. Always check for a defective spark plug(s) whenever a defective distributor cap or rotor is discovered. If a spark cannot jump to a spark plug, it tries to find a ground path wherever it can.

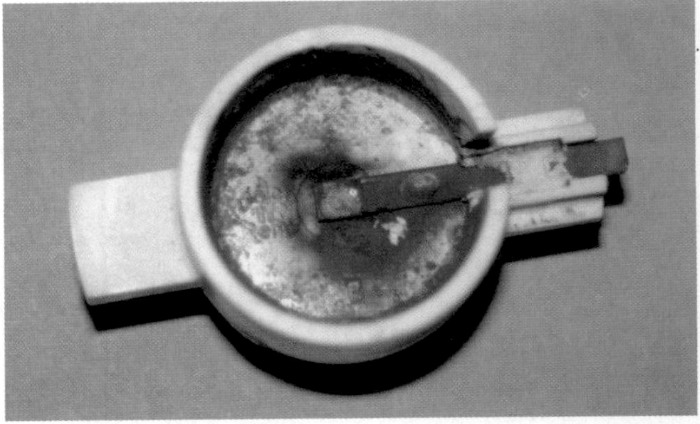

Figure 24–42 This rotor had arced through to the distributor shaft. The engine would not run above an idle speed, and the spark from the coil could easily fire a spark tester.

Figure 24–41 This distributor cap should be replaced because of the worn inserts and excessive dusting inside the cap.

Figure 24–43 Carbon track in a distributor cap. These faults are sometimes difficult to spot and can cause intermittent engine missing. The usual cause of a tracked distributor cap (or coil, if it is a distributorless ignition) is a defective (open) spark plug wire.

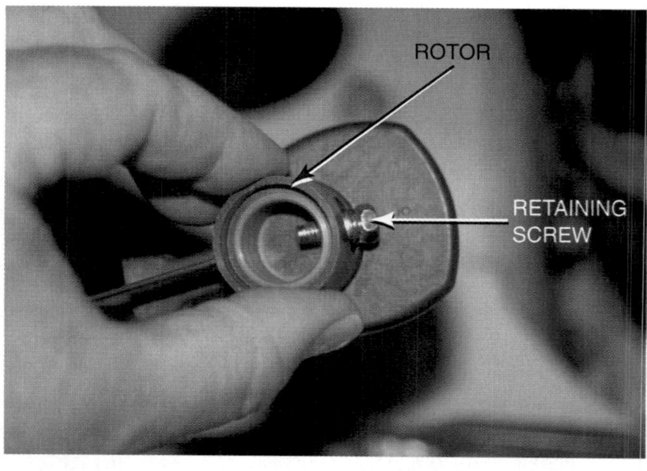

Figure 24–44 Some rotors are retained by a screw—look before you pry.

TECH TIP 

Look Before You Pry

Some distributor rotors are secured to the distributor shaft with a retaining screw, as shown in Figure 24–44. Serious damage can occur if excessive force is used to remove the rotor.

When replacing the distributor cap or spark plug wires, swap the wires one at a time to avoid mixing them.

SPARK PLUG WIRE INSPECTION

Spark plug wires should be visually inspected for cuts or defective insulation and checked for resistance with an ohmmeter. Good spark plug wires should measure less than 10 000 ohms per 300 mm (1 ft) of length. See Figures 24–45 and 24–46. Faulty spark plug wire insulation can cause hard starting or no starting in damp weather conditions.

TECH TIP 

Spark Plug Wire Pliers Are a Good Investment

Spark plug wires are often difficult to remove. Using good-quality spark plug wire pliers, such as shown in Figure 24–47, saves a lot of time and reduces the chance of doing harm to the wire during removal.

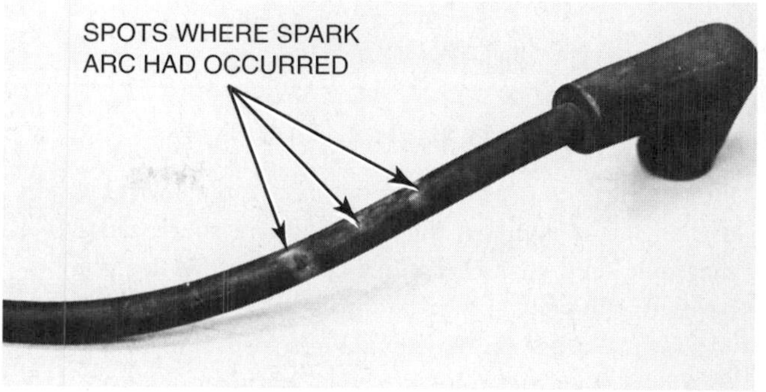

Figure 24–45 Careful visual inspection discovered this defective spark plug wire.

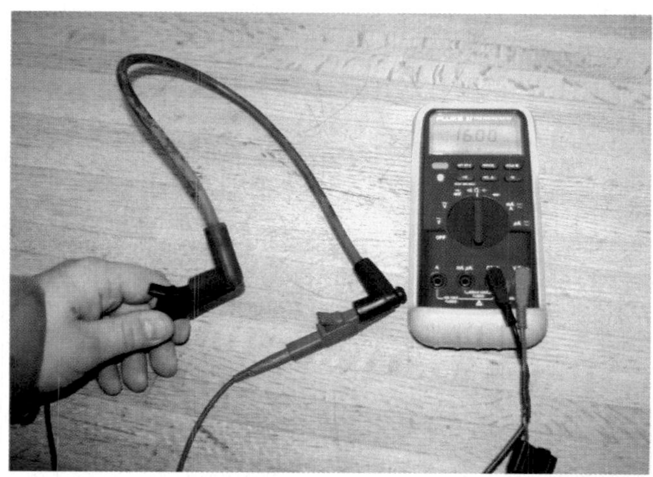

Figure 24–46 Measuring the resistance of a spark plug wire with a multimeter set to the ohms position. The reading of 16.03 kΩ (16 030 ohms) is okay because the wire is about 600 mm (2 ft) long. Maximum allowable resistance for a spark plug wire this long would be 20 kΩ (20 000 ohms). Always bend the wire gently while testing the resistance.

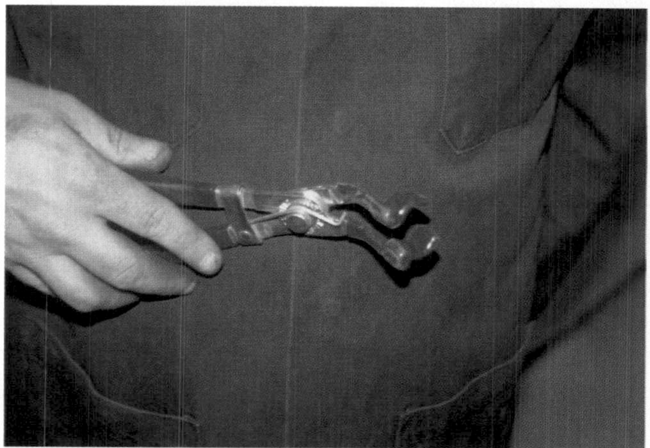

Figure 24–47 Spark plug wire boot pliers are a handy addition to any tool box.

TECH TIP 

Route the Wires Right!

High voltage is present through spark plug wires when the engine is running. Surrounding the spark plugs is a magnetic field that can affect other circuits or components of the vehicle. For example, if a spark plug wire is routed too close to the signal wire from a mass air flow (MAF) sensor, the induced signal from the ignition wire could create a false MAF signal to the computer. The computer, not knowing the signal was false, would act on the MAF signal and command the appropriate amount of fuel based on the false MAF signal.

Piston and piston ring damage may occur on some V-8 engines if the spark plug wires of certain cylinders are incorrectly positioned next to one another. The magnetic field around the firing cylinder wire crosses over the adjoining wire to induce voltage and crossfire.

To prevent any problems associated with high voltage spark plug wires, always be sure to route them the same way they were from the factory, using all the factory holding brackets and wiring combs. See Figure 24–48. Most factory service manuals show the correct routing if the factory method is unknown.

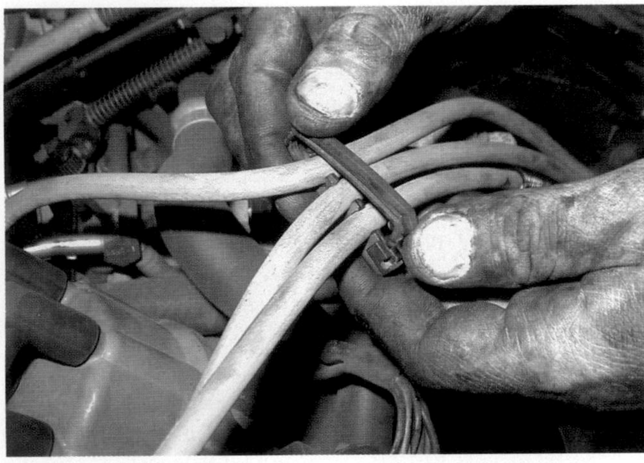

Figure 24–48 Always take the time to install spark plug wires back into the original holding brackets (wiring combs).

SPARK PLUG SERVICE

Spark plugs should be inspected when an engine performance problem occurs and should be replaced regularly to ensure proper ignition system performance. Many spark plugs have a service life of over 32 000 km (20 000 mi). Iridium and platinum-tipped original equipment spark plugs have a typical service life of 100 000 to 180 000 km (60 000 to 112 000 mi). Used spark plugs should *not* be cleaned and reused unless absolutely necessary. The labour required to remove and replace (R & R) spark plugs is the same whether the spark plugs are replaced or cleaned. Although cleaning spark plugs often restores proper engine operation, the service life of cleaned spark plugs is definitely shorter than that of new spark plugs. *Platinum-tipped spark plugs should not be regapped!* Using a gapping tool can break the platinum after it has been used in an engine.

The spark plug gap should be checked on all new plugs before they are installed. Some manufacturers recommend that only a tapered (ramp-style) spark plug gauge should be used to measure gap on platinum plugs. Wire-type gauges may damage the electrode.

Be certain that the engine is cool before removing spark plugs, especially on engines with aluminum cylinder heads. To help prevent dirt from getting into the cylinder of an engine while removing a spark plug, use compressed air or a brush to remove dirt from around the spark plug before removal. See Figures 24–49 and 24–50.

TECH TIP 

A Clean Engine Is a Happy Engine

Many technicians clean every engine before a tune-up or other engine service. Steam cleaners can be used, but steam tends to remove paint from the engine. A hot water wash, often found at coin-operated washes, does an excellent job of removing grease, oil, and dirt not only from the engine, but also from all underhood components, including the battery. Some technicians keep the engine running while cleaning it with hot water. If the engine stalls, yet restarts after drying of the spark plug wires and distributor cap, faulty spark plug wire insulation and/or a faulty distributor cap is indicated.

CAUTION: Avoid direct water spray to the air cleaner inlet and generator. Because water is thrown up on the engine components during normal driving on wet streets, no harm occurs from washing of these parts as long as direct water sprays are avoided. Some diesel engine manufacturers do not recommend engine cleaning, due to the close tolerances of the parts commonly found in the injection pump.

Beware of high pressure cleaning around both gasoline and diesel electronic engine components.

A clean engine will run cooler and is much easier to service. Oil leaks can also be easier to locate on a clean engine. Most customers are impressed to find a clean engine compartment—it is one of the few tune-up items that is visible to the average owner.

Figure 24–49 Whenever removing spark plugs, it is wise to arrange them so that they can be compared and any problem can be identified with a particular cylinder.

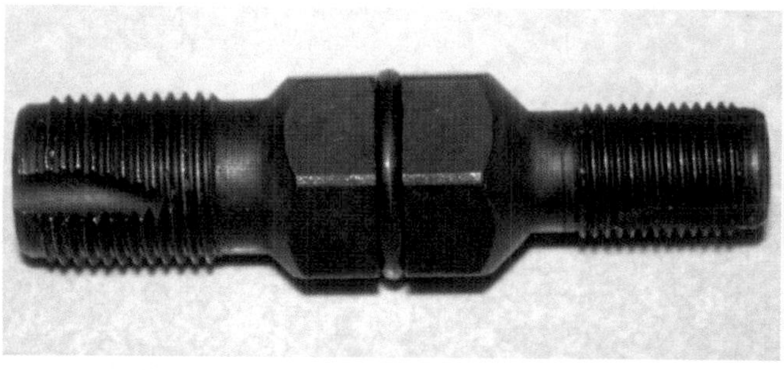

Figure 24–50 A spark plug thread chaser is one of those low cost tools that hopefully will not be used often, but is necessary to use to clean the threads before new spark plugs are installed. Lubricate the chaser threads with chassis grease before starting it in the head. Any material cleaned from the plug threads will stick to the grease instead of falling into the engine.

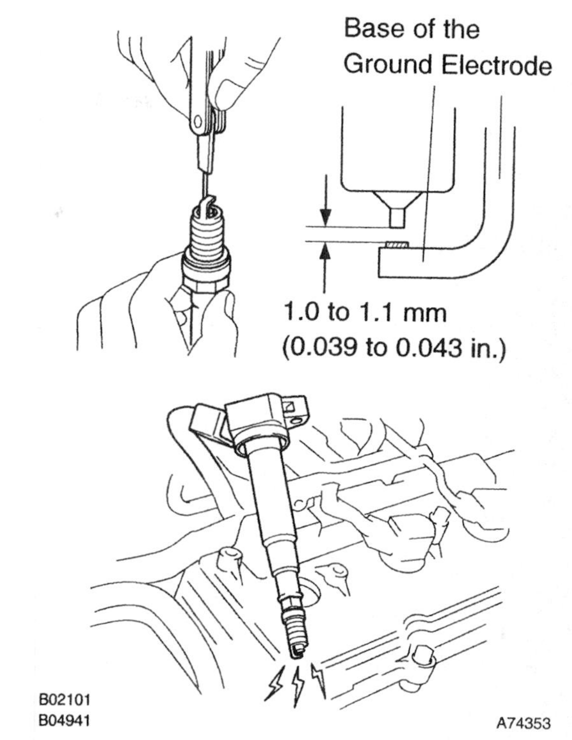

Figure 24–51 Checking the electrode spacing on a new iridium COP spark plug. (Courtesy Toyota Motor Co.)

Coil-on-plug ignitions mount the coil and extension on top of the spark plug. The coil is usually outside of the cam cover (for cooling) and the plug and seal are inside the cover. Use air to clean around the seal before removing the coil from the plug. Figure 24–51 shows a new iridium plug being regapped.

Spark Plug Inspection

Spark plugs are the windows to the inside of the combustion chamber. A thorough visual inspection of the spark plugs can often lead to the root cause of an engine performance problem. Two indications and their possible root causes include the following:

1. Carbon fouling. If the spark plug(s) has *dry black carbon* (soot), the usual causes include:
   - Excessive idling
   - Slow-speed driving under light loads that keeps the spark plug temperatures too low to burn off the deposits
   - Over rich air–fuel mixture
   - Weak ignition system output
2. Oil fouling. If the spark plug has *wet, oily* deposits with little electrode wear, oil may be getting into the combustion chamber from:
   - Worn or broken piston rings
   - Defective or missing valve stem seals

When removing spark plugs, place them in order so that they can be inspected to check for engine problems that might affect one or more cylinders. All the spark plugs should be in the same condition, and the colour of the centre insulator should be light tan or gray. If all the spark plugs are black or dark, the engine should be checked for conditions that could cause an overly rich air–fuel mixture or possible oil burning. If only one or a few spark plugs are black, check those cylinders for proper firing (possible defective spark plug wire) or an engine condition affecting only those particular cylinders. See Figures 24–52 through 24–55.

If all the spark plugs are white, check for possible overadvanced ignition timing or a vacuum leak causing a lean air–fuel mixture. If only one or a few spark plugs are white, check for a vacuum leak affecting the fuel mixture only to those particular cylinders.

Figure 24–52 An extended reach spark plug that shows normal wear. The colour and condition indicate that the cylinder is operating correctly.

Figure 24–53 Spark plug removed from an engine after a 800 km (500 mi) race. Note the clipped side (ground) electrode. The electrode design and narrow 0.625 mm (0.025 in.) gap are used to ensure that a spark occurs during extremely high engine speed operation. The colour and condition of the spark plug indicate that near-perfect combustion has been occurring.

Figure 24–54 Typical worn spark plug. Notice the rounded centre electrode. The deposits indicate that there may be an oil usage problem.

Figure 24–55 New spark plug that was fouled by a too-rich air–fuel mixture. The engine from which this spark plug came had a defective (stuck partially open) injector on this one cylinder only.

NOTE: The engine computer "senses" rich or lean air–fuel ratios by means of input from the oxygen sensor. If one cylinder is lean, the computer may make all other cylinders richer to compensate.

TECH TIP

Two-Finger Trick

To help prevent overtightening a spark plug when a torque wrench is not available, simply use two fingers on a 3/8 in. drive ratchet handle.

Inspect all spark plugs for wear by first checking the condition of the centre electrode. As a spark plug wears, the centre electrode becomes rounded. If the centre electrode is rounded, higher ignition system voltage is required to fire the spark plug. When installing spark plugs, always use the correct tightening torque to ensure proper heat transfer from the spark plug shell to the cylinder head.

NOTE: Extended life spark plugs (platinum and iridium) may remain in the cylinder head(s) up to 180 000 km (112 000 mi). In many cases, steel spark plugs seize in the aluminum head and the head is damaged when the plugs are removed. It is industry practice (in the field) to apply a very thin coat of anti-seize compound to the spark plug threads before installation to reduce seizing.

Do not touch the insulator with your fingers if you have touched the anti-seize compound; the compound is a conductor and can short the plugs. Beware of over-tightening the plug, as the compound reduces thread friction.

QUICK AND EASY SECONDARY IGNITION TESTS

Most engine running problems are caused by defective or out-of-adjustment ignition components. Many ignition problems involve the high-voltage secondary ignition circuit. Following are some quick and easy secondary ignition tests.

Test 1. If there is a crack in a distributor cap, coil, or spark plug, or a defective spark plug wire, a spark may be visible at night. Because high voltage is required during partial throttle acceleration, the technician's assistant should accelerate the engine slightly with the gear selector in "drive" or second gear (if manual transmission) and the brake firmly applied. If any spark is visible, the location should be closely inspected and the defective parts replaced. A blue glow or "corona" around the shell of the spark plug is normal and not an indication of a defective spark plug.

Test 2. For intermittent problems, use a spray bottle to apply a water mist to the spark plugs, distributor cap, and spark plug wires. See Figure 24–56. With the engine running, the water may cause an arc through any weak insulating materials and cause the engine to miss or stall.

TECH TIP

Use Original Equipment Manufacturer Spark Plugs

Original brand (original equipment manufacturer [OEM]) spark plugs should be installed in any vehicle experiencing plug heat-range problems with non-OEM plugs. The usual timing, fuel mixture, and EGR operation should be checked first. Even though the heat range of the replacement plug was close, the OEM plug is exact for that engine.

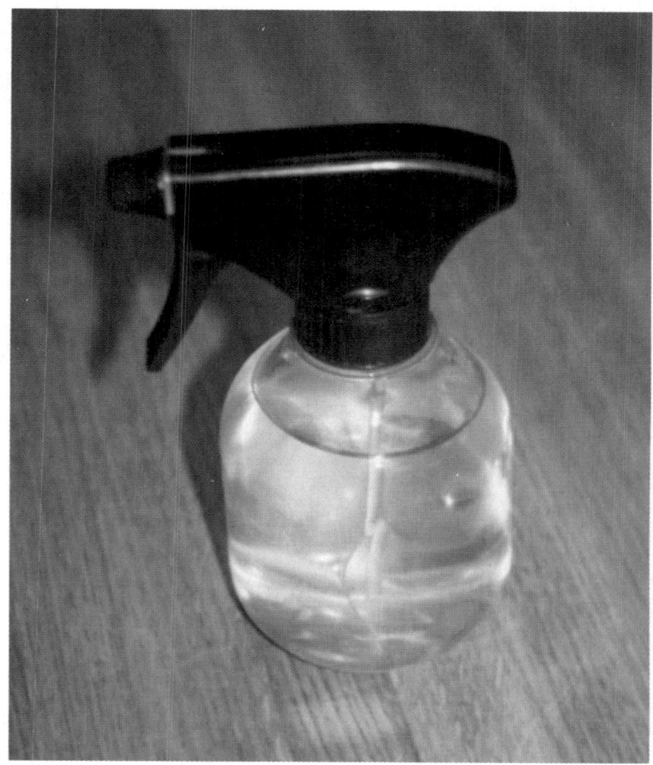

Figure 24–56 A water spray bottle is an excellent diagnostic tool to help find an intermittent engine miss caused by a break in a secondary ignition circuit component.

HINT: Adding a little liquid soap to the water makes the water more conductive, and also makes it easier to find those hard-to-diagnose intermittent ignition faults.

Test 3. To determine if the rough engine operation is due to secondary ignition problems, connect a 6 to

12 volt test light to the negative side (sometimes labeled "tach") of the coil. Connect the other lead of the test light to the positive lead of the coil. With the engine running, the test light should be dim and steady in brightness. If there is high resistance in the secondary circuit (such as that caused by a defective spark plug wire), the test light will pulse brightly at times. If the test light varies noticeably, this indicates that the secondary voltage cannot find ground easily and is feeding back through the primary windings of the coil. This feedback causes the test light to become brighter.

IGNITION TIMING

Ignition timing should be checked and adjusted according to the manufacturer's specifications and procedures for best fuel economy and performance, and lowest exhaust emissions. Generally, for testing, engines must be at idle with computer engine controls put into base timing. **Base timing** is the timing of the spark before the computer advances the timing. To be assured of the proper ignition timing, follow exactly the timing procedure indicated on the underhood emission decal. See Figure 24–57 for a typical ignition timing plate and timing mark.

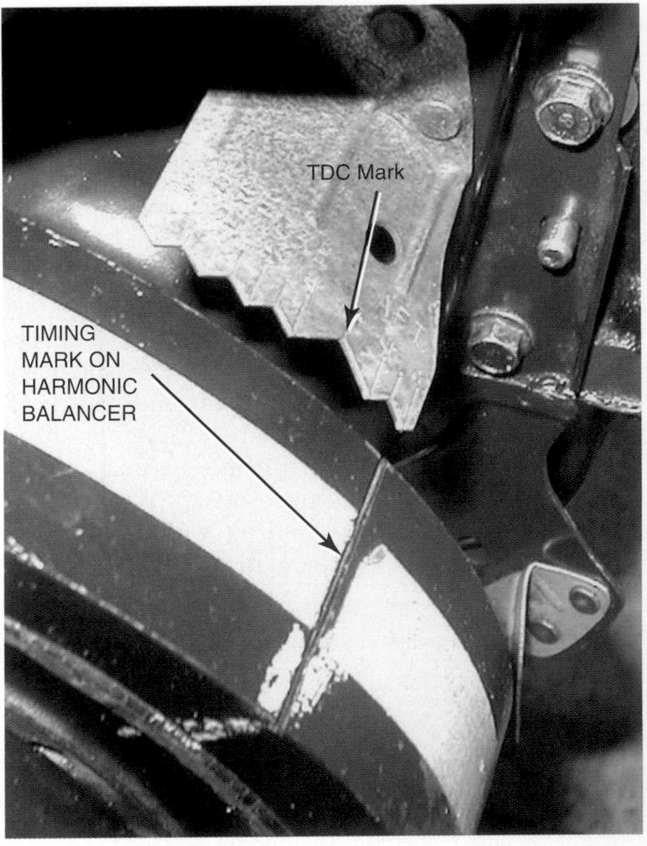

Figure 24–57 Typical timing marks. The numbers of the degrees are on the stationary plate and the notch is on the harmonic balancer. Touch up the two timing marks with a white felt pen; the marks will be easier to read with the timing light.

> **NOTE:** Most older engines equipped with a vacuum advance must have the vacuum hose removed and plugged before the timing is checked.

If the ignition timing is too far *advanced,* for example, if advanced ignition timing is set at 12 degrees before top dead centre (BTDC) instead of 8 degrees BTDC, the following symptoms may occur:

1. Engine ping or spark knock may be heard, especially while driving up a hill or during acceleration.
2. Cranking (starting) may be slow and jerky, especially when the engine is warm.
3. The engine may overheat if the ignition timing is too far advanced.

If the ignition timing is too far *retarded,* for example, if retarded ignition timing is timing set at 4 degrees BTDC instead of 8 degrees BTDC, the following symptoms may occur:

1. The engine may lack in power and performance.
2. The engine may require a long period of starter cranking before starting.
3. Poor fuel economy may result from retarded ignition timing.
4. The engine may overheat if the ignition timing is too far retarded.
5. The exhaust valves may burn. Retarded timing raises exhaust temperatures.

Pretiming Checks

Before the ignition timing is checked or adjusted, the following items should be checked to ensure accurate timing results:

1. The engine should be at normal operating temperature (the upper radiator hose should be hot and pressurized).
2. The engine should be at the correct timing RPM (check the specifications).
3. The vacuum hoses should be removed, and the hose from the vacuum advance unit on the distributor (if the vehicle is so equipped) should be plugged unless otherwise specified.
4. Computer-controlled engines trim the engine idle speed by constantly varying ignition timing; this

TECH TIP 

"Turn the Key" Test

If the ignition timing is correct, a warm engine should start immediately when the ignition key is turned to the start position. If the engine cranks for a long time before starting, the ignition timing may be retarded. If the engine cranks slowly or "kicks back", the ignition timing may be too far advanced. However, if the engine starts immediately, the ignition timing, although it may not be exactly set according to specification, is usually adjusted fairly close to specifications. When a starting problem is experienced, check the ignition timing first, before checking the fuel system or the cranking system for a possible problem. This procedure can be used to help diagnose a possible ignition timing problem quickly without tools or equipment.

obviously makes timing adjustments impossible. Each manufacturer has a different method of setting base timing; procedures may require disconnecting a "set timing" wire, grounding a diagnostic terminal, disconnecting a given connector, or commanding the computer to go into a backup or base timing mode. Always check the service manual for the correct procedure.

Many late-model DIS and COP ignitions have fixed crankshaft sensors; base timing adjustments are not required.

NOTE: General Motors specifies ten different pretiming procedures depending on the engine, type of fuel system, and type of ignition system. For example, many 4-cylinder engines use the *average* of the timing for cylinder #1 and cylinder #4! Always consult the emission decal under the hood or the shop manual for the exact procedure to follow.

Timing Light Connections

For checking or adjusting ignition timing, make the timing light connections as follows:

1. Connect the timing light battery leads to the vehicle battery: the red to the positive terminal and the black to the negative terminal.
2. Connect the timing light high-tension lead to the #1 spark plug cable.

Determining the #1 Cylinder

The following will help in determining the #1 cylinder:

1. *Four- or six-cylinder engines.* On all inline 4- and 6-cylinder engines, the #1 cylinder is the *most forward* cylinder.
2. *V-6 or V-8 engines.* Most V-type engines use the left front (driver's side) cylinder as the #1 cylinder, except for Ford engines and some Cadillacs, which use the right front (passenger's side) cylinder.
3. *Sideways (transverse) engines.* Most front-wheel drive vehicles with engines installed sideways use the cylinder to the far right (passenger's side) as the #1 cylinder (plug wire closest to the drive belt[s]).

Follow this rule of thumb: If the #1 cylinder is unknown for a given type of engine, it is the *most forward* cylinder as viewed from above (except in Pontiac V-8 engines). See Figure 24–58 for typical #1 cylinder locations.

NOTE: There are some engines that are not timed off the #1 cylinder. For example, Jaguar inline 6-cylinder engines before 1988 used cylinder #6, but the cylinders were numbered from the firewall (bulkhead) forward. Therefore, the #6 cylinder was the most forward cylinder. International Harvester (Navistar) V-8s usually time off the #8 cylinder. Always check for the specifications and procedures for the vehicle being tested.

HINT: If the #1 cylinder is difficult to reach, such as up against the bulkhead (firewall) or close to an exhaust manifold, simply use the opposite cylinder in the firing order (paired cylinder). The timing light will not know the difference and will indicate the correct position of the timing mark in relation to the pointer or degree mark.

Checking or Adjusting Ignition Timing

Follow these steps for checking or adjusting ignition timing:

1. Start the engine and adjust the speed to that specified for ignition timing.
2. With the timing light aimed at the stationary timing pointer, observe the position of the timing mark with the light flashing. Refer to the manufacturer's specifications on underhood decal for the correct setting. See Figure 24–59.

NOTE: If the timing mark appears ahead of the pointer, in relation to the direction of crankshaft rotation, the timing is advanced. If the timing mark appears after the pointer, in relation to the direction of crankshaft rotation, the timing is retarded.

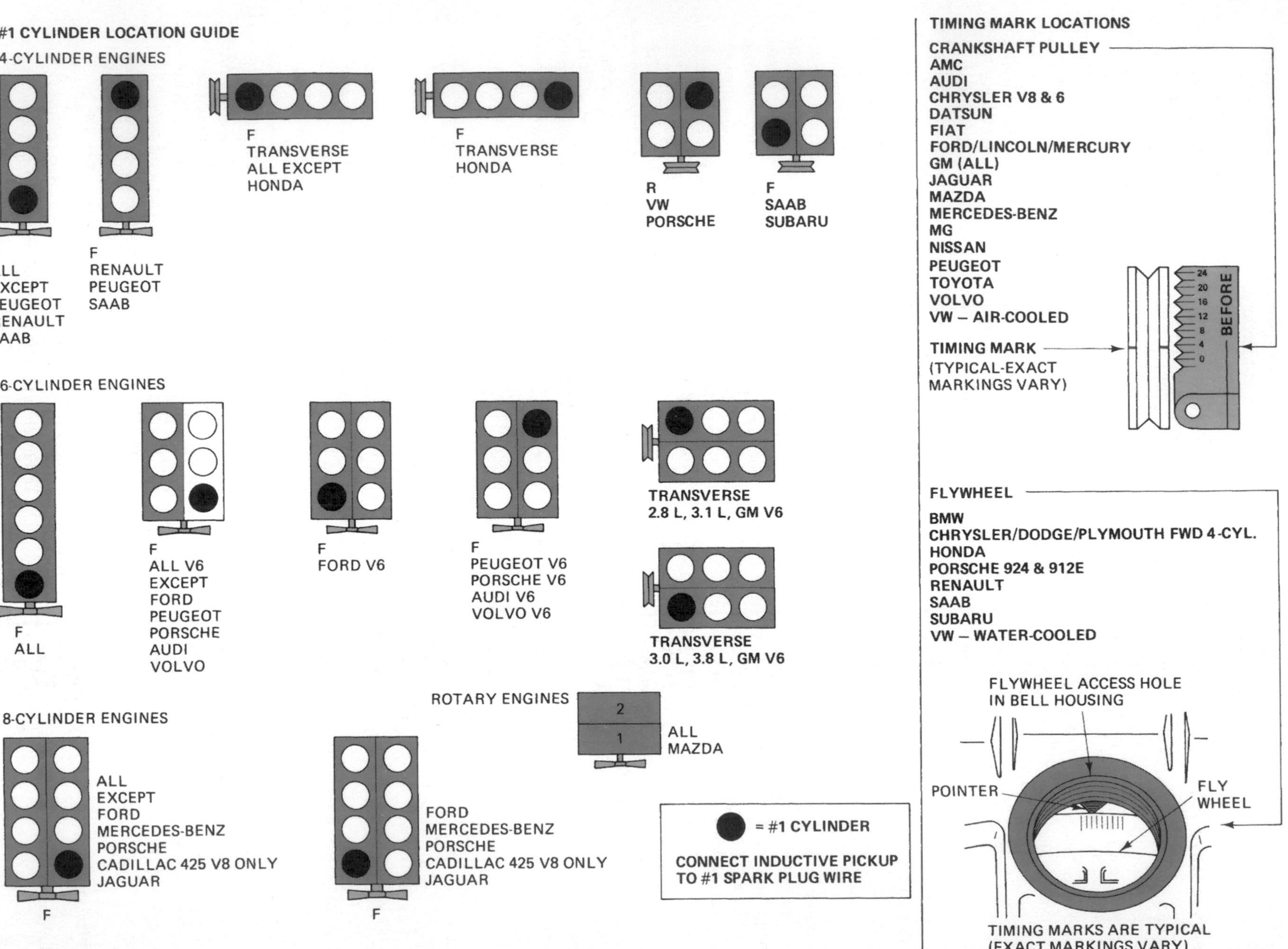

Figure 24–58 #1 cylinder and timing mark location guide.

(a)

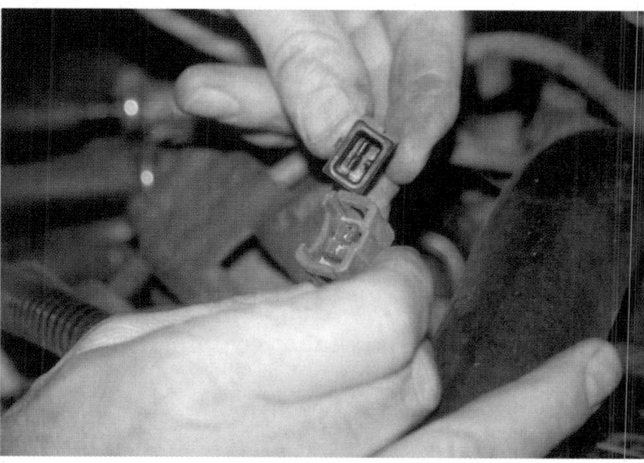

(b)

Figure 24–59 (a) Typical SPOUT (spark-output) connector as used on many Ford engines equipped with distributor ignition (DI). (b) The connector must be opened (disconnected) to check and/or adjust the ignition timing. On DIS/EDIS systems, the connector is called SPOUT/SAW (spark output/spark angle word).

TECH TIP

Two Marks Are the Key to Success

Whenever a distributor is removed from an engine, always mark the direction the rotor is pointing to be assured that the distributor is reinstalled in the correct position. Because of the helical cut on the distributor drive gear, the rotor rotates as the distributor is being removed from the engine. To help reinstall a distributor without any problems, simply make another mark where the rotor is pointing just as the distributor is lifted out of the engine. Then to reinstall, simply line up the rotor to the second mark and lower the distributor into the engine. The rotor should then line up with the original mark as a double check. See Figure 24–60.

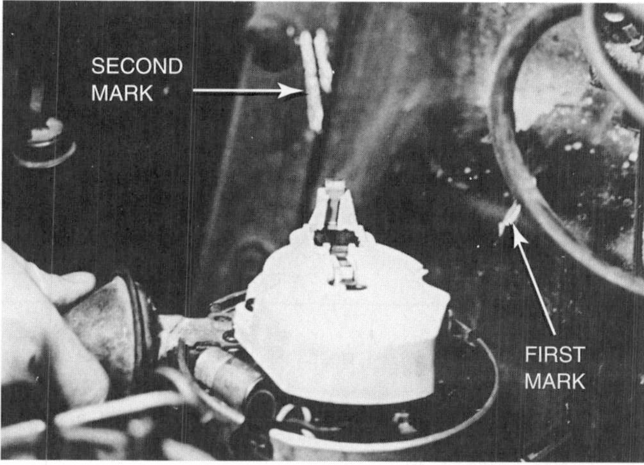

Figure 24–60 The first mark indicates the direction the rotor is pointing when the distributor is in the engine. The second mark indicates where the rotor is pointing just as it is pulled from the engine.

3. To adjust timing, loosen the distributor locking bolt or nut and turn the distributor housing until the timing mark is in correct alignment. Turn the distributor housing in the direction of rotor rotation to retard the timing and against rotor rotation to advance the timing.
4. After adjusting the timing to specifications, carefully tighten the distributor locking bolt. It is sometimes necessary to readjust the timing after the initial setting because the distributor may rotate slightly when the hold-down bolt is tightened.

AUTOMOTIVE OSCILLOSCOPES

An automotive scope is simply a voltmeter that displays ignition system voltages on a cathode ray tube (CRT) screen, much the same as a television picture tube. This voltage display is known as a waveform, a pattern, or a trace.

The vertical scale on the screen reads in kilovolts (kV) and the horizontal scale reads either in time (milliseconds), or degrees of distributor rotation. "Percent of dwell" is used instead of "degrees of dwell" on some models.

Voltage changes in the ignition system are indicated by the movement of a line (or lines) on the screen. See Figure 24–61.

Scope-Testing the Ignition System

Although both primary and secondary patterns are selected with contact-point ignition, only secondary

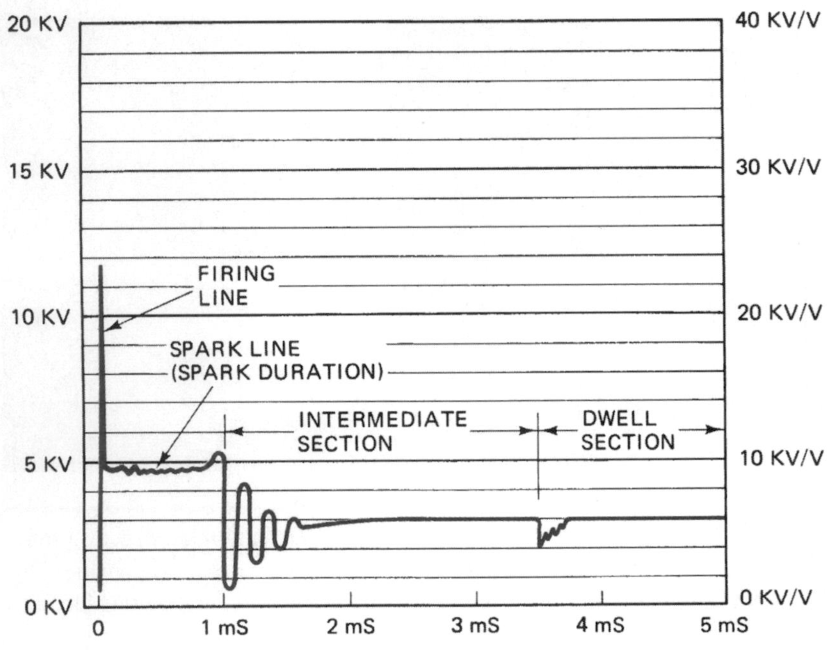

Figure 24–61 Typical secondary ignition oscilloscope pattern.

patterns are generally used to diagnose electronic ignition. A primary pattern provides an excellent window into contact-point and condenser condition; however, it is of less value with a transistor controlled primary circuit. The secondary circuit only will be used in our examples.

Oscilloscope Connections (Hookups)

The connector colours may differ between brands, however the basic hookup will be similar. See Figure 24–62.

1. Secondary pickup—measures voltage changes in the secondary circuit. This is an inductive pickup that may require an adaptor to match the type of coil. See Figure 24–63.
2. Number 1 spark plug—identifies the cylinder; once #1 is noted, the scope follows the firing order to determine cylinder location on the trace.
3. Primary pickup—measures voltages in the primary circuit; may also be used for engine RPM.
4. Ground lead—used to complete ground for scope connections; may also be used to ground the primary current of any cylinder the scope is instructed to "kill."

Firing Line

The leftmost vertical (upward) line is called the **firing** line. See Figure 24–64. The height of the firing line indicates voltage required to fire the spark plug. This voltage will change depending on the resistances in the secondary circuit, cylinder compression and air/fuel mixtures in the engine. See Figure 24–65. Firing line voltages should be between 7000 and 18 000 volts (7 kV and 18 kV) with no more than a 3 kV difference between the highest and lowest cylinders.

A higher than normal firing line height, or a height greater than that of the other cylinders, may be caused by one or more of the following:

1. Spark plug gap too wide.
2. A lean fuel mixture (vacuum leak or clogged fuel injector); it takes higher voltage to fire a lean mixture, as the molecules of fuel at the plug gap are farther apart.
3. An open or high resistance spark plug wire.

If the firing lines are higher than normal for *all* cylinders, then possible causes include one or more of the following:

1. A worn distributor cap and/or rotor (if the vehicle is so equipped)
2. Excessive wearing of all spark plugs
3. A defective coil wire (the high voltage could still jump across the open section of the wire to fire the spark plugs)
4. A lean mixture to all cylinders

Spark Line

The **spark line** is a short horizontal line connected to the firing line. The height of the spark line represents

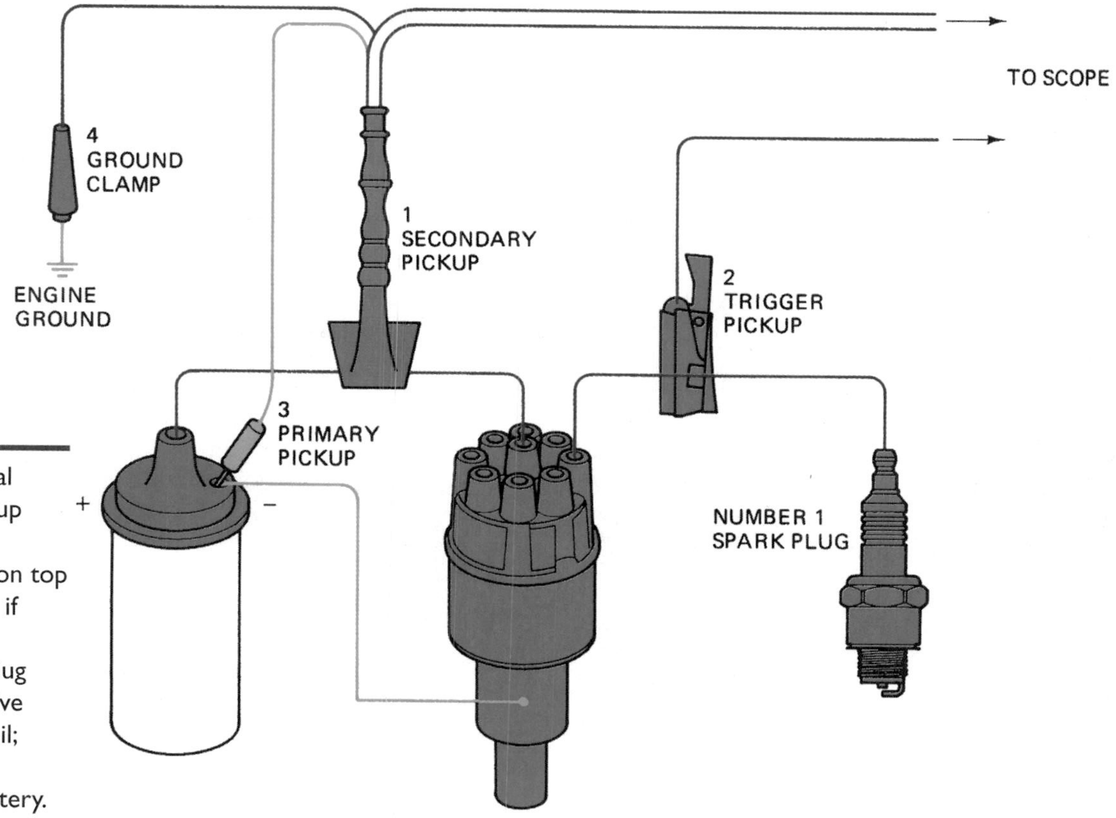

4 GROUND CLAMP

ENGINE GROUND

1 SECONDARY PICKUP

2 TRIGGER PICKUP

TO SCOPE

3 PRIMARY PICKUP

\+ –

NUMBER 1 SPARK PLUG

Figure 24–62 Typical engine analyzer hookup that includes a scope display. (1) Coil wire on top of the distributor cap if integral type of coil; (2) number 1 spark plug connection; (3) negative side of the ignition coil; (4) ground (negative) connection of the battery.

Vantage kVModule Coil–in–Cap Adapters

CIC-1 (EETM306A06)
Fits GM HEI coil-in-cap systems. This adapter works on caps with or without a plug wire retainer ring. Use the thumbscrew to reposition the clip for the cap configuration being tested.

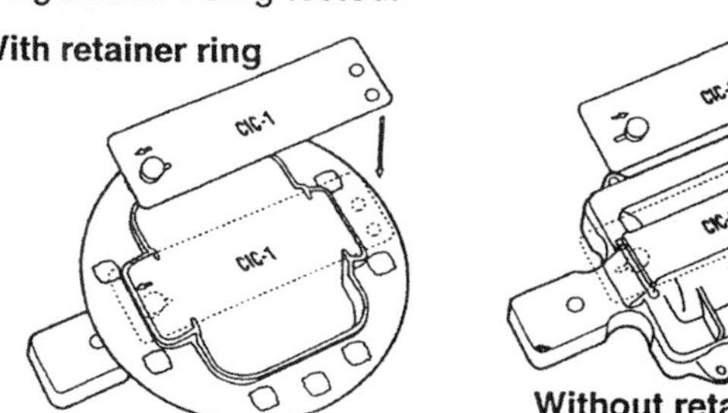

CIC-2 (EETM306A05)
Fits most Toyota and Honda models with coil-in-cap systems. One of the side clips is thumbscrew adjustable to accommodate a number of different size caps.

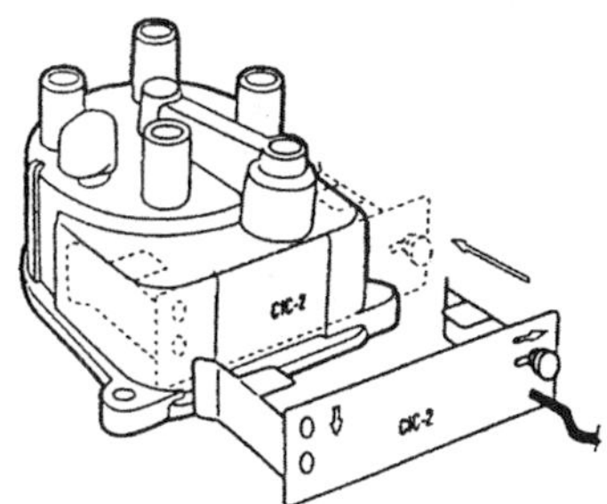

Vantage kVModule Coil–on–Plug Adapters

COP-1 (EETM306A03)
Fits the following Ford vehicles:

- 1996–2000 Taurus SHO 3.4L
- 1997–2000 E- and F-Series 5.4L and 6.8L.
- 1998 Mark VIII 4.6L
- 1998–2000 Crown Victoria, Grand Marquis, Town Car
- 1999–2000 Mustang

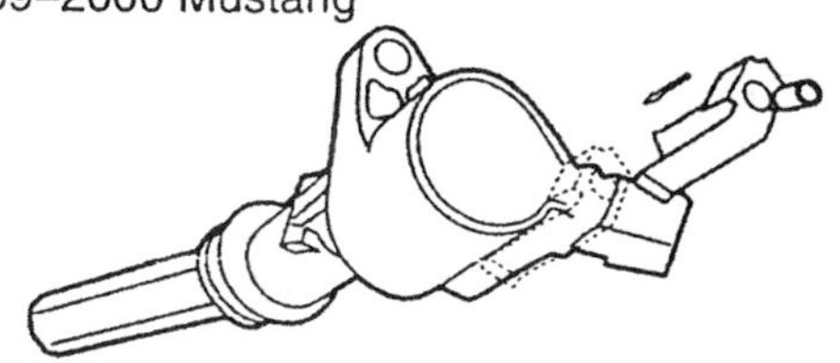

COP-4 (EETM306A08)
Fits the following Asian import vehicles:

- 1996–1999 Acura SLX
- 1996–1999 Honda Passport.
- 1997–1999 Isuzu Amigo, Rodeo, and Trooper.
- 1994–1999 Nissan Maxima, 3.0L, front bank

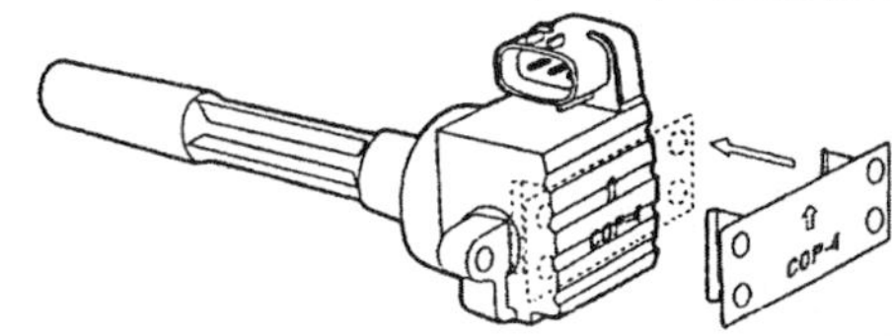

Figure 24–63 Clip-on adapters are used with an ignition system that uses an integral ignition coil. (Courtesy Snap-On Tools, Inc.)

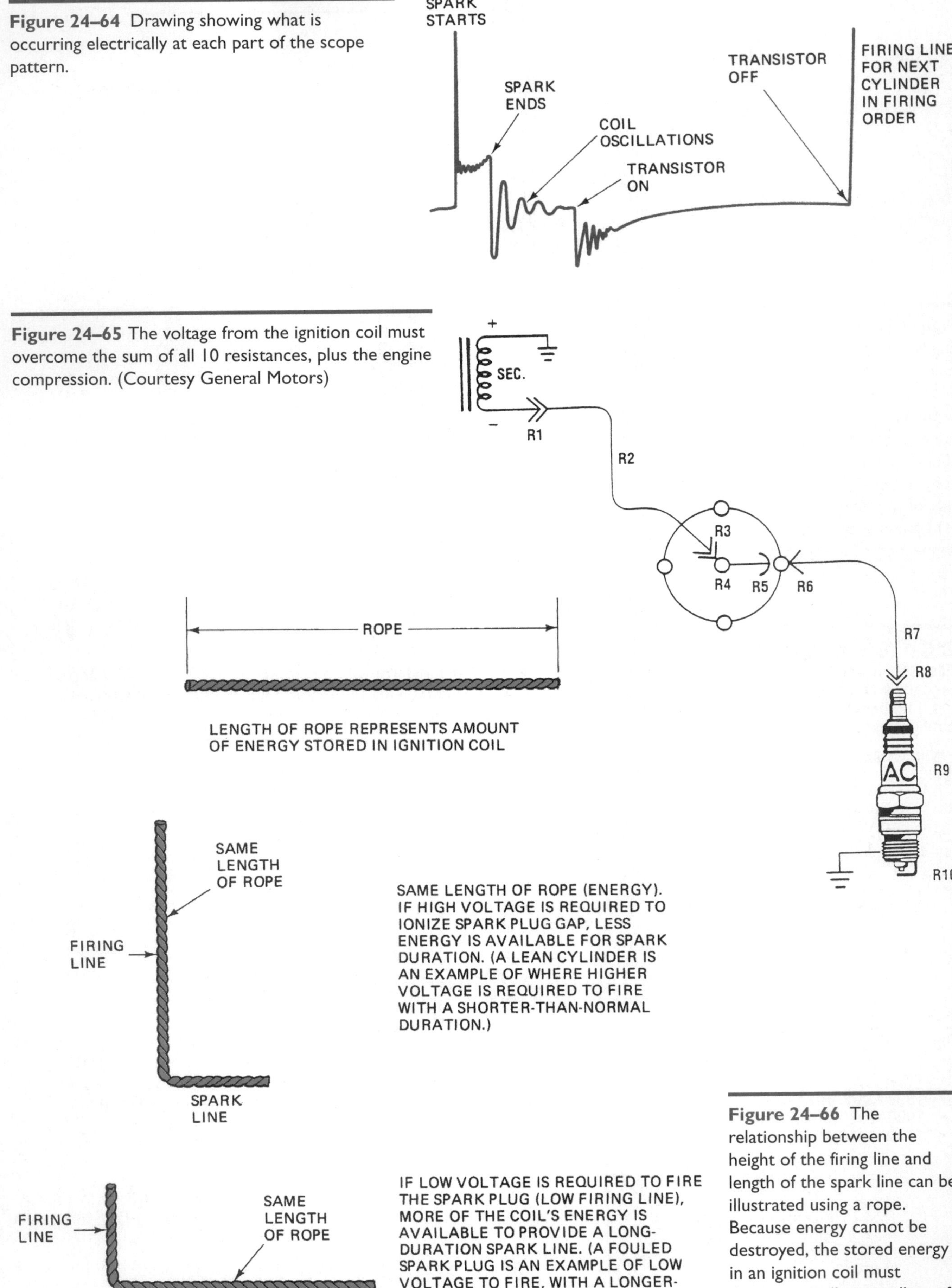

SPARK STARTS
SPARK ENDS
COIL OSCILLATIONS
TRANSISTOR ON
TRANSISTOR OFF
FIRING LINE FOR NEXT CYLINDER IN FIRING ORDER
+
SEC.
−
R1
R2
R3
R4
R5
R6
R7
R8
AC
R9
R10
ROPE
LENGTH OF ROPE REPRESENTS AMOUNT OF ENERGY STORED IN IGNITION COIL
SAME LENGTH OF ROPE
FIRING LINE
SPARK LINE
SAME LENGTH OF ROPE (ENERGY). IF HIGH VOLTAGE IS REQUIRED TO IONIZE SPARK PLUG GAP, LESS ENERGY IS AVAILABLE FOR SPARK DURATION. (A LEAN CYLINDER IS AN EXAMPLE OF WHERE HIGHER VOLTAGE IS REQUIRED TO FIRE WITH A SHORTER-THAN-NORMAL DURATION.)
FIRING LINE
SAME LENGTH OF ROPE
SPARK LINE
IF LOW VOLTAGE IS REQUIRED TO FIRE THE SPARK PLUG (LOW FIRING LINE), MORE OF THE COIL'S ENERGY IS AVAILABLE TO PROVIDE A LONG-DURATION SPARK LINE. (A FOULED SPARK PLUG IS AN EXAMPLE OF LOW VOLTAGE TO FIRE, WITH A LONGER-THAN-NORMAL DURATION.)

Figure 24–64 Drawing showing what is occurring electrically at each part of the scope pattern.

Figure 24–65 The voltage from the ignition coil must overcome the sum of all 10 resistances, plus the engine compression. (Courtesy General Motors)

Figure 24–66 The relationship between the height of the firing line and length of the spark line can be illustrated using a rope. Because energy cannot be destroyed, the stored energy in an ignition coil must dissipate totally, regardless of engine operating conditions.

the voltage required to maintain the spark across the spark plug after the spark has started. The height of the spark line should be one-fourth of the height of the firing line (between 1.5 and 2.5 kilovolts). The length (from left to right) of the line represents the length of time for which the spark lasts (duration). The spark duration should be between 0.8 and 2.0 milliseconds, approximately 1.5 milliseconds preferred. The spark stops at the end (right side) of the spark line as shown in Figure 24–64.

Firing Line versus Spark Line

The total energy (voltage) supplied by the coil can be used in one of two ways:

1. If high voltage is required to fire the plug (high firing line), less voltage is left to sustain (continue) the spark and the spark line will be shorter. See Figure 24–66.
2. If low voltage is required to fire the plug (low firing line), more voltage is left to sustain the spark and it continues for a longer period of time (long spark line).

Intermediate Oscillations

After the spark has stopped, there is still some remaining energy left in the coil. This remaining energy dissipates in the coil windings and the entire secondary circuit. The oscillations are also called the "ringing" of the coil as it is pulsed.

The secondary pattern amplifies any voltage variation occurring in the primary circuit because of the turns ratio between the primary and secondary windings of the ignition coil. A correctly operating ignition system should display five or more bumps (oscillations) (three or more for many variable dwell systems).

Transistor-On Point

After the intermediate oscillations, the coil is empty (not charged), as indicated by the scope pattern being on the zero line for a short period. When the transistor turns on an electronic system, the coil is being charged. Note that the charging of the coil occurs slowly (coil-charging oscillations) because of the inductive reactance of the coil.

Dwell Section

Dwell is the amount of time that the current is charging the coil from the transistor-on point to the transistor-off point. At the end of the dwell section is the beginning of the next firing line. This point is called "transistor off" and indicates that the primary current of the coil is stopped, resulting in a high-voltage spark out of the coil. Dwell remains constant on most contact-point and early electronic ignitions; primary current flow is usually controlled with a ballast resistor. Almost all late-model electronic, DIS and COP systems use variable dwell; long dwell increases current, short dwell reduces current. A hump (bump) in the middle of the dwell section indicates dwell switching. See Figure 24–67.

Pattern Selection

The entire pattern is not seen on a scope. Ignition oscilloscopes use three positions to view certain sections of the basic pattern more closely. These three positions are as follows:

1. **Superimposed.** This superimposed position is used to look at differences in patterns between cylinders in all areas except the firing line. There are no firing lines illustrated in superimposed positions. See Figure 24–68.
2. **Raster** (stacked). The #1 cylinder is at the bottom on most scopes. Use the raster position to look at the spark line length and transistor-on point. The raster (stacked) pattern shows all areas of the scope pattern except the firing lines. See Figure 24–69.
3. **Display** (parade). Display (parade) is the only position in which firing lines are visible. The firing line section for the #1 cylinder is on the far right side of the screen, with the remaining portions of the pattern on the left side. This selection is used to compare the height of firing lines among all cylinders. See Figure 24–70.

Reading the Scope on Display (Parade)

Start the engine and operate at approximately 1000 rpm to ensure a smooth and accurate scope pattern. Firing lines are visible only on the display (parade) position. The firing lines should all be 5 to 15 kilovolts in height and be within 3 kilovolts of each other. If one or more cylinders have high firing lines, this could indicate a defective (open) spark plug wire, a spark plug with too wide a gap, or a lean fuel mixture affecting only those cylinders.

Reading the Spark Lines

Spark lines can easily be seen on either superimposed or raster (stacked) position. On the raster (stacked) position, each individual spark line can be viewed.

The spark lines should be level and one-fourth as high as the firing lines (between 2.0 and 4.0 kilovolts). The spark line voltage is called the **burn kV.** The *length* of the spark line is the critical factor for determining

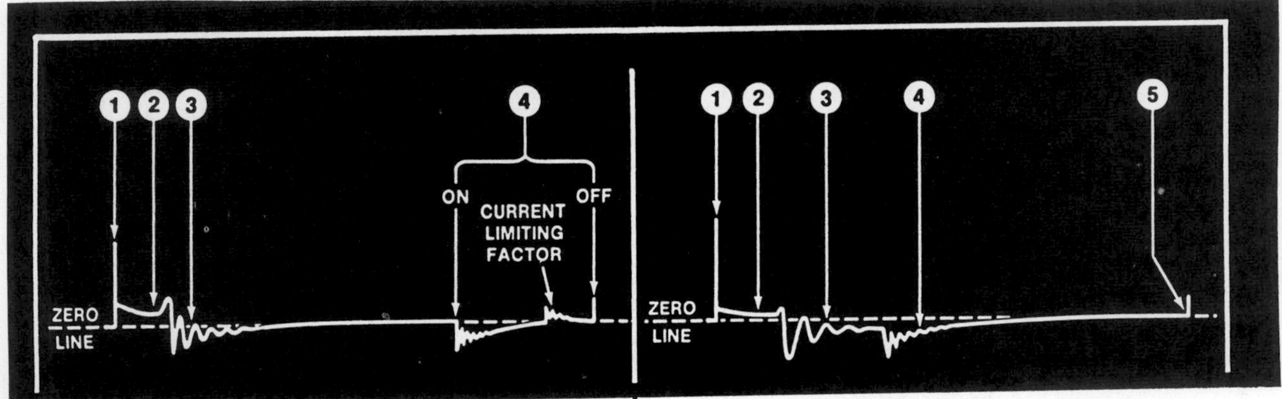

TYPICAL ELECTRONIC IGNITION SYSTEM PATTERN

1. **Firing line** from 7 to 18 kV with no more than 3 kV variation. Tests plug and rotor gap, broken wires and fuel mixture.
2. **Spark line** — with PATTERN SELECTOR in 5 ms position, spark duration should not be less than 0.8 ms nor more than 2.0 ms, approximately 1.5 ms preferred. The line should be level, between 2 and 4 kV. Tests plugs, wires, cap, rotor or engine condition affecting plug firing.
3. **Intermediate oscillations** should diminish gradually if coil is not shorted.
4. **Transistor opening and closing** indicates points at which transistor turns on and off. Tests control module and pickup coil in distributor cap.
5. **Current limiting** (on systems having saturation current limiting) tests for module condition and for high primary circuit resistance.

TYPICAL BREAKER POINT IGNITION SYSTEM PATTERN

1. **Firing line** from 5 to 15 kV with no more than 3 kV variation. Tests plug and rotor gap, broken wires and fuel mixture.
2. **Spark line** straight and level starting at 2 kV or less. Tests plugs, wires, cap, rotor, or engine condition affecting plug firing.
3. **Intermediate oscillations** test for coil, condenser or primary circuit defects. Should diminish gradually.
4. **Point closing**, short downward line followed by small oscillations. Tests for point condition and point spring tension.
5. **Point opening**, abrupt 90° angle to begin next firing line. Tests for pitted points or arcing caused by poor condenser action.

Figure 24–67 Typical ignition system waveform patterns. Note the dwell (current-limiting) hump with late electronic ignition. (Courtesy Sun Electric, a Division of Snap-On Tools, Inc.)

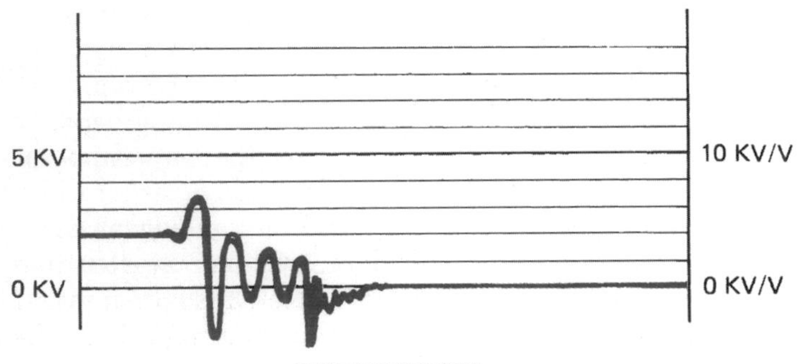

Figure 24–68 Typical secondary ignition pattern. Note the lack of firing lines on superimposed pattern.

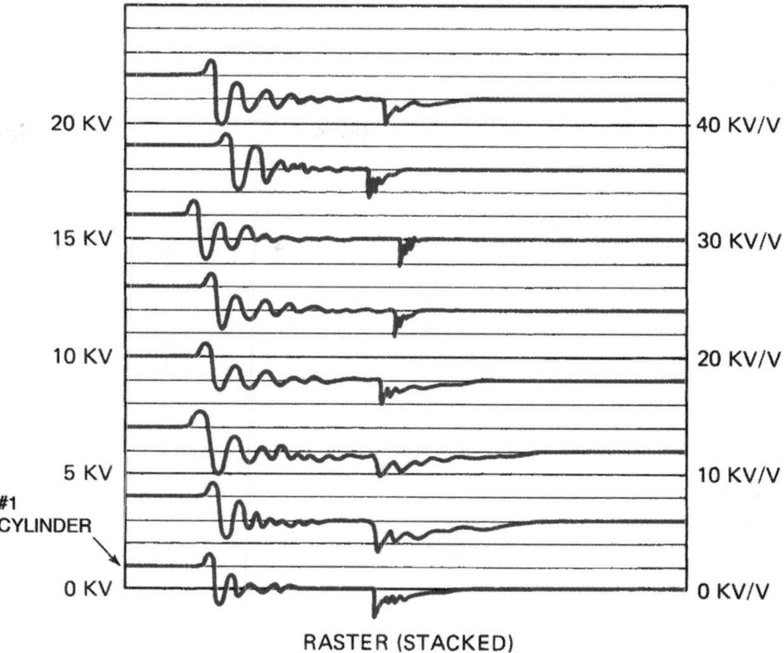

Figure 24–69 Raster is the best scope position to use to view the spark lines of all the cylinders to check for differences. Most scopes display the #1 cylinder at the bottom. The other cylinders are positioned by firing order above the #1 cylinder.

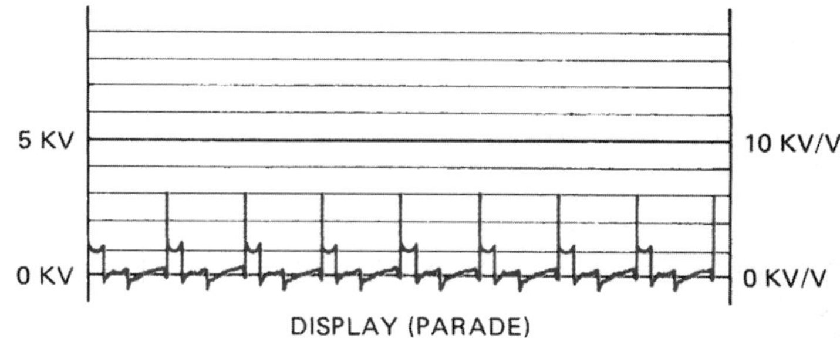

Figure 24–70 Display is the only position to view the firing lines of all cylinders. The #1 cylinder is displayed on the left (except for its firing line, which is shown on the right). The cylinders are displayed from left to right by firing order.

proper operation of the engine because it represents the spark duration time. There is only a limited amount of energy in an ignition coil. If most of the energy is used to ionize the air gaps of the rotor and the spark plug, there may not be enough energy remaining to create a spark of a duration long enough to completely burn the air–fuel mixture. Many scopes are equipped with a **millisecond (ms) sweep.** This means that the scope will sweep only that portion of the pattern that can be shown during a 5 or 25 ms setting. Spark line duration should not be lower than 0.8 ms or above 2.0 ms; approximately 1.5 ms is a good reading.

If the spark line is too short, possible causes include the following:

1. Spark plug(s) gapped too widely
2. Rotor tip to distributor-cap insert distance gapped too widely (worn cap or rotor)
3. High-resistance spark plug wire
4. Air-fuel mixture too lean (vacuum leak, clogged fuel injector, etc.)

If the spark line is too long, possible causes include the following:

1. Fouled spark plug(s)
2. Spark plug(s) gapped too closely
3. Shorted spark plug or spark plug wire

Spark Line Slope

Downward-sloping spark lines indicate that the voltage required to maintain the spark duration is decreasing during the firing of the spark plug. This downward slope usually indicates that the spark energy is finding ground through spark plug deposits (the plug is fouled) or other ignition problems. See Figure 24–71.

An upward-sloping spark line usually indicates a mechanical engine problem. A defective piston ring or valve would tend to seal better in the increasing pressures of combustion. As the spark plug fires, the effective increase in pressures increases the voltage

Figure 24–71 A downward-sloping spark line usually indicates high secondary ignition system resistance.

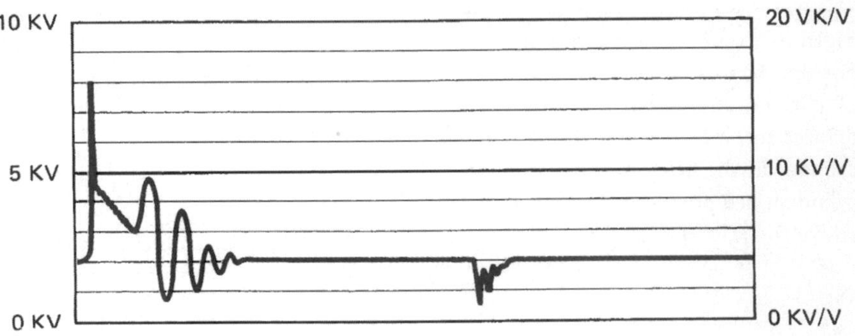

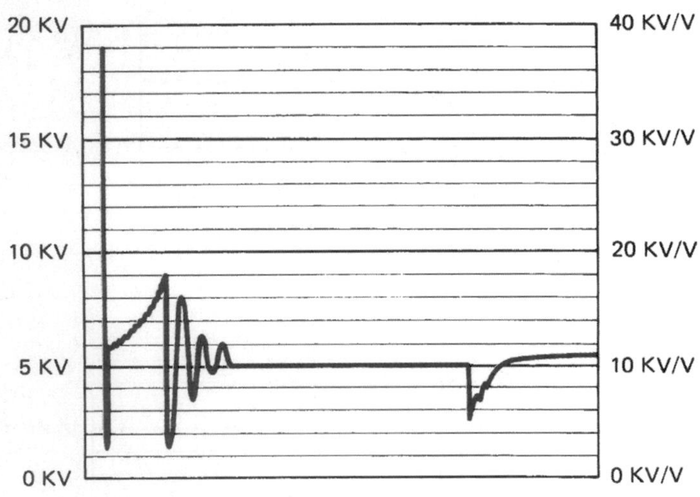

Figure 24–72 An upward-sloping spark line usually indicates a mechanical engine problem or a lean air–fuel mixture.

required to maintain the spark, and the height of the spark line rises during the duration of the spark. See Figure 24–72.

An upward-sloping spark line can also indicate a lean air–fuel mixture. Typical causes include:

1. Clogged injector(s)
2. Vacuum leak
3. Sticking intake valve

Reading the Intermediate Section

The intermediate section should have three or more oscillations (bumps) for a correctly operating ignition system. Because approximately 250 volts are in the primary ignition circuit when the spark stops flowing across the spark plugs, this voltage is reduced by about 75 volts per oscillation. Additional resistances in the primary circuit would decrease the number of oscillations. If there are fewer than three oscillations, possible problems include the following:

1. Shorted ignition coil
2. Leaky condenser (if point-type ignition)
3. Loose or high-resistance primary connections on the ignition coil or primary ignition wiring

Electronic Ignition and the Dwell Section

Electronic ignitions also use a dwell period to charge the coil. Dwell is not adjustable with electronic ignition; however, the dwell does increase with rising RPM in many electronic ignition systems. This change in dwell with RPM should be considered normal.

Dwell Variation (Electronic Ignition)

A worn distributor gear, worn camshaft gear, or other distributor problem may degrade engine performance because the signal created in the distributor will be affected by the inaccurate distributor operation. However, many electronic ignitions vary the dwell electronically in the module to maintain acceptable current flow levels through the ignition coil and module without the use of a ballast resistor.

> **NOTE:** Distributorless ignition systems also vary dwell time electronically within the engine computer or ignition module.

Coil Polarity

With the scope connected and the engine running, observe the scope pattern in the superimposed mode. If the pattern is upside down, the primary wires on the coil may be reversed, causing the coil polarity to be reversed.

> **NOTE:** Check the scope hookup and controls before deciding that the coil polarity is reversed.

SCOPE-TESTING A DISTRIBUTORLESS IGNITION SYSTEM

A handheld digital storage oscilloscope can be used to check the pattern of each individual cylinder. Some larger scopes can be connected to all spark plug wires and therefore are able to display both power and waste spark waveforms. See Figure 24–73. Because the waste spark does not require as high a voltage level as the cylinder on the power stroke, the waste form normally will be lower.

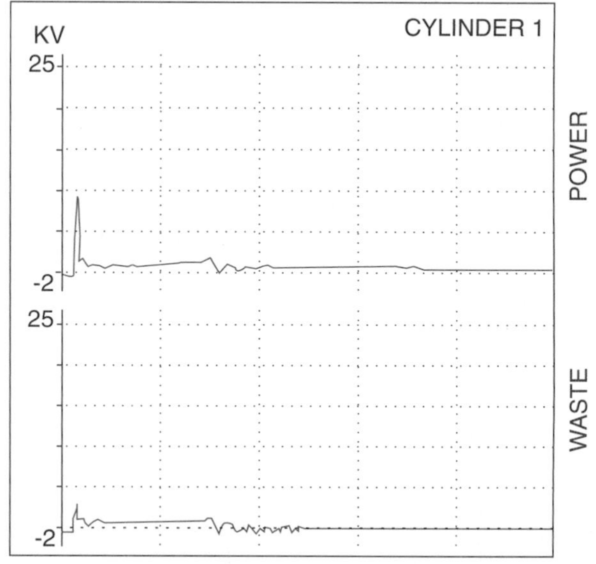

Figure 24–73 A dual trace scope pattern showing both the power and the waste spark from the same coil (cylinders #1 and #6). Note that the firing line is higher on the cylinder that is under compression (power); otherwise both patterns are almost identical.

IGNITION SYSTEM TROUBLESHOOTING GUIDE

Problem	Possible Causes and/or Solutions
No spark out of the coil	• Open in the ignition switch circuit • Defective ignition module (if electronic ignition coil) • Defective pickup coil or Hall-effect switch (if electronic ignition) • Shorted condenser
Weak spark out of the coil	• High-resistance coil wire or spark plug wire (DIS) • Poor ground between the distributor or module and the engine block
Engine missing	• Defective (open) spark plug wire • Worn or fouled spark plugs • Defective pickup coil • Defective module • Poor electrical connections at the pickup coil and/or module

PHOTO SEQUENCE 18 Ignition System Diagnosis

P18–1 The tools and supplies needed to test for a fault in the secondary ignition system include: spark plug boot removal pliers, spark tester, secondary ignition system voltage measuring tools, test light, short 50 mm (2 in.) long pieces of 4 mm (5/32 in.) ID vacuum hose and protective gloves to avoid getting burned around the hot exhaust system.

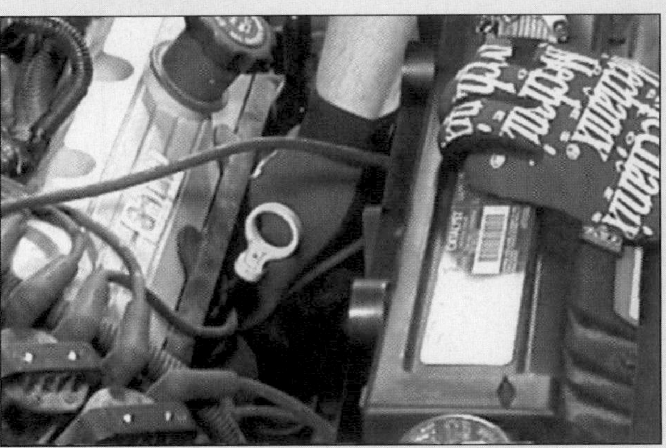

P18–2 The first step in the diagnosis of the ignition system is to check for adequate voltage from the coil(s). Using a spark plug wire boot removal tool, carefully remove the spark plug wire from the spark plug.

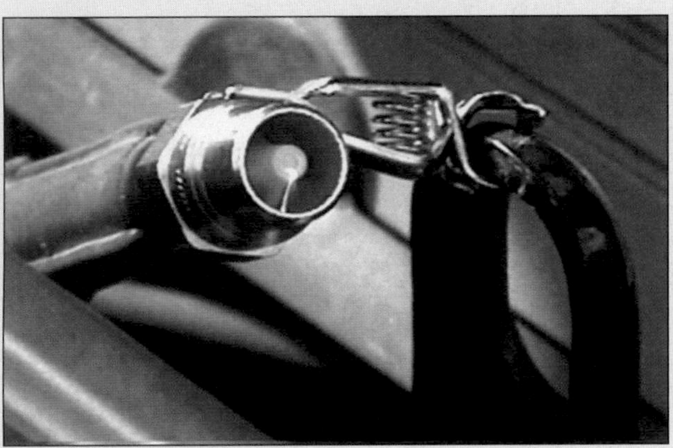

P18–3 Attach a spark tester to the end of the spark plug wire and then clip the spark tester to a good engine ground. Start the engine and observe the spark tester. A spark should consistently jump the gap, indicating that the system is capable of supplying at least 25 000 volts (25 kV).

P18–4 Engine faults as well as ignition system faults can often be detected by using a tester capable of measuring spark plug firing voltage such as this unit from Snap-On tools. Connect the ground clip to a good engine ground and clip the probe around a spark plug wire.

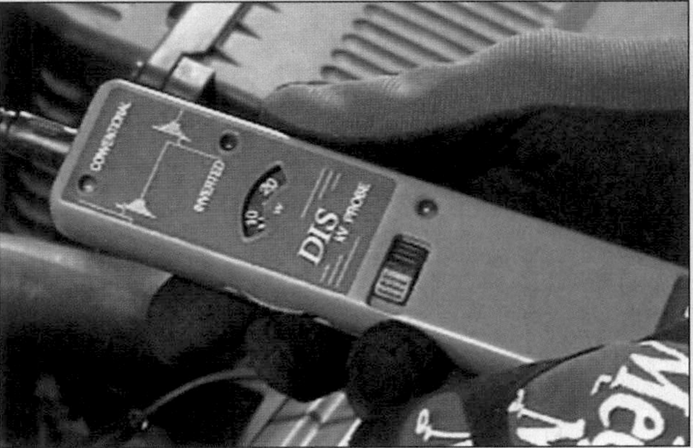

P18–5 Start the engine and rotate the thumb wheel until the red light emitting diode (LED) just flickers off and then read the firing voltage on the display. This cylinder shows about 13 kV with conventional firing. This reading is about normal (5 to 15 kV).

P18–6 This cylinder indicates a firing voltage of about 8 kV for the inverted spark on another cylinder. This cylinder is firing in the opposite polarity from the other cylinder (inverted). The firing voltage indicates a possible narrow gap or fouled spark plug.

P18–7 Another tester that can be used is one from OTC tools. To use this tester, connect the ground clip to a good engine ground and connect the test probe around a spark plug wire.

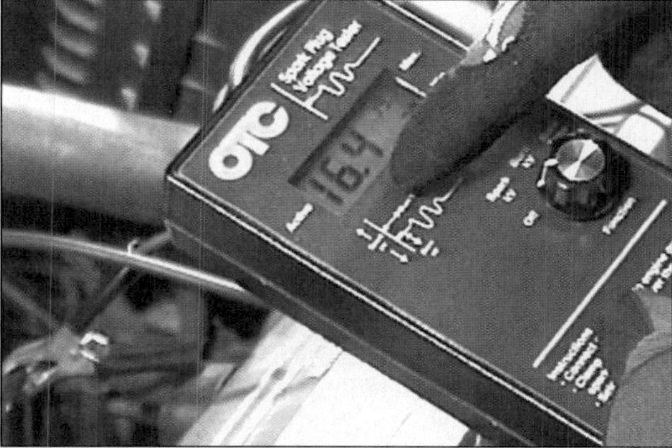

P18–8 Start the engine and select "spark kV." This is the voltage required to fire the spark plugs and this display indicates 16.4 kV. This is higher than normal and could be due to a high resistance spark plug wire or a wide gap spark plug.

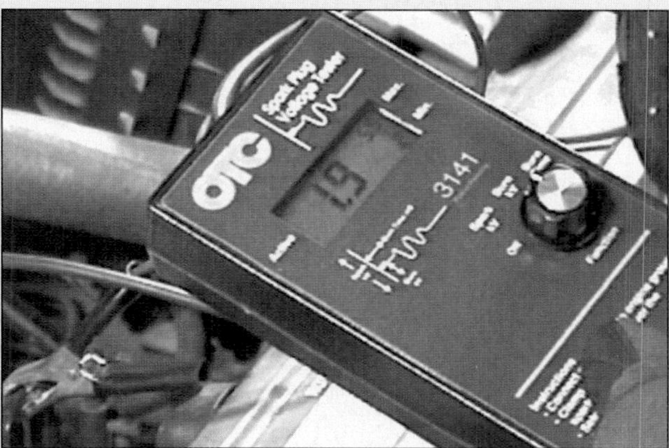

P18–9 Move the selector to read "burn kV" and the reading indicates 1.9 kV. This is the voltage necessary to keep the spark firing after it has been started. It should be less than 2 kV for most vehicles.

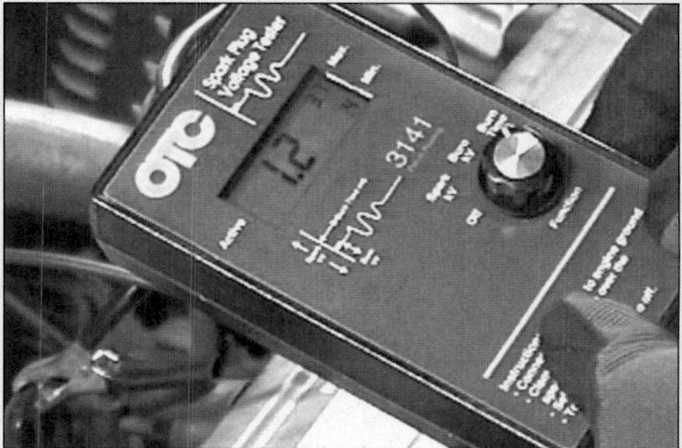

P18–10 Move the selector to "burn time" and the reading is 1.2 ms (milliseconds). This is the duration of the spark, and it should be between 1 and 2 ms.

P18–11 Ground out cylinders one at a time and observe if the engine speed or idle quality is affected. If one cylinder does not respond then this test can help pinpoint a fault in a particular cylinder. Insert 50 mm (2 in.) lengths of vacuum hose between the coil tower and the spark plug wires. This test can also be performed on vehicles equipped with a distributor.

P18–12 Use a grounded test light and touch the section of rubber hose with the tip. The high voltage will travel through the test light to ground and not fire the spark plug. This is an easy test to perform that does not require expensive test equipment and can be done quickly to help isolate a cylinder that has a fault.

SUMMARY

1. All inductive ignition systems supply battery voltage to the positive side of the ignition coil and pulse the negative side of the coil on and off to ground to create a high-voltage spark.
2. Always use a spark tester that requires at least 25 kilovolts (kV) to fire when checking for spark.
3. Ignition coils usually test at about 1 ohm across the primary winding and from 6000 to 30 000 ohms across the secondary winding.
4. A typical magnetic pickup coil should measure approximately in the middle of its specification for resistance and be able to produce an AC voltage of *at least* 0.25 volts while the engine is cranking.
5. An open spark plug wire can damage the ignition coil.
6. A thorough visual inspection should be performed of all ignition components when diagnosing an engine performance problem.
7. Platinum spark plugs should not be regapped after use in an engine.
8. A secondary ignition scope pattern includes a firing line, spark line, intermediate oscillations, and transistor-on and transistor-off points.
9. The slope of the spark line can indicate incorrect air–fuel ratio or other engine problems.

REVIEW QUESTIONS

1. Explain how 12 volts from a battery can be changed to 40 000 volts for ignition.
2. Discuss how a magnetic sensor works.
3. Discuss how a Hall-effect sensor works.
4. Explain why a spark tester should be used to check for spark rather than using a standard spark plug.
5. Explain how to test a pickup coil for resistance and AC voltage output.
6. Discuss what harm can occur if the engine is cranked or run with an open (defective) spark plug wire.
7. List the sections of a secondary ignition scope pattern.
8. Explain what the slope of the spark line can indicate about the engine.
9. Explain why a coil-on-plug ignition achieves longer spark plug life than DIS waste–spark ignition.

RED SEAL CERTIFICATION-TYPE QUESTIONS

1. Primary ignition current must be controlled to provide both a strong spark and long coil life. An ignition system with fixed dwell may use
   - **a.** A ballast resistor for current control
   - **b.** A current limiting circuit in the module
   - **c.** High primary circuit resistance to limit current
   - **d.** Variable dwell at high RPM
2. The ignition module has direct control over the firing of the coil(s) of an electronic ignition system. Which component(s) triggers (controls) the module?
   - **a.** Primary transistor
   - **b.** Ignition points
   - **c.** Reed switch
   - **d.** Pickup coil
3. Distributorless (waste spark) ignition systems can be triggered by a ________.
   - **a.** Reed switch
   - **b.** Camshaft sensor
   - **c.** Set of contact points
   - **d.** Hall-effect sensor
4. Pickup coils (pulse generators) can be tested with an ohmmeter or
   - **a.** By measuring the current flowing through the coil
   - **b.** A clamp-on spark tester
   - **c.** By measuring the voltage generated
   - **d.** By substituting a known good pickup coil
5. Typical primary coil resistance specifications usually range from _______.
   - **a.** 100 to 450 ohms
   - **b.** 500 to 1500 ohms
   - **c.** 1 to 3 ohms
   - **d.** 6000 to 30 000 ohms
6. Typical secondary coil resistance specifications usually range from _______.
   - **a.** 100 to 450 ohms
   - **b.** 500 to 1500 ohms
   - **c.** 1 to 3 ohms
   - **d.** 6000 to 30 000 ohms
7. An engine does not start. During cranking the fuel injector (electronic fuel injection) sprays fuel. This would indicate
   - **a.** A problem with the pickup coil
   - **b.** Grounding at the Hall-effect switch
   - **c.** An ignition primary pulse is present
   - **d.** The ignition module is triggering the secondary circuit
8. A light coating of anti-seize compound is put onto spark plug threads to reduce seizing in aluminum cylinder heads. The technician must be cautious when tightening the plugs as the compound
   - **a.** May cause cross-threading of the plug
   - **b.** Increases the torque required to tighten the plug
   - **c.** Makes the plugs difficult to remove
   - **d.** Reduces the torque required to tighten the plug
9. An engine can ping (spark knock) if the ignition timing is ______.
   - **a.** Too far advanced
   - **b.** Too far retarded
10. A secondary waveform is being analyzed. It has a lower than normal firing line and a longer than normal spark line on one cylinder. This could indicate
    - **a.** A high resistance spark plug wire
    - **b.** A fouled spark plug
    - **c.** A weak ignition coil
    - **d.** An excessive rotor air gap

25

Computers and Sensors—Operation, Diagnosis, and Service

OBJECTIVES: After studying Chapter 25, you should be able to:

1. Prepare for the interprovincial Red Seal certification examination in Appendix VIII (Engine Performance) on the topics covered in this chapter.
2. Explain the purpose, function and operation of on-board computers.
3. Discuss programming differences between a PROM and an EEPROM.
4. Discuss the operation and testing procedures for throttle position, manifold absolute pressure and coolant temperature sensors.
5. Explain the operation of heated and non-heated exhaust gas oxygen sensors.
6. Explain adaptive strategy.

COMPUTER CONTROL

Modern automotive control systems consist of a network of electronic sensors, actuators, and computer modules designed to regulate the powertrain and vehicle support systems. The **powertrain control module (PCM)** is the heart of this system. It coordinates engine and transmission operation, processes data, maintains communications, and makes the control decisions needed to keep the vehicle operating.

Automotive computers use voltage to send and receive information. Voltage is electrical pressure and does not flow through circuits, but voltage can be used as a signal. A computer converts input information or data into voltage signal combinations that represent number combinations. The number combinations can represent a variety of information—temperature, speed, or even words and letters. A computer processes the input voltage signals it receives by computing what they represent, and then delivering the data in computed or processed form.

NOTE: Standardized Emissions Terminology
In the early 1990s, the Society of Automotive Engineers developed a common list of terms (SAE J1930) for emission related parts, i.e., ignition, fuel delivery and emission control components. These terms, by law, have been used in all Canadian and U.S. automotive service and training publications since January 1, 1995. Many automobile manufacturers began using the new terms in 1993 when California adopted J1930.

As an example, the on-board computer had been known as a Micro-computer, a Processor, an Engine Control Assembly (ECA), or an Engine Control Unit (ECU) depending on the manufacturer. The new term, standard in the industry, is Powertrain Control Module (PCM).

It is important to note that older publications before the mid-1990s may use different terms than current texts.

THE FOUR BASIC COMPUTER FUNCTIONS

The operation of every computer can be divided into four basic functions. See Figure 25–1.

- Input
- Processing
- Storage
- Output

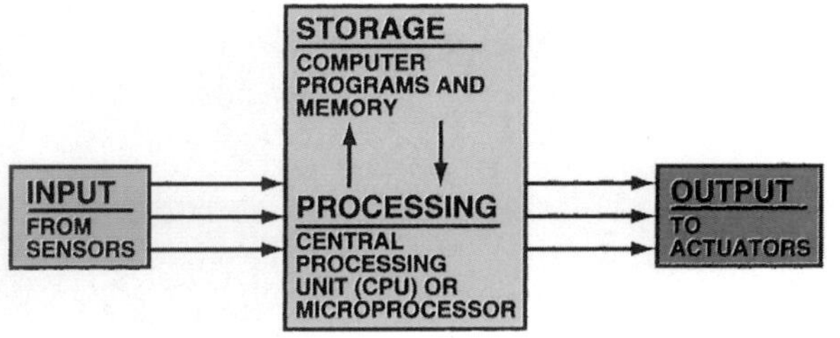

Figure 25–1 All computer systems perform four basic functions: input, processing, storage, and output.

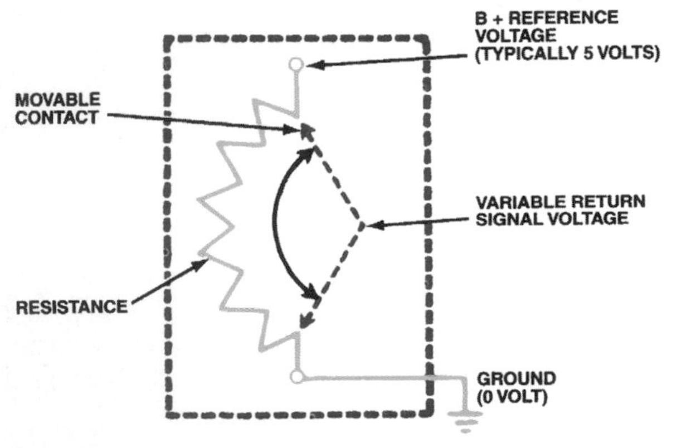

Figure 25–2 A potentiometer uses a movable contact to vary resistance and send an analog signal.

These basic functions are not unique to computers; they can be found in many noncomputer systems. However, we need to know how the computer handles these functions.

Input

First, the computer receives a voltage signal (input) from an input device. The device can be as simple as a button or a switch on an instrument panel, or a sensor on an automotive engine. See Figure 25–2 for a typical type of automotive sensor.

Vehicles use various mechanical, electrical, and magnetic sensors to measure factors such as vehicle speed, engine RPM, air pressure, oxygen content of exhaust gas, airflow, and engine coolant temperature. Each sensor transmits its information in the form of voltage signals. The computer receives these voltage signals, but before it can use them, the signals must undergo a process called **input conditioning.** This process includes amplifying voltage signals that are too small for the computer circuitry to handle. Input conditioners generally are located inside the computer, but a few sensors have their own input-conditioning circuitry.

Processing

Input voltage signals received by a computer are processed through a series of electronic logic circuits maintained in its programmed instructions. These logic circuits change the input voltage signals, or data, into output voltage signals or commands.

Storage

The program instructions for a computer are stored in electronic memory. Some programs may require that certain input data be stored for later reference or future processing. In others, output commands may be delayed or stored before they are transmitted to devices elsewhere in the system.

Output

After the computer has processed the input signals, it sends voltage signals or commands to other devices in the system, such as system actuators. An **actuator** is an electrical or mechanical device that converts electrical energy into a mechanical action, such as adjusting engine idle speed, altering suspension height, or regulating fuel metering.

Computers also can communicate with, and control, each other through their output and input functions. This means that the output signal from one computer system can be the input signal for another computer system.

DIGITAL COMPUTERS

In a **digital** computer, the voltage signal or processing function is a simple high/low, yes/no, on/off signal. The digital signal voltage is limited to two voltage levels: high voltage and low voltage. Since there is no stepped range of voltage or current in between, a digital binary signal is a square wave.

The signal is called digital because the on and off signals are processed by the computer as the digits or numbers 0 and 1. The number system containing only these two digits is called the **binary** system. Any number or letter from any number system or language alphabet can be translated into a combination of binary 0s and 1s for the digital computer.

A digital computer changes the analog input signals (voltage) to digital bits (*bi*nary digi*ts*) of information through an **analog-to-digital (AD) converter** circuit. The binary digital number is used by the computer in its calculations or logic networks. Output signals usually are digital signals that turn system actuators on and off.

The digital computer can process thousands of digital signals per second because its circuits are

Figure 25–3 Many electronic components are used to construct a typical vehicle computer. Notice all of the chips, resistors, and capacitors that are used in this computer.

able to switch voltage signals on and off in billionths of a second. See Figure 25–3.

Parts of a Computer

The software consists of the programs and logic functions stored in the computer's circuitry. The hardware is the mechanical and electronic parts of a computer.

Central Processing Unit (CPU) The microprocessor is the **central processing unit (CPU)** of a computer. Since it performs the essential mathematical operations and logic decisions that make up its processing function, the CPU can be considered the heart of a computer. Some computers use more than one microprocessor, called a coprocessor.

Computer Memory Other integrated-circuit (IC) devices store the computer operating program, system sensor input data, and system actuator output data, information necessary for CPU operation.

Computer Programs

By operating a vehicle on a dynamometer and manually adjusting the variable factors such as speed, load, and spark timing, it is possible to determine the optimum output settings for the best driveability, economy, and emission control. This is called **engine mapping.** See Figure 25–4.

Engine mapping creates a three-dimensional performance graph that applies to a given vehicle and powertrain combination. Each combination is permanently mapped digitally onto an IC chip called a **programmable read-only memory (PROM).** This allows an automaker to use one basic computer for all models; a unique PROM individualizes the computer for a particular model. Also, if a driveability problem can be resolved by a change in the program, the manufacturers can release a revised PROM to supersede the earlier part.

Some manufacturers use a single PROM that plugs into the computer. See Figure 25–5. Other computers use a non-replaceable calibration module that

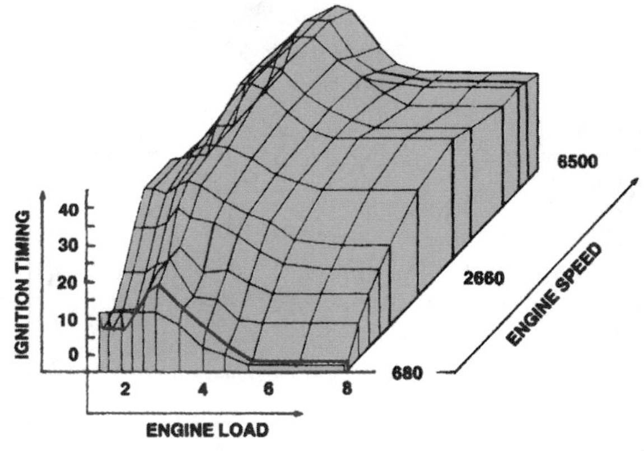

Figure 25–4 Typical ignition timing map developed from testing and used by the vehicle computer to provide the optimum ignition timing for all engine speeds and load combinations.

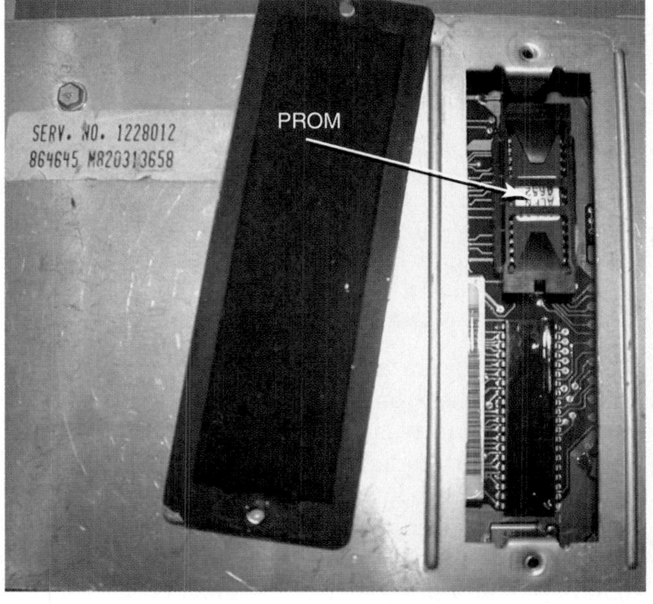

Figure 25–5 A replaceable PROM used in a General Motors computer. Notice that the sealed access panel has been removed to gain access.

contains the system PROM. If the on-board computer needs to be changed, the replaceable type of PROM or calibration module must be removed from the defective unit and installed in the replacement computer.

The original PROM was programmed to reduce emissions, improve fuel economy and provide acceptable power. Replacing the factory PROM with an aftermarket "hot" PROM to increase engine performance often increases engine emissions as well.

In order to reduce tampering and the use of aftermarket PROMs, the Environmental Protection Agency (EPA) mandated that the on-board computer be tamper resistant. As a result, beginning in 1994, PROMs are soldered into place and are not replaceable.

Some PROMs are made in a way that they can be erased by exposure to ultraviolet light and reprogrammed. These are called EEPROMs (electronically erasable), or EPROMs (erasable PROMs).

The new EEPROM chips allow technicians to reprogram them with special electronic service tools. Replacement computers must be programmed (either in the car or on the bench) before the vehicle will run; further updating can be done any time. This type of service is usually done by dealership technicians, although aftermarket reprogramming tools are becoming common.

Clock Rates and Timing

The microprocessor receives sensor input voltage signals, processes them by using information from other memory units, and then sends voltage signals to the appropriate actuators. The microprocessor communicates by transmitting long strings of 0s and 1s in a language called binary code. But the microprocessor must have some way of knowing when one signal ends and another begins. That is the job of a crystal oscillator called a **clock generator.** See Figure 25–6. The computer's crystal oscillator generates a steady stream of one-bit-long voltage pulses. Both the microprocessor and the memories monitor the clock pulses while they are communicating. Because they know how long each voltage pulse should be, they can distinguish between a 01 and a 0011. To complete the process, the input and output circuits also watch the clock pulses.

Computer Speeds

Not all computers operate at the same speed; some are faster than others. The speed at which a computer operates is specified by the cycle time, or clock speed, required to perform certain measurements. Cycle time or clock speed is measured in megahertz (4.7 MHz, 8.0 MHz, 15 MHz, 18 MHz, etc.).

Figure 25–6 The clock generator produces a series of pulses that are used by the microprocessor and other components to stay in step with each other at a steady rate.

Baud Rate

The computer transmits bits of a serial data stream at precise intervals. The computer's speed is called the baud rate, or bits per second. (It is named for J. M. E. Baudot [1845–1903], a French inventor and telegraphy expert.) Just as km/h helps in estimating the length of time required to travel a certain distance, the baud rate is useful in estimating how long a given computer will need to transmit a specified amount of data to another computer. Storage of a single character requires eight bits per byte, plus an additional two bits to indicate stop and start. This means that transmission of one character, or "word," requires 10 bits. Dividing the baud rate by 10 tells us the maximum number of words per second that can be transmitted. For example, if the computer has a baud rate of 600, approximately 60 words can be received or sent per minute.

Automotive computers have evolved from a baud rate of 160 used in the early 1980s to a baud rate as high as 60 500. The speed of data transmission is an important factor both in system operation and in system troubleshooting.

Control Module Locations

The on-board automotive computer has many names. It may be called an electronic control unit, module, controller, or assembly, depending on the manufacturer and the computer application. The Society of Automotive Engineers (SAE) bulletin J1930 standardizes the name as a **powertrain control module (PCM).** The computer hardware is

Figure 25–7 This powertrain control module (PCM) is located under the hood on this pickup truck.

Figure 25–8 This PCM on a Chrysler vehicle can only be seen by hoisting the vehicle because it is located next to the radiator in the airflow to help keep it cool.

all mounted on one or more circuit boards and installed in a metal case to help shield it from electromagnetic interference (EMI). The wiring harnesses that link the computer to sensors and actuators connect to multipin connectors or edge connectors on the circuit boards.

On-board computers range from single-function units that control a single operation to multifunction units that manage all of the separate (but linked) electronic systems in the vehicle. They vary in size from a small module to a notebook-sized box. Most early engine computers were installed in the passenger compartment either under the instrument panel or in a side kick panel where they can be shielded from physical damage caused by temperature extremes, dirt, and vibration, or interference by the high currents and voltages of various underhood systems. See Figures 25–7 and 25–8. Later model PCMs are larger, have increased memory and are usually located in the engine compartment where they are cooled by air from the radiator fan. Shorter wiring harnesses with fewer connections are another advantage.

FUEL CONTROL SYSTEM OPERATING MODES

A computer-controlled fuel metering system can be selective. Depending on the computer program, it may have different operating modes. The on-board computer does not have to respond to data from all of its sensors, nor does it have to respond to the data in the same way each time. Under specified conditions, it may ignore sensor input. Or, it may respond in different ways to the same input signal, based on inputs from other sensors. Most current control systems have two operating modes: open and closed loop. The most common application of these modes is in fuel-metering feedback control where the computer responds to a signal from the oxygen sensor and, if needed, changes the amount of fuel delivered; this is closed loop mode.

During periods of prolonged idle, cold engine operation, wide open throttle or no oxygen sensor signal, the computer only looks at ROM (read-only memory), permanent memory stored in the computer. This is open loop mode.

The latest PCMs have increased memory and operate in closed loop mode under many conditions that were not monitored on older systems.

BASIC COMPUTER OPERATION

Input

Battery power is supplied to the computer when the ignition switch is closed. Because (most) input sensors must operate with a fixed voltage in order to generate a reliable signal, battery voltage is reduced to 5 volts by an internal regulator before being sent to the major input sensors. See Figure 25–9. In our example, these are the throttle position, manifold absolute pressure, and the engine coolant temperature sensors.

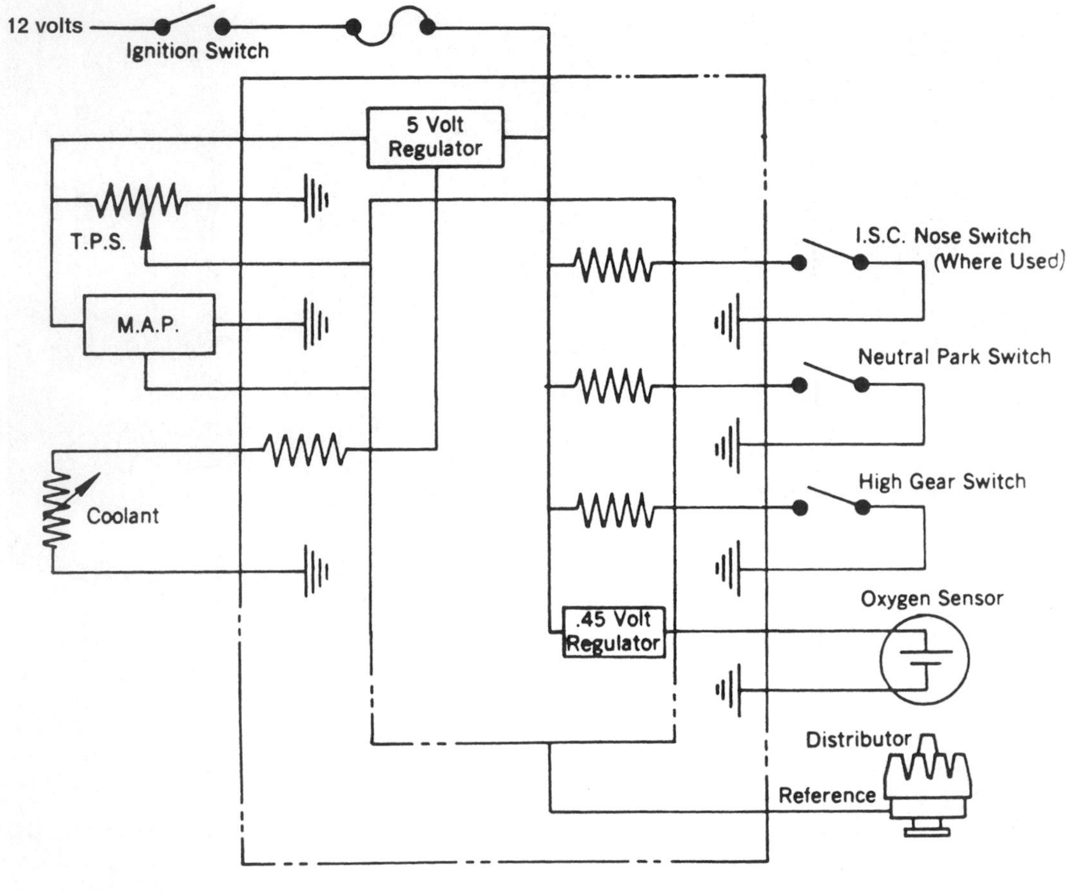

Figure 25–9 Basic computer inputs. (Courtesy General Motors)

THROTTLE POSITION SENSOR

Most computer-equipped engines use a **throttle position (TP)** sensor to signal the position of the throttle. See Figure 25–10 and 25–11. The TP sensor consists of a **potentiometer** variable resistor. A typical sensor uses three wires:

- A 5 volt reference feed wire from the computer
- A ground wire
- A voltage signal wire back to the computer; as the throttle is opened, the voltage to the computer changes

Normal throttle position voltage on most vehicles is about 0.5 volts at idle (closed throttle) and 4.5 volts at wide-open throttle (WOT). The TP sensor voltage at idle is usually about 10% of the TP sensor voltage when the throttle is wide open. The computer senses this change in throttle position and changes the fuel mixture and ignition timing. The actual change in fuel mixture and ignition timing is also partly determined by other sensors, such as the manifold pressure (engine vacuum), engine RPM, the engine coolant temperature, and oxygen sensor(s). Some throttle position sensors are adjustable and should be set according to the engine manufacturer's exact specifications. A defective or misadjusted throttle position sensor can cause hesitation on acceleration and other driveability problems. On some vehicles equipped with an automatic trans-

Figure 25–10 A typical throttle position (TP) sensor mounted on the throttle plate of this port-injected engine.

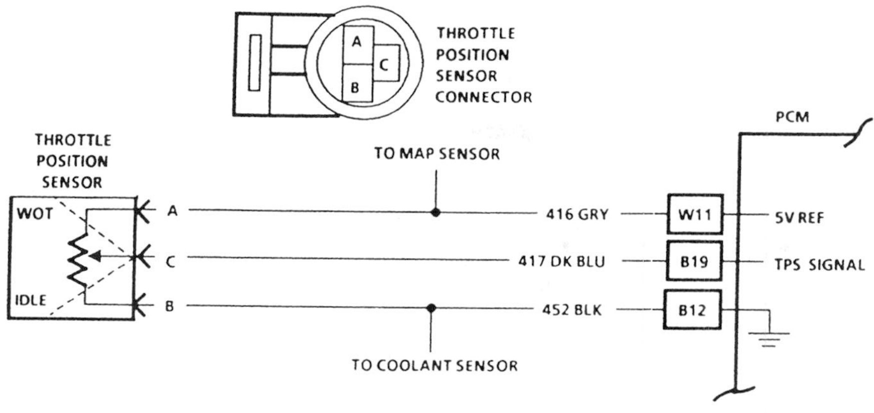

Figure 25–11 Schematic of a typical throttle position (TP) sensor circuit. Movement of the wiper on the potentiometer sends a voltage signal (0.5 to 4.5 volts) to the computer. (Courtesy General Motors)

mission, the throttle position sensor also affects the application of the torque converter clutch (TCC).

The throttle position (TP) sensor used on fuel-injected vehicles acts as an electronic accelerator pump. If the TP sensor is unplugged or defective, the engine may still operate satisfactorily, but hesitate upon acceleration as though the carburetor were in need of a new accelerator pump. Holding the throttle to the floor while cranking usually causes fuel injection to stop or reduce. This is called "clear flood" mode and is used to clear a flooded engine.

Manifold Absolute Pressure Sensor

The **manifold absolute pressure (MAP)** sensor is used by the engine computer to sense engine load. The typical MAP sensor consists of a ceramic or silicon wafer sealed on one side with a perfect vacuum, and exposed to intake manifold vacuum on the other side. See Figure 25–12. As the engine vacuum changes, the pressure difference on the wafer changes the output voltage (or frequency) of the MAP sensor.

Engine Load	Manifold Vacuum	Manifold Pressure	MAP Sensor Voltage Signal
Heavy	Low	High	High
(WOT)	(almost 0 mm Hg)	(almost atmospheric)	(4.6–4.8 V)
Light	High	Low	Low
(idle)	(430–530 mm Hg) (17-21 in. Hg)	(lower than atmospheric)	(0.8–1.6 V)

Figure 25–12 This MAP sensor is installed on the bulkhead with a vacuum hose attached that runs to the intake manifold. Some MAP sensors are attached directly to the intake manifold.

The PCM uses information from the MAP sensor to control ignition advance, timing, and fuel delivery. A typical MAP sensor uses three wires (see Figure 25–13), similar to a TPS.

- A 5 volt reference feed wire from the computer
- A ground wire
- A voltage (or frequency) wire back to the computer; as manifold vacuum changes, the voltage signal back to the computer also changes

Barometric Pressure Sensor

The **barometric pressure (BP** or **BARO)** sensor is used by the engine computer to sense the barometric pressure. This input not only allows the com-

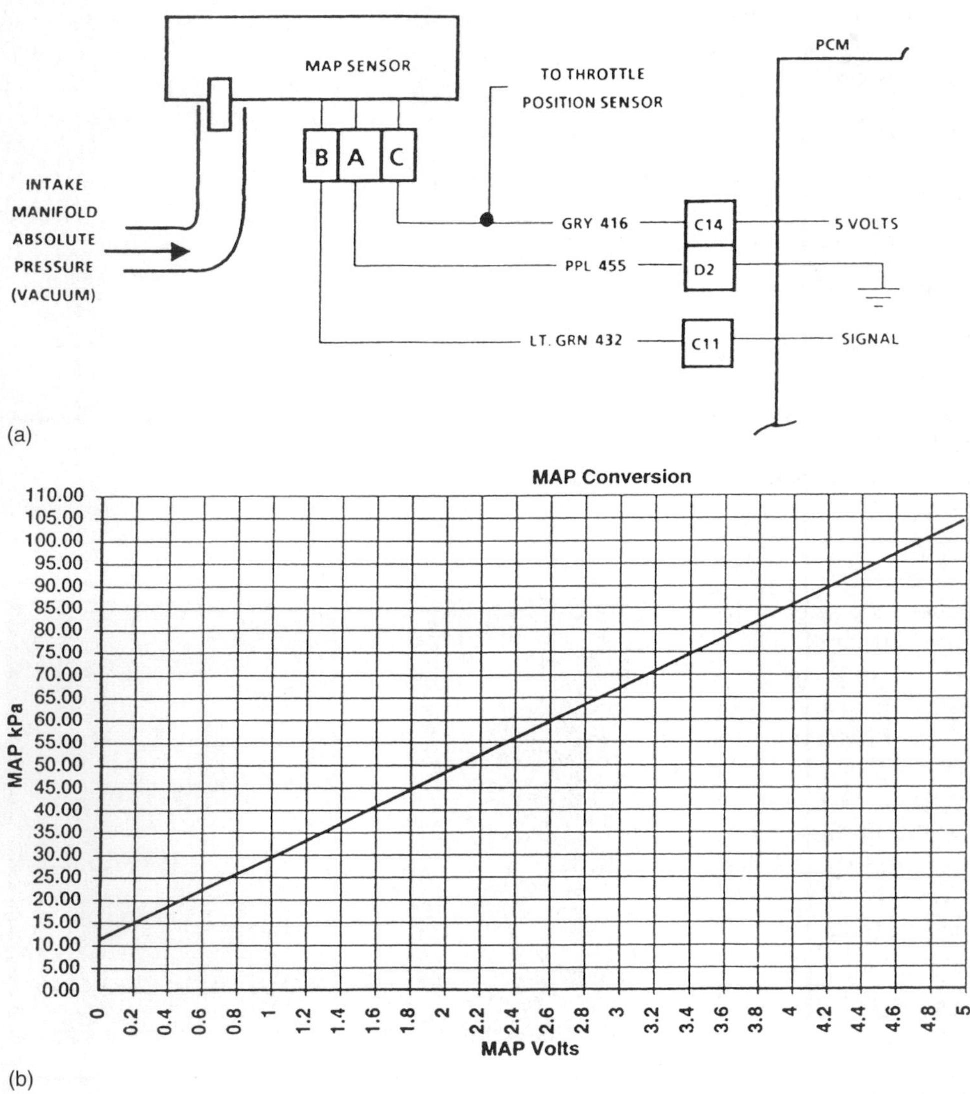

Figure 25–13 (a) Schematic of a typical manifold absolute pressure (MAP) sensor circuit. (b) As manifold pressure (vacuum) changes, the voltage signal to the computer also changes. (Courtesy General Motors)

puter to adjust for changes in atmospheric pressure due to weather, but also is the primary sensor used to determine altitude.

A MAP sensor and a BARO sensor are usually the same sensor. The MAP sensor is capable of reading barometric pressure just as the ignition switch is turned to the "on" position before the engine starts. Therefore, altitude and weather changes are available to the computer. During mountainous driving, it may be an advantage to stop and then restart the engine so that the engine computer can take another barometric pressure reading and recalibrate fuel delivery based on the new altitude. The computer on some vehicles will monitor the TP sensor and use the MAP sensor reading at wide-open throttle (WOT) to update the BARO sensor if it has changed during driving.

Engine Coolant Temperature Sensor

When the engine is cold, the fuel mixture must be richer to prevent stalling and engine stumble. When the engine is warm, the fuel mixture can be leaner to provide maximum fuel economy with the lowest possible exhaust emissions. Because the computer controls spark timing and fuel mixture, it will need to know the engine temperature. An engine coolant temperature sensor (ECT) threaded into the engine coolant passage will provide the computer with this information. See Figure 25–14. This will be the most important sensor while the engine is cold. The ignition timing can also be tailored to engine (coolant) temperature. A hot engine cannot have the spark timing as far advanced as a cold engine. Most coolant sensors have very high resistance when the coolant is cold and low resistance when the coolant is hot. This is referred to as having a **negative temperature coefficient (NTC),** which is opposite to the situation with most other electrical components. See Figure 25–15.

A typical CTS uses only two wires (see Figure 25–16):

- The computer sends a 5 volt signal through an internal resistor to the coolant temperature sensor and measures the voltage between the two resistors. The changing resistance in the sensor causes the voltage to be high with a cold engine and low with a warm engine.
- A ground wire.

If the coolant temperature sensor has a poor connection (high resistance at the wiring connector), the computer will supply a richer than normal fuel mixture based on the resistance of the coolant sensor. Therefore, poor fuel economy and a possible-rich trouble code can be caused by a defective sensor or high resistance in the sensor wiring. If the sensor was shorted or defective and has too low a resistance, a leaner-than-normal fuel mixture would be supplied to the engine. A too-lean fuel mixture can cause driveability problems and a possible lean diagnostic trouble code.

Oxygen Sensors

Most automotive computer systems use oxygen sensors (02S) in the exhaust system to measure the oxygen content of the exhaust. See Figure 25–17. If the

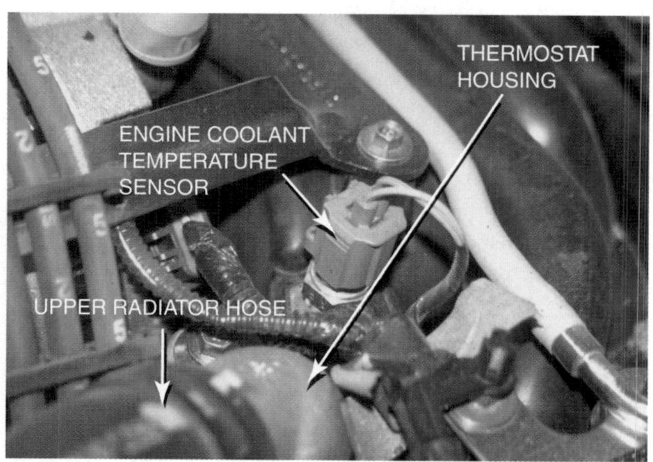

Figure 25–14 A typical engine coolant temperature (ECT) sensor. ECT sensors are located near the thermostat housing on most engines.

Coolant Sensor Temperature to Resistance Values (Approximate)

°C	°F	Ohms
100	210	185
70	160	450
38	100	1800
20	70	3400
4	40	7500
–7	20	13 500
–18	0	25 000
–40	–40	100 700

Figure 25–15 Engine coolant temperature resistance values. Note the resistance decreases as the temperature rises. These are typical values only; always refer to the vehicle specifications. (Courtesy General Motors)

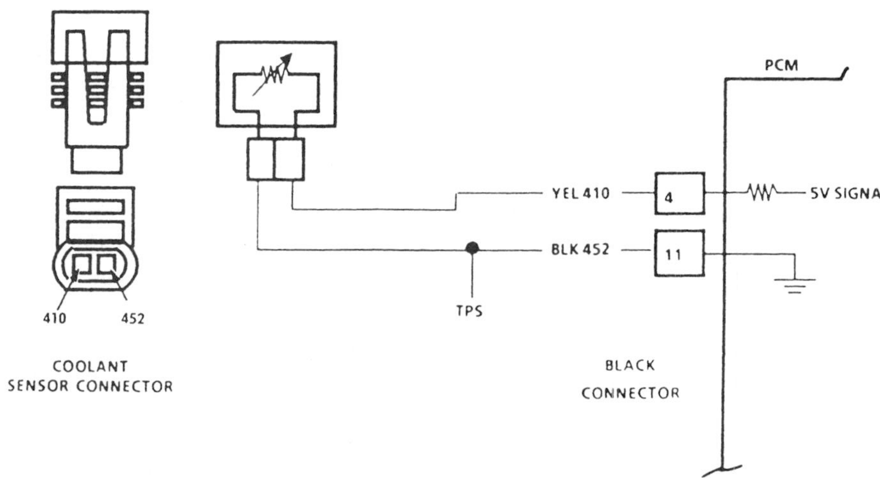

Figure 25–16 Schematic of a typical engine coolant temperature sensor circuit. The computer measures the voltage signal between the PCM resistor and the ECT resistance. (Courtesy General Motors)

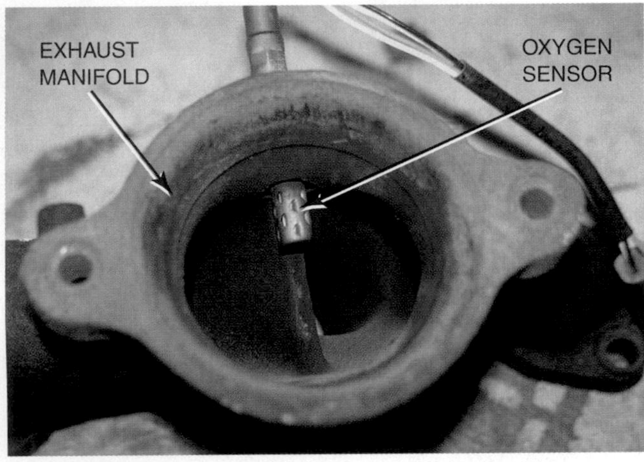

Figure 25–17 Many fuel control oxygen sensors are located in the exhaust manifold near its outlet so that the sensor can detect the presence or absence of oxygen in the exhaust stream for all cylinders that feed into the manifold.

exhaust contains very little oxygen (O_2), the computer assumes that the intake charge is rich (too much fuel) and reduces fuel delivery. On the other hand, when the oxygen level is high, the computer assumes that the intake charge is lean (not enough fuel) and increases fuel delivery. There are several different designs of oxygen sensors, including:

- **One-wire oxygen sensor**. This one wire of the one-wire oxygen sensor is the O2S signal wire. The ground for the O2S is through the shell and threads of the sensor and through the exhaust manifold.
- **Two-wire oxygen sensor.** The two-wire sensor has a signal wire and a ground wire for the O2S.
- **Three-wire oxygen sensor.** The three-wire sensor design uses an electric resistance heater to help get the O2S up to temperature more quickly and to help keep the sensor at operating temperature even at idle speeds. The three wires include the O2S signal, the power, and ground for the heater.
- **Four-wire oxygen sensor**. The four-wire sensor is heated O2S (HO2S) that uses an O2S signal wire and signal ground. The other two wires are the power and ground for the heater.

Zirconia Oxygen Sensors

The most common type of oxygen sensor is made from zirconia (zirconium dioxide). It is usually constructed using powder that is pressed into a thimble shape and coated with porous platinum material that acts as electrodes. See Figure 25–18 and 25–19. The oxygen sensor reacts with the exhaust gases to produce a voltage from 0 volts to 1 volt (0 mV to 1 000 mV) by comparing the oxygen content of the exhaust to the oxygen content of the outside air (21%).

Figure 25–18 Typical zirconia oxygen sensor.

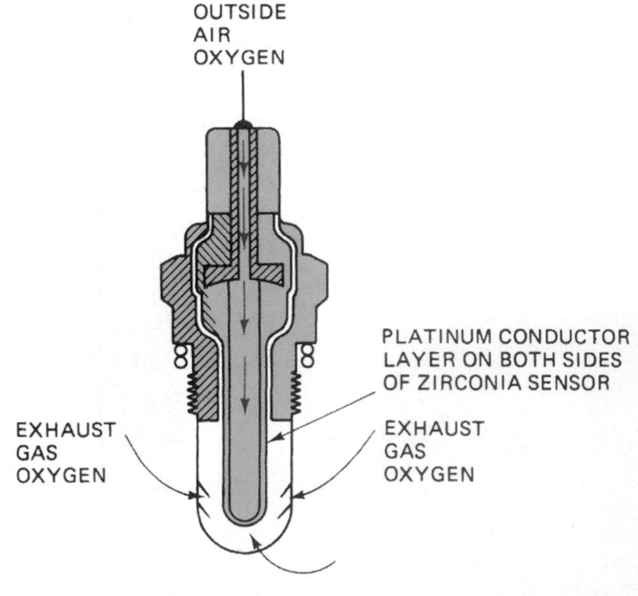

Figure 25–19 A cross-sectional view of a typical zirconia oxygen sensor.

Zirconia oxygen sensors (O2S) are constructed so that oxygen ions flow through the sensor when there is a difference between the oxygen content inside and outside the sensor. An ion is an electrically charged particle. The greater the differences in the oxygen content between the inside and outside of the sensor, the higher the voltage.

- **Rich mixture.** A rich mixture results in little oxygen in the exhaust stream. Compared to the outside air, this represents a large difference and the sensors create a relatively high voltage of about 1.0 volt (1000 mV).
- **Lean mixture.** A lean mixture leaves some oxygen in the exhaust stream that did not combine with the fuel. This leftover oxygen reduces the difference between the oxygen content of the exhaust compared to the oxygen content of the outside air. As a result, the sensor voltage is low or almost zero volts.
- **O2S** voltage above 450 mV is produced by the sensor when the oxygen content in the exhaust is

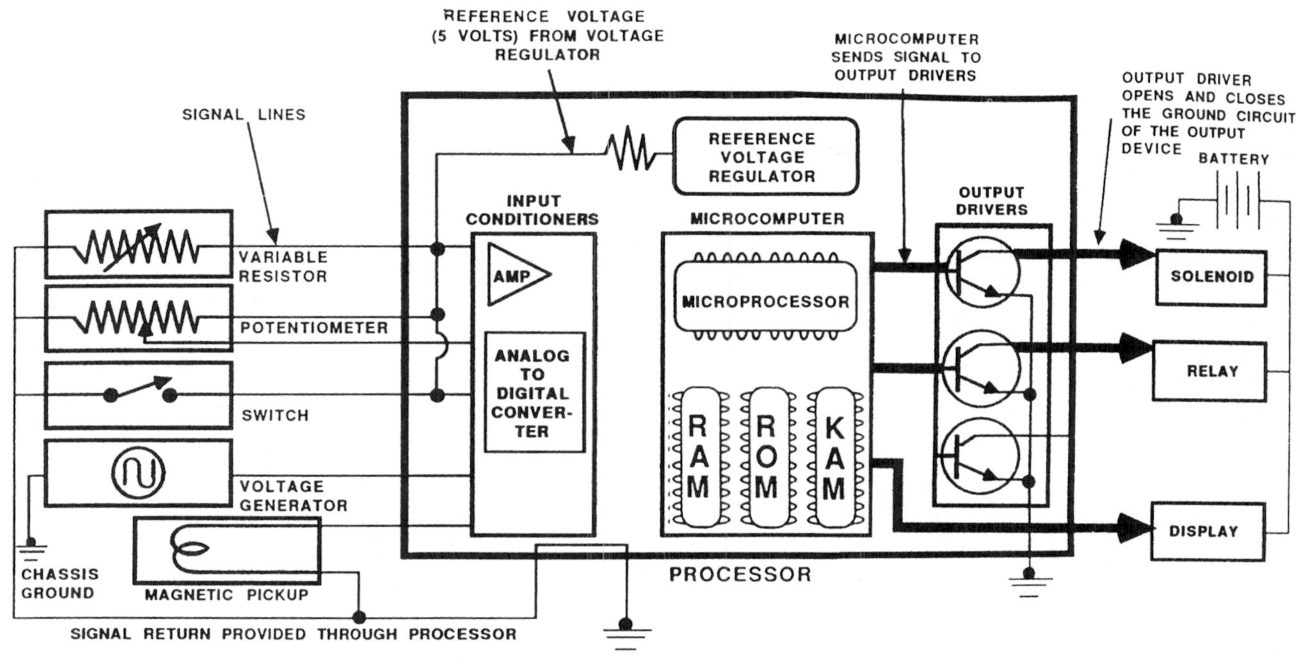

Figure 25–20 Microprocessor schematic showing input, processing, and output. Note that input sensors operate from a 5 volt reference signal and the output devices operate from battery voltage. (Courtesy Ford Motor Co.)

low. This is interpreted by the engine computer (PCM) as being a rich exhaust.

- **O2S** voltage below 450 mV is produced by the sensor when the oxygen content is high. This is interpreted by the engine computer (PCM) as being a lean exhaust.

Titania Oxygen Sensor

The titania (titanium dioxide) oxygen sensor does not produce a voltage but rather modifies one as it samples the presence of oxygen in the exhaust. All titania oxygen sensors use a four-terminal variable resistance unit with a heating element. A titania sensor samples exhaust air only and uses a reference voltage from the PCM. Titania oxide oxygen sensors use a 14-mm thread and are not interchangeable with zirconia oxygen sensors. One volt is applied to the sensor and the changing resistance of the titania oxygen sensor changes the voltage of the sensor circuit. As with a zirconia oxygen sensor, the voltage signal is about 450 mV when the exhaust is rich, and low (below 450 mV) when the exhaust is lean.

PROCESSING AND MEMORY

The microprocessor is the decision making part of the computer. It takes data from the various input sensors and compares it with information stored in memory. See Figure 25–20.

Computers have two types of memory: permanent and temporary. Permanent memory is called **read-only memory (ROM)** because the computer can only read the contents; it cannot change the data stored in it. This data is retained even when power to the computer is shut off. Part of the ROM is built into the computer, and the rest is located in an IC chip called a **programmable read-only memory (PROM)** or calibration assembly.

Temporary memory is called **random-access memory (RAM)** because the microprocessor can write or store new data into it as directed by the computer program, as well as read the data already in it. Automotive computers use two types of RAM memory: **volatile** and **nonvolatile.** Volatile RAM memory is lost whenever the ignition is turned off. However, a type of volatile RAM called **keep-alive memory (KAM)** can be wired directly to battery power. This prevents its data from being erased when the ignition is turned off. Both RAM and KAM have the disadvantage of losing their memory when disconnected from their power source. One example of RAM and KAM is the loss of station settings in a programmable radio when the battery is disconnected. Since all the settings are stored in RAM, they have to be reset when the battery is reconnected. System diagnostic trouble codes (DTC) are commonly stored in RAM and can be erased by disconnecting the battery.

Adaptive strategies that compensate for wear and aging are another function of KAM. The original computer program in ROM is written for the average engine operating under average conditions, but this is often not the case.

Fuel delivery calculations are based on information from the engine sensors; throttle position, air and coolant temperatures, engine speed and load are a few of these inputs. Based on these data, the computer refers to a look-up table stored in ROM and injects a given amount of fuel into the engine. The resulting air–fuel mixture is monitored by an exhaust-mounted oxygen sensor, which sends data back to the computer.

When the oxygen sensor detects a lean or rich condition, the computer increases or decreases fuel volume as a correction. When a major shift is determined over a period of time, the computer changes the original program to reflect different fuel requirements. This is called adaptive strategy and is stored in KAM. Many vehicles run well, even with low fuel pressure or restricted fuel injectors.

If the battery is disconnected, all adaptive information stored in KAM is lost; the computer now defaults to the original program and begins the relearning process.

Nonvolatile RAM memory can retain its information even when the battery is disconnected. One use for this type of RAM is the storage of odometer information in an electronic speedometer. The memory chip retains the distance accumulated by the vehicle. When speedometer replacement is necessary, the odometer chip is removed and installed in the new speedometer unit.

The computer processes the input voltage signals through a series of logic circuits maintained in its programmed instructions. The logic circuits change the input data into output voltage signals or commands that control output transistors.

OUTPUT

Actuators are electrical or mechanical devices that convert electrical energy into mechanical action. The computer sends a voltage signal to the base circuit of an output driver transistor which activates the device, usually a relay or solenoid. See Figure 25–21.

When the ignition switch is closed, battery voltage is supplied to the actuators; no current flows until ground is supplied by turning the transistor on. This is known as ground side control and is the most common circuit. Technicians often check output circuits by grounding the wire between the actuator and the microprocessor. Any actuator that runs at 100% duty cycle can be tested by grounding. Actuators such as fuel injector solenoids never run at 100% duty cycle and can be damaged by grounding. Follow the service instructions exactly when working with computer circuits.

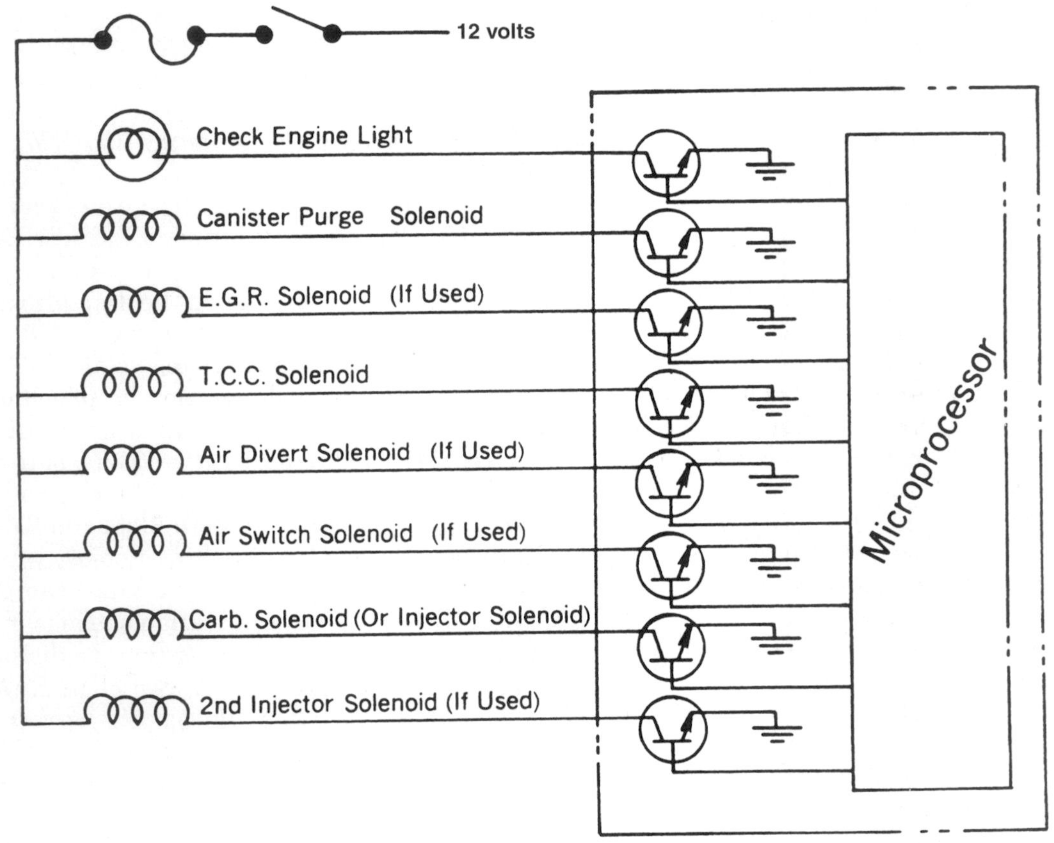

Figure 25–21 Basic computer outputs. (Courtesy General Motors)

Our basic computer shows only a single driver transistor for each device; most computers bank the transistors into a group of four called quad-drivers, but the function is the same.

Output devices are usually tested for resistance with an ohmmeter, or checked for current flow; a shorted solenoid coil, as an example, will allow excessive current to flow which could damage the driver transistor in the computer.

SENSOR TESTING

The correct operation of computerized engines depends on accurate and dependable sensors. Proper testing of sensors is an important part of computer problem diagnosis and troubleshooting.

Testing the Engine Coolant Temperature by Visual Inspection

The correct functioning of the engine coolant temperature (ECT) sensor depends on the following items that should be checked or inspected:

- **Properly filled cooling system.** Check that the radiator reservoir bottle is full and that the radiator itself is filled to the top.

> **CAUTION:** Be sure that the radiator is cool before removing the radiator cap to avoid being scalded by hot coolant.

The ECT sensor must be submerged in coolant to be able to indicate the proper coolant temperature.

- **Proper pressure maintained by the radiator cap.** If the radiator cap is defective and cannot allow the cooling system to become pressurized, air pockets could develop. These air pockets could cause the engine to operate at a hotter than normal temperature and prevent proper temperature measurement, especially if the air pockets occur around the sensor.
- **Proper antifreeze–water mixture.** Most vehicle manufacturers recommend a 50/50 mixture of antifreeze and water as the best compromise between freezing protection and heat transfer ability.
- **Proper operation of the cooling fan.** If the cooling fan does not operate correctly, the engine may overheat.

Testing the ECT Using a Multimeter

Both the resistance (in ohms) and the voltage drop across the sensor can be measured and compared with specifications. See Figure 25–22. See the following chart showing examples of typical engine coolant temperature sensor specifications. Some vehicles use a second resistor in the ECT circuit to provide a more accurate measure of the engine temperature. See Figure 25–23.

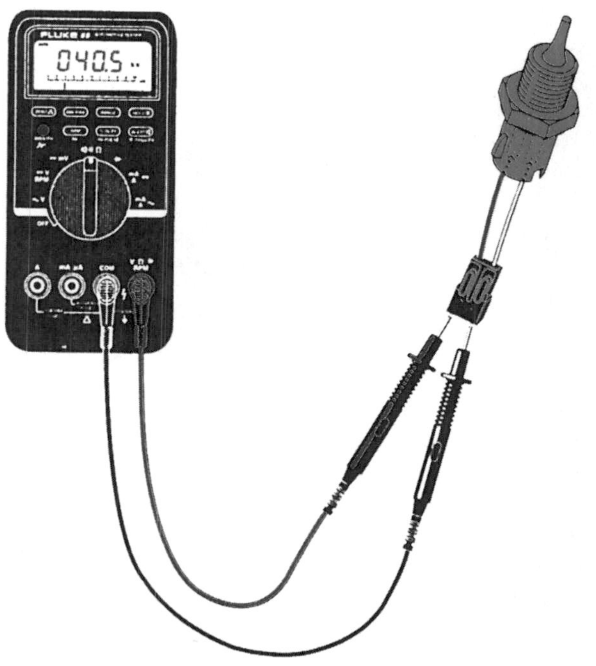

Figure 25–22 Measuring the resistance of the ECT sensor. The resistance measurement can then be compared with specifications. (Courtesy of Fluke Corporation)

General Motors ECT Sensor without Pull-Up Resistor

°C	°F	Ohms	Voltage Drop Across Sensor
−40	− 40	100 000+	4.95
−8	18	14 628	4.68
0	32	9420	4.52
10	50	5670	4.25
20	68	3520	3.89
30	86	2238	3.46
40	104	1459	2.97
50	122	973	2.47
60	140	667	2.00
70	158	467	1.59
80	176	332	1.25
90	194	241	0.97
100	212	177	0.75

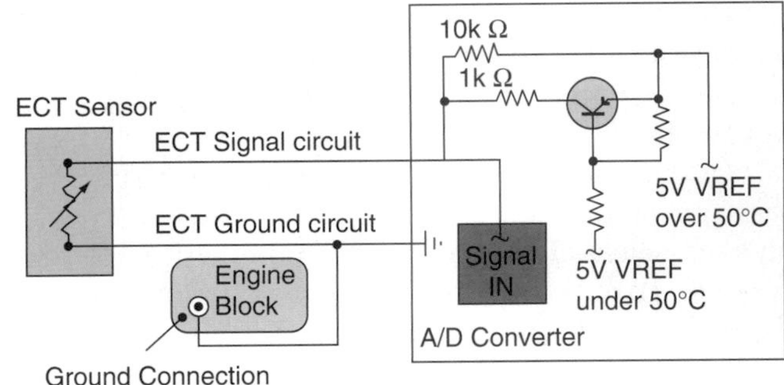

Figure 25–23 When the voltage drop reaches approximately 1.20 volts, the PCM turns on a transistor. The transistor connects a 1 kΩ resistor in parallel with the 10 kΩ resistor. Total circuit resistance now drops to around 909 ohms. This function allows the PCM to have full binary control at cold temperatures up to approximately 50°C (122°F), and a second full binary control at temperatures greater than 50°C (122°F).

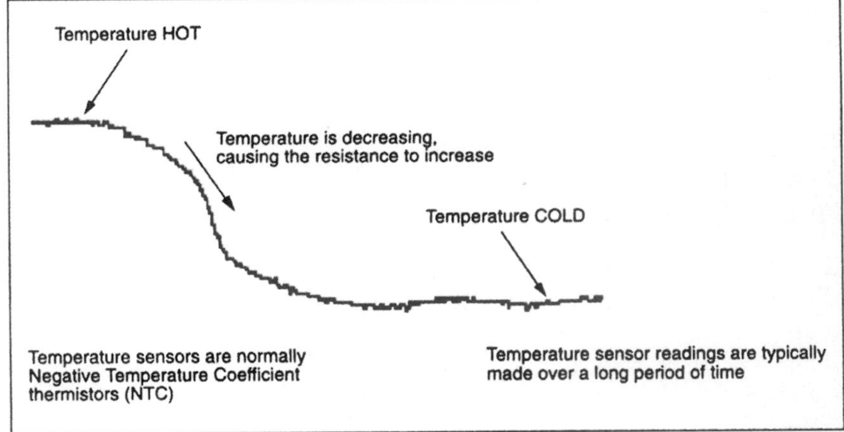

Figure 25–24 A typical ECT sensor being tested using a digital storage oscilloscope. The illustration shows the voltage of the sensor after the engine was stopped. As the resistance of the sensor increased, the voltage decreased. (Courtesy of Fluke Corporation)

If resistance values match the approximate coolant temperature and there is still a coolant sensor trouble code, the problem is generally in the wiring between the sensor and the computer. Always consult the manufacturer's recommended procedures for checking this wiring. If the resistance values do not match, the sensor may need to be replaced.

Normal operating temperature varies with vehicle make and model. Some vehicles are equipped with a thermostat with an opening temperature of 82°C (176°F), whereas other vehicles use a thermostat that is 90°C (195°F) or higher. Before replacing the ECT sensor, be sure that the engine is operating at the temperature specified by the manufacturer. Most manufacturers recommend checking the ECT sensor after the cooling fan has cycled twice, indicating a fully warmed engine. See Figure 25–24.

NOTE: Many manufacturers install a pull-up resistor inside the computer to change the voltage drop across the ECT sensor. This is done to expand the scale of the ECT sensor and to make the sensor more sensitive. Therefore, if measuring *voltage* at the ECT sensor, check with the service manual for the proper voltage at each temperature.

Testing the ECT Sensor Using a Scan Tool

Comparing the temperature of the engine coolant as displayed on a scan tool with the actual temperature of the engine is an excellent method to test an engine coolant temperature sensor.

1. Record the scan tool temperature of the coolant (ECT).
2. Measure the actual temperature of the coolant using an infrared pyrometer or contact-type temperature probe.

HINT: Often the coolant temperature gauge in the dash of the vehicle can be used to compare with the scan tool temperature. Although not necessarily accurate, it may help to diagnose a faulty sensor, especially if the temperature shown on the scan tool varies greatly from the temperature indicated on the dash.

The maximum difference between the two readings should be 5°C (10°F). If the actual temperature varies by more than 5°C (10°F) from the temperature indicated on the scan tool, check the

ECT sensor wiring and connector for damage or corrosion. If the connector and wiring are okay, replace the ECT sensor. If the connector and wiring are okay, check the sensor with a DVOM for resistance and compare to the actual engine temperature chart. If that checks out okay, check the computer.

> **NOTE:** Many manufacturers use two coolant sensors, one for the dash gauge and another one for the computer.

INTAKE AIR TEMPERATURE SENSOR

The intake air temperature (IAT) sensor is a negative temperature coefficient (NTC) thermistor that decreases in resistance as the temperature of the sensor increases. The IAT sensor can be located in one of the following locations:

- In the air cleaner housing
- In the air duct between the air filler and the throttle body as shown in Figure 25–25
- Built into the mass air flow (MAF) or air flow sensor

Figure 25–25 The IAT sensor on this General Motors 3800 V-6 engine is in the air passage duct between the air cleaner housing and the throttle plate.

- Threaded into the intake manifold where it senses the temperature of the air entering the cylinders

> **NOTE:** An IAT installed in the intake manifold is the most likely to suffer damage due to an engine backfire, which can often destroy the sensor.

The purpose and function of the intake air temperature sensor is to provide the engine computer (PCM) the temperature of the air entering the engine.

- **Cold air**—is more dense and contains more oxygen and therefore requires a richer mixture to achieve the proper air–fuel mixture. Air at 0°C (32°F) is 14% denser than air at 40°C (104°F).
- **Hot air**—is less dense and contains less oxygen and therefore requires a leaner mixture to achieve the proper air–fuel mixture.

The IAT sensor is a low-authority sensor and is used by the computer to modify the amount of fuel and ignition timing as determined by the engine coolant temperature sensor.

Engine temperature is most accurately determined by looking at the engine coolant temperature (ECT) sensor. In certain conditions, the IAT has an effect on performance and driveability. One such condition is a warm engine being stopped in very cold weather. In this case, when the engine is restarted, the ECT may be near normal operating temperature such as 93°C (200°F) yet the air temperature could be −30°C (−20°F). In this case, the engine requires a richer mixture due to the cold air than the ECT would seem to indicate.

Testing the Intake Air Temperature Sensor

If the intake air temperature sensor circuit is damaged or faulty, a diagnostic trouble code (DTC) is set and the malfunction indicator lamp (MIL) may or may not be on depending on the condition and the type and model of the vehicle. To diagnose the IAT sensor follow these steps:

Step 1 After the vehicle has been allowed to cool for several hours, use a scan tool and observe the IAT and compare it to the engine coolant temperature (ECT). The two temperatures should be within 3°C (5°F) of each other.

Step 2 Perform a thorough visual inspection of the sensor and the wiring. If the IAT is threaded into the intake manifold, remove the sensor and check for damage.

Step 3 Check the voltage and compare to the following chart.

Manifold/Intake Air Temperature Sensor Temperature vs. Resistance and Voltage Drop (Approximate)			
°C	°F	Ohms	Voltage Drop Across Sensor (V)
−40	−40	100 000	4.95
−8	+18	15 000	4.68
0	32	9400	4.52
10	50	5700	4.25
20	68	3500	3.89
30	86	2200	3.46
40	104	1500	2.97
50	122	1000	2.47
60	140	700	2.00
70	158	500	1.59
80	176	300	1.25
90	194	250	0.97
100	212	200	0.75

TECH TIP 

Poor Fuel Economy? Black Exhaust Smoke? Look at the IAT.

If the intake air temperature sensor is defective, it may be signaling the computer that the intake air temperature is extremely cold when in fact it is warm. In such a case the computer will supply a mixture that is much richer than normal.

If a sensor is physically damaged or electrically open, the computer will often set a diagnostic trouble code (DTC). This DTC is based on the fact that the sensor temperature did not change for a certain amount of time, usually about 8 minutes. If, however, the wiring or the sensor itself has excessive resistance, a DTC will not be set and the result will be lower than normal fuel economy, and in serious cases, black exhaust smoke from the tailpipe during acceleration.

Testing the Manifold Absolute Pressure Sensor

Most pressure sensors operate on 5 volts from the computer and return a signal (voltage or frequency) based on the pressure (vacuum) applied to the sensor. If a MAP sensor is being tested, make certain that the vacuum hose and hose fittings are sound and making a good, tight connection to a manifold vacuum source on the engine.

TECH TIP 

Check the Hose

A defective vacuum hose to a MAP sensor can cause a variety of driveability problems including poor fuel economy, hesitation, stalling, and rough idle. A small air leak (vacuum leak) around the hose can cause these symptoms and often set a trouble code in the vehicle computer. When working on a vehicle that uses a MAP sensor, make certain that the vacuum hose travels consistently *downward* on its route from the sensor to the source of manifold vacuum. Inspect the hose, especially if another technician has previously replaced the factory-original hose. It should not be so long that it sags down at any point. Condensed fuel and/or moisture can become trapped in this low spot in the hose and cause all types of driveability problems and MAP sensor codes.

Four different types of test instruments can be used to test a pressure sensor:

1. A digital voltmeter with three test leads connected in series between the sensor and the wiring harness connector (see Figure 25–26)
2. A scope connected to the sensor output, power, and ground
3. A scan tool or a specific tool recommended by the vehicle manufacturer
4. A breakout box connected in series between the computer and the wiring harness connection(s). A typical breakout box includes test points at which pressure sensor values can be measured with a digital voltmeter (or frequency counter, if a frequency-type MAP sensor is being tested)

NOTE: Always check service literature for the exact testing procedures and specifications for the vehicle being tested.

Use jumper wires, T-pins, or a breakout box to gain electrical access to the wiring to the pressure sensor. Most pressure sensors use three wires:

1. A 5 volt wire from the computer
2. A variable-signal wire back to the computer
3. A ground or reference low wire

The procedure for testing the sensor is as follows:

1. Turn the ignition on (engine off)
2. Measure the voltage (or frequency) of the sensor output
3. Using a hand-operated vacuum pump (or other variable vacuum source), apply vacuum to the sensor

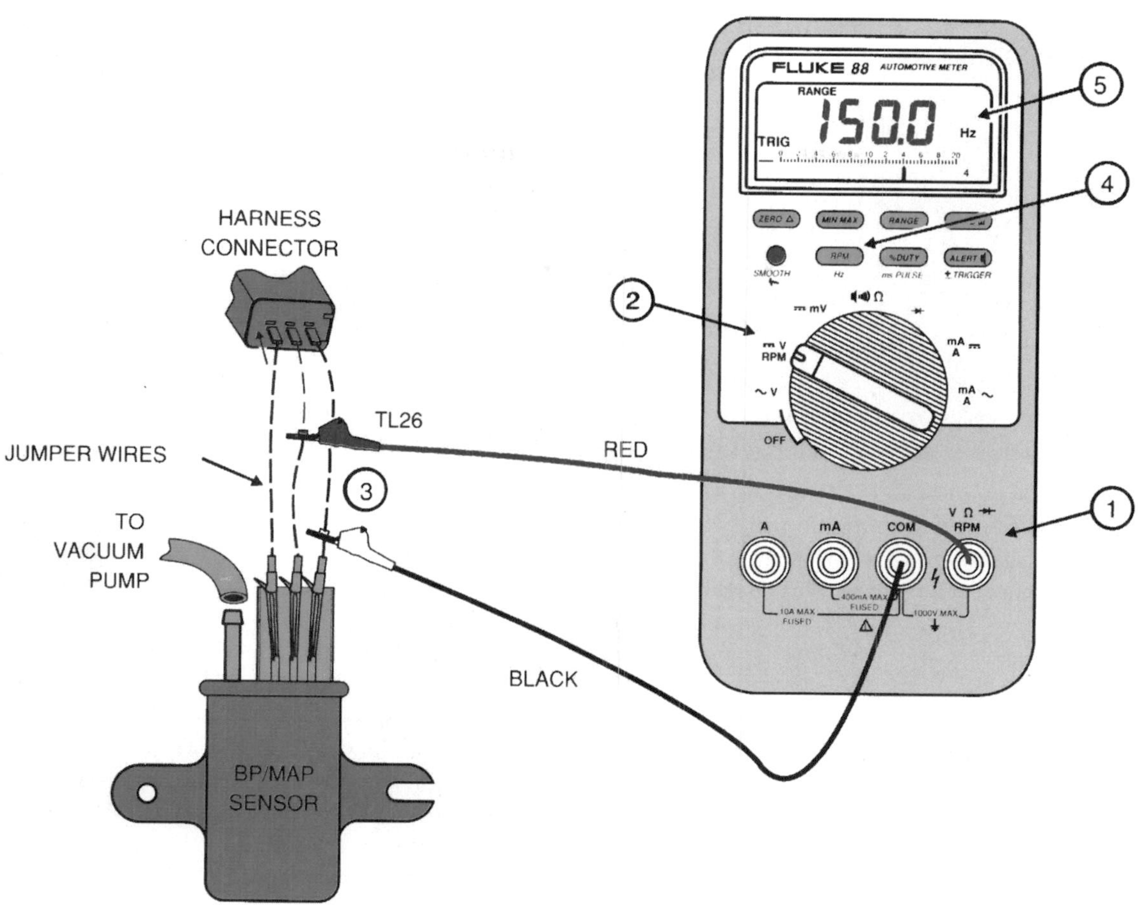

Figure 25–26 A digital multimeter set to test a MAP sensor. (1) Connect the red meter lead to the V meter terminal and the black meter lead to the COM meter terminal. (2) Select DC volts. (3) Connect the test leads to the sensor signal wire and the ground wire. (4) Select hertz (Hz) if testing a MAP sensor whose output is a varying frequency—otherwise keep it on DC volts. (5) Read the change of frequency as the vacuum is applied to the sensor. Compare the vacuum reading and the frequency (or voltage) reading to the specifications.

A good pressure sensor should change voltage (or frequency) in relation to the applied vacuum. If the signal does not change or the values are out of range according to the manufacturers' specifications, the sensor must be replaced.

Testing the Throttle Position Sensor

A TP sensor can be tested using one or more of the following tools:

- A digital voltmeter with three test leads connected in series between the sensor and the wiring harness connector or backprobing using T-pins.
- A scan tool or a specific tool recommended by the vehicle manufacturer.
- A breakout box that is connected in series between the computer and the wiring harness connector(s). A typical breakout box includes test points at which TP voltages can be measured with a digital voltmeter.
- An oscilloscope.

Use jumper wires, T-pins, or a breakout box to gain electrical access to the wiring to the TP sensor. See Figure 25–27.

> **NOTE:** The procedure that follows is the usual method used by many manufacturers. Always refer to service literature for the exact recommended procedure and specifications for the vehicle being tested.

The procedure for testing the sensor using a digital multimeter is as follows:

1. Turn the ignition switch on (engine off).
2. Measure the voltage between the signal wire and ground (reference low) wire. The voltage should be about 0.5 volt.

Figure 25–27 A meter lead connected to a T-pin that was gently pushed along the signal wire of the TP sensor until the point of the pin touched the metal terminal inside the plastic connector.

> **NOTE:** Consult the service literature for exact wire colours or locations.

3. With the engine still not running (but with the ignition still on), slowly increase the throttle opening. The voltage signal from the TP sensor should also increase. Look for any "dead spots" or open circuit readings as the throttle is increased to the wide-open position. See Figure 25–28 for an example of how a good TP sensor would look when tested with a digital storage oscilloscope (DSO).

> **HINT:** If TP sensor specifications are not available, remember that the TP sensor voltage at idle should be about 10% of the voltage at the **wide-open throttle (WOT)** position. Therefore, if the WOT voltage is 4.5 volts, then TP sensor voltage at idle should be about 0.45 volts.

4. With the voltmeter (or scan tool) still connected, slowly return the throttle down to the idle position. The voltage from the TP sensor should also decrease evenly on the return to idle.

The TP sensor voltage at idle should be within the acceptable range as specified by the manufacturer. Some TP sensors can be adjusted by loosening their retaining screws and moving the sensor in relation to the throttle opening. This movement changes the output voltage of the sensor.

All TP sensors should also provide a smooth transition voltage reading from idle to WOT and back to idle. Replace the TP sensor if erratic voltage readings are obtained or if the correct setting at idle cannot be obtained.

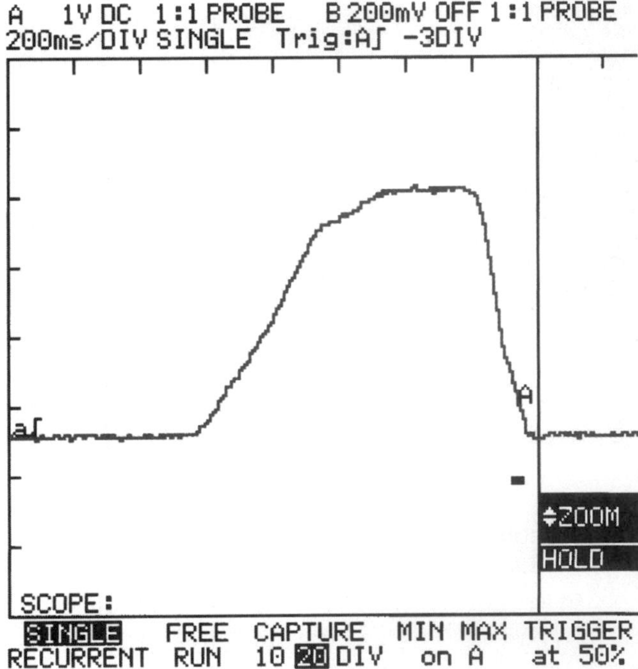

Figure 25–28 A typical waveform of a TP sensor signal as recorded on a DSO when the accelerator pedal was depressed with the ignition switch on (engine off). Clean transitions and the lack of any glitches in this waveform indicate a good sensor. (Courtesy of Fluke Corporation)

TECH TIP 

Check Power and Ground Before Condemning a Bad Sensor

Most engine sensors use a 5 volt reference and a ground. If the 5 volt to the sensor is too high (shorted to voltage) or too low (high resistance), then the sensor output will be **skewed** or out of range. Before replacing the sensor that did not read correctly, unplug the sensor and measure both the 5 volt reference and ground. To measure the ground, simply turn the ignition on (engine off) and touch one test lead of a DMM set to read DC volts to the sensor ground and the other to the negative terminal of the battery. Any reading higher than 0.6 volt (600 mV) represents a poor ground. See Figures 25–29 and 25–30.

Testing the Oxygen Sensor

Zirconia oxygen sensors produce a voltage (like a small battery) when in the *absence* of oxygen, when the sensor is hot (over 315°C or 600°F). The output

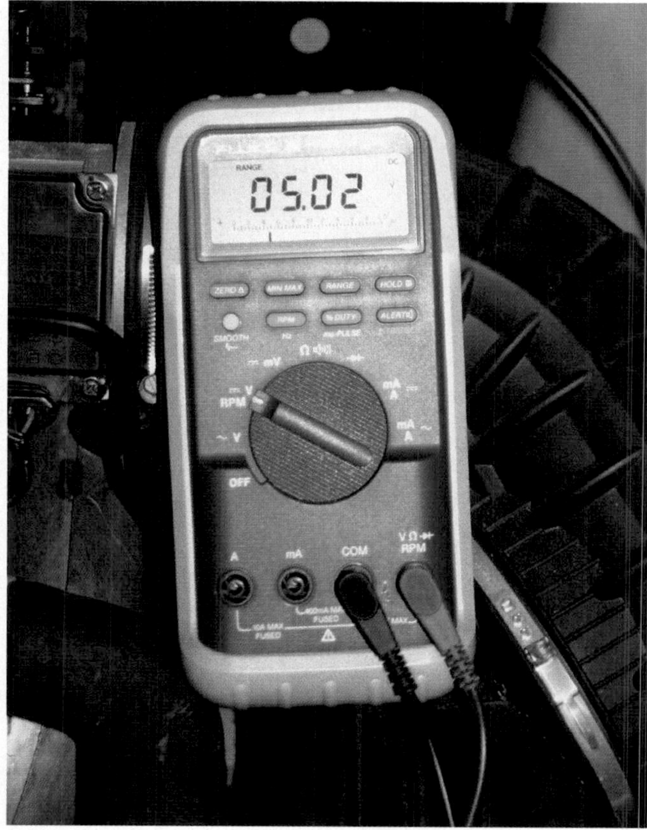

Figure 25–29 Checking the 5 volt reference from the computer being applied to the TP sensor with the ignition switch on (engine off).

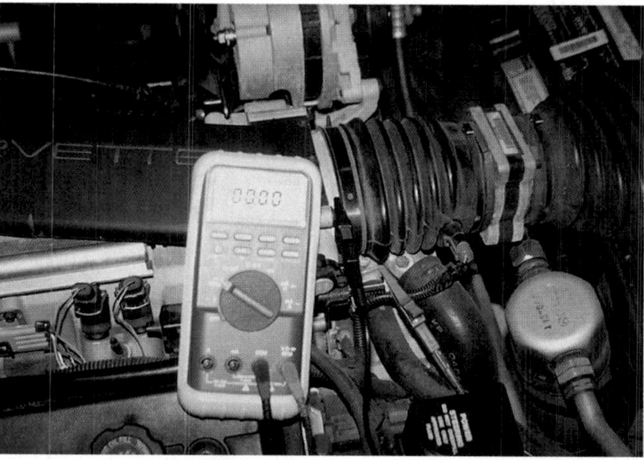

Figure 25–30 Checking the voltage drop between the TP sensor ground and a good engine ground with the ignition on (engine off). A reading of greater than 0.6 V (600 mV) represents a bad computer ground.

voltage of a typical oxygen sensor varies depending on the oxygen content of the exhaust gases passing the sensor.

Typical oxygen sensor values are as follows:

- **Rich exhaust.** Oxygen sensor voltage above 800 mV
- **Lean exhaust.** Oxygen sensor voltage below 200 mV

Testing an Oxygen Sensor Using a Digital Voltmeter

The oxygen sensor can be checked for proper operation using a digital high-impedance voltmeter.

1. With the engine off, connect the red lead of the meter to the oxygen sensor signal wire. See Figure 25–31.
2. Start the engine and allow it to reach closed-loop operation. To achieve closed-loop operation, the engine computer must have achieved three criteria including:
   a. The engine coolant temperature must be above a certain temperature, usually above 40°C (104°F).
   b. The oxygen sensor(s) must be producing a usable, variable voltage signal.
   c. A certain amount of time must elapse after engine start for closed loop to be achieved. This time could vary from a few seconds to several minutes depending on the vehicle and the temperature.
3. In closed-loop operation, the oxygen sensor voltage should be constantly changing as the fuel mixture is being controlled.

The results should be interpreted as follows:

- If the oxygen sensor fails to respond, and its voltage remains at about 450 millivolts, the sensor may be defective and require replacement. Before replacing the oxygen sensor, check the manufacturers' recommended procedures.
- If the oxygen sensor reads high all the time (above 550 millivolts), the fuel system could be supplying too rich a fuel mixture or the oxygen sensor may be contaminated.
- If the oxygen sensor voltage remains low (below 350 millivolts), the fuel system could be supplying too lean a fuel mixture. Check for a vacuum leak or partially clogged fuel injector(s). Before replacing the oxygen sensor, check the manufacturer's recommended procedures.

Testing the Oxygen Sensor Using the Min-Max Method

A digital meter set on DC volts can be used to record the minimum and maximum voltage with

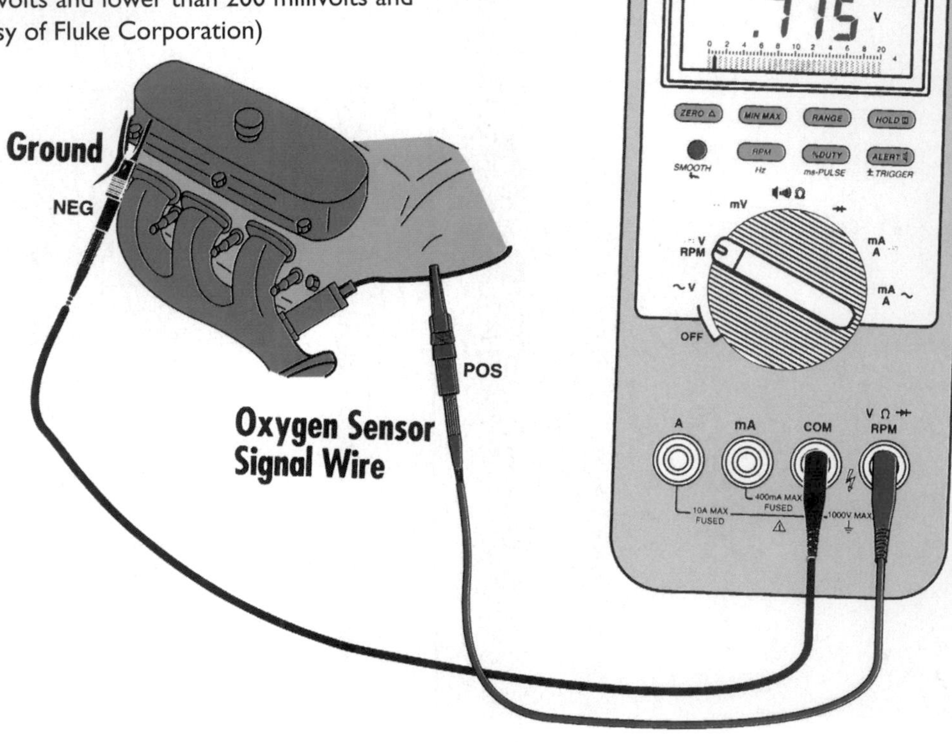

Figure 25–31 Testing an oxygen sensor using a digital multimeter set on DC volts. With the engine operating in closed loop, the oxygen voltage should read over 800 millivolts and lower than 200 millivolts and be constantly fluctuating. (Courtesy of Fluke Corporation)

the engine running. A good oxygen sensor should be able to produce a value of less than 300 millivolts and a maximum voltage above 800 millivolts. Replace any oxygen sensor that fails to go above 700 millivolts or lower than 300 millivolts.

Post-Catalytic Converter Oxygen Sensor Testing

The oxygen sensor located behind the catalytic converter is used on OBD II (On-Board Diagnostics—Generation II) vehicles to monitor converter efficiency.

Min/Max Oxygen Sensor Test Chart			
Minimum Voltage	**Maximum Voltage**	**Average Voltage**	**Test Results**
Below 200 mV	Above 800 mV	400 to 500 mV	Oxygen sensor is okay.
Above 200 mV	Any reading	400 to 500 mV	Oxygen sensor is defective.
Any reading	Below 800 mV	400 to 500 mV	Oxygen sensor is defective.
Below 200 mV	Above 800 mV	Below 400 mV	System is operating lean.*
Below 200 mV	Below 800 mV	Below 400 mV	System is operating lean. (Add propane to the intake air to see if the oxygen sensor reacts. If not, the sensor is defective.)
Below 200 mV	Above 800 mV	Above 500 mV	System is operating rich.
Above 200 mV	Above 800 mV	Above 500 mV	System is operating rich. (Remove a vacuum hose to see if the oxygen sensor reacts. If not, the sensor is defective.)
*Check for an exhaust leak upstream from the O2S or ignition misfire that can cause a false lean indication before further diagnosis.			

Frequently Asked Question ???

What Is the Difference Between a "False Lean" and a "Real Lean" Oxygen Sensor Reading?

A **false lean** signal is a result of oxygen flowing past the oxygen sensor that did not result from combustion inside the engine. Two examples of a false lean oxygen sensor indication include:

1. A cracked exhaust manifold or an exhaust leak upstream from the oxygen sensor (between the exhaust valve and the oxygen sensor) can cause a false lean. As an exhaust pulse occurs, an area of lower pressure develops behind the pulse of exhaust. This lower pressure area *draws* outside air into the exhaust stream and flows past the oxygen sensor. The oxygen sensor voltage drops as a result of this extra oxygen brought into the exhaust at the leak. The drop in oxygen sensor voltage is interpreted by the engine computer as a message that the mixture supplied to the engine is too lean, and it increases the amount of fuel supplied. As a result, the mixture now being supplied to the cylinder is too rich because the oxygen sensor was fooled and provided a false lean signal to the computer.
2. An ignition misfire as a result of a defective spark plug wire or fouled spark plug can cause a false lean. When a spark plug does not fire, the unburned gas and air inside the cylinder are pushed into the exhaust manifold by the piston(s) on the exhaust stroke. The unburned gas and air contain oxygen that is detected by the oxygen sensor as too lean a mixture.

NOTE: Remember, the oxygen sensor is a sensor to detect *oxygen,* not unburned fuel (hydrocarbons or HC)!

As a result of this oxygen being detected, the voltage produced by the oxygen sensor is lower. This lower-voltage signal is interpreted by the computer as a sign that the mixture being supplied is too lean. The computer then increases the amount of fuel delivered. This extra fuel can often cause more spark plug fouling and even more unburned oxygen passing the oxygen sensor.

Because a lean condition can be false, the wise service technician checks the exhaust system and the ignition system before trying to correct a lean indication.

DIAGNOSTIC STORY

The O_2 Sensor Is Lying to You

A technician was trying to solve a driveability problem with a V-6 passenger car. The car idled roughly, hesitated, and accelerated poorly. A thorough visual inspection did not indicate any possible problems, and there were no diagnostic trouble codes stored.

A check was made on the oxygen sensor activity using a DMM. The voltage stayed above 600 millivolts most of the time. If a large vacuum hose was removed, the oxygen sensor voltage would temporarily drop to below 450 millivolts and then return to a reading of over 600 millivolts. Remember:

- High O2S readings = rich exhaust (low O_2 content in the exhaust)
- Low O2S readings = lean exhaust (high O_2 content in the exhaust)

As part of a thorough visual inspection, the technician removed and inspected the spark plugs. All the spark plugs were white, indicating a lean mixture, not the rich mixture the oxygen sensor was indicating. The high O2S reading signalled the computer to reduce the amount of fuel resulting in an excessively lean operation.

After replacing the oxygen sensor, the engine ran great. But what killed the oxygen sensor? The technician finally learned from the owner that the head gasket had been replaced over a year ago. The silicone-silicate additives in the antifreeze coolant had coated the oxygen sensor. Because the oxygen sensor was coated, the oxygen content of the exhaust could not be detected—the result, a false rich signal from the oxygen sensor.

DIAGNOSTIC STORY

The Pickup Truck Story

The owner of a pickup truck complained that the engine ran terribly. It would hesitate and surge, yet there were no diagnostic trouble codes (DTCs). After hours of troubleshooting, the technician discovered while talking to the owner that the problem started after the transmission had been repaired. Before the transmission was repaired, the problem started, yet the transmission shop said that the problem was an engine problem and not related to the transmission.

A thorough visual inspection revealed that the front and rear oxygen sensor connectors had been switched. The computer was trying to compensate for an air–fuel mixture condition that did not exist. Reversing the OSS connectors restored proper operation of the truck.

A changing air–fuel mixture is required for the most efficient operation of the converter. If the converter is working correctly, the oxygen content after the converter should be fairly constant. See Figures 25–32 and 25–33.

SPEED DENSITY

Fuel-injection computer systems require a method for measuring the amount of air the engine is taking in, to be able to match the correct fuel delivery. There are two basic methods used:

1. Speed density method
2. Airflow method

The speed density method does not require an air quantity sensor, but rather calculates the amount of fuel required by the engine. The computer uses information from sensors such as the MAP and TP to calculate the needed amount of fuel.

- *MAP sensor.* The value of the intake (inlet) manifold pressure (vacuum) is a direct indication of engine load.
- *TP sensor.* The position of the throttle plate and its rate of change are used as part of the equation to calculate the proper amount of fuel to inject.
- *Temperature sensors.* Both engine coolant temperature (ECT) and intake air temperature (IAT) are used to calculate the density of the air and the need of the engine for fuel. A cold engine (low coolant temperature) requires a richer air–fuel mixture than a warm engine.

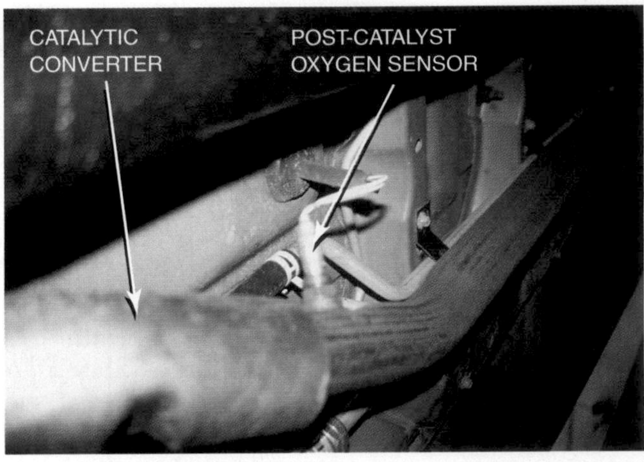

Figure 25–32 Most 1996 and newer vehicles use an oxygen sensor behind the catalytic converter. The purpose of the oxygen sensor is to sense the percentage of oxygen in the exhaust to check the efficiency of the catalytic converter.

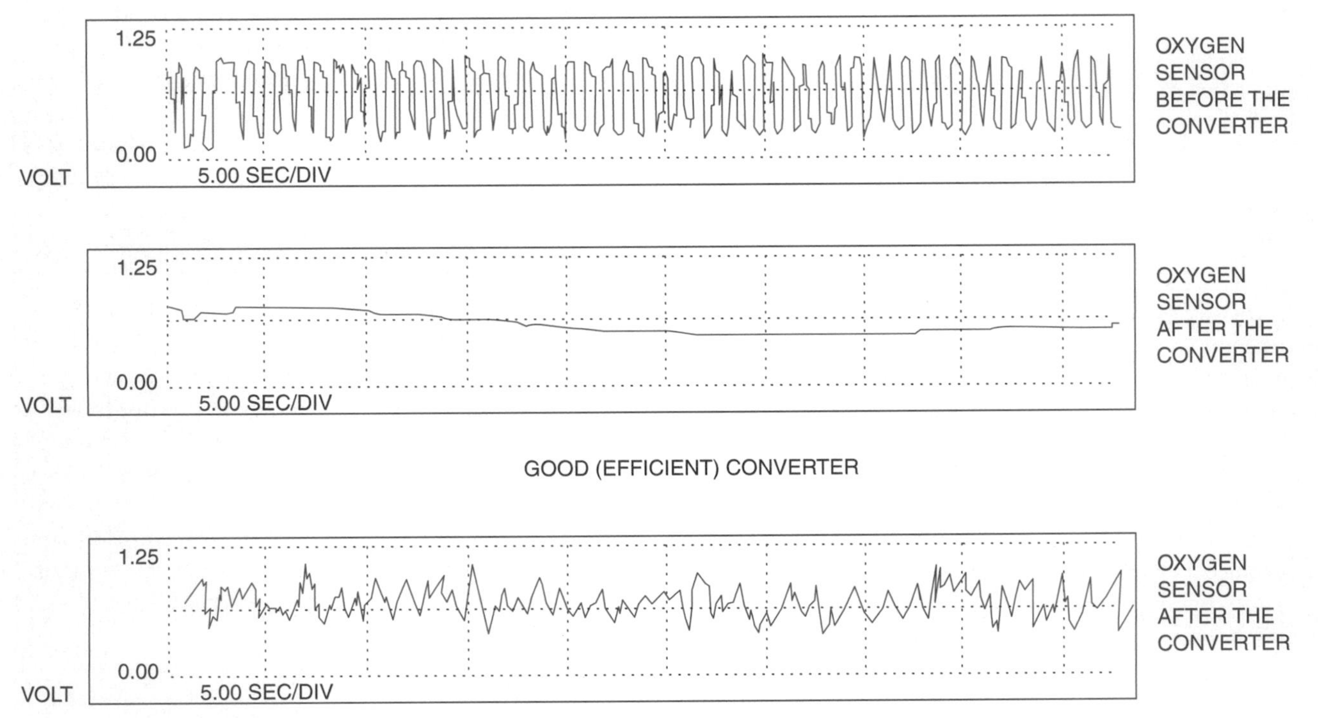

Figure 25–33 The post–catalytic converter oxygen sensor should display very little activity if the catalytic converter is efficient.

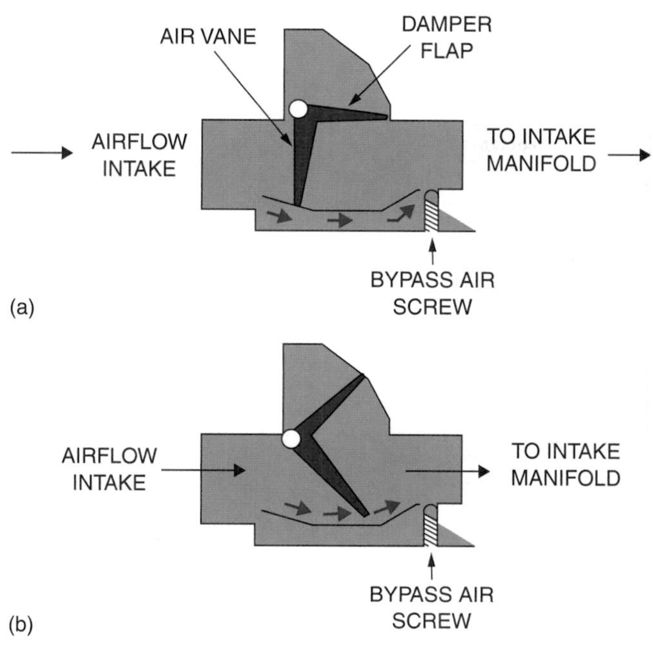

Figure 25–34 A typical air vane sensor. (a) At idle the air flows through a bypass passage. The bypass air screw is adjusted at the factory and should not require adjustment. (b) As the throttle is opened, the airflow moves the vane. The vane is attached to a potentiometer similar to a throttle position (TP) sensor.

Figure 25–35 A typical air vane sensor with the cover removed. The movable arm contacts a carbon resistance path as the vane opens. Many air vane sensors also have contacts that close to supply voltage to the electric fuel pump as the air vane starts to open when the engine is being cranked and air is being drawn into the engine.

AIRFLOW METHOD

The airflow method measures the amount of air as part of the computer input information necessary for accurate fuel delivery control. There are three basic types of airflow sensors used on port-injected engines: the air vane sensor, the hot film sensor, and the hot wire sensor.

AIR VANE SENSOR

This air vane sensor uses a movable vane that translates the amount of movement of the vane into the amount of air being drawn into the engine. An air vane sensor can be tested using a digital meter or an oscilloscope. See Figures 25–34 and 25–35.

HOT FILM SENSOR

The hot film sensor uses a temperature-sensing resistor (thermistor) to measure the temperature of the incoming air. Through the electronics within the sensor, a conductive film is kept at a temperature 75°C (165°F) above the temperature of the incoming air. See Figure 25–36.

Because the amount and density of the air both tend to contribute to the cooling effect as the air passes through the sensor, this type of sensor can actually produce an output based on the *mass* of the airflow. The output of this type of sensor is usually a frequency based on the amount of air entering the sensor. The more air that enters the sensor, the more the hot film is cooled. The electronics inside the sensor, therefore, increase the current flow through the hot film to maintain the 75°C (165°F) temperature differential between the air temperature and the temperature of the hot film. This change in current flow is converted to a frequency output that the computer can use as a measurement of airflow. Most of these types of sensors are referred to as **mass airflow (MAF) sensors** because unlike the air vane sensor, the MAF sensor takes into account relative humidity, altitude, and temperature of the air. The denser the air, the greater the cooling effect on the hot film sensor and the greater the amount of fuel required for proper combustion.

HOT WIRE SENSOR

The hot wire sensor is similar to the hot film type, but uses a hot wire to sense the mass airflow instead of the hot film. Like the hot film sensor, the hot wire sensor uses a temperature-sensing resistor (thermistor) to measure the temperature of the air entering the sensor. See Figure 25–37. The electronic circuitry within the sensor keeps the temperature of the wire at 75°C (165°F) above the temperature of the incoming air.

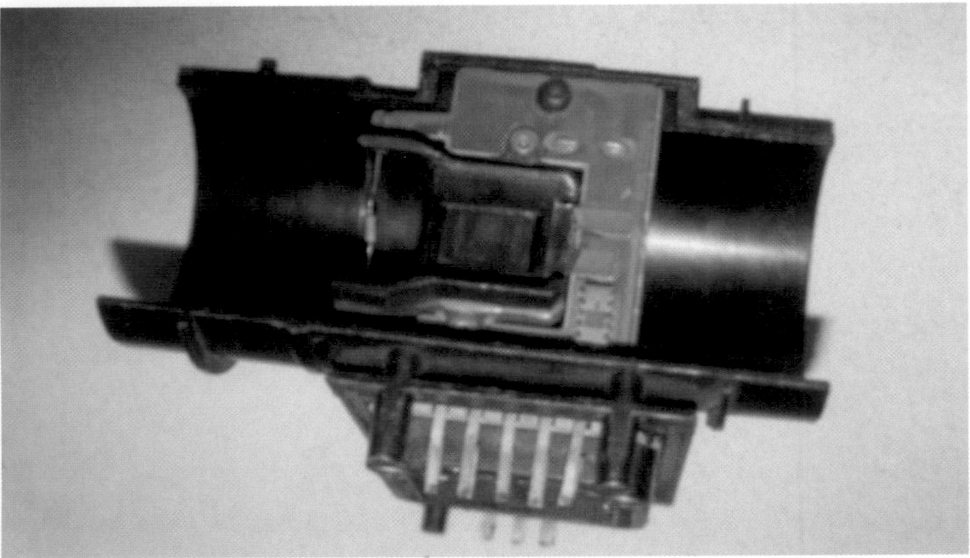

Figure 25–36 A GM hot film mass air flow (MAF) sensor that has been taken apart. The electronic circuit measures the cooling effect of the air entering the engine and generates a frequency output signal that is proportional to the amount of air passing through the sensor.

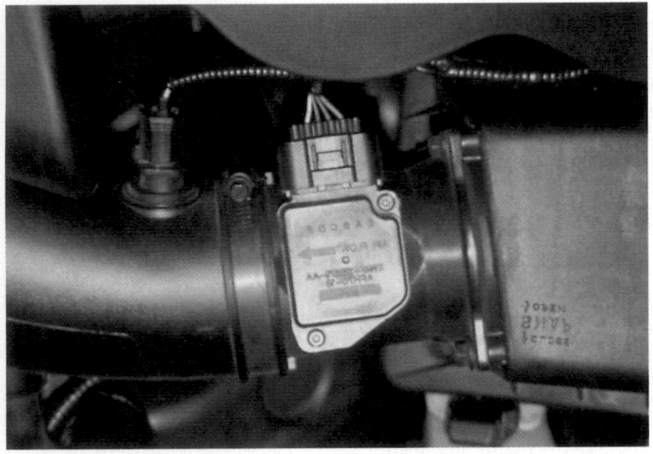

Figure 25–37 A typical hot wire MAF sensor located between the air filter and the throttle plate.

DIAGNOSTIC STORY

The Dirty MAF Sensor Story

The owner of a Buick Park Avenue complained that the engine would hesitate during acceleration, showed lack of power, and seemed to surge or miss at times. A visual inspection found everything to be like new, including a new air filter. There were no stored diagnostic trouble codes (DTCs). A look at the scan data showed airflow to be within the recommended 3 to 7 grams per second. A check of the frequency output showed the problem.

Idle frequency = 2.177 kHz (2177 Hz)

Normal frequency at idle speed should be 2.37 to 2.52 kHz. Cleaning the hot wire of the MAF sensor restored proper operation. The sensor wire was covered with what looked like fine fibres, possibly from the replacement air filter.

NOTE: Older AC MAF sensors operated at a lower frequency of 32 to 150 Hz, with 32 Hz being the average reading at idle and 150 Hz for wide-open throttle.

Testing Mass Airflow Sensors

Start the testing of a MAF sensor by performing a thorough visual inspection. Look at all the hoses that direct and send air, especially between the MAF sensor and the throttle body. Also check the electrical connector for:

- Corrosion
- Terminals that are bent or pushed out of the plastic connector
- Frayed wiring

False Air

Airflow sensors and mass airflow (MAF) sensors are designed to measure *all* the air entering the engine. If an air inlet hose was loose or had a hole, extra air

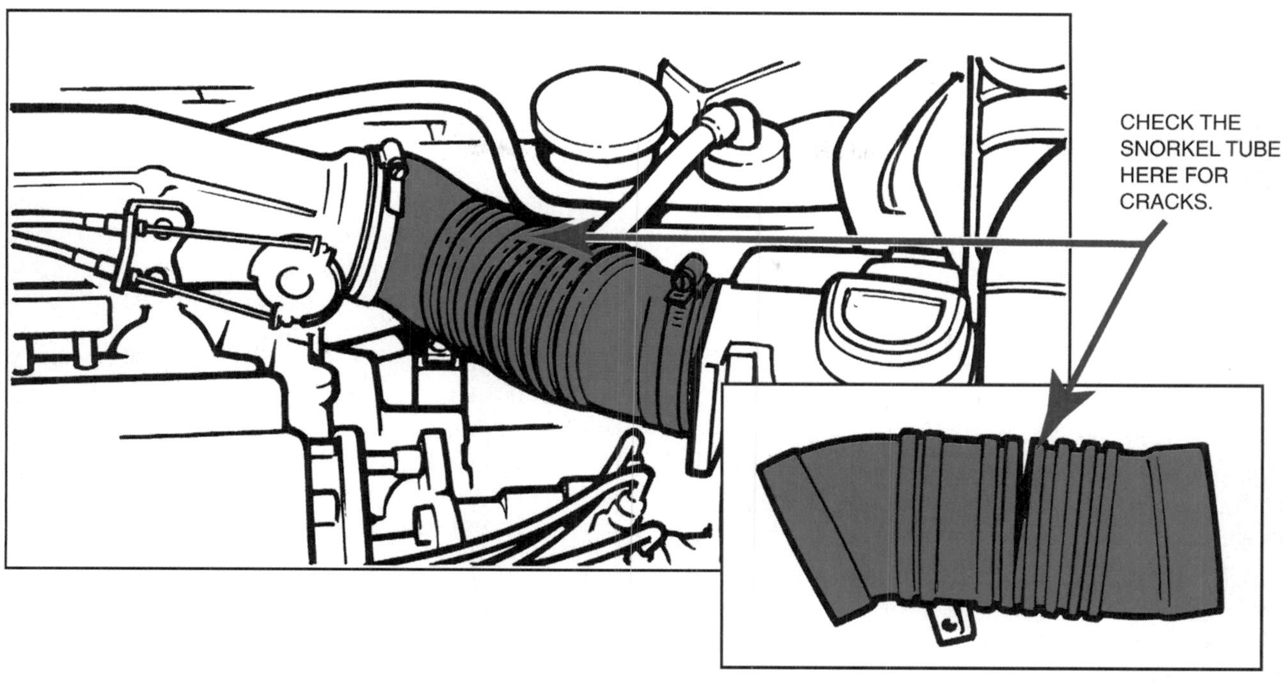
CHECK THE
SNORKEL TUBE
HERE FOR
CRACKS.

Figure 25–38 Carefully check the hose between the MAF sensor and the throttle plate for cracks or splits that could create extra (false) air in the engine that is not measured by the MAF sensor.

Frequently Asked Question ???

What Is Meant by a "High-Authority Sensor"?

A high-authority sensor is a sensor that has a major influence over the amount of fuel being delivered to the engine. For example, at engine start-up, the engine coolant temperature (ECT) sensor is a high-authority sensor and the oxygen sensor (O2S) is a low-authority sensor. However, as the engine reaches operating temperature, the oxygen sensor becomes a high-authority sensor and can greatly affect the amount of fuel being supplied to the engine. See the chart.

High-Authority Sensors	Low-Authority Sensors
ECT (especially when the engine starts and is warming up)	IAT (intake air temperature) sensors modify and back up the ECT
O2S (after the engine reaches closed-loop operation)	TFT (transmission fluid temperature)
MAP	PRNDL (shift position sensor)
MAF	KS (knock sensor)
TP	

could enter the engine without being measured. This extra air is often called **false air.** See Figure 25–38. Because this extra air is unmeasured, the computer does not provide enough fuel delivery and the engine operates too lean, especially at idle. A small hole in the air inlet hose would represent a fairly large percentage of false air at idle, but would represent a very small percentage of extra air at highway speeds.

To diagnose for false air, hook up a scan tool and look at long-term fuel trim numbers at idle and at 3000 rpm.

Tap Test

With the engine running at idle speed, *gently* tap the MAF sensor with the fingers of an open hand. If the engine stumbles or stalls, the MAF sensor is defective. This test is commonly called the **tap test.**

Digital Meter Test of a MAF Sensor

A digital multimeter can be used to measure the frequency (Hz) output of the sensor and compare the reading with specifications.

The frequency output and engine speed in RPM can also be plotted on a graph to check to see if the frequency and RPM are proportional, resulting in a straight line on the graph.

SENSOR TESTING USING DIAGNOSTIC TROUBLE CODES

Many vehicles display diagnostic trouble codes (DTCs), yet do not display scan data. To check if the problem is the sensor itself or the electrical sensor circuit that is at fault, follow these steps.

1. Clear the DTC.
2. Create the opposite sensor condition. For example, if the DTC indicates an open engine coolant temperature (ECT) circuit, unplug the sensor and, using a jumper wire, short the two terminals of the harness (not the sensor) together.

NOTE: If the ECT sensor wires are shorted together, the scan tool will display about 150°C (300°F) and about −40°C (−40°F) if the sensor wires are open (disconnected).

When checking three-wire sensors, such as the throttle position (TP) sensor, MAP, or MAF, use a jumper wire to jump the 5 volt reference back into the signal return after disconnecting the connector from the sensor.

Shorting the 5 volt reference to the signal should cause the vehicle computer to set a shorted sensor DTC. If a shorted sensor DTC is stored, simply clear the DTC and unplug the sensor. If the wiring is okay, the opposite (open) sensor DTC should be set.

TECH TIP 

The Unplug It Test

If a sensor is defective yet still produces a signal to the computer, the computer will often accept the reading and make the required changes in fuel delivery and spark advance. If, however, the sensor is not reading correctly, the computer will process this wrong information and perform an action assuming that the information being supplied is accurate. For example, if a mass airflow (MAF) sensor is telling the computer that 12 grams of air per second is going into the engine, the computer will then pulse the injector for 6.4 ms or whatever figure it is programmed to provide. However, if the air going into the engine is actually 14 grams per second, the amount of fuel supplied by the injectors will not be enough to provide proper engine operation. If the MAF sensor is unplugged, the computer knows that the sensor is not capable of supplying airflow information, so it defaults to a fixed amount of fuel based on the values of other sensors such as the TP and MAP sensors.

If the engine operates better with a sensor unplugged, then suspect that the sensor is defective. A sensor that is not supplying the correct information is said to be *skewed.* The computer will not see a diagnostic trouble code for this condition because the computer can often not detect that the sensor is supplying wrong information.

PHOTO SEQUENCE 19 Throttle Position Sensor Diagnosis

P19–1 Besides a scan tool, other equipment that can be used to check a throttle position (TP) sensor includes a scope or graphing multimeter, a digital multimeter equipped with MIN/MAX function, and T-pins to safely backprobe the sensor wires.

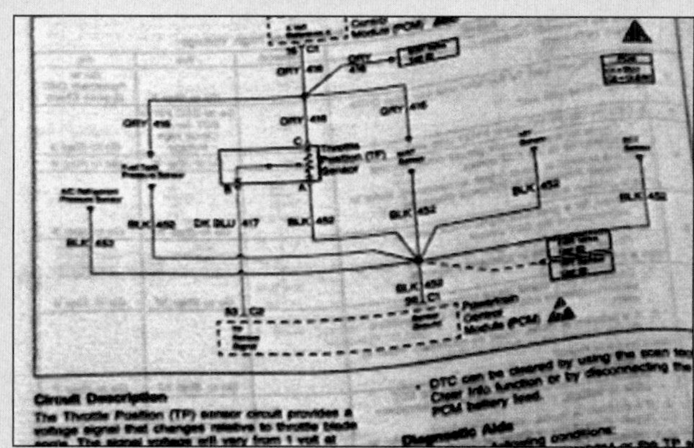

P19–2 Consult the factory service manual for the specifications and wire colors used for the TP sensor as well as the recommended testing procedure.

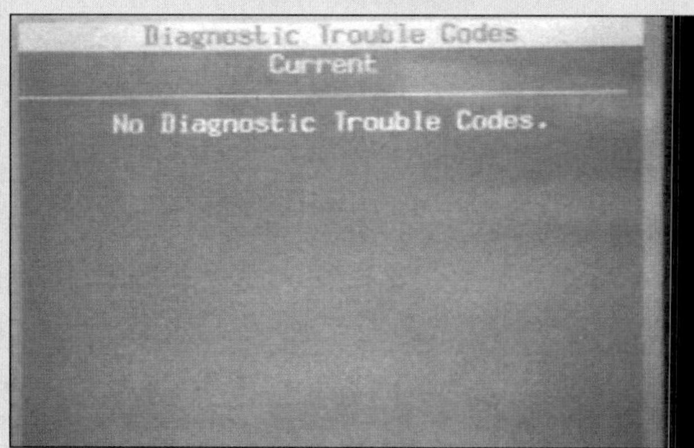

P19–3 A scan tool display showing no diagnostic trouble codes (DTCs). A fault could still exist even though a diagnostic trouble code is not set—it depends on what type of fault and when it occurs.

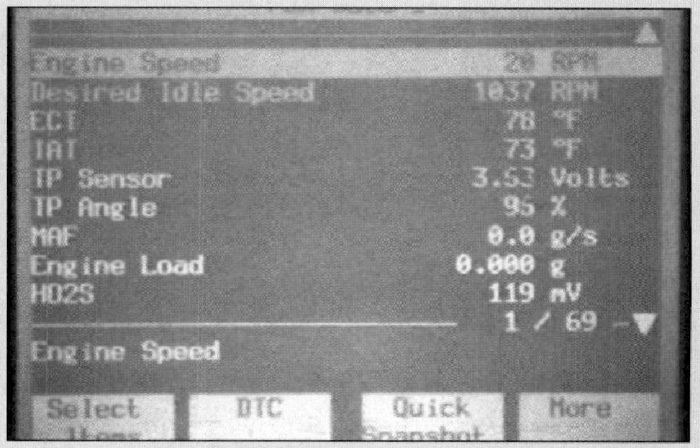

P19–4 A scan tool can be used to observe the output voltage and the calculated percentage (%) of throttle opening.

P19–5 Most throttle position sensors use a 5 volt reference voltage from the computer. To test that this signal is available at the sensor, carefully backprobe the 5 volt reference (grey on this General Motors vehicle) wire at the connector on the TP sensor. Simply push the T-pin alongside the wire until it touches the metal terminal inside the connector.

P19–6 Connect the red lead from the digital multimeter to the T-pin and attach the black meter lead to a good, clean engine ground.

Throttle Position Sensor Diagnosis—continued

P19–7 Select DC volts and turn the ignition key on (engine off). The meter reads slightly over 5 volts, confirming the computer is supplying the reference voltage to the TP sensor.

P19–8 Another important step when testing a TP sensor is to verify that the ground circuit is okay. To check the ground of the TP sensor, carefully backprobe the ground wire at the TP sensor connector (black on this General Motors vehicle) and connect the red meter lead to the T-pin.

P19–9 Attach the black meter lead to a good, clean engine ground.

P19–10 With the ignition on (engine off) and the digital meter still set to read DC volts, read the voltage drop of the TP sensor ground. The voltage drop is the difference in voltage between the leads of the meter. General Motors specifies that this voltage drop should not exceed 35 mV (0.035 V). This TP sensor ground shows 31.1 mV (0.0311 V).

P19–11 To measure the signal voltage, backprobe the signal wire (dark blue on this General Motors vehicle).

P19–12 Select DC volts and manually range the meter. This Fluke meter changes from the 4 volt scale to the 40 volt scale as the sensor voltage goes slightly higher than 4 volt. For an instant, "OL" appears on the display as it switches ranges. This OL could also indicate a fault.

Throttle Position Sensor Diagnosis—continued

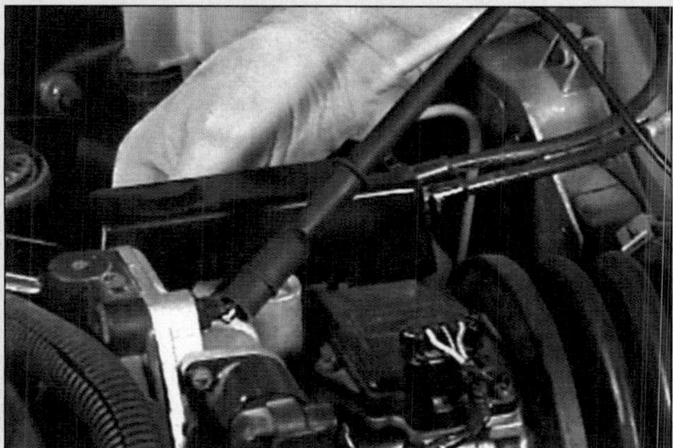

P19–13 Slowly move the throttle from idle speed to wide open and back to idle speed position. For best results, this test should be performed by depressing the accelerator pedal. This puts the same forces on the sensor as occurs during normal driving.

P19–14 The high reading for this sensor was 4.063 volts.

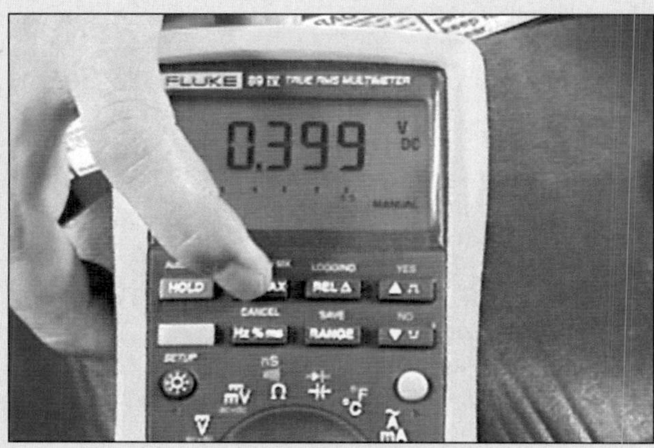

P19–15 Pushing the MIN/MAX button shows the minimum voltage the meter recorded during the test (0.399 volts).

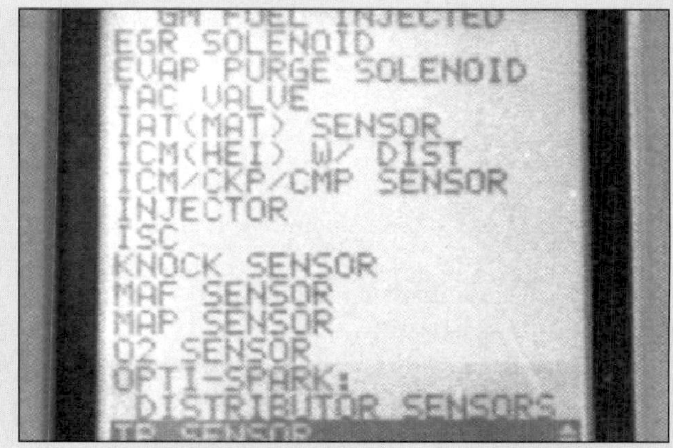

P19–16 A Snap-On Vantage graphing multimeter or digital storage oscilloscope can also be used to test a TP sensor. To test the sensor using the Snap-On Vantage, select TP sensor from the menu.

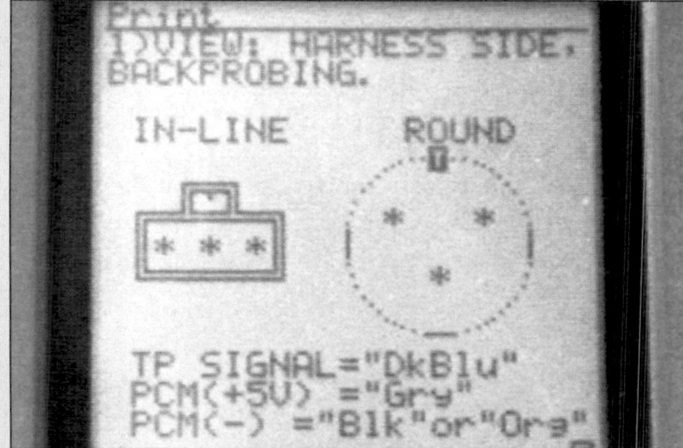

P19–17 The Vantage has a built-in database that can be accessed to show connector position and wire colour information.

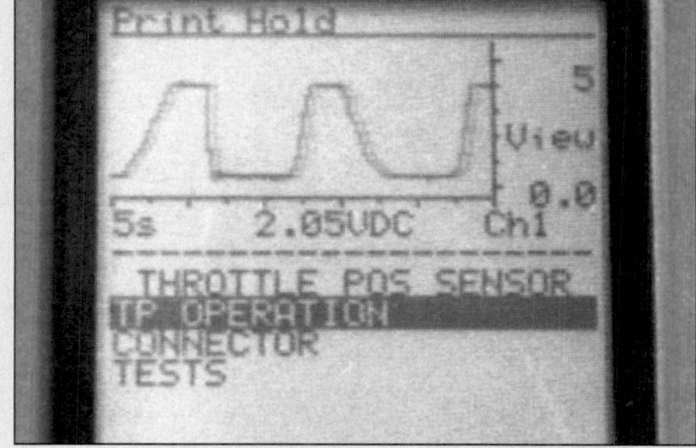

P19–18 After attaching the meter leads to the signal wire and ground (ignition key on, engine off), the graphing multimeter shows the waveform of the voltage signal as the throttle is depressed, released, and depressed again. These are normal for a TP sensor. A fault would show as a vertical line or dip in the waveform.

SUMMARY

1. The vehicle computer is called the powertrain control module (PCM) because it controls the engine and the transmission on most vehicles.
2. The four basic computer functions include: input, processing, storage, and output.
3. Permanent memory is called ROM, PROM, EPROM, or EEPROM.
4. Temporary memory is called RAM or KAM.
5. The central processing unit (CPU) is the "brains" of the computer and does all the calculations.
6. As the temperature of the engine coolant increases, the resistance of the ECT sensor decreases.
7. A throttle position sensor can best be checked with a voltmeter set on MIN/MAX or with a scope.
8. An oxygen sensor should switch rapidly from high to low on a fuel-injected engine operating in closed loop.

REVIEW QUESTIONS

1. List the four functions of a computer.
2. What is meant by the term Baud rate?
3. Explain how to test an engine coolant temperature sensor.
4. Describe the best method to test a MAP sensor.
5. Describe how a zirconia oxygen sensor works and how best to determine if it is operating correctly.

RED SEAL CERTIFICATION-TYPE QUESTIONS

1. Which of the following is an input sensor to the vehicle computer?
   - **a.** Fuel injector
   - **b.** Idle-speed control motor
   - **c.** Combustion chamber temperature sensor
   - **d.** Engine coolant sensor
2. Which part of the computer does the actual calculations?
   - **a.** PROM
   - **b.** RAM
   - **c.** CPU
   - **d.** KAM
3. Typical TP sensor voltage at idle is about _______.
   - **a.** 2.50 to 2.80 volts
   - **b.** 0.5 volts or 10% of WOT TP sensor voltage
   - **c.** 1.5 to 2.8 volts
   - **d.** 13.5 to 15.0 volts
4. The voltage output of a zirconia oxygen sensor when the exhaust stream is lean (excess oxygen) is _______.
   - **a.** Relatively high (close to 1 volt)
   - **b.** About in the middle of the voltage range
   - **c.** Relatively low (close to 0 volt)
   - **d.** Dependent on atmospheric pressure
5. The sensor that most determines fuel delivery when a fuel-injected engine is first started is the _______.
   - **a.** Oxygen sensor (O2S)
   - **b.** Engine coolant temperature (ECT) sensor
   - **c.** Engine MAP sensor
   - **d.** BARO sensor
6. The standardized name for the sensor that measures the temperature of the air being drawn into the engine is called a(n) _______.
   - **a.** Intake air temperature sensor (IAT)
   - **b.** Air temperature sensor (ATS)
   - **c.** Air charge temperature (ACT)
   - **d.** Manifold air temperature (MAT) sensor
7. Which sensor is generally considered to be the electronic accelerator pump of a fuel-injected engine?
   - **a.** Oxygen sensor
   - **b.** Coolant temperature sensor
   - **c.** Throttle position sensor
   - **d.** Engine manifold absolute pressure sensor
8. The sensor that must be warmed up and functioning before the engine management computer will go to the closed loop is the _______.
   - **a.** Oxygen sensor (O2S)
   - **b.** Engine coolant temperature (ECT) sensor
   - **c.** Engine MAP sensor
   - **d.** BARO sensor
9. Which of the following describes an acceptable oxygen sensor voltage range?
   - **a.** 0.5 to 0.7 volt
   - **b.** 200 mV to 800 mV
   - **c.** 300 mV to 500 mV
   - **d.** 400 mV to 800 mV
10. A pull-up resistor inside the computer (ECT circuit) is used to
    - **a.** Expand the scale of the ECT sensor
    - **b.** Dampen voltage fluctuation
    - **c.** Prevent amperage from back-feeding into other circuits
    - **d.** Compare resistance with the intake air temperature (IAT) sensor

26

Computers and On-Board Diagnostics

OBJECTIVES: After studying Chapter 26, you should be able to:

1. Prepare for the interprovincial Red Seal certification examination in Appendix VIII (Engine Performance) on the topics covered in this chapter.
2. Explain the purpose, function and operation of "flash" codes.
3. Describe the diagnostic procedures and routines relating to a trouble code.
4. Explain the purpose and operation of a scan tool.
5. Describe the differences between OBD I and OBD II.
6. Describe how the powertrain control module performs active and passive tests of the computerized engine control system.
7. Describe the standardized OBD II DTCs and terminology.
8. Explain the purpose behind one- and two-trip logic.

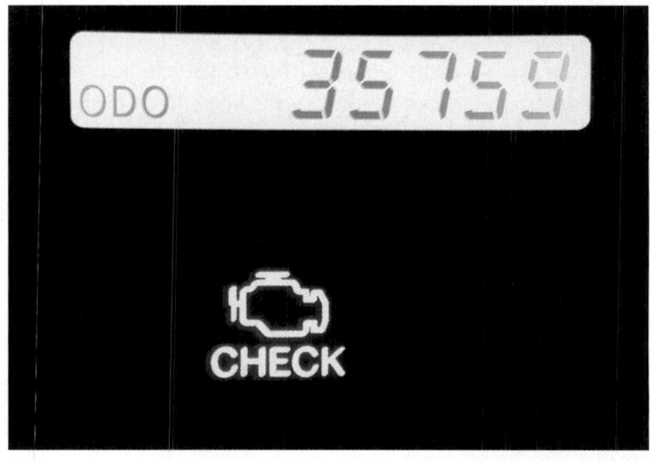

Figure 26–1 A typical malfunction indicator lamp (MIL), often labelled "Check Engine" or "Service Engine Soon."

ON-BOARD DIAGNOSTICS

During the 1980s, many manufacturers began equipping their vehicles with full-function control systems capable of alerting the driver of a malfunction and of allowing the technician to retrieve codes that identify circuit faults. These early diagnostic systems were meant to reduce emissions and assist the technician. The automotive industry calls these systems on-board diagnostics (OBD).

On-Board Diagnostics: Early Systems

The powertrain control module (PCM) has a built-in self-diagnosis program that detects failures or major faults in the engine management system and alerts the driver by illuminating a Malfunction Indicator Lamp (MIL). The MIL informs the driver to "Check Engine," "Service Engine Soon," or "Power Loss." See Figure 26–1.

The lamp will stay on if the problem is present (hard fault) and will go out if the problem no longer exists (soft fault). A *fault code* will set and remain in computer memory for approximately 25 to 30 engine starts (most vehicles). This is an aid to the technician when diagnosing the system.

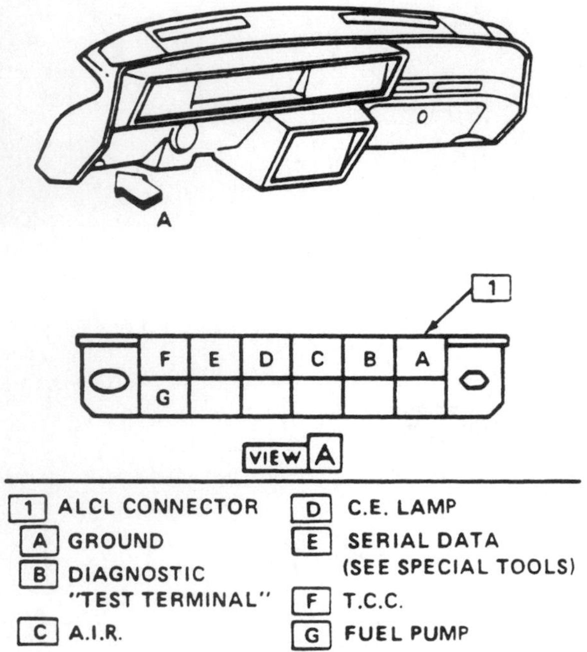

Figure 26–2 The data link connector (DLC) is located under the dash on this General Motors vehicle. It is known as the assembly-line communications link (ALCL) on early GM vehicles because it allowed the assembly plant to test engine operations before the vehicle left the factory. It is used by service technicians in the field to access trouble codes and read live data stream. (Courtesy General Motors of Canada Ltd.)

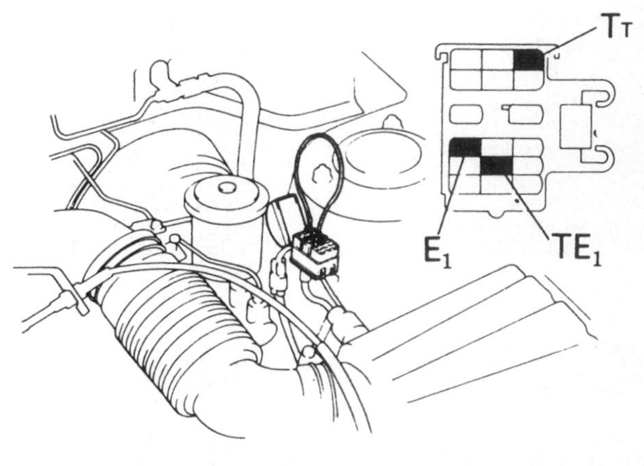

Figure 26–3 The data link connector on many Asian and domestic vehicles (non–OBD II) will cause the malfunction indicator lamp to flash trouble codes when the designated terminals are connected with a jumper wire. (Courtesy Toyota Canada Inc.)

Fault codes (diagnostic trouble codes—DTCs) are accessed through a diagnostic (data link connector—DLC) found in many different locations, e.g., under the hood, under the dash, in the console or the glove box. Often, the shop manual must be consulted for the exact location. See Figure 26–2. The DLC also varies in appearance among makes.

Flash Codes

The procedures for retrieving DTCs differs among makes. Many on-board computer diagnostics are entered by connecting two or more terminals in the DLC with a jumper (GM and many imports); see Figure 26–3. Chrysler cycles the ignition key a given number of times within 5 seconds. This will activate the MIL, which begins to flash; count the number of flashes.

Voltmeters are used with some Ford and Mitsubishi vehicles to identify trouble codes. Connecting a voltmeter into the system, as shown in Figure 26–4, will cause the meter needle to rise and fall; counting the number of needle sweeps will identify the DTC. Ford vehicles also go through a self-test, which checks the sensors and actuators before giving out trouble codes.

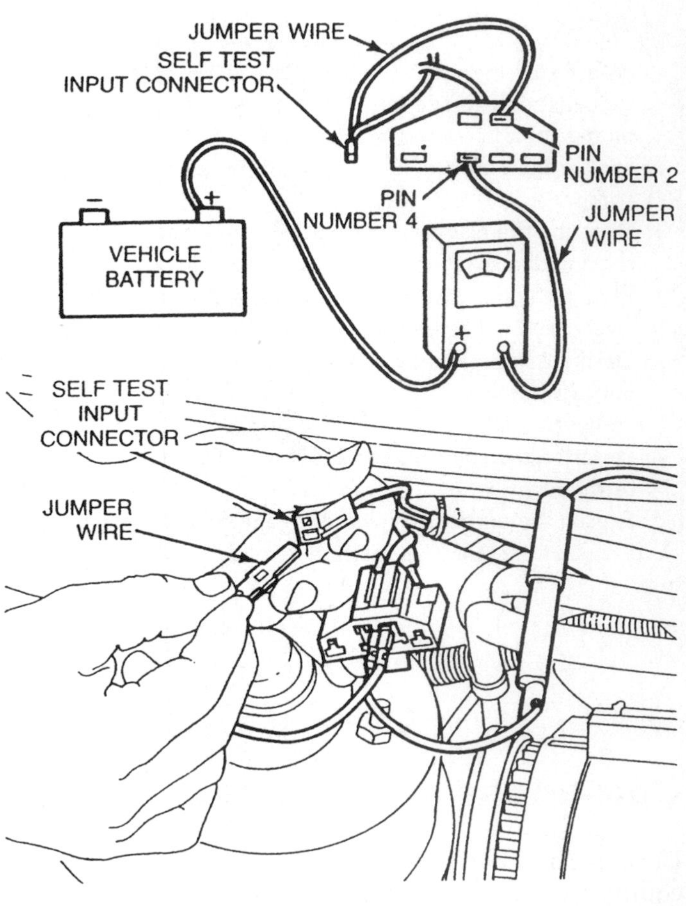

Figure 26–4 Analog voltmeters are used by Ford and some import vehicles to read diagnostic trouble codes. Counting the number of needle sweeps (pulses) will determine the code. (Courtesy Ford Motor Co. of Canada Ltd.)

PCM DIAGNOSTIC CODES

CODE	DESCRIPTION	ILLUMINATE SES
13	Oxygen Sensor - open circuit	YES
14	Coolant Temperatuare Sensor - high temp. indicated	YES
15	Coolant Temperature Sensor - low temp. indicated	YES
16	System Voltage high or low	YES
17	Spark Reference Circuit Problem	NO
21	Throttle Position Sensor voltage high	YES
22	Throttle Position Sensor voltage low	YES
23	Intake Air Temperature Sensor - low temp. indicated	NO
24	Vehicle Speed Sensor Circuit Problem	YES
25	Intake Air Temperature Sensor - high temp. indicated	NO
26	QDM Failure	YES
31	PRNDL Switch Circuit Problem	NO
34	MAF Sensor - low gm/sec indicated	YES
36	Trans Shift Circuit	NO
38	Brake Input Circuit Problem	NO
41	Cam Sensor Circuit Problem	YES
42	Electronic Spark Timing (EST) Circuit Problem	YES
43	Electronic Spark Control (ESC) Circuit Problem	YES
44	Oxygen Sensor - lean exhaust indicated	YES
45	Oxygen Sensor - rich exhaust indicated	YES
51	MEM-CAL Error	YES
58	PASS Key (VATS) Fuel Enable Circuit	NO
61	Cruise Vent Solenoid Circuit	NO
62	Cruise Vac Solenoid Circuit	NO
65	Cruise Servo Position Circuit	NO
66	Excessive A/C Cycling (low refrigerant charge)	NO
67	Cruise Switches Circuit	NO
68	Cruise System Problem	NO
69	A/C Head Pressure Switch Circuit Problem	NO

Figure 26–5 Typical list of early 1990s diagnostic trouble codes (DTC). It is important to use the shop manual (or data bank) when checking codes as they are different between car makers. On-board diagnostics, generation II (OBD II) standardized most trouble code numbers and terminology. (Courtesy General Motors of Canada Ltd.)

Diagnostic Trouble Codes

Trouble codes, known previously as fault codes, are usually listed in numerical order to identify the circuit. See Figure 26–5. The technician is then instructed to follow a set of diagnostic routines related to the trouble code. See Figures 26–6 and 26–7.

Clearing Trouble Codes

Trouble codes are cleared from computer memory by disconnecting a jumper wire, removing a fuse, or through the use of a scan tool. Refer to the shop manual since procedures differ. Disconnecting the vehicle battery to clear codes is not recommended, as this will also erase any adaptive strategy program changes

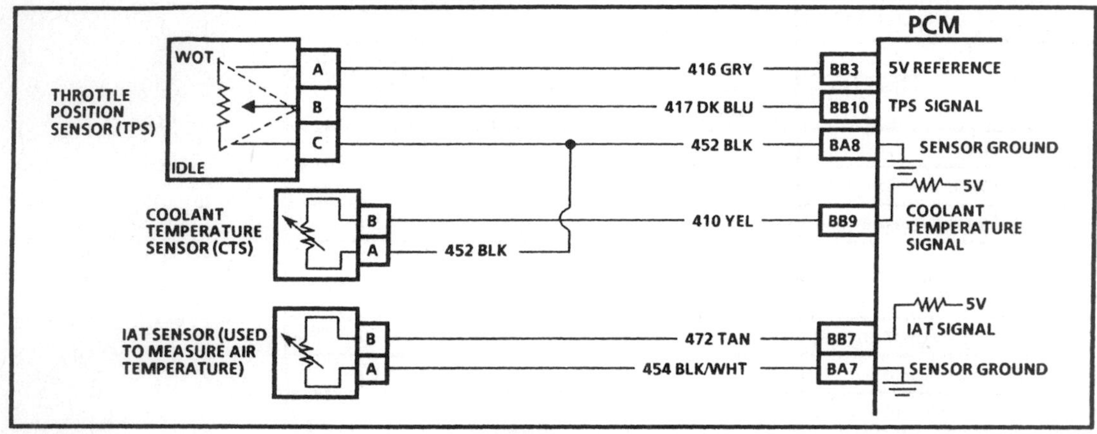

CODE 15

COOLANT TEMPERATURE SENSOR (CTS) CIRCUIT
(LOW TEMPERATURE INDICATED)
3800 (VIN L) (TPI)

Circuit Description:

The Coolant Temperature Sensor (CTS) uses a thermistor to control the signal voltage to the PCM. The PCM applies a voltage on CKT 410 to the sensor. When the engine is cold the sensor (thermistor) resistance is high, therefore, the PCM will see high signal voltage.

As the engine warms, the sensor resistance becomes less, and the voltage drops. At normal engine operating temperature 85°C to 95°C (185°F to 203°F), the voltage will measure about 1.5 to 2.0 volts.

Code 15 will set if:

- Engine is running over 2 seconds.
- Signal voltage indicates a coolant temperature less than -39°C (-36°F) for at least 4 seconds.

Test Description: Number(s) below refer to circled number(s) on the diagnostic chart.

1. Determines if conditions necessary to set Code 15 exist.
2. This test simulates a Code 14. If the PCM recognizes the low signal voltage, (high temperature) and the "Scan" reads 130°C (266°F) or more, the PCM and wiring are OK.
3. This test will determine if CKT 410 is open. There should be 5 volts present at sensor connector if measured with a DVM.

Diagnostic Aids:

A Tech 1 displays engine temperature in degrees. After engine is started the temperature should rise steadily to about 90°C (194°F) then stabilize when thermostat opens.

An intermittent may be caused by a poor connection, rubbed through wire insulation or a wire broken inside the insulation.

Check For:

- Poor Connection or Damaged Harness - Inspect PCM harness connectors for backed out terminal "BB9", improper mating, broken locks, improperly formed or damaged terminals, poor terminal to wire connection and damaged harness.
- Intermittent Test - With Tech 1, monitor coolant temperature while moving related connectors and wiring harness. If the failure is induced, the display will change. This may help to isolate the location of the malfunction.
- Shifted Sensor - The "Temperature To Resistance Value" scale may be used to test the coolant sensor at various temperature levels to evaluate the possibility of a "shifted" (mis-scaled) sensor which may result in driveability complaints.

A faulty connection, or an open in CKTs 410 or 452 will result in a Code 15.

Figure 26–6 Typical diagnostic early 1990s flow chart for a DTC. This section of the chart gives the circuit description, wiring schematic, and diagnostic aids. (Courtesy General Motors of Canada Ltd.)

stored in the computer. Other components such as the radio, which uses battery power to retain memory, will also lose their settings.

Scan Tools

Scanners are small hand-held computers that provide a major improvement over flash-code diagnostics. They typically plug into the data link connector and interface with the on-board computer. Power to operate the scanner is supplied through the lighter socket or a battery adaptor; late-model OBD II scanners receive power at the DLC. See Figure 26–8.

Scanners have the ability to read directly from live data stream; information from the input sensors and output actuators may be monitored during a road test. Many scan tools have a snap-shot mode, which allows the technician to freeze certain data at the point the

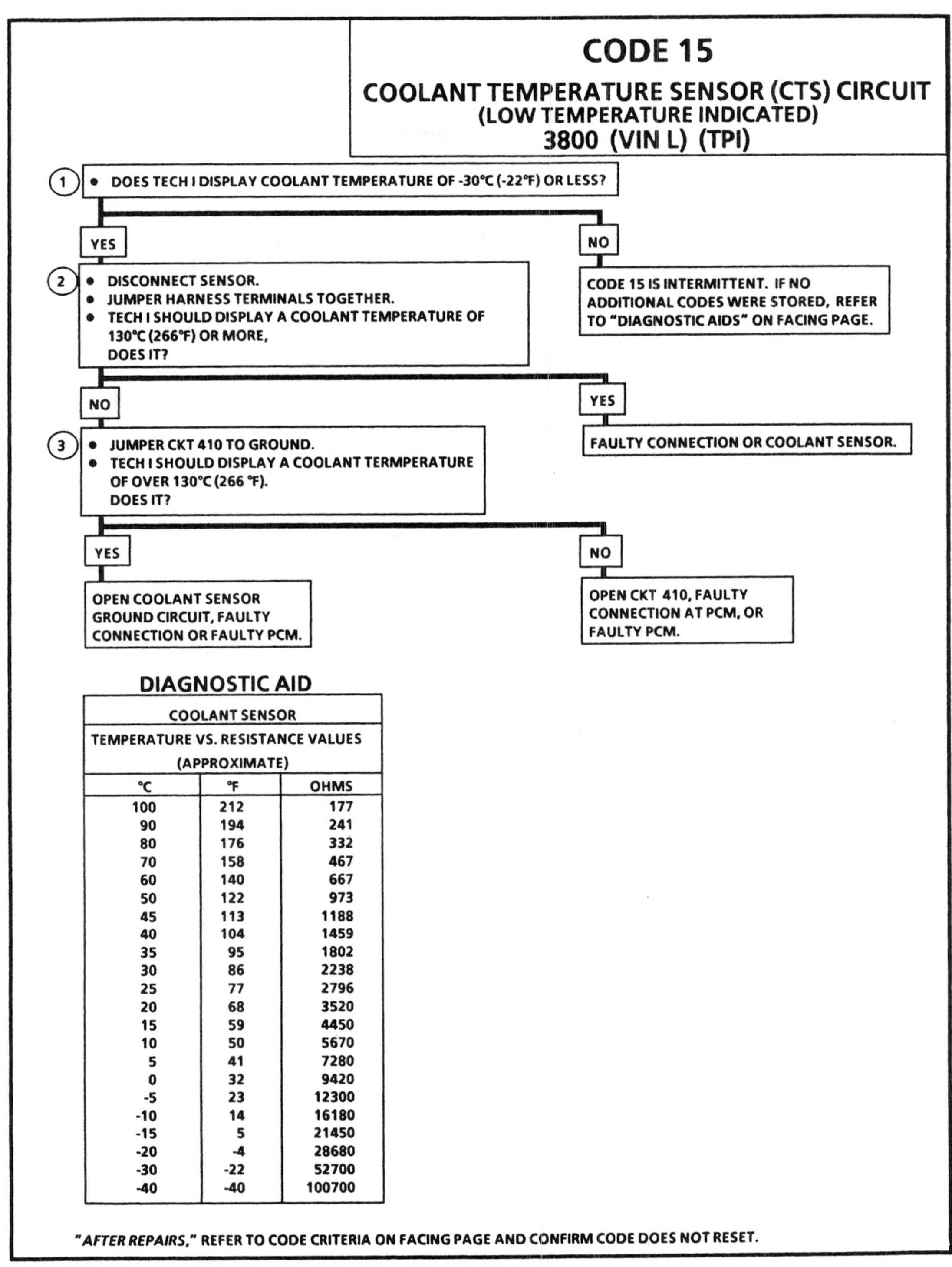

CODE 15
COOLANT TEMPERATURE SENSOR (CTS) CIRCUIT
(LOW TEMPERATURE INDICATED)
3800 (VIN L) (TPI)
1 • DOES TECH I DISPLAY COOLANT TEMPERATURE OF -30°C (-22°F) OR LESS?
YES
NO
2 • DISCONNECT SENSOR.
• JUMPER HARNESS TERMINALS TOGETHER.
• TECH I SHOULD DISPLAY A COOLANT TEMPERATURE OF 130°C (266°F) OR MORE, DOES IT?
CODE 15 IS INTERMITTENT. IF NO ADDITIONAL CODES WERE STORED, REFER TO "DIAGNOSTIC AIDS" ON FACING PAGE.
NO
YES
3 • JUMPER CKT 410 TO GROUND.
• TECH I SHOULD DISPLAY A COOLANT TERMPERATURE OF OVER 130°C (266 °F). DOES IT?
FAULTY CONNECTION OR COOLANT SENSOR.
YES
NO
OPEN COOLANT SENSOR GROUND CIRCUIT, FAULTY CONNECTION OR FAULTY PCM.
OPEN CKT 410, FAULTY CONNECTION AT PCM, OR FAULTY PCM.

DIAGNOSTIC AID

COOLANT SENSOR

TEMPERATURE VS. RESISTANCE VALUES (APPROXIMATE)

°C	°F	OHMS
100	212	177
90	194	241
80	176	332
70	158	467
60	140	667
50	122	973
45	113	1188
40	104	1459
35	95	1802
30	86	2238
25	77	2796
20	68	3520
15	59	4450
10	50	5670
5	41	7280
0	32	9420
-5	23	12300
-10	14	16180
-15	5	21450
-20	-4	28680
-30	-22	52700
-40	-40	100700

"AFTER REPAIRS," **REFER TO CODE CRITERIA ON FACING PAGE AND CONFIRM CODE DOES NOT RESET.**

Figure 26–7 Typical diagnostic flow chart. This section takes the technician, step by step, through the diagnostic routines. (Courtesy General Motors of Canada Ltd.)

driveability concern arrives. This information can then be reviewed and interpreted back in the service bay. The majority of Asian and European vehicles have no provisions for live data stream readouts with early on-board diagnostics. Today, virtually every automobile sold in Canada and the U.S. is equipped to provide running data.

Scanners also supply trouble code information in numerical form; there are no light flashes or needle sweeps to count.

Some scanners have the ability to control the output actuators and solenoids for test purposes. Performing a cylinder-balance test by interrupting the ignition spark is a common diagnostic routine used with

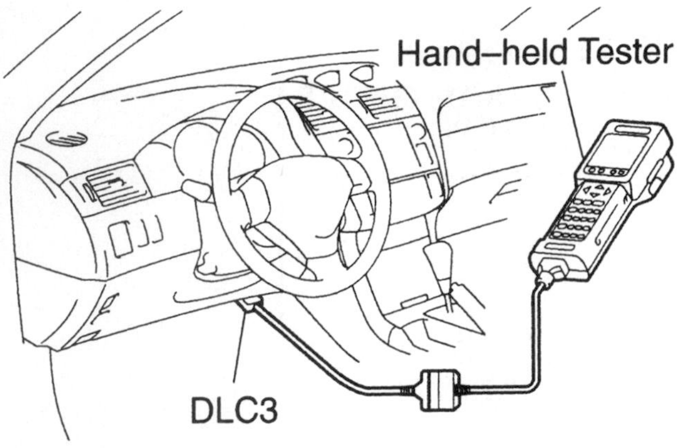

Figure 26–8 Hand-held scan tools interface with the on-board computer. They not only extract fault codes (DTC), they read live data from the sensors and actuators. Prior to OBD II, the scan tool required a different DLC adaptor and program cartridge when switching between makes. (Courtesy Toyota Canada Inc.)

many large oscilloscopes. This must be done very carefully, as the fuel and air from the dead cylinder will flow into the catalytic converter, causing it to overheat. Feeding the converter raw fuel and oxygen causes internal catalyst temperatures to rise quickly and the converter will begin to melt if the cylinder is "killed" for long. Vehicles with sequential (individual injector control) fuel injection often use scanners to cancel each fuel injector, instead of ignition, for cylinder balance testing. This protects the converter and eliminates any chance of a backfire in the exhaust pipes.

Many late vehicles have no provision for flash-code retrieval and a scanner must be used to extract trouble codes.

On-Board Diagnostics: Generation I (OBD I)

The California Air Resources Board (CARB) developed the first regulation requiring manufacturers selling vehicles in that state to install OBD. Called OBD Generation I (OBD I), OBD I applies to all vehicles sold in California beginning with the 1988 model year. It carries the following requirements:

1. An instrument panel warning lamp able to alert the driver of certain control system failures, now called a **malfunction indicator lamp (MIL).**
2. The system's ability to record and transmit **diagnostic trouble codes (DTCs)** for emission-related failures.
3. Electronic system monitoring of the HO2S, EGR valve, and evaporative purge solenoid. Although not EPA-required during this time, most manufacturers also equipped vehicles sold outside of California with OBD I.

These initial regulations failed to meet many expectations. By failing to monitor the catalytic converter, the evaporative system for leaks, and the presence of engine misfire, OBD I did not do enough to lower automotive emissions. In addition, the OBD I monitoring circuits that were installed lacked sufficient sensitivity.

Aside from OBD I's lack of emission-reduction effectiveness, another problem existed. Auto manufacturers implemented OBD I rules as they saw fit, resulting in a vast array of servicing tools and systems. Rather than simplifying the job of locating and repairing a failure, the aftermarket technician faced a tangled network of procedures often requiring the use of expensive special test equipment and dealer-proprietary information.

Soon it became apparent that more stringent measures were needed if the ultimate goal, reduced automotive emission levels, was to be achieved. This led to the development of OBD Generation II (OBD II).

OBD II Objectives

Generally an OBD II vehicle is defined by its ability to:

1. Detect component degradation or a faulty emission-related system that prevents compliance with federal emission standards.
2. Alert the driver of needed emission-related repair or maintenance.
3. Use standardized DTCs and accept a generic scan tool.

OBD II was first introduced on some 1994 vehicles; by 1998, all light-duty vehicles sold in Canada (U.S. 1996) were required to be OBD II compliant. The primary purpose of OBD II is emission-related, whereas the primary purpose of OBD I (1988) was to detect faults in sensors or sensor circuits. OBD II regulations require that not only must the sensors be tested but that all exhaust control devices be tested and verified for proper operation.

All new vehicles must pass the **Federal Test Procedure (FTP)** for exhaust emissions while being tested for 505 seconds on rollers that simulate the urban drive cycle around downtown Los Angeles, California.

NOTE: IM 240 is simply a shorter version of the 505-second-long federal test procedure.

The regulations for OBD II vehicles state that the vehicle computer must be capable of testing for exhaust emissions, and determining whether or not they are within 1 1/2 times the allowable standard for a new vehicle based on the FTP limits. In order to achieve this goal, the computer has to do all of the following:

1. Test all exhaust emission system components for correct operation.
2. Actively operate the system and measure the results.
3. Continuously monitor all aspects of the engine operation to be certain that the exhaust emissions do not exceed 1 1/2 times the FTP.
4. Check engine operation for misfire.
5. Turn on the malfunction indicator lamp (MIL) (check engine) if the computer senses a fault in a circuit or system.
6. Flash the MIL if an engine misfire occurs that could damage the catalytic converter.

Comprehensive Component Monitor

The **comprehensive component monitor (CCM)** is an internal program in the PCM designed to monitor a failure in any electronic component or circuit (including emission-related and non-emission-related circuits) that provide input or output signals to the PCM. The PCM considers that an input or output signal is inoperative when a failure exists due to an open circuit, out-of-range value or if an on-board rationality check fails. If an emission-related fault is detected, the PCM will set a code and activate the MIL (requires two consecutive trips). Some exceptions are (a) serious engine misfire that could damage the catalytic converter—this requires one trip only; (b) catalyst monitoring which requires three trips.

Many PCM sensors and output devices are tested at key on or immediately after engine startup. However, some devices, such as the idle air control (IAC), are only tested by the CCM after the engine meets certain engine conditions. The number of times the CCM must detect a fault before it will activate the MIL depends upon the manufacturer, but most require two consecutive trips to activate the MIL. The components tested by the CCM include:

- 4-wheel-drive low switch
- Brake switch
- Camshaft (CMP) and crankshaft (CKP) sensors
- Clutch switch (manual transmissions/transaxles only)
- Cruise servo switch
- Engine coolant temperature (ECT) sensor
- EVAP purge sensor or switch
- Fuel composition sensor
- Intake air temperature (IAT) sensor
- Knock sensor (KS)
- Manifold absolute pressure (MAP) sensor
- Mass airflow (MAF) sensor
- Transmission fluid temperature (TFT) sensor
- Transmission turbine speed sensor
- Vacuum sensor
- Vehicle speed (VS) sensor
- EVAP canister purge and EVAP purge vent solenoid
- Idle air control solenoid
- Ignition control system
- Transmission torque converter clutch solenoid
- Transmission shift solenoids

Main Monitors

On OBD II systems, the PCM incorporates a special segment of software. This software program is designed to manage the operation of all OBD II monitors by controlling the sequence of steps necessary to execute the diagnostic tests and monitors:

- Comprehensive component monitor
- Catalyst monitor
- EGR and EVAP system monitors
- Fuel system monitor
- Misfire monitor
- Oxygen sensor monitor
- Oxygen sensor heater monitor
- Secondary AIR system monitor

A list of devices or systems tested by OBD II comprehensive component monitor (CCM) and main monitors includes the devices in the following table.

Comprehensive Component Monitor	Main Monitors
BARO, ECT, and IAT sensor	Fuel control system (fuel trim)
MAF, MAP, or MDP sensors	Misfire detection
Oxygen sensor—voltage level, activity	Catalyst efficiency
CMP, CKP, and TP sensors	EGR system
EGR, EVAP solenoids	EVAP system
Idle speed control motor	Oxygen sensor—response time
Fuel injectors	Oxygen sensor heater
Some PCM switches	Secondary AIR system

NOTE: The number of trips required by the CCM and main monitors before a code is set and the MIL is activated varies among vehicle manufacturers.

See Figures 26-9 to 26-11.

OBD II Drive Cycle

The vehicle must be driven under a variety of operating conditions for all active tests to be performed. OBD II regulations also established a vehicle "drive cycle" pattern that would allow the CCM and main monitors to run and complete their individual diagnostic tests.

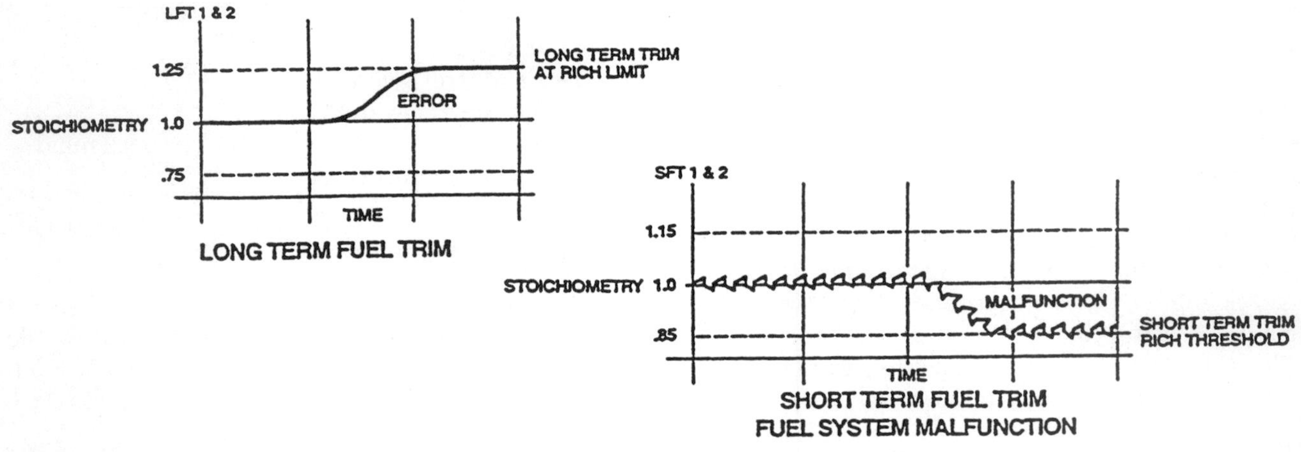

Figure 26–9 Fuel system monitor. The exhaust-gas oxygen sensor monitors the air-fuel ratio (in closed loop) and signals the on-board computer. If the mixture is incorrect, the computer adds or subtracts fuel to bring the mixture into range. This happens constantly and is known as short-term fuel trim. When short-term fuel trim is always rich (or lean), long-term fuel trim shifts from its original program and adjusts fuel delivery to bring the air-fuel mixture again back into range. If the correction needed reaches a pre-set limit, the MIL will illuminate. (Courtesy Ford Motor Co.)

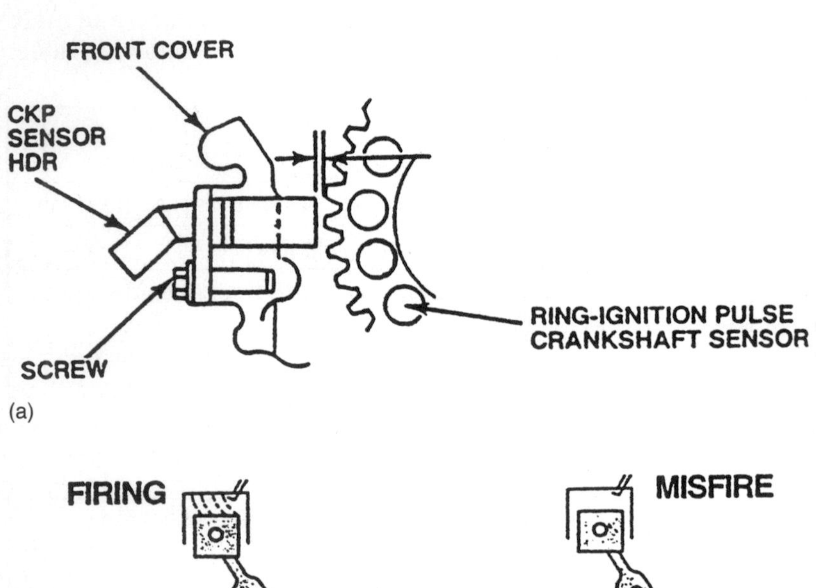

(a)

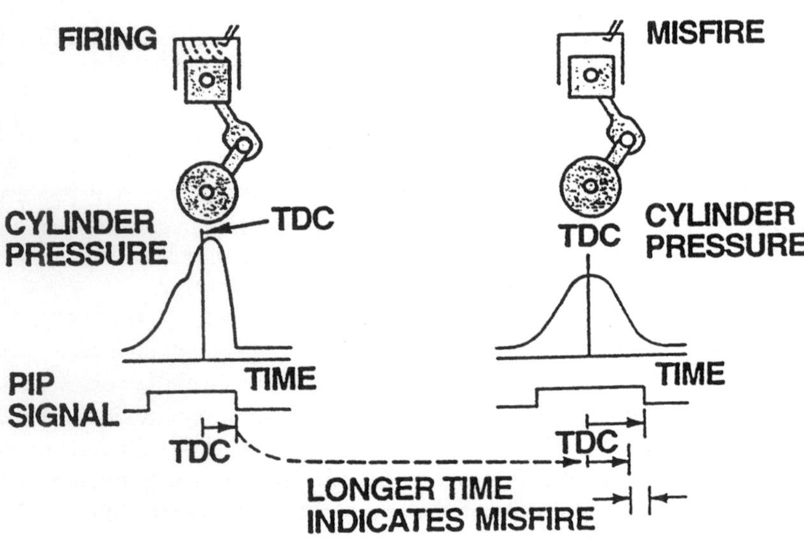

(b)

Figure 26–10 The misfire monitor reduces emissions and protects the catalytic converter. When a misfire occurs, raw hydrocarbons and unburned oxygen are pumped into the converter, raising internal temperatures. (a) The crankshaft position sensor (CKP), also used for ignition, sends a signal to the PCM for each pulse ring tooth. (b) A misfire will cause the crankshaft to slow. The increased time between pulses indicates a misfire. The fuel injector for the offending cylinder may be shut off by the PCM. (Courtesy Ford Motor Co.)

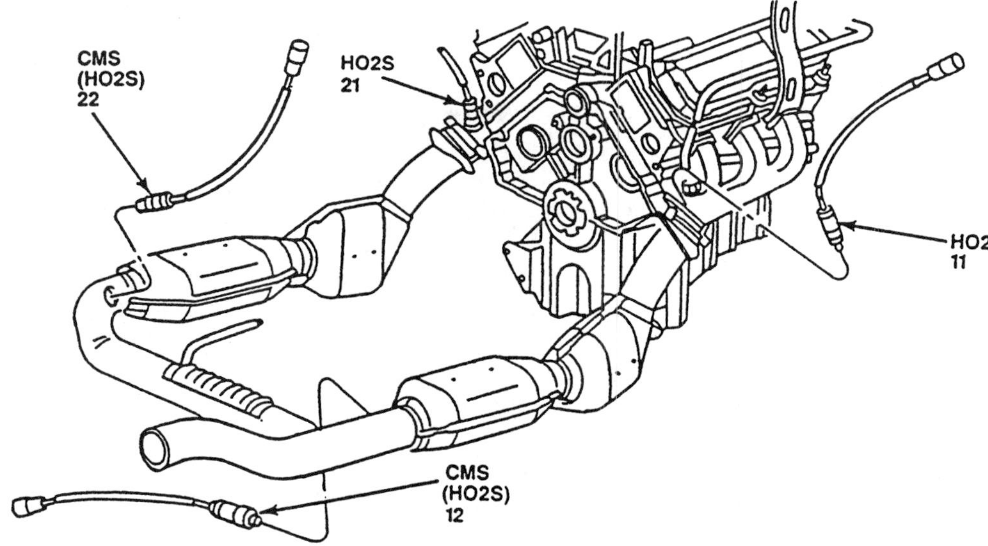

(a)

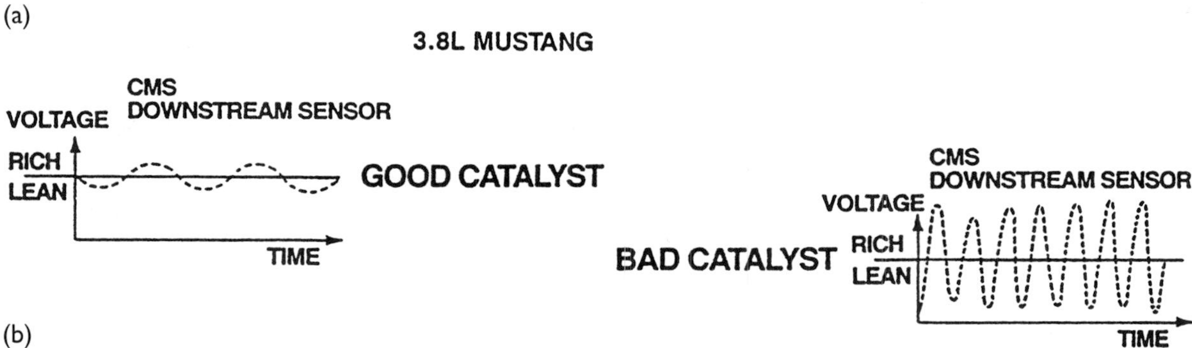

(b)

Figure 26–11 Catalyst efficiency. The efficiency of the catalytic converter(s) is determined by: (a) placing oxygen sensors before and after the converter; (b) comparing the downstream sensor reading with the upstream signal. If a malfunction is detected on three drive cycles, the MIL is illuminated. (Courtesy Ford Motor Co.)

The OBD II monitors that should run during the drive cycle include the CCM, EGR, EVAP, Fuel System, Misfire, Oxygen Sensor, and Secondary AIR System. One manufacturer has a special code (Ford—DTC P1000) that sets if all the main monitors have not been run to completion.

A trip is defined as an engine-operating drive cycle that contains the necessary conditions for a particular test to be performed. These conditions are called the enable criteria. For example, for the EGR test to be performed, the engine has to be at normal operating temperature and decelerating for a minimum amount of time. Some tests are performed when the engine is cold, whereas others require that the vehicle be cruising at a steady highway speed.

Frequently Asked Question ???

What Does "Rationality Check" Mean?

The power train control module (PCM) is programmed to detect faults that do not seem rational. For example, if the engine has been operating for 20 minutes and suddenly the engine coolant temperature changes from 90°C (195°F) to −40°C (−40°F), then the rationality test part of the computer program (CCM) determines that this is not possible (rational) and then defaults to a fail-safe operating temperature based largely on the intake air temperature (IAT) sensor. Before OBD II regulations, if the engine coolant temperature sensor became unplugged, the computer would increase the amount of fuel delivered to the engine because it assumed that the engine was in fact very cold. With rationality, the OBD II computer can reason that there must be a fault and continue to deliver fuel for proper operation and not too much, which could affect the exhaust emissions.

Warm-Up Cycle

The MIL will deactivate (turn off) if the PCM no longer detects a fault during three consecutive trips (warm-up cycles). Once a MIL is deactivated, the original code will remain in memory until 40 warm-up cycles are completed without the fault reappearing. A warm-up cycle is defined as a trip with an engine temperature increase of at least 22°C (40°F) and where engine temperature reaches at least 70°C (160°F).

MIL Condition: Off

This condition indicates that the PCM has not detected any faults in an emissions-related component or system, or that the MIL circuit is not working.

MIL Condition: On Steady

This condition indicates a fault in an emissions-related component or system that could affect the vehicle emission levels.

MIL Condition: Flashing

This condition indicates a misfire or fuel control system fault that could damage the catalytic converter.

> **NOTE:** In a misfire condition with the MIL on steady, if the driver reaches a vehicle speed and load condition with the engine misfiring at a level that could cause catalyst damage, the MIL would start flashing. It would continue to flash until engine speed and load conditions caused the level of misfire to subside. Then the MIL would go back to the on steady condition. This situation might result in a customer complaint of a MIL with an intermittent flashing condition.

MIL: Off

The PCM will turn off the MIL if any of these actions or conditions occur:

- The codes are cleared with a scan tool.
- Power to the PCM is removed at the battery or with the PCM power fuse for an extended period of time (may be up to several hours or longer).
- A vehicle is driven on three consecutive trips with a warm-up cycle and meets all code set conditions without the PCM detecting any faults.

The PCM will set a code if a fault is detected that could cause tailpipe emissions to exceed 1 1/2 times the FTP standard. However, the PCM will not deactivate the MIL until the vehicle has been driven on three consecutive trips with vehicle conditions similar to actual conditions present when the fault was detected. This is not merely three vehicle start-ups and trips. It means three trips where certain engine operating conditions are met so that the OBD II monitor that found the fault can run again and pass the diagnostic test.

Fuel Trim and Misfire Codes

If a fuel control system (fuel trim) or misfire-related code sets, then the vehicle must be driven under conditions similar to when the fault was detected before the PCM will deactivate the MIL. Similar conditions are:

- The vehicle must be driven with engine speed within 375 rpm of the engine speed stored in the freeze-frame data when the code set.
- The vehicle must be driven within engine load $\pm 10\%$ of the engine load value stored in the freeze-frame data when the code set.
- The vehicle must be driven with engine temperature conditions similar to the temperature value stored in freeze-frame data when the code set.

See Figure 26–12.

Frequently Asked Question ???

How Can All the Readiness Tests Be Set?

Readiness tests (sometimes called **flags**) are tests performed on all of the monitored systems as displayed on a scan tool. To run all tests, the engine coolant temperature should be less than 50°C (122°F) with the IAT within 6°C (11°F) of the ECT temperature and the fuel tank filled from 15% to 85% of capacity before starting the test. Proceed as follows:

1. *Start the engine and allow it to idle for 2 1/2 minutes.* This step tests the oxygen sensor heater, canister purge system, misfire, fuel trim, and time to closed loop operation.
2. *Accelerate at half throttle to 90 km/h (55 mph).* This step tests for misfire, fuel trim diagnostics, and canister purge.
3. *Hold the speed steady for 3 minutes.* This step tests the oxygen sensor, EGR system, canister purge, misfire, and fuel trim diagnostics.
4. *Decelerate without using the brake or clutch (if equipped).* This step tests the EGR system, canister purge, and fuel trim diagnostics.
5. *Accelerate at three-fourths throttle to 90 to 100 km/h (55 to 60 mph).* This step tests for misfire, fuel trim diagnostics, and canister purge.
6. *Hold steady speed for 5 minutes.* This step tests the catalytic converter.
7. *Decelerate without using the brake or clutch, if equipped.* This step tests the EGR system, canister purge, and fuel trim diagnostics.

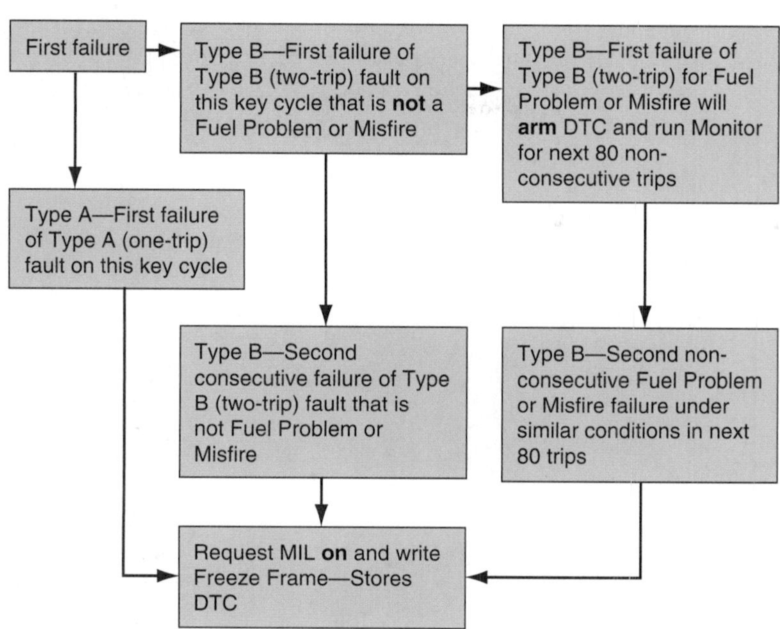

Figure 26–12 How a PCM turns on the MIL.

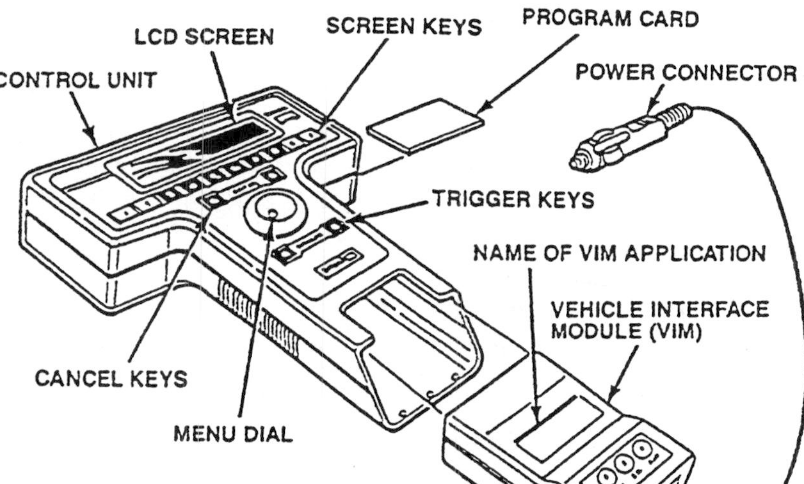

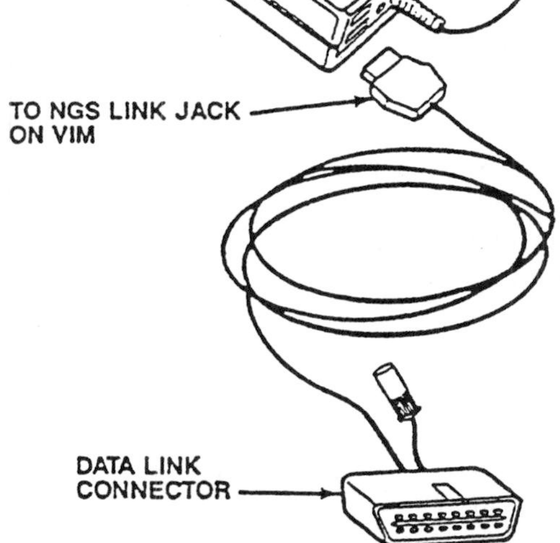

Figure 26–13 A typical scan tool set up for OBD II diagnostics. Ford calls this a New Generation Self-Test Automatic Readout tester (NG STAR or NGS). Most OBD II scan tools receive power through the DLC and do not require a separate power connector. (Courtesy Ford Motor Co.)

Retrieving OBD II Codes—16 Pin

A scan tool is required to retrieve DTCs from an OBD II vehicle. See Figure 26–13. Every OBD II scan tool will be able to read all generic Society of Automotive Engineers (SAE) DTCs from any vehicle. See Figures 26–14 and 26–15 for definitions and explanations of OBD alphanumeric DTCs. Although all data link connectors are the same on OBD II vehicles, some manufacturer-discretion pins are used for different purposes. See Figure 26–16. Generic scan tools often supply "personality keys" (small adaptors that fit into the scan tool plug) to match the pin use for the vehicle being tested.

DTC Numbering Explanation

The number in the hundredth position indicates the specific vehicle system or subgroup that failed. This position should be consistent for P0xxx and P1xxx

DTC FORMAT

Diagnostic Trouble Codes for EEC-V are formatted according to SAE J2012. SAE J2012 dictates a five-digit alphanumeric DTC with each digit defined as follows:

- Prefix letter of DTC indicates DTC function:
  - P — Powertrain
  - B — Body
  - C — Chassis
- First number indicates who was responsible for DTC definition:
  - 0 — SAE
  - 1 — Manufacturer
- Third digit of powertrain DTC indicates subgroup:
  - 0 — Total System
  - 1 — Fuel/Air Control
  - 2 — Fuel/Air Control
  - 3 — Ignition System/Misfire
  - 4 — Auxiliary Emission Controls
  - 5 — Idle/Speed Control
  - 6 — PCM and I/O
  - 7 — Transmission
  - 8 — Non-EEC Powertrain
- The fourth and fifth digit specify the area involved.

Let's take a possible DTC and break it into defined segments.

For Example: P1711

- P — First digit letter indicates a Powertrain DTC.
- 1 — Second digit indicates a manufacturer defined DTC.
- 7 — Third digit indicates a transmission sub-group concern.
- 11 — Fourth and fifth digits indicate a TOT Circuit out of range.

Figure 26–14 An alphanumeric DTC chart for OBD II. SAE (generic) codes are standardized for all vehicles. The example P1711 indicates a transmission oil temperature circuit out of range. (Courtesy Ford Motor Co.)

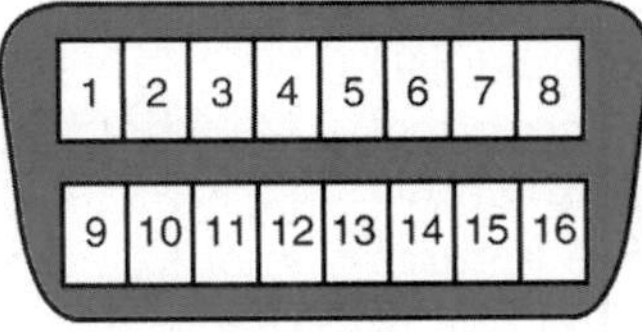

PIN NO.	ASSIGNMENTS
1.	MANUFACTURER'S DISCRETION
2.	BUS + LINE, SAE J1850
3.	MANUFACTURER'S DISCRETION
4.	CHASSIS GROUND
5.	SIGNAL GROUND
6.	MANUFACTURER'S DISCRETION
7.	K LINE, ISO 9141
8.	MANUFACTURER'S DISCRETION
9.	MANUFACTURER'S DISCRETION
10.	BUS–LINE, SAE J1850
11.	MANUFACTURER'S DISCRETION
12.	MANUFACTURER'S DISCRETION
13.	MANUFACTURER'S DISCRETION
14.	MANUFACTURER'S DISCRETION

Figure 26–15 Sixteen-pin OBD II DLC with terminals identified. Scan tools use the power (#16) pin and ground (#4) pin so that a separate cigarette lighter plug is not necessary on OBD II vehicles.

type codes. The following numbers and systems were established by SAE:

- P0100—air metering and fuel system fault
- P0200—fuel system (fuel injector only) fault
- P0300—ignition system or misfire fault
- P0400—emission control system fault
- P0500—idle speed control, vehicle speed sensor fault
- P0600—computer output circuit (relay, solenoid, etc.) fault
- P0700—transaxle, transmission faults

NOTE: The tens and ones numbers indicate the part of the system at fault.

OBD II Active Tests

The vehicle computer must run tests on the various emission-related components and turn on the malfunction indicator lamp (MIL). OBD II is an *active* computer analysis system because it actually tests the operation of the oxygen sensors, exhaust gas recirculation system, and other systems whenever conditions permit. It is the purpose and function of the powertrain control module (PCM) to monitor these components and perform these active tests.

For example, the PCM may open the EGR valve momentarily to check its operation while the vehicle is decelerating. A change in the manifold absolute pressure (MAP) sensor signal will indicate to the computer that the exhaust gas is, in fact, being introduced into the engine. Because these tests are active and certain conditions must be present before these tests can be run, the computer uses its internal diagnostic program to keep track of all the various conditions and to schedule active tests so that they will not interfere with each other.

Types of DTCs

Not all OBD II DTCs are of the same importance for exhaust emissions. Each type of DTC has different requirements for it to set, and the computer will only turn on the MIL for emissions-related DTCs.

Type A Codes A type A DTC is emission-related and will cause the MIL to be turned on on the *first trip* if the computer has detected a problem. Engine misfire or a very rich or lean air–fuel ratio, for example, would cause a type A DTC. These codes alert the driver to an emission problem that may cause damage to the catalytic converter.

Type B Codes A type B code will be stored and the MIL will be turned on during the *second consecutive trip,* alerting the driver to the fact that a diagnostic test was performed and failed.

> **NOTE:** Type A and B codes are emission-related codes that will cause the lighting of the malfunction indicator lamp, usually labelled "check engine" or "service engine soon."

Type C and D Codes Type C and D codes are for use with non-emission-related diagnostic tests; they will cause the lighting of a "service" lamp (if the vehicle is so equipped). Type C codes are also called type C1 codes, and D codes are also called type C0 codes.

OBD II Freeze-Frame

To assist the service technician, OBD II requires the computer to take a "snapshot" or freeze-frame of all data at the instant an emission-related DTC is set. A scan tool is required to retrieve this data.

What Are Each of the Pins for in the OBD II 16-Pin Data Link Connector (DLC)?

All OBD II vehicles use a 16-in connector that includes:

Pin 4 = chassis ground
Pin 5 = signal ground
Pin 16 = battery power (4A max)

Vehicles may use one of two major standards including:

- **ISO 9141-2 Standard** (ISO = International Standards Organization)
  Pins 7 and 15 (or wire at pin 7 and no pin at 2 or a wire at 7 and at 2 and/or 10)
- **SAE J-1850 Standard** (SAE = Society of Automotive Engineers)
  Two types: **VPW** (variable pulse width) or **PWM** (pulse width modulated)
  Pins 2 and 10 (no wire at pin 7)

DaimlerChrysler, European, and Asian vehicles use:

- ISO 9141-2 standard, which uses pins 4, 5, 7, 15, and 16
- **DaimlerChrysler Domestic OBD II**

  Pins 2 and 10—CCM
  Pins 3 and 14—OEM Enhanced—60 500 baud rate
  Pins 7 and 15—Generic OBD II—ISO 9141—10 400 baud rate

Ford vehicles use:

- SAE J-1850(PWM) (PWM - 41.6 kB) standard, which uses pins 2, 4, 5, 10, and 16
- **Ford Domestic OBD II**

  Pins 2 and 10—CCM
  Pins 6 and 14—OEM Enhanced—Class C—40 500 baud rate
  Pins 7 and 15—Generic OBD II—ISO 9141—10 400 baud rate

General Motors vehicles use:

- SAE J-1850 (VPW - Class 2 - 10.4 kB) standard, which uses pins 2, 4, 5, and 16 and not 10
- **GM Domestic OBD II**

  Pins 1 and 9—CCM (Comprehensive Component Monitor) slow baud rate—8192 UART
  Pins 2 and 10—OEM Enhanced—Fast Rate—40 500 baud rate
  Pins 7 and 15—Generic OBD II—ISO 9141—10 400 baud rate

Figure 26–16 OBD II DLC pin use.

NOTE: Although OBD II requires that just one freeze-frame of data be stored, the instant an emission-related DTC is set, vehicle manufacturers usually provide expanded data about the DTC beyond that required. However, to retrieve this enhanced data usually requires the use of the vehicle-specific scan tool.

Freeze-frame items include:

- Calculated load value
- Engine speed (RPM)
- Short-term and long-term fuel trim percent
- Fuel system pressure (on some vehicles)
- Vehicle speed (km/h or mph)
- Engine coolant temperature (ECT)
- Intake manifold pressure
- Closed/open loop status
- Fault code that triggered the freeze-frame
- If a misfire code is set, identify which cylinder is misfiring

Clearing OBD II DTCs

A DTC should not be cleared from the vehicle computer memory unless the fault has been corrected and the technician is so directed by the diagnostic procedure. If the problem that caused the DTC to be set has been corrected, the computer will automatically clear the DTC after 40 consecutive warm-up cycles with no further faults detected (misfire and excessively rich or lean condition codes require 80 warm-up cycles). The codes can also be erased by using a scan tool.

NOTE: Disconnecting the battery may not erase OBD II DTCs or freeze-frame data. Most vehicle manufacturers recommend using a scan tool to erase DTCs rather than disconnecting the battery because the memory for the radio, seats, and learned engine operating parameters are lost if the battery is disconnected.

Diagnostic Procedures

Diagnostic procedures for OBD I and OBD II vehicles are covered in Chapter 31, "Engine Performance Diagnosis and Testing."

DIAGNOSING COMPUTER PROBLEMS

If a computer fails, it is often difficult to determine if the computer itself is at fault or if there is a problem with some other system in the vehicle. For example, if the engine stalls, it could be the result of a fault in the ignition system, fuel system, or a failed sensor such as a crankshaft position sensor (CKP).

As part of the diagnostic process, check the computer grounds as shown in Figure 26–17. Also gently

TECH TIP 

Don't Forget—Three Clicks

OBD II requires that the fuel system integrity be checked for possible leakage. If the fuel (gas) cap is not securely tightened, then a DTC such as P0442 may be set. To help prevent such false codes and to ensure that the gas cap is properly tightened, General Motors Corporation has printed on the cap itself a note that the cap should be tightened until three clicks are heard. This also applies to other screw-thread-type gas caps of all years and makes to be assured that the cap is tight. Some vehicles are equipped with an amber "Check Gas Cap" lamp that will light if a system leak is detected.

NOTE: Gas caps are frequently tested as part of an exhaust emission test. Ask the person performing the test on your gas cap to tighten the cap three clicks to ensure proper tightness. This will help prevent false defective test results.

Frequently Asked Question ???

What Are Pending Codes?

Pending codes are set when operating conditions are met and the component or circuit is not within the normal range, yet the conditions have not yet been met to set a DTC. For example, a sensor may require two consecutive faults before a DTC is set. If a scan tool displays a pending code or a failure, a driveability concern could also be present. The pending code can help the technician try to determine the root cause before the customer complains of a check engine light indication.

Figure 26–17 Always check that the computer grounds are clean and tight.

Figure 26–18 Tap testing a vehicle computer. General Motors recommends that only the four fingers of an open hand be used to tap test any component to avoid causing damage.

tap on the computer with the engine running. If the engine stalls or changes the way it is operating, check the wiring connecter. If the wiring is OK, replace the computer. See Figure 26–18.

SUMMARY

1. Malfunction indicator lamp (MIL) is the name given to the amber check engine or "service engine soon" light.
2. On-board diagnostics second generation, called OBD II, is used on all vehicles sold in Canada since 1998.
3. OBD II requires that all emission-related components be checked and tested.
4. The vehicle must be driven with approximately the same speed, load, and temperature (similar conditions) before the PCM will deactivate the MIL for fuel trim and misfire codes.
5. The data link connector (DLC) and generic diagnostic trouble codes (DTC) are the same for all OBD II vehicles.

REVIEW QUESTIONS

1. List four components that are tested by the comprehensive component monitor (CCM).
2. What is the difference between a warm-up cycle and a trip?
3. What is a pending code?
4. What are "flash" codes?
5. How are codes cleared from PCM memory?

RED SEAL CERTIFICATION-TYPE QUESTIONS

1. All vehicles sold in Canada since _____ must be equipped with OBD II.
   - a. 1996 b. 1998
   - c. 2000 d. 2002
2. The primary purpose of OBD I is _____.
   - a. Emission related
   - b. Fuel injection control
   - c. To detect faults in sensors or circuits
   - d. Improving fuel economy
3. A loose gas cap can set a diagnostic trouble code (DTC).
   - a. True b. False
4. OBD II DTC PO172 (System Too Rich) will automatically clear from memory after _____ warm-up cycles when the problem is corrected.
   - a. 2 b. 3
   - c. 40 d. 80
5. A warm-up cycle has to achieve at least how many degrees of engine coolant temperature?
   - a. 15°C (60°F) b. 50°C (122°F)
   - c. 70°C (160°F) d. 80°C (177°F)
6. Which DTC represents an ignition or misfire fault?
   - a. P0100 b. P0200
   - c. P0300 d. P0400
7. An ignition misfire or fuel mix problem is an example of what type of DTC?
   - a. A b. B
   - c. C d. D
8. A type B DTC requires how many faults to turn on the MIL?
   - a. One b. Two
   - c. Three d. Four
9. A freeze-frame is generated on an OBD II vehicle _____.
   - a. Whenever a type C or D diagnostic trouble code is set
   - b. Whenever a type A or B diagnostic trouble code is set
   - c. Every other trip
   - d. Whenever the PCM detects a problem with the O2S
10. Terminal 16 of the OBD II DLC supplies volts to a scan tool, and terminal _____ supplies the signal ground.
    - a. 2 b. 5
    - c. 4 d. 1

27

Engine Fuels and Combustion

OBJECTIVES: After studying Chapter 27, you should be able to:

1. Prepare for the interprovincial Red Seal certification examination in Appendix VIII (Engine Performance) on the topics covered in this chapter.
2. Describe how the proper grade of gasoline affects engine performance.
3. List gasoline purchasing hints.
4. Explain how volatility affects driveability.
6. List the major fuels and byproducts refined from crude oil.
7. Describe the three categories of diesel fuel.

The quality of the fuel any engine uses is very important to its proper operation and long life. If the fuel is not right for the air temperature or if the tendency of the fuel to evaporate is incorrect, severe driveability problems can result. An engine burns about 15 parts of air to 1 part of gasoline (by weight). To achieve the same ratio in volume, it takes about 10 000 L of air for 1 L of gasoline (1350 cu ft of air for every gallon).

GASOLINE

Gasoline is a term used to describe a complex mixture of various hydrocarbons refined from crude petroleum oil for use as a fuel in engines. The word **petroleum** means *rock oil*. The refinery removes undesirable ingredients such as paraffins and puts in additives such as octane improvers. Most gasoline is blended to meet the needs of the local climates and altitudes. See Figure 27–1.

VOLATILITY

Volatility describes how easily the gasoline evaporates (forms a vapour). The definition of volatility assumes that the vapours will remain in the fuel tank or fuel line and will cause a certain pressure based on the temperature of the fuel.

Winter Blend

Reid vapour pressure (RVP) is the pressure of the vapour above the fuel when the fuel is at 38°C (100°F). Increased vapour pressure permits the engine to start in cold weather. Gasoline without air will not burn. Gasoline must be vaporized (mixed with air) to burn in an engine. Cold temperatures reduce the normal vaporization of gasoline; therefore, winter-blended gasoline is specially formulated to vaporize at lower temperatures for proper starting and driveability at low ambient temperatures. Standards for winter-blend gasoline allow volatility of up to 103 kPa (15 psi) RVP.

Summer Blend

At warm ambient temperatures, gasoline vaporizes easily. However, the fuel system (fuel pump, carburetor, fuel-injector nozzles, etc.) is designed to operate with liquid gasoline. The volatility of summer-grade gasoline should be about 50 kPa (7.3 psi) RVP and the maximum RVP should be 70 kPa (10.5 psi) for summer-blend gasoline.

Volatility Problems

At higher temperatures, liquid gasoline can easily vaporize and this can cause **vapour lock.** Vapour lock is a *lean* condition caused by vaporized fuel in the fuel

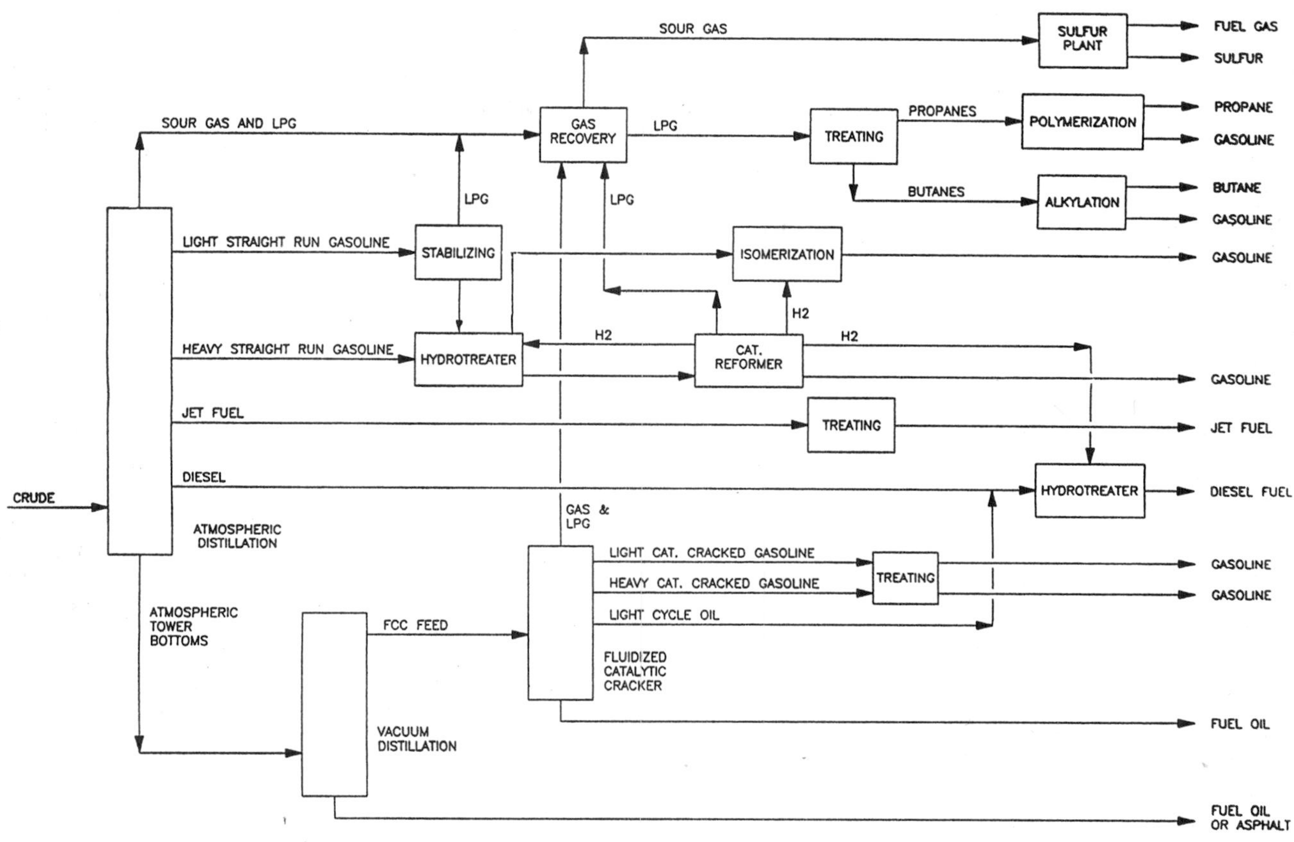

Figure 27-1 A typical oil refinery. Note the number of different fuels refined from a barrel of crude oil. (Courtesy Chevron Canada Ltd.)

system. This vaporized fuel takes up space normally occupied by liquid fuel and prevents normal fuel pump operation. Vapour lock is caused by bubbles that form in the fuel, preventing proper operation of the fuel pump, carburetor, or fuel-injection system.

Bubbles in the fuel can be caused by heat or by sharp bends in the fuel system. Heat causes some fuel to evaporate, thereby causing bubbles. Sharp bends cause the fuel to be restricted at the bend. When the fuel flows past the bend, the fuel can expand to fill the space after the bend. This expansion drops the pressure, and bubbles form in the fuel lines. When the fuel is full of bubbles, the engine is not being supplied with enough fuel and the engine runs lean. A lean engine will stumble during acceleration, will run rough, and may stall. Warm weather and alcohol-blended fuels both tend to increase vapour-lock and engine-performance problems.

If winter-blend gasoline (or high-RVP fuel) is used in an engine during warm weather, the following problems may occur:

1. Rough idle
2. Stalling
3. Hesitation on acceleration
4. Surging

The RVP can be tested using the test kit shown in Figure 27–2.

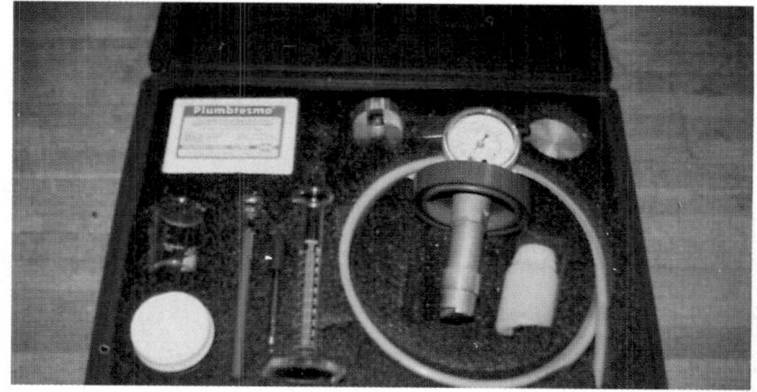

Figure 27–2 A gasoline testing kit. Included is an insulated container where water at 38°C (100°F) is used to heat a container holding a small sample of gasoline. The reading on the pressure gauge is the Reid vapour pressure (RVP).

TECH TIP

The Sniff Test

Problems can occur with stale gasoline from which the lighter parts of the gasoline have evaporated. Stale gasoline usually results in a no-start situation. If stale gasoline is suspected, smell the gasoline. If it smells rancid, replace the gasoline with fresh gasoline.

NOTE: If storing a vehicle, boat, or lawn mower over the winter, put some gasoline stabilizer into the gasoline to reduce the evaporation and separation that can occur during storage. Gasoline stabilizer is frequently found at lawn mower repair shops or marinas.

Some experts recommend that a diesel fuel additive be used to kill bacteria and fungi growth that occurs in fuels when there is some moisture present. To kill algae and stop bacterial growth, use from 8 to 15 mL (0.25 to 0.50 fl. oz.) additive in each 75 L (20 gallons) of fuel.

NORMAL AND ABNORMAL COMBUSTION

The **octane rating** of gasoline is the measure of its antiknock properties. **Engine knock** (also called **detonation, spark knock,** or **ping**) is a metallic noise an engine makes, usually during acceleration, resulting from abnormal or uncontrolled combustion inside the cylinder.

Normal combustion occurs smoothly and progresses across the combustion chamber from the point of ignition. See Figure 27–3. Normal combustion propagation is between 70 and 145 km/h (45 and 90 mph). The speed of the flame front depends on air–fuel ratio, combustion chamber design (determining amount of turbulence), and temperature.

During periods of spark knock (detonation), the combustion speed increases by up to 10 times to near the speed of sound. The increased combustion speed also causes increased temperatures and pressures, which can damage pistons, gaskets, and cylinder heads. See Figure 27–4.

One of the first additives used in gasoline was **tetraethyl lead (TEL).** TEL was added to gasoline in the early 1920s to reduce the tendency to knock. It was often called *ethyl* or *high-test* gasoline.

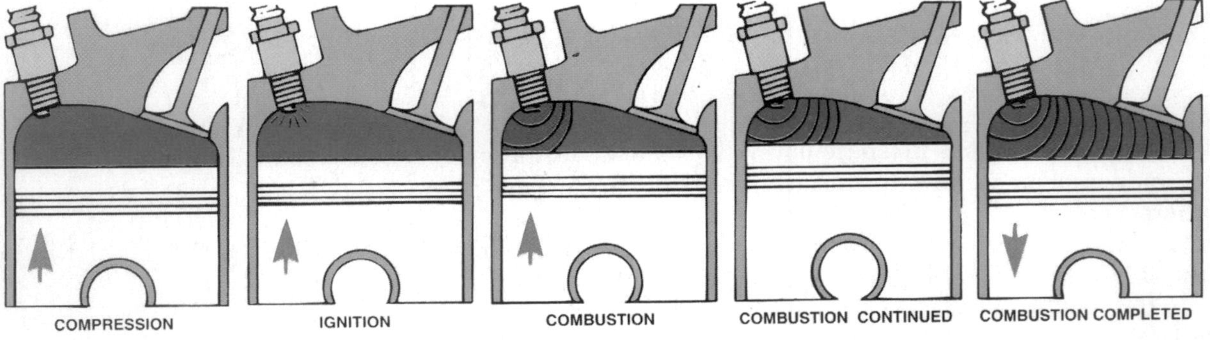

Figure 27–3 Normal combustion is a smooth, controlled burning of the air-fuel mixtue.

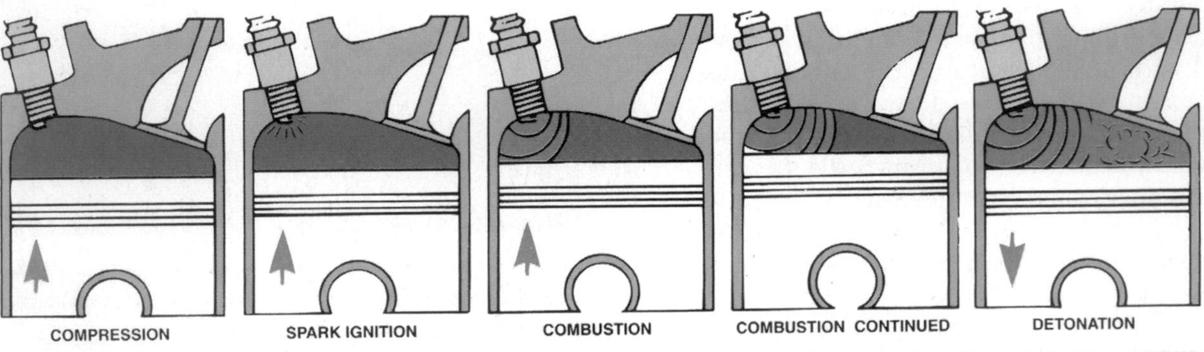

Figure 27–4 Detonation is a secondary ignition of the air–fuel mixture. It is also called *spark knock* or *pinging*.

OCTANE RATING

The antiknock standard or basis of comparison was the knock-resistant hydrocarbon isooctane, chemically called trimethylpentane (C_8H_{18}), also known as 2-2-4 trimethylpentane. If a gasoline tested had the exact same antiknock characteristics as isooctane, it was rated as 100-octane gasoline. If the gasoline tested had only 85% of the antiknock properties of isooctane, it was rated as 85 octane. Remember, octane rating is only a comparison test.

There are two basic methods used to rate gasoline for antiknock properties (octane rating): the *research method* and the *motor method*. Each uses a model of the special cooperative fuel research (CFR) single-cylinder engine. The research method and the motor method vary as to temperature of air, spark advance, and other parameters. The research method typically results in readings that are 6 to 10 points higher than those of the motor method. For example, a fuel with a research octane number (RON) of 93 might have a motor octane number (MON) of 85.

The octane rating posted on pumps in Canada and the U.S. is the average of the two methods and is referred to as (R + M)/2, meaning that, for the fuel used in the previous example, the rating posted on the pumps would be

$$\frac{\text{RON} + \text{MON}}{2} = \frac{93 + 85}{2} = 89$$

GASOLINE GRADES AND OCTANE NUMBER

The posted octane rating on gasoline pumps is the rating achieved by the average of the research and the motor methods. See Figure 27–5. Except in high-altitude areas, the grades and octane ratings are as follows:

Grades	Octane Rating
Regular	87
Mid-grade (also called Plus)	89
Premium	91 or higher

OCTANE IMPROVERS

When gasoline companies, under U.S. EPA regulations, removed tetraethyl lead from gasoline, other methods were developed to help maintain the antiknock properties of gasoline. Octane improvers (enhancers) can be grouped into three broad categories:

1. Aromatic hydrocarbons (hydrocarbons containing the benzene ring) such as xylene and toluene
2. Alcohols such as ethanol (ethyl alcohol), methanol (methyl alcohol), and tertiary butyl alcohol (TBA)
3. Metallic compounds such as methylcyclopentadienyl manganese tricarbonyl (MMT)

Figure 27–5 A typical fuel pump showing regular (87 octane), midgrade (89 octane), and premium (92 octane). These ratings can vary with brand as well as in different parts of the country, especially in high altitude areas, where the ratings are lower.

DIAGNOSTIC STORY

The Stalling Acura

On a warm day in March, a customer walked into an automotive repair shop and asked for help. The car was parked on the street just outside the shop. A service technician accompanied the owner to check out the situation. The owner complained that the engine would start, then immediately stall. The engine would again start, then stall during another attempt.

The service technician slid into the driver's seat and turned the ignition key. When the engine started, the technician depressed the accelerator slightly and the engine continued to run without any apparent problem. The car owner had never depressed the accelerator pedal and had never had any previous engine trouble.

The technician suspected winter-grade (high-RVP) gasoline was the problem. The owner replied that the present tank of fuel had been purchased during the last week in February. The technician explained that the uncommonly warm weather caused the fuel to vaporize in the fuel rail. Enough condensed fuel was available to start the engine, but the fuel injectors are designed to handle liquid fuel—not vapour—so the engine stalled.

The technician was probably lucky because by the third start enough of the remaining vapour had been drawn into the engine and all that remained was liquid gasoline.

NOTE: MMT, widely used as an octane improver, has been removed from Canadian gasolines beginning in 2004. The major automakers and the federal government claimed that MMT reduced oxygen sensor life, while the petroleum industry claimed otherwise. The oxygen sensor after the catalytic converter seemed to be the most susceptible. Some automakers allowed reflashing of the PCM to exclude the downstream oxygen sensor (OBD II).

Propane and butane, which are volatile byproducts of the refinery process, are also often added to gasoline as octane improvers. The increase in volatility caused by the added propane and butane often leads to hot weather driveability problems.

OXYGENATED FUELS

Oxygenated fuels contain oxygen in the molecule of the fuel itself. Examples of oxygenated fuels include methanol, ethanol, methyl tertiary butyl ether (MTBE), and ethyl tertiary butyl ether (ETBE).

Oxygenated fuels are commonly used in high-altitude areas to reduce carbon monoxide (CO) emissions. The extra oxygen in the fuel itself is used to convert harmful CO into carbon dioxide (CO_2). The extra oxygen in the fuel helps ensure that there is enough oxygen to convert all the CO into CO_2 during the combustion process in the engine or catalytic converter.

Methyl Tertiary Butyl Ether

Methyl tertiary butyl ether (MTBE) is manufactured by means of the chemical reaction of methanol and isobutylene. Unlike methanol, MTBE does not increase the volatility of the fuel, and is not as sensitive to water as are other alcohols. MTBE is currently being phased out due to concern with its contamination of drinking water if the MTBE is spilled from storage tanks.

Tertiary-Amyl Methyl Ether

Tertiary-amyl methyl ether (TAME) is often added to gasoline as an oxygenator.

Ethyl Tertiary Butyl Ether

Ethyl tertiary butyl ether (ETBE) is derived from ethanol. The maximum allowable volume level is 17.2%. The use of ETBE is the cause of much of the odour from the exhaust of vehicles using reformulated gasoline.

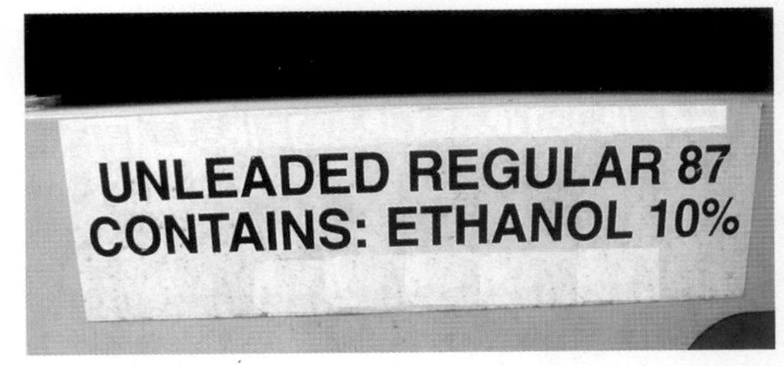

Figure 27–6 This fuel pump label indicates that the gasoline is blended with 10% ethanol (ethyl alcohol).

Ethanol

Ethyl alcohol is drinkable alcohol made from grain. Adding 10% ethanol (ethyl alcohol or grain alcohol) increases the (R + M)/2 octane rating by 3 points. The alcohol added to the base gasoline, however, also raises the volatility of the fuel about 3 kPa (0.5 psi). Most automobile manufacturers permit up to 10% ethanol if driveability problems are not experienced. The oxygen content of a 10% blend of ethanol in gasoline is 3.5% oxygen by weight. See Figure 27–6.

Methanol

Methyl alcohol is made from wood (wood alcohol), natural gas, or coal. Methanol is poisonous if ingested and tends to be more harmful to the materials in the fuel system, and it tends to separate when combined with gasoline unless used with a cosolvent. A cosolvent is another substance (usually another alcohol) that is soluble in both methanol and gasoline and is used to reduce the tendency of the liquids to separate.

Methanol can damage fuel system parts. Methanol is corrosive to lead (used as a coating of fuel tanks), aluminum, magnesium, and some plastics and rubber. Methanol can also cause rubber products (elastomers) to swell and soften. Methanol itself is 50% oxygen. Gasoline containing 5% methanol would have an oxygen content of 2.5% by weight.

CAUTION: All alcohols can absorb water, and the alcohol–water mixture can separate from the gasoline and sink to the bottom of the fuel tank. This is called **phase separation.** To help avoid engine performance problems, try to keep at least a quarter tank of fuel at all times, especially during seasons in which there is a wide temperature span between daytime highs and nighttime lows. These conditions can cause moisture to accumulate in the fuel tank as a result of condensation of the moisture in the air. See Figure 27–7.

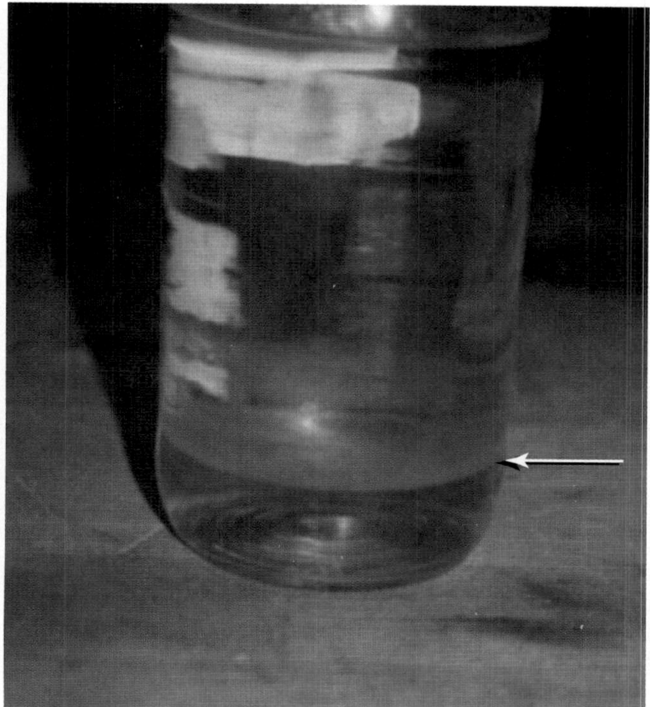

Figure 27–7 This container holds pure gasoline and water. Notice how the water separates and sinks to the bottom.

ALCOHOL ADDITIVES—ADVANTAGES AND DISADVANTAGES

The advantages and disadvantages of using alcohol as an additive to gasoline can be summarized as follows:

Advantages

1. Absorbs moisture in the fuel tank.
2. Ten percent alcohol added to gasoline raises the octane rating—(R + M)/2—by 3 points.
3. Alcohol cleans the fuel system.
4. The addition of alcohol reduces carbon monoxide (CO) emissions because alcohol contains oxygen.

Disadvantages

1. The use of alcohol can result in the clogging of fuel filters with dirt and so forth cleaned from fuel tank, pump, and lines.
2. Alcohol raises the volatility of fuel about 3 kPa (0.5 psi); this can cause hot weather driveability problems.
3. Addition of alcohol reduces the heat content of the resulting fuel mixture (alcohol has about one-half of the energy content of gasoline).
4. Alcohol absorbs water and then separates from the gasoline, especially as temperature drops. Separated alcohol and water on the bottom of the tank can cause hard starting during cold weather. Alcohol does not vaporize easily at low temperatures.

Frequently Asked Question ???

How Does Alcohol Content in the Gasoline Affect Engine Operation?

In most cases, the use of gasoline containing 10% or less of ethanol (ethyl alcohol) has little or no effect on engine operation. However, because the addition of 10% ethanol raises the volatility of the fuel slightly, occasional rough idle or stalling may be noticed, especially during warm weather. The rough idle and stalling may also be noticeable after the engine is started, driven, then stopped for a short time. Engine heat can vaporize the alcohol-enhanced fuel causing bubbles to form in the fuel system. These bubbles in the fuel prevent the proper operation of the fuel injection or carburetor and result in a hesitation during acceleration, rough idle, or in severe cases repeated stalling until all the bubbles have been forced through the fuel system and replaced by cooler fuel from the fuel tank.

TESTING GASOLINE FOR ALCOHOL CONTENT

Take the following steps when testing gasoline for alcohol content:

1. Pour suspect gasoline into a small clean beaker or glass container.

CAUTION: Do not smoke or run the test around sources of ignition!

2. Carefully fill the graduated cylinder to the 10-mL (milliliter) mark.
3. Add 2 mL of water to the graduated cylinder by counting the number of drops from an eyedropper. (Before performing the test, the eye dropper must be calibrated to determine how many drops equal 2.0 mL.)
4. Put the stopper in the cylinder and shake vigorously for 1 minute. Relieve built-up pressure by occasionally removing the stopper. Alcohol dissolves in water and will drop to the bottom of the cylinder.

5. Place the cylinder on a flat surface and let it stand for 2 minutes.
6. Take a reading near the bottom of the cylinder at the boundary between the two liquids.
7. For percent of alcohol in gasoline, subtract 2 from the reading and multiply by 10.

For example, if

The reading is 3.1 ml: $3.1 - 2 = 1.1 \times 10 = 11\%$ alcohol
The reading is 2.0 ml: $2 - 2 = 0 \times 10 = 0\%$ alcohol (no alcohol)

If the increase in volume is 0.2% or less, it may be assumed that the test gasoline contains no alcohol.

Figure 27–8 A gasoline pump in a high-altitude area. Note the lower than normal octane ratings. The "ethanol" sticker reads that all grades contain 10% ethanol from November 1 through February 28 each year to help reduce carbon monoxide (CO) exhaust emissions.

COMBUSTION CHEMISTRY

Internal combustion engines burn an organic fuel to produce power. The term **organic** refers to a product (gasoline) from a source that originally was alive. Because crude oil originally came from living plants and animals, all products of petroleum are considered organic fuels and are composed primarily of hydrogen (H) and carbon (C).

The combustion process involves the chemical combination of oxygen (O_2) from the air (about 21% of the atmosphere) with the hydrogen and carbon from the fuel. In a gasoline engine, a spark starts the combustion process, which takes about 3 ms (0.003 seconds) to be completed inside the cylinder of an engine. The chemical reaction that takes place can be summarized as follows: hydrogen (H) plus carbon (C) plus oxygen (O_2) plus nitrogen (N) plus spark equals heat plus water (H_2O) plus carbon monoxide (CO) plus carbon dioxide (CO_2) plus hydrocarbons (HC) plus oxides of nitrogen (NO_x) plus many other chemicals.

The heat produced by the combustion process is measured in calories or BTUs. One calorie is the amount of heat required to raise the temperature of one gram of water one Celsius degree. One BTU (British thermal unit) is the amount of heat required to raise the temperature of one pound of water one Fahrenheit degree.

Stoichiometric

If the combustion process is complete, all the gasoline or hydrocarbons (HC) will be completely combined with all the available oxygen (O_2). This total combination of all components of the fuel is called **stoichiometric air–fuel ratio.** The stoichiometric quantities for gasoline are 14.7 parts air for 1 part gasoline by weight. Different fuels have different stoichiometric proportions.

HIGH-ALTITUDE OCTANE REQUIREMENTS

As the altitude increases, atmospheric pressure drops. The air is less dense because a kilogram of air occupies more volume. The octane rating of fuel does not need to be as high because the engine cannot intake as much air. This process will reduce the combustion (compression) pressures inside the engine. In mountainous areas, gasoline (R + M)/2 octane ratings are 2 or more numbers lower than normal (according to SAE, about 1 octane number lower per 300 m (1000 ft) in altitude. See Figure 27–8. Some problems, therefore, may occur when driving out of high-altitude areas into lower-altitude areas where octane rating needs to be higher. Most computerized engine control systems can compensate for changes in altitude and modify the air–fuel ratio and ignition timing for best operation.

Because the combustion burn rate slows at high altitude, the ignition (spark) timing can be advanced to improve power. The amount of timing advance can be about 1 degree per 300 m (1000 ft) over 1500 m (5000 ft). Therefore, if driving at 2400 m (8000 ft) of altitude, the ignition timing can be advanced 3 degrees.

High altitude also allows fuel to evaporate more easily. The volatility of fuel should be reduced at higher altitudes to prevent vapour from forming in sections of the fuel system, which can cause driveability and stalling problems. The extra heat generated in climbing to higher altitudes plus the lower atmospheric pressure at higher altitudes combine to cause vapour lock problems as the vehicle goes to higher altitudes.

VALVE RECESSION AND UNLEADED FUEL

Unleaded fuel has been available since the early 1970s, and since that time there has been concern about valve problems related to using unleaded fuel. Back in the 1920s when leaded gasoline was first introduced, the main problem was with the valves. In the 1920s, the lead deposits in the engine prevented the valves from fully seating, which resulted in overheated valves because the valves get rid of the majority of their heat through the valve face or seat area. The solution to valve burning in the 1920s with leaded fuel was to increase the valve spring tension. This increased pressure smashed the lead deposits into a thin lubricating film, allowing the valve to fully close and thereby transfer heat to the seat area.

Without lead, the valve movement against the seat tears away tiny iron oxide particles during engine operation, especially during high load/high speed operation. The valve movement causes these particles of iron oxide to act like valve grinding compound, cutting into the valve seat surface. As the valve seat erodes, the valve recedes farther into the cylinder head.

Vehicle engines produced after the early 1970s (for sale in Canada and the U.S.) had to be able to operate on unleaded gasoline. Most engine manufacturers started induction hardening of valve seats to help prevent valve recession.

Natural gas and propane are two alternate fuels (vapours) that also provide no valve seat lubrication. Engines supplied by the automakers for CNG (compressed natural gas) or LPG (liquefied petroleum gas) vehicles usually have extremely hard valve seat inserts installed at the factory.

REFORMULATED GASOLINE

Reformulated gasoline (RFG) is used in some areas in an effort to reduce exhaust emissions. The gasoline refiners reformulate gasoline by using additives that contain at least 2% oxygen by weight and reducing the additive benzenes to a maximum of 1% by value. The two other major changes the refineries must make are:

1. **Reduce light compounds.** Refineries eliminate butane, pentane, and propane, which have a low boiling point and evaporate easily. These unburned hydrocarbons (HC) are released into the atmosphere during refuelling and through the fuel tank vent system, contributing to smog formation.
2. **Reduce heavy compounds.** Refineries eliminate heavy compounds with high boiling

Frequently Asked Question ???

Why Should I Keep the Fuel Gauge Above One-Quarter Tank?

The sock pickup inside the fuel tank can help keep water from being drawn into the fuel system unless water is all that is left at the bottom of the tank. Over time, moisture in the air inside the fuel tank can condense, causing liquid water to drop to the bottom of the fuel tank (water is about 35% more dense than gasoline). If alcohol-blended gasoline is used, the alcohol can absorb the water and the alcohol-water combination can be burned inside the engine. However, when water combines with alcohol, a separation layer occurs between the gasoline at the top of the tank and the alcohol-water combination at the bottom. When the fuel level is low, the fuel pump will draw mostly from this lower level of alcohol and water. Because alcohol and water do not burn as well as pure gasoline, severe driveability problems can occur such as stalling, rough idle, hard starting, and missing.

TECH TIP

Don't Overfill the Fuel Tank

Most gasoline fuel tanks have an expansion volume area at the top. The volume of this expansion area is equal to 10% to 15% of the volume of the tank. This area is normally not filled with gasoline, but rather it is designed to provide a place for the gasoline to expand, if the vehicle is parked in the hot sun and the gasoline expands. This prevents raw gasoline from escaping from the fuel system. A small constriction is usually present to control the amount of air and vapours that can escape the tank and flow to the charcoal canister.

This volume area could be filled with gasoline if the fuel is slowly pumped into the tank. Since it can hold an extra 10%, some people deliberately try to fill the tank completely. When this expansion volume is filled, liquid fuel (rather than vapours) can be drawn into the charcoal canister. When the purge valve opens, liquid fuel can be drawn into the engine, causing an excessively rich air-fuel mixture. Not only can this liquid fuel harm vapour recovery parts, overfilling the gas tank could cause the vehicle to fail an exhaust emission test. This is particularly true during an enhanced test where the tank could be purged during the test while on the rollers.

points such as aromatics and olefins. The purpose of this reduction is to reduce the amount of unburned hydrocarbons (HC) that go to the catalytic converter. Increased use of oxygen-containing MTBE (methyl tertiary butyl ether) helps the combustion process to reduce emissions.

Because many of the heavy compounds are eliminated, a drop in fuel economy of about 0.4 km/L (1 mpg) has been reported in areas where reformulated gasoline is being used. Formaldehyde is formed when RFG is burned, and the vehicle exhaust has a unique smell when reformulated gasoline is used.

GENERAL GASOLINE RECOMMENDATIONS

The fuel used by an engine is a major expense in the operating cost of the vehicle. The proper operation of the engine depends on clean fuel of the proper octane rating and vapour pressure for the atmospheric conditions.

To help ensure proper engine operation and keep fuel costs to a minimum, follow these guidelines:

1. Purchase fuel from a busy station. This helps ensure that the fuel is fresh and less likely to be contaminated with water or moisture.
2. Keep the fuel tank above one-quarter full, especially during seasons in which the temperature rises and falls by more than 10°C (18°F) between daytime highs and nighttime lows. This helps to reduce condensed moisture in the fuel tank and could prevent gas line freeze-up in cold weather.

NOTE: Gas line freeze-up occurs when the water in the gasoline freezes and forms an ice blockage in the fuel line.

DIAGNOSTIC STORY

The Cadillac Story

The owner of a Cadillac equipped with two-nozzle throttle body fuel injection came into a service facility complaining that the engine would miss and cut out at speeds above 60 km/h (37 mph). The technician assigned to the repair replaced many parts that could have contributed to the problem, including:

1. Distributor cap and rotor
2. Spark plugs
3. Spark plug wires
4. Fuel filter
5. Air filter
6. Ignition module

The replacement of each part did improve the operation of the engine slightly, but the problem still existed. The engine itself was determined to be in sound mechanical condition. A timing light was connected to the engine coil wire and the trigger taped in the on position. The timing light was then taped to the windshield so that the driver could see if the engine missing would cause the timing light to blink intermittently, indicating an ignition problem. The hood was carefully closed so that it did not disturb the timing light wiring. The vehicle was driven until it started missing. The timing light did not indicate an ignition problem.

Next, the technician connected separate LED test lights to each of the fuel-injector wiring connectors. The long leads were taped to the windshield and the vehicle was again test driven.

NOTE: If only one of the two fuel injectors had stopped functioning, the engine would only be getting fuel to every other cylinder and the engine would miss and cut out, especially at higher engine speeds. Some port-injected engines use two different injector circuits, each with its own fuse.

The LED test lights confirmed that both injectors were being pulsed by the computer all the time.

The next day, the technician added 40 L (10 gal) of gasoline to the tank because the "low fuel" lamp had come on during the last test drive. After the fuel was added, the engine started to operate better and better. Finally after about 10 km (6 mi) of driving, the engine ran well.

The customer later told the service manager that he had always kept the fuel level low and had never added more than a few dollars of gas at a time. Obviously, condensed moisture had accumulated in the bottom of the fuel tank and was being drawn through the fuel system. Because water does not burn, the engine would miss and run poorly. After the fuel tank was drained and cleaned, the vehicle was returned to the customer. The customer thanked the service manager for having finally found that "computer" and "fuel-injection" problem that no one else could find!

SAFETY TIP

Always Fill a Gas Can on the Ground

Many fires and some explosions have occurred when a metal gas can is filled while sitting in the bed of a pickup truck equipped with a plastic bed liner. Static electricity can build up and discharge from the metal can to the metal gas nozzle, creating a spark. This spark can cause a fire or explosion. To be safe, always place a metal gas can on the ground so that any static electricity created can be safely discharged to ground. Aircraft are always filled with fuel from a tanker truck after a ground strap is attached to both the plane and the truck and then attached to ground. See Figure 27–9.

3. Do not purchase fuel with a higher octane rating than is necessary. Try using premium high-octane fuel to check for operating differences. Most newer engines are equipped with a detonation (knock) sensor that signals the vehicle computer to retard the ignition timing when spark knock occurs. Therefore, an operating difference may not be noticeable to the driver when using a low-octane fuel, except for a decrease in power and fuel economy. In other words, the engine with a knock sensor will tend to operate knock-free on regular fuel, even if premium, higher-octane fuel is specified. Using premium fuel may result in more power and greater fuel economy. The increase in fuel economy, however, would have to be substantial to justify the increased cost of high-octane premium fuel. Some drivers find a good compromise by using midgrade (plus) fuel to benefit from the engine power and fuel economy gains without the cost of using premium fuel all the time.
4. Avoid using gasoline with alcohol in warm weather, even though many alcohol blends do not affect engine driveability. If warm-engine stumble, stalling, or rough idle occurs, change brands of gasoline.
5. Do not purchase fuel from a retail outlet when a tanker truck is filling the underground tanks. During the refilling procedure, dirt, rust, and water may be stirred up in the underground tanks. This undesirable material may be pumped into your vehicle's fuel tank.
6. Do not overfill the gas tank. After the nozzle clicks off, add just enough fuel to round up to the next dime. Adding additional gasoline will cause the excess to be drawn into the charcoal canister. This can lead to engine flooding and excessive exhaust emissions.
7. Be careful when filling gasoline containers.

Figure 27–9 Many gasoline service stations have signs posted warning customers to place portable fuel containers on the ground while filling. If placed in a trunk or pickup truck bed equipped with a plastic liner, static electricity could build up during fueling and discharge from the container to the metal nozzle, creating a spark and possible explosion. Some service stations have warning signs not to use cell phones while fueling to help avoid the possibility of an accidental spark creating a fire hazard.

DIESEL FUEL

Diesel fuel and gasoline are both refined from crude petroleum, but they have different characteristics. Diesel fuel burns at a slower rate, which results in combustion occurring for a longer period of time during the power stroke. This is one of the reasons diesel engines produce greater torque. The heat value of diesel fuel is higher than gasoline by about 10%; more heat generated results in more power.

A wax substance called paraffin is found in diesel fuel; it can result in wax crystals forming in the fuel at low temperatures. It is important in Canada and other areas that experience colder climates to use high quality fuel; low quality fuel begins to cloud (wax) earlier as the temperature drops. Some diesel fuel systems also include a fuel heater to prevent these crystals from forming.

Sulphur content, left behind after the refining process, increases engine wear, causes varnish and oil sludge, and damages late-model emission controls. In 1995, the federal government mandated low-sulphur diesel fuel. New regulations, expected in 2006, will reduce sulphur content even more.

Major categories of diesel fuel are:

- Number 1—winter fuel, lighter, easier flowing, less power
- Number 2—summer fuel, most often used, more powerful than Number 1
- High Arctic—extreme cold fuel, designed to flow at very low temperatures

Canadian diesel fuels are mixed (blended) for seasonal changes.

Gasoline engines require a fuel that burns slowly to resist pre-ignition and detonation; the higher the octane rating, the more resistance to knocking. The opposite is true with diesel fuel: The fuel should ignite quickly as it is injected into the combustion chamber.

Cetane rating is a measurement of the fuel's ignition quality; fuel with high cetane numbers will ignite at lower compression temperatures and have a very short delay (lag time) from the point of injection until ignition begins. See Figure 27-10.

Diesel fuels should never be stored in galvanized containers, as the galvanizing will flake off and cause fuel contamination. Fuel that is stored for long periods will go stale and, in some cases, form algae that may damage fuel and engine systems.

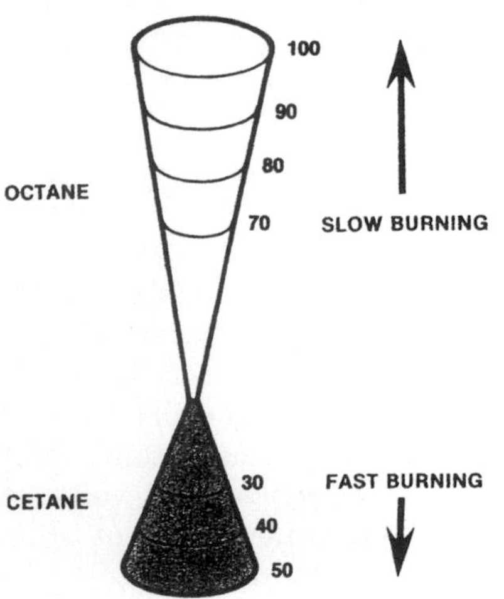

Figure 27-10 Cetane rating of diesel fuel compared to octane rating of gasoline. (Courtesy Ford Motor Co. of Canada Ltd.)

Bio-Diesel Fuel

A bio-diesel fuel mixture of 80% diesel fuel and 20% recycled biologicals (e.g., fish oil, cooking oil, animal fats, canola, or soy bean oil) has been shown to reduce emissions by 20% or more. The bio-fuel is being tested on a number of large commercial diesel fleets across Canada, from Halifax to Vancouver.

Initial reports are favourable in terms of lower emissions and exhaust odours; the downside is a reduction in fuel economy of up to 10%. It is also recommended that the fuel should not be stored for long periods as it can become rancid.

ALTERNATE FUELS

Propane

Propane, also known as liquefied petroleum gas (LPG) is one of the byproducts of the crude-oil refining process. Approximately 3% of crude oil becomes propane.

Propane remains a liquid at any temperature lower than −42°C (−43.7°F), or while under pressure in a sealed container. Releasing this pressure will cause the liquid to boil and turn into a vapour. Propane is sold and stored in the vehicle as a liquid; it is allowed to vaporize (by releasing the pressure) before it is fed into the engine. It has a higher octane rating (about 105 to 110) than gasoline and usually benefits from higher engine compression ratios. Fuel economy is close to that of gasoline.

Beware of any leak in the system; propane is heavier than air and does not dissipate easily. Canadian technicians must hold a provincial licence in order to service the high-pressure side of an LPG system.

Natural Gas

Natural gas, known as compressed natural gas (CNG) is also petroleum based and a byproduct of the crude-oil refining process; approximately 80% of natural gas is methane. It is dispensed and stored in the vehicle as a high-pressure vapour, at over 21 000 kPa (3000 psi). Vapour takes up more space than liquid, which limits the amount of fuel on board. A reduced driving range and lack of refuelling stations are major concerns with CNG. Although some dual-fuel gasoline-CNG retrofits are used, the majority are single-fuel dedicated systems; this includes original factory CNG vehicles. Most CNG use is with commercial vehicles, e.g., taxicabs and police cars.

Natural gas is very high octane, about 130, and burns cleanly. The combustion process is very smooth and easy on internal engine parts; a number of taxi engines have exceeded 1 million km (620 000 mi) before requiring replacement.

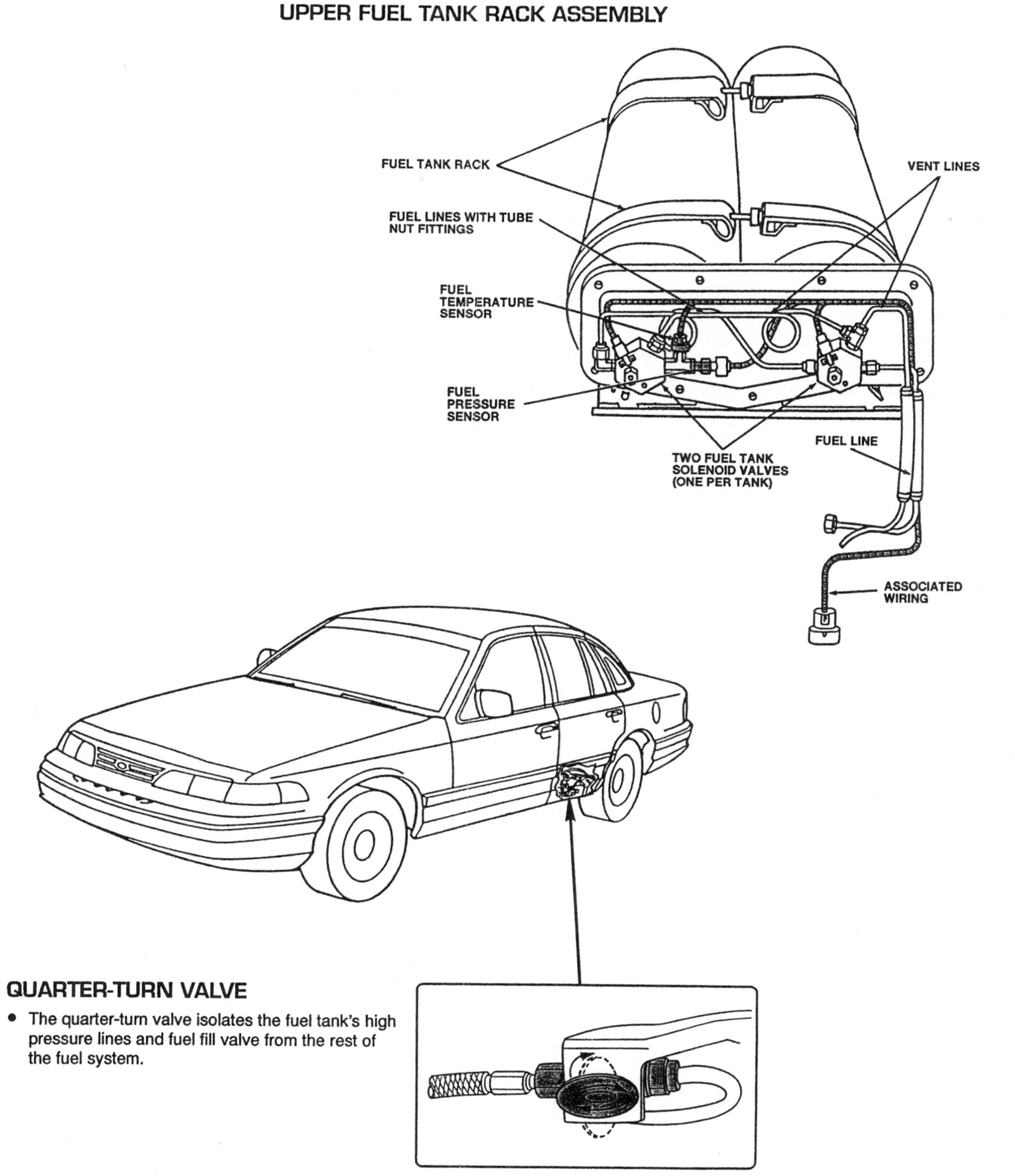

UPPER FUEL TANK RACK ASSEMBLY

FUEL TANK RACK
VENT LINES
FUEL LINES WITH TUBE NUT FITTINGS
FUEL TEMPERATURE SENSOR
FUEL PRESSURE SENSOR
FUEL LINE
TWO FUEL TANK SOLENOID VALVES (ONE PER TANK)
ASSOCIATED WIRING

QUARTER-TURN VALVE

- The quarter-turn valve isolates the fuel tank's high pressure lines and fuel fill valve from the rest of the fuel system.

Figure 27-11 This original-equipment natural gas system has automatic fuel tank shut-off solenoids. A quarter-turn manual valve is installed for system service or solenoid failure. (Courtesy Ford Motor Co. of Canada Ltd.)

Natural gas is lighter than air: leaking gas will rise and dissipate if the vehicle is outside. A natural gas leak inside a building is another matter: the gas collects at the highest point in the building and is very dangerous. Both propane tanks and natural gas cylinders have shut-off valves near the tank which should be closed if the vehicle is parked indoors. See Figure 27-11. Canadian technicians must hold a provincial licence in order to service the high-pressure side of a CNG system.

Hydrogen

Hydrogen, a very light vapour, is produced from natural gas, gasoline, crude oil, methanol or even water. The hydrogen is stripped by a number of methods including electrolysis where direct current applied to water (as an example) will split the water into hydrogen and oxygen.

Hydrogen, usually reformed from natural gas, is the fuel of choice for fuel-cell vehicles. Lack of refuelling facilities is a concern being addressed by the federal government. Funding is being made available for a network of hydrogen refuelling stations in two areas, Greater Toronto in Ontario and Vancouver to Whistler in British Columbia. The B.C.-based stations are expected to be in place for the 2010 Olympic games held at Whistler.

Honda has been producing hydrogen from water, using photovoltaic (solar-cell) powered electrolysis at their facility in Torrance, California. The hydrogen is used to power Honda fuel-cell vehicles.

SUMMARY

1. Gasoline is a complex blend of hydrocarbons. Gasoline is blended for seasonal usage for the correct volatility for easy starting and maximum fuel economy under all driving conditions.
2. Winter-blend fuel used in a vehicle during warm weather can cause a rough idle and stalling because of the higher RVP (Reid vapour pressure) of winter-grade fuel.
3. Abnormal combustion (also called detonation or spark knock) increases both the temperature and the pressure inside the combustion chamber.
4. Most regular-grade gasoline today, using the (R + M)/2 rating method, is 87 octane, midgrade (plus) is 89, and premium grade is 91 or higher.
5. Oxygenated fuels usually contain alcohol or MTBE that includes oxygen in its content to lower CO exhaust emissions.
6. Gasoline should always be purchased from a busy station, and the tank should not be overfilled.
7. Diesel fuel categories are Number 1 (winter), Number 2 (summer) and High Arctic (extreme cold).
8. A Provincial Gas Safety Branch Licence is required for any technician servicing the high-pressure side of CNG and LPG systems.

REVIEW QUESTIONS

1. Describe the difference between summer-blend and winter-blend gasoline.
2. Define *Reid vapour pressure.*
3. Define *vapour lock.*
4. Describe the (R + M)/2 gasoline pump octane rating.
5. Name five octane improvers that may be used during the refinery process.
6. Define *stoichiometrics.*
7. Describe how valves can recede into the head on engines using unleaded gasoline without hardened valve seats.
8. Describe the problems associated with storing diesel fuel.

RED SEAL CERTIFICATION-TYPE QUESTIONS

1. Winter-blend gasoline _____.
   - **a.** Vaporizes more easily than summer-blend gasoline
   - **b.** Has a higher RVP
   - **c.** Can cause engine driveability problems if used during warm weather
   - **d.** All of the above
2. Vapour lock
   - **a.** Can occur as a result of excessive heat near fuel lines
   - **b.** Can occur if a fuel line is restricted
   - **c.** Both a and b
   - **d.** Neither a nor b
3. Abnormal combustion, such as detonation, raises the temperature and pressure inside the combustion chamber and can cause _____.
   - **a.** Heavy carbon formation
   - **b.** Oil contamination
   - **c.** Severe engine damage
   - **d.** A decrease in fuel economy
4. The octane rating posted on gasoline pumps is a measurement of _____.
   - **a.** The research octane number
   - **b.** The motor octane number
   - **c.** An average of research and octane numbers
   - **d.** Adding the research and octane numbers together
5. Bio-diesel fuel uses a mixture of diesel fuel and fish oil or cooking oil to _____.
   - **a.** Improve fuel economy
   - **b.** Increase engine power
   - **c.** Reduce emissions
   - **d.** Decrease engine wear
6. Valve seat recession is most likely to occur with older engines not equipped with hardened valve seats if _____.
   - **a.** Driven at high speeds and with heavy loads
   - **b.** Driven at slow speeds and with light loads
   - **c.** Used at idle most or all of the time
   - **d.** Premium fuel is not used
7. Avoid driving a vehicle when the fuel level is below 1/4 tank because _____.
   - **a.** The vehicle weight is reduced
   - **b.** Any moisture sinks to the bottom of the tank

c. Pure gasoline can separate if exposed to air
d. Air may enter the fuel from sloshing

8. Reid vapour pressure is measured at _____.
a. 38°C (100°F)
b. 212°F (100°C)
c. −40°C (−40°F)
d. 16°C (60°F)

9. You should avoid topping off the fuel tank because _____,
a. It can saturate the charcoal canister
b. The extra fuel simply spills onto the ground
c. The extra fuel increases vehicle weight and reduces performance
d. The extra fuel goes into the expansion area of the tank and is not used by the engine

10. Using ethanol-enhanced or reformulated gasoline can result in reduced fuel economy.
a. True
b. False

28

Computerized Carburetor Operation, Diagnosis, and Service

OBJECTIVES: After studying Chapter 28, you should be able to:

1. Prepare for the interprovincial Red Seal certification examination in Appendix VIII (Engine Performance) on the topics covered in this chapter.
2. Explain how to test a mechanical fuel pump for pressure and volume.
3. Describe the symptoms of leaking main well plugs and explain how to correct the condition.
4. Discuss how to perform idle mixture and idle speed adjustments using a tachometer, dwell meter, voltmeter, and/or a vacuum gauge.
5. Explain how to test and adjust a choke using a choke angle gauge.

Computerized carburetors, also known as feedback carburetors, are common in the U.S., but very limited in Canada. In order to meet tighter 1980s emission standards, the U.S. went from conventional carburetors to feedback carburetors and then on to fuel injection. Most cars made for sale in Canada moved directly from conventional carburetors to fuel injection. The one major exception is General Motors, which supplied a number of vehicles with feedback carburetors (usually full-size, rear wheel drive).

Although Ford, G.M., Chrysler and Asian manufacturers, Nissan, Toyota and Mazda all produced computerized carburetors for North America, only G.M. has any appreciable numbers in Canada.

European vehicles, for the most part, had been using fuel injection since the mid 1970s and didn't become involved with feedback carburetors.

MECHANICAL FUEL PUMP

Mechanical fuel pumps are used on most vehicles equipped with a carburetor. Mechanical fuel pumps

DIAGNOSTIC STORY

"I Could Have Sworn It Was a Valve Lifter"

An experienced technician listened to a customer's V-8 engine noise and diagnosed the noise as coming from a hydraulic valve lifter. After the customer okayed the repair, the service technician replaced all the hydraulic lifters (to be sure). After reassembling the engine and starting it, the same noise was heard. Because the noise was at one-half engine speed, the technician was sure it was valve-train (camshaft, valve lifters, etc.) related. After careful listening using a stethoscope, the technician heard the noise the loudest at the mechanical fuel pump. When the pump was removed, a spring that kept the operating lever tightly against the eccentric was found to be broken. This broken spring caused the ticking sound that was transmitted through the entire length of the camshaft, making the noise sound like it could be due to a defective valve lifter. The fuel pump operated normally because the spring that broke simply kept the arm tightly against the eccentric and served no other purpose. Replacing the fuel pump finally cured the "valve noise."

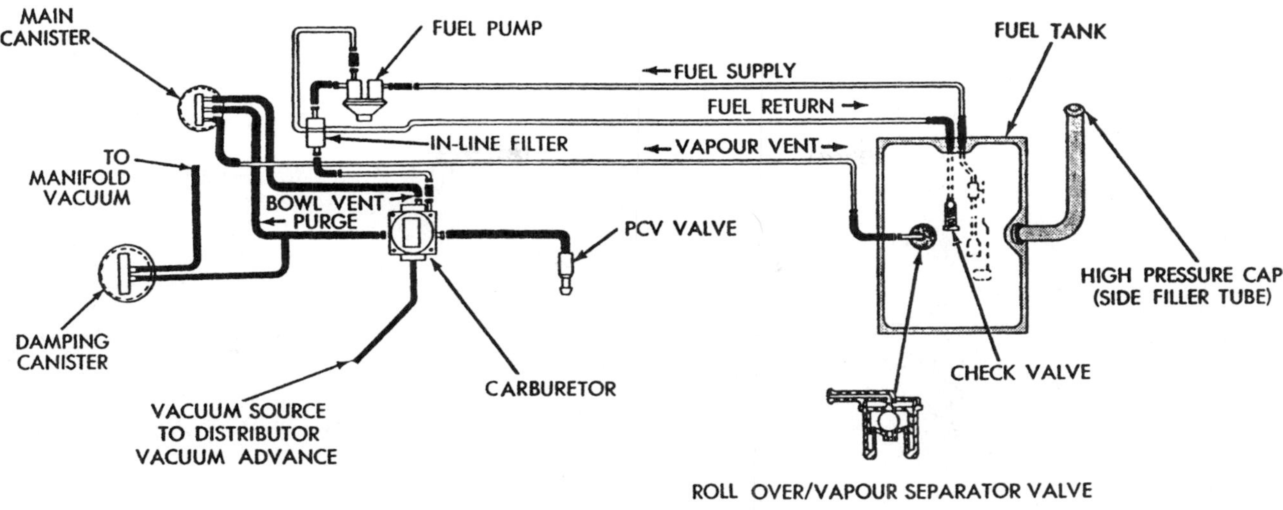

Figure 28–1 A typical gasoline fuel supply system. Note the engine-driven fuel pump. (Courtesy DaimlerChrysler Corporation)

are mounted on the engine itself and are operated by an eccentric or cam lobe at one-half engine (crankshaft) speed. The purpose of the pump is to draw fuel from the fuel tank and deliver the fuel to the carburetor. See Figure 28–1. A typical mechanical fuel pump consists of an actuating arm that contacts an eccentric driven by the camshaft or by a lobe on the camshaft itself. See Figures 28–2 and 28–3.

FUEL SYSTEM OPERATION

The fuel delivery system is designed to supply the carburetor(s) or fuel-injection system with clean fuel under pressure. The following are typical pressures for the carburetor-equipped engine (which usually uses a mechanical engine-driven fuel pump): 30 to 50 kPa (4 to 7 psi). Fuel pressure alone is not enough for proper engine operation. Sufficient fuel capacity (flow) should be at least 1 litre (2 pints) per minute, or 0.25 litre (0.5 pint) in 15 seconds.

NOTE: This amount of fuel delivery ensures that the needs of the engine are met at wide-open throttle, full load conditions.

All fuel must be filtered to prevent dirt and impurities from damaging the fuel system and/or engine. The first filter is inside the gas tank. See Figure 28–4. This filter, commonly called the **fuel sock filter,** is usually not replaceable separately, since it is attached to the fuel pump (if the pump is electric) and/or fuel gauge sending unit.

TECH TIP 

Change the Float

Older carburetors used floats made from stamped brass or hollow plastic. A leaking float was easy to diagnose; shake the float and listen for fuel inside.

Later floats are usually made of a phenolic material (plastic foam) that does not use a hollow core. Over a period of time, the float absorbs liquid fuel and becomes heavier, which in turn causes the float level to rise. High-volume carburetor rebuilders have special scales to weigh floats, but these are not often found in the field. It is common industry practice to replace phenolic floats when overhauling the carburetor.

The replaceable fuel filter is usually located between the fuel pump and the inlet to the carburetor. For long engine and fuel system life and optimal performance, the fuel filter should be replaced as often as every year or every 24 000 km (15 000 mi). (Consult vehicle manufacturer's recommendations for exact time and mileage intervals.) If the fuel filter becomes partially clogged, the following problems are likely to occur:

- There will be low power at higher engine speeds. The vehicle usually will not go faster than a certain speed (the engine acts as if it has a built-in speed limit governor).
- The engine will cut out or miss on acceleration, especially when climbing hills or during heavy-load acceleration.

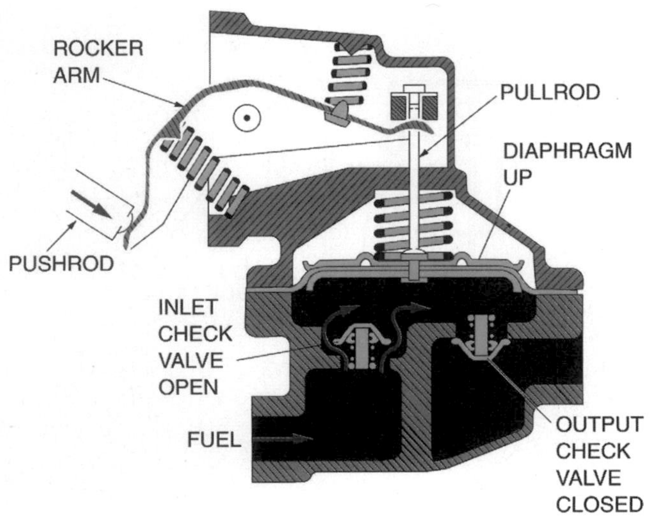

(a)

(b)

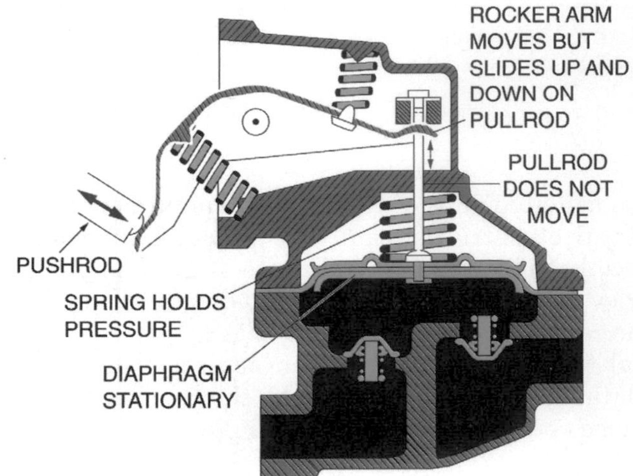

(c)

Figure 28–2 (a) Fuel is drawn through the inlet check valve into the pressure chamber of the pump as the diaphragm is moved upward. (b) When the pushrod moves inward, the pump spring pushes on the diaphragm and forces the fuel out the outlet check valve. (c) When the engine is at idle, the diaphragm remains in the upward position because the pump is capable of supplying far more fuel than the engine is able to consume at idle speed.

CONVENTIONAL CARBURETORS

All carburetors are pressure-differential devices. The difference between the air pressure of the atmosphere and the lower pressure (vacuum) at the venturi causes fuel to flow. Most gasoline carburetors designed for automotive use have six different, but related, circuits.

Float Circuit

The float circuit uses a float that sits in a bowl of gasoline (float bowl). See Figure 28–5. The float is mechanically connected to a needle valve used to control the level of the fuel in the float bowl. This level is critical for the proper operation of the carburetor because it determines the fuel pressure levels inside the carburetor. The relationship between float level and fuel delivery can be summarized as follows:

1. A higher-than-normal float level causes a richer-than-normal fuel delivery.
2. A lower-than-normal float level causes a leaner-than-normal fuel delivery.
3. About the only problem that can occur to a carburetor naturally is the float becoming saturated with fuel and thus heavier than normal. The fuel is then raised to a level that is higher than normal, which results in a richer-than-normal fuel delivery.

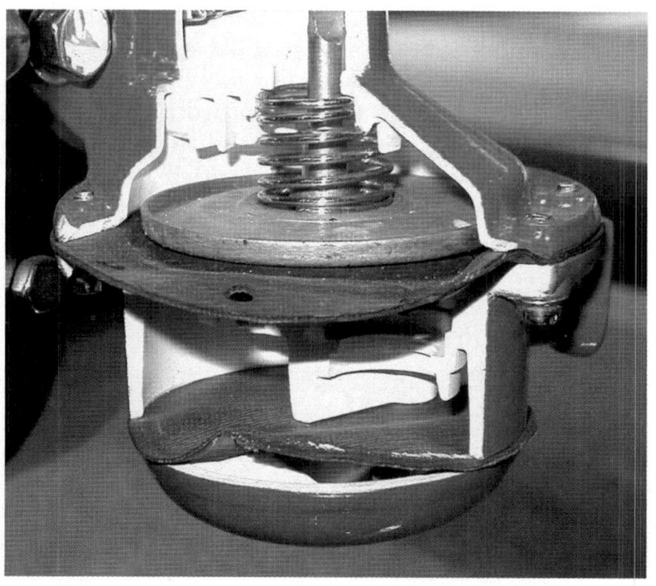

Figure 28–3 Cutaway of a typical mechanical fuel pump.

> **NOTE:** Float level can be adjusted by bending a tang on the float hinge, changing shims under the needle valve seat, or externally adjusting the height of the needle and seat assembly. Refer to specifications. Some carburetors have a glass "window" or "sight plug" in the side of the float chamber, which allows the float level to be checked without disassembling the carburetor.

Idle and Low-Speed Circuit

Some sources separate the operation of the idle and low-speed circuit into two separate circuits. Therefore, these sources indicate that a typical carburetor uses seven (instead of six) circuits. Because the operations of these two circuits are closely related, they are combined here for ease of discussion.

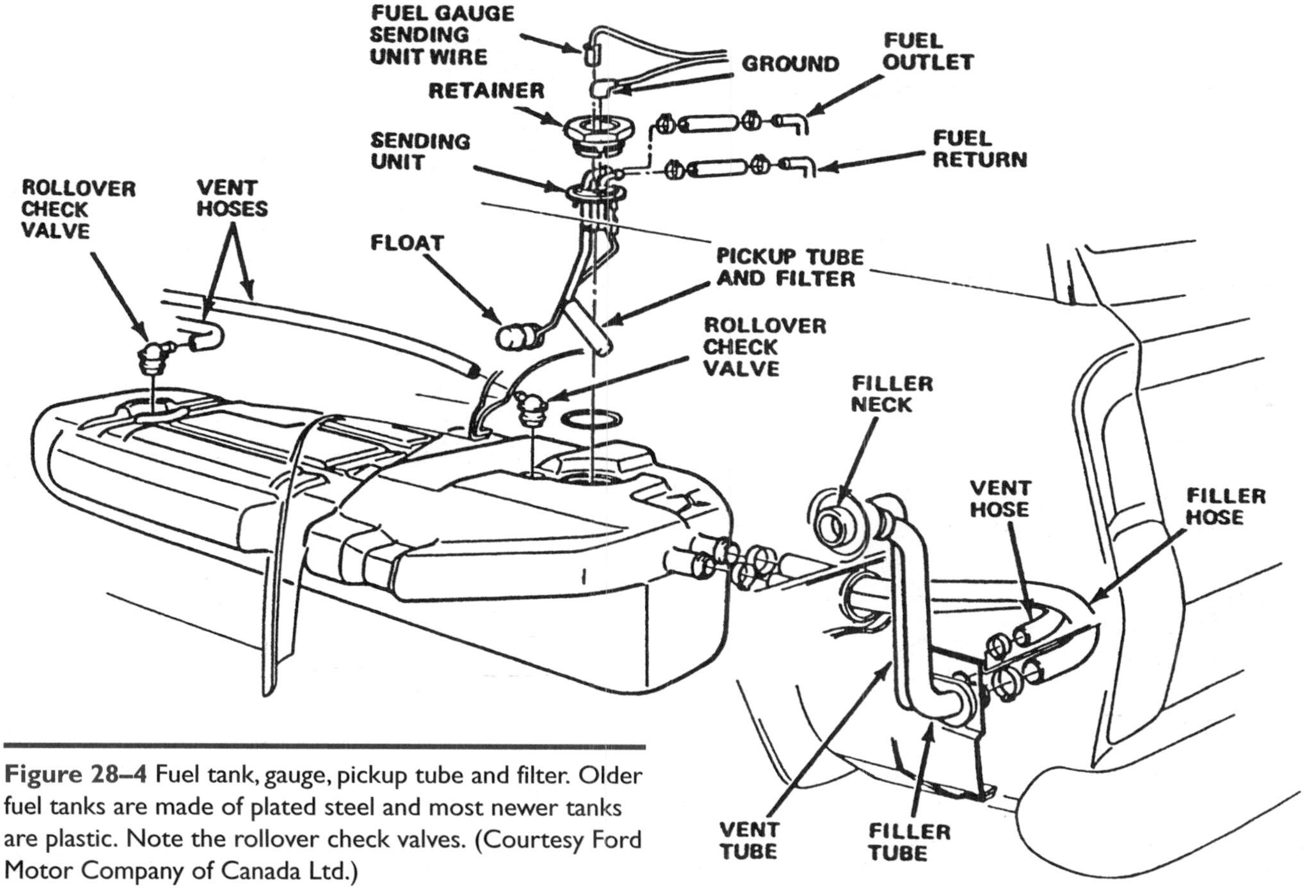

FUEL GAUGE SENDING UNIT WIRE
GROUND
FUEL OUTLET
RETAINER
SENDING UNIT
FUEL RETURN
ROLLOVER CHECK VALVE
VENT HOSES
FLOAT
PICKUP TUBE AND FILTER
ROLLOVER CHECK VALVE
FILLER NECK
VENT HOSE
FILLER HOSE
VENT TUBE
FILLER TUBE

Figure 28–4 Fuel tank, gauge, pickup tube and filter. Older fuel tanks are made of plated steel and most newer tanks are plastic. Note the rollover check valves. (Courtesy Ford Motor Company of Canada Ltd.)

Fuel delivery at idle must be richer to provide acceptable idle quality because the throttle is closed and the airflow through the carburetor is reduced. The fuel from the float bowl is drawn (pushed) through the main jet in the bottom of the bowl and through small drilled passages to be discharged below the throttle plate(s). To help **atomize** the fuel (make fuel droplets as small as possible to aid in the combustion process), small air passages called **air bleeds** are provided to premix air with the fuel before it leaves the idle discharge port below the throttle plate.

As the throttle is opened, additional passages are exposed to engine vacuum, which draws additional air–fuel mixture through the passages. This additional fuel delivery is commonly called the **low-speed circuit.** The slots or holes through which this additional fuel flows are called **transfer ports** or **transition ports.** See Figure 28–6.

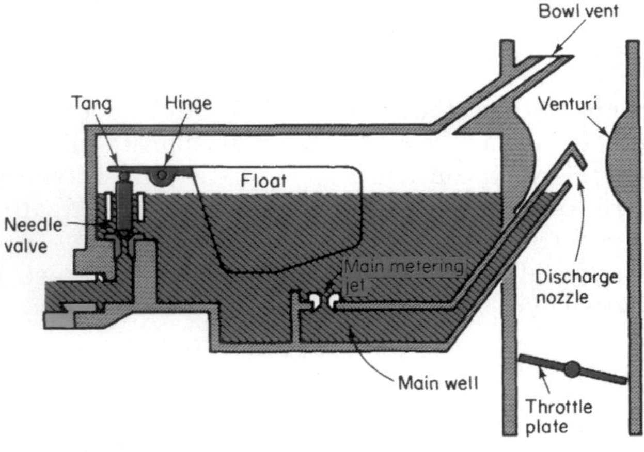

Figure 28–5 The float controls the level of fuel in the float bowl. Note the bowl vent extending into the air horn above the venturi. Air-horn pressure, which is higher than the low pressure at the venturi, pushes fuel out of the discharge nozzle into the venturi area.

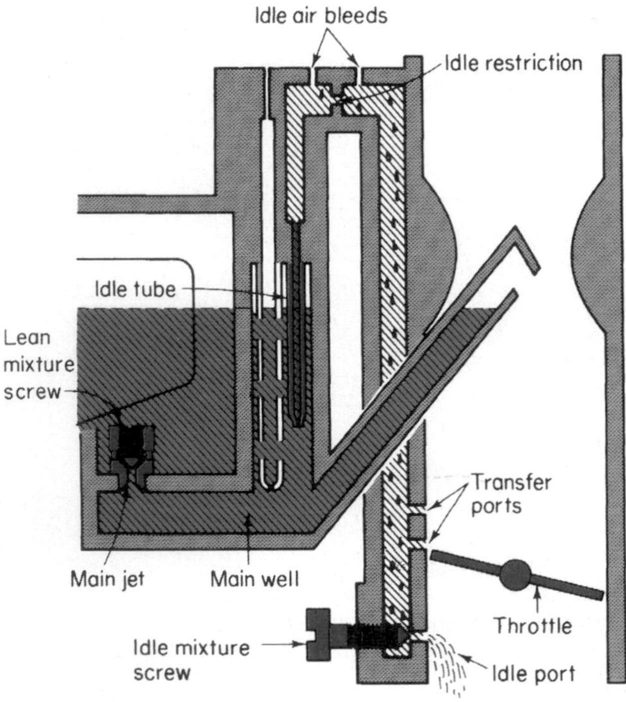

Figure 28–6 Idle air bleeds help atomize the liquid gasoline before it reaches the idle port. Note the location of the transfer ports. As the throttle is opened further, fuel will flow out of the transfer ports, adding to the fuel being delivered by the idle ports.

DIAGNOSTIC STORY

The Strawberry Ice Cream Story

A customer complained that every time he purchased strawberry ice cream at a local store, his vehicle was difficult to start. However, if he purchased vanilla ice cream, the engine started without a problem. This case really confused the service technician. A thorough visual inspection did not indicate any faults. Before continuing with the diagnostic procedure, the technician again asked the customer when the problem occurred. Again, the same story about how it only happened when he purchased strawberry ice cream. After patiently listening to where the driver travels, the technician finally discovered that the strawberry ice cream was hand-dipped, whereas the vanilla ice cream was prepackaged. As a result of the hand dipping, the customer spent more time in the store compared to when he purchased vanilla ice cream.

The technician was able to duplicate the condition. By waiting, the technician discovered that black soot poured from the exhaust, indicating a very rich condition. Further visual inspection showed that fuel was dripping from the discharge nozzle of the carburetor. Before removing the carburetor for overhaul or replacement, the technician tried one last simple trick. He revved the engine and placed a hand over the air horn (top) of the carburetor (see Figure 28–7). This created a low-pressure area under his hand and above the discharge nozzles and vents. After this procedure, the engine idled smoother than before. The vehicle was then driven and then allowed to sit, in an attempt to duplicate the original problem. This time the engine started quickly without any black smoke.

What did the "hand over the carburetor" do? By creating a low-pressure area above the idle and main metering vents, any dirt that had been drawn into this small opening was forced upward and out. These idle and main metering vent holes not only help in atomization of the fuel inside the passages but also act as a siphon breaker. When the engine was shut off, fuel could continue to flow from the float bowl and out the idle discharge nozzles if the vent hole was clogged. While the customer was waiting for the strawberry ice cream to be hand-dipped, the engine became flooded by the extra fuel being siphoned from the float bowl.

(a)

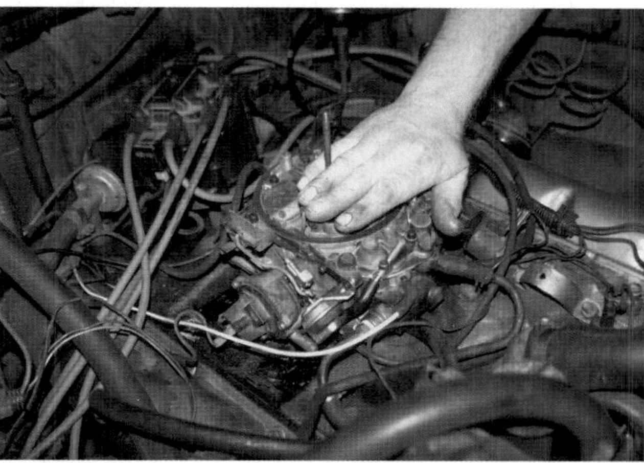

(b)

Figure 28–7 (a) To clean any dirt trapped in the idle air bleed holes, simply operate the engine at a fast idle with the air cleaner assembly removed. Then quickly place your hand over the air inlet. (b) The engine will start to stall and some gasoline may get on your hand. This is caused by the low-pressure area underneath your hand created when the top of the carburetor was covered. Placing your hand over the carburetor on a running engine also helps locate any vacuum leaks. If the engine runs better with your hand over the carburetor, air from another source is obviously getting into the engine.

Main Metering Circuit

Once the throttle plate (valve) opens to a point past the transfer ports, enough air flows through the venturi to cause a pressure drop that, in turn, causes fuel to be drawn (pushed) from the float bowl and discharged into the centre of the venturi. This fuel flow is controlled by the size of the main jet in the bottom of the float bowl. Tapered metering rods are often used to control the amount of fuel flow going out of the float bowl through the main jets. See Figure 28–8.

TECH TIP 

Epoxy the Main Well Plugs

Carburetors are manufactured with many drilled passages. Many of these passages carry fuel from the main well area under the main jets to the main discharge or idle discharge nozzles. Many of these passages travel at various angles. A straight drill bit cannot turn a corner. Therefore, two or more holes are drilled at the desired angle and the openings not needed are plugged. These plugs can leak fuel. Leaking main well plugs are a common problem with Rochester Quadrajets and Dualjet carburetors. The main well plugs are located above an open passage exposed to manifold vacuum. See Figure 28–9. When leaking, these plugs exhibit the following symptoms:

- A cold engine starts immediately—the extra fuel in the intake manifold provides the fuel to start.
- The engine then stalls—the fuel has leaked out of the float bowl and no fuel is available to keep the engine running.
- The engine has to be cranked a long time before the engine starts again—the engine must be cranked a long time because the fuel pump has to fill the float bowl before the engine restarts.

NOTE: The epoxy used to seal the main well plugs must be allowed enough time to cure before being exposed to gasoline. This may require that the carburetor sit unused for 24 hours.

If these symptoms occur, the carburetor will have to be repaired or replaced. These leaking main well plugs can be easily repaired by applying epoxy over the plugs.

Power Circuit

The power circuit involves those passages and components that provide additional fuel for high-load (low engine vacuum) conditions.

For an engine to produce more power, it must consume more fuel, and the power circuit is designed to provide this additional fuel yet shut off or become inoperative under light-load conditions to conserve fuel. Two basic types of power enrichment circuits are the:

- Power valve
- Metering rod

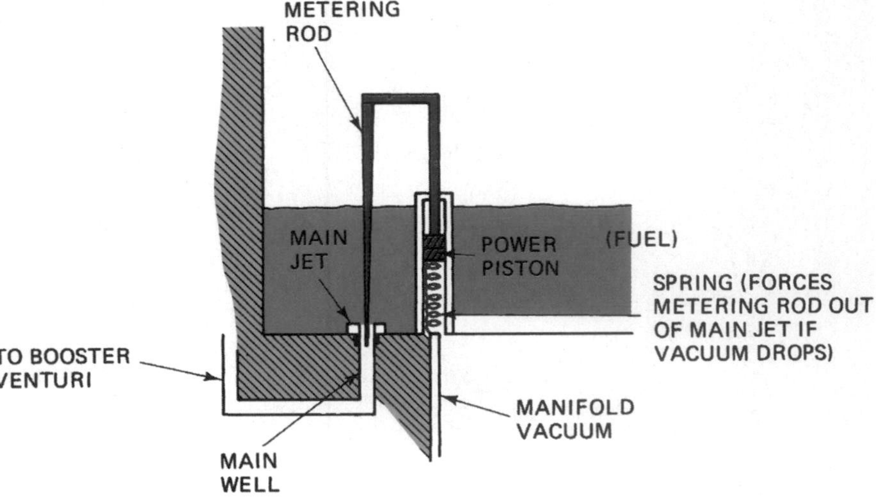

Figure 28–8 Cross-sectional view of a typical carburetor illustrating how the metering rods can control the air-fuel mixture. Strong manifold vacuum (light throttle) pulls the tapered metering rod down, which restricts fuel flow. As manifold vacuum depletes (throttle is opening) the spring pushes against the reduced vacuum and the metering rod rises. The thinner part of the rod now allows greater fuel flow.

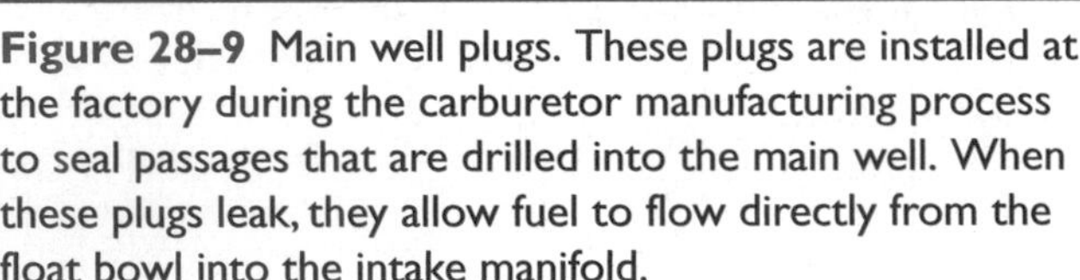

Figure 28–9 Main well plugs. These plugs are installed at the factory during the carburetor manufacturing process to seal passages that are drilled into the main well. When these plugs leak, they allow fuel to flow directly from the float bowl into the intake manifold.

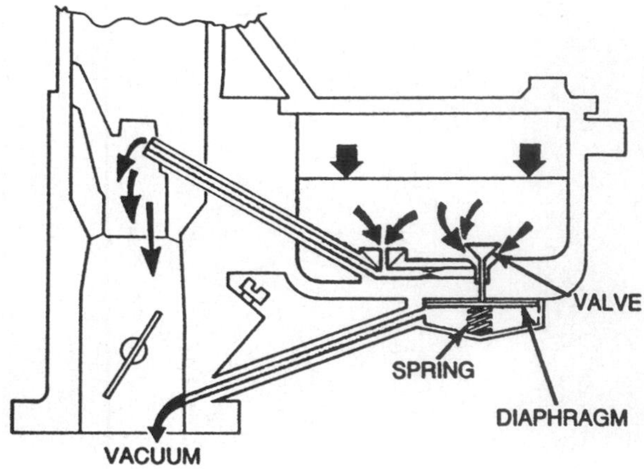

Figure 28–10 Typical vacuum operated power valve. A leak in the power valve diaphragm will allow raw fuel from the float bowl to pass directly into the intake manifold. Rough running, black smoke, and poor economy will result. (Courtesy Ford Motor Co. Ltd)

Power Valve A power-valve carburetor (such as most Holley-brand and older Ford carburetors) uses vacuum to keep the valve closed. During acceleration, the load on the engine decreases engine manifold vacuum, and the spring, which is part of the power valve, opens the valve. See Figure 28–10. Because the valve is located in the float bowl, additional fuel beyond that provided by the main jets flows into the main well and out through the booster venturi discharge ports.

Whether a power valve is on or off depends on the calibration of the closing spring. Engine vacuum acts on the diaphragm of the power valve and works against the force of the closing spring. Therefore, when vacuum is high (light engine load), the power valve is kept closed. When engine vacuum decreases (heavier engine load), the power valve spring opens the valve and allows additional fuel to flow from the carburetor. Some replacement power valves (such as those designed for use in Holley carburetors) are stamped with the opening vacuum level. (High numbers indicate valves that open sooner at higher vacuum settings than those marked with lower numbers.) See Figure 28–11.

NOTE: Power valves are often called **economy valves** or **economizer valves** because they remain closed much of the time for best fuel economy and only open when necessary for additional power.

Metering Rods A carburetor that uses metering rods for fuel control typically provides the best fuel economy because the tapered metering rod is gradually lifted (pushed) out of the main jet(s) in proportion to the increase in engine manifold vacuum. This method of fuel control provides the optimal arrangement because fuel control is directly related to engine load.

1. As engine load increases, manifold vacuum decreases and the metering rod is lifted out of the main jet.

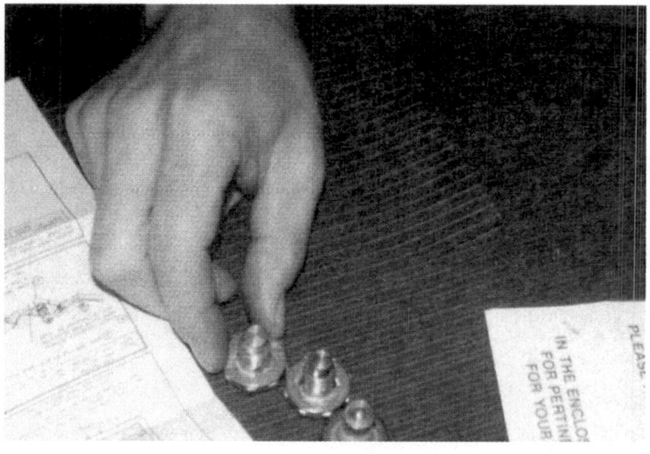

Figure 28–11 Typical assortment of power valves.

Figure 28–12 Accelerator pump being installed in a Rochester Quadrajet carburetor.

2. As engine load decreases, manifold vacuum increases and the metering rod is drawn down into the main jet, restricting the amount of fuel that can be drawn out of the discharge nozzle.

Accelerator Pump Circuit

When the accelerator is depressed, additional air can quickly be drawn into the engine through the throttle plates. However, because fuel weighs more than air, there is a slight delay period between the opening of the throttle and the delivery of additional fuel. The accelerator pump circuit is designed to provide a shot of fuel when the accelerator is first depressed to provide the fuel needed to prevent the hesitation that would otherwise occur during this delay.

The accelerator pump circuit consists of an inlet and outlet check valve and a rubber diaphragm or cup to pressurize the fuel when the accelerator pedal is depressed. See Figure 28–12. The fuel is discharged through an outlet nozzle(s) toward or near the booster venturi of the carburetor. The accelerator pump circuit is *not* controlled by the computer on vehicles equipped with a carburetor and a computer.

Choke Circuit

All engines require a richer air-fuel mixture to start. On carburetor-equipped engines, this is usually provided by a choke system that restricts the airflow through the carburetor during starting and cold-engine operation. This choke plate restriction causes a low-pressure area to develop beneath the choke plate and in the discharge nozzle area. This lower pressure draws additional fuel from the main jet and provides the richer mixture necessary for proper cold-engine operation. See Figure 28–13. Even though some thermostatic choke springs are electrically heated, the choke circuit is not computer controlled.

CHOKE OPERATION AND SERVICE

Vacuum Choke Pull-Off

A **vacuum choke pull-off,** also called a **vacuum break,** is designed to open the choke slightly after a cold start. See Figure 28–14. Because the choke valve is completely closed, the engine would stall once it started if the choke was not opened slightly. Therefore, symptoms of a defective or misadjusted vacuum choke pull-off include:

- Engine starts, then stalls
- Engine starts, then stalls again (this may be repeated several times until the engine warms enough and the choke finally starts to open)

Most vacuum choke pull-offs use a diaphragm that can be affected by gasoline fumes or alcohol-blended fuels. Therefore, a defective vacuum choke pull-off is a common problem. Most vacuum choke pull-offs are replaceable separately and are not included in a carburetor overhaul kit.

Adjusting a Vacuum Choke Pull-Off

Many vacuum choke pull-offs (vacuum breaks) are adjusted at the factory and do not require further adjustment. This is especially true of factory-original units that are purchased for a particular carburetor number. However, it is always wise to check the amount by which the unit opens the choke and adjust as needed. The usual steps include:

1. Setting the carburetor on a level surface and on a supporting stand or feet so as to permit all linkage to be free to move
2. Attaching a **choke angle gauge** to the choke valve and calibrating to the specified angle (see Figure 28–15)

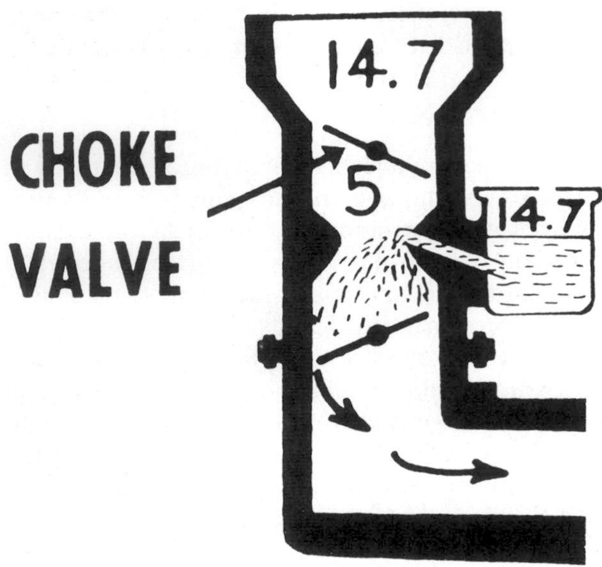

Figure 28–13 When the choke valve is closed, the throttle valve opens a small amount. Strong manifold vacuum passes by the partially opened throttle plate and acts on the discharge nozzle. This allows both the idle circuit and the main metering circuit to supply fuel. (Courtesy Ignition Manufacturer's Institute, *Automotive Emission Controls and Tune-Up Procedures,* Prentice Hall, 1980)

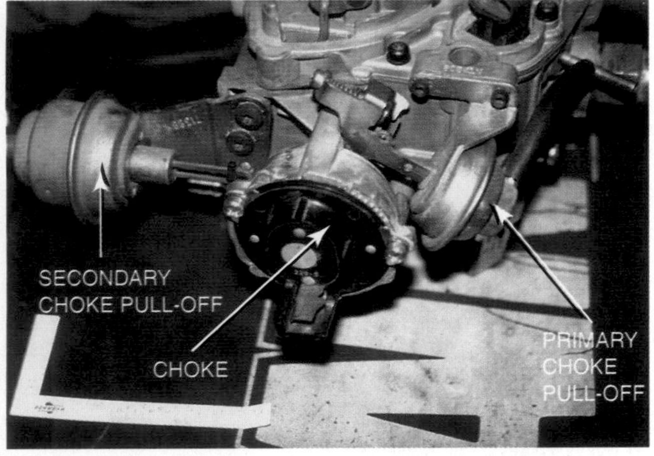

Figure 28–14 The choke on this Rochester Dualjet carburetor is controlled by both primary (front) and secondary (rear) vacuum choke pull-offs.

3. Applying vacuum to the vacuum choke pull-off from an external source such as a hand-operated vacuum pump
4. Adjusting the adjusting screw or slightly bending the linkage as necessary to accomplish the desired choke opening angle

An alternative to using a choke angle gauge is to use a gauging tool or drill bit of the specified diameter to measure the amount the choke is opened.

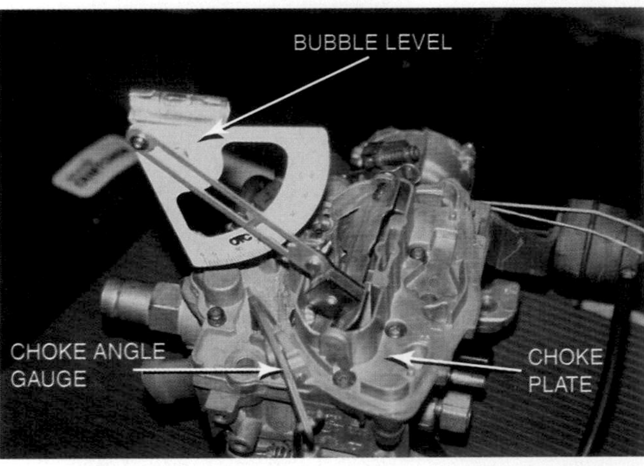

Figure 28–15 A choke angle gauge is an accurate method to adjust how far the choke is opened by the vacuum choke pull-off.

Diagnosing Automatic Choke Problems

The choke uses a bimetallic spring that expands as it gets hot. The heat to warm the choke can come from one or more of the following sources depending on the exact make and model of vehicle and carburetor:

1. **Exhaust heat.** This does not mean that exhaust is sent to the choke! There are several different methods for bringing the heat of the exhaust to the choke itself. These include:
   - A tube in the exhaust manifold to provide a passage for filtered outside air to be drawn by engine vacuum. As the air travels through the passage in the cast-iron exhaust manifold, it gets hot. This heated air travels through an insulated tube (or pipe) and into the choke spring housing.
   - Exhaust heat through the crossover passage in the intake manifold. The first step when testing for proper operation of a choke operated by exhaust heat is to check that the choke housing is getting hot. After the engine has reached operating temperature, check that the choke housing is too hot to touch. See Figure 28–16.

CAUTION: The choke housing should be *very hot!* Use care in checking. Use an infrared thermometer or contact-type pyrometer to safely check for proper choke temperature.

NOTE: The heat tube inside the exhaust manifold will often crack or burn through. This allows exhaust gases to enter the tube where they find their way into the choke housing. If the choke plate is sticking or frozen, remove the choke cap and check for exhaust contamination. This is a common problem on older Asian vehicles.

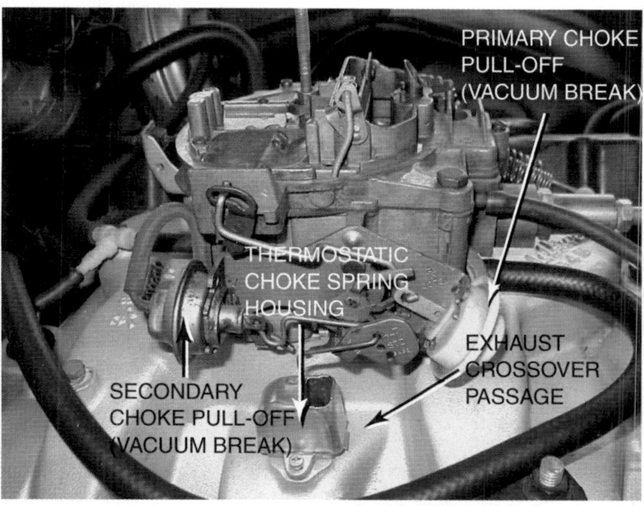

Figure 28–16 The choke spring gets warmed by the exhaust passing through a crossover passage on this V-8 engine.

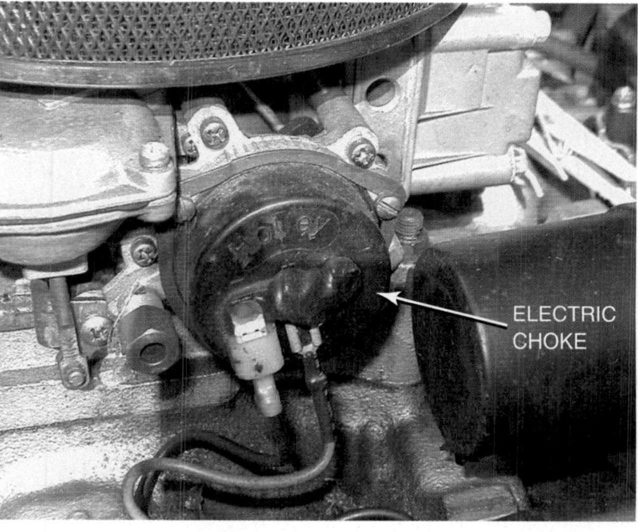

Figure 28–17 A typical electrically-heated choke assembly.

If the temperature of the choke housing is not hot, check the following:

- The heat tube should be connected to the exhaust heat source (exhaust manifold or intake manifold crossover).
- The heat tube should not be restricted.
- The vacuum passage to the choke housing should not be restricted.

2. **Electrically heated choke.** Voltage supplied through the ignition switch (or generator) is applied to a resistance coil inside the choke housing. See Figure 28–17.
   - Check for specified voltage at the choke connector with the engine running.
   - Check that the resistance coil has a good ground. Many electric chokes use a two-stage heater. When the thermostatic coil temperature is below 10°C (50°F), a terminal contacts the ceramic resistor which supplies heat to the choke. When the thermostatic spring is above 21°C (70°F), a second terminal contacts the ceramic resistor; this supplies additional heat to the choke spring and provides more rapid choke-valve opening.

NOTE: Some rebuilding kits include a gasket for use on the choke housing if the carburetor is equipped with an exhaust heat-type choke. If this gasket is used on a carburetor equipped with an electric choke, the gasket will insulate the choke coil from ground. Obviously, the choke coil will not work without a ground connection.

3. **Hot water choke.** Engine coolant can be used to heat the bimetallic choke spring. The hot-water (coolant-heated) choke requires the proper operation of the cooling system, including the cooling system thermostat. The first step in diagnosing a hot-water choke is to confirm that the upper radiator hose is hot and pressurized. If the cooling system is not reaching proper operating temperature, replace the engine thermostat. Check for a restriction in the passage leading to the choke housing if the choke is not reaching normal operating temperature.

NOTE: A restricted coolant hose to the choke is a common problem with some Chrysler minivans equipped with the 2.6 L 4-cylinder engine. The hose leading to the choke is a small formed hose. Often the hose can collapse internally, preventing hot water (coolant) from reaching the choke housing. This particular choke uses a thermo-wax that expands when in contact with heat. The restricted hose can prevent the wax from expanding and allow the choke to remain partially closed. The closed choke greatly reduces fuel economy and increases exhaust emissions.

Choke Adjustment

The choke adjustment itself determines how much heat is required to warm the choke and, therefore, the time it takes for the choke to be fully open. Manufacturers often publish choke settings in reference to a notch on the choke housing. A specification of 2NR means "2 notches rich," whereas a specification of 1NL means "1 notch lean." See Figure 28–18.

- If the choke is set too rich, the choke will remain closed too long, resulting in reduced fuel economy.
- If the choke is set too lean, the choke will open fully too soon, resulting in a possible hesitation or poor engine operation until the engine is fully warm.

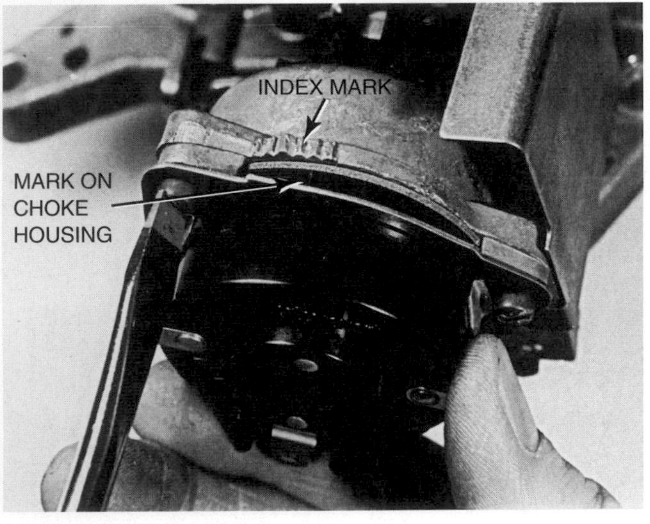

Figure 28–18 The mark on the choke housing must align with the specified notch for correct choke operation. Most computer-controlled carburetors use a choke housing that is not adjustable, to prevent anyone from changing the factory settings.

Choke Idle (Fast Idle) Adjustment

When the choke is open, the engine speed should be increased to higher than normal idle speed to be assured of smooth engine operation. This faster idle speed is accomplished by linkage and a **fast idle cam** that rests on an adjusting screw. The choke is set by depressing the accelerator pedal before starting the engine and the choke moves the fast idle cam.

- If the fast idle is set too low, the engine will run roughly and may stall when the engine is cold.
- If the fast idle is set too high, the engine will race when cold. This can also cause the vehicle equipped with an automatic transmission (transaxle) to creep while in gear.

To adjust the fast idle (choke idle), refer to the factory specifications and procedure. Usually the specifications will include which step of the fast idle cam is used for the adjustment, as well as the correct engine speed (RPM).

IDLE MIXTURE SCREW ADJUSTMENT

Idle mixture screws are adjusted at the factory for correct flow. Since about 1980, most carburetors have a seal that covers the idle mixture adjustment to prevent tampering, which may increase exhaust emissions. See Figure 28–19. The idle mixture screws mostly affect idle and off-idle engine operation. These adjustment screws are spring loaded to prevent engine vibrations from causing movement. An uneven air-fuel mixture can cause a rough idle and poor low-speed engine performance. First, determine if any vacuum (air) leaks are present that can affect the idle mixture. Second, try to determine if an engine condition such as a burned valve is present. See the Tech Tip "Carburetors Don't Get Misadjusted by Themselves" on p. 667.

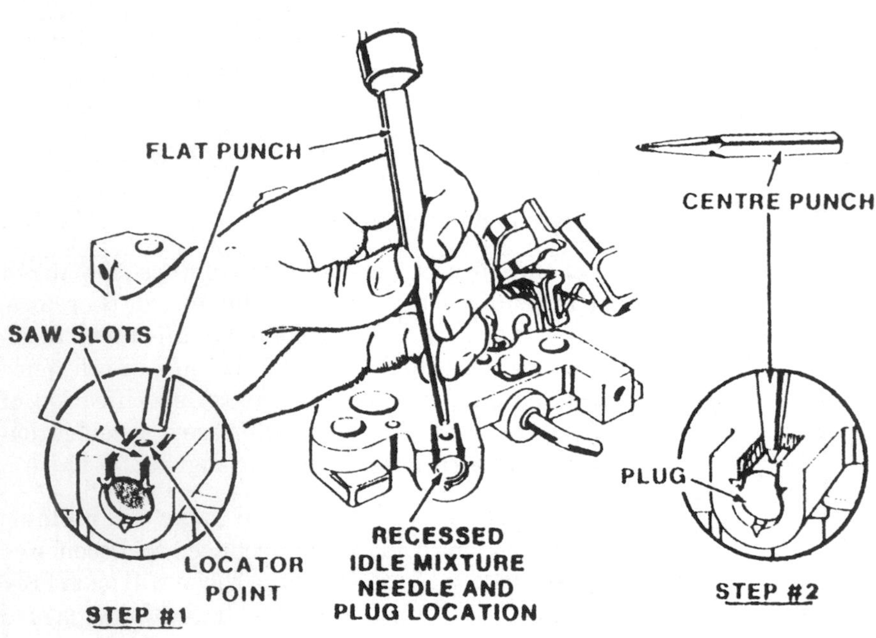

Figure 28–19 Removing the tamper-proof plugs from the idle circuit. The plugs can be removed by punching them from the casting (see above) or by drilling them out with a special hole saw. (Courtesy General Motors)

After being certain that the engine condition is okay and the ignition timing is correct, follow these steps to adjust the idle mixture screws:

1. Warm the engine to normal operating temperature.
2. Connect a tachometer to the engine to monitor engine speed.

NOTE: A vacuum gauge should also be connected to a manifold vacuum source.

3. Check that the idle speed is close to specifications.
4. Turn either idle mixture screw (if a two- or four-barrel carburetor) either way until the highest idle speed is observed. Repeat for the other screw. This step is called *peaking the idle mixture screws*.
5. This adjustment so far usually results in a mixture that is too rich for lowest exhaust emissions. Vehicle manufacturers recommend one of several ways to achieve acceptable exhaust emissions after the idle mixture screws have been peaked. These methods are discussed here.
   - *Idle Drop Method.* The idle drop method simply means that the idle mixture screws are turned equally inward (clockwise, which is leaner) a certain amount after peaking. This usually involves turning the idle mixture screws inward about 1/4 turn while noting the RPM drop on the tachometer. Follow the vehicle manufacturers' recommended procedures.
   - *Propane Enrichment Method.* The propane enrichment method requires that a certain amount of propane be added to the engine, then adjusting the idle mixture screws to obtain a certain RPM drop. Always follow the vehicle manufacturers' recommended procedures.
   - *Exhaust Analysis Method.* In the exhaust analysis method, the technician adjusts the idle mixture screws until the carbon monoxide (CO) *and* unburned hydrocarbons (HC) are both at their lowest levels. The carbon dioxide (CO_2) should also indicate its highest reading. The higher the CO_2 reading, the more efficiently the engine is operating. If the idle mixture screws are turned too far inward (too lean), then a lean misfire can occur, increasing the HC emissions. This method does not work on vehicles equipped with catalytic converters.

CARBURETOR TROUBLESHOOTING GUIDE

Problem	Possible Cause
Starts and stalls	• Vacuum choke pull-off is defective or misadjusted. • If the engine is equipped with a Rochester Quadrajet or Dualjet, problems can also be leaking main well plugs. If these are leaking, the engine usually starts then stalls, then extended cranking is necessary to get the engine to start again because the fuel in the float bowl has leaked through the main well plugs and into the intake manifold. With all the fuel in the intake manifold, the engine starts easily especially when cold, but stalls due to lack of fuel in the float bowl. Extended cranking causes the fuel pump to refill the float bowl and the engine continues to run okay.
Poor fuel economy	• Heavy, fuel-saturated float • Leaking main well plugs • Stuck closed (or partially closed) choke • High float level • Stuck open power valve • Plugged air bleed(s) • Defective power valve
Hesitation during initial acceleration	• Worn, misadjusted or defective accelerator pump • Too low an idle speed • Vacuum leak
Lack of power	• Restricted fuel filter • Weak or defective fuel pump • Too low a float level • Clogged gas cap or fuel tank vent • Engine mechanical or ignition problem • Stuck closed power valve
Dieseling (engine runs after the key is turned off)	• Idling too fast—misadjusted idle speed screw or stuck throttle linkage • Too lean—check for vacuum leaks

FEEDBACK-CARBURETOR MIXTURE CONTROL

Computerized carburetors are conventional (standard) carburetors that have one or more circuits modified for computer-controlled operation. See Figure 28–20. A feedback carburetor is designed to adjust the air-fuel mixture based on information (feedback) from the oxygen sensor. Although some feedback carburetors use a solenoid to control an air bleed (many Asian, some Ford and G.M., for example), most carburetors use a two-wire solenoid to control fuel flow. See Figure 28–21.

The mixture control solenoid is energized when the computer (PCM/ECM) provides a ground path for current to flow through the solenoid. This is ground-side control (see Chapter 25, Figure 25–21). Closing the ignition switch allows the current to flow through the mixture control solenoid to the driver transistor in the computer where it flows to ground if the transistor is switched on. The system is full lean. When the transistor turns off, the return spring pushes the metering rod up and the system is full rich. The mixture is controlled by varying the amount of on-time (duty cycle) during each cycle. See Figure 28–22.

Most vehicle computers control these solenoids at a rate of ten times per second (10 Hz). During open-loop operation, without feedback from the oxygen sensor, the computer controls the on-time of the solenoid based on the program inside the computer. Once the oxygen sensor reaches operating temperatures and the computer operates in closed loop, the on-time of the solenoid is shortened or lengthened to control the air-fuel mixture.

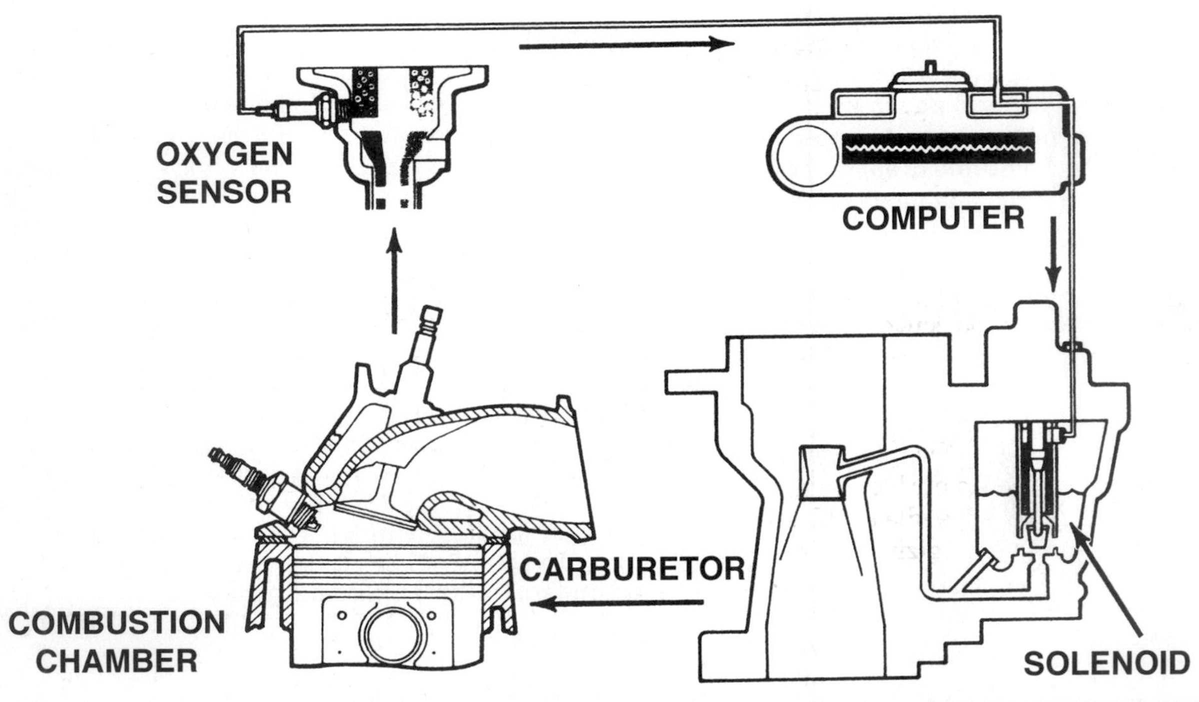

Figure 28–20 Schematic of a basic feedback circuit. Once the engine is at a predetermined temperature and the oxygen sensor is generating a signal (closed loop), the computer begins to control the feedback solenoid in the carburetor. Some systems operate at a preset duty cycle during open loop, others allow the solenoid to stay at full rich. (Courtesy DaimlerChrysler Corporation)

Figure 28–21 Most computer-controlled carburetors are designed to operate slightly rich without any computer control. The computer controls the mixture control solenoid to lean the mixture. The mixture is controlled by controlling the amount of time the solenoid is on. The metering rod is pushed up by the return spring and stays in that position (rich). When the solenoid is activated the metering rod is pulled down, restricting the jet (lean).

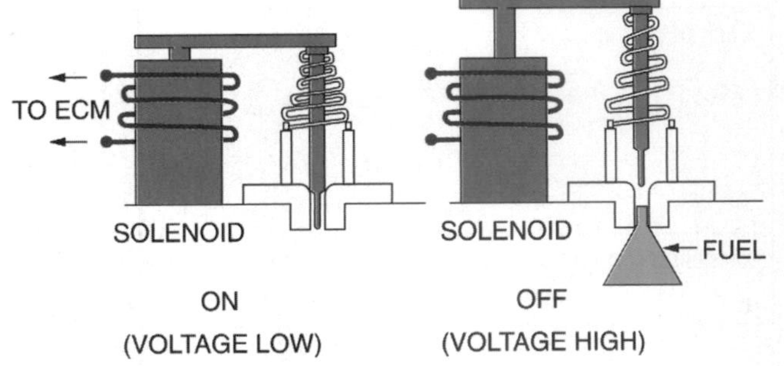

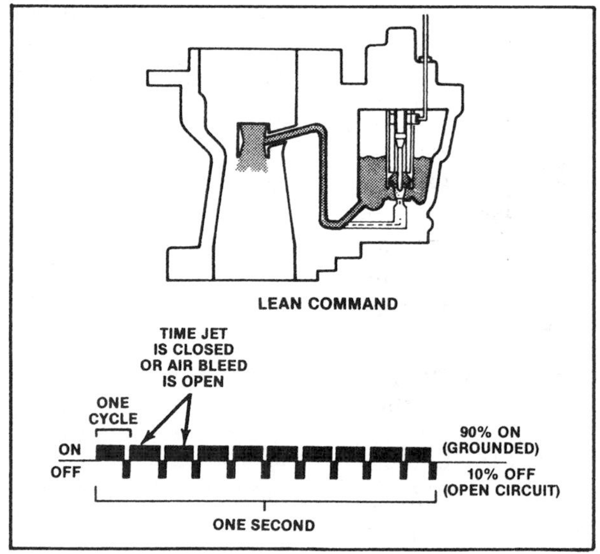

90% on = lean command

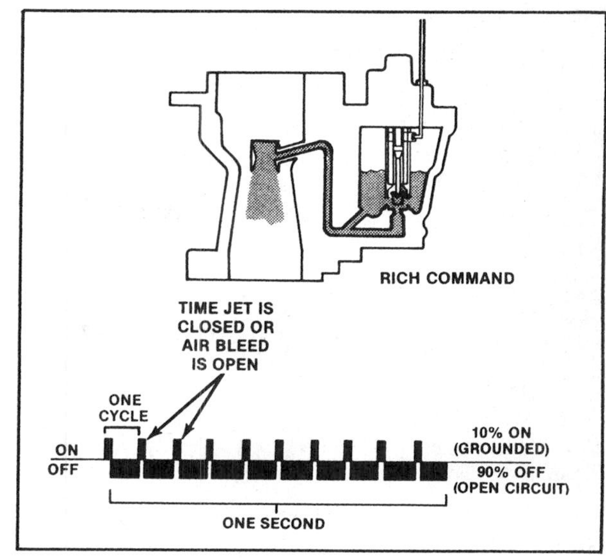

10% on = rich command

Figure 28–22 Mixture control solenoid duty cycle is controlled by the driver transistor in the computer. When the transistor is on (90% in our example), the rod is pulled down 90% of the cycle and the mixture is lean. A shorter on-time (10% in our example) allows the rod to be pulled down only 10% of the cycle and the mixture is rich. (Courtesy DaimlerChrysler Corporation)

Idle Mixture Control

Some feedback carburetors also control the idle circuit as well as the main metering circuit. See Figure 28–23. This example uses an air bleed valve, #2, to control the idle circuit air bleed. When the mixture control solenoid is energized, the plunger moves down. This allows the rod in the air bleed valve also to move down, which enlarges the idle air bleed. The idle mixture is now lean. De-energizing the solenoid allows the air bleed rod to move up, restricting the air bleed. The idle mixture goes rich. Control of the solenoid is exactly the same as for the main metering circuit.

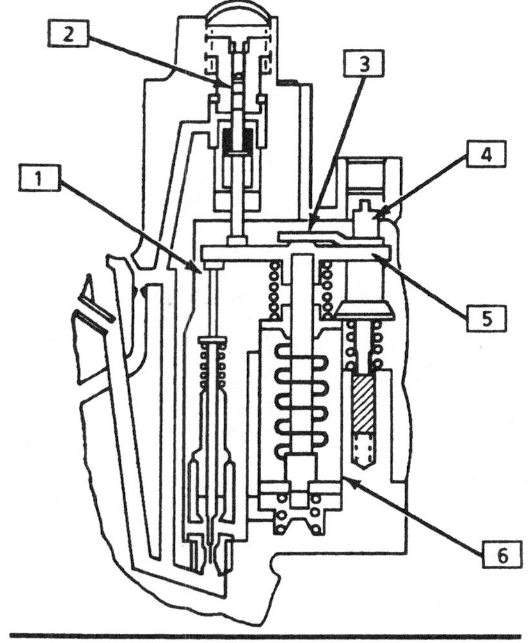

1 PRIMARY METERING ROD
2 AIR BLEED VALVE
3 RICH LIMIT STOP
4 SOLENOID ADJUSTING SCREW
5 SOLENOID PLUNGER
6 MIXTURE CONTROL SOLENOID

Figure 28–23 This mixture control solenoid adjusts fuel flow with a primary metering rod, #1, for the main metering circuit and an air bleed rod, #2, for the idle circuit. (Courtesy General Motors)

Testing the System Control

The duty cycle of the mixture control solenoid can be checked by measuring the varying duty cycle, dwell, or voltage in the circuit between the solenoid and the computer. A service connector is usually provided to attach the meter.

Using a Voltmeter

The computer controls the ground side of the circuit; if the computer grounds the circuit for 100% of the time, transistor on, the voltage (see Figure 28–24) will be close to zero. If the computer did nothing, transistor off, the voltage would read 14 volts (source voltage). A reading of 7 volts indicates a 50% duty cycle.

Figure 28–24 An analog voltmeter can be used to check the mixture control solenoid voltage. Notice that "lean" and "rich" have been added to the voltmeter scale to make it easier for the technician to understand the readings.

Higher voltage readings equal a rich command; low voltage readings equal a lean command. See Figure 28–25.

Using a Dwellmeter

General Motors uses a dwellmeter set on the 6-cylinder scale (0°–60°) to check the duty cycle. Hookup is the same as for the voltmeter. See Figure 28–26. A lean command would give a high dwell reading and a rich command would give a low dwell reading. See Figure 28–27. A reading of 30° equals a 50% duty cycle.

Diagnosing the Feedback System

The following procedures are typical of the steps required for system tests. The appropriate service manual or data source should always be consulted before beginning.

1. Connect a dwellmeter or voltmeter to the ground side of the circuit (between the mixture control solenoid and the computer).
2. Run the engine at 3000 rpm and note the meter reading. It should be fixed during open loop and varying during closed loop.
3. A closed loop reading of 30°, or 7 volts, is a 50% duty cycle. This indicates a correct air-fuel ratio of 14.7 to 1. The readings should vary back and forth, always crossing this mid-point. They may range from 6° to 54° or from 12 volts to 3 volts, but never staying above or below the mid-point. The system is operating as it should.

Dwell Fixed Under 10° or Voltage Fixed Over 12 Volts

This indicates a lean exhaust and the computer is driving the system to full rich.

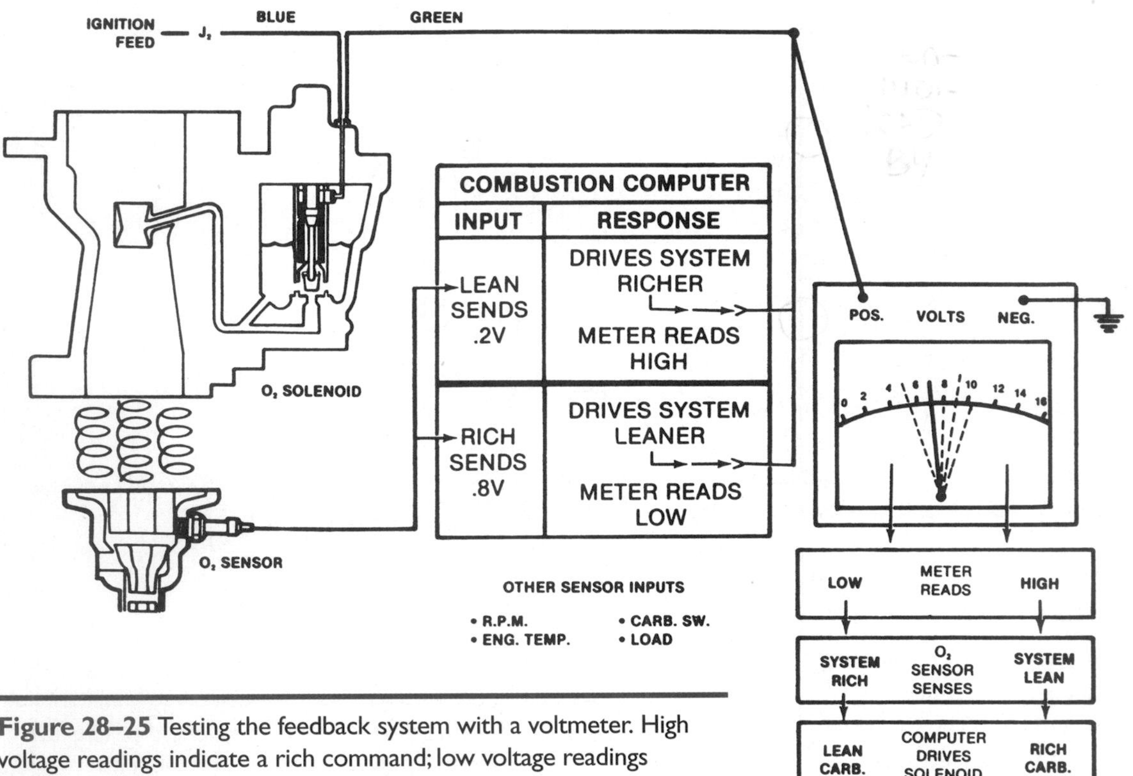

Figure 28–25 Testing the feedback system with a voltmeter. High voltage readings indicate a rich command; low voltage readings indicate a lean command. (Courtesy DaimlerChrysler Corporation)

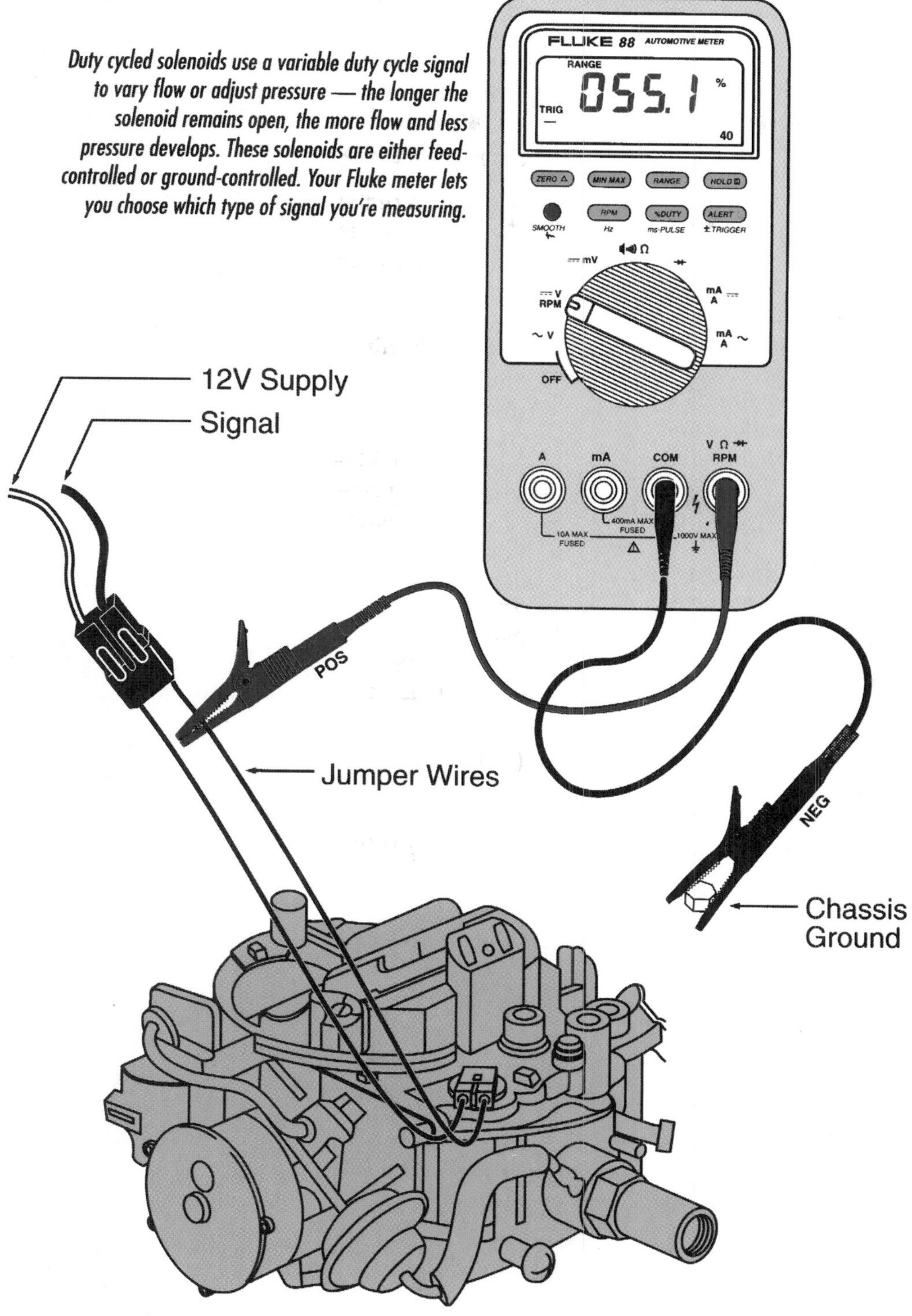
Duty cycled solenoids use a variable duty cycle signal to vary flow or adjust pressure — the longer the solenoid remains open, the more flow and less pressure develops. These solenoids are either feed-controlled or ground-controlled. Your Fluke meter lets you choose which type of signal you're measuring.
FLUKE 88 AUTOMOTIVE METER
055.1
12V Supply
Signal
POS
Jumper Wires
NEG
Chassis Ground

Figure 28–26 The engine must be at operating temperature and operating in closed-loop mode when measuring carburetor solenoid duty cycle. If no reading is observed on the meter, attach the red (positive) lead to the other solenoid wire. (Courtesy of Fluke Corporation)

Dwell Fixed Over 50° or Voltage Fixed Under 3 Volts

This indicates a rich exhaust and the computer is driving the system to full lean.

Further system testing will be required for both conditions to determine if the problem is electrical or mechanical. Continue to step 4.

4. Disconnect the oxygen sensor and connect a high-impedance voltmeter (or lab scope) to the sensor connector. Leave the sensor disconnected.
5. Start the engine and again run at 3000 rpm. Create a rich condition by closing the choke at the carburetor. The oxygen sensor reading should rise to about 1 volt. Open the choke and create a vacuum leak (don't let the engine stall) by slowly pulling off a vacuum hose. The voltage should drop to almost zero. This checks the oxygen sensor.
6. Ground the disconnected oxygen sensor wire (going to the computer); this simulates a lean exhaust. Watch the dwellmeter, or voltmeter, at the carburetor. The dwell readings should drop or the voltage reading should go high, indicating a rich command to compensate for the lean exhaust.
7. Apply power to the disconnected oxygen sensor wire going to the computer. Use a 1.5 volt flashlight battery (positive [+] to the computer, negative [−] to ground) or wet one finger, touch it to the positive terminal of the vehicle battery and place a wet finger from the other hand on the disconnected wire terminal. Either method will simulate a rich exhaust. The dwell reading should go high, or the voltage reading should go low, indicating a lean command, to compensate for the rich exhaust. This checks the computer.
8. Remove the dwellmeter, or voltmeter, from the mixture control ground circuit. Run the engine at 3000 rpm with the oxygen sensor disconnected. Connect a jumper wire from the mixture control circuit test connector to ground. This should drive the system to full lean and the rpm should drop. Disconnect the jumper and allow the rpm to stabilize. Unplug the solenoid connector at the carburetor. This will drive the system to full rich and the rpm should rise. This checks the mixture control solenoid.
9. If everything checks out electrically, look for a mechanical problem. A full lean command could be caused by excessive fuel from a high float level, heavy float, leaking needle and seat, saturated carbon canister, or a misadjusted carburetor. A full rich command could be caused by a large vacuum leak, a low float level, an air management system sending air to the wrong area or, again, a misadjusted carburetor. See Figure 28–28.

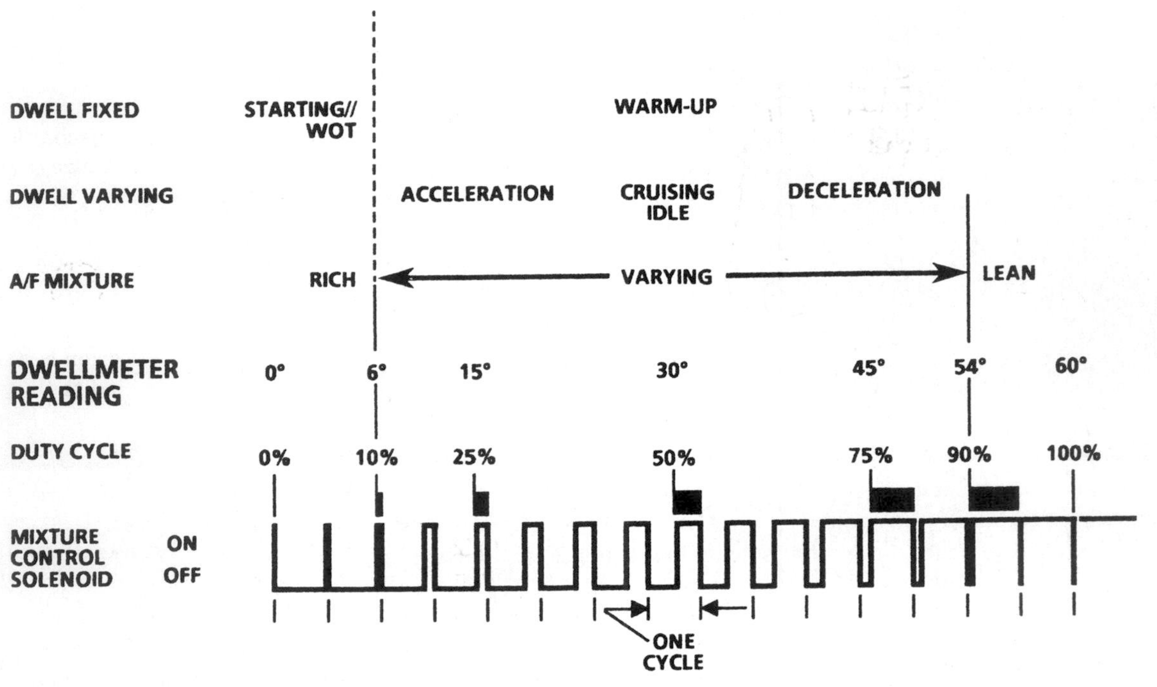

Figure 28–27 Dwellmeter relationship to duty cycle. (Courtesy General Motors Ltd.)

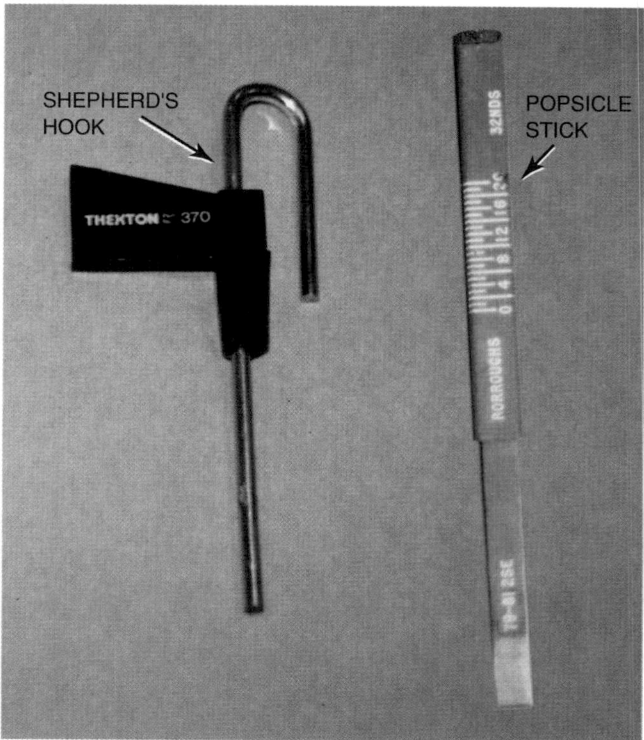

Figure 28–28 (a) A "shepherd's hook" and (b) a "popsicle stick" used on General Motors computer-controlled carburetors to measure and adjust the rich and lean stops as well as check for proper mixture control solenoid travel.

TECH TIP 

Three Turns To Be Sure

Whenever assembling any fuel line, brake line, or any other fitting, always turn the fitting at least three revolutions by hand before putting a wrench on it. This prevents the possibility of cross-threading the fitting. These fittings are usually constructed of brass or other soft metal that can be easily cross-threaded, especially if a wrench is used on the fitting.

IDLE SPEED CONTROL

Most computer-equipped engines include some type of engine **idle speed control (ISC).** Carburetor-equipped engines often use an idle-speed-control stepper motor operated by the computer. A stepper motor is a type of permanent-magnet motor that can be controlled precisely using the electronics of the computer. If the engine speed sensor detects a drop in engine speed (such as can happen when the steering wheel is turned if the vehicle is equipped with power steering), the ISC increases the throttle opening to maintain the proper idle speed.

TECH TIP 

Carburetors Don't Get Misadjusted By Themselves

Carburetors are carefully adjusted at the factory for correct flow. This does not mean that the two idle mixture screws (if a two- or four-barrel carburetor) are turned the same amount. All passages in a carburetor are flow tested. Passages are drilled and the diameters of these passages can vary slightly. By flow testing, the idle mixture screws can be adjusted to provide the correct (equal) amount of flow regardless of the position of the screws.

Once these screws are adjusted, most are sealed to prevent tampering. Some service technicians try to adjust the idle mixture screws to attempt to solve a low-engine-speed driveability problem. Adjusting these screws outward to provide more fuel helps solve the problem, but the richer mixture may only be covering up the real problem (root cause) such as a vacuum leak. Some technicians also believe that both screws should be adjusted exactly the same and they blame the factory when the screws are discovered to be unequally adjusted.

Before adjusting a carburetor, make sure there are no vacuum leaks. Remember, the carburetor did not get "out-of-adjustment" by itself, and therefore should not require adjustment unless it is being overhauled.

SUMMARY

1. Most carburetor-equipped engines use a mechanical fuel pump that should provide fuel at a pressure of between 28 to 55 kPa (4 and 8 psi) and at least 1 litre per minute (0.5 pint in 15 seconds).
2. A typical carburetor has six circuits. Only the idle and low-speed and the main metering circuits are computer controlled.
3. Placing a hand over the top of a carburetor on a running engine is one method that can be used to find a vacuum leak.
4. An excessively rich air-fuel mixture could be caused by leaking main well plugs.
5. The vacuum choke pull-off (vacuum break) opens the choke slightly after a cold start. A choke angle gauge is usually used to adjust exactly how much the choke is opened by the vacuum choke pull-off.
6. An electrically heated choke can be tested by measuring the amount of current in amperes it requires to operate.
7. Computer-controlled carburetors use a mixture control solenoid that is pulsed on and off to control the air-fuel mixture.

REVIEW QUESTIONS

1. List the six circuits of a carburetor.
2. Describe how to quickly determine if the engine has a vacuum leak.
3. Describe how to check an electric choke using an ammeter.
4. Explain how to connect a multimeter to the carburetor mixture control solenoid.
5. Explain the relationship between duty cycle in percentage (%) and dwell in degrees (°).

RED SEAL CERTIFICATION-TYPE QUESTIONS

1. How much fuel pressure should most mechanical fuel pumps produce?
   a. 7 to 21 kPa (1 to 3 psi)
   b. 14 to 28 kPa (2 to 4 psi)
   c. 28 to 55 kPa (4 to 8 psi)
   d. 55 to 69 kPa (6 to 10 psi)
2. What volume of gasoline should most mechanical fuel pumps be capable of pumping?
   a. 8 litres (2 gal) per minute
   b. 4 litres (1 gal) per minute
   c. 4 litres (1 gal) in 30 seconds
   d. 1 litre (2 pints) per minute
3. When a carburetor float absorbs gasoline, it gets heavier and causes the fuel level in the float bowl to be ________ than normal.
   a. Higher
   b. Lower
4. Clogged idle air bleeds can often be cleaned without removing the carburetor from the engine or disassembling the engine by performing what procedure?
   a. Spray the top of the carburetor with carburetor cleaner
   b. Remove the large vacuum hose and allow the engine to operate with a leaner-than-normal air–fuel mixture to burn the dirt
   c. Cover the top of the carburetor with the engine running
   d. Blow out the air bleed hole with compressed air
5. An engine equipped with a feedback carburetor is being tested at 3000 rpm with a dwellmeter. Dwell is fixed during warm-up (open loop) and varying from 6° to 54° when the engine is at operating temperature (closed loop). These readings indicate ________.
   a. A lean condition
   b. The system is normal
   c. A sticking metering rod
   d. A rich exhaust
6. An engine equipped with a carburetor (without metering rods) has a rough idle and delivers very poor fuel economy. The technician first checks the choke for being partially closed and the float level for being too high. Both are okay. What else could be at fault?
   a. A restricted main jet
   b. Contamination in the float bowl
   c. A leaking power valve diaphragm
   d. Dirt in the main discharge nozzle
7. The exhaust crossover passage on a V-8 engine is clogged with carbon. The engine has an automatic choke that uses the crossover heat to warm the choke. What operating condition will occur?
   a. Hard starting with a cold engine
   b. The choke may not open fully
   c. No fast-idle when cold
   d. The choke may not fully close
8. Turning the idle mixture screw(s) in too far may cause a lean misfire. This will increase ________ emissions.
   a. Hydrocarbon
   b. Carbon monoxide
   c. Oxides of nitrogen
   d. Particulate
9. A rough idle is being diagnosed. When the technician places one hand on top of the carburetor with the engine running, the engine speed increases. This indicates the engine is ________.
   a. Low on compression
   b. Idling too slow
   c. Running too lean
   d. Running too rich
10. The engine cuts out and lacks power during heavy-load, full-throttle acceleration. This could be caused by ________.
    a. Too high a float level
    b. A partially restricted fuel filter
    c. A power valve stuck in the open position
    d. A vacuum leak at the carburetor base

29

Gasoline and Diesel Fuel Injection: Operation, Diagnosis, and Service

OBJECTIVES: After studying Chapter 29, you should be able to:

1. Prepare for the interprovincial Red Seal certification examination in Appendix VIII (Engine Performance) on the topics covered in this chapter.
2. Describe how to check an electric fuel pump for proper pressure and delivery volume.
3. Explain how to check a fuel-pressure regulator.
4. Describe how to test fuel injectors.
5. Explain how to diagnose gasoline fuel-injection problems.
6. Explain the differences between throttle-body, port and direct fuel-injection.
7. Describe the operation of a diesel mechanical fuel-injection system.
8. Describe the operation of an electronic diesel fuel-injection system.

FUEL INJECTION

Electronic gasoline fuel-injection systems from the mid 1970s to the mid 1990s and later are all very similar in design and operation because they share a common beginning with Robert Bosch GmbH, a German company. Bosch is the largest supplier of fuel-injection systems in the world. It doesn't matter if it's a Fiat, Ferrari or a Ford, a Nissan, Toyota, Chevrolet, or a Chrysler, Bosch either designed or supplied the complete system or some components in the system. In the mid-1990s, automobile manufacturers began moving away from the original Bosch design and we now see many variations. However, Bosch is still a major component supplier for many of these late systems.

BASIC GASOLINE FUEL-INJECTION OPERATION

Most fuel-injection systems are closed loop, which means that any fuel sent to the injectors and not used in the engine will be returned to the fuel tank. See Figure 29–1.

Fuel Pump

The electric fuel pump delivers fuel from the tank to the system and develops fuel pressure. See Figure 29–2. The pump is usually located inside the fuel tank, where it is cooled by the surrounding fuel. Many pumps are incorporated with the fuel gauge sender unit. Some earlier vehicles, usually imports, mounted the pump outside the tank on the frame of the underbody. In-tank pumps are replaced by removing the fuel tank or, in some cases, through an access opening in the trunk floor.

The roller-cell pump, similar to power steering, is driven by a permanent-magnet electric motor. It provides high-pressure fuel, at about 200 to 350 kPa (30 to 50 psi) for port injection and low-pressure fuel, at about 70 kPa (10 psi) for throttle-body injection. Some Fords use port style injectors in their central fuel-injection (TBI type); system pressures are about 200 kPa (30 psi) for these units.

In the event of a restricted fuel filter or line blockage, the pump is capable of producing pressures of 700 kPa (100 psi) or higher. An excess pressure valve (relief valve) is built into the pump

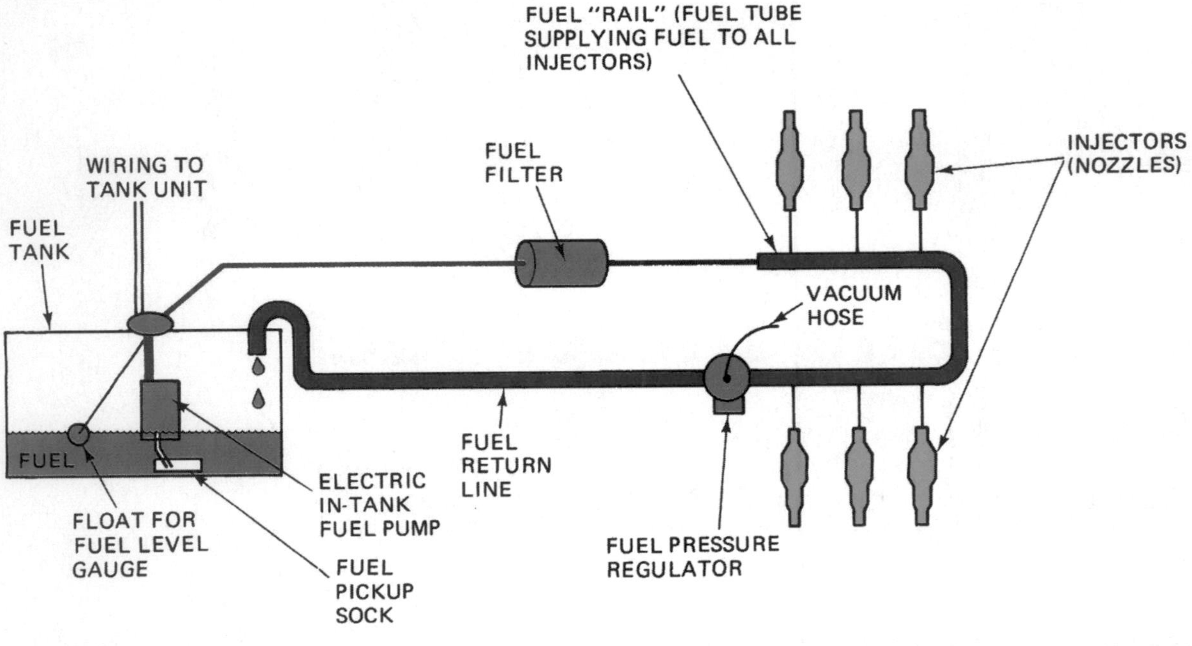

Figure 29–1 Typical port fuel-injection system, indicating the location of various components. Notice that the fuel pressure regulator is located on the fuel *return* side of the system. The computer does not control fuel pressure, but does control the operation of the electric fuel pump (on most systems) and the pulsing on and off of the injectors.

Electric fuel pump.

1 Suction side
2 Pressure limiter
3 Roller-cell pump
4 Motor armature
5 Non-return valve
6 Pressure side

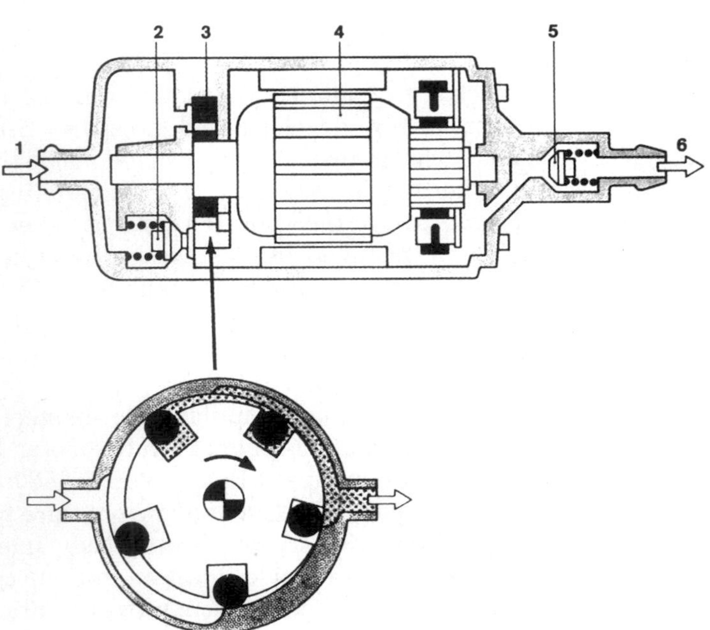

Figure 29–2 Schematic of a roller-cell fuel pump. Note #5 non-return valve, which prevents fuel pressure from bleeding back through the pump, and #2 pressure limiter (relief) valve, which acts as a safety valve if the fuel filter or line is restricted. (Courtesy Robert Bosch)

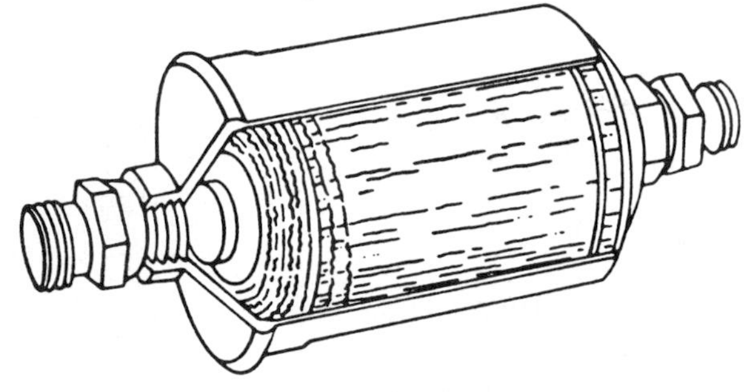

Figure 29–3 The fuel filter is located between the fuel pump and the fuel rail. Many filters are directional and have an arrow (or different sized fittings) to prevent incorrect installation. Most systems also have a filter "sock" at the fuel tank pick-up. (Courtesy Robert Bosch)

as a safety feature. A one-way check valve is also built into the pump outlet to prevent any fuel pressure in the lines or rail from bleeding back through the pump.

Fuel Filter

The fuel filter is a very important service item. See Figure 29–3. It prevents any rust or dirt in the fuel from reaching the fuel injectors where damage would occur; injector blockage, sticking or leakage are the usual result.

The filter is directional and may have an arrow or different sized fittings to prevent mounting backwards. Filters are normally replaced after a given number of kilometres or whenever major service is performed, e.g., fuel pump replacement or injector cleaning. Fuel system pressures *must* be released and the fuel tank cap removed before loosening filter lines. Pressurized fuel can spray for a long distance, causing personal injury or a fire.

Fuel Rail (Port Injection)

The fuel rail (or ring) acts as a manifold supplying fuel to each injector. See Figure 29–4. It also acts as a mounting point for the fuel-pressure regulator. Some domestic vehicles have the regulator riveted to the fuel rail; both are supplied if either needs replacing. The fuel injectors are sealed with O rings where they mount to the rail; the O rings should be replaced whenever the rail is removed from the injectors.

Domestic fuel rails usually have a fuel-pressure test fitting (Schrader valve) mounted on the rail, which makes servicing much easier. Many imported vehicles do not use Schrader valves and require special adaptors to test system pressures and fuel volume.

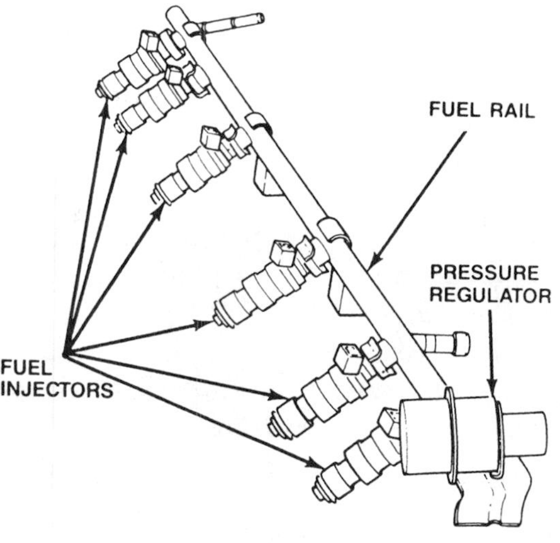

Figure 29–4 The fuel rail is a hollow manifold that supplies fuel to the injectors. Excess fuel not used in the engine flows through a pressure regulator (usually mounted on the rail) and returns to the tank. (Courtesy DaimlerChrysler Corporation)

Fuel Injectors

Electronic fuel injectors are liquid-control solenoids that open when electrically activated. See Figure 29–5. The injectors are pulsed on and off to control fuel volume. The longer the injectors are held open, the greater the amount of fuel injected into the manifold or intake port. Injectors are never operated at a 100% duty cycle. "On" time is called "pulse width"; the longer the pulse width, the greater the fuel flow; "on" time is usually in the 5 to 15 millisecond range.

Port Injection

Port injection systems used on gasoline-powered engines inject a fine mist of fuel into the *intake manifold* just above the intake valve. The pressure in the intake manifold is below atmospheric pressure on a running engine, and the manifold is therefore a vacuum. See Figure 29–6.

One major advantage of using port injection instead of the simpler throttle-body injection is that intake manifolds on port-injected engines only contain air, not a mixture of air and fuel. No pre-heating of the manifold is required to vaporize the fuel. This allows a cooler charge of intake air, which increases power. Another advantage is the equal volume of fuel provided to each cylinder. These "dry" manifolds also allow the engine design engineer the opportunity to design long, tuned intake-manifold runners that help the engine produce increased torque at lower engine speeds.

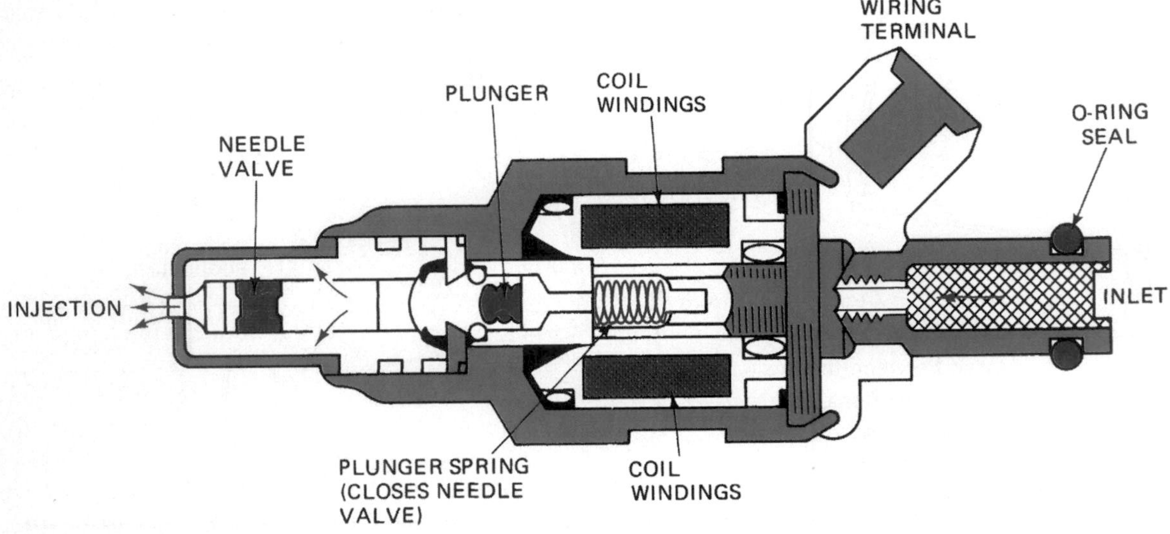

Figure 29–5 Cross-section of a typical port fuel-injection nozzle assembly. These injectors are serviced as an assembly only; no part replacement or service is possible other than cleaning or external O-ring replacement. Contamination at the needle valve area is a common problem, especially with older type injectors. Later injectors, called deposit-resistant, changed the tip design to reduce the formation of injector deposits.

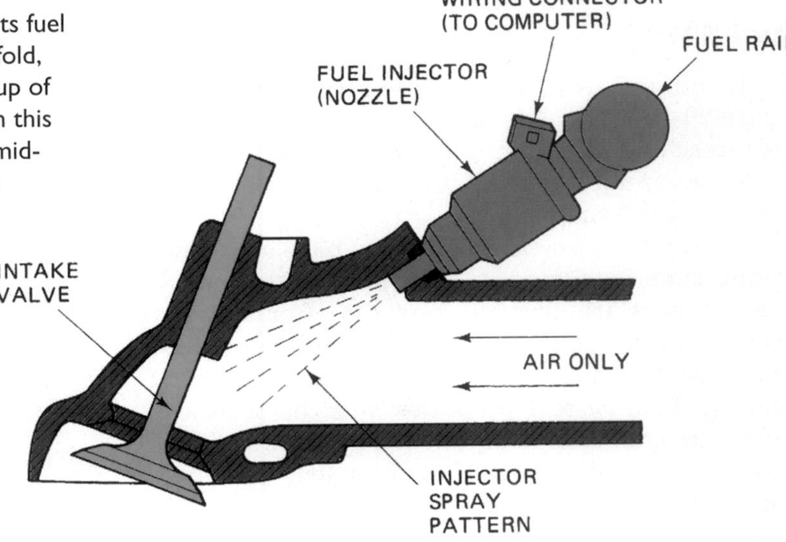

Figure 29–6 A typical port-injection system squirts fuel into the low pressure (vacuum) of the intake manifold, about 75 mm (3 in.) from the intake valve. A buildup of soft carbon on the intake valve often resulted from this design. The petroleum industry responded in the mid-1990s by increasing the percentage of detergent in gasoline. The detergent also reduced injector contamination.

NOTE: Some port-injection systems used on engines with four or more valves per cylinder may use two injectors per cylinder. One injector is used all the time, and the second injector is operated by the computer when high engine speed and high-load conditions are detected by the computer. Typically, the second injector injects fuel into the high-speed intake ports of the manifold. This system permits good low-speed power and throttle response as well as superior high-speed power.

Fuel Pressure Regulator: Port Injection

Fuel injectors that inject fuel into the intake port are influenced by intake manifold vacuum. At idle, manifold vacuum is very strong and a given amount of fuel flows. As the throttle opens, manifold vacuum diminishes (pressure in the manifold rises) and less fuel will flow because of the higher pressure at the injector tip. Vacuum-modulated pressure regulators increase fuel pressure about 35 kPa (5 psi) as the throttle is opened. See Figure 29–7. This compensates for the increase in manifold pressure.

Any excess fuel not injected into the engine returns to the tank via a return line.

The pressure regulator also prevents fuel pressure from bleeding into the return line when the engine is shut off; this maintains pressurized fuel at the rail and injectors for faster starting.

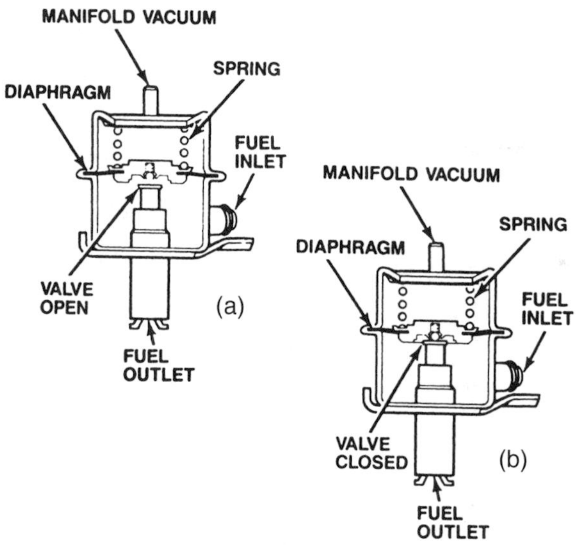

Figure 29–7 The vacuum-modulated pressure regulator controls system fuel pressure with a spring-loaded diaphragm. (a) Strong manifold vacuum (closed throttle) works against the spring and fuel pressure decreases. (b) As manifold vacuum drops (throttle opens), full spring pressure is now exerted on the diaphragm and fuel pressure rises. (Courtesy DaimlerChrysler Corporation)

Injector Firing Strategy

Fuel injectors have a number of operating strategies. They can all be fired at the same time (see Figure 29–8) with only one driver transistor. This is known as *simultaneous* injection; it is not timed. Some systems operate with two driver transistors; half of the injectors fire on one revolution, the other half fire on the second revolution; they also are not timed. *Sequential* injection, which requires a separate ground wire and transistor for each injector (ground side controlled), is timed. Injection usually occurs at the end of the exhaust stroke as the intake valve is opening.

Sequential injection has a number of advantages over simultaneous injection: 1) Emissions are reduced during low RPM and idle conditions. 2) It works with waste spark ignitions that fire the spark plug every revolution. 3) OBD II systems have the ability to cancel fuel delivery to any cylinder that is misfiring. This protects the catalytic converter.

Many imported vehicles use a resistor, which reduces the voltage at the injectors to approximately one-quarter of source voltage. This allows the use of low resistance injectors, which improves injector response. Domestic vehicles operate the injectors at source voltage and regulate injector response with the PCM.

Overspeed protection is also built into most computer programs. If the engine is operated above red line or is over-revved in neutral, the computer cuts off every second injector (or similar strategy) to bring the RPM down to a safe level.

Fuel Pump Electrical Circuits

The computer usually controls the operation of the electric fuel pump, located in (or near) the fuel tank. When the ignition switch is first turned on, the computer energizes the fuel pump relay and the pump operates. See Figure 29–9. If the computer does not receive a signal that the engine is rotating, the pump will be shut off after 2 to 3 seconds. When the computer receives information that the engine is being cranked, or has started, it continues to energize the fuel pump. The signal may come from one or more of the following:

- Movement inside the vane airflow sensor from air entering the engine.
- Oil pressure is noted at the oil pressure sender.
- An ignition tach signal (RPM) is present; this is the most common.

Figure 29–8 Wiring schematic for a simultaneous injection system. (Courtesy Toyota Canada Inc.)

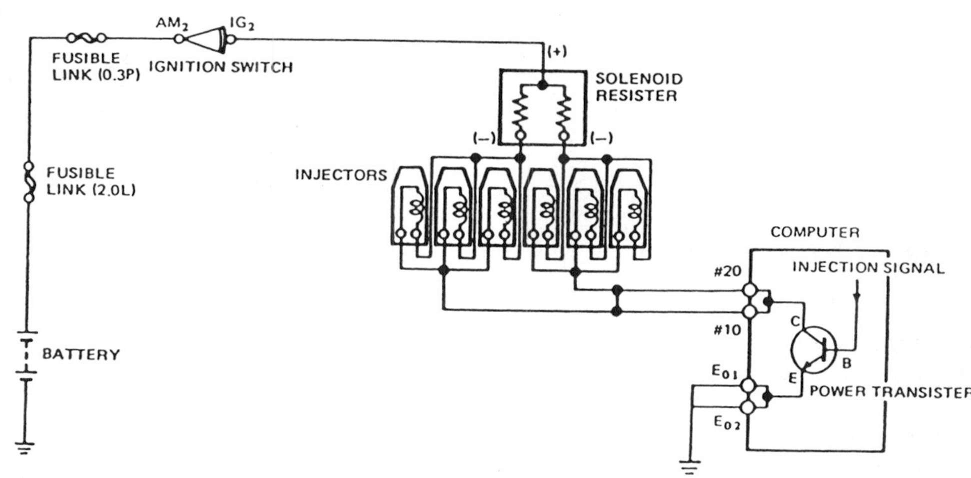

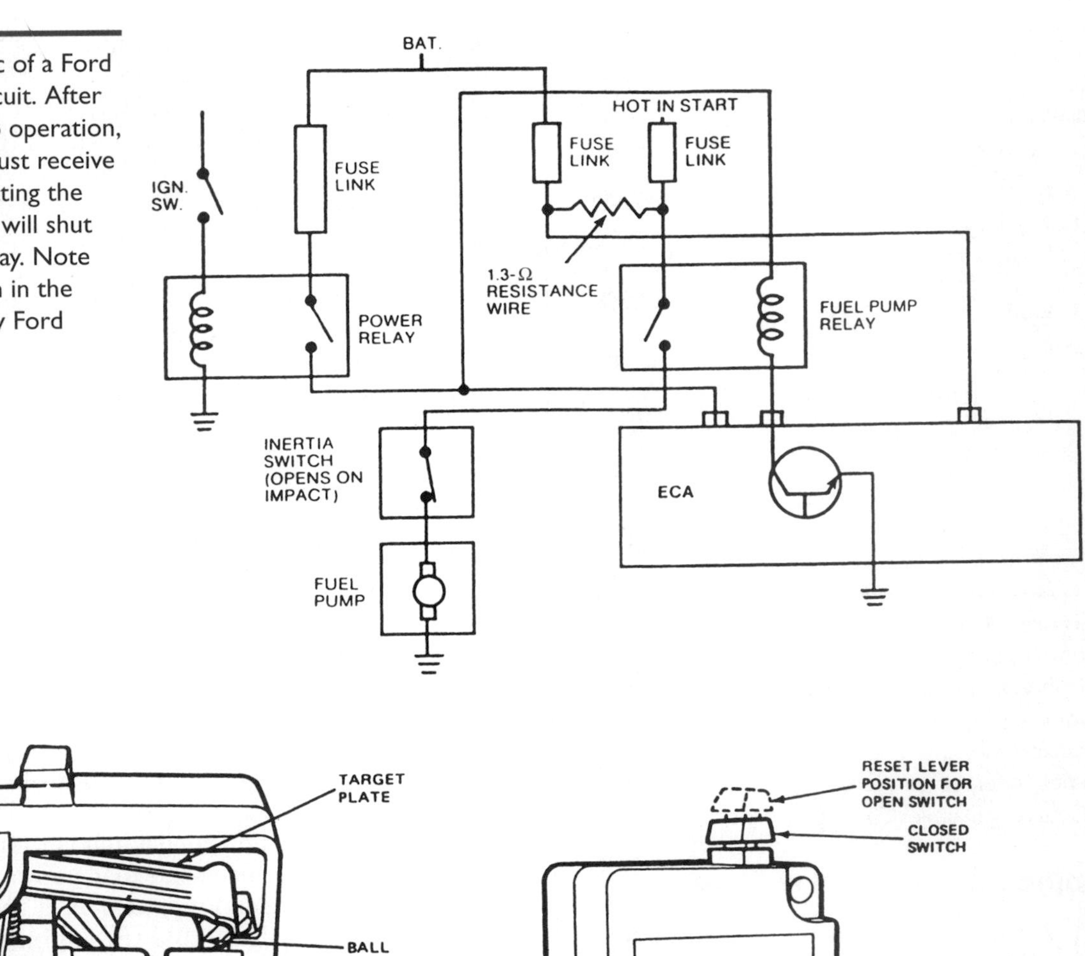

Figure 29–9 Schematic of a Ford fuel pump electrical circuit. After 2 to 3 seconds of pump operation, the computer (ECA) must receive an ignition signal (indicating the engine is rotating) or it will shut down the fuel pump relay. Note the inertia safety switch in the pump circuit. (Courtesy Ford Motor Co.)

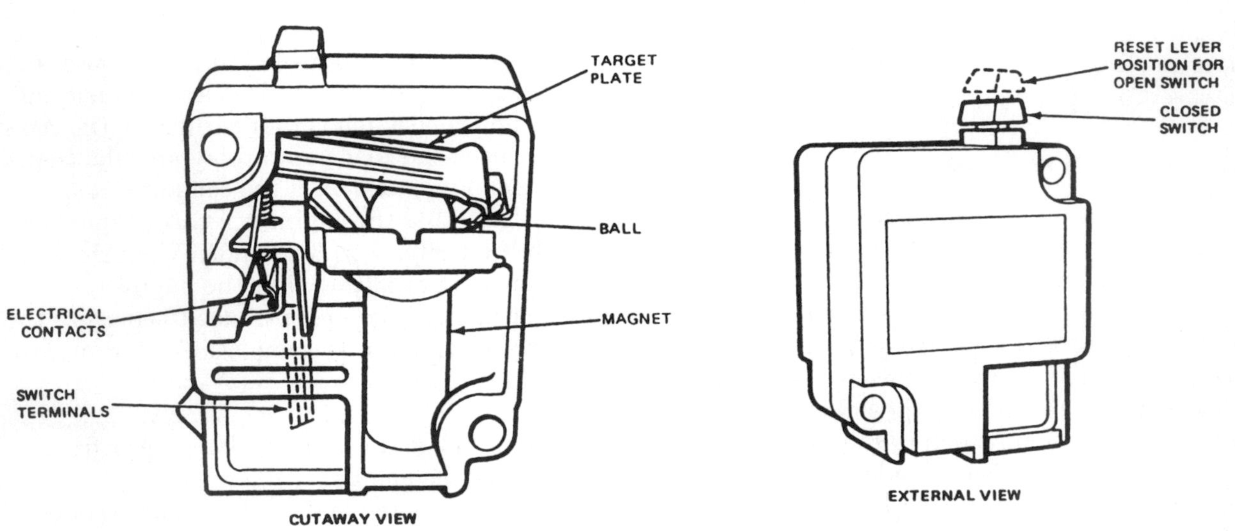

Figure 29–10 The inertia switch is used to shut off the electric fuel pump in case of an accident. Do not reset the switch before checking for fuel leaks at the tank, lines, or engine compartment. (Courtesy Ford Motor Co.)

NOTE: This is a safety feature: if the engine stalls and the tachometer (engine speed) signal is lost, the computer will shut off (de-energize) the fuel pump relay and stop the fuel pump.

Inertia Safety Switch

Ford, Jaguar and Fiat use an inertia switch in the fuel pump circuit to shut off the fuel pump in case of an accident. See Figure 29–10. A permanent magnet holds a steel ball in place; if an accident, or sharp impact, occurs, the steel ball breaks free and strikes a target plate, which opens the switch contacts, shutting off power to the pump. The switch is reset manually by depressing the reset button. Switch locations vary between vehicles; the switch may be in the trunk, on the firewall or behind a kick panel. Check the manual for location.

THROTTLE BODY INJECTION

Throttle-body injection (TBI) is also known as Central Fuel Injection (CFI) or Single-Point Injection. Throttle-body type of fuel injection uses one or two injectors (nozzles) to spray atomized fuel into the throttle body, which is similar to the base of a carburetor.

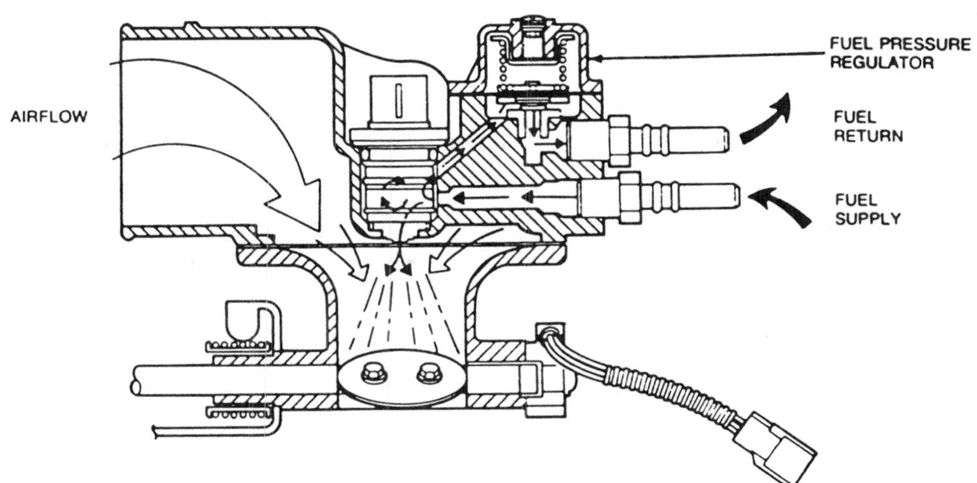

Figure 29–11 Fuel is injected above the throttle plate in this CFI system. The pressure regulator is not vacuum-modulated, as intake manifold vacuum does not have a major influence on injection rates. (Courtesy Ford Motor Co.)

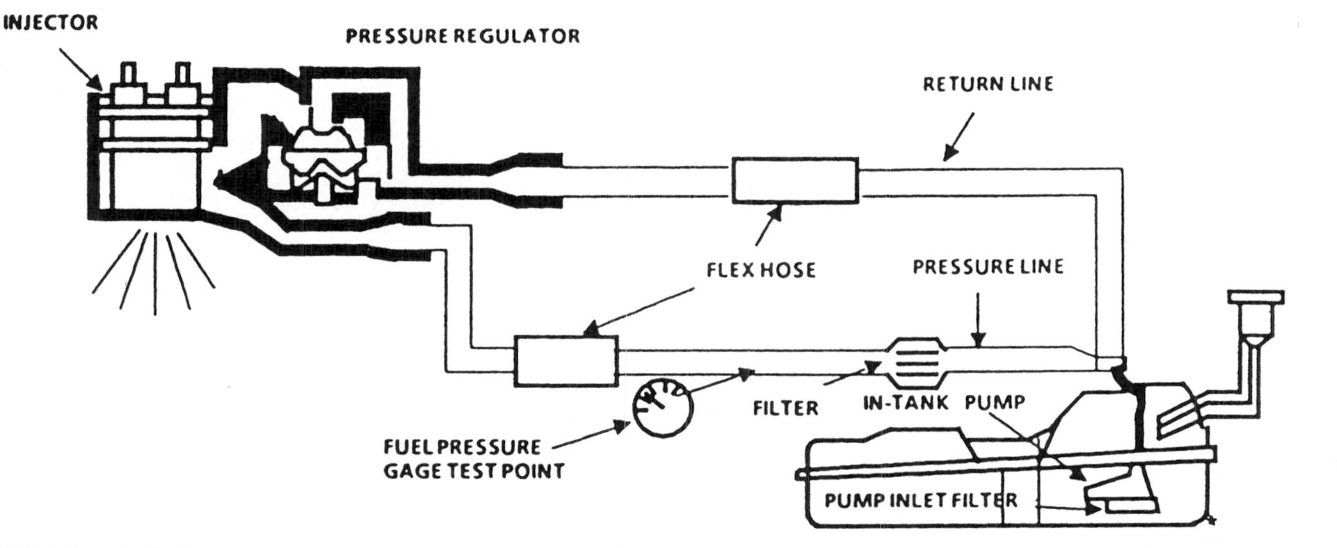

Figure 29–12 Fuel delivery and return lines on this TBI system are similar to port fuel injection. (Courtesy General Motors)

Air and fuel mix in the throttle-body unit and flow as a mixture down the intake manifold to the intake valves. See Figure 29–11. The fuel pump, filter, and lines are essentially the same as port injection. See Figure 29–12. Because fuel is injected above the throttle plate, intake manifold vacuum has no major influence on the injector. Fuel pressure regulators are not vacuum-modulated; fuel pressure is constant at 70 to 105 kPa (10 to 15 psi) depending on the model.

The ball-type tip of the TBI/CFI fuel injector is much larger than the needle tips of port injectors and it is prone to drip after the engine is shut off. See Figure 29–13. Some TBI pressure regulators (GM, Renault) have a bleed groove built into the pressure-regulator valve seat to relieve fuel pressure after the engine is turned off. Be aware of this condition when testing residual fuel pressure; there will be no pressure remaining after a few seconds.

A typical TBI system uses a throttle-position (TP) sensor and an **idle air-control (IAC)** valve. The TP is an input to the computer and the IAC is an output from the computer. The throttle-body injection unit costs less to manufacture, because it only uses one or two injectors (nozzles), whereas port-injection systems require an injector for every cylinder plus the additional computer capabilities to control all the injectors.

Throttle body injection provides better driveability and fuel economy than a mechanical (or electronically controlled) carburetor, however all of the distribution and vaporization problems associated with carburetted systems apply, as both air and fuel flow through the manifold. Unlike a port-injection system, many TBI units require that heated air be used with a heated intake manifold system to help vaporize the fuel that is injected into the incoming air inside the throttle-body unit.

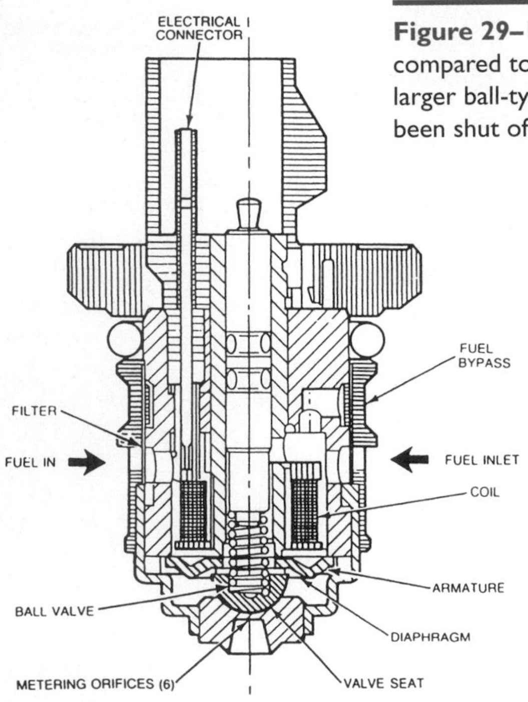

Figure 29–13 A low-pressure TBI/CFI fuel injector feeds all cylinders compared to a port fuel injector, which feeds only one cylinder. The larger ball-type injector tip is prone to leak or drip when the engine has been shut off. (Courtesy Ford Motor Co.)

BOSCH CONTINUOUS INJECTION (CIS)

Bosch continuous injection systems are also known as K-Jetronic injection: K stands for *konstant* in German. They are found on many 1970s to 1990s European vehicles (i.e., Audi, BMW, Mercedes, Volkswagen and Volvo, never on Asian or domestic automobiles).

Early CIS systems were mechanically operated; there is no computer. See Figure 29–14. Later systems, known as CIS-E, used a computer, a lambda (oxygen) sensor and a frequency valve to trim fuel mixtures. The frequency valve changes internal fuel pressures inside the fuel distributor to vary the mixture.

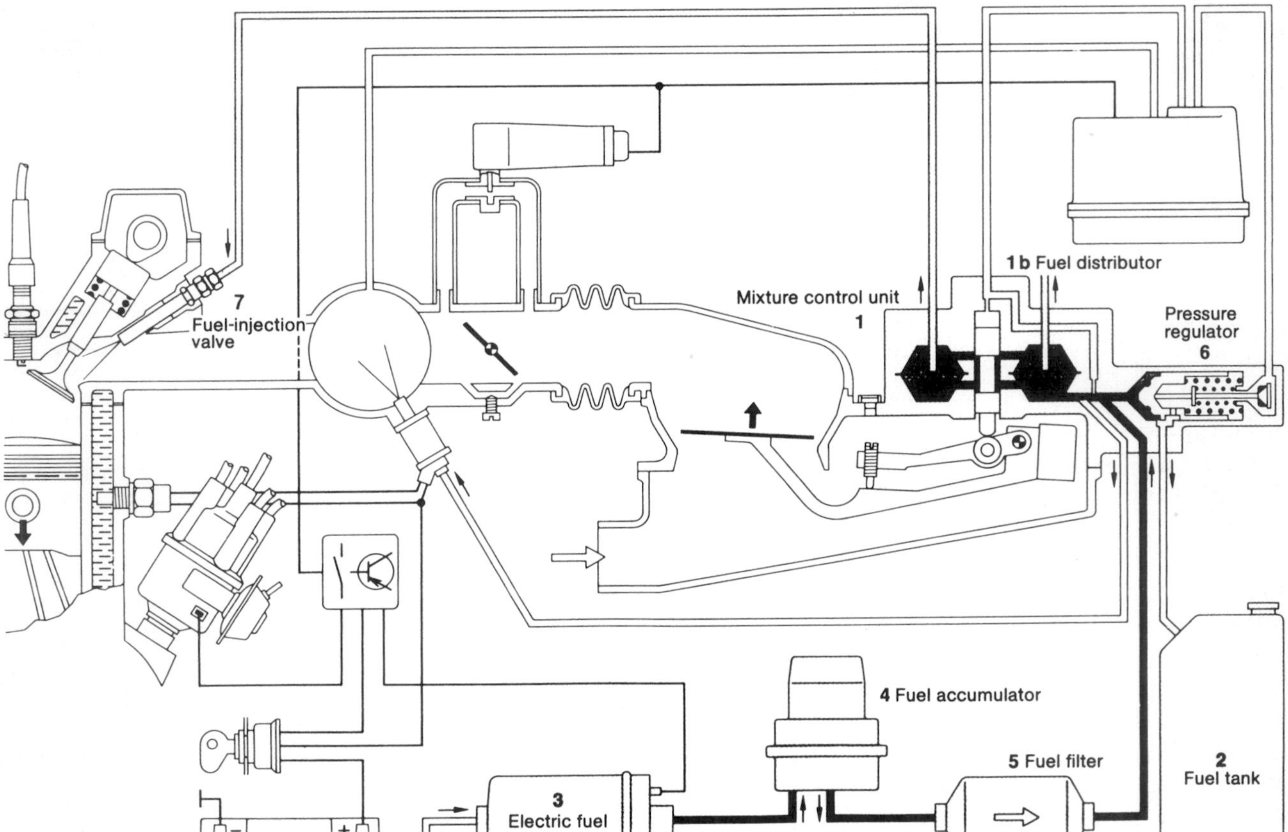

Figure 29–14 Schematic of a Bosch CIS mechanical injection system. These units are found only on European vehicles. (Courtesy Robert Bosch)

System Operation

Filtered fuel is pumped to the lower chamber of the mixture control unit where it is regulated to about 500 kPa (75 psi) by the pressure regulator. Excess fuel is returned to the tank.

Basic fuel control begins with an airflow sensor plate mounted next to the mixture control unit. Air entering the engine lifts the sensor plate; the greater the flow of air, the higher the plate is lifted. The arm on the airflow sensor plate contacts a fuel control valve called a control plunger. As the sensor plate lifts, it pushes on the control plunger, which also lifts, increasing fuel delivery. See Figure 29–15. Fuel flows from the mixture control unit to spring-loaded mechanical fuel injectors that open automatically when fuel pressure reaches 330 kPa (50 psi).

CENTRAL PORT INJECTION

The General Motors CPI system is a combination of a single electronic TBI-type injector and mechanical spring-loaded fuel injectors. See the manifold design in Chapter 9, Figure 9–42A.

The CPI fuel system is located inside a two-piece split intake manifold. Fuel arriving at the CPI unit is regulated by a built-in pressure regulator that returns unused fuel to the tank. The single maxi-injector (computer activated) injects fuel into a base, which contains six nylon tubes connected to six nylon fuel injectors (poppet nozzles). Fuel pressure at the injectors overcomes spring tension and fuel is injected into the ports. See Figure 29–16.

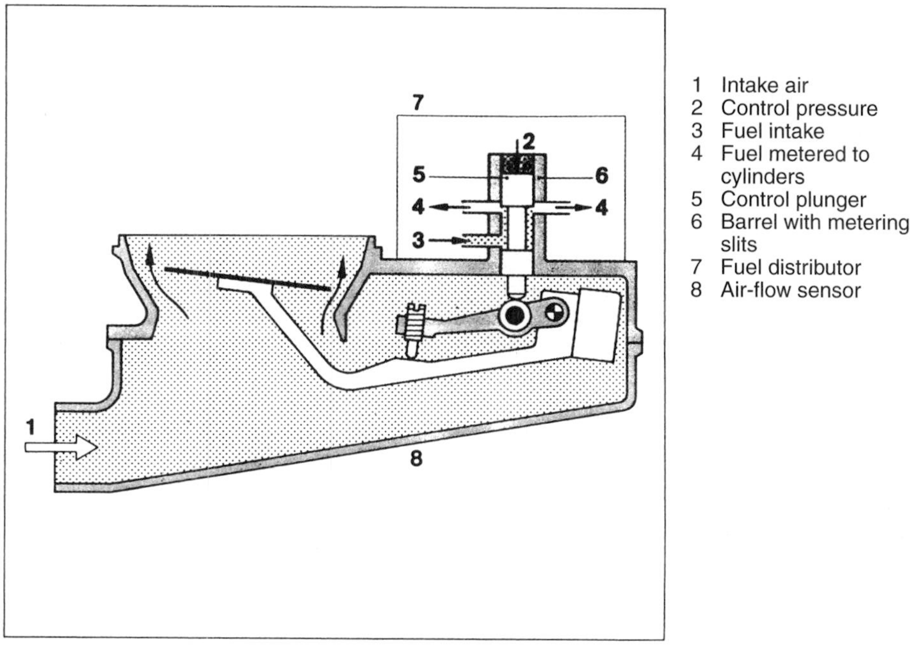

Figure 29–15 Fuel delivery in a Bosch CIS fuel distributor is metered by a control plunger, which is lifted by airflow at the sensor plate. (Courtesy Robert Bosch)

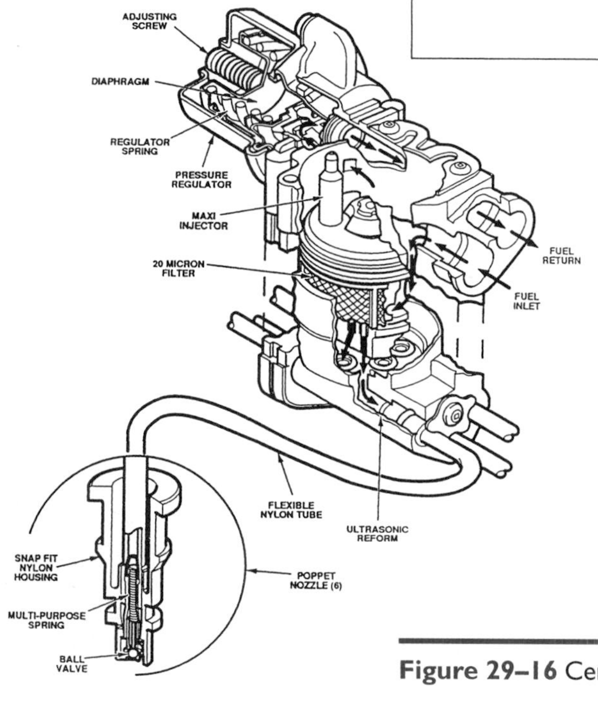

Figure 29–16 Central port injection (CPI) operation. (Courtesy General Motors)

Later designs use separate injector solenoids for each poppet valve, rather than a single maxi-injector. These systems are used primarily with V-6 and V-8 light truck engines.

RETURNLESS FUEL INJECTION

The most common injection system found from the mid 1990s to date is returnless fuel injection. An in-tank fuel pump module contains the pump, filter, pressure regulator, and fuel gauge, all in one unit. See Figure 29–17. There is nothing outside the tank, other than a single fuel line, rail, and injectors. See Figure 29–18. The extra computing memory of the OBD II processor allows fuel volume to be tailored to demand, regardless of changes in manifold vacuum.

Removing the rear seat (or trunk mat) and service-hole cover allows access to the unit without removing the tank in most instances.

DaimlerChrysler was one of the first (mid-1990s) to use returnless injection with their V-8 and V-10 engines. Since then it has been adopted by many domestic and import manufacturers and has become the standard around the world.

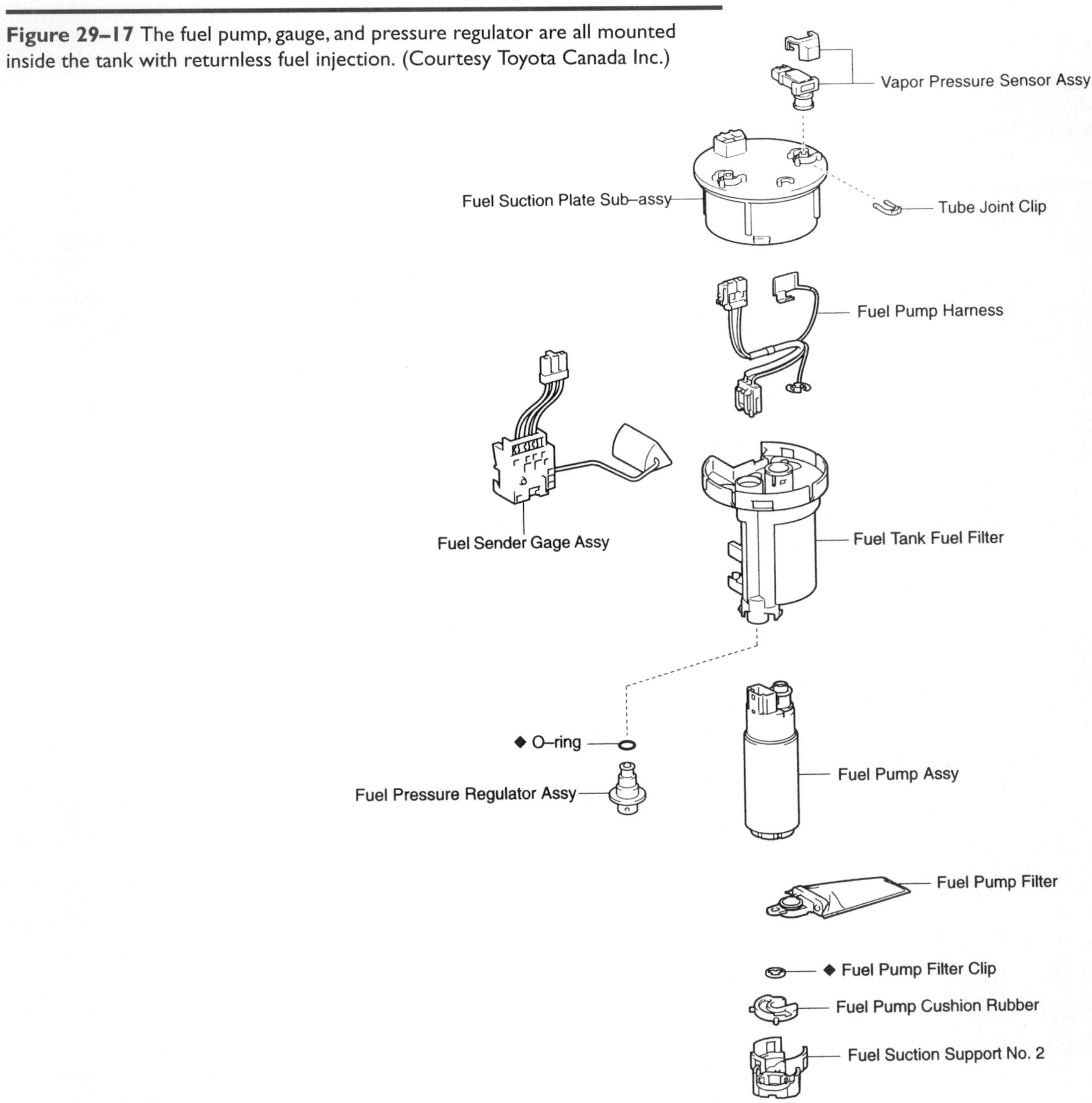

Figure 29–17 The fuel pump, gauge, and pressure regulator are all mounted inside the tank with returnless fuel injection. (Courtesy Toyota Canada Inc.)

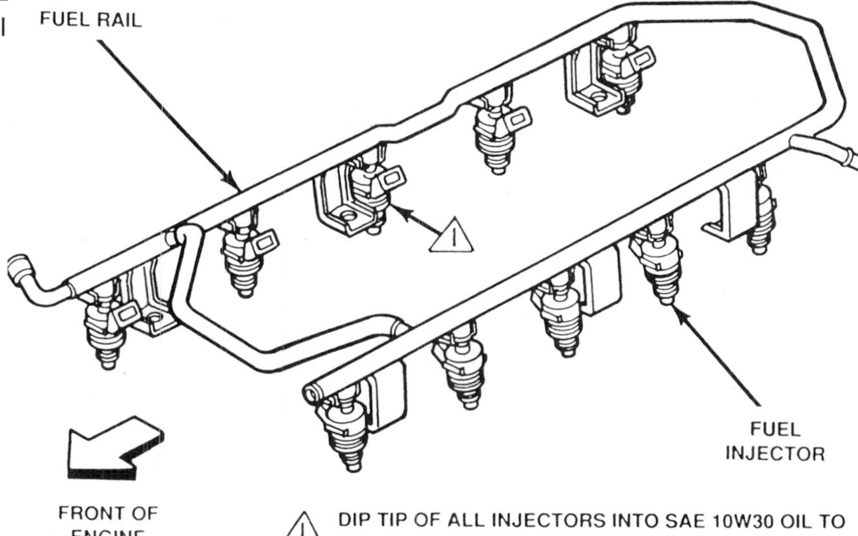

Figure 29–18 Fuel rails with returnless fuel injection contain an inlet fitting and pressure-gauge port. There is no return line. Pressure remains constant at 275 kPa (40 psi). (Courtesy DaimlerChrysler Corporation)

DIRECT FUEL INJECTION

A few Asian manufacturers—Mitsubishi, Toyota, and Isuzu—are using gasoline direct injection (GDI) with selected models. GDI sprays high-pressure fuel (8000 to 13 000 kPa, 1200 to 1950 psi) into the combustion chamber as the piston approaches the top of the compression stroke. See Figure 29–19.

The combination of high-pressure swirl injectors, with almost instant vaporization, and modified combustion chamber and port design allows the engine to run with a much leaner air/fuel mixture than conventional intake port injection. Fuel economy has shown a major improvement and engine emissions have been reduced.

Lean-burn engines traditionally lower hydrocarbon (HC) and carbon monoxide (CO) emissions; however, oxides of nitrogen (NO_x) emissions rise because of the elevated combustion temperatures created by lean mixtures. Increasing the amount of exhaust gas (EGR) fed into the incoming air and a special catalytic converter reduces NO_x to a very low level. It is expected that GDI engines will become more common as emission and fuel economy standards become more stringent.

Diagnosing Electronic Fuel-Injection Problems Using Visual Inspection

All fuel-injection systems require the proper amount of clean fuel delivered to the system at the proper pressure and the correct amount of filtered air. The following items should be carefully inspected before proceeding to more detailed tests.

- Check the air filter and replace as needed.
- Check the air induction system for obstructions.

TECH TIP 

No Spark, No Squirt

Most electronic fuel-injection computer systems use the ignition primary (pickup coil or crank sensor) pulse as the trigger for when to inject (squirt) fuel from the injectors (nozzles). If this signal were not present, no fuel would be injected. Because this pulse is also necessary to trigger the module to create a spark from the coil, it can be said that "no spark" could also mean "no squirt." Therefore, if the cause of a no-start condition is observed to be a lack of fuel injection, do not start testing or replacing fuel-system components until the ignition system is checked for proper operation.

- Check the condition of all vacuum hoses. Replace any hose that is split, soft (mushy), or brittle. Be sure to use the correct type of hose designed for use on a vacuum system. Using fuel line hose instead of vacuum hose can cause the hose to be sucked closed, creating more problems. This is especially true for the PCV valve hose.
- Check the positive crankcase ventilation (PCV) valve for proper operation or replacement as needed.

NOTE: The use of an incorrect PCV valve can cause a rough idle or stalling.

- Check all fuel-injection electrical connections for corrosion or damage.
- Check for gasoline at the vacuum port of the fuel pressure regulator if the vehicle is so equipped. Gasoline in the vacuum hose at the fuel pressure

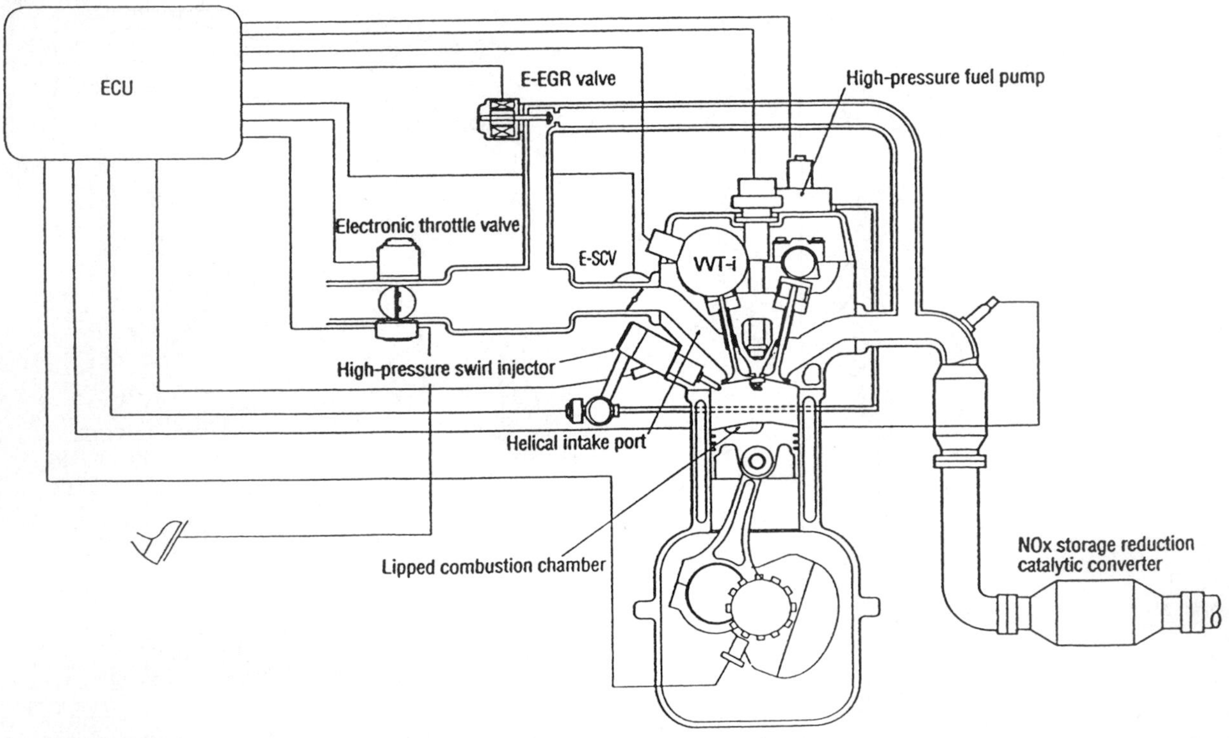

Figure 29–19 Gasoline direct injection (GDI). Note the high-pressure swirl fuel injector at the combustion chamber. (Courtesy Toyota Canada Inc.)

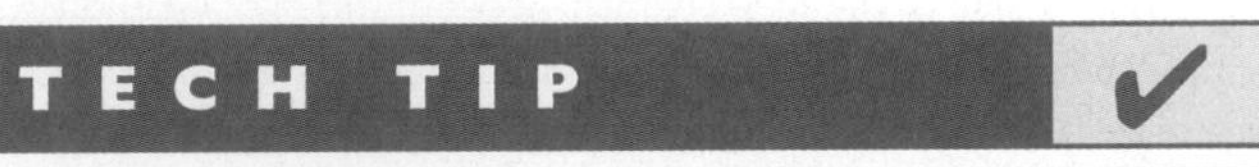

The Ear Test

No, this is not a test of your hearing, but rather using your ear to check that the electric fuel pump is operating. The electric fuel pump inside the fuel tank is often difficult to hear running, especially in a noisy shop environment. A commonly used trick to better hear the pump is to use a funnel in the fuel filter neck.

regulator indicates that the regulator is defective and requires replacement.

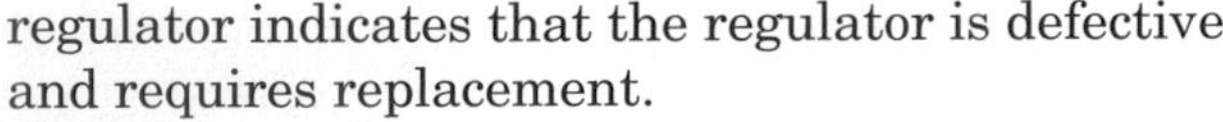

Test Connectors

Many vehicles have test procedures that allow the technician to operate the electric fuel pump without starting the engine; these vary between makes, but the following is typical:

- Open the meter plate at the vane airflow sensor. See Figure 29–20.
- Jumper two test terminals at the airflow sensor.
- Jumper specified terminals at the fuel pump relay.
- Ground the fuel-pump test connector (activates the relay).
- Power the test connector (powers the fuel pump).
- Activate the fuel pump relay with a scan tool.

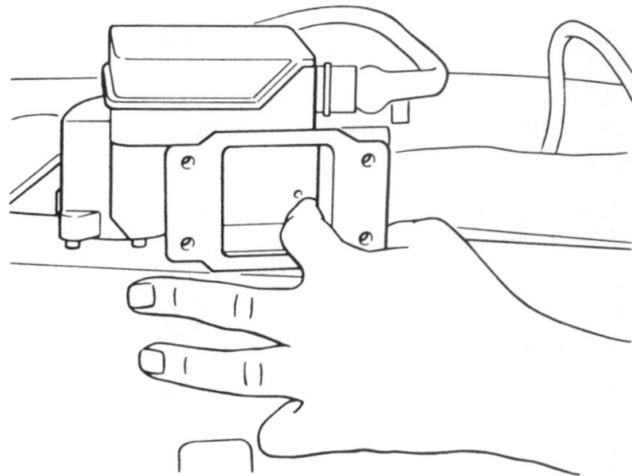

Figure 29–20 The vane airflow meter plate should open with light pressure to the fully open position and return to rest without dragging or binding. Many European and Asian vehicles (to mid-1990s) also incorporate fuel-pump safety contacts; opening the plate with a finger (engine key "on") will activate the fuel pump. Domestic vehicles with this type of meter use a tach signal, instead of contacts, for pump control. (Courtesy Robert Bosch)

Follow the manufacturer's instructions exactly; a wrong connection could ruin the computer, wiring or relay. See Figure 29–21.

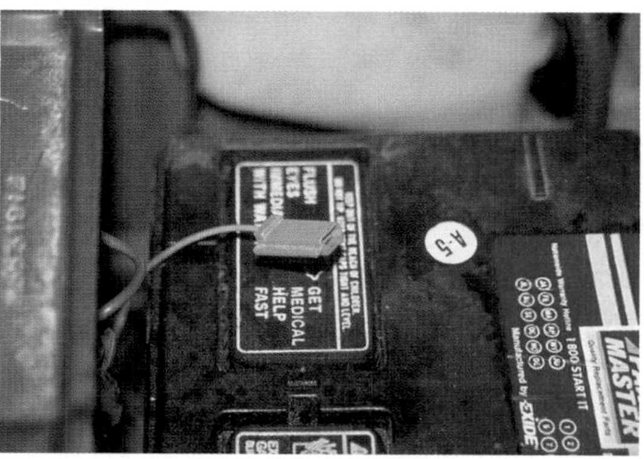

Figure 29–21 Most General Motors fuel-injected vehicles are equipped with a fuel pump test connector. The operation of the fuel pump can be checked by connecting a 12 volt test light to the positive (+) terminal of the battery and the point of the test light to the test connector. Turn the ignition to on (engine off). The light should either go out or come on for 2 seconds. This is a simple test to check to see if the computer can control the fuel pump relay.

Port Fuel-Injection System Diagnosis

To determine if a port fuel-injection system, including the fuel pump, injectors, and fuel pressure regulator, are operating okay, follow these steps:

1. Attach a fuel pressure gauge to the Schrader valve on the fuel rail.

NOTE: Some fuel rails may not have a Schrader valve on the rail and therefore, special adapters may be required.

2. Turn the ignition key on or start the engine to build up the fuel pump pressure (it should be about 210 to 350 kPa [30 to 50 psi]).
3. Wait 20 minutes and observe the fuel pressure retained in the fuel rail and note the value. (The fuel pressure should not drop more than 140 kPa [20 psi] in 20 minutes.) If the drop is less than 140 kPa (20 psi) in 20 minutes, everything is okay. If the drop is *greater* than 140 kPa (20 psi) in 20 minutes, there is a possible problem with:
   - The check valve in the fuel pump
   - Leaking injectors
   - A defective (leaking) fuel pressure regulator

To determine which unit is defective, perform the following with the gauges still connected:

- Re-energize the electric fuel pump for 10 seconds.
- Clamp the fuel *supply* line, wait 10 minutes (see Caution box on the next page). If the pressure drop does not occur, replace the fuel pump. If the pressure drop still occurs, continue with the next step.
- Repeat the pressure build-up of the electric pump and clamp the fuel return line. If the pressure drop time is now okay, replace the fuel pressure regulator.
- If the pressure drop still occurs, one or more of the injectors is leaking. Remove the injectors with the fuel rail and hold over paper. Replace those injectors that drip one or more drops after 10 minutes with pressurized fuel.

DIAGNOSTIC STORY

The Quad Four Story

A service technician was diagnosing a rough-running condition on a General Motors Quad Four engine. The paper test indicated a cylinder miss. To help determine which cylinder was possibly causing the problem, the technician disconnected the fuel-injector connectors one at a time. When the injector was disconnected from cylinder #2, the engine did not change in the way it was running. A compression test indicated that the cylinder had good compression. The technician removed the ignition cover and used conventional spark plug wires to connect the coils to the spark plugs. The technician then connected short lengths of rubber vacuum hose to each of the plugs. The technician then touched each rubber hose with a grounded test light to ground out each cylinder. Again, cylinder #2 was found to be completely dead.

Then the technician made a mistake by assuming that the fault had to be a defective fuel injector. A replacement fuel injector did not solve the problem. Further testing of the injectors revealed that injector #3 was shorted. Because both injectors #2 and #3 share the same driver inside the computer, the injector that was shorted electrically required more current than the normal good injector. Because the computer driver circuit controls and limits current flow, the defective (shorted) injector would fire (squirt), whereas the good injector did not have enough current to work.

CAUTION: The use of fuel-injector cleaner may damage the electrical windings of the fuel injector. Gasoline flows over the copper coil windings of an injector to help keep it cool. If a strong solvent is used in the fuel-injection cleaner, the varnish insulation on the coil may be damaged. As a result, the coil windings may short against each other, lowering the resistance of the injector.

TECH TIP

The Electric Fuel Pump Clue

The on-board computer controls the operation of the electric fuel pump, fuel-injection pulses, and ignition timing. With a distributorless ignition system, it is difficult at times to know what part in the system is not operating if there is no spark from any of the ignition coils. A fast-and-easy method for determining if the crankshaft sensor is operating is to observe the operation of the electric fuel pump. In most electronic fuel-injection systems, the computer will operate the electric fuel pump for only a short time (usually about 2 seconds) unless a crank pulse is received by the computer.

Most manufacturers provide a fuel pump test lead with which the technician can monitor the electrical operation of the pump. On most vehicles, if voltage is maintained to the pump during engine cranking for longer than 2 seconds, then the crankshaft sensor is working. If the pump only runs for 2 seconds then turns off during cranking of the engine, the crankshaft sensor, wiring, or computer may be defective.

NOTE: Another way of testing is to use a scan tool. If an RPM signal is processed and displayed by the computer, then the crank sensor is functioning.

DIAGNOSTIC STORY

The Rich-Running Chrysler

A four-cylinder Chrysler was running so rich that black smoke poured from the exhaust all the time. It was equipped with a TBI-type fuel-injector system, and the fuel pressure was fixed at about 260 kPa (38 psi)—the same as the maximum fuel-pump pressure. A replacement fuel-pressure regulator did not correct the higher-than-normal fuel pressure. The fuel return line was also carefully inspected for a kink or other obstruction that may have caused excessive fuel pressure. The technician discovered the root cause of the problem to be a stuck shuttle valve, a part of many Chrysler TBI systems used to close off the fuel return to the tank to keep the pressure high, permitting faster restarts when the engine is hot. The shuttle valve simply slides downward on an incline to close off the fuel regulator return passage. The technician removed the shuttle valve and cleaned it. Vehicle operation then returned to normal and both the technician and the customer were satisfied that a low cost and fast solution was found.

CAUTION: Do not clamp plastic fuel lines. Connect shut-off valves to the fuel system to shut off supply and return lines.

TESTING FUEL PUMP PRESSURE

The most common gasoline fuel injection systems operate with system pressures ranging from 70 kPa (10 psi) on low pressure TBI/CFI to 350 kPa (50 psi) on port injection. There are exceptions, so service specifications should always be checked before starting.

Typical System Pressures

Normal Operating Pressure	kPa (psi)	Maximum Pump Pressure kPa (psi)
Low-pressure TBI units	70 kPa (10 psi)	140 kPa (20 psi)
High- pressure TBI units	210 kPa (30 psi)	450 kPa (65 psi)
Port fuel-injection systems	350 kPa (50 psi)	700 kPa (100 psi)
Central port fuel injection	420 kPa (60 psi)	700 kPa (100 psi)
Bosch K-Jetronic (mechanical)	525 kPa (75 psi)	700 kPa (100 psi)
Returnless injection	280 kPa (40 psi)	550 kPa (80 psi)

Maximum fuel pressure should never be reached provided the fuel pressure regulator is operating and there is no blockage in the filter or lines; blockage before the gauge test fitting may not show a pressure rise at the gauge.

Closed loop injection returns excess fuel to the tank. The continuous flow of fuel cools the injector and helps prevent vapour from forming in the fuel system. Although vapour or foaming in a fuel system can affect engine operation, the cooling and lubricating flow of the fuel helps to ensure the durability of the injector nozzles.

Returnless injection systems cycle any excess fuel at the regulator inside the tank. The fuel is not exposed to high underhood temperatures (until it is used at the injectors) or heated by pumping it through the rail and back to the tank; the fuel remains cool.

To measure fuel-pump pressure, locate the Schrader valve, if equipped, or install a suitable adaptor. Attach a fuel pressure gauge as shown in Figure 29–22. Check the pressure while the engine idles. The fuel pressure should remain constant on all systems other than vacuum modulated port fuel injection where pressures vary with changes in manifold vacuum.

Figure 29–22 A fuel pressure gauge connected to the fuel pressure tap (Schrader valve) on a port-injected V-6 engine.

Port Fuel-Injection Pressure Regulator Diagnosis

Most port fuel-injected engines use a vacuum hose connected to the fuel pressure regulator. At idle, the pressure inside the intake manifold is low (high vacuum). Intake manifold vacuum is applied above the diaphragm inside the fuel pressure regulator. This reduces the pressure exerted on the diaphragm and results in a drop (about 35 kPa or 5 psi) in fuel pressure applied to the injectors. To test a vacuum-controlled fuel pressure regulator, follow these steps:

1. Connect a fuel pressure gauge to monitor the fuel pressure.
2. Locate the fuel pressure regulator and disconnect the vacuum hose from the regulator.

> **NOTE:** If gasoline drips out of the vacuum hose when removed from the fuel pressure regulator, the regulator is defective and will require replacement.

3. Using a hand-operated vacuum pump, apply vacuum, about 500 mm (20 in.) Hg to the regulator. The regulator should hold vacuum. If the vacuum drops, replace the fuel pressure regulator. See Figure 29–23.
4. With the engine running at idle speed, reconnect the vacuum hose to the fuel pressure regulator while watching the fuel pressure gauge. The fuel pressure should drop (about 35 kPa, 5 psi) when the hose is reattached to the regulator.

Testing Fuel-Pump Volume

Fuel pressure alone is not enough for proper engine operation. Sufficient fuel capacity (flow) must be at least 1 litre (2 pints) per minute (0.5 litre or 1 pint in 30 seconds).

Figure 29–23 If the vacuum hose is removed from the fuel pressure regulator when the engine is running, the fuel pressure should increase. If it does not increase, then the fuel pump is not capable of supplying adequate pressure or the fuel pressure regulator is defective. If gasoline is visible in the vacuum hose, the regulator is leaking and should be replaced.

All fuel must be filtered to prevent dirt and impurities from damaging the fuel-system components and/or engine. The first filter (sock) is inside the gas tank and is usually attached to the fuel pump (if the pump is electric) and/or fuel-gauge sending unit. The main fuel filter is usually located between the fuel tank and the fuel rail or inlet to the fuel-injection system. For long engine and fuel-system life and optimum performance, the main fuel filter should be replaced every year or every 24 000 km (15 000 mi). Consult vehicle manufacturers' recommendations for exact time and kilometre (mileage) intervals.

If the fuel filter becomes partially clogged, the following are likely to occur:

1. There will be low power at higher engine speeds. The vehicle usually will not go faster than a certain speed (engine acts as if it has a built-in speed governor).

TECH TIP

Stethoscope Fuel Injection Test

A commonly used test for injector operation is to listen to the injector with a stethoscope while the engine is operating at idle speed. See Figure 29–24. All injectors should produce the same clicking sound. If any injector sounds different from the others, further testing or replacement may be necessary. All injectors should make a "clicking" sound. If any injector makes a "clunking" or "rattling" sound, it should be tested further or replaced. With the engine still running, place the end of the stethoscope probe to the return line from the fuel pressure regulator. See Figure 29–25. The sound of fuel should be heard flowing back to the fuel tank. If no sound of fuel is heard, then the fuel pump, fuel filter, or the fuel pressure regulator is at fault.

2. The engine will cut out or miss on acceleration, especially when climbing hills or during heavy-load acceleration.

A weak or defective fuel pump can also be the cause of the symptoms just listed. If an electric fuel pump for a fuel-injected engine becomes weak, the engine may also be hard to start, or it will idle rough or stall.

CAUTION: Be certain to consult the vehicle manufacturer's recommended service and testing procedures before attempting to test or replace any component of a high-pressure electronic fuel-injection system.

NOTE: Most electric fuel pumps have a life expectancy of about 160 000 km (100 000 mi) before replacement. The usual cause of failure is brush wear at the commutator. Some manufacturers are now using brushless, permanent magnet fuel pumps, which provide a major improvement in service life.

SAFETY TIP

The arcing of the electric current from the fuel pump brushes to the armature commutator will not cause a gasoline fire or explosion, as there is insufficient oxygen in the pump while it is mounted on the vehicle.

This is not true if the pump has been removed from the vehicle; any remaining fuel vapours will mix with air if the pump is electrically activated (tested) off the vehicle. The pump could explode! Always follow the manufacturers' procedures when testing pumps.

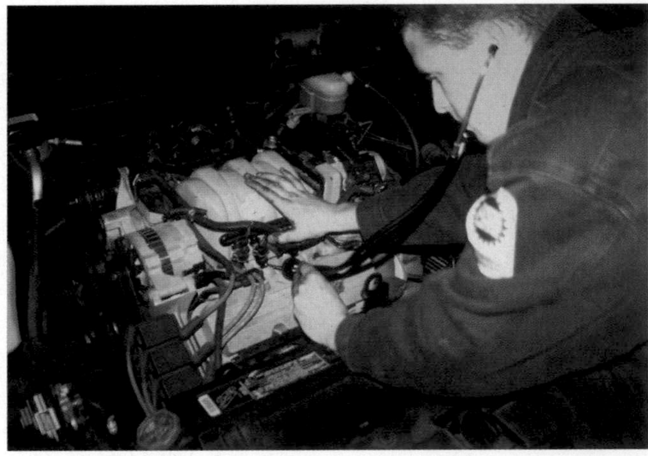

Figure 29–24 All fuel injectors should make the same sound with the engine running at idle speed. A lack of sound indicates a possible electrically open injector or a break in the wiring. A defective computer could also be the cause of a lack of clicking (pulsing) of the injectors.

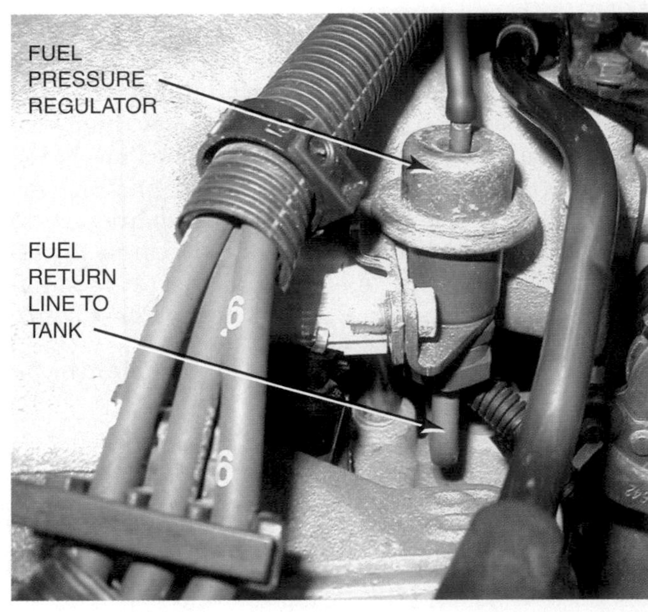

Figure 29–25 Fuel should be heard returning to the fuel tank at the fuel return line if the fuel pump and fuel pressure regulator are functioning correctly.

TECH TIP

Fuel-system pressure is controlled by a fuel pressure regulator at the fuel rail or throttle body. A restricted fuel filter or line will cause fuel pressure to increase, up to 700 kPa (100 psi) in some cases. The fuel pump slows down because of the added load and usually becomes noisier. A complaint of "whining noise in the rear" could be corrected by replacing the fuel filter. A fuel volume test (after the filter) will verify the diagnosis.

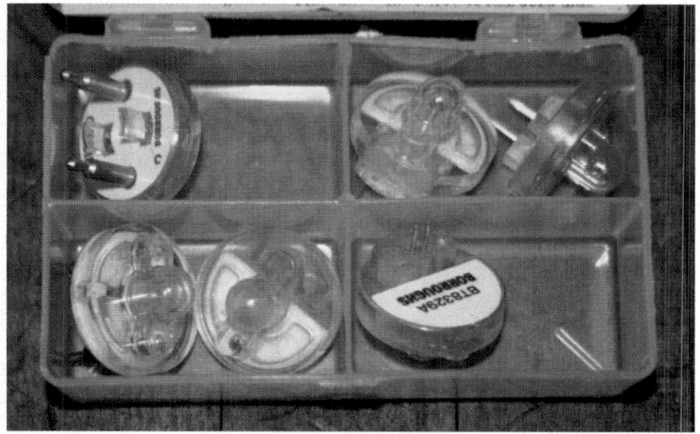

(a)

(b)

Figure 29–26 (a) Noid lights are usually purchased as an assortment so that one is available for any type or size of injector wiring connector. (b) The connector is unplugged from the injector and a noid light is plugged into the injector connector. The noid light should flash when the engine is being cranked if the power circuit and the pulsing to ground by the computer are functioning correctly.

Testing for an Injector Pulse

One of the first checks that should be performed when diagnosing a no-start condition is whether the fuel injectors are being pulsed by the computer. Checking for proper pulsing of the injector is also important in diagnosing a weak or dead cylinder.

A **noid** light is designed to electrically replace the injector in the circuit and to flash if the injector circuit is working correctly. See Figure 29–26. To use a noid light, disconnect the electrical connector at the fuel injector and plug the noid light into the injector harness connections. Crank or start the engine. The noid light should flash regularly.

> **NOTE:** The term *noid* is simply an abbreviation of the word *solenoid.* Injectors use a movable iron core and are therefore a solenoid. Therefore, a noid light is a replacement for the solenoid (injector).

Possible noid light problems and causes include the following:

1. **The light is off and does not flash.** The problem is an open in either the power side or ground side (or both) of the injector circuit.
2. **The noid light flashes dimly.** A dim noid light indicates excessive resistance or low voltage available to the injector. Both the power and ground side must be checked.
3. **The noid light is on and does not flash.** If the noid light is on, then both a power and a ground are present. Because the light does not flash (blink) when the engine is being cranked or started, then a short-to-ground fault exists either in the computer itself or in the wiring between the injector and the computer.

Checking Fuel-Injector Resistance

Each port fuel injector must deliver an equal amount of fuel or the engine will idle rough or perform poorly.

The electrical balance test involves measuring the injector coil-winding resistance. For best engine operation, all injectors should have the same electrical resistance. To measure the resistance, carefully release the locking feature of the connector and remove the connector from the injector.

Always check the service information for the exact specifications for the vehicle being checked.

> **NOTE:** Some engines require specific procedures to gain access to the injectors. Always follow the manufacturers' recommended procedures.

With an ohmmeter, measure the resistance across the injector terminals. Be sure to use the low-ohms feature of the digital ohmmeter to be able to read in tenths (0.1) of an ohm. See Figures 29–27 and 29–28. Subtract the lowest reading injector from the highest. For example,

$$\begin{aligned} \text{Highest-resistance injector} &= 17.4 \text{ ohms} \\ -\ \text{Lowest-resistance injector} &= \underline{17.2} \text{ ohms} \\ \text{Difference} &= \ \ 0.2 \text{ ohms} \end{aligned}$$

Acceptable maximum differences should be limited to 0.3 to 0.4 ohms. A greater difference in resistance indicates a possible problem. Further testing should be performed. The resistance of the

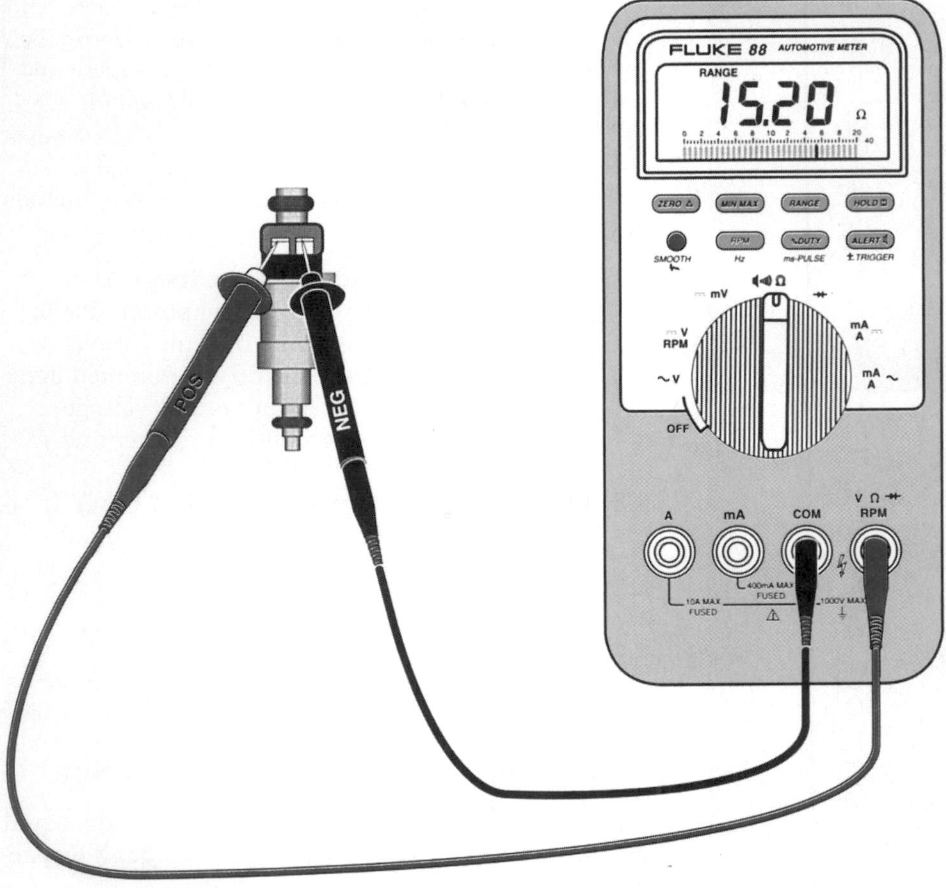

Figure 29–27 Connections and settings necessary to measure fuel-injector resistance. (Courtesy of Fluke Corporation)

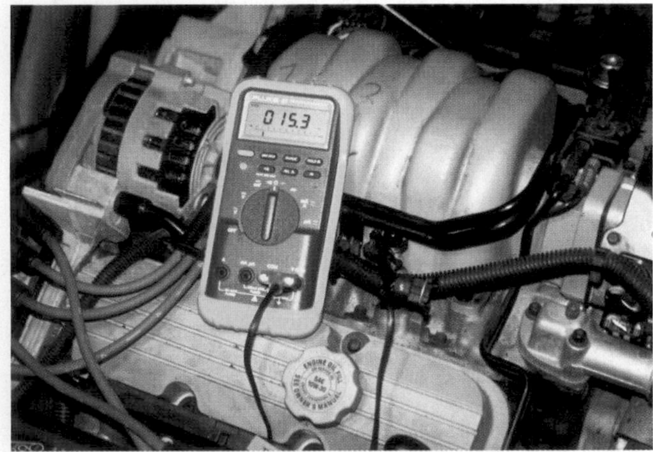

Figure 29–28 To measure fuel-injector resistance, a technician constructed a short wiring harness with a double banana plug that fits into the V and COM terminals of the meter and an injector connector at the other end. This setup makes checking resistance of fuel injectors quick and easy.

injectors should be measured twice—once when the engine (and injectors) are cold and once after the engine has reached normal operating temperature. If any injector measures close to or over 1.0 ohm different from the others, it must be replaced after making certain that the terminals of the injector are electrically sound.

Measuring Resistance of Grouped Injectors

Many vehicles are equipped with a port fuel-injection system that fires two or more injectors at a time. For example, a V-6 may group all three injectors on one bank to pulse on at the same time, then the other three injectors will be pulsed on. This sequence alternates. To measure the resistance of these injectors, it is often easiest to measure each group of three that is wired in parallel. The resistance of three injectors wired in parallel

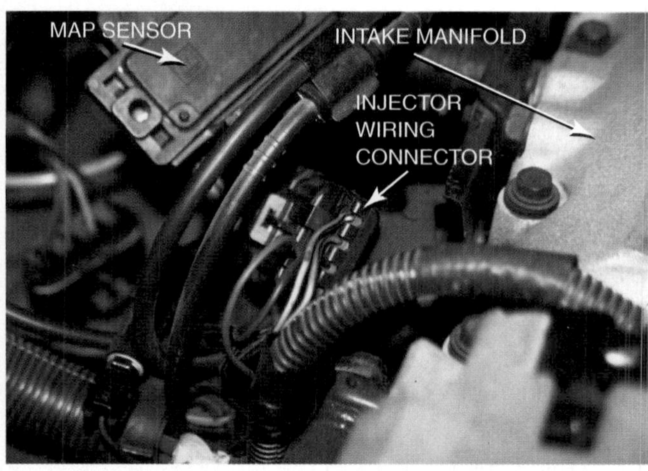
MAP SENSOR
INTAKE MANIFOLD
INJECTOR
WIRING
CONNECTOR

Figure 29–29 The fuel injector wiring connector on this General Motors 3.1-litre V-6 is hidden and attached to the rear of the intake manifold. Both groups of three injectors can be easily measured using an ohmmeter. Both groups of injectors should measure within 0.5 ohm of each other.

is one-third of the resistance of each individual injector. For example,

Injector resistance = 12 ohms
Three injectors in parallel = 4 ohms

A V-6 has two groups of three injectors. Therefore, both groups should measure the same resistance. If both groups measure 4 ohms, then it is likely that all six injectors are okay. However, if one group measures only 2.9 ohms and the other group measures 4 ohms, then it is likely that one or more fuel injectors are defective (shorted). This means that the technician now has reasonable cause to remove the intake manifold to get access to each injector for further testing. See Figure 29–29.

Pressure-Drop Balance Test

The pressure balance test involves using an electrical timing device to pulse the fuel injectors on for a given amount of time (usually 500 milliseconds) and observing the drop in pressure that accompanies the pulse. If the *fuel flow* through each injector is equal, the drop in pressure in the system will be equal. Most manufacturers recommend that the pressures be within about 10 kPa (1.5 psi) of each other for satisfactory engine performance. This test method not only tests the electrical functioning of the injector (for definite time and current pulse) but also tests for mechanical defects that could affect fuel flow.

Scope Testing Fuel Injectors

A scope such as a digital storage oscilloscope (DSO) can be attached to the pulse side of the injector and the waveform checked and compared to a known-good pattern. See Figures 29–30 and 29–31.

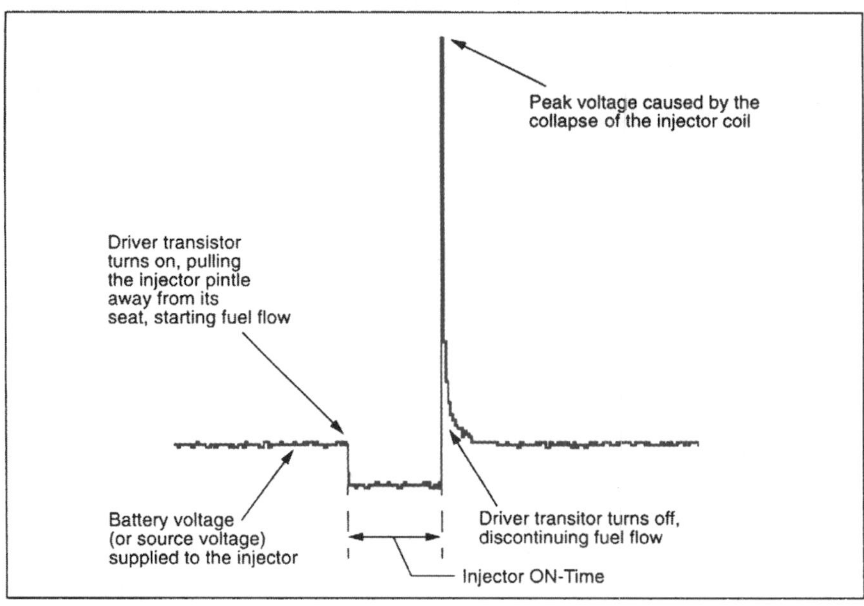
Conventional (Saturated Switch Driver) Fuel Injector
Peak voltage caused by the collapse of the injector coil
Driver transistor turns on, pulling the injector pintle away from its seat, starting fuel flow
Battery voltage (or source voltage) supplied to the injector
Driver transitor turns off, discontinuing fuel flow
Injector ON-Time

Figure 29–30 The injector on-time is called the *pulse width.* (Courtesy of Fluke Corporation)

Figure 29–31 A typical peak and hold fuel-injector waveform. Most fuel injectors that measure less than 6 ohms will display a similar waveform. (Courtesy of Fluke Corporation)

Current-Controlled (peak and Hold) Fuel Injector (Throttle Body and Port Fuel Injection Systems)

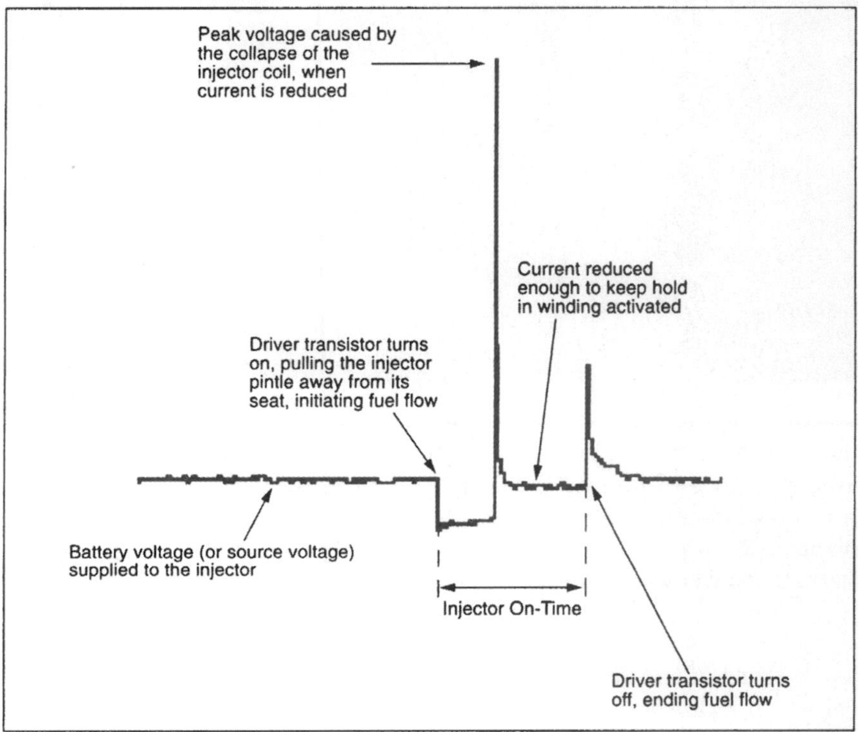
Peak voltage caused by the collapse of the injector coil, when current is reduced
Current reduced enough to keep hold in winding activated
Driver transistor turns on, pulling the injector pintle away from its seat, initiating fuel flow
Battery voltage (or source voltage) supplied to the injector
Injector On-Time
Driver transistor turns off, ending fuel flow

Figure 29–32 Fuel-injector cleaner is fed into the fuel system with this cleaning unit; shop air is attached to the regulator fitting. Aerosol cans, already pressurized and containing pre-mixed cleaner, are also used; however, they contain less cleaner and are often more expensive. (Courtesy OTC Division, SPX Corporation)

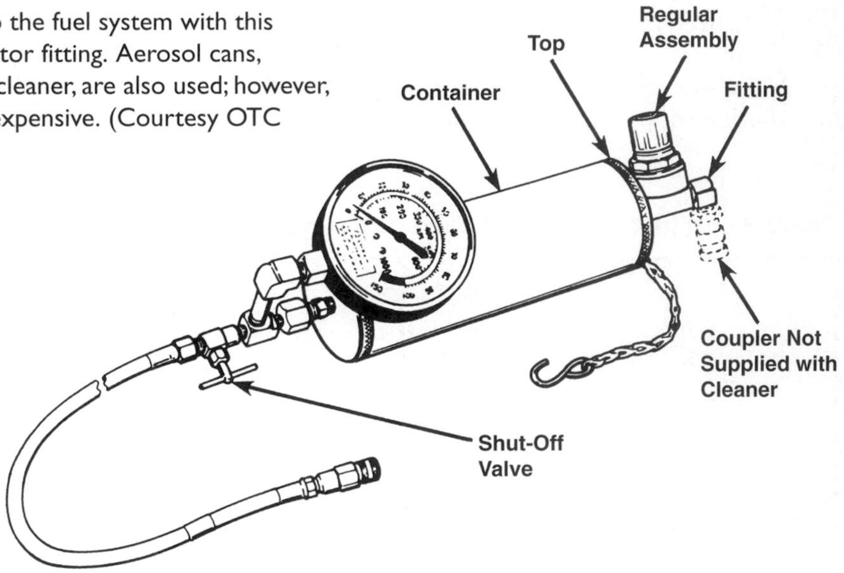

CLEANING FUEL INJECTORS

Most fuel injectors can be cleaned on the vehicle by feeding injector-cleaning liquid into the fuel rail, or TBI/CFI test port while the engine is running.

One common piece of equipment is shown in Figure 29–32. Liquid cleaner, which may require diluting with gasoline, is poured into the container after the top has been unscrewed. The top, containing an adjustable air pressure regulator, is reinstalled and a shop air hose is attached to the regulator. Ensure that the shut-off valve is closed and adjust the container pressure to 35 kPa (5 psi) lower than the fuel-injection-system operating pressure. TBI/CFI systems operate with low pressures; a 15 kPa (2 psi) lower setting is fine with these units.

Hang the cleaning unit under the hood and attach the supply hose to the Schrader valve (or adaptor) on the fuel rail or as directed in the operating instructions. Disconnect the wiring to the electric fuel pump on the vehicle. Block the fuel return line by clamping, if rubber, or by installing a shut-off valve if plastic or plastic-lined. See Figure 29–33.

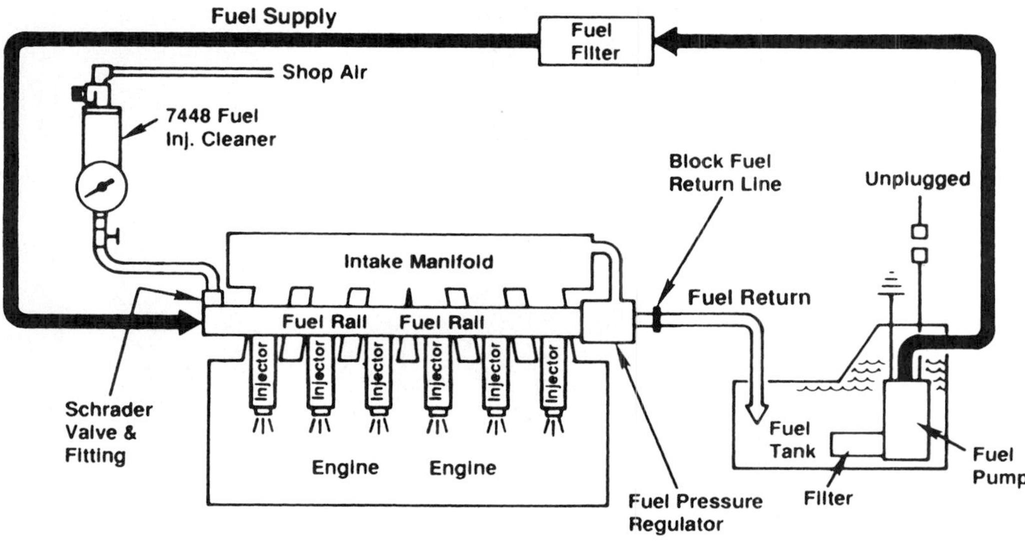

Figure 29–33 Typical hookup for on-vehicle injector cleaning. Note the blocked fuel return line and the unplugged wiring to the fuel pump. (Courtesy OTC Division, SPX Corporation)

Frequently Asked Question ???

If Three Out of Six Injectors Are Defective, Should I Also Replace the Other Three?

This is a good question. Many service technicians recommend that the three good injectors also be replaced along with the other three that tested as being defective. The reasons given by these technicians include:

- All six injectors have been operating under the same fuel, engine, and weather conditions.
- The labour required to replace all six is just about the same as replacing only the three defective injectors.
- Replacing all six at the same time helps ensure that all of the injectors are flowing the same amount of fuel so that the engine is operating most efficiently.

With these ideas in mind, the customer should be informed and offered the choice. Complete sets of injectors such as those in Figure 29–34 can be purchased at a reasonable cost.

Open the shut-off valve, start the engine and let it run until the container runs out of fluid. Some manufacturers recommend a fast idle only; others run the engine at various speeds. Remove the equipment, reconnect the pump, remove the return line shut-off, restart the engine and check the injector operation.

Cleaning the injectors on the vehicle will usually correct leaking or contamination at the injector tip; if this operation is not successful, the injectors must be removed for electronic cleaning (high frequency vibration) or replacement.

Figure 29–34 A set of six new injectors.

Remember always to keep a fire extinguisher, (suitable for gasoline) on hand whenever working with fuel injection.

IDLE AIR SPEED CONTROL

On an engine equipped with fuel injection (TBI or port injection), the idle speed is controlled by increasing or decreasing the amount of air bypassing the throttle plate. Again, an electronic stepper motor is used to maintain the correct idle speed. This control is often called the **idle air control (IAC).** See Figures 29–35 through 29–37.

When the engine stops, most IAC units will extend the conical valve until the valve bottoms in the air bypass passage. The computer notes this position and then moves the valve outward to get

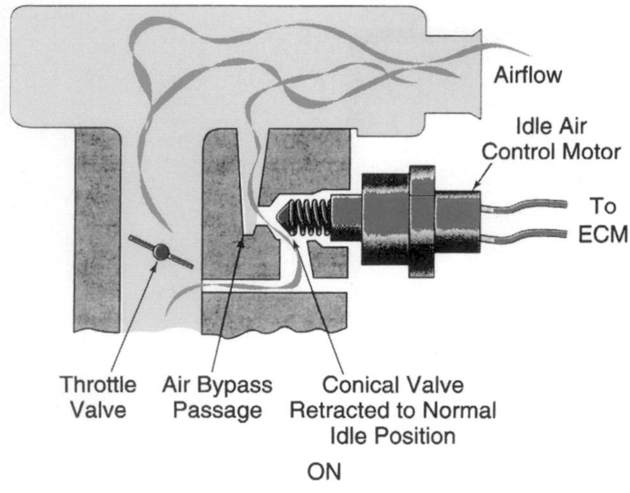

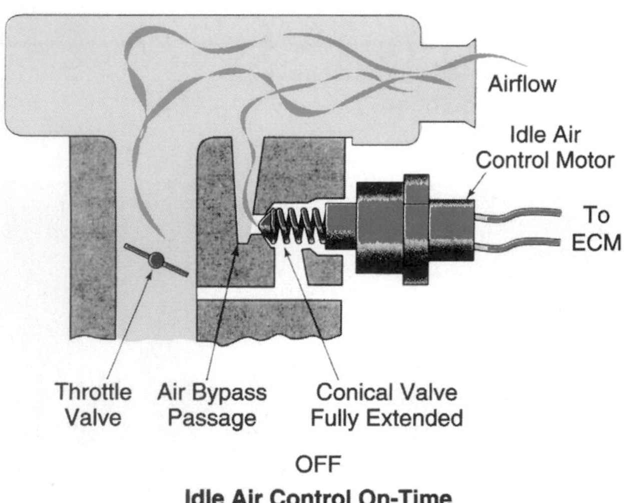

Figure 29–35 An idle air control (IAC) controls idle speed by controlling the amount of air that passes around the throttle plate. More airflow results in a higher idle speed. (Courtesy of Fluke Corporation)

Figure 29–36 A typical IAC.

Figure 29–37 Some idle air control units are purchased with the housing as shown. Carbon buildup in these passages can cause a rough or unstable idling or stalling.

ready for the next engine start. When the engine starts, the engine speed is high to provide for proper operation when the engine is cold. Then, as the engine gets warmer, the computer reduces engine idle speed gradually by reducing the number of counts or steps commanded by the IAC.

When the engine is warm and restarted, the idle speed should momentarily increase, then decrease to normal idle speed. This increase and then decrease in engine speed is often called an engine **flare.** If the engine speed does not flare, then the IAC may not be working (it may be stuck in one position).

Some air control valves (Ford, Hitachi) can be removed and disassembled for cleaning. Never use liquid cleaners on electrical components or plastic control valves as damage can occur.

THROTTLE BODIES: PORT FUEL INJECTION

Throttle Body Icing

Port fuel injection manifolds are not heated; air only passes through the runners. Under certain low temperature, high humidity conditions, moisture in the incoming air will freeze at the throttle plate area of the throttle body. Many current throttle bodies incorporate a pocket, or passage, for engine coolant to warm the body. See Figure 29–38.

Electronic Throttle Control

Most electronic throttle control systems do not use a throttle cable. An electric motor on the side of the throttle body operates the throttle plate when commanded by the PCM. An accelerator position sensor at

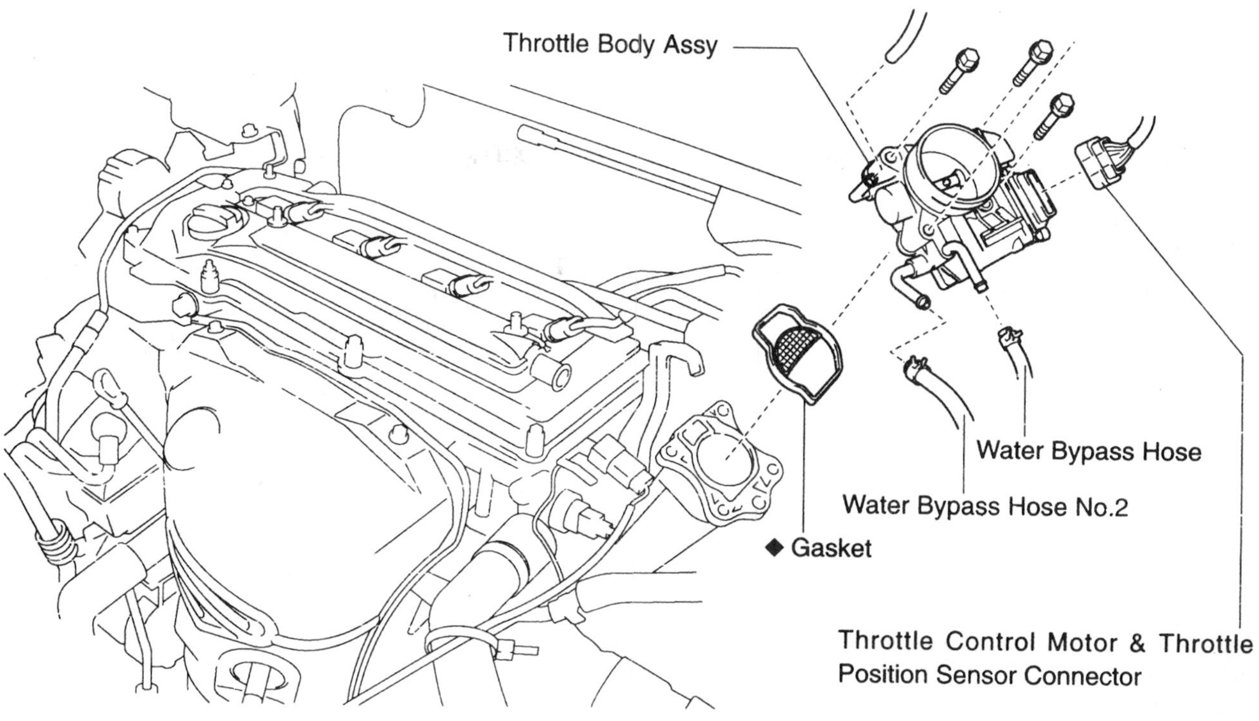

Figure 29–38 This electronic throttle body uses engine coolant to prevent throttle plate icing. Note the location of the throttle control motor and position sensor. (Courtesy Toyota Canada Inc.)

the accelerator pedal sends a signal to the PCM, which in turn, adjust the throttle motor to match the driver's input. The throttle position sensor on the throttle body sends throttle angle information to the PCM.

Electronic throttles originated with traction control systems where the computer reduces throttle opening when wheel spin is detected. Since then, it has become common with or without traction control.

Conditions of excessive RPM or engine overheating may also trigger reduced throttle opening.

Throttle Plate Contamination

The positive crankcase ventilation (PCV) system picks up ventilating air, usually between the mass airflow sensor and the throttle plate. See Figure 29–39. Crankcase fumes often backfeed into the throttle body causing a buildup of deposits at the throttle plate and bore. These deposits are normally removed during regular maintenance service or when a driveability concern is noted.

The throttle plates of a port fuel-injected engine may require cleaning, especially if the following conditions exist:

- Rough idle
- Stalling
- Surging at idle
- Hesitation during acceleration
- Higher than normal IAC counts as displayed on a scan tool.

See Figures 29–40 and 29–41.

FALSE AIR

Speed density fuel injection relies on information typically from MAP, CTS, ACT, RPM, and TPS for calculating fuel delivery. An air leak in the hose between the air cleaner and the throttle body usually will not affect driveability.

The opposite is true with mass-air systems; any air leaks could change the mass airflow sensor reading and cause hard starting and rough running. This usually occurs during open loop operation when fuel is not being trimmed by the oxygen sensor. See Figures 29–42 and 29–43.

DIESEL FUEL INJECTION

Diesel injection systems have seen many changes over the past few years, driven in part by new, more stringent emissions regulations and a call for increased economy. Earlier systems used a mechanical fuel injection pump to meter fuel delivery; however,

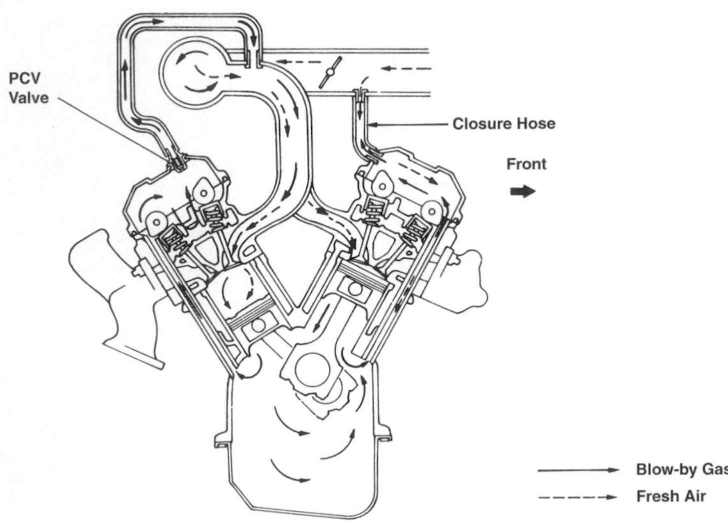

Figure 29–39 Airflow through the positive crankcase ventilation (PCV) system. Note the closure hose at the front cam cover; blow-by gases may back-flow into the air intake under certain driving conditions, i.e., full-throttle, high RPM operation. (Courtesy Toyota Canada Inc.)

(a)

(b)

Figure 29–40 (a) Dirty throttle plate. This throttle plate was so dirty that the technician removed the entire throttle body to be sure it was thoroughly cleaned. (b) Most throttle plates can be cleaned on the vehicle using a brush and throttle body cleaner. Be sure the cleaner is safe for oxygen sensors.

Figure 29–41 Some vehicles, such as this Ford, have labels on the throttle body warning not to clean the throttle plates. A slippery coating is placed on the throttle plate and throttle bore that prevents deposits from sticking. Cleaning this type of housing can remove this protective coating.

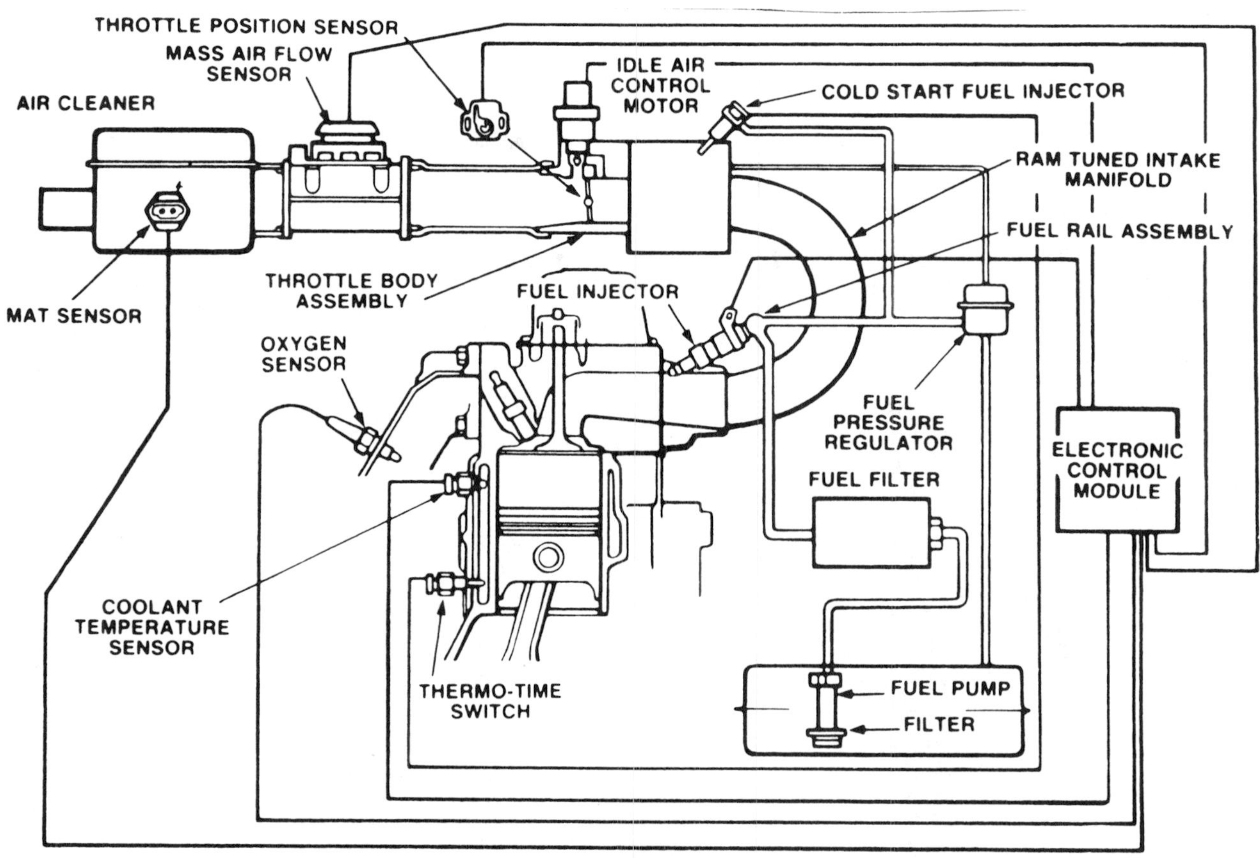

Figure 29–42 Schematic of a General Motors 2.8 litre gasoline fuel injection system with a mass airflow sensor. Many European and Asian vehicles use a cold-start fuel injector (as does this vehicle); however, cold-start injectors are not common in domestic vehicles, which typically use a major increase in injector pulse-width ("on" time) or a primer pulse (extra injector pulse) for cold engine starting. (Courtesy General Motors)

this did not allow the precise control required to meet new standards. Electronic systems were introduced in the mid to late 1990s. We will start with conventional fuel injection.

CONVENTIONAL (MECHANICAL) FUEL INJECTION

Conventional fuel injection uses, for the most part, all mechanical components. There is limited electrical use. Other than glow-plug circuits, solenoids, block heaters, and fuel heaters, fuel delivery is governed by a mechanical injection pump. See Figure 29–44. Although here are variations between makes and engine types, the following is common with most systems.

- Fuel tanks—Very similar to gasoline vehicles; multiple tanks are often used for long distance vehicles such as vans or pick-up trucks. The fuel supply line in the tank usually contains a pre-filter to limit large contaminants from entering the system.
- Lift pump—Transfers fuel from the fuel tank, through the fuel filter and on to the delivery system. This may be an electric pump or a mechanical pump driven by the engine.
- Fuel filter—Very important with a diesel engine as any small particles or abrasives that get past the filter may cause damage to the injection pump or injectors. See Figure 29–45. Hand priming pumps are often found on the fuel filter; they are used to remove trapped air from the fuel system and to force fuel to the injection pump. Many late-model systems remove air automatically.
- Water/fuel separators—Water in the fuel creates a number of driveability problems as well as system damage. Water is heavier than diesel fuel and will accumulate at the bottom of the separator, where it is drained as part of regular maintenance. Some separators have a sensor that illuminates a warning light on the instrument panel when the water reaches a given level. See Figure 29–46. Many late-model systems incorporate the fuel filter, water separator, and fuel heater in one unit.

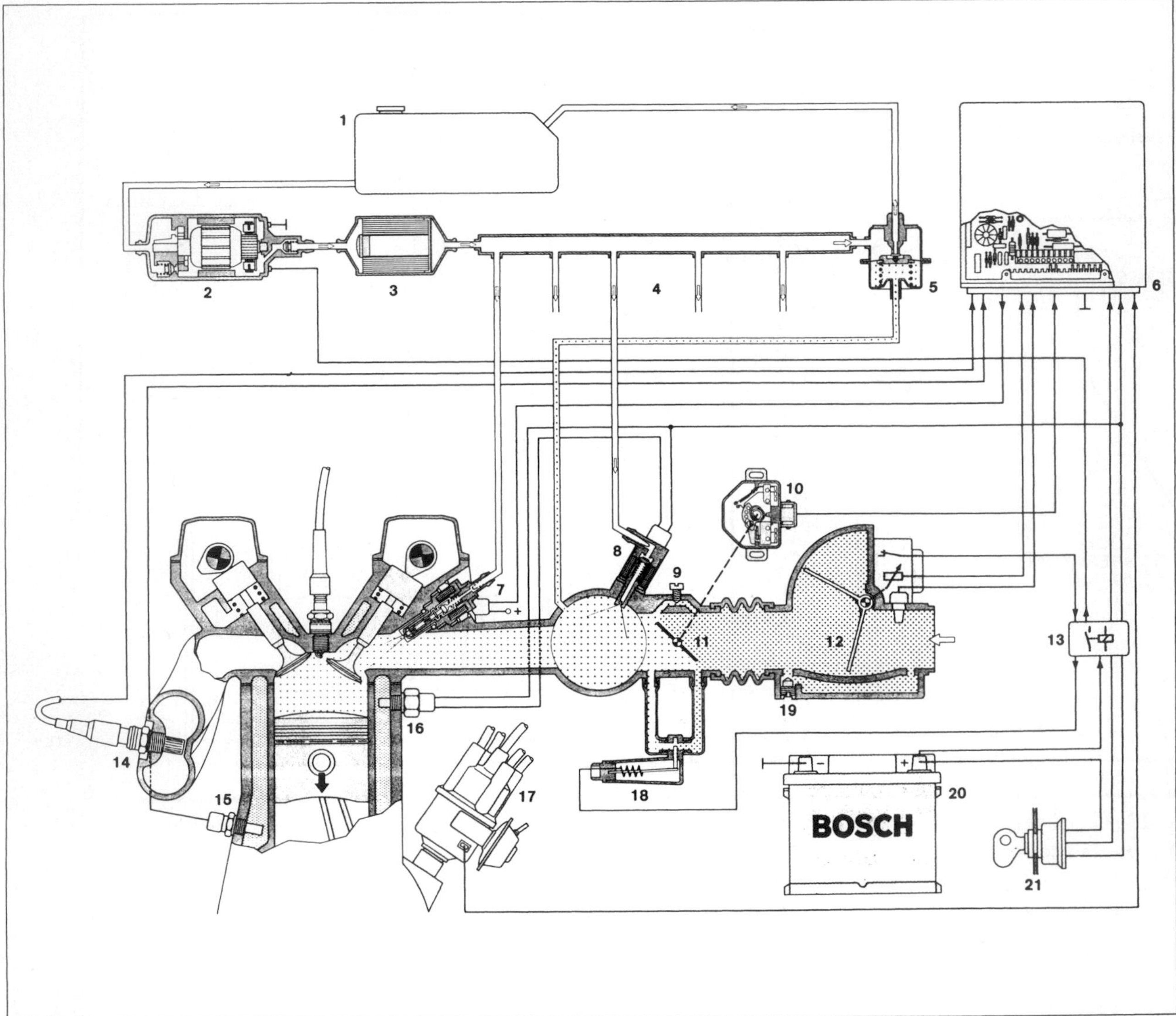

Summary of the L-Jetronic system
1 Fuel tank, 2 Electric fuel pump, 3 Fuel filter, 4 Distributor pipe, 5 Pressure regulator, 6 Control unit, 7 Injection valve, 8 Start valve, 9 Idle-speed adjusting screw, 10 Throttle-valve switch, 11 Throttle valve, 12 Air-flow sensor, 13 Relay combination, 14 Lambda sensor (only for certain countries), 15 Engine temperature sensor, 16 Thermo-time switch, 17 Ignition distributor, 18 Auxiliary-air device, 19 Idle-mixture adjusting screw, 20 Battery, 21 Ignition-starter switch

Figure 29–43 The Bosch L-Jetronic (L stands for *luft*, which is "air" in German) gasoline fuel injection system. The vane airflow sensor measures airflow, not mass. It is not as accurate as a mass air sensor, but it is a major improvement over speed-density systems. L-Jetronic injections are used on many European, Asian and some domestic vehicles from the mid-1970s to the mid-1990s. (Courtesy Robert Bosch)

- Fuel heaters—Because diesel fuel has a tendency to wax and thicken when cold, electric heaters are often used to warm the fuel. Canadian diesel fuels are also blended to match seasonal temperatures; a very light fuel is supplied for winter use.
- Fuel injection pump—Diesel fuel must be injected into the combustion chamber area at extremely high pressure, over 17 500 kPa (2500 psi), to overcome cylinder pressures.

An injection pump increases fuel pressure, controls speed and power by metering the volume of fuel injected, and directs the fuel to the correct injector. It may also contain a governor, which limits the maximum RPM of the engine, and a fuel shut-off.

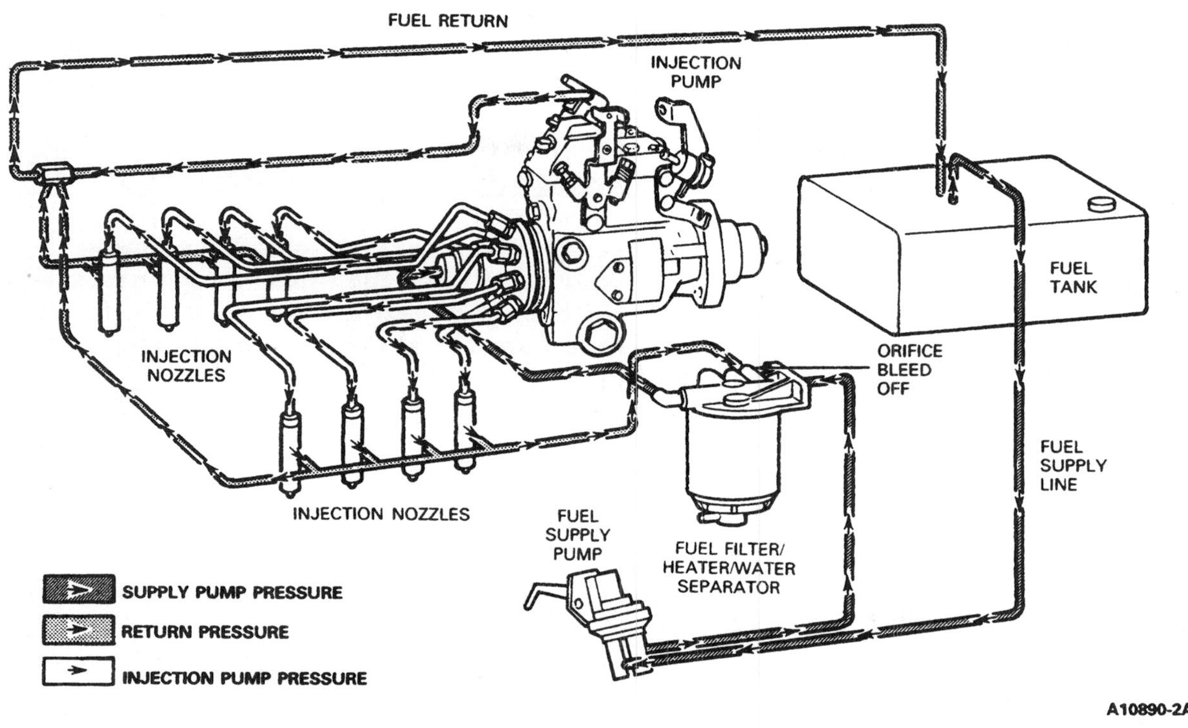

Figure 29–44 Schematic of the fuel delivery and return on a conventional (mechanical) diesel fuel injection. (Courtesy Ford Motor Co.)

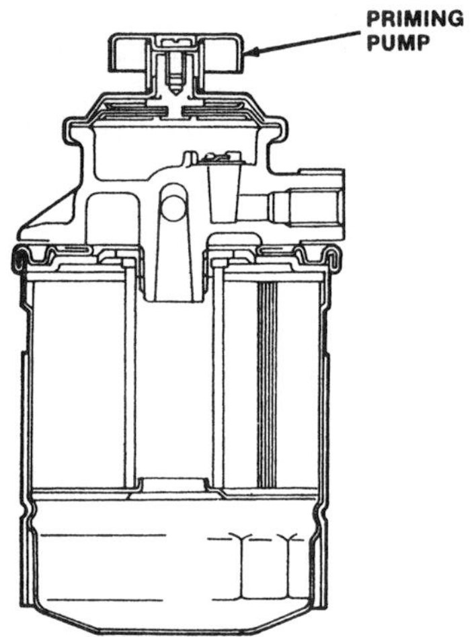

Figure 29–45 A diesel fuel filter with built-in priming pump. (Courtesy Ford Motor Co.)

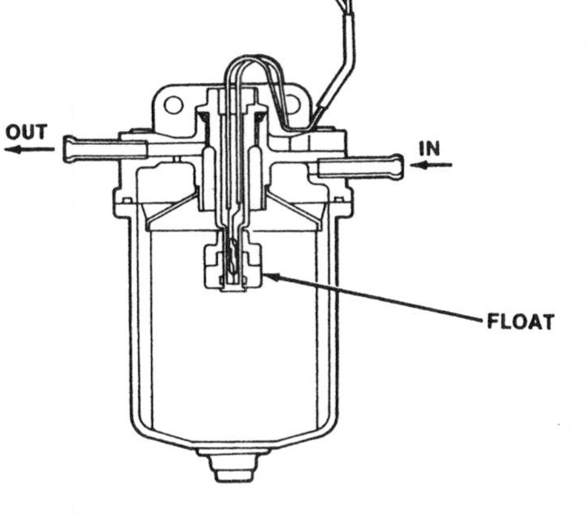

Figure 29–46 A water/fuel separator with a water level warning light. (Courtesy Ford Motor Co.)

FUEL INJECTION PUMPS

Two types of mechanical injection pumps are common with conventional systems: the in-line and the rotary.

In-line Injection Pumps (4-Cycle)

In-line pumps are usually found on large trucks and older passenger car/light truck applications. See Figure 29–47. The pump is driven at one-half the engine speed, which means the injection-pump camshaft makes one complete revolution for each two turns of the engine. When the pump cam lobe pushes up on the cam follower and plunger, the fuel above the plunger is put under very high pressure. See Figure 29–48. This high-pressure fuel opens the delivery valve spring, which allows fuel to move through steel lines to the injectors, where it is supplied to the engine. See Figure 29–49.

SAFETY TIP 

Never check for fuel leaks by running your hand over the lines—a high pressure leak could penetrate your skin, enter the blood stream and cause poisoning.

It is good practice, instead, to move a piece of light coloured cardboard along the lines, checking visually for signs of liquid fuel on the cardboard. See Figure 29–50.

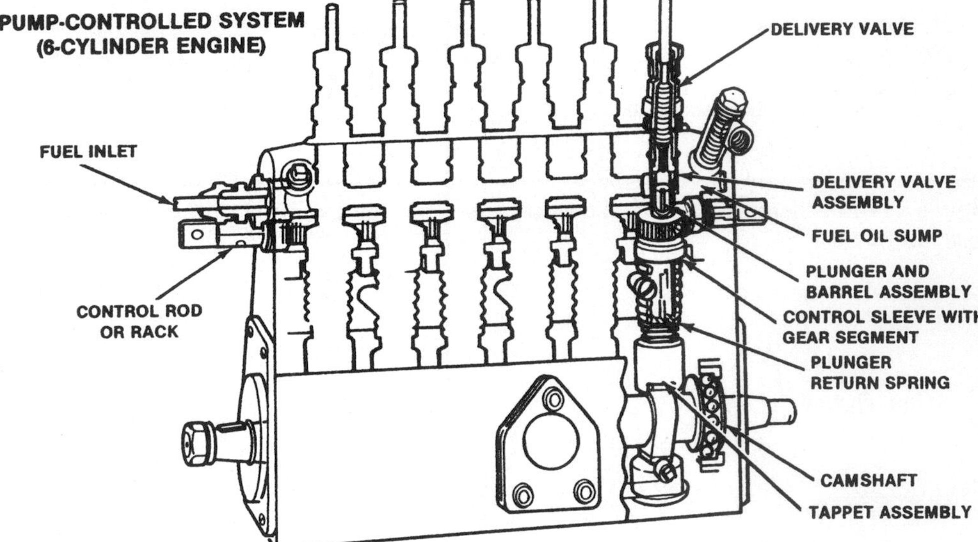

Figure 29–47 An in-line diesel injection pump. (Courtesy Ford Motor Co.)

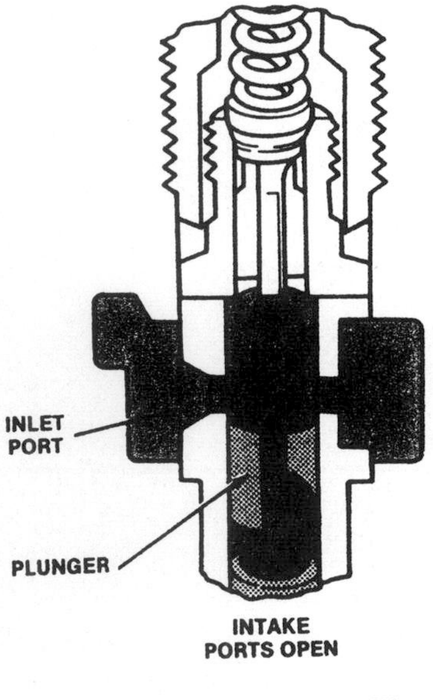

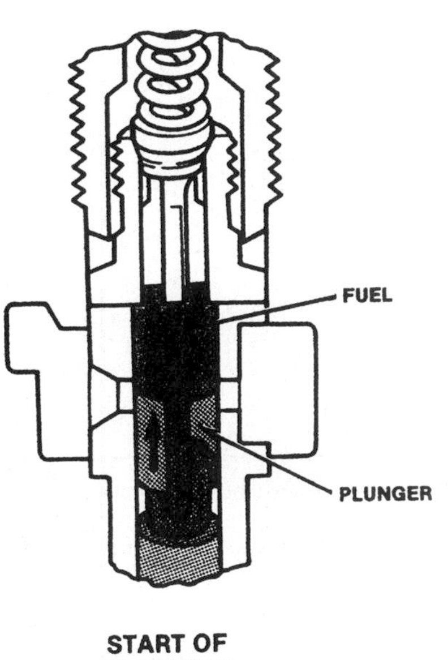

Figure 29–48 A diesel fuel injection pump: start of injection. (Courtesy Ford Motor Co.)

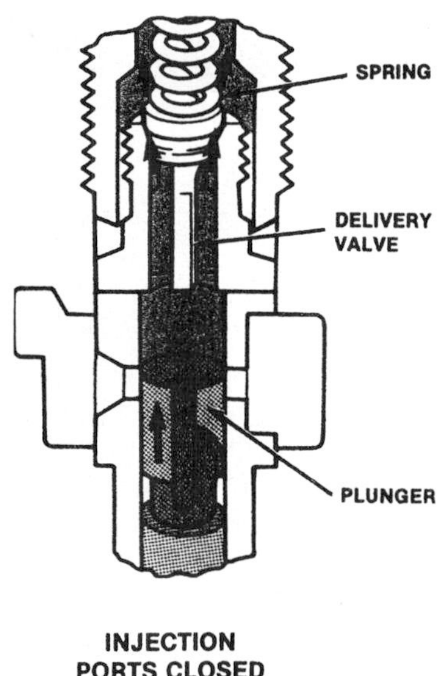

Figure 29–49 Fuel passing through the delivery valve to the injector. (Courtesy Ford Motor Co.)

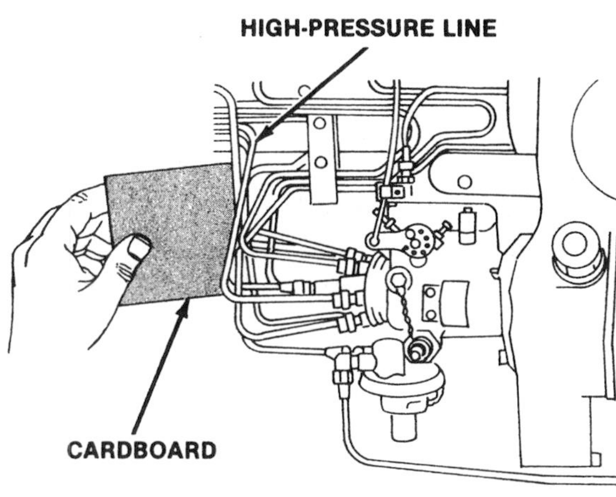

Figure 29–50 Diesel fuel leak testing. Use cardboard to test for leaks, NEVER your hand! (Courtesy Ford Motor Co.)

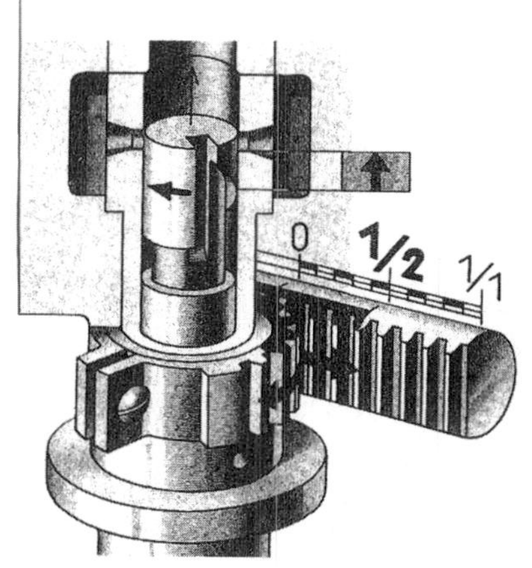

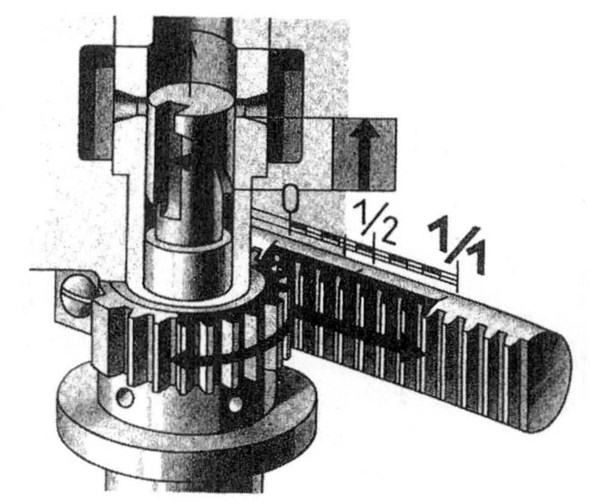

Figure 29–51 Movement of the control rack in an in-line injection pump changes the fuel delivery volume. (Courtesy Robert Bosch)

Fuel Control—In-line Injection Pump

Remember that diesels do not use a throttle plate; under most operating conditions the engine takes in far more air than it requires. Power and speed are controlled by the amount of fuel injected; more fuel equals higher speed and greater power.

Note the control rack in Figure 29–51, which is connected to the accelerator pedal. As the rack is moved in or out, it rotates a gear and control sleeve, which turns the plunger.

A tapered groove, called the helix, is machined into the plunger. This increases or decreases the amount of fuel as the plunger is rotated. The helix controls fuel volume by opening or restricting a passage to the spill port: a large opening means less fuel is left in the barrel for injection, a restricted opening leaves more fuel in the barrel and a greater volume of fuel is injected. See Figure 29–52.

Governors

Governors are usually incorporated into the fuel injection pump where engine speed is controlled by limiting the amount of fuel supplied to the injectors. The most common type of in-line pump governor uses flyweights, which are held in by spring pressure. See Figure 29–53. At higher RPM, centrifugal force causes the flyweights to move outward against the spring; this movement limits fuel-rack travel, which in turn restricts fuel delivery and prevents engine over-revving.

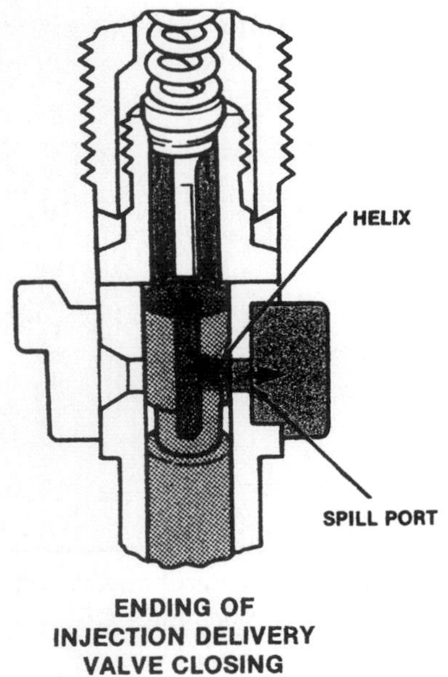

Figure 29–52 The helix controls fuel volume by varying the opening to the spill port. (Courtesy Ford Motor Co.)

Runaway Engines

A sticking governor, in extreme cases, may continue to supply fuel to the engine. This allows the RPM to build until the engine destroys itself. In order to stop the engine, turn off the fuel line shut-off valve (if equipped) or stuff rags into the air cleaner intake to shut off the air.

Diesel engine manufacturers generally caution against running the engine with the air intake hose disconnected from the intake manifold; not only could this allow dirt and foreign material to enter the engine, serious personal injury could result if a body part is pulled into the opening.

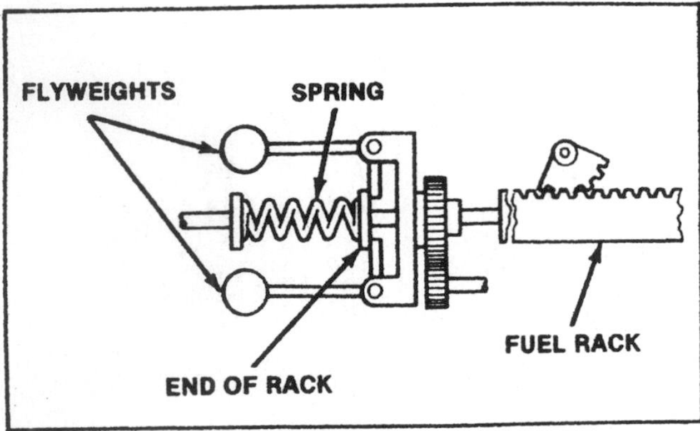

Governor operation:

Low RPM

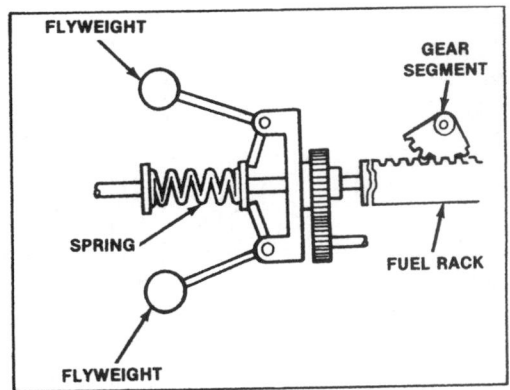

FLYWEIGHT
GEAR SEGMENT
SPRING
FUEL RACK
FLYWEIGHT

Governor operation:

High RPM

Figure 29–53 Governors control engine speed by limiting fuel at higher RPM. (Courtesy Ford Motor Co.)

ROTARY DIESEL FUEL INJECTION PUMPS

The common rotary pump, often called a distributor pump, uses a rotating motion rather than the reciprocating action of the in-line pump. Not only is the pressure of the incoming fuel raised, a controlled volume of fuel is sent to the proper cylinder. This type of pump normally contains a fuel metering valve, governor and a mechanical or electric fuel shut-off. See Figure 29–54.

Operation

Fuel enters the pump through a centre port, flows to a metering valve (controlled by the accelerator pedal and governor) and then, on to the pumping plungers where high pressure is developed. This pressurized fuel compresses the delivery spring, which now allows fuel movement to a rotor that distributes fuel to the correct injector. See Figure 29–55. Alignment of the rotor ports to the pump head determines which cylinder is being supplied with fuel. See Figure 29–56.

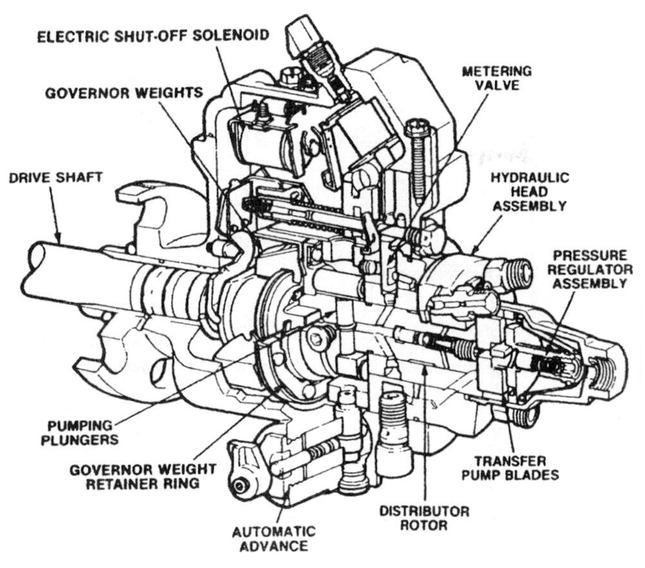

Figure 29–54 Ghost view of a rotary diesel fuel injection pump. (Courtesy General Motors)

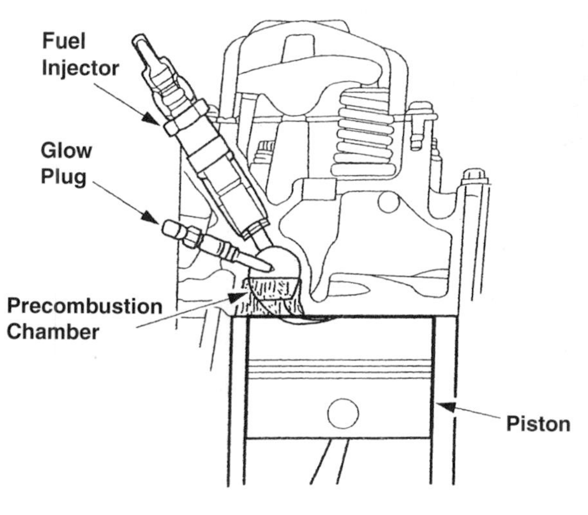

Figure 29–56 Indirect fuel injection injects fuel into a precombustion chamber. A glow plug is used to ignite the fuel during cold engine operation. (Courtesy Ford Motor Co.)

Figure 29–55 Fuel flow through a rotary pump fuel injection system. (Courtesy Ford Motor Co.)

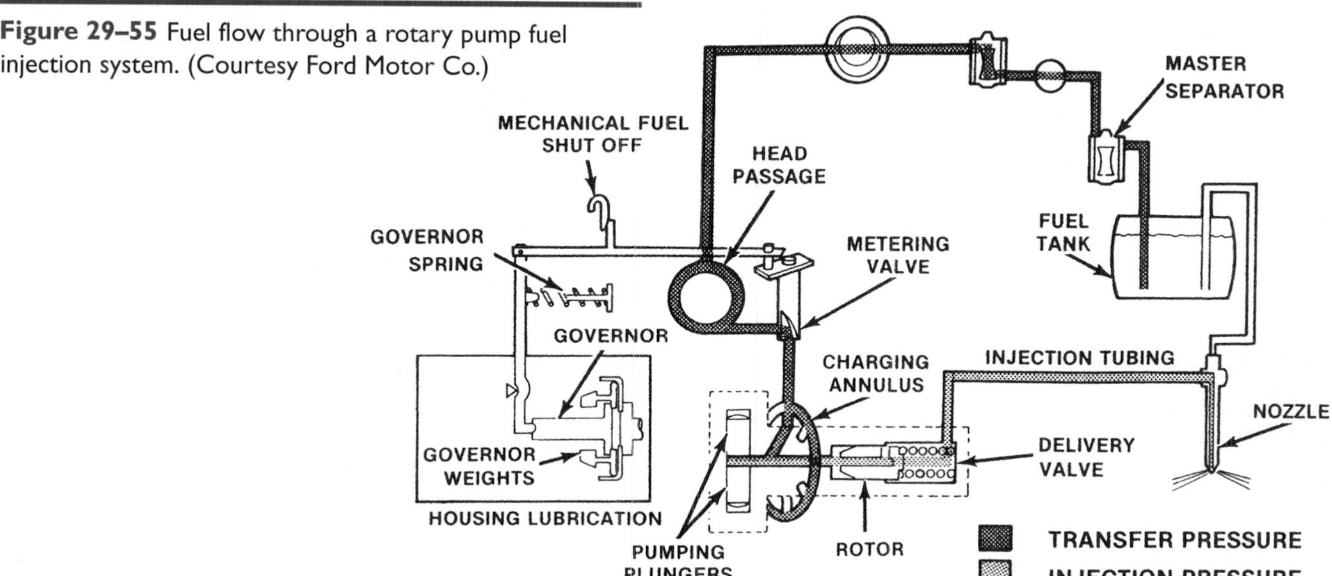

ELECTRONIC DIESEL FUEL INJECTION

EDFI more closely matches electronic gasoline fuel injection than the previous mechanical diesel injection systems. One type, the high pressure common-rail electronically controlled diesel injection, was introduced to Canada and North America in the later 1990s; pressures in this system may exceed 160 000 kPa (23 000 psi). It is used in both passenger car and light truck applications. See Figure 29–57.

Common-Rail Diesel Fuel Injection

Major components include:

- Fuel tanks
- Fuel lines
- Fuel injector control module
- Water separator
- Fuel filter
- Pump assembly
- Fuel rails
- Injectors

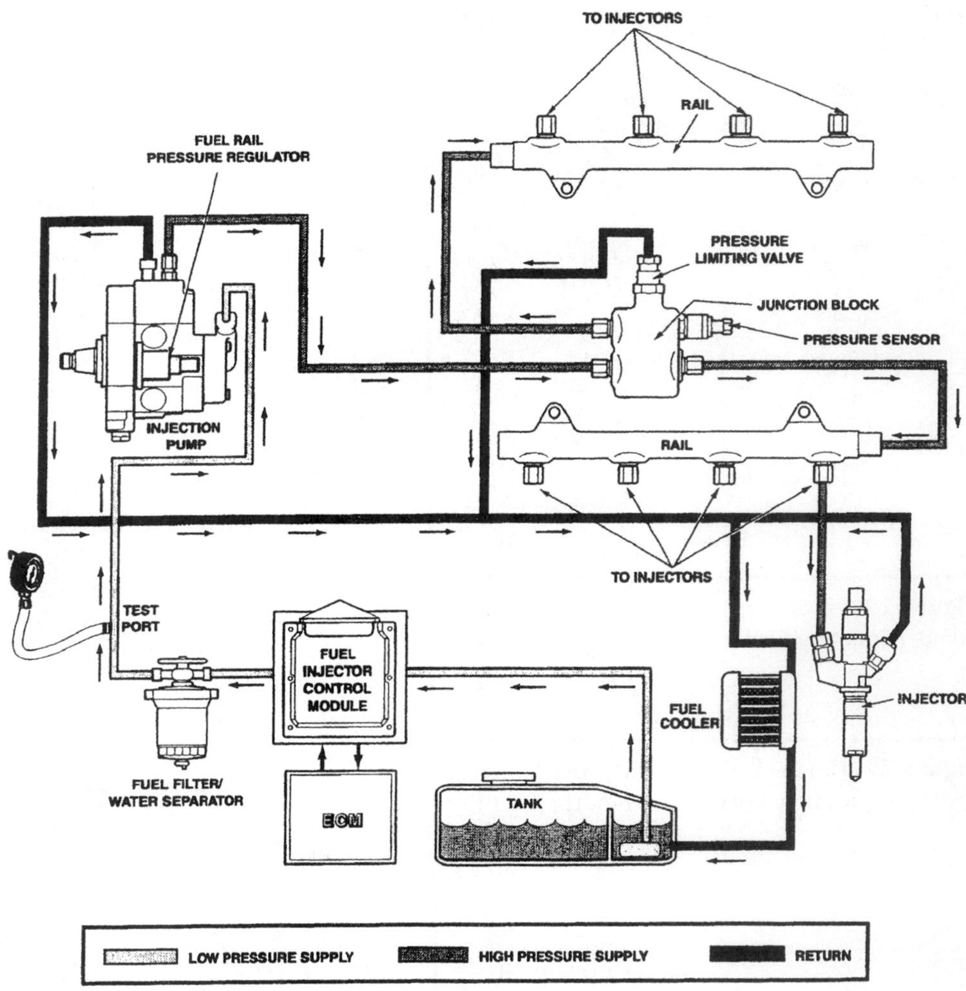

Figure 29–57 Schematic of an electronic diesel fuel injection system. (Courtesy General Motors)

Fuel Injector Control Module

Fuel delivery begins at the pick-up and pre-filter in the tank; it then flows to the base of the fuel injector control module (FICM). The module, which requires 93 volts and up to 20 amperes of current to drive the injectors, is cooled by the fuel flowing through the base. The FICM is operated by engine control module (ECM) commands.

Water Sensor-Separator/Primary Filter

Fuel continues to the WSS/PF where it is filtered; any water in the fuel is separated and collected in the lower housing. This unit may also contain an integrated hand pump used for priming and a fuel heater, which is activated in colder temperatures.

Fuel Filters

Fuel filter replacement is a common and essential service required with diesels as the typical paper element filter becomes restricted.

Injection Pump

The engine-driven fuel injection pump generates the high pressures required for system operation. It includes an ECM-controlled pressure regulator valve, which varies pump pressure with load: low pressure at idle, higher pressures with increasing engine load.

Function Block

Fuel moves from the high pressure pump to the function block, which contains both an excess-pressure limiting valve (acts as a fail-safe relief valve) and a pressure sensor, which sends fuel pressure readings to the ECM.

Common Rails

Pressurized fuel arrives at the rails which act as accumulators and reduce fuel pulsing.

Electrical Injectors

The injectors are electrical solenoids that function similarly to electronic gasoline injectors. See Figure

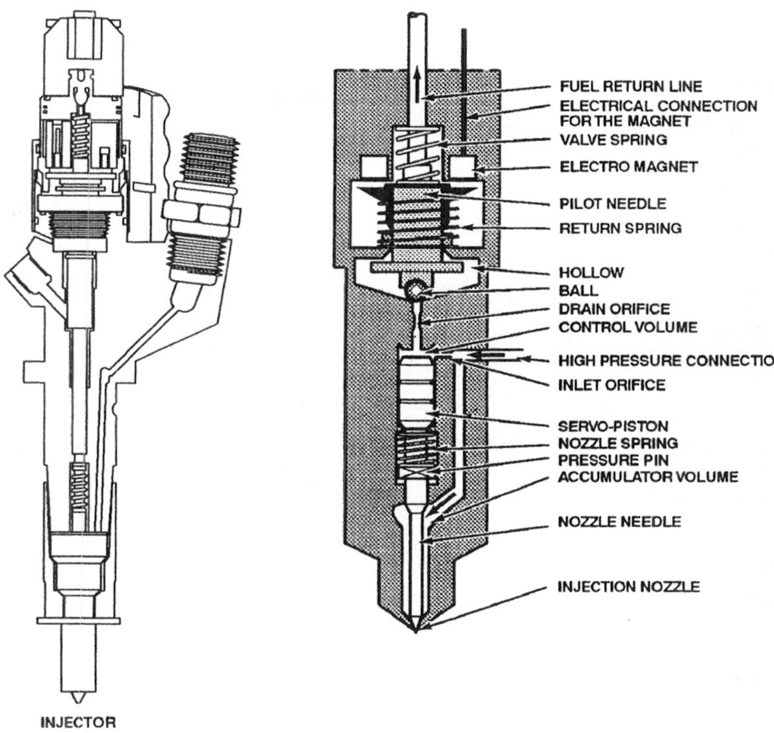

Figure 29–58 A diesel electrical fuel injector. Note the fuel return line. (Courtesy General Motors)

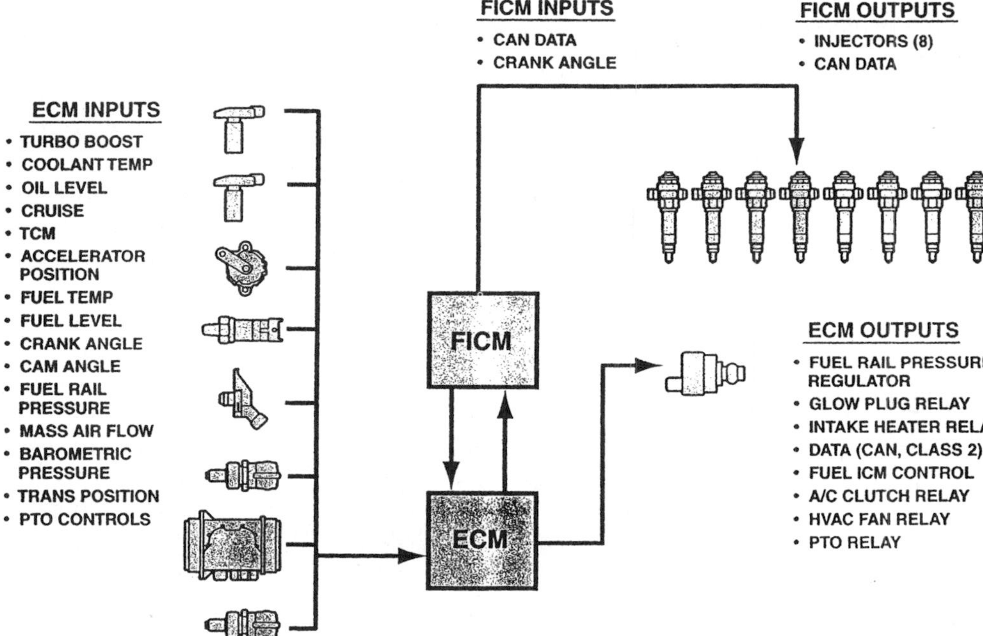

Figure 29–59. Diesel engine electronic management. Note the input sensors and the output actuators. (Courtesy General Motors)

29–58. When activated, the injector coil lifts the needle valve and fuel flows; injector fuel delivery varies with the on-time (duration) of injector opening.

DIESEL ENGINE MANAGEMENT—ECM CONTROL

The injectors are energized by an electronic control module (ECM) to begin injection. No power to the injector, no injection. The quantity of fuel delivered is determined by the on-time that the injector is held open; increasing the length of time the injector is opened increases the volume of fuel.

Major information inputs to the ECM (see Figure 29–59) would include data from the following sensors:

- Mass air flow (MAF)—Measures the intake air volume
- Intake air temperature (IAT) usually located in the MAF sensor

- Accelerator pedal position (APP)—Signals the driver's demand for speed and acceleration
- Barometric (BARO)—Senses barometric pressure for fine tuning fuel control
- Crankshaft (CKP) and camshaft (CMP) position sensors—Used to identify engine RPM and piston location

ENGINE COOLANT TEMPERATURE

Other input sensors can include fuel pressure, turbocharger (if used) boost, and fuel temperature; these vary with make and model. The ECM uses this information to control the fuel injectors and other various relays. A fuel-injector control module, managed by the ECM, may be used to supply large amounts of current to drive the injectors.

HYDRAULIC ELECTRONIC UNIT INJECTION

The HEUI system, used in some light truck applications, is unique in that it uses oil to develop the very high pressures required to inject diesel fuel. See Figure 29–60.

An engine driven high-pressure oil pump (not the lubrication pump) delivers oil to the upper end of the fuel injector. The oil, under high pressure, is blocked by a poppet valve located inside the injector. When injection is required, an electrical solenoid, controlled by the Powertrain Control Module (PCM), opens the poppet valve and oil enters the injector. This oil acts on the large upper end of a plunger, which through multiplication of force, injects fuel at pressures of 18 500 kPa (2700 psi) or higher.

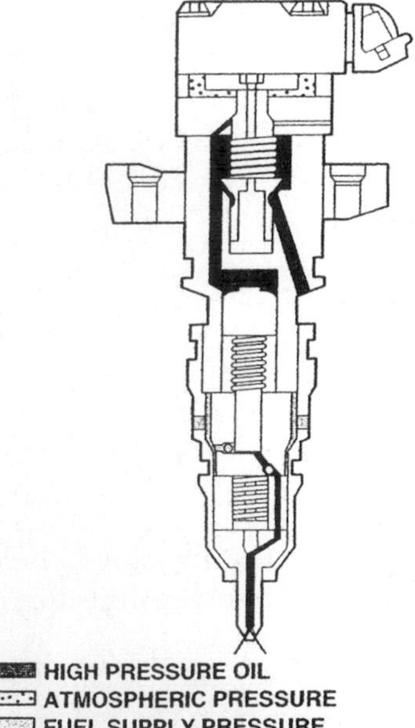

Figure 29–60 A high-pressure solenoid controlled fuel injector. (Courtesy Ford Motor Co.)

DIESEL ENGINE SERVICE

Diesel engines require normal service and maintenance for different reasons than gasoline engines: they have no ignition system, no carburetor to clean, and early diesels have limited emission controls. The following is a list of typical services that are required:

- Oil and filter change—Because of the high compression and combustion pressures, combustion residue (particulates) is blown past the piston rings and into the oil. Some diesels use two oil filters to remove contaminants.
- Fuel filter replacement—It is essential that water and foreign material are removed from the fuel, as they can damage the injection pump and injectors. Ford is now supplying a long-life fuel filter on selected models; it is incorporated into the fuel delivery module and requires no replacement or service for the life of the vehicle.
- Water drainage—Very common service; a warning light on the instrument panel may also be used to indicate excessive water in the fuel.
- Air filter replacement—Diesels take in far more air than they normally require because of no throttle plate; filters are larger than comparable displacement gasoline engines. An air filter restriction indicator may be found on the intake air hose on some models.
- Glow plug replacement—Testing of glow plugs and electrical circuits will be required for cold-start concerns.
- Compression testing—For weak piston rings and valve sealing; see Chapter 5 "Engine Condition Diagnosis" for details.
- Injection pumps and injectors—When a malfunction is noted with the pump or injectors, they are usually removed and sent to a diesel injection specialist for repair or exchange.
- The on-board computer (PCM) used with late model electronic injection, is required to monitor both engine operation and emission controls; using a scanner to access data stored in the PCM memory is also part of normal diesel service with these models.

PHOTO SEQUENCE 20 Testing a Gasoline Fuel Injector Using a Digital Storage Oscillocope

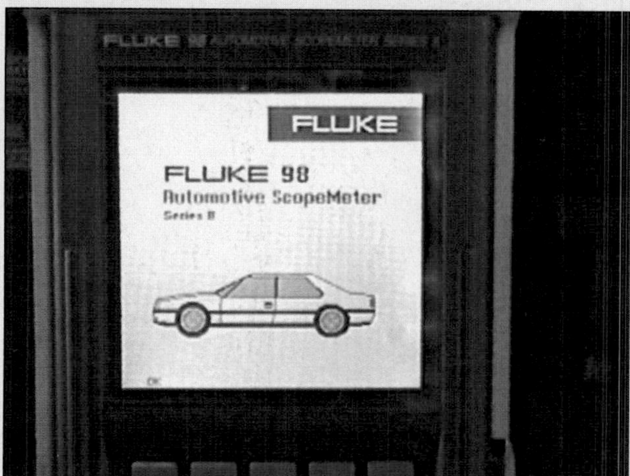

P20–1 This is the first screen you see when turning on a Fluke 98 scopemeter.

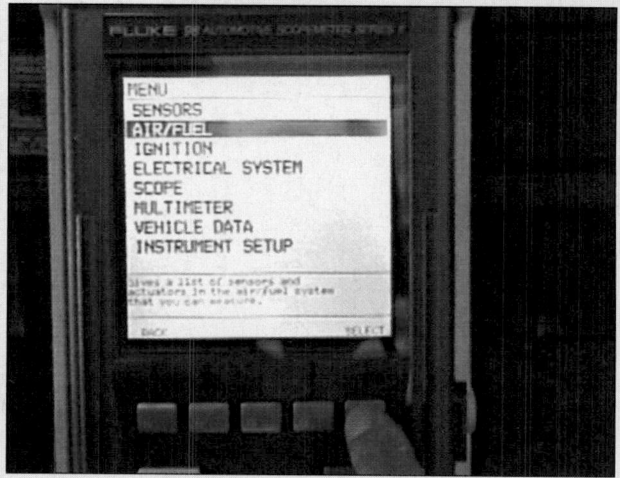

P20–2 Select "air/fuel" from the main menu.

P20–3 Select "fuel injector" from the air/fuel menu.

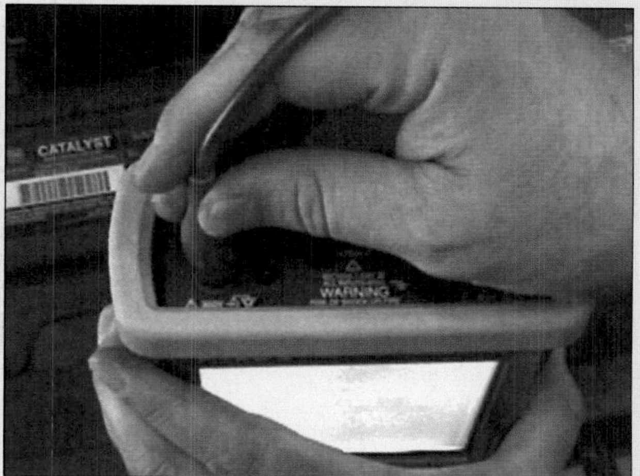

P20–4 The scopemeter will prompt you to connect the test lead into the input A terminal.

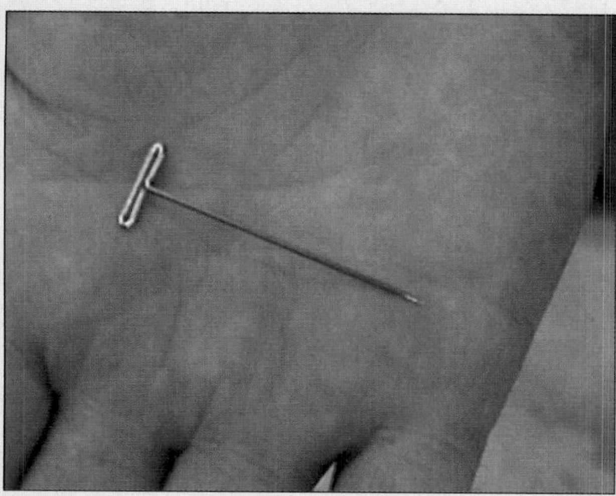

P20–5 Use a T-pin to backprobe the injector connector. These T-pins are usually available at discount stores and specialty shops in the craft area.

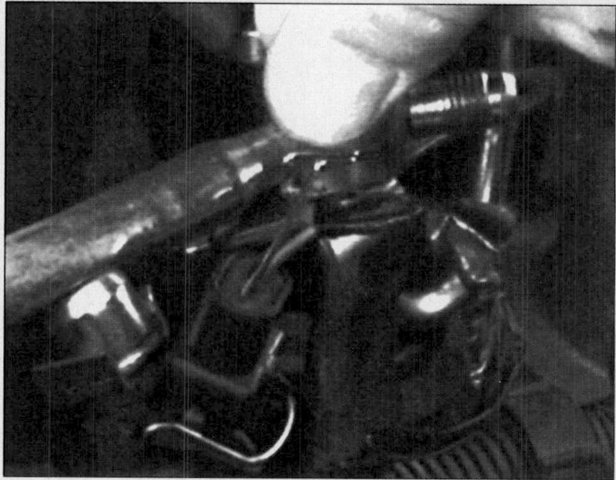

P20–6 Carefully insert the point of the T-pin into the back of the connector and lightly push on the T-pin until it contacts the metal terminal inside the connector.

Testing a Gasoline Fuel Injector Using a Digital Storage Oscillocope—continued

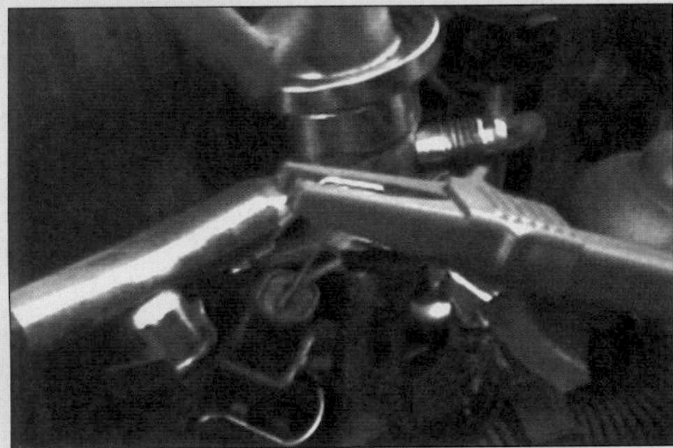

P20–7 Attach the test probe from the scopemeter to the T-pin.

P20–8 Attach the ground test lead to a good, clean engine ground.

P20–9 Start the engine.

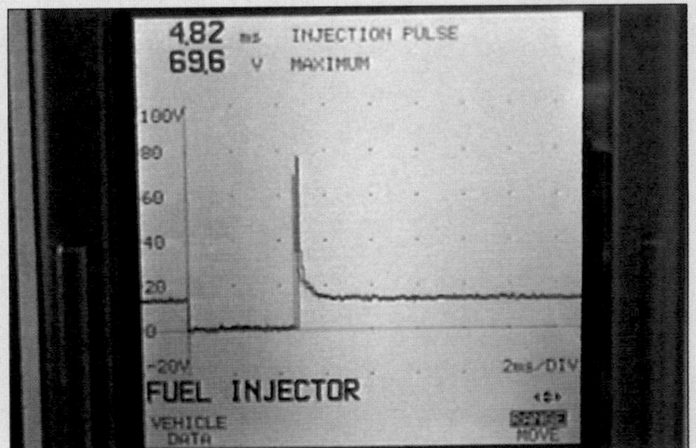

P20–10 Observe the waveform. If the waveform does not look similar to this, insert the T-pin into the other terminal of the connector. To achieve this pattern, the scopemeter should be connected to the terminal that is being pulsed on and off by the computer. The pulse width is longer than normal in this photo because the engine is cold and the computer is pulsing the injector on for a longer time to provide the engine with additional fuel.

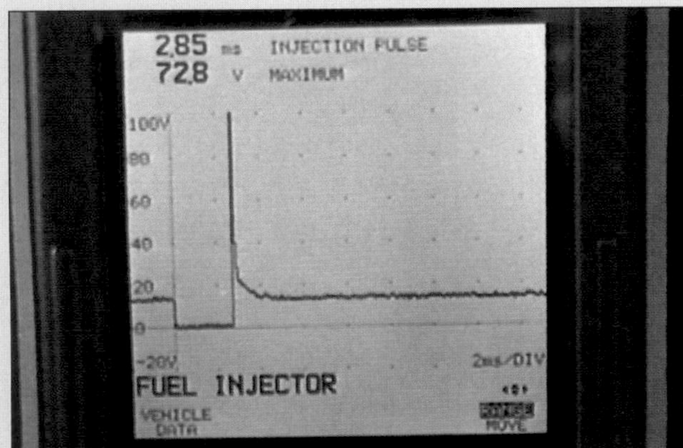

P20–11 Note the shortened pulse width compared to the previous photo. The engine is now at normal operating temperature and the injector pulse width should be 1.5 to 3.5 milliseconds. Also look for consistent inductive voltage spikes for all injectors, indicating that the injector coil is not shorted.

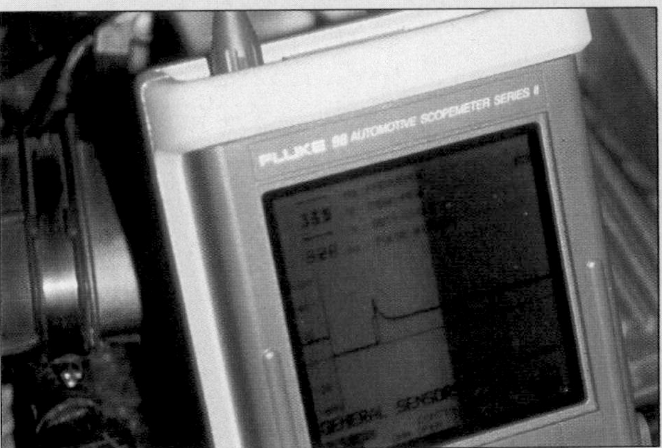

P20–12 Turn the engine off and disconnect the scopemeter.

SUMMARY

1. A typical throttle-body fuel injector uses a computer-controlled injector solenoid to spray fuel into the throttle-body unit above the throttle plates.
2. A typical port fuel-injection system uses an individual fuel injector for each cylinder and squirts fuel directly into the intake manifold about 75 mm (3 in.) from the intake valve.
3. Most electric fuel pumps can be tested for pressure, volume, and current flow.
4. A typical port fuel-injection system fuel pressure should not drop more than 140 kPa (20 psi) in 20 minutes.
5. A noid light can be used to check for the presence of an injector pulse.
6. Injectors can be tested for resistance and should be within 0.3 to 0.4 ohms of each other.
7. Different designs of injectors have different scope waveform depending on how the computer pulses the injector on and off.
8. An idle air-control unit controls idle speed and can be tested for proper operation using a scan tool or scope.
9. Conventional diesel fuel injection controls fuel delivery at the injection pump.
10. Scan tools are used to diagnose electronic diesel injection systems.

REVIEW QUESTIONS

1. List the ways fuel injectors can be tested.
2. Describe how to test an electric fuel pump.
3. List the steps necessary to test a fuel pressure regulator.
4. Explain why some vehicle manufacturers warn about using fuel-injector cleaner.
5. Describe why it may be necessary to clean the throttle plate of a port-injected engine.
6. Describe the operation of a conventional diesel injection system.
7. Explain the operation of an electronic diesel injection system.

RED SEAL CERTIFICATION-TYPE QUESTIONS

1. How much fuel pressure should most late-model port-injected engines be able to supply?
   a. 70 kPa (10 psi)
   b. 210 kPa (30 psi)
   c. 350 kPa (50 psi)
   d. 525 kPa (75 psi)
2. Fuel injectors can be tested using
   a. A cylinder balance test
   b. An ammeter
   c. Visual inspection
   d. An ohmmeter
3. Throttle body fuel-injection systems deliver fuel _____.
   a. Directly into the cylinder
   b. In the intake manifold, near the intake valve
   c. Above the throttle plate of the throttle-body unit
   d. Below the throttle plate of the throttle-body unit
4. Port fuel-injection systems deliver fuel _____.
   a. Directly into the cylinder
   b. In the intake manifold, near the intake valve
   c. Above the throttle plate of the throttle-body unit
   d. Below the throttle plate of the throttle-body unit
5. The vacuum hose was removed from a vacuum-modulated fuel pressure regulator and gasoline dripped from the hose. This could indicate a
   a. Leaking fuel injector
   b. Restricted return line
   c. Vacuum leak at the regulator hose
   d. Leaking pressure regulator diaphragm
6. Fuel pressure drops rapidly when the engine is turned off. This is normal on some TBI injection systems where the pressure regulator is equipped with _____.
   a. A vacuum line
   b. High-pressure fuel injectors
   c. A bleed orifice
   d. A fuel pressure sensor
7. In a typical port-injection system, the fuel pressure is regulated _____.
   a. By a regulator located on the fuel return side of the fuel rail
   b. By a regulator located on the pressure side of the fuel rail
   c. By the computer by pulsing the regulator on and off
   d. With the one-way check valve in the fuel pump
8. The airflow sensor plate on a K-Jetronic fuel injection system contacts the control plunger. As the plunger moves up, the mixture
   a. Becomes richer
   b. Shuts off because of high RPM
   c. Does not change
   d. Becomes leaner
9. Returnless fuel injection cycles excess fuel at the pressure regulator in/on the _____.
   a. Fuel rail
   b. TBI throttle body
   c. Fuel tank
   d. Fuel rail return line
10. Runaway diesel engines (with conventional injection) may be stopped by turning off the fuel line shut-off valve or by
    a. Tapping lightly on the injection pump
    b. Clamping the low-pressure supply line
    c. Opening the water separator drain
    d. Stuffing rags into the air intake

30

Emission Control Device Operation, Diagnosis, and Service

OBJECTIVES: After studying Chapter 30, you should be able to:

1. Prepare for the interprovincial Red Seal certification examination in Appendix VIII (Engine Performance) on the topics covered in this chapter.
2. Describe how the PCV system operates and how to diagnose a fault with the system.
3. List two methods for diagnosing problems with the AIR system.
4. Describe how the evaporative emission control system works and how to test for its proper operation.
5. Discuss the purpose and function of the EGR system and how to diagnose EGR operational problems.
6. Explain how to test a catalytic converter for obstructions and operating efficiency.
7. Describe the operation of a hybrid vehicle.
8. Explain the electrochemical reaction inside a fuel cell.

AIR POLLUTION AND EMISSIONS CONTROL

Motor vehicles are major contributors to air pollution, which causes a number of health-related and environmental concerns. High concentrations of contaminants and smog were first noted in larger cities, usually in areas with limited air movement.

Automobile manufacturers, in cooperation with the federal government, began researching the causes and effects of vehicle emissions in the early 1960s. They determined that there are three main sources of automobile emissions:

- Exhaust emissions - HC, CO and NO_x
- Crankcase vapours - HC
- Fuel evaporation - HC

The factory installation of emission-control systems first started with California vehicles in 1961; Canada and the remaining U.S. states joined in a few years later. Federal laws were enacted to ensure that all automobiles, domestic and imported, must meet federal control standards before being offered for sale in Canada and the U.S.

MAJOR POLLUTANTS

- **Hydrocarbons (HC).** Gasoline is made of hydrocarbons, which are consumed in the engine during the combustion process. Any condition that causes a misfire (or poor combustion) will raise HC levels. Ignition problems, very lean mixtures, and vacuum leaks are major causes of high HC. Fuel arrives at the engine as a hydrocarbon; if it leaves as unburned fuel, it's still a hydrocarbon.
- **Carbon monoxide (CO)** is formed when there is insufficient oxygen during combustion. CO is formed when one carbon atom from the fuel combines with one oxygen atom from the air. High CO readings are usually the result of an overly rich mixture.

  CO is a poisonous gas that kills by replacing the oxygen in red blood cells. Never run an engine inside without fitting adequate exhaust extraction hoses.
- **Oxides of nitrogen (NO_x)** are formed when nitrogen and oxygen from the air combine at

Figure 30–1 Smog is ground-level ozone that looks like either smoke or fog.

very high temperatures; major NO_x formation begins at temperatures above 1390°C (2500°F). Any condition that raises combustion chamber temperatures will increase NO_x, e.g., lean air-fuel mixtures, over-advanced ignition timing, and malfunctioning exhaust gas recirculation (EGR) systems.

- **Particulates,** composed mainly of carbon, are a major pollutant with diesel engines. The black smoke from a diesel under acceleration is usually caused by a rich air-fuel mixture or a restricted air cleaner.

SMOG

The common term used to describe air pollution is **smog,** a word that combines the two words *sm*oke and *fog*. See Figure 30–1. Smog is formed in the atmosphere when sunlight combines with unburned fuel (hydrocarbon, or HC) and oxides of nitrogen (NO_x) produced during the combustion process. Smog is ground-level ozone (O_3), a strong irritant to the lungs and eyes.

NOTE: Although upper-atmospheric ozone is desirable because it blocks out harmful ultraviolet rays from the sun, ground-level ozone is considered to be unhealthy smog.

CONTROL OF EMISSIONS

- **HC (unburned hydrocarbons).** Excessive HC emissions (unburned fuel) are controlled by the evaporative system (charcoal canister), the positive crankcase ventilation (PCV) system, the air-pump system, and the catalytic converter.

Figure 30–2 Notice the reddish-brown haze that is often seen over major cities.

- **CO (carbon monoxide).** Excessive CO emissions are controlled by the PCV system, the air-pump system, and the catalytic converter.
- **NO_x (oxides of nitrogen).** Excessive NO_x emissions are controlled by the exhaust gas recirculation (EGR) system and the catalytic converter. An oxide of nitrogen (NO) is a colourless, tasteless, and odourless gas when it leaves the engine, but as soon as it reaches the atmosphere and mixes with more oxygen, nitrogen oxides (NO_2) are formed, which appear as reddish-brown. See Figure 30–2.
- **Particulates.** Excessive particulate emissions are controlled (on very recent diesels) with electronic fuel injection and new catalytic converters designed to eliminate particulate matter.

HINT: Exhaust emissions depend on the condition of the engine, ignition system, and fuel system as well as the proper operation of exhaust emission-control devices. Proper vehicle maintenance, including regular oil and oil filter, air filter, and fuel filter changes and other scheduled service, contributes to the ability of the engine to operate properly and produce the lowest possible emissions.

POSITIVE CRANKCASE VENTILATION (PCV) SYSTEM

Most engines remove blow-by gases from the crankcase with a **positive crankcase ventilation (PCV)** system. This system pulls crankcase vapours

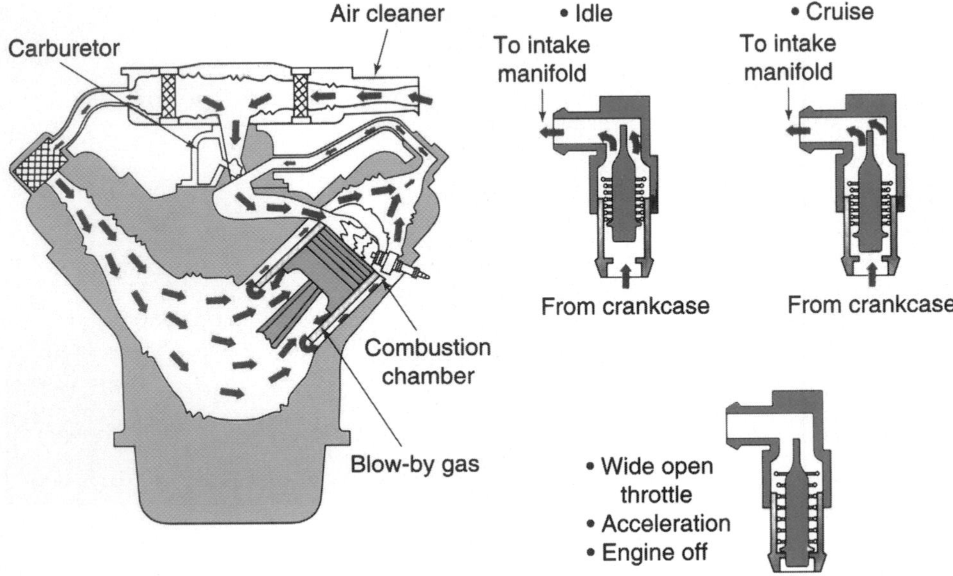

Figure 30–3 A positive crankcase ventilation (PCV) system includes a hose from the air-cleaner assembly so that filtered air can be drawn into the crankcase. This filtered air is then drawn by engine vacuum through the PCV valve and into the intake manifold, where the crankcase fumes are burned in the cylinder. The PCV valve controls and limits this flow of air and fumes into the engine. The valve shuts in the event of a backfire to prevent flames from entering the crankcase area. (Courtesy of Chrysler Corporation)

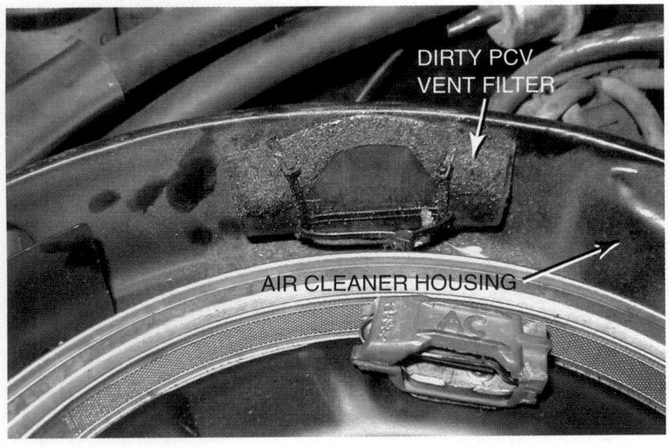

Figure 30–4 A dirty PCV vent filter inside the air cleaner housing. The air enters the crankcase through this filter and then is drawn into the engine through the PCV valve.

into the intake manifold, where they are sent to the cylinders with the intake charge. The vapours are then burned in the combustion chamber. Under some operating conditions, the blow-by gases are forced back through the inlet filter. See Figure 30–3.

NOTE: A blocked or plugged PCV system is a major cause of high oil consumption, and contributes to many oil leaks. Before expensive engine repairs are attempted, check the condition of the PCV system. See Figure 30–4.

TECH TIP 

Check for Oil Leaks with the Engine Off

The owner of an older vehicle equipped with a V-6 engine complained to his technician that he smelled burning oil, but only *after* shutting off the engine. The technician found that the rocker cover gaskets were leaking. But why did the owner only notice the smell of hot oil when the engine was shut off? Because of the positive crankcase ventilation (PCV) system, engine vacuum tends to draw oil away from gasket surfaces. But when the engine stops, engine vacuum disappears and the oil remaining in the upper regions of the engine will tend to flow down and out through any opening. Therefore, a good technician should check an engine for oil leaks not only with the engine running but also shortly after shut-down.

PCV System Performance Check

A properly operating positive crankcase ventilation system should be able to draw vapours from the crankcase and into the intake manifold. If the pipes, hoses, and PCV valve itself are not restricted, vacuum is applied to the crankcase. A slight vacuum is created in the crankcase (usually less than 25 mm [1 in.] Hg if measured at the dipstick) and is also applied to other areas of the engine. Oil drainback

Figure 30–5 A typical positive crankcase ventilation (PCV) valve. A defective or clogged PCV valve or hose can cause a rough idle or stalling problem. Because the airflow through the PCV valve accounts for about 20% of the air needed by the engine at idle, use of the incorrect valve for an application could have a severe effect on idle quality.

Figure 30–6 A typical PCV valve installed in a rubber grommet in the valve cover.

holes provide a path for oil to drain back into the oil pan. These holes also allow crankcase vacuum to be applied under the cam or rocker covers and in the valley area of most V-type engines. There are several methods that can be used to test a PCV system.

The Rattle Test

The rattle test is performed by simply removing the PCV valve and shaking it in your hand. See Figure 30–5.

- If the PCV valve does *not* rattle, it is definitely defective and must be replaced.
- If the PCV valve *does* rattle, it does not necessarily mean that the PCV valve is good. All PCV valves contain springs that can become weaker with age and heating and cooling cycles. Replace any PCV valve with the *exact* replacement according to vehicle manufacturers' recommended intervals, usually every 3 years or 60 000 km (36 000 miles).

The Card Test

Remove the oil-fill cap (usually in the valve cover) and start the engine. See Figure 30–6.

> **NOTE:** Use care on some overhead camshaft engines. With the engine running, oil may be sprayed from the open oil fill opening.

Hold a 75 × 125 mm (3 × 5 in.) card over the opening (any other piece of paper can be used for this test).

- If the PCV system, including the valve and hoses, is functioning correctly, the card should be held down on the oil-fill opening by the slight vacuum inside the crankcase.
- If the card will not stay, carefully inspect the PCV valve, hose(s), and manifold vacuum port for carbon build-up (restriction). Clean or replace as necessary.

> **NOTE:** On some 4-cylinder engines, the card may vibrate on the oil fill opening when the engine is running at idle speed. This is normal because of the longer time intervals between intake strokes on a 4-cylinder engine.

The Snap-Back Test

The proper operation of the PCV valve can be checked by placing a finger over the inlet hole in the valve when the engine is running and removing the finger rapidly. Repeat several times. The valve should "snap back." If the valve does not snap back, replace the valve.

AIR PUMP SYSTEM

An air pump provides the air necessary for the oxidizing process inside the catalytic converter. See Figure 30–7.

> **NOTE:** This system is commonly called AIR, meaning **air injection reaction.** Therefore, an AIR pump does pump air.

On late model systems, a computer controls the airflow from the pump by switching on and off various solenoid valves. When the engine is cold, the air pump output is directed to the exhaust manifold to

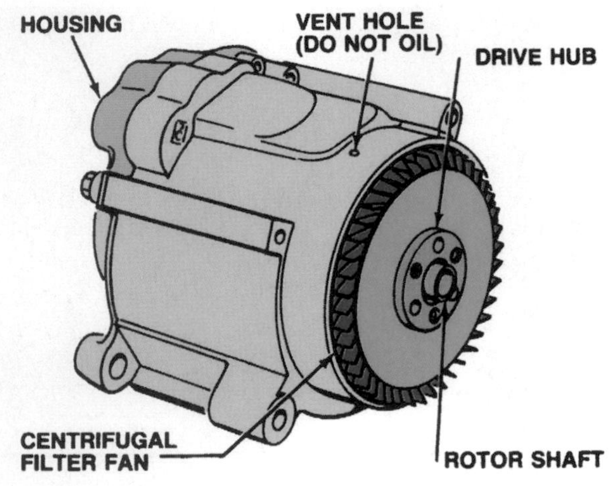

Figure 30–7 A typical belt-driven air pump. Air enters through the revolving fins. These fins act as a moving air filter because dirt is heavier than air and therefore the dirt in the air is deflected off the fins at the same time the air is drawn into the pump.

help provide enough oxygen to convert HC (unburned gasoline) and CO (carbon monoxide) to H_2O (water) and CO_2 (carbon dioxide). This also helps to heat the exhaust gas oxygen sensor. When the engine becomes warm and the engine is operating in closed loop, the computer operates the air valves to direct the air pump output to the catalytic converter. When the vacuum rapidly increases (above the normal idle level), as during rapid deceleration, the computer diverts the air pump output to the air cleaner assembly to silence the air. Diverting the air to the air cleaner prevents exhaust backfire during deceleration. See Figure 30–8. Three basic types of air pump are the belt-driven air pump, the pulse air-driven air pump, and the electric motor-driven air pump. All air-pump systems use one-way check valves to allow air to flow into the exhaust manifold and to prevent the hot exhaust from flowing into the valves on the air pump itself.

NOTE: These check valves commonly fail, resulting in excessive exhaust emissions (CO especially). When the check valve fails, hot exhaust can travel up to and destroy the switching valve(s) and air pump.

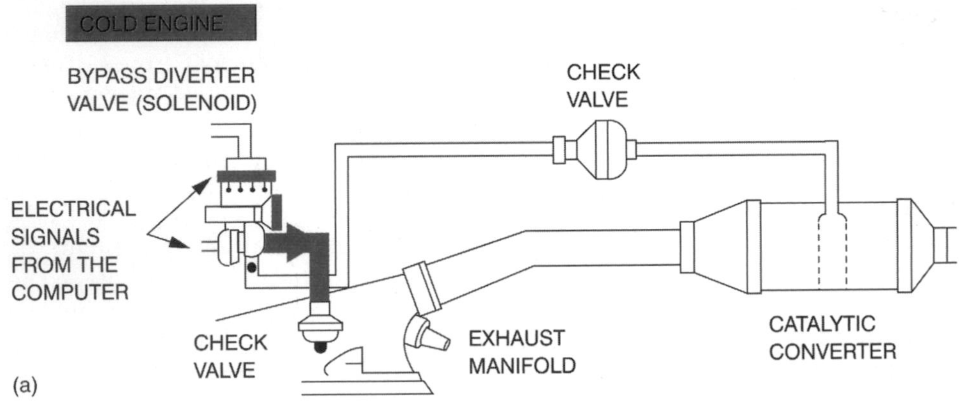

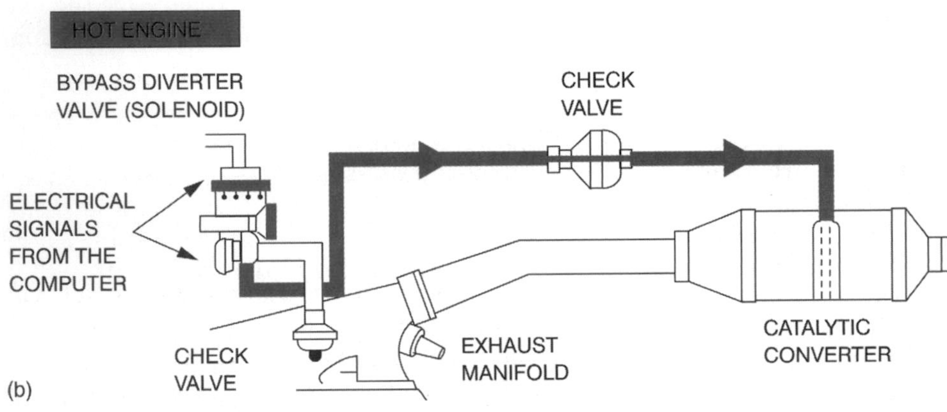

Figure 30–8 (a) When the engine is cold and before the oxygen sensor is hot enough to reach closed loop, the airflow is directed to the exhaust manifold(s) through one-way check valve(s). These valves keep exhaust gases from entering the switching solenoids and the air pump. (b) When the engine achieves closed loop, the airflow from the pump is directed to the check valve and catalytic converter.

Figure 30–9 A typical belt-driven air pump.

Belt-Driven Air Pumps

The belt-driven air pump uses a centrifugal filter just behind the drive pulley. As the pump rotates, underhood air is drawn into the pump and slightly compressed. See Figure 30–9. The air is then directed to

- The exhaust manifold when the engine is cold to help oxidize CO and HC into carbon dioxide (CO_2) and water vapour (H_2O)
- The catalytic converter on many models to help provide the extra oxygen needed for the efficient conversion of CO and HC into CO_2 and H_2O
- The air cleaner during deceleration or wide-open throttle (WOT) engine operation (see Figure 30–10)

Electric Motor-Driven Air Pumps

This style of pump is generally used only during cold engine operation.

Pulse Air Devices

The exhaust ports are normally under pressure from the burned exhaust leaving the cylinder. When the exhaust valve closes, the velocity of the escaping exhaust creates a vacuum in the port. This vacuum is used to draw fresh air from the air cleaner into the exhaust port. A one-way check valve prevents exhaust gases from reversing into the air cleaner when the exhaust valve opens and pressure returns. See Figure 30–11. Pulse air systems cannot be used with oxygen sensors.

Air Pump System Diagnosis

The air pump system should be inspected if an exhaust emissions test failure occurs. In some cases, the exhaust will enter the air cleaner assembly, resulting in a rough running engine because the extra exhaust displaces the oxygen needed for proper combustion. With the engine running, check for normal operation:

Engine Operation	Normal Operation of a Typical Air Injection Reaction (AIR) Pump System
Cold engine (open-loop operation)	Air is diverted to the exhaust manifold(s) or cylinder head
Warm engine (closed-loop operation)	Air is diverted to the catalytic converter
Deceleration	Air is diverted to the air cleaner assembly
Wide-open throttle	Air is diverted to the air cleaner assembly

Visual Inspection

Carefully inspect all air injection reaction (AIR) system hoses and pipes. Any pipes that leak air or exhaust require replacement. The check valve(s) should be checked when a pump has become inoperative. Exhaust gases could have leaked past the check valve and damaged the pump. Exhaust gas in the air cleaner is usually an indication of a leaking check valve. Check the drive belt on an engine-driven pump for wear and proper tension.

Four-Gas Exhaust Analysis

An AIR system can be easily tested using an exhaust gas analyzer. Follow these steps:

1. Start the engine and allow it to run until normal operating temperature is achieved.
2. Connect the analyzer probe to the tail pipe and observe the exhaust readings for hydrocarbons (HC) and carbon monoxide (CO).
3. Using the appropriate pinch-off pliers, shut off the airflow from the AIR system. Observe the HC and CO readings. If the AIR system is working correctly, the HC and CO should increase when the AIR system is shut off.
4. Record the O_2 reading with the AIR system still inoperative. Unclamp the pliers and watch the O_2 readings. If the system is functioning correctly, the O_2 level should increase by 1 to 4%.

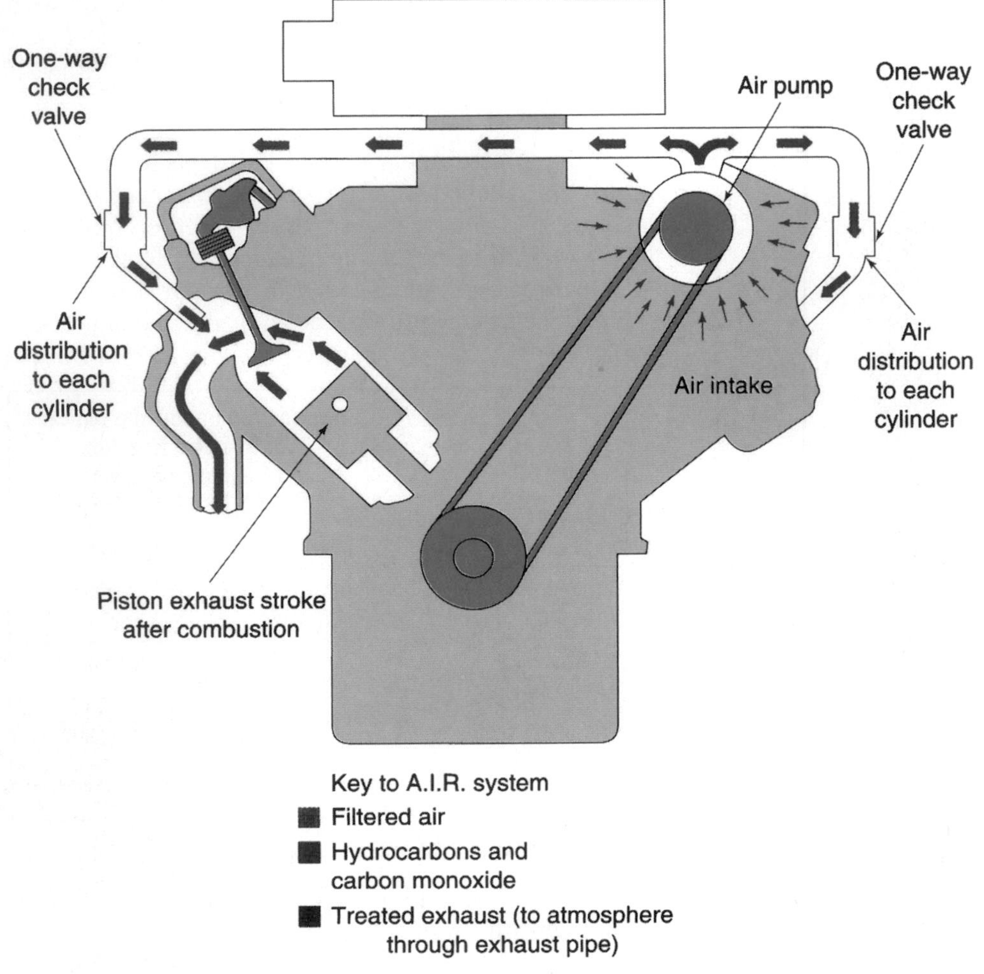

Figure 30–10 The air pump supplies air to the exhaust port of each cylinder. Unburned hydrocarbons (HC) are oxidized into carbon dioxide (CO_2) and water (H_2O), and carbon monoxide (CO) is converted to carbon dioxide (CO_2).

Figure 30–11 Cutaway of a pulse air-driven air device. It is used on many older engines to deliver air to the exhaust port through the use of the exhaust pulses acting on a series of one-way check valves. Air from the air cleaner assembly moves through the system and into the exhaust port, where the additional air helps reduce HC and CO exhaust emissions.

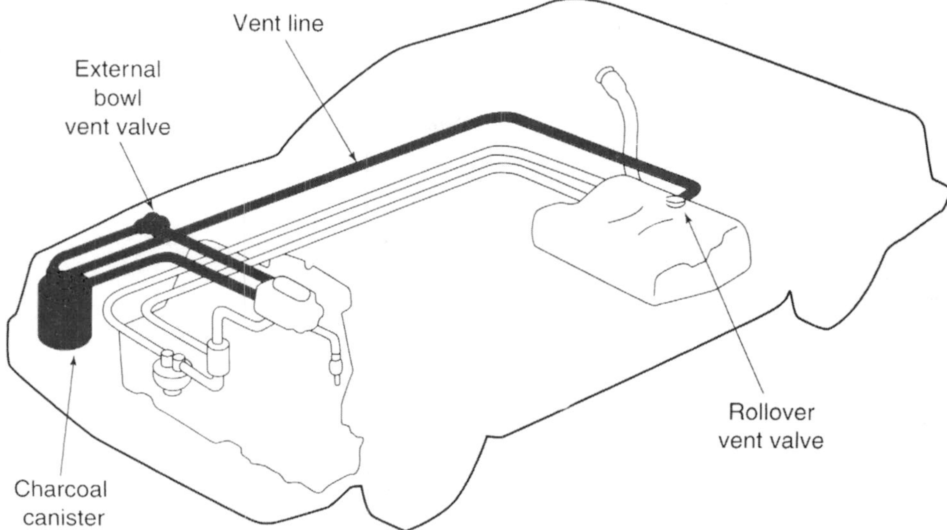

Figure 30–12 The evaporative emission control system includes all of the lines, hoses, and valves plus the charcoal canister. (Courtesy of Chrysler Corporation)

EVAPORATIVE EMISSION CONTROL SYSTEM

The purpose of the **evaporative (EVAP)** emission control system is to trap and hold gasoline vapours. The charcoal canister is part of an entire system of hoses and valves called the **evaporative control system.** See Figure 30–12. Before the early 1970s, most gasoline fumes were simply vented to the atmosphere.

Charcoal or carbon granules have a natural tendency to absorb gasoline fumes (vapours) because carbon attracts carbon. See Figure 30–13. After being absorbed by the canister, the gasoline vapours are drawn by the engine vacuum back into the intake manifold to be burned (see Figures 30–14 and 30–15). This process of drawing in vapours from the charcoal canister is called **purging.** How much should be purged and when is controlled by a vacuum valve or a computer-controlled solenoid.

Figure 30–13 Some vehicles, especially trucks equipped with a carburetor or TBI, use a charcoal (carbon) filter inside the regular air filter located in the air cleaner housing. The purpose and function of this charcoal insert is to absorb evaporating fumes that occur when the engine is turned off. These fumes can come from the carburetor or intake manifold. When the engine is started, the normal airflow through the charcoal insert draws the gasoline fumes into the engine, where they are burned. Many fuel injection systems (from 2004 on) use a hydrocarbon absorber in the hose between the air cleaner and throttle body. This hydrocarbon trap is a thin-wall honeycomb disc that holds HC until the engine starts.

Diagnosing the EVAP System

Before vehicle emissions testing began in many parts of the country, little service work was done on the evaporative emission system. Common engine-performance problems that can be caused by a fault in this system include:

- **Poor fuel economy.** A leak in a vacuum-valve diaphragm can result in engine vacuum drawing in a constant flow of gasoline vapours from the fuel tank. This usually results in a drop in fuel economy. Use a hand-operated vacuum pump to check that the vacuum diaphragm can hold vacuum.
- **Poor performance.** A vacuum leak in the manifold or ported vacuum section of vacuum hose in the system can cause the engine to run

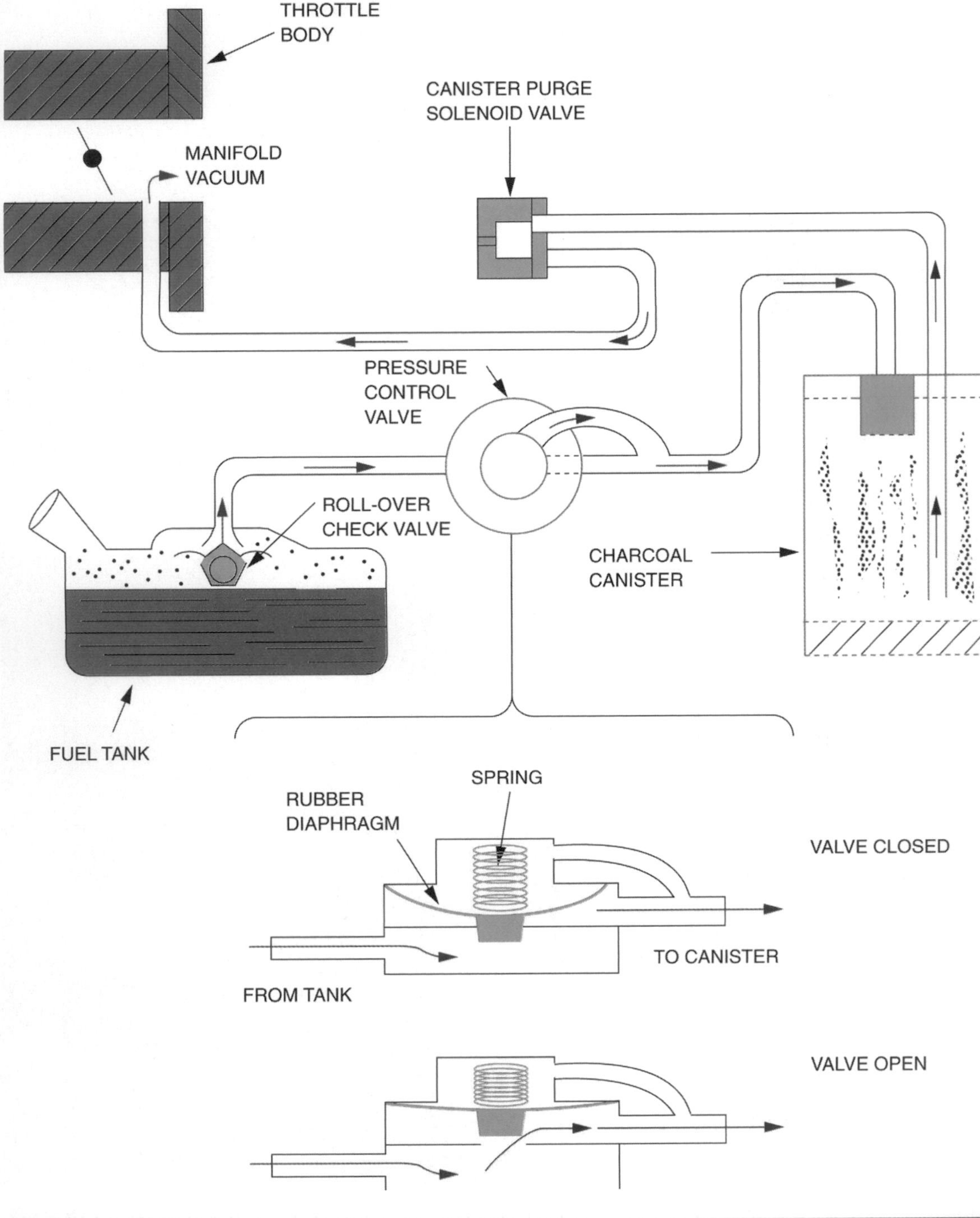

Figure 30–14 A typical evaporative emission control system. Note that when the computer turns on the canister purge solenoid valve, manifold vacuum draws any stored vapours from the canister into the engine. Manifold vacuum also is applied to the pressure control valve and when this valve opens, fumes from the fuel tank are drawn into the charcoal canister and eventually into the engine. When the solenoid valve is turned off (or the engine stops and there is no manifold vacuum), the pressure control valve is spring loaded shut to keep vapours inside the fuel tank from escaping to the atmosphere.

rough. Age, heat, and time all contribute to the deterioration of rubber hoses.

Enhanced exhaust emissions (I/M 240) testing tests the evaporative emission system. A leak in the system is tested by pressurizing the entire fuel system to 7 kPa (1 psi) with nitrogen, a nonflammable gas that makes up 78% of our atmosphere. The pressure in the system is then shut off and the pressure monitored. If the pressure drops below a set stan-

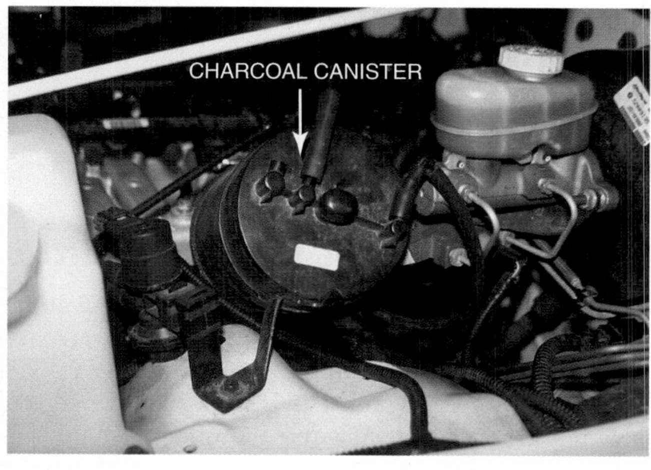

Figure 30–15 This charcoal canister is mounted under the hood. Not all charcoal canisters are this accessible; in fact, most are hidden away under the hood or in other locations on the vehicle.

dard, then the vehicle fails the test. This test determines if there is a leak in the system.

> **HINT:** To help diagnose leaks with the evaporative control system, start with a fuel tank that is three-quarters full, or more. Minor leaks will show up faster when the volume of air in the tank is small: The pressure drops more quickly.

To test for proper airflow in the EVAP system, a **flow gauge** is required as shown in Figure 30–16. Most vehicle emission test sites require at least 1 L of volume per purge during the 240 second (4 minute) test. Many vehicles today are capable of flowing up to 10 L or more per minute.

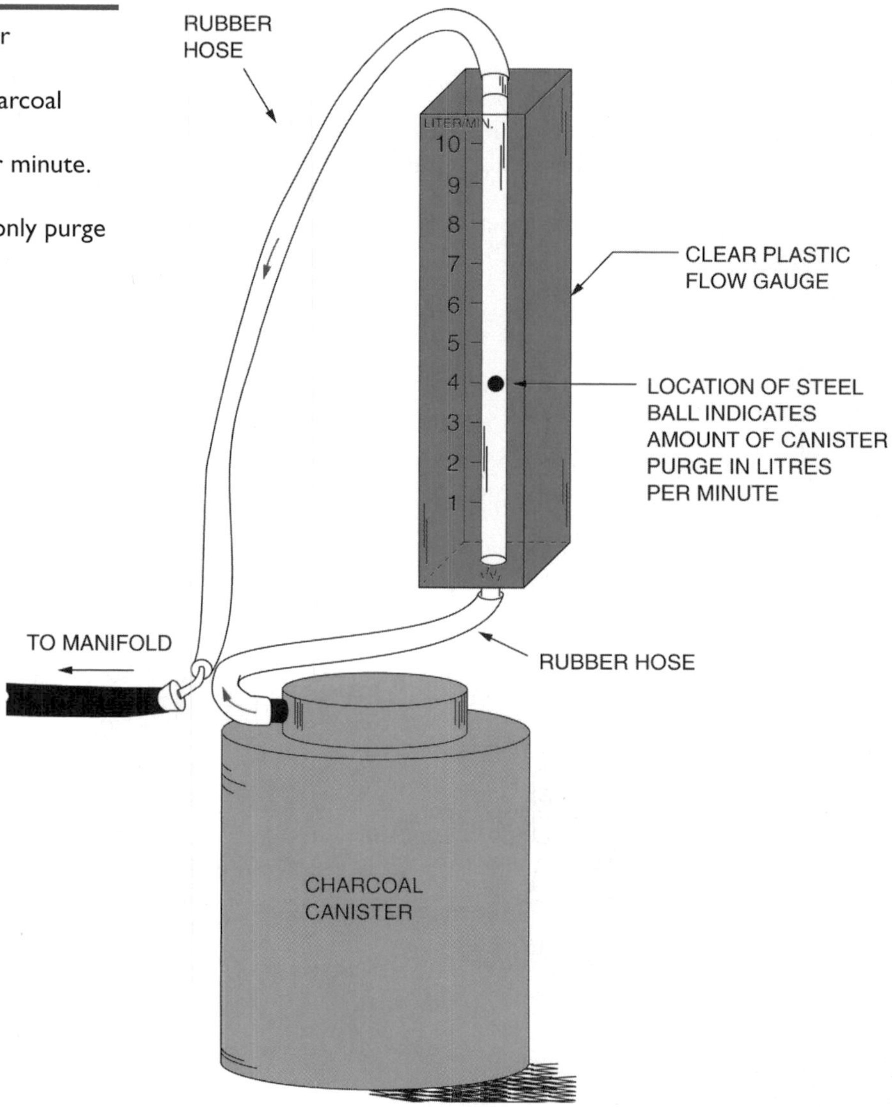

Figure 30–16 A typical purge flow tester connected in series between the intake manifold (or control solenoid) and the charcoal canister. Most working systems should be capable of flowing at least one litre per minute. Some vehicles have to be driven for testing because some vehicle computers only purge after a certain road speed has been achieved.

Frequently Asked Question ???

When Filling My Fuel Tank, Why Should I Stop When the Pump Clicks Off?

Every fuel tank has an upper volume chamber that allows for expansion of the fuel when hot. The volume of the chamber is between 10 and 20% of the volume of the tank. For example, if a fuel tank had a capacity of 80 litres (20 gallons), the expansion chamber volume would be from 8 to 16 litres (2 to 4 gallons). A hose is attached at the top of the chamber and vented to the charcoal canister. If extra fuel is forced into this expansion volume, liquid gasoline can be drawn into the charcoal canister. This liquid fuel can saturate the canister and create an overly rich air–fuel mixture when the canister purge valve is opened during normal vehicle operation. This extra-rich air–fuel mixture can cause the vehicle to fail an exhaust emissions test, reduce fuel economy, and possibly damage the catalytic converter. To avoid problems, simply add fuel to the next dime's worth after the nozzle clicks off. This will ensure that the tank is full, yet not overfilled.

OBD II EVAPORATIVE CONTROL SYSTEMS

Part of the on-board diagnostic second generation (OBD II) standards includes monitoring for a leak in the evaporative control system (EVAP).

OBD II Evaporative Systems Monitor

The EVAP system monitor tests for purge volume and leaks. Most applications purge the charcoal canister by venting the vapours into the intake manifold during cruise. To do this, the PCM typically opens a solenoid-operated purge valve installed in the purge line leading to the intake manifold.

A typical EVAP monitor first closes off the system to atmospheric pressure and opens the purge valve during cruise operation. See Figure 30–17. A fuel-tank pressure sensor then monitors the rate with which vacuum increases in the system. The monitor uses this information to determine the

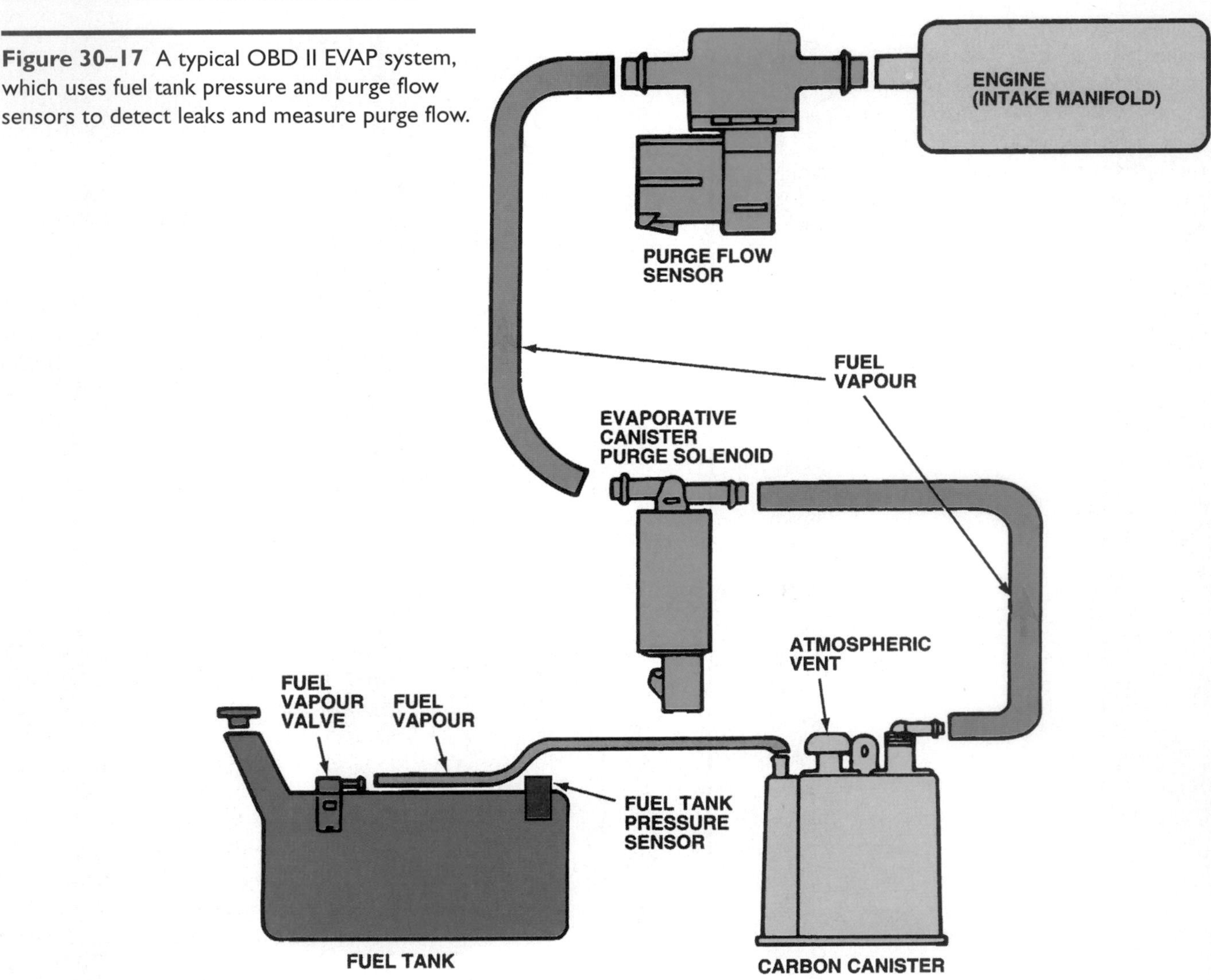

Figure 30–17 A typical OBD II EVAP system, which uses fuel tank pressure and purge flow sensors to detect leaks and measure purge flow.

purge volume flow rate. To test for leaks, the EVAP monitor closes the purge valve, creating a completely closed system. The fuel tank pressure sensor then monitors the leak-down rate. If the rate exceeds PCM-stored values, a leak greater than or equal to the OBD II standard of 1.0 mm (0.040 in.) exists. After two consecutive failed trips testing either purge volume or the presence of a leak, the PCM lights the MIL and sets a DTC.

DaimlerChrysler vehicles use an electric pump to pressurize the fuel system to check for leaks by having the PCM monitor the fuel-tank pressure sensor. See Figure 30–18. The fuel-tank pressure sensor is often the same part as the MAP sensor and instead of monitoring intake manifold absolute pressure, it is used to monitor fuel tank pressure.

Figure 30–18 A DaimlerChrysler electric EVAP pressure pump located at the rear of the vehicle is used to pressurize the fuel tank and the PCM monitors for leaks.

TECH TIP 

Always Tighten 3 Clicks

Many diagnostic trouble codes (DTCs) are set because the gas cap has not been properly installed. To be sure that a screw-type gas cap is properly sealed, tighten the cap until it clicks three times. The clicking is a ratchet device and the clicking does not harm the cap. Therefore, if a P0440 or similar DTC is set, check the cap. Test caps can also be used when diagnosing the system as shown in Figure 30–19.

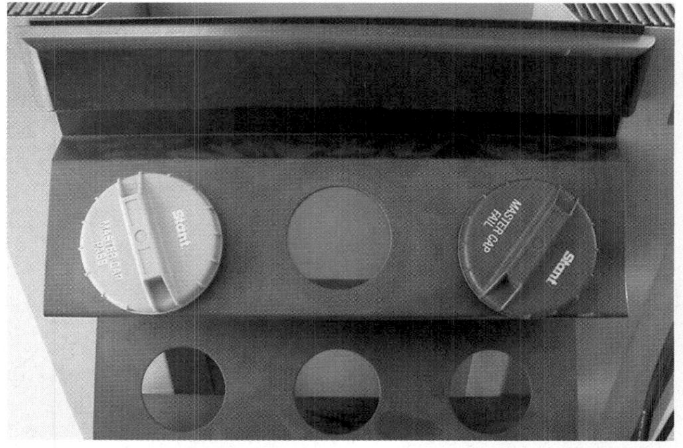

Figure 30–19 An assortment of gas caps used during testing of the EVAP system.

EXHAUST GAS RECIRCULATION SYSTEM

To reduce the emission of **oxides of nitrogen (NO_x)**, engines have been equipped with **exhaust gas recirculation (EGR)** valves. See Figure 30–20. From 1973 until recently, EGR valves were used on almost all vehicles. Because of the efficiency of computer-controlled fuel injection, some newer engines do not require an EGR system to meet emissions standards. Some engines use intake and exhaust valve overlap as a means of trapping some exhaust in the cylinder.

The EGR valve opens at speeds above idle on a warm engine. (NO_x emissions are not high on a cold engine). When open, the valve allows a small portion of the exhaust gas (up to about 7%) to enter the intake manifold. Here, the exhaust gas mixes with and takes the place of some intake charge. This leaves less room for the intake charge to enter the combustion chamber. The recirculated exhaust gas is **inert** (chemically inactive) and does not enter into the combustion process. The result is a lower peak combustion temperature. As the combustion temperature is lowered, the production of oxides of nitrogen is also reduced.

The EGR system has some means of interconnecting the exhaust and intake manifolds. See Figure 30–21. The interconnecting passage is controlled by the EGR valve. On V-type engines, the intake manifold crossover is used as a source of exhaust gas for the EGR system. A cast passage connects the exhaust crossover to the EGR valve. The gas is sent from the EGR valve to openings in the manifold. On inline-type engines, an external tube is generally used to carry exhaust gas to the EGR valve. This tube is often quite long so that the exhaust gas is cooled before it enters the EGR valve.

Figure 30–20 Typical vacuum-operated EGR valve. The operation of the valve is controlled by the computer by pulsing the EGR control solenoid on and off.

Positive and Negative Back Pressure EGR Valves

Many EGR valves are designed with a small valve inside that bleeds off any applied vacuum and prevents the valve from opening. Some EGR valves require a positive back pressure in the exhaust system. This is called a **positive back pressure** EGR valve. At low engine speeds and light engine loads, the EGR system is not needed, and the back pressure in it is also low. Without sufficient back pressure, the EGR valve does not open even though vacuum may be present at the EGR valve.

On each exhaust stroke, the engine emits an exhaust *pulse.* Each pulse represents a positive pressure. Behind each pulse is a small area of low pressure. Some EGR valves react to this low pressure area by closing a small internal valve, which allows the EGR valve to be opened by vacuum. This type of EGR valve is called a **negative back pressure** EGR valve. The following conditions must occur:

1. Vacuum must be applied to the EGR valve itself. This is usually ported vacuum on older, carburetor-equipped and some TBI fuel-injected systems. The vacuum source on later vehicles is often manifold vacuum controlled by the computer through a solenoid valve.
2. Exhaust back pressure must be present to close an internal valve inside the EGR to allow the vacuum to move the diaphragm.

Electronic EGR

Many engines since the mid-1990s have used computer-controlled solenoids or stepper motors (called linear EGR) to control the flow of exhaust into the intake manifold. See Figure 30–22 for an example of an assembly that uses three solenoids on a V-6 engine. The vehicle computer controls all three solenoids and can turn one, two, or all three on as necessary to provide the exact amount of EGR needed. Some vehicles use a linear EGR that contains a stepper motor to precisely regulate exhaust gas flow and a feedback potentiometer that signals the computer the actual position of the valve. See Figure 30–23.

Diagnosing a Defective EGR Valve or System

If the EGR valve is not opening or the flow of the exhaust gas is restricted, then the following symptoms are likely:

- Ping (spark knock or detonation) during acceleration or during cruise (steady-speed driving)
- Excessive oxides of nitrogen (NO_x) exhaust emissions

TECH TIP 

Watch Out for Carbon Balls!

Exhaust gas recirculation (EGR) valves can get stuck partially open by a chunk of carbon. The EGR valve or solenoid will test as defective. When the valve (or solenoid) is removed, small chunks or balls of carbon often fall into the exhaust manifold passage. When the replacement valve is installed, the carbon balls can be drawn into the new valve again, causing the engine to idle roughly or stall.

To help prevent this problem, start the engine with the EGR valve or solenoid removed. Any balls or chunks of carbon will be blown out of the passage by the exhaust. Stop the engine and install the replacement EGR valve or solenoid. Wear safety glasses or stay in the vehicle during this operation.

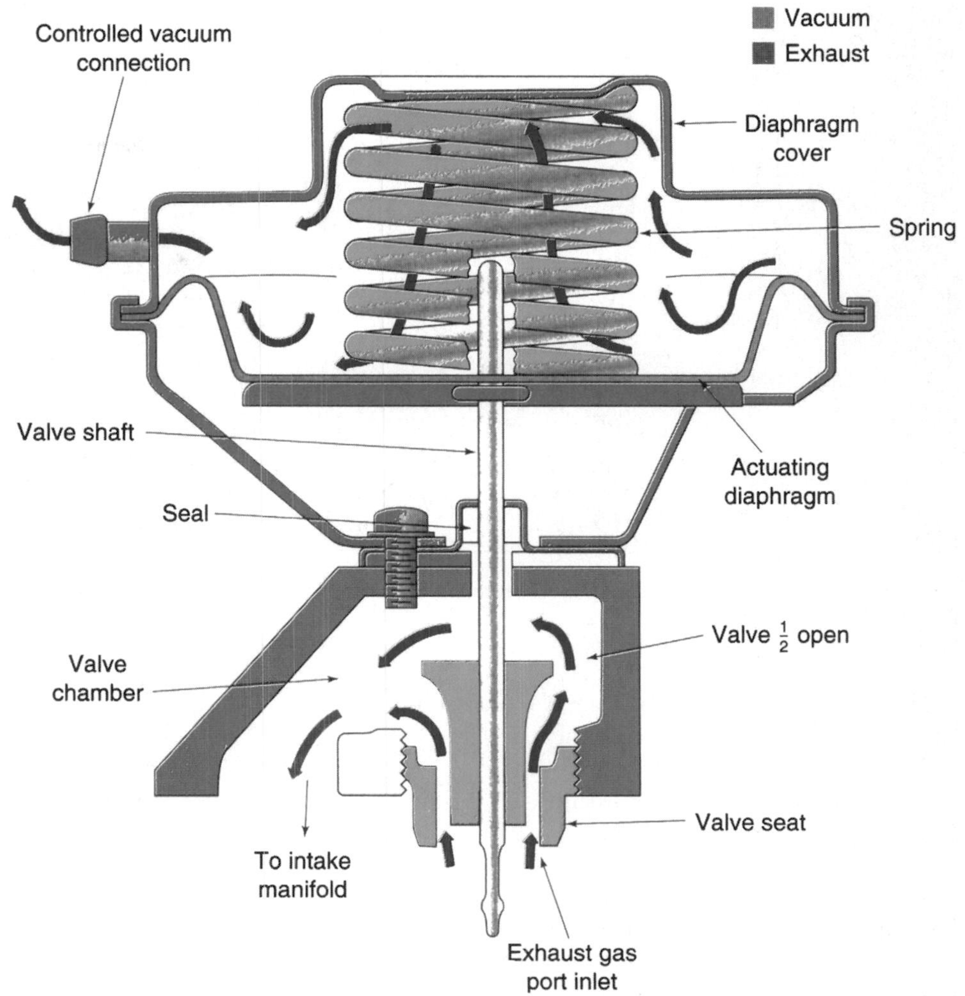

Figure 30–21 When the EGR valve opens, exhaust flows through the valve and into passages in the intake manifold.

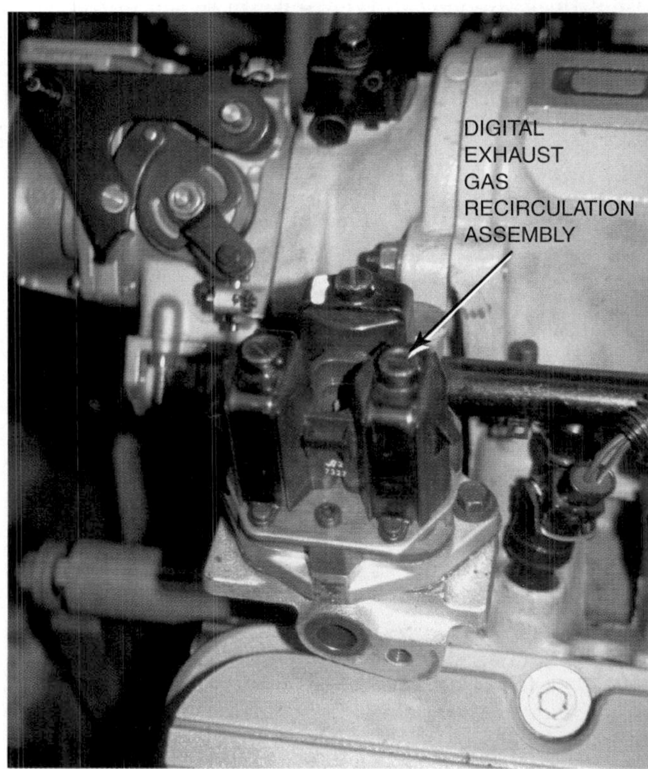

Figure 30–22 This V-6 uses three solenoids for EGR. A scan tool can be used to turn on each solenoid. This will check whether the valve is working and if the exhaust passages are capable of flowing enough exhaust to the intake manifold to affect engine operation when cycled.

Figure 30–23 A linear EGR valve.

If the EGR valve is stuck open or partially open, then the following symptoms are likely:

- Rough idle or frequent stalling
- Poor performance/low power

The first step in almost any diagnosis is to perform a thorough visual inspection. To check for proper operation of a vacuum-operated EGR valve, follow these steps:

1. Check the vacuum diaphragm to see if it can hold vacuum.

NOTE: Because many EGR valves require exhaust back pressure to function correctly, the engine should be running at the specified RPM.

2. Apply vacuum from a hand-operated vacuum pump and check for proper operation. The valve itself should move when vacuum is applied, and the engine operation should be affected. The EGR valve should be able to hold the vacuum that was applied. If the vacuum drops off, then the valve is likely to be defective.

NOTE: Positive back-pressure EGR valves require that a certain amount of exhaust restriction be present to allow the valve to operate correctly. If low-restriction aftermarket or custom exhaust systems have been installed, the EGR valve may not function correctly. If the valve does not open or does not open enough, the engine will likely ping or spark knock during acceleration. Exhaust NO_x exhaust emissions are also likely to occur.

DIAGNOSTIC STORY

The Blazer Story

The owner of a Chevrolet Blazer equipped with a 4.3 L, V-6 engine complained that the engine would stumble and hesitate at times. Everything seemed to be functioning correctly, except that the service technician discovered a weak vacuum going to the EGR valve at idle. This vehicle was equipped with an EGR valve-control solenoid, called an **electronic vacuum regulator valve** or **EVRV** by General Motors Corporation. The computer pulses the solenoid to control the vacuum that regulates the operation of the EGR valve. The technician checked the service manual for details on how the system worked. The technician discovered that vacuum should be present at the EGR valve only when the gear selector indicates a drive gear (drive, low, reverse). Because the technician discovered the vacuum at the solenoid to be leaking, the solenoid was obviously defective and required replacement. After replacement of the solenoid (EVRV), the hesitation problem was solved.

NOTE: The technician also discovered in the service manual that blower-type exhaust hoses should not be connected to the tail pipe on any vehicle while performing an inspection of the EGR system. The vacuum created by the system could cause false EGR valve operation to occur.

DIAGNOSTIC STORY

"I Was Only Trying to Help!"

On a Friday, an experienced service technician found that the driveability performance problem was a worn EGR valve. When vacuum was applied to the valve, the valve did not move at all. Additional vacuum from the hand-operated vacuum pump resulted in the valve popping all the way open. A new valve of the correct part number was not available until Monday, yet the customer wanted the vehicle back for a trip during the weekend.

To achieve acceptable driveability, the technician used a small hammer and deformed the top of the valve to limit the travel of the EGR valve stem. The technician instructed the customer to return on Monday for the proper replacement valve.

The customer did return on Monday, but now accompanied by his lawyer. The engine had developed a hole in one of the pistons. The lawyer reminded the technician and the manager that an exhaust emission control had been modified. The result was the repair shop paid for a new engine and the technician learned always to repair the vehicle correctly or not at all.

TECH TIP

The Snake Trick

The EGR passages on many intake manifolds become clogged with carbon, which reduces the flow of exhaust and the amount of exhaust gases in the cylinders. This reduction can cause spark knock (detonation) and increased emissions of oxides of nitrogen (NO_x).

To quickly and easily remove carbon from exhaust passages, cut an approximately 300 mm (1 ft) length from stranded wire, such as garage door guide wire or an old speedometer cable. Flare the end and place the end of the wire into the passage. Set your drill on reverse, turn it on, and the wire will pull its way through the passage, cleaning the carbon as it goes, just like a plumber's snake in a drain pipe.

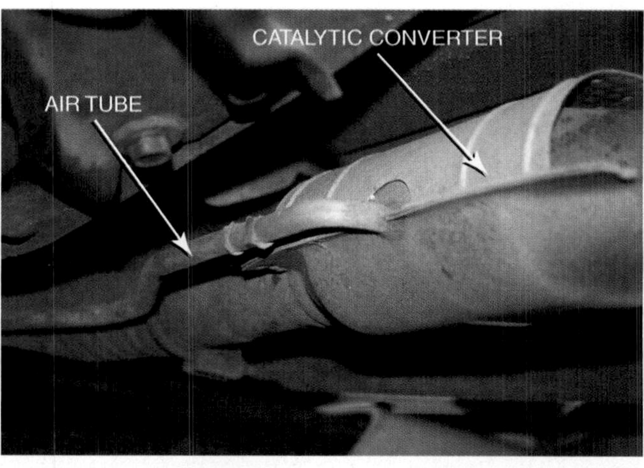

Figure 30–24 Typical catalytic converter. The small tube in the side of the converter comes from the air pump. The additional air from the air pump helps oxidize the exhaust into harmless H_2O (water) and CO_2 (carbon dioxide).

If the EGR valve is able to hold vacuum, but the engine is not affected when the valve is opened, then the exhaust passage(s) must be checked for restriction. See the Tech Tip "The Snake Trick." If the EGR valve will not hold vacuum, the valve itself is likely to be defective and require replacement.

OBD II EGR SYSTEM MONITOR

The OBD II EGR emission monitor uses a variety of methods to test EGR flow, depending on the manufacturer and the application. Most vehicles use the MAP sensor to test the EGR. During deceleration, the computer commands the EGR on and watches the MAP sensor response. The engine vacuum should decrease if the EGR flow is sufficient, and the MAP sensor should detect this drop in vacuum. If not enough change is noted, the test fails. The O2S sensor is also used by some systems to check the EGR. If the EGR efficiency level does not meet a predetermined standard after two consecutive trips, the computer lights the MIL and sets one or more DTCs.

CATALYTIC CONVERTERS

An exhaust pipe connected to the manifold or header carries gases through a catalytic converter to the muffler and resonator (if used). In single exhaust systems used on V-type engines, the exhaust pipe is designed to collect the exhaust gases from both manifolds using a Y-shaped design. Vehicles with dual exhaust systems have a complete exhaust system coming from each of the manifolds. In most cases, the exhaust pipe must be made up in several sections so that it can be assembled in the space available under the vehicle.

The **catalytic converter** is installed between the manifold and the muffler to help reduce exhaust emissions. The converter has a heat-resistant metal housing. See Figure 30–24. A bed of catalyst-coated pellets or a catalyst-coated honeycomb grid is inside the housing.

Catalytic Converter Operation

The converter contains small amounts of **rhodium, palladium,** and **platinum.** These elements act as **catalysts** (entities that start a chemical reaction without becoming a part of the chemical reaction). See Figure 30–25. As the exhaust gas passes through the catalyst, oxides of nitrogen (NO_x) are chemically reduced (that is, nitrogen and oxygen are separated) in the first section of the catalytic converter. This is called the reduction section. In the second section of the catalytic converter, most of the hydrocarbons and carbon monoxide remaining in the exhaust gas are oxidized to form harmless carbon dioxide (CO_2) and water vapour (H_2O). This is called the oxidizing section. An air-injection system or pulse air system is used on some engines to supply additional air that may be needed in the oxidation process. See Figure 30–26. Since the early 1990s, many converters also contain **cerium,** an element that can store oxygen. The purpose of the cerium is to provide oxygen to the oxidation bed of the converter when the exhaust is rich and lacks enough oxygen for proper oxidation. When

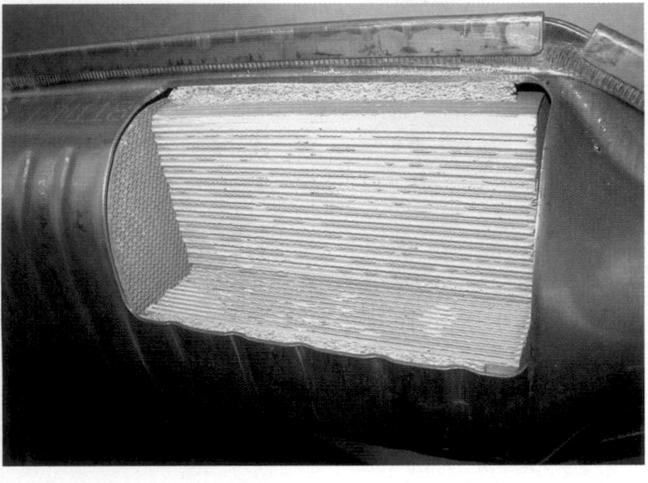

Figure 30–25 A cutaway of a monolith substrate converter.

Figure 30–26 A cutaway of a three-way catalytic converter showing the air tube in the centre of the reducing and oxidizing section of the converter. Note the small holes in the tube to distribute air from the AIR pump to the oxidizing rear section of the converter.

the exhaust is lean, the cerium absorbs the extra oxygen. The converter must have a varying rich-to-lean exhaust for proper operation:

- A rich exhaust is required for reduction—stripping the oxygen (O_2) from the nitrogen in NO_x
- A lean exhaust is required to provide the oxygen necessary to oxidize HC and CO (combining oxygen with HC and CO to form H_2O and CO_2)

Early catalytic converters are oxidizing only: helping to control HC and CO. They are know as two-way converters. Later converters added a reduction section that helps to control NO_x. These are known as three-way converters.

If the catalytic converter is not functioning correctly, check to see that the air-fuel mixture being supplied to the engine is correct and that the ignition system is free of defects.

Nitrogen-Oxide-Adsorptive Catalytic Converters

Conventional three-way converters are not effective in converting NO_x into nitrogen when excessive oxygen from lean mixtures is present. NOA converters attract NO_x molecules during lean operating conditions and release them when the mixture richens.

Figure 30–27 This catalytic converter blew up when gasoline from the excessively rich running engine ignited. Obviously, raw gasoline was trapped inside and all it needed was a spark. No further diagnosis of this converter is necessary.

Frequently Asked Question ???

Can a Catalytic Converter Be Defective Without Being Clogged?

Yes. Catalytic converters can fail by being chemically damaged or poisoned without being mechanically clogged. Therefore, the catalytic converter should not only be tested for physical damage (clogging) by performing a back-pressure or vacuum test and a rattle test but also for temperature rise, usually with a pyrometer or propane test, to check the efficiency of the converter.

Four-Way Converters

Late in 2004, California became the first state to approve a regulation reducing carbon dioxide (CO_2) emissions from vehicle exhaust. Canada and the other states are expected to follow. The new regulation becomes effective with 2009 vehicles.

The Tap Test

This simple test involves tapping (not pounding) on the catalytic converter using a rubber mallet. If the substrate inside the converter is broken, the converter will rattle when hit. If the converter rattles, a replacement converter is required. See Figure 30–27.

Testing Back Pressure with a Vacuum Gauge

A vacuum gauge can be used to measure manifold vacuum at a high idle (2000 to 2500 rpm). If the exhaust system is restricted, pressure increases in the exhaust system. This pressure is called **back pressure.** Manifold vacuum will drop gradually if the engine is kept at a constant speed and the exhaust is restricted.

The reason the vacuum will drop is that all the exhaust leaving the engine at the higher engine speed cannot get through the restriction. After a short time (within 1 minute), the exhaust tends to pile up above the restriction and eventually remains in the cylinder of the engine at the end of the exhaust stroke. Therefore, at the beginning of the intake stroke, when the piston traveling downward should be lowering the pressure (raising the vacuum) in the intake manifold, the extra exhaust in the cylinder *lowers* the normal vacuum. If the exhaust restriction is severe enough, the vehicle can become undriveable because cylinder filling cannot occur except at idle.

Testing Back Pressure with a Pressure Gauge

Exhaust system back pressure can be measured directly by installing a pressure gauge in an exhaust opening. This can be accomplished in one of the following ways:

1. To test at an oxygen sensor opening, remove the inside of an old, discarded oxygen sensor and thread in an adapter to connect it to a vacuum or pressure gauge.

> **NOTE:** An adapter can be easily made by inserting a metal tube or pipe. A short section of brake line works great. The pipe can be brazed to the oxygen sensor housing or it can be glued with epoxy. An 18 mm compression gauge adapter can also be adapted to fit into the oxygen sensor opening. See Figure 30–28.

2. To test at an exhaust gas recirculation (EGR) valve, remove the EGR valve and fabricate a plate.
3. To test at an air injection reaction (AIR) check valve, remove the check valve from the exhaust tubes leading to the exhaust manifold. Use a rubber cone with a tube inside to seal against the exhaust tube. Connect the tube to a pressure gauge.

At idle the maximum back pressure should be less than 10 kPa (1.5 psi), and it should be less than 15 kPa (2.5 psi) at 2500 rpm.

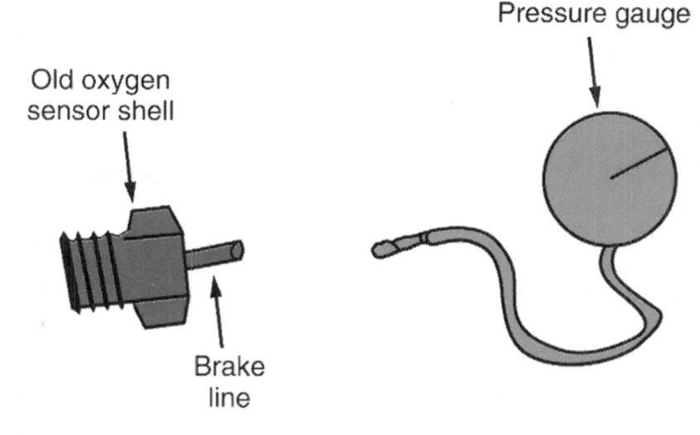

Figure 30–28 A back pressure tool can be easily made by attaching a short section of brake line to the shell of an old oxygen sensor. Braze or epoxy the tube to the shell.

Testing a Catalytic Converter for Temperature Rise

A properly working catalytic converter should be able to reduce NO_x exhaust emissions into nitrogen (N) and oxygen (O_2) and oxidize unburned hydrocarbon (HC) and carbon monoxide (CO) into carbon dioxide (CO_2) and water vapour (H_2O). During these chemical processes, the catalytic converter should increase in temperature at least 10% if the converter is working properly. To test, operate the engine at 2500 rpm for at least 2 minutes to fully warm up the converter. Measure the inlet and the outlet temperatures as shown in Figure 30–29.

> **NOTE:** If the engine is extremely efficient, the converter may not have any excessive unburned hydrocarbons or carbon monoxide to convert! In this case, a spark plug wire could be grounded out using a vacuum hose and a test light (see Chapter 21) to create some unburned hydrocarbon in the exhaust. This will heat the converter. Do not ground out a cylinder for longer than 10 seconds or the excessive amount of unburned hydrocarbon could overheat and damage the converter.

OBD II Catalytic Converter Monitor

The catalytic converter monitor of OBD II uses an upstream and downstream heated oxygen sensor (HO2S) to test catalytic efficiency. See Figure 30–30. When the engine combusts a lean air–fuel mixture, higher amounts of oxygen flow through the exhaust into the converter. The catalyst materials absorb this oxygen for the oxidation process, thereby removing it from the exhaust stream. If a converter cannot absorb enough oxygen, oxidation does not occur. Engineers established a correlation

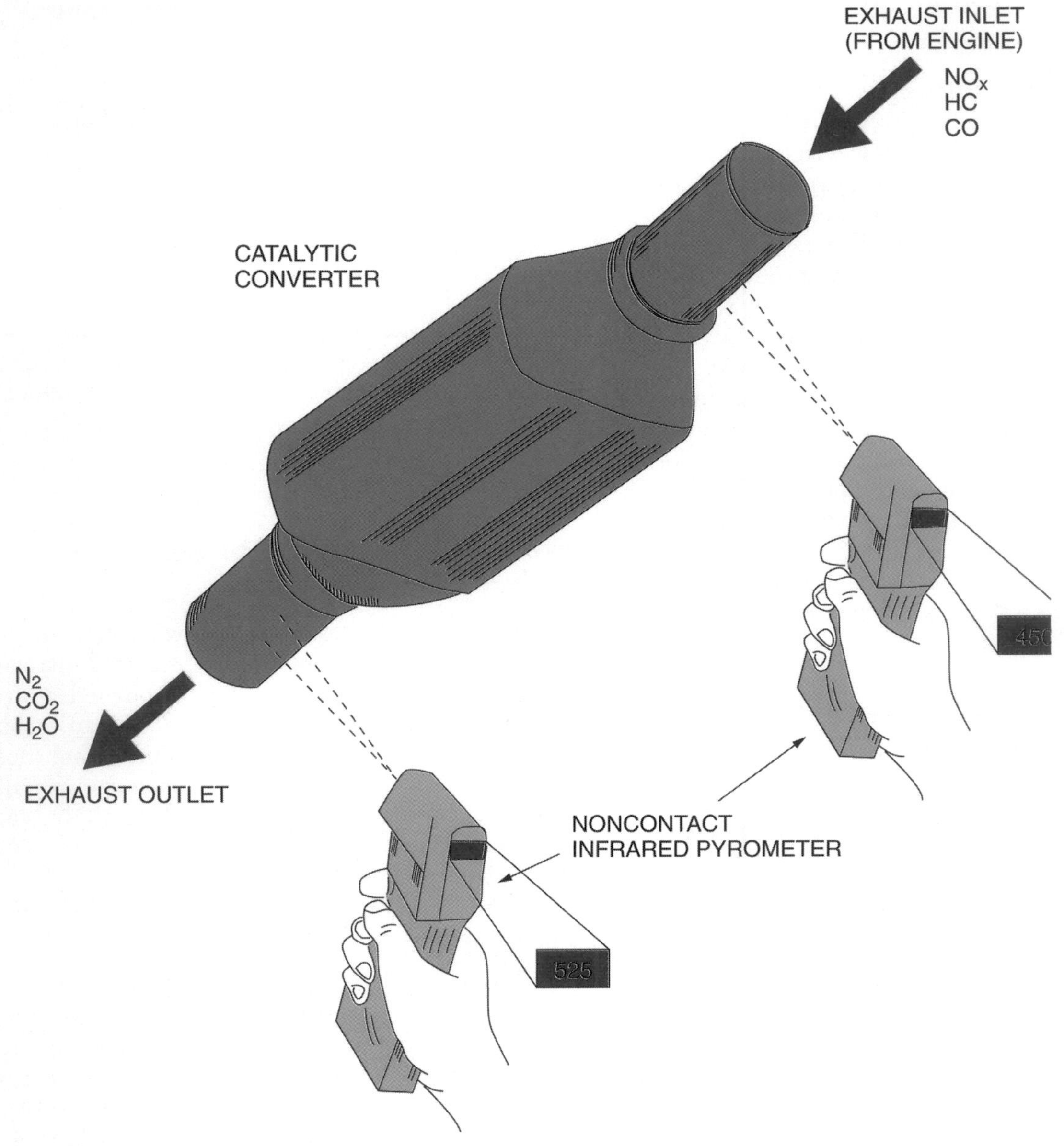

Figure 30–29 The temperature of the outlet should be at least 10% hotter than the temperature of the inlet. This converter is very efficient. The inlet temperature is 230°C (450°F). Ten percent of 230°C is 23°C (450°F, 45°F). In other words, the outlet temperature should be at least 253°C (495°F) for the converter to be considered okay. In this case, the outlet temperature of 274°C (525°F) is more than the minimum 10% increase in temperature. If the converter is not working at all, the inlet temperature will be hotter than the outlet temperature.

between the amount of oxygen absorbed and converter efficiency.

The OBD II system monitors how much oxygen the catalyst retains. A voltage waveform from the downstream HO2S of a good catalyst should have little or no activity. See Figure 30–31. A voltage waveform from the downstream HO2S of a degraded catalyst shows a lot of activity. In other words, the closer the activity of the downstream HO2S matches that of the upstream HO2S, the greater the degree of converter degradation. In operation, the OBD II monitor compares activity between the two exhaust oxygen sensors.

Diesel Particulate Catalytic Converters

Diesel exhaust contains some HC and NO_x, but excess particulates are the main emissions. There are a number of diesel converters that use high internal temperatures to incinerate the particulates and turn them into ash.

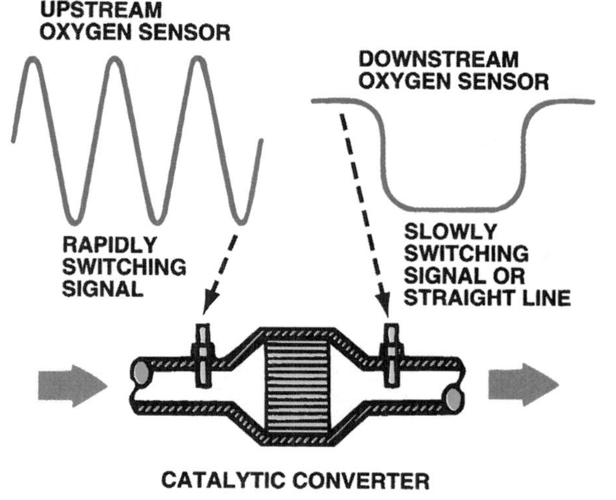

Figure 30–30 The OBD II catalytic converter monitor compares the signals of the upstream and downstream oxygen sensors to determine converter efficiency.

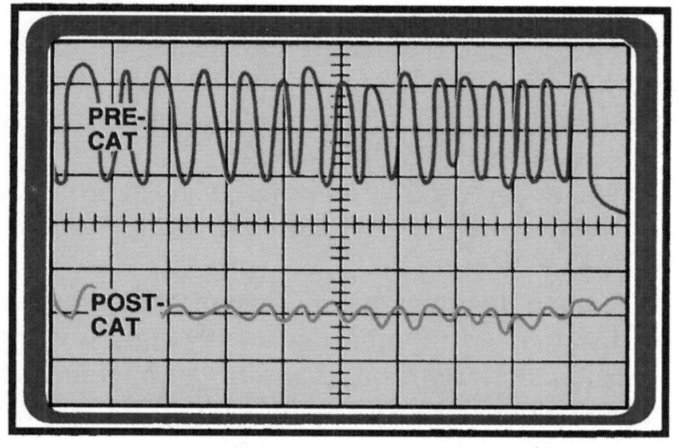

Figure 30–31 The waveform of an O2S downstream from a properly functioning converter shows little, if any, activity.

TECH TIP

Catalytic Converters Are Murdered

Catalytic converters start a chemical reaction but do not enter into the chemical reaction. Therefore, catalytic converters do not wear out and they do not die of old age. If a catalytic converter is found to be defective (nonfunctioning or clogged), look for the *root* cause. Remember this:

"Catalytic converters do not commit suicide—they're murdered."

Items that should be checked when a defective catalytic converter is discovered include all components of the ignition and fuel systems. Excessive unburned fuel can cause the catalytic converter to overheat and fail. The oxygen sensor must be working and fluctuating from 0.5 to 5 Hz to provide the necessary air–fuel mixture variations for maximum catalytic converter efficiency.

DIESEL EMISSION CONTROLS

Diesel engines have no throttle plate; they take in far more air than is needed, except during the maximum power demands. Because of this, combustion is very complete compared to a gasoline engine, and emissions differ. See Figure 30–32.

Hydrocarbons (HC) and carbon monoxide (CO) emissions are generally low. Oxides of nitrogen (NO_x) may be present because of the high temperatures and pressures during combustion; however, the worst emission is particulate matter. Particulates, composed primarily of carbon, are visible (black

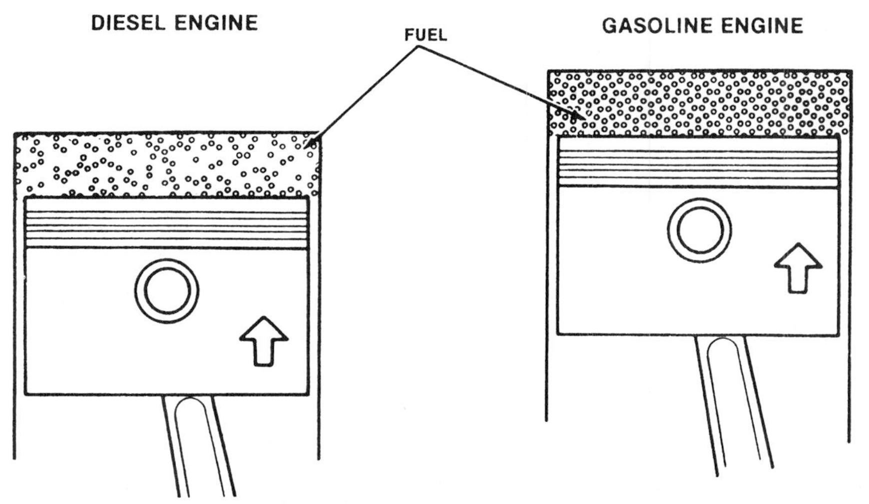

Figure 30–32 Excess air in a diesel engine contributes to a more complete combustion. (Courtesy Ford Motor Co.)

smoke) and are created by incomplete combustion. Rich fuel mixtures or an air intake restriction are common causes of increased particulate formation.

Federal emission standards for diesel engines began in 1988 and have become more stringent since that time. As an example, particulate emission limits were lowered from 60 grams per brake horsepower-hour in 1988 to 10 grams per horsepower-hour in 1994. This required the need for catalytic converters on some exhaust systems.

In 1997, OBD II standards for diesel engines were introduced; EGR systems were now monitored and in 1998, engine misfire and glow plug malfunctions were added. A malfunction indicator lamp (MIL) on the instrument panel turns on to indicate a system deterioration or failure.

Diesel engines are analyzed with an opacity meter (clamped to the exhaust pipe), which uses a light beam to measure exhaust density under different operating modes. Common emission controls include catalytic converters for particulates, EGR valves for NO_x, and crankcase depression regulator valves, a form of PCV valve used to control crankcase hydrocarbon emissions.

Diesel palladium-oxidation particulate-reduction converters require low-sulphur diesel fuel, which was mandated in Canada beginning in 1995. High-sulphur fuels will render the converter inactive. Bosch and a number of European manufacturers have developed a new sintered metal (vs. traditional ceramic) particulate-filter converter that is expected to last for the life of the vehicle. Production is expected to begin in 2005–2006.

The introduction of electronically controlled fuel injection assures a more precise fuel delivery that brings emissions to an even lower level.

EMISSIONS TESTING CENTRES

The British Columbia AirCare and the Ontario Drive Clean programs are designed to identify vehicles with high emissions, and to improve air quality by reducing harmful pollutants. Drive Clean inspects vehicles in southern and eastern Ontario, while AirCare covers the Greater Vancouver and Fraser Valley regions, areas in both provinces experiencing air pollution problems. Although there are differences between the two programs, they are similar. The following is typical.

- Older vehicles, prior to 1991 must be checked every year during a steady state 40 km/h (25 mph) tailpipe test.
- Newer vehicles, from 1992 to date, are inspected every two years. They go through a more comprehensive test. See Figure 30–33.
- Maximum allowable emissions, listed as parts per million (ppm), percent (%) or grams per kilometre (g/km), vary with the year and model of the vehicle. See Figure 30–34.
- New vehicles are exempt for the first year (or first two years).
- The vehicle must either pass the test or have a conditional pass before licence plates will be issued.

Vehicles brought to the test centre are checked visually for a catalytic converter, the gas cap is removed for pressure testing and the vehicle exhaust is measured for hydrocarbons (HC), carbon monoxide (CO) and oxides of nitrogen (NO_x) while running at speed on a dynamometer. Special dynamometers are often used for all-wheel drives. See Figure 30–35.

Owners of vehicles that fail the test will receive a conditional pass if they have the vehicle diagnosed and repaired by an AirCare Certified technician at an AirCare certified repair centre. There is a repair cost limit designed to ensure emissions are reduced while limiting the financial burden for the owner. Ontario has a fixed limit; British Columbia's limit is tied to the model year.

Vehicles repaired by a non-certified shop will not qualify for a conditional pass; the vehicle must be reinspected till it passes.

Certified technicians must pass a comprehensive examination on emissions control, gas analysis, diagnosing, electronics and engine management for gasoline engines. Diesel and alternate fuel examinations may be taken at the same time.

Older vehicles typically account for a high percentage of failed vehicles. Later vehicles, especially if equipped with OBD II on-board diagnostics, account for a very low percentage of failures; 2005 vehicles are 98% cleaner than 1970 vehicles.

Because of this, Ontario plans to phase out the Drive Clean program by 2008; AirCare is considering testing older vehicles only, starting in 2006.

ADVANCED VEHICLES

The Road to Zero Emissions

In 1990, the California Air Resources Board (CARB) adopted a requirement that 10% of the new cars offered for sale in California from 2003 on would have to be zero emission vehicles (ZEV): cars and trucks that produce no evaporative or exhaust emissions.

This was later reduced to 4% ZEVs, provided the remaining 6% are clean enough to qualify as partial ZEVs. The 4% ZEV level may be further reduced to 2% in the future.

Questions & Answers

What emissions are measured?

- AirCare tests vehicles for levels of hydrocarbons (HC), carbon monoxide (CO) and oxides of nitrogen (NOx). Emission readings above AirCare standards indicate that a problem exists with your vehicle's engine or emission control system.

Why should I be concerned about these emissions?

- CO is a toxic gas that is colourless and odourless. HC and NOx emissions contribute to the formation of ground-level ozone (the main ingredient in "smog"), which is harmful to our health and the environment. NOx, methane and carbon dioxide all contribute to climate change.

SAVING FUEL MEANS LESS GREENHOUSE GASES

- Combine Trips
- Reduce Speed
- Maintain proper tire pressure
- Keep your engine maintained

- **I maintain my vehicle and it is running fine, so why did I fail the test?**
  Generally, emission control devices have little impact on the drivability of a vehicle. Your vehicle may seem to be operating fine but still have an emissions defect. Even well maintained vehicles can experience AirCare failures. Please speak to your AirCare certified technician for more information.
- **Will the AirCare inspection tell me what's wrong with my vehicle?**
  The AirCare inspection determines whether your vehicle is emitting an excessive level of pollutants. However, the cause of the excess emissions cannot be identified by the inspection process alone or by the AirCare Inspectors who are not trained technicians. An automotive repair facility will be able to identify the cause of the high emissions and recommend the appropriate repair action.
- **Where do I take my vehicle to be repaired?**
  We recommend having your vehicle repaired by an AirCare Certified technician who has completed a specific training program to diagnose and repair emissions-related problems. Please see the list of Certified Repair Centres provided by the AirCare Lane Inspector or check it on our website at **www.aircare.ca**

For more information, read the *"What to Do if Your Vehicle Doesn't Pass?"* handout.

AirCare Online

Looking for information on:

- Odometer readings or pass/fail records for your vehicle?
- Station locations, directions and current wait times?
- Emissions repair information?
- List of AirCare Certified Repair Centres with performance ratings?
- AirCare technical reports?
- Important information about the impact that vehicle emissions have on health, regional air quality and the environment?

Visit our website at **www.aircare.ca** where you'll find the above information and answers to your questions about the AirCare program.

AirCare Works - Thanks to You!
Since 1992, vehicle emissions have been reduced significantly.

To get more information on the benefits of the AirCare program, visit our website at: **www.aircare.ca**

Light-Duty Vehicle Emission Reductions (1992-2002)

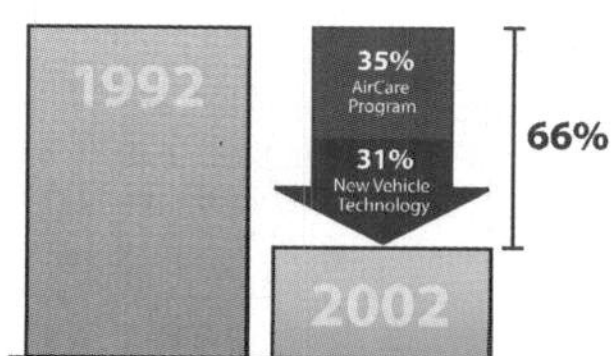

GAS CAP FAILURES

- If your vehicle has failed the gas cap test only, please have the gas cap repaired or replaced and return with the vehicle and replacement gas cap to the Manager's Office at the AirCare Inspection Centre for a free gas cap re-test. It is not necessary to line up in the lanes if you failed the gas cap only.

VEHICLES WITH ANTI-LOCK BRAKING SYSTEMS (ABS)

- Your ABS warning light may be on after a test. Normal braking performance will not be affected. The light should go out when the system detects equal front and rear speed signals.
- If the light does not go out after 24 hours, please call us at 604-436-2640 - Customer Service.

AIRCARE TEST SCHEDULE

- 1992 and newer vehicles are tested every 2 years - 726 day expiry date.
- 1991 and older vehicles are tested every year - 363 day expiry date.
- All vehicles receiving a conditional pass are tested every year. For more information on conditional passes, read the *"What to Do if Your Vehicle Doesn't Pass?"* handout or visit **www.aircare.ca**.

THIS INSPECTION WAS PERFORMED IN ACCORDANCE WITH DIVISION (40) MOTOR VEHICLE ACT REGULATIONS.

Figure 30–33 Emissions testing procedure. (Reprinted with permission from Pacific Vehicle Testing Technologies Ltd., operators of the BC AirCare Program. All rights reserved.)

AirCare® Vehicle Inspection Report

Thanks for doing your part for clean air! Since 1992, your efforts have reduced vehicle emissions by 66%.

TEST DATE	TEST TIME	AMOUNT PAID	INSPECTION RESULTS				FINAL RESULT
			EXHAUST EMISSIONS	CATALYTIC CONVERTER PRESENCE	GAS CAP PRESENCE	GAS CAP PRESSURE	
18-FEB-2004	15:36:18	$23.00	PASS	PASS	PASS	PASS	PASS

VEHICLE INFORMATION

Registration Number	Vehicle Year	Vehicle Make	Registered Curb Weight	Vehicle Identification Number (VIN)	Vehicle Type	Engine Size	Odometer	AIRCARE EXPIRY DATE:
7121374	1991	TOYT	1385	JT2VV22F3M	LDGV	2.5	71 ,000	15-FEB-2005

HOW TO UNDERSTAND YOUR AIRCARE VEHICLE INSPECTION REPORT

The "Maximum Allowables" indicate the point above which the results become a "Fail". The "Average Passing Reading" value represents the average result for vehicles of the same year, type (car or truck), make and engine as your vehicle, calculated from actual AirCare test results.

DRIVING TEST		Maximum Allowable	Vehicle Reading	Average Passing Reading	RESULT
Hydrocarbons (HC)	ppm	89.00	5.00	13.50	PASS
Carbon Monoxide (CO)	%	0.68	0.00	0.03	PASS
Oxides of Nitrogen (NOx)	ppm	1007	364.00	259.50	PASS
Opacity (Diesel Only)					

IDLE TEST		Maximum Allowable	Vehicle Reading	Average Passing Reading	RESULT
Hydrocarbons (HC)	ppm	107	2	8	PASS
Carbon Monoxide (CO)	%	0.81	0.00	0.02	PASS

Results close to, or better than, the "Average Passing Reading" level means your vehicle is a normal emitter for its age and type. Readings above the average, but still below the "Maximum Allowable", may indicate that key emission controls are degrading to the point where your vehicle may fail in the future.

GENERAL INFORMATION

-Your vehicle has passed.
-This report may be necessary when licensing this vehicle.

FOR OFFICE USE ONLY

For more information about your AirCare test, see reverse or visit www.aircare.ca FORM #7002 REV 6/2004

Figure 30–34 Vehicle emission inspection report. (Reprinted with permission from Pacific Vehicle Testing Technologies Ltd., operators of the BC AirCare Program. All rights reserved.)

(a) (b) (c) (d)

Figure 30–35. (a) Typical enhanced exhaust emission testing facility. The sign says to leave the engine running. (b) Vehicle being "driven" on the dynamometer. The driver is following a trace displayed on a television screen. (c) The gas cap is tested for leakage. (d) The final report is printed and given to the driver.

Electric Vehicles

Battery-powered electric vehicles were the first choice of most automakers to meet the new ZEV rules. Electric motors produce maximum power at 0 rpm and work well for around town transportation. The downside is a limited driving range of 80 to 160 km (50 to 100 mi), time for battery recharging, and the space required for a very heavy battery pack.

As an example, the Ford Ranger EV pickup truck (see Figure 30–36) has 39 8 volt lead-acid battery modules that weigh almost 900 kg (2000 lb). Connected in series, the battery pack produces over 300 volts to power the drive motor. See Figure 30–37. Switching to very expensive nickel-metal hydride batteries (25 12-volt modules) reduced the battery pack weight to 590 kg (1300 lb) and increased the driving range from 80 km (50 mi) to 130 km (80 mi). The Ranger was the only major EV imported into Canada. It is now discontinued.

By the year 2000, DaimlerChrysler, Ford, G.M., Honda, Nissan, and Toyota were all manufacturing electric vehicles. This ended shortly after for a number of reasons: relaxed CARB ZEV rules, low consumer demand, high initial costs, and concerns that ZEVs are not really zero emission vehicles, as emissions are often generated at the power company producing electricity to charge the batteries. These are called indirect emissions.

Hybrid Vehicles

Hybrids are the combination of a gasoline internal combustion engine and an electric motor. A smaller gasoline engine, which increases fuel economy and lowers emissions, can then be used; the electric motor power is brought in during high load conditions. The total power of the engine and the motor cannot be added together, as gasoline engines produce maximum

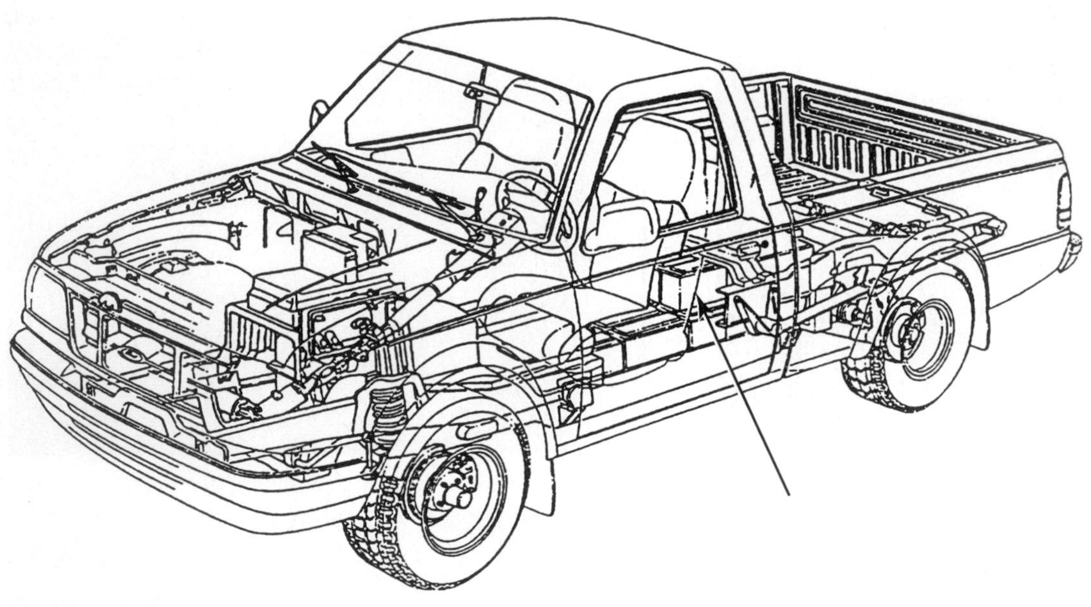

Figure 30–36 A Ford Ranger electric truck uses 39 batteries mounted under the pickup bed. (Courtesy Ford Motor Co.)

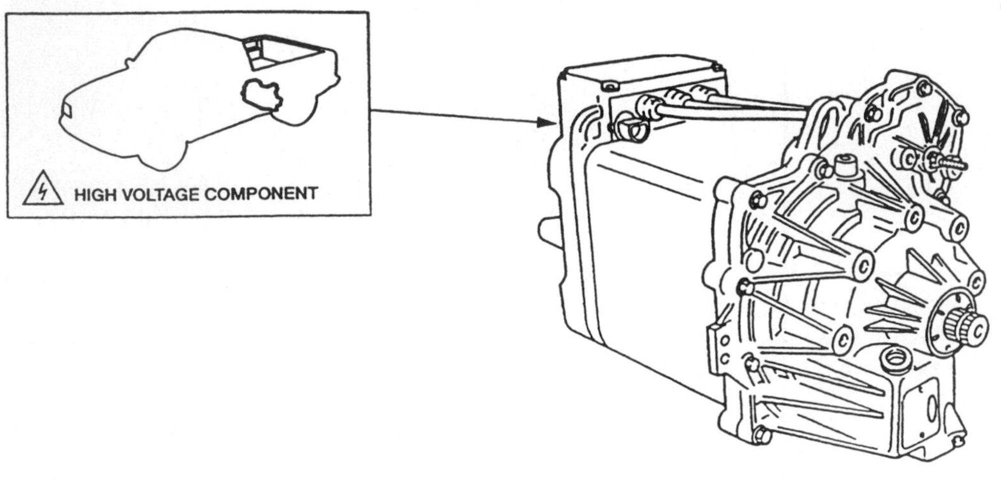

Figure 30–37 A typical motor/transaxle unit; torque is controlled by varying the amount of current flowing through the stator. The motor also charges (regenerates) the battery pack during braking. (Courtesy Ford Motor Co.)

power at higher RPM, while electric motors produce maximum power at 0 rpm. See Figure 30–38.

Series and Parallel Hybrids

Series hybrids use the engine to drive a generator, which in turn powers an electric motor that drives the wheels. Parallel hybrids use both the engine and the electric motor to propel the vehicle. See Figure 30–39.

Extensive Testing

Both Honda and Toyota carried out extensive testing in Japan before releasing the cars for sale in Canada and the U.S. Almost 50 000 hybrids were sold in Japan during the three years prior to North American introduction.

Honda Insight and Civic

Honda calls their system Integrated Motor Assist (IMA). The Insight uses a small 1.0-litre, 3-cylinder aluminum engine as the main power source; an electric motor mounted in the bell housing supplies additional power assist during high load conditions and acceleration. See Figures 30–40 and 30–41. The electric motor also functions as a generator during braking and deceleration to keep the 144 volt NiMH

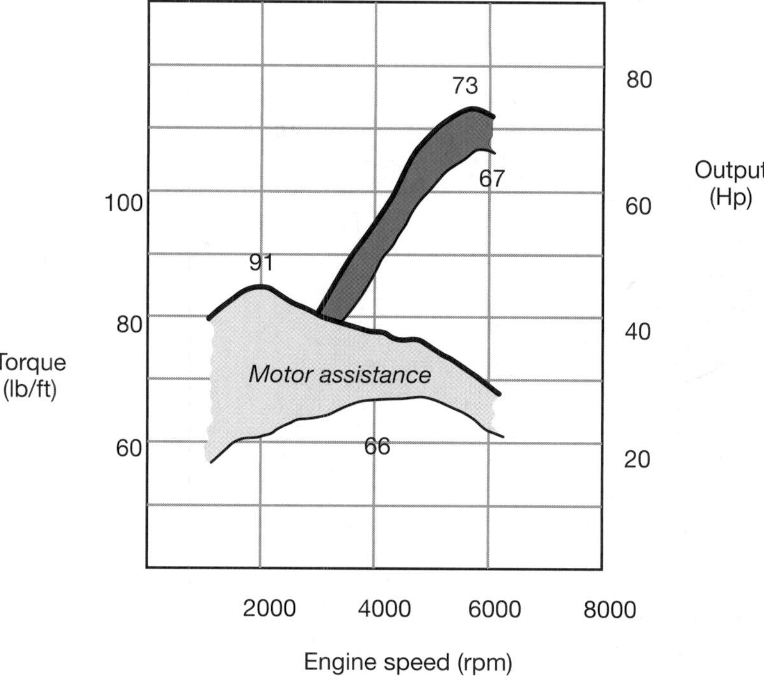

Figure 30–38 Combined power output of a Honda Integrated Motor Assist (IMA) hybrid. Note the electric motor produces maximum power at low RPM and the gasoline engine at high RPM. (Courtesy Honda Canada Inc.)

Series Hybrid System

In the series hybrid system, the engine runs a generator, and the generated electricity enables the electric motor to drive the wheels. This type of vehicle can be described as an electric car that is equipped with an engine-driven generator.

Equipped with a low-output engine, the engine is operated at a practically constant speed in its most effective range, in order to efficiently recharge the battery while the vehicle is in motion.

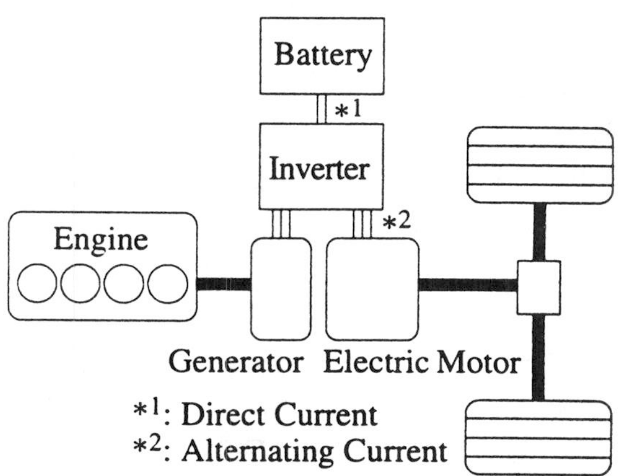

Parallel Hybrid System

This system, using both the engine and the electric motor to directly drive the wheels, is called the parallel hybrid system. In addition to supplementing the motive force of the engine, the electric motor in this system can also serve as a generator to recharge the battery while the vehicle is in motion.

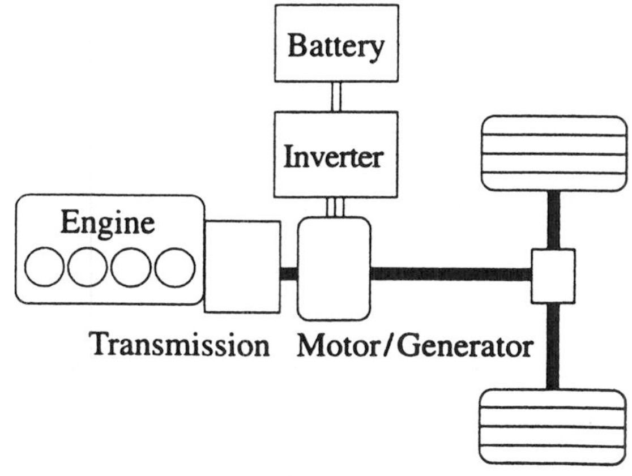

Figure 30–39 Series and parallel hybrid systems. (Courtesy Honda Canada Inc.)

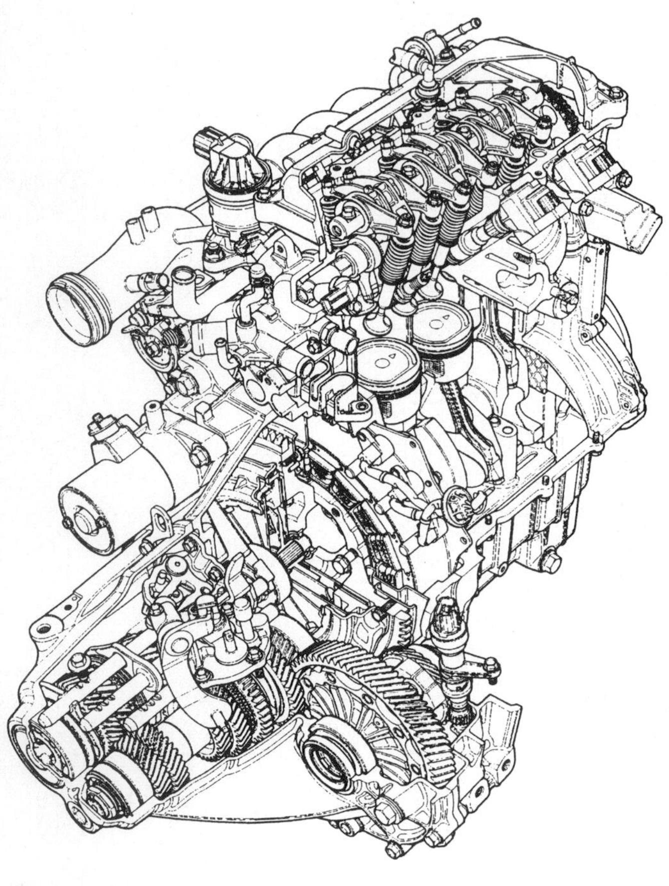

Figure 30–40 The Honda Insight IMA system mounts the ultra-compact electric motor in the bell housing. The motor functions as an assist motor, a generator and a starter. (Courtesy Honda Canada Inc.)

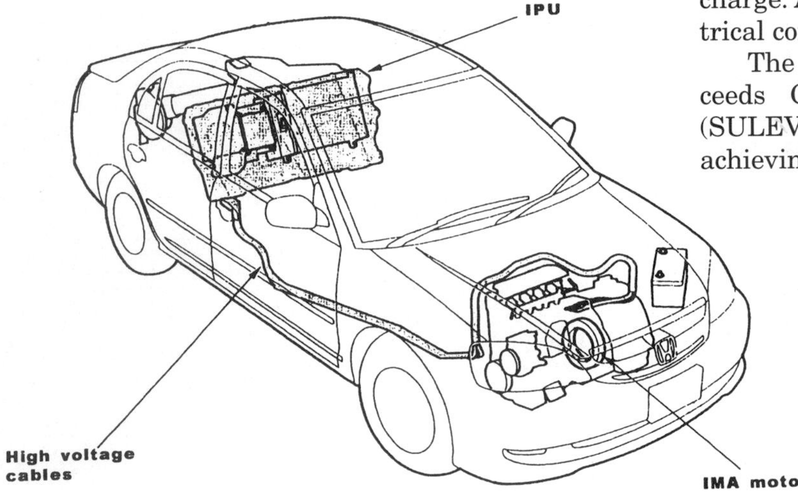

Figure 30–41 The major components of the Honda IMA system are the motor, the high voltage cables, and the Intelligent Power Unit (batteries and controls). (Courtesy Honda Canada Inc.)

battery pack charged. If the battery pack shows a low state of charge, the motor will continue the generator function at idle. No outside charging is required.

The engine will automatically shut off when coming to a stop unless the air conditioning is on, the batteries are low, or an electrical load exists (i.e., headlights on). The IMA motor will restart the engine when the accelerator pedal is depressed (with the clutch disengaged). A conventional 12 volt starter and battery are used only under abnormal conditions, such as a low battery-module state of charge.

The Insight is a lightweight aluminum-bodied two-seater that ranks as the most fuel-efficient gasoline-powered automobile sold in North America. See Figure 30–42.

The Civic is a larger four cylinder, four-seat automobile that also enjoys excellent fuel economy and low emissions. Most of the Insight IMA features also apply.

Toyota Prius

The Toyota Prius hybrid uses a slightly different concept. See Figures 30–43 and 30–44. Two electric motors mounted in the transaxle assembly are used to both drive the vehicle and charge the 274 volt NiMH battery pack. See Figure 30–45. One motor (MG2) drives the wheels on acceleration and charges the batteries during deceleration. The second motor (MG1) supplies electricity to MG2 to drive the wheels. It also functions both as a starter and a generator to charge the batteries. There is no auxiliary 12 volt starter. The Toyota hybrid has the ability to operate with only the electric motor or a combination of electric motor and engine. See Figure 30–46.

The engine stops automatically when the vehicle comes to a stop, unless the air conditioning is on, the engine is cold, or the batteries are at a low state of charge. A 12 volt battery is used to power body electrical components and lighting.

The Prius is an extremely clean vehicle that exceeds CARB super ultra-low emission vehicle (SULEV) standards for CO, HC and NO_x while still achieving excellent fuel economy and driveability.

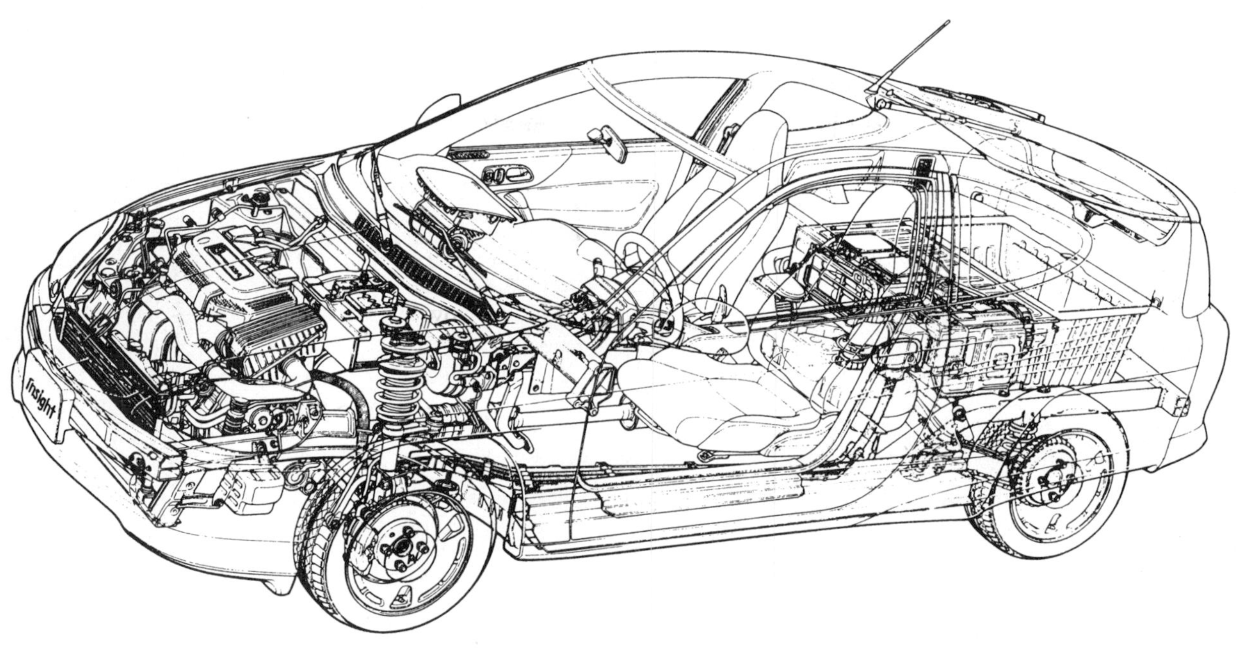

Figure 30–42 The Honda Insight battery pack is mounted in the trunk area. (Courtesy Honda Canada Inc.)

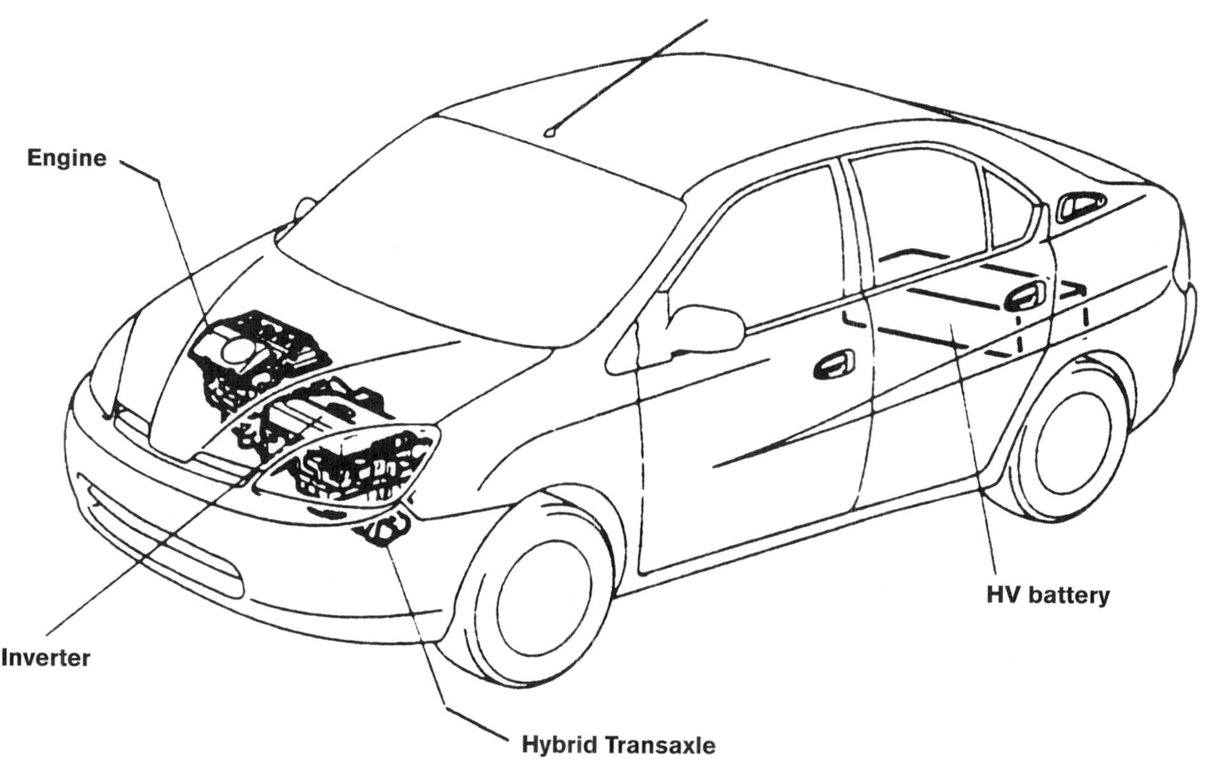

Figure 30–43 Toyota Prius: layout of main components. (Courtesy Toyota Canada Inc.)

Figure 30–44 The Toyota Prius combines the engine, transaxle and electric motors into a single powertrain assembly. (Courtesy Toyota Canada Inc.)

Inverter
HV battery
MG1
Power Splitting Device
Engine
MG2
Reduction gears
Hybrid transaxle
Mechanical power path
Electric path

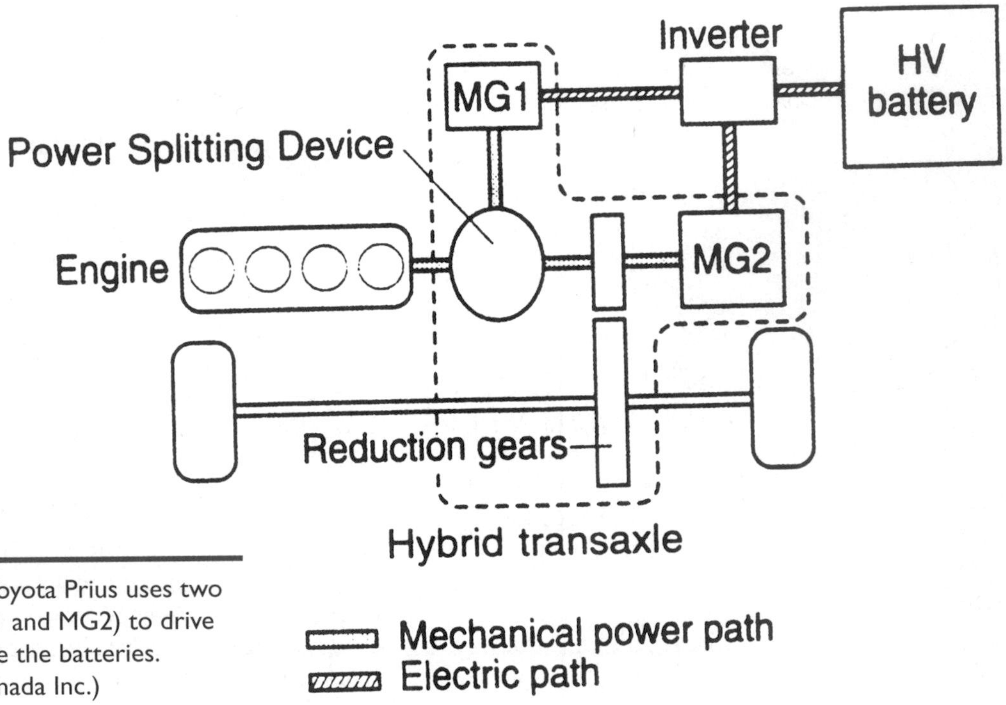

Figure 30–45 The Toyota Prius uses two electric motors (MG1 and MG2) to drive the wheels and charge the batteries. (Courtesy Toyota Canada Inc.)

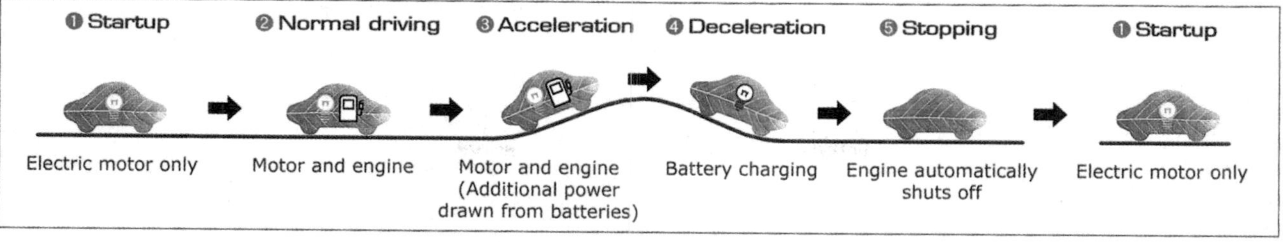

Figure 30–46 Operating modes of the Toyota Prius hybrid. (Courtesy Toyota Canada Inc.)

SAFETY

Only trained technicians are allowed to service the high voltage circuits in any hybrid. Special training, insulated wearing apparel and tools are needed to work safely in this area. In 2004, as an example, Toyota raised their hybrid operating voltage from 274 to almost 500 volts! Follow all safety instructions to the letter.

Industry Support

While Toyota and Honda were the first major manufacturers to build hybrids, many other domestic and import automakers have now joined their ranks. Ford released the Escape hybrid for 2005; GM joined with diesel/hybrid transit buses in 2004 and the Silverado hybrid pickup truck in 2005. GM also plans a hybrid Saturn Vue in 2006. DaimlerChrysler is currently testing this technology with the Dodge Durango and Jeep Liberty. Asian carmakers are moving into larger vehicles such as the Toyota Camry, Honda Civic, and Lexus SUV.

Fuel Cell Vehicles

Very simply put, a fuel cell vehicle is an electric vehicle powered by an electricity generating fuel cell, rather than a battery pack.

A fuel cell is a device that produces electricity from hydrogen (in our example), leaving nothing behind except heat and water. See Figures 30–47 and 30–48.

Fuel cells generate electricity from an electrochemical process using hydrogen as a fuel. See Figure 30–49. Compressed hydrogen is pumped into the fuel cell at the anode, the negative side of the cell. Oxygen (in the air) enters the cell from the opposite side at the cathode, the positive side of the cell. The oxygen attracts the hydrogen. The two are separated by a thin electrolytic membrane of polymer material.

A platinum powder catalyst in the cell begins a reaction that strips the hydrogen of its electrons; only the positive charged hydrogen ions (protons) can pass through the membrane into the positive side of the cell. This leaves the negative charged electrons behind. A voltage potential now exists between the two

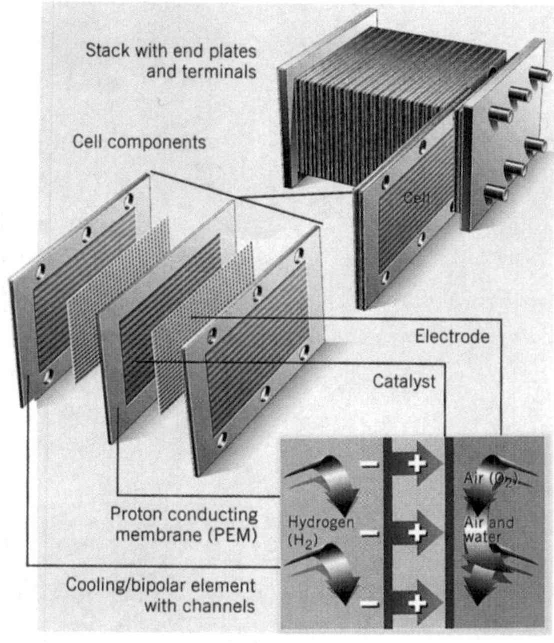

Figure 30–47 Individual fuel cells are combined into a stack, similar to a battery; each cell contributes to the total output voltage from the stack. (Courtesy DaimlerChrysler Corporation)

sides of the cell. Electrons (current) flowing through a circuit (connecting the positive and negative sides) power an electric motor to drive the wheels.

The electrons (−), now at the cathode, join with the hydrogen ions (+) and oxygen at a second platinum powder catalyst; a reaction occurs. Water and heat are the only products: no emissions.

When?

Almost every major automaker is developing a fuel cell vehicle. Some, such as Toyota and G.M., are using their own in-house technologies; others, such as Ford, DaimlerChrysler and Honda, are using fuel cells pioneered by a Canadian company, Ballard Power Systems of Burnaby, British Columbia.

Many of these car companies have working prototypes currently being tested; however, full production is still about ten years away. Reduced costs, improved reliability, and fuel availability are concerns still to be addressed.

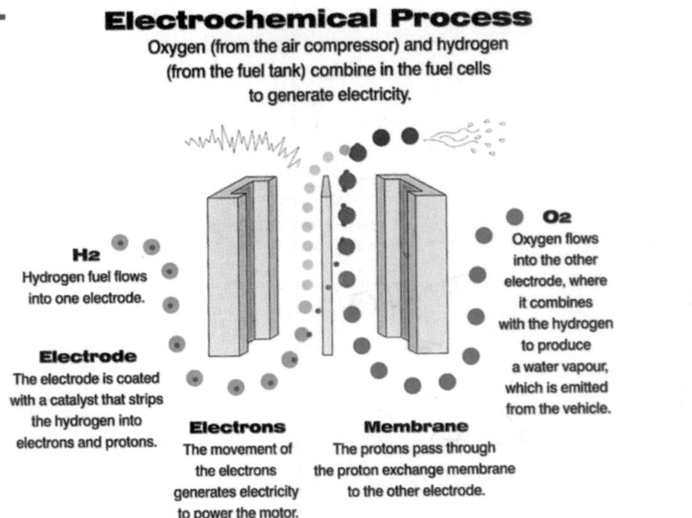
(a)
Electrochemical Process
Oxygen (from the air compressor) and hydrogen (from the fuel tank) combine in the fuel cells to generate electricity.
H2
Hydrogen fuel flows into one electrode.
Electrode
The electrode is coated with a catalyst that strips the hydrogen into electrons and protons.
Electrons
The movement of the electrons generates electricity to power the motor.
Membrane
The protons pass through the proton exchange membrane to the other electrode.
O2
Oxygen flows into the other electrode, where it combines with the hydrogen to produce a water vapour, which is emitted from the vehicle.
(b)
Direct Hydrogen Fuel Cell Vehicle
1. Hydrogen is supplied to the fuel cells.
2. Air is supplied to the fuel cells by the air compressor.
3. Oxygen from the air combines with hydrogen in the fuel cell to generate electricity, which is sent to the traction inverter module (TIM).
4. The traction inverter module converts the electricity for use by the motor/transaxle. The motor/transaxle converts the electric energy into the mechanical energy which turns the wheels.
5. Water vapour/droplets is/are the only byproduct of this process.
Pressurized H2 fuel tank
Fuel cell stack
Air compressor
Traction power
Electric motor/transaxle
Exhaust pipe

Figure 30–48 (a) Operation of a fuel cell. (b) Component layout. (Courtesy Ford Motor Co.)

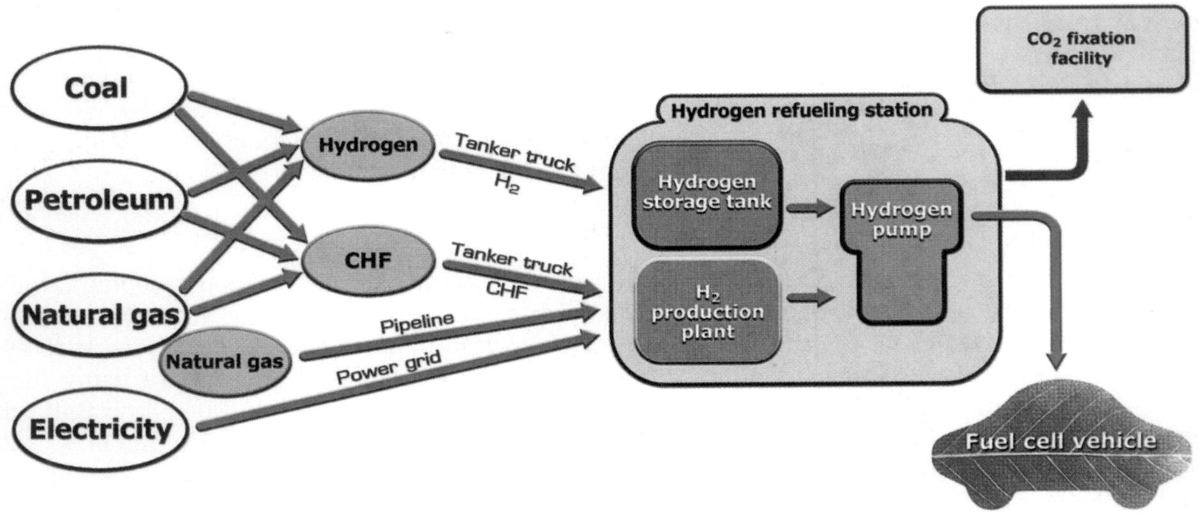
Fueling the Fuel Cell
Coal
Petroleum
Natural gas
Electricity
Hydrogen
CHF
Natural gas
Tanker truck H2
Tanker truck CHF
Pipeline
Power grid
Hydrogen refueling station
Hydrogen storage tank
H2 production plant
Hydrogen pump
CO2 fixation facility
Fuel cell vehicle

Figure 30–49 Compressed hydrogen, stored at a hydrogen refueling station, is pumped into a fuel tank in the vehicle. It initially arrives at the station as either compressed hyydrogen, clean hydrocarbon fuel or natural gas. (Courtesy Toyota Canada Inc.)

PHOTO SEQUENCE 21 Testing a Vacuum-Operated EGR Valve

P21–1 A cutaway of a typical vacuum-operated exhaust gas recirculation (EGR) valve.

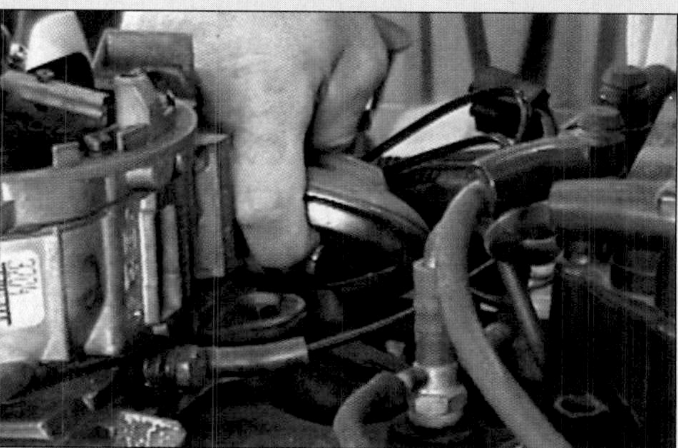

P21–2 When the engine operates at idle speed, it should stall if the EGR valve is opened by hand. The technician should use a glove or shop cloth to prevent the possibility of being burned on the hot EGR valve.

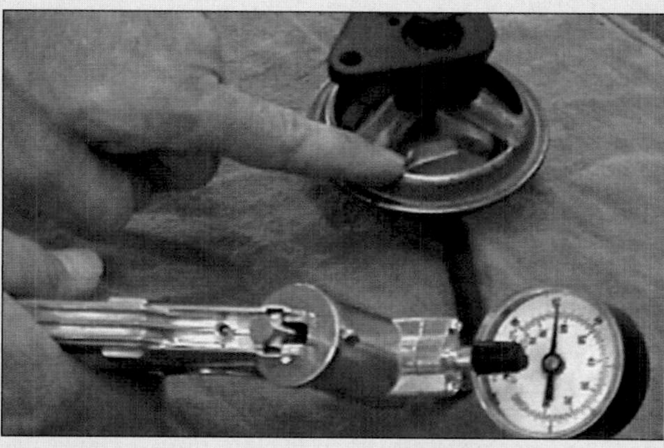

P21–3 An EGR valve can also be tested off the vehicle by applying vacuum from a hand-operated vacuum pump. The diaphragm of the valve should move when vacuum is applied, and the vacuum should hold if the valve is okay.

P21–4 This is a negative back-pressure EGR valve because the vacuum dropped to zero when shop air (compressed air) was blown over the end of the EGR valve pintle. A positive back-pressure EGR valve would require the air pressure to close an internal valve to allow the valve to open when vacuum was applied to the diaphragm.

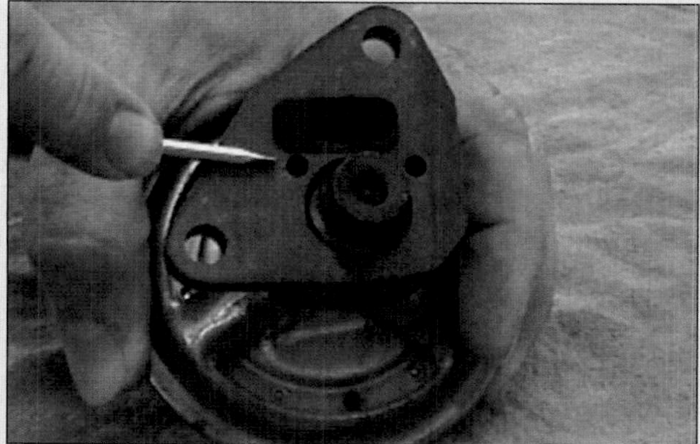

P21–5 All EGR valve passages should be checked for carbon blockages that can prevent the valve from flowing enough exhaust gas to reduce NO_x exhaust emissions.

P21–6 All EGR passages in the intake manifold should also be checked for carbon and cleaned out if restricted. Use a vacuum cleaner to help get all of the pieces of carbon out of the passages.

SUMMARY

1. The positive crankcase ventilation (PCV) system pulls blow-by gases and crankcase vapours into the intake manifold.
2. The PCV valve allows a metered amount of manifold vacuum to be applied to the crankcase. The valve can be tested by rattling the valve or by using a card over the oil fill opening.
3. An AIR pump supplies air to the exhaust manifold when the engine is cold and to the catalytic converter when the engine achieves closed-loop operation.
4. The evaporative emission control (EVAP) system uses a charcoal (carbon) canister and various hoses and lines to trap and hold gasoline fumes and to prevent these fumes from escaping into the atmosphere.
5. The exhaust gas recirculation (EGR) system bleeds some inert exhaust gases into the combustion chamber to prevent the higher peak temperature that could occur. The main purpose and function of the EGR system is to reduce the formation of oxides of nitrogen (NO_x) exhaust emissions.
6. A catalytic converter is used in the exhaust system to start a chemical reaction among the exhaust gases but the catalysts are not consumed by the reaction. Its function is to separate NO_x exhaust emissions into nitrogen (N) and oxygen (O_2). The other part of the converter is designed to oxidize hydrocarbons (HC) and carbon monoxides (CO) into harmless CO_2 and H_2O (water vapour).
7. Hybrid vehicles use a combination of a smaller internal combustion engine and an electric drive motor. Fuel cells convert hydrogen gas into electricity to power an electric drive motor.

REVIEW QUESTIONS

1. List three tests that can be performed to check the PCV system.
2. Describe how to test an AIR system using an exhaust gas analyzer.
3. Explain how to perform a pressure test on an evaporative control system.
4. List three methods that can be used to test an EGR valve and system.
5. Describe three tests that can be used to test the condition of a catalytic converter.

RED SEAL CERTIFICATION-TYPE QUESTIONS

1. Positive crankcase ventilation (PCV) systems help to control ______.
   - a. Particulates
   - b. Hydrocarbons
   - c. Oxides of nitrogen
   - d. Carbon dioxide
2. An air pump system with a defective one-way exhaust check valve could ______.
   - a. Create an external exhaust leak
   - b. Cause exhaust back-pressure to decrease
   - c. Cause the air pump to fail
   - d. Reduce engine power during cold operation
3. The charcoal canister can become saturated with gasoline by ______.
   - a. Overfilling the fuel tank
   - b. Leaking fuel injectors
   - c. Excessive fuel injection pressure
   - d. Leaving the gasoline filler cap loose
4. Positive back-pressure EGR valves
   - a. Operate at idle
   - b. Require low exhaust back pressure to open
   - c. Need exhaust back pressure to function
   - d. Operate only when the coolant temperature is below 50°C (122°F)
5. A partially clogged EGR passage could cause the vehicle to fail an emissions test for ______.
   - a. Oxides of nitrogen
   - b. Excessive hydrocarbons
   - c. Carbon monoxide
   - d. Particulates
6. Catalytic converters can be damaged by
   - a. Long periods of idle
   - b. Pulling a trailer
   - c. An ignition misfire
   - d. High engine RPM
7. A good catalytic converter should be
   - a. Hotter at the outlet than at the inlet
   - b. Hotter at the inlet than at the outlet
8. Smog is formed in the atmosphere when oxides of nitrogen combine with ______.
   - a. Carbon monoxide
   - b. Hydrocarbons
   - c. Carbon dioxide
   - d. Particulate matter
9. Diesel engines are tested with an opacity meter that passes a light beam through the exhaust gases at the tailpipe. This measures
   - a. Exhaust volume
   - b. Exhaust density
   - c. Carbon monoxide levels
   - d. Excessive back pressure
10. Hybrid vehicles reduce total exhaust emission because
    - a. The engines are very efficient
    - b. They only carry two passengers
    - c. The batteries are charged overnight
    - d. A smaller internal combustion engine can be used

31

Engine Performance Diagnosis and Testing

OBJECTIVES: After studying Chapter 31, you should be able to:

1. Prepare for the interprovincial Red Seal certification examination in Appendix VIII (Engine Performance) on the topics covered in this chapter.
2. List the steps of the diagnostic process.
3. Describe the simple preliminary tests that should be performed at the start of the diagnostic process.
4. List six items to check as part of a thorough visual inspection.
5. List the six fundamental troubleshooting principles.
6. List the precautions that should be taken when working on computerized engine control systems.
7. Explain the troubleshooting procedures to follow if a diagnostic trouble code has been set.
8. Explain the troubleshooting procedures to follow if no diagnostic trouble codes have been set.
9. Discuss the diagnosis of a vehicle equipped with the second generation of on-board diagnostics (OBD II).
10. List acceptable levels of HC, CO, CO_2, and O_2 with and without a catalytic converter.
11. List four possible causes of high readings for HC, CO, and NO_x.

It is important that all automotive service technicians know how to diagnose and troubleshoot engine computer systems. The diagnostic process is a specific method that eliminates known good components or systems in order to find the root cause of automotive engine performance problems. All vehicle manufacturers recommend a diagnostic procedure, and the plan suggested in this chapter combines most of the features of these plans plus additional steps developed over years of real-world problem solving.

THE EIGHT-STEP DIAGNOSTIC PROCEDURE

Many different things can cause an engine performance problem or concern. The service technician has to narrow the possibilities until the cause of the problem is found and corrected. A funnel is a way of visualizing a diagnostic procedure. See Figure 31–1. At the wide top are the symptoms of the problem; the funnel narrows as possible causes are eliminated until the root cause is found and corrected at the bottom of the funnel.

All problem diagnosis deals with symptoms that could be the result of many different causes. The wide range of possible solutions must be narrowed to the most likely and these must eventually be further narrowed down to the actual cause. The following section describes eight steps the service technician can take to narrow the possibilities to one cause.

Step #1. Verify the Problem

Before one minute is spent on diagnosis, be certain that a problem exists. If the problem cannot be

Figure 31–1 A funnel is a visual method of thinking of the diagnostic process. The goal, of course, is to find the root cause and to repair it in order to achieve customer satisfaction.

verified, the problem cannot be solved or tested to verify that the repair was complete. See Figure 31–2.

The driver knows the vehicle and how it is driven. *Before* diagnosis is started, always ask the following questions:

- Is the malfunction indicator light (check engine) on?
- What was the temperature outside?
- Was the engine warm or cold?
- Was the problem during starting, acceleration, cruise, etc.?
- How far had the vehicle been driven?
- Were any dash warning lights on? If so, which one?
- Has there been any service or repair work performed on the vehicle lately?

NOTE: This last question is very important! Many engine performance faults are often the result of something being knocked loose or a hose falling off during repair work, etc. Knowing that the vehicle was just serviced before the problem began may be an indicator.

TECH TIP 

"Original Equipment" Is Not a Four-Letter Word

Many problems can be traced to the use of an aftermarket part that has failed early in its service life. Technicians who work at dealerships usually go immediately to an aftermarket part that is observed during a visual inspection. It has been their experience that simply replacing the aftermarket part with the factory original equipment (OE) part often solves the problem.

Original equipment parts are *required* to pass quality and durability standards and tests that are not required of aftermarket parts. The technician should be aware that the presence of a new part does not necessarily mean that the part is good.

After the nature and scope of the problem are determined, the complaint should be verified before further diagnostic tests are performed. A sample of a form that customers could fill out with details of the problem can be seen in Figure 31–3. Perform a thorough test drive under similar conditions to verify the complaint (problem or concern).

Step #2. Perform a Thorough Visual Inspection and Basic Tests

The visual inspection is the most important aspect of diagnosis! Most experts agree that between 10 and 30% of all engine performance problems can be found simply by performing a *thorough* visual inspection.

NOTE: The purpose of any fault diagnosis is the elimination of known good components.

The inspection should include the following:

- **Check for obvious problems.**
  Fuel leaks
  Vacuum hoses disconnected or split (see Figure 31–4)
  Corroded connectors
  Unusual noises, smoke, or smell
  Check the air cleaner and air duct for restrictions. See Figure 31–5.

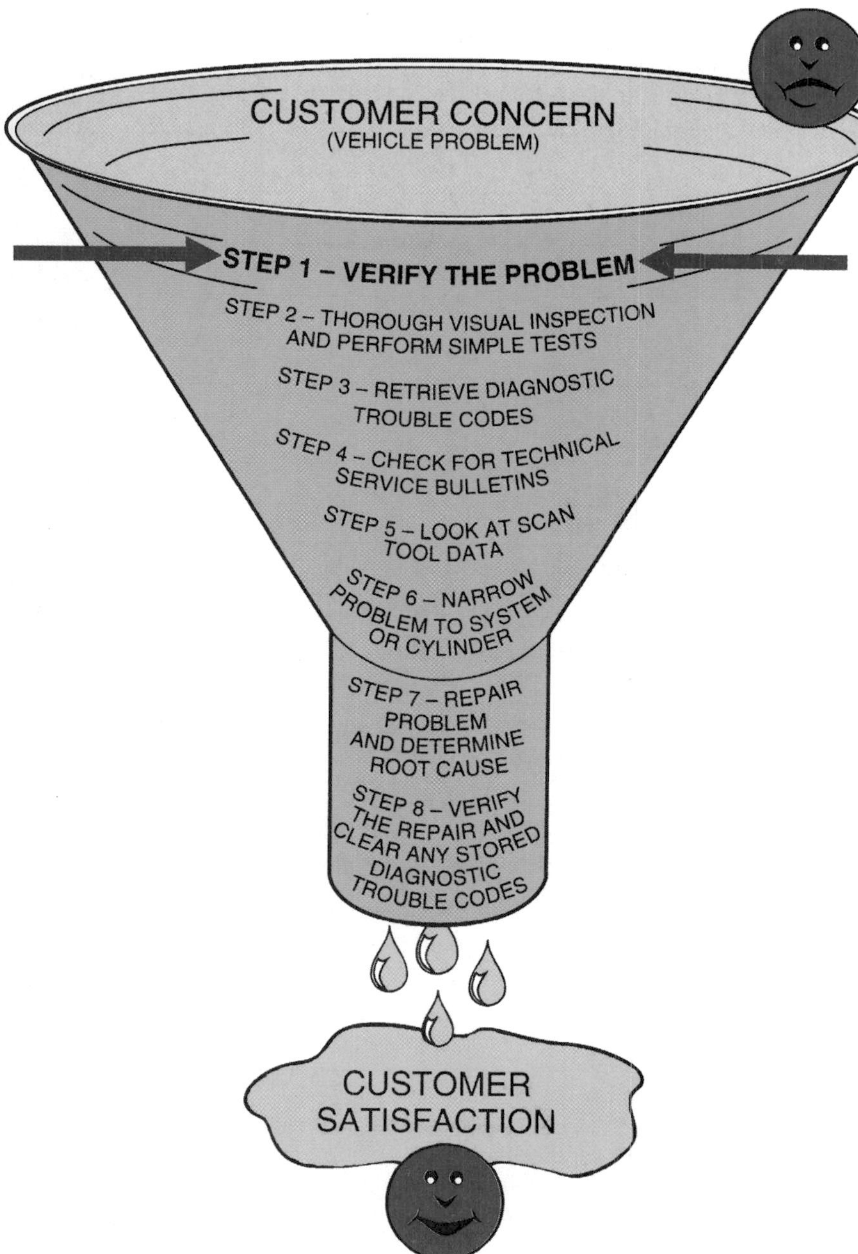
CUSTOMER CONCERN
(VEHICLE PROBLEM)
STEP 1 – VERIFY THE PROBLEM
STEP 2 – THOROUGH VISUAL INSPECTION AND PERFORM SIMPLE TESTS
STEP 3 – RETRIEVE DIAGNOSTIC TROUBLE CODES
STEP 4 – CHECK FOR TECHNICAL SERVICE BULLETINS
STEP 5 – LOOK AT SCAN TOOL DATA
STEP 6 – NARROW PROBLEM TO SYSTEM OR CYLINDER
STEP 7 – REPAIR PROBLEM AND DETERMINE ROOT CAUSE
STEP 8 – VERIFY THE REPAIR AND CLEAR ANY STORED DIAGNOSTIC TROUBLE CODES
CUSTOMER SATISFACTION

Figure 31–2 Diagnostic funnel. Step #1 is to verify the problem. If the problem cannot be duplicated, obviously the repair cannot be performed.

- **Check everything that does and does not work.** This step involves turning things on and observing that everything is working properly.
- **Look for evidence of previous repairs.** Any time work is performed on a vehicle, there is always a risk that something will be disturbed, knocked off, or left disconnected.
- **Check oil level and condition.** Another area for visual inspection is oil level and condition.
  Oil level—Oil should be to the proper level.
  Oil condition—Using a match or lighter, try to light the oil on the dipstick; if the oil flames up, gasoline is present in the engine oil. Drip some engine oil from the dipstick onto the hot exhaust manifold. If the oil bubbles or boils, coolant (water) is present in the oil. Check for grittiness by rubbing the oil between your fingers.

> **NOTE:** Gasoline in the oil will cause the engine to run rich by drawing fuel through the positive crankcase ventilation (PCV) system.

- **Check coolant level and condition.** Most mechanical engine problems are caused by overheating. The proper operation of the cooling system is critical to the life of any engine.

ENGINE PERFORMANCE DIAGNOSIS WORKSHEET

(To Be Filled Out By the Vehicle Owner)

Name: ______________________ Kilometres (Mileage): ______________ Date: ______________

Make: ______________ Model: ______________ Year: ______________ Engine: ______________

(Please Circle All That Apply in All Categories)	
Describe Problem:	
When Did the Problem First Occur?	• Just Started • Last Week • Last Month • Other ______________
List Previous Repairs in the Last 6 Months:	
Starting Problems	• Will Not Crank • Cranks, but Will Not Start • Starts, but Takes a Long Time
Engine Quits or Stalls	• Right after Starting • When Put into Gear • During Steady Speed Driving • Right after Vehicle Comes to a Stop • While Idling • During Acceleration • When Parking
Poor Idling Conditions	• Is Too Slow at All Times • Is Too Fast • Intermittently Too Fast or Too Slow • Is Rough or Uneven • Fluctuates Up and Down
Poor Running Conditions	• Runs Rough • Lacks Power • Bucks and Jerks • Poor Fuel Economy • Hesitates or Stumbles on Acceleration • Backfires • Misfires or Cuts Out • Engine Knocks, Pings, Rattles • Surges • Dieseling or Run-On
Auto. Transmission Problems	• Improper Shifting (Early/Late) • Changes Gear Incorrectly • Vehicle Does not Move When in Gear • Jerks or Bucks
Usually Occurs	• Morning • Afternoon • Anytime
Engine Temperature	• Cold • Warm • Hot
Driving Conditions During Occurrence	• Short—Less Than 3 km (2 mi) • 3–15 km (2–10 mi) • Long—More Than 15 km (2–10 mi) • Stop and Go • While Turning • While Braking • At Gear Engagement • With A/C Operating • With Headlights On • During Acceleration • During Deceleration • Mostly Downhill • Mostly Uphill • Mostly Level • Mostly Curvy • Rough Road
Driving Habits	• Mostly City Driving • Highway • Park Vehicle Inside • Park Vehicle Outside **Drive Per Day:** • Less Than 15 km (10 mi) • 15 to 80 km (10–50 mi) • More Than 80 km (50 mi)
Gasoline Used	**Fuel Octane:** • 87 • 89 • 91 • More Than 91 **Brand:** ______________
Temperature When Problem Occurs	• 0–13° C (32–55° F) • Below Freezing 0° C (32° F) • Above 13° C (55° F)
Check Engine Light/ Dash Warning Light	• Light On Sometimes • Light On Always • Light Never On
Smells	• "Hot" • Gasoline • Oil Burning • Electrical
Noises	• Rattle • Knock • Squeak • Other

Figure 31–3 Form that can be given to a customer to be filled out before attempting to diagnose an engine performance problem.

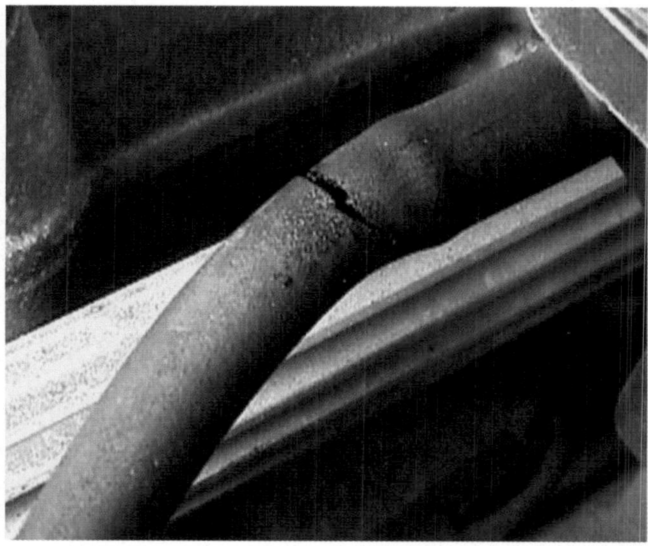

Figure 31–4 All vacuum hoses should be checked to see if they are cracked, swollen, or split.

TECH TIP 

Smoke Machine Testing

Vacuum (air) leaks can cause a variety of driveability problems and are often difficult to locate. One method that works well is to use a machine that generates a burst of smoke. Connecting the outlet of the machine to the hose removed from the vacuum brake booster allows smoke to enter the intake manifold. Any vacuum leaks will be spotted by observing smoke coming out of the leak. See Figure 31–6. A theatre smoke machine works well.

(a)

(b)

Figure 31–5 (a) This is what was found as the air filter housing was opened during service. The nuts were obviously deposited by squirrels (or some other animal). (b) Not only was the housing filled with nuts, but this air filter was extremely dirty, indicating that this vehicle had not been serviced for a long time.

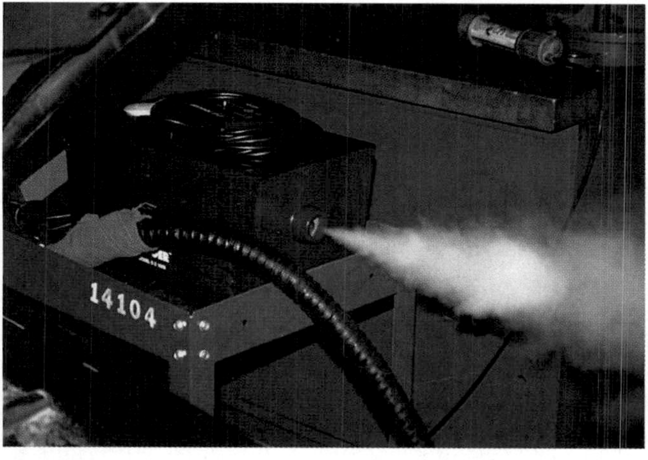

(a)

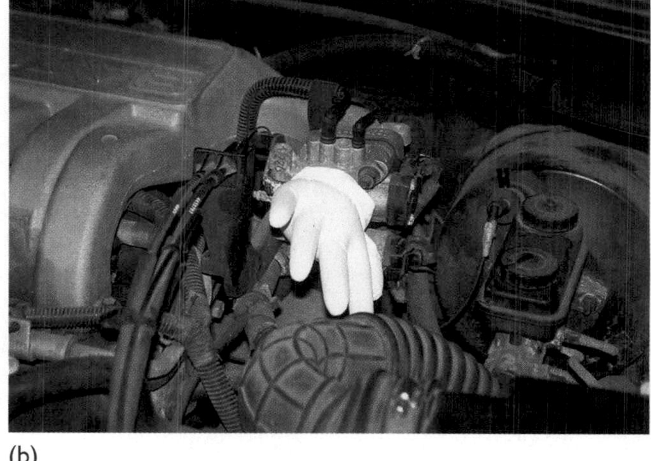

(b)

Figure 31–6 (a) A shot of smoke from a smoke machine. In actual use, this outlet is connected to a disconnected vacuum hose on the engine being tested. A convenient hose to use is the hose at the vacuum brake booster. The machine forces smoke into the intake manifold through the hose. (b) To keep the smoke from escaping through the throttle plate opening, a plastic bag can be used to seal the opening. Here a rubber glove is used, and while it looks strange, it worked well.

Figure 31–7 The paper test involves holding a piece of paper near the tailpipe with a warm engine at idle. A good engine should produce an even, outward flow of exhaust. If the paper is sucked in toward the tailpipe, a burned valve is a possibility.

NOTE: Check the coolant level in the radiator only if the radiator is cool. If the radiator is hot and the radiator cap is removed, the drop in pressure above the coolant will cause the coolant to boil immediately, which can cause severe burns because the coolant expands explosively upward and outward from the radiator opening.

- **Perform the paper test.** A soundly running engine should produce even and steady exhaust at the tail pipe. Hold a piece of paper or a 75 × 125 mm (3 × 5 in.) card within 25 mm (1 in.) of the tail pipe with the engine running at idle. See Figure 31–7. The paper should blow evenly away from the end of the tail pipe without puffing or being drawn inward toward the end of the tail pipe. If the paper is at times drawn *toward* the tail pipe, the valves in one or more cylinders could be burned. Other reasons why the paper might be drawn toward the tail pipe include the following:
  1. The engine could be misfiring because of a lean condition or an ignition system fault such as a bad spark plug wire.
  2. A faulty fuel injector.
  3. Pulsing of the paper toward the tail pipe could also be caused by a hole in the exhaust system. If exhaust escapes through a hole in the exhaust system, air could be drawn—in the intervals between the exhaust puffs—from the tail pipe to the hole in the exhaust, causing the paper to be drawn toward the tail pipe.
- **Ensure adequate fuel level.** Make certain that the fuel tank is at least one-fourth to one-half full; if the fuel level is low it is possible that any water or alcohol at the bottom of the fuel tank is more concentrated and can be drawn into the fuel system.

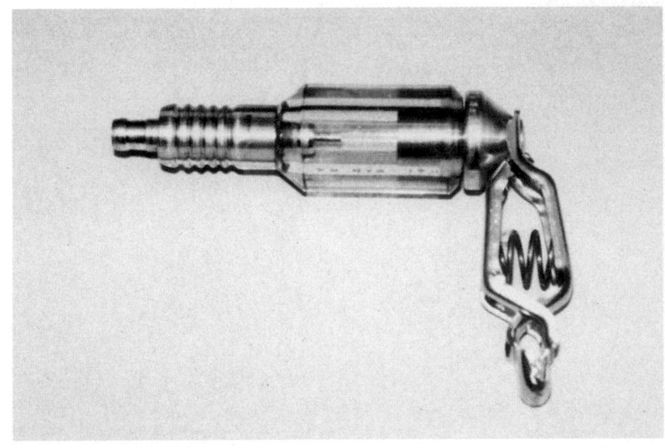

(a)

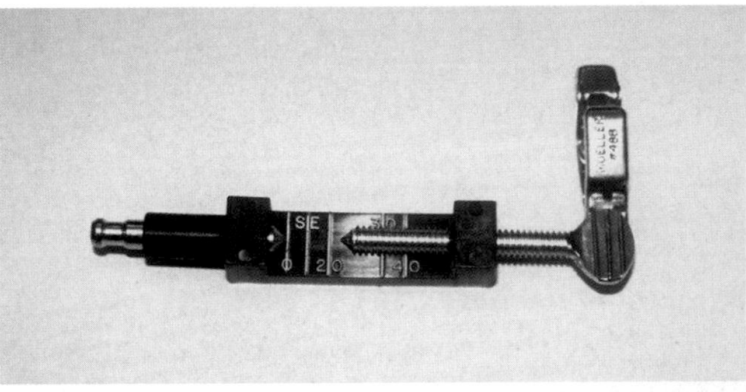

(b)

Figure 31–8 (a) A typical spark tester that uses a clear plastic shield that protects the spark from igniting any flammable substance that may be near while testing for spark. (b) A spark tester that is adjustable for different voltages. Most electronic ignition systems should be able to jump a 25 mm (1 in.) gap, which is equal to about 40 000 volts.

- **Check the battery voltage.** The voltage of the battery should be at least 12.4 volts and the charging voltage (engine running) should be 13.5 to 15.0 volts at 2000 rpm. Low battery voltage can cause a variety of problems including reduced fuel economy and incorrect (usually too high) idle speed.
- **Check the spark using a spark tester.** Remove one spark plug wire and attach the removed plug wire to the spark tester. Attach the grounding clip of the spark tester to a good clean engine ground, start or crank the engine, and observe the spark tester. See Figure 31–8. The spark at the spark tester should be steady and consistent. If an intermittent spark occurs, then this condition should be treated as a no-spark condition. If this test does not show satisfactory spark, carefully inspect and test all components of the primary and secondary ignition systems. See Chapter 24 for details.

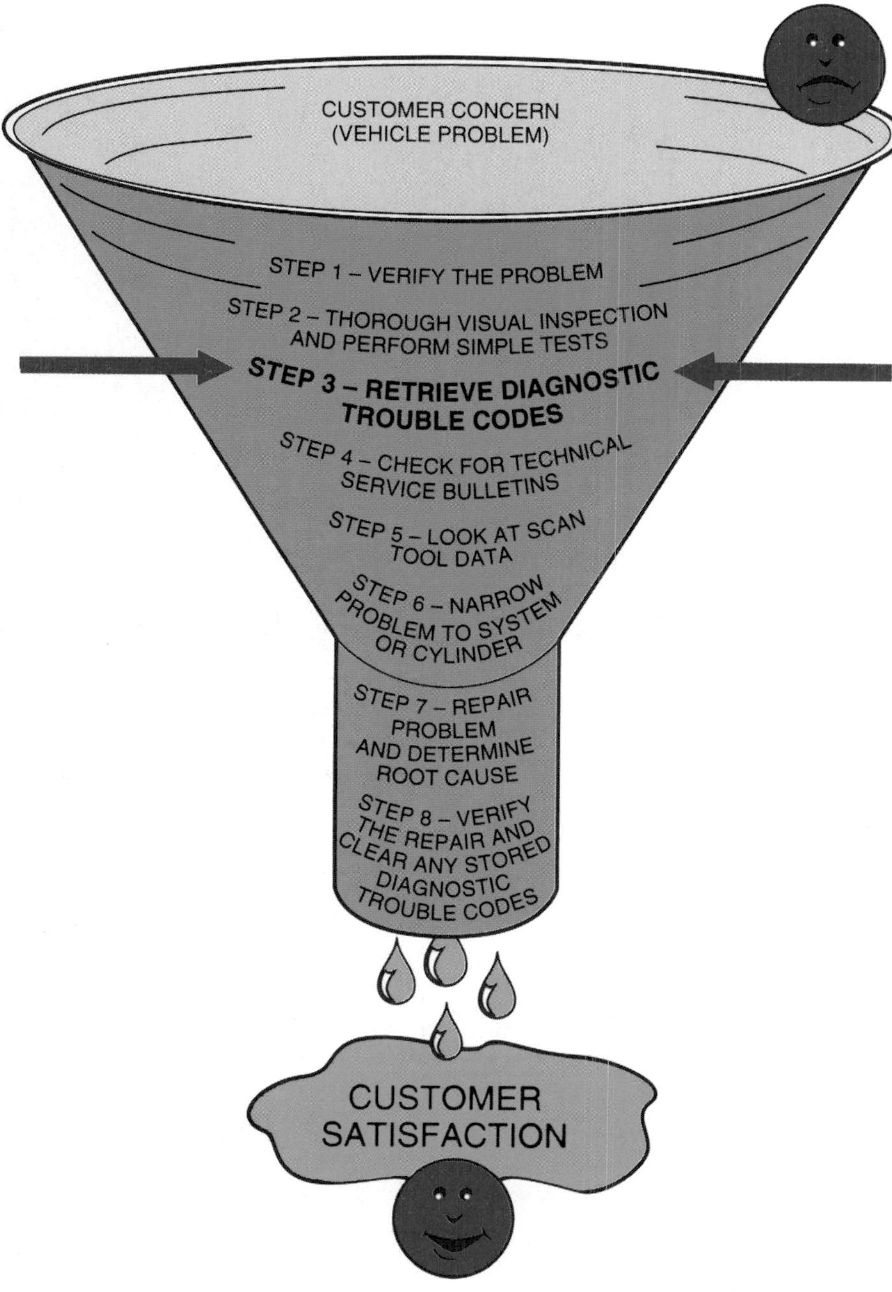
CUSTOMER CONCERN
(VEHICLE PROBLEM)
STEP 1 – VERIFY THE PROBLEM
STEP 2 – THOROUGH VISUAL INSPECTION AND PERFORM SIMPLE TESTS
STEP 3 – RETRIEVE DIAGNOSTIC TROUBLE CODES
STEP 4 – CHECK FOR TECHNICAL SERVICE BULLETINS
STEP 5 – LOOK AT SCAN TOOL DATA
STEP 6 – NARROW PROBLEM TO SYSTEM OR CYLINDER
STEP 7 – REPAIR PROBLEM AND DETERMINE ROOT CAUSE
STEP 8 – VERIFY THE REPAIR AND CLEAR ANY STORED DIAGNOSTIC TROUBLE CODES
CUSTOMER SATISFACTION

Figure 31–9 Step #3 in the diagnostic process is to retrieve any stored diagnostic trouble codes (DTCs). The vehicle computer is constantly monitoring all sensors and control devices and, therefore, if a DTC was stored, it makes sense to use the ability of the vehicle computer to help narrow the focus of what could be wrong.

NOTE: Do not use a standard spark plug to check for proper ignition system voltage. An electronic ignition spark tester is designed to force the spark to jump about 20 mm (0.75 in.). This amount of gap requires between 25 and 30 kilovolts (kV) at atmospheric pressure, which is enough voltage to ensure that a spark can occur under compression inside an engine.

- **Check the fuel pump pressure.** Checking the fuel pump pressure is relatively easy on many port fuel-injected engines. Often the cause of intermittent engine performance is due to a weak electric fuel pump. Checking fuel pump pressure early in the diagnostic process eliminates low fuel pressure as a possibility.

Step #3. Retrieve the Diagnostic Trouble Codes

If a diagnostic trouble code (DTC) is present in the computer memory, it is signalled by illuminating a malfunction indicator lamp (MIL), commonly labelled "check engine" or "service engine soon." See Figure 31–9. The code(s) displayed if the MIL is on is called a **hard code.** Any code(s) that is displayed when the MIL is *not* on is called a **soft code.** A soft code is sometimes called an **intermittent code** and indicates that the computer detected a fault in the circuit represented by the DTC. Because the MIL is not on, this indicates that the fault is no longer present. Although this soft code is helpful to let the technician know that a fault has, in the past, been detected, further testing will be needed to find the root cause of the problem. Most vehicle manufacturers state that the diagnostic procedure for a DTC is for a hard code only.

Step #4. Check for Technical Service Bulletins (TSBs)

Check for corrections in bulletins that match the symptoms. See Figure 31–10. According to studies performed by automobile manufacturers, as many as 30% of vehicles can be repaired following the information, suggestions, or replacement parts found in a service bulletin. (DTCs must be known before searching for service bulletins because bulletins often include information on solving problems that involve a stored diagnostic trouble code.)

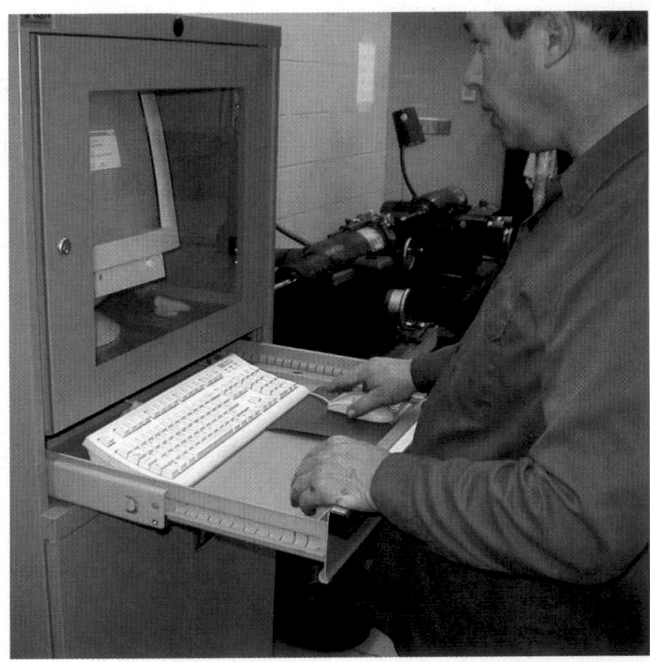

Figure 31–10 After checking for stored diagnostic trouble codes (DTCs), the technician checks to see if there are any technical service bulletins (TSBs) that relate to the vehicle being serviced.

Step #5. Look at Scan Tool Data

Starting in 1981, General Motors and Chrysler vehicle manufacturers have been giving the technician more and more data on a **scan tool** connected to the **data link connector** or **DLC.** See Figure 31–11. Beginning technicians are often observed scrolling through scan data without a real clue to what they are looking for. When asked, they usually reply that they are looking for something unusual, as if the screen will flash a big message "LOOK HERE—THIS IS NOT CORRECT." That statement does not appear on scan tool displays. See Figure 31–12. The best way to look at scan data is in a definite sequence and with specific, selected bits of data (also called **parameter identification** or **PID**) that can tell the most about the operation of the engine such as:

1. Engine coolant temperature (ECT) is the same as intake air temperature (IAT) after the vehicle sits for several hours.
2. Idle air control (IAC) valve is being commanded to an acceptable range.
3. Oxygen sensor (O2S) is operating properly:
   - Readings below 200 millivolts at times
   - Readings above 800 millivolts at times
   - Rapid transitions between rich and lean
   - At least eight cross counts on a fuel-injected engine

Step #6. Narrow the Problem to a System or Cylinder

Narrowing the focus to a system or individual cylinder is the hardest part of the entire diagnostic process.

TECH TIP 

The Five Whys

Whenever a problem is detected, the smart technician should ask, "Why did this part or component fail?" For example, consider a vehicle that misfired under load. A thorough inspection revealed a cracked spark plug. Replacing the spark plugs solved the misfire problem but only for a few weeks. Again, a spark plug was found to be cracked. Now the technician has to ask, "why?" Obviously, the cause of the engine misfire has been determined, but what can cause the recurring cracked spark plug? A missing inner-fender splash shield could be letting water splash onto a hot spark plug, causing it to crack. If the shield is missing, the technician could ask why it was missing. Perhaps some other body parts have been damaged by an accident or other cause.

Usually by the time the technician has asked "why" five times, the root cause of the problem has been determined. Asking yourself the five whys is being truly professional. Customers expect their vehicle to be repaired right the first time. Correcting the root cause is the key to customer satisfaction.

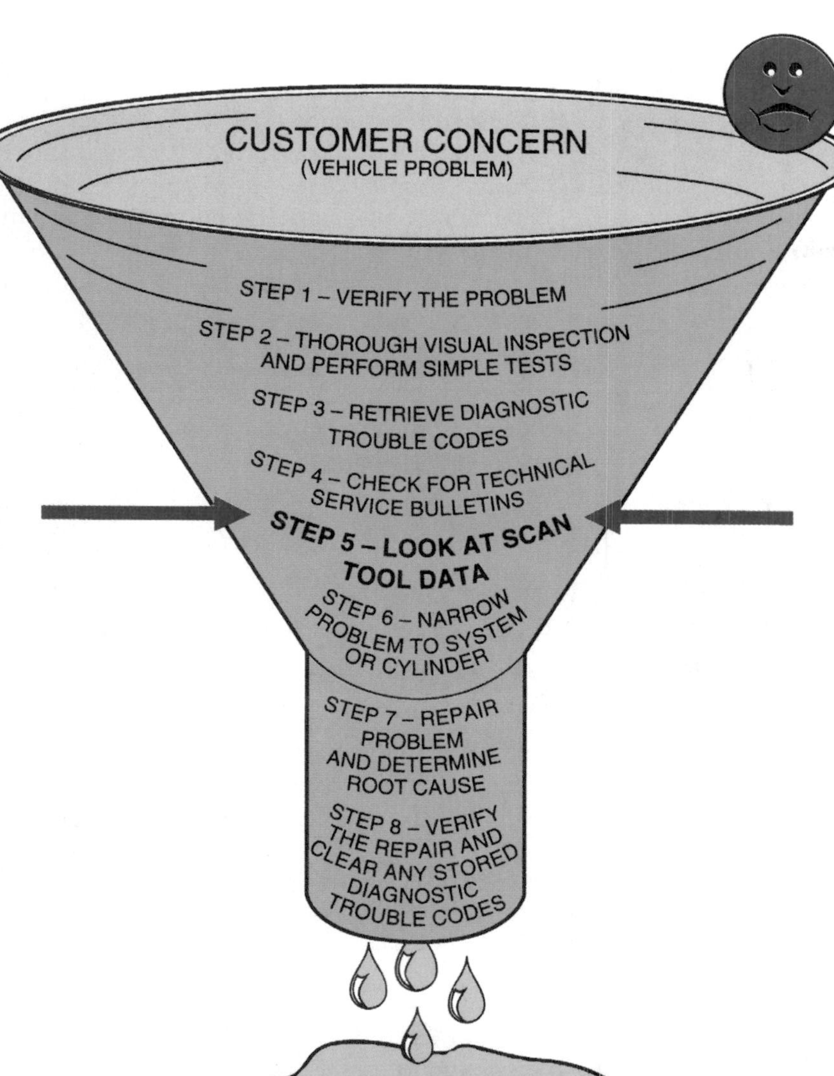

CUSTOMER CONCERN
(VEHICLE PROBLEM)
STEP 1 – VERIFY THE PROBLEM
STEP 2 – THOROUGH VISUAL INSPECTION AND PERFORM SIMPLE TESTS
STEP 3 – RETRIEVE DIAGNOSTIC TROUBLE CODES
STEP 4 – CHECK FOR TECHNICAL SERVICE BULLETINS
STEP 5 – LOOK AT SCAN TOOL DATA
STEP 6 – NARROW PROBLEM TO SYSTEM OR CYLINDER
STEP 7 – REPAIR PROBLEM AND DETERMINE ROOT CAUSE
STEP 8 – VERIFY THE REPAIR AND CLEAR ANY STORED DIAGNOSTIC TROUBLE CODES
CUSTOMER SATISFACTION

Figure 31–11 Scan tool data is a powerful tool to use to find engine performance malfunctions.

Figure 31–12 Using a Snap-On scan tool to check for engine data that may give an indication as to the root cause of the problem.

Figure 31–13 An engine analyzer can also be used to help narrow the problem to a particular cylinder or system.

- Perform a cylinder power balance test. See Figure 31–13.
- If a weak cylinder is detected, perform a compression and a cylinder leakage test to determine the probable cause (see Chapter 5 for details).

Step #7. Repair the Problem and Determine the Root Cause

The repair or part replacement must be performed following vehicle manufacturer's recommendations. Read the Tech Tip "The Five Whys" to be certain that the root cause of the problem has been found. Also follow manufacturers' recommended repair procedures and methods.

Step #8. Verify the Repair and Clear Any Stored DTCs

See Figure 31–14.

1. Test drive to verify that the original problem (concern) is fixed.
2. Verify that no additional problems have occurred during the repair process.
3. Clear all diagnostic trouble codes. (This step ensures that the computer will not make any changes based on any stored DTC.)
4. Before returning the vehicle to the customer double check that
    - The vehicle is clean.
    - The radio is turned off.
    - The clock is set to the right time and the radio stations have been restored if the battery was disconnected during the repair procedure.

TECH TIP 

One Test Is Worth 1000 "Expert" Opinions

Whenever any vehicle has an engine performance or driveability concern, certain people always say:

"Sounds like it's the ignition coil."

"I'll bet you it's a bad computer."

"I had a problem just like yours yesterday and it was a bad EGR valve."

Regardless of the skills and talents of those people, it is still more accurate to perform tests on the vehicle than to rely on feelings or opinions of others who have not even seen the vehicle. Even your own opinion should not sway your thinking. Follow a plan and perform tests and the test results will lead to the root cause.

DIAGNOSING USING DIAGNOSTIC TROUBLE CODES

Pinning down causes of the actual problem can be accomplished by trying to set the opposite code. For example, if a code indicates an open throttle position (TP) sensor (high resistance), clear the code and create a shorted (low-resistance) condition. This can be accomplished by using a jumper wire and connecting the signal terminal to the 5 volt reference terminal. This should set a diagnostic trouble code.

- *If the opposite code sets,* this indicates that the wiring and connector for the sensor is okay and the sensor itself is defective (open).
- *If the same code sets,* this indicates that the wiring or electrical connection is open (has high resistance) and is the cause of the setting of the DTC.

Methods for Clearing Diagnostic Trouble Codes

Clearing diagnostic trouble codes from a vehicle computer is an important procedure. The DTCs should be cleared whenever any of the following conditions exist.

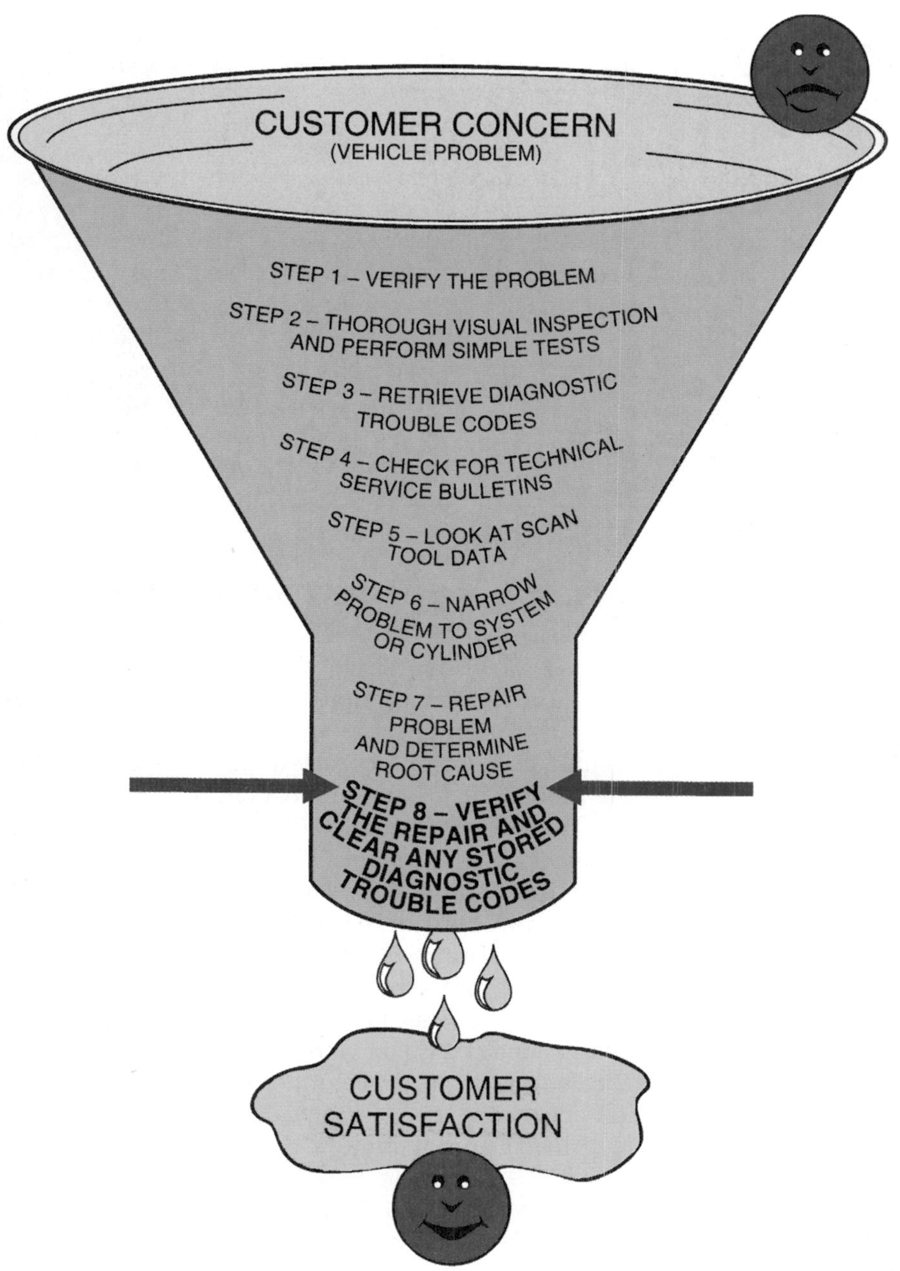
CUSTOMER CONCERN
(VEHICLE PROBLEM)
STEP 1 – VERIFY THE PROBLEM
STEP 2 – THOROUGH VISUAL INSPECTION AND PERFORM SIMPLE TESTS
STEP 3 – RETRIEVE DIAGNOSTIC TROUBLE CODES
STEP 4 – CHECK FOR TECHNICAL SERVICE BULLETINS
STEP 5 – LOOK AT SCAN TOOL DATA
STEP 6 – NARROW PROBLEM TO SYSTEM OR CYLINDER
STEP 7 – REPAIR PROBLEM AND DETERMINE ROOT CAUSE
STEP 8 – VERIFY THE REPAIR AND CLEAR ANY STORED DIAGNOSTIC TROUBLE CODES
CUSTOMER SATISFACTION

Figure 31–14 Step #8 is very important. Be doubly sure that the customer's concern has been corrected.

Before a Repair DTCs are often cleared before starting the diagnostic procedure to determine if the DTC will reset verifying the problem and the code. There are three methods that can be used to clear stored diagnostic trouble codes.

- **Clearing codes method #1.** The preferred method of clearing codes is by using a scan tool. This is the method recommended by most vehicle manufacturers if the procedure can be performed on the vehicle. The computer of some vehicles cannot be cleared with a scan tool.
- **Clearing codes method #2.** If a scan tool is not available or a scan tool cannot be used on the vehicle being serviced, the power to the computer can be disconnected.
  1. Disconnect the fusible link, if so equipped, that feeds the computer
  2. Disconnect the fuse or fuses that feed the computer

DIAGNOSTIC STORY

"Check Engine" Light On, But No Codes

A customer brought a GM vehicle to an independent service facility because the amber-coloured "check engine" light (malfunction indicator lamp or MIL) remained on all the time that the engine was running. This usually indicates a hard failure (a failure that is definite, not intermittent, and that affects the ability of the computer to properly operate the engine).

No trouble codes were found and no code 12 either, which would indicate a possible computer (**electronic control module [ECM]**) problem. After several hours of troubleshooting for loose or defective computer terminals, another technician came along and found that the 3 ampere fuse for the ECM was blown. After replacing the fuse, the computer (and the MIL) returned to normal operation. The customer later admitted that he may have been guilty of blowing the fuse when he attempted to install his own sound system into the existing wiring and fuses.

NOTE: The fuse may not be labelled as a computer fuse. For example, many Toyotas can be cleared by disconnecting the fuel-injection fuse. Some vehicles require that two fuses be disconnected to clear any stored codes.

- **Clearing codes method #3.** If the other two methods cannot be used, the negative (−) battery cable can be disconnected to clear stored diagnostic trouble codes.

NOTE: Because of the adaptive learning capacity of the computer, a vehicle may fail an exhaust emissions test if the vehicle is not driven enough to allow the computer to relearn.

CAUTION: By disconnecting the battery, the radio presets and clock information will be lost and they should be reset before returning the vehicle to the customer. If the radio has a security code, the code must be entered before the radio will function. Always check with the vehicle owner to be sure that the code is available *before* disconnecting the battery.

After a Repair DTCs should be cleared after a repair to prevent the computer from making adjustments to the operation of the engine as a result of a stored DTC.

TECH TIP

The Brake Pedal Trick

If a scan tool is not available and you must disconnect the battery to clear diagnostic trouble codes, it is more likely to be successful if an electrical load is applied to the electrical system of the vehicle to discharge any capacitors that are in the system. It is common for these capacitors to be able to supply the small amount of current needed to keep the memory from being erased. To safely discharge the capacitors, simply depress the brake pedal after removing the negative (−) battery cable. The brake lights will quickly drain any capacitors and the DTCs will be cleared.

FLASH CODE RETRIEVAL ON GENERAL MOTORS VEHICLES

Since 1981, many computer systems have had built-in on-board diagnostic capability. By checking the trouble codes, the technician can determine where the problem is located in most cases.

The GM system uses a "check engine" or "check engine soon" MIL to notify the driver of possible system failure. Under the dash (on most GM vehicles) is a **data link connector (DLC),** previously called an **assembly line communications link (ALCL)** or **assembly line diagnostic link (ALDL).** To retrieve DTCs, first locate the data link connector (DLC). Most DLCs on General Motors vehicles from 1981 to the present are underneath the dash to the left or right of the steering column.

Most General Motors diagnostic trouble codes (non OBD II vehicles) can be retrieved by using a metal tool and contacting terminals A and B of the 12-pin DLC. This method is called **flash code retrieval** because the MIL will flash to indicate diagnostic trouble codes. The steps are as follows:

1. Turn the ignition switch to on (engine off). The "check engine" light or "service engine soon" light should be on.
2. Connect terminals A and B at the DLC.
3. Observe the MIL. A code 12 (one flash, then a pause, then two flashes) reveals that the computer is receiving no engine speed indication because the engine is not running. This simply indicates that the computer diagnostic system is working correctly.
4. After code 12 is displayed three times, the MIL will flash any other stored DTCs in numeric order starting with the lowest-number code. If only code 12 is displayed another three times, the computer has not detected any other faults.

Typical General Motors Diagnostic Trouble Codes (DTC) (OBD-I)

DTC	Definition
13	O_2 sensor circuit
14	Engine coolant temperature (ECT)—high
15	ECT—low
16	Low voltage
17	Camshaft sensor circuit
21	TP sensor (voltage high)
22	TP sensor (voltage low)
23	Intake air temperature (IAT) sensor (low)
24	Vehicle speed (VS) sensor
25	IAT sensor (high)
26	Quad driver module circuit (MIL and gauges)
27	Quad driver module circuit (EVAP, SOL, and TCC)
28	Transmission range (TR) pressure switch assembly (4L80-E); or Quad driver module circuit (A/C clutch relays)
29	Quad driver module circuit for 4T60
33	MAP sensor circuit (low vacuum)
34	MAP sensor circuit (high vacuum)
35	Idle air control (IAC)—idle speed error
36	24 X signal circuit error (3.4 SFI)
37	Brake switch stuck on
38	Brake switch stuck off
39	Torque converter clutch (TCC) stuck off
42	Ignition control circuit error
43	Knock sensor (KS) circuit
44	O_2—lean exhaust
45	O_2—rich exhaust
51	EPROM error
52	System voltage high
53	Battery over voltage
54	Low voltage to fuel pump
55	Power enrichment too lean
58	Transmission fluid temperature (high)
59	Transmission fluid temperature (low)
65	Fuel injector (low current)
66	A/C refrigerant pressure sensor circuit (low)/or 3-2 shift control
67	TCC solenoid circuit fault
68	Transmission slipping
69	TCC stuck on
70	A/C refrigerant pressure sensor circuit (high)
72	Loss of transmission output speed signal
73	Transmission pressure control solenoid circuit
74	Transmission input speed (TIS) sensor circuit
75	Digital EGR #1 error/or system voltage low
76	Digital EGR #2 error
77	Digital EGR #3 error
79	VSS (high)/or transmission fluid over temperature
80	VSS (low)
81	Brake switch error/or 2-3 shift solenoid circuit
82	Ignition control 3 X signal error/or 1-2 shift solenoid circuit
83	TCC pulse width modulation (PWM) solenoid circuit fault
85	PROM error/or transmission ratio error
86	Transmission low ratio error
87	A/D error/or transmission high ratio error
87	Electronically erasable programmable read-only memory (EEPROM) error

See the OBD II DTCs for 1996 or newer vehicles. Refer to factory service information for a description of General Motors specific alphanumeric DTCs.

NOTE: Trouble codes can vary according to year, make, model, and engine. Always consult the service literature or service manual for the exact vehicle being serviced.

RETRIEVING FORD DIAGNOSTIC CODES

The best tool to use during troubleshooting of a Ford vehicle is a **self-test automatic readout (STAR)** tester or another scan tool with Ford capabilities. If a STAR tester or scan tool is not available, a needle (analog) type of voltmeter can be used. Connect a jumper lead and an analog voltmeter as illustrated in Figure 31–15. to obtain flash codes. A 12 volt test light may be substituted if a voltmeter is not available. See Figure 31–16. The test connector is usually located under the hood on the driver's side. See Figure 31–17.

Key On–Engine Off Test With the ignition key on (engine off), watch the voltmeter pulses, which should appear within 5 to 30 seconds. (Ignore any initial surge of voltage when the ignition is turned on.) The computer will send a two- or three-digit code that will cause the voltmeter to pulse or move from left to right. For example, if the voltmeter needle pulses two times, then pauses for 2 seconds, and then pulses three times, the code is 23. There is normally a 4-second pause between codes. The codes are then repeated. These are current (hard) faults.

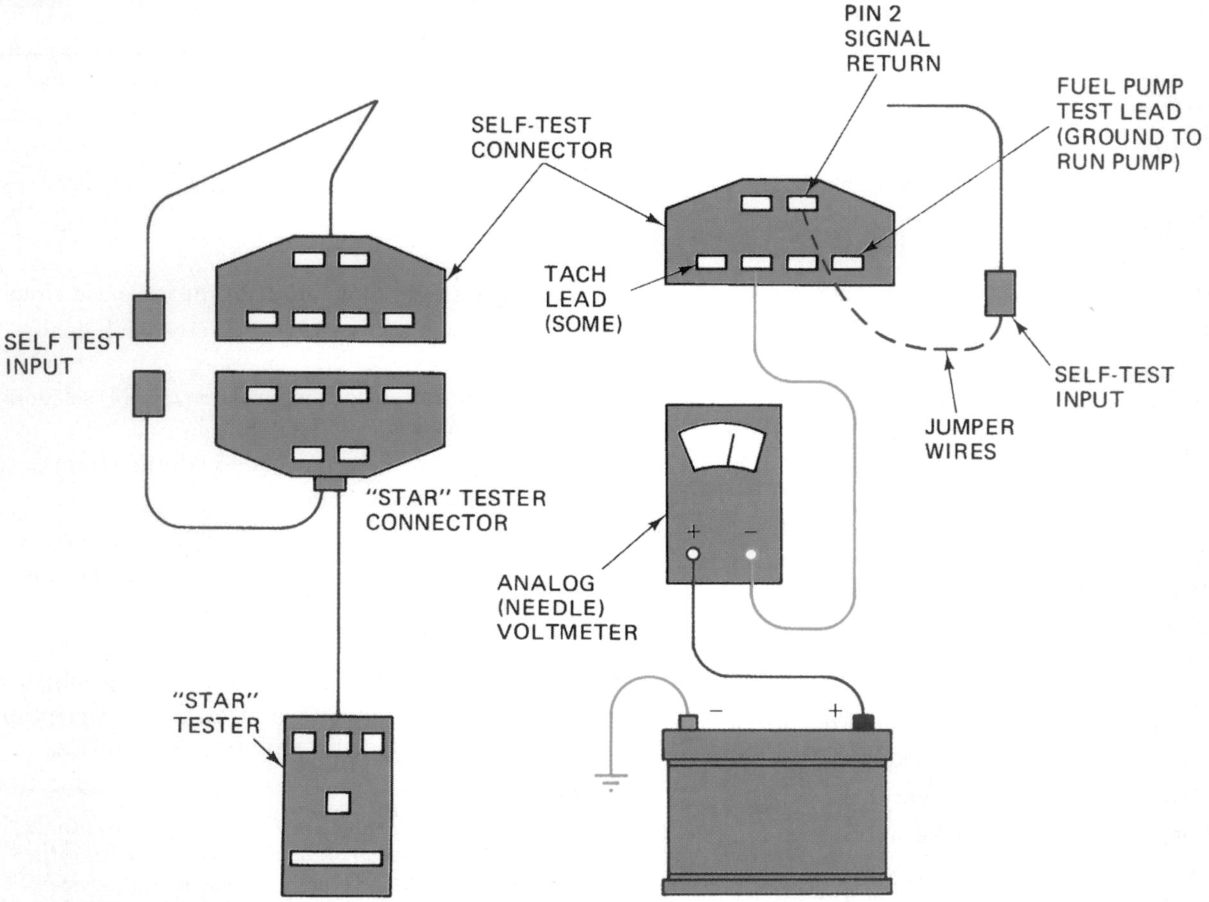

Figure 31–15 Typical connections needed to obtain Ford diagnostic trouble codes.

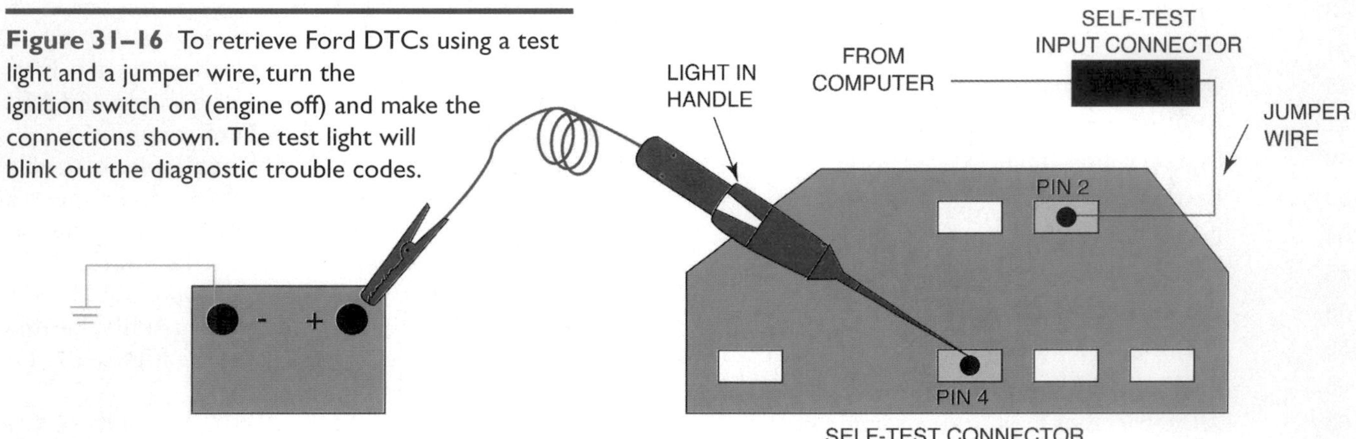

Figure 31–16 To retrieve Ford DTCs using a test light and a jumper wire, turn the ignition switch on (engine off) and make the connections shown. The test light will blink out the diagnostic trouble codes.

After all the codes have been reported, the computer will pause for about 6 to 9 seconds, then cause the voltmeter needle to pulse once (code 10), and then pause for another 6 to 9 seconds. This is the normal separation between current trouble codes and continuous memory codes (for intermittent problems). Code 11 is the normal pass code, which means that no fault has been stored in memory. Normal operation of the diagnostic procedure, using a voltmeter, should indicate the following if no codes are set: 1 pulse (2-second pause), 1 pulse (4-second pause), 1 pulse (2-second pause), and finally, 1 pulse. These two pulses separated by a 4-second interval represent a code 11, which is the code used for a "system pass." The code 11 was repeated twice.

After 6 to 9 seconds, the needle sweeps once. This is the separator (code 10), which precedes the continuous memory (soft) codes. Code 11 in contin-

TECH TIP 

The "Unplug It" Test

If a sensor is supplying *incorrect* data to the computer, the computer may respond with incorrect fuel delivery or ignition timing. The result is a poorly operating engine, possibly with no trouble codes stored in the computer. A common example involves the mass air flow (MAF) sensor used on many vehicles. If the MAF sensor is unplugged and the engine runs better (or starts, whereas it would not start before the sensor was unplugged), then the problem is a defective MAF sensor. As long as the sensor is supplying data within the parameters (guidelines) of the computer, the data will be processed. But if the suspected unit is unplugged, no data is received from the sensor and the computer substitutes a replacement value based on values of other related sensors. For example, the throttle position sensor and/or MAP sensor may back up a defective (or unplugged) MAF sensor. Therefore, if the engine does not start, but then starts if the MAF sensor is unplugged, the MAF sensor is defective.

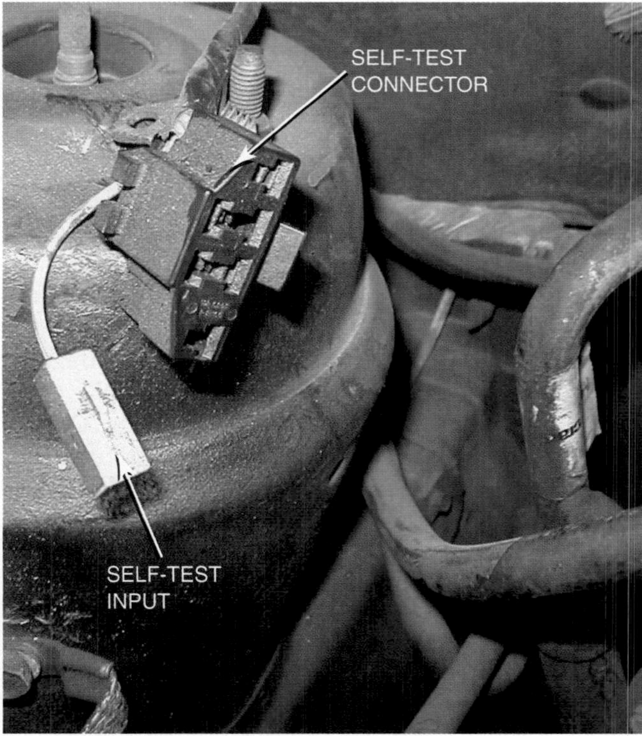

Figure 31–17 A Ford self-test connector. The exact location of this underhood connector varies with model and year of manufacture.

uous memory indicates the computer has not detected any faults in the past.

Engine Running Test Start the engine and raise the speed to 2500 to 3000 rpm within 20 seconds of starting. Hold a steady high engine speed until the initial pulses appear (2 pulses for a four-cylinder engine, 3 pulses for a six-cylinder, and 4 pulses for an eight-cylinder). Continue to hold a high engine speed until the code pulses begin (10 to 14 seconds). If any trouble codes appear, you must use the factory pinpoint tests (diagnostic flow charts) to trace the problem.

Refer to factory service information for a description of Ford-specific DTCs.

RETRIEVING CHRYSLER DIAGNOSTIC CODES

To put the computer into the self-diagnostic mode, the ignition switch must be turned on and off 3 times within a 5-second period (on-off-on-off-on). The computer will flash a series of fault codes in a manner similar to the GM system. Most Chrysler products flash the "power loss," "power limited," or "check engine" lamp on the dash. Refer to service information for a description of Chrysler-specific DTCs. See Figure 31–18 for the underhood Chrysler data link connector that is used to connect to a scan tool prior to OBD II.

NOTE: Unlike other makes, most Chrysler vehicles equipped with OBD II can still display codes (on the instrument cluster) by cycling the ignition key as previously performed on older vehicles.

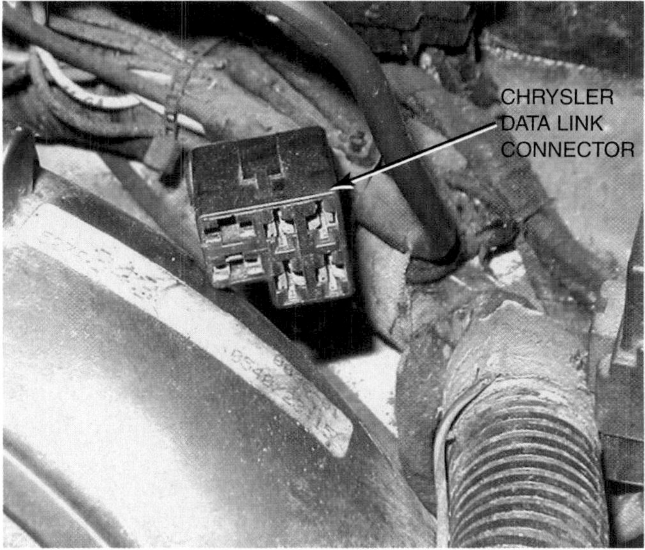

Figure 31–18 An underhood Chrysler data link connector used from 1981 until 1995 on OBD I vehicles.

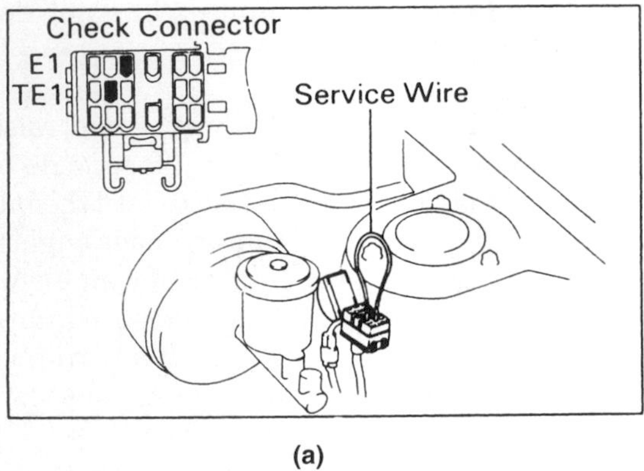

(a)

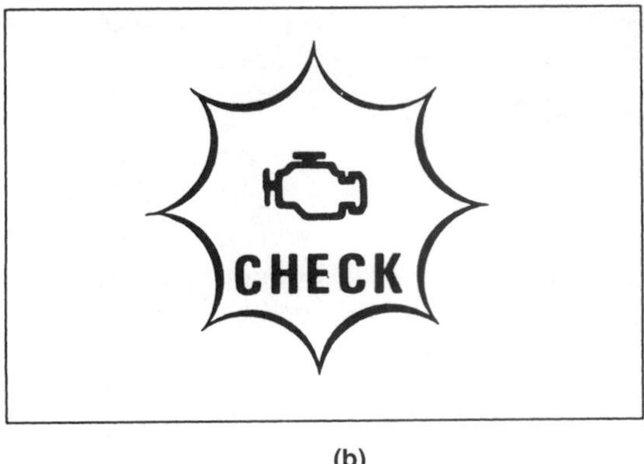

(b)

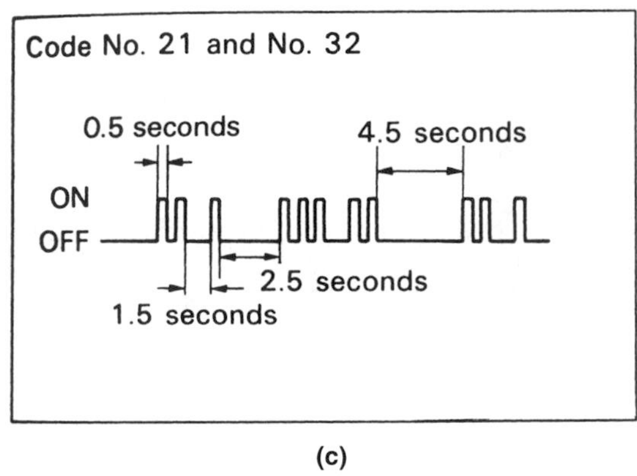

(c)

Figure 31–19 Many imports use a service wire (a) to connect the diagnostic terminals. The malfunction indicator lamp (MIL) will begin to flash (b). Read and note the number of flashes, and the spacing (c). (Courtesy Toyota Canada Inc.)

RETRIEVING DIAGNOSTIC CODES IN IMPORT VEHICLES

Early OBDI import and domestic vehicles use similar methods of retrieving DTCs. Generally a jumper wire is placed across two terminals of a diagnostic connector (see Figure 31–19) and a dash light flashes or a voltmeter (connected into the circuit) needle will rise and fall. Count the number of light flashes or needle sweeps to determine the code. See Figure 31–20. Follow the diagnostic routines in the shop manual. Import OBDII diagnostic systems are almost the same as domestic systems.

RETRIEVING OBD II CODES—16 PIN

A scan tool is required to retrieve diagnostic trouble codes from an OBD II vehicle. Every OBD II scan tool will be able to read all generic Society of Automotive Engineers (SAE) DTCs from any vehicle. Manufacturers' specific codes may require an adaptor (personality keys) for some scan tools. See Figure 31–21 for a typical OBD II data link connector (DLC) location. Except for Chrysler vehicles, all OBD II DTCs must be read using a scan tool. See Figure 31–22 for OBD II generic DTCs.

OBDII freeze-frame data such as "calculated load," "short and long-term fuel trim," and "cylinder identification for misfire" are invaluable for diagnosing problems.

When the repair is completed and the DTC is cleared, road test the vehicle again to confirm that the code does not reset. Although some OBDII codes require two or three trips to set, many scan tools have a program that allows codes to register with only one trip.

NOTE: Although OBD II requires that just one freeze-frame of data be stored, the instant an emission-related DTC is set, vehicle manufacturers usually provide expanded data about the DTC beyond that required. However, retrieving this enhanced data usually requires the use of the vehicle-specific scan tool.

DIAGNOSTIC CODES

Code No.	Number of check engine blinks	System	Diagnosis	Trouble area	See page
—	 ON OFF FI1401	Normal	This appears when none of the other codes (11 thru 71) are indentified.	—	—
11	 FI1388	ECU (+B)	Wire severance, however slight, in +B (ECU)	• IG switch circuit • IG switch • Main relay circuit • Main relay • ECU	FI-34
12	 FI1389	RPM Signal	No NE or G signal to ECU within several seconds after engine is cranked.	• Distributor circuit • Distributor • Starter signal circuit • ECU	IG-4
13	 FI1390	RPM Signal	No NE signal to ECU when the engine speed is above 1000 rpm.	• Distributor circuit • Distributor • ECU	—
14	 FI1391	Ignition Signal	No IGF signal to ECU 4 — 5 times in succession.	• Ignition circuit (+B, IGT, IGF) • Igniter • ECU	FI-44
21	 FI1609	Oxygen Sensor Signal	Detection of oxygen sensor deterioration.	• Oxygen sensor circuit • Oxygen sensor • ECU	FI-48
22	 FI1392	Water temp. Sensor Signal	Open or short circuit in water temp. sensor signal (THW).	• Water temp. sensor circuit • Water temp. sensor • ECU	FI-42
24	 FI1611	Intake air Temp. Sensor Signal	Open or short circuit in intake air temp. sensor signal (THA).	• Intake air temp. sensor circuit • Intake air temp. sensor • ECU	FI-41
*25	 FI2562	Air-fuel Ratio Lean Malfunction	When air-fuel ratio feedback compensation valve or adative control value continues at the upper (lean) or lower (rich) limit renewed for a certain priod of time.	• Injector circuit • Injector • Oxygen sensor circuit • Oxygen sensor • ECU • Fuel line pressure • Air flow meter • Water temp. sensor • Ignition system • ECU	—
*26	 FI2563	Air-fuel Ratio Rich Malfunction		• Injector circuit • Injector • Fuel line pressure • Cold start injector • Air flow meter • Water temp. ensor • ECU	—
*27	 FI3294	Sub-oxygen Sensor Signal	Open or short circuit in sub-oxygen sensor signal (OX2)	• Sub-oxygen sensor circuit • Sub-oxygen sensor • ECU	FI-48
31	 FI1394	Air flow Meter Signal	Open circuir in VC signal or short circuit between VC and E2 when idle contacts are closed.	• Air flow meter circuit • Air flow meter • ECU	FI-39
32	 FI1395	Air flow Meter Signal	Open circuit in E2 or short circuit between VC and VS.	Same as 31, above.	FI-39

*CALIF. only

Continued on next page

Figure 31–20 A typical OBD I diagnostic trouble code (DTC) chart for an import vehicle. Import OBD II charts are the same as generic fault codes for domestic vehicles. (Courtesy Toyota Canada Inc.)

DIAGNOSTIC CODES

Code No.	Number of check engine blinks	System	Diagnosis	Trouble area	See page
41	FI1396	Throttle Position Sensor Signal	(w/o ECT) IDL and PSW signals being output simulaneously for several seconds. (w/ ECT) Open or short circuit in throttle position sensor signal (VTA).	● Throttle position sensor circuit ● Throttle position sensor ● ECU	FI-36 or FI-37
42	FI1397	Vehicle Speed Sensor Signal	No SPD signal for several seconds when engine speed is between 2500–5500 rpm and coolant temp. is below 80°C (176°F) except when racing the engine.	● Vehicle speed sensor circuit ● Vehicle speed sensor ● ECU	—
43	FI1398	Starter Signal	No STA signal to ECU when behicle stopped and engine running over 800 rpm.	● IG switch circuit ● IG switch ● ECU	FI-43
*71	FI2622	EGR Malfunction	EGR gas temp. below predetermined level for during EGR control.	● EGR system (EGR valve, EGR hose etc.) ● EGR gas temp. sensor circuit ● EGR gas temp. sensor ● BVSV for EGR ● BVSV for EGR circuit ● ECU	FI-49
51	FI1399	Switch Signal	No IDL signal or A/C signal to ECU, with the check terminals TE1 and E1 connected.	● A/C switch circuit ● A/C amplifire ● Throttle position sensor circuit ● Throttle position sensor ● Accelerator pedal and cable	—

*CALIF. only

Figure 31–20 continued

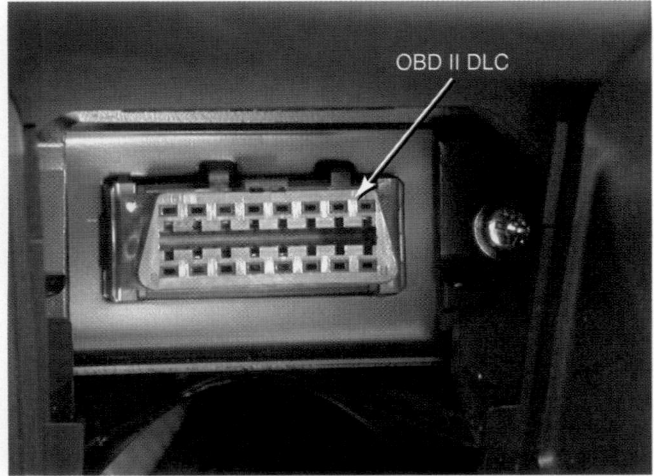

Figure 31–21 An OBD II data link connector (DLC). It is located under the dash and could be covered by a snap-in cover such as on this Acura TL.

EXHAUST ANALYSIS AND COMBUSTION EFFICIENCY

A popular method of engine analysis involves the use of five-gas exhaust analysis equipment. See Figure 31–23. The five gases analyzed and their significance are as follows.

Hydrocarbons

Hydrocarbons (**HC**) are unburned gasoline and are measured in parts per million (ppm). A correctly operating engine should burn (oxidize) almost all of the gasoline; therefore, very little unburned gasoline should be present in the exhaust. Acceptable levels of HC are 50 ppm or less. High HC levels are an indicator of poor combustion or a misfire. The most common cause of excessive HC emissions is a fault in the ignition system or a lean condition. Items that should be checked include:

- Spark plugs
- Spark plug wires
- Distributor cap and rotor (if the vehicle is so equipped)
- Ignition timing
- Ignition coil
- Vacuum leaks

Carbon Monoxide

Carbon monoxide (**CO**) is unstable and will easily combine with any oxygen to form stable carbon dioxide (**CO_2**). CO is a very poisonous gas. CO levels of a properly operating engine should be less than 0.5%.

Fuel and Air Metering System

P0100 Mass or Volume Airflow Circuit Problem
P0101 Mass or Volume Airflow Circuit Range or Performance Problem
P0102 Mass or Volume Airflow Circuit Low Input
P0103 Mass or Volume Airflow Circuit High Input
P0105 Manifold Absolute Pressure or Barometric Pressure Circuit Problem
P0106 Manifold Absolute Pressure or Barometric Pressure Circuit Range or Performance Problem
P0107 Manifold Absolute Pressure or Barometric Pressure Circuit Low Input
P0108 Manifold Absolute Pressure or Barometric Pressure Circuit High Input
P0110 Intake Air Temperature Circuit Problem
P0111 Intake Air Temperature Circuit Range or Performance Problem
P0112 Intake Air Temperature Circuit Low Input
P0113 Intake Air Temperature Circuit High Input
P0115 Engine Coolant Temperature Circuit Problem
P0116 Engine Coolant Temperature Circuit Range or Performance Problem
P0117 Engine Coolant Temperature Circuit Low Input
P0118 Engine Coolant Temperature Circuit High Input
P0120 Throttle Position Circuit Problem
P0121 Throttle Position Circuit Range or Performance Problem
P0122 Throttle Position Circuit Low Input
P0123 Throttle Position Circuit High Input
P0125 Excessive Time to Enter Closed-Loop Fuel Control
P0130 O2 Sensor Circuit Problem (Bank 1* Sensor 1)
P0131 O2 Sensor Circuit Low Voltage (Bank 1* Sensor 1)
P0132 O2 Sensor Circuit High Voltage (Bank 1* Sensor 1)
P0133 O2 Sensor Circuit Slow Response (Bank 1* Sensor 1)
P0134 O2 Sensor Circuit No Activity Detected (Bank 1* Sensor 1)
P0135 O2 Sensor Heater Circuit Problem (Bank 1* Sensor 1)
P0136 O2 Sensor Circuit Problem (Bank 1* Sensor 2)
P0137 O2 Sensor Circuit Low Voltage (Bank 1* Sensor 2)
P0138 O2 Sensor Circuit High Voltage (Bank 1* Sensor 2)
P0139 O2 Sensor Circuit Slow Response (Bank 1* Sensor 2)
P0140 O2 Sensor Circuit No Activity Detected (Bank 1* Sensor 2)
P0141 O2 Sensor Heater Circuit Problem (Bank 1* Sensor 2)
P0142 O2 Sensor Circuit Problem (Bank 1* Sensor 3)
P0143 O2 Sensor Circuit Low Voltage (Bank 1* Sensor 3)
P0144 O2 Sensor Circuit High Voltage (Bank 1* Sensor 3)
P0145 O2 Sensor Circuit Slow Response (Bank 1* Sensor 3)
P0146 O2 Sensor Circuit No Activity Detected (Bank 1* Sensor 3)
P0147 O2 Sensor Heater Circuit Problem (Bank 1* Sensor 3)
P0150 O2 Sensor Circuit Problem (Bank 2 Sensor 1)
P0151 O2 Sensor Circuit Low Voltage (Bank 2 Sensor 1)
P0152 O2 Sensor Circuit High Voltage (Bank 2 Sensor 1)
P0153 O2 Sensor Circuit Slow Response (Bank 2 Sensor 1)
P0154 O2 Sensor Circuit No Activity Detected (Bank 2 Sensor 1)
P0155 O2 Sensor Heater Circuit Problem (Bank 2 Sensor 1)
P0156 O2 Sensor Circuit Problem (Bank 2 Sensor 2)
P0157 O2 Sensor Circuit Low Voltage (Bank 2 Sensor 2)
P0158 O2 Sensor Circuit High Voltage (Bank 2 Sensor 2)
P0159 O2 Sensor Circuit Slow Response (Bank 2 Sensor 2)
P0160 O2 Sensor Circuit No Activity Detected (Bank 2 Sensor 2)
P0161 O2 Sensor Heater Circuit Problem (Bank 2 Sensor 2)
P0162 O2 Sensor Circuit Problem (Bank 2 Sensor 3)
P0163 O2 Sensor Circuit Low Voltage (Bank 2 Sensor 3)
P0164 O2 Sensor Circuit High Voltage (Bank 2 Sensor 3)
P0165 O2 Sensor Circuit Slow Response (Bank 2 Sensor 3)
P0166 O2 Sensor Circuit No Activity Detected (Bank 2 Sensor 3)
P0167 O2 Sensor Heater Circuit Problem (Bank 2 Sensor 3)
P0170 Fuel Trim Problem (Bank 1*)
P0171 System Too Lean (Bank 1*)
P0172 System Too Rich (Bank 1*)
P0173 Fuel Trim Problem (Bank 2)

Figure 31–22 Generic OBD II powertrain DTCs.

P0174 System Too Lean (Bank 2)
P0175 System Too Rich (Bank 2)
P0176 Fuel Composition Sensor Circuit Problem
P0177 Fuel Composition Sensor Circuit Range or Performance
P0178 Fuel Composition Sensor Circuit Low Input
P0179 Fuel Composition Sensor Circuit High Input
P0180 Fuel Temperature Sensor Problem
P0181 Fuel Temperature Sensor Circuit Range or Performance
P0182 Fuel Temperature Sensor Circuit Low Input
P0183 Fuel Temperature Sensor Circuit High Input

Fuel and Air Metering (Injector Circuit)

P0201 Injector Circuit Problem—Cylinder 1
P0202 Injector Circuit Problem—Cylinder 2
P0203 Injector Circuit Problem—Cylinder 3
P0204 Injector Circuit Problem—Cylinder 4
P0205 Injector Circuit Problem—Cylinder 5
P0206 Injector Circuit Problem—Cylinder 6
P0207 Injector Circuit Problem—Cylinder 7
P0208 Injector Circuit Problem—Cylinder 8
P0209 Injector Circuit Problem—Cylinder 9
P0210 Injector Circuit Problem—Cylinder 10
P0211 Injector Circuit Problem—Cylinder 11
P0212 Injector Circuit Problem—Cylinder 12
P0213 Cold Start Injector 1 Problem
P0214 Cold Start Injector 2 Problem

Ignition System or Misfire

P0300 Random Misfire Detected
P0301 Cylinder 1 Misfire Detected
P0302 Cylinder 2 Misfire Detected
P0303 Cylinder 3 Misfire Detected
P0304 Cylinder 4 Misfire Detected
P0305 Cylinder 5 Misfire Detected
P0306 Cylinder 6 Misfire Detected
P0307 Cylinder 7 Misfire Detected
P0308 Cylinder 8 Misfire Detected
P0309 Cylinder 9 Misfire Detected
P0310 Cylinder 10 Misfire Detected
P0311 Cylinder 11 Misfire Detected
P0312 Cylinder 12 Misfire Detected
P0320 Ignition or Distributor Engine Speed Input Circuit Problem
P0321 Ignition or Distributor Engine Speed Input Circuit Range or Performance
P0322 Ignition or Distributor Engine Speed Input Circuit No Signal
P0325 Knock Sensor 1 Circuit Problem
P0326 Knock Sensor 1 Circuit Range or Performance
P0327 Knock Sensor 1 Circuit Low Input
P0328 Knock Sensor 1 Circuit High Input
P0330 Knock Sensor 2 Circuit Problem
P0331 Knock Sensor 2 Circuit Range or Performance
P0332 Knock Sensor 2 Circuit Low Input
P0333 Knock Sensor 2 Circuit High Input
P0335 Crankshaft Position Sensor Circuit Problem
P0336 Crankshaft Position Sensor Circuit Range or Performance
P0337 Crankshaft Position Sensor Circuit Low Input
P0338 Crankshaft Position Sensor Circuit High Input

Auxiliary Emission Controls

P0400 Exhaust Gas Recirculation Flow Problem
P0401 Exhaust Gas Recirculation Flow Insufficient Detected
P0402 Exhaust Gas Recirculation Flow Excessive Detected
P0405 Air Conditioner Refrigerant Charge Loss
P0410 Secondary Air Injection System Problem
P0411 Secondary Air Injection System Insufficient Flow Detected
P0412 Secondary Air Injection System Switching Valve or Circuit Problem
P0413 Secondary Air Injection System Switching Valve or Circuit Open
P0414 Secondary Air Injection System Switching Valve or Circuit Shorted
P0420 Catalyst System Efficiency Below Threshold (Bank 1*)
P0421 Warm Up Catalyst Efficiency Below Threshold (Bank 1*)
P0422 Main Catalyst Efficiency Below Threshold (Bank 1*)
P0423 Heated Catalyst Efficiency Below Threshold (Bank 1*)
P0424 Heated Catalyst Temperature Below Threshold (Bank 1*)
P0430 Catalyst System Efficiency Below Threshold (Bank 2)
P0431 Warm Up Catalyst Efficiency Below Threshold (Bank 2)
P0432 Main Catalyst Efficiency Below Threshold (Bank 2)
P0433 Heated Catalyst Efficiency Below Threshold (Bank 2)
P0434 Heated Catalyst Temperature Below Threshold (Bank 2)
P0440 Evaporative Emission Control System Problem
P0441 Evaporative Emission Control System Insufficient Purge Flow

Figure 31–22 continued

P0442 Evaporative Emission Control System Leak Detected
P0443 Evaporative Emission Control System Purge Control Valve Circuit Problem
P0444 Evaporative Emission Control System Purge Control Valve Circuit Open
P0445 Evaporative Emission Control System Purge Control Valve Circuit Shorted
P0446 Evaporative Emission Control System Vent Control Problem
P0447 Evaporative Emission Control System Vent Control Open
P0448 Evaporative Emission Control System Vent Control Shorted
P0450 Evaporative Emission Control System Pressure Sensor Problem
P0451 Evaporative Emission Control System Pressure Sensor Range or Performance
P0452 Evaporative Emission Control System Pressure Sensor Low Input
P0453 Evaporative Emission Control System Pressure Sensor High Input

Vehicle Speed Control and Idle Control

P0500 Vehicle Speed Sensor Problem
P0501 Vehicle Speed Sensor Range or Performance
P0502 Vehicle Speed Sensor Low Input
P0505 Idle Control System Problem
P0506 Idle Control System RPM Lower than Expected
P0507 Idle Control System RPM Higher than Expected
P0510 Closed Throttle Position Switch Problem

Computer Output Circuit

P0600 Serial Communication Link Problem
P0605 Internal Control Module (Module Identification Defined by J1979)

Transmission

P0703 Brake Switch Input Problem
P0705 Transmission Range Sensor Circuit Problem (PRNDL Input)
P0706 Transmission Range Sensor Circuit Range or Performance
P0707 Transmission Range Sensor Circuit Low Input
P0708 Transmission Range Sensor Circuit High Input
P0710 Transmission Fluid Temperature Sensor Problem
P0711 Transmission Fluid Temperature Sensor Range or Performance
P0712 Transmission Fluid Temperature Sensor Low Input
P0713 Transmission Fluid Temperature Sensor High Input
P0715 Input or Turbine Speed Sensor Circuit Problem
P0716 Input or Turbine Speed Sensor Circuit Range or Performance
P0717 Input or Turbine Speed Sensor Circuit No Signal
P0720 Output Speed Sensor Circuit Problem
P0721 Output Speed Sensor Circuit Range or Performance
P0722 Output Speed Sensor Circuit No Signal
P0725 Engine Speed Input Circuit Problem
P0726 Engine Speed Input Circuit Range or Performance
P0727 Engine Speed Input Circuit No Signal
P0730 Incorrect Gear Ratio
P0731 Gear 1 Incorrect Ratio
P0732 Gear 2 Incorrect Ratio
P0733 Gear 3 Incorrect Ratio
P0734 Gear 4 Incorrect Ratio
P0735 Gear 5 Incorrect Ratio
P0736 Reverse Incorrect Ratio
P0740 Torque Converter Clutch System Problem
P0741 Torque Converter Clutch System Performance or Stuck Off
P0742 Torque Converter Clutch System Stuck On
P0743 Torque Converter Clutch System Electrical
P0745 Pressure Control Solenoid Problem
P0746 Pressure Control Solenoid Performance or Stuck Off
P0747 Pressure Control Solenoid Stuck On
P0748 Pressure Control Solenoid Electrical
P0750 Shift Solenoid A Problem
P0751 Shift Solenoid A Performance or Stuck Off
P0752 Shift Solenoid A Stuck On
P0753 Shift Solenoid A Electrical
P0755 Shift Solenoid B Problem
P0756 Shift Solenoid B Performance or Stuck Off
P0757 Shift Solenoid B Stuck On
P0758 Shift Solenoid B Electrical
P0760 Shift Solenoid C Problem
P0761 Shift Solenoid C Performance or Stuck Off
P0762 Shift Solenoid C Stuck On
P0763 Shift Solenoid C Electrical
P0765 Shift Solenoid D Problem
P0766 Shift Solenoid D Performance or Stuck Off
P0767 Shift Solenoid D Stuck On
P0768 Shift Solenoid D Electrical
P0770 Shift Solenoid E Problem
P0771 Shift Solenoid E Performance or Stuck Off
P0772 Shift Solenoid E Stuck On
P0773 Shift Solenoid E Electrical

Figure 31–22 continued

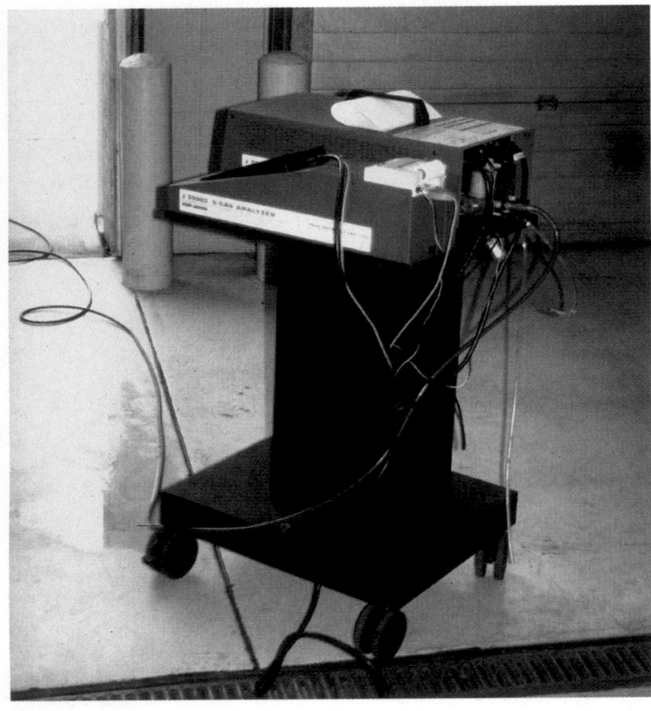

(a)

(b)

Figure 31–23 (a) Typical portable 5-gas exhaust analyzer. This particular unit can be removed from its stand and placed inside the vehicle to monitor the exhaust emission while driving. (b) A typical partial stream sample type of exhaust probe used to measure exhaust gases in parts per million (ppm) or percentage (%).

High CO is a good indicator of richness. High levels of CO can be caused by clogged or restricted crankcase ventilation devices such as the PCV valve, hose(s), and tubes. Other items that might cause excessive CO include:

- Sticking fuel injector
- Clogged air filter
- Incorrect idle speed
- Too-high fuel pressure
- Fuel saturated carbon canister
- Any other items that can cause a rich condition

Carbon Dioxide (CO_2)

Carbon dioxide (**CO_2**) is the result of oxygen in the engine combining with the carbon of the gasoline. An acceptable level of CO_2 is between 12 and 17%. A high reading indicates an efficiently operating engine. If the CO_2 level is low, the mixture may be either too rich or too lean. CO_2 emissions are considered a contributor to "greenhouse gases."

Oxygen

There is about 21% oxygen (**O_2**) in the atmosphere, and most of this oxygen should be used up during the combustion process to oxidize all the hydrogen and carbon (hydrocarbons) in the gasoline. Levels of O_2 should be very low (about 0.5%). O_2 readings are a good indicator of the air/fuel ratio (high O_2 = lean, low O_2 = rich).

Frequently Asked Question ???

What Do All These Emission Labels Mean?

TLEV	Transitional Low-Emission Vehicle, car exhaust hydrocarbon (HC) limited to 0.125 gram per mile (gpm).
LEV	Low-Emission Vehicle, car exhaust HC 0.075 gpm.
ULEV	Ultra Low-Emission Vehicle, car exhaust HC 0.040 gpm.
SULEV	Super Ultra Low-Emission Vehicle, car exhaust HC 0.010 gpm.
ZEV	Zero-Emission Vehicle.
CEV	City Electric Vehicle, a miniature car, which could earn minor credit against ZEV quota.
NEV	Neighborhood Electric Vehicle, very similar to golf cart, could earn minor credit against ZEV quota.
PZEV	A near-zero emissions category, P is for "partial." A PZEV would earn "partial credit" against manufacturers' ZEV quotas.
AT-PZEV	A near-zero-emissions category. AT is for "advanced technology," meeting PZEV requirements using, for example, a low-emissions fuel cell running on methanol or an internal-combustion engine running on natural gas.

> **NOTE:** Adding 10% alcohol to gasoline (gasohol) provides additional oxygen to the fuel and will result in lower levels of CO and higher levels of O_2 in the exhaust.

OXIDES OF NITROGEN (NO_X)

An oxide of nitrogen (NO) is a colourless, tasteless, and odorless gas when it leaves the engine, but as soon as it reaches the atmosphere and mixes with more oxygen, nitrogen oxides (NO_2) are formed. NO_2 is reddish-brown and has an acid and pungent smell. NO and NO_2 are grouped together and referred to as NO_x, where x represents any number of oxygen atoms. NO_x is the fifth gas commonly tested using a 5-gas analyzer. The exhaust gas recirculation (EGR) system is the major controlling device limiting the formation of NO_x. Because the formation of NO_x occurs mostly under load, the most efficient method to test for NO_x is to use a portable exhaust analyzer that can be carried in the vehicle while the vehicle is being driven under a variety of conditions. A maximum reading of 1,000 parts per million (ppm) of NO_x under loaded driving conditions will generally mean that the vehicle will pass an enhanced I/M roller test. A reading of over 100 ppm at idle should be considered excessive. Because NO_x is a good indicator of combustion temperatures, watch for overadvanced ignition timing or lean air/fuel ratios.

BASIC EXHAUST GAS ANALYSIS

Older gas analyzers give only two readings, carbon monoxide and hydrocarbons. See Figure 31–24. Note that hydrocarbons are high with both rich mixtures

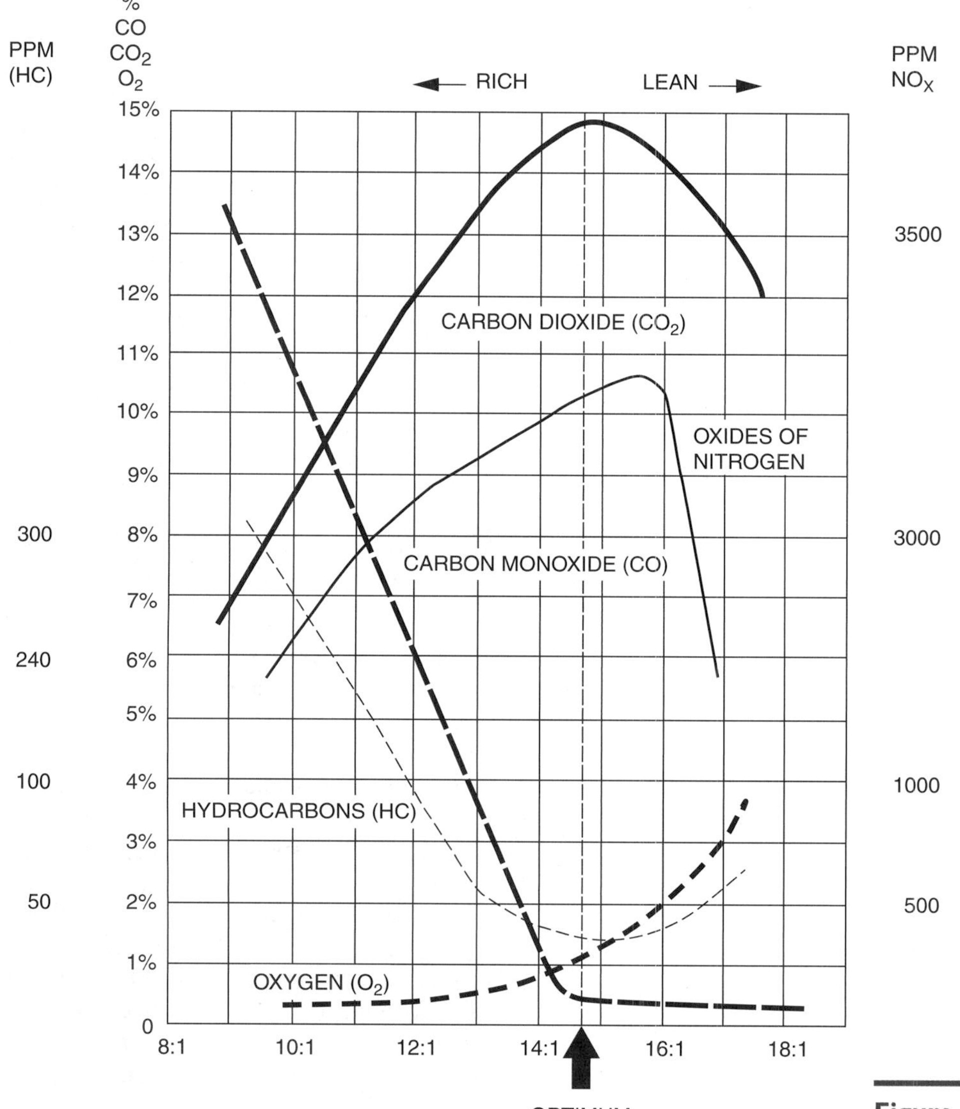

Figure 31–24 Exhaust emissions versus air/fuel ratio. (Courtesy DaimlerChrysler)

(too much fuel) and lean mixtures (not enough fuel). To determine the cause of a high hydrocarbon reading, look at the carbon monoxide reading. CO is a good indicator of richness. Therefore, if

HC and CO high = rich mixture
HC high, CO low = lean mixture
HC very high, CO low = possible misfire

Two-gas readings became obsolete when catalytic converters came into use; the converters mask both HC and CO. Some import vehicles have a removable plug ahead of the converter for "pre-cat" sampling, but these are not common.

Four-gas analyzers read both CO and HC, plus oxygen (O_2), which is a good indicator of rich/lean, and carbon dioxide (CO_2), an indicator of combustion efficiency.

High CO_2 = good combustion
Low CO_2 and high O_2 = too lean or misfire
Low CO_2 and low O_2 = too rich

The air injection system is sometimes disabled before taking tailpipe readings. Check your analyzer manual.

Five-gas analyzers include the above four gases, plus oxides of nitrogen (NO_x). Because NO_x increases under load, a chassis dynomometer or a portable gas analyzer must be used.

High NO_x = too lean, overadvanced timing, lack of EGR, etc.

Comparing the NO_x reading with the other gases will determine the problem area. Note that NO_x decreases with extremely lean mixtures when the engine misfires.

Low NO_x, high O_2 = misfire.

Acceptable exhaust emissions include:

	Without Catalytic Converter (pre-1975)	**With Catalytic Converter (post-1975)**
HC	300 ppm or less	30–50 ppm or less
CO	3% or less	0.3%–0.5% or less
O_2	0%–2%	0%–2%
CO_2	12%–17% or higher	12%–17% or higher

I/M 240

I/M 240 refers to inspection and maintenance (I/M), and the 240 means that the exhaust emissions test lasts 240 seconds (4 minutes). The I/M 240 test is a shorter version of the Federal Test Procedure (FTP) that takes 505 seconds. The I/M 240 procedure tests vehicle emissions under a loaded dynamometer that simulates actual highway usage. All the exhaust is analyzed and the results are given in grams per kilometre or per mile. See Figure 31–25.

Because many locations do not use the I/M 240 test, most vehicle exhaust emissions testing is referred to as **enhanced exhaust emission testing** or **enhanced I and M,** which refers to any of the various tests and variations of the tests used in different parts of the country.

Frequently Asked Question ???

How Can My Worn-Out, Old, High-Mileage Vehicle Pass an Exhaust Emissions Test?

Age and mileage of a vehicle are generally not factors when it comes to passing an exhaust emissions test. Regular maintenance is the most important factor for passing an enhanced I/M exhaust analysis test. Failure of the vehicle owner to replace broken accessory drive belts, leaking AIR pump tubes, defective spark plug wires, or a cracked exhaust manifold can lead to failure of other components, such as the catalytic converter. Tests have shown that if the vehicle is properly cared for, even an engine that has been operating for 480 000 km (300 000 mi) can pass an exhaust emissions test.

DIAGNOSTIC STORY

The Corvette Story

A Corvette failed an enhanced exhaust emissions test repeatedly. All of the exhaust gases, except hydrocarbons (HC), were well within limits. HC emissions were off the scale and a strong smell of gasoline was apparent. All of the fuel lines and the charcoal canister were replaced and the vehicle still failed. Finally, a technician used a hydrocarbon detector and located a small rust hole in the gas tank. The fumes were escaping from the hole in the tank and were picked up by the large exhaust hose during the testing on the rollers. A temporary plug of epoxy was applied to the hole and the Corvette then passed with flying colours. The customer was informed that a new gas tank is all that would be needed to complete the emission repair. See Figure 31–26.

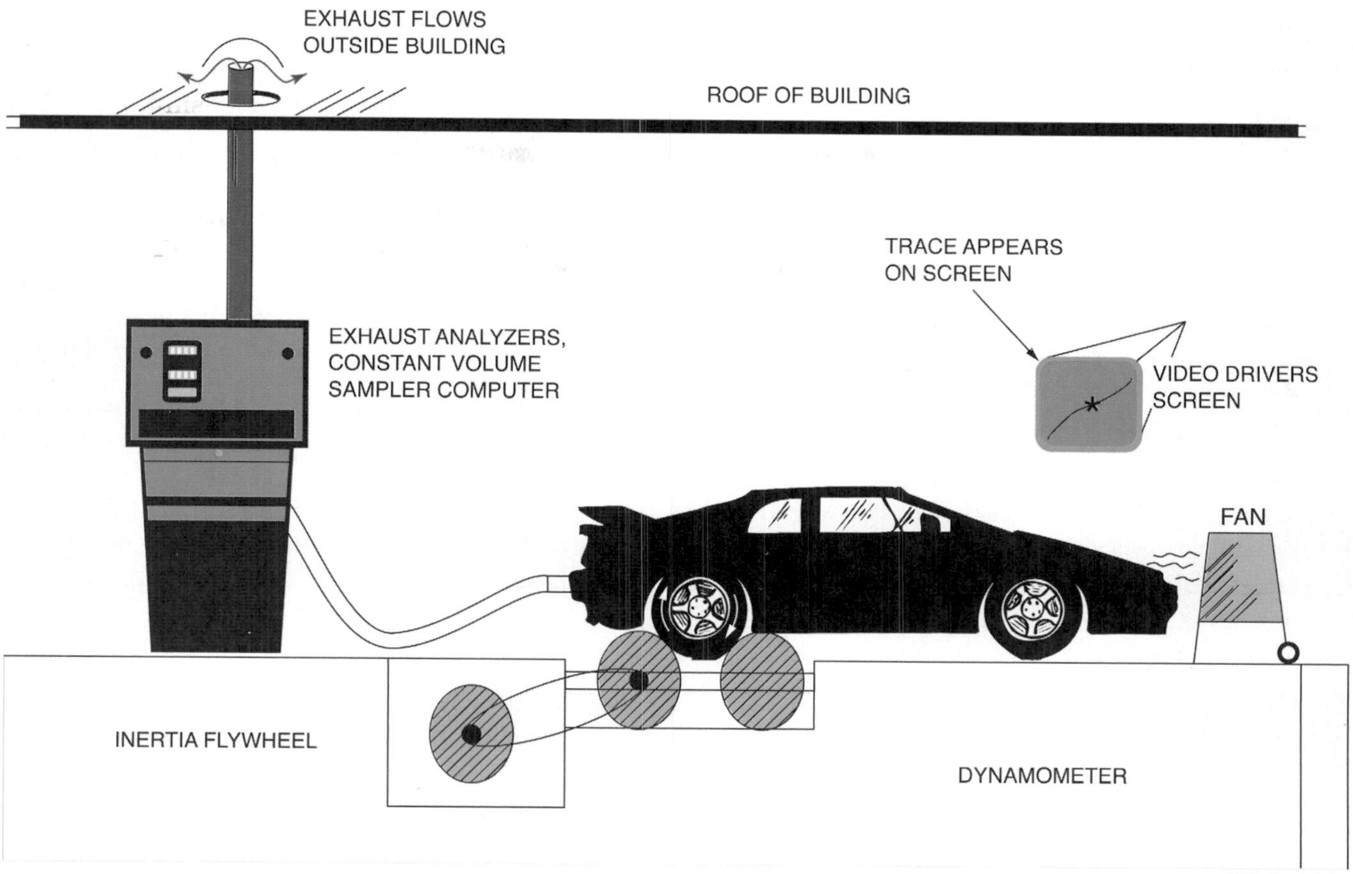

EXHAUST FLOWS OUTSIDE BUILDING

ROOF OF BUILDING

TRACE APPEARS ON SCREEN

EXHAUST ANALYZERS, CONSTANT VOLUME SAMPLER COMPUTER

VIDEO DRIVERS SCREEN

FAN

INERTIA FLYWHEEL

DYNAMOMETER

Figure 31–25 A line drawing representation of an enhanced I/M test setup. The vehicle's drive wheels rotate an inertia dynamometer that is loaded to match the inertia weight of the vehicle being tested. A driver "drives the trace," following the path deployed on an overhead monitor. The test measures all the exhaust, and the computer then calculates the amount of exhaust gases in grams per kilometre or grams per mile.

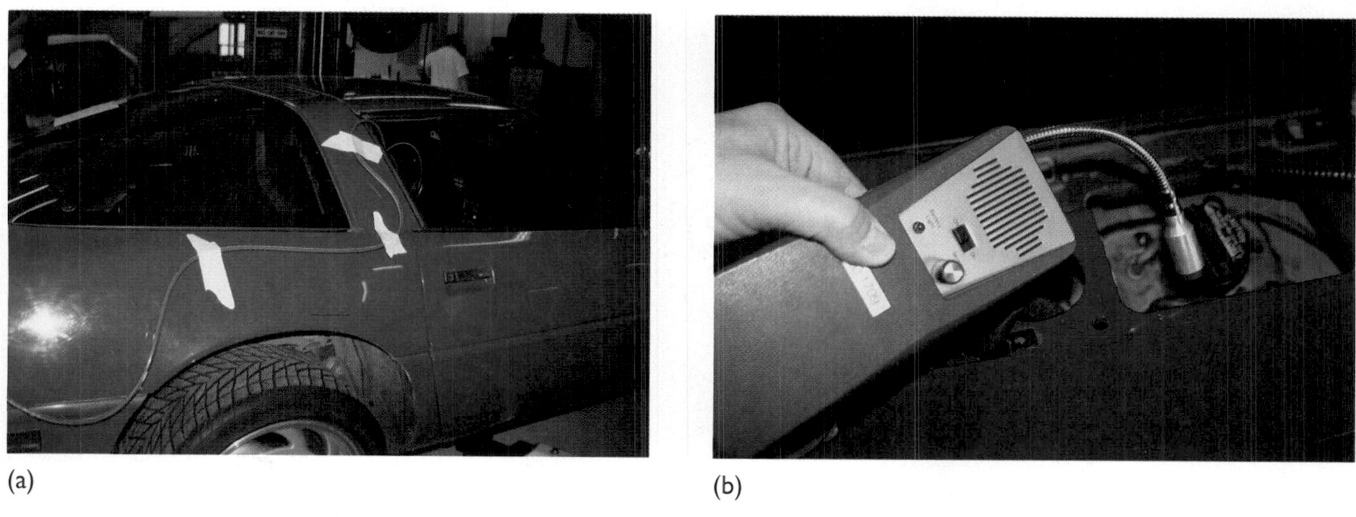

(a) (b)

Figure 31–26 (a) The first step during the diagnosis of the exhaust emissions from the Corvette was to test drive the vehicle with the 5-gas analyzer inside the vehicle. This allows the technician to monitor the exhaust emissions under conditions similar to those during an enhanced I/M test. Care should be taken not to damage the vehicle's paint when attaching the test hose. (b) A hydrocarbon tester finally found the gas tank leak.

TECH TIP

Your Nose Knows

Using the nose, a technician can often hone in on a major problem without having to connect the vehicle to an exhaust analyzer. For example:

- The strong smell of exhaust is due to excessive unburned hydrocarbon (HC) emissions. Look for an ignition system fault that could prevent the proper burning of the fuel. A vacuum leak could also cause a lean misfire and cause excessive HC exhaust emissions.
- If your eyes start to burn or water, suspect excessive oxides of nitrogen (NO_x) emissions. The oxides of nitrogen combine with the moisture in the eyes to form a mild solution of nitric acid. The acid formation causes the eyes to burn and water. Excessive NO_x exhaust emissions can be created by a vacuum leak, which causes higher-than-normal combustion chamber temperatures, over-advanced ignition timing, which also increases combustion chamber temperatures, or a malfunctioning exhaust gas recirculation system (EGR). EGR problems are usually noticed at higher RPM on most vehicles.
- Dizzy feeling or headache. This is commonly caused by excessive carbon monoxide (CO) exhaust emissions. Get out of the building and into fresh air as soon as possible. A probable cause of high levels of CO is an excessively rich air–fuel mixture.

TECH TIP

Hints for Passing an Emissions Test

While these hints will not permit a poorly-maintained or defective vehicle to pass an enhanced exhaust emissions test, it will help prevent a well-maintained vehicle from failing the test.

1. Only test your vehicle on a nice day—avoid very cold or windy days/nights. Cold weather requires that the engine be run longer for the engine coolant, oil, and catalytic converter to reach and maintain optimum operating temperature.
2. The battery must be in good condition. A weak or low voltage battery causes many fuel-injected engines to run too rich (too much fuel) due to battery voltage correction programs built into the PCM.
3. Change engine oil before having the vehicle tested. Dirty or contaminated oil increases exhaust emissions.
4. Use premium gasoline to help reduce oxides of nitrogen (NO_x) emission.
5. Do not overfill the gas tank. After the nozzle "clicks off," only add fuel to the next dime's worth. If the gas tank is overfilled, liquid gasoline can be drawn into the engine through the canister purge system during the test.
6. *Drive 30 km (20 mi) before having the vehicle tested.*
7. Arrive at the test centre with only one-fourth to one-half tank of gasoline.
8. While waiting for the inspection, place the gear selector in "park" or "neutral" and keep the engine running at a fast idle (about 2500 rpm).
9. Before testing begins, turn the air conditioning/heating or defroster to the off position.

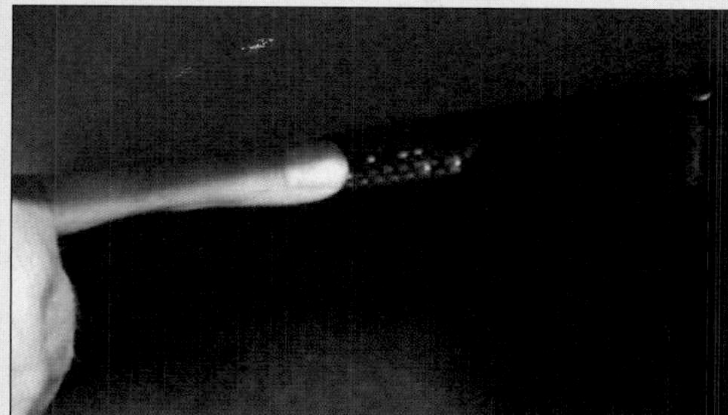

P22–1 All vehicles sold in Canada since 1998 (1996 in U.S.) use the OBDII 16-pin data link connector (DLC).

P22–2 Start the scan tool diagnosis by connecting the scan tool, a Tech 2 in this case, to the DLC. The DLC contains a 12 volt pin (Pin 16) and a chassis ground pin (Pin 4) to power the scan tool. An additional connection to the lighter plug or battery is not necessary on vehicles equipped with OBD II.

P22–3 Turn the power on to the scan tool before starting the engine. Much information can be learned if the scan tool is set up ready to go before the ignition is turned on or the engine is started.

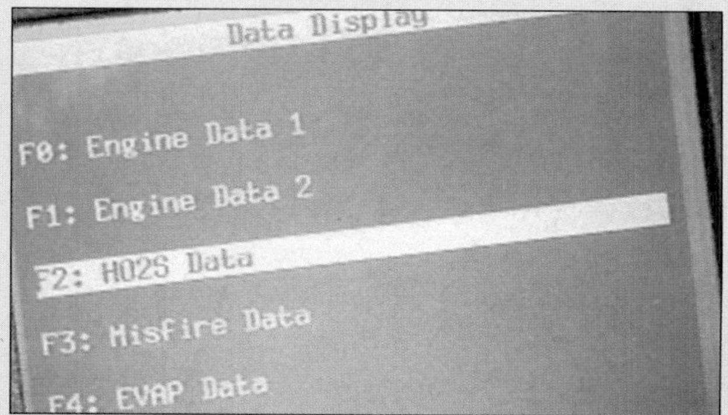

P22–4 Select heated oxygen sensor (HO2S) data before turning on the ignition.

P22–5 Turn the ignition key on (engine off) and observe the voltage readings of all the oxygen sensors. When the ignition is first turned on, the voltage of the oxygen sensors represents the bias voltage that the vehicle computer applies to the sensors.

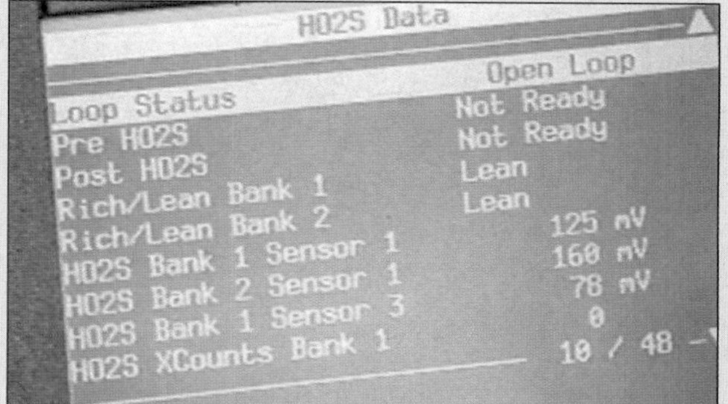

P22–6 After waiting several minutes, notice that the voltage has been lowered on all three oxygen sensors. As the electric heaters inside the oxygen sensors heat the sensors, they become more electrically conductive. Remember: The engine is off and the oxygen sensors are simply responding normally to the oxygen in the exhaust system. There may be a possible problem with bank 2 sensor 1 because it did not drop as far as the others.

P22–7 Another item to check before starting the engine is the engine coolant temperature (ECT). The temperature should be close to the surrounding temperature. In this case, the vehicle has been in the shop overnight and the temperature displayed is the temperature inside the building.

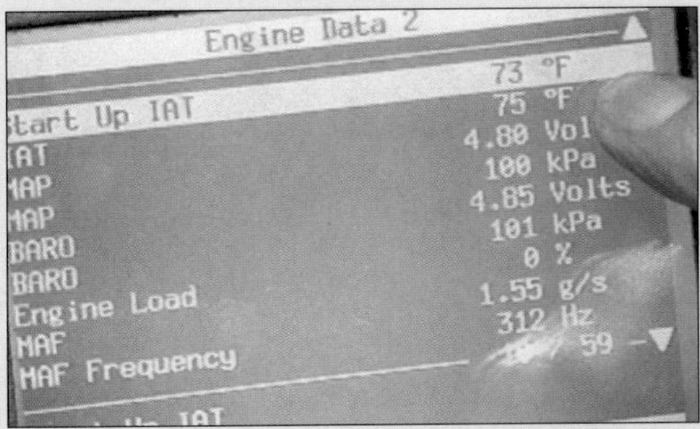

P22–8 To help check the ECT sensor, a scan tool can be used to check the intake air temperature (IAT) sensor. The two sensors (ECT and IAT) should be within 5° of each other. In this case, both show 73°F (22°C). Also notice that the manifold absolute pressure (MAP) sensor values match the barometric (BARO) sensor reading at key on/engine off. This value will vary according to altitude.

P22–9 After checking the temperature, pressure, and oxygen sensors, the engine can be started. With the engine running, notice that the injector pulse width is about the same for each bank of this 4.3 6L V-6 engine. Normal pulse width for most engines at operating temperature is 1.5 to 3.5 ms and should be higher when the engine is cold, as shown here.

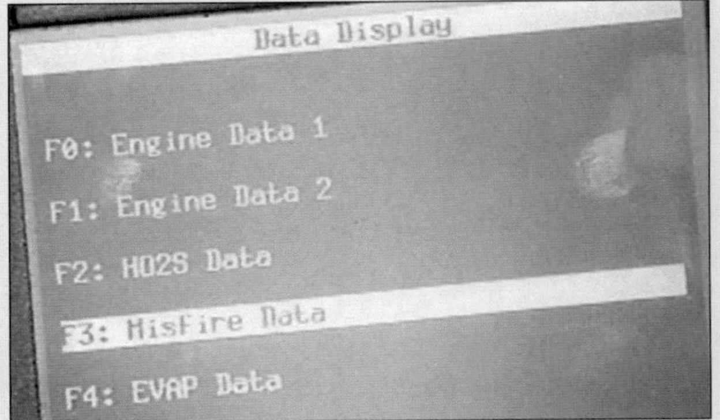

P22–10 Cylinder misfire data is available on most scan tools for vehicles equipped with OBD II. This helps determine if a fault exists in any particular cylinder.

P22–11 Misfire data shows no misfires for all six cylinders on this GM vechicle.

P22–12 The pre-catalytic converter oxygen sensor (sensor 1) should fluctuate from below 200 mV to above 800 mV. The post converter oxygen sensor should be steady if the converter is okay.

P22–13 Engine speed and idle speed control can also be maintained. The difference between the desired idle speed and the actual idle speed should be within 50 rpm. The idle air control (IAC) counts should also be checked. A lower-than-normal IAC count, such as zero, indicates a possible intake manifold or vacuum leak. A higher-than-normal reading could indicate dirty throttle plates or partially clogged fuel injectors.

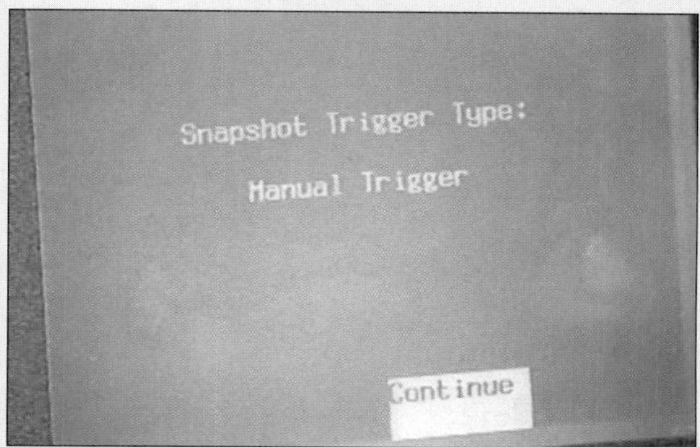

P22–14 The vehicle should also be checked for any stored diagnostic trouble codes (DTCs). If a DTC is stored, the engine controller (computer) could be compensating for the problem, and the scan data, also called **parameter identification data** or **PID,** could be misleading.

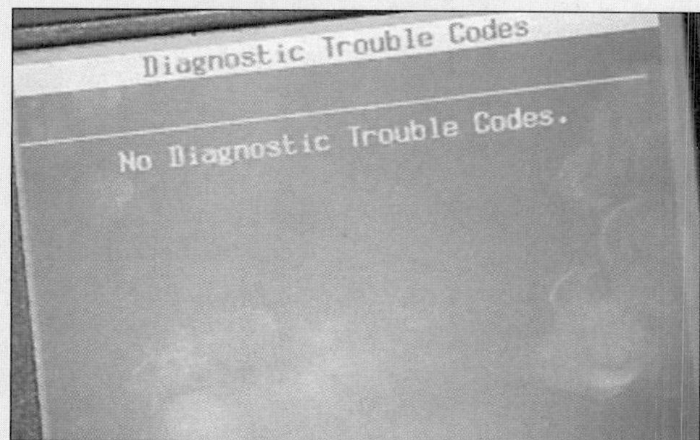

P22–15 The snapshot feature of most scan tools is useful to help find those intermittent problems. The scan tool can store and play back data about the engine even before the snapshot is triggered.

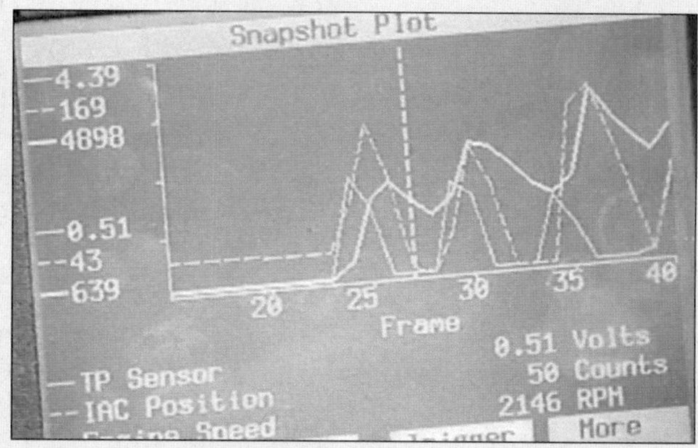

P22–16 When playing back snapshot data, it is useful to graph the value of several sensors to see if there is an obvious problem at one particular moment of time. The legend on the left side of the display shows the highest and the lowest value of the three sensors selected, displays which are also helpful when trying to see if a sensor is out of range.

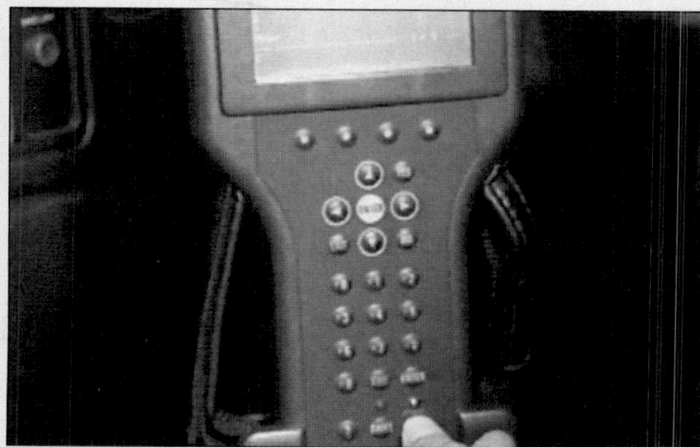

P22–17 After use, the scan tool should be used to clear any stored DTCs and then powered down.

P22–18 Disconnect the scan tool from the DLC and store it in its protective case.

P23–1 A typical portable exhaust gas analyzer that is capable of measuring unburned hydrocarbons (HC), carbon monoxide (CO), oxides of nitrogen (NO_x), carbon dioxide (CO_2), and oxygen (O_2).

P23–2 After turning the unit on, most exhaust analyzers require a warmup period.

P23–3 To test the exhaust of a vehicle, select "data display" from the main menu.

P23–4 Select "gases/RPM/oil temp" from the data display menu.

P23–5 Wait again! This is the reason why many service technicians turn on the exhaust gas analyzer at the beginning of each day and leave it on all day to avoid having to wait for the unit to become operational.

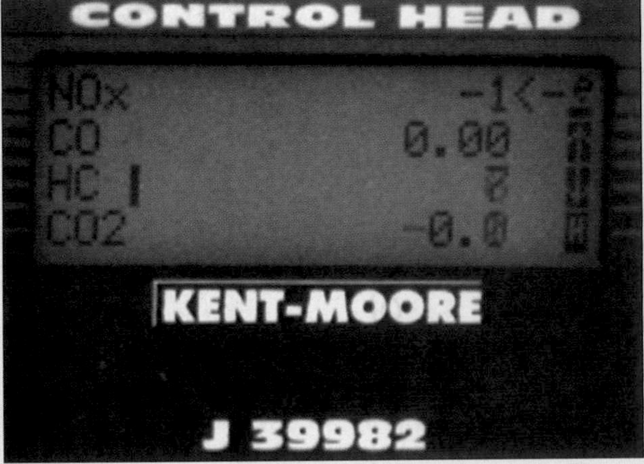

P23–6 The unit is now able to display exhaust gas readings. It has been about 15 minutes from the time the unit was first turned on!

P23–7 Insert the test probe into the tailpipe.

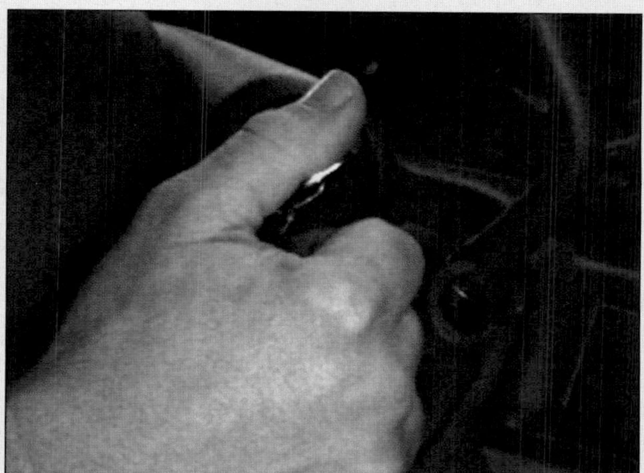

P23–8 Start the engine.

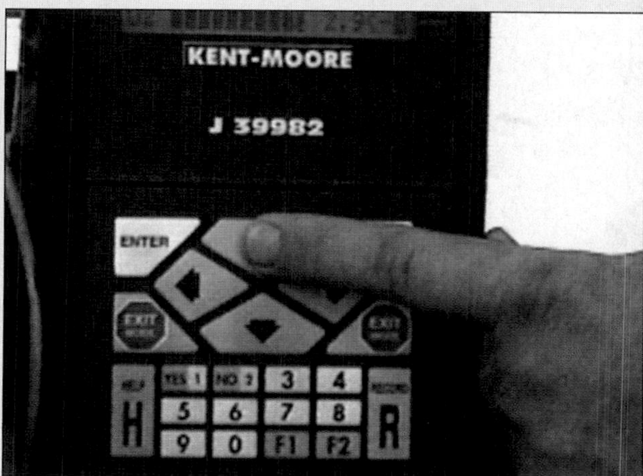

P23–9 Use the up and down arrow keys to scroll up and down the data list to observe the gases. This unit can only display four of the five gases at a time. Because we are not concerned with NO_x until the vehicle is driven, this technician selected this display showing CO, HC, CO_2 and O_2.

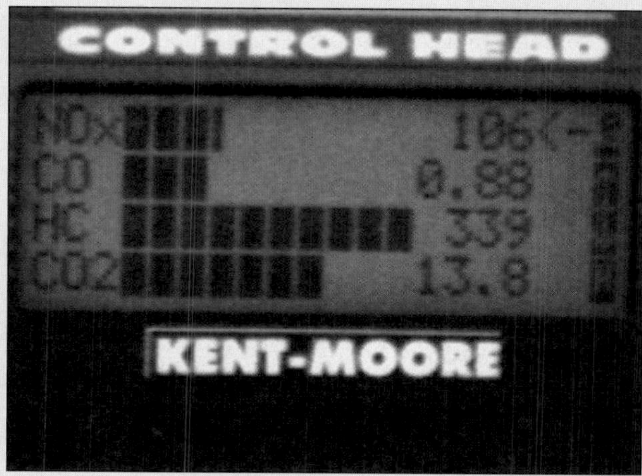

P23–10 This display shows a typical engine at idle after a cold start. Notice the higher-than-normal HC reading.

P23–11 To help get the engine, oxygen sensor, and catalytic converter up to operating temperature, operate the engine at 2000 rpm for several minutes.

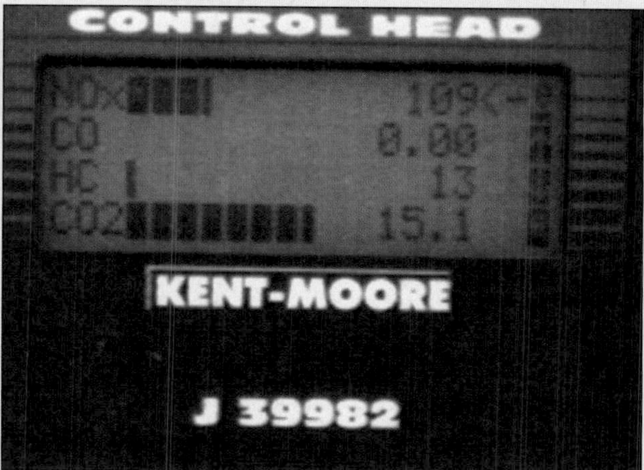

P23–12 After the engine has reached operating temperature, the HC readings are now 13 ppm—well within the normal allowable limit of less than 50 ppm.

SUMMARY

1. Funnel Diagnostics—Visual Approach to a Diagnostic Procedure
   Step #1. Verify the Problem (Concern)
   Step #2. Perform a Thorough Visual Inspection and Basic Tests
   Step #3. Retrieve the Diagnostic Trouble Codes (DTCs)
   Step #4. Check for Technical Service Bulletins (TSBs)
   Step #5. Look Carefully at Scan Tool Data
   Step #6. Narrow Focus of Problem to a System or Cylinder
   Step #7. Repair the Problem, Determine and Correct the Root Cause
   Step #8. Verify the Repair and Clear any Stored DTCs
2. Care should be taken not to induce high voltage or current around any computer or computer-controlled circuit or sensor.
3. A thorough visual inspection is the first step in the diagnosis and troubleshooting of any engine-performance problem or electrical malfunction.
4. If the MIL is on, retrieve the DTC and follow the manufacturer's recommended procedure to find the root cause of the problem.
5. All DTCs should be cleared after the repair.
6. OBD II vehicles use a 16-pin DLC and common DTCs.
7. Excessive hydrocarbon (HC) exhaust emissions are created by a lack of proper combustion, such as a fault in the ignition system, too lean an air–fuel mixture, or too cold engine operation.
8. Excessive carbon monoxide (CO) exhaust emissions are usually created by a rich air–fuel mixture.
9. Excessive oxides of nitrogen (NO_x) exhaust emissions are usually created by excessive heat or pressure in the combustion chamber or a lack of the proper amount of exhaust gas recirculation (EGR).
10. Carbon dioxide (CO_2) levels indicate efficiency—the higher the CO_2, the more efficient the engine operation.
11. Oxygen (O_2) is a lean indicator. The higher the O_2, the leaner the air-fuel mixture.
12. A vehicle should be driven about 30 km (20 mi), especially during cold weather, to allow the engine to be fully warm before an enhanced emissions test.

REVIEW QUESTIONS

1. Explain the procedure to follow when diagnosing a vehicle without any stored DTCs using a scan tool.
2. Discuss what the PCM does during a drive cycle to test emission-related components.
3. List three things that should be checked as part of a thorough visual inspection.
4. List the eight-step funnel diagnostic procedure.
5. Explain why a bulletin search should be performed after stored DTCs are retrieved.
6. Explain why a rich mixture is better for the engine than a lean mixture.
7. List the five exhaust gases and their maximum allowable readings for a fuel-injected vehicle equipped with a catalytic converter.

RED SEAL CERTIFICATION-TYPE QUESTIONS

1. The first step in the diagnostic process is
   a. Retrieve the diagnostic trouble codes
   b. Perform a thorough visual inspection
   c. Verify the problem
   d. Check the scan tool data
2. When testing a vehicle using a scan tool, what values should be the same before starting a cold engine?
   a. O2S and IAT
   b. ECT and IAT
   c. MAP and TP
   d. MAF and MAP
3. Before performing an exhaust gas analysis
   a. The computer should be scanned for codes
   b. The fuel tank should be full
   c. A cylinder balance test should be done
   d. The catalytic converter should be at temperature
4. After the customer complaint has been verified, what is the next step when diagnosing an engine performance problem?
   a. Checking for any stored diagnostic trouble codes
   b. Checking for any technical service bulletins (TSBs)
   c. Performing a thorough visual inspection
   d. Looking carefully at the scan tool data
5. A vehicle arrives with a DTC identifying an open TPS. The technician clears the code and installs a jumper wire between the 5 volt reference terminal and the signal terminal in the TPS wiring connector. The opposite code sets. The problem is with the
   a. Computer
   b. Wiring circuit
   c. Sensor
   d. Throttle cable
6. The preferred method to clear diagnostic trouble codes (DTCs) is to
   a. Disconnect the negative battery cable for 10 seconds
   b. Use a scan tool
   c. Remove the computer (PCM) power feed fuse
   d. Cycle the ignition key on and off 40 times

7. All OBD II vehicles use a _____ pin data link connector (DLC).
   a. 16
   b. 12
   c. 5
   d. 4
8. A port fuel-injected engine with a plugged fuel injector will show a rise in what emission?
   a. HC
   b. CO
   c. CO_2
   d. NO_x
9. HC and CO are high and CO_2 and O_2 are low. This could be caused by a
   a. Rich mixture
   b. Lean mixture
   c. Defective ignition components
   d. Clogged EGR passage
10. Which gas is generally considered to be the rich indicator? (The higher the level of this gas, the richer the air-fuel mixture.)
    a. HC
    b. CO
    c. CO_2
    d. O_2

SECTION **VI**

Brakes

32 Brake System Principles and Operation

33 Master Cylinders and the Hydraulic System

34 Wheel Bearings and Service

35 Drum Brake Operation, Diagnosis, and Service

36 Disc Brake Operation, Diagnosis, and Service

37 Machining Brake Drums and Rotors

38 Power-Assisted Brakes

39 Antilock Brakes

Chapter 32 covers the principles of operation of automotive brakes. Chapter 33 includes the master cylinder with details on brake fluid and how to properly bleed the air from the hydraulic system. Chapter 34 includes wheel bearings, rear axle bearings, and seals. Chapter 35 covers drum brake operation and service procedures. Chapter 36 covers disc brake operation and service procedures. Chapter 37 describes the machining of both brake drums and rotors with an emphasis on safety. Chapter 38 includes both vacuum- and hydraulically-operating brake assist units and Chapter 39 discusses theory and servicing of antilock braking systems (ABS).

32

Brake System Principles and Operation

OBJECTIVES: After studying Chapter 32, you should be able to:

1. Prepare for the interprovincial Red Seal certification examination in Appendix V (Brakes) on the topics covered in this chapter.
2. State the operating principles of the braking system.
3. List the parts and terms for disc and drum brakes.
4. Describe how the hydraulic brake system can be used to transfer pressure to each wheel.
5. Discuss the coefficient of friction and describe how the friction between the lining material and the drum or rotor stops wheels.
6. List the types of brake fluids and their application.
7. Discuss how ABS units help in braking and vehicle stability when stopping on slippery surfaces.

Brakes are by far the most important mechanism on any vehicle because the safety and lives of those riding in the vehicle depend on the proper operation of the braking system. It has been estimated that the brakes on the average vehicle are applied 50 000 times a year!

"Brakes stop wheels—not vehicles." This basic fact means that the best brakes in the world only stop the rotation of the tire/wheel assembly. It is the friction between the tire and the pavement that accomplishes the stopping or slowing of the vehicle. A vehicle being driven on an icy street will take an extremely long time to stop. Even a vehicle equipped with an antilock braking system (ABS) still has to have **friction (traction)** between the tire and the road for the vehicle to stop.

HOW BRAKES STOP VEHICLES

Brakes are an energy-absorbing mechanism to convert vehicle movement into heat while stopping the rotation of the wheels. All braking systems are designed to reduce the speed of and stop a moving vehicle and to keep it from moving if the vehicle is stationary. **Service brakes** are the main driver-operated brakes of the vehicle. See Figure 32–1. Service brakes are also called **base brakes** or **foundation brakes.**

Most vehicles built since the late 1920s use a brake on each wheel. To stop a wheel, the driver exerts force on a brake pedal. The force on the brake pedal pressurizes brake fluid in a master cylinder. This hydraulic force (liquid under pressure) is transferred through steel lines to a wheel cylinder or caliper at each wheel. Hydraulic pressure to each wheel cylinder or caliper is used to force friction materials against the brake drum or rotor. The friction between the stationary friction material and the rotating drum or rotor (disc) causes the rotating part to slow and eventually stop. Since the wheels are attached to the drums or rotors, the wheels of the vehicle also stop.

The heavier the vehicle and the higher the speed, the more heat the brakes have to be able to absorb. Long, steep hills can cause the brakes to overheat, reducing brake efficiency. See Figures 32–2 and 32–3.

Drum Brakes

Drum brakes are used on the rear of many rear-wheel-drive, front-wheel-drive, and four-wheel-drive

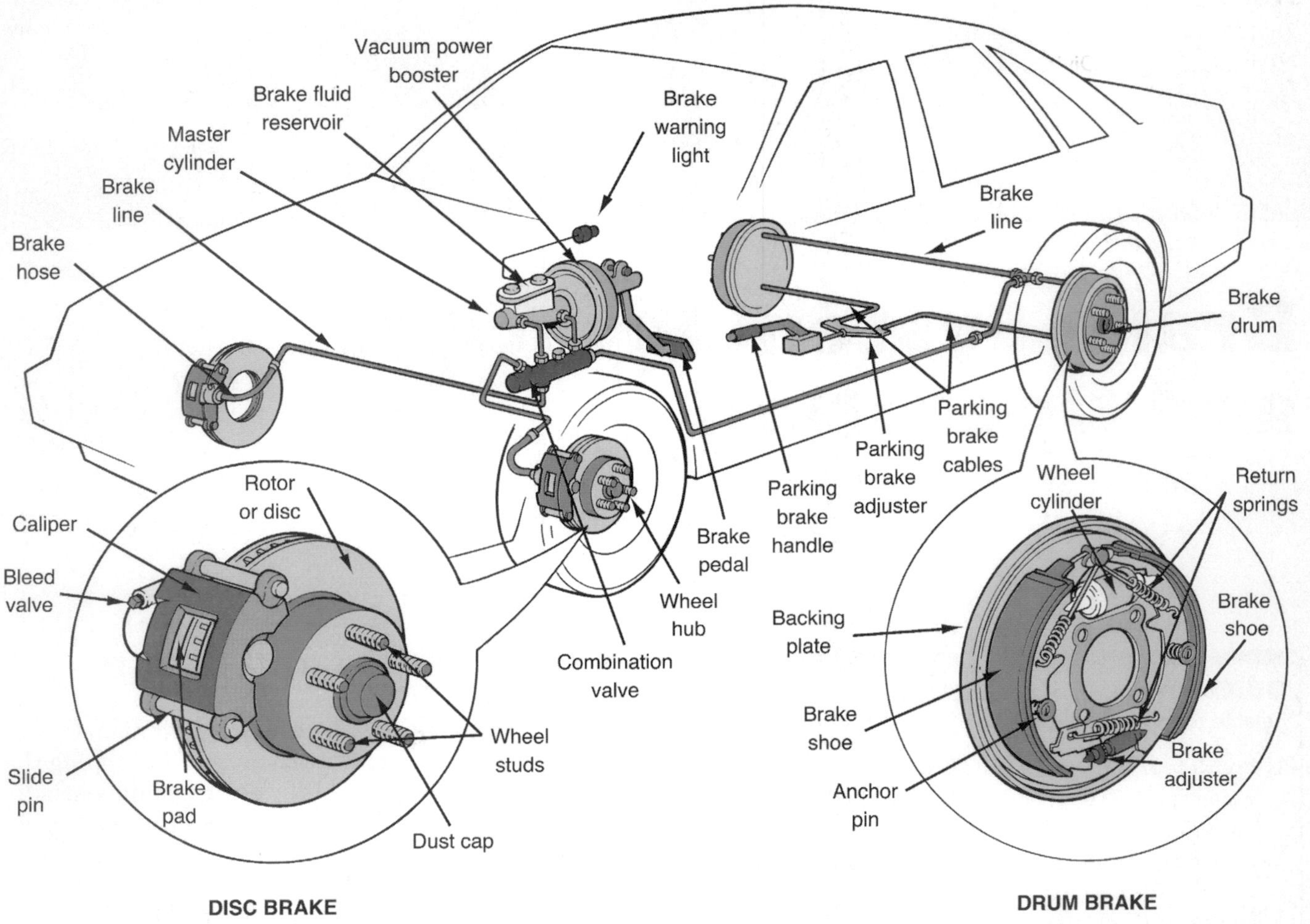

Figure 32–1 Typical vehicle brake system showing all typical components.

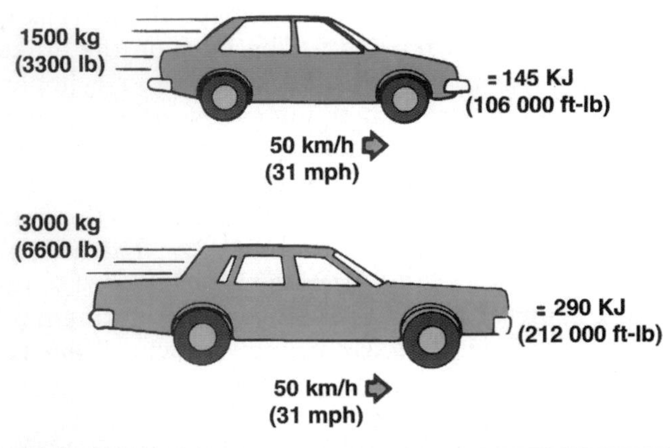

Figure 32–2 The kinetic (moving) energy increases in direct proportion to vehicle weight; 1 J = 1000 N·m.

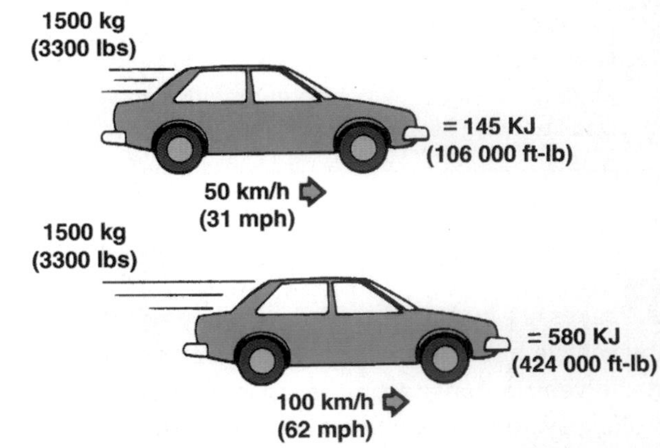

Figure 32–3 The kinetic (moving) energy increases as the square (speed times itself) of any increase in vehicle speed.

vehicles. Since the early 1970s few vehicles have used drum brakes on the front wheels. When drum brakes are applied, brake shoes are moved outward against a rotating brake drum. The wheel studs for the wheels are attached to the drum. When the drum slows and stops, the wheels also slow and stop.

Drum brakes are economical to manufacture, service, and repair. Parts for drum brakes are generally readily available and reasonably priced. On some vehicles, an additional drum brake is used as a parking brake on vehicles equipped with rear disc brakes. See Figure 32–4.

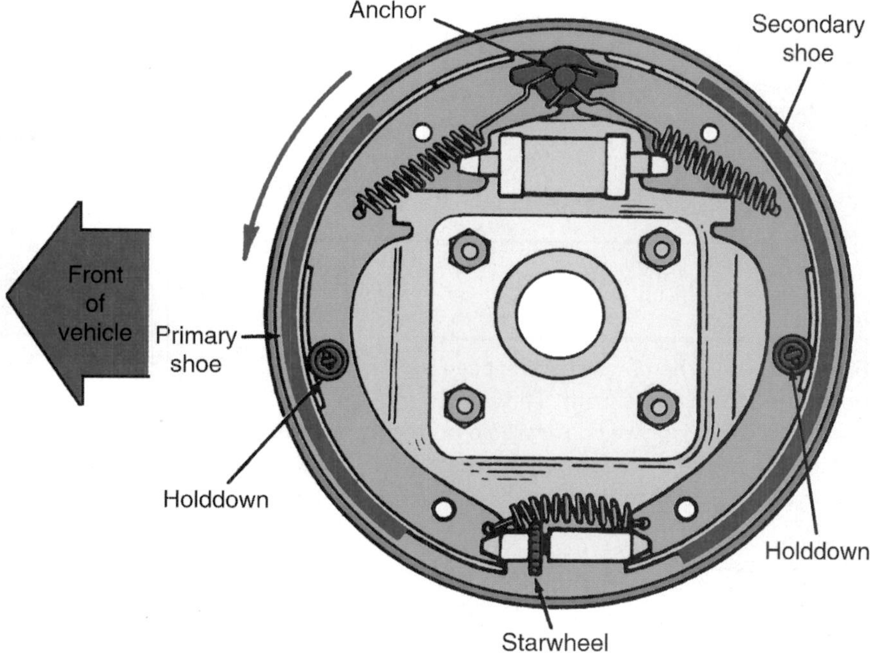

Figure 32–4 Typical drum brake assembly. (Wagner Division, Cooper Industries Inc.)

Disc Brakes

Disc brakes are used on the front of most vehicles built since the early 1970s and on the rear wheels of many vehicles. A disc brake operates by squeezing brake pads on both sides of a rotor or disc that is attached to the wheel. See Figure 32–5.

Type of Brake	Rotating Part	Friction Part
Drum brakes	Brake drum	Brake shoes
Disc brakes	Rotor or disc	Brake pads

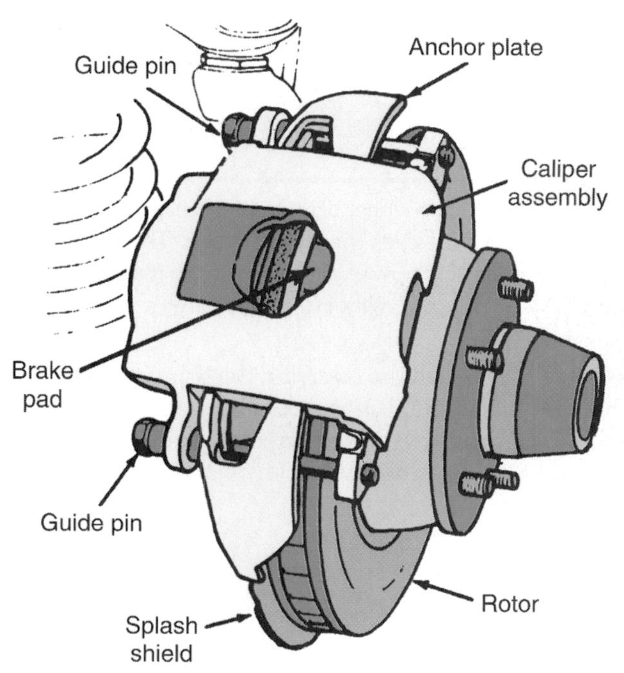

Figure 32–5 Typical disc brake assembly. (Wagner Division, Cooper Industries Inc.)

Due to the friction between the road surface and the tires, the vehicle stops. To summarize, the events necessary to stop a vehicle include:

1. The driver presses on the brake pedal.
2. The brake pedal force is transferred hydraulically to a wheel cylinder or caliper at each wheel.
3. Hydraulic pressure inside the wheel cylinder or caliper presses friction materials (brake shoes or pads) against rotating brake drums or rotors.
4. The friction slows and stops the drum or rotor. Since the drum or rotor is bolted to the wheel of the vehicle, the wheel also stops.
5. When the wheels of the vehicle slow and stop, the tires must have friction (traction) with the road surface to stop the vehicle.

WEIGHT TRANSFER DURING BRAKING

Whenever the brakes are applied on a vehicle in motion, the weight of the vehicle is transferred forward while driving forward. Most vehicles can be observed nosing downward whenever the brakes are applied. Greater braking power is required of the front brakes

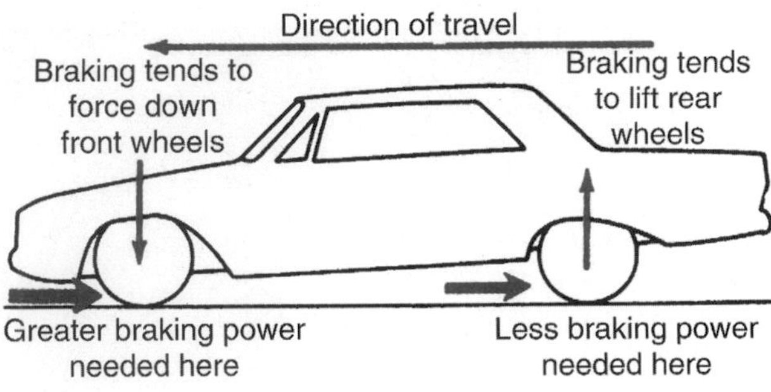

Figure 32–6 When brakes are applied, vehicle weight is transferred toward the front. This weight transfer requires that more braking power be available on the front wheels and less on the rear wheels to avoid rear-wheel lockup. (Courtesy of EIS Brake Parts)

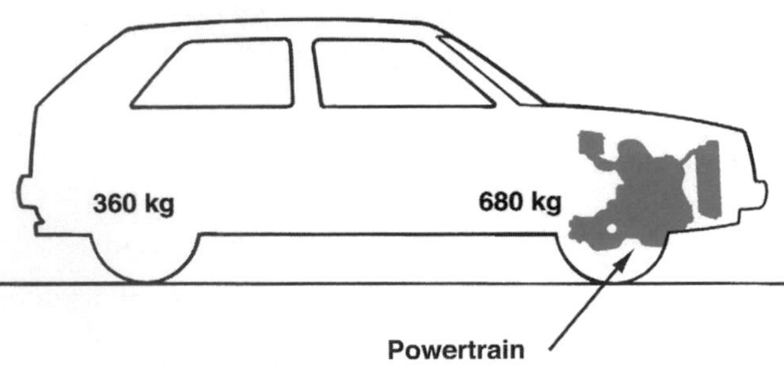

Figure 32–7 Front-wheel drive vehicles have much of their vehicle weight over the front wheels. This means that most of the braking power occurs with the front brakes. (Courtesy of Hunter Engineering Company)

because of this weight transfer. See Figure 32–6. It is estimated that the front brakes handle about 60% to 70% of the braking power on rear-wheel drive vehicles and 80% on front-wheel drive vehicles. See Figure 32–7.

FRICTION

Friction is the force that resists the motion between two objects that are in contact. See Figure 32–8. The amount of friction between two surfaces is called the **coefficient of friction** and is represented by a number from 0 to 1. The Greek letter **mu** (μ) is used to represent this factor.

$\mu = 0$ (no friction between surfaces)
$\mu = 1$ (maximum friction between surfaces)

To stop a vehicle there must be friction between the brake lining material and the rotating brake part such as the brake drum or rotor. Road surfaces also provide varying amounts of traction (friction) for the tires. On ice, tires cannot grip the road; even if the brakes are working perfectly, the vehicle will not stop quickly because of the lack of friction between the tires and the ice. Braking is especially dangerous when one side of the vehicle is travelling over normal high-friction road surfaces while the other wheel on the other side of the vehicle is running on gravel or ice. Brake engineers call these **split mu** conditions. Antilock braking systems are especially important during braking under these conditions.

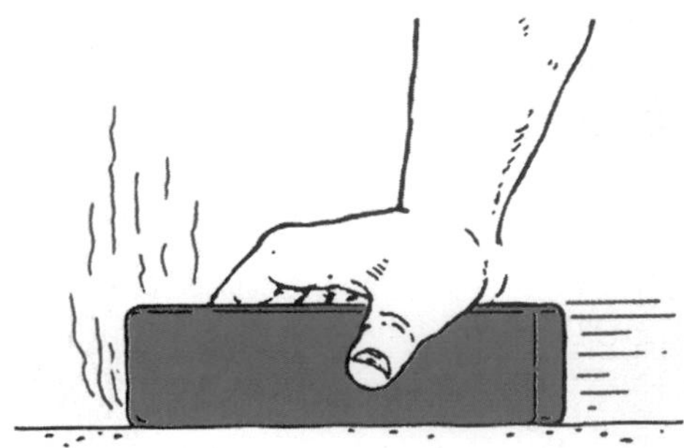

Figure 32–8 A brick being pushed against the floor creates heat from the friction between the two surfaces. (Courtesy of EIS Brake Parts)

BRAKE FLUID

Brake fluid is made from a combination of various types of glycol, a nonpetroleum-based fluid. Brake fluid is a polyalkylene-glycol-ether mixture called **polyglycol** for short. *All polyglycol brake fluid is clear to amber in colour.* Brake fluid has to have the following characteristics:

1. A high boiling point
2. A low freezing point
3. The ability not to damage rubber parts in the brake system

> **CAUTION:** DOT 3 brake fluid is a very strong solvent and can remove paint! Care is required when working with DOT 3 brake fluid to avoid contact with the vehicle's painted surfaces. It also takes the colour out of leather shoes.

DOT Brake Fluid Specifications

All automotive brake fluid must meet Federal Motor Vehicle Safety Standard 116. The Society of Automotive Engineers (SAE), the Canadian Standards Association (CSA), and the U.S. Department of Transportation (DOT) have established brake fluid specification standards.

	DOT 3	DOT 4	DOT 5
Dry boiling point	205°C (401°F)	230°C (446°F)	260°C (500°F)
Wet boiling point	140°C (284°F)	155°C (311°F)	180°C (356°F)

The wet boiling point is often referred to as ERBP, meaning **equilibrium reflux boiling point.** ERBP refers to the method in the specification (SAE J1703) for how the fluid is exposed to moisture and tested.

DOT 3 DOT 3 is the type of brake fluid most often used. It absorbs moisture. According to SAE, DOT 3 can absorb 2% of its volume in water per year. Moisture is absorbed by the brake fluid through microscopic seams in the brake system and around seals. Over time, the water will corrode the system and thicken the brake fluid. The moisture also can cause a spongy brake pedal due to reduced vapour-lock temperature. See Figure 32–9. DOT 3 must be used from a sealed (capped) container. If allowed to remain open for any length of time, DOT 3 will absorb moisture from the surrounding air.

DOT 4 DOT 4 is formulated for use by all vehicles, imported or domestic. It is commonly called LMA (low moisture absorption). DOT 4 does not absorb water as fast as DOT 3 but is still affected by moisture and should be used only from a sealed container. DOT 4 is approximately double the cost of DOT 3. *DOT 4 can be used wherever DOT 3 is specified.* See Figure 32–10.

DOT 5 DOT 5 is commonly called **silicone brake fluid** and is made from polydimethylsiloxanes. It does not absorb any water. DOT 5 brake fluid is purple (violet) in colour to distinguish it from DOT 3 or DOT 4 brake fluid.

DOT 5 brake fluid should not be mixed with any other type of brake fluid. Therefore, the entire braking system must be completely flushed and refilled with DOT 5. DOT 5 is approximately four times the cost of DOT 3 brake fluid.

NOTE: The ability of DOT 5 silicone brake fluid to absorb air is one of the major reasons why it is *not* recommended for use with antilock braking systems (ABS). In ABS, valves and pumps are used that can aerate the brake fluid. Brake fluid filled with air bubbles cannot properly lubricate the ABS components and will cause a low and soft brake pedal.

DOT 5.1 DOT 5.1 is a non-silicone-based polyglycol fluid and is clear to amber in colour. This severe duty fluid has a boiling point of over 260°C (500°F) equal to the boiling point of silicone-based DOT 5 fluid. Unlike DOT 5, DOT 5.1 can be mixed with either DOT 3 or DOT 4 according to the brake fluid manufacturer's recommendations.

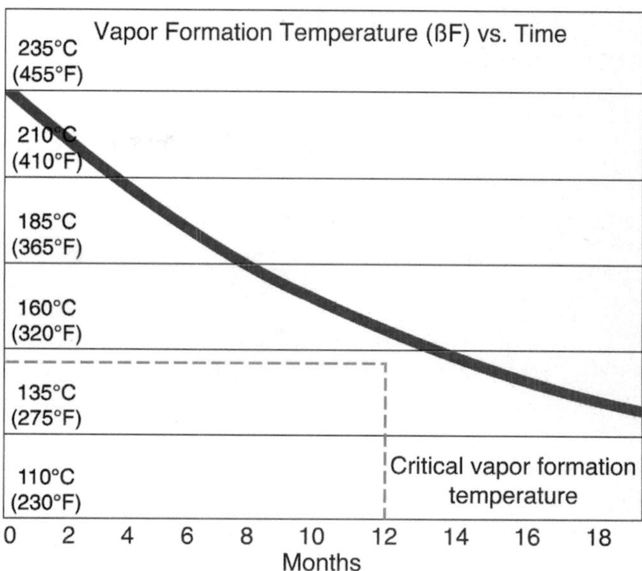

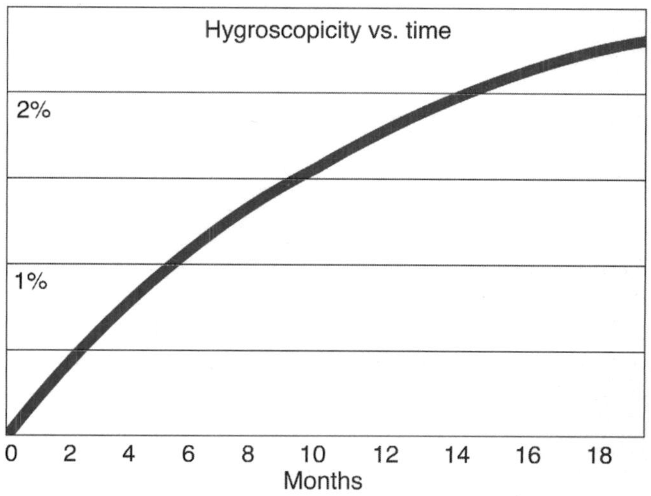

Figure 32–9 Brake fluid absorbs moisture from the air at the rate of about 2% per year. As the brake fluid absorbs water, its boiling temperature decreases.

CAUTION: Some vehicle manufacturers such as DaimlerChrysler do not recommend the use of or the mixing of other types of polyglycol brake fluid and specify the use of DOT 3 brake fluid only. Always follow the vehicle manufacturer's recommendation.

Hydraulic System Mineral Oil (HSMO)

Some French-built Citroen and British-designed Rolls Royce vehicles use hydraulic system mineral oil as part of their hydraulic control systems. The systems in these vehicle use a hydraulic pump to pressurize hydraulic oil for use in the suspension leveling and braking systems.

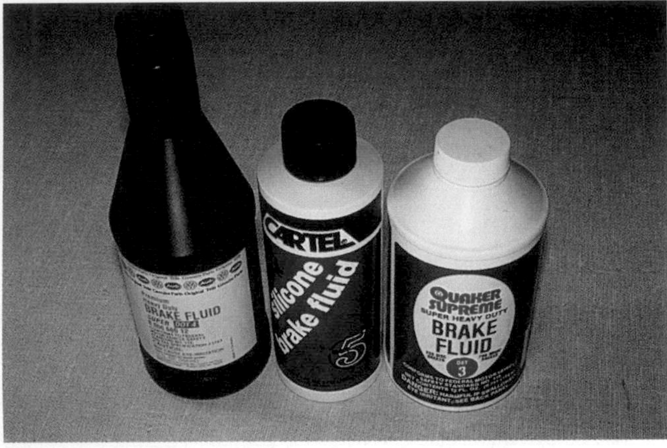

Figure 32–10 Brake fluid should be purchased in small containers to help prevent the possibility of contamination and moisture absorption after the container has been opened. On the left is DOT 4 brake fluid with DOT 5 in the middle and DOT 3 on the right.

Figure 32–11 Both rubber sealing cups were the exact same size. The cup on the left was exposed to mineral oil. Notice how the seal greatly expanded.

> **CAUTION:** Mineral hydraulic oil should never be used in a braking system that requires DOT 3 or DOT 4 polyglycol-base brake fluid. If *any* mineral oil such as engine oil, transmission oil, or automatic transmission fluid (ATF) gets into a braking system that requires glycol brake fluid, *every* rubber part in the entire braking system *must* be replaced. **Mineral oil causes the rubber compounds that are used in glycol brake fluid systems to swell.** See Figure 32–11.

To help prevent hydraulic system mineral oil from being mixed with glycol brake fluid, *hydraulic mineral oils are green.*

Figure 32–12 Brake fluid should be clear or amber in colour. If it looks dark, it may need to be changed.

Brake Fluid Testing

Most import brand vehicles specify a brake fluid replacement service interval. This recommendation is usually every 2 years or every 48 000 km (30 000 miles). Always check for the exact recommended brake fluid change interval. Most domestic vehicle manufacturers do not specify a brake fluid change interval. There are several ways to test/inspect the brake fluid including:

- **Visual**—The brake fluid should look clear or amber, as in Figure 32–12. If the brake fluid looks like black coffee or coffee with cream, it would be wise to replace the fluid.
- **Test strips**—Test strips are dipped into the brake fluid and change colour when contaminated as shown in Figure 32–13.
- **Brake fluid boiling point tester**—A brake fluid tester such as shown in Figure 32–14 can be used to test the boiling point of the brake fluid.

Brake Fluid Disposal

Brake fluid can cause irritation when it comes into direct contact with skin. The long-term effects of such contact are not known, but caution should be followed when handling brake fluid. Ensure you use protective eyewear and gloves when handling brake fluid and any hydraulic component. Brake fluid is a hazardous waste, and should be properly disposed of as per MSDS regulations in your province.

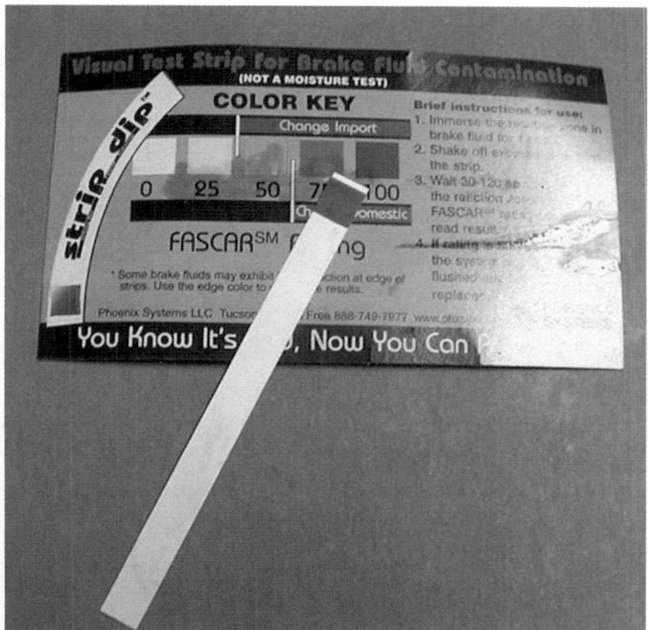

Figure 32–13 The colour of a test strip after being submerged in the brake fluid is used to indicate the level of contamination.

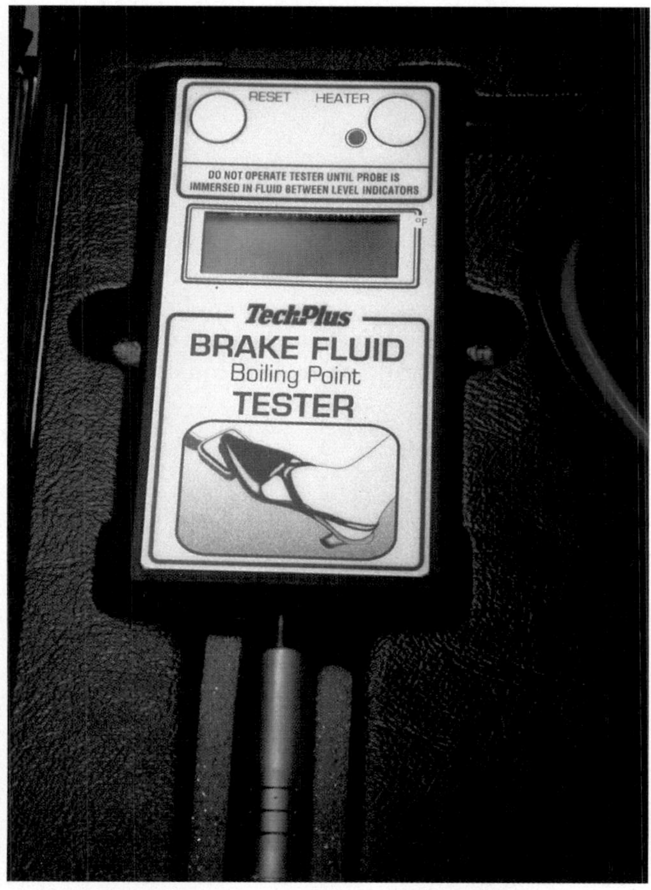

Figure 32–14 A brake fluid tester can test brake fluid for boiling point.

BRAKE LINING COMPOSITION

Friction material such as disc brake pads or drum brake shoes contains a mixture of ingredients. The various ingredients in brake lining are mixed and molded into the shape of the finished product. The fibres in the material are the only things holding this mixture together. A large press is used to force the

DIAGNOSTIC STORY 

The Pike's Peak Brake Inspection

All vehicles must stop about one-half way down Pike's Peak Mountain in Colorado (4300 m [14 000 ft]) for a brake inspection. When this author stopped at the inspection station, a uniformed inspector simply looked at the right front wheel and waved us on. I pulled over and asked the inspector what he was checking. He said that when linings and drums/rotors get hot, the vehicle loses brake effectiveness. But if the brake fluid boils, the vehicle loses its brakes entirely. The inspector was listening for boiling brake fluid at the front wheel and measuring the temperature of the front wheels using an infrared pyrometer. If the inspector felt the brakes were definitely too hot to continue, you would be instructed to pull over and wait for the brakes to cool. The inspector recommended placing the transmission into a lower gear, which uses the engine to slow the vehicle during the descent without having to rely entirely on the brakes.

DIAGNOSTIC STORY 

The Sinking Brake Pedal

This author experienced what happens when the brake fluid is not changed regularly. Just as many technicians will tell you, we do not always do what we know should be done to our own vehicles.

While driving a 4-year-old vehicle on vacation in very hot weather in mountainous country, the brake pedal sank to the floor. When the vehicle was cold, the brakes were fine. But after several brake applications, the pedal became soft and spongy and sank slowly to the floor if pressure was maintained on the brake pedal. Because the brakes were OK when cold, I knew it had to be boiling brake fluid. Old brake fluid (4 years old) often has a boiling point under 150°C (300°F). With the air temperature near 38°C (100°F), it does not take much more heat to start boiling the brake fluid. After bleeding over 1 litre of new brake fluid through the system, the brakes worked normally. I'll never forget again to replace the brake fluid as recommended by the vehicle manufacturers.

ingredients together to form a **brake block** that eventually becomes the brake lining. Many disc brake pads are **integrally moulded.**

Typical Compositions for Asbestos (Organic) Lining

Ingredient	Typical Formula Range (%)
Phenolic resin (binder)	9–15
Asbestos fibre	30–50
Organic friction modifiers (rubber scrap)	8–19
Inorganic friction (barytes, talc, whiting)	12–26
Abrasive particles (alumina)	4–20
Carbon	4–20

Semi-Metallic Friction Material Composition

The term semi-metallic, also called "semi-mets," refers to brake lining material that uses metal rather than asbestos in its formulation. It still uses resins and binders and is, therefore, not 100% metal, but rather semi-metallic. See Figure 32–15.

Ingredient	Formula Range (%)
Phenolic resin	15–40
Graphite or carbon particles	15–40
Steel fibres	0–25
Ceramic powders	2–10
Steel, copper, brass metal powders	15–40
Other modifiers (rubber scrap)	0–20

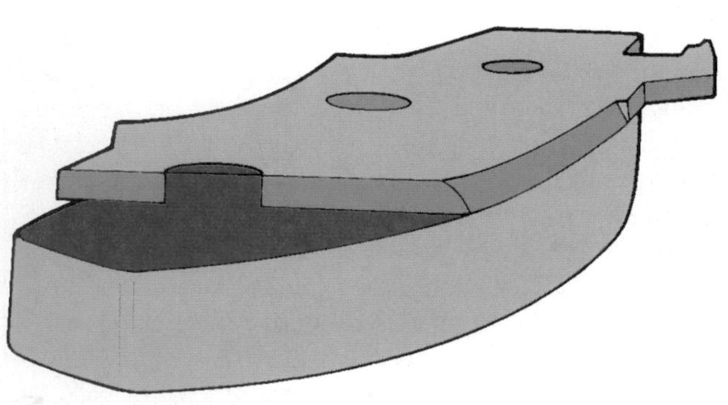

Figure 32–15 Cutaway shows friction material integrally moulded into steel backing plate.

Brake pads and linings that use synthetic material such as aramid fibres instead of steel are usually referred to as **nonasbestos, nonasbestos organic (NAO),** or **nonasbestos synthetic (NAS).** Disc brake pads that use nonferrous (nonsteel) and ceramic ingredients are often called **ceramic** pads.

LINING EDGE CODES

The edge coding contains three groups of letters and numbers. The first group is a series of letters that identify the manufacturer of the lining. The second group is a series of numbers, letters, or both that identify the lining compound or formula. The third group is two letters that identify the coefficient of friction. See Figure 32–16. The coefficient of friction is a pure number that indicates the amount of friction between two surfaces. For example, a material with a 0.55 coefficient of friction means it has more friction than a material with a coefficient of friction of 0.39. These codes were established by the SAE (Society of Automotive Engineers):

Code C = 0.00 to 0.15
Code D = 0.15 to 0.25
Code E = 0.25 to 0.35
Code F = 0.35 to 0.45
Code G = 0.45 to 0.55
Code H = 0.55 and above
Code Z = ungraded

The first letter, which is printed on the side of most linings, indicates the coefficient of friction when brakes are cold and the second letter indicates the coefficient of friction of the brake lining when the brakes are hot. (For example, FF indicates that the

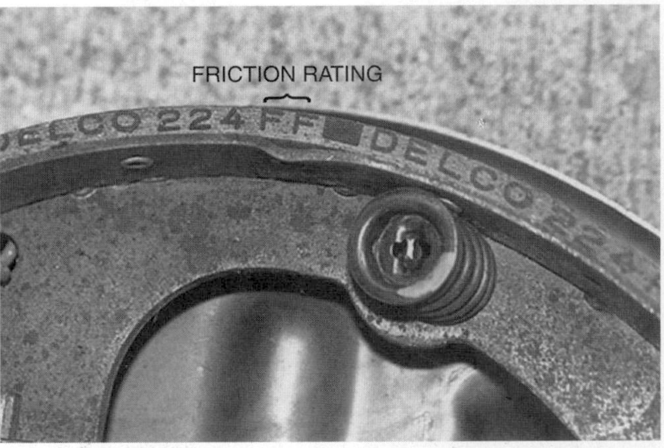

Figure 32–16 Typical drum brake lining edge code.

brake lining material has a coefficient of friction between 0.35 and 0.45 when both cold and hot.)

The code letters do not indicate the relative quality of the lining material. Lining wear, fade resistance, tensile strength, heat recovery rate, wet friction, noise, plus coefficient of friction, must be considered when purchasing quality linings. Unfortunately, there are no standards a purchaser can check regarding all of these other considerations. For best brake performance, always purchase the best-quality, name-brand linings you can afford.

HINT: While many brands of replacement brake lining provide acceptable stopping power and long life, purchasing factory brake lining from a dealer is usually the best opportunity to get lining material that meets all vehicle requirements. Aftermarket linings are *not* required by federal law to meet performance or wear standards that are required of original factory brake linings.

TECH TIP 

Competitively Priced Brakes

The term "competitively priced" means lower cost. Most brake manufacturers offer premium as well as lower-price linings to remain competitive with other manufacturers or importers of brake lining material produced overseas or in foreign countries. Organic asbestos brake lining is inexpensive to manufacture. In fact, according to warehouse distributors and importers, the box often costs more than the brake lining inside!

Professional brake service technicians should only install brake linings and pads that will give braking performance equal to that of the original factory brakes. This means that "competitive" asbestos linings should *never* be substituted for semi-metallic or NAO original linings or pads. For best results, always purchase quality brake parts from a known brand name manufacturer.

THE DANGERS OF EXPOSURE TO ASBESTOS

Friction materials such as brake and clutch linings often contain asbestos. While asbestos has been eliminated from most original equipment friction materials, the automotive service technician cannot know whether the vehicle being serviced is or is not equipped with friction materials containing asbestos. It is important that *all* friction material be handled as if it does contain asbestos.

Asbestos exposure can cause scar tissue to form in the lungs. This condition is called **asbestosis.** It causes gradually increasing shortness of breath, and the scarring to the lungs is permanent. Even low exposures to asbestos can cause **mesothelioma,** a type of fatal cancer of the lining of the chest or abdominal cavity. Asbestos exposure can also increase the risk of **lung cancer** as well as cancer of the voice box, stomach, and large intestines. It usually takes 15 to 30 years or more for cancer or asbestos lung scarring to show up after exposure.

Occupational Health and Safety Act

Handling of the Designated Substance (Asbestos), Regulation 837 The process refers to the handling of materials that generate airborne asbestos fibres. The process of handling asbestos fibres shall not proceed without the appropriate control measures such as ventilating or wet and damp processing being instituted where practical.

The following threshold limit value (TLV) is the time-weighted average concentration for a normal 8-hour workday, or 40-hour workweek, to which workers may be repeatedly exposed.

Asbestos Type	TLV
Crocidolite	0.2 fibres longer than 5 micometres per cubic centimetre of air
Amosite	0.5 fibres longer than 5 micrometres per cubic centimetre of air
Other forms	2 fibres longer than 5 micrometres per cubic centimetre of air

Asbestos Handling Guidelines

The air in the shop area can be tested by a testing laboratory, but this can be expensive. Tests have determined that asbestos levels can be easily kept below the recommended levels by using a solvent or a special vacuum.

NOTE: Even though asbestos is being removed from brake lining materials, the service technician cannot tell whether the old brake pads or shoes contain asbestos. Therefore, to be safe, the technician should *assume* that all brake pads or shoes contain asbestos.

HEPA Vacuum A special high efficiency particulate air (HEPA) vacuum system has been proven to be effective in keeping asbestos exposure levels below 0.1 fibre per cm^3.

Figure 32–17 All brakes should be washed with liquid to help keep brake dust from becoming air-borne.

Solvent Spray Many technicians use an aerosol can of brake cleaning solvent to wet the brake dust and prevent it from becoming air-borne. Commercial brake cleaners are available that use a concentrated cleaner that is mixed with water. See Figure 32–17. The waste liquid is filtered and, when dry, the filter can be disposed of as solid waste.

> **CAUTION:** Never use compressed air to blow brake dust. The fine talc-like brake dust can create a health hazard even if asbestos is not present or is present in dust rather than fibre form.

Disposal of Brake Dust and Brake Shoes The hazard of asbestos occurs when asbestos fibres are air-borne. Once the asbestos has been wetted down, it is considered to be solid waste and not hazardous waste. Old brake shoes and pads should be enclosed, preferably in a plastic bag, to help prevent any of the brake material from becoming air-borne.

Always follow current federal and local laws considering disposal of all waste.

ANTILOCK BRAKE SYSTEM (ABS) OPERATION

ABS means *antilock braking system.* The purpose of ABS is to prevent the wheels from locking during braking, especially on low friction surfaces such as wet, icy, or snowy roads. Remember, it is the friction between the tire tread and the road that does the actual stopping of the vehicle. Therefore, ABS does not mean that a vehicle can stop quickly on all road surfaces. ABS uses sensors at the wheels to measure the wheel speed. If one wheel is rotating slower than the others indicating possible lock-up (for example, on an icy spot), the ABS computer will control the brake fluid pressure to that wheel for a fraction of a second. **A locked wheel has less traction on the road surface than a rotating wheel.**

The ABS computer can reapply the pressure from the master cylinder to the wheel a fraction of a second later. Therefore, if a wheel *starts* to lock up, the purpose of the ABS system is to *pulse* the brakes on and off to maintain directional stability with maximum braking force. Many ABS units will cause the brake pedal to pulse if the unit is working in the ABS mode. The pulsating brake pedal is a cause for concern to some drivers. However, the pulsing brake pedal informs the driver that the ABS is being activated. Some ABS units use an isolator valve in the ABS unit to prevent brake pedal pulsations during ABS operation. With these types of systems, it is often difficult for the driver to know if and when the ABS unit is working to control a locking wheel. See Figure 32–18 for an overview of a typical ABS system.

Another symptom of normal ABS unit operation is the activation of the hydraulic pressure pump used by many ABS units. In some ABS units, the hydraulic pump is run every time the vehicle is started and moved. Other types of units operate randomly or whenever the pressure in the system calls for the pump to operate. See Chapter 39 for additional details on antilock braking systems.

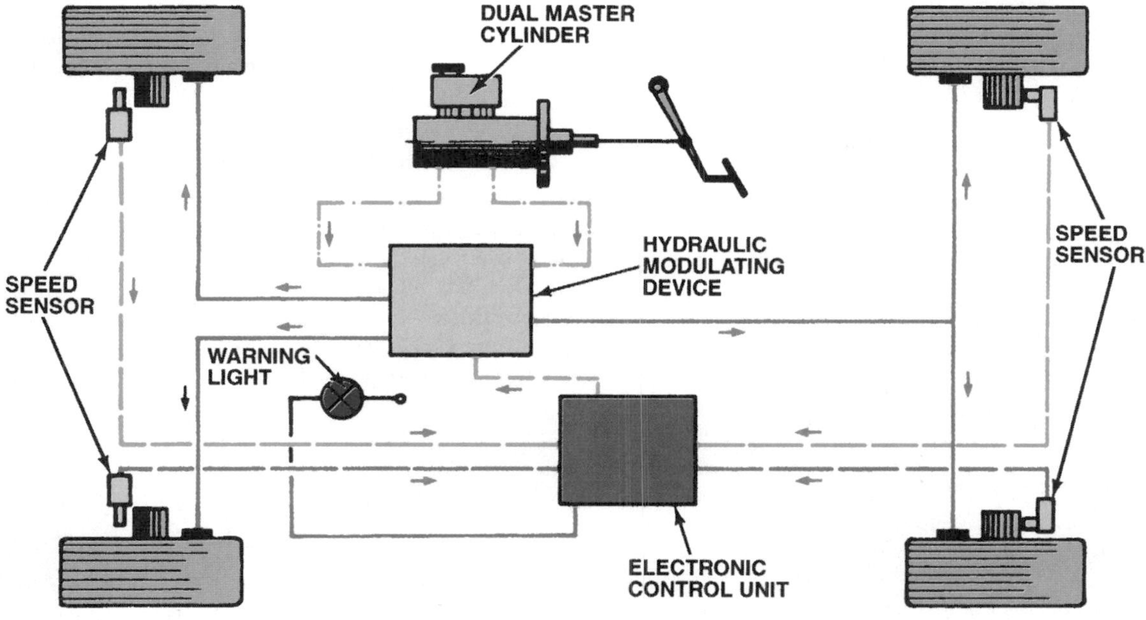

Figure 32–18 A typical antilock brake system.

SUMMARY

1. Brakes stop wheels—not vehicles.
2. Hydraulic pressure is sent to each wheel when the driver pushes on the brake pedal and creates a pressure build-up in the master brake cylinder.
3. The friction material for disc brakes are called pads, and for drum brakes they are called brake shoes.
4. All brake fluid is specified by DOT and SAE. DOT 3 brake fluid is the most commonly recommended brake fluid for all types of vehicles.
5. Brake pad/shoe edge codes indicate the coefficient of friction rating, not quality of materials.
6. ABS means antilock braking system. This system pulses the hydraulic force to the wheels to prevent the tires from locking up. A locked tire has lower friction than a rolling tire.

REVIEW QUESTIONS

1. Explain how hydraulic pressure is used to stop the rotation of the wheels.
2. List the coefficient of friction edge codes.
3. Describe brake fluid and how it should be used and handled.
4. Explain how ABS units prevent wheel lock-up.

RED SEAL CERTIFICATION-TYPE QUESTIONS

1. Disc brakes use replaceable friction material called
   - **a.** Linings
   - **b.** Pads
2. A wheel that locks up during braking
   - **a.** Has less friction than a rolling tire
   - **b.** Results in straighter stops
   - **c.** Results in shorter stops
   - **d.** Has more friction to the road than a rolling tire
3. Coefficient of friction is measured in what units?
   - **a.** A number from 0 to 1
   - **b.** A rating of A, B, or C
   - **c.** Pounds per square inch (psi)
   - **d.** Percentage
4. What type of disc brake pad should *not* be used to replace semi-metallic original equipment pads?
   - **a.** Semi-mets
   - **b.** NAO
   - **c.** Organic (asbestos)
   - **d.** NAS
5. The front brakes of a front-wheel-drive vehicle handle about what percentage of the braking power?
   - **a.** 50%
   - **b.** 60%
   - **c.** 70%
   - **d.** 80%

6. The letters "EF" on the edge of a brake lining mean
   - **a.** Wear resistance codes
   - **b.** Relative noise level codes
   - **c.** Coefficient of friction codes
   - **d.** Brake lining recipes
7. What type of brake fluid is recommended by almost every vehicle manufacturer?
   - **a.** DOT 2
   - **b.** DOT 3
   - **c.** DOT 4
   - **d.** DOT 5
8. DOT 3 brake fluid absorbs about what percentage of water per year?
   - **a.** 1%
   - **b.** 2%
   - **c.** 4%
   - **d.** 6%
9. What should be done with the dust from the brake system while performing service?
   - **a.** Nothing. The brake dust is not hazardous
   - **b.** Wash the brake shoes off with Varsol
   - **c.** Blow the brake dust off with compressed air
   - **d.** Wash the brake shoes off with water
10. When might it be okay to hear noises coming from the brake systems during brake application?
    - **a.** Braking on slippery roads
    - **b.** Braking on dry roads
    - **c.** Braking while moving in reverse
    - **d.** None of the above is correct. Brake systems should never make noises.

33

Master Cylinders and the Hydraulic System

OBJECTIVES: After studying Chapter 33, you should be able to:

1. Prepare for the interprovincial Red Seal certification examination in Appendix V (Brakes) on the topics covered in this chapter.
2. Describe the function, purpose, and operation of the master cylinder.
3. Explain how hydraulic force can be used to supply high pressures to each individual wheel brake.
4. Describe the process of troubleshooting master cylinders and related brake hydraulic components.
5. List the purposes and functions of the metering valve and proportional valve.
6. Discuss the methods that can be used to bleed the hydraulic braking system.

The master cylinder is the heart of the entire braking system. No braking occurs until the driver depresses the brake pedal. The brake pedal linkage is used to apply the force of the driver's foot into a closed hydraulic system.

BRAKE PEDAL MECHANICAL ADVANTAGE

The first thing that happens when the driver steps on the brake pedal is that the force measured in pounds (lb) or newtons (N) is transmitted through linkage to the master cylinder. The normal stroke distance of a brake pedal is about 3.8 cm (1.5 in.); the total pedal travel should not exceed 10 cm (4 in.). Because of the offset relationship of the pivot point (called the **fulcrum**) of the brake pedal mechanism, the force exerted into the master cylinder is increased up to 5 times (the average for all vehicles is about 3:1). See Figure 33–1.

THE HYDRAULIC BRAKING SYSTEM

All braking systems require that a driver's force be transmitted to the drum or rotor attached to each wheel. See Figure 33–2. The force that can be exerted

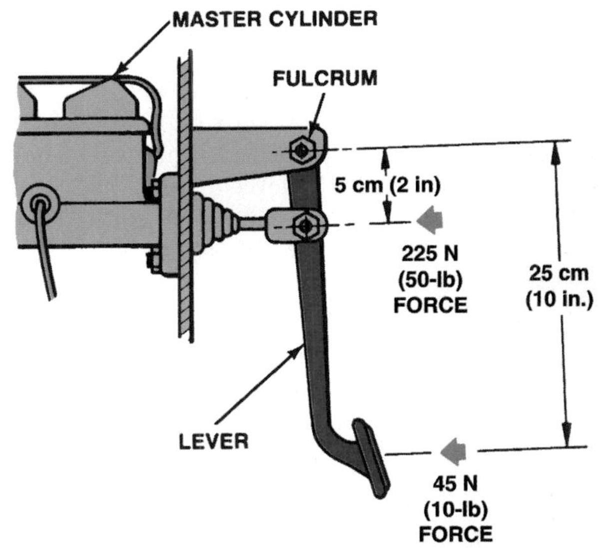

Figure 33–1 This brake pedal assembly provides a 5 to 1 mechanical advantage because a 45 N (10 lb) force input results in a 225 N (50 lb) force into the master cylinder.

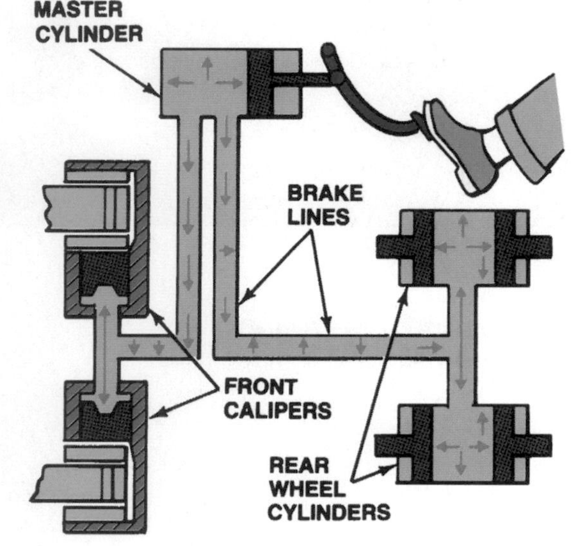

Figure 33–2 A simple hydraulically operated brake system.

on the brake pedal varies due to the strength and size of the driver. Engineers design braking systems to require less than 700 N (160 lb) of force from the driver, yet provide the force necessary to stop a heavy vehicle from high speed.

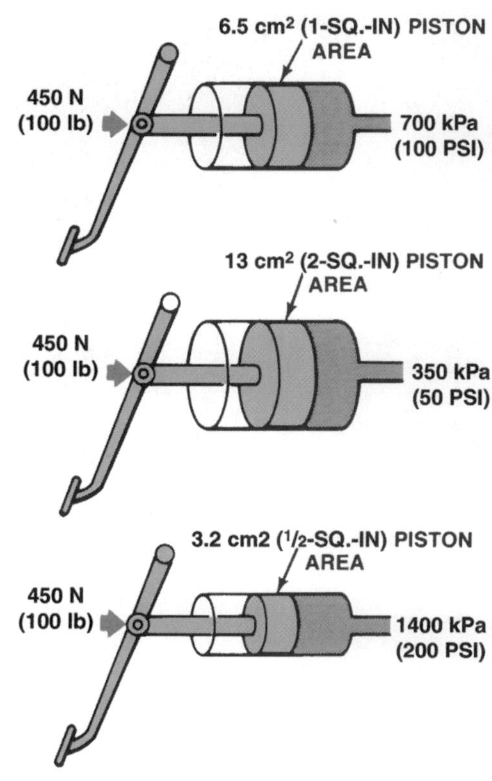

Figure 33–3 Mechanical force and master cylinder piston area determine hydraulic pressure within the brake system.

PASCAL'S LAW

The hydraulic principles that permit a brake system to function were discovered by a French physicist, Blaise Pascal (1632–1662). He discovered that "when force is applied to a liquid confined in a container or an enclosure, the pressure is transmitted equally and undiminished in every direction." To help understand this principle, assume that a force of 450 N (100 lb) is exerted on a piston with a surface area of 6.5 cm^2 (1 sq. in.). Since this *force* measured in newtons (N) (or pounds) is applied to a piston with an area measured in square centimetres (square inches), the *pressure* is the force divided by the area, or 450 N/ 6.5 cm^2 = 69 N/cm^2 = 690 kPa (100 psi). (*Note:* 1Pa = 1N/m^2.) It is this pressure that is transmitted, without loss, throughout the entire hydraulic system. See Figure 33–3.

Pascal's law can be stated mathematically:

$$P = F/A \text{ or } F = P \times A \text{ or } A = F/P$$

F = force in N or (lb.)
A = area in cm^2 (sq. in.)
P = pressure in N/cm^2 = 10 kPa (psi)

A practical example involves a master cylinder with a piston area of 6.5 cm^2 (1 sq. in.) and one wheel cylinder with an area of 5 cm^2 (3/4 sq. in.) and one disc brake caliper with a piston area of 25 cm^2 (4 sq. in.). See Figure 33–4.

What is nice about hydraulics is that the applied force can be sent to more than one wheel cylinder.

The real "magic" of a hydraulic brake system is the fact that different forces can be created at different wheel cylinders. More force is necessary for front brakes than for rear brakes because as the brakes are applied, the weight of the vehicle moves forward.

Larger (area) pistons are used in wheel cylinders (calipers, if disc brakes) on the front wheels to increase the force used to apply the front brakes.

Not only can hydraulics act as a "force machine" (by varying piston size), but the hydraulic system also can be varied to change piston stroke distances.

On a typical vehicle, a driver-input force of 660 N (150 lb) is boosted both mechanically (through the brake pedal linkage) and by the power booster to a fluid pressure of about 11 700 kPa (1700 psi). During a typical brake application only about *1 teaspoon* (5 mL) *of brake fluid* actually is moved from the master cylinder and into the hydraulic system to cause the pressure build-up to occur. With a drum brake, the wheel cylinder expands and pushes the brake shoes against a brake drum. *The distance the shoes move is only about 0.13–0.30 mm (0.005–0.012* in.*).* See Figure 33–5.

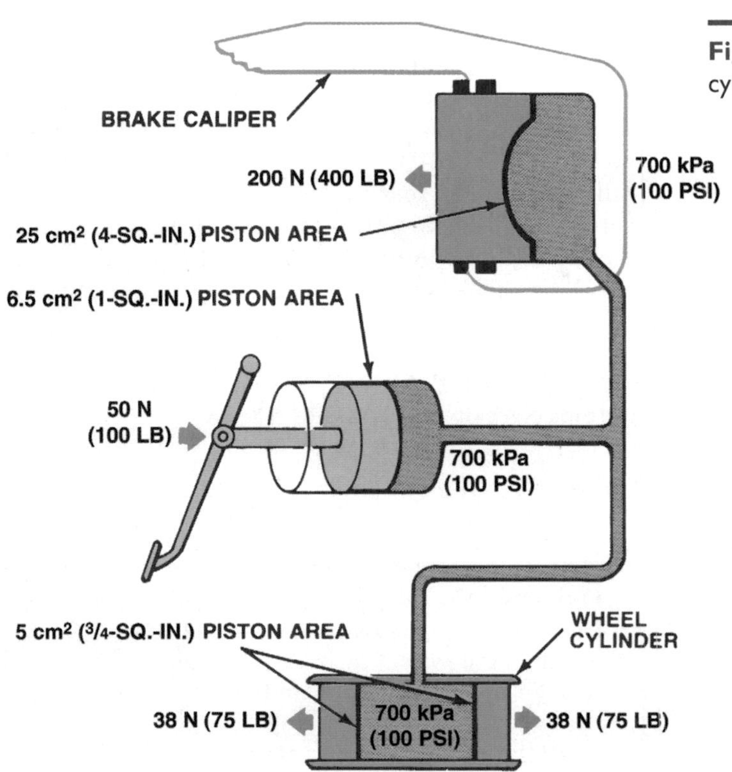

Figure 33–4 Differences in brake calipers and wheel cylinder piston area have a major effect on brake force.

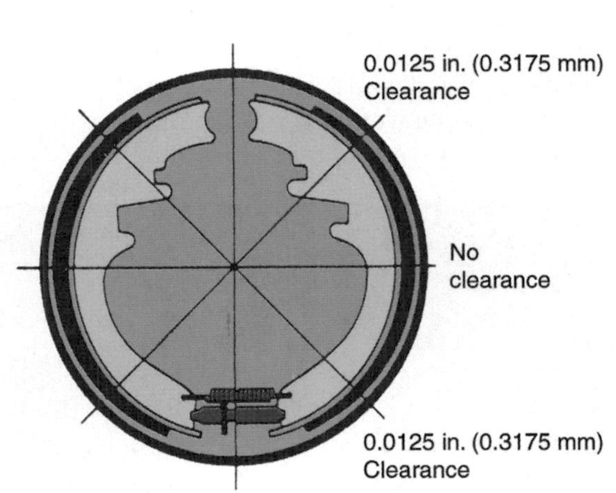

Figure 33–5 Drum brake illustrating the typical clearance between the brake shoes (friction material) and the rotating brake drum represented as the outermost black circle. (Courtesy of Cooper Industries)

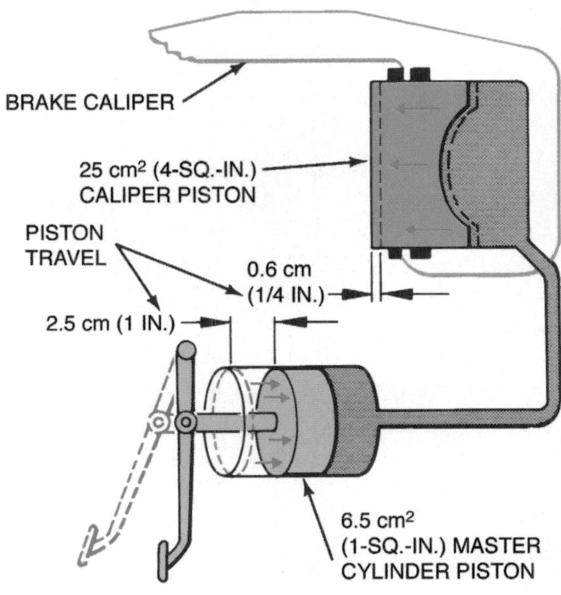

Figure 33–6 The increase in applied force created by the large disc brake caliper piston is offset by a decrease in piston travel.

With a disc brake, brake fluid pressure pushes on the piston in the caliper a small amount and causes a clamping of the disc brake pads against both sides of a rotor (disc). See Figure 33–6. *The typical distance the pads move is only about 0.025–0.076 mm (0.001–0.003 in.).*

MASTER CYLINDER RESERVOIRS

Most vehicles built since the early 1980s are equipped with see-through master cylinder reservoirs, which permit owners and service technicians to

DIAGNOSTIC STORY

Is Bigger Better?

A vehicle owner wanted better braking performance from his off-road race vehicle. Thinking that a larger master cylinder would help, a technician replaced the original 25.4 mm (1 in.) bore-diameter master cylinder with a larger master cylinder with a 28.6 mm (1 1/8 in.) bore-diameter master cylinder.

After bleeding the system, the technician was anxious to test drive the new brake system. During the test drive the technician noticed that the brake pedal grabbed much higher than with the original master cylinder. This delighted the technician. The owner of the vehicle was also delighted until he tried to stop from highway speed. *The driver had to use both feet to stop!*

The technician realized, after the complaint, that the larger master cylinder was able to move more brake fluid, but with *less* pressure to the wheel cylinders. The new master cylinder gave the impression of better brakes because the fluid was moved into the wheel cylinders (and calipers) quickly, and the pads and shoes contacted the rotor and drums sooner because of the greater volume of brake fluid moved by the larger pistons in the master cylinder.

To calculate the difference in pressure between the original (stock) master cylinder and the larger replacement, the technician used Pascal's law with the following results.

A typical force at the cylinder is 2000 N.

Original Master Cylinder (25.4 mm bore; $r = 12.7$ mm)	**Replacement Master Cylinder** (28.6 mm bore; $r = 14.3$ mm)
$P = F/A$	$P = F/A$
$P = 2000\ \text{N}/A$	$P = 2000\ \text{N}/A$
$A = \pi r^2$	$A = \pi r^2$
$= 3.14 \times (12.7\ \text{cm})^2$	$= 3.14 \times (14.3\ \text{mm})^2$
$A = 506.7\ \text{mm}^2$	$A = 641.4\ \text{mm}^2$
$P = 2000\ \text{N}/506.7\ \text{mm}^2$	$P = 2000\ \text{N}/641.4\ \text{mm}^2$
$P = 3.95\ \text{N/mm}^2 =$ 3950 kPa	$P = 3.12\ \text{N/mm}^2 =$ 3120 kPa

Since $1\ \text{N/mm}^2 = 1000$ kPa and $(3950 - 3120 = 830)$, the difference in pressure is 830 kPa less in the larger master cylinder, about 8 times atmospheric pressure (119 psi).

The stopping power of the brakes was reduced because the larger diameter master cylinder piston produced lower pressure (the same force was spread over a larger area, and this means that the pressure is less).

All master cylinders are sized correctly from the factory for the correct braking effort, pressure, pedal travel, and stopping ability. *A technician should never change the sizing of any hydraulic brake component on any vehicle!*

check the brake fluid level without having to remove the top of the reservoir. Some countries have laws that require this type of reservoir. See Figure 33–7.

The reservoir capacity is great enough to allow for the brakes to become completely worn out and still have enough reserve for safe operation. The typical capacity of the entire braking system is usually 1 to 1.5 L (2 to 3 pints). Vehicles equipped with four-wheel disc brakes usually hold 2 L (4 pints) or more.

MASTER CYLINDER RESERVOIR DIAPHRAGM

The entire brake system is filled with brake fluid up to the full level of the master cylinder reservoir.

CAUTION: The master cylinder should never be filled higher than the recommended full mark to allow for brake fluid expansion that occurs normally when the brake fluid gets hot due to the heat generated by the brakes.

The reservoir is vented to the atmosphere so the fluid can expand and contract without difficulty as would be the case if the reservoir were sealed.

Being open to the atmosphere, however, allows the possibility of moisture-laden air coming in contact with the brake fluid! This moisture in the air is readily and rapidly absorbed into the brake fluid because brake fluid has an affinity (attraction) to moisture (water).

Master cylinders use a rubber diaphragm or floating disc to help seal outside air from direct contact

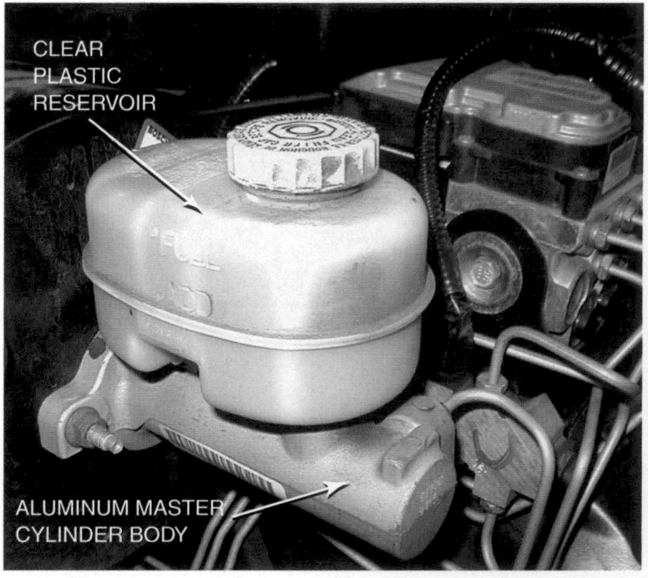

Figure 33–7 Master cylinder reservoirs are clear to allow viewing of the brake fluid level without having to remove the cover.

with brake fluid and still allow the brake fluid to expand and contract as the fluid heats up and cools down during normal brake system operation. This rubber diaphragm is vented between the steel cap and diaphragm. As the brake fluid level drops due to normal disc brake pad wear, the rubber diaphragm also lowers to remain like a second skin on top of the brake fluid.

Whenever adding brake fluid, push the rubber diaphragm back up into the cover. Normal atmospheric pressure will allow the diaphragm to return to its normal position on top of the brake fluid. Whenever servicing a brake system, be sure to check that the vent hole is clear on the cover to allow air to get between the cover and the diaphragm. See Figure 33–8.

MASTER CYLINDER OPERATION

The master cylinder is the heart of any hydraulic braking system. Brake pedal movement and force are transferred to the brake fluid and directed to wheel cylinders or calipers. The master cylinder is also separated into two pressure-building chambers (or circuits) to provide braking force to one-half of the brake in the event of a leak or damage to one circuit.

Both pressure-building sections of the master cylinder contain two holes from the reservoir. The Society of Automotive Engineers (SAE) term for the forward (tapered) hole is the **vent port,** and the rearward straight, drilled hole is called the **replenishing port.** See Figure 33–9.

Various vehicle and brake component manufacturers call these ports by various names. For example, the vent port is the high-pressure port. This tapered forward hole is also called the **compensating port** or **bypass** (a GM term).

The replenishing port is the low-pressure rearward, larger diameter hole. The inlet port is also called the **bypass port, filler port, breather port** or **compensating port** (a GM term).

The function of the master cylinder can be explained from the at-rest, applied, and released positions.

TECH TIP 

Too Much Is Bad

Some vehicle owners or inexperienced service people may fill the master cylinder to the top. Master cylinders should only be filled to the MAXIMUM level line or about 6 mm (1/4 in.) from the top to allow room for expansion when the brake fluid gets hot during normal operation. If the master cylinder is filled to the top, the expanding brake fluid has no place to expand and the pressure increases. This increased pressure can cause the brakes to "self-apply," shortening brake friction material life and increasing fuel consumption. Overheated brakes can result and the brake fluid may boil, causing a total loss of braking.

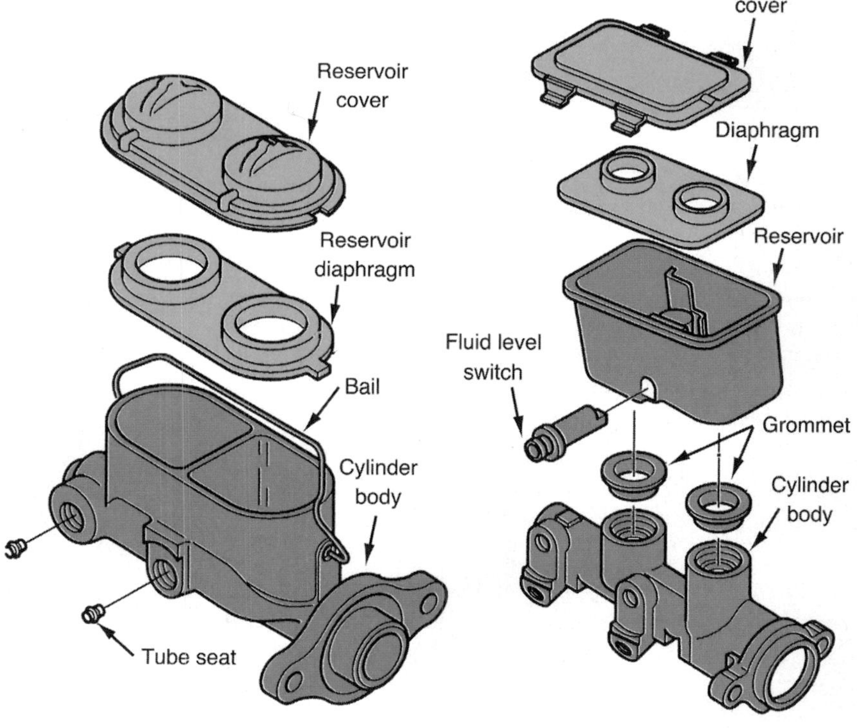

Figure 33–8 Note the cast iron master cylinder (left) uses a wire reservoir cover clamp called a **bail.** The composite master cylinder is made from two different materials—aluminum for the body and plastic materials for the reservoir and reservoir cover. This type of reservoir feeds both primary and secondary chambers, and therefore uses a fluid level switch that activates the red dash warning lamp if the brake fluid level drops.

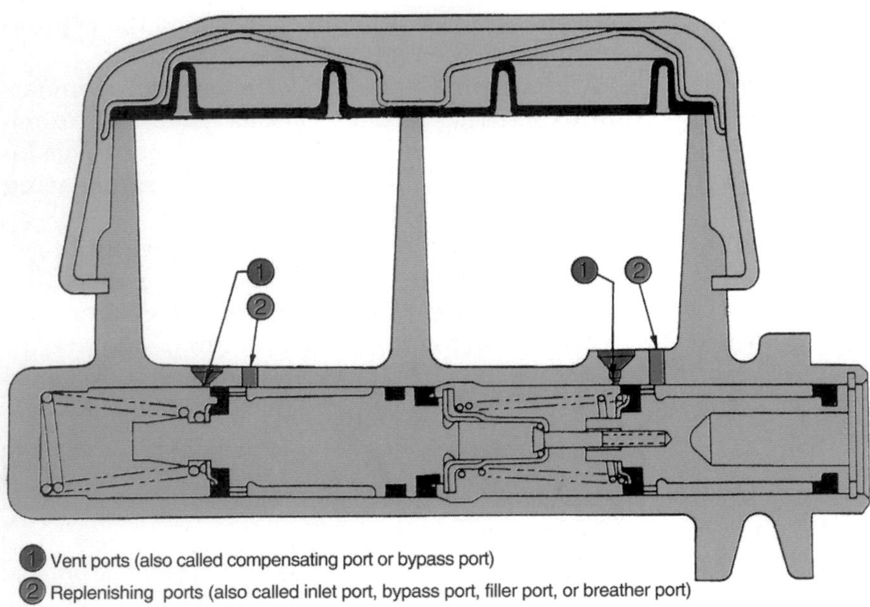

Figure 33–9 Note the various names for the vent port (front port) and the replenishing port (rear port). Names vary by vehicle and brake component manufacturer. The names *vent port* and *replenishing port* are the terms recommended by the Society of Automotive Engineers (SAE).

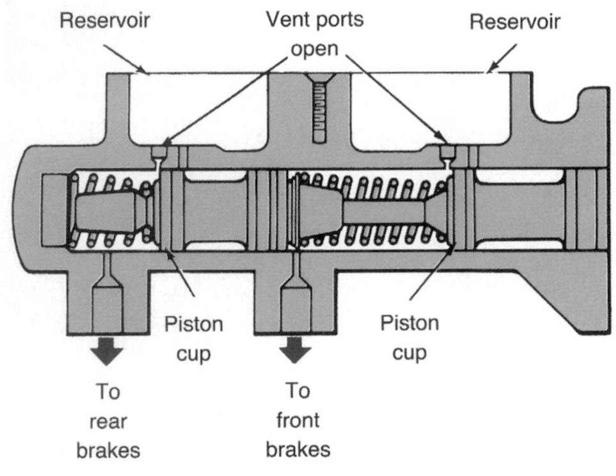

Figure 33–10 The vent ports must remain open to allow brake fluid to expand when heated by the friction material and transferred to the caliper and/or wheel cylinder. As the brake fluid increases in temperature, it expands. The heated brake fluid can expand and flow back into the reservoir through the vent ports. (Courtesy of Chrysler Corporation)

At-Rest Position The primary sealing cups are between the compensating port hole and the inlet port hole. In this position, the brake fluid is free to expand and move from the calipers, wheel cylinders, and brake lines up into the reservoir through the vent port (compensation port) if the temperature rises and the fluid expands. If the fluid was trapped, the pressure of the brake fluid would increase with temperature causing the brakes to **self-apply.** See Figure 33–10. The pistons (primary and secondary) are retained by a clip at the push rod end and held in position by return springs.

Applied Position When the brake pedal is depressed, the pedal linkage forces the push rod and primary piston down the bore of the master cylinder. See Figure 33–11. As the piston moves forward, the primary sealing cup covers and blocks off the vent port (compensating port). Hydraulic pressure builds in front of the primary seal as the push rod moves forward. The back of the piston is kept filled through the replenishing port. See Figure 33–12. This stops any suction (vacuum) from forming behind the piston. The secondary piston is moved forward as pressure is exerted by the primary piston. If, for any reason such as a leak, the primary piston cannot build pressure, a mechanical link on the front of the primary piston will touch the secondary piston and move it forward, as the primary piston is pushed forward by the push rod and brake pedal.

Released Position Releasing the brake pedal removes the pressure on the push rod and master cylinder pistons. A spring on the brake pedal linkage returns the brake pedal to its normal at-rest (up) po-

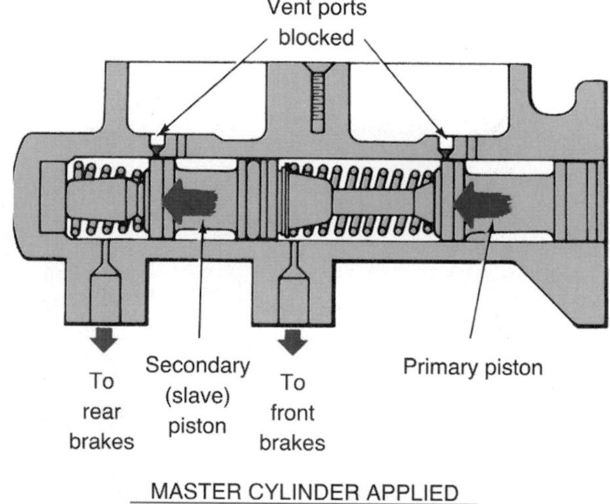

Figure 33–11 As the brake pedal is depressed, the push rod moves the primary piston forward, closing off the vent port. As soon as the port is blocked, pressure builds in front of the primary sealing cup, which pushes on the secondary piston. The secondary piston also moves forward, blocking the secondary vent port and building pressure in front of the sealing cup. (Courtesy of Chrysler Corporation)

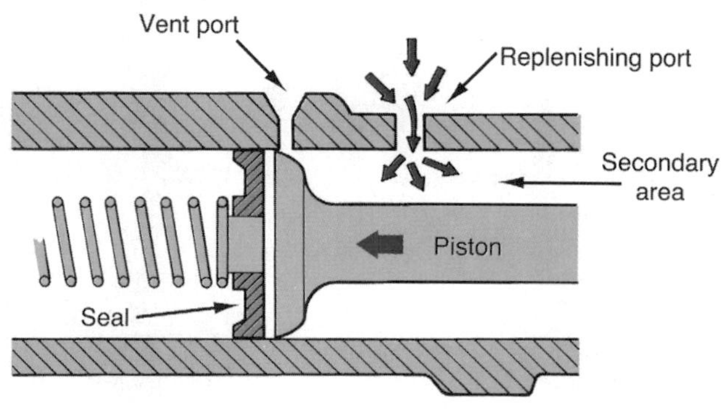

Figure 33–12 The purpose of the replenishing port is to keep the volume behind the primary piston filled with brake fluid from the reservoir as the piston moves forward during a brake application.

sition. The spring in front of the master cylinder piston expands, pushing the pistons rearward. At the same time, pressure is released from the entire braking system and the released brake fluid pressure is exerted on the master cylinder pistons, forcing them rearward. As the piston is pushed back, the lips of the seal fold forward allowing fluid to quickly move past the piston, as shown in Figure 33–13. Some pistons have small holes that allow the fluid to move more quickly. Once the primary seal passes the vent port, the remaining hydraulic pressure forces any excess fluid into the reservoir.

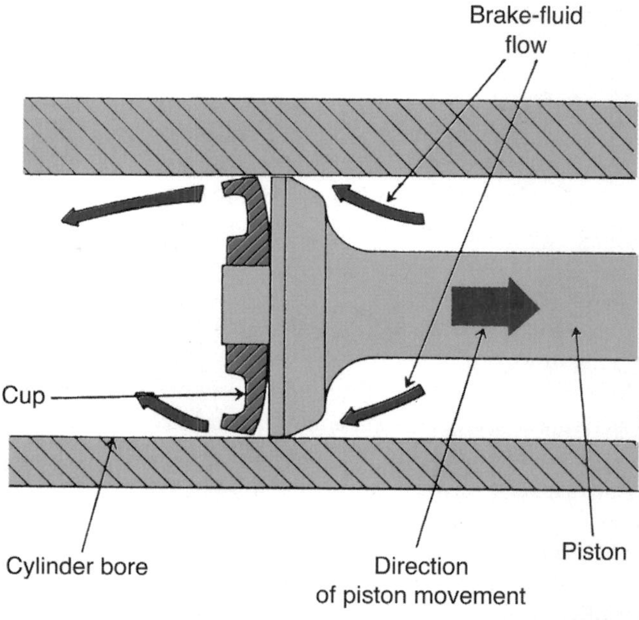

Figure 33–13 When the brake pedal is released, the master cylinder piston moves rearward. Some of the brake fluid is pushed back up through the replenishing port, but most of the fluid flows past the sealing cup. Therefore, when the driver pumps the brake pedal, the additional fluid in front of the pressure building sealing cup is available quickly.

Residual Check Valve

A residual check valve has been used on some drum brake systems to keep a slight amount of pressure on the entire hydraulic system for drum brakes (5–12 psi). This residual check valve is located in the master cylinder at the outlet for the drum brakes. The check ball and spring in the residual check valve permit all the brake fluid to return to the master cylinder until the designated pressure is reached.

This slight pressure prevents air leaks into the hydraulic system in the event of a small hole or leak. With a low pressure kept on the hydraulic system, any small hole will cause fluid to leak out rather than permit air to enter the system. This slight pressure also keeps the wheel cylinder sealing cups tight against the inside wall of the wheel cylinder.

Residual check valves are often *not* used on late model vehicles equipped with front disc/rear drum brakes. The residual check valve has been eliminated by equipping the wheel cylinder internal spring with a sealing cup **expander** to prevent sealing cup lip collapse.

Dual Split Master Cylinders

Dual split master cylinders use two separate pressure-building sections. One section operates the

TECH TIP 

Always Check for Venting

Whenever diagnosing any braking problem, start the diagnosis at the master cylinder—the heart of any braking system. Remove the reservoir cover and observe the brake fluid for spurting while an assistant depresses the brake pedal.

Normal operation (movement of fluid observed in the reservoir). There should be a squirt or movement of brake fluid out of the vent port of both the primary and secondary chambers. This indicates that the vent port is open and that the sealing cup is capable of moving fluid upward through the port before the cup seals off the port as it moves forward to pressurize the fluid. See Figure 33–14.

No movement of fluid observed in the reservoir in the primary piston. This indicates that brake fluid is not being moved as the brake pedal is depressed. This can be caused by:

- **a.** Incorrect brake pedal height—brake pedal or push rod adjustment could be allowing the primary piston to be too far forward, causing the seal cup to be forward of the vent port. Adjust the brake pedal height to a higher level and check for a too-long push rod length.
- **b.** A defective or swollen rubber sealing cup on the primary piston could cause the cup itself to block the vent port.

NOTE: If the vent port is blocked for any reason, the brakes of the vehicle may *self-apply* when the brake fluid heats up during normal braking. Since the vent port is blocked, the expanded hotter brake fluid has no place to expand and instead increases the pressure in the brake lines. The increase in pressure causes the brakes to apply. Loosening the bleeder valves and releasing the built-up pressure is a check that this is what is happening. Then check the master cylinder to see if it is venting.

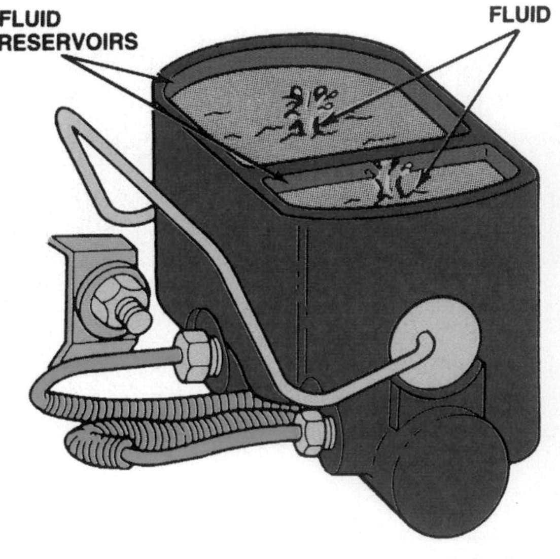

Figure 33–14 As the brakes are applied, a spurt of fluid occurs in the reservoir before the primary cup seal closes the vent (compensating) port.

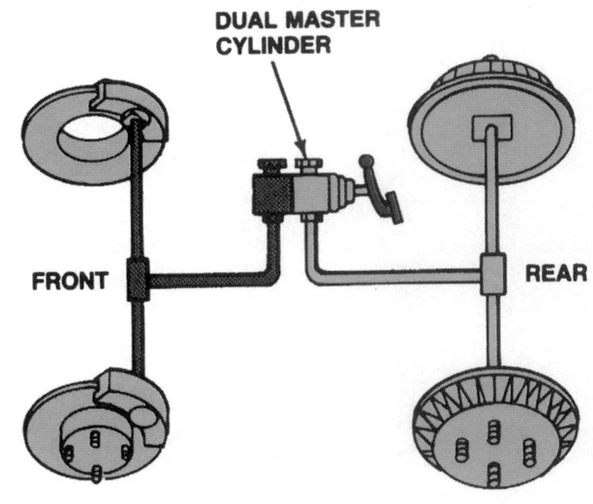

Figure 33–15 Rear-wheel-drive vehicles use a dual-split master cylinder.

front brakes and the other section operates the rear brakes on vehicles equipped with a front/rear split system. See Figure 33–15. The **nose end** of the master cylinder is the closed end toward the front of the vehicle. The open end is often called the **push rod end** of the master cylinder. Some manufacturers operate the front brakes (which do the most braking) from the nose end section (secondary piston end) of the master cylinder. The secondary piston has only one pressure-building seal. The primary piston (push rod end) requires two seals to build pressure. Therefore, the nose end of the master cylinder is considered the more reliable of the two master cylinder pressure-building sections.

NOTE: On vehicles equipped with front and rear split master cylinders, the front brakes may or may not be operated from the front chamber. General Motors typically uses the front (nose end) chamber for the front brakes and the rear (push rod end) for the rear brakes. Many other makes and models of vehicles use the rear chamber for the front brakes. If in doubt, consult the factory service manual for the exact vehicle being serviced.

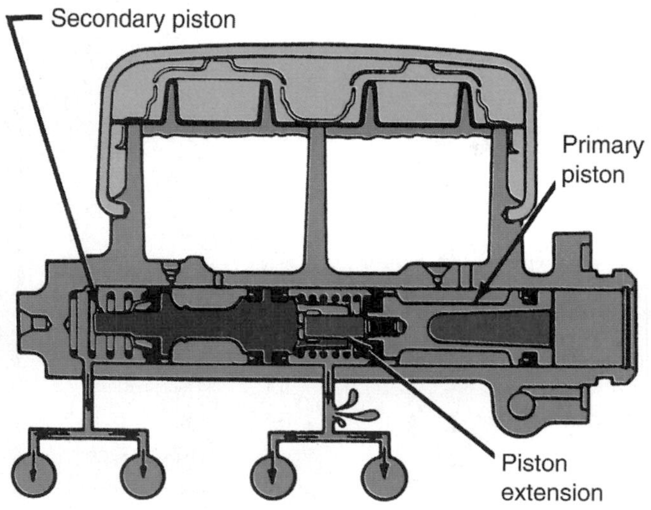

Figure 33–16 In the event of a primary system failure, no hydraulic pressure is available to push the secondary piston forward. As a result, the primary piston extension contacts the secondary piston and pushes on the secondary piston mechanically rather than hydraulically. The loss of pressure in the primary system is usually noticed by the driver by a lower-than-normal brake pedal and the lighting of the red brake warning lamp. (Wagner Division, Cooper Industries Inc.)

If the rear section of the hydraulic system fails, the primary piston will not build pressure to operate the secondary piston. To permit the operation of the secondary piston (nose end piston) in the event of a hydraulic failure of the rear section, the primary piston extension will mechanically contact and push on the secondary piston. See Figure 33–16. If there is a failure of the front section hydraulic system, the primary piston (push rod end) operates normally and exerts pressure on the secondary piston. The secondary piston, however, will not be able to build pressure because of the leak in the system.

Diagonal Split Master Cylinders

With front-wheel drive vehicles, the weight of the entire power train is on the front wheels and 80 to 90% of the braking force is achieved by the front brakes. This means that only 10 to 20% of the braking force is handled by the rear brakes. If the front brakes fail, the rear brakes alone will not provide adequate braking force. The solution is the diagonal split system. See Figures 33–17 and 33–18.

In a diagonal split braking system, the left front brake and the right rear brake are on one circuit, and the right front with the left rear is another circuit of the master cylinder. If one circuit fails, the remaining circuit can still stop the vehicle in a reasonable fashion because each circuit has one front brake. To prevent this one front brake from causing the vehicle to pull toward one side during braking, the front suspension is designed with negative scrub radius geometry. This effectively eliminates any handling problem in the event of a brake circuit failure.

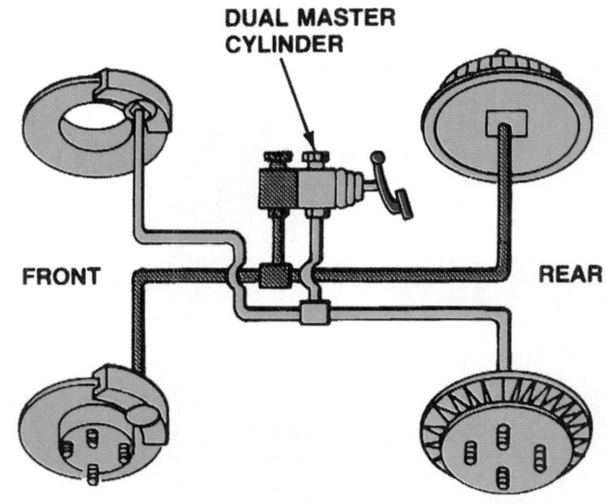

Figure 33–17 Front-wheel-drive vehicles use a diagonal split master cylinder. In this design, one section of the master cylinder operates the right front and the left rear brake and the other section operates the left front and right rear. In the event of a failure in one section, at least one front brake will still function. (Courtesy of Ford Motor Company)

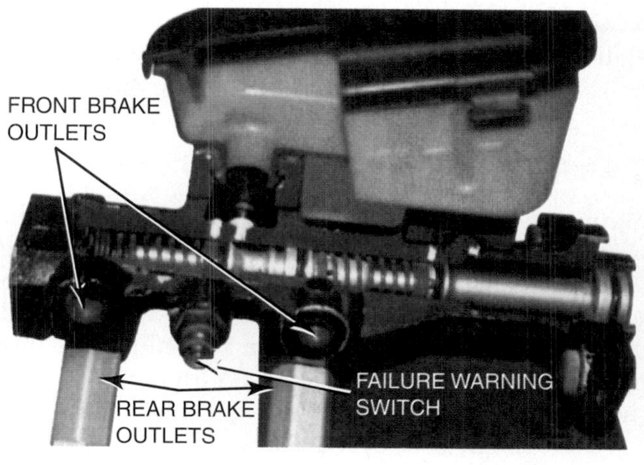

Figure 33–18 Typical General Motors diagonal split master cylinder. Notice the two aluminum proportioning valves. These valves limit and control brake fluid pressure to the rear brakes to help eliminate rear wheel lockup during a rapid stop.

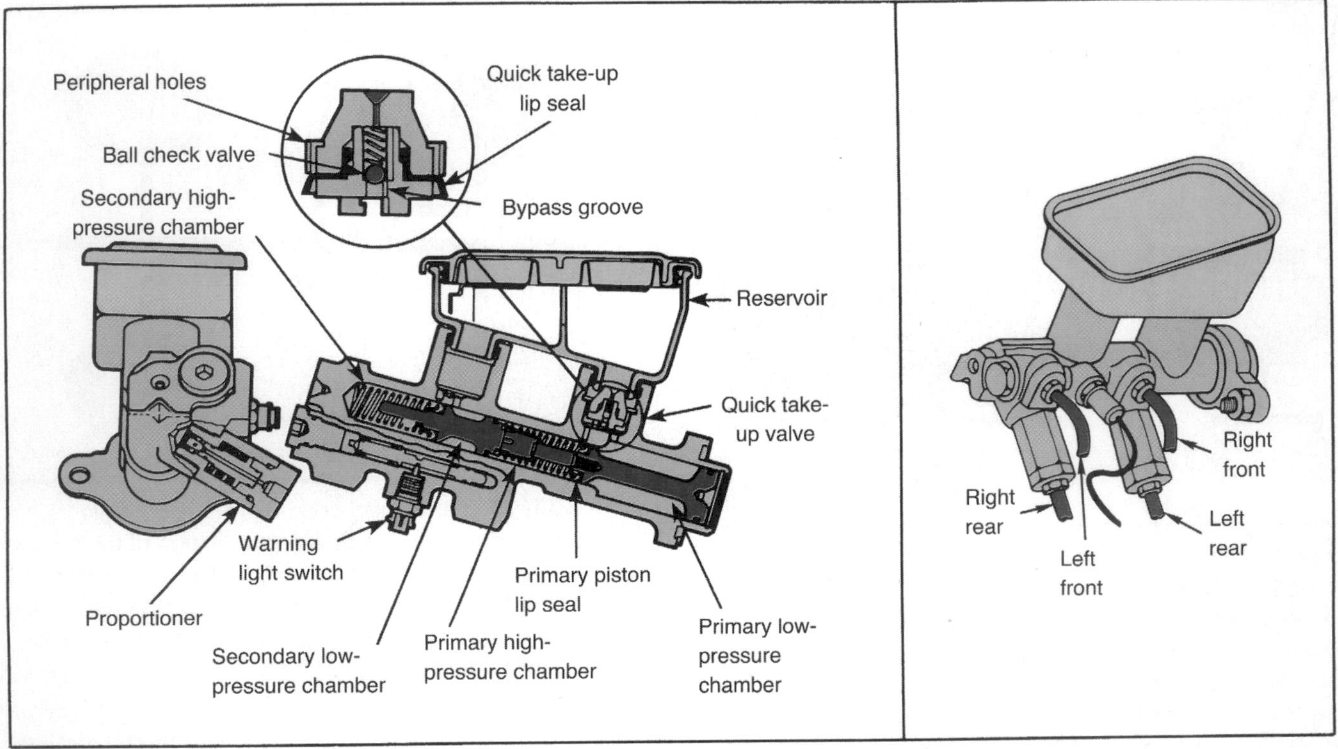

Figure 33–19 Typical quick take-up master cylinder showing the ball check valve and spring. (Courtesy of Allied Signal Automotive Aftermarket)

Quick Take-Up Master Cylinders

Many newer vehicles use low-drag disc brake calipers to increase fuel economy. However, due to the larger distance between the rotor and the friction pads, excessive brake pedal travel would be required before the pads touched the rotor. The solution to this problem is a master cylinder design that can take up this extra clearance.

The design of a quick take-up master cylinder includes a larger diameter primary piston (low-pressure chamber) and a quick take-up valve. This type of master cylinder is also called **dual-diameter bore, step-bore,** or **fast-fill** master cylinder.

A spring-loaded check ball valve holds pressure on the brake fluid in the large diameter rear chamber of the primary piston. When the brakes are first applied, the movement of the rear larger piston forces this larger volume of brake fluid forward past the primary piston seal and into the primary high-pressure chamber. This extra volume of brake fluid takes up the extra clearance of the front disc brake calipers without increasing the brake pedal travel distance. See Figure 33–19.

At 500–700 kPa (70–100 psi), the check ball valve in the quick take-up valve allows fluid to return to the brake fluid reservoir. Because the quick take-up works until 200 kPa (100 psi) is reached, a metering valve is not required to hold back the fluid pressure to the front brakes.

TECH TIP 

The Brake Pedal Depressor Trick

The master cylinder can be used to *block* the flow of brake fluid. Whenever any hydraulic brake component is removed, brake fluid tends to leak out because the master cylinder is usually higher than most other hydraulic components such as wheel cylinders and calipers.

To prevent brake fluid loss that can easily empty the master cylinder reservoir, simply *depress* the brake pedal slightly or prop a stick or other pedal depressor to keep the brake pedal down. When the brake pedal is depressed, the piston sealing cups move forward, blocking off the reservoir from the rest of the braking system. The master cylinder stays full and the brake fluid stops dripping out of brake lines that have been disconnected. See Figure 33–20.

HINT: Try this—put a straw into a glass of water. Use a finger to seal the top of the straw and then remove the straw from the glass of water. The water remains in the straw because air cannot get into the top of the straw. This is why the brake pedal depressor trick works to prevent the loss of brake fluid from the system even if the brake line is totally disconnected.

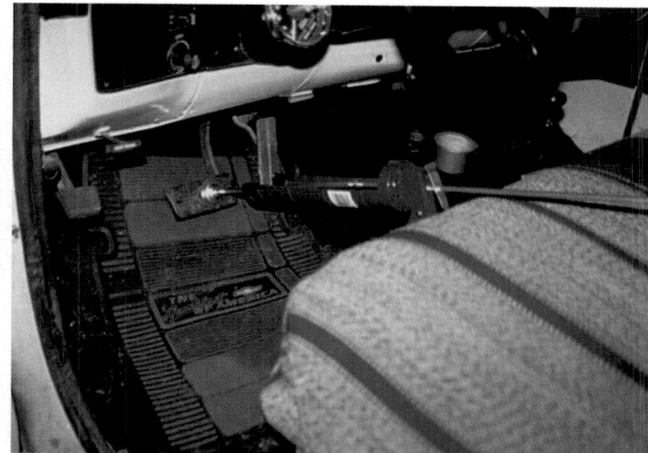

(a)

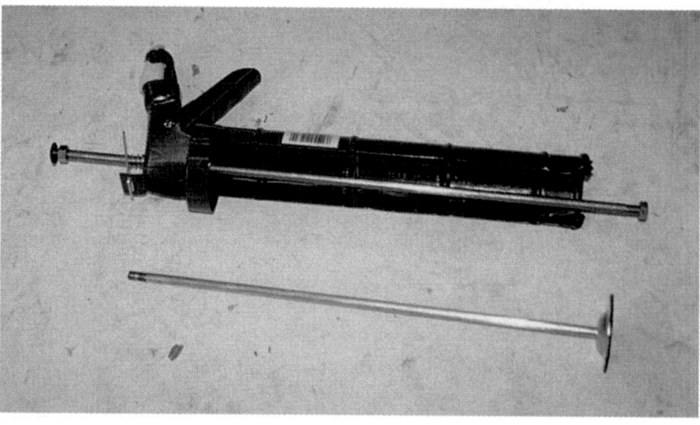

(b)

Figure 33–20 (a) A home-made brake pedal depressor. (b) A caulking gun with a removable extension rod is used. The removable extension rod allows the tool to be disassembled so that it can fit into a drawer of a tool box.

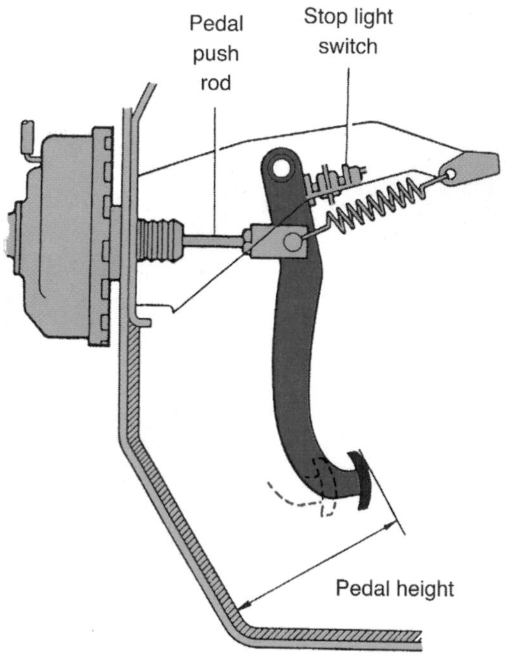

Figure 33–21 Pedal height is usually measured from the floor to the top of the brake pedal. Some vehicle manufacturers recommend removing the carpet and measuring from the asphalt matting on the floor for an accurate measurement. Always follow the manufacturer's recommended procedures and measurements.

Diagnosing and Troubleshooting Master Cylinders

A thorough visual inspection is important when inspecting any master cylinder. The visual inspection should include checking the following items:

1. Check the brake fluid for proper level and condition. (Brake fluid should not be rusty, thick, or contaminated.)
2. Check that the vent holes in the reservoir cover are open and clean.
3. Check that the reversion cover diaphragm is not torn or enlarged.

NOTE: If the cover diaphragm is enlarged, this is an indication that a mineral oil, such as automatic transmission fluid or engine oil, has been used in or near the brake system, because rubber that is brake-fluid resistant expands when exposed to mineral oil.

4. Check for any external leaks at the lines or at the pushrod area. After a thorough visual inspection, check for proper operation of **pedal height, pedal free play,** and **pedal reserve distance.** See Figures 33–21 and 33–22.

Proper brake pedal height is important for the proper operation of the stop (brake) light switch. If the pedal is not correct, the push rod may be in too far forward, preventing the master cylinder cups from uncovering the compensation port. If the pedal is too high, the free play will be excessive. Pedal reserve height is easily checked by depressing the brake pedal with the right foot and attempting to slide your left foot under the brake pedal. See Figure 33–23.

Free play is the distance the brake pedal travels before the primary piston in the master cylinder moves. *Most vehicles require brake pedal free play from 3 to 38 mm (1/8 to 1½ in.).* Too little or too much free play can cause braking problems that can be mistakenly attributed to a defective master cylinder.

Spongy Brake Pedal A spongy pedal with a larger than normal travel indicates air in the lines. Check for leaks and bleed the air from the system as discussed later in this chapter.

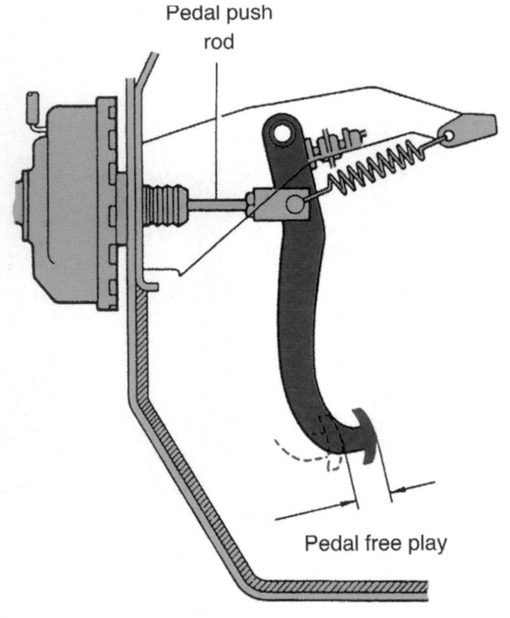

Figure 33–22 Brake pedal free-play is the distance between the brake pedal when fully released and the position of the brake pedal when braking resistance is felt.

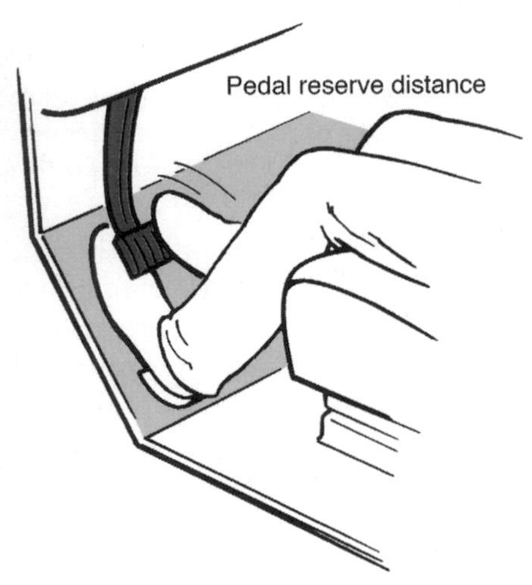

Figure 33–23 Brake pedal reserve is usually specified as the measurement from the floor to the top of the brake pedal with the brakes applied. A quick and easy test of pedal reserve is to try to place your left toe underneath the brake pedal while the brake pedal is depressed with your right foot. If your toe will not fit, then pedal reserve *may* not be enough.

Lower Than Normal Brake Pedal A brake pedal that travels downward more than normal and then gets firm is an indication that one circuit of the dual-circuit hydraulic system is probably not working. Check for leaks in the system and repair as necessary. Another possible reason is an out-of-adjustment drum brake, allowing too much pedal travel before the shoes touch the brake drum.

> **NOTE:** A lower than normal brake pedal may also be an indication of air in the hydraulic system.

See Chapter 35 for additional information on drum brakes.

Sinking Brake Pedal If the brake pedal sinks all the way to the floor, suspect a defective master cylinder that is leaking internally. This internal leakage is often called **bypassing** because the brake fluid is leaking past the sealing cup. See the Tech Tip, "Check for Bypassing."

DISASSEMBLY OF THE MASTER CYLINDER

Many master cylinders can be disassembled, cleaned, and restored to service.

> **NOTE:** Check vehicle manufacturer's recommendation before attempting to overhaul or service a master cylinder. Many manufacturers recommend replacing the master cylinder as an assembly.

Step 1. Remove the master cylinder from the vehicle, being careful to avoid dripping or spilling brake fluid onto painted surfaces of the vehicle. Dispose of all old brake fluid and clean the outside of the master cylinder.

Step 2. Remove the reservoir, if possible, as shown in Figure 33–24.

Step 3. Remove the retaining bolt that holds the secondary piston assembly in the bore.

Step 4. Depress the primary piston with a *blunt* tool such as a Phillips screwdriver, a rounded wooden dowel, or an engine push rod. Use of a straight-blade screwdriver or other nonrounded tool can damage and distort the aluminum piston.

> **CAUTION:** If holding the master cylinder in a vise, use the flange area; never clamp the body of the master cylinder.

Remove the snap ring and slowly release the pressure on the depressing tool. Spring pressure should push the primary piston out of the cylinder bore. See Figure 33–25.

Step 5. Remove the master cylinder from the vise and tap the open end of the bore against the top of a workbench to force the secondary piston out of the bore. If necessary, use compressed air in the outlet to force the piston out.

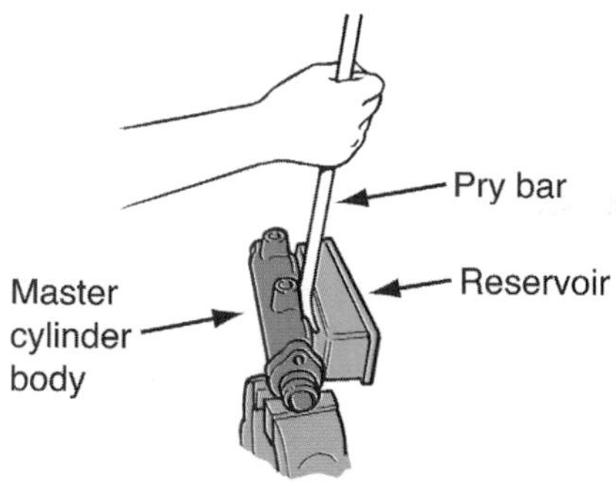

Figure 33–24 Using a pry bar to remove the reservoir from the master cylinder. (Courtesy of Allied Signal Automotive Aftermarket)

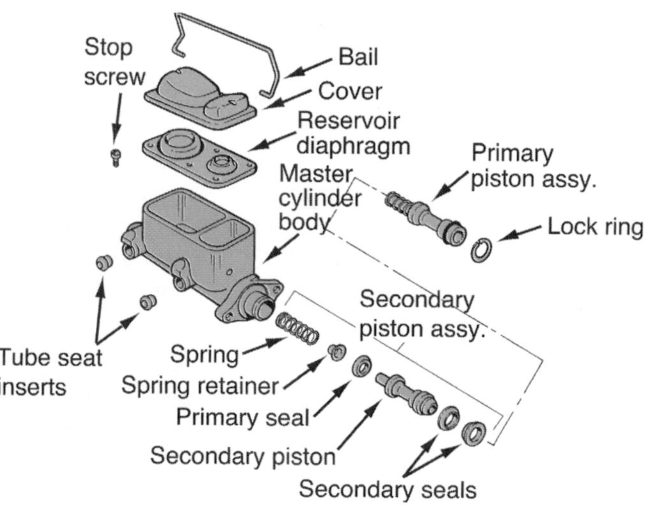

Figure 33–25 Whenever disassembling a master cylinder, note the exact order of parts as they are removed. Master cylinder overhaul kits (when available) often include entire piston assemblies rather than the individual seals. (Courtesy of Allied Signal Automotive Aftermarket)

CAUTION: Use extreme care when using compressed air. The piston can be shot out of the master cylinder with a great force.

Inspection and Reassembly of the Master Cylinder

Inspect the master cylinder bore for pitting, corrosion, or wear. Most cast iron master cylinders cannot be honed because of the special bearingized surface finish that is applied to the bore during manufacturing. Slight corrosion or surface flaws can usually be removed with a hone or crocus cloth; otherwise, the master cylinder should be replaced as an assembly. See Figure 33–26. Always follow the recommended procedures for the vehicle being serviced.

Figure 33–26 A cutaway master cylinder showing the corrosion that can occur in the cylinder bore.

Aluminum master cylinders cannot be honed. Aluminum master cylinders have an **anodized** surface coating applied that is hard and wear resistant. Honing would remove this protective coating.

Thoroughly clean the master cylinder and any other parts to be reused (except for rubber components) in clean denatured alcohol. If the bore is okay, replacement **piston assemblies** can be installed into the master cylinder after dipping them into clean brake fluid.

NOTE: While most master cylinder overhaul kits include the entire piston assemblies, some kits just contain the sealing cups and/or O-rings. Always follow the installation instructions that accompany the kit and always use the installation tool that is included to prevent damage to the replacement seals. Always use clean brake fluid from a sealed container or brake assembly fluid. See Figure 33–27.

Step 1. Install the secondary (smaller) piston assembly into the bore, spring end first. See Figure 33–28.

Step 2. Install the primary piston assembly, spring end first.

Step 3. Depress the primary piston and install the snap ring.

Step 4. Install the stop bolt.

Step 5. Reinstall the plastic reservoir, if equipped, as shown in Figure 33–29.

Step 6. Bench bleed the master cylinder. This step is very important. See Figure 33–30.

Figure 33–27 Brake assembly fluid or clean brake fluid should be used to lubricate brake parts during reassembly.

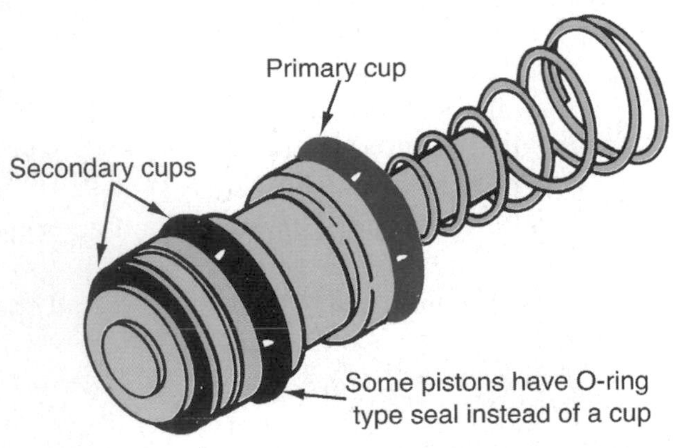

Figure 33–28 Piston assembly. (Courtesy of Allied Signal Automotive Aftermarket)

SAFETY TIP 

Avoid Using Compressed Air on Hydraulic Brake Parts

Compressed air often contains lubricating oil. While it is usual to use compressed air to disassemble a master cylinder, do not use compressed air to clean or assemble parts. If compressed air is used to dry hydraulic brake parts that contain rubber components, this oil in the compressed air could cause the rubber to swell. If the rubber components are then assembled into the master cylinder, caliper, or wheel cylinder, the oil can cause the brake system to fail.

TECH TIP 

Check for Bypassing

If a master cylinder is leaking internally, brake fluid can be pumped from the rear chamber into the front chamber of the master cylinder. This internal leakage is called *bypassing*. When the fluid bypasses, the front chamber can overflow while emptying the rear chamber. Therefore, whenever checking the level of brake fluid, do not think that a low rear reservoir is always due to an external leak. Also, a master cylinder that is bypassing (leaking internally) will usually cause a lower than normal brake pedal.

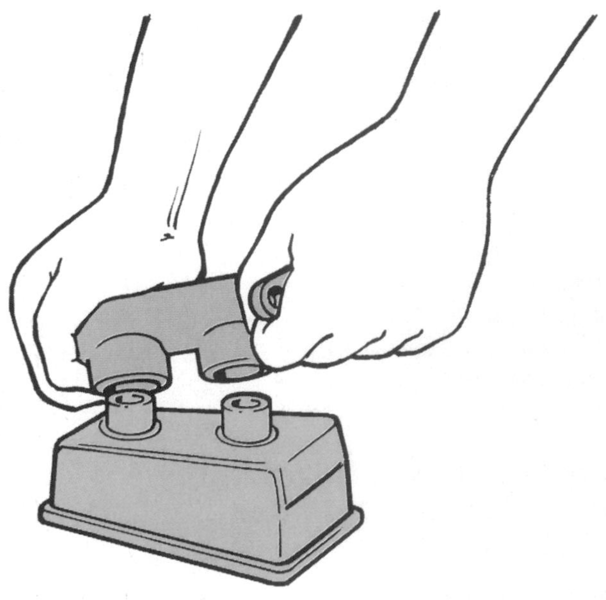

Figure 33–29 To reinstall the reservoir onto a master cylinder, place the reservoir on a clean, flat surface and push the housing down onto the reservoir after coating the rubber seals with brake fluid. (Courtesy of Allied Signal Automotive Aftermarket)

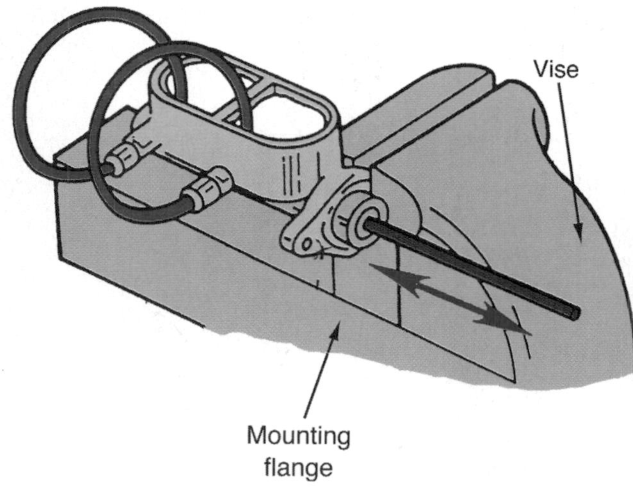

Figure 33–30 Bleeding a master cylinder before installing it on the vehicle. The master cylinder is clamped into a bench vise while using the rounded end of a breaker bar to push on the push rod end with bleeder tubes down into the brake fluid. Master cylinders should be clamped on the mounting flange as shown to prevent distorting the master cylinder bore.

Figure 33–31 A red brake warning lamp.

PRESSURE-DIFFERENTIAL SWITCH (BRAKE WARNING SWITCH)

A pressure-differential switch is used on all vehicles built after 1967 with dual master cylinders to warn the driver of a loss of pressure in one of the two separate systems by lighting the dashboard red brake warning indicator lamp as shown in Figure 33–31.

The brake lines from both the front and the rear sections of the master cylinder are sent to this switch, which lights the brake warning indicator lamp in the event of a difference in pressure between the two sections. See Figures 33–32 and 33–33.

A failure in one part of the brake system does not result in a failure of the entire hydraulic system. After the hydraulic system has been repaired and bled, moderate pressure on the brake pedal will centre the piston in the switch and turn off the warning lamp.

If the lamp remains on, it may be necessary to:

1. Apply light pressure to the brake pedal.
2. Momentarily open the bleeder valve on the side that did not have the failure.

This procedure should centre the pressure differential switch valve in those vehicles that are not equipped with self-centring springs.

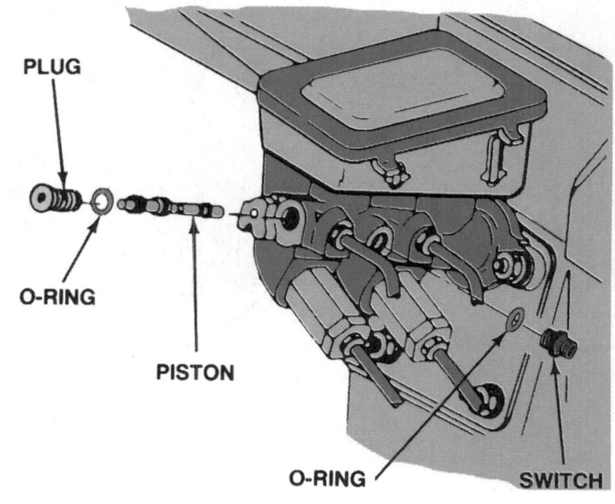

Figure 33–32 This pressure differential switch is integrated into the master cylinder.

Brake Fluid Level Sensor Switch

Many master cylinders, especially systems that are a diagonal split, use a brake fluid level sensor switch in the master cylinder reservoir. This sensor will light the red BRAKE warning lamp on the dash if low brake fluid level is detected. A float-type sensor or a magnetic reed switch are commonly used and provide a complete electrical circuit when the brake fluid level is low. After refilling the master cylinder reservoir to the correct level, the red BRAKE warning lamp should go out. See Figure 33–34.

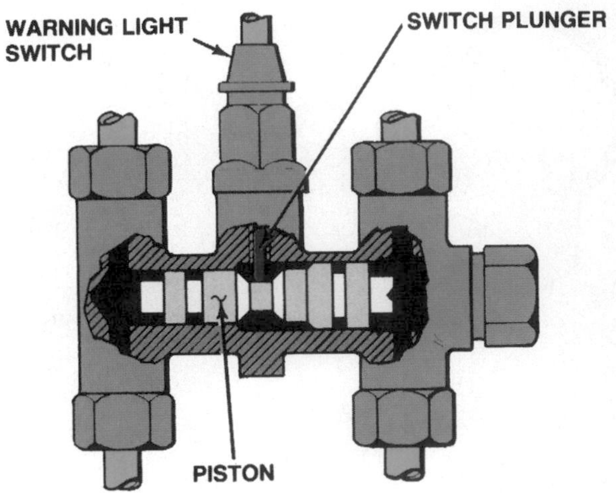

Figure 33–33 Pressure differential switches can be a separate part (as shown) or built into other hydraulic valves, becoming a combination valve. A leak in the hydraulic system causes unequal pressures between the two different brake circuits. This difference in pressure causes the plunger inside the switch to move, which completes the electrical circuit for the red brake warning lamp.

(a)

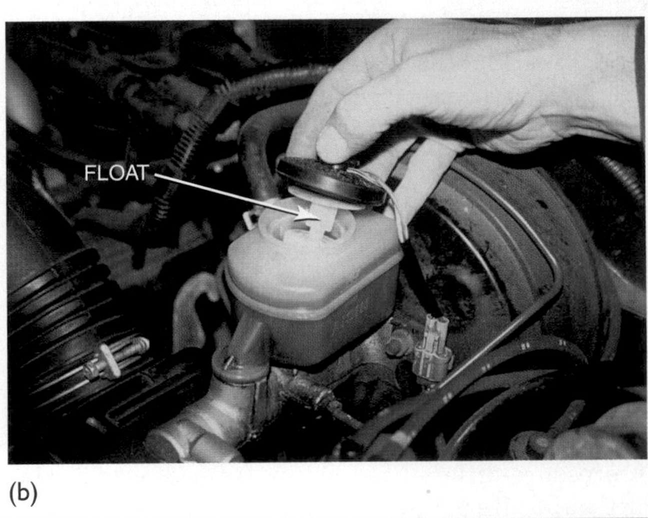

(b)

Figure 33–34 (a) This master cylinder cap has wires that lead to the brake fluid level sensor. (b) A float is part of the reservoir cap and is visible when the cap is lifted.

DIAGNOSING A RED BRAKE DASH WARNING LAMP

Activation of the red brake dash warning lamp can be for any one of several reasons:

1. *Parking brake on.* The same dash warning lamp is used to warn the driver that the parking brake is on.
2. *Low brake fluid.* This lights the red dash warning lamp on vehicles equipped with a master cylinder reservoir brake fluid level switch.
3. *Unequal brake pressure.* The pressure differential switch is used on most vehicles with a front/rear brake split system to warn the driver whenever there is low brake pressure to either the front or rear brakes.

> **NOTE:** Brake systems use *either* a pressure differential switch *or* a low brake fluid switch to light the dash red BRAKE lamp, but not both.

The most likely cause of the red BRAKE warning lamp being on is low brake fluid caused by a leaking brake line, wheel cylinder, or caliper. Therefore, the first step in diagnosis is to determine the cause of the lamp being on, then to repair the problem.

Step 1. *Check the level of the brake fluid.* If low, carefully inspect the entire hydraulic brake system for leaks and repair as necessary.

Step 2. *Disconnect the wire from the pressure-differential switch.* If the lamp is still on, the problem is due to the parking brake lever switch on or grounded, or the wire going to the switch is shorted to ground. If the red brake warning lamp is off after being disconnected from the pressure-differential switch, then the problem is due to a hydraulic failure (a low pressure in either the front or the rear system that creates a difference in pressure of at least 1035 kPa [150 psi]).

PROPORTIONING VALVE

Operation

A proportioning valve may or may not be used on all types of braking systems. When used, it prevents rear wheel lockup by limiting the amount of pressure sent to the rear wheels. A proportioning valve **reduces the pressure increase** to the rear brakes. A proportioning valve is also called a **pressure control valve** by some vehicle manufacturers.

A proportioning valve permits full master cylinder pressure to be sent to the rear brakes up to a certain point, called the **split point** or **change over pressure.** Above the split point, the pressure is reduced to a certain ratio, called the **slope,** of the front brake pressure. The split point is usually 1400–2100 kPa (200–300 psi), and the ratio (slope) could vary from 0.25 to 0.50. See Figure 33–35. With light brake-pedal applications, approximately the same brake pressure is sent to both front and rear brakes. However, when higher pressures are required to stop the vehicle, the pressure is controlled by this proportioning valve to limit the pressure sent to the rear brakes to less than half of the pressure being applied to the front brakes beyond the split point. This prevents rear wheel lockup due to weight transfer forward reducing the weight off the rear tires, plus allowing for the self-energizing forces of some rear drum brakes.

In the event of a front brake system failure, a bypass opens to allow full rear brake hydraulic pressure. Vehicles that use the diagonal split have a proportioning valve for each rear brake. This can be two separate units as shown in Figures 33–36 and 33–37 or one component part.

Height-Sensing Proportioning Valves

Many vehicles use a proportioning valve that varies the amount of pressure that can be sent to the rear brakes depending on the height of the rear suspension. If the vehicle is lightly loaded, the rear suspension is high, especially during braking. In this case, the amount of pressure allowed to the rear brakes is reduced. This *helps* prevent rear wheel lockup and possible skidding. Besides, a lightly loaded vehicle requires less braking force to stop than a heavily loaded vehicle.

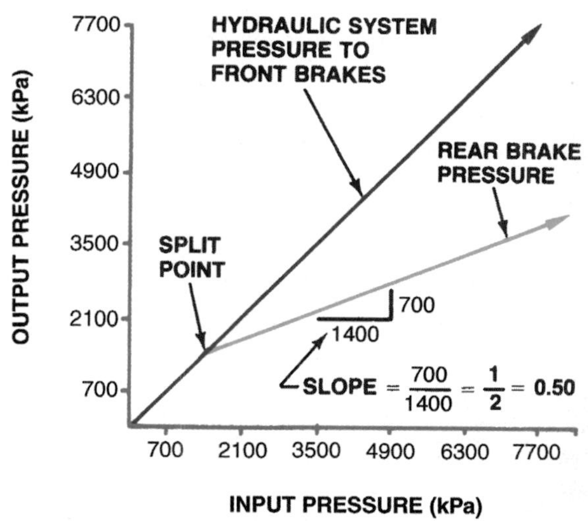

Figure 33–35 A typical proportioning valve pressure relationship. At low pressures, the pressure is the same to the rear brakes as to the front brakes. After the split point, only 50% (a percentage called the slope) of the master cylinder pressure is applied to the rear brakes.

TECH TIP 

The Master Cylinder One-Drip-Per-Second Test

Excessive brake wear is often caused by brake cylinder linkage or brake light switches keeping the brake pedal from fully releasing. If the brake pedal is not fully released, the primary piston sealing cup blocks the compensating port from the brake fluid reservoir. To test if this is the problem, loosen both lines from the master cylinder. Brake fluid should drip out of both lines about one drip per second. This is why this test is also called the master cylinder drip test. If the master cylinder does not drip, the brake pedal may not be allowing the master cylinder to fully release. Have an assistant pull up on the brake pedal. If the dripping starts, the problem is due to a misadjusted brake light or speed (cruise) control switch or pedal stop. If the master cylinder still does not drip, loosen the master cylinder from the power booster. If the master cylinder now starts to drip, the push rod adjustment is too long.

If the master cylinder still does not drip, the problem is in the master cylinder itself. Check for brake fluid contamination. If mineral oil, such as engine oil, power steering fluid, or automatic transmission fluid (ATF), has been used in the system, the rubber sealing cups swell and can block off the compensating port. If contamination is discovered, *every* brake component that contains rubber *must* be replaced.

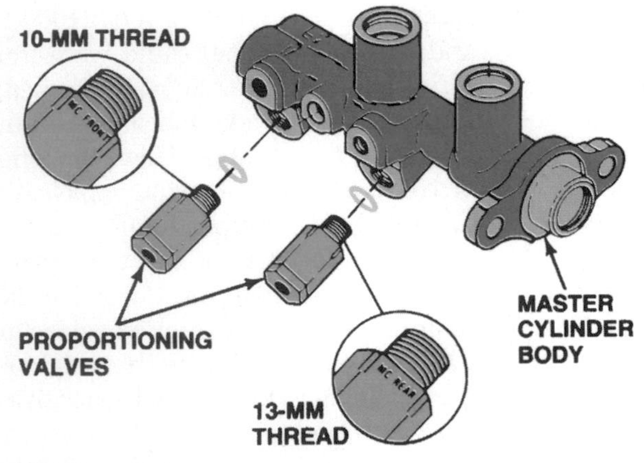

Figure 33–36 Many proportioning valves are mounted directly to the master cylinder in the outlet to the rear brakes.

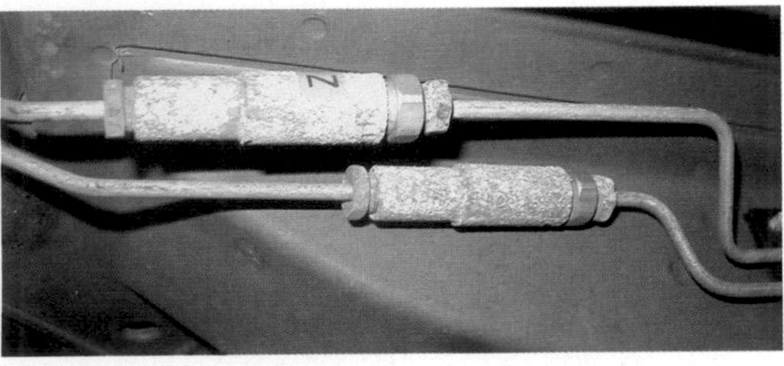

Figure 33–37 These two proportioning valves are found under the vehicle on this Dodge minivan.

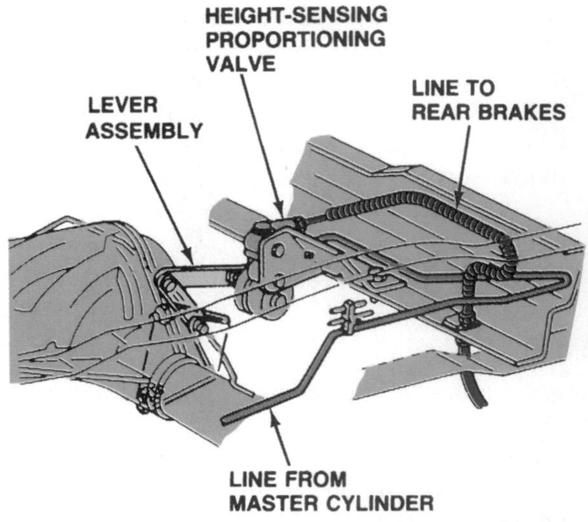

Figure 33–38 A height-sensing proportioning valve allows a higher pressure to be applied to the rear brakes when the vehicle is heavily loaded and less pressure when the vehicle is lightly loaded.

When the vehicle is loaded, the rear suspension is forced downward. The lever on the proportioning valve moves and allows a greater pressure to be sent to the rear brakes. See Figure 33–38. This greater pressure allows the rear brakes to achieve more braking force, helping to slow a heavier vehicle. When a vehicle is heavily loaded in the rear, the chances of rear wheel lockup are reduced.

CAUTION: Some vehicle manufacturers warn that service technicians should never install replacement air lift shock absorbers or springs that may result in a vehicle height different than specified by the vehicle manufacturer.

Height-sensing proportioning valves should be adjusted when replaced. The proper adjustment ensures that the proper pressure is applied to the rear brakes in relation to the loading of the vehicle.

Procedures vary from one vehicle to another. Always consult the factory service manual for the exact procedure.

TECH TIP 

Always Inspect Both Front and Rear Brakes

If a vehicle tends to lock up the rear brakes during a stop, many technicians may try to repair the problem by replacing the proportioning valve or servicing the rear brakes. Proportioning valves are simple spring-loaded devices that are usually trouble free. If the rear brakes lock up during braking, carefully inspect the rear brakes looking for contaminated linings or other problems that can cause the rear brakes to grab. Do not stop there—always inspect the front brakes, too. If the front brakes are rusted or corroded, they cannot operate efficiently and greater force must be exerted by the driver to stop the vehicle. Even if the proportioning valve is functioning correctly, the higher brake pedal pressure by the driver could easily cause the rear brakes to lock up.

A locked wheel has less traction with the road than a rotating wheel. As a result, if the rear wheels become locked, the rear of the vehicle often comes around or fishtails, causing the vehicle to skid. Careful inspection of the *entire* braking system is required to be assured of a safe vehicle.

METERING VALVE

Operation

The metering valve is used on all front-disc, rear-drum-brake-equipped vehicles. The metering valve prevents the full operation of (holds off) the disc brakes until between 520–861 kPa (75–125 psi) is sent to the rear drum brakes to overcome rear-brake return spring pressure. A metering valve is also called a **hold-off valve.** This allows the front and rear brakes to apply at the same time for even stopping. Most metering valves also allow for the pressure to the front brakes to be gradually blended up to the metering valve pressure to prevent front brake locking under light pedal pressures on icy surfaces.

The metering valve remains open at pressures below 20 to 200 kPa (3 to 30 psi) to allow the pressure to be equalized when the brakes are not applied. A metering valve is usually part of a **combination** valve as shown in Figure 33–39.

NOTE: Braking systems that are diagonal split, such as found on most front-wheel-drive vehicles, do *not* use a metering valve. A metering valve is only used on front/rear split braking systems such as those found on most rear-wheel-drive vehicles.

TECH TIP 

No Valves Can Cause a Pull

When diagnosing a pull to one side during braking, some technicians tend to blame the metering valve, proportional valve, the pressure differential switch, or the master cylinder itself.

Just remember that if a vehicle pulls during braking the problem *has* to be due to an individual wheel brake or brake line. The master cylinder and all the valves control front or rear brakes together or diagonal brakes and cannot cause a pull if not functioning correctly.

Metering Valve Diagnosis and Testing

A defective metering valve can leak brake fluid and/or cause the front brakes to apply before the rear brakes. This is most commonly noticed on slippery surfaces such as on snow or ice or on rain-slick roads.

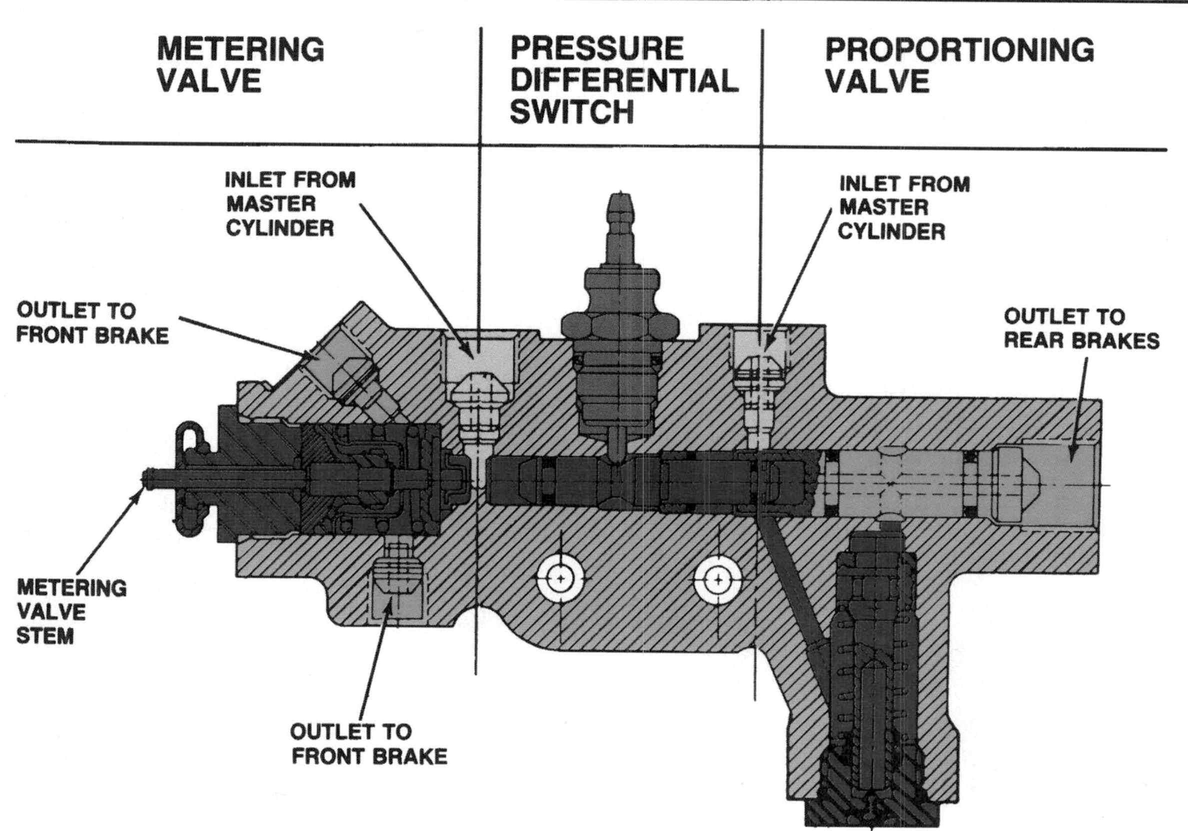

Figure 33–39 Combination valve containing metering, pressure differential (warning switch), and proportioning valves all in one unit. This style is often called a "pistol grip" design because the proportioning valve section resembles the grip section of a handgun.

If the front brakes lock up during these conditions, the front wheels cannot be steered. Inspect the metering valve for these two conditions:

1. *Leakage.* Look around the bottom on the metering valve for brake fluid leakage. (Ignore slight dampness.) Replace the metering valve assembly if leaking.
2. *Frozen stem.* As the pressure builds to the front brakes, the metering valve stem should move. If it does not, replace the valve.

BRAKE LINES

High-pressure double-walled steel brake lines or high-strength flexible lines are used to connect the master cylinder to each wheel. See Figure 33–40. The steel **brake lines** are also called **brake pipes** or **brake tubing** and are coated to help prevent corrosion. The steel brake lines leaving the master cylinder are usually coiled to allow for movement between the master cylinder and the mounting of the brake line to the frame, which could cause fatigue and brake line failure.

CAUTION: Copper tubing should *never* be used for brake lines. Copper tends to burst at a lower pressure than steel.

The ends of all steel brake lines should have a **double flare** or **ISO flare** at each end to ensure the connection will have the necessary strength. See Figures 33–41 and 33–42. **ISO** means **International Standards Organization.** ISO flare may also be called a **ball flare** or **bubble flare.** Whenever replacing steel brake line, new steel tubing can be used and a double lap flare or an ISO flare completed at each end using a special flaring tool. Brake line can also be purchased in selected lengths already correctly flared. They are available in different diameters, the most commonly used being 4.8 mm (3/16″), 6.4 mm (1/4″), and 7.9 mm (5/16″) outside diameter (O.D.). Always use two line wrenches

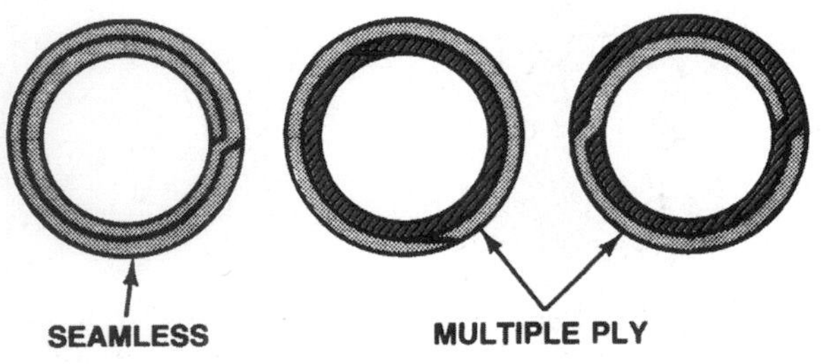

Figure 33–40 Steel brake lines are double-walled for strength and plated for corrosion resistance.

TECH TIP 

Push-In or Pull-Out Metering Valve?

Whenever bleeding the air out of the hydraulic brake system, the metering valve should be bypassed. The metering valve stops the passage of brake fluid to the front wheels until pressure exceeds about 860 kPa (125 psi). It is important not to push the brake pedal down with a great force so as to keep from dispersing any trapped air into small and hard to bleed bubbles. To bypass the metering valve, the service technician has to push or pull a small button located on the metering valve. An easy way to remember whether to push in or to pull out is to inspect the button itself. *If the button is rubber coated, then you push in. If the button is steel, then pull out.*

Special tools allow the metering valve to be held in the bypass position. Failure to remove the tool after bleeding the brakes can result in premature application of the front brakes before the rear drum brakes have enough pressure to operate.

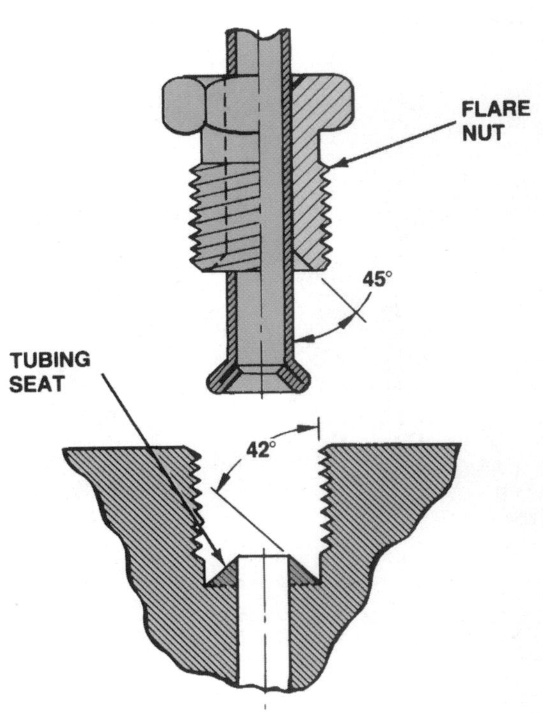

Figure 33–41 Because of the slight differences in flare angle, double-flare fitting seals cause a wedging action.

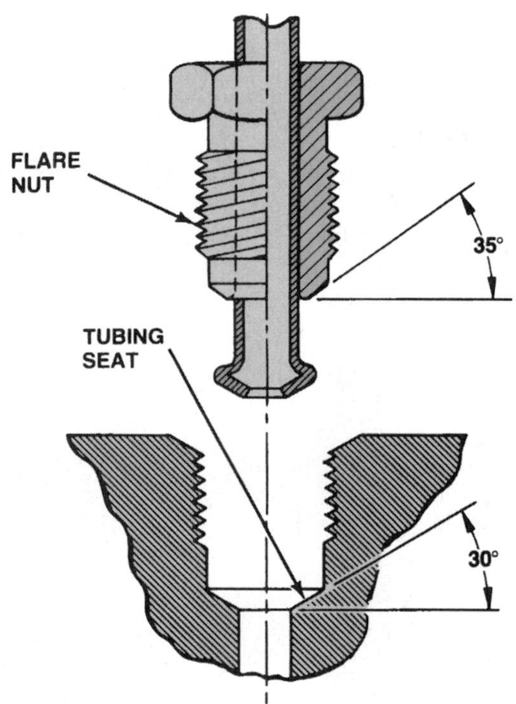

Figure 33–42 An ISO flare fitting.

when disconnecting or reattaching brake lines. See Figure 33–43. See Figures 33–44 and 33–45 for brake line flaring procedures.

CAUTION: According to vehicle manufacturers' recommended procedures, compression fittings should never be used to join two pieces of steel brake line. Only use double flare ends and connections, if necessary, when replacing damaged steel brake lines.

Coiled Brake Line

Steel brake line is often coiled as shown in Figure 33–46. The purpose of the coils is to allow movement between the brake components without stress that could lead to metal fatigue and brake line breakage. The typical master cylinder attaches to the bulkhead of the vehicle, and the combination valve is often attached to the frame. Because the body and frame are usually insulated from each other using rubber isolators, some movement occurs while driving.

Armoured Brake Line

In many areas of the brake system, the steel brake line is covered with a wire coil wrap as shown in Figure 33–47. This armour is designed to prevent damage from stones and other debris that could dent or damage the brake line. If a section of armoured brake line is to be replaced, armoured replacement line should be installed. Braided flexible brake line is also used on some vehicles to allow flexibility and protection against stone damage.

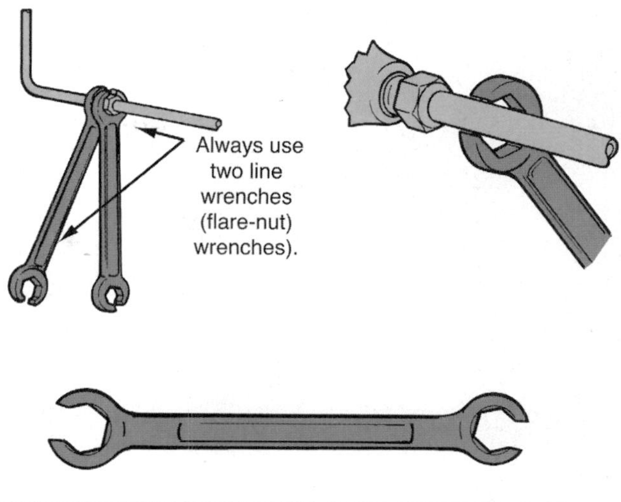

Figure 33–43 Whenever disconnecting or tightening a brake line, always use the correct size flare nut wrench. A flare nut wrench is also called a **tube nut wrench** or a **line wrench.**

TECH TIP 

Bend It Right the First Time

Replacing rusted or damaged brake line can be a difficult job. It is important that the replacement brake line be located in the same location as the original to prevent possible damage from road debris or heat from the exhaust. Often this means bending the brake line with many angles and turns. To make the job a lot easier, use a stiff length of wire and bend the wire into the exact shape necessary. Then use the wire as a pattern to bend the brake line. Always use a tubing bender to avoid kinking the brake line. A kink not only restricts the flow of brake fluid, but also weakens the line. To bend brake line without a tubing bender tool, use an old V-belt pulley. Clamp the pulley in a vise and lay the tubing in the groove and smoothly bend the tubing. Different diameter pulleys will create various radius bends. See Figure 33–48.

NOTE: Always use a tubing cutter instead of a hack saw when cutting brake line. A hacksaw will leave a rough and uneven end that will not flare properly.

(a)

(b)

(c)

(d)

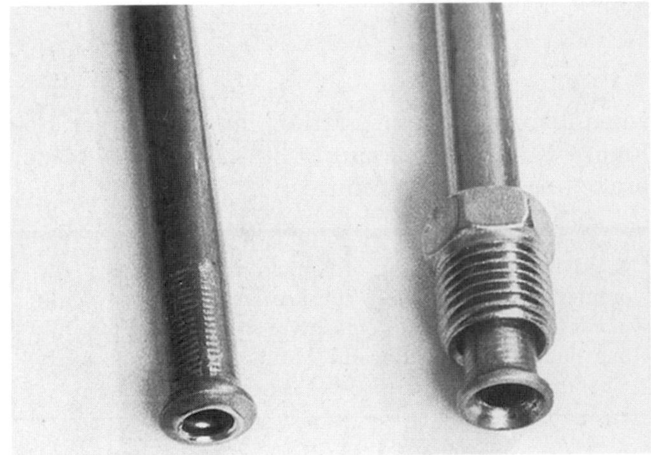

(e)

Figure 33–44 Double flaring the end of a brake line: (a) Clamp the line at the correct height above the surface of the clamping tool using the shoulder of the insert as a gauge. (b) The insert is pressed into the end of the tubing. This creates the first bend. (c) Remove the insert and use the pointed tool to complete the overlap double flare. (d) The completed operation as it appears while still in the clamp. (e) The end of the line as it appears after the first operation on the left and the completed double flare on the right.

(a)

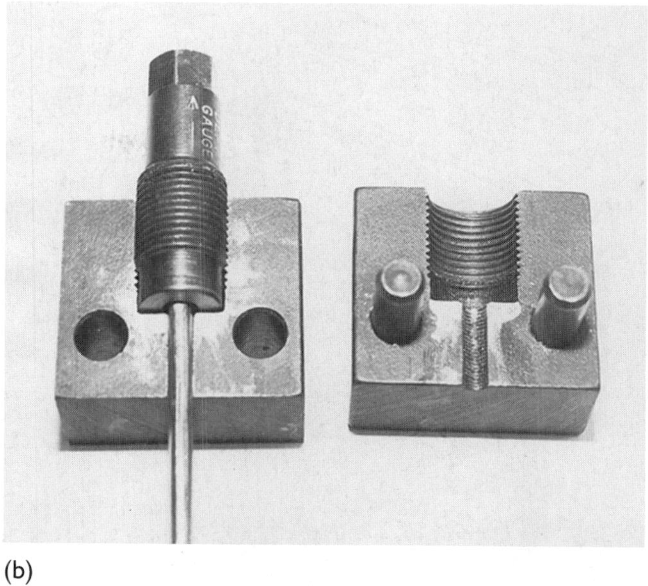

(b)

Figure 33–45 Making an ISO flare requires this special tool. (a) Position the brake line into the two-part tool at the correct height using the gauge end of the tool.
(b) Assemble the two blocks of the tool together and clamp in a vise. Turn the tool around and thread it into the tool block. The end of the threaded part of the tool forms the "bubble" or ISO flare.

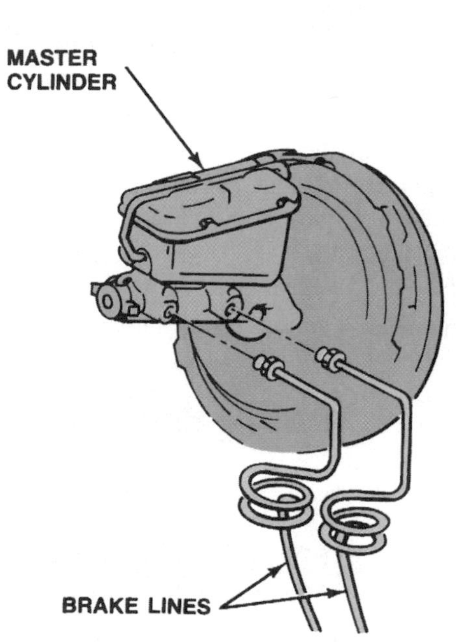

Figure 33–46 The coils in the brake line help prevent cracks caused by vibration.

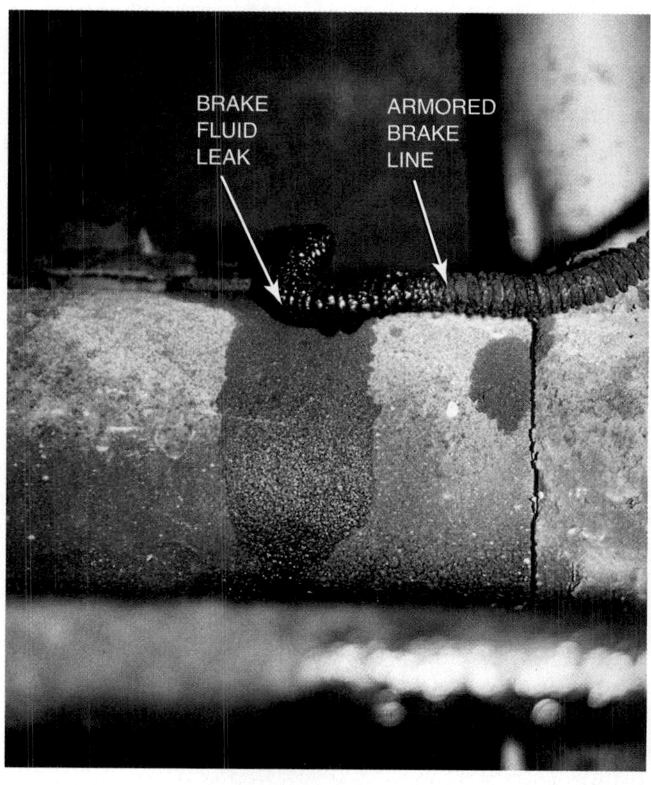

Figure 33–47 Armoured brake line is usually used in a location where the line may be exposed to rock or road debris damage. Even armoured brake line can leak, and a visual inspection is an important part of any brake service.

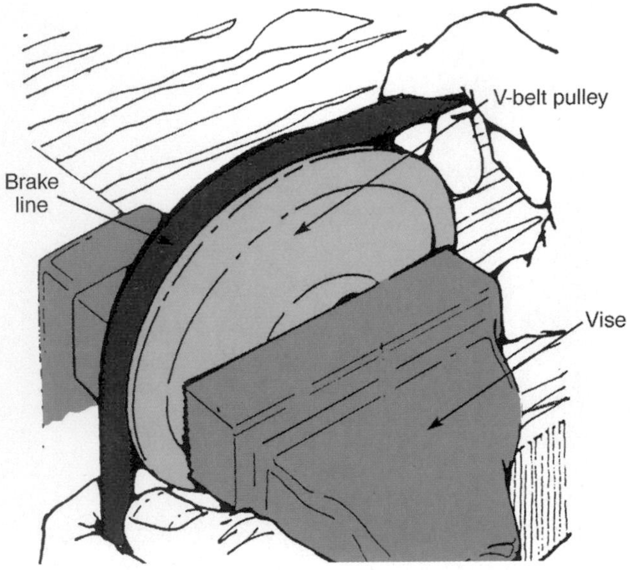

Figure 33–48 Using a V-belt pulley in a vise to bend brake line.

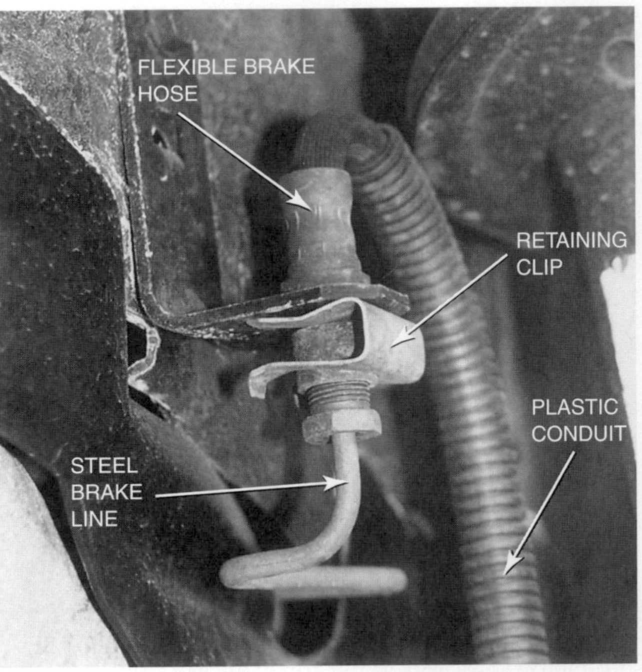

Figure 33–49 Flexible brake hoses are used between the frame or body of the vehicle and the wheel brakes. Because of suspension and/or steering movement, these flexible brake lines must be strong enough to handle high brake fluid pressures, yet remain flexible. Note that this flexible brake hose is further protected against road debris with a plastic conduit covering.

FLEXIBLE BRAKE HOSE

Flexible brake hoses are used on each front wheel to allow for steering and suspension movement and at the rear to allow for rear suspension travel. See Figure 33–49. These rubber high-strength hoses can crack, blister, or leak, and should be inspected at least every six months. Typical flexible brake hose is constructed of rubber hose surrounded by layers of braided synthetic yarn as shown in Figure 33–50. An outside jacket is made from rubber and protects the reinforcement fabric from moisture and abrasion. The outside covering is also ribbed so that a technician can see if the hose is twisted. It is not unusual for flexible brake lines to become turned around and twisted when the disc brake caliper is removed and then replaced during a brake pad change. See Figure 33–51.

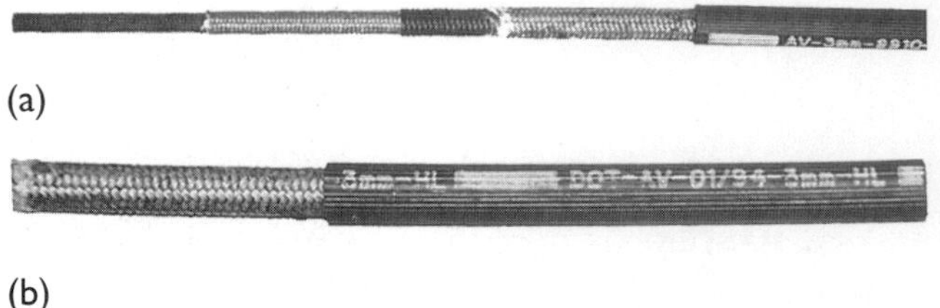

Figure 33–50 (a) Typical flexible brake hose showing the multiple layers of rubber and fabric. (b) The inside diameter (ID) is printed on the hose (3 mm) and the date it was manufactured (01/94).

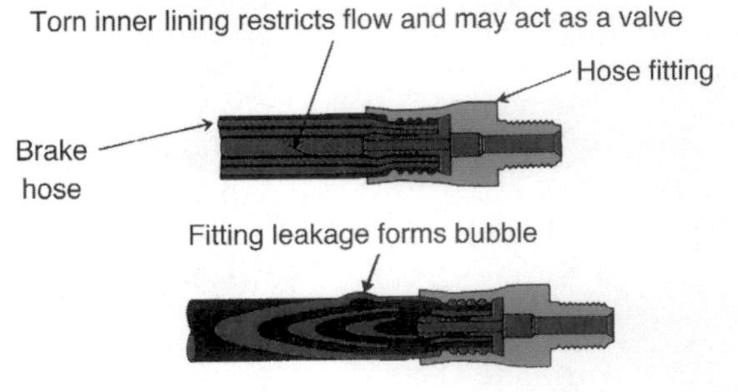

Figure 33–51 Typical flexible brake hose faults. Many faults cannot be seen, yet can cause the brakes to remain applied after the brake pedal is released.

BLEEDING PROCEDURE

Whenever the master cylinder is replaced or the hydraulic system has been left opened for several hours, the air may have to be bled from the master cylinder. Bleed the master cylinder on the bench before installing it on the vehicle. If bleeding the master cylinder after working on the hydraulic system, follow these steps:

Step 1. Fill the master cylinder with clean brake fluid from a sealed container up to the recommended full level.

TECH TIP

Don't Fill the Master Cylinder Without Seeing Me!

The boss explained to the beginning technician that there are two reasons why the customer should be told not to fill the master cylinder reservoir when the brake fluid is down to the minimum mark.

1. If the master cylinder reservoir is low, there may be a leak that should be repaired.
2. As the brakes wear, the disc brake piston moves outward to maintain the same distance between friction materials and the rotor. Therefore, as the disc brake pads wear, the brake fluid level goes down to compensate.

If the customer notices that the brake fluid is low in the master cylinder reservoir, the vehicle should be serviced—either for new brakes or to repair a leak.

TECH TIP

Bleeder Valve Loosening Tips

Attempting to loosen a bleeder valve often results in breaking (shearing off) of the bleeder valve. Several of these service procedures can be tried that help prevent the *possibility* of breaking a bleeder valve. Bleeder valves are tapered and become wedged in the caliper on the wheel cylinder housing. See Figures 33–52 and 33–53. All of these methods use shock to "break the taper" and to loosen the stuck valve.

Air Impact Method. Use a six-point socket for the bleeder valve and use the necessary adapters to fit an air impact wrench to the socket. Apply some penetrating oil to the bleeder valve and allow to flow around the threads. Turn the pressure down on the impact wrench to limit the force. The hammering effect of the impact wrench loosens the bleeder valve without breaking it off.

Hit and Tap Method

Step 1. Tap on the end of the bleeder valve with a steel hammer. This shock often "breaks the taper" at the base of the bleeder valve. The shock also breaks loose any rust or corrosion on the threads.

Step 2. Using a six-point wrench or socket, *tap* the bleeder valve in the clockwise direction (tighten).

Step 3. Using the same six-point socket or wrench, *tap* the bleeder valve counterclockwise to loosen and remove the bleeder valve.

NOTE: It is the *shock* of the tap on the wrench that breaks loose the bleeder valve. Simply pulling on the wrench often results in breaking off the bleeder.

If the valve is still stuck (frozen), repeat Step 1 through Step 3.

Air Punch Method. Use an air punch near the bleeder valve while attempting to loosen the bleeder valve at the same time.

The air punch creates a shock motion that often loosens the taper and threads of the bleeder valve from the caliper or wheel cylinder. It is also helpful to first attempt to turn the bleeder valve in the clockwise (tightening) direction, then turn the bleeder in counterclockwise direction to loosen and remove the bleeder valve.

Heat and Tap Method. Heat the area around the bleeder valve with a torch. The heat expands the size of the hole and usually allows the bleeder to be loosened and removed.

CAUTION: The heat from a torch will damage the rubber seals inside the caliper or wheel cylinder. Using heat to free a stuck bleeder valve will *require* that all internal rubber parts be replaced.

Wax Method

Step 1. Heat the bleeder valve itself with a torch. The heat causes the valve itself to expand.

Step 2. Remove the heat from the bleeder valve. As the valve is cooling, touch paraffin wax or candle wax to the hot valve. The wax will melt and run down around the threads of the bleeder valve.

Step 3. Allow the bleeder valve to cool until it can be safely touched with your hand. This assures that the temperature is low enough for the wax to return to a solid and provide the lubricating properties necessary for the easy removal of the bleeder valve. Again, turn the bleeder valve clockwise before turning the valve counterclockwise to remove.

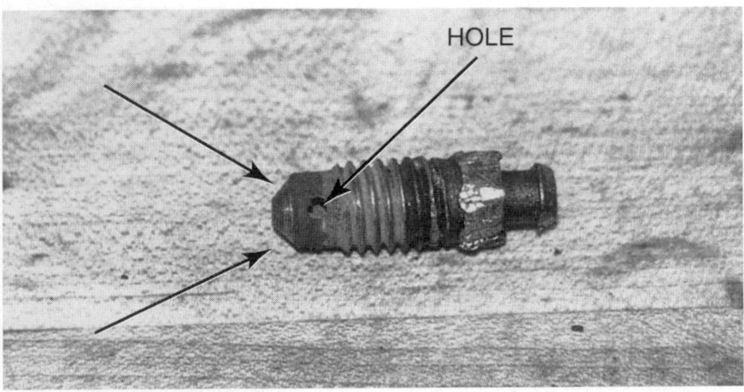

Figure 33–52 A typical bleeder valve from a disc brake caliper. The arrows point to the taper section that does the actual sealing. It is this taper that requires a shock to loosen. If the bleeder is simply turned with a wrench, the bleeder usually breaks off because the tapered part at the bottom remains adhered to the caliper or wheel cylinder. Once loosened, brake fluid flows around the taper and out through the hole in the side of the bleeder valve.

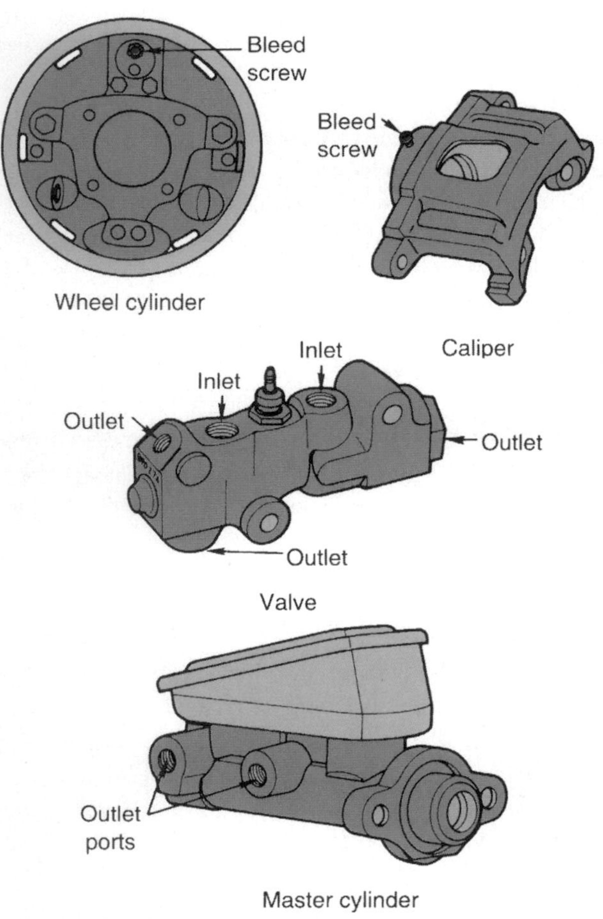

Figure 33–53 Typical bleeder locations. Note that the combination valve and master cylinder shown do not have bleeder valves; therefore, bleeding is accomplished by loosening the brake line at the outlet ports. (Courtesy of Allied Signal Automotive Aftermarket)

Step 2. Have an assistant slowly depress the brake pedal as you "crack open" the master cylinder bleed screw starting with the section closest to the bulkhead. It is very important that the primary section of the master cylinder be bled before attempting to bleed the air out of the secondary section of the master cylinder. Before the brake pedal reaches the floor, close the bleeder valve.

HINT: A proper manual bleeding of the hydraulic system requires that accurate communications occur between the person depressing the brake pedal and the person opening and closing the bleeder valve(s). The bleeder valve (also called a bleed valve) should be open only when the brake pedal is being depressed. The valve must be closed when the brake pedal is released to prevent air from being drawn into the system.

Step 3. Repeat the procedure several times until a solid flow of brake fluid is observed leaving the bleeder valve. If the master cylinder is not equipped with bleeder valves, the outlet tube nuts can be loosened instead.

TECH TIP

Do It Right—Replace the Brake Fluid

Often, used brake fluid looks like black coffee or coffee with cream. Both conditions indicate contaminated or moisture-laden brake fluid that should be replaced. The following steps will help assure a complete brake fluid change:

Step 1. Remove the old brake fluid from the master cylinder using a suction bulb. (Dispose of this old brake fluid properly.)

Step 2. Fill the master cylinder with new clean brake fluid from a sealed container.

Step 3. Bleed each wheel brake until the brake fluid is clean.

CAUTION: Do not allow the master cylinder to run out of brake fluid. Recheck and refill as necessary during the bleeding process.

This brake fluid replacement will fully restore the brake hydraulic system to as-new condition and help protect the system from rust and corrosion. Only replacing the friction pads and/or linings is not a complete and thorough brake system service. Customers should be educated as to the importance of this service procedure.

Bleeding Sequence

After bleeding the master cylinder, the combination valve should be bled if equipped. Follow the same procedure as when bleeding the master cylinder, being careful not to allow the master cylinder to run dry.

NOTE: The master cylinder is located in the highest section of the hydraulic braking system. Some master cylinders are equipped with bleeder valves. All master cylinders can be bled using the same procedure as that used for bleeding calipers and wheel cylinders. If the master cylinder is not equipped with bleeder valves, it can be bled by loosening the brake line fittings at the master cylinder.

Check the level in the master cylinder frequently and keep it filled with clean brake fluid throughout the brake bleeding procedure.

For most rear-wheel-drive vehicles equipped with a front/rear split system, start the bleeding with the wheel farthest from the master cylinder and work toward the closest.

For most vehicles, this sequence is:

1. Right rear
2. Left rear
3. Right front
4. Left front

NOTE: Before bleeding the front brakes, attach a holding tool to the stem or the metering valve to allow the brake fluid to flow through the valve unrestricted. See Figure 33–54.

NOTE: If the vehicle has two wheel cylinders on one brake, bleed the upper cylinder first.

For vehicles equipped with a diagonal split section, follow the brake bleeding procedure recommended in the service manual or service information for the vehicle you are servicing.

Manual Bleeding

Manual bleeding is the process of applying force (with the help from an assistant) to the brake pedal (service brakes) while the bleeder valve is opened slightly. The brake master cylinder applies pressure on the fluid that is forced out through the bleeder valve along with any trapped air.

In most cases, if only the one wheel cylinder or hydraulic line has been opened, only that wheel cylinder needs to be bled. If the brake system has been opened for an extended period of time or all four wheels have been opened, bleed the system in the sequence recommended by the vehicle manufacturer.

NOTE: See service manual for the exact brake bleeding procedure for the vehicle you are servicing.

To bleed the brakes, attach a hose to the bleeder screw. Place the other end of the hose into a glass jar, partially filled with fresh brake fluid. Be sure to keep the hose submerged in the brake fluid because it shows air bubbles as it comes out of the system and prevents air from accidentally being drawn into the system through the bleeder valve. See Figure 33–55.

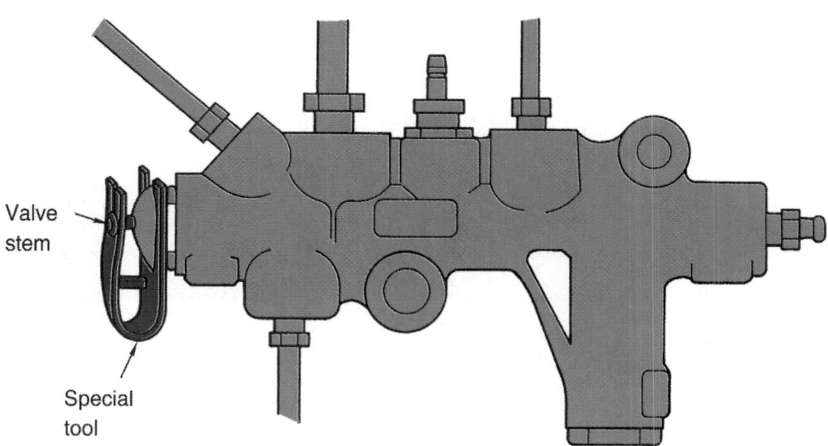

Figure 33–54 Special tool being used to hold out the valve stem on the metering valve. This allows brake fluid to flow unrestricted to the front brakes. If this valve was not released, a lot of brake pedal pressure would have to be used to overcome the metering valve.

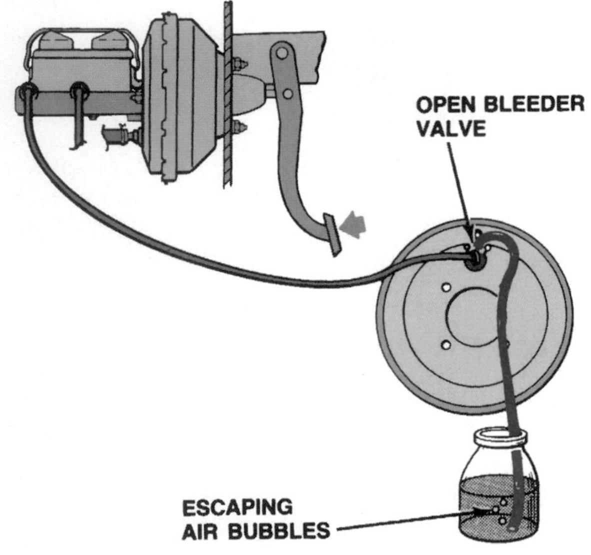

Figure 33–55 Manual bleeding can be used to flush the air from any brake system.

Have an assistant depress the brake pedal several times with the engine *off* to remove the power brake assist reserve. Press the brake pedal slowly and hold. Open the bleeder valve to purge the air from the system. Trapped air will hiss or spurt from the bleeder when the valve is opened. The bleeding sequence should be repeated as necessary until a solid stream of the brake fluid without air bubbles is observed flowing from the opened bleeder valve.

For best results do not allow the brake pedal to go to the floor. Some vehicle manufacturers recommend placing a block of wood about 25 mm (1 in.) thick under the brake pedal to keep it from bottoming. If the brake pedal is allowed to travel down to the floor, the sealing cups inside the master cylinder will be forced to travel farther down the bore of the master cylinder than normal. Because rust and dirt can accumulate in this area beyond the working range, the seals can be damaged.

All vehicle manufacturers and brake experts agree that the technician should wait at least 15 seconds before repeating the bleeding procedure. This wait time is important to allow time for any air bubbles present to reform into larger bubbles that can be more easily bled out of the system. See the Tech Tip "Tiny Bubbles" for details.

NOTE: Make certain all the brake components such as calipers and wheel cylinders are correctly installed, with the bleeder valve located on the highest section of the part. Some wheel cylinders and calipers (such as many Ford calipers) can be installed upside down! This usually occurs whenever both front calipers are off the vehicle and they accidentally get reversed left to right. If this occurs, the air will never be completely bled from the caliper.

TECH TIP

Tiny Bubbles

Do not use excessive brake pedal force while bleeding and never normally bleed the brake with the engine running! The extra assist from the power brake unit greatly increases the force exerted on the brake fluid in the master cylinder. The trapped air bubbles may be dispersed into tiny bubbles that often cling to the inside surface of the brake lines. These tiny air bubbles may not be able to be bled from the hydraulic system until enough time has allowed the bubbles to reform. To help prevent excessive force, do *not* start the engine. Without power assistance, the brake pedal force can be kept from becoming excessive. If the dispersal of the air into tiny bubbles is suspected, try tapping the calipers or wheel cylinders with a plastic hammer. After this tapping, simply waiting for a period of time will cause the bubbles to reform into larger and easier-to-bleed air pockets. Most brake experts recommend waiting *15 seconds or longer* between attempts to bleed each wheel. This waiting period is critical and allows time for the air bubbles to form.

HINT: To help prevent depressing the brake pedal too far, some experts recommend placing a wooden 2″ × 4″ under the brake pedal. This helps prevent the seals inside the master cylinder from travelling over unused sections inside the bore that may be corroded or rusty.

Frequently Asked Question ???

What Is Reverse Fluid Injection?

Reverse fluid injection is a procedure that uses an air- or hand-operated injection gun that pushes brake fluid from the bleeder valve into the hydraulic system. See Figure 33–56. By forcing brake fluid into the bleeder valve, any trapped air is forced upward into the master cylinder.

CAUTION: This procedure should only be done after a thorough flushing of the hydraulic system. Many experts warn that debris and sediment in the hydraulic system can be back-flushed into the ABS hydraulic unit and/or master cylinder. Many brake and ABS failures have been caused by forcing old brake fluid back into the system.

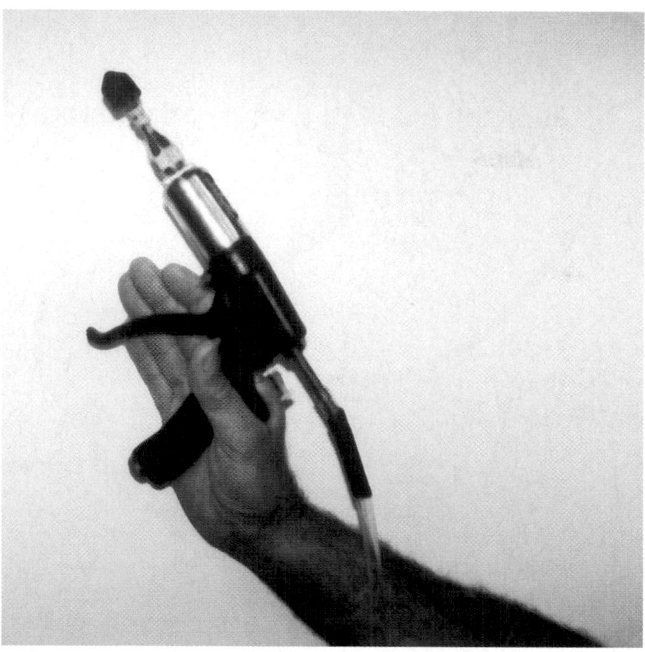

Figure 33–56 A reverse fluid injection unit that is used to bleed hydraulic brake and clutch systems by forcing brake fluid up from the bleeder valve into the master cylinder, thereby forcing any trapped air up and out of the system.

Pressure Bleeding

Pressure bleeding is a term used to describe the use of pressure on top of the master cylinder to rid the hydraulic brake system of trapped air. Pressure bleeders must use the correct master cylinder adapter. See Figures 33–57 and 33–58.

Whenever using a power bleeder, do not exceed 140 kPa of pressure (20 psi). Since the pressure is low, the button on the metering valve (if equipped) must be either pushed in or pulled out depending on the design and manufacturer. If the metering valve is not released, no fluid pressure will be applied to the front disc brakes. A major disadvantage to using the pressure bleeding method is the need to use the correct master cylinder reservoir adapter fitting. Using the wrong adapter or not installing it correctly can cause brake fluid to leak out under pressure, causing damage to the vehicle.

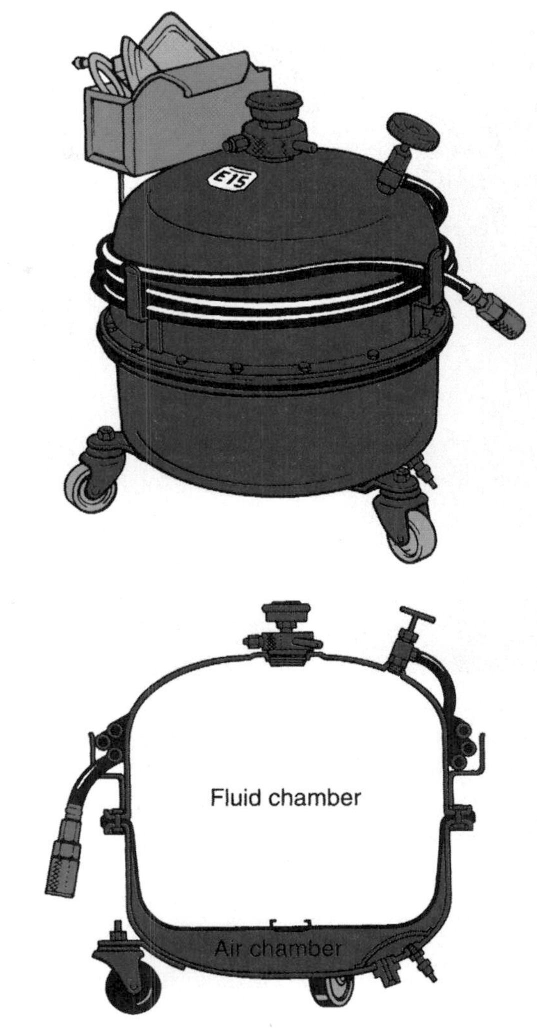

Figure 33–57 A typical pressure bleeder. The brake fluid inside is pressurized with air pressure in the air chamber. This air pressure is applied to the brake fluid in the upper section. A rubber diaphragm separates the air from the brake fluid. (Courtesy of EIS Brake Parts)

Vacuum Bleeding

Another popular bleeder uses a vacuum pump (either manual or electric) to draw the brake fluid from the bleeder valve and into a container. This type of bleeder can also be used to bleed the hydraulic brake system without the need of an assistant. See Figure 33–59.

Loosen the bleeder valve at least three-fourths of a turn and operate the vacuum bleeder. Continue bleeding until clean brake fluid flows into the bleeder container. Some air bubbles may be seen in the clear plastic tubing leading from the bleeder valve to the vacuum bleeder unit. Often these bubbles are the result of air being drawn in around the threads of the bleeder valve and do not indicate that there is air in the brake system.

Gravity Bleeding

Gravity bleeding is a slow, but effective, method that will work on many vehicles to rid the hydraulic system of air. The procedure involves simply opening the bleeder valve and waiting until brake fluid flows from the open valve. Any air trapped in the port being bled will rise and escape from the port when the valve is opened. It may take several minutes before brake fluid escapes. If no brake fluid comes out, remove the bleeder

Figure 33–58 Brake fluid under pressure from the power bleeder is applied to the top of the master cylinder. It is very important that the proper adapter be used for the master cylinder. Failure to use the correct adapter or failure to release the pressure on the brake fluid before removing the adapter can cause brake fluid to escape under pressure.

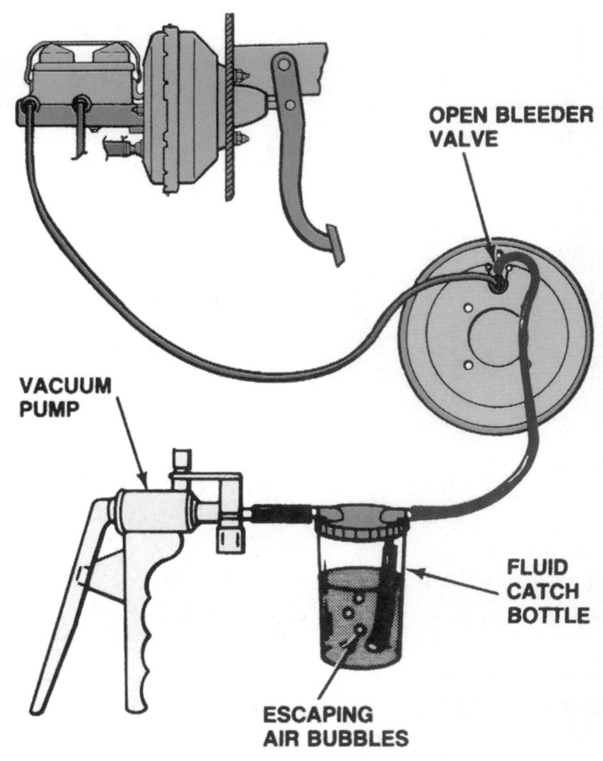

Figure 33–59 Vacuum bleeding uses atmospheric pressure to force brake fluid through the hydraulic system.

valve entirely—it may be clogged. Remember, nothing but air and brake fluid will be *slowly* coming out of the wheel cylinder or caliper when the bleeder valve is removed. *Do not press on the brake pedal with the bleeder valve out while gravity bleeding.*

Gravity bleeding works because any liquid tends to seek its own level. This means that the brake fluid in the master cylinder tends to flow downward toward the wheel cylinders or calipers. As long as the brake fluid level in the master cylinder is higher than the bleeder valve, the brake fluid will flow downward and out the open bleeder as shown in Figure 33–60.

TECH TIP

Quick and Easy Test for Air in the Lines

If air is in the brake lines, the brake pedal will be low and will usually feel spongy or mushy. To confirm that trapped air in the hydraulic system is the cause, perform this simple and fast test:

Step 1. Remove the cover from the master cylinder. Have an assistant pump the brake pedal several times and then hold the pedal down.

Step 2. Observe the squirts of brake fluid from the master cylinder when the brake pedal is quickly released. (This is best performed by allowing the foot to slip off the end of the brake pedal.)

Results: If the brake fluid squirts higher than 8 cm (3 in.) from the surface, then air is trapped in the hydraulic system. See Figure 33–61.

CAUTION: Always use a fender cover whenever performing this test. Brake fluid will remove paint if it gets onto the unprotected fender.

Explanation: Air can be compressed, whereas liquid cannot be compressed. When pumping the brake pedal, the assistant is compressing any trapped air. When the pedal is released quickly, the compressed air expands and takes up more volume, forcing the brake fluid upward through the compensation ports into the reservoir. Some upward movement is normal because of the return spring pressure on the valves in the master cylinder and springs in the wheel cylinders. If however, the spurt is higher than normal, this is a sure sign of air being trapped in the system. This test is also called the air entrapment test.

Figure 33–60 Gravity bleeding is simply opening the bleeder valve and allowing gravity to force the brake fluid out of the bleeder valve. Because air is lighter than brake fluid, all of the air escapes before the brake fluid runs out.

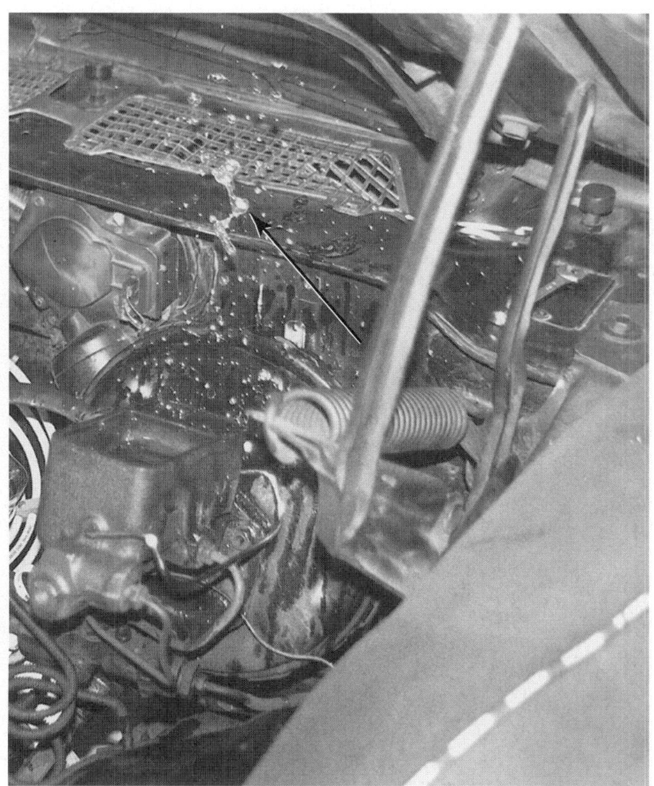

Figure 33–61 Note the large drops being squirted from the top of the master cylinder due to trapped air when the brakes were released.

This flow of brake fluid can even get past the metering valve and proportioning valve. The proportioning valve is normally open to the rear brakes until the pressure reaches a predetermined level when it starts to limit increasing pressure to the rear brakes. The metering valve used to control or delay the operation of the front brakes is open to the front wheels until the pressure exceeds 70 to 100 kPa (10 to 15 psi). Therefore, as long as no one is pushing on the brake pedal, the metering valve remains open to the front wheels and the brake fluid from the master cylinder can easily flow downward through the valve and out the open bleeder valve.

Since no pressure is exerted on the brake fluid, the large air bubbles remain large air bubbles and are not separated into smaller, harder-to-bleed air bubbles that can occur with manual bleeding.

SUMMARY

1. The brake pedal mechanism increases the force of the driver's foot and applies it to the master cylinder.
2. During a typical brake application only about 1 teaspoon (5 mL) of brake fluid actually is moved from the master cylinder into the hydraulic system.
3. Pascal's law states that: "When a force is applied to a liquid confined in a container or enclosure, the pressure is transmitted equally and undiminished in every direction."
4. Master cylinder reservoirs are large enough for the brakes to be worn completely down and still have a small reserve.
5. The front port of the master cylinder is called the compensating port and the rear port is called the inlet port.
6. A residual check valve was used on some older model vehicles with drum brakes. The purpose of the valve was to keep a slight positive pressure on the brake fluid in the wheel cylinder to keep the lip of the sealing cup from collapsing when the brakes were released.
7. Brake system diagnosis should always start with checking for venting (compensation).

8. Dual split master cylinders that separate the front brakes from the rear brakes are used on rear-wheel-drive vehicles.
9. Diagonal split master cylinders that separate right front and left rear from the left front and right rear brakes are used on front-wheel-drive vehicles.
10. Some master cylinders can be rebuilt, but the cylinder bore should not be honed unless recommended by the manufacturer.
11. A pressure differential or a brake fluid level sensor will light the red brake warning lamp if there is a leak in the hydraulic system.
12. A proportioning valve is used in braking systems to limit and control the pressure sent to the rear brakes to help prevent rear wheel lockup during heavy braking.
13. A metering valve (hold-off valve) delays the operation of the front disc brakes until enough pressure has been sent to the rear drum brakes to overcome return spring pressure. This valve helps prevent front wheel lockup during light braking on slippery surfaces.
14. Metal brake line should be double-wall steel tubing for strength and use either a double flare or an ISO flare at the ends.
15. Flexible brake line is made from many layers of fabric and rubber.
16. Air trapped in the hydraulic system is removed by bleeding the brakes. Bleeder valves are used to bleed the air from disc brake calipers and drum brake wheel cylinders.

REVIEW QUESTIONS

1. Explain Pascal's law.
2. Describe how a master cylinder works.
3. Discuss the difference between a dual split and a diagonal split master cylinder.
4. Explain the operation of the pressure-differential switch.
5. Describe the purpose of the metering and proportioning valves.
6. List the procedure for bleeding air from the hydraulic brake system.

RED SEAL CERTIFICATION-TYPE QUESTIONS

1. What might cause a brake pedal to slowly sink to the floor?
    - **a.** Defective master cylinder
    - **b.** Brake shoes adjusted with too little clearance
    - **c.** Restricted vent port
    - **d.** Insufficient pedal free play
2. What might cause a vehicle to pull to the right during brake application?
    - **a.** Low brake fluid
    - **b.** Drum brake adjusted with less clearance on left rear wheel than on the right
    - **c.** Defective quick-take-up valve
    - **d.** Drum brake adjusted with less clearance on right rear wheel than on left
3. If the brake pedal linkage is not adjusted correctly, brake fluid may not be able to expand back into the reservoir through the _____ port of the master cylinder when the brakes get hot.
    - **a.** Vent port (forward hole)
    - **b.** Replenishing port (rearward hole)
4. How might an external brake fluid leak affect brake operation?
    - **a.** Pedal slowly sinks to the floor when pressed
    - **b.** Firm pedal but lower than normal brake pedal
    - **c.** Higher than normal brake pedal
    - **d.** No effect on brake operation
5. What might be the result if the rear brake drum-to-shoe clearance was excessive?
    - **a.** The pedal could travel too far before the vehicle starts to slow
    - **b.** Brake shoes could overheat
    - **c.** Brake fluid leak
    - **d.** Firmer and higher than normal brake pedal
6. What could cause the rear brakes to lock up when brakes are applied?
    - **a.** Fluid leak in the rear brake circuit
    - **b.** Seized front disc calipers
    - **c.** Emergency brake cables seized
    - **d.** Plugged vent port
7. What could air in the hydraulic circuit cause?
    - **a.** External fluid leak
    - **b.** Spongy brake pedal
    - **c.** Out-of-adjustment emergency brake
    - **d.** Brake drag
8. The button on the _____ valve should be held when bleeding the brakes.
    - **a.** Metering
    - **b.** Proportioning
    - **c.** Pressure-differential
    - **d.** Residual check
9. A double lap flare and an ISO flare are interchangeable.
    - **a.** True
    - **b.** False
10. The brake bleeding procedure usually specified for a rear-wheel vehicle with a dual split master cylinder is
    - **a.** RR, LR, RF, LF
    - **b.** LF, RF, LR, RR
    - **c.** RF, LR, LF, RR
    - **d.** LR, RR, LF, RF

34

Wheel Bearings and Service

OBJECTIVES: After studying Chapter 34, you should be able to:

1. Prepare for the interprovincial Red Seal certification examination in Appendix V (Brakes) on the topics covered in this chapter.
2. Discuss the various types, designs, and parts of automotive antifriction wheel bearings.
3. Describe the symptoms of defective wheel bearings.
4. Explain wheel bearing inspection procedures and causes of spalling and brinelling.
5. List the installation and adjustment procedures for front wheel bearings.
6. Explain how to inspect, service, and replace rear-wheel bearings and seals.

Bearings allow the wheels of a vehicle to rotate and still support the weight of the entire vehicle.

ANTIFRICTION BEARINGS

Antifriction bearings use rolling parts inside the bearing to reduce friction. Four styles of rolling contact bearings include ball, roller, needle, and tapered roller bearings as shown in Figure 34–1. All four styles convert sliding friction into rolling motion. All of the weight of a vehicle or load on the bearing is transferred through the rolling part. In a ball bearing, all of the load is concentrated into small spots where the ball contacts the **inner** and **outer race (rings).** See Figure 34–2. While ball bearings cannot support the same weight as roller bearings, there is less friction in ball bearings and they generally operate at higher speeds. A roller bearing, having a greater (longer) contact area, can support heavier loads than a ball bearing. See Figure 34–3. A needle bearing is a type of roller bearing that uses smaller rollers, called **needle rollers.** The clearance between the diameter of the ball or straight roller is manufactured into the bearing to provide the proper **radial clearance** and is *not adjustable.*

Figure 34–1 Rolling contact bearings include (left to right): ball, roller, needle, and tapered roller.

Tapered Roller Bearings

The most commonly used automotive wheel bearing is the tapered roller bearing. Not only is the bearing itself tapered, but the rollers are also tapered. By design, this type of bearing can withstand **radial** (up and down) as well as **axial** (thrust) loads in one direction. See Figure 34–4.

Most non-drive-wheel bearings use tapered roller bearings. The taper allows more weight to be handled by the friction-reducing bearings because

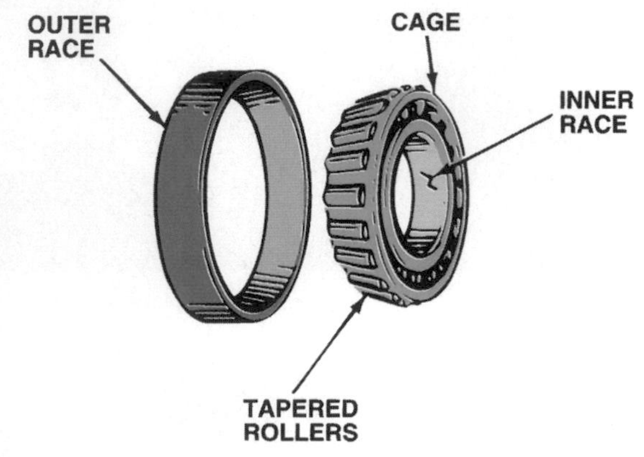

Figure 34–2 The tapered roller bearing is a common type of wheel bearing.

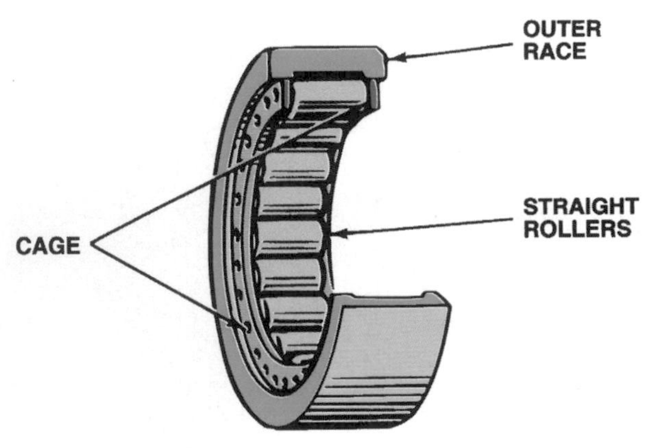

Figure 34–3 Straight roller bearings are used only on rear-drive axles.

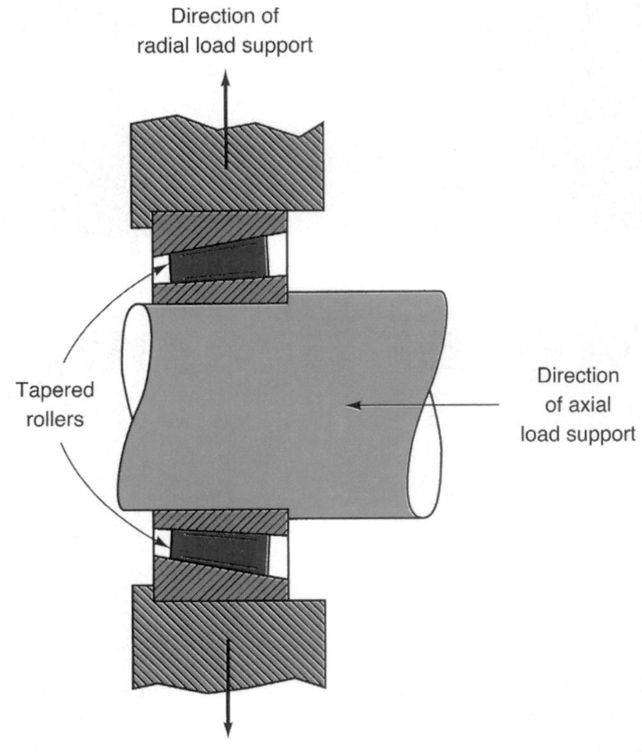

Figure 34–4 A tapered roller bearing will support a radial load and an axial load in only one direction.

the weight is directed over the entire length of each roller rather than concentrated on a small spot as with ball bearings. Because of the taper, these bearings are called tapered roller bearings. The rollers are held in place by a **cage** between the inner race (also called the **inner ring** or **cone**) and the outer race (also called the **outer ring** or **cup**). Tapered roller bearings must be loose in the cage to allow for heat expansion. Tapered roller bearings should always be adjusted for a certain amount of free play to allow for heat expansion. On non-drive-axle vehicle wheels, the cup is tightly fitted to the wheel hub and the cone is loosely fitted to the wheel spindle. New bearings come packaged with rollers, cage, and inner race all assembled with the outer race wrapped with moisture-resistant paper. See Figure 34–5.

Figure 34–5 Many tapered roller bearings use a plastic cage to retain the rollers.

Inner and Outer Wheel Bearings

Most rear-wheel-drive vehicles use an inner and an outer wheel bearing on the front wheels. The inner wheel bearing is always the larger bearing because

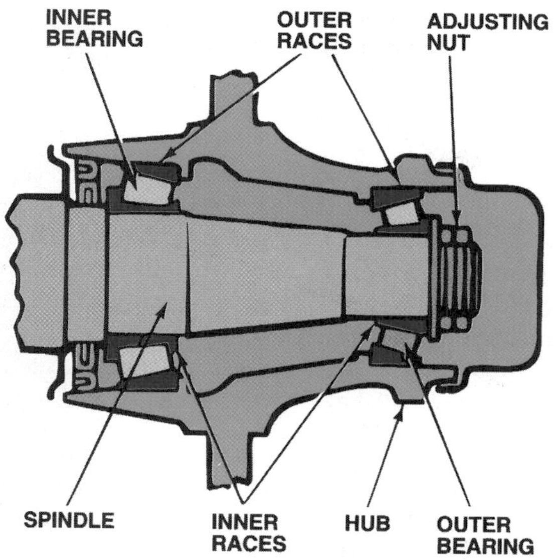

Figure 34–6 Tapered roller bearings are used in pairs for wheel bearing service.

it is designed to carry most of the vehicle weight and transmit the weight to the suspension and through to the spindle. See Figure 34–6. Between the inner wheel bearing and the spindle, there is a grease seal that prevents grease from getting onto the braking surface and dirt and moisture from entering the bearing.

Standard Bearing Sizes

Bearings use standard dimensions for inside diameter, widths, and outside diameter. The standardization of bearing sizes permits interchangeability. The dimensions that are standardized include bearing bore size (inside diameter), bearing series (light to heavy usage), and external dimensions. When replacing a wheel bearing, note the original bearing brand name and number. Replacement bearing catalogs usually have cross-over charts from one brand to another. The bearing number is usually the same because of the interchangeability and standardization within the wheel bearing industry.

Sealed Front-Wheel-Drive Bearings

Most front-wheel-drive (FWD) vehicles use a sealed, nonadjustable front wheel bearing. This type of bearing can include either two preloaded tapered roller bearings or a double-row ball bearing. Double row ball bearings are often used because of their reduced friction and greater seize resistance. This type of sealed bearing is also used on the rear of many front-wheel-drive vehicles. See Figures 34–7 and 34–8.

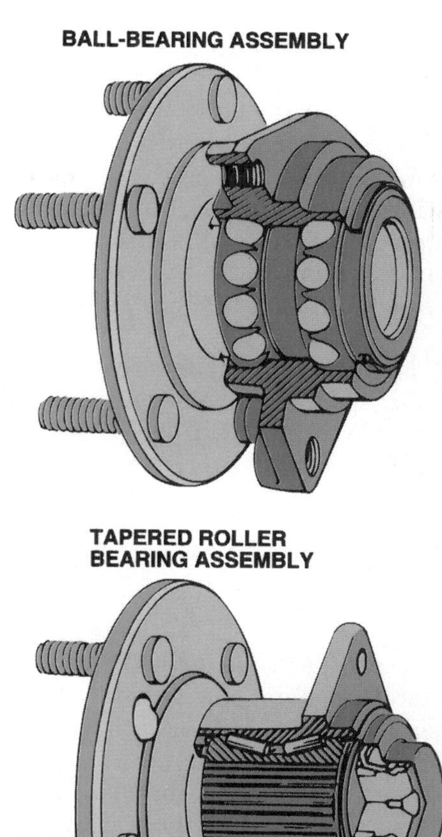

Figure 34–7 Sealed bearing and hub assemblies are used on the front and rear wheels of many vehicles.

Figure 34–8 Sealed bearing and hub assemblies are serviced as a complete unit as shown. This assembly includes the wheel speed sensor.

BEARING GREASES

Vehicle manufacturers specify the type and consistency of grease for each application. The technician should know what these specifications mean. Grease is an oil with a thickening agent to allow it to be installed in places where a liquid lubricant would not stay. Greases are named for their thickening agent, such as aluminum, barium, calcium, lithium, or sodium.

The **American Society for Testing Materials (ASTM)** specifies the consistency using a **penetration** test. The **National Lubricating Grease Institute (NLGI)** specifies grease by designation as to its use:

GC designation is acceptable for wheel bearings.

LB designation is acceptable for chassis lubrication.

Many greases are labelled with both GC and LB and are therefore acceptable for both wheel bearings and chassis use, such as in lubrication ball joints and tie rods. NLGI also uses the penetration test as a guide to assign the grease a number. Low numbers are very fluid and higher numbers are more firm. For example, a typical grease used for wheel bearings is labeled NLGI #2 6C. See the chart.

National Lubricating Grease Institute (NLGI) Numbers	
NLGI Number	**Relative Consistency**
000	Very fluid
00	Fluid
0	Semi-fluid
1	Very soft
2	Soft (typically used for wheel bearings.)
3	Semi-firm
4	Firm
5	Very firm
6	Hard

The Timken OK Load label is from a test that determines the maximum load the lubricant will carry. The OK Load is the maximum weight that can be applied without scoring on the test block.

More rolling bearings are destroyed by overlubrication than by under-lubrication because the heat generated in the bearings cannot be transferred easily to the air through the excessive grease. Bearings should never be filled beyond one-third to one-half of their grease capacity by volume. Molybdenum disulfide is added to grease in amounts up to 10% for use as a multipurpose lubrication on automotive equipment parts, such as chassis joints, steering joints, U-joints, and kingpins.

SAFETY TIP 

Smoking Can Kill You

Some greases contain polymers such as Teflon® that turn to a deadly gas when burned. Always wash your hands thoroughly after handling grease that contains these ingredients before smoking. If some of the grease is on the cigarette paper and is burned, these polymers turn into nitrofluoric acid—a deadly toxin.

SEALS

Seals are used in all vehicles to keep lubricant, such as grease, from leaking out and to prevent dirt, dust, or water from getting into the bearing or lubricant. Two general applications of seals include static and dynamic. **Static seals** are used between two surfaces that do not move. **Dynamic seals** are used to seal between two surfaces that move. Wheel bearing seals are dynamic-type seals that must seal between rotating axle hubs and the stationary spindles or axle housing. Most dynamic seals use a synthetic rubber lip seal encased in metal. The lip is often held in contact with the moving part with the aid of a **garter spring,** as seen in Figure 34–9. The sealing lip should be installed toward the grease or fluid being contained. See Figure 34–10.

Figure 34–9 Typical lip seal with a garter spring.

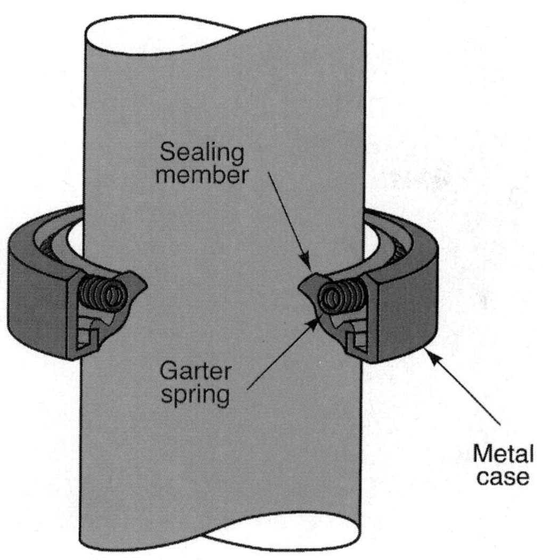

Figure 34–10 A garter spring helps hold the sharp lip edge of the seal tight against the shaft. (Courtesy of Dana Corporation)

SYMPTOMS AND DIAGNOSIS OF DEFECTIVE BEARINGS

Wheel bearings control the positioning and reduce the rolling resistance of vehicle wheels. Whenever a bearing fails, the wheel may not be kept in position and noise is usually heard. Symptoms of defective wheel bearings include:

1. A hum, rumbling, or growling noise that increases with vehicle speed

> **HINT:** A noisy bearing will often sound like noisy tires, such as aggressive mud and snow or off-road tires. Therefore, whenever you hear what sounds like a noisy tire, think of a wheel bearing as the cause. The sound a tire makes changes with different road surfaces, whereas the sound a wheel bearing makes remains the same regardless of road surfaces.

2. Roughness felt in the steering wheel that changes with the vehicle speed or cornering
3. Looseness or excessive play in the steering wheel, especially while driving over rough road surfaces
4. In severe cases, a loud grinding noise, indicating a defective front wheel bearing
5. Pulling during braking
6. Bearing roughness, heard and felt when, with the vehicle off the ground, rotating the wheel by hand.
7. Bearing looseness felt when grasping the wheel at the top and bottom and wiggling it back and forth.

TECH TIP

Watch Out for Bearing Overload

It is not uncommon for vehicles to be overloaded. This is particularly common with pickup trucks and vans. Whenever there is a heavy load, the axle bearings must support the entire weight of the vehicle including its cargo. If a bump is hit while driving with a heavy load, the balls of a ball bearing or the rollers of a roller bearing can make an indent in the race of the bearing. This dent or imprint is called **brinelling,** named after Johann A. Brinell, a Swedish engineer, who developed a process of testing for surface hardness by pressing a hard ball with a standard force into a sample of material to be tested.

Once this imprint is made, the bearing will make noise whenever the roller or ball rolls over the indent. Continued use causes wear to occur on all of the balls or rollers and eventual failure. While failure may take months, the *cause* of the bearing failure is often overloading of the vehicle. Avoid shock loads and overloading for safety and for longer vehicle life.

> **NOTE:** Excessive looseness in the wheel bearings can cause a low brake pedal.

If any of the symptoms above are present, carefully clean and inspect the bearings.

NON-DRIVE WHEEL BEARING INSPECTION AND SERVICE

1. Hoist the vehicle safely.
2. Remove the wheel.
3. Remove the brake caliper assembly and support it with a coat hanger or other suitable hook to avoid allowing the caliper to hang by the brake hose.
4. Remove the grease cap (dust cap). See Figure 34–11.
5. Remove the old cotter key and discard.

> **NOTE:** The term "cotter" as in *cotter key* or *cotter pin* is derived from the old English verb meaning "to close or fasten."

6. Remove the spindle nut (castle nut).
7. Remove the washer and the outer wheel bearing. See Figure 34–12.
8. Remove the bearing hub from the spindle. The inner bearing will remain in the hub and may be

Figure 34–11 Removing the grease cap with grease-cap pliers.

Figure 34–12 After wiggling the brake rotor slightly, the washer and outer bearing can be easily lifted out of the wheel hub.

removed (simply lifted out) after the grease seal is pried out. See Figure 34–13.

9. Most vehicle and bearing manufacturers recommend cleaning the bearing thoroughly in solvent or acetone. If there is no acetone, clean the solvent off the bearings with denatured alcohol to make certain that the thin solvent layer is completely washed off and dry. *All solvent must be removed or allowed to dry from the bearing because the new grease will not stick to a layer of solvent.*
10. Carefully inspect the bearings and the races for the following:
    a. The cage for roundness. If the round cage has straight sections, this is an indication of an over-tightened adjustment or that the cage has been dropped. See Figure 34–14. If any of the above are observed, then the bearing, including the outer race, must be replaced. Failure to replace the outer race (which is included when purchasing a bearing) could lead to rapid failure of the new bearing.

Figure 34–13 Some technicians remove the inner wheel bearing and the grease seal at the same time by jerking the rotor off the spindle after reinstalling the spindle nut. While this is a quick-and-easy method, sometimes the bearing is damaged (deformed) from being jerked out of the hub using this procedure.

Figure 34–14 This bearing should be replaced because it has been dropped or damaged and the cage is distorted.

Figure 34–15 Thoroughly clean and inspect the outer race before installing the wheel bearing.

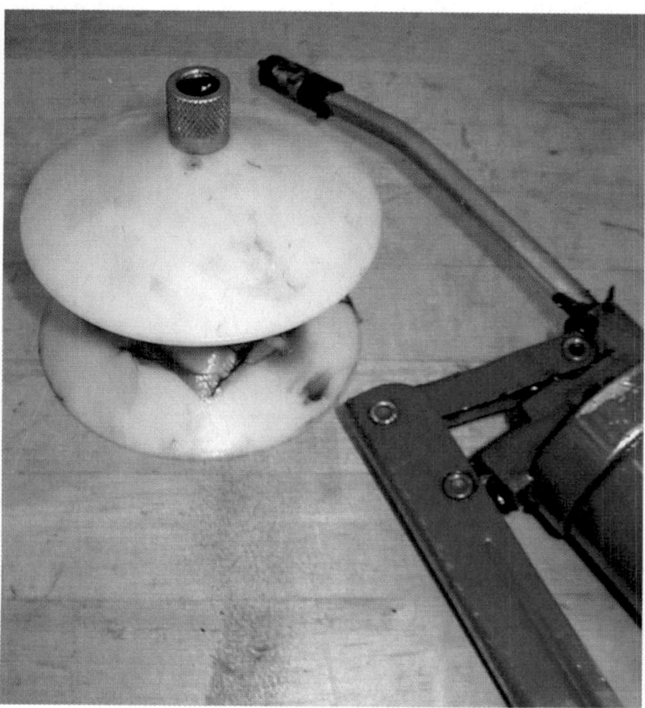

Figure 34–16 A typical wheel-bearing packer. A hand-operated grease gun is used to inject grease between the cones of the packer and into the bearing.

b. The outer race for lines, scratches, or pits. See Figure 34–15.

11. Pack the cleaned or new bearing thoroughly with clean, new, approved wheel-bearing grease using hand packing or a wheel-bearing packer. Always clean out all of the old grease before applying the recommended type of new grease. *Because of compatibility problems, it is not recommended that greases be mixed.* See Figure 34–16.

Figure 34–17 Installing a grease seal with a special tool after installing the inner bearing.

NOTE: Some vehicle manufacturers do *not* recommend that "stringy-type" wheel-bearing grease be used. Centrifugal force can cause the grease to be thrown outward from the bearing. Because of the stringy texture, the grease may not flow back into the bearing after it has been thrown outward. The final result is lack of lubrication and eventual bearing failure.

12. Place a thin layer of grease on the outer race.
13. Apply a thin layer of grease to the spindle, being sure to cover the outer bearing seat, inner bearing seat, and shoulder at the grease seal seat.
14. Install a new **grease seal** (also called a **grease retainer**) flush with the hub using a grease seal installation tool as shown in Figure 34–17.
15. Place approximately 45 mL (3 tablespoons) of grease into the grease cavity of the wheel hub. Excessive grease could cause the inner grease seal to fail with the possibility of grease getting on the brakes. Place the rotor with the inner

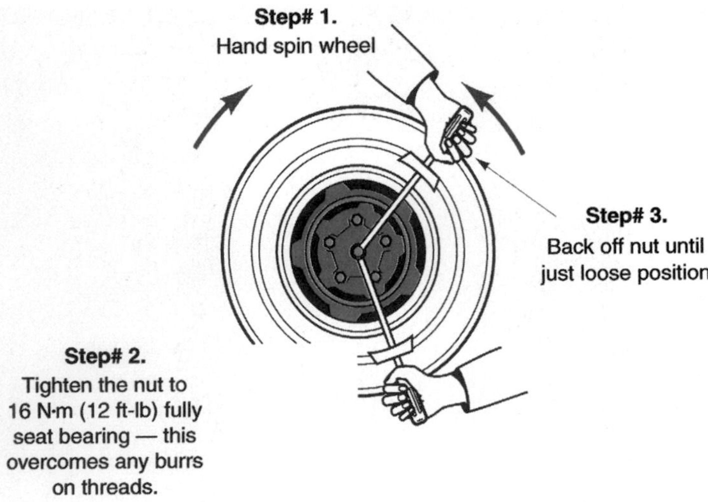

Step# 1.
Hand spin wheel
Step# 3.
Back off nut until just loose position
Step# 2.
Tighten the nut to 16 N·m (12 ft-lb) fully seat bearing — this overcomes any burrs on threads.

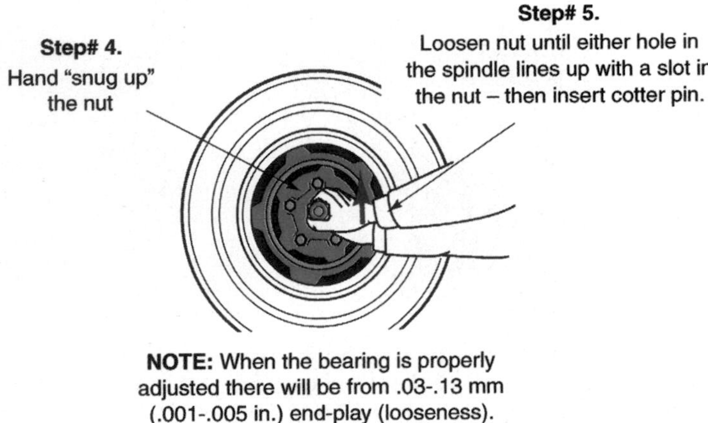

Step# 4.
Hand "snug up" the nut
Step# 5.
Loosen nut until either hole in the spindle lines up with a slot in the nut – then insert cotter pin.
NOTE: When the bearing is properly adjusted there will be from .03-.13 mm (.001-.005 in.) end-play (looseness).

Figure 34–18 The wheel bearing adjustment procedure as specified for rear-wheel-drive General Motors vehicles. (Courtesy of General Motors Service Technology Group)

bearing and seal in place over the spindle until the grease seal rests on the grease seal shoulder.

16. Install the outer bearing and the bearing washer.
17. Install the spindle nut, and while rotating the tire assembly, tighten to about 16–40 N·m (12–30 lb.-ft.) with a wrench to "seat" the bearing correctly in the race (cup) and on the spindle. See Figure 34–18.
18. While still rotating the tire assembly, loosen the nut approximately one-half turn and then *hand tighten only* (about 0.6 N·m or 5 in.-lb.).

NOTE: If the wheel bearing is properly adjusted, the wheel will still have about 0.03 to 0.13 mm (0.001 to 0.005 in.) end play. This looseness is necessary to allow the tapered roller bearing to expand when hot and not bind or cause the wheel to lock up.

19. Install a new cotter key. (An old cotter key could break a part off where it was bent and lodge in the bearing, causing major damage.)

HINT: Most vehicles use a cotter key that is 3 mm (1/8″) in diameter by 38 mm (1 1/2″) long. If the cotter key does not line up with the hole in the spindle, loosen slightly (no more than 1/16 of a turn) until the hole lines up. *Never tighten more than hand tight.*

20. Bend the cotter key ends up and around the nut, not over the end of the spindle where the end of the cotter key could rub on the grease cap, causing noise. See Figure 34–19.
21. Install the grease cap (dust cap) and the wheel cover.

CAUTION: Clean grease off disc brake rotors or drums after servicing the wheel bearings. Use a brake cleaner and a rag. Even a slight amount of grease on the friction surfaces of the brakes can harm the friction lining and/or cause brake noise.

TECH TIP 

Wheel Bearing Looseness Test

Looseness in a front-wheel bearing can allow the rotor to move whenever the front wheel hits a bump, forcing the caliper piston in, and the brake pedal to kick back, causing the feeling that the brakes are locking up.

Loose wheel bearings are easily diagnosed by removing the cover of the master cylinder reservoir and watching the brake fluid as the front wheels are turned left and right with the steering wheel. If the brake fluid moves while the front wheels are being turned, caliper piston(s) are moving in and out because of loose wheel bearing(s). If everything is OK, the brake fluid should not move.

Figure 34–19 Properly installed cotter key.

FRONT-WHEEL-DRIVE SEALED BEARING REPLACEMENT

Most front-wheel drive vehicles use a sealed bearing assembly that is bolted to the steering knuckle and supports the drive axle. This design incorporates a splined drive hub that transfers power from the drive axle to the wheels that are bolted to the hub. See Figures 34–20 and 34–21. Many front-wheel-drive vehicles use a bearing that must be pressed off the steering knuckle. Special aftermarket tools are

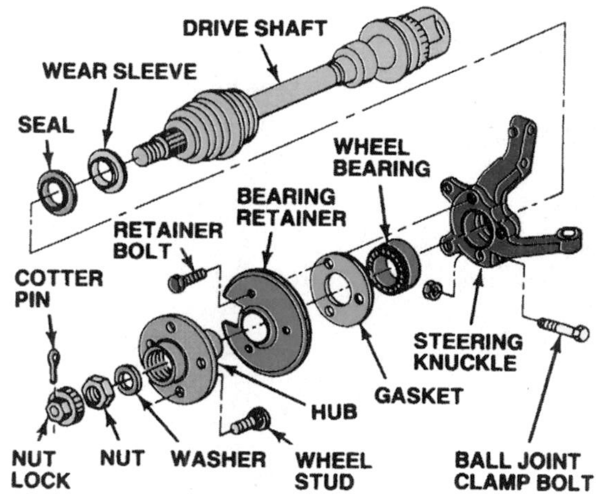

Figure 34–20 A typical sealed wheel bearing assembly.

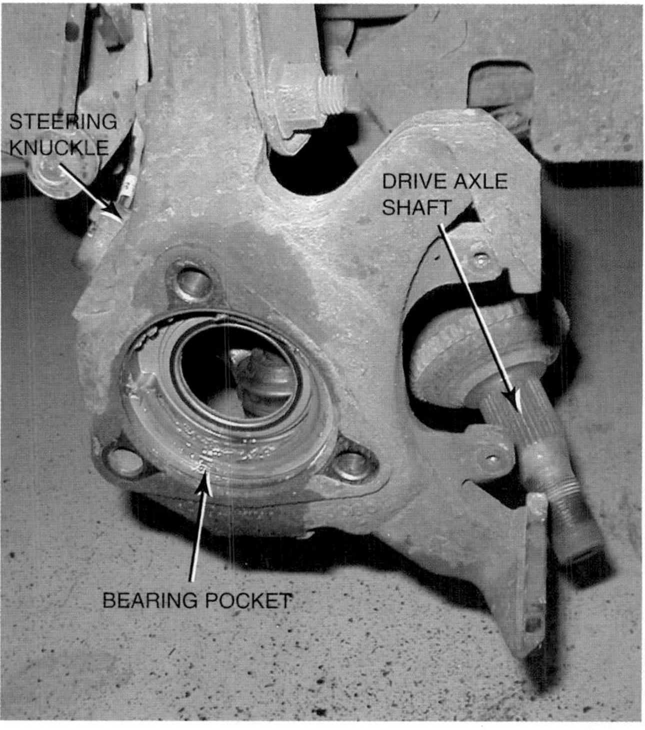

Figure 34–21 A steering knuckle with the sealed bearing-hub assembly removed.

also available to remove many of the bearings without removing the knuckle from the vehicle. Check the factory service manual and tool manufacturers for exact procedures for the vehicle being serviced.

Diagnosing a defective front bearing on a front-wheel-drive vehicle is sometimes confusing. A defective wheel bearing is usually noisy while driving straight, and the noise increases with vehicle speed (wheel speed). A drive axle shaft U-joint (CV joint) can also be the cause of noise on a front-wheel-drive vehicle but usually makes *more noise* while turning and accelerating. See Chapter 46 for further CV joint analysis.

REAR AXLE BEARING AND SEAL REPLACEMENT

The rear bearings used on rear-wheel-drive vehicles are constructed and serviced differently from other types of wheel bearings. Rear-axle bearings are either sealed or lubricated by the rear-end lubricant. The rear axle must be removed from the vehicle to replace the rear-axle bearing. There are two basic types of axle retaining methods, **retainer plate-type** and the **C-lock.**

The retainer plate-type rear axle uses four fasteners that retain the axle in the axle housing. To remove the axle shaft and the rear axle bearing and seal, the retainer bolts or nuts must be removed.

HINT: If the axle flange has an access hole, then a retainer plate-type axle is used. See Figure 34–22.

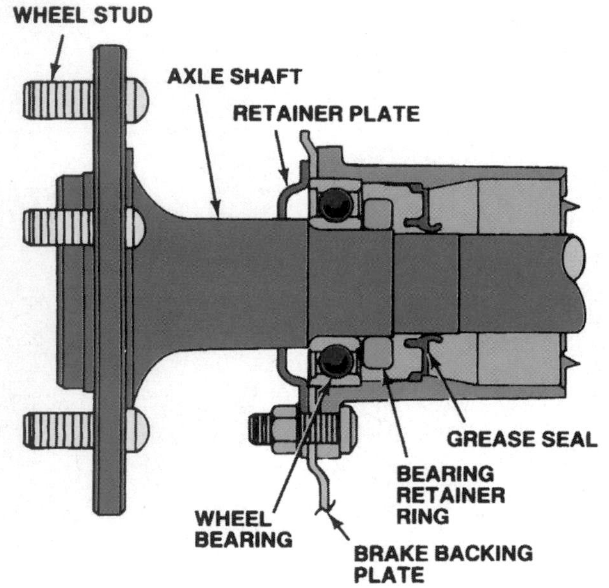

Figure 34–22 A typical retainer-plate-type rear axle.

TECH TIP

The Brake Drum Slide-Hammer Trick

To remove the axle from a vehicle equipped with a retainer-plate-type rear axle, simply use the brake drum as a slide hammer to remove the axle from the axle housing. See Figure 34–23. If the brake drum does not provide enough force, a slide hammer can also be used to remove the axle shaft.

The hole or holes in the wheel flange permit a socket wrench access to the fasteners. After the fasteners have been removed, the axle shaft must be removed from the rear-axle housing. With the retainer-plate-type rear axle, the bearing and the retaining ring are press fit onto the axle, and the bearing cup (outer race) is also a tight fit into the axle housing tube.

Vehicles that use C-clips use a straight roller bearing supporting a semi-floating axle shaft inside the axle housing. The straight rollers do not have an inner race. The rollers ride on the axle itself. If a bearing fails, both the axle and the bearing usually need to be replaced. The outer bearing race holding the rollers is pressed into the rear axle housing. The axle bearing is usually lubricated by the rear-end lubricant and a grease seal is located on the outside of the bearing.

NOTE: Some replacement bearings are available that are designed to ride on a fresh, unworn section of the old axle. These bearings allow the use of the original axle, saving the cost of a replacement axle.

The C-clip-type rear axle retaining method requires that the differential cover plate be removed. See Figure 34–24. After removal of the cover, the differential pinion shaft has to be removed before the C-clip that retains the axle can be removed. See Figure 34–25.

NOTE: When removing the differential cover, rear-axle lubricant will flow from between the housing and the cover. Be sure to dispose of the old rear-axle lubricant in the environmentally approved way, and refill with the proper type and viscosity (thickness) of rear-end lubricant. Check the vehicle specifications for the recommended grade.

Once the C-clip has been removed, the axle is simply pulled out of the axle tube. Axle bearings with inner races are pressed onto the axle shaft and

(a)

(b)

Figure 34–23 (a) To remove the axle from this vehicle equipped with a retainer plate-type rear axle, the brake drum was placed back onto the axle studs backwards so that the drum itself can be used as a slide hammer to pull the axle out of the axle housing. (b) A couple of pulls and the rear axle is pulled out of the axle housing.

Figure 34–24 The C-clip (C washer) can be seen after removing the differential cover plate. The C-clip fits into a groove in the axle.

(a)

(c)

(b)

Figure 34–25 (a) Removing the pinion-shaft lock bolt. (b) After the lock bolt has been removed, the pinion shaft can be removed. (c) The axle can be pushed inward slightly to allow the C-clip to be removed. After the C-clip has been removed, the axle can be easily pulled out of the axle housing.

must be pressed off using a hydraulic press. A bearing retaining collar should be chiselled or drilled into to expand the collar to allow it to be removed. See Figure 34–26.

Always follow the manufacturer's recommended bearing removal and replacement procedures. Always

What's That Sound?

Defective wheel bearings usually make noise. The noise most defective wheel bearings make sounds like noisy *winter tires.* Wheel-bearing noise will remain constant while driving over different types of road surfaces, while tire-tread noise usually changes with different road surfaces. In fact, many defective bearings have been ignored by vehicle owners and technicians because they thought that the source of the noise was the aggressive tread design of the mud and snow tires. Always suspect defective wheel bearings whenever you hear what seems to be extreme or unusually loud tire noise.

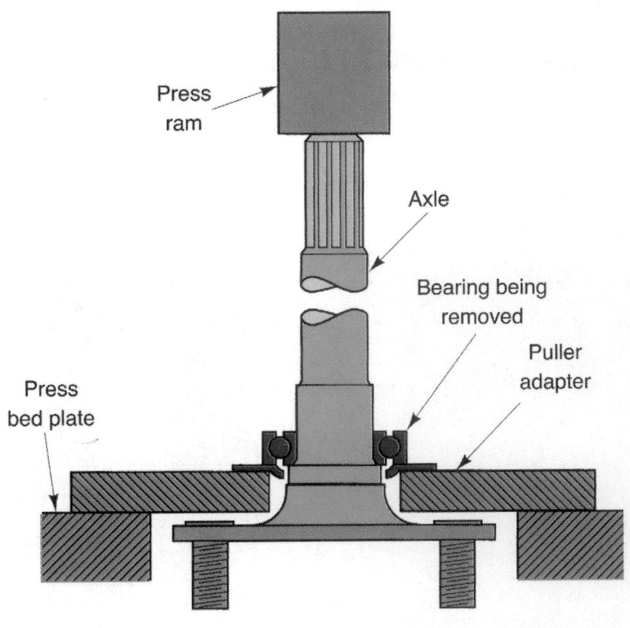

Figure 34–26 Using a hydraulic press to press an axle bearing from the axle. When pressing a new bearing back onto the axle, pressure should only be on the inner bearing race to prevent damaging the bearing.

replace the rear-axle seal whenever replacing a rear-axle bearing. See Figure 34–27 for an example of seal removal.

See Figure 34–28 for an example of a rear-axle bearing with a broken outer race.

When refilling the differential, check for a tag or lettering as to the correct lubricant. Always check the differential vent to make sure it is clear. A clogged vent can cause excessive pressure to build up inside the differential and cause the rear-axle seals to leak. If rear-end lubricant gets on the brake linings, the brakes will not have the proper friction and the linings themselves will be ruined and must be replaced.

BEARING FAILURE ANALYSIS

Whenever a bearing is replaced, the old bearing must be inspected and the cause of the failure eliminated. See Figures 34–29 through 34–37 for examples of normal and abnormal bearing wear.

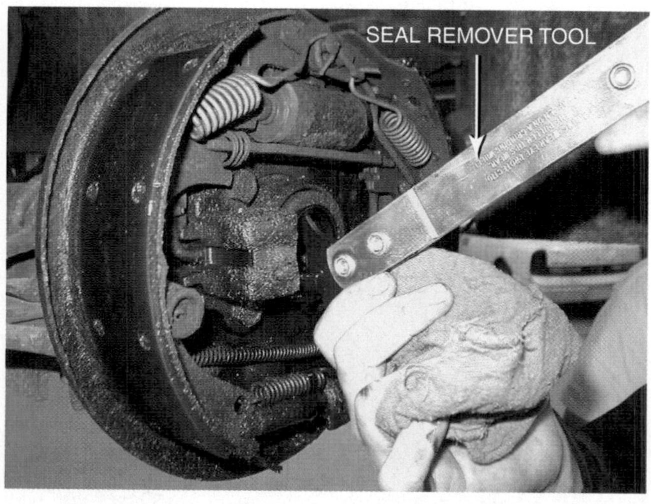

Figure 34–27 Using a grease seal remover tool to remove a seal from the rear axle housing.

Figure 34–28 This axle bearing came from a high-mileage vehicle. Noise was first noticed when turning because weight transfer increased the load on the bearing. Later, a rumbling sound occurred all the time, increasing in noise level as the vehicle speed increased.

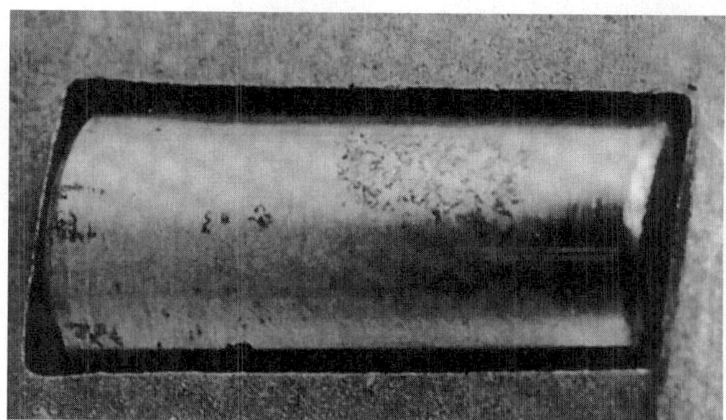

(a)

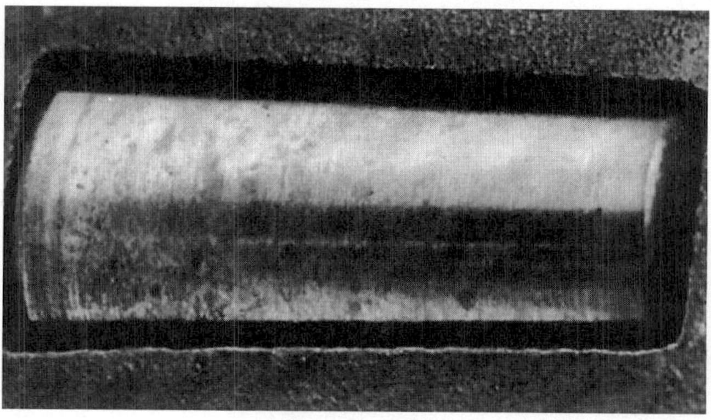

(b)

Figure 34–29 (a) When corrosion etches into the surface of a roller or race, the bearing should be discarded. (b) If light corrosion stains can be removed with an oil-soaked cloth, the bearing can be reused. (Courtesy of SKF, USA, Inc.)

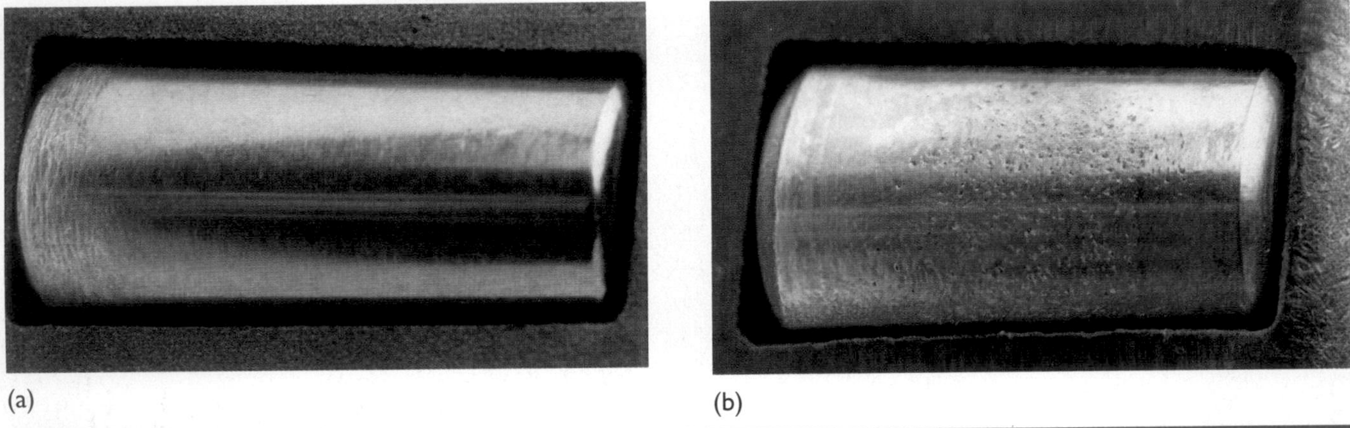
(a) (b)

Figure 34–30 (a) When just the end of a roller is scored, it is because of excessive preload. Discard the bearing. (b) This is a more advanced case of pitting. Under load, it will rapidly lead to spalling. (Courtesy of SKF, USA, Inc.)

(a) (b)

Figure 34–31 (a) Always check for faint grooves in the race. This bearing should not be reused. (b) Grooves like this are often matched by grooves in the race (above). Discard the bearing. (Courtesy of SKF, USA, Inc.)

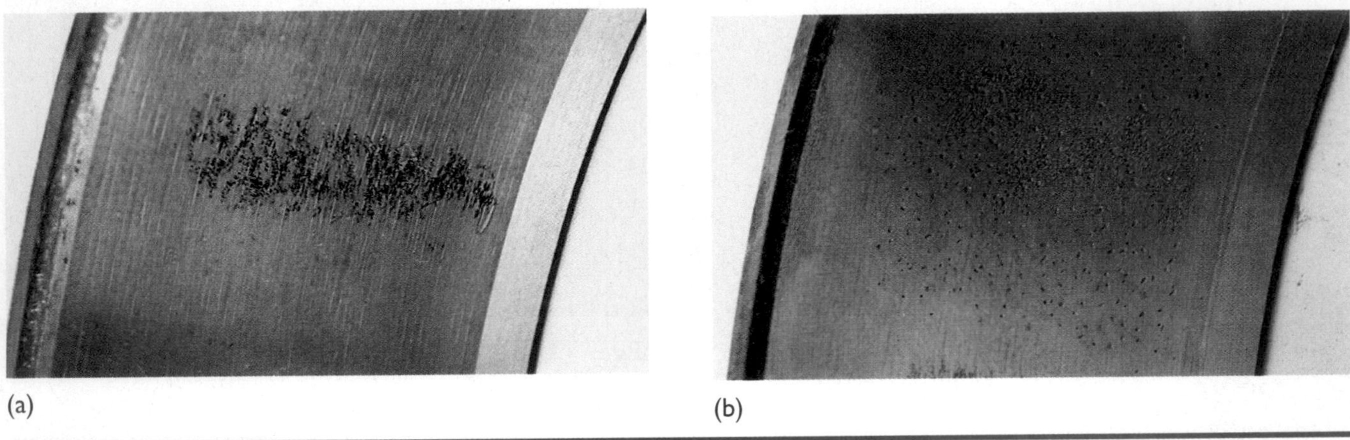
(a) (b)

Figure 34–32 (a) Regular patterns of etching in the race are from corrosion. This bearing should be replaced. (b) Light pitting comes from contaminants being pressed into the race. Discard the bearing. (Courtesy of SKF, USA, Inc.)

(a) (b)

Figure 34–33 (a) This bearing is worn unevenly. Notice the stripes. It should not be reused. (b) Any damage that causes low spots in the metal renders the bearing useless. (Courtesy of SKF, USA, Inc.)

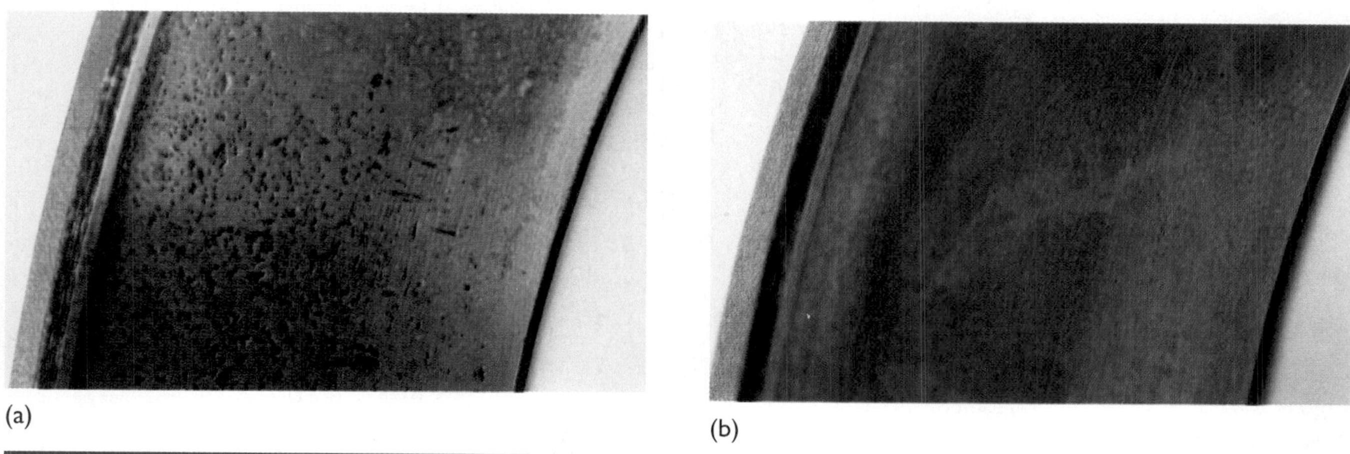
(a) (b)

Figure 34–34 (a) In this more advanced case of pitting, you can see how the race has been damaged. (b) Discolouration is a result of overheating. Even a lightly burned bearing should be replaced. (Courtesy of SKF, USA, Inc.)

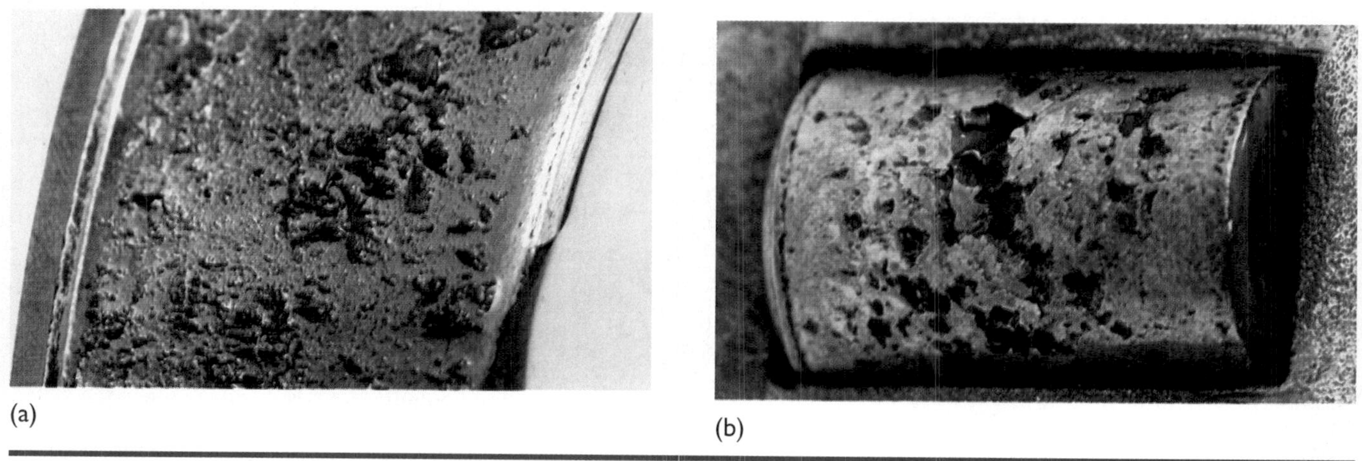
(a) (b)

Figure 34–35 (a) Pitting eventually leads to spalling, a condition where the metal falls away in large chunks. (b) In this spalled roller, the metal has actually begun to flake away from the surface. (Courtesy of SKF, USA, Inc.)

Figure 34–36 These dents result from the rollers hammering against the race, a condition called brinelling. (Courtesy of SKF, USA, Inc.)

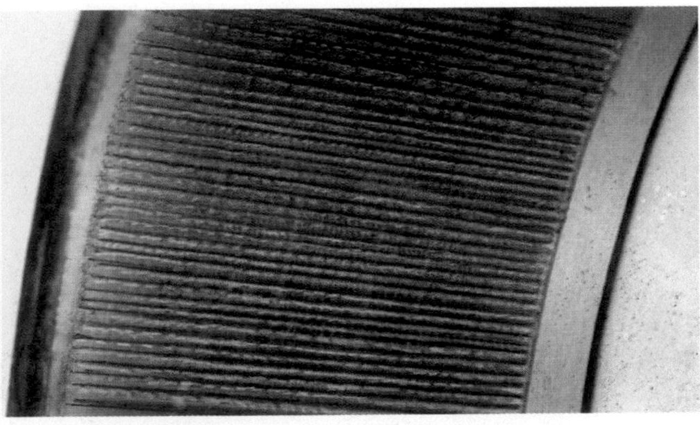

Figure 34–37 This condition results from an improperly grounded arc welder. Replace the bearing. (Courtesy of SKF, USA, Inc.)

SUMMARY

1. Wheel bearings support the entire weight of a vehicle and are used to reduce rolling friction.
2. Ball and straight roller-type bearings are nonadjustable, while tapered roller-type bearings must be adjusted for proper clearance.
3. Most front-wheel-drive vehicles use sealed bearings, either two preloaded, tapered roller bearings or double-row ball bearings.
4. Most wheel bearings have standardized sizes.
5. A defective bearing can be caused by metal fatigue that leads to spalling or by shock loads that cause brinelling, or by bearing damage from electrical arcing due to poor body ground wires or improper electrical welding on the vehicle.
6. Bearing grease is an oil with a thickener. The higher the NLGI number of the grease, the thicker or harder the grease consistency.
7. Tapered wheel bearings must be adjusted by hand-tightening the spindle nut after properly seating the bearings. A new cotter key must always be used.
8. Defective wheel bearings usually make more noise while turning because more weight is applied to the bearing as the vehicle turns.
9. All bearings must be serviced, replaced, and/or adjusted using the vehicle manufacturer's recommended procedures as stated in the service manual.

REVIEW QUESTIONS

1. List three common types of automotive anti-friction bearings.
2. Explain the adjustment procedure for a typical tapered roller wheel bearing.
3. List four symptoms of a defective wheel bearing.
4. Describe how the rear axle is removed from a C-clip-type axle.

RED SEAL CERTIFICATION-TYPE QUESTIONS

1. Which type of automotive bearing can withstand radial and thrust loads, yet must be adjusted for proper clearance?
   - **a.** Roller bearing
   - **b.** Tapered roller bearing
   - **c.** Ball bearings
   - **d.** Needle roller bearing
2. Most sealed bearings used on the front wheels of front-wheel drive vehicles are usually which type?
   - **a.** Roller bearing
   - **b.** Single tapered roller bearing
   - **c.** Double-row ball bearing
   - **d.** Needle roller bearing
3. On a bearing that has been shock loaded, the race (cup) of the bearing can be dented. This type of bearing failure is called
   - **a.** Spalling
   - **b.** Arcing
   - **c.** Brinelling
   - **d.** Fluting
4. The bearing grease most often specified is rated NLGI
   - **a.** #00
   - **b.** #0
   - **c.** #1
   - **d.** #2
5. A non-drive-wheel-bearing adjustment procedure includes a final spindle nut tightening torque of
   - **a.** Finger tight
   - **b.** 0.6 N·m (5 in.-lb.)
   - **c.** 16–40 N·m (12–30 lb.-ft.)
   - **d.** 14–20 N·m (10–15-lb.-ft. plus 1/16 turn)

6. After a non-drive-wheel-bearing has been properly adjusted, the wheel should have how much end play?
   a. 0
   b. 0.03 to 0.13 mm (0.001 to 0.005 in.)
   c. 0.25 to 0.75 mm (0.10 to 0.30 in.)
   d. 1.6 to 2.4 mm (1/16″–3/32″)
7. The differential cover must be removed before removing the rear axle on which type of axle?
   a. Retainer plate
   b. C-clip
   c. Press fit
   d. Welded tube
8. What part *must* be replaced when servicing a wheel bearing on a non-drive wheel?
   a. The bearing cup
   b. The grease seal
   c. The cotter key
   d. The retainer washer
9. Axle grease seals can be removed ____________.
   a. Before the axle is removed
   b. With a hammer and chisel
   c. Using a grease seal removal tool
   d. Seals are never removed
10. A defective wheel bearing usually sounds like
   a. Marbles in a tin can
   b. A noisy tire
   c. A baby rattle
   d. A clicking sound—like a ball-point pen

35

Drum Brake Operation, Diagnosis, and Service

OBJECTIVES: After studying Chapter 35, you should be able to:

1. Prepare for the interprovincial Red Seal certification examination in Appendix V (Brakes) on the topics covered in this chapter.
2. Identify drum brake component parts.
3. Describe the operation of dual-servo and leading-trailing brakes.
4. Discuss the procedure recommended for brake drum removal.
5. Discuss the inspection and lubrication points of the backing plate.
6. Explain the importance of proper drum-brake hardware.
7. Disassemble and reassemble a drum-brake assembly.
8. Properly adjust a parking brake.

Drum brakes were the first type of brakes used on motor vehicles. Even today, over 100 years after the first horseless carriages, drum brakes are still used on the rear of many vehicles, as shown in Figure 35–1.

DRUM BRAKE PARTS

Drum brakes use two **brake shoes** mounted on a stationary **backing (back) plate** (also called a **support plate**). See Figures 35–2 and 35–3. Hydraulic force from the master cylinder to the **wheel cylinder** pushes brake shoes against the rotating drum, as shown in Figure 35–4.

Dual Servo (DUO Servo) Drum Brakes

Drum brakes use outward expanding brake shoes that contact the rotating brake drum when the driver depresses the brake pedal. Since the wheels of the vehicle are attached to the drums, the wheels also slow and stop when the brakes are applied. Because of the curved surface of the brake lining and the rotating brake drum, a wedging action occurs whenever the brakes are applied. This action is called **self-energizing** and increases the amount of force applied to the drums beyond that provided by hydraulic pressure alone. During braking, the primary lining wedges into the drum and tends to pivot in the direction of rotation. This movement is transmitted through a lower connecting link to the secondary lining, which is forced into the drum with even greater force. This type of braking action is called servo-self-energizing or **Dual-Servo** or **Duo-Servo.** (Duo-Servo is a trade name of the Bendix Corporation.) See Figures 35–5, 35–6, and 35–7. This self-energizing effect depends on the free movement of the linings against the backing plate. This is the reason the rear (secondary) lining is usually longer and made from a different mix of materials—to be able to handle the greater forces and heat.

Leading-Trailing Drum Brakes

In a leading-trailing-type drum brake system, the forward shoe is held stationary at the bottom and pushed against the drum by the wheel cylinder at the top. As the drum rotates, this leading shoe is pulled tighter into the drum and tends to rotate with the drum. But, because the shoe is anchored at the

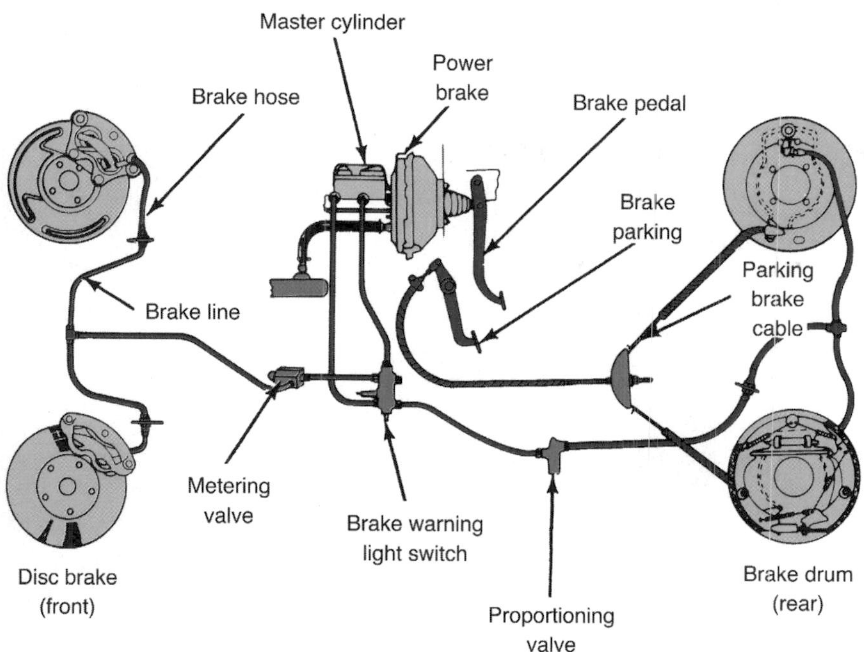

Figure 35–1 Typical brake system components showing disc brakes on the front and drum brakes on the rear. (Courtesy of Chrysler Corporation)

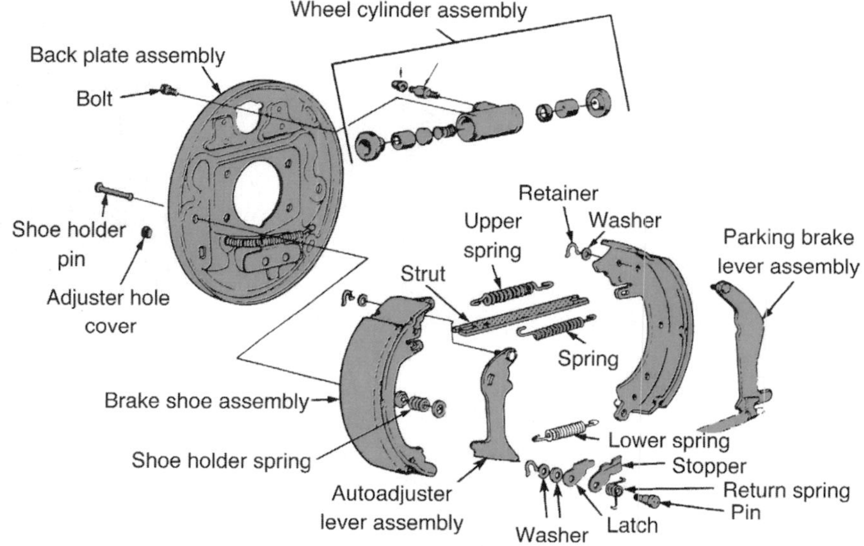

Figure 35–2 Exploded view of a typical drum brake, showing all parts. (Courtesy of Allied Signal Automotive Aftermarket)

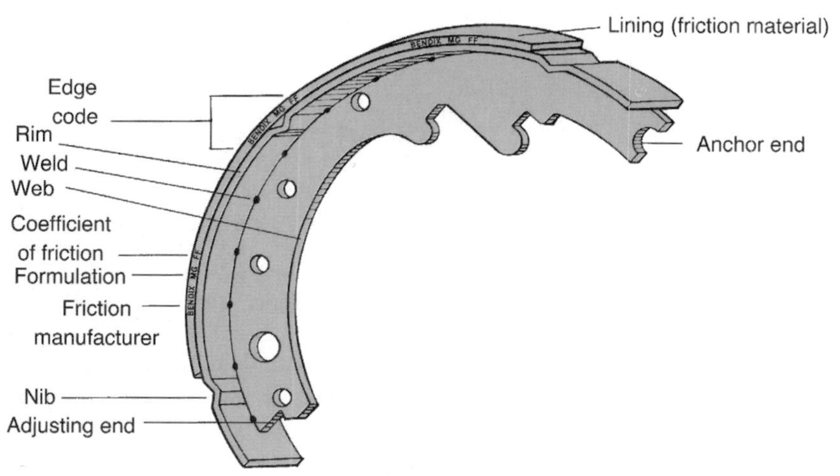

Figure 35–3 Typical drum brake shoe and the names of the parts. (Courtesy of Allied Signal Automotive Aftermarket)

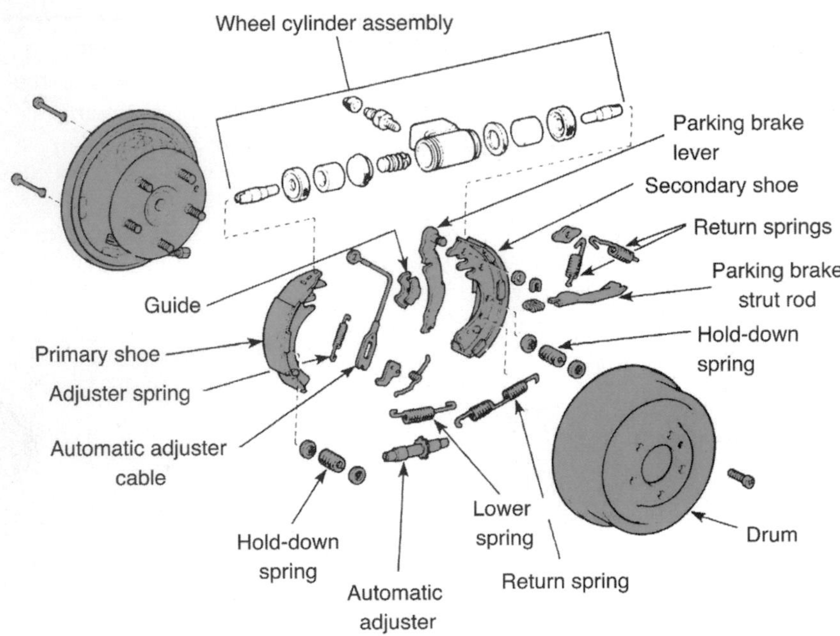

Figure 35–4 The drum rotates with the wheels. The brake shoes are attached to the vehicle. When the brake shoes expand outward, friction between the brake shoes and the rotating brake drum slows and stops the wheels. (Courtesy of Allied Signal Automotive Aftermarket)

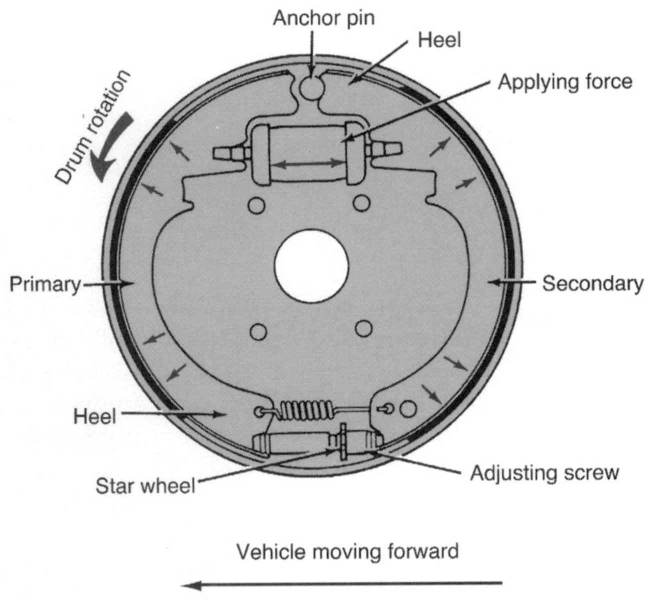

Figure 35–5 The rotation of the brake drum causes the curved brake shoe to wedge tighter into the drum. (Courtesy of Chrysler Corporation)

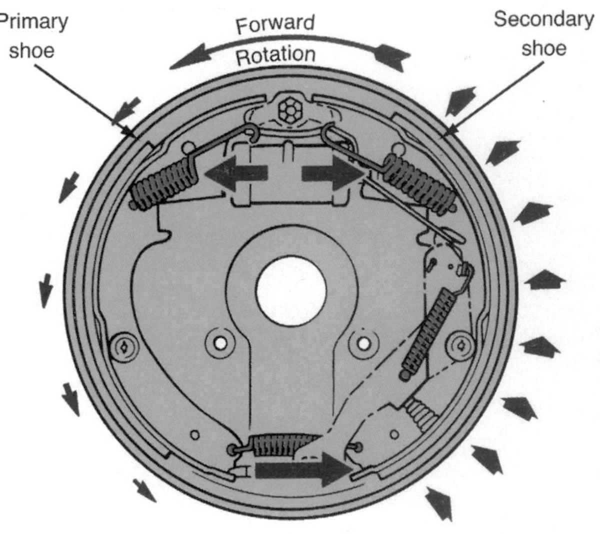

Figure 35–6 The primary shoe on the left exerts a force on the secondary shoe on the right.

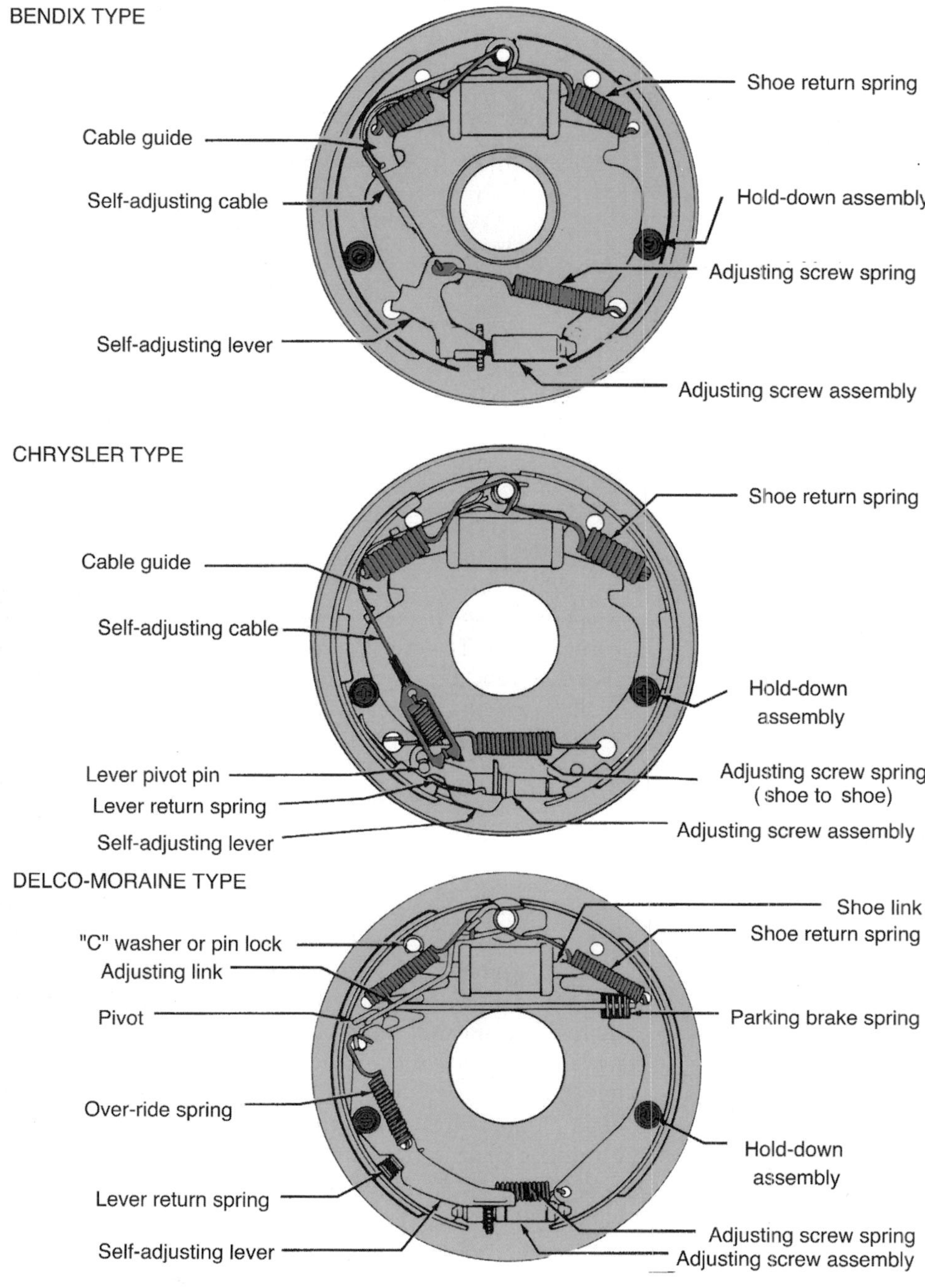

Figure 35–7 Typical drum brake assemblies. (Courtesy of Cooper Automotive Company)

bottom, the shoe simply wedges itself into the drum. This **leading shoe** is also called the **forward shoe** or the **energized shoe.** See Figure 35–8.

The **trailing shoe** is attached to the backing plate at the leading end of the shoe and pushed against the drum at the trailing end of the shoe. When the wheel cylinder pushes against the trailing shoe, the drum rotation tends to push the shoe away from the drum, reducing the application pressure. The trailing shoe is also called the **de-energized shoe** or the **reverse shoe.** Leading-trailing drum brakes are also called a **nonservo** brake.

BRAKE DRUM REMOVAL

The drum has to be removed before an inspection or repair of the drum brake can start. There are two basic types of drums, and the removal procedure depends on which type is being serviced. With either

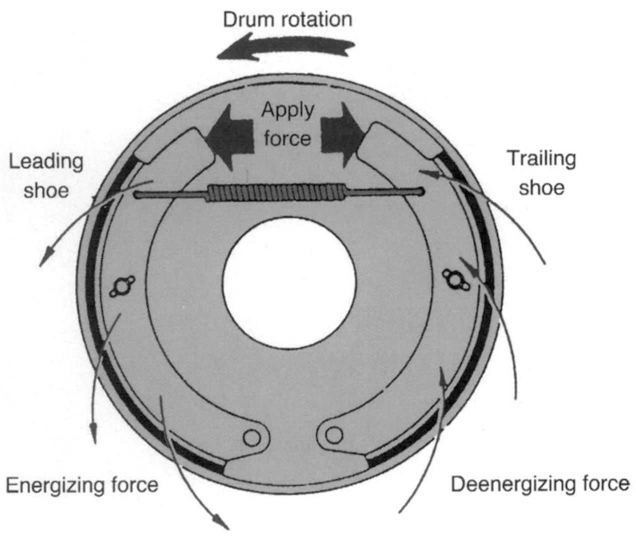

Figure 35–8 A leading-trailing design drum brake uses two brake shoes, but both are the same length and are not connected. The applying force is provided by the wheel cylinder.

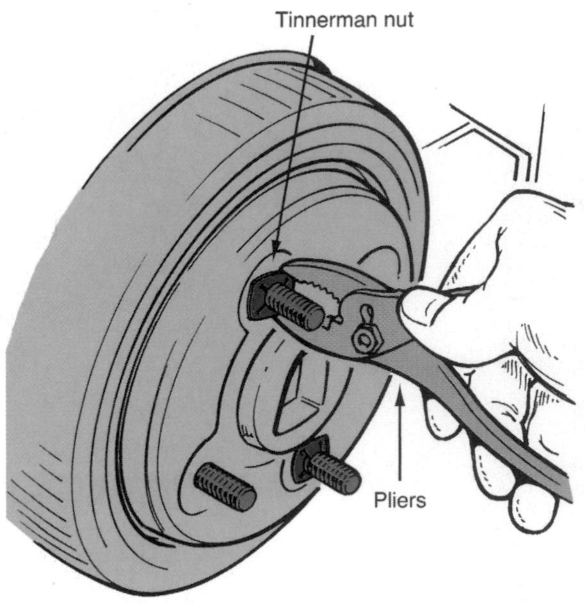

Figure 35–9 Tinnerman nuts are used at the vehicle assembly plant to prevent the brake drum from falling off until the wheels can be installed. These sheet-metal retainers can be discarded after removal.

type, it is usually recommended that the drums be marked with an "L" for left or an "R" for right so they can be replaced in the same location.

CAUTION: Proper precaution should be taken to prevent any asbestos that may be present in the brake system from becoming airborne. Removal of the brake drum should occur inside a sealed vacuum enclosure equipped with a HEPA filter, or the drum brake should be washed with water or solvent.

Hub or Fixed Drums

A fixed or hub-mounted drum is often used on the rear of front-wheel-drive vehicles. The drum has a hub for inner and outer bearings and is retained by a spindle nut. To remove the brake drum, remove the dust cap and cotter key that is used to retain the spindle nut. Remove the spindle nut and washer and then the brake drum can be carefully pulled off the spindle.

See Chapter 34 for details on wheel bearings, grease, and bearing adjustment.

Hubless or Floating Drums

Floating or hubless drums are usually used on the rear of a rear-wheel-drive vehicle. The drums are secured to the axle flange by the wheel and lug nuts. After the wheel has been removed, the drum *should* simply pull off over the wheel studs. New vehicles have **tinnerman nuts (clips),** also called **speed nuts,** installed on the stud when the vehicle is being assembled. These thin sheet-metal nuts keep the brake drum from falling off during shipping and handling prior to the installation of the rear wheels. See Figure 35–9. These tinnerman nuts can be discarded because they are not needed after the vehicle leaves the assembly plant. After removing the wheels, the drum *should* move freely on the hub and slip off over the brake shoes. Some brake drums have two threaded holes in the drum that allow bolts to be installed. See Figure 35–10. By tightening the bolts, the drum is forced off of the hub.

HINT: Rust and corrosion often cause the drum to seize to the hub. Striking the area inside the wheel studs will usually "break loose" the drum from the hub. An air hammer with a flat-headed driver used against the hub also works well to break loose the drum from the hub. Use caution not to distort the drum.

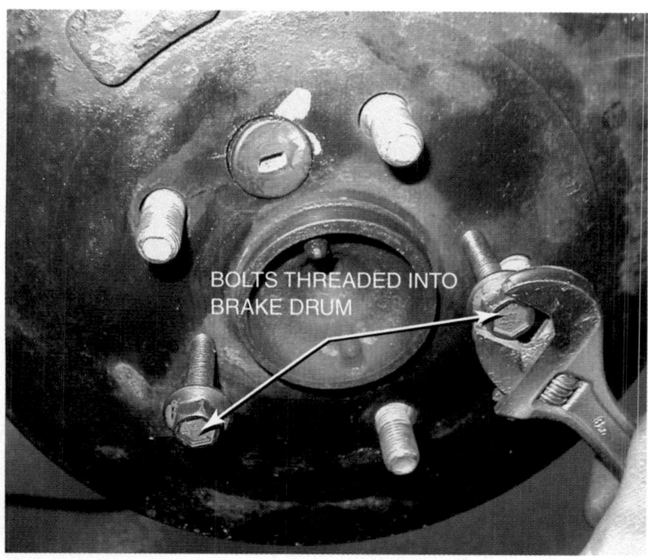

Figure 35–10 Turning the bolts that are threaded into the brake drum forces the drum off the hub.

Even if the pilot hole is loose, many brake drums cannot be removed because the inner edge of the brake drum catches on the lining. Pulling outward on the drum often bends the backing plate or breaks some of the mounting hardware. To prevent damage, remove the adjuster plug from the backing plate or drum and back off the adjuster. See Figure 35–11.

NOTE: Be sure to reinstall the adjuster opening plugs. These plugs help keep water and debris out of the brakes.

TECH TIP

Cutting the Nails Trick

Many times a brake drum cannot be removed because the linings have worn a groove into the drum. Attempting to adjust the brakes inward is often a frustrating and time-consuming operation. The easy solution is to use a pair of diagonal side-cut pliers and cut the heads off the hold-down pins (nails) at the backing plate. This releases the brake shoes from the backing plate and allows enough movement of the shoes to permit the removal of the brake drum without bending the backing plate.

The hold-down pins (nails) must obviously be replaced, but they are included in most drum brake hardware kits. Since most brake experts recommend replacing all drum brake hardware anyway, this solution does not cost any more money than normal and may save the backing plate from damage and the service technician lots of time. See Figure 35–12.

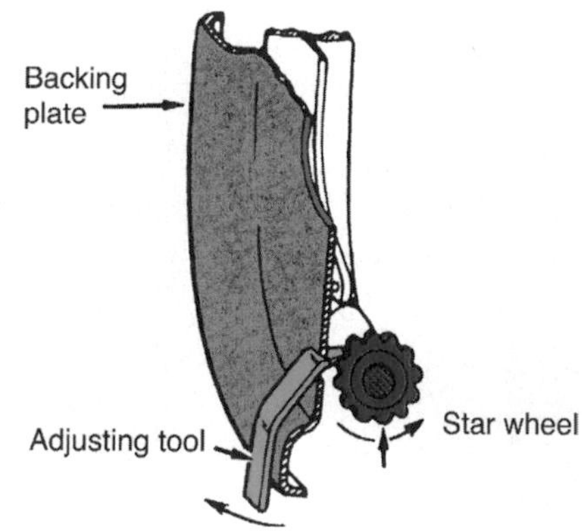

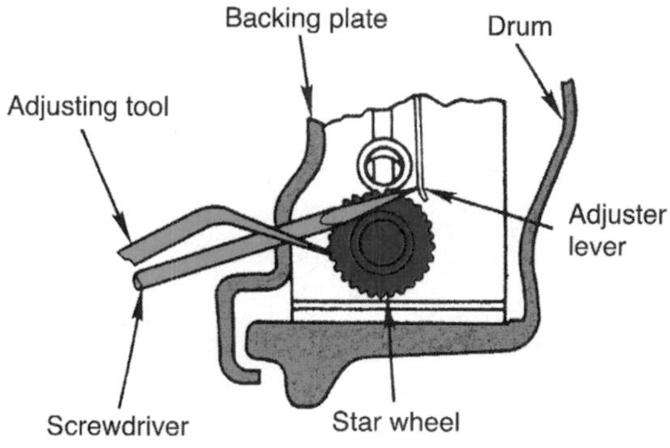

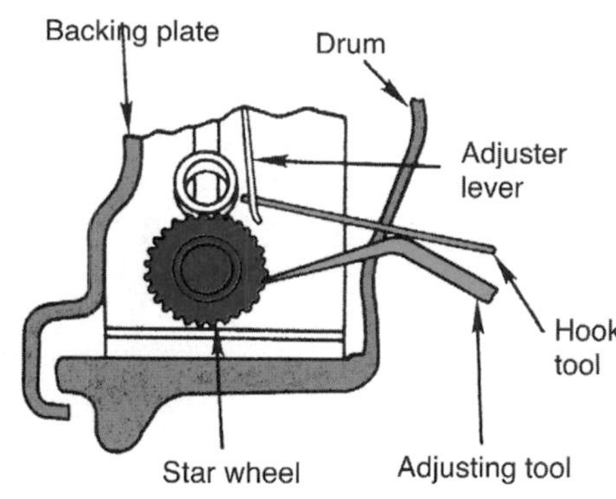

Figure 35–11 If the brake shoes have worn into the brake drum, the adjuster can be backed in after removing the access plug. Often, the plug is an outline on the brake drum that must be knocked out. After removing the plug, use another wire or screwdriver to move the adjusting lever away from the star wheel, then turn the star wheel with a brake adjusting tool, often called a brake spoon. (Courtesy of Allied Signal Automotive Aftermarket)

After removing the brake drums, they should be cleaned, inspected, measured, and possibly machined before being returned to service. See Chapter 37 for measuring and machining procedures.

Figure 35–12 Using side-cut pliers to cut the heads off the hold-down spring pins (nails) from the backing plate to release the broken drum from the shoes.

Figure 35–13 All brakes should be moistened with solvent or disassembled in an approved enclosure to prevent possible asbestos dust from becoming airborne.

DRUM BRAKE DISASSEMBLY AND INSPECTION

After removal of the brake drum, the brake shoes and other brake hardware should be wetted down with a solvent or enclosed in an approved evacuation system to prevent possible asbestos release into the air. Usually the first step in the disassembly of a drum brake system is the removal of the return (retracting) springs. See Figure 35–13. After the return springs have been removed, the hold-down springs and the other brake hardware can be removed. See Figures 35–14 and 35–15.

NOTE: There are generally no "exact" disassembly or reassembly procedures specified by the manufacturer. The order for the parts to be disassembled or reinstalled is based on experience and personal preference of the technician. A good hint is to leave one side assembled while servicing the other.

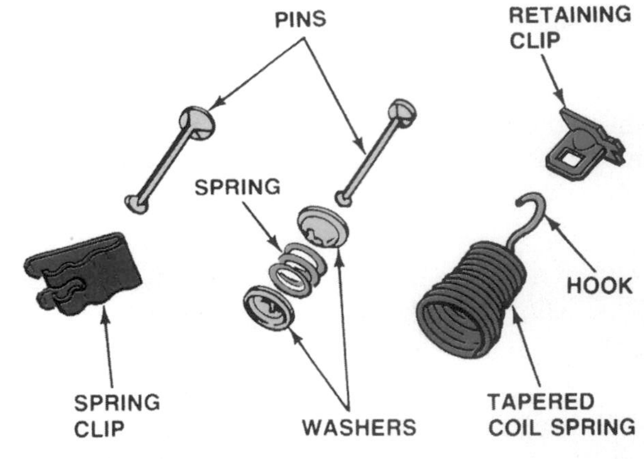

Figure 35–14 Brake shoe hold-down springs come in a variety of styles and shapes.

When brakes are serviced, the six raised contact surfaces, called **pads, ledges,** or **shoe contact area,** of the backing plate should be inspected because they rub against the sides of the shoes. See Figure 35–16. If the pads are worn more than 1.5 mm (1/16″), the backing plate should be replaced. The raised pads should be cleaned and lubricated. See Figures 35–17 and 35–18. **Silicone brake grease, lithium high temperature brake grease, synthetic brake grease,** or **antiseize lubricant** can be used to lubricate drum brake parts.

Both primary (front-facing) and secondary (rear-facing) lining material must be thicker than 1.5 mm (0.060 in.).

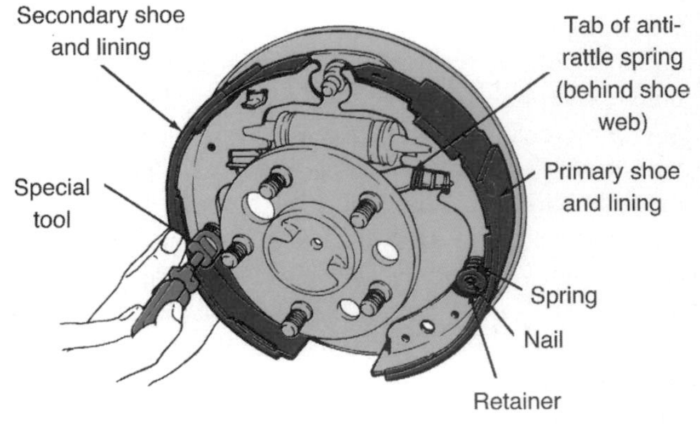

Figure 35–15 A special tool called a hold-down spring tool being used to depress and rotate the retainer. (Courtesy of Chrysler Corporation)

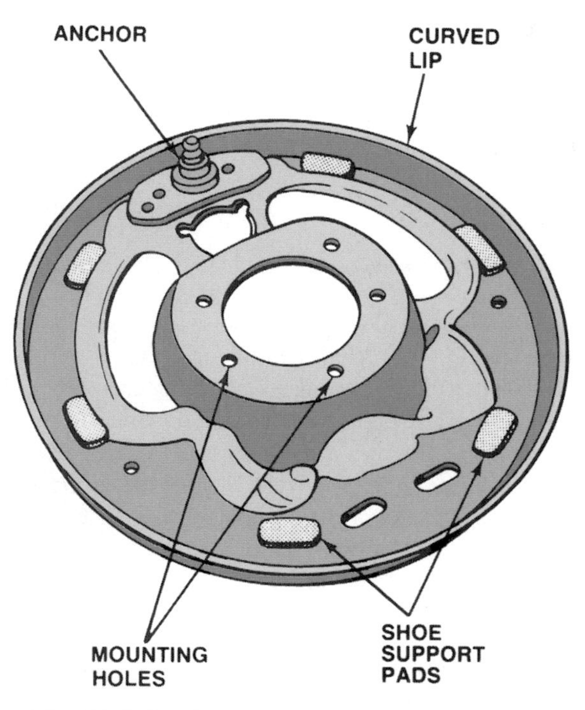

Figure 35–16 Most drum brakes use six shoe contact pads or ledges.

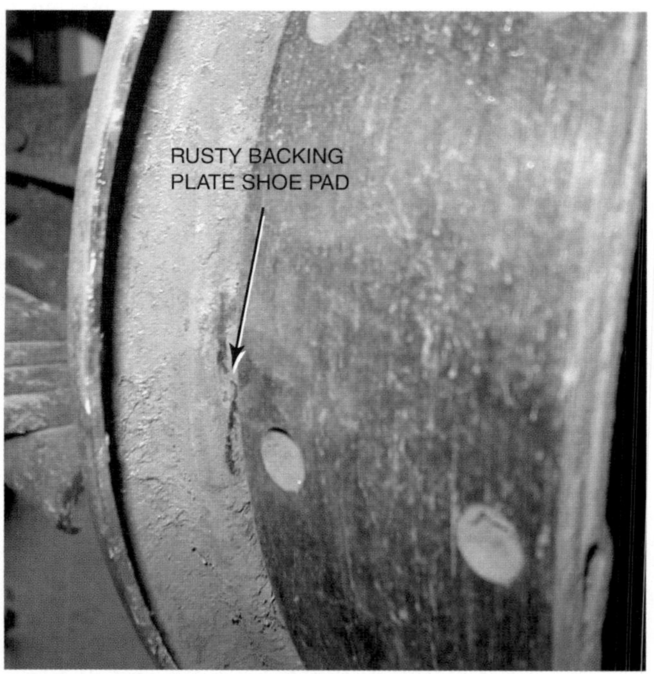

Figure 35–17 A typical rusting backing plate shoe pad. This can cause the brakes to squeak when the shoes move outward during a brake application and again when the brake pedal is released.

Figure 35–18 Lithium high-temperature brake grease is used by many service technicians to lubricate metal-to-metal contact surfaces of a drum brake. A small metal-handled acid brush is stuck through a hole cut into the lid of this container of grease to make the application of grease easy and less messy. Avoid using too much grease. Excessive grease can get onto the friction surfaces of the brake shoes or drum and affect braking performance.

TECH TIP 

A Nickel's Worth of Lining

Most vehicle manufacturers recommend replacing the brake lining when its thickness reaches 1.5 mm (0.060 in.). This measurement should be determined using a micrometer or vernier caliper. A quick way to guide yourself, as a technician, is to compare the brake lining thickness with the thickness of a nickel coin, which is about 1.5 mm thick—hence the phrase "a nickel's worth of lining".

The lining must be replaced if cracked as shown in Figure 35–19.

CAUTION: Be sure to place old worn brake shoes back into the replacement brake shoe box. The old shoes (called a **core**) should be returned to the parts store, which will send them to be relined with new brake friction material. The box helps prevent any brake dust from being released into the air.

Return Spring Inspection

Each lining has a return spring (retracting spring), which returns the brake shoes back from the drums

Figure 35–19 Cracked brake lining must be replaced.

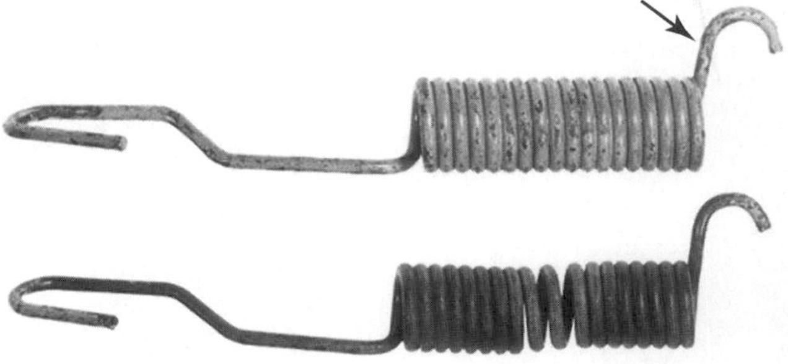

Figure 35–20 The top spring is a good looking spring because all coils of the spring are touching each other. The bottom spring is stretched and should be discarded. The arrow points to the back side of the spring that goes into a hole in the brake shoe. The open loop of the spring is not strong enough to keep from straightening out during use. Using the back side of the hook provides a strong, long-lasting hold in the brake shoe.

TECH TIP 

The Drop Test

Brake return (retracting) springs can be tested by dropping them to the floor. A good spring should thud when the spring hits the ground. This noise indicates that the spring has not been stretched and that all coils of the springs are touching each other. If the spring "rings" when dropped, the spring should be replaced because the coils are not touching each other. See Figure 35–20.

While this drop test is often used, many experts recommend *replacing* all brake springs every time the brake linings are replaced. Heat generated by the brake system often weakens springs enough to affect their ability to retract brake shoes, especially when hot, yet they may not ring when dropped.

whenever the brakes are released. The springs are called the **primary return spring** and **secondary return spring.** The primary return spring attaches to the primary brake shoe and the secondary return spring attaches to the secondary brake shoe. These springs should be tested prior to a brake overhaul and especially when uneven lining wear is discovered.

Some drum brakes use a spring that connects the primary and secondary shoes, commonly called a **shoe-to-shoe spring.** Some of these springs will be on solid pieces of spring steel bent in the shape of a U. Return springs can get weak due to heat and time and can cause the linings to remain in contact with the drum. See Tech Tip "The Drop Test" for one testing method.

Hold-Down Springs

Hold-down springs (one on each shoe) are springs used with a retainer and a hold-down **spring pin** (or **nail**) to keep the linings on the backing plate. Other types of hold-down springs include U-shape, flat-spring-steel-type, and the combination return and hold spring. These springs still permit the freedom of movement necessary for proper braking operation.

Self-Adjusting Mechanisms

In the early 1960s, vehicle manufacturers began adding self-adjusting parts to drum brakes. The first to introduce self-adjusting brakes was Ford, who used an adjusting cable attached to the anchor pin going to an adjusting lever over a cable guide. See Figure 35–21. The operation of the adjusting lever on the star-wheel adjuster occurs when applying the brakes while driving in reverse. See Figures 35–22 and 35–23. Because of the free movement built into drum brakes, the forces that cause the servo-self-energizing action cause the secondary lining to be-

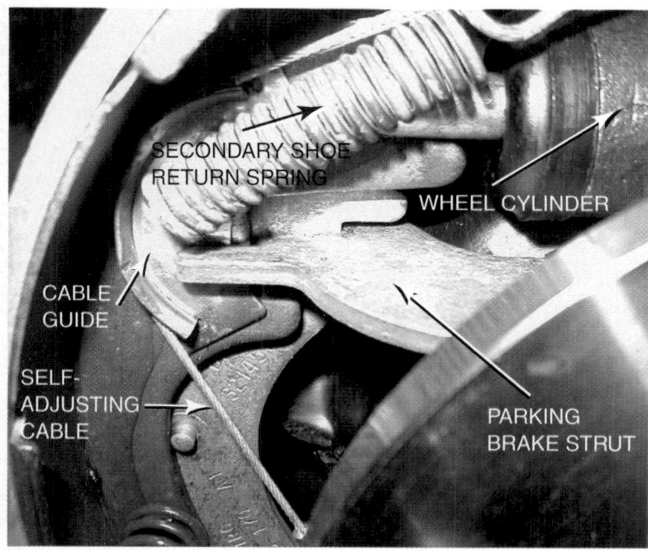

Figure 35–21 Close-up view of an adjuster cable and cable guide.

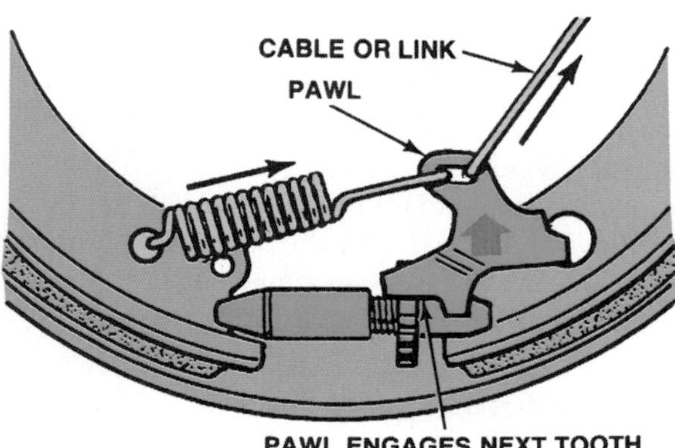

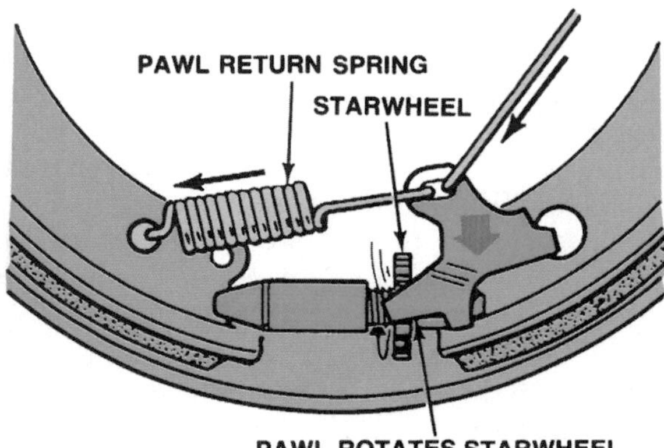

Figure 35–22 This self-adjusting mechanism operates only when the brake pedal is depressed while travelling in reverse. If the secondary brake shoe travels far enough, the adjusting lever is raised up enough to cause the star wheel to move when the brake pedal is released.

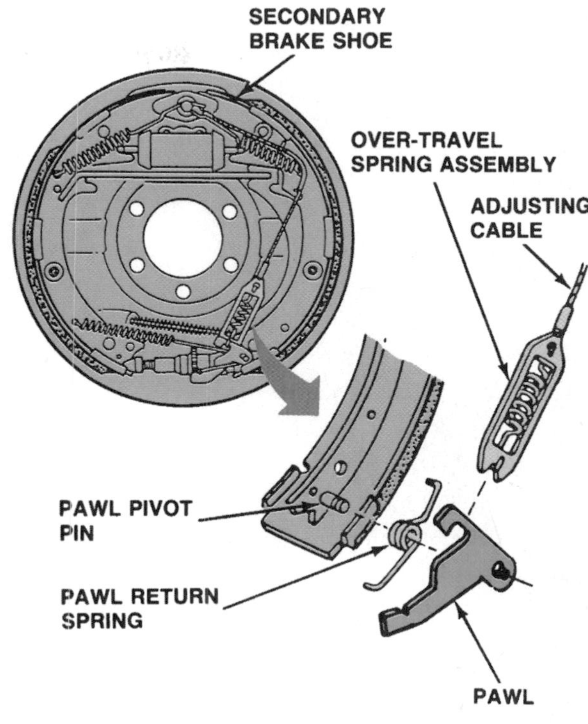

Figure 35–23 A cable-actuated star-wheel automatic adjuster equipped with an over-travel spring.

come the primary lining in reverse gear, which causes the rotation of the linings. This action pulls on the adjusting lever and, upon release of the brakes, causes this lever to move one tooth of the star-wheel adjuster if there is enough movement (slack) to need adjustment. Some details of and precautions for self-adjusting brakes include:

- Self-adjusting brakes will only adjust if there is enough clearance between the lining and the drum to require adjustment.
- The star-wheel adjusters are threaded for left- or right-side operation. Make certain that the correct-side star-wheel adjuster is always used. If the incorrect star wheel is used, the brakes would tend to adjust inward rather than outward toward the drum.
- Self-adjusting parts can be purchased individually or in a self-adjusting kit that includes all self-adjuster parts. The star-wheel adjuster can be purchased separately. The star-wheel adjuster should be replaced if the points of the star wheel are rounded. When purchasing self-adjusting parts, you must specify left (driver's side) or right (passenger's side). See Figures 35–24 and 35–25.
- Be careful backing up when drums are hot. Hot drums have expanded outward and the self-adjusting mechanism will try to adjust to this larger drum if the brakes are applied several

Figure 35–24 This star-wheel adjuster is damaged and must be replaced. A lack of proper lubrication can cause the star wheel to become frozen in one place and not adjust properly.

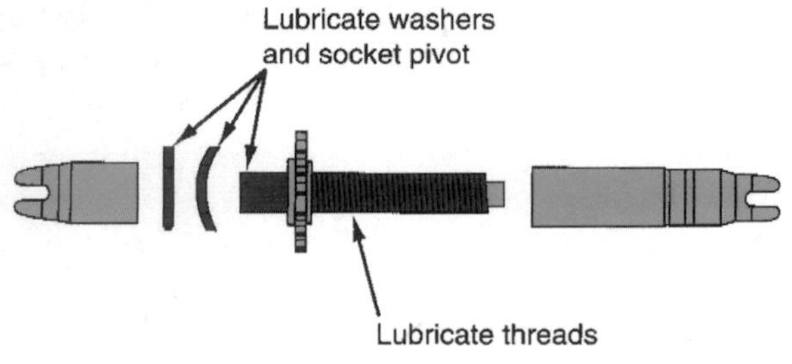

Figure 35–25 Star-wheel adjusters are designed with left- and right-handed threads. They are not interchangeable from side to side! Using an adjuster on the wrong side of the vehicle would cause the brake to self-adjust inward (farther from the brake drum) instead of closer to the brake drum. The wavy washer acts on the flat thrust washer to help prevent noise. The threads and end caps should be cleaned and lubricated before reuse.

times. This could overadjust the brakes and cause a lock-up situation after the drums have cooled.

- Some drum brakes do not use a cable to operate their self-adjusters, but rather a steel lever called the **activating lever,** which is connected to the anchor pin by the actuator link and adjusts the steering wheel adjusting screw by an adjusting lever called a **pawl.**
- Some manufacturers use the parking brake as the self-adjusting mechanism. Whenever the parking brake is used, a lever or a ratchet mechanism works to maintain the proper brake-shoe-to-brake-drum clearance to compensate for wear.

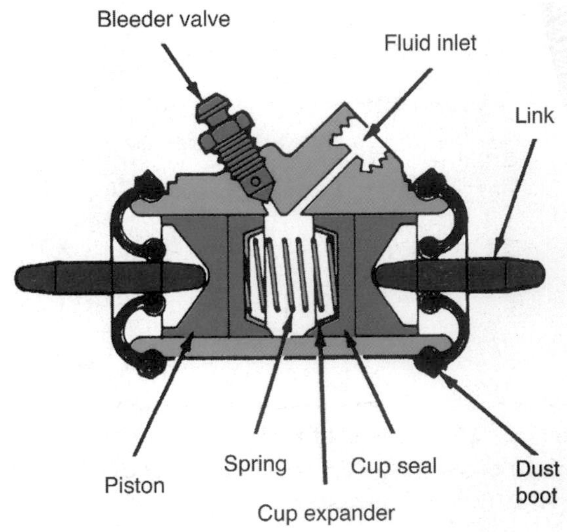

Figure 35–26 Cross-sections of a wheel cylinder that shows all of its internal parts. The brake line attaches to the fluid inlet. The cup expander prevents the cup seal lip from collapsing when the brakes are released.

- On some vehicles, a spring connected to the self-adjusting mechanism prevents binding of the mechanism in the event the star-wheel adjuster could not rotate. This spring is called an **over-travel, override,** or **overload spring.**

Wheel Cylinders

Hydraulic pressure is transferred from the master cylinder to each wheel cylinder through brake fluid. The force exerted on the brake fluid by the driver forces the piston inside the wheel cylinder to move outward. Through **push rods** or **links,** this movement acts on the brake shoes, forcing them outward against the brake drum. See Figure 35–26.

Drum-brake wheel cylinders are cast iron with a bore (hole) drilled and finished to provide a smooth finish for the wheel-cylinder seals and pistons. This special finish is called **bearingized.** The final step in the manufacture of the wheel cylinder is to force a hardened steel ball through the bore to bend over any opening in the "grain" of the metal and to smooth the inner surface.

CAUTION: It is because of this bearingized surface finish that most manufacturers do not recommend that wheel cylinders be honed. Be sure to follow the vehicle manufacturer's recommended procedures. Some manufacturers state that the wheel cylinders can be overhauled using new (replacement) sealing cups and dust shields after *cleaning* the cylinder bore only.

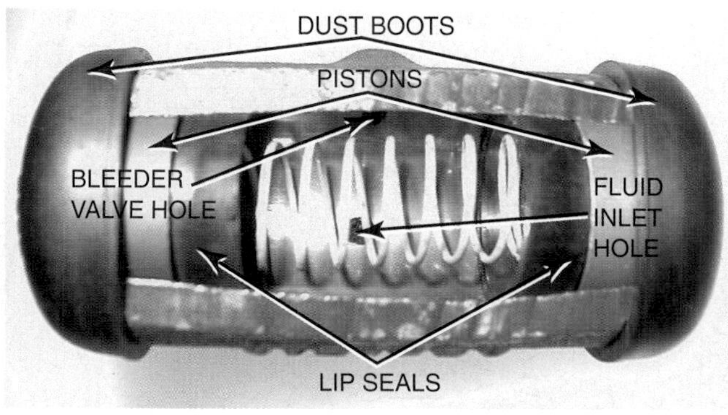

Figure 35–27 Cutaway of a wheel cylinder showing the lips of the sealing cups facing each other and the flat part of the cups against the piston.

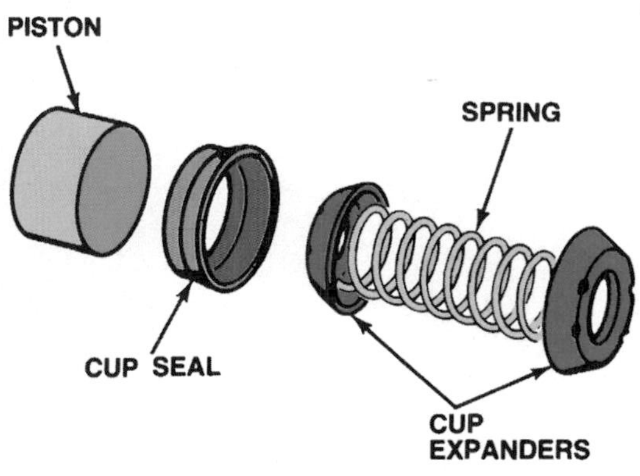

Figure 35–28 Cup expanders mechanically hold the cup sealing lip against the wheel cylinder bore.

Dust boots are installed outside of each wheel-cylinder piston to keep dirt out of the cylinder bore. See Figure 35–27. Between both piston seals, there is a spring with piston **seal expanders** to keep the seals from collapsing toward each other and to keep force exerted on the lips of both seals to ensure proper sealing. See Figure 35–28.

On the back of each wheel cylinder there is a threaded hole for the brake line and a bleeder valve, which can be loosened to remove (bleed) air from the hydraulic system. The wheel cylinder is bolted or clipped to the backing plate.

The wheel cylinders should be checked regularly for possible brake fluid leakage past the piston seals. With a dull tool, pry aside slightly the wheel-cylinder dust boots and check for any wetness. Remember, the dust boots are not designed to hold hydraulic pressure, but they do act as a small reservoir for seeping fluid.

TECH TIP 

Time, Not Distance, Is Important

Many brake experts recommend rebuilding or replacing wheel cylinders at every *other* brake job. Some experts recommend that the wheel cylinders be overhauled or replaced every time the brake linings are replaced. If the wheel cylinders are found to be leaking, they *must* be replaced or overhauled. The most important factor is *time*, not distance, when determining when to repair or replace hydraulic components.

The longer the time, the more moisture is absorbed by the brake fluid. The greater the amount of moisture absorbed by the brake fluid, the greater the corrosion to metal hydraulic components. For example, a vehicle that is used all day every day will likely wear out the brakes much sooner than a vehicle driven only a short distance every week. In this example, the high-mileage vehicle may need replacement brake linings every year, whereas the short-distance vehicle will go several years before replacement brakes are needed. The service technician should try to determine the amount of time the brake fluid has been in the vehicle. The longer the brake fluid has been in the system, the greater the chances that the wheel cylinders need to be replaced or overhauled.

TECH TIP 

Brake Parts Cleaning Tips

Denatured alcohol or "brake clean" should be used to clean only brake parts that are disassembled. When individual parts are cleaned, they can dry in the air before being assembled. **Never clean or flush *assembled* brake components with denatured alcohol or brake clean.** Often the alcohol cannot evaporate entirely from an assembled component. This trapped alcohol will evaporate inside the brake system, causing contamination. The trapped alcohol vapours also act like trapped air in the braking system and can cause a spongy brake pedal. Always clean *assembled* brake components with brake fluid or brake assembly fluid.

NOTE: When inspecting a drum brake wheel cylinder, look for brake fluid under the dust boot. According to vehicle manufacturers, a slight amount of brake fluid behind the boot is normal and serves to lubricate the pistons. However, if there is enough fluid to run or spill out when the boot is pried back, excessive leakage is indicated and the wheel cylinder must be rebuilt or replaced.

REASSEMBLING THE DRUM BRAKE

Carefully clean the backing plate. Check the anchor pin for looseness. Clean and lubricate the shoe contact surfaces (shoe pads) and star-wheel adjuster with antiseize, brake grease, or synthetic grease. See Figure 35–29. Reassemble the primary and secondary shoes and brake strut along with all springs.

> **HINT:** Many technicians preassemble the primary and secondary shoes as a unit with the connecting (lower retracting) spring before installing them onto the backing plate. See Figure 35–30.

Finish assembling the drum brake, being careful to note the correct location of all springs and parts. See Figure 35–31. Most self-adjusters operate off the rear (secondary) shoe and should, therefore, be assembled toward the rear of the vehicle.

Adjusting Drum Brakes

Most drum brakes are adjusted by rotating a star-wheel or rotary adjuster. As the adjuster is moved, the brake shoes move toward the drum. If the brakes have been assembled correctly and with the parking brake fully released, both brake shoes should make contact with the anchor pin at the top. See Figure 35–32 for an example of one shoe not making contact with the anchor pin.

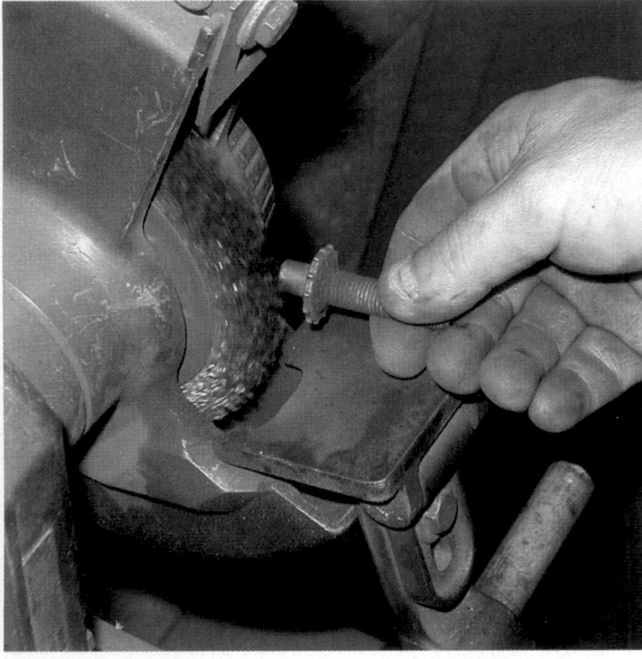

Figure 35–29 All brake parts should be cleaned and lubricated before reassembly.

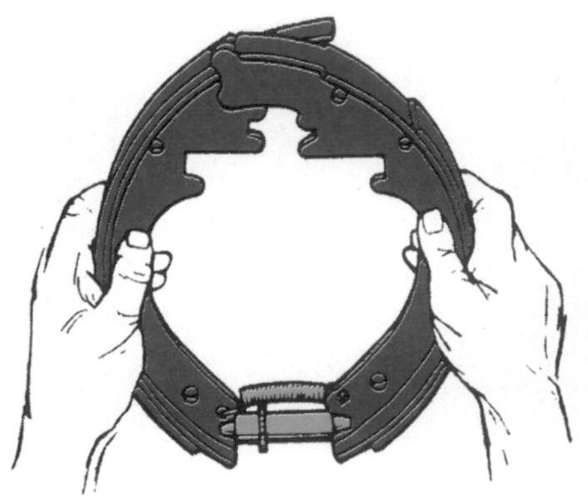

Figure 35–30 Sometimes it is necessary to cross the shoes when preassembling the star wheel adjuster and connecting spring. (Courtesy of Allied Signal Automotive Aftermarket)

Figure 35–31 Using the long handle of brake spring pliers to install a return spring over the anchor pin.

Figure 35–32 Notice that the brake shoe is not contacting the anchor pin. This often occurs when the parking brake cable is stuck or not properly adjusted.

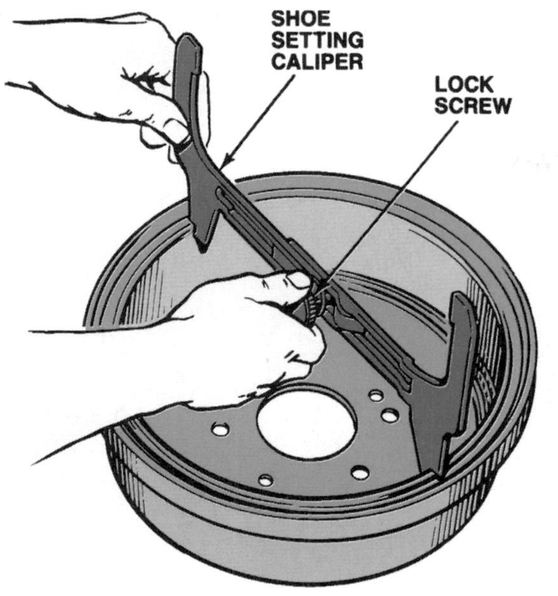

Figure 35–33 The first step in using a brake shoe clearance gauge is to adjust it to the drum inside diameter and tighten the lock screw.

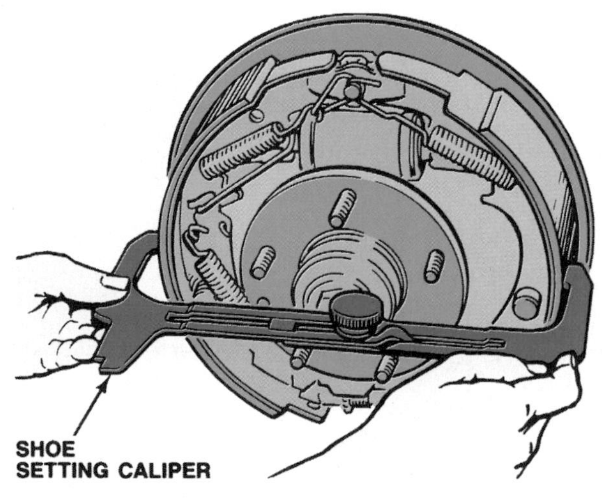

Figure 35–34 Place the gauge over the shoes and adjust the brakes until they contact the inside of the gauge.

If the clearance between the brake shoes and the brake drum is excessive, a low brake pedal results. The wheel cylinder travel may not be adequate to cause the lining to contact the drums. Often, the driver has to pump the brakes to force enough brake fluid into the wheel cylinder to move it enough for braking action to occur. Many technicians use a **brake shoe clearance gauge** to adjust the brake shoes before installing the drum. See Figures 35–33 and 35–34.

TECH TIP 

The Masking Tape Trick

Some technicians cover the friction material with masking tape to prevent contaminating the linings with dirt or grease during installation. After everything has been installed and double checked, the masking tape is removed and the brake drums installed.

CAUTION: Before installing the brake drum, be sure to clean any grease off the brake lining. Do not use sandpaper on the lining to remove grease. The sandpaper may release asbestos fibre into the air. Grease on the linings can cause the brakes to grab. See the tech tip "The Masking Tape Trick."

THE PARKING BRAKE

According to Federal Motor Vehicle Safety Standard (FMVSS) 105, the parking brake must hold a fully loaded (laden) vehicle stationary on a slope of 30% (for a manual transmission-equipped vehicle) or a slope of 20% (if equipped with an automatic transmission). The hand force required cannot exceed 350 N (80 lb.); the foot force required cannot be greater than 450 N (100 lb.). See Figure 35–35 for a typical parking brake system. Parking brakes can be applied using either a hand lever or foot-operated pedal.

Some foot-operated parking brakes use a ratchet mechanism that requires the driver to push the pedal down several times. This type of parking brake is commonly called "pump to set." The lever or foot-pedal mechanism is designed to apply the required force on the parking brake using normal driver effort.

All parking brakes lock into a slot or notch that keeps the parking brake applied until it is released. Some vehicles are equipped with a mechanism connected to the shifter mechanism that automatically releases the parking brake when the transmission is moved from park to a drive gear (either forward or reverse). See the service manual for the exact service procedures.

Parking Brake Warning Lamp

Whenever the parking brake is engaged, a red BRAKE warning lamp lights on the dash. On most vehicles, this is the same lamp that lights when there is a hydraulic or brake-fluid-level problem. The warning lamp for the parking brake warns the driver

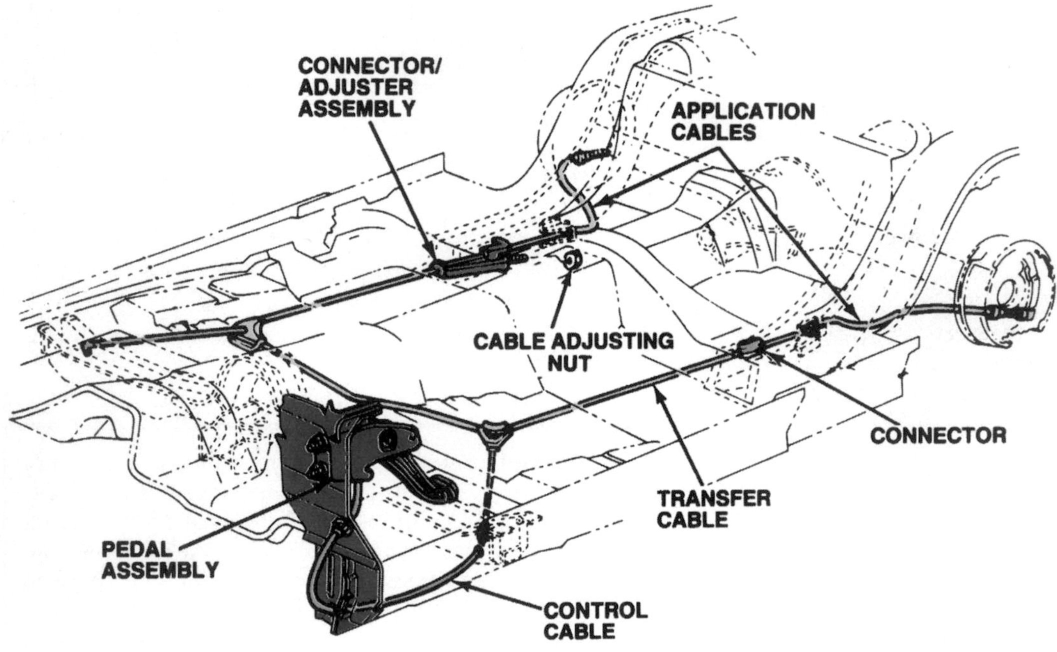

Figure 35–35 Typical parking brake cable system showing the foot-operated parking brake lever and cable routing.

that the parking brake is applied or partially applied. This warning helps prevent damage or overheating to the brake drums and linings that could occur if the vehicle was driven with the parking brake applied. If the red BRAKE warning lamp is on, check the parking brake to see if it is fully released. If the BRAKE lamp is still on, then the parking brake switch may be defective or out of adjustment, or there may be a hydraulic problem.

Parking Brake Cables

Parking brake cables run through protective housing. The cable attaches to the hand lever or foot-operated pedal and runs to a junction. This front section of parking brake cable is usually called the **control cable.** The control cable then attaches to an **equalizer,** which attaches to a second cable or pair of cables that run to each rear brake. These individual wheel-brake cables are often called **application cables** or left or right **parking brake cables.** See Figure 35–36.

The parking brake equalizer is normally located under the vehicle. Most vehicles since the mid-1980s use wire strand cables covered with nylon for corrosion resistance. The housing or conduit contains plastic seals that help keep out dirt and water to prevent the cables from sticking and to reduce parking brake effort.

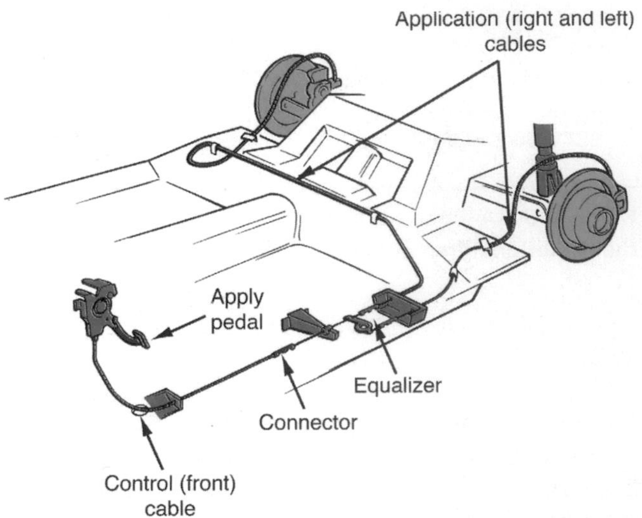

Figure 35–36 The cable from the activating lever to the equalizer is commonly called the *control cable.* From the equalizer, the individual brake cables are often called *application cables.* These individual cables can usually be purchased separately.

TECH TIP 

Look for Swollen Parking Brake Cables

Always inspect parking brake cables for proper operation. A cable that is larger in diameter in one section indicates that it is rusting inside and has swollen. See Figure 35–37. A rusting parking brake cable can keep the rear brake applied even though the parking brake lever has been released. This can cause dragging brakes, reduced fuel economy, and possible vehicle damage due to overheated brakes.

Figure 35–37 Notice how rust inside the covering of this parking brake cable has caused the cable to swell.

Parking Brake on Drum Brakes

Most parking brakes move steel woven cables attached to the rear brakes only and operate through the **parking brake lever,** which is attached to the cable and the secondary shoe. The parking brake force is transferred to the primary shoe through a flat steel bar called a **parking brake strut.** Around the end of the slotted strut is a spring called an **antirattle spring** (or **strut spring**), which prevents the strut from rattling whenever the parking brake is not applied. See Figure 35–38.

Parking Brake Cable Adjustment

Most manufacturers specify a minimum of three or four and a maximum of eight to ten clicks when applying the parking brake. Consult the service manual for the vehicle being serviced on the exact specification and adjustment procedures. Most vehicle manufacturers specify that the rear brakes be inspected and correctly adjusted before attempting to adjust the parking brake cable. Always follow the manufacturer's recommended procedure exactly.

Below is a general procedure for a parking brake adjustment.

1. Make certain that the rear service brakes are adjusted correctly and the lining is serviceable.

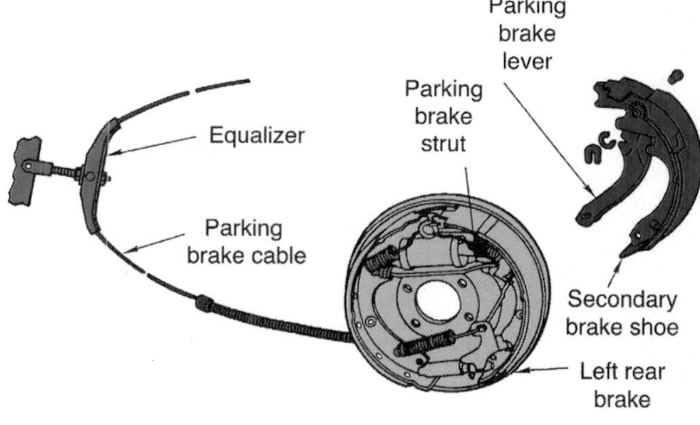

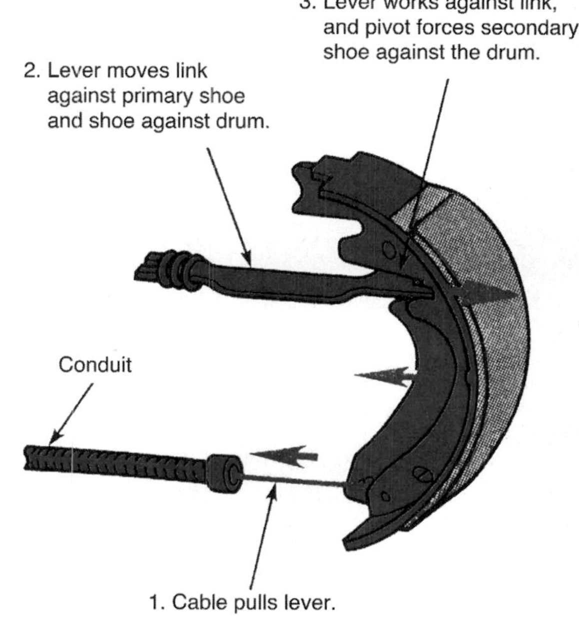

Figure 35–38 Notice the spring at the end of the parking brake strut. This antirattle spring keeps tension on the strut. The parking brake lever is usually attached with a pin and spring (wavy) washer and retained by a horseshoe clip.

2. With the drums installed, apply the parking brake three to four clicks. There should be a slight drag on both rear wheels.
3. Adjust the cable at the equalizer (equalizes one cable's force to both rear brakes) if necessary until there is a slight drag on both rear brakes. See Figures 35–39 and 35–40.
4. Release the parking brake. Both rear brakes should be free and not dragging. Repair or replace rusted cables or readjust as necessary to ensure that the brakes are not dragging.

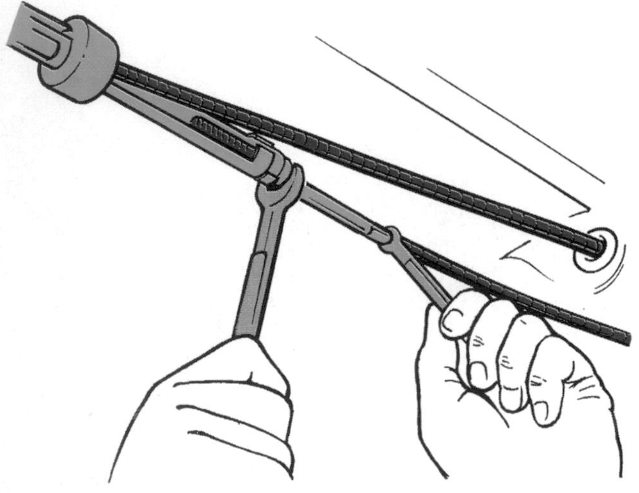

Figure 35–39 After checking that the rear brakes are okay and properly adjusted, the parking brake cable can be adjusted. Always follow the manufacturer's recommended procedure.

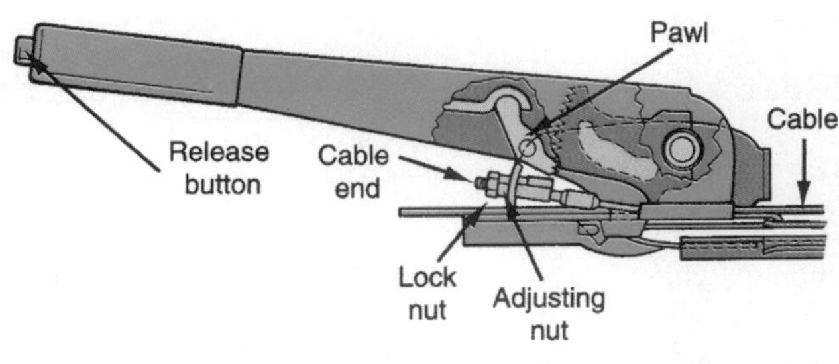

Figure 35–40 Many hand-operated parking brakes are adjusted inside the vehicle.

DRUM BRAKE TROUBLESHOOTING GUIDE

Problem	Possible Causes
Low pedal or the pedal goes to the floor	• Excessive clearance between linings and drum • Automatic adjusters not working • Leaking wheel cylinder • Air in the system
Springy, spongy pedal	• Drums worn below specifications • Air in the system
Excessive pedal pressure required to stop the vehicle	• Grease or fluid-soaked linings • Frozen wheel cylinder pistons • Linings installed on wrong shoes
Light pedal pressure—brakes too sensitive	• Brake adjustment not correct • Loose backing plate • Lining loose on the shoe • Excessive dust and dirt in the drums • Scored, bell-mouthed, or barrel-shaped drum • Improper lining contact pattern
Brake pedal travel decreasing	• Weak shoe retracting springs • Wheel cylinder pistons sticking
Pulsating brake pedal (parking brake apply pulsates also)	• Drums out-of-round
Brakes fade (temporary loss of brake effectiveness when hot)	• Poor lining contact • Drums worn below the discard dimension • Charred or glazed linings
Shoe click	• Shoes lift off the backing plate and snap back • Hold-down springs weak • Shoe bent • Grooves in the backing plate pads
Snapping noise in the front end	• Grooved backing plate pads • Loose backing plates
Thumping noise when brakes are applied	• Cracked drum; hard spots in the drum • Retractor springs unequal—weak
Grinding noise	• Shoe hits the drum • Bent shoe web • Brake improperly assembled

DRUM BRAKE TROUBLESHOOTING GUIDE, continued

Problem	Possible Causes
One wheel drags	• Weak or broken shoe retracting springs • Brake-shoe-to-drum clearance too tight—brake shoes not adjusted properly • Brake assembled improperly • Wheel cylinder piston cups swollen and distorted • Pistons sticking in the wheel cylinder • Drum out-of-round • Loose anchor pin/plate • Parking brake cable not free • Parking brake not adjusted properly
Vehicle pulls to one side	• Brake adjustment not correct • Loose backing plate • Linings not of specified kind; primary and secondary shoes reversed or not replaced in pairs • Water, mud, or other material in brakes • Wheel cylinder sticking • Weak or broken shoe retracting springs • Drums out-of-round • Wheel cylinder size different on opposite sides • Scored drum
Wet weather: brakes grab or will not hold	• Bent backing plate flange • Incorrect or abused shoe and linings
Brakes squeak	• Backing plate is bent or shoes twisted • Shoes scraping on backing plate pads • Weak or broken hold-down springs • Loose backing plate, anchor, or wheel cylinder • Glazed linings • Dry shoe pads and hold-down pin surfaces
Brakes chatter	• Incorrect lining-to-drum clearance • Loose backing plate • Weak or broken retractor spring • Drums out-of-round • Tapered or barrel-shaped drums • Improper lining contact pattern

TECH TIP 

The Parking Brake Click Test

When diagnosing any brake problem, apply the parking brake and count the "clicks." This method works for hand-operated, as well as foot-operated, parking brakes.

> **CAUTION:** Do not adjust the parking brake cable until the rear brakes have been thoroughly inspected and adjusted. Most vehicle manufacturers specify a maximum of ten clicks. If the parking brake travel exceeds this amount, then the rear brakes may be worn or out of adjustment.

If the rear brake lining is usable, check for the proper operation of the self-adjustment mechanism. If the rear brakes are out of adjustment, the service brake pedal will also be low. This ten-click test is a fast-and-easy way to determine if the problem is due to the rear brakes.

SUMMARY

1. Brake shoes are forced outward against a brake drum by hydraulic action working on the brake shoes through the piston of a wheel cylinder.
2. The curved arch of the brake shoe causes a wedging action between the brake shoe and the rotating drum. This wedging action increases the amount of force applied to the drum.
3. Dual-servo brakes use primary and secondary brake shoes that are connected at one end. The wedge action on the front (primary) shoe forces the secondary shoe into the drum with even greater force. This action is called servo-self-energizing.
4. Leading-trailing brakes use two brake shoes that are *not* connected. Leading-trailing brakes operate on a more linear basis and are, therefore, more suited for ABS than dual-servo.
5. Care should be exercised when removing a brake drum so as not to damage the drum, backing plate, or other vehicle components.

6. After disassembly of the drum brake component, the backing plate should be inspected and cleaned.
7. Most experts recommend replacing the wheel cylinder as well as all brake springs as part of a thorough drum-brake overhaul.
8. When a drum brake is properly assembled, both shoes should contact the anchor pin.

REVIEW QUESTIONS

1. Describe the difference between a dual-servo and a leading-trailing drum-brake system.
2. List all the parts of a typical drum brake.
3. List all items that should be lubricated on a drum brake.
4. Explain how a self-adjusting brake mechanism works.

RED SEAL CERTIFICATION-TYPE QUESTIONS

1. What is the purpose of the Tinnerman nut?
   - **a.** To hold the brake rotor on during factory assembly
   - **b.** To hold the brake drum on during factory assembly
   - **c.** To retain the wheel cylinder to backing plate
   - **d.** It is a type of nut used to hold the brake bleeder screw
2. The backing plate should be replaced if the shoe contact areas (pads or ledges) are worn more than
   - **a.** 13 mm (1/2″)
   - **b.** 6 mm (1/4″)
   - **c.** 3 mm (1/8″)
   - **d.** 1.5 mm (1/16″)
3. To what point of the drum brake system does the brake lever attach?
   - **a.** Front or primary brake shoe
   - **b.** Rear or secondary brake shoe
   - **c.** Middle of the backing plate
   - **d.** Front of the hydraulic wheel cylinder
4. Most brake experts and vehicle manufacturers recommend replacing the brake lining when the lining thickness is
   - **a.** 0.8 mm (0.030 in.)
   - **b.** 1.0 mm (0.040 in.)
   - **c.** 1.3 mm (0.050 in.)
   - **d.** 1.5 mm (0.060 in.)
5. What is the purpose of the star wheel adjuster?
   - **a.** To move out the bottom of the brake shoes mechanically
   - **b.** To move out the top of the brake shoes hydraulically
   - **c.** To hold the brake lever to the brake shoe
   - **d.** To hold the brake shoes together
6. What is the purpose of the seal expander inside the wheel cylinder?
   - **a.** It holds the dust seal in place
   - **b.** It prevents the cup seal from moving in or out
   - **c.** It holds the cup seal in place during pedal release
   - **d.** It prevents dirt from returning to the master cylinder
7. Most manufacturers recommend that brake parts should be cleaned with
   - **a.** Carburetor cleaner
   - **b.** Denatured alcohol
   - **c.** Stoddard solvent
   - **d.** Detergent and water
8. Old brake shoes are often returned to the manufacturer, who installs new friction material. These old shoes are usually called the
   - **a.** Core
   - **b.** Web
   - **c.** Rim
   - **d.** Nib
9. What could cause the drum brake shoes to drag?
   - **a.** Too much drum to shoe clearance
   - **b.** Too little drum to shoe clearance
   - **c.** Air in the hydraulic system
   - **d.** The star wheel adjuster is seized
10. What can be done to keep the brake shoes cleaner during servicing?
   - **a.** Place masking tape over the brake shoe friction material before installation
   - **b.** Wash the brake shoes with solvent
   - **c.** Use water-soluble grease
   - **d.** Nothing. Grease helps the shoes break in

36

Disc Brake Operation, Diagnosis, and Service

OBJECTIVES: After studying Chapter 36, you should be able to:

1. Prepare for the interprovincial Red Seal certification examination in Appendix V (Brakes) on the topics covered in this chapter.
2. Describe how disc brakes function.
3. Name the parts of a typical disc brake system.
4. Identify the types of disc brake pads.
5. Explain how to disassemble and reassemble a disc brake caliper assembly.
6. Describe how to prevent disc brake noise.

DISC BRAKE OPERATION AND PARTS

Disc brakes use a piston(s) to squeeze friction material (pads) on both sides of a rotating disc (rotor). The rotor is attached to and stops the wheel. The disc and pads are usually mounted where air can quickly cool the parts. In fact, over 80% of the rotor is exposed to the air. Also, as the rotor becomes hotter, the rotor expands toward the friction pads, not away from the shoes as happens with drum brakes. See Figure 36–1.

Fixed Calipers

The first disc brakes on American vehicles often used four pistons, two on each side of the rotors. The caliper (containing the four pistons with rubber

TECH TIP 

Wax the Wheels?

Brake dust from semimetallic brake pads often discolours the front wheels. Customers often complain to service technicians about this problem, but it is normal for the front wheels to become dirty because the iron and other metallic and nonmetallic components wear off the front disc brake pads and adhere to the wheel covers. A coat of wax on the wheels or wheel covers helps prevent damage and makes it easier to wash off the brake dust.

Figure 36–1 Disc brakes can absorb and dissipate a great deal of heat. During this demonstration, the brakes were gently applied as the engine drove the front wheels until the rotor became cherry red. During normal braking, the rotor temperature can exceed 180°C (350°F) and about 800°C (1500°F) on a race vehicle.

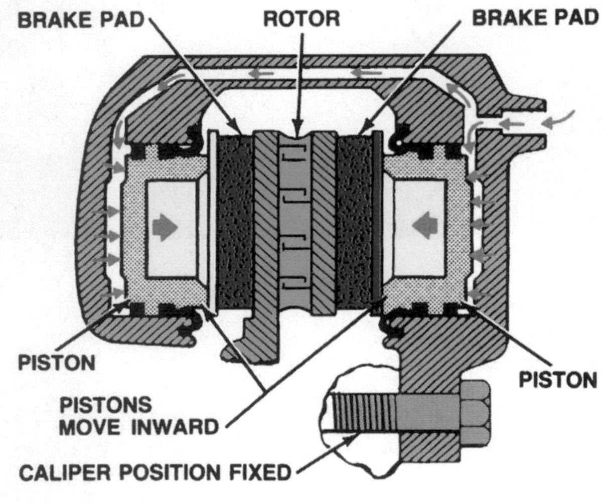

Figure 36–2 Fixed calipers apply the brakes by forcing pistons toward the rotor from both sides.

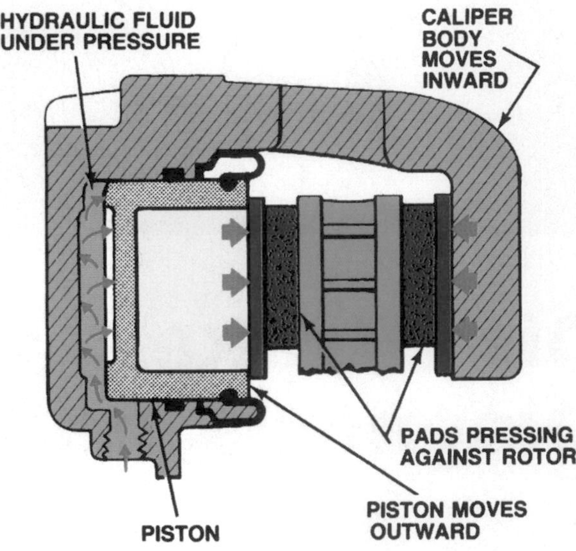

Figure 36–3 Sliding and floating calipers apply the brakes by forcing the piston in one direction and the caliper body in the other direction. If the caliper piston and slides can move freely, equal force is exerted on both sides of the rotor.

piston seals on each) was bolted directly to the steering knuckle and did not move. This is called a **fixed caliper.** See Figure 36–2. When the brake pedal is depressed, hydraulic brake fluid is forced into the caliper cylinder bores. This forces the pistons outward and against the pads.

When the brake pedal is released, a small amount of brake fluid returns to the master cylinder, lowering the hydraulic pressure on the piston. The clamping action of the brake pads against the rotor is released and the caliper pistons retract slightly back into the caliper bore.

Floating and Sliding Calipers

Most disc brake calipers use only one large piston in a caliper that moves slightly, allowing it to squeeze the rotor between the two disc pads. This type of caliper is called a **floating caliper** or **sliding caliper.** See Figures 36–3 and 36–4.

When the brakes are applied, the hydraulic pressure in the caliper bore is exerted equally against the bottom of the piston and on the back of the caliper itself. The pressure on the piston forces the inside pad against the rotor. At the same time the piston is pushing against the rotor, the caliper itself is being forced toward the center of the vehicle. Since the outboard pad is attached to this inward, moving caliper, it contacts the outer surface of the rotor with the same force that is being exerted on the inboard pad, as shown in Figure 36–5. When the brake pedal is released, the hydraulic force against the piston is released. The caliper seal that was deformed during the brake application forces the piston to return to its original at-rest position. See Figure 36–6. The entire caliper then returns to its released position and all pressure against the brake pads is removed.

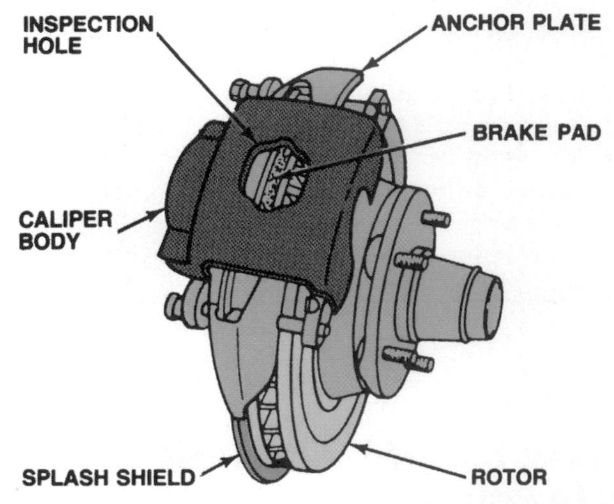

Figure 36–4 A typical single-piston floating caliper. In this type of design, the entire caliper moves when the single piston is pushed out of the caliper during a brake application. When the caliper moves, the outboard pad is pushed against the rotor.

Low-Drag Calipers

Many front-wheel-drive vehicles use a low-drag caliper design that uses a different O-ring groove in

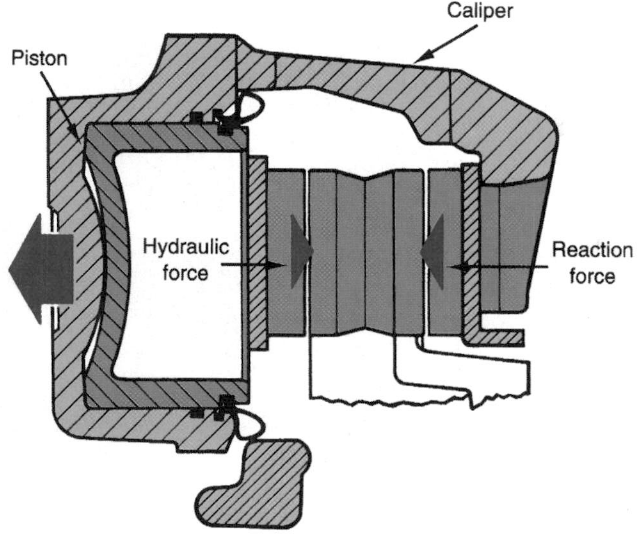

Figure 36–5 Hydraulic force on the piston (left) is applied to the inboard pad and the caliper housing itself. The reaction of the piston pushing against the rotor causes the entire caliper to move toward the inside of the vehicle (large arrow). Since the outboard pad is retained by the caliper, the reaction force of the moving caliper applies pressure to the outboard pad against the outboard surface of the rotor.

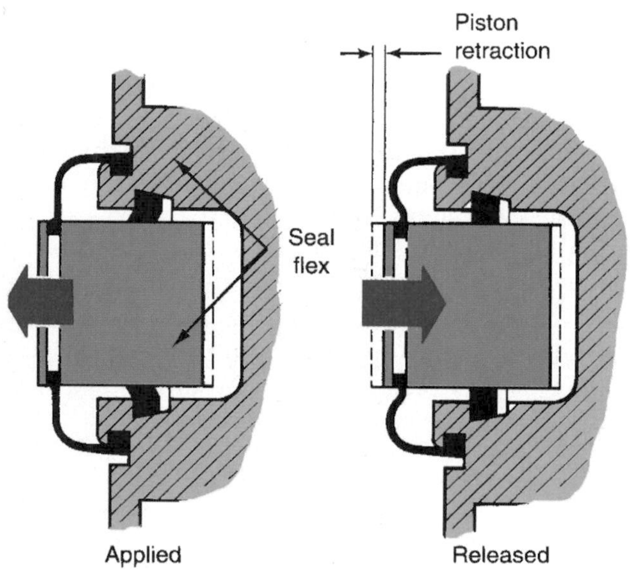

Figure 36–6 The square-cut O-ring not only seals hydraulic brake fluid but also retracts the caliper piston when the brake pedal is released.

TECH TIP 

The Bleed-and-Squirt Test (for non-ABS brakes)

If you suspect a brake is not being fully released, simply loosen the bleeder valve. If brake fluid squirts out under pressure, then the brake is being kept in the applied position. Look for a defective flexible brake hose.

If the vehicle is off the ground, the wheels should be able to rotate with the brakes off. If a wheel is difficult or hard to turn by hand and is easy to turn after opening the bleeder valve, then there is a brake fluid restriction between the master cylinder and the brake.

the caliper to help keep the pads from rubbing against the rotor when the brake is released. See Figure 36–7.

NOTE: If a floating caliper is stuck and cannot easily move when the brakes are applied, the inboard pad will wear more than the outboard pad. Uneven pad wear will also occur if the piston is stuck ("frozen") inside the caliper. Therefore, when uneven disc brake pad wear occurs, carefully inspect the caliper piston(s) and caliper slides.

Brake Pad Wear Compensation

As the disc brake pad wears, the caliper piston moves out closer to the rotor. As the wear occurs and the piston moves, additional brake fluid is needed behind the piston. This additional brake fluid comes from the master cylinder, and the brake fluid level drops as the disc brake pads wear.

Disc Brake Pads

Disc brake pads have friction material attached to a steel backing. See Chapter 32 for details on friction material composition. There are three methods of attaching the friction material to the steel backing:

- **Riveted.** Holes are drilled through the friction material block, and brass rivets hold the block to the steel backing. See Figure 36–8.
- **Bonded.** Friction blocks are glued to the steel backing.
- **Integrally moulded.** The friction material is moulded with the steel backing, rather than moulded separately and then attached to the steel backing. Integrally molded linings use holes in the steel backing to allow the friction material

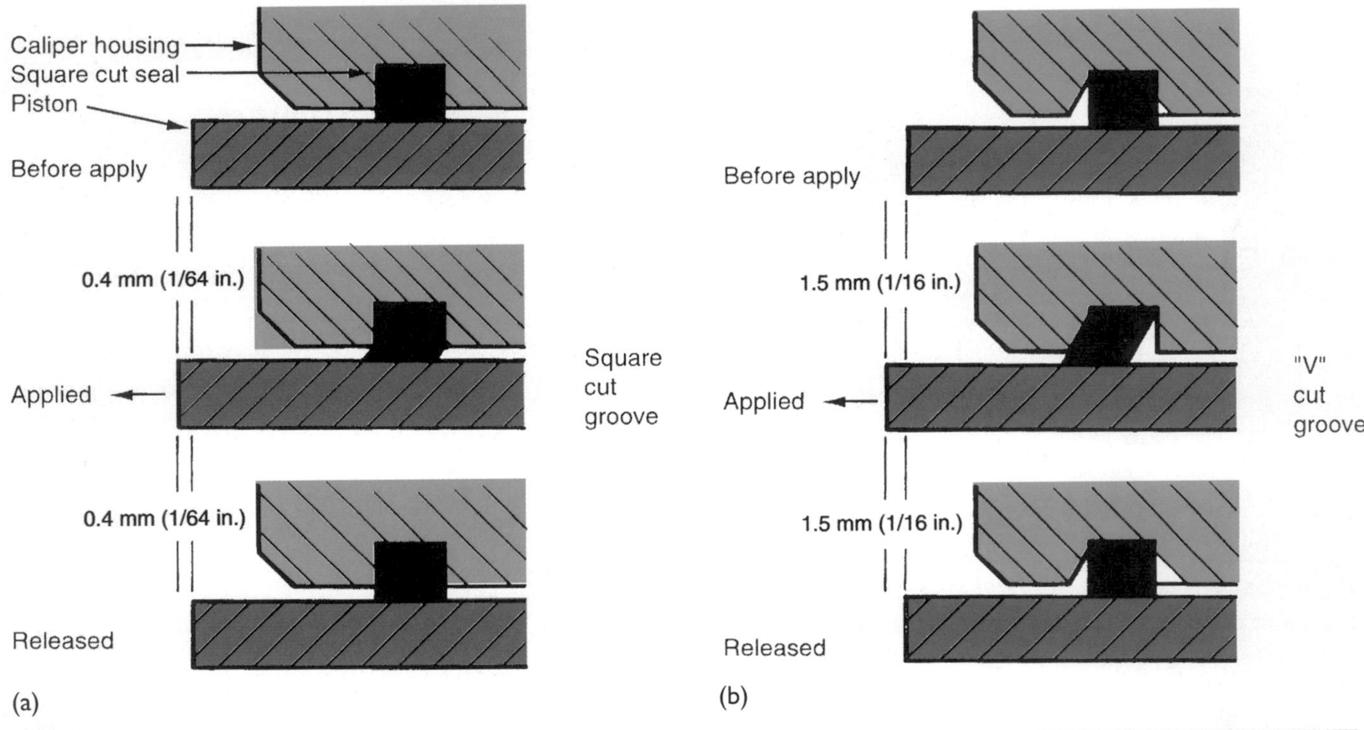

Figure 36–7 (a) In a standard disc brake caliper, the square-cut O-ring deforms when the brakes are applied and returns the piston to its original (released) position due to the elastic properties of the rubber seal. (b) In a low-drag caliper design, the groove for the square-cut O-ring is V-shaped, allowing for more retraction. When the brake pedal is released, the piston is moved away from the rotor, further resulting in less friction between the disc brake pads and the rotor when the brakes are released.

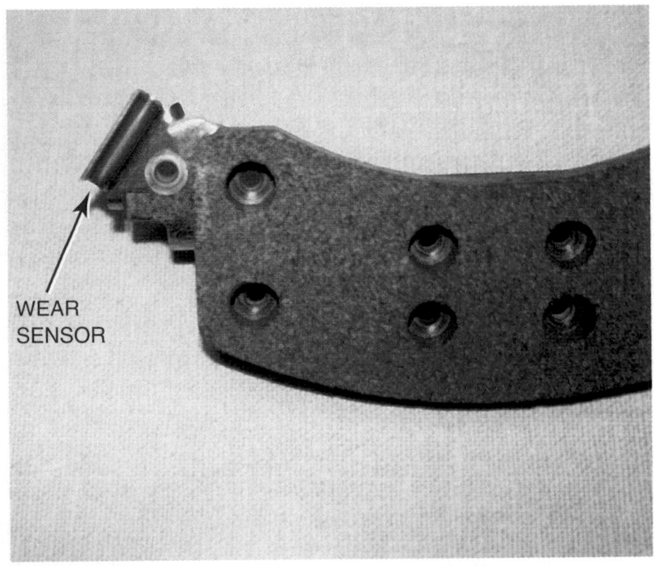

Figure 36–8 A riveted disc brake pad with a wear sensor.

to become a part of the steel backing. This process results in a brake pad that has a lot of strength and is resistant to the shearing of the friction material from the steel backing.

Wear Sensors

Many disc brake pads are equipped with a groove or notch moulded into the pad, as shown in Figure 36–9. When the pads are worn down to the depth of the notch, the pads should be replaced. Another type of wear indicator uses a soft metal tang that contacts the rotor when the pad is worn down to the thickness requiring replacement. These wear indicators make a high-pitched squeal sound when the wheels are rotating and the ends of the metal tang are rubbing against the rotor. See Figure 36–10.

> **NOTE:** With many vehicles, the wear indicator noise *stops* when the brakes are applied. The fact that the noise disappears when the brakes are applied has wrongly convinced many drivers (and some service technicians) that the problem is *not* due to the brakes. Some vehicles have indicators that only make noise while the vehicle is being driven in reverse. Other vehicles have sensors that tend to make the most noise during braking. Any noise while driving should be investigated.

Some manufacturers position the sensors on the brake pads so that the rotor touches the sensor be-

Figure 36–9 These replacement pads have a wear indicator groove and are integrally moulded.

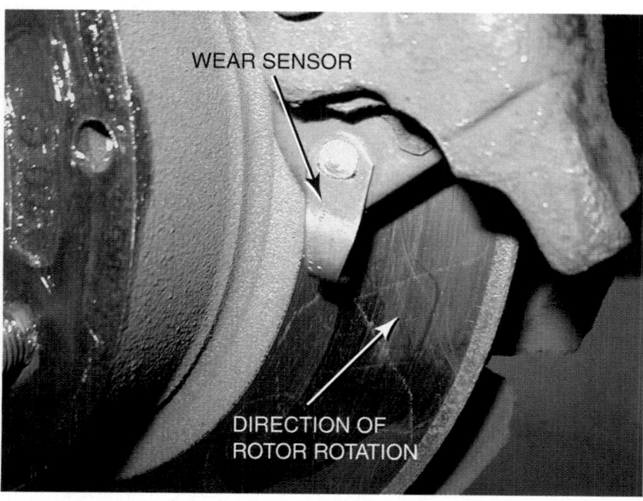

Figure 36–10 Most wear sensors are designed to contact the rotor before the friction material so that it bends slightly toward the pad and then springs back in position, creating a squeaking sound.

fore passing across the friction material. Other manufacturers position the sensor on the trailing edge of the pad.

Electrical Brake Wear Indicators

Some vehicle manufacturers use electrical brake lining wear indicators. A typical installation involves an electrical wire leading to a sensor at the edge of the friction pad. When the lining material wears down to the point of replacement, the electrical sensor touches the disc brake rotor. When the sensor touches the metal rotor, the electrical circuit is completed and lights a dash warning lamp.

TECH TIP 

Brake Pads Should be Thicker than the Steel Backing

Although the *exact* thickness of allowable brake lining varies with the vehicle manufacturer, most experts agree that the lining should be thicker than a nickel coin. This is about 1.5 mm (0.060 in.).

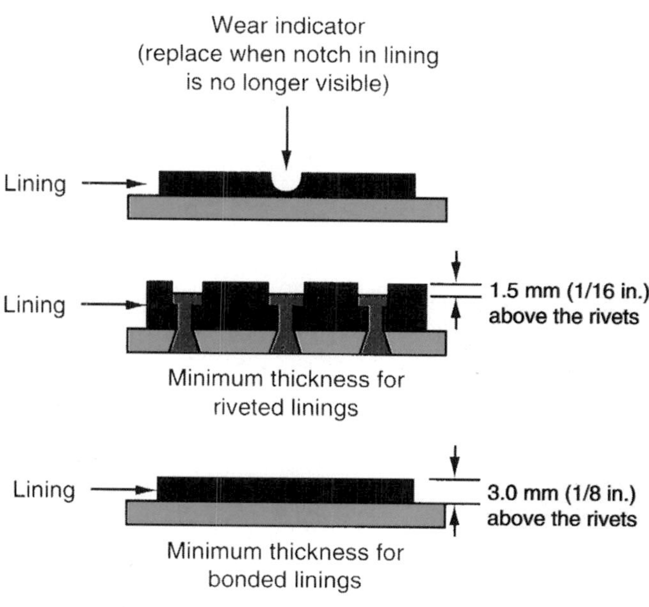

Figure 36–11 Minimum thickness for various types of disc brake pads. Disc brake pads, of course, can be replaced before they wear down to the factory recommended *minimum* thickness.

Whenever servicing this type of system, be sure to purchase the correct pads for the vehicle. Failure to reinstall the original-equipment sensor-type pads could cause the lining to be completely worn down until metal-to-metal contact occurs between the steel backing plate of the disc brake pads and the rotor.

DIAGNOSIS AND SERVICE

Visual Inspection

Even with operating wear sensors, a thorough visual inspection is very important. See Figure 36–11. A lining thickness check should not be the only inspection performed on a disc brake. *A thorough visual inspection can only be accomplished by removing the*

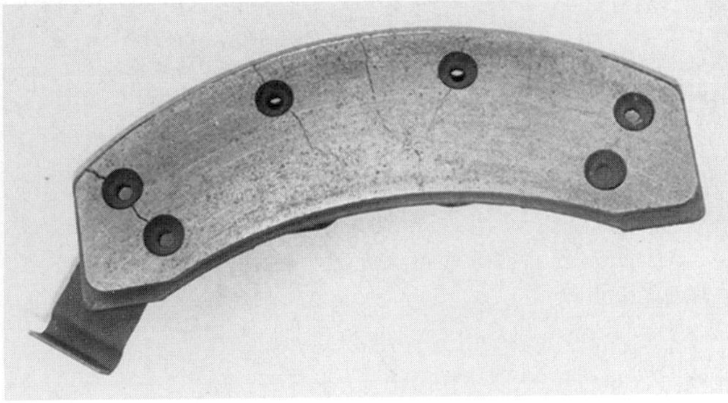

Figure 36–12 This cracked disc brake pad must be replaced even though it is thicker than the minimum allowable by the vehicle manufacturer.

friction pads. See Figure 36–12 for an example of a disc brake pad that shows usable lining thickness but is severely cracked and *must* be replaced.

NOTE: Some disc brake pads use a heat barrier (thermo) layer between the steel backing plate and the friction material. The purpose of the heat barrier is to prevent heat from transferring into the caliper piston where it may cause the brake fluid to boil. Do not confuse the thickness of the barrier with the thickness of the friction lining material. The barrier material is usually a different colour and usually can be distinguished from the lining material.

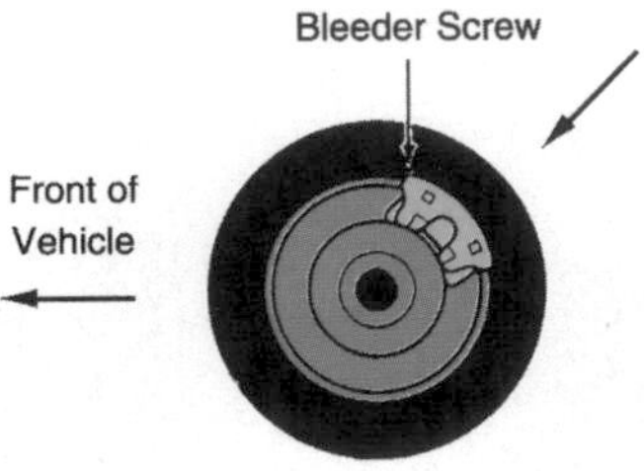

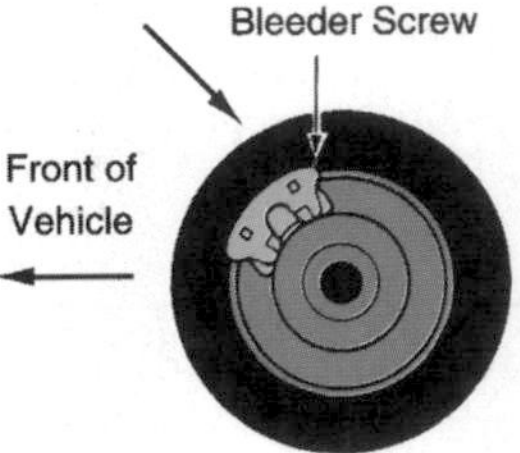

Figure 36–13 Both rear-mount and forward-mount calipers have the bleeder valve at the top. Some calipers *will* fit on the wrong side of the vehicle, yet not be able to be correctly bled because the bleeder valve would point down, allowing trapped air to remain inside the caliper bore. If both calipers are being removed at the same time, mark them left and right.

Disc Brake Calipers

Removal Hoist the vehicle and remove the wheel(s). Note the caliper mount position, as shown in Figure 36–13, before removing the caliper. Knowing whether the caliper is "rear-mount" position or "forward-mount" position is often necessary when purchasing replacement calipers. Remove the caliper following the steps in Figures 36–14 through 36–17.

Inspection and Disassembly Check for brake fluid in and around the piston boot area. If the boot is damaged or a fluid leak is visible, then make the repair or replace the caliper assembly. See Figures 36–18 and 36–19 for steps to follow to disassemble a disc brake caliper.

Phenolic Caliper Pistons

Phenolic caliper pistons are made from a phenol-formaldehyde resin combined with various reinforcing fibres. Phenolic brake caliper pistons were first used in the 1970s on many Chrysler vehicles. The

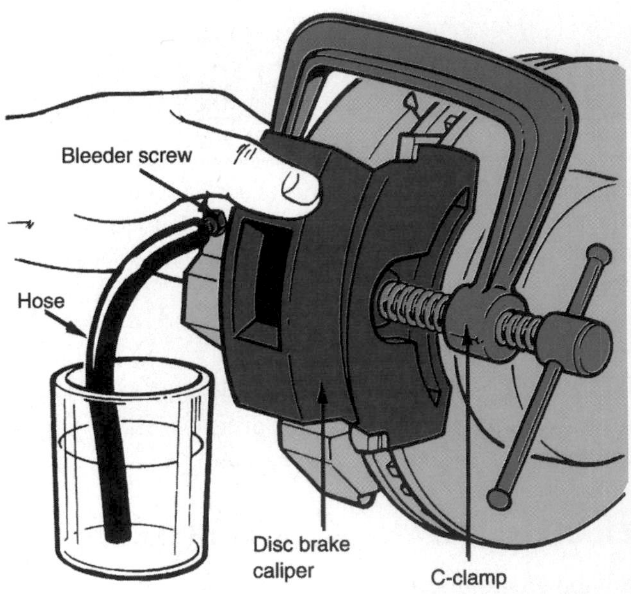

Figure 36–14 Most manufacturers recommend that the bleeder valve be opened and the brake fluid forced into a container rather than back into the master cylinder reservoir. This helps prevent contaminated brake fluid from being forced into the master cylinder, where the dirt and contamination could cause problems.

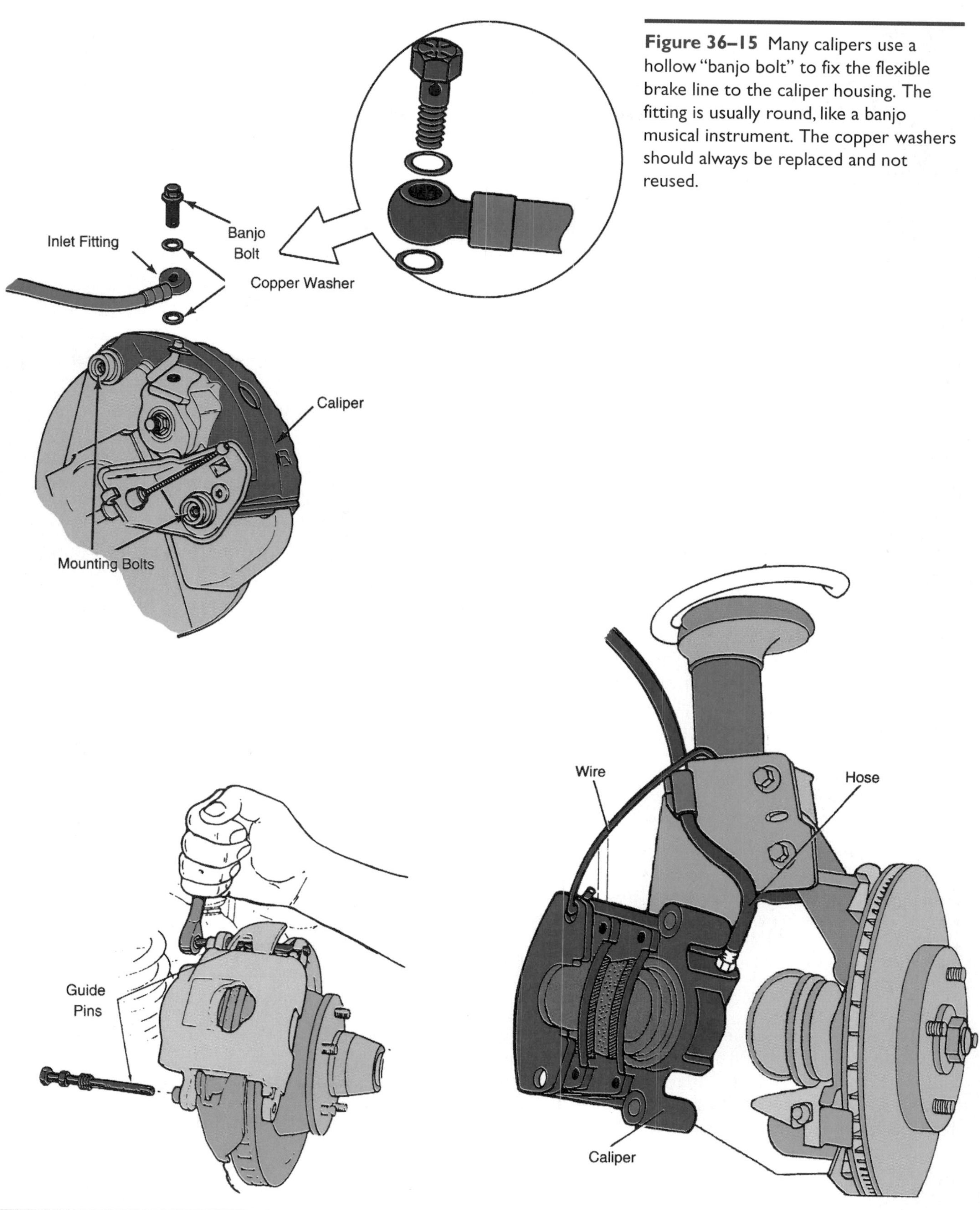

Figure 36–15 Many calipers use a hollow "banjo bolt" to fix the flexible brake line to the caliper housing. The fitting is usually round, like a banjo musical instrument. The copper washers should always be replaced and not reused.

Figure 36–16 Caliper retaining bolts are often called *guide pins*. These guide pins are used to fix the caliper to the steering knuckle. These pins also slide through metal bushings and rubber O-rings. (Courtesy of EIS Brake Parts)

Figure 36–17 If the caliper is not being removed, it must be properly supported so that the weight of the caliper does not pull on the flexible rubber brake line. A suitable piece of wire such as a coat hanger may be used.

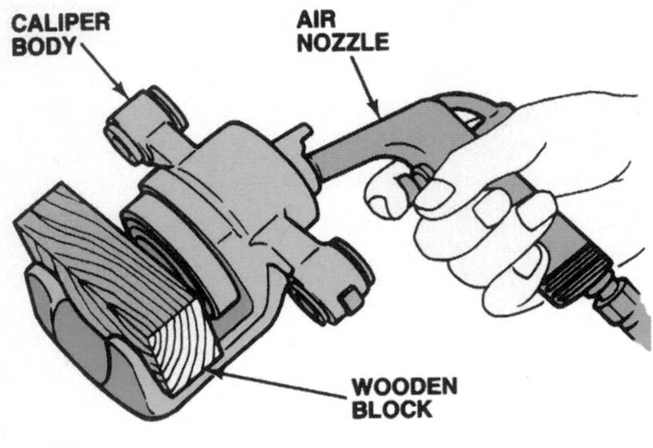

Figure 36–18 A wooden block or a folded shop cloth helps prevent damage when caliper pistons are removed.

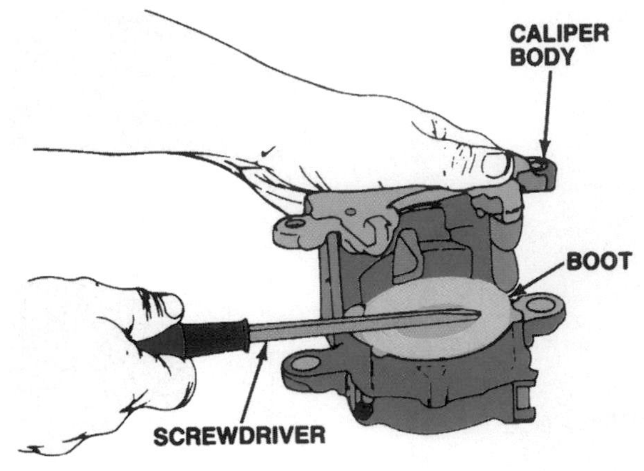

Figure 36–19 Removing a dust boot that is a press fit in the caliper body.

NOTE: Mechanic's wire is not sturdy enough to use to support a caliper. Double the mechanic's wire to ensure that it is study enough to support the various brake calipers.

results were not good and problems were blamed on plastic pistons. What happened was that the pistons were becoming stuck in the caliper, which caused the brake pads to remain applied. This caused the brake pads to wear out very rapidly. The problem occurred because the phenolic pistons absorbed moisture and swelled.

NOTE: Brake engineers in the 1970s did not realize that phenolic materials were hygroscopic (absorbed moisture). As the phenolic material absorbed water over a long period of time, the diameter of the piston grew until it became stuck in the caliper bore.

By reducing the diameter of the pistons 0.025 to 0.050 mm (0.001 to 0.002 in.) and improving the caliper boot seal, the sticking problem has been solved. Since the mid-1980s, phenolic caliper pistons have been used as original equipment by many vehicle manufacturers. Phenolic caliper pistons are natural thermal insulators and help keep heat generated by the disc brake pads from transferring through the caliper piston to the brake fluid. Phenolic brake caliper pistons are also lighter in weight than steel caliper pistons and are usually brown in colour. See Figure 36–20.

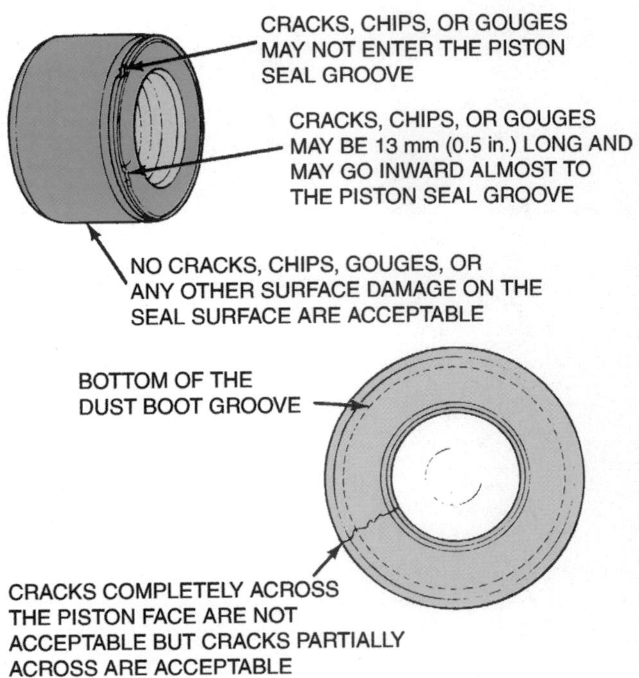

Figure 36–20 Phenolic (plastic) pistons should be carefully inspected.

Steel Caliper Pistons

Many manufacturers still use steel pistons. The stamped steel pistons are plated first with nickel, then chrome to achieve the desired surface finish. See Figure 36–21. Unlike phenolic caliper pistons, steel pistons can transfer heat from the brake pads to the brake fluid. The surface finish on a steel piston is critical. Steel can rust and corrode. Any surface pitting can cause the piston to stick.

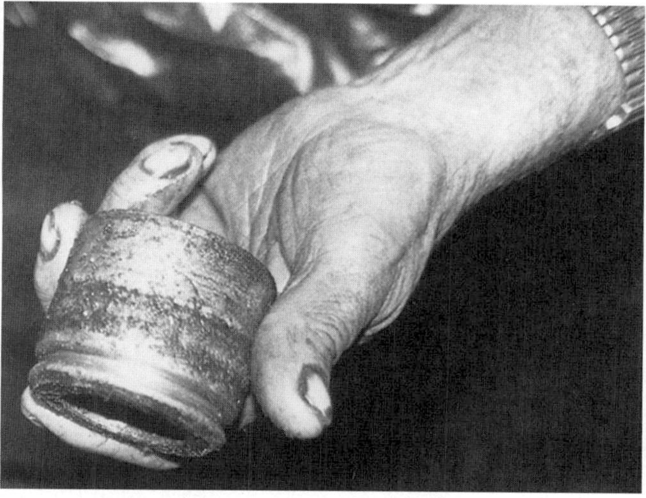

(a)

(b)

Figure 36–21 (a) The outside surface of caliper pistons should be carefully inspected. The square-cut O-ring inside the caliper rides on this outside surface of the piston. Sometimes dirty pistons can be cleaned and reused. (b) If there are any surface flaws such as rust pits on the piston, it should be replaced.

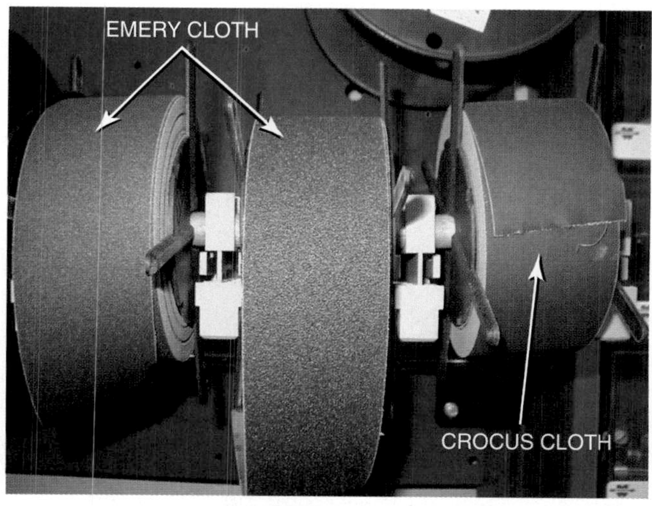

Figure 36–22 Crocus cloth (far right) is a fine abrasive polishing cloth.

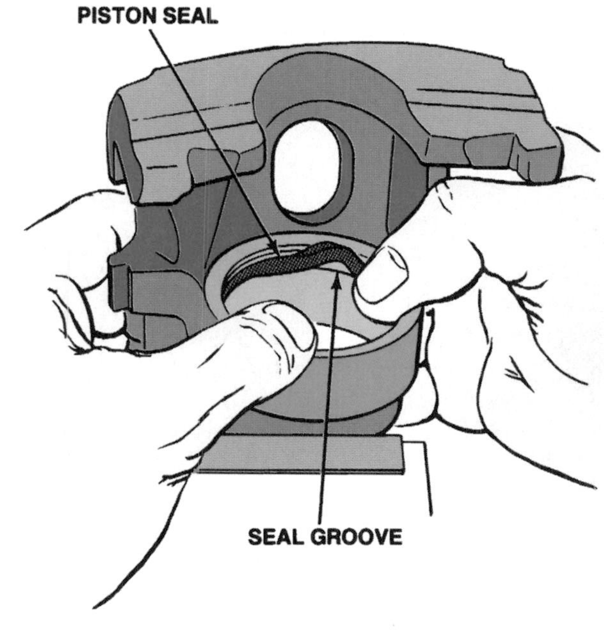

Figure 36–23 Installing a new piston seal. Never reuse rubber parts.

Frequently Asked Question ???

What Is Crocus Cloth?

Crocus cloth is a very fine emery cloth used to clean surface rust or stains from surfaces such as steel caliper pistons without harming the finish. See Figure 36–22. Crocus cloth is so fine that if you hold it in your hand and close your eyes, you should not be able to feel any difference between the front and the back.

REASSEMBLING DISC BRAKE CALIPERS

After disassembly, the caliper should be thoroughly cleaned in denatured alcohol and closely examined.

Carefully clean the caliper bore with clean brake fluid from a sealed container. Coat a new piston seal with clean brake fluid and install it in the groove inside the caliper bore, as shown in Figure 36–23.

Check the piston-to-caliper-bore clearance. Typical piston-to-caliper-bore clearance is

- Steel piston: 0.05–0.13 mm clearance (0.002 in.–0.005 in.)
- Phenolic piston: 0.13–0.25 mm clearance (0.005 in.–0.010 in.)

Coat a new dust boot with brake fluid and install the piston into the caliper. Some caliper boots require a special boot seating tool as shown in Figure 36–24.

Always lubricate caliper bushings, shims, and other brake hardware as instructed by the manufacturer. See Figure 36–25.

The pads should be securely attached to the caliper, as shown in Figures 36–26 and 36–27.

> **CAUTION:** Installing disc brake pads on the wrong side of the vehicle (left versus right) will often prevent the wear sensor from making noise when the pads are worn down.

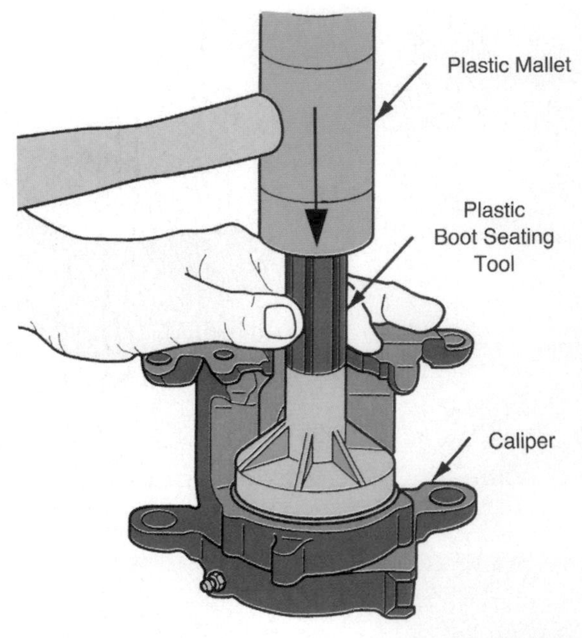

Figure 36–24 Seating the dust boot into the caliper housing using a special plastic seating tool.

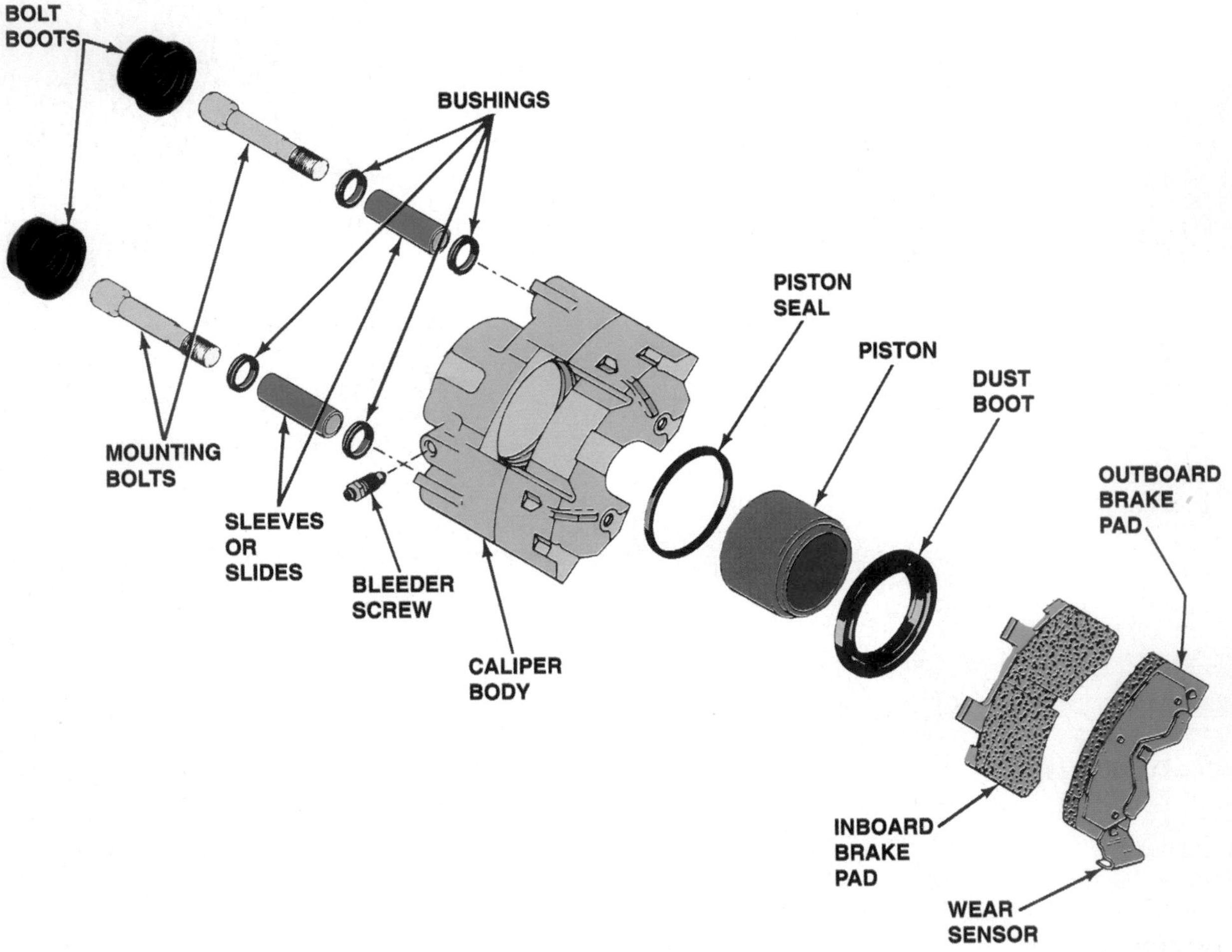

Figure 36–25 All rubber bushings should be lubricated with silicone brake grease for proper operation.

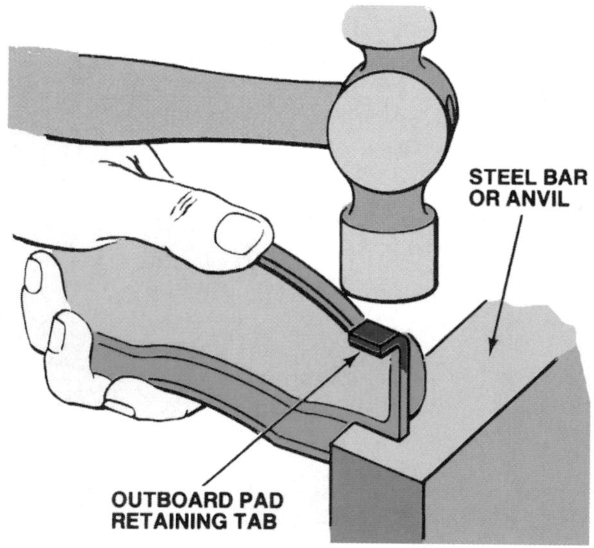

Figure 36–26 Often, a hammer is necessary to bend the retainer flange to make certain that the pads fit tightly to the caliper. If the pads are loose, a click may be heard every time the brakes are depressed. This click occurs when the pads move and then hit the caliper or caliper mount. If the pads are loose, a clicking noise may be heard while driving over rough road surfaces.

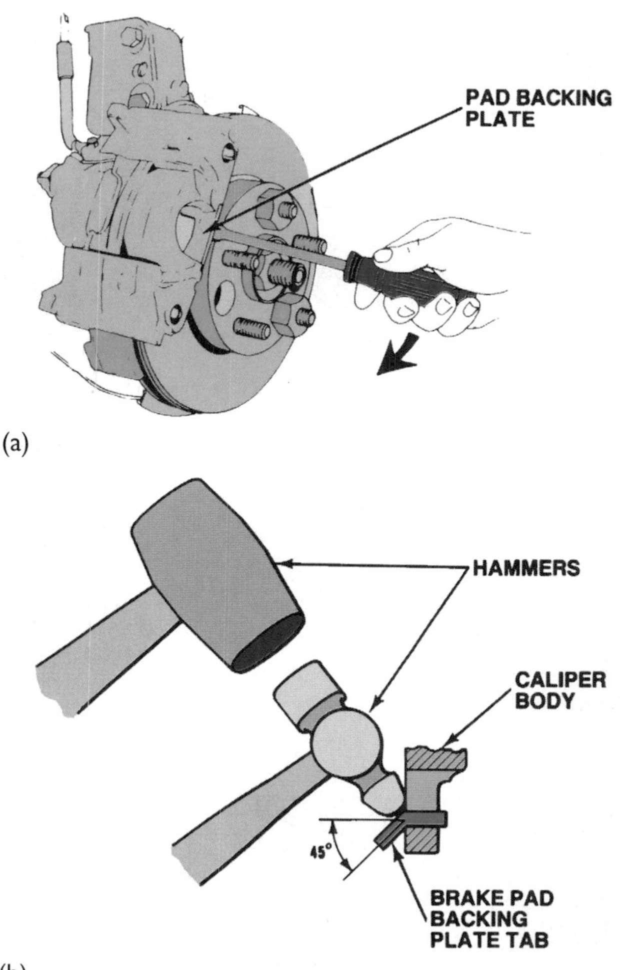

Figure 36–27 (a) Using a small pry-bar to force the outboard pad into proper position before bending the retaining tabs. (b) Use two hammers to bend the tab where it extends through the hole in the caliper body. Be sure to use one hammer that is soft-faced.

TECH TIP 

Using "Loaded Calipers" Saves Time

Many technicians find that disassembly, cleaning, and rebuilding calipers can take a lot of time. Often the bleeder screw breaks off or the caliper piston is too corroded to reuse. This means that the technician has to get a replacement piston, caliper overhaul kit (piston seal and boot), plus the replacement friction pads and hardware kit.

To save time (and sometimes money), many technicians are simply replacing the old used calipers with "loaded calipers." Loaded calipers are remanufactured calipers that include (come loaded with) the correct replacement friction pads and all the necessary hardware. See Figure 36–28. Therefore, only one part number is needed for each side of the vehicle for a complete disc brake overhaul.

Figure 36–28 A loaded caliper includes all hardware and shims with the correct pads all in one convenient package ready to install on the vehicle.

Caliper Mounts

When the hydraulic pressure from the master cylinder applies force to the disc brake pads, the entire caliper tends to be forced in the direction of rotation of the rotor. All calipers are mounted to the steering knuckle or axle housing. See Figure 36–29.

All braking force is transferred through the caliper to the mount. The points where the caliper contacts the caliper mount are called the **abutments,**

Figure 36–29 Floating calipers must be able to slide during normal operation. Therefore, there must be clearance between the caliper and the caliper mounting pads (abutments). Too little clearance will prevent the caliper from sliding and too much clearance will cause the caliper to make a clunking noise when the brakes are applied.

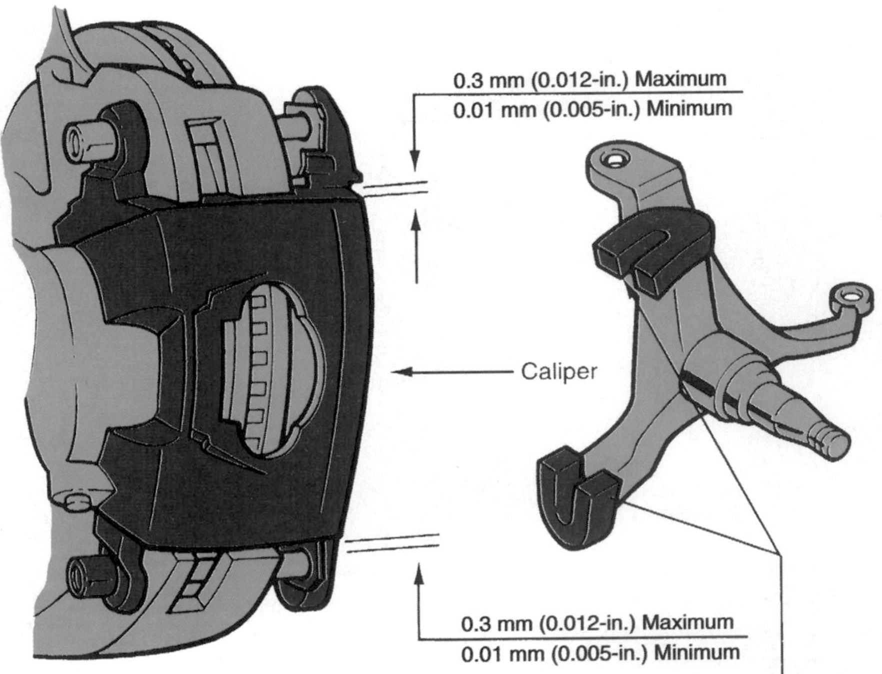

(a)

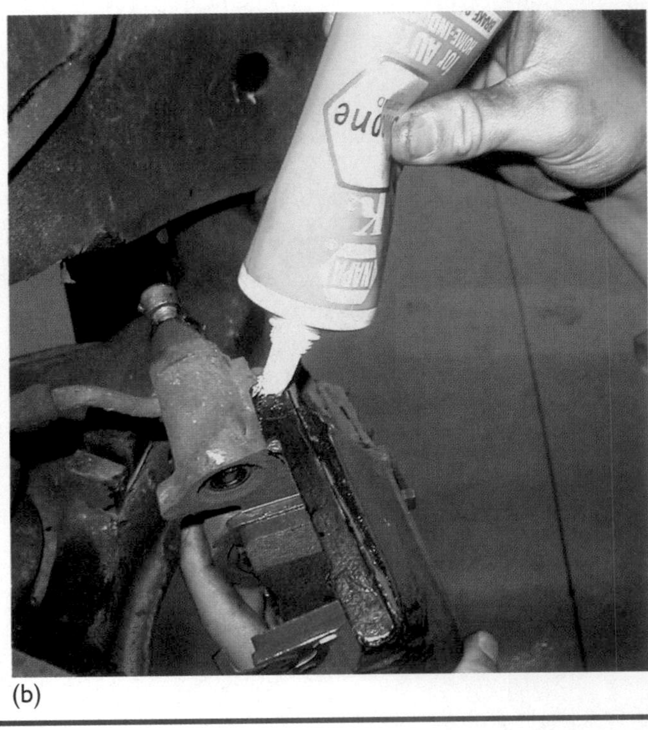
(b)

Figure 36–30 (a) Using an air-powered sanding disc to clean the caliper mount pads. (b) Applying silicone brake grease to the slides assures proper caliper operation.

reaction pads, or **ways.** The sliding surfaces of the caliper support should be cleaned with a wire brush and coated with a synthetic grease or silicone grease according to manufacturers' recommendations. See Figure 36–30. As the vehicle ages and the brakes are used thousands of times, these abutments (pads) can wear, causing too much clearance between the caliper and the mounting. When this occurs, the caliper often rotates against the abutment when the brakes are first applied making a loud knocking noise. If this occurs, the service technician can repair this type of wear by either replacing the entire steering knuckle or by using a knuckle kit.

SAFETY TIP 

Always Double Check Your Work

Whenever reassembling brakes, it is easy to twist the flexible brake hose as shown in Figure 36–31. To prevent possible brake hose failure and possibly an accident, always double check that the ribs on the brake hose are straight. The ribs are designed to allow the service technician to spot easily if the hose has been twisted.

Test Drive After Brake Replacement

After installing replacement disc brake pads or any other brake work, depress the brake pedal several times before driving the vehicle. This is a very important step! New brake pads are installed with the caliper piston pushed all the way into the caliper. The first few brake pedal applications usually result in the brake pedal going all the way to the floor. The brake pedal must be depressed (pumped) several times before enough brake fluid can be moved from the master cylinder into the calipers to move the piston tight against the pads and the pads against the rotors.

CAUTION: Never allow a customer to be the first to test drive the vehicle after brake work has been performed.

Bedding-in Replacement Brake Pads

Some manufacturers recommend that their replacement brake pads be "bedded-in" or burnished

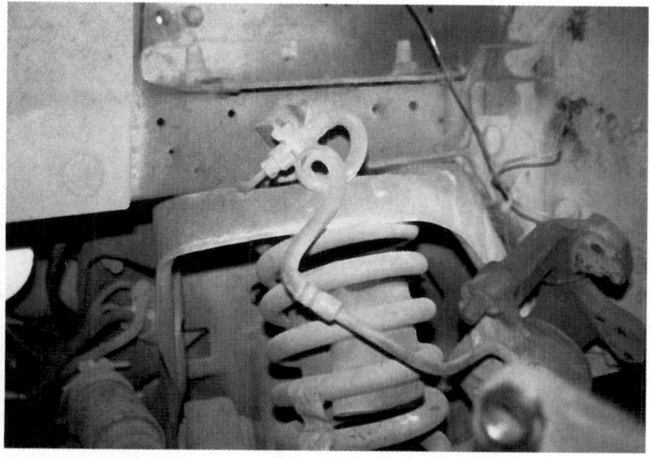

Figure 36–31 Note the twisted flexible brake line. This can cause brake hose failure if not corrected.

TECH TIP 

Foot Power Is Stronger than Air Pressure

Many times, a caliper piston becomes so stuck that normal shop air pressure is not powerful enough to pop the piston out of a caliper. Hydraulic pressure using the service brake pedal is often able to easily remove even the most corroded caliper piston.

If compressed air has been tried with the caliper off the vehicle, reattach the caliper to the brake line. Bleed the brakes by opening the bleeder valve as normal to rid the caliper of any trapped air. Use a wood board or shop rag in front of the caliper piston and apply the brake. Pump the brake pedal as necessary to force the piston out.

CAUTION: Pump the brake pedal *slowly*. The piston normally will be gently pushed from the caliper. If the pedal is pushed hard, the caliper piston could be forced out of the caliper bore with tremendous force. Position the caliper so that no damage will occur when the piston does pop free.

Some technicians will not try to overhaul a caliper but will simply replace it if compressed air pressure will not remove the piston.

before returning the vehicle to the owner. This break-in process varies with the manufacturer but usually involves stopping the vehicle from 50 km/h (30 mph) up to 30 times, allowing the brakes to cool 2–3 minutes between stops. This break-in procedure helps the replacement pads conform to the rotor and helps cure the resins used in the manufacture of the pads. Failure to properly break in new pads according to the manufacturer's recommended procedure could result in a hard brake pedal complaint from the driver and/or reduced braking effectiveness.

Even if the brake pad manufacturer does not recommend a break-in procedure, high-speed stops and overheating of the brakes should be avoided as much as possible during the first 50 to 100 stops.

Correcting Disc Brake Squeal

Brake squeal can best be *prevented* by careful attention to details whenever servicing any disc brake. Some of these precautions include

- *Keep the disc brake pads clean and grease free.*
- *Use factory-type clips and anti-squeal shims.* See Figure 36–32.

TECH TIP 

Increasing Pad Life

Many vehicles seem to wear out front disc brakes more often than normal. Stop-and-go city-type driving is often the cause. Driving style, such as rapid stops, also causes a lot of wear to occur.

The service technician can take some actions to increase brake pad life that are easier than trying to cure the driver's habits. These steps include:

1. Make sure the rear brakes are properly adjusted and working correctly. If the rear brakes are not functioning, all of the braking is accomplished by the front brakes alone.

HINT: Remind the driver to apply the parking brake regularly to help maintain proper rear-brake clearance on the rear brakes.

2. Use factory brake pads or premium brake pads from a known manufacturer. Tests performed by vehicle manufacturers show that many aftermarket replacement brake pads fail to deliver original equipment brake pad life.

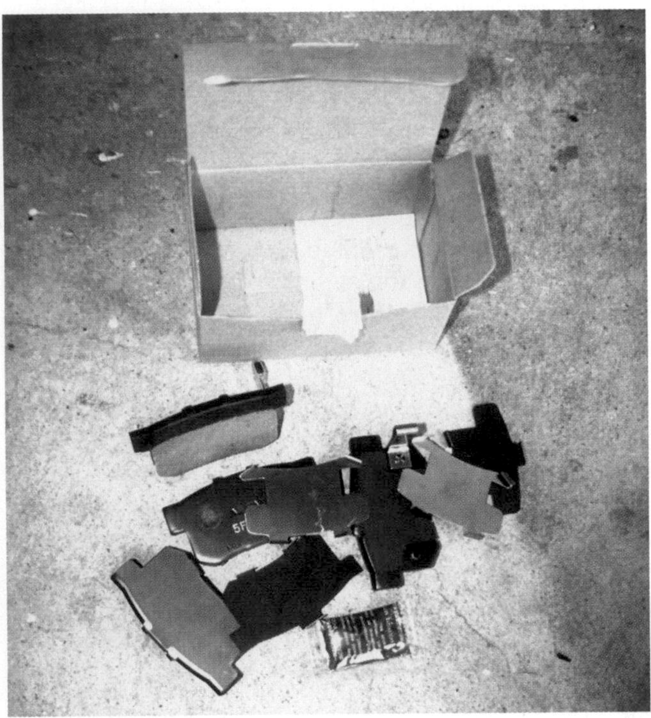

Figure 36–32 For best braking performance, purchase replacement disc brake pads that include all clips and shims specified by the vehicle manufacturer. Some pads even come with a package of the specified grease to use on the shims to reduce the possibility of brake noise.

NOTE: Many aftermarket disc brake pads do *not* include replacement hardware, which usually includes noise-reducing shims and clips. One of the advantages of purchasing original equipment (OE) disc brake pads is that they usually come equipped with all necessary shims and often with special grease that is recommended for use on metal shims.

CAUTION: Grease should only be applied to the non-friction (steel) side of the disc brake pads. Avoid getting grease on the friction side of any brake pad or shoe. Use only approved grease for disc brakes such as silicone brake grease or synthetic brake grease. Always follow the vehicle manufacturer's recommendations.

- *Lubricate all caliper slide points following the manufacturer's recommendation.*

REAR DISC BRAKES

Rear disc brakes are used on many vehicles. A parking brake is more difficult to use with disc brakes. Rear disc brakes are commonly found on high-performance and many production vehicles. Most vehicles equipped with rear disc brakes use one of two different styles of parking brake:

Style 1. An integral parking brake built into the piston assembly. See Figures 36–33 and 36–34.

Style 2. A more conventional disc brake that uses a small drum brake for the parking brake function. See Figure 36–35.

Figure 36–33 Cutaway of a General Motors rear disc brake with an integral parking brake.

TECH TIP

Bleed the Brakes at Every Oil Change?

An experienced technician started cracking open bleeder valves and allowing some brake fluid to escape whenever a vehicle was in the shop for an oil change. The technician started the practice because more and more customers' vehicles were equipped with aluminum calipers, especially rear disc brake calipers. Service work on these calipers had shown the technician that the steel bleeder valves often corroded to the aluminum caliper, resulting in broken-off bleeder valves. To prevent this from happening, the technician opened each bleeder valve and allowed some brake fluid to drip out as part of an under-vehicle inspection. The major reason for opening the bleeder valves was to keep them free, since the escaping brake fluid would help lubricate the threads of the bleeder valve and prevent them from corroding.

Almost every time the bleeder valve was opened on rear disc brake calipers, a spurt of air would come out before the brake fluid would start to flow. Customers noticed that every time the oil was changed, the brakes felt firmer. Now the technician includes this service for all customers as long as the bleeder is free to open.

Rotating Pistons Back into the Caliper

Many disc brake calipers used on the rear wheels require that the pistons be rotated to reseat them. When the parking brake is applied, the actuating screw moves the piston outward, forcing the pads against the disc brake rotor. The piston is kept from rotating because of an antirotation device or notches on the inboard pad and piston.

When the disc brake pads are being replaced, use a special tool to rotate the piston back into the brake calipers. Insert the tip of the tool in the holes or slots in the piston. Exert inward pressure while turning the piston. Make sure that the piston is retracting into the caliper and continue to turn the piston until it bottoms out.

NOTE: Some pistons are activated with left-handed threads.

After putting the pads back into the caliper, check that the clearance does not exceed 1.5 mm (1/16 in.) from the rotor. Clearance greater than 1.5 mm (1/16 in.) may allow the adjuster to be pulled out of the piston when the service brake is applied. If the clearance is greater than 1.5 mm (1/16 in.), readjust by rotating the piston outward to reduce the clearance. See Figure 36–36 on page 870.

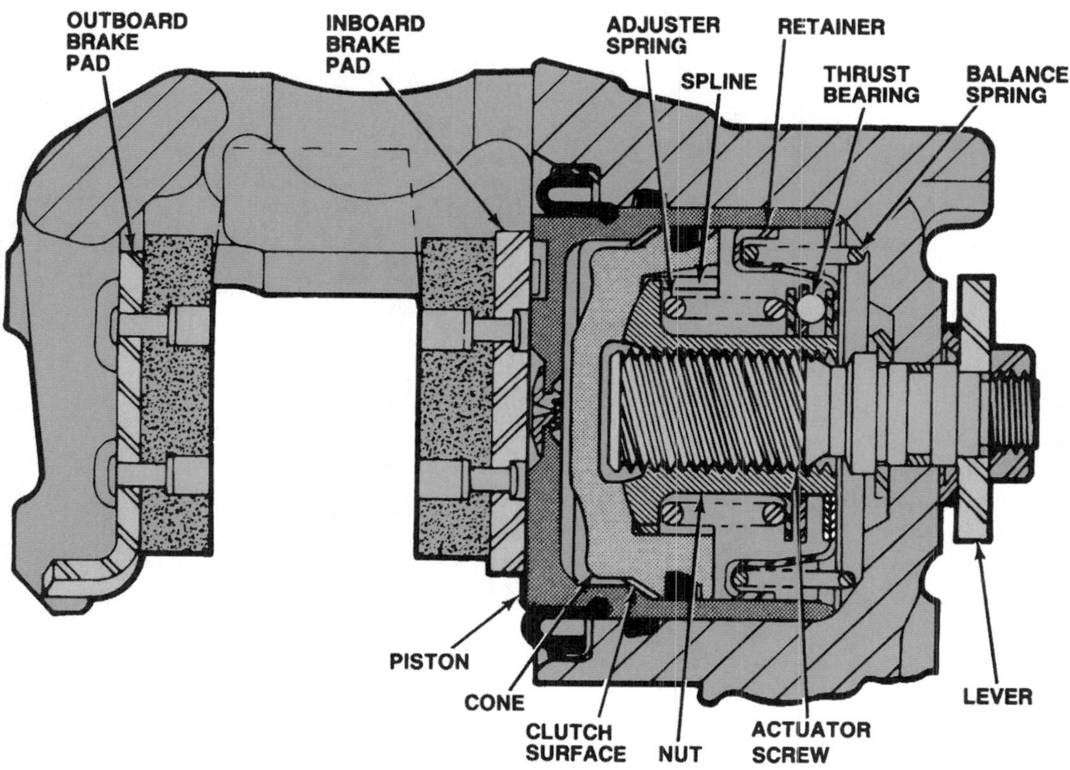

Figure 36–34 A cross-sectional view of a General Motors rear disc brake caliper showing the screw, nut, and cone parking brake components.

(a)

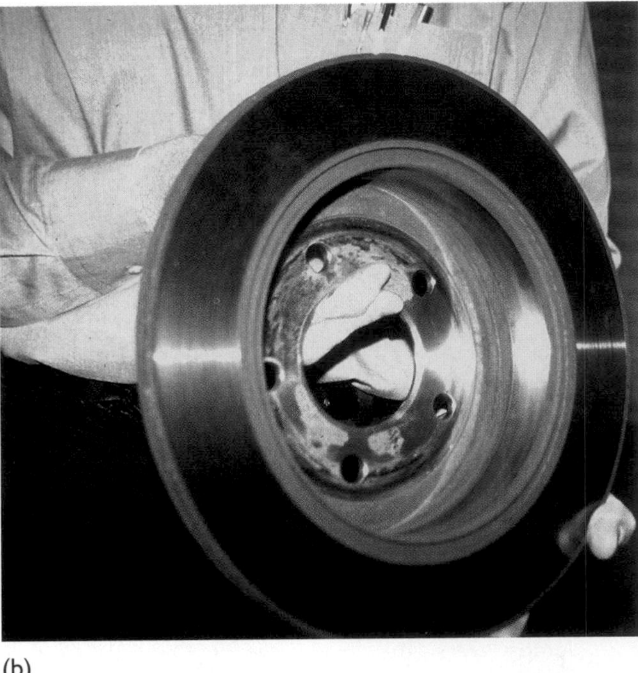

(b)

Figure 36–35 (a) Removing the disc brake rotor from this Chrysler minivan reveals a small drum brake used for the parking brake. (b) The inside "hat" of the rotor is the friction surface for the drum brake shoes.

TECH TIP

The Screwdriver Trick

A low brake pedal on GM vehicles equipped with rear disc brakes is a common customer complaint. Often the reason is a lack of self-adjustment that *should* occur whenever the brake pedal (or parking brake) is released. During brake release, the pressure is removed from the caliper piston and the spring inside the caliper piston is free to adjust. Often this self-adjustment does not occur and a low brake pedal results.

A common trick used on the vehicle assembly line is to use a screwdriver to hold the piston against the rotor while an assistant releases the brake pedal. See Figure 36–37. As the brake pedal is released, the adjusting screw inside the caliper piston is free to move. Sometimes, it may be necessary to tap on the caliper itself with a dead blow hammer to free the adjusting screw. Repeat the process as necessary until the proper brake pedal height returns. If this method does not work, replace the caliper assembly.

In summary:

Step 1. Have an assistant depress the brake pedal.

Step 2. Using a small pry-bar inserted through the hole in the top of the caliper, hold the piston against the rotor.

NOTE: Be careful not to damage the dust boot.

Step 3. While still holding the piston against the rotor, have the assistant release the brake pedal. The adjusting screw adjusts when the brake pedal is *released,* and a slight vibration or sound will be noticed as the brake is released. This vibration or sound is created by the self-adjusting mechanism inside the caliper piston taking up the excess clearance.

DISC BRAKE TROUBLESHOOTING GUIDE	
Problem	**Possible Causes**
Pulls to one side during braking	• Incorrect or unequal tire pressures • Front end out of alignment • Unmatched tires on the same axle • Restricted brake lines or hoses • Stuck or seized caliper or caliper piston • Defective or damaged shoe and lining (grease or brake fluid on the lining, or a bent shoe) • Malfunctioning rear brakes • Loose suspension parts • Loose calipers
Brake roughness or chatter (pedal pulsates)	• Excessive lateral runout of rotor • Parallelism of the rotor not within specifications • Wheel bearings not adjusted correctly • Rear drums out of round • Brake pads worn to metal backing plate
Excessive pedal effort	• Binding or seized caliper suspension • Binding brake pedal mechanism • Improper rotor surface finish • Malfunctioning power brake • Partial system failure • Excessively worn shoe and lining • Piston in the caliper stuck or sluggish • Fading brakes due to incorrect lining
Excessive pedal travel	• Partial brake system failure • Insufficient fluid in the master cylinder • Air trapped in the system • Bent shoe and lining • Excessive pedal effort • Excessive parking brake travel (four-wheel disc brakes, except Corvette)
Dragging brakes	• Pressure trapped in the brake lines. To diagnose, momentarily open the caliper bleeder valve to relieve the pressure. • Restricted brake tubes or hoses • Improperly lubricated caliper suspension system • Improper clearance between the caliper and torque abutment surfaces • Check valve installed in the outlet of the master cylinder to the disc brakes instead of to the outlet to the drum brakes
Front disc brakes very sensitive to light brake applications	• Metering valve not holding off the front brake application • Incorrect lining material • Improper rotor surface finish • Check other causes listed under "Pulls"
Rear drum brakes skidding under hard brake applications	• Proportioning valve • Contaminated rear brake lining • Caliper or caliper piston stuck or corroded

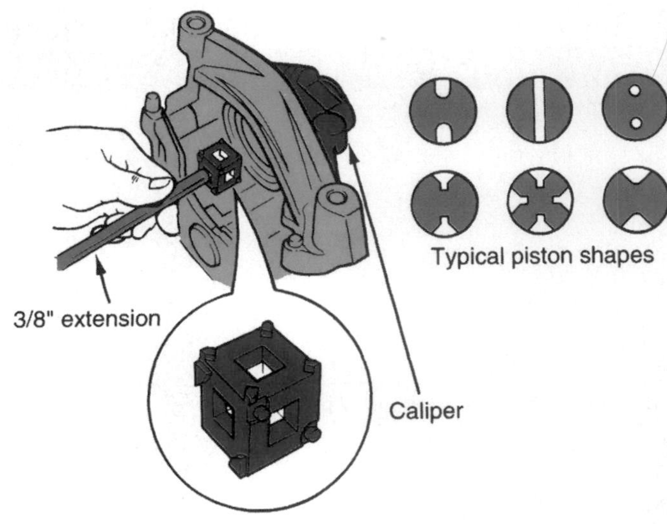

Figure 36–36 Determine which face of the special tool best fits the holes or slots in the piston. Sometimes needle-nose pliers can be used to rotate the piston back into the caliper bore.

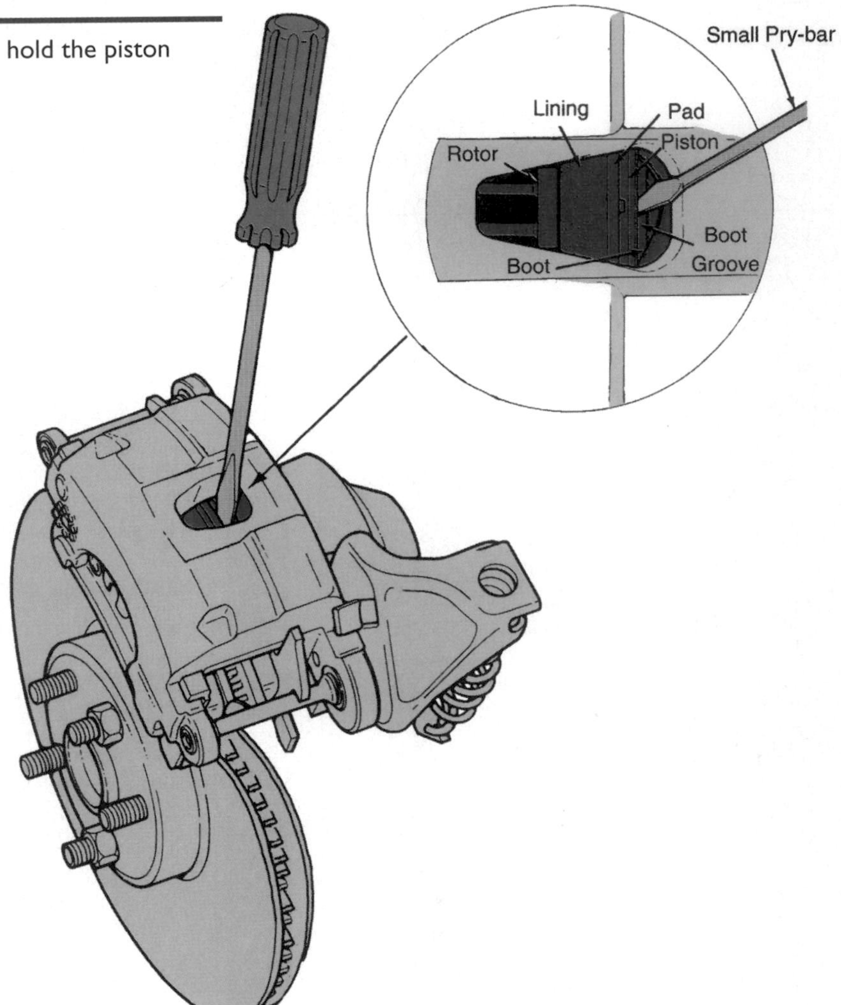

Figure 36–37 Using a screwdriver to hold the piston against the rotor as an assistant releases the brake pedal.

PHOTO SEQUENCE 24 Disc Brake Pad Replacement

P24–1 After safely hoisting the vehicle, remove the wheels. To help break loose a bleeder valve, tap on the caliper at the base of the bleeder valve.

P24–2 Often a blow to the top of the bleeder valve is also necessary to "break the taper" at the base of the bleeder valve.

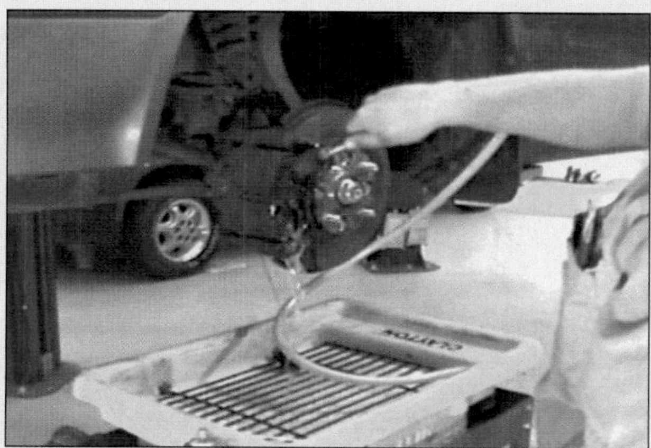

P24–3 Before loosening the bleeder valve, attempt to tighten the valve first. Again, this helps break the bleeder valve loose.

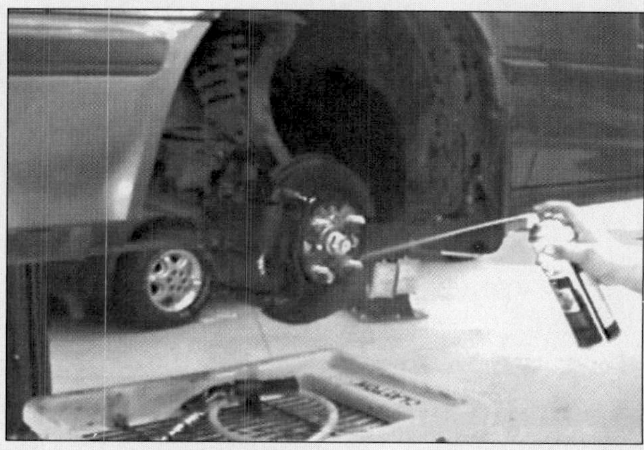

P24–4 The bleeder valve should be able to be loosened without breaking.

P24–5 With the bleeder valve open, use a pry-bar or screwdriver against the inboard pad to force the caliper piston back into its bore to provide clearance so that the caliper can be removed.

P24–6 A C-clamp can also be used to compress the caliper piston. Be sure the bleeder valve is open to prevent the old brake fluid from being forced up into the ABS hydraulic unit and/or the master cylinder.

Disc Brake Pad Replacement—continued

P24–7 After the caliper piston has been pushed back into its bore, the caliper guide pins (caliper retaining pins) can be removed.

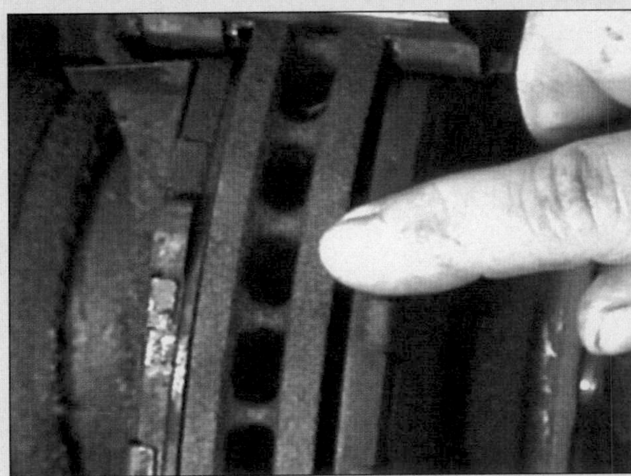

P24–8 It may be necessary to use a screwdriver or pry bar to lift the caliper off of its support.

P24–9 Lift the caliper assembly off the rotor.

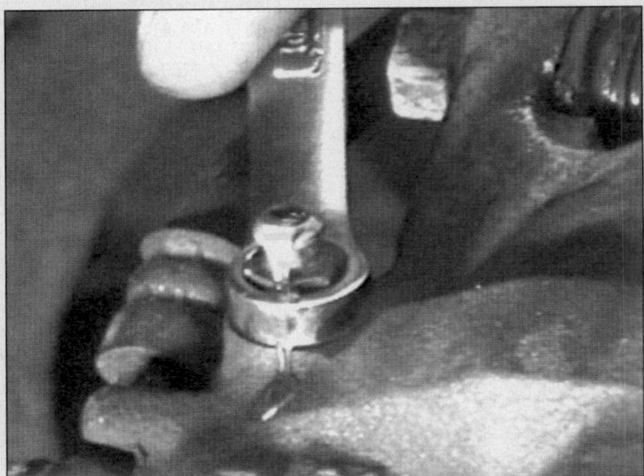

P24–10 Hang the caliper by a wire, or in this case, the service technician simply hung the caliper on the strut. This support is necessary to prevent damage to the flexible brake lines that could occur if the caliper were allowed to hang by the hoses.

P24–11 Use a micrometer and measure the thickness of the rotor. Machine or replace the rotor as necessary.

P24–12 Remove the disc brake pads.

P24–13 If necessary, open the bleeder valve and use a C-clamp to push the caliper piston all the way into the caliper.

P24–14 During reassembly, use silicone brake grease to lubricate any part(s) that contains both rubber and metal, such as this guide pin.

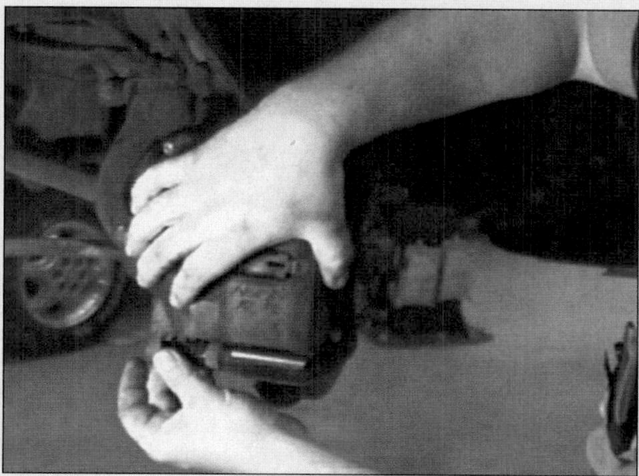

P24–15 Thoroughly clean the caliper slides.

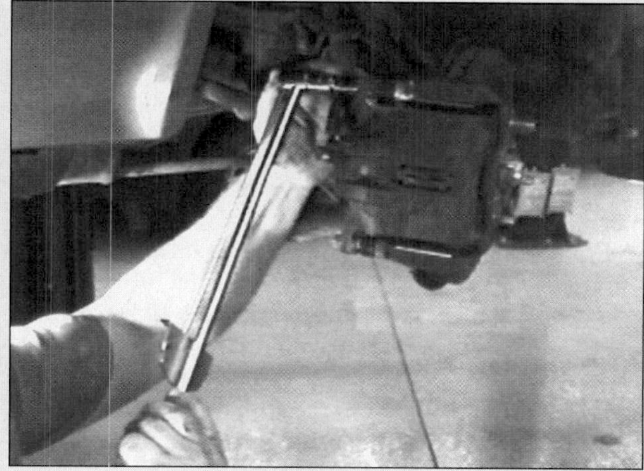

P24–16 Apply disc brake dampening material on the back of the pads especially if they are not equipped with noise-dampening shims.

P24–17 Install the pads. Be sure to use all the clips and noise-reduction shims and install properly.

P24–18 Install the caliper and torque the guide pins (or caliper retaining bolts) to specifications. Be sure to depress the brake pedal several times before test driving the vehicle.

SUMMARY

1. Disc brakes are used on the front and on the rear wheels of many vehicles. Disc brake calipers are either fixed or floating.
2. When a disc brake is applied, the square-cut O-ring is deformed. When the brakes are released, the rubber O-ring returns to its original shape and draws the caliper piston back into the caliper and away from the rotor.
3. As the disc brake pad wears, the caliper piston moves through the square-cut O-ring to compensate for the wear. Because the piston is now moved outward, brake fluid fills the space and the brake fluid level in the master cylinder drops.
4. Disc brake wear indicators can be a metal tag that touches the rotor and makes noise or can be a groove moulded into the pad itself. Some wear indicators are electrical and light a dash indicator lamp when the brakes are worn.
5. Caliper pistons are either chrome-plated steel or plastic (phenolic). Any damaged piston must be replaced. Both the square-cut O-ring and the dust boot must be replaced when the caliper is disassembled.
6. All metal-to-metal contact points of the disc brake assembly should be coated with an approved brake lubricant such as synthetic grease, "moly" grease, or antiseize compound.
7. After a brake overhaul, the brake pedal should be depressed several times until a normal brake pedal height is achieved before performing a thorough test drive.
8. Many rear disc brake systems use an integral parking brake. Regular use of the parking brake helps maintain proper rear brake clearance.

REVIEW QUESTIONS

1. Describe how a single caliper works.
2. List what parts are included in a typical overhaul kit for a single piston floating caliper.
3. List three types of disc brake pad wear sensors.
4. Describe how to remove caliper pistons and perform a caliper overhaul.
5. Explain what causes disc brake squeal and list what a technician can do to reduce or eliminate the noise.

RED SEAL CERTIFICATION-TYPE QUESTIONS

1. Uneven disc brake pad wear could be caused by
   a. Seized caliper slides
   b. Air in the hydraulic system
   c. A seized caliper piston
   d. A seized emergency brake cable
2. What could be the cause of a chirping noise from the wheel area while driving, but that stops once the brake is depressed?
   a. A defective wheel bearing
   b. Wear sensor on the brake pad
   c. Normal sound for metallic pads
   d. Phenolic caliper piston expanding from heat
3. What part causes the disc brake caliper piston to retract when the brakes are released?
   a. Return (retracting) spring
   b. The rotating rotor (disc) which pushes the piston back
   c. The square-cut O-ring
   d. The caliper bushings
4. What could be the cause of the brake fluid reservoir being low?
   a. Internal leak in the master cylinder
   b. Blocked brake line
   c. Brake pad wear
   d. Seized caliper piston
5. What is the minimum thickness of the brake pad friction material?
   a. Twice the thickness of the steel backing
   b. 3.0 mm or more with bonded pads
   c. 3.0 mm or more with riveted pads
   d. 1.5 mm or more with bonded linings
6. A typical disc brake caliper overhaul (OH) kit usually includes what parts?
   a. Square-cut O-ring seal and dust boot
   b. Replacement caliper piston and dust boot
   c. Dust boot, return spring, and caliper seal
   d. Disc brake pad clips, dust boot, and caliper piston assembly
7. What could be the cause of a knocking sound when the brake is first applied?
   a. Seized brake caliper piston
   b. Low brake fluid
   c. Too much clearance between the brake caliper and knuckle
   d. Too little clearance between the brake caliper and knuckle
8. What is the correct method to remove a caliper piston?
   a. Compressed air
   b. Slide hammer
   c. Channel lock pliers
   d. Manufacturers' specialty tool
9. Which is *not* a recommended type of grease to use on brake parts?
   a. Silicone grease
   b. Wheel bearing (chassis) grease
   c. Synthetic grease
   d. Antiseize lubricant
10. What causes the brake pad to contact the rotor when applying the emergency brakes on a four-wheel disc vehicle?
    a. Hydraulic pressure
    b. A screw thread inside the caliper piston
    c. Vacuum booster operation
    d. Air pressure

37

Machining Brake Drums and Rotors

OBJECTIVES: After studying Chapter 37, you should be able to:

1. Prepare for the interprovincial Red Seal certification examination in Appendix V (Brakes) on the topics covered in this chapter.
2. Discuss the construction of brake drums and rotors.
3. Explain the formation of hard spots in drums and rotors.
4. Describe how to measure and inspect drums and rotors before machining.
5. Discuss how surface finish is measured and its importance to satisfactory brake service.
6. Demonstrate how to machine a brake drum and rotor correctly.

Brake drums and rotors are the major energy-absorbing parts of the braking system. Friction between the friction material and the drum or rotor creates heat. As energy continues to be absorbed, the drum or rotor increases in temperature. Air flow across the drum or rotor helps to dissipate the heat and keep the temperature rise under control. See Figures 37–1 and 37–2 for examples of how drums and rotors are cooled.

BRAKE DRUMS

Where the lining contacts the drum, brake drums are constructed of cast iron; otherwise, they have mild steel centres. The drum is drilled for the lug studs. Cast iron is approximately 3% carbon content, which makes the drum hard, yet brittle. This 3% carbon content of the cast iron also acts as a lubricant, which prevents noise during braking. Also, the rubbing surface can be machined without the need of a coolant (as would be required if constructed of mild steel). Because of these properties, cast iron is used on the friction surface of all drums. See Figure 37–3. Even aluminum brake drums use cast iron for the friction surface area. Besides saving

Figure 37–1 An aluminum brake drum with a cast iron friction surface. The cooling fins around the outside help dissipate the heat from the friction surface to the outside air. Note the "MAX DIA 243.5 mm" cast into the drum.

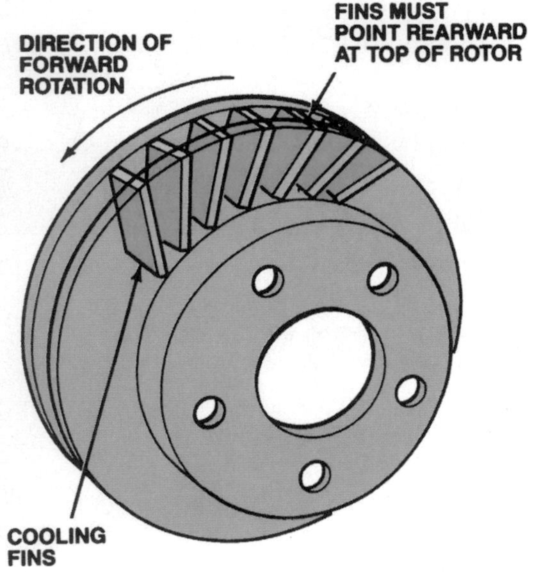

Figure 37–2 The airflow through cooling vents helps keep brakes from overheating.

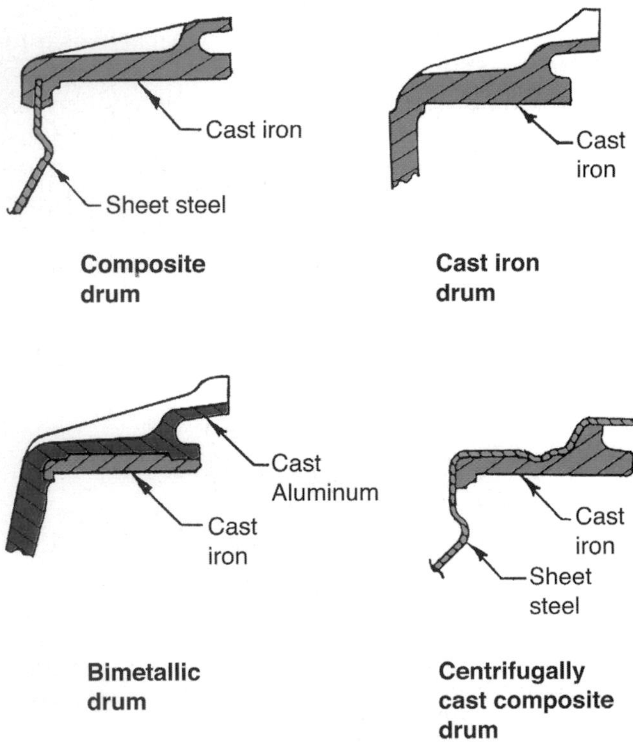

Figure 37–3 Types of brake drums. Regardless of the design, all types use cast iron as a friction surface.

weight, aluminum brake drums transfer heat to the surrounding air faster than cast iron or steel.

One inspection step after removing a brake drum is to check it for warpage using a straight edge, as shown in Figure 37–4.

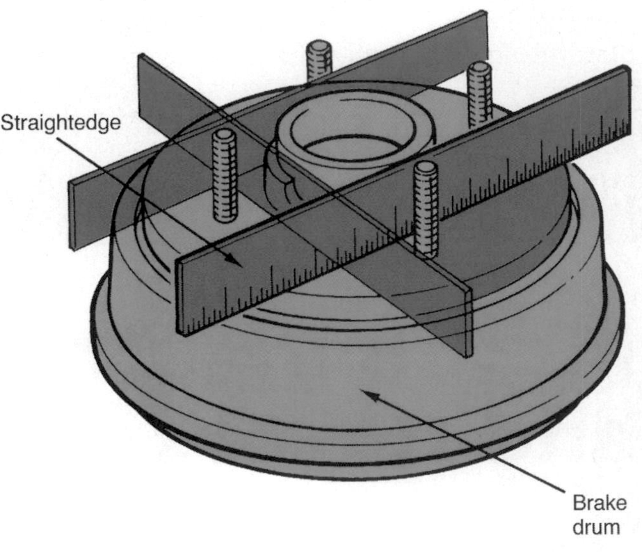

Figure 37–4 A straightedge can be used to check for brake drum warpage.

TECH TIP 

Mark It to Be Sure

Most experts recommend that brake rotors, as well as drums and wheels, be marked *before* removing them for service. Many disc brake rotors are directional and will only cool properly if replaced in the original location. A quick-and-easy method is to use correction fluid. This alcohol-based liquid comes in small bottles with a small brush inside making it easy to mark rotors with an "L" for left and an "R" for right. Correction fluid (also called "white out" or "liquid paper") can also be used to make marks on wheel studs, wheels, and brake drums to help ensure reinstallation in the same location.

A warped drum is often a source of vibration. A brake drum that is out-of-round can cause a brake pedal pulsation during braking.

HINT: To help diagnose if the front disc brakes or rear drum brakes are the cause of the vibration, try slowing the vehicle using the parking brake. If the vibration occurs, the problem is due to the rear brakes.

Hard Spots

Hard spots are created by heat. Vehicles that are stopped from high speed or long braking down a hill or mountain can generate excessive temperatures. The metal on the surface, being at a much higher temperature, tends to expand and raise a small bump. As the spot cools, the crystallized structure of the cast iron changes to a hard steel so that the metallurgy actually becomes different in the hard spot than the surrounding areas. See Figure 37–5.

Some experts recommend using a grinding stone to remove hard spots. However, most experts and vehicle manufacturers agree that these hard spots have "memory" and will tend to return as soon as the brakes are subjected to severe service again and recommend that drums or rotors with hard spots be replaced.

"Machine to" versus "Discard Dimension"

Brake drums can usually be machined a maximum of 1.5 mm (0.060 in.) oversize (for example, a 241.3 mm (9.500 in.) drum new could wear or be machined to a maximum inside diameter of 242.8 mm (9.560 in.) unless this is otherwise prohibited (indicated by a stamp on the drum). Most brake experts recommend that both drums on the same axle be within 0.25 mm (0.010 in.) of each other. *The maximum specified inside diameter (I.D.) means the maximum wear inside diameter.* Always leave at least 0.4 mm (0.015 in.) after machining (resurfacing) for wear. Many manufacturers recommend that 0.8 mm (0.030 in.) be left for wear. Be certain to follow manufacturers' specifications for turning.

TECH TIP 

Brake Drum Chamfer

Look at the chamfer on the outer edge of most brake drums. When the chamfer is no longer visible, the brake drum is usually at or past its maximum I.D. See Figure 37–6. Although this chamfer is not an accurate gauge of the inside diameter of the brake drum, it still is a helpful indicator to the technician.

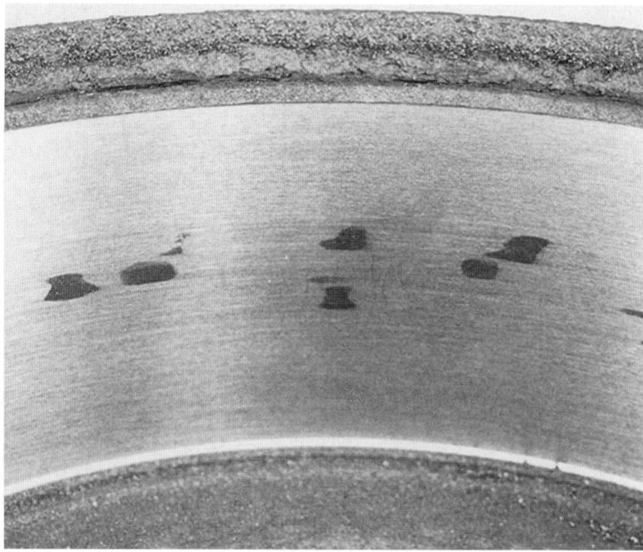

Figure 37–5 These dark hard spots are created by heat that actually changes the metallurgy of the cast-iron drum. Most experts recommend replacement of any brake drum that has these hard spots.

Measuring and Inspecting Brake Drums

Brake drums are usually measured using a micrometer especially designed for brake drums. See Figure 37–7. The drum should be checked for roundness, bell mouth, taper, and deep scoring. See Figure 37–8.

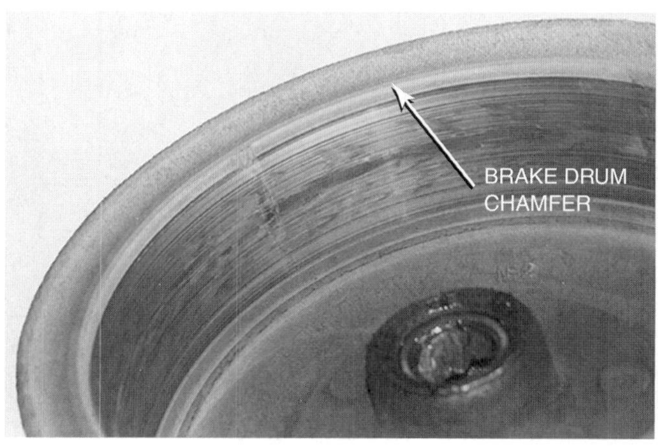

Figure 37–6 Most brake drums have a chamfer around the edge. If the chamfer is no longer visible, then the drum is usually worn (or machined) to its maximum allowable inside diameter.

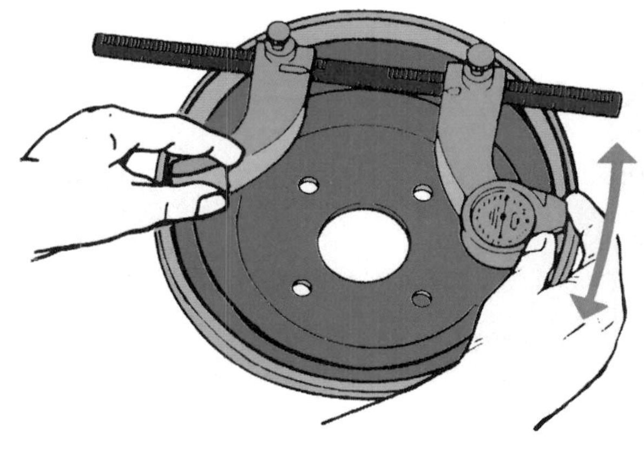

Figure 37–7 A typical needle-dial brake drum micrometer. The left movable arm is set to the approximate drum diameter and the right arm to the more exact drum diameter. This dial indicator (gauge) reads in thousandths of an inch.

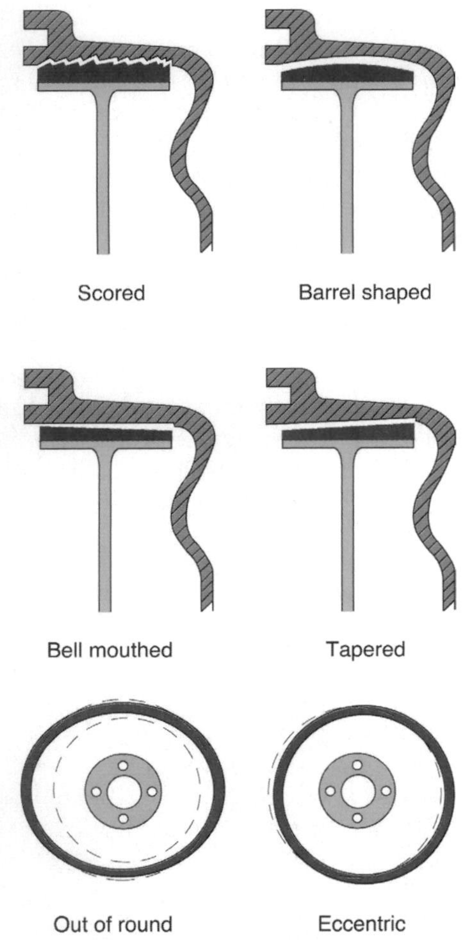

Figure 37–8 Typical brake drum wear problems.

> **HINT:** Hold a brake drum in the centre with one hand and tap the outside of the drum with a light steel hammer. The drum should ring like a bell. If the drum produces a dull thud, it is probably cracked and needs to be replaced.

MACHINING DRUMS

If the drum has a hub with bearings, check the outer bearing races (cups) for wear and replace as necessary before placing the drum on the brake lathe. Also, carefully inspect and clean the lathe spindle shaft and cones before use. Use a **self-aligning spacer (SAS)** to make sure even force will be applied to the drum by the spindle nut. Always follow the instructions for the lathe you are using.

Hubless drums use a hole in the centre of the brake drum for centring. Always check that the centre hole is clean and free of burrs or nicks. Typical drum brake machining steps include

Step 1. Mount the drum on the lathe and install the silencer band as shown in Figures 37–9 and 37–10.

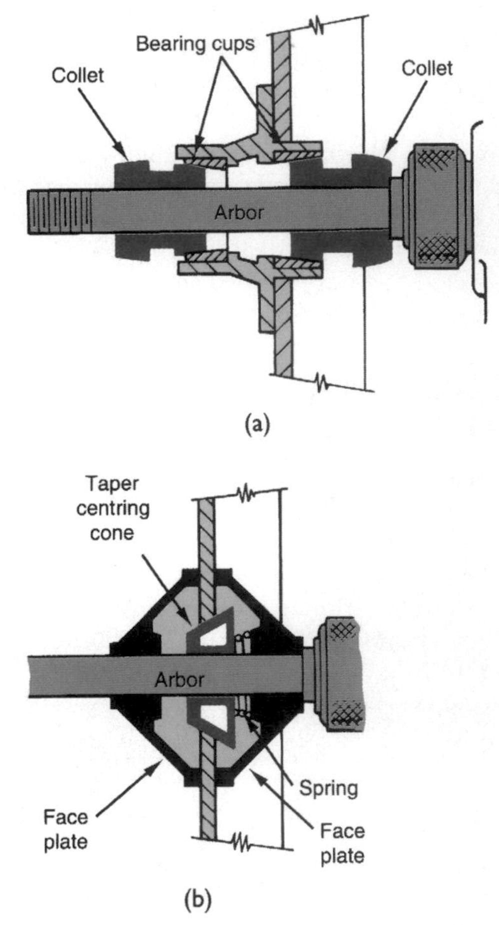

Figure 37–9 (a) A rotor or brake drum with a bearing hub should be installed on a brake lathe using the appropriate size collets that fit the bearing cups (races). (b) A hubless rotor or brake drum requires a spring and a tapered centring cone. A face plate should be used on both sides of the rotor or drum to provide support.

Step 2. Turn the drum by hand before turning on the lathe to be sure everything is clean. Advance the tool bit manually until it just contacts the drum. This is called a **scratch cut.** See Figure 37–11.

Step 3. Stop the lathe and back off the tool bit. Loosen the arbor nut and rotate the drum one-half turn (180°) on the arbor. Turn the lathe on and make a second scratch cut.

a. If the scratch cuts are side by side, the lathe is okay and machining can begin.

b. If the scratch cuts are opposite, remove the drum and check for nicks, burrs, or chips on the mounting surfaces.

Step 4. Start the lathe and set the depth of the cut. See Figure 37–12. The maximum rough cut depends on the lathe type. The minimum cut is usually specified as no less than 0.05 mm (0.002 in.). A shallower cut usually causes the tool bit to slide over the surface of the metal rather than cut into the metal. See Figure 37–13 for an example of a drum

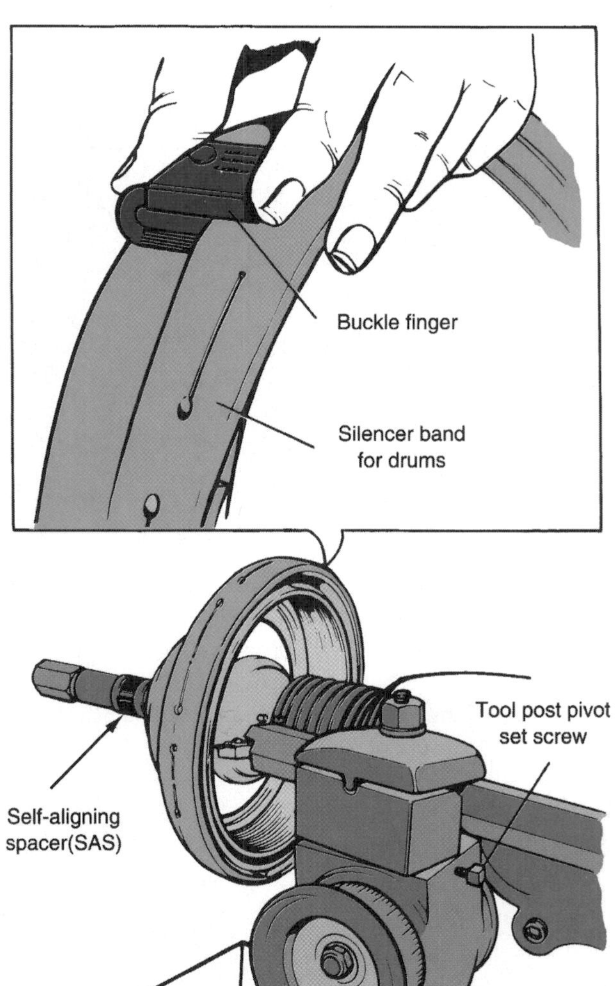

Figure 37–10 A self-aligning spacer (SAS) should always be used between the drum or rotor and the spindle retaining nut to help assure an even clamping force and to prevent the adapters and cone from getting into a bind. A silencer band should always be installed to prevent turning-tool chatter and to assure a smooth surface finish. (Courtesy of AMMCO Tools, Inc.)

Figure 37–11 After installing a brake drum on the lathe, turn the cutting tool outward until the tool just touches the drum. This is called a *scratch cut.* (Courtesy of AMMCO Tools, Inc.)

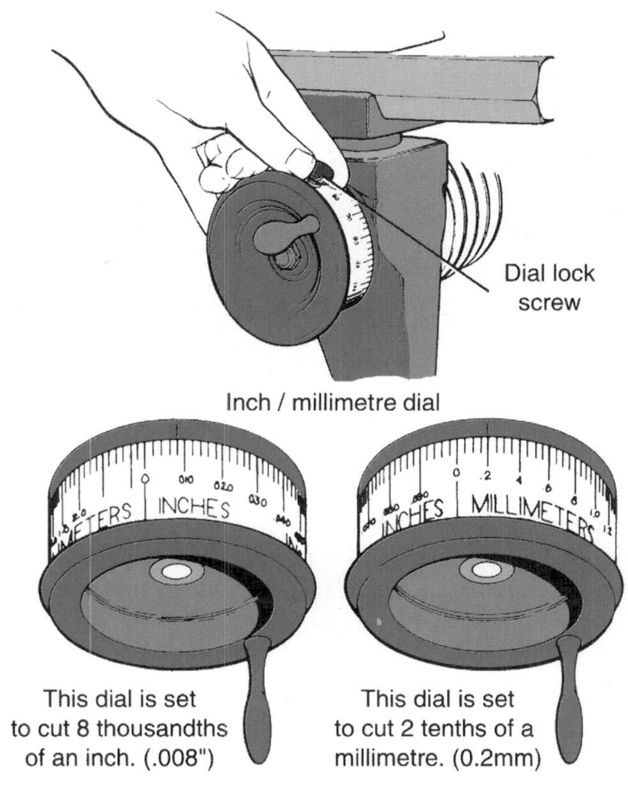

Figure 37–12 Set the depth of the cut indicator to zero just as the turning tool touches the drum. (Courtesy of AMMCO Tools, Inc.)

Figure 37–13 Notice the chatter marks at the edge of the friction-area surface of the brake drum. These marks were caused by vibration of the drum because the technician failed to wrap the dampening strap (silencer band) over the friction-surface portion of the brake drum.

Figure 37–14 This excessively worn (thin) rotor was removed from the vehicle in this condition. It is amazing that the vehicle was able to stop with such a thin rotor.

machined without properly positioning the antichatter (vibration) strap.

DISC BRAKE ROTORS

Cast-Iron Rotors

Disc brake rotors use cast gray iron at the area that contacts the friction pad. Rotors are made in several styles including:

1. **Solid**—used on the rear of many vehicles equipped with rear disc brakes and on the front of some small and mid-size vehicles. Solid rotors are much thinner than vented rotors. See Figure 37–14 for an example of an extremely worn solid rotor.
2. **Vented**—used on the front of most vehicles. The internal vanes allow air to circulate between the two friction surfaces of the rotor. Rotors can be either straight-vane design or a directional-vane design, as shown in Figure 37–15.

Composite rotors use a steel centre section with a cast iron wear surface. These composite rotors are lighter in weight than conventional cast iron rotors. See Figure 37–16. The light weight of composite rotors makes them popular with vehicle manufacturers. However, technicians should be aware that full contact adapters that simulate the actual wheel being bolted to the rotor must be used when machining composite rotors. If composite rotors are incorrectly machined, they usually must be replaced.

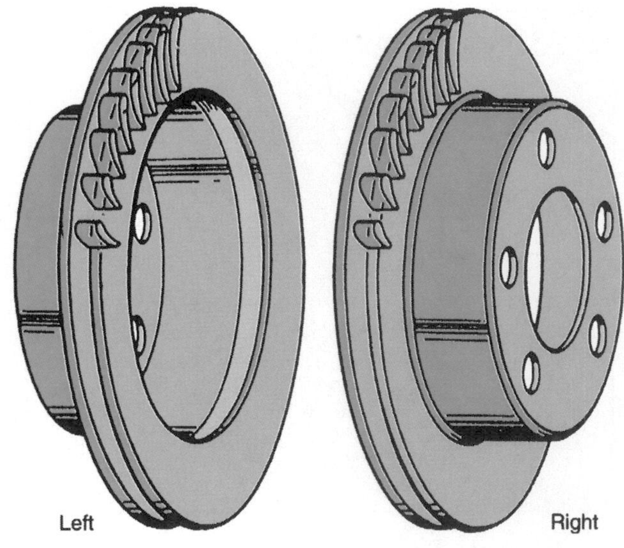

Figure 37–15 Directional-vane-vented disc brake rotors. Note that the fins angle toward the rear of the vehicle. It is important that this type of rotor be reinstalled on the correct side of the vehicle. (Courtesy of Allied Signal Automotive Aftermarket)

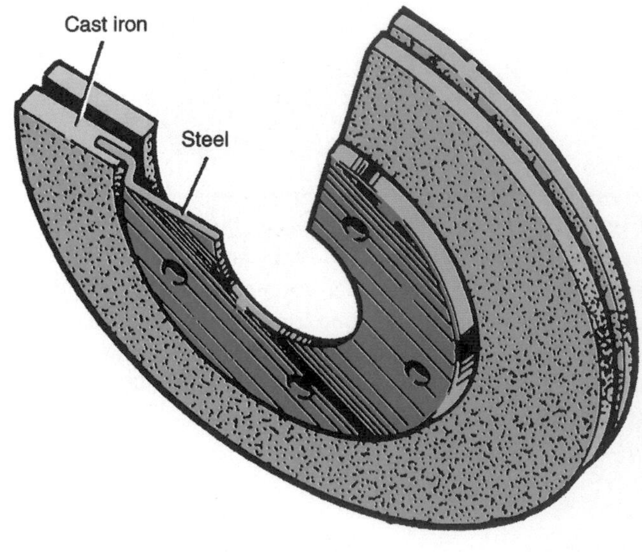

Figure 37–16 A typical composite rotor that uses cast-iron friction surfaces and a steel centre section.

Aluminum Metal Matrix Composite Rotors

Some disc brake rotors are manufactured from an aluminum metal matrix composite alloy reinforced with 20% silicon carbide particulate. These rotors can be distinguished from conventional cast-iron rotors in several ways. They will show no signs of rust

Frequently Asked Question ???

What Do "Cross-Drilled" and "Slotted" Mean?

The expressions "cross-drilled" and "slotted" refer to two separate processes. The first procedure involves drilling rows of holes through the friction surfaces of the rotor. The second procedure refers to milling a series of specially machined grooves from the centre of the disc towards the edge. When the friction surfaces of a rotor are smooth and flat, there is no means of escape for the gases and dust, which build up between pad and rotor. This is not a huge problem in normal driving, but is an important consideration in street performance applications.

The drill holes (which are sometimes called "gas relief openings") provide an exit route for the dust and gas. The holes are also commonly labelled "cooling holes" because of the improvements they make in this area. Better cooling means less fade during repeated heavy brake application. They also help dissipate water when driving in poor weather. See Figure 37–17.

Slotting increases the bite of the pads and is even more effective than cross-drilling in combatting the problem known as "out-gassing." This is when, at very high braking temperatures, the bonding agents used in some brake pads produce a gas. Under extreme conditions, this gas can create a gas cushion between pad and rotor, giving a driver a normal pedal feel but reducing the amount of friction being generated. The slots pump away gas and restore full contact. The "micro-shaving" effect of the slots also serves to deglaze the pads, which is why the edges of the slots are not chamfered or "radiused." It also tends to even out the wear across the brake pad faces, increasing the effective contact area.

Figure 37–17 A Corvette equipped with high-performance brakes including cross-drilled brake rotors.

and are nonmagnetic, unlike cast iron. When removed from the vehicle, the aluminum composite rotors can be further distinguished by their light weight (usually under 2.7 kg [6 lb] versus over 5.4 kg [12 lb] for cast-iron rotors on the typical passenger vehicle). See Figure 37–18.

Servicing these rotors is slightly different from servicing cast-iron rotors. The dark transfer layer on the rubbing surface does not harm rotor performance and should *not* be removed unless the rotor needs to be machined for dimensional reasons (warped, etc). *Aluminum metal matrix composite disc brake rotors cannot be machined with steel cutting tools!* Carbide tools *can* be used to machine a single set of aluminum composite rotors. If a shop receives these rotors on a regular basis, a polycrystalline diamond-tipped (PCD) tool is a good investment. Although more expensive initially, the PCD tool can last one hundred times longer than a carbide tool.

Lateral Runout

A disc brake rotor should have a maximum of 0.05–0.13 mm (0.002 in.–0.005 in.) runout depending upon the manufacturer's specifications for total lateral runout. See Figure 37–19.

Figure 37–18 An aluminum metal matrix composite rear rotor for a Chrysler Plymouth Prowler. (Courtesy of Duralcan, USA)

Figure 37–19 Excessive lateral runout can cause uneven wear. To help prevent excessive runout, always use a torque wrench or torque absorbing adapters with an impact wrench when tightening lug nuts.

NOTE: The diameter of a human hair is about 0.05 to 0.08 mm (0.002 in. to 0.003 in.). Therefore, the maximum allowable rotor runout is about equal to the thickness of a human hair. This small a measurement requires the use of an accurate measuring gauge.

Excessive rotor runout is also called **wobble** and causes disc brake rotor wear that can cause uneven thickness variations. The procedure for checking lateral runout follows:

1. If the rotor is installed on a wheel where bearings are adjustable, temporarily tighten the wheel bearings to remove all end play.
2. With a hubless rotor, install and torque the lug nuts to retain the rotor.
3. Attach a dial indicator to the end of the spindle and observe the reading through one complete revolution, as shown in Figure 37–20.
4. Total dial indicator movement should not exceed the specifications. If greater than specifications, machine the rotor.
5. Readjust the front wheel bearing for proper end play.

Rotor Thickness (Parallelism)

Excessive rotor runout does lead to rotor thickness variations as the rotor wears. Measure rotor thickness, using a micrometer, at four or more equally spaced locations on the rotor.

Figure 37–20 Rotate the disc brake rotor one complete revolution while observing the dial indicator (gauge). Most vehicle manufacturers specify a maximum runout of 0.08 mm (0.003 in.).

Figure 37–21 The rotor should be measured with a micrometer at four or more equally spaced locations around the rotor.

NOTE: Some manufacturers specify that eight or more measurements be made to check for parallelism. See Figures 37–21 and 37–22.

Each measurement must not vary more than 0.013 mm (0.0005 in.) and must be greater than the minimum allowable thickness. *It is the excessive rotor thickness variation that causes brake shudder or steering wheel shimmy.*

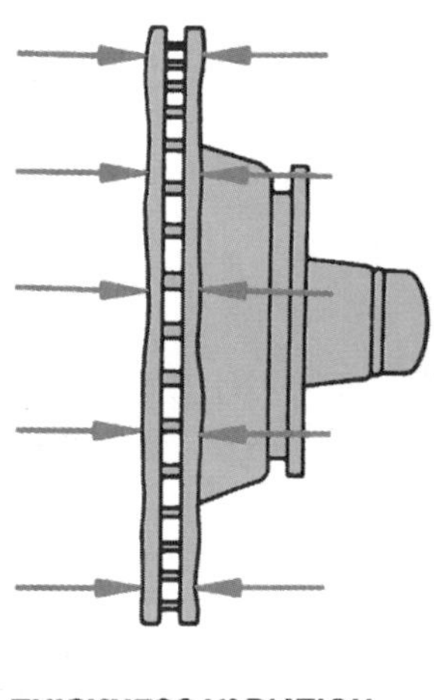

Figure 37–22 Thickness variation in a disc brake rotor causes the brake pedal to pulsate during braking.

Figure 37–23 A heavily rusted rotor. This rotor will likely need to be replaced because the surface flaws could be deeper than can be removed by machining and still maintain the minimum allowable thickness.

Minimum Thickness

Most rotors have a minimum thickness cast or stamped into the rotor. This thickness is minimum wear thickness. At least 0.4 mm (0.015 in.) must remain after machining to allow for wear. (Some vehicle manufacturers, such as General Motors, specify that 0.8 mm [0.030 in.] be left for wear.) Whenever machining (resurfacing) a rotor, an equal amount of material must be removed from each side of the rotor.

When the Rotors Should Be Machined

According to brake design engineers, a worn rotor has a very smooth friction surface that is ideal for replacement (new) disc brake pads. Often when the rotors are machined, the surface finish is not as smooth as specified. Therefore, a rotor should *only* be machined if one of the following conditions exists:

1. Grooves deeper than 1.5 mm (0.060 in.). This is the approximate thickness of a nickel coin! See Figure 37–23.
2. Thickness variation exceeding specifications and a brake pedal pulsation complaint.
3. Heavy rust that has corroded the friction surface of the rotor.

Therefore, if there is no complaint of a pulsating brake pedal during braking and the rotor is not deeply grooved or rusted, it should not be machined. Each time a rotor is machined, material is removed and the rotor can then absorb less heat causing it to operate at a higher temperature. New disc brake pads perform best against a smooth surface and a used disc brake rotor is often smoother than a new rotor.

TECH TIP 

Brown = Semimetallic

Brake rotors that have used semimetallic brake pads during operation are brown in colour on the friction surface. The reason for the brown colour is the rust from the steel used in the manufacture of the pads. If the friction surface of the disc brake rotor is shiny, then organic (asbestos), nonasbestos organic (NAO), or nonasbestos synthetic (NAS) pads have been used on the rotor.

This information is helpful to know, especially if the vehicle being serviced is to be equipped with semimetallic pads as specified by the manufacturer and the rotors are shiny. In this case, the incorrect lining may have been installed during a previous service. The colour of the friction surface is a quick-and-easy way to determine whether semimetallic pads have been used.

Rotor Finish

The smoothness of the rotor is called **rotor finish** or **surface finish.** Surface finish is measured in units called micro-inches, abbreviated **μin.** (the symbol in front of in. is the Greek letter mu). One micro-inch equals 0.000 001 in. (0.025 μm). The finish classification of micro-inch indicates the distance between the highest peak and the deepest valley. The usual method of expressing surface finish is the

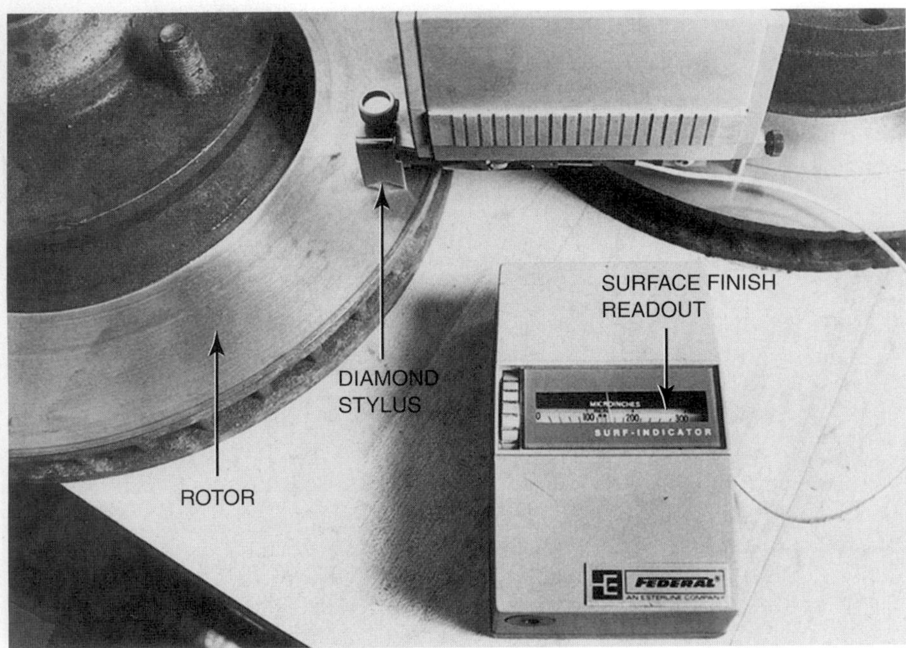

Figure 37–24 An electronic surface finish machine. The reading shows about 140 μin. This is much too rough for use but is typical for a rough-cut surface.

arithmetic-average roughness height, abbreviated **Ra,** which is the average of all peaks and valleys from the mean (average) line. This surface finish is measured using a machine with a diamond stylus, as shown in Figure 37–24.

Often a machined rotor will not be as smooth as a new rotor, resulting in a hard-stopping complaint after new brakes have been installed. Most new rotors have a surface finish of 45 to 60 μin. Ra.

MACHINING A DISC BRAKE ROTOR

Before machining a rotor, make sure that it can be machined by comparing the minimum thickness specification and the measured thickness of the rotor.

CAUTION: Some original-equipment and replacement disc brake rotors are close to the minimum allowable thickness when new. Often these rotors cannot be safely machined at all!

The following is an example of the steps necessary to machine a disc brake rotor. Always follow the instructions for the equipment you are using.

Step 1. Mount the disc brake rotor to the spindle of the lathe using the recommended cones and adapters. See Figures 37–25 and 37–26.

Figure 37–25 Typical adapter to properly mount a composite rotor onto a brake lathe.

Step 2. Install a rotor damper and position the cutting tools close to the rotor surface as shown in Figures 37–27 and 37–28.

NOTE: Failure to install the damper causes vibrations to occur during machining that create a rough surface finish.

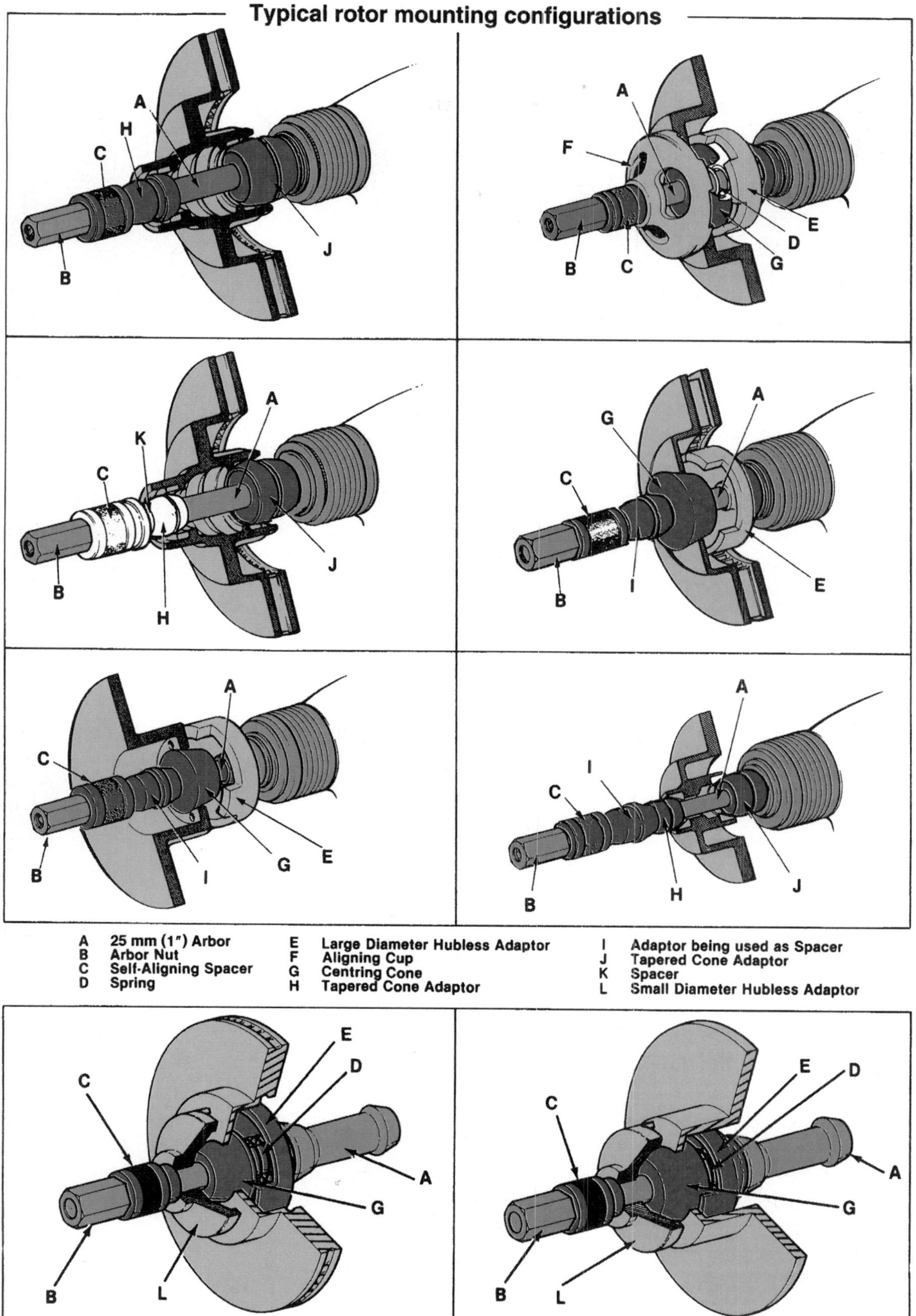

Figure 37–26 Typical rotor mounting configurations. (Courtesy of Hennessy Industries)

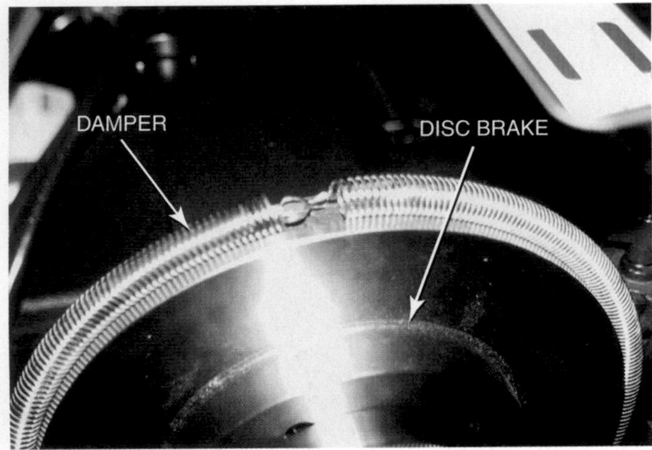

Figure 37–27 A damper is necessary to reduce cutting-tool vibrations that can cause a rough surface finish.

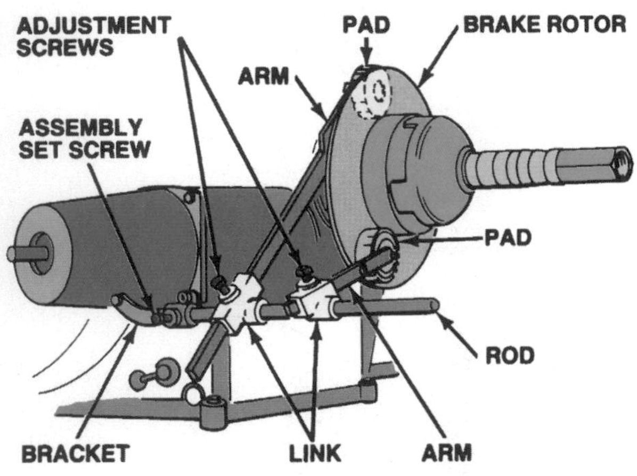

Figure 37–28 "Ear muff"-type disc brake rotor damper used to reduce vibration during machining.

Step 3. Make a scratch cut on the rotor face as shown in Figure 37–29.

Step 4. To check that the rotor is correctly mounted, loosen the retaining nut and turn the rotor one-half turn (180°) and retighten the nut. Make another scratch cut.

  a. The second scratch cut should be side by side with the first scratch cut if the rotor is properly installed.

  b. If the second scratch cut is on the opposite side (180°) from the first scratch cut, the rotor may not be correctly installed on the lathe.

NOTE: The runout as measured with a dial indicator on the brake lathe should be the same as the runout measured on the vehicle. If the runout is *not* the same, then the rotor is not correctly installed on the brake lathe.

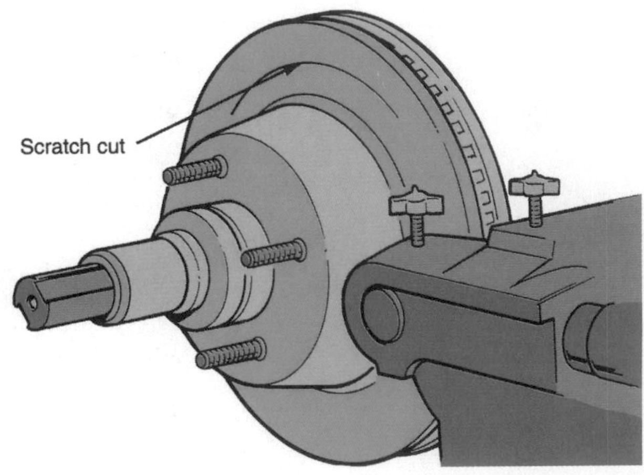

Figure 37–29 After installing the rotor on the brake lathe, turn the cutting tool in just enough to make a scratch cut.

After proper installation of the disc brake rotor on the brake lathe, proceed with machining the rotors. For best results do not machine any more material from the rotor than is absolutely necessary. Always follow the recommendations and guidelines as specified by the vehicle manufacturer.

Rough Cut

A rough cut on a lathe involves cutting 0.13 mm (0.005 in.) per side with a feed of 0.2 mm (0.008 in.) per revolution and 150 rpm spindle speed. This usually results in a very coarse surface finish of about 150 μin. Ra.

NOTE: Some brake lathes, such as the Accuturn®, have the ability to provide a finish cut to almost any depth in a single cut. The cutter on these lathes is angled upward (positive rack) rather than downward (negative rack) like other types of brake lathes.

Finish Cut

A finish cut involves removing 0.05 mm (0.002 in.) per side with a feed of 0.05 mm (0.002 in.) per revolution and 150 rpm spindle speed. Although this cut usually looks smooth, the surface finish is about 90 to 100 μin. Ra. Even a typical finish cut is still not nearly as smooth as a new rotor.

Nondirectional Finish

Most vehicle and brake component manufacturers recommend a nondirectional finish to help prevent the grooves machined into the rotor from acting like record grooves, which would force the pads to move outward while the rotor rotates. See Figure 37–30.

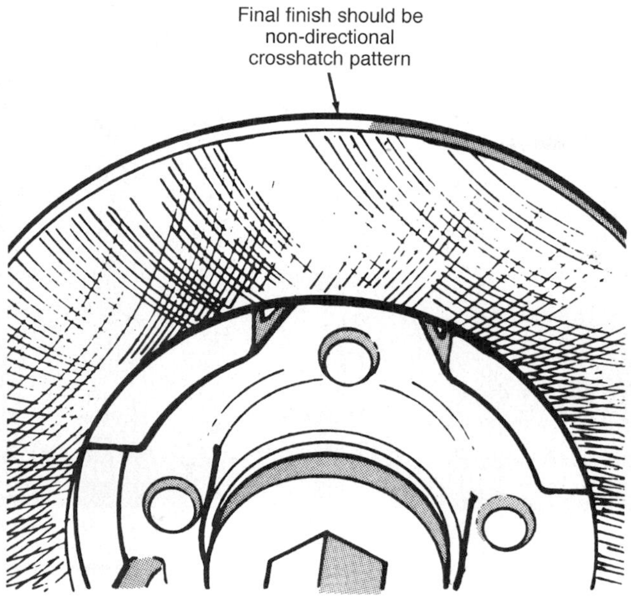
Final finish should be non-directional crosshatch pattern

Figure 37–30 The correct final surface finish should be smooth and nondirectional. (Courtesy of Chrysler Corporation)

Surface Finishing the Rotor

The goal of any brake repair or service should be to restore the braking effectiveness to match new vehicle brakes. This means that the rotor finish should be as smooth or smoother than a new rotor for maximum brake pad contact. Research conducted at the Delco Chassis Brake Division of General Motors has shown that like-new rotor finish can be easily accomplished by using a block and sandpaper. After completing the finish cut, place 150-grit aluminum oxide sandpaper on a block and apply steady pressure against the rotor surface for 60 seconds on *each* side of the rotor. See Figure 37–31. The aluminum oxide is hard enough to remove the highest ridges left by the lathe cutting tool. This results in a surface finish ranging from 20 to 80 μin. and usually less than 40 μin., which is smoother than a new rotor. See Figure 37–32.

NOTE: Many commercial rotor-finish products may also give as smooth a surface finish. See Figure 37–33. Always compare rotor finish to the rotor finish of a *new* rotor. Micro-inch finish is often hard to distinguish unless you have a new rotor with which to compare.

Cleaning Rotors

Disc brake rotors (and drums) should be thoroughly cleaned after machining. Because the machining particles can lodge into the surface of the rotor, many experts agree that hot, soapy water should be used to clean any dirt or grit from the surface. Even new rotors should be cleaned as shown in Figure 37–34 to remove any rust preventative that may be on the surface before they contact the new disc brake pads.

(a)

(b)

Figure 37–31 (a) This technician uses two sanding blocks each equipped with 150-grit aluminum-oxide sandpaper. (b) With the lathe turned on, the technician presses the two sanding blocks against the surface of the rotor after the rotor has been machined to achieve a smooth micro-inch surface finish.

On-the-Vehicle Rotor Machining

Many vehicle manufacturers recommend on-the-vehicle machining for rotors *if* the disc brake rotor *must* be machined due to deep scoring or a pulsating brake pedal complaint. This is especially true of composite rotors or for vehicles such as many Hondas that require major disassembly to remove the rotors.

Caliper-mount on-the-vehicle lathes require that the disc brake caliper be removed. The cutter attaches to the steering knuckle or caliper support

(a)

(b)

Figure 37–32 (a) After machining and sanding the rotor, it should be cleaned. In this case brake cleaner from an air pressurized spray can is used. (b) With the lathe turning, the technician stands back away from the rotor and sprays both sides of the rotor to clean it of any remaining grit from the sanding process. This last step assures a clean, smooth surface for the disc brake pads and a quality brake repair.

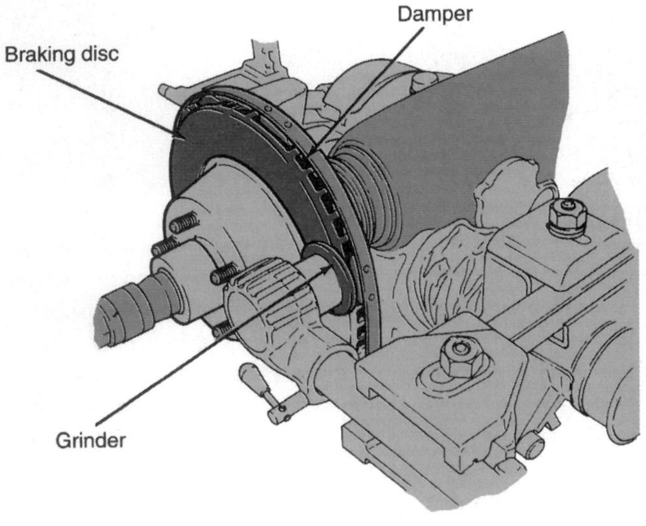

Figure 37–33 A grinder with sandpaper can be used to give a smooth nondirectional surface finish to the disc brake rotor. (Courtesy of Chrysler Corporation)

Figure 37–34 Washing a new rotor with spray brake cleaner to remove any protective film that may be on the surface.

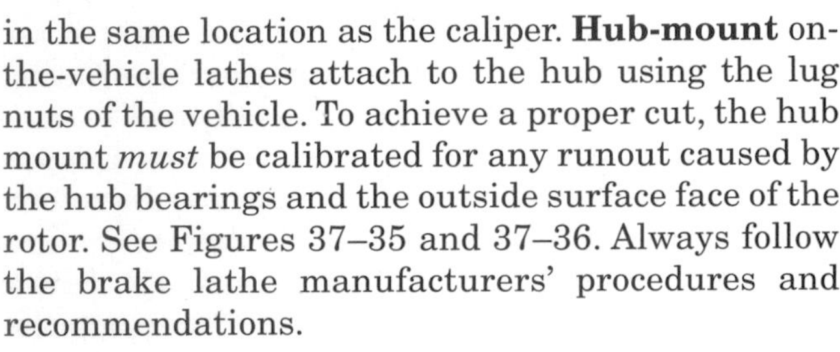

in the same location as the caliper. **Hub-mount** on-the-vehicle lathes attach to the hub using the lug nuts of the vehicle. To achieve a proper cut, the hub mount *must* be calibrated for any runout caused by the hub bearings and the outside surface face of the rotor. See Figures 37–35 and 37–36. Always follow the brake lathe manufacturers' procedures and recommendations.

NOTE: All on-the-vehicle lathes require that the wheel be removed. For best results, always use a torque wrench when tightening lug nuts or lathe adapters. Unequal torque on the bolts causes stress and distortion that can cause warped rotors and a pulsating brake pedal.

Figure 37–35 Rust should always be cleaned from both the rotor and the hub whenever the rotors are machined or replaced. An air-powered die grinder with a sanding disc makes quick work of cleaning this hub.

Figure 37–36 A typical hub-mount on-the-vehicle lathe. This particular lathe oscillates while machining the rotor, thereby providing a smooth and nondirectional finish at the same time.

SUMMARY

1. Brake drums and rotors must absorb the heat generated by the friction of slowing and stopping a vehicle.
2. All rotors should be marked before removing them from the vehicle to make sure that they will be reinstalled in the same position and on the same side of the vehicle.
3. All brake drums should be machined only enough to restore proper braking action. Brake drums should be the same size on the same axle to help prevent unequal braking.
4. Disc brake rotors should be machined so that up to 0.8 mm (0.030 in.) is allowed for wear.
5. To ensure proper braking, all rotors should be machined to a very smooth finish of less than 60 microinches.

REVIEW QUESTIONS

1. Explain the difference between "machine to" specifications and the "discard" dimension.
2. List the steps for machining a brake drum.
3. Describe how to measure a disc brake rotor for lateral runout and thickness variation.
4. List the steps for machining a disc brake rotor.
5. Describe what is necessary to achieve "like new" disc brake rotor finish.

RED SEAL CERTIFICATION-TYPE QUESTIONS

1. What type of friction surface is used when a vehicle is equipped with aluminum drums?
   - **a.** Cast iron
   - **b.** Aluminum
   - **c.** Steel
   - **d.** Phenolic resin
2. What is the correction for hard spots on a brake drum?
   - **a.** Machine the drum to remove them
   - **b.** Replace the drum due to the potential of "memory" in the material
   - **c.** Rub hard spot with emery cloth to remove
   - **d.** Rub hard spot with crocus cloth to remove
3. What is the maximum allowable drum diameter difference for drums on the same axle?
   - **a.** 0.10 mm
   - **b.** 0.25 mm
   - **c.** 0.15 mm
   - **d.** 0.4 mm
4. A hubless brake drum cannot be machined because it cannot be held in a lathe.
   - **a.** True
   - **b.** False
5. The major reason for brake pedal pulsation during braking is excessive rotor thickness variation.
   - **a.** True
   - **b.** False
6. Rotor finish is measured in
   - **a.** mm
   - **b.** inches
   - **c.** micro-inches
   - **d.** centimetres

7. The lower the Ra of a rotor, the _____ the surface.
    a. Smoother
    b. Rougher
    c. Higher
    d. Lower
8. When machining a rotor you find the cutting bit leaves a scratch on only half the rotor, even after repositioning. What does this indicate?
    a. The rotor needs further machining
    b. The rotor needs to be remounted
    c. The rotor is cracked
    d. The vibration dampener is missing
9. Typical maximum rotor runout specifications are
    a. 0.008 to 0.013 mm (0.0003 in. to 0.0005 in.).
    b. 0.08 to 0.13 mm (0.003 in. to 0.005 in.).
    c. 0.8 to 1.3 mm (0.030 in. to 0.050 in.).
    d. 8.0 to 13 mm (0.300 in. to 0.500 in.).
10. Typical maximum rotor thickness variation (parallelism) specifications are
    a. 0.008 to 0.013 mm (0.0003 in. to 0.0005 in.).
    b. 0.08 to 0.13 mm (0.003 in. to 0.005 in.).
    c. 0.8 to 1.3 mm (0.030 in. to 0.050 in.).
    d. 8.0 to 13 mm (0.300 in. to 0.500 in.).

38

Power-Assisted Brakes

OBJECTIVES: After studying Chapter 38, you should be able to:

1. Prepare for the interprovincial Red Seal certification examination in Appendix V (Brakes) on the topics covered in this chapter.
2. List the parts of a vacuum brake booster.
3. Describe how a vacuum brake booster operates.
4. Explain how to test a vacuum brake booster.
5. Describe how a hydraulic or electro-hydraulic brake booster operates.

Power-assisted brakes reduce the effort the driver has to use to apply the necessary stopping force to the vehicle. Power-assisted brakes were once considered a luxury and were first available on large, heavy cars and trucks. Without power-assisted brakes, the entire braking force was achieved by mechanical and hydraulic leverage, as explained in Chapter 32.

VACUUM BOOSTER OPERATION

Most power-brake boosters are vacuum operated, the vacuum supplied from the intake manifold of the engine. See Figure 38–1. When running, any gasoline-powered engine creates vacuum in the intake manifold, that is, a pressure below atmospheric pressure (101 kPa or 30 in. Hg). A well running engine should produce a vacuum of 60 to 70 kPa (18 to 21 in. Hg) at sea level.

DIAGNOSTIC STORY

Check the Vacuum, Then the Brakes

A customer complained of a very rough idle and an occasional pulsating brake pedal. The customer was certain that the engine required serious work since it did have over 250 000 km. During the troubleshooting procedure, a spray cleaner was used to find any vacuum (air) leaks. A large hole was found melted through a large vacuum hose next to the vacuum hose feeding the vacuum-operated power-brake booster.

After repairing the vacuum leak, the vehicle was test driven again to help diagnose the cause of the pulsating brake pedal. The engine idled very smoothly after the vacuum leak was repaired *and* the brake pulsation was also cured. The vacuum leak resulted in lower-than-normal vacuum being applied to the vacuum booster. During braking, when engine vacuum is normally higher (deceleration), the vacuum booster would assist, then not assist when the vacuum was lost. This on-and-off-again supply of vacuum to the vacuum booster was noticed by the driver as a brake pulsation. Always check the vacuum at the booster whenever diagnosing any brake problems. Most vehicle manufacturers specify a minimum of 50 kPa (15 in.) of Hg of vacuum at the booster. The booster *should* be able to provide at least two or three power-assisted stops even if the engine stops running and providing additional vacuum. The booster should also be checked to see if it can hold a vacuum after several hours. A good vacuum booster, for example, should be able to provide power assist after sitting all night without starting the engine.

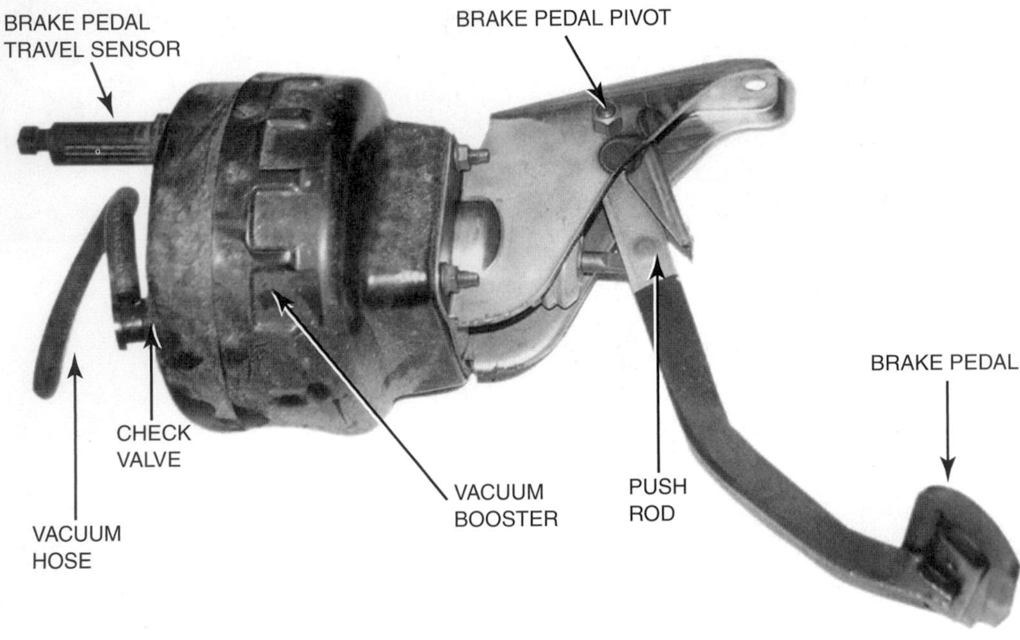

Figure 38–1 A typical vacuum-brake-booster assembly. The vacuum hose attaches to the intake manifold of the engine. The brake pedal travel sensor is an input sensor for the antilock braking system.

NOTE: Most manufacturers specify that the minimum engine vacuum necessary for the proper operation of a vacuum power-assist unit is 50 kPa (15 in. Hg) If the engine is producing less than 50 kPa (15 in. Hg) at idle, the cause of the low vacuum should be found and repaired before further brake-system diagnosis is performed. See the Tech Tip "Check the Vacuum, Then the Brakes" for an example of how vacuum affects braking performance.

Charcoal Filter

The vacuum hose leading from the engine to the power booster should run downward without any low places in the hose. If a dip or sag occurs in the vacuum hose, condensed fuel vapours and/or moisture can accumulate that can block or restrict the vacuum to the booster. Many manufacturers use a small charcoal filter in the vacuum line between the engine and booster, as shown in Figure 38–2. The charcoal filter attracts and holds gasoline vapours and keeps the fumes from entering the vacuum booster.

Vacuum Check Valve

All vacuum boosters use a one-way vacuum check valve. This valve allows air to flow in only one direction—from the booster and toward the engine. This valve prevents the loss of vacuum when the engine stops. See Figure 38–3.

Vacuum Brake Booster

A vacuum power-brake booster contains a rubber diaphragm that is connected to the brake pedal at one end and the master cylinder at the other end. The vacuum power unit contains the power-piston assembly, which houses the control valve and reaction mechanism, and the power-piston return spring. The control valve is composed of the air valve (valve plunger), the floating control-valve assembly, and the push rod. The reaction mechanism consists of a hydraulic piston-reaction plate and a series of reaction levers. The push rod that operates the air valve projects out of the end. See Figures 38–4 and 38–5.

Released-Position Operation At the released position (brake pedal up), the air valve is seated on the floating control valve, which shuts off the air. The floating control valve is held away from the valve seat in the power-piston insert. Vacuum from the engine is present in the space on both sides of the power piston. Any air in the system is drawn through a small passage in the power piston, over the seat in the power-piston insert, and then through a passage in the power-piston insert. There is a vacuum on both sides of the power piston and it is held against the rear of the housing by the power-piston return spring. At rest, the hydraulic reaction plate is held against the reaction retainer. The air-valve spring holds the reaction lever against the hydraulic reaction plate and also holds the air valve against its stop

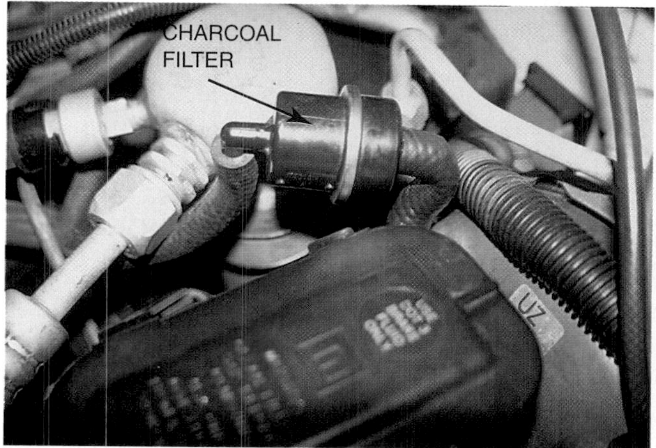

Figure 38–2 The charcoal filter traps gasoline vapours that are present in the intake manifold and prevents them from getting into the vacuum chamber of the booster.

(a)

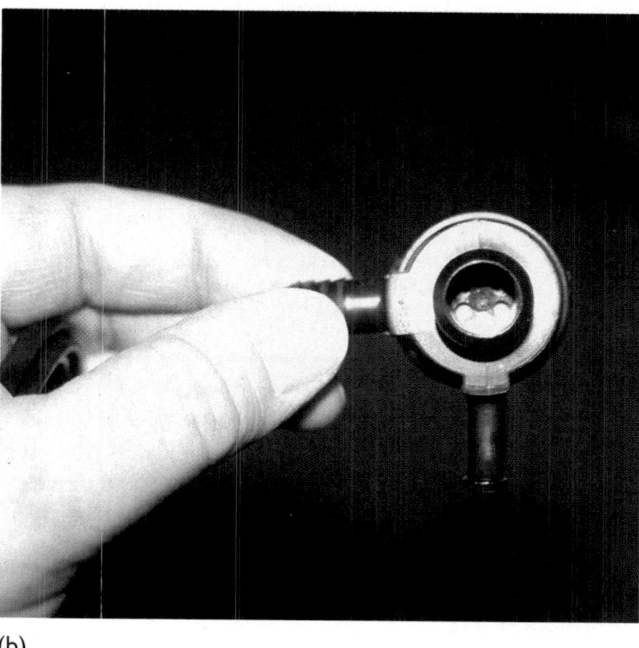
(b)

Figure 38–3 (a) Many vacuum-brake-booster check valves are located where the vacuum hose from the engine (vacuum source) attaches to the vacuum booster. (b) This one-way valve prevents the loss of vacuum when the engine is off. The diaphragm inside allows air to flow in one direction only.

in the tube of the power piston. The floating control-valve assembly is held against the air-valve seat by the floating control-valve spring. See Figure 38–6.

Applied-Position Operation As the brake pedal is depressed, the valve push rod moves the air valve away from the floating control valve. The floating control valve will follow until it is in contact with the raised seat in the power-piston insert. When this occurs, vacuum is shut off to the rear of the power piston, and air under atmospheric pressure enters through the air filter and travels past the seat of the air valve and through a passage into the housing at the rear of the power piston. Since there is still vacuum on the front side of the power piston, the atmospheric air pressure at the rear of the piston will force the power piston to travel forward.

NOTE: This movement of air into the rear chamber of the brake booster may be heard inside the vehicle as a hissing noise. The loudness of this air flow varies from vehicle to vehicle and should be considered normal.

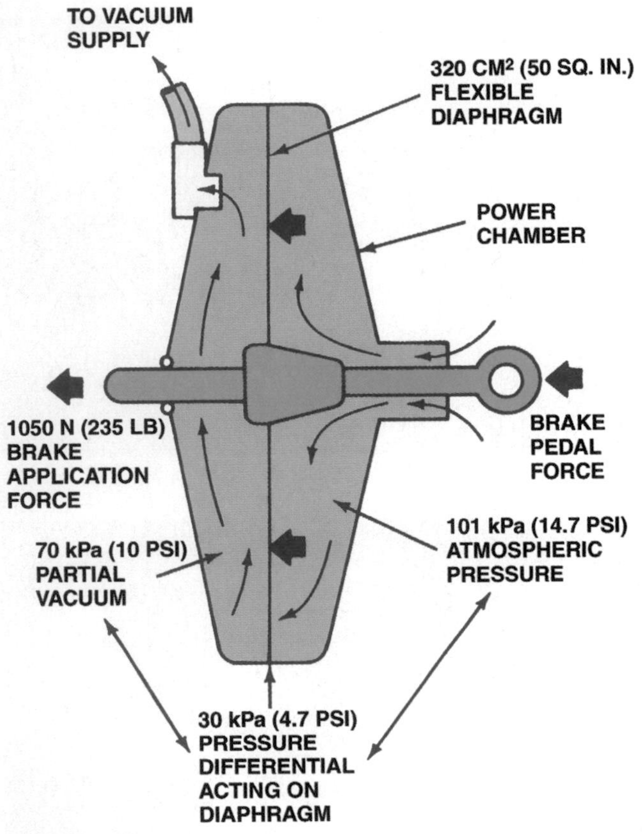

Figure 38–4 Vacuum power-brake boosters operate on the principle of pressure differential. The engine manifold vacuum supplies the vacuum on the front section of a flexible diaphragm and atmospheric pressure is applied to the rear section of the diaphragm when the brake pedal is depressed.

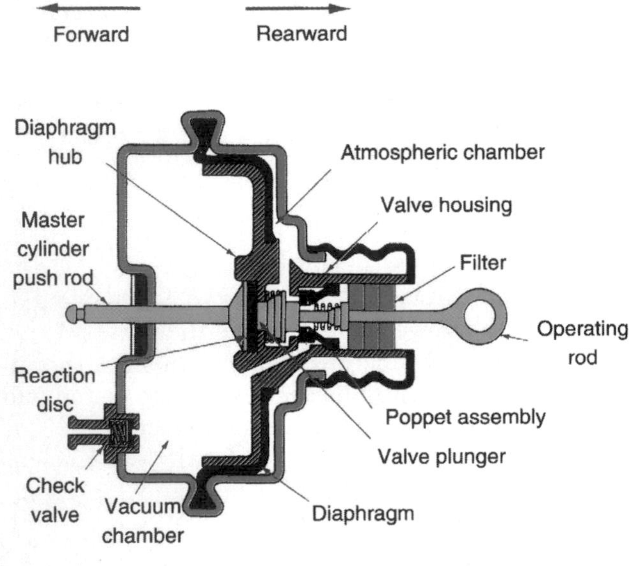

Figure 38–5 Cross-section view of a typical vacuum-brake-booster assembly.

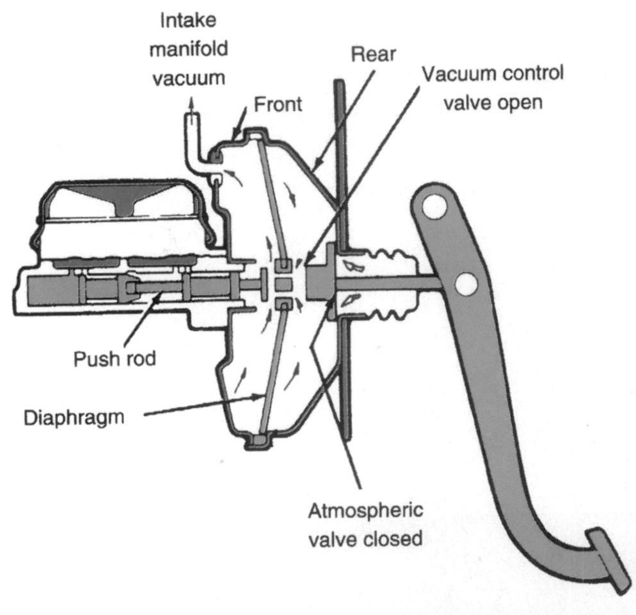

Figure 38–6 In the release position (brake pedal up), the vacuum is directed to both sides of the diaphragm. (Courtesy of Chrysler Corporation)

As the power piston travels forward, the master-cylinder push rod pushes the master-cylinder primary and secondary pistons forward. As back-pressure builds up on the end of the master-cylinder piston, the hydraulic reaction plate is moved off its seat on the power piston and presses against the reaction levers. The reaction lever pushes against the end of the air-valve rod assembly. Approximately 30% of the load on the hydraulic master-cylinder piston is transferred back through the reaction system to the brake pedal. This gives the driver feedback proportional to the degree of brake application. See Figure 38–7.

Hold-Position Operation When the desired brake pedal pressure is reached, the power piston moves forward until the floating control valve, which is still on the power piston, again seats on the air valve. The power piston will now remain stationary, until either additional force is applied or released at the brake pedal. See Figure 38–8. As the pressure at the brake pedal is released, the air-valve spring forces the air valve back to its stop on the power piston. As it returns, the air valve pushes the floating control valve off its seat on the power-piston insert. The air valve seating on the floating control valve has shut off the outside air source. When it lifts the floating control valve from its seat on the power-piston insert it opens the space at the rear of the power-piston insert to the vacuum source. The power-piston return spring will return the piston to its released position against the rear housing, since both sides of the piston are now under a vacuum. As this occurs, the master cylinder releases its pressure and the brakes are released.

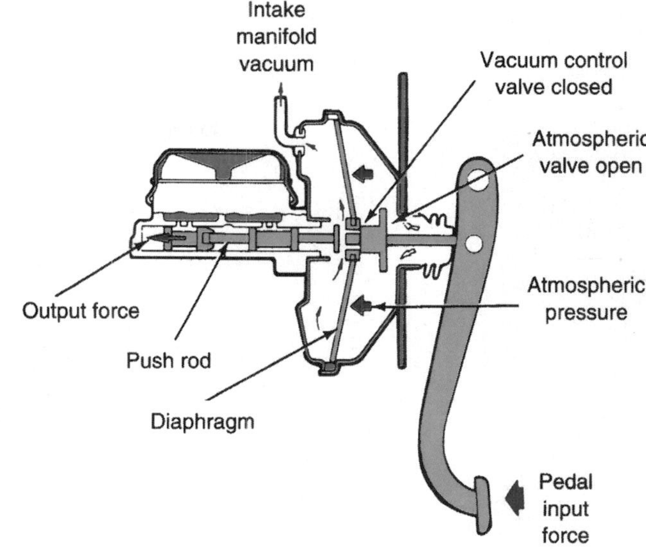

Figure 38–7 A simplified diagram of a vacuum brake booster in the apply position. Notice that the atmospheric valve is open and air pressure is being applied to the diaphragm. (Courtesy of Chrysler Corporation)

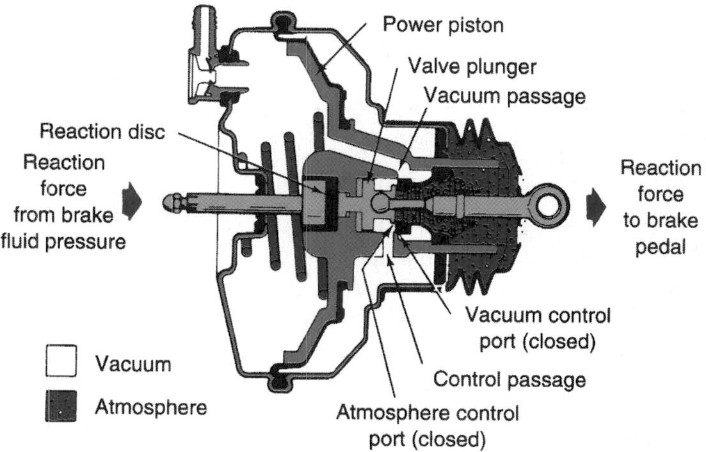

Figure 38–8 Cross-section of a vacuum brake booster in hold position with both vacuum and atmospheric valves closed. Note that the reaction force from the brake fluid pressure is transferred back to the driver as a reaction force to the brake pedal. (Courtesy of Chrysler Corporation)

Vacuum-Failure Mode In case of vacuum source interruption, the brake operates as a standard brake as follows: As the pedal is pushed down, the end of the air valve contacts the reaction levers and pushes, in turn, against the hydraulic reaction plate, which is fastened to the master-cylinder piston rod, which applies pressure in the master cylinder.

For safety, in the event of a stalled engine and a loss of vacuum, a power brake should have adequate storage of vacuum for several power-assisted stops.

Dual Diaphragm (Tandem) Vacuum Boosters

To provide power assist, air pressure must work against a rubber diaphragm. The larger the area of the diaphragm, the more force can be exerted. Instead of increasing the diameter, some vacuum-booster manufacturers use two smaller-diameter di-

TECH TIP 

A Low, Soft Brake Pedal Is Not a Power-Booster Problem

Some service technicians tend to blame the power-brake booster if the vehicle has a low, soft brake pedal. A defective power-brake booster causes a hard brake pedal, not a soft brake pedal. A soft or spongy brake pedal is usually caused by air being trapped somewhere in the hydraulic system. Many times, a technician has bled the system and therefore thinks that the system is free of any trapped air. According to remanufacturers of master cylinders and power-brake boosters, most of the returned parts under warranty are not defective. Incorrect or improper bleeding procedures account for much of the problem.

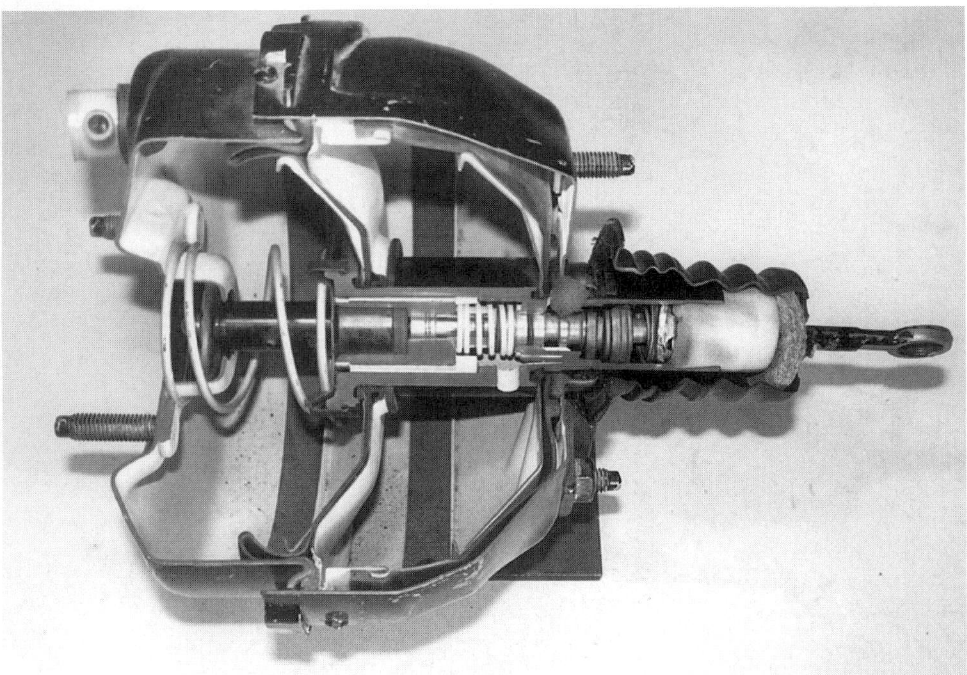

Figure 38–9 Cutaway showing a dual-diaphragm (tandem) vacuum brake booster.

aphragms and place one in front of the other. This design increases the total area without increasing the physical diameter of the booster. This style is called a **dual-diaphragm** or **tandem-diaphragm** vacuum booster. See Figure 38–9.

DIAGNOSING VACUUM-BOOSTER PROBLEMS

Vacuum-Booster Operation Test

With the engine off, apply the brakes several times to deplete the vacuum. With your foot on the brake pedal, start the engine. The brake pedal *should* drop. If the brake pedal does *not* drop, check for proper vacuum source to the booster. If there is proper vacuum, then repair or replacement of the power booster is required.

Vacuum-Booster Leak Test

To test if the vacuum booster can hold a vacuum, run the engine to build up a vacuum in the booster, then turn the engine off. Wait one minute, then depress the brake pedal several times. There should be two or more power-assisted brake applications.

If applications are not power assisted, either the vacuum check valve or the booster is leaking. To test the check valve, remove the valve from the booster and blow through the check valve. If air passes through, the valve is defective and must be replaced. If the check valve is okay, the vacuum booster is leaking and should be repaired or replaced based on manufacturer's recommendations.

Hydraulic-System Leak Test

An internal or external hydraulic leak can also cause a brake system problem. To test if the hydraulic system (and not the booster) is leaking, with the engine off, depress and release the brake pedal (service brakes) several times. This should deplete any residual power assist. On some ABS units, this may require depressing the brake pedal twenty or more times! After depleting the power-assist unit, depress and then hold the brake pedal depressed with medium force (90 to 150 N or 20 to 35 lb.). The brake pedal should *not* fall away. If the pedal falls, the hydraulic brake system is leaking. Check for external leakage at wheel cylinders, calipers, hydraulic lines, and hoses. If there is no external leak, there may be an internal leak inside the master cylinder. Repair or replace components as needed to correct the leakage.

Push-Rod Clearance Adjustment

Whenever the vacuum brake booster or master cylinder is replaced, the push-rod length should be checked. The length of the push rod must match correctly with the master cylinder. See Figure 38–10. If the push rod is too long and the master cylinder is installed, the rod may be applying a force on the primary piston of the master cylinder even though the brake pedal is not applied. This can cause the brakes to overheat and then

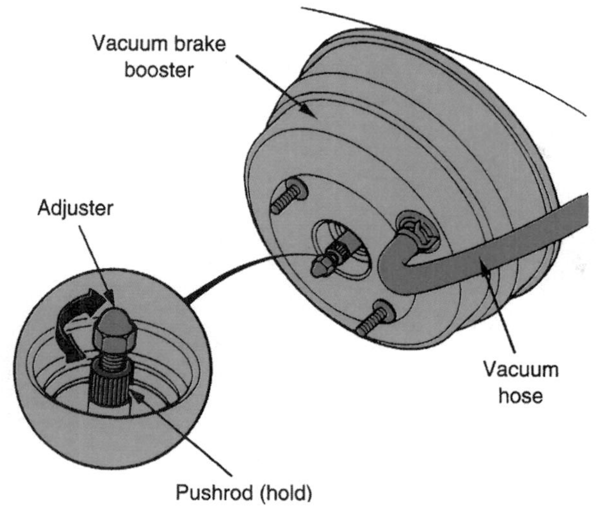

Figure 38–10 Typical adjustable pushrod.

cause the brake fluid to boil. If the brake fluid boils, a total loss of braking force can occur. Obviously, this push-rod clearance check and adjustment is very important. A gauge is often used to measure the position of the master cylinder piston and then, with the other end of the gauge, to determine the proper push-rod clearance. See Figure 38–11.

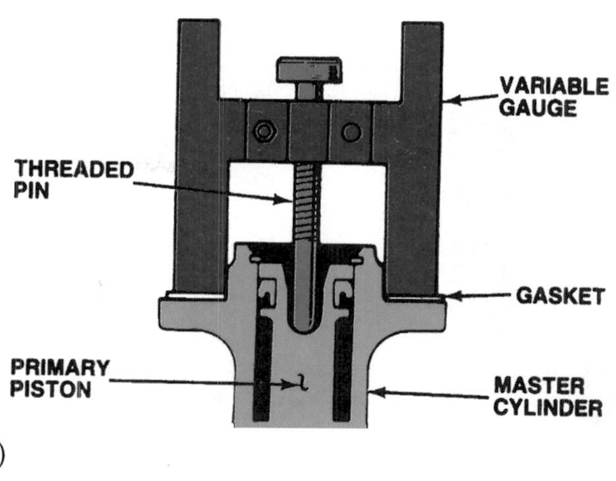

(a)

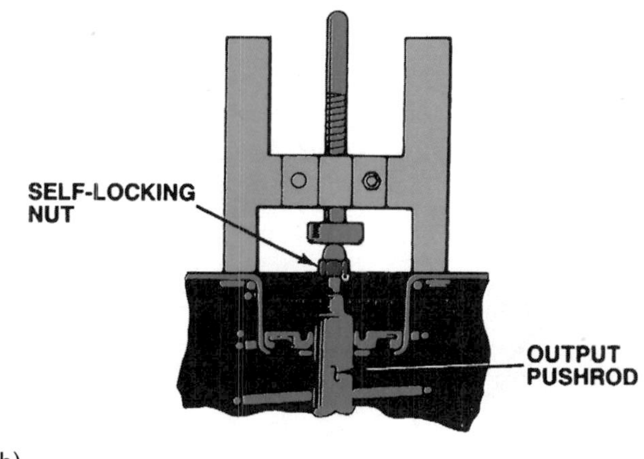

(b)

Figure 38–11 (a) A gauge being used to check the proper push rod clearance. The knob is turned until the threaded pin touches the primary piston of the master cylinder. (b) After the gauge has been set, it is turned upside down and placed on the vacuum booster output push rod end. The proper clearance is achieved when the self-locking nut is rotated until it just touches the gauge.

HYDRO-BOOST HYDRAULIC BRAKE BOOSTER

Hydro-boost is a hydraulically operated power-assist unit built by Bendix. The hydro-boost system uses the pressurized hydraulic fluid from the vehicle's power-steering pump as a power source rather than engine vacuum as with vacuum boosters. See Figures 38–12 and 38–13. The hydro-boost unit is used on vehicles that lack enough engine vacuum, such as turbo-charged or diesel-engine vehicles.

Operation

Fluid pressure from the power steering pump enters the unit and is directed by a spool valve. See Figure 38–14. When the brake pedal is depressed, the lever and primary valve are moved. The valve closes off the return port, causing pressure to build in the boost pressure chamber. The hydraulic pressure pushes on the power piston, which then applies force to the output rod that connects to the master cylinder piston. In the event of a power-steering-pump failure, power assist is still available for several brake applications. During operation, hydraulic fluid under pressure from the power steering pump pressurizes an **accumulator.** Although some units use a spring inside the accumulator, most hydro-boost units use nitrogen gas. The fluid trapped in the accumulator under pressure is used to provide power-assisted stops in the event of a hydraulic system failure.

Diagnosis

The power source for hydro-boost units is the power-steering pump. The first step of troubleshooting is to perform a thorough visual inspection, including:

1. Checking for proper power steering fluid level
2. Checking for leaks from the unit or power-steering pump
3. Checking the condition and tightness of the power-steering drive belt
4. Checking for proper operation of the base brake system

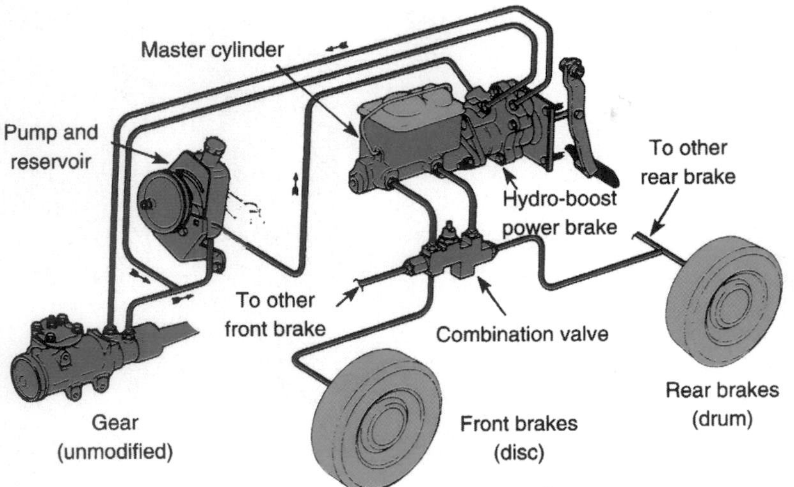

Figure 38–12 A hydro-boost unit attaches between the bulkhead and the master cylinder and is powered by the power steering pump. (Courtesy of Allied Signal Automotive Aftermarket)

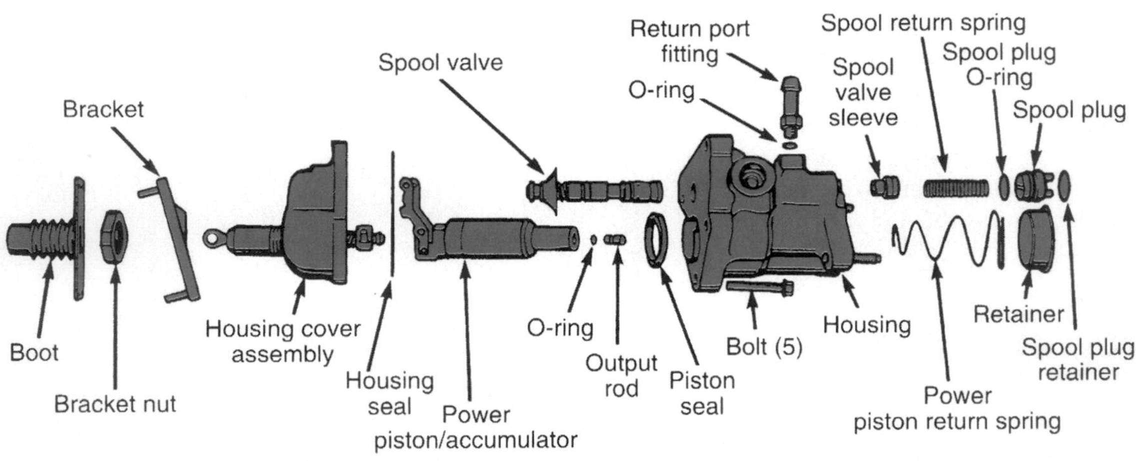

Figure 38–13 Exploded view of the hydro-boost unit. (Courtesy of Allied Signal Automotive Aftermarket)

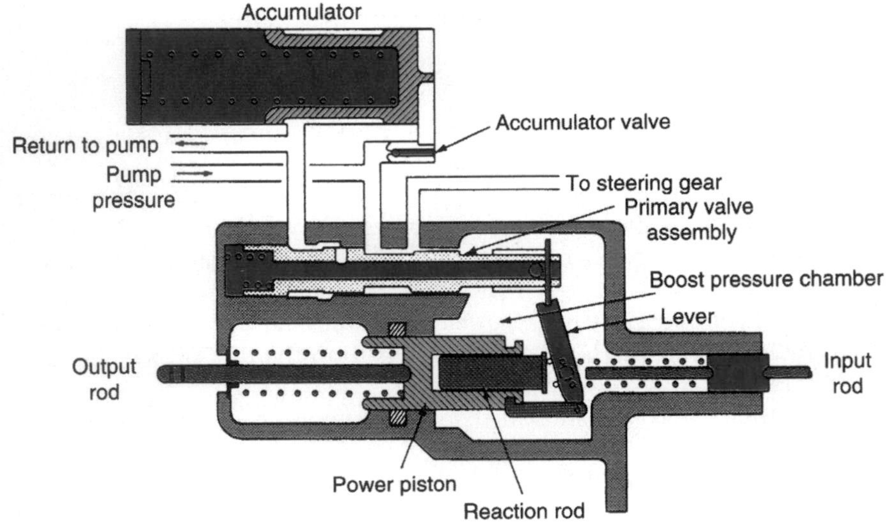

Figure 38–14 Simplified drawing of a hydro-boost power-brake unit. Note that the hydraulic pressure from the power-steering pump enters the unit and goes around the primary valve assembly then back out and to the steering gear.

After checking all of the visual components, check for proper pressure and volume from the power steering pump using a power-steering-pump tester, as shown in Figure 38–15. The pump should be capable of producing a minimum of 8 L (2 gal) with a *maximum* pressure of 1000 kPa (150 psi) with the steering assembly in the straight-ahead position. With the engine off, the accumulator should be able to supply a minimum of two power-assisted brake applications.

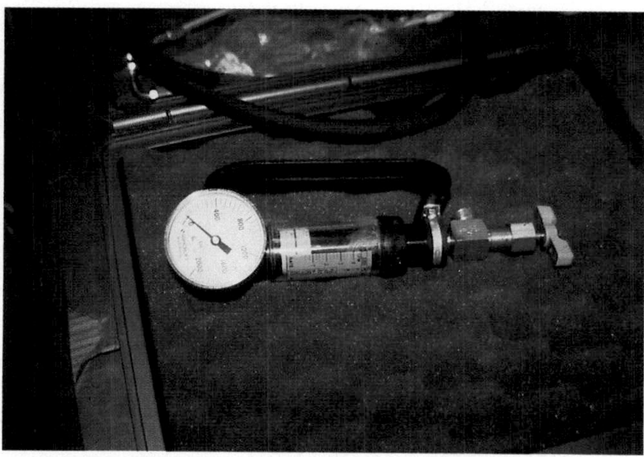

Figure 38–15 A power steering pressure and volume tester is used to test a hydro-boost power brake unit. The power steering pump should be capable of producing a minimum of 8 L (2 gal) per minute for the proper operation of the unit.

Hydro-Boost Function Test

With the engine off, apply the brake pedal several times until the accumulator is completely depleted. Depress the service brake pedal and start the engine. The pedal should fall and then push back against the driver's foot.

TECH TIP 

The Hydro-Boost Accumulator Test

The accumulator stores hydraulic fluid under pressure to provide a reserve in the event of a failure of the power steering system. The accumulator is designed to provide three or more power-assisted stops with the engine off. See Figure 38–16. If the accumulator fails, it does not hold pressure. To easily check whether the accumulator has lost its charge, simply grasp the accumulator with your hand and try to twist or move it. The accumulator should have so much pressure on it that it should not move or wiggle. If the accumulator moves, it has lost its ability to hold pressure and the hydro-boost unit should be replaced.

HYDRO-BOOST TROUBLESHOOTING GUIDE

Problem	Possible Causes
Excessive brake pedal effort	• Loose or broken power steering pump belt • No fluid in the power steering reservoir • Leaks in the power steering, booster, or accumulator hoses • Leaks at tube fittings, power steering, booster, or accumulator connections • External leakage at the accumulator • Faulty booster piston seal, causing leakage at the booster flange vent • Faulty booster cover seal with leakage between housing and cover • Faulty booster spool plug seal
Slow brake pedal return	• Excessive seal friction in the booster • Faulty spool action • Broken piston return spring • Restriction in the return line from the booster to the pump reservoir • Broken spool return spring
Grabby brakes	• Broken spool return spring • Faulty spool action caused by contamination in the system
Booster chatters—pedal vibrates	• Power steering pump belt slipping • Low fluid level in the power steering pump reservoir • Faulty spool operation caused by contamination in the system

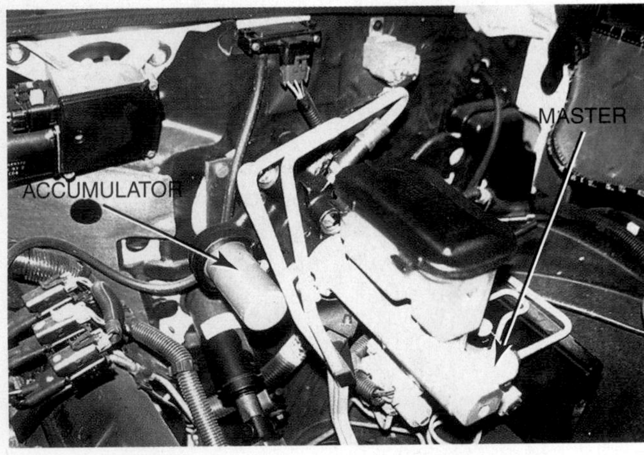

Figure 38–16 The accumulator should be able to hold pressure and feel tight when hand force is used to try to move it.

SUMMARY

1. Vacuum brake boosters use air pressure acting on a diaphragm to assist the driver's force on the brake master cylinder.
2. At rest, there is vacuum on both sides of the vacuum-booster diaphragm. When the brake pedal is depressed, atmospheric air pressure is exerted on the back side of the diaphragm.
3. The use of two diaphragms in tandem allows a smaller-diameter booster with the same area. The larger the area of the booster diaphragm, the more air-pressure force can be applied to the master cylinder.
4. When replacing a vacuum brake booster, always check for proper push rod clearance.
5. Hydraulic-operated brake boosters use the engine-driven power-steering pump.
6. To make sure of power-assisted brake application in the event of failure, hydraulic power-assisted brake systems use an accumulator to provide pressure to the system.

REVIEW QUESTIONS

1. Describe the purpose and function of the one-way check valve used on vacuum-brake booster units.
2. Explain how vacuum is used to assist in applying the brakes.
3. Describe how to perform a vacuum-booster leak test and hydraulic-system leak test.
4. Explain how a hydro-boost system functions.

RED SEAL CERTIFICATION-TYPE QUESTIONS

1. What could be the cause of a low soft brake pedal?
   a. The brake booster unit
   b. The brake booster check valve
   c. Air in the hydraulic brake system
   d. Charcoal filter
2. What is indicated by a brake pedal falling towards the floor when it is depressed and the engine is started?
   a. Normal operation
   b. Defective master cylinder
   c. Leak vacuum booster
   d. Low engine vacuum
3. Brake pedal feedback to the driver is provided by the
   a. Vacuum check-valve operation
   b. Reaction system
   c. Charcoal filter unit
   d. Vacuum diaphragm
4. The proper operation of a vacuum brake booster requires that the engine be capable of supplying at least
   a. 50 kPa (15 in. Hg vacuum)
   b. 57 kPa (17 in. Hg vacuum)
   c. 64 kPa (19 in. Hg vacuum)
   d. 70 kPa (21 in. Hg vacuum)
5. The purpose of the charcoal filter in the vacuum hose between the engine and the vacuum brake booster is to
   a. Filter the air entering the engine
   b. Trap gasoline vapours to keep them from entering the booster
   c. Act as a one-way check valve to help keep a vacuum reserve in the booster
   d. Direct the vacuum
6. A defective vacuum brake booster will cause a
   a. Hard brake pedal
   b. Soft (spongy) brake pedal
   c. Low brake pedal
   d. Slight hissing noise when the brake pedal is depressed
7. An accumulator as is used on hydraulic brake boosters
   a. Reduces brake pedal noise
   b. Provides a higher pressure being fed back to the driver's foot
   c. Provides a reserve in the event of a failure
   d. Works against engine vacuum
8. The first step in diagnosing a hydro-boost problem is
   a. A pressure test of the pump
   b. A volume test of the pump
   c. Tightening the power-steering drive belt
   d. A thorough visual inspection
9. What could cause the brake pedal to vibrate when depressed if the system is equipped with hydro boost?
   a. Too much power steering fluid
   b. Too much brake fluid
   c. Too little brake fluid
   d. Too little power steering fluid
10. The engine has to be running for the hydro-boost to provide any power assist for the brakes.
    a. True
    b. False

39

Antilock Brakes

OBJECTIVES: After studying Chapter 39, you should be able to:

1. Prepare for the interprovincial Red Seal certification examination in Appendix V (Brakes) on the topics covered in this chapter.
2. Explain the reason for ABS.
3. Describe the purpose and function of the ABS components such as wheel speed sensors, the electro-hydraulic unit, and the electronic controller.
4. Discuss how the ABS components control wheel slippage.
5. Explain how the ABS components control acceleration traction control.
6. Describe normal ABS dash lamp operation.
7. Discuss the procedure to follow to locate an ABS problem.
8. Explain how to retrieve trouble codes.
9. Explain the various methods for bleeding ABS systems.
10. Discuss the methods and tools needed to diagnose an ABS-equipped vehicle.

Antilock braking systems help prevent the wheels from locking during sudden braking, especially on slippery surfaces. This helps the driver maintain control.

THEORY OF OPERATION

When the wheels stop turning during a stop, the friction (traction) between the road surface and the tires decreases by almost 40%. At the surface of the road, a locked tire creates heat that generally softens the rubber of the tire. The tread rubber becomes almost liquid and loses its traction grip on the road surface.

A total loss of traction, called **100% slip,** means the tire is sliding across the road surface with the wheels locked. See Figure 39–1. Maximum traction occurs when the slip is controlled to between 10% and 20%. See Figure 39–2. This is accomplished in an antilock braking system by using electronic and hydraulic controls to monitor wheel slip and pulse the brakes on and off just the right amount to achieve maximum possible traction without wheel lockup. A typical ABS vehicle pulses the brakes on and off between ten and twenty times per second. This is much faster than any driver is capable of doing.

Steering Control

When a front tire loses traction, the vehicle cannot be steered. Steering of the vehicle requires that the tires have traction, but a locked wheel has little or no traction with the road. As a result, the vehicle will continue travelling in a straight line even though the front wheels are being turned by the driver. See Figure 39–3.

Skid Control

A vehicle equipped with ABS can still get into a skid; therefore, the term *skid control* is no longer used when describing antilock braking systems. ABS systems can prevent wheel lockup but cannot prevent the vehicle from skidding. See Figure 39–4.

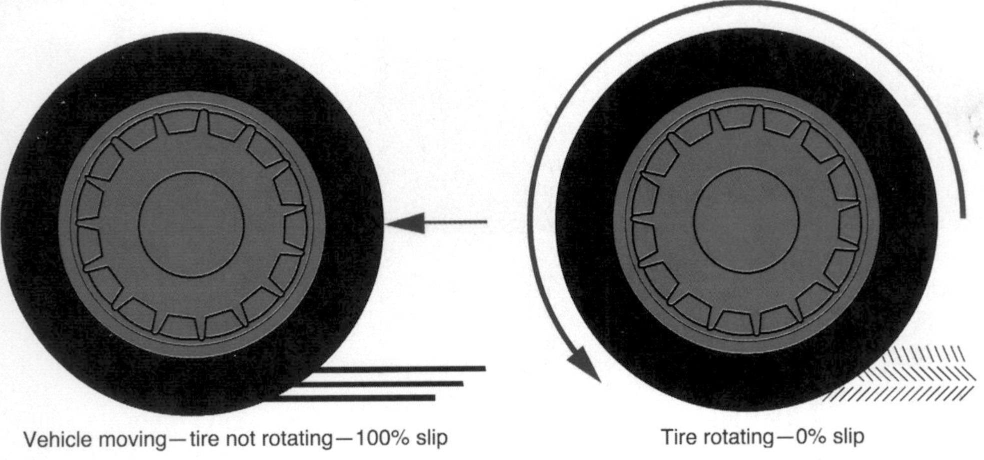

Figure 39–1 Maximum braking traction occurs when tire slip is between 10% and 20%. A rotating tire has 0% slip and a locked-up wheel has 100% slip.

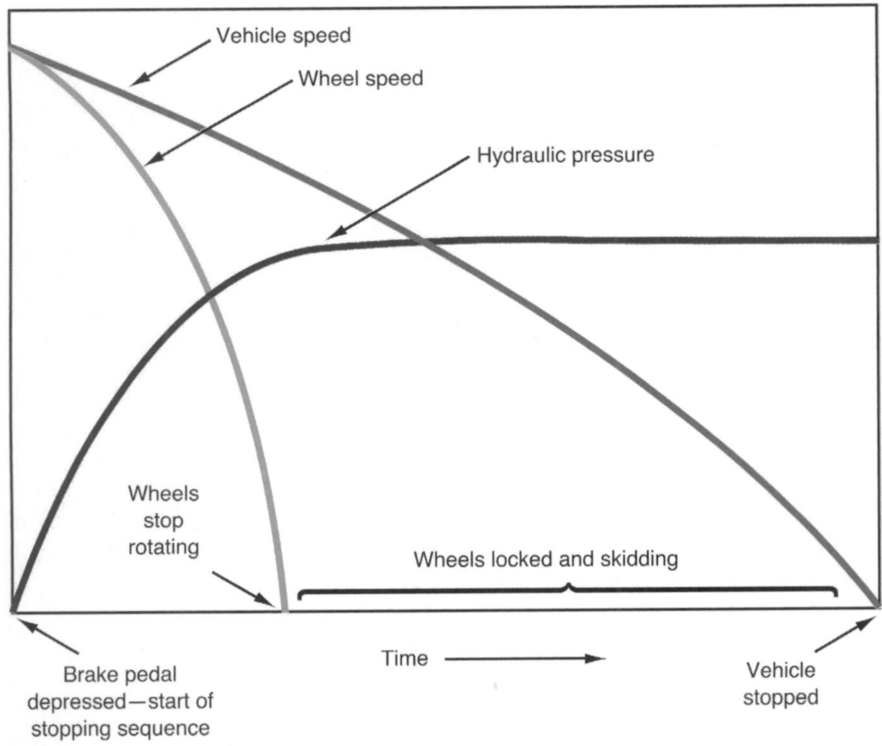

Figure 39–2 Typical stop on a slippery road surface without antilock brakes. Notice that the wheels stopped rotating before the vehicle finally came to a stop.

PURPOSE AND FUNCTION OF ABS COMPONENTS

All ABS systems use three basic subsystems, including:

- **Wheel speed sensors.** These electromagnetic sensors, often abbreviated **WSS,** produce a speed signal for the electronic controller.
- **Electronic control unit.** This is the brain, computer, or controller of any ABS unit. The controller receives wheel-speed information from the wheels and controls the hydraulic control unit if one or more wheels is slowing down at a faster rate than the other wheels. The electronic control unit is also called **controller antilock brake (CAB)** or **electronic brake control module (EBCM).**

Figure 39–3 Being able to steer and control the vehicle during rapid braking is one major advantage of an antilock braking system.

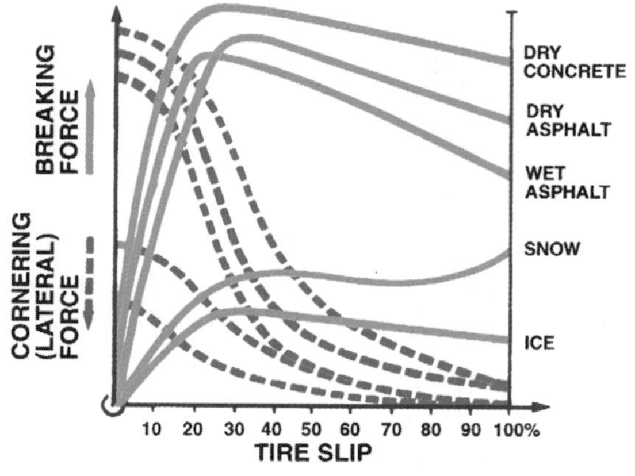

Figure 39–4 Traction is determined by pavement conditions and tire slip.

Frequently Asked Question ???

Does a Vehicle Equipped with ABS Brakes Stop Quicker?

Most experts agree that it is usually possible to stop in less distance *without* ABS. Antilock brakes are designed primarily for *control* rather than to simply shorten stopping distances.

Responsible drivers should continue to drive within the limits of their vehicle, including vehicle speed and weather and tire conditions. See Figure 39–5.

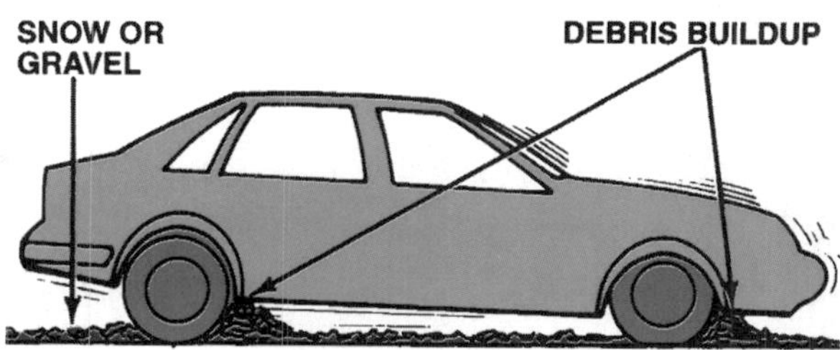

Figure 39–5 A wedge of gravel or compressed snow in front of a locked wheel can help stop a vehicle faster than if it were equipped with ABS.

- **Electro-mechanical hydraulic unit.** This unit does the actual work of controlling brake line pressures to keep the wheels from locking during a stop. See Figure 39–6.

ABS HYDRAULIC OPERATION

All ABS units use solenoid valves or rotary valves to control the brake fluid pressure at the wheels. The three stages of ABS operation that are controlled by the hydraulic control unit are described next.

Pressure Build-up (Normal Braking) The hydraulic system functions the same as any other hydraulic braking system. The driver has complete control of the pressure applied to the wheel cylinders and calipers. When greater braking force is required, the driver simply depresses the brake pedal farther, which increases hydraulic pressure build-up in the master cylinder and in all wheel cylinders and calipers. This stage is also called **pressure increase.** See Figure 39–7.

NOTE: Antilock braking systems cannot increase brake fluid pressure higher than the force applied by the driver.

Pressure Holding Pressure holding means that the ABS controller has detected a rapid slowing of a wheel during braking. To help prevent the wheel from locking, the controller commands that a valve be closed between the master cylinder and the wheel brake drum or caliper. See Figure 39–8. By closing off the master cylinder, the pressure to the brake is held at the present level. Even if the driver pushes down farther on the brake pedal, the increase in pressure at the master cylinder is blocked. This stage is also called **pressure maintain.**

Pressure Reduction The ABS controller can reduce the hydraulic pressure on the wheel cylinder or

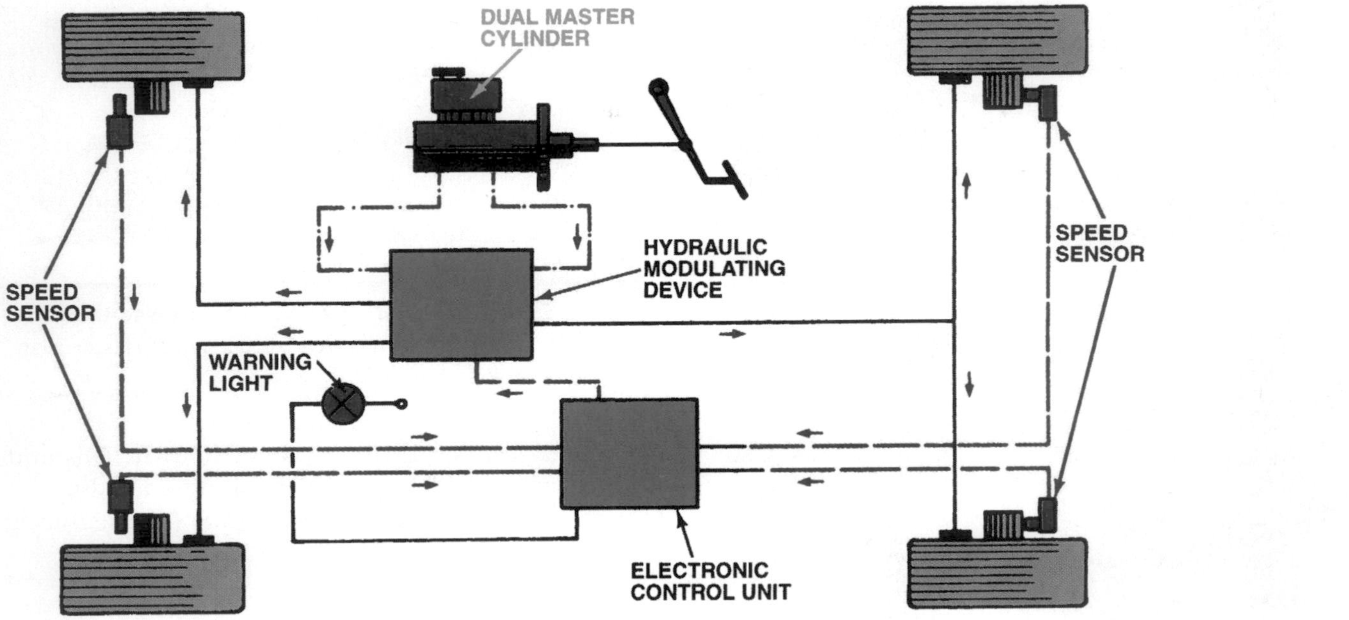

Figure 39–6 A schematic drawing of a typical antilock braking system (ABS).

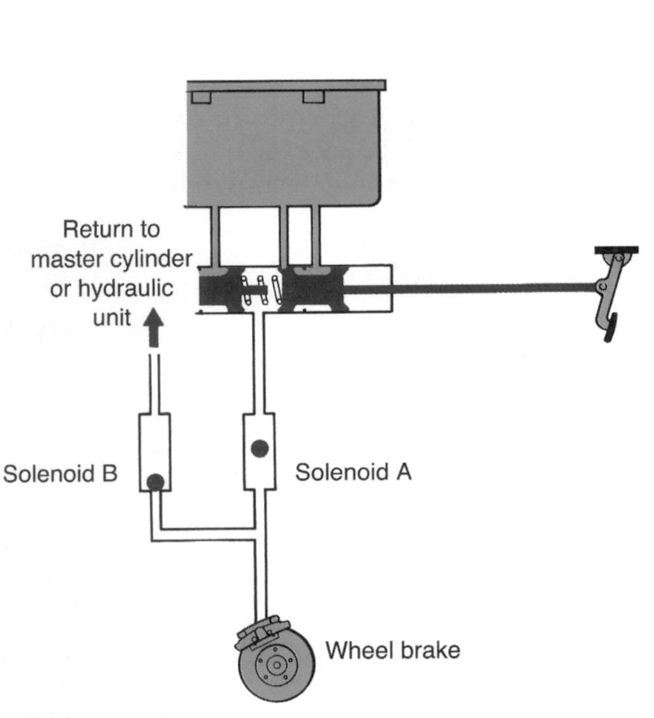

Figure 39–7 In a typical antilock braking system, the flow of brake fluid is controlled by valves or solenoids. During normal braking, solenoid A is open, allowing normal pressure building to occur from the master cylinder during a normal non-ABS stop. Solenoid B is closed to maintain master cylinder pressure at the wheel brake.

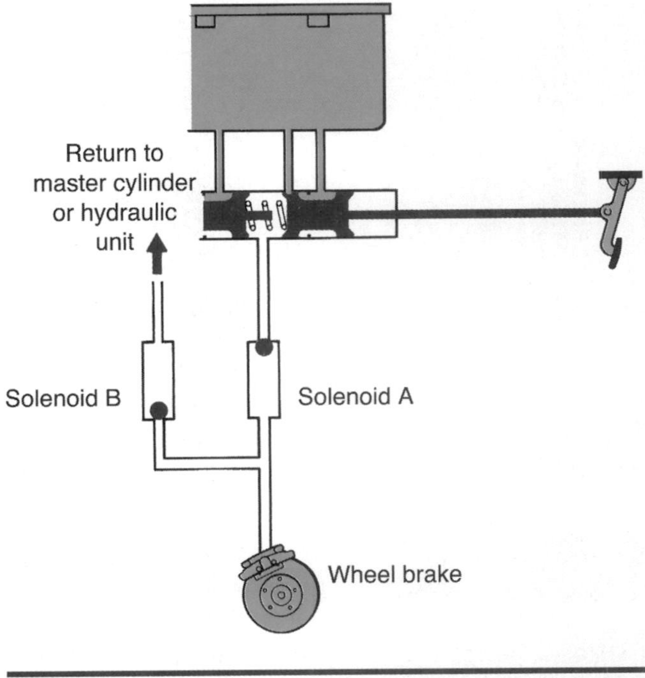

Figure 39–8 If a wheel is starting to slow down too fast, the ABS controller will command that solenoid A block off the master cylinder from the wheel brake. This prevents the driver from exerting additional pressure on the wheel brake. This stage is called **pressure holding.** This solenoid is called the *inlet* or *isolating* solenoid because it is used to control the movement of brake fluid to the wheel brake and, if closed, isolate any pressure from the wheel brake.

caliper by opening a valve and allowing the pressurized brake fluid to escape into a low pressure area of the system. When this occurs, the pressure is reduced and it is called the **pressure reduction** stage. See Figure 39–9. See Figure 39–10 for a graph showing vehicle speed, wheel speed, and hydraulic pressure during a typical ABS stop. The hydraulic pump delivers brake fluid to the master cylinder to decrease fluid pressure in the caliper. The accumulator (reservoir) temporarily stores brake fluid returning from the calipers as required in order to provide a smooth pressure decrease in the caliper. See Figure 39–11. This stage is also called the **pressure decrease, pressure decay,** or **pressure dump** stage.

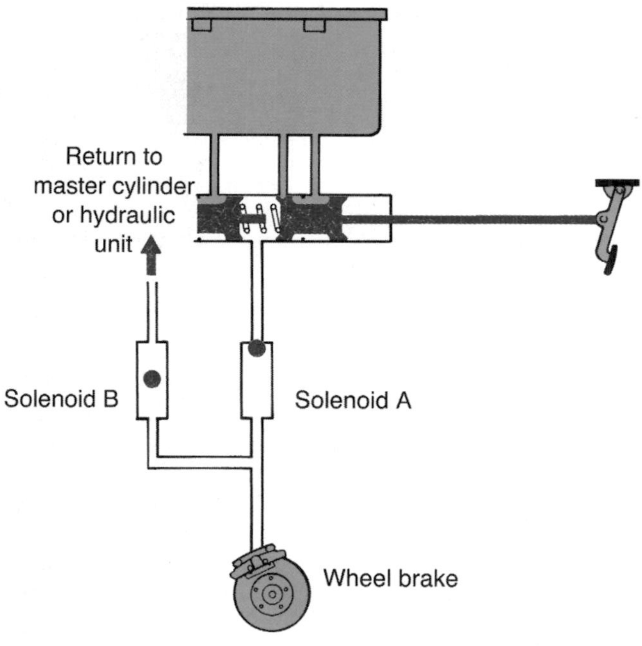

Figure 39–9 If a wheel is still slowing too fast and is about to lock up, solenoid B is opened, allowing the trapped pressurized brake fluid at the wheel brake to escape. This stage is called pressure reduction (release).

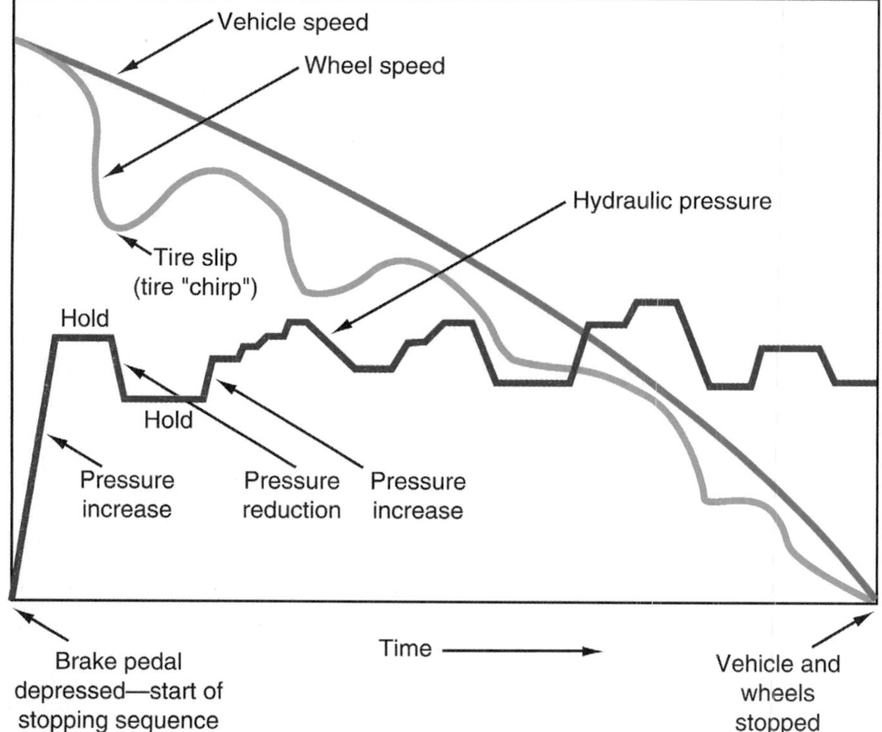

Figure 39–10 Typical stop with antilock brakes. Notice how the pressure increase, hold, and release are all used to bring the vehicle to a safe stop. ABS is not active below about 8 km/h (5 mph).

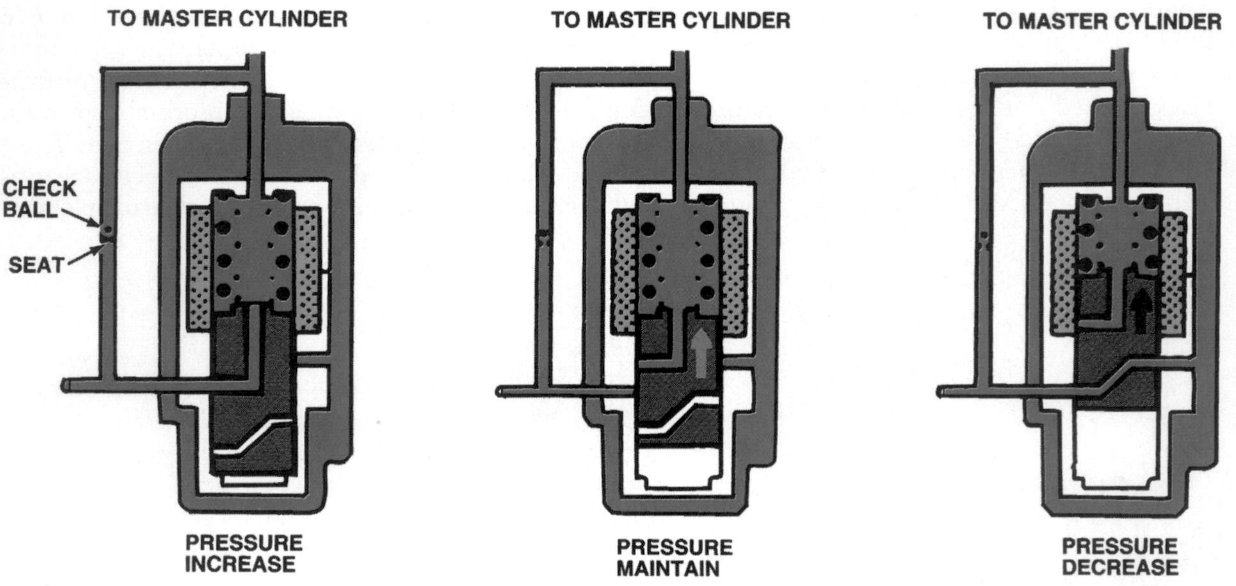

Figure 39–11 An ABS 3-way solenoid can increase, maintain, or decrease brake pressure to a given brake circuit.

Brake Pedal Feedback

Many ABS units force brake fluid back into the master cylinder under pressure during an ABS stop. This pulsing brake fluid return causes the brake pedal to pulsate. Some vehicle manufacturers use the pulsation of the brake pedal to inform the driver that the wheels are tending toward lockup and that the ABS is pulsing the brakes.

> **NOTE:** A pulsating brake pedal may be normal only during an ABS stop. It is not normal for a vehicle with ABS to have a pulsating pedal during normal braking. If the brake pedal is pulsating during a non-ABS stop, the brake drums or rotor may be warped. See Chapter 37 for details.

Some manufacturers use an **isolation valve** that prevents brake pedal pulsation even during an ABS stop.

Brake Pedal Travel Switch (Sensor)

Some ABS systems, such as the TEVES Mark IV system, use a brake pedal travel switch (sensor). See Figure 39–12. The purpose of the switch is to turn on the hydraulic pump when the brake pedal has been depressed 40% of its travel. The pump pumps brake fluid back into the master cylinder, which raises the brake pedal until the switch closes again, turning off the pump.

> **NOTE:** Some early ABS systems did not use a brake switch. Without a brake switch to signal the electronic controller that the brake pedal was being depressed, the ABS controller would activate the ABS when the vehicle was being driven over rough roads. The rough roads caused the wheels to rotate at different speeds and the hydraulic unit attempted to prevent the sudden slowing of the wheels. The brake switch can be the same as the brake light switch *or* a separate switch when the ABS could be activated while driving over rough roads.

The brake pedal switch is an input for the electronic controller. When the brakes are applied, the electronic controller gets ready to act if ABS needs to initialize the starting sequence of events.

> **CAUTION:** If the driver pumps the brakes during an ABS event, the controller will reset and reinitialization starts over again. This resetting process can disrupt normal ABS operation. The driver need only depress and hold the brake pedal down during a stop for best operation.

Wheel Speed Sensors

Wheel speed sensors are small electromagnetic generators. A toothed wheel is called a **tone ring, toothed ring,** or **reluctor.** See Figures 39–13 through 39–15.

The speed sensor contains a coil of wire surrounding a permanent magnet. As each tooth passes

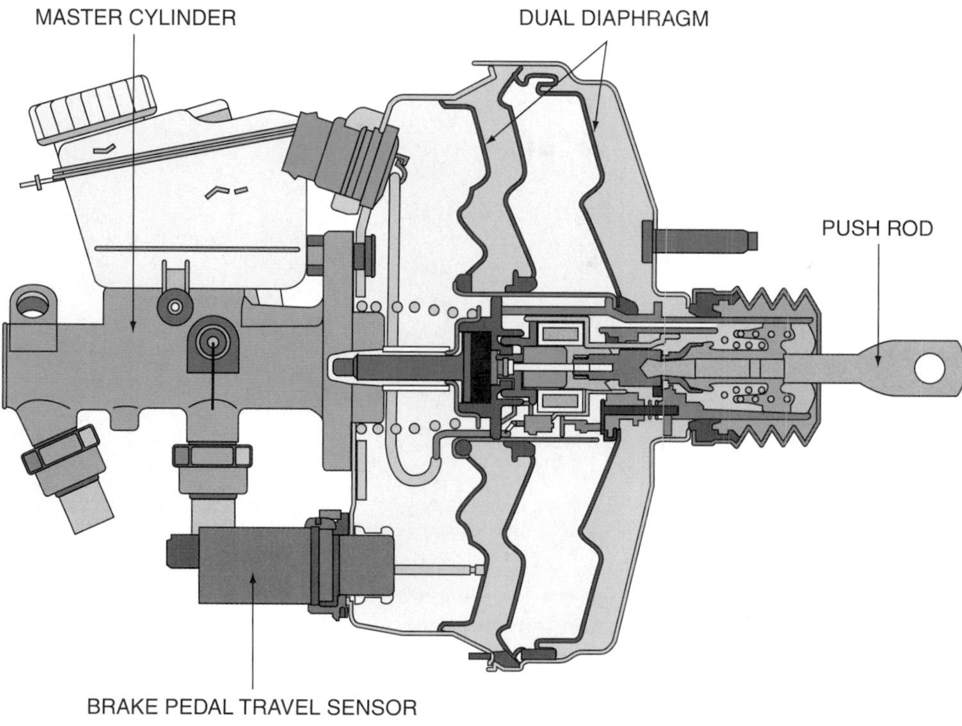

Figure 39–12 A cutaway of a vacuum power brake unit showing the brake pedal travel sensor. Notice that the plunger contacts the diaphragm inside the booster.

Figure 39–13 The wheel speed sensor and wiring are exposed on the front wheels of this four-wheel-drive vehicle. Road debris could damage the wiring or nick the tone wheel, especially if the vehicle is used off road.

TECH TIP 

KISS

KISS means "Keep It Stock, Stupid," and it is important to remember when replacing tires. Vehicles equipped with antilock brakes are "programmed" to pulse the brakes at just the right rate for maximum braking effectiveness. A larger tire rotates at a slower speed, and a smaller-than-normal tire rotates at a faster speed. Therefore, tire size affects the speed and rate-of-change in speed of the wheels as measured by the wheel speed sensors.

Although changing tire size will not prevent ABS operation, it *will* cause less effective braking during hard braking with the ABS activated. Using the smaller spare tire can create such a difference in wheel speed compared to the other wheels that a false wheel speed sensor code may be set and an amber ABS warning lamp on the dash may light. However, most ABS systems will still function with the spare tire installed, but the braking performance will not be as effective. For best overall performance, always replace tires with the same size and type as specified by the vehicle manufacturer.

(a)

(b)

Figure 39–14 (a) The tone ring is part of the front disc brake rotor on this Ford four-wheel-drive pickup truck. (b) The wheel speed sensor is visible after removing the hub assembly.

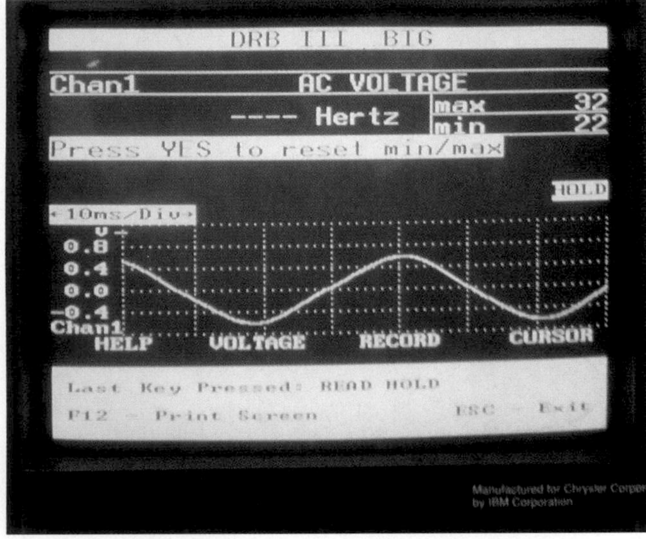

Figure 39–15 The wheel speed sensor generates a varying voltage as the wheel revolves. As the speed of the wheel increases, the voltage and the frequency (number of voltage cycles per second) also increase. This wheel-speed-sensor scope pattern was produced by simply rotating the tire by hand.

by the magnet, the magnetic field around the coil is increased. Then, as the tooth moves away, the magnetic field strength weakens. It is this *changing* magnetic field strength that produces a *changing* voltage (electrical pressure) in the coil of wire surrounding the magnet. This rapidly changing voltage signal is sent to the electronic controller. The electronic controller uses the *frequency* of the high and low voltages as a measure of the wheel speed. Frequency means the number of times the voltage changes per second, and it is measured in hertz. The electronic controller looks at the frequency of all wheel speed sensors and activates the antilock control if one or more sensors indicates that a wheel is slowing down a lot faster than the others.

> **NOTE:** Even motorcycles are equipped with ABS and wheel speed sensors. See Figure 39–16.

Lateral Acceleration Sensor

Some ABS-equipped vehicles include a lateral acceleration sensor or switch that measures the vehicle's cornering force. The signal is sent from the lateral acceleration sensor to the electronic brake-control module (EBCM) to modify its control logic to account for hard-cornering conditions.

Electronic Controller Operation

The electronic controller is the computer in the system that controls all parts of the ABS operation, including a **self-test** of all of its components every time the ignition is turned on or the vehicle starts to move.

> **NOTE:** Since an antilock braking system is a safety-related system, people can be injured if it malfunctions. This is one reason why the system does a complete system check every time the ignition is cycled.

The controller looks at the deceleration rate of all wheels. If a wheel is slowing down too fast, the controller activates the necessary hydraulic pressure controls. See Figure 39–17.

REAR-WHEEL ANTILOCK SYSTEMS

Antilock brakes are especially important for use on the rear wheels. Rear-wheel antilock systems are commonly used on pickup trucks, sport utility vehicles (SUVs), and vans. See Figure 39–18. Rear-wheel antilock systems may be abbreviated:

Figure 39–16 Notice that this motorcycle is equipped with a wheel speed sensor tone ring and is equipped with an antilock braking system (ABS).

RWAL—rear-wheel antilock

RABS—rear antilock braking system

Rear-wheel antilock systems will hold or decrease hydraulic pressure to *both* rear-wheel brakes if *either* wheel starts to lock up. Some rear-wheel ABS systems use just one speed sensor located in the differential or a vehicle speed sensor located on the output shaft of the transmission. Other systems use a wheel speed sensor at each rear wheel. In other words, both rear wheels are handled as one, and it does not matter to the electronic controller which wheel brake is about to lock. Rear-wheel antilock braking systems are also called **one-channel systems** because the hydraulic controls just one hydraulic circuit to both rear wheels.

Three-Channel Systems

Most rear-wheel-drive and many front-wheel-drive vehicles use a three-channel antilock braking system. Each front-wheel brake is controlled separately and both rear brakes are controlled together. A three-channel ABS system may use three or four wheel-speed sensors. In other words, even though a front-wheel-drive vehicle is equipped with four wheel speed sensors, it can be equipped with a three-channel ABS

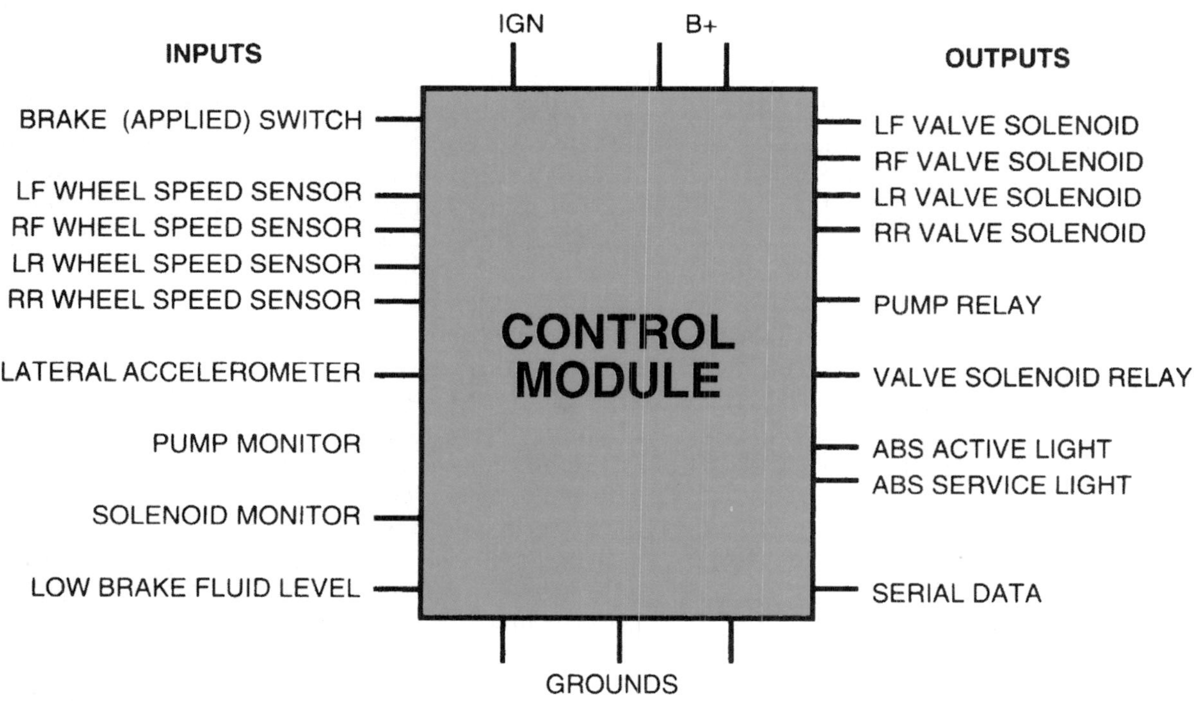

Figure 39–17 Typical inputs and outputs for brake control modules.

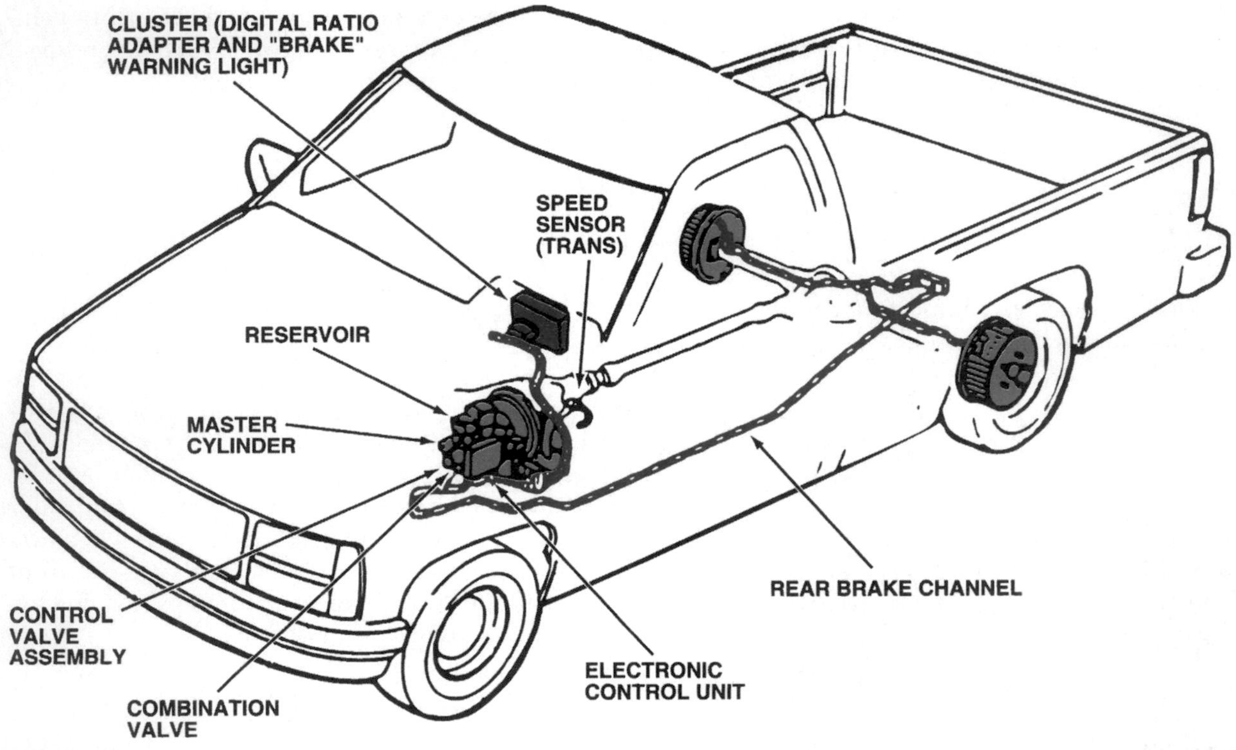

Figure 39–18 The Kelsey-Hayes RWAL system.

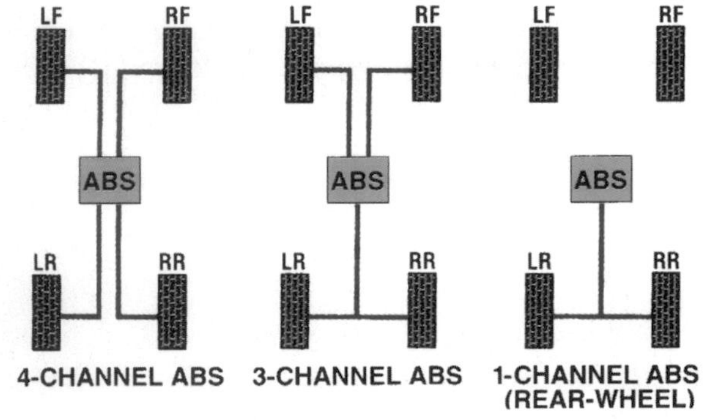

Figure 39–19 ABS systems include four-channel, three-channel, and single-channel.

unit. The two rear wheel speed sensors are monitored by the antilock controller and if just one of the rear brakes starts to slow down at too rapid a rate, both rear wheels are pulsed on and off together regardless of which rear wheel had lost traction. This strategy for controlling both rear brakes, based on the needs of the tire with the least traction, is called the **select-low principle.**

Four-Channel Systems

Four-channel antilock braking systems control all four wheel brakes individually. This is the most expensive type of system and requires that each wheel have a wheel speed sensor (WSS). See Figure 39–19.

INTEGRAL AND NONINTEGRAL

Integral systems combine the brake master cylinder and ABS hydraulic modulator, pump, and accumulator into one assembly. See Figure 39–20. Integral systems do not have a vacuum booster for power assist and rely instead on pressure generated by the electric pump for this purpose. The accumulators in these systems can contain over 18 000 kPa (2700 psi). See Safety Tip "Depress the Brake Pedal 40 Times to Be Safe." Most of the older ABS applications are integral systems. Integral ABS systems include the Bendix 10 and Bendix 9 (Jeep) ABS systems, Bosch 3, Delco Moraine Powermaster III, and Teves Mark 2.

Nonintegral ABS systems, which are sometimes referred to as add-on systems, have become the predominant type of ABS system because of their lower cost and simplicity. See Figure 39–21. Nonintegral ABS systems have a conventional brake master cylinder and vacuum power booster with a separate hydraulic modulator unit. Some also have an electric pump for ABS braking (to reapply pressure during the ABS hold-release-reapply cycle), but do not use the pumps for normal power assist.

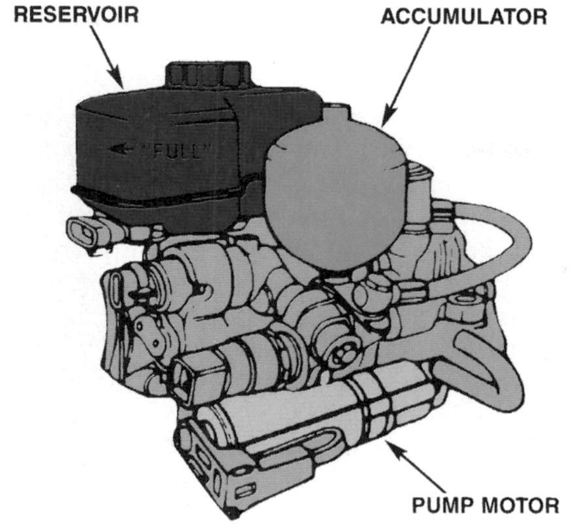

Figure 39–20 An integral ABS unit with a pump motor to provide power assist during all phases of braking and brake pressure during ABS braking.

> **SAFETY TIP**
>
> **Depress the Brake Pedal 40 Times to Be Safe**
>
> Whenever servicing a vehicle equipped with an integral ABS unit, depress the brake pedal 40 times to make sure that the accumulator has discharged all of its pressurized brake fluid back into the reservoir. If the brake fluid reservoir were to be filled to the MAX line without discharging the accumulator, the fluid level could overflow the reservoir during the next ABS stop when the accumulator discharges brake fluid into the reservoir.

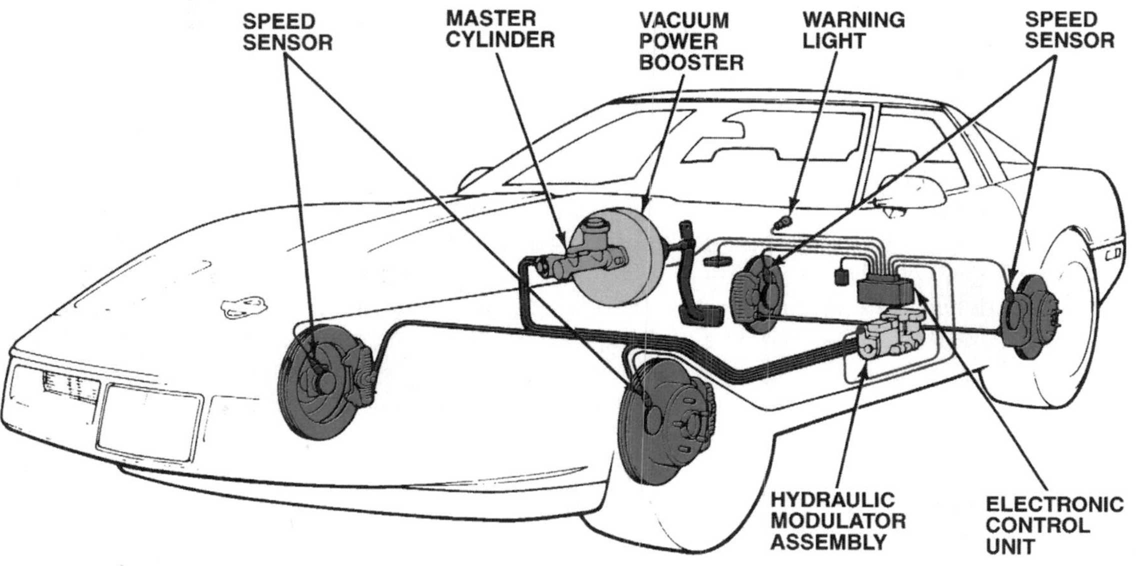

Figure 39–21 A nonintegral ABS system. This type of system uses a conventional master cylinder, and the ABS components are connected to the system to control brake fluid pressure to the wheel brakes.

Nonintegral (add-on) systems include Bendix 3, Bendix 6, Bendix ABX-4, Bendix Mecatronic, Bosch 2, Bosch 2S Micro, Bosch 2U, Bosch 2E, Bosch 5, Delco Moraine ABS-VI, Kelsey-Hayes RABS/RWAL, 4WAL, EBC-5 and EBC-10, Sumitomo ABS, Teves Mark 4 ABS and MK20, and Toyota rear-wheel ABS.

INTEGRAL ANTILOCK BRAKING SYSTEMS

Integral ABS means that the hydraulic control unit includes:

- A master cylinder with reservoir
- A hydraulic brake booster
- A brake pressure pump and motor
- A pressure accumulator
- Pressure monitoring switches
- Brake pressure modulator valves
- A brake fluid level sensor

Because this system functions as a brake booster as well as an antilocking braking unit, the hydraulic pump can run even in normal braking applications. If the pump fails, there will be no rear brakes and the brake pedal will be hard because of a lack of power assist.

Integral ABS units are usually serviced as complete units on an assembly. The operation of each unit varies with the individual vehicle and year. All integral systems are used on front-wheel-drive vehicles because if the rear brakes are lost, it is not as severe as with a rear-wheel-drive vehicle. On a front-wheel-drive vehicle, only about 20% of the braking force occurs on rear brakes.

NONINTEGRAL (REMOTE) ABS

Nonintegral systems are added to a base brake system and are often called "remote" or "add-on" ABS. Their only function is to provide antilock braking. These systems use a hydraulic system that is remote (removed) from the master cylinder. The ABS hydraulic unit is added in series with the hydraulic brake lines. Some nonintegral systems use a hydraulic pump for fluid circulation.

TRACTION CONTROL

Like seat belts and airbags, **traction control** is a safety feature that is being installed in today's automobiles as more and more manufacturers make traction control or **acceleration slip reduction** (ASR) available in their new vehicles. Traction control makes it easier for drivers to manoeuvere a vehicle in adverse road conditions. But what is traction control, and how does it work?

The word **traction** refers, in general, to your car's ability to maintain traction between its tires and the road. There are different kinds of traction: one kind occurs when the vehicle brakes, another when it accelerates, and still another when it turns.

Traction control deals specifically with front or back tire loss of traction during acceleration. In other words, when your car accelerates from a dead stop, or speeds up while passing another vehicle, traction control works to ensure maximum contact between the road surface and your tires under adverse road conditions. A wet or icy road surface will significantly reduce the traction between your tires and the road, and since your tires are the only part of your vehicle that actually touch the ground, any resulting loss of friction can have serious consequences.

Traction control, or ASR, is part of the car's braking technology. The changes in anti-lock brakes have occurred as follows: ABS was introduced in 1978, traction control in 1985, and stability control in 1995. Stability control provides operators with the benefit of stopping and starting their vehicle without a lot of dedication on their part.

Traction control works in a way opposite to ABS, dealing with *acceleration* rather than deceleration. The components are very similar to ABS since many of the same principles apply to both systems. On a wet road, traction control senses slippage between the wheel and the road. When this happens the brake will be applied to the wheel that is slipping, forcing it to slow and increasing static friction. This will help provide maximum static friction between the tire and the road; and by continually adjusting the braking pressure the system will ensure maximum contact between the wheel and the road. You can actually hear a shuddering sound and feel the pedal pulsate when the system is working.

ABS and traction control operate similarly. In fact, the ABS control unit is the basic building block for both traction control *and* stability control. By adding extra controllers and more inputs and outputs, the system can be expanded to include the necessary parts for traction control.

When designing traction control systems, the basic ABS system and other components in the vehicle will be modified. The accelerator cable will be replaced by another means to control vehicle acceleration—in other words, the direct connection between the accelerator pedal and the throttle ceases to exist. Instead, a sensor converts the position of the accelerator pedal to an electrical signal, which the control unit uses to generate a control voltage. The ABS hydraulic modulator is also redesigned to include a traction control component.

The various inputs and outputs work as a team to activate the traction control system.

Consider an example in which one wheel is on a slippery surface and that wheel starts to spin. The traction control system instantaneously kicks in, sensing that the wheel has begun to slip. Within a split second, this data is fed back to the control unit, which will reduce throttle input and apply the brakes to the faster-turning wheel. The wheel is then prevented from spinning and the car maintains maximum traction (see Figure 39–22).

NOTE: The ABS controller only supplies the necessary pressure to the wheel brake that is required to prevent tire slipping during acceleration. The amount of pressure varies according to the condition of the road surface and the amount of engine power being delivered to the drive wheels. A program inside the controller will disable traction control if brake-system overheating is likely to occur. The driver should either wait for the brakes to cool down or use less accelerator pedal while driving.

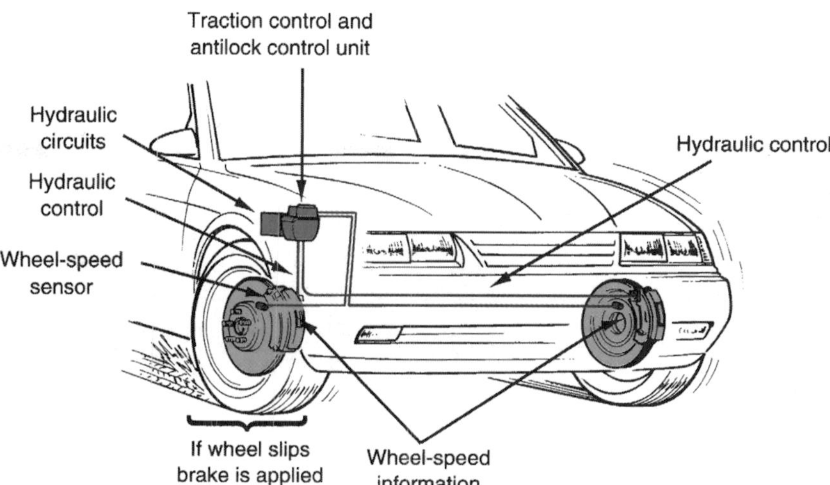

Figure 39–22 Brake-system-only traction control uses information from wheel speed sensors to the traction control unit. If the drive wheel is accelerating too fast, indicating wheel slip, the control unit applies hydraulic control to the wheel brake to stop the wheel slip.

VEHICLE STABILITY SYSTEM

Some vehicles are equipped with a vehicle stability system that can automatically apply one wheel brake to prevent a slide and to aid in vehicle stability, especially under slippery road conditions. A four-channel ABS system must be used because the system must be able to control each wheel brake individually. Some systems can be turned off but will be automatically turned back on when the engine is started the next time. See Figure 39–23. A hydraulic fault with the base brakes or an ABS fault will disable the vehicle stability system.

Figure 39–23 Most vehicle stability systems can be switched off but will be reactivated at the next ignition cycle. This Acura is equipped with an off switch. The system is called vehicle stability assist (VSA), and it includes traction control in its operation.

Frequently Asked Question ???

Is Tire Chirp Normal with ABS?

Many owners of vehicles complain that their antilock braking system is not working correctly because their tires chirp and occasionally experience tire lockup during hard braking, especially at low speed. These conditions are perfectly normal because for maximum braking between 12% and 20% of slip means that the tire will slip or skid slightly during an ABS stop.

It is also normal for vehicles with ABS to have the tires lock and skid slightly when the speed of the vehicle is below 8 km/h (5 mph). This occurs because the wheel speed sensors cannot generate usable speed signals for the electronic controller. This low-speed wheel lockup seldom creates a problem.

Before attempting to troubleshoot or diagnose an ABS problem, be sure the problem is not just normal operation of the system.

ABS DIAGNOSIS AND SERVICE

Brake Warning Lamp Operation

The first step in the correct diagnosis of an antilock braking system problem is to check the status of the brake warning lamps.

Red Brake Warning Lamp This lamp warns of a possible dangerous failure in the base brakes, such as low brake fluid level or low pressure in half of the hydraulic system. The red brake warning lamp will also light if the parking brake is applied and may light due to an ABS failure, such as low brake pressure on an integral system. See Figure 39–24.

SEQUENCE NUMBER	LAMP SEQUENCE	SYMPTOM DESCRIPTION	PERFORM TEST
1	LAMPS: IGNITION ON, CRANKING, RUNNING, MOVING, BRAKING, STOPPED, IDLE; "ANTI-LOCK"; BRAKE	NORMAL LAMP SEQUENCE WITH -EXCESSIVE PEDAL TRAVEL OR SPONGY PEDAL -ANTILOCK BRAKING OPERATION OR VALVE CYCLING DURING NORMAL STOPS ON DRY PAVEMENT -POOR VEHICLE TRACKING DURING ANTILOCK BRAKING	H C D
2	LAMPS: IGNITION ON, CRANKING, RUNNING, MOVING, BRAKING, STOPPED, IDLE; "ANTI-LOCK"; BRAKE	CONTINUOUS "ANTILOCK" LAMP NORMAL "BRAKE" LAMP	A
3	LAMPS: IGNITION ON, CRANKING, RUNNING, MOVING, BRAKING, STOPPED, IDLE; "ANTI-LOCK"; BRAKE	"ANTILOCK" LAMP COMES ON AFTER VEHICLE STARTS MOVING NORMAL BRAKE LAMP	C
4	LAMPS: IGNITION ON, CRANKING, RUNNING, MOVING, BRAKING, STOPPED, IDLE; "ANTI-LOCK"; BRAKE	NO "ANTILOCK" LAMP WHILE CRANKING NORMAL "BRAKE" LAMP	E
5	LAMPS: IGNITION ON, CRANKING, RUNNING, MOVING, BRAKING, STOPPED, IDLE; "ANTI-LOCK"; BRAKE	NO "ANTILOCK" LAMP NORMAL "BRAKE" LAMP	F
6	LAMPS: IGNITION ON, CRANKING, RUNNING, MOVING, BRAKING, STOPPED, IDLE; "ANTI-LOCK"; BRAKE	INTERMITTENT "ANTILOCK" LAMP WHILE DRIVING NORMAL "BRAKE" LAMP	G
7	LAMPS: IGNITION ON, CRANKING, RUNNING, MOVING, BRAKING, STOPPED, IDLE; "ANTI-LOCK"; BRAKE	CONTINUOUS "ANTILOCK" LAMP CONTINUOUS "BRAKE" LAMP	B
8	LAMPS: IGNITION ON, CRANKING, RUNNING, MOVING, BRAKING, STOPPED, IDLE; "ANTI-LOCK"; BRAKE	"ANTILOCK" AND "BRAKE" LAMPS COME ON WHILE BRAKING	B
9	LAMPS: IGNITION ON, CRANKING, RUNNING, MOVING, BRAKING, STOPPED, IDLE; "ANTI-LOCK"; BRAKE	NORMAL "ANTILOCK" LAMP CONTINUOUS "BRAKE" LAMP	B
10	LAMPS: IGNITION ON, CRANKING, RUNNING, MOVING, BRAKING, STOPPED, IDLE; "ANTI-LOCK"; BRAKE	NORMAL OR CONTINUOUS "ANTILOCK"LAMP FLASHING "BRAKE" LAMP	B

Figure 39–24 This lamp sequence chart refers you to a specific troubleshooting procedure. To use it properly, the driving conditions and which lamps are on must be known.

> **NOTE:** Some antilock braking systems will light the red brake warning lamp through a resistor. This results in a dim red brake warning lamp. To check if the lamp is dim or at full brightness, simply apply the parking brake. If the warning lamp gets brighter, you know that the red brake warning lamp is indicating an ABS problem and not a hydraulic problem.

Amber ABS Warning Lamp The amber lamp usually comes on after a start during the initialization or start-up self-test sequence. The exact time the amber lamp remains on after the ignition is turned on varies with the vehicle and the ABS design. Most ABS systems will not function if a diagnostic trouble code (DTC) has been set and the amber warning light is illuminated. The base brake system will perform normally. See Figure 39–25.

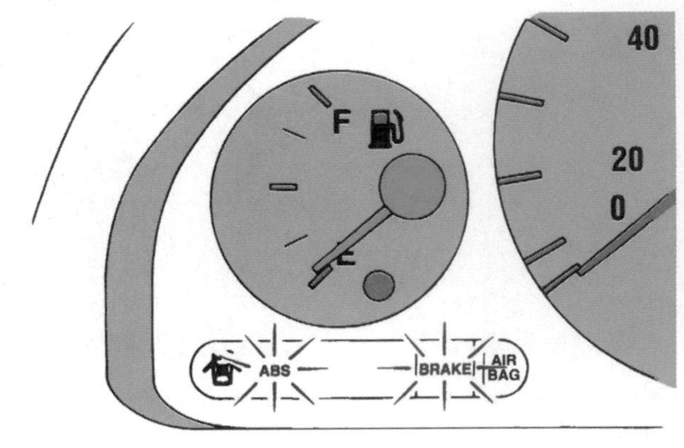

Figure 39–25 On most vehicles equipped with ABS, the ABS and the BRAKE warning lamps should come on as a bulb check when the ignition is first switched on.

Frequently Asked Question ???

What's That Noise and Vibration?

Many vehicle owners and service technicians have been disturbed to hear and feel an occasional groaning noise. It usually is heard and felt through the vehicle after it is first started and driven. Because this occurs when first being driven in forward or reverse, many technicians have blamed the transmission or related drive-line components. But the noise is common in many ABS vehicles as part of a system check. As soon as the ABS controller senses speed from the wheel speed sensors after an ignition cycles on, the controller will run the pump either every time or whenever the accumulator pressure is below a certain level. This can occur while the vehicle is being backed out of a driveway or being driven forward because wheel sensors can only detect speed, not direction.

Before serious and major repairs are attempted to cure a noise, make sure it is not the normal ABS self-test activation sequence of events.

DIAGNOSTIC STORY

RWAL Diagnosis

The owner of an S-10 pickup truck complained that the red brake warning lamp on the dash remained on even when the parking brake was released. The problem could be

1. A serious hydraulic problem
2. Low brake fluid
3. A stuck or defective parking brake switch
4. RWAL trouble if the brake lamp is dim

The technician found that the brake lamp was on dimly, indicating an antilock braking problem was detected. The first step in diagnosing an antilock braking problem *with* a dash lamp on is to check for stored trouble codes. When the technician used a jumper between terminal A and H on the DLC (old ALCL), four flashes of the brake lamp indicated a code 4.

Checking a service manual, code 4 was found to be a grounded switch inside the hydraulic control unit. The hardest part about the repair was getting access to and replacing the defective (electrically grounded) switch. After bleeding the system and a thorough test drive, the lamp sequence and RWAL functioned correctly.

Visual Inspection

Many ABS-related problems can be more easily diagnosed if all of the basics are carefully inspected. A thorough visual inspection should include the following items:

- Brake fluid level—check the conditions and level in the reservoir.
- Brake fluid leaks—check for cracks in flexible lines or other physical damage.
- Fuses and fusible links—check all ABS-related fuses.
- Wiring and connections—check all wiring, especially wheel-speed-sensor leads for damage.
- Wheel speed sensors—check that the sensor ring teeth are not damaged. Clean debris from the sensor if possible.

NOTE: Most wheel speed sensors are magnetic and therefore can attract and hold metallic particles. Be sure to remove any metallic debris from around the magnetic wheel speed sensor.

- Base brake components—all base brake components such as disc brake calipers, drum brake wheel cylinders, and related components must be in proper working condition.
- Parking brake—check that the parking brake is correctly adjusted and fully released.
- Wheel bearings—all wheel bearings must be free of defects and properly adjusted.
- Wheels and tires—check for correct size, proper inflation, and legal tread depth.

Test Drive and Verify the Fault

A test drive is a very important diagnostic procedure. Many ABS systems and diagnostic trouble codes (DTC) will not set unless the vehicle is moving. Often, the driver has noticed something like the self-test while driving and thinks it may be a fault in the system.

NOTE: Some ABS units will cause the brake pedal to move up and down slightly during the cycling of the valves during the self-test. Each system has its own unique features. The service technician will have to be aware of these to avoid attempting to repair a problem that is not a fault of the system.

Before attempting to diagnose and repair an ABS vehicle, be certain to verify that there is actually a problem and that the customer is not complaining about normal operation of the system.

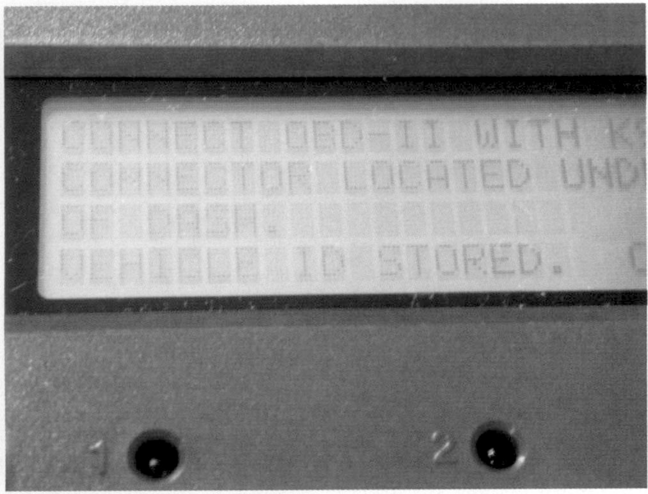

Figure 39–26 A scan tool such as this Snap-On MT2500 can be used to read diagnostic trouble codes (DTCs) and display data stream information as well as perform functional tests on some systems.

(a)

(b)

Figure 39–27 (a) A breakout box is being used to diagnose an ABS problem. The controller (computer) is located in the trunk of this vehicle, and a digital multimeter is being used to measure resistance and voltage at various points in the system, following the service manual procedure. (b) Another vehicle being tested for an ABS fault. In this vehicle, the computer is located under the passenger seat, which has been removed to gain better access to the wiring and terminals.

Before driving, start the engine and observe the red and amber brake warning lamps. If the red brake warning lamp is on, the base brakes may not be functioning correctly. Do not drive the vehicle until the base brakes are restored to proper operation.

ABS Problem Diagnosis

Most ABS problems set a diagnostic trouble code (DTC). Although some older systems flash the ABS amber light a number of times to indicate a code, most ABS systems require the use of a scan tool. The scan tool will be able not only to read the codes but also clear any stored DTCs. A scan tool is also necessary to bleed air from the hydraulic control unit on many systems. See Figure 39–26.

After the DTC has been displayed, the service manual may direct the service technician to check voltages at various parts to help pinpoint the actual cause of the problem. See Figure 39–27.

Hydraulic ABS Service

Before doing any brake work on a vehicle equipped with antilock brakes, always consult the appropriate service information for the exact vehicle being serviced. For example, some manufacturers recommend depressurizing the hydraulic accumulator by depressing the brake pedal many times before opening any bleeder valves. Many service checks require that a pressure gauge be installed in the system.

Brake Bleeding ABS

After depressurizing the unit as per the manufacturer's recommended procedures, the brakes can be bled using the same procedure as for a vehicle without ABS (see Chapter 33). Air trapped in the ABS hydraulic unit may require that a scan tool be used to cycle the valves. See the Tech Tip "Don't Forget to Bleed the E-H Unit" for details.

TECH TIP 

Don't Forget to Bleed the E-H Unit

Air can easily get trapped in the ABS electronic-hydraulic (E-H) assembly whenever the hydraulic system is opened. Even though the master cylinder and all four wheel cylinders/calipers have been bled, sometimes the brake pedal will still feel spongy. Some E-H units can be bled through the use of a scan tool where the valves are pulsed in sequence by the electronic brake controller (computer). Some units are equipped with bleeder valves, where others must be bled by loosening the brake lines. Bleeding the E-H unit also purges out the older brake fluid that can cause rust and corrosion damage. Only DOT 3 brake fluid is specified for use in an antilock braking system. Always check the label on the brake fluid reservoir and/or service manual or owner's manual.

CAUTION: Some ABS units require that the brake pedal be depressed up to 40 times to fully discharge brake fluid from the accumulator. Failure to fully discharge the accumulator can show up as too low brake fluid level. If brake fluid is added, it could overflow the reservoir during an ABS stop when the accumulator discharges brake fluid back into the reservoir.

SAFETY TIP 

ABS Safety Precautions

- Avoid mounting the antenna for a transmitting device near the ABS control unit. Transmitting devices, such as cellular (cell) telephones, citizen band radios, etc. can often interfere with the electronics in the unit.
- Avoid mounting tires of different diameter than the original tires. Different size tires generate different wheel-speed-sensor frequencies that may not be usable by the ABS controller.
- Never open a bleeder valve or loosen a hydraulic line while the ABS is pressurized. The accumulator must be depressurized according to the manufacturer's recommended procedures.
- Do not pry against or hit the wheel-speed-sensor ring.

PHOTO SEQUENCE 25 Bleeding a Teves Antilock Braking System

P25–1 Prepare to bleed the brake hydraulic system by checking the hydraulic system including the master cylinder.

P25–2 Always use DOT 3 brake fluid in any vehicle equipped with ABS.

P25–3 Be sure the brake fluid level in the reservoir is filled to the maximum line. Do not overfill.

P25–4 Hoist the vehicle safely and raise to a good working level to service the wheel brakes.

P25–5 Remove the wheels.

P25–6 The Chrysler service manual specifies that the base brakes be manually bled before using the scan tool to bleed the air in the hydraulic unit. Tapping on the bleeder valve helps break the taper of the bleeder valve.

P25–7 Use a six-point wrench or socket and loosen the bleeder valve.

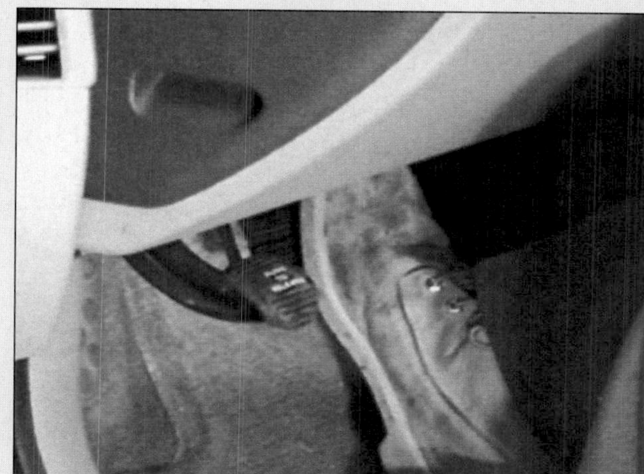

P25–8 Have an assistant depress the brake pedal slowly to bleed the air from each wheel starting at the right rear, then the left rear, right front, and finally the left front wheel.

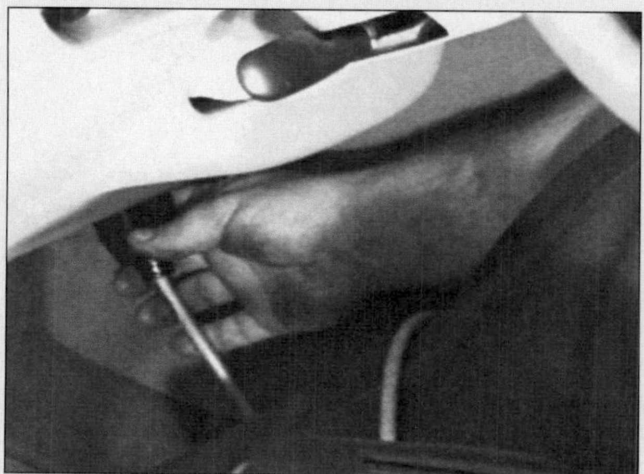

P25–9 After manually bleeding all four wheels, connect the Chrysler DRB III scan tool to the data link connector (DLC) located under the dash.

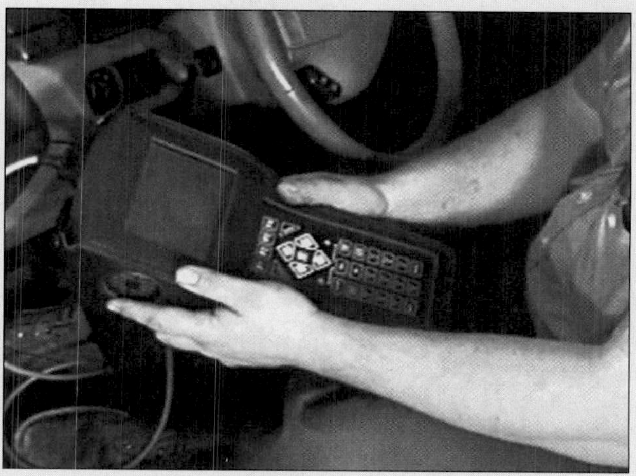

P25–10 Turn the scan tool on and follow the directions on the display.

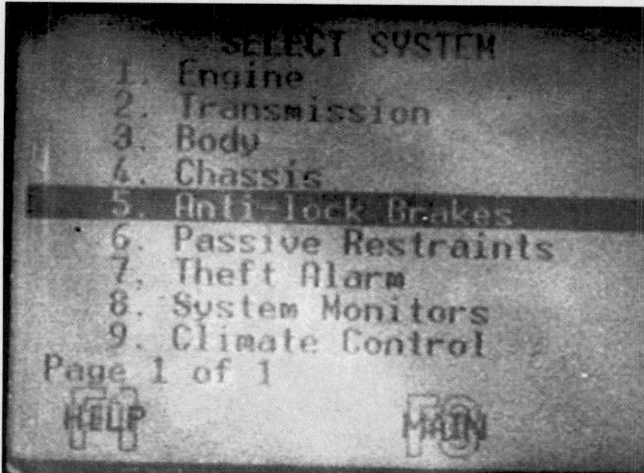

P25–11 Select "antilock brakes" from the menu.

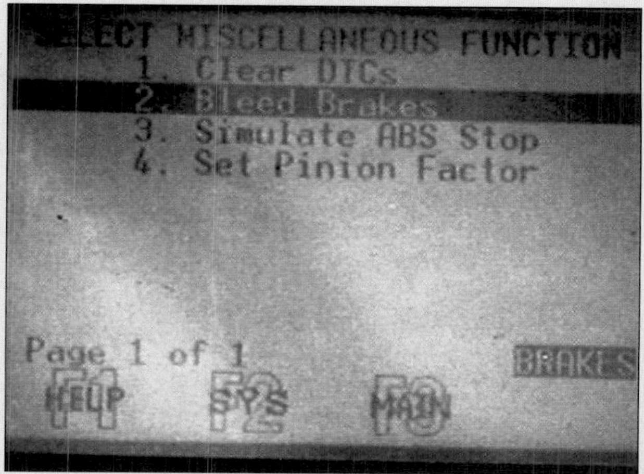

P25–12 Select "bleed brakes" from the selection menu.

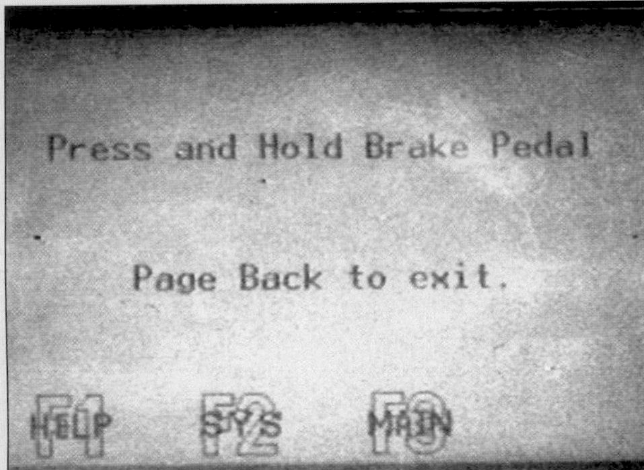

P25–13 The scan tool now instructs the service technician to press and hold the brake pedal.

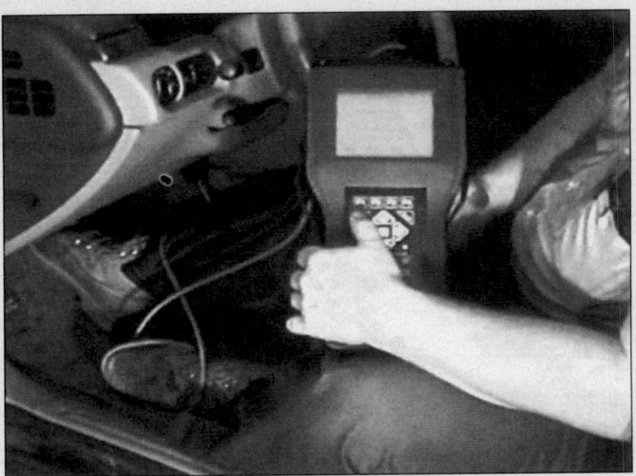

P25–14 With the brake pedal depressed, the scan tool commands the ABS pump motor to operate.

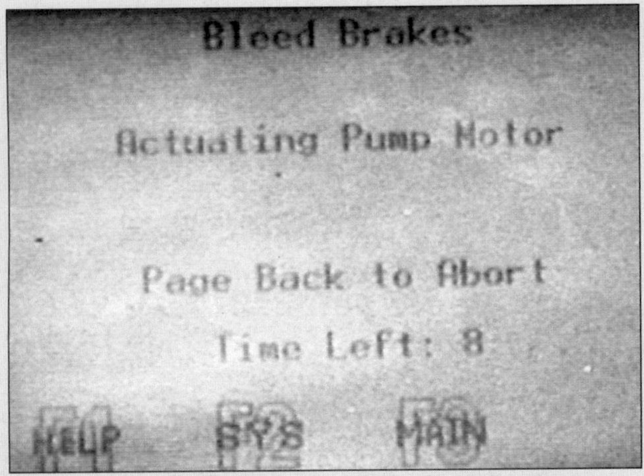

P25–15 The pump motor will run until the countdown on the display reads zero.

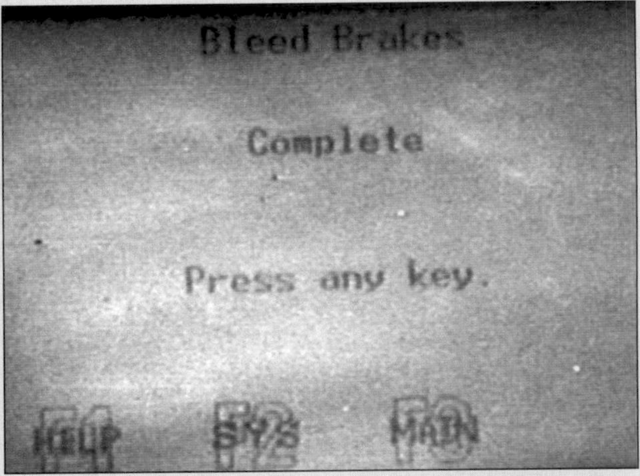

P25–16 Finally the scan tool display indicates that the brake bleeding process is complete.

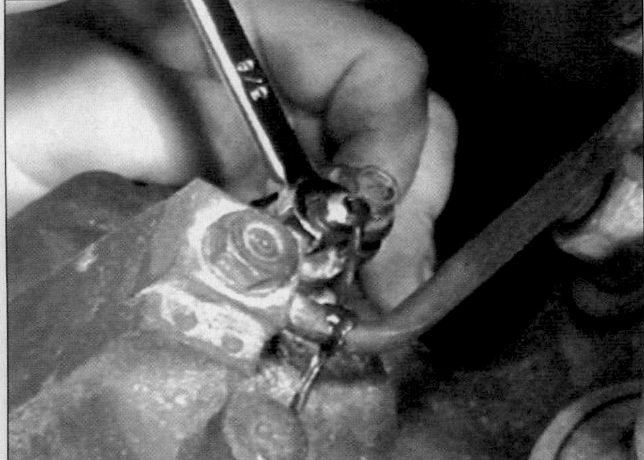

P25–17 After the scan tool bleeding is complete, fill the master cylinder if necessary and bleed the base brakes again following the same procedure as before. Be sure to refill the master cylinder after bleeding.

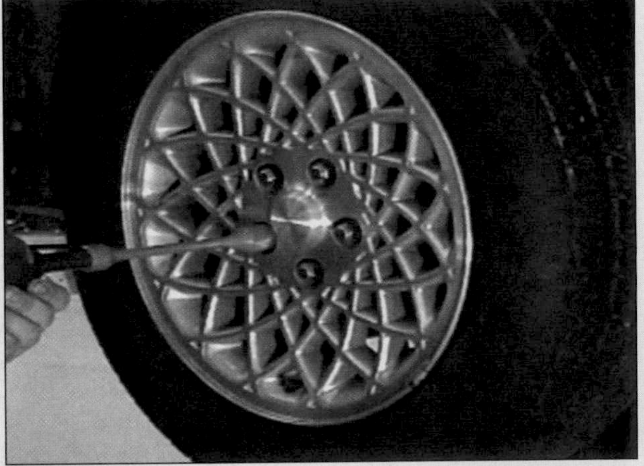

P25–18 Install all four wheels and torque the lug nuts to factory specifications. Test drive the vehicle to ensure proper braking before returning the vehicle to the customer.

PHOTO SEQUENCE 26 4-WAL ABS Diagnosis

P26–1 A Chevrolet pickup truck is being driven into the shop with an antilock brake system (ABS) problem.

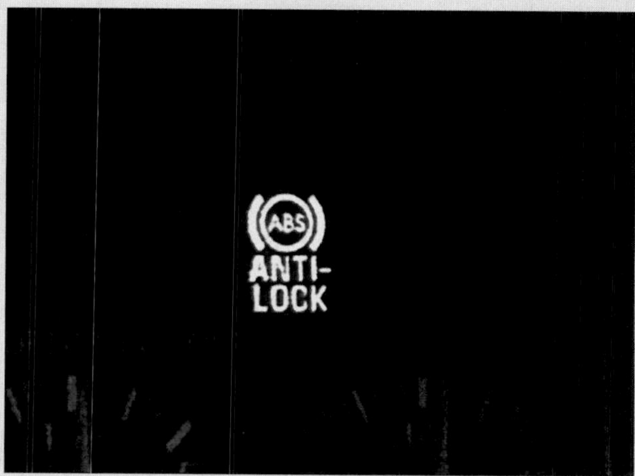

P26–2 The amber ABS warning light remains on whenever the ignition is on.

P26–3 The first step of almost any diagnostic procedure is to perform a thorough visual inspection, including checking the level and condition of the brake fluid in the master cylinder reservoir.

P26–4 A visual inspection should also include an inspection of the wiring and all hydraulic components under the hood.

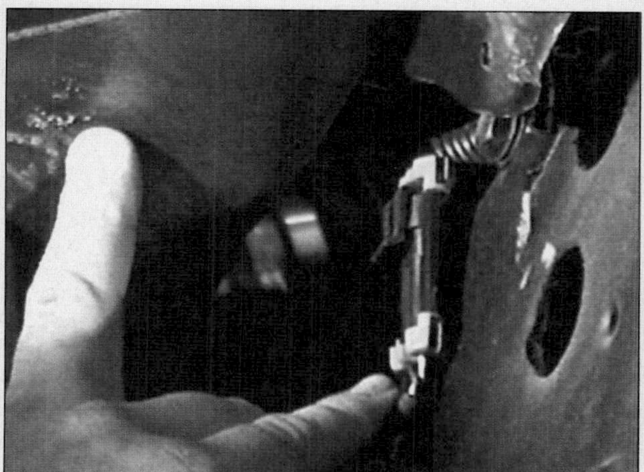

P26–5 A thorough visual inspection should also include checking all wheel speed sensor wiring and connectors.

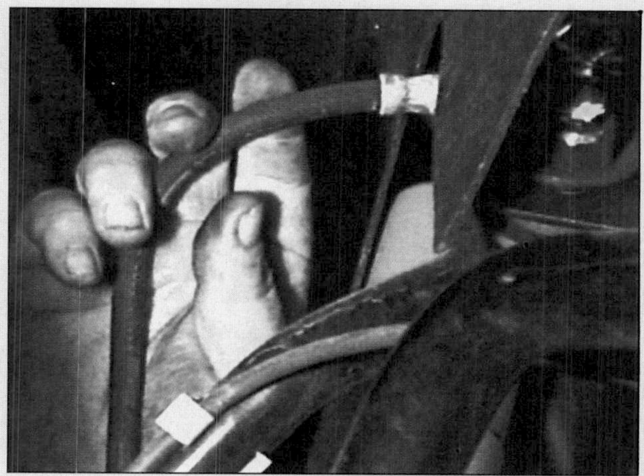

P26–6 The hydraulic system should also be inspected for obvious faults or damage that could have been caused by road debris such as a cut flexible brake line.

P26–7 After a thorough visual inspection, a scan tool should be used to retrieve any stored diagnostic trouble codes (DTCs). A Tech 2 is being used on this Chevrolet truck.

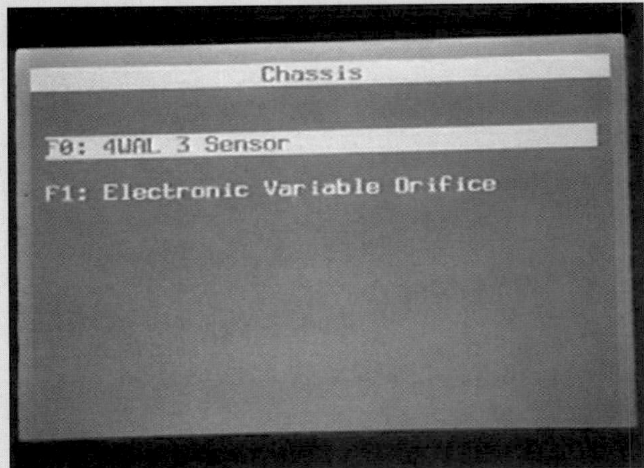

P26–8 From "chassis" select "4WAL, 3 sensor" ABS on the Tech 2 scan tool.

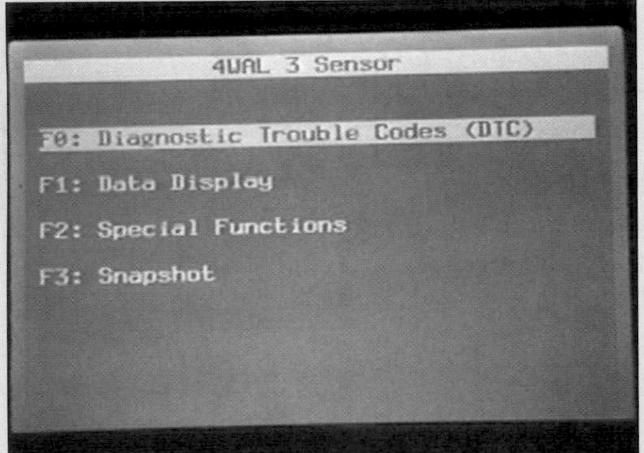

P26–9 Select "diagnostic trouble codes (DTC)" from the selection menu.

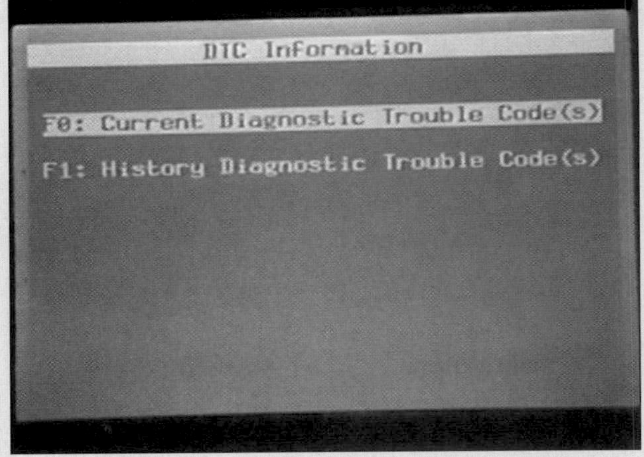

P26–10 Select "current diagnostic trouble code(s)" from the selection menu.

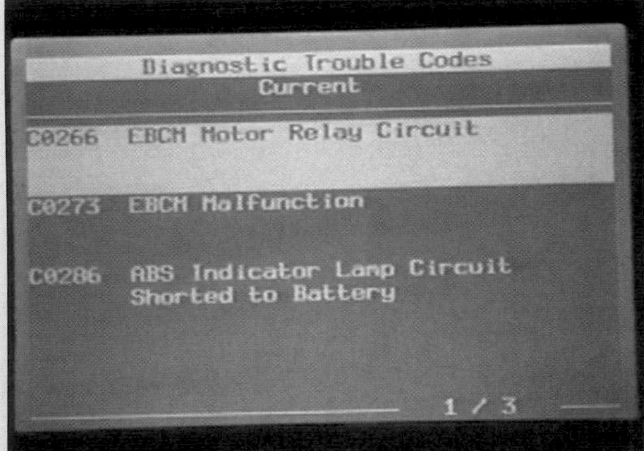

P26–11 There are three DTCs stored including C0266. The "C" means that it is a chassis code and the "0" indicates that this is an SAE-specified OBD II DTC.

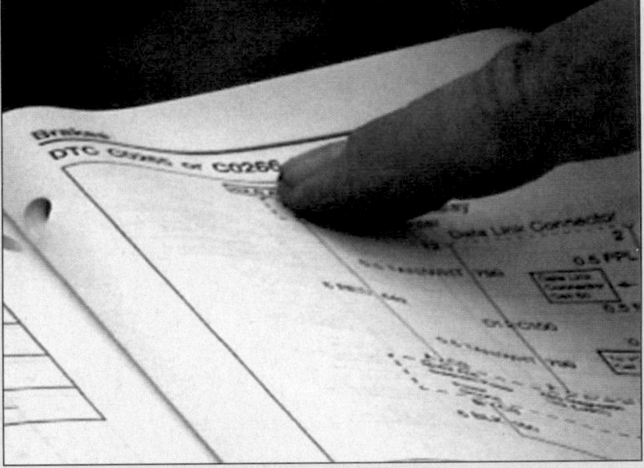

P26–12 The service manual is checked for DTC C0266.

P26–13 By following the service manual test procedure, the technician is led to the conclusion that the fault is due to a defective ABS controller (computer), which also explains the multiple codes found.

P26–14 The technician disconnected the battery before replacing the ABS computer. The old computer was returned to the parts store as a core to be rebuilt.

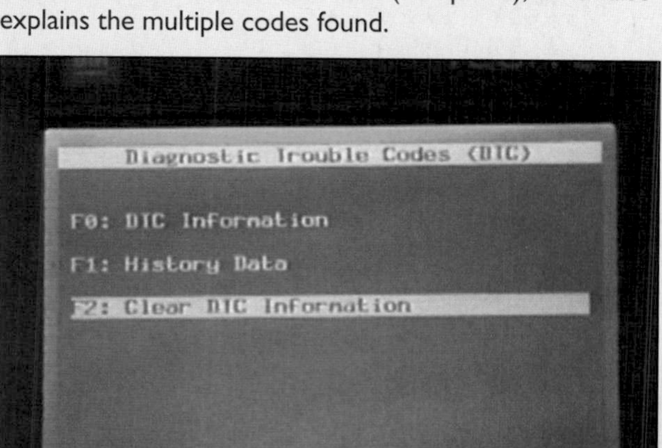

P26–15 The battery was reconnected and the vehicle driven to check for proper operation of the ABS amber dashboard warning light and for proper ABS brake operation. The Tech 2 was connected again. If another fault had been found, the scan tool would be used to clear the stored DTC and the vehicle driven to confirm that the problem has been corrected.

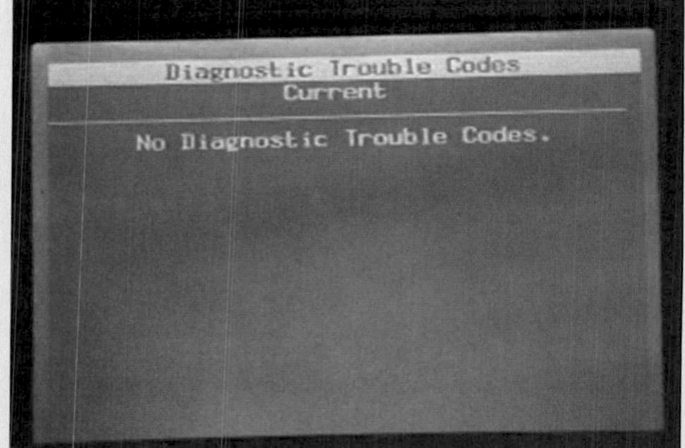

P26–16 After test driving the vehicle, a quick check using the Tech 2 indicates no stored DTCs.

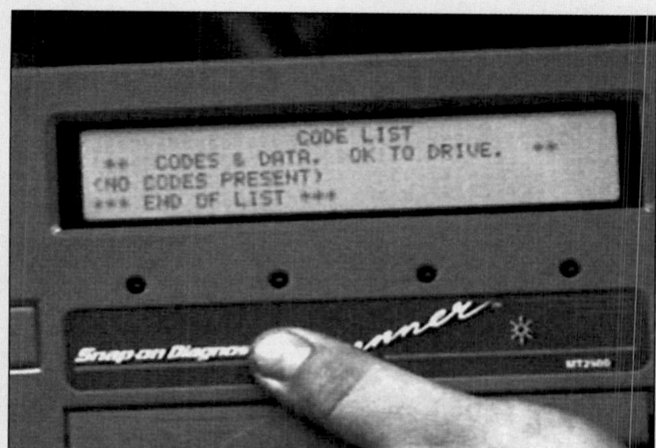

P26–17 If a Tech 2 is not available, a Snap-on Scanner can also be used on this vehicle to retrieve and clear ABS DTCs.

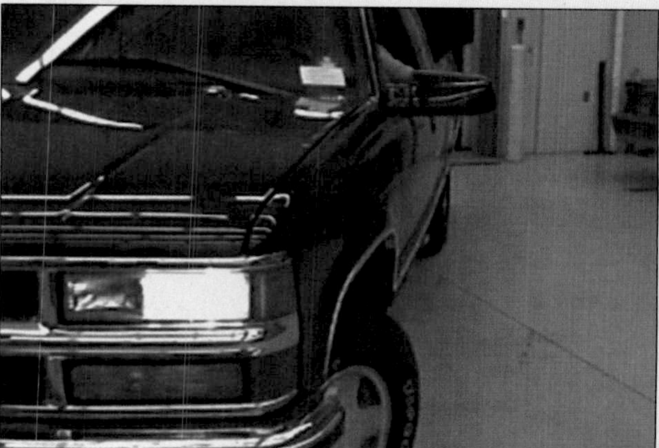

P26–18 After double-checking that everything is okay with the antilock braking system, the vehicle can be driven out of the stall and returned to the customer.

SUMMARY

1. Antilock brake systems are designed to limit the amount of tire slip by pulsing the wheel brake on and off up to twenty times per second.
2. Steering control is possible during an ABS stop if the tires still maintain traction with the road surface.
3. The three stages of ABS operation are pressure build-up, pressure holding, and pressure reduction.
4. The heart of an antilock braking system is the electronic controller (computer). Wheel speed sensors produce an electrical frequency that is proportional to the speed of the wheel. If a wheel is slowing down too fast, the controller controls the pressure of the wheel brake through an electro-hydraulic unit.
5. Antilock braking systems that control the drive-wheel brakes can also be used for acceleration traction control.
6. ABS diagnosis starts with checking the status of both the red brake warning lamp and the amber ABS warning lamp, followed by a thorough visual inspection and a test drive to verify the fault.
7. Always consult the factory service information for the exact vehicle being serviced for the proper procedure.
8. Hydraulic service on most integral-type ABS units requires that the brake pedal be depressed up to 40 times with the ignition key off to depressurize the hydraulic system.

REVIEW QUESTIONS

1. Describe how an antilock braking system works.
2. List the three stages of ABS operation.
3. Explain how wheel speed sensors work.
4. Describe the difference between a three- and four-channel system.
5. Explain how ABS can be used to prevent wheel slippage during acceleration.
6. Describe the proper operation of the red and amber brake warning lamps.
7. List the items that should be checked as part of a thorough visual inspection.

RED SEAL CERTIFICATION-TYPE QUESTIONS

1. What might cause the brake pedal to pulsate on a vehicle equipped with anti-lock brakes?
   - **a.** The brake shoes are out of adjustment
   - **b.** Stopping on dry roads
   - **c.** Stopping on slippery roads
   - **d.** Ruptured accumulator for the anti-lock brakes
2. What could be the cause of wheel chirp during hard braking on dry roads?
   - **a.** Low tire air pressure
   - **b.** Normal anti-lock brake operations
   - **c.** Drum brake adjustment too tight
   - **d.** Tire pressure too high
3. When monitoring the crown gear, what speed does a wheel speed sensor indicate?
   - **a.** Fastest axle speed
   - **b.** Slowest axle speed
   - **c.** Drive shaft speed
   - **d.** Average speed of both axles
4. What does the anti-lock brake self-test accomplish?
   - **a.** Verifies solenoid and pump operation
   - **b.** Verifies brake light operation
   - **c.** Complete pedal travel
   - **d.** Brake fluid condition
5. What action does the scan tool provide as the system is being bled?
   - **a.** It pumps the pedal
   - **b.** It opens the passageway for fluid
   - **c.** It turns on the RBWL (red brake warning light)
   - **d.** It turns on the low fluid indicator
6. What could cause the red brake warning lamp to illuminate?
   - **a.** Wheel speed sensor failure
   - **b.** Parking brake adjusted too tightly
   - **c.** Integral system pressure too low
   - **d.** Traction control system failure
7. The wheel speed sensor produces 0 V when the sensor is unplugged. What does this indicate?
   - **a.** A defective WSS
   - **b.** A defective computer
   - **c.** The system is in diagnostic mode
   - **d.** Continuity between WSS and computer
8. What is the most common way to retrieve ABS codes?
   - **a.** Turn key to accessory position to display codes
   - **b.** Scan tools will retrieve codes
   - **c.** Disconnect ABS fuse
   - **d.** Cycle key twice to retrieve codes
9. When the ABS system malfunctions, the vehicle service or base brakes will
   - **a.** Lock up the wheels when the brake pedal is pressed
   - **b.** React the same way as a non-ABS system
   - **c.** Not work at all
   - **d.** Cause the ABS light to flash
10. The key input that is needed for the ABS system to operate is
    - **a.** The red brake warning lamp
    - **b.** The fluid control solenoid
    - **c.** The brake pedal switch
    - **d.** The fluid level indicator

SECTION **VII**

Suspension and Steering

This section includes those systems and components that provide vehicle steering control and ride comfort, and handling. Chapter 40 covers tires, including tire balancing techniques. Chapter 41 describes how parallelogram and rack and pinion steering systems work and how to diagnose and repair the various parts involved. Chapter 42 covers all types of suspension systems including short-long arm and McPherson struts as well as how to diagnose and service suspension-related problems. Chapter 43 details the terms and alignment angles needed to be able to properly perform a complete four-wheel alignment. Vehicle handling problems that may be related to alignment are also discussed.

40

Tires and Wheels

OBJECTIVES: After studying Chapter 40, you should be able to:

1. Prepare for the interprovincial Red Seal certification examination in Appendix IV (Suspension and Steering) on the topics covered in this chapter.
2. List the various parts that make up a tire.
3. Explain how a tire is manufactured.
4. Discuss tire sizes and ratings.
5. Describe tire purchasing considerations and maintenance.
6. Explain the construction and sizing of steel and alloy wheels and attaching hardware.
7. Define sprung and unsprung weight.
8. Demonstrate the correct lug nut tightening procedure and torque.

PURPOSES OF TIRES AND WHEELS

The combination of tires and wheels provides a variety of services to the rest of the vehicle. The primary purpose of the front tires and wheels is to steer the vehicle. The tire will carry the weight of the vehicle and transfer it to the road surface for traction during steering manoeuveres. The rubber compound in the tire helps to absorb small amounts of road shock.

The drive axle on the vehicle will use the tire and wheel assembly to connect the axle to the road in order to provide traction, which is used to propel the vehicle.

All tires are assembled by hand from many different component parts consisting of various rubber compounds, steel, and various types of fabric material. Tires are available in many different designs and sizes. All tires sold in Canada must meet Transport Canada 1995 Motor Vehicle Tire Safety Regulations.

PARTS OF A TIRE

Tread Tread refers to the part of the tire which contacts the ground. **Tread rubber** is chemically different from other rubber parts of a tire, and is compounded for a combination of traction and tire wear. **Tread depth** is usually 8.77 mm (11/32 in.) deep on new tires (this could vary, depending on manufacturer, from 7.1 mm (9/32 in.) to 11.9 mm (15/32 in.). Figure 40–1 shows a tread depth gauge.

NOTE: A tread depth is always expressed in thirty-secondths of an inch, even if the fraction can be reduced to sixteenths or eighths, etc.

Wear indicators are also called **wear bars.** When tread depth is down to the legal limit of 1.6 mm (2/32 in.), bald strips appear across the tread (see Figure 40–2).

Grooves Grooves are large, deep recesses molded in the tread and separating the tread blocks. These grooves are called **circumferential grooves** or **kerfs.** Grooves running sideways across the tread of a tire are called **lateral grooves. Sipes** are small slits in the tread area to increase wet and dry traction. See Figure 40–3.

Grooves in both directions are necessary for wet traction. The trapped water can actually cause the tires to ride up on a layer of water and lose contact with the ground, as shown in Figure 40–4. This is

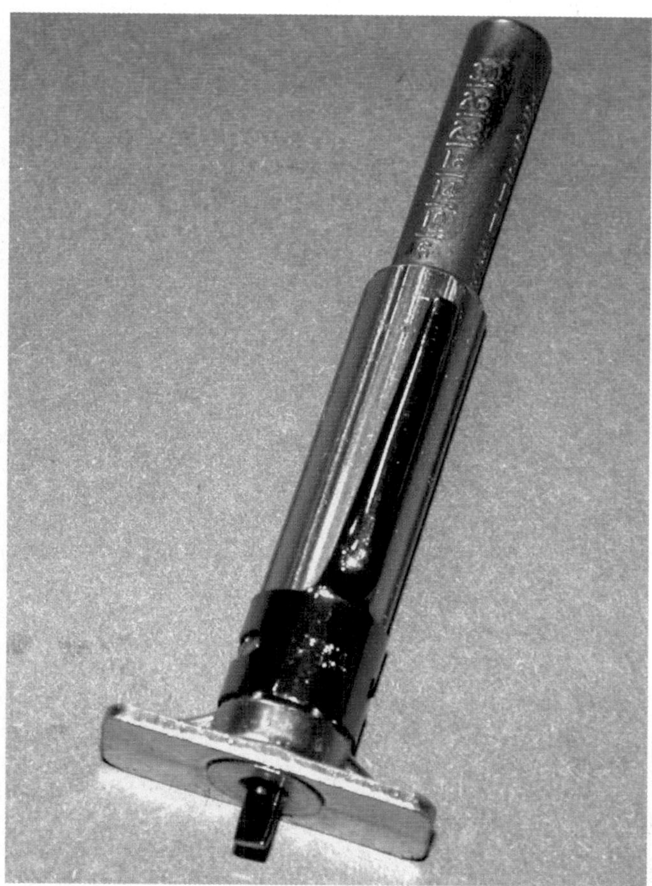

Figure 40–1 A tire tread depth gauge. The depth is read at the junction of the movable plunger that is inserted into the groove of the tire and is usually displayed in thirty-secondths of an inch.

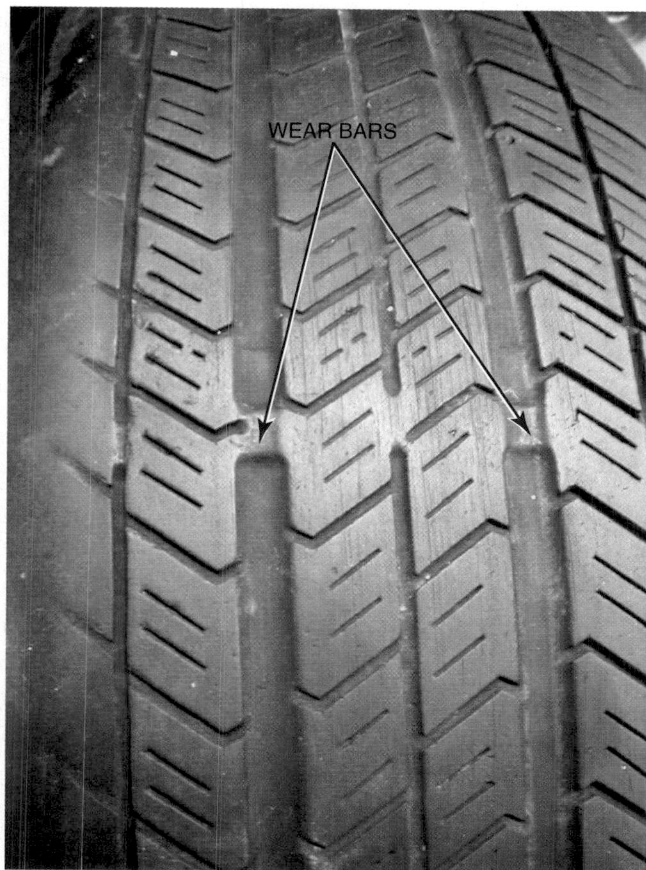

Figure 40–2 Wear indicators (wear bars) are strips of bald tread that show when the tread depth is down to 1.6 mm (2/32 in.), the legal limit in many provinces.

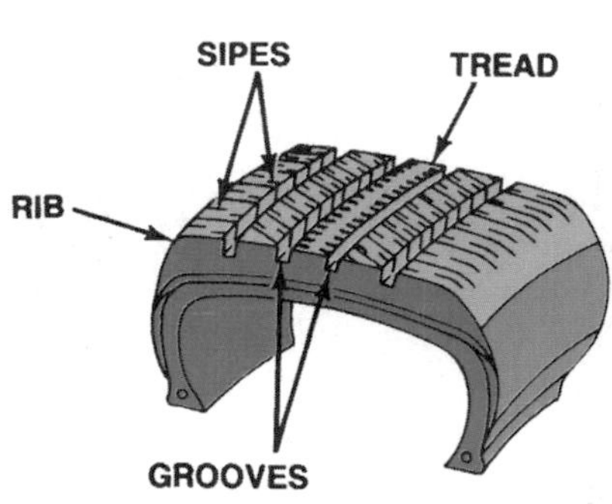

Figure 40–3 The tire tread runs around the circumference of the tire, and its pattern helps maintain traction. The ribs provide grip, while the grooves direct any water on the road away from the surface. The sipes help the tire grip the road.

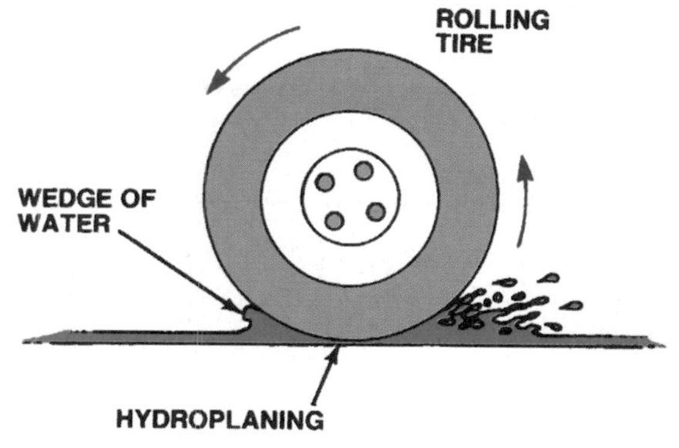

Figure 40–4 Hydroplaning can occur at speeds as low as 50 km/h (30 mph). If the water is deep enough and the tire tread cannot evacuate water through its grooves fast enough, the tire can be lifted off the road surface by a layer of water. Hydroplaning occurs at lower speeds as the tire becomes worn.

called **hydroplaning.** With worn tires, hydroplaning can occur at speeds as low as 50 km/h (30 mph) on wet roads. Stopping and cornering is impossible when hydroplaning occurs.

Sidewall The sidewall is that part of the tire between the tread and the wheel. The sidewall has moulded all the size and construction details of the tire into it.

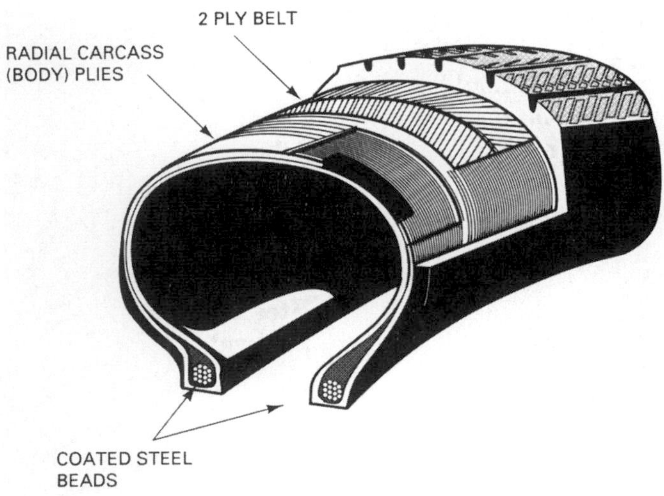

Figure 40–5 Typical construction of a radial tire. Some tires have only one body ply, and some tires use more than two belt plies.

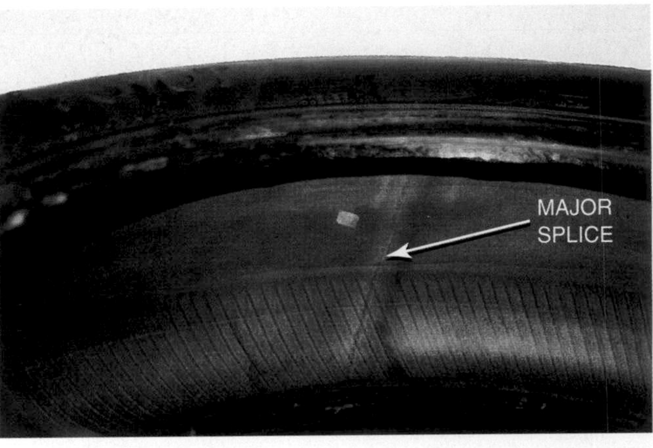

Figure 40–6 The major splice of a tire can often be seen and felt on the inside of the tire. The person who assembles (builds) the tire usually places a sticker near the major splice as a means of identification for quality control.

Some tires turn brown on the sidewalls after a short time. This is due to ozone (atmosphere) damage which actually causes the rubber to oxidize. Premium quality tires contain an anti-oxidizing chemical additive blended with the sidewall rubber to prevent this discoloration.

Bead The bead is the foundation of the tire and is located where the tire grips the inside of the wheel rim. The bead is constructed of many turns of copper- or bronze-coated steel wire. The main body plies (layers of material) are wrapped around the bead. Most radial ply and all truck tires wrap the bead with additional material to add strength.

> **CAUTION:** If the bead of a tire is cut or damaged, the tire must be replaced!

Body Ply A tire gets its strength from the layers of material wrapped around both beads under the tread and sidewall rubber. This creates the main framework, or "carcass," of the tire; these body plies are often called **carcass plies.** A 4-ply tire has 4 separate layers of material. If the body plies overlap at an angle (bias), the tire is called a **bias ply** tire. If only one or two body plies are used and they do not cross at an angle, but lie directly from bead to bead, then the tire is called **radial ply.** Materials used for body plies include rayon, nylon, aramid (Kevlar®), and polyester.

Belt As shown in Figure 40–5, a tire belt is two or more layers of material applied over the body plies and under the tread area only, to stabilize the tread and increase tread life and handling. Belt material can be steel mesh, nylon, rayon, fibreglass, or aramid.

> **NOTE:** Most tires rated for high speed use a nylon *overlay* or *cap belt* between the 2-ply belt and the tread of the tire. This overlay helps stabilize the belt package and helps hold the tire together at high speeds, when centrifugal force acts to tear a tire apart.

Inner Liner The inner liner is the soft rubber lining (usually a butyl rubber compound) on the inside of the tire which protects the body plies and helps provide for self-sealing of small punctures.

Frequently Asked Question ???

Why Do I Get Shocked by Static Electricity When I Drive a Certain Vehicle?

Static electricity builds up in insulators due to friction of the tires with the road. Newer tires use silica and contain less carbon black in the rubber, which makes the tires electrically conductive. Because the tires cannot conduct the static electricity to the ground, static electricity builds up inside the vehicle and is discharged through the body of the driver and/or passenger whenever the metal door handle is touched.

> **NOTE:** Toll booth operators report being shocked by many drivers as money is being passed between the driver and the toll booth operator.

Newer tire sidewall designs that use silica usually incorporate carbon sections that are used to discharge the static electricity to ground. To help reduce the static charge buildup, spray the upholstery with an antistatic spray available at hardware and grocery stores.

Major Splice When the tire is assembled by a craftsman on a tire-building machine, the body plies, belts and tread rubber are spliced together. The fabric is overlapped approximately five threads. The point where the majority of these overlaps occur is called the **major splice,** which represents the stiffest part of the tire. This major splice is visible on most tires on the inside, as shown in Figure 40–6.

> **NOTE:** On most new vehicles and/or new tires, the tire manufacturer paints a dot on the sidewall near the bead, indicating the largest diameter of the tire. The largest diameter of the tire usually is near the major splice. The wheel manufacturer either marks the wheel or drills the valve core hole at the smallest diameter of the wheel. Therefore, the dot should be aligned with the valve core or marked for best balance and minimum radial runout.

TIRE VALVES

All tires use a tire valve, called a **Schrader valve,** to hold air in the tire. The Schrader valve was invented in New York in 1844 by August Schrader for the Goodyear brothers: Charles, Henry, and Nelson. Today, Schrader valves are used not only as valves in tires but on fuel injection systems, air-conditioning systems, and air-shock (ride-control) systems. Most tire experts agree that the valve stem (which includes the Schrader valve) should be replaced whenever tires are replaced: tires can last four or more years, and in that time the valve stem can become brittle and crack. A defective or leaking valve stem is a major cause of air loss.

> **CAUTION:** Incorrect installation of a hubcap or beauty ring can push the valve stem sideways and cause the stem to leak. Low tire pressure can cause the tire to become overheated. Replacement valve stems are, therefore, a wise investment whenever purchasing new tires. Aluminum (alloy) wheels often require special metal valve stems that use a rubber washer and are actually bolted to the wheel. See Figure 40–7.

Tire Pressure

Tire pressures should be checked when the tires are cold. This means that they should be checked before the vehicle is driven more than a couple of kilometres. The tires should be inflated to the pressure specified by the vehicle manufacturer. The specification is usually on a placard located on the driver's door or in the owner's manual. See Figure 40–8.

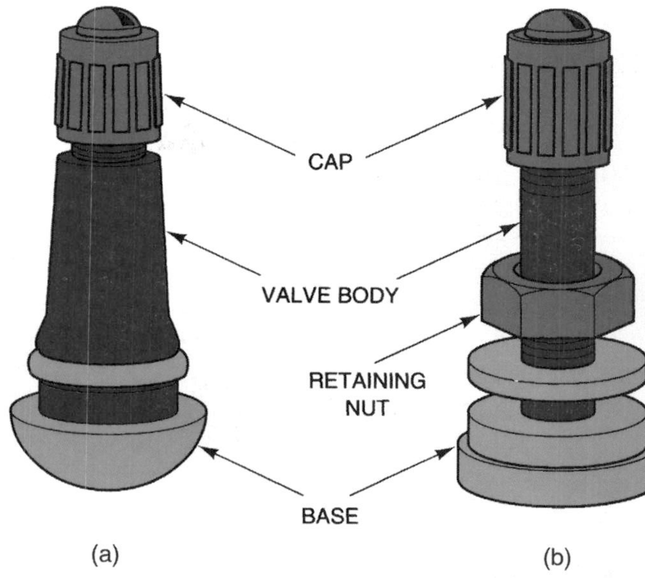

Figure 40–7 (a) A rubber snap-in style tire valve assembly. (b) A metal clamp-type tire valve assembly used on most high-pressure (over 400 kPa [60 psi]) tire applications, such as are found on many trucks, RV's, and trailers. The internal Schrader valve threads into the valve itself and can be replaced individually, but most experts recommend replacing the entire valve assembly every time the tires are replaced to help prevent air loss.

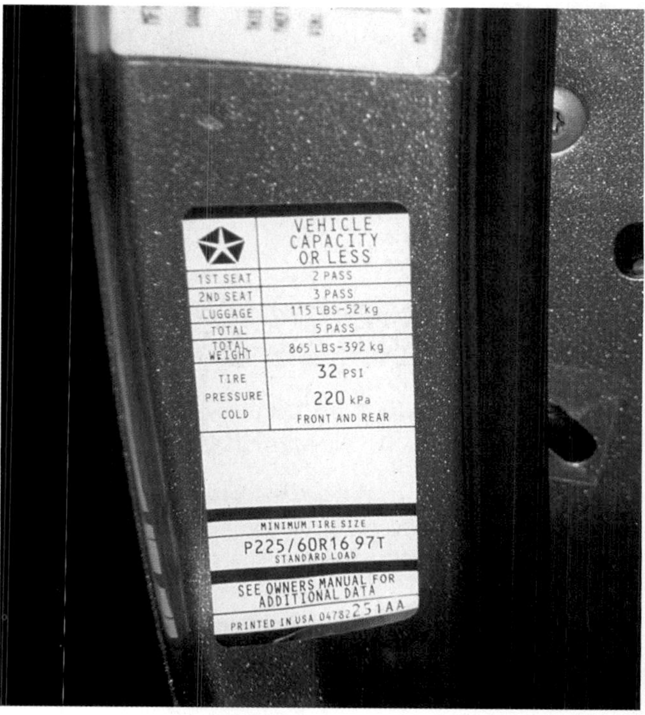

Figure 40–8 The proper air pressure is often printed on a decal or placard on the edge of the driver's door or post. The owner's manual also includes the recommended tire pressure.

HIGH PERFORMANCE TIP

How Much Bigger Can I Go?

Many owners think they can improve their vehicle by upgrading the tire size over the size that comes from the factory to make their vehicle look sportier and ride and handle better. When changing tire size, there are many factors to consider:

1. The tire should be the same outside diameter as the original to maintain the proper suspension, steering, and ride height specifications.
2. Tire size affects vehicle speed sensor values, ABS brake wheel sensor values that can change automatic transmission operation, and ABS operation.
3. The tire should not be so wide as to contact the inner wheel well or suspension components.
4. Generally, a tire that is 10 mm wider is acceptable. For example, an original equipment tire size 205/75 × 15 (outside diameter = 688 mm [27.1 in.]) can be changed to 215/75 × 15 (outside diameter = 701 mm [27.6 in.]). This much change is less than 13 mm (1/2 in.) in width and increases the outside diameter by 13 mm (1/2 in.).

> **NOTE:** Outside diameter is calculated by adding the wheel diameter to the cross-sectional height of the tire multiplied by 2.

5. Whenever changing tires, make sure that the load capacity is the same or greater than that of the original tires.
6. If wider tires are desired, a lower aspect ratio is required to maintain the same, or close to the same, overall outside diameter of the tire.

Old	**New**
P205/75 × 15	P215/70 × 15
205 × 0.75 = 154 mm	215 × 0.70 = 151 mm

Notice that the overall sidewall height is generally maintained. If even larger tires are needed, then 225/60 × 15s may be OK—let's check the math:

$$225 \times 0.60 = 135 \text{ mm}$$

Notice that this is much too short a sidewall height when compared with the original tire (see #6).

7. Use the "plus 1" or "plus 2" concept. When specifying wider tires, the sidewall height must be reduced to maintain the same or close to the same as original equipment specifications. The "plus 1" concept involves replacing the wheels with wheels 1 inch larger in diameter to compensate for the lower aspect of wider tires.

Original	**Plus 1**
205/75 × 15	225/60 × 16

The overall difference in outside diameter is only 13 mm (0.5 in.), even though the tire width has increased from 205 mm to 225 mm and the wheel diameter has increased by 1 in. If money is no object and all-out performance is the goal, a "plus 2" concept can also be used (use a P245/50 × 17 tire and change to 17 in. diameter wheels). (See Figure 40–9.)

Here the overall diameter is within 13 mm (1/2 in.) of the original tire/wheel combination, yet the tire width is 40 mm (1.6 inches) wider than the original tire. Refer to the section entitled "Wheels" later in this chapter for proper wheel back spacing and offset when purchasing replacement wheels.

Frequently Asked Question ???

How Much Does Tire Pressure Change with a Change in Temperature?

As the temperature of a tire increases, the pressure inside the tire also increases. The general amount of pressure gain (when temperatures increase) or loss (when temperatures decrease) is as follows:

5°C change causes 6 kPa change
10°F change causes 1 psi change

For example, if a tire is correctly inflated to 240 kPa (35 psi) when cold and then driven on a highway, the tire pressure may increase 35 kPa (5 psi) or more.

Always check the tire pressures on a vehicle that has been driven fewer than 3.2 km (2 mi).

> **CAUTION:** DO NOT LET AIR OUT OF A HOT TIRE! If air is released from a hot tire to bring the pressure down to specifications, the tire will be *underinflated* when the tire has cooled. The tire pressure specification is for a cold tire.

Air pressure in the tires also affects fuel economy. If all four tires are underinflated (low on air pressure), fuel economy is reduced about 0.06 km/L for each 10 kPa low pressure (0.1 mpg for each 1 psi). For example, if all four tires were inflated to 175 kPa (25 psi) instead of 245 kPa (35 psi), fuel economy is reduced by about 0.42 km/L (70/10 × 0.06 = 0.42) or 1 mpg (10/1 × 0.1 = 1).

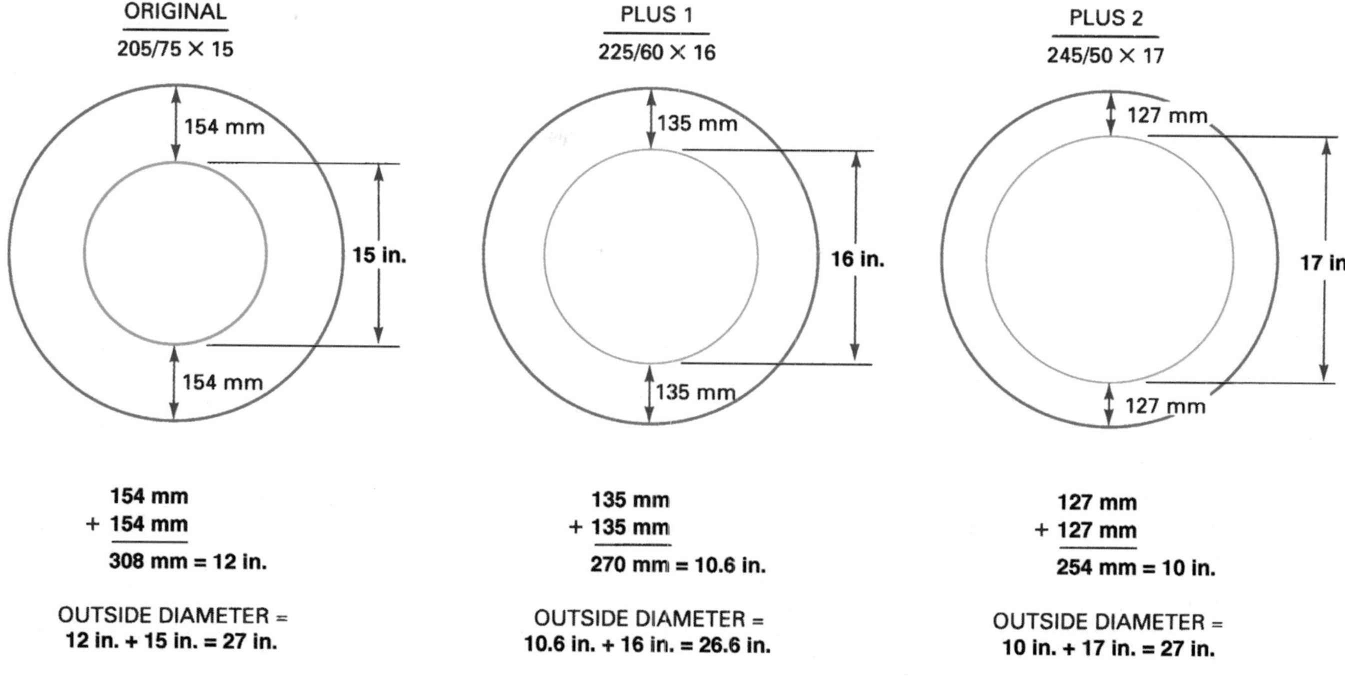

Figure 40–9 Notice that the overall outside diameter of the tire remains almost the same when the aspect ratio is decreased and the rim diameter is increased.

- If overinflated, the tires will tend to wear mostly in the centre of the tread.
- If underinflated, the tires will tend to wear on both edges.

> **CAUTION:** Do not inflate a tire to a pressure greater than that imprinted on the sidewall of the tire.

Canadian Metric Tire Size Designations

After 1980, Canadian tires were also designated using the metric system. For example, P205/75R × 14 means

P = passenger vehicle

205 = 205 mm cross-sectional width

75 = 75% aspect ratio. The height of the tire (from the wheel to the tread) is 75% as great as its cross-sectional width (the width measured across its widest part). *This percentage ratio of height to width is called the "aspect ratio."* (A 60 series tire is 60% as high as it is wide.)

R = radial

14 = 14 in. diameter wheel

SERVICE DESCRIPTION

Tires built after 1990 use a service description method of sidewall information in accordance with ISO 4000 (International Standards Organization) that includes size, load, and speed rating together in one easy-to-read format. See Figure 40–10.

P-Metric Designation P205/75 HR × 15	**Service Description 205/75R × 15 92 H**
P = passenger vehicle	205 = cross-sectional width in mm
205 = cross-sectional width in mm	75 = aspect ratio
75 = aspect ratio	R = radial construction
H = speed rating (130 mph/210 km/h)	15 = rim diameter in inches
R = radial construction	92 = load index
15 = rim diameter in inches	H = speed rating (130 mph/210 km/h)

HIGH-FLOTATION TIRE SIZES

High-flotation light truck tires are designed to give improved off-road performance on sand, mud, and soft soil and still provide acceptable hard-road surface performance. These tires are usually larger than conventional tires and usually require a wider than normal wheel width. High-flotation tires have a size designation such as 33 × 12.50 R × 15 LT:

33 = approximate overall tire diameter in inches

12.50 = approximate cross-sectional width in inches

R = radial-type construction

15 = rim diameter in inches

LT = light truck designation

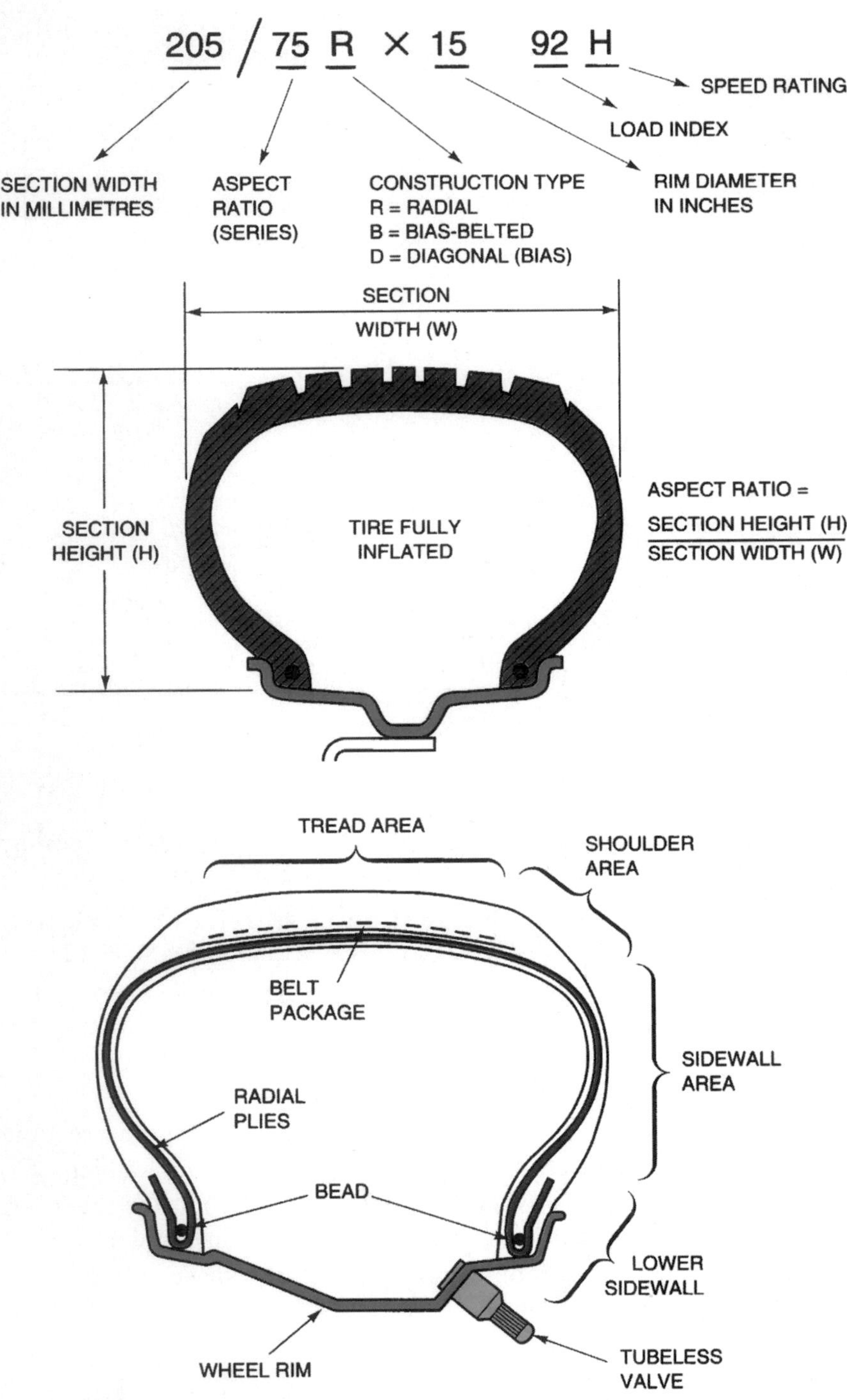

Figure 40–10 Cross-sectional view of a typical tire and the terms used for the various parts and sizes of the tire.

LOAD INDEX AND EQUIVALENT LOADS

The load index is an abbreviated method to indicate the load-carrying capabilities of a tire. The weights listed in the chart represent the weight that *each tire* can safely support. Multiply this amount by 4 to get the maximum that the vehicle should weigh fully loaded with cargo and passengers.

Load Index	Load (kg)	Load (lb)
75	387	853
76	400	882
77	412	908
78	425	937
79	437	963
80	450	992
81	462	1019
82	475	1047
83	487	1074
84	500	1102
85	515	1135
86	530	1168
87	545	1201
88	560	1235
89	580	1279
90	600	1323
91	615	1356
92	630	1389
93	650	1433
94	670	1477
95	690	1521
96	710	1565
97	730	1609
98	750	1653
99	775	1709
100	800	1764
101	825	1819
102	850	1874
103	875	1929
104	900	1934
105	925	2039
106	950	2094
107	975	2149
108	1000	2205
109	1030	2271
110	1060	2337
111	1090	2403
112	1120	2469
113	1150	2535
114	1180	2601
115	1215	2679

SPEED RATINGS

Tires are rated according to the maximum *sustained* speed. A vehicle should never be driven faster than the speed rating of the tires.

Frequently Asked Question ???

What Effect Does Tire Size Have on Overall Gear Ratio?

Customers often ask what effect changing tire size has on fuel economy and speedometer readings. If larger (or smaller) tires are installed on a vehicle, many other factors change also. These include:

1. **Speedometer reading.** *If larger diameter tires are used, the speedometer will read slower* than you are actually travelling. This can result in speeding tickets!
2. **Odometer reading.** Even though larger tires are said to give better fuel economy, just the opposite can be calculated! Since a larger diameter tire travels farther than a smaller diameter tire, the larger tire will cause the odometer to read a shorter distance than the vehicle actually travels. For example, if the odometer reads 100 miles travelled on tires that are 10% oversized in circumference, then the actual distance traveled is 110 miles.
3. **Fuel economy.** If fuel economy is calculated on distance travelled, the result will be *lower* fuel economy than for the same vehicle with the original tires.

Calculations:

$$\text{km/h} \propto \frac{\text{rpm} \times \text{diameter} \times 3.14}{\text{gear ratio}}$$

$$\text{rpm} \propto \frac{\text{km/h} \times \text{gear ratio}}{\text{diameter} \times 3.14}$$

$$\text{gear ratio} \propto \frac{\text{rpm} \times \text{diameter} \times 3.14}{\text{km/h}}$$

CAUTION: A high speed rating does not guarantee that the tires will not fail, even at speeds much lower than the rating. Tire condition, inflation, and vehicle loading also affect tire performance.

As the speed rating of a tire increases, fewer compromises exist for driver comfort and low noise level. The higher speed rating does not mean a better tire. To survive, a high-speed tire must be built with stiff tread compounds, reinforced body (carcass) construction, and fabric angles that favour high speed and high performance over other

Frequently Asked Question ???

If I Have an Older Vehicle, What Size Tires Should I Use?

Newer radial tires can be used on older model vehicles if the size of the tires is selected that best matches the original tires. See the following cross-reference chart.

NOTE: Vehicles designed for older bias ply tires may drive differently when equipped with radial tires.

Cross-Reference Chart
(This chart does not imply complete interchangeability.)

Pre-1964	'65 to '72	80 Series Metric	Alpha Numeric 78 Series	P-Metric 75 Series Radial	P-Metric 70 Series Radial
590-13	600-13	165-13	A78-13	P165/75R13	P175/70R13
640-13	650-13	175-13	B78-13	P175/75R13	P185/70R13
725-13	700-13	185-13	D78-13	P185/75R13	P205/70R13
590-14	645-14	155-14	B78-14	P175/75R14	P185/70R14
650-14	695-14	175-14	C78-14	P185/75R14	P195/70R14
700-14	735-14	185-14	E78-14	P195/75R14	P205/70R14
750-14	775-14	195-14	F78-14	P205/75R14	P215/70R14
800-14	825-14	205-14	G78-14	P215/75R14	P225/70R14
850-14	855-14	215-14	H78-14	P225/75R14	P235/70R14
590-15	600-15	165-15	A78-15	P165/75R15	P175/70R15
650-15	685-15	175-15	C78-15	P175/75R15	P185/70R15
640-15	735-15	185-15	E78-15	P195/75R15	P205/70R15
670-15	775-15	195-15	F78-15	P205/75R15	P215/70R15
710-15	815-15	205-15	G78-15	P215/75R15	P225/70R15
760-15	855-15	215-15	H78-15	P225/75R15	P235/70R15
800-15	885-15	230-15	J78-15	P225/75R15	P235/70R15
820-15	900-15	235-15	L78-15	P235/75R15	P255/70R15

considerations. For example, a V-rated tire often has less tread depth than a similar tire with an H speed rating and, therefore, will often not give as long a service life. Since the speed ratings were first developed in Europe, the letters correspond to metric speed in kilometres per hour, with a conversion to miles per hour.

Letter	Maximum Rated Speed
L	120 km/h (75 mph)
M	130 km/h (81 mph)
N	140 km/h (87 mph)
P	150 km/h (93 mph)
Q	160 km/h (99 mph)
R	170 km/h (106 mph)

Letter	Maximum Rated Speed
S	180 km/h (112 mph)
T	190 km/h (118 mph)
U	200 km/h (124 mph)
H	210 km/h (130 mph)
V	240 km/h (149 mph)
W	270 km/h (168 mph)
Y	300 km/h (186 mph)
Z	open-ended *

*The exact speed rating for a particular Z-rated tire is determined by the tire manufacturer and may vary according to size. For example, not all Z-rated tires of a certain brand are rated at 270 km/h, even though one size may be capable of these speeds.

Frequently Asked Question ???

How Should Tires Be Stored?

Tires that are not being used should be stacked on the side wall, not the tread, and kept in a cool and dry location. Many experts recommend placing the tires in a plastic trash bag and then stacking them on wood.

TIRE CONICITY

Tire conicity can occur during the construction of any radial or belted tire when the parts of the tire are badly positioned, causing the tire to be smaller in diameter on one side. When this tire is installed on a vehicle, it can cause the vehicle to pull to one side of the road due to the cone shape of the tire. See Figure 40–11.

Since the cause of conicity is due to the construction of the tire itself, there is nothing the service technician can do to correct the condition. The exact cause of the conicity is generally the slight movement of the belt and tread in the mould during inflation. If a vehicle pulls to one side of the road, the service technician should switch tires left to right (left-side tires to the right side and the right-side tires to the left side of the vehicle). If this swap of tires corrects the pulling condition, or causes the vehicle to pull in the opposite direction, then tire conicity was the possible cause.

NOTE: *Radial pull* or *radial tire pull* are other terms often used to describe tire conicity.

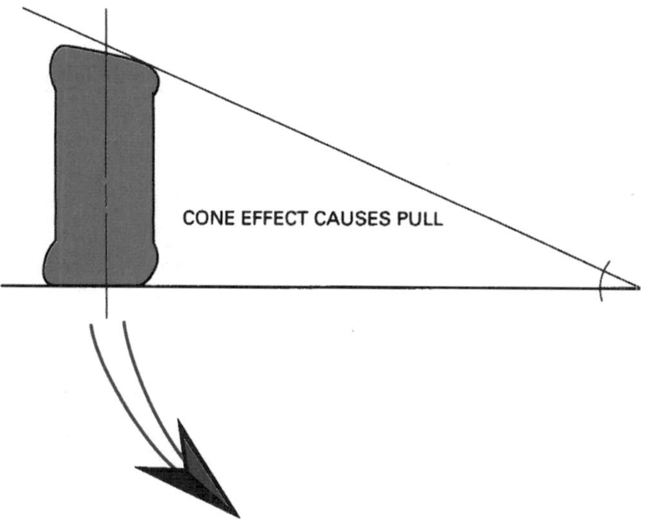

Figure 40–11 Conicity is a fault in the tire that can cause the vehicle to pull to one side due to the cone effect (shape) of the tire.

NOTE: Whenever a wheel and tire assembly are switched from one side of a vehicle to the other, the tire revolves in the opposite direction.

RIM WIDTH AND TIRE SIZE

As a general rule, for a given rim width it is best not to change tire width more than 10 mm (either wider or narrower). For a given tire width, it is best not to vary rim width more than 13 mm (1/2 in.) in either direction. For example, if the original tire size is 195/70 × 14, then either a 185/70 × 14 (−10 mm) or a 205/70 × 14 (+10 mm) *could* be used on the original rim (wheel) without undue harm *if* the replacement tire has proper clearance with the body and suspension components.

Installing a tire on too narrow a wheel will cause the tire to wear excessively in the centre of the tread. Installing a tire on too wide a wheel will cause excessive tire wear on both edges.

See a knowledgeable tire retailer for recommended tire sizes that can be safely installed on your rims.

UNIFORM TIRE QUALITY GRADING SYSTEM

The Transport Canada and the **Motor Vehicle Safety Act** use a system of tire grading to help customers better judge the relative performance of tires. The three areas of tire performance are tread wear, traction, and temperature resistance, as shown in Figure 40–12.

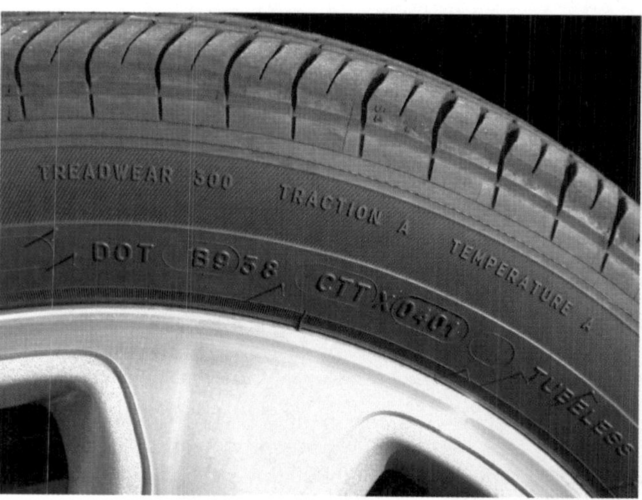

Figure 40–12 Typical Uniform Tire Quality Grading System (UTQGS) ratings imprinted on the tire sidewall.

Frequently Asked Question ???

Is There a Rule-of-Thumb for Rim Size?

According to the Tire and Rim Association, Inc., the answer is no. Each tire size has a designated rim width on which it is designed to be mounted so as to provide the best performance and wear. The width of the specified rim also varies with rim diameter. A 235/45 × 17 tire may require a 7.5 in. rim but a 235/45 × 19 tire may require an 8.0 in. rim. A rule-of-thumb that has been used is to multiply the width of the rim by 33.55 to determine the approximate tire size for the rim. For example,

Rim width 5.0 in. × 33.55 = 167.85 (165 mm) tire
Rim width 5.5 in. × 33.55 = 184.50 (185 mm) tire
Rim width 6.0 in. × 33.55 = 201.30 (195 mm) tire
Rim width 6.5 in. × 33.55 = 218.00 (215 mm) tire
Rim width 7.0 in. × 33.55 = 234.90 (235 mm) tire
Rim width 7.5 in. × 33.55 = 252.00 (245 mm) tire
Rim width 8.0 in. × 33.55 = 268.00 (265 mm) tire
Rim width 8.5 in. × 33.55 = 285.00 (285 mm) tire
Rim width 9.0 in. × 33.55 = 302.00 (305 mm) tire
Rim width 10.0 in. × 33.55 = 335.60 (335 mm) tire

Always check with the tire manufacturer as to the specified tire rim width that should be used.

NOTE: All tires sold in Canada must have uniform tire quality grading system ratings moulded into the sidewall.

Tread Wear

The tread wear grade is a comparison rating based on the wear rate of a standardized tire, tested under carefully controlled conditions, which is assigned a value of 100. A tire rated 200 should have a useful life twice as long as the standard tire's.

HINT: The standard tire has a rating for tread wear of 100. This value has generally been accepted to mean a useful life of 30 000 km of normal driving. Therefore, a tire rated at 200 could be expected to last 60 000 km, etc.

Tread Wear Rating Number	Approximate Number of km (mi)
100	30 000 (19 000)
150	50 000 (31 000)
200	65 000 (40 000)
250	80 000 (50 000)
300	100 000 (62 000)
400	130 000 (80 000)
500	160 000 (100 000)

The tread wear life of any tire is affected by driving habits (fast stops, starts, and cornering will decrease tread life), tire rotation (or lack of tire rotation), inflation, wheel alignment, road surfaces, and climate conditions.

Traction

Traction performance is rated by the letters AA, A, B, or C, with AA the highest.

IMPORTANT NOTE: The traction rating is for **wet braking** distance only! It does not include cornering traction or dry braking performance.

The traction rating is only one of many other factors that affect wet braking traction, including air inflation, tread depth, vehicle speed, and brake performance.

Temperature Resistance

Temperature resistance is rated by letters A, B, or C, with A the highest rating and C the lowest rating. This rating is determined by how hot a tire becomes when subjected to high-speed operation under full load conditions.

ALL-SEASON TIRE DESIGNATION

Most all-season tires are rated and labelled as *M & S, MS* or *M + S,* and therefore must adhere to general design features as specified by the Rubber Manufacturers Association (RMA).

Tires labelled M & S are constructed with an aggressive tread design as well as tread compounds and internal construction that are designed for mud and snow. One design feature is that the tire has at least 25% void area. This means that the tread blocks have enough open space around them to allow the blocks to grab and clean themselves of snow and mud. Block angles, dimensional requirements, and minimum cross-sectional width are also a requirement for the M & S designation.

The tread rubber used to make all-season tires is also more flexible at low temperatures. This rubber compound is low-bounce (called **high-hysteresis**) and is more likely to remain in contact with the road surface. The rubber compound is also called *hydrophilic,* meaning that the rubber has an affinity for water (rather than being *hydrophobic* rubber, which repels water).

NOTE: Most vehicle manufacturers recommend that the same *type* of tire be used on all four wheels even though the size of the tire may vary front and rear on some high-performance vehicles. Therefore, if all-season replacement tires are purchased, a complete set of four should be used for proper handling and uniform traction characteristics. While *tire* manufacturers have been recommending this for years—since the late 1980s—most *vehicle* manufacturers are now also recommending that all four tires be of the same construction and tread type to help ensure proper vehicle handling.

DOT TIRE CODE

All tires sold in Canada must meet Transport Canada's Motor Vehicle Safety Act Schedules IV and V. All tires sold in the United States must be approved by the U.S. Federal Department of Transportation (DOT). Specified tire requirements include resistance to tire damage that could be caused by curbs, chuckholes, and other common occurrences for a tire used on public roads.

NOTE: Most race tires are *not* DOT-approved and must never be used on public streets or highways.

Each tire that is DOT-approved has a DOT number moulded into the sidewall of the tire.

This number is usually imprinted on only one side of the tire and is usually on the side *opposite the whitewall.* The DOT code includes letters and numbers such as **MJP2CBDX264.**

The first two letters identify the manufacturer and location. For this example, the first two letters (MJ) mean that the tire was made by the Goodyear Tire and Rubber Company in Topeka, Kansas, USA. The last three numbers are the build date code. The last of these three numbers is the year (1994), and the 26 means that it was built during the 26th week of 1994. The last number is the same for 1984 and 2004, but the style and design of the tire usually change enough after ten years so that it is easy enough to correctly identify the decade in which the tire was built.

DIAGNOSTIC STORY

Tire Date Code Information Saved Me Money!

This author was looking to buy a three-year-old vehicle when I noticed that the right rear tire had a build date code newer than the vehicle. I asked the owner, "How badly was this vehicle hit?" The owner stumbled and stuttered a little, then said, "How did you know that an accident occurred?" I told the owner that the right rear tire, while the exact same tire as the others, had a date code indicating that it was only one year old, whereas the original tires were the same age as the vehicle. The last three numbers of the DOT code on the sidewall indicate the week of manufacture (the first two numbers of the three-digit date code) followed by the last number of the year. See Figure 40–13.

The owner immediately admitted that the vehicle slid on ice and hit a curb damaging the right rear tire and wheel. Both the tire and wheel were replaced and the alignment checked. The owner then dropped the price of the vehicle $500! Knowing the date code helps you be sure that you purchase fresh tires and can also help the technician determine if the tires have been replaced. For example, if new tires are found on a vehicle with 30 000 km, then the technician should check to see if the vehicle may have been involved in an accident or have more kilometres than indicated on the odometer.

NOTE: Tires manufactured after January 1, 2000, will include four digits rather than three digits. The new code such as 3498 would distinguish the 34th week of 1998 from the 34th week of 2008 (3408).

Figure 40–13 Typical DOT date code. This tire was built the 4th week of 2001.

SPARE TIRES

Most vehicles today come equipped with space-saver spare tires that are smaller than the wheels and tires that are on the vehicle. The reason for the small size is to reduce the size and weight of the entire vehicle and to increase fuel economy by having the entire vehicle weigh less by not carrying a heavy spare tire and wheel around. The style and type of these spare tires have changed a great deal over the last several years, and different makes and types of vehicles use various types of spare tires.

CAUTION: Before using a spare tire, always read the warning label (if so equipped) and understand all use restrictions. For example, some spare tires are not designed to exceed 50 mph (80 km/h) or be driven more than 500 miles (800 km).

Many small space-saving spare tires use a higher than normal air inflation pressure, usually 400 kPa (58 psi). Even though the tire often differs in construction, size, diameter, and width from the vehicle's original tires, it is amazing that the vehicle usually handles the same during normal driving. Obviously, these tires are not constructed with the same durability as a full-size tire and should be removed from service as soon as possible.

RUN-FLAT TIRES

Run-flat tires are designed to operate without any air for a limited distance (usually 80 km at 90 km/h). This feature allows vehicle manufacturers to build vehicles without the extra room and weight of a spare tire and jack assembly.

A typical run-flat tire (also called *extended mobility tire [EMT]* or *zero pressure [ZP] tire*) requires the use of an air pressure sensor/transmitter and a dash-mounted receiver to warn the driver that a tire has lost pressure. Because of the reinforced sidewalls, the vehicle handles almost the same with or without air pressure. See Figure 40–14.

CAUTION: Tire engineers warn that rapid cornering should be avoided if a run-flat tire has zero air pressure. The handling during quick manoeuvres is often unpredictable and could be dangerous.

SAFETY TIP 

Check Your Spare Tire Regularly

When was the last time you checked the tire pressure in your spare tire? The spare tire pressure should be checked regularly. Always inflate the spare to the recommended pressure.

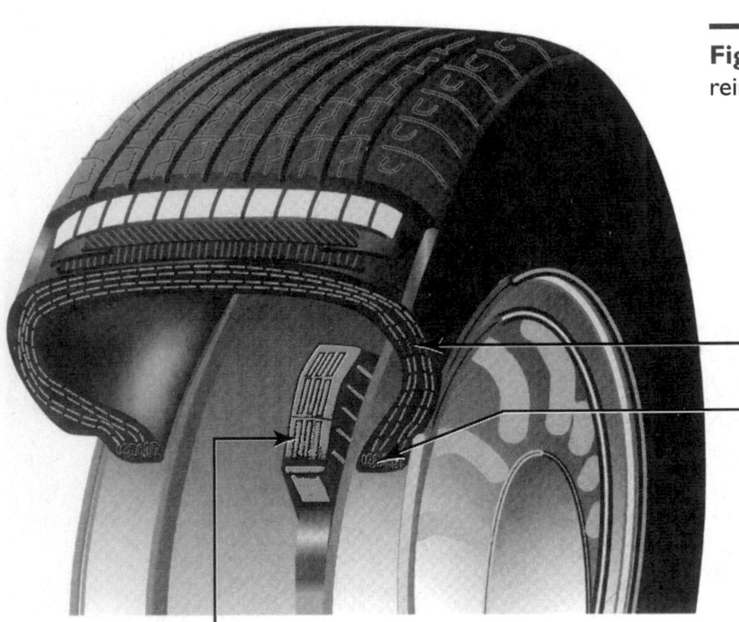
SIDEWALLS ARE REINFORCED
BEAD KEEPS TIRE ON RIM AT ZERO PRESSURE
TIRE-PRESSURE MONITORING SYSTEM

Figure 40–14 Cutaway of a run-flat tire showing the reinforced sidewalls and the required pressure sensor.

WHEELS

The concept of a wheel has not changed in the last 5000 years, but the style and materials used have changed a lot. Early automotive wheels were constructed from wood with a steel band as the tire.

Today's wheels are constructed of steel or aluminum alloy. The centre section of the wheel that attaches to the hub is called the **centre section** or **spider** because early wheels used wooden spokes that resembled a spider's web. The rubber tire attaches to the rim of the wheel. The rim has two **bead flanges** where the bead of the tire is held against the wheel when the tire is inflated.

- Rim width is the distance across the rim flanges at the bead seat.
- Rim diameter is the distance across the centre of the rim from bead seat to bead seat.

The shape of this flange is very important and is designated by Tire and Rim Association letters. For example, a wheel designated 14 × 6JJ means that the diameter of the wheel is 14 in. and it is 6 in. wide measured from inside to inside of the flanges. The letters JJ indicate the *exact* shape of the flange area. This flange area shape and the angle that the rim drops down from the flange are important because:

- They permit a good seal between the rim and the tire.
- They help retain the tire on the rim in the event of loss of air. This is the reason why modern wheels are called a safety rim wheel. See Figure 40–15.

Frequently Asked Question ???

Wheel Offset Is Confusing—Can You Help?

The owner of a Honda Accord wanted to purchase high-performance wheels and tires. The stock wheel offset is +55 mm. This means that the centre of the wheel is 55 mm outboard from the centreline of the tire. The owner was able to find a set of wheels that had a +40 mm and another set with a +48 mm offset. Both of these offsets will cause the wheel to be extended outward toward the wheel well the amount of the difference between the original and the replacement offset. If the +40 mm wheel were selected, the outside edge of the wheel (and tire, of course) would be moved out 15 mm (about 0.6 in.). If the +48 mm rim were selected, the wheel would extend 7 mm (0.3 in.). Always select wheels that are recommended by wheel manufacturers to correctly fit your vehicle.

- Run-flat tires (tires that are designed to operate without air for a limited distance without damage) often require a specific wheel rim shape.

Wheel Offset

Offset is a very important variable in wheel design. If the centre section (spider) is centred on the outer rim, the offset is zero. See Figure 40–16. The distance from the centreline is called offset, and it is usually specified in millimetres (mm).

Positive Offset

The wheel has a positive offset if the centre section is outward from the wheel centreline. Front-wheel-drive vehicles commonly use positive offset wheels to improve the loading on the front wheels.

Negative Offset

The wheel has a negative offset if the centre section is inboard (or "dished") from the wheel centreline. See Figure 40–17. Avoid using replacement wheels that differ from the original offset.

Back Spacing

Back spacing, also called **rear spacing** or **backside setting,** is the distance between the back rim edge and the wheel centre section mounting pad. *This is not the same as offset.* Back spacing can be measured directly with a ruler, as shown in Figure 40–18.

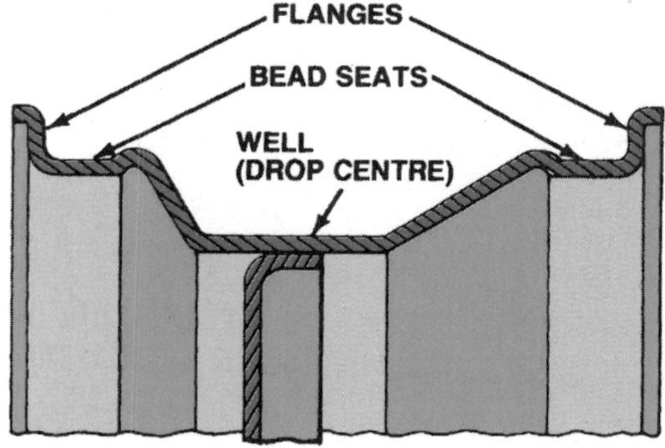

Figure 40–15 The wheel rim well provides a space for the tire to fit during mounting; the bead seat provides a tire-to-wheel sealing surface; the flange holds the beads in place.

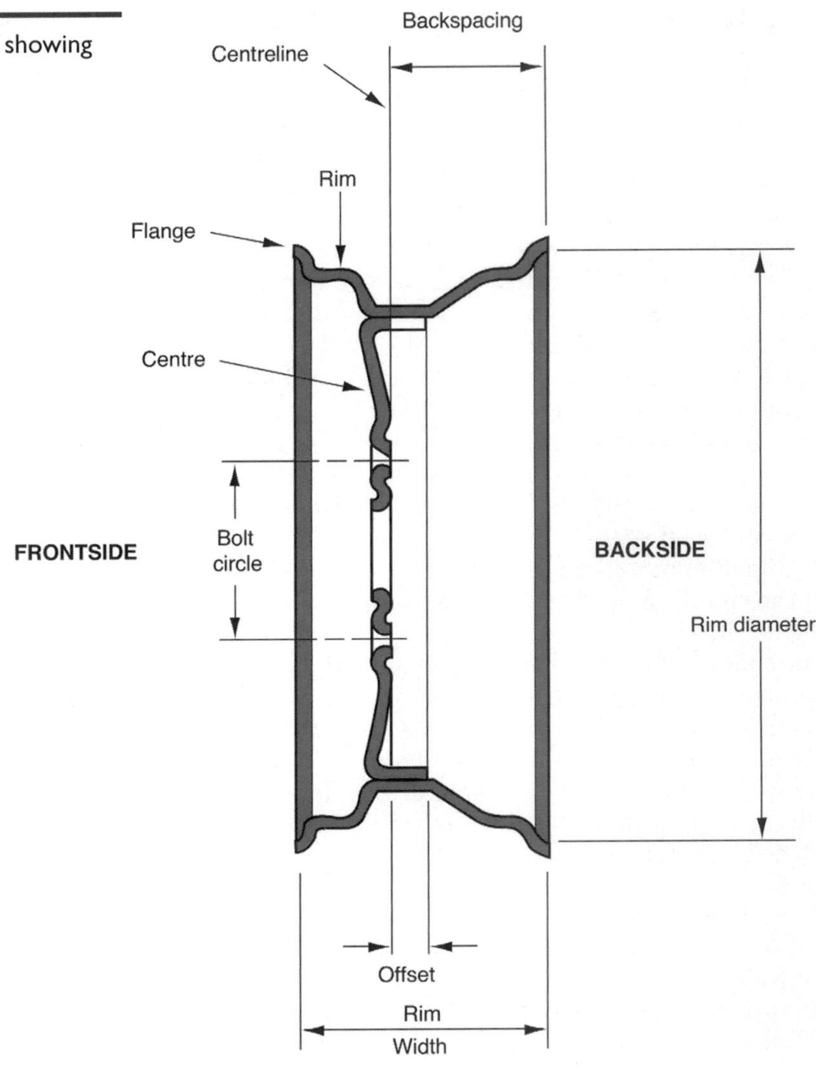

Figure 40–16 Cross-sectional view of a wheel showing the terms and where the sizes are measured.

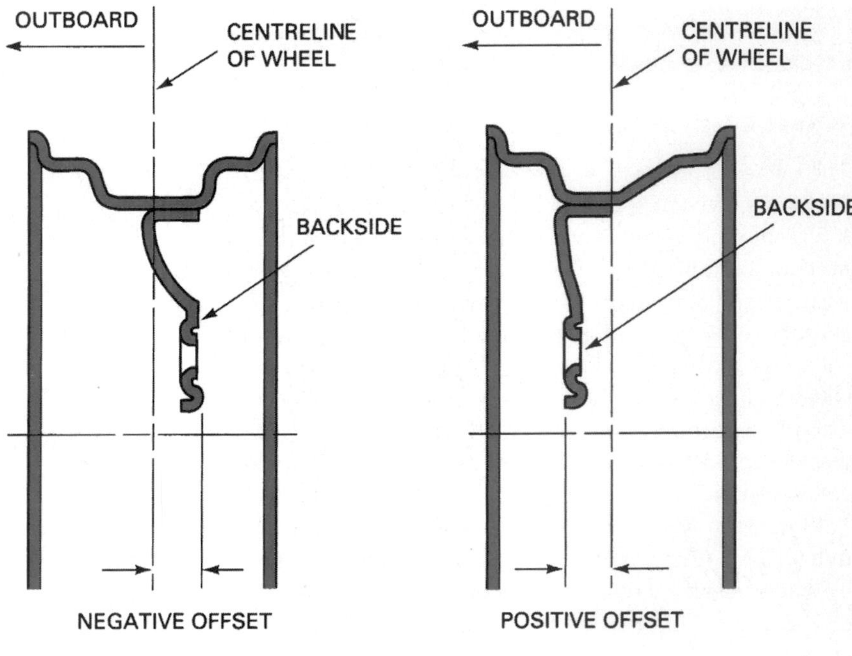

Figure 40–17 Offset is the distance between the centreline of the wheel and the wheel mounting surface.

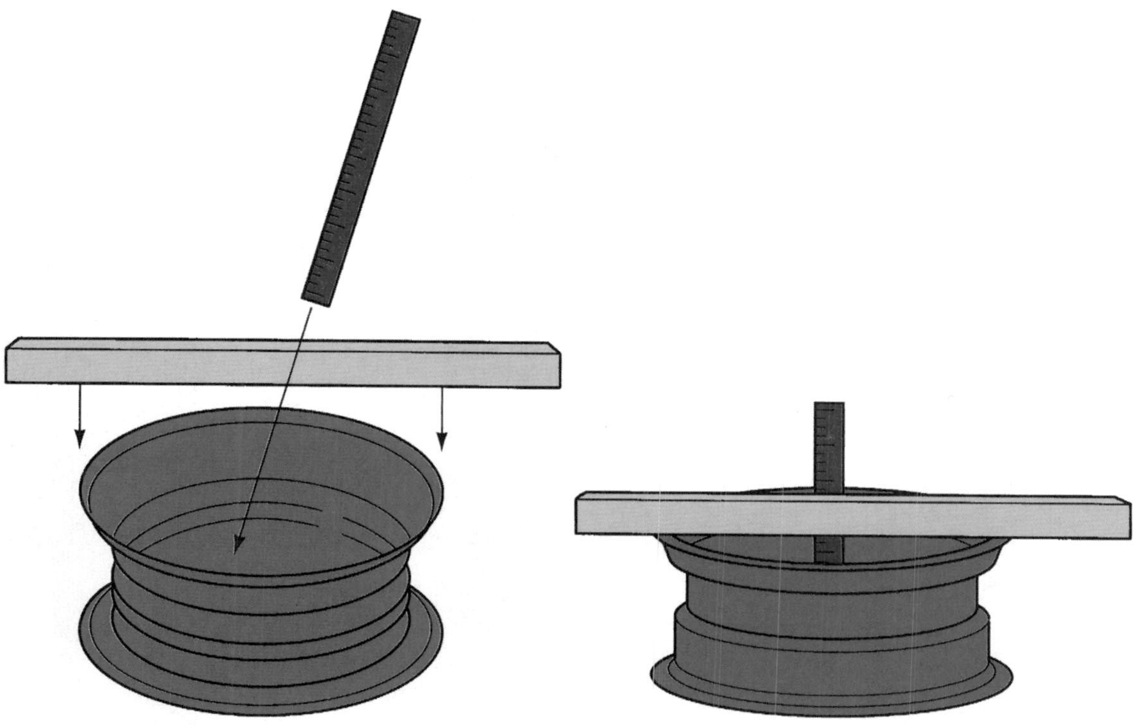

Figure 40–18 Back spacing (rear spacing) is the distance from the mounting pad to the edge of the rim. Most custom wheels use this measurement method to indicate the location of the mounting pad in relation to the rim.

Determining Bolt Circle

On four-lug axles and wheels, the measurement of bolt circle is simply taken from centre to centre on opposite studs or holes, as shown in Figure 40–19.

Steel Wheels

Steel is the traditional wheel material. A steel wheel is very strong due to its designed shape and the fact that it is work hardened during manufacturing. In fact, most of the strength of a steel wheel is due to its work hardening. Painting and baking cycles also increase the strength of a steel wheel. Steel wheels are formed from welded hoops, flared and joined to stamped spiders.

TECH TIP 

Easy Method to Determine the Bolt Circle of a 5-Lug Wheel

An easy method to determine the approximate bolt circle of a five-lug bolt circle wheel is to use a tape measure and place the end of the tape over the edge of one lug. Then measure the distance to the centre of the opposite bolt. See Figure 40–20.

HIGH PERFORMANCE TIP 

Wheel/Tire Weight Is Important

Many owners replace their original equipment wheels with wheels that are larger in diameter, such as replacing 16 in. diameter rims with 17 in. or 18 in. diameter wheels.

Even though they purchased tires that had a lower aspect ratio to maintain the same overall diameter of the factory wheels/tires, the performance of the vehicle can suffer.

There is an old saying in the high-performance field that states: "Two kilograms extra on the wheel is equal to adding 20 kg to the vehicle." While this statement has not been scientifically proven to be accurate, it is true that adding weight to the wheels not only hurts handling due to the increased weight, but also hurts acceleration. The engine has to create torque to rotate the tires and wheels to accelerate the vehicle with the added weight of a heavier tire/wheel assembly and is therefore unable to accelerate the vehicle as rapidly as with the lighter tire/wheel assembly. Lower priced aluminum alloy wheels are usually much heavier than stock wheels, especially when the diameter has been increased.

The solution is to check the actual weight of the wheels and tires and compare them to the weight of the original wheels and tires. Most forged wheels are usually lighter, yet much more expensive than cast wheels.

Aluminum Wheels

Forged and cast aluminum wheels are commonly used on cars and trucks. *Forged* means that the aluminum is hammered or forged under pressure into shape. A forged aluminum wheel is much stronger than a *cast* aluminum wheel.

A cast aluminum wheel is constructed by pouring liquid (molten) aluminum into a mould. After the aluminum has cooled, the cast aluminum wheel is removed from the mould and machined. Aluminum wheels are usually thicker than steel wheels and require special wheel weights when balancing. Most aluminum wheels use an alloy of aluminum. Aluminum can be combined (alloyed) with copper, manganese, silicon, or other elements to achieve the physical strength and characteristics for the exact product.

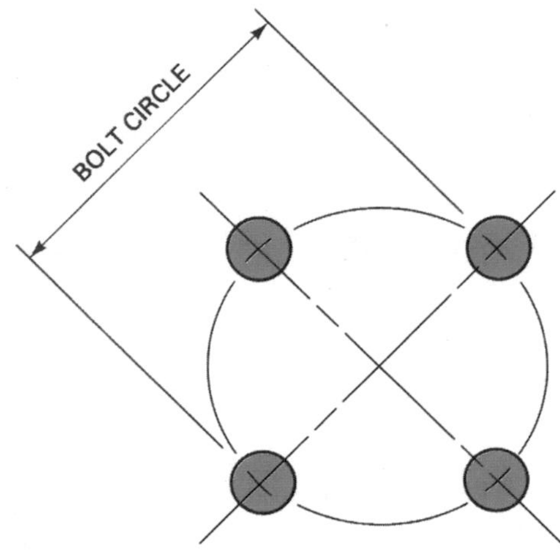

Figure 40–19 The bolt circle is the diameter of a circle that can be drawn through the centre of each lug hole or stud.

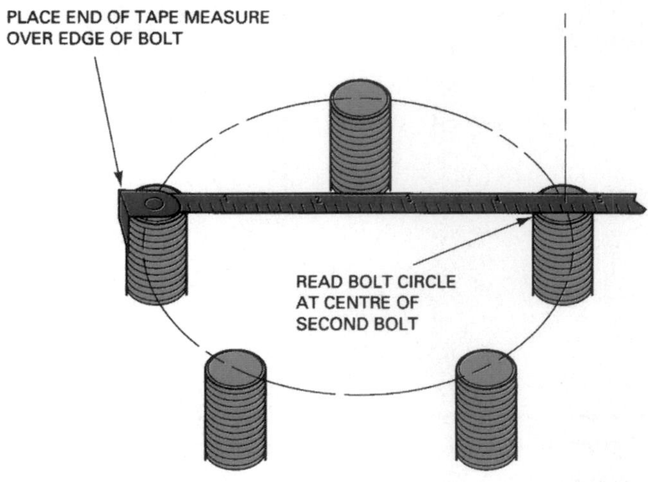

Figure 40–20 The easiest method to determine the approximate bolt circle of a five-lug bolt circle.

Frequently Asked Question ???

What Width Rim Should Be Used with What Size Tire?

For best overall vehicle operation and handling, the same size tires should be used that come on the vehicle when new. If a change of tire size is necessary, refer to the tire guide available at most stores that sell or service tires for the recommended alternative size that will fit the width of the rim.

NOTE: Interchangeability does not mean that it is always possible because of differences in rim size, wheel well clearance, and load ratings.

P-75 Series Metric	85 Series Bias	P-70 Series Metric	80 Series Metric	78 Series Alphanumeric	Rim Width (inches)
P195/75R14	700-14, 735-14	P205/70R14	185-14	E78-14	5–7 in.
P205/75R14	750-14, 775-14	P215/70R14	195-14	F78-14	5–7.5 in.
P215/75R14	800-14, 825-14	P225/70R14	205-14	G78-14	5.5–7.5 in.
P225/75R14	850-14, 855-14	P235/70R14	215-14	H78-14	6.8 in.
P195/75R15	640-15, 735-15	P205/70R15	175-15	E78-15	5–7 in.
P205/75R15	670-15, 775-15	P215/70R15	185-15	F78-15	5–7.5 in.
P215/75R15	710-15, 825-15	P225/70R15	205-15	G78-15	5.5–7.5 in.
P225/75R15	760-15, 855-15	P235/70R15	215-15	H78-15	6–8 in.
P235/75R15	820-15, 900-15	P255/70R15	230-15	L78-15	6–8.5 in.

Some racing wheels are made from a lighter weight metal called magnesium. These wheels are called *mag* wheels (an abbreviation for magnesium). True magnesium wheels are not practical for production wheels because their cost and corrosion are excessive compared with steel or aluminum alloy wheels. The term *mag wheel,* however, is still heard when referring to alloy (aluminum) wheels.

HINT: If purchasing replacement aftermarket wheels, check that they are certified by SFI. SFI is the Specialty Equipment Manufacturers Association (SEMA) Foundation, Incorporated. SEMA and SFI are nongovernment agencies that were formed by the manufacturers themselves to establish standards for safety.

Metric Wheels

Several vehicle manufacturers, including Ford Motor Company, equip vehicles with wheels that are 365 mm or 390 mm in diameter rather than the more conventional 14 in., 15 in., or 16 in. wheels.

Metric Code Bead Diameter Tire and Rim

Tire Size	Rim Size
185/65R *365*	*365* × 135 TR
195/65R *390*	*390* × 150 TR

Note that the rim in this example is 365 mm or 390 mm in diameter and 135 mm or 150 mm wide.

WARNING: Do not attempt to mount an inch code tire on a metric code rim or vice versa. A mismatch of tire size and rim size may result in tire failure and serious or fatal injury.

UNSPRUNG WEIGHT

The lighter the wheel and tire assembly, the faster it can react to bumps and dips in the road surface and the better the ride. The chassis and the body of any vehicle is supported by some sort of spring suspension system. It is the purpose of the suspension system to isolate the body of the vehicle from the road surface. Also, for best handling, all four tires must remain in contact with the road. After all, a tire cannot grip the road if it leaves the ground after hitting a bump. The wheel and tire are **unsprung weight** because they are not supported by the vehicle's springs. If heavy wheels or tires are used, every time the vehicle hits a bump, the wheel is forced upward. The heavy mass of the wheel and tire would transmit this force through the spring of the vehicle and eventually to the driver and passengers. Obviously, a much lighter wheel and tire assembly reacts faster to bumps and dips in the road surface. The end result is a smoother riding vehicle with greater control.

LUG NUTS

Lug nuts are used to hold a wheel to the brake disc, brake drum or wheel bearing assembly. Most manufacturers use a stud in the brake or bearing assembly with a lug nut to hold the wheel. Some models of VW, Audi, and Mazda use a lug *bolt* that is threaded into a hole in the brake drum or bearing assembly.

NOTE: Some aftermarket manufacturers offer a stud conversion kit to replace the lug bolt with a conventional stud and lug nut.

Typical lug nuts are tapered so that the wheel stud will centre the wheel onto the vehicle. Another advantage of the taper of the lug nut and wheel is to provide a suitable surface to prevent the nuts from loosening. The taper, usually 60°, forms a wedge that helps ensure that the lug nut will not loosen. Steel wheels are deformed slightly when the lug nut is torqued down against the wheel mounting flange; be certain that the taper is *toward* the vehicle.

NOTE: Many Chrysler-made products from the late 1950s to the early 1970s had left-handed threads on the wheel studs on the left side of the vehicle and right-handed threads on the right side of the vehicle. More than one technician has broken off wheel studs trying to remove lug nuts from the left side of an old Chrysler vehicle. The reason for using left-handed threads on the left side is that the normal direction of rotation tends to tighten, rather than loosen, the lug nuts.

Frequently Asked Question ???

What Does This Mark on a Wheel Mean?

A symbol (JWL) for the Japan Wheel Light Metal Standard Mark means that the wheel meets the technical standards for passenger car light alloy disk wheels. See the mark in Figure 40–21.

The manufacturer is responsible for conducting the inspections set in the technical standard, and the JWL mark is displayed on those products which pass the inspection.

Many alloy wheels use a *shank-nut*-type lug nut that has straight sides without a taper. This style of nut must be used with wheels designed for this nut type. If replacement wheels are used on any vehicle, check with the wheel manufacturer for the proper type and style lug nut. Figure 40–22 shows several of the many styles of lug nuts that are available.

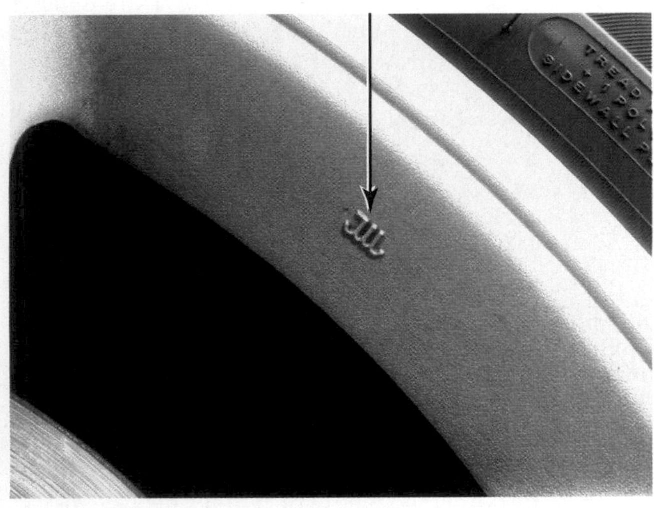

Figure 40–21 A typical JWL symbol for the Japan Wheel Light Metal Standard Mark.

Size

Lug nuts are sized to the thread size of the studs onto which they screw. The diameter and the number of threads per inch are commonly stated. Since some vehicles use left-hand threads, RH and LH are commonly stated, indicating right-hand and left-hand threads. A typical size is 7/16-20 RH, where the 7/16 indicates the diameter of the wheel stud and 20 indicates that there are 20 threads per inch. Another common fractional size is 1/2-20. Metric sizes such as M12 × 1.5 use a different sizing method.

M	metric
12	12 mm diameter of stud
1.5	1.5 mm distance from one thread peak to another

Other commonly used metric lug sizes include M12 × 1.25 and M14 × 1.5. Obviously, metric wheel studs require metric lug nuts.

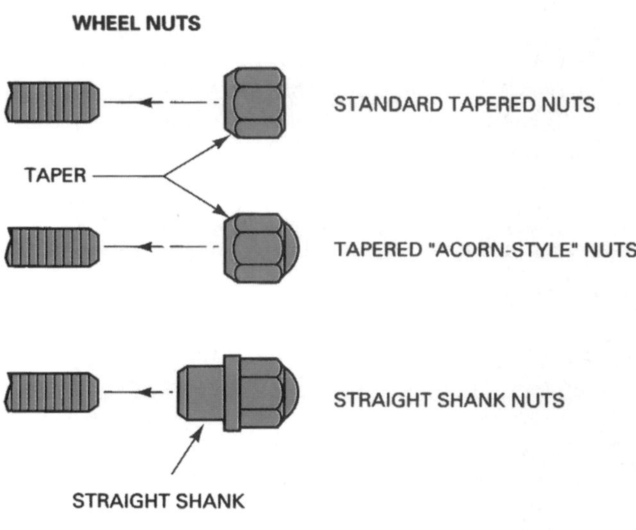

Figure 40–22 Various types of lug nuts.

Tightening Torque

All wheels must be tightened in a star pattern to a specified torque. Always use a torque wrench or torque-absorbing adapters. Proper tightening sequence and tightness is important to prevent possible damage to the wheel and/or brake rotor or drum. **Never use an air impact wrench to install wheels, except when using torque-absorbing adapters!** See Figures 40–23 and 40–24. Tests performed by skilled technicians using their own air impact wrenches show that tightening torque can vary as much as 25 N·m (19 lb-ft). This uneven torque puts unequal stress on the wheel studs and the wheel mounting surface.

DIAGNOSTIC STORY

"I Thought the Lug Nuts Were Tight!"

Proper wheel nut torque is critical, as one technician discovered when a customer returned complaining of a lot of noise from the right rear wheel. See Figure 40–25 for a photo of what the technician discovered. The lug (wheel) nuts had loosened and ruined the wheel.

CAUTION: Most vehicle manufacturers also specify that the wheel studs/nuts should *not* be lubricated with oil or grease. The use of a lubricant on the threads could cause the lug nuts to loosen.

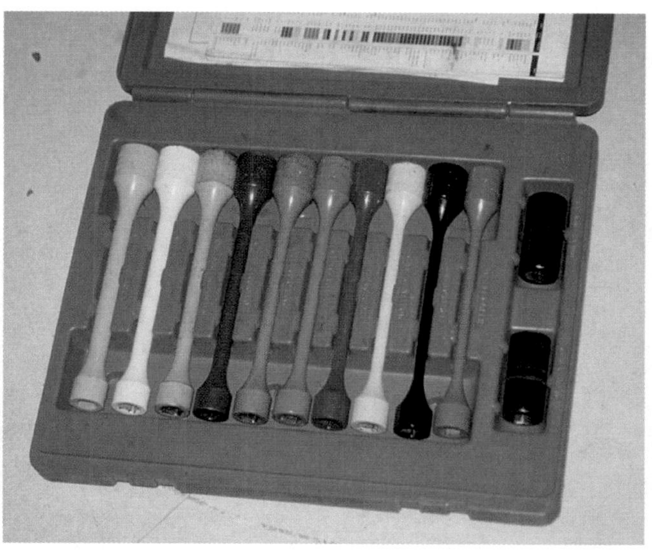

(a)

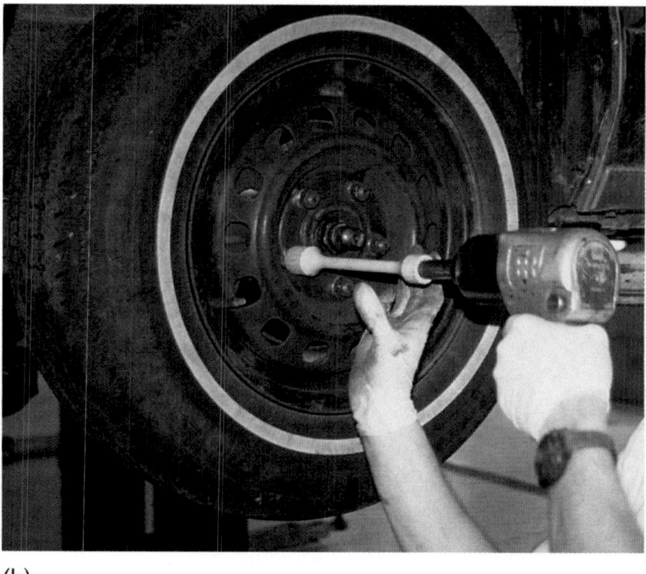

(b)

Figure 40–23 (a) A typical assortment of torque-limiting adapters to use with an air impact wrench to properly torque wheel lug nuts. (b) Proper torque is achieved by using an air-impact wrench with a torque-limiting socket and keeping the impact on until the lug nut end of the adapter stops rotating. Repeating the torque sequence also helps assure proper wheel nut torque.

Figure 40–24 Proper wheel nut torque is essential. Always use a torque wrench or use torque-limiting adapters to tighten wheel nuts. The use of an impact wrench will distort the wheel, hub, and rotor, resulting in vibration and brake pedal pulsations.

Figure 40–25 This wheel was damaged because the lug nuts were not properly torqued.

TIRE MOUNTING RECOMMENDATIONS

1. When removing a wheel from a vehicle for service, mark the location of the wheel and lug stud to ensure that the wheel is replaced in the exact same location. This ensures that the tire balance will be maintained if the tire/wheel assembly was balanced on the vehicle.
2. Make certain that the wheel has a good and clean metal-to-metal contact with the brake drum or rotor. Grease, oil, or dirt between these two surfaces could cause the wheel lug nuts to loosen while driving.
3. Rim flanges must be free of rust, dirt, scale, or loose or flaked rubber build-up prior to mounting the tire. See Figure 40–26.

(a)

(b)

Figure 40–26 (a) Cleaning the bead area of an aluminum (alloy) wheel using a hand-held wire brush. The technician is using the tire changer itself to rotate the wheel as the brush is used to remove any remnants of the old tire. (b) Using an electric or air-powered wire brush speeds the process, but care should be exercised not to remove any of the aluminum itself. (Remember, steel is harder than aluminum and a steel wire brush could cause recesses to be worn into the aluminum wheel, which would prevent the tire from proper seating in the bead area.)

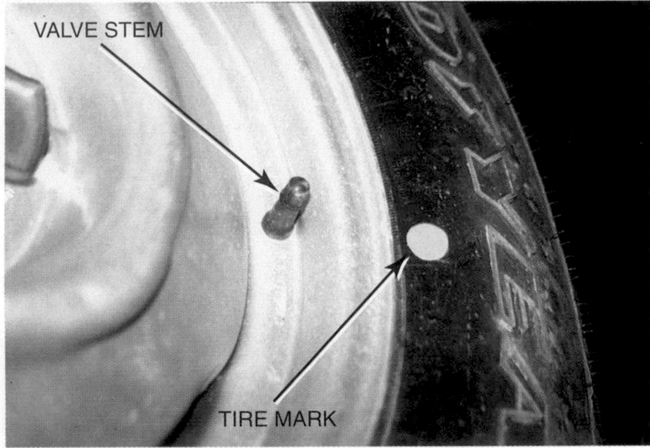

Figure 40–27 This tire on a new vehicle has been match mounted at the factory. The yellow sticker is placed at the largest diameter of the tire. The valve core hole in the wheel is usually drilled at the smallest diameter of the wheel. The best way to make sure the assembly is as round as possible and to reduce the number of wheel weights needed to balance the tire is to align the sticker with the valve core.

DIAGNOSTIC STORY

The Greased Wheel Causes a Vibration

Shortly after an oil change and a chassis lubrication, a customer complained of a vibration at highway speed. The tires were checked for excessive radial runout to be certain the cause of the vibration was not due to a defective out-of-round tire. After removing the wheel assembly from the vehicle, excessive grease was found on the inside of the rim. Obviously, the technician who greased the lower ball joints had dropped grease on the rim. After cleaning the wheel, it was checked for proper balance on a dynamic computer balancer and found to be properly balanced. A test drive confirmed that the problem was solved.

4. Many tires are marked with a paint dot or sticker, as shown in Figure 40–27. This mark represents the largest diameter (high point) and/or stiffest portion of the tire. (Variation is due to the overlapping of carcass and belt fabric layers as well as tread and sidewall rubber splices.) The tire should be mounted to the rim with this mark lined up with the valve stem. The valve stem hole is typically drilled at the smallest diameter (low point) of the wheel. Mount the tires on the rim with the valve stem matched (lined up next to) the mark on the tire. This is called **match mounting.**
5. Never use more than 275 kPa (40 psi) to seat a tire bead.
6. When mounting new tires, do *not* use silicone lubricant on the tire bead. Use special rubber lubricant to help prevent tire rotation on the rim. This rubber lube is a water-based soap product that is slippery when wet (coefficient of friction less than 0.3) and almost acts as an adhesive when dry (coefficient of friction dry of over 0.5 for natural products and over 1.0 for synthetic products).

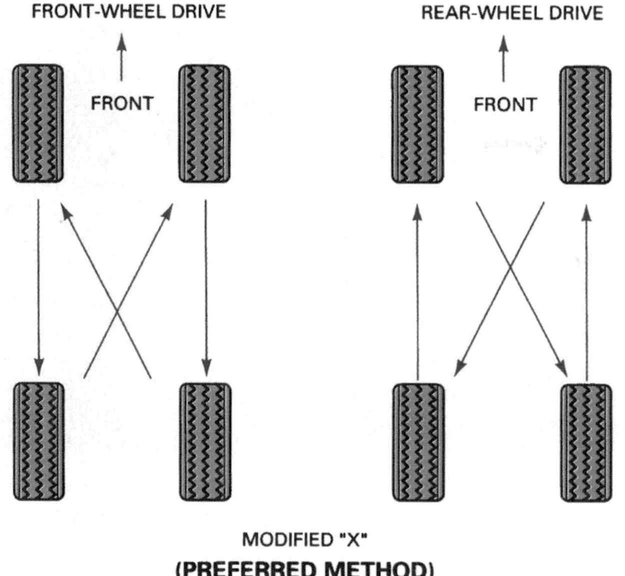

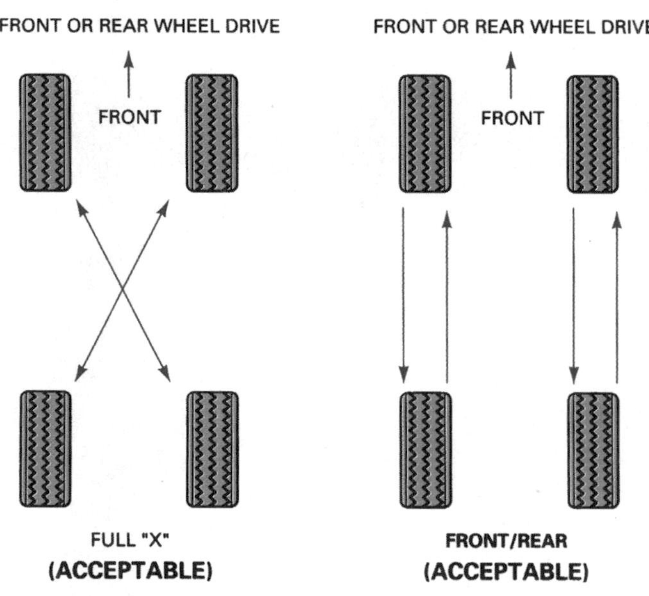

Figure 40–28 The method most often recommended is the modified X method. Using this method, each tire eventually is used at each of the four wheel locations. An easy way to remember the sequence, whether front-wheel-drive or rear-wheel-drive, is to say to yourself "drive wheels straight, cross the nondrive wheels."

TIRE ROTATION

To assure long life and even tire wear, it is important to rotate each tire to another location. For best results, tires should be rotated every 10 000 km (6000 mi) or six months. See Figure 40–28 for suggested methods of rotation.

Frequently Asked Question ???

"I Thought Radial Tires Couldn't Be Rotated!"

When radial tires were first introduced by American tire manufacturers in the 1970s, rotating tires side to side was *not* recommended because of concern over a belt or tread separation. Since the late 1980s, most tire manufacturers throughout the world including Canada use tire-building equipment specifically designed for radial ply tires. These newer radial tires are constructed so that the tires can now be rotated from one side of the vehicle to the other without fear of a separation being caused by the resulting reversal of the direction of rotation.

Figure 40–29 Tire showing excessive shoulder wear resulting from underinflation and/or high-speed cornering.

HINT: To help remember when to rotate the tires, just keep in mind that it should be done at every other oil change. Most manufacturers recommend changing the engine oil every 5000 km (3000 mi) or every three months, and tire rotation is recommended every 10 000 km (6000 mi) or every six months.

TIRE INSPECTION

All tires should be carefully inspected for faults in the tire itself or for signs that something may be wrong with the steering or suspension system of the vehicle. See Figures 40–29 through 40–31 for examples of common problems.

Figure 40–30 Tire showing excessive wear in the centre indicating overinflation or heavy acceleration on a drive wheel.

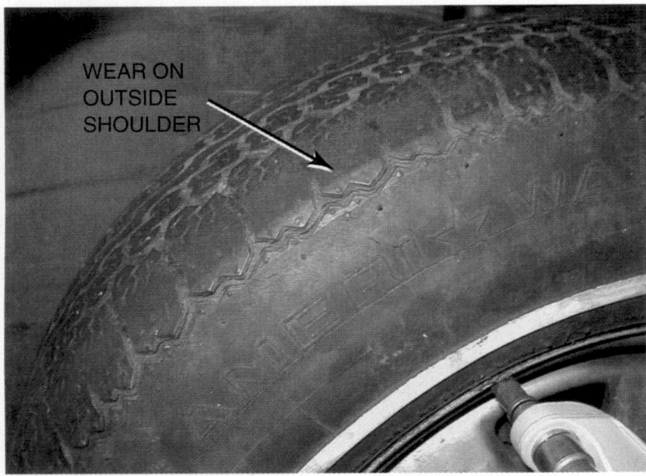

Figure 40–31 Wear on the outside shoulder only is an indication of an alignment problem.

Figure 40–32 A tire runout gauge being used to measure the radial runout of a tire.

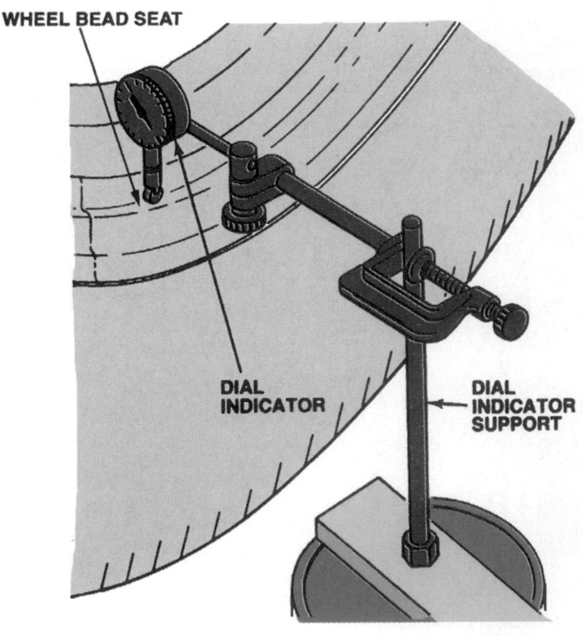

Figure 40–33 To check wheel radial runout, the dial indicator plunger tip rides on a horizontal surface of the wheel, such as the bead seat.

Radial Runout

Even if a tire has no visible faults, it can be the cause of a vibration. If a vibration is felt above 70 km/h (45 mph), regardless of the engine load, the usual cause is due to an out-of-balance or defective out-of-round tire. Both of these problems cause a **tramp** or **up-and-down**-type vibration. **Radial runout** can be checked using a runout gauge (see Figure 40–32). Maximum radial runout should be less than 1.5 mm (0.060 in.). Little, if any, tramp will be noticed with less than 0.8 mm (0.030 in.) runout. If the reading is over 3.2 mm (0.125 in.), check the runout of the wheel to see if the wheel is round before replacing the tire. See Figure 40–33.

Lateral Runout

Another problem that tires can cause is a type of vibration called **shimmy.** This rapid back-and-forth motion can be transmitted through the steering linkage to the steering wheel. Excessive runout usually is noticeable by the driver of the vehicle as a side-to-side vibration, especially at low speeds between 8 and 70 km/h (5 and 45 mph). Shimmy can be caused by an internal defect of the tire or a bent wheel. **Lateral runout** can be checked using a runout gauge on the side of the tire or wheel.

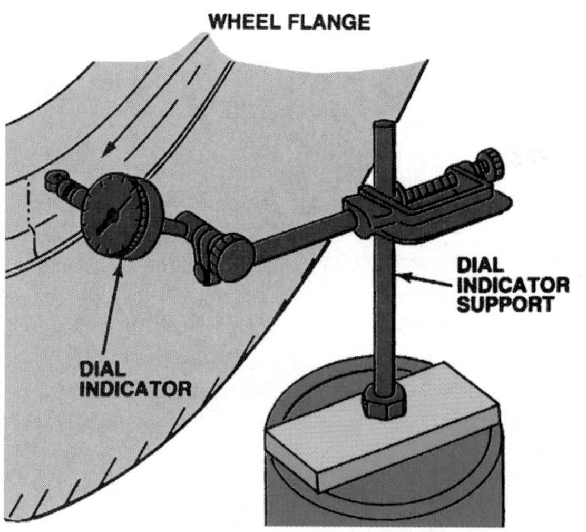

Figure 40–34 To check lateral runout, the dial indicator plunger tip rides on a vertical surface of the wheel, such as the wheel flange.

The runout gauge is placed against the side of the tire and the wheel is rotated. The maximum allowable reading is 1.1 mm (0.045 in.). If the reading is close to or above 1.1 mm (0.045 in.), the edge of the wheel should be checked to see if the cause of the lateral runout is due to a bent wheel, as shown in Figure 40–34. Most manufacturers specify a maximum lateral runout of 0.9 mm (0.035 in.) for alloy wheels and 1.1 mm (0.045 in.) for steel wheels. See Figure 40–35.

DIAGNOSTIC STORY

The Vibrating Ford

A technician was asked to solve a vibration problem on a rear-wheel drive Ford. During a test drive, the vibration was felt everywhere—the dash, in the steering wheel, the front seat, the shoulder belts—everything was vibrating! The technician balanced all four tires on a computer balancer. Even though wheel weights were put on all four wheels and tires, the vibration was even worse than before. The technician rebalanced all four wheels time after time, but the vibration was still present. The shop supervisor then took over the job of solving the vibrating Ford. The supervisor balanced one wheel/tire assembly and then tested it again after installing the weights. The balance was way off! The supervisor broke the tire down and found about one quart (1 liter) of liquid in the tire! Liquid was found in all four tires. No wonder the tires couldn't be balanced! Every time the tire stopped, the liquid would settle in another location.

The customer later admitted to using a tire stop-leak liquid in all four tires. Besides stop leak, another common source of liquid in tires is water that accumulates in the storage tank of air compressors, which often gets pumped into tires when air is being added. All air compressor storage tanks should be drained of water regularly to prevent this from happening. See Figure 40–37.

TIRE BALANCING

Proper tire balance is important for tire life, ride comfort, and safety.

Static Balance

The term **static balance** means that the weight mass is evenly distributed around the axis of rotation.

1. For example, if a wheel were spun and it stopped at different places with each spin, then the tire is statically balanced.
2. *If the static balance is not correct, wheel-tramp-(vertical-shake) type vibration and uneven tire wear can result.*

Dynamic Balance

The term **dynamic balance** means that the centre line of weight mass is in the same plane as the centre line of the wheel. See Figure 40–36.

1. Dynamic balance must be checked with the tire and the wheel rotated to determine side-to-side out-of-balance as well as up-and-down.
2. *Incorrect dynamic balance causes shimmy.* Shimmy-type vibration causes the steering wheel to shake side to side.

Wheel Weights

Wheel weights are available in a variety of styles and types (see Figure 40–38) including:

1. Clip-on lead weights for standard steel rims
2. Clip-on weights for alloy (aluminum) wheels:
   a. Uncoated—generally *not* recommended by wheel or vehicle manufacturers because corrosion often occurs where the lead weight contacts the alloy wheel surface
   b. Coated—lead weights that are painted or coated with a plastic material are usually the *recommended* type weight to use on alloy wheels, as shown in Figure 40–39. Weights are usually coated with a nylon or polyester-type material that often matches the color of aluminum wheels.
3. Stick-on weights come with an adhesive backing that is most often used on alloy wheels.

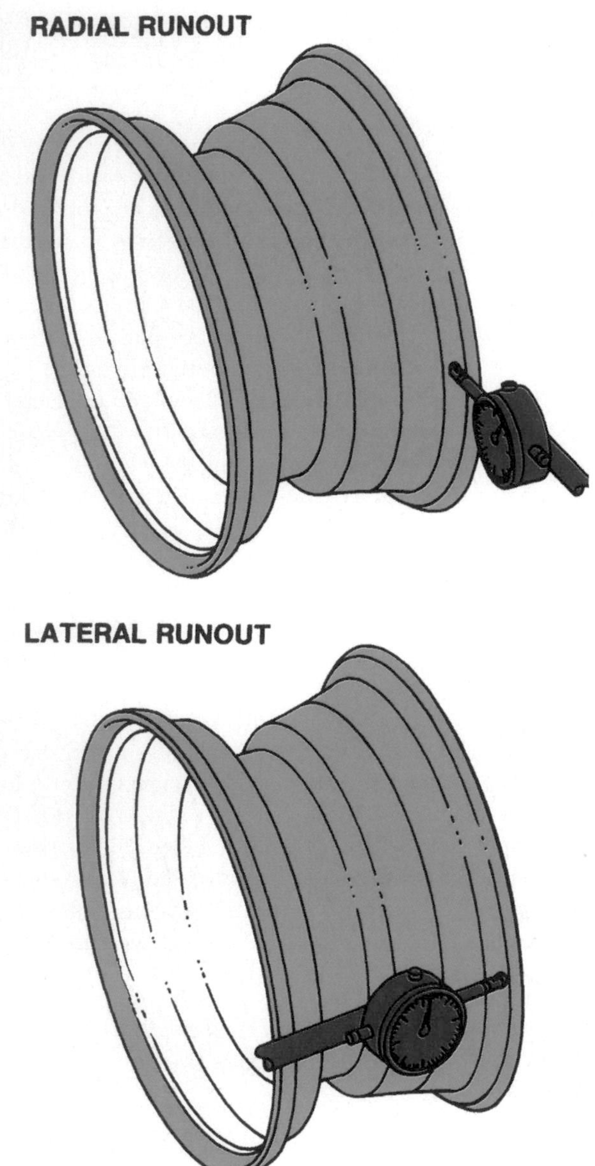

Figure 40–35 The most accurate method of measuring wheel runout is to dismount the tire and take dial indicator readings on the inside of the wheel rim.

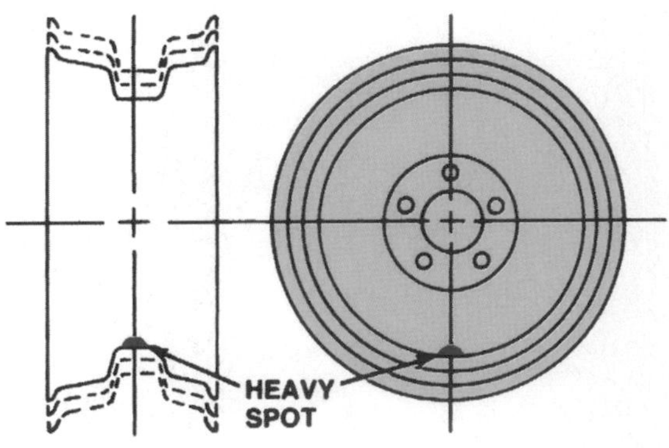

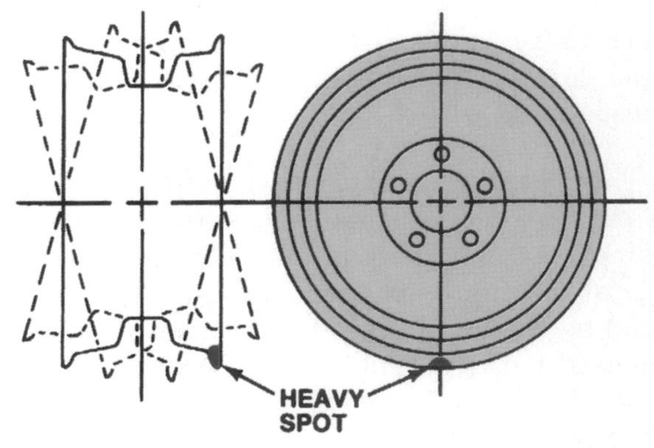

Figure 40–36 A wheel balancer detects heavy spots on the wheel and tire, and most indicate where to place weights to offset both static and dynamic imbalances.

Bubble Balancer

A bubble balancer is a type of static balancer that is commonly used and it is accurate if calibrated and used correctly. A bubble balancer is portable and can be easily stored away when not in use. It is also easy to use and relatively inexpensive.

Computer Balancer

Most computer balancers are designed to balance wheels and tires off the vehicle. Computer dynamic balancers spin the tire at a relatively slow speed (approximately 30 km/h [20 mph]). Sensors

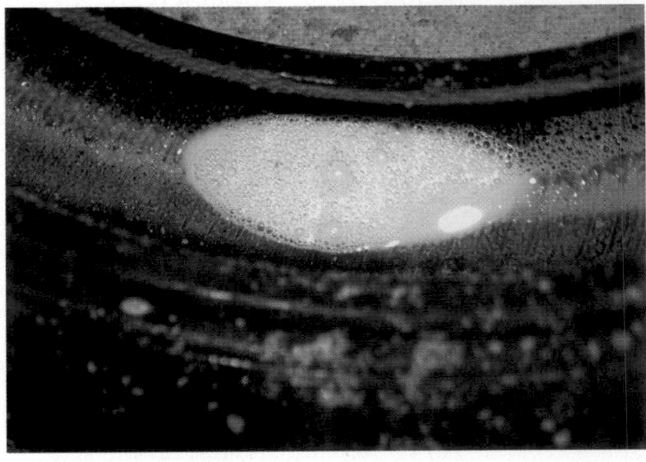

Figure 40–37 Liquid-tire stop leak was found in all four tires. This liquid caused the tires to be out-of-balance.

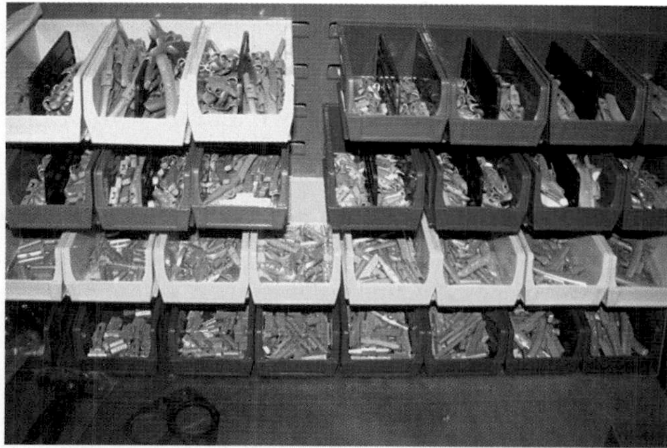

Figure 40–38 Each different colour bin contains a different style of wheel weight designed for specific models of vehicles or types of wheels.

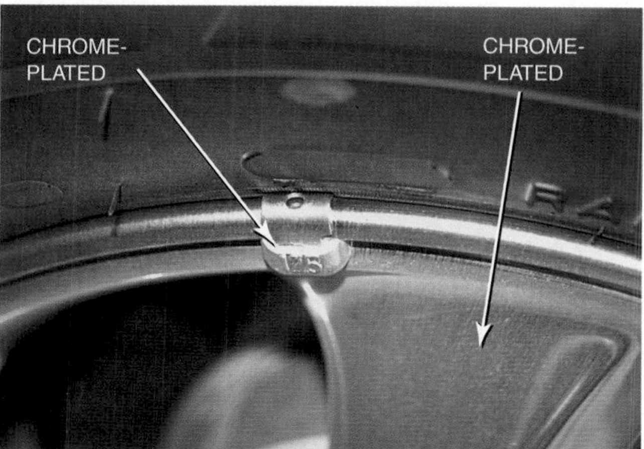

(a)

(b)

Figure 40–39 (a) A chrome-plated wheel weight used on a new vehicle equipped with chrome-plated aluminum (alloy) wheels. (b) Note the corrosion on this alloy wheel caused by the use of standard lead wheel weights. Using a coated wheel weight would have prevented this damage to an expensive wheel.

Figure 40–40 A tire balancer that can also detect radial force variation and instruct the operator where to rotate the tire to achieve the best ride.

attached to the spindle of the balancer determine the amount and location of weights necessary to dynamically balance the tire. All computer balancers must be "programmed" or "instructed" with actual rim size and tire location for the electronic circuits to calibrate the required weight locations. Computer balancers are the most expensive type of balancer. See Figure 40–40 for an example of a radial force measuring-type balancer. Most computer balancers will be accurate to within 7 g (0.25 oz), while some are accurate to within 3.5 g (0.125 oz). (Most drivers can "feel" an out-of-balance of 1 oz or more, but few can feel a vibration caused by just 7 g [0.25 oz].)

TIRE LEAK DETECTION

A tire can leak air in several locations, including:

- A hole caused by a nail, glass, or other debris
- A leaking tire valve or stem
- A leak around the tire bead-to-bead seat junction of the wheel

To locate a tire air leak, try spraying soapy water from a spray bottle over the suspected area. An air leak will cause the solution to bubble.

HINT: Glass cleaner can also be used to locate an air leak in a tire if soapy water is not available.

TIRE REPAIR

Tread punctures, nail holes, or cuts up to 6 mm (1/4 in.) can be repaired. Repairs should be done from the inside of the tire using plugs or patches. The tire should be removed from the rim to make the repair. With the tire off the wheel, inspect the wheel and the tire for hidden damage. The steps to follow for a proper tire repair include:

1. Mark the location of the tire on the wheel.
2. Dismount the tire and inspect and clean the punctured area with a prebuff cleaner. DO NOT USE GASOLINE!
3. Buff the cleaned area with sandpaper or a tire buffing tool until the rubber surface has a smooth velvet finish (see Figure 40–41).
4. Ream the puncture with a fine reamer from the inside and cut and remove any loose wire material from the steel belts.
5. Fill the puncture with contour filling material and cut or buff the material flush with the inner liner of the tire.
6. Apply chemical vulcanizing cement and allow it to dry.

NOTE: Most vulcanizing (rubber) cement is highly flammable. Use out of the area of an open flame. Do not smoke when making a tire repair.

7. Apply the patch and use a **stitching tool** from the centre toward the outside of the patch to work any air out from between the patch and the tire (see Figure 40–42). Another excellent tire repair procedure uses a rubber plug. Pull the stem through the hole in the tire, as shown in Figure 40–43.
8. Remount the tire on the rim and align the marks made in Step 1 above. Inflate to recommended pressure and check for air leaks.

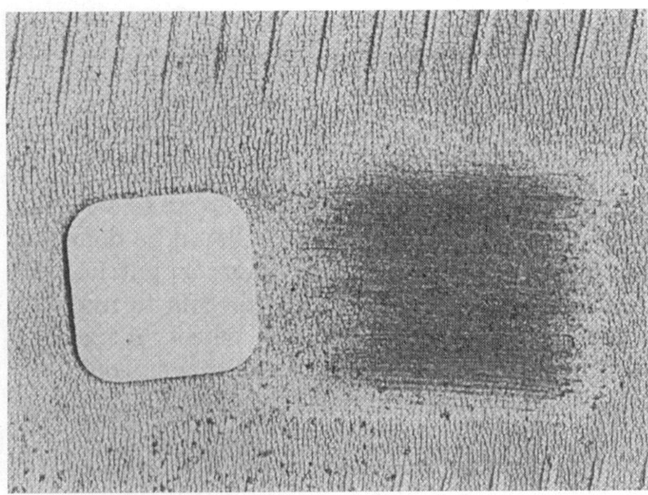

Figure 40–41 The area of the repair should be buffed slightly larger than the patch to be applied.

There are many tire repair products on the market. Always follow the installation and repair procedures exactly as per manufacturer's instructions.

CAUTION: Most experts agree that tire repairs should be done from the inside. Many technicians have been injured and a few killed when the tire they were repairing exploded as a steel reamer tool was inserted into the tire. The reamer can easily create a spark as it is pushed through the steel wires of a steel-belted tire. This spark can ignite a combustible mixture of gases inside the tire that resulted from using stop-leak or inflator cans. Since there is no way a technician can know if a tire has been inflated with a product that uses a combustible gas, always treat a tire as if it could explode.

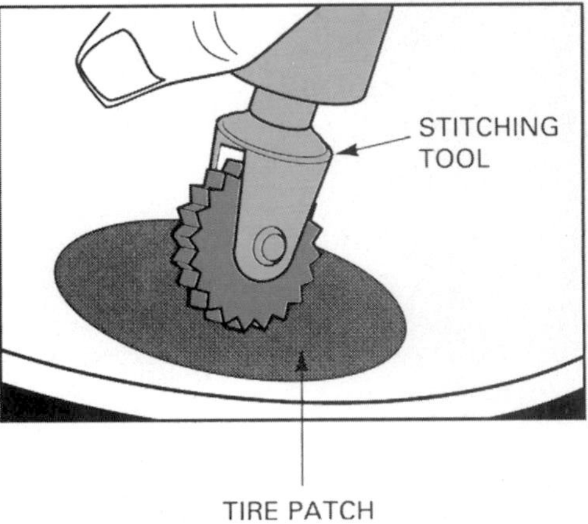

Figure 40–42 A stitching tool being used to force any trapped air out from under the patch.

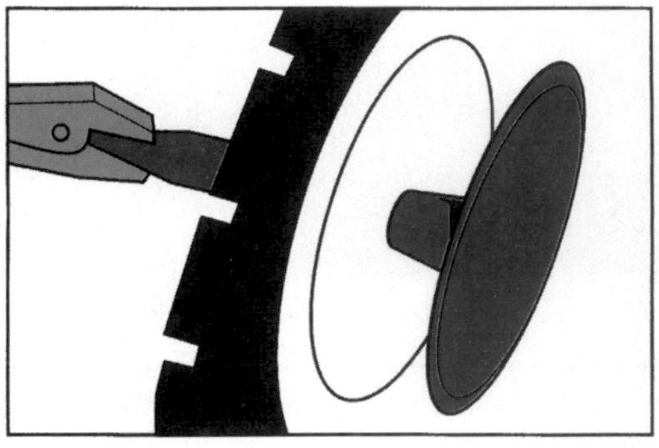

Figure 40–43 A rubber plug being pulled through a hole in the tire. The stem is then cut off flush with the surface of the tire tread.

DIAGNOSTIC STORY

It Happened to Me— It Could Happen to You

During routine service, I rotated the tires on a Pontiac TransAm. Everything went well and I even used a torque wrench to properly torque all of the lug nuts. Then, when I went to drive the car out of the service stall, I heard a horrible grinding sound. When I hoisted the car to investigate, I discovered that the front wheels were hitting the outer tie rod ends (see Figure 40–44). The 16-inch wheels had a different back spacing front and rear, and therefore these wheels could not be rotated. Always check replacement or aftermarket wheels for proper fit before driving the vehicle.

Figure 40–44 Notice that the rim touches the tie rod end when a wheel with the wrong back spacing is installed.

PHOTO SEQUENCE 27 Tire Inspection

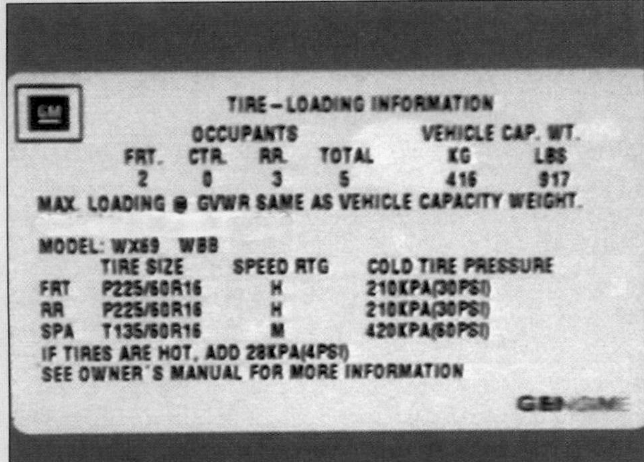

P27–1 Before checking and adjusting tire pressure, check the tire loading information decal or placard usually located on the driver's door or door jamb.

P27–2 Do not inflate a tire higher than the maximum pressure rating on the tire sidewall.

P27–3 Use a good-quality tire pressure gauge to be assured of accurate tire pressure readings. Be sure the vehicle has not been driven to ensure that the tires are cool when checking tire pressure.

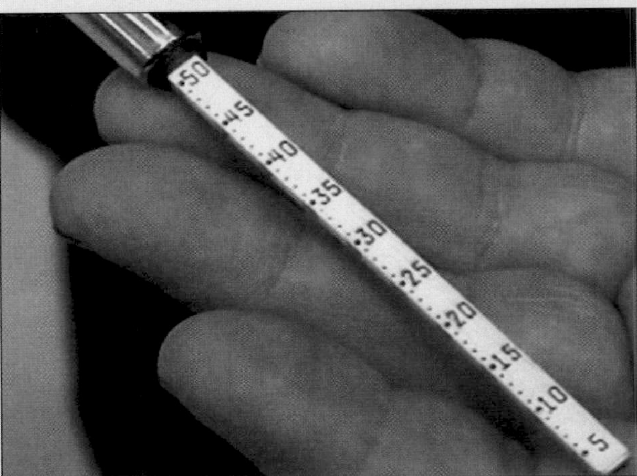

P27–4 This tire pressure gauge reads from 5 to 50 psi and is a good choice because most passenger car tires fall within the range of this gauge.

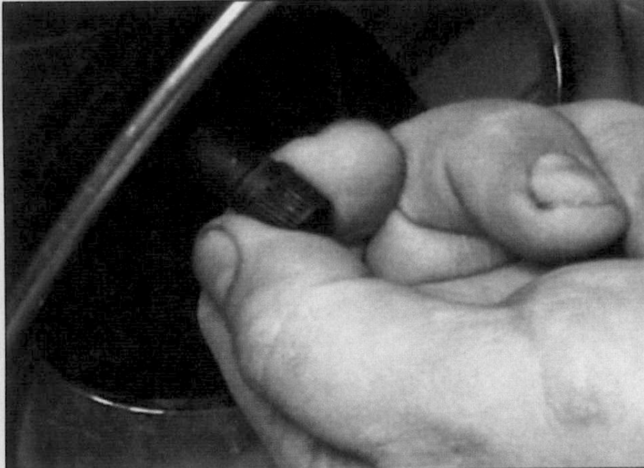

P27–5 Remove the cap from the tire valve (Schrader valve).

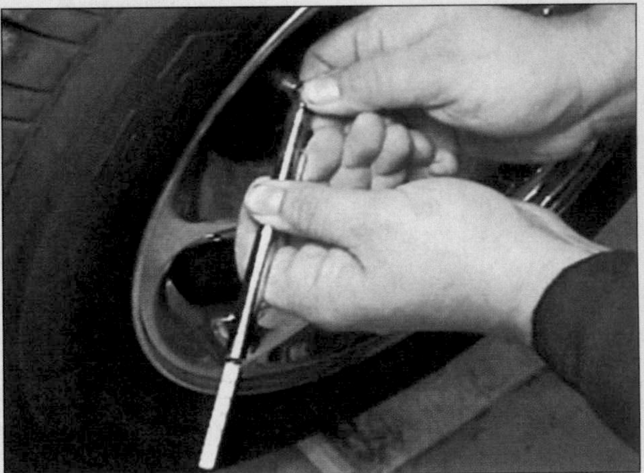

P27–6 To get accurate tire pressure results, be sure to press the tire gauge straight onto the end of the tire valve in one smooth motion.

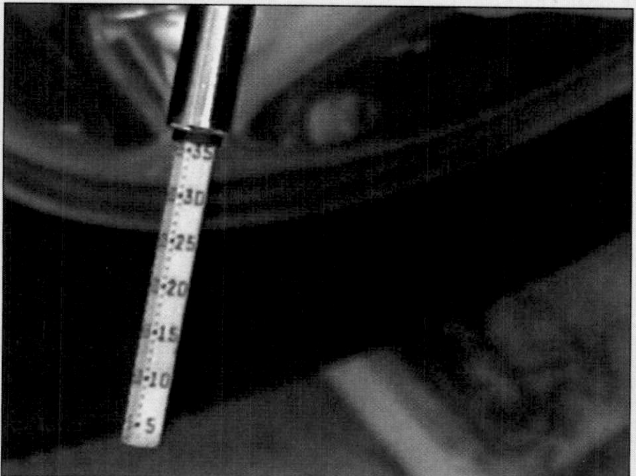

P27–7 The tire pressure is read at the junction between the housing of the gauge and the movable plunger.

P27–8 A combination tire inflator with gauge can be used to measure tire pressure and add air if necessary.

P27–9 The tire pressure is read through a window on the inflator handle.

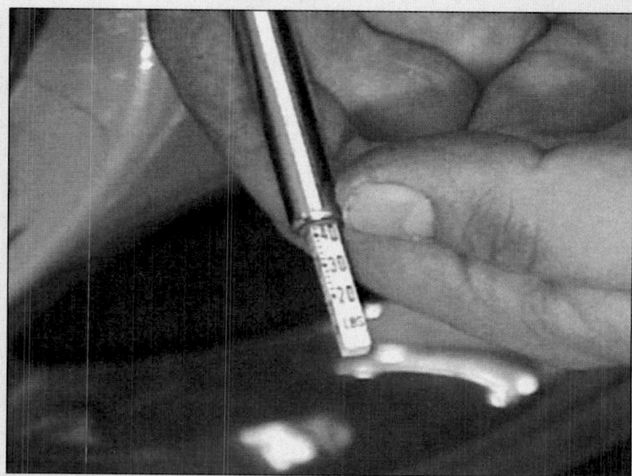

P27–10 Repeat testing each tire to be sure that all four tires are inflated to the factory recommended inflation. Many vehicle tire information decals specify different tire pressures for front and rear tires.

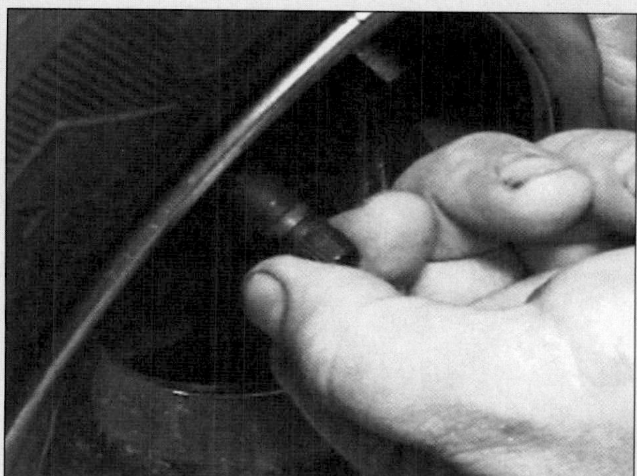

P27–11 Be sure to check the tire pressure in the spare tire and to re-install all tire valve caps.

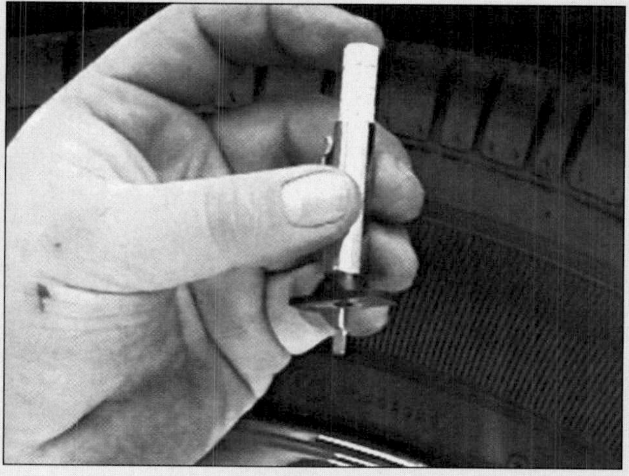

P27–12 A typical tire tread depth gauge.

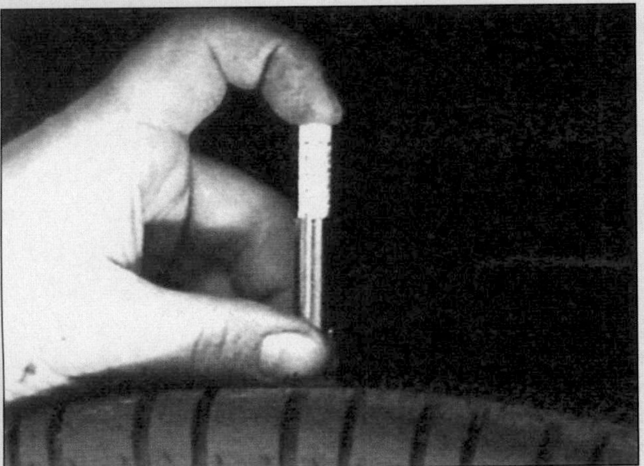

P27–13 To use a tire tread depth gauge, position the gauge over a groove in the tire and depress the top of the gauge.

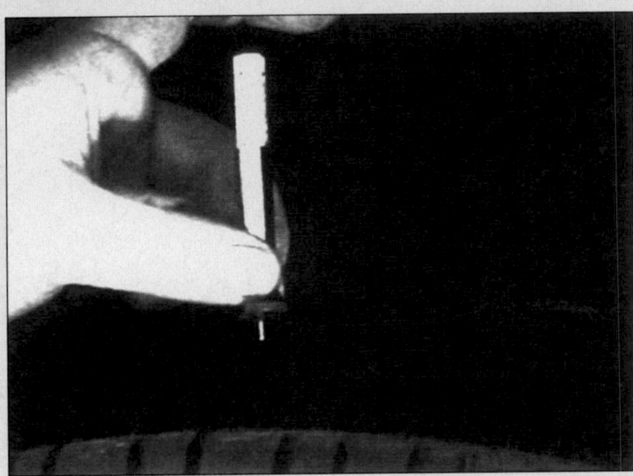

P27–14 Lift the gauge off the tire to read the depth.

P27–15 Read the tread depth at the junction between the housing and the plunger. The number that is closest to the junction is the depth of the tread.

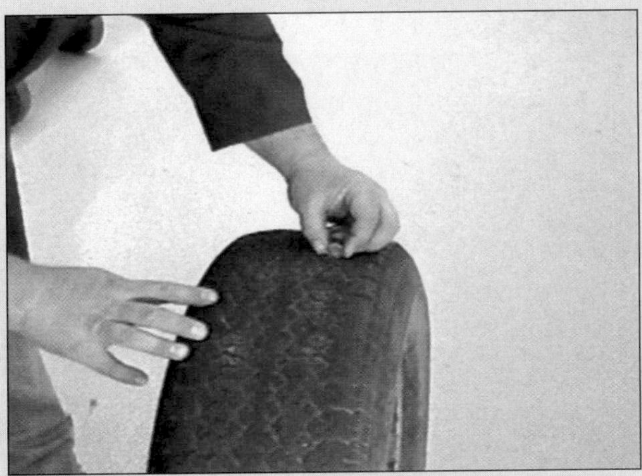

P27–16 A penny can also be used to check to see if there is at least 1.6 mm (2/32 in.) of tread remaining, an amount often specified by governments as the minimum allowable legal tread depth.

P27–17 On a U.S. penny, the top of Lincoln's head is visible, then the tread depth is less than 1.6 mm (2/32 in.).

P27–18 The same tire is measured using a U.S. penny, but in another location. In this location, the tread depth is deep enough that the tip of Lincoln's head is just starting to be covered. All tires should be measured at the minimum tread depth, not at a point of maximum tread depth.

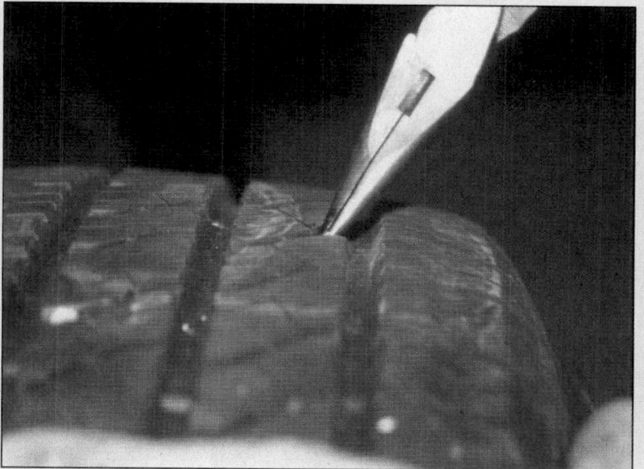

P28–1 The source of the leak was detected by spraying soapy water on the inflated tire. Needle nose pliers are being used to remove the object that caused the leak.

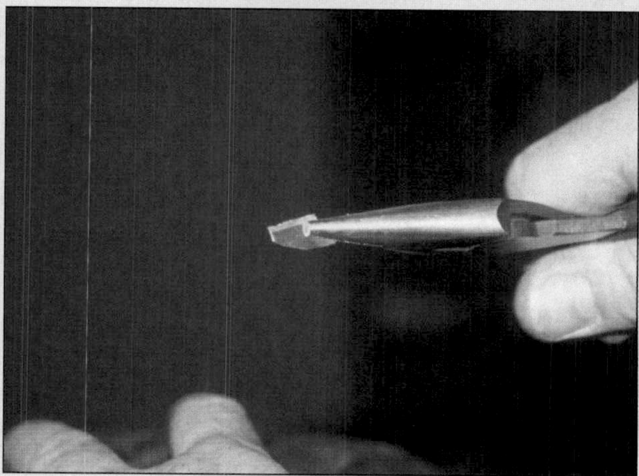

P28–2 A part of a razor blade was found to be the cause of the flat tire.

P28–3 A reamer is being used to clean the puncture hole.

P28–4 A method used by some technicians is to hold the beads apart with two open-end wrenches. In this case, two line wrenches were used, and this provided more than enough room to gain access to the inside of the tire.

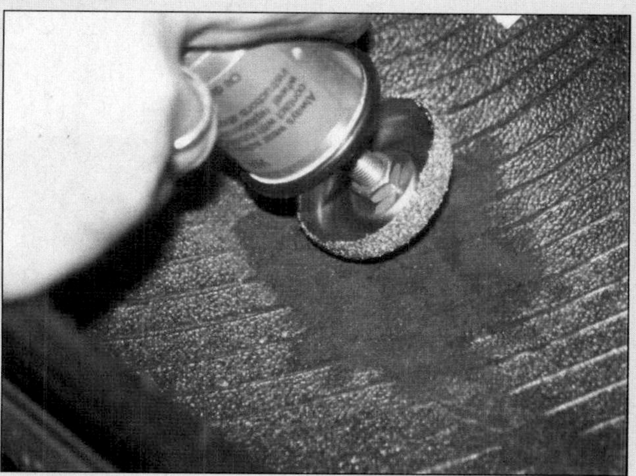

P28–5 The surrounding area is being buffed using an air-powered die grinder equipped with a special buffing tool specifically designed for this process.

P28–6 Rubber cement is then applied to the buffed area.

P28–7 The brush included with the rubber cement makes the job easy. Be sure to cover the entire area around the puncture.

P28–8 Peel off the paper from the adhesive on the patch and insert the tip of the patch through the puncture from the inside of the tire.

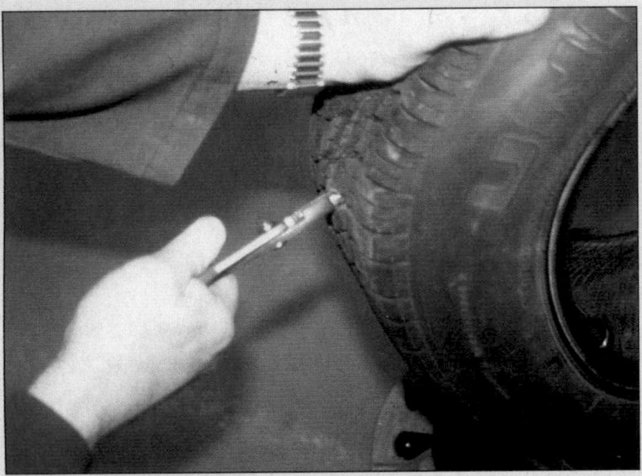

P28–9 Use a pair of pliers to pull the plug of the patch through the puncture.

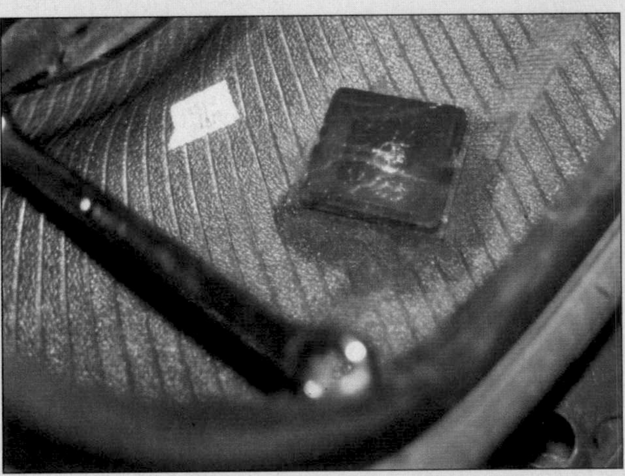

P28–10 A view of the patch on the inside of the tire.

P28–11 To be assured of an air-tight patch, the adhesive of the patch should be "stitched" to the inside of the tire using a serrated roller called a stitching tool.

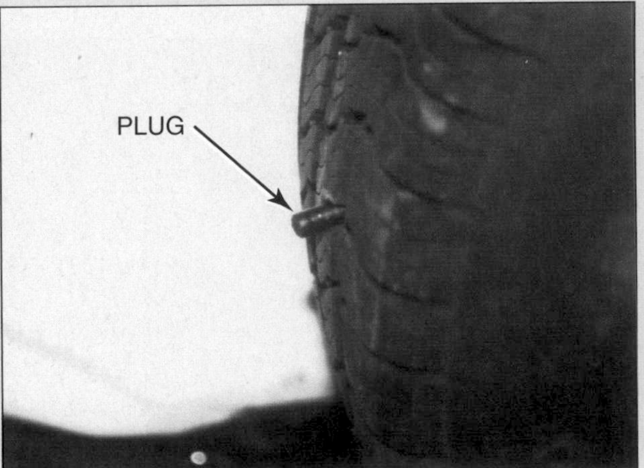

P28–12 A view of the plug from the outside of the tire after the metal covering used to pierce the puncture is removed from the patch plug. The plug can be trimmed to the level of the tread using side cutters or a knife.

SUMMARY

1. All tires are assembled by hand from many different materials and chemical compounds. After the "green" tire is assembled, it is placed into a mould under heat and pressure for about 30 minutes. The tread design and the tire shape are determined by the mould design.
2. New tires have between 7.1 mm (9/32 in.) and 11.9 mm (15/32 in.) tread depth. Wear bars (indicators) show up as a bold strip across the tread of the tire when the tread depth gets down to 1.6 mm (2/32 in.).
3. A 205/75R × 14 92S tire is 205 mm wide at its widest section and is 75% as high as it is wide. The *R* stands for radial-type construction and the tire is designed for a 14 in.-diameter rim. The number 92 is the load index of the tire (the higher the number, the more weight the tire can safely support). The *S* is the speed rating of this tire (S = 180 km/h [112 mph] maximum sustained).
4. The uniform tire-quality grading system is a rating for tread wear (100, 150, etc.), traction (AA, A, B, C), and temperature resistance (A, B, C).
5. Replacement wheels should have the same offset as the factory wheels to prevent abnormal tire wear and/or handling problems.
6. Tires should be rotated every 8000–11 000 km (5000–7000 mi) or at every other oil change.
7. Wheels should always be tightened to the proper torque in a star pattern with a torque wrench.
8. Properly balanced tires prolong tire life. Wheel tramp or an up-and-down-type of vibration results if the tires are statically out of balance or if the tire is out-of-round.
9. Only coated or stick-on type wheel weights should be used on alloy wheels to prevent corrosion damage.

REVIEW QUESTIONS

1. List the various parts of a tire and explain how a tire is constructed.
2. Explain the three major areas of the uniform tire-quality grading system.
3. Explain how to determine the proper tire pressure.
4. Explain bolt circle, wheel diameter, and wheel width.
5. Describe the difference between static and dynamic balance.

RED SEAL CERTIFICATION-TYPE QUESTIONS

1. The *T* in a tire labeled 215/60R × 15 92T means:
   - **a.** Its speed rating
   - **b.** Its tread wear rating
   - **c.** Its load rating
   - **d.** Its temperature resistance rating
2. The 92 in the tire designation in question 1 refers to
   - **a.** Speed rating
   - **b.** Tread wear rating
   - **c.** Load rating
   - **d.** Temperature resistance rating
3. Radial tires can cause a vehicle to pull to one side while driving. This is called "radial tire pull" and is often due to the
   - **a.** Angle of the body (carcass) plies
   - **b.** Tire conicity
   - **c.** Tread design
   - **d.** Bead design
4. Tire inflation is very important to the safe and economical operation of any vehicle. The maximum pressure should be the pressure imprinted
   - **a.** On the door placard
   - **b.** In the owner's manual
   - **c.** In the service manual
   - **d.** All of the above
5. When purchasing replacement tires, do not change tire width by more than
   - **a.** 10 mm stock
   - **b.** 15 mm stock
   - **c.** 20 mm stock
   - **d.** 25 mm stock
6. Wheel lug nuts must be tightened
   - **a.** By hand
   - **b.** With a torque wrench
   - **c.** With an air impact wrench
   - **d.** By hand plus 1/4 turn
7. A tire is worn excessively on both edges. The most likely cause of this type of tire wear is
   - **a.** Overinflation
   - **b.** Underinflation
   - **c.** Excessive radial runout
   - **d.** Excessive lateral runout
8. When seating a bead of a tire, never exceed _____ psi.
   - **a.** 200 kPa (30 psi)
   - **b.** 270 kPa (40 psi)
   - **c.** 335 kPa (50 psi)
   - **d.** 400 kPa (60 psi)
9. For best tire life, most vehicle and tire manufacturers recommend tire rotation every
   - **a.** 5000 km (3000 mi)
   - **b.** 10 000 km (6000 mi)
   - **c.** 15 000 km (9000 mi)
   - **d.** 20 000 km (12 000 mi)
10. The recommended type of wheel weight to use on aluminum (alloy) wheels is
    - **a.** Lead with plated spring steel clips
    - **b.** Coated (painted) lead weights
    - **c.** Lead weights with longer than normal clips
    - **d.** Aluminum weights

41

Steering System Diagnosis and Service

OBJECTIVES: After studying Chapter 41, you should be able to:

1. Prepare for the interprovincial Red Seal certification examination in Appendix IV (Suspension and Steering) on the topics covered in this chapter.
2. Identify steering system components.
3. Describe the operation of a power rack-and-pinion steering system.
4. Describe how to perform a dry park test to determine the condition of steering system components.
5. Perform an under-the-vehicle inspection of the steering system components.
6. Explain how to replace steering linkage parts.
7. Describe manual and power steering diagnosis and repair procedures.

PURPOSE OF STEERING SYSTEMS

The purpose of the steering system is to make the steering wheel and column, steering gear and linkages turn the directional actions of the operator into reality. The steering column will also house systems not related to directional control, like the signal light switch, horn, and other driver safety systems. In the last 12 years, supplemental restraint systems (airbags) have been built into the steering wheel. These will be discussed in other chapters.

The main purpose of the steering wheel and column is to provide the driver with an easy connection to the steering gear, along with a mechanical advantage due to the size of the steering wheel.

The steering gear will convert the radial motion of the steering wheel into an axial motion.

The steering gear will connect to various linkages connected to the steering spindle assembly. This linkage will allow for angle changes caused by uneven road surfaces and steering actions while turning corners.

Some road shock is absorbed through the linkage and gear and in the power assist inside the hydraulic system that can be made part of the steering gear.

THE STEERING COLUMN

The typical vehicle requires about three complete revolutions (turns) of the steering wheel to rotate the front wheels from full left to full right. The front wheels rotate up to 45° while turning. The steering wheel is bolted to a splined shaft in the steering column. Since the late 1960s, the steering column and shaft are sectional and are designed to collapse in the event of an accident. See Figures 41–1 and 41–2 for an example of the many different sections and parts contained in a typical steering column.

Intermediate Shaft

Steering forces are transferred from the steering column to an **intermediate shaft** and a **flexible coupling** and then to the stub shaft of the steering gear or rack-and-pinion unit. The flexible coupling is also called a **rag joint** or **steering coupling disc** and is used to prevent the transfer of noise, vibration, and harshness from the steering components up through the steering column to the driver. Many steering systems use one or more U-joints between the steering column and the steering gear, as shown in Figure 41–3.

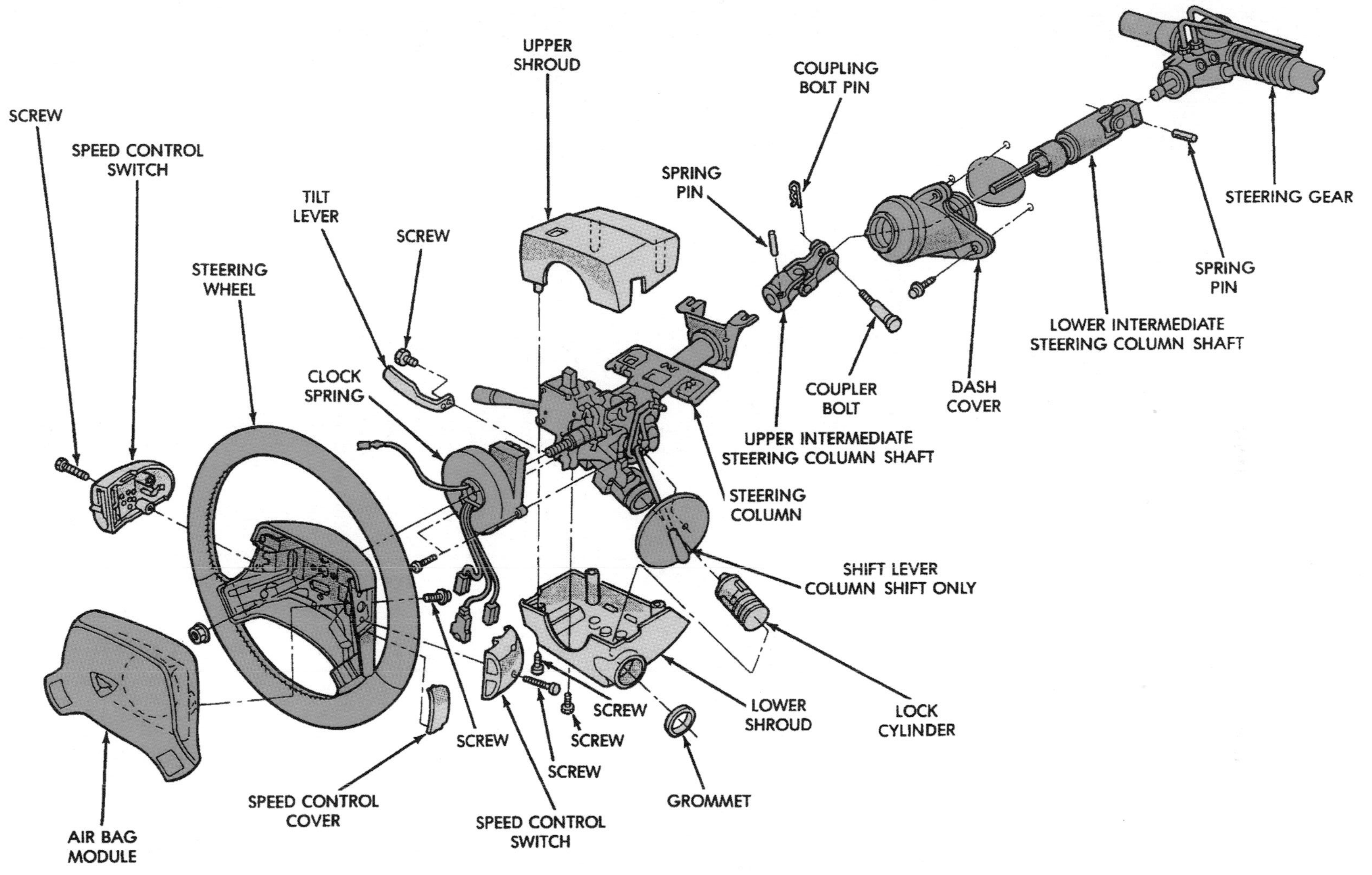

Figure 41–1 Typical steering column and related components. (Courtesy of Chrysler Corporation)

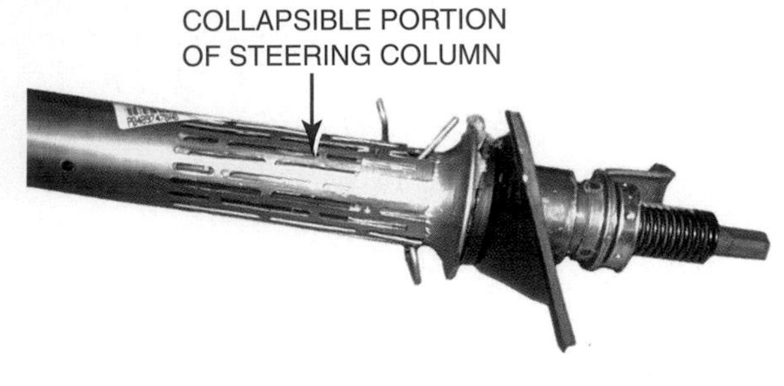

Figure 41–2 The outer housing of many steering columns is designed to collapse in the event of a frontal collision.

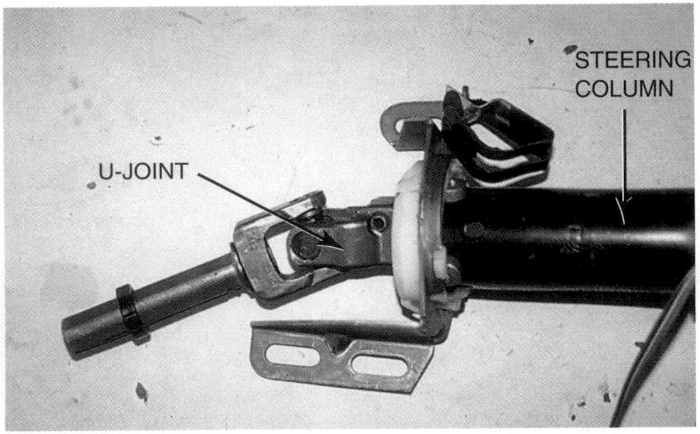

Figure 41–3 The left end of the steering column slips over the input shaft of the steering gear. The U-joint allows the steering column to align with the steering gear.

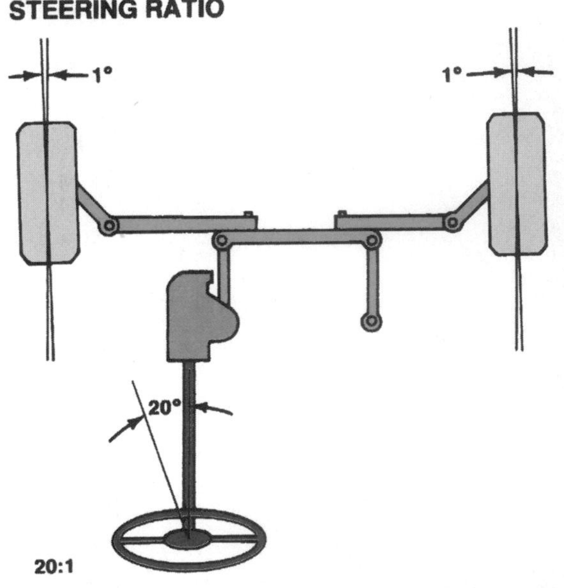

Figure 41–4 Steering ratios allow for easy steering of the front wheels. Low ratios such as 12:1 give quick but stiff steering, whereas high ratios such as 20:1 shown here provide slow but easier steering.

CONVENTIONAL STEERING GEAR

The rotation of the steering wheel is transferred to the front wheels through a steering gear and linkage. See Figure 41–4. The intermediate shaft is splined to a **worm gear** inside a conventional steering gear. Around the worm gear is a nut with gear teeth that mesh with the teeth on a section of a gear called a **sector gear.** The sector gear is part of a **pitman shaft,** also known as a **sector shaft.** Ball, roller, or needle bearings support the sector shaft and the worm gear shaft depending on the make and model of gear assembly.

As the steering wheel is turned, the movement is transmitted through the steering gear to an arm attached to the bottom end of the pitman shaft. This arm is called the **pitman arm.** Whenever the steering wheel is turned, the pitman arm moves. Since the late 1950s and early 1960s, most manufacturers have used a recirculating ball nut-type design. The term *recirculating ball* comes from the series of ball bearings placed between the input worm shaft and the ball nut. See Figure 41–5.

As the steering wheel turns, the worm shaft rolls inside a set of ball bearings. The movement of the bearings causes the ball nut to move. The ball nut has gear teeth that mesh with the gear teeth of the sector shaft. The sector gear and shaft rotate and move the pitman arm. The pitman arm is connected to steering linkage that moves and steers the front wheels. The rotating steel balls in the ball nut reduce friction by rolling in the nut along the groove in the steering shaft and through a ball guide.

Steering Linkage

Steering linkage relays steering forces from the steering gear to the front wheels. Most conventional steering linkages use the **parallelogram-type design.** A parallelogram is a geometric box shape whose opposite sides are parallel and at an equal distance from one another. A parallelogram-type linkage uses two **tie rods** (left and right), a **centre link** (between the tie rods), an **idler arm** on the passenger side, and a **pitman arm** attached to the steering gear output shaft (pitman shaft). See Figure 41–6.

Other types of steering linkage often used on light trucks and vans include the **cross-steer linkage** and the **Haltenberger linkage.** See Figure 41–7 for a comparison of parallelogram, cross-steer, and Haltenberger-type steering linkage arrangements.

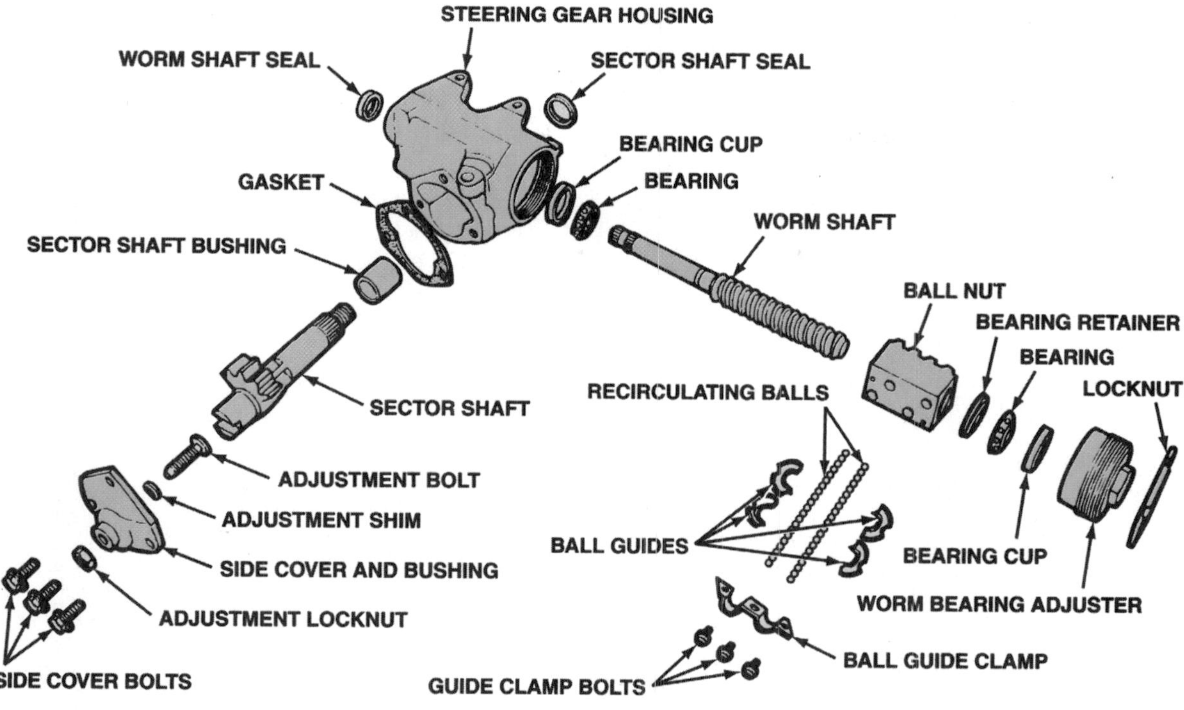

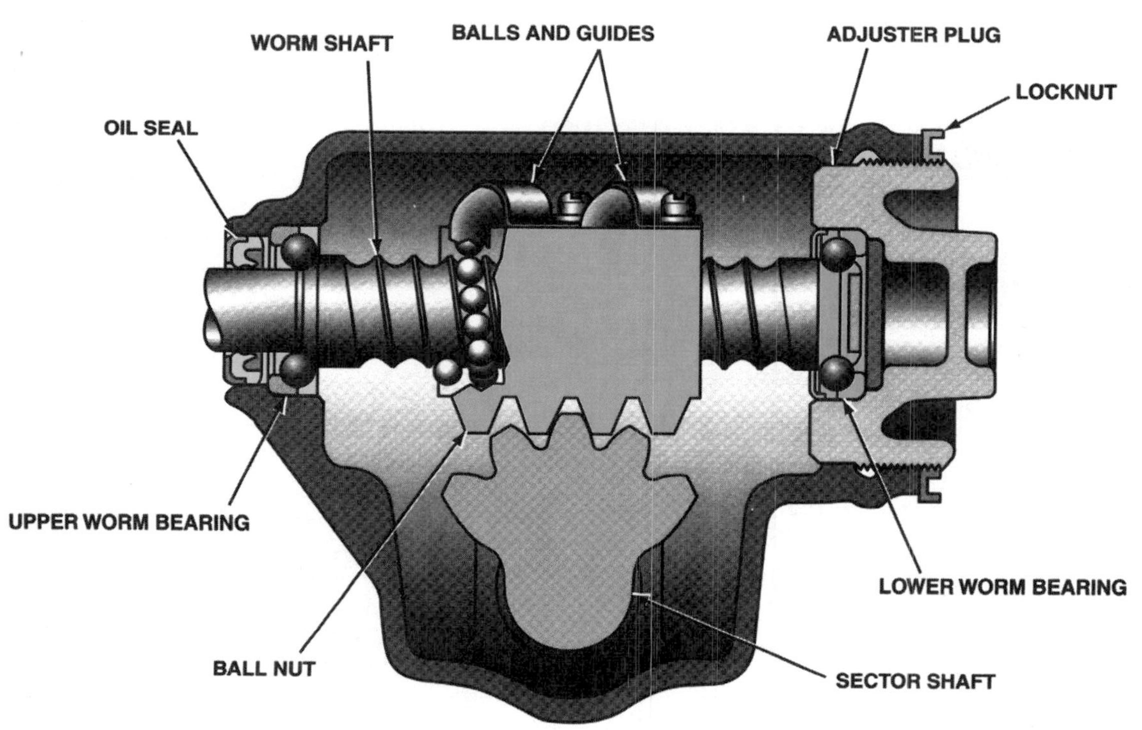

Figure 41–5 Recirculating (moving) steel balls reduce the friction between the worm gear teeth and the ball nut.

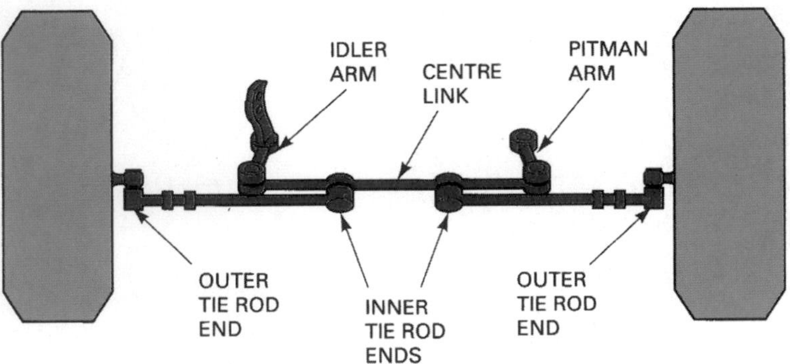

Figure 41–6 Steering movement is transferred from the pitman arm that is splined to the sector shaft (pitman shaft) through the centre link and tie rods to the steering knuckle at each front wheel. The idler arm supports the passenger side of the centre link and keeps the steering linkage level with the road. (Courtesy of Dana Corporation Perfect Circle Products)

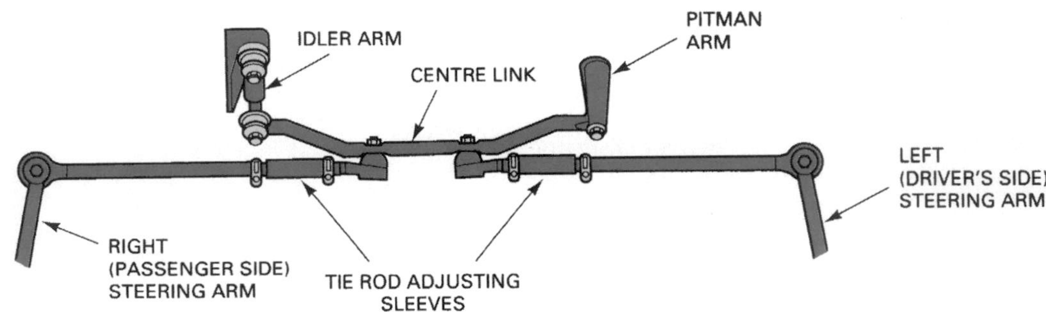

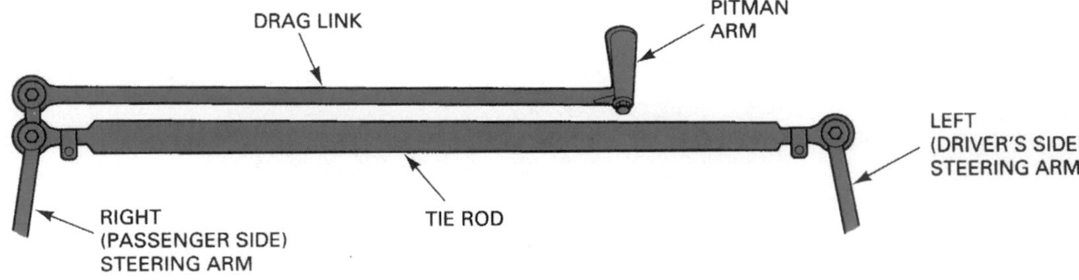

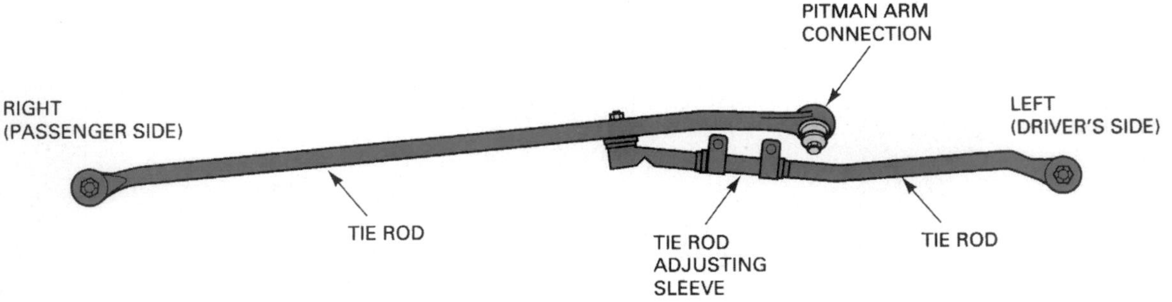

Figure 41–7 Types of steering linkage. Parallelogram steering linkage is commonly used on most rear-wheel drive passenger cars and light trucks. The cross-steer and Haltenberger linkage designs are used on some trucks and vans.

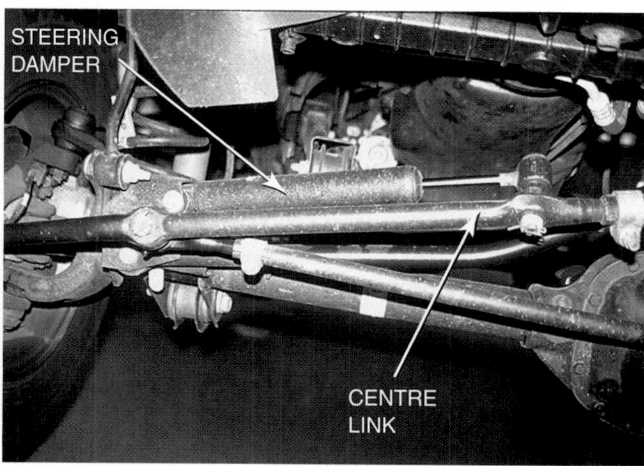

Figure 41–8 This Jeep is equipped with a steering dampener to help prevent steering wheel kickback when the front tires hit uneven ground or rocks or logs that may be encountered during off-road driving.

NOTE: Many light trucks, vans, and some luxury cars use a steering dampener attached to the linkage. A *steering dampener* is similar to a shock absorber, and it absorbs and dampens sudden motions in the steering linkage. See Figure 41–8.

Connections between all steering component parts are constructed of small ball-and-socket joints. These joints allow movement from side to side to provide steering of both front wheels plus the up-and-down movement of joints, which is required for normal suspension travel. It is important that all these joints be lubricated with chassis grease through a **grease fitting,** also called a **zerk fitting,** at least every six months or as per vehicle manufacturer's specifications. See Figure 41–9.

NOTE: The zerk fitting was developed in 1922 by Oscar U. Zerk, an employee of the Alamite Corporation, a manufacturer of pressure lubrication equipment. A zerk or grease fitting is also known as an Alamite fitting.

Some vehicles come equipped with sealed joints and do not require periodic servicing. Since the early 1980s, Ford Motor Company has used tie rod ends that have rubber bonded to the steel ball stud. Since there is no sliding friction inside the tie rod end, no lubrication is needed or required. This type of tie rod end is called **RBS,** meaning **rubber-bonded socket.** See Figure 41–10.

CAUTION: RBS tie rods should never be lubricated. The grease will cause the rubber to deteriorate in the joint and can cause the tie rod to separate.

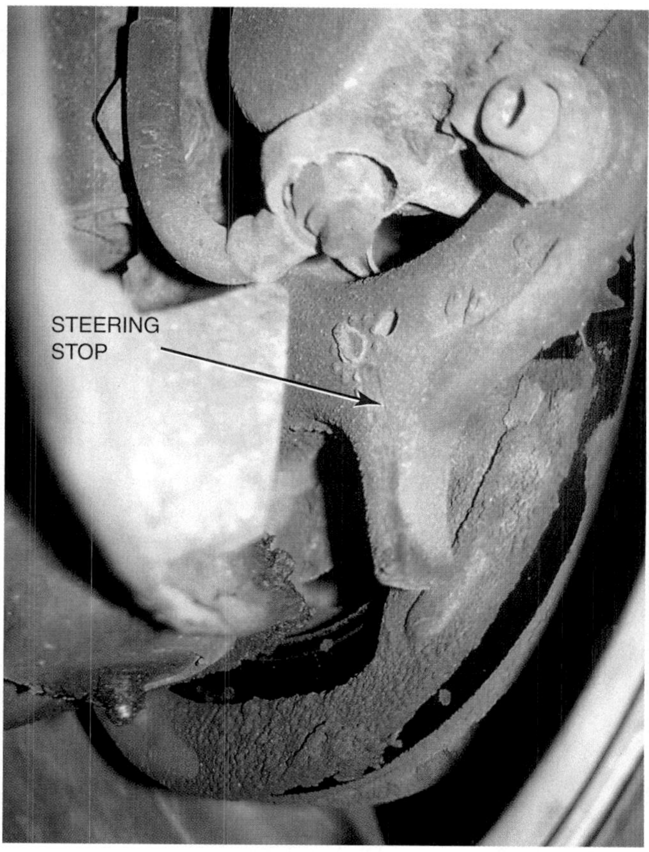

Figure 41–9 Part of steering linkage lubrication is applying grease to the steering stops. If these stops are not lubricated, a grinding sound may be heard when the vehicle hits a bump when the wheels are turned all the way one way or the other. This often occurs when driving into or out of a driveway that has a curb.

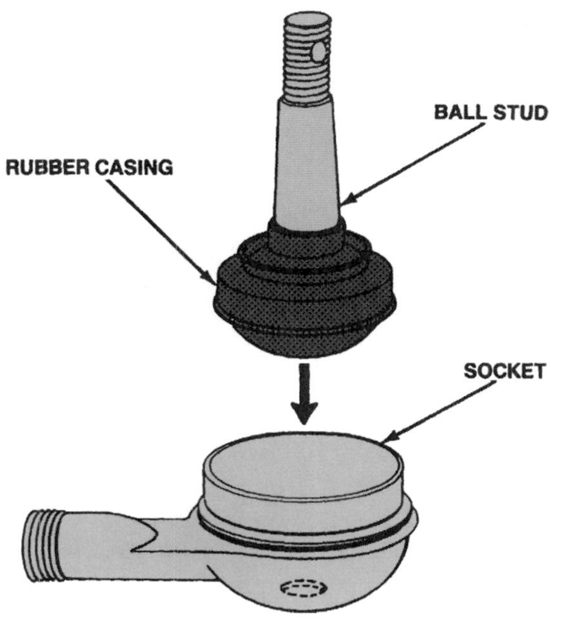

Figure 41–10 The ball stud of a rubber bonded socket (RBS) joint fits tightly into the socket. The hole in the socket allows air to escape as the ball stud is installed.

MANUAL RACK-AND-PINION STEERING

A rack-and-pinion steering unit consists of a **pinion gear** that is in mesh with a flat gear called a **rack.** The ends of the rack are connected to the front wheels through tie rods. Turning the steering wheel rotates the pinion and causes the rack to move left and right in the housing. The rack housing attaches to the body or frame of the vehicle by rubber bushings to help isolate noise and vibration. The steering forces act in a straight line and provide direct steering action with no wasted motion. See Figures 41–11 and 41–12.

Rack-and-pinion steering is lightweight and small in size. The inner tie rod ends attach to the rack with a ball-and-socket joint. This ball-and-socket joint is held to the end of the rack by a soft pin, a roll pin, or a stacked flange. See Figure 41–13.

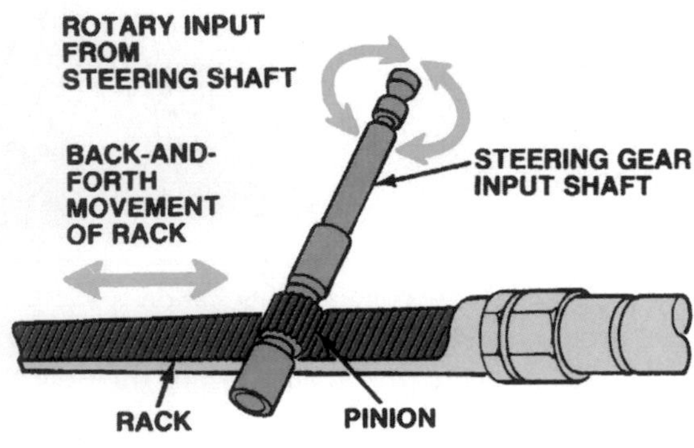

Figure 41–11 As the driver rotates the steering wheel, the input shaft and the pinion gear also rotate. The pinion gear is in mesh with flat teeth cut into the rack, which is connected to the front wheels.

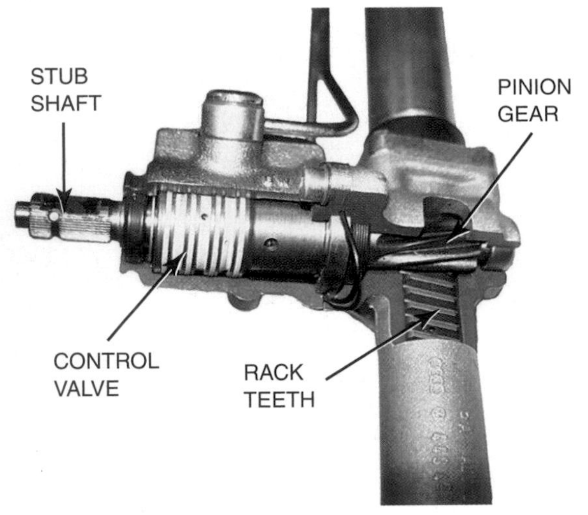

Figure 41–12 A cutaway showing the inside of a typical power rack and pinion steering gear.

POWER STEERING PUMPS

Power-assisted steering, commonly called *power steering,* allows the use of faster steering ratios and reduced steering wheel turning force. A typical power steering system only requires 0.9 to 1.6 kg (2 to 3.5 lb) of effort to turn the steering wheel.

Most power steering systems use an engine-driven hydraulic pump. Power steering hydraulic pumps are usually belt driven from the front crankshaft pulley of the engine, as shown in Figure 41–14.

The drive pulley of the power steering pump is usually fitted to a chrome-plated shaft with a press fit. The shaft is applied to a **rotor** with **vanes** that rotate between a **thrust plate** and a **pressure plate.** See Figure 41–15. Some power steering pumps are of the slipper or roller design instead of the vane type. See Figure 41–16. With a vane-type pump, centrifugal force and hydraulic pressure push the vanes of the rotor outward into contact with the **pump ring.** The shape of the pump ring causes a change in the volume of fluid between the vanes. As the volume increases, the pressure is decreased in the space between the vanes and draws in fluid from the pump reservoir. When the volume between the vanes decreases, the pressure is increased and flows out the pump discharge port. See Figure 41–17.

Flow Control Valve Operation

Between the pump discharge ports and the outlet fitting of the pump is the **flow control valve.** The operation of the flow control valve is determined by the needs of the power steering gear or rack. When the engine speed is increased, the volume and pressure output of the power steering pump increases.

Recirculating the power steering fluid back through the pump reduces the power required by the pump and keeps the fluid temperature from increasing, while still supplying adequate flow for proper power steering operation. The power steering fluid temperature still can reach 150°C (300°F), and a power steering fluid cooler is used on many vehicles. See Figure 41–18.

When the steering wheel is turned all the way to the left or right, the valve in the steering gear is closed off, shutting off flow from the pump. This causes the pressure to rise rapidly. A pressure relief valve inside the flow control valve prevents the pressure from building higher and acts as a safety valve.

INTEGRAL POWER STEERING GEAR OPERATION

With power-assisted steering, the driver effort is always in proportion to the force necessary to turn the front wheels. The hydraulic pump pressurizes

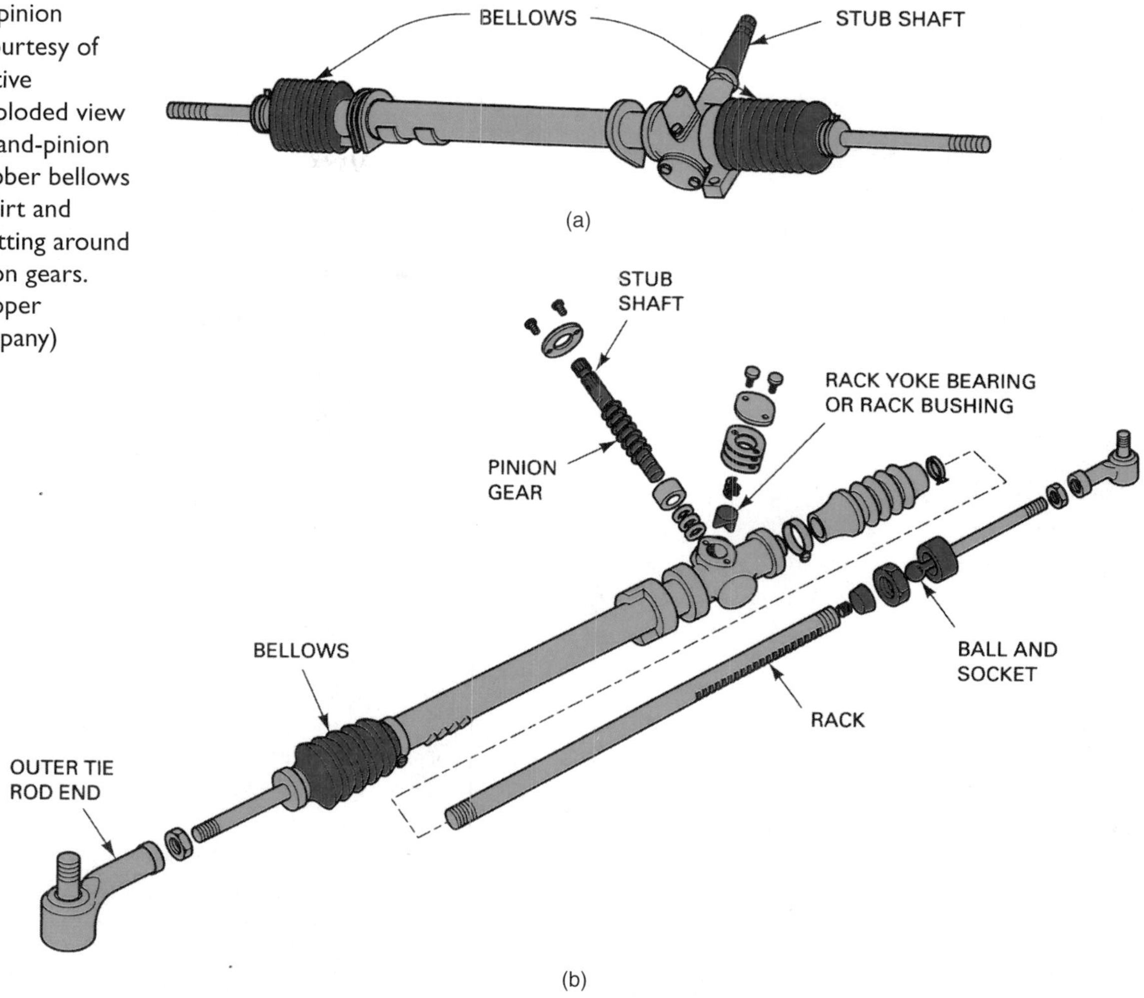

Figure 41–13 (a) Typical manual rack-and-pinion steering unit. (Courtesy of Cooper Automotive Company) (b) Exploded view of a manual rack-and-pinion assembly. The rubber bellows (boots) prevent dirt and moisture from getting around the rack and pinion gears. (Courtesy of Cooper Automotive Company)

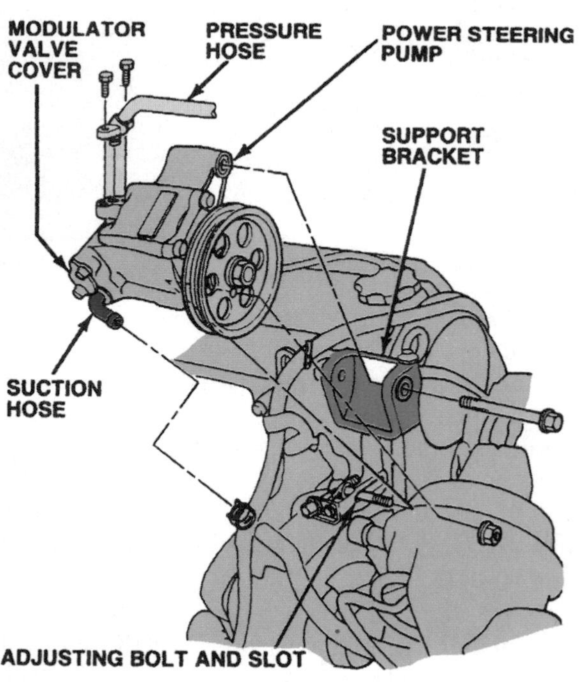

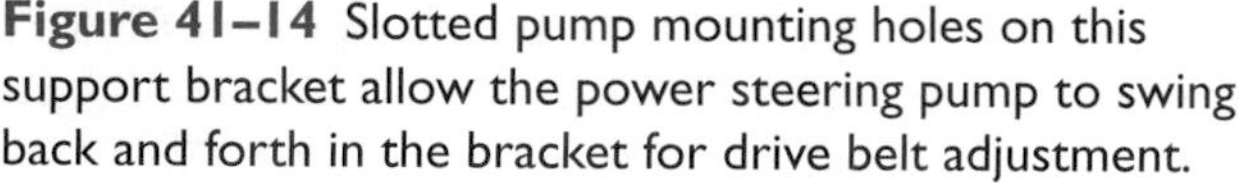

Figure 41–14 Slotted pump mounting holes on this support bracket allow the power steering pump to swing back and forth in the bracket for drive belt adjustment.

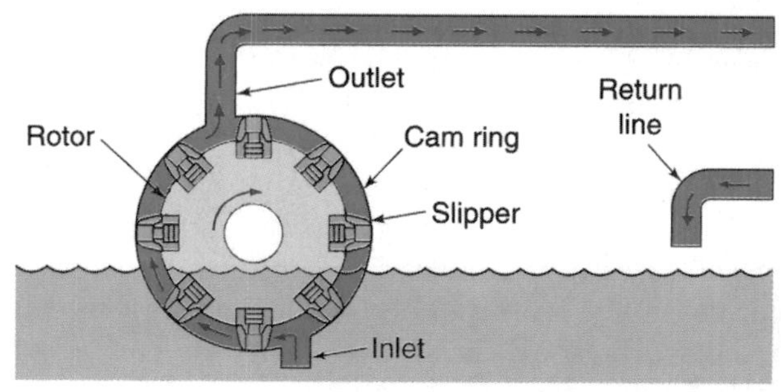

Figure 41–15 Cross sectional view of a submerged power steering pump showing the interior parts. The pump itself is inside (submerged) in the power steering fluid reservoir. (Courtesy of Ford Motor Company)

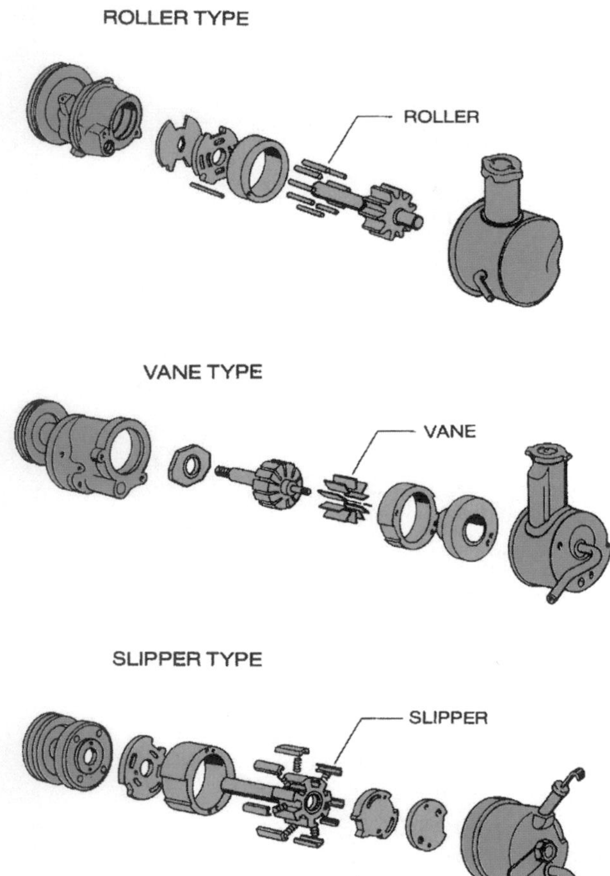

Figure 41–16 Exploded views of the three types of power steering pumps, showing the design and shape of the pumps and reservoirs. (Courtesy of Cooper Automotive Company)

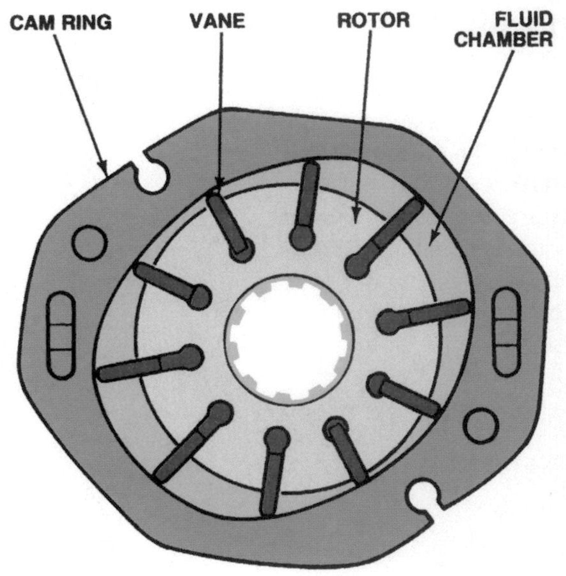

Figure 41–17 Fluid is being driven into the pump around the vanes as volume increases and the pressure is lowered. As the vanes rotate around toward a smaller volume, the pressure of the fluid trapped between the vanes increases as it approaches the discharge port.

Figure 41–18 A typical power steering fluid cooler.

the power steering fluid and sends it through a pressure hose to the steering gear. Manual steering is available if the engine stops running or if there is a loss of hydraulic assist.

Power steering gears are usually called **integral gears** because the power piston or actuator for the power assist is inside (integrated into) the steering gear box. The driver's steering effort is transferred from the steering wheel through the steering column and intermediate shafts to the **stub shaft** or **input shaft** of the gear assembly. (The stub shaft is sometimes called the **spool shaft.**)

The stub shaft connects to the rotary (spool) valve inside the steering gear and directs and controls the flow of pressurized power steering fluid within the gear assembly. The other end of the valve is connected to the worm gear through the torsion bar. As the driver applies force to the steering wheel, the resistance of the tires on the road surface creates a resistive force and the torsion bar twists. This causes a change between the input shaft and the control sleeve, which restricts the flow of power steering fluid and directs the high pressure fluid to one end of the piston in the gear housing. This high pressure forces the piston to move the **sector gear (gear nut** or **rack piston),** which in turn rotates the pitman shaft and pitman arm and assists the turning effort. See Figure 41–19.

POWER RACK-AND-PINION STEERING

Power rack-and-pinion steering is used in many passenger cars as well as in light trucks and vans. Its light weight and small size make it possible to be mounted in a variety of locations. There are two basic designs of rack and pinion used today: the **end-take-off** (Figure 41–20) and the **centre-take-off** (Figure 41–21).

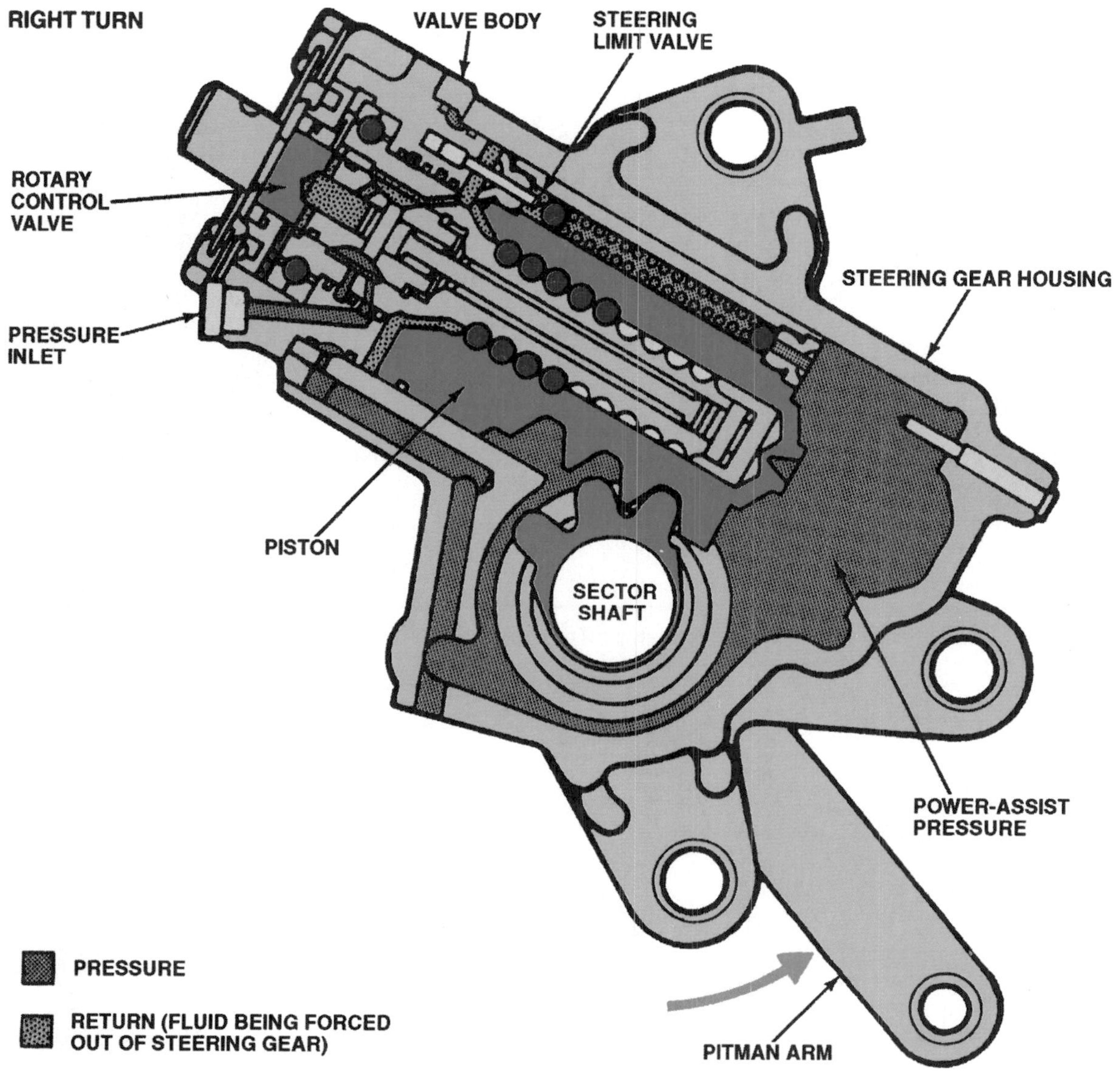

Figure 41–19 The high-pressure fluid from the power steering pump pushes the piston up the worm gear, thereby moving the sector shaft and pitman arm to provide assist during a right turn. The fluid is directed to the top of the piston during a left turn by the control valve.

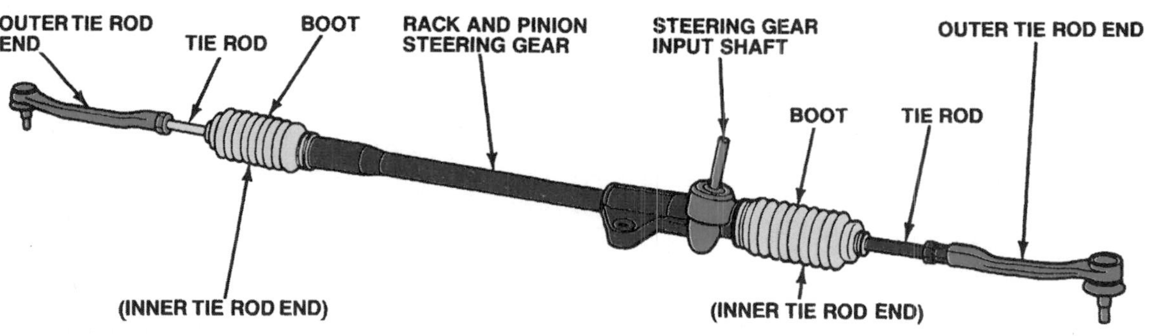

Figure 41–20 This end-take-off rack consists of two tie rod ends and the steering gear. The inner tie rod ends are also called **ball-socket assemblies** on most units.

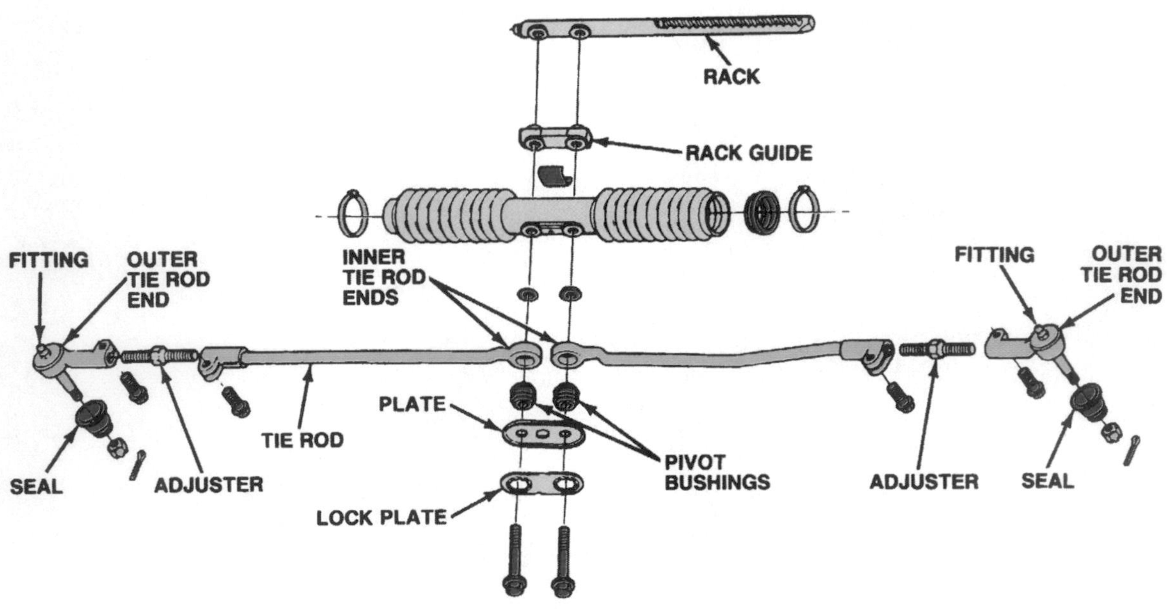

Figure 41–21 The inner tie rod ends attach to the centre rather than the ends on this centre-take-off rack assembly.

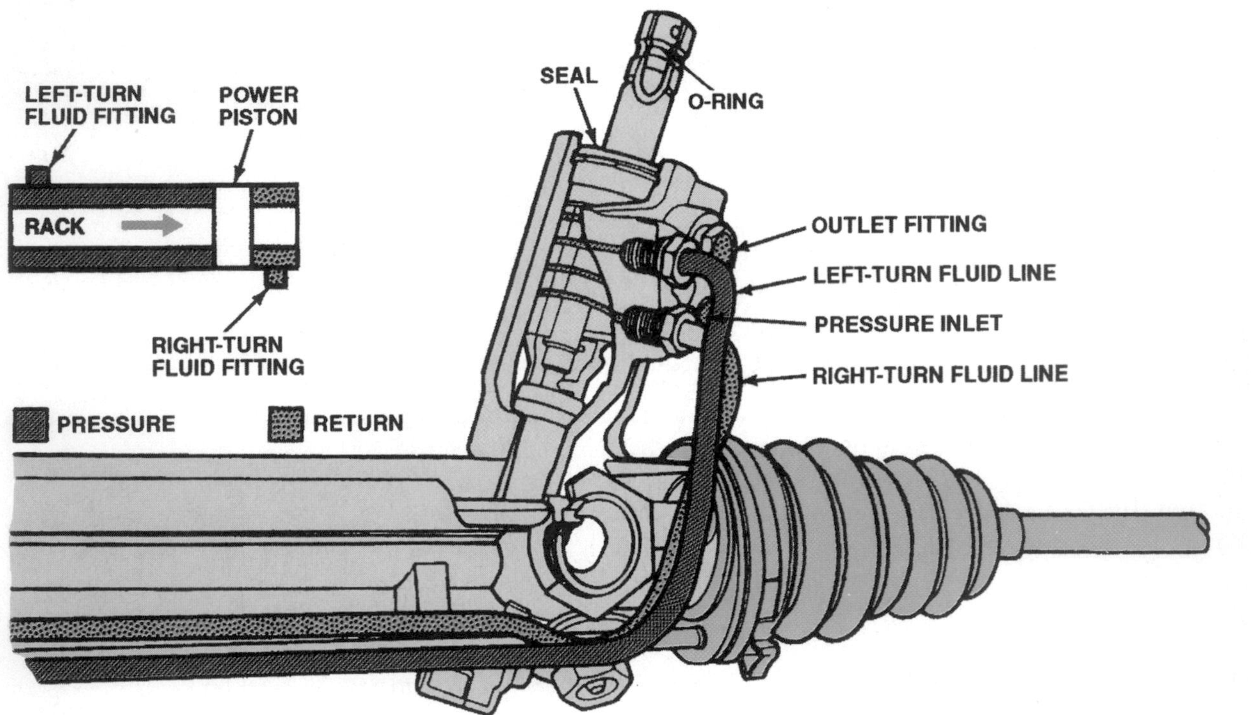

Figure 41–22 During a left turn, the control valve directs high-pressure power steering fluid from the pump into the left-turn fluid line and the rack moves toward the left. Fluid pushed out of the right-turn fluid chamber travels back to the return circuit.

The power steering pump supplies pressurized hydraulic fluid to the top or "hat" section of the unit. The steering column attaches to the stub shaft and turns a rotary spool valve just as in a conventional integral power steering gear. The spool valve assembly directs the pressurized fluid to one side of the rack piston, as shown in Figures 41–22 and 41–23. Fluid from the other side of the rack piston returns to the spool valve area as return fluid. Some power rack-and-pinion steering units use a variable ratio rack. See Figure 41–24.

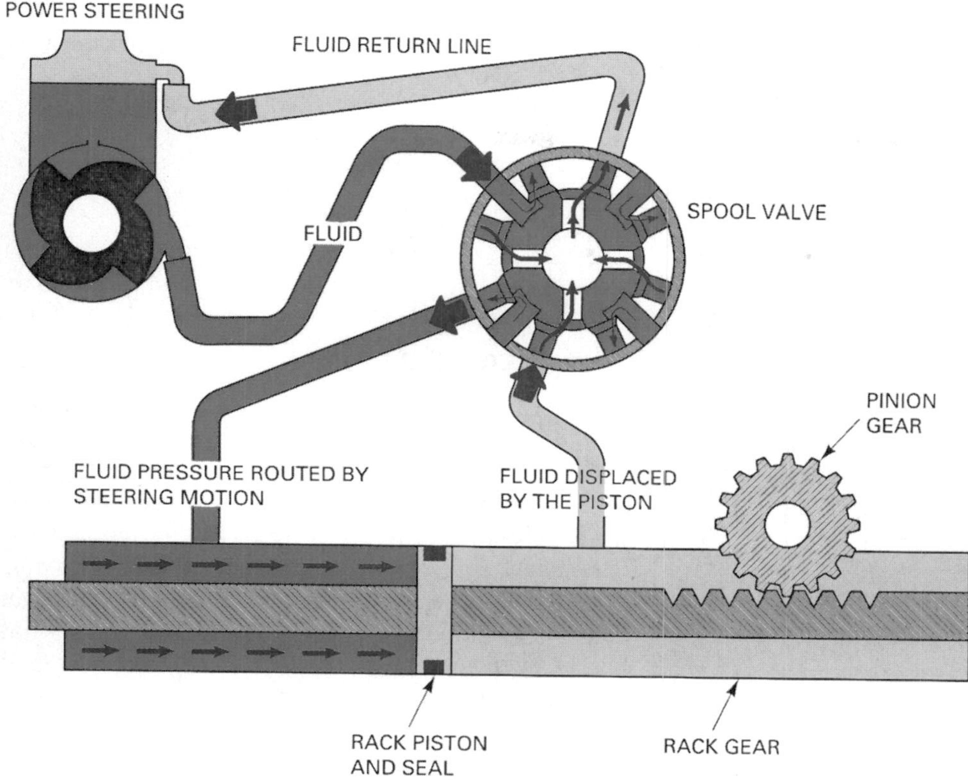

Figure 41–23 An end view of the control (spool) valve showing how pressurized power steering fluid is routed to one side of the rack piston. (Courtesy of John Bean Company)

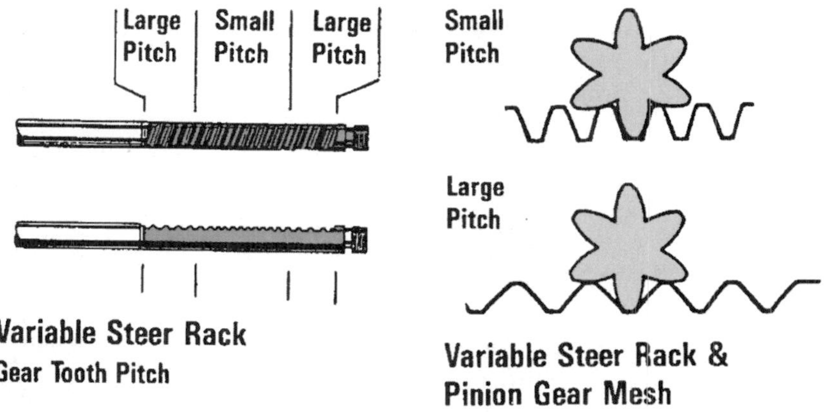

Figure 41–24 Variable ratio in a rack-and-pinion steering unit is accomplished by varying the gear tooth pitch on the rack. (Courtesy of TRW Inc.)

VARIABLE-EFFORT POWER STEERING

Variable-effort power steering uses an electrical control solenoid or motor to control the output volume of the power steering pump. There are two basic designs being used today, the **variable-effort-** and the **two-flow-** or **switched-type.** Figure 41–25 shows a General Motors Magnasteer system that uses a magnetic actuator to control steering wheel effort. Most systems control the outlet flow rate between the power steering pump and the steering gear or rack-and-pinion assembly.

Some variable-effort power steering systems *gradually* change the amount of power steering

Figure 41–25 The vehicle computer controls the effort on this General Motors vehicle equipped with the Magnasteer variable-effort power steering. A scan tool such as the Tech 2 is used to diagnose this system.

DIAGNOSTIC STORY

Simple Answer to a Difficult Problem

An owner of a Japanese sports coupe complained of stiff steering. While driving straight ahead, the steering felt stiff but would suddenly loosen when the steering wheel was turned slightly. This caused the car to dart back and forth and made it difficult to track straight ahead. After many wheel alignments and changes of tires, the real problem was discovered. The U-joint in the steering shaft between the steering column and the flexible steering shaft coupling was defective and binding. This problem was discovered after all other steering components had been replaced at great expense, including the rack-and-pinion steering assembly. It is always best to check everything, including the obvious and the simple items, first before starting to replace parts—especially expensive parts.

assist as the vehicle speed changes, thereby providing a less noticeable change in steering effort. Besides vehicle speed, many *variable-effort* systems use a **steering wheel rotation sensor** to measure rapid steering-wheel movement.

NOTE: The default mode of most variable-effort power steering systems is to allow maximum power assist at all speeds. If, for example, the electrical connector were to become disconnected from the output actuator of the power steering pump, maximum steering assist is available because the orifice size is set to its largest opening.

Power Steering Computer Sensor

The typical power steering sensor switch is a pressure switch that completes an electrical circuit to the computer (controller) whenever the power steering pressure exceeds a certain point, usually about 2000 kPa (300 psi). As the pressure of the power steering increases, the load on the engine increases. The purpose of the switch is to signal the computer that an additional load is being placed on the engine so that the idle speed can be increased to prevent the engine from stalling during slow-speed parking or steering manoeuvres.

STEERING SYSTEM INSPECTION

Dry Park Test

Since many steering (and suspension) components do *not* have *exact* specifications for replacement purposes, it is extremely important that the beginning service technician work closely with an experienced technician. Although most technicians can determine when a steering component such as a tie rod end is definitely in need of replacement, often marginally worn parts are hard to spot and can lead to handling problems. One of the most effective yet easy-to-perform steering-component-inspection methods is called the **dry park test.**

This simple test is performed with the vehicle on the ground or on a drive-on ramp-type hoist by moving the steering wheel back and forth *slightly* while an assistant feels for movement at each section of the steering system. The technician can check for any looseness in the steering linkage starting either at the outer tie rod ends and working toward the steering column or from the steering column toward the outer tie rod ends. It is important to check each and every joint and component of the steering system. See Figure 41–26.

Under-Vehicle Inspection

After checking the steering system components as part of a dry park test, hoist the vehicle and perform

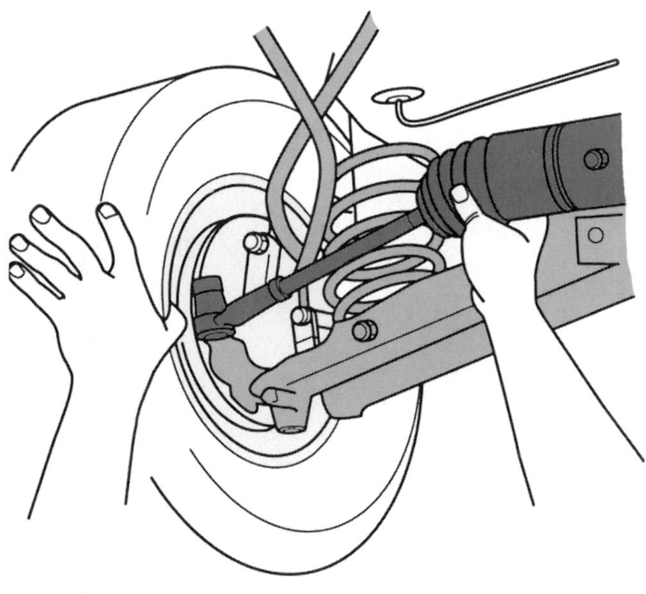

Figure 41–26 All joints should be felt during a dry park test. Even inner tie rod ends (ball-socket assemblies) can be felt through the rubber bellows on many rack-and-pinion steering units.

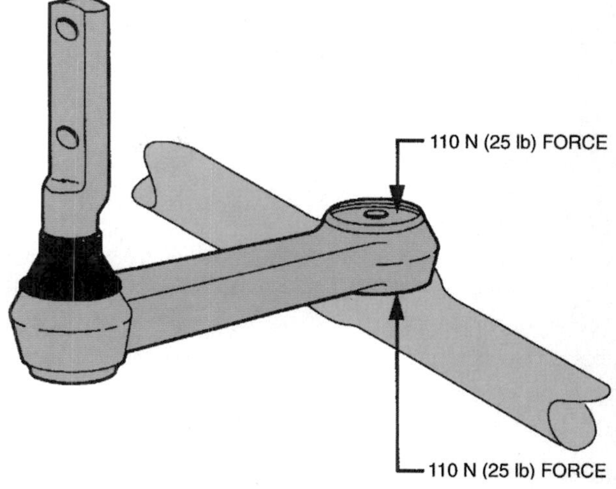

Figure 41–27 Idler arms should be checked by hand only. Do not use a pry bar to check for excessive wear or too much force will be exerted, which could cause the arm to move more than specified (usually 6 mm [1/4 in.] total). (Courtesy of Dana Corporation, Perfect Circle Products)

TECH TIP

The Killer B's

The three B's that can cause steering and suspension problems include bent, broken, or binding components. Always inspect each part under the vehicle for each of the killer B's.

a thorough part-by-part inspection. This thorough inspection includes

1. Inspecting each part for damage due to accident or bending due to hitting an object in the roadway.

CAUTION: Never straighten bent steering linkage. Always replace with new parts.

2. Inspecting the idler arm by using *hand* force of 110 N (25 lb) up and down on the arm. If the movement exceeds 6 mm (1/4 in.), the idler arm should be replaced. See Figure 41–27.
3. Testing all other steering linkage *by hand* for any vertical or side-to-side looseness. It is normal for tie rods to rotate in their sockets when the tie rod sleeve is rocked. *End play in any tie rod should be zero.* Many tie rods are spring loaded to help keep the ball-and-socket joint free of play as the joint wears.
4. Testing all steering components with the wheels in the straight-ahead position. When the wheels are turned, some apparent looseness may be noticed due to the angle of the steering linkage.

CAUTION: Do not turn the front wheels of the vehicle while it is suspended on a lift to check for looseness in the steering linkage. The extra leverage of the wheel and tire assembly can cause a much greater force being applied to the steering components than can be exerted by hand alone. This extra force may cause some apparent movement in good components that may not need to be replaced.

Steering Linkage Replacement

When replacing any steering system component, it is best to replace all defective and marginally good components at the same time. Replacing steering system components involves these steps:

Step 1. Hoist the vehicle safely with the wheels in the straight-ahead position. Remove the front wheels, if necessary, to gain access to the components.

Step 2. Loosen the retainer nut on tapered components, such as tie rod ends. Use a tie rod re-

DIAGNOSTIC STORY

Bump Steer

Bump steer or *orbital steer* are terms used to describe what occurs when the steering linkage is not level, causing the front tires to turn inward or outward as the wheels and suspension move up and down. (Automotive chassis engineers call it *roll steer.*) The vehicle's direction is changed *without moving the steering wheel* whenever the tires move up and down over bumps, dips in the pavement, or even over gentle rises!

This author experienced bump steer once and will never forget the horrible feeling of not having control of the vehicle. After replacing an idler arm and aligning the wheels, everything was okay until about 65 km/h (40 mph); then the vehicle started darting from one lane of the freeway to another. Because there were no bumps as such, bump steer was not considered as a cause. Even when holding the steering wheel perfectly still and straight ahead, the vehicle would go left then right. Did a tie rod break? It certainly felt like that's exactly what happened. I slowed down to below 50 km/h (30 mph) and returned to the shop.

After several hours of checking everything, including the alignment, I discovered that the idler arm was not level with the pitman arm. This caused a pull on the steering linkage whenever the suspension moved up and down. As the suspension compressed, the steering linkage pulled inward on the tie rod on that side of the vehicle. As the wheel moved inward (toed in), it created a pull just as if the wheel was turned by the driver.

This is why all steering linkage *must* be parallel with the lower control arm. The reason for the bump steer was that the idler arm bolted to the frame was slotted vertically. I didn't pay any attention to the location of the original idler arm and simply bolted the replacement to the frame. After raising the idler arm back up where it belonged (about 1.3 cm or 1/2 in.), the steering problem was corrected. See Figure 41–28.

Other common causes of bump steer are worn or deteriorated rack mounting bushings, noncentred steering linkage, or a bent steering linkage. If the steering components are not level, any bump or dip in the road will cause the vehicle to steer in one direction or the other.

Always carefully check the steering system whenever a customer complains about any weird handling problem.

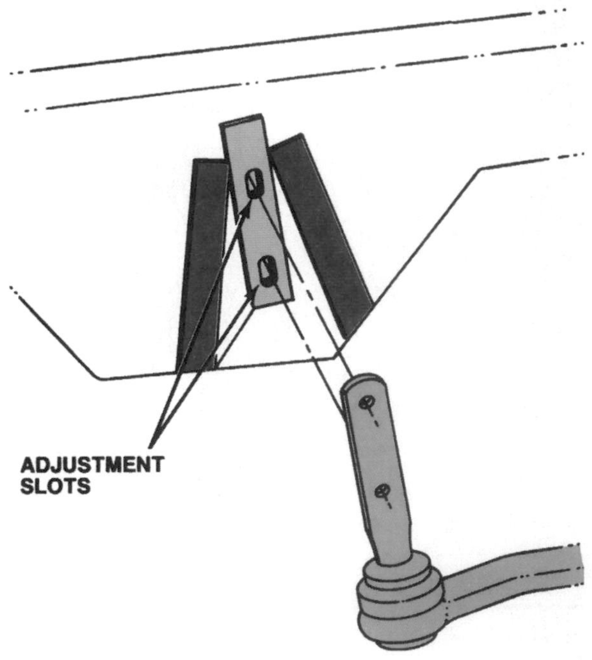

Figure 41–28 On some vehicles, elongated mounting bolt holes in the frame permit changing the position of the idler arm so the steering linkage is level. This is called parallelism and is used to correct bump steer.

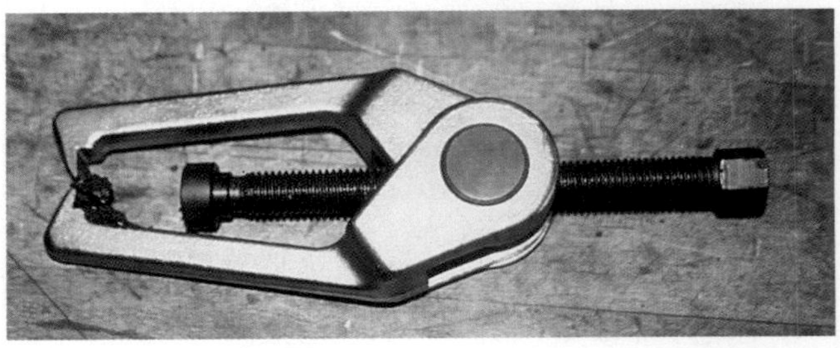

Figure 41–29 A typical tie rod end removal tool. After the attaching nut has been loosened and removed, the tool is used to separate the tapered tie rod end from the steering knuckle by simply tightening the screw on the puller with a wrench or socket.

moval puller or taper breaker, as shown in Figure 41–29.

Two hammers can also be used to separate tie rod ends. Place one hammer behind the tie rod as a backing support while tapping the side of the tie rod end with the other hammer. The shock from the hammer blows will distort the taper and the tie rod end will be knocked loose. Do not pound on the bolt.

CAUTION: Vehicle manufacturers often warn about using a tapered "pickle fork" tool to separate tapered parts. The wedge tool can tear the grease seal and damage both the part being removed and the adjoining part.

Pitman arms require a large puller to remove the pitman arm from the splines of the pitman shaft. See Figure 41–30.

Step 3. Replace the part using the hardware and fasteners supplied with the replacement part.

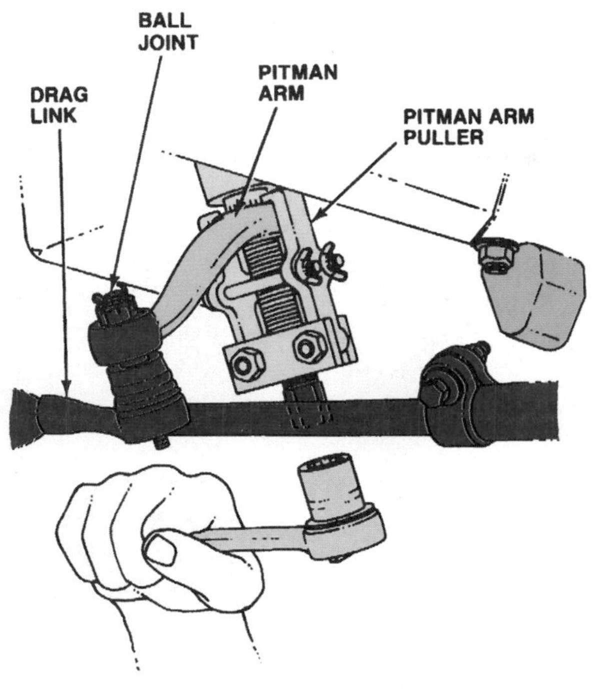

Figure 41–30 A pitman arm puller is used to separate the splined fitting between the pitman arm and the steering gear sector shaft.

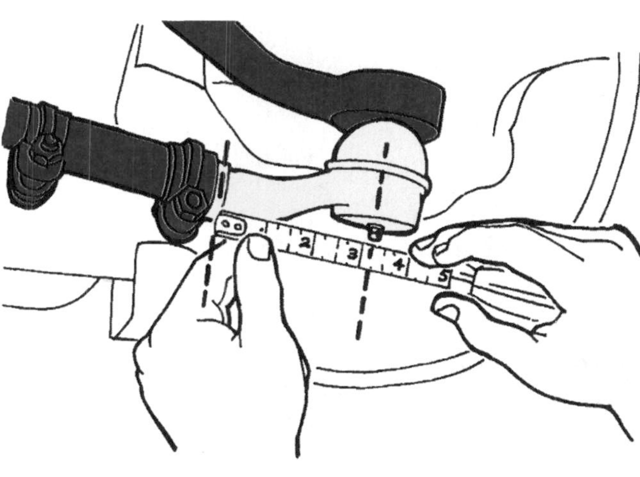

Figure 41–31 Replacement tie rods should be installed with the same length as the originals. Measure from the edge of the tie rod sleeve to the centre of the grease fitting. When the new tie rod is threaded to this dimension, the toe setting will be close to the original. (Courtesy of Dana Corporation, Perfect Circle Products)

CAUTION: Do not reuse precrimped torque prevailing nuts used as original factory equipment on many tie rod ends.

CAUTION: Whenever tightening the nuts of tapered parts, such as tie rods, DO NOT loosen them after reaching the proper assembly torque in order to align the cotter key hole. If the cotter key does not fit, TIGHTEN the nut further until the hole lines up for the cotter key.

When replacing tie rod ends, use the adjusting sleeve to adjust the total length of the tie rod to the same position and length as the original. Measure the original length of the tie rods and assemble the replacement tie rod(s) to the same overall length. See Figures 41–31 through 41–33.

NOTE: On Ford vehicles that use rubber-banded socket-type (RBS) tie rods, be sure that the wheels are pointed straight ahead when the tie rods are installed and tightened. If the wheels were turned, the vehicle may pull in the direction the wheels were turned because the rubber has a "memory" and can apply force to the steering linkage.

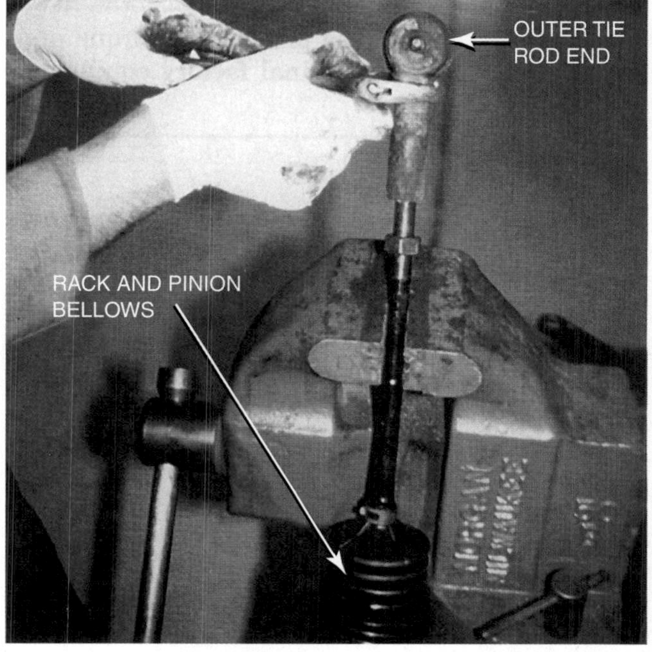

Figure 41–32 Installing an outer tie rod end on a rack-and-pinion steering gear unit. This is being done on a workbench because the rack-and-pinion unit is new and the outer tie rod ends were replaced just six months before it was discovered that the rack and pinion unit was leaking from many different places.

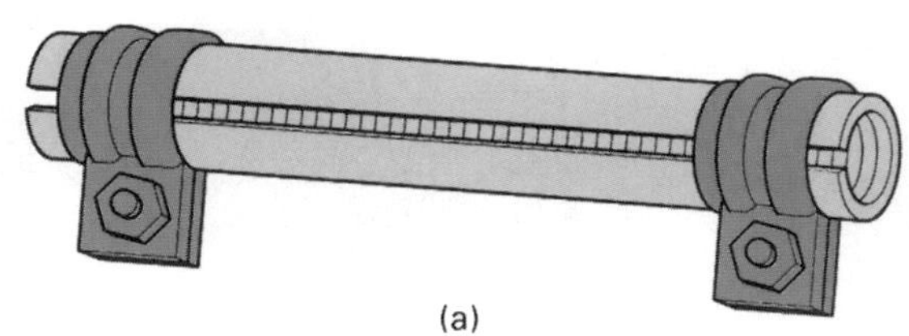

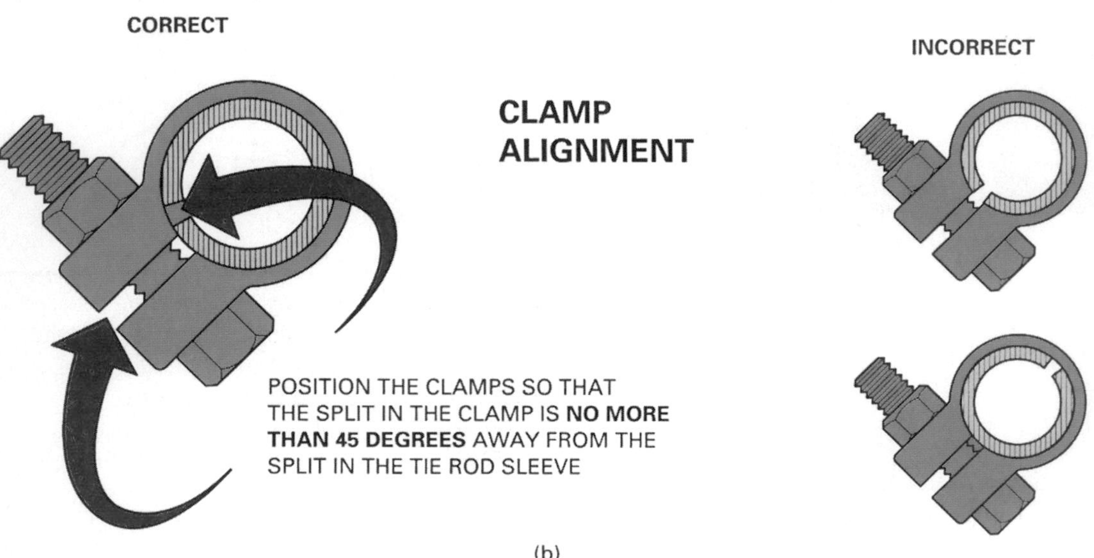

Figure 41–33 (a) Tie rod adjusting sleeve. (Courtesy of Dana Corporation, Perfect Circle Products) (b) Be sure to position the clamp correctly on the sleeve. (Courtesy of John Bean Company)

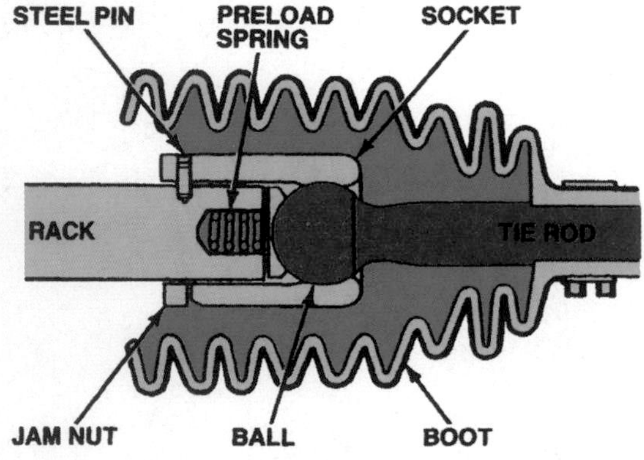

Figure 41–34 On rack and pinion steering, the end of the inner tie rod forms the ball and a separate socket fits over the ball and anchors the tie rod to the rack. This is called a ball-socket assembly.

Inner tie-rod end assemblies used on rack-and-pinion steering units require special consideration and often special tools. The inner tie rod end (ball socket assembly) should be replaced whenever there is any noticeable free play in the ball-and-socket joint. See Figure 41–34.

TECH TIP 

Jounce/Rebound Test

All steering linkage should be level and work at the same angle as the suspension arms. A simple test to check these items is performed as follows:

1. Park on a level, hard surface with the wheels straight ahead and the steering wheel in the unlocked position.
2. Bounce or jounce the vehicle up and down at the front bumper while watching the steering wheel. The steering wheel should *not* move.

If the steering wheel moves while the vehicle is being bounced, look for a possible bent steering linkage, suspension arm, or steering rack.

POWER STEERING DIAGNOSIS AND TROUBLESHOOTING

Power steering systems are generally very reliable, yet many problems are caused by not correcting simple service items such as

1. *A loose, worn, or defective power steering drive belt,* including serpentine belts. This can cause jerky steering and belt noise, especially when turning.

> **NOTE:** Do not guess at the proper belt tension. Always use a belt tension gauge or observe the marks on the tensioner. Always apply force on the pump at the proper location to prevent damage to the pump. See Figures 41–35 and 41–36.

2. *A bent or misaligned drive pulley* usually caused by an accident or improper reassembly of the power steering pump after an engine repair procedure. This can cause a severe grinding noise whenever the engine is running and may sound like an engine problem.
3. *Low or contaminated power steering fluid* usually caused by a slight leak at the high-pressure hose or defective inner rack seals on a power rack-and-pinion power steering system. This can cause a loud whining noise and lack of normal power steering assist.

TECH TIP 

The "Pinky" Test

Whenever diagnosing any power steering complaint, always check the level *and* condition of the power steering fluid. Often this is best accomplished by putting your finger (pinky) down into the power steering fluid reservoir and pulling it out to observe the texture and colour of the fluid. See Figure 41–37.

A common problem with some power rack-and-pinion units is the wearing of grooves in the housing by the Teflon sealing rings of the spool (control) valve. When this wear occurs, aluminum particles become suspended in the power steering fluid, giving it a grayish colour and also thickening the fluid. Normally, clear power steering fluid is clear, and when it is found to be grayish in colour and when steering is difficult when cold these are clear indications as to what has occurred and why the steering is not functioning correctly.

> **NOTE:** Some vehicles use power steering reservoir caps with *left-hand threads.* Always clean the top of the cap and observe and follow all directions and cautions. Many power steering pump reservoirs and caps have been destroyed by technicians attempting to remove a cap in the wrong direction using large pliers.

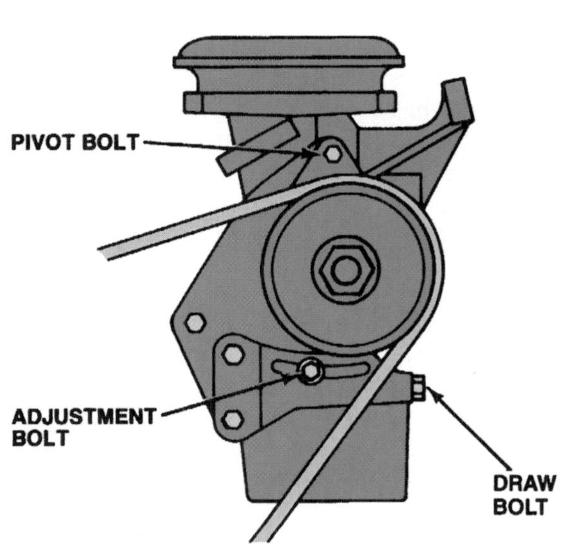

Figure 41–35 To adjust belt tension on this pump, loosen the adjustment bolt and turn the draw bolt to pivot the assembly on its bracket.

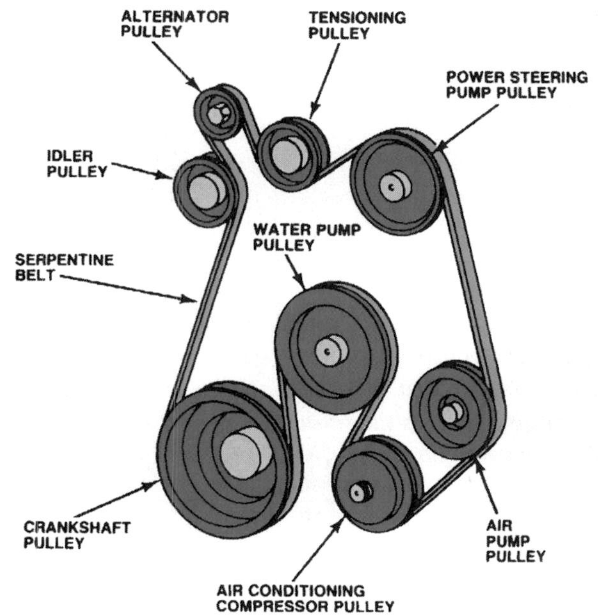

Figure 41–36 On this serpentine belt system, spring force of an automatic belt tensioning pulley applies pressure to the belt to ensure correct tension.

Figure 41–37 If the power steering fluid is black or silver, it is contaminated with aluminum worn from the steering gear.

4. *Broken or loose power steering pump mounting brackets.* In extreme cases, the pump mounting bolts can be broken, which can cause jerky steering. It is important to carefully inspect the pump mounting brackets and hardware when diagnosing a steering-related problem. The brackets tend to crack at the adjustment points and pivot areas. Tighten all the hardware to ensure that the belt will remain tight and not slip and cause noise or a power-assist problem.
5. *Under-inflated tires.*
6. *Engine idle speed below specifications.*
7. *A defective power steering pressure switch.* If this switch fails, the computer will not increase engine idle speed while turning.
8. *Internal steering gear mechanical binding.*

As part of a complete steering system inspection and diagnosis, a steering wheel turning effort test should be performed. The power steering force, as measured by a spring scale during turning, should be less than 2.3 kg (5 lb).

Power Steering Fluid

The correct power steering fluid is *critical* to the operation and service life of the power steering system! The *exact* power steering fluid to use varies as to vehicle manufacturer and sometimes from model to model of the same manufacturer because of differences among steering component manufacturers. See Figures 41–38 and 41–39.

NOTE: Remember, multiple purpose power steering fluid does not mean *all*-purpose power steering fluid. Always consult the power steering reservoir cap, service manual, or owner's manual for the exact fluid to be used in the vehicle being serviced.

Bleeding Air out of the Power Steering System

If the power steering fluid is pink (if ATF is the power steering fluid) or tan (if clear power steering fluid is

Figure 41–38 Some power steering fluid is unique to the climate, such as this cold climate fluid recommended for use in General Motors vehicles when temperatures are low.

Figure 41–39 Refilling a power steering reservoir after replacing the rack-and-pinion steering gear assembly. Notice that the technician is pouring the clean power steering fluid from a container with the outlet toward the top. This is the correct way to pour from a container of this design because it allows air to get into the container, which allows the liquid in the container to flow smoothly.

used), there may be air bubbles trapped in the fluid. Stop the engine and allow the air to "burp" out to the surface for several minutes. Lift the front tires off the ground and rotate the steering wheel left and right with the engine off. This prevents the breaking up of large air bubbles into thousands of smaller bubbles, which are more difficult to bleed out of the system.

NOTE: Some vehicle manufacturers recommend that the engine be cranked or started and allowed to idle during the bleeding procedure. All vehicle manufacturers recommend bleeding the system with the front tires off the ground.

Power Steering Pump Service

Some power steering pump service can usually be performed without removing the pump, including replacing the high-pressure and return hoses, and removing and cleaning the flow control valve assembly (see Figure 41–40). Most power steering pump service requires the removal of the pump from the engine mounting and/or removal of the drive pulley. See Figure 41–41.

NOTE: Most replacement pumps are not equipped with a pulley. The old pulley must be removed and installed on the new pump. The old pulley should be carefully inspected for dents, cracks, or warpage. If the pulley is damaged, it must be replaced. The pulley must be removed and installed with a pulley removal and installation tool.

CAUTION: Do not hammer the pump shaft or pulley in an attempt to install the pulley. The shock blows may damage the internal components of the pump or cause the pump to fail due to mislocation of its internal parts.

Pressure Testing

Using a power steering pressure tester,

1. Disconnect the pressure hose at the pump.
2. Connect the leads of the tester to the pump and the disconnected pressure line (see Figure 41–42).
3. Open the valve on the tester.
4. Start the engine; allow the power steering system to reach operating temperatures.
5. The pressure gauge should register 550 to 860 kPa (80 to 125 psi); if the pressure is greater than 1400 kPa (200 psi), check for restrictions in the system, including the operation of the poppet valve located in the inlet of the steering gear.

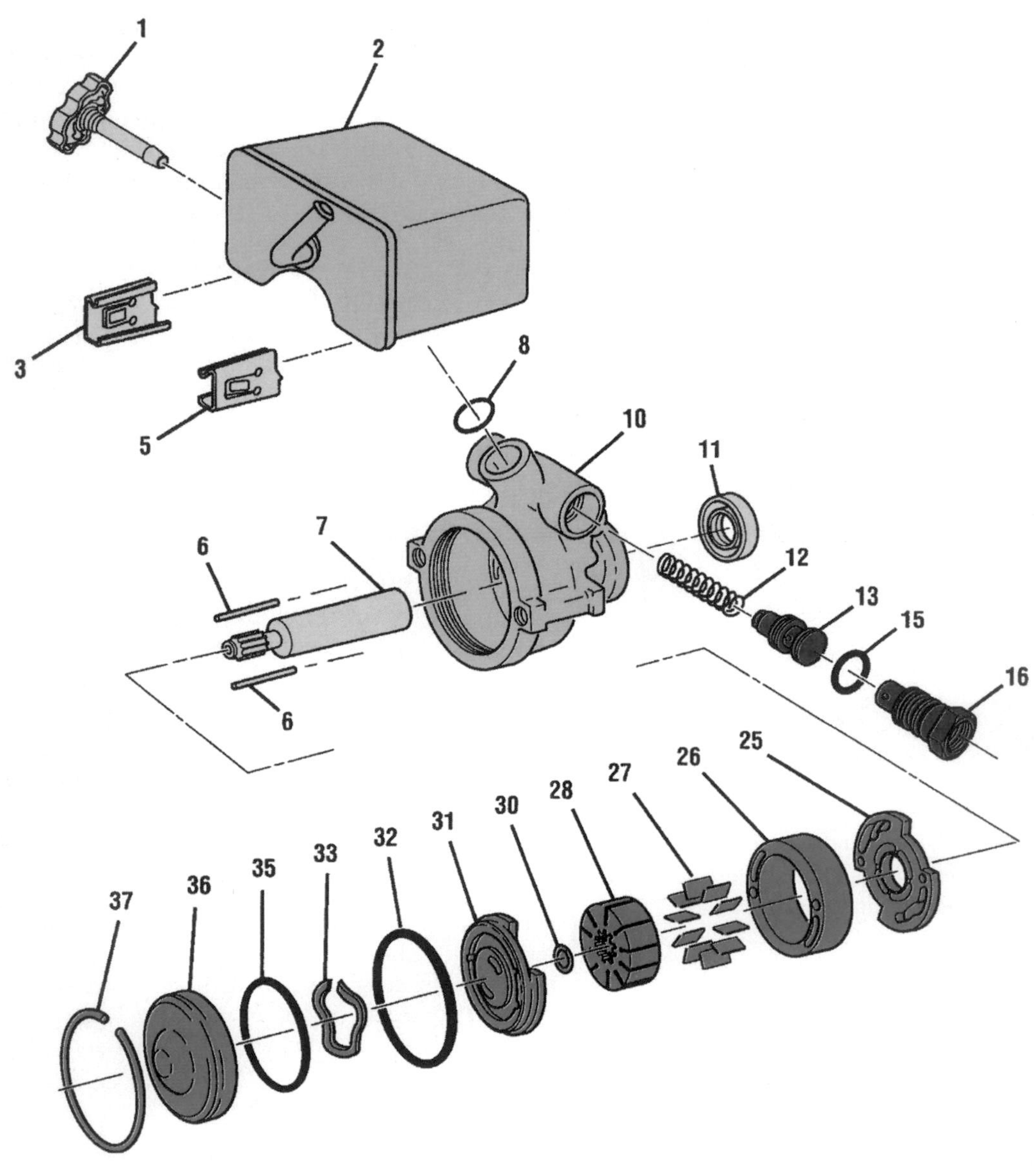

Key No.	Part Name
1	CAPSTICK ASM, RESERVOIR
2	RESERVOIR ASM, HYD PUMP (TYPICAL)
3	CLIP, RESERVOIR RETAINING (LH)
5	CLIP, RESERVOIR RETAINING (RH)
6	PIN, PUMP RING DOWEL
7	SHAFT, DRIVE
8	SEAL, O-RING
10	HOUSING ASM, HYD PUMP
11	SEAL, DRIVE SHAFT
12	SPRING, FLOW CONTROL
13	VALVE ASM, CONTROL
15	SEAL, O-RING

Key No.	Part Name
16	FITTING, O-RING UNION
25	PLATE, THRUST
26	RING, PUMP
27	VANE
28	ROTOR, PUMP
30	RING, SHAFT RETAINING
31	PLATE, PRESSURE
32	SEAL, O-RING
33	SPRING, PRESSURE PLATE
35	SEAL, O-RING
36	COVER, END
37	RING RETAINING

Figure 41–40 Typical power steering pump showing the order of assembly. The high pressure (outlet) hose attaches to the fitting (#16). The flow control valve can be removed from the pump by removing the fitting. (Courtesy of General Motors Corporation)

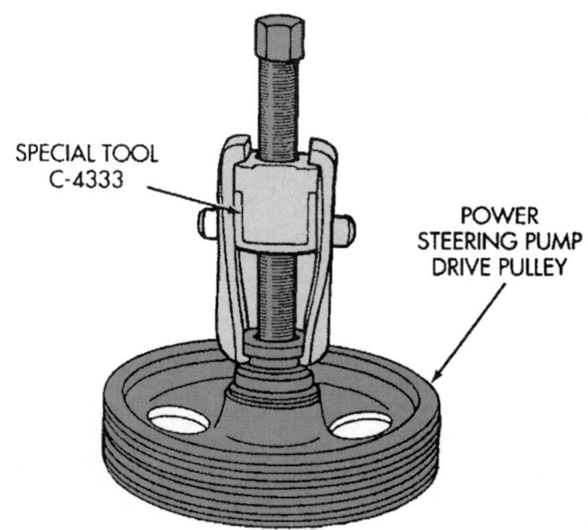

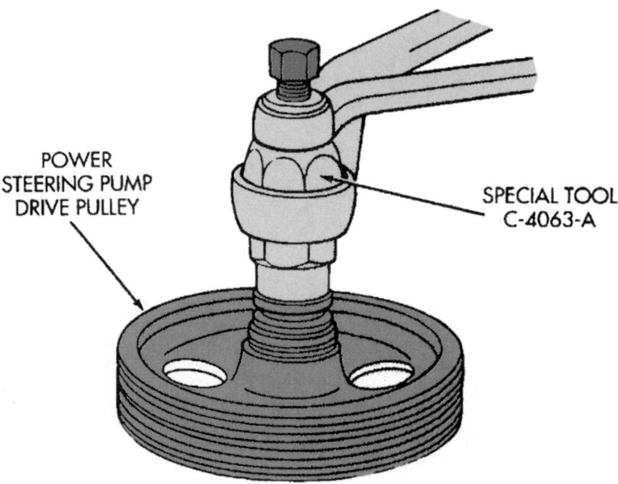

Figure 41–41 A special puller and installation tool are usually required to remove and install a power steering pump drive pulley. (Courtesy of Chrysler Corporation)

6. Fully close the valve three times *(do not leave the valve closed for more than five seconds!)*; all three readings should be within 350 kPa (50 psi) of each other, and the peak pressure should be higher than 7000 kPa (1000 psi).
7. If the pressure readings are high enough *and* within 350 kPa (50 psi) of each other, the pump is okay.
8. If the pressure readings are high enough, yet not within 350 kPa (50 psi) of each other, the flow control valve is sticking.
9. If the pressure readings are less than 7000 kPa (1000 psi), replace the flow control valve and recheck. If the pressures are still low, replace the rotor and vanes in the power steering pump.
10. If the pump is okay, turn the steering wheel to both stops. If the pressure at both stops is not the same as the maximum pressure, the steering gear (or rack and pinion) is leaking internally and should be repaired or replaced.

Many vehicle manufacturers recommend using a pressure gauge that also measures volume, as shown in Figure 41–43.

Frequently Asked Question ???

What Can Be Done About Hard Steering Only When Cold?

Many technicians are asked to repair hard steering that occurs only when the vehicle is cold, usually first thing in the morning. After a couple of minutes, normal steering effort returns. As the vehicle gets older, the problem tends to get worse at higher and higher temperatures until the steering remains hard to turn even when warm. This condition is often referred to as "morning sickness" and occurs when the Teflon sealing rings cause wear grooves in the aluminum spool valve area of the rack and pinion steering unit. See Figure 41–44. During cold weather, these Teflon seals are stiff and the power steering fluid leaks past them. As the power steering fluid heats up, the Teflon seals become more pliable and seal correctly, thereby restoring proper steering effort.

NOTE: The power steering fluid leaking past the Teflon sealing rings of the spool valve will not cause or create an external power steering fluid leak. This leakage around the spool valve area is an internal leak only that causes the power steering fluid, under pressure, to be applied to the wrong end of the rack piston. External power steering fluid leaks are commonly caused by leaking seals on the rack itself.

There are several methods that many technicians use to cure morning sickness:

Method 1. Replacing the entire rack and pinion steering unit. Even though this is the most expensive method, it is also the most commonly used repair.

Method 2. Replacement of the Teflon sealing rings with lap-joint Teflon seals. This procedure is usually performed when the vehicle is under warranty and involves the removal, disassembly, and replacement of the seals followed by reinstallation in the vehicle.

Method 3. Flushing the old power steering fluid and refilling with new fluid. This method costs least and is recommended for mild cases of cold weather reduction of power assist. Cold-climate power steering fluid is also available from General Motors dealers for use in General Motors rack-and-pinion steering gear units.

Method 4. Flushing the system and using special additives is another commonly used technique.

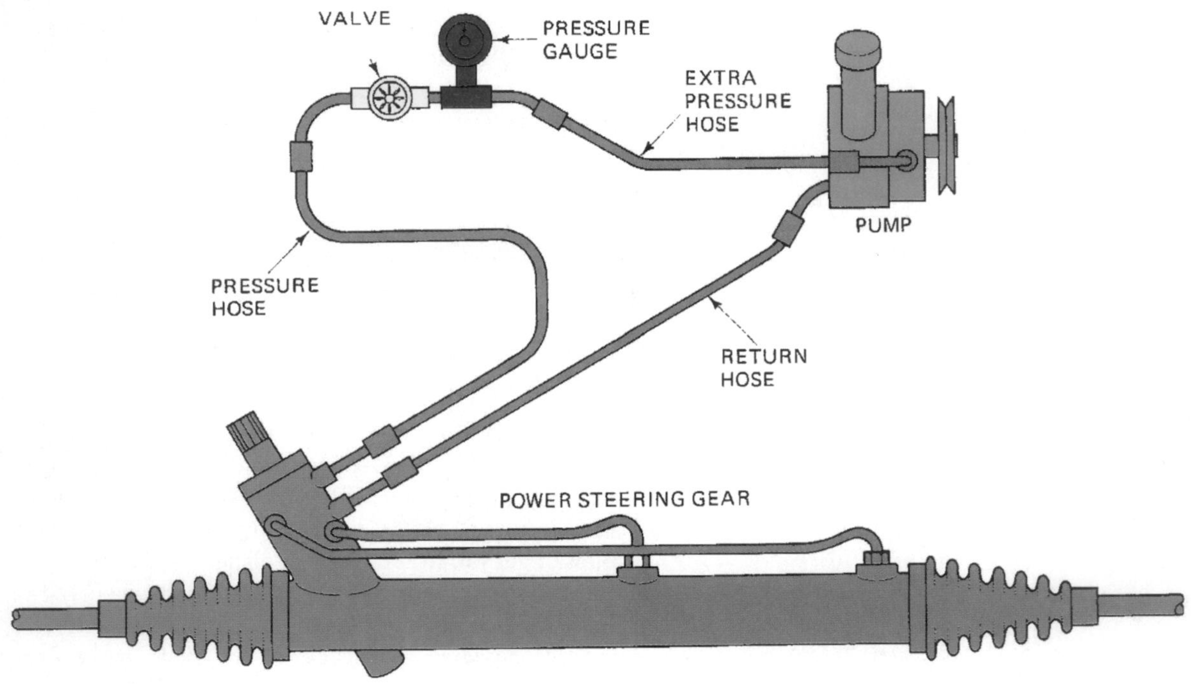

Figure 41–42 A power steering pressure gauge is installed on the high-pressure side of the power steering system between the pump and the gear.

Figure 41–43 A power steering analyzer that measures both pressure and volume. The shutoff valve at the right is used to test the maximum pressure of the pump.

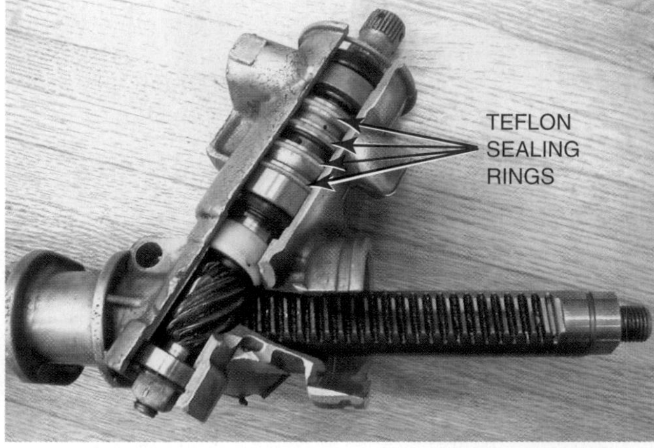

Figure 41–44 Hard steering when cold is usually caused by the Teflon sealing rings wearing grooves in the aluminum housing.

P29–1 The first step is to safely hoist the vehicle to a comfortable working position and remove both front wheels.

P29–2 Remove the cotter key (if equipped) from the outer tie rod end attaching nut and remove the nut.

P29–3 A tie rod end puller can be used to separate the tapered tie rod end from the tapered hole in the steering knuckle.

P29–4 Many technicians simply use a large ball-peen hammer to separate the tie rod end from the steering knuckle by striking the steering knuckle.

P29–5 After the tapered tie rod end has been separated, the tie rod can be disconnected.

P29–6 Use a line (flare nut) wrench to loosen the hydraulic lines from the control valve area of the rack and pinion steering gear assembly.

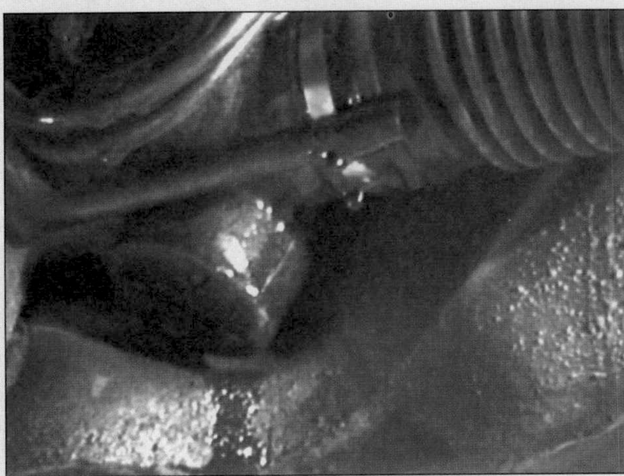

P29–7 Be sure to have a drain pan positioned under the vehicle when the lines are loosened from the rack, because power steering fluid will leak out.

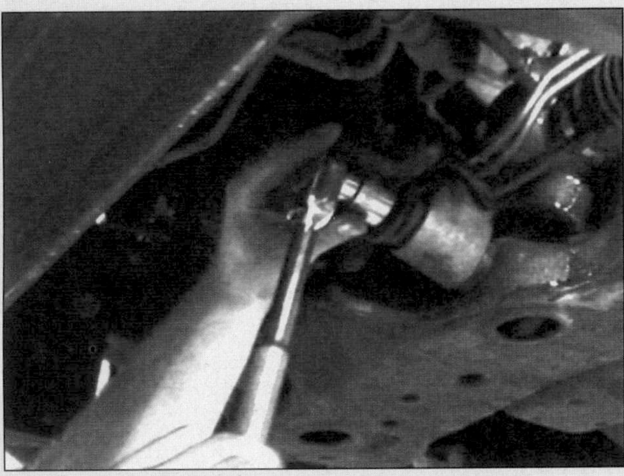

P29–8 After the hydraulic lines have been removed from the control valve area of the rack and pinion, the rack attaching bolts can be removed.

P29–9 A pinch bolt holds the intermediate steering shaft to the stub shaft (input shaft) of the rack and pinion steering gear assembly. The bolt has to be completely removed before the two can be separated.

P29–10 The rack and pinion steering gear assembly can now be removed from the vehicle. The replacement rack and pinion assembly is then reinstalled, reversing the procedure.

P29–11 After the rack and pinion assembly has been installed and the hydraulic lines have been attached and torqued to specifications, power steering fluid is added to the reservoir.

P29–12 To bleed any trapped air from the power steering system, be sure the wheels are off the ground and simply turn the steering wheel from one side to the other with the engine off.

P29–13 After turning the steering wheel several times to force the power steering fluid throughout the system, check the level of the fluid and add more if necessary.

P29–14 Start the engine and turn the steering wheel from side to side, checking for any leaks or abnormal noise. After this step, the vehicle can be lowered and the steering checked with the weight of the vehicle on the ground. After adjusting the alignment (toe) and a thorough test drive to verify proper operation, the vehicle can be returned to the owner.

SUMMARY

1. The driver's movement of the steering wheel is transmitted through the steering column to the intermediate shaft and flexible coupling to the steering gear or rack-and-pinion unit.
2. Most steering system components use greaseable ball-and-socket joints to allow for suspension travel and steering. Some manufacturers use rubber-bonded sockets (RBS) that are not to be greased.
3. Most conventional steering gears use a recirculating ball nut-type design.
4. Power steering pumps supply hydraulic fluid to the steering gear, power piston assembly, or rack and pinion unit. The spool (rotary) valve controls and directs the high-pressure fluid to the power piston to provide power-assisted steering.
5. In a rack-and-pinion steering unit, the stub shaft connects to the small pinion gear. The pinion gear meshes with gear teeth cut into a long shaft called a rack.
6. The dry park test is very important in detecting worn or damaged steering parts. While the vehicle is on the ground, an assistant moves the steering wheel back and forth while the technician feels for any looseness in every steering system part.
7. The idler arm usually is the first steering system component to wear out in a conventional parallelogram-type steering system. Following the idler arm in wear are the tie rods, centre link, and then the pitman arm.
8. The steering system must be level side-to-side to prevent unwanted bump steer. Bump steer occurs when the vehicle's direction is changed when travelling over bumps or dips in the road.
9. Always use a belt tension gauge when checking, replacing, or tightening a power steering drive belt. The proper power steering fluid should always be used to prevent possible seal or power steering hose failure.
10. Trapped air in a power steering system should be bled by hoisting the front tires off the ground and simply turning the steering wheel several times from full left to full right.

REVIEW QUESTIONS

1. List all the parts that move when the steering wheel is turned with a conventional steering unit and with a rack-and-pinion steering unit.
2. Describe the hydraulic fluid flow from the pump through the flow control valve and to the steering gear.
3. Describe how to perform a dry park test.
4. Explain the procedure for bleeding air out of a power steering system.

RED SEAL CERTIFICATION-TYPE QUESTIONS

1. Which type of steering linkage component must *not* be lubricated?
   - **a.** Zerk fittings
   - **b.** Alamite fittings
   - **c.** RBS tie rods
   - **d.** Ball guides
2. What steering component is between the intermediate shaft from the steering column and the stub shaft of the steering gear on a rack-and-pinion unit?
   - **a.** Pitman shaft
   - **b.** Flexible coupling
   - **c.** Sector shaft
   - **d.** Tie rod
3. A dry park test to determine the condition of the steering components and joints should be performed with the vehicle
   - **a.** On level ground
   - **b.** On turn plates that allow the front wheels to move
   - **c.** On a frame contact lift with the wheels off the ground
   - **d.** Lifted off the ground about 5 cm (2 inches)
4. What driving symptoms result from "bump steer"?
   - **a.** Vehicle pulls to the left only
   - **b.** Vehicle pulls to the right only
   - **c.** Steering wheel will vibrate
   - **d.** Vehicle darts from lane to lane (is unstable to steer)
5. Which statement is correct when discussing bleeding the power steering system?
   - **a.** The back wheels should be raised off the ground
   - **b.** The engine must be running at 3500 rpm
   - **c.** The engine should be stopped
   - **d.** The steering gear must be disconnected
6. When testing the power steering pump pressure, what could cause a situation where the pressure is too low?
   - **a.** Excessive fluid level
   - **b.** Restricted pressure hose
   - **c.** Fluid level is too low
   - **d.** Engine RPM too high
7. A vehicle with power rack-and-pinion steering is hard to steer when cold (temporary loss of power assist when cold). The most likely cause is
   - **a.** Leaking rack seals
   - **b.** A defective or worn power steering pump
   - **c.** Worn grooves in the housing by the spool valve seals
   - **d.** Using the incorrect power steering fluid
8. Integral power steering gears use _____ for lubrication of the unit.
   - **a.** SAE 80W-90 gear lube
   - **b.** Chassis grease (NLGI #2)
   - **c.** Power steering fluid in the system
   - **d.** Molybdenum disulfide
9. When must the steering rack be replaced?
   - **a.** When the rack gear is damaged
   - **b.** When the outer tie rod is defective
   - **c.** When the power steering pump is defective
   - **d.** When the inner tie rod is defective
10. When installing a slotted nut on a tie rod end or ball joint
    - **a.** Do not use the cotter pin if the hole does not line up with the slot
    - **b.** Always torque the nut to 75 N·m; then install cotter pin
    - **c.** Torque the nut to specifications; then back the nut off to the first slot the hole lines up with
    - **d.** Torque to minimum specification; then tighten until the next slot lines up with a hole

42

Suspension System Diagnosis and Service

OBJECTIVES: After studying Chapter 42, you should be able to:

1. Prepare for the interprovincial Red Seal certification examination in Appendix IV (Suspension and Steering) on the topics covered in this chapter.
2. List various types of suspensions and their component parts.
3. Describe how the front suspension components function to allow wheel movement up and down and provide for turning.
4. Discuss rear suspension function for both front-wheel-drive and rear-wheel-drive as well as four-wheel-drive vehicles.
5. Explain how to perform diagnosis of problems in the suspension system.
6. Discuss the procedures for testing load-carrying and follower-type ball joints.
7. Describe ball joint replacement procedures.

PURPOSE OF SUSPENSION SYSTEMS

The suspension system is attached to the frame or body and carries most of the vehicle's weight. The suspension will transmit this weight to the tire and wheel assembly while providing a comfortable ride for the vehicle's occupants.

The suspension will assist in cushioning the road irregularities from the driver and help hold the wheels to the road during aggressive steering manoeuvres.

TYPES OF SUSPENSIONS

Early suspension systems on old horse wagons, buggies, and older vehicles used a solid axle for the front and rear wheels. If one wheel hit a bump, the other wheel was affected, as shown in Figure 42–1. Today, most vehicles use a separate control-arm type of suspension for each front wheel, which allows for movement of one front wheel without affecting the other front wheel. This type of suspension is called **independent** front suspension, as shown in Figure 42–2. Many rear suspensions also use independent-type systems. Regardless of the design, all suspensions use springs in one form or another.

Coil Springs

Coil springs are made of special round spring steel wrapped in a helix shape. Coil springs are used in front and/or rear suspensions.

Variable Rate Coil Springs Many coil springs are designed to provide a variable spring rate. This

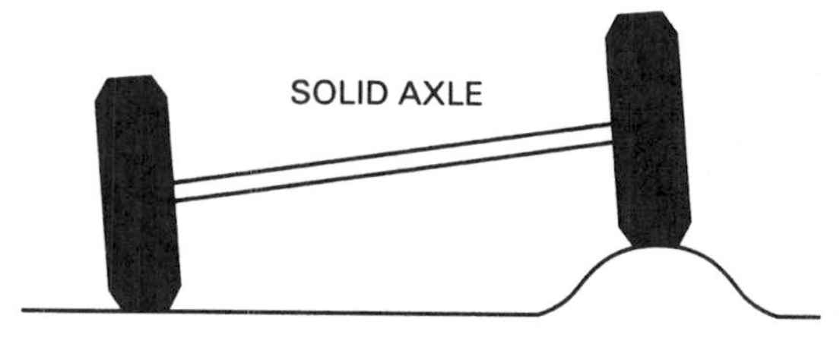

Figure 42–1 In a solid-axle suspension system, when one wheel hits a bump or drops into a hole, both left and right wheels are moved. Because both wheels are affected, the ride is often harsh and stiff feeling.

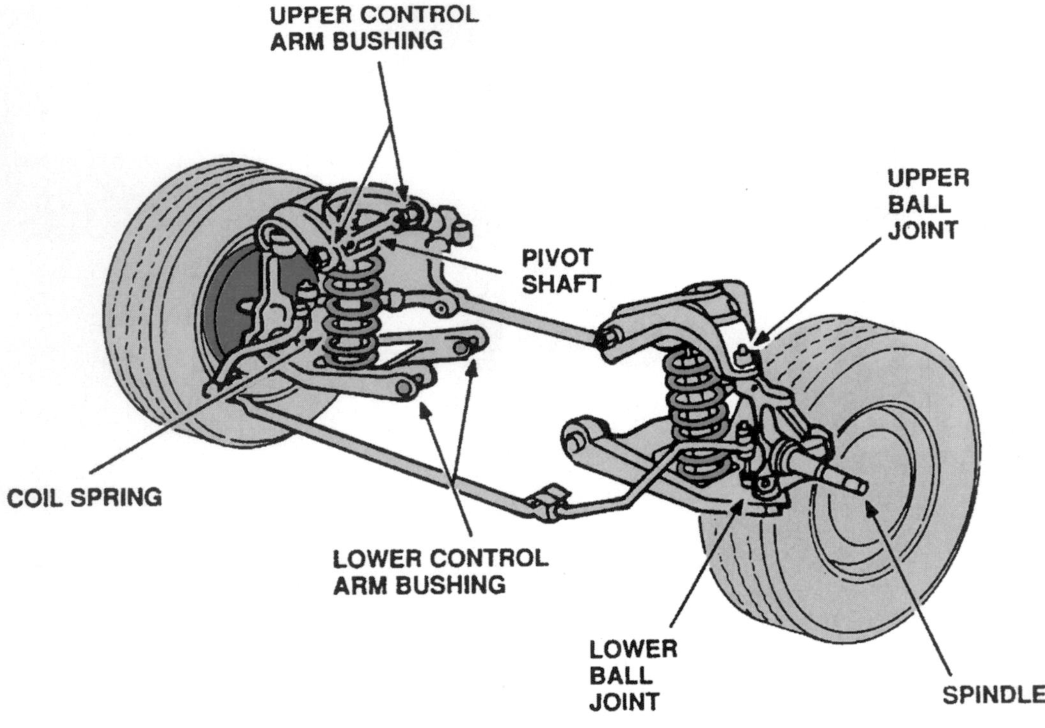

Figure 42–2 A typical independent front suspension used on a rear-wheel-drive vehicle. Each wheel can hit a bump or hole in the road *independently* without affecting the opposite wheel. (Courtesy of Hunter Engineering Company)

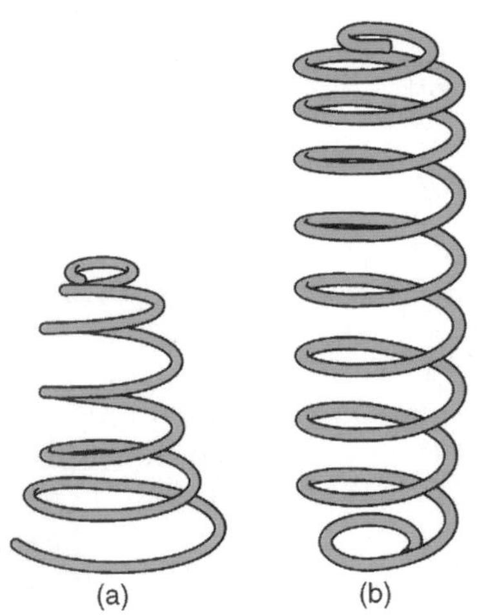

Figure 42–3 (a) A semiconical spring used in the rear suspension of passenger cars. It provides a variable rate because it is designed so that the coils bottom out on the spring seat. Because the coil can compress into itself (nest), it conserves space. (b) Typical application on the rear coil suspensions of light trucks. This cylindrical spring is manufactured from tapered wire to achieve a variable rate.

means that as the spring is compressed, it becomes stiffer. This allows for a smooth ride when bumps and dips in the road are small and provides load-carrying capacity and resistance to bottoming out when travelling over rough roads. See Figure 42–3.

Coil Spring Mounting Coil springs are usually installed in a **spring pocket** or **spring seat.** Hard rubber or plastic **cushions** or **insulators** are usually mounted between the coil spring and the spring seat. See Figures 42–4 and 42–5.

> **CAUTION:** All springs are painted or coated with epoxy to help prevent breakage. A scratch, nick, or pit caused by corrosion can cause a **stress riser** that can lead to spring failure. Always use a tool that will not scratch or nick the surface of the spring.

Leaf Springs

Leaf springs are constructed of one or more strips or leaves of long, narrow, spring steel. These metal strips, called *leaves,* are assembled with plastic or synthetic rubber insulators between the leaves allowing freedom of movement during spring operation. See Figure 42–6. The ends of the main leaf

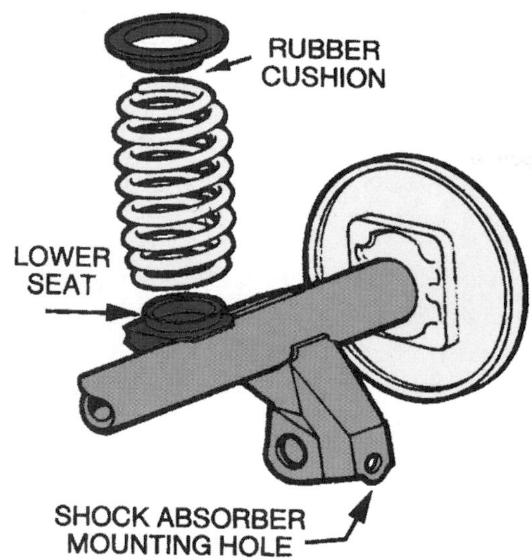

Figure 42–4 Rubber cushions are usually placed between the coil spring and the body of the vehicle to help prevent noise from being transmitted into the passenger compartment. (Courtesy of Cooper Automotive Company)

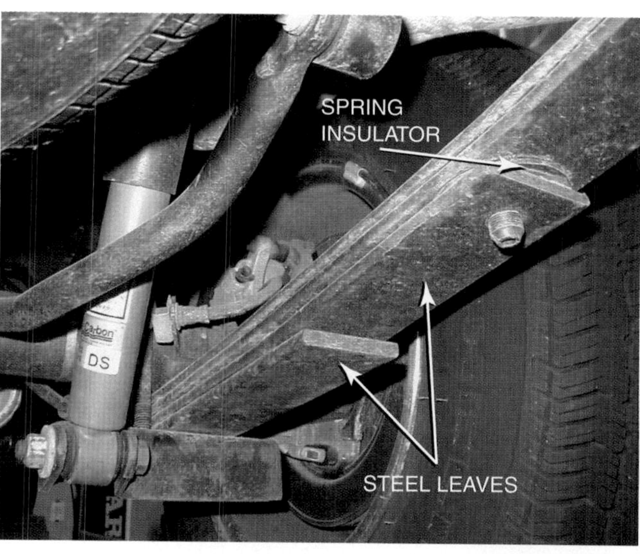

Figure 42–6 Typical leaf spring used on the rear of a rear-wheel-drive vehicle.

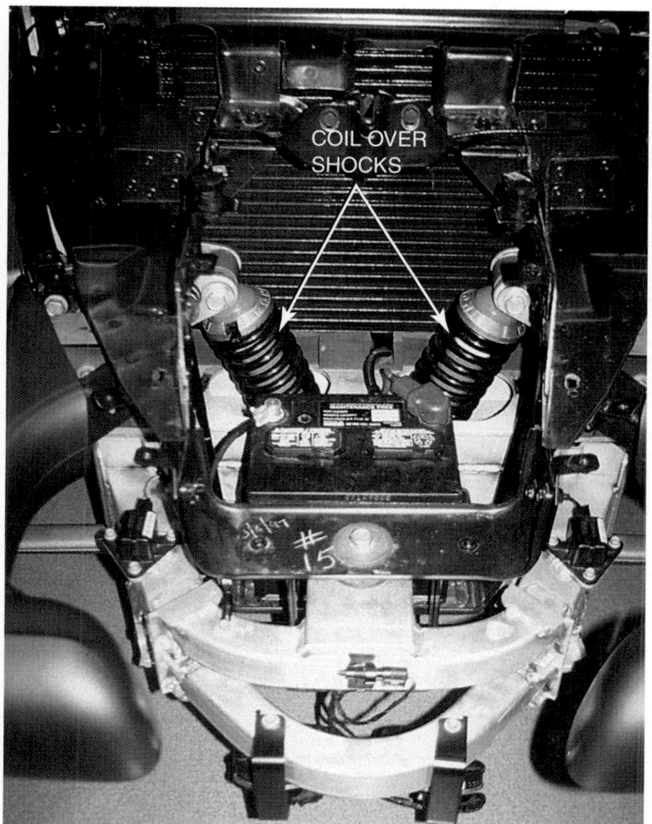

Figure 42–5 Coil springs can be used for many different types of front and rear suspensions. This is the front suspension of a Plymouth Prowler, showing how the shock absorbers are inside the coil springs. This arrangement is called "coil-over-shocks."

spring are rolled or looped to form eyes. Rubber bushings are installed in the eyes of the spring and act as noise and vibration insulators.

The leaves are held together by a **centre bolt,** also called a **centring pin.** See Figure 42–7. One end of a leaf spring is mounted to a hanger with a bolt and rubber bushings directly on the frame and the other end of the leaf spring is attached to the frame with movable mounting hangers called **shackles,** as shown in Figure 42–8. **Rebound clips** or **spring alignment clips** help prevent the leaves from separating whenever the leaf spring is rebounding from hitting a bump or rise in the roadway. See Figure 42–9. Single-leaf steel springs are used on some vehicles and are called **mono leaf.**

NOTE: If the centring bolt were to break, the axle could move forward or rearward. This condition can cause the vehicle to track sideways, often called "dog tracking."

Composite Leaf Springs

Since the early 1980s, fibreglass-reinforced epoxy plastic leaf springs have been used on production vehicles. They save weight since an eight-pound plastic spring can replace a conventional forty-pound steel leaf spring. The single-leaf composite spring helps isolate road noise and vibrations. See Figure 42–10 (p. 991).

Figure 42–7 The centre bolt is used to hold the leaves of a leaf spring together. However, the hole for the centre bolt also weakens the leaf spring. The crack shown is what a technician discovered when the leaf spring was removed during the diagnosis of a sagging rear suspension.

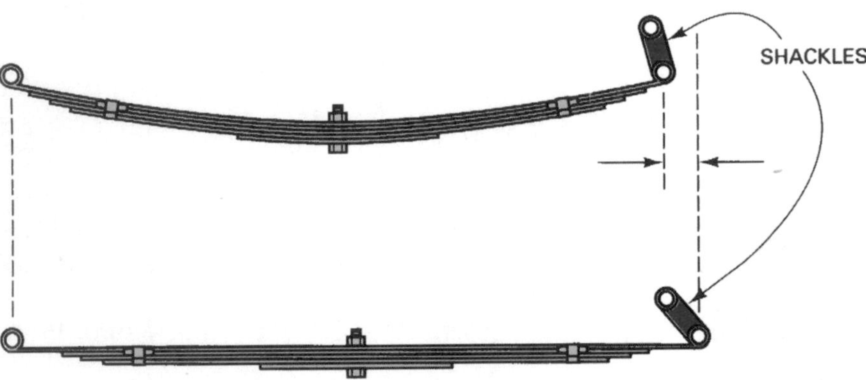

Figure 42–8 When a leaf spring is compressed, the spring flattens and becomes longer. The shackles allow for this lengthening.

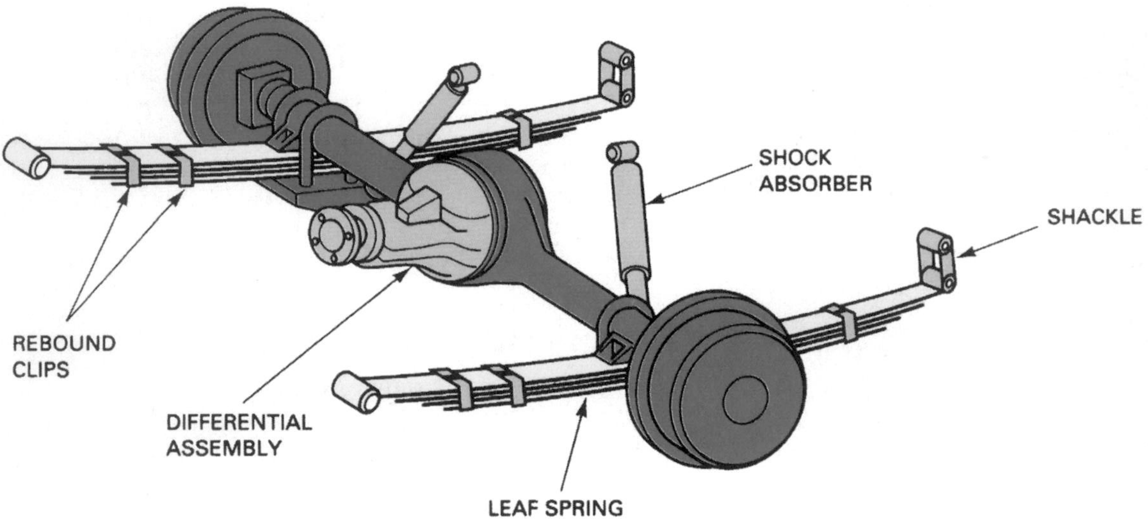

Figure 42–9 Typical rear leaf-spring suspension of a rear-wheel-drive vehicle.

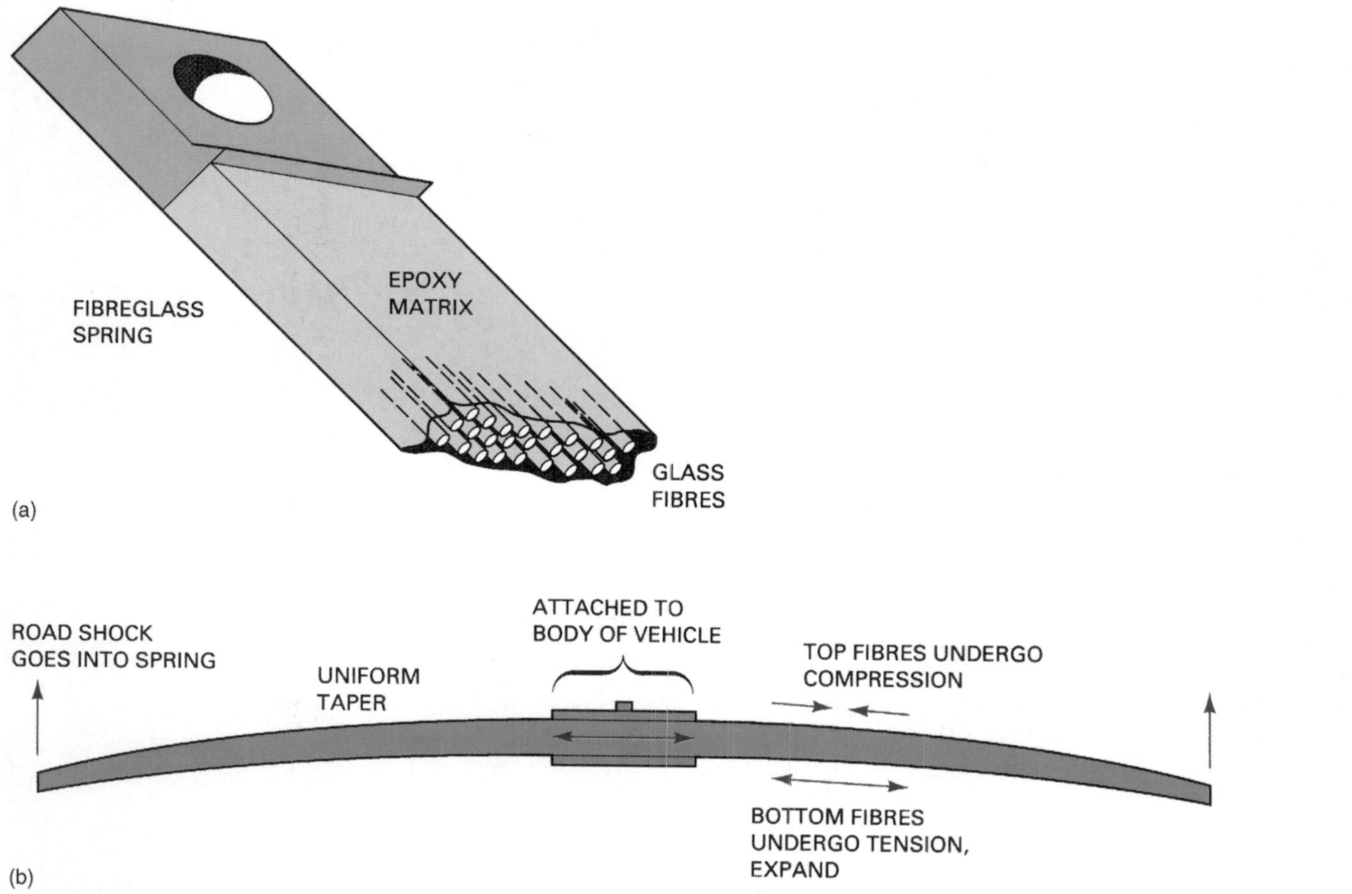

Figure 42–10 (a) A fibreglass spring is composed of long fibres locked together in an epoxy (resin) matrix. (b) When the spring compresses, the bottom of the spring expands and the top compresses.

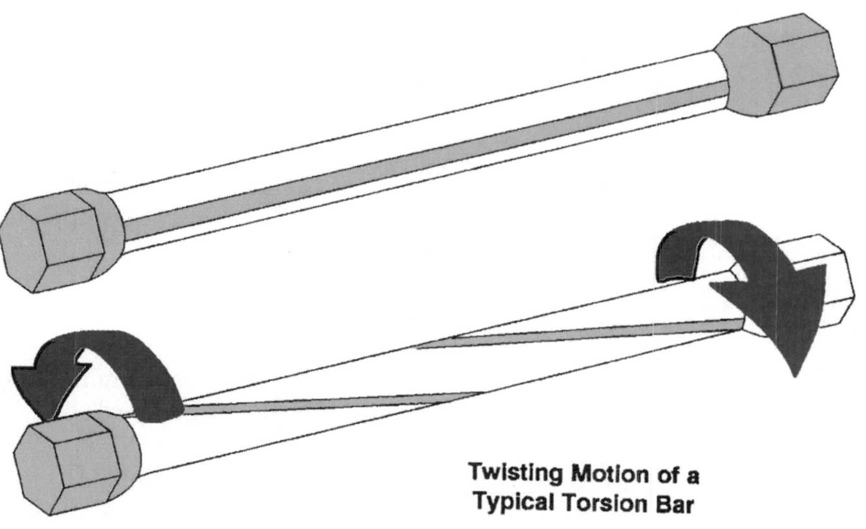

Figure 42–11 A torsion bar twists when a vehicle hits a bump in the road. (Courtesy of John Bean Company)

Torsion Bars

A torsion bar is a spring which is a long, *round* hardened straight steel bar, as shown in Figure 42–11. One end is attached to the lower control arm of a front suspension and the other end to the frame. When the wheels hit a bump, the bar twists and then untwists. Chrysler Corporation cars use torsion bar front suspension both longitudinally and transversely.

Many manufacturers of pickup trucks currently use torsion-bar type suspensions, especially on their

HIGH PERFORMANCE TIP

Don't Cut Those Coil Springs!

Chassis service technicians are often asked to lower a vehicle. One method is to remove the coil springs and cut off one-half or more coils from the spring. Although this *will* lower the vehicle, the method is generally not recommended because

1. A coil spring could be damaged during the cutting-off procedure, especially if a torch is used to do the cutting.
2. The spring will get stiffer when shortened, often resulting in a very harsh ride.

Instead of cutting springs to lower a vehicle, there are several other, preferred methods available if the vehicle *must* be lowered:

1. Using replacement springs designed to lower the specific vehicle. A change in shock absorbers may be necessary because the shorter springs change the operating height of the stock (original) shock absorbers. Consult spring manufacturers for exact installation instructions and recommendations.
2. Using replacement spindles designed to *raise* the location of the wheel spindle, thereby lowering the body in relation to the ground. Except for ground-clearance problems, this method is the one recommended by many chassis service technicians. Replacement spindles keep the same springs, shock absorbers, and ride, while lowering the vehicle.

(a)

(b)

Figure 42–12 (a) The front end of the torsion bar attaches to the lower control arm on the pickup truck. (b) The other end of the torsion bar attaches to the cross member through an adjustable socket. The suspension height can be adjusted by turning the adjusting bolt.

four-wheel-drive models. Torsion bars allow room for the front drive axle and constant velocity joint and still provide for a strong suspension. Unlike other types of springs, torsion bars are *adjustable* for correct ride height. See Figure 42–12.

CAUTION: Torsion bars are marked left and right at the factory and should not be switched side-to-side. The bars are manufactured the same, but become work hardened by being twisted during normal service life. If a used torsion bar is switched to the other side of the vehicle, it will be twisting in the opposite direction and can break. If a torsion bar breaks, the entire suspension can collapse, causing a collision and possible personal injury.

SUSPENSION PRINCIPLES AND TYPES

Suspensions use various links, arms, and joints to allow the wheels to move up and down freely. Front suspensions also have to allow the front wheels to turn. All suspensions must provide for all of the following supports:

1. **Transverse (or side-to-side) wheel support.** As the wheels of the vehicle move up and down, the suspension must allow for this movement and still hold the wheel from moving away from the vehicle or inward toward the centre of the vehicle. See Figure 42–13.
2. **Longitudinal (front-to-back) wheel support.** As the wheels of the vehicle move up and down, the suspension must allow for this movement and still hold the wheels from moving backward whenever a bump is hit. At least two suspension links or arms are required in order to provide for freedom of movement up or down and *prevent* any in-out or forward-back movement. See Figure 42–14.

UPPER
CONTROL
ARM
SPINDLE
LOWER
CONTROL ARM

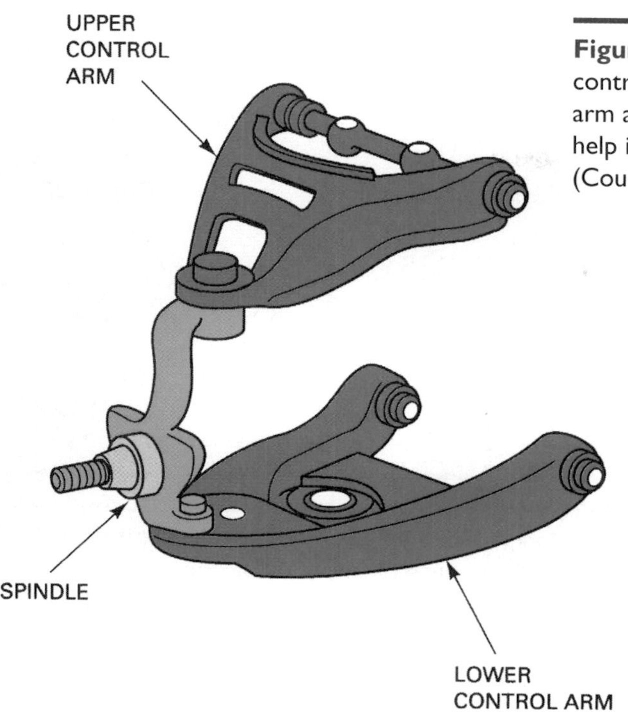

Figure 42–13 The spindle supports the wheels and attaches to the control arm with ball-and-socket joints called ball-joints. The control arm attaches to the frame of the vehicle through rubber bushings to help isolate noise and vibration between the road and the body. (Courtesy of Cooper Automotive Company)

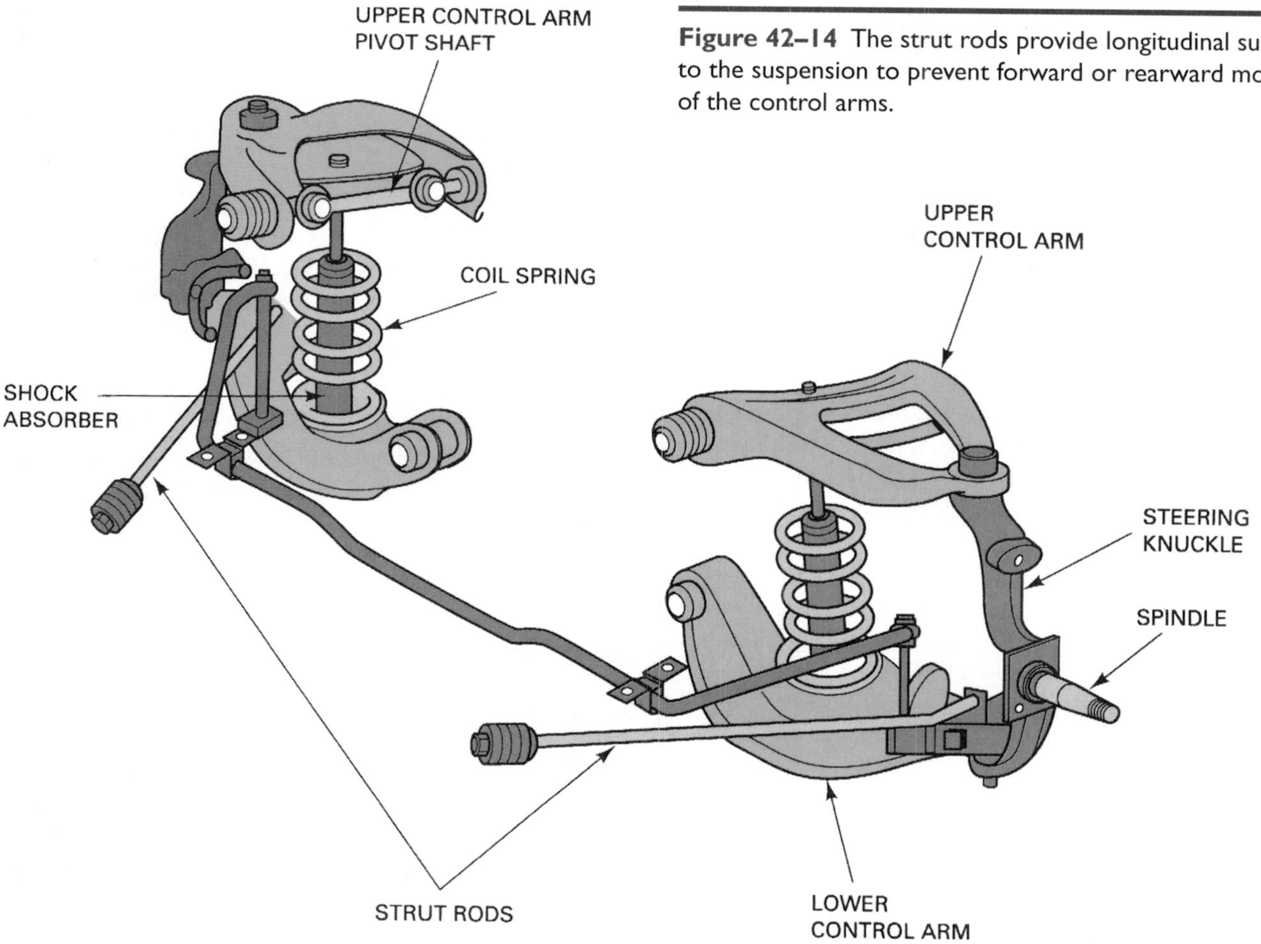

UPPER CONTROL ARM
PIVOT SHAFT
COIL SPRING
SHOCK
ABSORBER
UPPER
CONTROL ARM
STEERING
KNUCKLE
SPINDLE
STRUT RODS
LOWER
CONTROL ARM

Figure 42–14 The strut rods provide longitudinal support to the suspension to prevent forward or rearward movement of the control arms.

TECH TIP 

Radius Rod Bushing Noise

When the radius rod bushing (see Figure 42–16) on a Ford truck or van deteriorates, the most common complaint from the driver is noise. Besides causing tire wear, a worn or defective radius-rod bushing can cause

1. A clicking sound when braking (sounds as if the brake caliper may be loose).
2. A clunking noise when hitting bumps.

When the bushing deteriorates, the axles can move forward and backward with less control. The noise is the first sign that something is wrong. Without proper axle support, handling and cornering can also be affected.

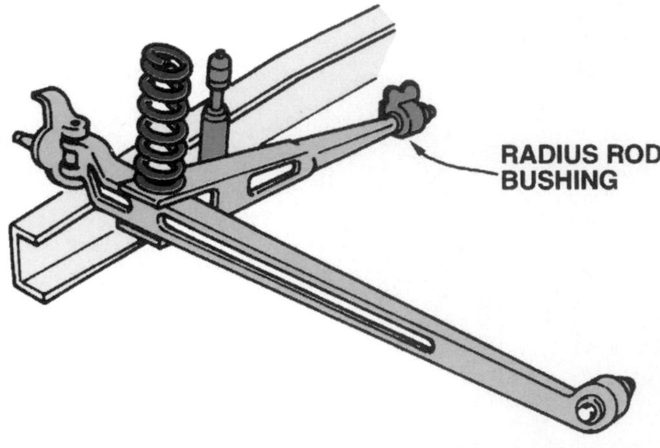

Figure 42–16 Radius rod bushings are used between the radius rod and the frame to isolate noise, vibration, and harshness from the passenger compartment.

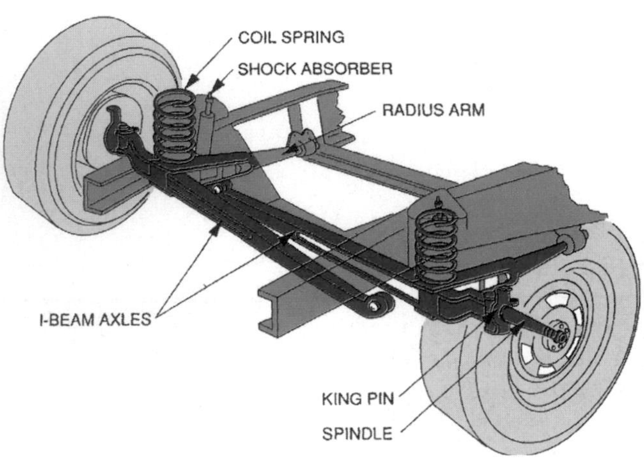

Figure 42–15 Twin I-beam front suspension. (Courtesy of Dana Corporation, Perfect Circle Products)

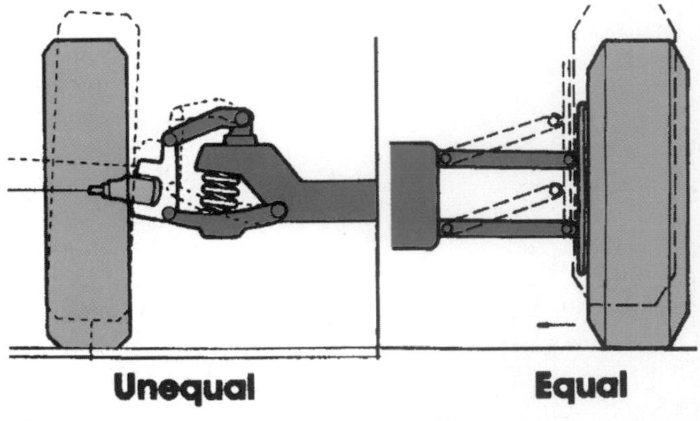

Figure 42–17 If the control arms were both the same length, the tire would move side to side as the wheels moved up and down, as illustrated on the right. To keep the wheel moving straight up and down as the suspension moves, the upper control arm is shorter, as shown on the left. (Courtesy of Cooper Automotive Company)

Twin I-Beams

Since the mid 1960s a twin I-beam front suspension has been used on Ford pickup trucks and vans. Strong steel twin beams that cross provide independent front suspension operation with the strength of a solid front axle. See Figure 42–15. To control longitudinal (front-to-back) support, a **radius rod** is attached to each beam and anchors to the frame of the truck using rubber bushings. These bushings allow the front axle to move up and down while still isolating the frame and body from road noise and vibration.

Short/Long Arm Suspensions

This type of suspension uses a short upper control arm and a larger lower control arm, and is usually referred to as the **SLA** type (abbreviation for short, long arm). See Figure 42–17. SLA-type suspension can be used with either coil springs or torsion bars. Most vehicles use two A-shaped steel arms connected to the frame by rubber bushings at the bottom of the A, and the other end connected to the steering knuckle by ball joints at the top of the A. See Figure 42–18.

These **A arms** are usually called **control arms** because they "control" the location of the front wheels and allow for the up-and-down movement of the front wheels plus turning of the front wheels for steering.

NOTE: SLA-type suspension is also called a double wishbone suspension because both control arms often resemble the shape of a chicken or turkey wishbone. See Figure 42–19.

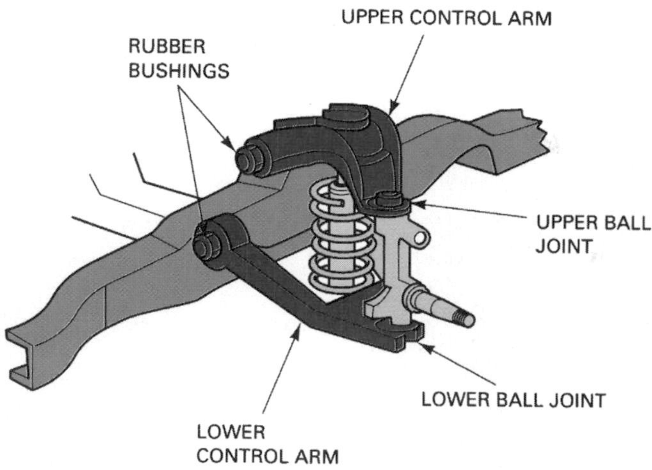

Figure 42–18 An SLA-type suspension. Note the lower control arm is longer than the upper control arm. (Courtesy of Cooper Automotive Company)

Figure 42–19 All components of this Corvette front suspension are aluminum alloy, including the upper and lower control arms.

Figure 42–20 A robot arm welds an automotive suspension system on an assembly line.

The top control arm is called the **upper control arm;** the bottom control arm is called the **lower control arm.** The same terms also apply to the other parts of the control arms, such as **lower ball joint, upper ball joint, upper control arm bushings, and lower control arm bushings.**

The upper control arm is shorter than the lower control arm. This permits the tires to remain as vertical as possible during suspension travel. Short/long arm suspensions are used in the front as well as the rear of many rear-wheel-drive and front-wheel-drive vehicles. While some high-performance vehicles use forged aluminum control arms, most production vehicles use stamped-steel arms that are welded. See Figure 42–20.

MacPherson Struts

The **MacPherson strut** suspension was patented in 1958 by Earle S. MacPherson, a vice president of engineering at Ford Motor Company. The most commonly used strut suspension combines the coil spring and the shock absorber into one structural suspension component, as shown in Figure 42–21. A MacPherson strut suspension is lightweight and saves space in the vehicle because only one control arm is needed and the top of the strut simply attaches to the body of the vehicle. *The entire strut rotates when the front wheels are turned.* The pivot points of a strut are at the lower ball joint and at a bearing assembly at the top of the strut. Some vehicles use a modified strut suspension, as shown in Figure 42–22.

Figure 42–21 Typical MacPherson strut front suspension on a front-wheel-drive vehicle. Note the drive axle shaft and CV joints.

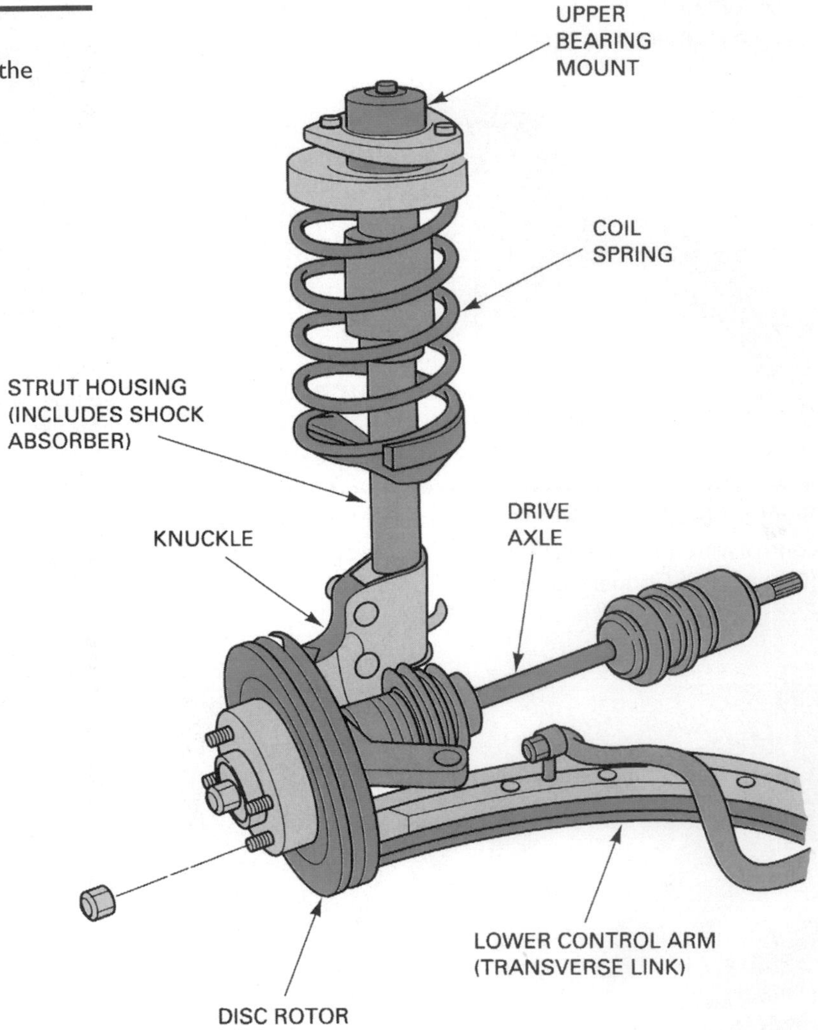

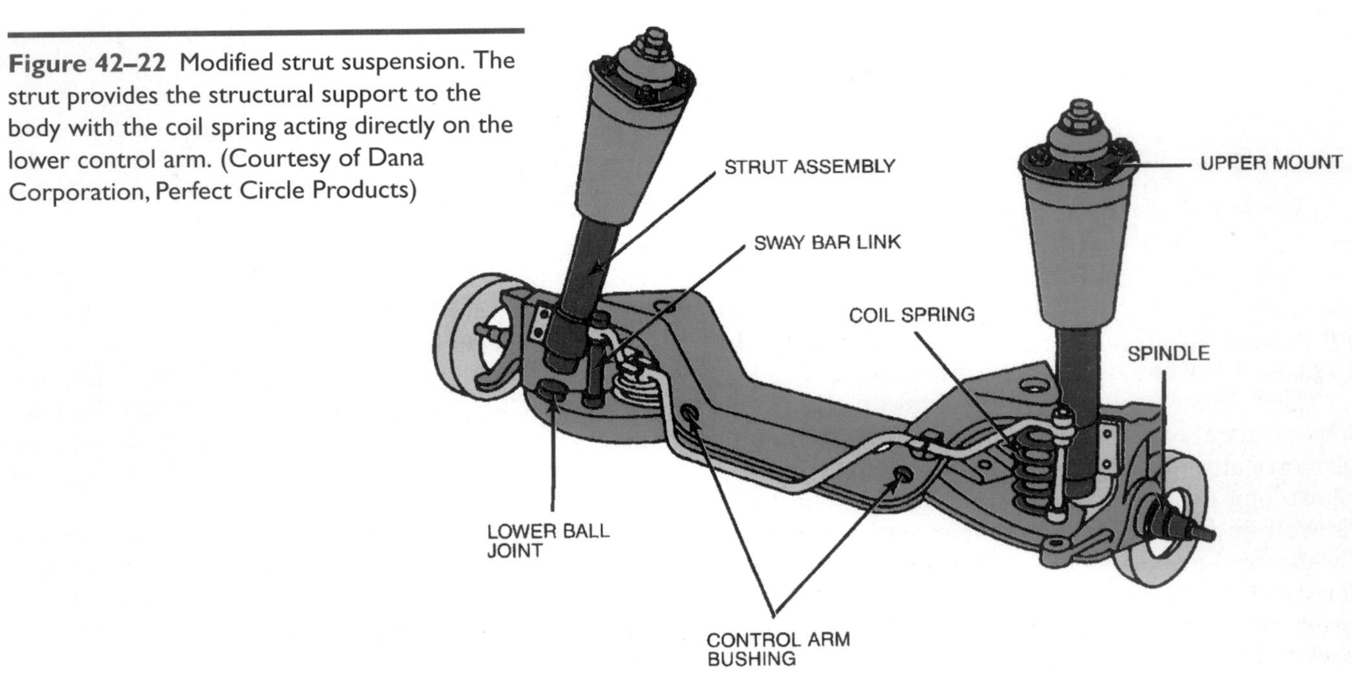

Figure 42–22 Modified strut suspension. The strut provides the structural support to the body with the coil spring acting directly on the lower control arm. (Courtesy of Dana Corporation, Perfect Circle Products)

PARTS OF A SUSPENSION SYSTEM

Ball Joints

Ball joints are actually ball-and-socket joints, similar to the joints in a person's shoulder. Ball joints allow the front wheels to move up and down as well as side to side for steering.

A vehicle can be equipped with coil springs, mounted either above the upper control arm *or* mounted on the lower control arm. If the coil spring is attached to the top of the upper control arm, then the upper ball joint is carrying the weight of the vehicle and is called the **load-carrying ball joint.** The lower ball joint is called the **follower ball joint.** If the coil spring is attached to the lower control arm, then the lower ball joint is the load-carrying ball joint and the upper ball joint is the follower ball joint. See Figure 42–23.

If a torsion-bar type spring is used, the lower ball joint is the load-carrying ball joint because the torsion bar is attached to the lower control arm on most vehicles that use torsion bars. On vehicles equipped with a twin I-beam front suspension with ball joints, *both* ball joints are load-carrying and must, therefore, be replaced together if worn or defective. MacPherson struts use a ball joint on the lower control arm. Since the weight of the vehicle is applied to the upper strut mount, the ball joint is non-load carrying. See Figure 42–24.

A specific amount of turning resistance to the strut is built into each ball joint to stabilize steering. The ball joints that do not support the weight of the vehicle and the outer suspension pivot are often called follower ball joints or **friction** ball joints. The load-carrying (weight-carrying) ball joint is subjected to the greatest amount of wear and is the most frequently replaced. See Figure 42–25.

Strut Rods

Some vehicles are equipped with round steel rods attached with rubber bushings called **strut rod bushings** between the lower control arm at one end and the frame of the vehicle at the other end. The purpose of these strut rods is to provide forward/backward support to the control arms. See Figure 42–26. Strut rods are also called **tension** or **compression** rods or simply **TC rods.** If a strut rod has a nut on *both* sides of the bushings, then the strut rod is used to adjust *caster,* an alignment angle discussed in Chapter 43.

Stabilizer Bars

Most cars and trucks are equipped with a stabilizer bar on the front suspension, a round, hardened steel bar which is attached to both lower control arms

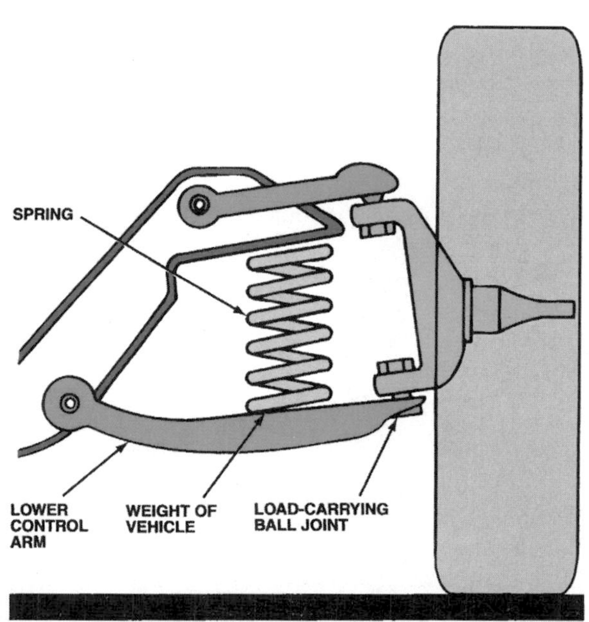

Figure 42–23 The lower ball joint is load carrying in this type of suspension because the weight of the vehicle is applied through the spring, lower control arm, and ball joint to the wheel.

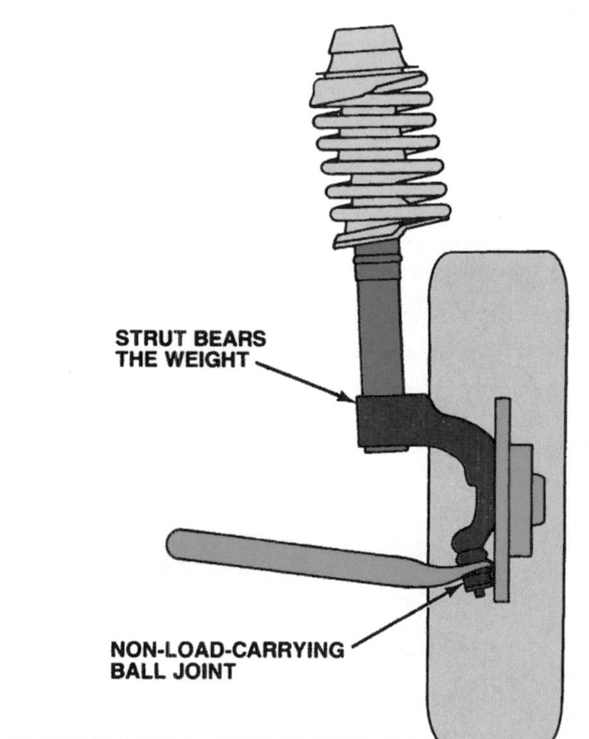

Figure 42–24 The ball joint used in a MacPherson-type suspension is non-load carrying. The vehicle weight is transferred through the spring and upper strut mount plate.

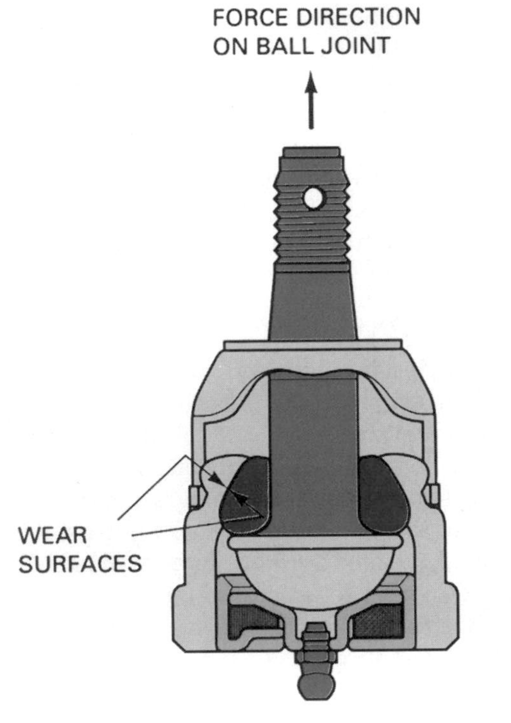

Figure 42–25 In this tension-design ball joint, the wear surface is above the pivot ball and socket, as shown.

with bolts and rubber bushing washers called **stabilizer bar bushings.** See Figure 42–27. A stabilizer bar is also called an **antisway bar (sway bar)** or **antiroll bar (roll bar).** Its purpose is to prevent excessive body roll while cornering and to add to stability while driving over rough road surfaces. See Figure 42–28.

The stabilizer bar is also used as a longitudinal (front/back) support to the lower control arm on many vehicles equipped with MacPherson struts. The **stabilizer links** or **rubber bushings** that connect the ends of the stabilizer bar to the lower control arm are commonly found to be defective (cracked rubber washers or broken spacer bolts) because of the great amount of force that is transmitted through the links and the bushings. See Figure 42–29.

Frequently Asked Question ???

What Is the Difference Between a Strut Bar and a Sway Bar?

A strut bar, also called a strut tie bar, is a bar that connects the top of the strut towers together under the hood. See Figure 42–30. A sway bar, also called a stabilizer bar or antiroll bar, is located under the vehicle and twists as the body leans into a corner to help keep the body from leaning.

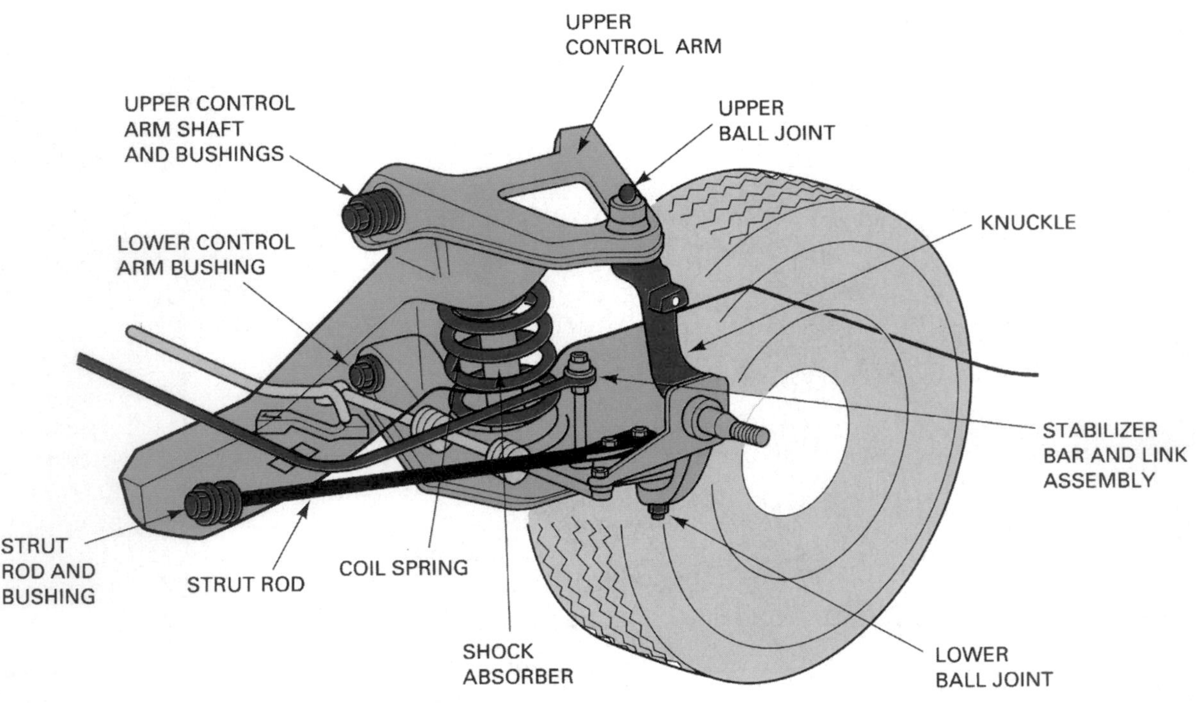

Figure 42–26 A strut rod is a longitudinal support to prevent front-to-back wheel movement.

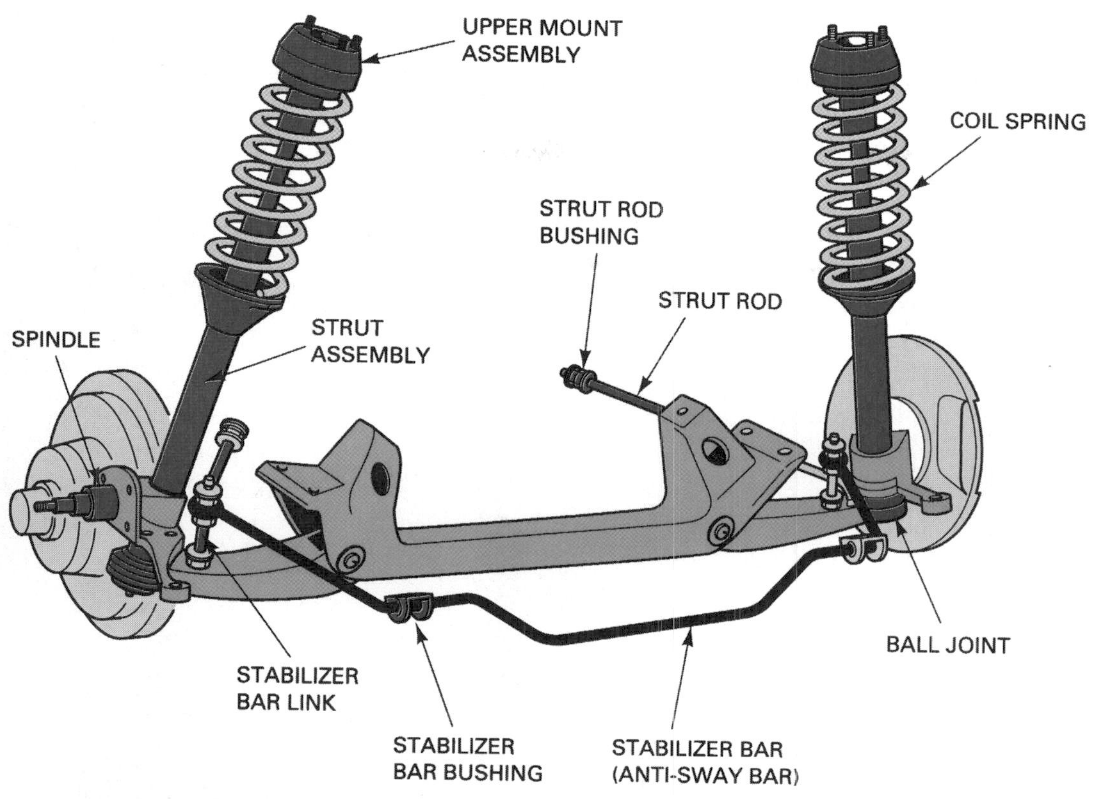

Figure 42–27 Typical stabilizer bar installation.

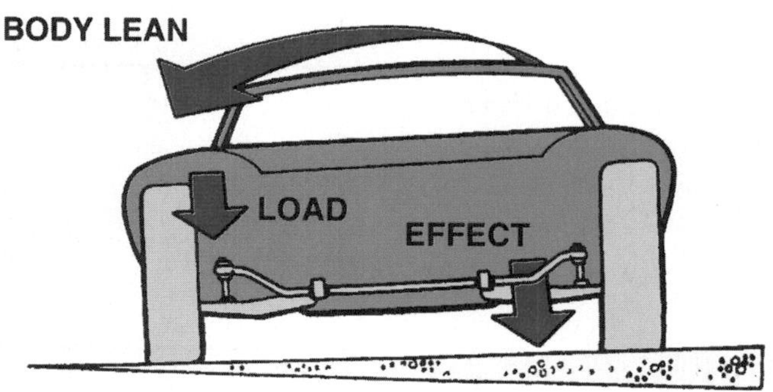

Figure 42–28 As the body of the vehicle leans, the stabilizer bar is twisted. The force exerted by the stabilizer bar counteracts the body lean. (Courtesy of Cooper Automotive Company)

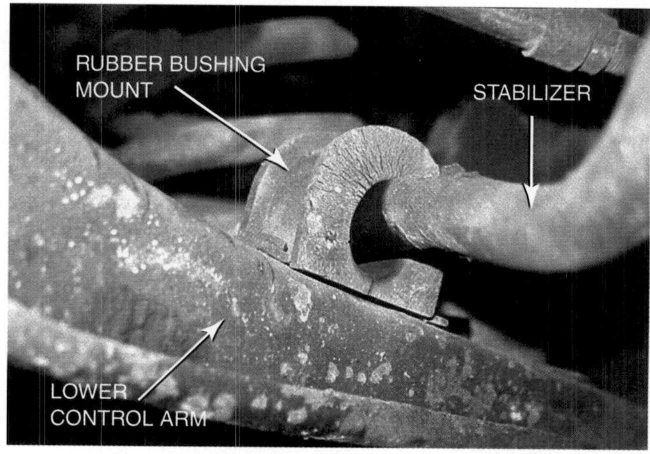

Figure 42–29 Notice how the stabilizer bar pulls down on the mounting bushing when the vehicle is hoisted off the ground, allowing the front suspension to drop down. These bushings are a common source of noise, especially when cold. Lubricating the bushings with paste silicone grease often cures the noise.

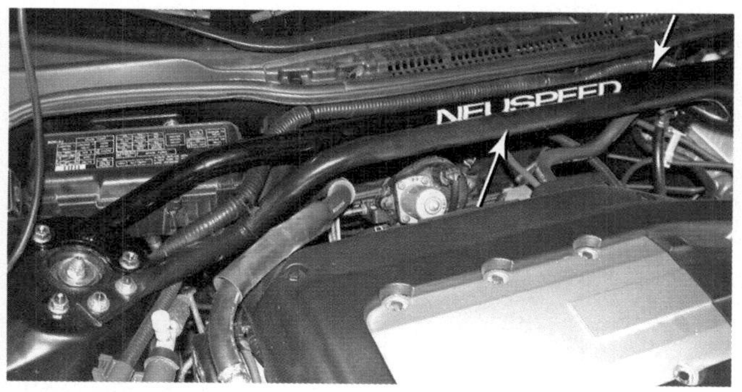

Figure 42–30 This vehicle is equipped with two strut bars—the original factory installed unit and an additional aftermarket version.

Shock Absorbers

Shock absorbers are used on all conventional suspension systems to dampen and control the motion of the vehicle's springs. Without shock absorbers (dampers), the vehicle would continue to bounce after hitting bumps. See Figure 42–31. Struts are shock absorbers that are part of a MacPherson strut assembly. *The major purpose of any shock or strut is to control ride and handling.* Standard shock absorbers *do not* support the weight of a vehicle. *The springs support the weight of the vehicle and the shock absorbers control the actions and reactions of the springs.*

Most shock absorbers are direct acting because they are connected directly from the vehicle frame or body to the axles. See Figure 42–32. The shock absorber helps dampen the rapid up-and-down movement of the vehicle springs by converting the energy of movement into heat by forcing hydraulic fluid through small holes inside the shock absorber. See Figure 42–33.

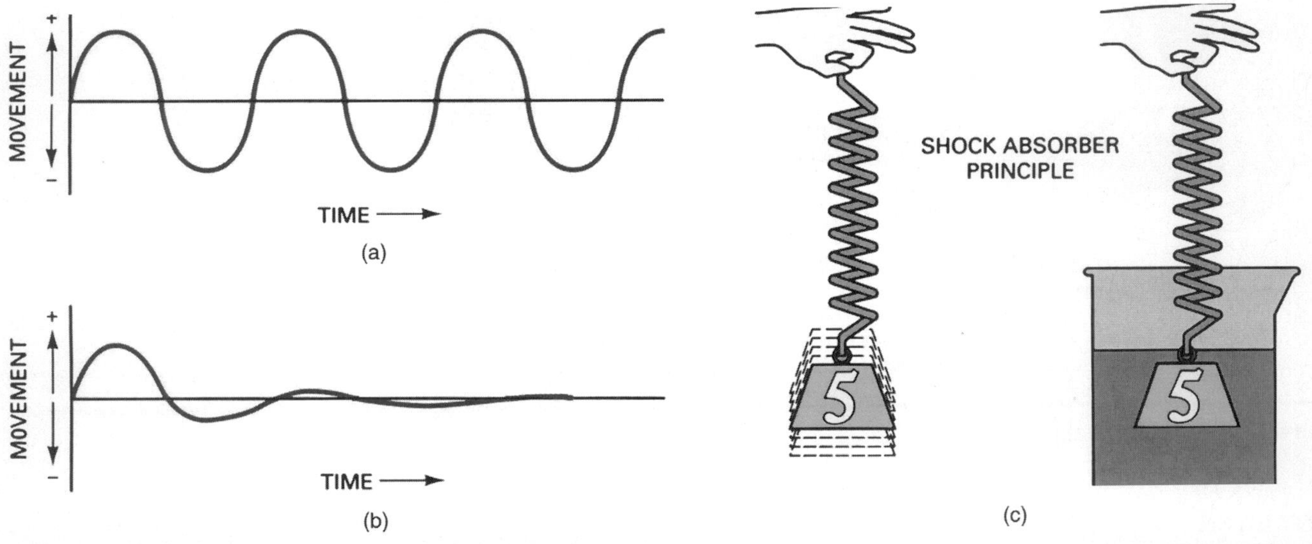

Figure 42–31 (a) The movement of a vehicle is supported by springs without a dampening device. (b) Spring action dampened with a shock absorber. (c) The function of any shock absorber is to dampen the movement or action of a spring in a way similar to using a liquid to control the movement of a weight on a spring. (Courtesy of John Bean Company)

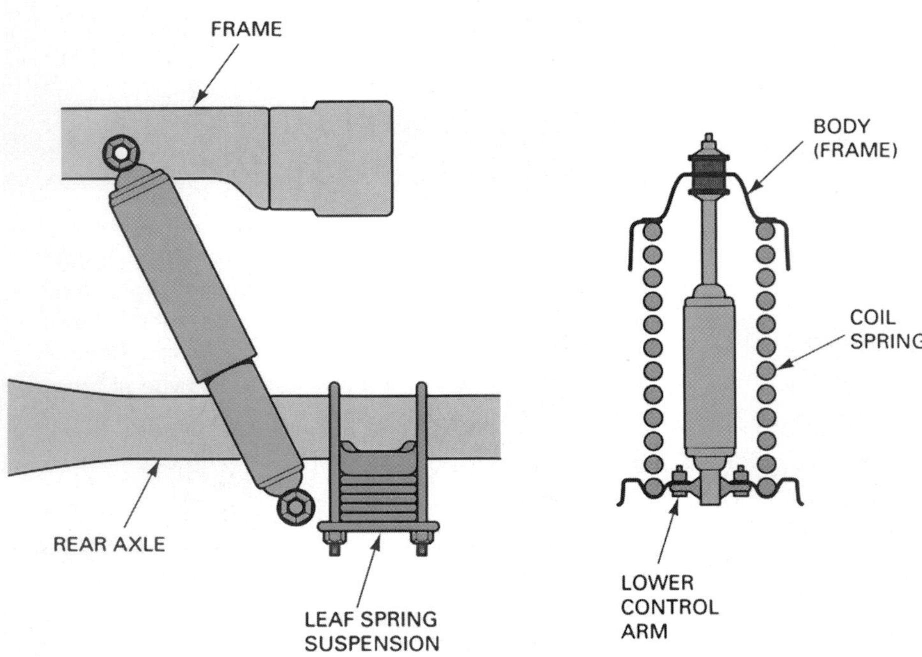

Figure 42–32 Shock absorbers work best when mounted as close to the spring as possible. Shock absorbers that are mounted straight up and down offer the most dampening.

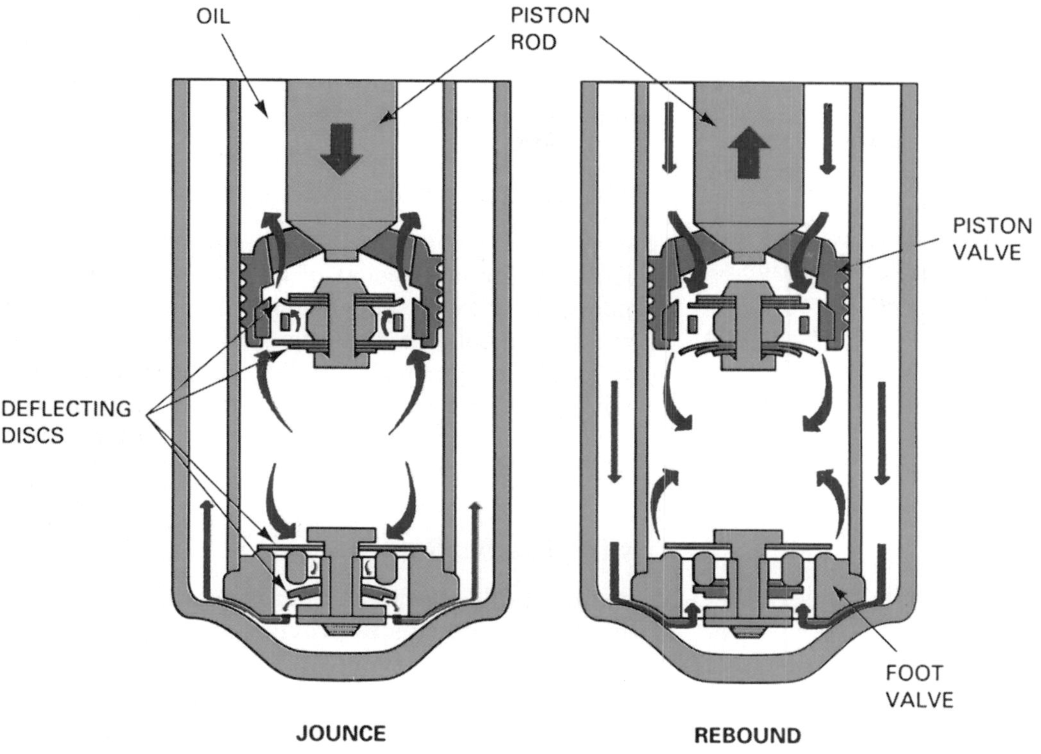

Figure 42–33 Oil flow through a deflected disc-type piston valve. The deflecting disc can react rapidly to the movement of the suspension. For example, if a large bump is hit at high speed, the disc can deflect completely and allow the suspension to reach its maximum jounce distance while maintaining a controlled rate of movement.

Gas-Charged Shocks Most shock absorbers and MacPherson struts on new vehicles are gas charged. Pressurizing the oil inside the shock absorber helps smooth the ride over rough roads. The pressure helps prevent air pockets from forming in the shock absorber oil as it passes through the small passages in the shock. Typical gas-charged shocks are pressurized with nitrogen at 900–1000 kPa (130–150 psi) to aid in both handling and ride control.

Some gas-charged shock absorbers and MacPherson struts use a single tube containing two pistons that separate the high-pressure gas from the working fluid. Single-tube shocks are also called **monotube** or **DeCarbon,** after the French inventor of the principle and manufacturer of suspension components. See Figure 42–34.

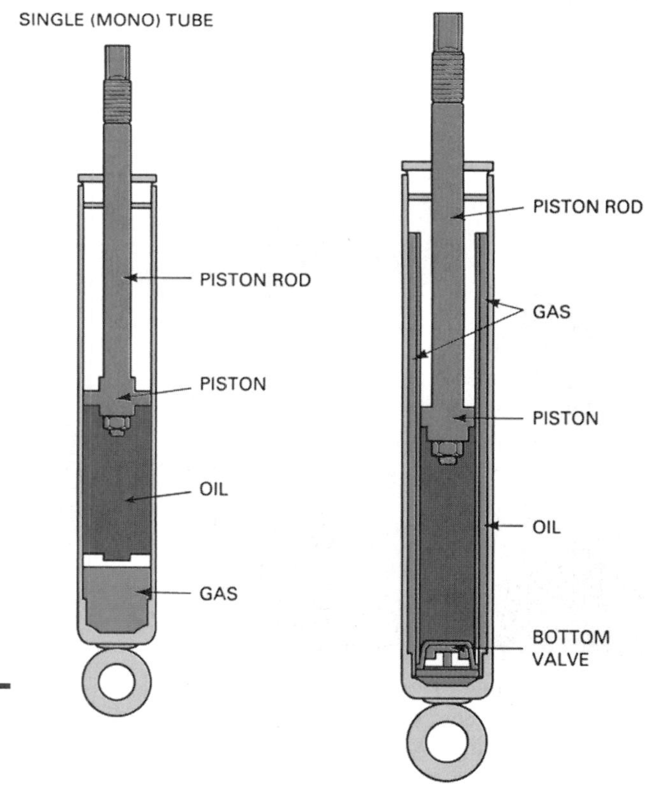

Figure 42–34 Gas-charged shock absorbers are manufactured with a double-tube design similar to conventional shock absorbers and also with a single- or monotube design.

REAR SUSPENSIONS

Solid-Axle Rear Suspensions

Solid- or straight-axle rear suspensions can use coil springs or leaf springs. See Figures 42–35 and 42–36. Leaf springs function as a load-carrying member as well as provide side-to-side support and stability. Coil springs, however, can only function as load-carrying members and must depend on various other suspension members to provide side-to-side (lateral) as well as front-to-back rear axle support.

Longitudinal (back-and-forth) support is provided by rear **control arms,** also called **trailing arms** because the rear axle trails behind the control-arm frame mounts. These rear control arms are usually angled to provide transverse (side-to-side) support as well as longitudinal support. Some manufacturers add an additional rear support member to ensure that the centre of the body is kept directly over the centre of the rear axle. These horizontal rear bars are called **track rods** or **panhard rods** and are bolted to the rear axle at one end and the vehicle frame at the other end. See Figure 42–37.

Figure 42–35 A semi-independent axle-beam rear suspension. It is called *semi-independent* because as a wheel hits a bump in the road, the trailing arm moves upward and twists the axle beam. This twisting of the axle beam helps isolate one side of the vehicle from the other. (Courtesy of Dana Corporation, Perfect Circle Products)

Figure 42–36 The rear suspension of a Dodge Caravan minivan. Note the use of a single-leaf spring and an axle-beam rear axle.

Independent Rear Suspensions

Most newer front-wheel-drive vehicles use an independent rear suspension, often abbreviated **IRS.** An independent rear suspension provides a smoother ride than a solid axle suspension because each rear wheel can react to bumps and dips in the road without moving the entire rear axle. Many front-wheel-drive vehicles with IRS also provide for some alignment adjustments. See Figure 42–38.

Air Shocks/Struts

Air-inflatable shock absorbers or struts are used in the rear of vehicles to provide proper vehicle ride height while carrying heavy loads. Many air shock/strut units are original equipment and are often combined with a built-in air compressor and ride height sensor(s) to provide automatic ride-height control. Air-inflatable shocks are standard shock absorbers that have an air chamber with a rubber bag built into the dust cover (top) of the shock. See Figure 42–39. Air pressure is used to inflate the bag, which raises the installed height of the shock. *It is important that the load capacity of the vehicle not be exceeded or serious damage can occur to the vehicle's springs, axles, bearings, and shock support mounts.*

Electronically Controlled Suspensions

Many vehicle manufacturers offer some type of electronically controlled suspension. Most use conventional springs or air springs.

Electronically Controlled Rear Air-Inflatable Shock Absorbers The main purpose of this system is to maintain controlled rear ride (trim) height under all vehicle load conditions. Some vehicles are equipped with rear air shocks that can be controlled electronically to adjust the ride height of the vehicle regardless of vehicle load. See Figure 42–40. An air dryer is usually attached to the pump to remove moisture from the air before it is sent to the shocks and back through the dryer (to dry the chemical dryer) during the release of air from the shocks. The height sensor operates the compressor or exhaust solenoid based on the height of the rear of the vehicle.

Four-Wheel Ride Height Control Four-wheel ride height control uses air-inflatable springs to

TRACK ROD
(PANHARD ROD)
SHOCK ABSORBER
UPPER
CONTROL ARM
LOWER
CONTROL ARM
COIL SPRING

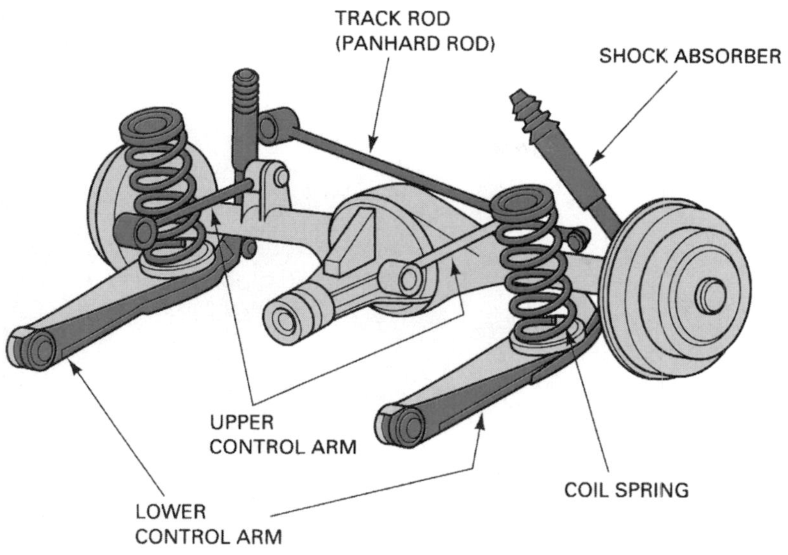

Figure 42–37 A track rod attaches to the frame (or body) on one end and to the axle itself on the other end. This rod helps keep the rear axle centred on the vehicle.

31
27
11
10
9
31
2
32
A
41
FRT
12
33
A REAR CROSSMEMBER
2 TUBING ASSEMBLY
9 AIR HOSE
10 AIR FILTER ASSEMBLY
11 BRACKET
12 BRACKET
27 HEIGHT SENSOR ASSEMBLY
31 CLIP
32 RIGHT HAND AIR ADJUSTABLE SHOCK
33 LEFT HAND AIR ADJUSTABLE SHOCK

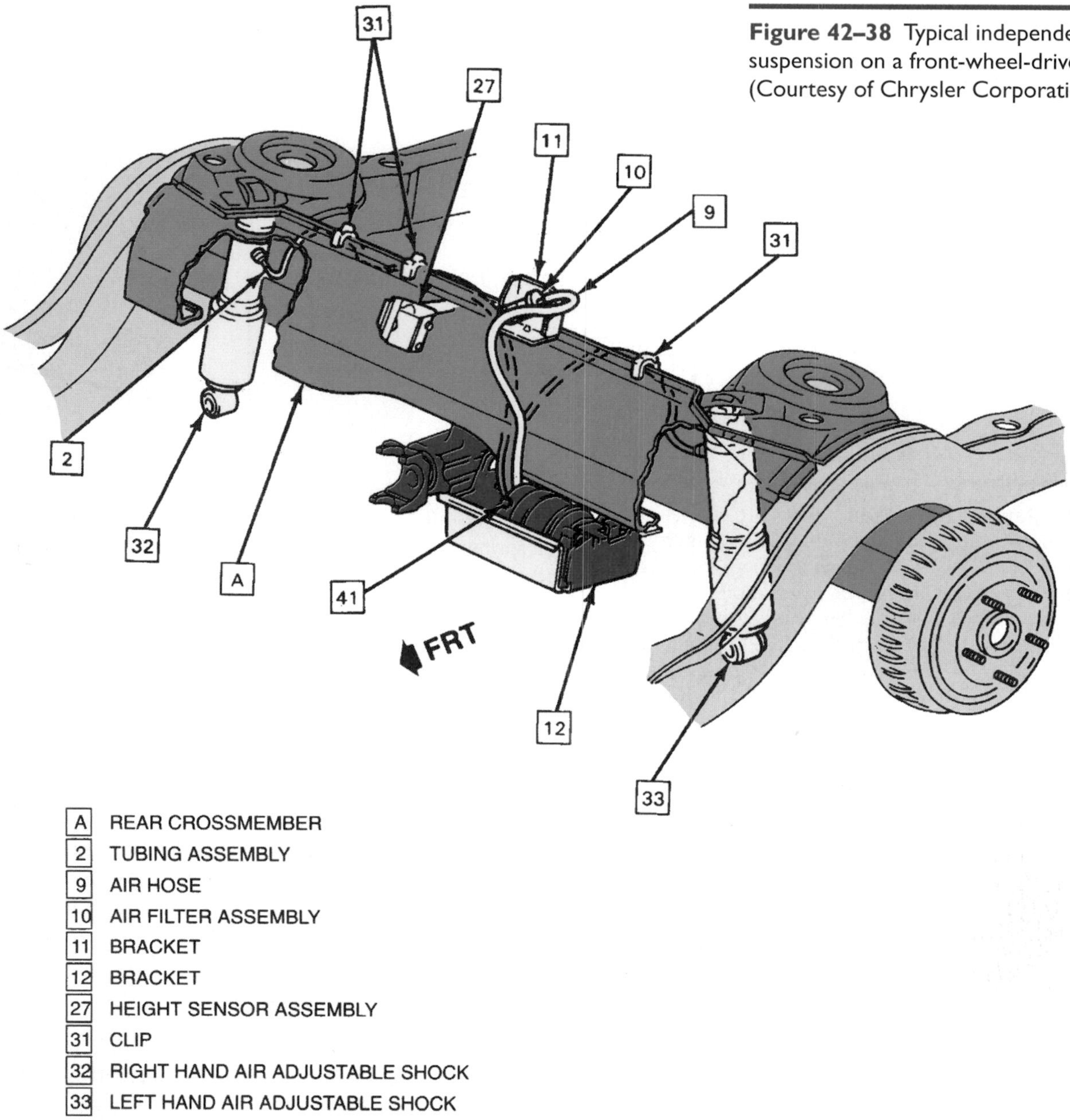

Figure 42–38 Typical independent rear suspension on a front-wheel-drive vehicle. (Courtesy of Chrysler Corporation)

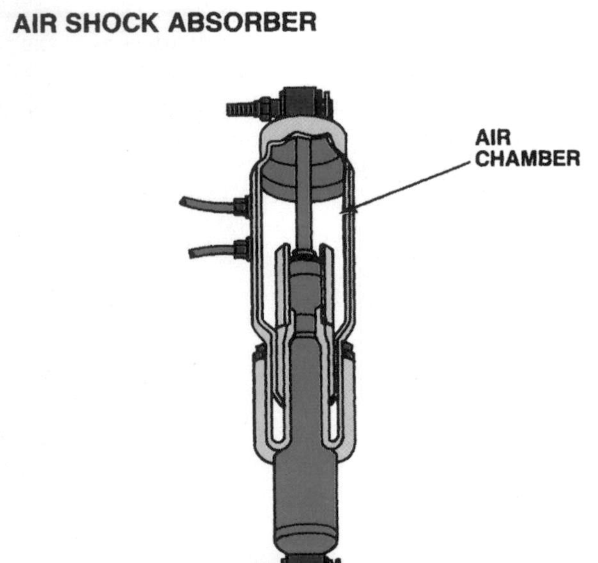

Figure 42–39 A rubber tube forms an inflatable air chamber at the top of an air shock. The higher the air pressure in the chamber, the stiffer the shock.

support vehicle weight; the inflation pressure is varied by an electronic controller. The main purpose of this type of system is to maintain the same ride height both front and rear as well as side-to-side under all driving conditions. See Figure 42–41.

> **CAUTION:** Many vehicles equipped with air suspension, such as many Lincoln automobiles, have a trunk-mounted on/off switch. Before servicing, hoisting, jacking, or towing, this switch must be in the off position. If the switch is not turned off, the height sensor will indicate that the vehicle is too high when it is hoisted and release all of the air from the air springs. The vehicle's suspension will be at the lowest possible level when the vehicle is lowered. Proper height will usually be restored when the engine is started and the sensor determines that the level is too low. See Figure 42–42.

Computer-Controlled Shock Absorbers Computer-controlled shock absorbers are used with conventional metal or fibreglass composite springs. The main purpose of this type of system is to permit a smoother ride over rough road surfaces yet still permit a stiffer ride at higher speeds or to stiffen the shocks during braking, accelerating, or cornering.

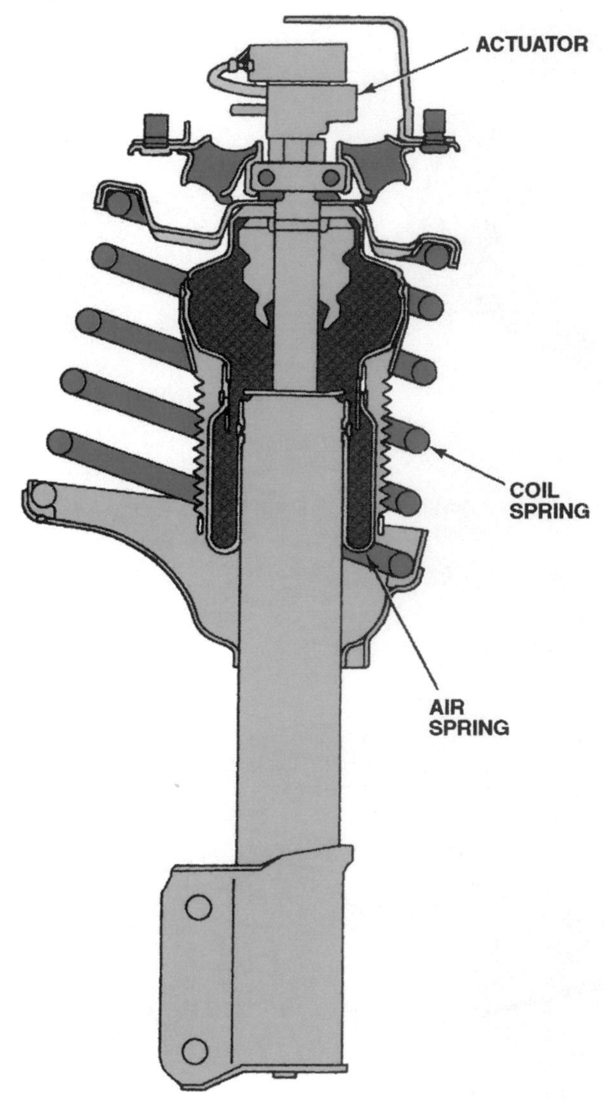

Figure 42–40 Some air springs are auxiliary units to the coil spring and are used only to control ride height, while the coil spring is the weight-carrying component.

SUSPENSION SYSTEM DIAGNOSIS

Suspension systems are designed and manufactured to provide years of trouble-free service with a minimum amount of maintenance. The smart technician should always road test any vehicle before and after servicing. (See the Tech Tip "Road Test Before and After" for details.) *The purpose of any diagnosis is to eliminate known-good components.*

Road-Test Diagnosis

If possible, perform a road test of the vehicle with the owner of the vehicle. It is also helpful to have the owner drive the vehicle. A proper road test for any

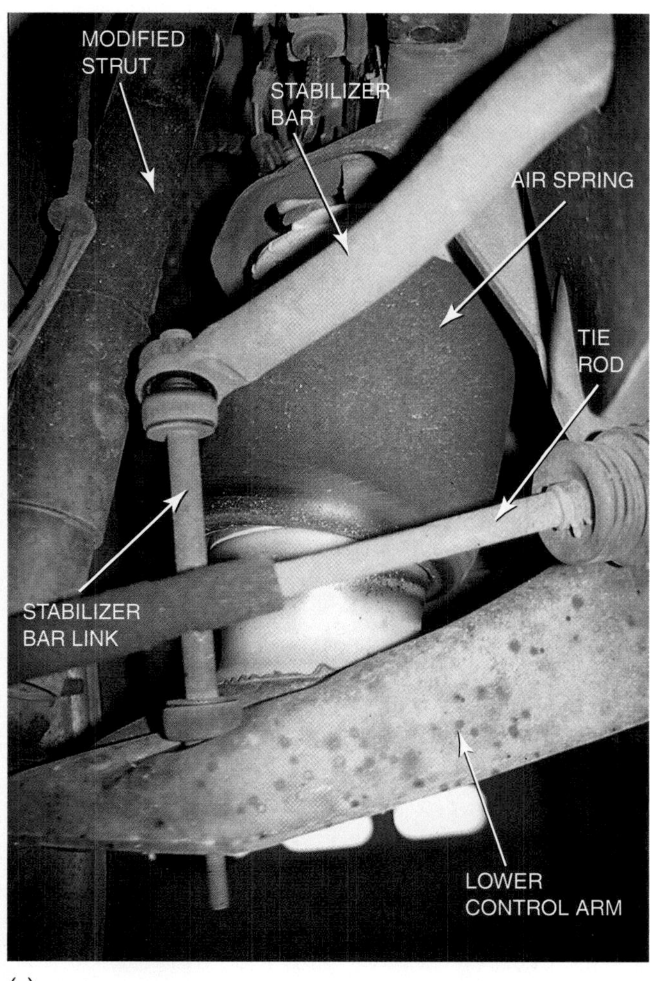

(a)

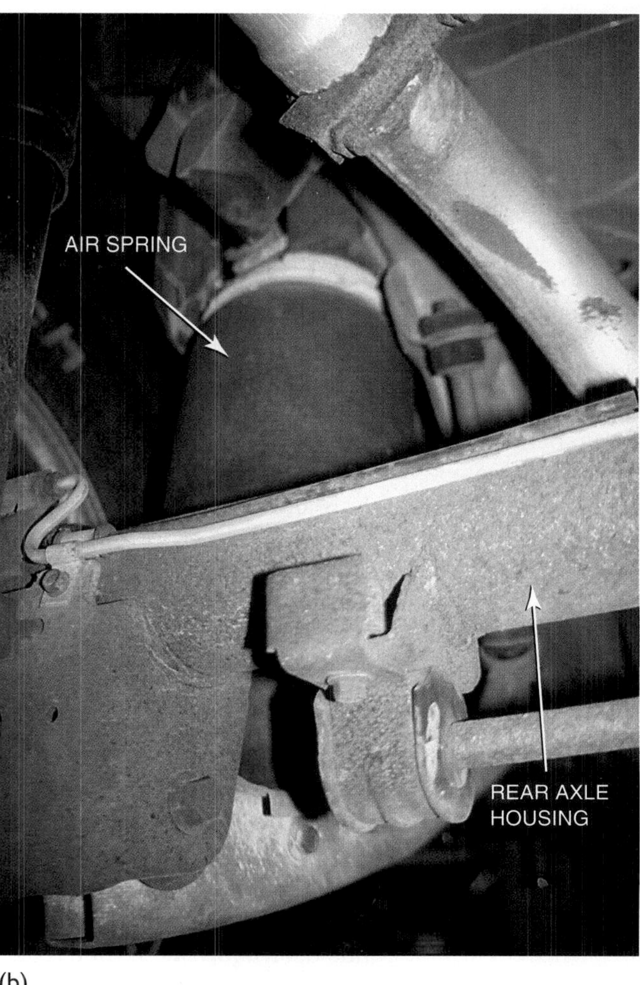

(b)

Figure 42–41 (a) The front suspension of a Lincoln with an air-spring suspension. (b) The rear suspension of the same Lincoln.

Figure 42–42 Always check in the trunk for a cutoff switch for a vehicle equipped with an air suspension before hoisting or towing the vehicle.

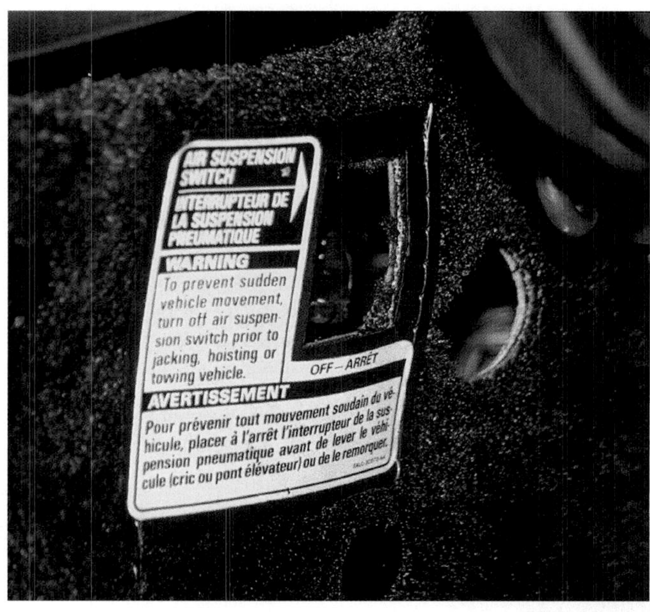

suspension system problem should include the following measures:

- *Driving beside parked vehicles.* Any noise generated by the vehicle suspension or tires is reflected off solid objects, such as a row of vehicles parked along a street. Repeat the drive for the right side. Defective wheel bearings or power steering pumps usually make noise and can be heard during this test.
- *Driving into driveways.* Suspension problems often occur when turning at the same time the suspension hits a bump. The curb causes the suspension to compress while the wheels are turned. Defective stabilizer bar bushings, control arm bushings, and ball joints will usually make noise during this test procedure.
- *Driving in reverse while turning.* This technique is usually used to find possible defective outer CV joints on the drive axle shaft of front-wheel-drive vehicles.
- *Driving over a bumpy road.* Worn or defective suspension (and steering) components can cause the vehicle to bounce or dart side-to-side while travelling over bumps and dips in the road. Worn or defective ball joints, control arm bushings, stabilizer bar bushings, stabilizer bar links, as well as worn shock absorbers, can be the cause.

Once the problem has been confirmed, then a further inspection can be performed in the service bay.

Visual Inspection

All suspension components should be carefully inspected for signs of wear or damage. For example, there could be worn shock absorbers or saggy springs if the jounce bumpers (stops) are damaged, worn, or missing. While an assistant bounces the vehicle up and down, check if there is any free play in any of the suspension components. See Figure 42–43. Many load-carrying ball joints have wear indicators with a raised area around the grease fitting. See Figure 42–44.

> **NOTE:** Always check ball joints with wear indicators with the wheels of the vehicle on the ground. If the raised area around the grease fitting is flush to or recessed from the surrounding area, the ball joint is worn more than 1.3 mm (0.050 in.) and must be replaced.

> **HINT:** Most ball joints must be replaced if the joint has more than 1.3 mm (0.050 in.) axial (up-and-down) movement. To help visualize this distance, consider that the thickness of a nickel coin is about 1.5 mm (0.060 in.). See Figure 42–45.

Figure 42–43 It was easy to see that this worn bushing on a Ford pickup needed to be replaced. The new bushing is shown next to the original.

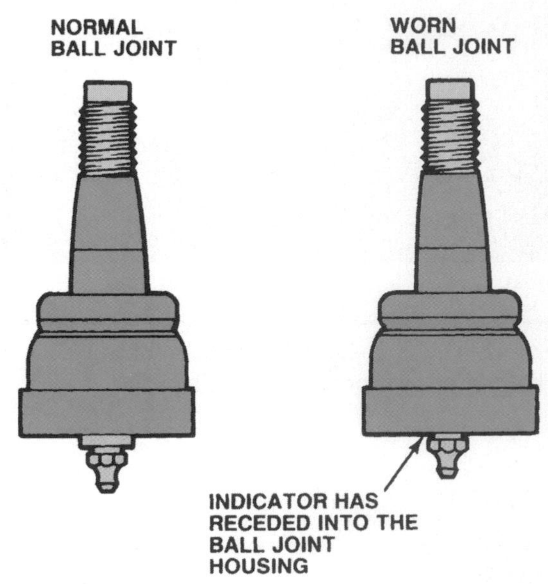

Figure 42–44 As a ball joint with a wear indicator wears, the shoulder around the grease fitting moves inward toward the joint.

To perform a proper ball joint inspection, the force of the vehicle's springs *must* be *unloaded* from the ball joint. If this force is not relieved, the ball-and-socket joint will be forced tightly together and thus prevent wear from being detected by movement.

> **HINT:** The location of the load-carrying ball joint is closest to the seat of the spring or torsion bar.

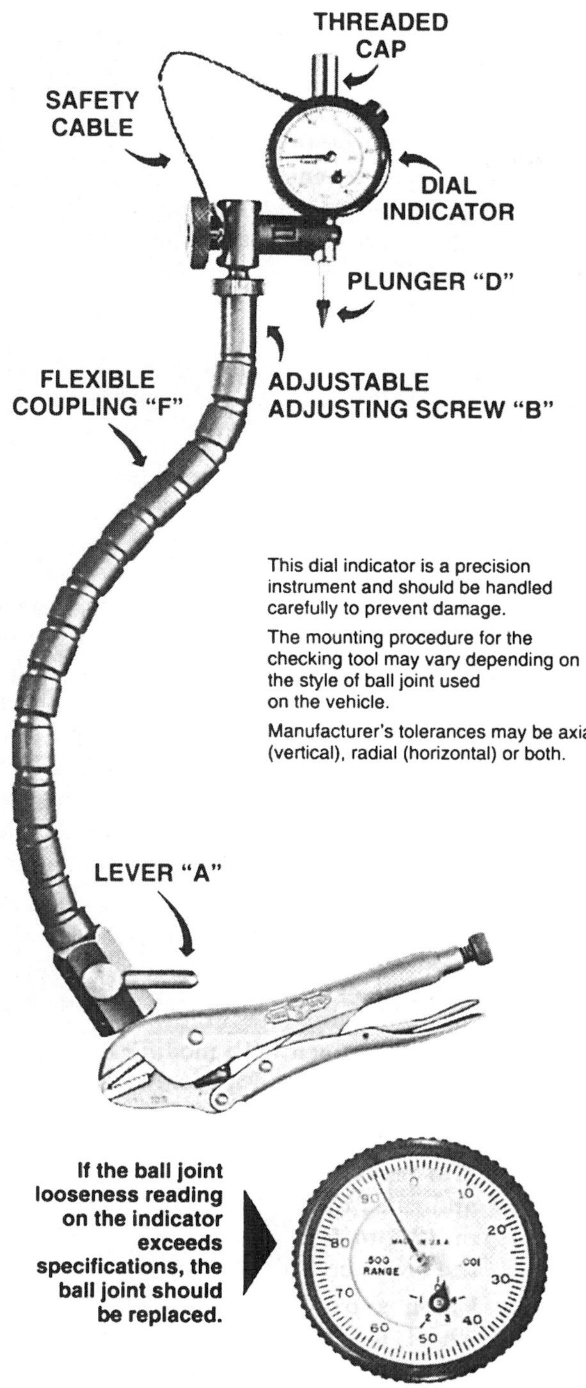
THREADED CAP
SAFETY CABLE
DIAL INDICATOR
PLUNGER "D"
FLEXIBLE COUPLING "F"
ADJUSTABLE ADJUSTING SCREW "B"
This dial indicator is a precision instrument and should be handled carefully to prevent damage.
The mounting procedure for the checking tool may vary depending on the style of ball joint used on the vehicle.
Manufacturer's tolerances may be axial (vertical), radial (horizontal) or both.
LEVER "A"
If the ball joint looseness reading on the indicator exceeds specifications, the ball joint should be replaced.

Figure 42–45 Typical dial indicator used to measure suspension component movement. The locking pliers attach the gauge to a stationary part of the vehicle, and the flexible coupling allows the dial indicator to be positioned at any angle. (Courtesy of Cooper Automotive Company)

TECH TIP 

Road Test Before and After

Many times technicians will start to work on a vehicle based on the description of the problem from the driver or owner. A typical conversation was overheard in which the vehicle owner complained that the vehicle handled "funny," especially when turning. The vehicle owner wanted a wheel alignment and therefore the vehicle was aligned, yet the problem was still present. The real problem was a defective tire. The service technician should have road tested the vehicle *before* any service work was done to confirm the problem and try to determine its cause. Every technician should test drive the vehicle *after* any service work is performed to confirm that the service work was performed correctly and that the customer complaint has been solved. This is especially true for any service work involving the steering, suspension, or braking systems.

If the coil spring or torsion bar is attached to the *lower* control arm, the *lower* ball joint is the load-carrying ball joint. See Figure 42–46. This includes vehicles equipped with modified MacPherson strut-type suspension. See Figure 42–47.

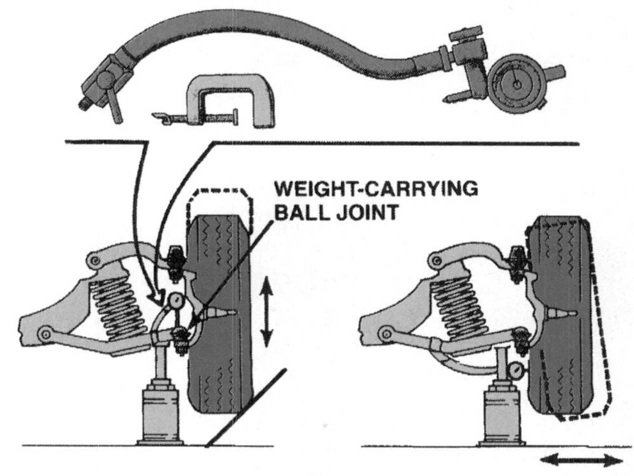
WEIGHT-CARRYING BALL JOINT

Figure 42–46 If the spring is attached to the lower control arm, as in this SLA suspension, the jack should be placed under the lower control arm as shown. A dial indicator should be used to measure the amount of free play in the ball joints. Be sure that the looseness measured is not due to normal wheel-bearing end play. (Courtesy of Dana Corporation, Perfect Circle Products)

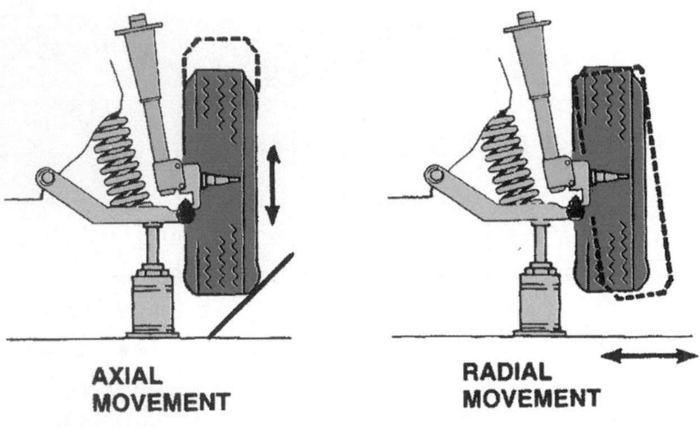

Figure 42–47 The jack should be placed under the lower control arm of this modified MacPherson-type suspension. (Courtesy of Dana Corporation, Perfect Circle Products)

TECH TIP 

Always Inspect the Spring Seat Indicator Holes

Most vehicles equipped with a coil spring front suspension have two holes in the spring seat of the lower control arm that are used to check that the spring is correctly seated. One hole must be completely covered and the other hole should be partially or completely covered. See Figure 42–48.

This fact came in handy one day when inspecting a vehicle for a handling problem. Someone had installed replacement front springs upside down. Neither hole was covered by the spring. Removing the springs and installing them correctly solved the problem.

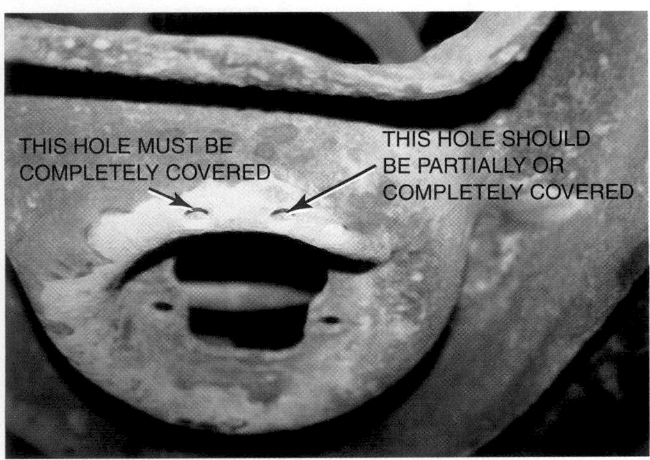

Figure 42–48 The holes at the bottom of the spring seat not only allow water to drain, but also indicate whether the spring is correctly installed.

TECH TIP 

The Chrysler Minivan Ball Joint Test

Minivans manufactured by Chrysler Corporation, including the Dodge Caravan and the Plymouth Voyager, are easily checked for worn ball joints. Simply grasp the grease fitting and attempt to move it with your fingers. If the grease fitting moves, the ball joint is worn and requires replacement. This simple test should be done with the weight of the vehicle on the floor—in other words, there is no need to raise or support the vehicle to do this simple test.

Ball Joint Removal

Take care to avoid damaging grease seals when separating ball joints from their mounts. *The preferred method of separating tapered parts is to use a puller-type tool that applies force to the tapered joint as the bolt is tightened on the puller.* See Figure 42–49. Sometimes a hammer can be used to separate the ball joint from the steering knuckle. For best results, another hammer should be used as a backup while striking the joint to be separated on the side with a heavy hammer.

CAUTION: Using tapered "pickle forks" should be avoided, unless the part is to be replaced, because they often damage the grease seal of the part being separated.

Some ball joint studs have a slot or groove where a **pinch bolt** is used to hold the ball joint to the steering knuckle. See Figure 42–50. When removing

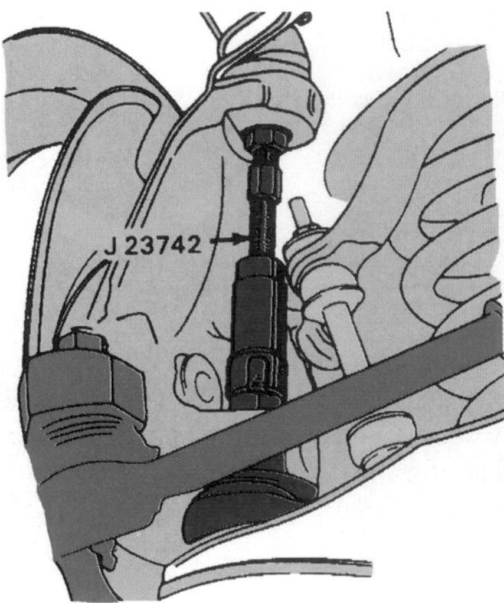

Figure 42–49 Taper-breaker tool being used to separate the upper ball joint from the steering knuckle. (Courtesy of General Motors Corporation)

ball joints that are riveted in place, always cut off or drill rivet heads before separating the ball joint from the spindle. This provides a more solid base for removing rivets. *The preferred method of removing rivets from ball joints is to centre punch and drill out the centre of the rivet using the specified drill bit size before using a drill or an air-powered chisel to remove the rivet heads.* Be careful not to drill or chisel into the control arms. See Figure 42–51. Use only the bolts that came with the replacement ball joints. Press-in ball joints are removed and installed using a special C-clamp-type tool. See Figure 42–52.

NOTE: Many replacement press-in ball joints are slightly larger in diameter (about 1.3 mm [0.050 in.]) than the original ball joint to provide the same press fit. If the ball joints have been replaced before, then the control arm may need to be replaced.

SAFETY TIP

Always Tighten—Never Loosen—Tapered Parts

Always follow the manufacturer's recommended installation instructions whenever replacing any suspension or other chassis component part. Tie rod ends and ball joints use a taper to provide the attachment to other components. When installing a replacement tie rod end or ball joint, be sure to seat the taper so that the nut will tighten. Whenever a nut is used to tighten a tapered part, it is important to not back off (loosen) the nut after tightening. As the nut is tightened, the taper is being pulled into the taper of the adjoining part. The specified torque on the nut assures that the two pieces of the taper are properly joined. If the cotter key does not line up with the hole in the tapered stud when the nut has been properly torqued, *tighten* it more to line up a hole—never loosen the nut.

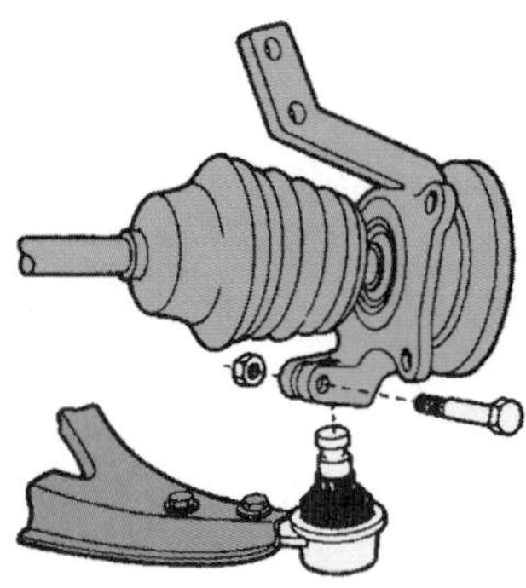

Figure 42–50 A pinch bolt attaches the steering knuckle to the ball joint. Remove the pinch bolt by turning the nut, not the bolt. (Courtesy of Cooper Automotive Company)

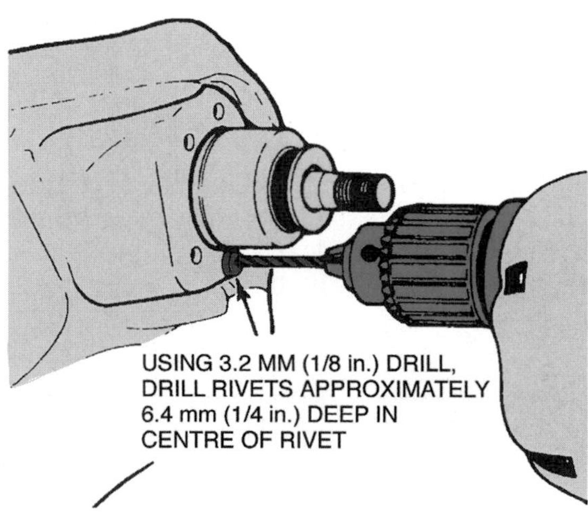

USING 3.2 MM (1/8 in.) DRILL,
DRILL RIVETS APPROXIMATELY
6.4 mm (1/4 in.) DEEP IN
CENTRE OF RIVET

Figure 42–51 By drilling into the rivet, the holding force is released. (Courtesy of General Motors Corporation)

IMPORTANT

Figure 42–52 Press-in ball joints are best removed using a large C-clamp press, as shown. The same tool is used to remove the old and install the new ball joint by using different adapters and sleeves for the tool.

DIAGNOSTIC STORY 

The Rattle Story

A customer complained that a rattle was heard every time the vehicle hit a bump. The noise sounded as if it came from the rear. All parts of the exhaust system and suspension system were checked. Everything seemed okay until the vehicle was raised with a frame-type hoist instead of a drive-on type. Then, whenever the right rear wheel was lifted, the noise occurred. The problem was a worn (elongated) shock absorber mounting hole. A washer with the proper size hole was welded over the worn lower frame mount, and the shock absorber was bolted back into place.

Avoid using heat to remove suspension or steering components. Many chassis parts use rubber and plastic that can be damaged if heated with a torch. *If heat is used to remove a part, it must be replaced.* Many vehicles are equipped with nonreplaceable ball joints, so the entire control arm must be replaced if the ball joint is worn or defective.

Shock Absorber and Strut Diagnosis

Replacement shock absorbers may be required when any or all of the following symptoms appear:

1. *Ride harshness.* Worn shocks can cause ride harshness and yet not cause the vehicle to bounce after hitting a bump.
2. *Frequent "bottoming out" on rough roads.* Shock absorbers provide a controlled movement of the axle whenever the vehicle hits a bump or dip in the road.

NOTE: Frequent bottoming out is also a symptom of reduced ride height due to sagging springs. Before replacing the shock absorbers, always check for proper ride height as specified in the vehicle service manual or any alignment specification booklet available from suppliers or companies manufacturing alignment or chassis parts and equipment.

3. *Extended vehicle movement after driving on dips or a rise in the road.* The most common shock absorber test is the **bounce test.** Push down on the body of the vehicle and let go. The vehicle should return to its normal ride height and stop. If the vehicle continues to bounce two or three times, then the shocks or struts are worn and must be replaced.

DIAGNOSTIC STORY 

It's Not Far—It Can Take It

An automotive instructor needed to transport several V-8 engines just a couple of kilometres. A truck was not available so the instructor carried the three engines in a station wagon. The rear of the station wagon sagged under the load. After the engines were unloaded, the rear of the station wagon remained lower than normal. The steel of the coil spring had exceeded its "yield point" and did not return to its original position. As a result, the rear coil springs took a set due to the excessive load and were ruined. The rear coil springs had to be replaced to restore the proper ride height.

NOTE: Leaf springs, too, can be easily overloaded and take a set or break! Overloading *any* vehicle can also damage the wheel bearings.

Never carry a load in any vehicle that exceeds its design capacity.

4. *Cuppy-type tire wear.* Defective shock absorbers can cause **cuppy**-type tire wear. Cuppy wear means that indentations are worn into the tread caused by the tire bouncing up and down as it rotates.
5. *Leaking hydraulic oil.* When a shock or strut leaks oil externally, this indicates a defective seal. The shock absorber or strut cannot function correctly when low on oil inside.

Shock absorbers should be replaced in pairs. Both front or both rear shocks should be replaced together to provide the best handling and control. See Figure 42–53.

NOTE: Shock absorbers do not affect ride height except where special air shocks or coil overload carrying shocks are used. If a vehicle is sagging on one side or in the front or the rear, the springs should be checked and replaced if necessary.

HINT: Shock absorbers are filled with fluid and sealed during production. A slight amount of fluid may bleed by the rod seal in cold weather and deposit a light film on the upper area of the shock absorber. This condition will not hurt the operation of the shock and should be considered normal.

Figure 42–53 Whenever replacing shock absorbers (especially rear shock absorbers) be sure to support the rear axle. The rear axle assembly could drop and cause damage to the vehicle and possible personal injury if the axle is not supported when the shock absorber attaching bolt (or nut) is removed.

HIGH PERFORMANCE TIP

Urethane Bushings and Teflon® Tape

The replacement of the rubber suspension bushings with urethane bushings stiffens the chassis and makes steering more responsive. The disadvantage of using urethane bushings is that they tend to make squeaking sounds unless constantly lubricated with silicone grease. One way to help prevent the need to keep lubricating stabilizer bar bushings is to first wrap the bar with Teflon® tape and then place the bushing on the tape. Stabilizer bars work by twisting, and the Teflon® tape will lubricate the space between the bar and the urethane bushing. See Figure 42–54.

(a)

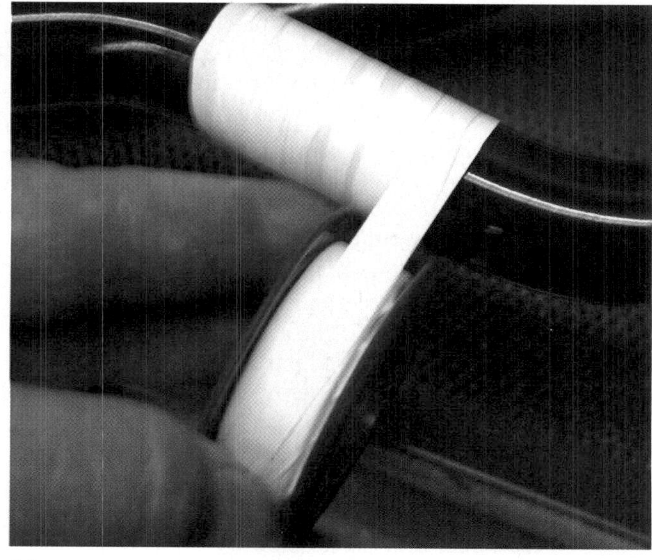

(b)

Figure 42–54 (a) Harder urethane bushings are frequently used with larger diameter high performance stabilizer bars. (b) Teflon® tape being used on the stabilizer bar to help reduce noise that often occurs when urethane bushings are used.

SUMMARY

1. Spring types include coil, leaf, and torsion bar.
2. Suspension designs include a straight or solid axle design and two control arm-types, an SLA suspension and a MacPherson strut.
3. All shock absorbers dampen the motion of the suspension to control ride and handling.
4. Ball joints attach to control arms and allow the front wheels to move up and down as well as turn.
5. Active (or reactive) suspension systems use sensors and a hydraulic pump to maintain ride height under all vehicle manoeuvres.
6. A thorough road test of a suspension problem should include driving beside parked vehicles and into driveways in an attempt to determine when and where the noise occurs.
7. Defective shock absorbers can cause ride harshness as well as frequent bottoming out on rough roads.
8. Ball joints must be unloaded before testing. The ball joints used on vehicles with a MacPherson strut suspension are *not* load carrying. Wear-indicator ball joints are to be observed with the wheels on the ground.
9. Always use a taper breaker puller or two hammers to loosen tapered parts to remove them. Never use heat unless you are replacing the part, because heat from a torch can damage rubber and plastic parts.
10. When installing a tapered part, always tighten the attaching nut to specifications and never loosen the nut to install a cotter key. If the cotter key will not line up with a hole in the tapered part, tighten the nut more until the cotter key hole lines up with the nut and stud.
11. Always follow manufacturers' recommended procedures whenever replacing springs or MacPherson struts. Never remove the strut end nut until the coil spring is compressed and the spring force is removed from the upper bearing assembly.

REVIEW QUESTIONS

1. List the types of suspensions and name their component parts.
2. Describe the purpose and function of a stabilizer bar.
3. Describe how to perform a proper road test for the diagnosis of suspension related problems.
4. List four symptoms of worn or defective shock absorbers.
5. Describe the testing procedure for ball joints.

RED SEAL CERTIFICATION-TYPE QUESTIONS

1. How is the ride height adjusted on a vehicle equipped with torsion bars?
   - **a.** By inserting shims
   - **b.** With an adjustment bolt
   - **c.** With air pressure
   - **d.** With rubber blocks
2. What can cause a rattling sound heard from the rear of the vehicle when travelling over bumps?
   - **a.** Loose steering gear
   - **b.** The rubber bushing around the shock is missing
   - **c.** Over-inflated tires
   - **d.** The power steering pressure-relief valve is loose
3. What does the typical MacPherson strut connect to near the wheel?
   - **a.** The brake caliper
   - **b.** The lower control arm
   - **c.** The upper control arm
   - **d.** The knuckle or wheel hub
4. What component can be used to change vehicle ride height?
   - **a.** Air shocks
   - **b.** Hydraulic shocks
   - **c.** The control arm
   - **d.** The stabilizer bar
5. What is the primary purpose of the shocks?
   - **a.** To support vehicle weight
   - **b.** To dampen the vehicle suspension when going over bumps
   - **c.** To dampen the vehicle suspension when turning
   - **d.** To provide a extra reservoir for power steering fluid
6. What is one advantage of electronically controlled air shocks?
   - **a.** Ride height is controlled automatically
   - **b.** They are more cost-efficient to build
   - **c.** There is less chance of leakage in cold weather
   - **d.** Noises are not transmitted as easily through air
7. The lower ball joint on the SLA suspension with the spring mounted on the lower control arm is
   - **a.** The load carrier
   - **b.** Always compression loaded
   - **c.** Inspected for wear by lifting on the frame of the vehicle
   - **d.** The follower
8. The preferred method for separating tapered chassis parts is to use
   - **a.** A "pickle fork" tool
   - **b.** A torch to heat the joint until it separates
   - **c.** Two hammers to shock and deform the taper or a puller tool
   - **d.** A drill to drill out the tapered part
9. The principle of operation of a standard hydraulic shock relies on
   - **a.** Hydraulic fluid being pushed through a small passage
   - **b.** Air being compressed in a closed capsule
   - **c.** Oil being compressed in a closed capsule
   - **d.** Nitrogen being compressed in a closed capsule
10. What could result from a broken rear leaf spring centre bolt?
    - **a.** The tire could separate from the vehicle
    - **b.** The rear wheels could "dog track"
    - **c.** Steering would be slow to respond
    - **d.** The shock absorber would rattle over bumps

43

Wheel Alignment Principles, Diagnosis, and Service

OBJECTIVES: After studying Chapter 43, you should be able to:

1. Prepare for the interprovincial Red Seal certification examination in Appendix IV (Suspension and Steering) on the topics covered in this chapter.
2. Define camber, caster, toe, SAI, included angle, turning radius, thrust line, and set back.
3. Explain how camber, caster, and toe affect the handling and tire wear of the vehicle.
4. List the many checks that should be performed before aligning a vehicle.
5. Describe the proper alignment setup procedure.

ALIGNMENT PURPOSE

A wheel alignment is the adjustment of the suspension and steering to ensure proper vehicle handling with minimum tire wear. A change in alignment angles may result from one or more of the following factors:

1. Wear of the steering and the suspension components
2. Bent or damaged steering and suspension parts
3. Sagging springs, which can change the ride height of the vehicle and therefore the alignment angles

By adjusting the suspension and steering components, the proper alignment angles can be restored. An alignment includes checking and adjusting, if necessary, both front and rear wheels.

ALIGNMENT-RELATED PROBLEMS

Most alignment diagnosis is symptom based. The following definitions of alignment symptom terms are used in this book:

Pull A pull is generally defined as a definite tug on the steering wheel toward the left or the right while driving straight on a level road.

Lead or Drift A lead or drift is a mild pull that does not cause a force on the steering wheel that the driver must counteract. When the vehicle moves toward one side or the other, this is called a *lead* or *drift.* A lead or drift could be caused by the crown of the road, as shown in Figure 43–1.

CAUTION: When test driving a vehicle for a lead or a drift, make sure that the road is free of traffic and that your hands remain close to the steering wheel. Your hands should simply be held away from the steering wheel for just a second or two—just long enough to check for a lead or drift condition.

Wander A wander is a condition in which almost constant steering wheel corrections by the driver are necessary to maintain a straight-ahead direction on a straight, level road.

Camber

Camber is the inward or outward tilt of the wheels from true vertical as viewed from the front or rear of the vehicle. See Figure 43–2.

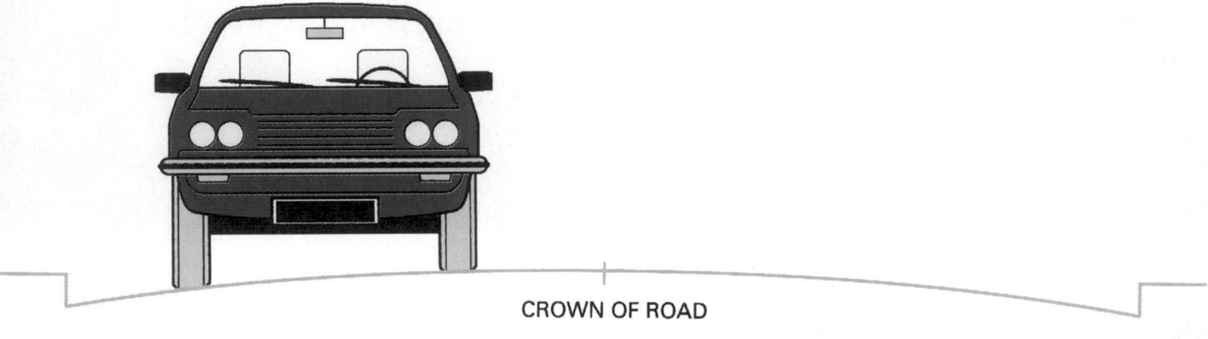

Figure 43–1 The crown of the road refers to the angle or slope of the roadway needed to drain water off the pavement. (Courtesy of Hunter Engineering Company)

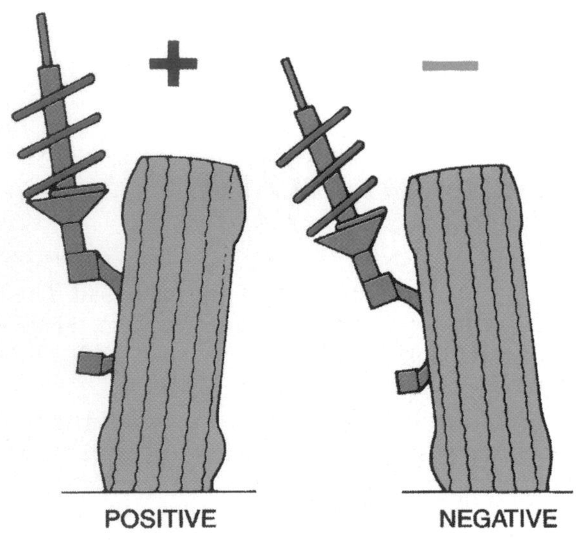

Figure 43–2 Positive and negative camber. (Courtesy of Hunter Engineering Company)

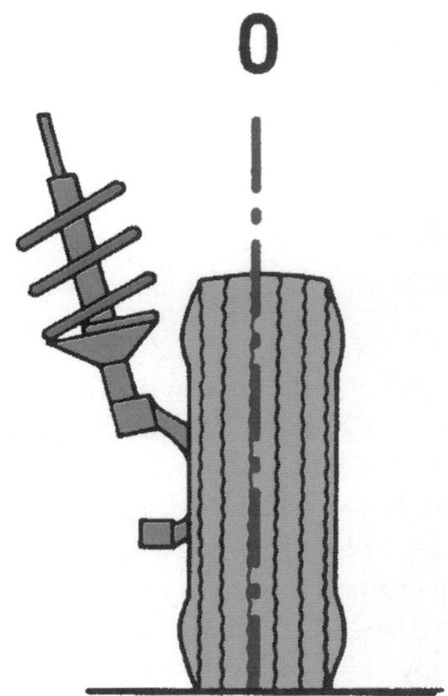

Figure 43–3 Zero camber. (Courtesy of Hunter Engineering Company)

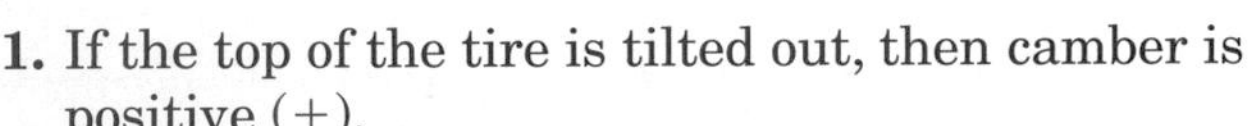

1. If the top of the tire is tilted out, then camber is positive (+).
2. If the top of the tire is tilted in, then camber is negative (−).
3. Camber is zero (0°) if the tilt of the wheel is truly vertical, as shown in Figure 43–3.
4. Camber is measured in degrees or fractions of degrees.
5. *Camber can cause tire wear if not correct.*
   a. Excessive positive camber causes scuffing and wear on the outside edge of the tire
   b. Excessive negative camber causes scuffing and wear on the inside edge of the tire
6. Camber can cause pull if it is unequal side to side. *The vehicle will pull toward the side with the **most positive** (or **least negative**) camber.* A difference of more than half a degree from one side to the other will cause the vehicle to pull. See Figure 43–4.
7. Incorrect camber can cause excessive wear on wheel bearings, as shown in Figure 43–5. Many vehicle manufacturers specify positive camber so that the vehicle's weight is applied to the larger inner wheel bearing and spindle. As the vehicle is loaded or when the springs sag, camber usually decreases. If camber is kept positive, then the running camber is kept near zero degrees for best tire life.

NOTE: Many front-wheel-drive vehicles that use sealed wheel bearings often are manufactured to have negative camber.

8. Camber is *not* adjustable on many vehicles.
9. If camber is adjustable, the change is made by moving the upper or the lower control arm or

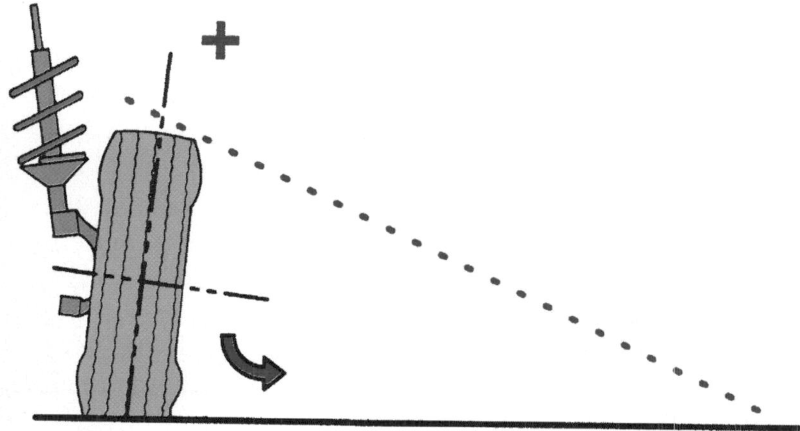

Figure 43–4 Camber tilts the tire and forms a cone shape that causes the wheel to roll away or pull outward toward the point of the cone. (Courtesy of Hunter Engineering Company)

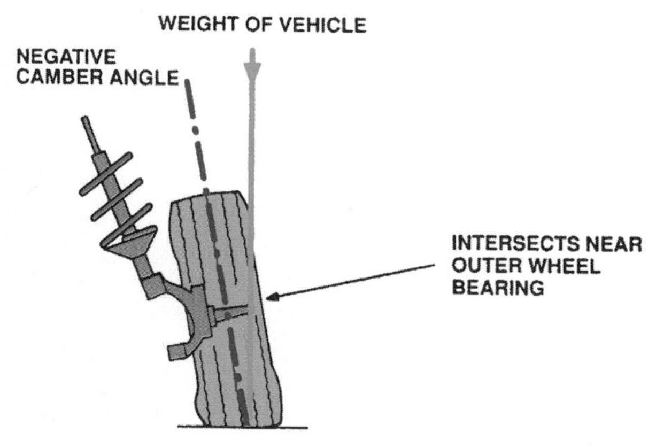

Figure 43–5 Negative camber applies the vehicle weight to the smaller outer wheel bearing. Excessive negative camber, therefore, may contribute to outer wheel bearing failure. (Courtesy of Hunter Engineering Company)

strut assembly by means of one of the following methods:
   a. Shims
   b. Eccentric cams
   c. Slots

10. Camber should be equal on both sides; however, if camber cannot be adjusted to be exactly equal, make certain that there is more camber on the front of the left side to help compensate for the road crown (half a degree maximum difference).

Toe

Toe is the difference in distance between the front and rear of the tires. As viewed from the top of the vehicle (bird's-eye view), zero toe means that both wheels on the same axle are parallel, as shown in Figure 43–6. If the front of the tires is closer than the rear of the same tires, then the toe is called *toed-in* or positive (+) toe. See Figure 43–7. If the front of the tires are farther apart than the rear of the same tires, then the wheels are *toed-out* or have negative (−) toe. See Figure 43–8.

The purpose of the correct toe setting is to provide maximum stability with the minimum of tire wear when the vehicle is being driven.

1. Toe can be measured in both angular and length units. A toe of 0.25° is the same as 3.2 mm, 0.125 in., or 1/8 in.
2. *Incorrect toe is the major cause of excessive tire wear!*

NOTE: If the toe is improper by just 3 mm (1/8 in.) the resulting tire wear is equivalent to dragging a tire sideways 5.3 m for each kilometre travelled (28 ft per mi).

Toe causes camber-type wear on one side of the tire if not correct, as shown in Figure 43–9 (p. 1017).

3. *Incorrect **front** toe does **not** cause a pull condition.* Incorrect toe on the front wheels is split equally as the vehicle is driven because the forces acting on the tires are exerted through the tie rod and steering linkage to both wheels.
4. *Incorrect (unequal) **rear** toe can cause tire wear.* See Figures 43–10 and 43–11 (p. 1017). If the toe of the rear wheels is not equal, the steering wheel will not be straight and will pull toward the side with the most toe-in.
5. Front toe adjustment must be made by adjusting the tie rod sleeves correctly. See Figure 43–12 (p. 1017).

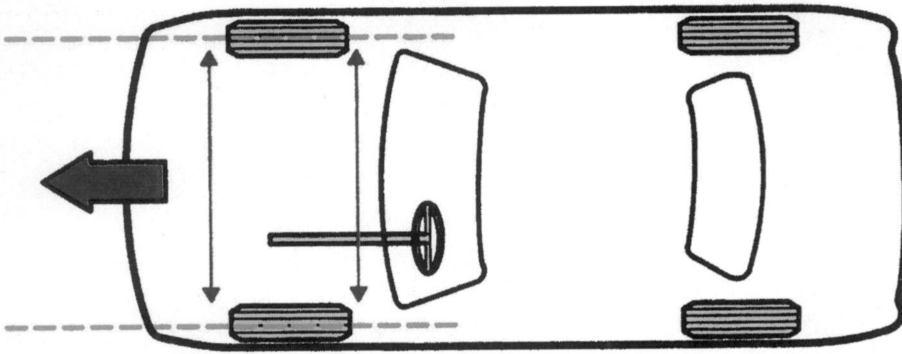

Figure 43–6 Zero toe. (Courtesy of Hunter Engineering Company)

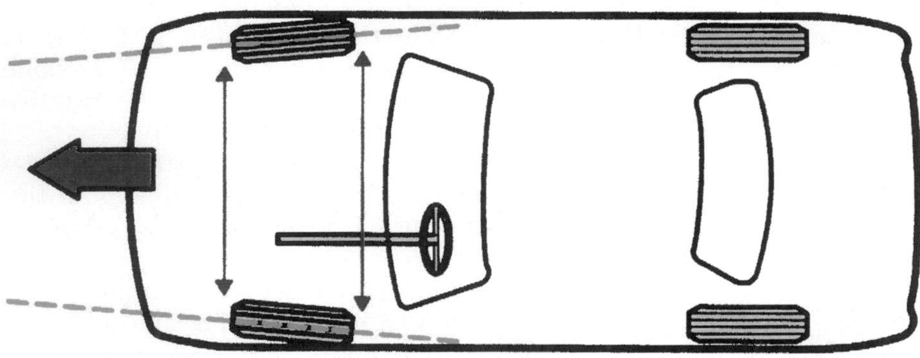

Figure 43–7 Toe-in, also called positive (+) toe. (Courtesy of Hunter Engineering Company)

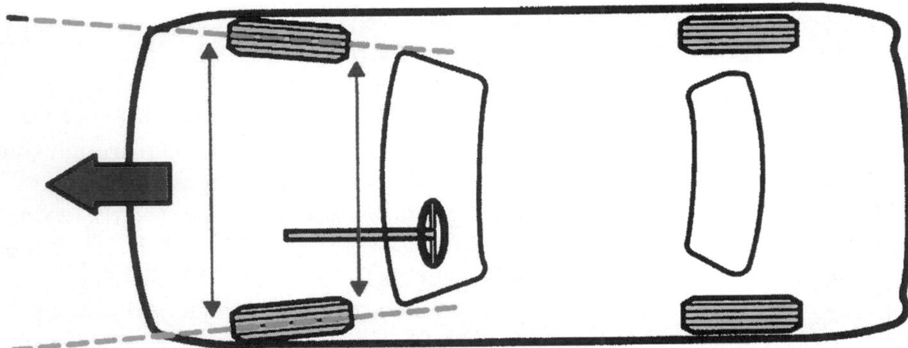

Figure 43–8 Toe-out, also called negative (−) toe. (Courtesy of Hunter Engineering Company)

Figure 43–9 This tire is just one month old! It was new and installed on the front of a vehicle that had about 6 mm (1/4 in.) of toe out. By the time the customer returned to the tire store for an alignment, the tire was completely bald on the inside. Note the almost new tread on the outside.

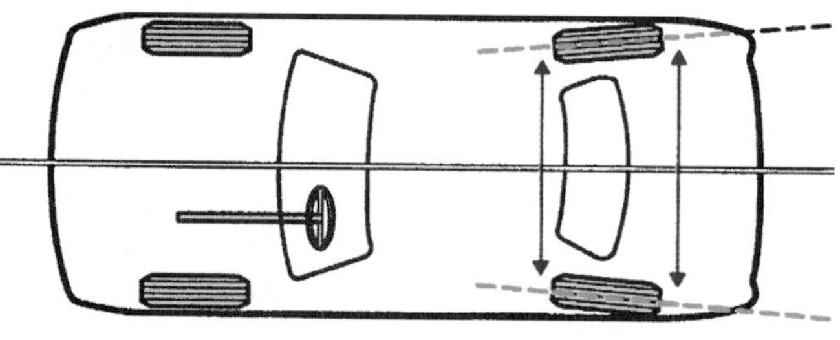

Figure 43–10 Rear toe-in (+). (Courtesy of Hunter Engineering Company)

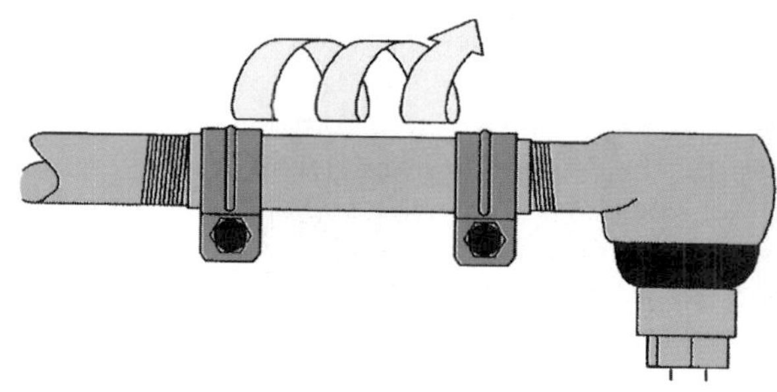

Figure 43–12 Toe on the front of most vehicles is adjusted by turning the tire rod sleeve as shown. (Courtesy of John Bean Company)

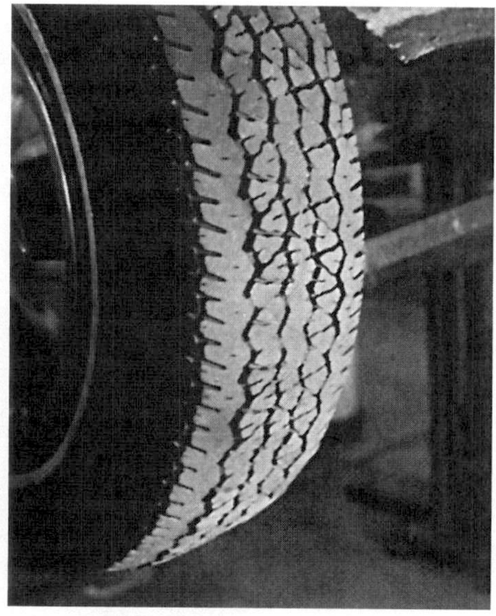

Figure 43–11 Diagonal wear such as shown here is usually caused by incorrect toe on the rear of a front-wheel-drive vehicle.

6. Most vehicle manufacturers specify a slight amount of toe-in to compensate for the natural tendency of the front wheels to spread apart (become toed-out) due to the centrifugal force of the rolling wheels acting on the steering linkage.

> **NOTE:** Some manufacturers of front-wheel-drive vehicles specify a toe-out setting to compensate for the toe-in forces created by the engine drive forces on the front wheels.

7. Normal wear to the tie rod ends and other steering linkage parts usually causes toe-out.

Caster

Caster is the forward or rearward tilt of the steering axis in reference to a vertical line as viewed from the side of the vehicle. The steering axis is defined as the

Frequently Asked Question ???

Why Doesn't Unequal Front Toe on the Front Wheels Cause the Vehicle to Pull?

Each wheel could have individual toe, but as the vehicle is being driven, the forces on the tires tend to split the toe, causing the steering wheel to cock at an angle as the front wheels both track the same. If the toe is different on the rear of the vehicle, the rear will be steered similar to a rudder on a boat because the rear wheels are not tied together as are the front wheels.

TECH TIP

Smooth In, Toed-In— Smooth Out, Toed-Out

Whenever the toe setting is not zero, a rubbing action on the tire tread causes a feather-edge-type wear. See Figure 43–13. A quick-and-easy method to determine if incorrect toe could be the cause of excessive tire wear or other problems is to simply rub your hand across the tread of the tire. If it feels smoother when you move your hand toward the centre of the vehicle than when you move your hand toward the outside, then the cause is excessive toe-in. The opposite effect is caused by toe out. This method may be used on all types of tires including radial ply tires, where the wear may not appear as a feather edge. Just remember this simple saying, "smooth in, toed-in—smooth out, toed-out."

Feathered or sawtooth tire wear pattern
Sharp edges point in the direction of the toe problem
(IN - Toe In / OUT Toe Out)

Figure 43–13 Feather-edge-type tire wear is usually caused by an incorrect toe setting. (Courtesy of John Bean Company)

line drawn through the upper and lower steering pivot points. On an SLA suspension system, the upper pivot is the upper ball joint and the lower pivot is the lower ball joint. On a MacPherson strut system, the upper pivot is the centre of the upper bearing mount and the lower pivot point is the lower ball joint. Zero centre means that the steering axis is straight up and down, also called *zero degrees* or *perfectly vertical,* as shown in Figure 43–14.

1. Positive (+) caster is present when the upper suspension pivot point is behind the lower pivot point (ball joint) as viewed from the side. See Figure 43–15.
2. Negative (−) caster is present when the upper suspension pivot point is ahead of the lower pivot point (ball joint) as viewed from the side.
3. Caster is measured in degrees or fractions of degrees.
4. Caster is not a tire wearing angle, but positive caster does cause changes in camber during a turn. See Figure 43–16. This condition is called **camber roll.** (See the Tech Tip "Caster Angle Tire Wear.")
5. Caster is a stability angle:
   a. If caster is excessively positive, vehicle steering will be very stable (will tend to be straight with little steering wheel correction needed) and help with steering wheel **returnability** after a turn.
   b. If the caster is positive, the steering effort will increase with increasing positive caster.

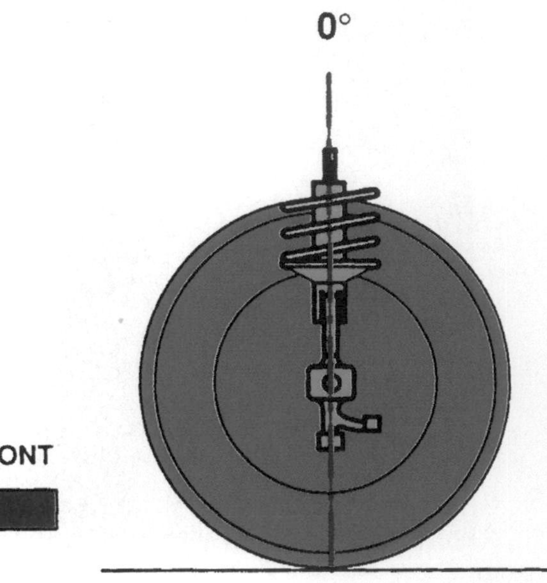
0°
FRONT

Figure 43–14 Zero caster. (Courtesy of Hunter Engineering Company)

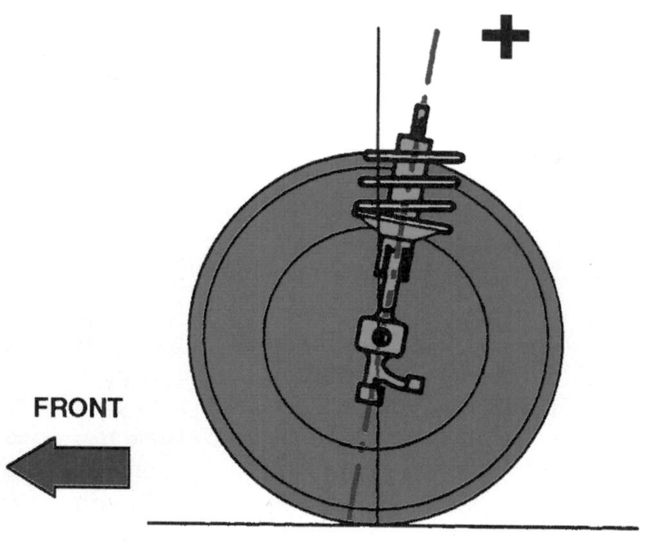

Figure 43–15 Positive (+) caster. (Courtesy of Hunter Engineering Company)

Figure 43–16 As the spindle rotates, it lifts the weight of the vehicle due to the angle of the steering axis. (Courtesy of Hunter Engineering Company)

Greater road shocks will be felt by the driver when driving over rough road surfaces. Vehicles with as high as eleven degrees of positive caster usually use a steering dampener to control possible shimmy at high speeds and to dampen the snap-back of the spindle after a turn.

c. If caster is negative, or excessively unequal, the vehicle will not be as stable and will tend to wander. If a vehicle is heavily loaded in the rear, caster increases, as shown in Figure 43–17.

6. Caster could cause pull if unequal. *The vehicle will pull toward the side with the least positive caster.*

7. Caster is *not* adjustable on many vehicles.

8. If caster is adjustable, the change is made by moving either the lower or the upper pivot point forward or backward by means of one of the following methods:

a. Shims
b. Eccentric cams
c. Slots
d. Strut rods

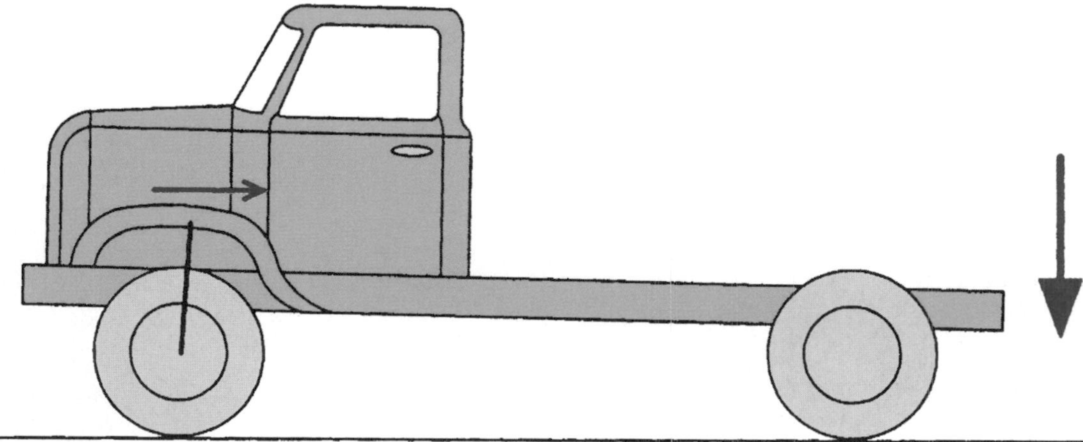

Figure 43–17 As the load increases in the rear of a vehicle, the top steering axis pivot point moves rearward, increasing positive (+) caster. (Courtesy of Hunter Engineering Company)

NOTE: Caster is only measured on the front turning wheels of the vehicle. Although some caster is built into the rear suspension of many vehicles, rear caster is not measured as part of a four-wheel alignment.

TECH TIP 

Caster Angle Tire Wear

The caster angle is generally considered to be a *non*-tire-wearing angle. Even though this statement is true, excessive or unequal caster can *indirectly* cause tire wear. When the front wheels on a vehicle with a lot of positive caster are turned, they become angled, which is called **camber roll.** (The caster angle is a measurement of the difference in camber angle from when the wheel is turned inward compared to when the wheel is turned outward.) Many vehicle manufacturers design positive caster into the suspension system. This positive caster has increased the directional stability of these vehicles. However, if the vehicle is used exclusively in city-type driving, the positive caster can cause tire wear to the outside shoulders of both front tires, as seen in Figure 43–18.

Steering Axis Inclination (SAI)

The steering axis is the angle formed between true vertical and an imaginary line drawn between the upper and lower pivot points of the spindle. See Figure 43–19. *Steering axis inclination (SAI) is the inward tilt of the steering axis.* SAI is also known as *kingpin inclination* (KPI) and is the imaginary line drawn through the kingpin as viewed from the front.

Included Angle The included angle is the SAI added to the camber reading of the front wheels only. *The included angle is determined by the design of the steering knuckle, or strut construction.* See Figure 43–20. Included angle is an important angle to measure when diagnosing vehicle handling or tire-wear problems.

Turning Radius (Toe-Out on Turns)

Whenever a vehicle turns a corner, the inside wheel has to turn at a sharper angle than the outside wheel because the inside wheel has a shorter distance to travel, as shown in Figure 43–21. Turning radius is also called **toe-out on turns,** abbreviated **TOT** or, more commonly, **TOOT,** and is determined by the

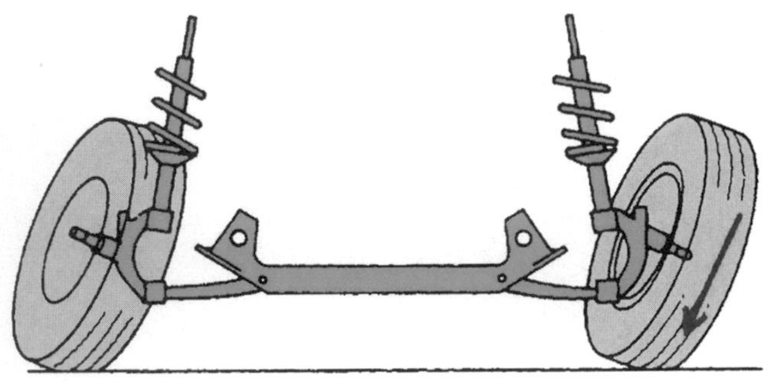

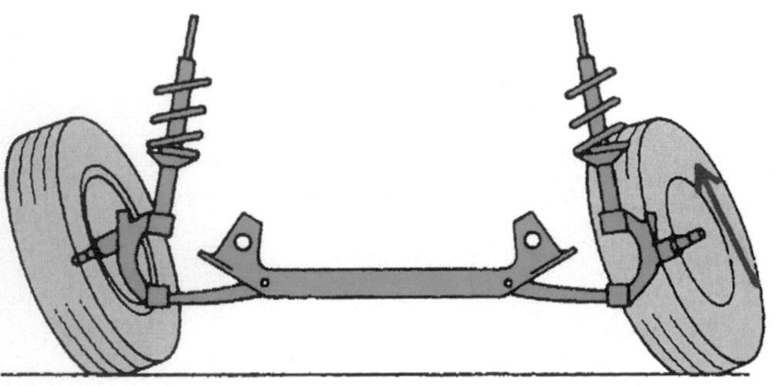

Figure 43–18 As the front wheels on a vehicle with a lot of positive caster are turned, the wheel tilts at an angle. This is called *camber roll* and can cause tire wear to both the inside and outside edges of the tire.

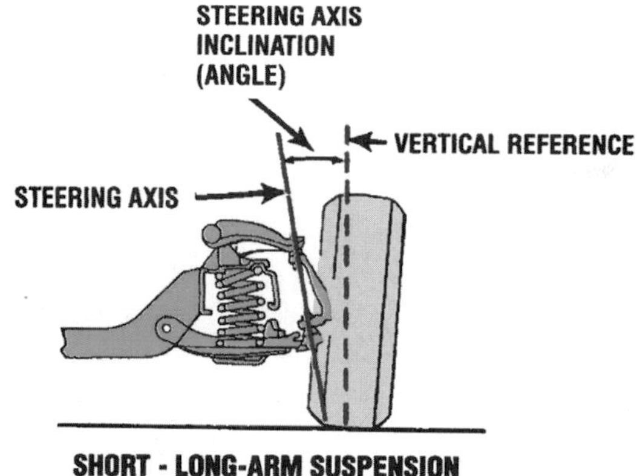

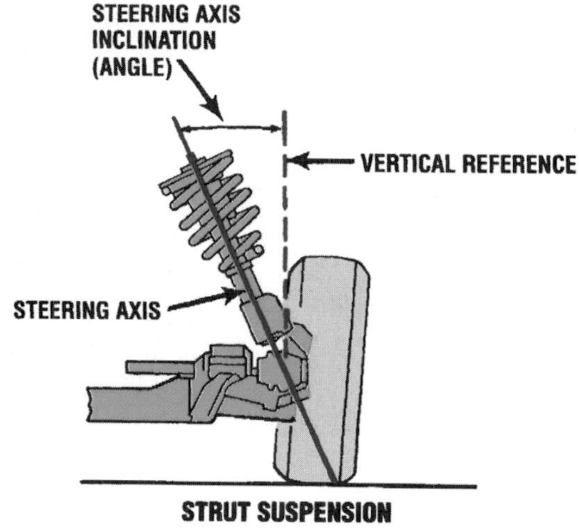

Figure 43–19 SAI is an imaginary line through the upper and lower suspension pivot points.

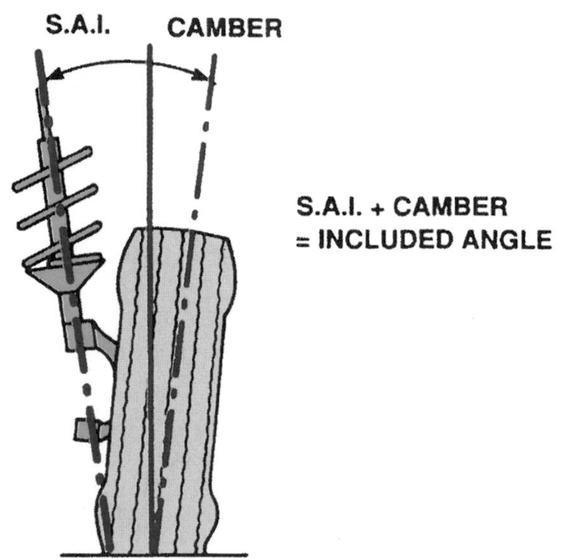

Figure 43–20 Included angle on a MacPherson strut-type suspension. (Courtesy of Hunter Engineering Company)

angle of the steering knuckle arms. *Turning radius is a nonadjustable angle.* The turning radius can and should be measured as part of an alignment to check if the steering arms are bent or damaged. Symptoms of out-of-specification turning angle include tire squeal noise during normal cornering even at low speeds and/or scuffed tires.

This angle is also called the *Ackerman effect,* named for its promoter, the English publisher Rudolph Ackerman, circa 1898.

Setback

Setback is the angle formed by a line drawn perpendicular (90°) to the front axles. See Figure 43–22. *Setback is a nonadjustable measurement even though it may be corrected.* Positive setback means the right front wheel is set back farther than the left. Negative setback means the left front wheel is set back farther than the right.

Thrust Angle

Thrust angle is the angle of the rear wheels as determined by the total rear toe. If both rear wheels have zero toe, then the thrust angle is the same as the geometric centre line of the vehicle. The total of the rear toe setting determines the **thrust line,** or the direction the rear wheels are pointed. See Figure 43–23 (p. 1023). On vehicles with an independent rear suspension, if both wheels do not have equal toe, the vehicle will pull in the direction of the side with the most toe-in.

Tracking

Tracking is the term used to describe the fact that the rear wheels should track directly behind the front wheels. If the vehicle has been involved in an accident, it is possible that the frame or rear axle mounting could cause dog tracking.

PREALIGNMENT CHECKS

Before checking or adjusting the front end alignment, the following items should be checked and corrected if necessary:

1. Check all the tires for proper inflation pressures and approximately the same size and tread depth and that they are the recommended size for the vehicle.
2. Check the front wheel bearings for proper adjustment.

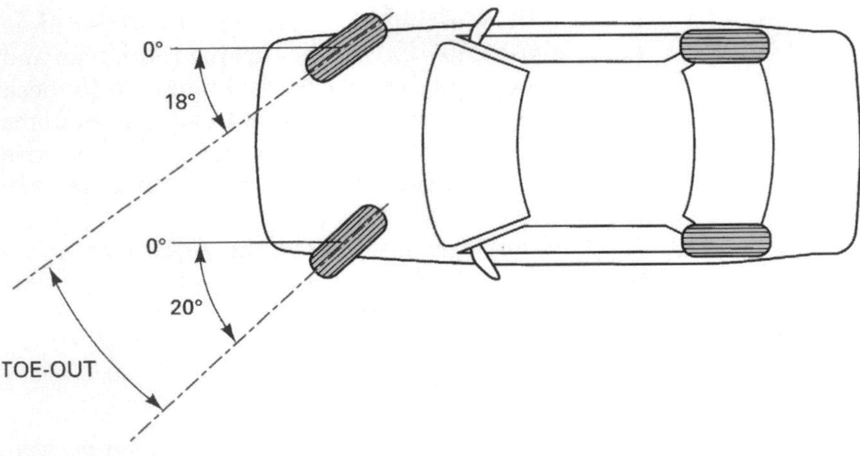

Figure 43–21 To provide handling, the inside wheel has to turn at a greater turning radius than the outside wheel.

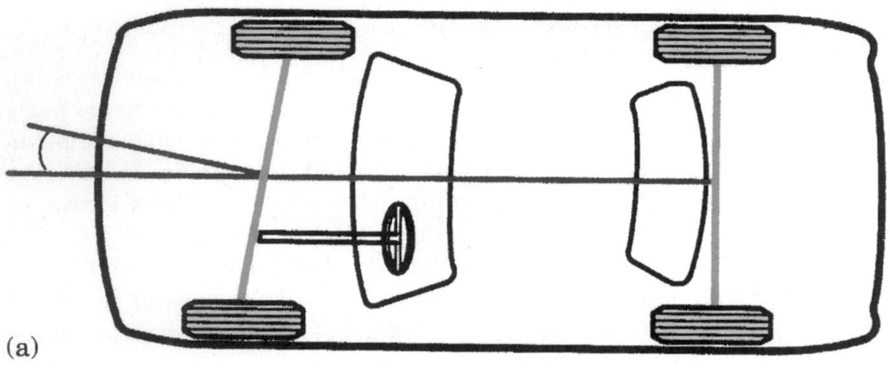

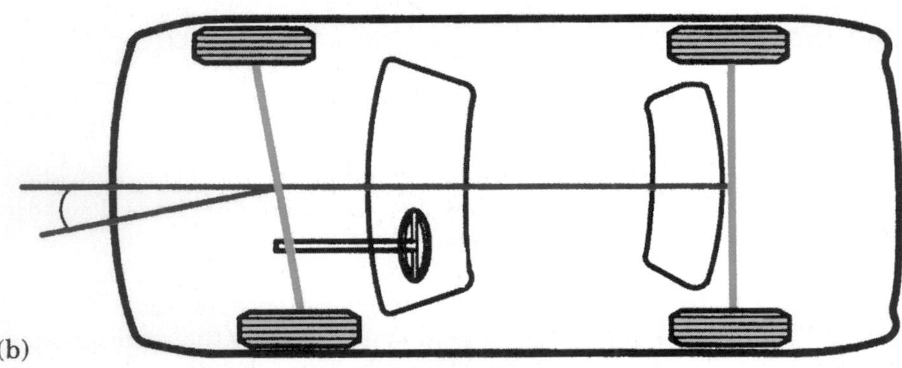

Figure 43–22 (a) Positive setback. (b) Negative setback. (Courtesy of Hunter Engineering Company)

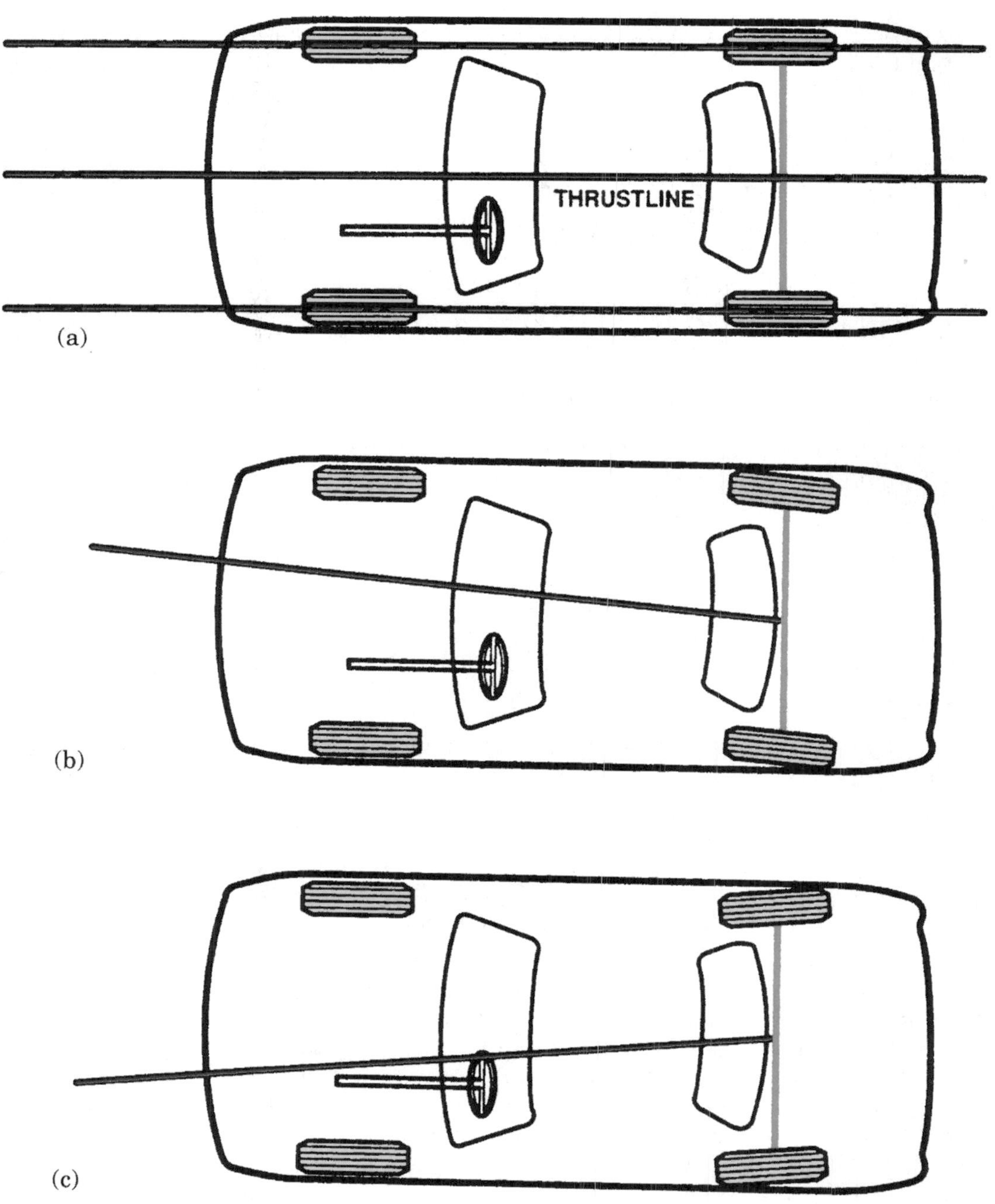

Figure 43–23 (a) Zero thrust angle. (b) Thrust line to the right. (c) Thrust line to the left. (Courtesy of Hunter Engineering Company)

3. Check for loose ball joints or torn ball joint boots. See Figure 43–24.
4. Perform a dry park test to check the:
   - Tie rod ends for damage or looseness
   - Centre link or rack bushings for play
5. Check the pitman arm for any movement.
6. Check for run-out of the wheels and the tires.
7. Check for vehicle ride height (should be level front-to-back as well as side-to-side). Make sure that the factory load levelling system is functioning correctly, if so equipped. Check height according to the manufacturer's specifications. See Figures 43–25 and 43–26.

NOTE: Manufacturers often have replacement springs or spring spacers that can be installed between the coil spring and the spring seat to restore proper ride level. Ride (trim) is also called *chassis height*.

Figure 43–24 The owner of this Honda thought that all it needed was an alignment. Obviously, something more serious than an alignment caused this left rear wheel to angle inward at the top.

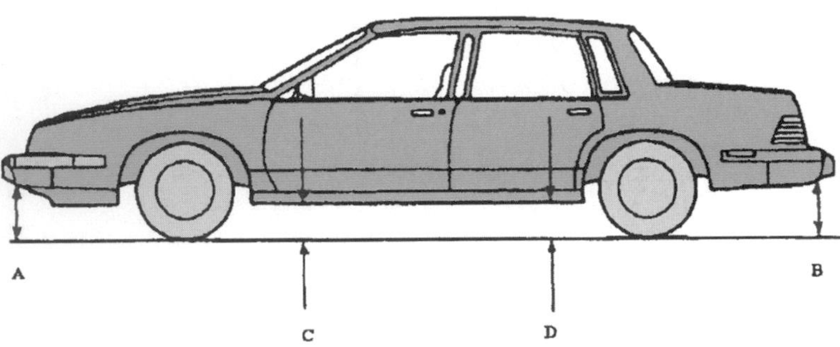

Figure 43–25 Measuring points for ride (trim) height vary by manufacturer. (Courtesy of Hunter Engineering Company)

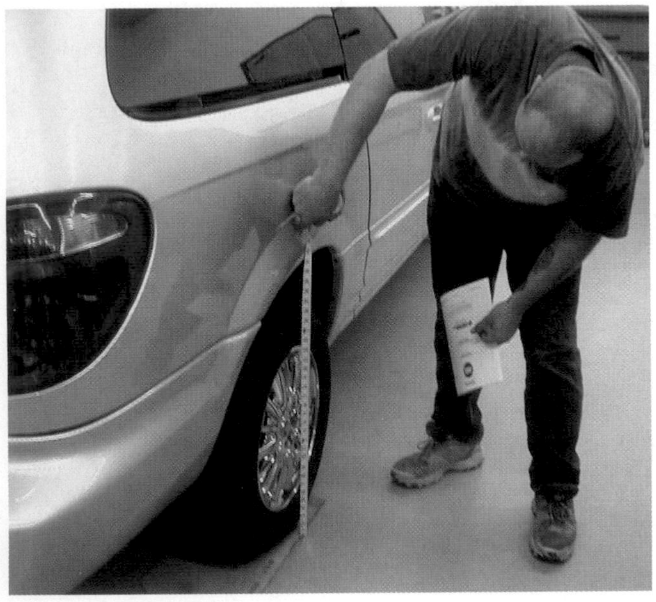

Figure 43–26 Measuring to be sure the left and right sides of the vehicle are equal heights. If this measurement is not equal side-to-side by as little as 3 mm (1/8 in.), it can affect the handling of the vehicle.

8. Check for steering gear looseness at the frame.
9. Check for improperly operating shock absorbers.
10. Check for worn control arm bushings or ball joints.
11. Check for loose or missing stabilizer bar attachments.
12. Check the trunk for excess loads.
13. Check for dragging brakes.

> **NOTE:** Checking for dragging brakes is usually performed when installing alignment heads to the wheels prior to taking an alignment reading. A dragging brake can cause the vehicle to pull or lead toward the side with the dragging brake.

READING ALIGNMENT SPECIFICATIONS

There are several methods used by vehicle manufacturers and alignment equipment manufacturers to specify alignment angles.

DIAGNOSTIC STORY 

The Five-Wheel Alignment

The steering wheel should always be straight when driving on a straight, level road. If the steering wheel is not straight, the customer will often think that the wheel alignment is not correct. One such customer complained that the vehicle pulled to the right while driving on a straight road. The service manager test drove the vehicle and everything was perfect, except that the steering wheel was not perfectly straight, even though the toe setting was correct. Whenever driving on a straight road, the customer would "straighten the steering wheel" and, of course, the vehicle went to one side. After correctly adjusting toe with the steering wheel straight, the customer and the service manager were both satisfied. The technician learned that regardless of how accurate the alignment, the steering wheel *must* be straight because it is this "fifth wheel" that the customer notices most.

NOTE: Many vehicle manufacturers now include the maximum allowable steering wheel angle variation from straight. This specification is commonly ±3° (plus or minus three degrees) or less.

TECH TIP 

"Set Everything to Zero?"

An apprentice service technician observed that the experienced alignment technician seldom looked at the specifications for the vehicle being aligned. When questioned, the technician said that for best tire life, the tires should rotate perpendicular to the road. After studying alignment specifications, the technician noticed that almost every camber and toe specification for both front and rear included zero within the range of the specifications. Caster, of course, varies from one vehicle to another and should be checked and adjusted to specifications. The beginning technician learned that zero camber and zero toe will be acceptable and "within specifications" on almost all vehicles and is easy to remember!

Maximum/Minimum/ Preferred Method

This method indicates the preferred setting for each alignment angle and the minimum and maximum allowable value for each. The alignment technician should always attempt to align the vehicle to the preferred setting. See Figure 43–27.

Plus or Minus Method

This method indicates the preferred setting with the lowest and highest allowable value, indicated by a negative (−) and positive (+) sign as in the specifications. For example, if a camber reading is specified as $+1/2°$ with a + and − value of $1/2°$, it could be written as $+1/2° \pm 1/2°$. The minimum value would be 0° ($1/2° - 1/2° = 0°$) and the maximum value would be +1° ($+1/2° + 1/2° = 1°$). The range would be from 0° to 1°.

NOTE: The angle is assumed to be positive unless it is labelled with a negative (−) sign in front of the number.

Specifications are often published in fractional or decimal degrees or in degrees and minutes. There are sixty minutes (written as 60′) in one degree. See the angle-unit conversion table below.

Angle–Unit Conversions

Units	Conversions		
Fractional degrees	$1/4°$	$1/2°$	$3/4°$
Decimal degrees	0.25°	0.50°	0.75°
Degrees and minutes	0°15′	0°30′	0°45′

ALIGNMENT SETUP PROCEDURES

After confirming that the tires and all steering and suspension components are serviceable, the vehicle is ready for an alignment. The exact setup procedures for the equipment being used must always be followed. Typical alignment procedures include the following steps:

Step 1. Drive onto the alignment rack straight and adjust the ramps and/or turn plates so that they are centred under the tires of the vehicle. Use chocks (blocks) for the wheels to prevent the vehicle from accidentally rolling off the alignment rack.

Step 2. Raise the vehicle off the alignment rack. See Figure 43–28.

Step 3. Attach and calibrate the wheel sensors to each wheel as specified by the alignment equipment manufacturer, as shown in Figure 43–29.

Step 4. Unlock all rack or turn plates.

Step 5. Lower the vehicle and jounce the vehicle by pushing down on the centre of the front and then the rear bumper of the vehicle. This motion allows the suspension to become centred.

Step 6. Following the procedures for the alignment equipment, determine all alignment angles.

ALIGNMENT SPECIFICATIONS AT CURB HEIGHT

FRONT WHEEL ALIGNMENT	ACCEPTABLE ALIGNMENT RANGE AT CURB HEIGHT	PREFERRED SETTING
CAMBER . . All* *Side To Side Differential	-0.6° to +0.6° 0.7° or less	+0.0° 0.0°
TOTAL TOE All Vehicles (See Note) Specified In Degrees	0.4° In to 0.0°	0.2° In
CASTER*	REFERENCE ANGLE	
All Models *Side To Side Caster Differential Not to Exceed	+2.0° to +4.0° 1.0° or less	+3.0° 0.0°
REAR WHEEL ALIGNMENT	**ACCEPTABLE ALIGNMENT RANGE AT CURB HEIGHT**	**PREFERRED SETTING**
CAMBER . . All Models	-0.6° to +0.4°	-0.1°
TOTAL TOE* All Vehicles (See Note) Specified In Degrees	0.2° Out to 0.4° In	0.1° In
THRUST ANGLE *TOE OUT When Backed On Alignment Rack Is TOE IN When Driving.	-0.15° to +0.15°	
NOTE: Total toe is the arithmetic sum of the left and right wheel toe settings. Positive is Toe-in, negative is Toe-out. Total Toe must be equally split between each front wheel to ensure a centred steering wheel. Left and Right toe must be equal to within 0.02 degrees.		

Figure 43–27 Typical alignment specifications for a vehicle at the proper curb height. Curb height is ride height or trim height as measured at the curb weight. Curb weight is the weight of the vehicle with a full tank of fuel and all other fluids filled. (Courtesy of Chrysler Corporation)

Figure 43–28 Using the alignment rack hydraulic jacks, raise the tires off the rack so that they can be rotated as part of the compensating process.

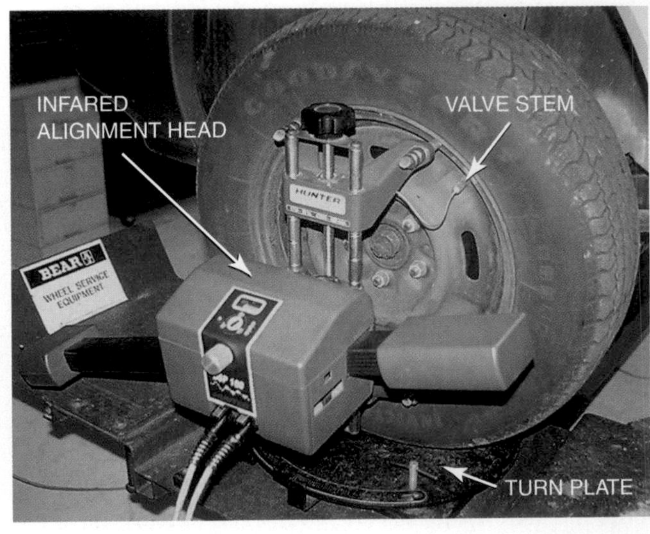

Figure 43–29 This wheel sensor has a safety wheel that screws to the valve stem to keep the sensor from falling onto the ground if the clamps slip on the wheel lip.

TECH TIP

Using a Two-Wheel Alignment Rack for a Four-Wheel Alignment

Alignment racks designed for total four-wheel alignment are equipped with movable plates under the rear wheels. Older racks used for front-end-only alignment do not move and therefore will not allow the rear suspension to become settled. This freedom of movement is necessary to correctly perform a four-wheel alignment, especially on a vehicle with independent rear suspension. One commonly used trick of the trade is to place a two-layer plastic garbage bag under each rear wheel before lowering the vehicle onto the rack. As the vehicle is lowered, the rear wheels will easily *slide* over the plastic-on-plastic surface. The rear wheels will resume the normal position, the same as if the vehicle were lowered onto movable turn plates. Another method that is often used is to roll the vehicle back about 1.2 m (4 ft) and then forward to allow the rear independent suspension to settle.

NOTE: Some alignment machines do not have cables long enough to allow this method to be used.

Measuring Camber, Caster, SAI, Toe, and TOOT

Camber Camber is measured with the wheels in the straight-ahead position on a level platform. Since camber is a vertical reference angle, alignment equipment reads camber directly.

Caster Caster is measured by moving the front wheels through an arc both inward, then outward, from straight ahead. This necessary movement of the front wheels to measure caster is called **caster sweep.** What the alignment measuring equipment is actually doing is measuring the camber at one wheel sweep and measuring the camber again at the other extreme of the caster sweep. *The caster angle itself is the difference between the two camber readings.*

SAI Steering axis inclination (SAI) is also measured by performing a caster sweep of the front wheels. When measuring SAI separately, the usual procedure involves raising the front wheels off the ground and leveling and locking the wheel sensors before performing a caster sweep. When the suspension is extended, the SAI is more accurately determined because the angle itself is expanded.

Toe Toe is determined by measuring the angle of both front and/or both rear wheels from the straight ahead (0°) position. Most alignment equipment reads the toe angle for each wheel *and* the combined toe angle of both wheels on the same axle. This combined toe is called **total toe.** Toe angle is more accurate than the centre-to-centre distance, especially if oversize tires are installed on the vehicle. See Figure 43–30.

TOOT Toe out on turns (TOOT) is a diagnostic angle that is normally not measured as part of a regular alignment, but it is recommended that this measurement be made as a part of a total alignment check. TOOT is measured by recording the angle of the front wheels as indicated on the front turn plates. See Figure 43–31. If, for example, the inside wheel is turned 20°, then the outside wheel should

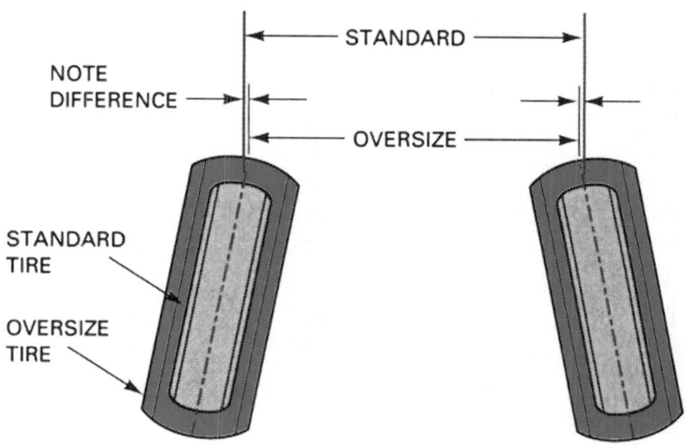

Figure 43–30 If toe for an oversize tire is set by distance, the toe angle will be too small. Toe angle is the same regardless of tire size.

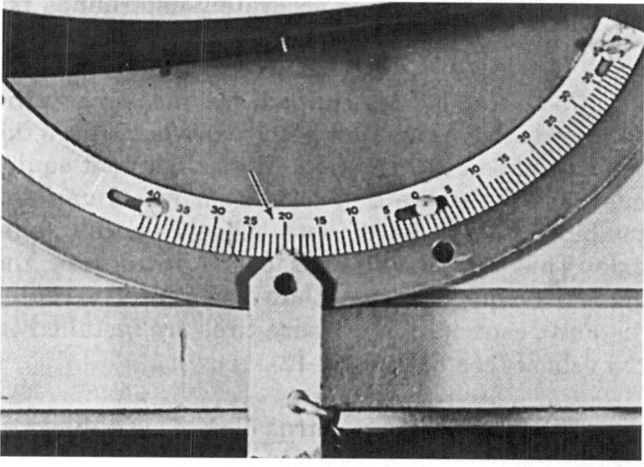

Figure 43–31 The protractor scale on the front turn plates allows the technician to test the turning radius by turning one wheel to an angle specified by the manufacturer and observing the angle of the other front wheel.

TECH TIP 

Ask Yourself These Three Questions

An older technician told a beginning technician that the key to success in doing a proper alignment is to ask yourself three questions about the alignment angles:

Question 1. *"Is it within specifications?"* For example, if the specification reads 1° ±1/2°, any reading between +1/2° and +1 1/2° is within specifications. All vehicles should be aligned to within this range.

Question 2. *"Is it within 1/2° of the other side of the vehicle?"* Not only should the alignment be within specifications, it should also be as equal as possible from one side to the other. The difference between the camber from one side to the other side is called **cross camber. Cross caster** is the difference between the caster angle from one side to another.

Question 3. *"If the camber and caster cannot be* ***exactly*** *equal side-to-side in the front, is there more camber on the left and more caster on the right to help compensate for road crown?* Seldom, if ever, are the alignment angles perfectly equal. Sometimes, one side of the vehicle is more difficult to adjust than the other side. Regardless of the reasons, if there *has* to be a difference in front camber and/or caster angle, follow this advice to avoid a possible lead or drift problem even if answers to the first two questions are "yes." See Figure 43–32.

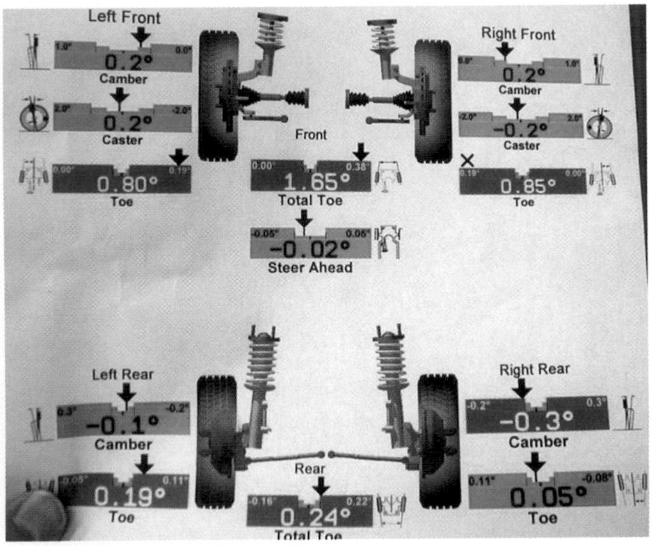

Figure 43–32 This computer alignment printout is very useful for determining which angles are OK (in green) and which angles need to be adjusted (in red).

indicate about 18° on the turn plate. The exact angles are usually specified by the vehicle manufacturer. The turning angle should only be checked after the toe is correctly set. *The turning angle for the wheel on the outside of the turn should not vary more than* $1\frac{1}{2}°$ *from specifications.*

Checking Frame Alignment of Front-Wheel-Drive Vehicles

Many front-wheel-drive vehicles mount the drive train (engine and transaxle) and lower suspension arms on a subframe or cradle. If the frame is shifted either left or right, that can cause differences in SAI, included angle, and camber. See Figures 43–33 and 43–34. Adjust the frame if SAI and camber angles are different on the left and right, yet the included angles are equal.

TYPES OF ALIGNMENTS

There are three types of alignment: geometric centreline, thrust line, and total four-wheel alignment.

Geometric Centreline This type of alignment is simply an alignment that uses the geometric centreline of the vehicle as the basis for all measurements of toe (front or rear). See Figure 43–35. This method is now considered to be obsolete.

Thrust Line A thrust line alignment uses the thrust angle of the rear wheels and sets the front wheels parallel to the thrust line. See Figure 43–36.

HINT: It has often been said that while the front wheels steer the vehicle, the rear wheels determine the direction the vehicle will travel. Just think of the rear wheels as being like a rudder of a boat. As the rudder turns, the front of the boat turns.

Thrust line alignment is *required* for any vehicle with a nonadjustable rear suspension. If a vehicle has an adjustable rear suspension, then a total four-wheel alignment is necessary to ensure proper tracking.

Total Four-Wheel Alignment A total four-wheel alignment is the most accurate method and is necessary to ensure maximum tire wear and vehicle handling. The major difference between a thrust line alignment and a total four-wheel alignment is that the rear toe is adjusted to bring the thrust line to zero. In other words, the rear toe on both rear wheels is adjusted equally so that the actual direction the rear wheels are pointed is the same as the geometric centreline of the vehicle. See Figure 43–37.

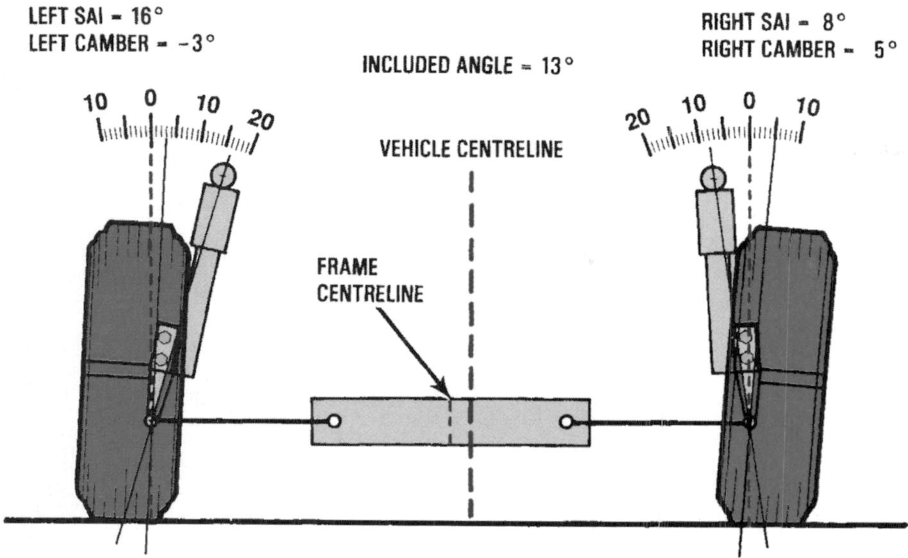

Figure 43–33 In this example both SAI and camber are way off from being equal side-to-side. However, both sides have the same included angle, indicating that the frame may be out of alignment. An attempt to align this vehicle by adjusting the camber on both sides either with factory or aftermarket kits would result in a totally incorrect alignment. (Courtesy of General Motors Corporation Service Technology Group)

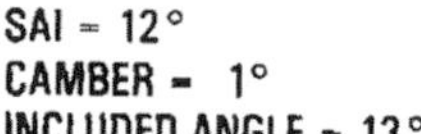

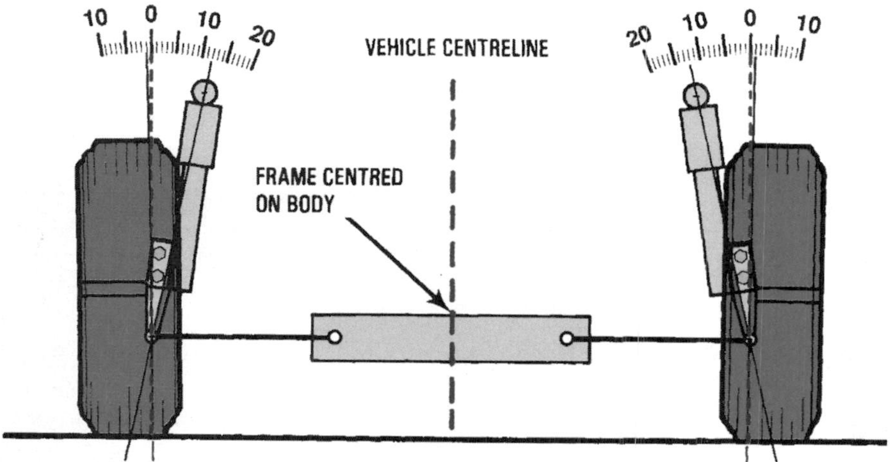

Figure 43–34 This is the same vehicle as shown in Figure 43–33, except now the frame (cradle) has been shifted over and correctly positioned. Notice how both the SAI and camber become equal without any other adjustments necessary. (Courtesy of General Motors Corporation Service Technology Group)

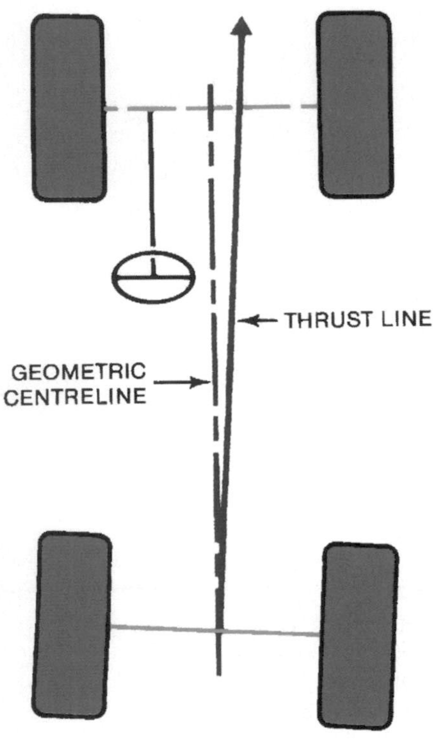

Figure 43–35 Geometric centreline alignment sets the front toe readings based on the geometric centreline of the vehicle and does not consider the thrust line of the rear wheel toe angles. (Courtesy of Hunter Engineering Company)

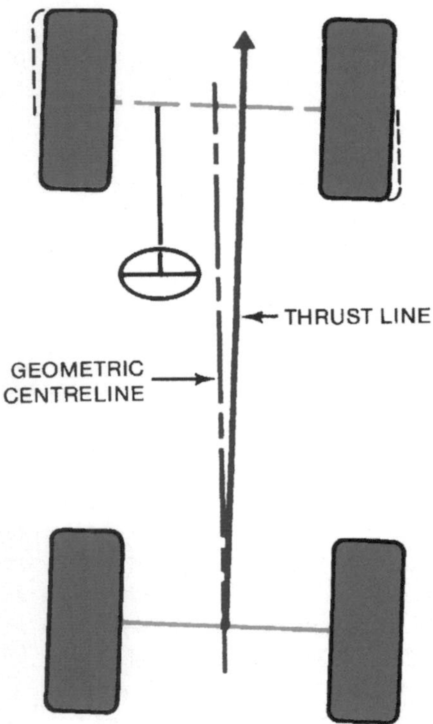

Figure 43–36 Thrust line alignment sets the front toe parallel with the rear wheel toe. (Courtesy of Hunter Engineering Company)

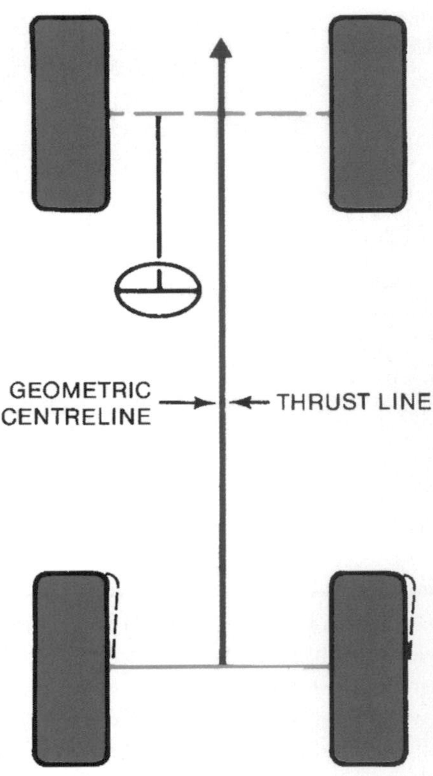

Figure 43–37 Four-wheel alignment corrects for any rear-wheel toe to make the thrust line and the geometric centreline of the vehicle the same. (Courtesy of Hunter Engineering Company)

Four-Wheel Alignment Procedure

The procedure for a total four-wheel alignment includes these steps:

1. Adjust the rear camber (if applicable). See Figure 43–38.
2. Adjust the rear toe (this should reduce the thrust angle to near zero). See Figure 43–39.
3. Adjust the front caster and camber.
4. Adjust the front toe, making sure that the steering wheel is in the straight-ahead position.

The Gritty Solution

Many times it is difficult to loosen a TORX bolt, especially those used to hold the backing plate onto the rear axle on many GM vehicles. See Figure 43–40. A technique that always seems to work is to place some **valve grinding compound** on the fastener. The gritty compound keeps the TORX socket from slipping up and out of the fastener and more force can be exerted to break loose a tight bolt. Valve grinding compound can also be used on Phillips-head screws as well as other types of bolts, nuts, and sockets.

Figure 43–38 The rear camber is adjustable on this vehicle by rotating the eccentric cam and watching the alignment machine display.

TECH TIP

Locking Pliers to the Rescue

Many vehicles use a jam nut on the tie rod end. This jam nut must be loosened to adjust the toe. Because the end of the tie rod is attached to a tie rod end that is movable, loosening the nut is often difficult. Every time force is applied to the nut, the tie rod end socket moves and prevents the full force of the wrench from being applied to the nut. To prevent this movement, simply attach locking pliers (Vise Grips®) to hold the tie rod. Wedge the pliers against the control arm to prevent any movement of the tie rod. By preventing the tie rod from moving, full force can be put on a wrench to loosen the jam nut without doing any harm to the tie rod end.

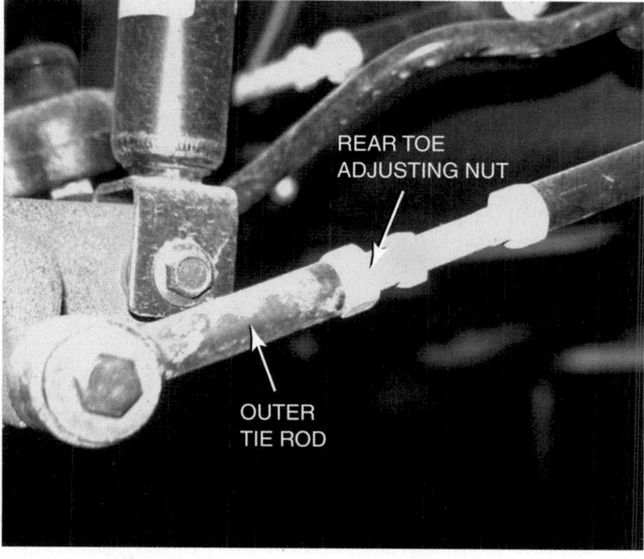

Figure 43–39 The rear toe was easily set on this vehicle. The adjusting nuts were easy to get to and turn. Rear toe is not this easy on every vehicle.

Adjusting Front Camber/Caster Most SLA-type suspensions can be adjusted for caster and camber. Most manufacturers recommend adjusting caster, then camber before adjusting the toe. As the caster is changed, the camber and toe also change. See Figure 43–41. If the camber is then adjusted, the caster is unaffected. Many technicians adjust caster and camber at the same time using shims, slots, or eccentric cams. *Always follow the manufacturer's recommended alignment procedure.* Regardless of the methods or procedures used, toe is always adjusted after all the angles are set because caster and camber both affect the toe.

Setting Toe Front toe is the last angle that should be adjusted and is the most likely to need correction. Most newer alignment equipment displays in degrees of toe instead of inches of toe. (See the toe unit conversion table on page 1033.)

$$+ \text{ toe} = \text{toe-in}$$
$$- \text{ toe} = \text{toe-out}$$

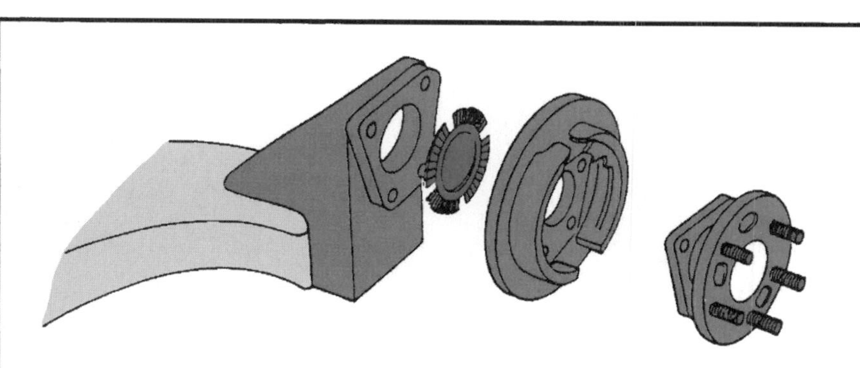

Figure 43–40 Full contact plastic or metal shims can be placed between the axle housing and the brake backing plate to change rear camber or toe or both. (Courtesy of Northstar Manufacturing Company, Inc.)

METHODS OF ADJUSTMENT

Tools and adjustment devices may be available from aftermarket suppliers to perform adjustments in cases where manufacturers do not make such provisions.

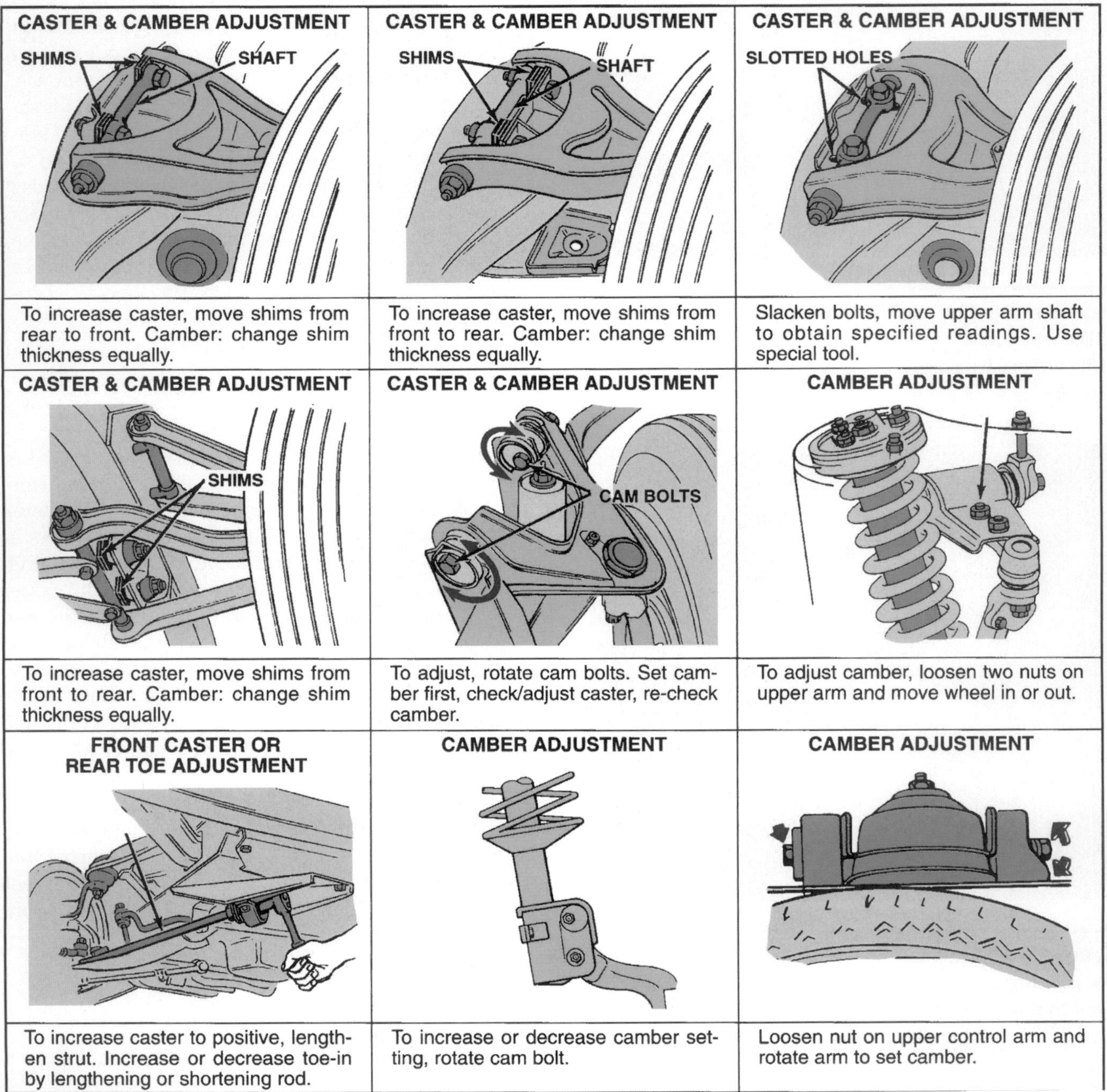

CASTER & CAMBER ADJUSTMENT
SHIMS
SHAFT
To increase caster, move shims from rear to front. Camber: change shim thickness equally.
CASTER & CAMBER ADJUSTMENT
SHIMS
SHAFT
To increase caster, move shims from front to rear. Camber: change shim thickness equally.
CASTER & CAMBER ADJUSTMENT
SLOTTED HOLES
Slacken bolts, move upper arm shaft to obtain specified readings. Use special tool.
CASTER & CAMBER ADJUSTMENT
SHIMS
To increase caster, move shims from front to rear. Camber: change shim thickness equally.
CASTER & CAMBER ADJUSTMENT
CAM BOLTS
To adjust, rotate cam bolts. Set camber first, check/adjust caster, re-check camber.
CAMBER ADJUSTMENT
To adjust camber, loosen two nuts on upper arm and move wheel in or out.
FRONT CASTER OR REAR TOE ADJUSTMENT
To increase caster to positive, lengthen strut. Increase or decrease toe-in by lengthening or shortening rod.
CAMBER ADJUSTMENT
To increase or decrease camber setting, rotate cam bolt.
CAMBER ADJUSTMENT
Loosen nut on upper control arm and rotate arm to set camber.

Figure 43–41 Typical methods of adjusting caster and camber. (Courtesy of John Bean Company)

Toe Unit Conversions

Units	Conversions			
Fractional inches	1/16 in.	1/8 in.	3/16 in.	1/4 in.
Decimal inches	0.062 in.	0.125 in.	0.188 in.	0.250 in.
Millimetres	1.60 mm	3.18 mm	4.76 mm	6.35 mm
Decimal degrees	0.125°	0.25°	0.375°	0.5°
Degrees and minutes	0°8′	0°15′	0°23′	0°30′
Fractional degrees	1/8°	1/4°	3/8°	1/2°

Toe is adjusted by turning the tie rod(s) or tie rod end sleeve(s). See Figures 43–42 and 43–43.

To make sure the steering wheel is straight after setting toe, the steering wheel *must* be locked in the straight-ahead position while the toe is being adjusted. To lock the steering wheel, always use a steering wheel lock that presses against the seat and the outer rim of the steering wheel. *Do not* use the locking feature of the steering column to hold the steering

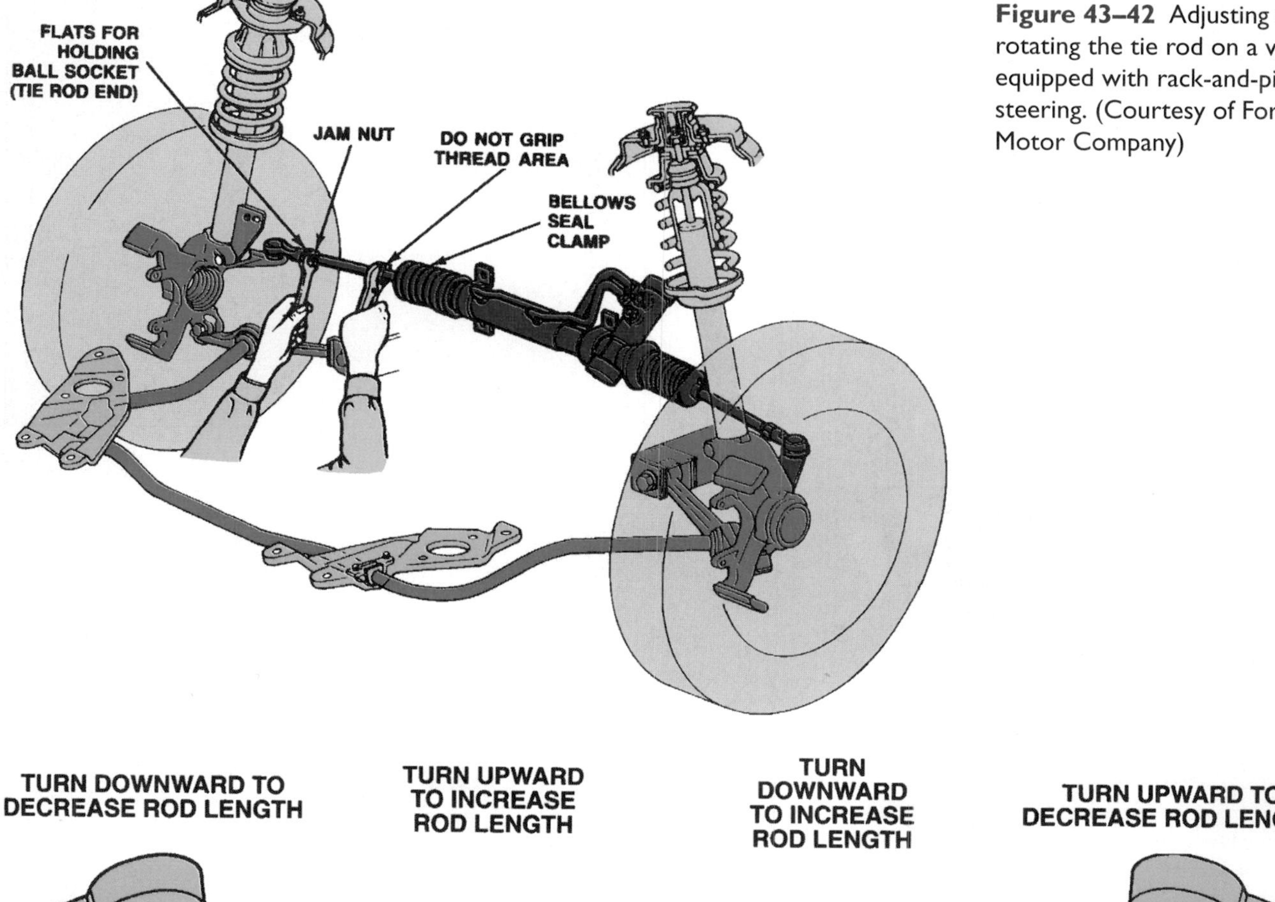

Figure 43–42 Adjusting toe by rotating the tie rod on a vehicle equipped with rack-and-pinion steering. (Courtesy of Ford Motor Company)

Figure 43–43 Toe is adjusted on a parallelogram-type steering linkage by turning adjustable tie rod sleeves. Special tie rod sleeve adjusting tools should be used that grip the slot in the sleeve and will not crush the sleeve while it is being rotated. (Courtesy of Ford Motor Company)

wheel straight. Always "unlock" the steering column, straighten the steering wheel, and install the steering wheel lock.

NOTE: If the vehicle is equipped with power steering, the engine must be started and the steering wheel straightened with the engine running to make sure the steering wheel is straight. Lock the steering wheel with the steering lock tool before stopping the engine. See Figure 43–44.

After straightening the steering wheel, turn the tie rod adjustment until the toe for both wheels is within specifications.

Many alignment machines include a screen that shows straight-ahead steering. Simply adjust the tie rod adjusters until the reading shows that the toe is correct *and* the front wheels will result in a straight steering wheel. This is often called **centreline steering** and means that the steering wheel will be centred when the vehicle is travelling a straight course. Test drive the vehicle for proper handling and centreline steering.

DIAGNOSTIC STORY

Left Thrust Line, But a Pull to the Right!

A new four-door sport sedan had been aligned several times at the dealership in an attempt to solve a pull to the right. The car had front-wheel-drive and had four-wheel independent suspension. The dealer rotated the tires but it made no difference. The alignment angles of all four wheels were in the centre of specifications. The dealer even switched all four tires from another car in an attempt to solve the problem.

In frustration, the owner took the car to an alignment shop. Almost immediately, the alignment technician discovered the right rear wheel was slightly toed-in. Even though the right rear being toed-in usually causes a thrust line to the left, in this particular car, it caused a pull to the right. See Figure 43–45. The alignment technician adjusted the toe on the right rear wheel, which was adjustable, and reset the front toe. The car drove beautifully.

The owner was puzzled why the new car dealer was unable to correct the problem. It was later discovered that the alignment machine at the dealership was out of calibration by the exact amount that the right rear wheel was out of specification. The car pulled to the right because the independent suspension created a rear steering force toward the left that caused the front to pull to the right. Alignment equipment manufacturers recommend that alignment equipment be calibrated regularly.

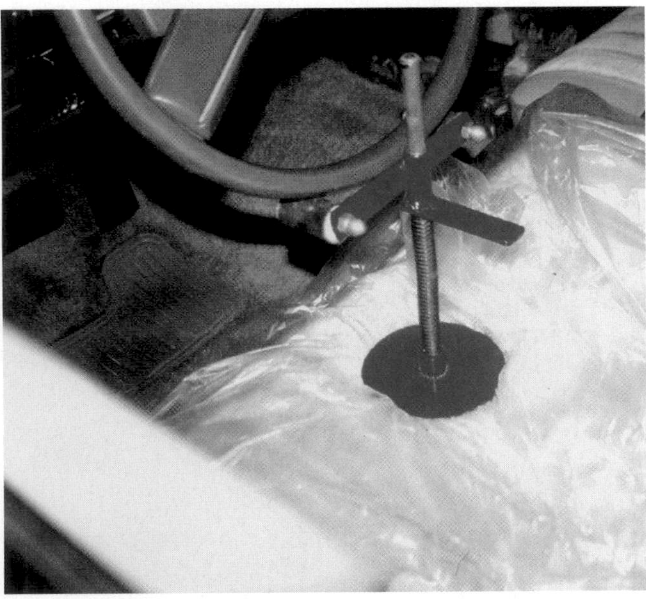

Figure 43–44 Many procedures for setting toe specify that the steering wheel be held in the straight-ahead position using a steering wheel lock, as shown. One method recommended by Hunter Engineering sets toe without using a steering wheel lock.

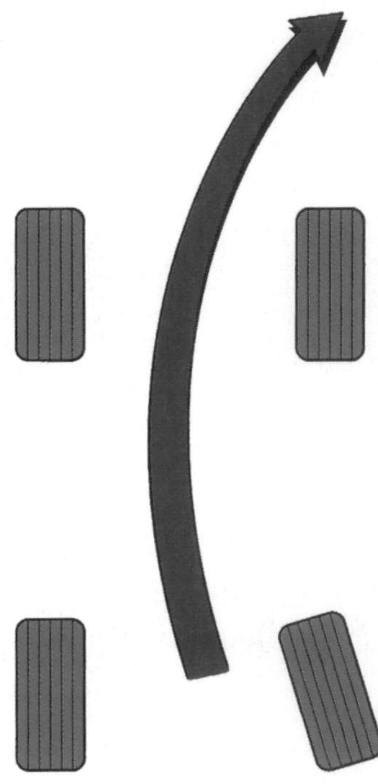

Figure 43–45 The toe-in on the right wheel creates a turning force toward the right.

AFTERMARKET ALIGNMENT METHODS

Accurate alignments are still possible on vehicles without factory methods of adjustment by using alignment kits or parts. Aftermarket alignment kits are available for most vehicles. Even with factory alignment methods, sometimes the range of adjustment is not enough to compensate for sagging frame members or other normal or accident-related faults. See Figures 43–46 and 43–47.

(a)

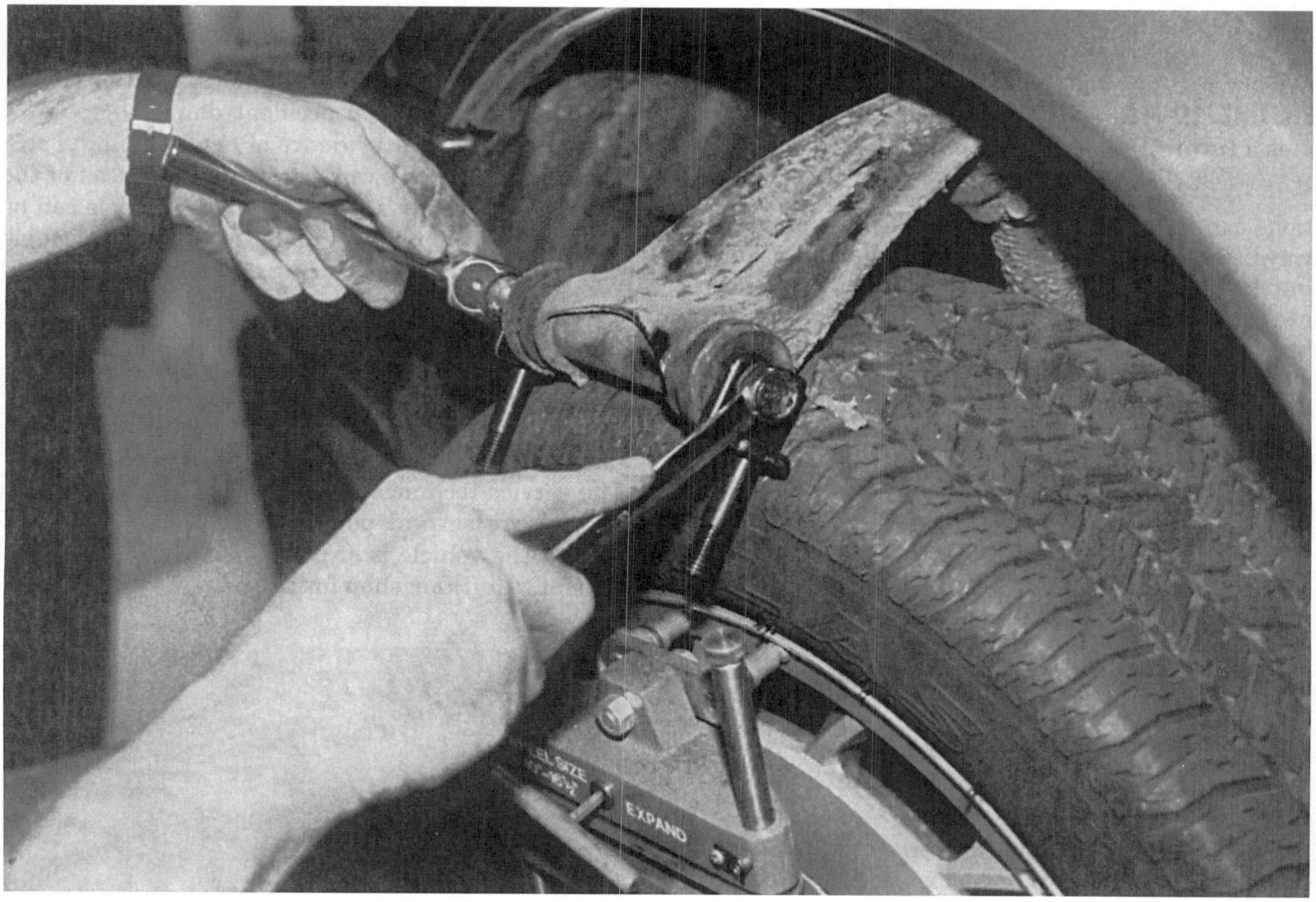

(b)

Figure 43–46 (a) Aftermarket camber kit designed to provide some camber adjustments for a vehicle that does not provide for any adjustment. (b) Installation of this kit requires that the upper control arm shaft be removed. Note that the upper control arm was simply rotated out over the wheel pivot on the upper ball joint.

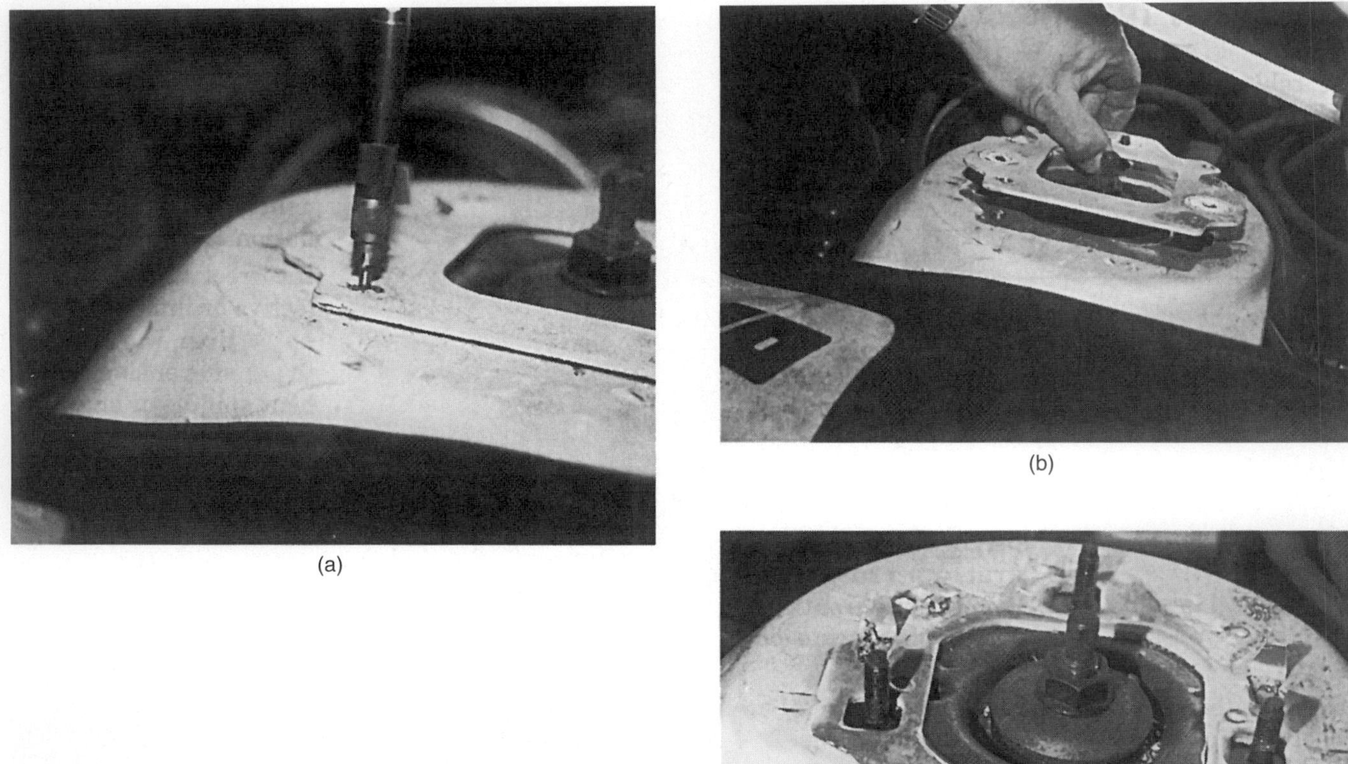

(a)

(b)

(c)

Figure 43–47 (a) The installation of some aftermarket alignment kits requires the use of special tools such as this cutter, which is being used to drill out spot welds on the original alignment plate on a strut tower. (b) Original plate being removed. (c) Note the amount of movement the upper strut bearing mount has around the square openings in the strut tower. An aftermarket plate can now be installed to allow both camber and caster adjustment.

P30–1 Begin the alignment procedure by first driving the vehicle onto the alignment rack as straight as possible.

P30–2 Position the front tires in the centre of the turn plates. These turn plates can be moved inward and outward to match any width vehicle.

P30–3 Check and adjust tire pressures and perform the other prealignment checks necessary to be assured of a proper alignment.

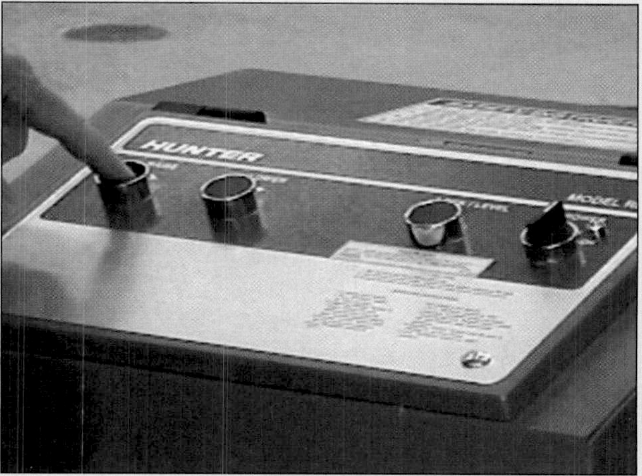

P30–4 Raise the vehicle and perform a dry park test to determine whether steering and/or suspension parts may need replacement before continuing with the alignment.

P30–5 Position both the front and rear rack jacking systems under the suspension system.

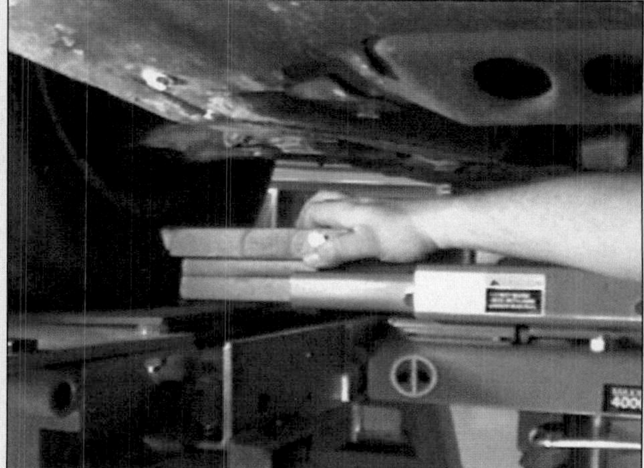

P30–6 Move the pads of the lifting unit under the suspension so that the vehicle can be raised off the drive-on surface of the alignment rack.

P30–7 Lower the alignment rack floor supports before lowering the alignment rack.

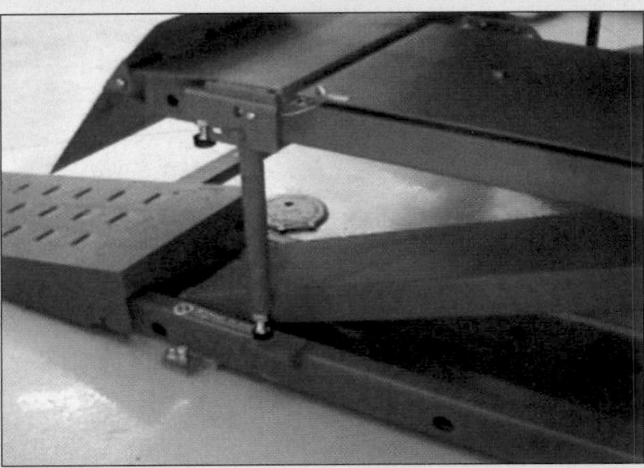

P30–8 When the alignment rack is lowered, the support arms should contact the floor or the bottom of the hoist in the case of this scissor-type alignment rack.

P30–9 With the alignment rack firmly supported by the support legs, raise the vehicle off the alignment rack using the air/hydraulic jacks previously placed under the front and rear suspension.

P30–10 With the wheels off the rack, install the alignment heads. Position the alignment heads with the valve core located in the 1 o'clock position so that the safety cable can be installed to the valve core.

P30–11 Remove the tire valve cap and either put it in your pocket or place it in a location where it will not be lost. Screw the safety cable for the alignment head to the tire valve.

P30–12 Connect all of the cables and lines necessary. In this situation, the alignment heads are battery powered and communicate to the alignment machine via radio frequency signals. To power up this type of alignment head, simply turn it on.

P30–13 The bubble level and three lights in the circle are used during the compensation process.

P30–14 Compensate all four alignment heads according to the alignment machine specified procedures. This compensation process allows for correct alignment of the wheels even if the alignment heads are not all installed to exactly the same depth or if there is a bent wheel.

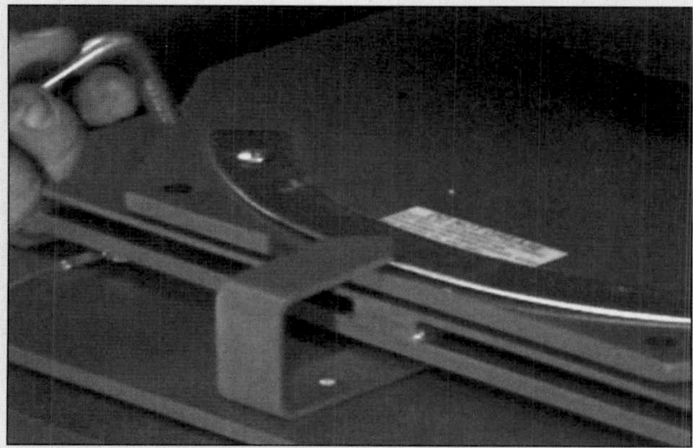

P30–15 Remove the pins from the turn plates (both front and rear).

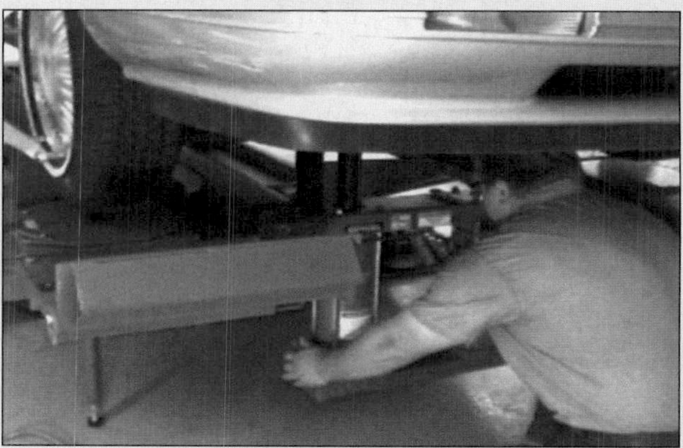

P30–16 Lower the vehicle onto the turn plates.

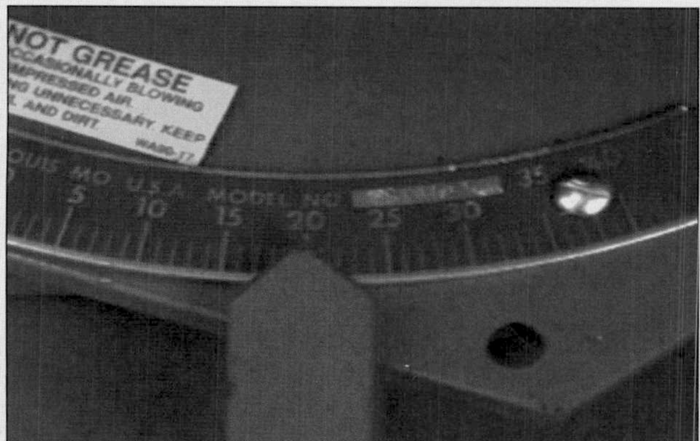

P30–17 Now is a good time to check for toe-out on turns (TOOT). The front wheels are turned until the turn plate under the outside wheel reads 20°.

P30–18 A check on the other side of the vehicle indicates that the inside turn plate had rotated 18°, which was within specifications for this vehicle. A bent or damaged steering arm (knuckle) is the most likely cause if the TOOT is not within specifications, and a problem of tire squeal while turning a corner at low speeds is the usual symptom.

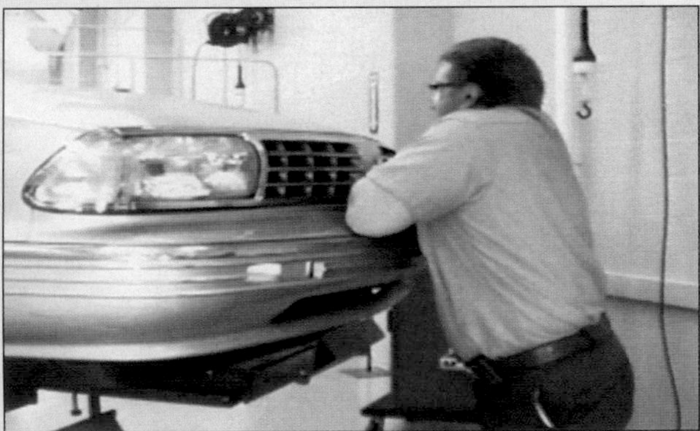

P30–19 After lowering the vehicle and making sure the wheels are turned in the straight-ahead position, jounce (bounce) the vehicle at both front and rear to centre the suspension.

P30–20 Some alignment machines such as this Hunter P211 have a built-in ride height gauge. The readout shows the actual measurement and the specifications so the technician will know if replacement springs are necessary before the alignment is begun.

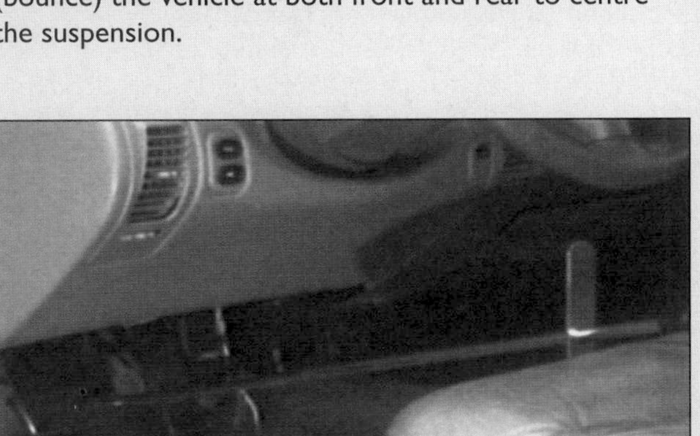

P30–21 To prevent the wheels from rotating during the checking procedures, most alignment equipment manufacturers specify that the brakes should be kept applied. A brake pedal depressor tool connects between the seat and the brake pedal.

P30–22 Whenever the brake pedal is depressed, the brake lights will also be on with most vehicles. To prevent the brake lights from draining the battery, the brake light fuse could be removed or the connector to the rear lights disconnected.

P30–23 To measure caster, the front wheels must be steered first in one direction, then the other direction as directed by on-screen instructions. Most experts recommend that the front wheels be turned using the steering wheel because this creates the same forces on the steering system as is normally exerted during vehicle operation.

P30–24 After the caster angle has been determined, raise the front wheels off the rack and allow the wheels to droop. This allows a more accurate measurement for SAI than if the vehicle was kept on the rack.

P30–25 The front wheels are again rotated to the right and then to the left following the directions on the alignment machine display to measure the steering axis inclination (SAI).

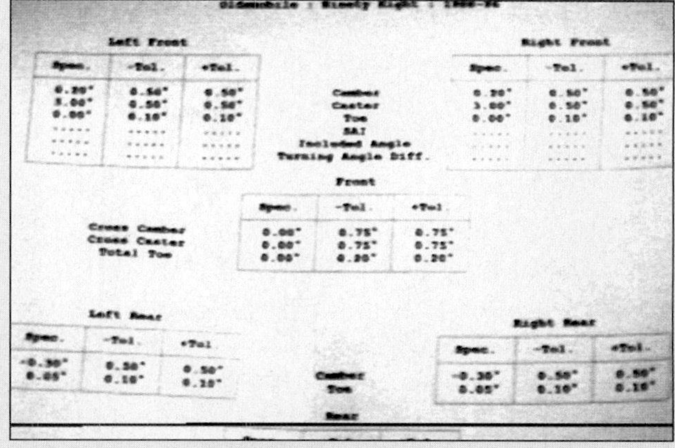

Left Front

Spec.	-Tol.	+Tol.		Spec.	-Tol.	+Tol.
0.20°	0.50°	0.50°	Camber	0.20°	0.50°	0.50°
3.00°	0.50°	0.50°	Caster	3.00°	0.50°	0.50°
0.00°	0.10°	0.10°	Toe	0.00°	0.10°	0.10°
-----	-----	-----	SAI	-----	-----	-----
-----	-----	-----	Included Angle	-----	-----	-----
-----	-----	-----	Turning Angle Diff.	-----	-----	-----

Right Front

Front

	Spec.	-Tol.	+Tol.
Cross Camber	0.00°	0.75°	0.75°
Cross Caster	0.00°	0.75°	0.75°
Total Toe	0.00°	0.20°	0.20°

Left Rear

Spec.	-Tol.	+Tol.		Spec.	-Tol.	+Tol.
-0.30°	0.50°	0.50°	Camber	-0.30°	0.50°	0.50°
0.05°	0.10°	0.10°	Toe	0.05°	0.10°	0.10°

Right Rear

Rear

P30–26 After all of the angles have been measured, the alignment results can be printed out and compared to specifications.

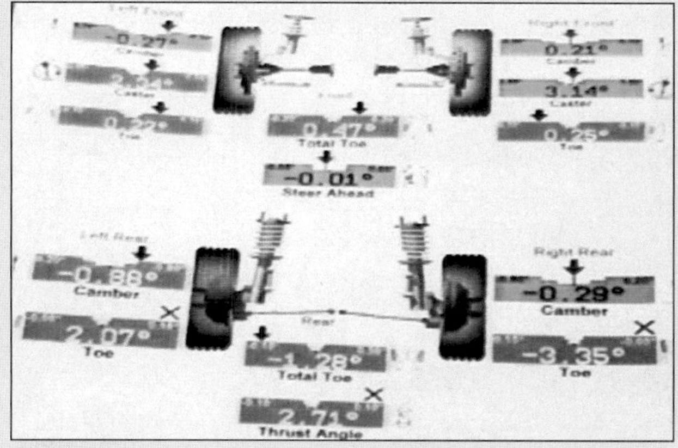

P30–27 This printout shows that most angles are out of specification—not unusual for this training vehicle that has been used by students practicing replacing suspension and steering components.

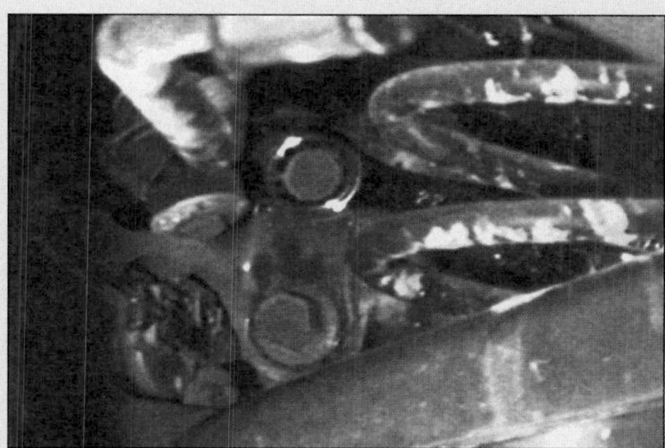

P30–28 Start correcting the alignment by adjusting rear camber. The rear camber is adjusted on this vehicle by loosening the strut attachments bolts and moving the bottom portion of the rear strut.

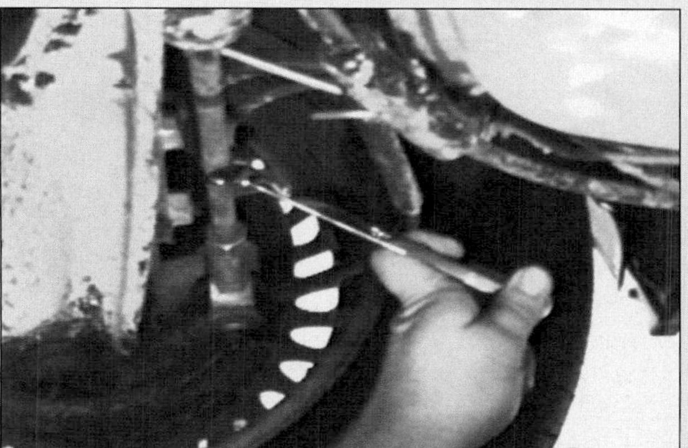

P30–29 After the rear camber has been adjusted, the rear toe is then brought back into factory specifications by rotating the rear tie-rod after loosening the jam nut. Many vehicles require aftermarket shims to adjust the rear toe and/or camber.

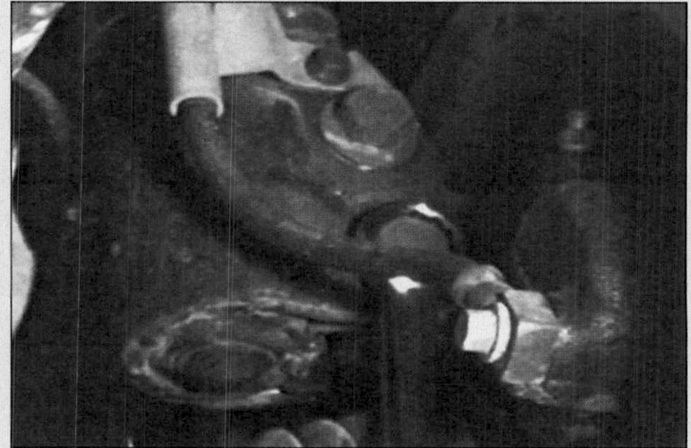

P30–30 After the rear camber and toe have been adjusted, the front camber is now being adjusted by loosening and moving the lower strut mount. The caster on this vehicle was OK and did not require adjustment. If it had required adjustment, the caster should be adjusted before adjusting the camber.

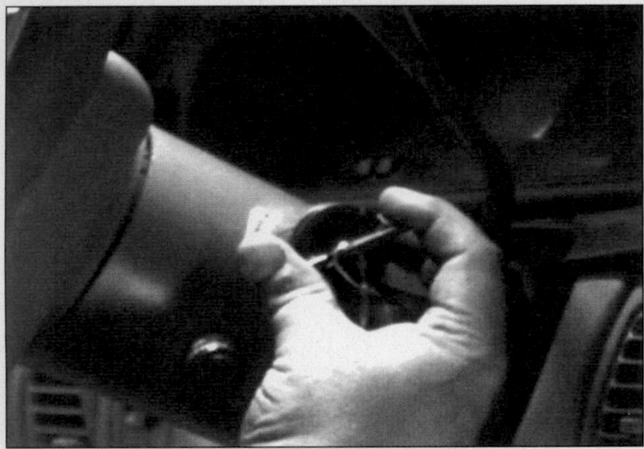

P30–31 Before setting the front toe, start the engine if the vehicle is equipped with power steering.

P30–32 Straighten the steering wheel and use a steering wheel lock to hold the steering wheel in the straight-ahead position as shown. Some methods of adjusting front toe do not require that the steering wheel be locked. Follow the recommended procedures as specified by the alignment equipment manufacturer.

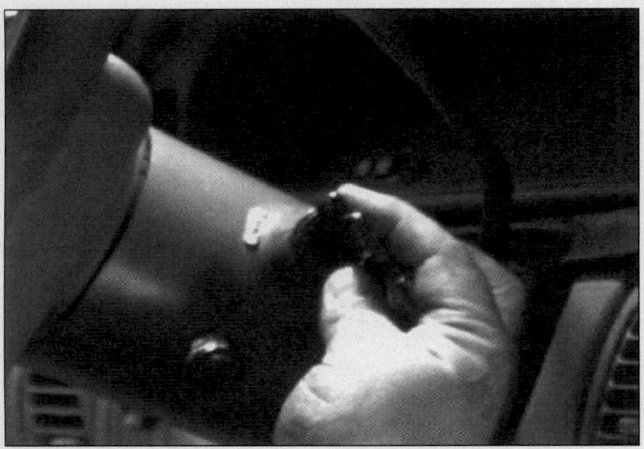

P30–33 After centring the steering wheel and locking it in the straight-ahead position, turn the engine and ignition off.

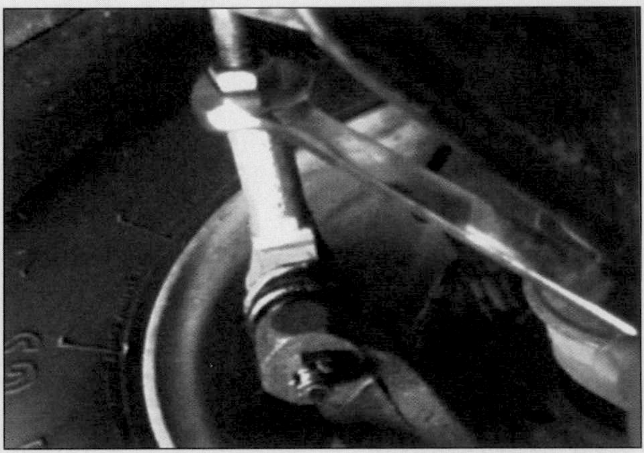

P30–34 Loosen the jam nut to allow the tie-rod to be lengthened or shortened to adjust the front toe.

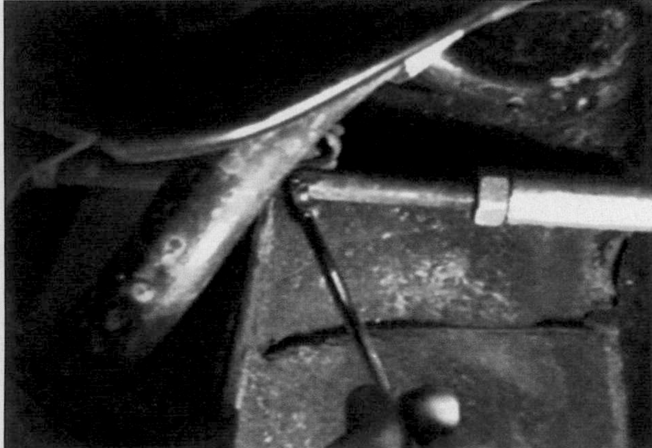

P30–35 Use a wrench or the flats of the tie-rod (if equipped) to rotate the tie-rod to bring the toe into factory specifications.

P30–36 After the toe has been adjusted, hold the tie-rod with a wrench while tightening the lock (jam) nut to prevent any change in the toe setting.

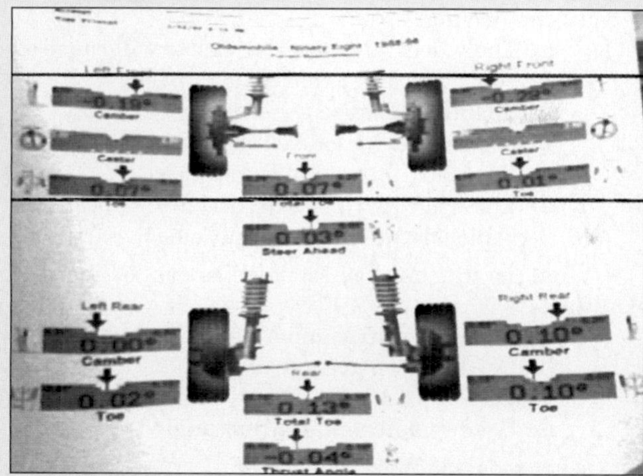

P30–37 After the alignment is completed, print out the results so the customer can see that all angles are within factory specifications.

P30–38 After completing the alignment, carefully disconnect the alignment heads from the wheels. Reinstall the valve caps and wheel covers if necessary.

P30–39 Lower the vehicle.

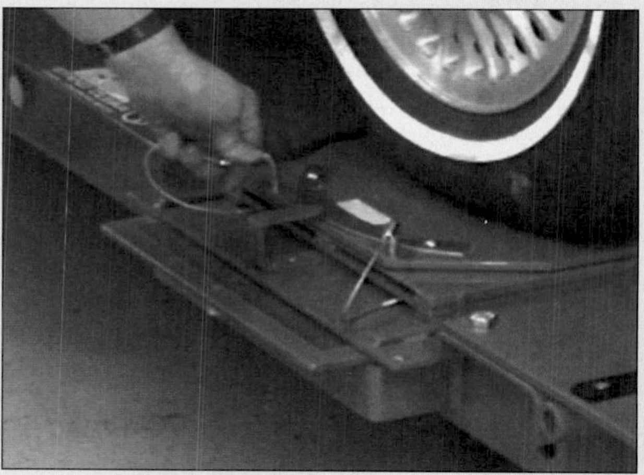

P30–40 Install the pins in the turn plates before driving the vehicle off the alignment rack.

P30–41 Remove any chocks (blocks) used to keep the vehicle from moving on the rack.

P30–42 Carefully drive the vehicle off the alignment rack. The vehicle should be driven to check for proper vehicle handling and double-check that the steering wheel is straight before returning the vehicle to the customer.

SUMMARY

1. Toe is the most important alignment angle because toe is usually the first alignment angle needing correction and when incorrect causes severe tire wear.
2. Caster is the basic stability angle yet does not cause tire wear (directly) if not correct or equal side-to-side.
3. Camber is both a pulling angle if not equal side-to-side as well as a tire-wearing angle if not set to specifications.
4. SAI and included angle (SAI and camber added together) are important diagnostic measurements.
5. If the toe-out-on-turns (TOOT) reading is not within specifications, a bent steering spindle (steering knuckle) is the most likely cause.
6. A four-wheel alignment includes aligning all four wheels of the vehicle, whereas a thrust line alignment sets the front toe equal to the thrust line (total rear toe) of the rear wheels.
7. Before attempting to align any vehicle, it must be checked for proper ride height (trim height), tire conditions, and tire pressures as well as thoroughly inspected for the condition of all steering and suspension components.
8. The proper sequence for a complete four-wheel alignment is
   - **a.** Rear camber
   - **b.** Rear toe
   - **c.** Front caster and camber
   - **d.** Front toe

REVIEW QUESTIONS

1. Explain the three basic alignment angles of camber, caster, and toe.
2. Explain how knowing SAI, TOOT, and included angle can help in the correct diagnosis of an alignment problem.
3. List ten prealignment checks that should be performed before the wheel alignment is checked and/or adjusted.
4. List the steps necessary to follow for a four-wheel alignment.

RED SEAL CERTIFICATION-TYPE QUESTIONS

1. How does toe affect the direction a vehicle would pull toward?
   - **a.** Pulls toward the side with the most positive toe on the rear wheel
   - **b.** Pulls toward the side with the most negative toe on the rear wheel
   - **c.** Pulls toward the side with the positive toe on the front wheel
   - **d.** Pulls toward the side with the negative toe on the front wheel
2. How does caster angle affect vehicle directional stability and driving?
   - **a.** The wheel with positive caster will cause a vehicle to pull toward that wheel
   - **b.** Caster will cause the tire to wear badly
   - **c.** Positive caster causes the vehicle to wander on the road
   - **d.** The wheel with negative caster will cause a vehicle to pull toward that wheel
3. What is the purpose of verification of toe-out-on-turns?
   - **a.** Used to verify camber angle
   - **b.** Used to verify caster angle
   - **c.** Used to check steering spindle for bends
   - **d.** Used to determine thrust angle
4. Strut rods (if adjustable) adjust
   - **a.** Toe
   - **b.** Camber
   - **c.** Caster
   - **d.** Toe-out on turns
5. If metal shims are used for alignment adjustment in the front, they adjust
   - **a.** Camber
   - **b.** Caster
   - **c.** Toe
   - **d.** a and b only
6. What alignment angle is identified by the inward or outward tilt of the tire at the top viewed from the front of the vehicle?
   - **a.** Caster
   - **b.** Camber
   - **c.** Toe
   - **d.** Thrust

Use the Following Information to Answer Question 7

Specifications:	Minimum	Preferred	Maximum
Camber (degree)	0	1.0	1.4
Caster (degree)	.8	1.5	2.1
Toe (mm)	−2.5	1.5	3.8

Results:	L	R
Camber (degree)	−.1	.6
Caster (degree)	1.8	1.6
Toe (mm)	2.8	+3

7. The vehicle above will
   - **a.** Pull toward the right and feather edge both tires
   - **b.** Pull toward the left
   - **c.** Wear the outside of the left tire and the inside of the right tire
   - **d.** None of the above

Use the Following Information to Answer Questions 8 and 9

Specifications:	Minimum	Preferred	Maximum
Camber (degree)	$-^1/_4$	$+^1/_2$	1
Caster (degree)	0	+2	+4
Toe (inch)	$-^1/_{16}$	$^1/_{16}$	$^3/_{16}$

Results:	L	R
Camber (degree)	−0.3	−0.1
Caster (degree)	3.6	1.8
Toe (inch)	−0.16	+0.32

8. The vehicle at the left will
- **a.** Pull toward the left
- **b.** Pull toward the right
- **c.** Wander
- **d.** Lead to the left slightly

9. The vehicle at the left will
- **a.** Wander
- **b.** Wear tires, but not pull
- **c.** Pull, but not wear tires
- **d.** Pull toward the left and cause feather-edge tire wear

10. Which alignment angle is most likely to need correction and cause the most tire wear?
- **a.** Toe
- **b.** Camber
- **c.** Caster
- **d.** SAI/KPI

SECTION **VIII**

Manual Drive Train and Axles

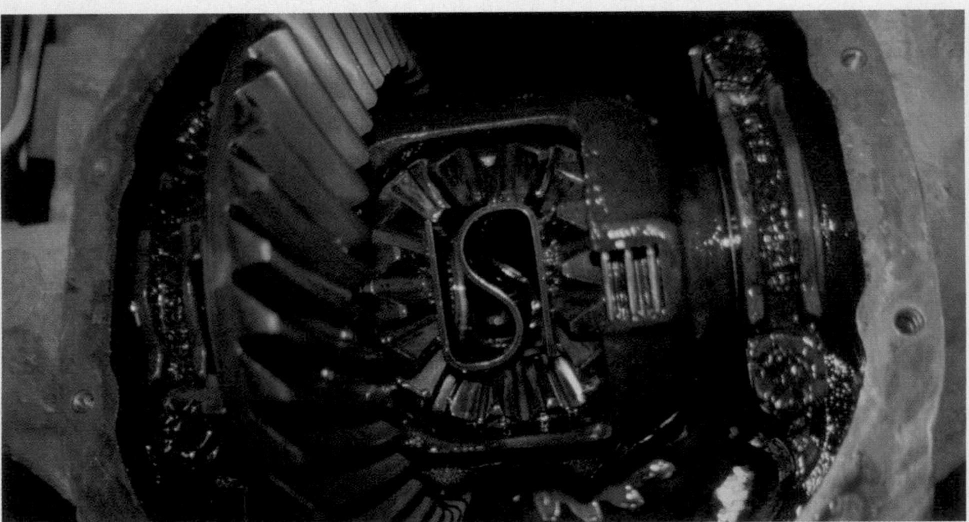

Chapter 44 includes clutch construction, problem diagnosis, and service procedures. Chapter 45 contains details on both rear-wheel-drive manual transmissions as well as front-wheel-drive transaxles. Chapter 46 covers Cardan universal joints and constant velocity (CV) joints plus details on drive shafts. Chapter 47 describes operation and servicing of differential assemblies and Chapter 48 covers all aspects of four-wheel-drive and all-wheel-drive systems including transfer cases.

44

Clutches

OBJECTIVES: After studying Chapter 44, you should be able to:

1. Prepare for the interprovincial Red Seal certification examination in Appendix III (Manual Drive Trains and Axles) on the topics covered in this chapter.
2. List the parts that are included in the clutch system.
3. Describe how the clutch works.
4. Explain the importance of proper clutch pedal freeplay.
5. List the steps necessary to replace a clutch.
6. Describe the characteristic noise each clutch component part makes when defective.

PURPOSE AND FUNCTION OF A CLUTCH

The clutch assembly is located between the engine and the transmission/transaxle.

NOTE: The term *transmission* refers to rear-wheel-drive vehicles and the term *transaxle* usually refers to front-wheel-drive vehicles that have a differential built into the unit. A separate differential is used with a transmission.

The purpose and function of a clutch include the following:

- To disconnect the engine from the transmission/transaxle to permit the engine to remain running when the vehicle is stopped and to permit the transmission/transaxle to be shifted
- To connect and transmit engine torque to the transmission/transaxle
- To dampen and absorb engine impulses and drive train vibration
- To provide a smooth engagement and disengagement between the engine and the transmission/transaxle

COMPONENT PARTS AND OPERATION OF A CLUTCH ASSEMBLY

A clutch assembly consists of a **clutch disc** that is splined to the input shaft of the transmission/transaxle. When the driver depresses the clutch pedal, a **throwout bearing (release bearing)** is forced against the fingers of the **pressure plate.** The pressure plate is bolted to and rotates with the flywheel. See Figure 44–1. When force is exerted on the centre of the pressure plate, the pressure is released from the clutch disc that has been forced against the engine flywheel. With the pressure removed from the clutch disc, the engine can be operated without transferring torque to the transmission/transaxle. This also permits the transmission/transaxle to be shifted because a shift cannot be made if the transmission/transaxle is transferring engine torque.

When the driver reduces force on the clutch pedal, the pedal return spring and the pressure plate spring combine to return the clutch pedal to its at-rest position (clutch-engaged position). When the clutch pedal moves up, the pressure on the throwout bearing is released and the force against

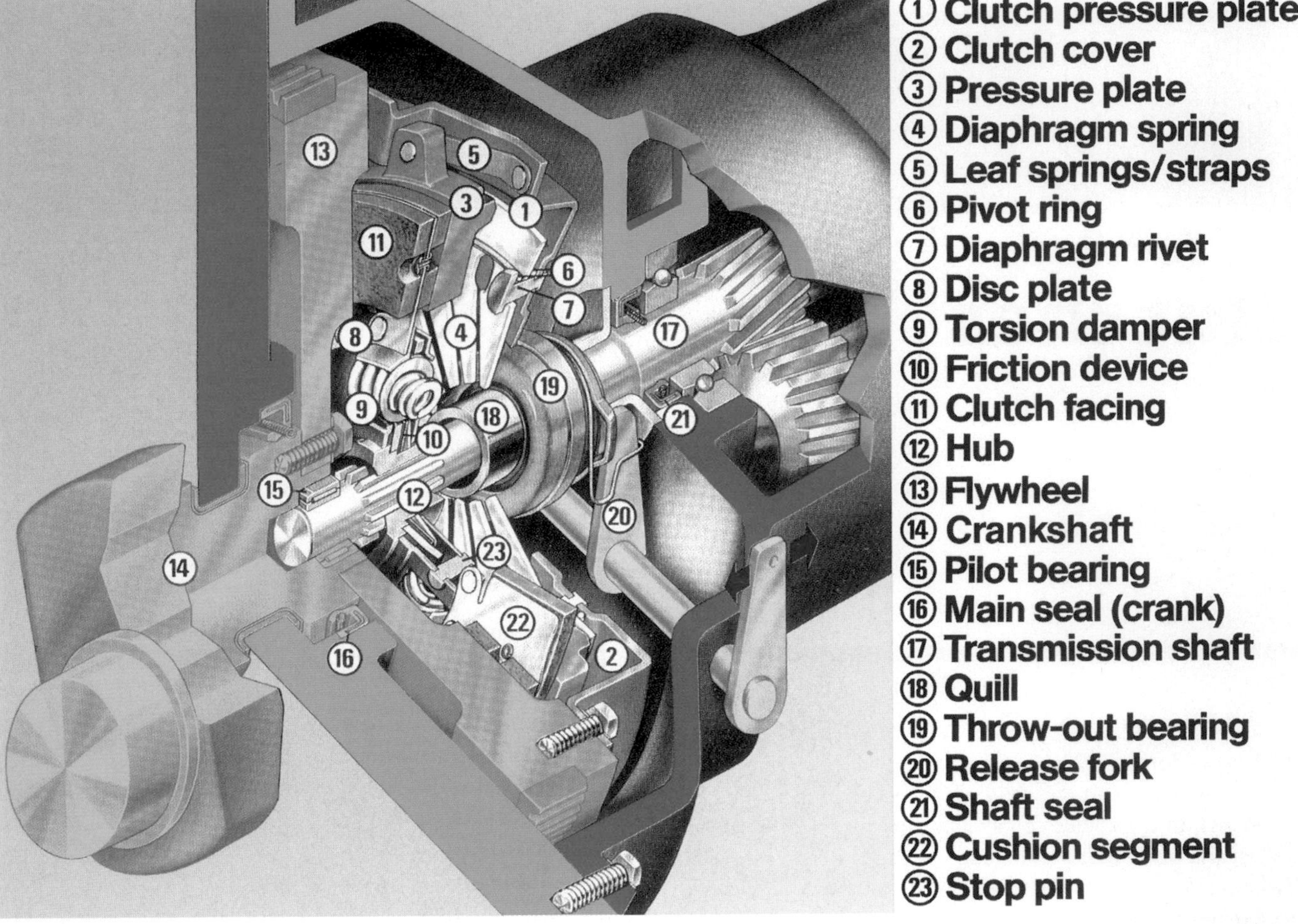

Figure 44–1 Typical automotive clutch assembly showing all related parts. (Courtesy of LUK)

the pressure plate spring(s) is released, allowing the force of the pressure plate to clamp the clutch tightly between the flywheel and the pressure plate. See Figure 44–2.

Additional related parts include the **pilot bearing** (or **bushing**) that supports the front of the transmission input shaft. See Figure 44–3. The throwout bearing is often supported and rides on the transmission/transaxle **front bearing retainer** (also called the **quill**).

> **NOTE:** Most front-wheel-drive transaxles do not use a pilot bearing.

To summarize:

- When the clutch pedal is up, the clutch is engaged.
- When the clutch pedal is down, the clutch is disengaged.

Clutch Pedal Linkage

There are three methods of transferring the force of the driver's foot to the throwout (release) bearing, including

- **Levers and rods.** Through a series of levers and rods, the release fork is forced against the throwout bearing. This method was commonly used on many older vehicles.
- **Cable operation.** A cable is used similar to a brake cable used on a bicycle. See Figure 44–4.
- **Hydraulic.** A small master cylinder and a slave cylinder located near the throwout bearing is a very common method of connecting the clutch pedal to the release fork on vehicles equipped with a manual transmission. See Figures 44–5 (p. 1050) and 44–6 (p. 1051).

Clutch Disc

The clutch disc is round with a splined centre hole that slips over the splines of the input shaft of the

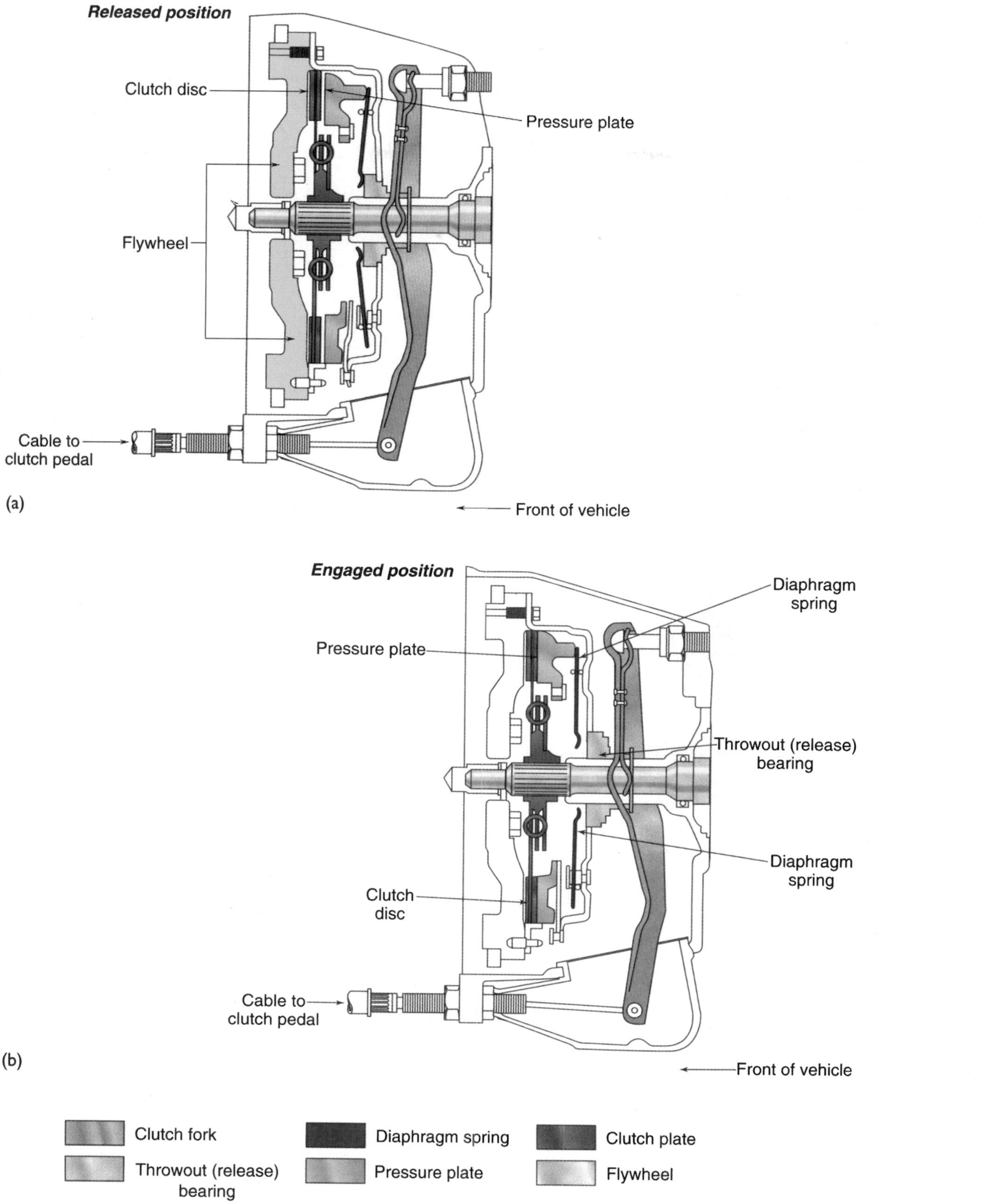

Released position

Clutch disc

Pressure plate

Flywheel

Cable to clutch pedal

(a)

Front of vehicle

Engaged position

Diaphragm spring

Pressure plate

Throwout (release) bearing

Diaphragm spring

Clutch disc

Cable to clutch pedal

(b)

Front of vehicle

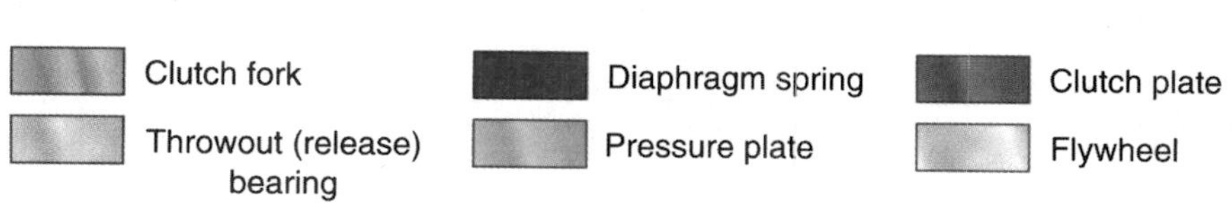

Figure 44–2 (a) When the clutch is in the released position (clutch pedal depressed), the clutch fork is applying a force to the throwout (release) bearing, which pushes on the diaphragm spring, releasing the pressure on the friction disc. (b) When the clutch is in the engaged position (clutch pedal up), the diaphragm spring exerts force on the clutch disc, holding it between the flywheel and the pressure plate.

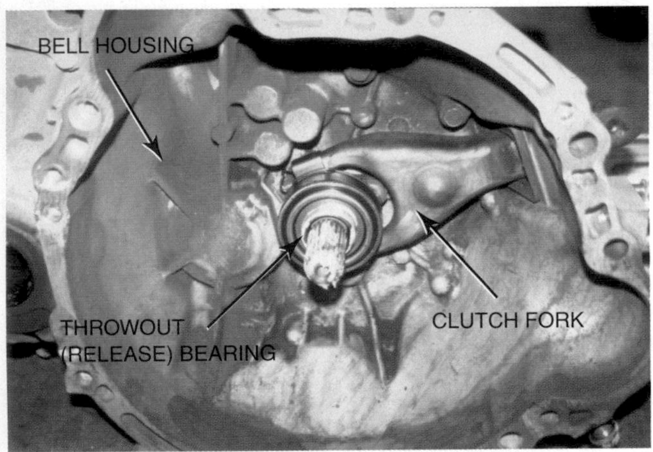

Figure 44–3 The transmission has just been removed. Note that this type of transmission incorporates the bell housing, which was therefore removed at the same time as the transmission. The clutch fork and throwout (release) bearing also came off together. All that remained attached to the engine was the flywheel, clutch disc, and pressure plate.

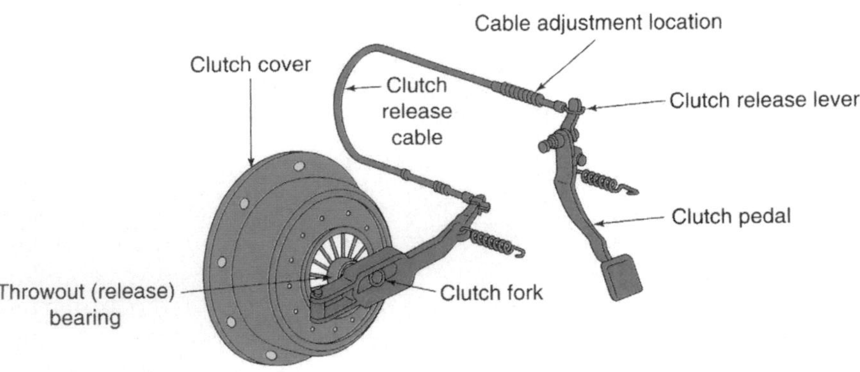

Figure 44–4 A typical cable-operated clutch.

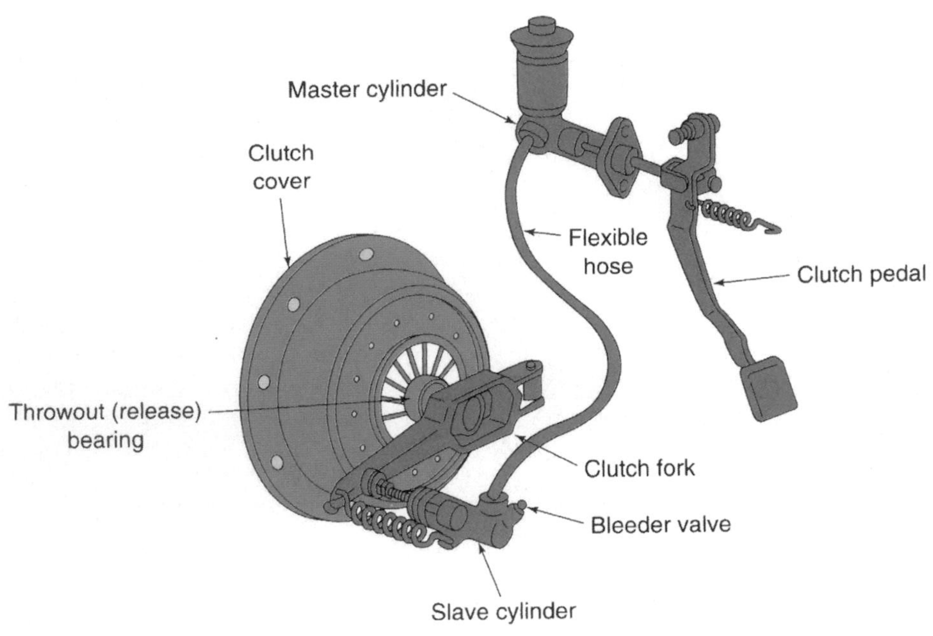

Figure 44–5 A hydraulic clutch linkage uses a master cylinder and a slave cylinder.

Figure 44–6 A typical clutch master cylinder and reservoir mounted on the bulkhead on the driver's side of the vehicle. Brake fluid is used in the hydraulic system to operate the slave cylinder located on the bell housing.

transmission/transaxle. Friction material is riveted to both sides of the clutch disc—one side touches the flywheel of the engine and the other side touches the friction surface of the pressure plate.

Friction material is either woven or moulded from a mixture of other materials. Woven materials are softer and help cushion clutch engagement, but they may not last as long as moulded materials.

Friction materials operate in high heat and pressure. For many years, asbestos was the most common material used in both clutch and brake linings. However, it is no longer used because inhaling tiny particles of asbestos causes lung damage. Today, clutch friction material may contain paper, cotton, and bits of copper or brass wire with resin holding the mixture together.

CAUTION: Always take precautions when working around clutch lining material and assume that it contains asbestos. These precautions should include wetting the friction disc before removal and preventing any dust from the lining from becoming airborne.

High Performance Clutch Disc

Another type of friction material is a ceramic and metallic mixture. This creates a hard, long-lasting lining, but is more expensive and does not cushion clutch engagement as much as a softer lining. Instead of a full circle of softer friction material, the disc may have only a few segments or buttons of this ceramic-metallic material. Clutches that use these discs, which are sometimes called *button clutches,* are found in racing applications where strength and durability are a greater concern than smooth engagement. See Figure 44–7.

Stock Clutch Disc

Around the centre hub of the clutch disc are **torsional dampers** that absorb the initial shock of engagement and help dampen engine-firing in pulses being transmitted into and through the transmission/transaxle. See Figure 44–8. The torsional dampers are either coil springs or are made of rubber. In the space between the friction surfaces is a wavy spring steel material called a **cushioning spring** or **marcel spring.** See Figure 44–9. The marcel spring also helps to absorb the initial shock of engagement and allows for a smooth engagement of the clutch.

HINT: The larger centre hub section of the disc must be installed with the thicker portion facing the pressure plate. See Figure 44–10.

Pressure Plates

The purpose of the pressure plate is to exert a force on the clutch disc so that engine torque can be transmitted from the engine to the transmission/transaxle. A strong spring(s) is required to provide adequate clamping force on the clutch disc. However, a strong pressure plate spring force must be released by the force of the driver's foot to disengage the clutch. The pressure plate, like the flywheel, is usually made of nodular cast iron. A smooth, machined area on one side forms the friction disc contact surface. When the clutch engages, spring force pushes the pressure plate toward the flywheel so the friction disc is clamped between the flywheel

Figure 44–7 A racing or high-performance clutch disc lacks the features of a stock clutch disc that help provide smooth engagement.

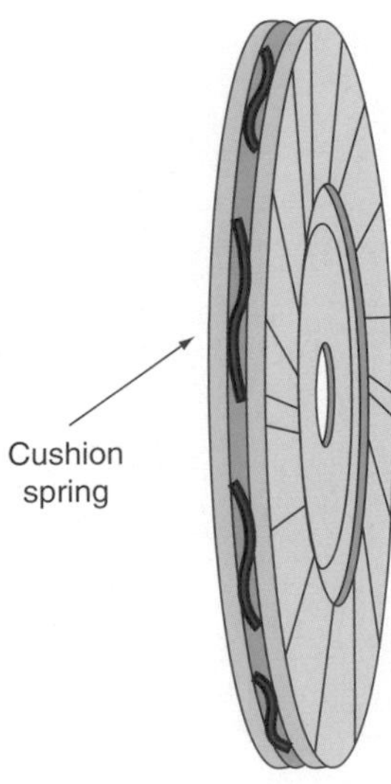

Figure 44–9 A cushion spring is a wavy spring that is placed between the two friction surfaces to cushion the clutch engagement.

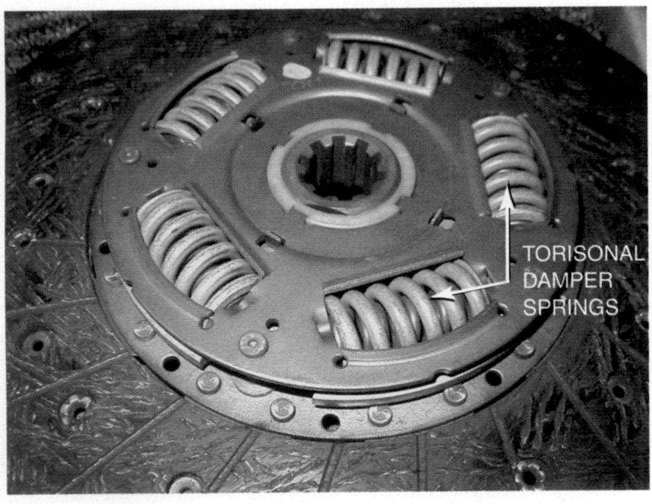

Figure 44–8 A typical stock clutch friction disc that uses coil spring torsional dampers.

Figure 44–10 Cutaway of the centre section of a clutch plate showing the various layers of steel plates used in the construction.

and the pressure plate. Engine torque flows through the clutch to the transmission input shaft. Three or four drive straps or clips connect the pressure plate to the clutch cover. These spring-steel straps or clips help hold the pressure plate away from the flywheel when the clutch disengages. Several styles of pressure plates have been used, including

- **Coil spring style.** This style of pressure plate uses coil springs and three release arms. A coil-spring-style pressure plate is also called the **lever style** because it uses levers to compress the coil springs. See Figure 44–11.
- **Diaphragm spring style.** This style is the most commonly used pressure plate design. One large, round, spring-steel spring is used to apply even force on the clutch disc. See Figure 44–12. These tend to be smaller assemblies, weigh less, and have fewer parts than coil spring assemblies. The one-piece diaphragm spring does the job of all the release levers and coil springs in a coil spring clutch.

The driver must push harder on the clutch pedal to disengage a **coil spring clutch** than to disengage a comparable diaphragm spring design. The

Figure 44–11 A coil spring (lever style) clutch pressure plate.

Figure 44–12 Typical diaphragm-style pressure plate that uses a Belleville spring.

pedal effort for a coil spring clutch increases the farther down the pedal is pushed. The pedal effort for a diaphragm spring clutch decreases during the second half of pedal travel.

As the friction disc wears, coil springs expand and lose some of their clamping force. In contrast, the design of the diaphragm spring tends to increase its clamping force as the friction disc wears to half its original thickness. Then, as the friction disc continues to wear, the clamping force of the spring gradually returns to its original level. This happens without any obvious change in clutch pedal effort.

In many cases, aftermarket clutch parts manufacturers supply a diaphragm spring pressure plate assembly when an original coil spring assembly must be replaced. If so, carefully compare the new pressure plate to the old one to make sure it is the correct replacement. Physical characteristics, such as dimensions and bolt-hole patterns, must be identical for the assembled clutch to operate properly. Check that the inner edges of the diaphragm spring fingers are the same height as the release levers on the original unit.

Flywheels

The engine flywheel serves four basic purposes:

- Smoothes out or dampens engine power pulses.
- Absorbs some of the heat created by clutch operation.
- Provides the connection point for the starter motor to crank the engine.
- Provides the application surface for the clutch friction disc.

A flywheel is heavy, or has a large mass, which creates inertia. This inertia acts upon crankshaft rotation to smooth out or dampen engine power pulses. On a running engine, the crankshaft speeds up as a cylinder fires, then slows due to internal engine friction until the next cylinder fires. The inertia provided by the flywheel mass tends to keep crankshaft speed more constant.

Whenever friction exists between two moving parts, heat is generated. The flywheel absorbs some of the heat created by clutch operation by acting as a heat sink for the clutch friction disc.

An external ring gear is pressed or welded onto the flywheel along its outer circumference. When the starter motor is engaged, the starter-drive gear meshes with the flywheel ring gear. Through gear reduction, the flywheel transfers starter motor rotation to the crankshaft to crank the engine.

The face on the transmission side of the flywheel has a smooth, machined area that creates the application surface for the clutch friction disc. This surface must be properly finished to allow adequate slippage as the clutch engages and disengages, and to prevent slippage when the clutch is engaged. See Figure 44–13.

The flywheel is constructed of cast iron and attaches to the end of the engine crankshaft. The carbon content of the cast iron (about 3%) provides a suitable surface for the clutch disc. The carbon, in the form of graphite, acts as a lubricant to provide a smooth engagement of the clutch. The weight of the flywheel helps to absorb and smooth out engine-firing impulses. A starter ring gear is welded or pressed onto the outside diameter of the flywheel. Often the ring gear can be replaced separately without having to replace the flywheel in the event of a

Figure 44–13 A flywheel after it has been machined (ground) to provide the correct surface finish for the replacement clutch disc.

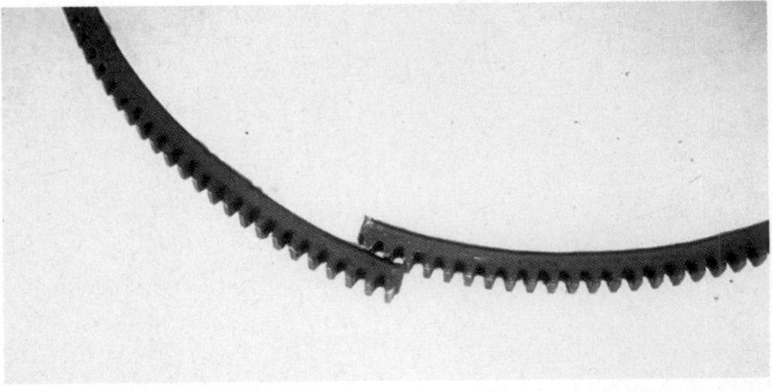

Figure 44–14 The starter motor will spin but the engine will not crank if the ring gear on the flywheel is broken.

failure, as shown in Figure 44–14. The pilot bearing is often installed in the centre of the flywheel (or in the end of the crankshaft) to support the end of the input shaft of the transmission.

Dual-mass Flywheels Some vehicles, especially high-performance vehicles and vehicles equipped with diesel engines, use a dual-mass flywheel. The purpose of a dual-mass flywheel is to dampen engine vibrations and keep them from being transmitted to the passenger compartment through the transmission and shift linkage. A dual-mass flywheel consists of two separate flywheels attached with damper springs, friction material, and ball bearings to allow some movement between the primary and secondary flywheel. By allowing a very slight amount of movement between the two flywheels, the damper absorbs engine torque peaks and normal vibration to provide smoother drive train operation. The damper assembly is completely sealed, because it also contains a fluid or lubricant, typically silicone-based, which also helps absorb vibration and transmit torque. Typically, the two flywheels twist out of phase with each other by up to about 60 degrees to absorb torsional oscillations. The starter ring gear mounts on the primary flywheel. Power from the starter motor does not have to flow through the damper assembly to reach the engine crankshaft. The ring gear and pilot bearing are usually attached to the primary flywheel, and the clutch friction surface is usually the secondary flywheel. See Figure 44–15.

NOTE: If the dual-mass flywheel fails, the symptom is the same as a slipping clutch. The torque-limiting friction material connecting the primary and secondary flywheels can fail. This failure requires the replacement of the flywheel assembly.

TECH TIP 

Shim It or Replace It

Whenever replacing a clutch, most experts agree that the flywheel should be removed from the engine and resurfaced. When material is removed from the surface of the flywheel, the geometry (relationship) of the clutch parts changes because the pressure plate is now closer to the rear of the engine by the amount removed from the flywheel. Ask your parts supplier for a shim equal in thickness to the amount of material removed during resurfacing. Generally, these round shims are available in 0.50 mm (0.020 in.) to 2.5 mm (0.100 in.) thicknesses. The shim is installed between the crankshaft flange and the flywheel. If a shim is not used, the flywheel may have to be replaced to properly restore proper clutch operation and service life.

TECH TIP 

Repair the Oil Leaks Before Replacing the Clutch

If engine oil or transmission lube gets onto the friction surface of the clutch, the clutch will chatter when engaged. This grabbing and releasing of the clutch is not only harmful to the drive train (transmission, drive shaft, etc.) but also is disturbing to the driver when the vehicle vibrates and shakes while driving. To avoid the possibility of a chattering clutch, always repair oil leaks as soon as possible. Rocker (valve) cover gaskets, intake manifold gaskets, oil galley plugs, rear main seals, as well as the input shaft seal on the transmission/transaxle itself can all lead to clutch contamination. See Figure 44–16 (p. 1056).

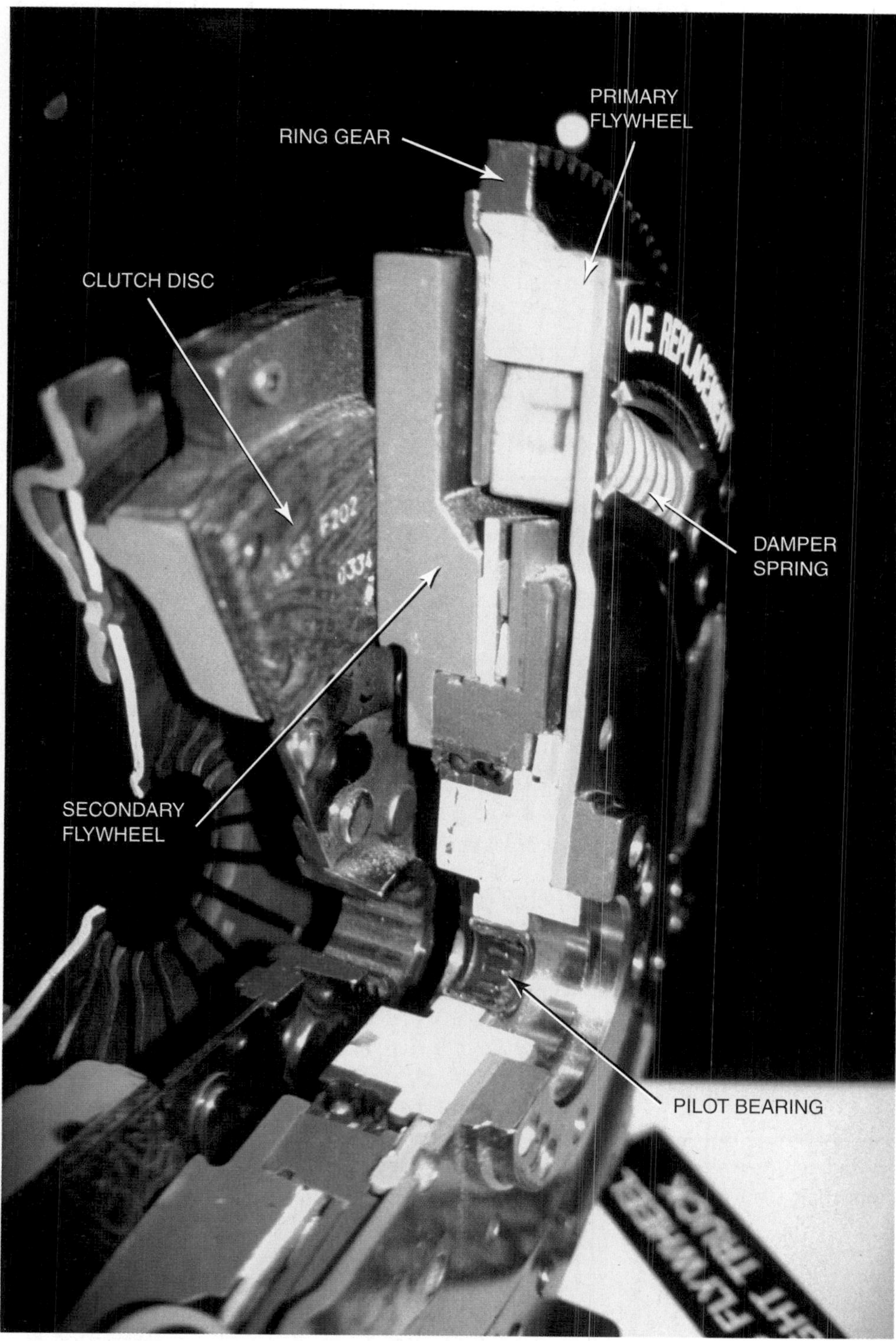

Figure 44–15 A cutaway of a dual-mass flywheel used on a Ford diesel pickup truck.

Pilot Bearing or Bushing

The transmission input shaft goes all the way from the transmission, through the clutch assembly, to the engine. Transmission bearings support the transmission end of the shaft. Depending on the length of the input shaft, it may also need a pilot bearing or bushing to support it at the engine end.

A front-wheel-drive vehicle with a stepped flywheel, compact clutch assembly, and a transaxle has a short input shaft that may not reach all the way to the flywheel. This design does not need a pilot bushing or bearing to support the engine end of the input shaft. See Figure 44–17.

Other designs, such as a rear-wheel-drive vehicle with a flat flywheel, have a much longer transmission

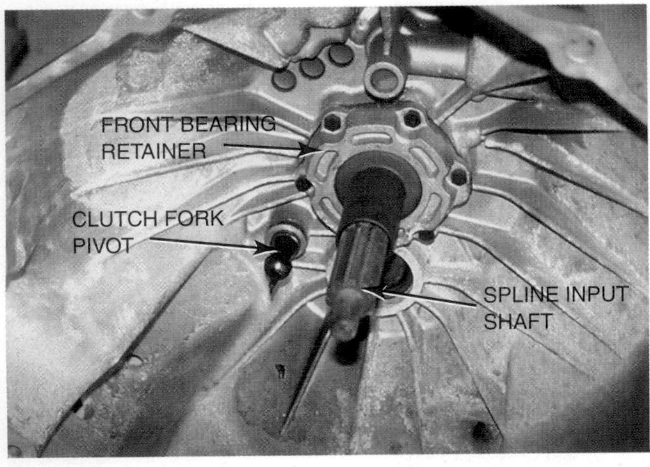

(a)

(b)

Figure 44–16 (a) Before replacing the clutch, the bell housing should be cleaned and the clutch fork pivot lightly lubricated. (b) The input shaft seal should also be replaced to prevent the possibility of getting transmission lubricant on the friction surfaces of the clutch.

Figure 44–17 A transaxle assembly has been removed to replace the clutch. Note the short input shaft. This vehicle did not use a pilot bearing (bushing).

input shaft. At the engine, the transmission input shaft rests inside a small bore in the flywheel or crankshaft flange. The pilot bearing or bushing, which is pressed into this bore, supports the engine end of the input shaft and provides a low-friction surface for the shaft to ride on. This keeps the shaft and friction disc perfectly aligned with the flywheel and pressure plate.

The pilot bearing or bushing rotates with the crankshaft when the engine is running. At times, the input shaft does not rotate when the engine is running. The pilot bearing or bushing lowers the friction between these two moving parts. Some pilot bearings use ball bearings while other applications use a caged-needle bearing. The outer race of the bearing is pressed into the crankshaft or flywheel. The input shaft slides freely into the inner race. Pilot bushings are usually a sintered metal sleeve pressed into the bore in the crankshaft flange.

DIAGNOSTIC STORY

The Mazda Pickup Truck Story

The driver of a Mazda pickup truck complained that it was difficult to shift the manual transmission into first gear and reverse. The hydraulic clutch system was checked and bled and seemed to be operating as designed. A defective clutch was not suspected because the clutch did not slip. The problem continued to worsen. Finally, when the driver had trouble shifting into all gears, the technician decided that the transmission had to be removed and the clutch inspected. When the transmission was removed, the clutch assembly including the pressure plate, throwout bearing, and clutch disc all appeared to be worn but not enough to cause any trouble. Then the pilot bearing was inspected. The needle bearings were broken. The input shaft of the transmission is supported by the pilot bearing located in the centre of the flywheel. Apparently, what had happened was that the pilot bearing failed and the pieces of the bearing kept the input shaft to the transmission rotating whenever the engine was running whether or not the clutch was depressed or released. The technician replaced the pilot bearing and the other clutch components at the request of the owner and everything worked perfectly.

Always follow the manufacturer's lubrication instructions. Excess lubricant leaks out onto the clutch friction disc, which causes clutch slippage and early failure. Too little lubricant leads to noisy operation and input shaft damage.

Replacement pilot bearings may need to be packed before installation. Sometimes, the bottom of the bore behind the bearing is also packed with grease. Other pilot bearings are permanently lubricated at the factory. Prelubricated bearings have an oil seal to hold the lubricant. If only one side is sealed, that side faces the transmission when installed.

Some pilot bushings need to be soaked in oil before installation. Others have a permanent lubricant built into the bushing material. With this type, adding another lubricant actually increases friction, by preventing the permanent lubricant from doing its job.

Figure 44–18 The clutch pedal linkage moves the clutch fork, which then applies a force against the release bearing, which then releases the clamping force the pressure plate is exerting on the clutch disc.

Release Bearing

The throwout (release) bearing is attached to the clutch fork and rides on the fingers of the pressure plate. The clutch operating system moves the clutch release bearing when the driver presses or releases the clutch pedal. Most systems move the release bearing toward the flywheel to disengage the clutch. See Figure 44–18. However, some systems have a pull-type mechanism that moves the bearing away from the flywheel to disengage the clutch. The release bearing presses against the diaphragm spring fingers or coil spring levers. This takes spring force off the pressure plate so that it no longer clamps the friction disc against the flywheel.

The diaphragm spring fingers or coil spring levers rotate at crankshaft speed, but the clutch operating system is a part of the vehicle chassis and does not rotate. The release bearing is the point where the fixed, stationary clutch operating system meets the rapidly spinning clutch assembly. See Figure 44–19.

Figure 44–19 The release bearing rubs against the tips of the diaphragm spring.

Release Bearing Construction

Most clutch release bearings are ball bearings. The bearing absorbs a thrust load when its outer race presses against the diaphragm spring fingers or coil spring levers. When the outer race contacts the spring fingers or levers, it must rotate with them at engine crankshaft speed. The inner bearing race is pressed onto an iron hub, or sleeve. In some designs, the inner bearing race and sleeve are machined as one piece. The inner bearing race and sleeve are stationary and do not spin when the outer race spins.

Release Bearing Installation

The transmission front bearing retainer has a long, hollow tube extending toward the engine. The release bearing sleeve slides on the outer surface of this tube, which is commonly called the **quill, quill shaft,** or **candlestick.**

In a typical system, the outside of the release bearing sleeve has grooves or raised flat surfaces that fit into the clutch release fork. A snap ring, spring clips, or lock pins secure the release bearing to the release fork. The clutch operating system pivots the release fork back and forth when the driver presses and releases the clutch pedal. The pivoting motion of the fork slides the release bearing away from or toward the engine to engage or disengage the clutch.

Types of Release Bearings

If the clutch operating system self-adjusts, then there is no clearance between the release bearing outer race and the diaphragm spring fingers or coil spring levers. The release bearing outer race constantly turns at engine crankshaft speed. This is called a constant-running release bearing. In some self-adjusting systems, a snap ring holds the outer race to the spring fingers. This design is typical of pull-type clutch operating systems that move away from the flywheel to disengage the clutch.

If the clutch operating system does not self-adjust, then there must be some clearance between the release bearing outer race and the spring fingers when the clutch is engaged. The outer race does not contact the spring fingers and so it does not turn. As the driver depresses the clutch pedal, the release bearing moves into contact with the fingers and the outer race begins to rotate with them. This type of release bearing is not designed to rotate constantly. If the clutch is not adjusted properly and there is no clearance, the release bearing spins constantly and wears out quickly.

Release Bearing Lubrication

The ball bearing portion of the release bearing is usually permanently lubricated and sealed during manufacture. This part of the bearing should not be lubricated during service.

The sleeve, or quill shaft, often needs lubrication during clutch service. Typically, a thin film of high-temperature grease coats the sliding surfaces. Always follow the manufacturer's recommendations for release bearing lubrication, and avoid overlubricating. As with pilot bearings, too much lubricant here can lead to early clutch failure.

CLUTCH PROBLEM DIAGNOSIS

If the clutch is slipping, it cannot transfer engine torque to the transmission or drive wheels. A common method used to check for a slipping clutch is the following:

1. Drive the vehicle to a safe location where it can be accelerated safely.
2. Rapidly accelerate the vehicle in first or second gear and rapidly shift the transmission into a higher gear.

The engine speed should drop as the clutch is released after selecting a higher gear. If the clutch is slipping, the engine speed will either rise or not drop after the clutch pedal is released (clutch is engaged).

Another common problem with a clutch is that it sometimes will not fully disengage. The following symptoms will occur if there is a fault in the clutch or in the linkage or hydraulic system that could prevent the clutch from being fully disengaged:

- The transmission will be difficult (or impossible) to shift into reverse.
- The transmission will be difficult (or impossible) to shift.

See Figures 44–20 through 44–28 for examples of worn clutch components.

Figure 44–20 Heavy chatter marks on the pressure plate indicate that oil or grease has gotten onto the clutch facing. (Courtesy of LUK)

Figure 44–21 Hot spots on the pressure plate indicate that this clutch has been slipping or that oil/grease has gotten onto the clutch facing. (Courtesy of LUK)

Figure 44–22 Friction material (facing) worn down to the rivets. Normal wear can cause this or improper clamping force from a defective pressure plate. (Courtesy of LUK)

Figure 44–23 Friction material (facing) only makes contact with the flywheel on the inner and outer edge. The likely cause is that the flywheel was not resurfaced or replaced during a previous repair. (Courtesy of LUK)

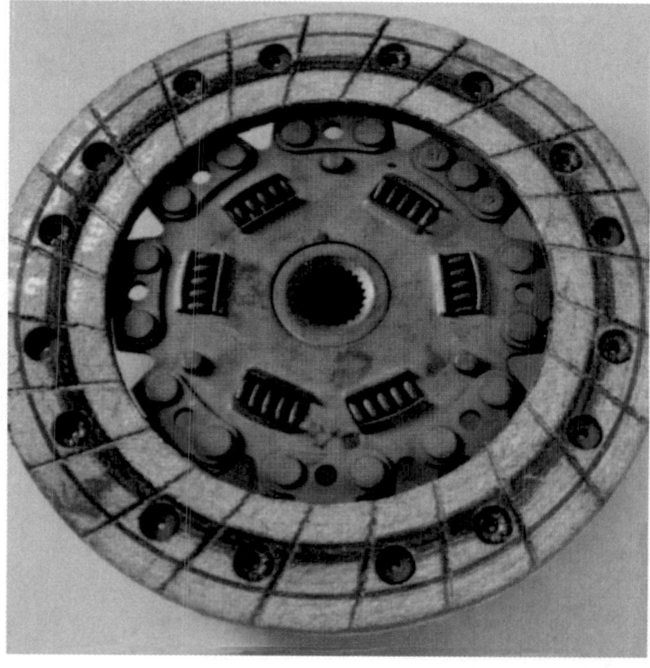

Figure 44–24 Deep scoring in the friction material (facing) on the flywheel side indicates that the flywheel was not resurfaced or replaced during a previous repair. (Courtesy of LUK)

Figure 44–25 A broken cushion segment caused by movement between the engine and transmission. The most likely cause is a missing or defective pilot bearing. (Courtesy of LUK)

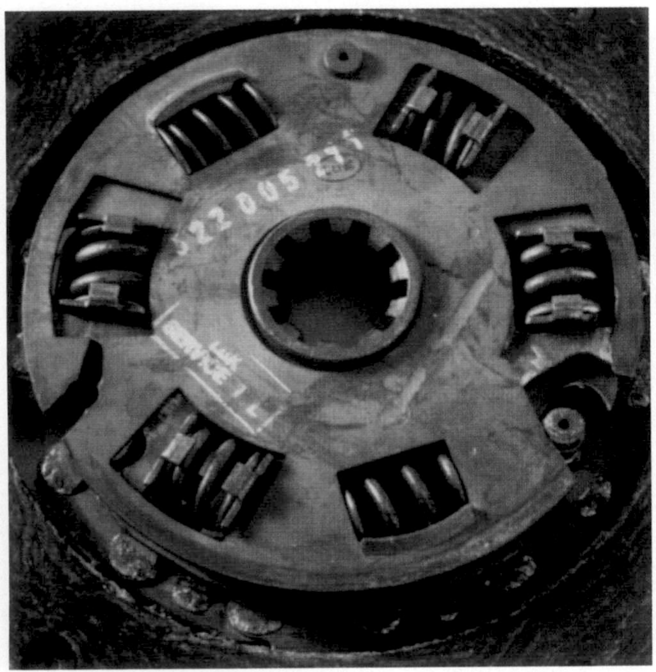

Figure 44–26 A destroyed torsional damper is usually caused by driving at too low an engine speed, which would cause too much strain on the torsional damper. (Courtesy of LUK)

Figure 44–27 A worn down or broken diaphragm is often caused by a faulty release bearing or a linkage problem that keeps the clutch from fully releasing. (Courtesy of LUK)

Figure 44–28 Rusting hub splines indicate that the transmission shaft was not lubricated, which can cause the clutch to not disengage correctly. (Courtesy of LUK)

Frequently Asked Question ???

What Part Causes What Noise and When?

Many service technicians try to determine which part causes noise before the clutch assembly is removed from the vehicle. Start your noise analysis by starting the engine with the manual transmission in neutral and the clutch engaged (foot off the clutch pedal). If you hear a growl or grinding sound, the cause is the input shaft bearing in the transmission.

If you are hearing a chirping noise, slowly depress the clutch pedal. If the noise stops, the problem is lack of lubrication at the fork and pivot. If the noise gets louder as you depress the clutch, the throwout (release) bearing is the problem.

The pilot bearing is the cause of a squealing noise if the sound changes as the clutch pedal is depressed or released. The sound will be loudest when the difference in speed between the engine and the input shaft is greatest.

DIAGNOSTIC STORY

Best to Double Check Your Parts Before Installation

A beginning technician installed a new clutch in a Chevrolet S-10 pickup truck. After the transmission was installed and the driveshaft connected, the technician started the engine to check the operation of the clutch with the truck still on the lift and off the ground. The drive wheels never turned even though the clutch was released. It was almost as if the clutch disc had been left out completely, although the clutch pedal felt normal.

The transmission was removed and the clutch parts inspected. Everything looked okay until the technician slid the clutch disc over the splines of the transmission input shaft. The diameter of the hole in the clutch disc was a lot larger than the diameter of the shaft. The clutch also simply revolved without even touching the input shaft. Obviously, the technician received the wrong clutch disc from the parts department. The experienced technician explained that not only should all parts be carefully inspected before installation but that the clutch disc should have been slid over the splines of the input shaft to check for any possible burrs that could prevent the clutch disc from disengaging.

CLUTCH REPLACEMENT

The clutch replacement for a typical rear-wheel-drive vehicle includes the following steps.

1. Hoist the vehicle safely and mark and remove the drive shaft. This step ensures that the drive shaft will be reinstalled correctly and in phase.

SAFETY TIP

Disconnect the Battery Before Work Begins

It is always a safe idea to disconnect the negative (−) battery cable before performing major work on the vehicle as a safety precaution.

2. Disconnect the shift linkage, speedometer connections, and reverse light switch connection.
3. Support the transmission with a transmission jack and then remove the rear crossmember and bell housing bolts.
4. Carefully move the transmission toward the rear. Try to keep the transmission level to avoid causing damage to the pilot bearing or clutch components. A slight wiggling of the transmission is usually necessary to allow the input shaft to slide over the spline of the clutch disc.
5. After the transmission has cleared the clutch, it can be lowered and inspected before being reinstalled after the clutch assembly has been replaced.
6. Mark the pressure plate and flywheel if they are to be reused to allow them to be reinstalled in the same location to maintain assembly balance.
7. Remove the clutch pressure plate retaining bolts, and remove the clutch assembly including the release bearing, pressure plate, and clutch disc.
8. Clean and inspect the flywheel.

NOTE: Most experts recommend that the flywheel be removed and resurfaced. Always use new flywheel bolts and torque to factory specifications.

9. Replace or lightly lubricate the pilot bearing/bushing.
10. Install the clutch disc and pressure plate using an aligning tool to centre the clutch disc and then torque the pressure plate bolts to factory specifications. See Figure 44–29.
11. Inspect the clutch release lever and replace if necessary.
12. Attach the replacement release bearing and install the transmission and torque the retaining bolts to factory specifications.
13. Reconnect the clutch linkage and place the transmission into high gear and have an assistant depress the clutch pedal. Grasp the output shaft and turn it with your hand.
    a. The transmission output shaft should be easy to rotate if the clutch is fully disengaged with the clutch pedal held down. See Figure 44–30.

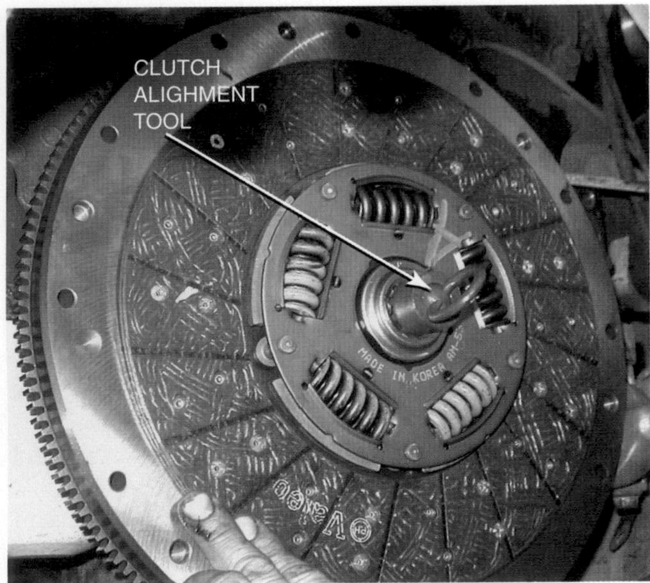

Figure 44–29 A clutch alignment tool is inserted into the pilot bearing and over the splines of the clutch disc to keep the disc properly centred before installing the pressure plate. After the pressure plate has been installed and torqued to factory specifications, the alignment tool can be removed because the pressure plate spring force holds the friction disc tightly against the flywheel.

b. If the output shaft cannot be rotated, double check that the clutch linkage and clutch is correctly installed.

14. Reinstall the rear crossmember and torque the retaining bolts to factory specifications.
15. Reconnect the shift linkage, speedometer, and reverse light connections.
16. Install the drive shaft and torque the U-joint retaining fastener to factory specifications.
17. Lower the vehicle and test drive it to verify correct clutch operation.

CLUTCH PEDAL ADJUSTMENT

As the clutch disc wears, the pressure plate moves closer to the flywheel. This causes the clutch to engage when the clutch pedal is higher and higher. Eventually, the clutch will start to slip if the linkage is not adjusted to compensate for the normal wear. Most hydraulic clutch linkage is self-adjusting and does not require any adjustment in normal service. Some cable-operated clutches are either self-adjusting or are adjusted easily. For example, one style of clutch linkage is adjusted by simply pulling upward on the clutch pedal until it stops. Some cable-operated clutch linkage is adjusted either at the bulkhead (firewall) where the cable exits the passenger compartment or at the clutch fork. Follow the adjustment procedures specified for the exact vehicle being serviced.

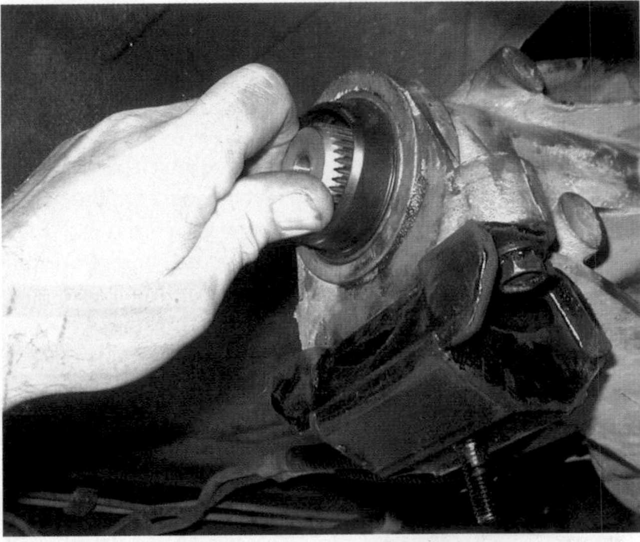

Figure 44–30 To check that the clutch is properly installed before replacing all of the components, try to turn the output shaft with the transmission in gear and the clutch pedal depressed by an assistant.

TECH TIP 

Check for Bulkhead Flex

Many cable-operated clutch linkage problems are caused by flexing of the bulkhead (firewall) as the clutch pedal is depressed. This movement of the bulkhead can cause the clutch to slip. To prevent unnecessary clutch repairs, have an assistant observe the bulkhead near the clutch cable while the clutch pedal is depressed. If there is movement of the sheet metal bulkhead, add reinforcing steel plate to the area.

Most adjustment procedures specify a clutch pedal freeplay of 12 to 25 mm (0.5 to 1.0 in.). Freeplay is the distance the clutch pedal can be depressed without encountering any noticeable resistance. This slight amount of freeplay assures that the clutch is fully engaged and not partially engaged, as could occur if there is no freeplay in the pedal linkage.

BLEEDING THE HYDRAULIC CLUTCH

If the hydraulic system has been opened to replace either a clutch slave cylinder or master cylinder or both, air has to be bled from the system. See Figures 44–31 and 44–32. Fill the master cylinder with DOT 3 brake fluid and open the bleeder valve at the slave cylinder. Gravity should force the brake fluid to flow downward, expelling any trapped air that may be in the system. When brake fluid starts to drip from the bleeder valve, close the bleeder valve and check the clutch for normal operation. Sometimes depressing the clutch pedal slowly as an assistant opens the bleeder valve at the slave cylinder will force any trapped air out of the system. This is called *manual bleeding* and should be repeated as necessary until the normal operation of the clutch returns.

Figure 44–31 The clutch slave cylinder is often corroded because of moisture absorbed by the brake fluid used in the hydraulic clutch. This slave cylinder was disassembled to see if it could be overhauled rather than replaced.

(a)

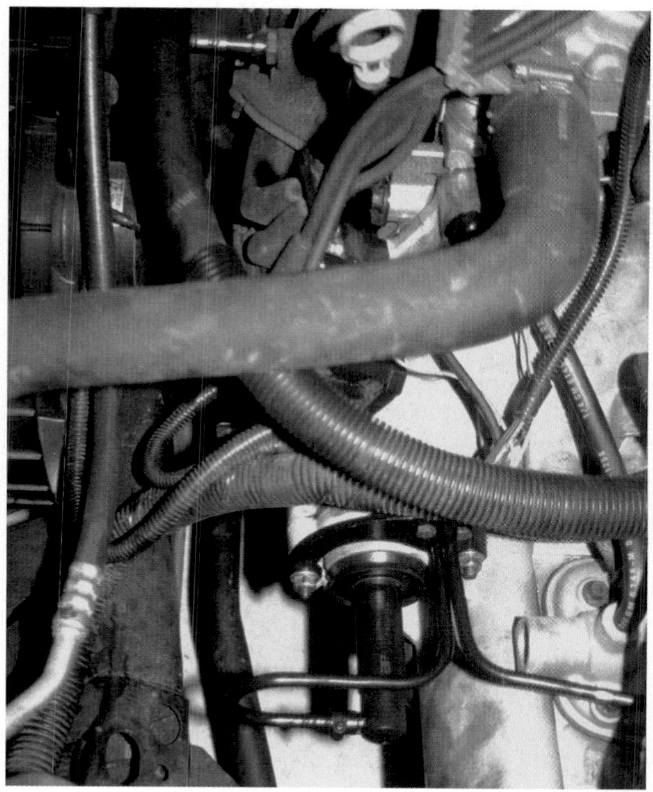
(b)

Figure 44–32 (a) The replacement hydraulic clutch for a Saturn includes the master cylinder (shown) with the line and the slave cylinder as an assembly. The assembly is even filled with brake fluid! Do not open the master cylinder cap on this unit because Saturn did not provide any method of bleeding air out of the ignition. (b) The slave cylinder attaches to the bell housing of the transaxle.

CLUTCH TROUBLESHOOTING GUIDE

Problem	Possible Causes
Clutch slips	• Clutch is worn • Clutch disc has oil on the surface • Flywheel height is out-of-specification
Clutch grabs	• Clutch disc has oil on the surface • Clutch linkage is binding
Clutch noises	• Pilot bearing is defective or worn • Release bearing is defective or worn

SUMMARY

1. The clutch not only transmits engine torque from the flywheel to the transmission/transaxle, it also absorbs engine-firing impulses to reduce the vibration felt by the driver through the shift linkage.
2. The clutch has to be depressed (clutch disengaged) to keep the engine running with the transmission in gear and to shift from one gear to another.
3. The clutch disc has friction material on both sides and is clamped between the engine flywheel and the pressure plate.
4. The pressure plate bolts to and revolves with the flywheel.
5. A throwout (release) bearing is used to disengage the clutch by depressing a lever or spring, which removes the clamping force from the clutch disc.
6. The pilot bearing is supported by the front bearing retainer of the transmission.
7. The linkage between the clutch pedal and the clutch fork can be levers and rods, a cable, or a hydraulic connection.
8. The flywheel attaches to the engine and not only provides the friction surface for one side of the clutch disc but also dampens engine-firing impulses.
9. A dual-mass flywheel is used on many import, luxury, and diesel vehicles to help dampen engine and driveline vibrations.
10. The clutch linkage can be adjusted on some vehicles to provide about 12 to 25 mm (1/2 to 1 in.) of clutch pedal freeplay.
11. It is a normal service procedure to replace the clutch disc, pressure plate, and throwout bearing as well as the pilot bearing every time the clutch is replaced. The flywheel should also be removed from the engine and resurfaced or replaced.

REVIEW QUESTIONS

1. List the parts of a typical clutch assembly.
2. Describe what happens when the driver depresses the clutch pedal.
3. Describe how to determine which of the following is the cause of a noise: pilot bearing, throwout (release) bearing, or input shaft bearing.
4. Explain why a dual-mass flywheel is used on some vehicles.
5. What is meant by clutch pedal freeplay?

RED SEAL CERTIFICATION-TYPE QUESTIONS

1. What could too little clutch freeplay cause?
   - **a.** Noisy release bearing
   - **b.** Clutch slip during acceleration
   - **c.** Clutch pedal hard to press
   - **d.** Gear clash when going into gear from a stop
2. What is the purpose of a dual mass flywheel?
   - **a.** Reduce engine noise being transmitted to the transmission
   - **b.** Reduce engine vibrations being transmitted to the transmission
   - **c.** Used to extend clutch disc life
   - **d.** Used to replace the clutch release bearing
3. What might be the cause of a growling noise only when the clutch pedal is pressed down fully?
   - **a.** Crankshaft main bearing
   - **b.** Input shaft bearing
   - **c.** Pilot bearing or bushing
   - **d.** Output shaft bearing
4. Which part does *not* rotate when the engine is running and the clutch is depressed?
   - **a.** Clutch disc
   - **b.** Pilot bearing
   - **c.** Pressure plate
   - **d.** Flywheel
5. What could be the cause of the clutch grabbing when the pedal is released?
   - **a.** Too little clutch freeplay
   - **b.** Oil contamination on the clutch disc
   - **c.** Defective output shaft bearing
   - **d.** Shift fork worn
6. What part is often *not* used on a front-wheel-drive vehicle with a manual transaxle?
   - **a.** Flywheel
   - **b.** Throwout (release bearing)
   - **c.** Clutch fork
   - **d.** Pilot bearing
7. Most hydraulic clutch systems use what hydraulic fluid?
   - **a.** Mineral (hydraulic) oil
   - **b.** SAE 80W-90
   - **c.** DOT 3
   - **d.** ATF
8. What takes place as the clutch disc wears?
   - **a.** Transmission shifting becomes more difficult
   - **b.** Pedal play decreases
   - **c.** Pedal play increases
   - **d.** Unable to shift transmission into reverse
9. What could be the cause of hot spots on the flywheel?
   - **a.** Too little clutch pedal freeplay
   - **b.** Pilot bearing seized
   - **c.** Bent shift linkage
   - **d.** Pressure plate springs too strong
10. What type of fluid do most hydraulic clutches use?
    - **a.** Engine oil
    - **b.** Dot 3 brake fluid
    - **c.** Transmission fluid
    - **d.** Antifreeze

45

Manual Transmissions/Transaxles

OBJECTIVES: After studying Chapter 45, you should be able to:

1. Prepare for the interprovincial Red Seal certification examination in Appendix III (Manual Drive Trains and Axles) on the topics covered in this chapter.
2. Explain how to calculate gear ratios.
3. Name the parts of a typical manually shifted transmission/transaxle.
4. Describe how the synchronizer assembly allows for smooth, clash-free shifting.
5. Describe the different types of lubricants that may be used in a manual transmission/transaxle.
6. Diagnose a difficult-to-shift manual transmission/transaxle.

THE NEED FOR A TRANSMISSION

Manual transmissions are used mostly on rear-wheel-drive vehicles and transaxles are used primarily on front-wheel-drive vehicles. The engine that attaches to a transmission or a transaxle can be longitudinal- or transverse-mounted, but usually a transaxle is attached to a transverse-mounted engine.

The transmission/transaxle has three purposes: to multiply torque and to provide neutral and reverse functions. The neutral function is accomplished by moving the internal components of the transmission in order to disconnect the input shaft from the output shaft, allowing the engine to stay running with the clutch disengaged and the vehicle not moving. The reverse function is accomplished by the introduction of an idler gear, which allows the output shaft to rotate opposite to the input shaft. Internal combustion engines power curve varies according to engine RPM and the transmission will allow the engine RPM to stay in the best torque range for the type of driving being done.

A vehicle requires a lot of torque to start off and to climb hills. It does not require as much torque to move on level ground. The source of the torque is the engine. Torque is a twisting or turning force that is exerted on the input shaft of a transmission/transaxle. An engine produces increasing torque as its speed increases up to a certain point where the torque output starts to decrease. Therefore, to get a vehicle moving or to accelerate up a hill, it is desirable to use a transmission that allows the engine speed to be increased even though the vehicle speed may be low. Using gears allows the engine speed to increase at low vehicle speeds yet still permits it to drop at higher speeds to save fuel and reduce exhaust emissions.

Frequently Asked Question ???

What Is the Difference Between a Transmission and a Transaxle?

A transmission is used on rear-wheel-drive vehicles, whereas a transaxle is usually used on front-wheel-drive vehicles. A vehicle equipped with a transmission uses a separate differential to split the torque equally to the drive wheels. A transaxle includes a differential assembly. In a transaxle, the differential, sometimes called the *final drive unit,* is incorporated in the construction of the transmission.

For example,

1st gear: Vehicle speed is low, engine speed is high.

2nd gear: Vehicle speed increases, engine speed decreases as shift is made.

3rd gear: Vehicle speed continues to increase, engine speed is kept in a narrow range.

4th gear: Again, the vehicle speed is increasing, yet engine speed is about the same as in 3rd gear.

GEAR TYPES

The simplest type of gear is the **spur gear.** See Figure 45–1. A spur gear consists of a gear blank with straight-cut teeth around its entire circumference. All gear teeth lie parallel to the centreline, or **axis,** of the gear. The teeth are shaped so they can mesh without slippage with a second spur gear's teeth positioned along a parallel axis.

Spur gear design permits 1.5 to 2.5 gear teeth to mesh at a time. The gear teeth make contact with each other over their full width at the same instant. The fact that the gear teeth are in full contact increases the strength of the gear, but also causes spur gear operation to be noisy. Due to their strength, most heavy-duty truck transmissions use spur gears.

A **helical gear,** although similar to a spur gear, has its teeth cut at an angle to the axis of the gear. See Figure 45–2. This enables more teeth, 2.5 to 3.5, to mesh at a time than the spur gear. Additionally, the angle allows the teeth to mesh gradually, rather than all at once. As a result, helical gears run quieter than spur gears. Helical gears, however, have two disadvantages. Each gear pushes against its shaft parallel to its axis. Special bearings are needed to protect the gearbox from this type of axial, or thrust, loading. Furthermore, because of the increased contact area, helical gears create more friction than spur gears. See Figure 45–3.

Spur and helical gears have gear teeth on their outside circumference and, for this reason, are

Figure 45–1 Spur gears have straight-cut teeth.

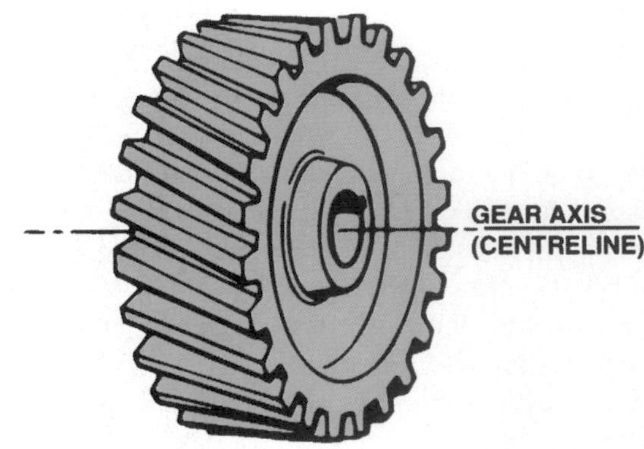

Figure 45–2 The teeth of a helical gear are cut at an angle to the gear axis.

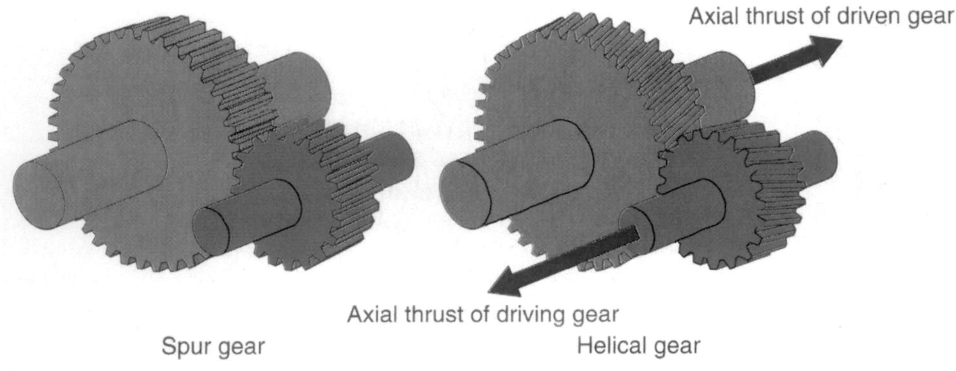

Figure 45–3 A spur gear has straight-cut teeth. This design is very strong and is used where strength is important. Spur gears are noisy during operation. Helical-cut gears, on the other hand, operate quietly but create a force in line with the axis of the gears due to the angle of the gear teeth.

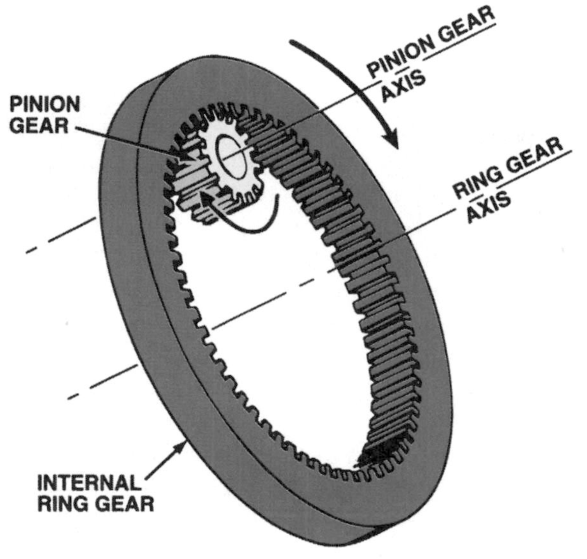

Figure 45–4 A pinion gear meshed with an internal ring gear rotates in the same direction around a parallel axis of rotation.

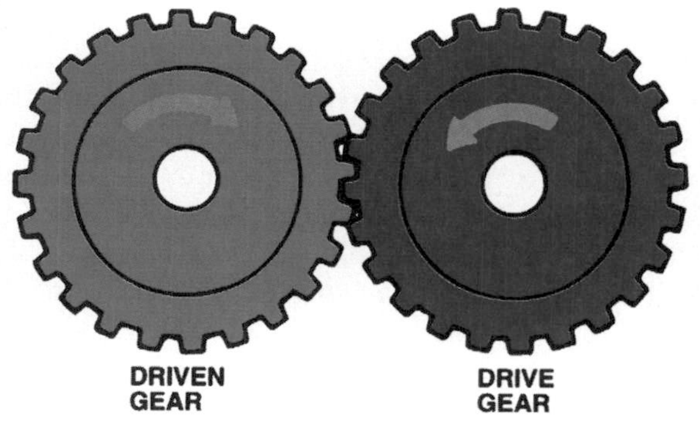

Figure 45–5 When two external gears mesh, they rotate in opposite directions.

called **external gears.** This type of gear is the most commonly used in manual transmissions and transaxles.

Gears having teeth along the inside circumference are called **internal ring** gears. See Figure 45–4. The teeth of an internal ring gear may be spur or helical teeth. An internal ring gear may mesh with a smaller external gear designed to rotate as it travels around the inside of the internal ring gear. This type of external gear is called a **pinion gear** because of its smaller diameter.

When an external gear meshes with an internal ring gear, both gears rotate in the same direction, but when an external gear meshes with another external gear, the gears rotate in opposite directions as shown in Figure 45–5.

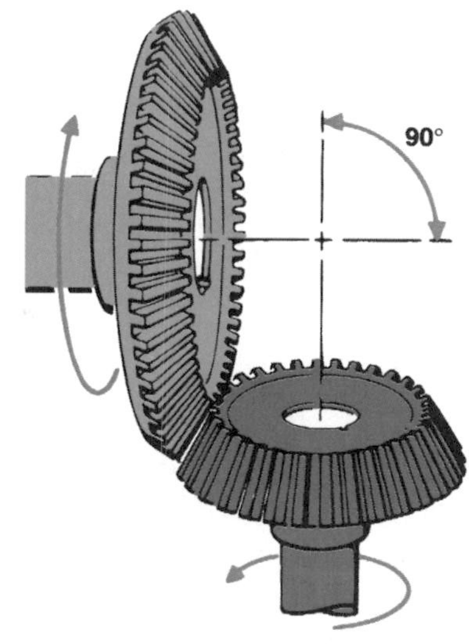

Figure 45–6 Bevel gears are often used to change the direction of rotation and are typically used in differentials.

Figure 45–7 A differential uses a hypoid gear set to provide a change in the direction of torque and for gear reduction (torque increases) to the drive wheels.

Bevel Gears

The teeth of a **bevel gear** are cut at an angle to the outside gear surface. Simple bevel gears have straight-cut teeth similar to those on a spur gear. See Figure 45–6. Special gears used in a differential, called spider gears, are a common example of the simple bevel gear.

Hypoid Gears

Hypoid gear sets have gear teeth that are curved much like the teeth of a spiral bevel gear. The pinion gear is offset below the centreline of the ring gear as shown in Figure 45–7. This design provides maximum gear tooth contact for strength, gradual tooth engagement, and quiet operation. Hypoid gears are generally available only as a matched set.

Hypoid gears are commonly used as the final drive gears in rear axles where load-carrying ability and low noise are important. The offset pinion allows the driveshaft to be positioned lower in the vehicle, reducing the size of the hump in the vehicle's interior. See Chapter 47 for details about differentials.

GEAR RATIOS

When one gear turns another, the speed that the two gears turn in relation to each other is the gear ratio. Gear ratio is expressed as the number of rotations the **drive gear** must make in order to rotate the **driven gear** through one revolution. To obtain a gear ratio, simply divide the number of teeth on the driven gear by the number of teeth on the drive gear. Gear ratios, which are expressed relative to the number one, fall into three categories:

- Direct drive
- Gear reduction
- Overdrive

Direct Drive

If two meshed gears are the same size and have the same number of teeth, they will turn at the same speed. Since the drive gear turns once for each revolution of the driven gear, the gear ratio is 1:1; this is called a **direct drive.** When a transmission is in direct drive, the engine and transmission turn at the same speed.

Gear Reduction

If one gear drives a second gear that has three times the number of teeth, the smaller drive gear must travel three complete revolutions in order to drive the larger gear through one rotation. See Figure 45–8. Divide the number of teeth on the driven gear by the number of teeth on the drive gear and you get a 3:1 gear ratio (pronounced three to one). This type of gear arrangement, where driven gear speed is slower than drive gear speed, provides **gear reduction.** Gear reduction may also be called underdrive as drive speed is less than, or under, driven speed. Both terms mean the same thing and use is a matter of preference.

Gear reduction is used for the lower gears in a transmission. First gear in a transmission is called *low* gear because output speed, not gear ratio, is low. Low gears have numerically high gear ratios. That is, a 3:1 gear ratio is a lower gear than those with a 2:1 or 1:1 gear ratio. These three ratios taken in order represent a typical upshift pattern from low gear (3:1), to second gear (2:1), to drive gear (1:1).

Overdrive

Overdrive is the opposite of a gear reduction condition and occurs when a driven gear turns faster than its drive gear. For the gears shown in Figure 45–9, the driven gear turns three times for each turn of the drive gear. The driven gear is said to overdrive the drive gear. For this example, the gear ratio is 0.33:1. Overdrive ratios of 0.65:1 and 0.70:1 are typical of those used in automotive applications.

> **NOTE:** Ratios always end in 1 with a colon in between. Therefore, the first number is less than 1 if it is an overdrive ratio and greater than 1 if it is a gear reduction ratio.

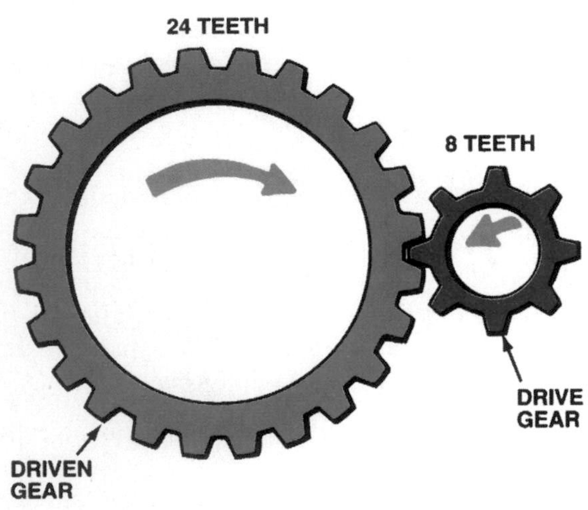

Figure 45–8 This gear combination provides a gear reduction of 3:1.

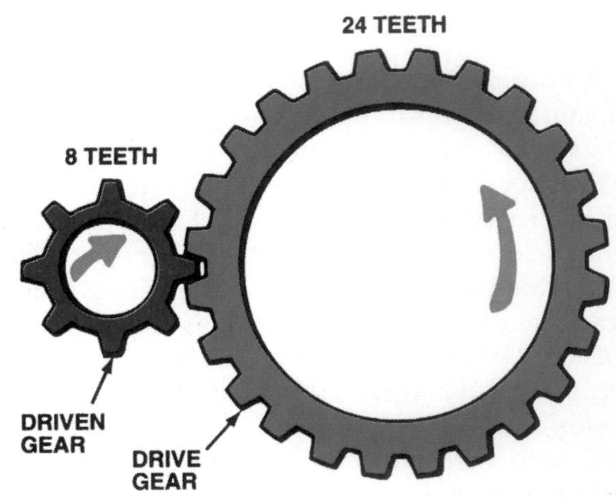

Figure 45–9 This gear combination provides an overdrive ratio of 0.33:1.

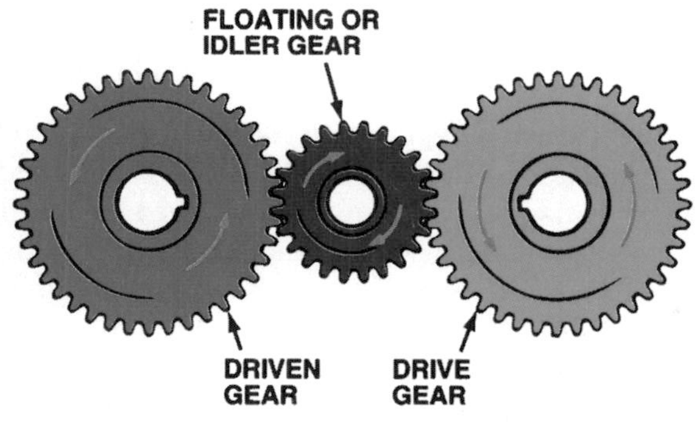

Figure 45–10 Idler gears affect the direction of rotation in a gear train, but not the final drive ratio.

Idler Gears

In a gear train, a gear that operates between the drive and driven gears is called a floating gear, or idler gear. See Figure 45–10. Idler gears do not affect the speed relationship between the drive and driven gears, although they do affect the direction of rotation. Reverse gear on an automatic transmission often uses an idler gear to change the direction of rotation.

When a drive and driven gear mesh directly, they rotate in opposite directions. When an idler gear is installed between the drive and driven gears, both gears rotate in the same direction. The presence of idler gears in the gear train does not affect the gear ratio.

TORQUE, SPEED, AND POWER

Torque is a twisting force commonly expressed in pound-feet (lb-ft) or Newton-meters (N·m). Gears apply torque much like a wrench does; each tooth of a gear is actually a lever. On a gear with a 60 cm (2 ft) radius, applying a force of 45 N (10 lb) to one gear tooth exerts 27 N·m (20 lb-ft) of torque on the centre of the shaft to which the gear attaches. See Figure 45–11.

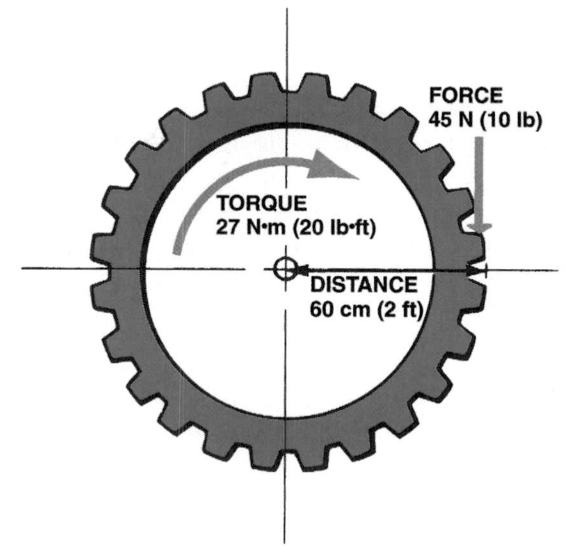

Figure 45–11 Gears apply torque in the same way a wrench applies torque—the force applied multiplied by the distance from the centre of the gear equals the torque.

Torque and Speed Relationship

Torque and speed have an inverse relationship: as one goes up, the other goes down. With a constant input speed, transmission torque decreases as output speed increases. The opposite also applies; assuming a constant input speed, transmission torque increases as output speed decreases.

Torque Multiplication

Levers can be used to increase or multiply torque. For example, a wheel that is too heavy for a person to turn by muscle power alone turns easily when that same person uses a lever and fulcrum to multiply the applied force. See Figure 45–12. The force, or torque, increases at one end, but the lever must be moved a greater distance at the opposite end to obtain the increase in force. Either distance or speed must always be given up in order to increase, or multiply, torque.

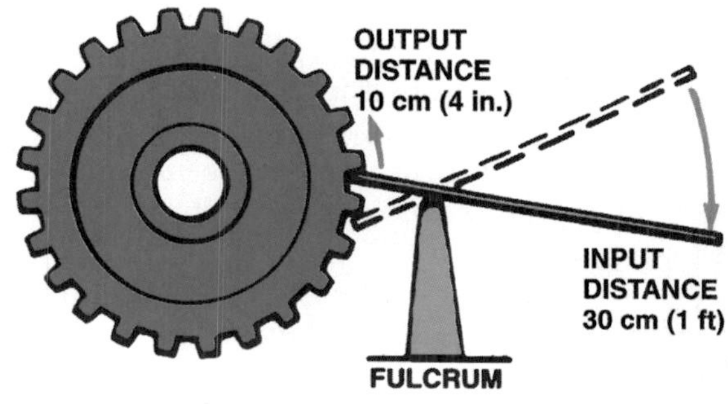

Figure 45–12 A lever can be used to multiply torque, but it does so at the expense of distance or speed.

Gears can be used in the same way as levers to multiply torque. When two gears of the same diameter are meshed, the driven gear will turn at the same speed as the drive gear. Since there is no difference in speed, there is no difference in torque between the two gears.

If the drive gear is one-third the diameter of the driven gear, it must rotate three times for each rotation of the larger gear. This means that the larger gear will turn three times slower than the smaller gear. At the same time, the larger gear will exert three times the torque of the smaller gear. When speed decreases, torque increases.

Torque multiplication and gear ratios are directly related. When a gear system is in reduction, there is more torque available at the driven gear, but less speed. When the gear system is in overdrive, there is less torque available at the driven gear, but greater speed.

Engine Torque Characteristics

The torque curve of an engine shows how much torque is available at different points within a range of engine speeds.

Because of these characteristics, torque multiplication must be provided between the crankshaft and drive axles to enable a vehicle to begin moving from a standstill and to accelerate at low speeds. Once engine RPM rises beyond the torque peak, a change in gear ratio brings engine speed back within the most efficient torque producing range.

POWER TRAIN GEAR RATIOS

A transmission enables a vehicle to maximize engine torque, allowing the vehicle to move more efficiently. The transmission is aided in this task by the final drive gearing. These components work together to provide select gear ratios that take maximum advantage of engine torque available through various speed ranges.

A gear ratio, to repeat, is determined by dividing the number of teeth on the driven gear (output) by the number of teeth on the driving gear (input). See Figure 45–13.

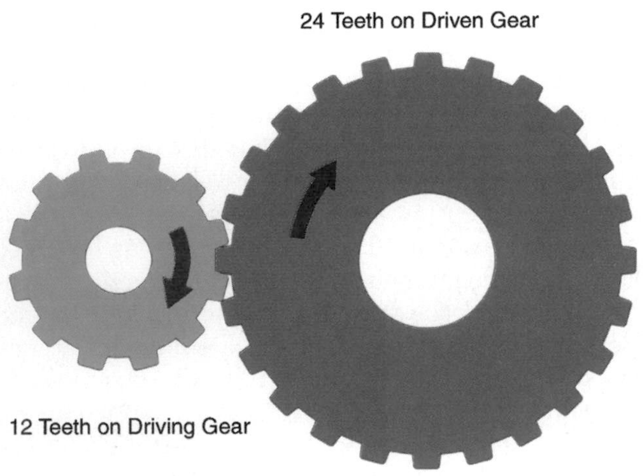

Figure 45–13 Gear ratio is determined by dividing the number of teeth of the driven (output) gear (24 teeth) by the number of teeth on the driving (input) gear (12 teeth). The ratio illustrated is 2:1.

$$\frac{\text{Number of teeth on the driven gear (24)}}{\text{Number of teeth on the driving gear (12)}} = 2{:}1$$

The gear ratio represents the number of turns of the input gear to one turn of the output gear. A transmission/transaxle usually uses two pairs of gears to achieve each gear ratio, and there may be four, five, or six forward gears plus reverse. When two pairs of gears are used to create a gear, simply multiply the two ratios together to get the gear ratio.

A low first-gear (high numerical) ratio creates a high amount of torque applied to the drive wheels to get the vehicle moving. To summarize what is occurring if the engine speed is constant:

1st gear:

- Output shaft speed is a lot lower than engine speed.
- Output torque is a lot higher than the engine is producing.

5th gear:

- Output shaft speed is faster than the engine speed.
- Output torque is lower than the engine is producing.

TRANSMISSION CONSTRUCTION

A transmission is usually constructed of cast aluminum machined to accept the internal parts and strong enough to be a structural member of the drive train. The front of the transmission attaches to a separate **bell housing** or includes the bell housing as part of the casting of the transmission itself at the front of the transmission (toward the engine) in the **front bearing retainer** (sometimes called the **quill**) that supports the clutch throwout (release) bearing and usually houses the front grease seal. The rear of the transmission usually includes a separate casting called the **extension housing.** The centre housing is usually referred to as the **transmission case.** See Figure 45–14.

The **input shaft** is splined to the clutch disc and is also referred to as the **main gear, clutch gear,** or **main drive pinion assembly.** See Figure 45–15. The **main shaft,** also called the **output shaft,** is splined at the end and transmits engine torque to the drive shaft (propeller shaft) through a yoke and universal shaft.

All manual transmissions/transaxles use a **countershaft** (also called a **lay shaft** or **cluster shaft**) to provide the other set of gears necessary to achieve the changes in gear ratios. The gears on the countershaft are called **cluster gears** or **counter gears.**

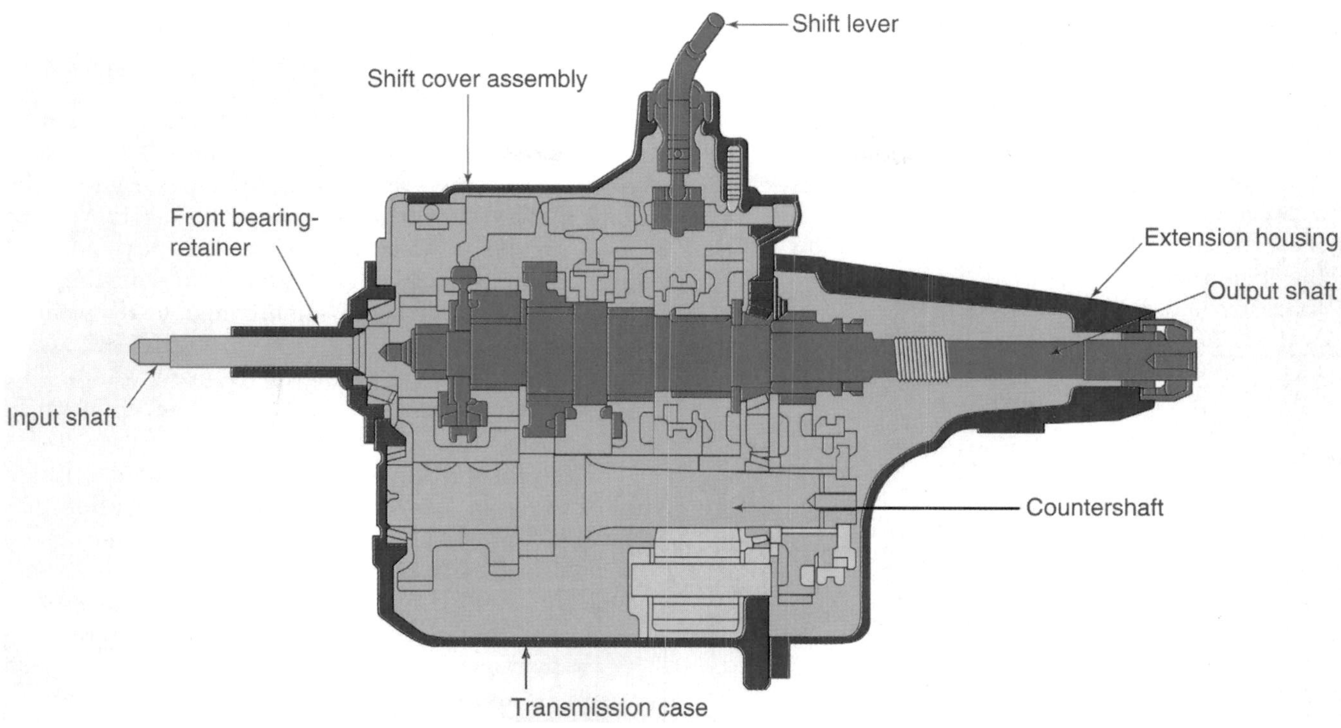

Figure 45–14 Cross section of a five-speed manual transmission showing the main parts.

Figure 45–15 Cutaway of a six-speed manual transmission showing all of its internal parts.

Frequently Asked Question ???

What Is Meant by a 77 mm Transmission?

The size (77 mm or about 3 inches) is the distance between the centre of the input shaft and the centre of the countershaft. The greater this distance, the larger the transmission and the more torque it is capable of handling due to the larger gears.

TORQUE FLOW THROUGH A MANUAL TRANSMISSION

The engine torque is applied to the input shaft when the clutch is engaged (clutch pedal up). This torque is applied to the main gear, which is in constant mesh with the countershaft gear.

HINT: The fact that the countershaft is revolving any time the clutch is engaged makes transmission noise diagnosis easier.

The engine torque is multiplied by the ratio difference between the main gear and the cluster gear. The engine torque is then transferred and multiplied again when first gear is in mesh with the corresponding first gear on the main (output) shaft. Again, the torque is multiplied by the ratio difference between the two gears. The engine torque then is applied to the drive wheels through the drive shaft, differential, and drive axles.

SPEED GEARS

All gears on the countershaft are permanently attached to the shaft. When the countershaft rotates, all gears on the countershaft rotate. The input shaft gear is also part of the input shaft. However, the gears on the main shaft are free to move on the shaft

Figure 45–16 Notice that the countershaft and the main shaft both use gears of increasing size that mesh together.

and are connected to the main shaft through the synchronizer hub when a shift is made. All speed gears use bearings that allow the speed gears to move independently of the main shaft.

> **HINT:** When assembling the main shaft and the countershaft, just remember that each shaft should look like a Scotch pine (tapered downward from the top). When installed in the transmission, these two Scotch pines are meshed together with the small gear end of one shaft meshing with the large gear end of the other shaft. See Figure 45–16.

SYNCHRONIZER PARTS AND OPERATION

Most vehicles today in a manually shifted transmission use a floor-mounted shifter to change gears. The shifting lever either moves cables that transfer the shifting motion to the transmission or transaxle or move the shift forks directly. Inside the transmission/transaxle are shift forks that control shifts between two gears, such as first and second or second and third. Interlocks either in the shifter linkage itself or inside the transmission/transaxle prevent the accidental selection of reverse except when shifting from neutral and also prevent selecting two gears at the same time. See Figure 45–17.

Synchronizers are used in manual transmissions/transaxles to make shifting easier. To synchronize means to make two or more events occur at the same time. When the driver depresses the clutch pedal, torque is no longer being transmitted to the input shaft and the drive wheels are driving the main shaft of the transmission/transaxle. To achieve a clash-free (no grinding sound) shift, the shift speed must match the speed of the rotating gears. The detents and interlocks hold the shift mechanism in position.

The real shifting in a synchromesh transmission takes place in the **synchronizer assemblies,** not the gears. Most synchronizer assemblies ride on the output shaft between two gears. A synchronizer assembly is named for the gears on either side of it, which are the two speeds that it engages. For example, a five-speed transmission with constant-mesh reverse uses a 1-2 synchronizer, 3-4 synchronizer, and a 5-reverse synchronizer.

Synchronizer Construction

Although there are number of design variations, all are similar and include a hub, a **sliding sleeve,** a **stop ring** (or **blocker rings** or **synchronizer ring**), **keys,** and **springs.** In addition, the tapered cone and coupling teeth machined on the speed gear are part of the synchronizer assembly. See Figure 45–18. In a typical synchronizer:

- Splines attach the centre hub of the synchronizer to the output shaft, so the hub and output shaft rotate together. There are also splines machined on the outer circumference of the hub.
- An outer sleeve rides on the external hub splines with enough clearance so that it slides freely. The splines on the sleeve also match the small coupling teeth of the stop ring and speed gear. Coupling teeth are also called engagement or clutch teeth. The sleeve is splined to the hub, so it rotates with the output shaft.
- A **stop ring** sits between the speed gear and the sleeve. The coupling teeth on the stop ring match those on both the sleeve and the speed gear. The stop ring also has a tapered cone to match the cone machined on the speed gear.
- Small, spring-loaded detent keys, also called **synchronizer keys** or **struts,** ride in slots on the outer sleeve. The stop ring has slots to match these keys. This allows the stop ring to rotate slightly, relative to the sleeve, before the keys hit the sides of their slots and stop the stop ring. As the sleeve moves, the synchronizer keys move

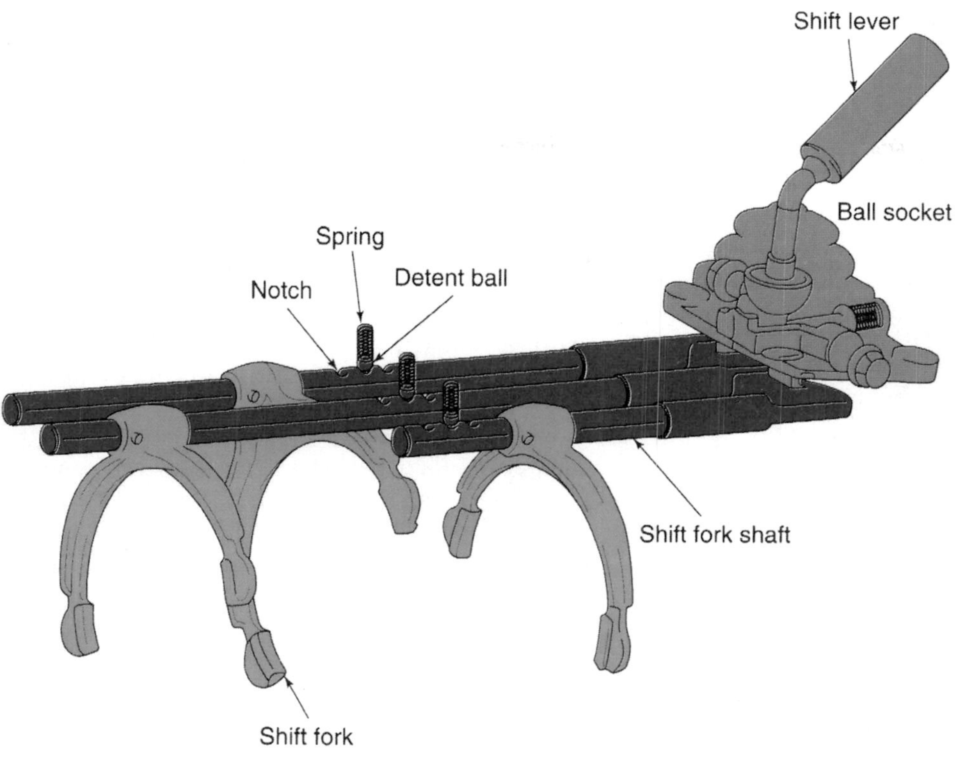

Figure 45–17 A typical shift mechanism showing the shift detents designed not only to give the driver a solid feel when shifting but also to prevent two gears from being selected at the same time.

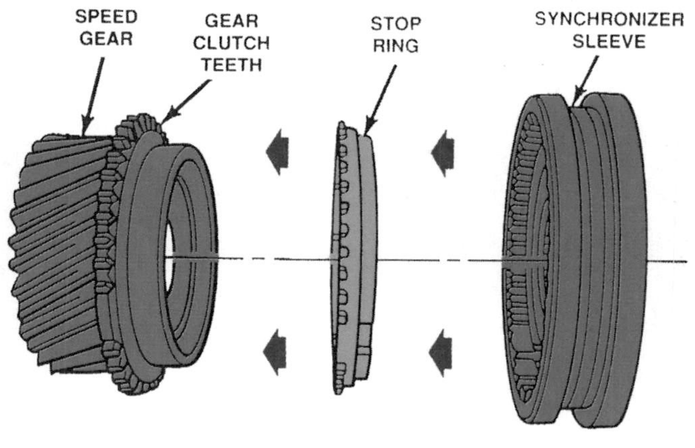

Figure 45–18 The shifter fork fits into the groove of the synchronizer sleeve. When a shift is made, the sleeve is moved toward the speed gear. The sleeve presses the stop ring (synchronizer ring) against the cone area of the speed gear. The friction between the stop ring and the speed gear causes the speed of the two to become equal, permitting the sleeve to engage the gear clutch teeth of the speed gear. When this engagement occurs, the shift is complete. (Courtesy of Chrysler Corporation)

with it, which pushes the blocking ring onto the tapered cone of the speed gear.

Synchronizer Operation

When the outer sleeve is centred on the hub, the synchronizer is in its neutral position—it does not contact either of the speed gears. See Figure 45–19. To shift into gear, the driver disengages the clutch and moves the shift linkage. The shift linkage, which is described later in this chapter, pushes the sleeve toward one of the speed gears. As the sleeve moves, the detent keys push the stop ring toward the speed gear. This causes the ring cone to slide onto the tapered cone of the speed gear.

The speed gear is turning because it is in constant mesh with a countershaft gear. However, the gear may not be turning at the same speed as the synchronizer assembly even though both are on the same shaft. When the clutch is disengaged, the engine is no longer driving the transmission, so there is no torque applied to the input shaft, and the countershaft, or cluster gear, simply freewheels. As the

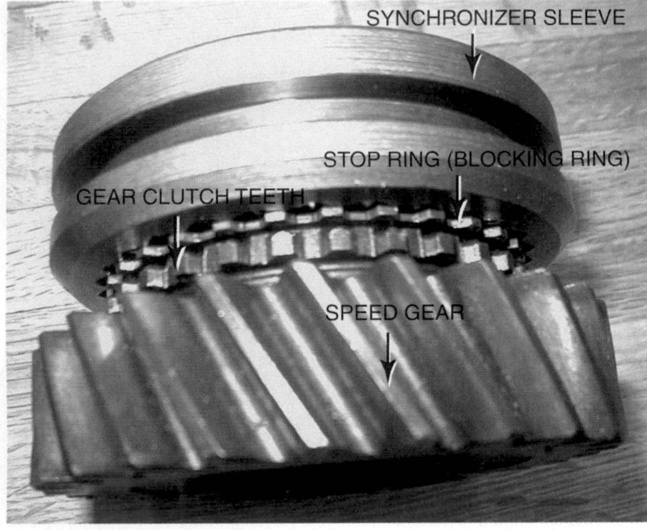

Figure 45–19 Typical synchronizer assembly.

shift is made, the stop ring acts as a brake to slow down the gear so that its speed matches the speed of the synchronizer assembly. That is, it synchronizes the shift. This matched speed allows the internal hub splines to easily engage the coupling teeth on the stop ring and speed gear. When the clutch disengages, the crankshaft drives the input shaft, which drives the countershaft, which drives the output shaft through the selected gear.

The synchronizer goes through three stages during a shift:

1. The tapered surface, or cone, of the stop ring touches the speed gear first. As the two conical surfaces begin riding against each other, friction is created. See Figure 45–20. This causes the stop ring to move with the speed gear, but it moves only slightly until the detent keys hit the sides of their slots. This aligns the coupling teeth on the stop ring with the sleeve splines. Friction between the stop ring and cone slows the gear.
2. The sleeve overcomes the force of the detent key springs as the shift linkage continues to move it toward the gear. This allows the stop ring to relax and move slightly so that the sleeve splines begin to engage the coupling teeth on the stop ring. At this point, the coupling teeth on the stop ring and the speed gear may not line up with each other. However, friction continues to build between the ring and the cone, so the gear continues to slow down.
3. Once the sleeve, stop ring, and gear are all turning at the same speed, it takes just a small movement between the stop ring and gear to align the coupling teeth and allow the sleeve to slip completely over both sets. The speed gear is now locked to the output shaft through the synchronizer stop ring and sleeve. See Figure 45–21.

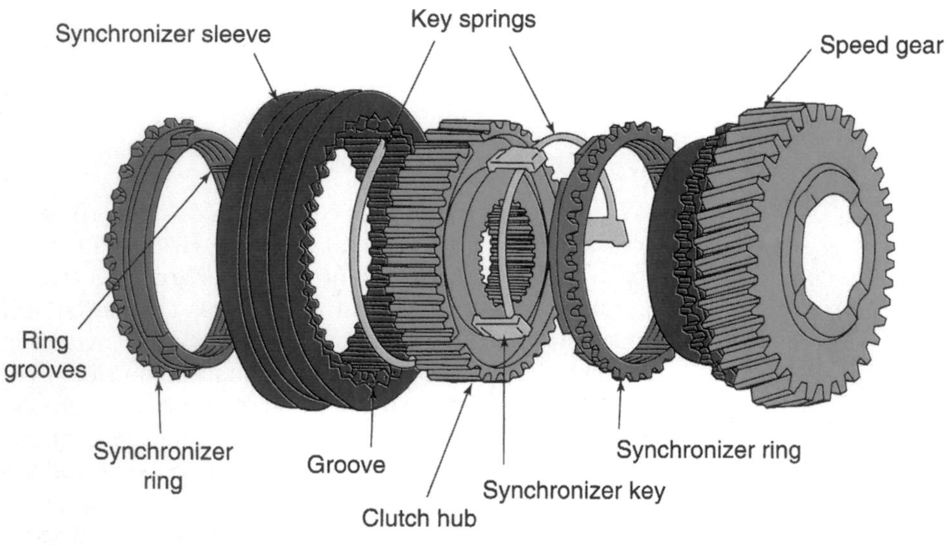

Figure 45–20 Synchronizer keys are attached to the clutch hub and push against the synchronizer ring when the sleeve is being moved during a shift. Notice the grooves on the sychronizer ring. These grooves prevent lubricating oil from becoming trapped between the ring and the cone surface of the speed gear. The grooves also help the ring release from the cone surface when a shift is made out of a gear. (Courtesy of Chrysler Corporation)

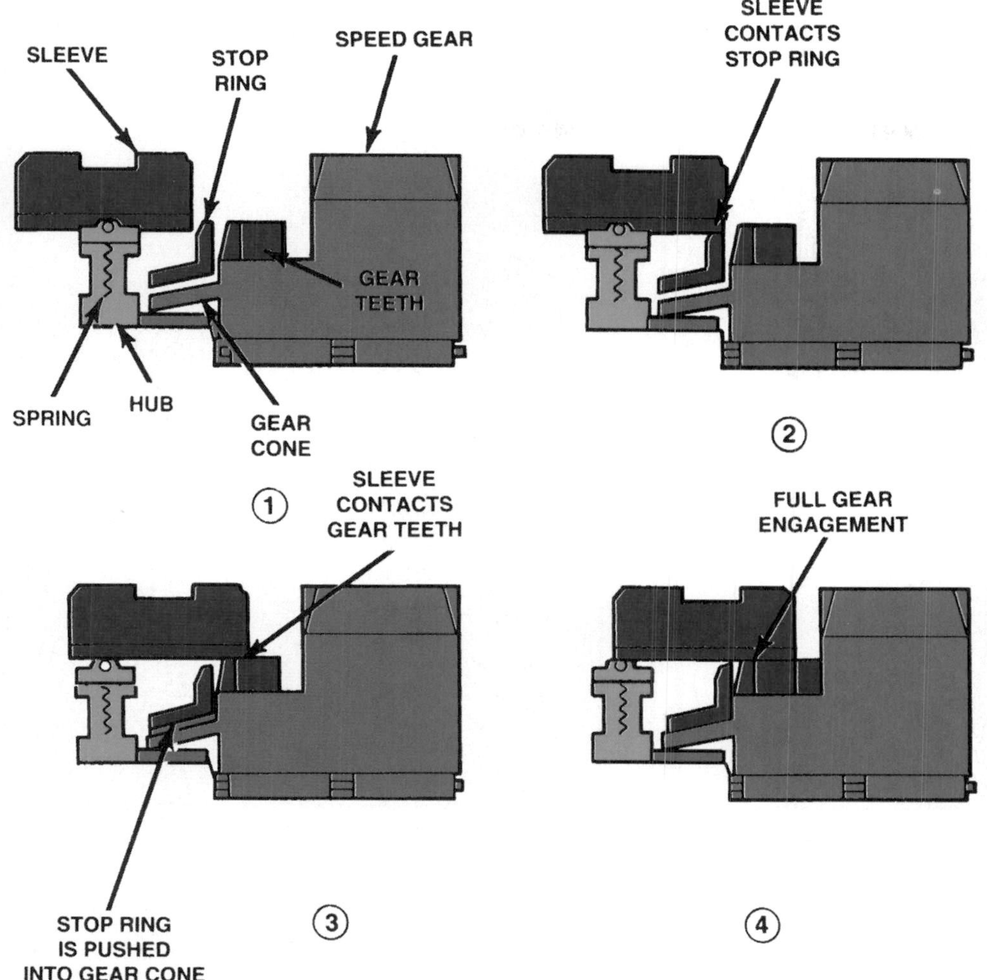

Figure 45–21 A shift sequence starts when the shift fork is moved by the driver, (1) applying a force on the sleeve that moves it toward the speed gear. (2) The sleeve and the inserts contact the stop ring (blocking ring). (3) The synchronizer ring (stop ring) engages the cone on the speed gear, causing both assemblies to reach the same speed. (4) The shift is completed when the internal teeth of the sleeve mesh with the gear clutch teeth of the speed gear. (Courtesy of Chrysler Corporation)

Synchronizer stop rings are a simple type of clutch, called a cone clutch for the shape of the mating surfaces. Some manufacturers refer to the synchronizer action as *clutching.*

Synchronizer sleeves and hubs are gear-quality steel. Stop rings are a softer metal—usually brass, copper, or a sintered metal—to absorb the friction of synchronizer operation. The tapered cone is relieved, that is, grooves are machined into its contact surface. These grooves serve two purposes; they

- Channel excess lubricant out from between the two pieces for better contact.
- Retain a small amount of lubricant. This decreases wear when the cone clutch must slip slightly during coupling tooth alignment.

The internal splines on the synchronizer sleeve and the coupling gear teeth on stop rings and speed gears have a special shape that works to hold the gear engaged once the driver releases the shift lever. The ends of the gear teeth are chamfered, giving them a triangular shape. These pointed ends allow easier sleeve-to-gear alignment as the angles tend to centre the splines between the teeth. Once aligned, a back taper machined behind the chamfered end of the teeth and splines tends to keep the sleeve in place until the linkage pushes the sleeve away for another shift. **Back taper** is an angle cut opposite to the chamfer so that spline or tooth narrows just behind the chamfered end. See Figure 45–22. The back taper creates resistance to motion to keep the splines from sliding off the coupling teeth. This is

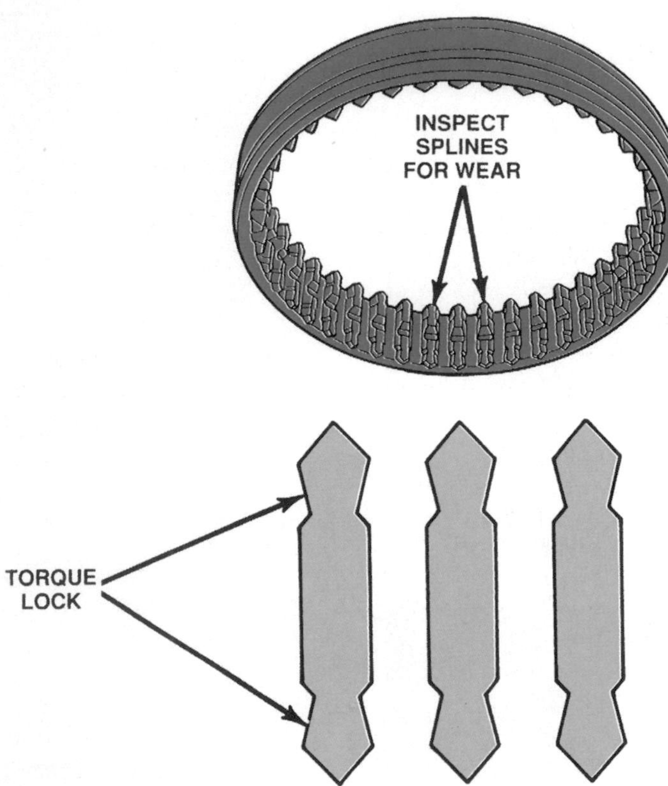

Figure 45–22 Before reassembling the transmission/transaxle, carefully inspect the splines on the synchronizer sleeves for wear. The shape of the splines helps prevent the transmission/transaxle from jumping out of gear during acceleration and deceleration. (Courtesy of Chrysler Corporation)

especially important when there is no torque load, such as coasting, to help keep the parts meshed. Worn back taper may cause the transmission to jump out of gear, usually when the throttle is released.

Some synchronizer stop rings have friction material on the cone surface. This paper-friction material is the same as used on automatic transmission clutch plates, and provides a smoother synchronizing action than metal-to-metal contact. A manual transmission with paper stop rings must use automatic transmission fluid (ATF). Other lubricants damage the paper ring surface. See Figure 45–23.

Figure 45–23 A three-piece synchronizer assembly. This type of synchronizer uses two cones, which helps achieve a smooth shift with less driver effort. Many newer transmissions/transaxles use a paper lining similar to that of the clutches in an automatic transmission. The transmissions/transaxles that have these paper linings must use automatic transmission fluid (ATF) for proper operation and long life.

FIVE-SPEED GEARBOX TORQUE FLOW

This section describes how power is transmitted through a typical five-speed gearbox. Although minor differences exist among different designs, the basic pattern of torque flow, also called power flow, is similar for most gearboxes. The concept of torque flow, or torque transfer, is the same for any transmission, regardless of the number of gear ratios available. The differences are in how the parts assemble and where they are located in the transmission.

Five-Speed Transmission

A five-speed transmission has six gear sets that provide five forward speeds and one reverse speed. Either a sliding gear or constant-mesh gears may be used for reverse. All forward gears are the constant-mesh type. The Borg-Warner T5 manual transmission serves as an example of a contemporary five-speed design. In addition to reverse, the T5 provides three gear reduction ratios (first, second, and third), direct drive (fourth), and an overdriven ratio (fifth). A sliding idler gear is used to change output shaft direction and provide reverse.

Neutral In **neutral,** all of the synchronizer sleeves are centred on their hubs as shown in Figure 45–24. Note that in this and the following illustrations the reverse idler shaft and sliding gear have been repositioned for clarity. In actuality, the assembly is positioned so it meshes with the reverse gears of the countershaft and output shaft simultaneously.

With the clutch engaged, the drive gear of the input shaft turns the cluster gear, or countershaft. The speed gears are driven by the cluster gears, but rotate freely, on the output shaft. The output shaft may turn if the vehicle is moving or coasting, but no engine torque is being transferred through the transmission.

First Gear In **first gear,** the shift linkage slides the 1–2 synchronizer sleeve rearward toward the first speed gear. See Figure 45–25. The synchronizer assembly locks the speed gear to the output shaft.

With the clutch engaged, the input shaft drives the countershaft, delivering engine torque to the gearbox. Torque transfers from the first counter gear to the first speed gear, which drives the output shaft through the 1–2 synchronizer hub splines. Torque flows through the transmission in gear reduction at the first gear ratio.

Second Gear In **second gear,** the shift linkage slides the 1–2 synchronizer sleeve forward, away from the first speed gear and toward the second speed gear. See Figure 45–26. The synchronizer assembly releases first gear, then locks the second speed gear to the output shaft.

With the clutch engaged, the input shaft is driven at crankshaft speed and turns the countershaft. Engine torque transfers from the second counter gear to the second speed gear, which drives the output shaft through the 1–2 synchronizer hub splines. Torque flows through the transmission in gear reduction at the second gear ratio.

Third Gear In **third gear,** the shift linkage centres the 1–2 synchronizer sleeve and moves the 3–4 synchronizer sleeve back toward the third speed

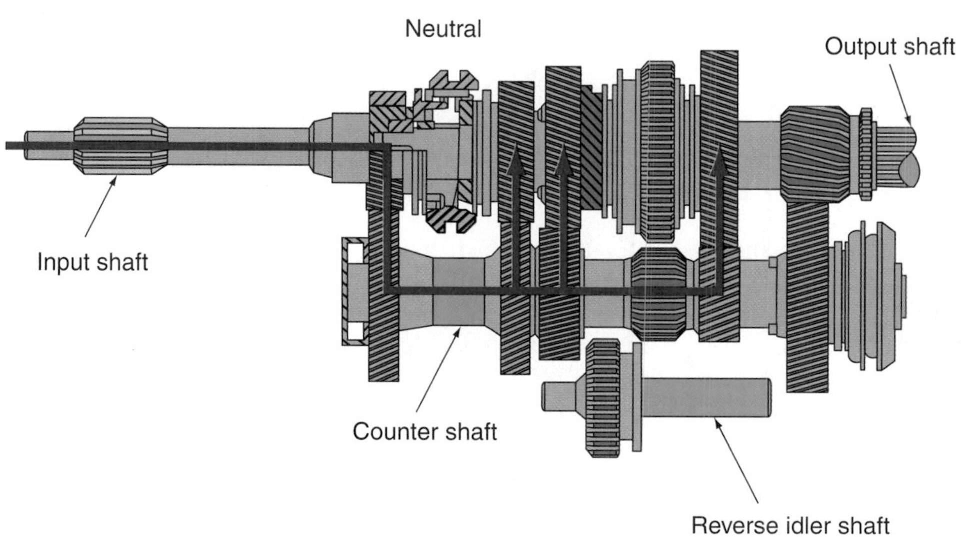

Figure 45–24 In neutral, the input shaft and the countershaft are rotating if the clutch is engaged (clutch pedal up), but no torque is being transmitted through the transmission.

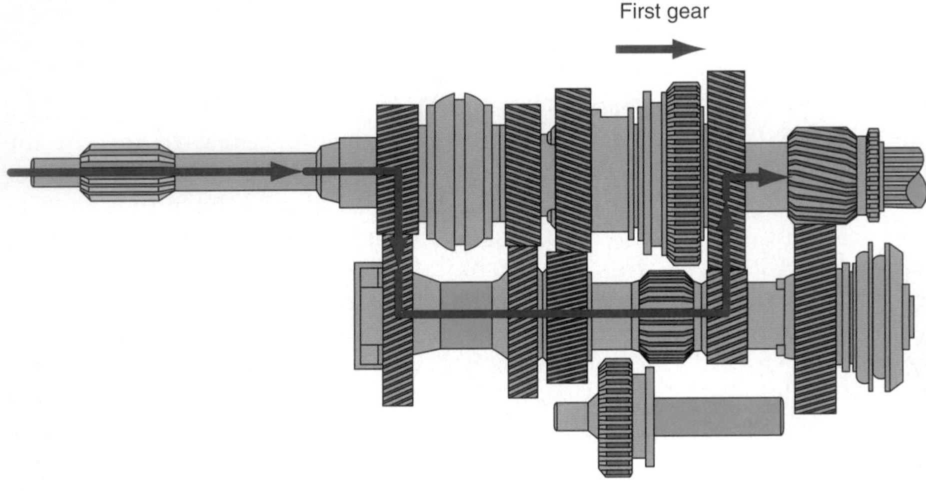

Figure 45–25 In first gear, the 1–2 synchronizer sleeve is moved rearward, locking the speed gear to the output shaft. Torque is transmitted from the input shaft to the countershaft and then to the output shaft.

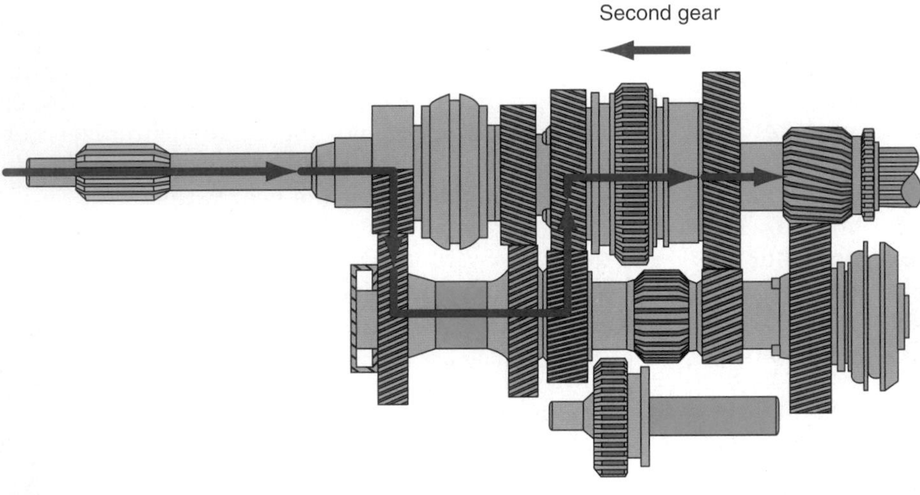

Figure 45–26 In second gear, the 1–2 synchronizer sleeve is moved forward, which locks the second speed gear to the output shaft.

gear. See Figure 45–27. The synchronizer assembly locks the third speed gear to the output shaft.

With the clutch engaged and the input shaft driving the countershaft, the third counter gear transfers torque to the third speed gear. The speed gear drives the output shaft through the 3–4 synchronizer hub splines. Torque flows through the transmission in gear reduction at the third gear ratio.

Fourth Gear In **fourth gear,** the shift linkage moves the 3–4 synchronizer sleeve forward, away from the third speed gear and toward the input shaft drive gear. See Figure 45–28. The synchronizer assembly locks the input shaft drive gear to the output shaft.

With the clutch engaged, the input shaft drives the output shaft through the 3–4 synchronizer hub splines and both shafts rotate at crankshaft speed. Torque flows straight through the transmission at a 1:1 ratio, delivering engine torque to the drive shaft. This is called direct drive because there is no gear reduction through the transmission. The counter gears also turn because they are in constant mesh, but they do not affect torque flow because all of the speed gears are freewheeling on the output shaft.

Fifth Gear In **fifth gear,** the shift linkage centres the 3–4 synchronizer sleeve and moves the fifth

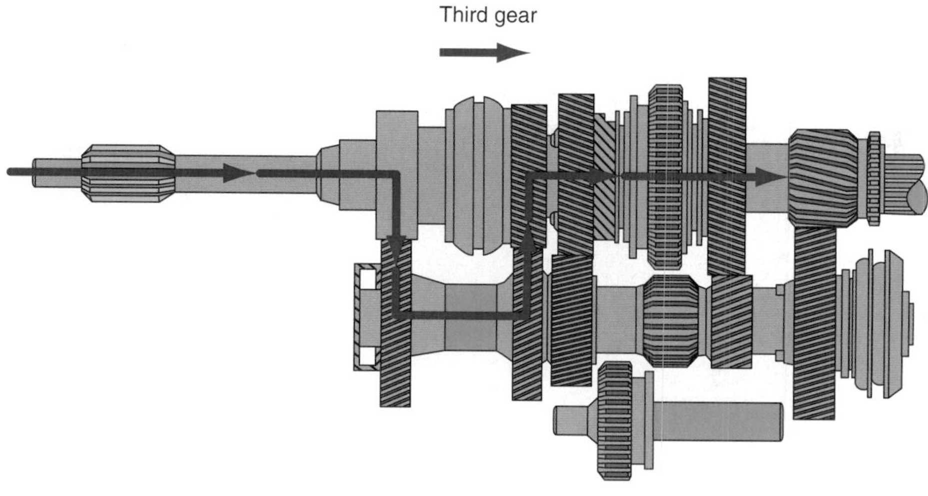

Figure 45–27 To achieve third gear, the shaft linkage first centres the 1–2 synchronizer sleeve and then moves the 3–4 synchronizer sleeve rearward, locking third gear to the output shaft.

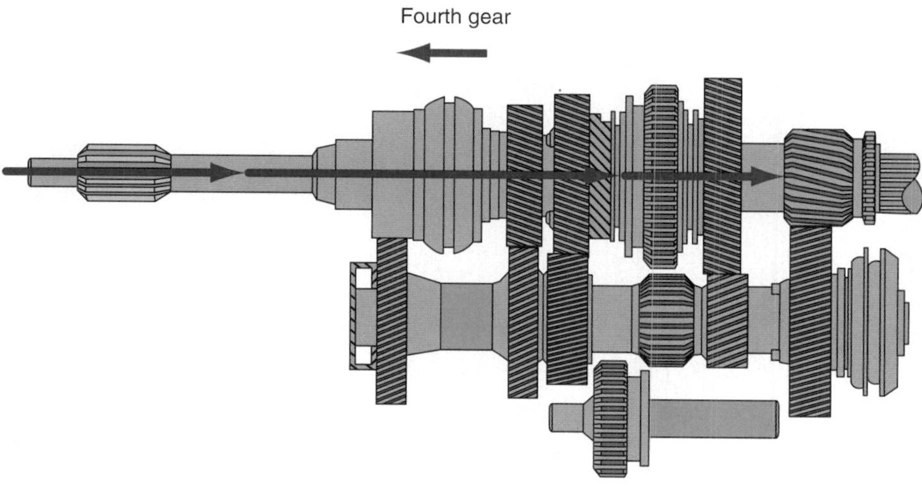

Figure 45–28 In fourth gear, the 3–4 synchronizer sleeve is moved forward, which locks the fourth speed gear to the output shaft.

synchronizer sleeve toward the fifth speed gear. See Figure 45–29. Note that on the T5 transmission the synchronizer assembly locks the fifth speed gear to the countershaft. The speed gear drives a fixed gear on the output shaft.

With the clutch engaged, the input shaft drives the countershaft. The fifth synchronizer hub is splined to the countershaft, so it is driven and driving the speed gear when fifth gear is engaged. This transfers engine torque to the output shaft through the fixed fifth gear. Note the countershaft gear is larger than the output shaft gear. Therefore, fifth gear is overdriven. Torque flows through the transmission at the fifth gear, or overdrive, ratio. Typical overdrive gear ratios are between 0.6:1 and 0.8:1. This lowers engine speed for economical highway cruising.

On some five-speed transmissions, the fifth speed gear is on the output shaft with the other speed gears. This type of arrangement is typically used with constant-mesh reverse gears. In these designs, fifth and reverse gears share a synchronizer assembly. The fixed countershaft gear drives the speed gear, which drives the output shaft through the hub splines when the sliding sleeve is engaged. Torque flow through the transmission is similar to any of the gear reduction forward speeds detailed above, but the speed gear is generally overdriven.

Reverse There are two common **reverse** gear designs used on transmissions:

1. Sliding gear
2. Constant-mesh gear.

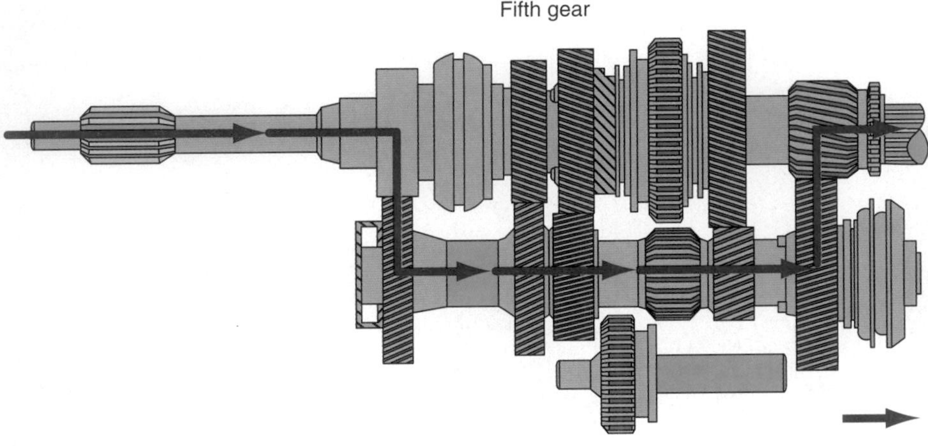

Figure 45–29 To achieve fifth gear, the shift linkage first centres the 3–4 synchronizer sleeve and then moves the fifth synchronizer sleeve toward the fifth speed gear, locking it to the output shaft.

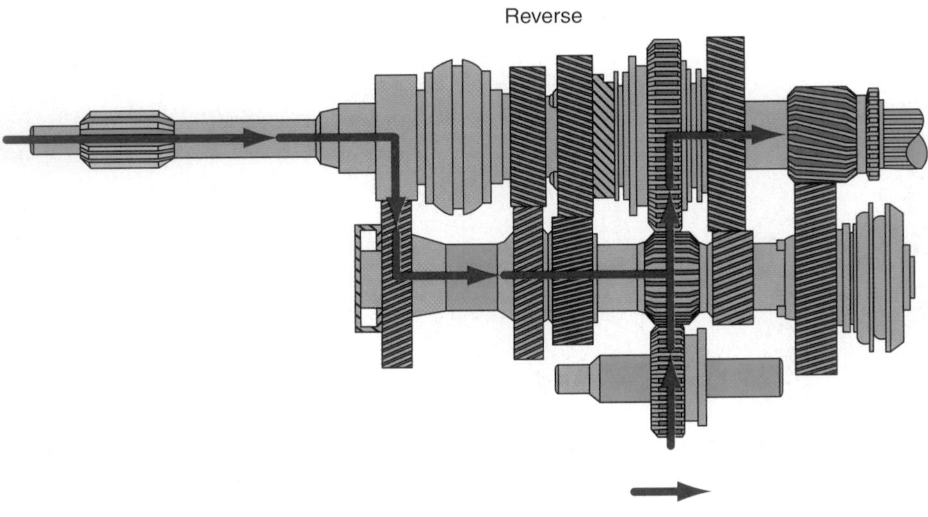

Figure 45–30 Torque flows through the transmission in reverse gear. Note that the idler gear drives the 1–2 synchronizer sleeve gear, which is splined to the output shaft.

With a **sliding reverse gear** design, such as on the T5, the shift linkage slides the reverse idler gear on its shaft until it engages the reverse gears on the countershaft and output shaft gear. Both gears are fixed to their respective shafts. This design uses spur gears for reverse, not helical gears, because the gear teeth must move into and out of mesh. On some gearboxes, the sliding gear splines to the output shaft. The linkage moves the gear along the output shaft splines to engage the reverse idler gear.

An unusual feature of the Borg-Warner T5 is that it does not have a separate reverse output shaft gear. See Figure 45–30. Instead, spur teeth machined around the outside of the 1–2 synchronizer sleeve act as the reverse output gear. When the T5 is shifted into reverse, the linkage moves the reverse idler gear rearward so it simultaneously meshes with the countershaft reverse gear and the gear on the synchronizer sleeve.

When the clutch is engaged, the countershaft is driven and the reverse gear drives the idler gear, which rotates in the opposite direction of the countershaft. The idler gear drives the 1–2 synchronizer sleeve, so there is another directional change in rotation. Although the sleeve is not engaged to a speed gear, it remains splined to the output shaft, so the sleeve drives the output shaft when the idler gear is engaged. The output shaft rotates in the opposite direction of the input shaft because the idler gear is between them.

With **constant-mesh gears,** the shift linkage moves the 5-reverse synchronizer sleeve away from the fifth speed gear and toward the reverse speed gear when reverse is selected. Typically, no stop ring is used between the synchronizer sleeve and the reverse gear, so the output shaft must be stopped to engage reverse without grinding the sleeve splines against the coupling teeth of the reverse gear. The synchronizer assembly locks the reverse speed gear to the output shaft.

With the clutch engaged, the input shaft drives the countershaft. The reverse counter gear drives the reverse idler gear, which drives the reverse speed gear in the direction opposite normal rotation. The reverse speed gear drives the output shaft through the 5-reverse synchronizer hub splines. Torque flows through the transmission in gear reduction at the reverse gear ratio. The output shaft turns opposite its normal direction of rotation, so the vehicle moves to the rear. See Figure 45–31.

Figure 45–31 Cutaway of a T5 five-speed transmission showing all of its internal parts.

MANUAL TRANSAXLE CONSTRUCTION

A manually shifted transaxle includes an input shaft, an output shaft, and a differential assembly all in one case. The input shaft is attached to the clutch, which transfers engine torque from the engine flywheel to the input shaft when the clutch is engaged.

Most transaxles use speed gears and synchronizers on both the input and output shafts, as shown in Figure 45–32. The **differential assembly,** also called a **final drive assembly,** attaches to the output shaft and splits the torque to both front drive axles. See Figure 45–33. See Chapter 47 for additional information on differentials.

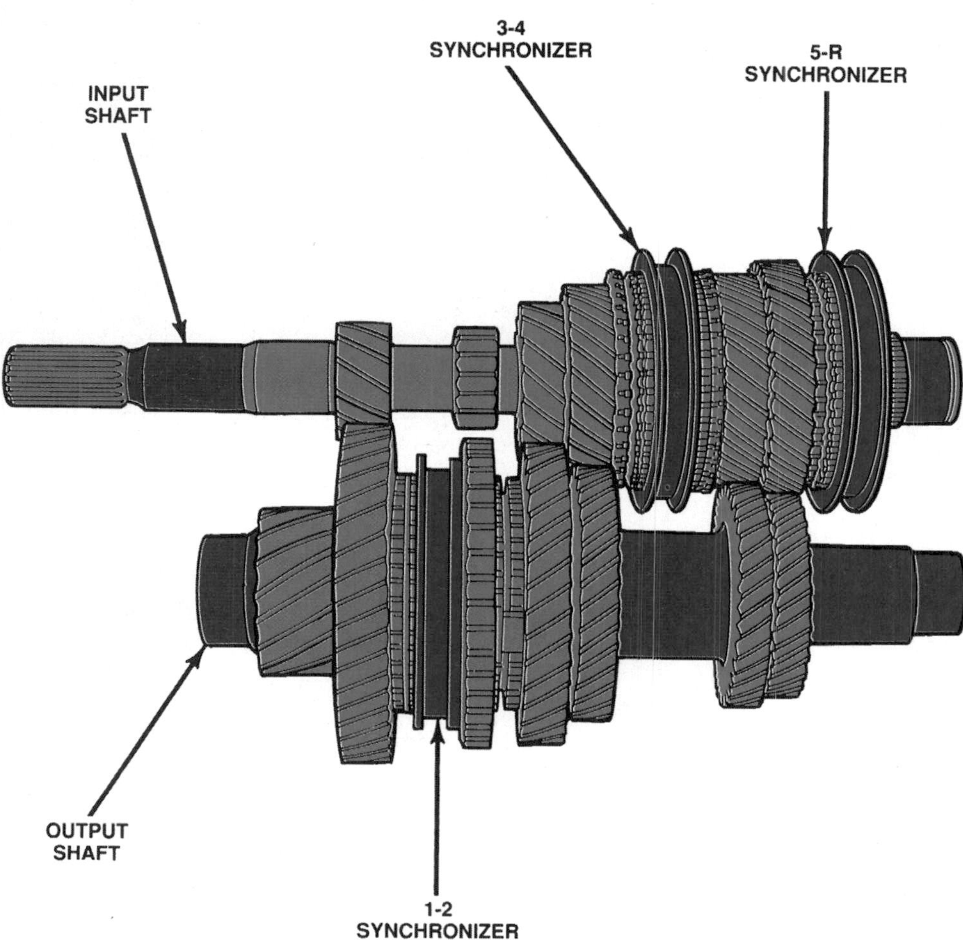

Figure 45–32 Notice that this five-speed transaxle from a Dodge/Plymouth Neon uses synchronizers on both the input and output shafts. (Courtesy of Chrysler)

Figure 45–33 Cutaway of a typical manual transaxle showing all of its internal parts, including the final drive assembly.

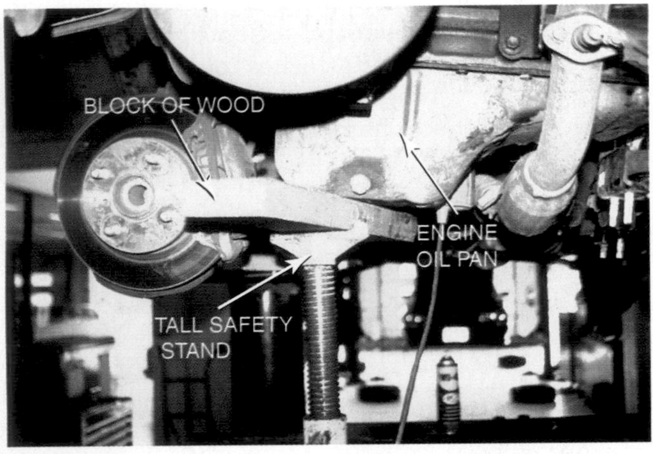

Figure 45–34 When the transmission/transaxle is removed from the vehicle, the engine must be supported. In this case, the engine oil pan is supported with a block of wood to spread the load across the entire oil pan to prevent damage. The block of wood is placed on top of a tall safety stand that allows room for the service technician to work while standing.

Figure 45–35 A transmission from a restored muscle car from the 1970s. Notice the use of external control rod shift linkage.

Figure 45–36 Typical cable-operated shift linkage used on a front-wheel-drive transaxle.

TRANSMISSION/TRANSAXLE REMOVAL

Before removing the transmission/transaxle for service, double check that the problem is not due to any malfunction of the clutch or shift linkage. To remove a transmission or transaxle, always follow the procedure in the service manual to be assured of doing no harm to either the vehicle or to yourself. Steps typically involved in the removal and disassembly include

- Disconnecting the negative battery cable
- Safely hoisting and supporting the vehicle
- Supporting the engine with a holding fixture or other support (front-wheel-drive) (see Figure 45–34)
- Removing the drive axle shafts or drive shaft (rear-wheel-drive)
- Removing the clutch linkage and shift linkage (see Figures 45–35 and 45–36)
- Disconnecting the vehicle speed sensor and reverse (backup) light connectors
- Removing the attaching bolts/nuts from the engine and transmission/transaxle mounts and then removing the unit from the vehicle

Sometimes it is easier to remove the entire power train (engine and transaxle as an assembly) from the vehicle, as shown in Figure 45–37. When the entire assembly has been removed from the vehicle, often the transaxle can then be removed from the engine.

(a)

(b)

Figure 45–37 (a) Saturn drive train is removed as an assembly along with the cradle. (b) The transaxle can now be easily removed from the cradle and the engine.

TRANSMISSION/TRANSAXLE DISASSEMBLY

Before disassembling the transmission/transaxle, drain any remaining gear lubricant from the unit and dispose of it properly.

> **CAUTION:** Most extreme pressure (EP) lubricants contain sulfur compounds that can cause skin irritation. Either wear protective gloves or wash your hands thoroughly using soap and water after exposure to used gear lubricant.

Mount the transmission/transaxle on a holding fixture or place it on a large clean work surface. Many vehicle manufacturers recommend removing the shift housing before further disassembly. The removal of the shifter housing allows the technician to see any obvious damage as well as providing the opportunity to check the shift forks, which are frequently worn in manually-shifted transmissions/transaxles. See Figures 45–38 and 45–39.

The disassembly and reassembly of a manual transaxle is similar to that for a manual transmission except for the addition of the final drive unit. Some transaxles require two people for disassembly and reassembly because often the shift linkage has to be held in place while assembled components are placed into the case, as shown in Figure 45–40.

Check the service manual for the exact disassembly procedures to follow for the unit being serviced. Sometimes the main shaft is removed through the rear of the transmission and sometimes it is removed through the top of the case. Also look for hidden snap rings. See Figures 45–41 and 45–42. Also see the Tech Tip titled "Manual Transmission Service Tips."

Figure 45–38 The shift forks should be inspected for wear.

Figure 45–39 The cost to replace these gears may exceed the cost of a replacement transmission.

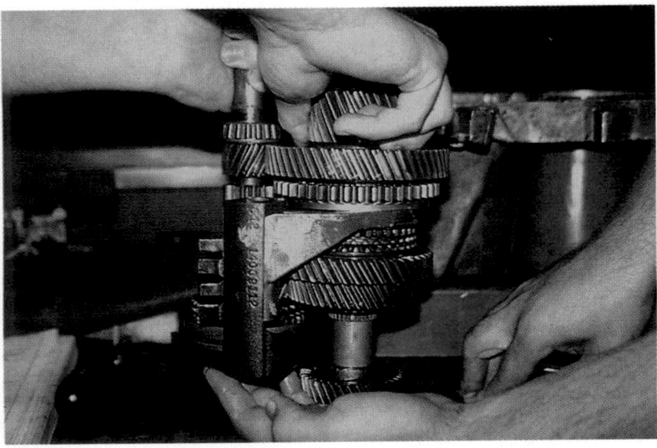

Figure 45–40 It often requires two people to assemble a transaxle because the shaft with the shifter forks needs to be placed into the case as an assembly, as on this unit.

TECH TIP 

Manual Transmission Service Tips

A wise technician once told a beginning technician to remember these items when working with transmissions:

- Always use a *brass* or *plastic* hammer when pounding on a steel or aluminum component.
- If using a steel hammer, always use a *brass* or *aluminum* punch or place wood between the steel components and the hammer.
- Many parts can be installed in either direction but usually only one way is correct.
- If you are exerting a lot of force, you are probably doing something wrong.
- Many drive train parts are pulled or pressed off and pressed or driven on.

(a)

(b)

(c)

Figure 45–41 (a) During the disassembly of any manual transmission/transaxle, carefully check for the location of the snap rings. Often they are hidden. Consult the factory service manual or unit repair manual for information and procedures for the unit being serviced. (b) Using snap-ring pliers to remove a snap ring. Many snap rings have an "up" side. Be sure to reinstall any snap rings in the correct direction. (c) After the snap ring is removed, some components can be simply lifted off the main shaft, while other gears may require the use of a press.

(a)

(b)

(c)

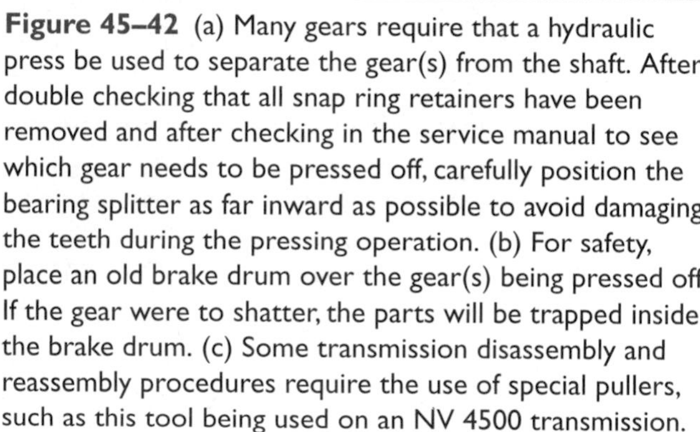

Figure 45–42 (a) Many gears require that a hydraulic press be used to separate the gear(s) from the shaft. After double checking that all snap ring retainers have been removed and after checking in the service manual to see which gear needs to be pressed off, carefully position the bearing splitter as far inward as possible to avoid damaging the teeth during the pressing operation. (b) For safety, place an old brake drum over the gear(s) being pressed off. If the gear were to shatter, the parts will be trapped inside the brake drum. (c) Some transmission disassembly and reassembly procedures require the use of special pullers, such as this tool being used on an NV 4500 transmission.

HARD-TO-SHIFT PROBLEM DIAGNOSIS

Several items that could be worn or defective can cause a manual transmission/transaxle to be difficult to shift, including:

- **Clutch not fully disengaging.** If the clutch linkage is not properly adjusted or if there is a leak in the hydraulic clutch linkage, the clutch may not be fully disengaged. A shift is very difficult, if not impossible, if engine torque is being transferred through the transmission/transaxle as a shift is being attempted.
- **Worn synchronizer.** If the synchronizer rings are worn, the rings will be unable to properly match the speed gear speed, making the shift difficult and/or creating gear clash (noise) when shifting.
- **Worn, cracked, or loose shift forks.** If there is any problem with the shift forks, the synchronizer cannot be properly moved during a shift attempt, making shifting difficult, if not impossible. If only one fork is worn or defective, usually engaging two gears instead of one is likely.
- **Excessive input- or main-shaft endplay.** Excessive endplay in the input or main shaft will cause the gears to move away from the synchronizer assembly, resulting in grinding during shifts or shifts that are difficult or impossible to complete.
- **Improper lubrication.** Many of today's manual transmissions use synchronizer rings (blocking rings) that are lined with compounds, paper, or other friction material. All of these transmissions/transaxles must be filled with the proper fluid formulated for proper shifting.

DIAGNOSTIC STORY

The Worn Shift Fork Mystery

A vehicle equipped with a manual transmission had to be repaired several times for worn shift forks. Even though the vehicle warranty paid for the repair, both the customer and the service department personnel were concerned about the repeated failures. All technical service bulletins (TSBs) were checked to see if there was an updated, improved shift fork. No luck. Even the manufacturer's technical assistance personnel were unable to determine why the shift forks were wearing out. After the third repair, the service technician rode with the customer to see if the cause could be determined. As the woman driver got into the driver's seat, she placed the handle of her purse over the shifter on the floor and allowed the purse to hang from the shifter. The technician asked the owner if she always placed her purse on the shifter and when she said yes, the technician knew immediately the cause of the worn shift forks. The purse exerted a force on the shifter all the time. This force pushed the shift forks against the synchronizer sleeve. Because the sleeve rotates all the time the vehicle is in motion, the shift forks were quickly worn. The service technician should have determined the root cause of the problem after the *first* repair. The customer agreed to find another location for her purse so that the transmission problem would not reoccur.

NOTE: A worn synchronizer sleeve and/or blocking ring can cause the transmission/transaxle to pop out of gear while accelerating or decelerating.

MANUAL TRANSMISSION INSTALLATION

When installing a repaired or replacement transmission/transaxle, the clutch should be carefully inspected and replaced as necessary. The clutch friction disk must be held in position using an alignment tool (sometimes called a *dummy shaft*) that is secured in the pilot bearing. This holds the disk in position while the pressure plate is being installed. Finally, the engine bell housing is put on the engine, if it was not installed before. The alignment of this type of bell housing is then checked.

CAUTION: Perfectly round cylinders can be distorted whenever another part of the engine is bolted and torqued to the engine block. For example, it has been determined that after the cylinders are machined, the rear cylinder bore can be distorted as much as 0.15 mm (0.006 in.) out of round after the bell housing is bolted onto the block! To help prevent this distortion, always apply the specified torque to all fasteners going into the engine block and tighten in the recommended sequence.

The clutch release yoke should be checked for free movement. Usually, the clutch release bearing is replaced, ensuring that the new bearing is securely attached to the clutch release yoke. The transmission can then be installed.

The transmission clutch shaft must be guided straight into the clutch disk and pilot bearing. See the Tech Tip "The Headless Bolt Trick." The transmission clutch shaft is rotated, as required, to engage in the splines of the clutch disk. The assembly bolts are secured when the transmission fully mates with the bell housing.

CAUTION: Always adjust the clutch freeplay *before* starting the engine to help prevent thrust bearing damage.

Complete the installation by attaching the transmission/transaxle mount, drive shaft (drive axle shafts), vehicle speed sensor, and reverse (backup) light switch.

GEAR LUBRICATION

After the installation of the transmission/transaxle, the unit should be filled with the correct lubricant. The various lubricants, their general use, and their American Petroleum Institute (API) rating include:

GL-1 Straight mineral oil

GL-2 Worm-type gear lubricant

GL-3 Mild-type EP lubricant (will not protect hypoid gears)

GL-4 EP-type lubricant (okay for manual transmissions/transaxles)

GL-5 EP-type okay for hypoid gears and for Mil-L2150B (military)

Manual transmissions/transaxles require one of the following lubricants:

- SAE 80W-90 (GL-4) gear lube

- STF (synchromesh transmission fluid) with friction characteristics designed for manual transmissions (see Figure 45–43)
- ATF (automatic transmission fluid)
- Engine oil (usually SAE 5W-30)

CAUTION: Failure to use the specified manual transmission/transaxle lubricant could cause hard shifting and possible severe transmission damage.

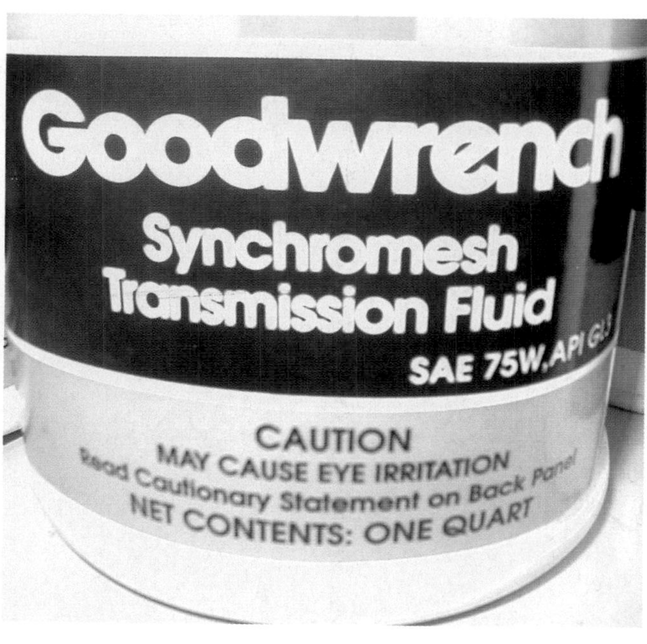

Figure 45–43 Some manual transmissions/transaxles require synchromesh transmission fluid.

TECH TIP 

The Headless Bolt Trick

Sometimes parts do not seem to line up correctly. Try this tip the next time. Cut the head off extra-long bolts that are of the same diameter and thread as those being used to retain the part, such as a transmission. See Figure 45–44. Use a hacksaw to cut a slot in the end of these guide bolts for a screwdriver slot. Install the guide bolts; then install the transmission. Use a straight-blade screwdriver to remove the guide bolts after securing the transmission with the retaining bolts.

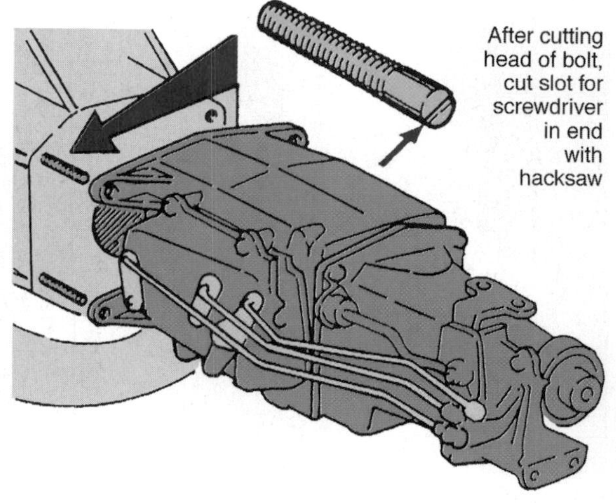

Figure 45–44 Headless, long bolts can be used to help install a transmission to the engine.

P31–1 A NV-1500 five-speed manual transmission is used in two-wheel drive applications only.

P31–2 The shifter assembly has been removed. Notice the roll pin in the centre of the shift lever socket.

P31–3 Snap-ring pliers are being used to remove the snap ring retaining the input shaft bearing.

P31–4 The upside-down case is being separated showing the countershaft (top) and shift forks.

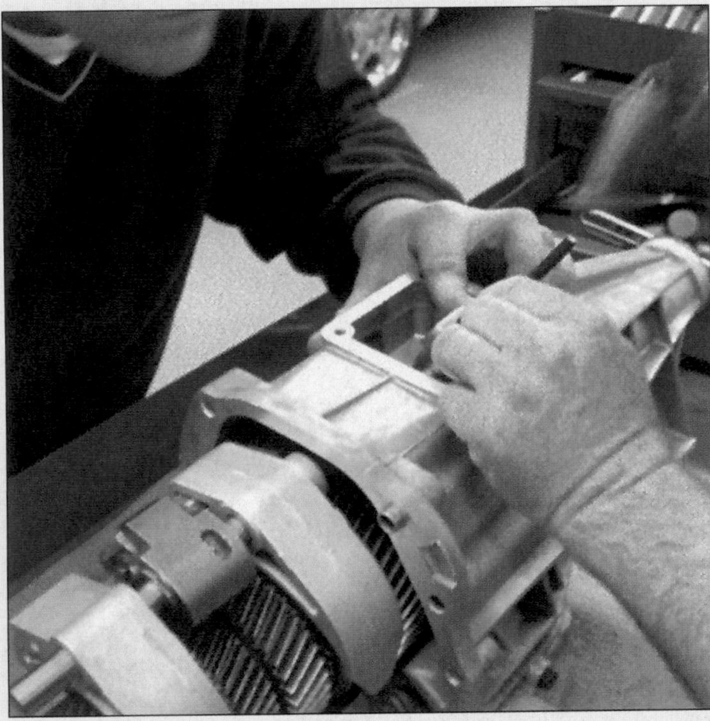

P31–5 Before further disassembly can be accomplished, the shift lever socket roll pin must be driven out using a punch and a hammer.

P31–6 The shift shaft and forks can now be removed.

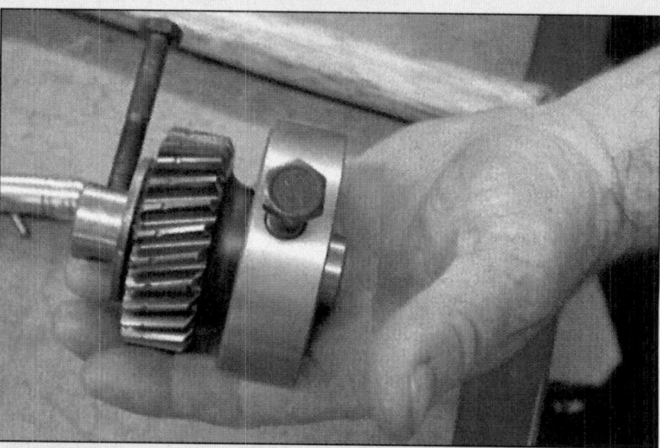

P31–7 The reverse idle gear is unbolted from the case and removed.

P31–8 A special tool is required to be bolted to the case to hold the output shaft bearing retainer before removal of the output shaft. The output shaft assembly showing fifth gear (far left) and the synchronizer assemblies.

P31–9 The bearing is being removed using a bearing splitter and a hydraulic press.

P31–10 A speed gear (bottom) along with the double row needle bearing used between the shaft and the speed gear. The hub (centre) is splined and rotates with the output shaft.

P31–11 A synchronizer assembly being reassembled. It often takes several hands to hold the hub (centre) and the sleeve (outer ring) as the strut, spring, and detent ball are installed into the three notches as shown.

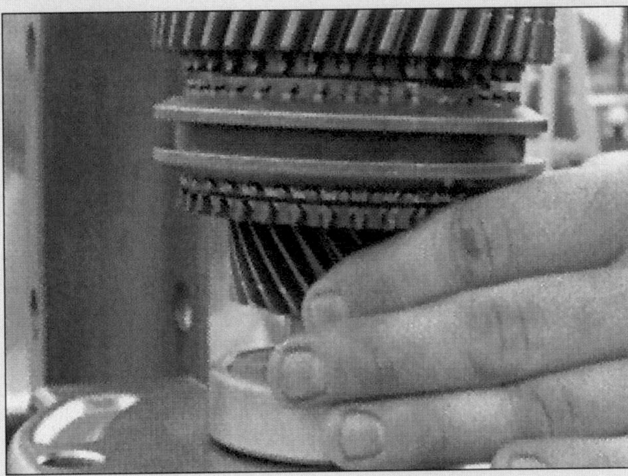

P31–12 A hydraulic press is used to reassemble the output shaft and bearing.

P31–13 The assembled output shaft is held against the countershaft to double check that all of the gears have been correctly assembled.

P31–14 The assembled output shaft and countershaft are being reinstalled in the transmission case.

P31–15 The case halves are bolted together.

P31–16 The roll pin is reinstalled in the shift lever socket. The last component in the installation of the countershaft bearing cup (background on the table) which also provides the countershaft bearing preload.

P32–1 After the transaxle has been removed from the vehicle and the fluid drained, place the transaxle on a clean work surface. Disassembly starts by removing the bolts from the bell housing case half.

P32–2 The bell housing case half contains the large output shaft front bearing (centre) and the input shaft front bearing (smaller bearing on the left).

P32–3 The differential assembly is simply lifted out of the other half of the case.

P32–4 The input and output shafts are a press fit into the bearings and are also retained with a snap ring, which must be removed.

P32–5 Using a special tool, the input and output shafts are pressed out of the housing using a hydraulic press.

P32–6 The input shaft can be disassembled using a bearing splitter and a press, or two screwdrivers to pry the gears off the shaft.

P32–7 This transaxle uses both brass and powdered metal synchronizer rings with a fibre (paper) inner cone surface. It is this paper surface that requires the use of automatic transmission fluid (ATF).

P32–8 Synchronizer ring gaps are being measured using a feeler (thickness) gauge. A new synchronizer will have a large gap and a worn synchronizer will have a smaller gap. The factory specifications are usually about 1.00 to 1.75 mm (0.040 to 0.069 in.).

P32–9 The gear clutch teeth should be inspected for wear.

P32–10 An assembled synchronizer assembly containing a sleeve, struts, springs, and detent balls.

P32–11 The input shaft (left) and the output shaft (right) are checked for proper assembly before being installed into the case.

P32–12 The differential bearing preload is determined by measuring for zero endplay, then adding the specified thickness shim under the bearing cup.

P32–13 The bearing cup is being installed using an installation tool and a hammer.

P32–14 All of the shift forks and shift arms must be aligned properly before installing the components into the case.

P32–15 All of the components, including the differential (right), the output shaft (centre), and the input shaft (left), plus the shift linkage are installed in the case and checked for proper positioning.

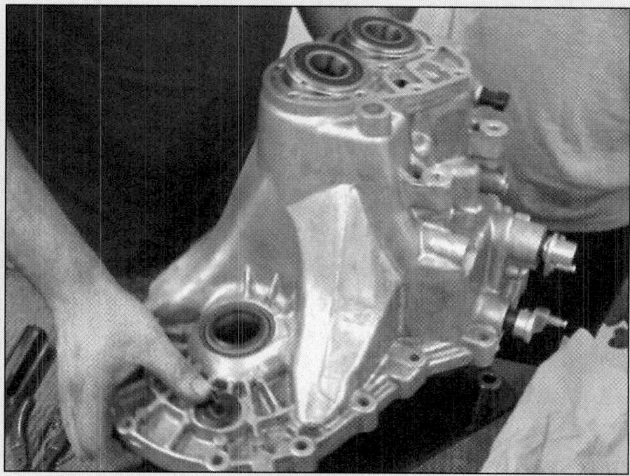

P32–16 The case halves being reinstalled. The bearings (top) must be pressed back onto the input and output shafts using a press.

P32–17 The bell housing case being reattached.

P32–18 The completed assembly. Notice the bearing cover (top) has already been installed.

SUMMARY

1. A transmission is required both to provide the torque necessary to the drive wheels to get the vehicle moving from a stop and to provide economical cruising on the highway.
2. A gear ratio is determined by dividing the number of teeth on the driven gear (output) by the number of teeth on the driving gear (input). A ratio is always expressed as a number relative to one rotation of the output gear.
3. An overdrive ratio is a ratio that results in the output gear rotating faster than the input gear; the first number of this ratio is less than 1.
4. A spur gear is a gear with straight teeth, and a helical-cut gear is a gear with angled teeth.
5. The input shaft is splined to the clutch disc. The output shaft is also called the main shaft.
6. A countershaft is another shaft inside a transmission/transaxle which provides another set of gears to produce the necessary gear ratios.
7. Care should be taken not to damage the parts of the transmission/transaxle during disassembly. Always consult the factory service manual for the exact procedures to follow, especially regarding using a hydraulic press to press gears off or onto the shafts.
8. A synchronizer assembly permits a shift to be made without gear clash. The parts of a typical synchronizer include the synchronizer sleeve, hub, and ring.
9. A transaxle includes a final drive unit that splits the torque to the two front-drive wheels and allows the drive wheels to rotate at different speeds while travelling around a corner or over bumpy roads.
10. A manual transmission/transaxle may use one of four possible lubricants including gear lube, synchromesh transmission fluid (STF), automatic transmission fluid (ATF), or engine oil.

REVIEW QUESTIONS

1. Calculate the gear ratio if the driven gear has 36 teeth and the driving gear has 12 teeth.
2. Explain what is meant by an overdrive ratio.
3. List the parts of a manual transmission.
4. Explain how a synchronizer assembly is able to allow a clash-free shift.
5. List four possible causes for a manual transmission/transaxle being difficult to shift.
6. List the possible lubricants that a manual transmission/transaxle may require.

RED SEAL CERTIFICATION-TYPE QUESTIONS

1. How does changing gears from second to third affect torque to the output shaft?
   - **a.** Torque is increased
   - **b.** Torque is decreased
   - **c.** Torque stays the same
   - **d.** None of the above
2. What would the gear ratio be if the driving gear had 15 teeth and the driven gear had 29 teeth?
   - **a.** 3.86:1
   - **b.** 2.5:1
   - **c.** 1.93:1
   - **d.** 1:1
3. Which part is splined to the clutch disc?
   - **a.** Main shaft
   - **b.** Countershaft (lay shaft)
   - **c.** Cluster shaft
   - **d.** Main gear
4. With what does the input shaft mesh inside the rear-wheel-drive transmission?
   - **a.** Reverse idler
   - **b.** Countershaft gear
   - **c.** Output shaft gear
   - **d.** Flywheel
5. Which component cannot be removed before removing the transmission/transaxle from the vehicle?
   - **a.** Vehicle speed sensor
   - **b.** Reverse (backup) light connector
   - **c.** Front bearing retainer (quill)
   - **d.** Drive axle shaft(s)
6. Which statement is most correct?
   - **a.** Snap rings hold the clutch disc from turning on the input shaft
   - **b.** Snap rings hold bearings from sliding on the output shaft
   - **c.** Snap rings must be replaced after being used once
   - **d.** Snap rings are best removed using a small screwdriver
7. What could be the cause of hard to shift into first and reverse?
   - **a.** Worn 2/3 synchronizer
   - **b.** Too much clutch freeplay
   - **c.** Damaged speed gear
   - **d.** Countershafts main drive gear
8. Which part of a synchronizer is splined to a shaft?
   - **a.** Synchronizer sleeve
   - **b.** Hub
   - **c.** Synchronizer ring (blocking ring)
   - **d.** Speed gear
9. What might be the cause of hard to shift when transmission is cold?
   - **a.** Synchronizer brass blocker ring
   - **b.** Shift fork worn
   - **c.** Incorrect transmission lubricant
   - **d.** Pilot bearing seized
10. Which type of lubricant is usually *not* used in a manual transmission/transaxle?
   - **a.** Automatic transmission fluid (ATF)
   - **b.** High-temperature chassis grease
   - **c.** SAE 80W-90 gear lube
   - **d.** Engine oil

46

Drive Shafts and CV Joints

OBJECTIVES: After studying Chapter 46, you should be able to:

1. Prepare for the interprovincial Red Seal certification examination in Appendix III (Manual Drive Trains and Axles) on the topics covered in this chapter.
2. Name drive-shaft and U-joint parts and describe their purpose, function, and operation.
3. Explain how the working angles of the U-joints are determined.
4. Describe how CV joints work.
5. Explain how to perform a U-joint inspection.
6. Describe the service procedures for replacing CV joints and boots.

A drive axle shaft transmits engine power from the transmission or transaxle (if front wheel drive) to the rear axle assembly or drive wheels. See Figures 46–1 and 46–2. **Drive shaft** is the term used by the Society of Automotive Engineers (SAE) to describe the shaft between the transmission and the rear axle assembly on a rear-wheel-drive vehicle. General Motors, Chrysler, and some other manufacturers use the term **propeller shaft** or **prop shaft** to describe this same part. The SAE term will be used throughout this textbook.

A typical drive shaft is a hollow steel tube. U-joints are attached to both ends of the drive shaft. The front U-joint is attached to a splined yoke that slips over the output shaft of the transmission. See Figure 46–3. Beyond about 165 cm (65 in.) in length, a **centre support bearing** must be used, as shown in Figure 46–4. A centre support bearing is also called a **steady bearing** or **hanger bearing.**

Some vehicle manufacturers use aluminum drive shafts, which can be as long as 230 cm (90 in.) without requiring a support bearing. Composite drive shafts are also used in some vehicles. These carbon fibre-plastic drive shafts are very strong yet lightweight and can be made in long lengths without the need for a centre support bearing.

To dampen drive shaft noise, it is common to line the inside of the hollow drive shaft with cardboard. This helps eliminate the tinny sound when shifting between drive and reverse in a vehicle equipped with an automatic transmission. See Figure 46–5.

U-JOINT DESIGN AND OPERATION

Universal joints (U-joints) are used at both ends of a drive shaft. U-joints allow the wheels and the rear axle to move up and down and remain flexible and still transfer power to the drive wheels. A simple universal joint can be made from two Y-shaped yokes connected by a cross member called a **cross** or **spider.** The four arms of the cross are called **trunnions.** See Figure 46–6 for a line drawing of a simple U-joint with all part names identified. A similar design is the common U-joint used with a socket wrench set.

Most U-joints are called **cross yoke** or **Cardan universal joints.** The Cardan joint takes its name

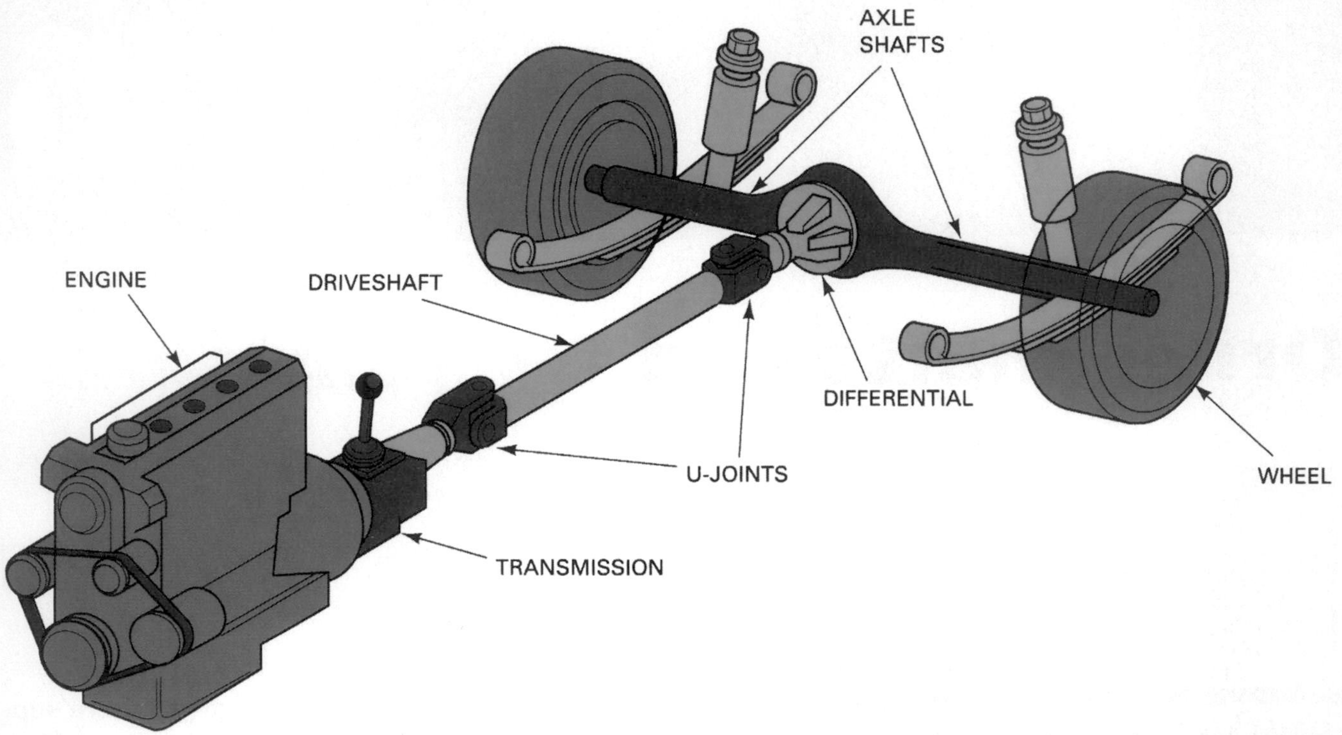

Figure 46–1 Typical rear-wheel-drive power train arrangement. The engine is mounted longitudinally (lengthwise) in the vehicle.

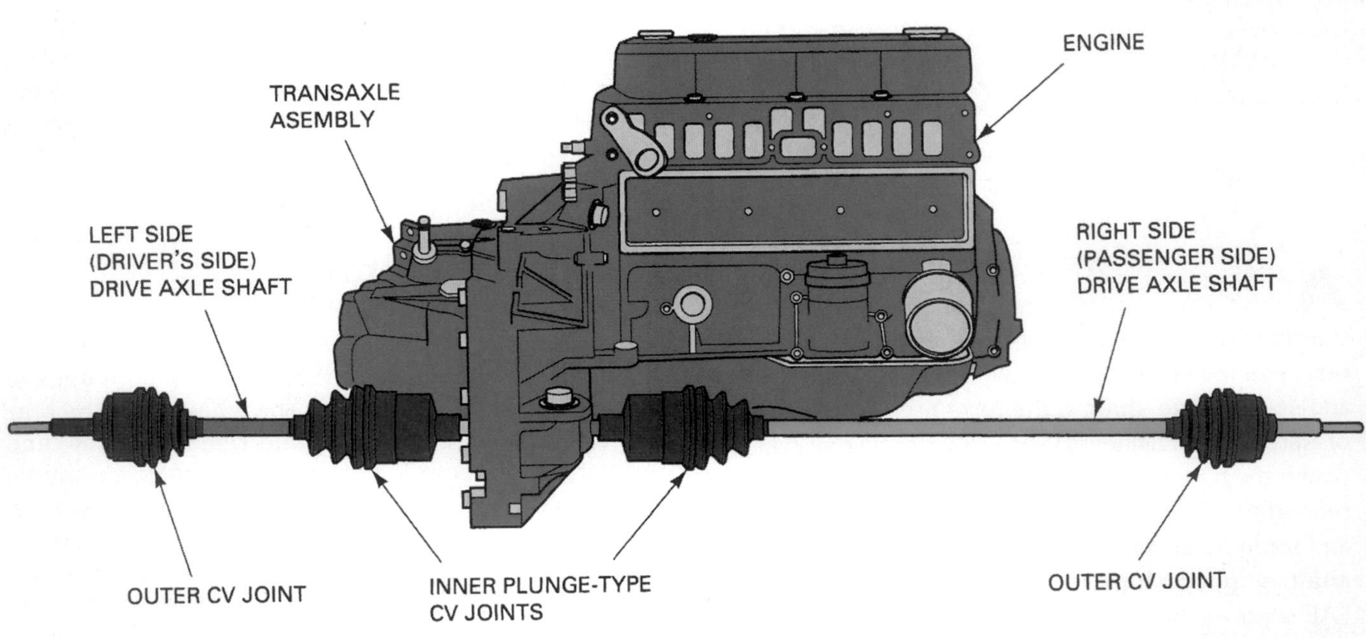

Figure 46–2 Typical front-wheel-drive power train arrangement. The engine is usually mounted transversely (sideways) in the vehicle.

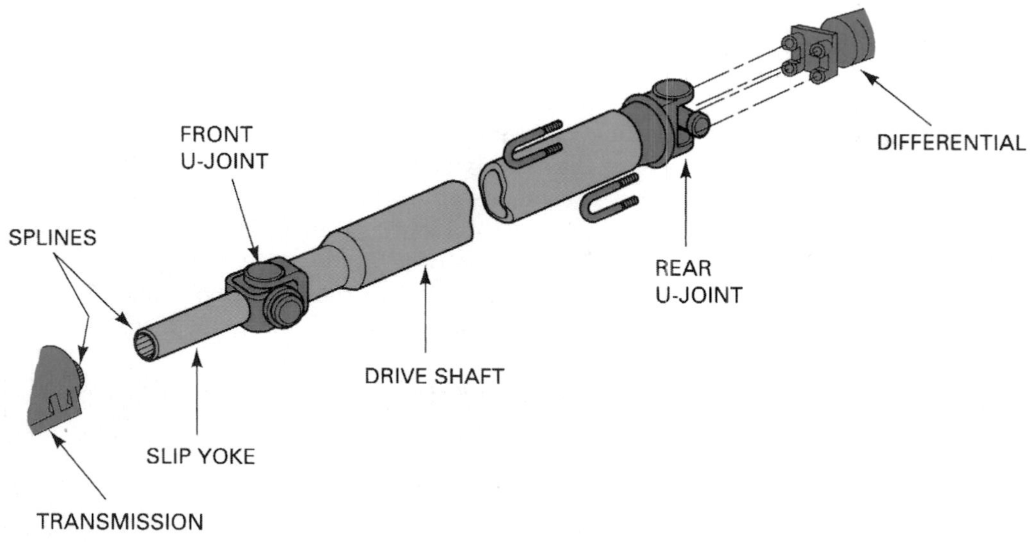

Figure 46–3 Typical drive shaft (also called a propeller shaft). The drive shaft transfers engine torque from the transmission to the differential.

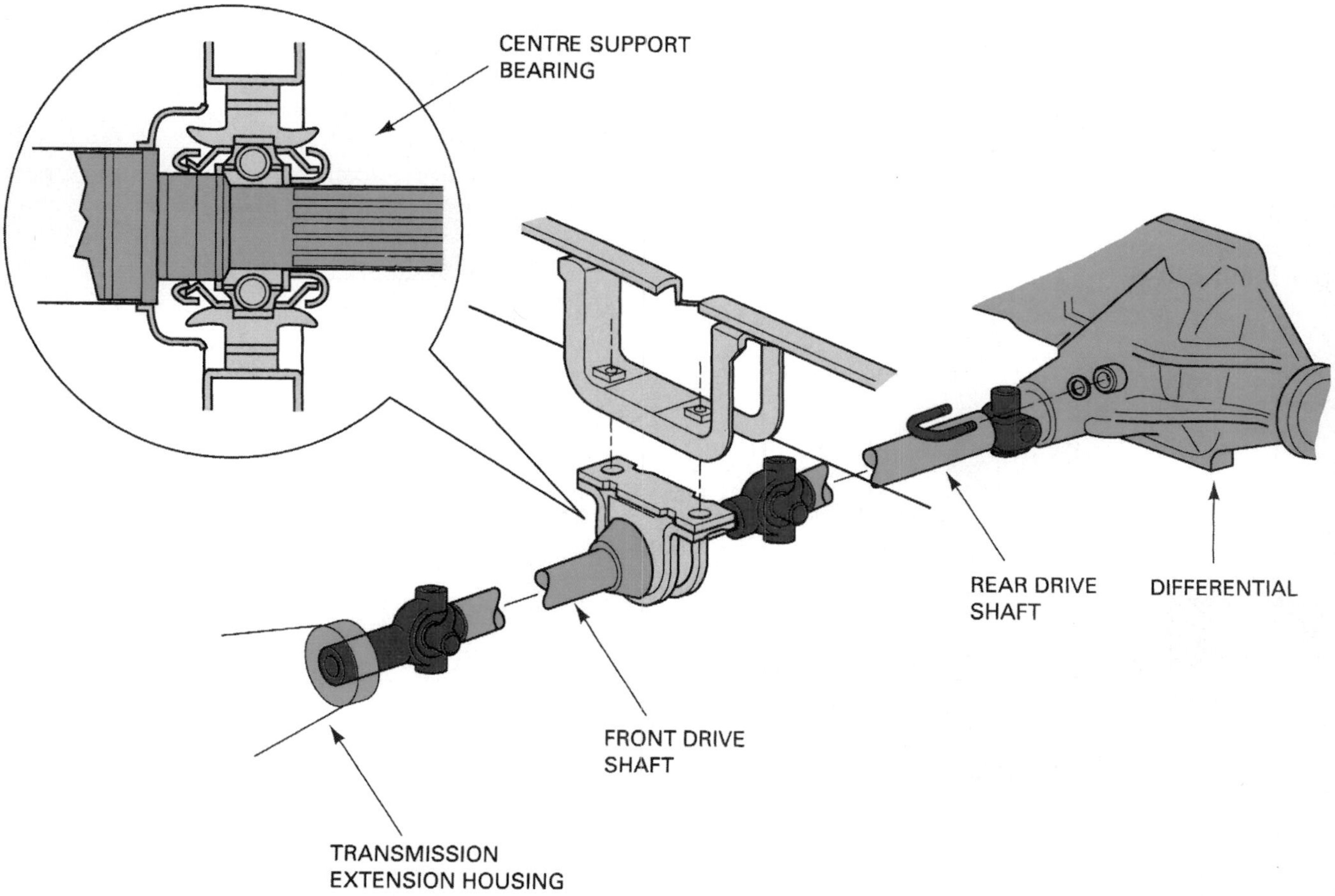

CENTRE SUPPORT
BEARING

REAR DRIVE
SHAFT

DIFFERENTIAL

FRONT DRIVE
SHAFT

TRANSMISSION
EXTENSION HOUSING

Figure 46–4 A centre support bearing is used on many vehicles with long drive shafts.

Figure 46–5 Some drive shafts use rubber between an inner and outer housing to absorb vibrations and shocks to the drive line.

from a sixteenth century Italian mathematician who worked with objects that moved freely in any direction. Torque from the engine is transferred through the U-joint. The engine drives the U-joint at a constant speed, but the output speed of the U-joint changes because of the angle of the joint. The speed changes twice per revolution. *The greater the angle, the greater the change in speed (velocity).* This causes torque losses due to friction, heat, and vibration and results in needle bearing, bearing cap, and trunnion wear. See Figure 46–7. *It is very important that both U-joints are operating at about the same angle to prevent excessive driveline vibration.* See Figure 46–8.

Angle Cancellation and U-Joint Phasing

Design engineers use two techniques to reduce driveline vibration caused by these speed fluctuations. The first involves making sure that changes in speed between the front and rear U-joints match.

On many drivelines the driving and driven yokes must be 90° out-of-phase besides having a matching speed. This allows the rear driving U-joint to slow down as the front driving U-joint speeds up. To check

DIAGNOSTIC STORY

One Vehicle, Two Problems, One Solution

The owner of an older-model Chrysler rear-wheel-drive vehicle complained that the rear was sitting down and that a vibration was felt, only during acceleration. A careful inspection of the suspension system determined that the rear leaf springs had sagged and required replacement. After the rear leaf springs were replaced, the correct ride (suspension) height was restored. Now the technician attempted to verify the vibration complaint. However, now the car did not vibrate during acceleration. This type of vibration during acceleration only is often called **launch shudder.** Could it be that the sagging leaf springs caused a vibration? How?

The answer was that sagging rear springs did cause the rear driveshaft U-joint angle to change, resulting in the vibration during acceleration. Restoring the proper ride height restored the proper drive shaft angles, thus solving two problems at the same time.

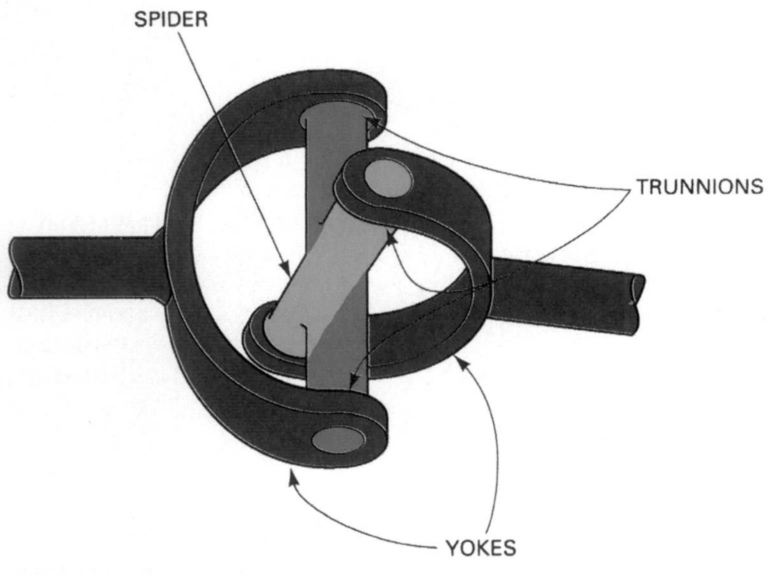

Figure 46–6 A simple universal joint (U-joint).

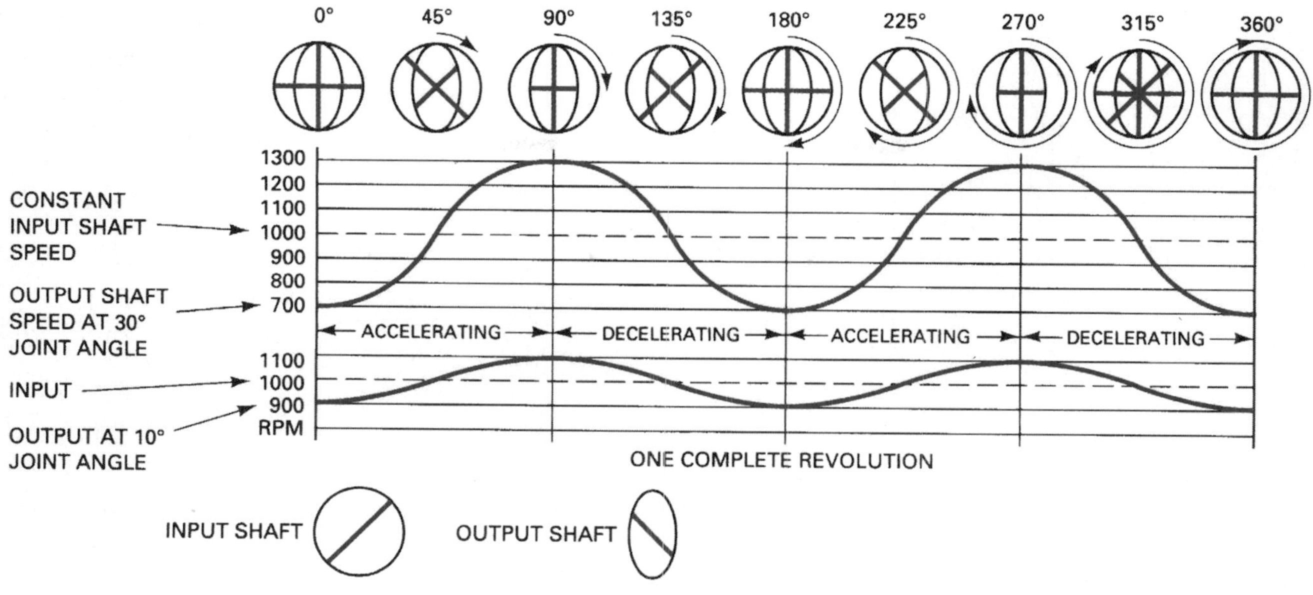

Figure 46–7 Graphic showing how the speed difference on the outset of a typical U-joint varies with the speed and the angle of the U-joint. At the bottom of the chart, the input speed is a constant 1000 rpm, while the output speed varies from 900 rpm to 1100 rpm when the angle difference in the joint is only 10°. At the top part of the chart, the input speed is a constant 1000 rpm, yet the output speed varies from 700 to 1200 rpm when the angle difference in the joint is changed to 30°. (Courtesy of Dana Corporation, Perfect Circle Products)

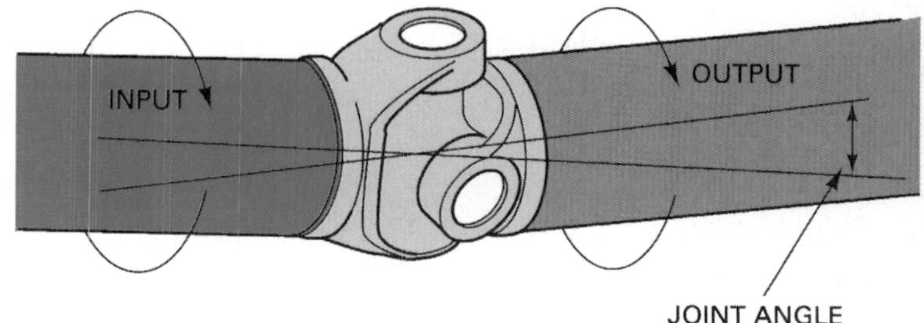

Figure 46–8 The joint angle is the difference between the angles of the joint. (Courtesy of Dana Corporation, Perfect Circle Products)

driveline phasing on a rear-wheel-drive vehicle, place the transmission in neutral and raise the vehicle on a lift. Rotate the rear wheels until the driving yoke attached to the transmission output shaft has its ears in the 12 and 6 o'clock positions. The driving yoke attached to the rear end of the propeller shaft will be in the 3 and 9 o'clock positions, exactly 90 degrees out-of-phase from the other yoke.

Double Cardan Joint

On some vehicles, propeller shafts, and other drive shafts must transfer torque at angles greater than the U-joints can handle. To solve this problem and lessen vibration, engineers developed a **double Cardan joint** with no speed fluctuations, making it a type of constant velocity (CV) joint. Manufacturers use it in drivelines of some rear-wheel-drive vehicles and on the front drive shafts of some four-wheel-drive pickups.

This joint uses two single U-joints joined in the middle with a ball and socket using a coupling or centre yoke. The first front-wheel-drive U-joints were double Cardan. See Figure 46–9. The coupling yoke transfers power from the driving to the driven cross, phasing each 90° apart. The ball and socket, along with a centring pin, makes sure the centrelines of the driving and driven shafts intersect in the coupling yoke's centre. See Figure 46–10. Since the ball and socket split the angles equally between the two yokes, the speed fluctuations created by one shaft cancels the other.

Slip Joint

The rear axle moves closer and farther from the vehicle frame as the rear tires ride over potholes, ruts, and speed bumps. Since the transmission is in a fixed position, this also means that the distance be-

Figure 46–9 The front-wheel-drive double Cardan U-joints used on the 1929 Cord.

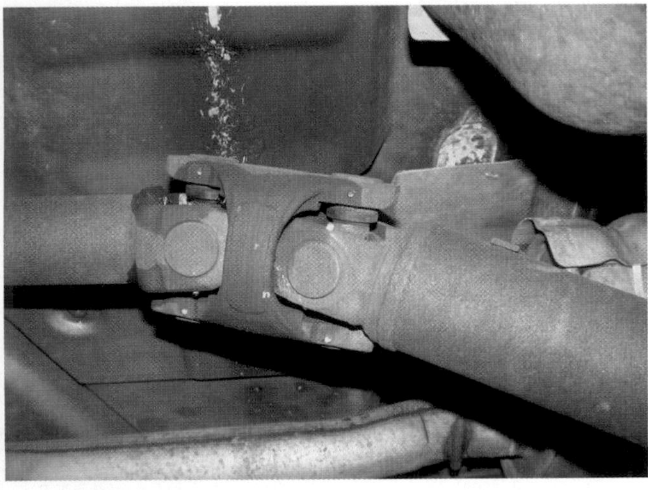

Figure 46–10 A double Cardan U-joint.

tween the axle and the transmission is continually changing. The slip joint allows the driveline to collapse and expand its effective length.

In most applications, the slip joint transfers torque from the transmission output shaft to the front end of the drive shaft. The slip joint, however, may be installed in the centre of the drive shaft, or at the rear between a drive shaft and the drive pinion flange. Regardless of the installation, slip joints are hardened steel tubes splined internally at one end with a yoke attached to the other. Usually, the end with the internal splines fits over the externally splined transmission output shaft. The meshing splines allow torque transfer. When the nose of the rear axle moves up, toward the vehicle frame, it pushes the drive shaft toward the transmission, causing the slip joint to slide

Figure 46–11 A drive pinion flange (yoke) with the drive shaft removed.

up the external splines of the transmission output shaft into the extension housing.

Inside the extension housing of the transmission, a bushing supports the machined outer circumference of the slip joint tube. An oil seal attached between the yoke and the extension housing prevents lubricant from leaking past the yoke. At the rear of the driveline, the rear axle pinion flange (yoke) attached to the drive pinion shaft drives the final drive pinion gear. Internal splines on the yoke mesh with the external splines of the drive pinion shaft. See Figure 46–11.

Driveline Types

Drivelines found in late-model vehicles may be grouped into two types: torque tube and Hotchkiss. Functionally, they differ in how they control rear axle twist and what paths they allow forces applied to the wheels to travel to the chassis. This twisting action is also called rear-end torque. As torque is applied to the drive shaft, the nose of the rear axle housing rises. When the drive pinion gear first starts moving, it must overcome the resistance of the ring gear. This force presses against the drive pinion bearings in a direction opposite to wheel rotation. Since the pinion is moving clockwise as seen from the front of the vehicle, the rear axle housing nose rises.

At the same time, the clockwise rotation of the drive pinion gear uses the ring gear as leverage, turning the axle housing around the driveline axis. Since the drive pinion gear turns into the ring gear, toward the driver's left, the right side of the rear axle rises. Manufacturers seek to minimize this twisting motion, which changes the angle and length of the driveline, to prevent drive shaft, differential, and axle failure.

Figure 46–12 Many motor sports sanctioning groups require that a drive shaft hoop be installed on all race vehicles.

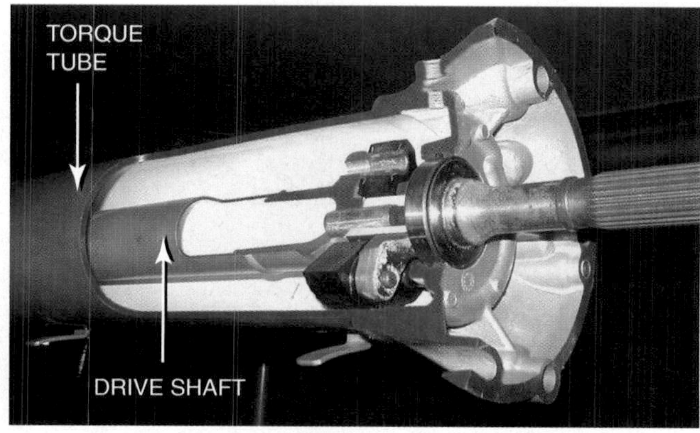

Figure 46–13 A torque tube is used on the 1997 and newer Chevrolet Corvette. The outer tube (torque tube) is attached to the engine at the front and the transmission in the rear. The drive shaft is smaller in diameter than most drive shafts because all of the torque multiplication of the torque converter and the transmission is performed at the rear of the vehicle. Only the actual torque of the engine is applied to the drive shaft.

SAFETY TIP 

Drive Shaft Hoop

Many motor sport sanctioning organizations require the use of a drive shaft hoop. See Figure 46–12. This hoop (loop) is used to retain the drive shaft and keep it from dropping from underneath the vehicle in the event of U-joint failure.

Always follow the safety regulations.

Torque tube drivelines, commonly used on vehicles with a rear-mounted transmission, such as the 1997 and newer Chevrolet Corvette, virtually eliminate the effects of rear-end torque on the rear axle. They use drive shafts of solid steel 25 to 38 mm (1 to 1.5 in.) in diameter that turn inside a steel or aluminum tube bolted to the rear-mounted transmission, transaxle, or rear axle.

These drivelines control rear-end torque by using the hollow steel tube as a brace against the force exerted against the drive pinion bearing when the vehicle drive train is under load. This tube allows the drive shaft to maintain alignment with the drive pinion at all times. See Figure 46–13.

Most rear-wheel-drive vehicles use a **Hotchkiss,** or **open,** driveline. Unlike the torque tube driveline, the Hotchkiss drive shaft is not aligned with the drive pinion shaft. The Hotchkiss driveline *minimizes* the effects of rear-end torque on the rear axle by transferring most of the forces exerted against the drive pinion bearing to the vehicle's rear suspension. While normal Hotchkiss drivelines use leaf springs, **modified Hotchkiss drivelines** use rear axle control arms supported by coil springs. The suspension components in both types allow the rear axle to twist.

The up-and-down movement of the wheel in all Hotchkiss drivelines exerts a pushing force on the axle that travels to the wheel bearings and axle housing. In a normal Hotchkiss driveline, the force then travels through the leaf springs to the chassis or unibody. In a modified Hotchkiss driveline, however, the force then travels through the control arms to the chassis or unibody.

Some vehicles use **split Hotchkiss drivelines** that have two drive shafts. Most are larger trucks and long-bed pickups. If only one drive shaft were to be used in these vehicles, it would arc in the middle while spinning, like a jump rope. Splitting the driveline in these vehicles corrects this condition by supporting the drive shaft close to the centre, allowing the drive shaft to operate at the proper angles.

Usually, the inner race of the support bearing is pressed or bolted onto the end of the first drive shaft. Manufacturers usually insert the outer race of the bearing into a large rubber ring supported by a bracket attached to the vehicle underbody. The rubber ring dampens driveline vibrations. In most applications, the manufacturer lubricates and seals the centre bearing prior to installation.

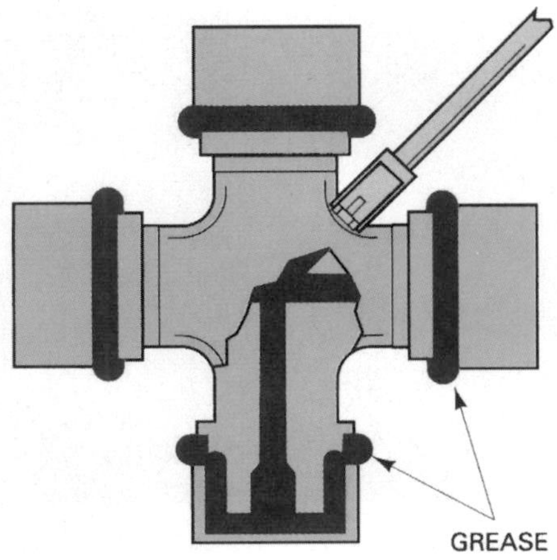

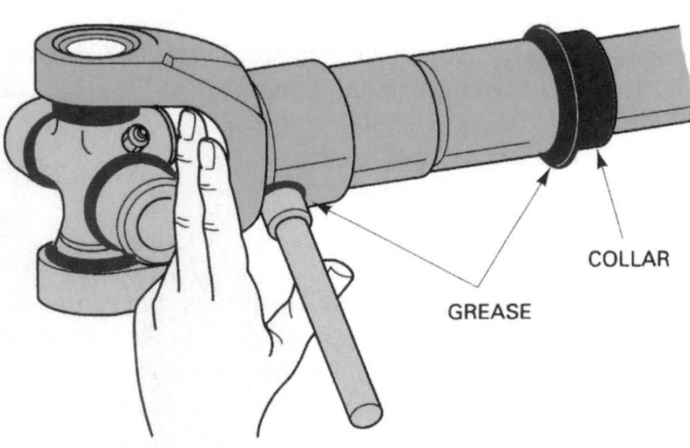

Figure 46–14 All U-joints and spline collars equipped with a grease fitting should be greased four times a year as part of a regular lubrication service. (Courtesy of Dana Corporation, Perfect Circle Products)

DRIVE SHAFT AND U-JOINT INSPECTION

The drive shaft should be inspected for the following:

1. Any dents or creases caused by incorrect hoisting of the vehicle or by road debris.

CAUTION: A dented or creased drive shaft can collapse, especially when the vehicle is under load. This collapse of the drive shaft can cause severe damage to the vehicle and may cause an accident.

2. Undercoating, grease, or dirt build-up on the drive shaft can cause a vibration. Undercoating should be removed using a suitable solvent and a shop cloth. Always dispose of used shop cloths properly.

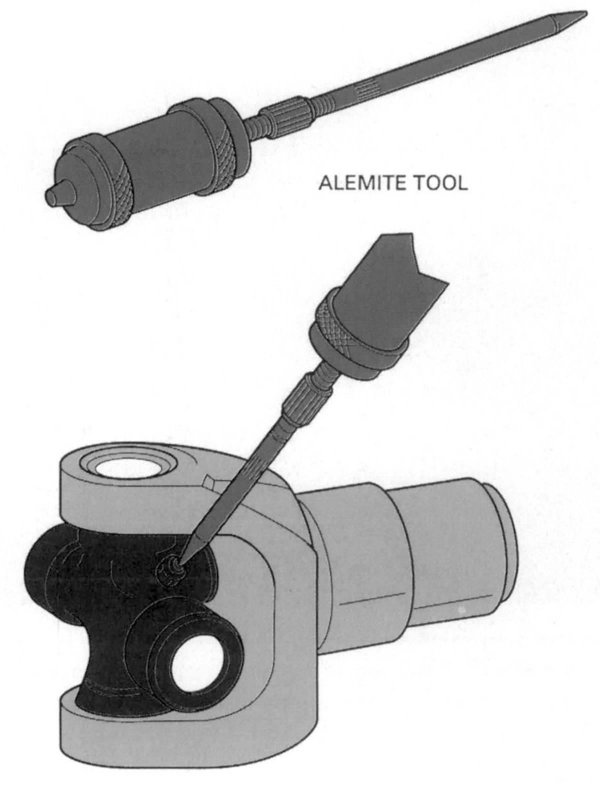

Figure 46–15 Many U-joints require a special grease gun tool to reach the grease fittings. (Courtesy of Dana Corporation, Perfect Circle Products)

The U-joints should be inspected every time the vehicle chassis is lubricated or four times a year. Most original equipment (OE) U-joints are permanently lubricated and have no provision for greasing. If there is a grease fitting, the U-joint should be lubricated by applying grease with a grease gun. See Figures 46–14 and 46–15.

Beside periodic lubrication, the drive shaft should be grabbed and moved to see if there is any movement of the U-joints. If *any* movement is noticed when the drive shaft is moved, the U-joint is worn and must be replaced.

NOTE: U-joints are not serviceable items and cannot be repaired. If worn or defective, they must be replaced.

U-joints can be defective and still not show noticeable free movement. *A proper U-joint inspection can only be performed by removing the drive shaft from the vehicle.* Before removing the drive shaft, always mark the position of all mating parts to ensure proper reassembly. White correction fluid, also known as White Out or Liquid Paper, is an easy and fast-drying marking material. See Figure 46–16. To remove the drive shaft from a rear-wheel-drive vehicle, first remove the four fasteners at the rear

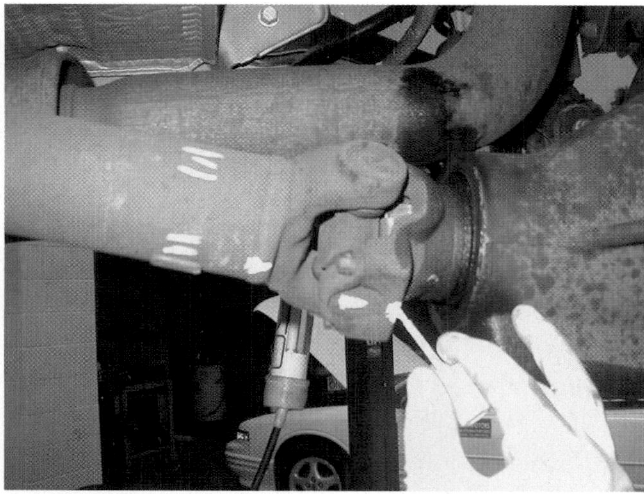

Figure 46–16 Always mark the original location of U-joints before disassembly.

U-joint at the differential. See Figure 46–17. Push the drive shaft forward toward the transmission and then down and toward the rear of the vehicle. The drive shaft should slip out of the transmission spline and can be removed from underneath the vehicle.

> **HINT:** With the drive shaft removed, transmission lubricant can leak out of the rear extension housing. To prevent a mess, use an old spline the same size as the one being removed or place a plastic bag over the extension housing to hold any escaping lubricant. A rubber band can be used to hold the bag onto the extension housing.

To inspect U-joints, move each joint through its full travel, making sure it can move (articulate) freely and equally in all directions. See Figure 46–18.

DIAGNOSTIC STORY

The Squeaking Pickup Truck

The owner of a pickup truck complained that a squeaking noise occurred while driving in reverse. The "eeeee-eeeee-eeee" sound increased in speed as the truck increased in speed, yet the noise did not occur when driving forward.

Because there was no apparent looseness in the U-joints, the service technician at first thought that the problem was either inside the transmission or the rear end. When the drive shaft was removed to further investigate the problem, it became obvious where the noise was coming from. The U-joint needle bearing had worn the cross shaft bearing surface of the U-joint. The noise occurred only in reverse because the wear had occurred in the forward direction and, therefore, only when the torque was applied in the opposite direction did the needle bearing become bound up and start to make noise. A replacement U-joint solved the squeaking noise in reverse.

U-JOINT REPLACEMENT

All movement in a U-joint should occur between the trunnions and the needle bearings in the end caps. The end caps are press-fitted to the yokes, which are welded to the drive shaft. Three types of retainers are used to keep the bearing caps on the U-joints: the outside snap ring, the inside retaining ring, or injected synthetic (usually nylon).

U-joints that use synthetic retainers must be separated using a press and a special tool that presses on both sides of the joint in order to shear the

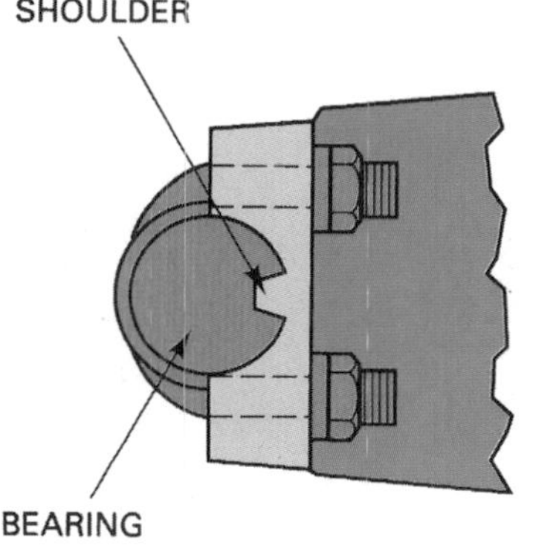

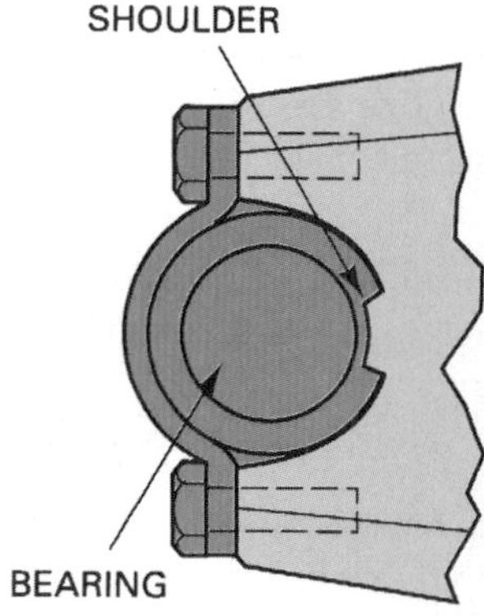

Figure 46–17 Two methods of attaching a U-joint to a drive shaft yoke. (Courtesy of Dana Corporation, Perfect Circle Products)

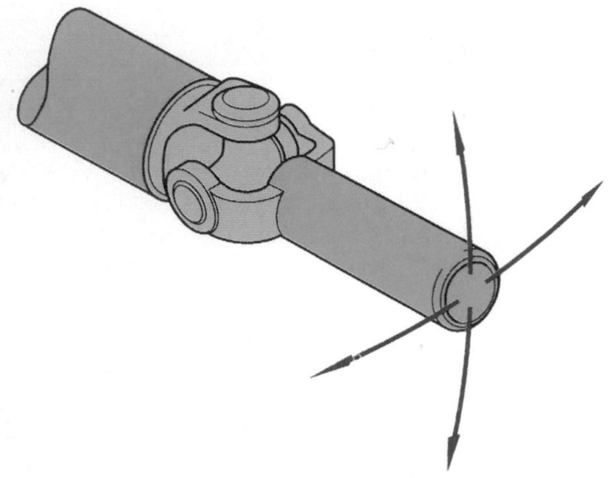

Figure 46–18 The best way to check any U-joint is to remove the drive shaft from the vehicle and move each joint in all directions. A good U-joint should move freely without binding. (Courtesy of Dana Corporation, Perfect Circle Products)

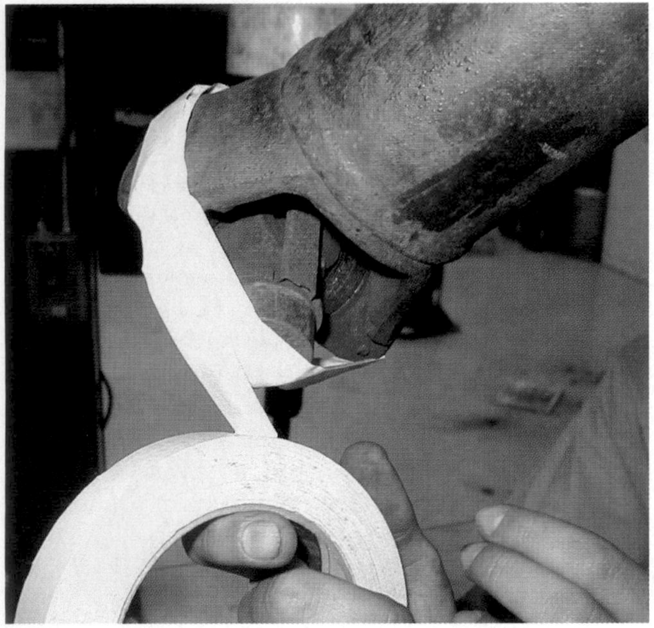

Figure 46–19 Taping the U-joint to prevent the caps from coming off.

TECH TIP

Use Tape to Be Safe

When removing a drive shaft, use tape to prevent the rear U-joint caps from falling off. If the caps fall off the U-joint, all of the needle bearings will fall out and scatter all over the floor. See Figure 46–19.

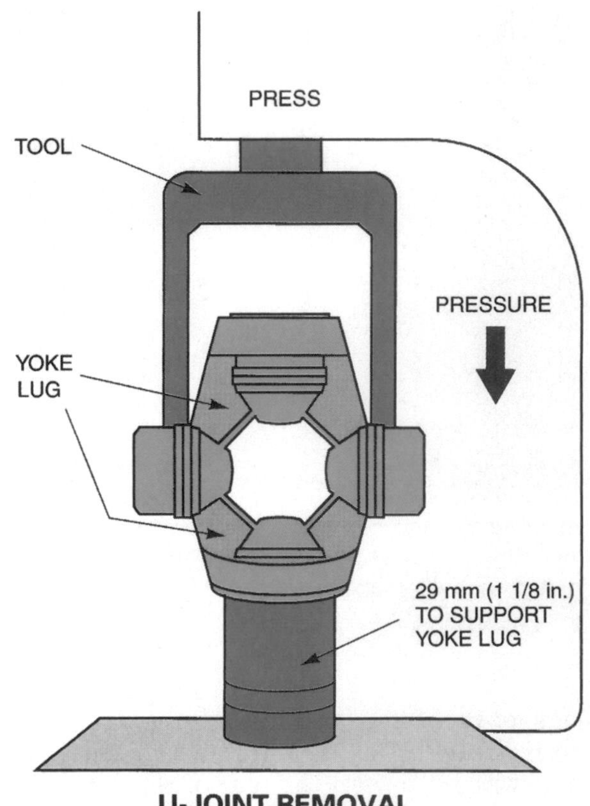

Figure 46–20 A special tool being used to press apart a U-joint that is retained by injected plastic. Heat from a propane torch may be necessary to soften the plastic to avoid exerting too much force on the U-joint.

plastic retainer, as shown in Figure 46–20. Replacement U-joints use spring clips instead of injected plastic. Remove the old U-joint from the yoke and replace it with a new U-joint.

HINT: If a U-joint is slightly stiff after being installed, strike the U-joint with a brass punch and a light hammer. This often frees a stiff joint and is called "relieving the joint." The shock aligns the needle bearings in the end caps.

MEASURING DRIVE SHAFT ANGLES

To measure U-joint and drive shaft angles, the vehicle must be hoisted using an axle contact or drive-on-type lift so as to maintain the same drive shaft angles as the vehicle has while being driven. The working angles of the two U-joints on a drive shaft should be within 0.5° of each other in order to cancel out speed changes. See Figure 46–21. To measure the working angle of a U-joint, follow these steps:

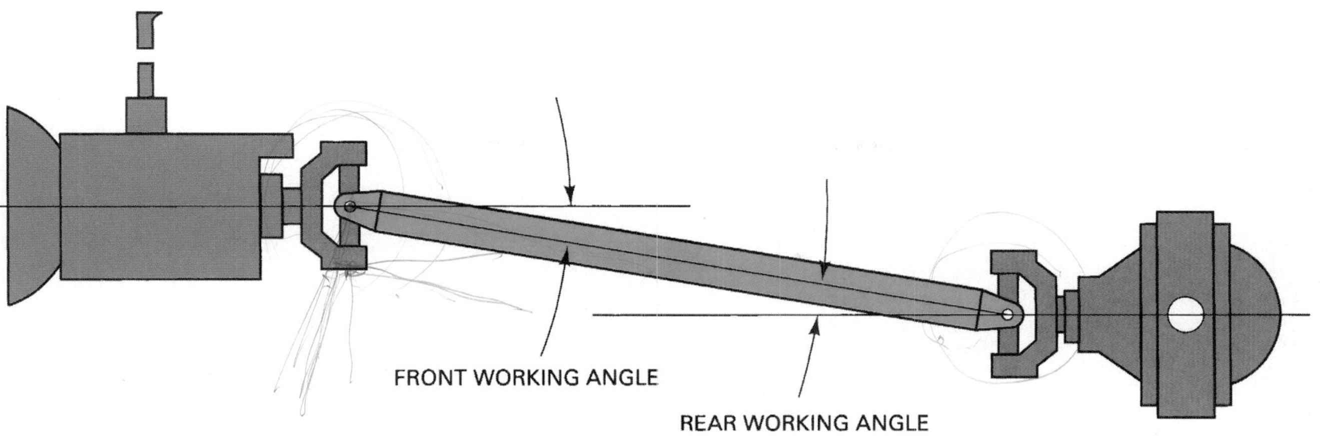

Figure 46–21 Front and rear U-joint angles should be within 0.5° of each other. (Courtesy of General Motors)

Figure 46–22 The inclinometer reads 19.5° at this rear U-joint.

Step 1. Place an **inclinometer** (a tool used to measure angles) on the rear U-joint bearing cap. Level the bubble and read the angle. See Figure 46–22. The reading is 19.5°.

Step 2. Rotate the drive shaft 90° and read the angle of the rear yoke. For example, this reading is 17°.

Step 3. Subtract the smaller reading from the larger reading to obtain the working angle of the joint. In this example it is 2.5° (19.5° − 17° = 2.5°).

Repeat the same procedure for the front U-joint. The front and rear working angles should be within 0.5° of each other. If the two working angles are not within 0.5°, shims can be added to bring the two

TECH TIP 

Spline Bind Cure

Drive line clunk often occurs in rear-wheel-drive vehicles when shifting between drive and reverse or when accelerating from a stop. Often the cause of this noise is excessive clearance between the teeth of the ring and pinion in the differential. Another cause is called *spline bind* and occurs when the changing rear pinion angle creates a binding in the spline as the rear springs change in height. For example, when a pickup truck stops, the weight transfers toward the front and unloads the rear springs. The front of the differential noses downward and forward as the rear springs unload. When the driver accelerates forward, the rear of the truck squats downward causing the drive shaft to be pulled rearward when the front of the differential rotates upward. This movement on the spline often causes the spline to bind and make a loud clunk when the bind is finally released.

NOTE: This spline bind is not to be confused with launch shudder, which is the vibration felt during acceleration when the front and rear drive shaft angles are not equal. Launch shudder is usually caused by weak rear springs or an overloaded vehicle. See the Diagnostic Story, "One Vehicle, Two Problems, One Solution."

The method recommended by vehicle manufacturers to solve this noise is to follow these steps:

1. Remove the drive shaft.
2. Clean the splines on both the drive shaft yoke and the transmission output shaft.
3. Remove any burrs on the splines with a small metal file (remove all filings).
4. Apply a high-temperature grease to the spline teeth of the yoke. Apply grease to each spline, but do not fill the splines. Synthetic chassis grease is preferred because of its high temperature resistance properties.
5. Reinstall the drive shaft.

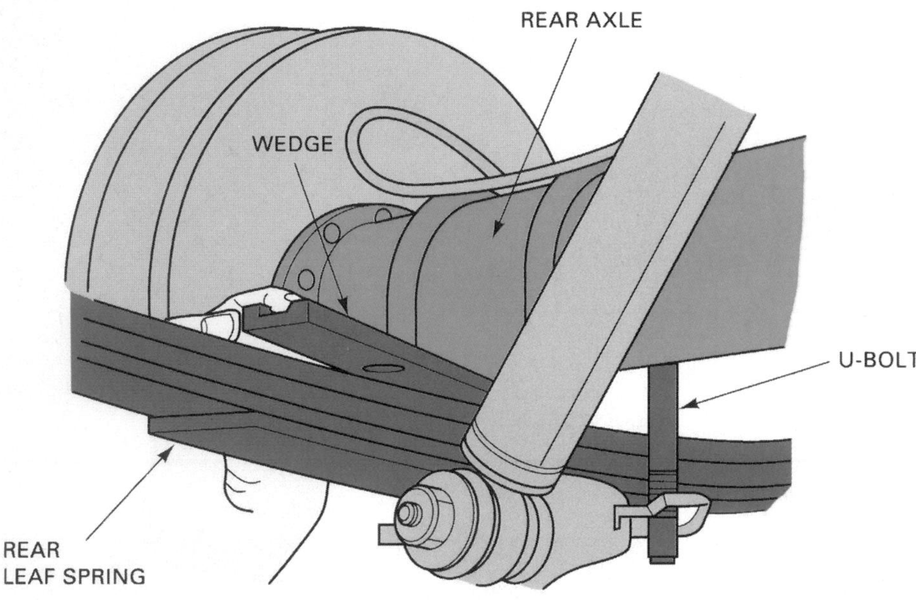

Figure 46–23 Placing a tapered metal wedge between the rear leaf spring and the rear axle pedestal to correct rear U-joint working angles.

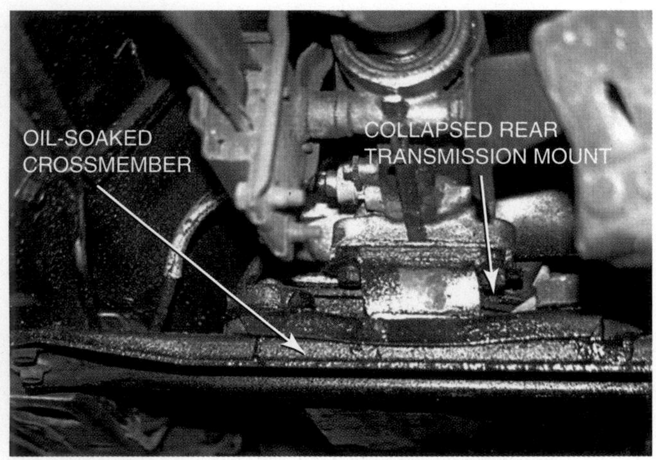

Figure 46–24 A transmission oil pan gasket leak allowed automatic transmission fluid (ATF) to saturate the rear transmission mount rubber, causing it to collapse. After replacing the defective mount, proper drive shaft angles were restored and the drive line vibration was corrected.

angles closer together. The angle of the rear joint is changed by installing a tapered shim between the leaf spring and the axle, as shown in Figure 46–23. The angle of the front joint is changed by adding or removing shims from the mount under the transmission or by replacing the rear transmission mount if collapsed, as shown in Figure 46–24.

CONSTANT VELOCITY JOINTS

Regular U-joints are usually designed to work at up to 12° of angularity. If two Cardan style U-joints are joined together, the angle at which this double Cardan joint can function is about 18° to 20°. Constant velocity joints (commonly called CV joints) are designed to rotate without changing speed.

NOTE: Many four-wheel-drive light trucks use standard Cardan style U-joints in the front drive axles. If the front wheels are turned sharply and then accelerated, the entire truck often shakes due to the pulsations created by the speed variations through the U-joints. This vibration is normal and cannot be corrected. It is characteristic of this type of design and is usually not noticeable in normal driving.

The first constant velocity joint was designed by Alfred H. Rzeppa (pronounced *shep'pa*) in the mid-1920s. The **Rzeppa joint** transfers power through six round balls that are held in position midway between the two shafts. This design resulted in the angle between the shafts being equally split regardless of the degree of the angle. See Figure 46–25. Because the angle is always split equally, power is transferred equally without the change in speed (velocity) that occurs in Cardan U-joints. This Rzeppa joint results in a constant velocity between driving and driven shafts and can also function at greater angles, up to 40°, than simple U-joints.

NOTE: CV joints are also called *LÖBRO* joints after the brand name of an original equipment manufacturer.

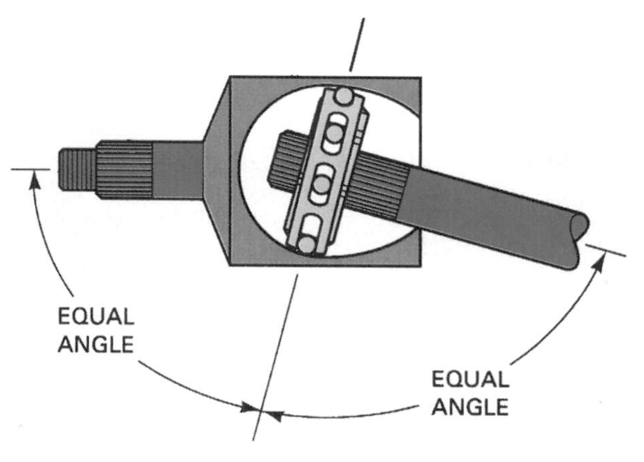

Figure 46–25 A constant velocity (CV) joint can operate at high angles without a change in velocity (speed) because the joint design results in equal angles between input and output.

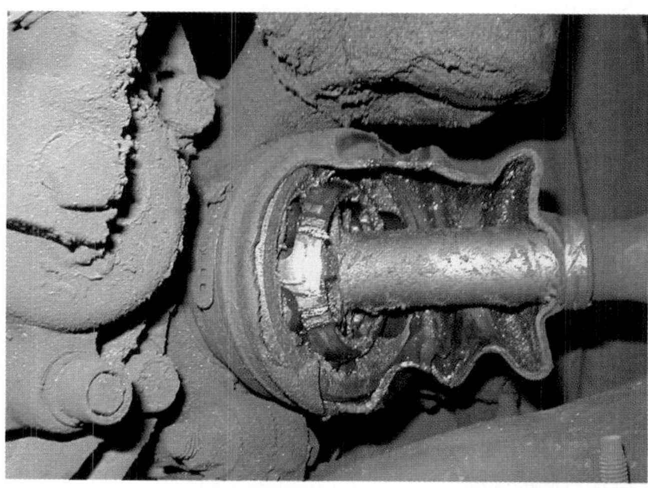

Figure 46–27 The protective CV joint boot has been torn away on this vehicle and all of the grease has been thrown outward onto the brake and suspension parts. The driver of this vehicle noticed a "clicking" noise, especially when turning.

Outer CV Joints

The Rzeppa-type CV joint is most commonly used as an outer joint on most front-wheel-drive vehicles. See Figure 46–26. The outer joint must allow turning up to 40° while the front wheels move up and down and still be able to transmit engine power to drive the front wheels. Outer CV joints are called "fixed." The outer joints are also attached to the front wheels. They are more likely to suffer from road hazards that often can cut through the protective outer flexible boot. See Figure 46–27. Once this boot has been split open, the special high quality grease is thrown out and contaminants such as dirt and water can enter.

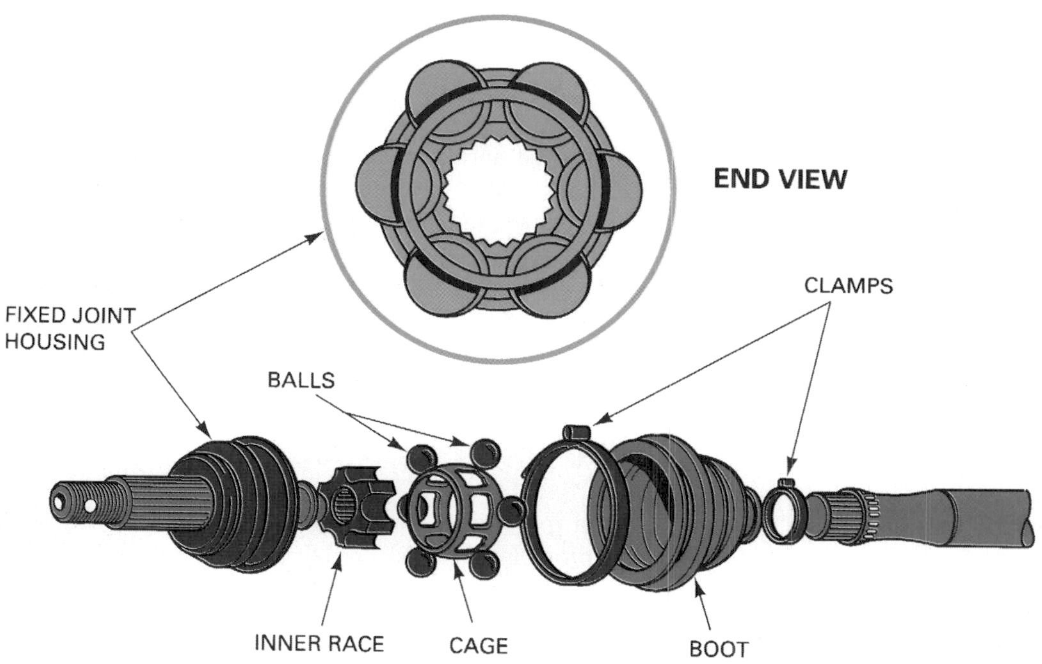

Figure 46–26 A Rzeppa fixed joint. This type of CV joint is commonly used at the wheel side of the drive axle shaft. It can operate at high angles to compensate for suspension travel and steering angle changes. (Courtesy of Dana Corporation, Perfect Circle Products)

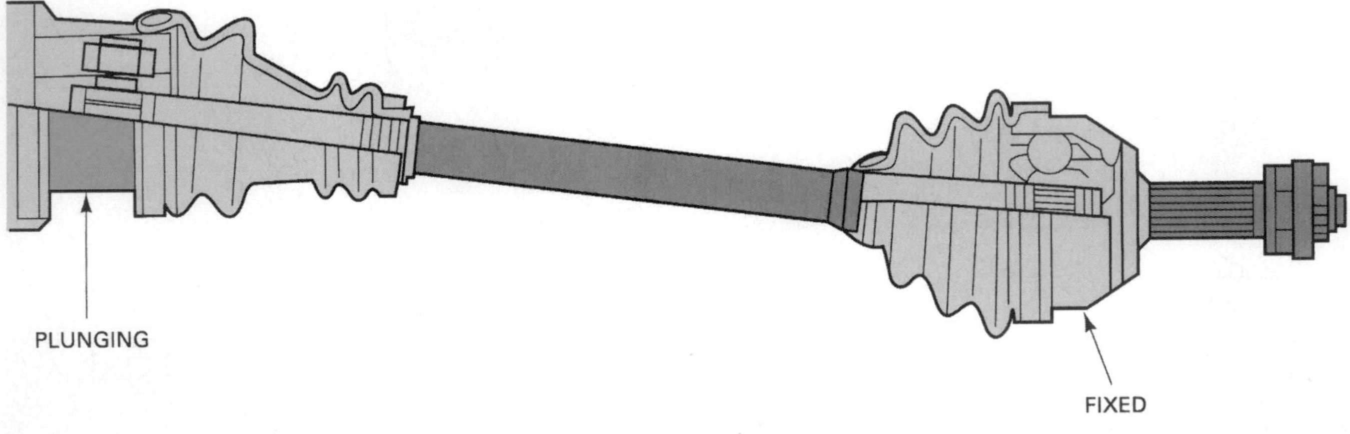

Figure 46–28 The fixed outer joint is required to move in all directions because the wheels must turn for steering as well as move up and down during suspension movement. The inner joint has to be able not only to move up and down, but also to plunge in and out as the suspension moves up and down. (Courtesy of Dana Corporation, Perfect Circle Products)

Inner CV Joints

Inner CV joints attach the output of the transaxle to the drive axle shaft. Inner CV joints are therefore inboard, or toward the centre of the vehicle. See Figure 46–28. Inner CV joints have to be able to allow the drive axle shaft to move up and down and change length as required during vehicle suspension travel movements. Unequal-length drive axle shafts (also called **half shafts**) result in unequal drive axle shaft angles to the front drive wheels. See Figure 46–29.

This unequal angle often results in a pull on the steering wheel during acceleration. This pulling to one side during acceleration, which is due to unequal engine torque being applied to the front drive wheels, is called **torque steer.** To help reduce the effect of torque steer, some vehicles are manufactured with an intermediate shaft that results in equal drive axle shaft angles. Both designs use fixed outer CV joints with plunge-type inner joints. See Figures 46–30 through 46–32 for examples of each type. CV joints are also used in rear-wheel-drive vehicles and in many four-wheel-drive vehicles.

> **NOTE:** Some aftermarket companies offer a split-style replacement CV joint boot. Being split means that the boot can be replaced without having to remove the drive axle shaft. Vehicle manufacturers usually do *not* recommend this type of replacement boot because the joint cannot be disassembled and properly cleaned with the drive axle still in the vehicle.

The pliable boot surrounding the CV joint must be able to remain flexible under all weather conditions and still be strong enough to avoid being punctured by road debris. There are four basic types of boot materials used over CV joints, including **natural rubber** (black), **silicone rubber** (usually grey), **hard thermoplastic** (black), and **urethane** (often blue). See Figures 46–33 and 46–34.

DIAGNOSTIC STORY

The Vibrating Buick

The owner of a front-wheel-drive Buick complained that it vibrated during acceleration only. The vehicle would also pull toward one side during acceleration. An inspection discovered a worn (cracked) engine mount. After replacing the mount, the CV joint angles were restored and both the vibration and the pulling to one side during acceleration were solved. See Figure 46–35.

CV JOINT DIAGNOSIS

When a CV joint wears or fails, the most common symptom is noise while driving. An outer, fixed CV joint will most likely be heard when turning sharply and accelerating at the same time. This noise is usually a clicking sound. Although inner joint failure is less common, a defective inner CV joint often creates a loud clunk noise while accelerating from rest. To help verify a defective joint, drive the vehicle in reverse while turning and accelerating. This almost always will reveal a defective outer joint.

UNEQUAL LENGTH DRIVESHAFT

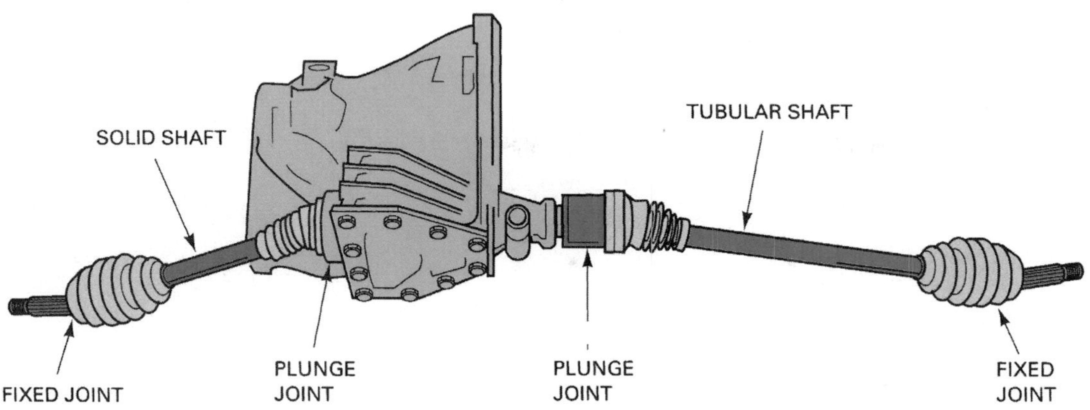

EQUAL LENGTH DRIVESHAFT

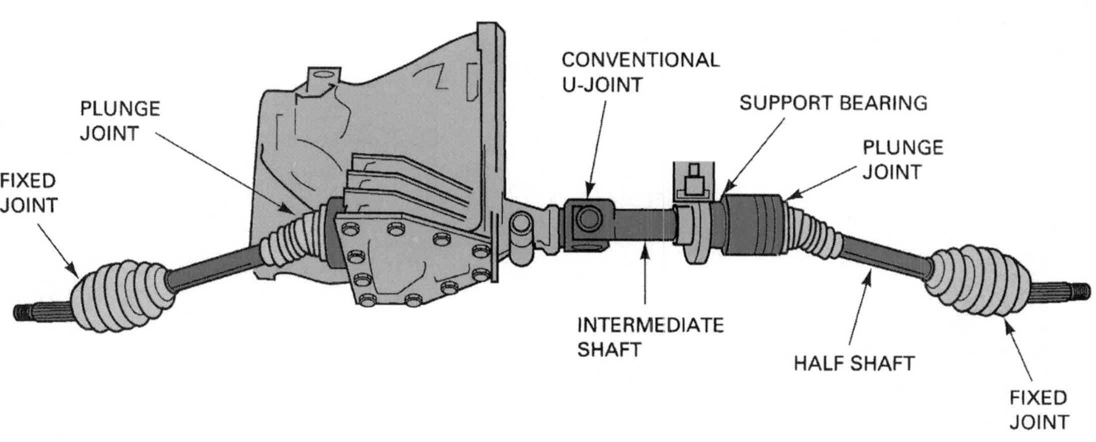

Figure 46–29 Unequal length drive shafts result in unequal drive axle shaft angles to the front drive wheels. This unequal angle side-to-side often affects the steering of the vehicle during acceleration, called *torque steer.* By using an intermediate shaft, both drive axles are the same angle and the torque steer effect is reduced. (Courtesy of Dana Corporation, Perfect Circle Products)

Frequently Asked Question ???

What Is That Weight for on the Drive Axle Shaft?

Some drive axle shafts are equipped with what looks like a balance weight (see Figure 46–36). It is actually a dampener weight used to dampen out certain drive line vibrations. The weight is not used on all vehicles and may or may not appear on the same vehicle depending on engine, transmission, and other options. The service technician should always try to replace a defective or worn drive axle shaft with the exact replacement, so when replacing an entire drive axle shaft, the technician should always follow the manufacturers' instructions regarding either transferring or not transferring the weight to the new shaft.

CV JOINT SERVICE

The hub nut must be removed whenever servicing a CV joint or shaft assembly on a front-wheel-drive vehicle. Since these nuts are usually torqued to almost 250 N·m (185 lb-ft), keep the vehicle on the ground until the hub nut is loosened (see Figure 46–37, p. 1113) and then follow these steps:

Step 1. Remove the front wheel and hub nut.

NOTE: Most manufacturers warn against using an air impact wrench to remove the hub nut. The impacting force can damage the hub bearing.

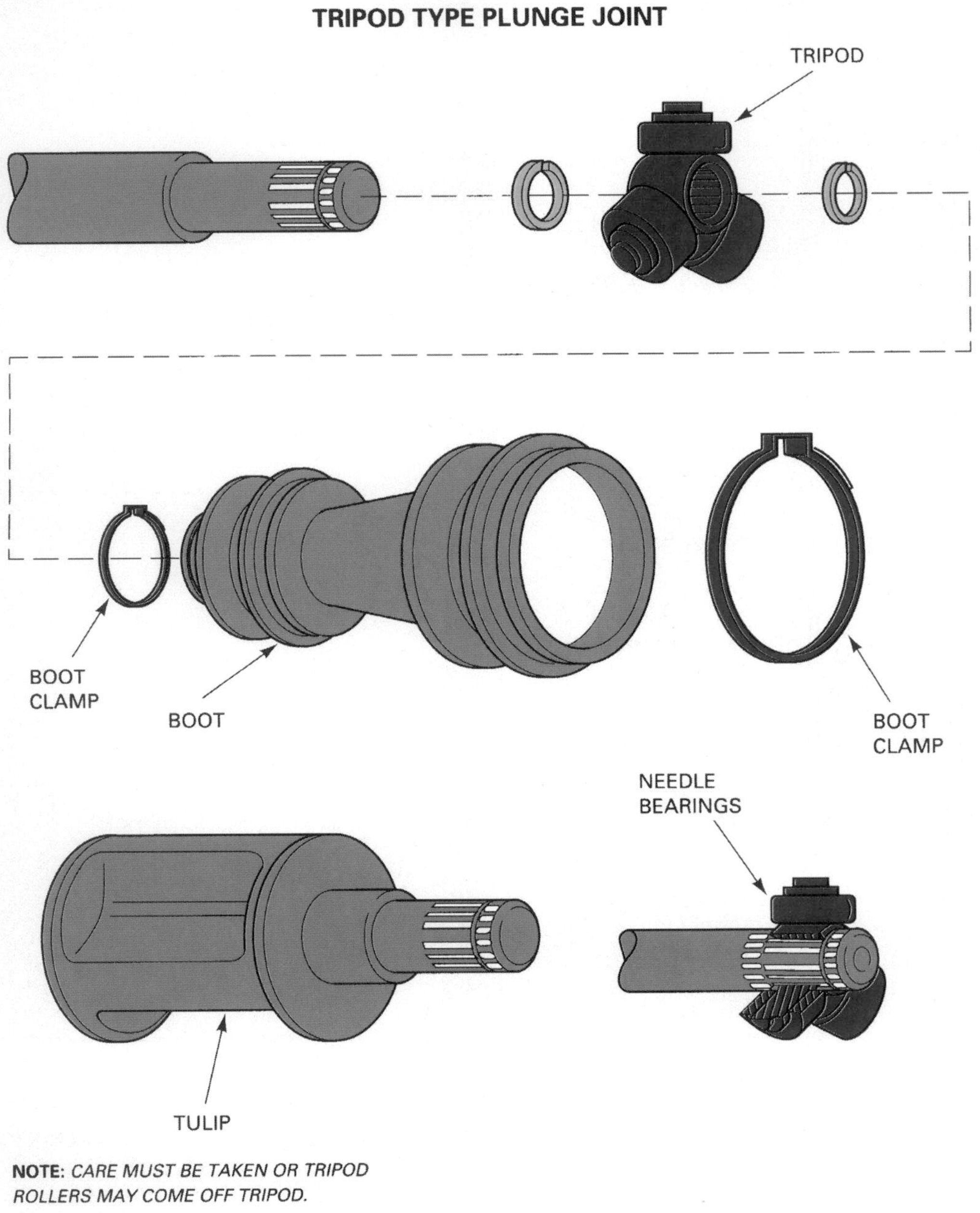

TRIPOD TYPE PLUNGE JOINT
TRIPOD
BOOT CLAMP
BOOT
BOOT CLAMP
NEEDLE BEARINGS
TULIP
NOTE: CARE MUST BE TAKEN OR TRIPOD ROLLERS MAY COME OFF TRIPOD.

Figure 46–30 A tripod joint is also called a *tri-pot, tripode,* or *tulip* design. (Courtesy of Dana Corporation, Perfect Circle Products)

CROSS GROOVE PLUNGE JOINT
PLUNGE JOINT OUTER RACE
BALLS
CAGE
INNER RACE

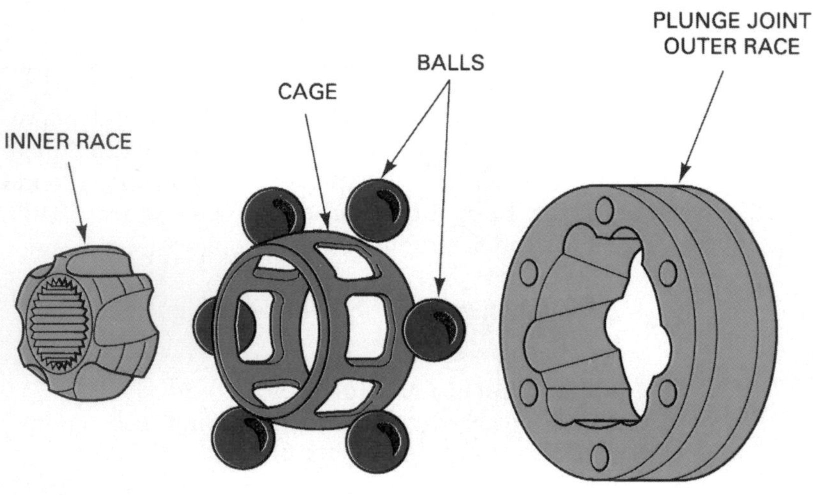

Figure 46–31 A cross-groove plunge joint is used on many German front-wheel-drive vehicles and as both inner and outer joints on the rear of vehicles with an independent-type rear suspension. (Courtesy of Dana Corporation, Perfect Circle Products)

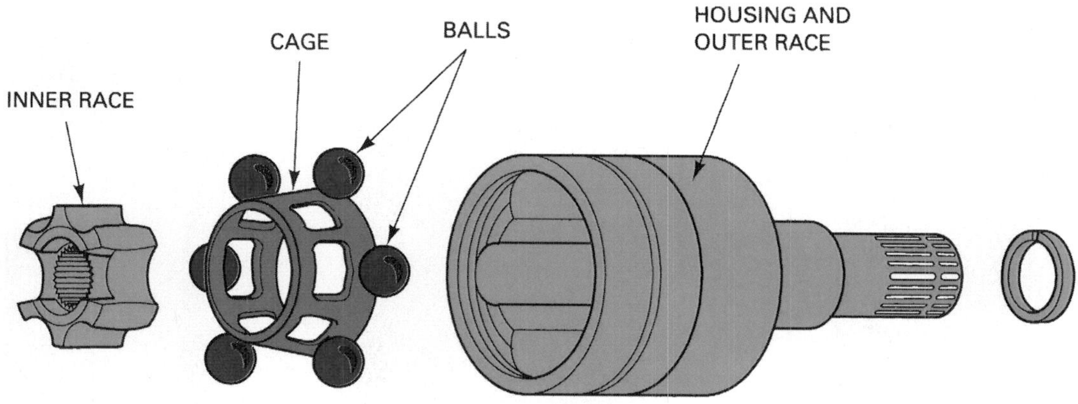

Figure 46–32 Double offset ball-type plunge joint. (Courtesy of Dana Corporation, Perfect Circle Products)

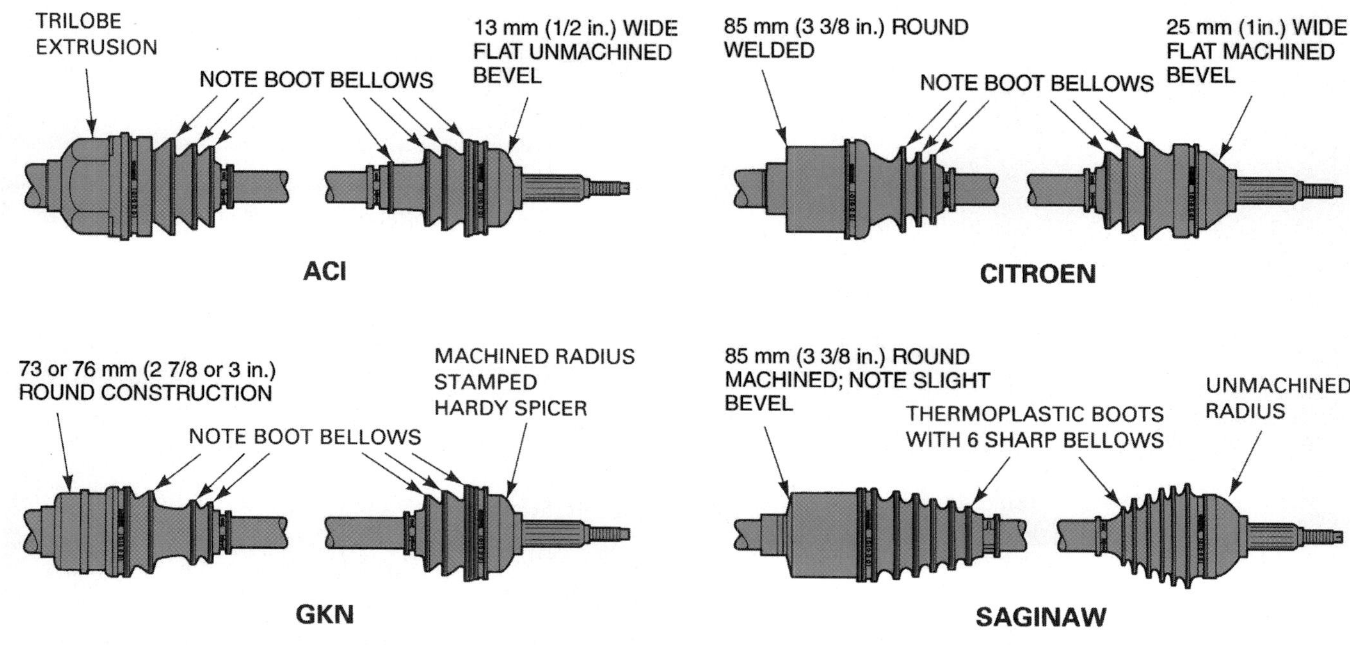

Figure 46–33 Getting the correct boot kit or parts from the parts store is more difficult on many Chrysler front-wheel-drive vehicles because Chrysler has used four different manufacturers for their axle shaft assemblies. (Courtesy of Dana Corporation, Perfect Circle Products)

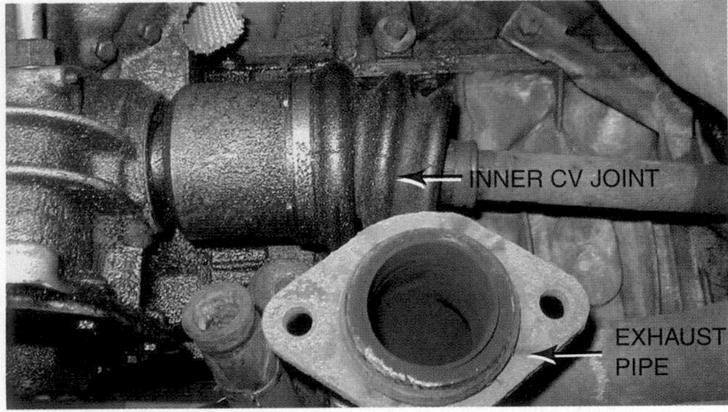

Figure 46–34 Notice how close the exhaust system is to this inner CV joint. It is important to always use the factory recommended replacement boots and grease to be able to survive under this intense heat.

(a)

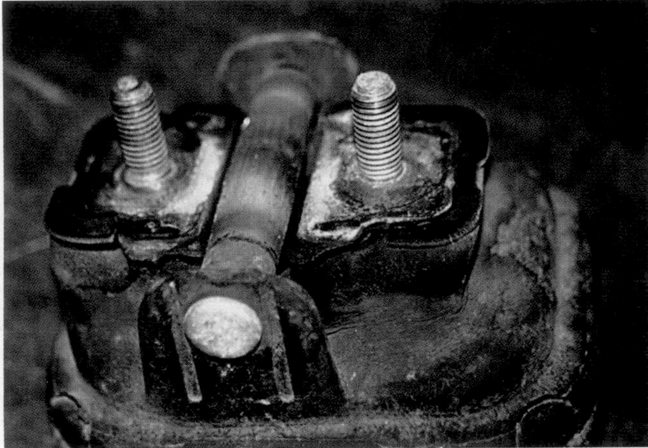

(b)

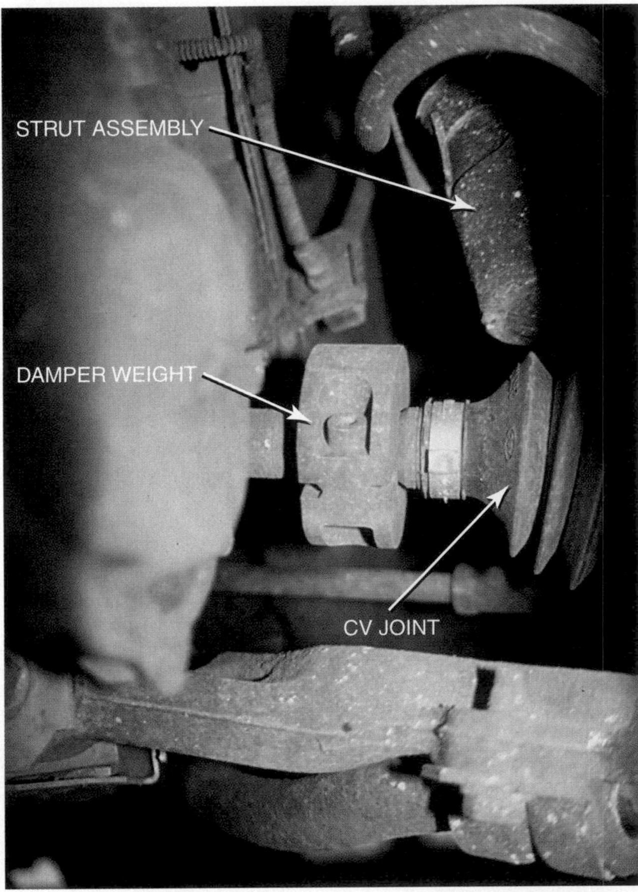

Figure 46–36 A typical drive axle shaft with dampener weight.

(c)

Figure 46–35 (a) Before the engine mount could be replaced, the vehicle was hoisted and a tall safety stand was placed under the engine. The stand was adjustable, thereby allowing the technician to raise the engine slightly to get the old mount out. (b) The old engine mount was torn and shorter than the replacement. (c) The engine had to be raised higher to get the new (noncollapsed) engine mount installed.

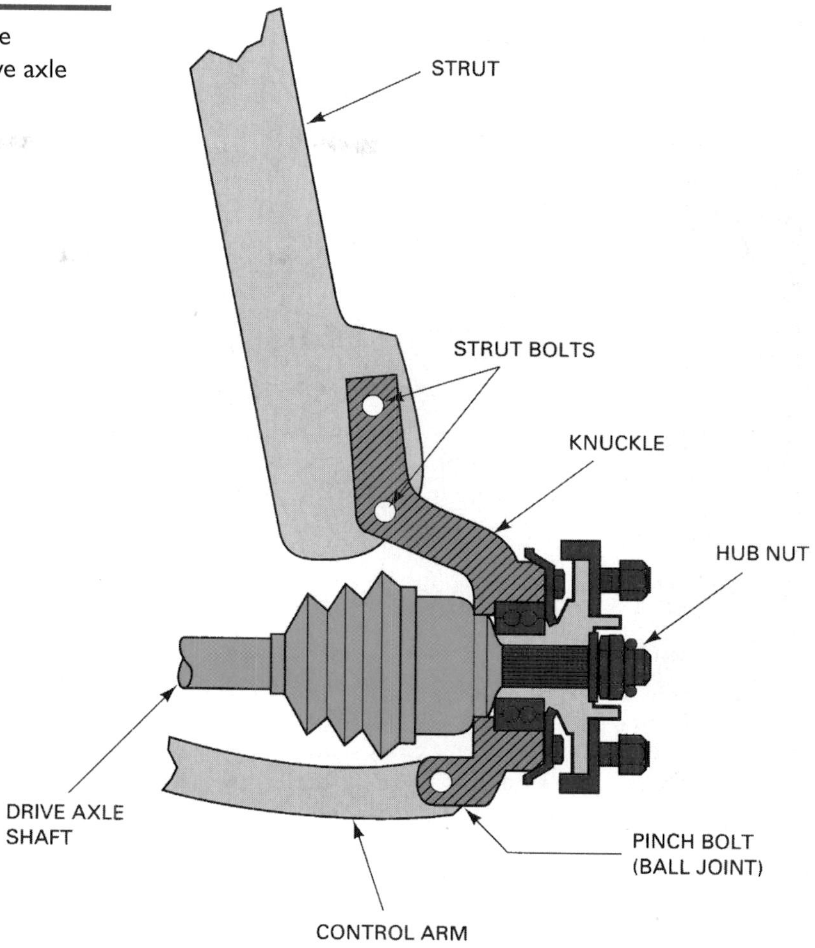

Figure 46–37 The hub nut (spindle nut) must be removed before the hub bearing assembly or drive axle shaft can be removed from the vehicle.

Step 2. To allow the knuckle room to move outward far enough to remove the drive axle shaft, some or all of the following will have to be disconnected:

a. Lower ball joint or **pinch bolt** (see Figure 46–38)

b. Tie rod end (see Figure 46–39)

c. Stabilizer bar link (if equipped)

d. Front disc brake caliper

Step 3. Remove the splined end of the axle from the hub bearing.

Step 4. Use a pry bar or special tool with a slide hammer, as shown in Figure 46–40, and remove the inner joint from the transaxle. See Figure 46–41.

Figure 46–38 Many knuckles are attached to the ball joint on the lower control arm by a pinch bolt.

CAUTION: Some vehicles such as many Fords use the drive axle shafts to retain the side gears inside the transaxle. See Figure 46–42. It is generally okay to remove one drive axle at a time, but if the second axle is removed, the side gears will fall into the transaxle case. Always follow the vehicle manufacturer's recommended service procedures.

Step 5. Disassemble, clean, and inspect all components. See Figures 46–43 through 46–48.

Step 6. Replace the entire joint if there are *any* worn parts. Pack *all* the grease that is supplied into the assembly or joint. Most CV joint grease is a molybdenum-disulfide type grease, commonly referred to as **moly** grease. Depending on the CV joint manufacturer, the exact composition of

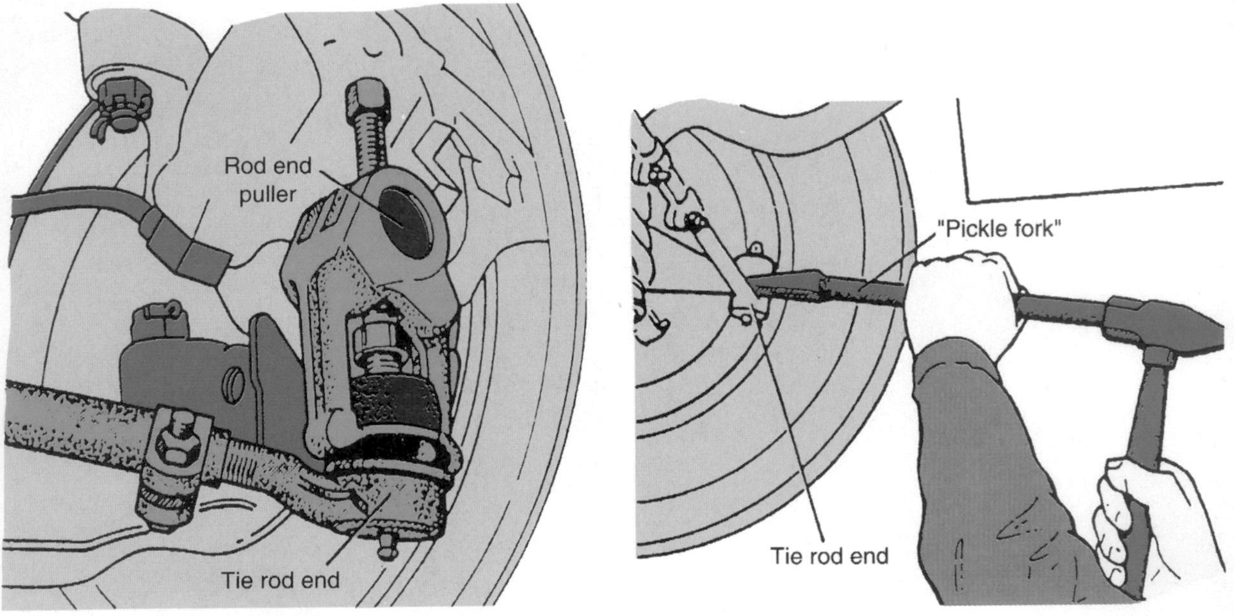

Figure 46–39 The preferred method for separating the tie rod end from the steering knuckle is to use a puller such as the one shown. A pickle-fork type tool should be used only if the tie rod end is going to be replaced. A pickle-fork type tool can damage or tear the rubber grease boot.

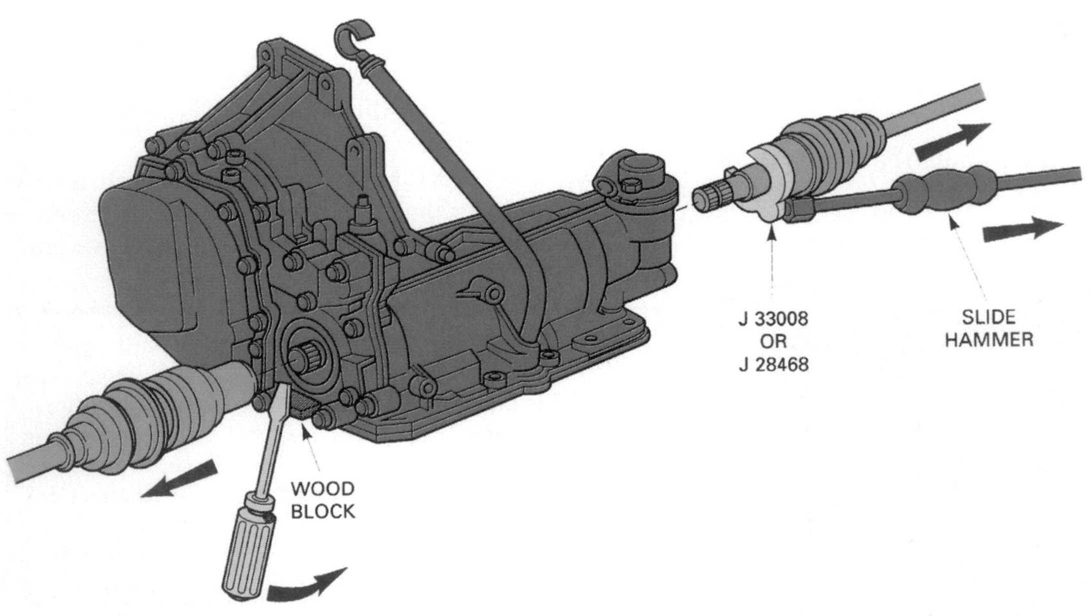

Figure 46–40 Most inner CV joints can be separated from the transaxle with a pry bar. (Courtesy of General Motors)

(a)

(b)

(c)

Figure 46–41 (a) A hub bearing puller is being used to remove the hub bearing assembly after the retaining nut has been removed. (b) The hub bearing is now ready to be pulled off the end of the drive axle shaft. (c) The drive axle shaft being removed from the vehicle. Note that the spindle did not need to be separated from the lower control arm to remove the drive axle assembly using this method.

Figure 46–42 The splines of the side gear are visible inside this transaxle after the drive shaft has been removed.

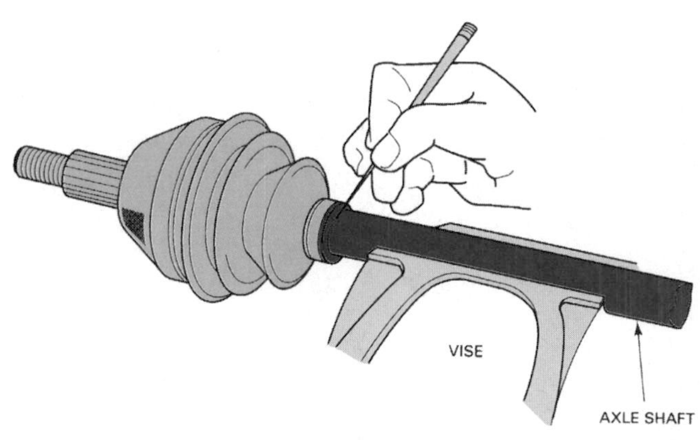

Figure 46–43 Mark the location of the boots with a scribe before removal. The replacement boots must be in the same location.

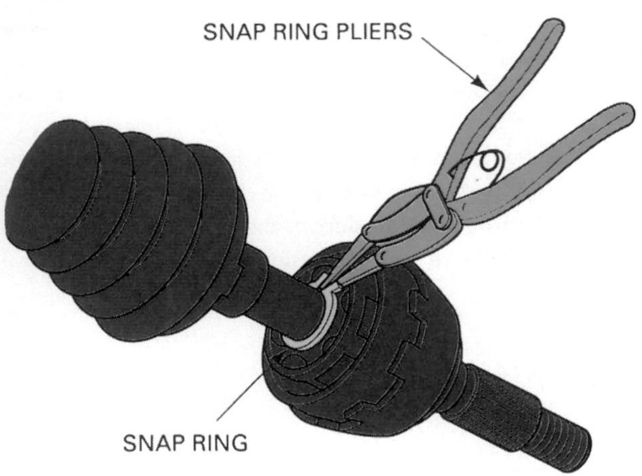

Figure 46–44 Most CV joints use a snap ring to retain the joint on the drive axle shaft.

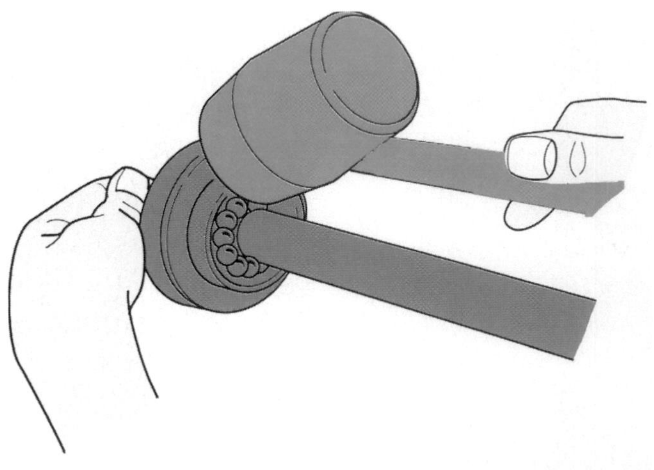

Figure 46–45 After releasing the snap ring, most CV joints can be tapped off the shaft using a brass or shot-filled plastic (dead blow) hammer.

Figure 46–46 Typical outer CV joint after removing the boot and the joint from the drive axle shaft. This joint was removed from the vehicle because a torn boot was found. After disassembly and cleaning, this joint was found to be okay and was put back into service. Even though the grease looks terrible, there was enough grease in the joint to provide lubrication to prevent any wear from occurring.

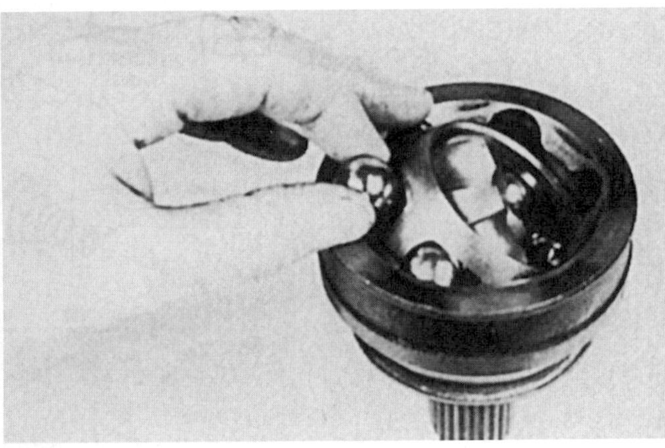

Figure 46–47 The cage of this Rzeppa-type CV joint is rotated so that one ball at a time can be removed. Some joints require that the technician use a brass punch and a hammer to move the cage.

Frequently Asked Question ???

What Do Different Colour Greases Mean?

Nothing. According to grease manufacturers, grease is coloured for identification, marketing, and for consistency colour reasons. See Figure 46–49 for an example of a red CV joint grease.

- **Identification.** The colour is often used to distinguish one type of grease from another within the same company. The blue grease from one company may be totally different from the blue grease produced or marketed by another company.
- **Marketing.** According to grease manufacturers, customers tend to be attracted to a particular colour of grease and associate that colour with quality.
- **Consistency of colour.** All greases are produced in batches, and the colour of the finished product often varies in colour from one batch to another. By adding colour to the grease, the colour can be made consistent.

Always use the grease recommended for the service being performed.

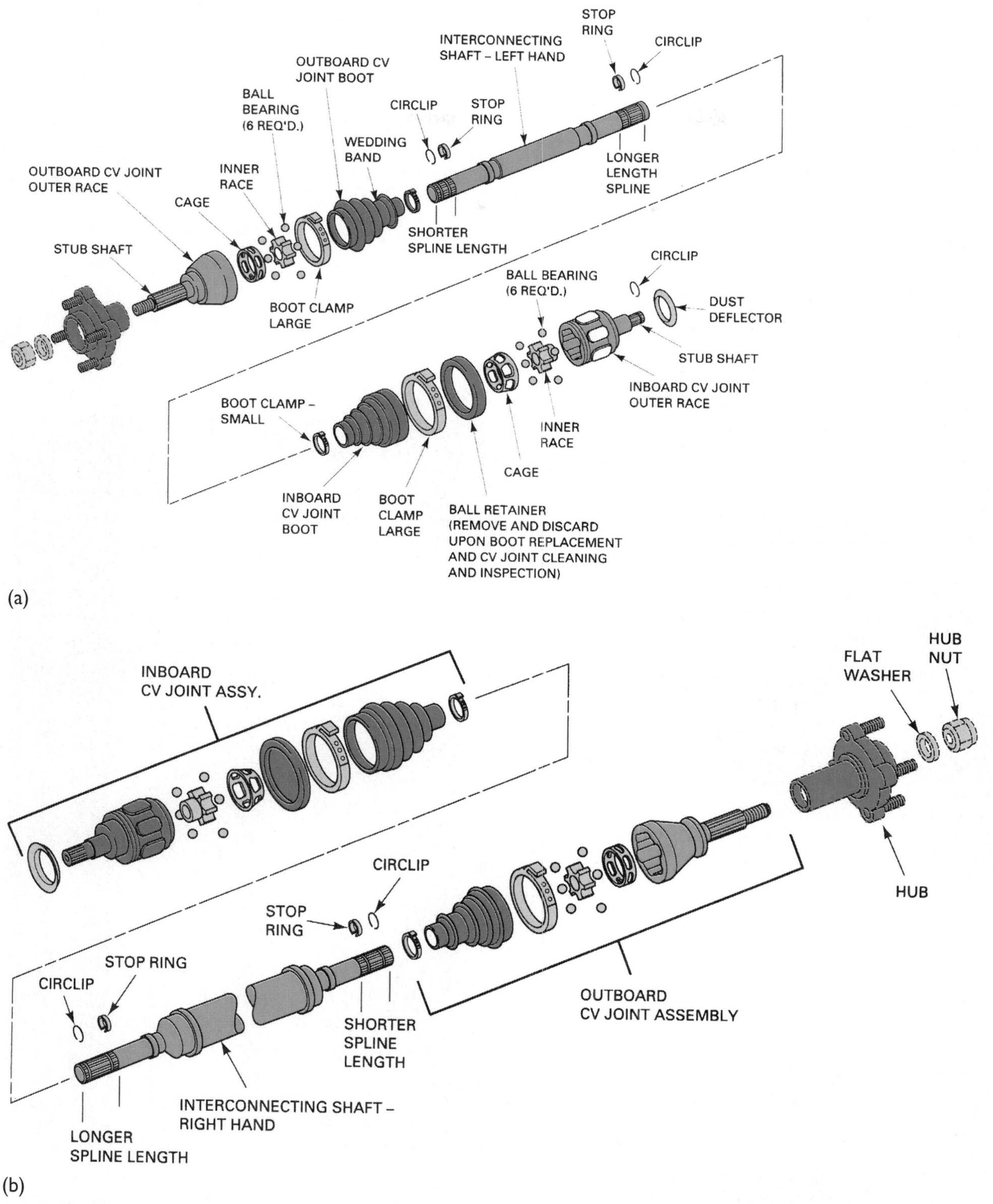

Figure 46–48 Typical left and right drive axle shaft assemblies showing all parts, including the location of stop rings and circlips. (Courtesy of Ford Motor Company)

grease can vary. *The grease supplied with a replacement CV joint or boot kit should be the only grease used.* Assemble the joint and position the boot in the same location as marked before disassembly. Before clamping the last seal on the boot, be sure to release trapped air to prevent the boot from expanding when heated and collapsing when cold. This is sometimes called "burping the boot." Clamp the boot according to the manufacturer's specifications. See Figure 46–50.

Step 7. Reinstall the drive axle shaft in the reverse order of removal and be sure to torque the drive axle spindle nut to specifications, as shown in Figure 46–51.

Figure 46–49 The colour of a grease is not an indication of quality.

Figure 46–50 Special pliers are often necessary to achieve the proper crimp on CV joint boot clamps.

Figure 46–51 A screwdriver placed into the cooling slots of the rotor and wedged against the caliper is being used to keep the drive axle from rotating as the drive axle spindle nut is being torqued to specifications using a torque wrench. An alternative method would involve installing the spindle nut snugly, installing the wheel and tire assembly, and then lowering the vehicle to the ground before torquing the spindle nut to specifications. Most vehicle manufacturers also recommend using a *new* replacement spindle nut.

PHOTO SEQUENCE 33 Drive Axle Shaft Replacement

P33–1 Start the servicing of a drive axle shaft by positioning the hoist correctly under the vehicle.

P33–2 Remove the hub cap or lug nut cover.

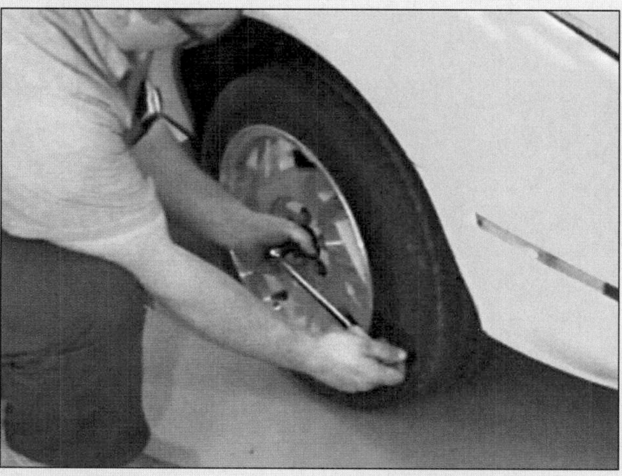

P33–3 Loosen the drive axle shaft nut using a breaker bar while the vehicle is still resting on the ground. This axle shaft nut is often tightened to 250 N·m (185 lb.-ft) of torque, which makes it difficult to remove, especially after the vehicle is raised on a hoist.

P33–4 After loosening the drive axle shaft retaining nut, hoist the vehicle to a good working height.

P33–5 Remove the front wheel(s).

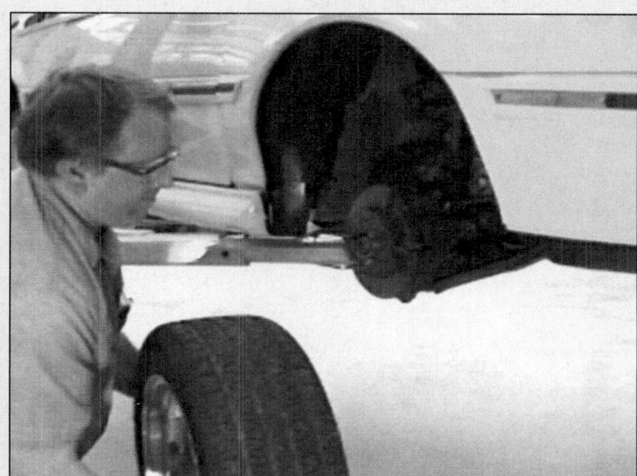

P33–6 Place the wheels out of the work area for safety.

P33–7 Remove the drive axle shaft nut that was loosened when the vehicle was still on the ground. Discard the nut.

P33–8 Separate the lower arm from the steering knuckle by disconnecting the lower ball joint. After removing the retaining nut, use a pry bar and exert a downward force on the lower control arm as an assistant strikes the knuckle around the ball joint with a hammer to separate.

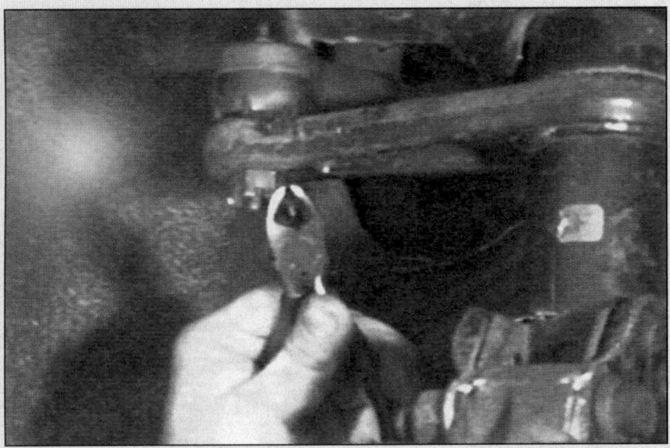

P33–9 To allow room to remove the drive axle shaft on this vehicle, it is necessary to disconnect the outer tie-rod end from the strut assembly. Start the separation process by removing (and discarding) the cotter key from the outer tie-rod retaining nut.

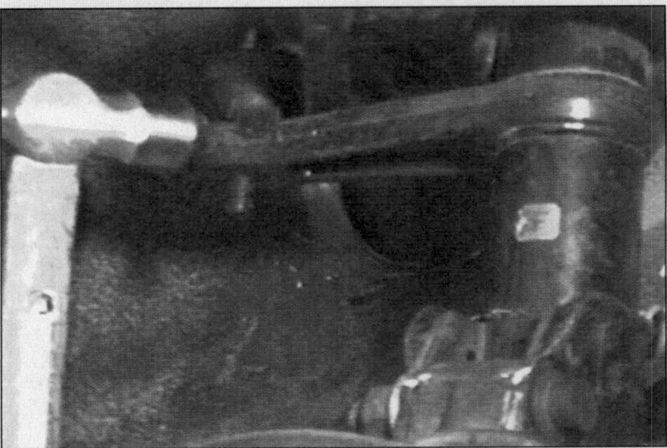

P33–10 After removing the retaining nut, tap the joint with a hammer to break the taper of the joint.

P33–11 A special tool is often necessary to push the drive axle shaft through the splines in the bearing hub.

P33–12 The hub assembly including the disc brake caliper and rotor can be pulled outward off the splines of the drive axle shaft.

P33–13 Use a pry bar to separate the inboard CV joint from the transaxle. Use a block of wood against the transaxle to prevent damage to the case of the transaxle. A special slide hammer tool is recommended by some vehicle manufacturers to separate the drive axle shaft from the transaxle.

P33–14 After the circlip at the end of the drive axle shaft has been released from the transaxle, the entire drive axle shaft assembly can be removed from the vehicle.

P33–15 After repairing or replacing the boot on the drive axle shaft, it can be replaced in the vehicle.

P33–16 Carefully insert the splines of the drive axle shaft into the splines of the side gear inside the transaxle.

P33–17 Guide the front hub over the outboard end of the drive axle shaft. In this case the strut is still attached to the body and is supporting the weight of the caliper, rotor, and hub assembly, so this procedure is relatively easy.

P33–18 After the drive axle shaft has been installed through the bearing hub, use a pry bar to lower the lower control arm to help reinstall the lower ball joint into the steering knuckle.

P33–19 A tap with a hammer is often necessary to seat the tapered ball joint stud into the tapered hole in the steering knuckle. If this step is not performed, the entire ball joint stud can turn instead of the nut when the retaining nut is being installed.

P33–20 Reinstall the outer tie-rod end to the strut assembly.

P33–21 Install a new cotter key everywhere a cotter key is used.

P33–22 Install a new drive axle shaft retaining nut, but do not torque it to its final reading until the vehicle is lowered to the ground.

P33–23 Install the front wheel(s) and torque the lug nuts to specifications, or use the correct torque-absorbing adapter and an air impact as shown here.

P33–24 After the vehicle is lowered to the ground, use a torque wrench and torque the drive axle shaft retaining nut to factory specifications. Reattach the lug nut cover and test-drive the vehicle to check for proper operation.

SUMMARY

1. The drive shaft of a rear-wheel-drive vehicle transmits engine power from the transmission to the differential.
2. Universal joints (U-joints) allow the drive shaft to transmit engine power while the suspension and the rear axle assembly are moving up and down during normal driving conditions.
3. Acceptable working angles for a Cardan-type U-joint are 0.5° to 3°. Some degree of angle is necessary to allow the roller bearings to rotate. A working angle of greater than 3° can lead to driveline vibrations.
4. Constant velocity joints (CV joints) are used on all front-wheel-drive vehicles and many four-wheel-drive vehicles to provide a smooth transmission of power to the drive wheels regardless of the angularity of the wheel or joint.
5. Outer or fixed CV joints commonly use a Rzeppa design, while inner CV joints are the plunging or tri-pot type.
6. A defective U-joint often makes a clicking sound when the vehicle is driven in reverse. Severely defective U-joints can cause driveline vibrations or a clunk sound when the transmission is shifted from reverse to drive or drive to reverse.
7. Incorrect drive shaft working angles can result from collapsed engine or transmission mounts.
8. A clunk noise in the driveline can often be corrected by applying high-temperature chassis grease to the splines of the front yoke on the drive shaft.
9. CV joints require careful cleaning, inspection, and lubrication using specific CV joint grease.

REVIEW QUESTIONS

1. Explain why Cardan-type U-joints on a drive shaft must measure within 0.5° working angles of each other.
2. What makes a constant velocity joint able to transmit engine power through an angle at a constant velocity?
3. What type of grease must be used in CV joints?
4. List two items that should be checked when inspecting a drive shaft.
5. Describe how to replace a Cardan-type U-joint.
6. Explain the proper steps to perform when replacing a CV joint.

RED SEAL CERTIFICATION-TYPE QUESTIONS

1. A rear-wheel-drive vehicle shudders or vibrates when first accelerating from a stop. The vibration is less noticeable at higher speeds. The most likely cause is
   - **a.** Drive shaft unbalance
   - **b.** Excessive U-joint working angles
   - **c.** Unequal U-joint working angles
   - **d.** Brinelling of the U-joint
2. What might be the cause of a vibration when turning a corner in an all-wheel-drive vehicle?
   - **a.** Seized drive shaft universal joint
   - **b.** Defective axle shaft universal joint
   - **c.** Damaged ring gear tooth
   - **d.** Damaged pinion gear tooth
3. The outer CV joints used on front-wheel-drive vehicles are
   - **a.** Fixed type
   - **b.** Plunging type
4. The proper grease to use with a CV joint is
   - **a.** Black chassis grease
   - **b.** Dark blue EP grease
   - **c.** Red moly grease
   - **d.** The grease that is supplied with the boot kit
5. A faulty double Cardan universal joint on the drive shaft would be felt
   - **a.** As a high-speed vibration
   - **b.** As a low-speed clunking noise
   - **c.** As a vibration only when accelerating
   - **d.** As a vibration when turning
6. Incorrect or unequal U-joint working angles are most likely to be caused by
   - **a.** A bent drive shaft
   - **b.** A collapsed engine or transmission mount
   - **c.** A dry output shaft spline
   - **d.** Defective or damaged U-joints
7. A defective outer CV joint will usually make a
   - **a.** Rumbling noise
   - **b.** Growling noise
   - **c.** Clicking noise
   - **d.** Clunking noise
8. The last step before installing a replacement CV joint or boot is to
   - **a.** "Burp the boot"
   - **b.** Lubricate the CV joint with chassis grease
   - **c.** Mark the location of the boot on the drive axle shaft
   - **d.** Separate the CV joint before installation
9. What will the drive shaft working angle be?
   - **a.** The difference in joint angles on the shaft should be no more than 0.5°
   - **b.** The angle measured between the transmission output shaft centreline and pinion gear centreline
   - **c.** The difference in the angle measured between the two U-joints on the drive shaft
   - **d.** The angle of the differential axle shaft
10. The splines of the drive shaft yoke should be lubricated to prevent
    - **a.** A vibration
    - **b.** Spline bind
    - **c.** Rust
    - **d.** Transmission fluid leaks from the extension housing

47

Differentials

OBJECTIVES: After studying Chapter 47, you should be able to:

1. Prepare for the interprovincial Red Seal certification examination in Appendix III (Manual Drive Trains and Axles) on the topics covered in this chapter.
2. Describe how the differential allows engine torque to be applied to both drive wheels and still allow a difference in the speed of the drive wheels during cornering.
3. Determine the rear axle ratio.
4. Perform a tooth contact pattern check and determine corrective action.
5. Describe how to determine proper drive pinion gear depth.
6. Explain how to achieve proper drive pinion bearing preload.
7. Describe how to adjust the ring gear position to provide the proper backlash.

PURPOSE AND FUNCTION OF A DIFFERENTIAL

The differential allows engine torque to be applied to both drive axles, which rotate at varying speeds during cornering and while travelling over bumps and dips in the road. The differential also changes the direction of engine torque 90° from the rotation of the drive shaft lengthwise with the vehicle. These two purposes of a differential can be summarized as follows:

- To change the direction of engine torque (see Figure 47–1).
- To allow the drive wheels to rotate at different speeds (see Figure 47–2).

A differential is a mechanical addition and subtraction assembly. By splitting the engine torque to the drive wheels when the vehicle is turning a corner, the torque forces cause the side gear and pinion mate gears to subtract torque from one side and add torque to the opposite side. See Figure 47–3.

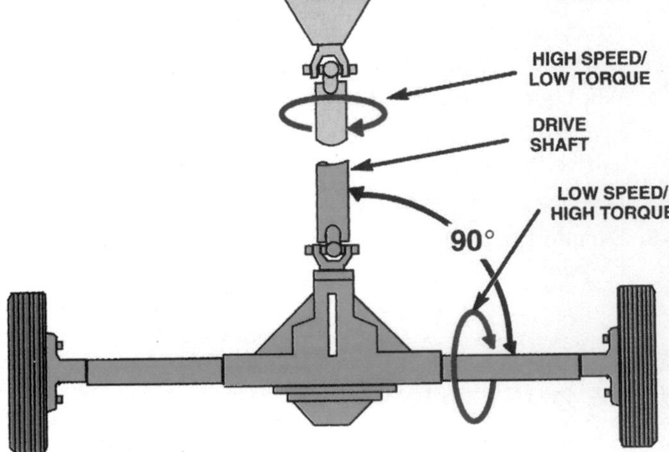

Figure 47–1 The differential assembly changes the direction of engine torque and increases the torque to the drive wheels. (Courtesy of Chrysler Corporation)

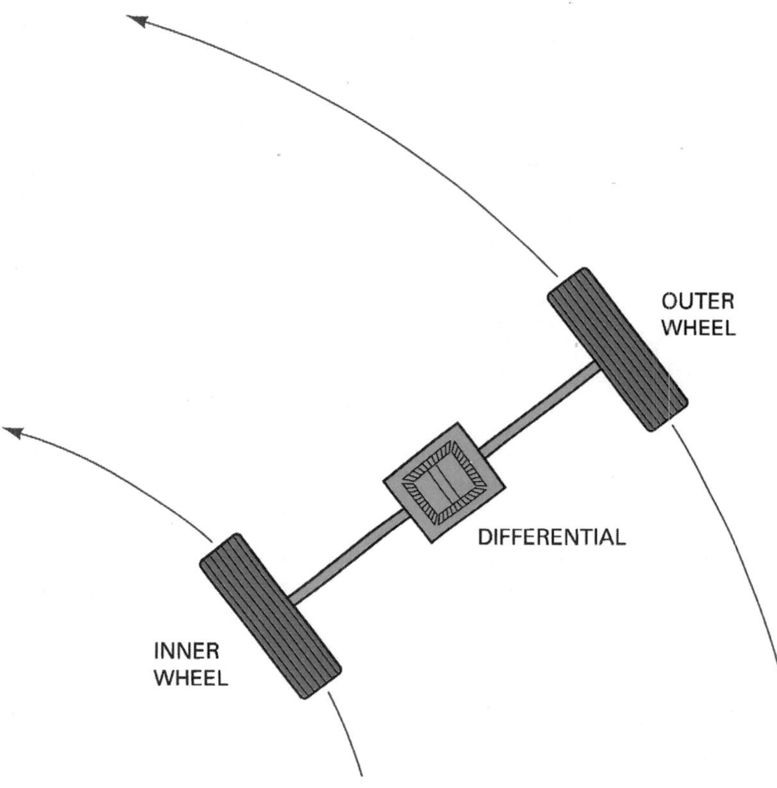

Figure 47–2 The difference between the travel distance of the drive wheels is controlled by the differential. (Courtesy of General Motors Corporation, Service Technology Group)

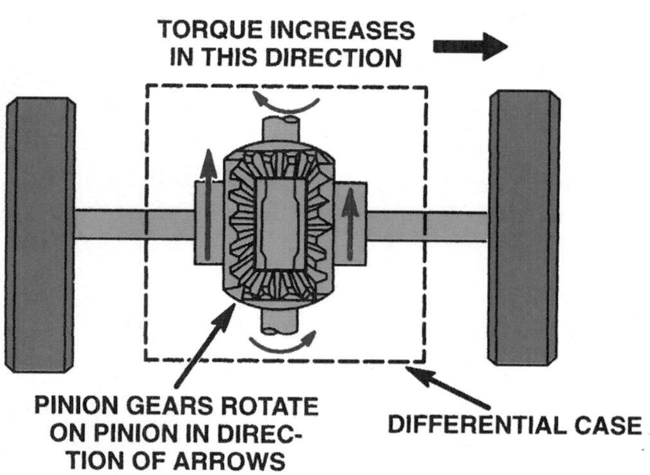

Figure 47–3 When the vehicle turns a corner, the inner wheel slows and the outer wheel increases in speed to compensate. This difference in rotational speed causes the pinion gears to "walk" around the slower side gear. (Courtesy of Chrysler Corporation)

PARTS OF A DIFFERENTIAL

A differential is also called a **rear end** or abbreviated simply as a **diff.** Whenever any vehicle makes a turn, the outside wheel must travel a greater distance than the inside wheel. The drive shaft applies torque to the **drive pinion gear** that meshes below the centre line of a **ring gear** as shown in Figure 47–4. This type of gear set is called a **hypoid gear set** and requires gear lubrication specifically designed for this type of service. The ring gear is attached to a **differential case** that also contains small bevelled **spider gears** or **pinion gears.** A **pinion shaft** passes through the two pinion gears in the case. In mesh with the pinion gears are two **side gears** that are splined to the inner ends of the axles. See Figure 47–5.

The Pinion and Ring Gears During Operation

During operation, the position of the drive pinion gear on the ring gear changes. The ring gear mounts

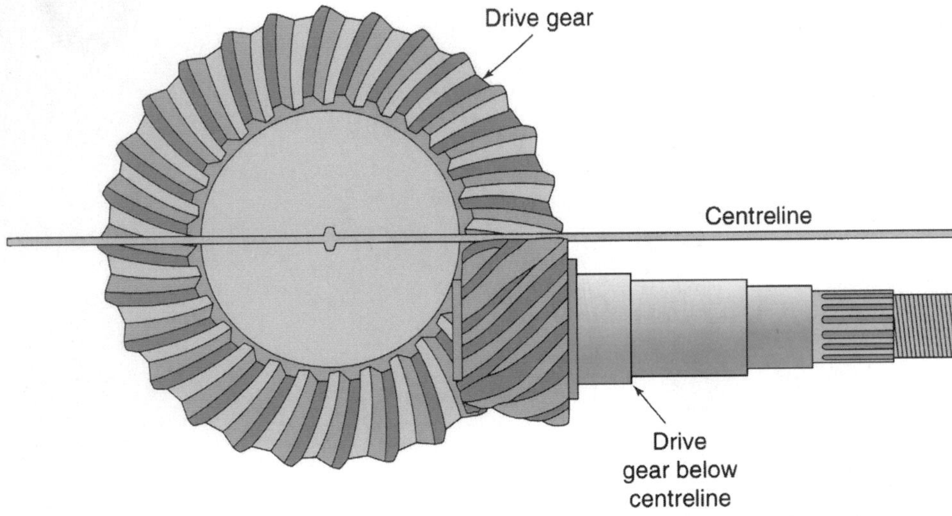

Figure 47–4 A hypoid gear set uses a drive pinion that meshes with the ring gear below the centreline of the ring gear. (Courtesy of Chrysler Corporation)

Figure 47–5 The differential case provides the support for the ring gear, side bearings, and side gears.

onto the differential case as shown in Figure 47–6. Each slanted ring gear tooth has two ends. Its **toe** is closest to the ring gear centre; its **heel,** closest to the outside circumference. The tooth **root** is the depression lying between two teeth, and the **crown** is the very top of each tooth.

While a vehicle accelerates, the drive pinion contacts the ring teeth on its **drive,** or **convex side.** While decelerating, the drive pinion contacts the ring teeth on its **coast,** or **concave side.** See Figure 47–7. The intermediate position between drive and coast, when neither the ring gear nor the pinion is driving each other, is called the **floating position.**

DIFFERENTIAL GEAR RATIOS

The final gear reduction in the drive train occurs in the differential assembly. The amount of torque a gear set delivers depends on the gear ratio between the drive pinion gear and the driven ring gear. The gear ratio of the final drive (differential) is called the **axle ratio.** To determine the axle ratio, divide the number of teeth of the ring gear (driven gear) by the number of teeth of the drive pinion gear (driving gear):

$$\frac{\text{Driven}}{\text{Driving}} = \frac{\text{Ring gear (41 teeth)}}{\text{Pinion gear (10 teeth)}} = 4.10 \text{ (Axle ratio)}$$

The higher the axle ratio number, the faster the engine rotates for each rotation of the drive wheels. See the High-Performance Tip "Change the Axle Ratio."

Ring and Pinion Gear Set Types

The final drive gear ratio determines how many times a drive pinion tooth will make contact with a particular ring gear tooth during one revolution. This affects final-drive-gear-set manufacture and service.

Final drive gear sets may be divided into three types, depending on the final drive gear ratio.

1. **Hunting gear sets** are gear sets with final drive ratios expressible in a fraction that

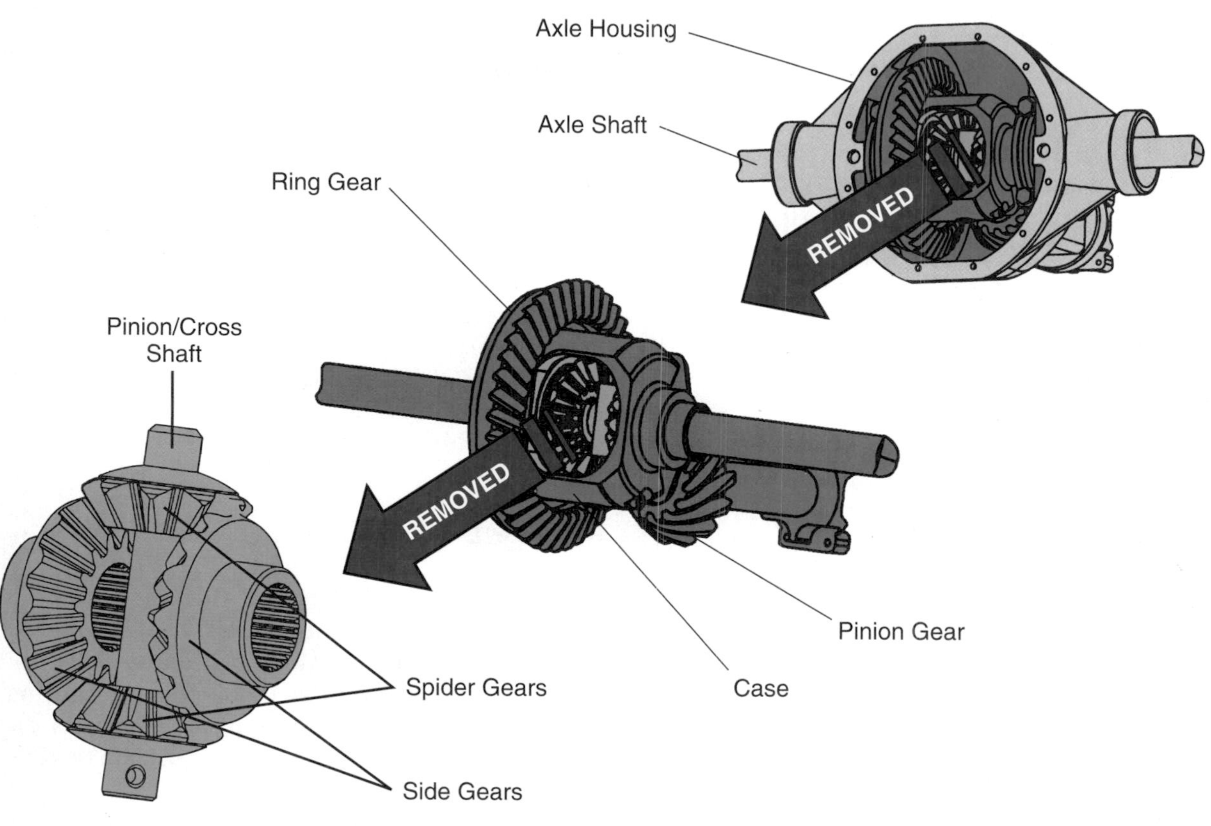

Figure 47–6 The relationship among the ring gear and drive pinion as well as the side and spider gears.

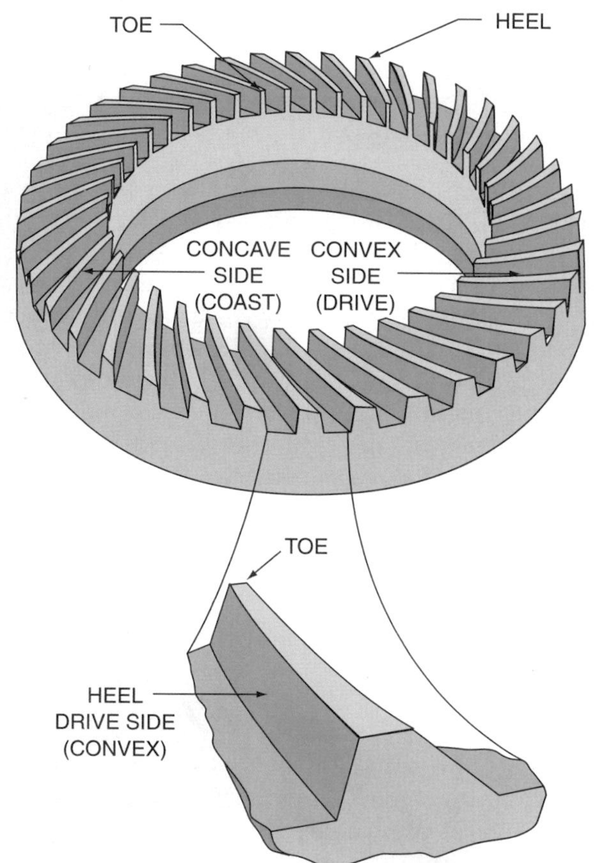

Figure 47–7 The drive side is the convex side of the ring gear except for some front axles used in four-wheel vehicles, and they often use the concave side on the drive side.

HIGH PERFORMANCE TIP 

Change the Axle Ratio

To increase vehicle performance, replace a high ratio (lower number) rear axle ratio with a lower ratio (higher number) rear axle. For example,

Stock rear end = 3.23:1 (drive pinion has 13 teeth and the ring gear has 42 teeth)

Replacement rear end = 3.73:1 (drive pinion has 11 teeth and the ring gear has 41 teeth)

The high-performance axle ratio (3.73:1) allows the engine to rotate faster than the stock 3.23:1 ratio. Because most engines produce greater torque with increasing RPM (up to a point), this allows more torque to be applied to the drive wheels. Not only is the engine producing more torque, but the higher-number gear ratio also multiplies the available torque times 3.73 instead of the original 3.23. However, there are several disadvantages associated with changing the rear end ratio:

- Decreased fuel economy
- Incorrect speedometer and odometer readings that can affect the shifting of the automatic transmission unless changes are made to the computer or vehicle speed sensors
- Increased engine noise due to the higher engine speed
- Increased engine wear, again due to the increased engine speed

If you can live with these disadvantages, a change in the rear end ratio generates a real performance gain.

cannot be reduced to any lower terms. An example of a hunting gear set is one that has 41 teeth on the ring gear and 11 teeth on the drive pinion. This combination creates a 3.73:1 axle ratio. This type of gear set requires no timing marks or alignment during assembly. As the pinion gear drives the ring gear, each pinion tooth will hunt for, or seek, contact with every ring gear tooth.

2. **Non-hunting gear sets** are gear sets with final drive ratios expressible as a whole number. Non-hunting gear sets require timing marks. As the pinion gear drives the ring gear, each pinion tooth contacts only a few ring gear teeth during each revolution.
3. **Partially non-hunting gear sets** are gear sets with final drive ratios expressible as a reducible fraction not equalling a whole number.

Partially non-hunting gear sets also require timing marks. During final drive operation, each pinion tooth contacts only some of the ring pinion teeth. For the pinion teeth to make contact with the highest number of ring gear teeth, the pinion gear must drive the ring gear more than one revolution.

On non-hunting and partially non-hunting gears, manufacturers **lap** the contacting gear teeth to decrease wear. For this reason, these gear sets are marked to ensure proper alignment during assembly procedures. To preserve the wear patterns, the gear sets should be reassembled using the same alignment. This prolongs the life of the gear set and decreases operational noise.

DIFFERENTIALS

While a vehicle travels straight ahead, the speed of each driven wheel must be allowed to vary slightly as they go over bumps, potholes, railroad tracks, and other road surface irregularities. While cornering, the wheels must be able to turn at much greater differences in speed. Without some mechanism to allow for a difference in speed between the wheels, the left wheel would skid through the turn.

Inside the differential gear housing four to six bevel gears help drive the axles. In most rear axles, two of these bevel gears are smaller pinions mounted on a shaft. They drive two side gears splined with each inner axle end.

Torque Flow Through a Standard Open Differential

Open differentials deliver equal torque to both wheels at all times. As the case rotates (driven by the engine through the ring and pinion gears), the cross-shaft applies a drive force to the spider gears. The two side gears apply reaction forces that counter this drive force. See Figure 47–8. Because the spider gear is free to rotate about the cross-shaft, the two reaction forces are equal. As the side gear applies a force to the spider gear, the spider gear applies an equal and opposite force to the side gear. It is this force, on the side gear, that supplies the torque to the axle that drives the wheel. Because the force on each side gear is equal, the torque supplied to each wheel is also equal. This is true regardless of whether one wheel is rotating faster than the other or at the same speed.

Travelling Straight-Ahead Assuming that a vehicle has equal traction at both wheels, differential action does not occur. In other words, when travelling straight on smooth road surfaces the ring gear, carrier, and the drive axles are travelling at the same speed; they rotate as a unit.

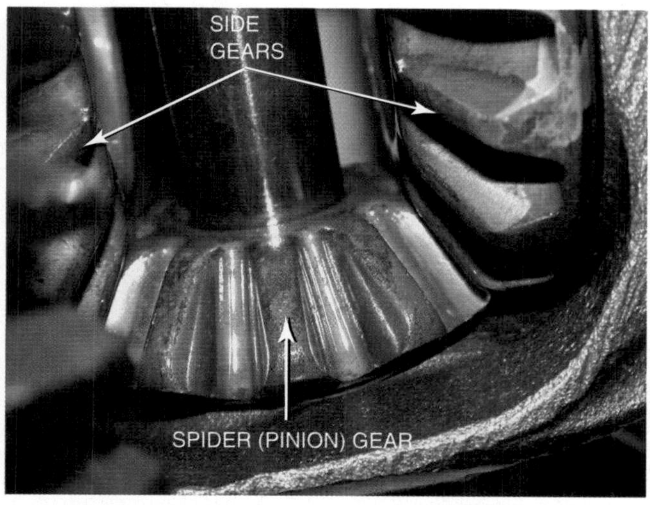

Figure 47–8 A close-up view of the side gears and spider (pinion) gear. Note the ridges on the gear teeth. These ridges are manufactured into the gear teeth to help retain lubricant so that no metal-to-metal contact occurs.

Traveling Around Corners The ability of the differential pinion gears to spin on their shafts allows each axle to rotate at a different speed.

Case speed is always equal to the average speed of the two side gears. Since the ring gear rotates with the case and each side gear rotates with its axle, when a vehicle corners, the outside wheel gains the same number of RPMs that the wheel on the inside loses, while ring gear RPM remains constant.

Limited Slip Differentials

When a vehicle equipped with a standard differential spins a tire, the opposite wheel does not receive enough torque to move the vehicle. To solve this problem, most manufacturers use differentials that direct more power to the side gear attached to the spinning axle. Many differentials do this by forcing the side gear against the revolving case. This bypasses differential action, allowing the case to drive the side gear directly.

A limited-slip differential distributes torque to both wheels equally or unequally, allowing the wheels to turn at the same or at different speeds. See Figure 47–9.

The only means of having the standard differential apply different amounts of torque to each axle is to have the case drive the side gear directly, bypassing the pinion gears. One means of accomplishing this is to literally push the side gear out of mesh with the pinion gears against the rotating case.

Preloaded clutches use two mechanisms to accomplish this action. First, a coil, Belleville, or leaf spring cocks the two side gears. See Figure 47–10. Second, a multi-disc clutch pack (or cones) lie behind one or both of the side gears. Vehicle manufacturers refer to these differentials using various brand names, such as **Positive Traction, Sure-Grip, Anti-Spin,** and **Traction-Lok.**

When forces inside the differential push the side gear against the case, the clutch pack allows the gear to lock smoothly without jerking. The pack, lying between at least one of the backs of the side gears and the case, consists of two types of alternatively stacked steel discs with holes through their middle sections. The first is coated with friction material and the second is not. The interior splines of the friction disc holes mesh with the splines on the centre hub protruding from the backside of the side gear. The holes of the steel discs are not splined. Instead, they have two or three tabs along their outside

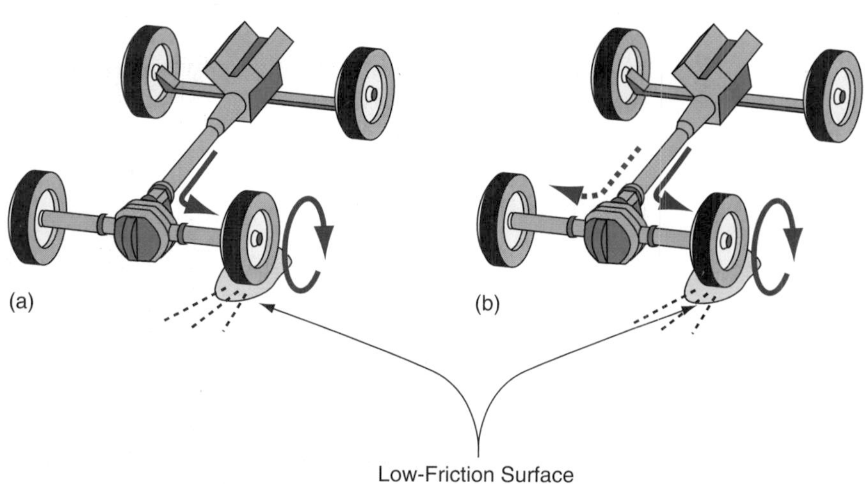

Figure 47–9 (a) A two-wheel-drive vehicle equipped with an open differential. (b) A two-wheel-drive vehicle equipped with a limited-slip differential.

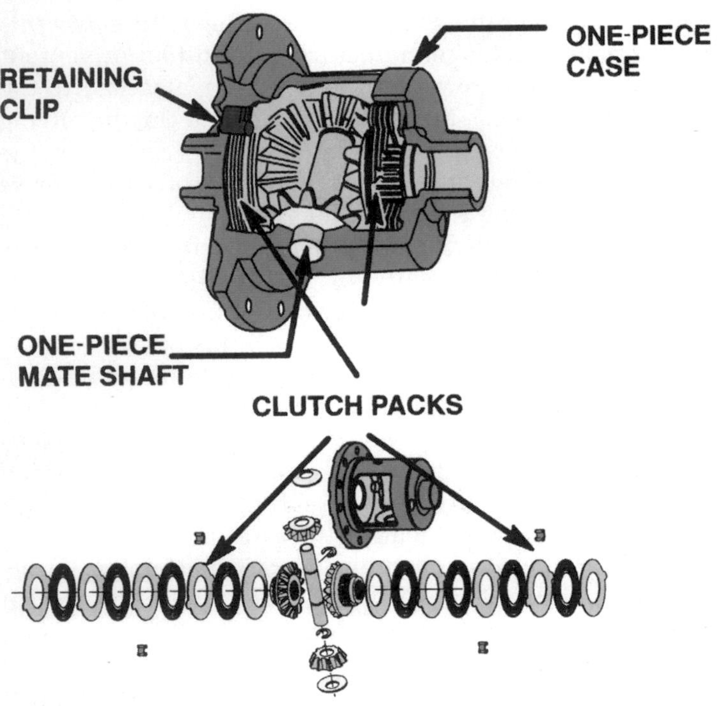

Figure 47–10 Trac-loc limited-slip differential. This type of limited-slip differential uses the preload force from a spring and the torque generated by the side gears as the two axles rotate at different rates to apply the clutches and limit the amount of difference in the speed of two axles.

diameter that fit into slots machined into the differential case.

As the side gear is pushed farther against the case, each friction plate rubs against the steel plate in front of and behind it, gradually slowing the side gear's rotation until it smoothly locks against the case.

Two forces help to push the side gear out of mesh from the differential pinions and to lock it against the differential case.

1. The rotating differential pinions apply pressure against the side gear. The amount of pressure depends on the traction beneath the tire connected to the side gear.
2. The spring applies the second force that allows the preloaded clutch to work. This spring, whether a coil, leaf, or Belleville, preloads the clutch discs, narrowing the clearances between them. Tighter springs cause the differential to lock up sooner than looser springs.

To vary the amount of traction a tire must have before its axle's side gear locks up, many differentials use adjustment shims. Available in different thicknesses, manufacturers install them between the rear of the clutch packs and the differential case. The thicker the shims, the sooner the differential locks up. Some differentials rely on the preload spring alone to determine when the side gear locks up. They use no shims.

During operation, the clutch discs slide against each other every time the vehicle turns and corners. This action creates friction, making it important to add the manufacturer-recommended lubricant that contains a friction modifier. This lubricant may already be included in the gear oil or may be a special additive. Using improper lubricants may cause the discs to wear prematurely and vibrate during turns.

Cone Type

The second type of preloading clutch differential uses two tapered cones instead of multi-disc clutch packs. Positioned between the side gears and the case, the cone's tapered end fits inside a dished receptacle machined into the case. The same forces that push the side gears against the case in the clutch pack differential push the side gears against the case in the tapered-cone differential. When these forces press the cones into their dished receptacles, they come to a stop smoothly, locking the side gears to the case.

Viscous Coupled Limited-Slip Units

Differentials can be designed to work on the principle of a **viscous coupling.** This design uses a series of closely positioned plates, which do not physically touch one another. Half of the plates are splined to the case, and the other half are alternately splined to each side gear. The plates are housed in a sealed chamber, which is filled with a thick and viscous silicone-based fluid. The silicone allows normal speed differences between two shafts, resisting high-speed differences associated with wheel spin on one shaft.

This type of viscous-coupled differential is used in the front differentials of some Japanese front-wheel-drive vehicles and in four-wheel-drive vehicles. See Chapter 48 for details.

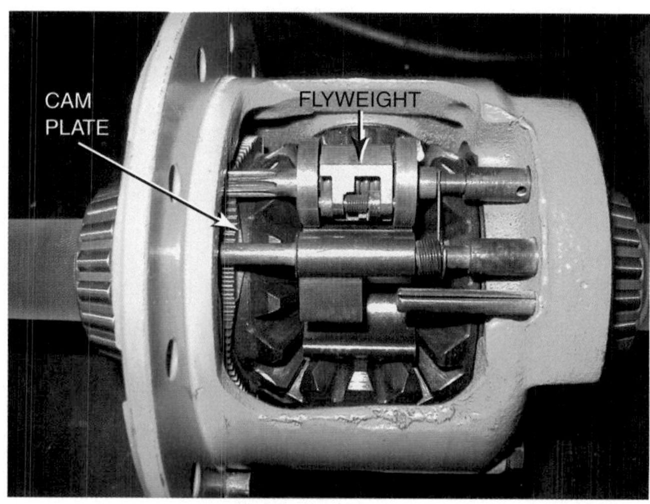

Figure 47–11 An Eaton-locker differential.

The Eaton "Locker" Differential

The Eaton locker's sturdier design makes it more efficient in transferring torque from the driveline to the axles while in the locked position than the clutch-type multi-disc differential.

When a vehicle spins a rear wheel, both the preloaded multi-disc differential and the Eaton locker compress their clutch packs lying between the side gears and the case. This allows the case to directly drive the axles, bypassing the effect of the rotating differential pinions.

The Eaton and preloaded multi-disc differentials differ in how they compress their clutch packs. The preloaded multi-disc uses either a coil, leaf, or Belleville spring to apply initial pressure against the side gears and the clutch pack. As the rotating pinion gears push against a slower moving side gear, it is forced against the case, thereby compressing the discs in the clutch pack together.

The Eaton differential, on the other hand, uses a unique mechanism to collapse the clutch packs. See Figure 47–11. It has four parts:

- A governor with two flyweights
- A cam plate and cam side gear on the left side
- A latching bracket
- A thrust block.

These parts allow the Eaton to momentarily shift into the locked mode when side gear and case rotational speeds differ by more than 100 rpm.

DIAGNOSTIC STORY 

"I Used to Have a Limited-Slip Differential"

The owner of a Chevrolet S-10 pickup truck equipped with a V-6 and five-speed manual transmission complained that he used to be able to spin both rear tires on dry pavement, but lately only one tire spins. The service technician assigned to the repair order was very familiar with what might have occurred. Many General Motors pickup trucks are equipped with an Eaton locking differential that uses a torque limiting disc. The teeth of this disc are designed to shear to prevent the possibility of breaking an axle. See Figure 47–12.

The service procedure to correct the customer's concern is to replace the left-hand clutch plates. Usually, the shearing of the torque-linking teeth is associated with a loud bang in the rear axle. The differential will continue to operate normally as a standard (open) differential.

Torsen Differentials

The Torsen differential is a torque sensing, locking design that uses a set of worm side gears in mesh with individual worm wheel pinions that are supported by the differential case. See Figure 47–13. The pinions have spur gear sections machined on them at each end, which form the connection between left and right side pinions. Because of the worm and worm wheel configurations, the side gears can turn the pinions, but the pinions cannot turn the side gears. The result is a complex operation, which meets all drive requirements without excessive wheel slip.

This unit has been available as original equipment on several vehicles as well as for many aftermarket applications.

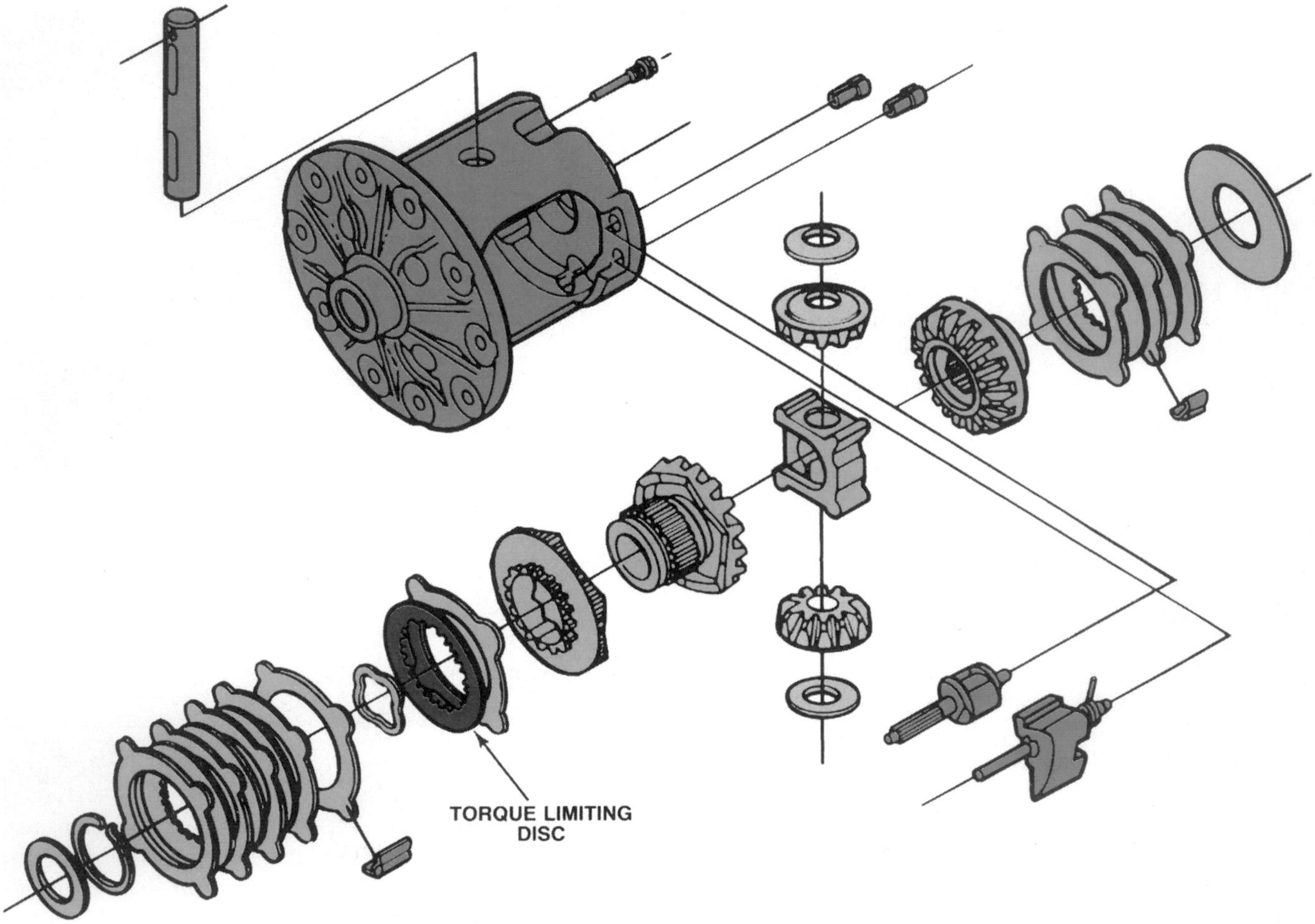

TORQUE LIMITING DISC

Figure 47–12 This Eaton design differential uses a torque-limiting disc to prevent the possibility of breaking an axle in the event of a high-torque demand. When the disc tangs shear, the differential will continue to function but as an open rather than as a limited-slip differential.

Figure 47–13 A Torsen differential. This type of differential provides torque to both drive wheels even if one tire is on ice. The complex system of gears allows this smooth transfer of torque without the use of clutches.

Drive Pinion

The drive pinion is driven by a flange often called a **companion flange.** The heavy bulk of the companion flange helps dampen vibrations and absorb shocks in the driveline. See Figure 47–14. The final drive pinion shaft may be supported by bearings using one of two methods.

1. The first method, and most common, uses two opposed taper roller bearings, with a collapsible (compressible) spacer separating the two inner races to support an overhung pinion. See Figure 47–15. This term means all of the bearings supporting the pinion shaft lie on one side of the pinion gear. The bearings are preloaded, a state that minimizes wobble and endwise movement while the drive pinion shaft rotates.
2. The second method uses two opposed taper roller bearings to support a **straddle-mounted**

Figure 47–14 This pinion flange is equipped with a damper weight to help dampen driveline vibrations.

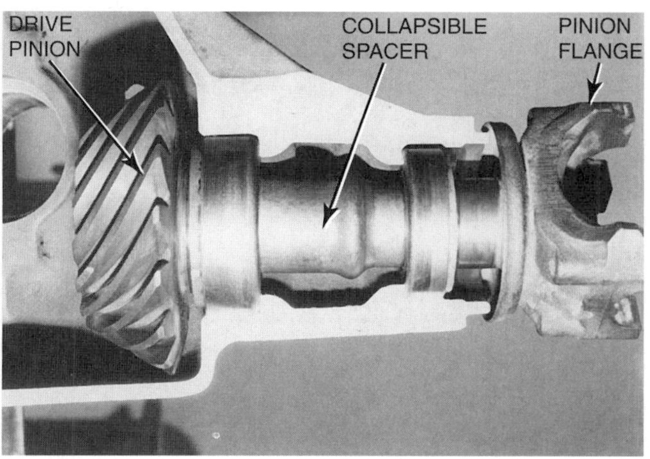

Figure 47–15 A collapsible spacer-type drive pinion shaft.

pinion, but the distance between them is smaller than in the overhung design. Most noticeably, a third smaller bearing attaches to a stem-like machined pilot protruding from the gear-end of the drive pinion shaft. This third bearing, usually a straight roller type, fits into a bore in the carrier. Unlike the overhung design, bearings supporting a straddle-mounted pinion lie on both sides of the pinion gear. Like the overhung design, a straddle-mounted pinion shaft usually has a compressible preloaded spacer positioned between the two larger differential case bearings. Straddle-mounted pinions are usually mounted in a pinion housing that can be removed from the carrier.

Figure 47–16 Side bearings are press fit on the differential case.

Drive Pinion Gear Adjustment Depth

The pinion shaft mounting method also determines how deeply the pinion gear meshes into the ring gear. This is called pinion depth and helps adjust the precise gear tooth relationship between the ring and pinion gears. You can vary the pinion depth adjustment by changing the thickness of a shim (spacer). This shim is located between the rear preloaded bearing and the pinion gear, or between the removable pinion housing and the carrier.

Side Bearings

The differential case is supported by two side bearings pressed onto its sides. See Figure 47–16. These are usually tapered roller bearings and are preloaded to ensure case rotation without axial or radial movement.

Side bearing preload is adjusted either by threaded adjusting nuts as shown in Figure 47–17, or by placement of adjusting shims (spacers) on either side of the case between the bearing outer races and the inside of the carrier. The method used to adjust side bearing preload is also used to adjust ring gear-to-pinion backlash (tooth clearance between one gear and the other). This is necessary to ensure enough space between the teeth of the two gears to allow for expansion of the gear tooth dimensions as the unit warms up to operating temperature. When the unit is warm, there must be just enough space between the gear teeth to allow adequate lubrication of the tooth surfaces and still allow full tooth contact for good transfer of torque from one gear to the other. Too much clearance between the gears will allow one

Figure 47–17 Some side bearings use threaded adjusters to adjust preload.

to travel too far before contacting the other when the power train goes from drive to coast and back again. Excess clearance can result in final drive noise and gear tooth damage.

BALL BEARINGS/REAR AXLES

If ball bearings are used, the bearing itself absorbs the radial forces. The bearing is placed on the axle and retained by a pressed-on collar. A stamped steel plate bolts to the axle housing and keeps the axle in place. The bearing is pre-lubricated when it is manufactured. An oil seal is located on the inboard side of the bearing retainer collar, and keeps the hypoid lubricant from reaching the bearing or the brake assembly. In this design, there is no axle shaft endplay (thrust) adjustment.

STRAIGHT ROLLER BEARINGS/REAR AXLES

If a straight roller bearing is used, the axle surface serves as the inner race. See Figure 47–18. The outer race is pressed into the housing, and a grease seal is pressed in afterward. The bearing is lubricated by the hypoid lubricant. This design uses a C-washer on the inboard end of the axle, which prevents the axle from moving outward. Outward thrust forces are taken by the C-washer through the axle's side gear and thrust washer, to the differential case and side bearing. Inward thrust forces are taken by the axle shaft inner end pushing on the spider pinion shaft, and passed on to the differential case and the opposite side bearing. There is no axle shaft endplay adjustment with this design.

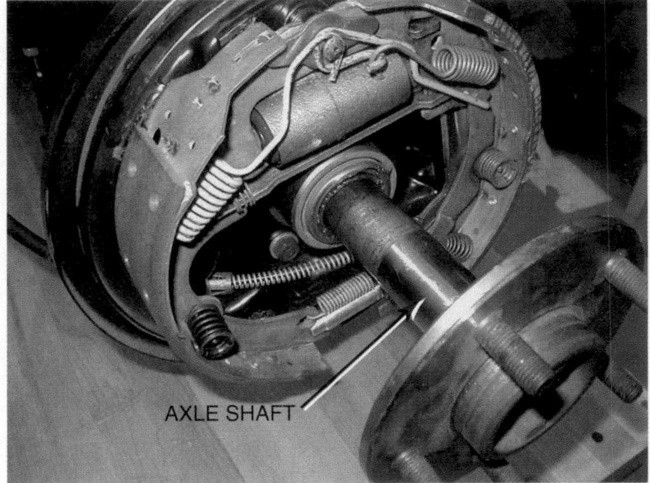

(a)

(b)

Figure 47–18 (a) The axle shaft itself is the inner race if a straight roller bearing is used. (b) The straight roller bearings are lubricated by the rear axle fluid, and a leak at the rear axle seal can cause this fluid to get onto brake components.

TAPERED ROLLER BEARINGS/REAR AXLES

If a tapered roller bearing is used, axle shaft endplay is adjustable. The bearing is pre-lubricated before it is installed, and is held in place by a pressed collar behind it. The axle is prevented from moving outward by a stamped steel retainer plate that bolts to the axle housing. The inner diameter of the plate is threaded to accept a bearing-adjusting nut, which is similar in appearance and function to a differential side bearing adjuster. A variation of this design has the endplay adjustment made by shims between the axle housing and the brake backing plate. Thrust is taken from the inner end of the axle by a thrust block

TECH TIP ✔

Don't Spin Those Wheels!

While driving on ice or snow-covered roads, it is common to see drivers moving slowly up a hill by simply spinning one drive wheel. However, when one wheel is spinning and the other wheel is stationary (or close to stationary), the pinion gears are spinning twice as fast as the drive wheel. This spinning of the drive wheel has been known to completely wear down the pinion gear thrust washers in less than one minute! See Figure 47–19. The same wear can occur if different size tires are used on the same drive axle. Therefore, to prevent expensive repairs, avoid unnecessary tire spinning and check that both tires on the same axle are the same size, brand name, and condition.

Figure 47–19 The pinion gear thrust washers can be destroyed by spinning one wheel for an extended period of time.

mounted on the spider pinion shaft, and passed on to the opposite axle, through its length to the opposite wheel bearing.

DIFFERENTIAL IDENTIFICATION

Before any service work is performed on a differential assembly, the *exact* axle specification must be determined. Vehicle manufacturers often use differentials from more than one axle manufacturer, and each manufacturer has its own individual ratios, parts, service procedures, and specifications. Differential assembly identification includes

- **Visual identification**—usually identifies the manufacturer and size only
- **Axle assembly number**—usually stamped in the axle tube of the differential assembly and identifies the gear ratio and other information
- **Limited-slip identification tag**—often the only external identification whether or not the axle assembly is an open design or limited-slip design

DETERMINING THE AXLE RATIO OF A DIFFERENTIAL

To determine the axle ratio of a differential without having to remove the axle housing cover, simply follow these steps:

Step 1. Hoist the vehicle safely.

Step 2. Mark the rear tires with masking tape at the 12 o'clock position.

Step 3. Mark the drive shaft with masking tape.

Step 4. Have an assistant hold one drive tire to keep it from moving and slowly rotate the other drive tire exactly ten times while the assistant counts the drive shaft revolutions.

Step 5. Multiply the drive shaft revolutions by 2 (except for a limited-slip differential), and then move the decimal point one place to the left. For example, if ten turns of the tire result in 18.5 turns of the drive shaft, that multiplied by 2 equals 37.0; then, moving the decimal point to the left one place equals a 3.70:1 gear ratio.

REAR END NOISE DIAGNOSIS

One of the major reasons why differentials are serviced is to correct a noise problem. Knowing when and under what conditions the noise is noticeable is a big help in identifying which bearing or component is the likely cause. Typical noise and its sources include:

- **Grinding or growling noise while turning**—usual cause is a defective axle bearing.
- **Whine noise during cruise**—drive pinion bearings are the likely causes of this type of noise.

TECH TIP 

A Quick-and-Easy Backlash Test

Excessive clearance (lash) between the drive pinion and the ring gear can cause driveline clash noise during a gear selector change. To check if the cause is due to the differential, simply hoist the vehicle and, while one wheel and the drive shaft are being held stationary, use your hand to move the opposite wheel. The maximum amount the tire should move is 2.5 cm (1 in.) measured at the tread of the tire. If backlash is greater than this, then further inspection of the differential assembly is required. Beside excessive clearance between the drive pinion and the ring gear, the wear may also be between the pinion and the side gears.

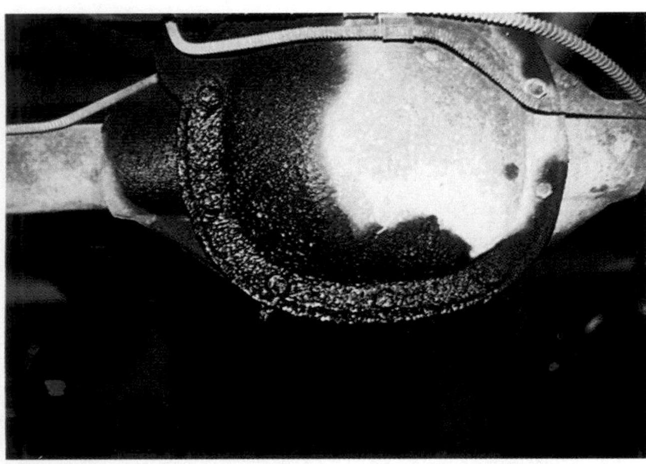

Figure 47–20 This differential has obviously been leaking. If the differential lubricant is low, wear may have occurred that would require further inspection.

DIFFERENTIAL INSPECTION

Carefully inspect the ring gear, side, and pinion gears for obvious damage or wear. See Figure 47–20. Check the backlash. The backlash is the amount of clearance between the drive pinion and the ring gear; excessive backlash could indicate excessive wear. Use a dial indicator as shown in Figure 47–21 to check and compare the results with specifications. Also see the Tech Tip "Click-Click Is Okay—Clunk-Clunk Is Not."

Also use a dial indicator to check **ring gear runout** (see Figure 47–22). If any of the visual measurement tests indicate a problem or a noise analysis indicates a bearing problem, the axle assembly should be disassembled for further analysis and service.

(a)

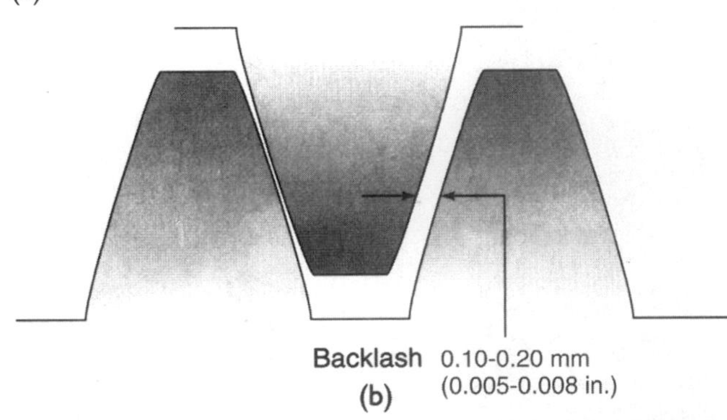

(b)

Figure 47–21 (a) Backlash is determined by mounting a dial indicator to the differential housing and placing the button of the gauge against a tooth of the ring gear. Moving the ring gear back and forth will indicate on the dial indicator the amount of backlash. (b) Backlash is the clearance between the drive pinion and the ring gear teeth.

TOOTH CONTACT PATTERN TEST

A tooth contact pattern test is an excellent method for checking proper drive pinion depth as well as proper backlash between the drive pinion and the ring gear. Any faults in these areas will be reflected in the pattern. The pattern test involves the following steps:

Step 1. Clean the gear teeth of the ring gear and the drive pinion.

Step 2. Using a small brush, apply a light coating of iron oxide compound.

Step 3. Use a small pry bar to apply a load to the ring gear to achieve a more accurate contact pattern. See Figure 47–23.

Figure 47–22 Ring gear runout should be less than 0.05 mm (0.002 in.) as measured by a dial indicator.

Figure 47–23 Force has to be applied to the ring gear to achieve a proper contact pattern.

Step 4. Rotate the drive pinion until the ring gear turns one revolution (about three revolutions of the drive pinion gear).

Step 5. Repeat rotating the drive pinion in the opposite direction. This will create a contact pattern on both the **drive side** and the **coast side** of the ring gear.

> **NOTE:** The drive side is the convex surface of the ring gear teeth. The coast side is the concave side of the ring gear. This is true except for many differentials used on the front of four-wheel-drive vehicles. In this case, the drive side in the front differential is the concave surface and the coast side is the convex surface of the ring gear teeth. Always check the service information for the vehicle being serviced for the correct interpretation of the pattern results.

See Figure 47–24 for good and bad tooth contact patterns and what could have caused them.

Condition:

- Pinion depth correct.
- Backlash incorrect – too much clearance between the pinion and ring gears.

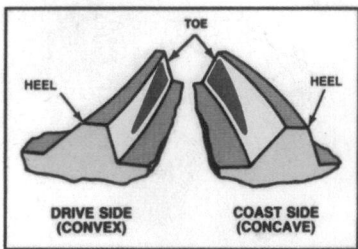

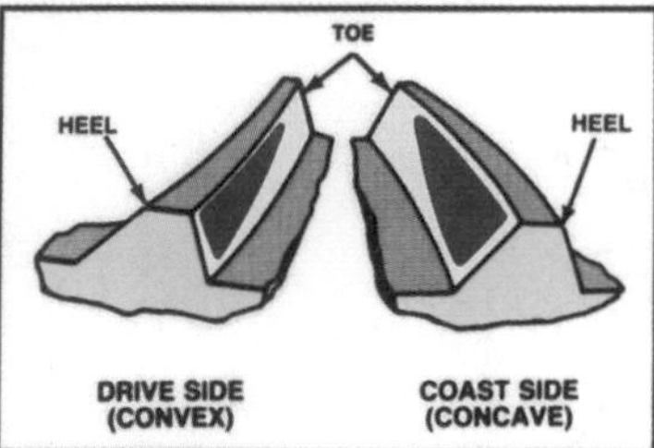

Correction:

Increase the thickness of the left (ring gear side) shim and decrease the thickness of the right shim an equal amount.

Service Hints:

How to check patterns:

- Brush gear marking compound on the ring gear teeth.
- Apply brakes so that 67 N•m (50 lb.-ft.) is needed to rotate the pinion.
- Rotate the pinion six times clockwise and six times counterclockwise.
- Observe the tooth contact pattern and make any necessary corrections.

Condition:

- Pinion depth correct.
- Backlash correct.

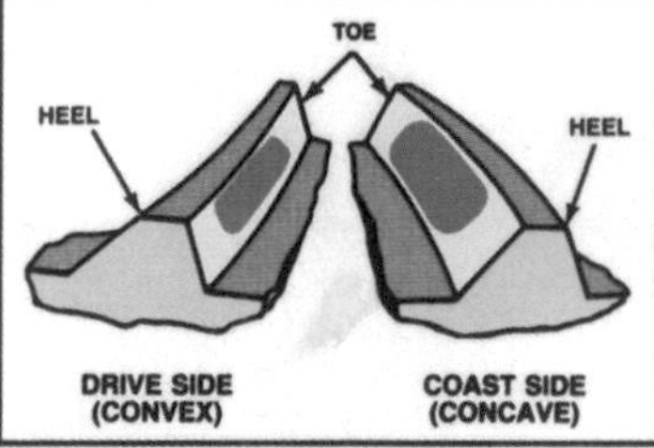

Correction:

None.

Service Hints:

Patterns that vary may be caused by loose bearings on the pinion or the differential case. Check these bearing preload settings:

- Total assembly
- Differential case
- Pinion

If these settings are good, look for damaged or incorrectly assembled parts.

Condition:

- Pinion depth correct.
- Backlash incorrect – too little clearance betweer the pinion and ring gears.

Correction:

Increase the thickness of the right shim and decrease the thickness of the left (ring gear side) shim.

Service Hints:

Side bearing shim locations:

- Between the side bearing cones and the differential case
- Between the side bearing cups and the rear axle housing

Condition:

- Backlash correct.
- Pinion depth incorrect – pinion gear is too far away from ring gear.

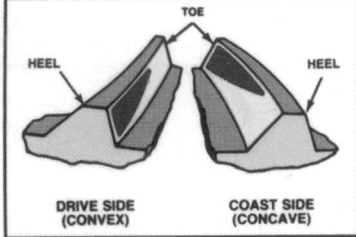

Correction:

Increase the pinion shim thickness.

Service Hints:

How to check patterns:

- Brush gear marking compound on the ring gear teeth.
- Apply brakes so that the pinion can be rotated with 67 N•m (50 lb.-ft.) effort.
- Rotate the pinion six times clockwise and six times counterclockwise.
- Observe the tooth contact pattern and make any necessary corrections.

Condition:

- Backlash correct.
- Pinion depth correct.

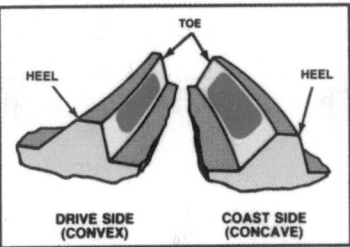

Correction:

None.

Service Hints:

Patterns that vary may be caused by loose bearings on the pinion or the differential case. Check these bearing preload settings:

- Total assembly
- Differential case
- Pinion

If these settings are good, look for damaged or incorrectly assembled parts.

Condition:

- Backlash correct.
- Pinion depth incorrect – pinion gear is too close to ring gear.

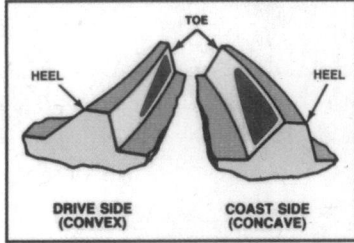

Correction:

Decrease the pinion shim thickness.

Service Hints:

Pinion depth shim locations:

- Between the inner pinion bearing cone and the head of the pinion gear
- Between the inner pinion bearing cup and the rear axle housing

Figure 47–24 Tooth contact pattern. (Courtesy of General Motors Corporation, Service Technology Group)

DIFFERENTIAL DISASSEMBLY

Start the differential disassembly by removing the axle housing cover. Be sure that the old rear end lubricant is drained into a disposal container according to local, provincial, and federal laws and regulations. After the cover has been removed, complete the disassembly by following these steps:

Step 1. Remove the drive shafts and inspect the axle bearing and seals for damage.

Step 2. Remove the third member by unbolting it from the housing or by removing the side bearing caps, as shown in Figure 47–25.

Step 3. Remove the drive pinion by first removing the pinion nut. See Figure 47–26. Discard the drive pinion nut. Always replace it with a new one.

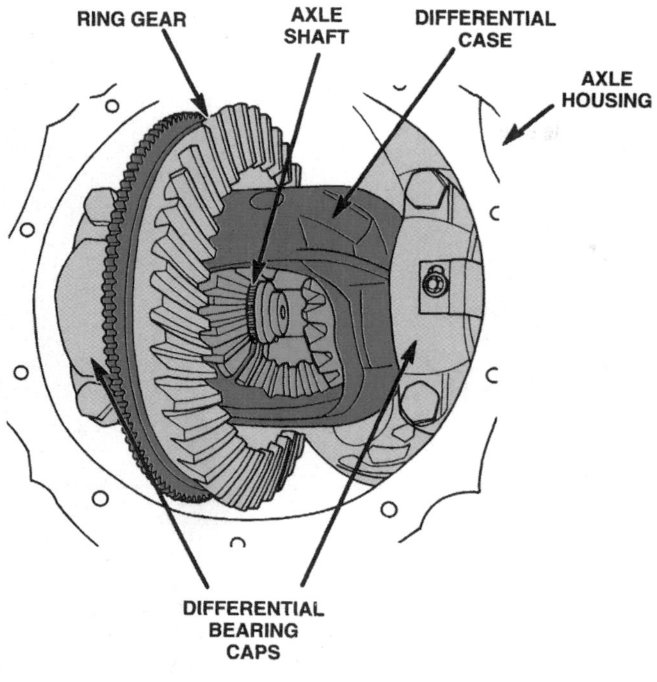

Figure 47–25 Mark the differential bearing caps before removing them to make sure that they are replaced in the same location.

> **CAUTION:** Do not use an air impact wrench to remove or install the drive pinion nut. The hammer action of the impact wrench can cause the roller bearings to be pounded into the race. This denting of the race is called *brinelling* and can cause premature bearing failure.

PINION SHAFT BEARING REPLACEMENT

The pinion shaft usually has two tapered roller bearings; the small diameter of each bearing faces the other. This arrangement allows the two bearings to absorb thrust load in both directions. When tapered roller bearings are used in a differential, it is very important that they have the proper preload. If a tapered roller bearing is too loose (too little preload), then the bearing cannot properly support and position the pinion shaft. If the preload is too great, excessive heat will quickly destroy the bearing as it expands with heat during normal operation of the rear axle assembly. Two methods are used to ensure proper drive pinion gear preload (see Figure 47–27).

- Preload shims
- Collapsible spacer

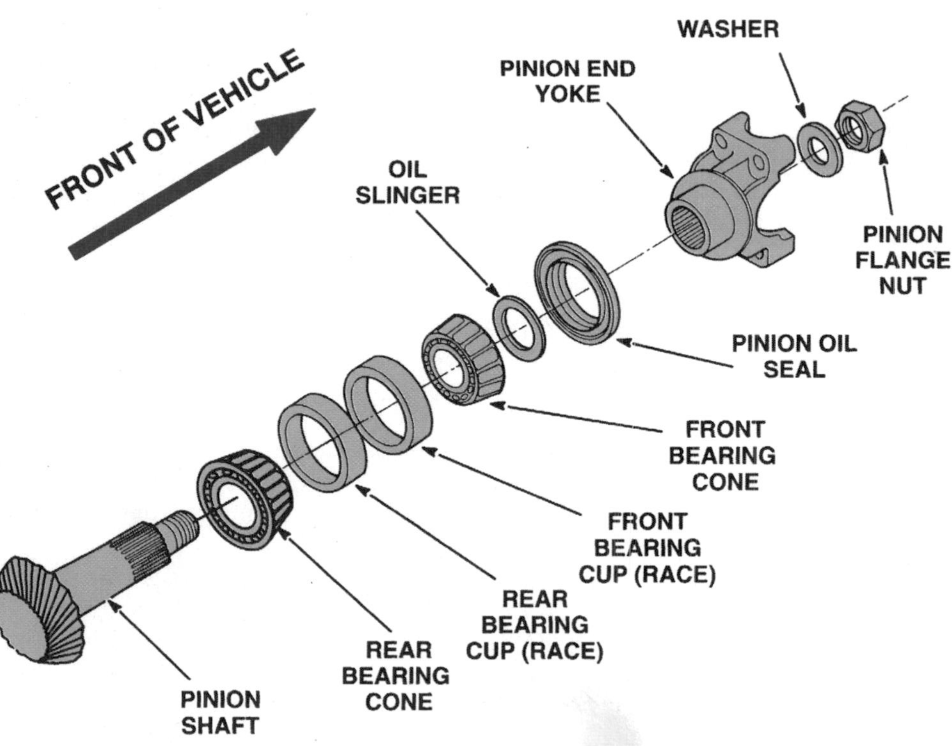

Figure 47–26 Pinion gear and associated parts. The pinion end yoke is also called the *pinion flange*. (Courtesy of Chrysler Corporation)

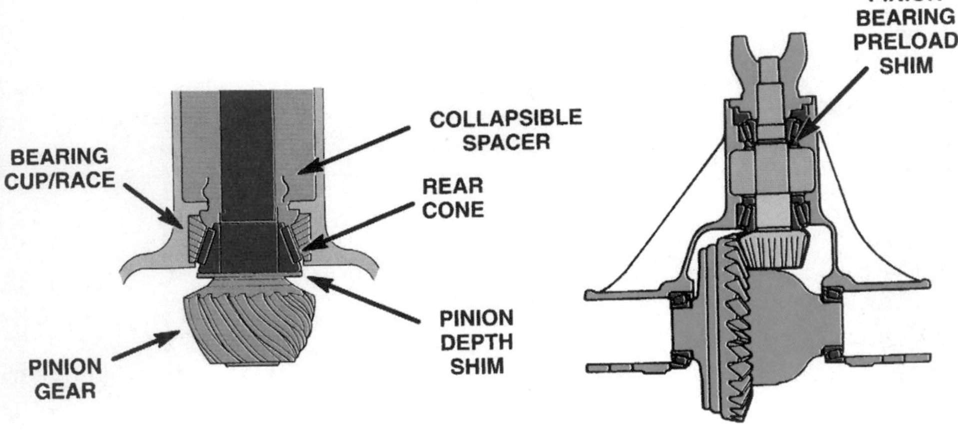

Figure 47–27 The pinion on the left uses a collapsible spacer, and the pinion on the right uses shims to provide the necessary preload to the pinion shaft bearings. (Courtesy of Chrysler Corporation)

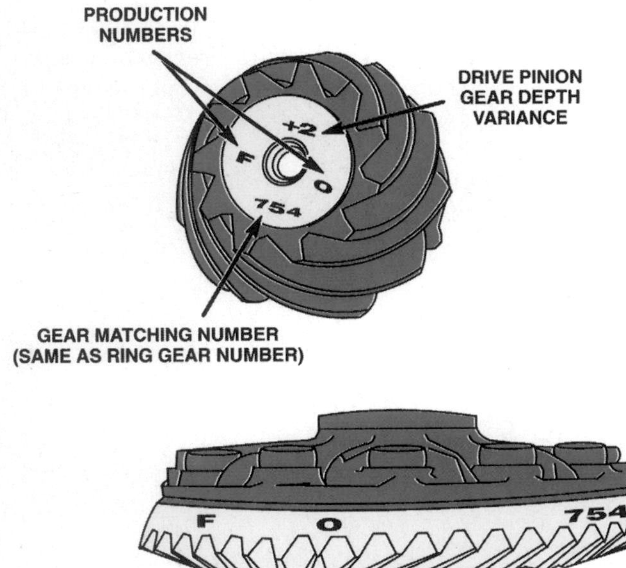

Figure 47–28 The ring and pinion gears are a matched set and are marked for correct pinion depth variance.

The rear pinion shaft bearing (closest to the drive pinion gear) is usually pressed out of the drive pinion. A shim is usually located between the drive pinion gear and the rear drive pinion bearing to properly position the drive pinion in relation to the ring gear. The ring gear and pinion are manufactured as a matched pair and must be installed correctly to be assured of quiet operation and long service life. See Figure 47–28. The drive pinion bearing must be pressed off using a hydraulic press or a special tool.

DRIVE PINION DEPTH

The drive pinion gear and ring gear are manufactured as a matched set and must be installed as a set. Due to variances in the production of these gears, it is often necessary to vary the thickness of a shim (thin metal spacer) between the rear pinion bearing and the pinion gear to provide the correct contact tooth pattern when the gears are assembled. Correct drive pinion depth measurement can be determined in several different ways:

- **Wear pattern analysis.** This method is useful as a first step and a last step to verify correct setup (discussed earlier in the chapter). It is time consuming to use this method to determine the thickness of the drive pinion shim because the rear pinion bearing must be pressed off and then back on for each shim change.
- **Plus (+) and minus (−) markings on the drive pinion.** The end of the pinion gear is usually marked as to the variance needed to create the proper ring gear-to-drive pinion pattern:

  A plus (+) sign means the gear is too long and removing a shim(s) is required when assembling the drive pinion into the axle housing.

  A minus (−) sign means that the gear is too short and a shim(s) will be needed when assembling the drive pinion into the axle housing.
- **A gauging set and depth micrometer.** This is a common method used to determine the correct shim thickness necessary to provide the proper gear pattern; see Figure 47–29.

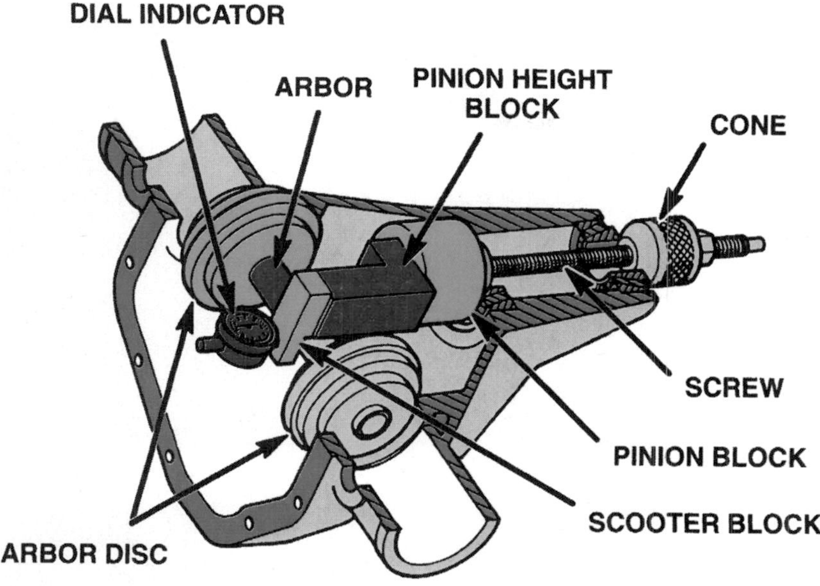

Figure 47–29 Special tool kit used for determining the correct pinion shaft shim thickness. (Courtesy of Chrysler Corporation)

PINION GEAR PRELOAD

After the proper drive pinion depth has been determined, the correct size shim is installed and the rear drive pinion bearing is pressed onto the drive pinion. The outer races of the pinion bearing should be replaced in the axle housing and the pinion shaft placed in the housing. It is then necessary to apply the specified preload to the pinion bearings. A new drive pinion nut should be used and tightened to specifications. After the nut has been tightened, torque needed to rotate the drive pinion should be measured using a beam-type torque wrench. The drive pinion nut is then tightened further until the **turning torque** is within specifications. See Figure 47–30.

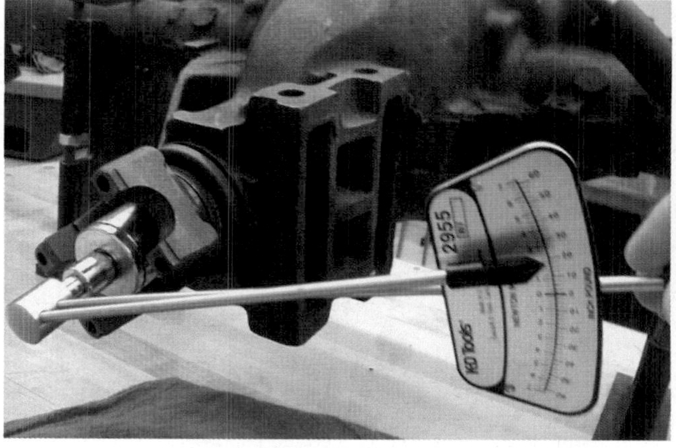

Figure 47–30 Using a torque wrench to check the rotating torque of the drive pinion. This procedure is very important if the axle uses a collapsible spacer. The drive pinion nut should be gradually tightened and the rotating torque checked to prevent overtightening the nut. If the rotating torque is higher than specifications, the collapsible spacer will require replacement and the installation procedure must be repeated.

CHECKING AND CORRECTING BACKLASH

If the ring gear and pinion are being replaced, the bolts that hold the ring gear to the differential case *must* be replaced. See Figure 47–31. The differential case with the ring gear is then placed into the differential housing. Backlash is the clearance between the drive pinion gear and the ring gear. A dial indicator is used to measure backlash, as shown in Figure 47–32. The backlash should be checked at three or four points around the ring gear and the lash should not vary over 0.05 mm (0.002 in.). Backlash normally is between 0.10 and 0.20 mm (0.005 and 0.008 in.) for most axle assemblies. Always check the specifications for the differential being serviced. See Figure 47–33.

Backlash is corrected by moving the ring gear either closer or farther away from the drive pinion gear. The correction is made by either of two methods

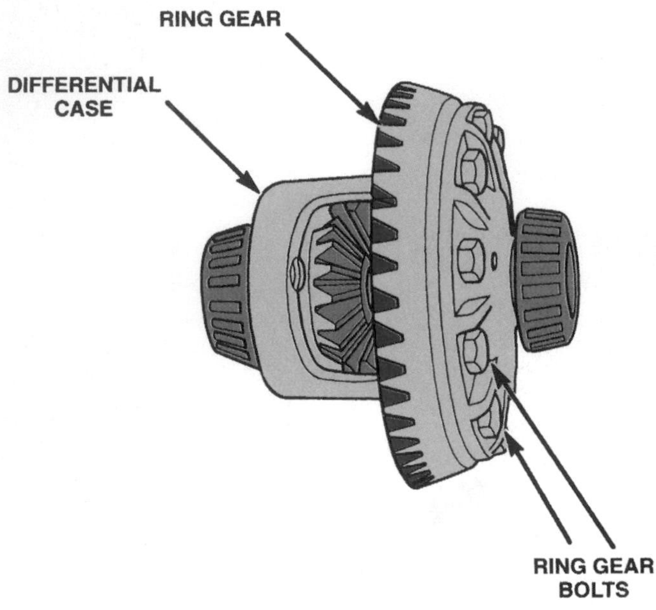

Figure 47–31 If the ring gear has been removed from the differential case or if a new ring gear is being installed, always replace the ring gear bolts. (Courtesy of Chrysler Corporation)

Figure 47–33 (a) Some vehicle manufacturers recommend using a housing spreader tool that fits into the round openings on both sides. (b) The spreader tool being installed. The housing is spread a specified amount and the differential is then installed into the housing.

Figure 47–32 Backlash should be between 0.13 and 0.20 mm (0.005 and 0.008 in.) on most differentials. If the backlash is too great, add shim thickness to the ring gear side and subtract shim thickness from the opposite side.

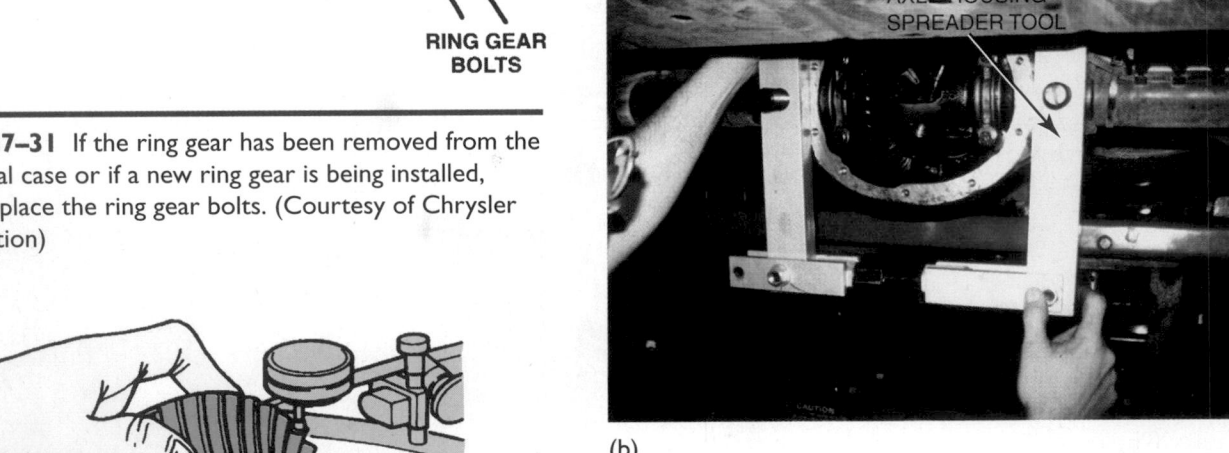

depending on the manufacturer and the type of differential:

- Transferring shims from one side of the axle housing to the other
- Turning threaded adjusters located in the differential housing bores, as shown in Figure 47–34

SETTING SIDE BEARING PRELOAD

After the correct backlash has been determined, the side bearing must be correctly preloaded. To accomplish the proper preload, thicker shims than were used to set proper backlash are placed between the housing and the differential to provide for the proper

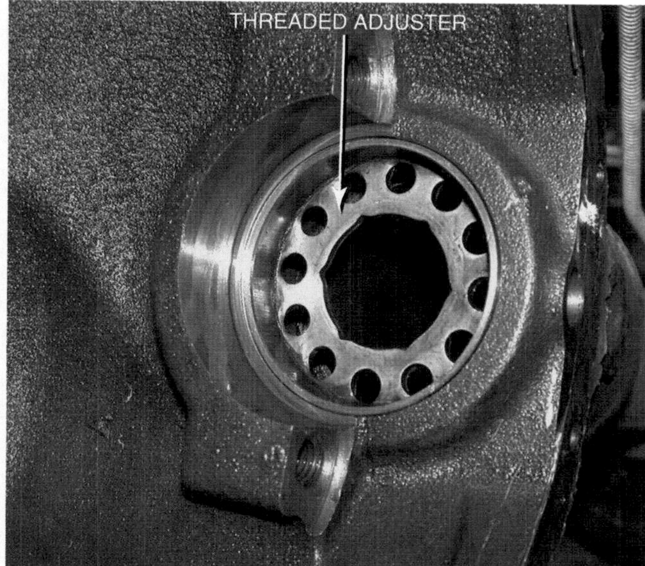

(a)

(b)

Figure 47–34 (a) Note the hex shape of the threaded adjuster used to adjust side bearing preload and ring gear backlash on a Dodge Dakota truck. (b) A long handled adjuster tool is needed to turn the side bearing adjuster on this truck.

preload on the side bearings. See Figure 47–35. Always follow the procedures specified for the axle being serviced. A typical axle may require the installation of a shim 0.10 mm (0.004 in.) thicker on both sides. After setting the preload, double check that the backlash is within specification.

TECH TIP

Click-Click Is Okay—Clunk-Clunk Is Not

An experienced service technician was observed checking the backlash on a differential. The technician was simply turning the drive pinion by grasping the pinion flange and using wrist action to quickly rotate it first in one direction and then the other. The technician explained that if it made a "click-click" sound, the backlash was usually between 0.13 and 0.20 mm (0.005 and 0.008 in.), which is usually within specifications for most differentials. If, however, the sound made was more like a "clunk-clunk," then the backlash was greater than 0.25 mm (0.010 in.) and had to be corrected. To summarize what the sounds mean when the drive pinion is moved back and forth:

- **No sound when moved back and forth**—too little or no backlash; backlash must be adjusted.
- **A click-click sound**—backlash is usually within specifications; double check with a dial indicator and compare against specifications for the axle being serviced.
- **A clunk-clunk sound**—usually too much backlash; correction is required to restore proper backlash.

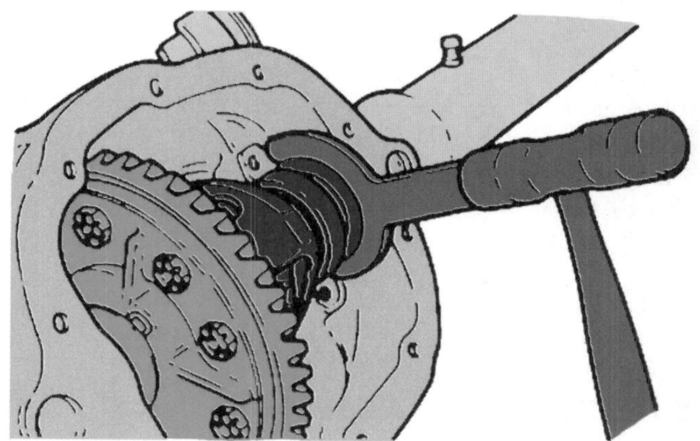

Figure 47–35 On many axles, it is necessary to use a special tool to install steel spacers (shims) to achieve the specified backlash and side bearing preload. (Courtesy of General Motors Corporation, Service Technology Group)

Frequently Asked Question ???

What Do I Do About Drive Pinion Bearing Preload When I Replace Just the Pinion Seal?

To replace a pinion seal, the drive pinion nut pinion flange must be removed.

> **CAUTION:** Do not use an air impact wrench on the drive pinion nut. The pinion bearings can be damaged by the impact of the wrench.

Before the nut is removed, make a mark on the pinion nut and on the axle housing. After the new pinion seal is installed, tighten the pinion nut to the same position it was in before disassembly and then rotate the nut 1.5 mm (1/16 in.) farther. This extra rotation makes sure that the collapsible space (crush sleeve) is still able to maintain the proper preload on the pinion bearing. Another method is to measure the rotating torque of the drive pinion using an inch-pound beam-type torque wrench after removing both rear wheels and brake drums. After installing the replacement pinion shaft seal, tighten the drive pinion nut until the rotating torque is 4 to 7 N·m (3 to 5 in-lb) more than the reading obtained before the pinion nut was removed.

Frequently Asked Question ???

What Is a Spool Rear End?

A spool is a solid piece of metal that takes the place of the side gears and pinion gears in a differential assembly (see Figure 47–36). A spool used in drag racing is not suitable for street driving because the spool does not allow for any differences in the speeds of the drive wheel during cornering. Obviously, drag vehicles do not turn corners while racing and the spool rear end is one of the reasons they bounce when turning around at the end of the strip to return to the pits.

REASSEMBLY OF THE DIFFERENTIAL ASSEMBLY

After the backlash has been checked to be within factory specifications, the axle shafts can be installed. See Figure 47–37. Install the retaining C clip or bolt the retainer to the axle housing. Clean and install the differential cover and fill with the specified differential lubrication.

Figure 47–36 A spool used in a rear end for drag racing only.

Figure 47–37 Install the axle shaft, being careful not to damage the seal.

DIFFERENTIAL LUBRICANT

Because all differentials use hypoid gear sets, a special lubricant is necessary because the gears both roll and slide between their meshed teeth. Gear lubes (GL) are specified by the American Petroleum Institute (API):

GL-1 Straight mineral oil

GL-2 Worm gear lubricant

GL-3 Mild EP lubricant (will *not* protect hypoid gears)

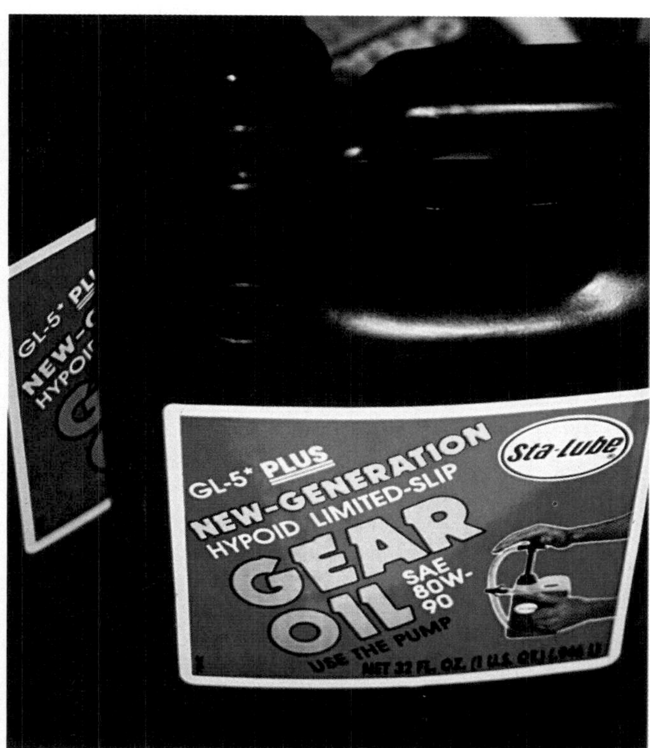

Figure 47–38 A container of GL-5 SAE 80W-90 gear lubricant.

GL-4 Mild EP lubricant suitable for manual transmissions/transaxles

GL-5 EP lubricant okay for hypoid gears (meets military Mil-L2150B requirements) See Figure 47–38.

NOTE: EP additives contain sulphurized esters and organic sulphur phosphorous compounds. These ingredients give the lubricant a very strong pungent smell. To avoid possible skin irritation, always wear protective gloves or wash your hands thoroughly with soap and water if exposed to differential lubricant.

Most differentials require

1. SAE 80W-90 GL-5
2. SAE 75W-90 GL-5
3. SAE 80W GL-5

NOTE: Always check the *exact* specification before adding or replacing rear axle lubricant.

Limited-slip differentials (often abbreviated LSD) usually use an additive that modifies the friction characteristics of the rear axle lubricant to prevent chattering while cornering.

DIAGNOSTIC STORY

I Didn't Know It Would Fit the Wrong Way!

An automotive student changed the differential lubricant by removing the housing cover. The cover was reinstalled and then filled with the correct lubricant. However, when the student drove the vehicle it made a grinding sound that was not there before the differential service. When the cover was removed, it was discovered that the cover had been installed with the raised area on the right side of the housing instead of on the left side and the ring gear had rubbed a groove in the cover, as shown in Figure 47–39. Installing the cover correctly stopped the grinding sound.

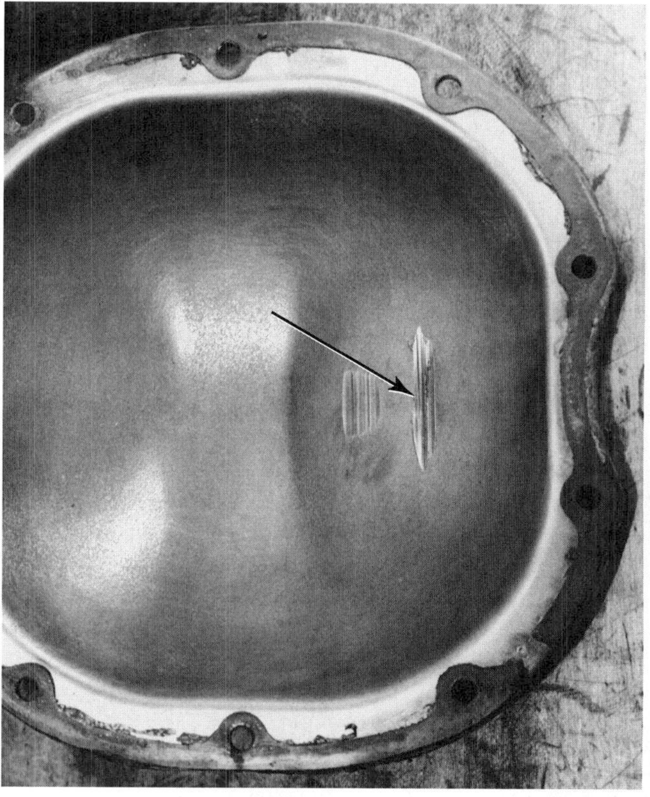

Figure 47–39 The beginning automotive student did not realize that the axle housing cover could fit the wrong way. The only problem was that the ring gear scraped against the cover.

HINT: If chattering becomes noticeable while cornering, replace the old differential lubricant with the correct lubricant and add limited-slip additives if specified by the vehicle manufacturer. After refilling the differential, drive the vehicle in a figure-eight pattern at least four times to help all of the lubricant and additives get into the clutch plates. This usually stops the chattering-while-cornering problem.

SUMMARY

1. A differential allows the drive wheels to rotate at different speeds while travelling around a corner or over bumps and dips in the road.
2. The drive pinion transfers torque to the ring gear, which is attached to the differential case. The case revolves with the ring gear. The case is equipped with pinion gears that mesh with side gears. The side gears are splined to the axles.
3. When one wheel is rotating faster than the other, the pinion gears "walk around" the side gears.
4. The gear ratio of a differential is determined by dividing the number of teeth of the drive pinion into the number of teeth of the ring gear.
5. Most axle assemblies have numbers and/or letters stamped into the axle housing as an identification.
6. A tooth contact pattern test is important to determine if the relationship between the drive pinion and ring gear is correct.
7. The depth of the drive pinion in the differential housing is critical to the proper operation of the differential.
8. A shim pack or a collapsible spacer is used to provide the proper drive pinion shaft bearing preload.
9. Backlash should be about 0.13 to 0.20 mm (0.005 to 0.008 in.) for most differentials.
10. Many limited-slip differentials use clutches to limit the amount of slippage that can occur between the two drive axles.

REVIEW QUESTIONS

1. Explain how to determine the axle ratio without removing the housing cover.
2. Describe how to perform a ring gear tooth contact pattern test.
3. List three methods that may be used to determine the proper drive pinion gear depth.
4. Explain how to achieve proper drive pinion gear bearing preload.
5. Describe how to adjust the position of the ring gear to achieve the proper backlash.
6. List the steps for replacing a drive pinion gear seal while still maintaining proper preload on the drive pinion bearing.

RED SEAL CERTIFICATION-TYPE QUESTIONS

1. On what side of the differential gear's teeth is the drive side of a front differential of a sports utility vehicle when it is moving forward?
   - **a.** Concave
   - **b.** Hypoid
   - **c.** Convex
   - **d.** Toe
2. The drive pinion gear is positioned with a shim that is too thick. This will cause contact with the ring gear teeth too close to the
   - **a.** Toe
   - **b.** Heel
   - **c.** Flank
   - **d.** Face
3. The backlash exceeds specifications. The technician should position the ring gear
   - **a.** Closer to the drive pinion gear
   - **b.** Farther from the drive pinion gear
4. The backlash is less than specifications (too low). This will cause the ring gear tooth pattern to be too close to the
   - **a.** Heel
   - **b.** Flank
   - **c.** Toe
   - **d.** Face
5. A collapsible spacer is used in some differentials to provide
   - **a.** A lubrication path to the drive pinion bearing
   - **b.** The proper preload for the side bearings
   - **c.** The proper preload for the drive pinion bearings
   - **d.** The proper amount of slippage in a limited-slip differential
6. What could cause a noise from the differential only while cornering?
   - **a.** Pinion gear
   - **b.** Crown gear
   - **c.** Side bearings
   - **d.** Axle bearing
7. The spacer used on a drive pinion gear is used to properly position the gear so that it can correctly mesh with the
   - **a.** Ring gear
   - **b.** Side gear
   - **c.** Differential pinion gears
   - **d.** Both b and c
8. What part(s) wears rapidly if a vehicle equipped with an open differential spins one wheel on ice or snow for an extended period of time?
   - **a.** Ring gear and pinion
   - **b.** Side gear
   - **c.** Pinion bearings
   - **d.** Pinion and side gear thrust washers
9. What type of lubricant can be used in a rear axle with a hypoid gear set?
   - **a.** SAE 10W-30 oil
   - **b.** Dextron oil
   - **c.** 525 mineral oil
   - **d.** SAE 80W-90 oil
10. What compound is used to verify crown gear to pinion gear tooth contact pattern?
    - **a.** Iron oxide compound
    - **b.** Valve lapping compound
    - **c.** Toothpaste
    - **d.** Anti-seize compound

48

Four-Wheel Drive and All-Wheel Drive

OBJECTIVES: After studying Chapter 48, you should be able to:

1. Prepare for the interprovincial Red Seal certification examination in Appendix III (Manual Drive Trains and Axles) on the topics covered in this chapter.
2. Explain the difference between a mode shift and a range shift.
3. Describe the purpose and function of the centre differential.
4. Explain the purpose and function of a viscous coupling.
5. Describe the difference between four-wheel drive and all-wheel drive.
6. Explain how the front axle is disconnected when two-wheel drive is selected.

PURPOSE AND FUNCTION OF FOUR-WHEEL AND ALL-WHEEL DRIVE

The increase in four-wheel drive systems has resulted from the popularity of sports utility vehicles. Manufacturers provide operators the choice of transferring torque either only to the rear wheels or to all four wheels at once. The transfer case can be shifted between two-wheel drive and four-wheel drive applications. In doing so the transfer case splits the engine torque between the front and rear wheels. All this is achieved with very little effort or inconvenience to the driver.

FOUR-WHEEL-DRIVE SYSTEMS

Two-wheel-drive vehicles use engine torque to turn either the front or the rear wheels. A differential is required to allow the drive wheels to travel different distances and speeds while cornering or driving over bumps or dips in the road. A four-wheel-drive vehicle, therefore, requires two differentials—one for the front wheels and one for the rear wheels.

NOTE: The term *4 × 4* means a four-wheeled vehicle that has engine torque applied to all four wheels (four-wheel drive). A *4 × 2* means a four-wheeled vehicle that has engine torque applied to only two wheels (two-wheel drive).

Four-wheel-drive vehicles require more than just two differentials. The front and the rear wheels of a four-wheel-drive vehicle also travel different distances and speeds whenever cornering or running over dips or rises in the road. There are three different methods used to allow for front-to-rear driveline speed variation.

Method 1—Locking Hubs

Engine torque from the transmission is applied directly to the rear differential through the transfer case. See Figure 48–1. The transfer case permits the driver to select a low-speed, high-power gear ratio inside the transfer case while in four-wheel drive. These positions and their meanings include

4H four-wheel drive with no gear reduction in the transfer case.

4L four-wheel drive with gear reduction. Use of this position is usually restricted to low speeds on slippery surfaces.

2H two-wheel drive (rear wheels only) in high range, meaning no gear reduction in the transfer case.

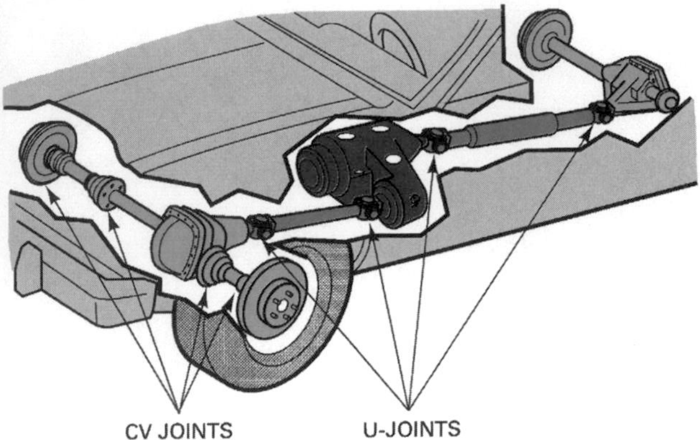

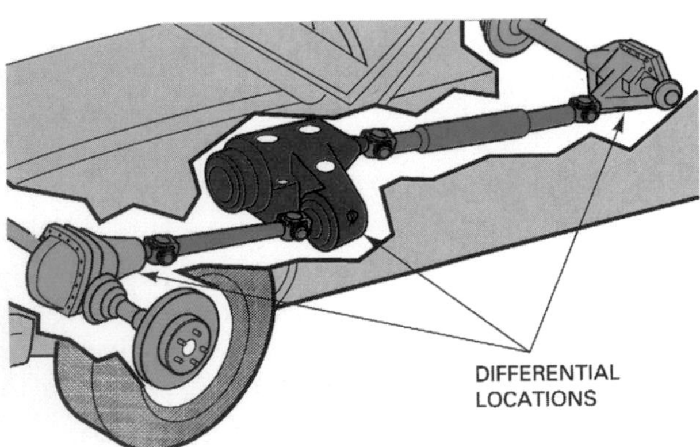

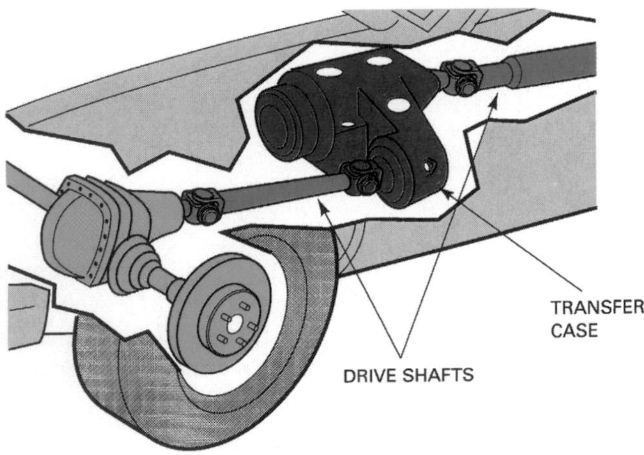

Figure 48–1 Many light trucks and sport utility vehicles use a transfer case to provide engine torque to all four wheels and to allow a gear reduction for maximum power to get through mud or snow. (Courtesy of Dana Corporation, Perfect Circle Products)

> **CAUTION:** Check the owner's manual or service manual for the recommended procedure to follow when changing from one position to another in the transfer case. Some vehicles require that the vehicle be stopped before selecting between two- and four-wheel drive and between high and low range.

Figure 48–2 Cutaway of a manually-operated locking hub.

The transfer case also applies power to the front differential. Power is then applied to the front wheels through the drive axles to the **locking hubs.** In normal 4H driving on hard surfaces, the front hubs *must* be in the unlocked position. The front hubs are locked whenever driving on loose road surfaces to absorb and allow for tire slippage due to the different tire speeds front to back. This type of four-wheel-drive system is called **part-time four-wheel drive** because it can only be driven in four-wheel drive on slippery surfaces. See Figure 48–2.

> **CAUTION:** Failure to unlock the front wheel hubs while driving on a hard road surface can cause serious driveline vibrations and damage to drive shafts, U-joints, and bearings as well as to the transfer case, transmission, and even the engine.

Method 2—Autolocking Hubs

Another method of locking the hubs on a part-time four-wheel-drive system is with a clutch arrangement built into the hub assembly. Whenever driving on smooth, hard road surfaces, the hubs free-wheel and allow the front wheels to rotate at different speeds from the rear wheels. When the speed difference between the wheels and the front drive axle is great, the hubs will automatically lock and allow engine torque to be applied to the front wheels. Figure 48–3 shows an autolocking hub with the cover removed. Automatic-locking hubs are unlocked by disengaging four-wheel drive at the transfer case and driving in reverse for several metres.

> **NOTE:** One of the disadvantages of automatic locking hubs is that they do not transfer torque to the front wheels when the vehicle is in reverse.

Figure 48–3 Manual locking hubs require that the hubs be rotated to the locked position by hand to allow torque to be applied to the front wheels. Automatic locking hubs enable the driver to shift into four-wheel drive from inside the vehicle.

TECH TIP 

How to Tow a Four-Wheel-Drive Vehicle Without Doing Harm

If any of the drive wheels are on the ground, the wheels are turning the axles. Depending on the exact type of four-wheel-drive vehicle being towed, this rotation of the wheels can cause severe wear; therefore most experts suggest the following options:

- **Placing the vehicle on a flatbed or trailer.** This keeps all four wheels off the ground and is the safest method for transporting a four-wheel-drive (or all-wheel-drive) vehicle without doing any harm.
- **Hoisting the rear wheels off the ground and placing the front wheels on a dolly.** This procedure also keeps all wheels off the ground and therefore prevents any damage being done to the power train as a result of towing. See Figure 48–4.

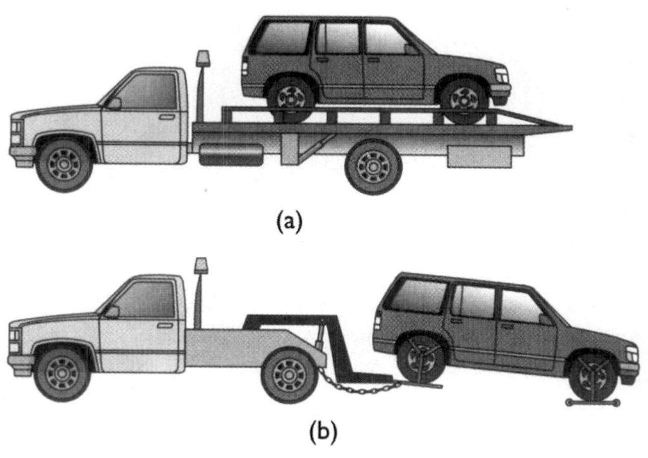

Figure 48–4 If a four-wheel-drive vehicle must be towed, it should be either on (a) a flatbed truck or (b) a dolly.

Method 3—Full-Time Four-Wheel Drive

This method uses a centre differential to allow front and rear wheels to travel at different speeds under all operating conditions, as shown in Figure 48–5. Although this drive train design is the easiest to operate both on and off the road, the centre differential can cause the vehicle to get stuck in mud or snow even though it is a four-wheel-drive vehicle.

All open-style differentials allow for speed differences and torque is applied equally, so if one wheel is on ice or mud, the other wheel receives the same low torque. This is why many vehicles spin just one wheel when stuck on ice or snow. But if one rear wheel starts to spin, the vehicle may not move forward at all!

There are two methods used to lock the centre differential to prevent this from happening.

- A **viscous coupling** is commonly used on many four-wheel-drive vehicles to provide an automatic lockup of the centre differential. A viscous coupling is a type of fluid clutch. When the speed difference between the front and rear wheels is high enough, the silicon fluid inside the coupling stiffens to reduce the speed difference between the front and rear drive shafts. See Figures 48–6 and 48–7.
- An **electronically controlled clutch assembly** is actuated by the vehicle's computer based on inputs from the ABS wheel speed sensors. If a wheel starts to spin, the computer can pulse the clutch on and off as necessary to control the amount of wheel slippage.

Frequently Asked Question ???

What Is Brake-Actuated Traction Control?

The engine torque of a full-time four-wheel-drive vehicle (with the centre differential unlocked) is split into four nearly equal parts. One quarter of the torque is applied to each wheel. If a brake is applied to a spinning wheel, the torque to that wheel is increased, which will increase the torque to all of the other wheels. The increased torque applied to the wheels that have contact with a surface that has some traction will enable the vehicle to proceed. This is the principle involved in brake-controlled traction control such as is used on the Mercedes M4 sport utility vehicle (SUV).

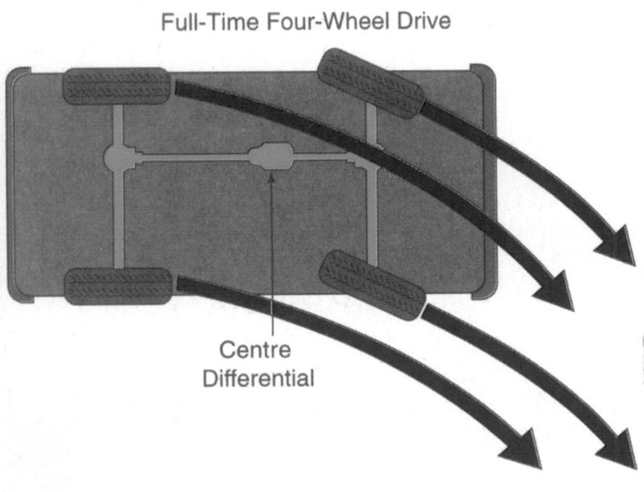

Figure 48–5 When turning a corner, each wheel takes a slightly different path and rotates at a slightly different speed. Unlike a part-time four-wheel-drive system, which when engaged locks the front and rear axles together, a full-time system uses a centre differential that allows for any speed differences between the front and rear axles. It can therefore be activated on any surface—slippery or dry.

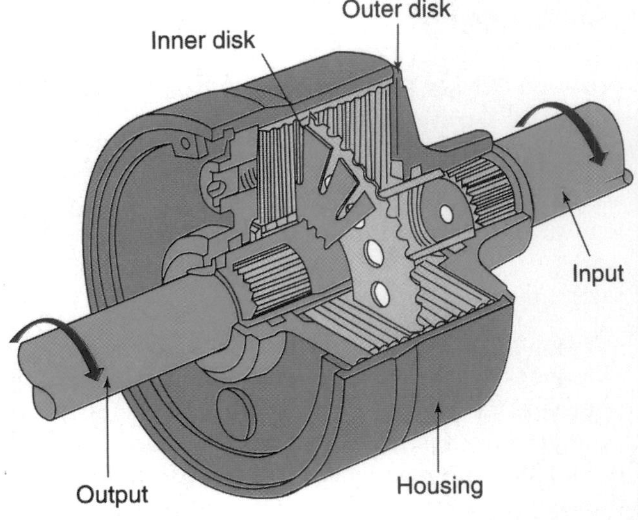

Figure 48–6 A viscous coupling is a sealed unit containing many steel discs. One-half of them are splined to the input shaft, with every other disc splined to the output shaft. Surrounding these discs is a thick (viscous) silicone fluid that expands when hot and effectively locks the discs together.

(a)

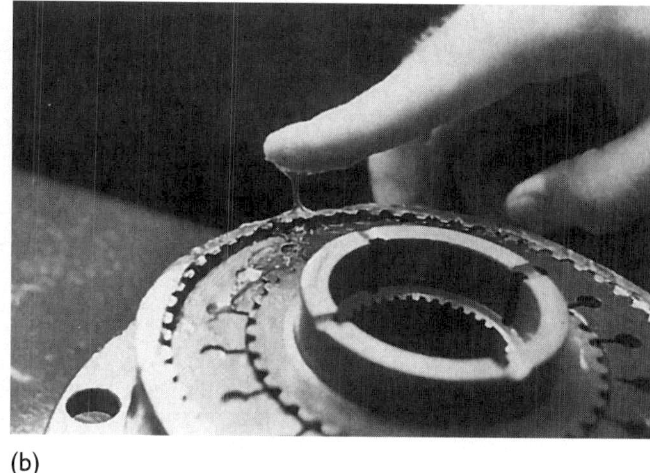

(b)

Figure 48–7 (a) The inside of the viscous coupling consists of thin metal discs. (b) Viscous silicone fluid is used between the metal discs.

Figure 48–8 The centre differential is the heart of a typical all-wheel-drive system. All-wheel drive systems do not use a low range, and therefore the vehicle may not be able to go off-road like a vehicle equipped with a four-wheel drive with a low range.

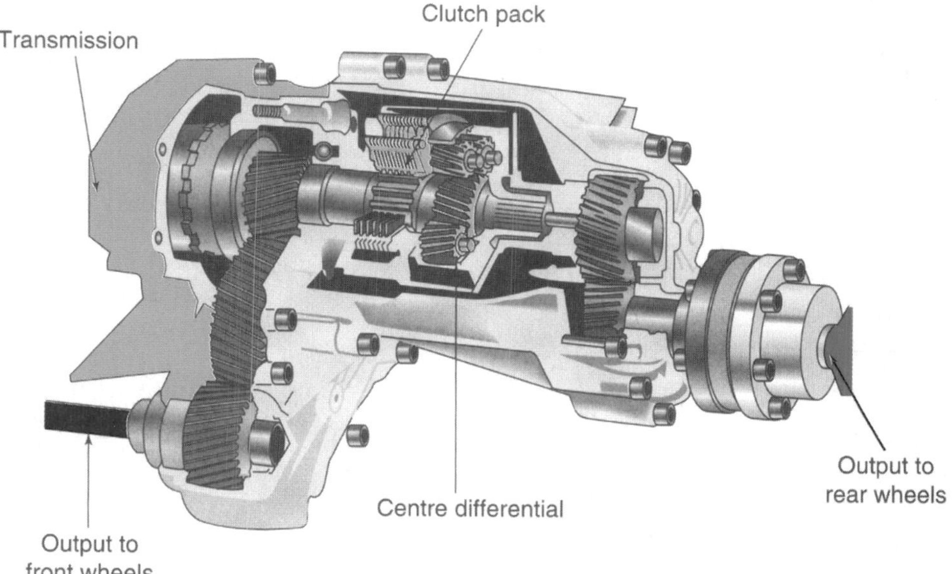

ALL-WHEEL DRIVE

Some cars and light trucks are equipped with an all-wheel-drive system that uses a transfer case with a centre differential and only one speed (high). Low-range gear reduction is not used. A viscous coupling is usually incorporated into the centre differential to provide superior all-weather traction. Combined with a limited-slip differential in the rear, and sometimes also in the front, an all-wheel-drive system can provide ideal road traction under all driving conditions without any action by the driver. See Figure 48–8.

Frequently Asked Question ???

What Is the Difference Between Four-Wheel Drive (4WD) and All-Wheel Drive (AWD)?

The major difference between four-wheel drive and all-wheel drive is that four-wheel-drive units contain a transfer case with a low range. Most all-wheel-drive vehicles do not have low range and are in high four-wheel drive all the time. Both use a centre (interaxle) differential and both usually use a viscous coupling or an electronically controlled clutch to control (lock) the centre differential.

FRONT AND REAR DIFFERENTIAL AXLE RATIOS

In most four-wheel-drive vehicles, the overall gear ratio of the front differential is slightly higher than the overall ratio of the rear differential. The overall ratio is determined by multiplying the gear ratio by the differential ratio. See the following chart comparing the ratios for the front and rear differentials of a typical four-wheel-drive vehicle equipped with a manual five-speed transmission.

Manual Transmission and Final-Drive Gear Ratios			
Speed	Gear Ratio	Final-Drive Ratio	Overall Ratio
1st	3.083:1	4.933 front 4.927 rear	15.208 front 15.190 rear
2nd	1.684:1	4.933 front 4.927 rear	8.307 front 8.297 rear
3rd	1.115:1	4.933 front 4.927 rear	5.500 front 5.494 rear
4th	0.833:1	4.933 front 4.927 rear	4.109 front 4.104 rear
5th	0.666:1	4.933 front 4.927 rear	3.285 front 3.281 rear

Although the difference between the ratios is small, the purpose is to prevent the drive train from binding. With the front differential ratio being just slightly higher, the tendency is for the front of the vehicle to pull the vehicle thereby eliminating the problem of having the rear pushing at the exact same ratio as the front is pulling. The different ratios also help reduce resonant vibration and noise created in the driveline.

TRANSFER CASE

The purpose and function of the transfer case is to direct engine torque to the front and rear axle assemblies. See Figure 48–9. A four-wheel-drive transfer case is basically an auxiliary 2-speed transmission. It uses the transmission output as an input to a secondary gear train or planetary gear set, which provides a low and high range. The transfer of torque to the front axle output shaft can be accomplished either by a gear-to-gear transfer or a gear and chain transfer. The gear ranges can be engaged a number of ways, such as a manual lever, electrical, or vacuum actuators. A transfer case has one input shaft (connected to the output of the transmission) and two output shafts (see Figure 48–10). The two output shafts are connected to the drive shafts and

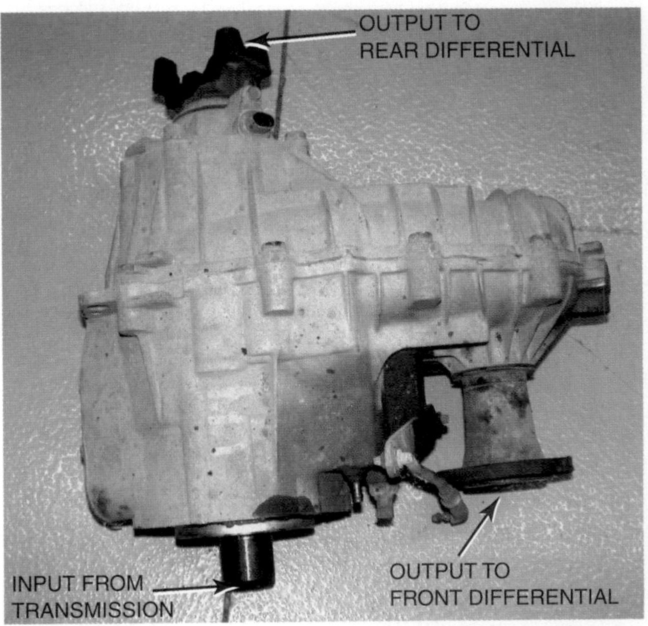

Figure 48–9 A typical transfer case is attached to the output of the transmission and directs engine torque to the rear or to the front and rear differentials.

transfer torque to the front and rear differentials. Most transfer cases also provide for two types of shifts:

- **Mode shift.** Either two-wheel drive or four-wheel drive may be selected. Many transfer cases also have a neutral position. The mode shift is achieved by the use of a floor-mounted lever to engage and disengage a clutch inside the transfer case. This shift is usually performed when the vehicle is stopped. However, new designs allow the mode shift to be performed under most driving conditions.

NOTE: The mode shift is not available on all-wheel-drive vehicles.

- **Range shift.** A **low range** may be selected to deliver high torque at low speeds to the drive wheels. Low range usually provides a 2:1 and 3:1 gear reduction. High range (usually 1:1) simply transfers engine torque at the same speed as the output shaft of the transmission.

NOTE: Part-time four-wheel drive means that the transfer case does not include a differential.

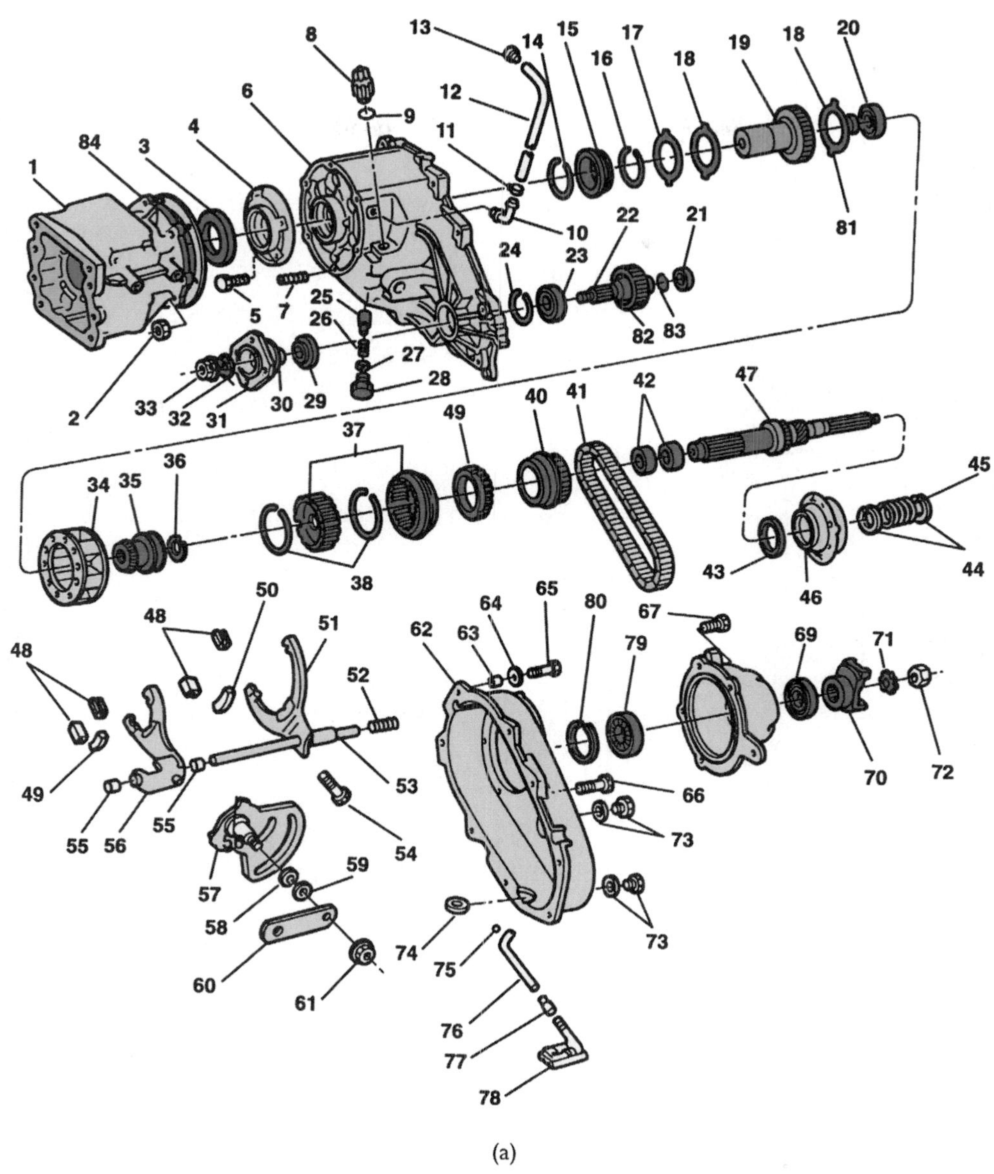

(a)

NEW VENTURE 241 TRANSFER CASE COMPONENTS

1. Adapter
2. Locknut
3. Front retainer seal
4. Front bearing retainer
5. Retainer screw
6. Front case
7. Case stud
8. Vacuum switch
9. Vacuum switch O-ring
10. Vent
11. Vent hose clamp
12. Vent hose
13. Vent hose end cap
14. Input bearing retainer snap ring
15. Input gear bearing
16. Input gear snap ring
17. Input gear retainer
18. Input gear thrust washer
19. Input gear
20. Input gear pilot bearing
21. Output shaft rear bearing
22. Output shaft
23. Output shaft front bearing
24. Front output shaft, front bearing snap ring
25. Shift detent plunger
26. Shift detent plunger spring
27. O-ring seal
28. Shift detent plug
29. Yoke oil seal
30. Yoke oil slinger
31. Front output shaft yoke
32. Yoke washer
33. Yoke nut
34. Low range gear
35. Range fork shift hub
36. Synchronizer hub snap ring
37. Synchronizer assembly
38. Synchronizer springs
39. Synchronizer stop ring
40. Drive chain sprocket
41. Drive chain
42. Drive sprocket bearing
43. Oil pump seal
44. Speedometer gear, snap ring
45. Speedometer gear
46. Oil pump assembly
47. Transfer case mainshaft
48. Shift fork pads
49. Range fork, centre pad
50. Mode fork, centre pad
51. Shift mode fork
52. Shift rail spring
53. Shift rail
54. Mode fork pin
55. Range fork bushings
56. Range fork assembly
57. Shift sector
58. Sector O-ring seal
59. Sector O-ring retainer
60. Range lever
61. Range lever, nut
62. Rear case
63. Case alignment dowels
64. Dowel bolt washer
65. Dowel bolt
66. Case bolt
67. Rear retainer screw
68. Rear retainer
69. Rear retainer seal
70. Rear yoke
71. Rear spline seal
72. Rear yoke nut
73. Plug and washer
74. Magnet
75. O-ring, tube seal
76. Oil pick-up tube
77. Tube connector
78. Oil pick-up screen
79. Rear output bearing
80. Snap ring, output bearing
81. Input gear plug
82. Front output shaft
83. Sprocket snap ring
84. Gasket

(b)

Figure 48–10 An exploded view of a New Venture-241 transfer case. (Courtesy of Chrysler Corporation)

Gear-to-Gear Transfer Cases

Gear-to-gear transfer cases are simple in design. Three gear shafts are in mesh within the transfer case. One gear shaft is attached to the transmission output shaft. The second shaft acts as an idler, and the third shaft is the output to the front axle. Gear-to-gear transfer cases, in most cases, have two speeds. The first, 4-wheel-drive low, is a gear reduction that is usually around 2:1. The second gear in the transfer case is a direct drive. The gears are engaged by sliding collars or synchronizers to lock the gears to the shaft. Neutral is accomplished when neither gear collar is locking a gear in place.

Two-Wheel-Drive Operation When the transfer case controls are in two-wheel drive, the front differential assembly is disconnected from the transfer case. This disconnection is usually accomplished by disconnecting one of the drive axles, as shown in Figures 48–11 and 48–12. The disconnect mechanism in the front axle and a synchronizer assembly in the transfer case combine to remove torque from the front wheels.

Four-Wheel-Drive Operation To achieve four-wheel drive, two things must occur:

- A synchronizer assembly connects the torque from the engine to the front drive shaft in the transfer case.
- The drive axles must be connected to allow the torque from the front differential to be applied to the drive wheels. See Figure 48–13.

Planetary Gear Set Transfer Cases

Many transfer cases use a planetary gear set for gear reduction in low range. A planetary gear set includes the following three elements:

1. **Sun gear.** This gear is in the centre like the position of the sun is in our solar system.
2. **Planet pinions.** The planet pinion gears rotate around the sun gear, like the planets around the sun, and are attached by a **planet carrier.**
3. **Ring gear.** The outer ring gear has teeth on the inside that mesh with the teeth of the

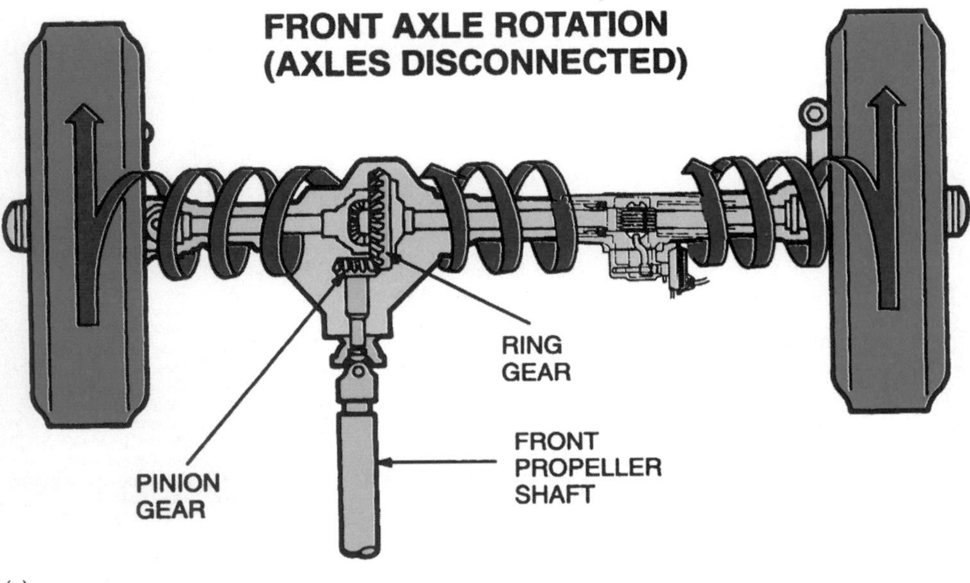

Figure 48–11 (a) When one axle shaft is disconnected, both front wheels can rotate independently, reducing excessive tire wear. (Courtesy of Chrysler Corporation)

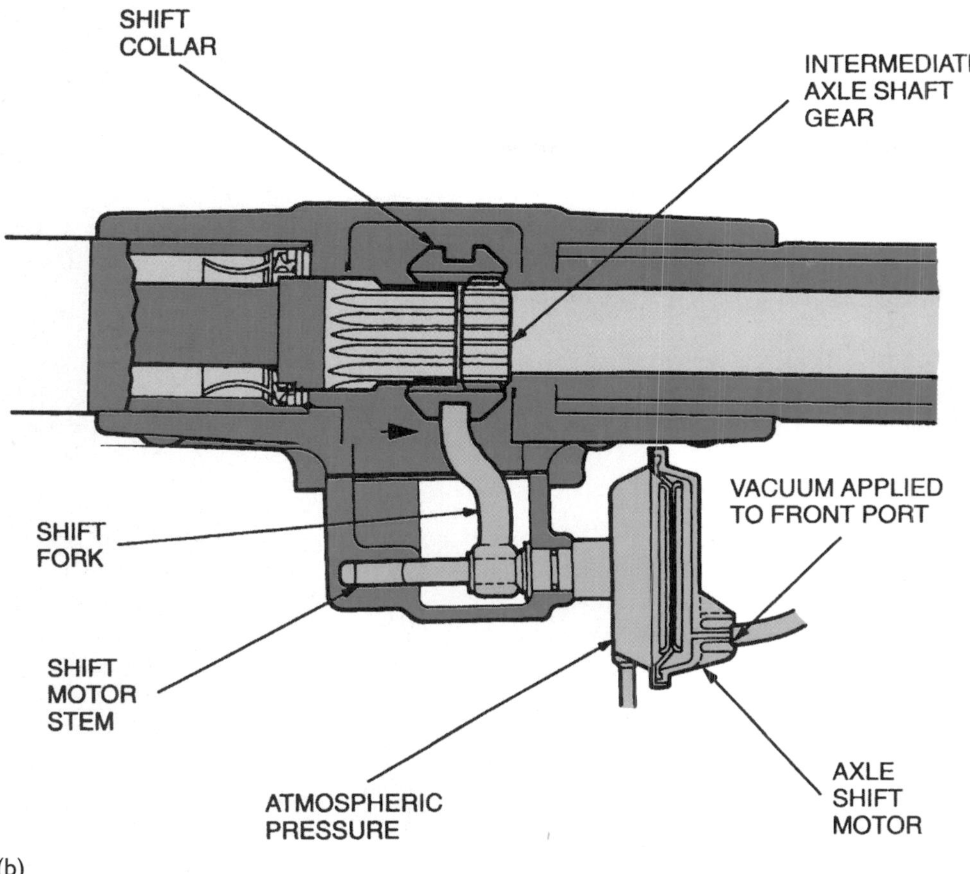

Figure 48–11 (b) In four-wheel-drive mode, vacuum is applied to the front part and the opposite side is vented to atmospheric pressure, retracting the shift motor stem. The shift fork and collar move into engagement with both axle shaft gears. Engine torque from the front differential can now be applied to both front axles. When the transfer case is placed in two-wheel drive, the vacuum is applied to the other side of the diaphragm and the shift collar moves, unlocking the front axles. (Courtesy of Chrysler Corporation)

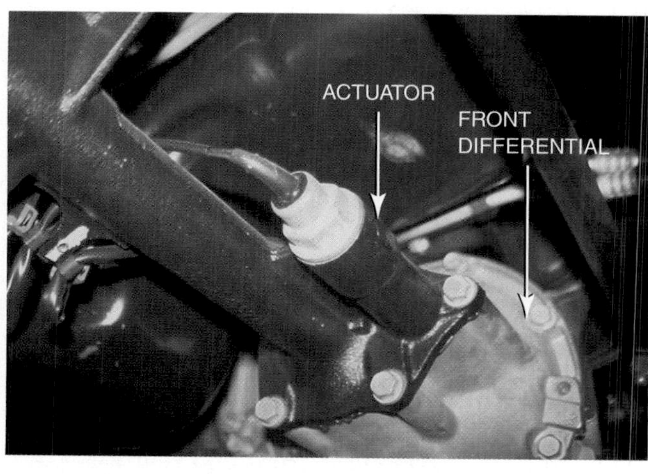

Figure 48–12 A General Motors sport utility vehicle front axle showing the electric axle disconnect actuator.

Figure 48–13 The range shift selector on an AM General Hummer sport utility vehicle. This vehicle is always in four-wheel drive, but the driver can select neutral (N) or low range.

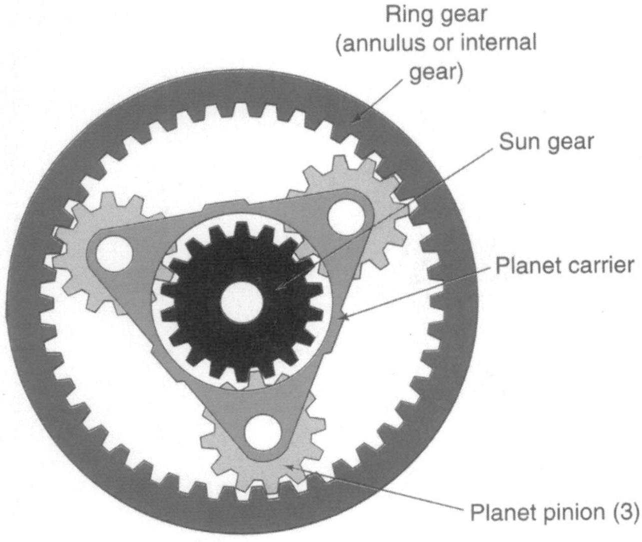

Figure 48–14 A typical planetary gear set used in a transfer case.

planet pinion gears. The ring gear is also called the **annulus gear** or **internal gear** because the gear teeth are on the inside (rather than the outside) portion of the gear.

The gear teeth of a planetary gear set remain in constant mesh. When gear reduction is needed, the sun gear is often the drive gear and the planet carrier is often the driven gear. The gear ratio reduction depends on the number of teeth on the various gears used in a planetary gear set. See Figures 48–14 and 48–15. To achieve direct 1:1 output from the transfer case, any two of the three elements can be locked together and the entire assembly will rotate as a unit.

Power flows through a planetary gear set in several steps to get from the drive action of the first member to the driven action of the last member. The terms "drive" and "driven" simply describe how any two gears work together. When three or more gears are involved, the second gear is a *driven* gear in relation to the first, but a *drive* gear in relation to the third. For this reason, the drive member of a planetary gear set is called the **input member,** the held member, the **reaction member,** and the driven member, the **output member.** See Figures 48–16 through 48–18.

INTERAXLE DIFFERENTIAL

All-the-time 4-wheel-drive, all-wheel-drive, and full-time 4-wheel-drive systems use an **interaxle differential (centre differential)** to prevent driveline harshness and vibration, commonly referred to as driveline windup. An interaxle differential can be found in various configurations including:

Figure 48–15 Cutaway of a planetary gear set transfer case.

- Standard bevel gear differential
- Planetary gear differential
- Viscous coupling

Although they are different in appearance, interaxle differentials serve the same purpose, to maintain smooth operation while making turns in a 4-wheel-drive/all-wheel-drive vehicle. The **bevel gear differential** uses two bevel gears or spider gears attached to the output shaft of the transmission. Two to four differential pinion gears are attached to a carrier, which is attached to the transfer gears. In other words, it operates in the same fashion as the differential in a rear axle; power is transferred to the tire with the least traction. When there is unequal traction between the front and rear axles, the axle with the most traction is allowed to slip enough to prevent damage to driveline components. See Figure 48–19 (p. 1159).

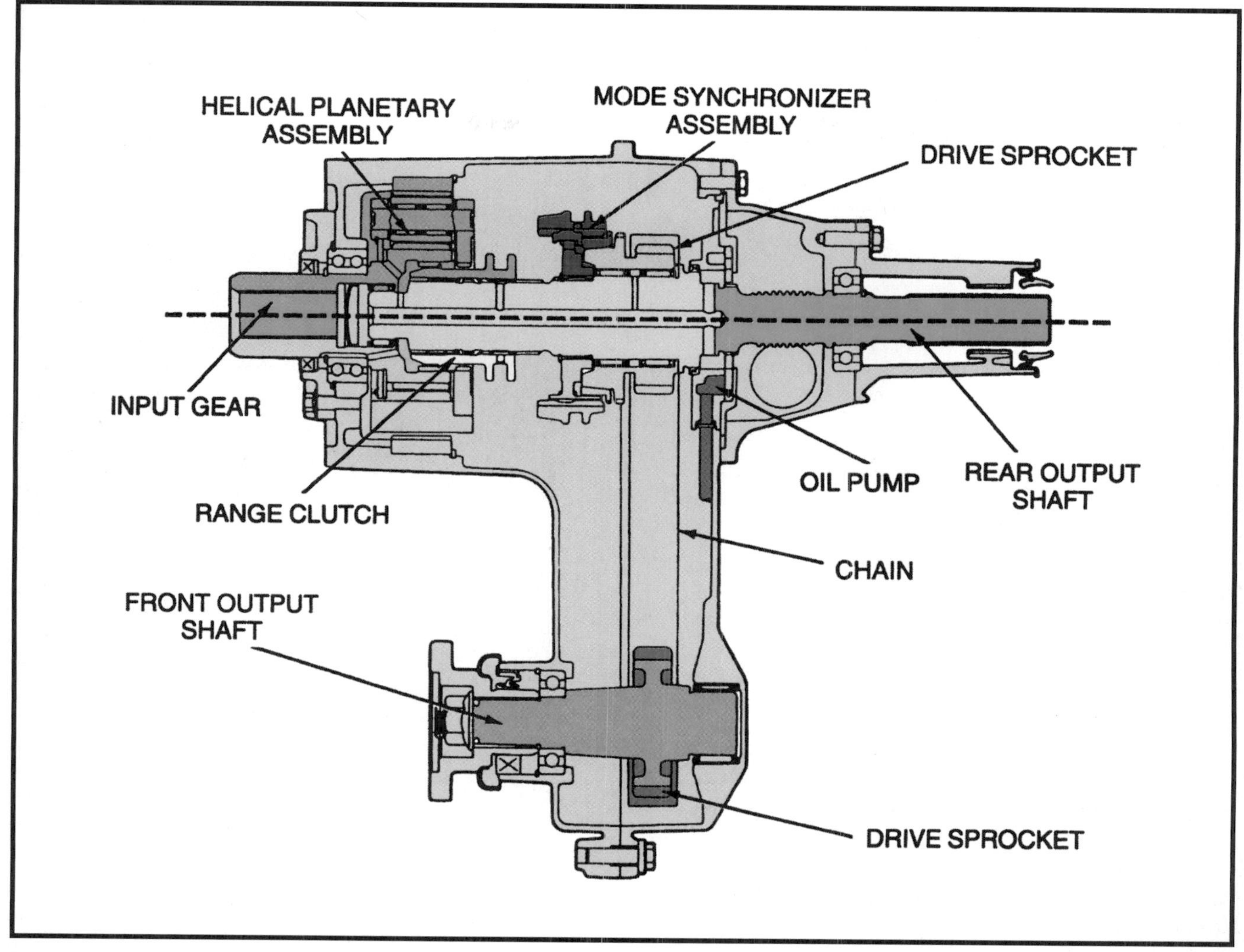

Figure 48–16 Two-wheel-drive/high-range torque flow in an NV231 transfer case. The sliding range clutch is shifted to the forward position by the range lever and fork, which connects the input gear to the output shaft and rear axle. The mode synchronizer sleeve is moved out of engagement from the drive sprocket to remove torque from the front axle. (Courtesy of Chrysler Corporation)

With this setup, the loss of traction at one wheel could effectively disable the vehicle. For example, if one wheel had zero traction, the majority of engine torque would be applied to that wheel. In a standard bevel gear setup, torque is split between the front and rear axles. If there is a loss of traction in the front, the transfer of torque to the rear axle will be significantly lowered. To remedy this condition, auto manufacturers incorporate an internal clutch mechanism, much like a limited slip unit, to increase torque transfer and still lessen driveline vibration and harshness.

A planetary gear set is often incorporated in transfer cases to act as a differential.

A **viscous coupling** is nothing more than a selection of steel plates housed in a sealed steel drum. See Figure 48–20. The viscous coupling is not active during equal traction conditions. The viscous coupling does actively transfer torque during light to moderate cornering, but there is a certain amount of slippage under these conditions to prevent driveline windup. If there is a significant loss of traction, the speed differences between the front and rear axles increase, and this increase in plate speed heats the silicon fluid in the viscous coupling, causing it to thicken to the point that it transfers more torque to the axle that is losing traction. During a severe loss of traction, the viscous fluid thickens enough to lock

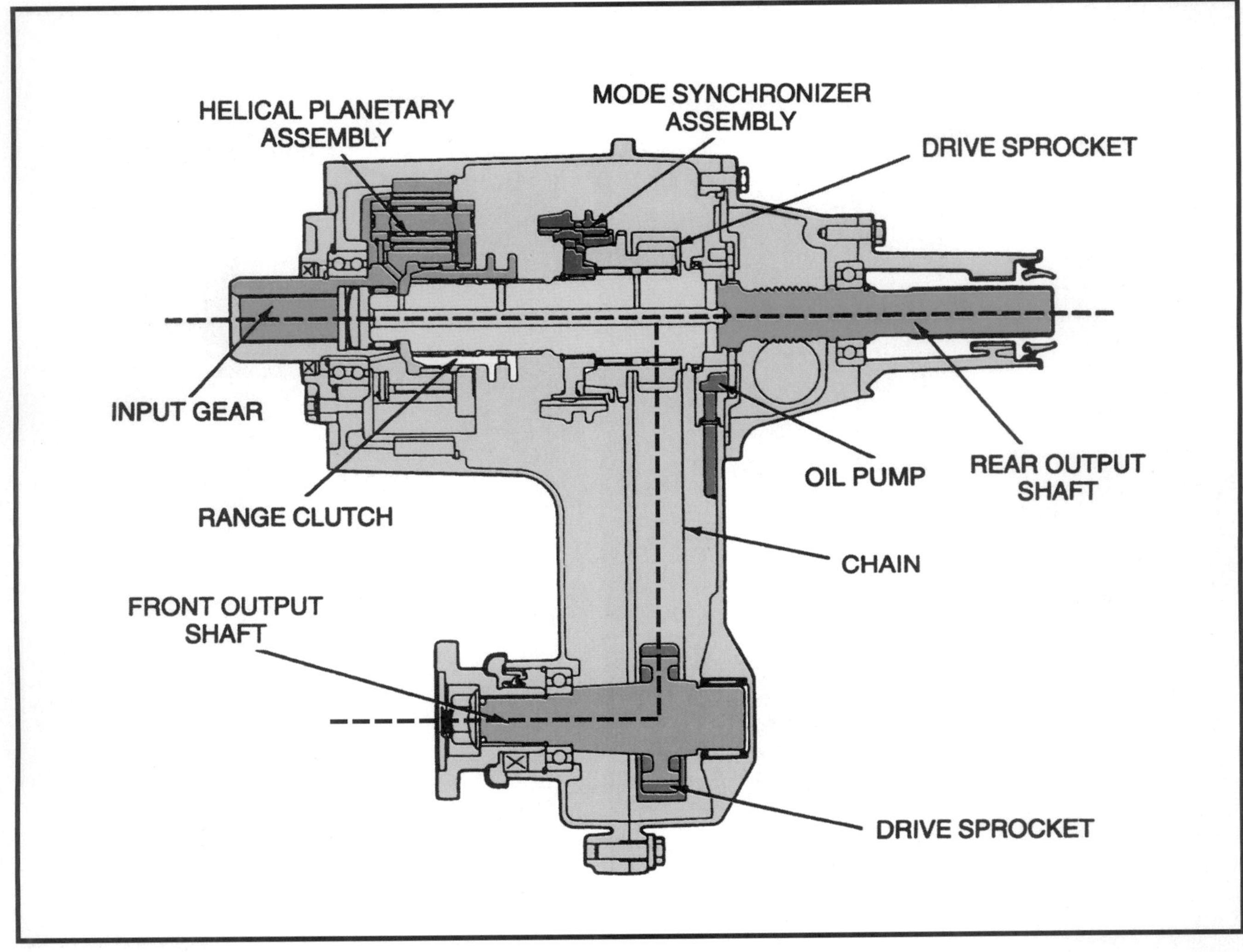

Figure 48–17 Four-wheel-drive/high-range torque flow in an NV231 transfer case. The range clutch position remains the same as in two-wheel drive/high-range, but the synchronizer sleeve is moved rearward and engages the drive sprocket clutch teeth. This action connects the drive sprocket to the rear output shaft, thereby applying equal torque to both front and rear output shafts. (Courtesy of Chrysler Corporation)

the plates together, dividing engine torque equally 50/50 between the front and rear axles.

FOUR-WHEEL-DRIVE AXLES

Four-wheel-drive vehicles use a variety of drive shafts and U-joint designs:

- **Standard Cardan-type U-joints.** See Figure 48–21. If this type of U-joint is used on the front wheels of a four-wheel-drive vehicle, the different speeds it creates can cause the front wheels to skip, hop, and shake if engine torque is applied while on dry pavement and turning a corner at the same time. This is normal for this type of U-joint used on the front wheels of a four-wheel-drive vehicle.
- **Constant velocity (CV) joints.** The use of CV joints at the front wheels allows engine torque to be applied without changes in wheel speed, as can often occur if standard U-joints are used. See Figure 48–22.

NOTE: Constant velocity (CV) joints are commonly used on vehicles that have the differential assembly attached to the frame of the vehicle. This design reduces the amount of weight that has to move up and down during suspension movement and helps provide a smooth ride.

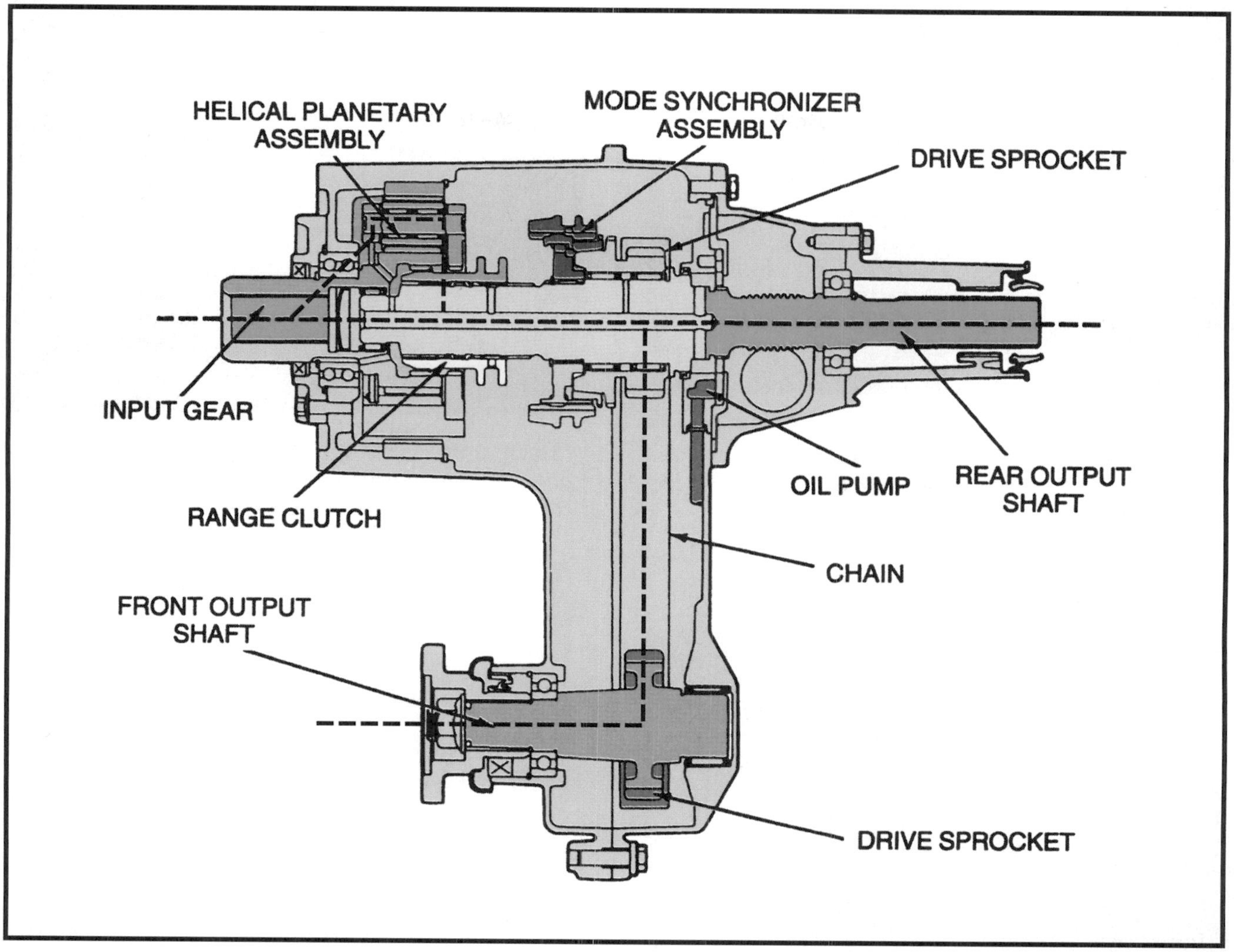

Figure 48–18 Four-wheel-drive/low-range torque flow in an NV231 transfer case. The mode synchronizer assembly remains engaged and the range clutch is moved to the rearward position. The annulus (ring) gear is fixed to the case and the input (sun) gear drives the pinion gears, which walk around the stationary annulus gear and drive the planetary carrier and output shaft at a speed lower than the input gear. (Courtesy of Chrysler Corporation)

Figure 48–19 A bevel gear-type interaxle differential.

Figure 48–20 A viscous coupling. Note that the unit is attached to the output shaft between the transfer case (or transaxle) and the rear differential. A typical viscous coupling in a sealed unit is serviced as a complete assembly.

Figure 48–22 Constant velocity (CV) joints are used on the front axles of many four-wheel-drive vehicles like this Chevrolet Blazer.

(a)

(b)

Figure 48–21 (a) A standard Cardan U-joint used on the output drive shaft from the transfer case to the front differential assembly. (b) A Cardan-type U-joint at the front drive wheels on a Jeep Wrangler.

TRANSFER CASE SERVICE AND PROBLEM DIAGNOSIS

Four-wheel-drive transfer cases and related components are usually built strong enough for heavy-duty use. However, there is some preventative maintenance that may need to be done:

- **Draining and refilling the transfer case.** Most transfer cases require automatic transmission fluid (ATF), yet some (especially older) units require SAE 80W-90 GL-4 gear lube. Obviously, any fluid leaks should be corrected as soon as possible to avoid damage from low lubricant level. See Figure 48–23.
- **Drive chain.** The chain in chain-drive transfer cases can stretch and start hitting the inside of the transfer case. See Figure 48–24. This occurs most frequently in vehicles that use four-wheel drive under heavy loads for extended periods of time. The noise the chain makes is very loud, and the chain should be replaced as soon as possible to avoid excessive damage to the case.
- **Bearings.** Transfer case bearings may cause noise whenever the input shaft is rotating even if the transfer case is in neutral. Consult the factory service information for details on transfer case bearing noise diagnosis procedures.
- **Shifting.** Shifting problems can be caused by several items: shift linkage bent or binding, worn shift fork or synchronizer assembly (see Figure 48–25), or incorrect transfer case lubricant.

Figure 48–23 Most transfer cases use an internal oil pump to force the lubricant throughout the unit. Using the correct lubricant is critical to the proper operation of the transfer case.

Figure 48–24 A cutaway view of a transfer case showing the drive chain.

TECH TIP 

Please Install Snap Rings Correctly

Many snap rings are tapered at their opening, as shown in Figure 48–26. This allows the snap ring pliers to grasp the points of the snap ring so that it can be expanded and easily removed. If the points are facing down, it is very difficult for snap ring pliers to grasp the end of the snap ring. Therefore, to make it easier to disassemble a transfer case later, always install snap rings as they were designed to be installed.

(a)

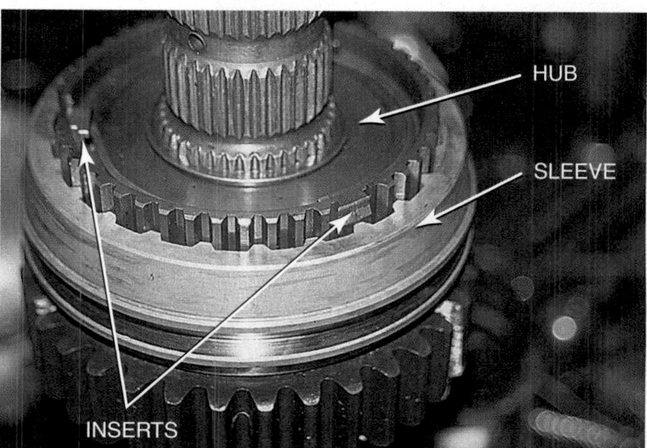

(b)

(c)

Figure 48–25 (a) The transfer case shift forks attach to the synchronizer sleeve. (b) The sleeve, hub, and inserts are similar in design except larger than those used in a manual transmission/transaxle. (c) The blocking ring should be carefully inspected for wear if hard shifting is the customer complaint.

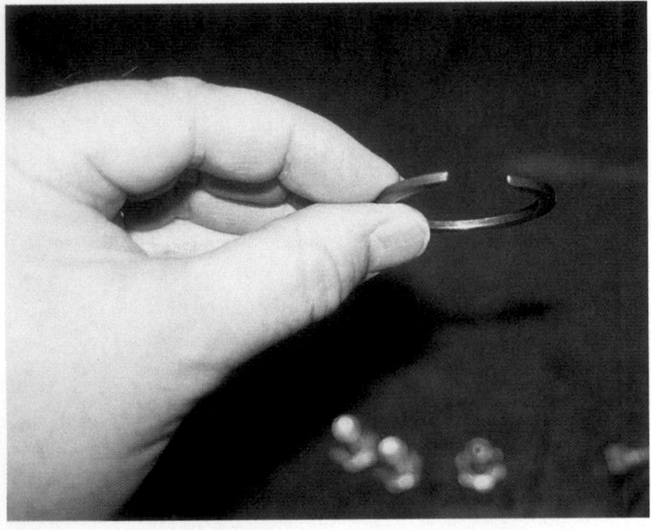

Figure 48–26 When reassembling a transfer case (or another automotive component) that includes a snap ring, always be sure that the upper opening is tapered from the top to allow snap ring pliers room to get a grip on the open end.

NOTE: The transfer case may be difficult to shift if the recommended procedure is not followed. For example, many manufacturers recommend that the vehicle be completely stopped before attempting to make a mode and/or a range shift. Verify proper shifting procedures before further testing or disassembly.

DIAGNOSING AND SERVICING LOCKING HUBS

Locking front hubs should be cleaned periodically, especially if the vehicle has been driven under water or in dusty conditions. Most vehicle manufacturers recommend that the hubs be cleaned and lightly coated with grease at the same time the front wheel bearings are serviced. Check the service information for the exact procedure for the vehicle being serviced. See Figure 48–27.

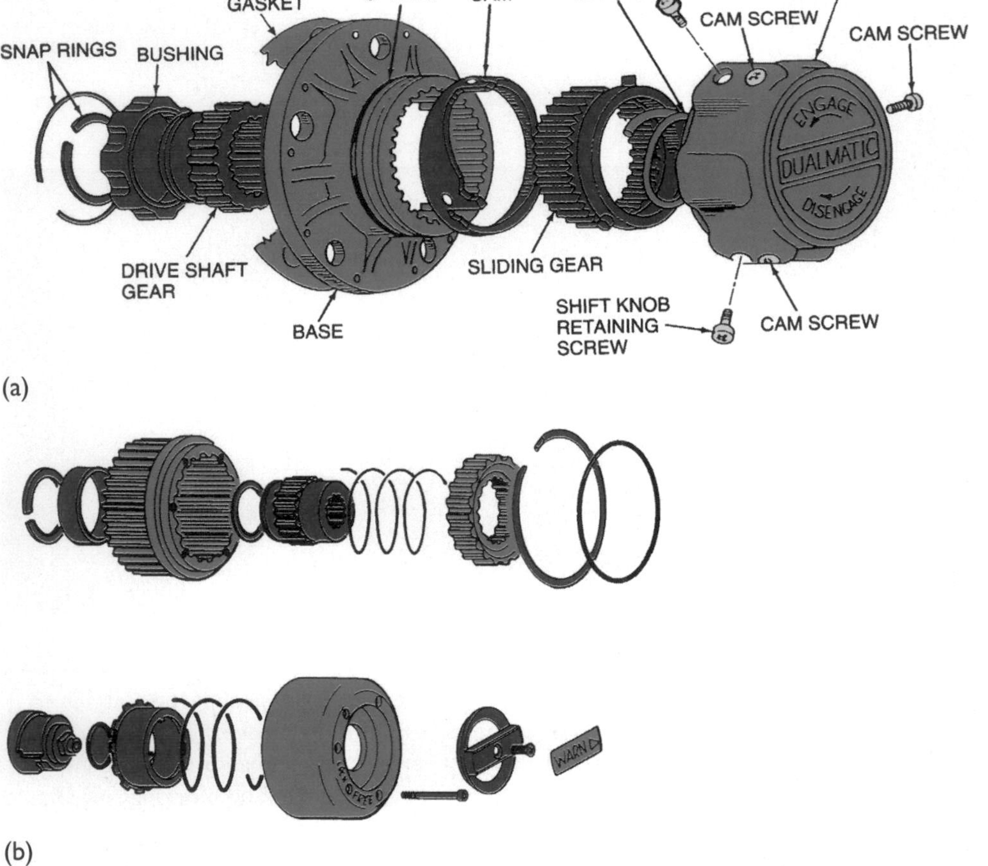

Figure 48–27 (a) An exploded view of a Dualmatic® manual locking hub. (b) A Warn® manual locking hub. (Courtesy of Chrysler Corporation)

Start the inspection of the front hubs by removing the cover plate. Many problems associated with locking hubs can be corrected by cleaning and lubricating the components. If noise is heard from the hubs, carefully inspect the inner components on both sides of the vehicle. A damaged part can cause noise in the hub on the other side. Service kits are often available for the hubs. These kits contain the gaskets, seals, and retaining rings necessary for installing the hubs correctly after wheel bearing or front brake work has been completed.

NOTE: Check the amount of axle end play. Excessive end play caused by defective bearings can cause the drive axle to move enough to damage the hubs.

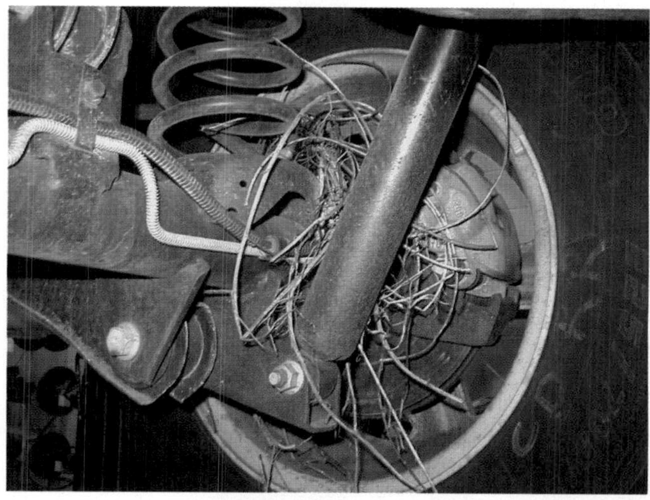

Figure 48–28 Every diagnosis of a transfer case problem should start with a thorough visual inspection. Mud, weeds, and other debris can affect the operation of the wheel speed sensors as well as wheel brakes and Cardan-type U-joints.

TRANSFER CASE SERVICE

Transfer cases usually require occasional lubricant change during normal service life. However, driver abuse often causes parts to break, requiring the overhaul or replacement of the entire assembly. See Figures 48–28 through 48–35 for typical items to check when a transfer case is disassembled and inspected. Always follow the vehicle manufacturer's recommended servicing procedure.

TECH TIP 

Keep the Differential Vents Clear

All differentials are vented to allow for expansion and contraction of differential lubricant in all temperature ranges. Typically, these vents are shielded openings near the top of the differential. Most trucks, especially four-wheel-drive vehicles, use an extended vent hose to prevent water from getting into the differential if the vehicle is driven in deep water.

If mud gets into the vent, pressure can build up inside the differential and cause lubricant leakage past the rear axle seals. Therefore, whenever replacing rear axle seals, always check to make sure that the differential vent is clear. Remember that four-wheel-drive vehicles use two differentials and that both the front and rear vents plus the vent on the transfer case should be checked.

Figure 48–29 Before any driveline component is removed, it should be marked so that it can be reinstalled in the exact same location.

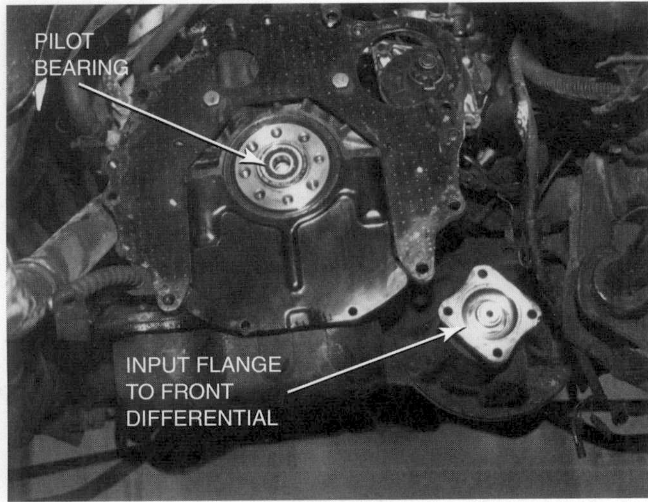

Figure 48–30 Having to remove the transfer case and the manual transmission makes replacing a clutch in a four-wheel-drive vehicle more difficult than with a two-wheel-drive vehicle. The flywheel on this Isuzu Trooper has been sent out to be resurfaced.

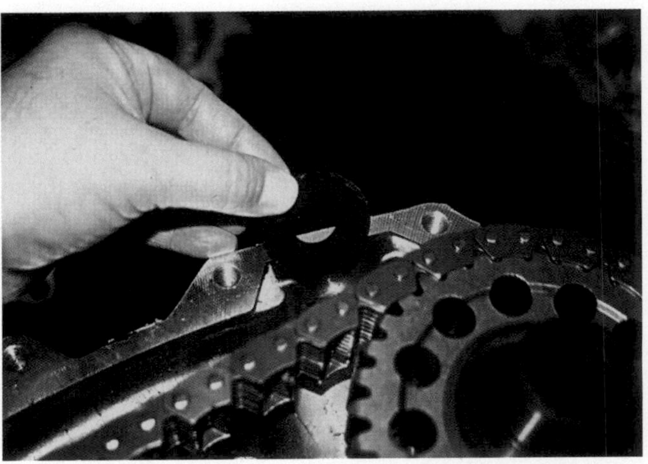

Figure 48–32 Most transfer cases have a magnet to trap and hold steel debris to keep it from being circulated throughout the case and causing harm. If metal particles are discovered on this magnet, severe damage may have already occurred.

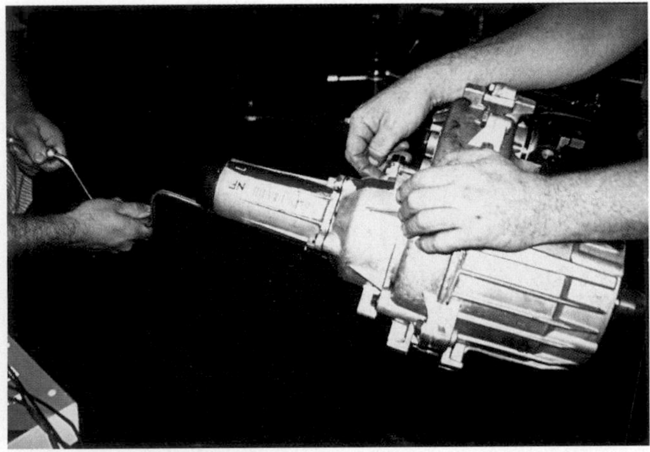

Figure 48–31 This New Venture 241 transfer case is being disassembled on a workbench.

Figure 48–33 The chain and sprockets being removed from the case.

Figure 48–34 All component parts such as this planetary gear set should be thoroughly inspected for wear.

Figure 48–35 Reassembly of a typical transfer case often includes checking for proper shaft end play using a dial indicator.

DIAGNOSTIC STORY

The Differential Lubricant Story

A four-wheel-drive vehicle was serviced and both differentials were drained and refilled as recommended by the vehicle manufacturer. The owner returned shortly after picking up the vehicle and complained that the vehicle drove as if the parking brake was still applied. The vehicle lacked power and would decelerate rapidly whenever the accelerator pedal was released. Careful inspection of the parking brake revealed that everything was functioning correctly. Because all that was done was the differential fluid service, the fluid level was checked and again, the level was correct and not overfull. Then the technician checked the container of gear lubricant that was used and discovered that the parts store had accidentally sent SAE 80W-140 instead of the requested, and more commonly used, SAE 80W-90. Both lubricants were listed GL-5, meaning that they were acceptable for differentials. The container of lubricant had been installed in the portable lubricating dispenser when it was delivered, and therefore the label on the container was not visible to the technician. The correct lubricant was installed in the differential and normal vehicle performance was restored. The technician and the parts store learned to double check the product before shipping or using it.

PHOTO SEQUENCE 34 NV-242 Transfer Case Service

P34–1 The identification plate on the housing indicates that the transfer case is a New Venture (New Process Gear) model #242 and has a low-range gear ratio of 2.72:1.

P34–2 Rear output shaft housing being removed.

P34–3 Before the case can be separated, the bearing retaining snap ring must be removed using snap-ring pliers.

P34–4 The lubricating oil pump is visible after the cover and bearing assembly have been removed.

P34–5 The two case halves are being separated.

P34–6 The oil pump assembly, pickup screen, and tube are visible on the backside of the case cover.

P34–7 The rear output shaft and sprocket are visible on the right. The front output shaft and sprocket are visible on the left, connected by the drive chain.

P34–8 View of the shift levers and the centre differential after the chain has been removed.

P34–9 Differential being removed.

P34–10 Centre differential assembly after removal from the transfer case.

P34–11 The mode shift fork (upper fork) is used to change between two-wheel drive and four-wheel drive. The lower fork is attached to the range hub, which changes from four-wheel drive high to four-wheel drive low.

P34–12 Main shaft showing the range hub (left), which changes the transfer case between four-wheel high and four-wheel low.

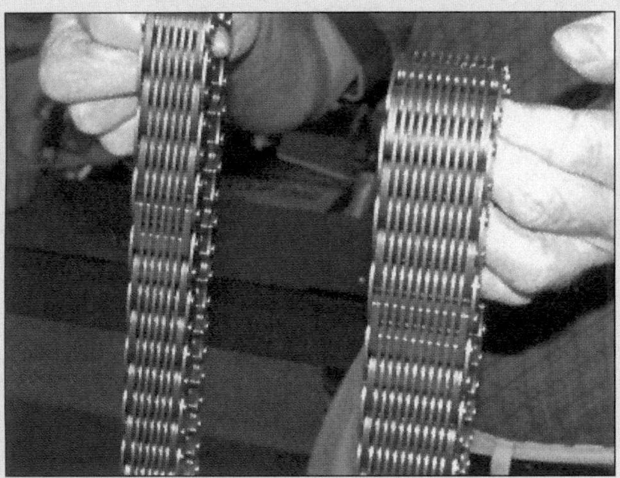

P34–13 The chain used on the NV-242 (right) is larger than the chain used in the smaller version NV-231 (left).

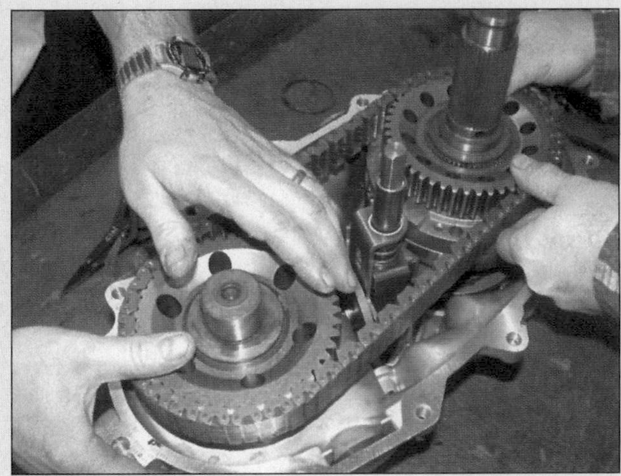

P34–14 Reinstalling the components and the drive chain.

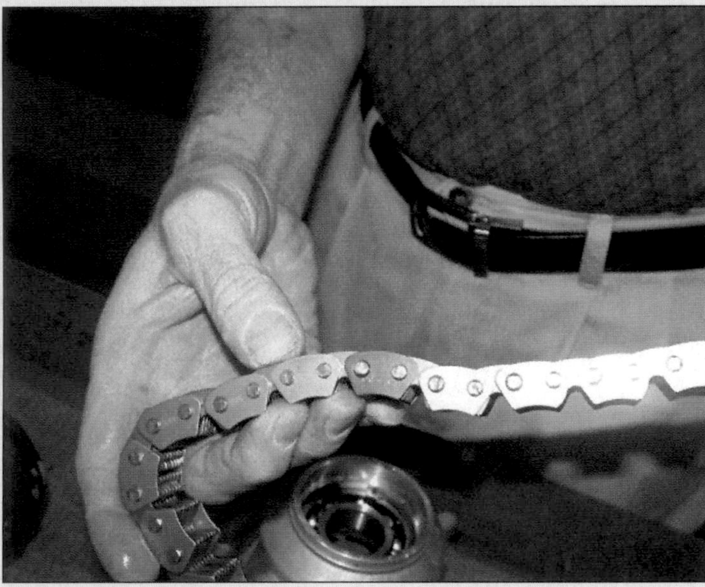

P34–15 The drive chain should be installed with the black (dark) link(s) up.

P34–16 Install all snap rings so that the sharpest tips face up so snap-ring pliers can grab onto the tips for easier removal.

P34–17 Assembling the case halves.

P34–18 The parting surface should be sealed with RTV silicone. Do not use too much or the oil pump screen can become clogged.

P34–19 After attaching the oil pump and tube, the rear output shaft housing is installed.

P34–20 The output shaft speed sensor drive gear is correctly installed in this photo. The slip yoke of the drive shaft slips onto the splines and inside the nylon gear.

P34–21 The electronically-shifted version of the transfer case is identical except that the shifting is achieved using an electric motor, shown here installed in a vehicle.

SUMMARY

1. A 4 × 4 is a four-wheel vehicle that has engine torque applied to all four wheels, whereas a 4 × 2 is a four-wheel vehicle that has engine torque applied to just two wheels.
2. Part-time four-wheel drive means that four-wheel drive should only be used on a slippery surface because the transfer case does not include a centre differential to allow for differences in front-to-rear wheel rotational speeds.
3. Most part-time four-wheel-drive vehicles use either manual- or automatic-locking front hubs.
4. All four-wheel-drive vehicles should be towed with all four wheels off the ground if possible to avoid possible drive train damage.
5. Full-time four-wheel-drive vehicles use a centre differential.
6. All-wheel-drive vehicles usually do not have a low range transfer case and are therefore not suited for serious off-road usage.
7. The centre differential can be locked to provide additional traction by the use of either a viscous coupling or an electronically controlled clutch assembly.
8. A mode shift selects two-wheel drive or four-wheel drive, whereas a range shift selects either low range, neutral, or high range.
9. Some four-wheel-drive vehicles use Cardan-type U-joints for the front wheels, which may cause drive line vibration during rapid acceleration while cornering.
10. Transfer cases may use either automatic transmission fluid (ATF) or SAE 80W-90 gear lube.

REVIEW QUESTIONS

1. Explain the difference between four-wheel drive and all-wheel drive.
2. Explain why part-time four-wheel drive vehicles use locking front hubs.
3. Describe the difference between a mode shift and a range shift in a transfer case.
4. Describe how a viscous coupling works.
5. List the elements of the planetary gear set used in many transfer cases.

RED SEAL CERTIFICATION-TYPE QUESTIONS

1. While turning on dry pavement in four-wheel drive, what can a vibration indicate?
   - **a.** Defective transfer case
   - **b.** Cardan "U" joint normal operation
   - **c.** Constant velocity joint normal operation
   - **d.** Drive shaft out of balance
2. When comparing gear ratios used in front and rear differentials, which numbers would be most correct?
   - **a.** Front—3:73; rear—3:71
   - **b.** Front—3:71; rear—3:73
   - **c.** Front—4:11; rear—5:11
   - **d.** Front—3:73; rear—3:73
3. What is the reason to drive a four-wheel-drive vehicle in reverse after shifting from four-wheel drive to two-wheel drive?
   - **a.** It helps to release the front differential from the transfer case
   - **b.** It helps to release the rear differential from the transfer case
   - **c.** It helps release the front hubs from the differential
   - **d.** It helps release the transfer case from the transmission
4. What is the purpose of the centre differential in the transfer case?
   - **a.** Provides over-drive ratio to front axle
   - **b.** Provides over-drive ratio to rear axle
   - **c.** Provides the ability of front and rear axles to turn at different speeds
   - **d.** Provides a direct connection between front and rear axles
5. Which type of system uses a one-speed transfer case and a centre differential with a viscous coupling?
   - **a.** Part-time four-wheel drive
   - **b.** Full-time four-wheel drive
   - **c.** Full-time four-wheel drive with automatic locking front hubs
   - **d.** All-wheel drive
6. What type of lubricant will be used in transfer cases?
   - **a.** Automatic transmission fluid
   - **b.** Engine oil
   - **c.** Chassis lubricant
   - **d.** Mineral oil
7. When might the transfer case input shaft bearings be noisy?
   - **a.** Only when the vehicle is coasting
   - **b.** Anytime the output shaft turns
   - **c.** Anytime the input shaft turns
   - **d.** Anytime the engine is running
8. What might be the cause of a transfer case being hard to shift?
   - **a.** Worn synchronizer assemblies
   - **b.** Transfer case fluid too full
   - **c.** Transmission is in neutral and engine RPM is too high
   - **d.** Transmission is in neutral and engine RPM is too low
9. What is the best procedure for towing a four-wheel-drive vehicle?
   - **a.** Transport the vehicle with the front wheels off the ground
   - **b.** Transport the vehicle with the rear wheels off the ground
   - **c.** Transport the vehicle with all wheels off the ground
   - **d.** Transport the vehicle any way, as long as the speed does not exceed 40 km/h
10. Snap rings that are used to hold gears inside the transfer case can be
    - **a.** Installed in one direction only
    - **b.** Installed in any position
    - **c.** Installed with vise-grip pliers
    - **d.** Installed with needle-nose pliers

SECTION **IX**

Automatic Transmissions and Transaxles

Chapter 49 describes how automatic transmissions/transaxles work, including details on torque converters, planetary gear sets, clutches, and bands as well as the valve body operation on hydraulically shifted and computer-controlled electronically shifted units. Chapter 50 includes diagnosis of automatic transmission/transaxle problems as well as disassembly, testing, and reassembly techniques.

49

Automatic Transmission/ Transaxle Principles

OBJECTIVES: After studying Chapter 49, you should be able to:

1. Prepare for the interprovincial Red Seal certification examination in Appendix II (Automatic Transmission/Transaxle) on the topics covered in this chapter.
2. Explain how a torque converter can transmit and multiply engine torque.
3. Describe how a planetary gear set can be used for gear reduction and reverse.
4. List three planetary gear set holding devices.
5. Describe how shift points are achieved with a hydraulically shifted automatic transmission/transaxle.
6. Explain how solenoids are used to control the shifting on electronically shifted automatic transmissions/transaxles.

Figure 49–1 A cross-sectional view of a Chrysler Power Flight 2-speed automatic transmission used in the 1950s. Most of the heat generated in an automatic transmission is created in the torque converter. This air-cooled unit has a vent to allow hot air to escape.

Automatic transmissions were first used on a large scale in the late 1940s, and now about 85% of the vehicles in North America are so equipped. Unlike manual transmissions, most automatic transmissions do not actually "shift gears" but apply clutches (or bands) to hold various sections of two or more planetary gear sets. See Figure 49–1. The torque converter is attached between the engine and the transmission/transaxle and transmits and multiplies engine torque.

PURPOSE AND FUNCTION OF AUTOMATIC TRANSMISSIONS AND TRANSAXLES

The automatic transmission/transaxle was originally installed in automobiles to free the driver from having to use the clutch and shift lever to change gears. The transmission uses gears, hydraulic clutches and bands to provide various gear ratios. The transmission provides torque multiplication and the ability to stop the vehicle while still in gear without the engine stalling.

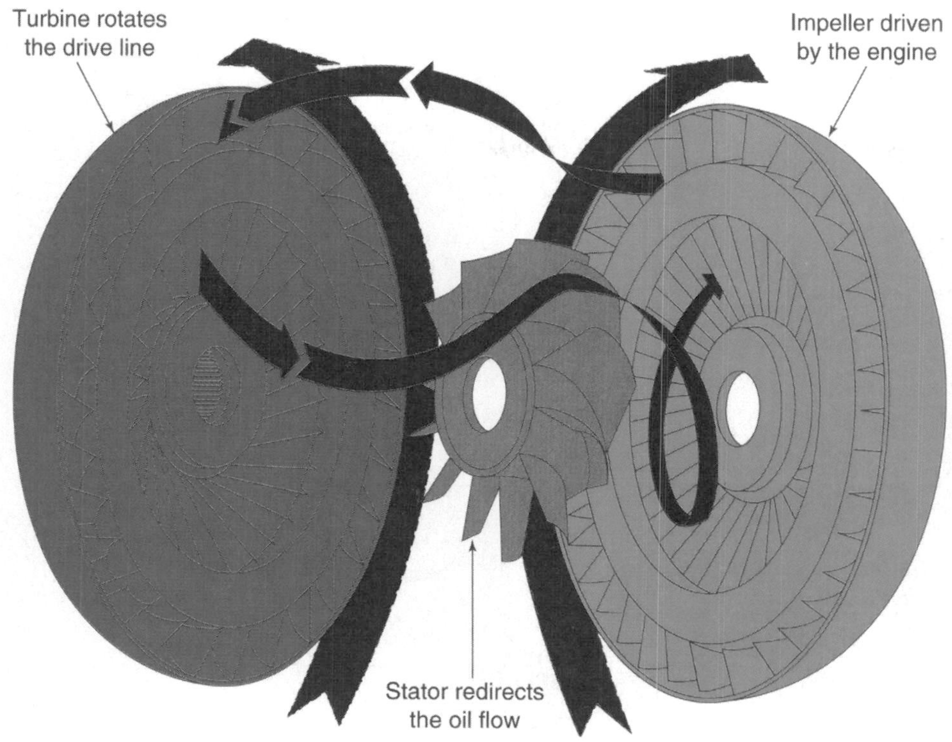

Figure 49–2 Fluid flow within a torque converter. The stator redirects the fluid that is thrown out by the turbine, thereby improving efficiency.

The transmission is usually used in rear wheel drive and longitudinally mounted engines. The transaxle is used with transverse mounted engines with front wheel drive.

TORQUE CONVERTERS

The **impeller,** also known as the **pump,** is the driving member and rotates with the engine. The impeller vanes pick up fluid in the converter housing and direct it toward the **turbine.** Fluid flow drives the turbine, and when the flow between the impeller and turbine is adequate, the turbine rotates and turns the transmission input shaft. A torque converter also contains the **stator,** or reactor, which is a reaction member mounted on a one-way clutch.

The vanes used in each of the three elements of a torque converter are curved to increase the diversion angle of the fluid. This also increases the force exerted by the fluid and improves the hydraulic advantage. The outlet side of the impeller vanes accelerates the fluid as it leaves the impeller to increase torque transfer to the turbine. See Figure 49–2. The inlet side of the turbine vanes absorb shock and limit power loss that occurs when flow between the impeller and turbine suddenly changes. The curve of the stator vanes is opposite to the curve of the impeller and turbine vanes. See Figure 49–3. Since the stator

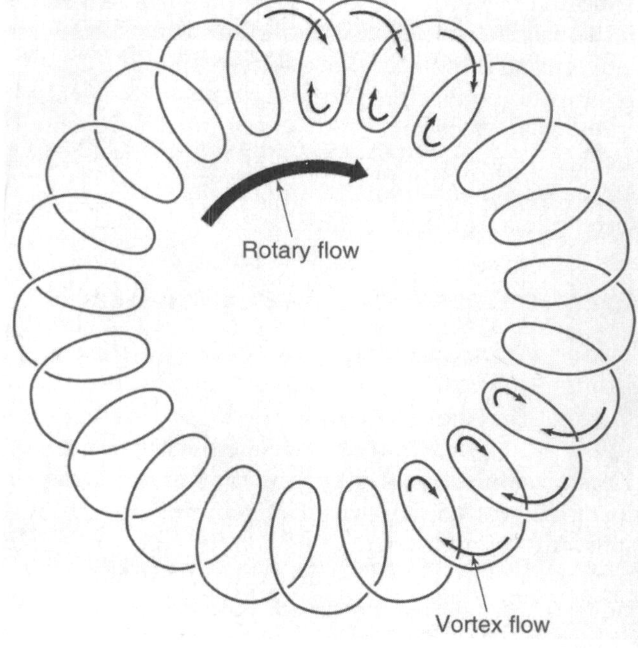

Figure 49–3 Fluid pumped into the turbine by the impeller not only creates rotary fluid flow but also vortex flow that increases the efficiency of the torque converter.

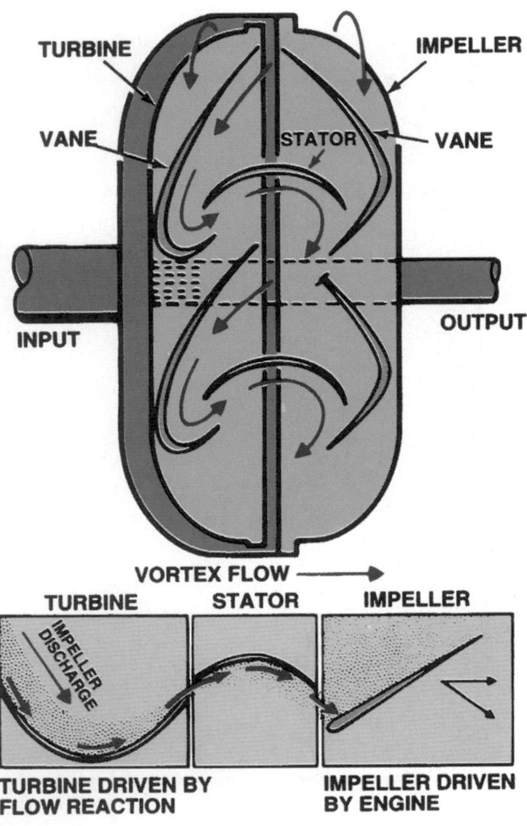

Figure 49–4 The vane curvature of each element in a torque converter helps maintain efficient fluid flow.

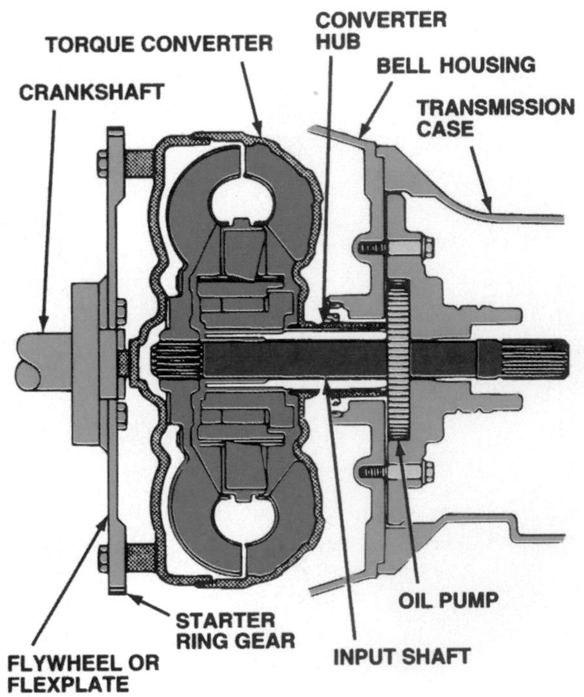

Figure 49–5 The torque converter bolts to the flexplate, which is attached to the crankshaft and rotates at engine speed. The hub of the converter drives the oil pump directly on most rear-wheel-drive transmissions.

is located between the impeller and turbine, it adds to the original impeller flow and multiplies the force delivered to the turbine. See Figure 49–4.

Torque converters are single-piece, welded assemblies that cannot be disassembled or repaired easily. Although they can be rebuilt using specialized equipment, most shops simply replace welded converters as a unit if they fail.

Torque Converter Attachments

The torque converter normally attaches to the engine through a **flexplate** that mounts on the crankshaft flange of the engine. See Figure 49–5. The flexplate replaces the heavy flywheel used with a manual transmission. An important function of a flywheel is to smooth out engine pulsations and dampen vibrations. An automatic transmission does not require a conventional flywheel because the fluid in the torque converter provides enough mass to dampen engine vibrations.

An external ring gear generally attaches to the outer rim of the flexplate. This ring gear engages the starter motor pinion gear to turn the engine during starting.

> **NOTE:** On some older applications, such as the Ford C4 and Chrysler Torqueflite, the ring gear may be welded to the outside of the torque converter cover.

To ensure the pump will deliver fluid to the transmission whenever the engine turns, an integral hub is located on the converter housing and directly engages the pump. See Figure 49–6. Oil pump drive shafts generally pass through the converter inside a hollow input or transfer shaft and internally connect to the converter housing by splines.

Most rear-wheel-drive transmissions use an in-line method to drive the converter and provide a direct mechanical connection between the turbine and the transmission input shaft. In a typical design, splines on the turbine connect it to the transmission input shaft and the stator hub mounts on a one-way overrunning clutch. The one-way clutch mounts on splines to a stationary extension of the oil pump called the stator support, or reaction shaft. See Figure 49–7. The converter drive hub at the rear of the torque converter housing passes over the stator support and through the front oil seal to drive the oil pump.

Many transaxles, and a few rear-wheel-drive transmissions, use an offset drive arrangement to conserve space. An offset drive design generally uses a drive chain to provide the mechanical connection

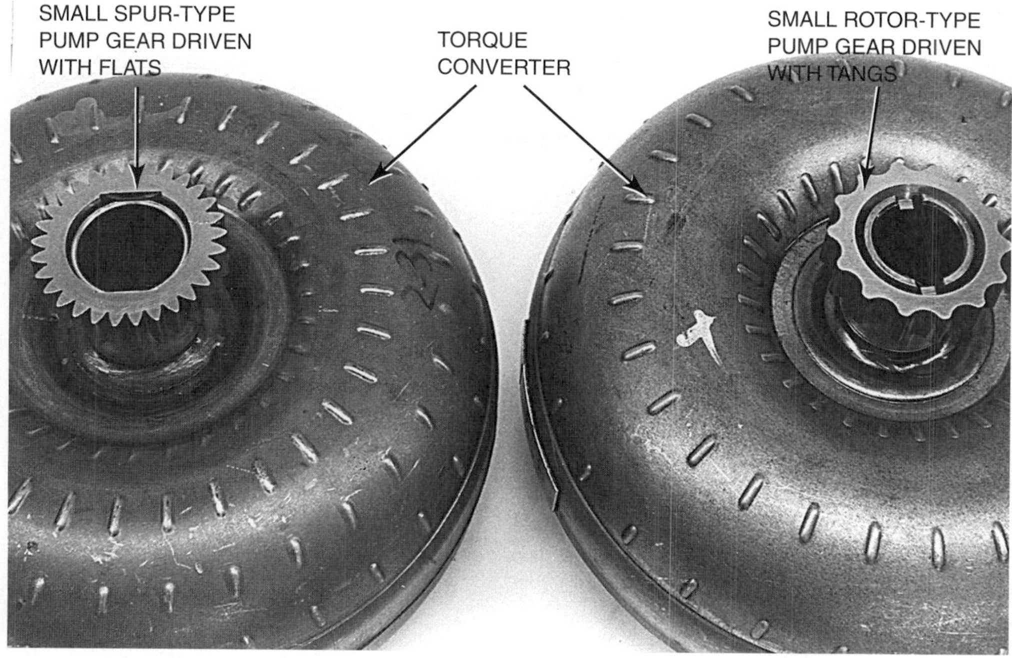

Figure 49–6 The inner oil pump gear is keyed to the hub of the torque converter, which drives the pump. Notice that the hub does not engage the full depth of the gear. This is the major reason why the torque converter *must* be fully installed. Failure to fully engage the oil pump gear can cause serious damage to both the pump and the torque converter.

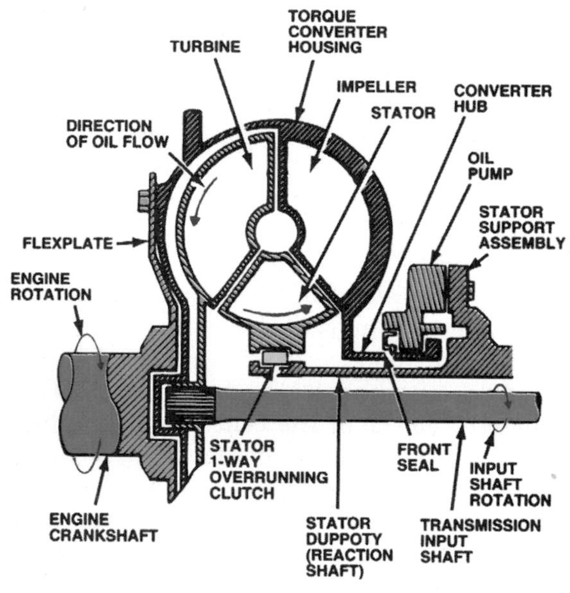

Figure 49–7 The transmission input shaft connects directly to the turbine through splines in most rear-wheel-drive transmissions.

between the turbine and the input shaft. See Figure 49–8. The oil pump may be driven directly by the converter housing or by a separate drive shaft.

Torque Converter Operation

Fluid sent to the torque converter from the transmission oil pump is picked up by the rotating vanes of the impeller and transferred to the turbine vanes through rotary and vortex flow paths.

Torque Multiplication Phase

Torque multiplication phase occurs when fluid leaving the turbine vanes strikes the concave, or front side, of the stator vanes. The stator vanes redirect this fluid so that it joins the fluid flow being delivered from the impeller to the next turbine vane. See Figure 49–9. The force of the fluid from the stator adds to the force of the fluid flowing from the impeller to increase the overall torque being transferred from the impeller to the turbine.

Torque multiplication occurs whenever the vortex flow makes a full cycle from impeller to turbine, then through the stator and back to the impeller. A torque converter multiplies torque in relation to the speed ratio. At low speed ratios, the impeller is turning much faster than the turbine, so vortex flow is high and torque multiplication occurs. As turbine speed

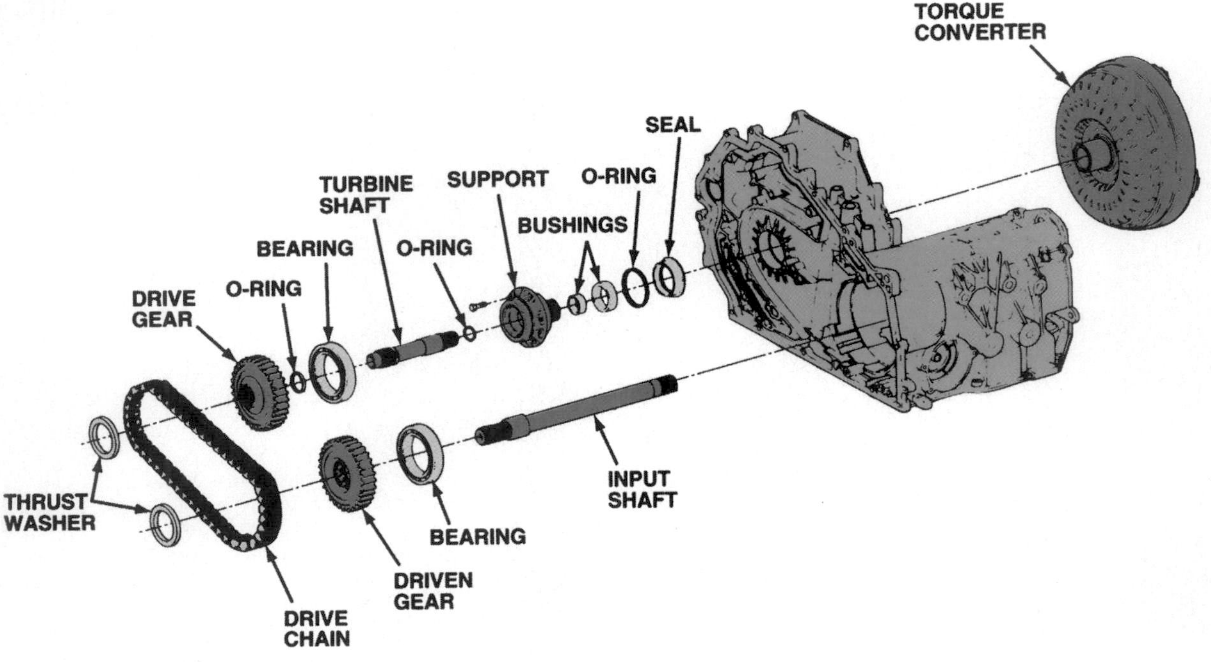

Figure 49–8 On a transaxle, the turbine drives the input shaft through a drive chain assembly.

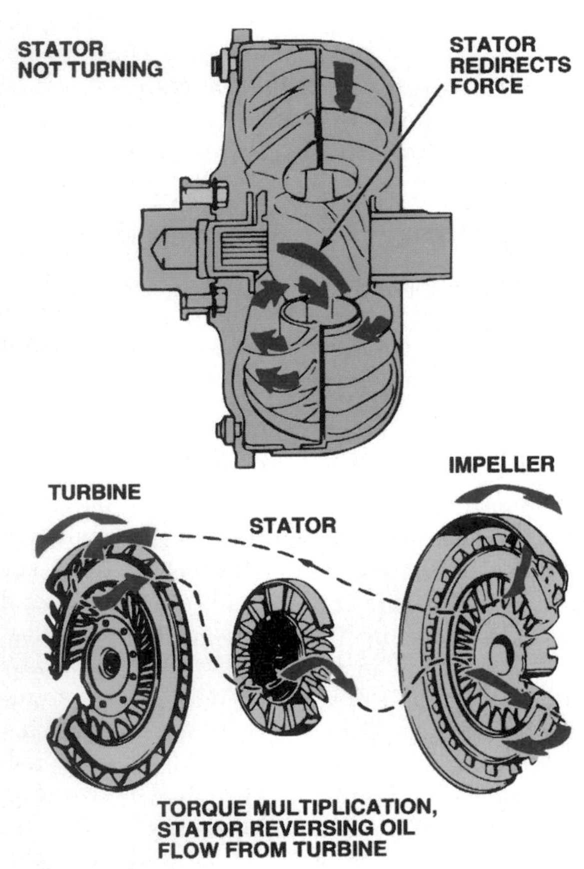

Figure 49–9 Torque multiplication occurs when fluid leaving the turbine strikes the front of the stator vanes and is redirected back to the impeller.

increases and approaches impeller speed, rotary flow increases, which reduces both vortex flow and torque multiplication. As the speed ratio approaches 90%, torque multiplication becomes minimal and a torque converter functions like a fluid coupling.

The stator redirects fluid flow because it remains stationary during the torque multiplication phase. The stator hub mounts on a one-way clutch, freewheeling in a clockwise direction, but locking when driven in a counterclockwise direction. See Figure 49–10. When fluid from the turbine strikes the concave face of the stator vanes, it tries to drive the stator counterclockwise. By locking the stator it can redirect the fluid back to the impeller.

Coupling Phase

When the speed ratio is 90% or more, fluid flow in the torque converter is mostly rotary flow and the angle of flow from turbine to stator increases. Fluid eventually strikes the convex side, or backside, of the stator vanes rather than the concave. As the force of fluid striking the backside becomes great enough to drive the stator clockwise, the one-way clutch overruns. With the clutch overrunning the turbine, impeller, and stator, all rotate in the same direction and at approximately the same speed. This is called the **coupling phase.** The stator unlocks and freewheels once the angle of fluid flow changes enough to strike the opposite side of the stator vanes and rotate the stator clockwise.

Figure 49–10 A stator contains a one-way roller clutch, which locks it from rotating in one direction and allows it to rotate freely in the opposite direction.

Torque multiplication drops as the torque converter approaches the coupling phase because the stator no longer redirects fluid to increase the flow from impeller to turbine. When the torque converter reaches coupling speed, the turbine is travelling at nearly the same speed as the impeller, rotary flow is much greater than vortex flow, and the torque converter simply transmits torque like a fluid coupling.

Stall Speed

During converter stall, the impeller rotates but the turbine does not. This occurs just before the drive wheels of a vehicle begin to move. The greatest amount of stall occurs when the engine drives the impeller at the maximum speed possible without moving the turbine. The engine speed at which this occurs is called the torque converter **stall speed.** When the impeller rotates but the turbine does not, the speed ratio is zero. This is the lowest possible speed ratio and the greatest possible torque multiplication. Most modern torque converters multiply torque in the range of 2:1 to 2.5:1 at the stall speed.

Torque Converter Diameter

The outside diameter of a torque converter and the angle of its stator blades determines the stall speed of the converter. When both a small and large diameter converter share the same stator blade angle and turn at the same speed, the smaller converter creates less centrifugal force to move the fluid inside. As a result, the small diameter converter has a higher stall speed, multiplies torque at higher engine speeds, and will not couple until the engine reaches high speeds. In comparison, the large diameter converter has a lower stall speed, multiplies torque at lower engine speeds, and also couples at a lower engine speed.

Vehicle manufacturers select torque converters to match the powertrain requirements and operating demands of each application. A vehicle with a large engine that produces a lot of torque at low RPM will often use a torque converter that couples at low speeds for greater fuel economy. Vehicles with smaller engines that produce less torque at low RPM will use a torque converter that allows the engine to operate higher in its torque curve, where more power is available. High-performance vehicles with automatic transmissions use small diameter converters for the same reason.

Lockup Torque Converter

Even the most efficient torque converters slip 3% to 6% during operation. This is because the fluid that transmits torque exhibits a type of slippage known as fluid shear. Fluid shear creates friction heat, but performs no work when the different layers of fluid slide past each other.

Eliminating torque converter slippage can improve fuel economy approximately 4% to 5% during freeway cruising. With the increased emphasis on fuel economy for late-model vehicles, this became an important goal for automotive engineers. An additional benefit to no slippage is a reduction of transmission operating temperature, which increases transmission life expectancy. Lockup torque converters reduce slippage by using a **torque converter clutch (TCC)** to lock the impeller to the turbine. Similar to a clutch for a manual transmission, a TCC uses a friction disc operated by a hydraulic piston to mechanically couple the turbine to the impeller. See Figure 49–11. Engaging the clutch creates mechanical connection between the engine and transmission, resulting in a direct, 1:1, drive ratio.

Converter Clutch Control

The first hydraulic lockup converters were controlled entirely by hydraulic pressure and spool valves in the transmission valve body. Some later designs added simple electric switches and solenoids to control pressure to the converter clutch. Late-model hydraulic TCCs use an electronic control system to regulate the timing and application of the clutch.

Early hydraulic converter clutches will engage only in high gear because lockup in the lower gears reduces the torque multiplication needed for acceleration. Lockup may also be limited to specific vehicle speeds or operating conditions. For most vehicles, lockup can occur at speeds over 40–48 km/h (25–30 mph) after the transmission upshifts into high gear. Once lockup occurs, the clutch may

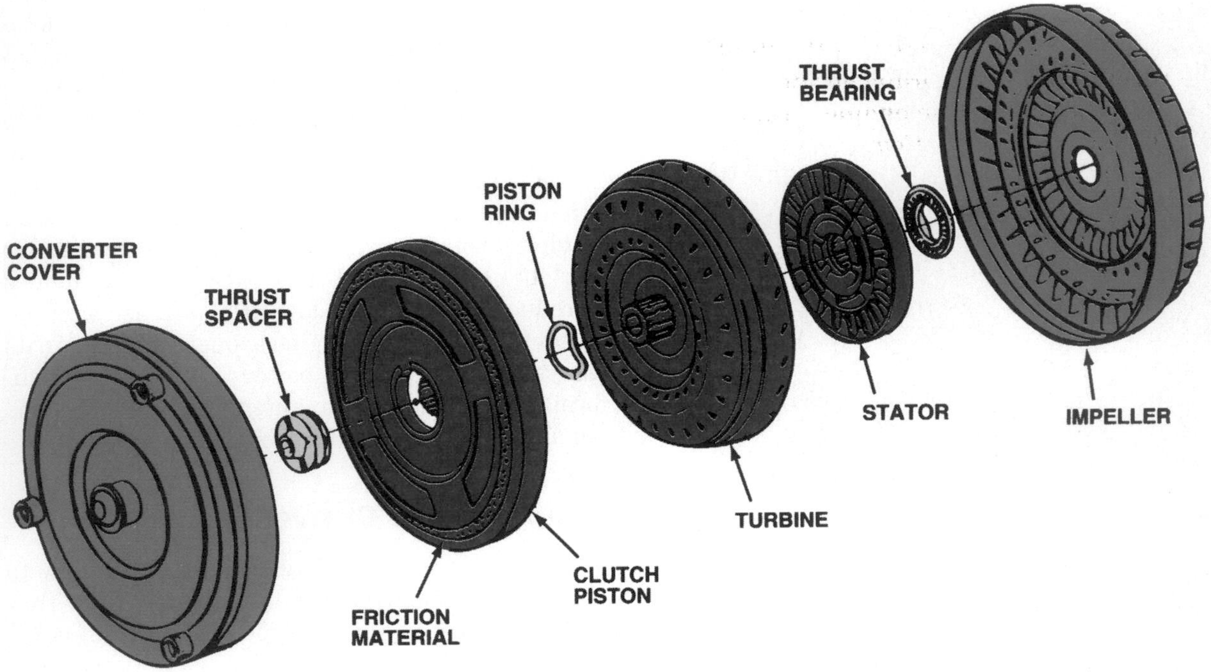

Figure 49–11 An expanded view of a typical General Motors torque converter clutch (TCC).

disengage automatically during certain operating conditions such as part- or full-throttle downshift. At these times, the increased acceleration requirements generally override the need for better fuel economy.

The more sophisticated electronic control systems can lock and unlock a converter clutch hundreds of times per minute to meet the vehicle demands of the moment. Some recent systems also allow partial lockup of the torque converter. Traditional lockup torque converters operate either locked or unlocked. Partial lockup converters allow a regulated amount of slippage at the clutch. See Figure 49–12 , which shows that each type of torque converter clutch control requires a certain type of friction material to be used on the TCC clutch. This allows the converter to lock up smoothly, improving fuel economy and performance, without the drawback of shock to the driveline.

The summary of torque converter operation is as follows:

- *Engine speed is low* with the vehicle in gear and stopped. At low engine speeds, automatic transmission fluid does not exert enough force on the turbine to permit the vehicle to move at a *creep*.
- *Engine speed increases and vehicle speed starts to increase.* As more engine torque is applied to the torque converter, the torque is transmitted through the movement of the fluid to the turbine. The stator is locked (prevented from

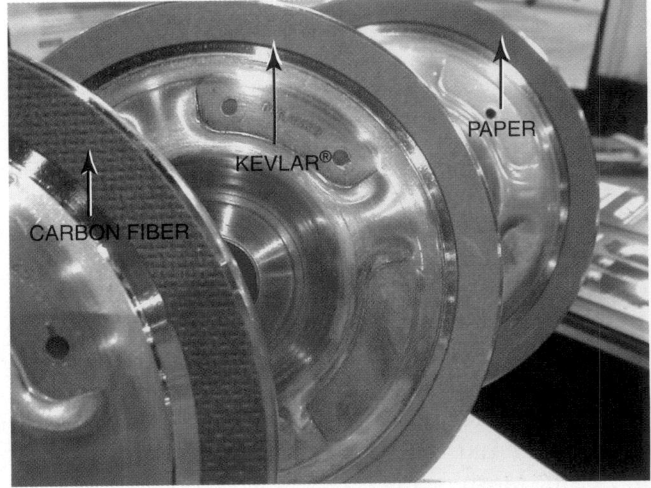

Figure 49–12 The type of torque converter clutch control determines the type of friction material that is used on a torque converter clutch. A paper friction material is usually used on clutches that are turned on or off, whereas Kevlar® or carbon fibre friction materials are used where the clutch is pulse-width modulated.

moving) and redirects the fluid flow back against the turbine. The redirection of the fluid back to the turbine creates a torque on the turbine that is greater than the engine torque. This is called *torque multiplication.* Most torque converters are capable of doubling the applied engine torque due to redirection of the fluid by the stator.

- *Engine speed is steady and vehicle speed is steady.* When the speed of both the impeller and the turbine reach about the same speed (85–90%), the one-way clutch in the stator unlocks and the stator is free to rotate. This point is called the *coupling point.*
- *Vehicle is accelerated rapidly.* During periods of rapid acceleration, the engine speed and therefore the impeller speed are a great deal faster than the turbine speed. The greatest amount of torque multiplication occurs when the turbine is stopped and the impeller is turning as fast as the engine will turn it. This speed is called the *stall speed.* The maximum torque multiplication at stall speed is about 2:1, meaning that the amount of torque applied to the input shaft of the transmission/transaxle is double the amount that the engine is producing.

NOTE: The fact that the torque converter can double the torque to the transmission is the major advantage of using an automatic transmission. A clutch used in a manual transmission/transaxle can only transmit engine torque.

- *Vehicle speed is above 55 km/h (35 mph) and steady.* To improve fuel economy, the impeller and the turbine are mechanically connected by a *torque converter clutch (TCC),* also known as a *lockup torque converter.* See Figure 49–13. Except for some rare cases, the torque converter clutch is applied by the vehicle computer. The computer senses vehicle speed (VS), engine load (MAP), and throttle position (TP) and applies the torque converter clutch. This lockup can occur in second, third, or fourth (overdrive) gear if the conditions are right. When the torque converter clutch engages, the engine RPM usually drops by 150 to 250 rpm. This reduction in engine speed and the elimination of the normal slippage in the torque converter improves fuel economy. The torque converter clutch is released during rapid acceleration for maximum torque multiplication through the torque converter for best acceleration.

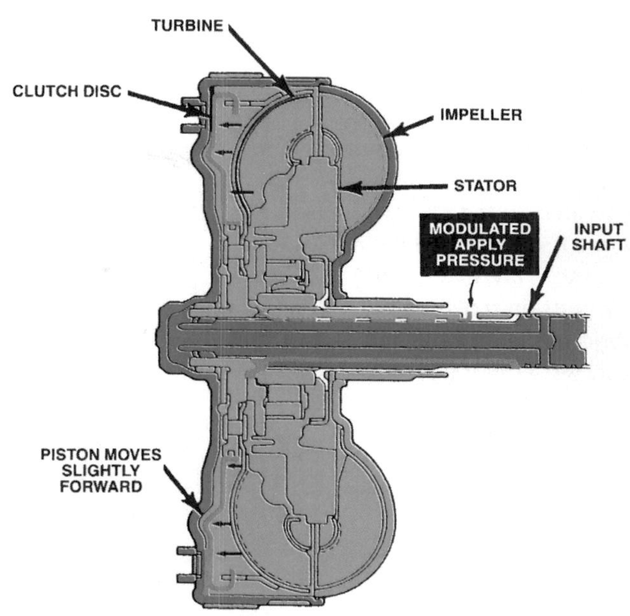

Figure 49–13 A cross-sectional view of a computer-controlled (modulated) torque converter clutch. The vehicle computer is capable of pulsing the solenoid that controls the fluid flow on and off to apply the torque converter clutch. (Courtesy of Chrysler Corporation)

NOTE: The application of the torque converter clutch feels like a normal shift to most drivers. Therefore, a three-speed automatic transaxle will feel to many drivers like shifting three times (1-2, 2-3, and TCC engagement).

Automatic Transmission Fluid Cooler

The torque converter generates a lot of heat due to the slippage and torque multiplication that occurs inside. The greatest amount of heat is generated when the vehicle is operating under a heavy load and the torque converter clutch is disengaged. The automatic transmission fluid (ATF) can reach high temperatures (120°C [over 250°F]) very quickly. This is the reason an automatic transmission fluid cooler is used. Most vehicles use a small section of the engine radiator to cool the ATF. Automatic transmissions/transaxles use a pump to circulate ATF and to provide the necessary hydraulic pressure to operate the hydraulic components of the unit. The ATF is pumped from the torque converter (greatest source of heat) to the cooler. The ATF flows through the cooler and returns to the transmission/transaxle to passages that lubricate the bearings and bushings of the unit. This returned fluid is called **lube oil.** See Figures 49–14 and 49–15.

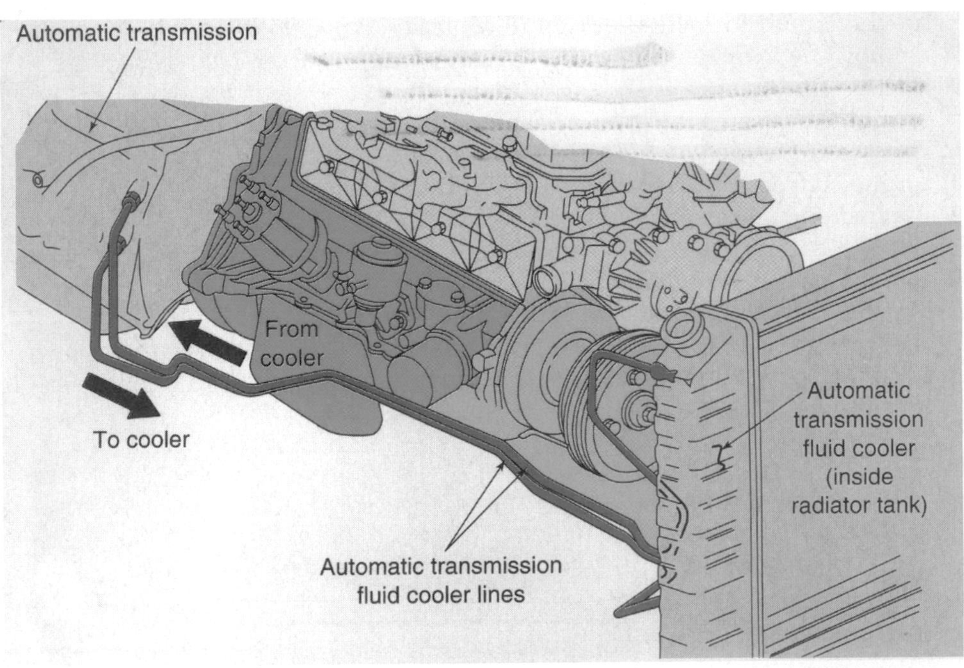

Figure 49–14 Automatic transmission fluid is routed from the torque converter, where most of the heat in an automatic transmission is generated, to the radiator, where it is cooled. The cooled fluid then returns to the transmission/transaxle to lubricate the bearings and bushings.

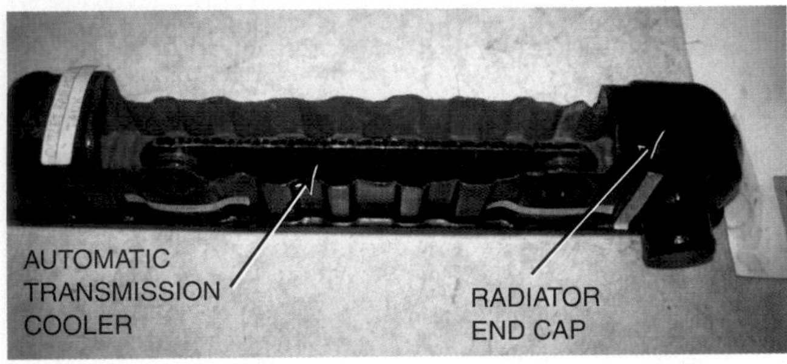

Figure 49–15 A cutaway section of a typical radiator showing the automatic transmission fluid cooler. The heat from the automatic transmission fluid is released to the engine coolant. The engine coolant also warms the automatic transmission fluid after a cold start.

CAUTION: Because the lube oil uses the ATF flowing from the cooler, if there is a blockage in the cooler, the transmission/transaxle may not have enough fluid to properly cool or lubricate the bearings and bushings inside the unit, leading to wear and eventually premature failure.

HIGH PERFORMANCE TIP 

Use a Smaller Diameter Torque Converter for Improved Performance

A smaller-than-stock-diameter torque converter will not be capable of absorbing as much torque as a larger (stock) torque converter. As a result, the stall speed is increased. Because an engine develops more torque with increased speed (up to a point), the smaller torque converter will allow the engine to increase to a higher speed and create more torque to the transmission than would be capable with the stock torque converter.

This is especially helpful for modified engines because an engine having a camshaft with increased lift and duration usually lacks low RPM torque. By using a smaller torque converter, the stall speed is increased to better match the engine torque.

CAUTION: Using a nonstock torque converter is likely to increase exhaust emissions and decrease fuel economy.

PLANETARY GEAR SETS

In a manual transmission, different gear ratios are obtained by sliding the gears into mesh. However, torque flow must be momentarily interrupted (accomplished by using a clutch) before the gears are shifted. With an automatic transmission there is no driver-operated clutch, so gear shifts are not made by sliding gears into mesh. Automatic transmissions use a planetary gear set system that does not require manual gear shifting or an interruption of torque flow to change gear ratios. A simple planetary gear set consists of three primary components:

- Sun gear
- Planet carrier assembly
- Ring gear

As discussed in the last chapter, the sun gear gets its name from its position at the centre of the gear set. The planet carrier assembly holds the pinion gears, also known as planet gears, which revolve around the sun gear. The outermost member of the gear set is the ring gear, which is the internal type with the teeth inside. The pinion gears are in simultaneous mesh with both the sun and ring gear.

The pinion gears are free to rotate on pins that are part of the carrier, and the entire assembly rotates to direct torque flow. The simple planetary gear set as seen in Figure 49–16 has only two planet pinions, but most transmission gear sets use three or four. The pinions are fully meshed with both the sun gear and internal ring gear *at all times.* The planetary gears never disengage to change gear ratios; torque is simply redirected.

All gears in a planetary gear set are in constant mesh. The torque flow through a planetary gear set, both input and output, occurs along a single axis. The parts in a planetary gear system may be known by several different names. The internal ring gear is sometimes called an annulus gear or a ring gear. The planet pinion gears are often called planet gears or pinion gears. The planet carrier assembly is commonly referred to as the "carrier."

Planetary Gear Set Torque Flow

In any planetary gear set, each gear always meshes with several other gears. Therefore, driving one gear will drive all of the other gears as well. This allows the gear set to provide different gear ratios, depending upon how torque is distributed through the assembly. To transmit torque through a planetary gear set, a drive member rotates while a second member is held, which causes a third member to be driven. See Figure 49–17. Each member of a planetary gear set can play any one of these three roles to transmit torque. The various combinations of drive, held, and driven members result in the number of gear ratios available. Certain combinations of drive, held, and driven can change the direction of rotation as well. As discussed in Chapter 48, torque flows through a planetary gear set in several steps to get from the drive action of the first member to the driven action of the last member. The terms "drive" and "driven" simply describe how any two gears work together. When three or more gears are involved, the second gear is a *driven* gear in relation to the first, but a *drive* gear in relation to the third. For this reason, the drive member of a planetary gear set is known as the **input member,** the held member is the **reaction member,** and the driven member is the **output member.**

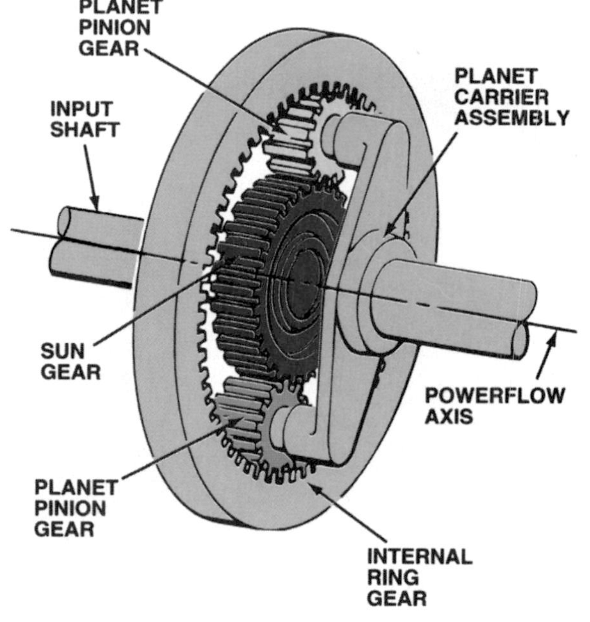

Figure 49–16 The three members of a simple planetary gear set are the sun gear, internal ring gear, and planet carrier assembly.

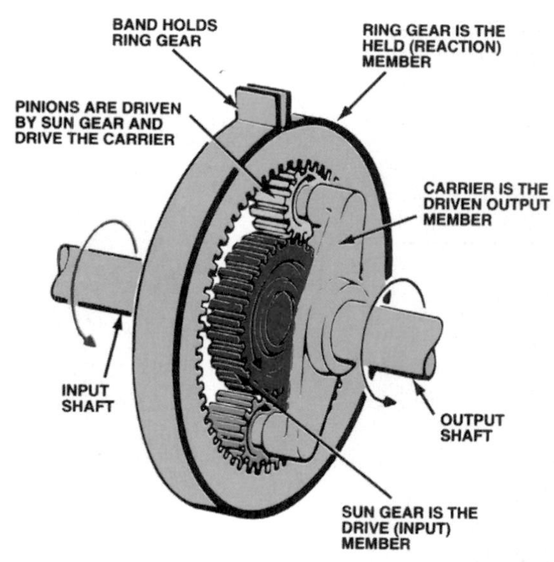

Figure 49–17 To transmit torque through a planetary gear set, one (input) member drives, another (reaction) member is held, and the third (output) member is driven.

See Figure 49–18 for the possible gear ratios and how they are achieved.

Simple Planetary Gear Set Systems

A simple planetary gear set system consists of one sun gear, carrier, and ring gear. A single planetary gear set can provide all of the necessary gear ratios for a basic automatic transmission.

Using a simple planetary gear set along with a brake band and multiple disc clutch as apply devices, you can design a 2-speed automatic transmission. The transmission provides neutral and reverse gearing, and performs low-to-drive gear changes without any input from the driver.

Simple planetary gear systems like this were used in some early automatic transmissions. However, they are no longer used because they do not provide enough usable gear ratios for present-day applications. They also present design problems for the particular gear set members that must be driven or held. However, the simple planetary gear set remains the foundation upon which the compound planetary gear sets used in modern transmissions are built. In fact, a simple planetary gear set is often used together with a compound planetary gear set to provide additional overdrive gearing.

Compound Planetary Gear Set Systems

A **compound planetary gear set** system is a configuration that contains more than just the three basic members of a simple planetary system. Compound planetary gear sets are capable of providing various combinations of gear reduction, direct drive, neutral, reverse, and overdrive.

Simpson Gear Set

The most popular compound planetary design is the **Simpson gear set.** Named for its inventor, the Simpson gear set consists of two simple planetary

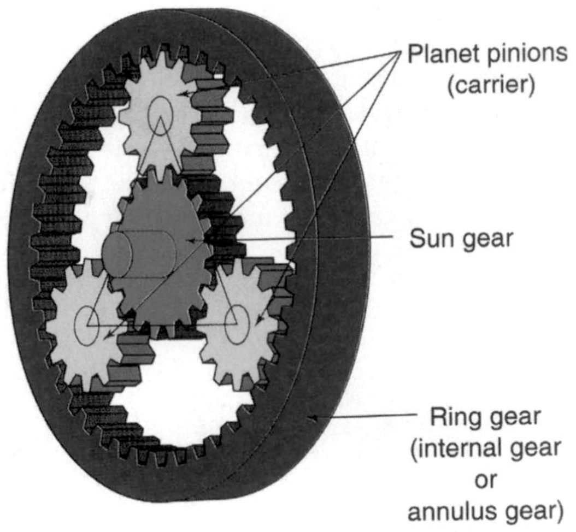

Planetary Gear Chart

Input	Output	Held	Results
Planet Carrier	Ring Gear	Sun Gear	Reduction
Sun Gear	Ring Gear	Planet Carrier	Reduction
Ring Gear	Planet Carrier	Sun Gear	Overdrive
Ring Gear	Sun Gear	Planet Carrier	Overdrive
Planet Carrier	Sun Gear	Ring Gear	Reduction and Reversal

Figure 49–18 Different modes of transferring torque through a planetary gear set.

gear sets that share a common sun gear. See Figure 49–19. This combination is capable of providing three forward gears, as well as neutral and reverse. Basic operation, construction, and methods of obtaining various gear ratios with a simple planetary gear set also apply to the Simpson gear set. The main difference is the number of gear ratios.

Ravigneaux Gear Set

Another popular compound planetary design is the **Ravigneaux gear set.** The Ravigneaux system has two sun gears: two sets, one longer than the other, of planet pinions supported in one carrier; and a single ring gear. See Figure 49–20. This design provides four forward gears, two in reduction, one direct, and one overdrive, as well as neutral and reverse. Basic planetary gear set operation, construction, and control methods also apply to the Ravigneaux gear set.

Both of these compound planetary gear set designs have been used over the years by import and domestic manufacturers.

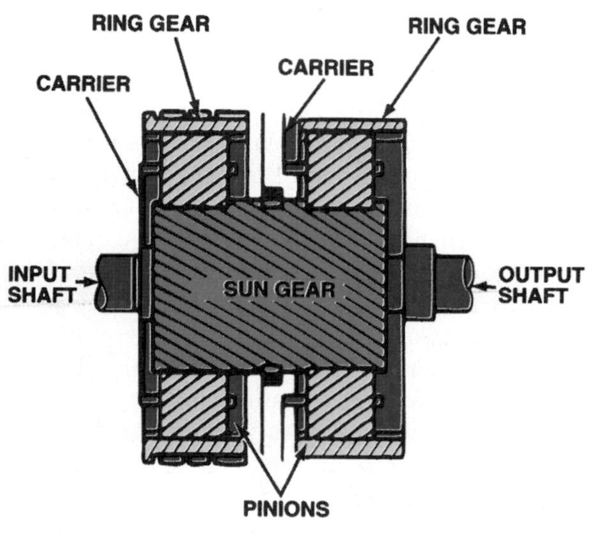

Figure 49–19 A Simpson planetary gear set is composed of two ring gears and two planet carrier assemblies that share a common sun gear.

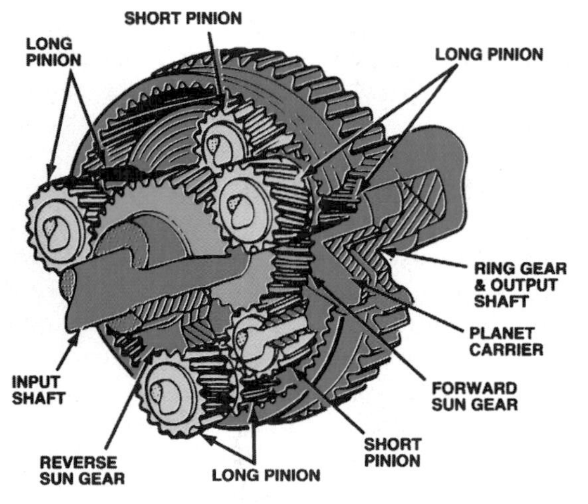

Figure 49–20 A Ravigneaux gear set is composed of two sun gears, one carrier that supports two sets of pinion gears, and a single ring gear.

APPLY DEVICES

Apply devices are the mechanical assemblies that provide these holding and driving forces. Automatic transmissions typically use transmission bands, multiple-disc clutches, and one-way clutches as apply devices.

Transmission bands are holding devices. While bands always provide a holding force, they cannot provide a driving force. The planetary gear set member held by the band is known as a **reaction member.**

A **transmission band** stops and holds one planetary gear set member so that another member can react against the held member and develop output motion. The reaction member has a control surface for the band to ride on known as a drum. See Figure 49–21. The band provides holding force around the outside of the drum, closing tightly to keep it from turning. To repeat, a transmission band is a holding device and is not capable of driving any member of the planetary gear set.

Transmission bands are made of cast iron or steel with friction material lining the inside surface. Transmission design and component size dictate the type of band used. Bands fall into one of two categories:

- Single-wrap
- Double-wrap

The single-wrap band is a simple one-piece design, while the double-wrap band is a split band with overlapping ends. Bands may also be classified as either flexible or fixed depending on how well they hold their shape when they are off the drum. See Figure 49–22.

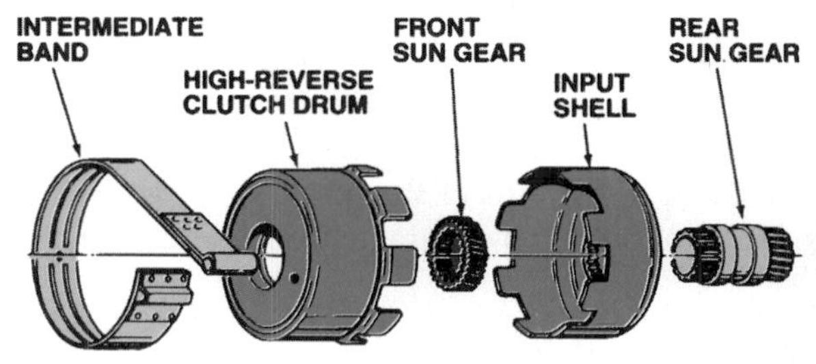

Figure 49–21 Gear set members are attached to a drum and are held stationary when the band applies.

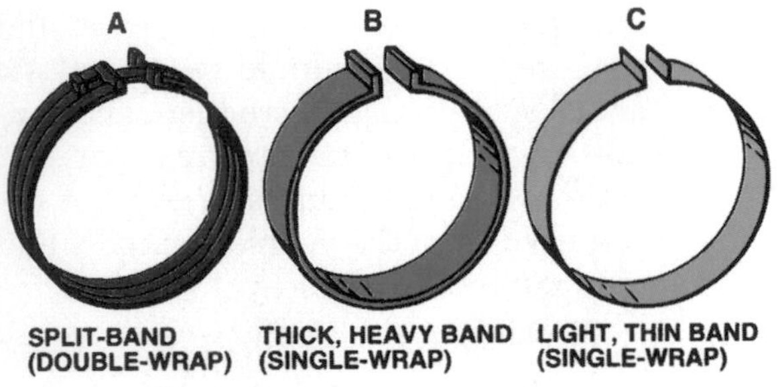

Figure 49–22 Transmission bands come in several designs and thicknesses.

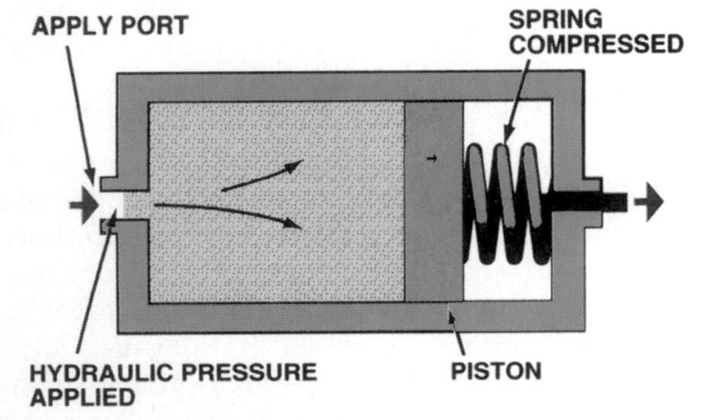

Figure 49–23 A servo uses hydraulic pressure to move a piston, which applies a band.

HYDRAULIC SERVOS

A hydraulically operated piston that travels inside a machined cylinder bore applies the transmission band. This piston and cylinder assembly is known as a **servo.** See Figure 49–23. A piston return spring normally holds the servo piston in its unapplied position. To apply the band, hydraulic fluid under pressure enters the servo cylinder and acts on the piston. The piston begins moving once hydraulic pressure overcomes spring force. A mechanical rod and linkage attaches to the piston and connects it to the band. As the piston moves, the linkage applies the band by tightening it around the drum.

Servo Linkages

Servo **rods** and **struts** transfer the servo apply force to the transmission band. Rods are round metal bars and struts are flat metal plates. These may be used at either, or both, ends of the band. Linkages connect the band to the servo or an anchor. See Figure 49–24.

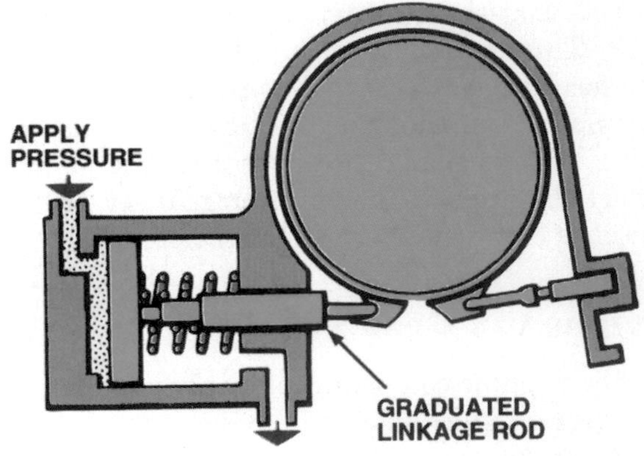

Figure 49–24 Notice that one end of the band is held stationary and the other end is attached to the servo.

ACCUMULATORS

An accumulator cushions, or dampens, hydraulic pressure surges by temporarily diverting part of the fluid flow in a hydraulic circuit into a parallel circuit or chamber. The diversion allows pressure in the main apply circuit to increase gradually and provides a smooth engagement of the band or clutch. Accumulators fit into two classifications: piston- or valve-type. Piston-type accumulators look and function much like servo pistons. In fact, some piston-type accumulators share a bore with one of the transmission servos. This common bore design is known as an **integral accumulator.** See Figure 49–25. Piston accumulators that install in a dedicated bore in the transmission case are known as **independent accumulators.**

As hydraulic pressure enters both circuits, the accumulator piston offers much less resistance than the servo piston because it represents a much lighter load. As a result, the accumulator piston moves first and absorbs any surges as the fluid fills the accumulator cylinder. Once the accumulator piston reaches the end of its travel, cushioning is complete and pressure begins to build in the servo cylinder. This pressure acts on the servo piston to apply the band.

MULTIPLE-DISC CLUTCHES

Like a transmission band, a multiple-disc hydraulic clutch is a type of apply device. Clutches have more friction area so they can develop more force and handle more torque than a band, and they are self-adjusting.

The **multiple-disc clutch** consists of plates, a piston, drum, and snap ring. The piston returns to an unapplied position via a return spring assembly. Some transmissions use a special wave-type spring to return the piston and cushion clutch applications. The entire assembly is commonly known as a **clutch pack.** See Figure 49–26.

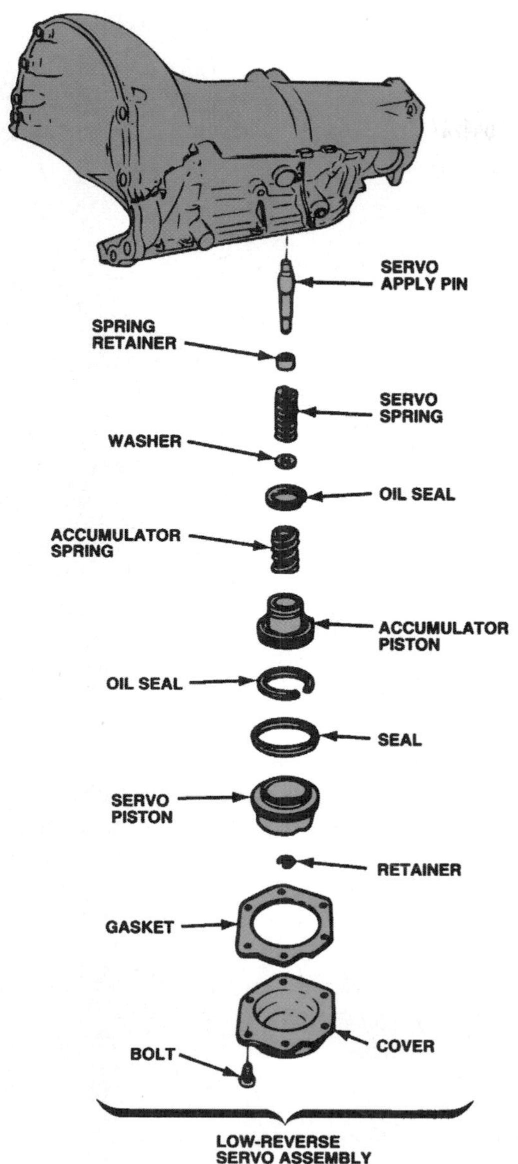

Figure 49–25 An integral accumulator is combined with a servo in a single bore.

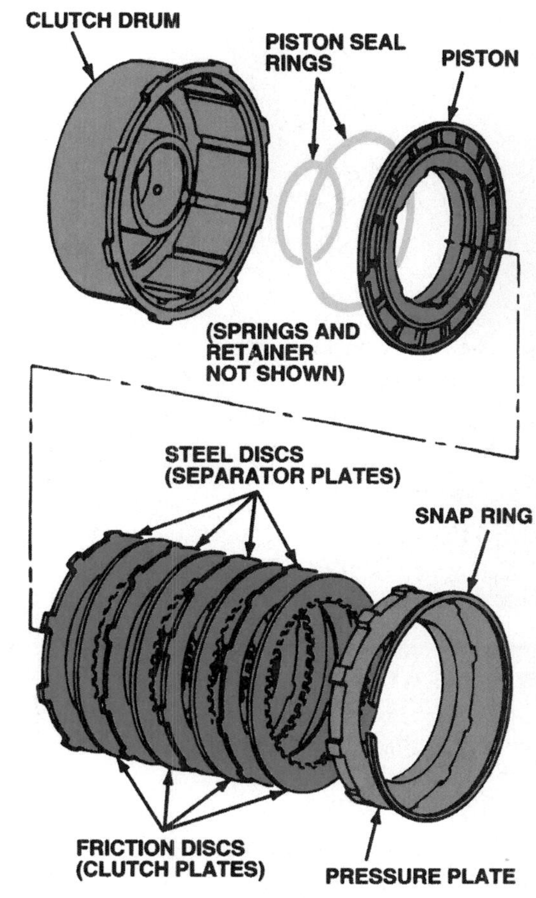

Figure 49–26 An exploded view of a multiple-disc clutch pack assembly.

The plates of a multiple-disc clutch assembly consist of friction discs alternated with steel discs. The friction discs have a rough surface friction material applied to both faces. The steel discs have a smooth, flat surface finish without any friction material. At times you may see them referred to as separator plates, apply plates, drive plates, or simply "steels." Collectively, the friction and steel discs are called the **clutch plates.**

Generally, the steel plates have splines on their outer edge, while the friction discs have splines on their inner edge. Each set of splines engages matching splines on a shaft, drum, planetary gear set member, or the transmission case. When the clutch applies, hydraulic pressure acting on the piston squeezes the two sets of plates together to mechanically connect the two components that engage the splines of the discs.

The piston compresses the clutch plates against a thicker reaction plate known as the **pressure plate.** Pressure plates may be used at one or both ends of the clutch pack and are available in selective sizes for adjusting clutch pack clearance. The pressure plate and clutch assembly components fit into either a **clutch drum** or a machined bore in the transmission case. Snap rings retain all the clutch assembly components and are available in selective sizes for adjusting clearance. See Figure 49–27. Although a multiple-disc clutch is an apply device similar to a transmission band, it differs from a band because it can be used to drive members of planetary gear sets as well as hold them. There are two types of multiple-disc clutches:

- Holding
- Driving

Figure 49–27 A typical clutch pack assembly.

Holding Clutches

An example of a holding clutch is shown in Figure 49–28. In this arrangement, splines on the inner edge of the friction discs engage matching splines on the outside of the clutch drum. The steel discs, alternated with the friction discs, have splines on their outer edge that engage matching splines machined into the transmission case.

A holding clutch is an open design and usually fits into either a machined area of the case or in a special support that bolts to the case. Internal passages in the case route fluid to the apply piston.

Driving Clutches

There are two types of multiple-disc driving clutches, and both types are commonly used in automotive transmissions. In one configuration, splines connect a set of friction discs to the transmission input shaft so that these discs function as the driving member. The alternating set of steel discs spline to the inside of the clutch drum and serve as the driven member. When the clutch is released, the drive discs rotate with the input shaft, but they do not drive the driven discs that spline to the drum.

When the clutch applies, the piston takes up clearance and forces both sets of discs firmly together. Now, the input shaft and drum rotate together at the same speed and torque transfers from one gear set member to another. A passage inside the input shaft carries fluid to the clutch apply piston. See Figure 49–29.

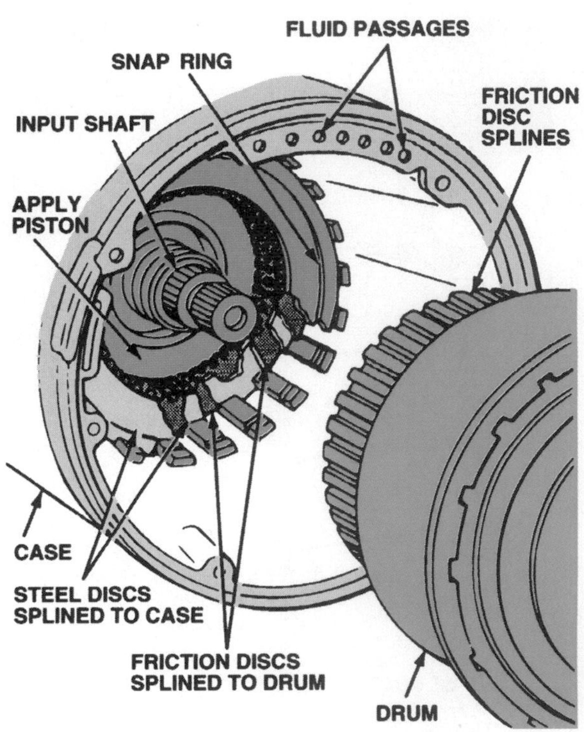

Figure 49–28 In a holding clutch, one set of discs engages splines on the transmission case and the other set engages splines on the drum. By applying the clutch, the drum is locked to the case.

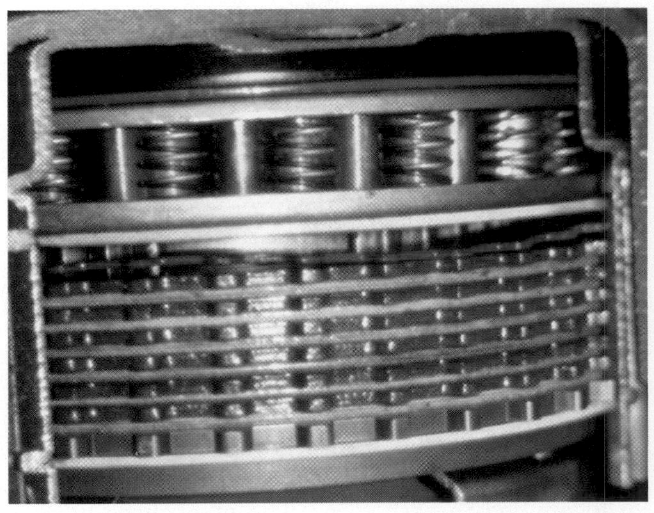

Figure 49–29 Cutaway of a clutch housing on a GM 4T60 (440-T4) transaxle.

With the second driving clutch configuration, the drum connects directly to the input shaft so the drum always rotates with the shaft. Splines connect the steel discs to the inside of the drum and the friction discs to the outside of a clutch hub. When the clutch applies, hydraulic pressure compresses the clutch pack to lock the drum and clutch hub together.

The input shaft then drives the output shaft and both turn at the same speed.

Clutch Operation

To apply the clutch, pressurized fluid enters the drum through an internal passage in the input shaft. The fluid acts on the piston and moves it against return spring force to clamp the clutch plates together and hold them against the pressure plate. See Figure 49–30. The friction between the discs then locks the clutch drum to the hub, causing them to turn as one unit.

To release the clutch, hydraulic fluid is cut off to the apply side of the piston and exhausted. The piston-return springs, which were compressed when the clutch was applied, are now free to expand and move the piston back, allowing the clutch discs to disengage.

ONE-WAY CLUTCHES

Another type of automatic transmission device in common use is the **one-way clutch,** or overrunning clutch. Like a transmission band, a one-way clutch is always a holding device. However, it can work together with a drive clutch to provide input. One-way clutches are either roller or sprag clutches. However, the roller clutch is more common.

One-Way Roller Clutch

A one-way roller clutch consists of a hub, rollers, and springs that fit inside a drum. See Figure 49–31. The inner circumference of the drum has a series of machined ramps, or cam cuts, to accommodate the rollers and springs. Each ramp is narrower at one end than it is at the other.

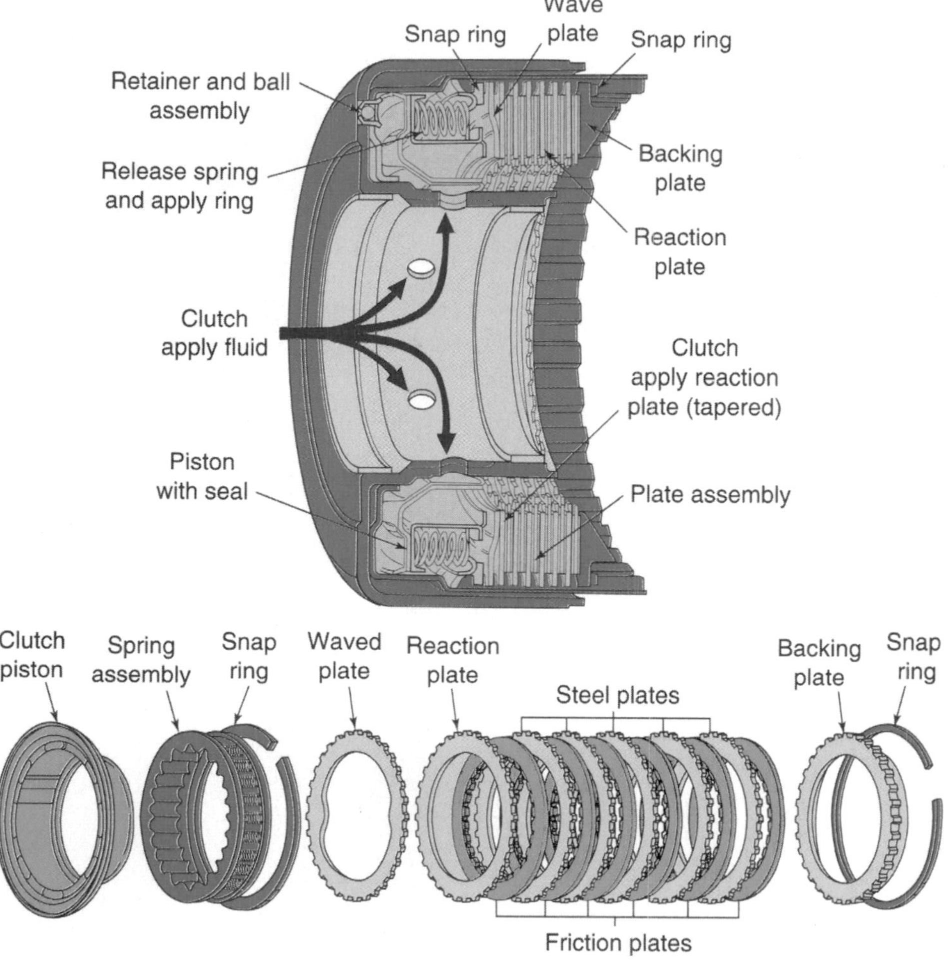

Figure 49–30 Hydraulic fluid under pressure enters the clutch housing and exerts a force on the clutch piston. The clutch piston forces the steel plates and the friction plates together, creating a shift.

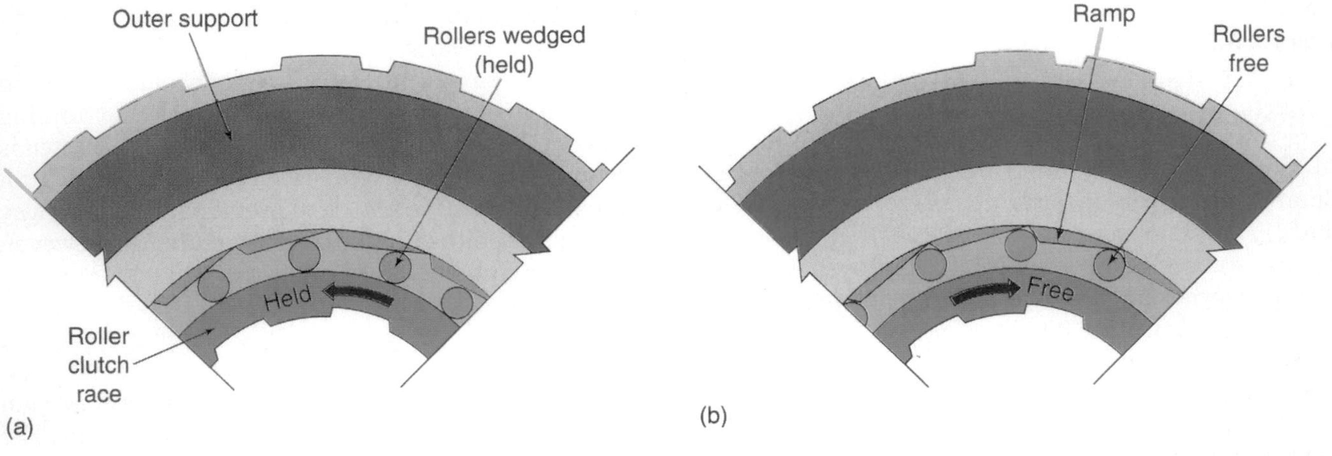

Figure 49–31 (a) A roller one-way clutch in the locked (held) position. Note how the rollers are wedged into the ramp machined into the outer support. (b) A roller one-way clutch in the released (free) position. When the inner roller clutch race rotates faster than the outer support, the rollers move out of the wedge and are free to rotate, thereby unlocking the one-way clutch.

If you hold the drum while rotating the hub clockwise, the rollers will compress their springs and move toward the larger end of the ramps. This unlocks the clutch because there is enough clearance between the rollers and the drum for the hub to freewheel.

Rotate the hub counterclockwise while holding the drum. The rollers move toward the narrow end of the ramp, wedging themselves between the hub and drum to lock the clutch. With the rollers at the narrow end of the ramp there is no roller-to-drum clearance. Therefore, the hub cannot turn counterclockwise because the drum is being held.

One-Way Sprag Clutch

Less commonly used is a **one-way sprag clutch** that consists of a hub and a drum separated by a number of figure-eight-shaped metal pieces called **sprags.** See Figure 49–32. Sprags lock and unlock the clutch in a manner similar to the rollers in a one-way roller clutch. The shape of a sprag provides two effective working lengths. The direction in which the sprag tilts determines if working length is short or long.

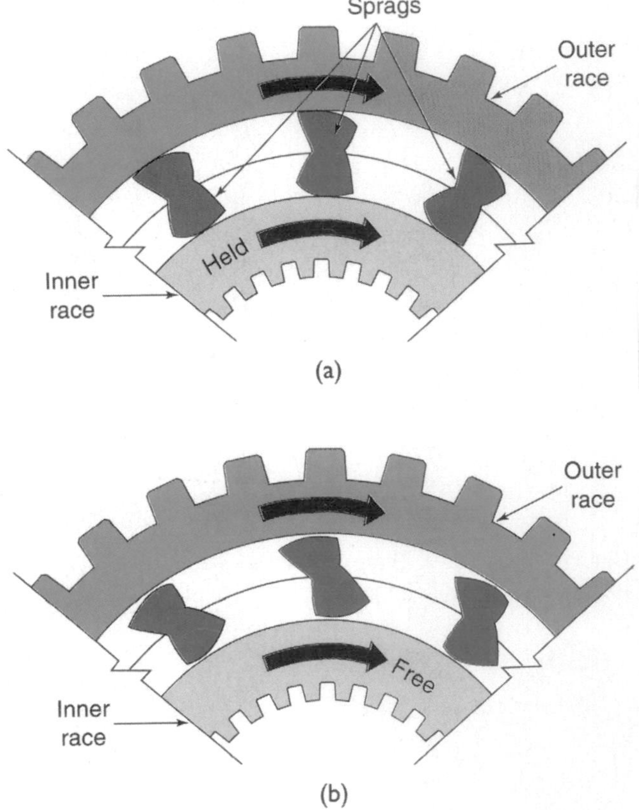

Figure 49–32 (a) The sprag is in the holding (locked) position. Note how the long portion of the sprag is wedged between the inner and outer race. (b) The sprag is released. The inner race is free to rotate faster than the outer race.

PUMP

Every hydraulic system requires a pump to supply fluid flow and pressurize the system. However, the pump itself does not develop pressure. Pressure occurs only when there is a resistance to flow. Initially, fluid flows freely when a hydraulic circuit is empty or partially filled. Once the circuit is completely full, there is a resistance to further flow. At this point, pressure begins to build up in the circuit as the pump continues to create flow.

Most oil pumps mount directly behind the torque converter and are usually driven by the converter drive hub. See Figure 49–33. This connects the pump to the engine and allows it to respond quickly to engine demand. This type of oil pump operates whenever the engine is running.

Pressure Regulation

Transmission oil pumps are capable of creating an excessive amount of pressure quickly, which could easily damage the transmission. Therefore, every transmission has at least one valve that opens to relieve any excess pressure the pump generates. These pressure regulator valves maintain constant pressure within the system. Valves that regulate system pressure are directly in line with the oil pump output flow. All transmission operating pressures derive from the regulated output flow of the oil pump. The **primary spring** combines with the pressure regulator valve to control mainline pressure.

Pressure Regulating Valves

Pressure regulating valves control the amount of pressure that the transmission hydraulic system, or a particular hydraulic circuit, develops. An automatic transmission uses two types of valves, pressure regulator and pressure relief, to control hydraulic pressure.

The **pressure regulator valve,** or pressure control valve, is usually a spool valve and spring combination that regulates the main hydraulic system pressure. This pressure, commonly known as mainline or simply line pressure, is the working pressure for the entire hydraulic system. The pressure regulator valve is directly in line with the output flow of the transmission oil pump.

Most pressure regulator valves balance pump pressure on one side of the valve against a preset

(a)

(b)

(c)

Figure 49–33 (a) A gear-type pump. (b) Gerotor-type pump. (c) A vane-type pump.

spring force acting on the other side of the valve. See Figures 49–34 and 49–35. When hydraulic pressure is greater than spring force, the valve moves in its bore far enough to uncover an exhaust port. The exhaust port provides a low-pressure path to the sump. Excess pressurized fluid flowing through this port reduces system pressure. When hydraulic pressure drops below spring pressure, the regulator valve closes the port and pressure begins to build up again.

In operation, this sequence of events opening and closing the exhaust port occurs many times per second. This achieves a steady pressure as the forces working on each end of the valve hold it in balance. Because of this action, this type of valve is sometimes called a **balanced valve.**

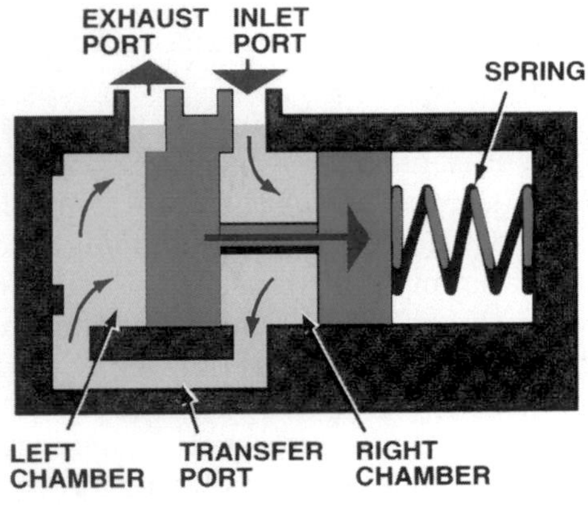

Figure 49–34 When pressure on the face of a pressure regulator valve overcomes spring force, the valve moves to open the exhaust port.

Electronic Pressure Regulation

Electronic automatic transmissions often regulate hydraulic system pressure using computer-controlled solenoids called **pressure control solenoids, variable force solenoids (VFS),** or simply **force motors.** An on-board computer switches the solenoids on and off very quickly using pulse-width modulation (PWM). This pulsed switching positions an internal ball valve in the solenoid, which opens and closes the hydraulic circuit it regulates. See Figure 49–36. Electronic pressure control allows precise hydraulic system pressure regulation and can also be used to modify the timing and feel of transmission shifting.

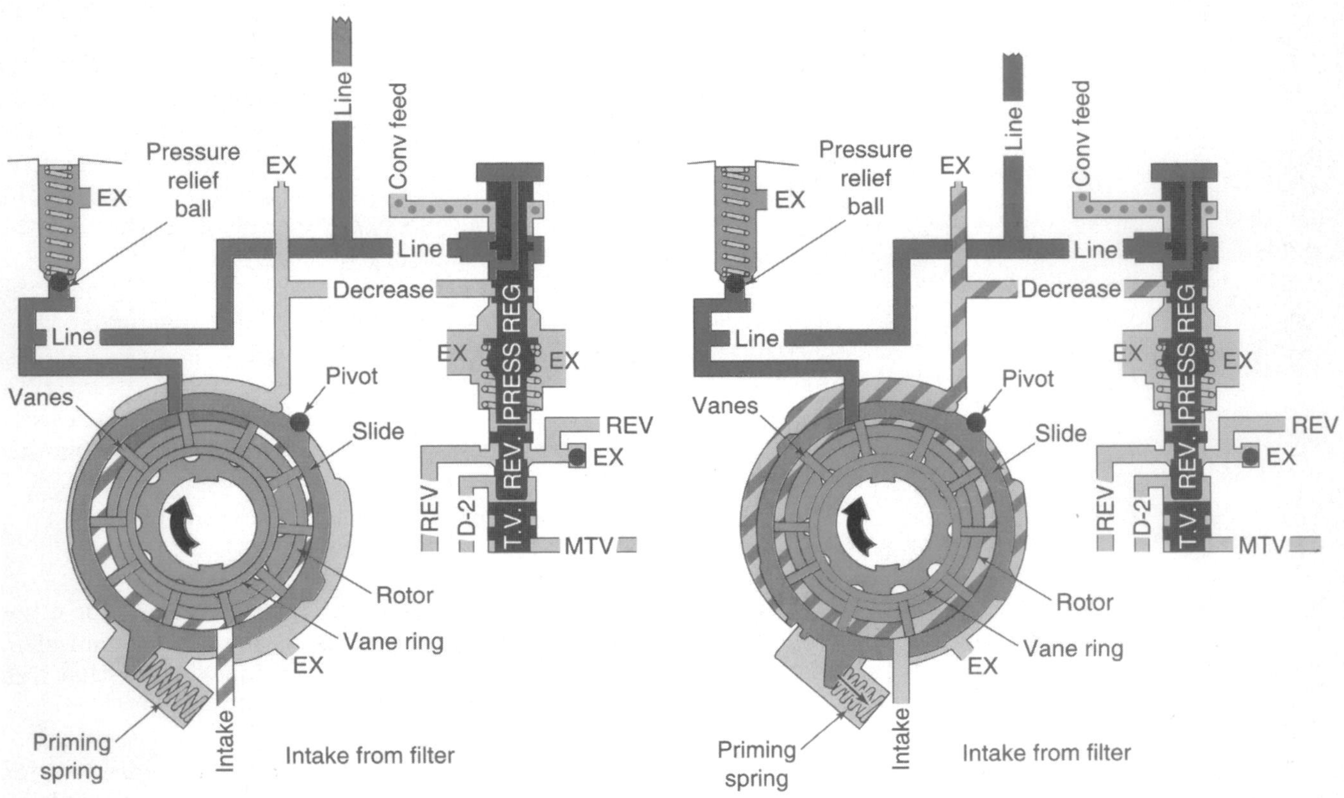

Figure 49–35 The variable pump is at the maximum pump output position until the regulator valve moves enough to decrease volume by rotating the slide against the force of the priming spring. The position of the pump constantly varies depending on the needs of the transmission/transaxle and driving conditions.

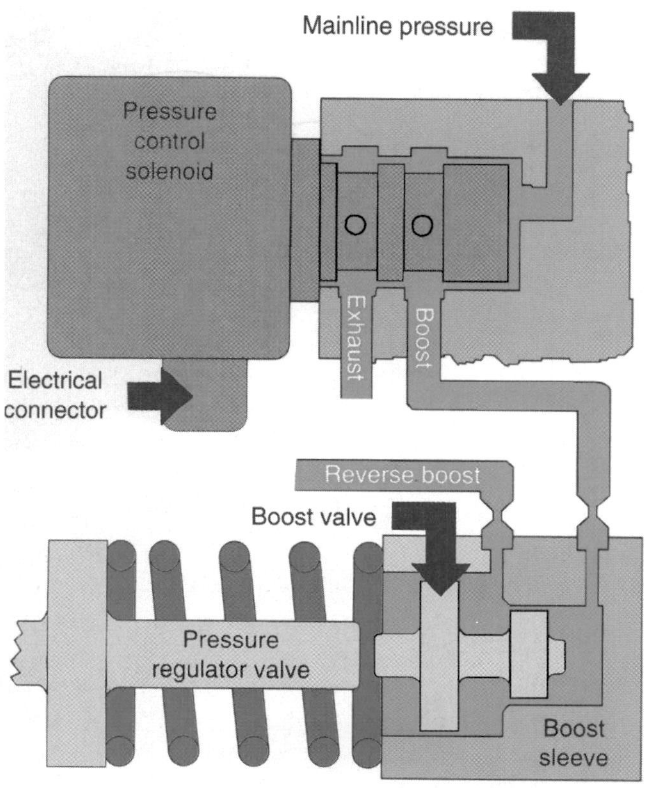

Figure 49–36 The pressure control solenoid controls mainline pressure, which is controlled by the vehicle computer by applying fluid pressure to the spring side of the pressure regulator valve.

Flow Directing Valves

Flow directing valves, or switching valves, control the direction and distribution of fluid flow in the hydraulic system. These valves may open or close passages, fill hydraulic circuits, apply or release clutches and bands, and control the direction of fluid flow from one passage or circuit to another.

One-way Valves A **one-way valve** allows fluid to flow in one direction. The spring-loaded ball check valve is an example of one type of one-way valve. Valve operation is similar to that of a poppet valve. The spring holds the ball against its seat at the inlet port until fluid pressure overcomes spring force to push the ball from its seat. Fluid flows through the valve as long as hydraulic pressure exceeds the force of the spring.

Spring-loaded ball check valves are used as pressure-relief valves, and work well on bypass circuits because they provide a fast apply rate with a slow release. A second type of one-way valve is a simple gravity valve, as commonly used in transmission valve bodies.

The **check balls** in these valves are usually made of steel, but they can be nylon, rubber, or some composite material as well. Which material is used depends on the manufacturer and application. Steel balls generally hold up better, but cause greater seat wear because of their hardness. The softer composite balls are easier on seats and they cannot be magnetized. See Figure 49–37.

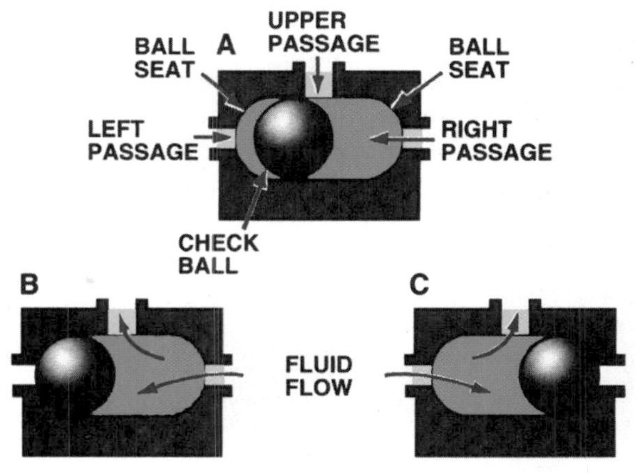

Figure 49–37 Some check balls are used in the valve body to allow hydraulic circuits to share a common passage.

Manual Valve

The **manual valve** is the primary flow-directing valve in an automatic transmission. See Figure 49–38. This valve connects to a shift lever in the transmission, which in turn connects to the gear selector lever through a mechanical linkage. The driver controls manual valve position through the gear selector and shift linkage.

Mechanical linkage physically positions the manual valve in its bore for the particular gear range selected. This aligns the lands on the valve so they uncover ports feeding the correct hydraulic circuits. The manual valve receives mainline pressure from the pump output and distributes it to the hydraulic circuits uncovered by the valve lands.

Transmission Pressure Valves

These valves use mainline pressure to develop other hydraulic circuit pressures within the transmission. Pressure valves are normally spool valves that link to external components.

Throttle Valve The throttle valve senses engine load and uses that operating signal to develop throttle pressure on hydraulically-shifted automatic transmissions. Some throttle valves have linkage that connects them mechanically to the throttle plates, and the throttle valve responds directly to engine load. See Figure 49–39. A low engine load develops low throttle

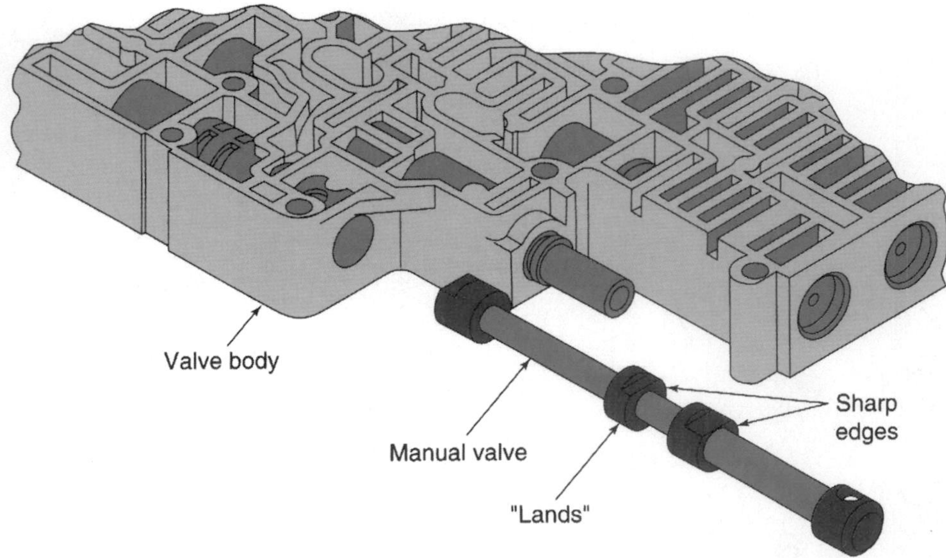

Figure 49–38 The manual valve in the valve body is moved by shift linkage. All valves in a valve body should have sharp edges on the lands. Any dirt in this area can cause shifting problems due to the close tolerances between the valves and the bores in the valve body.

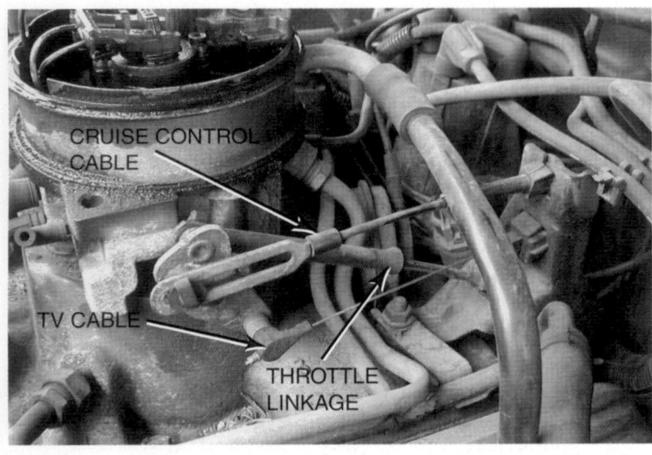

Figure 49–39 The throttle valve (TV) cable adjustment on the 700-R4 (4T60) is very sensitive and greatly affects the shifting.

pressure, while a higher load develops higher throttle pressure. The throttle position (TP) sensor has replaced the need for these valves in electronically-shifted automotive transmissions/transaxles.

Vacuum Modulator Valve A vacuum modulator is used to convert engine manifold vacuum into a signal pressure that increases as engine vacuum decreases. A vacuum modulator is used on hydraulically shifted transmissions/transaxles to help determine the shift point based on engine load. See Figures 49–40 and 49–41. For example,

- **Light engine load—**manifold vacuum is high, shifts occur at lower speeds.
- **Heavy engine load—**manifold vacuum is low, shifts occur at higher speeds.

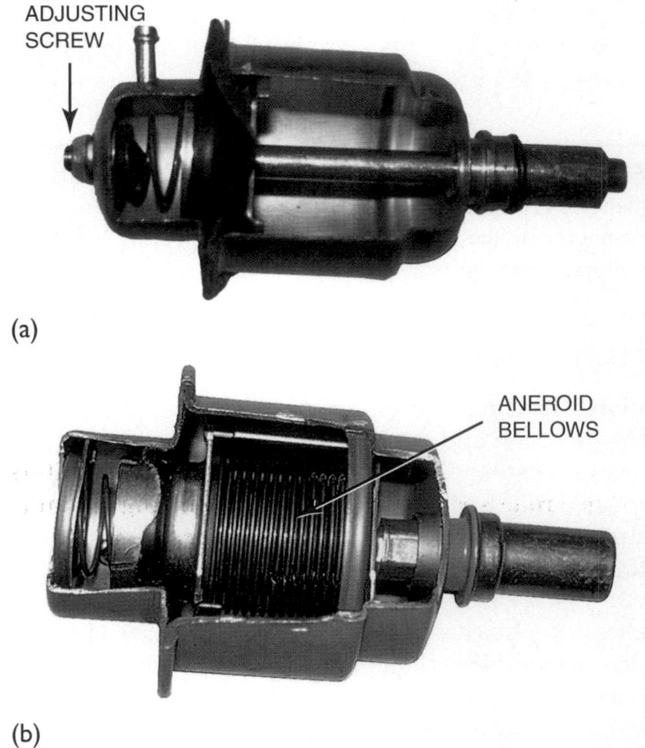

Figure 49–40 (a) A cutaway of a modulator valve. A vacuum line runs from the intake manifold to the modulator valve, where changes in engine load (vacuum) move the diaphragm in the valve. The diaphragm is connected to a valve in the valve body to delay the shift points whenever the engine is under a heavy load (low vacuum). The screw at the end allows the service technician to make minor corrections to the shift points. This is a replacement modulator valve. Most original equipment modulator valves are not adjustable. (b) This modulator valve is cut away to show the altitude compensating aneroid bellows.

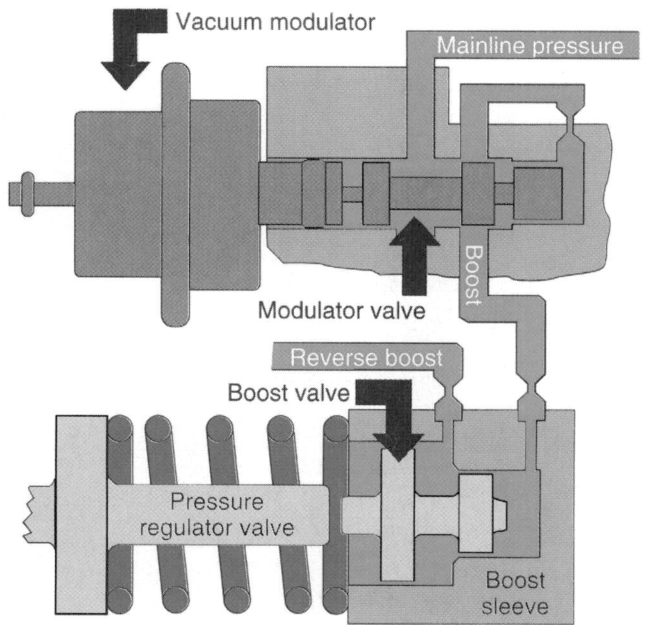

Figure 49–41 The vacuum modulator moves the modulator spool valve in the valve body that applies mainline pressure to the boost sleeve of the pressure regulator valve. Because this force is acting in the same direction as the pressure regulator spring, the mainline pressure is increased.

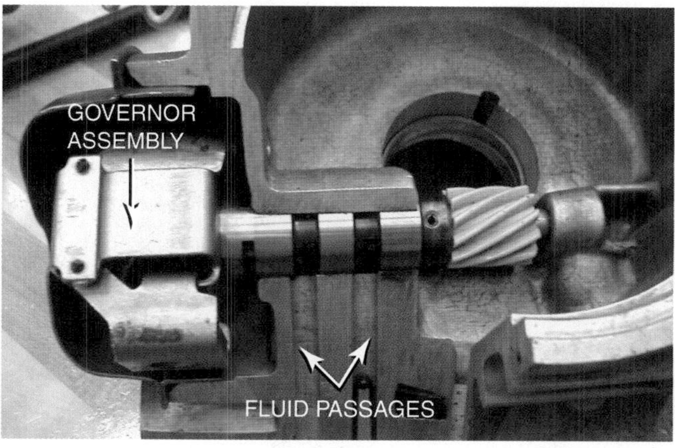

Figure 49–42 A governor assembly is used on older automatic transmissions/transaxles to control shift points based on vehicle speed as determined by the drive gear on the output shafts that rotate the governor assembly.

The manifold absolute pressure (MAP) sensor and throttle position (TP) sensor serve in place of the vacuum modulator valve in measuring engine load on computer-controlled electronically shifted automatic transmissions/transaxles.

Governor Valve The **governor valve** monitors vehicle road speed and uses that operating signal to develop governor pressure. The governor valve normally follows transmission output shaft rotation speed, which increases with vehicle speed. As the output shaft speed increases, governor pressure also increases. Governor pressure opposes throttle pressure at the shift valves to control upshifts and downshifts in relation to vehicle speed. See Figure 49–42.

Pressure valves develop rather than simply route hydraulic pressures. Electronic transmissions often replace these pressure valves with solenoids that can develop hydraulic pressure directly from electronic speed sensor signals.

Shift Valves

A **shift valve** is a spring-loaded spool valve that controls the transmission upshift and downshift circuits. See Figure 49–43. Throttle pressure works against one side of the valve, while governor pressure works against the other side. When one pressure is greater than the other, the valve moves to the upshift or downshift position and the valve lands uncover the ports to the relative circuits. Transmission shift valves may be referred to as "snap valves" because they shift almost instantly in response to pressure differential changes. Since these valves cause upshifts and downshifts, they are also known as "event-causing valves." There are only two positions for a shift valve—fully to the right or to the left. Otherwise, hydraulic pressure could apply control devices for two gears at once and damage the transmission.

In an electronically-shifted automotive transmission/transaxle, solenoids replace shift valves. See Figure 49–44.

Valve Body

Most of the valves in a transmission are located in the valve body. See Figures 49–45 and 49–46. Valve bodies can be either cast aluminum or cast iron and bolt up to the case. The valve body in most rear-wheel-drive transmissions is inside the oil pan at the bottom of the case. A transaxle valve body may be at the bottom of the case, on the backside of the torque converter housing, or on the top or side of the transaxle housing depending on the specific application.

Valve bodies have many fluid passages for the various transmission hydraulic circuits cast into them. These are sometimes called **worm holes** or **worm tracks.** Some of these passages may be widened to form pockets that contain steel, nylon, or rubber check balls.

Most valve bodies consist of two or more cast sections that bolt together with a flat metal separator

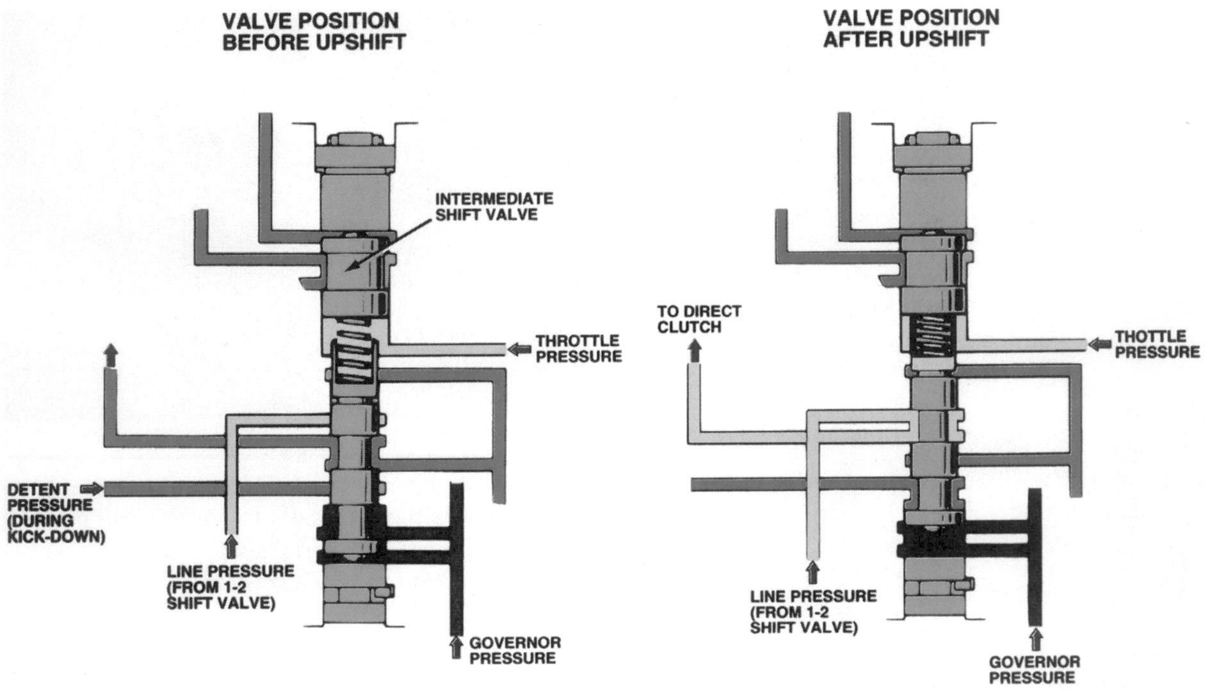

Figure 49–43 Shift valves move when there is a difference in pressure. In a hydraulically shifted transmission, the shift valves balance governor pressure against throttle pressure to determine when to upshift or downshift.

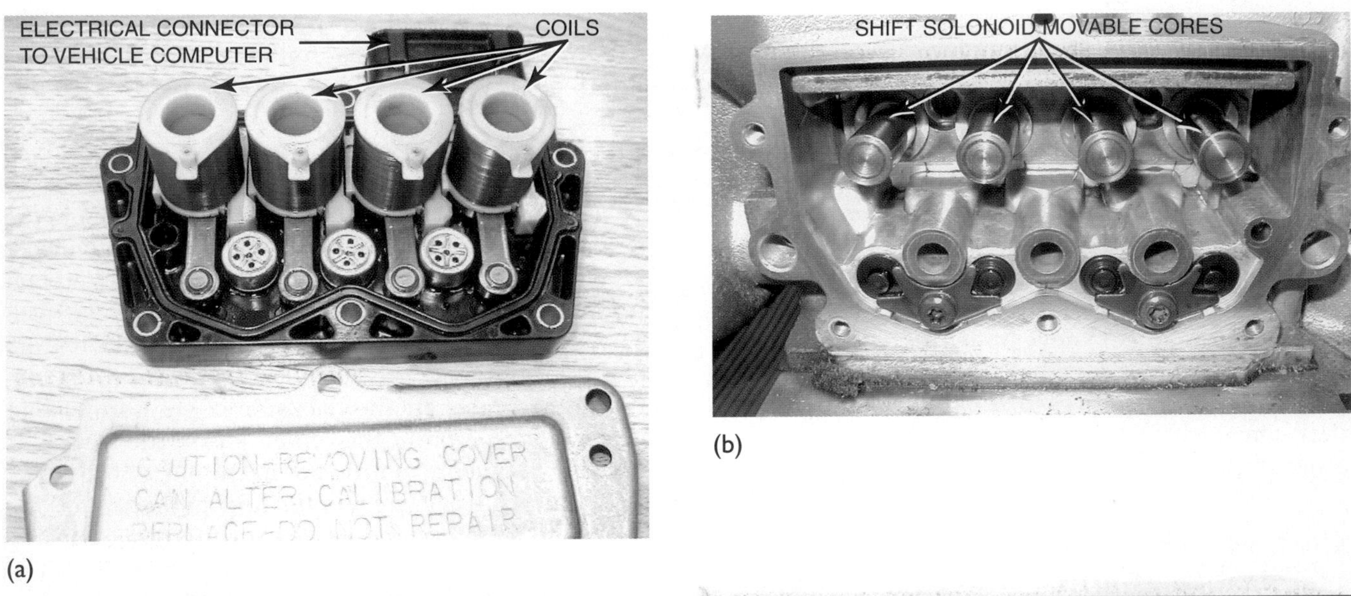

Figure 49–44 (a) The four electric coils represent the electromagnetic part of the shift control solenoid pack on this Chrysler 41TE transaxle. (b) The cores of the shift solenoids move when the coil(s) is engaged by the vehicle or transmission control computer.

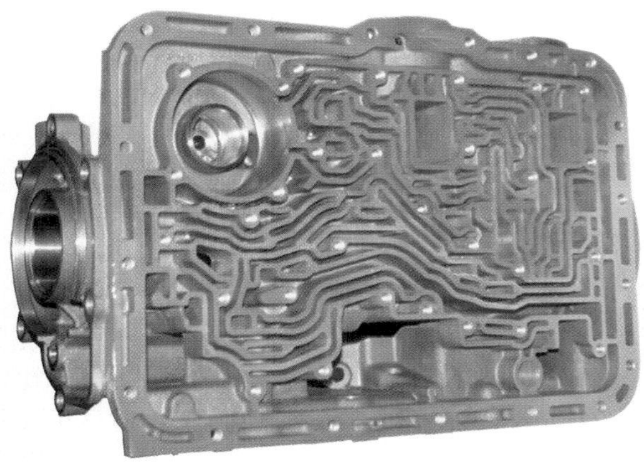

Figure 49–45 A typical valve body with all of the valves and servos removed.

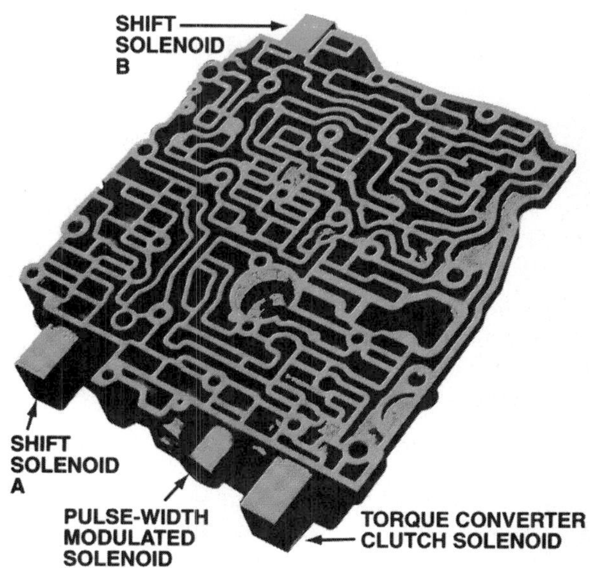

Figure 49–47 Solenoids are used to direct fluid flow through the hydraulic passages of this General Motors 4L80-E valve body.

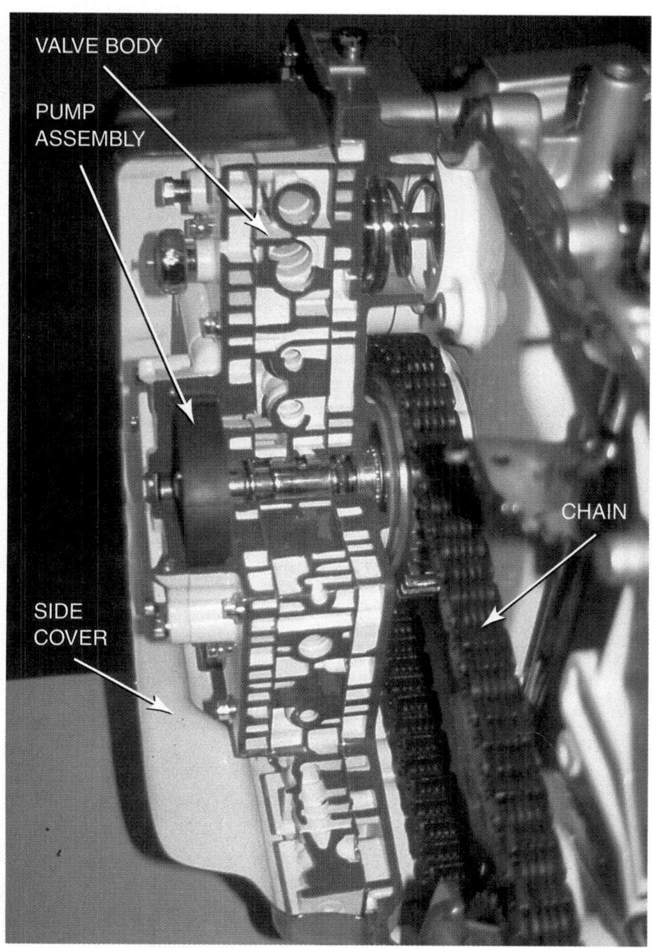

Figure 49–46 A cutaway of a valve body on a transaxle. Notice the relationship to the pump assembly and the drive chain used to transfer engine torque to the planetary gear sets. The edges of the valve body are painted red. Access to the valve body is achieved by removing the side cover.

plate between them. The upper section of the valve body is part of the transmission case casting. The separator plate provides rigidity and contains calibrated drill holes and openings that help manage fluid flow. Valve bodies contain specialized valves and circuits that are particular to a specific transmission. Electronic solenoids are used in place of some valves on electronically-shifted transmissions/transaxles. See Figure 49–47.

Shift Solenoids

Shift solenoids are computer controlled—they open passages in the valve body to the clutch band to achieve a shift. Shift solenoids may be labelled 1 and 2 or A and B. Using a combination of the two shift solenoids prevents the actuation of four forward gears—one being the **default gear,** a gear that the transmission defaults to if there is a failure in the electronic or computer system. If neither solenoid is engaged, then either second or third gear is actuated, depending on the exact make and model of the transmission/transaxle. See the following charts for examples of two General Motors transmissions.

General Motors 4T60-E (Front-Wheel-Drive Transaxle)		
Gear Range	**Solenoid A**	**Solenoid B**
1st gear	on	on
2nd gear	off	on
3rd gear	off	off
4th gear	on	off

TECH TIP 

Parking Brake Before Parking Pawl

To prevent possible damage to the transmission/transaxle case or other internal components, most experts agree that the parking brake should be applied *before* placing the gear selector into the park position, especially when parking on a hill. This procedure keeps the weight of the vehicle from being exerted entirely on the parking pawl and makes it easier to move the gear selector out of the park position.

In the following example, the vehicle would start out in second gear if there were a fault with the computer or wiring and the transaxle would not make any upshifts.

General Motors 4L80-E (Rear-Wheel-Drive Transmission)

Gear Range	Solenoid A	Solenoid B
1st gear	on	off
2nd gear	off	off
3rd gear	off	on
4th gear	on	on

TYPICAL TORQUE FLOW

The General Motors 4L60-E can provide an example of how a typical electronically-shifted rear-wheel drive automatic transmission works. See Figure 49–48.

Park and Neutral

With the gear selector level in P or N, there is no torque flow through the gear set, even though the low-reverse clutch applies in the 4L60-E. The clutch holds the reaction carrier stationary, but torque input to the gear set stops at the input housing.

The torque converter cover and impeller rotate clockwise at engine speed to hydraulically drive the turbine and mechanically drive the oil pump. The transmission input drum assembly rotates clockwise at turbine speed to drive the gear set. Turbine speed is slightly less than engine crankshaft speed. However, there is nothing connecting the input drum assembly to drive the gear sets and transfer torque at this time.

In neutral, the output shaft is free to rotate in either direction, and the vehicle can be pushed or towed. In park, a mechanical pawl engages a sprag on the reaction internal gear and locks the output shaft to the transmission case, preventing the vehicle from moving in either direction.

RANGE	GEAR	SHIFT SOLENOIDS		2-4 BAND	REVERSE INPUT CLUTCH	OVERRUN CLUTCH	FORWARD CLUTCH	FORWARD SPRAG CL. ASSEMBLY	3-4 CLUTCH	LOW ROLLER CLUTCH	LOW REVERSE CLUTCH
		"A"	"B"								
PARK		ON	ON								APPLIED
REVERSE		ON	ON		APPLIED						APPLIED
NEUTRAL		ON	ON								
Ⓓ	FIRST	ON	ON				APPLIED	HOLDING		HOLDING	
	SECOND	OFF	ON	APPLIED			APPLIED	HOLDING			
	THIRD	OFF	OFF				APPLIED	HOLDING	APPLIED		
	FOURTH	ON	OFF	APPLIED			APPLIED		APPLIED		
D	FIRST	ON	ON				APPLIED	HOLDING		HOLDING	
	SECOND	OFF	ON	APPLIED			APPLIED	HOLDING			
	THIRD	OFF	OFF			APPLIED	APPLIED	HOLDING	APPLIED		
2	FIRST	ON	ON			APPLIED	APPLIED	HOLDING		HOLDING	
	SECOND	OFF	ON	APPLIED		APPLIED	APPLIED	HOLDING			
1	FIRST	ON	ON			APPLIED	APPLIED	HOLDING		HOLDING	APPLIED
	SECOND	OFF	ON	APPLIED		APPLIED	APPLIED	HOLDING			

Figure 49–48 The General Motors 4L60-E electronically-shifted rear-wheel-drive automatic transmission clutch, band, and solenoid application chart.

Overdrive First

With the gear selector lever in overdrive, the transmission starts off in first gear, then upshifts into second, third, and fourth gears as the vehicle continues to accelerate. To engage first gear, the forward clutch applies, transferring engine torque from the input shaft to the input sun gear through the forward sprag clutch, and driving the sun gear clockwise.

With the input sun gear turning clockwise, the input pinion gears spin counterclockwise in the stationary carrier and attempt to drive the input internal gear and reaction carrier counterclockwise. However, the forward sprag clutch is holding, so the pinions walk clockwise inside the internal gear, turning the input carrier clockwise. Then, the input carrier drives the output shaft clockwise in gear reduction. See Figure 49–49.

The reaction internal gear turns clockwise along with the output shaft and drives the reaction pinions clockwise on the stationary reaction carrier. Pinion action drives the reaction sun gear counterclockwise. However, the reaction sun gear is not connected to a gear set member, so the reaction gear set simply freewheels. The low roller clutch prevents the reaction carrier from turning counterclockwise.

As long as the vehicle continues to accelerate in overdrive first, torque transfers through the gear set to the output shaft. During closed-throttle coasting, the clockwise torque load on the forward sprag clutch and the counterclockwise torque load on the low roller clutch are released. Both one-way clutches overrun so the gear sets freewheel on deceleration, and engine braking is not available.

Overdrive Second

As the vehicle continues to accelerate in the overdrive range, the transmission upshifts to second gear by applying the 2–4 band. The band holds the reverse drum, input shell, and reaction sun gear stationary. The forward clutch remains applied, while the input shaft drives the input sun gear clockwise through the forward sprag clutch. See Figure 49–50.

As in first gear, the input sun gear rotates clockwise and drives the input pinions counterclockwise. Since the 2–4 band is holding, the input pinions walk inside the internal gear, driving the input carrier and output shaft clockwise in gear reduction.

At the same time, the output shaft drives the reaction ring and pinion gears clockwise. With the reaction sun gear held, the pinion gears walk clockwise and drive the reaction carrier clockwise with them.

Clockwise rotation of the reaction carrier transfers to the input internal gear through the reaction carrier shaft. With the input internal gear turning clockwise, the input pinions spin counterclockwise and drive the input carrier clockwise. This removes the counterclockwise torque load from the low roller clutch so that it overruns at this time. There is no engine compression braking available in overdrive second because the forward sprag clutch overruns.

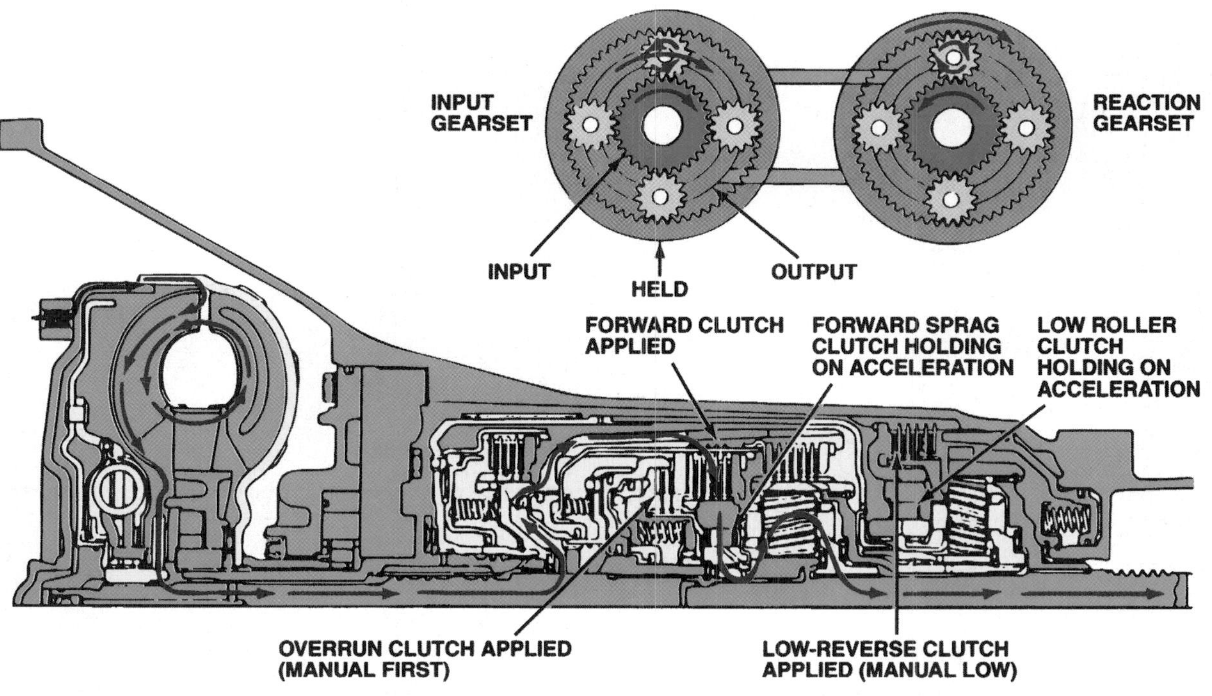

Figure 49–49 A 4L60-E torque flow in overdrive first gear.

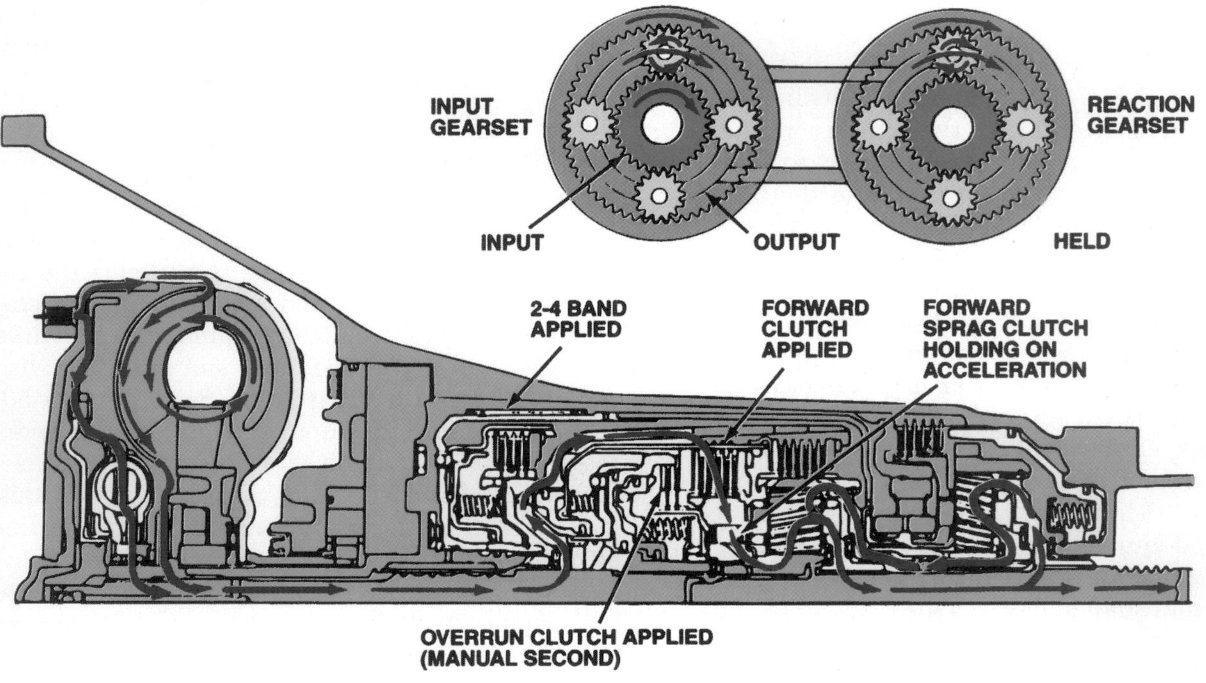

Figure 49–50 A 4L60-E torque flow in overdrive second gear.

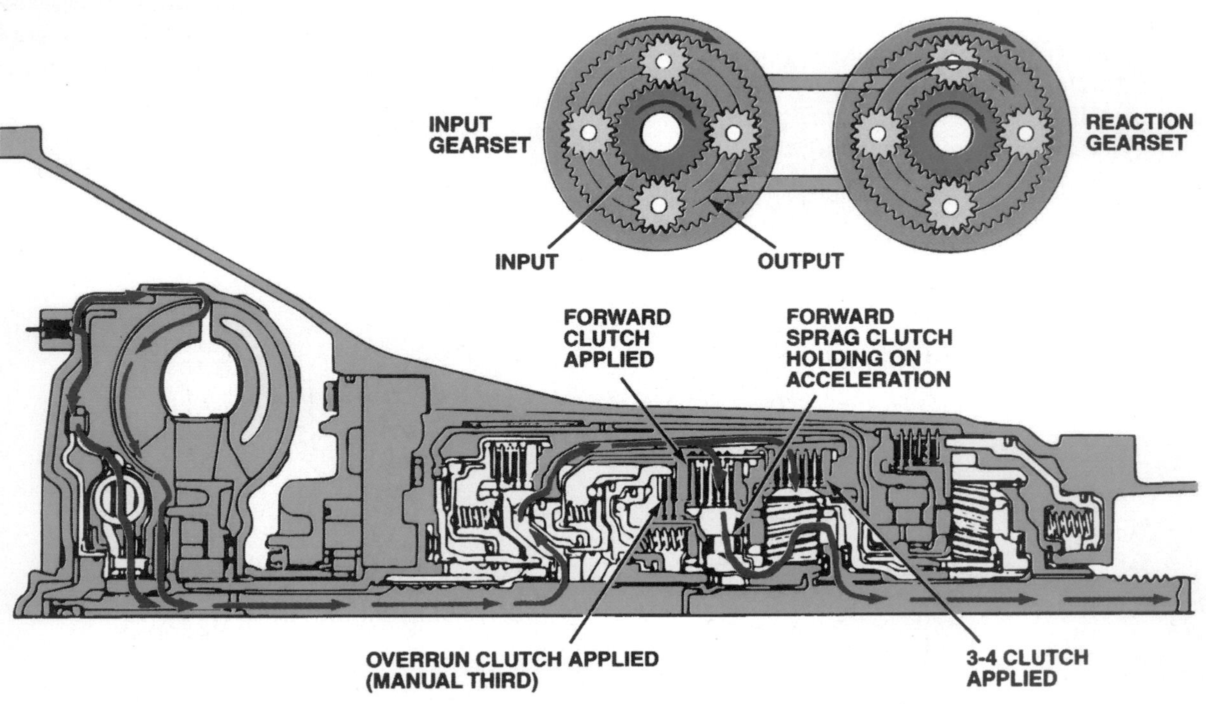

Figure 49–51 A 4L60-E torque flow in overdrive third gear.

Overdrive Third

To automatically upshift into third gear as the vehicle continues to accelerate, the transmission releases the 2–4 band and applies the 3–4 clutch. Also, the forward clutch remains applied so the input shaft drives the input sun gear clockwise through the forward sprag clutch. See Figure 49–51.

Applying the 3–4 clutch connects the input shaft to the input internal gear, which drives the internal gear clockwise at turbine speed. Now that two members of the input gear set—sun and internal—are being driven at turbine speed, the gear set provides direct drive as it locks up and turns as a unit.

As long as the vehicle is accelerating in overdrive third, torque transfers through the planetary gear set to the output shaft. There is no engine braking because the forward one-way clutch overruns and allows the input sun gear to freewheel.

Overdrive Fourth

The transmission upshifts into fourth gear by applying the 2–4 band as the vehicle continues to accelerate in overdrive range. The 2–4 band holds the reverse drum and reaction sun gear stationary. Both the 3–4 and forward clutches remain applied, and the input drum continues to drive the input internal gear clockwise. See Figure 49–52.

This drives the reaction carrier clockwise, as well, since it is in common with the input internal gear. As the carrier turns, the reaction pinions walk clockwise around the stationary reaction sun gear. This drives the reaction internal gear and output shaft clockwise at an overdrive ratio.

In fourth gear, the input internal gear turns at input shaft speed, while the input carrier turns at a faster output shaft speed; both gears turn clockwise. As a result, the input pinions turn counterclockwise and drive the sun gear clockwise faster than input speed. This causes the forward sprag clutch to overrun and renders the forward friction clutch, which remains applied, ineffective.

When the transmission is operating in fourth gear, the input member, the reaction carrier, is being driven by a multiple-disc clutch, while a band prevents the held member, the reaction sun gear, from turning in either direction. Therefore, engine compression braking is available. However, due to the overdrive gear ratio, the braking effect is not noticeable to the driver.

Reverse

With the gear selector lever in reverse, the low-reverse clutch applies to drive the reaction sun gear clockwise with the input shaft. The reaction carrier and input internal gear are held stationary by the applied reverse input clutch. This turns the reaction pinions counterclockwise and drives the carrier counterclockwise in gear reduction. See Figure 49–53.

In reverse gear, the input internal gear is held, while the input carrier is driven counterclockwise. This causes the input pinions to rotate clockwise and drive the input sun gear counterclockwise. However, the forward sprag clutch overruns, so the input gear set freewheels.

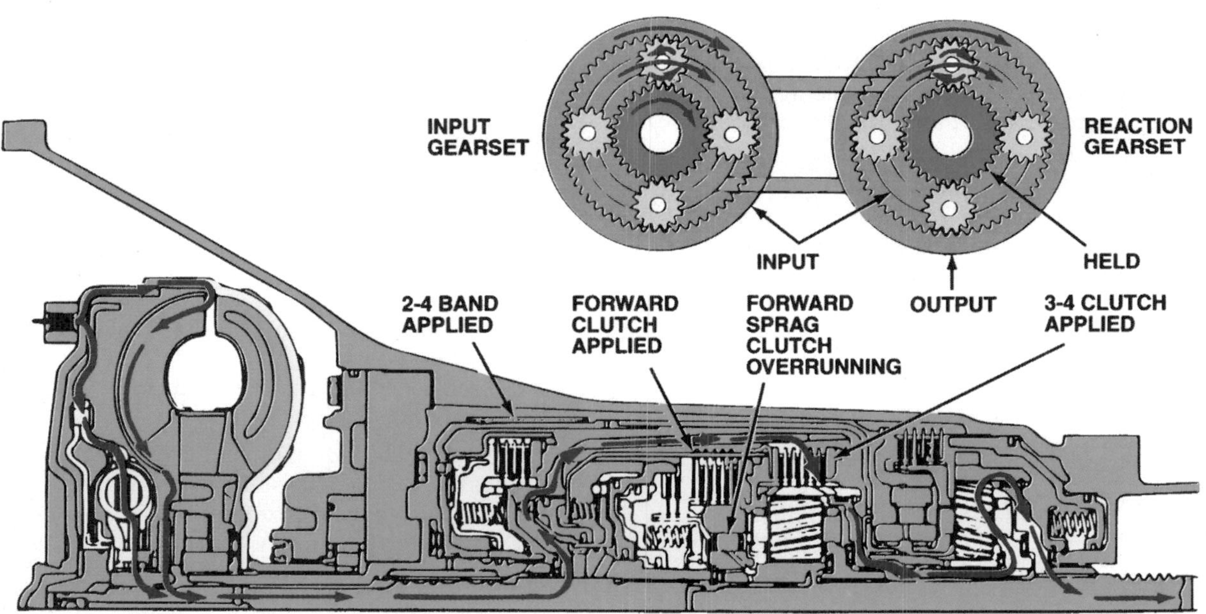

Figure 49–52 A 4L60-E torque flow in overdrive fourth gear.

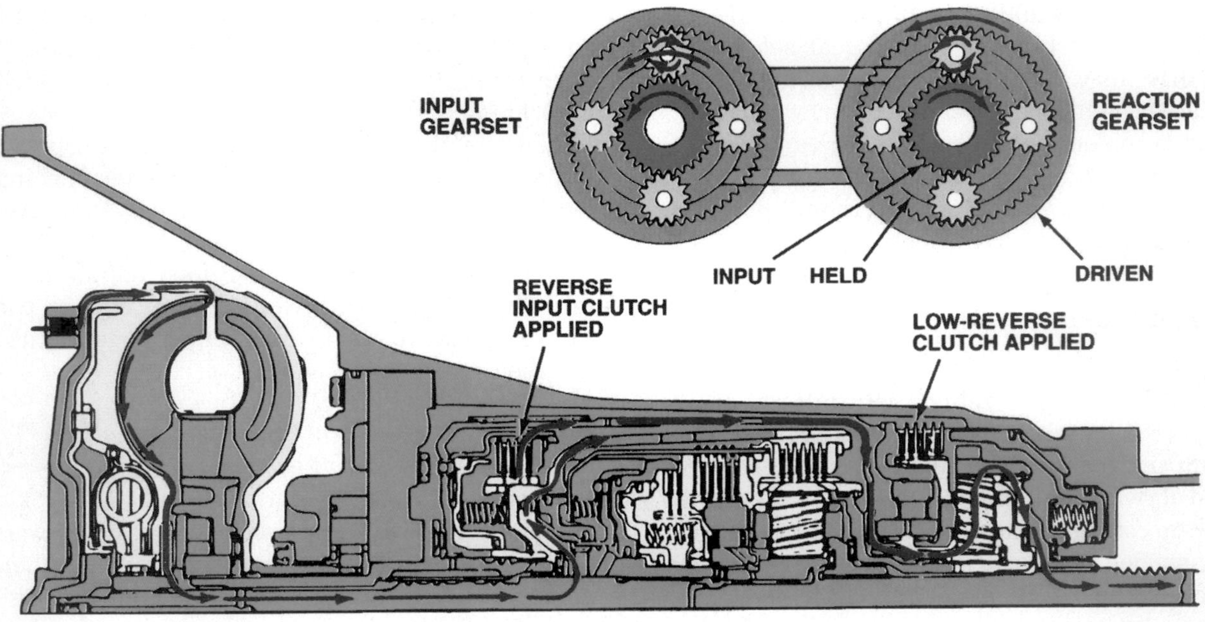

Figure 49–53 A 4L-60E torque flow in reverse.

SUMMARY

1. The torque converter attaches to the engine and transmits engine torque to the automatic transmission/transaxle assembly.
2. The torque converter consists of three major components: the impeller (driving member), turbine (driven member), and the stator, which helps the torque converter double the available engine torque at stall speed.
3. Since the early 1980s, a torque converter clutch has usually been used on most automatic transmissions/transaxles to increase fuel economy by locking the input and output members of the torque converter together.
4. A typical planetary gear set includes a sun gear in the centre surrounded by planet pinions attached to a planet carrier assembly and a ring gear on the outside where internal teeth mesh with the teeth of the planet pinions.
5. Most automatic transmissions/transaxles use a compound planetary gear set to achieve the various forward gears as well as reverse.
6. Automatic transmissions/transaxles use compound planetary gear sets called Simpson or Ravigneaux.
7. Certain members of a gear set must be held to achieve a particular gear ratio and direction. Two types of holding devices include multiple-disc clutches and bands.
8. One-way clutches are used in most automatic transmissions/transaxles as holding devices. Two types of one-way clutches include the sprag and the roller.
9. Most newer automatic transmissions/transaxles use a variable displacement pump to create the necessary mainline pressure to actuate the clutches and bands necessary to complete a shift.
10. The governor is used on hydraulically shifted automatic transmissions/transaxles to control when a shift is made in relation to vehicle speed.
11. A vacuum modulator or a throttle valve (TV) is used to control shift points based on engine load (vacuum) or throttle opening.
12. The valve body is the brains of any automatic transmission/transaxle. The passages connect all of the sensors to the apply servos and clutch packs to actually make the shift.
13. A transaxle uses a chain or gears to transfer engine torque from inline with the engine to parallel to the engine. Transaxles include the final drive (differential) assembly.
14. Electronically shifted automatic transmissions/transaxles usually use two shift solenoids and a pressure control solenoid plus a torque converter clutch solenoid, which are all computer controlled.

REVIEW QUESTIONS

1. Describe how a torque converter can double engine torque.
2. List the three members of a planetary gear set.
3. Explain how various gear ratios and reverse can be obtained by using a compound planetary gear set.
4. List the parts of a typical clutch pack assembly.
5. Explain the purpose of the priming spring used in a variable displacement vane pump.
6. List the solenoids used in a typical electronically shifted automatic transmission/transaxle.

RED SEAL CERTIFICATION-TYPE QUESTIONS

1. A very common cause of "stop sign creeping" in a car equipped with an automatic transmission is
   - **a.** The ATF level is too high
   - **b.** A defective governor
   - **c.** An incorrect idle speed
   - **d.** Multiple clutch disc wear
2. When a lock-up torque converter is locked, the
   - **a.** Impeller is locked to the drive shell
   - **b.** Stator is locked to the turbine
   - **c.** Turbine is locked to the drive shell
   - **d.** Stator is locked to the reaction shaft
3. In most automatic transmissions the oil is picked up by the front pump and directed to the
   - **a.** Pressure regulator valve
   - **b.** The torque converter
   - **c.** Manual valve
   - **d.** Shift valve
4. If the rear planetary gear is input and the sun gear is held by a Simpson planetary gear set, the gear selected is
   - **a.** First
   - **b.** Reverse
   - **c.** Second
   - **d.** Overdrive
5. The automatic selection of the most efficient gear ratio for each car speed is controlled by
   - **a.** The driver
   - **b.** The planetary units
   - **c.** The front oil pump
   - **d.** The centrifugal governor or electronic control system
6. When road testing an automatic transmission it was found that the unit shifted too soon. The possible problem could be
   - **a.** Governor and throttle valve pressure is too high
   - **b.** The vacuum modulator hose is cracked or missing
   - **c.** The throttle valve pressure is too high
   - **d.** Governor pressure is too high or throttle pressure is too low
7. Overrunning clutches are used in automatic transmission/transaxles to
   - **a.** Provide engine braking when the band is not applied
   - **b.** Override hydraulic clutch operation
   - **c.** Restrict rotation to one direction only
   - **d.** Prevent band rotation
8. A variable displacement pump is used in some transmissions and transaxles to
   - **a.** Increase hydraulic fluid requirements
   - **b.** Reduce power requirements and fuel consumption
   - **c.** Reduce shift harshness
   - **d.** Increase space requirements
9. Vehicles equipped with automatic transmissions/transaxles that tow trailers should also be equipped with
   - **a.** A higher capacity torque converter
   - **b.** A higher capacity hydraulic pump
   - **c.** A larger capacity hydraulic pump
   - **d.** An auxiliary oil cooler
10. When going up a steep hill, line pressure is increased by
    - **a.** Road speed
    - **b.** 1–2 boost pressure
    - **c.** The throttle opening
    - **d.** Governor pressure

50

Automatic Transmission/Transaxle Diagnosis and Service

OBJECTIVES: After studying Chapter 50, you should be able to:

1. Prepare for the interprovincial Red Seal certification examination in Appendix II (Automatic Transmission/Transaxle) on the topics covered in this chapter.
2. Describe what to look for during a test drive.
3. List the steps necessary to follow when removing an automatic transmission/transaxle assembly.
4. Explain how to perform a system pressure test.
5. Describe how to properly remove and install an aluminum pump in an automatic transmission/transaxle.
6. Describe how to test a vacuum modulator.
7. Explain how to flush an automatic transmission fluid cooler.

PRELIMINARY AUTOMATIC TRANSMISSION/TRANSAXLE PROBLEM DIAGNOSIS

The first step in diagnosing any problem is to test drive the vehicle and verify the customer complaint (concern). (See the Tech Tip, "Quick-and-Easy Automatic Transmission/Transaxle Diagnosis.") Before test driving the vehicle, check the level and condition of the automatic transmission/transaxle fluid. Follow the procedure for checking the level as published in the owner's manual or factory information. See Figures 50–1 and 50–2. If the fluid level is low, add fluid until the proper level is achieved before test driving the vehicle. See Chapter 3 for details on automatic transmission fluids.

Figure 50–1 Typical automatic transmission fluid level indicator (dipstick). The clip on this indicator keeps the dipstick from being forced upward due to pressure changes inside the transmission. The seal also helps prevent water from getting into the fluid, which can cause severe damage to the friction discs and other components inside the transmission.

TECH TIP 

Use Manual First Gear as a Diagnostic Aid

If the transmission/transaxle slips during acceleration when the shift lever is placed in the *drive* position, try placing the gear selector in the manual first position. If the internal holding clutch is slipping, the additional pressure applied to the clutch when the manual first gear is selected may be enough to allow the vehicle to move. If the vehicle moves when manual first gear is selected and will not move when *drive* is selected, then the clutches are worn and must be replaced.

This information is helpful during diagnosis, when learning as much information as possible about the transmission/transaxle before disassembly is important so that the known problem areas can be carefully checked.

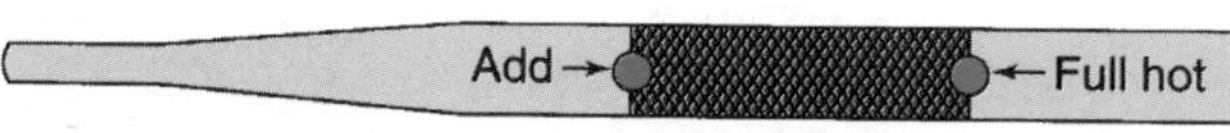

Figure 50–2 A typical automatic transmission/transaxle fluid level indicator (dipstick). The add mark usually indicates that the fluid level is down 0.5 L. Always measure the fluid level according to the instructions usually imprinted on the dipstick itself.

Road Testing

After checking the fluid, perform a thorough test drive and note the following:

- *Note how the shifts feel.* The shifts may be too harsh or too soft. This could indicate a fluid pressure problem or worn clutch or bands.
- *Note when the shifts occur.* The shifts may occur too early or too late. Either of these concerns could be caused by a defective governor or vehicle speed sensor, vacuum modulator (if so equipped), or TV cable adjustment (if so equipped). For example, a defective vacuum modulator will likely cause a delayed upshift and often a harsh downshift.

Stall Testing the Torque Converter

A stall test is often performed to verify the proper operation of the torque converter.

CAUTION: Some vehicle manufacturers do not recommend performing a stall test. Always follow the manufacturer's recommended service procedures.

TECH TIP 

Quick-and-Easy Automatic Transmission/Transaxle Diagnosis

An experienced technician told the beginning technician that automatic transmission/transaxle diagnosis is often very easy. For example:

- *If the vehicle does not move in drive or reverse*—remove the transmission/transaxle for service because the problem is likely mechanical rather than hydraulic (valve body) or electrical (computer, solenoids, or sensors). If the unit will not power the vehicle, the unit will more than likely require removal for a thorough mechanical inspection and repair.
- *If the vehicle moves, but does not shift correctly*—the problem is likely electrical (computer, solenoid, or sensor) or hydraulic (valve body) rather than mechanical. This is usually true because if the vehicle is able to move forward and backward, the major mechanical components, though not in like-new condition, are at least able to function. Therefore, correcting the nonmechanical problem should be the technician's first consideration.

Performing a stall test includes the following steps:

Step 1. Drive the vehicle until normal operating temperature is achieved.

Step 2. Check the stall speed specifications for the vehicle being serviced and connect a tachometer to the engine.

Step 3. With your left foot firmly applied to the brake pedal, move the shift selector in the drive position and depress the accelerator pedal to the floor. Observe the maximum engine speed. This engine speed is the stall speed. See Figure 50–3.

Step 4. Release the accelerator as soon as possible to avoid the possibility of overheating the automatic transmission fluid. Repeat the test with the gear selector in reverse.

Step 5. Compare the results with the specifications.

- *If the engine speed is higher than specifications,* a holding clutch or band is slipping.
- *If the engine speed is lower than specifications,* the torque converter is defective (one-way clutch or stator is slipping) or the engine is not producing normal output.

Both conditions can result in reduced vehicle performance and slow acceleration.

DIAGNOSTIC STORY

The Stalling Lumina

The owner of a Chevrolet Lumina complained that the vehicle would occasionally stall when slowing to a stop. The problem only occurred after at least 30 km and occurred more frequently in warm weather. The owner also indicated even though this vehicle was equipped with an automatic transmission it felt like the clutch not being depressed on a manual transmission. Thankfully, the service technician was aware of this common problem and installed a new torque converter clutch solenoid. See Figure 50–4. When the original solenoid got hot, it became stuck in the applied position. Even though the voltage was removed from the solenoid when the brakes were applied, the solenoid and the torque converter clutch (TCC) remained applied.

Figure 50–3 This four-cylinder General Motors vehicle has a stall speed of about 2350 rpm. Notice that the gear selector is in drive and the speedometer is reading zero.

Figure 50–4 Typical torque converter clutch (TCC) solenoid. This TCC solenoid on a General Motors vehicle can be replaced without having to remove the transmission/transaxle from the vehicle.

DIAGNOSTIC STORY

The Rough Idle Story

The owner of a Chevrolet pickup truck equipped with a V-6 engine complained of a rough idle. The idle was smooth when the transmission was in park or neutral but became rough when the gear selector was placed in any drive gear position. The service technician could not find the cause of the problem but did notice that the engine seemed to be under a heavy load at idle speed due to the MAP sensor reading. The customer was questioned again about the possibility of a previous repair that may have had an effect on the idle. The customer said that the automatic transmission had been replaced recently but didn't think that could have an effect on the rough idle problem. A quick check of the stall speed indicated a much lower stall speed than normal—1400 rpm versus 1850 rpm normal stall speed. Obviously, either the torque converter was defective or a torque converter for a V-8 was installed in the V-6 truck. After returning to the transmission shop and getting a replacement torque converter installed, the rough idle problem was solved.

TECH TIP

Vibration—Engine or Transmission?

A vibration is often difficult to diagnose. One method is to separate (unbolt) the torque converter from the engine drive plate. Push the torque converter as far toward the transmission/transaxle as possible, then start the engine. If the vibration is gone, the problem is due to a fault in the torque converter, pump assembly, or other component that is constantly rotating with the engine running. If the vibration is still present, then the cause is due to an engine or accessory problem.

NOTE: There are many other possible causes of poor performance or slow acceleration besides a fault with the automatic transmission/transaxle. The stall test is just one test that can be performed to help narrow the problem to the root cause.

Torque Converter Clutch Diagnosis

The torque converter clutch is usually applied above 50 km/h (30 mph) when the automatic transmission/

transaxle is in second, third, or overdrive gear, depending on the vehicle speed and the throttle position. It is often difficult to distinguish between a normal shift and the application of the torque converter clutch. The torque converter clutch (TCC) may not even be applying due to a fault in the computer sensors, wiring, or the TCC solenoid.

NOTE: If the torque converter clutch does not apply, a drop in fuel economy of 0.8 L/100 km (4 mpg) is commonly reported. If the TCC fails to apply on an automatic transmission/transaxle, the automatic transmission fluid is likely to become overheated due to the torque converter operating under the increased load of an overdrive gear ratio. The higher fluid temperature can cause the automatic transmission/transaxle to fail.

To test for proper operation of the torque converter clutch, simply drive the vehicle and watch either the tachometer on the dash or connect a scan tool to observe the engine RPM.

Step 1. Drive the vehicle until the engine has reached normal operating temperature.

Step 2. Drive the vehicle on a flat, level road away from any traffic about 80 km/h (50 mph).

Step 3. While maintaining constant speed with your right foot on the accelerator, gently apply the brake pedal with your left foot to open the electrical circuit for the torque converter clutch through the brake switch. The TCC will disengage and the RPM should increase about 150 to 250 rpm and then drop back when the brake pedal is released. This RPM change is your proof that the TCC is, in fact, working.

If the torque converter clutch is not operating, consult the factory information for the steps necessary to find and correct the problem.

Scan Tool Testing the Automatic Transmission/Transaxle

A scan tool can display information about the various sensors and components that can assist the service technician in determining the cause of many automatic transmission/transaxle problems. See Figure 50–5. A weak or missing engine can cause the vehicle to lack power, jerk, and hesitate. These symptoms are often blamed on an incorrectly shifting or slipping automatic transmission/transaxle.

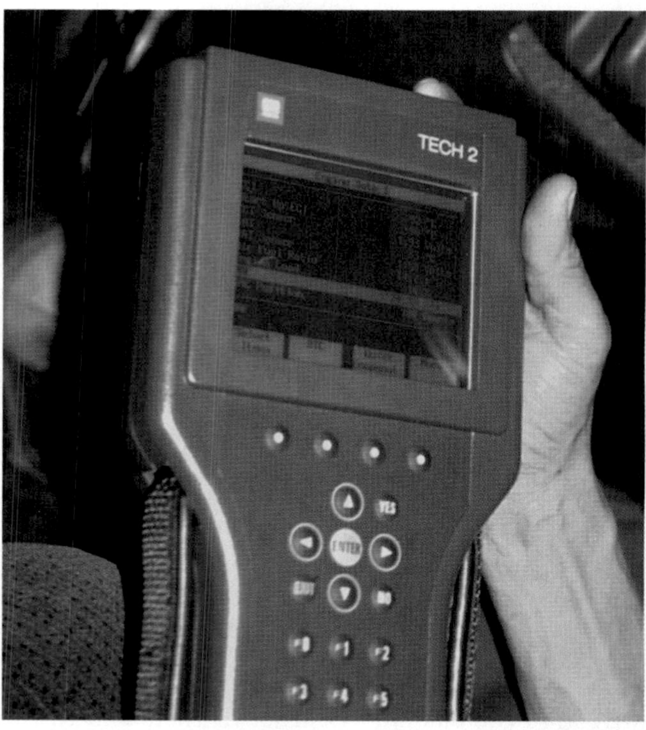

Figure 50–5 A Tech 2 scan tool being used to check for diagnostic trouble codes (DTCs) and data stream information that may affect the operation of the automatic transmission/transaxle.

Diagnostic Trouble Codes (DTCs) Obviously, if there are any DTCs stored in the memory of the vehicle computer, a problem has been detected that should be corrected before further testing.

Scan Data A properly operating engine should display the following readings with the engine at idle and operating in closed loop:

- **Engine coolant temperature (ECT)—** between 80° to 100°C (175° to 212°F).
- **Throttle position (TP) sensor—**usually between 0.5 to 4.5 V and varying directly with throttle movement.
- **Fuel injector pulse width—**1.5 to 3.5 ms.
- **O2S—**200 to 800 mV.
- **Transmission fluid temperature—**less than 135°C (275°F).
- **Brake switch—**scan data should show a change when the break pedal is pressed and released.
- **Manifold absolute pressure (MAP) sensor—** with the engine idling in park or neutral, the voltage should be within 0.88 and 1.62 V or between 102 and 109 Hz for a Ford MAP sensor.

If any of the engine information is not within these ranges, consult the factory information for procedures to follow to determine the cause before proceeding with the analysis of the automatic transmission/transaxle.

NOTE: If the temperature of the automatic transmission fluid (ATF) is too high, the computer will modify the shift pattern (usually disabling overdrive) and engage the TCC at slower speeds in an attempt to drop the temperature of the ATF to less harmful temperatures. This computer control of the shifting may be noticeable to the driver as a fault.

Shift Solenoids Observe the operation of the command for the shift solenoids and the TCC solenoid while driving the vehicle. This information confirms that the computer is commanding the operation; it does not mean that the solenoids are working correctly. Therefore, if the scan data indicates that a particular solenoid is being commanded on and nothing occurs, then the problem more likely is a defective solenoid or a fault in the wiring to the solenoid or from the solenoid to the computer.

NOTE: Shift solenoids vary in resistance, yet may look the same. An on/off solenoid usually has twice as much electrical resistance as a pulse width modulated shift solenoid. Always double check that the correct replacement solenoids are used.

Commanding the Shifts Many test tools can be used to actually cause the automatic transmission/transaxle to shift electrically. The tester is connected to the electrical connector at the automatic transmission/transaxle after disconnecting the factory connector. To perform this simple test, safely hoist the vehicle, start the engine, and place the gear selector in the drive position. The tester can now command the various shift solenoids to actuate. If the shift occurs when commanded, the hydraulic system is functioning. If the tester commands a shift to occur and a shift does not occur, the service technician knows that the problem is either in the solenoid itself or the hydraulic system that actuates the clutch or band to accomplish the shift.

Testing the Vacuum Modulator

A vacuum modulator is used on many hydraulically shifted automatic transmissions/transaxles. To check for proper operation of the vacuum modulator, follow these steps:

Step 1. Hoist the vehicle safely and locate the vacuum modulator (if equipped).

NOTE: The vacuum modulator used on the General Motors 4T60 (formerly called 440-T4) is located toward the front of the vehicle and is accessible from under the hood without the need to hoist the vehicle. See Figure 50–6. This vacuum modulator is not used to control shift points, but is rather used to control shift feel. Higher engine loads (lower vacuum to the vacuum modulator) result in a firmer shift; at light engine loads, the shift is softened.

Step 2. Remove the vacuum hose from the vacuum modulator. If automatic transmission fluid drips out when the hose is removed, the vacuum modulator is defective and must be replaced.

Step 3. Use a hand-operated vacuum pump to apply vacuum to the vacuum modulator. If the modulator is okay, the vacuum reading will hold steady and not drop. If the vacuum modulator will not hold vacuum, the modulator should be replaced.

Step 4. Connect a vacuum hose to the vacuum line from the intake manifold and have an assistant start the engine. The vacuum reading at the vacuum modulator should be 430 to 530 mm (17 to 21 in.) Hg with a minimum vacuum reading of

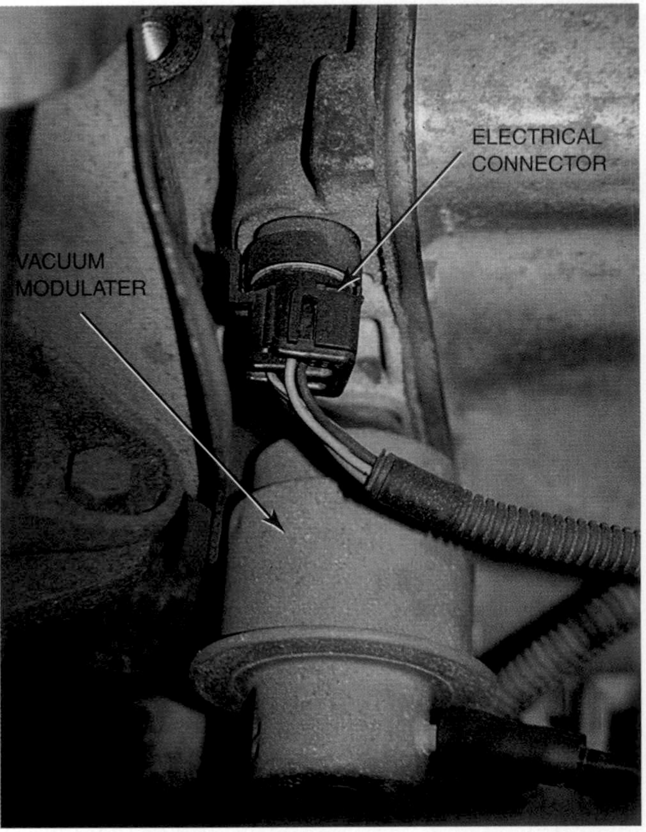

Figure 50–6 A view of a General Motors 4T60 (440-T4) automatic transaxle showing the electrical connector and the vacuum modulator.

TECH TIP 

White Exhaust Smoke Is Not Necessarily Due to a Blown Head Gasket

A defective vacuum modulator can cause automatic transmission fluid (ATF) to be drawn by engine vacuum into the intake manifold. When ATF burns, it produces white smoke. The white smoke is often confused with steam. Therefore, the smart technician should check to see if the vehicle is equipped with a properly functioning vacuum modulator before continuing the diagnosis for steam coming from the tail pipe.

380 mm (15 in.) Hg to be assured of proper shifting of the automatic transmission/transaxle.

Range Charts

All vehicle manufacturers publish range charts that indicate which holding device is applied or holding for each gear selection. Knowing which component is being used when helps the service technician determine the cause of a failure or problem. See Figure 50–7 for a sample chart for a hydraulically shifted automatic transmission.

Pressure Testing

Pressure testing involves connecting a pressure gauge to pressure taps located on the outside of the automatic transmission/transaxle, as shown in Figure 50–8. After connecting the pressure gauge(s) to the transmission/transaxle, start the engine and select the gear being monitored. If the pressure is not within specifications, then the technician knows that the fault is internal and usually involves either removing the valve body, or in many cases, removing the automatic transmission/transaxle from the vehicle. See Figures 50–9 and 50–10.

Removing the Automatic Transmission Pan for Inspection

The inspection of the fluid and the transmission pan should be part of any thorough transmission/transaxle diagnosis. Removing the pan from an automatic transmission/transaxle can be a dirty and messy job. To make the job as easy as possible, follow these steps:

Step 1. Hoist the vehicle safely.

Step 2. Use a large drain pan and position it under the transmission pan.

Step 3. Loosen all of the oil pan bolts. ATF will start to flow out from around the gasket.

Range	Gear	2-4 Band	Reverse input clutch	Overrun clutch	Forward clutch	Forward sprag cl. assembly	3-4 clutch	Lo-roller clutch	Lo-rev. clutch
Park-neutral									
Overdrive	First gear				Applied	Holding		Holding	
	Second gear	Applied			Applied	Holding			
	Third gear				Applied	Holding	Applied		
	Fourth gear	Applied			Applied		Applied		
Drive	First gear			Applied	Applied	Holding		Holding	
	Second gear	Applied		Applied	Applied	Holding			
	Third gear			Applied	Applied	Holding	Applied		
Manual 2nd	First gear			Applied	Applied	Holding		Holding	
	Second gear	Applied		Applied	Applied	Holding			
Manual 1st	First gear			Applied		Holding		Holding	Applied
Reverse	Reverse		Applied						Applied

Figure 50–7 A range chart for a General Motors 4L60 (formerly called the 700-R4) rear-wheel-drive transmission. Notice that the forward clutch is applied in all forward gears. Also notice that if the low-reverse clutch were to fail, it would prevent the vehicle from moving in both reverse and manual first.

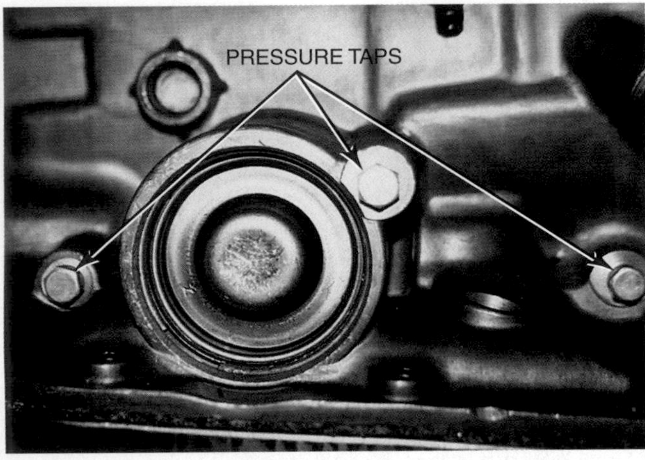

Figure 50–8 The location (tap) for connecting a pressure gauge to measure the pressure of the various hydraulic circuits are usually on the sides of the automatic transmission/transaxle. Some may not be very accessible. Check factory service information for the exact locations for the vehicle being serviced.

Figure 50–10 Six pressure gauges are installed on this vehicle to show students at a college how the pressures vary and how the gauges can be used to find faults or possible problem areas before the unit is removed and disassembled.

Figure 50–9 A pressure gauge connected to check mainline pressure.

Figure 50–11 This is a normal amount of wear material in the bottom of an automatic transmission oil pan.

SAFETY TIP 

Hot Fluid

The automatic transmission fluid may be hot enough to cause personal injury. Wear protective clothing and avoid contact with the hot fluid.

Step 4. Remove all of the oil pan bolts except for two at one end. This will allow the pan to drop and empty most of the ATF into the drain container without falling. After most of the ATF has drained, remove the remaining bolts and remove the pan.

Step 5. Inspect the inside of the pan for excessive friction material and wear metals (such as lead and copper from bushings). Use a magnet to check for steel particles, which would indicate serious wear to major components. See Figure 50–11.

DIAGNOSTIC STORY

The Customized Van Story

The owner of a customized General Motors van equipped with an electrically shifted automatic transmission (4L80-E) complained that the automatic transmission downshifted into second gear and stayed in second gear whenever the headlights were turned on. The transmission shifted okay when the headlights were turned off. After hours of troubleshooting, including the replacement of the vehicle computer (which did not help), it was discovered that 4 volts DC were on the one wire leading from the vehicle speed (VS) sensor to the vehicle computer whenever the headlights were turned on. Obviously, there was a short to voltage between a light wire and the sensor wire. Instead of totally disassembling the van, it was decided to replace the wire with a new one, and the problem was solved. The 4 volts DC apparently shut down the computer. When the computer stopped controlling the shifts, both A and B solenoids were shut off. With both solenoids A and B off, the transmission was in second gear. This is the default gear or the limp-in-mode gear for this transmission. After replacing the wire, the automatic transmission returned to manual operation, allowing the driver to drive at night and in the daytime.

NOTE: The presence of wear metals in the pan of an automatic transmission/transaxle does not necessarily mean that a part has failed or needs to be replaced. Some wear is normal. If there are a lot of metallic particles in the pan, then this may be an indication of severe gear failure that may require replacement. Use a magnet to check for steel particles. Ask the advice of an experienced transmission expert, if in doubt, about whether the wear should be considered normal.

Band Adjustment

Some automatic transmissions/transaxles allow the technician to adjust the clearance between the band and the drum inside the unit. The procedure usually involves tightening the adjustment nut or bolt to a specified torque reading and then backing off the adjustment nut or bolt a specified number of times. See Figure 50–12. Some bands are adjusted using selective length push rods and some bands are not adjustable at all. The band(s) should be adjusted whenever the fluid is changed or whenever recommended by the vehicle manufacturer.

Frequently Asked Question ???

What Is Wrong When My Automatic Transmission Does Not Upshift at All?

There are several things that can cause the automatic transmission/transaxle to fail to upshift, including:

- **A defective governor** (if so equipped) will often not allow any automatic transmission/transaxle to shift out of first gear.
- **A defective vacuum modulator** (if so equipped) will often delay the shift until a very high speed is achieved.
- **A fault in the computer or sensor.** On electronically shifted automatic transmissions/transaxles, one gear, usually second or third, is selected and the unit will not shift out of that gear.

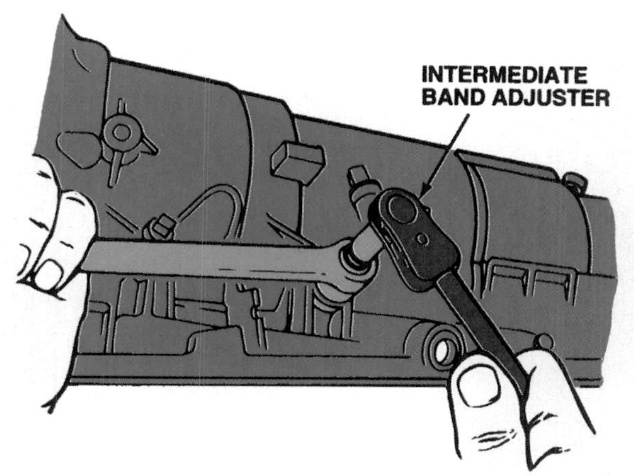

Figure 50–12 Adjusting the intermediate band on a Ford A4LD transmission.

Linkage Adjustment

The linkage between the shift selector and the automatic transmission should be checked for proper adjustment whenever there is a transmission-related problem. The linkage may need to be adjusted to compensate for worn linkage components. Before adjusting the linkage, check the engine and transmission/transaxle mounts carefully because a defective mount is a common reason for needing a linkage adjustment.

REMOVING THE AUTOMATIC TRANSMISSION/TRANSAXLE FOR SERVICE

Removing an automatic transmission/transaxle from a vehicle includes many steps to avoid doing damage to the vehicle or harm to yourself. Always follow the vehicle manufacturer's recommended procedures. Most procedures include the following steps.

Step 1. Disconnect the negative (−) battery cable from the battery. This prevents the possibility of an accidental short circuit that could damage the vehicle or cause a spark that could start a fire.

Step 2. Disconnect the drive shaft or drive axle shafts.

Step 3. Disconnect all cooler lines, linkage, and electrical connections. Be sure to label each to ensure proper reinstallation.

Step 4. Disconnect the torque converter from the flex (drive) plate of the engine.

Step 5. Support the engine before disconnecting the automatic transmission/transaxle, as shown in Figure 50–13.

Step 6. Remove the transmission/transaxle mounting fasteners.

Step 7. Support the transmission/transaxle on a jack and remove the attaching bolts at the bell housing of the engine, as shown in Figure 50–14. Remove the transmission/transaxle from the vehicle.

TECH TIP 

The Chain Trick

If two slide hammers are not available to remove a cast iron pump from an automatic transmission, try using a length of chain. Attach each end of a chain to the pump and jerk the chain. The pump should come out.

CAUTION: Do not attempt this procedure with an aluminum pump or damage could result.

(a)

(b)

Figure 50–13 (a) A tall safety stand with a block of wood on top being used to support the engine to permit the removal of the automatic transmission without doing harm to the engine or its accessories. (b) A chain and holding fixture being used on this front-wheel-drive vehicle to support the engine when the transaxle is removed.

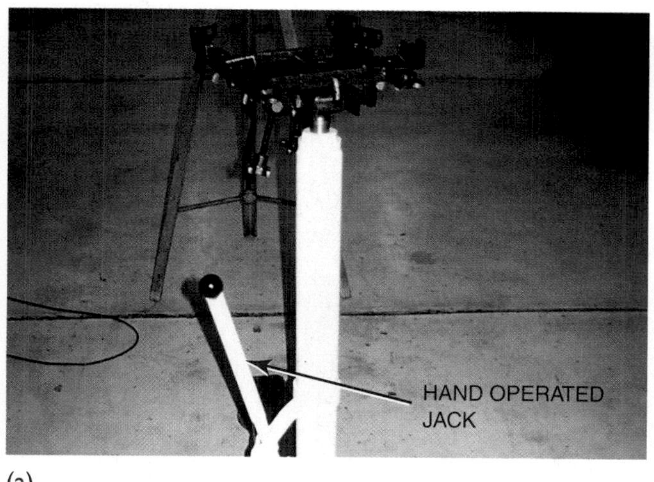

(a)

(b)

Figure 50–14 (a) A typical transmission jack. The top portion of the jack can be raised by pumping the lever on the side. (b) A transmission jack in position during the removal of the transaxle assembly.

AUTOMATIC TRANSMISSION/TRANSAXLE DISASSEMBLY

For best results, the automatic transmission/transaxle should be attached to a holding fixture that allows the unit to be rotated yet properly supported during disassembly and reassembly.

Torque Converter Check

Check the torque converter for internal end play of the stator. See Figure 50–15.

> **NOTE:** Many automotive transmission/transaxle experts recommend that the torque converter be replaced when the automatic transmission is rebuilt or replaced. This is because the torque converter is generally considered to be the "garbage pit" of the entire unit in that it often collects wear particles from the clutch and bands that can cause future problems. According to remanufacturers of torque converters, the majority of the torque converters being turned in as cores have little, if any, friction material remaining for the torque converter clutch. See Figure 50–16.

Figure 50–15 Special tool being used to help measure the end play of the stator inside the torque converter.

Pump Assembly

Remove the pump assembly using the proper removal tool to avoid damaging it. See Figures 50–17 and 50–18. Check the pump for wear as shown in Figure 50–19.

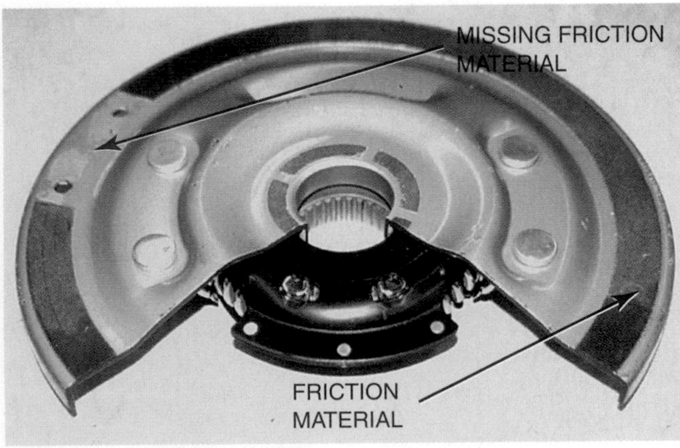

Figure 50–16 A cutaway of a torque converter clutch showing the thin paper friction material.

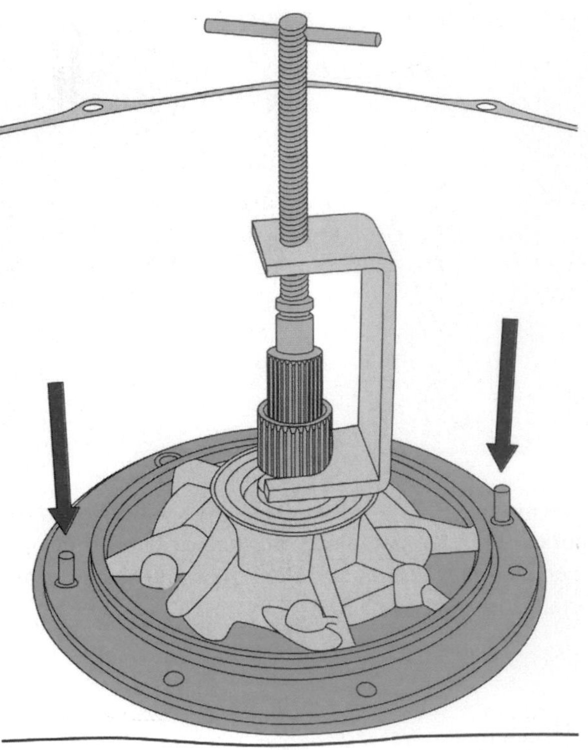

Figure 50–18 A special puller is usually specified to remove aluminum pumps from automatic transmissions/transaxles. Alignment pins (arrows) are used to properly align the gasket and pump on the case during reassembly.

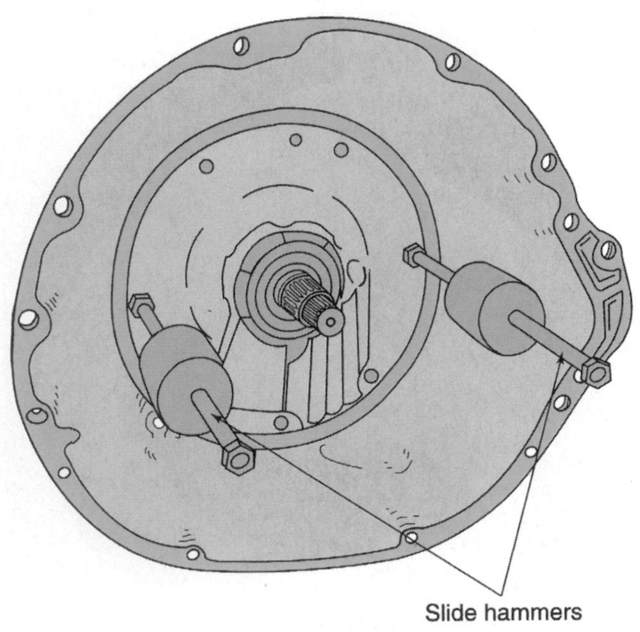

Figure 50–17 Two slide hammers are usually used to remove a cast-iron pump assembly from older automatic transmissions.

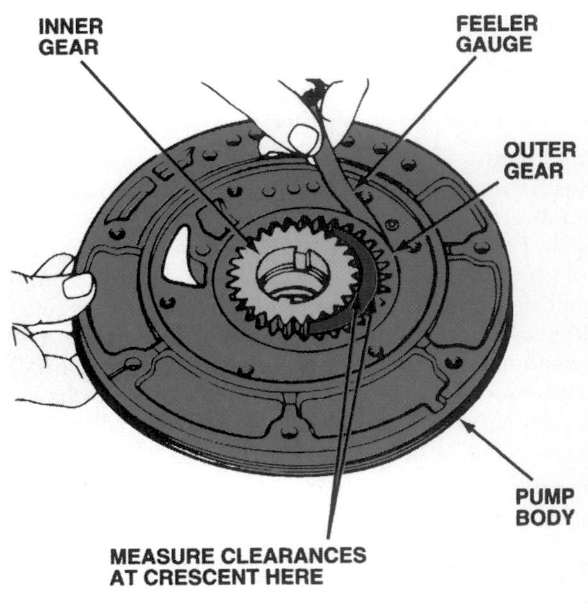

Figure 50–19 Checking a transmission pump assembly for wear using a feeler gauge. Compare the readings to factory specifications.

Valve Body

Remove the valve body and check all valves for proper operation. See Figure 50–20. To service a valve body, disassemble all the parts and identify them for reassembly. See Figure 50–21. Save the old gaskets to match with the new ones. Clean all parts in a solvent that removes all gum, varnish, dirt, and grease. Rinse clean parts in hot, running water, then immerse them in clean mineral spirits or a similar solvent to separate water from the parts. Finish cleaning by blow drying with low-pressure, filtered, compressed air. Once clean, inspect the valve body and its components and look for:

- Scored, cracked, or burred plugs and valves
- Broken, bent, or worn springs
- Scored or rusted bores
- Plugged or restricted fluid passages
- Bent or rusted separator plates
- Stuck check valves
- Bent manual valves
- Cracked castings and distorted or nicked mating surfaces.

Shiny areas on valve lands indicate friction between the spool valve and body. On steel valves, these areas can be polished carefully with 400- to 600-grit wet or dry sandpaper, crocus cloth, or polishing stone. Take care not to round off the edges of the valve lands while polishing. Aluminum valves cannot be polished. If a valve needs polishing, the bore it rides in also requires servicing. Polish the valve bore by inserting and turning loosely rolled wet or dry sandpaper or crocus cloth. Avoid rounding the edge of the bore. Attach a piece of crocus cloth to a slotted dowel rod or bent welding rod to reach the bottom of a deep bore. Rewash and dry any valves and bores that are polished.

After polishing and washing, lubricate the spool valve with ATF and slide it into its bore to check fit and operation. The valve should slide back and forth freely of its own weight.

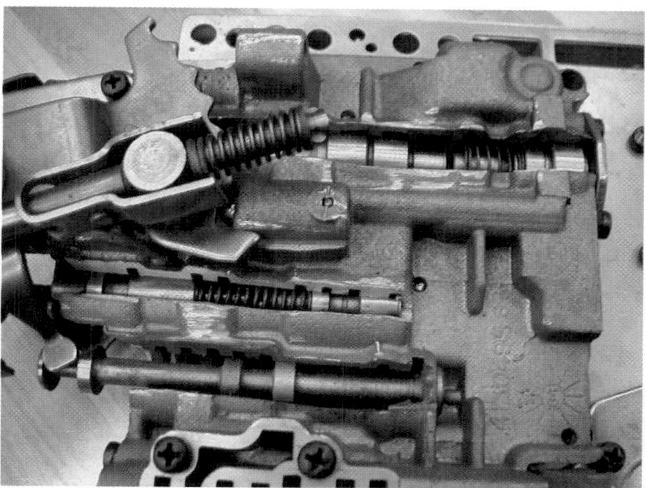

Figure 50–20 A cutaway of an auxiliary valve body showing the valves and springs that should be checked for smooth operation.

Clutch Packs

Begin disassembling a clutch pack by removing the snap ring that holds the discs in the housing. Remove the snap ring from most clutches by prying one end of it free from its groove with a small screwdriver. Then, slide the screwdriver around the drum and the snap ring removes easily.

Figure 50–21 Sometimes unique tools make the job go smoother. An engine valve spring compressor is being used to compress a servo piston so the snap ring can be removed.

Friction Disc Inspection

Wipe each friction disc with a dry, lint-free cloth. Inspect for:

- Excessive wear
- Cracks in the lining material
- Charred, burned, or glazed lining surface
- Pitting, flaking, or scoring
- Chips or particles embedded in the lining
- Scoring or burns on disc serrations
- Distortion

Friction discs tend to discolour in use, which is normal. However, if any friction disc shows signs of one or more of the defects above, replace the entire set. Replace the set of friction discs if they do not fit freely in the clutch hub serrations or if there is wear or damage to their splines.

Steel Disc Inspection

Also clean steel discs by wiping with a dry, lint-free cloth. Once clean, inspect each disc for:

- Uneven heat discolouration
- Surface scuffing or scoring
- Drive lug damage
- Distortion

TECH TIP 

Smooth Is In; Rough Is Out

It used to be common practice in the automatic transmission business for the rebuilder to use sandpaper to roughen up the surface of the steel discs to achieve a good clutch apply. This is not true now. Sanding creates grooves and sharp peaks that decrease the oil film between the paper on the friction plate and the steel plates. There should be a thin oil film between the paper and the steel to create a holding bond and make it possible for a clutch pack to apply and release thousands of times without wear. Therefore, for consistent shifts and long-lasting transmissions/transaxles, do not sand the steel discs. Used steel discs are often smoother than new steel discs due to normal wear. As long as the steel discs are not discoloured, heat checked, or warped, used steel discs should be reused.

NOTE: Be sure to soak all the friction discs in ATF before assembling the clutch pack.

Replace the entire set of steels if you note a rough surface or there is uneven or spotty discolouration on any of the discs. Also replace steel discs if they do not fit freely into the clutch drum serrations.

Clutch Piston Removal and Inspection

To remove the snap ring holding the clutch piston in place, compress the piston return springs, which is done with a compressor tool. See Figure 50–22.

Tightening a nut onto the shaft draws the fingers of the tool down, compressing the spring, and allowing the snap ring to be removed. After removing the snap ring, release and remove the spring compressor, then remove and inspect the return springs.

Return Spring Inspection

Coil springs should be straight and provide proper pressure. Check for broken, distorted, or collapsed

Figure 50–22 A compressor tool is usually necessary to compress the springs of the clutch piston to remove the snap ring.

springs. If one or more of the springs requires replacement, discard them all and install a complete set of new springs.

Some coil springs are permanently attached to their retaining collar and can only be serviced as a set. When individual coil springs are used, be sure to note their exact location. There will be vacant spring seats in some applications. This allows the manufacturer to use the same piston but vary the number and location of springs to precisely match spring return rate to the requirements of a particular vehicle. In these cases, reinstall return springs in *exactly the same vacancy* pattern.

Clutch Piston Inspection

Remove the clutch piston from the hub. The drag of the piston seal can make it hard to remove the piston from its bore. Should this be the case, apply low-pressure compressed air through the hydraulic apply hole in the housing to force the piston from its bore.

Do not use high air pressure and be careful to avoid pinching your hand or dropping the piston as it pops from its bore. Once you remove the piston, check for:

- Cracks or scoring in the piston bore
- Nicks, scores, burrs, or signs of wear on the piston
- Seal damage
- Fluid passage obstructions or restrictions

If the piston contains a check valve, make sure it is functional. Remove and discard seals.

Hubs, Drums, Shells, and Planetaries

Clutch hubs, drums, and shells transfer the torque load to the various combinations of planetary gear set members to provide different gear ratios. Hubs, drums, shells, and planetaries are *hard parts* that do not wear out under normal conditions, so they can be reused unless they are damaged. Wash with solvent, dry with compressed air and then inspect. Planetary gear sets should be checked for proper pinion gear end play and compared to factory specifications. See Figure 50–23.

SAFETY TIP

Always Use CCOHS Approved Air Nozzles

Compressed air can be very dangerous. The Canadian Centre for Occupational Health and Safety has specified an air nozzle that diverts some air outward that helps reduce the full force of the compressed air able to be applied to a clutch pack. Be sure to always use a CCOHS approved air nozzle.

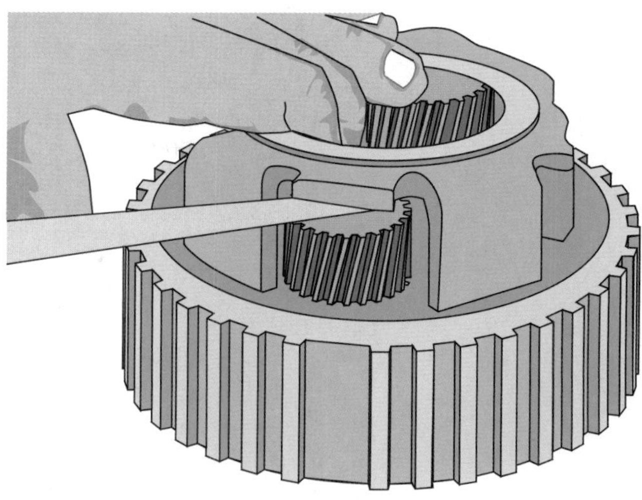

Figure 50–23 Pinion gear end play can be checked using a feeler gauge.

REASSEMBLING AN AUTOMATIC TRANSMISSION/TRANSAXLE

Air Pressure Checks

Reassembly of an automatic transmission/transaxle involves assembling the various subassemblies, such as a clutch pack, before final assembly is completed. See Figures 50–24 and 50–25 for how to check for proper clutch pack clearance. Air pressure checks are used to verify that components such as clutch packs perform correctly. Use a rubber-tipped air nozzle and regulate the air supply to about 240 kPa (35 psi). Use the factory service information regarding where to air check and what the results should be. A typical result is a dull thud or clunk heard when air pressure is applied to a clutch pack or servo piston. See Figure 50–26. When the air pressure is removed, the unit should release. If there is a seal leak, air can usually be heard hissing from around the seal.

All bushings should be inspected and replaced if necessary, as shown in Figure 50–27. Follow the vehicle manufacturer's recommended procedures. For example, a special clamp is often necessary to properly assemble a pump, as shown in Figure 50–28. Special tools are often specified by the vehicle manufacturer. These tools allow the service technician to

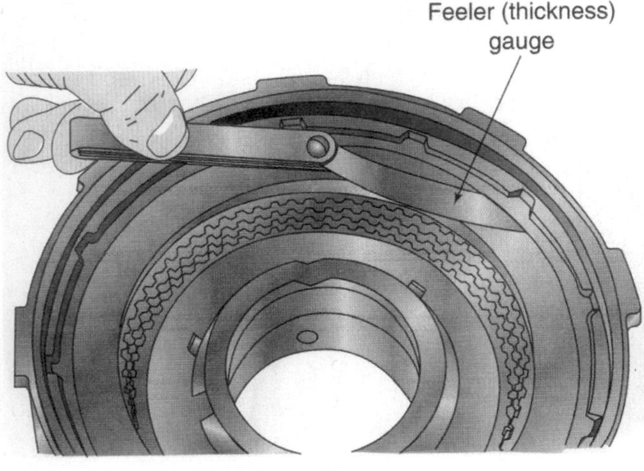

Figure 50–24 All clutch packs should be checked with a feeler (thickness) gauge to be certain that the clearance is within factory specifications.

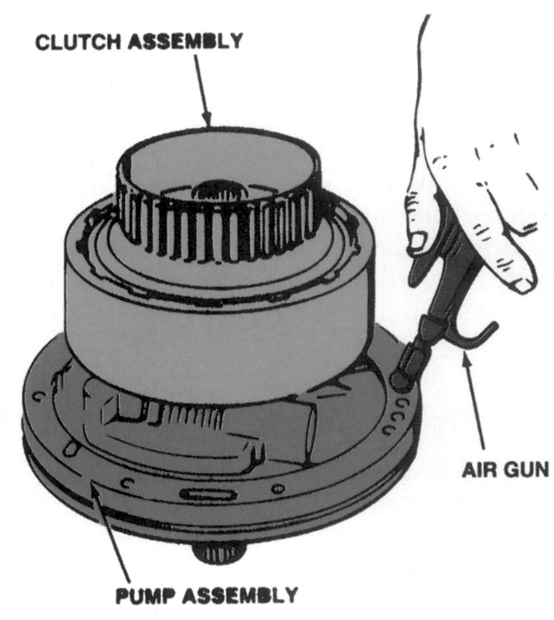

Figure 50–26 Air testing a clutch pack on the bench before it is installed into the transmission/transaxle.

Figure 50–25 Checking clutch pack clearance using a dial indicator. This method is used when a feeler gauge cannot be inserted to check for proper clearance.

Figure 50–27 A typical brass bushing used in an automatic transmission/transaxle assembly.

disassemble and reassemble the transmission/ transaxle more easily and without doing any harm. See Figure 50–29. Also perform all end play checks during assembly to ensure that the unit was properly assembled and that the proper internal clearances are achieved. See Figure 50–30.

CAUTION: When assembling the valve body, double check that all the valves move by gently prying each valve with a plastic tool. If any valve is stuck, carefully clean with a crocus cloth and avoid rounding the sharp edges of the valves. Also avoid using gasket sealer that could clog small passages.

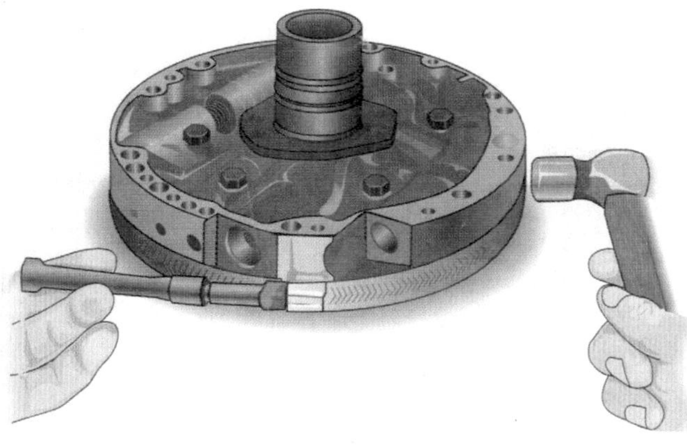

Figure 50–28 Using an alignment clamp to assemble both pump halves. To ensure proper alignment, many experts recommend lightly tapping around the outside edges of the pump while tightening the clamp.

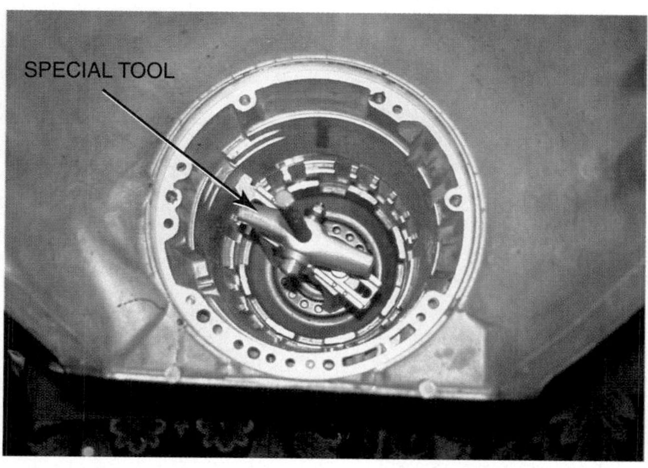

Figure 50–29 A special clamp makes removal and reinstallation of the clutch pack easier.

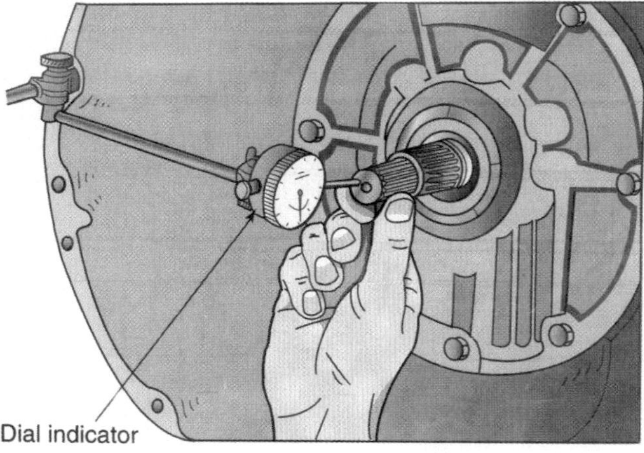

Figure 50–30 A dial indicator being used to measure the end play of the input shaft. If the end play is not within factory specifications, the unit may not have been assembled correctly.

Valve Body Checks

The valve body can be checked using a tester especially designed to check valve bodies. See Figure 50–31. Adapters are available for all commonly serviced automatic transmissions/transaxles, and the pressure gauges that are part of the tester are used to monitor the movement and flow through the valve body. This unit also heats the automatic transmission fluid so that the valve body is being tested under the same conditions as will be occurring in the vehicle. It is easier to repair a fault with the valve body than wait until the valve body and the transmission are installed in the vehicle.

Flushing the Cooler and Torque Converter

All vehicle manufacturers recommend that the automatic transmission fluid cooler be flushed or replaced when a replacement or overhauled automatic transmission/transaxle is installed in a vehicle. Debris from the old unit could quickly cause excessive wear in the replacement unit if not thoroughly flushed.

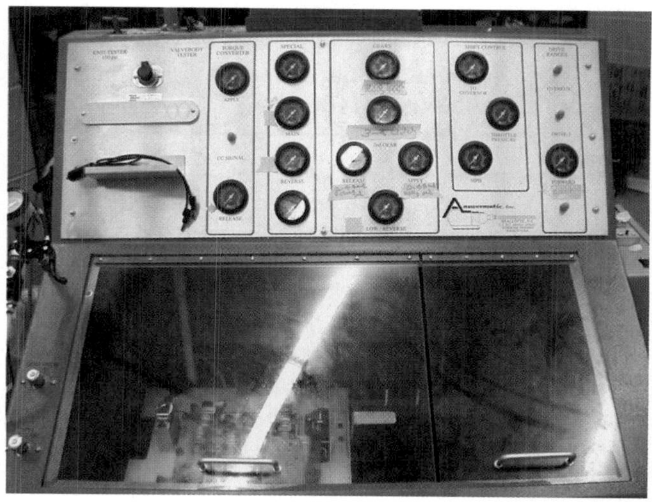

Figure 50–31 Valve body tester.

Change the Bolts and Washers

Whenever reassembling an automatic transmission, always replace the pump bolts and washers to avoid the possibility of a leak. A leak in the area of the pump can cause quite a headache for the technician because the entire assembly must be removed from the vehicle again to fix it.

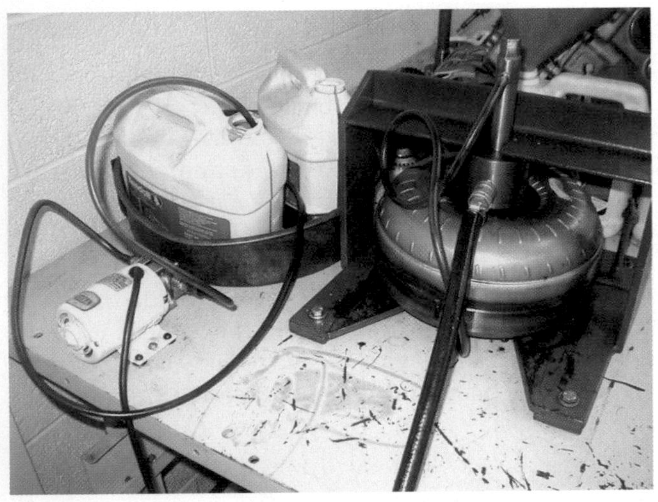

Figure 50–32 Setup used to flush a torque converter.

Most commercial flushing units use compressed air and a solvent or ATF to flush the cooler. See Figure 50–32 for an example of a setup used to flush a torque converter before being installed into the vehicle.

CAUTION: Most experts agree that water-based flushing solutions should be avoided. The water may contaminate the new fluid when the cooler lines are reattached and the ATF flows through the cooler.

NOTE: At least 2 L of ATF should flow through the cooler every 30 seconds; if not, the cooler and/or the lines are restricted.

To flush the cooler, determine which cooler line from the transmission/transaxle is flowing to the cooler. See the following chart for the placement of many of the cooler-out lines on the most commonly used transmissions/transaxles.

Cooler-Out Lines	
Transmission	**Cooler-Out Line on the Transmission/Transaxle**
General Motors	
125 (3T40)	Bottom
180	Bottom
200/200-4R	Top
325/325-4L	Bottom
350	Bottom
400 (4L80)	Bottom
440-T4 (4T60)	Bottom
700-R4 (4L60)	Bottom
Ford	
A4LD	Bottom
AOD	Top
ATX	Bell housing end
AXOD	Top
C3, C4, C5, C6	Front
Chrysler	
904, 727	Front
FWD	Bottom
Import Brand	
Honda	Over the bell housing
Jatco (RWD)	Front
Mitsubishi	Inner
Renault	Top
Nissan RL3F01A	Top
Nissan RL4F02A	Front
Subaru	Top of the differential
Toyota FWD	Top
Toyota RWD	Front

Dyno Testing the Automatic Transmission/Transaxle

A rebuilt automatic transmission/transaxle can be tested on a dynamometer powered by an electric motor as shown in Figure 50–33 or by a gasoline engine as shown in Figure 50–34. Most dynamometers are equipped with pressure gauges as well as providing a load, so the operation of the unit can be checked before being installed in the vehicle.

REINSTALLING THE AUTOMATIC TRANSMISSION/TRANSAXLE

After the unit has been reassembled and all end play checks indicate that the unit is properly assembled, reinstall the automatic transmission/transaxle in the vehicle. Many experts recommend that new transmission/transaxle mounts be installed to assure proper drive shaft/drive axle shaft angles.

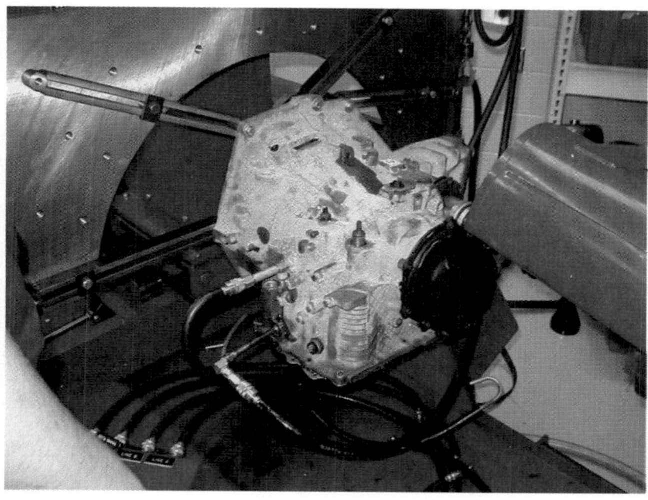

Figure 50–33 A motor-driven dynamometer being used to check the operation of a 41TE transaxle.

Figure 50–34 A gasoline engine-powered dynamometer being set up to test a rear-wheel-drive transmission.

NOTE: New mounts are particularly important if the unit was leaking automatic transmission fluid (ATF). The ATF can soften and cause the rubber used in the mounts to deteriorate.

Before installing the unit into the vehicle, flush the torque converter with clean ATF. Carefully install the torque converter onto the input shaft, being sure to fully engage the pump gear.

Carefully install the unit and use a torque wrench to torque the bolts to the bell housing. Attach the torque converter to the flex (drive) plate. Reattach all electrical connections. Lower the vehicle and add enough ATF to properly fill the unit. Consult factory information for the recommended amount to avoid under- or overfilling.

TECH TIP 

Avoid Using Red Assembly Lube

Assembly lube is used during the reassembly of automatic transmissions. If red assembly lube is used on seals, it may look like an automatic transmission fluid leak when the transmission gets hot and the lube melts. If you use blue, green, brown, or clear assembly lube, then the colour will immediately identify it as assembly lube. See Figure 50–35.

Many transmissions have been disassembled because the service technician thought that the red liquid dripping from parts of the transmission was automatic transmission fluid, while in fact it was just assembly lube that melted and ran when the transmission reached normal operating temperature.

Figure 50–35 Blue assembly lube.

ROAD TEST

Start the engine and check the level of the ATF. Carefully test drive the vehicle, checking for proper operation and shift points. Hoist the vehicle and check for any possible ATF leaks before returning the vehicle to the customer.

TECH TIP

Install a Transmission Cooler

An auxiliary transmission fluid cooler is recommended by most experts to help keep the temperature from becoming excessive, especially when towing or performing other heavy-duty vehicle operation. See Figure 50–36.

Most experts recommend that the cooler be connected so that the hot fluids travel through the auxiliary cooler and then through the factory cooler and return to the transmission/transaxle. Using this method of plumbing allows the radiator to warm the transmission fluid in cold weather as well as provide additional cooling of the fluid when the fluid temperature is high.

Figure 50–36 An auxiliary transmission cooler installed on a Chevrolet tow vehicle.

SUMMARY

1. The first step in the diagnosis of an automatic transmission/transaxle problem is to verify the complaint.
2. The automatic transmission fluid level should be checked before performing a thorough road test.
3. A stall test involves accelerating the engine at wide-open throttle with the automatic transmission/transaxle gear selector in drive and your foot on the brake. The maximum attainable engine speed is called the *stall speed.*
4. A stuck torque converter clutch solenoid can cause the engine to stall when the vehicle slows to a stop.
5. A scan tool can be helpful in the diagnosis of electronically shifted automatic transmissions/transaxles. All engine-related diagnostic trouble codes (DTCs) should be corrected before further diagnosis of the transmission/transaxle is attempted.
6. A vacuum modulator should be able to hold a vacuum applied by a hand-operated vacuum pump.
7. Most automatic transmissions/transaxles are equipped with pressure taps that allow a service technician to check mainline and other hydraulic pressures in the unit.
8. The transmission pan should be carefully inspected for evidence of excessive wear material. Use a magnet to check for any particles of steel that could be the result of serious internal damage such as a defective planetary gear set.
9. The engine should be properly supported before the automatic transmission/transaxle is removed from the vehicle.
10. When reassembling an automatic transmission/transaxle, the clutch pack clearances should be checked with a feeler gauge and air checked.
11. End play should be checked according to the vehicle manufacturer's recommendations. This check is also used as a double check for the service technician that the unit was properly assembled.
12. All vehicle manufacturers recommend that the automatic transmission fluid cooler be flushed when rebuilding or replacing an automatic transmission/transaxle.

REVIEW QUESTIONS

1. List the tests that can be performed on an automatic transmission/transaxle to determine any faults while the unit is still in the vehicle.
2. Explain how a defective torque converter clutch solenoid can cause the vehicle to stall when the vehicle is slowing to a stop.
3. Explain how automatic transmission fluid could reach the intake manifold of the engine and be burned in the engine.
4. Describe how to perform a test of the mainline and other pressures of an automatic transmission/transaxle.
5. List the procedures to follow to remove an automatic transmission/transaxle from a vehicle.
6. Describe two methods of checking a clutch pack.
7. Explain why it is important to perform an end play check of an automatic transmission/transaxle during the reassembly process.
8. Explain why it is important to flush the automatic transmission fluid cooler when a rebuilt or replacement automatic transmission/transaxle is being installed in a vehicle.

RED SEAL CERTIFICATION-TYPE QUESTIONS

1. A correct shift cable or gearshift linkage adjustment in an automatic transmission will
   - **a.** Position the governor valve
   - **b.** Position the throttle valve
   - **c.** Position the kick-down valve
   - **d.** Position the manual valve
2. Torque multiplication in a torque converter is not at its highest point
   - **a.** When the one-way clutch is locked
   - **b.** When the one-way clutch is freewheeling
   - **c.** When the vehicle is accelerating
   - **d.** When the vehicle is at stall speed
3. An automatic transmission that delays shifting into reverse or drive when cold and operates normally when hot may have a
   - **a.** Plugged filter
   - **b.** Stuck throttle valve
   - **c.** Stuck governor valve
   - **d.** Accumulator piston stuck in its bore
4. The oil from the governor is directed to the
   - **a.** Torque converter
   - **b.** Servos
   - **c.** Clutches
   - **d.** Shift valves
5. The valve which produces a pressure in direct proportion to vehicle speed is the
   - **a.** Pressure regulator valve
   - **b.** Governor valve
   - **c.** Modulator valve
   - **d.** Shift valve
6. The clutch plates in an automatic transmission/transaxles are held in the disengaged position by
   - **a.** Spring force
   - **b.** Hydraulic pressure
   - **c.** Servo release pressure
   - **d.** Oil pressure and spring force
7. The driving member of the fluid coupling or torque converter is connected to the
   - **a.** Front drive gear
   - **b.** Flywheel or flexplate
   - **c.** Main shaft of the transmission
   - **d.** Input shaft of the transmission
8. If the vacuum modulator line were cracked or missing, TV (throttle valve) pressure would
   - **a.** Increase
   - **b.** Decrease
   - **c.** Stay the same
   - **d.** Decrease main line or system pressure
9. An accumulator is used to
   - **a.** Cushion the application of a clutch pack
   - **b.** Cushion the application of a band
   - **c.** Prevent excessive main line pressure
   - **d.** Upshift the transmission
10. Air pressure checking is used to test
    - **a.** Clutch packs
    - **b.** TV adjustment
    - **c.** Vacuum modulators
    - **d.** Governors

Answers to Even Numbered End-of-Chapter Red Seal Certification-Type Questions

Chapter 1
2. c **4.** c **6.** c **8.** b **10.** a

Chapter 2
2. d **4.** b **6.** b **8.** b **10.** a

Chapter 3
2. b **4.** d **6.** b **8.** a **10.** b

Chapter 4
2. b **4.** a **6.** b **8.** b **10.** a

Chapter 5
2. c **4.** b **6.** c **8.** c **10.** c

Chapter 6
2. b **4.** b **6.** b **8.** c **10.** c

Chapter 7
2. a **4.** a **6.** c **8.** c **10.** a

Chapter 8
2. a **4.** b **6.** a **8.** c **10.** c

Chapter 9
2. a **4.** d **6.** b **8.** c **10.** c

Chapter 10
2. a **4.** b **6.** d **8.** c **10.** c

Chapter 11
2. c **4.** b **6.** b **8.** d **10.** b

Chapter 12
2. c **4.** c **6.** d **8.** c **10.** b

Chapter 13
2. a **4.** b **6.** b **8.** b **10.** d

Chapter 14
2. c **4.** b **6.** c **8.** a **10.** b

Chapter 15
2. d **4.** a **6.** b **8.** d **10.** b

Chapter 16
2. b **4.** a **6.** d **8.** a **10.** b

Chapter 17
2. c **4.** c **6.** c **8.** b **10.** d

Chapter 18
2. c **4.** c **6.** c **8.** a **10.** d

Chapter 19
2. a **4.** a **6.** c **8.** a **10.** a

Chapter 20
2. d **4.** c **6.** d **8.** c **10.** b

Chapter 21
2. d **4.** b **6.** a **8.** a **10.** b

Chapter 22
2. a **4.** a **6.** b **8.** a **10.** a

Chapter 23
2. c **4.** c **6.** a **8.** c **10.** a

Chapter 24
2. d **4.** c **6.** d **8.** d **10.** b

Chapter 25
2. c **4.** c **6.** a **8.** a **10.** a

Chapter 26
2. a **4.** d **6.** c **8.** b **10.** b

Chapter 27
2. c **4.** c **6.** a **8.** a **10.** a

Chapter 28
2. d **4.** c **6.** c **8.** a **10.** b

Chapter 29
2. d **4.** b **6.** c **8.** a **10.** d

Chapter 30
2. c **4.** c **6.** c **8.** b **10.** d

Chapter 31
2. b **4.** c **6.** b **8.** a **10.** b

Chapter 32
2. a **4.** c **6.** c **8.** b **10.** a

Chapter 33
2. d **4.** a **6.** b **8.** a **10.** a

Chapter 34
2. c **4.** c **6.** b **8.** c **10.** b

Chapter 35
2. c **4.** d **6.** c **8.** a **10.** a

Chapter 36
2. b **4.** c **6.** a **8.** a **10.** b

Chapter 37
2. b **4.** a **6.** c **8.** a **10.** a

Chapter 38
2. a **4.** c **6.** c **8.** b **10.** a

Chapter 39
2. b **4.** a **6.** c **8.** b **10.** c

Chapter 40
2. c **4.** d **6.** b **8.** b **10.** b

Chapter 41
2. b **4.** d **6.** c **8.** c **10.** d

Chapter 42
2. b **4.** a **6.** a **8.** c **10.** b

Chapter 43
2. d **4.** c **6.** b **8.** b **10.** a

Chapter 44
2. b **4.** a **6.** d **8.** c **10.** b

Chapter 45
2. c **4.** a **6.** b **8.** b **10.** b

Chapter 46
2. b **4.** d **6.** b **8.** a **10.** b

Chapter 47
2. a **4.** c 6. d **8.** d **10.** a

Chapter 48
2. b **4.** c **6.** c **8.** d **10.** d

Chapter 49
2. c **4.** d **6.** d **8.** b **10.** c

Chapter 50
2. d **4.** d **6.** a **8.** a **10.** a

APPENDIX I

Engine Repair: Sample Interprovincial Red Seal Examination Questions

1. A grade 8 UNF capscrew has ______ lines on the head.
   - **a.** 2
   - **b.** 4
   - **c.** 6
   - **d.** 8
2. A metric bolt size of M8 means that ______.
   - **a.** The bolt is 8 mm long
   - **b.** The bolt is 8 mm in diameter
   - **c.** The pitch (the distance between the crest of the threads) is 8 mm
   - **d.** The bolt is 8 cm long
3. On a metric bolt sized M8 × 1.5, the 1.5 means that _____.
   - **a.** The bolt is 1.5 mm in diameter
   - **b.** The bolt is 1.5 cm long
   - **c.** The bolt has 1.5 mm between the crest of the threads
   - **d.** The bolt has a strength grade of 1.5
4. Four-stroke cycle engines fire once ______ crankshaft revolution/s.
   - **a.** Every two
   - **b.** Every four
   - **c.** Every
   - **d.** Every one-half
5. If the bore of an engine is increased without any other changes except for the change to oversize replacement pistons, the displacement will ______ and the compression rate will ______.
   - **a.** Increase; increase
   - **b.** Increase; decrease
   - **c.** Decrease; increase
   - **d.** Decrease; decrease
6. An engine has low oil pressure. Installing a new oil pump and the correct grade of oil made no difference. What is the most likely problem?
   - **a.** Worn engine bearings
   - **b.** Worn piston rings
   - **c.** Loose valve clearance (lash)
   - **d.** Plugged PCV system
7. The stroke of the engine is determined by the
   - **a.** Connecting rod length
   - **b.** Piston pin location in the piston
   - **c.** Crankshaft
   - **d.** Height of the piston head
8. Air, at a pressure of 830 kPa (120 psi), is fed into a spark plug opening with a cylinder leakage tester. Air is heard escaping from the oil fill opening in the camshaft cover. This could indicate
   - **a.** A burned valve
   - **b.** A leaking head gasket
   - **c.** Broken piston rings
   - **d.** Cracks in the cylinder head
9. Checking compression on a diesel engine is done
   - **a.** At the spark plug opening
   - **b.** With a crankcase pressure test
   - **c.** At the glow plug opening
   - **d.** With a cylinder balance test
10. Most oil pressure tests are done at idle speed and ______ rpm.
    - **a.** 500
    - **b.** 1250
    - **c.** 2500
    - **d.** 3500

11. Engine oil leaks are often located by adding fluorescent dye to the oil and checking with an/a
    a. Aerosol powder spray
    b. Shop trouble light
    c. Black light
    d. Visual inspection
12. When removing a cylinder head, which order should the bolts/nuts be loosened?
    a. From the front of the engine to the rear
    b. The lower (or outer) row first
    c. In the reverse order of assembly
    d. Start in the middle and work to both ends
13. Removing the ring ridge before removing the piston/rod assembly is done to prevent damage to the
    a. Piston ring lands
    b. Cylinder block
    c. Piston rings
    d. Piston skirt
14. In what area does most cylinder wall wear take place?
    a. In the centre of the cylinder
    b. Varies with engine loading
    c. Near the top of the cylinder
    d. At the bottom, due to connecting rod loading
15. Squirting oil into the cylinders (wet test) before checking the compression is done to test
    a. Piston rings
    b. Valve sealing
    c. Head gasket leakage
    d. The cylinder head for cracks
16. The crankshaft harmonic balancer should be removed by pulling on
    a. The outer ring
    b. The crankshaft snout
    c. The damper hub
    d. Both the ring and the hub at the same time
17. If a notch is found on the head of a piston, the notch usually faces the
    a. Rear of the engine
    b. Major thrust side
    c. Front of the engine
    d. Minor thrust side
18. Piston pin offset is used to
    a. Reduce piston skirt temperature
    b. Reduce piston slap
    c. Lower piston crown temperature
    d. Reduce piston pin clearance
19. The valve timing on a single overhead camshaft engine is retarded because of a stretched timing belt. How will this affect performance?
    a. High RPM power will be reduced
    b. No change in performance
    c. Low RPM power will be reduced
    d. Power will be reduced at all engine speeds
20. Low compression in two cylinders that are side by side is likely caused by
    a. Two burned exhaust valves
    b. Two burned intake valves
    c. A leaking intake manifold gasket
    d. A leaking head gasket
21. Before removing the piston/rod assemblies from the engine, the connecting rods should be checked for
    a. Proper marking for location
    b. Free movement of the piston pin
    c. Big-end elongation
    d. Rod bolt torque values
22. Connecting rods are resized by grinding the parting surfaces of the rod and honing the bore back to standard. This cannot be done with most ______ rods
    a. Forged steel
    b. Powdered metal
    c. Full-floating
    d. Press-fit
23. Piston rings are installed on the piston with a
    a. Piston ring compressor
    b. Pair of snap-ring pliers
    c. Piston ring expander
    d. Piston press
24. A bearing shell is being installed in a connecting rod. The ends of the bearing are slightly above the parting line. This is called bearing ______.
    a. Spread
    b. Oil clearance
    c. Crush
    d. Side play
25. Press-fit piston pins are often installed in the connecting rod by
    a. Cooling the piston pin in dry ice
    b. Soaking the rod eye in boiling water
    c. Heating the eye of the connecting rod with a rod heater
    d. Pushing the pin with a vise and soft jaws
26. Crankshaft rod journal damage during piston/rod installation is prevented by using
    a. Rod bolt protectors
    b. The old bearing while installing the rod
    c. Heavy grease on the crank journal
    d. A wooden hammer handle to push the piston into the cylinder
27. A scored or cracked cylinder wall in a cast-iron block can be repaired by
    a. Welding the cylinder wall
    b. Installing cast-iron threaded plugs
    c. Reboring for a larger piston
    d. Installing a dry cylinder sleeve
28. Piston ring end gap is usually about 0.10 mm (0.004 in.)
    a. On most engines
    b. Per 25 mm (1 in.) of bore size
    c. Per 100 mm (4 in.) of bore size
    d. To prevent blowby
29. Piston ring end gap should be measured ______ in a worn cylinder
    a. At the top of the cylinder
    b. At the bottom of the cylinder
    c. Above the ring travelled area
    d. In the centre of the cylinder
30. Oil holes in main bearing shells should
    a. Be in both upper and lower bearings
    b. Face the block

c. Be small enough to retain high oil pressure
d. Face the cap

31. Most engine bearing clearance specifications are in the range of
a. 0.00 to 0.05 mm (0.000 to 0.002 in.)
b. 0.025 to 0.075 mm (0.001 to 0.003 in.)
c. 0.05 to 0.10 mm (0.002 to 0.004 in.)
d. 0.075 to 0.125 mm (0.003 to 0.005 in.)

32. RTV silicone sealant cures from
a. Evaporation in the air
b. The moisture in the air
c. The absence of air
d. Pressure of the two components

33. The heat shield has been removed from the bottom of a carbureted V-8 intake manifold. This may cause
a. The manifold to run cooler
b. Engine oil to coke (harden)
c. An increase in high RPM power
d. The engine to overheat

34. A cast-iron V-8 cylinder head is checked for warpage using a straightedge and a feeler (thickness) gauge. Maximum warpage is 0.05 mm (0.002 in.). What should be done?
a. Straighten the head in a press
b. Resurface the head
c. Replace the head
d. Reinstall as is

35. Many automakers recommend that torque-to-yield head bolts should
a. Be measured for overall length
b. Be thread checked with a thread pitch/gauge
c. Not be reused
d. Be lubricated only with anti-seize lubricant

36. All valve train components should be kept together because
a. They can be inspected for wear
b. They should always be replaced as a set
c. Parts wear into each other
d. They are easier to measure for wear when they are a pair

37. A valve being removed from a cylinder head begins to bind as the tip enters the guide. What should be done?
a. Apply penetrating oil to the guide
b. Tap the valve through with a brass punch
c. The valve tip edges should be filed
d. Cut the valve stem off with a hacksaw

38. Timing chains are usually replaced when chain slack exceeds
a. 6 mm (1/4 in.)
b. 13 mm (1/2 in.)
c. 19 mm (3/4 in.)
d. 25 mm (1 in.)

39. The timing belt breaks on a free wheeling overhead camshaft engine. What will happen?
a. All intake valves will be bent
b. The piston and valves collide
c. The exhaust valves are bent
d. The engine will quit

40. Before the valve seats are reconditioned, the ______.
a. Valves must be refaced
b. Valve guides must be reconditioned
c. Valve installed height must be measured
d. Valve spring assembled height must be measured and noted

41. Typical valve stem to guide clearance should be
a. 0.012 to 0.025 mm (0.0005 to 0.001 in.)
b. 0.025 to 0.075 mm (0.001 to 0.003 in.)
c. 0.125 to 0.250 mm (0.005 to 0.010 in.)
d. 0.250 to 0.380 mm (0.010 to 0.015 in.)

42. Some manufacturers recommend that valves be ground with an interference angle. This angle is the difference between the ______.
a. Valve margin and valve face angles
b. Valve guide and stem angle
c. Valve face and valve seat angles
d. Margin angle and valve head

43. Valve margin should be at least ______ with most valves
a. 0.38 mm (1/64 in.)
b. 0.75 mm (1/32 in.)
c. 1.50 mm (1/16 in.)
d. 3 mm (1/8 in)

44. Integral valve guides are reconditioned by installing bronze guide liners or by
a. Installing oversize valve guides
b. Installing undersize valve stems
c. Reaming the guide for an oversize valve stem
d. Pressing out the old valve guide and installing a new guide

45. To narrow and lower a 45° valve seat, the technician should use a ______ stone
a. 75°
b. 60°
c. 45°
d. 30°

46. To widen a 45° valve seat without lowering or raising its position, the technician should use a ______ stone
a. 45°
b. 60°
c. 75°
d. 90°

47. Valve springs are checked for ______, free height and squareness
a. Tension
b. Out of round
c. Open valve height
d. Twist

48. Multiple valve springs (dual springs) generally have both coils
a. Wound in the same direction
b. With exactly the same tension
c. Wound in opposite directions
d. With the same number of coil turns

49. Excessive valve stem height is usually corrected by
a. Replacing the valve
b. Grinding the valve seat
c. Grinding material from the valve tip
d. Replacing the valve seat

50. Valve spring installed height is usually adjusted by
  a. Replacing the valve spring retainers
  b. Installing longer valve springs
  c. Installing valve spring inserts (shims)
  d. Installing shorter valves

51. Which type of valve seal moves up and down with the valve?
  a. Umbrella seals
  b. Rubber and teflon seals
  c. Positive valve seals
  d. All teflon positive seals

52. Cylinder head bolts are generally lubricated with
  a. SAE 80W-90 gear lube
  b. Never-seize compound
  c. Silicone spray lubricant
  d. Engine oil

53. The freezing and boiling point of engine coolant is measured with a/an
  a. Spectrograph
  b. Coolant hydrometer
  c. Infared pyrometer
  d. Scan tool

54. Radiator cores are made of sheet brass or
  a. Aluminum
  b. Copper
  c. Steel
  d. Plastic

55. A cooling system with a 100 kPa (15 psi) radiator pressure cap has raised the coolant boiling point to
  a. 100°C (212°F)
  b. 125°C (257°F)
  c. 150°C (302°F)
  d. 175°C (347°F)

56. Checking the radiator coolant level should be done when the engine is
  a. Warm
  b. Cold
  c. At operating temperature
  d. Idling

57. Engines that use reverse cooling pump the coolant from the
  a. Engine block into the cylinder head
  b. Cylinder head into the radiator
  c. Engine block into the radiator outlet
  d. Radiator into the cylinder head

58. A leaking water pump may show coolant flowing from the
  a. Bypass hose
  b. Water pump weep hole
  c. Bearing assembly
  d. Radiator overflow container

59. The cooling fan on most transverse engine vehicles is driven by
  a. A belt from the crankshaft
  b. A serpentine (one piece) drive belt
  c. An electric motor
  d. Hydraulic oil pressure

60. Radiator pressure caps are tested with
  a. An air hose and adaptor
  b. A radiator pressure tester
  c. A scan tool readout of cooling system pressure
  d. The pressure cap mounted on the radiator

61. The top radiator hose collapses flat whenever the engine is allowed to cool. The most likely problem is
  a. A leaking pressure valve seal at the cap
  b. Insufficient coolant in the coolant recovery container
  c. Low coolant level
  d. A sticking pressure cap vent valve

62. If the level of the coolant in the overflow container is correct, the radiator coolant level must also be correct.
  a. False
  b. True
  c. Only with a cold engine
  d. Only at operating temperature

63. Radiators that use an integral transmission oil cooler locate the cooler in the
  a. Overflow tank
  b. Inlet tank
  c. Outlet tank
  d. Opening to the radiator core

64. Oil pumps are usually driven by the camshaft or
  a. Timing chain
  b. Camshaft sprocket
  c. Crankshaft snout
  d. Timing belt

65. Lubricating oil moves from the oil pump to the
  a. Main oil gallery for the bearings
  b. Valve train
  c. Oil filter
  d. Hydraulic valve lifters

66. A vehicle is towed in with an oil filter that has blown open. After replacing the filter and oil, the technician should
  a. Check the maximum oil pressure
  b. Run the engine at high RPM
  c. Check the minimum oil pressure
  d. Check the original oil for the correct weight

67. When an oil pump drive shaft breaks, the usual cause is
  a. Excess oil in the engine
  b. Debris in the oil pump
  c. Lack of lubrication
  d. A worn oil pump

68. The oil pump relief valve (pressure regulating valve) controls
  a. Maximum oil pressure
  b. Oil pressure to the valve train
  c. Minimum oil pressure
  d. Return oil from the bearings

69. A new or rebuilt engine should be broken in during the first road test by
  a. Keeping maximum speed under 50 km/h (30 mph)
  b. Light throttle acceleration

c. Full throttle acceleration from 50 to 80 km/h (30 to 50 mph)
d. Driving at higher speeds: over 80 km/h (50 mph)

70. The first oil and filter change on a rebuilt engine should be done in ______ kilometres (______ miles)
a. 80 (50)
b. 500 (300)
c. 800 (500)
d. 1500 (1000)

ANSWERS

1. c
2. b
3. c
4. a
5. a
6. a
7. c
8. c
9. c
10. c
11. c
12. c
13. a
14. c
15. a
16. c
17. c
18. b
19. c
20. d
21. a
22. b
23. c
24. c
25. c
26. a
27. d
28. b
29. b
30. b
31. b
32. b
33. b
34. d
35. c
36. c
37. c
38. b
39. d
40. b
41. b
42. c
43. b
44. c
45. d
46. a
47. a
48. c
49. c
50. c
51. a
52. d
53. b
54. a
55. b
56. b
57. d
58. b
59. c
60. b
61. d
62. a
63. c
64. c
65. c
66. a
67. b
68. a
69. c
70. c

APPENDIX 2

Automatic Transmission/ Transaxles: Sample Interprovincial Red Seal Examination Questions

1. If the input to a Simpson planetary gear set is the front ring gear, and the rear planetary is the held member, the automatic transmission is in?
   - **a.** Manual second
   - **b.** Intermediate range
   - **c.** Low range
   - **d.** Reverse range
2. The purpose of the multiple disc clutches in an automatic transmission is to
   - **a.** Drive planetary gear members only
   - **b.** Hold planetary gear members only
   - **c.** Hold a planetary gear or drive a planetary gear member
   - **d.** Engaged only to provide for gear reduction
3. A servo in an automatic transmission
   - **a.** Applies clutches
   - **b.** Cushions the application of a clutch pack or a band
   - **c.** Applies a band
   - **d.** Holds the one way clutch
4. Excessive clutch pack clearance can cause
   - **a.** Insufficient clutch application (slippage)
   - **b.** Too much clutch apply pressure
   - **c.** Poor clutch release
   - **d.** Too little shift lag time
5. A customer complains of a clank when her car is shifted into reverse. The likely cause is
   - **a.** Worn axle bearing
   - **b.** Worn rear axle traction clutches
   - **c.** Excessive ring gear run-out
   - **d.** Excessive ring gear and pinion backlash
6. When the driving force is delivered to the road wheels, the rear axle assembly
   - **a.** Tends to rotate with the wheels
   - **b.** Tends to rotate opposite to the wheels
   - **c.** Tends to move from side to side
   - **d.** Is not affected
7. Hydraulic control pressure after it leaves the front pump is controlled first by the
   - **a.** Modulator valve
   - **b.** Regulator valve
   - **c.** Governor valve
   - **d.** Manual valve
8. Automatic transmission/transaxle bands,
   - **a.** Hold various planetary units
   - **b.** Drive various planetary units
   - **c.** Hold or drive various planetary units as required
   - **d.** Drive various planetary units
9. The neutral safety switch
   - **a.** Allows engine to start only in park or neutral
   - **b.** Prevents gear damage in neutral
   - **c.** Prevents clutch damage in neutral
   - **d.** Prevents brake application in neutral
10. Multiple disc clutches can be used as
    - **a.** Both holding and driving members
    - **b.** Holding members only
    - **c.** Driving members only
    - **d.** Reaction members
11. Pressure regulating valves are identified as
    - **a.** Downshift valve and accumulator
    - **b.** Manual valve and shift valve
    - **c.** Manual valve and governor valve
    - **d.** Relief valve and throttle valve

12. The shafts and drums of an automatic transmission limit endplay movement by
- **a.** Hydraulic pressure and thrust washers driving lugs
- **b.** Thrust washers
- **c.** Ball bearings
- **d.** Driving lugs

13. What is the name of a holding device that would release the instant that torque reversal occurs?
- **a.** Piston clutch
- **b.** Servo-operated band
- **c.** Linkage operated band
- **d.** Sprag clutch

14. In a three-speed automatic transmission, the direct drive is in effect when
- **a.** Bands are engaged and the clutches are released
- **b.** Clutches are engaged and the bands are released
- **c.** Clutches and bands are engaged
- **d.** Clutches and bands are released

15. An orifice can be used to
- **a.** Direct pressure more positively
- **b.** Increase apply pressure
- **c.** Increase upstream pressure
- **d.** Cushion and/or delay unit application

16. The valve which directs oils to operating valves used in the driving range selected is the
- **a.** Balanced valve
- **b.** Pressure regulator valve
- **c.** Accumulator valve
- **d.** Manual valve

17. An automatic transmission equipped with a lock-up torque converter appears to hunt in and out of gear at about 60 km/h (37 mph). The problem is most likely to be
- **a.** Pump pressure fluctuating (press. reg. valve)
- **b.** Converter apply valves out of calibration
- **c.** Detent linkage out of adjustment
- **d.** Band adjusted too tight

18. The valve which controls and maintains pump output pressure is called the
- **a.** Manual valve
- **b.** Pressure relief valve
- **c.** Pressure regulator valve
- **d.** Pressure metering valve

19. The valve which is balanced between spring load plus TV (throttle valve) pressure on one end and governor pressure on the other end is called the
- **a.** Shift valve
- **b.** Detent valve
- **c.** Throttle valve
- **d.** Governor valve

20. In the three-speed Simpson gear set, which two units are usually splined to the output shaft?
- **a.** Forward ring gear and rear carrier assembly
- **b.** Forward sun gear and forward ring gear
- **c.** Rear ring gear and forward carrier assembly
- **d.** Forward carrier assembly and rear carrier assembly

21. The front pump in an automatic transmission/transaxle is driven by the
- **a.** Torque converter hub
- **b.** Input shaft
- **c.** Turbine hub
- **d.** Reaction shaft

22. Multiple disc clutch packs are made up of
- **a.** Alternating internally and externally toothed composition plates
- **b.** Alternating internally and externally toothed plates
- **c.** Various types of steel plates
- **d.** Alternating steel and friction plates

23. When pressurized transmission fluid is directed up the input shaft of a lockup converter, the torque converter is
- **a.** At stall speed (vortex flow)
- **b.** Released (unlocked)
- **c.** Locked up
- **d.** Being cooled down (rotary flow)

24. A Simpson compound gear set consists of
- **a.** Two carriers, two ring gears, two sun gears
- **b.** Two sun gears, two sets of pinions, one ring gear
- **c.** One common sun gear, two carriers, two ring gears
- **d.** One carrier, two ring gears, two sun gears

25. Bands in automatic are anchored through a strut to the
- **a.** Extension housing
- **b.** Stator
- **c.** Carrier
- **d.** Transmission/transaxle case

26. An automatic transmission/transaxle shift valve
- **a.** Is a pressure regulating valve
- **b.** Is a control valve operated by oil pressure
- **c.** Must be manually preset
- **d.** Is a diaphragm-type valve

27. Dynamic oil seals are used to prevent leaks from occurring
- **a.** From around moving parts or shafts
- **b.** Between two stationary parts
- **c.** Between oil pan and case
- **d.** Between pump and case

28. Following removal of the control valve body, air pressure can be used to check the operation of the
- **a.** Clutch and servo
- **b.** Converter and pump
- **c.** Manual valve and throttle valve
- **d.** Relief valve

29. Broken engine mounts could have an effect on the operation of the
- **a.** Manual valve
- **b.** Throttle valve
- **c.** Modulator valve
- **d.** Governor valve

30. Pressure tests are used on automatic transmissions/transaxles to check
- **a.** Release pressures only
- **b.** Converter operation
- **c.** Apply and release pressures
- **d.** Apply pressures only

31. An engine speed that is too high during a stall test indicates
- **a.** That torque multiplication in the converter is too great
- **b.** That bands and/or clutches are slipping
- **c.** The stator overrunning clutch is not holding
- **d.** That clutches and bands are not releasing

32. Transfer of energy from one torque converter member to another is the result of
- **a.** Vortex flow of oil
- **b.** Dynamic flow of oil
- **c.** Cavitation of oil
- **d.** Rotary flow of oil

33. End play within the transmission/transaxles is usually measured with a
- **a.** Micrometer
- **b.** Dial indicator
- **c.** Feeler gauge
- **d.** Straight edge ruler

34. The arrangement of clutch discs in a clutch pack should be such that piston applies against the
- **a.** Friction plate
- **b.** Snap ring
- **c.** Steel plate
- **d.** Pressure plate

35. A slipping one-way clutch in the stator during a stall test would result in
- **a.** Delayed engagement
- **b.** No effect on engine performance
- **c.** High engine rpm
- **d.** Low engine rpm

36. To measure operating clearance in a clutch pack, use a
- **a.** Micrometer
- **b.** Feeler gauge
- **c.** Vernier micrometer
- **d.** Metal ruler

37. The device in the converter that prevents excessive turbulence from developing is the
- **a.** Split ring
- **b.** Vanes
- **c.** Stator
- **d.** Rotor

38. An engine that will start with the automatic transmission gear selector in any position will likely have
- **a.** An open neutral safety switch
- **b.** A grounded transmission regulator spark switch
- **c.** A shorted ignition switch
- **d.** A shorted neutral safety switch

39. Gear train end play can be corrected with the use of
- **a.** Selective gear sizes
- **b.** Oversize shafts
- **c.** Selective carrier sizes
- **d.** Selective thrust washers

40. A 1–2 upshift takes place when
- **a.** Throttle pressure overcomes governor pressure
- **b.** Governor pressure overcomes throttle pressure
- **c.** Main line pressure overcomes throttle pressure
- **d.** Main line pressure overcomes governor pressure

41. A coupling stage in the converter is reached when the
- **a.** Turbine reaches 9/10 impeller speed
- **b.** Impeller reaches 9/10 turbine speed
- **c.** Stator ceases rotation
- **d.** Turbine turns faster than the impeller

42. The force acting on the main pressure regulator to increase line pressure for high torque loads is
- **a.** Governor pressure
- **b.** Converter stator pressure
- **c.** Throttle pressure
- **d.** Accumulator pressure

43. For automatic upshifts, the shift valves are moved by
- **a.** Main line pressure
- **b.** Exhaust pressure
- **c.** Modulator pressure
- **d.** Governor pressure

44. The throttle valve can be made to sense torque by use of
- **a.** Engine manifold vacuum
- **b.** A spring force
- **c.** Governor pressure
- **d.** Main line pressure

45. In a simple 3-speed, if the car will drive forward in neutral range
- **a.** The rear one-way clutch will not release
- **b.** The low/reverse band will not reverse
- **c.** The high/reverse clutches will not release
- **d.** The forward clutches will not release

46. Bands in an automatic transmission
- **a.** Are used to lock two members of an elliptic gear together
- **b.** Are applied when the transmission is in park
- **c.** Are used to connect a gear to the transmission case
- **d.** Are usually a double wrap type

47. Stators provide most torque conversion when the speed difference between the impeller and the
- **a.** Turbine is the same
- **b.** Stator is the lowest
- **c.** Turbine is lowest
- **d.** Turbine is highest

48. The front pump
- **a.** Drives the output shaft and clutch pack assembly
- **b.** Produces pressure for all uses in the transmission
- **c.** Directs pressure to the manual valve
- **d.** Has a low volume output

49. Most late model automatic transmissions cannot be push started because
- **a.** The stator in the torque converter freewheels in the wrong direction
- **b.** There is no rear pump incorporated in the transmission

c. The engine will be turning in the wrong direction
d. The vortex flow in the torque converter will be in the wrong direction

50. In an internal-external gear pump
a. The two gears turn in the same direction
b. The two gears turn in opposite directions
c. There is no crescent in this pump
d. The internally toothed gear is the drive gear

ANSWERS

1. d
2. c
3. c
4. a
5. d
6. b
7. b
8. c
9. a
10. a
11. d
12. b
13. d
14. b
15. d
16. d
17. b
18. c
19. a
20. c
21. a
22. d
23. b
24. c
25. d
26. b
27. a
28. a
29. b
30. c
31. b
32. a
33. b
34. c
35. d
36. b
37. a
38. d
39. d
40. b
41. a
42. c
43. d
44. a
45. d
46. c
47. d
48. c
49. b
50. a

APPENDIX 3

Manual Drive Trains and Axles: Sample Interprovincial Red Seal Examination Questions

1. A clutch engages close to the floor and often will not disengage. What is the most likely cause?
   - **a.** Worn clutch disc
   - **b.** Misadjusted clutch linkage
   - **c.** Weak pressure plate
   - **d.** Worn flywheel
2. A ring gear and pinion are being replaced. Which part(s) *must be* replaced?
   - **a.** Ring gear bolts
   - **b.** Differential side bearings
   - **c.** Axle seals
   - **d.** Drive pinion preload spacer
3. Which rating of a lubricant means that it is suitable to use in a differential using a hypoid gear set?
   - **a.** SAE
   - **b.** 80W-90
   - **c.** GL-5
   - **d.** API
4. A vehicle is equipped with different-size tires on the same drive axle (P205/75RX15 on the left rear and P215/75RX15 on the right rear). What part may wear due to this tire-size mismatch?
   - **a.** Drive pinion bearings
   - **b.** Side gear bearings
   - **c.** Rear axle bearings
   - **d.** Pinion gear thrust washers
5. Different designs, styles, weights and lengths of front wheel drive CV half-shafts have been designed for the purpose of
   - **a.** Durability
   - **b.** Strength
   - **c.** Torque steer
   - **d.** Vibration
6. A removable-carrier differential is being rebuilt. A pattern check shows the drive pinion is not deep enough on the ring gear. What is the correct adjustment?
   - **a.** Remove the drive pinion assembly and install a thinner shim
   - **b.** Remove the ring gear and case assembly and install a thicker shim
   - **c.** Remove the rear drive pinion bearing and install a thicker shim
   - **d.** Remove the drive pinion assembly and install a thicker shim
7. A differential is being rebuilt. The technician tightens the companion flange nut too tight when setting the "crush." What should be done?
   - **a.** Back off the flange nut
   - **b.** Loosen the cap adjusters and re-torque
   - **c.** Replace the companion flange
   - **d.** Replace the collapsible spacer
8. The end of the ring gear teeth that is closest to the centre of the gear is called the
   - **a.** Heel
   - **b.** Toe
   - **c.** Convex
   - **d.** Concave
9. What is the ratio of a differential that has 39 teeth on the ring gear and 11 teeth on the drive pinion?
   - **a.** 4.11:1
   - **b.** 3.78:1
   - **c.** 3.54:1
   - **d.** None of the above
10. The outer CV joint must be able to work with angles in excess of
    - **a.** 80°
    - **b.** 40°

c. 60°
d. 50°

11. The correct name for the most common type of outboard CV joint is the
a. Cross and roller
b. Carden
c. Tripod
d. Rzeppa

12. A linkage style clutch pedal freeplay is correctly adjusted
a. If the pedal has approximately one half to one inches of freeplay
b. If the transmission can be shifted without clashing
c. If the clutch does not slip
d. Has no adjustment

13. When the clutch is disengaged
a. The disc has maximum slippage
b. The disc has minimum slippage
c. The pedal is furthest from the floor
d. The flywheel is stopped

14. The pilot bearing or bushing is located
a. On the rear of the output shaft
b. On the main shaft
c. Behind the main drive gear
d. In the end of the crankshaft

15. Crankshaft and driveline torsional vibrations are absorbed by
a. The clutch pressure plate springs
b. The clutch torsion springs
c. The wave spring between the two clutch faces
d. The input shaft bearings

16. The clutch's driven disc is splined to the
a. Engine crankshaft
b. Transmission input shaft
c. Transmission output shaft
d. Transmission counter shaft

17. Excessive shuddering of the clutch on initial take-up is caused by
a. Weak disc torsion springs
b. A bad release bearing
c. Too much linkage freeplay
d. An overheated, weakened wave spring

18. In a hydraulic system, if the clutch self engages while the pedal is fully depressed
a. The pressure plate springs are weak
b. There is insufficient clutch pedal freeplay
c. The clutch master cylinder primary cup is leaking
d. The transmission is in neutral

19. In gear systems, to achieve a torque increase
a. The input shaft must turn slower than the output shaft
b. Both shafts must turn in the same direction
c. The input gear must be smaller than the output gear
d. An idler gear is needed

20. When a constant mesh transmission is in neutral with the clutch engaged and the engine running
a. Only the input shaft drive gear and the cluster revolve
b. All gears in the transmission revolve
c. Only the mainshaft gears revolve
d. No gears revolve

21. A helical toothed gear has its teeth
a. Parallel to the gear's axis
b. In a helix around the outer face of the gear
c. Radiating out from the centre of the gear
d. Perpendicular to the gear's axis

22. In a conventional RWD transmission, the synchromesh units are
a. Splined to the input shaft
b. Splined to the main shaft
c. Meshed to the sliding gears
d. Splined to the counter shaft

23. A transmission's forward gear ratios are shown below. Select second gear.
a. 0.78:1
b. 1:1
c. 1.73:1
d. 2.89:1
e. 3.28:1

24. In a constant mesh standard transmission, when the output shaft revolves
a. The input shaft must also revolve
b. The synchromesh units must also revolve
c. The cluster gears must also revolve
d. All gears in the transmission must revolve

25. In a RWD four speed transmission, the largest gear on the counter shaft is in constant mesh with
a. Main shaft second gear
b. Reverse idle gear
c. First main shaft gear
d. Input shaft main drive gear

26. A 38 tooth gear on the main shaft is in mesh with a 12 tooth gear on the counter shaft. What is the correct gear ration?
a. 0.3158:1
b. 3.166:1
c. 1.90:1
d. 1:3.166

27. When inspecting a transmission for grinding during shifting, one should check
a. The grooves inside the synchronizer ring
b. The splines on the shifter hub
c. The condition of the constant mesh gear teeth
d. The condition of the cluster shaft bearings

28. To prevent the possibility of engaging two gears at the same time
a. A detent mechanism is used
b. A synchromesh unit is used in all forward gears
c. An interlock mechanism is used
d. Helical gears are used

29. Most manufacturers recommend that a disabled, RWD vehicle not be towed beyond a certain distance or speed with its drive wheels on the ground. Why?
   - **a.** The counter shaft is not spinning therefore not providing lubrication
   - **b.** The input shaft is not turning therefore the oil pump is not running
   - **c.** The clutch can be severely damaged
   - **d.** None of the above.

30. A conventional RWD transmission makes noise in all gears except fourth. What is the most likely problem?
   - **a.** All synchros except fourth are worn out
   - **b.** The release bearing is damaged
   - **c.** The rear bearing on the input shaft is damaged
   - **d.** Fourth gear main shaft bearing is damaged

31. When is a bad pilot bearing most likely to make itself evident?
   - **a.** Hard acceleration in first or reverse
   - **b.** Steady cruise in fifth
   - **c.** Standing still, engine off, moving the clutch pedal up and down
   - **d.** Sitting at a red light in first gear

ANSWERS

1. b
2. d
3. b
4. d
5. d
6. c
7. d
8. b
9. c
10. b
11. d
12. a
13. a
14. d
15. b
16. b
17. d
18. c
19. c
20. a
21. b
22. b
23. d
24. b
25. d
26. b
27. a
28. c
29. a
30. c
31. d

APPENDIX 4

Suspension and Steering: Sample Interprovincial Red Seal Examination Questions

1. Steering axis inclination is
   - **a.** The inward tilt of the steer axis at the top from true vertical
   - **b.** The included camber and caster angles
   - **c.** Where the steering axis and wheel centreline intersect
   - **d.** The distance between wheel centrelines at spindle height
2. Final toe adjustment check
   - **a.** Must be performed after camber and caster adjustment
   - **b.** Must be performed before the caster adjustment
   - **c.** Must be performed with wheels off the ground
   - **d.** Wheels must be turned at a 20° angle
3. When performing a rear wheel alignment, each wheel must have equal amounts of toe to
   - **a.** Maintain riding height at rear
   - **b.** Provide a toe-out on turn condition
   - **c.** Provide a 0° thrust angle
   - **d.** Provide rear body to frame alignment
4. With rack and pinion steering, how much play is allowed in the inner tie rod end?
   - **a.** 0.25 mm (0.010 inch) vertical movement
   - **b.** .050 mm (0.020 inch) lateral movement
   - **c.** .075 mm (0.030 inch) vertical movement
   - **d.** Zero vertical and zero lateral movement
5. If the bottom coil of the left front spring is broken, this will probably cause
   - **a.** No loss of directional control or stability
   - **b.** No change in the spring rate
   - **c.** A condition known as toe change
   - **d.** The right rear of the body to be low
6. The pump in a hydraulic power-steering system operates
   - **a.** Only when needed
   - **b.** When the engine is started, shutting off when pressure is built up
   - **c.** Continuously when engine running
   - **d.** Only when the steering wheel is turned
7. In the linkage type of power steering system, the swing end of the Pitman arm actuates
   - **a.** A tie rod
   - **b.** An oil pump
   - **c.** An idler valve
   - **d.** A valve assembly
8. The energy used to operate most automatic power steering systems is
   - **a.** Hydraulic pressure
   - **b.** Air pressure
   - **c.** Atmospheric pressure
   - **d.** Vacuum
9. With power steering pump pressure 100 psi, the output force on a 0.5 sq. in. piston is
   - **a.** 90.9 kg
   - **b.** 56.8 kg
   - **c.** 45.5 kg
   - **d.** 22.7 kg
10. Because the power steering pump is driven at various speeds, it must include a
    - **a.** Warning device for extreme pressure
    - **b.** Bypass tube returning oil to the reservoir

c. Flow control valve
d. Centrifugal governor control

11. In a manual rack and pinion steering gear the pinion gear is connected to the
a. Gear housing
b. Steering shaft
c. Rack end
d. Tie rod

12. To measure suspension height the following conditions should be met
a. Vehicle on level floor, at curb weight with correct tire pressure
b. Vehicle on level floor, all passengers in vehicle, correct tire pressure
c. Vehicle at curb weight, on a level floor, spare in place and all passengers in car
d. No passengers in car, spare removed, curb weight and on a level floor

13. When unusual wear of the rear tires is noticed
a. Switch tires to front wheels
b. Check alignment of rear wheels
c. Rear brake adjustment is probably unequal
d. Rear shock absorbers are probably required

14. A negative caster reading indicates
a. That the top ball joint is forward at the top from the vertical
b. That the top ball joint is back at the top from the vertical
c. That the top ball joint is inward at the top of the vertical
d. That the reading is outside the manufacturer's specification

15. Which of the following would you consider to be a typical automobile front-end camber specification?
a. +1/4 degree
b. −41/2 degrees
c. +6 degrees
d. 1/8 in.

16. When performing a wheel alignment, which adjustment is made first?
a. SAI
b. Turning radius
c. Caster
d. Toe-in

17. Unsprung weight refers to
a. The GVW rating
b. Weight not attached to the springs
c. Weight supported by the springs
d. Weight not supported by the springs

18. When the rear of the front tires are closer together than at the front, the tires have
a. Positive camber
b. Toe-in
c. Toe-out
d. Negative camber

19. The purpose of the steering axis inclination is
a. To allow for steering radius
b. To keep the camber and caster angles constant when the vehicle is in motion
c. To help offset road crown pull
d. To help reduce the need for excessive camber

20. A non-integrated anti-lock brake system
a. Uses a special master cylinder with a booster piston
b. Uses s conventional dual master cylinder
c. Does not need wheel speed sensors
d. Works only on two wheels

21. The axial wear measurement of a ball joint is the movement
a. Up and down
b. In a horizontal direction
c. Sideways
d. In a radial direction

22. The caster on the left wheel has been set at 1¾ in. negative. The right wheel caster has been set at 7/8 degrees negative. What would result?
a. The car would pull to the right
b. The car would travel straight ahead
c. The left tire would show second rib wear
d. The car would pull to the left

23. Which of the following is not considered a tire wearing angle?
a. Camber
b. Caster
c. Toe-in
d. Turning radius

24. You have just aligned the front end of a car and the owner, who weighs 110 kg (250 lb), sits down behind the steering wheel; the
a. Camber on the left wheel will increase toward positive
b. Camber on both wheels becomes more positive
c. Camber on the right wheel will increase toward positive
d. Camber on both wheels becomes more negative

25. Which of the following items is not a means of adjusting camber on a vehicle?
a. Shims
b. A sliding control arm shaft
c. A cam-bolt assembly
d. A strut rod

26. The centre bolt
a. Holds the leaf spring to the axle housing
b. Holds the leaf spring together
c. Holds the leaf spring together and locates the spring
d. Positions the shackle assembly in the spring eye bushing

27. A negative scrub radius tends to force the front wheel to
a. Toe-out
b. Steer to the right
c. Toe-in
d. Steer to the left

28. Steering will pull to the side with
a. Most negative camber or most positive caster
b. Most positive camber or most positive caster

c. Most negative camber or most negative caster
d. Most positive camber or most negative caster

29. Tire wear on the outside edge of the right front tire only could be caused by
- **a.** Under-inflation
- **b.** Too much positive camber
- **c.** Over-inflation
- **d.** Too much negative camber

30. Rubber suspension components such as control arm bushings, tie rod ends and idler arms must be tightened in their normal operating position because
- **a.** They make a noise
- **b.** They have a position memory
- **c.** They prevent premature failure of rubber
- **d.** This is the only way to get a wrench on the bolts

31. Toe-out on turns is
- **a.** A built-in feature of the steering to allow wheels to turn at different angles
- **b.** Measurement that must be adjusted
- **c.** The ability of steering to return to centre after cornering
- **d.** The angle of the rear wheels during cornering

32. The reference line used to check horizontal distances on a frame is called a
- **a.** Comparable measurement
- **b.** Geometric centre line
- **c.** Datum line
- **d.** Thrust line

33. A frame that is separate from the body, but forms a border around the passenger compartment, is known as a
- **a.** Unitized frame
- **b.** Ladder frame
- **c.** Unitized frame with sub-bolt on assembly
- **d.** Perimeter frame

34. A tire tread has sharp edges when the hand is dragged across it from outside to inside, but, the tread feels smooth in the opposite direction. The problem is
- **a.** Incorrect toe-out on turns
- **b.** Dynamic imbalance
- **c.** Excessive toe-in
- **d.** Excessive toe-out

SMOOTH IN – TOE IN
SMOOTH OUT – TOE OUT.

35. To check for internal wear in the outer tie rod end, you should
- **a.** Only twist the tie rod and feel for looseness
- **b.** Have the steering wheel rotated and check the end for free play
- **c.** Use a steel bar and pry up and down next to the end
- **d.** Compress the end with small vise grips and observe

36. A vehicle has manual steering and the caster for both wheels is 1° positive. If both wheels are set to a 3° positive, what would be the result?
- **a.** Decreased directional control
- **b.** Outside tire tread wear
- **c.** Improved directional control
- **d.** Excessive wander and weave

37. If a vehicle has a negative setback of 19 mm (0.75 in.) and the rear axle thrust line points left, the vehicle will
- **a.** Steer straight down the road
- **b.** Have a longer wheel base measurement on the left
- **c.** Only need to have the steering wheel re-centred
- **d.** Constantly steer to the left

38. All other factors being equal, a vehicle will drift to the side whose wheel has
- **a.** The most camber and the most caster
- **b.** The most positive camber and least negative caster
- **c.** The most camber and the most negative caster
- **d.** The most positive caster and the least amount of scrub radius

39. A front-wheel-drive vehicle pulls toward the right during acceleration. The most likely cause is
- **a.** Worn or defective tires
- **b.** Leaking or defective shock absorbers
- **c.** Normal torque steer
- **d.** A defective power steering rack and pinion steering assembly

40. Defective outer CV joints usually make a clicking noise
- **a.** Only when backing
- **b.** While turning and moving
- **c.** While turning only
- **d.** During braking

ANSWERS

1. a
2. a
3. c
4. d
5. a
6. c
7. d
8. a
9. d
10. c
11. b
12. a
13. b
14. a
15. a
16. c
17. d
18. c
19. a
20. b
21. a
22. a
23. b
24. d
25. b
26. c
27. a
28. d
29. b
30. b
31. a
32. a
33. a
34. c
35. b
36. c
37. d
38. b
39. c
40. b

APPENDIX 5

Brakes: Sample Interprovincial Red Seal Examination Questions

1. To test a vacuum power booster for leaks
   a. Connect a pressure gauge to the exhaust pipe
   b. Stop engine, wait three minutes, then apply brakes
   c. Pressure test in a pail of water
   d. Stop engine and apply brake
2. The wheel speed sensor used on the anti-lock system
   a. Produces an electrical pulse to the anti-lock control module
   b. Controls hydraulic pressure in the faster rotating wheel cylinder
   c. Controls pressure in the total hydraulic system
   d. Monitors brake shoe retracting speed
3. When a vehicle is being braked to a stop
   a. Kinetic energy is being produced
   b. Energy is being destroyed
   c. Heat energy is being changed to kinetic energy
   d. Kinetic energy is being changed to heat energy
4. The amount of resistance developed by any two bodies in contact is referred to as
   a. Frictional tolerance
   b. Coefficient of friction
   c. Frictional horsepower
   d. Frictional heat value
5. To test a vacuum power booster for operation you can
   a. Connect a vacuum gauge to booster inlet
   b. Exhaust vacuum, apply brakes, start engine, note reaction of brake pedal
   c. Measure stopping distance
   d. Stop engine, wait, then apply brakes
6. A vacuum suspended power assist brake diaphragm chamber has
   a. Air pressure on either side at the diaphragm
   b. Vacuum and atmospheric pressure on each side in the released position
   c. Vacuum only on one side when in the released position
   d. Vacuum on both sides when in the released position
7. The hydraulic control unit used in integral recirculating ball power steering is part of the
   a. Steering shaft
   b. Steering gear
   c. Linkage
   d. Steering sleeve
8. The purpose of the vacuum check valve used on the power assist booster is to
   a. Hold vacuum in the booster, should manifold vacuum drop
   b. Remove moisture
   c. Prevent dirt from entering the unit
   d. Open the atmospheric apply port in the event of engine failure
9. The open center spool valve of a hydro-boost power brake unit
   a. Provides accumulator pressure on a stall test condition
   b. Provides a balanced braking action to disc and drum units

   c. Closes the boost chamber area to the reservoir on apply
   d. Provides the driver a reaction force for more braking efficiency

10. Fluid is used in the brake system to transmit
   a. Leverage and heat
   b. Motion and force
   c. Force and friction
   d. Motion and friction

11. When a liquid is subjected to pressure, its volume will be
   a. Increased
   b. Decreased
   c. The same
   d. Increased if pumped

12. The purpose of a residual check valve in a cylinder is to
   a. Maintain a constant low pressure
   b. Allow pumping of the brakes
   c. Allow the fluid to return to the reservoir
   d. Control the speed of the returning fluid

13. Master cylinder piston travel must be carefully adjusted because
   a. It provides for the amount the brake pedal will be depressed before the brakes are applied
   b. Incorrect adjustment can cause brakes to drag
   c. It determines how much of the braking effort will be delivered to the front or rear wheels
   d. The master cylinder primary cup must clear the bypass port in the retracted position

14. A brake pedal that pulsates during braking may be caused by
   a. Leaking hoses
   b. Brakes out of adjustment
   c. Rotor run-out or eccentric drum
   d. High fluid

15. Insufficient clearance between the master cylinder pushrod and master cylinder piston can cause brake
   a. Drag
   b. Fade
   c. Fluid leak
   d. Grab

16. Grease soaked or glazed brake lining will
   a. Increase the co-efficiency of friction
   b. Have a tendency to cause the brake to slip or grab
   c. Require less pressure to apply the brake
   d. Have no noticeable effect on stopping

17. In order to stop a car when the power booster is not working, it is necessary to increase
   a. Pedal force
   b. Vacuum tank capacity
   c. Hydraulic pressure
   d. Vacuum line size

18. Single channel anti-lock braking acts only on
   a. Both front wheels
   b. A single front wheel
   c. A single rear wheel
   d. Both rear wheels

19. An integrated anti-lock brake system
   a. Does not require a vacuum brake booster
   b. Has electric power brakes
   c. Uses a vacuum brake booster
   d. Has its own air compressor

20. The modulator valves in the hydraulic control assembly of integrated anti-lock brakes regulate
   a. Power brake assist pressure
   b. Master cylinder input pressure
   c. Master cylinder output pressure
   d. Power brake input pressure

21. A non-integrated anti-lock brake system
   a. Uses a special master cylinder with a booster piston
   b. Uses a conventional dual master cylinder
   c. Does not need wheel speed sensors
   d. Works only on two wheels

22. Some anti-lock brake systems work together with
   a. The automatic speed control
   b. A variable volume vacuum modulator
   c. A traction control system
   d. A traction booster system

23. Hydraulic accumulator pressures may reach
   a. 140 000 kPa (20 000 psi)
   b. 140 kPa (200 psi)
   c. 14 kPa (20 psi)
   d. 14 000 kPa (2000 psi)

24. Before disconnecting ABS hydraulic lines
   a. Depressurize the accumulator
   b. Disconnect the computer
   c. Bleed the brakes
   d. Add brake fluid

25. In the rear wheel anti-lock brake systems (RWAL) the hydraulic controller has
   a. One isolation and one dump solenoid
   b. Two solenoid valves that are both normally open
   c. Two solenoid valves and two accumulators
   d. Two isolation solenoids that are both normally open

26. When first working on a hydro-boost brake system, which of these should you do first?
   a. Disconnect hydraulic lines at the booster
   b. Disconnect hydraulic lines at the steering pump
   c. Release master cylinder pressure
   d. Release accumulator pressure

27. The pedal pulsates only during hard braking on a car equipped with an anti-lock system. This is an indication of
   a. An out-of-round drum
   b. Normal system function
   c. A warped rotor
   d. A bad actuator

28. On a hydro-boost system brake pedal feedback to the driver is provided by the
   a. Reaction system
   b. Vacuum check valve operation
   c. Charcoal filter unit
   d. Vacuum diaphragm

29. If a power brake booster has a vacuum leak, all of the following conditions would exist except
   a. Pedal pulsation
   b. Rough engine idle
   c. Hissing sound
   d. Hard pedal

30. The RWAL/RABS system operates in three phases of ABS operation
   a. Hold, maintain and release
   b. Maintain, decrease and hold
   c. Maintain, decrease and increase
   d. Release, delay and decrease

31. A technician holds the power brake pedal in the depressed position. When the engine is started, the pedal sinks slightly. What does this indicate?
   a. A bad reaction disc
   b. A leaking check valve
   c. A defective control valve
   d. A normal operating booster

32. In general, anti-lock brake systems do not
   a. Improve steering control during an emergency braking situation
   b. Operate at vehicle speeds below 5 to 10 km/h
   c. Operate at speeds above 5 to 10 km/h
   d. Reduce stopping distances on wet pavement

33. When the anti-lock system malfunctions, the vehicle's brake system will
   a. Lock up the wheel during a normal stop
   b. Perform as a normal brake system
   c. Become inoperative
   d. The parking brake needs to be adjusted

34. The accumulator in a hydro-boost system
   a. Accumulates power steering fluid in pump reservoir
   b. Distributes pressure to the booster and steering gear
   c. Regulates pressure in the boost activity
   d. Stores pressure to provide power assisted brake application, in case engine stalls

35. A vehicle has a vacuum suspended power brake unit. When the engine is running and the brake pedal is not applied, there is
   a. Vacuum in the front and rear chambers
   b. Vacuum in the front chamber and atmospheric pressure in the rear chamber
   c. Atmospheric pressure only in the front chamber
   d. Vacuum present only in the front chamber

36. When a vehicle is equipped with a power brake unit
   a. Gasoline will not cause the flexible diaphragm to become porous
   b. The check valve must keep a small amount of fluid inside the unit
   c. The vacuum line should be installed lower than the booster
   d. The brakes should be bled with the engine off

37. When a wheel is turned by hand, this wheel speed sensor output should be at least
   a. 5 V DC
   b. 1 V AC
   c. 12 V AC
   d. 2.5 V DC

38. In what way does a hydro-boost differ from a vacuum brake booster?
   a. It uses a power steering pump as a power source
   b. It uses electricity instead of vacuum
   c. It uses no vacuum at low speeds
   d. They are the same but have different names

39. The _______ maintains a storage of vacuum in the booster when the engine is off, or when manifold vacuum drops.
   a. Diaphragm assembly
   b. Air valve
   c. Floating control valve
   d. Check valve

40. When working on a vehicle, safety experts recommend that the technician
   a. Wear safety glasses
   b. Wear a bump cap
   c. Wear gloves
   d. All of the above

41. Rear brakes tend to lock up during hard braking before front brakes because
   a. The rear brakes are larger
   b. The vehicle weight transfers forward away from the rear wheels
   c. The rear tires have less traction
   d. Drum brakes cool better than disc

42. Most fluid manufacturers recommend using _______.
   a. DOT 2
   b. DOT 3
   c. DOT 4
   d. DOT 5

43. Used brake fluid should be disposed of
   a. According to local or provincial regulations
   b. As hazardous waste
   c. By burning in an MOE certified facility
   d. By recycling

44. The rubber used in most brake system components will swell if exposed to
   a. Engine oil or ATF
   b. Moisture in the air
   c. DOT 5 brake fluid
   d. Water

45. The edge-code lettering on the side of friction material tells the technician
   a. The coefficient of friction code
   b. The quality of the friction material
   c. The temperature of the resistance rating
   d. Material water resistance

46. Brakes failing to release can occur if
   a. The master cylinder is overfilled
   b. The vent port is clogged or covered
   c. The replenishing port is clogged or covered
   d. Master cylinder cap is missing

47. The proper brake-bleeding sequence for a front/rear split hydraulic system is
   a. Right front, right rear, left front, left rear
   b. Right rear, left rear, right front, left front

c. Left front, left rear, right front, right rear
d. Left rear, right rear, left front, right front

48. After a disc brake pad replacement, the brake pedal went to the floor the first time the brake pedal was depressed. The most likely cause was
a. Air in the lines
b. Improper disc brake pad installation
c. Lack of proper lubrication of the caliper slides
d. Normal operation

49. Disc brake rotors should be machine if rusted.
a. True
b. False

50. Before checking the brake fluid level in a typical integral ABS, the technician should pump the brake pedal
a. 2 or 3 times
b. 3 or 4 times
c. 5 to 10 times
d. 25 times or more

51. A brake lining with a high coefficient of friction generally
a. Is called a hard lining
b. Resists fade better than a lining with a low friction coefficient
c. Requires less pedal pressure than a lining with a low friction coefficient
d. Wears more slowly than a low friction coefficient lining

52. Drum brakes must be periodically adjusted to compensate for
a. Loose wheel bearings
b. Brake fluid evaporation
c. Poor design
d. Lining wear

53. When brake fluid absorbs moisture, the moisture
a. Has no effect on the fluid's boiling point
b. Raises the fluid's boiling point
c. Lowers the fluid's boiling point
d. Lowers the fluid's ability to be compressed

54. The amplitude of the WSS output voltage will increase
a. As the air gap at the WSS decreases
b. The speed of rotation of the wheel decreases
c. As battery strength decreases
d. As battery strength increases

55. A solenoid valve doesn't seem to operate. The correct way to test it is
a. With an ohmmeter
b. By putting 12 V to one side and grounding the other
c. By substituting the solenoid with a test light
d. Connecting an ammeter in place of the solenoid

ANSWERS

1. b
2. a
3. d
4. b
5. b
6. d
7. b
8. a
9. c
10. b
11. c
12. a
13. d
14. c
15. a
16. b
17. a
18. d
19. a
20. c
21. b
22. c
23. d
24. a
25. a
26. d
27. b
28. a
29. a
30. a
31. d
32. b
33. b
34. d
35. a
36. d
37. b
38. a
39. d
40. d
41. b
42. b
43. a
44. a
45. a
46. b
47. b
48. d
49. b
50. d
51. d
52. d
53. c
54. a
55. a

APPENDIX 6

Electrical/Electronic Systems: Sample Interprovincial Red Seal Examination

1. The resistance of copper wire _______ as its temperature increases.
   a. Increases
   b. Stays the same
   c. Decreases
   d. Fluctuates
2. A load test is being performed on a battery that has just been charged. The technician removes the surface charge and tests the battery with a load of _______ for 15 seconds.
   a. One-half of the CCA rating
   b. One-half of the reserve-capacity rating
   c. Twice the CCA rating
   d. One-half of the CA rating
3. On a negative ground battery system, ________.
   a. Disconnect the ground cable first and reconnect the positive cable last
   b. Disconnect the ground cable first and reconnect the positive cable first
   c. Disconnect the positive cable first and reconnect the ground cable first
   d. Disconnect the positive cable first and reconnect the ground cable last
4. Normal battery drain (parasitic drain) on a vehicle with many computer and electronic circuits is
   a. 150 to 300 milliamperes
   b. 2 to 3 amperes
   c. 20 to 30 milliamperes
   d. 0.3 to 0.4 ampere
5. The battery open circuit voltage measures 13.0 volts when the engine is first shut off. This indicates _______.
   a. Overcharging
   b. Undercharging
   c. Normal surface charge
   d. A sulphated battery
6. When the key is turned to the start position, the solenoid chatters and the interior lights flicker. The most likely cause is
   a. Low battery voltage
   b. A defective pull-in winding
   c. A defective hold-in winding
   d. A defective starter motor
7. A rebuilt starter cranks the engine too slowly for starting. The battery has been charged and passes a load test. The problem could be
   a. A defective ignition switch
   b. Lack of engine compression
   c. High resistance at the battery cable connections
   d. Lack of resistance at the battery cable connections
8. Whenever jump-starting ______.
   a. The last connection should be the positive post of the dead battery
   b. The bumpers of the two vehicles should touch to provide a good ground
   c. The AC generator wiring should be disconnected on both vehicles
   d. The last connection should be the engine block of the dead vehicle

9. When making the jumper cable connections to jump-start a computer-equipped vehicle with another computer-equipped vehicle ______.

a. The ignition switch on the dead vehicle should be in the "off" position
b. The ignition switches on both vehicles should be in the "on" position
c. The ignition switch on the service vehicle should be in the "on" position
d. The ignition switches on both vehicles should be in the "off" position

10. A starter draws too many amperes on a current draw test. This could be due to

a. A defective starter motor
b. An overcharged battery
c. High resistance in the starter cables
d. A poor ground at the starter

11. The engine cranks slowly: the battery passes all tests and a starter current draw test shows low amperage flow to the starter. The technician suspects high resistance in the battery cables. What test is next?

a. Test each cable with an ohmmeter
b. Remove each cable for visual inspection
c. Voltage drop the starter insulated and ground circuits
d. Substitute the suspected items with known good cables

12. The first check for a cranking problem (after verifying the condition) is

a. A starter current draw test
b. Voltage drop the starter circuits
c. Test the battery
d. Test the control circuit

13. Many manual transmissions use a switch to prevent starter operation, unless the

a. Transmission is in neutral
b. Clutch is engaged
c. Parking brake is on
d. Clutch pedal is depressed

14. A rebuilt starter rotates at high speed, but the engine does not turn. The most likely cause is

a. A missing solenoid return spring
b. A defective starter drive
c. The solenoid contact disc is installed backwards
d. Rough teeth on the flywheel ring gear

15. Starter motor brushes should be replaced if worn to less than ______% of their original length.

a. 10
b. 25
c. 50
d. 75

16. The wire at the output terminal of an AC generator connects to the ______.

a. Ignition switch
b. Starter solenoid "S" terminal
c. Battery positive terminal or junction
d. Fuse panel

17. The charge light does not come on when the key is turned to the "run" position. This could be caused by

a. A burned-out bulb
b. An open circuit to the sending unit
c. An open diode
d. A short inside the AC generator

18. Which of the following is the correct range for charging voltage when measured across the battery terminals?

a. 12.5 to 14 V
b. 13 to 14 V
c. 13.5 to 15 V
d. 14.5 to 16.5 V

19. A fusible line between the battery and AC generator is hot to the touch. The charging system voltage is 9.8 V. This could indicate

a. Overcharging
b. Undercharging
c. A poor connection at the battery
d. High resistance at the fusible link

20. Charging system amperage output is lower than specified by the vehicle manufacturer. The technician suspects a faulty voltage regulator. What test should be performed next?

a. Voltage drop testing of the regulator wiring
b. Determine if the correct regulator has been installed
c. Bypass the regulator, if possible
d. Test for a poor regulator ground

21. Maximum voltage output from the AC generator is regulated by

a. Controlling the field circuit
b. Controlling the stator circuit
c. Adding resistance at the output terminal
d. The action of the diodes

22. The regulator is bypassed (full-field) on a "B" circuit by

a. Disconnecting the regulator
b. Connecting a jumper wire from "battery +" to the "field" terminal
c. Grounding the field circuit before the regulator
d. Connecting a jumper wire from the "field" terminal to ground

23. The regulator is bypassed (full-field) on a "A" circuit by

a. Connecting a jumper wire from the "stator" terminal to the "field" terminal
b. Grounding the field circuit (after the rotor) before the regulator
c. Connecting a jumper wire from "battery +" to the "field" terminal
d. Removing the regulator from the AC generator

24. Regulators can be bypassed by full-fielding on all AC generators.

a. Yes, except delta-wound stators
b. Only on some systems
c. Not with heavy-duty AC generators
d. Only with wye wound stators

25. When voltage drop testing the AC generator insulated and ground circuits, the charging circuit is loaded to produce ______ amperes.
- **a.** 20
- **b.** 30
- **c.** 40
- **d.** Maximum

26. Maximum current output tests are usually performed at ______.
- **a.** Idle speed
- **b.** 2000 rpm
- **c.** 3000 rpm
- **d.** 4000 rpm

27. Delta connected stators produce higher output at ______ than a wye connected stator.
- **a.** Idle
- **b.** Higher speeds
- **c.** Lower RPM
- **d.** All speeds

28. Wye connected stators produce higher output at ______ compared to a delta-connected stator.
- **a.** Very high RPM
- **b.** High speeds
- **c.** All speeds
- **d.** Low speed

29. A rotor is being tested with an ohmmeter by measuring the resistance between the slip rings. Specifications call for the value of 4 to 4.5 ohms: this rotor measures 3 ohms. The rotor is
- **a.** Open
- **b.** Grounded
- **c.** Shorted
- **d.** Serviceable

30. Delta wound stators usually cannot be tested for ______ with an ohmmeter.
- **a.** Opens
- **b.** Grounds
- **c.** Output resistance
- **d.** Shorts to ground

31. Diodes may be checked with a 12-volt battery and test light or a digital multi-meter with a "diode-check" function. A good diode should
- **a.** Block current flow in both directions
- **b.** Allow current flow in both directions
- **c.** Allow current flow in only one direction
- **d.** Light the test light in both directions

32. An ohmmeter on the 30 K scale reads 1.93 on a digital face. How many ohms of resistance is being measured?
- **a.** 193
- **b.** 1 930
- **c.** 19.30
- **d.** 19 300

33. In a parallel 12 V circuit with 3 bulbs (each 10 Ω resistance), which statement below would be correct if one of the bulbs burned out (had an open)?
- **a.** The total resistance would be the same
- **b.** The total resistance would be lower
- **c.** The current would increase in the circuit
- **d.** The current would decrease in the circuit

34. A meter reads OL. This means the component or circuit being measured ______.
- **a.** Is shorted
- **b.** Is open
- **c.** Is grounded
- **d.** Has low resistance

35. What makes a meter a high-impedance tester?
- **a.** The amount of current the meter can safely carry
- **b.** The effective resistance of the meter circuit
- **c.** The maximum voltage that can be measured
- **d.** The maximum resistance that can be measured

36. When the parking lights are turned on, the left light is dim while the right light is a normal brightness. When the brake is applied, the left light totally goes out, while the right side works properly. What is the problem?
- **a.** A bad ground at the left bulb
- **b.** A shorted left bulb
- **c.** A bad switch
- **d.** A shorted right bulb

37. On a single-headlight system, the right-side high beam does not work: low beam is working. The probable cause is ______.
- **a.** A bad dimmer switch
- **b.** A bad headlight ground
- **c.** An open wire to the switch
- **d.** A bad headlight

38. A vehicle's reverse lights are always on, even in "drive." The most likely cause is
- **a.** The wrong bulb was installed for the reverse lights
- **b.** A misadjusted neutral safety switch
- **c.** An open neutral safety switch
- **d.** A grounded neutral safety switch

39. A corroded light socket would likely cause
- **a.** A fuse to blow in the circuit
- **b.** A feedback to occur to another circuit
- **c.** The light to be dim as a result of reduced current flow
- **d.** Damage to the bulb as a result of decreased voltage

40. The technician is checking a headlight door motor with an ammeter, which shows excessive current draw. The most likely cause is
- **a.** A binding headlight door
- **b.** A bad ground
- **c.** A corroded connection
- **d.** Worn brushes in the motor

41. The blower is running slow at all speeds. The most likely cause is
- **a.** A blown resistor
- **b.** Dry bearings in the motor
- **c.** An open blower switch
- **d.** A plugged defroster vent hose

42. Airbag wiring is coloured ______.
- **a.** Red
- **b.** Orange

c. Yellow
d. Blue

43. Only _______ solder should be used to join electrical wiring.
a. Rosin-core
b. Flux-core
c. Acid-core
d. Pure lead

44. Technicians must be very careful when repairing deployed dual-stage airbag systems as
a. Only one stage may have been deployed and the system is still "alive"
b. The airbag powder is very toxic
c. Broken plastic from the airbag mounting is sharp and may cause personal injury
d. Diagnostic trouble codes (DTC), still in memory, may prevent the new airbag from deploying

45. Many "low tire" warning systems use wheel mounted pressure sensors or _______ to monitor tire pressures.
a. The ABS wheel speed sensors
b. The engine speed (RPM) signal
c. Vehicle height sensors
d. Driveshaft speed on rear-wheel-drive vehicles

46. The most effective auto-theft deterrent is the
a. Shifter lever lock
b. Brake pedal lock
c. Vehicle immobilizer
d. Steering wheel locking bar

47. Damaged vehicles that are to be scrapped should have the airbags deployed by using a 12 V battery, remote switch, and wiring. How long should the technician wait before handling the deployed module?
a. 10 minutes
b. 20 minutes
c. 30 minutes
d. One hour

48. It is important to never touch the glass of a halogen bulb with bare fingers, because
a. The sharp glass may cause finger injury
b. The bulb will go "cloudy"
c. Oils from the skin may cause the bulb to break
d. Oils from the skin will reduce the light intensity

49. Many in-tank fuel pump modules also include a
a. Fuel tank pressure sensor
b. Fuel temperature sensor
c. Fuel-level gauge
d. Kilometres (miles) to zero sensor

50. A battery that becomes totally discharged (and then recharged or replaced) may cause the PCM to lose DTCs and
a. The radio to "lock"
b. Erase all odometer information
c. Require PCM resetting
d. Limit vehicle speed for 30 km (20 mi) until the PCM "relearns"

ANSWERS

1. a	18. c	35. b
2. a	19. d	36. a
3. b	20. c	37. d
4. c	21. a	38. b
5. c	22. b	39. c
6. a	23. b	40. a
7. c	24. b	41. b
8. d	25. a	42. c
9. d	26. b	43. a
10. a	27. b	44. a
11. c	28. d	45. a
12. c	29. c	46. c
13. d	30. a	47. a
14. b	31. c	48. c
15. c	32. b	49. c
16. c	33. d	50. a
17. a	34. b	

APPENDIX 7

Heating and Air Conditioning: Sample Interprovincial Red Seal Examination Questions

1. The amount of heat from the heater changes with engine speed. The most likely cause is
   a. A defective thermostat
   b. A defective water pump
   c. A low coolant level
   d. Incorrect water/antifreeze ratio
2. The blower motor only operates on high speed. The most likely cause is due to a defective
   a. Blower motor
   b. Resistor pack
   c. Blower motor ground
   d. Electrical connector
3. An engine overheats (temperature gauge approaches 125°C (260°F) if driven at slow speeds, but does not overheat at highway speeds. The most likely cause is
   a. Low coolant level
   b. Inoperative cooling fan
   c. Defective water pump
   d. Incorrect water/antifreeze ratio
4. The heater blows barely warm air. The technician touches the upper radiator hose after the engine has been running for 30 minutes. The hose is warm, but not hot. What is the problem?
   a. The engine thermostat is defective
   b. Incorrect coolant has been installed
   c. The water pump is defective
   d. The heater core is plugged
5. What is the default position of the heater dampers (doors) in the event of a failure with the vacuum supply to the control head?
   a. Defrost
   b. Panel
   c. Floor
   d. Vent
6. Where are the bleeder valves (if used) located in the cooling system?
   a. In the heater hoses
   b. Near the high points of the system
   c. On the radiator side of the thermostat
   d. At the lowest point of the system
7. What position should the heater control valve be in when the air conditioning is on and the panel controls are in the "max air" setting?
   a. Fully open
   b. Almost closed
   c. About 50% open
   d. Fully closed
8. Both heater hoses are very hot to the touch. This confirms that the
   a. Heater control valve is closed
   b. Water pump is defective
   c. The engine thermostat is sticking closed
   d. Heater core is clear

9. Clear water is dropping out of the heater/evaporator housing when the air conditioning is being used: this indicates
  a. A leak in the heater core or hoses
  b. Condensation from the heater core
  c. Normal evaporator condensation
  d. That the heater control valve is still in the "open" position

10. The extra heat required to transform a substance from one state to another is called _____.
  a. Energy heat
  b. Latent heat
  c. Vaporization heat
  d. Kinetic heat

11. Increasing the pressure on a vapour by compression
  a. Lowers the temperature
  b. Increases the volume
  c. Increases the temperature
  d. Decreases the liquid volume

12. Relative humidity is the percentage of how much moisture is present in the air compared to
  a. Zero humidity
  b. How much moisture the air is capable of holding
  c. A solid column of pure water
  d. The moisture level at 20°C (68°F)

13. The purpose of an air conditioning compressor is to
  a. Pressurize the liquid refrigerant
  b. Add lubricant to the vapour
  c. Raise the pressure and temperature of the refrigerant
  d. Raise the pressure and lower the temperature of the refrigerant

14. The purpose of the condenser is to
  a. Allow outside air to heat the refrigerant
  b. Act as a refrigerant reservoir
  c. Change the refrigerant vapour into a liquid
  d. Change the refrigerant liquid into a vapour

15. The discharge line from the compressor is also known as the
  a. Low side
  b. Vapour side
  c. Suction side
  d. High side

16. The purpose of the thermostatic expansion valve (TXV) or the orifice tube is to
  a. Reduce the refrigerant pressure in the evaporator
  b. Increase the refrigerant pressure in the evaporator
  c. Ensure that evaporator pressure does not exceed compressor pressure
  d. Prevent any moisture in the system from reaching the evaporator

17. The purpose of the evaporator is to
  a. Evaporate any moisture (humidity) inside the vehicle
  b. Allow the refrigerant to evaporate and absorb heat
  c. Allow the refrigerant to boil and give up heat
  d. Allow the refrigerant to condense back into a liquid

18. The international agreement to limit production and import of new CFCs is called the
  a. Montreal Protocol
  b. Canadian Accord
  c. Canadian Protocol
  d. Quebec Accord

19. The accumulator or receiver-drier contains a drying agent called _______ to absorb any water in the refrigerant.
  a. Drying powder
  b. Silica paper
  c. Desiccant
  d. Condensing media

20. Accumulators are located on the low side of the system, receiver-driers are located
  a. On the high side
  b. Also on the low side
  c. Either on the high or low sides
  d. Always between the evaporator and the compressor

21. An H-valve is a form of
  a. Orifice tube
  b. Oil separator valve
  c. Condenser control valve
  d. Thermostatic expansion valve

22. CFC-12 (R-12) is no longer used in new air conditioning systems because
  a. The chlorine in the CFC-12 attacks the ozone layer
  b. The hydrogen in the CFC-12 attacks the ozone layer
  c. The R-12 is corrosive to aluminum condensers and evaporators
  d. Chlorine for the R-12 refrigerant is no longer available

23. The air conditioning compressor is lubricated by oil circulating with the refrigerant. The oil recommended by the automakers for an HFC-134a system is
  a. Polyalkeline glycol (PAG) oil
  b. Mineral refrigerant oil
  c. Gel-based petroleum oil
  d. Compressor oil

24. The cycling-clutch switch shuts off the _____ when the evaporator temperature is close to 0° C (32° F).
  a. Thermostatic expansion valve (TXV)
  b. Compressor
  c. Evaporator fan
  d. Electric condenser fan

25. The low-pressure switch shuts off the compressor if the refrigerant charge is lost, or very low. The switch also prevents the compressor from operating when
  a. Outside temperatures are very hot
  b. High side pressures are too high
  c. Outside temperatures are very low
  d. The compressor clutch is slipping

26. HFC-134a pressure gauges have a blue face. What colour is the HFC-134a refrigerant container?
    a. White
    b. Green
    c. Blue
    d. Red
27. Variable displacement compressors do not shut off. They control the volume of refrigerant flowing through the evaporator by
    a. Bypassing refrigerant back to the compressor inlet
    b. Storing excessive refrigerant in the accumulator
    c. Changing the swash plate angle
    d. Varying the inlet orifice at the compressor
28. Before connecting the pressure gauges or discharging the system
    a. Test the operation of the gauge set
    b. Check the cycling clutch apply rates
    c. Identify the refrigerant
    d. Hook up a recovery station to the gauge set
29. Both high-pressure and low-pressure gauges are connected to the service ports; the controls are set to "max air" and the engine speed is 1500 rpm. Both high side and low side pressures are too low. This could indicate
    a. Low refrigerant charge
    b. Restricted airflow past the condenser
    c. Evaporator fan not functioning
    d. A plugged orifice tube
30. Both high-side and low-side pressures are too high. This could indicate the system is overcharged or
    a. Insufficient air is passing through the evaporator
    b. The orifice tube is plugged
    c. Insufficient air is passing through the condenser
    d. The compressor did not shut off
31. The technician can test for trapped air inside the refrigerant container by
    a. Checking the outside of the container for frost
    b. Checking the pressure versus temperature of the container
    c. Weighing the container
    d. Sending the container to a special laboratory for analysis
32. An oily area is discovered around the front clutch assembly of the air conditioning compressor. This indicates
    a. A slipping compressor clutch
    b. A piston leak inside the compressor
    c. A refrigerant leak at the compressor seal
    d. Excessive oil in the compressor
33. The air conditioning compressor on an orifice tube system constantly cycles on and off every 10 seconds. This would indicate
    a. The system is operating normally
    b. The air conditioning compressor clutch wiring has a short circuit
    c. The system is low on refrigerant
    d. Moisture in the system
34. To check for a plugged orifice tube, connect gauges to the high and low side ports. Run the A/C system for 10 minutes, shut off the system and observe the pressures. If the orifice tube is functioning normally, then
    a. Both high and low side pressures should equalize quickly
    b. The low side pressure will stay low and the high side pressure will stay high
    c. The low side pressure should exceed the high side pressure
    d. The low side pressure must be at least 140 kPa (20 psi) lower than the high side pressure
35. Refrigerant leaks are best located with
    a. A halide torch
    b. Dye sprayed on the suspected area
    c. An electronic leak detector
    d. A scan tool set on "leak detection"
36. When discharging the refrigerant into a recovery station, any oil discharged with the refrigerant should be
    a. Kept with the recovery station as it contains refrigerant
    b. Used to lubricate any new components
    c. Measured to ensure the same amount of new oil is added when recharging
    d. Retained for filtering and reuse
37. Some manufacturers recommend that mineral refrigerant oil be used to lubricate any "O" rings replaced on an HFC-134a system, since PAG oil
    a. Does not lubricate well
    b. Attracts moisture
    c. Hardens with oxygen contact
    d. Has poor sealing qualities
38. An A/C system has been open to the atmosphere for three days; what should be replaced?
    a. The refrigerant oil
    b. The accumulator or receiver drier
    c. Any non-barrier hoses
    d. The orifice tube or TXV
39. The system is put under a deep vacuum (evacuated) to remove
    a. Any remaining oil
    b. Dirt or contamination
    c. Any moisture in the system
    d. Any loose desiccant
40. Service valves used on all HFC-134a systems are
    a. Quick-disconnect
    b. Only on the low side
    c. Schrader type
    d. On the high-side only
41. The amount of refrigerant required will be found either in the service manual or
    a. On a tag or sticker located on the vehicle
    b. Listed on the recovery station
    c. On a chart based on engine size
    d. Based on a small, medium or large system
42. Recharging procedures vary between makes. Some automakers recommend a liquid charge with the engine shut off. If the total amount of refrigerant did not

go into the system, start the engine, engage the compressor and
   a. Liquid charge the low side at the compressor
   b. Liquid charge the high side
   c. Vapour charge the low side
   d. Vapour charge the high side

43. Other manufacturers recommend a vapour charge only. Install a small amount of refrigerant to lubricate the compressor, close the low pressure switch (if installed), start the engine, engage the compressor and
   a. Liquid charge the low side at the compressor
   b. Liquid charge the high side
   c. Vapour charge the low side
   d. Vapour charge the high side

44. The operation of the system can be best checked by
   a. Noting the cycling rate of the compressor
   b. Measuring the outlet temperature at the center A/C vent
   c. Inspecting the sight glass at the accumulator
   d. Feeling the temperature of the hoses

45. The necessary parts to retrofit a CFC-12 system to an HFC-134a system are
   a. Always ordered separately
   b. Often included in a kit
   c. The same for domestic vehicles and the same for imports
   d. Often not available for many vehicles

46. The CFC-12 service fitting are replaced (during a retrofit) with HFC-134a fitting to match the HFC-134a equipment and
   a. Prevent leakage
   b. Allow the PAG oil to be installed during charging
   c. To prevent cross-contamination of the refrigerants
   d. To prevent the use of the wrong pressure gauges

47. The correct amount of HFC-134a installed during a retrofit is
   a. 90% of the CFC-12 capacity plus 115 grams (4 ounces)
   b. 90% of the CFC-12 capacity minus 115 grams (4 ounces)
   c. 90% of the CFC-12 capacity
   d. Equal to the CFC-12 capacity minus 115 grams (4 ounces)

48. The recovered CFC-12 is not added to the next CFC-12 repair because
   a. It may be contaminated
   b. Mineral refrigerant oil is mixed in with the CFC-12
   c. It is illegal to charge a CFC-12 system
   d. New CFC-12 refrigerant is more efficient

49. Using only mineral refrigeration oil in an HFC-134a system will cause
   a. Damage to the compressor
   b. Damage to the barrier hoses
   c. A restriction in the accumulator
   d. Loss of at least 10% of A/C cooling efficiency

50. Canadian technicians who service air conditioning must complete a __________ on Environmental Awareness for ODS Control.
   a. One-day course
   b. 5-day course of studies
   c. 30-hour certification course
   d. 3-day certification course

ANSWERS

1. c	**18.** a	**35.** c
2. b	**19.** c	**36.** c
3. b	**20.** a	**37.** b
4. a	**21.** d	**38.** b
5. a	**22.** a	**39.** c
6. b	**23.** a	**40.** a
7. d	**24.** b	**41.** a
8. d	**25.** c	**42.** c
9. c	**26.** c	**43.** c
10. b	**27.** c	**44.** b
11. c	**28.** c	**45.** b
12. b	**29.** a	**46.** c
13. c	**30.** c	**47.** b
14. c	**31.** b	**48.** c
15. d	**32.** c	**49.** a
16. a	**33.** c	**50.** a
17. b	**34.** a	

APPENDIX 8

Engine Performance: Sample Interprovincial Red Seal Examination Questions

1. Retarded ignition timing reduces engine power; exhaust temperatures will
   a. Cool
   b. Remain the same
   c. Rise
   d. Fluctuate
2. The burning rate of the air/fuel mixture varies with ratio changes, such that
   a. Richer mixtures burn slower, lean mixtures burn faster
   b. Richer mixtures burn slower, lean mixtures burn very slow
   c. Richer mixtures burn faster, lean mixtures burn slower
   d. Richer mixtures burn faster, lean mixtures burn very fast
3. If the base ignition timing is set incorrectly with an extra 10° of advance at idle speed
   a. Only the idle timing will be incorrect
   b. Maximum advance, at high RPM, will not change
   c. Timing will be advanced 10° too far at any RPM
   d. The advance rate gradually decreases as the RPM rises
4. Computer-controlled engines often "trim" engine idle speeds by constantly varying the ignition timing. Setting the base timing (if adjustable) requires
   a. Adjusting the timing at a higher RPM
   b. Subtracting 10° from the crankshaft damper reading
   c. Lowering the idle speed to 400 rpm, which is below the point where the computer is influencing the timing
   d. Following the exact procedures in the service manual for removing the computer influence
5. Base timing on most DIS and COP ignition systems is
   a. Set at the crankshaft sensor
   b. Not adjustable
   c. Not required unless the ignition module is replaced
   d. Checked through an access port in the bell housing
6. A pickup coil is being measured with a digital multimeter set to the kilo ohm position. The specification for the resistance is 500 to 1500 Ω. The digital face reads 0.826. This indicates that the pickup coil is
   a. Okay
   b. Shorted
   c. Open
   d. Grounded
7. A random misfire diagnostic trouble code (PO300) has been set on a V-6, dual-overhead camshaft, port-injected engine. This code may be caused by
   a. A cracked spark plug insulator
   b. Using fuel with too high an octane
   c. An incorrect base timing adjustment
   d. An EGR valve that does not open
8. The engine has a rough idle but runs well when above idle speed. This could be caused by
   a. An EGR valve stuck partially open
   b. An EGR valve that does not open

c. A weak ignition system
d. A restriction in the air cleaner

9. The engine misses on hills or on hard acceleration. When viewing the scope, the technician sees that the #5 firing line is about 5 to 6 kV higher than the rest, and the spark line slants down from the firing line to the coil oscillations. What is the most likely cause?
   a. A fuel-fouled plug on #5
   b. A high-resistance plug wire on #5
   c. A plug with a worn electrode on #5
   d. High resistance at the coil to cap high tension wire
10. The PCV valve is frozen in the closed position. What is the most likely result?
   a. Oil film in the air intake
   b. Spark knock during acceleration
   c. High idle
   d. Blue exhaust smoke from the tailpipe
11. The PCM tests many components for correct operation on an OBD II equipped vehicle. It tests the EGR valve by opening the valve and monitoring the change at what sensor/s?
   a. The engine coolant temperature (ECT)
   b. The oxygen sensor (O2S) and/or manifold absolute pressure (MAP)
   c. Mass airflow (MAF)
   d. Both the upstream and downstream oxygen sensors
12. The technician connects a scan tool to a vehicle equipped with port fuel injection. Long-term fuel trim is +20%. This could be caused by
   a. An exhaust leak in front of the oxygen sensor
   b. A dripping fuel injector
   c. Fuel pressure too high
   d. A saturated carbon canister
13. HC and CO are high and CO_2 and O_2 are low. The most likely cause is
   a. Too rich
   b. EGR stuck open
   c. Ignition misfire
   d. Too lean
14. The spark lines are short in duration (.60 ms maximum) and the firing lines are low on all cylinders. What is the most likely cause?
   a. The coil secondary is shorted between windings
   b. The rotor to cap air gap is too close
   c. Excessive resistance at the cap to rotor button
   d. Excessive dwell in the primary
15. High O2S voltage could be due to
   a. A lean exhaust
   b. A rich exhaust
   c. A restricted catalytic converter
   d. An open PCV valve
16. Checking for an injector pulse signal is done with a
   a. Noid light
   b. Vacuum hose and 12 V test lamp
   c. Spark tester
   d. DVOM on "pulse CK"
17. Ballast resistors were used on some early electronic ignition systems to control primary current. Current is now controlled with
   a. In-line resistors
   b. Not required with computerized ignition
   c. Variable dwell
   d. Resistor wires
18. The injector "clicks" during cranking when a "no start" problem is being diagnosed; this indicates
   a. The fuel injector is okay
   b. The problem must be ignition
   c. The crankshaft sensor (or pickup) signal is present
   d. That the ignition module is providing a signal
19. Ignition coils are often tested with an/a
   a. Ohmmeter
   b. Voltmeter
   c. Ammeter
   d. Scan tool
20. Waste-spark ignition systems (also known as DIS) fire the spark plugs every crankshaft revolution. Coil-on-plug ignitions fire the plugs __________.
   a. Once every revolution
   b. Twice each revolution
   c. Once every two revolutions
   d. Twice every two revolutions
21. Platinum and iridium spark plugs should be regapped (if needed) only
   a. After being retorqued once
   b. On the first plug inspection
   c. When they are new
   d. The gap is never changed
22. A highway vehicle is experiencing short spark plug life. OE plugs are being used, fuel mixtures and ignition timing are correct. What is usually the next step?
   a. Install plugs that are one heat range colder
   b. Richen the fuel mixture
   c. Install plugs one heat range hotter
   d. Retard the ignition timing
23. An oscilloscope pattern shows a "hump" in the dwell section. This indicates
   a. High resistance in the ignition primary
   b. A cross-fire between primary and secondary circuits
   c. The action of current-limiting variable dwell
   d. Transistor leakage
24. Throttle position sensor (TPS) voltage at closed throttle is usually about ____% of the TPS input voltage.
   a. 90
   b. 0
   c. 10
   d. 3
25. The manifold absolute pressure (MAP) sensor is used by the computer to sense
   a. Throttle plate position
   b. Intake valve opening
   c. Engine load
   d. Heated air cleaner operation

26. MAP sensors are often not used with _______ fuel injection.
- **a.** Mass air
- **b.** Throttle-body
- **c.** Speed-density
- **d.** Port

27. Barometric pressure (BARO) sensors are used to sense barometric pressure. They are usually incorporated with the ________ sensor.
- **a.** MAF
- **b.** ACT
- **c.** MAP
- **d.** O2S

28. The engine coolant temperature (ECT) sensor is usually checked with a scan tool or tested by measuring voltage at the signal wire. As the engine warms up, the voltage (on a single stage sensor) should
- **a.** Decrease
- **b.** Increase
- **c.** Not change
- **d.** Stay at 5 V

29. Unplugging the ECT sensor will send a _______ signal to the computer.
- **a.** Warm engine
- **b.** Boiling coolant
- **c.** Very cold engine
- **d.** Hot engine

30. A poor connection at the coolant temperature sensor could cause ________ with some engines.
- **a.** Engine misfire at high RPM
- **b.** A richer fuel mixture
- **c.** The engine to overheat
- **d.** A leaner fuel mixture

31. Speed-density fuel injection systems do not use a/an _______ sensor
- **a.** Manifold absolute pressure (MAP)
- **b.** Throttle position (TPS)
- **c.** Mass airflow (MAF)
- **d.** Engine coolant temperature (ECT)

32. Diagnostic trouble codes (DTC) are stored in ______ and can be erased if the battery is disconnected.
- **a.** EEPROM
- **b.** ROM
- **c.** PROM
- **d.** RAM

33. Adaptive strategies that compensate for wear and aging are a function of KAM. The adaptive information stored in KAM will be lost if
- **a.** A scan tool is connected to the system
- **b.** The vehicle is not driven for 10 days, or more
- **c.** The battery is disconnected
- **d.** Any DTCs are displayed

34. "Flash codes" are often used to diagnose OBD I vehicles. OBD II vehicles normally require the use of _________ to retrieve codes.
- **a.** An analog voltmeter
- **b.** A scan tool
- **c.** A meter that reads frequency
- **d.** A laptop computer

35. OBD II catalytic converters are monitored by
- **a.** Oxygen sensors in both exhaust manifolds
- **b.** Oxygen sensors before and after the converter
- **c.** A temperature sensor in the converter
- **d.** Pressure sensors in the exhaust headpipe/s

36. When testing a catalytic converter with an infared pyrometer, the converter outlet temperature should be _____ than the inlet temperature if the converter is functioning.
- **a.** The same as
- **b.** Cooler than
- **c.** Much cooler than
- **d.** Hotter than

37. A restricted exhaust can be diagnosed with a vacuum gauge or by
- **a.** Road testing at wide-open throttle
- **b.** Measuring the back-pressure with a pressure gauge
- **c.** Comparing the exhaust manifold temperature with the headpipe temperature
- **d.** Measuring exhaust volume at the tailpipe

38. Number 2 diesel fuel is used
- **a.** In extreme cold
- **b.** All year round in cold climates
- **c.** In the winter
- **d.** In the summer

39. Diesel fuel should never be stored in ______ containers.
- **a.** Stainless steel
- **b.** Plastic
- **c.** Galvanized
- **d.** Non-galvanized

40. Carburetors that use phenolic floats should have the floats replaced when the carburetor is overhauled because
- **a.** Cracks often appear on the float
- **b.** The float becomes lighter
- **c.** The float absorbs fuel
- **d.** The phenolic plastic becomes soft and spongy

41. A feedback carburetor fuel system is being tested with a dwellmeter. The engine is running at 3000 rpm and the dwellmeter is fixed at 54°. This would indicate that the exhaust is
- **a.** Lean
- **b.** Normal
- **c.** Rich
- **d.** Extremely lean

42. Inertia safety switches are designed to ______ in the event of an accident.
- **a.** Shut off the electric fuel pump
- **b.** Kill the ignition system
- **c.** Shut down the fuel injectors
- **d.** Isolate the battery from the vehicle

43. Fuel pressure is being checked on a port fuel injection system that uses a vacuum modulated pressure regulator. When the throttle is opened quickly, fuel pressure should
- **a.** Rise
- **b.** Drop
- **c.** Not change
- **d.** Go down and then rise

44. A ground-side controlled sequential fuel injection system is being tested. When the technician grounds the injector wiring harness and the injector "clicks," then
 a. The injector is faulty
 b. The injector is serviceable
 c. This test could burn out the injector
 d. The injector must be grounded for at least 5 seconds for the test to be valid

45. The fuel pressure on a port fuel injection system is being tested. When the engine is shut off, the fuel pressure drops to zero within 20 seconds. If the fuel line from the tank to the rail is squeezed shut (or a shut-off valve is installed) the fuel pressure does not drop. This indicates
 a. A leak in the pressure regulator
 b. The injectors are leaking
 c. The non-return valve in the fuel pump is leaking
 d. The system is normal

46. The technician removes the vacuum hose from a fuel pressure regulator and fuel squirts out of the regulator: What is the most likely cause?
 a. One or more fuel injectors are leaking
 b. Fuel pressure is too high
 c. The pressure regulator diaphragm is leaking
 d. The fuel return line is plugged

47. The idle air control (IAC) valve is open further (higher count) than specifications. What is the most likely cause?
 a. A vacuum leak
 b. Dirty throttle plate or throttle bore
 c. An open PCV valve
 d. A defective MAF sensor

48. Black exhaust smoke from a gasoline engine is an indication of
 a. Weak piston rings
 b. A defective PCV system
 c. A leaking head gasket
 d. Too rich an air/fuel mixture

49. A cylinder power balance test is done on an inline 6-cylinder engine. The RPM drop is within 50 rpm of each other for the first 5 cylinders while #6 does not drop at all. This would indicate that
 a. #6 cylinder is "dead"
 b. Cylinders #1 to #5 are weak
 c. #6 cylinder has a fuel delivery problem
 d. #6 is the strongest cylinder

50. The flow of air from the air pump is directed to the exhaust manifold during
 a. Closed loop engine operation
 b. Periods of deceleration
 c. Open loop engine operation
 d. Hard acceleration

51. The engine misfires when loaded. The technician locates carbon tracks (to ground) inside the distributor cap. What could cause this problem?
 a. Fouled spark plugs
 b. Insufficient resistance in the spark plug wires
 c. Too rich an air/fuel mixture
 d. High resistance in one or more spark plug leads

52. Why is "one-trip logic" used for engine misfire on an OBD II vehicle?
 a. Misfires cause a major rise in emissions
 b. Fuel economy will suffer
 c. The extra fuel and air from the misfiring cylinder/s could damage the catalytic converter
 d. The extra fuel and air from the misfiring cylinder could cause engine overheating

53. A four-cylinder port-injected engine has a rich DTC. This could be caused by
 a. Low fuel pressure
 b. A defective MAP sensor
 c. A restricted fuel filter
 d. Contamination in the throttle body

54. A coil-on-plug ignition system has a defective coil which causes a cylinder misfire. How is the misfiring cylinder located?
 a. OBD II diagnostics list cylinder misfire data
 b. Perform a power balance test
 c. Connect an oscilloscope to the ignition system
 d. Swap coils with a known good coil

55. The vacuum hose to the MAP sensor becomes disconnected. This could cause the computer to
 a. Drive the system lean
 b. Shut the system down
 c. Provide a rich mixture
 d. Add 20° more ignition advance

56. The first step of the eight-step diagnostic procedure is
 a. Verify the problem
 b. Perform a thorough visual inspection
 c. Retrieve the diagnostic trouble codes
 d. Look for scan tool data

57. A noisy electric fuel pump is often caused by
 a. Low fuel pressure
 b. Lack of lubrication at the pump
 c. A restricted fuel filter
 d. Excessive fuel in the return line

58. I/M 240 refers to inspection and maintenance (I/M), and the 240 means the test
 a. Lasts for 240 seconds
 b. Is performed at 39 km/h (24 mph)
 c. Lasts for 24.0 minutes
 d. Is number 240 in federal standards

59. Carbon dioxide (CO_2) is an indicator of combustion efficiency. What CO_2 percentage listed here is the most efficient?
 a. 6%
 b. 10%
 c. 14%
 d. 3%

60. Parallel hybrid vehicles use ______ to drive the wheels.
 a. the electric motor only
 b. 274-volt batteries only
 c. both the engine and electric motor
 d. generated electricity from the engine

61. Typical late model port fuel injection uses pressures in the range of
 a. 350 kPa (50 psi)
 b. 280 kPa (40 psi)

c. 210 kPa (30 psi)
d. 70 kPa (10 psi)

62. The worst emission from many diesel engines is
a. Carbon monoxide
b. Carbon dioxide
c. Hydrocarbons
d. Particulate matter

63. Oxides of nitrogen (NO_x) emissions are high during
a. Idle
b. Heavier engine loads
c. Cold engine operation
d. Periods of deceleration

64. Positive back-pressure EGR valves require engine vacuum (usually controlled by the computer through a solenoid valve) and ________ to operate.
a. Intake manifold pressure
b. Catalytic converter pressure
c. Exhaust back pressure
d. Compression pressure

65. A fuel injector pressure drop test checks the drop in fuel rail pressure when the injector is electrically activated for 500 milliseconds. The maximum variation between injectors is
a. 40 kPa (6.0 psi)
b. 30 kPa (4.5 psi)
c. 20 kPa (3.0 psi)
d. 10 kPa (1.5 psi)

66. An EGR valve that is held partially open by a small piece of carbon will usually cause
a. NO_x emissions to rise
b. Rough running at cruise
c. A rough idle and stalling
d. A misfire under load

67. "False air" is a term used to describe a vacuum leak
a. At the air injection pump
b. After the MAF sensor
c. After the air cleaner
d. Before the MAF sensor

68. The rear (oxidizing) section of a three-way catalytic converter helps to control hydrocarbons and
a. Carbon dioxide (CO_2)
b. Carbon monoxide (CO)
c. Oxides of nitrogen (NO_x)
d. Particulate matter

69. Idle air control (IAC) valves control idle speed by controlling the amount of air
a. Passing around the throttle plate
b. Feeding into the PCV circuit
c. Feeding directly into the intake manifold
d. Bypassing the MAF sensor

70. The power to operate an OBD II scan tool is taken from ________.
a. The lighter socket
b. An underhood battery adaptor
c. The data link connector
d. A 12 V lantern battery

ANSWERS

1. c	**25.** c	**49.** a
2. c	**26.** a	**50.** c
3. c	**27.** c	**51.** d
4. d	**28.** a	**52.** c
5. b	**29.** c	**53.** b
6. a	**30.** b	**54.** a
7. a	**31.** c	**55.** c
8. a	**32.** d	**56.** a
9. b	**33.** c	**57.** c
10. a	**34.** b	**58.** a
11. b	**35.** b	**59.** c
12. a	**36.** d	**60.** c
13. a	**37.** b	**61.** a
14. a	**38.** d	**62.** d
15. b	**39.** c	**63.** b
16. a	**40.** c	**64.** c
17. c	**41.** c	**65.** d
18. c	**42.** a	**66.** c
19. a	**43.** a	**67.** b
20. c	**44.** c	**68.** b
21. c	**45.** c	**69.** a
22. a	**46.** c	**70.** c
23. c	**47.** b	
24. c	**48.** d	

Glossary

4 × 2 The term used to describe a two-wheel-drive truck. The "4" indicates the number of wheels of the vehicle and the "2" indicates the number of wheels that are driven by the engine.
4 × 4 The term used to describe a four-wheel-drive vehicle. The first "4" indicates the number of wheels of the vehicle and the second "4" indicates the number of wheels that are driven by the engine.
4WAL Four-wheel antilock.

ABS Antilock brake system.
Absorbent glass mat (AGM) batteries Sponge-like plate separators that absorb and hold the electrolyte.
AC coupling A signal that passes the AC signal component to the meter, but blocks the DC component. Useful to observe an AC signal that is normally riding on a DC signal; for example, charging ripple.
AC generator Produces AC voltage but the output is rectified by diodes to produce DC voltage. Also called an *alternator.*
ACI Automotive Components Inc.
Ackerman principle The angle of the steering arms causes the inside wheel to turn more sharply than the outer wheel when making a turn. This produces toe-out on turns (TOOT).
Adaptive strategy The ability of the on-board computer to compensate for wear and aging of system components.
Additive A substance added in small amounts to something, such as gasoline or oil to enhance existing properties.
AIR Air injection reaction emission control system.
Alamite fitting See *Zerk.*
ALCL Assembly line communications link.
ALDL Assembly line diagnostic link.
Align To bring the parts of a unit into the correct position.
Alloy A metal that contains one or more other elements usually added to increase strength or give the base metal important properties.
Alternating current (AC) An electrical signal in which current and voltage vary in a repeating sequence.
Alternator An electric generator that produces alternating current but is rectified to DC current by diodes. Also called an *AC generator.*
Altitude Elevation as measured in relationship to the earth's surface at sea level.
AM Amplitude modulation.
Ambient air temperature The temperature of the air surrounding an object.
Ammeter An electrical test instrument used to measure amperes (unit of the amount of current flow).
Ampere The unit of the amount of current flow. Named for André Ampère (1775–1836).
Amplitude The difference between the highest and lowest level of a waveform.
Analog A type of dash instrument that indicates values by use of the movement of a needle or similar device. An analog signal is continuous and variable.
Anchor pin A steel stud firmly attached to the backing plate of a drum brake.

Anchor pin

Annulus gear Another name for a ring gear that has internal teeth used in a planetary gear set or internal gear. Also called a *ring gear.*

Anode The positive electrode; the electrode toward which electrons flow.

ANSI American National Standards Institute.

Anti-dive A term used to describe the geometry of the suspension that controls the movement of the vehicle during braking. It is normal for a vehicle to nosedive slightly during braking and this is designed into most vehicles.

Antiknock index A measure of a fuel's ability to resist engine knock, stated as a number, is called the octane number.

Antimony A metal added to nonmaintenance-free or hybrid battery grids to add strength.

Anti-roll bar See *stabilizer bar.*

Anti-squat A term used to describe the geometry of the suspension that controls the movement of the vehicle body during acceleration. A body that remains level during acceleration has 100% anti-squat. Less than 100% indicates that the body "squats down" or lowers in the rear during acceleration.

Anti-sway bar See *stabilizer bar.*

API American Petroleum Institute.

APRA Automotive Parts Rebuilders Association.

Aramid Generic name for aromatic polyamide fibers developed in 1972. Kevlar is the Dupont brand name for aramid.

Armature The rotating unit inside a DC generator or starter consisting of a series of coils of insulating wire wound around a laminated iron core.

Articulation test A test specified by some vehicle manufacturers that tests the amount of force necessary to move the inner tie rod end in the ball socket assembly. The usual specification for this test is greater than 0.5 kg (1 lb.) and less than 2.7 kg (6 lbs.) of force.

Asbestosis A health condition where asbestos causes scar tissue to form in the lungs causing shortness of breath.

ASE Abbreviation for the National Institute for Automotive Service Excellence, a nonprofit organization for the testing and certification of vehicle service technicians.

ASME American Society of Mechanical Engineers.

Aspect ratio The ratio of height to width of a tire. A tire with an aspect ratio of 60 (a 60 series tire) has a height (from rim to tread) of 60% of its cross-sectional width.

ASTM American Society for Testing Materials.

ATC After top centre.

ATDC After top dead centre.

ATe Alfred Teves Engineering, a manufacturer of brake system components and systems.

Atmospheric pressure Pressure exerted by the atmosphere on all things based on the weight of the air.

Atom An atom is the smallest unit of matter that still retains its separate unique characteristics.

Atomize To reduce or separate into fine or minute particles.

Auto range Activates automatic settings of the test tool to the input signal.

AWG American Wire Gauge system.

Axial In line along with the axis or centerline of a part or component. Axial play in a ball joint means looseness in the same axis as the ball joint stud.

Back pressure The exhaust system's resistance to flow. Measured in pounds per square inch.

Back spacing The distance between the back rim edge and the center section mounting pad of a wheel.

Backing plate A steel plate upon which the brake shoes are mounted.

Backlight Light that illuminates the test tool's display from the back of the LCD or the rear window of a vehicle.

Baffle A plate or shield used to direct the flow of a liquid or gas.

Bakelite A brand name of the Union Carbide Company for phenolformaldehyde resin plastic.

Balance shaft A shaft in the engine that is designed so that, as it rotates, it reduces or cancels out any vibration.

Ball socket assembly An inner tie rod end assembly that contains a ball-and-socket joint at the point where the assembly is threaded onto the end of the steering rack of a rack-and-pinion steering gear.

Ballast resistor A variable resistor used to control the primary ignition current through the coil.

Ball-joint A flexible joint having a ball-and-socket type of construction used in suspension systems.

BARO sensor A sensor used to measure barometric pressure.

Barometric pressure The measure of atmospheric pressure, in inches of mercury (Hg), that reflects altitude and weather conditions.

Barrel-shaped A brake drum having a frictional surface that is larger in the center than at the open end or the rear of the drum.

Barrier hose A type of air-conditioning hose that includes a barrier layer on the inside to help prevent the loss of refrigerant through the hose. Barrier hoses are usually required for use with HFC-134a refrigerant.

Base The name for the section of a transistor that controls the current flow through the transistor.

Base brakes See *service brakes.*

Battery A chemical device that produces a voltage from two dissimilar metals submerged in an electrolyte.

Battery

Battery electrical drain test A test to determine if a component or circuit is draining the battery with everything electrical turned off.

Baud rate The speed at which bits of computer information are transmitted on a serial data stream; measured in bits per second (bps).

Bed plate A support plate that often joins the main bearing caps.

Bell housing A bell-shaped housing attached between the engine and the transmission.

Bell-mounted A brake drum with a frictional surface larger at the open end of the drum than at any other point toward the rear of the drum.

Belt Fabric or woven steel material over the body plies of a tire, and just under the tread area, to help keep the tread from squirming.

Bendix drive An inertia-type starter engagement mechanism not used on vehicles since the early 1960s.

Bias voltage In electrical terms, bias is the voltage applied to a device or component to establish the reference point for operation.

Bias-belted A bias-ply tire with additional belt material just under the tread area.

Bias-ply The body plies cover the entire tire and are angled as they cross from bead to bead.

Bidirectional communication Computer communication that uses serial data as both an input and an output.

Bit The individual voltage signal of a serial data stream; also, the smallest unit of measurement recognized by a computer.

Bittering agent A chemical added to antifreeze to discourage animals from drinking any spilled coolant.

Bleeder screw A valve in wheel cylinders (and other locations) for bleeding air from the hydraulic system.

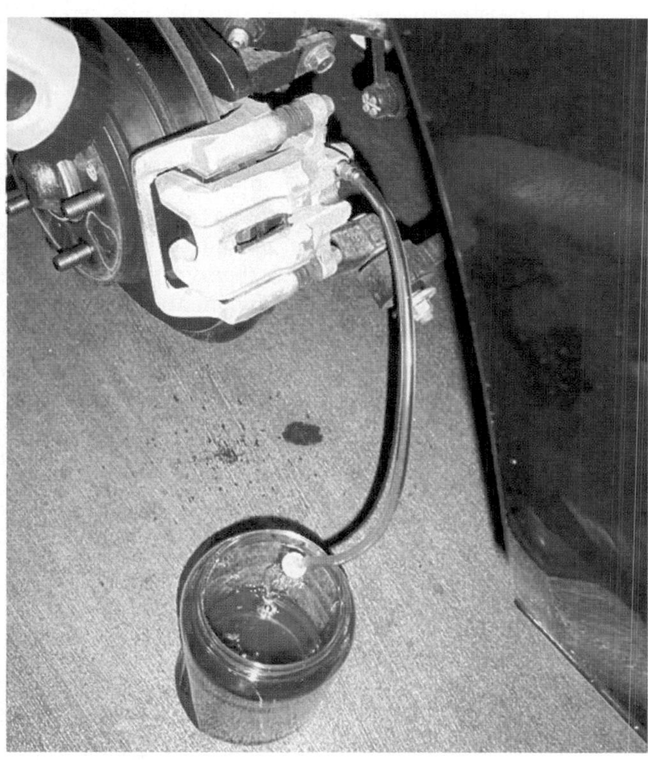

Bleeder screw

Blocking ring Part of a synchronizer assembly used in manual transmissions/transaxles. Also called a *stop ring, blocker ring,* or *synchronizer ring.*

Blow-by gases Combustion gases that leak past the piston rings into the crankcase during the compression and combustion strokes of the engine.

Blower-motor An electric motor and squirrel-cage type of fan that moves air inside the vehicle for heating, cooling, and defrosting.

BNC connector Coaxial-type connector usually used on oscilloscopes. Named for its inventor, Baby Neil Councilman.

Bolt circle The diameter (in inches or millimeters) of a circle drawn through the center of the bolt holes in a wheel.

Boost An increase in air pressure above atmospheric; measured in pounds per square inch (psi).

Boots Rubber dust protectors on the ends of a wheel cylinder, or caliper; also used to cover and protect a drive axle shaft constant velocity (CV) joint.

Bottom dead center (BDC) The lowest position in the cylinder that a piston can travel without reversing its direction.

Bounce test A test used to check the condition of shock absorbers.

BPMV Brake pressure modulator valve.

Brake fade A result of heat buildup. It is the reduction in braking force due to loss of friction between the brake shoes and the drum or between the disc brake pads and the rotor.

Brake lining A friction material fastened to the brake shoes.

Brake shoe The part of the drum brake to which the brake lining is attached.

Breather tube A tube that connects the left and right bellows of a rack-and-pinion steering gear.

Brinelling A type of mechanical failure used to describe a dent in metal such as what occurs when a shock load is applied to a bearing. Named after Johann A. Brinell, a Swedish engineer.

Brinelling

British thermal unit (BTU) The amount of heat required to raise 1 pound of water 1° F at sea level.

Brushes A copper or carbon conductor used to transfer electrical current from or to a revolving electrical part such as that used in an electrical motor or generator.
BTDC Before top dead center.
Buffer A component or circuit used to reduce the interaction between two electronic circuits.
Bump steer A term used to describe what occurs when the steering linkage is not level, causing the front tires to turn inward or outward as the wheels and suspension move up and down. Also called *orbital steer.*
Bump stop See jounce bumper.
Byte Eight bits of computer information that are processed as a unit and are transmitted in sequence on the serial data stream. Also known as a *word.*

CAFE Corporate average fuel economy.
Calcium A metallic chemical element added to the grids of a maintenance-free battery to increase strength.
Caliper The U-shaped housing that contains the hydraulic pistons and holds the pads on disc brake applications.
Camber The inward or outward tilt of the wheels from true vertical.
Candlepower A measure of the amount of light produced by a bulb.
Capacitance A term used to measure or describe how much charge can be stored in a capacitor (condenser) for a given voltage potential difference. Capacitance is measured in farads or smaller increments of farads such as microfarads.
Capacitor Also called a *condenser.* An electrical unit that can pass alternating current yet block direct current; used in electrical circuits to control fluctuations in voltage.
Carbon dioxide (CO_2) A colourless, odourless, nonflammable gas produced during the combustion process. The amount (%) in the exhaust can be used to evaluate the efficiency of an engine's combustion process.
Carbon monoxide (CO) A colourless, odourless, and highly poisonous gas. It is formed by the incomplete combustion of gasoline.
Carbon pile An electrical test instrument used to provide an electrical load for testing batteries and the charging circuit.
Cardan joint A type of universal joint named for a sixteenth century Italian mathematician.
Caster The forward or backward tilt of an imaginary line drawn through the steering axis as viewed from the side of the vehicle.
Caster sweep A process used to measure caster during a wheel alignment procedure where the front wheels are rotated first inward, then outward, a specified amount.
Catalytic converter An emission control device located in the exhaust system that changes HC and CO into harmless H_2O and CO_2. In a three-way catalyst, NO_x is also divided into harmless nitrogen (N_2) and oxygen (O_2).
Cathode The negative electrode.
Cavitation The formation and collapse of bubbles that contain vapor or gas.
CCC Computer command control is the name of General Motors' Computer Control System that uses a carburetor.
CCOT An abbreviation often used to identify an air-conditioning system that uses a cycling clutch orifice tube.
Cell A group of negative and positive plates capable of producing 2.1 V.
CEMF Counterelectromotive force.
Centre bolt A bolt used to hold the leaves of a leaf spring together in the centre. Also called a *centring pin.*
Centre support bearing A bearing used to support the centre of a long drive shaft on a rear-wheel-drive vehicle. Also called a *steady bearing* or *hanger bearing.*

Centre support bearing

Centreline steering A term used to describe the position of the steering wheel while driving on a straight, level road. The steering wheel should be centred or within plus or minus 3 degrees as specified by many vehicle manufacturers.
Centi-Stoke (cSt) centimeter per gram per second; unit of measure of viscosity.
Cetane Diesel fuel rating.
CFC-12 Air conditioning refrigerant; also called R-12, whose chemical name is diclorodifluoromethane.
CFRC Carbon fibre reinforced carbon.
Charging circuit Electrical components and connections necessary to keep a battery fully charged.
Chassis The frame, suspension, steering and machinery of a motor vehicle.
Chassis ground In electrical terms, a ground is the desirable return circuit path.
Chatter Sudden grabbing and releasing of the drum when brakes are applied.
Check engine light A dashboard warning light that is controlled by the vehicle computer; also called the *malfunction indicator light* or *MIL.*
Circuit A circuit is the path that electrons travel from a power source, through a resistance, and back to the power source.
Circuit breaker A mechanical unit that opens an electrical circuit in the event of excessive current flow.
Cluster gears Gears on the cluster shaft; also see *countershaft.*

Cluster shaft See *countershaft.*
Clutch gear See *input shaft.*
CO Carbon monoxide.
Coefficient of friction A measure of the amount of friction, usually in increments from 0 to 1. A low number (0.3) indicates low friction, and a high number (0.9) indicates high friction.
Coil spring A spring steel rod wound in a spiral (helix) shape; used in both front and rear suspension systems.
Coil-on-plug ignition system An ignition system without a distributor where each spark plug has its own ignition coil.

Coil-on-plug ignition system

Cold cranking amperes (CCA) The rating of a battery's ability to provide battery voltage during cold weather operation.
Collector The name of one section of a transistor.
Combustion The rapid burning of the air–fuel mixture in the engine cylinders.
Combustion chamber The space left within the cylinder when the piston is at the top of its stroke.
Combustion recess A form of combustion chamber used in rotary engines.
Commutator The name for the copper segments of the armature of a starter or DC generator.
Compensating port The port located in the master cylinder that allows excess fluid to return to the reservoir. See also *vent port.*
Compensation A process used during a wheel alignment procedure where the sensors are calibrated to eliminate errors in the alignment readings that may be the result of a bent wheel or unequal installation of the sensor on the wheel of the vehicle.
Composite A term used to describe the combining of individual parts into a larger component. For example, a composite leaf spring is constructed of fibreglass and epoxy, and a composite master brake cylinder contains both plastic parts (reservoir) and metal parts (cylinder housing).
Composite headlights A type of headlight that uses a separate, replaceable bulb.
Compression bumper See *jounce bumper.*
Compression ratio The ratio of the volume in the engine cylinder with the piston at bottom dead center (BDC) to the volume at top dead center (TDC).
Compression rod See *strut rod.*
Compressor A device used in air-conditioning systems to raise the pressure and the temperature of the refrigerant.
Computer Any device that can perform high-speed mathematical or logical calculations.
Computer command control (CCC or C^3) The name of General Motors' computer engine control system that uses a carburetor.
Concentric Perfectly round; the relationship of two round parts on the same center.
Condenser A radiator-like device used to condense the air-conditioning system refrigerant.
Conductor A material that conducts electricity and heat. A metal that contains fewer than four electrons in its atom's outer shell.
Cone The inner race or ring of a bearing.
Constant velocity joint Commonly called CV joints. CV joints are driveline joints that can transmit engine power through relatively large angles without a change in the velocity, as is usually the case with conventional Cardan-type U-joints.
Continuity Instrument setup to check wiring, circuits, connectors, or switches for breaks (open circuit) or short circuits (closed circuit).
Controller A name commonly used to describe a computer or an electronic control module.
Conventional ignition system Ignition system that uses a distributor, also called *distributor ignition* (DI).
Conventional theory The theory that electricity flows from positive (+) to negative (−).
Coolant The liquid mixture of antifreeze and water in the engine cooling system.
Corrosion Wear by chemical or electrochemical reaction.
Cotter key A metal loop used to retain castle nuts by installation through a hole. Size is measured by diameter and length (for example, 1/8″ × 1 1/2″). Also called a *cotter pin.* Named for the old English verb meaning "to close or fasten."
Coulomb A coulomb is 6.28 billion electrons.
Countershaft A shaft in a manual transmission that is below the mainshaft. Also called a *lay shaft* or *cluster shaft.* The gears on the countershaft are called *cluster gears* or *counter gears.*
Coupling disc See *flexible coupling.*
Coupling point The speed when both the turbine and the impeller in a torque converter reach about the same speed.
Courtesy light General term used to describe all interior lights.
Cow catcher A large spring seat used on many General Motors MacPherson strut units. If the coil spring breaks, the cow catcher is designed to prevent one end of the spring from moving outward and cutting a tire.
Cranking circuit Electrical components and connections required to crank the engine to start.
Cross camber/caster The difference of angle from one side of the vehicle to the other. Most manufacturers recommend a maximum difference side-to-side of 1/2° for camber and caster.

Cross steer A type of steering linkage commonly used on light and medium trucks.
CRT Cathode ray tube.
Cup The outer race or ring of a bearing.
Current Electron flow through an electrical circuit; measured in amperes.
Cushioning spring See *marcel spring.*
CV joints Constant velocity joints.
Cylinder hone A tool that uses an abrasive to smooth out and bring to exact measurement such things as wheel cylinders.

Data Information used as a basis for mechanical or electronic computation.
DC Direct current.
DC coupling A signal transmission that passes both AC and DC signal components to the meter. Also see *AC coupling.*
Deep cycling The full discharge and then the full recharge of a battery.
Default setup The setup that exists as long as there are no changes made to the settings.
Deflection A bending or distorting motion; usually applied to a brake drum when it is forced out-of-round during brake application.
Delta wound A type of stator winding where all three coils are connected in a triangle shape.
Density Mass per unit of volume; specific gravity.
Desiccant A drying agent used in air-conditioning systems, usually silica alumina or silica gel.
Detonation A violent explosion in the combustion chamber created by uncontrolled burning of the air–fuel mixture; often causes a loud, audible knock.
Diagnostic trouble code (DTC) An alphanumeric or numeric sequence indicating a fault in a vehicle operating system.
Dielectric strength Resistance to electrical penetration.
Diesel Engines that rely on the heat of compression for ignition.
Diff An abbreviation or slang for *differential.*
Differential A mechanical unit containing gears that provides gear reduction and a change of direction of engine power and permits the drive wheels to rotate at different speeds, as is required when turning a corner.
Digital A method of display that uses numbers instead of a needle or similar device.
Digital signal An electrical signal that is either on or off with no in between.
Dimmer switch An electrical switch used to direct the current to either bright or dim headlight filaments.
Diode An electrical device that allows current to flow in one direction only.
Diode trio Three diodes grouped together with one output used to put out the charge indicator lamp and provide current for the field from the stator windings on many alternators.
Direct current (DC) A constant electric current that flows in one direction only.
Directional stability Ability of a vehicle to move forward in a straight line with a minimum of driver control. Crosswinds and road irregularities will have little effect if directional stability is good.

Differential

DIS Distributorless ignition system; also called *direct-fire ignition system.*
Distributor Electromechanical unit used to help create and distribute the high voltage necessary for spark ignition.
Division A specific segment of a waveform as defined by the grid on the display.
Dog See *key.*
Dog tracking A term used to describe the condition where the rear wheels do not follow directly behind the front wheels; named for the way many species of dogs run with their rear paws offset toward one side so that they will not hit the front paws while running.
Doping The adding of impurities to pure silicon or germanium to form either P- or N-type material.
DOT Abbreviation for the Department of Transportation.
Double Cardan A universal joint that uses two conventional Cardan joints together to allow the joint to operate at greater angles.

Double Cardan

Double flare A tubing end made such that the flare area has two-wall thickness.

DPDT switch Double-pole, double-throw switch.

Drag link A term used to describe a link in the center of the steering linkage, usually called a *center link.*

Drag rod See *strut rod.*

Drift A mild pull that does not cause a force on the steering wheel that the driver must counteract (also known as lead). Also refers to a tapered tool used to centre a component in a bolt hole prior to installing the bolt.

Drive plate See *flex plate.*

Driveability The general evaluation of an engine's operating qualities, including idle smoothness, cold and hot starting, throttle response, and power delivery.

Dropping point The temperature at which a grease passes from a semisolid to a liquid state under conditions specified by ASTM.

Dry park test A test of steering and/or suspension components. With the wheels in the straight-ahead position and the vehicle on level ground, the steering wheel is turned while all steering and suspension components are inspected for any looseness.

Dual-mass flywheel A flywheel that consists of two parts separated by springs used to absorb vibration in the driveline.

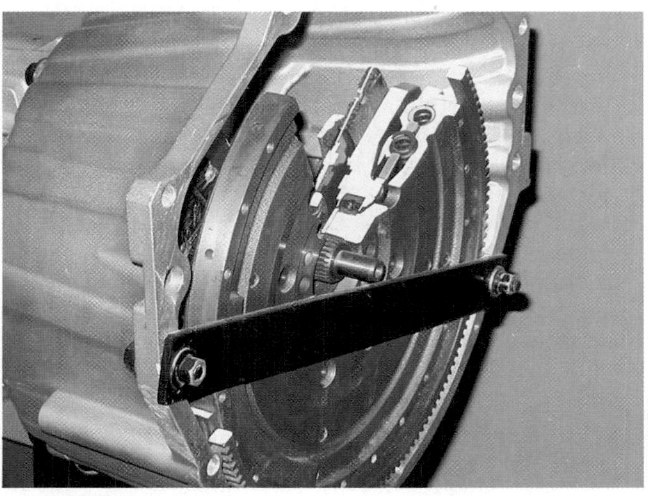

Dual-mass flywheel

Dual master cylinder A two-compartment master cylinder.

Dual overhead camshaft (DOHC) An engine design with two camshafts above each line of cylinders—one for the exhaust valves and one for the intake valves.

Dual-stage airbags Airbags whose deployment force varies with crash intensity. Only one stage may deploy with low-speed crashes.

Duo-servo The brand name of a Bendix dual-servo drum brake.

Duration A rating system applied to engine camshafts that determines how long the valve will be open relative to crankshaft movement in degrees.

Durometer The hardness rating of rubber products named for an instrument used to measure hardness that was developed about 1890.

Dual overhead camshaft

Dust cap A functional metal cap that keeps grease in and dirt out of wheel bearings. Also called a *grease cap.*

Duty cycle On-time or off-time to period-time ratio expressed in a percentage.

Dwell The amount of time, recorded on a dwell meter in degrees, that voltage passes through a closed switch.

Dynamic balance The balance achieved when the weight mass centreline of a tire is in the same plane as the centerline of the object.

EBCM Electronic brake control module.

Eccentric The relationship of two round parts having different centres; a part which contains two round surfaces, not on the same centre.

ECM Electronic control module.

ECU Electronic control unit.

EEPROM Electronically erasable programmable read-only memory.

EFI Electronic fuel injection.

EGR Exhaust gas recirculation. An emission control device to reduce NO_x (oxides of nitrogen).

EHCU Electro-hydraulic control unit.

Elastomer Another term for rubber.

Electricity The movement of free electrons from one atom to another.

Electrode A solid conductor through which current enters or leaves a substance, such as a gas or liquid.

Electrolyte Any substance which, in solution, is separated into ions and is made capable of conducting an electric current; the acid solution of a lead-acid battery.

Electromagnetic gauges A type of dash instrument gauge that uses small electromagnetic coils.

Electromagnetic induction The generation of a current in a conductor that is moved through a magnetic field. Electromagnetic induction was discovered in 1831 by Michael Faraday.

Electromagnetic interference (EMI) An undesirable electronic signal.

Electromagnetism A magnetic field created by current flow through a conductor.

Electromotive force (EMF) The force (pressure) that can move electrons through a conductor.

Electron A negative-charged particle 1/1800 the mass of a proton.

Electron theory The theory that electricity flows from negative (−) to positive (+).

Electronic circuit breaker See *PTC.*

Electronic ignition A general term used to describe any of various types of ignition systems that use electronic instead of mechanical components such as contact points.

Electronic spark control (ESC) The computer system equipped with a knock sensor that can retard spark advance if necessary to eliminate spark knock.

Electronic spark timing (EST) The control of spark timing advance by computer.

Element Any substance that cannot be separated into different substances.

Emergency brake See *parking brake.*

EMF Electromotive force.

EMI Electromagnetic interference.

Emissions Gases and particles left over after the combustion event of an engine. The primary emissions of concern are hydrocarbons, carbon monoxide, and oxides of nitrogen.

Emitter The name of one section of a transistor. The arrow used on a symbol for a transistor is on the emitter and points toward the negative section of the transistor.

Emulsion Dispersion of globules of one liquid in another.

Energized shoe A brake shoe that receives greater applied force from wheel rotation.

Energy Capacity for performing work.

Engine control module (ECM) The on-board computer of the engine management system that controls fuel and emissions, as well as diagnostics, for the vehicle's engine management system.

Enleanment The act of reducing fuel delivery to the air–fuel mix to create a leaner mixture.

Enrichment The act of adding fuel to the air–fuel mix to create a richer mixture.

Environmental Protection Agency (EPA) A federal government agency that oversees the enforcement of laws related to the environment. Included in these laws are regulations on the amount and content of automotive emissions.

EP lubricant Extreme pressure lubricant.

EPA Environmental Protection Agency.

EPR Ethylene propylene rubber; also an abbreviation of an air-conditioning valve called the *evaporator pressure regulator.*

EPROM Erasable programmable read-only memory.

ESC A computer system equipped with a knock sensor that can retard spark advance if necessary to eliminate spark timing advance.

EST Electronic spark timing.

Ester oil A type of refrigerant oil.

Ethanol (grain alcohol) An octane enhancer added, at a rate of up to 10%, to gasoline that increases the octane rating of the fuel by 2.5 to 3.0 points. Ethanol is a fuel oxygenate because it contains oxygen.

Ethylene glycol A common form of antifreeze that is very poisonous if ingested.

Ethyl tertiary butyl ether (ETBE) An octane enhancer for gasoline. It is also a fuel oxygenate that is manufactured by reacting isobutylene with ethanol, which results in high octane and low volatility. ETBE can be added to gasoline up to a level of approximately 13%.

Evaporative (EVAP) emissions A control system used to prevent fuel vapors in the tank from entering the atmosphere as HC emissions.

Evaporator A radiator-like device used to absorb heat and cause the refrigerant to change from a liquid to a gas.

Exhaust gas recirculation (EGR) The process of passing a small, measured amount of exhaust gas back into the engine to reduce combustion temperatures and formation of NO_x (oxides of nitrogen).

Extension housing The rear housing of a manual or automatic transmission.

Fade To grow weak; describes brakes that are becoming less effective.

Farad A unit of capacitance named for Michael Faraday (1791–1867), an English physicist. A farad is the capacity to store 1 coulomb of electrons at 1 volt of potential difference.

Feedback The reverse flow of electrical current through a circuit or electrical unit that should not normally be operating. This feedback current (reverse-bias current flow) is most often caused by a poor ground connection for the same normally operating circuit.

Fibre optics The transmission of light through special plastic that keeps the light rays parallel even if the plastic is tied in a knot.

Field coils Coils or wire wound around metal pole shoes to form the electromagnetic field inside an electric motor.

Filament The light-producing wire inside a light bulb.

Filler vent A breather hole in the filler cap on the master cylinder.

Filter An electrical device that only passes or blocks certain signal frequencies. An application can be removing noise from a signal.

Final drive A differential in a transaxle.

Flex plate The flywheel used on an engine equipped with an automatic transmission/transaxle. Also called a *drive plate.*

Flexible coupling A part of the steering mechanism between the steering column and the steering gear or rack-and-pinion assembly. Also called a *rag joint* or *steering coupling disc.* The purpose of the flexible coupling is to prevent the transmission of noise, vibration, and harshness from the road and steering to the steering wheel.

Floating caliper A type of caliper used with disc brakes that moves slightly to assure equal pad pressure on both sides of the rotor.

Flow control valve A valve that regulates and controls the flow of power steering pump hydraulic fluids to the steering gear or rack-and-pinion assembly. The flow control valve is usually part of the power steering pump assembly.

FM Frequency modulation.

FMSI Friction Materials Standards Institute.

Follower ball joint A ball joint used in a suspension system to provide support and control without having the weight of the vehicle or the action of the springs transferred through the joint itself. Also called a *friction ball joint.*

Foot-pound A measurement of work. A one-pound load, moved one foot.
Force motor See *pressure control solenoid.*
Forward bias Current flow in normal direction.
Forward steer See *front steer.*
Foundation brakes See *service brakes.*
Free play The distance that the steering wheel moves without moving the front wheels. The maximum allowable amount of free play is less than 2″ for a parallelogram-type steering system and 3/8″ for a rack-and-pinion steering system.
Freeze-frame Data that is stored in computer memory at the instant an emissions-related DTC is set.
Freon Dupont trade name for CFC-12 refrigerant.
Frequency The number of times a waveform repeats in one second, measured in hertz (Hz), in a frequency band.
Friction The resistance to sliding of two bodies in contact with each other.
Friction ball joint The outer suspension pivot that does not support the weight of the vehicle. Also called a *follower ball joint.*
Front steer A construction design of a vehicle that places the steering gear and steering linkage in front of the centerline of the front wheels. Also called *forward steer.*
Fuel cell A device that converts a chemical, such as hydrogen, into electricity.
Fuel injector A liquid control valve that sprays fuel into the intake manifold or combustion chamber.
Fuel trim A computer function that adjusts fuel delivery during closed-loop operation to bring the air–fuel mixture as close to 14.7:1 as possible.
Full fielding The method of supplying full battery voltage to the magnetic field of a generator as part of the troubleshooting procedure for the charging system.
Fuse An electrical safety unit constructed of a fine tin conductor that will melt and open the electrical circuit if excessive current flows through it.

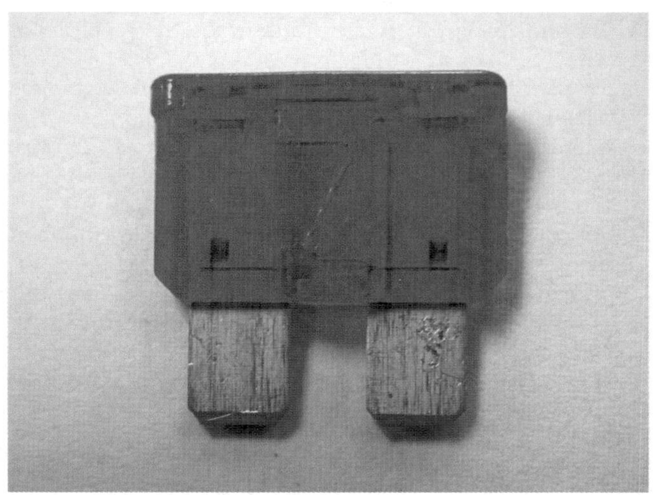

Fuse

Fusible link A type of fuse that will melt and open the protected circuit in the event of a short circuit, which could cause excessive current flow through the fusible link. Most fusible links are actually wires that are four gauge sizes smaller than the wire of the circuits being protected.
FWD Front-wheel drive.

Galvanized steel Steel with a zinc coating to help protect the steel from rust and corrosion.
Garter spring A spring used in a seal to help keep the lip of the seal in contact with the moving part.
Gassing The release of hydrogen and oxygen gas from the plates of a battery during charging or discharging.
Gauge Wire sizes as assigned by the American Wire Gauge system; the smaller the gauge number, the larger the wire.
Gauss A unit of magnetic induction or magnetic intensity named for Karl Friedrich Gauss (1777–1855), a German mathematician.
Gear ratio The relationship between two gears determined by dividing the number of teeth on the driving gear by the number of teeth on the driven gear and expressed as a ratio to one.
Generator A device that converts mechanical energy into electrical energy.
GKN Guest, Keene, and Nettelfolds.
Gland nut The name commonly used to describe the large nut at the top of a MacPherson strut housing. This gland nut must be removed to replace a strut cartridge.
Glazed drum A drum surface hardened excessively by intense heat.
Glitch A momentary spike in a waveform. This can be caused by a momentary disruption in the tested circuit.
Glow plugs Electrical heating elements that extend into the combustion chamber area on diesel engines.
Grab Seizure of the drum on linings when brakes are applied.
Grease Lubricant composed of an oil thickener for a solid or semi-solid consistency.
Grease cap A functional metal cap that keeps grease in and dirt out of wheel bearings. Also called a *dust cap.*
Grease seal A seal used to prevent grease from escaping and to prevent dirt and moisture from entering.
Grid The lead-alloy framework (support) for the active materials of an automotive battery.
Grommet An eyelet usually made from rubber used to protect, strengthen, or insulate around a hole or passage.
Ground The lowest possible voltage potential in a circuit. In electrical terms, a ground is the desirable return circuit path. Ground can also be undesirable and provide a shortcut path for a defective electrical circuit.
Growler Electrical tester designed to test starter and DC generator armatures.
GVW Abbreviation for gross vehicle weight. GVW is the weight of the vehicle plus the weight of all passengers and cargo up to the limit specified by the manufacturer.

Half shaft Drive axles on a front-wheel-drive vehicle or a shaft running from a stationary differential to the drive wheels.
Hall-effect switch The sensor operates by moving a magnetic field relative to a semiconductor creating a square-wave output; usually used to determine position.

Named for Edwin H. Hall, who discovered the Hall effect in 1879.

Halogenated compounds Chemicals containing chlorine, fluorine, bromine, or iodine. These chemicals are generally considered to be hazardous, and any product containing them should be disposed of using approved procedures.

Haltenberger linkage A type of steering linkage commonly used on some light trucks.

Hand brake See *parking brake.*

Hanger bearing See *centre support bearing.*

Hash An unclear or a messy section of a scope pattern.

Hazard flasher Emergency warning flashers; lights at all four corners of the vehicle that flash on and off.

HC Hydrocarbons (unburned fuel) that when combined with NO_x and sunlight form smog.

HD Heavy duty.

Heat checked Cracks in the braking surface of a drum caused by excessive heat.

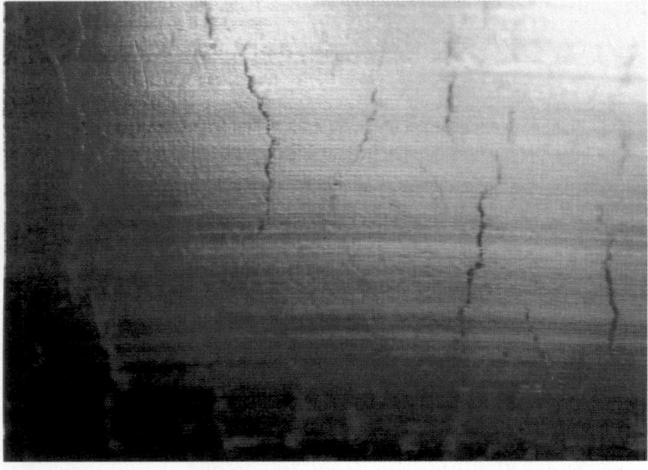

Heat checked

Heat riser valve A damper valve placed at the exhaust manifold to divert exhaust heat through the intake manifold.

Heat sink Usually, a metallic-finned unit used to keep electronic components cool.

HEI General Motors' name for its high energy ignition.

Helical-cut gears Gears that have teeth cut at an angle.

Helper springs Auxiliary or extra springs used in addition to the vehicle's original springs to restore proper ride height or to increase the load carrying capacity of the vehicle.

HEPA High Efficiency Particulate Air filter.

Hertz A unit of measurement of frequency, abbreviated Hz. One hertz is one cycle per second. Named for Heinrich R. Hertz, a nineteenth century German physicist.

HFC-134a Automotive air conditioning refrigerant, also called R-134a, whose chemical name is tetrofluorolthene.

High-intensity discharge (HID) headlamps Headlamps that give off a white light that provides better road illumination.

High pressure switch A switch used in an air-conditioning system to stop the operation of the compressor when the pressure reaches a dangerous level.

Hold-in winding One of two electromagnetic windings inside a solenoid; used to hold the movable core in the solenoid.

Hooke's law The force characteristics of a spring, discovered by Robert Hooke (1635–1703), an English physicist. Hooke's law states "the deflection (movement or deformation) of a spring is directly proportional to the applied force."

Horsepower A unit of power equivalent to 33 000 foot-pounds per minute. One horsepower equals 746 W.

HSS High strength steel, a low carbon alloy steel that uses various amounts of silicon, phosphorus, and manganese.

Hub cap A functional and decorative cover over the lug nut portion of the wheel. Also see *wheel cover.*

HVAC An abbreviation often used for heating, ventilation, and air conditioning.

Hybrid Something (such as a battery) made from more than one element.

Hybrid vehicle Vehicle powered by a combination of an electric motor and an internal combustion engine.

Hydraulic lifter A valve lifter that, using simple valving and the engine's oil pressure, can adjust its length slightly, thereby maintaining zero clearance in the valve train. Hydraulic lifters reduce valve train noise and are maintenance-free.

Hydro cracking Cracking or thermal degradation of petroleum in the presence of hydrogen.

Hydrocarbons (HC) Any of a number of compounds of carbon and hydrogen used as fuel, such as gasoline. High levels of hydrocarbons in tail pipe emissions are a result of unburned fuel. When combined with NO_x and sunlight, they form smog.

Hydrometer An instrument used to measure the specific gravity of a liquid. A battery hydrometer is calibrated to read the expected specific gravity of battery electrolyte.

Hydrophilic A term used to describe a type of rubber used in many all-season tires that has an affinity for water (rather than repels).

Hydrophobic A term used to describe the repelling of water.

Hydroplaning A condition that occurs when driving too fast on wet roads where the water on the road gets trapped between the tire and the road, forcing the tire onto a layer of water and off the road surface. All traction between the tire and the road is lost.

Hydroscopic A term used to describe the absorption of water, especially from moisture in the air.

Hypoid gear set A ring gear and pinion gear set that meshes together below the centreline of the ring gear. This type of gear set allows the drive shaft to be lower in the vehicle but requires special hypoid gear lubricant.

IAC Idle air control.

Icing Formation of ice on or around the throttle plate due to atmospheric conditions and the lowering of temperatures as the air–fuel mixture passes through the throttle opening.

Ignition circuit Electrical components and connections that produce and distribute high-voltage electricity to ignite the air–fuel mixture inside the engine.

Ignition coil An electrical device consisting of two separate coils of wire—a primary and a secondary winding. The purpose of an ignition is to produce the high-voltage (20 000 to 40 000 V), low-amperage (about 80 mA) current necessary for spark ignition.

Ignition timing The exact point of ignition in relation to piston position.

ILC Idle load control.

Immobilizer An electronic security system that "shuts down" the fuel injection and cranking systems.

Included angle SAI angle added to the camber angle of the same wheel.

Independent suspension A suspension system that allows a wheel to move up and down without undue effect on the opposite side.

Inductance The signal caused by the sudden change of a magnetic field. For example, the turning off of the current through a solenoid generates a voltage spike across the solenoid.

Inductive reactance An opposing current created in a conductor whenever there is a charging current flow in a conductor.

Inlet port See *replenishing port.*

Input shaft The shaft that is splined to the clutch shaft. Also known as the *main gear, clutch gear,* or *main drive pinion assembly.*

Insulator A material that does not readily conduct electricity and heat. A nonmetal material that contains more than four electrons in its atom's outer shell.

Intake air temperature (IAT) sensor A sensor that measures the air temperature of the air entering the engine.

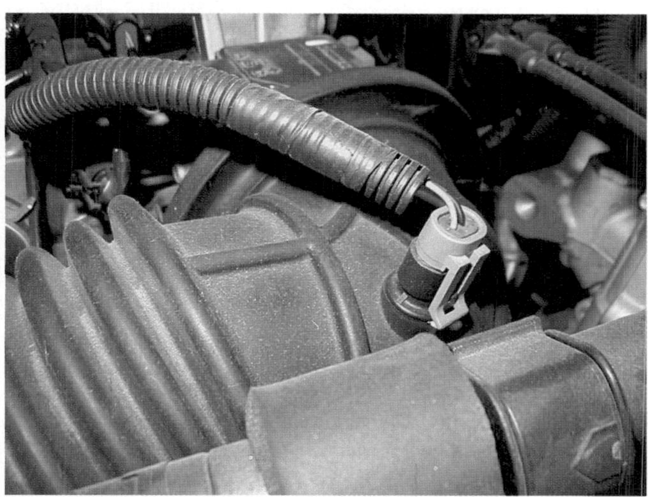

Intake air temperature (IAT) sensor

Integrated Motor Assist (IMA) An internal electric motor assists the gasoline engine for more power.

Intercooler A heat exchanger mounted on the intake of a supercharged or turbocharged engine.

Intermittent Irregular; a condition that happens with no apparent or predictable pattern.

Internal gear A gear with internal teeth used in a planetary gear set. Also called a *ring gear* or *annulas gear.*

Ion An atom with an excess or deficiency of electrons, forming either a negatively or a positively charged particle.

Iron Refined metal from iron ore (ferrous oxide) in a furnace. Also see *steel.*

IRS Independent rear suspension.

ISC Idle speed control.

ISO International Standards Organization.

Isolator bushing The rubber bushing used between the frame and the stabilizer bar. Also known as a *stabilizer bar bushing.*

IVR Instrument voltage regulator.

Jounce Up-and-down movement or to cause up-and-down motion.

Jounce bumper A rubber or urethane stop to limit upward suspension travel. Also called a *bump stop, a strike-out bumper, suspension bumper,* or *compression bumper.*

Jumper cables Heavy-gauge (4 to 00) electrical cables with large clamps used to connect a vehicle that has a discharged battery to a vehicle that has a good battery.

Kevlar Dupont brand name of aramid fibers.

Key Part of a synchronizer used in manual transmissions/transaxles. Also called a *strut* or a *dog.*

Kicker A throttle kicker is used on some computer engine control systems to increase engine speed (RPM) during certain operating conditions, such as when the air-conditioning system is on.

Kilo 1000; abbreviated k or K.

Kinetic energy The energy in any moving object. The amount of energy depends on the weight (mass) of the object and its speed.

King pin A pivot pin commonly used on solid axles or early model twin I-beam axles that rotate in bushings and allow the front wheels to rotate. The knuckle pivots about the king pin.

King pin inclination The inclination of the tops of the king pins toward each other to create a stabilizing force to the vehicle.

Knock sensor A sensor that can detect engine spark knock.

KPI King pin inclination (also known as *steering axis inclination, SAI*).

Ladder frame A steel frame for a vehicle that uses crossbraces along the length similar to the rungs of a ladder.

Lambda sensor Oxygen sensor or O_2 sensor. Lambda is the Greek letter that represents ratio, as in air–fuel ratio.

Lateral runout A measure of the amount a tire or wheel is moving side-to-side while being rotated. Excessive lateral runout can cause a shimmy-type vibration if the wheels are on the front axle.

Lay shaft See *countershaft.*

LCD Liquid-crystal display.

Lead A mild pull that does not cause a force on the steering wheel that the driver must counteract (also known as *drift*).

Lead peroxide The positive plate of an automotive-style battery; the chemical symbol is PbO_2.

Lead sulfate Both battery plates become lead sulfate when the battery is discharged. The chemical symbol for lead sulfate is $PbSO_4$.

Leaf spring A spring made of several pieces of flat spring steel.
LED Light-emitting diode.
Liquid crystal display (LCD) A display that uses liquid crystals to display waveforms and text on its screen.
Live axle A solid axle used on the drive wheels and containing the drive axles that propel the vehicle.
LMA Low moisture absorption type of brake fluid (DOT 4).
Load index An abbreviated method that uses a number to indicate the load-carrying capabilities of a tire.
Load-carrying ball joint A ball joint used in a suspension system to provide support and control and through which the weight (load) of the vehicle is transferred to the frame.
LÖBRO joint A brand name of a CV joint.
Lock nut See *prevailing torque nut.*
Lockup torque converter See *torque converter clutch.*
Low pressure switch Used in an air-conditioning system to prevent the operation of the compressor when the pressure in the system is too low for safe operation.
LSD An abbreviation commonly used for limited slip differentials.
LT Light truck.
Lubricant Any substance introduced between two surfaces for the purpose of friction reduction.
Lumbar The lower section of the back.

M & S Mud and snow.
M/C solenoid Mixture control solenoid.
MacPherson strut A type of front suspension with the shock absorber and coil spring in one unit that rotates when the wheels are turned. The assembly mounts to the vehicle body at the top and to one ball joint and control arm at the lower end. It is named for its inventor, Earle S. MacPherson.
Magnetic timing A method of measuring ignition that uses a magnetic pickup tool to sense the location of a magnet on the harmonic balancer.
Main drive pinion assembly See *input shaft.*
Main gear See *input shaft.*
Main shaft The main shaft inside a manual transmission/transaxle, also called the *output shaft.*
Malfunction indicator lamp (MIL) This amber dashboard warning light may be labeled "check engine" or "service engine soon."
Manifold absolute pressure (MAP) A sensor used to measure the pressure inside the intake manifold compared to a perfect vacuum.
Manifold vacuum Low pressure (vacuum) measured at the intake manifold of a running engine (normally between 17 and 21 inches Hg at idle).
MAP Manifold absolute pressure.
Marcel spring A part of a clutch friction disc used to absorb the instant shock of clutch engagement.
Mass air flow (MAF) The volume of air passing into the engine; varies with temperature and humidity and used in calculating injector operation and spark timing.
Master cylinder The part of the brake hydraulic system where the pressure is generated.
Match mount The process of mounting a tire on a wheel and aligning the valve stem with a mark on the tire. The mark on the tire represents the high point of the tire and the valve stem location represents the smallest diameter of the wheel.
Memory steer Memory steer is the lead or pull of a vehicle caused by faults in the steering or suspension system. If after making a turn the vehicle tends to pull in the same direction as the last turn, then the vehicle has memory steer.
Metering valve (Hold-off valve) A valve installed between the master cylinder and front disc brakes that prevents operation of the front disc brakes until 75–125 psi is applied to overcome rear drum-brake return-spring pressure.
Methanol (wood alcohol) Typically manufactured from natural gas. Methanol content, including cosolvents, in unleaded gasoline is limited by law to 5%.
Methyl tertiary butyl ether (MTBE) A fuel oxygenate that is permitted in unleaded gasoline up to a level of 15%.
Micron Unit of measure equal to one millionth of a meter.
MIL See *malfunction indicator lamp.*
Millisecond One thousandth (1/1000) of one second.
Mineral oil A refined hydrocarbon without animal or vegetable additives.
Minutes A unit of measure of an angle; sixty minutes equal one degree.
Miscible A term that means "capable of being mixed."
Misfire A circumstance that occurs when complete combustion does not happen in one or more cylinders due to fuel, ignition, or cylinder compression.
MLS Multi-layered steel head gasket.
Mode shift A selection of either two-wheel-drive or four-wheel-drive in a transfer case.
Module A group of electronic components functioning as a component of a larger system.
Moly grease Grease containing molybdenum disulfide.
Monograde Single grade; an engine oil that meets the requirements for only one SAE viscosity grade or classification.
Morning sickness A slang term used to describe temporary loss of power steering assist when cold caused by wear in the control valve area of a power rack-and-pinion unit.
MSDS Material safety data sheets.
μ (Mu) The Greek letter that represents the coefficient of friction.
Multigrade An engine oil that meets the requirements for more than one SAE viscosity grade or classification.
Multiplexing A system that allows a number of computers to share information on a single wire.
Mutual induction The generation of an electric current due to a changing magnetic field of an adjacent coil.

NAO Nonasbestos organic.
NAS Nonasbestos synthetic.
Negative temperature coefficient (NTC) Usually used in reference to a temperature sensor (coolant or air temperature). As the temperature increases, the resistance of the sensor decreases.
Neutron A neutral-charged particle; one of the basic particles of the nucleus of an atom.
Nickel metal hydride (NiMH) battery A special battery usually found in hybrid and electric vehicles.

Nitrile A type of rubber that is okay for use with petroleum.

NLGI National Lubricating Grease Institute. Usually associated with grease. The higher the NLGI number, the firmer the grease: #000 is very fluid, whereas #5 is very firm. The consistency most recommended is NLGI #2 (soft).

Nonvolatile memory Computer memory capability that is not lost when power is removed. See also *read-only memory (ROM).*

NO_x Oxides of nitrogen which, when combined with HC and sunlight, form smog.

NTC Negative temperature coefficient. Usually used in reference to a temperature sensor (coolant or air temperature). As the temperature increases, the resistance of the sensor decreases.

N-type material Silicon or germanium doped with phosphorus, arsenic, or antimony.

Nucleus The central part of an atom, which has a positive charge and contains almost all the mass of the atom.

NVH Abbreviation for noise, vibration, and harshness.

NVRAM Nonvolatile random-access memory.

O_2 sensor Oxygen sensor; also called *O2S.*

Octane Gasoline fuel rating.

Octane rating The measurement of a gasoline's ability to resist engine knock. The higher the octane rating, the less prone the gasoline is to cause engine knock (detonation).

OE Original equipment.

OEM Original equipment manufacturer.

Offset The distance the centre section (mounting pad) is offset from the centreline of the wheel.

Ohm The unit of electrical resistance; named for Georg Simon Ohm (1787–1854).

Ohmmeter An electrical test instrument used to measure ohms (unit of electrical resistance).

Ohm's law An electrical law that requires 1 volt to push 1 ampere through 1 ohm of resistance.

Ω (Omega) The last letter of the Greek alphabet; a symbol for ohm, the unit for electrical resistance.

On-board diagnostics A self-diagnosis program built into the Powertrain Control Module (PCM).

OnStar System The General Motors system of satellite tracking and navigation for their vehicles.

Open circuit Any circuit that is not complete and in which no current flows.

Orbital steer See *bump steer.*

Oscilloscope A visual display of electrical waves on a fluorescent screen or cathode ray tube.

OSHA Occupational Safety and Health Administration.

Output shaft See *main shaft.*

Over-centre adjustment An adjustment made to a steering gear while the steering is turned through its center straight-ahead position. Also known as a *sector lash* adjustment.

Overdrive A gear ratio where the driving gear turns at a speed slower than the driven gear.

Overinflation A term used to describe a tire with too much tire pressure (greater than maximum allowable pressure).

Overlap The number of crankshaft degrees that the intake and exhaust valves are open at same time.

Oversteer A term used to describe the handling of a vehicle where the driver must move the steering wheel in the opposite direction from normal while turning a corner. Oversteer handling is very dangerous. Most vehicle manufacturers design their vehicles to understeer rather than oversteer.

Oxidation Chemical deterioration of a petroleum product by addition of oxygen atoms.

Oxidation catalysts Platinum and palladium used in the catalytic converter to combine oxygen (O_2) with hydrocarbons (HC) and carbon monoxide (CO) to form nonharmful tail pipe emissions of water (H_2O) and carbon dioxide (CO_2).

Oxides of nitrogen (NO_x) A primary emission produced in the combustion chamber under high temperatures when nitrogen combines with oxygen. Oxides of nitrogen contribute to the formation of smog (ground level ozone [O_3]) when combined with HC and sunlight.

Oxygenate An octane component containing hydrogen, carbon, and oxygen in its molecular structure. Types of oxygenates include ethers, such as MTBE, and alcohols, such as ethanol and methanol.

Oz.-in. Measurement of imbalance: 3 oz.-in. means that an object is out-of-balance to the degree that it would require a 1 oz. weight placed 3 inches from the center of the rotating object, or a 3 oz. weight 1 inch from the centre, or any other combination that when multiplied equals 3 oz.-in.

Ozone Oxygen rich (O_3) gas created by sunlight reaction with unburned hydrocarbons (HC) and oxides of nitrogen (NO_x); also called *smog.*

PAG An abbreviation for polyalkeline glycol.

Panhard rod A horizontal steel rod or bar attached to the rear axle housing at one end and the frame at the other to keep the center of the body directly above the center of the rear axle during cornering and suspension motions. Also called a *track rod.*

Parallelogram A geometric box shape where opposite sides are parallel (equal distance apart).

Parking brake Components used to hold a vehicle on a 30° incline. The parking brake is also called the *hand brake* if hand force is used to apply it.

Partitions Separations between the cells of a battery. Partitions are made of the same material as the outside case of the battery.

Pasting The process of applying active battery materials onto the grid framework of each plate.

Pawl A lever for engaging in a notch; used to rotate the notched star wheel on self-adjusting brakes.

PCM Powertrain Control Module.

PCV Positive crankcase ventilation.

Peak value The highest and lowest value of a waveform.

Peak-and-hold A method for regulating the current flow through electronic fuel injectors. Supplies the higher current necessary to energize the injector, then drops to a level just low enough to keep the injector energized.

Perimeter frame A steel structure for a vehicle that supports the body of the vehicle under the sides as well as the front and rear.

Permalloy A permanent-magnet alloy of nickel and iron.

Permeability The measure of a material's ability to conduct magnetic lines of force.

Phenolic brake pistons A hard type of plastic disc-brake caliper pistons that do not rust or corrode.

Phenolic brake pistons

Photoelectric principle The production of electricity created by light striking certain sensitive materials, such as selenium or cesium.

Pickle fork A tapered fork used to separate chassis parts that are held together by a nut and a taper. Hitting the end of the pickle fork forces the wedge portion of the tool between the parts to be separated and "breaks the taper." A pickle fork tool is generally *not* recommended because the tool can tear or rip the grease boot of the part being separated.

Piezoelectric principle The principle by which certain crystals become electrically charged when pressure is applied.

Pilot bearing A bearing located in the end of the engine crankshaft to support the end of the manual transmission input shaft. Also called a *pilot bushing.*

Ping Secondary rapid burning of the last 3–5% of the air–fuel mixture in the combustion chamber causing a second flame front that collides with the first flame front producing a knock noise. Also called *detonation* or *spark knock.*

Pinion gear A small gear on the end of the starter drive that rotates the engine flywheel ring gear for starting.

Pitch The pitch of a threaded fastener refers to the number of threads per inch.

Pitman arm A short lever arm that is splined to the steering gear cross shaft. It transmits the steering force from the cross shaft to the steering linkage.

Pitman shaft See *sector shaft.*

Planet pinions Pinion gears attached to a planet carrier that surround a sun gear in a planetary gear set.

Plastigage A soft, plastic-like thread used to check bearing clearances.

Platform The platform of a vehicle includes the basic structure (frame and/or major body panels) as well as the basic steering and suspension components. One platform may be the basis for several different brand vehicles.

Plenum A chamber located between the throttle body and the runners of the intake manifold used to distribute the intake charge more evenly and efficiently.

PM motor A permanent-magnet electric motor.

POA An abbreviation for an air-conditioning valve called the *pilot-operated absolute.*

Polarity The condition of being positive or negative in relation to a magnetic pole.

Polymer Substance formed by the linking of two or more simple molecules to form a single, heavier molecule.

Porous lead Lead with many small holes to make a porous surface for use in battery negative plates; the chemical symbol for lead is Pb.

Ported vacuum Low pressure (vacuum) measured above the throttle plates. As the throttle plates open, the vacuum increases and becomes of the same value as the manifold vacuum.

Positive crankcase ventilation (PCV) A system used to prevent corrosive blowby gases (by products of combustion) in the crankcase from entering the atmosphere.

Positive temperature coefficient (PTC) Usually used in reference to a conductor or electronic circuit breaker. As the temperature increases, the electrical resistance also increases.

Potentiometer A three-terminal variable resistor that varies the voltage drop in a circuit.

Powdered metal Sintered metal used to form engine components.

Power In electrical terms, amperes × volts (Power = $I \times E$), expressed in watts.

Power train control module (PCM) The on-board computer that controls both the engine management and transmission functions of the vehicle.

PPM Parts per million.

Preignition Ignition of the air–fuel mix before the timed ignition spark occurs.

Pressure bleeder A device that forces pressure into the master cylinder, so that when the bleeder screws are opened at the wheel cylinder, air will be forced from the system.

Pressure control solenoid A computer-controlled solenoid that controls mainline pressure in an electronically shifted automatic transmission/transaxle. Also called a *variable force solenoid* or *force motor.*

Pressure-differential switch A switch installed between the two separate braking circuits of a dual master to light the red dashboard brake running light in the event of a brake system failure caused by a *difference* in brake pressure in the hydraulic system.

Pressure regulator A regulating device that maintains a specified pressure in a system.

Prevailing torque nut A special design of nut fastener that is deformed slightly or has other properties that permit the nut to remain attached to the fastener without loosening.

Primary shoe A brake shoe installed facing the front of the vehicle.

PROM Programmable read-only memory.

Prop shaft An abbreviation for propeller shaft.

Propeller shaft A term used by many manufacturers for a drive shaft.

Proportioning valve A valve installed between the master cylinder and rear brakes that limits the amount of pressure to the rear wheels to prevent rear wheel lockup.

Proton A positively charged particle; one of the basic particles of the nucleus of an atom.

PSI Pounds per square inch.

PTC See *positive temperature coefficient.*

P-type material Silicon or germanium doped with boron or indium.

Pull Refers to vehicles that tend to go left or right while traveling on a straight, level road.

Pull-in windings One of two electromagnetic windings inside a solenoid used to move a movable core.

Pulse A voltage signal that increases or decreases from a constant value then returns to the original value.

Pulse generators An electromagnetic unit that generates a voltage signal used to trigger the ignition control module that controls (turns on and off) the primary ignition current of an electronic ignition system.

Pulse train A DC voltage that turns on and off in a series of pulses.

Pulse width The amount of "on" time of an electronic fuel injector or other electrical component.

Pulse width modulation (PWM) Operation of a device by an on/off digital signal that is controlled by the time duration the device is turned on and off.

Push rod The link rod connecting the brake pedal to the master cylinder piston.

Pyrometer A test instrument used to measure temperatures.

Quill Another name for a manual transmission front-bearing retainer.

R-12 Air-conditioning refrigerant, also called *CFC-12;* the chemical name is diclorodifluoromethane.

R134a Automotive air-conditioning refrigerant; also called *HFC-134a;* the chemical name is tetrafluorolthene.

RABS Rear antilock braking system.

Race Inner and outer machined surface of a ball or roller bearing.

Range shift A selection of high range or low range in a transfer case.

Rack and pinion A type of lightweight steering unit that connects the front wheels through tie rods to the end of a long shaft called a *rack.* When the driver moves the steering wheel, the force is transferred to the rack-and-pinion assembly, inside of which is a small pinion gear that meshes with gear teeth cut into the rack.

Radial grid A lead-alloy framework for the active materials of a battery that has radial support spokes to add strength and to improve battery efficiency.

Radial runout A measure of the amount a tire or wheel is out of round. Excessive radial runout can cause a tramp-type vibration.

Radial tire A tire whose carcass plies run straight across (or almost straight across) from bead to bead.

Radio frequency interference (RFI) A high-frequency type of EMI that is in the radio frequency band.

Radius rod A suspension component to control longitudinal (front-to-back) support, usually attached with rubber bushings to the frame at one end and the axle or control arm at the other end. Also see *strut rod.*

Rag joint See *flexible coupling.*

RAM Random access memory.

Ratio The expression for proportion. For example, in a typical rear-axle assembly, the drive shaft rotates three times faster than the rear axles, which is expressed as a ratio of 3:1. Power train ratios are always expressed as driving gear divided by driven gear.

Ravigneaux gear set A type of compound planetary gear set used in many automotive transmissions/transaxles.

RBS Rubber-bonded socket.

RBWL Red brake warning lamp.

Reaction disc A feature built into a power brake unit to provide the driver with a "feel" of the pedal.

Read-only memory (ROM) A permanent type of computer memory programmed by the computer manufacturer to store the operating instructions and parameters of the computer.

Rear spacing See *back spacing.*

Rear steer A construction design of a vehicle that places the steering gear and steering linkage behind the centerline of the front wheels.

Rebuilt See *remanufactured.*

Receiver dryer A device used as a reservoir and container for desiccant in some automotive air-conditioning systems.

Recirculating ball-steering gear A steering gear that uses a series of ball bearings that feed through and around the grooves in the worm and nut.

Rectifier An electronic device that converts alternating current into direct current.

Rectifier bridge A group of six diodes, three positive (+) and three negative (−), commonly used in alternators.

Reference voltage A voltage applied to a circuit.

Reid vapor pressure (RVP) A method of determining vapor pressure of gasoline and other petroleum products; widely used in the petroleum industry as an indicator of the volatility of gasoline.

Relative humidity The percentage of water vapour (actually) in the air relative to the actual amount that could be in the air.

Relay An electromagnetic switch that uses a movable arm.

Release bearing See *throwout bearing.*

Reluctance The resistance to the movement of magnetic lines of force.

Remanufactured A term used to describe a component that is disassembled, cleaned, inspected, and reassembled using new or reconditioned parts. According to the Automotive Parts Rebuilders Association (APRA), this same component is also called *rebuilt.*

Renewal A part built to be used as a replacement for the original equipment (OE) part.

Replenishing port The Society of Automotive Engineers (SAE) term for the rearward low-pressure master cylinder port. Also called *inlet port, bypass port, filler port,* or *breather port.*

Reserve capacity The number of minutes a battery can produce 25 A and still maintain a battery voltage of 1.75 V per cell (10.5 V for a 12 V battery).

Residual check valve A valve in the outlet end of the master cylinder to keep the hydraulic system under a light pressure on drum brakes only.

Residual magnetism Magnetism remaining after the magnetizing force is removed.

Resistance The opposition to current flow, measured in ohms.

Resonator A small secondary muffler used to reduce exhaust resonance.

Reverse bias Current flow in the opposite direction from normal.

Revolutions per minute (RPM) A measure of how fast an object is rotating around an axis.

RFG Reformulated gasoline.

Rheostat A two-terminal variable resistor.

Ring gear An outer gear in a planetary gear set or the large gear used in the differential.

Rise time The time, measured in microseconds, for the output of a coil to rise from 10% to 90% of its maximum output.

Road crown A roadway where the center is higher than the outside edges. Road crown is designed into many roads to drain water off the road surface.

Roll bar See *stabilizer bar.*

Roll steer See *bump steer.*

ROM Read-only memory.

Root mean square (RMS) Conversion of AC voltages to the effective DC value.

Rotary engine Engine using a revolving three-sided rotor instead of pistons and connecting rods.

RPM Engine speed expressed in revolutions per minute of the crankshaft.

RTV Room-temperature vulcanization.

Run-flat tires Tires specially designed to operate for reasonable distances and speeds without air inside to support the weight of the vehicle.

RWAL Rear-wheel antilock.

RWD Rear-wheel drive.

SAE Society of Automotive Engineers.

SAI Steering axis inclination (same as KPI).

SBR Styrene butadiene rubber.

Scan tool A small computer used to extract information from the on-board Powertrain Control Module.

Schrader valve A spring-loaded valve used in the service ports of the fuel rail and air-conditioning system. Invented in 1844 by August Schrader.

Scoring Grooves worn into the drum or disc braking surface.

Scrub radius An imaginary line drawn through the steering axis intersecting the ground at a point compared to the center line of the tire. "Zero scrub radius" means the line intersects at the center line of the tire. "Positive scrub radius" means that the line intersects below the road surface, and "negative scrub radius" means the line intersects above the road surface. Also called *steering offset* by some vehicle manufacturers.

Secondary pickup An accessory that can be clamped on the high-voltage coil wire used to measure secondary ignition patterns.

Secondary shoe The brake shoe installed facing the rear of the vehicle.

Sector lash Clearance (lash) between a section of gear (sector) on the pitman shaft in a steering gear. Also see *over-centre adjustment.*

Sector shaft The name for the output shaft of a conventional steering gear; part of the sector shaft in a section of a gear that meshes with the worm gear and is rotated by the driver when the steering wheel is turned. Also called a *pitman shaft.*

Self-adjusting brakes Brakes that maintain the proper lining-to-drum clearance by an automatic adjusting mechanism.

Self-energizing A brake shoe that, when applied, develops a wedging action that assists the braking force applied by the wheel cylinder.

Self-induction The generation of an electric current in the wires of a coil created when the current is first connected or disconnected.

SEMA Specialty Equipment Manufacturers Association.

Semiconductor A material that is neither a conductor nor an insulator and has exactly four electrons in the atom's outer shell.

Semimets Semimetallic brake linings.

Separators In a battery, nonconducting, porous, thin materials used to separate positive and negative plates.

Series wound In a starter motor, the field coils and the armature are wired in series. All the current flows through the field coils, the hot brushes, the armature, and then to the ground through the ground brushes.

Service brake The main driver-operated vehicle brakes.

Servo action Brake construction in which the end of the primary shoe bears against the secondary shoe. When the brakes are applied, the primary shoe applies force to the secondary shoe.

Servo unit A vacuum-operated unit on a cruise control system that attaches to the throttle linkage to move the throttle.

Setback The amount the front wheels are set back from true parallel with the rear wheels. Positive setback means the right front wheel is set back farther than the left.

Shackle A mounting that allows the end of a leaf spring to move forward and backward as the spring moves up and down during normal operation of the suspension.

Shelf life The length of time that something can remain on a storage shelf and not be reduced in performance level from that of a newly manufactured product.

Shim A thin metal spacer.

Shimmy A vibration that results in a rapid back-and-forth motion of the steering wheel. A bent wheel or a wheel assembly that is not correctly balanced dynamically are common causes of shimmy.

Shock absorber A device used to control spring movement in the suspension system.

Shoe pad A raised support on the backing plate against which the shoe edge rests; also called a *shoe ledge.*

Short circuit A circuit in which current flows but bypasses some or all of the resistance in the circuit; a connection that results in a "copper-to-copper" connection.

Short to ground A short circuit in which the current bypasses some or all of the resistance in the circuit and flows to ground. Because ground is usually steel in automotive electricity, a short to ground (grounded) is a "copper-to-steel" connection.

Short/long arm suspension (SLA) A suspension system with a short upper control arm and a long lower control arm. The wheel changes very little in camber with a vertical deflection.

Shunt A device used to divert or bypass part of the current from the main circuit.

Simpson gear set A type of compound planetary gear set used in many automatic transmissions/transaxles.

Sintering A process in which metal particles are fused together without melting.

Sipes Small traction-improving slits in the tread of a tire.

SLA Abbreviation for short/long arm suspension. Also called *double wishbone-type suspension.*

Slip angle The angle between the true centerline of the tire and the actual path followed by the tire while turning.

Smog The term used to describe a combination of *smoke* and *fog.* Formed by NO_x and HC with sunlight.

Society of Automotive Engineers (SAE) A professional organization made up of automotive engineers and designers that establishes standards and conducts testing for many automotive-related functions.

Solenoid An electromagnetic switch that uses a movable core.

Solid axle A solid supporting axle for both front or both rear wheels. Also referred to as a *straight axle* or *nonindependent axle.*

Space-frame construction A type of vehicle construction that uses the structure of the body to support the engine and drive train as well as the steering and suspension. The outside body panels are nonstructured.

Spalling A term used to describe a type of mechanical failure caused by metal fatigue. Metal cracks then break out into small chips, slabs, or scales of metal.

Spark knock Secondary rapid burning of the last 3%–5% of the air–fuel mixture in the combustion chamber causing a second flame front that collides with the first flame front and produces a knock noise.

Specific gravity The ratio of the weight of a given volume of a liquid divided by the weight of an equal volume of water.

Speed gears Gears used in a manual transmission/transaxle that are free to move on bearings on the main shaft and are locked to the shaft through the synchronizer hub when a shift is completed.

Spider Center part of a wheel; also known as the *center section.*

Spike A (high) voltage pulse during a short period of time (sharp pulse).

Spindle nut A nut used to retain and adjust the bearing clearance of the hub to the spindle.

Spiral-wound batteries The battery cells are wound in a cylindrical shape, rather than flat plates.

Splayed crank The crankpins are offset to provide equal firing impulses, usually on V-6 engines.

Split mu A term used to describe two different friction (μ) surfaces under the wheels of a vehicle; (μ) is the Greek letter for coefficient of friction.

Split system A divided hydraulic brake system.

Sponge lead Lead made with many small holes to make its surface porous or sponge-like for use in battery negative plates; the chemical symbol for lead is Pb.

Spongy pedal When there is air in the brake lines, the pedal will have a springy or spongy feeling when applied.

Sprag A type of one-way clutch commonly used in automatic transmissions/transaxles.

Sprung weight The weight of a vehicle supported by the suspension.

Spur gears Gears with straight-cut teeth.

Squeal A high-pitched noise caused by high-frequency vibrations when brakes are applied.

Stabilizer bar A hardened steel bar connected to the frame and both lower control arms to prevent excessive body roll. Also called an *antisway* or *antiroll bar.*

Stabilizer links A bolt, spacer, and nut connecting (linking) the end of the stabilizer bar to the lower control arm.

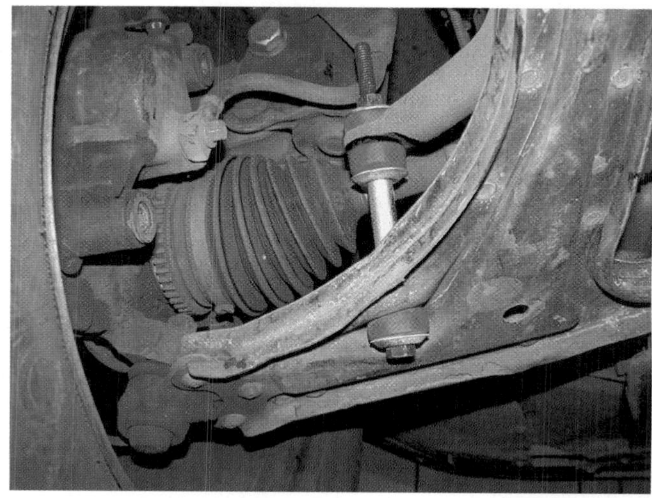

Stablizer links

Stall speed The maximum engine RPM that can be achieved with an automatic transmission/transaxle with the gear selector in a drive gear, brakes held, and the accelerator wide open.

Star wheel A notched wheel with a left- or right-hand threaded member for adjusting brake shoes.

Starter drive A term used to describe the starter motor drive pinion gear with overrunning clutch.

State of charge The degree or the amount that a battery is charged. A fully charged battery would be 100% charged.

Static balance Describes a tire that has an even distribution of weight about its axis.

Stator A name for three interconnected windings inside an alternator. A rotating rotor provides a moving magnetic field and induces a current in the windings of the stator.

Steady bearing See *centre support bearing.*

Steel Refined iron metal with most of the carbon removed.

Steering arms Arms bolted to or forged as a part of the steering knuckles. They transmit the steering force from the tie rods to the knuckles, causing the wheels to pivot.

Steering coupling disc See *flexible coupling.*

Steering gear Gears on the end of the steering column that multiply the driver's force to turn the front wheels.

Steering knuckle The inner portion of the spindle that pivots on the kingpin or ball joints.

Steering offset See *scrub radius.*

Step-bore cylinder A wheel cylinder having a different diameter at each end.

Stepper motor A motor that moves a specified amount of rotation.

Stoichiometric Describes an air–fuel ratio of exactly 14.7: 1. At this specific rate, all the gasoline is fully oxidized by all the available oxygen.

Stop ring See *blocking ring.*

Straight axle See *solid axle.*

Strike-out bumper See *jounce bumper.*

Stroboscopic A very bright, pulsing light triggered from the firing of one spark plug used to check and adjust ignition timing.

Strut rod Suspension member used to control forward/backward support to the control arms. Also called *tension* or *compression rod (TC rod),* or *drag rod.*

Strut rod bushing A rubber component used to insulate the attachment of the strut rod to the frame on the body of the vehicle.

Stud A short rod with threads on both ends.

Sun gear The centre gear in a planetary gear set.

Suspension Parts or linkages by which the wheels are attached to the frame or body of a vehicle. These parts or linkages support the vehicle and keep the wheels in proper alignment.

Sway bar Shortened name for antisway bar; see *stabilizer bar.*

Synchronizer An assembly containing the sleeve, hub, keys, and ring used to make a clash-free change of gear ratio in a manual transmission/transaxle.

Synchronizer

Synchronizer assembly Parts that allow a shift to occur in a manual transmission/transaxle without gear clash. The parts in the assembly include the *synchronizer sleeve, synchronizer keys (struts),* and *synchronizer ring (blocking ring).*

Synchronizer ring See *blocking ring.*

Tachometer (tach) Instrument or gauge used to measure RPM (revolutions per minute).

Tandem cylinder A master cylinder with two pistons arranged one ahead of the other; one cylinder operates the rear brakes and the other the front brakes.

TBI Throttle body injection.

TC rod See *strut rod.*

TDC Top dead centre.

Tell-tale light Dash warning light (sometimes called an *idiot light*).

Tension rod See strut rod.

TEV An abbreviation for an air-conditioning system that uses a thermostatic expansion valve.

TFI Thick-film integration.

Thermistor A resistor that changes resistance with temperature. A positive-coefficient thermistor has increased resistance with an increase in temperature. A negative-coefficient thermistor has increased resistance with a decrease in temperature.

Thermoelectric principle The production of current flow created by heating the connection of two dissimilar metals.

Thermostat A device that controls the flow in a system such as the engine cooling system based on temperature.

Thick-film integration (TFI) A type of Ford electronic ignition system.

Throttle body A housing containing a valve to regulate the airflow through the intake manifold.

Throttle-By-Wire A throttle plate operated by an electric motor.

Throttle position (TP) sensor A sensor that signals the computer as to the position of the throttle.

Throwout bearing A bearing that rides on the pressure plate and transfers the driver's foot force to disengage the clutch. Also called a *release bearing.*

Throwout bearing

Thrust angle The angle between the geometric centerline of the vehicle and the thrust line.

Thrust line The direction the rear wheels are pointed as determined by the rear-wheel toe.

Tie rod A rod that connects the steering arms.

Time base The time defined per each horizontal division on the display.

Toe-in The difference in measurement between the front of the wheels and the back of the wheels (the fronts of the tires are closer than the backs of the tires).

Toe-out The backs of the tires are closer than the fronts of the tires.

Top dead centre (TDC) The highest point in the cylinder that the piston can travel. The measurement from bottom dead centre (BDC) to TDC determines the stroke length of the crankshaft.

Torque A twisting force measured in pounds-feet (lb-ft) or Newton-metres (N·m) that may or may not result in motion.

Torque converter A special form of fluid coupling in which torque is increased.

Torque converter clutch A clutch located inside the torque converter that locks the turbine and the impeller together to prevent any slippage. Also called a *lockup torque converter.*

Torque steer Torque steer occurs in front-wheel-drive vehicles when engine torque causes a front wheel to change its angle (toe) from straight ahead. The resulting pulling effect of the vehicle is most noticeable during rapid acceleration, especially when upshifting of the transmission creates a sudden change in torque.

Torque wrench A wrench that registers the amount of applied torque.

Torsen™ A brand name of a type of differential that applies torque to both drive wheels. The name is a combination of torque and sensing.

Torsion bar A type of spring in the shape of a straight bar; one end is attached to the frame of the vehicle and the opposite end is attached to a control arm of the suspension. When the wheels hit a bump, the bar twists and then untwists.

Torsional dampers Springs (steel or rubber) used in the hub of a clutch friction disc to absorb the shock of engagement and help dampen engine firing pulses.

Torx A type of fastener that features a star-shaped indentation for a tool. A registered trademark of the Camcar Division of Textron.

Track The distance between the centerline of the wheels as viewed from the front or rear.

Track rod A horizontal steel rod or bar attached to the rear axle housing at one end and the frame at the other to keep the centre of the rear axle centred on the body. Also known as a *panhard rod.*

Tracking A term used to describe the fact that the rear wheels should track directly behind the front wheels.

Trade number The number stamped on an automotive light bulb. All bulbs of the same trade number have the same candlepower and wattage, regardless of the manufacturer of the bulb.

Tramp A vibration usually caused by up-and-down motion of an out-of-balance or out-of-round wheel assembly.

Transducer An electrical and mechanical speed sensing and control unit used on cruise control systems.

Transfer case Used in four-wheel-drive vehicles to transfer engine torque to both the front and the rear differential.

Transistor A semiconductor device that can operate as an amplifier or an electrical switch.

Trigger A current level that determines the beginning point of a waveform.

Trigger slope The voltage direction that a waveform must have to start display. A positive slope requires the voltage to be increasing as it crosses the trigger level; a negative slope requires the voltage to be decreasing.

TRW, Inc. Thompson Ramo Wooldridge Inc.

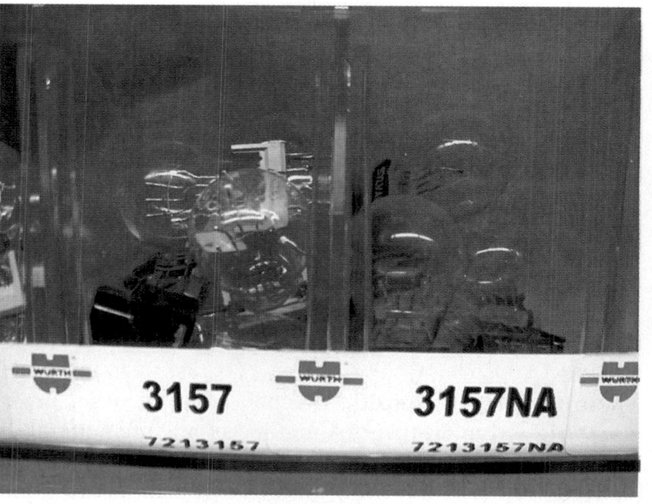

Trade number

Turbocharger An exhaust-powered supercharger.

Turbulence The state of being violently disturbed, as in an engine; the rapid swirling motion of the air–fuel mixture entering the cylinder.

Turning radius The angle of the steering knuckles that allows the inside wheel to turn at a sharper angle than the outside wheel whenever turning a corner. Also known as *toe out on turns* (TOOT) or the *Ackerman angle.*

TXV An abbreviation for an air-conditioning system that uses a thermostatic expansion valve.

UNC Unified national coarse.

Underinflation A term used to describe a tire with too little tire pressure (less than minimum allowable pressure).

Understeer A term used to describe the handling of a vehicle where the driver must turn the steering wheel more and more while turning a corner.

UNF Unified national fine.

Unit-body A type of vehicle construction, first used by the Budd Company of Troy, Michigan, that does not use a separate frame. The body is built strongly enough to support the engine and the power train as well as the suspension and steering system. The outside body panels are part of the structure. Also see *space-frame construction.*

Unsprung weight The parts of a vehicle not supported by the suspension system. Examples of items that are typical unsprung weight include wheels, tires, and brakes.

VAC Vacuum sensor.

VIR An abbreviation of an air-conditioning system in one unit called *valves in receiver.*

Vacuum Negative pressure (below atmospheric); measured in units of inches or centimetres of mercury (Hg).

Vacuum booster A vacuum power brake unit.

Vacuum kicker A computer-controlled throttle device used to increase idle RPM during certain operating conditions, such as when the air-conditioning system is operating.

Vacuum, manifold Vacuum in the intake manifold that develops as a result of the intake stroke of the cylinders.

Vacuum, ported A vacuum that develops on the intake side of the throttle plate as air moves past it.

Valve overlap The amount of time, in degrees of crank rotation, the intake and exhaust valves are both open.

Valve train The collection of parts that make the valves operate. The valve train includes the camshaft(s), related drive components, the various parts that convert the camshaft's rotary motion into reciprocating motion, and the valves and their associated parts.

Vapour lock Vaporized fuel, usually in the fuel line, that prevents or retards the necessary fuel delivery to the cylinders.

Variable cylinder engine An engine that reduces the number of working cylinders by keeping the valves closed.

Variable force solenoid See *pressure control solenoid.*

Variable valve timing A method of advancing and retarding the camshaft to match engine demand.

Vehicle control module (VCM) The on-board computer that controls the engine management, transmission, and other vehicle systems such as antilock brakes.

Vehicle identification number (VIN) Alphanumeric number identifying vehicle type, assembly plant, powertrain, etc.

Vent port The Society of Automotive Engineers (SAE) term for the front port of a master cylinder, also called the *compensating port* or *bypass.*

Vibration An oscillation, shake, or movement that alternates in opposite directions.

Viscosity Thickness, or body, of a fluid.

Viscous coupling A clutch-like device on some four-wheel-drive and most all-wheel-drive vehicles that uses thin metal disks and thick silicone fluid to connect the front and rear differentials if there is a difference in speed between the two drive shafts.

VOC Volatile organic compounds.

Volatility A measurement of the tendency of a liquid to change to vapour.

Volt The unit of measurement for the amount of electrical pressure; named for Alessandro Volta (1745–1827).

Voltage drop Voltage loss across a wire, connector, or any other conductor. Voltage drop equals resistance in ohms times current in amperes (Ohm's law).

Voltage regulator An electronic or mechanical unit that controls the output voltage of an electrical generator or alternator by controlling the field current of the generator.

Voltmeter An electrical test instrument used to measure volts (unit of electrical pressure). A voltmeter is connected in parallel with the unit or circuit being tested.

Volumetric efficiency The ratio between the amount of air–fuel mixture that actually enters the cylinder and the amount that could enter under ideal conditions expressed as a percentage.

VSS Vehicle speed sensor.

VTF Vacuum-tube fluorescent.

Vulcanization A process in which heat and pressure combine to change the chemistry of rubber.

W/O Without.

Wander A type of handling requiring constant steering wheel correction to keep the vehicle going straight.

Warning light A light on the instrument panel that alerts the driver when one-half of a split hydraulic system fails as determined by the pressure differential switch.

Wastegate A form of pressure bypass valve used with turbochargers.

Watt An electrical unit of power; one watt equals current (amperes) × voltage (1/746 hp). Named after James Watt, a Scottish inventor.

Watt's link A type of track rod that uses two horizontal rods pivoting at the center of the rear axle.

Waveform The pattern defined by an electrical signal.

Wear bars See *wear indicators.*

Wear indicator ball joint A ball joint design with a raised area around the grease fitting. If the raised area is flush to or recessed from the surrounding area of the ball joint, the joint is worn and must be replaced.

Wear indicators Bald areas that appear across the tread of a tire when only 2/32″ or less of tread depth remains.

Weight-carrying ball joint See *load-carrying ball joint.*

Wheel cover A functional and decorative cover over the entire wheel. Also see *hub cap.*

Wheel cylinder The part of the hydraulic system that receives pressure from the master cylinder and applies the brake shoes to the drums.

Wheelbase The distance between the centerline of the two wheels as viewed from the side.

Wishbone suspension See *SLA.*

Worm and roller A steering gear that uses a worm gear on the steering shaft. A roller on one end of the cross shaft engages the worm.

Worm and sector A steering gear using a worm gear to engage a sector gear on the cross shaft.

WOT Wide-open throttle.

WSS Wheel speed sensor.

Wye wound A type of stator winding in which all three coils are connected to a common center connection. Called a *wye* because the connections look like the letter Y.

Zener diode A specially constructed (heavily doped) diode designed to operate with a reverse-bias current after a certain voltage has been reached. Named for Clarence Melvin Zener.

Zerk A name commonly used for a grease fitting. Named in 1922 for its developer, Oscar U. Zerk, an employee of the Alamite Corporation. A grease fitting is also called an *Alamite fitting.*

Zerk

Index

"AS IS" LICENSE AGREEMENT AND LIMITED WARRANTY

READ THIS LICENSE CAREFULLY BEFORE OPENING THIS PACKAGE. BY OPENING THIS PACKAGE, YOU ARE AGREEING TO THE TERMS AND CONDITIONS OF THIS LICENSE. IF YOU DO NOT AGREE, DO NOT OPEN THE PACKAGE. PROMPTLY RETURN THE UNOPENED PACKAGE AND ALL ACCOMPANYING ITEMS TO THE PLACE YOU OBTAINED THEM. THESE TERMS APPLY TO ALL LICENSED SOFTWARE ON THE DISK EXCEPT THAT THE TERMS FOR USE OF ANY SHAREWARE OR FREEWARE ON THE DISKETTES ARE AS SET FORTH IN THE ELECTRONIC LICENSE LOCATED ON THE DISK:

1. GRANT OF LICENSE and OWNERSHIP: The enclosed computer programs and any data ("Software") are licensed, not sold, to you by Pearson Education Canada Inc. ("We" or the "Company") in consideration of your adoption of the accompanying Company textbooks and/or other materials, and your agreement to these terms. You own only the disk(s) but we and/or our licensors own the Software itself. This license allows instructors and students enrolled in the course using the Company textbook that accompanies this Software (the "Course") to use and display the enclosed copy of the Software for academic use only, so long as you comply with the terms of this Agreement. You may make one copy for back up only. We reserve any rights not granted to you.

2. USE RESTRICTIONS: You may not sell or license copies of the Software or the Documentation to others. You may not transfer, distribute or make available the Software or the Documentation, except to instructors and students in your school who are users of the adopted Company textbook that accompanies this Software in connection with the course for which the textbook was adopted. You may not reverse engineer, disassemble, decompile, modify, adapt, translate or create derivative works based on the Software or the Documentation. You may be held legally responsible for any copying or copyright infringement that is caused by your failure to abide by the terms of these restrictions.

3. TERMINATION: This license is effective until terminated. This license will terminate automatically without notice from the Company if you fail to comply with any provisions or limitations of this license. Upon termination, you shall destroy the Documentation and all copies of the Software. All provisions of this Agreement as to limitation and disclaimer of warranties, limitation of liability, remedies or damages, and our ownership rights shall survive termination.

4. DISCLAIMER OF WARRANTY: THE COMPANY AND ITS LICENSORS MAKE NO WARRANTIES ABOUT THE SOFTWARE, WHICH IS PROVIDED "AS-IS." IF THE DISK IS DEFECTIVE IN MATERIALS OR WORKMANSHIP, YOUR ONLY REMEDY IS TO RETURN IT TO THE COMPANY WITHIN 30 DAYS FOR REPLACEMENT UNLESS THE COMPANY DETERMINES IN GOOD FAITH THAT THE DISK HAS BEEN MISUSED OR IMPROPERLY INSTALLED, REPAIRED, ALTERED OR DAMAGED. THE COMPANY DISCLAIMS ALL WARRANTIES, EXPRESS OR IMPLIED, INCLUDING WITHOUT LIMITATION, THE IMPLIED WARRANTIES OF MERCHANTABILITY AND FITNESS FOR A PARTICULAR PURPOSE. THE COMPANY DOES NOT WARRANT, GUARANTEE OR MAKE ANY REPRESENTATION REGARDING THE ACCURACY, RELIABILITY, CURRENTNESS, USE, OR RESULTS OF USE, OF THE SOFTWARE.

5. LIMITATION OF REMEDIES AND DAMAGES: IN NO EVENT, SHALL THE COMPANY OR ITS EMPLOYEES, AGENTS, LICENSORS OR CONTRACTORS BE LIABLE FOR ANY INCIDENTAL, INDIRECT, SPECIAL OR CONSEQUENTIAL DAMAGES ARISING OUT OF OR IN CONNECTION WITH THIS LICENSE OR THE SOFTWARE, INCLUDING, WITHOUT LIMITATION, LOSS OF USE, LOSS OF DATA, LOSS OF INCOME OR PROFIT, OR OTHER LOSSES SUSTAINED AS A RESULT OF INJURY TO ANY PERSON, OR LOSS OF OR DAMAGE TO PROPERTY, OR CLAIMS OF THIRD PARTIES, EVEN IF THE COMPANY OR AN AUTHORIZED REPRESENTATIVE OF THE COMPANY HAS BEEN ADVISED OF THE POSSIBILITY OF SUCH DAMAGES. SOME JURISDICTIONS DO NOT ALLOW THE LIMITATION OF DAMAGES IN CERTAIN CIRCUMSTANCES, SO THE ABOVE LIMITATIONS MAY NOT ALWAYS APPLY.

6. GENERAL: THIS AGREEMENT SHALL BE CONSTRUED AND INTERPRETED ACCORDING TO THE LAWS OF THE PROVINCE OF ONTARIO. This Agreement is the complete and exclusive statement of the agreement between you and the Company and supersedes all proposals, prior agreements, oral or written, and any other communications between you and the company or any of its representatives relating to the subject matter.

Should you have any questions concerning this agreement or if you wish to contact the Company for any reason, please contact in writing: Editorial Manager, Pearson Education Canada, 26 Prince Andrew Place, Don Mills, Ontario M3C 2T8.